AN A TO Z OF almost EVERYTHING

Author's note

This is the second A–Z of Everything. I hope you are entertained and edified by it. There are three points I ought to make about the book. First, there is often a time lag in the compilation of statistics – especially government figures – but those I have presented are the latest available to me. Second, since this is a British book there may be a preponderance of British data, but I have attempted to give the book a global reach. Finally, and most important, although I have done my utmost to achieve 100 per cent accuracy, with a project of this magnitude covering such a wide range of facts, it seems unavoidable that mistakes will be made, for which I apologise. I would be delighted to have these pointed out to ensure that future editions of *An A–Z of Almost Everything* are as correct as can be. If you wish to do so or wish to suggest new ideas for the book, please write to Trevor Montague c/o Time Warner Books.

AN **A** TO **Z**

OF *almost* EVERYTHING

A COMPENDIUM OF
GENERAL KNOWLEDGE

TREVOR MONTAGUE

LITTLE, BROWN

A *Little, Brown* Book

First published in Great Britain in 2001 by Little, Brown
This edition first published in 2003
Reprinted 2004

A CIP catalogue record for this book
is available from the British Library.

Hardback with jacket ISBN 0 316 72557 9
Laminated with board ISBN 0 316 72587 0

Typeset by M Rules
Printed and bound in Great Britain by
CPI Bath

Little, Brown
An imprint of
Time Warner Book Group UK
Brettenham House
Lancaster Place
London WC2E 7EN

wwwtwbg.co.uk

CONTENTS

ABOUT THE AUTHOR

Trevor Montague is perhaps one of the best-known general knowledge buffs in the country. A veteran of numerous radio and television programmes, in 1997 alone he won a dozen shows, including the Grand Finals of both *15-to-1* (Channel 4) and *Today's the Day* (BBC). Despite also winning a holiday to Barbados that year, Trevor cites his highlight as partnering Emma Noble (now Emma Major) in a fun quiz on the *This Morning* with Richard and Judy show, which was the envy of all his friends. Trevor won a Gold Medal at the 1998 Mind Sports Olympiad and the following year founded the British Quiz Association, which held its first-ever championship in 1999 at Olympia in London. The second British Quiz Championship was held at Alexandra Palace in 2000, and Trevor set the questions for both events as well as co-hosting them alongside Magnus Magnusson.

Also in 2000, Trevor's crack quiz team, made up of four former *Mastermind* contestants, swept all before them by winning the South London Quiz League title (now the Quiz League of London), and, yet again, despite this success Trevor lists his highlight of 2000 as taking part in a television fun quiz partnering the delightful Kate Robbins – once again the bonus of a kiss from Kate (no puns please) held sway over other achievements of that year.

The all-consuming demands of the *A to Z* have meant that Trevor has had to retire from many of his active quiz commitments but he did come out of hibernation to take part in the 2002 British Quiz Championships where he managed the bronze medal behind Kevin Ashman and John Wilson. Trevor was also a member of the celebrated 'Dream Team' put together by the *Guardian* newspaper for the purpose of raiding London quizzes for one week last February, suffice to say with a team including multiple *15- to-1* champion Daphne Fowler, *Mastermind* champions Christopher Hughes and Gavin Fuller, and *Millionaire* and *Mastermind* champion David Edwards, success was guaranteed. Trevor also sets questions for television quiz shows, Big Brother 3 being his most interesting recent offering, and he compiles quizzes for Internet companies, charities and corporate concerns.

Trevor has had a very successful sporting career but lists his proudest moments as his third place in the Peugeot Zest National Fitness Championship in 2000, from an entry of over 10,000 (and at the age of 46!) and his tenth place in his first-ever open cycle race in March 2001, a result that made the pages of Cycling Weekly Magazine, a coup for any budding cyclist.

Acknowledgements

I would like to thank the following people for their help in the compilation of this work: Kevin Ashman, Mike Billson, Mark Bytheway, Eric Carden, Peter Chitty, Bob Collier, Patricia Cowley, Andy Curtis, Peter Ediss, Robert Edwards, Brian Ennis, Keith Fawdry, Gavin Fuller, Gavin Gaughan, Phillida Grantham, Paul Henderson, Christopher Hughes, June Humphries, Ann Kelly, Phil Lewis, Magnus Magnusson, Angelita March, Christine Moorcroft, Mike O'Sullivan, Anita Oxley, Fiona Redmond, Craig Scott, Leo Stevenson, Rob Sutherland, Geoff Thomas, Gordon Troughton, Ritchie Venner, Tim Westcott, Neil White and John Wilson.

Introduction to the First Edition by Magnus Magnusson KBE

Trevor Montague is a Masterminder. That is to say, in 1995 he became one of the 1,231 bravehearts who appeared on the television *Mastermind* during its twenty-five-year run. But Trevor Montague is much more than that: he is that not-quite-so-rare-now animal, a quiz addict.

Trevor is also a begetter of quiz-teams. There is an unofficial *Mastermind* mafia which meets every month in the Grape Street wine bar in London, and from its regulars Trevor puts together formidable scratch teams of veteran Masterminders to take part in all and any quiz challenges. Trevor is also the question-setter of the fledgling British Quiz Championship which is a part of the annual Mind Sports Olympiad at London's Olympia.

That in itself is a sign of the immense and growing popularity of quizzes of all kinds on television, on radio, in pubs, in the Civil Service, and now even on the Internet. And it has given rise to Trevor's most ambitious project yet – *An A–Z of Almost Everything*: a massive factfile of information calculated to be of value to anyone and everyone interested in quizzes.

But how does one define 'General Knowledge' as opposed to 'Specialised Knowledge'? Indeed, when does 'Specialised Knowledge' become 'General Knowledge'? With the staggering growth of pub quiz-teams and television game-shows over recent years, the reservoir of what used to be considered 'General Knowledge' has expanded out of all recognition. Over the twenty-five years of *Mastermind*, for instance, questions which would once have come into the specialised category became demoted to the General Knowledge sets. I tried to make that very point, as subtly as possible, in the last round of the last Final of the last *Mastermind* series (in Kirkwall Cathedral, Orkney, in 1997): the last question echoed the very first question I had asked, in the University of Liverpool back in 1972:

Q: During the Spanish Civil War, which town in the Basque country was destroyed by German bombers, an event which was commemorated in a painting by Picasso?

A: Guernica

When that question was first asked in 1972, it was in a set of specialised questions on 'The Visual Arts'; in 1997 it was in a General Knowledge set.

So, what exactly makes up an A–Z of Everything? For Trevor, everything is grist to his insatiable mill. He has produced a monster factfile on an astonishing array of subjects from abbreviations to zodiac, embracing Americanisms, animal adjectives, assassination attempts, *Carry On* films, dubbed singing voices, famous dogs, gestation periods, London postal areas, middle names, nursery rhymes, obituaries, pub names, quantum theory, Schrödinger's cat, sculptors, trains, Visigoth rulers and zip codes.

I can think of few subjects which have been omitted, except perhaps for some of the classic *Mastermind* offerings which never made it to the screen: 'orthopaedic bone cement in total hip-replacement'; 'self-service petrol stations from 1963–68'; 'perfect squares from 992–9801'; and 'motorway routes to anywhere in mainland Britain from Letchworth'.

To put together this weighty tome, Trevor called upon his network of friends and colleagues in the Mastermind Club – that remarkable association of survivors of the Black Chair. The Club membership represents an astonishing reservoir of knowledge which its owners are always ready to impart to others. Many is the time I found myself marooned in a hotel without reference books and phoned friends in the Club to check on some vital detail which I needed for an occasion in the next morning.

The quiz cognoscenti who will avidly devour this book may well start off feeling superior ('I know that, of course!'), but I am pretty sure that even they will find much to intrigue them in this shrine of serendipity.

ABBREVIATIONS

A & P   Advertising and Promotion
A & R   Artists and Repertoire / Recording
AA   Automobile Association; Alcoholics Anonymous
AAA   Amateur Athletic Association; Anti-Aircraft Artillery
AAM   Air-to-Air Missile
ABC   Atomic, Biological and Chemical; American Broadcasting Company; Australian Broadcasting Commission
ABM   Anti-Ballistic Missile
ABRACADABRA   ABbreviations and Related ACronyms Associated with Defense, Astronautics, Business and RAdio-electronics
ABS   Anti-lock Braking System
ABTA   Association of British Travel Agents
AC   Alternating Current
A/C   Account
ACAS   Advisory Conciliation and Arbitration Service
ACCA   Association of Certified and Corporate Accountants
ACLU   American Civil Liberties Union
ACM   Air Chief Marshal
ACPO   Association of Chief Police Officers
ACT   Advance Corporation Tax
ACTT   Association of Cinematograph, Television and Allied Technicians
ACV   Air-Cushion Vehicle
AD   Anno Domini
ADC   Aide-De-Camp
ADCM   Archbishop of Canterbury's Diploma in Church Music
AEEU   Amalgamated Engineering and Electrical Union
AEGIS   Aid for the Elderly in Government InstitutionS
AEU   Amalgamated Engineering Union
AFP   Agence France Press
AFV   Armoured Fighting Vehicle
AG   Attorney General; Adjutant General
AGM   Air-to-Ground Missile; Annual General Meeting
AGR   Advanced Gas-cooled Reactor
AH   Anno Hegirae (from 622 AD, the start of the Muslim calendar)
AI   Artificial Intelligence; Amnesty International; Artificial Insemination
AID   Artificial Insemination by Donor
AIDS   Acquired Immune Deficiency Syndrome
AIM   Alternative Investment Market
AKA   Also Known As
ALGOL   ALGOrithmic Language
ALICE   Autistic and Language-Impaired Children's Education
ALWR   Advanced Light Water Reactor
AM   Ante Meridiem; Amplitude Modulation
AMCST   Associate, Manchester College of Science and Technology
AMICE   Associate Member of the Institute of Civil Engineers
ANC   African National Congress
ANZAC   Australian and New Zealand Army Corps
AOL   America On Line

AONB   Area of Outstanding Natural Beauty
AP   Associated Press, Artist's Proof
APEX   Advance Purchase EXcursion; Association of Professional, EXecutive, Clerical and Computer Staff
APR   Annual / Annualised Percentage Rate
APT   Advanced Passenger Train
APWR   Advanced Pressurised Water Reactor
ARCO   Associate of the Royal College of Organists
ARCS   Associate of the Royal College of Science
ARP   Association of Retired Persons; Air-Raid Precautions
ASA   Advertising Standards Authority; Amateur Swimming Association
ASAP   As Soon As Possible
ASB   Alternative Service Book
ASBM   Air-to-Surface Ballistic Missile
ASCII   American Standard Code for Information Interchange
ASDA   ASsociated DAiries
ASDE   Airport Surface Detection Equipment
ASDIC   Anti-Submarine Detection Investigation Committee
ASEAN   Association of South East Asian Nations
ASH   Action on Smoking and Health
ASLEF   Associated Society of Locomotive Engineers and Firemen
ASSC   Accounting Standards Steering Committee
ASSR   Autonomous Soviet Socialist Republic
ASTMS   Association of Scientific, Technical and Managerial Staff
AT & T   American Telephone and Telegraph Company
ATC   Air Traffic Control; Air Training Corps
ATOL   Air Travel Organisers Licence
ATS   Auxiliary Territorial Service
ATV   Associated TeleVision
AUC   Anno Urbis Conditae (in the year of the founding of the city); Ab Urbe Condita (years since the foundation of Rome)
AUEW   Amalgamated Union of Engineering Workers (now AEU)
AUT   Association of University Teachers
AVR   Army Volunteer Reserve
AWACS   Airborne Warning And Control System
AWOL   Absent WithOut Leave / Absent Without Official Leave
AWP   Amusement With Prizes
AWRE   Atomic Weapons Research Establishment

BA   Bachelor of Arts; British Airways
BAA   British Airports Authority
BAC   British Aircraft Corporation
BACS   Bankers' Automated Clearing Service
BACUP   British Association of Cancer-United Patients
BAF   British Athletics Federation
BAFTA   British Academy of Film and Television Arts
BALPA   British AirLine Pilots' Association
BANANA   Build Absolutely Nothing Anywhere Near Anyone
BAOR   British Army Of the Rhine

BARB   British Audience Research Bureau; Broadcasters' Audience Research Board
BART   Baronet
BART   Bay Area Rapid Transit
BASIC   Beginners All-Purpose Symbolic Instruction Code
BAT   British American Tobacco Company
BBBC   British Boxing Board of Control
BBC   British Broadcasting Corporation
BBFC   British Board of Film Censors / Classification (new title)
BC   Before Christ; British Colombia
BCC   British Chamber of Commerce
BCE   Before Common / Christian Era
BCh(D) / BDS   Bachelor of Dental Surgery
BEC   Building Employers' Confederation
BECTU   Broadcasting, Entertainment and Cinematograph Technicians Union
BEF   British Expeditionary Force
BEM   British Empire Medal
BES   Business Expansion Scheme
BEST   British Expertise in Science and Technology
BFI   British Film Institute
BFPO   British Forces Post Office
BHF   British Heart Foundation
BHI   British Horological Institute
BIFU   Banking, Insurance and Finance Union
BIM   British Institute of Management
BIT   BInary DigiT
BLitt   Bachelor of Letters
BMA   British Medical Association
BMJ   British Medical Journal
BMR   Basal Metabolic Rate
BMX   Bicycle Motocross
BOAC   British Overseas Airways Corporation
BPD   Barrels Per Day
BPS   Bits Per Second; Bytes Per Second
BRCS   British Red Cross Society
BSA   Birmingham Small Arms
BSAD   British Sports Association for the Disabled
BSB   British Satellite Broadcasting
BSc   Bachelor of Science
BSE   Bovine Spongiform Encephalopathy
BSI   British Standards Institution
BST   British Summer Time
BSW   British Standard Whitworth
Bt   Baronet
BTEC   Business and Technology Education Council
BUNA   BUtadiene and NAtrium (synthetic rubber)
BUPA   British United Provident Association
BUS   Broadcast and Unknown Server
BVM   Blessed Virgin Mary
BWIA   British West Indian Airways
BWR   Boiling Water Reactor
BYO   Bring Your Own

CAA   Civil Aviation Authority
CAB   Citizens Advice Bureau
CAD   Computer Aided Design
CADD   Computer Aided Design and Drafting
CAFOD   CAtholic Fund for Overseas Development
CAL   Computer Aided Learning
CAMRA   CAMpaign for Real Ale
CAN   Christian Advertising Network
Cantab   Cantabrigiensis (of Cambridge)

CAP   Computer Aided Publishing; Common Agricultural Policy
CARE   Co-operative for American Relief Everywhere
CAT   Computerised Axial Tomography
CB   Companion of the order of the Bath
CBC   Canadian Broadcasting Corporation
CBE   Commander of the Order of the British Empire
CBI   Confederation of British Industry
CBS   Columbia Broadcasting System
CCTV   Closed Circuit TeleVision
CDI   Compact Disc Interactive
CDS   Chief of the Defence Staff
CE   Christian Era; Common Era
CERN   Conseil Européen pour la Recherche Nucléaire
CET   Central European Time; Common External Tariff
CFC   ChloroFluoroCarbon
CFS   Chronic Fatigue Syndrome (see ME)
CGM   Conspicuous Gallantry Medal
CGS   Centimetre-Gramme-Second; Chief of General Staff
CH   Companion of Honour
CHP   Combined Heat and Power
CIA   Central Intelligence Agency
CICB   Criminal Injuries Compensation Board
CID   Criminal Investigations Department
CIS   Commonwealth of Independent States (former Soviet republics)
CITES   Convention on International Trade in Endangered Species
CIWF   Compassion In World Farming
CLA   Country Landowners' Association
CM   Chirurgiae Magister (Master of Surgery)
CMEA   Council for Mutual Economic Assistance
CND   Campaign for Nuclear Disarmament
CNN   Cable News Network
COBOL   COmmon Business-Oriented Language
COD   Cash On Delivery
COI   Central Office of Information
COMECON   COuncil for Mutual ECONomic aid / assistance
COMINTERN   COMmunist INTERNational
CPRE   Council for the Protection of Rural England
CPS   Crown Prosecution Service; Characters Per Second
CPSA   Civil and Public Services Association
CPU   Central Processing Unit
CRE   Commission for Racial Equality
CRT   Cathode Ray Tube
CS (gas)   Carson and Staughton
CSA   Child Support Agency
CSE   Certificate of Secondary Education
CSO   Central Statistical Office
CTO   Cancelled To Order (Philately)
CTT   Capital Transfer Tax
CURE   Care, Understanding, REsearch
CVD   Compact Video Disc
CVO   Commander of the Royal Victorian Order
CVP   Climate, Vegetation and Productivity
CWU   Communication Workers' Union

DA   District Attorney
DAB   Digital Audio Broadcasting
DAGMAR   Defining Advertising Goals for Measured Advertising Results

D & C Dilatation and Curettage
DAR Daughters of the American Revolution
DAT Digital Audio Tape
DBE Dame Commander of the Order of the British Empire
DBS Direct Broadcasting by Satellite
DC Direct Current; District of Columbia
DCL Doctor of Civil Law
DCM Distinguished Conduct Medal
DCMG Dame Commander of the Order of St Michael and St George
DD Doctor of Divinity
DDS Doctor of Dental Surgery
DDT DichloroDiphenylTrichloroethane
DEFRA Department for Environment, Food and Rural Affairs
DERV Diesel-Engined-Road Vehicle
DFC Distinguished Flying Cross
DFM Distinguished Flying Medal
DINKY Double Income No Kids Yet
DipSW Diploma in Social Work
DLitt Doctor of Letters
DLR Docklands Light Railway
DNA DeoxyriboNucleic Acid
DOA Dead On Arrival
DORA Defence Of the Realm Act (1914)
DOS Disc Operating System
DQL Data Query Language
DSA Driving Standards Agency
DSC Distinguished Service Cross
DSM Distinguished Service Medal
DSO Distinguished Service Order
DSS Department of Social Security
DTI Department of Trade and Industry
DTLR Department of Transport, Local Government and the Regions
DTP Desk-Top Publishing
DVD Digital Versatile / Video Disc
DVM Doctor of Veterinary Medicine
DWI Drinking Water Inspectorate
DWP Department for Work and Pensions
DWT Denarius WeighT (pennyweight); Dead Weight Tonnage

EAROM Electrically Alterable Read Only Memory
EBRD European Bank for Reconstruction and Development
EBV Epstein-Barr Virus
ECG ElectroCardioGram / Graph
ECGD Export Credit Guarantee Department
ECHR European Court of Human Rights
ECJ European Court of Justice
ECO English Chamber Orchestra
ECSC European Coal and Steel Community
ECT Electro-Convulsive Therapy
ECU European Currency Unit
EDM Early Day Motion
EDP Electronic Data Processing
EEC European Economic Community
EEG ElectroEncephaloGram / Graph
EFA European Fighter Aircraft; Extended File Attribute
EFTA European Free Trade Association
EFTS Electronic Funds Transfer System
e.g. exempli gratia (for example)
EHF Extremely High Frequency

EIB European Investment Bank
EIS Educational Institute of Scotland
E-Mail Electronic Mail
EMF Electro-Motive Force; European Monetary Fund
EMI Electro-Magnetic Interference
EMS European Monetary System
EMU ElectroMagnetic Unit; European Monetary Union
ENEA European Nuclear Energy Agency
ENG Electronic News Gathering
ENIAC Electronic Numerical Integrator Analyser and Computer
ENO English National Opera
ENSA Entertainments National Service Association
ENT Ear, Nose and Throat
EOC Equal Opportunities Commission
EPCOT Experimental Prototype Community Of Tomorrow
ER Elizabeth Regina
ERA Engine Room Artificer (navy)
ERM Exchange Rate Mechanism
ERNIE Electronic Random Number Indicator Equipment
EROM Erasable Read Only Memory
ESA European Space Agency
ESF European Social Fund
ESP ExtraSensory Perception
ESSO Standard Oil
et seq. et sequentia (and the following)
ETA Estimated Time of Arrival; Euzkadi Ta Askatasuna (Basque separatist organisation)
ETD Estimated Time of Departure
EU European Union
EVA ExtraVehicular Activity
EWCB England and Wales Cricket Board
E-ZINE Electronic magaZINE

FANY First Aid Nursing Yeomanry
FAO Food and Agriculture Organisation
FAP File Access Protocol
FAQ Frequently Asked Questions
Fax Facsimile transmission
FBI Federal Bureau of Investigation
FBOU Fellow of the British Ornithologists' Union
FCO Foreign and Commonwealth Office
FGS Fellow of the Geographical Society
FHS Fellow of the Heraldry Society
FIA Fellow of the Institute of Actuaries
FICE Fellow of the Institution of Civil Engineers
FIFA Fédération Internationale de Football Association
FIFO First In, First Out
FILO First In, Last Out
FIRST Fixed Interest Rate Savings Tax free
FMCG Fast Moving Consumer Goods
FOIA Freedom Of Information Act
FOREST Freedom Organisation for the Right to Enjoy Smoking Tobacco
FORTRAN Formula Translation
FRAM Fellow of the Royal Academy of Music
FRAS Fellow of the Royal Astronomical Society
FRBS Fellow of the Royal Botanical Society
FRCGP Fellow of the Royal College of General Practitioners
FRCM Fellow of the Royal College of Music
FRCOG Fellow of the Royal College of Obstetricians and Gynaecologists

A B B R E V I A T I O N S

FRCP Fellow of the Royal College of Physicians
FRHS Fellow of the Royal Horticultural Society
FTP File Transfer Protocol
FTSE Financial Times Stock Exchange
FWTK FireWall Tool Kit
FYI For Your Information

GAA Gaelic Athletic Association
GATT General Agreement on Tariffs and Trade
GBE Knight or Dame Grand Cross of the Order of the British Empire
GC George Cross
GCB Knight or Dame Grand Cross of the Order of the Bath
GCHQ Government Communications Headquarters
GCSE General Certificate of Secondary Education
GCVO Knight or Dame Grand Cross of the Royal Victorian Order
GDBA Guide Dogs for the Blind Association
GDP Gross Domestic Product
Gestapo GEheime STAatsPOlizei
GIF Graphics Interchange Format
GIFT Gamete IntraFallopian Transfer
GMB Grand Master Bowman
GMT Greenwich Mean Time
GNP Gross National Product
GNVQ General National Vocational Qualification
GPMU Graphical, Paper and Media Union
GPS Global Positioning System
GRAS Generally Regarded As Safe
GRU Glavnoye Razvedyvatelnoye Upravleniye (military counterpart of KGB in former Soviet Union)

HB Hard Black (pencil)
HBM Her / His Britannic Majesty
HCF Highest Common Factor
HDRA Henry Doubleday Research Association (Gardening)
HDTV High-Definition TeleVision
HF High Frequency
HGV Heavy Goods Vehicle
HIV Human Immunodeficiency Virus
HJ Hic Jacet (here lies, seen on gravestones)
HOLMES Home Office Large Major Enquiry System (police computer system)
HMSO Her / His Majesty's Stationery Office
HOTOL HOrizontal Take-Off and Landing
HRH Her/His Royal Highness
HSH Her / His Serene Highness
HSV Herpes Simplex Virus
HTHL Horizontal Take-Off Horizontal Landing
HTML HyperText Mark-up Language
HTTP HyperText Transfer Protocol
HTVL Horizontal Take-Off Vertical Landing
HWM High Water Mark

IATA International Air Transport Association
ib. ibidem (in the same place)
IBA International Broadcasting Authority
ibid. Ibidem (in the same place)
ICAEW Institute of Chartered Accountants of England and Wales
ICAO International Civil Aviation Organisation
ICBM InterContinental Balistic Missile
IDDS Insulin Dependent Diabetic Syndrome

i.e. id est (that is)
IFAW International Fund for Animal Welfare
IFOR Implementation FORce
IFS Institute for Fiscal Studies
IGC Inter-Governmental Conference
IGY International Geophysical Year
ILO International Labour Organisation
IMO International Maritime Organisation
INRI Iesus Nazarenus Rex Iudaeorum (Jesus of Nazareth King of the Jews)
INSET INSErvice Training
INST INSTant (current month)
INTEGRAL INTErnational Gamma-Ray Astrophysics Laboratory
INTERPOL INTERnational Criminal POLice Organisation
IOM Isle Of Man
IOTA Infrared-Optical Telescope Array; International Occultation Timing Association
IOW Isle Of Wight
IPA International Phonetic Alphabet
IQ Intelligence Quotient
IRC International Red Cross
IRS Internal Revenue Service
IRSF Inland Revenue Staff Federation
ISBN International Standard Book Number
ISH Information Super Highway
ISP Internet Service Provider
ISY International Space Year
IT Information Technology
ITA Initial Teaching Alphabet
ITC Independent Television Commission
ITU International Telecommunications Union
ITV Independent TeleVision
IV Intra Vires (within power); IntraVenous
IVF In Vitro Fertilisation
IWC International Whaling Commission

J & B Justerini and Brooks
JCR Junior Common Room
JCS Joint Chiefs of Staff
JP Justice of the Peace
JPEG Joint Photographic Experts Group
JPL Jet Propulsion Laboratory
JRDF Joint Rapid Deployment Force

KBE Knight Commander of the Order of the British Empire
KCVO Knight Commander of the Royal Victorian Order
KG Knight of the Order of the Garter
KGB Komitet Gosudarstvennoi Bezopasnosti (State Security Committee in former Soviet Union)
KT Knight of the Order of the Thistle

LACS League Against Cruel Sports
LAN Local Area Net (computer Internet)
LASER Light Amplification by Stimulated Emission of Radiation
LAUTRO Life Assurance and Unit Trust Regulatory Organisation
LBO Leveraged BuyOut
LCE London Commodities Exchange
LCJ Lord Chief Justice
LCM Lowest Common Multiple
LDOS Lord's Day Observance Society

LDV Local Defence Volunteers (Home Guard)
LED Light Emitting Diode
LEM Lunar Excursion Module
LH Liquid Hydrogen
LIDAR Light Detection And Ranging
LIFFE London International Financial Futures and options Exchange
LIFO Last In, First Out
LIFT London International Festival Theatre
LILO Last In, Last Out
LLD Doctor of Laws
LMS / LMSR London, Midland and Scottish Railway
LNER London and North Eastern Railway
LORAN Long RAnge Navigation
LOX Liquid OXygen
LSD Librae Solidi Denarii; LySergic Acid Diethylamide
LSE London School of Economics
LSO London Symphony Orchestra
LULU Locally Unacceptable Land Use
LWM Low Water Mark

M & B May and Baker (forerunner of antibiotics)
MADD Mothers Against Drunk Driving
MAFF Ministry of Agriculture Fisheries and Food
MANWEB Merseyside And North Wales Electricity Board
MASER Microwave Amplification by Stimulated Emission of Radiation
MBA Master of Business Administration
MBE Member of the Order of the British Empire
MBO Management BuyOut
MCC Marylebone Cricket Club
MCS Marine Conservation Society
ME Myalgic Encephalomyelitis (see CFS)
MEP Member of the European Parliament
MFH Master of Fox Hounds
MFN Most Favoured Nation
M. ft. mistura fiat (let a mixture be made)
MIDAS Missile Defence Alarm System
MIG Mortgage Indemnity Guarantee
MIPS Millions of Instructions Per Second
MIRAS Mortgage Income Relief At Source
MIRV Multiple Independently targeted Re-entry Vehicle
MIT Massachusetts Institute of Technology
MKS Metre Kilogram Second
MLR Minimum Lending Rate
MM Messieurs; Military Medal
MNR Marine Nature Reserve
MOBO MOther BOard; Music Of Black Origin
MOMA Museum Of Modern Art
MOMI Museum Of Moving Image
MORI Market and Opinion Research Institute
MoT Ministry of Transport
MP Member of Parliament; Military Police
MPLA Movimento Popular de Libertação de Angola (Popular Movement for the Liberation of Angola)
MPV Multi-Purpose Vehicle
MRSA Methicillin Resistant Staphylococcus Aureus
MSF Manufacturing, Science and Finance (Union)
MSP Member of Scottish Parliament
MST Mountain Standard Time
MWA Member of the Welsh Assembly
MWGM Most Worthy Grand Master (Masons)

NAACP National Association for the Advancement of Colored People
NAAFI Navy, Army, and Air Force Institutes
NACODS National Association of Colliery Overmen, Deputies and Shotfirers
NACRO National Association for the Care and Resettlement of Offenders
NAO National Audit Office
NARAS National Academy of Recording Arts and Sciences
NASA National Aeronautics and Space Administration
NASDAQ National Association of Securities Dealers Automatic Quotation
NAS / UWT National Association of Schoolmasters / Union of Women Teachers
NATO North Atlantic Treaty Organisation
NB Nota Bene (note well)
NBC National Broadcasting Company
NBL National Book League
NCCL National Council for Civil Liberties
NCDL National Canine Defence League
NCIS National Criminal Intelligence Service
NCVO National Council for Voluntary Organisations
NCVQ National Council for Vocational Qualifications
NEDC National Economic Development Council (Neddy)
NFT National Film Theatre
NFU National Farmers' Union
NGA National Graphical Association (now merged with SOGAT to form GPMU)
NHI National Health Insurance
NIDDS Non-Insulin-Dependent Diabetic Syndrome
NIMBY Not In My Back Yard
NIREX Nuclear Industry Radioactive waste EXecutive
NORWICH (K)Nickers Off Ready When I Come Home
NP Notary Public
NPT Non-Proliferation Treaty
NRA National Rifle Association; National Rivers Authority
NSPCC National Society for the Prevention of Cruelty to Children
NUCPS National Union of Civil and Public Servants (now the PCS)
NUJ National Union of Journalists
NUMAST National Union of Marine, Aviation and Shipping Transport Officers
NUS National Union of Students
NUT National Union of Teachers
NYO National Youth Orchestra
NYT National Youth Theatre

O & M Organisation and Method
OAPEC Organisation of Arab Petroleum-Exporting Countries
OAS Organisation of American States
OAU Organisation of African Unity
OBE Officer of the Order of the British Empire; Out-of-Body Experience
OBO Ore Bulk Oil (carrier)
OCR Optical Character Recognition
OECD Organisation for Economic Co-operation and Development
OED Oxford English Dictionary
OFFER OFFice of Electricity Regulation

OFGAS OFfice of GAS Supply
OFSTED OFfice for STandards in EDucation
OFTEL OFfice of TELecommunications
OFWAT Office of Water Services
OHMS On Her / His Majesty's Service
OM Order of Merit
OMOV One Member One Vote
ONO Or Near Offer
OP Opposite Prompt side (theatre); Out of Print (publishing)
OPCS Office of Population Censuses and Surveys
OPEC Organisation of Petroleum-Exporting Countries
OS Old Style; Ordnance Survey
OST Office of Science and Technology
OT Old Testament
OUDS Oxford University Dramatic Society
OXFAM OXford Committee for FAMine Relief
Oxon Oxoniensis (of Oxford)

P & O Peninsular and Oriental Steamship Company
PABX Private Automatic Branch eXchange
PACE Police And Criminal Evidence act
parSec parallax second (3.26 light-years)
PAS Power-Assisted Steering
PAYE Pay As You Earn
PBX Private Branch eXchange
PC Personal Computer; Privy Council; Police Constable; Prince Consort; Politically Correct
PCA Police Complaints Authority
PCB Printed Circuit Board
PCS Public and Commercial Services Union
PDF Portable Document File; Package Definition File
PDSA People's Dispensary for Sick Animals
PEP Personal Equity Plan
pH potential of Hydrogen ions
PIA Personal Investment Authority (replaced LAUTRO)
PIN Personal Identification Number
PIPO Parallel In, Parallel Out
Pixel Picture Element
PLA Port of London Authority
PLC Public Limited Company
PLO Palestine Liberation Organisation
PLR Public Lending Rights
PMT Pre-Menstrual Tension
PNMPB Police National Missing Persons Bureau
POS Point Of Sale
POW Prisoner Of War
PP Per Procurationem (by proxy); Parallel Port
PPS Parliamentary Private Secretary
PPV Pay Per View
pro tem. pro tempore (for the time being)
PROM Programmable Read Only Memory
PRP Profit-Related Pay
PRS Performing Rights Society
PS Post Scriptum
PSBR Public Sector Borrowing Requirement
PSDR Public Sector Debt Repayment
PSV Public Service Vehicle
PTI Physical Training Instructor
PTO Please Turn Over
PTSD Post-Traumatic Stress Disorder
PVC PolyVinylChloride

QA Quantitative Analysis; Quality Assurance
QANTAS Queensland And Northern Territory Aerial Service
QARANC Queen Alexandra's Royal Army Nursing Corps
QARNNS Queen Alexandra's Royal Naval Nursing Service
QBD Queen's Bench Division
QC Queen's Counsel; Quality Control
QED Quod Erat Demonstrandum (which was to be demonstrated)
QGM Queen's Gallantry Medal
QMG QuarterMaster General
QMV Qualified Majority Voting
QPM Queen's Police Medal
QSO Quasi-Stellar Object (quasar)
QUANGO QUasi-Autonomous Non-Governmental Organisation
qv quod vide (which see)

RAC Royal Automobile Club
RADA Royal Academy of Dramatic Art
RADAR RAdio Detection And Ranging
RAEC Royal Army Educational Corps
RAFVR Royal Air Force Voluntary Reserve
RAM Random-Access Memory
RAMC Royal Army Medical Corps
RAOC Royal Army Ordnance Corps
RAVC Royal Army Veterinary Corps
RBA Royal Society of British Artists
RC Roman Catholic; Red Cross
RCA Radio Corporation of America
RCM Royal College of Music
RCMP Royal Canadian Mounted Police
RCN Royal College of Nursing
REM Rapid Eye Movement
REME Royal Electrical and Mechanical Engineers
RFA Royal Fleet Auxiliary
RFDS Royal Flying Doctor Service
RH Relative Humidity
RHA Regional Health Authority
RHS Royal Historical / Horticultural / Humane Society
RIBA Royal Institute of British Architects
RKO Radio-Keith-Orpheum
RMT (National Union of) Rail, Maritime and Transport Workers
RNA RiboNucleic Acid
RNAS Royal Naval Air Service
RNIB Royal National Institute for the Blind
RNID Royal National Institute for the Deaf
RNLI Royal National Lifeboat Institution
RNR Royal Naval Reserve
ROC Royal Observer Corps
ROI Return On Investment
ROM Read-Only Memory
ROSPA ROyal Society for the Prevention of Accidents
RP Received Pronunciation
RPI Retail Price Index
RRP Recommended Retail Price
RSC Royal Shakespeare Company
RSI Repetitive Stress Injury
RSM Regimental Sergeant Major
RSPB Royal Society for the Protection of Birds
RSPCA Royal Society for the Prevention of Cruelty to Animals

RSV Revised Standard Version (Bible)
RSVP Répondez S'il Vous Plaît
RTE Radio Telefis Eireann
RTS Royal Television Society
RTZ Rio Tinto Zinc Corporation Ltd
RUC Royal Ulster Constabulary
RYS Royal Yacht Squadron

SA Sociedad Anónima (Spanish: limited company); Société Anonyme (French: limited company)
SAD Seasonal Affective Disorder
SAE Stamped Addressed Envelope
SAFE Saving Animals From Extinction
SALT Strategic Arms Limitation Talks
SANE Schizophrenia – A National Emergency
SARS Severe Acute Respiratory Syndrome
SAS Special Air Service
SATB Soprano, Alto, Tenor, Bass
SBS Special Boat Squadron; Sick Building Syndrome
SCM State Certified Midwife
SCO Scottish Chamber Orchestra
SCR Senior Common Room
SCREAM Society for the Control and Registration of Estate Agents and Mortgage brokers
SCUBA Self-Contained Underwater Breathing Apparatus
SDA Severe Disability Allowance
SDI Strategic Defence Initiative
SDLP Social Democratic and Labour Party
SDP Social Democratic Party
SEA Single European Act
SEC Securities Exchange Commission
SEN Special Educational Needs; State Enrolled Nurse
SERPS State Earnings-Related Pension Scheme
SETI Search for Extra-Terrestrial Intelligence
SFO Serious Fraud Office
SHAPE Supreme Headquarters Allied Powers in Europe
SHF Super High Frequency
SI Système International (of units)
SIB Securities and Investments Board
SIG Special Interest Group
SJ Society of Jesus (Jesuits)
SLBM Submarine-Launched Ballistic Missile
SLDP Social and Liberal Democratic Party
SLR Single Lens Reflex
SMMT Society of Motor Manufacturers and Traders
SMP Statutory Maternity Pay
SNAFU Situation Normal All Fouled / Fucked Up
SNCF Société Nationale des Chemins de Fer français
SNP Scottish National Party
SOGAT Society Of Graphical and Allied Trades (now merged with NGA to form GPMU)
SOM Start Of Message
SONAR SOund Navigation And Ranging
SOS Save Our Souls
SOWETO SOuth WEstern TOwnships (South Africa)
SP Sine Prole (without issue)
SPCK Society for Promoting Christian Knowledge
SPF Sun Protection Factor
SPG Special Patrol Group
SPQR Senatus PopulusQue Romanus (the Senate and People of Rome)
SRA Squash Rackets Association
SRN State Registered Nurse

SS SchutzStaffel
SSP Statutory Sick Pay
SSSI Site of Special Scientific Interest
SST SuperSonic Travel
START STrategic Arms Reduction Talks
STD Subscriber Trunk Dialling; Sexually Transmitted Disease
STOL Short TakeOff and Landing
STRIVE Society for The Preservation of Rural Industrial and Village Enterprises
STROBE Satellite TRacking Of Balloons and Emergencies
STV Single Transferable Vote
SVQ Scottish Vocational Qualification
SWALK Sealed With A Loving Kiss
SWAPO South West African People's Organisation
SWAT Special Weapons And Tactics

TA Territorial Army
TAMBA Twins And Multiple Births Association
TASS Technical, Administrative and Supervisory Section (of AUEW); Telegrafnoye Agentsvo Sovetshkovo Soyuza (news agency)
TAURUS Transfer and AUtomated Registration of Uncertified Stock
TAVR Territorial and Army Volunteer Reserve
TAVRA Territorial Auxiliary and Volunteer Reserve Association
TBA To Be Advised / Agreed / Announced / Arranged
TCCB Test and County Cricket Board
TEC Training and Enterprise Corporation
TEFL Teaching English as a Foreign Language
TELEX TELeprinter EXchange
TES Times Educational Supplement
TGWU Transport and General Workers Union
3GL Third Generation Language
TIFF Tag Image File Format (computing)
TIROS Television and InfraRed Observation Satellite
TLD Top Level Domain
TLR Twin Lens Reflex
TLS Times Literary Supplement
TM Transcendental Meditation; Trade Mark
TNT TriNitroToluene
Toc H Talbot House (Christian aid organisation)
TT Tuberculin Tested; Tourist Trophy
TUC Trades Union Congress
TVP Textured Vegetable Protein
TWAIN Technology Without Any Interesting Name
24/7 Twenty-Four Hours a Day, Seven Days a Week

UAE United Arab Emirates
UCAS Universities and Colleges Admissions Service (replaced UCCA in 1993)
UCATT Union of Construction, Allied Trades and Technicians
UCCA Universities Central Council on Admissions (replaced by UCAS in 1993)
UCLA University of California Los Angeles
UDA Ulster Defence Association
UDC Urban Development Corporation (e.g. Docklands) Urban District Council
UDI Unilateral Declaration of Independence
UDM Union of Democratic Mineworkers
UDP United Democratic Party; Ulster Democratic Party

UDR Ulster Defence Regiment
UEFA Union of European Football Associations
UFC Universities' Funding Council
UFO Unidentified Flying Object
UGC University Grants Committee
UHF Ultra High Frequency
UHT Ultra High Temperature; Ultra Heat Treatment
UKAEA United Kingdom Atomic Energy Authority
ULCC Ultra Large Crude Carrier
ULTRA Unrelated Live Transplant Regulatory Authority
UMIST University of Manchester Institute of Science and Technology
UNCTAD United Nations Conference on Trade And Development
UNESCO United Nations Educational, Scientific and Cultural Organisation
UNHCR United Nations High Commission for Refugees
UNICEF United Nations Children's Fund
UNITA União Nacional para a Independencia Total de Angola (National Union for the Total Independence of Angola)
UNITAR United Nations Institute for Training And Research
UNPROFOR United Nations Protection Force
UNRRA United Nations Relief and Rehabilitation Administration
UPC Universal Product Code
UPU Universal Postal Union
URL Uniform Resource Locator
USB Universal Serial Bus
USDAW Union of Shop, Distributive and Allied Workers
USM Unlisted Securities Market
USSR Union of Soviet Socialist Republics
UUP Ulster Unionist Party
UV Ultra Violet
UVF Ulster Volunteer Force

VASCAR Visual Average Speed Computer And Recorder
VAT Value Added Tax
VC Victoria Cross
VDU Video / Visual Display Unit
VHF Very High Frequency
VHS Video Home System
vix. vixit (she / he lived)
viz. videlicet (namely)
VLF Very Low Frequency
VLT Very Large Telescope
VOD Video On Demand
VR Virtual Reality
VRY ViceRoY
VSO Voluntary Service Overseas
VSOP Very Special Old Pale

VTOL Vertical TakeOff and Landing

WAN Wide Area Net (computer Internet)
WASP White Anglo-Saxon Protestant
WCC World Council of Churches
WDCS Whales and Dolphins Conservation Society
WEA Workers' Educational Association
WEU Western European Union
WFP World Food Programme
WFTU World Federation of Trade Unions
WHAM Winning Hearts And Minds (Vietnam propaganda slogan)
WHO World Health Organisation
WIBF Women's International Boxing Federation
WIMP Windows Icons Menus Pointing (computing); Weakly Interacting Massive Particle
WMO World Meteorological Organisation
WOMAN World Organisation for Mothers of All Nations
WORM Write Once Read Many (times)
WPBSA World Professional Billiards and Snooker Association
WRAC Women's Royal Army Corps
WRAF Women's Royal Air Force
WRNS Women's Royal Naval Service
WRP Worker's Revolutionary Party
WRVS Women's Royal Voluntary Service
WSPA World Society for the Protection of Animals
WTO World Trade Organisation
WVS Women's Voluntary Service
WWF World Wide Fund for Nature (formerly World Wildlife Fund)
WWW World Weather Watch; World Wide Web
WYSBYGI What You See Before You Get It
WYSIWYG What You See Is What You Get

YCNAC Young Conservative National Advisory Committee
YHA Youth Hostels Association
YMCA Young Men's Christian Association
YOC Young Ornithologists' Club
Y2K Year 2000
YTD Year To Date
YUPPIE Young Upwardly mobile / Urban Professional
YWCA Young Women's Christian Association

ZANU Zimbabwe African National Union
ZAPU Zimbabwe African People's Union
ZEBRA Zero-Energy Breeder-Reactor Assembly
ZEG Zero Economic Growth
ZENITH Zero-Energy NITrogen-Heated thermal reactor
ZIP Zone Improvement Plan; Zigzag In-line Package
ZPG Zero Population Growth

NB: For Internet chat-room abbreviations please see the Computer section.

ARCHITECTURE

Famous Architects

Aalto, Alvar (1898–1976)   Finnish architect and designer whose work included the Hall of Residence, Massachusetts Institute of Technology, the Finlandia Concert Hall, Helsinki and Nordic Centre in Reykjavik. He also invented bent plywood furniture in 1932.

Abercrombie, (Sir) Patrick (1879–1957)   English architect and pioneer of town planning in Britain, brother of the poet Lascelles Abercrombie. His major work was the replanning of London (County of London Plan, 1943, and Greater London Plan, 1944).

Adam, Robert (1728–92)   Scottish architect and interior designer, leader of the British Neo-Classical revival. Famous works include the interiors of Harewood House, Luton Hoo, Syon House and Osterley Park. He worked with his brother James Adam, on the Adelphi near Charing Cross, largely rebuilt in 1936.

Archer, Thomas (1668–1743)   Along with Vanbrugh and Hawksmoor, the third member of the great triumvirate of English Baroque architects. The north elevation at Chatsworth with its pilastered bow front is his best-known remaining work. Born in Tamworth, Archer's work was chiefly in ecclesiastical architecture. He designed the church of St Paul's, Deptford (1712-30), the church of St John's, Westminster (1714-28) and Birmingham Cathedral (1709-15).

Barry, (Sir) Charles (1795–1860)   British architect of the Neo-Gothic Houses of Parliament (1840–60), which were completed after his death by his son Edward Middleton Barry. Other works included the church of St Peter, Brighton; Travellers' Club, Pall Mall; the Reform Club, London; King Edward's School, Birmingham, and the Manchester Athenaeum. His fifth son Sir John Wolfe-Barry (1836–1918) was engineer of Tower Bridge and Barry Docks.

Bramante, Donato (1444–1514)   Italian High Renaissance architect, born near Urbano. Designed the new Basilica of St Peter's as well as the Belvedere courtyard, the Tempietto di S Pietro in Montorio and the Palazzo Caprini.

Brown, Lancelot (1716–83)   English landscape-gardener and architect, nicknamed 'Capability' due to his stock reply to clients that their gardens had 'excellent capabilities'. Works include the gardens at Blenheim, Kew, Stowe, and Warwick Castle.

Brunel, Isambard Kingdom (1806–59)   English engineer and inventor, born in Portsmouth, son of Sir Marc Isambard Brunel. His numerous works include the original Thames Tunnel, Clifton and Hungerford Suspension Bridges, and the Saltash Bridge over the Tamar. His ship designs include the *Great Western* (1838), the *Great Britain* (1845) and the *Great Eastern*, in collaboration with John Scott Russell.

Chambers, (Sir) William (1723–96)   Swedish-born, Scottish architect. He popularised Chinese influence (Kew Garden pagoda) and designed Somerset House, London (1776).

Cockerell, Charles Robert   (1788–1863)   English architect, son of Samuel Pepys Cockerell. He designed the Taylorian Institute at Oxford, Fitzwilliam Museum at Cambridge, and Ashmolean Museum, Oxford.

Foster, Norman (Lord Foster of Thames Bank) (1935–)   British architect of the high-tech school. His best-known buildings include the Willis Faber office, Ipswich (1975), the Sainsbury Centre for the visual arts, Norwich (1978), and the Hong Kong and Shanghai Bank, Hong Kong (1986).

Fuller, Richard Buckminster (1895–1983)   American architect who invented the Geodesic Dome. Examples of his works are at the Union Tank Car Repair Shop, Louisiana (1958), and the US Pavilion, Montreal Exhibition (1967).

Gaudí, Antonio (1852–1926)   Spanish architect, noted for his flamboyant style. His work on the Church of the Holy Family in Barcelona begun in 1883 was unfinished at his death.

Gibbs, James (1682–1754)   Scottish Neo-Classical architect whose works include St Martin-in-the-Fields, London (1722), and the Radcliffe Camera, Oxford (1737).

Hawksmoor, Nicholas (1661–1736)   English Baroque architect born in Nottingham. He designed many London churches including St George's, Bloomsbury, and Christ Church, Spitalfields. Assisted Vanbrugh at Blenheim Palace and Castle Howard and was clerk to Wren.

Jones, Inigo (1573–1652)   English architect, born in London. The founder of Classical English architecture whose innovations include the introduction of the proscenium arch and movable scenery to the English stage. In 1616 he designed the Queen's House at Greenwich. Other commissions included the rebuilding of the Banqueting Hall at Whitehall, the nave and transepts and a large Corinthian portico of old St Paul's, Marlborough Chapel, the Double-Cube room at Wilton, and possibly the York Water Gate. Jones also laid out Covent Garden and Lincoln's Inn Fields.

Kent, William (1684–1748)   Born in Yorkshire. After studying painting in Rome became a leading light in the introduction of the Palladian style of architecture into Britain. He designed many public buildings in London, including the Royal Mews in Trafalgar Square, the Treasury buildings and the Horse Guards block in Whitehall (1745). An example of his gardens is at Stowe House in Buckinghamshire and his artistry is visible in the Gothic screens at Westminster Hall and Gloucester Cathedral. He also designed the interiors of Burlington House and Chiswick House in London.

Lasdun, (Sir) Denys Louis (1914–2001)   English architect whose works include the Royal College of Physicians, London; University of East Anglia, Norwich; National Theatre, London; and the European Investment Bank in Luxembourg.

Le Corbusier (1887–1965)   Pseudonym of Charles Édouard Jeanneret, Swiss-born French architect, famous for his proclamation that the house is a habitable machine to be designed to functional criteria. His works include the Palace of the Nations, Geneva; and Cité Radieuse, Marseilles; as well as the town plan for Chandigarh, India.

Lutyens, (Sir) Edwin Landseer (1869–1944)   English architect whose designs ranged from the picturesque of his early country houses, including

Marsh Court, Stockbridge, and the restoration of Lindisfarne Castle, which owed much to the Arts and Crafts movement, to those in the Renaissance style such as Heathcote, Ilkley and Salutation, Sandwich. He finally evolved a classical style exhibited in the Cenotaph, Whitehall, which reached its height in his design – never built – for Liverpool Roman Catholic Cathedral. Other works include the Viceroy's House, New Delhi, and the British Embassy in Washington.

Mackintosh, Charles Rennie (1868–1928)   Scottish architect, designer, and water colourist. Outstanding exponent of the Art Nouveau style in Scotland. Born in Glasgow, the son of a police superintendent, he married Margaret Mackintosh in 1900. His output included the Glasgow School of Art, Cranston tearooms, and houses such as Hill House in Helensburgh. By the end of World War I he had given up architecture for a career in water colours, mainly in France.

Mies Van Der Rohe, Ludwig (1886–1969)   German-born American architect, born in Aachen. A pioneer of glass skyscrapers and high-rise flats, he also designed tubular-steel furniture, particularly the 'Barcelona Chair'. Became professor of architecture at the Illinois Institute of Technology in Chicago and designed two glass apartment towers on Lake Shore Drive, and the Seagram Building in New York. He also designed the Washington DC Public Library and two art galleries in Berlin.

Nash, John (1752–1835)   British architect who designed Regent's Park and its terraces, Regent Street and Marble Arch. He also recreated Buckingham Palace from old Buckingham House and rebuilt Brighton Pavilion in oriental style. Trafalgar Square and St James's Park were also laid out by Nash.

Paxton, (Sir) Joseph (1801–65)   British architect and garden superintendent to the Duke of Devonshire. By far his most famous work was the design of the Great Exhibition Building of 1851, the Crystal Palace, the first example of a prefabricated industrialised building on a large scale.

Pei, Ieoh Meng (1917–)   Chinese-born American architect whose works include the John Hancock Tower, Boston; the Mile High Center, Denver and the glass pyramid at the Louvre.

Rogers, Richard (Lord Rogers of Riverside) (1933–) Florence-born British architect whose works include the Pompidou Centre in Paris (1977) and the Lloyd's building, London (1986). Founder member with Norman Foster and their wives of 'Team 4'.

Saarinen, Eero (1910–61)   Finnish-born American architect whose works include the American Embassy in London and Dulles Airport near Washington DC.

Scott, (Sir) George Gilbert (1811–78)   English architect, born in Gawcott, Bucks. His works include the Albert Memorial, St Pancras station, and the Episcopal Cathedral in Edinburgh.

Scott, (Sir) Giles Gilbert (1880–1960)   English architect, grandson of Sir George Gilbert Scott. Won a competition in 1903 for the design of the Anglican Cathedral in Liverpool (consecrated 1924). Other works include the new Bodleian Library at Oxford and the new Cambridge University Library. He also planned the new Waterloo Bridge and was responsible for the rebuilding of the House of Commons after World War II.

Shaw, Norman (1831–1912)   English architect born in Edinburgh. Worked with his partner William Eden

Nesfield (1835–88) in many styles ranging from Gothic Revival to Neo-Baroque, but became an acknowledged leader in the trend away from the Victorian style back to traditional Georgian design, leading to the English Domestic Revival. His major buildings include the Old Swan House, Chelsea (1876), New Scotland Yard (1888), the Gaiety Theatre, Aldwych (1902, now demolished), and Piccadilly Hotel (1905). He also designed the garden suburb at Bedford Park, London.

Smirke, (Sir) Robert (1781–1867)   English architect, son of Robert Smirke (1752–1845) the painter and book illustrator. His works in London include Covent Garden Theatre (destroyed), British Museum, King's College and the Royal College of Physicians (now Canada House).

Soane, (Sir) John (1753–1837)   English architect, born near Reading, the son of a mason. His works included the Bank of England, the Dulwich Picture Gallery and his own house in Lincoln's Inn Fields, London which he bequeathed to the nation.

Spence, (Sir) Basil Urwin (1907–76)   Scottish architect, born in India. His works include the conversions at Queen's College, Cambridge; the pavilions for the Festival of Britain and the British Embassy in Rome. His best-known work is his prize design for the new Coventry Cathedral (1951).

Sullivan, Louis (1856–1924)   Architect born in Boston, Massachusetts but studied in Paris. Won the New Exposition building contract (1886) with Dankmar Adler (1844–1900). Sullivan was an early pioneer of the skyscraper: e.g. the Wainwright building in St Louis (1891). His experimental, functional skeleton constructions of skyscrapers and office blocks, particularly the Stock Exchange, Chicago, earned him the title 'Father of Modernism'.

Tange, Kenzo (1913–)   Japanese architect who designed the National Gymnasium for the Tokyo Olympics and the city plan for the new Nigerian capital of Abuja (completed 1986).

Utzon, Jorn (1918 –)   Danish architect born in Copenhagen. Came to prominence after winning a competition to design Sydney Opera House in 1956. The building, completed between 1957 and 1973, is one of the most famous landmarks of the 20th century. Other works include the Municipal Theatre in Zurich (1964) and the Kuwait Parliamentary Building (1983). His awards include the gold medal of the Royal Institute of British Architects (1978), the Alvar Aalto medal (1982) and the Fritz Schumacher prize (1988).

Vanbrugh, (Sir) John (1664–1726)   English playwright and Baroque architect, born in London, the son of a tradesman. Educated in France and commissioned into Lord Huntingdon's regiment, he suffered imprisonment in the Bastille as a suspected spy. His major architectural work was Blenheim Palace at Woodstock, Oxfordshire, which was so disliked by the Duchess of Marlborough that she refused to pay him for some time.

Wilkins, William (1778–1839)   Son of an architect, he was educated at Cambridge and established a reputation as an enthusiastic Greek revivalist with the publication of his *Antiquities of Magna Graecia*. In London he built St George's Hospital at Hyde Park Corner (1827–8) and the National Gallery in Trafalgar Square (1832).

Wren, Christopher (1632–1723)   Wren was educated at Westminster School and Wadham College, Oxford, and became a fellow of All Souls, Oxford. He became professor of astronomy at

Gresham College, London, 1657, before returning to Oxford to take up a similar position. The chapel at Pembroke College, Cambridge, 1663, was the first design of Wren's to be built and later that year he began designs for Sheldonian Theatre at Oxford. Following the Great Fire he designed over 50 London churches including St Paul's (1675–1710). Other works included the Ashmolean Museum at Oxford, Chelsea Hospital, Greenwich Observatory, parts of Hampton Court Palace, Royal Exchange, and parts of the Royal Naval College, Greenwich. Wren was a founder of the Royal Society, was knighted in 1673, and became MP for Plympton in 1685, Windsor in 1689, and finally, Weymouth in 1701.

Wright, Frank Lloyd (1867–1959)   American architect, born in Richland Center, Wisconsin. Studied civil engineering at Wisconsin University, but the collapse of a newly-built wing of the Wisconsin

State Capitol caused him to apply engineering principles to architecture. After setting up in practice in Chicago he became known for low-built prairie-style bungalows like Robie House. His best-known public buildings include the Imperial Hotel in Tokyo (1916–20), the 'Falling Water' weekend retreat at Mill Run in Pennsylvania (1936), the Johnson Wax office block in Racine, Wisconsin (1936), Florida Southern College (1940) and the Guggenheim Museum of Art in New York (1959), in which the exhibits line the walls of a continuous spiral ramp.

Wyatt, James (1746–1813)   Born in Staffordshire, he closely followed the style of Robert Adam in his early days, so much so that Adam accused him of plagiarism. Wyatt won a competition to redesign the Pantheon in Oxford Street (1772) and his reputation was made. Fonthill Abbey in Wiltshire displays the extravagant Gothic Revival country house he built for William Thomas Beckford.

Architectural Terms

Abacus   The top member of a capital, usually a square or rounded slab of stone or marble

Acanthus   Conventionalised acanthus leaf used to decorate Corinthian and Composite capitals

Adobe   Sun-dried brick mainly of clay; also the name of buildings constructed of such bricks

Architrave   Lowest part of an entablature, resting immediately upon the abacus (flat slab) on the capital of a column. The term also describes the moulding around the exterior of an arch or the various parts surrounding a door or window

Art Deco   Popular design style of the 1920s and at its height in the 1930s, characterised by geometrical shapes, bold outlines and zigzag forms

Ashlar   Hewn and squared stones prepared for building

Astragal   Small convex moulding usually with a semi-circular cross-section

Atrium   Inner courtyard of a home or other building that is open to the sky or covered by a skylight

Baluster   Short post or pillar in a series that supports a rail, thus forming a balustrade

Bauhaus   German school of architecture and design founded by Walter Gropius in 1919 and closed in 1933

Bay, bow and oriel windows   These windows project out from the front or side of a house. Oriel windows generally project from an upper storey, supported by a bracket. Bay windows are angled projections that rise up from the ground on the first floor. Bow windows are rounded projections, often formed of the window glass itself

Brickwork: Types   English Bond: Bricklaying with alternate courses of headers and stretchers. Flemish Bond: Bricklaying with courses of alternate headers and stretcher. Monk Bond: Bricklaying with courses alternating with pairs of stretchers

Buildings, New   Bridgewater Hall, Manchester: International concert hall opened in September 1996. Experimental Office Building for Building Research Establishment, Garston, near Watford, Herts: latest addition to the BRE site. River and Rowing Museum, Henley, Oxfordshire: opened in 1997. St Barnabas Church, Dulwich, London: rebuilding of Victorian church destroyed by fire in 1992. Waterfront Hall, Lanyon Place, Laganside

Belfast: conference centre opened 17 Jan 1997. Greater London Authority Headquarters, Southwark, London, opened by The Queen on 23 July 2002 and designed by Foster and Partners

Buttress   Structure of wood, stone or brick built against a wall to strengthen or support it

Campanile   A free-standing bell-tower

Cantilever   Horizontal projection from a building, such as a step, beam, balcony or canopy, that is without external bracing and appears self-supporting

Capital   Head of a column, usually featuring mouldings or carvings

Cartouche   Scroll-shaped ornament or corbel. Term also describes a tablet representing a scroll with rolled-up ends or edges, with or without an inscription

Caryatid   Female figure used as a pillar to support an entablature

Clerestory   Row of windows in the upper part of the wall of a church that divides the nave from the aisle, set above the aisle roof

Column   Tall, often slightly tapering, cylinder usually surmounted by an entablature and forming part of an arcade or colonnade, or standing alone as a monument

Console   Ornamental flat-sided bracket or corbel, usually incorporating a volute at each end

Corbel   Projection of stone or timber jutting out from a wall to support weight

Corinthian Column   One of the five classical orders of architecture, characterised by a bell-shaped capital having carved ornamental decorations of acanthus leaves

Cornice   Horizontal, usually moulded projection crowning the outside of a building or structure, especially the uppermost part of an entablature, above the frieze. Term also applies to an ornamental moulding running round the wall of a room near the ceiling

Cupola   Rounded vault or dome forming part of a roof of a building. Term also describes the ceiling of a dome

Curtain Wall   External non-loadbearing wall composed of repeated modular elements generally of glass in metal framing. These are prefabricated then erected on site.

Cyma   Moulding in a section of two contrasting curves, either cyma recta or cyma reversa

ARCHITECTURE

Dado   The plain portion of a pedestal between the base and the cornice. Term also describes the lower part of an interior wall when faced or coloured differently from the upper part

Dome: Geodesic   Invented by Richard Buckminster Fuller, the geodesic dome, built with lightweight rods arranged as linked hexagons, is the only practical kind of building that has no limiting dimensions, i.e. beyond which the structural strength must be insufficient

Doric Column   Greek-style column with only a simple decoration around the top, usually a smooth or slightly rounded band of wood, stone or plaster

Dormer Window   Window placed vertically in a sloping roof that has a tiny roof of its own. Most often seen in second-floor bedrooms

Ell   Single-storey extension to a building, usually at right angles

Engaged Column   Column that is attached to the wall so that only a half to three-quarters of its circumference stands visible

Entablature   The part of a classical temple above the columns, having an architrave, a frieze, and a cornice

Fanlight   Fan-shaped window over a door or other window

Flute   Vertical channelling in the shaft of a column

Flying Buttress   Buttress, usually on an arch, which slants upwards to a wall from a pier or other support

Frieze   Central member of the classical entablature

Gable   Triangular upper portion of a wall at the end of a pitched roof

Gargoyle   Grotesque carving, usually in the form of a human or real or fantastic animal mouth, head, or body projecting from the gutter of a building, especially in Gothic architecture, and used as a spout to drain off rainwater

Gazebo   Building or structure that commands a view, i.e. a summer-house or balcony

Gothic   Style of architecture prevalent in western Europe from the 12th to the 16th century, of which familiar features include the pointed arch and the flying buttress

Greek Orders   The three original classical orders of architecture, i.e. Doric, Ionic and Corinthian

Groin   The edge formed by the intersection of two vaults. Term also describes an arch supporting a vault

Hammerbeam   Horizontal beam in timber roof situated as a tie beam but in two sections with main opening in the centre

Hypocaust   Hollow space under the floor where hot air was sent from a furnace to provide heating in Roman houses

Keystone   The wedge-shaped block or central voussoir at the summit of an arch built of stone

Kouros   Sculptured representation of a youth on Ionic architecture

Lancet   High, narrow window with a lancet arch

Lancet Arch   An arch with a head resembling the blade of a lancet (surgical knife)

Lintel   Horizontal stone slab or timber beam spanning an opening and supported on columns or walls

Loggia   Covered area on the side of a building that opens on one or more sides

Lunette   Semicircular panel, often ornamented in the form of stone, wood or glass

Mansard   Roof in which each face has two slopes, the lower one steeper than the upper

Mezzanine   Low storey between two others in a building, usually between the ground floor and the floor above. Term also describes the floor beneath the stage in a theatre, from which the traps are worked

Mullion   Vertical bar dividing the lights in a window, especially in Gothic architecture

Niche   Artificially constructed wall recess often holding a statue or urn

Ogee   Moulding consisting of a continuous double curve, especially with the upper part concave and the lower part convex

Ogee Arch   Arch formed by two contrasted ogees which meet at its apex, often called a pointed or Gothic arch

Ogive   The diagonal groin or rib of a vault, two of which cross each other at the vault's centre; or any pointed arch

Oriel   Porch or balcony at the head of an outdoor staircase

Oriel Window   Large polygonal recess with a window, projecting from upper storey of a building, and supported from the ground or on corbels

Palladian Window   A window with three openings, the central one arched and wider than the others

Pediment   Triangular part crowning the front of a building in the classical style, usually situated over a portico and consisting of a flat recessed field, framed by a cornice and often ornamented with sculptures

Pergola   Covered walk in a garden, usually formed by a double row of posts or pillars with joists above and covered by climbing plants

Pier   Solid support designed to sustain vertical pressure, e.g. a doorpost or gatepost; also a massive supporting column, holding up a nave or a bridge

Porte-cochere   Large covered entrance for vehicles leading into a courtyard

Portico   Formal entrance to a classical temple, church, or other building, consisting of columns at regular intervals supporting a roof often in the form of a pediment, a covered walkway

Porticus   Addition on north or south side of a church of the Anglo-Saxon period, resembling an aisle or transept and containing a chapel

Prefabrication   The manufacture of whole buildings or components cast in a factory or on site before being placed in position

Purlin   Horizontal beam along the length of a roof, resting on principals (pairs of angled supporting beams that meet at the top) and supporting the common rafters

Quoin   Dressed stones at the corners of a building

Rib   A curved member supporting a vault or defining its form. The term also describes the curved pieces of stone, timber or metal strips forming the framework of a dome or the arched or flat beam or girder supporting a bridge

Roman Orders   The two classical orders of architecture, i.e. Tuscan and Composite, which were added to the earlier Greek orders

Rotunda   Building with a circular interior and plan, especially one with a dome, e.g. the Pantheon in Rome

Rustication   Style of masonry in which the surface of the blocks is roughened. Rustication also refers to masonry cut in massive blocks separated from each other by deep joints

Soffit   Underside of any architectural element such as an arch, beam or stair

Spandrel Originally, a space between timbers supporting a building, but now refers to the almost triangular space between one side of the outer curve of an arch and the rectangle formed by the mouldings enclosing it. The term also applies to the area of support between a set of steps and the ground

Stucco Fine plaster usually made from gypsum and pulverised marble, for covering walls and ceilings

Stupa Domed structure erected as a Buddhist burial mound

Styles Regency, Baroque, Palladian, Rococo, International

Telamon Male figure used as a pillar to support an entablature or other structure

Terrazzo Floor or wall finish made by setting marble or other stone chips into a layer of mortar and polishing the surface

Tracery Ornamentation in the upper part of a Gothic window, consisting of a perforated design or of an intersecting pattern, formed by the elaboration of the mullions. Tracery also refers to the interlaced work of a vault or panel

Transom Horizontal supporting or strengthening crossbar in any structure but usually refers to a window frame

Tuscan Order Simplest of the five classical orders of architecture, resembling the Doric, but devoid of all ornaments

Tympanum Triangular space between the sloping and horizontal cornices of a classical pediment

Vault Continuous arch, or a series of arches radiating from a central point or line, used to form a roof over a space inside a building

Venetian Window Composite window with three separate openings, the central one being arched and taller than the others

Volute Spiral scroll characteristic of Ionic capitals and also used in Corinthian and Composite capitals

Voussoir Each of the wedge-shaped or tapered stones forming an arch or vaulting

Wainscoting Decorative panelling applied to the lower half of an interior wall; usually wood in a plain design but may be painted

Wattle-and-Daub Walling made from vertical timber stakes woven horizontally with branches and reeds. The whole is then surfaced with mud

Wonders of the World: Ancient Colossus of Rhodes: bronze statue of Apollo erected c 280 BC; Hanging Gardens of Babylon: adjoining Nebuchadnezzar's palace 60 miles south of Baghdad; Pharos of Alexandria: lighthouse erected c 270 BC; Pyramids of Gizeh (Giza) near Cairo: Zoser, at Saqqara built c 2650 BC; Cheops built c 2580 BC (both still standing); Statue of Zeus: marble statue, built by Phidias c 430 BC, in the plains of Elis, Olympia; Temple of Artemis at Ephesus: Ionic temple built c 350 BC and burned by the Goths in AD 262; Tomb of Mausolus at Halicarnassus: built by the widowed Queen Artemisia c 350 BC

Wonders of the World: Modern The seven modern wonders of the world are the Colosseum of Rome; Catacombs of Alexandria; Great Wall of China; Stonehenge; Leaning Tower of Pisa; Porcelain Tower of Nanking; Mosque of St Sophia at Constantinople

ARCHITECTURE

ART

Famous Artists

Abbate, Niccolo dell' (c1512–71)   Italian Mannerist landscapist.
Selected work: *Rape of Proserpine* (Louvre, Paris).

Albers, Josef (1888–1976)   German Bauhaus painter who founded the American Bauhaus in 1933 and took US citizenship in 1939.
Selected work: *Homage to the Square* series (Museum of Modern Art, New York).

Alma-Tadema, (Sir) Lawrence (1836–1912)   Dutch-born British painter of Classical genre paintings.
Selected works: *The Visit* (Victoria and Albert Museum, London); *Pheidias and the Frieze of the Parthenon, Athens* (Birmingham City Gallery).

Altdorfer, Albrecht (c1480–1538)   German landscape painter and engraver, a pioneer of copperplate etching.
Selected work: *Landscape with a Bridge* (National Gallery, London); *St George* (Alte Pinakothek, Munich).

Andrea del Sarto (1486–1530)   Florentine High Renaissance painter. His original name was Andrea D'Agnolo, but his father's family (from Lanfranchi) were tailors, hence del Sarto.
Selected works: *Madonna of the Harpies* (Uffizi, Florence); *St John the Baptist* (Pitti Palace, Florence); *A Young Man* (National Gallery, London).

Angelico, Fra (c1387–1455)   Florentine religious painter and Dominican (monastic name Giovanni da Fiesole).
Selected works: *Annunciation* (Convent of San Marco, Florence); *St Lawrence Receiving the Treasure of the Church* (Vatican Museum, Rome).

Antonello da Messina (c1430–79)   Sicilian Renaissance landscapist and master of the oil-painting rather than tempera.
Selected works: *St Sebastian* (Gemäldegalerie, Dresden); *Salvator Mundi* his first dated work (1465); *A Man* (both National Gallery, London).

Appel, Karel (1921–)   Dutch Abstract Expressionist who founded the CoBrA group.
Selected work: *The Horseman* (Stedelijk Van Abbe-Museum, Eindhoven).

Avercamp, Hendrick (1585–1634)   Deaf and dumb Dutch landscapist who specialised in winter scenes.
Selected works: *Ice Skating in a Village* (Rijksmuseum Kröller-Müller, Otterlo); *Winter Landscape with Ice Skaters* (Rijksmuseum, Amsterdam); *Winter Scene* (National Gallery, London).

Bacon, Francis (1909–92)   Dublin-born figurative painter, influenced by Surrealism and violent imagery; studied under Graham Sutherland. A good collection of his work is in the Tate Gallery, London, including *Three Studies for a Crucifixion*.
Selected work: triptych inspired by the *Oresteia* trilogy of Aeschylus (Scottish National Gallery of Modern Art, Edinburgh).

Baldung (aka Grien), Hans (1484–1545)   German religious painter of the macabre.
Selected works: *A Man* (National Gallery, London); *Allegorical Figure* (Alte Pinakothek, Munich).

Balla, Giacomo (1871–1958)   Italian Futurist who signed the Futurist Manifesto (1910) but by 1930 adopted a more conventional style of painting.
Selected work: *Dynamism of a Dog on a Leash* (Museum of Modern Art, New York).

Barocci, Federico (1530–1612)   Religious painter from Urbino who developed a very personal colour scheme of vivid reds and yellows.
Selected works: *The Circumcision* (Louvre, Paris); *Madonna of the Rosary* (Ashmolean Museum, Oxford); *Ecce Homo* (Pinacoteca di Brera, Milan).

Bassano, Jacopo (c1510/17–92)   Italian Mannerist and specialist in religious scenes. An important collection of his works and those of his followers is in the Museo Civico, Bassano del Grappa.
Selected works: *The Holy Family* (Castle Howard, North Yorkshire); *The Adoration of the Magi* (National Gallery of Scotland, Edinburgh); *The Good Samaritan* (National Gallery, London).

Beardsley, Aubrey Vincent (1872–98)   English illustrator, born in Brighton. Became famous for his fantastic posters and illustrations for *Morte d'Arthur*, Wilde's *Salome*, *Pope's Rape of the Lock*, as well as for the *Yellow Book* magazine (1894–6) and his own *Book of Fifty Drawings*. With Wilde he is regarded as leader of the 'Decadents' of the 1890s. Died of TB at Menton, France, having embraced Catholicism.

Beckmann, Max (1884–1950)   German Expressionist figurative painter and draughtsman who emigrated to the USA in 1947.
Selected work: *Night* (Kunstsammlung Nordrhein-Westfalen, Düsseldorf).

Bellini Family (fifteenth-century)   Jacopo (c1400–70) was founder of Venetian Renaissance art. His sons were Gentile (1429–1507), a portrait and panorama painter, and Giovanni (c1430–1516), the first Renaissance master of Venetian art, who taught both Giorgione and Titian.
Selected works (Giovanni):   *Descent into Limbo* (City of Bristol Art Gallery); *Doge Leonardo Loredan* (National Gallery, London); *Pietà* (Brera, Milan).

Bellotto, Bernardo (1720–80)   Venetian topographical artist, nephew of Canaletto. Painted a masterly interior of King's College Chapel, Cambridge.
Selected work: *View of Dresden* (Gemäldegalerie, Dresden).

Bernini, Gian Lorenzo (1598–1680)   Italian sculptor, architect and painter, born in Naples. Patronised by Cardinal Scipione Borghese. He designed the monumental baldacchino (choir canopy) for Saint Peter's in the Vatican. Although frequently used by Pope Urban VIII he was less popular with Innocent X, who preferred Alessandro Algardi. His most famous works include the Cornaro Chapel in the church of Santa Maria della Vittoria, the tomb of Alexander VII in Saint Peter's and the small Jesuit church of San Andrea al Quirinale, all in Rome. He was buried in Rome in the church of Santa Maria Maggiore.

Bewick, Thomas (1753–1828)   English wood engraver, born a farmer's son in Ovingham, Northumberland. His *History of British Birds* (1797–1804) was his masterpiece and the Bewick's Swan was named in his honour shortly after his death.

Blake, Peter (1932–) British Pop artist during the 1960s and now more conventional.

Selected work: *Toy Shop* (Tate Gallery, London).

Blake, William (1757–1827) English Romantic painter, poet and visionary.

Selected works: 20 illustrations to Dante's *Divine Comedy* (Tate Gallery, London); *Heads of the Poets* (18 pictures) (Manchester City Art Gallery); *The Circle of the Lustful* (Birmingham City Art Gallery).

Bonington, Richard Parkes (1802–28) English topographical watercolourist.

Selected work: *View of Normandy* (Tate Gallery, London).

Bonnard, Pierre (1867–1947) French landscape painter who also specialised in domestic scenes. Bonnard joined the Nabis, who included Denis and Vuillard, with whom he formed the Intimiste group.

Selected work: *Women with a Dog* (Phillips Collection, Washington DC).

Bosch, Hieronymus (c1450–1516) Netherlandish painter of the macabre and master of fantasy.

Selected works: *The Ship of Fools* (Louvre, Paris); *Christ Mocked* (National Gallery, London); altarpiece *The Garden of Earthly Delights* (Prado, Madrid).

Botticelli, Sandro (1445–1510) Florentine Renaissance allegorical painter with distinctive linear style.

Selected works: *Mars and Venus* (National Gallery, London); *La Primavera*; *The Birth of Venus* (both Uffizi, Florence).

Boucher, François (1703–70) French Rococo court painter and decorator to Louis XV; also director of the famous French tapestry workshop the Gobelins.

Selected works: *Diana after her Bath* (Louvre, Paris); *Reclining Girl* (Alte Pinakothek, Munich); *Madame de Pompadour* (Wallace Collection, London).

Boudin, Eugène Louis (1824–98) French 'plein-airiste', painting in particular the fashionable French resorts of Trouville and Deauville in the 1860s. Collections of his work are in the Musée de Doctor Faure, Aix-les-Bains, and the Musée des Beaux-Arts Jules Chéret, Nice.

Selected works: *Deauville* (Tate Gallery, London); *Harbour of Trouville* (National Gallery, London); *Corvette Russe* (Luxembourg, Paris); *Beach Scene* (Leeds Castle, Kent).

Brancusi, Constantin (1876–1957) Romanian sculptor, born in Pestisani, near Turgujiu. In his youth he was a shepherd boy in the Carpathians. Brancusi worked in Rodin's atelier and produced his *The Kiss* (1908) 22 years after Rodin's. His *Sleeping Muse* (1910) also shows Rodin's influence, but is the first of his characteristic highly polished egg-shaped carvings. The *Prodigal Son* (1925) shows the influence of African sculpture. Brancusi was a pioneer of modern abstract sculpture.

Selected works: *Adam and Eve*; *Flying Turtle* (both Guggenheim Museum, New York).

Brangwyn, Sir Frank (1867–1956) Welsh painter, initially apprenticed to the Socialist designer William Morris. He presented a collection of his work to the city of Bruges in 1936 which is now housed in the Brangwyn Museum, and there is a substantial collection in the McManus Gallery, Dundee, and Brangwyn Hall, Swansea.

Selected work: *British Empire Panels* (Swansea Guildhall).

Braque, Georges (1882–1963) French pioneer of Cubism, with Picasso, who designed scenes for two Diaghilev ballets, *Les Fâcheux* and *Zéphyr et Flore*. Braque was a Grand Officier of the Légion d'Honneur and was awarded an honorary doctorate by Oxford University in 1956. He was the first man to have his work exhibited in the Louvre during his lifetime.

Selected works: *Still Life* (Musée National d'Art Moderne, Paris); *Still Life with Playing Cards* (Rijksmuseum Kröller-Müller, Otterlo); *The Woman Musician* (Kunstmuseum, Basel); *The Candlestick* (Scottish National Gallery of Modern Art, Edinburgh).

Bronzino, Agnolo (1503–72) Florentine Mannerist and portraitist.

Selected works: *Noli Me Tangere* (Louvre, Paris); *Venus, Cupid, Folly and Time* (National Gallery, London); *Portrait of Don Garzia de Medici* (Ashmolean Museum, Oxford); *Eleanora da Toledo with Her Son*; *Christ in Limbo* (both Uffizi, Florence).

Brouwer, Adriaen (c1605–38) Flemish-born low-life painter who studied at Haarlem under Frans Hals and is regarded as 'culturally' Dutch, although eventually settling in Antwerp, where he died of the plague.

Selected works: *A Boor Asleep* (Wallace Collection, London); *Interior of an Alehouse* (Dulwich Picture Gallery, London); *Man with a Pointed Hat* (Museum Boymans-van Beuningen, Rotterdam).

Brown, Ford Madox (1821–93) French-born British painter associated with Pre-Raphaelites and William Morris in particular. He completed twelve frescoes for Manchester Town Hall, just before his death. His most famous picture, *Work,* was first exhibited at a retrospective exhibition held in London but is now hung in Manchester. Brown was the early tutor of Dante Gabriel Rossetti.

Selected work: *The Last of England* (Birmingham Museum & Art Gallery).

Brueghel, Jan (1568–1625) Flemish landscape and flower painter; son of 'Peasant' Brueghel.

Selected works: *The Tower of Babel* (Koninklijk Museum voor Schone Kunsten, Antwerp); *Still Life with Garland of Flowers* (Musées Royaux des Beaux Arts, Brussels); *Vase of Flowers* (Ashmolean Museum, Oxford).

Brueghel the Elder, Pieter (c1520–69) Flemish allegorical and religious painter, nicknamed 'Peasant' Brueghel.

Selected works: *Adoration of the Magi* (National Gallery, London); *Peasant Dance* (Kunsthistorisches Museum, Vienna).

Brueghel the Younger (c1564–1638) Flemish painter nicknamed 'Hell' because he painted scenes of diablerie; son of Pieter 'Peasant' Brueghel.

Burne-Jones, Sir Edward Coley (1833–98) British painter associated with Pre-Raphaelites and the Arts and Crafts Movement.

Selected works: *Perseus* series (Southampton Art Gallery); *The Legend of the Briar Rose* series (Buscot Park, Oxfordshire); *King Cophetua and the Beggar Maid* (Tate Gallery, London).

Canaletto, Antonio (1697–1768) Venetian topographical artist who was the uncle of Bellotto. Canaletto was associated with his views of London and Venice, where the entrepreneur Joseph Smith was responsible for popularising his work.

Selected works: *View of the Grand Canal, Venice* (Uffizi, Florence); *View of the City of London from Richmond House* (Goodwood House, Sussex); *Stonemason's Yard* (National Gallery, London).

Caravaggio, Michelangelo Merisi da (c1573–1610) Italian Baroque painter who specialised in painting chiaroscuro. He fled Rome in 1606 after killing a man and spent the rest of his life as a refugee, moving between Naples, Sicily and Malta.

Selected works: *The Young Bacchus* (Uffizi, Florence); *Beheading of St John* (Cathedral of St John, Valletta, Malta); *Supper at Emmaus* (National Gallery, London).

(Sir) Anthony Caro (1924–) English sculptor. Assistant to Henry Moore between 1951 and 1953 and specialising in clay figures. From 1953 he was influenced by the American sculptor David Smith and began to use steel as his medium. He was knighted in 1987.

Selected works: *The Tower of Discovery* (Tate Gallery, London).

Carpaccio, Vittore (c1450–1525) Venetian early Renaissance religious painter. His most characteristic work is seen in the nine subjects from the life of St Ursula, and in his masterpiece, *the Presentation in the Temple*, both now in the Accademia, Venice.

Selected works: *The Preaching of St Stephen* (Louvre, Paris); *Courtesans* (Civico Museo Correr, Venice).

Carrà, Carlo (1881–1966) Italian Futurist who founded the Metaphysical School with de Chirico in 1917.

Carracci, Annibale (1560–1609) Most important of the family of Bolognese Mannerists.

Selected works: *The Butcher's Shop* (Christchurch Picture Gallery, Oxford); *Bacchus and Silenus* (National Gallery, London); *Coronation of the Virgin* (Staatliche Museen, Berlin).

Castagno, Andrea del (c1420–57) Florentine Early Renaissance fresco painter.

Selected works: *Dante* (Convent of S. Apollonia, Florence); *The Youthful David* (National Gallery of Art, Washington DC).

Cézanne, Paul (1839–1906) French Post-Impressionist who married Hortense Fiquet (subject of many of his paintings) in 1886, the year his friendship with Émile Zola ended, due to the publication of Zola's *L'Oeuvre*, in which the central figure is unflatteringly Cézanne.

Selected works: *Self portrait* (National Gallery, London); *The Lake at Annecy* (Courtauld Institute Galleries, London); *Card Players* (Metropolitan Museum of Art, New York).

Chagall, Marc (1887–1985) Russian-born figurative painter, active in France and the USA. The Musée Marc Chagall in Nice is entirely devoted to his work.

Selected works: *The Dead Man* (Marc Chagall Collection, Saint-Paul, France); *I and the Village* (Museum of Modern Art, New York); *Self Portrait with Seven Fingers* (Stedelijk Museum, Amsterdam).

Champaigne, Philippe de (1602–74) Brussels-born, French Baroque court painter to Louis XIII who was patronised by Cardinal Richelieu. After 1647 he was associated with the Jansenists, a strict Roman Catholic sect.

Selected works: *Ex Voto of 1662*; *Cardinal Richelieu* (both Louvre, Paris).

Chardin, Jean-Baptiste Siméon (1699–1779) French still-life genre painter.

Selected works: *Grace before Meat*; *Housewife* (both Louvre, Paris); *The Young Schoolmistress* (National Gallery, London); *Still Life* (Badische Kunsthalle, Karlsruhe).

Chirico, Giorgio de (1888–1978) Italian Surrealist and co-founder of Metaphysical School with Carlo Carrà.

Selected work: *The Pink Tower* (Guggenheim Foundation, Venice).

Cimabue, Giovanni (c1240–1302) Florentine fresco painter who is accepted as the teacher of Giotto.

Selected work: *Madonna and Child* (Louvre, Paris).

Claude (le) Lorrain (1600–82) French Classical landscapist (born Claude Gellée).

Selected works: *Village Fête* (Louvre, Paris); *Aeneas at Delos* (National Gallery, London); *Ascanius Shooting the Stag of Sylvia* (Ashmolean Museum, Oxford).

Clouet the Younger, Jean (c1485–1541) French court painter to François I.

Selected work: *Guillaume Budé* (Metropolitan Museum of Art, New York).

Clouet, François (c1510–72) French court painter to Francis I, Henri II, Francis II, and Charles IX.

Selected works: *Elizabeth of Austria* (Louvre, Paris); *Mary Queen of Scots* (Scottish National Portrait Gallery, Edinburgh); *Portrait of Henri II* (Uffizi, Florence).

Constable, John (1776–1837) English landscapist, born in East Bergholt, Suffolk, the county where many of his most famous works are set.

Selected works: *Dedham Vale* (National Gallery of Scotland, Edinburgh); *The Haywain* (National Gallery, London); *Harnham Ridge from Archdeacon Fisher's House, Salisbury* (National Gallery of Ireland, Dublin).

Copley, John Singleton (1738–1815) American portraitist and history painter working in England from 1775.

Selected works: *Hugh Montgomery, 12th Earl of Eglinton* (Scottish National Portrait Gallery, Edinburgh); *The Siege of Gibraltar* (Guildhall Art Gallery, London); *The Copley Family* (National Gallery of Art, Washington DC); *Brook Watson and the Shark* (National Gallery of Art, Washington DC).

Corot, Jean-Baptiste Camille (1796–1875) French landscapist.

Selected works: *Louis Robert as a Child* (Louvre, Paris); *Avignon* (National Gallery, London).

Correggio, Antonio Allegri da (c1490–1534) Italian High Renaissance painter, active mainly in Parma.

Selected works: *Ecce Homo* (National Gallery, London); *The Agony in the Garden* (Wellington Museum, London); *St Mary Magdalen* (National Gallery, London); *Danae* (Borghese Gallery, Rome).

Cortona, Pietro Berrettini da (1596–1669) Italian painter and architect, creator of Roman High Baroque.

Selected works: *The Rape of the Sabines* (Capitoline Gallery, Rome); *Allegory of Divine Providence and Barbarian Power* (ceiling frescoe in the Galleria Nazionale, Rome).

Cotman, John Sell (1782–1842) English landscapist, co-founder of the Norwich School.

Selected works: *The Devil's Elbow* (Castle Museum, Norwich); *Greta Bridge* (British Museum, London); *Seashore with Boats* (Tate Gallery, London).

Courbet, Gustave (1819–77) French Realist who joined the Paris Commune, was imprisoned for his part in the destruction of the Vendôme Column and died in exile in Switzerland.

Selected works: *Studio of the Painter: an Allegory of Realism* (Louvre, Paris); *Les Demoiselles de Village* (Leeds City Art Gallery); *Bonjour, Monsieur Courbet* (Musée Fabre, Montpellier); *Stream in a Ravine* (Louvre, Paris); *Young Women on the Banks of the Seine* (Musée du Petit Palais, Paris).

Cranach the Elder, Lucas (1472–1553) German court painter to the Elector of Saxony. A number of his works are in the collection at Jagdschloss Grunewald, Berlin. He had three sons, one of them Lucas the Younger (1515–86), whose works are hard to distinguish from his father's.

Selected works: *A Young Girl* (Louvre, Paris); *Adam and Eve* (Courtauld Institute Galleries, London); *A Crucifixion* (Stadtkirche, Weimar); *Martin Luther* (Bristol City Art Gallery).

Crome, John (1768–1821) English topographical artist and founding member of the Norwich Society (1803), now known as the Norwich School.

Selected works: *Yarmouth Jetty* (Castle Museum, Norwich); *The Beaters* (National Gallery of Scotland, Edinburgh); *Marlingford Grove* (Lady Lever Art Gallery, Port Sunlight).

Cuyp, Aelbert (1620–91) Dutch landscapist who was greatly influenced by Jan van Goyen. He also painted animals, seascapes and still lifes.

Selected works: *River Scene with a View of Dordrecht* (Manchester City Art Gallery); *River Scene with a View of Dordrecht* (Wallace Collection, London); *Sunset after Rain* (Fitzwilliam Museum, Cambridge); *Resting Horsemen in a Landscape* (Dordrecht Museum).

Daddi, Bernardo (c1290–1348) Florentine Early Renaissance contemporary of Giotto.

Selected works: *Virgin and Child* (Museu de Arte de São Paolo 'Assis Chateaubriand', Brazil).

Dali, Salvador (1904–89) Spanish Surrealist. Born in Figueras but lived in Paris and, from 1940, in the USA. Dali collaborated with Luis Buñuel on such Surrealist films as *Le Chien Andalou* (1928) and *L'Age d'Or* (1930). His painting *The Persistence of Memory* in New York's Museum of Modern Art was known as 'The Limp Watches'.

Selected works: *Christ of St John of the Cross* (Glasgow Art Gallery & Museum); *Inventions of the Monsters* (Art Institute of Chicago); *Galacidalacideoxyribonucleicacid* (New England Merchant Bank, Boston, Mass.).

Daubigny, Charles-François (1817–78) French landscapist of the Barbizon School who was a pupil of Paul Delaroche.

Selected work: *Evening Landscape* (Metropolitan Museum of Art, New York).

David, Gerard (c1460–1523) Netherlandish painter who became dean of the Painters' Guild of Bruges in 1501.

Selected works: *The Transfiguration* (Lieve Vrouwkerk, Bruges); *The Marriage at Cana* (Louvre, Paris); *The Tree of Jesse* (Musée des Beaux-Arts, Lyons).

David, Jacques-Louis (1748–1825) French Neo-classicist who voted in the National Convention for the death of Louis XVI and after Robespierre's death was twice imprisoned. He produced his masterpiece *The Rape of the Sabines* in 1799 and in 1804 became court painter to Napoleon, but was eventually banished as a regicide after the Bourbon restoration.

Selected works: *The Death of Marat* (Musées Royaux des Beaux Arts, Brussels); *Death of Socrates* (Metropolitan Museum of Art, New York); *Madame Récamier* (Louvre, Paris); *Napoleon Crowning Josephine* (Musée de l'Histoire de la France, Versailles).

Degas, Edgar (1834–1917) French Impressionist painter and sculptor who specialised in dancers.

Selected works: *Miss La La at the Cirque Fernando* (National Gallery, London); *The Dancing Class* (Musée du Jeu de Paume, Paris); *L'Absinthe* (Louvre, Paris).

Delacroix, Eugène (1798–1863) French Romantic painter. Delacroix's Paris studio-apartment is now a museum for his work.

Selected works: *The Death of Sardanapalus* (Louvre, Paris); *Battle of Taillebourg* (Galerie des Batailles, Versailles); *Baron Schwiter* (National Gallery, London; *The Massacre at Chios* (Louvre, Paris); *The Execution of Faliero* (Wallace Collection, London); *Liberty Leading the People* (Louvre, Paris).

Delaunay, Robert (1885–1941) French Cubist and exponent of Orphism, husband of the pioneer abstract painter Sonia Delaunay Terk (1885–1979).

Selected works: *La Tour Eiffel* (Kunstmuseum, Basel); *L'Equipe de Cardiff* (Scottish National Gallery of Modern Art, Edinburgh).

Delvaux, Paul (1897–1994) Belgian Neo-Impressionist, Expressionist and Surrealist.

Selected work: *Sleeping Venus* (Tate Gallery, London).

Denis, Maurice (1870–1943) French painter, founder of the 'Nabis' group.

Selected work: *Hommage à Cézanne* (Musée d'Art Moderne, Paris).

Derain, André (1880–1954) French Fauvist painter and sculptor.

Selected works: *Mountains at Collioure* (Scottish National Gallery of Modern Art, Edinburgh); *Blackfriars* (Glasgow Art Gallery & Museum).

Dix, Otto (1891–1969) German Expressionist painter, a leader of the Neue Sachlichkeit group.

Selected works: *Sylvia von Harden* (Musée National d'Art Moderne, Paris); *Nude Girl in a Fur* (Scottish National Gallery of Modern Art, Edinburgh).

Dobson, William (c1610–46) English portrait painter who succeeded Van Dyck as painter to the exiled Charles I (1641).

Selected work: *Endymion Porter* (Tate Gallery, London).

Doesburg, Theo van (1883–1931) Dutch artist and architect. Leader of De Stijl movement with Mondrian and devotee of a severe form of geometrical abstraction known as Neo-Plasticism. He was originally called Christian Emil Marie Kupper.

Domenichino (1581–1641) Bolognese landscapist and portrait painter.

Selected works: *Portrait of Monsignor Agucchi* (York Art Gallery); *Sibyl* (Borghese Gallery, Rome); *Last Communion of St Jerome* (Vatican Palace, Rome); *Tobias* (National Gallery, London).

Domenico Veneziano (c1400–61) Florentine Early Renaissance painter.

Selected work: *St Lucy Altarpiece* (Uffizi, Florence).

Dongen, Kees van (1877–1968) Dutch painter active in Paris. Fauvist and member of Die Brücke (The Bridge).

ART

Selected work: *Women on the Balcony* (Musée del'Annonciade, St Tropez).

Dossi, Dosso (c1479–1542) Ferrarese fresco painter.

Selected work: *The Christ Child Learning to Walk* (Nottingham Castle); *The Sorceress Circe* (Borghese Gallery, Rome).

Dou, Gerrit (or Gerard) (1613–75) Dutch painter and former collaborator with Rembrandt. Started the 'Fijnschilder' (fine painter) School in Leiden.

Selected works: *A Woman at a Window* (Fitzwilliam Museum, Cambridge); *Rembrandt's Mother, Self Portrait* (both Rijksmuseum, Amsterdam); *A Poulterer's Shop* (National Gallery, London); *The Astronomer* (Stedtlijk Museum 'De Lakenhal', Leiden).

Duccio di Buoninsegna (c1260–c1318) Sienese painter.

Selected works: *Maestà* (Cathedral Museum, Siena); *Rucellai Madonna* (Uffizi, Florence); *Christ Healing the Blind Man*; *The Annunciation* (both National Gallery, London).

Duchamp, Marcel (1887–1968) French-born American painter and sculptor, brother of Jacques Villon. Inventor of the 'Ready-Made' and leader of the New York Dadaists.

Selected work: *The Bride Stripped Bare by her Bachelors, Even*, also known as *The Large Glass* (Philadelphia Museum of Art).

Dufy, Raoul (1877–1953) French artist and designer, born in Le Havre. Dufy played a big part in popularising Fauvism. In 1911 he illustrated Guillaume Apollinaire's *Bestiary*.

Selected work: *Château and Horses* (Philips Collection, Washington DC).

Dürer, Albrecht (1471–1528) German painter and graphic artist, born in Nuremberg, the son of a Hungarian goldsmith. Dürer is often considered the inventor of etching and was a supreme master of the woodcut.

Selected works: *Self Portrait in a Fur-collared Robe* (Alte Pinakothek, Munich); *A Young Man* (Hampton Court Palace, London); *Adoration of the Magi* (Uffizi, Florence).

Dyck, (Sir) Anthony van (1599–1641) Anglo-Flemish court painter to Charles I of England and pupil of Rubens.

Selected works: *Triple Portrait of Charles I* (Windsor Castle); *Portrait of the Earl of Strafford* (Petworth House, Sussex); *The Lornellini Family* (National Gallery of Scotland, Edinburgh).

Eakins, Thomas (1844–1916) American painter and photographer, born in Philadelphia. His composite plates inspired Duchamp's *Nude Descending a Staircase*.

Selected works: *Max Schmitt in a Single Scull*; *Chess Players* (both Metropolitan Museum of Art, New York).

Elsheimer, Adam (1578–1610) German painter on copper, of night scenes and landscapes.

Selected works: *St Paul on Malta* (National Gallery, London); *Judith and Holofernes* (Wellington Museum, London); *Tobias and the Angel* (Historisches Museum, Frankfurt am Main).

Emin, Tracey (1963–) British modern artist, who may be best described as Controversalist. Typical work includes *The Hut* and *My Bed*. Her best-selling autobiography was entitled *Exploration of the Soul*.

Selected work: *Every Part of Me's Bleeding* (Lehman Maupin Gallery, New York).

Ensor, James (1860–1949) Belgian painter of the macabre and precursor of Surrealism.

Selected work: *Entry of Christ into Brussels* (Casino Communal, Belgium).

Epstein, (Sir) Jacob (1880–1959) American-born British sculptor, born a Russian-Polish Jew in New York. His early commissions included 18 nude figures for the façade of the British Medical Association building in the Strand (1907–8) and *Night and Day* (1929) for the London Transport Building in Westminster. These and later symbolic sculptures, such as the marble *Genesis* (1930), the *Ecce Homo* (1934) and the alabaster *Adam* (1939), resulted in accusations of indecency and blasphemy. His last two large commissioned works were *Christ in Majesty* (Llandaff Cathedral) and *St Michael and the Devil* (Coventry Cathedral).

Ernst, Max (1891–1976) German painter and sculptor who was a founder of the Surrealist movement. He invented the technique of frottage (pencil rubbings on canvas).

Selected works: *The Elephant Celebes* (Tate Gallery, London); *Le Grand Amoureux* (Scottish National Gallery of Modern Art, Edinburgh).

Etty, William (1787–1849) English portrait painter who specialised in nudes.

Selected works: *Monk Bar, York* (York City Art Gallery); *The Combat* (National Gallery of Scotland, Edinburgh); *Somnolency* (Aberdeen Art Gallery); *The Fairy of the Fountain* (Tate Gallery, London).

Eyck, Jan van (c1389–1441) Netherlands painter, probably born near Maastricht; successively in the service of John of Bavaria, the Count of Holland and Philip the Good of Burgundy.

Selected works: *The Arnolfini Wedding* (National Gallery, London); *Adoration of the Lamb* (Church of St Bavo, Ghent); *The Madonna with Chancellor Rolin* (Louvre, Paris); *Man in a Red Turban* (National Gallery, London).

Fabritius, Carel (1622–54) Dutch painter of still lifes and street-scenes. Worked under Rembrandt around 1641 and lived mainly at Delft, where he was killed in the explosion of the municipal ammunition depot.

Selected works: *View of Delft* (National Gallery, London); *An Old Man* (Walker Art Gallery, Liverpool); *The Goldfinch* (Mauritshuis, The Hague); *Self-portrait* (Museum Boymans-van Beuningen, Rotterdam).

Fantin-Latour, Henri (1836–1904) French genre, still-life and Symbolist painter, born in Grenoble.

Selected works: *Flowers and Fruit* (Louvre, Paris); *Homage to Delacroix* (Musé du Jeu de Paume, Paris).

Feininger, Lyonel (1871–1956) American artist and cartoonist, born in New York of German immigrant parents. Taught at the Bauhaus at Weimar and Dessau, but when the Nazis came to power he returned to the USA and, with Gropius and Mies van der Rohe, founded the Chicago Bauhaus.

Selected works: *Sailing Boats* (Collection Tannahill, Detroit); *Gelmeroda III* (Scottish National Gallery of Modern Art, Edinburgh).

Fouquet, Jean (c1420–81) French court painter to Louis I. Pope Eugenius IV commissioned a portrait from him, now lost.

Selected works: *Etienne Chevalier with St Stephen* (Staatliche Museen, Berlin); *Madonna and Child* (Musée des Beaux Arts, Antwerp); *Charles VII* (Louvre, Paris).

Fragonard, Jean-Honoré (1732–1806)   French Rococo painter.

Selected works: *The Swing* (Wallace Collection, London); *Bathers* (Louvre, Paris).

Frankenthaler, Helen (1928–)   American Abstract Expressionist painter, who devised a technique for staining unprimed canvases with washes of colour.

Selected work: *Blue Territory* (Whitney Museum, New York City).

Freud, Lucien (1922–)   German-born, English figurative painter. In his early years he was one of the Neo-Romantic group along with Minton, Craxton, Sutherland and Piper; but from the 1950s he developed a realist style. One of the most respected artists since World War II. Freud's work does not lend itself to be pigeon-holed in any particular style and includes portraits ranging from *Francis Bacon* in the Tate (stolen in 1988 whilst on exhibition in Germany) to the painting of a man in a raincoat with a yucca – *Interior in Paddington* (Walker Art Gallery, Liverpool). Sigmund Freud was the artist's grandfather.

Friedrich, Caspar David (1774–1840)   German Romantic painter of nature, and particularly forest scenes. His works are included in the German Romantic collection in the Schinkel Pavilion at Schloss Charlottenburg and in the Neue National Galerie, both in Berlin.

Selected works: *Man and Woman Gazing at the Moon* (Staatliche Museen, Berlin); *Wreck of the Hope* (Kunsthalle, Hamburg).

(Dame) Elizabeth Frink (1930–1993)   English sculptress. The horror of war ran through her entire oeuvre and is best depicted in *Gogglehead*.

Selected works: *Arrival at Canterbury* (Royal Museum and Art Gallery, Canterbury).

Frith, William Powell (1819–1909)   English genre painter who became the wealthiest painter of his time by selling both paintings and their copyright.

Selected works: *The Derby Day* (Tate Gallery, London); *The Railway Station* (Royal Holloway College, Egham, Surrey).

Fuseli, Henry (1741–1825)   Swiss Romantic fantasy painter who took British citizenship and became professor of painting at the Royal Academy, and Keeper in 1804.

Selected works: *Lady Macbeth Sleepwalking* (Louvre, Paris); *Titania and Bottom* (Tate Gallery, London); *The Three Witches from Macbeth* (Kunsthaus, Zurich); *The Nightmare* (Detroit Institute of Art).

Gaddi, Taddeo (c1300–66)   Florentine painter and mosaicist who was Giotto's best pupil and also his godson.

Selected works: *Life of the Virgin* (Baroncelli Chapel, Church of S. Croce, Florence).

Gainsborough, Thomas (1727–88)   English portrait and landscape painter, born in Sudbury, Suffolk. Married Margaret Burr, the illegitimate daughter of the 4th Duke of Beaufort.

Selected works: *Harvest Wagon* (Barber Institute, University of Birmingham); *Self Portrait* (National Portrait Gallery, London); *Portrait of Mary, Countess Howe* (Iveagh Bequest, Kenwood House, London); *The Watering Place* (Tate Gallery, London); *Mrs Graham* (National Gallery of Scotland, Edinburgh); *George III and Queen Charlotte* (Windsor Castle).

Gaudier-Brzeska, Henri (1891–1915)   French Cubist sculptor born in St Jean de Braye. Henri Gaudier came to England in 1911 with his childhood

sweetheart Sophie Brzeska and founded the London Group of Sculpture. In 1914 he signed the Vorticist Manifesto. He joined the French army at the outbreak of WWI and was killed in action.

Selected work: *Armour* (Tate Gallery, London).

Gauguin, Paul (1848–1903)   French Post-Impressionist who gave up a stockbroking career to devote himself to painting. He evolved a style known as 'Synthetism' in a reaction against Impressionism. Lived in Tahiti 1891–1901 and then the Marquesas Islands. Fell out with his friend Van Gogh at Arles in 1888.

Selected works: *The Vision after the Sermon* (National Gallery of Scotland, Edinburgh); *Tahitian Women* (Metropolitan Museum of Art, New York); *La Seine au Pont d'Iéna* (Louvre, Paris).

Gentile da Fabriano (c1370–1427)   Italian International Gothic painter (properly, Niccolo di Giovanni di Massio).

Selected work: *Adoration of the Magi* (Uffizi, Florence).

Gentileschi, Artemisia (c1597–c1651)   Italian painter, daughter of the Bolognese painter Orazio Gentileschi.

Selected works: *Self-portrait as Pittura* (Kensington Palace, London); *Susannah and the Elders* (Schloss Eisenstein, Pommersfelden).

Géricault, Théodore (1791–1824)   French Romantic history painter. He died following a fall from his horse. His tomb in Père Lachaise cemetery, Paris, has a brass relief of *The Raft of the Medusa*.

Selected works: *The Raft of the Medusa*; *The Wounded Cuirassier* (both Louvre, Paris); *Mad Woman with a Mania of Envy* (Musée des Beaux Arts, Lyons).

Gheeraerts, Marcus, the Younger (c1561–1636)   Flemish portraitist. Court painter to Elizabeth I and James I of England (VI of Scotland). Portrait of Arabella Stuart in the Scottish National Portrait Gallery is possibly by Gheeraerts.

Selected works: *The Ditchley Portrait of Elizabeth I* (National Portrait Gallery, London); *Sir Thomas Lee* (Tate Gallery, London); *William Camden* (Bodleian Library, Oxford).

Ghirlandaio, Domenico (1449–94)   Florentine Renaissance fresco painter (properly, Domenico di Tommaso Bigordi).

Selected works: *Life of the Virgin* (Strozzi Chapel, S. Maria Novella, Florence); *Visitation of the Virgin* (Louvre, Paris); *Old Man and His Grandson* (Louvre, Paris).

Gilbert, (Sir) Alfred (1854–1934)   English sculptor and goldsmith who was a leader of the New Sculpture movement. The Clarence Memorial in Windsor is considered the climax of his work. Other works include the Alexandra Memorial in Marlborough Road, London, and the *Queen Victoria* statue in Winchester.

Selected works: *Eros* (Piccadilly Circus, London); *Perseus Arming* (Victoria and Albert Museum, London); *Joule* (Manchester Town Hall).

Gill, Eric (1882–1940)   English sculptor, engraver, writer and typographer, born in Brighton, the son of a clergyman. In 1909 he carved his first stone figure *The Madonna and Child*. Through the influence of Augustus John he exhibited at the Chenil Galleries, Chelsea (1911). He maintained a steady output for the rest of his life, during which he designed the classic typeface Gill. Joined the Fabian movement and eventually became Catholic.

A
R
T

Selected works: *Mankind* (Tate Gallery, London); *Stations of the Cross* (Westminster Cathedral, London); *Prospero and Ariel* (BBC Broadcasting House, London).

Gillray, James (1756–1815) English political and social caricaturist and printmaker, born in Chelsea, the son of a Lanark trooper. Gillray had a life-long partnership with the publisher Mrs Humphrey. From 1810 until his death he was hopelessly insane.

Giordano, Luca (1634–1705) Neapolitan decorative painter, precursor of Rococo and court painter to Charles II of Spain. Renowned for his speed of working, hence his nickname 'Luca Fa Presto' (Luke Go Quickly).

Selected work: *Apotheosis of the Medici* (ballroom ceiling, Palazzo Medici-Riccardi, Florence).

Giorgione (c1478–1510) Venetian Renaissance painter (properly, Giorgio Barbarelli).

Selected works: *The Adulteress before Christ* (Glasgow Art Gallery & Museum); *The Adoration of the Magi* (National Gallery, London); *The Tempest* (Galleria dell'Accademia, Venice).

Giotto di Bondone (c1266–1337) Florentine painter who introduced sculptural solidity into painting and heralded the Renaissance. He was a pupil of Cimabue, but because of confusion as to his early life it is not known for sure if the St Francis of Assisi frescoes were attributable to him. Often called the 'Father of Modern Painting'. Both he and Cimabue are mentioned by Dante. Legend says he drew a perfect circle freehand for the Pope.

Selected works: the Arena Chapel murals (S. Maria Annunziata dell'Arena, Padua); *Ognissanti Madonna* (Uffizi, Florence).

Giulio Romano (1492–1546) Roman Mannerist painter and architect. An indication of his fame is a mention in Shakespeare's *Winter's Tale*.

Selected works: *Isabella d'Este* (Hampton Court Palace, London); *Allegory of Immortality* (Alnwick Castle, Northumberland); fresco decorations at the Palazzo del Te, Mantua.

Goes, Hugo van der (c1440–82) Flemish master painter, mostly of religious subjects.

Selected works: *Adoration of the Shepherds* (Uffizi, Florence); *Death of the Virgin* (Musée Communal, Bruges); *Adoration of the Magi* (Museum Dahlem, Berlin).

Gogh, Vincent van (1853–90) Dutch Post-Impressionist. The Rijksmuseum Vincent van Gogh in Amsterdam houses over 700 of his paintings and drawings.

Selected works: *Cornfield and Cypress Trees* (National Gallery, London); *Self Portrait* (Saint-Rémy, 1889: Louvre, Paris); *The Potato Eaters* (Rijksmuseum Vincent van Gogh, Amsterdam); *Sunflowers* (Tate Gallery, London).

Gore, Spencer Frederick (1878–1914) English painter, born in Epsom, Surrey. Gore was a founder member and first president of the Camden Town Group (1911).

Selected work: *From a Window in Cambrian Road, Richmond* (Tate Gallery, London).

Gorky, Arshile (1904–48) Armenian-born US painter influenced by Cubism, Surrealism and Abstract Expressionism. Original name: Vosdanig Manoog Adoian.

Selected work: *The Liver Is the Cock's Comb* (Albright-Knox Art Gallery, Buffalo, NY State).

Gormley, Antony (1950 –) At the forefront of a generation of British artists who emerged during the 1980s. He has exhibited work around the world and has major public works in Australia, Ireland, Japan, Norway and the USA. Public work in Britain can be seen in locations as diverse as the crypt at Winchester Cathedral and Birmingham city centre. In 1994 he won the Turner Prize and in 1997 was awarded the OBE for services to sculpture. His best-known work is *The Angel of the North* in Gateshead.

Goya y Lucientes, Francisco (1746–1828) Spanish Romantic artist who was court painter to Charles IV of Spain. His series of etchings, *The Disasters of War*, describe the horrors of the Penninsular war in Spain.

Selected works: *Family of Charles IV*; *The Naked Maja* (both Prado, Madrid); *The Duke of Wellington* (National Gallery, London).

Goyen, Jan van (1596–1656) Dutch realistic landscapist.

Selected works: *Cottages and Fishermen by a River* (Glasgow City Art Gallery); *Leiden from the North-East* (Stedelijk Museum 'De Lakenhal', Leiden); *View of Dordrecht from Papendrecht* (Mauritshuis, The Hague).

Gozzoli, Benozzo (c1421–97) Florentine fresco painter, a pupil of Fra Angelico.

Selected works: frescoes (Medici Palace, Florence); *Journey of the Magi* (chapel of the Palazzo Medici-Riccardi, Florence).

Greco, El (1541–1614) Cretan-born Spanish Mannerist (properly, Domenico Theotocopoulos).

Selected works: *The Saviour* (National Gallery of Scotland, Edinburgh); *The Tears of St Peter* (Bowes Museum, Barnard Castle, Durham); *The Disrobing of Christ* (Toledo Cathedral).

Greuze, Jean-Baptiste (1725–1805) French genre and portrait painter.

Selected works: *The Broken Pitcher* (Louvre, Paris); *Girl with Doves* (Wallace Collection, London).

Gris, Juan (1887–1927) Spanish Cubist (properly, José Victoriano González).

Selected works: *Still Life with Dice* (Musée National d'Art Moderne, Paris); *The Glass* (Glasgow Art Gallery & Museum).

Grosz, George (1893–1959) German-born American Expressionist and Dadaist whose depictions of the depravity of war were so graphic that the Nazis called them 'Cultural Bolshevist Number One'. Although starting as a Dadaist, he was a co-founder of the Neue Sachlichkeit movement.

Selected works: *Kristallnacht* (Leicester Museum & Art Gallery, Leicester); *To Oskar Panizza* (Staatsgalerie, Stuttgart).

Grünewald, Matthias (c1470/80–1528) German visionary artist (properly, Mathis Gothardt – although he occasionally added his wife's surname Neithardt to his own). Grünewald is the 'Mathis der Maler' of Hindemith's opera of that name.

Selected works: *The Isenheim Altarpiece* (Musée d'Unterlinden, Colmar, France); *The Mocking of Christ* (Alte Pinakothek, Munich); *The Miracle of the Snow* (Aschaffenburg Altarpiece, Augustinermuseum, Freiburg-in-Breisgau).

Guardi, Francesco (1712–93) Italian topographical artist, born in Pinzolo. Pupil of Canaletto, and like his master famous for his views of Venice.

Selected works: *Ascent in a Balloon* (Staatliche Museen, Berlin); *The Doge Embarking on the Bucintoro* (Louvre, Paris); *The Doge's Palace* (National Gallery, London).

Guercino (1591–1666) Bolognese early Baroque painter (properly, Gian-Francesco Barbieri).

Selected works: *The Incredulity of St Thomas* (National Gallery, London); *Susanna Bathing* (Prado, Madrid).

Hals, Frans (c1580–1666) Dutch genre and portrait painter, born in Antwerp.

Selected works: *The Laughing Cavalier* (Wallace Collection, London); *Married Couple in a Garden* (Rijksmuseum, Amsterdam); *Aletta Hannemans* (Mauritshuis, The Hague); *The Merry Toper* (Rijksmuseum, Amsterdam).

Hamilton, Richard (1922–) English artist who became a pioneer of Pop Art after attending the *This is Tomorrow* exhibition in Whitechapel Art Gallery, London, in 1956. He reconstructed Duchamp's *Bride Stripped Bare by her Bachelors, Even*, by consulting the original notes and studies by the artist (Tate Gallery, London).

Selected work: *Just What Is It That Makes Today's Homes So Different, So Appealing* (Private Collection, California).

Hepworth, (Dame) Jocelyn Barbara (1903–75) English sculptor, born in Wakefield, West Yorkshire. Her first marriage was to fellow sculptor John Skeaping and her second to painter Ben Nicholson. Hepworth was noted for the strength and formal discipline of her carving, e.g. *Contrapuntal Forms*, exhibited at the Festival of Britain, 1951. Such pieces as *Wave* (1944) and *Mr & Mrs Ashley* (Havinden Collection, England) became increasingly open, hollowed out and variously perforated, so that the interior space became as important as the mass surrounding it.

Selected works: *Pelagos* (Tate Gallery); *Pendour* (Hirshhorn Museum, Washington DC).

Hilliard, Nicholas (1537–1619) English miniature-painter at the courts of Elizabeth I and James I of England.

Selected works: *Young Man among Roses* (Vicoria and Albert Museum, London); *Elizabeth I Playing a Lute* (Berkeley Castle, Gloucester); *Self-portrait Aged 31* (Drumlanrig Castle, Dumfriesshire).

Hirst, Damien (1965–) Avant-garde artist, born in Bristol. Following a disappointing 'D' in his A-Level art exam went on to train at Goldsmiths College, London. Became known for his works which made use of parts or all of dead animals preserved in formaldehyde, such as *Mother and Child Divided* – four tanks containing the severed halves of a cow and calf. His 1994 exhibition contained a dead lamb 'Away from the flock' suspended within a tank. In 1995 he was awarded the Turner Prize and in 1996 his New York exhibition 'No Sense of Absolute Corruption' contained several large paintings, as well as earlier works.

Hobbema, Meindert (1638–1709) Dutch landscapist and pupil of Jacob von Ruysdael.

Selected works: *The Avenue at Middleharnis* (National Gallery, London); *A Watermill* (Rijksmuseum, Amsterdam); *A Peasant Cottage on a Water Course* (Historisches Museum, Amsterdam).

Hockney, David (1937–) English Pop artist, born in Bradford.

Selected works: *My Parents and Myself* (Cartwright Hall Art Gallery, Bradford); *Rocky Mountains and Tired Indians* (Scottish National Gallery of Modern Art, Edinburgh).

Hogarth, William (1697–1764) English painter and satirist, born in Smithfield, the son of a teacher. Studied under Sir James Thornhill and married Thornhill's daughter in 1729.

Selected works: *Lord George Graham in His Cabin* (National Maritime Museum, London); *The Rake's Progress* series (Sir John Soane's Museum, London); *Self-portrait with His Pug* (Tate Gallery, London).

Hokusai, Katsushika (1760–1849) Japanese engraver and watercolourist whose work became extremely popular in England after the Anglo-Japanese trade agreements of the 1880s. His work influenced Whistler.

Selected work: *Thirty-six Views of Mount Fuji* series (Art Institute of Chicago).

Holbein the Younger, Hans (c1497–1543) German realist portraitist who was court painter to Henry VIII. His father, Hans Holbein the Elder (c1460–1524), was also a painter of note.

Selected works: *The Ambassadors* (National Gallery, London); *Sir Thomas Moore* (Frick Collection, New York); *Jane Seymour* (Mauritshuis, The Hague).

Homer, Winslow (1836–1910) American painter, born in Boston. Began as an illustrator for magazines such as *Harper's Weekly* and *Ballou's Pictorial*. Worked for many years at his Prouts Neck studio in Maine, where the local sea area became a favourite subject for depiction.

Selected works: *Fog Warning* (Museum of Fine Arts, Boston, Mass.); *Pitching Quoits* (Fogg Art Museum, Cambridge, Mass.).

Honthorst, Gerrit van (1590–1656) Dutch genre and night-scene painter who was the court painter to the Stadholder of Holland and Charles I of England.

Selected works: *Winter Queen* (Elizabeth of Bohemia) (National Portrait Gallery, London); *Willem II, Prince of Orange* (Mauritshuis, The Hague); *The Death of Seneca* (Centraal Museum, Utrecht).

Hooch (or Hoogh), Pieter de (1629–84) Dutch genre painter.

Selected works: *A Musical Party* (Wellington Museum, Apsley House, London); *Interior with a Woman Delousing a Child's Hair* (Rijksmuseum, Amsterdam); *A Courtyard in Delft* (Mauritshuis, The Hague).

Hopper, Edward (1882–1967) American realist painter, mostly of urban scenes, born in New York.

Selected works: *Early Sunday Morning* (Whitney Museum of American Art, New York); *Room in Brooklyn* (Museum of Fine Arts, Boston, Mass.).

Hunt, William Holman (1827–1910) English painter and founder member of the Pre-Raphaelite Brotherhood.

Selected works: *The Scapegoat* (Lady Lever Gallery, Port Sunlight); *Claudio and Isabella* (Tate Gallery, London); *The Light of the World* (Keble College, Oxford).

Hunt, William Morris (1824–79) American Romantic painter who created a fashion in the USA for the luminous, atmospheric painting of the Barbizon School.

Selected work: *Girl at a Fountain* (Metropolitan Museum of Art, New York).

Huysum, Jan van (1682–1749) Dutch still-life painter.

Selected work: *Fruit, Flowers and Insects* (Alte Pinakothek, Munich).

Ingres, Jean Auguste Dominique (1780–1867) French Classical painter of portraits and history pictures. Ingres bequeathed much of his work to his home town of Montauban, and the collection is now housed in the town's Musée Ingres. His motto was 'A thing well drawn is well enough painted'. Ingres was awarded the Légion d'Honneur and made a senator in 1862.

Selected works: *Madame Moitessier* (National Gallery, London); *The Turkish Bath* (Louvre, Paris).

Inness, George (1825–94)   American landscapist, later influenced by the Barbizon School.

Selected works: *The Delaware Valley* (Metropolitan Museum of Art, New York); *Rainbow after a Storm* (Chicago Art Institute).

Jawlensky, Alexej von (1864–1941)   Russian Expressionist working in Munich from 1896 and France from 1905. In 1924 he co-founded Der Blaue Vier (Blue Four group) with Kandinsky, Klee and Feininger.

Selected work: *Head of a Woman* (Scottish National Gallery of Modern Art, Edinburgh).

John, Augustus Edwin (1878–1961)   Welsh painter, born in Tenby. Graduated from the Slade School of Art, London, with his elder sister, Gwen John. His favourite themes were gypsies, fishing folk and wild, lovely, yet regal women.

Selected works: *Smiling Woman* (Tate Gallery, London); *Richard Hughes* (Tenby Museum & Picture Gallery).

John, Gwen (1876–1939)   Welsh painter and elder sister of Augustus John. Worked as an artist's model and became Rodin's mistress.

Selected works: *Self-portrait* (Tate Gallery, London); *A Corner of the Artist's Room* (Cannon Hall, Barnsley).

Johns, Jasper (1930–)   American Neo-Dadaist painter and sculptor, a strong influence on Pop Art, whose sculptures are of everyday items.

Selected work: *Zero Through Nine* (Tate Gallery, London).

Jordaens, Jacob (1593–1678)   Flemish low-life and religious painter. Pupil of Rubens.

Selected works: *Commerce and Industry Protecting the Fine Arts* (Koninklijk Museum voor Schone Kunsten, Antwerp); *Presentation in the Temple* (Rubenshuis, Antwerp); *The Fruit Seller* (Glasgow City Art Gallery).

Jorn, Asger Oluf (1914–73)   Danish Expressionist (properly, Asger Jorgensen). Founded the CoBrA group, which was named after COpenhagen, BRussels, Amsterdam.

Selected work: *The Lost World* (Stedelijk Van Abbe-Museum, Eindhoven).

Kandinsky, Wassily (1866–1944)   Russian pioneer of abstract art who was influenced by the Fauves, Bauhaus, and Surrealists. He founded Der Blaue Reiter group with Franz Marc.

Selected works: *First Abstract Watercolour* (Nina Kandinsky Collection, Neuilly-sur-Seine); *First Abstract Watercolour* (Musée National d'Art Moderne, Paris); *Blue Mountain* (Solomon R. Guggenheim Museum, New York).

Kapoor, Anish (1954–)   Born in Bombay but lives and works in London. Renowned for his enigmatic sculptural forms that permeate physical and psychological space. His versatility and inventiveness have resulted in works ranging from powdered pigment sculptures and site-specific interventions on wall or floor, to gigantic installations both in and outdoors. Throughout, he has explored what he sees as deep-rooted metaphysical polarities: presence and absence, being and non-being, place and non-place and the solid and the intangible.

Best-known work to date is *Marsyas*, the third in the Unilever series of commissions for the Turbine Hall at the Tate Modern.

Kauffmann, Angelica (1741–1807)   Swiss Neo-classical painter in England who co-founded the Royal Academy (1768). She married the Venetian painter Antonio Zucchi.

Selected works: *Self Portraits* (National Portrait Gallery & Tate Gallery, London); *Rinaldo and Armida* (Kenwood House, London); *Euphrosyne Complains to Venus of the Wounds of Cupid* (Attingham Park, Shropshire).

Kirchner, Ernst Ludwig (1880–1938)   German Expressionist, influenced by Neo-Impressionism, Fauvism and Primitive art.

Selected works: Die Brücke painters – portraits of Otto Muller, Erich Heckel, Schmidt-Rotluff and Kirchner (Wallraf-Richartz Museum / Museum Ludwig, Cologne); *Japanisches Theater* (Scottish National Gallery of Modern Art, Edinburgh).

Kitaj, Ron B. (1932–)   American Pop artist, introducing cultural and political elements. Active in the UK.

Selected work: *If Not . . . Not* (Scottish National Gallery of Modern Art, Edinburgh).

Klee, Paul (1879–1940)   Swiss painter and etcher. Blaue Reiter member and teacher at the Bauhaus. Described his work as 'taking a line for a walk'. A large collection of his work from 1906 to 1938 is housed in the Kunstsammlung Nordrhein-Westfalen at Düsseldorf.

Selected works: *Death and Fire* (Kunstmuseum, Berne); *Around the Fish* (Museum of Modern Art, New York); *Ad Marginem* (Kunstmuseum, Basel).

Klein, Yves (1928–62)   French revolutionary Minimalist, painting only in blue. Klein was a celebrated exponent of judo and lived in Japan in 1952–3.

Selected work: *ANT 143 The Handsome Teuton* (London Arts Gallery).

Klimt, Gustav (1862–1918)   Austrian Art Nouveau painter, founder member of the Vienna Secession, 1898, artists who resigned as a group from conventional academic bodies.

Selected works: *Salome* (Galleria d'Arte Moderna, Ca' Pesaro, Venice); *The Kiss* (Österreichische Galerie, Vienna).

Kneller, (Sir) Godfrey (1646–1723)   German portrait painter in England, court painter to William III and George I. Famous for painting 42 portraits of the members of the literary association called the Kit-Kat Club, now in the National Portrait Gallery, London. These pictures were painted between 1700 and 1720 and are of a size (36" x 28") now known as 'Kit-Kat' size.

Selected works: *Isaac Newton* (National Gallery, London); *James, Duke of Monmouth* (Goodwood House, Sussex).

Knight, (Dame) Laura (1877–1970)   British artist best known for her beautifully tranquil beach and seaside paintings, paintings of the circus and of ballet. She was elected a Royal Academician in 1936. Dame Laura was an official war artist who was sent to make portraits at the Nuremberg Trials.

Kokoschka, Oskar (1886–1980)   Austrian Expressionist working in England and Switzerland.

Selected works: *Still Life with Tortoise and Hyacinth* (Österreichische Galerie, Vienna); *The Tempest* (Kunstmuseum, Basel).

Koninck, Philips de (1619–88)   Dutch panoramic landscapist.

Selected work: *Landscape* (Hunterian Art Gallery, Glasgow).

Kooning, Willem de (1904–97) Dutch-born American Abstract Expressionist.

Selected work: *Woman I* (Museum of Modern Art, New York).

La Tour, Georges de (1593–1652) French painter of candle-lit scenes, active entirely in Lorraine.

Selected works: *St Joseph the Carpenter* (Louvre, Paris); *The Dice Players* (Middlesbrough Art Gallery); *St Jerome* (Musée de Grenoble).

La Tour, Maurice Quentin de (1704–88) French pastellist and portrait painter whose works are celebrated in the Musée Antoine Lecuyer in Saint-Quentin, France.

Selected works: *Mr and Mrs Angerstein*; *Madame de Pompadour* (both Louvre, Paris).

Lancret, Nicholas (1690–1743) French Rococo genre and *fêtes galantes* painter in the style of Watteau.

Selected work: *Mademoiselle Camargo Dancing* (Wallace Collection, London).

Landseer, (Sir) Edwin Henry (1802–73) English animal painter and engraver – a favourite of Queen Victoria. Landseer is famous for his *Monarch of the Glen* and for sculpting the lions at the foot of Nelson's Column. Buried in St Paul's Cathedral, London.

Selected works: *Dignity and Impudence*; *The Rout of Comus* (both Tate Gallery, London).

Lawrence, (Sir) Thomas (1769–1830) English painter, born in Bristol, the son of an innkeeper. In 1792 he became painter to George III.

Selected work: *Queen Charlotte* (National Gallery, London).

Le Nain Brothers Antoine (c1588–1648), Louis (c1593–1648) and Mathieu (c1607–77). French painters, born in Laon. All painted scenes of peasant life but did not sign work with their initials, thus making attributions almost impossible.

Selected works: *Peasant Children* (Burrell Collection, Glasgow); *A Blacksmith in His Forge* (Louvre, Paris).

Léger, Fernand (1881–1955) French Cubist who has a museum dedicated to him at Boit on the Côte d'Azur.

Selected works: *Homage to David* (Musée National d'Art Moderne, Paris); *Woman and Still Life* (Scottish National Gallery of Modern Art, Edinburgh).

Leighton, (Lord) Frederick (1830–96) English painter of classical subjects, who became the 1st Baron Leighton of Stretton, the first British artist to be awarded a peerage; Leighton is buried in St Paul's Cathedral, London.

Selected work: *The Garden of the Hesperides* (Lady Lever Gallery, Port Sunlight).

Lely, (Sir) Peter (1618–80) Dutch portrait painter working in England. Court painter to Charles II.

Selected works: *Ladies of the Lake Family* (Tate Gallery, London); *The Windsor Beauties* (Hampton Court Palace, London).

Leonardo da Vinci (1452–1519) Italian painter, sculptor, scientist and creator of the High Renaissance style. Worked in the pay of Cesare Borgia, son of Pope Alexander VI, as senior military architect and general engineer, and then for François I of France.

Selected works: *Mona Lisa* (aka *La Gioconda*) (Louvre, Paris); *The Virgin of the Rocks* (National Gallery, London); *The Last Supper* (Convent of S. Maria delle Grazie, Milan).

Leyster, Judith (1609–60) Dutch genre and portrait painter, pupil of Hals. She married and worked with the painter Jan Molenaer (c1609–68).

Selected work: *The Lute-Playing Fool* (Rijksmuseum, Amsterdam).

Lichtenstein, Roy (1923–97) American Pop artist, whose works were inspired by comic strips.

Selected works: *Whaam!* (Tate Gallery, London); *In the Car* (Scottish National Gallery of Modern Art, Edinburgh).

Limbourg Bothers (early 15th-century) Flemish family of miniature painters in the International Gothic style. The three brothers were Pol, Jehanequin and Hermann de Limbourg.

Selected work: *Les Très Riches Heures* (Musée Condé, Chantilly).

Lippi, Filippino (c1457–1504) Florentine painter of the transition from Early to High Renaissance. Son of Fra Filippo Lippi.

Selected work: *Vision of St Bernard* (Badia, Florence).

Lippi, Fra Filippo (c1406–69) Florentine fresco painter, influenced by Masaccio and Gothic art. Aka 'Fra Lippo Lippi'.

Selected works: *Annunciation* (Church of S. Lorenzo, Florence); *The Adoration of the Magi* (National Gallery, Washington DC).

Lissitzky, Eleazar M (1890–1941) Russian Constructivist painter, influenced by Malevich.

Selected work: *Victory over the Sun* (Tate Gallery, London).

Lorenzetti, Ambrogio (c1290/1300–c1348) Sienese landscapist and realist.

Selected work: frescoes in the Palazzo Pubblico, Siena.

Lotto, Lorenzo (c1480–1556) Italian Renaissance painter.

Selected works: *Portrait of Andreas Odoni* (Hampton Court Palace, London); *Madonna and Child with Saints* (National Gallery, Rome); *A Gentleman in His Study* (Galleria dell'Accademia, Venice).

Louis, Morris (1912–62) American Cubist until 1952 and then influenced by Jackson Pollock. He pioneered Colorfield painting, using bands of colour. Louis was further influenced by Helen Frankenthaler's *Mountains and Sea*, which prompted him to throw acrylic paint onto unprimed canvases to create brilliant patches of abstract colour.

Selected work: *Alpha-Phi* (Tate Gallery, London).

Low, (Sir) David (1891–1963) New Zealand-born British political cartoonist. Joined the *Evening Standard* in 1927. His most famous creation was 'Colonel Blimp', an embodiment of the die-hard British bigot.

Lowry, Laurence Stephen (1887–1976) Salford painter famous for his matchstick-like men and women. Lowry was only ever a part-time painter and worked most of his life as a clerk.

Selected work: *The Pond* (Tate Gallery, London).

Mabuse, Jan (c1478–1532) Flemish Mannerist allegorical painter (properly, Jan Gossaert).

Selected work: *The Adoration of the Kings*; *Little Girl* (both National Gallery, London).

Maes, Nicolaes (1634–93) Dutch portrait and genre painter, pupil of Rembrandt.

Selected works: *The Idle Servant* (National Gallery, London).

Magritte, René (1898–1967) Belgian Surrealist, influenced by de Chirico.

Selected work: *Black Flag* (Scottish National Gallery of Modern Art, Edinburgh).

ART

Malevich, Kasimir (1878–1935)   Russian Suprematist, producing the first strictly geometrical art of the 20th century.

Selected work: *Woman with Water Pails* (Museum of Modern Art, New York).

Manet, Edouard (1832–83)   French precursor of Impressionism.

Selected works: *Music in the Tuileries Garden* (Hugh Lane Municipal Gallery, Dublin); *A Bar at the Folies Bergère* (Courtauld Institute Galleries, London); *Olympia* (Musée du Jeu de Paume, Paris); *Déjeuner sur l'herbe* (Louvre, Paris).

Mantegna, Andrea (1431–1506)   Italian Renaissance painter working in Padua and Mantua. Mantegna married a daughter of Jacopo Bellini.

Selected works: *The Triumph of Caesar* (Hampton Court Palace, London); *Crucifixion* (Louvre, Paris); frescoes in the Camera degli Sposi, Palazzo Ducale, Mantua.

Marc, Franz (1880–1916)   German Expressionist and leading member of Der Blaue Reiter. Marc was killed at Verdun.

Selected works: *Large Blue Horses* (Walker Art Center, Minneapolis); *Red Woman* (Leicester Museum and Art Gallery).

Martini, Simone (c1280–1344)   Artist of the Sienese School.

Selected works: *Madonna with Angels and Saints, Maesta* (Palazzo Pubblico, Siena); *Christ Returns to his Parents* (Walker Art Gallery, Liverpool).

Masaccio (1401–28)   Florentine painter (properly Tommaso di Ser Giovanni di Simone dei Guidi), whose nickname literally means 'Hulking Tom'.

Selected works: frescoes in the Brancacci Chapel, S. Maria del Carmine, Florence; *Madonna and Child* (National Gallery, London); *Crucifixion* (Capodimonte, Naples).

Massys, Quentin (c1465–1530)   Netherlandish portrait and religious-subject painter, influenced by Italian art.

Selected works: *Jesus and the Infant St John Embracing* (Chatsworth House, Derbyshire); *The Virgin and Child with Angels* (National Gallery, London); *Altarpiece of the Lamentation* (Koninklijk Museum voor Schone Kunsten, Antwerp).

Matisse, Henri (1869–1954)   French painter who was leader of the Fauves, 1905–6, before changing his style. The Chapelle de Rosaire in Vence, France, was entirely designed and decorated by him. The Musée Matisse in Nice houses a collection donated by the artist's family.

Selected works: *The Painting Lesson* (Scottish National Gallery of Modern Art, Edinburgh); *Interior with Aubergines* (Musée de Peinture, Grenoble).

Memling, Hans (c1430–94)   Flemish biblical and portrait painter. A good collection of his work is housed in the Memlingmuseum in Bruges.

Selected works: *Bathsheba* (Staatsgalerie, Stuttgart); *St John* (National Gallery, London); *The Adoration of the Magi* (Memlingmuseum, Bruges).

Mengs, Anton-Raphael (1728–79)   German painter, born in Bohemia, the son of a Danish artist. Precursor of Neo-Classicism.

Selected works: *Maria Luisa of Parma* (Prado, Madrid); *Richard Wilson* (National Museum of Wales, Cardiff).

Metsu, Gabriel (1629–67)   Dutch genre painter, particularly of domestic scenes, a pupil of Dou.

Selected work: *The Sick Child* (Rijksmuseum, Amsterdam); *The Music Lesson* (National Gallery, London); *Woman at the Spinet* (Museum Boymans-van Beuningen, Rotterdam).

Michelangelo Buonarotti (1475–1564)   High Renaissance and later Mannerist painter, sculptor and architect, born near Florence, where he grew up. Patronised by Pope Julius II, for whom he decorated the ceiling of Sistine Chapel (1508–12).

Selected works: *The Last Judgement* (Sistine Chapel, Vatican Palace, Rome); *Holy Family* (Uffizi, Florence); *The Entombment* (National Gallery, London); *David* (Accademia, Florence).

Millais, (Sir) John Everett (1829–96)   English co-founder of the Pre-Raphaelite Brotherhood. Born in Southampton. In 1840 he became the youngest ever student at the Royal Academy, and in 1896 its President.

Selected works: *The Blind Girl* (Birmingham City Museum & Art Gallery); *Christ in the House of His Parents* (Tate Gallery, London); *The Return of the Dove to the Ark* (Ashmolean Museum, Oxford); *Ophelia* (Tate Gallery, London); *Autumn Leaves* (Manchester City Art Gallery).

Millet, Jean François (1814–75)   French realist painter of peasant life. Worked at Barbizon from 1849.

Selected works: *The Gleaners* (Louvre, Paris); *La Famille du Paysan* (National Museum of Wales, Cardiff).

Miró, Joan (1893–1983)   Spanish Abstract painter, sculptor and ceramicist, influenced by Cubism and Surrealism.

Selected works: *Samurai* (Cannon Hall, Barnsley); *The Egg* (Fondation Maeght, Saint-Paul-de Vence).

Modigliani, Amedeo (1884–1920)   Italian painter and sculptor, working in Paris from 1906.

Selected work: *Seated Nude* (Courtauld Institute, London).

Moholy-Nagy, László (1895–1946)   Hungarian-born, American experimental artist and photographer, influenced by Lissitzky and Constructivism. He developed kinetic art and taught at the Bauhaus and in Chicago.

Selected work: *Z IV* (Marlborough Gallery, London).

Mondrian, Piet (1872–1944)   Dutch member of De Stijl and developer of Neo-Plasticism, who influenced the Bauhaus School.

Selected works: *Broadway Boogie Woogie* (Museum of Modern Art, New York); *Composition in Black and White* (Rijksmuseum Kröller-Müller, Otterlo); *The Grey Tree* (Haags Gemeentemuseum, The Hague).

Monet, Claude (1840–1926)   Father of Impressionism, whose *Impression: Sunrise* gave its name to the movement. Monet's *Déjeuner sur l'herbe* (Luncheon on the Grass) should not be confused with Manet's.

Selected works: *Field with Poppies* (Louvre, Paris); *The Beach at Trouville* (Tate Gallery, London); *Rouen Cathedral: Sunset* (Museum of Fine Arts, Boston, Mass.).

Moore, Henry Spencer (1898–1986)   English sculptor, born in Castleford, Yorkshire, the son of a coal-miner. Moore is best known for his reclining female figures, carved in wood and stone or cast in bronze. He was an official war artist 1940–42, during which time he produced a famous series of drawings of air-raid shelter scenes. His principal commissions included the *Madonna and Child* in St Matthew's

Church, Northampton; the decorative frieze on the Time-Life building, London; and the massive reclining figures for the UNESCO building in Paris and the Lincoln Center in New York. Moore was awarded the Order of Merit in 1963.

Moreau, Gustave (1826–98) French Symbolist painter whose Paris home and studio is now the Musée Gustave Moreau.

Selected work: *The Apparition* (Louvre, Paris).

Morisot, Berthe (1841–95) French Impressionist, granddaughter of Fragonard, who married Eugène, the brother of Manet.

Selected work: *Cradle* (Louvre, Paris).

Moro, Antonio (c1519–76) Dutch court painter to the Habsburgs and Mary I of England, who knighted him as Sir Anthony More.

Selected works: *Queen Anna of Spain* (Kunsthistorisches Museum, Vienna); *Sir Henry Lee* (National Portrait Gallery, London).

Morse, Samuel (1791–1872) American painter and first President of the National Academy (1826), but better known for his invention of the electric telegraph.

Selected works: *House of Representatives* (Corcoran, Washington DC); *Lafayette* (Brooklyn Museum, New York).

Motherwell, Robert Burns (1915–91) American Abstract Expressionist who married fellow Expressionist Helen Frankenthaler in 1955.

Selected works: *Elegy to the Spanish Republic XXXIV* (Albright-Knox Art Gallery, Buffalo, NY).

Mucha, Alphonse (1860–1939) Czech painter, graphic artist and designer, chiefly known for his Art Nouveau illustration style, especially the posters for the actress Sarah Bernhardt.

Selected work: *Job and Lorenzaccio* (Victoria and Albert Museum, London).

Munch, Edvard (1863–1944) Norwegian Expressionist. Important collections of his work are at the Rasmus Meyers Samlinger, Bergen, and the Munch Museum and the National Gallery, Oslo.

Selected works: *The Scream* (Nasjonalgalleriet, Oslo); *Vampire* (Munch-Museet, Oslo); *Ashes* (Nasjonalgalleriet, Oslo).

Murillo, Bartolomé Esteban (c1618–82) Spanish Baroque painter of religious and genre subjects. Born in Seville, Murillo fell from a scaffold when painting an altarpiece at Cadiz, and died shortly afterwards in Seville.

Selected works: *Virgin of the Rosary* (Archbishop's Palace, Seville); *The Two Trinities*, aka *The Holy Family* (National Gallery, London); *Boys with Fruit* (Alte Pinakothek, Munich).

Nash, Paul (1889–1946) English painter and co-founder of the Modern Movement. Nash was an official war artist in both world wars.

Selected works: *Landscape of the Vernal Equinox* (Scottish National Gallery of Modern Art, Edinburgh); *Pillar and Moon*; *Totes Meer* (Dead Sea) (both Tate Gallery, London).

Nicholson, Ben (1894–1982) English Abstract painter who used a restricted palette of greys and muted tones. Married three times; his second wife was the sculptor Barbara Hepworth.

Selected works: *Still Life* (Glasgow Art Gallery & Museum); *White Relief* (Tate Gallery, London).

Nolde, Emil (1867–1956) German Expressionist and printmaker (properly, Emil Hansen). His Art Nouveau house in Seebull, Germany, is now a museum.

Selected works: *Doubting Thomas* (Nolde-Museum, Seebull); *Death of Mary* (Museum Folkwang, Essen); *The Flower Garden* (Wallraf-Richartz Museum, Cologne).

Ofili, Chris (1968–) Born in Manchester but heavily influenced by his African roots. His controversial collage *The Holy Virgin Mary*, which featured a black Virgin Mary with elephant dung on one breast and cutouts from pornographic magazines glued in the background, created a stir when exhibited in New York.

O'Keeffe, Georgia (1887–1986) American Surrealist and Abstract painter who married photographer Alfred Stieglitz.

Selected work: *Black Iris* (Metropolitan Museum of Art, New York).

Oliver, Isaac (c1560–1617) French-born English miniaturist who married the half-sister of Marcus Gheeraerts the Younger. Oliver's work included a famous miniature of Elizabeth I of England that displeased her immensely.

Selected work: *Self Portrait* (National Portrait Gallery, London).

Opie, John (1761–1807) Cornish portrait and history painter, son of a carpenter. Nicknamed the 'Cornish Wonder'.

Patronised by John Wolcot (the political satirist Peter Pindar). His first exhibited historical work was *The Assassination of James I of Scotland* (1786), followed by *The Murder of Rizzio* (1787), both destroyed by bombing in 1941.

Selected work: *Mary Wollstonecraft* (Tate Gallery, London).

Oudry, Jean-Baptiste (1686–1755) French still-life painter.

Selected works: *The Dog* (Burrell Collection, Glasgow); *The Calling of the Hounds* (tapestry) (Pitti Palace, Florence).

Palma Vecchio (c1480–1528) Venetian painter of *sacra conversazione* altarpieces (properly, Jacopo Palma).

Selected works: *Venus and Cupid* (Fitzwilliam Museum, Cambridge); *Polyptych of St Barbara* (S. Maria Formosa, Venice); *The Assumption* (Galleria dell'Accademia, Venice).

Palmer, Samuel (1805–81) English landscapist and etcher, influenced by William Blake.

Selected work: *Coming from Evening Church* (Tate Gallery, London).

Parmigianino, Il (1503–40) Italian early Mannerist (properly, Girolamo Francesco Maria Mazzola).

Selected works: *The Marriage of St Catherine* (National Gallery, London); *Madonna with the Long Neck* (Uffizi, Florence); frescoes in S. Maria della Steccata, Parma.

Pasmore, Victor (1908–98) English portrait, still-life and landscape painter. Co-founder of the Euston Road School. In the late 1940s he turned towards abstract art.

Selected works: *Inland Sea* (Tate Gallery, London); *Wine Red* (Bristol City Art Gallery).

Pechstein, Max Hermann (1881–1955) Co-founder of German Expressionism and member of Die Brücke from 1906 before helping to found the rival Neue Sezession (New Secession).

Selected work: *Indian and Woman* (Morton D. May Collection).

Perugino, Pietro (c1445–1523) Umbrian Renaissance painter (properly, Pietro di Cristoforo

A
R
T

Vannucci). Perugino was the master of Raphael.

Selected work: *Virgin and Child* (National Gallery, London).

Piazzetta, Giovanni Battista (1682–1754) Venetian painter, illustrator and designer.

Selected works: *Fortune Teller* (Galleria dell' Accademia, Venice); fresco *The Crucifixion* (Church of S. Maddalena de' Pazzi, Florence).

Picabia, Francis (1879–1953) French Cubist, Dadaist and Surrealist who also dabbled in Futurism. Married Gabrielle Buffet in 1909.

Selected work: *Udnie* (Musée d'art Moderne, Paris).

Picasso, Pablo (1881–1973) Spanish painter and sculptor who embraced Cubism, Surrealism and Expressionism. Born in Malaga, Picasso, along with Braque, pioneered Cubism. Picasso's blue period was from 1902 to 1904, followed by his pink period (1904–6) and a short brown period (1905–6). He was director of the Prado during the Spanish Civil War and joined the Communist Party in 1944. Picasso died in Mougins, France. The Musée Picasso in Antibes was decorated by him in 1946, and many works are in the Musée Picasso, Paris. His mural *War and Peace* is housed in the Musée National Picasso in Vallauris, and *Man with a Lamb* is in the public square. The Museo Pablo Picasso in Barcelona holds early works donated by the painter in 1970.

Selected works: *Three Dancers* (Tate Gallery, London); *Les Demoiselles d'Avignon* (Museum of Modern Art, New York); *Guernica* (Prado, Madrid).

Piero della Francesca (c1419–92) Umbrian painter, scientist and mathematician.

Selected works: *The Nativity* (National Gallery, London); *Constantine's Dream* (Legend of the Holy Cross) (S. Francesco, Arezzo); *Federigo da Montefeltro* (Uffizi, Florence).

Piper, John (1903–92) English artist, born in Epsom, Surrey. Originally an abstract painter, he turned to Romantic realism under the influence of Palmer and the earlier English topographical painters. As an official war artist (1940–42), he painted many successful war pictures, but his design of the stained glass windows for Coventry Cathedral and Eton are his best-known works.

Pisanello, Antonio (c1390–1455) Italian painter and follower of the International Gothic style of Gentile da Fabriano.

Selected works: *The Vision of St Eustace* (National Gallery, London); *Lionello d'Este* (Accademia Carrara, Bergamo); *St George and the Princess* (Church of S. Anastasia, Verona).

Pisano, Andrea (c1290–c1349) Italian sculptor born in Pontadera and trained in Pisa. Considered the founder of the Florentine School of sculpture. Best known for his relief panels on the bronze south door of the Florence Baptistry.

Selected works: *Weaver* (Campanile, Florence cathedral); *Noah* (Museo dell'Opere del Duomo, Florence).

Pissarro, Camille (1830–1903) French Impressionist and Pointillist, born in St Thomas, West Indies.

Selected works: *Boulevard Montmartre by Night*; *Lower Norwood, London, Snow* (both National Gallery, London).

Pollaiuolo, Antonio (c1431–c1498) Florentine painter, sculptor, goldsmith and engraver, properly Antonio di Jacopo d'Antonio Benci, but took his name from his father's profession as a poulterer. Collaborated with his brother Piero (c1443–c1496) on the bronze tomb of Sixtus IV and the monument to Pope Innocent VIII, both in Saint Peter's, Rome. Other notable works include the bronze statuette *Hercules and Antaeus* in the Bargello, Florence, and the signed engraving *Battle of the Ten Nude Gods*. It is not always clear which brother should be credited with some of their oeuvre, but Piero, principally a painter, is thought to be responsible for at least three of the *Seven Virtues* in the Uffizi, Florence; three others were probably collaborations with Antonio, and the seventh by Botticelli.

Pollock, Jackson (1912–56) American Abstract Expressionist and early exponent of tachisme (action painting). *Full Fathom Five* was probably the first work of this controversial 'poured painting' style. Alcoholism and his death in a car crash added to Pollock's notoriety.

Selected works: *Enchanted Wood* (Guggenheim Foundation, Venice); *Summertime: Number 9a* (Tate Gallery, London).

Pontormo, Jacopo Carrucci (1494–1557) Florentine early Mannerist.

Selected works: *Four Scenes from the Life of Joseph* (National Gallery, London); frescoes in S. Felicità, Florence; *Cosimo I de Medici* (Uffizi, Florence).

Poussin, Nicolas (1594–1665) French Classical landscapist who was court painter to Louis XIII. His oeuvre included mythological works and biblical subjects; he was an early exponent of history painting.

Selected works: *The Nurture of Jupiter* (Dulwich Gallery, London); *Tancred and Erminia* (Barber Institute, University of Birmingham); *Inspiration of the Poet* (Louvre, Paris); *The Adoration of the Golden Calf* (National Gallery, London).

Primaticcio, Francesco (1504–70) Italian Mannerist painter, sculptor and architect. A collection of his drawings is in the Louvre.

Selected works: *The Rape of Helen* (Bowes Museum, Barnard Castle); Fontainebleau Palace decorations, France.

Puvis de Chavannes, Pierre (1824–98) French decorative, symbolic painter, noted for his murals. A number of huge canvases are set in to the walls of the grand staircase of the Musée de Picardie, Amiens.

Selected work: *Poor Fisherman* (Louvre, Paris).

Raeburn, (Sir) Henry (1756–1823) Scottish portraitist, elected to the Royal Academy in 1815 and Selected works: *Reverend Robert Walker Skating on Duddingston Loch* (National Gallery of Scotland, Edinburgh); *Self Portrait* (National Gallery of Scotland, Edinburgh); *Lady Dalrymple* (Tate Gallery, London).

Raphael (1483–1520) Italian High Renaissance painter who worked on a number of Papal commissions. Raphael (properly, Raffaello Santi or Sanzio) was born in Urbino. Leo X selected him to succeed Donato Bramante (a relative) as architect of St Peter's in 1514. His last work, the *Transfiguration* was left unfinished when he died.

Selected works: *Pope Julius II* (National Gallery, London); *The Madonna of the Goldfinch* (Uffizi, Florence); frescoes in the Vatican Palace, Rome.

Redon, Odilon (1840–1916) French Symbolist painter and graphic artist; a precursor of Surrealism.

Selected work: *Violette Heyman* (Cleveland Museum of Art, Ohio).

Rembrandt Harmenszoon van Rijn (1606–69) Dutch painter, etcher and graphic artist whose home is now a museum in Amsterdam. Born in Leiden, the son of a prosperous miller, his first wife was Saskia van Ulenburgh (d. 1642). He failed to achieve financial security and, despite being the most famous painter of his time, died a pauper.

Selected works: *Self Portrait* (Walker Art Gallery, Liverpool); *Portrait of Titus* (Wallace Collection, London); *The Night Watch – The Militia Company of Captain Frans Banning Cocq* (Rijksmuseum, Amsterdam).

Reni, Guido (1575–1642) Bolognese Classical painter of Baroque religious works.

Selected work: *St John the Baptist* (Dulwich Gallery , London).

Renoir, Pierre Auguste (1841–1919) French Impressionist, born in Limoges. He visited Italy in 1880 and during the next few years painted a series of *Bathers* in a colder, more classical style, influenced by Ingres and Raphael. He then returned to hot reds, orange and gold to portray nudes in sunlight. Renoir's hands were crippled by arthritis in later years. His son Jean (1894–1979) became a great film director.

Selected works: *Umbrellas* (Hugh Lane Municipal Gallery of Modern Art, Dublin); *Umbrellas* (National Gallery, London); *Moulin de la Galette* (Louvre, Paris); *Madame Charpentier and Her Children* (Metropolitan Museum of Art, New York).

Reynolds, (Sir) Joshua (1723–92) English portraitist and art theorist. Co-founder and first President of the Royal Academy, 1768. Principal painter to George III of England, 1784.

Selected works: *Self-portrait*, c1753 (National Portrait Gallery, London); *Three Ladies Adorning a Term of Hymen: The Montgomerie Sisters* (Tate Gallery, London); *Admiral Lord Anson* (Shugborough, Staffordshire).

Ribera, Jusepe de (c1591–1652) Spanish Baroque painter, known as Lo Spagnoletto (The Little Spaniard).

Selected work: *Martyrdom of St Bartholomew* (Prado, Madrid).

Richter, Hans (1888–1976) American painter, sculptor and film-maker, born in Berlin. Member of the Zurich Dadaists, 1917.

Rigaud, Hyacinthe (1659–1743) French Rococo painter. Portraitist to Louis XIV and Louis XV of France. A small collection of his works is housed in the Musée Rigaud, Perpignan.

Selected works: *Cardinal de Bouillon* (Musée Rigaud, Perpignan); *Louis XIV*; *Louis XV* (both Musée de l'Histoire de la France, Versailles).

Riley, Bridget (1931–) English Op artist since the early 1960s.

Selected work: *Crest* (Rowan Gallery, London).

Rodin, Auguste (1840–1917) French sculptor, born in Paris, the son of a clerk. Produced his first great work in 1864, *L'Homme au nez cassé*. In 1877 he made a tour of the French cathedrals and published *Les Cathédrales de la France* in 1914. From 1886 to 1895 he worked on *Les Bourgeois de Calais*. His statues include a nude Victor Hugo and Balzac in a dressing gown. His works are represented in the Musée Rodin, Paris; the Rodin Museum, Philadelphia; and the Victoria and Albert Museum, London, where there is a collection of his bronzes

that he presented to the British nation in 1914.

Selected works: *Le Penseur* (The Thinker) (Musée Rodin, Paris); *Le Baiser* (The Kiss) (Tate Gallery, London).

Romney, George (1734–1802) English portraitist and history painter, born in Lancashire. At the height of his fame he rivalled both Reynolds and Gainsborough and his later history paintings and portraits of Emma Hart (later Lady Hamilton) enhanced his reputation, but he eventually died insane.

Selected work: *Self-portrait* (National Gallery, London).

Rosa, Salvator (1615–73) Neapolitan Baroque and macabre painter.

Selected work: *Landscape* (National Gallery, London).

Rossetti, Dante Gabriel (1828–1882) Anglo-Italian painter and poet, brother of the poet Christina Rossetti. DG Rossetti was born in London and his mother was Frances Mary Lavinia Polidori, daughter of Gaetano Polidori and sister of Lord Byron's physician, Dr John Polidori. Rossetti was fascinated by the Middle Ages and was a co-founder of the Pre-Raphaelite Brotherhood.

Selected works: *St George and the Princess Sabra*; *Ecce Ancilla Domini* (both Tate Gallery, London); *The Blessed Damozel* (Lady Lever Art Gallery, Port Sunlight).

Rothko, Mark (1903–70) American Abstract Expressionist and co-founder of Colorfield painting. Latvian-born (properly, Marcus Rothkovitch).

Selected work: *Two Openings in Black over Wine* (Tate Gallery, London).

Rouault, Georges (1871–1958) French Expressionist painter often on religious themes. Many of his works were acquired by the art dealer Ambroise Vollard.

Selected works: *Head of Christ* (Musée National d'Art Moderne, Paris); *Two Nudes* (Metropolitan Museum of Art, New York).

Rousseau, Henri (1844–1910) French Primitive painter, known as 'Le Douanier' due to his early occupation as a tax collector in the Paris customs office.

Selected works: *The Child among Rocks* (Philadelphia Museum of Art); *The Sleeping Gypsy* (Museum of Modern Art, New York).

Rubens, (Sir) Peter Paul (1577–1640) Enormously successful and productive Flemish Baroque painter and diplomat. Rubens's Antwerp home is now a museum. He married his first wife, Isabella Brandt, in 1609 (d. 1626) and his second, Helen Fourment, in 1630.

Selected works: *The Judgement of Paris* (National Gallery, London); *Descent from the Cross* (Antwerp Cathedral); *Peace and War* (National Gallery, London); *Portrait of Isabella Brandt* (Wallace Collection, London); *Apotheosis of James I* (Whitehall Banqueting House, London); *Helen Fourment with Two of Her Children* (Louvre, Paris).

Ruysdael, Jacob van (1628–82) Dutch landscapist whose work was only appreciated after his death.

Selected works: *The Jewish Cemetery* (Gemäldegalerie, Dresden); *View on the Amstel Looking toward Amsterdam* (Fitzwilliam Museum, Cambs); *The Windmill at Wijk bij Duurstede* (Rijksmuseum, Amsterdam).

Ruysdael, Salomon van (c1600–70) Dutch realist landscapist, properly, Salomon de Goyer. Uncle of Jacob van Ruysdael.

A
R
T

Selected works: *River Scene* (Leicester City Art Gallery); *River Scene near Utrecht* (Gemeentemuseum, Arnhem); *Landscape with a Carriage and Horsemen at a Pool* (National Gallery, London).

Saenredam, Pieter Janszoon (1597–1665) Dutch architectural painter.

Selected works: *Interior of the Grote Kerk at Haarlem* (National Gallery, London); *Interior of the Nieuwe Kerk* (Frans Hals Museum, Haarlem); *Interior of the Janskerk*, Utrecht (Centraal Museum, Utrecht).

Sargent, John Singer (1856–1925) American portraitist of fashionable London society from 1884. Born in Florence, Sargent was an official war artist during World War I.

Selected works: *Carnation, Lily, Lily, Rose* (Tate Gallery, London); *Madame Gautreau* (Metropolitan Museum of Art, New York); *The Three Vickers Sisters* (Mappin Art Gallery, Sheffield); *Gassed* (Imperial War Museum, London).

Sassetta, Stefano di Giovanni (c1392–1450) Sienese painter of large altarpieces.

Selected works: *St Francis Renounces His Earthly Father* (National Gallery, London); *Journey of the Magi* (Metropolitan Museum of Art, New York).

Sebastiano del Piombo (c1485–1547) Venetian painter influenced by Giorgione and Michelangelo.

Selected works: *The Raising of Lazarus* (National Gallery, London); *The Madonna and Child with SS. Catherine and John the Baptist* (Galleria dell'Accademia, Venice).

Seurat, Georges Pierre (1859–91) French Neo-Impressionist and developer of Pointillism.

Selected works: *Sunday Afternoon on the Island of the Grande Jatte* (Art Institute of Chicago); *Circus* (Louvre, Paris); *Bathers at Asnières* (National Gallery, London).

Sickert, Walter Richard (1860–1942) German-born, English painter, influenced by Degas and Whistler. Co-founder of the Camden Town Group.

Selected works: *The Lion of St Mark* (Fitzwilliam Museum, Cambridge); *View at Ramsgate* (Huddersfield Art Gallery).

Sisley, Alfred (1839–99) French landscape Impressionist of British parentage, noted for his subtle treatment of skies.

Selected works: *Flood at Port Marly*; *The Boat during the Flood* (both Louvre, Paris).

Snyders, Frans (1579–1657) Flemish painter, born in Antwerp. Pupil of Pieter Brueghel the Younger. He specialised in still life and animals, often assisting Rubens in hunting scenes. In 1611 he married Margaretha de Vos, the sister of the Flemish painters Cornelis and Paul de Vos.

Selected work: *Stag Hunt* (Prado, Madrid).

Soutine, Chaim (1893–1943) Lithuanian painter, in Paris from 1913, influenced by Cézanne and Die Brücke group.

Selected work: *Les Gorges du Loup sur Vence* (Scottish National Gallery of Modern Art, Edinburgh).

Spencer, (Sir) Stanley (1891–1959) English painter of portraits, landscapes and religious works. Born in Cookham, Berkshire. Spencer was an official war artist in World War II.

Selected works: *Sandham Memorial Chapel* murals, Burghclere; *The Garden at Cookham Rise* (Huddersfield Art Gallery).

Steen, Jan (c1626–79) Dutch painter of low-life scenes and still-life subjects.

Selected works: *The Effects of Intemperance*

(National Gallery, London); *Self-portrait* (Rijksmuseum, Amsterdam); *Romping Couple* (Stedelijk Museum 'De Lakenhal', Leiden).

Steer, Philip Wilson (1860–1942) English landscapist. Member of the New English Art Club.

Selected works: *Mrs Cyprian Williams and Her Daughters* (Tate Gallery, London); *The Last Chapter* (Cartwright Hall, Bradford); *Self Portrait, The Music Room* (Tate Gallery, London).

Stella, Frank (1936–) American Abstract Expressionist and Minimalist.

Selected work: *Hyena Stomp* (Tate Gallery, London).

Streeter, Robert (1624–79) Pepys's famous history painter who became Charles II's serjeant-painter in 1660. The ceiling of Oxford's Sheldonian Theatre is one of his few remaining decorative works.

Stubbs, George (1724–1806) English animal painter and engraver, born in Liverpool. Stubbs specialised in painting horses.

Selected works: *Mares and Foals in a River Landscape* (Tate Gallery, London); *Self-portrait* (National Portrait Gallery, London); *Molly Long Legs with a Jockey* (Walker Art Gallery, Liverpool).

Sutherland, Graham Vivian (1903–80) English portraitist and official war artist, WW2. His official portrait of Sir Winston Churchill was destroyed by Lady Churchill, as she detested it. The Graham Sutherland Gallery in Haverfordwest was devoted almost entirely to his work until 1996, when it was closed, and the nearly 800 works have been displayed at Tenby Art Gallery (1996), Bodelwyddan Castle (1997) and the Turner House Gallery, Penarth (1998 and 2000-1). At time of writing Pembrokeshire Coast National Park is pursuing a new home near its visitors centre at St Davids.

Selected work: *Somerset Maugham* (Tate Gallery, London); *Christ in Majesty* (tapestry in Coventry Cathedral).

Tanguy, Yves (1900–55) French Surrealist in the USA from 1939, influenced by de Chirico.

Selected work: *The Furniture of Time* (Collection Soby, New Canaan, Connecticut).

Teniers the Younger, David (1610–90) Flemish genre painter. Curator of Archduke Leopold Wilhelm's picture gallery in Brussels, and copyist of many of its masterpieces.

Selected works: *Archduke Leopold Wilhelm in His Gallery* (Musées Royaux des Beaux Arts, Brussels); *The Dentist* (Manchester City Art Gallery); *Interior with a Peasant* (Nottingham Castle Museum).

Terborch, Gerard (1617–81) Dutch genre painter of domestic scenes.

Selected works: *A Man* (Museum de Waag, Deventer); *A Woman Playing a Theorbo to Two Men* (National Gallery, London); *Woman at a Mirror* (Rijksmuseum, Amsterdam).

Terbrugghen, Hendrick (c1588–1629) Dutch religious and genre painter, influenced by Caravaggio.

Selected work: *Jacob, Laban and Leah* (National Gallery, London).

Thornhill, (Sir) James (1675–1734) English Baroque painter, born in Melcombe Regis, Dorset. His paintings for the dome of St Paul's (1707), the hall at Blenheim Palace, Hampton Court and the Painted Hall at Greenwich Hospital – on a scale unrivalled in Britain in the 15th century – made his reputation. He was the father-in-law of William

Hogarth. Knighted by George I (1720) and appointed serjeant-painter; from 1722 became MP for Melcombe Regis.

Thornycroft, (Sir) William Hamo (1850–1925) English sculptor, born in London.

Selected works: public statues of General Gordon in Trafalgar Square; John Bright in Rochdale; and Cromwell outside the Houses of Parliament.

Tiepolo, Giambattista (1696–1770) Venetian Rococo decorative painter. His work is prominent in palaces and churches throughout Europe.

Selected works: *Finding of Moses* (National Gallery of Scotland, Edinburgh); frescoes in the Residenz, Würzburg, and the Royal Palace, Madrid.

Tintoretto (1518–94) Venetian Mannerist (properly, Jacopo Robusti). The son of a silk dyer (*tintore*), hence his nickname of Tintoretto (Little Dyer).

Selected works: *St George Killing the Dragon* (National Gallery, London); *Miracle of S. Marco* (Galleria dell'Accademia, Venice); *The Washing of the Feet* (Wilton House, Wiltshire).

Titian (c1487–1576) Venetian painter (properly, Tiziano Vecellio); renowned for his use of colour. The Prado in Madrid has a superb collection of his work, particularly the paintings done under the patronage of the Holy Roman Emperor, Charles V. Titian was buried in the Church of S. Maria dei Frari, Venice.

Selected works: *The Three Ages of Man* (National Gallery of Scotland, Edinburgh); *Venus, Cupid and a Lute Player* (Fitzwilliam Museum, Cambridge); *Ecce Homo* (National Gallery of Ireland); *The Assumption* (S. Maria dei Frari, Venice).

Toulouse-Lautrec, Henri de (1864–1901) French painter, graphic artist and lithographer who forsook his noble origins for the cafés of Montmartre. He was influenced by Degas and by Japanese prints. Much of his work is housed in the Musée Toulouse-Lautrec et Galerie d'Art Moderne, Albi, France.

Selected works: *Jane Avril at the Moulin Rouge* (Courtauld Institute, London); *La Toilette* (Louvre, Paris); *The Artist's Mother* (Musée Toulouse-Lautrec, Albi); *At the Moulin Rouge*; *In the Circus Fernando: The Ringmaster* (both Art Institute of Chicago); *At the Moulin de la Galette* (Stedelijk Museum, Amsterdam); *Jane Avril Dansant* (Louvre, Paris).

Turner, Joseph Mallord William (1775–1851) English Romantic landscapist and precursor of Impressionism. A superb collection of Turner's work is in the Clore Gallery, attached to the Tate Gallery, London. Turner entered the Royal Academy at the age of 14 and was patronised by Lord Egremont of Petworth. He died in temporary lodgings in Chelsea under the assumed name of Booth.

Selected works: *Battle of Trafalgar* (National Maritime Museum, London); *Norham Castle, Sunrise* (Tate Gallery, London); *The Fall of the Clyde* (Lady Lever Art Gallery, Port Sunlight).

Uccello, Paolo (1397–1475) Florentine painter noted for his sophisticated use of perspective.

Selected works: *The Hunt* (Ashmolean Museum, Oxford); *The Battle of San Romano* (National Gallery, London); *The Deluge* (Church of S. Maria Novella, Florence).

Utrillo, Maurice (1883–1955) French painter, born in Montmartre, Paris, the illegitimate son of painter Suzanne Valadon. Adopted by the Spanish writer Miguel Utrillo, he began to paint at Montmagny in 1902. Utrillo specialised in Paris street scenes. Despite acute alcoholism and drug addiction, his output was astonishing. His 'White Period' paintings

of about 1908–14 are much sought after. He signed his works 'Maurice Utrillo V', incorporating the initial of his mother's family name.

Vasarely, Victor (1908–97) Hungarian-born, French precursor of Op art. The 16th-century Château de Gordes in Vaucluse, France, is now the Musée Didactique Vasarely.

Selected works: *Sirius II* (Galerie Denise René, Paris); *Ondho* (Museum of Modern Art, New York); *Supernovae* (Tate Gallery, London).

Vasari, Giorgio (1511–74) Italian Mannerist fresco painter, architect and biographer. His *Lives of the Artists* was first published in Florence in 1550. The Casa Vasari in Arezzo was decorated by him.

Selected works: *Allegory of the Immaculate Conception* (Ashmolean Museum, Oxford); *Lorenzo the Magnificent* (Uffizi, Florence).

Velazquez, Diego Rodriguez de Silva y (1599–1660) Spanish Baroque genre and royal portrait painter to Philip IV of Spain. Born in Seville and pupil of Francisco Pacheco, whose daughter he married in 1618.

Selected works: *Las Meninas* (aka *Maids of Honour*) (Prado, Madrid); *An Old Woman Cooking Eggs* (National Gallery of Scotland, Edinburgh); *The Toilet of Venus*, known as *The Rokeby Venus* (National Gallery, London).

Velde, Esaias van de (c1591–1630) Dutch realistic landscapist who was the master of Jan van Goyen.

Selected work: *Ice Scene* (Alte Pinakothek, Munich).

Vermeer, Jan (1632–75) Dutch genre painter of domestic scenes. Born in Delft, the son of an art dealer, he married Caterina Bolnes, who was to bear him eleven children. Fewer than 40 of his paintings are known. During World War II, forged Vermeers were produced by Jan Van Meegeren, who for some time deceived the experts.

Selected works: *A Young Woman Standing at a Virginal* (National Gallery, London); *A Lady Reading a Letter* (Rijksmuseum, Amsterdam); *Head of Girl with a Pearl Earring* (Mauritshuis, The Hague).

Veronese (c1528–88) Venetian biblical and allegorical painter (properly, Paolo Caliari).

Selected works: *Hermes, Herse and Aglauros* (Fitzwilliam Museum, Cambridge); *Mars and Venus* (National Gallery of Scotland, Edinburgh); frescoes in the Palazzo Ducale, Venice.

Vigée-Lebrun, Elisabeth Louise (1755–1842) French painter famous for her female subjects such as Marie Antoinette. She did paint male subjects, notably the Prince of Wales and Lord Byron.

Villon, Jacques (1875–1963) French painter (real name Gaston Duchamp) who specialised in Cubist works.

Vlaminck, Maurice de (1876–1958) French Fauve who was also a noted violinist, author and racing cyclist.

Selected work: *Woody River Scene* (Glasgow Art Gallery and Museum).

Vouet, Simon (1590–1649) French Baroque history and portrait painter who was influenced by Caravaggio. Court painter to Louis XIII.

Selected work: *La Richesse* (Louvre, Paris).

Vuillard, Edouard (1868–1940) French portrait and domestic genre painter. Member of the Nabis in the 1890s.

Selected works: *The Mantelpiece* (National Gallery, London); *The Open Window* (Scottish National Gallery of Modern Art, Edinburgh).

ART

Warhol, Andy (1928–87) American Pop Art painter, graphic artist and film-maker who was famous for the Campbell soup-can labels and magazine illustrations directly reproduced by silk-screen. His controversial films included *Sleep* (1963) and *Chelsea Girls* (1966). In 1968 he was shot and wounded by Valerie Solanis, an actress in one of his films.

Selected work: *Green Coca-Cola Bottles* (Whitney Museum of American Art, New York).

Watteau, Jean-Antoine (1684–1721) French Rococo painter of *fêtes galantes*.

Selected works: *The Music Party* (Wallace Collection, London); *Gilles* (Louvre, Paris); *Mezzetin* (Metropolitan Museum of Art, New York); *L'Enseigne de Gerseint* (Gerseint's Signboard) (Schloss Charlottenburg, Berlin).

Watts, George Frederick (1817–1904) English portrait and allegorical painter who first drew attention with his cartoon of Caractacus in the competition for murals for the new Houses of Parliament. In 1864 he married actress Ellen Terry but parted from her within a year.

Selected works: *Found Drowned* (Watts Gallery, Compton, Surrey); *Hope* (Tate Gallery, London).

West, Benjamin (1738–1820) American Neo-classical painter, in England from 1763. Founding member of the Royal Academy and its President in 1792. Court painter to George III of England, who patronised him for 40 years.

Selected works: *The Death of General Wolfe* (National Gallery of Canada, Ottawa); *The Apotheosis of Lord Nelson* (National Maritime Museum, London); *Mrs Worrall as Hebe* (Tate Gallery, London).

Westmacott, (Sir) Richard (1775–1856) A leading Neo-classical sculptor of public monuments and statues. After studying in Italy he returned to London and became a favourite sculptor of the Committee of Taste. His most accomplished monument was a public subscription commission commemorating Charles James Fox, in Westminster Abbey. His bronze public monuments include the *Achilles* at Hyde Park Corner, Park Lane.

Weyden, Rogier van der (c1399–1464) Netherlandish painter of portraits and altarpieces, noted for his technical brilliance and emotional intensity.

Selected works: *Lamentation (Pietà) over the dead Christ* (National Gallery, London); *Antoine de Bourgogne* (Musées Royaux des Beaux Arts, Brussels); *Deposition* (Prado, Madrid); *Bladelin Altarpiece* (Museum Dahlem, Berlin).

Whistler, James Abbott McNeill (1834–1903) American painter who lived in London and Paris. The critic John Ruskin's vitriolic criticism of his contributions to the Grosvenor Gallery exhibition of 1877, accusing him of 'flinging a pot of paint in the public's face', provoked the famous lawsuit in which Whistler was awarded a farthing's damages. Famous for his evening scenes, called nocturnes, such as the well-known impression of Battersea Bridge in the Tate Gallery, London. Whistler often dressed as the typical stereotype of an artist.

Selected works: *Thomas Carlyle* (Glasgow Art Gallery); *Little White Girl: Symphony in White No. II* (Tate Gallery, London); *Arrangement in Grey and Black, No. I: The Artist's Mother* (Louvre, Paris).

Wilson, Richard (1714–82) Welsh Classical landscapist, influenced by Claude and Poussin. The National Museum of Wales, Cardiff, holds an important collection of his British and Italian landscapes. In 1776 he became librarian to the Royal Academy.

Selected works: *Caernarvon Castle* (National Museum of Wales, Cardiff); *Flora Macdonald* (Scottish National Portrait Gallery, Edinburgh); *Hadrian's Villa* (Tate Gallery, London, and Manchester City Art Gallery).

Wright, Joseph (1734–97) English genre and portrait painter who specialised in fireside portraits and industrial scenes. A large number of his works are in his home town at Derby Art Gallery; he is known as Wright of Derby.

Selected works: *A Philosopher Giving a Lecture on the Orrery* (Derby Museum & Art Gallery); *An Experiment on a Bird in the Air Pump* (National Gallery, London); *Sir Brooke Boothby* (Tate Gallery, London).

Wyeth, Andrew Newell (1917–97) American figurative painter of scenes in Pennsylvania. His *Christina's World* in the Museum of Modern Art, New York, is probably the most famous American picture of the 20th century.

Selected work: *Young America* (Pennsylvania Academy of Fine Arts, Philadelphia).

Yeats, Jack Butler (1870–1957) Irish painter, born in London, brother of the poet William Butler Yeats. Jack Yeats is considered as his country's greatest modern artist.

Selected works: *Grief* (National Gallery of Ireland, Dublin); *The Two Travellers* (Tate Gallery, London).

Zoffany, Johann (1733–1810) German portraitist working in England from 1758, Italy from 1772 and India from 1783. Patronised by George III of England and a founder member of the Royal Academy.

Selected works: *Garrick, Ackman and Bransby in Lethe* (Birmingham City Art Gallery); *Self Portrait* (National Portrait Gallery, London); *The Bradshaw Family* (Tate Gallery, London); *Charles Towneley among His Marbles* (Towneley Hall Art Gallery, Burnley).

Zurbarán, Francisco de (1598–1664) Spanish Baroque religious painter whose earliest known painting, *Immaculate Conception* dated 1616, suggests he was schooled in the same naturalistic style as his contemporary Velazquez.

Selected works: *The Vision of St Peter Nolasco* (Prado, Madrid); *Death of St Bonaventure* (Louvre, Paris).

Painting Movements and Terms

Abstract Art Non-representational forms, relying on line, form and colour, rather than realistic depiction. Originally formulated by Kandinsky c1912, the art form was embraced by all media, including sculpture. The early years of English Abstract art are represented in the Jim Ede collection at Kettle's Yard, Cambridge, which includes a large collection by Henri Gaudier-Brzeska and works by Nicholson and Brancusi.

Abstract Expressionism American painting movement developed in the 1940s from Surrealism, in which the idea is to make painting a spontaneous act, devoid of premeditation. Jackson Pollock and Willem de Kooning are the foremost exponents of Action Painting (or Tachisme, as it is called in France), using riotous swirls and splatters of colour. Rothko, Motherwell and Gorky were also Abstract Expressionists.

Academic Painting Traditional and figurative painting, often representing the work of a school or academy.

Action Painting see Abstract Expressionism.

Alla Prima Describes the technique, general since the 19th century but considered freakish and slapdash before then, of completing the picture surface in one session in full colour and with such opacity that neither any previous drawing nor underpainting (if in existence) modifies the final effect. The French term is 'Au Premier Coup'.

Altarpiece Decorated screen or panel placed behind an altar. The number of panels is indicated by the words diptych (2), triptych (3) or polyptych (many).

Armory Show, 1913 This exhibition introduced New York to modern European painting and sculpture, including the work of Marcel Duchamp.

Arts and Crafts English aesthetic movement that grew out of disenchantment at the mass-produced and trite decorative arts that followed the Industrial Revolution. By 1861, the social reformer, poet and designer William Morris had co-founded a firm of interior decorators dedicated to recapturing the essence and quality of medieval craftmanship. Together with artists Edward Burne-Jones and Ford Madox Brown, and architect Philip Webb, Morris set out to produce hand-crafted jewellery, wallpaper, textiles, furniture and books. Many of Morris's wallpaper and furniture designs continue to be popular today.

Art Brut (Raw Art) Term coined by Jean Dubuffet, referring to spontaneous and untrained artworks, often by criminals or the mentally ill.

Art Nouveau (New Art) Art and design style developed at the end of the 19th century, incorporating angular or sinuous vegetable forms into furniture and architecture. The style had its roots in the Arts and Crafts Movement and was popular all over Europe and North America. Samuel Bing coined the term when he opened his Paris gallery under the name L'Art Nouveau in 1895, although in Germany it was known as 'Jugendstil', in Italy as 'Stile Floreale' or 'Stile Liberty', in Spain as 'Modernismo' and in Austria as 'Sezession'. Leading exponents included René Lalique (glassware), Louis Comfort Tiffany (lamps and jewellery), Alphonse Mucha (graphic design), Alfred Gilbert (sculpture), Charles Rennie Mackintosh (interiors, buildings, furniture), Victor Horta and Hector Guimard (architecture), and Klimt, Beardsley, Jan Toorop and Ferdinand Hodler (art).

Ashcan School Painting group preoccupied with depicting the low-life of New York in the early 20th century. George Wesley Bellows and his master, Robert Henri, were leading exponents.

Attribution An artwork is 'attributed' to an artist when its provenance has not been proven.

Au Premier Coup see Alla Prima.

Automatism The method of producing a painting spontaneously and without conscious control. Used by Surrealists such as Miró and Abstract Expressionists such as Pollock.

Avant-garde Literally 'Vanguard'. In the forefront of artistic development, often with a conscious rejection of traditional methods or prior art forms.

Barbizon School Mid-19th-century French school of landscape painting based in the village of Barbizon, near Fontainebleau. Members included Théodore Rousseau, Narcisse Diaz, Daubigny and Millet. As the precursors of Impressionism they painted *en plein air* observing light.

Baroque European style of art and architecture following the High Renaissance and Mannerism, c1600–1740. It was a particularly Catholic style, popular in Italy, France and Spain in churches and public buildings, and encouraged as an integral part of the Counter-Reformation to appeal to the emotions and the senses of a still largely illiterate population. It was also eminently suitable for dramatising the idea of the divine right of kingship, and was fostered by many monarchs, such as Louis XIV of France. Exponents included the sculptor Bernini and the painters Rubens and da Cortona.

Bauhaus School of modern art and design originally based in Weimar, founded and headed by the architect Walter Gropius in 1919. Its policy was to explore the avant-garde and to reforge the link between art and design and industry, which the Arts and Crafts Movement had largely surrendered. The Bauhaus moved to Dessau in 1925, and then to Berlin, where it was closed by the Nazis in 1933. The new Bauhaus was set up by László Moholy-Nagy in Chicago in 1937.

Blaue Reiter, Der (Blue Rider) German Expressionist group that exhibited in Munich in 1911 and 1912. Among its members was the Russian émigré Kandinsky, who developed one of the earliest forms of abstract painting, and Franz Marc. It was an early titlework of Kandinsky's which provided the name. Other key members were Georges Braque, Robert Delaunay, André Derain, Paul Klee, August Macke, Henri Rousseau and Maurice de Vlaminck. Representative works are at the Kunsthalle, Bielefeld, Germany.

Bloomsbury Group British group of the 1920s and 1930s, influenced by French Post-Impressionism and later developments. Members included Vanessa Bell, Roger Fry and Duncan Grant. Roger Fry staged the first Post-Impressionist exhibition in London in 1910.

Brücke, Die (The Bridge) Among the earliest of the German Expressionist groups, Die Brücke was founded in Dresden in 1905, and included the artists van Dongen, Erich Heckel, Kirchner, Nolde and Karl Schmidt-Rottluff. The group disbanded in 1913. Two of the best collections of artworks by Die Brücke are housed in the Brücke-Museum, Berlin, and the Kunsthalle at Bielefeld. Kirchner's portrait series of the Die Brücke members is in the Wallraf-Richartz Museum / Ludwig Museum, Cologne.

Cabinet Picture Small easel picture, usually not more than about 3 or 4 feet across, and often much less. The minor Dutch masters were the principal painters of this type of furniture picture at its best.

Camera Obscura Mechanical means of securing accuracy in drawing, particularly of topographical detail. Invented in the 16th century and consisting of an arrangement of lenses and mirrors in a darkened tent or box. The view seen through the lens is reflected through the mirrors on to a sheet of paper, so that all the observer has to do is to trace round the edges. Canaletto is known to have used the

ART

device in making studies for his 'Vedute' (views). Camera Lucida is a more sophisticated optical instrument incorporating a prism.

Camden Town Group British group formed in 1911 and influenced by the Post-Impressionists. Members included Sickert, Gore, Augustus John, Harold Gilman, Charles Ginner, Lucien Pissaro and Robert Bevan.

Capriccio A picture in which real scenes, forms and figures are rearranged to suit a particular composition.

Caravaggisti Those artists heavily influenced by the style of Caravaggio, particularly in his use of chiaroscuro – contrasting light and dark. A strong Dutch Caravaggist school in the 17th century included van Honthorst, Terborch and Dirk van Baburen.

Cartoon Originally a full-size preparatory drawing of an intended artwork (painting, fresco or tapestry).

Chiaroscuro (Italian, light and dark) Defined contrast of light and dark most particularly in candle-lit scenes. Term used to describe works by Rembrandt and Caravaggio.

Classicism The imitation of Classical art, i.e. the style of Ancient Greece or Rome. An ordered style based on the harmony of perspective and composition, devised in the early Renaissance period by Filippo Brunelleschi. Classicism influenced thinking in the Renaissance period, leading to the philosophies of Platonism and Humanism, and the stories of Homer and other ancients provided a host of popular subjects which were applied to portraits, history subjects (Titian, Jacques-Louis David) and landscape (Poussin, Claude) into the 18th century. The Stoicism of ancient Rome provided the inspiration for the Neo-classical reaction to the Rococo style in the 1780s. In the 19th century the more mundane details of life in ancient Greece or Rome became the vehicle for finely executed decorative works by Leighton, Alma-Tadema and Albert Moore.

CoBrA Painting group that drew members from Copenhagen, Brussels and Amsterdam, including Appel and Jorn; founded in 1948. Their style incorporated violent figurative forms with Action Painting. Collections are in the Stedelijk Museum, Amsterdam, the Stedelijk Van Abbe-Museum, Eindhoven, and the Museum voor Schone Kunsten, Ghent.

Collage Picture built up wholly or partly from pieces of paper, cloth or other material stuck on to the canvas or other ground. The word comes from the French *coller* (to stick). The device was much used by the early Cubists and by the Dadaists, such as Kurt Schwitters. In his last years Matisse used pieces of coloured paper as a complete substitute for painting.

Colorfield Painting American offshoot of Abstract Expressionism and Minimalism, exploring monochromes or restricted contrasts in paint. The original of this idea was Malevich's *Black Square* of 1913. Rothko and Klein were typical exponents.

Constructivism Russian abstract sculptural and architectural movement from 1917 to 1921, founded by Vladimir Tatlin and developed by Naum Gabo and Antoine Pevsner, whose interest centred on movement in space and a reflection of the modern age.

Counterproof Mirror-image reproduction made by damping an original drawing or engraving, laying a damp sheet of clean paper on it, and then running both through a press. It is sometimes done by an artist in order to bring a fresh eye to his/her work by seeing it in reverse, but it is also the commonest method of faking 'original' drawings. Such fakes are obviously easily detectable because of the reversal. An offset is the same as a counterproof but has a wider meaning, for example in printing.

Cubism In 1907 Picasso and Braque began what was perhaps the first major development in painting away from figurative art. They were influenced by African tribal masks and by Cézanne, who looked at the world in terms of subtle coloured planes. This was the basis of Facet Cubism (1907–9). Analytical Cubism (1910–12) further fragmented basic shapes from all angles, and Synthetic Cubism (1913–14) totally recreated new objects. Delaunay (see Orphism), Léger and Gris were prominent Cubists. Although, as a particular style of art, Cubism developed into other things, it changed forever the way objects, and even the human form, were looked at.

Dada Formulated as an anarchic form of Expressionism during World War I in Zurich, 1916, possibly by the poet Tristan Tzara. The main centres of Dada in Germany were in Berlin, Hanover and Cologne. Its purpose was to discomfit and enrage the viewer. One of its major exponents was Kurt Schwitters, whose *Elterwater Merz* is in the Hatton Gallery at the University of Newcastle upon Tyne. Other exponents included Man Ray, Jean Arp, Duchamp, Ernst, Hannah Hoch and Picabia. Dada eventually developed into Surrealism.

Euston Road School Originally known as the Fitzroy Street School, this was a London-based school of painting and drawing, 1937–9, established by Pasmore, Claude Rogers and William Coldstream. It aimed to counteract the tendencies of Surrealism and abstract art by returning to more figurative and natural forms of expression. Exponents included Vanessa Bell, Eric Gill, Duncan Grant, Augustus John, Kenneth Martin, John Nash and Fred Uhlman.

Expressionism Early 20th-century painting movement that expressed highly charged emotions and thoughts through colour, violence, distortion and exaggeration. The German Expressionist groups were among the first so to characterise their work, which itself developed further into Dada and Abstract Expressionism.

Fauves (Wild Beasts) An initially derogatory label applied by the critics of artists such as Derain, Matisse, Rouault and Vlaminck when their work was exhibited in one room at the Paris Salon d'Automne of 1905. The distortion and flat patterns, along with the intensity of the colour, created a furore, and the Fauves were born. Matisse came to be regarded as their leader, although the movement itself had fallen apart by 1908 as a number of its members defected to Cubism.

Fête champêtre Typical Rococo scene of lovers in an ideal setting, as epitomised by Lancret and Fragonard.

Fête galante Pastoral masquerade in dreamlike setting, as painted by Lancret and Watteau.

Figurative Art Artworks that contain recognisable objects.

Found Object (objet trouvé) A Dadaist and Surrealist technique of taking any given object and displaying it as an art form, as in *Bicycle Wheel*.

Fresco Wall-painting using water-based paints on damp plaster, particularly in European churches and ancient Greek and Egyptian temples. Giotto was one of the masters of fresco painting.

Futurism Italian art movement developed in Venice c1909–15, embracing the machine and new technology. Balla, Carrà, Umberto Boccioni and Gino Severini were its leading exponents. The term was born in Paris, in an article in *Le Figaro* by the poet Filippo Marinetti (1876–1944). Although Futurism is sometimes used to mean any art more recent than 1900, as a discrete aesthetic movement it died early in World War I.

Genre Type of subject painting or, more particularly, paintings of everyday life in a naturalistic style, reported without idealisation. Extremely popular in 17th-century Holland.

German Expressionism Much of German Expressionism grew out of a painterly reaction to modernity, but most particularly to the horrors of World War I. Die Brücke was one of the first Expressionist groups, and the movement also embraced Der Blaue Reiter and Dada. Representative artists include Ernst Barlach, Beckmann, Grosz, Kirchner and Nolde.

German Romantic Painting Early 19th-century forerunner of the English Pre-Raphaelite school. Artists were inspired by the collection of 14th and 15th century painting at the home of Bernhard August von Lindenau, now the Staatliches Lindenau-Museum, Altenburg. Friedrich, Philip Otto Runge and the Nazarenes are typical exponents.

Gothic A generic term first used in the Renaissance period to describe the style of the 11th to 15th centuries. It was initially a critical term implying barbarism because the style made no reference to Classical precedents. In the 19th century medieval architecture and painting 'pre-Raphael' became the inspiration for a Victorian resurgence, led by the critic John Ruskin and the architect-designer A. W. Pugin, which produced 'Gothic' fantasies far removed from the original inspiration. William Morris, whilst also taking the medieval Gothic period for inspiration, went back to basics and developed the culture of craftsmanship and simple forms.

Grisaille A painting done in tones of grey to define shadows or modelling. Often used in *trompe l'oeil*.

Happening An art form developed from the 1960s in which an artist participates in an action that encompasses the whole purpose of the piece, and once over is gone. Similar to Performance Art. Largely developed by Joseph Beuys.

High Victorian Art The British art of the 1870s until the turn of the century, epitomised by the languid classical beauties of Albert Moore, Leighton and Alma-Tadema – fabulously painted, very beautiful and often low on meaning. Fine collections are in the Lady Lever Art Gallery, Port Sunlight; Birmingham Museum and Art Gallery; and the Tate Gallery, London, as well as at Leighton's House in Holland Park Road, London.

History Painting After portraiture, the painting of uplifting scenes from history, the Bible or allegory was the highest form of art according to Reynolds. It was also used very effectively for propaganda purposes by the Neo-Classical painters such as Jacques-Louis David. (See his *Death of Marat*.)

Hudson River School 19th-century American landscape painting school, highly Romantic in feeling and glorifying the wonders of nature. The name is properly applied to the period after 1825 when leading exponent Thomas Cole, painter of *The Voyage of Life*, settled in New York. Other members include Albert Bierstadt, Asher B. Osmond and Frederick Church.

Impasto Word used to describe the thickness of the paint applied to a canvas or panel. When the paint is so heavily applied that it stands up in lumps, with the tracks of the brush clearly evident, it is said to be 'heavily' impasted.

Impressionism Essentially the painting of light and its effects on nature and objects. Developed in France in the late 19th century and influential all over Europe. Monet's *Impression: Sunrise* (Musée Marmottan, Paris) of 1872 was the work that suggested the name of the movement. Other leading protagonists included Cézanne, Degas, Morisot, Pissarro, Renoir and Sisley. The Impressionist exhibitions were held between 1874 and 1886. Seurat and Paul Signac took Impressionism a stage further with Pointillism.

International Gothic Late 14th-century form of Gothic which spread throughout Europe. Leading exponents were Gentile da Fabriano and Pisanello.

Kinetic Art Art that relies on real or apparent movement.

Land Art, Earth Art Arrangements of earth mounds or natural elements in situ, often in rural areas. Developed in the USA from the 1960s as a reaction to materialistic Pop Art. Richard Long is a leading exponent. Grizedale Forest in Cumbria is one of the foremost sculpture parks here, specialising in sculpture within natural settings.

Maestà (Majesty) A term used to describe a painting of the Virgin and Child enthroned, with saints or angels.

Mannerism The style that succeeded the High Renaissance, c1520–1600, exemplified by exaggerated figure drawing. Bronzino, El Greco, Michelangelo, Parmigianino and Pontormo were all Mannerists.

Metaphysical School Surrealist art group formed in Ferrara in 1917 by de Chirico and Carrà, which survived until 1920.

Minimalism American art movement in painting and sculpture, essentially paring ideas down to bare essentials. Exponents include Carl André and Richard Serra.

Mobile A form of sculpture invented in 1932 by Alexander Calder, and named by Marcel Duchamp. Usually a mobile consists of a number of shapes cut from wood, cardboard, plastic or metal, connected by wires or rods and suspended so that a gentle touch will cause the whole to revolve and produce transforming 3D patterns of planes, solids and colours, and sometimes sounds.

Modern Art Accepted as the course of art in the 20th century from Impressionism up to the present day, embracing all major artistic developments including Cubism, Expressionism, Surrealism, Abstract Art, Pop Art, Minimalism and Performance Art. Excellent British public collections are in the Tate Galleries in London, Liverpool and St Ives; and the Scottish National Gallery of Modern Art in Edinburgh.

Nabis (Prophets) French anti-Impressionist art group inspired by Paul Gauguin's use of outline and flat colour which exhibited from 1892 to 1899. Members included Bonnard, Denis, Paul Sérusier and Vuillard.

Nazarenes Group of early 19th-century German and Austrian Romantic religious painters, founded by Friedrich Overbeck and Franz Pforr.

Neo-classicism Often described as the art of the French Revolution, it was a late 18th-century

ART

reaction to the fussiness of the Rococo, embracing noble simplicity and stoic grandeur. Jacques-Louis David was its leading exponent in painting, and Antonio Canova in sculpture.

Neo-Impressionism A pre-Cubist movement which examined Impressionism from a scientific standpoint rather than an aesthetic one. An offshoot of Neo-Impressionism was Pointillism.

Neo-Plasticism Mondrian's term for his style of pure abstract art, first used in *De Stijl* magazine in 1917.

Neue Sachlichkeit An inter-war German brutal realism art style represented by Dix, Grosz and Christian Schad. The literal meaning is 'New Objectivity'.

Newlyn School Group of British painters based in the fishing village near Penzance, Cornwall, and dedicated to Plein air, following the lead in France. The school was founded by Stanhope Forbes (1857-1947) and his wife Elizabeth (1857–1912). Other members included Walter Langley (1852–1922) and Laura Knight (née Johnson) and her husband Harold.

New English Art Club British art group founded in 1886, which included George Clausen, Stanhope Forbes, Sargent, Steer and Edward Stott's work. The Club is well represented in the collection at Cartwright Hall, Bradford.

Norwich School A group of early 19th-century landscape painters led by Cotman and Crome.

Objet trouvé see Found Object.

Omega Workshops Co-operative workshop-cum-showroom at 33 Fitzroy Square, London, run by Roger Fry from 1913 to 1919, for the production of painted furniture, textiles, artefacts and decorative commissions.

Op Art (short for Optical Art) is a style of painting which manipulates overall patterns, using repeated shapes or undulating lines which give an optical illusion of movement and often dazzles the beholder. Victor Vasarely (1908–97) is often considered a precursor of the op art movement with his black and white geometrical paintings but the movement became established in the early 1960s by Bridget Riley when she began to use colour in her optical paintings. The term became popularised following the 1965 New York City exhibition 'The Responsive Eye' at the Museum of Modern Art.

Perspective Quasi-mathematical system for the representation of three-dimensional objects in spatial recession on a two-dimensional surface, i.e. for the creation of an independent pictorial space as a microcosm of nature. The basic assumption of all perspective systems is that parallel lines never meet, but they appear to do so; and that, further, all parallel lines going in any one direction meet at a single point on the horizon, known as a vanishing point.

Pietà (Pity) Painting or sculpture showing the dead Christ cradled in the lap of the Virgin Mary.

Plein air 19th- and 20th-century landscape painting carried out in the open air, depicting nature and light as realistically as possible, as opposed to the deliberate Classicism of Old Masters such as Claude Lorrain and Poussin. Plein airists included the Barbizon School, the Impressionists, the Pre-Raphaelites, Millais, Ford Madox Brown and William Holman Hunt.

Pointillism Also known as 'Divisionism'. Seurat developed the Neo-Impressionist technique of using tiny dots of colour to build up form and subject; most notably used in his *Sunday Afternoon on the Island of the Grand Jatte*.

Pop Art American-formulated art form embracing painting, graphic design and sculpture, and preoccupied with modern technology, materialism and advertising. Exponents included Warhol, Blake, Johns, Robert Rauschenberg, Hamilton, Hockney, Lichtenstein and Claes Oldenburg.

Post-Impressionism Roger Fry of the Bloomsbury Group coined the term when he staged the 'Manet and the Post-Impressionists' Exhibition in London in 1910. They were artists whose chief feature in common was that they had rejected naturalism in various ways, through form, colour and subject, and included Cézanne, Denis, Gauguin, van Gogh, Picasso, Rouault, Seurat, Paul Sérusier, and Vlaminck.

Pre-Raphaelite Brotherhood The dream of a new generation to return art to its original purity of form and colour by preferring truth to nature to the stylised ideals of the Royal Academy and the ground rules laid down by its first president, Reynolds. The group was formed in London in 1848 by the painters Dante Gabriel Rossetti, William Holman Hunt, Millais and James Collinson, the art critics William Michael Rossetti and Frederick Stephens, and the sculptor Thomas Woolner. The group itself was shortlived, as its members were following separate artistic paths by 1853, but its impact on contemporary Victorian art was far more long-lasting. Pre-Raphaelitism strongly influenced Ford Madox Brown, Burne-Jones, Augustus Egg, Frith, Hubert Herkomer, Watts, among others, and formed the basis of High Victorian Art. It was also a foundation stone of the Arts and Crafts Movement, led by William Morris, and the English Art Nouveau of Charles Rennie Mackintosh and the Glasgow School, Scottish painters of the late 19th century. The style also opened the way for a new class of art collectors in the form of major industrialists based in the north, important contemporary art galleries such as the Grosvenor Gallery, and satire in the form of Gilbert and Sullivan's *Patience* and the cartoons in *Punch*. Subject matter varies from the willowy and lush allegorical beauties of Rossetti and Burne-Jones to the real-life and religious subjects of Holman Hunt and Ford Madox Brown. Major collections of Pre-Raphaelite art are in the Tate Gallery, London; Walker Art Gallery, Liverpool; Lady Lever Art Gallery, Port Sunlight; Birmingham Museum and Art Gallery, and Manchester City Art Gallery.

Primitive Term applied to pre-Renaissance art and provincial or naive art by untrained artists.

Provenance The documented history – and hence authenticity – of an artwork: who created it, who owned it, etc.

Ready-Made Term coined by Duchamp for his found objects, such as the urinal he exhibited at the 1913 Armory Show, signed 'R. Mutt'.

Realism Term applied to the realistic painting of artists such as Courbet, using a precision of detail and natural colour without idealisation.

Renaissance The 'rebirth' of art and ideas in Italy after the Dark Ages and Gothic art, starting in the 14th century. It had repercussions around the European world on artistic expression, intellectual discussion, religious thought and scientific experiment. It was inspired by the rediscovery of the Classicism of the ancient civilisations of Rome and Greece in Italy and the rise of humanism. The Early Renaissance period, up to c1500, includes the artists Giotto, Duccio and Uccello, and the first experiments in art with perspective and painterly modelling. The High Renaissance saw the development of architecture, sculpture and painting by men such as Michelangelo, Leonardo, Raphael and Titian, leading to Mannerism and the late

Renaissance of Correggio, Veronese and the sculptor Benvenuto Cellini. Dürer was responsible for introducing new ideas into Germany, and Holbein the Younger into England. France embraced Renaissance ideals following the rise of Italian influence after the marriage of Catherine de' Medici to the future Henri II in 1533.

Rococo 18th-century French decorative style, epitomised by the paintings of Rigaud, Boucher, Fragonard and Watteau. It illustrated the dream world in which the nobility wished to live, of sunlit *fêtes galantes*, garden swings, cherry-picking and whimsical shepherdesses. The French Revolution forced them to face an unpleasant reality. Rococo also influenced painters, architects and sculptors in Austria , Germany and Italy.

Romanticism The early 19th-century reaction to the cold formality of Neo-classicism, the style introduced a new depth of colour, expression and passion into painting not seen since Titian, particularly in the works of Delacroix and Géricault. Stylistically different Romanticists were William Blake, Constable, Friedrich, Fuseli, Turner, the Nazarenes and the Pre-Raphaelites.

Sacra conversazione A painting of the Virgin and Child, often with saints or family in an informal setting, first depicted by Fra Angelico in the 15th-century. The term literally means 'Holy Conversation'.

Slade School of Art London art school, founded 1871, that in the 1890s and under the professorship in 1918–30 of Henry Tonks produced some of the most important painters of British 20th-century art. Slade teachers and graduates included David Bomberg, Mark Gertler, Harold Gilman, Spencer Gore, Duncan Grant, Augustus John, Gwen John, Wyndham Lewis, Ambrose McEvoy, Paul Nash, C.R.W. Nevinson, Ben Nicholson, William Orpen, William Rothenstein, Matthew Smith, Stanley Spencer and Edward Wadsworth.

Socialist Realism A realistic if stylised art form officially sponsored and sanctioned for propaganda purposes in the Soviet Union, where it was first defined in 1932, and later in China and Cuba.

Stijl, De ('The style') Dutch 20th-century art movement which embraced painting, sculpture, graphic design, interior design and architecture. Exponents include Mondrian, van Doesburg, Bart van der Leck and the architects Rietveld and Jacobus Oud. De Stijl architecture includes the Zonnestraal Sanatorium by Johannes Duiker, and Rietveld's Schröder house at Utrecht.

Suprematism Malevich produced his first non-representational Suprematist painting in 1913, *Black Square*, exploring elementary forms and restricted contrasts of colour which in turn influenced Expressionism, Abstract Art and Colorfield Painting.

Surrealism Art of the inner reality, of objects out of context, and spontaneous writing, developed from Dada, founded in 1924 by the poet André Breton and influenced by Sigmund Freud's ideas. Exponents included de Chirico, Dali, Duchamp, Ernst, Klee, Magritte, Miró, Man Ray and Tanguy.

Symbolism Late figurative style of painting, associated with the Art Nouveau period. Jan Toorop, Johan Thorn Prikker, Munch, Arnold Böcklin, Redon, Puvis de Chavannes, Rouault and Moreau were all exponents.

Tempera Although this term actually means any kind of binder which will serve to 'temper' powder colour and make it workable, in practice it is confined to egg tempera (using the yolk of the egg), which was until the late 15th century the commonest technique of painting easel pictures.

Tenebrism Sombrely atmospheric painting particularly as seen in the works of those early 17th-century painters, mostly Neapolitan and Spanish, who were much influenced by Caravaggio. The term literally means 'Dark colouring'.

Trompe l'oeil Illusionistic painting effect, such as painting a ceiling to look as if it is open to the sky. The term literally means 'Deceive the eye'.

Veduta (View) Detailed topographical painting of an existing place. Leading 'Vedutisti' were Guardi and Canaletto.

Vernissage The practice – once common, now discontinued – by which painters would enter an exhibition after the pictures had been hung but before it was open to the public, so that they could varnish and also retouch their pictures. Turner would often submit his pictures incomplete and take advantage of Vernissage (Varnishing Day). Nowadays the custom is merely to invite favoured patrons to see the pictures before the public are allowed in.

Vorticism Brief English movement from 1914 with similar influences to Futurism, led by Percy Wyndham Lewis.

Watercolour The English landscapists were particularly strong in their use of watercolour, especially the artists of the Norwich School, William Blake, Girtin, Bonington and Turner. Dante Gabriel Rossetti brought a new jewel-like richness to watercolour painting in the 1850s, which raised the medium from insipidity.

A
R
T

Artists (not listed in main table)

Amigoni, Jacopo (c1682–1752) Venetian history and portrait painter. The altarpiece of Emmanuel College, Cambridge, is his.

André, Carl (1935–) American Minimalist sculptor famous for his 120 bricks (*Equivalent VIII*) in the Tate.

Arp, Jean (1887–1966) French artist and co-founder of Dadaism.

Avercamp, Hendrick (1585–1634) Dutch landscape painter who specialised in winter scenes.

Baily, Edward Hodges (1788–1867) English sculptor whose most famous work is his *Nelson* for the column in Trafalgar Square.

Beechey, Sir William (1753–1839) English portraitist who was knighted for *George III and the*

Prince of Wales Reviewing Troops.

Beerbohm, Max (1872–1956) English writer and caricaturist famous for his watercolours of Oscar Wilde and Edward VII.

Bell, Vanessa (1879–1961) English painter and decorative designer, sister of the writer Virginia Woolf.

Calder, Alexander (1898–1976) American kinetic sculptor, abstract painter and illustrator of children's books. Calder invented the mobile.

Canova, Antonio (1757–1822) Venetian Neoclassicist sculptor whose work includes *The Three Graces* and *Daedalus and Icarus*.

Christo (1935–) Bulgarian-born, American sculptor famous for his 'wrappings', e.g. of the

Reichstag building. His full name is Javacheff Christo.

Cooper, Samuel (c1608–72) English miniaturist whose *Oliver Cromwell* (Buccleuch College) was his most famous work.

Cuyp, Jacob (1594–1651) Dutch landscape and animal painter, many of whose works are housed in the Dulwich Gallery, London.

Dadd, Richard (1817–86) English literary painter whose *Fairy Feller's Master-Stroke* is in the Tate. He murdered his father and was confined in an asylum.

Daumier, Honoré (1808–79) French caricaturist and political satirist.

Delaroche, Paul (1797–1859) French history painter whose *Children of King Edward* is housed in the Louvre.

Donatello (c1386–1466) Florentine sculptor whose work included his *David* and *St George Killing the Dragon* (properly, Donato di Niccolò.)

Dyce, William (1806–64) Scottish painter and pioneer of state art education in Great Britain.

Eyck, Hubert van (c1366–1426) Flemish painter; the brother of Jan van Eyck.

Gabo, Naum (1890–1977) Russian born, US artist; the brother of Antoine Pevsner, with whom he founded Constructivism.

Gérard, Baron François (1770–1837) French artist, born in Rome; his *Cupid and Psyche* is housed in the Louvre.

Giacometti, Alberto (1901–66) Swiss sculptor and painter best known for his attenuated sculptures of solitary figures.

Gibson, John (1790–1866) Welsh Neo-classical sculptor whose *Tinted Venus* is in the Walker Art Gallery, Liverpool.

Gilbert & George (1943– / 1942–) English avant-garde artists, noted for painting their faces gold and wearing identical outfits. Their full names are Gilbert Proesch and George Passmore.

Guardi, Giovanni (1699–1760) Venetian painter, born in Vienna, brother of Francesco Guardi.

Hamilton, Gavin (1723–98) Scottish painter in Rome, who pioneered the depiction of Homeric subjects in a severe manner.

Heartfield, John (1891–1968) German painter, originally Helmut Herzfelde, a leading member of Berlin Dada and a lifelong pacifist.

Hoppner, John (1758–1810) English portraitist whose masterpiece was *The Countess of Oxford.*

Hughes, Arthur (1830–1915) English painter associated with the Pre-Raphaelite Brotherhood, although never formally.

Ibbetson, Julius Caesar (1759–1817) English landscapist who specialised in the scenery of the Lakes and his native Yorkshire.

Judd, Donald (1928–1994) American Minimalist artist and sculptor who has geometric boxes built especially to use in his work.

Kiefer, Anselm (1945–) German avant-garde artist whose work tends to concentrate on German history.

Kline, Franz Joseph (1910–62) American artist who became an Abstract Expressionist around 1950, using black shapes on white canvas.

Le Brun, Charles (1619–90) French historical painter; the first director of the Gobelins tapestry works (1662).

Lear, Edward (1812–88) English landscape painter,

youngest of 21 children, famous for his nonsense verse.

Liebermann, Max (1847–1935) German painter and etcher, leader of the German Impressionist school.

Lorenzo, Monaco (the Monk) (c1370–1425) Sienese painter in the International Gothic style who took holy orders in 1391.

Macke, August (1887–1914) German painter and leader of Der Blaue Reiter group killed in action in WWI.

Masson, André (1896–1987) French Surrealist painter and graphic artist who was famous for working whilst in a state of trance.

Moses, Anna Mary ('Grandma') (1860–1961) American Primitive artist who did not start to paint until she was 75 years old.

Newman, Barnett (1905–70) American painter who founded the 'subject of the Artist' school with William Baziotes, Rothko and Motherwell.

Nolan, (Sir) Sidney (1917–92) Australian artist noted for his series of Ned Kelly paintings, begun in 1946.

Oldenburg, Claes Thure (1929–) Swedish-born, US sculptor specialising in representing giant foodstuffs, such as hamburgers.

Pevsner, Antoine (1886–1962) Russian-born French Constructivist painter, brother of Naum Gabo.

Quelling, Arnold (1653–1686) English sculptor who collaborated with Grinling Gibbons on many works.

Rackham, Arthur (1867–1939) English artist best known for his illustrations of *Peter Pan* and of Hans Christian Andersen's fairy tales.

Ramsay, Allan (1713–84) Scottish portrait painter to George III of England.

Rauschenberg, Robert (1925–) American avant-garde artist specialising in works constructed from everyday rubbish. Also a noted Pop silk-screenist.

Ray, Man (1890–1976) American painter, photographer and film-maker; he co-founded the New York Dadaist movement.

Rousseau, Théodore (1812–67) French landscape painter whose best known work was *The Forest of Compiègne.*

Schiele, Egon (1890–1918) Austrian Expressionist painter who died in the influenza epidemic of 1918.

Signac, Paul (1863–1935) French painter akin to Seurat, but using mosaic-like patches of colour as opposed to dots.

Smith, David Roland (1906–65) American sculptor who specialised in welded metal pieces.

Tàpies, Antoni (1923–) Spanish painter; a founder member of the Dau al Set (Die with the Seven) and El Paso groups.

Tatlin, Vladimir (1885–1953) Russian painter and designer, the founder of Constructivism, whose model *Monument to the Third International* was never built.

Teniers, the Elder, David (1582–1649) Flemish genre painter whose best-known work is *Temptation of St Anthony.*

Tenniel, (Sir) John (1820–1914) English illustrator and political satirist (especially in *Punch*), best known for his illustrations of Lewis Carroll's *Alice in Wonderland* and *Through the Looking Glass.*

Tinguely, Jean (1925–91) Swiss sculptor who pioneered kinetic and auto-destructive art.

Twygge, Richard (1476–1510) English painter on

glass whose work can be seen in many Malvern buildings.

Van Loo, Charles André (Carle) (1705–65) Prolific French artist and Rococo decorator; principle painter to Louis XV from 1762; the most talented of the artistic Van Loo family.

Van Loo, Jean-Baptiste (1684–1745) French portrait painter in England also notable for historical subjects. Brother of Charles André.

Wilkie, (Sir) David (1785–1841) Scottish painter famous for his genre pictures in the Dutch style, eg, *Card Players*, and *Penny Wedding*.

Zincke, Christian Frederick (c1683–1767) German enamel portraitist in London from 1714.

Famous Works of Art

Paintings	Artist	Location
Abduction of Rebecca, The	Delacroix	Louvre, Paris
Absinthe Drinker, The	Manet	Copenhagen
Accommodations of Desire	Dali	Mr & Mrs Julien Levy Collection, Bridgewater, Connecticut
Adam and Eve	Dürer	Prado, Madrid
Adam and Eve in Paradise	Brueghel	Mauritshuis, The Hague
Adoration of the Kings, The	Brueghel the Elder (Pieter)	Musées Royaux des Beaux-Arts, Brussels
Adoration of the Kings, The	Correggio	Brera, Milan
Adoration of the Kings, The	Veronese	National Gallery, London
Adoration of the Lamb, The	Jan van Eyck	Altarpiece of St Bavo Cathedral, Ghent
Adoration of the Magi, The	Bassano	Kunsthistorisches Museum, Vienna
Adoration of the Magi, The	Bosch	Johnson Collection, Philadelphia
Adoration of the Magi, The	Botticelli	Uffizi, Florence (1475) & Washington National Gallery, DC (1482)
Adoration of the Magi, The (1500)	Dürer	Uffizi, Florence
Adoration of the Magi, The	Leonardo da Vinci	Uffizi, Florence
Adoration of the Magi, The (1446)	Lippi	National Gallery, Washington DC
Adoration of the Magi, The (1479)	Memling	Memling Museum, Bruges
Adoration of the Magi, The	Velazquez	Prado, Madrid
Adoration of the Magi, The (tapestry)	Burne-Jones	Exeter College, Oxford
Adoration of the Shepherds, The	Bassano	Hampton Court Palace, London
Adoration of the Shepherds, The	Caravaggio	Museo Nazionale, Messina
Allegory of Fortitude and Wisdom	Tiepolo	Ca' Rezzonico, Venice
Allegory of Spring (aka La Prima vera)	Botticelli	Uffizi, Florence
Ambassadors, The	Holbein the Younger	National Gallery, London
Anatomy Lesson of Dr Jan Deyman	Rembrandt	Rijksmuseum, Amsterdam
Anatomy Lesson of Dr Nicolaes Tulp	Rembrandt	Mauritshuis, The Hague
Andromeda	Rembrandt	Mauritshuis, The Hague
Angelus, The	Millet	Louvre, Paris
Anna Selbdritt	Dürer	Metropolitan Museum of Art, New York
Anne of Cleves	Holbein the Younger	Victoria and Albert Museum, London
Annunciation, The	Duccio di Buoninsegna	National Gallery, London
Annunciation, The	Jan van Eyck	National Gallery, Washington DC
Annunciation, The	Goya	Private Spanish Collection
Annunciation, The	Leonardo da Vinci	Versions in the Uffizi, Florence and Louvre, Paris
Anthony and Cleopatra	Steen	Kunstsammlung der Universität, Göttingen, Germany
Antibes	Monet	Toledo Museum of Art
Aristotle Contemplating the Bust of Homer	Rembrandt	Metropolitan Museum of Art, New York
Arnolfini Wedding, The	van Eyck, Jan	National Gallery, London
Around the Fish	Klee	Museum of Modern Art, New York
Arrangement in Grey and Black; No. 1: The Artist's Mother	Whistler	Louvre, Paris
Arrangement in Grey and Black; No. 2: Thomas Carlyle	Whistler	Glasgow Art Gallery
Artist and His Wife, The	Metsu	Metropolitan Museum of Art, New York
Ascension of Christ, The	Correggio	San Giovanni Church, Parma
Assumption	Titian	S. Maria dei Frara, Venice
Assumption of the Virgin	Correggio	Parma Cathedral

ART

Paintings	Artist	Location
Assumption of the Virgin	El Greco	Church of Santo Domingo el Antiguo, Toledo, Spain
At the Bar	Toulouse-Lautrec	Kunsthaus, Zurich
At the Linen Closet	Hooch	Rijksmuseum, Amsterdam
At the Moulin Rouge	Toulouse-Lautrec	Art Institute of Chicago
At the Nouveau Cirque: Five Stuffed Shirts	Toulouse-Lautrec	Philadelphia Museum of Art
At the Races	Degas	Fogg Art Museum, Cambridge, Mass.
Avenue at Middelharnis, The	Hobbema	National Gallery, London
Backgammon Players	de Hooch	National Gallery of Ireland, Dublin
Balaam's Ass and the Angel	Rembrandt	Cognacq-Jay Museum, Paris
Ballet Scene, The	Degas	National Gallery, Washington DC
Banker Jabach and His Family, The	Le Brun	Staatliche Museen Preussischer Kulturbesitz, Berlin
Banks of the Seine, The	Henri Rousseau	Private Collection, Paris
Banquet of Anthony and Cleopatra	Tiepolo	Palazzo Labia, Venice
Baptism of Christ, The	Piero della Francesca	National Gallery, London
Bar at the Folies-Bergère, A	Manet	Courtauld Institute Galleries, London
Baron Schwiter	Delacroix	National Gallery, London
Bather	Renoir	Albright-Knox Art Gallery, Buffalo, NY (1879–90) and Sterling and Francine Clark Art Institute, Williamstown, Mass. (1881)
Bather, The	Cézanne	Museum of Modern Art, New York
Bathers	Renoir	Tyson Collection, Philadelphia
Bathsheba	Rembrandt	Louvre, Paris
Battle between Two Stags	Courbet	Louvre, Paris
Battle of Austerlitz	François Gérard	Versailles
Beach at Trouville, The	Monet	Tate Gallery, London
Beggar's Opera, The	Hogarth	Tate Gallery, London
Belle Jardinière, La	Raphael	Louvre, Paris
Belshazzar's Feast	Rembrandt	National Gallery, London
Bentheim Castle	Jacob van Ruysdael	National Gallery of Ireland, Dublin
Bicycle Wheel	Duchamp	Museum of Modern Art
Birth of Venus, The	Botticelli	Uffizi, Florence
Blind Girl, The	Millais	Birmingham City Museum & Art Gallery
Blonde with Bare Breasts	Manet	Louvre, Paris
Blue Boy, The	Gainsborough	Huntington Library & Gallery, San Marino, California
Blue Mountain	Kandinsky	Guggenheim Museum, New York
Blue Rider, The	Kandinsky	Ernst Bührle Collection, Zürich
Blue Vase, The	Cézanne	Louvre, Paris
Boat during the Flood, The	Sisley	Louvre, Paris
Boatbuilding near Flatford Mill	Constable	Victoria and Albert Museum, London
Boy Bitten by a Lizard	Caravaggio	Louvre, Paris
Boy in a Red Waist-Coat	Cézanne*	Mr & Mrs Paul Mellon Collection, Upperville, Vancouver
Boyhood of Raleigh, The	Millais	Tate Gallery, London
Breaking Wave of Kanagawa, The	Hokusai	One of 36 Views of Mt Fuji series, Art Institute of Chicago
Broadway Boogie Woogie	Mondrian	Museum of Modern Art, New York
Bubbles	Millais	Lever Foundation Collection
Burial of the Count de Orgaz	El Greco	Church of Santo Tomé, Toledo, Spain
Calling of St Matthew, The	Caravaggio	Contarelli Chapel, S. Luigi dei Francesci, Rome
Calvary	Bassano	Fitzwilliam Museum, Cambridge
Capt Woodes Rogers and Family	Hogarth	National Maritime Museum, Greenwich
Capture of Samson	Rembrandt	Dahlem Museums, Berlin
Card Players	Cézanne	Metropolitan Museum of Art, New York
Cardinal Richelieu	Champaigne	Louvre, Paris
Carrying of the Cross	Van Dyck	St Paul's, Antwerp
Cascade, The	Henri Rousseau	Art Institute of Chicago
Chair and the Pipe, The (aka Van Gogh's Chair)	Van Gogh	Tate Gallery, London
Chancellor Séguier, The	Le Brun	Louvre, Paris
Charge of the Mamelukes, The	Goya	Prado, Madrid

Paintings	Artist	Location
Charging Chasseur, The	Géricault	Louvre, Paris
Charles Brandon	Holbein the Younger	Windsor Castle
Charles I and Henrietta Maria with Their Children	Van Dyck	Windsor Castle
Charles I, King of England	Van Dyck	Louvre, Paris
Charles VII	Fouquet	Louvre, Paris
Chess Players, The	Duchamp	Philadelphia Museum of Art
Child among Rocks, The	Henri Rousseau	Philadelphia Museum of Art
Children of Edward	Delaroche	Louvre, Paris
Christ among the Doctors	Veronese	Prado, Madrid
Christ before Pilate	Rembrandt	National Gallery, London
Christ Crowned With Thorns	Titian	Louvre, Paris
Christ Healing the Blind Man	Duccio	National Gallery, London
Christ in the House of His Parents	Millais	Tate Gallery, London
Christ Nailed to the Cross	Gerard David	National Gallery, London
Christ on the Cross	Goya	Prado, Madrid
Christ on the Cross	Velazquez	Prado, Madrid
Christ Taking Leave of His Mother	Correggio	National Gallery, London
Christina of Denmark, Duchess of Milan	Holbein the Younger	National Gallery, London
Church at Auvers, The	Van Gogh	Louvre, Paris
Church at Blainville	Duchamp	Philadelphia Museum of Art
Clothed Maja, The	Goya	Prado, Madrid
Colossus, The	Goya	Prado, Madrid
Composition in Black and White	Mondrian	Rijksmuseum Kröller-Müller, Otterlo, Netherlands
Composition in Diamond Shape	Mondrian	Rijksmuseum Kröller-Müller, Otterlo, Netherlands
Composition II	Kandinsky	State Tretyakov Gallery, Moscow
Conversion of St Paul, The	Michelangelo	Pauline Chapel, Vatican
Conversion of St Paul, The	Caravaggio	Sta Maria del Popolo, Rome
Conversion of St Paul, The	Brueghel the Elder (Pieter)	Kunsthistorisches Museum, Vienna
Cornfield (etching)	Jacob van Ruysdael	Petit-Palais, Paris
Cornfield, The	Constable	National Gallery, London
Coronation of the Virgin, The	Fra Angelico	Uffizi, Florence
Coronation of the Virgin, The	Raphael	Vatican Museum, Rome
Country Festival near Antwerp	Teniers the Younger	National Gallery, London
Cripples, The	Brueghel the Elder (Pieter)	Louvre, Paris
Crowning with Thorns, The	Bosch	Versions in the National Gallery, London & Escorial, Madrid
Crucifixion of St Peter	Caravaggio	Sta Maria del Popolo, Rome
Crucifixion of St Peter	Michelangelo	Pauline Chapel, Vatican
Cupid and Psyche	Van Dyck	Buckingham Palace, London
Cupid and Psyche	François Gérard	Louvre, Paris
Cure of Folly, The	Bosch	Prado, Madrid
Danae	Correggio	Borghese Gallery, Rome
Danae	Rembrandt	Hermitage, St Petersburg
Dance of Four Breton Women	Gauguin	Neue Pinakothek, Munich
Dancer	Renoir	National Gallery of Art, Washington DC
Dancers, The	Degas	Toledo Museum of Art, Toledo, Ohio
Dead Man, The	Chagall	Marc Chagall Collection, Saint-Paul, France
Death and Fire	Klee	Kunstmuseum, Berne
Dead Marat, The	Jacques-Louis David	Louvre, Paris
Death of the Virgin	Brueghel the Elder (Pieter)	National Gallery, London
Death of the Virgin	Caravaggio	Louvre, Paris
Dedham Lock and Mill	Constable	Victoria and Albert Museum, London
Déjeuner sur l'herbe, Le	Manet	Louvre, Paris
Demoiselles d'Avignon, Les	Picasso	Museum of Modern Art, New York
Deposition in the Tomb, The	Weyden	Uffizi, Florence
Descent from the Cross	Rembrandt	Alte Pinakothek, Munich
Descent from the Cross	Rubens	Antwerp Cathedral
Dignity and Impudence	Landseer	Tate Gallery, London
Dinner Table, The	Matisse	Stavros Niarchos Collection, London
Duchess of Cleveland	Lely	Courtauld Institute, London
Duet, The	Metsu	National Gallery, London
Duke of Wellington, The	Goya	National Gallery, London
Dunes	Jacob van Ruysdael	Louvre, Paris

Paintings	Artist	Location
Early Sunday Morning	Hopper	Whitney Museum of American Art, New York
Ecce Homo	Bosch	Stadelsches Kunstinstitut, Frankfurt-am-Main
Ecce Homo	Caravaggio	Galleria di Palazzo Rosso, Genoa
Ecce Homo	Correggio	National Gallery, London
Ecstasy of St Diego of Alcalá	Murillo	Louvre, Paris
Education of Cupid	Correggio	National Gallery, London
Emmanuel Philibert	Van Dyck	Dulwich Gallery, London
Entombment of the Lord, The	Massys	Musée Royal des Beaux-Arts, Antwerp
Entry into Jerusalem, The	Van Dyck	Herron Museum of Art, Indianapolis
Erasmus	Holbein the Younger	Louvre, Paris
Erasmus in the Roundel	Holbein the Younger	Kunstmuseum, Basel,
(L') Estaque, l'embarcadère	Braque	Musée National d'Art Moderne, Paris
Evening Hour, The	Munch	Munch Museet, Oslo
Ex Voto of 1662	Champaigne	Louvre, Paris
Execution of Faliero	Delacroix	Wallace Collection, London
Fable of Arachne, The (aka The Spinners)	Velazquez	Prado, Madrid
Feast of the Rose Garlands, The	Dürer	St Bartholomew Church, Venice
Field of Waterloo, The	Turner	Tate Gallery, London
Fight between Carnival and Lent, The	Brueghel the Elder (Pieter)	Kunsthistorisches Museum, Vienna
Fighting Temeraire, The	Turner	National Gallery, London
First Abstract Watercolour	Kandinsky	Nina Kandinsky Collection, Neuilly-sur-Seine
Fishing Party, A	Hogarth	Dulwich Gallery, London
Flatford Mill on the River Stour	Constable	Tate Gallery, London
Flight into Egypt	Bassano	Bassano, Italy
Football Players	Henri Rousseau	Guggenheim Museum, New York
Fortune-Teller (aka La Zingara)	Caravaggio	Louvre, Paris
Four Saints	Correggio	Metropolitan Museum of Art, New York
Frau Adele Bloch-Bauer	Klimt	Österreichische Galerie, Vienna
Frau Fritza Riedler	Klimt	Österreichische Galerie, Vienna
Fuji in Spring	Hokusai	Art Institute of Chicago
Galacidalacideoxyribonucleicacid	Dali	New England Merchant Bank, Boston, Mass.
Garden of Earthly Delights, The	Bosch	Prado, Madrid
Gardener, The	Cézanne	Tate Gallery, London
Garrick in the Character of Richard III	Hogarth	Earl of Feversham Collection
Gilles and His Family	Watteau	Wallace Collection, London
Gioconda, La (aka Mona Lisa)	Leonardo da Vinci	Louvre, Paris
Girl Asleep, A	Vermeer	Metropolitan Museum of Art, New York
Girl Balancing on a Ball	Picasso	Pushkin Museum, Moscow
Girl Drinking Wine with a Gentleman	Vermeer	Staatliche Museen Preussischer Kulturbesitz, Berlin
Girl in the Artist's Studio	Toulouse-Lautrec	Kunsthalle, Bremen
Girl with Bare Feet	Picasso	Picasso Museum, Paris
Gleaners, The	Millet	Louvre, Paris
Golconda	Magritte	D and J de Menil Collection, Houston, Texas
Goldfish and Sculpture	Matisse	Museum of Modern Art, New York
Good Samaritan, The	Hogarth	St Bartholomew's Hospital, London
Graham Children, The	Hogarth	National Gallery, London
Greenwich Hospital from the North Bank of the Thames	Canaletto	National Maritime Museum, Greenwich
Grey Tree, The	Mondrian	Haags Gemeentemuseum, The Hague
Guernica	Picasso	Prado, Madrid
Guillaume Budé	Clouet the Younger	Metropolitan Museum of Art, New York
Gypsy Girl	Hals	Louvre, Paris
Half-Past Three	Chagall	Philadelphia Museum of Art
Hamlet (aka Young Man Holding a Skull)	Hals	Richard Proby Collection, Peterborough
Hay Wain, The	Bosch	Prado, Madrid
Haywain, The	Constable	National Gallery, London

Paintings	Artist	Location
Haystacks at Giverny	Monet	Josef Rosensaft Collection, New York
Henry VIII	Holbein the Younger	Thyssen-Bornemisza Collection, Castagnola, Switzerland
Hercules and Antaeus	Cranach the Elder	Private Collection, Garmisch-Partenkirchen, Germany
Hercules Killing the Stymphalian Birds	Dürer	Germanisches Nationalmuseum, Nürnberg
Holy Family	Michelangelo	Uffizi, Florence
Holy Family	Turner	Tate Gallery, London
Holy Family on the Steps	Poussin	National Gallery, Washington DC
Holy Family with St James	Correggio	Hampton Court Palace, London
Holy Family (aka The Two Trinities)	Murillo	National Gallery, London
Hope	Watts	Tate Gallery, London
Horatius Cocles Defending Rome	Le Brun	Dulwich Gallery, London
House by the Railroad	Hopper	Museum of Modern Art, New York
Hunters in the Snow	Brueghel the Elder (Pieter)	Kunsthistorisches Museum, Vienna
Hyde Park, London	Monet	Philadelphia Museum of Art
I and the Village	Chagall	Museum of Modern Art, New York
L'île de Cythère	Watteau	J Heugel Collection, Paris
Impression: Sunrise	Monet	Musée Marmottan, Paris
In the Circus Fernando: The Ringmaster	Toulouse-Lautrec	Art Institute of Chicago
In the Field	Van Gogh	Rijksmuseum, Vincent Van Gogh, Amsterdam
Inventions of the Monsters	Dali, Salvador	Art Institute of Chicago
Jane Seymour	Holbein the Younger	Kunsthistorisches Museum, Vienna
Jewish Bride, The	Rembrandt	Rijksmuseum, Amsterdam
Jewish Cemetery	Jacob van Ruysdael	Gemäldegalerie, Dresden
Job and His Wife	Dürer	Wallraf-Richartz-Museum, Cologne
Josephine Bonaparte	François Gérard	Louvre, Paris
Judgement of Paris, The	Cranach the Elder	Kunsthalle, Karlsruhe,
Judgement of Paris, The	Rubens	National Gallery, London
Judgement of Solomon	Giorgione	Uffizi, Florence
Juggler, The	Chagall	Art Institute of Chicago
Jupiter and Io	Correggio	Kunsthistorisches Museum, Vienna
King Charles on Horseback	Van Dyck	National Gallery, London
King Cophetua and the Beggar Maid	Burne-Jones	Tate Gallery, London
King's Wife, The (aka Women with Mangoes)	Gauguin	Pushkin Museum, Moscow
Kiss, The	Klimt	Österreichische Galerie, Vienna
Kitchen-Maid, The (1658)	Vermeer	Rijksmuseum, Amsterdam
Liberty Leading the People	Delacroix	Louvre, Paris
Lady Reading a Letter at an Open Window, A	Vermeer	Gemäldegalerie, Dresden
Lamentation	Giotto	S. Maria Annunziata dell'Arena, Padua
Lamentation for Christ	Van Dyck	Alte Pinakothek, Munich
Lamentation over St Sebastian	La Tour	Staatliche Museen Preussischer Kulturbesitz, Berlin
Landscape with a Bridge	Altdorfer	National Gallery, London
Large Glass, The	Duchamp	Philadelphia Museum of Art; replica by Richard Hamilton in the Tate Gallery, London
Last Judgement, The	Michelangelo	Sistine Chapel, Vatican
Last Supper, The	Dali	National Gallery, Washington DC
Last Supper, The	Holbein the Younger	Kunstmuseum, Basel, Switzerland
Last Supper, The (mural)	Leonardo da Vinci	Convent of S. Maria delle Grazie, Milan
Laughing Cavalier, The	Hals	Wallace Collection, London
Leaping Horse, The	Constable	Royal Academy of Arts, London
Leda	Correggio	Berlin Museum
Light of the World, The	Holman Hunt	Keble College, Oxford
Linlithgow Palace	Turner	Walker Gallery, Liverpool
Little Street, The	Vermeer	Rijksmuseum, Amsterdam
Loge, La (aka The Theatre Box)	Renoir	Courtauld Institute, London
Lucretia	Dürer	Alte Pinakothek, Munich
Luncheon, The	Manet	Neue Staatsgalerie, Munich
Luncheon of the Boating Party, The	Renoir	Phillips Collection, Washington DC
Lute Player, The	Caravaggio	Hermitage, St Petersburg

ART

Paintings	Artist	Location
MacNab, The	Raeburn	John Dewar & Sons Collection
Mad Woman with a Mania of Envy	Géricault	Musée des Beaux-Arts, Lyons
Madame Charpentier and Her Children	Renoir	Metropolitan Museum of Art, New York
Mademoiselle Gachet at the Piano	Van Gogh	Kunstmuseum, Basel
Madhouse, The	Goya	Dallas, Texas
Madonna in Glory, The	Giotto	Uffizi, Florence
Madonna of St Jerome, The	Correggio	National Gallery, Parma
Madonna of the Basket, The	Correggio	National Gallery, London
Madonna of the Goldfinch, The	Raphael	Uffizi, Florence
Madonna of the Rosary	Van Dyck	Oratorio del Rosario, Palermo
Madonna of the Star	Fra Angelico	Museo di San Marco, Florence
Madonna with Angels and Saints	Gerard David	Musée des Beaux-Arts, Rouen
Madonna with Chancellor Rolin, The	Jan van Eyck	Louvre, Paris
Madonna with Musical Angels	Dürer	Staatliche Museen Preussischer Kulturbesitz, Berlin
Madonna with the Carnation	Leonardo da Vinci	Alte Pinakothek, Munich
Maestà	Duccio di Buoninsegna	Cathedral Museum, Siena
Maids of Honour, The (aka Las Meninas)	Velazquez	Prado, Madrid
Man with a Straw Hat, The	Cézanne	Metropolitan Museum of Art, New York
Market Cart, The	Gainsborough	Tate Gallery, London
Marriage at Cana	Veronese	Louvre, Paris
Marriage of Isaac and Rebecca, The (aka The Mill)	Claude Lorrain	National Gallery, London
Mars and Venus	Botticelli	National Gallery, London
Marsh in the Woods	Jacob van Ruysdael	Hermitage, St Petersburg
Massacre at Chios, The	Delacroix	Louvre, Paris
Massacre of the Innocents, The	Brueghel the Elder (Pieter)	Hampton Court Palace, London
Meninas, Las (aka Maids of Honour)	Velazquez	Prado, Madrid
Merlin and Nimue	Burne-Jones	Victoria and Albert Museum, London
Merry Company, The	Hals	Metropolitan Museum of Art, New York
Merry Drinker, The	Hals	Rijksmuseum, Amsterdam
Militia Company of Captain Frans Banning Cocq, The (aka Night Watch)	Rembrandt	Rijksmuseum, Amsterdam
Milkmaid, The (1844)	Millet	Louvre, Paris
Milkmaid of Bordeaux, The	Goya	Prado, Madrid
Mill, The (aka The Marriage of Isaac and Rebecca)	Claude Lorrain	National Gallery, London
Miracle of St Bavo	Rubens	St Bavo Cathedral, Ghent
Miss Cicely Alexander: Harmony in Grey and Green	Whistler	Tate Gallery, London
Miss Harriet Cholmondeley	Hoppner	Tate Gallery, London
Mocker Mocked, The	Klee	Museum of Modern Art, New York
Model Reading	Hopper	Art Institute of Chicago
Mona Lisa (aka La Gioconda)	Leonardo da Vinci	Louvre, Paris
Mona Lisa with Moustache and Goatee	Duchamp	Ready Made (photograph) – various venues
Money Changer and His Wife, The	Massys	Louvre, Paris
Morning Walk, The	Gainsborough	National Gallery, London
Mother beside a Cradle, A	Hooch	Staatliche Museen Preussischer Kulturbesitz, Berlin
Moulin Rouge, The	Toulouse-Lautrec	Národni Gallery, Prague
Mr and Mrs Andrews	Gainsborough	National Gallery, London
Mrs Robinson (aka Perdita)	Gainsborough	Wallace Collection, London
Mrs Siddons	Gainsborough	National Gallery, London
Mrs Siddons as the Tragic Muse	Reynolds	Henry E. Huntington Library, San Marino, California
Music Lesson, The	Metsu	Metropolitan Museum of Art, New York
Naked Maja, The	Goya	Prado, Madrid
Nativity	Correggio	Brera, Milan
Night-School	Gerrit Dou	Rijksmuseum, Amsterdam
Night Watch, The (aka The Militia)	Rembrandt	Rijksmuseum, Amsterdam
Nighthawks	Hopper	Art Institute of Chicago
Nocturne in Black and Gold: The Falling Rocket	Whistler	Detroit Institute of Arts
Nocturne in Blue and Gold: Old Battersea Bridge	Whistler	Tate Gallery, London
Nude Descending a Staircase, Nos 1–4	Duchamp	Philadelphia Museum of Art

Paintings	Artist	Location
		(No. 2 is most famous)
Nurse and Child	Hals	Staatliche Museen Preussischer Kulturbesitz, Berlin
Oath of the Tennis Court	David	Louvre, Paris
Odalisque	Renoir	National Gallery of Art, Washington DC
Oedipus and the Sphinx	Ingres	Louvre, Paris
Officer and Laughing Girl	Vermeer	Frick Collection, New York
Old Man and the Courtesan, The	Massys	Pourtalès Collection, Paris
Old Walton Bridge	Canaletto	Dulwich Gallery, London
Old Woman Cooking Eggs, An	Velázquez	National Gallery of Scotland, Edinburgh
Old Woman Praying	Rembrandt	Residenz Gallery, Salzburg
Old Women of Arles	Gauguin	Art Institute of Chicago
Open Window	Matisse	John Hay Whitney Collection, New York
Order of Release, The	Millais	Tate Gallery, London
Oswolt Krel	Dürer	Alte Pinakothek, Munich
Painter's Daughters Chasing a Butterfly, The	Gainsborough	National Gallery, London
Pantry, The	Hooch	Rijksmuseum, Amsterdam
Paradise	Cranach the Elder	Kunsthistorisches Museum, Vienna
Parapluies, Les (aka Umbrellas)	Renoir	National Gallery, London
Paris through the Window	Chagall	Guggenheim Museum, New York
Parting of Hero and Leander, The	Turner	National Gallery, London
Pastoral	Bassano	Lugano, Switzerland
Payment, The	Cranach the Elder, Lucas	Nationalmuseum, Stockholm
Peasant Wedding	Brueghel the Elder (Pieter)	Kunsthistorisches Museum, Vienna
Peasant Woman in a Red Bonnet	Van Gogh, Vincent	Rijksmuseum Vincent Van Gogh, Amsterdam
Peasants Playing Music	Teniers the Younger	Alte Pinakothek, Munich
Peasants Returning from Market	Gainsborough	Toledo Museum of Art, Ohio
Pembroke Family, The	Reynolds	Wilton House, Wiltshire
Perdita (aka Mrs Robinson)	Gainsborough	Wallace Collection, London
Peter Denying Christ	Rembrandt	Rijksmuseum, Amsterdam
Pheidias and the Frieze of the Parthenon, Athens	Alma-Tadema	Birmingham City Gallery
Piano and Lute	Braque	Guggenheim Museum, New York
Piazza San Marco and the Colonnade of the Procuratie Nuove	Canaletto	National Gallery, London
Piazza San Marco Looking East from South of the Central Line	Canaletto	Fogg Art Museum, Cambridge, Mass.
Pipe and Bandaged Ear (Self-portrait)	Van Gogh	Leigh B. Block Collection, Chicago
Pluto and Proserpina	Rembrandt	Dahlem Museums, Berlin
Portrait of a Young Man	Dürer	Alte Pinakothek, Munich
Potato Eaters, The	Van Gogh	Rijksmuseum Vincent Van Gogh, Amsterdam
Poulterer's Shop, A	Dou	National Gallery, London
Primavera, La (aka Allegory of Spring)	Botticelli	Uffizi, Florence
Princess Charlotte and her Two Sisters (aka Three Eldest Princesses)	Gainsborough	Buckingham Palace, London
Rabbi of Vitebsk (aka The Praying Jew)	Chagall	Art Institute of Chicago
Raft of the Medusa, The	Géricault	Louvre, Paris
Rain, Steam and Speed	Turner	National Gallery, London
Raising of Lazarus	Rembrandt	Los Angeles County Museum of Art
Raisng the Cross	Rubens	Antwerp Cathedral
Rake's Progress, The	Hogarth	Sir John Soane's Museum, London
Rape of Proserpine	dell Abbate	Louvre, Paris
Rape of the Sabine Women, The	Poussin	Louvre, Paris
Red Cloud, The	Mondrian	Haags Gemeentemuseum, The Hague
Red Tree, The	Mondrian	Haags Gemeentemuseum, The Hague
Rembrandt's Mother	Dou	Rijksmuseum, Amsterdam
Republic, The	Daumier	Louvre, Paris
Repudiation of Hagar	Tiepolo	Rasini Collection, Milan
Rest on the Flight into Egypt	Bassano	Milan
Return of the Dove to the Ark, The	Millais	Ashmolean Museum, Oxford
Return of the Prodigal Son	Rembrandt	Hermitage, St Petersburg

ART

Paintings	Artist	Location
Rio dei Mendicanti	Guardi	Accademia Carrara, Bergamo
River, The	Monet	Art Institute of Chicago
Roffey Family	Reynolds	City of Birmingham Museum and Art Gallery
Rokeby Venus, The (aka The Toilet of Venus)	Velázquez	National Gallery, London
Room in Brooklyn	Hopper	Museum of Fine Arts, Boston, Mass.
Rouen Cathedral: Sunset	Monet	Museum of Fine Arts, Boston, Mass.
Rout of Comus, The	Landseer	Tate Gallery, London
Rout of San Romano, The	Uccello	National Gallery, London
Rucellai Madonna	Ducio	Uffizi, Florence
Ruins of Brederode Castle, The	Hobbema	National Gallery, London
Sabines, Les	Jacques-Louis David	Louvre, Paris
Sacrifice of Abraham (aka Sacrifice of Isaac)	Tiepolo	S. Maria dei Derelitti, Venice
Sacrifice of Isaac	Caravaggio	Uffizi, Florence
Sacrifice of Isaac	Rembrandt	Hermitage St Petersburg, and Alte Pinakothek, Munich
Sacrifice of Isaac (aka Sacrifice of Abraham)	Tiepolo	S. Maria dei Derelitti, Venice
Sad Young Man in a Train	Duchamp	Peggy Guggenheim Collection, Venice
St Ildefonso	El Greco	Hospital de la Caridad, Illescas, Spain
St Jerome Curing the Lion	Dürer	Kunstmuseum, Basel
St Joseph the Carpenter	La tour	Louvre, Paris
St Lawrence Receiving the Treasure of the Church	Fra Angelico	Vatican Museum, Rome
St Luke Painting the Virgin	Weyden	Museum of Fine Arts, Boston, Mass.
St Mawes at the Pilchard Season	Turner	Tate Gallery, London
St Michael Vanquishing Satan	Raphael	Louvre, Paris
Salisbury Cathedral from the Bishop's Grounds	Constable	Victoria and Albert Museum, London
Salisbury Cathedral from the Meadows	Constable	Lord Ashton of Hyde Collection, Moreton-in-Marsh
Salvator Mundi	Antonello da Messina	National Gallery, London
Samson and Delilah	Van Dyck	Kunsthistorisches Museum, Vienna
School of Athens	Raphael	Stanza della Segnatura, the Vatican, Rome
School of Love, The	Correggio	National Gallery, London
Scream, The	Munch	Nasjonalgalleriet, Oslo
Seine au Pont d'Iéna, La	Gauguin	Louvre, Paris
Self Portrait with Seven Fingers	Chagall	Stedelijk Museum, Amsterdam
Semiramis Founding Babylon	Degas	Louvre, Paris
Serenade	Steen	Národní Galerie, Prague
Seven Deadly Sins, The	Boschs	Prado, Madrid
Shoeing	Landseer	Tate Gallery, London
Shrimp Girl, The	Hogarth	National Gallery, London
Sick Child, The	Munch	Nasjonalgalleriet, Oslo
Sir Stanley Unwin	Kokoschka	Allen and Unwin Collection, London
Sir Thomas More	Holbein the Younger	Frick Collection, New York
Sistine Chapel ceiling	Michelangelo	Sistine Chapel, Vatican
Skating	Manet	Fogg Art Museum, Cambridge, Mass.
Skittle Players outside an Inn	Steen	National Gallery, London
Skull with a Cigarette	Van Gogh	Rijksmuseum Vincent Van Gogh, Amsterdam
Sleeping Gypsy, The	Henri Rousseau	Museum of Modern Art, New York
Smiling Woman	Augustus John	Tate Gallery, London
Snow, Moon and Flowers	Hokusai	Art Institute of Chicago
Soldier Drinks, The	Chagall	Guggenheim Museum, New York
Solitude	Chagall	Tel Aviv Museum
Sojourn in Egypt, The	Correggio	Uffizi, Florence
Soup, The	Picasso	Art Gallery of Ontario, Toronto
Sower, The	Millet	Various locations
Spanish Singer	Manet	Metropolitan Museum of Art, New York
Spinners, The (aka The Fable of) Arachne	Velázquez	Prado, Madrid

Paintings	Artist	Location
Stag Hunt of the Elector Frederick the Wise	Cranach the Elder	Kunsthistorisches Museum, Vienna
Starry Night, The	van Gogh	Museum of Modern Art, New York
Still Life with Gingerpot	Mondrian	Haags Gemeentemuseum, The Hague
Still Life with Playing Cards	Braque	Rijksmuseum Kröller-Müller, Otterlo
Still Life with Tortoise and Hyacinth	Kokoschka	Österreichische Galerie, Vienna
Stoning of St Stephen	Rembrandt	Museum of Fine Arts, Lyons
Storm at Sea, The	Bruege the Elder (Pieter)	Kunsthistorisches Museum, Vienna
Street in Tahiti	Gauguin	Toledo Museum of Art, Ohio
Street Singer, The	Manet	Museum of Fine Arts, Boston, Mass.
Suicide's House, The	Cézanne	Louvre, Paris
Sunday Afternoon on the Island of La Grande Jatte	Seurat	Art Institute of Chicago
Sunflowers and Pears	Gauguin	Private Collection, Paris
Susannah and the Elders	Bassano	Bassano, Italy
Swineherd, The	Gauguin	N. Simon Collection, Los Angeles
Symphony in Grey and Green: The Ocean	Whistler	Frick Collection, New York
Symphony in White No. 1: The White Girl	Whistler	National Gallery, Washington DC
Taking of Christ, The	Van Dyck	Prado, Madrid
Tempered Elan	Kandinsky	Nina Kandinsky Collection, Neuilly-sur-Seine
Tempest, The	Kokoschka	Kunstmuseum, Basel
Tête-à-Tête Supper, The	Toulouse-Lautrec	Courtauld Institute, London
Theatre Box, The (aka La Loge)	Renoir	Courtauld Institute, London
Thirty-Six Views of Mt Fuji (series)	Hokusai	Art Institute of Chicago
Threatening Weather	Magritte	Penrose Collection, London
Three Dancers	Picasso	Tate Gallery, London
Three Eldest Princesses (aka Princess Charlotte and Her Two Sisters)	Gainsborough	Buckingham Palace, London
Three Graces	Raphael	Musée Condé, Chantilly
Three Lawyers in Conversation	Daumier	Phillips Collection, Washington DC
Three Women of Ghent	Jacques-Louis David	Louvre, Paris
Toilet of Venus, The (aka The Rokeby Venus)	Velázquez	National Gallery, London
Toilette, La	Toulouse-Lautrec	Louvre, Paris
Topers, The (aka Triumph of Bacchus)	Velázquez	Prado, Madrid
Tour Eiffel, La	Delaunay	Kunstmuseum, Basel
Tower of Babel	Brueghel the Elder (Pieter)	Kunsthistorisches Museum, Vienna
Transfiguration	Duccio	National Gallery, London
Trial of Moses	Giorgione	Uffizi, Florence
Trinity	El Greco	Prado, Madrid
Triumph of Bacchus (aka The Topers)	Velázquez	Prado, Madrid
Triumph of the Innocents, The	Holman Hunt	Tate Gallery, London
Tropical Forest with Monkeys	Rousseau, Henri	John Hay Whitney Collection, New York
Tuna Fishing	Dali	Paul Ricard Collection, Paris
Turkish Bath, The	Ingres	Louvre, Paris
Twittering Machine	Klee	Museum of Modern Art, New York
Two Haystacks	Monet	Art Institute of Chicago
Two Trinities, The (aka Holy Family)	Murillo	National Gallery, London
Ugolino	Reynolds	Knole House, Sevenoaks, Kent
Umbrellas (aka Les Parapluies)	Renoir	National Gallery, London
Uncle Dominic as a Monk	Cézanne	Private Collection, New York
Vampire	Munch	Munch-Museet, Oslo
Van Gogh's Chair	Van Gogh	National Gallery, London
Venus and Adonis	Titian	Prado, Madrid
Venus and Adonis	Turner	Tate Gallery, London
Venus and Cupid	Cranach the Elder	Staatliche Museen Preussischer Kulturbesitz, Berlin
Venus of Urbino	Titian	Uffizi, Florence
Victory Boogie Woogie	Mondrian	Burton Tremaine Collection, Meriden, Conn.
View of Delft	Vermeer	Mauritshuis, The Hague
View of Naples	Brueghel the Elder (Pieter)	Galleria Doria-Pamphili, Rome
Village Fête, The	Teniers the Younger, David	Hermitage, St Petersburg
Violin and Jug	Braque	Kunstmuseum, Basel

A
R
T

Paintings	Artist	Location
Virgin and Child with Saints	Duccio di Buoninsegna	National Gallery, London
Virgin and Child with Saints and Donor	Gerard David	National Gallery, London
Virgin in Prayer, The	Massys	Musée Royal des Beaux-Arts, Antwerp
Virgin of the Rocks	Leonardo da Vinci	Louvre, Paris and National Gallery, London
Virgin of the Rosary	Murillo	Archbishop's Palace, Seville
Vision of St Bernard	Lippi, Filippino	Badia, Florence
Visit, The	Alma-Tadema	Victoria and Albert Museum, London
Washerwoman, The	Daumier, Honoré	Louvre, Paris
Water-Lily Pool	Monet	Louvre, Paris
Water Mill, The	Hobbema	Wallace Collection, London
Way to Calvary, The	Brueghel the Elder, Pieter	Kunsthistorisches Museum, Vienna
Wedding Dance, The	Brueghel the Elder, Pieter	Detroit Institute of Arts
Wedding of Stephen Beckingham & Mary Cox	Hogarth	Metropolitan Museum of Art, New York
Whaam!	Lichtenstein	Tate Gallery, London
Wheatfields	van Ruysdael, Jacob	Metropolitan Museum of Art, New York
When Shall We Be Married	Gauguin	Kunstmuseum, Basel
Whistler's Mother (aka Arrangement in Grey and Black No. 1)	Whistler	Louvre, Paris
White Crucifixion	Chagall	Art Institute of Chicago
White Line	Kandinsky	Nina Kandinsky Collection, Neuilly-sur-Seine
Wild Poppies	Monet	Louvre, Paris
William Warham, Archbishop of Canterbury	Holbein the Younger	Louvre, Paris
Windmill in Sunlight	Mondrian	Haags Gemeentemuseum, The Hague
Windsor Beauties, The	Lely	Hampton Court Palace, London
Woman and Her Maid in a Court	Hooch	National Gallery, London
Woman in an Armchair	Picasso	Picasso Museum, Paris
Woman Musician, The	Braque	Kunstmuseum, Basel
Woman Weighing Gold, A	Vermeer	National Gallery of Art, Washington DC
Woman with Pears	Picasso	Pushkin Museum, Moscow
Woman with the Hat	Matisse	Walter A Haas Collection, San Francisco
Women in a Brothel	Toulouse-Lautrec	Szépmüvészeti Museum, Budapest
Women of Algiers in Their Apartment	Delacroix	Louvre, Paris
Women with Mangoes (aka The King's Wife)	Gauguin	Pushkin Museum, Moscow
Woodcutter Courting a Milkmaid, The	Gainsborough	Woburn Abbey, Bedfordshire
Woods near Oele	Mondrian	Haags Gemeentemuseum, The Hague
World Upside-down, The	Steen	Kunsthistorisches Museum, Vienna
Wounded Cuirassier, The	Géricault	Louvre, Paris
Wounded Heron, The	Watts	Watts Gallery, Compton, Surrey
Wreck of a Transport Ship	Turner	Gulbenkian Foundation, Lisbon
Young Bacchus, The	Caravaggio	Uffizi, Florence
Young Lady with a Pearl Necklace	Vermeer	Staatliche Museen Preussischer Kulturbesitz, Berlin
Young Man Holding a Skull (aka Hamlet)	Hals	Richard Proby Collection, Peterborough
Young Man in a Garden	Hilliard	Victoria and Albert Museum, London
Young Mother, The	Dou	Mauritshuis, The Hague
Young Virgin Auto-Sodomized by Her Own Chastity	Dali	Carlos B Alemany Collection, New York
Young Woman Holding a Powder-Puff	Seurat	Courtauld Institute, London
Young Woman Standing at a Virginal, A	Vermeer	National Gallery, London
Yellow Christ, The	Gauguin	Albright-Knox Art Gallery, Buffalo, NY
Young Woman with a Water Jug, A	Vermeer	Metropolitan Museum of Art, New York

Paintings	Artist	Location
Young Women on the Banks of the Seine	Courbet	Musée du Petit Palais, Paris
Zingara, La (aka The Fortune-Teller)	Caravaggio	Louvre, Paris
Zoological Garden	Klee	Klee Foundation, Berne

NB: There are a number of points to be considered with reference to this section. The history of art is a complex subject and although it is traditional to fix a label on artists and their works, in fact not only is it often impossible to identify a painter with any one group, it is also just as precarious to attach one term to the whole oeuvre of an artist. Even the historical styles overlap in many instances. The problem is that painters do not like to be pigeonholed, as styles and moods change and very often one style or school may become defunct or develop into something else. In researching this section I have also found that the nationalities of artists, especially those of the Low Countries, are open to interpretation, dependent not only on place of birth or naturalisation but also on style. I have endeavoured to qualify any contentious entries so as to give a more complete picture of the nature of the artist and his or her work.

A problem when listing artworks is that not only are particular subjects covered as 'stock' pieces by numerous artists (such as *The Adoration of the Magi*) but also many individual artists often paint more than one version of a particular work – for example, Cézanne painted several versions of *The Card Players* and Millet painted several versions of *The Sower*. The final observation I have to offer in this web of intrigue is that when I came to list paintings in alphabetical order it occurred to me that many have alternative titles. For instance Vermeer's *The Kitchen-Maid* is listed in reputable sources with the alternative titles of *The Milkmaid, The Maid with a Milk Jug, The Cook, The Maid-Servant Pouring Milk* and *The Servant Pouring Milk*. I have listed only the most common variants in the table.

Art Movements and Schools: Some Members and Founders

Members / Founders (F)	Art Movements & Schools	Members / Founders (F)	Art Movements & Schools
Arp, Jean (F)	Dada	Fry, Roger (F)	Omega Workshops
Ball, Hugo	Dada	Funi, Achille	Novecento Italiano
Beardsley, Aubrey	Art Nouveau	Gauguin, Paul	Pont-Aven School
Bell, Vanessa	Omega Workshops	Gauguin, Paul	Post-Impressionism
Bellows, George	Ashcan School	Gilman, Harold (F)	Camden Town Group
Blake, Peter	Pop Art	Ginner, Charles (F)	Camden Town Group
Bleyl, Fritz (F)	Die Brücke (The Bridge)	Giulio Romano	Mannerism
Bomberg, David	Kitchen Sink School	van Gogh, Vincent	Post-Impressionism
Bonnard, Pierre	Nabis	Goncharova, Natalia	Rayonnism
Braque, Georges (F)	Cubism	Gore, Spencer (F)	Camden Town Group
Braque, Georges (F)	Fauvism	Gowing, Lawrence	Euston Road School
Bratby, John	Kitchen Sink School	Grant, Duncan	Omega Workshops
Brown, Ford Madox	Pre-Raphaelite Brotherhood	El Greco	Mannerism
Brueghel the Elder, Pieter	Antwerp School	Grosz, George	Neue Sachlichkeit
Burne-Jones, Edward	Arts and Crafts Movement	Hamilton, Richard	Pop Art
Burne-Jones, Edward	Pre-Raphaelite Brotherhood	Heckel, Erich (F)	Die Brücke (The Bridge)
Carrà, Carlo (F)	Metaphysical school	Hepworth, Barbara	St Ives Painters
Cézanne, Paul	Impressionism	Hunt, William Holman (F)	Pre-Raphaelite Brotherhood
Cézanne, Paul	Post-Impressionism	Kandinsky, Wassily (F)	Blaue Reiter (Blue Rider)
de Chirico, Giorgio	Metaphysical School	Kirchner, Ernst Ludwig (F)	Die Brücke (The Bridge)
Church, F. E.	Hudson River School	Klee, Paul	Blaue Reiter (Blue Rider)
Coldstream, William (F)	Euston Road School	Knight, Laura	Newlyn School
Cole, Thomas	Hudson River School	'Grandma' Moses	Primitivism
Cotman, John (F)	Norwich School	Kokoschka, Oscar	Expressionism
Crome, John (F)	Norwich School	Kooning, Willem de (F)	Abstract Expressionism
Dali, Salvador	Surrealism	Ladbrooke, Robert	Norwich School
Degas, Edgar	Impressionism	Larionov, Mikhail (F)	Rayonism
Delaunay, Robert (F)	Orphism	Léger, Fernand	Cubism
Delaunay, Robert	Synchronism	Lewis, Wyndham (F)	Vorticism
Delaunay Terk, Sonia (F)	Orphism	Lichtenstein, Roy (F)	Pop Art
Denis, Maurice (F)	Nabis	Mackintosh, Charles Rennie (F)	Glasgow School
Derain, André (F)	Fauvism	Magritte, René	Surrealism
Dix, Otto	Neue Sachlichkeit	Malevich, Kasimir (F)	Suprematism
van Doesburg, Theo (F)	De Stijl	Manet, Edouard	Impressionism
van Doesburg, Theo	Neo-Plasticism	Marc, Franz (F)	Blaue Reiter (Blue Rider)
van Dongen, Kees	Post-Impressionism	Matisse, Henri (F)	Fauvism
Duccio di Buoninsegna (F)	Sienese School	Millais, John Everett (F)	Pre-Raphaelite Brotherhood
Duchamp, Marcel	Dada	Mondrian, Piet	Cubism
van Dyck, Anthony	Antwerp School	Mondrian, Piet (F)	De Stijl
Ernst, Max	Dada	Mondrian, Piet (F)	Neo-Plasticism
Ernst, Max	Surrealism	Monet, Claude (F)	Impressionism
Forbes, Stanhope	Newlyn School		

A
R
T

Members / Founders (F)	Art Movements & Schools	Members / Founders (F)	Art Movements & Schools
Moreau, Gustave	Symbolism	Rouault, Georges	Expressionism
Morris, William	Arts and Crafts Movement	Rouault, Georges (F)	Fauvism
Morris, William	Pre-Raphaelite Brotherhood	Rousseau, Henri	Primitivism
Munch, Edvard	Expressionism	Rousseau, Théodore	Barbizon School
Nicholson, Ben	St Ives Painters	Rubens, Peter Paul	Antwerp School
Overbeck, Friedrich (F)	Nazarenes	Schmidt-Rottluff, Karl (F)	Die Brücke (The Bridge)
Parmigianino, Francesco	Mannerism	Seurat, Georges (F)	Pointillism
Pasmore, Victor (F)	Euston Road School	Sickert, Walter (F)	Camden Town Group
Pechstein, Max	Expressionism	Sisley, Alfred	Impressionism
Pforr, Franz	Nazarenes	Sluijters, Jan	Post-Impressionism
Picasso, Pablo (F)	Cubism	Stella, Frank	Post-Painterly Abstraction
Piper, John	Neo-Romanticism	Stokes, Adrian	St Ives Painters
Pissarro, Camille	Impressionism	Sutherland, Graham	Neo-Romanticism
Pollock, Jackson (F)	Abstract Expressionism	Tatlin, Vladimir (F)	Constructivism
Puvis de Chavannes,	Symbolism	Tintoretto	Mannerism
Redon, Odilon	Symbolism	de Vlaminck, Maurice (F)	Fauvism
Renoir, Pierre	Impressionism	Vuillard, Edouard	Nabis
Riley, Bridget (F)	Op Art	Warhol, Andy (F)	Pop Art
Rossetti, Dante Gabriel (F)	Pre-Raphaelite Brotherhood	Watteau, Jean-Antoine	Rococo
Rothko, Mark	Abstract Expressionism		

NB: The table above should be taken as a quick reference for identifying artists and groups. As has been stated previously, there is a distinct grey area in attempting to categorise painters – e.g. although Peter Blake was certainly identified with Pop Art in his early career, whether he would consider himself as such nowadays is debatable.

Art: General Information

Action Painting: aka	Abstract Expressionism
Adoration of the Magi (Botticelli)	The Medici family are depicted as the Magi
Angel of the North: details	Sculpted by Antony Gormley and situated on the site of an old coal mine next to the A1 at Eighton Banks, Gateshead, Tyne and Wear. The 20m (65ft) high figure in steel with a copper mixture has a wingspan of 54m (175ft), a weight of 200 tonnes (100 tonnes for the body and 50 tonnes per wing), and cost £800,000 to construct, largely funded by National Lottery donations. As the surface oxidises to form a patina the sculpture has become a rich brown colour
Arrangement in Grey and Black: nickname	Whistler's Mother
Art Deco	Refers to a decorative style of the 1920s and 1930s
Art Gallery: largest	The Hermitage in St Petersburg
Beggarstaff Brothers	Sir William Nicholson (1872–1949) and James Pryde (1866–1941), still-life and poster painters
Blue Boy: depiction of	Master Jonathan Buttall, a friend of the artist Gainsborough
Blue Period: Picasso	Between 1901 and mid-1904
Brueg(h)el: nicknames	Pieter (The Elder) – Peasant, Pieter (The Younger) – Hell, Jan – Velvet
Brueg(h)el: spelling	Pieter the Elder spelt the name with an 'H' until 1559 and his children resorted back to original spelling
Bubbles: subject	Millais' grandson, the future Admiral William James
Churchill Portrait (Sutherland)	Destroyed by Churchill's wife
Cire Perdue	Modern bronzes are made either in sand moulds or by the 'cire perdue' (lost wax) method, which consists of a model smaller than the mould, the space between being filled with wax and vent pipes inserted. The molten bronze is poured in the top and takes the place of the wax which has been melted out
Claude Lorrain Glass	Black convex glass used by artists to reflect the landscape in miniature and, in doing so, to merge details and reduce the strength of colour so that the artist is presented with a broad picture of the scene
Collage	Objects such as newspaper, string or cloth which are pasted onto paper or canvas. Picasso's *Still Life with Chair Caning* may have been the first example of collage
Constructivism	Russian art movement initiated by Vladimir Tatlin in 1913 and favouring the use of a 'Culture of Materials' which resulted in an art which had social purpose
Correggio	Named from the town in Modena where he was born
Cranach the Elder, Lucas: epitaph	Pictor Celerrimus (swiftest of painters) is how Cranach is described on his tombstone

Cubism: first picture	*Les Demoiselles d'Avignon* by Picasso
Customs Officer: former	Henri Rousseau (hence his byname 'Le Douanier')
Dada: formed where	In a nightclub in Zurich (Cabaret Voltaire) 1916
Duke of Wellington (Goya)	Stolen in 1961 but later found
Fakers: famous	Tom Keating faked Samuel Palmer paintings; Hans van Meegeren faked Vermeers
Frottage	Technique employed by Surrealists such as Max Ernst, which involves placing a piece of paper over an object and rubbing the paper with chalk or charcoal
Hay-Wain, The: farm	Willy Lott's farm
I Want You: Recruiting Poster	James Montgomery Flagg
Intaglio	Term used to describe types of printing such as etching and engraving whereby the design is incised as opposed to relief printing, such as wood cutting, where the raised portion creates the design
Killed a man in argument	Caravaggio in 1606 forced to flee Rome after killing a man in fit of temper
Knighted by Britain & Spain	Sir Peter Paul Rubens
Libel Action Against John Ruskin	James Whistler, for Ruskin's attack on his *Falling Rocket* (won the case but received only one farthing)
Madonna Rucellai	Now attributed to Duccio Di Buoninsegna: formerly thought to be a work of Cimabue (Vasari's attribution)
Magic Realism	Refers to a type of painting which combines a realistic technique with fanciful designs, as in the paintings of René Magritte and other surrealists. In its strict sense it refers to German realist art of the 1920s
Marsyas: details	The title refers to a satyr in Greek mythology who was flayed alive by the god Apollo. The PVC membrane has a fleshy quality and the dark red colour suggests something 'of the physical, of the earthly, of the bodily'. *Marsyas* confounds spatial perception, immersing the viewer in a monochromatic field of colour. It is impossible to view the entire sculpture from any one position. The sculpture comprises three steel rings joined together by a single span. The flute-shaped structure is 500ft long and 10 storeys high, filling the entire space of the Tate Modern's Turbine Hall
Montage	Form of collage but refers specifically to the use of components which are complete in themselves
Murdered His Father	Richard Dadd
Myra (Hindley): painter	Marcus Harvey painted this controversial painting on display at the 'Sensations' exhibition of 1997
Neo-Expressionism	Refers to an International art movement of the late 1970s and 1980s involving revival of expressionist concerns
Neo-Plasticism	Name used by Mondrian & van Doesburg for a type of art which avoids representation in favour of abstraction
Neo-Romanticism	British art movement existing before the Second World War which revived the interest in the Romantic landscapes of William Blake and Samuel Palmer
New Objectivity	Name coined by G.F. Artlaub to describe a group of German artists who rejected abstract culture of the 1920s
Novecento Italiano	Italian art movement of the 1920s which encouraged a return to the renaissance art
Novembergruppe	Formed in Berlin 1918 and advocating art for the masses
Obscene: exhibition closed as	Modigliani
Old Masters: highest prices at auction	1 Rubens *(Massacre of the Innocents)* £49.5m ($76.6m)
	2 Pontormo *(Portrait of Duke Cosimo I, de Medici)* $35.2m
	3 Rembrandt *(Portrait of a Lady aged 62, perhaps AP Uylenburgh)* $29.04m
	4 Canaletto *(The Old Horse Guards)* $17.6m
	5 Guardi *(Veduta della Giudecca e della Zattere a Venezia)* $15.3m
	6 Titian *(Venus & Adonis)* $13.61m
	7 Hals *(Portrait of Tieleman Roosterman)* $12.7m
	8 Rembrandt *(Portrait of a Bearded Man in a Red Doublet)* $12.6m
	9 Canaletto *(Le Retour du Bucentaure Ader)* $12.43m
	10 Michelangelo *(The Risen Christ* – drawing) $12.28m
Orphism	Term coined by poet Apollinaire in 1912 to distinguish the fragmented use of colour from the Cubist approach

ART

Painting: highest price at auction	Van Gogh's *Portrait of Dr Gachet* fetched £44,378,696 in May 1990
Patina	Term used to describe the beautiful greenish surface alteration on a bust or statue caused by age
Pears Soap Advertisement	*Bubbles* by Sir John Everett Millais
Pentimento	Phenomenon of earlier painting showing through a layer or layers of paint on a canvas
Pop Art: term coined by	The critic Lawrence Alloway
Post-Painterly Abstraction	Term coined by the critic Clement Greenberg in 1964 to refer to non-objective artists who were not members of the Abstract Expressionist movement
Primary Colours	The colours from which all other colours are made up i.e. Blue, Yellow and Red
Purism	Term coined in 1918 by Amédée Ozenfant in 'Après le Cubisme' which rejected decorative qualities of Cubism
Putto	A plump naked boy used as a decorative addition to painting and sculpture, especially in the Baroque
Quattrocento	The 15th century, especially with reference to Renaissance Italian Art (literally four hundred, i.e. short for 14 hundred)
Rayonism	Russian art movement described as a combination of Cubism, Futurism and Orphism
Renoir's Nude Sitter	Renoir's maid, Gabrielle, would often sit as nude model for his paintings
Rheumatism Sufferer	In later life Renoir was forced to paint with the brush tied to his fingers
Rokeby Venus (Velázquez)	Slashed by suffragette in the National Gallery
Rose Period: Picasso	Late 1904 to 1906
Saturday Evening Post	Norman Rockwell was famous for the covers
Scumbling	Term used to describe the effect when an opaque colour is applied over another colour but allows the original colour to show through
Secondary Colours	Aka Complementary Colours; produced when two primary colours are mixed together, i.e. Green, Orange & Violet
Sensation	Charles Saatchi's controversial 1997 exhibition at the Royal Academy which includes such items as Damien Hirst's *Tiger Shark*, *Bisected Pig* & *Thousand Years*; Marcus Harvey's *Myra*, and Tracey Emin's *Everyone I have ever slept with*
Signed Paintings 'OK'	Oscar Kokoschka signed many of his paintings 'OK' making them look like they had been vandalised
Stole Mona Lisa 1914	Vincenzo Perugia (sentenced to one year, 15 days imprisonment)
Stolen from National Gallery	*The Scream* (stolen in 1994 but returned 2 months later)
Surrealism	Term coined in 1922 by André Breton to describe the real and unreal world of waking and dreaming as depicted by the artist. Breton chose term from earlier description of a Chagall work by Guillaume Apollinaire
Tachisme	Term often used synonymously with Abstract Expressionism, but it strictly refers to a French movement of the 1950s which consisted of paintings composed of large blobs of colour
Tempest, The (Kokoschka)	Depicts the artist and Alma Mahler resting in a huge cockleshell in the midst of a raging sea
Thousand Years	Damien Hirst's rotting cow head in a smear of blood, beset by flies
Turner Prize winners	Sponsored by Channel 4 and awarded to a British artist under 50. Inaugurated in 1984, the prize is worth £20,000 to the winner. The full list of previous winners are Malcolm Morley (1984), Howard Hodgkin (1985), Gilbert and George (1986), Richard Deacon (1987), Tony Cragg (1988), Richard Long (1989), Prize suspended (1990), Anish Kapoor (1991), Grenville Davey (1992), Rachel Whiteread (1993), Antony Gormley (1994), Damien Hirst (1995), Douglas Gordon (1996), Gillian Wearing (1997), Chris Ofili (1998), Steve McQueen (1999), Wolfgang Tillmans (2000), Martin Creed (2001), Keith Tyson (2002)
Van Gogh: only painting sold	*Red Vineyard* was the only painting he sold in his lifetime

ASTRONOMY

Constellations

Latin name	English name	Latin name	English name	Latin name	English name
Andromeda	Andromeda	Crux	Southern Cross	Orion	Orion
Antlia	Air Pump			Pavo	Peacock
Apus	Bird of Paradise	Cygnus	Swan	Pegasus	Winged Horse
		Delphinus	Dolphin	Perseus	Perseus
Aquarius	Water Bearer	Dorado	Swordfish or Goldfish	Phoenix	Phoenix
Aquila	Eagle			Pictor	Painter
Ara	Altar	Draco	Dragon	Pisces	Fishes
Aries	Ram	Equuleus	Foal	Piscis Austrinus	Southern Fish
Auriga	Charioteer	Eridanus	River Eridanus	Puppis	Poop or Stern
Boötes	Herdsman	Fornax	Furnace	Pyxis	Mariner's Compass
Caelum	Chisel	Gemini	Twins		
Camelopardalis	Giraffe	Grus	Crane	Reticulum	Net
Cancer	Crab	Hercules	Hercules	Sagitta	Arrow
Canes Venatici	Hunting Dogs	Horologium	Clock	Sagittarius	Archer
Canis Major	Great Dog	Hydra	Sea Serpent	Scorpius	Scorpion
Canis Minor	Little Dog	Hydrus	Water Snake	Sculptor	Sculptor
Capricornus	Sea Goat	Indus	Indian	Scutum	Shield
Carina	Keel	Lacerta	Lizard	Serpens	Serpent
Cassiopeia	Cassiopeia	Leo	Lion	Sextans	Sextant
Centaurus	Centaur	Leo Minor	Little Lion	Taurus	Bull
Cepheus	Cepheus	Lepus	Hare	Telescopium	Telescope
Cetus	Whale	Libra	Scales	Triangulum	Triangle
Chamaeleon	Chameleon	Lupus	Wolf	Triangulum Australe	Southern Triangle
Circinus	Compasses	Lynx	Lynx		
Columba	Dove	Lyra	Lyre	Tucana	Toucan
Coma Berenices	Berenice's Hair	Mensa	Table	Ursa Major	Great Bear
		Microscopium	Microscope	Ursa Minor	Little Bear
Corona Australis	Southern Crown	Monoceros	Unicorn	Vela	Sails
		Musca	Fly	Virgo	Virgin
Corona Borealis	Northern Crown	Norma	Level	Volans	Flying Fish
		Octans	Octant	Vulpecula	Fox
Corvus	Crow	Ophiuchus	Serpent Bearer		
Crater	Cup				

The Planets

Planetary data	Diameter km	miles	Maximum distance from Sun (millions) km	miles	Minimum distance from Sun (millions) km	miles	Sidereal period	Axial rotation period
Mercury	4878	3031	69.4	43	46.8	29	88 days	58d 16h
Venus	12104	7521	109	67.6	107.6	66.7	224.7 days	243 days
Earth	12756	7927	152.6	94.6	147.4	91.4	365.26 days	23h 56m
Mars	6794	4222	249.2	154.5	207.3	128.5	687 days	24h 37m 23s
Jupiter	142800	88700	817.4	506.8	741.6	459.8	11.86 years	9h 50m 30s
Saturn	120000	74600	1512	937.6	1346	834.6	29.46 years	10h 14m
Uranus	52000	32300	3011	1867	2740	1699.0	84.01 years	16-28 hours
Neptune	48400	30000	4543	2817	4466	2769.0	164.79 years	18-20 hours
Pluto	2300	1430	7364	4566	4461	2766.0	248.5 years	6d 9h

Astronomers Royal

John Flamsteed	1675–1719	Sir Frank Dyson	1910–1933	Until 1972 the title of Astronomer Royal was given to the director of Greenwich Observatory. It is now an honorary title for an outstanding astronomer, who receives a stipend of approximately £100 per year.
Edmund Halley	1720–1742	Sir Harold Jones	1933–1955	
James Bradley	1742–1762	Sir Richard Woolley	1956–1971	
Nathaniel Bliss	1762–1764	Sir Martin Ryle	1972–1982	
Nevil Maskelyne	1765–1811	Sir Francis Graham–Smith	1982–1990	
John Pond	1811–1835	Sir Arnold Wolfendale	1991–1995	
Sir George Airy	1835–1881	Sir Martin Rees	1995–	
Sir William Christie	1881–1910			

Planetary Satellites

		Discovered	Diameter km	miles				Discovered	Diameter km	miles
Earth	Moon		3476	2160			Pandora	1980	100	60
Mars	Phobos	1877	27	17			Atlas	1980	40	25
	Deimos	1877	15	9			Calypso	1980	30	19
Jupiter	Ganymede	1610	5260	3270			Telesto	1980	24	15
	Callisto	1610	4800	3000			Dione B	1982	15	9
	Io	1610	3650	2268			Prometheus	1980	10	6
	Europa	1610	3138	1950		Uranus	Oberon	1787	1600	1000
	Amalthea	1892	270	168			Titania	1787	1600	1000
	Himalia	1904	180	110			Ariel	1851	1300	800
	Elara	1905	80	50			Umbriel	1851	1100	700
	Pasiphae	1908	50	30			Miranda	1948	400	250
	Sinope	1914	40	25			Puck	1986	170	105
	Carme	1938	40	25			Portia	1986	90	55
	Lysithea	1938	40	25			Cressida	1986	70	40
	Metis	1979	40	25			Juliet	1986	70	40
	Ananke	1951	30	19			Belinda	1986	50	30
	Adrastea	1979	24	15			Bianca	1986	50	30
	Leda	1974	20	12			Desdemona	1986	50	30
	Thebe	1979	100	62			Rosalind	1986	50	30
Saturn	Titan	1655	5150	3200			Ophelia	1986	20	12
	Rhea	1672	1530	950			Cordelia	1986	15	9
	Iapetus	1671	1440	900		Neptune	Triton	1846	2700	1678
	Dione	1684	1120	700			Proteus	1989	415	260
	Tethys	1684	1050	650			Nereid	1949	300	190
	Enceladus	1789	500	310			Larissa	1989	190	118
	Hyperion	1848	400	250			Galatea	1989	160	100
	Mimas	1789	390	240			Despina	1989	150	95
	Phoebe	1898	220	135			Naiad	1989	50	30
	Janus	1966	200	120			Thalassa	1989	50	30
	Epimetheus	1980	140	90		Pluto	Charon	1978	1000	620
	Helene	1980	100	60						

Astronomy and Space: Selected Data

Albedo　Reflecting power of a planet or other non-luminous body

American in Space: 1st　Alan Shepard in Freedom 7 (5 May 1961); duration of flight 15 minutes 28 seconds

American to Orbit the Earth: 1st　John Glenn in Friendship 7 (20 Feb 1962); for 3 orbits, duration of flight 4 hrs 55 mins 23 secs

Aphelion　Furthest distance of a planet from the Sun

Apogee　Furthest point of the Moon from the Earth

Apollo 13: Crew　James Lovell, Jack Swigert and Fred Haise. The service module exploded 55 hrs into the mission to the Moon, but the lunar module was used to reach home safely on 17 Apr 1970

Appleton Layer　Highest region of the Ionosphere, extending from a height of about 150 to about 1,000 kilometres. It contains the highest proportion of free electrons and is the most useful region for long-range radio transmission. The layer is also called the F-region

Artificial Satellite: 1st　Sputnik 1, launched by Soviet Union on 4 October 1957. Sputnik was an 83.6 kg metal sphere, transmitting signals for three weeks before failing batteries caused it to fall to Earth on 4 January 1958

Asteroid　Another name for a minor planet. Eros, discovered in 1898, comes closer to the Earth (every 37 years) than anything except the Moon

Asteroid: brightest　Vesta

Asteroid: largest　1. Ceres 2. Pallas 3. Vesta 4. Hygeia

Asteroid Belt　The 4,000-plus minor planets (asteroids) that orbit the Sun between Mars and Jupiter

Astrolabe　Ancient instrument used to measure altitudes of celestial bodies

Astronomical Unit　Mean distance between the Earth and the Sun: 149,598,500 km

Baikonur　Launch site for manned Soviet space flights in Kazakhstan

Baily's Beads　Brilliant points seen around the Moon just before and after a total solar eclipse

Big Bang Theory　First advanced by Georges Lemaître: the idea that the universe began, around 15 to 17 billion years ago, as a point of superdense matter that exploded and has been expanding ever since

Black Hole　Region of immense gravitational pull around a massive collapsed star from which not even light can escape

Bolide　A brilliant exploding meteor

Brightest Stars　1. Sirius 2. Canopus 3. Alpha Centauri 4. Arcturus 5. Vega

British National Space Centre　Head Office at 151 Buckingham Palace Road, London SWI 9SS

Cassini's Division　Dark gap between rings A and B of Saturn discovered by Gian Domenico Cassini, among others

Celestial Equator　Projection of the Earth's equator on to the celestial sphere

Celestial Sphere Imaginary sphere surrounding the Earth on which all heavenly bodies appear to move, and whose centre is the same as that of the Earth's globe

Challenger US space shuttle exploded 72 seconds after lift-off on 28 Jan 1986, killing all 7 crew members, including schoolteacher Christa McAuliffe

Chromosphere Part of the Sun's atmosphere that lies above the Photosphere

Coldest Planet Pluto

Comet: Shortest known orbital period Encke's Comet, 3.3 years

Comet: meaning From the Latin 'Coma', which means hair

Constellations 31 in Northern and 52 in Southern hemisphere, with 5 'floaters' overlapping. **Largest:** Hydra. **Smallest:** Crux Australis

Corona Outermost part of the Sun's atmosphere visible with the naked eye only during a total solar eclipse

Cosmogony Study of the origin and evolution of the universe

Cosmology Study of the universe considered as a whole

Declination Angular distance of celestial body north or south of celestial equator, corresponding to latitude on the Earth

Doppler Effect Apparent change in wavelength of the light from a luminous body in motion relative to the observer

D-region Lowest layer of the Ionosphere. Extends from a height of about 60 to about 90 kilometres, contains a low concentration of free electrons, and reflects low-frequency radio waves

Earth: mean distance from Sun 150 million kms (93 million miles)

Ecliptic Apparent yearly path of the Sun among the stars

Ephemeris Table showing the predicted positions of a celestial body such as a planet, comet or asteroid

Equinox Equinoxes are two points at which the ecliptic cuts the celestial equator; vernal equinox 21 Mar, autumnal 22 Sep

European Space Agency Created 1975 by merger of European Space Research Organisation and European Launcher Development Organisation. Members are Austria, Belgium, Denmark, Finland, France, Germany, Ireland, Italy, Netherlands, Norway, Spain, Sweden, Switzerland and the UK. Canada being non-European is deemed a co-operating state. Head Office is at 8–10 Rue Mario Nikis, 75738 Paris, France

Exosphere Outermost part of a planet's atmosphere

Expanding Universe Observation made by Edwin Hubble in 1929 that the universe appears to be expanding; this confirms the Big Bang Theory

Flocculi Patches on the Sun's surface: bright (calcium) and dark (hydrogen)

Galaxies Systems made up of stars, nebulae and interstellar matter, forming star families held together by their own gravitational pull and separate from other such galaxies

Gibbous Phase Phase of the Moon or planet when between half and full

Great Red Spot Enormous red feature in the atmosphere of Jupiter, visible since the 17th century

Heaviside Layer Region of the Ionosphere, extending from a height of 90 to about 150 kilometres. It reflects radio waves of medium wavelength. This layer is also called the E-region

Hertzsprung-Russell Diagram Diagram in which stars are plotted according to their spectral types and their absolute magnitudes

Hottest Planet Venus

Hubble Space Telescope Placed in the Earth's orbit by the space shuttle *Discovery* (24 April 1990)

Inferior Planets Mercury and Venus: closer to the Sun than the Earth is

Inner Planets The 4 planets that orbit the Sun within the Asteroid Belt; i.e. Mercury, Venus, Earth, Mars

Ionosphere Region of the Earth's atmosphere lying above the Stratosphere

Jupiter Mean distance from Sun: 778.34 million km (486 million miles). Galileo discovered satellites Callisto, Europa, Ganymede and Io. Atmosphere: hydrogen, ammonia and methane. Temperature can be as low as -200º C. Probes: *Pioneer 10* and *11* (1973/4); *Voyagers 1* and *2* (1979); *Galileo* (1995)

Largest Planet Jupiter

Light Year Distance travelled by light in one year: 9.4607 million million km. Light travels at 186,000 miles per second (7 1/2 times round the Earth)

Local Group Group of more than two dozen galaxies, including our own galaxy. Largest member is the Andromeda Galaxy, M.31

Lunar Eclipse Passage of the Moon through the shadow cast by the Earth

Magnitude Measurement unit for the brightness of a star or planet

Mariner 9 US space probe to Mars in 1971

Mars Mean distance from the Sun: 227.94 million km (142 million miles). Atmosphere nearest to our own, but there is no water on Mars. Probes: *Mariner 4, 6, 7, 8, 9* (1965–71); and *1* and *2* landed 1976; *Pathfinder* landed 1997

Mercury Mean distance from the Sun: 57.9 million kms (36.2 million miles). Atmosphere: non-existent – burnt off by closeness to Sun. Probe: *Mariner 10* (1974 & 1975)

Mesosphere Region of the Earth's atmosphere between the Stratosphere and the Thermosphere, sometimes called the D-region and characterised by a rapid decrease in temperature with height

Meteor Particle or small rock moving around Sun and destroyed when entering atmosphere

Meteorite Larger object that reaches the ground without being destroyed

Milky Way The galaxy of which our Sun is a member. It contains approximately 100,000 million stars, of which 5,776 are visible to the naked eye

Mir Advanced type of space station 1st launched by the Soviet Union in 1986

Moon Mean distance from Earth: 384,000 km (239,900 miles). Diameter: 3,476 km (2,160 miles). Revolves around the Earth from west to east. First soft landing by Soviet *Luna 9*, launched on 31 Jan 1966, landed 3 Feb. First manned flight around the Moon: *Apollo 8* in Dec 1968. First manned landing and walk: *Apollo 11* on 20 Jul 1969. Last man on the Moon was Eugene Cernan in *Apollo 17* on 11 Dec 1972

Moon Walks 12 men, all American, have walked on the surface of the Moon, Neil Armstrong and Buzz Aldrin *(Apollo 11)*, Charles Conrad Jr and Alan Bean *(Apollo 12)*, Alan Shepard and Edgar Mitchell *(Apollo 14)*, David Scott and James Irwin *(Apollo 15)*, John Young and Charles Duke *(Apollo 16)*, Eugene Cernan and Harrison Schmitt *(Apollo 17)*

Moon's Rotation Rotates about its own axis in 29 1/2 days, which is about the same time it takes to orbit the

ASTRONOMY

Earth. Hence the same face of the Moon is always presented to the Earth

Nadir Point on the celestial sphere directly below the observer, diametrically opposite the zenith

Nearest Galaxy Andromeda (2.3 million light years)

Nearest Planet to Earth Venus

Nearest Star to Earth Sun

Nearest Stars to Sun 1. Proxima Centauri (4.26 light years) 2. Alpha Centauri (4.34) 3. Barnard's Star (5.88)

Nebula Cloud of gas and dust in space

Neptune Mean distance from the Sun: 4,496.7 million km (2,810 million miles). Discovered by JG Galle in 1846. Atmosphere: hydrogen, helium, methane, ammonia. First suggested name was 'Janus'. Probe: *Voyager 2* (1989)

Neutron Star Remnant of a massive star that once exploded as a supernova

Nova Star that suddenly flares up to many times its normal brilliancy and then fades back to obscurity

Occultation The obscuring of one celestial body by another

Ophiuchus Often called the 13th constellation of the Zodiac

Orrery Model showing the Sun and the orbiting planets, capable of being moved mechanically to scale

Outer Planets The 5 planets that orbit the Sun beyond the Asteroid belt; i.e. Jupiter, Saturn, Uranus, Neptune, Pluto

Ozone Layer Located in the Stratosphere, between c19 and 30 km above the surface of the Earth. Ozone is created when energetic solar radiation strikes molecules of oxygen and causes the oxygen atoms to split apart. These atoms can then reform with O_2 molecules to form ozone (O_3) – a process known as photolysis. Ozone absorbs most of the incoming solar UV radiation which can be harmful to life on Earth

Parsec Basic unit used to measure large astronomic distances: 3.26 light years

Perigee Position of the Moon in its orbit when closest to the Earth

Perihelion Position in orbit of a planet when closest to the Sun

Photosphere The bright surface of the Sun

Planet Large body orbiting a star; the name means 'Wanderer' in Greek

Pluto Mean distance from the Sun: 5,900 million km (3,687 million miles). Atmosphere: tenuous. Discovered by Clyde Tombaugh 1930; named by Venetia Burney

Polaris Also called the Pole Star, it is 680 light years from the Earth

Quadrant Ancient astronomical instrument used for measuring the apparent positions of celestial bodies

Reversing Layer Gaseous layer above the Sun's photosphere

Rings of Saturn Discs composed of ice and rock, in sizes ranging from tiny particles to massive boulders, orbiting Jupiter, Neptune and Uranus, and most spectaculary Saturn

Rotating Backwards Venus (east to west)

Saturn Mean distance from the Sun: 1,427 million km (891 million miles). Atmosphere: mostly hydrogen and helium, some methane and ammonia. Christiaan Huygens discovered the rings in 1655. Cassini discovered 4 of the satellites. The satellite Phoebe revolves in the opposite direction to the others. Probes: *Voyager 1* and *2*, 1980–81

Sirius Also called the 'Dog Star', it is 8.7 light years from the Earth

Solar Cycle Discovered by H. Schwabe in 1826. He found that there is an 11-year solar cycle of sunspot activity

Solar Eclipse Blotting out of the Sun by the Moon, so that the Moon is directly between the Earth and the Sun

Solar Flares Brilliant eruptions of hydrogen in outer part of Sun's atmosphere

Solar Wind Flow of ionised hydrogen and helium from the Sun

Solstices Times when Sun is at its maximum declination of 23 1/2 degrees

Space Flight: 1st Yuri Gagarin in *Vostok 1* (12 Apr 1961); duration of flight 1 hr 48 mins

Space Flight: 1st Briton Helen Sharman (18 May 1991)

Space Walk: 1st American Ed White (June 1965 from *Gemini IV*)

Space Walk: 1st American Woman Dr Kathryn Sullivan (Oct 1984 from *Challenger*)

Space Walk: 1st Briton Michael Foale

Space Walk: 1st Untethered Bruce McCandless of the USA (3 Feb 1984)

Space Walk: 1st Woman Svetlana Savitskaya of the USSR (17 Jul 1984)

Stratosphere Region of the Earth's atmosphere lying above the Troposphere and below the Ionosphere

Sun Distance from the Earth: 149,597,900 km on average. Diameter: 1,392,000 km. Light takes 8 minutes 14.2 seconds to reach the Earth

Sunspot Region of lower temperature and therefore less brilliance, on the surface of the Sun

Superior Planets Those whose orbits lie outside the Earth's: Mars, Jupiter, Saturn, Uranus, Neptune, Pluto.

Supernova Cataclysmic explosion of a very massive star, which ends its career as a patch of expanding gas with a neutron star at its centre

Syzygy Position of the Moon in its orbit when new or full

Telescope: Largest Mount Semirodriki, Caucasus, with a 600 cm (236.2 in) reflector

Troposphere Lowest part of the Earth's atmosphere, reaching to about 11km

Umbra Main cone of shadow cast by Earth. Also darkest part of a sunspot

Unmanned Moon Landing: 1st *Lunik 2* (USSR) 1959. First US landing, *Ranger 4* in 1962, although this was a crash-landing

Uranus Mean distance from Sun: 2,869.6 million km (1,793 million miles). Atmosphere: hydrogen and helium. Discovered by William Herschel 1781. Probe: *Voyager 2* (1986)

Van Allen Radiation Belts Zones of charged particles around the Earth, held captive by the Earth's magnetic field

Venera Space Probes Russian series commencing with *Venera 4* in 1967 to explore Venus, the first planetary probe

Venus Mean distance from Sun: 108.2 million km (67.2 million miles). Atmosphere is largely carbon dioxide. Probes: Russian *Venera* series (1962–71); US *Mariners 2, 5,* and 10; *Magellan* (1990). Other names: Hesperus (evening star), Phosphorus (morning star)

Voyager A pair of unmanned US interplanetary probes launched to observe and transmit to Earth data about the outer planetary system. *Voyager* runs out of power around 2020. *Voyager 1* was Launched on 5 Sep

1977, flew by Jupiter in March 1979, reached Saturn in Nov 1980, then proceeded out of the solar system. *Voyager 2* was launched on 20 Aug 1977. It flew by Jupiter (Jul 1979), Saturn (Aug 1981), Uranus (Jan 1986) and Neptune (Aug 1989), then on into interstellar space

Walk in Space: 1st   Alexei Leonov (18 Mar 1965)

Woman in Space: 1st   Valentina Tereshkova (16 June 1963)

Zenith   Point on the celestial sphere directly above the observer (altitude 90 degrees)

Zodiac   Belt stretching around the sky 8 degrees to either side of ecliptic. The constellations Aries, Taurus, Gemini, Cancer, Leo, Virgo, Libra, Scorpius, Sagittarius, Capricornus, Aquarius and Pisces lies within this belt, and so do the apparent paths of the Sun and all the planets except Pluto, which sometimes moves outside it

ASTRONOMY

BRITAIN

United Kingdom: Administration Centres

A restructure of the old County boundaries has been ongoing throughout the UK. Formerly there were 46 English County Councils, but this has been reduced to 34, all of which have the same Administrative Headquarters as before.

The other twelve Counties, along with parts of still existing Counties, have been restructured and are now known officially as Unitary Authorities. There are 82 such authorities at present, plus the 32 London Boroughs and the City of London Corporation.

A similar position exists in Scotland, Wales and Northern Ireland, although it remains unclear if all the district councils are to become Counties.

Northern Ireland's six Counties have been rationalised across 26 districts (the same number as there are Counties of the Irish Republic), although at present only the traditional six Counties plus Belfast City and Londonderry City have Lord-Lieutenants.

As this is an area of uncertainty none of the District Councils and their respective Administration Headquarters have been entered in the very comprehensive list of 'Capitals', and only the long-established Counties have been listed.

English County Councils (as at 31 December 2002)

County	Admin Headquarters	County	Admin Headquarters
Bedfordshire	Bedford	Lincolnshire	Lincoln
Buckinghamshire	Aylesbury	Norfolk	Norwich
Cambridgeshire	Cambridge	Northamptonshire	Northampton
Cheshire	Chester	Northumberland	Morpeth
Cornwall	Truro	North Yorkshire	Northallerton
Cumbria	Carlisle	Nottinghamshire	Nottingham
Derbyshire	Matlock	Oxfordshire	Oxford
Devon	Exeter	Shropshire	Shrewsbury
Dorset	Dorchester	Somerset	Taunton
Durham	Durham	Staffordshire	Stafford
East Sussex	Lewes	Suffolk	Ipswich
Essex	Chelmsford	Surrey	Kingston-upon-Thames
Gloucestershire	Gloucester		
Hampshire	Winchester	Warwickshire	Warwick
Hertfordshire	Hertford	West Sussex	Chichester
Kent	Maidstone	Wiltshire	Trowbridge
Lancashire	Preston	Worcestershire	Worcester
Leicestershire	Leicester		

NB: The five inhabited islands of the Scillies, i.e. St Mary's (Admin HQ), Tresco, Bryher, St Agnes and St Martin's, although not constituting a separate County, do however have their own Council.

London Boroughs

(these are also Unitary Authorities)

Council	Admin Headquarters	Council	Admin Headquarters
Barking & Dagenham	Dagenham	Hounslow	Hounslow
Barnet	Hendon	* Islington	Islington
Bexley	Bexleyheath	* Kensington and Chelsea #	Kensington
Brent	Wembley	Kingston-upon-Thames #	Kingston-upon-Thames
Bromley	Bromley		
* Camden	Camden	* Lambeth	Brixton
City of London	Guildhall, London	* Lewisham	Catford
Croydon	Croydon	Merton	Morden
Ealing	Ealing	Newham	East Ham
Enfield	Enfield	Redbridge	Ilford
* Greenwich	Woolwich	Richmond-upon-Thames	Twickenham
* Hackney	Hackney	* Southwark	Southwark
* Hammersmith & Fulham	Hammersmith	Sutton	Sutton
Haringey	Wood Green	* Tower Hamlets	Tower Hamlets
Harrow	Harrow	Waltham Forest	Walthamstow
Havering	Romford	* Wandsworth	Wandsworth
Hillingdon	Uxbridge	* Westminster City	Westminster

* denotes Inner London Borough

# denotes Royal Borough

Unitary Authorities (as at 31 December 2002)

Authority	Headquarters	Authority	Headquarters
Barnsley*	Barnsley	Oldham*	Oldham
Bath and North East Somerset	Bath	Peterborough	Peterborough
Birmingham*	Birmingham	Plymouth	Plymouth
Blackburn with Darwen	Blackburn	Poole	Poole
Blackpool	Blackpool	Portsmouth	Portsmouth
Bolton*	Bolton	Reading	Reading
Bournemouth	Bournemouth	Redcar and Cleveland	Redcar
Bracknell Forest	Bracknell	Rochdale*	Rochdale
Bradford*	Bradford	Rotherham*	Rotherham
Brighton and Hove	Brighton	Rutland	Oakham
Bristol	Bristol	St Helens*	St Helens
Bury*	Bury	Salford*	Swinton
Calderdale*	Halifax	Sandwell*	West Bromwich
Coventry*	Coventry	Sefton*	Southport
Darlington	Darlington	Sheffield*	Sheffield
Derby	Derby	Slough	Slough
Doncaster*	Doncaster	Solihull*	Solihull
Dudley*	Dudley	Southampton	Southampton
East Riding of Yorkshire	Beverley	Southend	Southend
Gateshead*	Gateshead	South Gloucestershire	Thornbury
Halton	Widnes	South Tyneside*	South Shields
Hartlepool	Hartlepool	Stockport*	Stockport
Herefordshire	Hereford	Stockton-on-Tees	Stockton-on-Tees
Isle of Wight	Newport		
Kingston-upon-Hull	Kingston-upon-Hull	Stoke-on-Trent	Stoke-on-Trent
Kirklees*	Huddersfield	Sunderland*	Sunderland
Knowsley*	Huyton	Swindon	Swindon
Leeds*	Leeds	Tameside*	Ashton-under-Lyme
Leicester	Leicester		
Liverpool*	Liverpool	Telford and Wrekin	Telford
Luton	Luton	Thurrock	Grays
Manchester*	Manchester	Torbay	Torquay
Medway Towns	Rochester	Trafford*	Stretford
Middlesbrough	Middlesbrough	Wakefield*	Wakefield
Milton Keynes	Milton Keynes	Walsall*	Walsall
Newcastle-upon-Tyne*	Newcastle-upon-Tyne	Warrington	Warrington
		West Berkshire	Newbury
North East Lincolnshire	Grimsby	Windsor and Maidenhead	Maidenhead
North Lincolnshire	Brigg	Wigan*	Wigan
North Somerset	Weston-Super-Mare	Wirral*	Wallasey
		Wokingham	Wokingham
North Tyneside*	North Shields	Wolverhampton*	Wolverhampton
Nottingham	Nottingham	York	York

* denotes Metropolitan Authority

Scottish Districts
(Unitary Authorities)

Council	Admin Headquarters	Council	Admin Headquarters
Aberdeen	Aberdeen	Highland	Inverness
Aberdeenshire	Aberdeen	Inverclyde	Greenock
Angus	Forfar	Midlothian	Dalkeith
Argyll and Bute	Lochgilphead	Moray	Elgin
Clackmannanshire	Alloa	North Ayrshire	Irvine
Comhairlenan Eilean Siar	Stornoway	North Lanarkshire	Motherwell
Dumfries and Galloway	Dumfries	Orkney	Kirkwall
Dundee	Dundee	Perth and Kinrosshire	Perth
East Ayrshire	Kilmarnock	Renfrewshire	Paisley
East Dunbartonshire	Kirkintilloch	Scottish Borders	Melrose
East Lothian	Haddington	Shetland	Lerwick
East Renfrewshire	Glasgow	South Ayrshire	Ayr
Edinburgh	Edinburgh	South Lanarkshire	Hamilton
Falkirk	Falkirk	Stirling	Stirling
Fife	Glenrothes	West Dunbartonshire	Dunbarton
Glasgow City	Glasgow	West Lothian	Livingston

BRITAIN

Welsh Districts
(Unitary Authorities)

District Council	Admin Headquarters	District Council	Admin Headquarters
Anglesey	Llangefni	Merthyr Tydfil	Merthyr Tydfil
Blaenau Gwent	Ebbw Vale	Monmouth	Cwmbran
Bridgend	Bridgend	Neath Port Talbot	Port Talbot
Caerphilly	Hengoed	Newport	Newport
Cardiff	Cardiff	Pembrokeshire	Haverfordwest
Carmarthenshire	Carmarthen	Powys	Llandrindod Wells
Ceredigion	Aberystwyth	Rhondda, Cynon, Taff	Cardiff
Conwy	Conwy	Swansea, City and County	Swansea
Denbighshire	Ruthin	Torfaen	Pontypool
Flintshire	Mold	Vale of Glamorgan	Barry
Gwynedd	Caernarfon	Wrexham	Wrexham

Northern Irish Districts
(Unitary Authorities)

District Council	Admin Headquarters	District Council	Admin Headquarters
Antrim	Antrim	Down	Downpatrick
Ards	Newtownards	Dungannon	Dungannon
Armagh	Armagh	Fermanagh	Enniskillen
Ballymena	Ballymena	Larne	Larne
Ballymoney	Ballymoney	Limavady	Limavady
Banbridge	Banbridge	Lisburn	Hillsborough
Belfast	Belfast	Magherafelt	Magherafelt
Carrickfergus	Carrickfergus	Moyle	Ballycastle
Castlereagh	Cregagh	Newry and Mourne	Newry
Coleraine	Coleraine	Newtownabbey	Ballyclare
Cookstown	Cookstown	North Down	Bangor
Craigavon	Craigavon	Omagh	Omagh
Derry	Derry	Strabane	Strabane

Shopping Centres
by Towns and Cities

Aberdeen	Bredero	Colchester	Culver Square; St John's Walk
Aldershot	The Arcade	Coventry	Cannon Park; West Orchard
Ashford	Park Mall	Crawley	County Mall
Aylesbury	Hale Leys	Croydon	Whitgift
Barnstaple, Devon	Green Lanes	Dartford	Orchards
Bath	Green Park	Derby	Eagle
Bayswater	Whiteleys Centre	Dorking	St Martin's Walk
Bedford	Harpur	Dudley	Trident
Belfast	Castle Court	Dundee	Wellgate
Birmingham	Bull Ring, City Plaza	Durham	Milburngate
Blackpool	Hounds Hill	Eastbourne	Arndale
Bolton	Crompton Place	Ellesmere Port	Cheshire Oaks
Bradford	Kirkgate Mall	Epsom	Ashley Centre
Brighton	Churchill Square	Exeter	Guildhall
Bristol	Galleries, Clifton Arcade	Farnborough	Kingsmead
Bromley	Glades	Gateshead	MetroCentre
Burgess Hill	The Martletts	Glasgow	St Enoch; Sauchiehall Centre
Burnley	Charter Walk	Gloucester	Kings Square
Bury	Millgate	Greenhithe, Kent	Bluewater
Cambridge	Grafton Centre	Grimsby	Freshney Place
Cardiff	St Davids	Guildford	Friary, White Lion Walk
Carlisle	The Lanes	Harlow	Harvey Centre
Caterham	Church Walk	Hartlepool	Middleton Grange
Chelmsford	Meadows	Havant	Meridian Centre
Cheltenham	Regent Arcade	Hereford	The Atrium
Chester	Grosvenor	High Wycombe	Chilterns

Hinckley, Leics	Britannia	Portsmouth	Bridge
Horsham	Swan Walk	Preston	Fishergate
Hounslow	Treaty Centre	Redhill	Belfry
Hull	North Point	Romford	Liberty 2
Ilford	Exchange	Scarborough	Brunswick; Balmoral
Ipswich	Tower Ramparts	Sheffield	Forum, Meadowhall
Kingston Upon		Shrewsbury	Darwin
Thames	Bentalls	Skipton, North Yorks	Craven Court
Lancaster	St Nicholas; Markgate	Slough	Queensmere
Leatherhead	Swan Centre	Southampton	Marland
Leeds	Bramley Centre; Crossgates;	Southend	Victoria Plaza, Royals
	Merrion Centre	St Albans	Christopher Place; The Maltings
Leicester	Shires	Stevenage	Westgate
Lincoln	Waterside	St Helens	St Mary's Arcade
Liverpool	Clayton Square; St John's	Stockton	Teeside Park
	Precinct	Stoke-on-Trent	Potteries
Lowestoft	The Britten Centre	Street, Somerset	Clarks Village
Maidenhead	The Nicholsons Centre	Sunderland	Bridges
Maidstone	The Corn Exchange	Sutton Coldfield	Sainsbury Centre; Gracechurch
Manchester	Arndale		Centre
Mansfield	Four Seasons	Sutton (Surrey)	St Nicholas, Times Square
Morecambe	Arndale	Swansea	St Davids
Newcastle	Eldon Gardens	Swindon	Brunel
Northampton	Grosvenor Centre, Weston	Thurrock	Lakeside
	Favell; Peacock Place	Torquay	Fleet Walk
Norwich	Castle Mall, Dixons	Tunbridge Wells	Royal Victoria Place
Nottingham	Broadmarsh; Victoria	Wakefield	The Ridings
Nuneaton	Abbey Gate	Wandsworth	Arndale
Oldham	Spindles	Warrington	Cockhedge
Oxford	Westgate	Watford	Harlequin Centre
Peterborough	Queensgate	Winchester	Brooks
Piccadilly, London	The London Pavilion	York	Coppergate; Swinegate;
Plymouth	The Armada Centre		Monks Cross
Poole	Dolphin		

NB: Many cities have more than one shopping precinct, e.g. Leeds. This is purely a list of some of the best-known.

B
R
I
T
A
I
N

Pub Names

Blind Beggar	Situated in Whitechapel Road, London and famous as the site of Ronald Kray's murder of George Cornell.
Crown	Second most popular pub name in Britain.
Five Alls	Sign depicts a king with the caption 'I rule for all', a parson with 'I pray for all', a lawyer with 'I plead for all' a soldier with 'I fight for all' and a labourer with 'I work for all'.
Greyhound	Situated in Tinsley Green, Crawley and famous for hosting the World Marbles Championships at Easter.
Marquis of Granby	Named after John Manners, Marquis of Granby (1721–70). C-in-C of the British army in 1766.
Red Lion	Most popular pub name in Britain.
Royal Oak	Named after the oak tree that Charles II hid in after the battle of Worcester in 1651, the third most popular pub name in Britain.
Tan Hill Inn	Situated in Arkengarthdale, near Reeth, N. Yorks, the highest pub in Britain.
Trip to Jerusalem	Situated in the Brewhouse Yard, Nottingham, possibly the oldest pub in Britain.
White Hart	Named after Richard II's heraldic symbol.
White Lion	Named after Edward IV's heraldic symbol.

There are approximately 55,000 pubs in Britain, and since 1988 they can remain open any time between 11am and 11pm.

Prisons

Name	Location	Name	Location
* Aberdeen	Aberdeen	Grendon	Aylesbury, Bucks
Acklington	Morpeth, Northumberland	Guys Marsh	Shaftesbury, Dorset
Albany	Newport, Isle of Wight	Haslar	Gosport, Hants
Aldington	Ashford, Kent	Hatfield	Hatfield, Doncaster
** Altcourse	Liverpool	Haverigg	Millom, Cumbria
Armley	Leeds	Hewell Grange	Redditch, Worcs
Ashfield	Bristol	High Down	Sutton, Surrey
Ashwell	Oakham, Leics	* Highpoint	Newmarket, Suffolk
* Askham Grange	Askham Richard, York	Hindley	Wigan, Lancs
Aylesbury	Aylesbury, Bucks	Hollesley Bay	Woodbridge, Suffolk
Barlinnie	Glasgow	* Holloway	Parkhurst Rd, London
	(holds the most prisoners in	Holme House	Stockton-on-Tees
	Scotland, approx 1,150)	Hull	Hull, Yorks
Bedford	Bedford	Hydebank Wood	Belfast
Belmarsh	Thamesmead, London	** Kilmarnock	Kilmarnock
** Blakenhurst	Redditch, Worcs	Kingston	Portsmouth
Blantyre House	Cranbrook, Kent	Kirkham	Preston, Lancs
Blundeston	Lowestoft, Suffolk	Kirklevington Grange	Yarm, Cleveland
Brinsford	Wolverhampton	Lancaster	Lancaster
Bristol	Bristol	Lancaster Farms	Lancaster
Brixton	Brixton, London	Latchmere House	Richmond, Surrey
* Brockhill	Redditch, Worcs	Leicester	Leicester
** Buckley Hall	Rochdale, Lancs	Lewes	Lewes, East Sussex
Bullingdon	Bicester, Oxon	Leyhill	Wotton-under-Edge, Glos
* Bullwood Hall	Hockley, Essex	Lincoln	Lincoln
Camp Hill	Newport, Isle of Wight	Lindholme	Doncaster
Cardiff	Cardiff, South Wales	Littlehey	Huntingdon
Castington	Morpeth	Liverpool	Liverpool (holds on average
Castle Huntly	Longforgan, nr Dundee		most prisoners in Europe,
Channings Wood	Newton Abbott, Devon		approx 1216)
* Chelmsford	Chelmsford, Essex	Long Lartin	Evesham, Worcs
Coldingley	Woking, Surrey	Longport	Canterbury, Kent
* Cookham Wood	Rochester, Kent	Longriggend	Airdrie
* Cornton Vale	Stirling	** Lowdham Grange	Lowdham, Notts
Crumlin Road	Belfast	Low Moss	Glasgow
Dartmoor	Princetown, Yelverton,	* Low Newton	Brasside, Durham
	Devon	Maghaberry	Lisburn, Co Antrim
Deerbolt	Barnard Castle	Magilligan	Londonderry
** Doncaster	Marshgate, Doncaster	Maidstone	Maidstone
Dorchester	North Square, Dorchester	Manchester	Manchester
Dover	Dover, Kent	Maze (formerly	Lisburn, Co Antrim
Downview	Sutton, Surrey	'Long Kesh')	
* Drake Hall	Eccleshall, Staffs	Moorland	Doncaster
* Dumfries	Dumfries	Morton Hall	Lincoln
Dungavel	Strathaven, Lanark	Mount	Hemel Hempstead
* Durham	Old Elvet, Durham	Mountjoy	Dublin
* East Sutton Park	Maidstone, Kent	Mousehold	Norwich
* Eastwood Park	Falfield	* New Hall	Wakefield, Yorks
Edinburgh	Edinburgh	Noranside	Angus
Elmley	Sheerness, Kent	Northallerton	Northallerton, N. Yorks
Erlestoke House	Devizes, Wilts	North Sea Camp	Boston, Lincs
Everthorpe	Brough, Yorks	Norwich	Norwich
Exeter	Exeter	Nottingham	Nottingham
Featherstone	Featherstone,	Onley	Rugby, Warks
	Wolverhampton	** Parc	Bridgend, S. Wales
Ford	Arundel, West Sussex	Parkhurst	Newport, Isle of Wight
* Foston Hall	Ashbourne, Derby	Penninghame	Newton Stewart
Frankland	Brasside, Durham	Pentonville	London
Friarton	Perth	Perth	Perth
Full Sutton	Full Sutton, Yorks	Peterhead	Aberdeenshire
Garth	Preston, Lancs	Polmont	Falkirk
Gartree	Market Harborough, Leics	Portland	Portland, Dorset
Gateside	Greenock	* Porterfield	Inverness
Glenochil	Clackmannanshire	Prescoed	Pontypool
Glen Parva	Leicester	Preston	Preston, Lancs
Gloucester	Barrack Square,	Ranby	Retford, Notts
	Gloucester	Reading	Reading

Name	Location	Name	Location
* Risley	Warrington	Wandsworth	London
Rochester	Rochester, Kent	Wayland	Thetford, Norfolk
Send	Woking, Surrey	Wealston	Wetherby, W. Yorks
Shepton Mallet	Somerset	Weare	Portland Harbour, Dorset
Shotts	Shotts		
Shrewsbury	The Dana, Shrewsbury	Wellingborough	Wellingborough, Northants
Stafford	Gaol Rd, Stafford		
Standford Hill	Sheerness, Kent	Werrington	Stoke-on-Trent
Stocken	Stretton, Leics	Wetherby	Wetherby, Yorks
Stoke Heath	Market Drayton, Shrops	Whatton	Notts
* Styal	Wilmslow, Cheshire	Whitemoor	March, Cambs
Sudbury	Sudbury, Derbyshire	* Winchester	Winchester, Hants
Swaleside	Isle of Sheppey, Kent	Winson Green	Birmingham
Swansea	Swansea	** Wolds, The	Brough, Yorks
Swinfen Hall	Lichfield, Staffs	Woodhill	Milton Keynes
Thorn Cross	Warrington	Wormwood Scrubs	DuCane Rd, London (built in 1874, the Scrubs is the largest prison in GB)
Usk	Usk, Gwent		
Verne, The	Portland, Dorset		
Wakefield	Wakefield, Yorks	Wymott	Preston, Lancs

* denotes women's prison (or women's wing attached)
** denotes private prison

British Castles

Name	Location	General Information
Abergavenny	Gwent	Norman Motte & Bailey castle founded by Hamelin of Ballon between 1087 & 1100, rebuilt in stone C12, captured by Welsh. c1172, recaptured by William de Braose c1175, ordered to be destroyed by Charles I in 1645.
Aberystwyth	Dyfed	Edwardian concentric castle erected 1277–90 under aegis of Edmund Crouchback and Master Giles of St George (after destruction in 1282 by Welsh). Held by Glyndwr 1404–9, slighted by Parliament in 1649.
Abinger	Surrey	Norman Motte & Bailey castle erected c1100. Wooden Donjon on stilts, excavated 1947–9.
Aboyne	Grampian	Motte castle erected C13, stone additions by 1300.
Acton Burnell	Shropshire	Fortified manor founded by Bishop Burnell c1284–90.
Airlie	Tayside	Enclosure castle founded by Ogilvy family c1432.
Allington	Kent	Founded by Stephen of Penchester 1281 beside site of Norman Motte & Bailey. Altered at end of C15 by Sir Henry Wyatt, restored by Lord Conway 1905–30. Now a Carmelite nunnery.
Alnwick	Northumberland	Norman castle founded by Gilbert de Tesson, C12 shell keep, seat of Percy family since 1309, remodelled by Salvin C19.
Amberley	West Sussex	Built for the Bishops of Chichester, licence to crenellate 1377. Partially ruined, now a private residence.
Anstey	Herts	C12 Motte & Bailey, now lost.
Appleby	Cumbria	Norman castle erected C12 by Henry II, restored by Lady Anne Clifford 1651.
Ardrossan	Strathclyde	Courtyard castle founded late C13, gatehouse improved C15/16.
Arundel	West Sussex	Norman castle, founded 1069 by Roger of Montgomery, C12 shell keep, seat of Dukes of Norfolk.
Ashby de la Zouch	Leicestershire	Norman hall founded C12 by Zouch family. Converted into a castle 1474 by Lord Hastings, slighted by Parliament 1648. Now owned by English Heritage.
Auchen	Dumfries & Galloway	Castle founded C13, slighted by Bruce, rebuilt C14 as quadrangular castle.
Ayr	Strathclyde	Castle founded C12 by William the Lion, besieged by English 1298.
Balvenie	Grampian	Enclosure castle founded late C13 by Douglases, remodelled C16 by 4th Earl of Atholl.
Bamburgh	Northumberland	Norman castle with C12 tower keep erected by Henry II, besieged in 1095, 1462 and 1464, 'restored' by Lord Armstrong 1894–1905.
Bampton	Oxfordshire	Quadrangular castle founded 1315 by Aymer de Valence, now lost.
Banbury	Oxfordshire	Norman castle built early C12 by Bishops of Lincoln, extended 1400 into concentric plan, now lost.
Barnard Castle	Durham	Norman castle erected by Guy de Balliol c1100, C13 round keep,

BRITAIN

Name	Location	General Information
		dismantled 1630 by Sir Henry Vane, now owned by English Heritage.
Barnstaple	Devon	Norman Motte & Bailey castle erected C11 by Judhael, C12 shell keep now lost.
Barnwell	Northants	Norman castle founded 1132 by Reginald de Moine. Rebuilt c1265, now ruined.
Bass of Inverurie	Grampian	Motte & Bailey castle founded c1180 by David, Earl of Huntingdon.
Beaumaris	Gwynedd	Concentric Edwardian castle erected by Master James of St George 1295–1330.
Bedford	Bedfordshire	Norman Motte & Bailey castle founded late C11, modified and enlarged C12, besieged by Henry III 1224 and destroyed shortly after.
Beeston	Cheshire	Built by Ranulf of Chester c1220, slighted in Civil War, owned by English Heritage.
Belvoir	Lincolnshire	Gothic style C19 castle, seat of Dukes of Rutland on site of Norman Motte & Bailey castle founded by Robert de Todeni C11, destroyed by King John.
Berkeley	Gloucestershire	Norman castle founded by William Fitz Osbern pre-1086, current building erected 1154 by Robert Fitzhardinge.
Berkhamsted	Hertfordshire	Norman Motte & Bailey castle founded by Robert of Mortain, rebuilt by Thomas Becket 1155–65 and King John, rare double moat, now owned by English Heritage.
Berry Pomeroy	Devon	Norman castle probably founded C12.
Bickleigh	Devon	Norman Motte & Bailey castle dismantled mid-C12; Courtenay family built fortified mansion on site C14.
Bishop's Stortford	Hertfordshire	Norman Motte & Bailey castle, now lost.
Blackness	Lothian	Tower castle founded C15, extended C16 with plan resembling that of a ship.
Blair	Tayside	Tower founded c1270, last castle to be besieged (1746), C18 mansion, seat of Dukes of Atholl.
Bodiam	East Sussex	Quadrangular moated castle built by Edward Dalyngrigge 1386, restored by Lord Curzon. National Trust property.
Bolingbroke	Lincolnshire	Built by Ranulf, Earl of Chester, c1220, now ruined.
Bolsover	Derbyshire	Norman castle founded by William Peverel, rebuilt by Smythson in Jacobean Romantic style, owned by English Heritage.
Bolton	North Yorkshire	Quadrangular castle built by Lord Scrope c1381–99, slighted during Civil War.
Bothwell	Strathclyde	Castle founded in 1270s by Moravia family, captured by Scots 1297, English 1301 & 1331, dismantled by Sir Andrew de Moravia 1337, rebuilt by Black Douglas in 1360s.
Bowes	County Durham	Tower castle built by the Earl of Richmond 1170–87, now owned by English Heritage.
Bramber	West Sussex	Norman castle founded by William de Braose c1070, slighted during Civil War, now owned by National Trust.
Brecon	Powys	Norman castle founded 1090 by Bernard de Neufmarche, extended and fortified in stone C12, unsuccessfully besieged by Welsh 1216, 1233 & 1404.
Bridgnorth	Shropshire	Norman castle founded by Robert de Belleme C11, C12 keep erected by Henry II, slighted during Civil War.
Bristol	Avon	Norman Motte & Bailey castle founded after Conquest; Tower Keep erected C12 by Stephen, destroyed in 1650s.
Bronllys	Powys	Norman Motte & Bailey castle founded C12, cylindrical tower added c1176 after a fire.
Brough	Cumbria	Norman castle founded by William Rufus c1095 in ruins of a Roman fort, destroyed 1174 by William the Lion, rebuilt by Theobald de Valoires, restored C17 by Lady Anne Clifford. Now owned by English Heritage.
Brougham	Cumbria	Norman castle built C12 by Hugh d'Albini, pulled down c1700, now owned by English Heritage.
Buckingham	Buckinghamshire	Norman Motte & Bailey castle now covered by a church.
Builth	Powys	Norman Motte & Bailey castle founded by Philip de Braose c1100, destroyed by Llywelyn ap Gruffyd 1260, rebuilt 1277–82 by Edward I under direction of Master James of St George, severely damaged by Glyndwr.
Bungay	Suffolk	Norman castle founded by Roger Bigod c1105, demolished 1176, shell keep & bailey erected c1295 by Roger Bigod.
Caerlaverock	Dumfries	Built c1280 to a triangular plan, captured by Edward I 1300, slighted by Bruce, rebuilt C15, now owned by Historic Scotland.
Caerleon	Gwent	Norman Motte & Bailey castle erected c1086, great tower added. 1158–73.

Name	Location	General Information
Caernarvon	Gwynedd	Norman Motte & Bailey castle erected 1093 by Earl Hugh of Chester, destroyed by Welsh 1115, Edwardian castle on site constructed by Master James of St George 1283–1330, designed to resemble walls of Constantinople.
Caerphilly	Mid Glamorgan	Built by Gilbert de Clare, Earl of Gloucester, 1271–80 after original castle of 1267–70 destroyed by Llywelyn, now owned by Welsh Historic Mons.
Cainhoe	Bedfordshire	Norman castle founded by Nigel d'Albini, motte and 3 bailleys.
Caister	Norfolk	Built by Sir John Fastolf 1432–36, made of brick and surrounded by a moat.
Caldicot	Gwent	Norman Motte & Bailey castle founded by Walter Fitzroger early C12, developed by de Bohun Earls of Hereford late C12/early C13, gatehouse extended c1385, repaired late C19.
Cambridge	Cambs	Norman castle founded by William I 1068, rebuilt 1284–98, slighted in 1647.
Canterbury	Kent	Norman Motte & Bailey castle founded by William I 1066, Keep erected early C12.
Cardiff	South Glamorgan	Norman Motte built C1080 by Robert Fitzhamon on site of Roman fort, shell keep erected C12, further additions by Gilbert de Clare C13, castle remodelled by William Burges for 3rd Marquess of Bute C19.
Cardigan	Dyfed	Norman castle founded c1093, captured by Welsh c1170 and converted to stone, sold to John 1199, destroyed by Llywelyn the Great 1231, new castle built near original site by English in 1240s.
Carew	Dyfed	Norman Motte & Bailey castle founded by Gerald de Windsor 1105, extended by Nicholas de Carew in C13, damaged by Parliamentary forces in 1645.
Carisbrooke	Isle of Wight	Norman castle founded by William Fitz Osbern c1070, extended by Baldwin de Redvers in 1130s gatehouse erected c1335, now owned by English Heritage.
Carlisle	Cumbria	Norman castle built by William Rufus in 1192, improved by David I of Scotland, rebuilt 1541 for Henry VIII by Stefan von Hashenperg, now owned by English Heritage.
Carmarthen	Dyfed	Norman Motte & Bailey castle founded early C12, captured by Llywelyn the Great 1215, rebuilt and extended by English during C13, held by Glyndwr 1403–9.
Carreg Cennen	Dyfed	Courtyard castle built in C13 on site of Roman fort, demolished by Yorkists 1462.
Castell y Bere	Gwynedd	Enclosure castle founded c1221 by Llywelyn the Great, captured by Edward I 1283, restored 1286–90, abandoned by 1300.
Castle Acre, priory	Norfolk	Norman castle founded by William de Warenne C11, stone keep rebuilt C1140, now owned by English Heritage.
Castle Bytham	Lincolnshire	Norman castle founded c1169, besieged and demolished 1221, rebuilt by William de Colville 1220s.
Castle Drogo	Devon	Granite castle designed by Edwin Lutyens 1910–30.
Castle Hedingham	Essex	Tower keep built by Aubrey de Vere III 1141 on site of late C11 timber castle, now owned by English Heritage.
Castle Rising	Norfolk	Tower keep built by William II d'Albini c1140, now owned by English Heritage.
Castle Rushen	Castletown, I.O.M.	Probably the best-preserved medieval castle in the British Isles. Built c1200; partly destroyed in a siege by Robert the Bruce in 1313, but rebuilt by Sir William Montacute in c1344. The castle chapel houses a clock presented by Queen Elizabeth I in 1597.
Cause	Shropshire	Norman Motte & Bailey castle founded by Roger Fitz Corbet, fortified in stone C12, demolished 1645.
Cawdor	Inverness	Built 1454, seat of Earls of Cawdor.
Chepstow	Gwent	Norman castle with stone keep founded by William Fitz Osbern 1070, extended C13, disused from 1690, now owned by Welsh Historic Monuments.
Chester	Cheshire	Norman Motte & Bailey castle built on site of Roman fortress, improved C13, now lost.
Chilham	Kent	Norman castle founded by Fulbert of Dover, octagonal keep built for Henry II 1171–5.
Chirk	Clwyd	Motte & Bailey castle founded mid-C12, new castle founded nearby by Roger Mortimer 1274–1310.
Christchurch	Dorset	Norman Motte & Bailey castle founded by Richard de Redvers c1100, ruins now owned by English Heritage.
Cilgerran	Dyfed	Norman enclosure castle founded by Gerald of Windsor c1110, rebuilt and extended c1233.
Clare	Suffolk	Norman Motte & Bailey castle founded by Richard Fitzgilbert,

Name	Location	General Information
		improved by Gilbert de Clare.
Clavering	Essex	Norman castle founded by Robert Fitz Wimarc c1050.
Claypotts	Tayside	Built C16.
Clifford's Tower	York	Quatrefoil keep on motte founded by Henry III 1245 on site of Norman castle of 1069, burnt down 1190 whilst housing Jewish refugees, rebuilt and blown down 1228, now owned by English Heritage.
Clitheroe	Lancashire	Norman castle founded by Roger de Poitou.
Clun	Shropshire	Norman castle founded by Roger de Say, tower keep built in motte C12 by William Fitz Alan.
Cockermouth	Cumbria	Built C13 by William de Fortibus, rebuilt by Anthony de Lucy in 1360, slighted in Civil War.
Coity	Mid Glamorgan	Norman castle founded by Payn de Turberville, extended late C12, altered C14.
Colchester	Essex	Norman castle founded by William the Conqueror 1076–80; largest Norman tower keep, partly demolished 1683.
Conisborough	Yorkshire	Norman castle founded by William de Warenne, rebuilt with cylindrical tower keep by Hamelin, Earl of Surrey c1180, now owned by English Heritage.
Conwy	Gwynedd	Edwardian castle erected by Master James of St George 1283–7.
Cooling	Kent	Double quadrangular castle founded in 1380s, erected by Henry Yevele.
Corfe	Dorset	Norman castle founded by William I c1080, great tower erected by Henry I, gloriette erected by John, dismantled in Civil War (1646), now owned by National Trust.
Coulthalley	Strathclyde	Founded C12, rebuilt c1375, altered c1415 and c1520, rebuilt after siege 1557.
Craignethan	Strathclyde	Built in C16 by Sir James Hamilton, fortified courtyards with provision for artillery surrounding tower house, slighted 1579.
Criccieth	Gwynedd	Enclosure castle founded early C13, probably by Llywelyn the Great, Edwardian additions to site 1290, ruined by Glyndwr 1404.
Crichton	Lothian	Castle founded by John de Crichton late C14, extended C15.
Croft	Herefordshire	Medieval quadrangular castle of C14, named after family who built it, now owned by National Trust.
Cruggleton	Dumfries & Galloway	Motte & Bailey castle founded C12, reinforced in stone C13.
Dartmouth	Devon	Artillery fort built 1481 by Dartmouth corporation to protect town, now owned by English Heritage.
Deal	Kent	Henrician artillery fort built in 1539–40, besieged 1648, now owned by English Heritage.
Deganwy	Gwynedd	Double Motte & Bailey castle founded c1090, taken by Henry III 1241 and rebuilt/extended, destroyed by Llywelyn 1257.
Denbigh	Clywd	Edwardian castle built by Henry de Lacy, designed by Master James of St George, 1282–1311, destroyed in 1650s.
Devizes	Wiltshire	Norman castle founded late C11, used as prison by Henry II and Henry III, demolished in Civil War.
Dinefwr	Dyfed	Castle founded C12, rebuilt with cylindrical donjon C13, damaged by fire C18, modern castle constructed 1856.
Dirleton	Lothian	Founded by de Vaux family C12, stone buildings built C13, extended C14/C15.
Dolbadarn	Gwynedd	Castle with cylindrical donjon erected by Llywelyn the Great early C13, partially dismantled by Edward I in 1284.
Dolwyddelan	Gwynedd	Castle founded by Iorwerth Trwyndwn c1170, captured by English 1282 and repaired.
Donnington	Berkshire	Enclosure castle founded late C14 by Richard de Adderbury, destroyed in 1646, now owned by English Heritage.
Doune	Perth & Kinrosshire	Enclosure castle founded by Duke of Albany late 14th Century.
Dover	Kent	Norman castle founded 1066 by William I, rebuilt with tower keep designed by Maurice the Engineer for Henry II in 1180–9, concentric fortifications built at same time, besieged 1216, extra fortifications added C19.
Dudley	West Midlands	Norman Motte & Bailey castle founded by William Fitzansculf, destroyed by Henry II 1175, rebuilt c1270 by John de Somery, extended early C14 by John de Somery, slighted 1647.
Duffus	Grampian	Motte & Bailey castle founded by Freskin de Moravia C12, rebuilt c1300 in stone, north-west corner of Donjon slid down motte late C14.
Dumbarton	Strathclyde	Built upon Dumbarton Rock.
Dundonald	Strathclyde	Founded by Walter Stewart c1250, expanded by Robert II, 1371–90.
Dunstaffnage	Strathclyde	Enclosure castle built by MacDougall in the 13th century.
Dunstanburgh	Northumberland	Enclosure castle founded by Thomas, 2nd Earl of Lancaster

Name	Location	General Information
		1313–16, altered by John of Gaunt, now owned by English Heritage.
Dunster	Somerset	Norman castle founded by William de Mohun, fortified manor built on site C14, owned by Luttrells from 1376, remodelled by Salvin C19, now owned by National Trust.
Dunvegan	Skye	Home of the Chiefs of Clan Macleod since foundation in C13.
Durham	County Durham	Norman castle founded by William I c1072, rebuilt C12 in stone, keep C14, rebuilt 1840, now used by University of Durham.
Edinburgh	Lothian	Wooden fortress founded by Malcolm III C11, rebuilt C12/13, taken by Edward I 1296, taken by Earl of Moray and destroyed 1313, rebuilt C14.
Edlingham	Northumberland	Castle founded by Sir William Felton late C12, triangular enclosure with separate great tower.
Egremont	Cumbria	Norman castle built by William de Meschines in 1130.
Eilean Donan	Western Ross	Built in C13, probably by Alexander II, rebuilt in C20.
Etal	Northumberland	Castle with donjon and gatehouse tower at opposing corners, founded 1342 by Manners family, captured 1513 by James IV.
Ewloe	Clwyd	Castle founded 1146 by Owain Gwynedd, rebuilt in stone c1200 by Llywelyn the Great.
Ewyas Harold	Herefordshire	Norman castle built c1050, refortified by William FitzOsbern.
Exeter	Devon	Norman castle founded by William I in 1067 in corner of Roman walls, largely demolished in 1744, stone gatehouse c1068 still extant.
Eynsford	Kent	Norman enclosure castle fortified in stone c1088, extended C12.
Farleigh Hungerford	Somerset	Castle erected c1370–83 by Sir Thomas Hungerford, enlarged C15 by Walter Hungerford, now owned by English Heritage.
Farnham	Surrey	Norman Motte & Bailey castle founded by Henry de Blois C12, slighted by Henry II 1155, rebuilt late C12 with stone encasing motte, slighted 1648, now owned by English Heritage.
Flint	Clwyd	Edwardian castle erected by Master James of St George 1277–80, donjon separate from rest of castle, slighted 1646.
Ford	Northumberland	Quadrangular castle founded 1338 by William Heron, attacked by Scots 1385, 1513, 1549, rebuilt 1861 by Marchioness of Waterford.
Fotheringhay	Northants	Norman Motte & Bailey castle, famous as the site of Mary Queen of Scots' beheading.
Framlingham	Suffolk	Norman castle founded c1100 by Roger Bigod, destroyed by Henry II 1175, rebuilt as enclosure castle by Roger II Bigod c1189–1200.
Gloucester	Gloucestershire	Norman Motte & Bailey castle founded by William I, Great Tower built by Henry I c1112.
Goodrich	Hereford and Worcester	Keep built mid-C12, converted into quadrangular castle by de Valence family late C13. Barbican erected C14, slighted 1646, now owned by English Heritage.
Grosmont	Gwent	Castle founded late C11, rebuilt in stone c1210, extended by Hubert de Burgh 1220–40.
Guildford	Surrey	Norman Motte & Bailey castle, keep erected on side of motte mid-C12.
Hadleigh	Essex	Enclosure castle founded by Hubert de Burgh C13, extended by Edward III 1361–70, now owned by English Heritage.
Hailes	Lothian	Founded C13, owned from C14 by Hepburns, who extended castle, besieged by Percys c1400.
Hallaton	Leicestershire	Norman Motte & Bailey castle, motte almost as large as bailey.
Harbottle	Northumberland	Motte & Bailey castle with shell keep erected 1159–60 by Robert d'Umfraville.
Harlech	Gwynedd	Edwardian concentric castle erected 1283–9 by Master James of St George, besieged 1294, 1401–5, 1408–9, 1468, 1647, now owned by Welsh Historic Monuments.
Hastings	East Sussex	Norman Motte & Bailey castle founded by William I 1066, appears in Bayeux Tapestry, later converted to stone, only C13 ruins extant.
Haughley	Suffolk	Norman Motte & Bailey castle, one of largest in Britain, dismantled by Henry II c1173.
Haverfordwest	Dyfed	Norman castle founded c1120 by Gilbert de Clare, strengthened by William de Valence C13, besieged by Glyndwr 1405.
Hawarden	Clwyd	Norman Motte & Bailey castle, fortified in stone early C13, destroyed by Llywelyn 1265, rebuilt 1277, slighted 1647/8.
Hay–on–Wye	Powys	Norman Motte & Bailey castle founded early C12 by William Revell, destroyed by King John, C13 replacement built on different site, destroyed by Glyndwr.
Helmsley	North Yorkshire	Norman castle founded by Robert de Mortain, held by Walter l'Espec and de Roos family, who constructed current structure 1186–1227. Enclosure castle with keep, keep heightened early

Name	Location	General Information
		C14, slighted 1644/5.
Hereford	Hereford and Worcester	Norman Motte & Bailey castle possibly founded c1050, held by William Fitz Osbern 1066–71, stoneworks C13 with tower on motte, now destroyed.
Hermitage	Borders	Founded early C14, captured by Scots 1338, owned by the Douglases, who extended it C14/15.
Herstmonceux	East Sussex	Brick quadrangular castle founded 1441 by Sir Roger Fiennes, restored C20.
Hertford	Herts	Norman Motte & Bailey castle founded c1067 by William I, major works on castle C15, demolished C17.
Hever	Kent	Manor house founded 1270s, fortified 1340 by William de Hever and in 1384 by Sir John Cobham, bought by Boleyn family 1462 and modified, restored by Viscount Astor 1903–7.
Holt	Clwyd	Edwardian enclosure castle founded by John de Warenne 1280s, demolished late C17.
Hopton	Shropshire	Norman Motte & Bailey castle founded C12, donjon built on motte by Walter de Hopton c1300.
Huntingdon	Cambridgeshire	Norman Motte & Bailey castle founded 1069 by William I, 2nd motte added C12, demolished 1174 by Henry II.
Huntly	Grampian	Motte & Bailey castle founded C12, rebuilt in stone and extended by 1st Earl of Huntly C15, blown up by James VI 1594, rebuilt by 1st Marquis of Huntly c1600–06.
Inverlochy	Highland	Enclosure castle founded c1270–80.
Inverness	Highland	Founded C12, later reclad in stone. Destroyed by Young Pretender 1746.
Jedburgh	Borders	Motte & Bailey castle founded C12 by David I, destroyed c1410 by Regent Albany.
Kenilworth	Warwickshire	Enclosure castle with motte & donjon founded c1120 by William de Clinton, donjon rebuilt later C12, water defences added C13, besieged for 6 months 1266, remodelled by John of Gaunt 1370s, slighted 1649, now owned by English Heritage.
Kidwelly	Dyfed	Norman castle founded by Roger, Bishop of Salisbury c1106, burnt by Welsh 1215, enclosure castle built 1270s, concentric curtain added C14.
Kiessimut	Barra, Western Isles	Enclosure castle of late C12/early C13, restored by MacNeils.
Kildrummy	Grampian	Enclosure castle of C13 on site of C12 Motte & Bailey castle.
Kirby Muxloe	Leicestershire	Unfinished quadrangular castle built by Lord Hastings c1480–3, now owned by English Heritage.
Knaresborough	North Yorkshire	Norman castle built C12 by Eustace Fitzjohn, improved by Edward II and III 1307–50, slighted 1648.
Lancaster	Lancashire	Norman castle built early C12 by Roger de Poitou, extended by King John, improved by Henry IV, partially demolished 1649.
Laugharne	Dyfed	Castle founded C12, rebuilt in C13 and 14 including cylindrical keep.
Launceston	Cornwall	Norman Motte & Bailey castle of Dunheved, built by Robert of Mortain, rebuilt with shell keep C13 by Richard of Cornwall. George Fox imprisoned in gatehouse 1656, owned by English Heritage.
Leeds	Kent	Norman castle founded by the de Crevecoeur family, rebuilt by Edward I after 1278, restored C19.
Leicester	Leicestershire	Norman Motte & Bailey castle founded c1068, fortified in stone by 2nd Earl of Leicester mid-C12, improved by Henry IV and V.
Lewes	East Sussex	Norman double Motte & Bailey castle built by William de Warenne c1069–70, shell keep added C13, barbican added C14.
Lincoln	Lincolnshire	Norman Double Motte & Bailey castle founded by William 1 1068, shell keep (Lucy Tower) added C12.
Llandovery	Dyfed	Norman Motte & Bailey castle founded early C12 by Robert Fitzpons, captured by Welsh 1116, recovered c1158, stonework added late C12, slighted by Cromwell.
Llanstephan	Dyfed	Enclosure castle founded C12, captured by Welsh 1146, retaken by Henry II, given to William de Camville, strengthened c1192, extended C13, captured by Glyndwr 1403.
Loch Doon	Strathclyde	Enclosure castle of late C13 erected on an island; moved to western shore of loch 1934–5.
Longtown	Hereford & Worcester	Norman Motte & Bailey castle founded late C11, cylindrical donjon added on motte early C14.
Ludgershall	Wiltshire	Norman Motte & Bailey castle founded late C11, unfinished donjon added mid-C12, replacement tower added c1200, now owned by English Heritage.
Ludlow	Shropshire	Norman enclosure castle with flanking towers erected c1086 by

Name	Location	General Information
		Roger de Lacy.
Lydford	Devon	Norman castle founded C11, donjon added C12 and extended with motte built around base C13.
Lympne	Kent	Norman castle founded 1080s, reconstructed C14.
Manorbier	Dyfed	Norman enclosure castle founded by Otto de Barri late C11, strengthened C12, birthplace of Giraldus Cambrensis 1146.
Marlborough	Wiltshire	Norman Motte & Bailey castle, extended by Henry II, shell keep added by King John and added to by Henry III.
Middleham	North Yorkshire	Norman Motte & Bailey castle founded c1086, tower keep built on nearby site by Robert Fitzranulph c1170, quadrangular curtain added C13, slighted in Civil War, now owned by English Heritage.
Monmouth	Gwent	Norman Motte & Bailey castle founded by William FitzOsbern c1070, keep added on motte c1120–30, birthplace of Henry V 1387, slighted during Civil War.
Montacute	Somerset	Norman Motte & Bailey castle founded by Robert of Mortain 1069/70, dismantled C12 by Cluniac monks of Montacute Priory.
Montfichet	London	Norman Motte & Bailey castle founded by William I 1066/7, dismantled C13.
Montgomery (I) (Hen Domen)	Powys	Norman Motte & Bailey castle built by Roger de Montgomery c1071, dismantled C12.
Montgomery (II)	Powys	Enclosure castle founded 1223 by Baldwin de Boller, slighted 1649.
Morpeth	Northumberland	Norman Motte & Bailey castle founded late C11, destroyed by King John 1215, castle rebuilt in bailey mid-C13.
Mountsorrell	Leicestershire	Norman Motte & Bailey castle, dismantled 1217.
Neroche	Somerset	Norman enclosure castle founded C11 by Robert of Mortain, motte added early C12, shell keep added mid-C12.
Nether Stowey	Somerset	Norman Motte & 2 Bailey castle, tower keep added on motte mid-C12.
Newark	Nottinghamshire	Norman enclosure castle built by Bishop of Lincoln 1130s, major reconstruction early C13, slighted 1646.
New Buckenham	Norfolk	Built by William II d'Albini c1140, cylindrical tower keep (first in Britain), demolished by Sir Philip Knyvey 1649.
Newcastle	Tyne & Wear	Norman Motte & Bailey castle founded c1080, rebuilt with keep designed by Maurice the Engineer 1068–77.
Newport	Gwent	Norman castle founded C12, rebuilt C13, sacked by Glyndwr and rebuilt C15.
Norham	Northumberland	Norman Motte & Bailey castle founded c1120 by Ranulf Flambard, destroyed by Scots 1140s, rebuilt by Bishop Hugh of Durham 1158–74, taken by Scots 1513, now owned by English Heritage.
Northampton	Northants	Norman Motte & Bailey castle founded c1080, enlarged by Henry I. tower keep added c1170.
Norwich	Norfolk	Norman Motte & Bailey castle founded by William FitzOsbern for William I 1067, tower keep added on motte 1125–30, stone curtain added 1268–70, keep restored by Salvin 1834–9, now serving as museum (since 1894).
Nottingham	Nottinghamshire	Norman Motte & Bailey castle founded 1068 by William I, modified by Henry II. Keep built 1213, demolished 1651 by Colonel Hutchinson, renovated 1878 by the Corporation and now a museum.
Nunney	Somerset	Rectangular moated Great Tower with cylindrical towers at corners built 1373 by Sir John de la Mare, slighted 1645, now owned by English Heritage.
Oakham	Rutland	Norman Motte & Bailey castle, stone added C12, Great Hall built by Wakelin de Ferrers c1180 still extant.
Odiham	Hampshire	Octagonal keep built by King John 1207–12.
Ogmore	Mid–Glamorgan	Norman castle founded c1110, stone donjon built late C12, fortified in stone C13.
Okehampton	Devon	Norman Motte & Bailey castle founded by Baldwin Fitzgilbert c1070, extended and tower built on motte early C14.
Ongar	Essex	Norman Motte & Bailey castle founded early C12 by de Lucy family, stone tower built on motte 1150s.
Orford	Suffolk	Castle with polygonal keep founded by Henry II 1165–72, now owned by English Heritage.
Oswestry	Shropshire	Norman Motte & Bailey castle founded late C11 by Rainald de Bailleul, shell keep built C12.
Oxford	Oxfordshire	Norman Motte & Bailey castle founded c1071 by Robert d'Oilly, St George's Tower built on motte late C11, shell keep built on motte C12.
Oystermouth	West Glamorgan	Norman castle built c1100, destroyed 1215, rebuilt C13 by William

Name	Location	General Information
		de Braose.
Peel Castle	Peel, I.O.M.	Situated on St Patrick's Isle near Peel harbour and built by William Le Scrope in 1392. The castle houses the ruins of St German's Cathedral, named from Germanus a disciple of Patrick who is thought to have brought Christianity to the island.
Peel of Lumphanan	Grampian	Motte & Bailey castle founded C12, shell keep erected early C13.
Pembridge	Hereford & Worcester	Castle founded C13 by Ralph de Pembridge, includes moat and cylindrical donjon, ruined in Civil War.
Pembroke	Dyfed	Norman enclosure castle founded c1090 by Arnulf de Montgomery, extended and cylindrical donjon built by William Marshal early C13, slighted by Cromwell 1648/9.
Pendennis	Cornwall	Henrician artillery fort built to protect Falmouth, now owned by English Heritage.
Penhow	Gwent	Enclosure castle founded early C13 by Sir William St Maur.
Penrice	West Glamorgan	Norman enclosure castle founded c1100, stone castle raised on nearby site mid-C13, cylindrical donjon.
Penrith	Cumbria	Tower built C14, quadrangular castle erected on site c1397–9 by William Strickland, Bishop of Carlisle.
Pevensey	East Sussex	Norman castle built within the site of old Roman fort, founded C11 by Robert of Mortain, donjon added c1100 by William of Mortain, strengthened early C13, now owned by English Heritage.
Peveril	Derbyshire	Norman castle founded by William Peverel, also known as Peak Castle, improved by Henry II, tower keep erected 1176, now owned by English Heritage.
Pickering	North Yorkshire	Norman Motte & Bailey castle founded c1100, shell keep built c1218–36, improved early C14.
Picton	Dyfed	Norman Motte & Bailey castle founded c1090 by William de Picton, enclosure castle built on nearby site mid-C13.
Pleshey	Essex	Norman Motte & Bailey castle founded early C12, destroyed 1157, refortified 1167–80, donjon on motte.
Pontefract	West Yorkshire	Norman Motte & Bailey castle founded 1069 by Ilbert de Lacy, improved by Thomas, Earl of Lancaster, and John of Gaunt C14, destroyed 1649.
Portchester	Hampshire	Norman castle founded by Henry I c1120 in corner of old Roman fort, keep raised by Henry II, palace constructed for Richard II 1396–9, now owned by English Heritage.
Powis	Powys	Castle founded C13 by Gruffydd, Baron de la Pole, destroyed in 1270s by Llywelyn the Last and rebuilt, modified by the Herberts after purchase in 1587, now owned by the National Trust.
Raglan	Gwent	Norman Motte & Bailey castle founded c1070 by the Bloet family, major reconstruction C15, hexagonal Yellow Tower of Gwent constructed by Sir William ap Thomas, other works 1450–69 by Sir William Herbert, slighted 1646, now owned by Welsh Historic Monuments.
Ravenscraig	Fife	Coastal artillery fortress founded 1460 by James II, erected 1460–3.
Restormel	Cornwall	Norman castle founded C11 by Baldwin FitzUrstin, C12 shell keep built by Robert of Cardinham, now owned by English Heritage.
Rhuddlan	Clwyd	Norman Motte & Bailey castle founded c1070, Edwardian concentric castle erected nearby by Master James of St George 1282, slighted 1648.
Richards Castle	Hereford & Worcester	Norman Motte & Bailey castle founded by Richard Fitzscrub pre-Conquest, stone tower built on motte c1175.
Richborough	Kent	Roman fort situated near Sandwich and thought to be the landing point of the Roman invasion armies in AD 43.
Richmond	North Yorkshire	Norman enclosure castle founded by Count of Penhievre 1071, late C11 stone hall (Scolland's Hall) built by Alan the Red, great tower added by Conan, Duke of Brittany, c1150–70, now owned by English Heritage.
Ripley	Harrogate, North Yorks	C19 castle owned by Sir Thomas Ingilby, a baronet, who inherited the stately home on his 18th birthday.
Rochester	Kent	Norman Motte & Bailey castle founded c1080 and built by Bishop Gundulf, stone curtain added c1088, stone keep built c1126–40 by William de Corbeuil, besieged and taken by John 1215, recaptured by Louis of France 1216, keep repaired c1225 with cylindrical corner added, besieged by de Montfort 1264, captured by Wat Tyler 1381, now owned by English Heritage.
Rockingham	Northants	Norman Motte & Bailey castle founded by William I, improved by Henry II, gatehouse built by Edward I c1280, damaged in Civil War, alterations by Salvin C19.

Name	Location	General Information
Rothesay	Isle of Bute, Strathclyde	Motte & Bailey castle founded C12, shell keep erected C13.
Roxburgh	Borders	Motte & Bailey castle founded early C12, captured 1314 by Scots and demolished, rebuilt by Edward III 1335–7, extended by Richard II, taken by Scots 1460 with loss of James II and destroyed.
Ruthin	Clwyd	Edwardian castle founded 1277, held by Prince Dafydd to 1282 when taken by Reginald de Grey, slighted 1647, converted into a hotel C19.
Saffron Walden	Essex	Norman Motte & Bailey castle founded C11 by Geoffrey de Mandeville, flint tower added C12.
St Andrews	Fife	Castle founded late C12, slighted by Andrew Moray 1337, rebuilt late C14, extended early C16, besieged and damaged 1546–7, John Knox amongst besieged.
St Briavels	Gloucestershire	Norman enclosure castle founded C12 by Milo Fitzwalter, tower added mid-C12, gatehouse built by Edward I c1292–3, keep collapsed 1752.
St Donats	South Glamorgan	Double enclosure castle founded by the Stradlings c1300.
St Mawes	Cornwall	Henrician artillery fort built 1540 to protect Falmouth, now owned by English Heritage.
Saltwood	Kent	Norman enclosure castle founded by Henry of Essex c1150–60, improved by Archbishop Courtenay of Canterbury 1380s, designed by Henry Yevele, rendered uninhabitable by an earthquake 1580, formerly owned by Alan Clark MP.
Sandal	West Yorkshire	Norman Motte & Bailey castle founded c1157, converted to stone c1200–80, besieged 1645 and slighted 1646.
Sauvey	Leicestershire	Motte & Bailey castle founded by King John early C13, disused from 1260s.
Scarborough	North Yorkshire	Norman castle founded c1136 by William of Aumale, keep built by Henry II, barbican added c1240, Piers Gaveston besieged 1312, now owned by English Heritage.
Scotney	Kent	Moated castle founded late C14 by Roger Ashburnham, only cylindrical turret remaining, now owned by National Trust.
Sherborne	Dorset	Norman enclosure castle founded by Roger, Bishop of Salisbury, c1107–35, I-shaped donjon added mid-C12, besieged and ruined 1645, now owned by English Heritage.
Shrewsbury	Shropshire	Norman Motte & Bailey castle founded by Roger de Montgomery c1067–9, converted to stone by Henry II, tower on motte collapsed c1270, altered by Thomas Telford C18 for Sir William Pulteney.
Skenfrith	Gwent	Norman Motte & Bailey castle founded late C11, cylindrical donjon and stone curtain walls built c1220–40 by Hubert de Burgh.
Skipsea	East Yorkshire	Norman Motte & Bailey castle founded c1086, motte separated from bailey by a marsh, destroyed by Henry III.
Skipton	North Yorkshire	Norman D-shaped enclosure castle founded c1080, extended with six round towers added by Robert Clifford c1310–14, besieged and severely damaged 1645, renovated by Lady Anne Clifford C17.
Southampton	Hampshire	Norman Motte & Bailey castle founded early C12, refortified C14 by Richard II with tower built by Henry Yevele.
South Mimms	Hertfordshire	Norman Motte & Bailey castle founded c1140–2 by Geoffrey de Mandeville, motte built around base of tower.
Stafford	Staffordshire	Norman Motte & Bailey castle founded c1070, destroyed by 1086, restored late C11, tower built on motte 1348 by Ralph, 1st Earl of Stafford, decayed C16.
Stamford	Lincolnshire	Norman Motte & Bailey castle founded late C11, shell enclosure built on motte C12, extended late C12.
Stirling	Stirling	Timber castle founded C12, taken 1296, 1297, 1298, 1299, 1304, 1314 (whence dismantled), rebuilt under the Stewarts C15.
Stogursey	Somerset	Norman enclosure castle founded late C11, improved by de Courcys C12, demolished c1216.
Stokesay	Shropshire	Fortified manor house crenellated by Lawrence de Ludlow 1291.
Sulgrave	Northants	Norman triangular enclosure castle founded late C11, stone tower added early C12.
Sutton Valence	Kent	Castle founded mid-C12 with great tower, altered by William de Valence C13.
Swansea	West Glamorgan	Norman Motte & Bailey castle founded by Henry Beaumont, burned 1115/6, C12 enclosure castle constructed nearby, rebuilt early C14, damaged by Glyndwr.
Sween	Strathclyde	Castle founded by McSwine family early C12, earliest stone castle in Scotland. Remodelled by Earls of Menteith C13 and extended by Lords of the Isles C14.
Tamworth	Staffordshire	Norman castle with shell enclosure founded early C12 by the Marmions.

BRITAIN

Name	Location	General Information
Tantallon	Lothian	Founded by the 1st Earl of Douglas c1360, besieged by Stewarts 1492 and 1526, damaged by General Monck 1651.
Tattershall	Lincolnshire	Castle with Great Tower built in brick by Ralph, Lord Cromwell 1433–43, rescued by Lord Curzon 1911, now owned by National Trust.
Taunton	Somerset	Norman enclosure castle founded c1110 by William Gifford, tower and other buildings raised by Henry de Blois mid-C12, improved 1207.
Tenby	Dyfed	Norman castle founded after 1153, sacked by Welsh 1187 and 1260.
Thetford	Norfolk	Norman Motte & Bailey castle founded C11, destroyed by Henry II 1174.
Thornbury	Avon	Last military castle built in England c1511 by Edward Stafford, Duke of Buckingham, never completed.
Threave	Dumfries and Galloway	Founded by Archibald, 3rd Earl of Douglas, c1370, extended c1454, taken by James II 1455.
Tickhill	South Yorkshire	Norman Motte & Bailey castle founded late C11 by Robert de Belleme, 11-sided tower built on motte c1178–80 by Henry II.
Tintagel	Cornwall	Norman castle built c1145 by Reginald, Earl of Cornwall, modified by Richard, Earl of Cornwall, C13, now owned by English Heritage.
Tonbridge	Kent	Norman Motte & Bailey castle founded 1080s by Richard Fitzgilbert, shell enclosure added C12, gatehouse built by Gilbert de Clare C13.
Totnes	Devon	Norman Motte & Bailey castle founded C11 by the Nonants, shell keep added C13.
Tower of London	London	Norman enclosure castle founded by William I 1067, White Tower built by Gundulf of Rochester 1078–c1100, concentric fortifications added C13 by Henry III & Edward I.
Trematon	Cornwall	Norman Motte & Bailey castle founded C11, shell keep added C12.
Tretower	Powys	Norman Motte & Bailey castle founded by Sir Miles Picard c1100, shell keep added by Simon Picard mid-C12, cylindrical donjon added by Roger Picard c1220.
Turnberry	Strathclyde	Cylindrical Tower castle of C13, childhood home of Robert Bruce.
Tutbury	Staffordshire	Norman Motte & Bailey castle founded by Henry de Ferrers, improved by John of Gaunt from 1350, added to C15, slighted 1646.
Tynemouth	Tyne and Wear	Enclosure castle crenellated by Robert de Mowbray 1296, gatehouse added 1390s.
Urquhart	Highland	Motte & Bailey castle founded c1150, taken by Edward I, in 1313 passed to Randolph, Earl of Moray, extended C14.
Usk	Gwent	Norman earthwork castle founded by de Clares c1138, rebuilt C14, slighted in Civil War.
Wakefield	West Yorkshire	Motte & 2 Bailey castle erected c1140–50, possibly by William de Warenne.
Wallingford	Oxfordshire	Norman Motte & Bailey castle erected c1071, stonework added C12, demolished 1652.
Wardour	Wiltshire	Old Wardour castle – hexagonal construction founded by John, 5th Lord Lovell, 1393, damaged after siege 1644. New Wardour 'Castle' built 1769–76.
Wareham	Dorset	Norman castle with keep founded by Henry I, destroyed in Civil War.
Wark	Northumberland	Norman Motte & Bailey castle dismantled by David I of Scotland 1138, rebuilt by Henry II 1158, decayed C14.
Warkworth	Northumberland	Norman Motte & Bailey castle founded by Henry, Earl of Northumberland, c1140, taken by William the Lion 1173, rebuilt by Clavering family C13, multiangular tower added by Henry Percy mid-C14, owned by Percys 1332–1922, now owned by English Heritage.
Warwick	Warwickshire	Norman Motte & Bailey castle founded by William I 1068, shell keep added C12, rebuilt C14 by Thomas Beauchamp, unfinished additions by Richard III C15, repaired by Fulke Greville C17.
West Malling	Kent	Stone tower built c1100 by Bishop Gundulf of Rochester, now ruined.
White Castle	Gwent	Norman castle founded by Pain Fitzjohn, stone fortifications built c1184–6 by William de Braose, refortified by Edward I 1260s.
Whittington	Shropshire	Norman Motte & Bailey castle, improved by Fulke de Warenne from 1219 with tower built on motte.
Wigmore	Hereford & Worcester	Norman Motte & Bailey castle founded c1067 by William FitzOsbern, shell keep built C12, reconstructed C14.
Winchester	Hampshire	Norman Motte & Bailey castle founded 1067 by William I, Domesday Book originally housed in castle, site destroyed 1141,

Name	Location	General Information
		rebuilt shortly after, donjon added by Henry II, cylindrical tower on motte and Great Hall added by Henry III, only the Great Hall presently remains.
Windsor	Berkshire	Norman Motte & 2 Bailey castle founded 1067 by William I, shell keep added by Henry I, site rebuilt in stone and keep improved by Henry II, major rebuilding by Edward III c1350–77 with keep raised, alterations by Wyatville for George IV C19, damaged by fire 1992.
Wolvesey	Hampshire	Ecclesiastical castle-palace founded c1100, rebuilt in quadrangular form with great tower by Henry of Blois c1135–70.
Worcester	Hereford & Worcester	Norman Motte & Bailey castle founded c1069, burned down 1113, rebuilt C12, motte levelled 1830.
Wressle	East Yorkshire	Quadrangular enclosure castle founded c1380 by Sir Thomas Percy, damaged in Civil War.
Yester	Lothian	Motte & Bailey castle founded C12, C13 tower erected on motte, extended C15.
York	North Yorkshire	Norman Motte & Bailey castle on Baile Hill founded by William I 1068–9, destroyed 1069 and rebuilt, now lost.

Castles: General Information

Adulterine Castles	Unlicensed private castles built by barons primarily during the Anarchy (1135–54) of King Stephen's reign
Berkeley Castle	Edward II murdered in south tower
Bolingbroke Castle	Henry IV born Apr 1366
Caernarfon Castle	Edward II born 25 Apr 1284
Cardiff Castle	Built on the site of a Roman fort. Robert Curthose imprisoned for 28 years
Carisbrooke Castle	Prison of Charles I 1647–8
Carlisle Castle	Prison of Mary Queen of Scots when she first entered England
Castle: Terms	
allure	Wall-walk along the top of the battlements: the basic fighting platform for archers and crossbowmen
bailey	A courtyard in a castle
barbican	An outer fortification in front of the gate of a castle
bartizan	Turret projecting from a tower or wall
bastion	Tower projecting from a wall length or junction of two walls, designed to cover dead ground
battlement	Parapet or wall with indentures or embrasures, originally for shooting through
berm	Space between curtain wall and moat
buttery	One of the 2 service rooms (the other is the kitchen), used for dispensing drinks
caponier	A covered gallery running across a ditch, housing guns to fire along the ditch
casemate	Armoured compartment in which guns are mounted
concentric	Possessing more than one curtain wall
counterscarp	Outer side of the moat
crenel	Openings formed in top of a wall or parapet between the merlons, having slanting sides as in a battlement
curtain wall	Wall around the perimeter of a castle or one of its courtyards
drawbridge	Bridge that may be raised to prevent access
embrasure	The opening in a wall behind a window or an arrow loop
forebuilding	Structure protecting the entrance to a tower
garderobe	Latrine
gatehouse	Guarded building above or beside an entrance gate
great tower	Most important tower also called the donjon and, since the 16th century, the keep
hourd	(also hoarding) Timber gallery carried on beams outside the battlements. Stones could be dropped on attackers via holes in the floor
keep	see great tower
loop	Slit in wall for firing arrows
machicolation	Permanent stone version of a hourd
mangonel	Stone-throwing siege machine
merlon	Length of protective parapet between the openings of a battlement
mews	Building or yard where the hawks are kept
moat	Wide, often water-filled ditch surrounding a castle preventing land access
motte	Large, usually round flat-topped mound which supported a tower
murder hole	Opening over an entrance passage
oubliette	Dungeon or pit under the floor, usually below ground level, reached by a trap-door
palisade	Strong wooden fence
portcullis	Iron or wooden grating hanging vertically in gateway of castle, set in grooves and able to be raised and lowered
postern	Subsidiary gate in the outer wall

BRITAIN

rampart	Surrounding embankment of a castle
revetment	Facing of stones or sandbags to protect a wall or embankment
scarp	Side of a moat surrounding a castle cut nearest to and immediately below a rampart
trebuchet	Stone-throwing siege engine powered by counterpoise weights; successor to the mangonel, and far more powerful
turret	Small tower that projects from the wall of a castle
ward	Courtyard in a castle
Dover Castle	Known as the 'Key of England'
First Castles	Imported by the Normans after 1066, although four possible sites c1050 built by Norman friends of Edward the Confessor
Flint Castle	Richard II formally surrendered his crown to Henry Bolingbroke
Fotheringhay Castle	Richard III born 2 Oct 1452; Mary Queen of Scots executed 8 Feb 1587
Framlingham Castle	Mary Tudor proclaimed Queen while staying there
Henry VIII's reign: built	Calshot, Camber, Deal, Hurst, Pendennis, St Mawes, Sandgate, Southsea, Walmer
Keep: largest	Colchester castle
Largest Castle : England	Windsor
Scotland	Doune
Wales	Caerphilly
Leaning Keep	Bridgnorth, Shropshire
Lewes Castle	Two mottes
Ludlow Castle	King Edward IV made Royal property when he ascended the throne
Marlborough Castle	John Lackland was married in the castle chapel and Henry III was married in the chapel
Newark Castle	King John died of dysentery 19 Oct 1216
Oldest inhabited, UK	Berkeley, Gloucestershire
Pembroke Castle	Birthplace of Henry VII
Pontefract Castle	Richard II died c14 Feb 1400
Powys Castle	Clive of India Museum
Roman forts: built in	Pevensey and Portchester Castles built within old Roman forts
Sherborne Castle	Once owned by Sir Walter Raleigh
Stone-built: first	Chepstow, Gwent
Stone keep: first	Tower of London (White Tower) 1078; Colchester built c1087
Thornbury Castle	Last built for military purposes
Tintagel Castle	Linked with Arthurian legend
Towers of similar design :	Colchester and White Tower, London
	Castle Rising, Norwich and Falaise (Normandy)
	Castle Hedingham and Rochester
	Dover and Newcastle
Walmer Castle	Lord Warden of the Cinque Ports resides there; it houses a Madame Tussaud's Waxworks
Windsor Castle	Queen Mary's dolls' house, St George's Chapel, Royal Mausoleum Frogmore. Oldest royal residence still in regular use. Edward III born 13 Nov 1312. George III, George IV, William IV all died there

British Cathedrals

Name	Location	General Information
Aberdeen	Grampian	Dedicated to St Andrew. Seat of Episcopal diocese of Aberdeen and Orkney.
Aberdeen	Grampian	Dedicated to St Machar. Presbyterian cathedral founded 1424.
Aberdeen	Grampian	Dedicated to St Mary. RC Gothic revival Victorian cathedral.
Arundel	West Sussex	Dedicated to Our Lady and St Philip Howard. RC since 1965 for see of Arundel and Brighton, designed by J.A. Hansom.
Ayr	Ayrshire	RC cathedral, seat of Bishop of Galloway.
Bangor	Gwynedd	Founded by and dedicated to St Deiniol and extensively restored in 1866.
Beverley Minster	Humberside	Destroyed by Danes, refounded by King Athelstan c935.
Birmingham	West Midlands	Dedicated to St Philip. Built by Thomas Archer 1715, became a cathedral 1905.
Birmingham	West Midlands	Dedicated to St Chad. RC cathedral from 1850, designed by Augustus Pugin 1841.
Blackburn	Lancashire	Dedicated to St Mary, became Anglican cathedral 1927.
Bradford	West Yorkshire	Dedicated to St Peter, designed by Sir Edward Maufe, became Anglican cathedral 1914.
Brecon	Powys	Benedictine priory of St John the Evangelist became cathedral 1923 for the see of Swansea and Brecon.
Brentwood	Essex	Dedicated to St Mary and St Helen, RC cathedral from 1917.
Bristol	Avon	Dedicated to the Holy Trinity, Anglican cathedral founded 1142 but rebuilt by G.E. Street.
Bristol	Avon	Dedicated to SS. Peter and Paul, RC cathedral, seat of Bishop of Clifton since 1850.

Name	Location	General Information
Bury St Edmunds	Suffolk	Dedicated to St James, Anglican cathedral designed by John Wastell / Gilbert Scott 1914, seat of Bishop of St Edmonsbury and Ipswich.
Canterbury	Kent	Dedicated to Christ, rebuilt 1174 by William of Sens.
Cardiff	Glamorgan	Dedicated to St David, RC cathedral from 1920, replacing Belmont, designed by Edward Pugin.
Carlisle	Cumbria	Dedicated to the Holy Trinity, original site of Church of the Augustinian priory, founded 1093.
Chelmsford	Essex	Dedicated to SS. Mary, Peter and Cedd, refurbished by Charles Nicholson 1913, became cathedral 1914.
Chester	Cheshire	Dedicated to Christ and Blessed Virgin Mary, Henry VIII gave cathedral status in 1541.
Chichester	West Sussex	Dedicated to the Holy Trinity, founded by Bishop Ralph de Luffa 1108.
Coventry	West Midlands	Dedicated to St Michael, designed by Basil Spence, dedicated 1962.
Derby	Derbyshire	Dedicated to All Saints, became Anglican cathedral 1927, designed by James Gibbs.
Dundee	Central	Dedicated to St Paul. Seat of Episcopal Bishop of Brechin.
Dundee	Central	RC cathedral, seat of Bishop of Dunkeld.
Durham	Durham	Dedicated to Christ and Blessed Mary the Virgin c1093.
Edinburgh	Lothian	Dedicated to St Giles. High Kirk & National Church of Scotland.
Edinburgh	Lothian	Dedicated to St Mary. Episcopal cathedral.
Edinburgh	Lothian	RC cathedral, seat of Bishop of St Andrews and Edinburgh.
Elgin	Moray	Founded in 1224, rebuilt in form of Jerusalem cross, now ruined.
Ely	Cambridgeshire	Dedicated to the Holy Trinity, founded by Simeon, Abbot of Ely, became cathedral 1109.
Exeter	Devon	Dedicated to St Peter, consecrated 1133 and rebuilt c1275.
Glasgow	Strathclyde	Dedicated to St Mary. Seat of Episcopal Bishop of Glasgow and Galloway.
Glasgow	Strathclyde	Dedicated to St Mungo (St Kentigern). Built in C12.
Gloucester	Gloucestershire	Dedicated to St Peter and Holy Trinity, founded 681, became cathedral 1541.
Guildford	Surrey	Dedicated to the Holy Spirit, Anglican cathedral designed by Sir Edward Maufe, completed 1968.
Hereford	Hereford and Worcester	Dedicated to the Blessed Virgin Mary and St Ethelbert, founded 676 by Bishop Putta, restored 1908.
Inverness	Highland	Dedicated to St Andrew. Seat of Episcopal Bishop of Moray, Ross and Caithness. Part of the worldwide Anglican Communion.
Kirkwall	Orkney	Dedicated to St Magnus. Founded in 1137 by St Rognvald, a Viking ruler, in honour of his martyred uncle.
Lancaster	Lancashire	Dedicated to St Peter, built 1859, became RC cathedral 1924.
Leeds	West Yorkshire	Dedicated to St Anne, RC cathedral from 1878.
Leicester	Leicestershire	Dedicated to St Martin, redesigned by Sir Charles Nicholson 1927.
Lichfield	Staffordshire	Dedicated to the Blessed Virgin Mary and St Chad. Built in C13/14.
Lincoln	Lincolnshire	Dedicated to the Blessed Virgin Mary. Norman cathedral built by Geoffrey de Noiers.
Liverpool	Merseyside	Dedicated to Christ. Neo-Gothic Anglican cathedral founded 1904 but completed 1978.
Liverpool	Merseyside	Dedicated to Christ the King. Roman Catholic Metropolitan cathedral completed 1967. Nicknamed 'Paddy's Wigwam'. Original design by Lutyens rejected on grounds of cost.
Llandaff	Cardiff	Dedicated to St Peter and St Paul. Founded by St Teilo, rebuilt by Bishop Urban C12.
London	London	Dedicated to St Paul. Designed by Sir Christopher Wren, built 1675–1710.
Manchester	Greater Manchester	Dedicated to St Mary, St Denys and St George. Cathedral founded 1847.
Middlesbrough	Cleveland	Dedicated to St Mary. RC cathedral completed 1986.
Millport	Great Cumbrae Island, Ayrshire	Collegiate Church of the Holy Spirit. Anglican church known as the Cathedral of the Isles.
Motherwell	Strathclyde	Roman Catholic cathedral designed by Edward Pugin.
Newcastle	Tyne & Wear	Dedicated to St Nicholas. C14 cathedral rebuilt by R.J. Johnson.
Newcastle	Tyne & Wear	Dedicated to St Mary. RC cathedral from 1850, seat of Bishop of Hexham and Newcastle.
Newport	Newport	Dedicated to St Woolos. Seat of Bishop of Monmouth.
Northampton	Northamptonshire	Dedicated to Our Lady and St Thomas. RC cathedral completed in 1864.
Norwich	Norfolk	Dedicated to the Holy Trinity. Norman cathedral founded by William I in 1068.

BRITAIN

\Name	Location	General Information
Norwich	Norfolk	Dedicated to St John the Baptist. RC cathedral from 1976, seat of Bishop of East Anglia.
Nottingham	Nottinghamshire	Dedicated to St Barnabas. RC cathedral from 1850, designed by Augustus Pugin 1842.
Oban	Strathclyde	Dedicated to St John. Seat of Episcopal Bishop of Argyll and the Isles.
Oban	Strathclyde	Roman Catholic cathedral, seat of Bishop of Argyll and the Isles.
Oxford	Oxfordshire	Dedicated to St Frideswide. Smallest cathedral in England, also known as Christ Church.
Paisley	Glasgow	Roman Catholic cathedral built in the 1930s.
Perth	Perthshire	Dedicated to St Ninian. Seat of Episcopal Bishop of St Andrews, Dunkeld & Dunblane. Built between 1850 and 1890.
Peterborough	Cambs	Dedicated to St Peter, St Paul and St Andrew. Consecrated 1238 and became cathedral 1541.
Plymouth	Devon	Dedicated to St Mary and St Boniface. RC cathedral completed 1858.
Portsmouth	Hampshire	Dedicated to St Thomas of Canterbury. Founded in C12, became a cathedral in 1927.
Portsmouth	Hampshire	Dedicated to St John the Evangelist. RC cathedral from 1882.
Ripon	North Yorkshire	Dedicated to St Peter and St Wilfred. Built in the C15.
Rochester	Kent	Dedicated to Christ and the Blessed Virgin Mary. Medieval church renovated by Bishop Gundulf 1125–30.
Salford	Greater Manchester	Dedicated to St John the Evangelist. RC cathedral from 1850, designed by Matthew Hadfield.
Salisbury	Wiltshire	Dedicated to the Blessed Virgin Mary. Founded 1220 by Richard Poore replacing prior foundation at Old Sarum.
Sheffield	South Yorkshire	Dedicated to St Peter and St Paul. Built by Charles Nicholson.
Sheffield	South Yorkshire	Dedicated to Saint Marie. RC cathedral from 1980, designed by Matthew Hadfield. Seat of the Bishop of Hallam.
Shrewsbury	Shropshire	Dedicated to Our Lady Help of Christians and St Peter of Alcontara. RC cathedral built by Edward Pugin, completed 1856.
Southwark	London	Dedicated to St Saviour and St Mary Overie. Sir Arthur Blomfield rebuilt 1890s.
Southwark	London	Dedicated to St George. RC cathedral from 1850, rebuilt 1858.
Southwell	Nottinghamshire	Dedicated to the Blessed Virgin Mary.
St Albans	Hertfordshire	Dedicated to St Alban. Built in 1077 and designated a cathedral in 1877.
St Andrews	Fife	Medieval cathedral completed in 1144, now ruined.
St Asaph	Clwyd	Dedicated to St Asaph. Restored C19 by Gilbert Scott.
St Davids	Dyfed	Dedicated to St David & St Andrew. Norman cathedral restored in C19.
Swansea	Swansea	Dedicated to St Joseph. RC cathedral 1875, seat of Bishop of Menevia.
Truro	Cornwall	Dedicated to St Mary. Designed by J.L. Pearson 1879–1910.
Wakefield	West Yorkshire	Dedicated to All Saints. Designed by J.L. Pearson.
Wells	Somerset	Dedicated to St Andrew. Built C12 by Reginald de Bohun.
Westminster	London	Dedicated to the Most Precious Blood. RC cathedral designed by James Bentley 1895.
Winchester	Hampshire	Dedicated to Holy Trinity, St Peter, St Paul and St Swithin. Restored by Bishop Walkelin c1090.
Worcester	Hereford and Worcester	Dedicated to Christ and Blessed Virgin Mary. Wulfstan restored Worcester cathedral 1084, improved C19.
Wrexham	Clwyd	Dedicated to Our Lady of Sorrows. RC cathedral built by Edward Pugin.
York Minster	North Yorkshire	Dedicated to St Peter. Thomas of Bayeux built St Peter's church c1070; restored C13.

NB: Although St Giles is known as Edinburgh Cathedral it does not have a cathedra so is technically a church. However, it is included in the listing because it has the same standing in Scotland as Westminster Abbey in England.

British Cathedrals: General Information

Arundel Screen Part of Chichester cathedral.

Bell Harry Tower Tower of Canterbury cathedral erected 1490.

Bell-tower: detached Chichester.

Birmingham Cathedral Edward Burne-Jones designed four windows in 1880 and William Morris made them.

Bishop's eye window Lincoln cathedral.

Black stone fonts Lincoln and Winchester both have black stone fonts from Belgium.

Canterbury Cathedral Tombs for Henry IV and Edward the Black Prince and Trinity Chapel Shrine of Thomas Becket. William of Sens fell from scaffolding and work completed by William the Englishman. T.S. Eliot's play *Murder in the Cathedral* first performed in the Chapter House in 1935. Destroyed by fire in 1174, rebuilt by William of Sens with stone from Caen. Based on the Monastic Church of St Etienne in Caen where Lanfranc had been Abbot.

Carlisle Cathedral Sir Walter Scott was married there.

Cathedral: definition Church that contains a cathedra, or throne of the bishop of the diocese.

Cathedral: longest Winchester 556 ft.

Cathedral: widest in England Manchester at 114 ft.

Cathedrals: shape Cruciform, traditionally.

Chichester Cathedral Houses tomb for Bishop Robert Sherburne, who died in 1536. Houses monument for Walter Huskisson, Chichester MP (dressed as Roman).

Chichester: windows Designed by Marc Chagall.

Christ Church Gateway Canterbury cathedral.

Clock with no face Salisbury cathedral.

Coventry Cathedral Tapestry of the Risen Christ by Graham Sutherland 1952. Statue of Christ being doomed (behold the man) by Jacob Epstein. Windows by John Piper. Benjamin Britten's *War Requiem* first performed.

Coventry Cathedral: Old Destroyed by bombing 1940.

Durham Cathedral Completed by Ranulf Flambard and houses tomb of St Cuthbert.

Gloucester Cathedral Contains tomb of Edward II, murdered in Berkeley castle; also tomb of Robert Curthose, Duke of Normandy.

Great Paul 17-ton bell in St Paul's.

Hedda Stone: Sculpture Peterborough Cathedral.

Hereford Cathedral Map of the World (Mappa Mundi) by Richard of Haldingham and Lafford C13, based on C5 work of Orosius. Africa is labelled as Europe, and vice versa. Jerusalem is centre of the world. Largest chained library (1,450 books) includes *Anglo-Saxon Chronicle*. Restored by Lewis Cottingham and Sir George Gilbert Scott. Houses shrine of St Thomas Cantilupe. Highpoint of Hereford is a tower, not a spire.

Highest Spire Salisbury cathedral 404 ft; 2nd highest spire is Norwich at 315 ft.

Inverted Arches Wells cathedral.

Largest Gothic Church York Minster, in England.

Lichfield Cathedral Houses the *Sleeping Children* statue. Three spires named The Ladies of the Vale. Name means Field of the Dead (Emperor Diocletian martyred 1,000 Christians). Previous name – Bishopric called the diocese of 'Lichfield and Coventry' until 1836.

Lincoln Highest spire 524 ft until it was blown down in 1584.

Liverpool Anglican Designed by Sir Giles Gilbert Scott after winning competition.

Llandaff Cathedral Houses *Christ in His Majesty* by Jacob Epstein.

Longest Nave St Albans has England's longest nave at 275½ feet.

Magna Carta: copies Lincoln and Salisbury cathedrals; the other two are in the British Library.

Mostyn Christ Bangor cathedral.

Nelson's Column Hereford cathedral had a Nelson's Column long before the London monument.

New Cathedrals of 1927 Isle of Wight and South Hampshire became Anglican Diocese, creating many new cathedrals.

Norwich Cathedral Edith Cavell buried. It also has the largest cloisters in England.

Old St Paul's The Norman cathedral was 600 ft long; its spire was 490 ft high.

Oldest clock (1380) Salisbury cathedral (no dial).

Peterborough Cathedral Catherine of Aragon buried there 1536 and Mary Queen of Scots 1587 (moved to Westminster Abbey).

Priest and people: face East, traditionally.

Ribbed Vault 1st Durham cathedral.

Ripon Cathedral Crypt by St Wilfred and Reredos by Ninian Comper.

Scott, Sir George Gilbert Restored Westminster Abbey, Ely, Lichfield and Salisbury cathedrals.

Smallest Cathedral St Asaph's, Clwyd.

Southwark Cathedral John Harvard, founder of Harvard University, baptised 1607. Bunyan and Chaucer windows.

St Albans: dedicatee St Alban, Britain's first Christian martyr (executed circa 209).

St Augustine's Chair Canterbury cathedral.

St David's Cathedral Based on the Spanish Santiago de Compostela.

St Giles Cathedral Jenny Geddes flung stool at preacher for reading an Anglican text. John Knox, the religious reformer, was buried there in 1572. White stork's nest was recorded on roof in 1416, the only British brooding occurrence.

St Lucy's Chapel Oxford cathedral.

St Paul's Cathedral Henry Moore's statue *Mother and Child*. Bombed in December 1940. Statue of Queen Anne outside. St Paul's destroyed by fire in 1666. All Souls Chapel is memorial to Kitchener and other casualties of World War I. Whispering Gallery is famous for its acoustics. Frescoes on the inside of the dome by Sir James Thornhill. Houses Wellington's monument by Alfred Stevens and Nelson's statue by John Flaxman.

Three Spires Lichfield, Truro and St Mary's Edinburgh.

Triforium 1st Canterbury cathedral.

Twenty-four-hour clock Wells cathedral.

Wastell's Tower Canterbury cathedral.

Westminster Abbey Not a cathedral as such, as it lacks a Bishop's Throne. Official name is the Collegiate Church of St Peter. George II was last Sovereign to be buried in the Abbey, as Windsor Castle was subsequently used. Tombs include Henry III, Edward I, Edward III, Henry V, Elizabeth I, Mary Queen of Scots and the Unknown Warrior.

Westminster Cathedral Houses Eric Gill's *14 Stations of the Cross*.

BRITAIN

Whispering Gallery St Paul's cathedral.
Winchester Cathedral Canute and other Danish kings are buried here. So are Jane Austen and Izaak Walton. When St Swithin's remains were transferred in 971 it rained for 40 days. Nave was built C14 by William of Wykeham and William of Edington.

Worcester Cathedral Houses the tomb of King John.
Wren's tomb inscription Lector, si monumentum requiris, circumspice – 'Reader, if you seek his monument, look around you.'
York Minster Great East window by John Thornton 1405–8; St Cuthbert's (bishop in 685) window 1440.

UK's Top Ten Visitors' Pay Attractions of 2002

1 London Eye (3,850,000)
2 Tower of London (2,019,210)
3 Eden Project (1,700,000)
4 Natural History Museum (1,696,176)
5 Legoland (1,632,000)
6 Victoria and Albert Museum (1,446,344)
7 Science Museum (1,352,649)
8 Flamingoland (1,322,000)
9 Windermere Lake Cruises (1,241,918)
10 Canterbury Cathedral (1,151,099)

UK's Top Ten Visitors' Free Attractions of 2002

1 Blackpool Pleasure Beach (6,500,000)
2 National Gallery (4,918,985)
3 British Museum (4,800,938)
4 Tate Modern, London (3,551,885)
5 Pleasureland Theme Park, Southport (2,100,000)
6 Clacton Pier (1,750,000)
7 York Minster, York (1,600,000)
8 Pleasure Beach, Great Yarmouth (1,500,000)
9 National Portrait Gallery, London (1,269,819)
10 Poole Pottery, Poole (1,063,499)

UK's Top Ten Mobile Ringtones of 2002

(compiled by the official UK ringtone chart)

1 *Phoenix Nights* Theme
2 Logical Song – Scooter
3 *Mission Impossible* Theme
4 Round Round – Sugababes
5 I Need A Girl – P. Diddy
6 The Tide is High – Atomic Kitten
7 Without Me – Eminem
8 *Italian Job* – Theme
9 *Scooby Doo* – Theme
10 Romeo Dunn – Romeo

UK's Top Ten Places to Live 2002

1 Alnwick, Northumberland
2 Midhurst, West Sussex
3 Fowey, Cornwall
4 Tetbury, Gloucestershire
5 Crail, Fife
6 Presteigne, Welsh Borders
7 Fakenham, Norfolk
8 Richmond, North Yorkshire
9 Framlingham, Suffolk
10 Wimborne, Dorset

UK's Top Ten Cars 2002

(compiled by the Society of Motor Manufacturers and Traders)

1 Ford Focus
2 Vauxhall Corsa
3 Vauxhall Astra
4 Peugeot 206
5 Ford Fiesta
6 Renault Clio
7 VW Golf
8 Ford Mondeo
9 Renault Megane
10 BMW 3 Series

UK's Top Ten Hardback Non-Fiction 2002

1 *What Not to Wear* by Susannah Constantine & Trinny Woodall
2 *Guinness Book of World Records 2003*
3 *Delia's How to Cook: Book Three* by Delia Smith
4 *Keane* by Roy Keane
5 *Sahara* by Michael Palin
6 *Unless I'm Very Much Mistaken* by Murray Walker
7 *Jamie's Kitchen* by Jamie Oliver
8 *How to Be a Gardener: Book One* by Alan Titchmarsh
9 *Berlin: The Downfall, 1945* by Antony Beevor
10 *Delia's Vegetarian Collection* by Delia Smith

UK's Top Ten Paperback Fiction 2002

1 *How to Be Good* by Nick Hornby
2 *Atonement* by Ian McEwan
3 *Dead Famous* by Ben Elton
4 *A Painted House* by John Grisham
5 *One for My Baby* by Tony Parsons
6 *Five Quarters of the Orange* by Joanne Harris
7 *About a Boy* by Nick Hornby
8 *On Green Dolphin Street* by Sebastian Faulks
9 *The Fellowship of the Ring* by JRR Tolkien
10 *Violets Are Blue* by James Patterson

Radio Times List of the Most powerful Persons in Comedy 2002

1 Ricky Gervais – *The Office*
2 Steve Coogan – *Alan Partridge*
3 Graham Norton
4 Lorraine Heggessey – BBC Controller
5 Jane Root – BBC Controller
6 Talkback Productions – Griff Rhys Jones and Mel Smith
7 Paul Whitehouse – *The Fast Show*
8 Sacha Baron Cohen – Ali G
9 Danielle Lux – Channel 4 Head of Entertainment
10 Jonathan Ross

UK's Top Ten Boys' and Girls' Names 2002

Boys
1 Jack
2 Joshua
3 Thomas
4 James
5 Daniel
6 Benjamin
7 William
8 Samuel
9 Joseph
10 Oliver

Girls
1 Chloe
2 Emily
3 Jessica
4 Ellie
5 Sophie
6 Megan
7 Charlotte
8 Lucy
9 Hannah
10 Olivia

British Museum's Top Ten Artefacts Discovered in Britain

1 Vindolanda Tablets (oldest handwritten documents in the UK)
2 Sutton Hoo (burial of Anglo-Saxon king's boat)
3 Hoxne Hoard (jewellery, gold & silver coins, tableware)
4 Snettisham Torcs (gold and silver deposits)
5 Lewis Chessmen (walrus and whale ivory chessmen)
6 Mold Gold Cape (made from one ingot)
7 Mildenhall Treasure (engraved Roman silver tableware)
8 Fishpool Hoard (15th century jewellery, gold & silver coins)
9 Cuerdale Hoard (Viking Age silver hoard)
10 Ringlemere/Rillaton Cups (Cornish gold vessels)

BBC Viewers Top Ten Artefacts in the British Museum

1 Sutton Hoo (6th to 7th century Anglo-Saxon boat)
2 Vindolanda Tablets (1st / 2nd century Northumberland script)
3 Lewis Chessmen (Norway 1150 AD, found in Lewis)
4 Snettisham Torcs (c. 70 BC Norfolk, from Europe's Iron Age)
5 Mildenhall Treasure (4th century, Suffolk, silver tableware)
6 Mold Gold Cape (Bronze Age c. 750 BC)
7 Ringlemere/Rillaton Cups (Bronze Age, 1700–1500 BC)
8 Hoxne Hoard (late Roman, c. 407 AD, Suffolk)
9 Fishpool Hoard (hoard from England and Flanders)
10 Cuerdale Hoard (largest Viking Age silver hoard in W. Europe)

Ten Highest-Paid Directors in the FTSE 100 (2002 fiscal year)

1 Dr Jean-Pierre Garnier (Glaxo SmithKline) £20.27m
2 Sir Christopher Gent (Vodafone) £12.3m
3 Bart Becht (Reckitt Benckiser) £11.2m
4 Lord Browne of Madingley (BP) £7.87m
5 Tom Glocer (Reuters) £6.78m
6 Tony Ball (BSkyB) £6.10m
7 Charles Brady (Amvescap) £4.52m
8 Ben Verwaayen (BT Group) £3.94m
9 Graham Wallace (Cable & Wireless) £3.84m
10 Stanley Fink (Man Group) £3.83m

BRITAIN

Top 100 Greatest Britons of all time, as voted by internet and BBC viewers

1 Winston Churchill
2 Isambard Kingdom Brunel
3 Diana, Princess of Wales
4 Charles Darwin
5 William Shakespeare
6 Isaac Newton
7 Elizabeth I
8 John Lennon
9 Horatio Nelson
10 Oliver Cromwell
11 Ernest Shackleton
12 James Cook
13 Robert Baden Powell
14 Alfred the Great
15 1st Duke of Wellington
16 Margaret Thatcher
17 Michael Crawford
18 Queen Victoria
19 Paul McCartney
20 Alexander Fleming
21 Alan Turing
22 Michael Faraday
23 Owain Glyndwr
24 Elizabeth II
25 Stephen Hawking
26 William Tyndale
27 Emmeline Pankhurst
28 William Wilberforce
29 David Bowie
30 Guy Fawkes
31 Leonard Cheshire
32 Eric Morecambe
33 David Beckham
34 Thomas Paine
35 Boudicca
36 Steve Redgrave
37 Thomas More
38 William Blake
39 John Harrison
40 Henry VIII
41 Charles Dickens
42 Frank Whittle
43 John Peel
44 John Logie Baird
45 Aneurin Bevan
46 Boy George
47 Douglas Bader
48 William Wallace
49 Francis Drake
50 John Wesley
51 King Arthur (mythical king)
52 Florence Nightingale
53 TE Lawrence
54 Robert Falcon Scott
55 Enoch Powell
56 Cliff Richard
57 Alexander Graham Bell
58 Freddie Mercury
59 Julie Andrews
60 Edward Elgar
61 Queen Elizabeth, the Queen Mother
62 George Harrison
63 David Attenborough
64 James Connolly
65 George Stephenson
66 Charlie Chaplin
67 Tony Blair
68 William Caxton
69 Bobby Moore
70 Jane Austen
71 William Booth
72 Henry V
73 Aleister Crowley (occult leader)
74 Robert the Bruce
75 Bob Geldof
76 The Unknown Soldier
77 Robbie Williams
78 Edward Jenner
79 David Lloyd George
80 Charles Babbage
81 Geoffrey Chaucer
82 Richard III
83 JK Rowling
84 James Watt
85 Richard Branson
86 Bono
87 John Lydon
88 Montgomery of Alamein
89 Donald Campbell
90 Henry II
91 James Clerk Maxwell
92 JRR Tolkien
93 Walter Raleigh
94 Edward I
95 Barnes Wallis
96 Richard Burton (actor)
97 Tony Benn
98 David Livingstone
99 Tim Berners Lee (WWW inventor)
100 Marie Stopes

CALENDAR

Wedding Anniversaries

1	Cotton / Paper	8	Bronze / Pottery	15	Crystal	50	Golden
2	Paper / Cotton	9	Pottery / Willow	20	China	55	Emerald
3	Leather	10	Tin	25	Silver	60	Diamond
4	Fruit / Flowers	11	Steel	30	Pearl	65	Blue Sapphire
5	Wood	12	Silk / Linen	35	Coral	70	Platinum
6	Sugar	13	Lace	40	Ruby	75	Gold or Diamond
7	Wool / Copper	14	Ivory	45	Sapphire		

NB: Wedding anniversaries are an area of frustration for quiz players because there are slight variations to many of the gifts that are traditionally given on wedding anniversaries, and to complicate matters even more, some of the gifts have changed over the years: e.g. diamonds were traditionally given on a 75th wedding anniversary but after Queen Victoria celebrated her 'Diamond' Jubilee in 1897, this became the established gift for a 60th anniversary, and the 75th which was previously Diamond then became Gold, as opposed to 'Golden' for a 50th. A more common cause of frustration is the gift for a first anniversary. Cotton was traditionally given, as the 'binding' of two people who have tied the knot, but as in the case of so many infrequently used customs it has become traditional to think of a first anniversary as a paper one, after the certificate of marriage. Neither is right or wrong, as they have never been observed for any reason other than a convenient question to ask in a quiz. In fairness, it would be better for quiz-setters to avoid the more controversial anniversaries – e.g. 1st, 2nd, 75th – or if insisting on using them, it would be advisable to phrase the question in the form 'If paper is a first anniversary, what is a second?'

Months of the French Revolutionary Calendar

Vendémiaire	(Grape harvest)	23 Sep –22 Oct	Germinal	(Buds)	22 Mar –20 Apr
			Floréal	(Flowers)	21 Apr –20 May
Brumaire	(Mist)	23 Oct –21 Nov	Prairial	(Meadows)	21 May –19 Jun
Frimaire	(Frost)	22 Nov –21 Dec	Messidor	(Harvest)	20 Jun –19 Jul
Nivôse	(Snow)	22 Dec –20 Jan	Thermidor	(Heat)	20 Jul –18 Aug
Pluviôse	(Rain)	21 Jan –19 Feb	Fructidor	(Fruit)	19 Aug –22 Sep
Ventôse	(Wind)	20 Feb –21 Mar			

Months of the Jewish Calendar

Tishri	30 days	Adar*	29 days	Tammuz	29 days
Marheshvan	29 / 30 days	Ve-Adar†	30 days	Av	30 days
Kislev	29 / 30 days	Nisan	30 days	Elul	29 days
Tevet	29 / 30 days	Iyyar	29 days		
Shevat	30 days	Sivan	30 days		

*30 days in a leap year
†13th month every 3rd, 6th, 8th, 11th, 14th, 17th, & 19th year of a 19-year cycle
NB: The Jewish calendar places the creation at 3761 BCE.

Months of the Muslim Calendar

1	Muharram	30 days	5	Jumâda I	30 days	9	Ramadan	30 days
2	Safar	29 days	6	Jumâda II	29 days	10	Shawwal	29 days
3	Rabia I	30 days	7	Rajab	30 days	11	Dhâl-Qa'da	30 days
4	Rabia II	29 days	8	Shaaban	29 days	12	Dhâl-Hijja	29 days*

*30 days in a leap year
NB: The Muslim calendar starts in 622 CE. 1 Muharram of the year I was 16 July 622; it marks the Prophet's move from Mecca to Medina.

Other Calendars

Indian	Vikrama Era	Dates from 23 Feb 57 BC	**Japanese Days**	Nichiyobi	Sun-day
	Saka Era	Dates from 3 Mar AD 78	(months are	Getsuyobi	Moon-day
	Buddhist Era	Dates from 543 BC	numbered)	Kayobi	Fire-day
	Jain Era	Dates from 527 BC		Suiyobi	Water-day
		(death of Vardhamana)		Mokuyobi	Wood-day
	Parsee Era	Dates from 16 Jun AD 632		Kinyobi	Metal-day
				Doyobi	Earth-day
Coptic	Egypt and Ethiopia; dates from 29 Aug AD 284				

Commemorative Days

Advent Sunday	Sunday nearest to 30 Nov
All Saints' Day	1 Nov
All Souls' Day	2 Nov
Andrew's Day, St	30 Nov
Ascensiontide	Ascension day to Whitsun Eve (10 days)
Ash Wednesday	The 1st day of Lent
Assumption	15 Aug
Australia Day	26 Jan
Barnabas's Day, St	11 Jun
Bartholomew's Day, St	24 Aug
Bastille Day	14 Jul
Burns Night	25 Jan
Calends / Kalends	First day of each month in ancient Roman Calendar
Cecilia's Day, St	22 Nov
Commonwealth Day	2nd Monday in March
Corpus Christi	Thursday after Trinity Sunday
Crispin's Day, St	25 Oct
David's Day, St	1 Mar
Easter Sunday	The 1st Sunday after the full moon following the vernal equinox
Epiphany	6 Jan
First day of year pre-1752	25 Mar
Francis of Assisi's Day, St	4 Oct
George Washington Day (USA)	17 Feb
George's Day, St	23 Apr
Giles' Day, St	1 Sept
Good Friday	Day before Easter Saturday
Holy Saturday	Last day of Lent
Immaculate Conception Day	8 Dec
Independence Day (USA)	4 Jul
John the Baptist's Day, St	24 Jun
John the Evangelist's, St	27 Dec
Labor Day (USA)	Equivalent to our May Day, First Monday of September
Lady Day	25 Mar
Lent	The 40 days between Ash Wednesday and Easter Saturday
Low Sunday	excluding Sundays The 1st after Easter
Luke's Day, St	18 Oct
Maggie Thatcher Day	10 Jan on Falkland Islands
Mark's Day, St	25 Apr
Martin Luther King Day (USA)	15 Jan
Martin's Day, St	11 Nov
Matthew's Day, St	21 Sept
Maundy Thursday	Day before Good Friday
May Day	Became public holiday in 1978
Michael's Day, St	29 Sept
Mothering Sunday	4th in Lent and 3rd before Easter
New Year's Day	Became public holiday in 1974
Nicholas' Day, St	6 Dec
Nones (Roman Calendar)	The 9th day before the ides of each month i.e. 7th of March, May, July and October and 5th of other months
Orangeman's Day	Celebrated by Irish protestants on 12 July
Palm Sunday	Sunday before Easter Sunday
Passion Sunday	Sunday before Palm Sunday
Patrick's Day, St	17 Mar
Paul's Day, St	29 Jun
Pentecost (Whit Sunday)	7th Sunday after Easter Sunday
Peter's Day, St	29 Jun
Shrove Tuesday	Day before Ash Wednesday
Stephen's Day, St	26 Dec
Swithin's Day, St	15 Jul
Sylvester's Day, St	31 Dec
Thomas' Day, St	21 Dec
Trafalgar Day	21 Oct
Trinity Sunday	1st Sunday after Whitsun
Twelfth Night	5 Jan
United Nations Day	24 Oct
Valentine's Day, St	14 Feb

English Quarter Days

Lady Day	25 March
Midsummer Day	24 June
Michaelmas	29 September
Christmas Day	25 December

NB: A useful mnemonic for remembering English Quarter Days is that three of the days end with the same number as letters in the month e.g. March has five letters so Lady Day is the 25th, June has four letters so Midsummer Day is 24th, September has nine letters so Michaelmas is 29th. Christmas Day should never be forgotten.

Scottish Quarter Days

Candlemas	28 February
Whitsuntide	28 May
Lammas	28 August
Martinmas	28 November

NB: Although the names of the four Scottish Quarter Days have remained the same, the dates changed in 1991. Candlemas used to be on 2 Feb, Lammas was 1 Aug and Martinmas was on 11 Nov. The date of Whitsuntide varied.

Birthstones

January	Garnet
February	Amethyst
March	Bloodstone or Aquamarine
April	Diamond
May	Emerald
June	Pearl, Agate Moonstone, or Alexandrite
July	Ruby or Cornelian
August	Sardonyx or Peridot
September	Sapphire or Chrysolite
October	Opal or Tourmaline
November	Topaz
December	Turquoise or Zircon

NB: Birthstones are also controversial, as once again some months have more than one stone. Attempts to introduce birthstones for each sign of the Zodiac have fallen largely out of use.

Chinese Years

Snake (serpent)	1989
Horse	1990
Sheep (ram)	1991
Monkey	1992
Chicken (cock)	1993
Dog	1994
Pig	1995
Rat	1996
Ox	1997
Tiger	1998
Rabbit	1999
Dragon	2000

NB: The calendar goes in 12-year cycles, so it continues Snake, 2001; Horse, 2002; and so on.

Watches at Sea

First Watch	8pm–midnight
Middle Watch	midnight–4am
Morning Watch	4am–8am
Forenoon Watch	8am midday
Afternoon Watch	midday–4pm
First Dog Watch	4pm–6pm
Last Dog Watch	6pm–8pm

NB: A bell is rung every half-hour during a watch, which therefore ends on eight bells or four for a dog watch. The New Year is brought in with 16 bells. Incidentally 'Dog' is thought to be a corruption of 'dodge', which was introduced to enable easier rostering.

Zodiac

Aries	21 Mar–19 Apr
Taurus	20 Apr–20 May
Gemini	21 May–21 Jun
Cancer	22 Jun–22 Jul
Leo	23 Jul–22 Aug
Virgo	23 Aug–22 Sep
Libra	23 Sep–23 Oct
Scorpio	24 Oct–21 Nov
Sagittarius	22 Nov–21 Dec
Capricorn	22 Dec–19 Jan
Aquarius	20 Jan–18 Feb
Pisces	19 Feb–20 Mar

CALENDAR

CINEMA (A–Z OF OUTSTANDING FILMS)

A.I. Artificial Intelligence (2001)   Haley Joel Osment (David), Jude Law (Gigolo Joe), William Hurt, Brendan Gleeson, Frances O'Connor. Child robot searches for the mother who abandoned him. *Dir.* Steven Spielberg.

À Nous la Liberté (1931)   Raymond Cordy, Henri Marchand. Factory owner is blackmailed about his past and is helped by an old prison friend. US title: *Freedom for Us. Dir.* René Clair.

Abbott & Costello Go to Mars (1953)   Bud Abbott, Lou Costello, Mari Blanchard, Martha Hyer, Robert Paige. Despite the title, they land first in Louisiana and then on Venus! *Dir.* Charles Lamont.

Abbott & Costello Meet Captain Kidd (1952)   Bud Abbott, Lou Costello, Charles Laughton, Leif Erickson. *Dir.* Charles Lamont.

Abbott & Costello Meet Dr Jekyll & Mr Hyde (1953)   Bud Abbott, Lou Costello, Boris Karloff, Craig Stevens. This film starring Boris Karloff was given an 'X' certificate in its day. *Dir.* Charles Lamont.

Abbott & Costello Meet Frankenstein (1948)   Bud Abbott, Lou Costello, Bela Lugosi, Lon Chaney Jnr. Dracula and the Wolf Man also feature. GB title: *Abbott & Costello Meet the Ghosts. Dir.* Charles Barton.

Abbott & Costello Meet the Killer, Boris Karloff (1948)   Bud Abbott, Lou Costello, Boris Karloff, Gary Moore. Boris Karloff is not the killer and appears very little. *Dir.* Charles Barton.

Abe Lincoln in Illinois (1940)   Raymond Massey (Abraham Lincoln), Ruth Gordon. GB title: *Spirit of the People. Dir.* John Cromwell.

Abominable Dr Phibes, The (1971)   Vincent Price, Joseph Cotten, Terry-Thomas. Dr Phibes, a disfigured musical genius, avenges his wife's death at the hands of surgeons. Sequel: *Dr Phibes Rises Again* (1972), starred Price, Terry-Thomas, Beryl Reid, John Thaw. *Dir.* Robert Fuest.

Abominable Snowman, The (1957)   Peter Cushing, Forrest Tucker, Richard Wattis. US title: *The Abominable Snowman of the Himalayas. Dir.* Val Guest.

About a Boy (2002)   Hugh Grant, Nicholas Hoult, Sharon Small, Madison Cook, Jordan Cook, Toni Collette, Rachel Weisz. Layabout philanderer exploits single mothers but has responsibility, in the form of a 12-year-old boy, thrust upon him. Based on a Nick Hornby novel. *Dir.* Chris and Paul Weitz.

Above and Beyond (1952)   Robert Taylor (Colonel Paul Tibbets, who dropped the first atomic bomb on Japan). *Dir.* Melvin Frank and Norman Panama.

Absence of Malice (1981)   Paul Newman, Sally Field. *Dir.* Sydney Pollack.

Absent-Minded Professor, The (1961)   Fred MacMurray, Tommy Kirk, Keenan Wynn, Ed Wynn. Lighter than air substance called 'Flubber' allows the Professor's Model-T Ford to fly. Sequel *Son of Flubber. Dir.* Robert Stevenson.

Absolute Beginners (1986)   Eddie O'Connell, Patsy Kensit, David Bowie (Vendice Partners), Ray Davies, James Fox, Steven Berkoff, Mandy Rice Davies, Robbie Coltrane, Irene Handl, Eric Sykes, Lionel Blair. Teen life in 1958 London. *Dir.* Julien Temple.

Absolute Power (1997)   Clint Eastwood, Gene Hackman (President Richmond), Ed Harris, EG Marshall, Laura Linney, Judy Davis. *Dir.* Clint Eastwood.

Accident (1967)   Dirk Bogarde, Stanley Baker, Vivien Merchant, Michael York. Screenplay by Harold Pinter. *Dir.* Joseph Losey.

Accidental Hero (1992)   Dustin Hoffman (Bernie Laplante), Geena Davis (Gale Gayley), Andy Garcia (John Bubber). Screenplay by David Webb Peoples, the writer of *Unforgiven* and *Blade Runner. Dir.* Stephen Frears.

Accidental Tourist, The (1988)   William Hurt, Kathleen Turner, Geena Davis. Geena Davis won Academy Award for Best Supporting Actress. *Dir.* Lawrence Kasdan.

Accused, The (1988)   Kelly McGillis (Kathryn Murphy), Jodie Foster (Sarah Tobias), Bernie Coulson. Jodie Foster won Academy Award for Best Actress. *Dir.* Jonathan Kaplan.

Ace in the Hole (1951)   Kirk Douglas (Chuck Tatum), Jan Sterling (Lorraine), Porter Hall (Boot), Ray Teal (Sheriff). In order to boost newspaper sales a journalist delays the rescue of a man trapped in a cave. Aka: *The Big Carnival. Dir.* Billy Wilder.

Ace Ventura, Pet Detective (1994)   Jim Carrey, Courteney Cox, Sean Young, Tone Loc. Ace is hired to recover the Miami Dolphins' dolphin mascot. *Dir.* Tom Shadyac.

Ace Ventura, When Nature Calls (1995)   Jim Carrey, Ian McNeice, Simon Callow, Adewalé. Ace goes to Africa to find a sacred white bat. *Dir.* Steve Oedekerk.

Across the Pacific (1942)   Humphrey Bogart (Rick Leland), Mary Astor (Alberta Marlow), Sydney Greenstreet (Dr Lorenz). Huston was called up mid-film and it was eventually completed by Vincent Sherman. *Dir.* John Huston.

Actress, The (1928)   Norma Shearer, Ralph Forbes. This film was the opening attraction at London's Empire Theatre, Leicester Square. GB title: *Trelawney of the Wells. Dir.* Sidney Franklin.

Adam's Rib (1949)   Spencer Tracy, Katharine Hepburn, Judy Holliday. *Dir.* George Cukor.

Addams Family, The (1991)   Anjelica Huston (Morticia), Raul Julia (Gomez), Christopher Lloyd (Uncle Fester). Impostor arrives at the Addams family home purporting to be a long-lost elder brother. *Dir.* Barry Sonnenfeld.

Addams Family Values (1993)   Anjelica Huston (Morticia), Raul Julia (Gomez), Christopher Lloyd (Uncle Fester). Sequel in which the Addams children try, unsuccessfully, to kill the new baby. *Dir.* Barry Sonnenfeld.

Addicted To Love (1997)   Meg Ryan (Maggie), Matthew Broderick (Sam), Kelly Preston (Linda), Tcheky Karyo (Anton) *Dir.* Griffin Dunne.

Addiction, The (1996)   Christopher Walken, Lili Taylor. *Dir.* Abel Ferrara.

Admirable Crichton, The (1957)   Kenneth More, Cecil Parker, Sally Ann Howes, Diane Cilento, Peter Graves, Gerald Harper. US title: *Paradise Lagoon. Dir.* Lewis Gilbert.

Adolf Hitler – My Part In His Downfall (1972)   Jim Dale (Spike Milligan), Spike Milligan (Milligan's father), Arthur Lowe, Bill Maynard. Notable for appearance of Spike Milligan playing the part of his father. *Dir.* Norman Cohen.

Adventure of Sherlock Holmes' Smarter Brother,

The (1975)   Gene Wilder, Marty Feldman, Madeline Kahn, Thorley Walters. *Dir.* Gene Wilder.

Adventures of Arsène Lupin, The (1956)   Robert Lamoureux, Liselotte Pulver, Otto Hasse. Based on the Jewel Thief character created by Maurice Leblanc. *Dir.* Jacques Becker.

Adventures of Baron Munchausen (1989)   John Neville, Eric Idle, Sarah Polley, Oliver Reed, Uma Thurman. *Dir.* Terry Gilliam.

Adventures of Barry Mackenzie, The (1972)   Barry Crocker, Barry Humphries (Edna Everage), Peter Cook, Spike Milligan, Dennis Price. *Private Eye* comic strip fantasy. (The 1974 sequel was called *Barry Mackenzie Holds His Own*.) *Dir.* Bruce Beresford.

Adventures of Captain Marvel (1941)   Tom Tyler (Billy Batson alias Captain Marvel). Assistant radio operator on scientific trip to Siam is endowed with superpowers by the mysterious 'Shazam' and battles against the evil 'Scorpion'. *Dir.* John English & William Witney.

Adventures of Mark Twain (1944)   Fredric March (Twain), Alexis Smith, Alan Hale. *Dir.* Irving Rapper.

Adventures of Milo and Otis (1986)   Narrated by Dudley Moore, the tale of a puppy in search of his friend, a kitten. This film was the second most popular film ever made in Japan. *Dir.* Masanori Hata.

Adventures of Pinocchio, The (1996)   Martin Landau, Jonathan Taylor Thomas, Geneviève Bujold, Griff Rhys Jones, Dawn French. *Dir.* Steve Barron.

Adventures of Priscilla Queen of the Desert (1994)   Terence Stamp, Hugo Weaving, Bill Hunter, Guy Pearce. Two transvestites and a transsexual drive a bus from Sydney to Alice Springs for a cabaret gig. *Dir.* Stephan Elliott.

Adventures of Robin Hood, The (1938)   Errol Flynn (Robin), Basil Rathbone (Guy of Gisbourne), Claude Rains (Prince John), Olivia de Havilland (Marian), Alan Hale (Little John), Ian Hunter (King Richard), Melville Cooper (Sheriff of Nottingham). Won Academy Awards for Music and Editing. *Dir.* William Keighley and Michael Curtiz.

Adventures of Robinson Crusoe, The (1953)   Dan O'Herlihy (Crusoe), Jaime Fernandez (Friday). *Dir.* Luis Buñuel.

Adventures of Sherlock Holmes, The (1939)   Basil Rathbone, Nigel Bruce, George Zucco (Moriarty), Mary Gordon (Mrs Hudson). GB title: *Sherlock Holmes*. *Dir.* Alfred Werker.

Adventures of Tom Sawyer, The (1938)   Tommy Kelly (Tom), Jackie Moran (Huck), Ann Gillis (Becky Thatcher). *Dir.* Norman Taurog.

Advise and Consent (1962)   Charles Laughton, Henry Fonda, Walter Pidgeon, Don Murray. *Dir.* Otto Preminger.

African Queen, The (1951)   Humphrey Bogart (Charlie Allnutt), Katharine Hepburn (Rose Sayer), Robert Morley. Based on the CS Forester novel. Humphrey Bogart awarded the Best Actor Oscar. *Dir.* John Huston.

Agatha (1979)   Vanessa Redgrave (Agatha Christie), Dustin Hoffman, Timothy Dalton. Tells the story of Agatha Christie's disappearance in 1926. *Dir.* Michael Apted.

Age of Innocence, The (1993)   Daniel Day-Lewis, Michelle Pfeiffer, Winona Ryder, Richard E Grant. Wealthy lawyer falls in love with his wife's cousin. *Dir.* Martin Scorsese.

Agony and the Ecstasy, The (1965)   Charlton Heston (Michelangelo), Rex Harrison (Pope Julius II). Based on the Irving Stone novel. *Dir.* Carol Reed.

Aida (1953)   Sophia Loren, Lois Maxwell. Based on Verdi's opera. *Dir.* Clemente Fracassi.

Airborne (1993)   Shane McDermott, Seth Green, Brittney Powell. Surfer moves to Cincinnati and becomes a rollerblade champion. *Dir.* Rob Bowman.

Airforce One (1997)   Harrison Ford (President James Marshall), Jurgen Prochnow (General Radek), Gary Oldman (Korshunov) *Dir.* Wolfgang Petersen.

Airplane! (1980)   Robert Stack, Lloyd Bridges, Leslie Nielsen, Peter Graves, Kareem Abdul-Jabbar, Julie Hagerty. (The 1982 sequel, *Airplane II*, was directed by Ken Finkleman.) *Dir.* J. Abrahams, David and Jerry Zucker.

Airport (1970)   Burt Lancaster, Dean Martin, Jean Seberg, Helen Hayes (Best Supporting Actress Oscar). Based on the Arthur Hailey novel. *Dir.* George Seaton.

Al Capone (1959)   Rod Steiger (Capone), Fay Spain, Nehemiah Persoff, Martin Balsam. *Dir.* Richard Wilson.

Aladdin (1992)   Voices of Robin Williams (Genie), Linda Larkin (Jasmine), Scott Weinger (Aladdin). 'Whole New World' won Best Song Oscar (music by Alan Menken, lyrics by Tim Rice) *Dir.* John Musker and Ron Clements.

Alamo, The (1960)   John Wayne (Davy Crockett), Richard Widmark (Jim Bowie), Laurence Harvey (Travis), Frankie Avalon (Smitty), Richard Boone (Houston) *Dir.* John Wayne.

Albert RN (1953)   Jack Warner, Anthony Steel, Robert Beatty, Anton Diffring. POWs build a life-like dummy to cover the absence of escapers. US title: *Break to Freedom*. *Dir.* Lewis Gilbert.

Albino Alligator (1997)   Faye Dunaway, Matt Dillon. Villains hold a group of New Yorkers hostage in a bar. *Dir.* Kevin Spacey.

Alexander the Great (1956)   Richard Burton (Alexander), Fredric March, Claire Bloom. *Dir.* Robert Rossen.

Alexander's Ragtime Band (1938)   Tyrone Power, Alice Faye, Don Ameche, Ethel Merman. *Dir.* Henry King.

Alf Garnett Saga, The (1972)   Warren Mitchell, Dandy Nichols. The Una Stubbs and Tony Booth parts were played by Adrienne Posta and Mike Angelis. *Dir.* Bob Kellett.

Alfie (1966)   Michael Caine (Alfie), Vivien Merchant, Shirley Anne Field, Jane Asher, Millicent Martin, Shelley Winters. Theme song sung by Cher. *Dir.* Lewis Gilbert.

Alfie Darling (1975)   Alan Price, Jill Townsend, Joan Collins, Annie Ross, Hannah Gordon, Rula Lenska. Alan Price takes over the Michael Caine role as well as contributing the music. *Dir.* Ken Hughes.

Algiers (1938)   Charles Boyer, Hedy Lamarr, Alan Hale. The famous line 'Come with me to the Casbah' was never actually said in this film. *Dir.* John Cromwell.

Ali (2001)   Will Smith (Ali), Jamie Foxx (Drew 'Bundini' Brown), Jon Voight (Howard Cosell), Mario Van Peebles (Malcolm X), Ron Silver (Angelo Dundee), Mykelti Williamson (Don King), LeVar Burton (Martin Luther King Jr), Albert Hall (Elijah Muhammad), Giancarlo Esposito (Ali's father), Michael Michele (Veronica), Nona Gaye (Belinda). *Dir.* Michael Mann.

Ali G Indahouse (2002)   Sacha Baron Cohen, Michael Gambon, Charles Dance, Kellie Bright (Me Julie), Martin Freeman. Black rapper becomes a national hero after becoming an MP. *Dir.* Mark Mylod.

Alice (1990)   Mia Farrow, Joe Mantegna, Alec Baldwin, William Hurt. *Dir.* Woody Allen.

Alice Doesn't Live Here Any More (1974) Ellen Burstyn, Kris Kristofferson, Jodie Foster, Diane Ladd, Alfred Lutter. Ellen Burstyn won Academy Award for Best Actress. *Dir.* Martin Scorsese.

Alice in Wonderland (1933) Charlotte Henry (Alice), WC Fields (Humpty Dumpty), Cary Grant (Mock Turtle), Gary Cooper (White Knight). Ida Lupino was brought from the UK for the title role but ultimately not used. *Dir.* Norman Z McLeod.

Alice's Adventures in Wonderland (1972) Fiona Fullerton (Alice), Michael Crawford (White Rabbit), Robert Helpmann (Mad Hatter), Dudley Moore (Dormouse), Spike Milligan (Gryphon), Peter Sellers (March Hare), Michael Hordern (Mock Turtle), Ralph Richardson (Caterpillar) *Dir.* William Sterling.

Alice's Restaurant (1969) Arlo Guthrie, Pat Quinn, James Broderick. *Dir.* Arthur Penn.

Alien (1979) Tom Skerritt, Sigourney Weaver, John Hurt, Ian Holm, Harry Dean Stanton. *Dir.* Ridley Scott.

Alien Resurrection (1997) Sigourney Weaver, Winona Ryder, Dominique Pinou, Ron Perlman. *Dir.* Jean-Pierre Jeunet.

Aliens (1986) Sigourney Weaver, Carrie Henn, Michael Biehn, Bill Paxton. Sequel to *Alien* which won Academy Award for Special Visual Effects. *Dir.* James Cameron.

Alien 3 (1992) Sigourney Weaver, Charles S Dutton, Charles Dance, Paul McGann. *Dir.* David Fincher.

All about Eve (1950) Bette Davis (Margo Channing), George Sanders (Addison de Witt; Best Supporting Actor, Anne Baxter (Eve), Marilyn Monroe (Miss Caswell). Won Best Film Oscar. As well as Oscars above, Joseph L Mankiewicz won Academy Awards for Writing & Directing. *Dir.* Joseph L Mankiewicz.

All Creatures Great and Small (1974) Anthony Hopkins, Simon Ward, TP McKenna. Sponsored by *Reader's Digest. Dir.* Claude Whatham.

All of Me (1984) Steve Martin (Roger Cobb), Lily Tomlin (Edwina Cutwater), Victoria Tennant (Terry Hoskins) *Dir.* Carl Reiner.

All or Nothing (2002) Timothy Spall, Lesley Manville, Alison Garland, James Cordon, Ruth Sheen, Marion Bailey. *Dir.* Mike Leigh.

All Quiet on the Western Front (1930) Lew Ayres (Paul Baumer), Louis Wolheim (Katczinsky). Based on novel by Erich Maria Remarque. *Dir.* Lewis Milestone.

All That Jazz (1979) Roy Scheider, Jessica Lange, Ann Reinking, Leland Palmer, Ben Vereen. Semi-autobiographical musical of Fosse's life which won Oscars for Editing, Art Direction, Musical Adaptation & Costume Design. *Dir.* Bob Fosse.

All That Money Can Buy (1941) Walter Huston (Mr Scratch), Edward Arnold (Daniel Webster). Bernard Herrmann won Oscar for his music for this Faustian version of Stephen Vincent Benet's *The Devil and Daniel Webster. Dir.* William Dieterle.

All the Fine Young Cannibals (1960) Robert Wagner, Natalie Wood, Pearl Bailey. A fine young pop group took their name from the title of this film. *Dir.* Michael Anderson.

All the King's Men (1949) Broderick Crawford, Joanne Dru, John Ireland, Mercedes McCambridge (Best Film Oscar). Academy Awards for Broderick Crawford (Best Actor) and Mercedes McCambridge (Best Supporting Actress). *Dir.* Robert Rossen.

All the President's Men (1976) Robert Redford, Dustin Hoffman, Jason Robards Jnr. Reconstruction of the White House link with the Watergate affair by the *Washington Post. Dir.* Alan J Pakula.

Almost an Angel (1990) Paul Hogan (Terry Dean), Elias Koteas (Steve), Linda Kozlowski (Rose Garner) *Dir.* John Cornell.

Alphabet Murders, The (1965) Tony Randall, Robert Morley, Anita Ekberg, Margaret Rutherford (cameo role as Miss Marple). Based on *The ABC Murders* by Agatha Christie. This film is notable for the fact that Tony Randall plays several characters as well as Poirot. *Dir.* Frank Tashlin.

Always (1989) Richard Dreyfuss, Holly Hunter, Audrey Hepburn. Remake of the 1944 film *A Guy Named Joe* about a dead pilot's ghostly return to matchmake his girlfriend. *Dir.* Steven Spielberg.

Amadeus (1984) F Murray Abraham (Salieri), Tom Hulce (Mozart), Elizabeth Berridge (Constance Mozart). Filmed mainly in Prague. The part of Constance was originally Meg Tilly's but she was injured in a soccer match the day before shooting began. *Dir.* Milos Forman.

Amélie (2001) Audrey Tautou (Amélie), Mathieu Kassovitz (Nino Quincampoix), Rufus (Raphael Poulain). A young woman full of joie de vivre has a rejuvenating effect on the people of a French town. French title: *Le Fabuleux Destin d'Amélie Poulain. Dir.* Jean-Pierre Jeunet.

American Beauty (1999) Kevin Spacey (Lester Burnham), Annette Bening, Thora Birch, Wes Bentley. *Dir.* Sam Mendes.

American Gigolo (1980) Richard Gere, Lauren Hutton. Music by Giorgio Moroder. Christopher Reeve allegedly refused $1 million to play the lead. *Dir.* Paul Schrader.

American Graffiti (1973) Richard Dreyfuss, Ron Howard, Candy Clark. Film was set in 1962 California. *Dir.* George Lucas.

American in Paris, An (1951) Gene Kelly, Oscar Levant, Leslie Caron. *Dir.* Vincente Minnelli.

America's Sweethearts (2001) Julia Roberts, Billy Crystal, Catherine Zeta-Jones, John Cusack, Christopher Walken. *Dir.* Joe Roth.

Amityville Horror, The (1979) James Brolin, Margot Kidder, Rod Steiger, Don Stroud. (The 1982 film *Amityville II: The Possession* was in fact a prequel.) *Dir.* Stuart Rosenberg.

Anaconda (1997) Jennifer Lopez, Ice Cube, Jon Voight, Eric Stoltz. *Dir.* Luis Llosa.

Anastasia (1956) Ingrid Bergman, Yul Brynner, Helen Hayes. Bergman's award-winning performance was all the more noteworthy as this was her comeback after being ostracised for 'immoral behaviour'. *Dir.* Anatole Litvak.

Anchors Aweigh (1945) Frank Sinatra, Gene Kelly, Katherine Grayson. Notable for the homophonic spelling of the title and a memorable dance scene between Gene Kelly and Jerry Mouse. *Dir.* George Sidney.

And God Created Woman (1988) Rebecca DeMornay (Robin Shay), Frank Langella (Jim Tiernan), Donovan Leitch (Pete Moran). Remake of the 1957 classic starring Brigitte Bardot. *Dir.* Roger Vadim.

And Soon The Darkness (1970) Michele Dotrice, Pamela Franklin, Sandor Eles, John Nettleton. Cult film about 2 young nurses on a cycling holiday in France. *Dir.* Robert Fuest.

And Then There Were None (1945) Walter Huston, Barry Fitzgerald, Richard Haydn, Queenie Leonard. GB title: *Ten Little Niggers* (after the novel it was based on by Agatha Christie) *Dir.* René Clair.

And Then There Were None (1974) Oliver Reed, Richard Attenborough, Elke Sommer, Charles Aznavour, Herbert Lom. US title: *Ten Little Indians.*

The writer Peter Welbeck is in fact Harry Alan Towers, a curious character who has made a living out of remaking this film. *Dir.* Peter Collinson.

Angela's Ashes (1999) Emily Watson (Angela), Robert Carlyle, Joe Breen (Young Frank), Ciaran Owen (Adolescent Frank), Michael Legge (Grown-up Frank). Based on Frank McCourt bestseller about the life of a Roman Catholic writer brought up in poverty-stricken Limerick. Ultimately fails to capture the spirit and sense of identity of the Irish people but a touching story of triumph over adversity. *Dir.* Alan Parker.

Angels With Dirty Faces (1938) James Cagney, Pat O'Brien, Dead End Kids, Ann Sheridan, Humphrey Bogart. Memorable final scenes when the gangster goes to the electric chair. *Dir.* Michael Curtiz.

Animal Crackers (1930) Groucho Marx (Captain Spaulding), Chico, Harpo, Zeppo, and Margaret Dumont. Thieves covet a valuable oil painting unveiled at a swank party. *Dir.* Victor Heerman.

Anna and the King of Siam (1946) Irene Dunne, Rex Harrison, Linda Darnell. In 1862 an English governess arrives in Bangkok to teach the 67 children of the King. *Dir.* John Cromwell.

Anna Christie (1930) Greta Garbo, Charles Bickford, Marie Dressler. Prostitute falls in love with a seaman. This was the film in which Garbo first talked. *Dir.* Clarence Brown.

Anna Karenina (1935) Greta Garbo (Anna), Fredric March (Count Vronsky). Based on the Tolstoy novel. A 1948 British version starring Vivien Leigh was less successful. *Dir.* Clarence Brown.

Anne of Green Gables (1934) Anne Shirley (Anne), Tom Brown. Based on the LM Montgomery novel set on Prince Edward Island and notable for the fact that its star changed her name from Dawn O'Day to Anne Shirley to play the part. *Dir.* George Nicholls Jnr.

Anne of the Thousand Days (1969) Richard Burton (Henry VIII), Geneviève Bujold (Boleyn) John Colicos (Thomas Cromwell). Highly acclaimed film with many Oscar nominations but no awards. *Dir.* Charles Jarrott.

Annie Get Your Gun (1950) Betty Hutton (Annie Oakley), Howard Keel, Edward Arnold. Judy Garland was originally cast but was fired after her displays of temperament. *Dir.* George Sidney.

Annie Hall (1977) Woody Allen, Diane Keaton, Paul Simon, Shelley Duvall. Oscars for Best Picture, Script, Direction Actress. Classic line by Woody Allen: 'Hey, don't knock masturbation. It's sex with someone I love'. *Dir.* Woody Allen.

Another Woman (1988) Gena Rowlands, Mia Farrow, Ian Holm, Gene Hackman. *Dir.* Woody Allen.

Anthony Adverse (1936) Fredric March, Olivia de Havilland, Claude Rains, Akim Tamiroff. Based on the novel by Hervey Allen, this film won minor Academy Awards. *Dir.* Mervyn Le Roy.

Antonia's Line (1995) Willeke van Ammelrooy, Els Dottemans, Jan Decleir. *Dir.* Marleen Gorris.

Antony and Cleopatra (1972) Charlton Heston, Hildegarde Neil, Fernando Rey, John Castle (Octavius). Based on Shakespeare's play. Both Olivier and Orson Welles were sought for the lead. *Dir.* Charlton Heston.

Antz (1998) Voices of Woody Allen, Dan Aykroyd, Anne Bancroft, Sharon Stone, Sylvester Stallone. *Dir.* Eric Darnell and Tim Johnson.

Anything Goes (1936) Bing Crosby, Ethel Merman, Charles Ruggles, Ida Lupino. PG Wodehouse adapted much of the script from the successful Broadway show but only 3 of Cole Porter's songs were retained. *Dir.* Lewis Milestone.

Anything Goes (1956) Bing Crosby, Donald O'Connor, Zizi Jeanmaire, Mitzi Gaynor. Same story of the stars of a musical comedy each signing a different female lead. *Dir.* Robert Lewis.

Apartment, The (1960) Jack Lemmon (CC Baxter), Shirley Maclaine (Fran Kubelik), Fred MacMurray (Jeff D Sheldrake). Insurance co. name: Consolidated Life. Last line of film by Miss Kubelik: 'Shut up and deal'. *Dir.* Billy Wilder.

Apocalypse Now (1979) Martin Sheen, Robert Duvall, Marlon Brando, Harrison Ford. Vittorio Storaro won Oscar for Photography. Harvey Keitel originally played Willard but was replaced by Martin Sheen. *Dir.* Francis Coppola.

Apollo 13 (1995) Tom Hanks, Bill Paxton, Kevin Bacon, Ed Harris, Emile Ann Lloyd. Won Oscar for Sound Effects. *Dir.* Ron Howard.

Aria (1987) Theresa Russell, Nicola Swain, Jack Kyle, Marion Peters, Beverley D'Angelo, Elizabeth Hurley, John Hurt, Bridget Fonda. Ten episodes each based on a different opera. *Ten Directors*: Nicolas Roeg, Jean-Luc Godard, Charles Sturridge, Julien Temple, Bruce Beresford, Robert Altman, Franc Roddam, Ken Russell, Derek Jarman, Bill Bryden.

Around the World in Eighty Days (1956) David Niven, Cantinflas, Robert Newton, Shirley Maclaine. Although, winning a Best Film Oscar, this film is more notable for the galaxy of stars that had cameos., e.g. Sinatra, George Raft, John Mills, Noël Coward, Buster Keaton, Marlene Dietrich. *Dir.* Mike Anderson and Kevin McClory.

Arsenic and Old Lace (1942) released 1944. Cary Grant (Mortimer Brewster), Josephine Hull (Abby), Jean Adair (Martha), Raymond Massey (Jonathan), John Alexander (Teddy), Peter Lorre (Dr Einstein), Grant Mitchell (Rev Harper). Two old ladies poison unsuspecting visitors with elderberry wine and have their mad brother, who believes they are yellow fever victims, bury them in the cellar. Raymond Massey was imitating Boris Karloff. *Dir.* Frank Capra.

Arthur (1981) Dudley Moore (Arthur Bach), John Gielgud (Hobson), Liza Minnelli (Linda Marolla). Gielgud won Oscar as Best Supporting Actor and 'Best That You Can Do' won Best Song Oscar. *Dir.* Steve Gordon.

Arthur 2: On the Rocks (1988) Dudley Moore (Arthur Bach), John Gielgud (Hobson), Liza Minnelli (Linda Marolla Bach). Brogan Lane, the ex-Mrs Moore, appears briefly as 'Cindy'. *Dir.* Bud Yorkin.

As Good As It Gets (1997) Jack Nicholson (Best Actor Oscar), Helen Hunt (Best Actor Oscar), Greg Kinnear. *Dir.* James L Brooks.

Ashanti (1979) Michael Caine, Omar Sharif, Peter Ustinov, Rex Harrison, William Holden. Wife of a member of the World Health Organisation is seized by slave traders in West Africa. *Dir.* Richard Fleischer.

Ask a Policeman (1938) Will Hay, Graham Moffatt, Moore Marriott. Classic written by Val Guest and remade by him in 1983 as the somewhat less popular *The Boys in Blue* starring Cannon and Ball. *Dir.* Marcel Varnel.

Asphalt Jungle, The (1950) Sterling Hayden (Dix Handley), Louis Calhern (Alonzo D Emmerich), Marilyn Monroe (Angela Phinlay) *Dir.* John Huston.

Assassination Bureau, The (1968) Oliver Reed, Diana Rigg, Telly Savalas, Curt Jurgens. In 1906, a woman journalist breaks up an international gang of professional killers by falling in love with their leader. *Dir.* Basil Dearden.

Assassins (1995) Sylvester Stallone, Antonio Banderas, Julianne Moore. Hitman decides to quit but is menaced by a younger rival. *Dir.* Richard Donner.

Associate, The (1996)   Whoopi Goldberg (Laurel Ayres and 'male' alter ego Robert S Cutty), Dianne Wiest (Sally), Tim Daly, Eli Wallach. *Dir.* Donald Petrie.

Asterix and the Big Fight (1989)   Voices of Bill Oddie, Bernard Bresslaw, Ron Moody, Sheila Hancock, Brian Blessed, Peter Hawkins. Asterix attempts to restore the village soothsayer's memory in order to make a potion to defeat the invading Romans. *Dir.* Philippe Grimond.

Atlantis: The Lost Empire (2001)   Voices of Michael J Fox (Milo Thatch), Claudia Christian (Helga Sinclair), James Garner (Commander Rourke), John Mahoney (Preston B Whitmore), Corey Burton (Mole), Cree Summer (Princess Kida). Animated film in which a polyglot leads an expedition to discover Atlantis in 1914. *Dir.* Gary Trousdale and Kirk Wise.

Attila the Hun (1954)   Anthony Quinn, Sophia Loren. *Dir.* Pietro Francisci.

August (1995)   Anthony Hopkins, Leslie Phillips, Kate Burton. *Dir.* Anthony Hopkins.

Austin Powers in Goldmember (2002)   Mike Myers (Austin Powers/Goldmember/Fat Bastard/Dr Evil), Beyoncé Knowles (Foxxy Cleopatra), Michael Caine (Nigel Powers), Seth Green (Scott Evil), Verne Troyer (Mini-Me), Michael York (Basil Exposition), Robert Wagner (No. 2), Mindy Sterling (Frau Farbissina). *Dir.* Jay Roach.

Austin Powers: International Man of Mystery (1997)   Mike Myers, Elizabeth Hurley, Michael York, Mimi Rogers, Robert Wagner, Seth Green. *Dir.* Jay Roach.

Austin Powers: The Spy Who Shagged Me (1999)   Mike Myers (Austin Danger Powers/Dr Evil/Fat Bastard), Robert Wagner (No 2), Elizabeth Hurley (Vanessa Kensington Powers), Heather Graham (Felicity Shagwell), Michael York (Basil Exposition), Rob Lowe (Young No. 2), Seth Green (Scott Evil). *Dir.* Jay Roach.

Autumn Leaves (1956)   Joan Crawford, Cliff Robertson, Lorne Greene, Vera Miles. Spinster marries a young man who turns out to be a pathological liar and tries to murder her. *Dir.* Robert Aldrich.

Awakening, The (1980)   Charlton Heston, Susannah York, Jill Townsend, Stephanie Zimbalist. Based on the Bram Stoker novel *Jewel of the Seven Stars* about an archaeologist who believes the spirit of an Egyptian queen has entered the soul of his daughter. *Dir.* Mike Newell.

Awakenings (1990)   Robert De Niro (Leonard Lowe) Robin Williams (Dr Sayer) Max Von Sydow (Dr Ingham). Based on factual development in treatment of mental illness. Robin Williams broke De Niro's nose accidentally. *Dir.* Penny Marshall.

Awfully Big Adventure, An (1994)   Georgina Cates, Hugh Grant, Alan Rickman, Peter Firth, Prunella Scales, Nicola Pagett. Romance in a Liverpool repertory theatre in 1947. *Dir.* Mike Newell.

Babe (1995)   James Cromwell, Magda Szubanski, Roscoe Lee Browne (Narrator). Orphaned piglet is adopted by a sheepdog. Based on a book by Dick King-Smith. *Dir.* Chris Noonan.

Babe, The (1992)   John Goodman, Kelly McGillis, Bruce Boxleitner. *Dir.* Arthur Hiller.

Babette's Feast (1987)   Stéphane Audran, Jean-Philippe Lafont, Jarl Kulle, Birgitte Federspiel. Best Foreign Language Oscar for this Danish film about a Lottery winner laying on an enormous banquet. The original story on which the film was based was written by Karen Blixen. *Dir.* Gabriel Axel.

Baby Doll (1956)   Karl Malden, Eli Wallach, Carroll Baker. *Dir.* Elia Kazan.

Back to the Future (1985)   Michael J Fox (Marty McFly), Christopher Lloyd (Dr Emmett Brown), Crispin Glover (George McFly). Notable for cameo roles by Billy Zane as Match, and Huey Lewis, who sings 'Power of Love'. *Dir.* Robert Zemeckis.

Back to the Future II (1989)   Michael J Fox (Marty McFly), Christopher Lloyd (Dr Emmett Brown), Lea Thompson (Lorraine Baines). Crispin Glover refused to take part for less than $1 million so lookalikes were used. *Dir.* Robert Zemeckis.

Back to the Future III (1990)   Michael J Fox (Marty / Seamus McFly), Christopher Lloyd (Dr Emmett Brown), Lea Thompson (Lorraine Baines / Maggie McFly). Set in the Wild West of the 1880s. *Dir.* Robert Zemeckis.

Backdraft (1991)   Kurt Russell (Stephen McCaffrey), William Baldwin (Brian McCaffrey), Rebecca DeMornay (Helen McCaffrey) Robert De Niro (Donald Rimgale) Donald Sutherland (Ronald Bartel). Two brothers track down an arsonist and expose corruption in the fire department. *Dir.* Ron Howard.

Bad and the Beautiful, The (1952)   Kirk Douglas (Jonathan Shields), Lana Turner (Georgia Lorrison), Walter Pidgeon (Harry Pebbel), Dick Powell (James Lee Bartlow). A director, a star, a screenwriter and an executive recall their experiences at the hands of a go-getting Hollywood producer. *Dir.* Vincente Minnelli.

Bad Day at Black Rock (1955)   Spencer Tracy, Robert Ryan, Lee Marvin, Walter Brennan. Action takes place within 24 hours and concerns a one-armed stranger greeted with hostility by a town with something to hide. *Dir.* John Sturges.

Bad Influence (1990)   Rob Lowe (Alex), James Spader (Michael Ball). Notable scene where Lowe tries to blow up a car by connecting a broken tail-light with a petrol tank is apparently a terrorist trick from which one important step was omitted. *Dir.* Curtis Hanson.

Badlands (1973)   Martin Sheen, Sissy Spacek, Warren Oates. Teenage girl and garbage collector wander across America leaving a trail of murder. *Dir.* Terrence Malick.

Ballad of the Sad Café, The (1991)   Vanessa Redgrave (Miss Amelia Evans), Keith Carradine (Marvin Macy), Rod Steiger (Reverend Willin). Tale of a Southern town run by the despotic Redgrave, based on the novella by Carson McCullers. The film was shot at Willie Nelson's farm. *Dir.* Simon Callow.

Bananas (1971)   Woody Allen, Louise Lasser, Carlos Montalban, Sylvester Stallone (walk-on as mugger). When asked why he called the film *Bananas*, Allen replied, 'Because there are no bananas in it.' *Dir.* Woody Allen.

Bandit Queen (1994)   Seema Biswas, Nirmal Pandey, Manjoj Baipal. Story of Phoolan Devi, a real-life Indian bandit and rape victim. *Dir.* Sheka Kapur.

Bandits (2001)   Bruce Willis, Billy Bob Thornton, Cate Blanchett, Troy Garity. *Dir.* Barry Levinson.

Bank Dick, The (1940)   WC Fields, Franklin Pangborn, Shemp Howard, Jack Norton. Fields wrote the script using his nom de plume of Mahatma Kane Jeeves, which derived from characters in old English plays. They would say 'M'Hat, M'cane, Jeeves'. GB title: *The Bank Detective. Dir.* Eddie Cline.

Barabbas (1962)   Anthony Quinn, Silvano Mangano, Ernest Borgnine, Jack Palance. The eclipse of the Sun at the beginning was a real one filmed in Nice. *Dir.* Richard Fleischer.

Barb Wire (1996)   Pamela Anderson Lee, Temuera Morrison, Victoria Rowell. Set in civil-war-ravaged USA in the year 2017. *Dir.* David Hogan.

Barbarella (1967)   Jane Fonda, John Phillip Law, Milo O'Shea, David Hemmings, Marcel Marceau. Beautiful 40th-century astronaut prevents positronic ray from getting into the wrong hands. *Dir.* Roger Vadim.

Barbarosa (1981)   Willie Nelson (Barbarosa), Gary Busey (Karl), Isela Vega (Josephina). Old-style Western that was well received by critics. *Dir.* Fred Schepisi.

Barbary Coast (1935)   Edward G Robinson, Miriam Hopkins, Joel McCrea, Walter Brennan. Set during the San Francisco gold rush. *Dir.* Howard Hawks.

Barefoot Contessa, The (1954)   Humphrey Bogart (Harry Dawes), Ava Gardner (Maria Vargas), Edmond O'Brien (Muldoon). O'Brien won Best Supporting Actor Oscar. *Dir.* Joseph L Mankiewicz.

Barefoot in the Park (1967)   Robert Redford (Paul Bratter), Jane Fonda (Corie Bratter), Charles Boyer (Victor Velasco), Mildred Natwick (Ethel Banks). Based on Neil Simon's play. *Dir.* Gene Saks.

Barkleys of Broadway, The (1949)   Fred Astaire, Ginger Rogers, Oscar Levant. Judy Garland was originally cast but withdrew through illness. *Dir.* Charles Walters.

Barretts of Wimpole Street, The (1934)   Norma Shearer (Elizabeth Barrett), Fredric March (Robert Browning), Charles Laughton (Edward Moulton-Barrett), Maureen O'Sullivan (Henrietta). The 1956 remake starred Jennifer Jones and Bill Travers. *Dir.* Sidney Franklin.

Basic Instinct (1992)   Michael Douglas (Nick Curran), Sharon Stone (Catherine Tramell), George Dzundza (Gus), Jeanne Tripplehorn (Dr Beth Garner), Leilani Sarelle (Roxy). Famous for a scene where the knickerless Stone crosses her legs. *Dir.* Paul Verhoeven.

Basket Case (1982)   Kevin Van Hentenryck, Terri Susan Smith, Beverly Bonner. First of 3 (to date) cult films – followed by *Basket Case II* (1990) and *Basket Case 3: The Progeny* (1992) – depicting Siamese twins with attitude. *Dir.* Frank Henenlotter.

Batman (1989)   Michael Keaton (Batman), Jack Nicholson (Joker), Kim Basinger (Vicki Vale), Jerry Hall (Alicia) Jack Palance (Grissom). *Batman Returns* (1992) starred Danny De Vito as Penguin (Oswald Cobblepot). *Dir.* Tim Burton.

Batman and Robin (1997)   George Clooney (Batman), Chris O'Donnell (Robin), Alicia Silverstone (Batgirl), Arnold Schwarzenegger (Mr Freeze), Uma Thurman (Poison Ivy). Schwarzenegger line: 'Revenge is a dish best served cold' originally heard in *Star Trek: The Wrath of Khan*. *Dir.* Joel Schumacher.

Batman Forever (1995)   Val Kilmer (Batman), Tommy Lee Jones (Harvey Two-Face), Jim Carrey (Riddler), Chris O'Donnell (Robin), Nicole Kidman, Drew Barrymore. *Dir.* Joel Schumacher.

Battle of Britain (1969)   Laurence Olivier (Dowding), Robert Shaw, Michael Caine, Christopher Plummer, Kenneth More, Susannah York, Trevor Howard, Ralph Richardson, Michael Redgrave, Edward Fox. *Dir.* Guy Hamilton.

Battle of the Bulge (1965)   Henry Fonda, Robert Shaw, Robert Ryan, Telly Savalas, Ty Hardin. Story of the German counter-attack in the Ardennes in December 1944. *Dir.* Ken Annakin.

Battle of the River Plate (1956)   John Gregson, Anthony Quayle, Peter Finch. US title: *Pursuit of the Graf Spee*. *Dir.* Emeric Pressburger & Michael Powell.

Beach, The (2000)   Leonardo DiCaprio (Richard), Tilda Swinton (Sal), Virginie Ledoyen (Françoise), Guillaume Canet (Etienne), Robert Carlyle (Duffy), Peter Youngblood Hills (Zeph). American traveller discovers a hippy community living by a perfect beach on a remote island in Thailand. *Dir.* Danny Boyle.

Beaches (1988)   Bette Midler (CC Bloom), Barbara Hershey (Hillary Whitney Essex). Singer visits her dying friend, a lawyer, and recalls their long and volatile friendship. *Dir.* Garry Marshall.

Bean (1997)   Rowan Atkinson, Peter MacNicol, Pamela Reed, Burt Reynolds, John Mills, Peter Egan, Harris Yulin, Richard Gant, Tricia Vessey, Peter Capaldi, Andrew Lawrence. *Dir.* Mel Smith.

Beau Brummell (1954)   Stewart Granger, Elizabeth Taylor, Robert Morley (George III), Peter Ustinov (Prince of Wales). Remake of the 1924 film starring John Barrymore and Mary Astor. *Dir.* Curtis Bernhardt.

Beau Geste (1939)   Gary Cooper, Ray Milland, Brian Donlevy, Susan Hayward. Remake of the 1926 film starring Ronald Colman and based on PC Wren's novel. *Dir.* William Wellman.

Beautiful Mind, A (2001)   Russell Crowe (John Nash), Jennifer Connelly, Ed Harris, Christopher Plummer, Paul Bettany. Biopic of Nobel Prize-winning mathematician John Nash's struggle against mental illness. Multiple Oscar-winning film. *Dir.* Ron Howard.

Beauty and the Beast (1991)   Voices of Robby Benson (Beast), Paige O'Hara (Belle), Angela Lansbury (Mrs Potts). Disney classic which became the best-selling video of all time in the USA. *Dir.* Gary Trousdale & Kirk Wise.

Beavis and Butthead Do America (1996)   Created by animator Mike Judge. Voices include Robert Stack and Bruce Willis. *Dir.* Mike Judge.

Becket (1964)   Richard Burton (Becket), Peter O'Toole (Henry II), John Gielgud, Sian Phillips. Based on Jean Anouilh's bitter stage play. *Dir.* Peter Glenville.

Bed Sitting Room, The (1969)   Ralph Richardson, Rita Tushingham, Michael Hordern, Arthur Lowe, Spike Milligan, Harry Secombe, Peter Cook, Dudley Moore. After a nuclear war, motley survivors turn into bed sitting rooms, cupboards and parakeets. *Dir.* Richard Lester.

Bedazzled (1967)   Peter Cook, Dudley Moore, Michael Bates, Raquel Welch, Eleanor Bron. *Dir.* Stanley Donen. Short-order cook is saved from suicide by Mr Spiggott, who offers him seven wishes in exchange for his soul.

Bedknobs and Broomsticks (1971)   Angela Lansbury, David Tomlinson, Bruce Forsyth, Tessie O'Shea. *Dir.* Robert Stevenson.

Beetlejuice (1988)   Alec Baldwin (Adam), Geena Davis (Barbara), Michael Keaton (Betelgeuse), Winona Ryder (Lydia Deetz). *Dir.* Tim Burton.

Beguiled, The (1971)   Clint Eastwood, Geraldine Page, Elizabeth Hartman, Darleen Carr. Wounded Union soldier hides out in a Confederate girls' school. *Dir.* Don Siegel.

Behind Enemy Lines (2001)   Owen Wilson, Gene Hackman, Gabriel Macht, Charles Malik Whitfield, David Keith, Joaquim de Almeida. US naval pilot is shot down over Bosnia and hunted by Serbian troops. *Dir.* John Moore.

Beijing Bastards (1993)   Cui Jian, Li Wei, Wu Gang, Bian Tianshuo. Original title: *Beijing Zazhong*. Story of disillusionment by the young Chinese. *Dir.* Zhang Yuan.

C
I
N
E
M
A

Being Human (1994)   Robin Williams, John Turturro, Anna Galiena, Theresa Russell (as narrator). Box office flop about a father who fails to provide for his family in five historic eras. *Dir.* Bill Forsyth.

Being John Malkovich (1999)   John Cusack, Cameron Diaz, Catherine Keener, John Malkovich. *Dir.* Spike Jonze.

Being There (1979)   Peter Sellers, Shirley MacLaine, Melvyn Douglas. Melvyn Douglas won Best Supporting Actor Oscar for this film about a simple gardener who becomes philosopher and sage to the American people. *Dir.* Hal Ashby.

Bell, Book and Candle (1958)   James Stewart, Kim Novak, Jack Lemmon, Hermione Gingold. Publisher slowly realises that his girlfriend is a witch. *Dir.* Richard Quine.

Belles of St Trinian's, The (1954)   Alastair Sim, George Cole (Flash Harry), Joyce Grenfell, Beryl Reid, Irene Handl. Based on Ronald Searle's cartoons. *Dir.* Frank Launder.

Bells of St Mary's, The (1945)   Bing Crosby (Father O'Malley), Ingrid Bergman (Sister Benedict). Sequel to *Going My Way*. *Dir.* Leo McCarey.

Belstone Fox, The (1973)   Eric Porter, Rachel Roberts, Dennis Waterman, Jeremy Kemp, Bill Travers. Based on the novel *The Ballad of the Belstone Fox* by David Rook. *Dir.* James Hill.

Ben Hur (1925)   Ramon Novarro, Francis X Bushman, Carmel Myers. Based on the Lew Wallace novel. Originally, Charles Brabin was director and George Walsh the star; both were replaced when Louis Mayer saw the first rushes. *Dir.* Fred Niblo.

Ben Hur (1959)   Charlton Heston, Haya Harareet, Jack Hawkins, Stephen Boyd, Hugh Griffith. Multi-award-winning film but critics generally regard the 1925 silent epic as definitive. *Dir.* William Wyler.

Bend it Like Beckham (2002)   Parminder K Nagra, Keira Knightley, Jonathan Rhys-Meyers, Anupam Kher, Shaznay Lewis. Teenage London girl wants to become a professional footballer but is thwarted by her Punjabi Sikh parents, who want her to study law. *Dir.* Gurinder Chadha.

Beneath the Planet of the Apes (1970)   James Franciscus, Charlton Heston, Linda Harrison, Kim Hunter. Sequel to *Planet of the Apes*. *Dir.* Ted Post.

Benji (1974)   Peter Breck, Edgar Buchanan, Christopher Connelly. Popular film about a stray mongrel dog who saves two kidnapped children. *Dir.* Joe Camp.

Benny Goodman Story (1955)   Steve Allen (Goodman), Donna Reed, Berta Gersten, Harry James, Gene Krupa, Sammy Davis Snr. Steve Allen went on to host one of America's leading variety shows on television. *Dir.* Valentine Davies.

Bequest to the Nation (1973)   Peter Finch, Glenda Jackson, Michael Jayston, Margaret Leighton, Anthony Quayle. US title: *The Nelson Affair*. Story of Nelson's long affair with the tempestuous Lady Hamilton. *Dir.* James Cellan Jones.

Bespoke Overcoat, The (1956)   Alfie Bass, David Kossoff. Won Academy Award for Best Short Film and launched its stars as successful TV actors. *Dir.* Jack Clayton.

Best Years of Our Lives, The (1946)   Fredric March, Myrna Loy, Teresa Wright, Dana Andrews, Virginia Mayo, Hoagy Carmichael. Multi-award-winning film notable for the performance of Harold Russell, a veteran who had lost his hands; he had no previous acting experience. *Dir.* William Wyler.

Beverly Hillbillies, The (1993)   Diedrich Bader, Dabney Coleman, Erika Eleniak, Cloris Leachman, Buddy Ebsen, Zsa Zsa Gabor, Dolly Parton. *Dir.* Penelope Spheeris.

Beverly Hills Cop (1984)   Eddie Murphy (Axel Foley), Judge Reinhold (Det Billy Rosewood), Steven Berkoff (Victor Maitland). Detroit cop races to Los Angeles to track down the killers of his best friend. *Dir.* Martin Brest.

Beverly Hills Cop 2 (1987)   Eddie Murphy (Axel Foley), Judge Reinhold (Det Billy Rosewood), Brigitte Nielsen (Karla Fry). Ironically Sylvester Stallone was to play Axel Foley in the original film and his ex Brigitte Nielsen appears in this sequel. *Dir.* Tony Scott.

Beverly Hills Cop 3 (1994)   Eddie Murphy (Axel Foley), Judge Reinhold (Det Billy Rosewood), John Saxon. Cop discovers that the head of security at a Los Angeles theme park is a murderer. *Dir.* Tony Scott.

Beyond Bedlam (1994)   Craig Fairbrass, Elizabeth Hurley, Keith Allen, Anita Dobson, Georgina Hale. *Dir.* Vadim Jean.

Beyond the Poseidon Adventure (1979)   Michael Caine, Telly Savalas, Karl Malden, Sally Field. Not so much a sequel, more an alternative ending to the original. *Dir.* Irwin Allen.

Bible, The (1966)   Michael Parks (Adam), Ulla Bergryd (Eve), Richard Harris (Cain), John Huston (Noah), George C Scott (Abraham), Peter O'Toole (the 3 Angels). Remembered for Huston's whispered commentary and the eye-catching photography as well as Toshiro Mayuzumi's musical interpretation. *Dir.* John Huston.

Big (1988)   Tom Hanks (Josh Baskin), Elizabeth Perkins (Susan), Robert Loggia (MacMillan). Story of 12-yr-old who wishes he were 'Big' and wakes up 20 yrs older. Steven Spielberg was originally going to direct and Harrison Ford to star. *Dir.* Penny Marshall.

Big Business (1929)   Oliver Hardy, Stan Laurel, James Finlayson. Laurel & Hardy classic about their failure to sell a Christmas tree to a belligerent householder. Memorable for the scene of mutual destruction. *Dir.* James W Horne.

Big Business (1988)   Bette Midler (Sadie Shelton / Ratcliff), Lily Tomlin (Rose Shelton / Ratcliff). Story of twins mixed up at birth. *Dir.* Jim Abrahams.

Big Chill, The (1983)   Tom Berenger (Sam), Glenn Close (Sarah), William Hurt (Nick), Jeff Goldblum (Michael), Kevin Kline (Harold), Meg Tilly (Chloe). Story of a students' reunion after the suicide of one of them. Kevin Costner plays the corpse, Alex, although only his hands, torso and legs are seen in the final version. *Dir.* Lawrence Kasdan.

Big Country, The (1958)   Gregory Peck, Jean Simmons, Charlton Heston, Burl Ives, Carol Baker, Charles Bickford, Chuck Connors. Story of the Terrills' and the Hannesseys' feud over water rights. Burl Ives won Best Supporting Actor Oscar. *Dir.* William Wyler.

Big Fat Liar (2002)   Frankie Muniz, Paul Giamatti, Amanda Bynes, Amanda Detmer, Lee Majors. *Dir.* Shawn Levy

Big Hand for the Little Lady, A (1966)   Henry Fonda, Joanne Woodward, Jason Robards, Kevin McCarthy, Charles Bickford, Burgess Meredith. GB title: *Big Deal at Dodge City* (though the action, in fact, takes place in Laredo). *Dir.* Fielder Cook.

Big Man, The (1990)   Liam Neeson, Joanne Whalley-Kilmer, Billy Connolly, Ian Bannen. Unemployed miner becomes a bare-knuckle fighter. *Dir.* David Leland.

Big Sleep, The (1946)   Humphrey Bogart (Philip Marlowe), Lauren Bacall (Vivian Sherwood

Rutledge), John Ridgely (Eddie Mars), Martha Vickers (Carmen Sternwood). Based on Raymond Chandler's Novel but adapted by William Faulkner, Leigh Brackett and Jules Furthman. (Alternative version with 18 minutes of different footage exists.) *Dir.* Howard Hawks.

Big Sleep, The (1978)   Robert Mitchum (Philip Marlowe), Sarah Miles, Richard Boone, Candy Clark, James Stewart, Edward Fox, Oliver Reed, Richard Todd. Remake of the 1946 film but set in London. *Dir.* Michael Winner.

Big Trouble in Little China (1986)   Kurt Russell (Jack Burton), Kim Cattrall (Gracie Law). *Dir.* John Carpenter.

Bill and Ted's Excellent Adventure (1989)   Keanu Reeves (Ted 'Theodore' Logan), Alex Winter (Bill S Preston). Napoleon, Billy the Kid, Socrates, Freud, Genghis Khan, Joan of Arc and Abe Lincoln are some of the famous people met on their journey. *Dir.* Stephen Herek.

Billy Bathgate (1991)   Dustin Hoffman, Nicole Kidman, Bruce Willis. Based on EL Doctorow's novel. Teenager becomes an assistant to top gangster Dutch Schultz. *Dir.* Robert Benton.

Billy Budd (1962)   Peter Ustinov, Robert Ryan, Terence Stamp, Melvyn Douglas, David McCallum. Based on Herman Melville's novel about the young Billy Budd, who kills the sadistic master-at-arms of a British warship in 1797. *Dir.* Peter Ustinov.

Billy Elliot (2000)   Julie Walters (Mrs Wilkinson), Jamie Bell (Billy Elliot), Gary Lewis (Billy's Dad), Jamie Draven (Tony). Young son of a working-class miner has aspirations to become a ballet dancer. *Dir.* Stephen Daldry.

Billy Liar (1963)   Tom Courtenay, Julie Christie, Wilfred Pickles, Leonard Rossiter. Written by Keith Waterhouse and inspired by *The Secret Life of Walter Mitty*. *Dir.* John Schlesinger.

Birdcage, The (1996)   Robin Williams, Nathan Lane, Gene Hackman, Dianne Wiest. Remake of French film, *La Cage aux Folles*. Son of a homosexual club-owner persuades his father to act the heterosexual with his future very conservative in-laws. *Dir.* Mike Nichols.

Birdman of Alcatraz (1962)   Burt Lancaster (Robert Stroud), Karl Malden, Thelma Ritter, Edmond O'Brien, Neville Brand, Telly Savalas. True story of Robert Stroud, who spent nearly 60 years in prison and made a name for himself as an ornithologist. *Dir.* John Frankenheimer.

Birds, The (1963)   Rod Taylor, Tippi Hedren, Jessica Tandy, Suzanne Pleshette. Birds turn against humans. Action takes place at Bodega Bay, California. *Dir.* Alfred Hitchcock.

Birdy (1984)   Matthew Modine (Birdy), Nicolas Cage (Al Columbato). *Dir.* Alan Parker.

Birth of a Nation (1915)   Lillian Gish, Henry B Walthall, Mae Marsh, Donald Crisp. Originally *The Clansman*, this story of US Civil War strife was the first big screen epic. *Dir.* DW Griffith.

Black Beauty (1994)   Alan Cummings (voice), Sean Bean, David Thewlis, Jim Carter, Peter Davison, Eleanor Bron, Peter Cook. Story is told by the horse itself. *Dir.* Caroline Thompson.

Black Hawk Down (2001)   Josh Hartnett, Eric Bana, Tom Sizemore, Ewan McGregor, Sam Shepard, William Fichtner. Graphic war film set in 1993 troubled Mogadishu. Won Oscars for sound and editing. *Dir.* Ridley Scott.

Black Narcissus (1946)   Deborah Kerr, Sabu, Jean Simmons, Flora Robson. Anglo-Catholic nuns in the Himalayas have trouble with climate and morale. *Dir.* Michael Powell & Emeric Pressburger.

Black Robe (1991)   Lothaire Bluteau, Aden Young, Sandrine Holt. Jesuit priest travels through Quebec to convert the Indians in the 17th century. *Dir.* Bruce Beresford.

Blackboard Jungle, The (1955)   Glenn Ford, Anne Francis, Louis Calhern, Sidney Poitier, Vic Morrow. Notable for the music of Bill Haley and the Comets. *Dir.* Richard Brooks.

Blackmail (1929)   Anny Ondra, Sara Allgood, Charles Paton. Hitchcock's first talkie involves a Scotland Yard inspector who finds his girl is involved in a murder but conceals the fact and is blackmailed. *Dir.* Alfred Hitchcock.

Blade Runner (1982)   Harrison Ford (Deckard), Rutger Hauer (Roy Batty), Sean Young (Rachel), Daryl Hannah (Pris). Set in LA in 2019. Ridley Scott released his 'Director's Cut' in 1992 which had a more satisfactory conclusion. Based on the novel *Do Androids Dream of Electric Sheep?* by Philip K Dick. *Dir.* Ridley Scott.

Blair Witch Project, The (1999)   Heather Donahue, Michael C Williams, Joshua Leonard. *Dir.* Daniel Myrick and Eduardo Sanchez.

Blair Witch 2: Book of Shadows (2000)   Tristen Skyler, Stephen B Turner, Jeffery Donovan. *Dir.* Joe Berlinger.

Blazing Saddles (1974)   Cleavon Little, Gene Wilder, Slim Pickens, Mel Brooks, Madeline Kahn. Black railroad worker and an alcoholic ex-gunfighter foil a crooked attorney. Famous for its beans scene. *Dir.* Mel Brooks.

Blob, The (1958)   Steve McQueen, Aneta Corseaut, Earl Rowe. *Dir.* Irwin S Yeaworth.

Blockheads (1938)   Oliver Hardy, Stan Laurel, Billy Gilbert. Twenty years after WW1, Stan is still guarding a trench because nobody told him to stop. *Dir.* John G Blystone.

Blondie (1938)   Arthur Lake, Penny Singleton, Daisy the Dog, Jonathan Hale. Mr & Mrs Small Town America, Dagwood Bumstead and wife Blondie, spawned many sequels. *Dir.* Frank R Strayer.

Blow (2001)   Johnny Depp (George Jung), Penelope Cruz, Franka Potente, Rachel Griffiths, Jordi Molla. True-life story of a Boston boy who grows up in the 1970s to become the biggest smuggler of cocaine into the United States from Colombia. *Dir.* Ted Demme.

Blow Up (1966)   David Hemmings, Sarah Miles, Vanessa Redgrave. London fashion photographer thinks he sees a murder, but the evidence disappears. *Dir.* Michelangelo Antonioni.

Blue Angel, The (1930)   Emil Jannings, Marlene Dietrich (Lola). Story of a professor's infatuation with a nightclub singer. *Dir.* Josef von Sternberg.

Blue Bird, The (1940)   Shirley Temple, Johnny Russell, Gale Sondergaard (the cat), Eddie Collins (the dog). Two children of a poor woodcutter seek the bluebird of happiness. *Dir.* Walter Lang.

Blue Bird, The (1976)   Elizabeth Taylor (Mother, Maternal Love, Light & The Witch), Ava Gardner, Jane Fonda, George Cole. Remake of the 1940 classic. *Dir.* George Cukor.

Blue Dahlia (1946)   Alan Ladd, Veronica Lake, William Bendix, Howard de Silva. Raymond Chandler story of a returning war veteran who finds his faithless wife murdered and himself suspected. *Dir.* George Marshall.

Blue Lagoon (1949)   Jean Simmons, Donald Houston, Cyril Cusack. Shipwrecked boy and girl grow up on a desert island. *Dir.* Frank Launder.

Blue Lagoon (1980)   Brooke Shields, Christopher Atkins, Leo McKern. Remake of the 1949 film. *Dir.* Randal Kleiser.

Blue Lamp, The (1949)   Jack Warner, Jimmy Hanley, Dirk Bogarde, Dora Bryan. Famous for its opening shooting scene and the subsequent reincarnation of George Dixon for *Dixon of Dock Green*, which ran for 20 years on Television. *Dir.* Basil Dearden.

Blue Max, The (1966)   George Peppard, James Mason, Ursula Andress, Jeremy Kemp. *Dir.* John Guillermin.

Blues Brothers, The (1980)   John Belushi (Jake), Dan Aykroyd (Elwood), Carrie Fisher, Cab Calloway. *Dir.* John Landis.

Bob and Carol and Ted and Alice (1969)   Robert Culp, Natalie Wood, Elliott Gould, Dyan Cannon. *Dir.* Paul Mazursky.

Body Heat (1981)   William Hurt, Kathleen Turner, Richard Crenna, Ted Danson. Florida lawyer becomes involved with a married woman and they plot to kill her husband. *Dir.* Lawrence Kasdan.

Bodyguard, The (1992)   Kevin Costner (Frank Farmer), Whitney Houston (Rachel Marron), Gary Kemp (Sy Spector). *Dir.* Mick Jackson.

Bonfire of the Vanities (1990)   Tom Hanks (Sherman McCoy), Bruce Willis (Peter Fallow), Melanie Griffith (Maria Ruskin). Based on Tom Wolfe's novel of the same name. *Dir.* Brian de Palma.

Bonnie and Clyde (1967)   Warren Beatty (Clyde Barrow), Faye Dunaway (Bonnie Parker), Gene Hackman (Buck), Estelle Parsons, Michael J Pollard, Gene Wilder. Estelle Parsons won Academy Award for Best Supporting Actress. *Dir.* Arthur Penn.

Boom! (1968)   Elizabeth Taylor, Richard Burton, Noël Coward. Based on Tennessee Williams's play *The Milk Train Doesn't Stop Here Anymore*. *Dir.* Joseph Losey.

Born on the Fourth of July (1989)   Tom Cruise (Ron Kovic), Kyra Sedgwick (Donna), Willem Dafoe, Tom Berenger. *Dir.* Oliver Stone.

Bourne Identity, The (2002)   Matt Damon, Franka Potente, Chris Cooper, Clive Owen, Brian Cox. Story of a secret agent trying to piece together the threads of his life whilst suffering total amnesia. *Dir.* Doug Liman.

Box of Moonlight (1996)   John Turturro (Al Fountain), Sam Rockwell (The Kid). *Dir.* Tom DiCillo.

Boxing Helena (1993)   Julian Sands, Sherilyn Fenn, Bill Paxton, Art Garfunkel. Most memorable for Kim Basinger being sued for changing her mind over starring in it. Court ordered her to pay $8 million but studio settled for $3 million. *Dir.* Jennifer Chambers Lynch.

Boys Don't Cry (1999)   Peter Sarsgaard (John), Brendan Sexton III (Tom), Alison Folland (Kate). *Dir.* Kimberly Peirce.

Boys from Brazil, The (1978)   Gregory Peck (Josef Mengele), Laurence Olivier, James Mason, Lilli Palmer. Based on the Ira Levin novel. *Dir.* Franklin Schaffner.

Brassed Off (1996)   Peter Postlethwaite (Danny), Tara Fitzgerald (Gloria), Ewan McGregor. *Dir.* Mark Herman.

Braveheart (1995)   Mel Gibson, Sophie Marceau, Patrick McGoohan, Ian Bannen. *Dir.* Mel Gibson.

Brazil (1985)   Jonathan Pryce, Robert De Niro, Michael Palin, Peter Vaughan, Bob Hoskins. *Dir.* Terry Gilliam.

Breaking the Waves (1996)   Emily Watson, Stellan Skarsgard, Katrin Cartlidge, Jean-Marc Barr. Award-winning film set in Scotland, it concerns a woman who humiliates herself in the hope of saving the life of her husband, paralysed in an oil rig accident. *Dir.* Lars von Trier.

Bridge on the River Kwai (1957)   Alec Guinness (Colonel Nicholson), Sessue Hayakawa (Colonel Saito), William Holden (Shears), Jack Hawkins (Major Warden). Based on the novel by Pierre Boulle. *Dir.* David Lean.

Bridges of Madison County (1995)   Clint Eastwood, Meryl Streep, Annie Corley. Written by Richard LaGravenese. *Dir.* Clint Eastwood.

Bridget Jones's Diary (2001)   Renée Zellweger, Hugh Grant, Colin Firth, Gemma Jones, Jim Broadbent. Cameo performances by Jeffrey Archer and Salman Rushdie. *Dir.* Sharon Maguire

Brief Encounter (1945)   Celia Johnson (Laura Jesson), Trevor Howard (Alec Harvey), Stanley Holloway, Joyce Carey. Based on a Noël Coward play, *Still Life*. The theme music was Rachmaninov's Piano Concerto No 2 and the railway station was Carnforth. *Dir.* David Lean.

Brigadoon (1954)   Gene Kelly, Cyd Charisse, Van Johnson. Scottish village awakens only once every hundred years. *Dir.* Vincente Minnelli.

Bringing Up Baby (1938)   Katharine Hepburn (Susan), Cary Grant (David Huxley), May Robson. The baby of the title was, in fact, a leopard. *Dir.* Howard Hawks.

Broken Arrow (1996)   John Travolta, Christian Slater, Samantha Mathis. *Dir.* John Woo.

Browning Version, The (1951)   Michael Redgrave, Jean Kent, Nigel Patrick, Wilfrid Hyde-White, Bill Travers. Based on Terence Rattigan's one-act play. *Dir.* Anthony Asquith.

Browning Version, The (1994)   Albert Finney, Greta Scacchi, Matthew Modine, Julian Sands, Michael Gambon. Ronald Howard's adaptation of Terence Rattigan play. *Dir.* Mike Figgis.

Brubaker (1980)   Robert Redford, Yaphet Kotto, Jane Alexander, Morgan Freeman, Murray Hamilton. Setting: Wakefield Prison Farm. *Dir.* Stuart Rosenberg.

Bugsy Malone (1976)   Scott Baio, Jodie Foster, Florrie Dugger. All the parts are played by children and the guns fire ice cream. *Dir.* Alan Parker.

Bullitt (1968)   Steve McQueen, Jacqueline Bisset, Robert Vaughn, Robert Duvall. Based on the novel *Mute Witness* by Robert L Pike. *Dir.* Peter Yates.

Burbs, The (1989)   Tom Hanks, Bruce Dern, Carrie Fisher, Corey Feldman. *Dir.* Joe Dante.

Buster (1988)   Phil Collins, Julie Walters (June Edwards), Larry Lamb, Stephanie Lawrence, Martin Jarvis. *Dir.* David Green.

Butch Cassidy and the Sundance Kid (1969)   Paul Newman, Robert Redford, Katharine Ross. 'Raindrops Keep Falling on My Head' won Oscar for Best Song. *Dir.* George Roy Hill.

Butterfield 8 (1960)   Elizabeth Taylor, Laurence Harvey, Eddie Fisher. Taylor won Best Actress Oscar for her role as a society call girl. The title *Butterfield 8* was her telephone number. *Dir.* Daniel Mann.

Cabaret (1972)   Liza Minnelli, Joel Grey, Michael York. Based on the novel *Goodbye to Berlin* by Christopher Isherwood and John Van Druten's play *I Am a Camera*. *Dir.* Bob Fosse.

Cabin in the Sky (1943)   Eddie 'Rochester' Anderson (Little Joe), Lena Horne (Georgia Brown), Ethel Waters (Petunia), Louis Armstrong. All black cast. *Dir.* Vincente Minnelli.

Cable Guy, The (1996)   Jim Carrey, Matthew Broderick, George Segal. *Dir.* Ben Stiller.

Cactus Jack (1979)   Kirk Douglas, Arnold Schwarzenegger, Ann-Margret. US title: *The Villain*. *Dir.* Hal Needham.

Caesar and Cleopatra (1945)   Claude Rains, Vivien Leigh, Stewart Granger, Flora Robson. Britain's most expensive film to this date was based on George Bernard Shaw's comedy. *Dir.* Gabriel Pascal.

Caine Mutiny, The (1954)   Humphrey Bogart (Capt Queeg), José Ferrer (Lt Barney Greenwald), Van Johnson (Lt Steve Maryk), Fred MacMurray (Lt Tom Keefer), Lee Marvin (Meatball), Claude Akins (Horrible). Based on Herman Wouk's novel. *Dir.* Edward Dmytryk.

Calamity Jane (1953)   Doris Day, Howard Keel. Memorable for its opening rendition of 'The Deadwood Stage' and the Oscar-winning song 'Secret Love'. *Dir.* David Butler.

California Suite (1978)   Michael Caine, Maggie Smith, Walter Matthau, Alan Alda, Jane Fonda, Bill Cosby, Richard Pryor. Misadventures of 4 groups of guests at the Beverly Hills Hotel. *Dir.* Herbert Ross.

Caligula (1979)   Malcolm McDowell, John Gielgud, Peter O'Toole, Helen Mirren. *Dir.* Tinto Brass.

Callan (1974)   Edward Woodward, Eric Porter, Carl Mohner, Catherine Schell, Peter Egan, Russell Hunter. Aka: *The Neutralizer. Dir.* Don Sharp.

Camille (1936)   Greta Garbo (Marguerite Gautier), Robert Taylor (Armand Duval), Lionel Barrymore, Henry Daniell. Based on Alexandre Dumas' novel. *Dir.* George Cukor.

Candyman (1992)   Virginia Madsen, Tony Todd, Xander Berkeley, Vanessa Williams. Story of a mythical hook-handed serial killer which had an unsuccessful 1995 sequel *Candyman: Farewell to the Flesh. Dir.* Bernard Rose.

Cape Fear (1991)   Robert De Niro (Max Cady), Nick Nolte (Sam Bowden), Jessica Lange (Leigh Bowden), Robert Mitchum (Lt Elgart), Gregory Peck (Lee Heller). Notable for cameo roles of Mitchum, Peck and Martin Balsam, who were all in original 1962 film. *Dir.* Martin Scorsese.

Captain America (1944)   Dick Purcell, Lionel Atwill, Lorna Gray. District Attorney in guise of Capt America battles The Scarab (in guise of a museum curator). *Dir.* John English.

Captain America (1989)   Matt Salinger, Ronny Cox, Ned Beatty, Bill Mumy. Captain America is freed from his deep-ice captivity to battle arch-enemy The Red Skull. *Dir.* Albert Pyun.

Captain Corelli's Mandolin (2001)   Nicholas Cage (Corelli), Penelope Cruz, John Hurt, Christian Bale, David Morrissey. *Dir.* John Madden.

Captains Courageous (1937)   Spencer Tracy, Lionel Barrymore, Freddie Bartholomew, Mickey Rooney. Spoiled rich boy falls off a cruise liner and lives for a while among fisherfolk. *Dir.* Victor Fleming.

Caravaggio (1986)   Nigel Terry, Sean Bean, Tilda Swinton, Robbie Coltrane. *Dir.* Derek Jarman.

Caretaker, The (1964)   Alan Bates, Robert Shaw, Donald Pleasence. Based on Pinter's play about 2 men who invite a tramp to share their attic. US title: *The Guest. Dir.* Clive Donner.

Carnal Knowledge (1971)   Jack Nicholson, Art Garfunkel, Candice Bergen, Ann-Margret, Rita Moreno. *Dir.* Mike Nichols.

Carousel (1956)   Gordon Macrae, Shirley Jones, Cameron Mitchell. *Dir.* Henry King.

Carpetbaggers, The (1964)   George Peppard, Alan Ladd, Carroll Baker, Martin Balsam, Elizabeth Ashley, Lew Ayres, Archie Moore, Leif Erickson. *Dir.* Edward Dmytryk.

Carrie (1952)   Laurence Olivier, Jennifer Jones, Eddie Albert. Based on Theodore Dreiser's novel *Sister Carrie. Dir.* William Wyler.

Carrie (1976)   Sissy Spacek, Piper Laurie, Amy Irving, John Travolta. Based on the Stephen King novel. *Dir.* Brian De Palma.

Carrington (1995)   Emma Thompson (Carrington), Jonathan Pryce (Strachey), Janet McTeer (Vanessa Bell). Based on Lytton Strachey's book. *Dir.* Christopher Hampton.

Carry On Columbus (1992)   Jim Dale (Chris Columbus), Bernard Cribbins (Mort), Maureen Lipman (Countess Esmerelda), Alexei Sayle, Julian Clary, Rik Mayall. Last of the series of Carry Ons. *Dir.* Gerald Thomas.

Carry On Sergeant (1958)   Bob Monkhouse, William Hartnell, Kenneth Williams, Charles Hawtrey, Shirley Eaton, Kenneth Connor. First of the series of 30 *Carry Ons. Dir.* Gerald Thomas.

Carve Her Name With Pride (1958)   Virginia McKenna (Violette Szabo), Paul Scofield, Jack Warner, Sydney Tafler. Based on RJ Minney's book about young British WW2 spy shot by a German firing squad. *Dir.* Lewis Gilbert.

Casablanca (1942)   Humphrey Bogart (Rick Blaine), Ingrid Bergman (Ilse Lund), Paul Henreid (Victor Laszlo), Claude Rains (Captain Louis Renault), Sydney Greenstreet (Ferrari), Peter Lorre (Ugarte), Conrad Veidt (Major Strasser), Dooley Wilson (Sam). Closing line, 'Louis, I think this is the beginning of a beautiful friendship.' Ronald Reagan and Ann Sheridan were originally cast as the leads. *Dir.* Michael Curtiz.

Casanova (1976)   Donald Sutherland, Tina Aumont, Cicely Browne. Aka *Fellini's Casanova. Dir.* Federico Fellini.

Casino (1995)   Sharon Stone, Robert De Niro, Joe Pesci, James Woods. *Dir.* Martin Scorsese.

Casino Royale (1967)   David Niven, Deborah Kerr, Orson Welles, Peter Sellers, Ursula Andress, Woody Allen, William Holden, Charles Boyer, Jean-Paul Belmondo, Peter O'Toole, John Huston, George Raft. Sir James Bond is called out of retirement to tackle the power of 'SMERSH'. Joe McGrath was originally the sole director but was fired after Sellers walked out and Huston, Ken Hughes, Robert Parrish, Val Guest and Richard Talmadge finished the film. This was the first James Bond book but clearly not the first film. *Dir.* John Huston & others.

Cassandra Crossing, The (1976)   Sophia Loren, Richard Harris, Ava Gardner, Burt Lancaster, Martin Sheen, OJ Simpson. *Dir.* George Pan Cosmatos.

Cast a Dark Shadow (1955)   Dirk Bogarde, Margaret Lockwood. Wife-murderer marries an ex-barmaid and tries again. *Dir.* Lewis Gilbert.

Cast a Giant Shadow (1966)   Kirk Douglas, Angie Dickinson, Chaim Topol, John Wayne, Frank Sinatra, Yul Brynner, Gordon Jackson, Jeremy Kemp, Michael Hordern. Biopic of Colonel David Marcus's fight against the Arabs in the Israel of 1947. *Dir.* Melville Shavelson.

Castaway (1987)   Oliver Reed (Gerald Kingsland), Amanda Donohue, Georgina Hale, John Sessions. Based on Lucy Irvine's autobiographical book. *Dir.* Nicolas Roeg.

Casualties of War (1989)   Michael J Fox (Eriksson), Sean Penn (Sgt Meserve). Story of the gang rape of a Vietnamese girl. *Dir.* Brian De Palma.

Cat and the Canary, The (1939)   Bob Hope (Wally Campbell), Paulette Goddard (Joyce Norman), Gale Sondergaard (Miss Lu). *Dir.* Elliott Nugent.

Cat Ballou (1965)   Jane Fonda, Lee Marvin, Nat King Cole, Stubby Kaye. Oscar-winning performances by Lee Marvin as twin brothers. *Dir.* Elliot Silverstein.

Cat on a Hot Tin Roof (1958)   Paul Newman (Brick), Burl Ives (Big Daddy), Elizabeth Taylor (Maggie). Based on the play by Tennessee Williams. *Dir.* Richard Brooks.

Cat People (1942)   Simone Simon, Tom Conway, Kent Smith. Yugoslavian girl believes she can turn into a panther and deaths follow, although the monster is never seen. *Dir.* Jacques Tourneur.

Cat People (1982)   Nastassja Kinski, Malcolm McDowell. Kinky version of the 1942 classic. *Dir.* Paul Schrader.

Catch My Soul (1973)   Richie Havens, Lance LeGault, Season Hubley, Tony Joe White. Rock and country musical version of *Othello*. *Dir.* Patrick McGoohan.

Catch 22 (1970)   Alan Arkin (Yossarian), Martin Balsam, Richard Benjamin, Art Garfunkel, Bob Newhart, Orson Welles, Martin Sheen, Jon Voight, Anthony Perkins. Based on Joseph Heller's novel. *Dir.* Mike Nichols.

Catholic Boys (1985)   Donald Sutherland (Brother Thadeus), John Heard (Brother Timothy). Originally called *Heaven Help Us*. *Dir.* Michael Dinner.

Cats & Dogs (2001)   Jeff Goldblum (Professor Brody), Elizabeth Perkins (Mrs Brody), Alexander Pollock (Scott Brody), Miriam Margolyes (Sophie). Story of a Persian cat's attempt to conquer the world, mixing actors and animation. Voices of Tobey Maguire (Lou), Alec Baldwin (Butch), Susan Sarandon (Ivy), Charlton Heston (The Mastiff), Sean Hayes (Mr Tinkles), Joe Pantoliano (Peek), Jon Lovitz (Calico). *Dir.* Lawrence Guterman.

Celebrity (1998)   Kenneth Branagh, Hank Azaria, Judy Davis, Leonardo DiCaprio, Melanie Griffith, Winona Ryder. *Dir.* Woody Allen.

Celia (1989)   Rebecca Smart (Celia), Nicholas Eadie (Ray). *Dir.* Ann Turner.

Cemetery Man (1994)   Rupert Everett, François Hadji-Lazaro, Anna Falci. *Dir.* Michele Soavi.

Central Station (1998)   Fernanda Montenegro, Marilia Pera, Vinicius de Oliveira, Soia Lira, Othon Bastos. *Dir.* Walter Salles.

Chain Reaction (1996). Keanu Reeves, Morgan Freeman, Rachel Weisz. *Dir.* Andrew Davis.

Chamber, The (1996)   Gene Hackman (Sam Cayhall), Chris O'Donnell (Adam Hall), Faye Dunaway. *Dir.* James Foley.

Champ, The (1931)   Wallace Beery, Jackie Cooper. Frances Marion won Oscar for Best Original Story. *Dir.* King Vidor.

Champ, The (1979)   Jon Voight, Faye Dunaway, Ricky Schroeder. Remake of the 1931 classic. *Dir.* Franco Zeffirelli.

Champions (1983)   John Hurt (Bob Champion), Edward Woodward (Josh Gifford). Story of a jockey's fight against cancer and his subsequent Grand National success in 1981. *Dir.* John Irvin.

Chance of a Lifetime (1950)   Bernard Miles, Kenneth More, Hattie Jacques. *Dir.* Bernard Miles.

Changing Lanes (2002)   Ben Affleck, Samuel L Jackson, Kim Staunton, Toni Collette, Sydney Pollack, William Hurt, Amanda Peet. *Dir.* Roger Michell.

Chaplin (1992)   Robert Downey Jnr, Dan Aykroyd (Mack Sennett), Geraldine Chaplin (Hannah Chaplin), Kevin Dunn (J Edgar Hoover), Kevin Kline (Douglas Fairbanks), John Thaw (Fred Karno), Marisa Tomei (Mabel Normand). *Dir.* Richard Attenborough.

Chariots of Fire (1981)   Ben Cross (Harold Abrahams), Ian Charleson (Eric Liddell), Nigel Havers. Oscars include: Best Film, Costume Design, Music and Script (Colin Welland). *Dir.* Hugh Hudson.

Charley Varrick (1973)   Walter Matthau, Joe Don Baker. Story of a bank robber who discovers he has stolen mafia money. *Dir.* Don Siegel.

Charley's Aunt (1941)   Jack Benny, Kay Francis, Anne Baxter, Laird Cregar. Based on play by Brandon Thomas. *Dir.* Archie Mayo.

Charlie Chan (Series)   Warner Oland (1931–37), Sidney Toler (1938–47), Roland Winters (1947–49). Based on Earl Derr Biggers's character. *Dir.* Various.

Charlotte Gray (2001)   Cate Blanchett (Charlotte), Billy Crudup, Michael Gambon, James Fleet, Jack Shepherd. Based on a Sebastian Faulks bestseller about a young Scotswoman who becomes a spy in France during the Second World War. *Dir.* Gillian Armstrong.

Che! (1969)   Omar Sharif (Che Guevara), Jack Palance (Castro). *Dir.* Richard Fleischer.

Cheech and Chong's Next Movie (1980)   Cheech Marin, Thomas Chong, Evelyn Guerrero. GB title: *High Encounters of the Ultimate Kind*. *Dir.* Thomas Chong.

Cheyenne Autumn (1964)   Richard Widmark, Carroll Baker, Karl Malden, Dolores del Rio, Sal Mineo, Edward G Robinson, James Stewart (Wyatt Earp). *Dir.* John Ford.

Chicago (2002)   Richard Gere (Billy Flynn), Renée Zellweger (Roxie Hart), Catherine Zeta-Jones (Velma Kelley), Queen Latifah, Taye Diggs. Adaptation of Bob Fosse's 1975 Broadway musical about two dreamers Velma Kelley and Roxie Hart. Velma is the Windy City's top nightclub star until the night she guns down her cheating husband, after which she becomes an even bigger celebrity, thanks to smooth lawyer Billy Flynn. Roxie also desperately wants fame, so decides to shoot her abusive lover dead. After Roxie replaces her, an outraged Velma plots Roxie's demise. *Dir.* Rob Marshall.

Chicago Joe and the Showgirl (1990)   Kiefer Sutherland (Ricky Allen), Emily Lloyd (Georgina Grayson), Patsy Kensit (Joyce Cook). *Dir.* Bernard Rose.

Children of a Lesser God (1986)   William Hurt (James), Marlee Matlin (Sarah), Piper Laurie (Mrs Norman). Deaf woman falls in love with her speech therapist. *Dir.* Randa Haines.

Child's Play (1988)   Catherine Hicks (Karen Barclay), Chris Sarandon (Mike Norris). Dying killer Brad Dourif's soul passes into a Chucky Doll. *Dir.* Tom Holland.

China Syndrome, The (1979)   Jane Fonda, Jack Lemmon, Michael Douglas. *Dir.* James Bridges.

Chinatown (1974)   Jack Nicholson, Faye Dunaway, John Huston, Roman Polanski, Diane Ladd. *Dir.* Roman Polanski.

Chitty Chitty Bang Bang (1968)   Dick Van Dyke, Sally Ann Howes (Truly Scrumptious), Lionel Jeffries, Benny Hill, Robert Helpmann, Gert Frobe, James Robertson Justice. Roald Dahl adapted the original Ian Fleming story. *Dir.* Ken Hughes.

Chocolat (2000)   Juliette Binoche (Vianne Rocher), Alfred Molina (Comte de Reynaud), Carrie-Anne Moss (Caroline Clairmont), Johnny Depp (Roux), Judi Dench (Armande Voizin), Lena Olin (Josephine Muscat). Based on Joanne Harris bestseller. *Dir.* Lasse Hallstrom.

Chorus Line, A (1985)   Michael Douglas (Zach), Alyson Reed (Cassie), Terrence Mann (Larry). *Dir.* Richard Attenborough.

Chorus of Disapproval (1989)   Anthony Hopkins (Dafydd Ap Llewellyn), Jeremy Irons (Guy Jones), Prunella Scales (Hannah), Jenny Seagrove (Fay Hubbard). *Dir.* Michael Winner.

Christmas Carol: The Movie (2001)   Simon Callow (Charles Dickens), voices of Kate Winslet (Belle), Nicolas Cage (Jacob Marley), Jane Horrocks (Ghost

of Christmas Past), Simon Callow (Scrooge),
Michael Gambon (Ghost of Christmas Present),
Rhys Ifans (Cratchit), Juliet Stevenson (Mrs
Cratchit/Mother Gimlet). Animated version – other
than Callow's Dickens. *Dir.* Jimmy T Murakami.
Christopher Columbus: The Discovery (1992)
Marlon Brando (Torquemada), Tom Selleck (King
Ferdinand), Georges Corraface (Columbus), Rachel
Ward (Queen Isabella), Catherine Zeta Jones
(Beatriz). *Dir.* John Glen.
Cincinnati Kid, The (1965)   Steve McQueen, Edward
G Robinson, Karl Malden, Ann-Margret, Tuesday
Weld. Based on Richard Jessup's novel concerning
battle for supremacy among stud poker experts.
Dir. Norman Jewison.
Citadel, The (1938)   Robert Donat, Rosalind Russell,
Ralph Richardson, Rex Harrison. Based on AJ
Cronin's novel, which also spawned the TV series *Dr
Finlay's Casebook*. *Dir.* King Vidor.
Citizen Kane (1941)   Orson Welles (Kane), Joseph
Cotten (Jedediah Leland), Agnes Moorehead (Kane's
mother). Based loosely on the newspaper magnate
William Randolph Hearst. Welles also co-wrote the
script with Herman J Mankiewicz. *Dir.* Orson Welles.
City Hall (1996)   Al Pacino, John Cusack, Bridget
Fonda, Danny Aiello. *Dir.* Harold Becker.
City Heat (1984)   Clint Eastwood (Lt Speer), Burt
Reynolds (Mike Murphy), Madeline Kahn (Caroline
Howley). Reynolds broke his jaw when a prop chair
turned out to be a real one!. *Dir.* Richard Benjamin.
City of Industry (1997)   Harvey Keitel, Stephen
Dorff, Timothy Hutton. *Dir.* John Irvin.
City Slickers (1991)   Billy Crystal (Mitch Robbins),
Daniel Stern (Phil Berquist), Jack Palance (Curly).
Oscar for Jack Palance as Best Supporting Actor.
Dir. Ron Underwood.
Class Act (1992)   Christopher Reid, Christopher
Martin, Karyn Parsons. Two students swap identities.
Dir. Randall Miller.
Class Action (1991)   Gene Hackman, Mary
Elizabeth Mastrantonio, Colin Friels. Father and
daughter, both lawyers, find themselves on opposing
sides in the courtroom. *Dir.* Michael Apted.
Cleopatra (1934)   Claudette Colbert, Henry Wilcoxon
(Antony), Warren William (Caesar). *Dir.* Cecil B de
Mille.
Cleopatra (1963)   Elizabeth Taylor, Richard Burton,
Rex Harrison. *Dir.* Joseph L Mankiewicz.
Clockers (1995)   Harvey Keitel, John Turturro, Delroy
Lindo, Mekhi Phifer, Pee Wee Love, Sticky Fingaz. A
clocker is a small-time crack dealer working on the
streets. *Dir.* Spike Lee.
Clockwise (1986)   John Cleese (Timpson), Alison
Steadman (Gwenda), Penelope Wilton (Pat Garden).
Dir. Christopher Morahan.
Clockwork Orange, A (1971)   Malcolm McDowell,
Adrienne Corri, Patrick Magee, Michael Bates,
Warren Clarke. Based on Anthony Burgess's novel.
Dir. Stanley Kubrick.
Close Encounters of the Third Kind (1977)   Richard
Dreyfuss, François Truffaut, Teri Garr. *Dir.* Steven
Spielberg.
Coal Miner's Daughter (1980)   Sissy Spacek (Loretta
Lynn), Tommy Lee Jones. *Dir.* Michael Apted.
Cocktail (1988)   Tom Cruise (Brian Flanagan), Bryan
Brown (Doug Coughlin), Elizabeth Shue (Jordan
Mooney). *Dir.* Roger Donaldson.
Cocoanuts, The (1929)   Four Marx Brothers,
Margaret Dumont. First of the Marx Brothers films.
Dir. Robert Florey and Joseph Santley.
Cocoon (1985)   Don Ameche (Art Selwyn), Steve
Guttenberg (Jack Bonner), Jessica Tandy (Alma

Finley), Tahnee Welch, (Kitty). There was a 1988
sequel *Cocoon: The Return*. *Dir.* Ron Howard.
Cold Comfort Farm (1995)   Kate Beckinsale (Flora
Poste), Joanna Lumley, Stephen Fry, Eileen Atkins,
Ian McKellen. *Dir.* John Schlesinger.
Color of Money, The (1986)   Paul Newman (Eddie
Felson), Tom Cruise (Vincent), Mary Elizabeth
Mastrantonio (Carmen). Sequel to *The Hustler*.
Dir. Martin Scorsese.
Color of Night (1994)   Bruce Willis, Jane March,
Ruben Blades, Lesley Ann Warren, Scott Bakula.
Psychiatrist takes over a group that includes the
person who murdered a colleague. *Dir.* Richard
Rush.
Color Purple, The (1985)   Whoopi Goldberg (Celie),
Danny Glover (Albert Johnson) Oprah Winfrey
(Sofia), Willard Pugh (Harpo). Based on the novel by
Alice Walker. *Dir.* Steven Spielberg.
Comfort and Joy (1984)   Bill Paterson (Alan),
Eleanor David (Maddy), CP Grogan (Charlotte). Ice
cream empires are called 'Mr McCool' and 'Mr
Bunny' and the music is by Mark Knopfler. *Dir.* Bill
Forsyth.
Coming Home (1978)   Jane Fonda, Jon Voight,
Bruce Dern. *Dir.* Hal Ashby.
Commitments, The (1991)   Robert Arkins (Jimmy
Rabbitte), Andrew Strong (Deco Cuffe), Michael
Aherne (Steve Clifford). Story of a Dublin soul band.
Dir. Alan Parker.
Con Air (1997)   Nicolas Cage, John Cusack, John
Malkovich. *Dir.* Simon West.
Conspiracy Theory (1997)   Mel Gibson (Jerry
Fletcher), Julia Roberts (Alice Sutton). *Dir.* Richard
Donner.
Contact (1997)   Jodie Foster (Ellie). Based on Carl
Sagan's book. *Dir.* Robert Zemeckis.
Cook, the Thief, His Wife and Her Lover, The (1989)
Richard Bohringer (Richard the Cook), Michael
Gambon (Albert the Thief), Helen Mirren (Georgina,
His Wife), Alan Howard (Michael, Her Lover).
Dir. Peter Greenaway.
Cool Hand Luke (1967)   Paul Newman (Lucas
Jackson), George Kennedy, Jo Van Fleet. Luke was
imprisoned for sawing off a parking meter. Famous
scene where Luke swallows 50 eggs in an hour.
Dir. Stuart Rosenberg.
Cotton Club, The (1984)   Richard Gere (Dixie
Dwyer), Gregory Hines (Sandman Williams), Bob
Hoskins (Owney Madden), Nicolas Cage (Vincent
Dwyer). *Dir.* Francis Ford Coppola.
Courage under Fire (1996)   Denzel Washington
(Colonel Serling), Meg Ryan (Captain Karen
Walden). *Dir.* Edward Zwick.
Courtneys of Curzon Street, The (1947)   Anna
Neagle, Michael Wilding, Michael Medwin.
Dir. Herbert Wilcox.
Cousins (1989)   Ted Danson (Larry Kozinski),
Isabella Rossellini (Maria Hardy), Sean Young (Tish
Kozinski), Lloyd Bridges (Uncle Vince). *Dir.* Joel
Schumacher.
Cowboy Way, The (1994)   Woody Harrelson, Kiefer
Sutherland, Ernie Hudson. *Dir.* Gregg Champion.
Craft, The (1996)   Robin Tunney, Fairuza Balk.
Dir. Andrew Fleming.
Crash (1996)   James Spader (James), Deborah
Unger (Catherine), Holly Hunter (Helen). *Dir.* David
Cronenberg.
Crimes and Misdemeanors (1989)   Caroline Aaron
(Barbara), Alan Alda (Lester), Woody Allen (Cliff
Stern), Claire Bloom (Miriam Rosenthal), Mia Farrow
(Halley Reed), Anjelica Huston (Dolores Paley).
Dir. Woody Allen.

Crimes of the Heart (1986) Diane Keaton (Lenny Magrath), Jessica Lange (Meg), Sissy Spacek (Babe). Three kooky sisters argue about which one of them is going to go completely mad, first. *Dir.* Bruce Beresford.

Critters (1986) Dee Wallace Stone, M Emmet Walsh, Billy Green Bush. Hair-ball creatures arrive from an asteroid and devastate Kansas. *Dir.* Stephen Herek.

Crocodile Dundee (1986) Paul Hogan (Mick Dundee), Linda Kozlowski (Sue Charlton), John Meillon (Wally Reilly). As so often the case with sequels, *Crocodile Dundee II* was not as big a hit. *Dir.* Peter Faiman.

Crocodile Dundee in Los Angeles (2001) Paul Hogan, Linda Kozlowski, Jere Burns, Jonathan Banks, Mike Tyson (as himself). Second sequel made 13 years after the previous one but similar plot. *Dir.* Simon Wincer.

Cromwell (1970) Richard Harris, Alec Guinness, Frank Finlay, Robert Morley. *Dir.* Ken Hughes.

Crossing Guard, The (1995) Jack Nicholson, David Morse, Anjelica Huston, Piper Laurie. Alcoholic jeweller plans to kill the man who killed his daughter in a drink driving incident. *Dir.* Sean Penn.

Crossroads (2002) Britney Spears (Lucy), Zoe Saldana (Kit), Justin Long, Dan Aykroyd, Anson Mount, Kim Cattrall, Taryn Manning (Mimi). Three girls go to Los Angeles following their graduation. *Dir.* Tamara Davis.

Crouching Tiger, Hidden Dragon (1999) Michelle Yeoh, Chang Chen, Zhang Ziyi, Chow Yun-Fat. *Dir.* Ang Lee.

Crow, The (1994) Brandon Lee, Ernie Hudson, Michael Wincott. Brandon Lee died in a shooting accident during filming. *Dir.* Alex Proyas.

Cruel Sea, The (1953) Jack Hawkins, Donald Sinden, Stanley Baker. Eric Ambler adapted the novel of Nicholas Monsarrat. *Dir.* Charles Frend.

Crumb (1994) Robert Crumb, Charles Crumb, Maxon Crumb, Dana Crumb, Beatrice Crumb, Aline Kominsky. Documentary about the creator of Fritz the Cat and Mr Natural. *Dir.* Terry Zwigoff.

Cry Freedom (1987) Kevin Kline (Donald Woods), Denzel Washington (Steve Biko). *Dir.* Richard Attenborough.

Cry in the Dark, A (1988) Meryl Streep (Lindy Chamberlain), Sam Neill (Michael). True story of a mother, convicted of killing her baby, who maintained a dingo had run off with it. *Dir.* Fred Schepisi.

Crying Freeman (1995) Mark Dacascos, Julie Condra (Emu O'Hara). *Dir.* Christophe Gans.

Crying Game, The (1992) Stephen Rea (Fergus), Miranda Richardson (Jude), Forest Whitaker (Jody). *Dir.* Neil Jordan.

Curse of the Pink Panther, The (1983) David Niven (Sir Charles Litton), Robert Wagner (George Litton), Herbert Lom (Dreyfus), Joanna Lumley (Chandra), Capucine (Lady Litton). David Niven's voice was dubbed by Rich Little. *Dir.* Blake Edwards.

Cutthroat Island (1995) Geena Davis (Morgan), Matthew Modine (William Shaw), Frank Langella. *Dir.* Renny Harlin.

Cyrano de Bergerac (1990) Gérard Depardieu, Anne Brochet, Vincent Perez. *Dir.* Jean-Paul Rappeneau.

Daddy Longlegs (1931) Janet Gaynor, Warner Baxter. Orphan girl grows up to fall in love with a mysterious benefactor. *Dir.* Alfred Santell.

Daddy Longlegs (1955) Fred Astaire, Leslie Caron, Fred Clark. Musical remake of the 1931 film. *Dir.* Jean Negulesco.

Daleks: Invasion Earth 2150 AD (1966) Peter Cushing, Bernard Cribbins. *Dir.* Gordon Flemyng.

Dam Busters, The (1954) Michael Redgrave (Barnes Wallis), Richard Todd (Guy Gibson). *Dir.* Michael Anderson.

Damien: Omen Two (1978) William Holden, Lee Grant, Jonathan Scott-Taylor, Sylvia Sidney. *Dir.* Don Taylor.

Dance with a Stranger (1985) Miranda Richardson (Ruth Ellis), Rupert Everett (David Blakely), Ian Holm, Stratford Johns. *Dir.* Mike Newell.

Dances with Wolves (1990) Kevin Costner (Lt John J Dunbar), Mary McDonnell (Stands With a Fist), Graham Greene (Kicking Bird). *Dir.* Kevin Costner.

Dangerous Ground (1997) Elizabeth Hurley, Ice Cube. *Dir.* Darrell James Roodt.

Dangerous Liaisons (1988) Glenn Close (Marquise de Merteuil), John Malkovich (Vicomte de Valmont), Michelle Pfeiffer (Madame de Tourvel), Keanu Reeves (Chevalier Danceny), Uma Thurman (Cecile de Volanges). *Dir.* Stephen Frears.

Danny the Champion of the World (1989) Jeremy Irons (William Smith), Samuel Irons (Danny), Robbie Coltrane (Victor Hazell). Based on a Roald Dahl book. *Dir.* Gavin Millar.

Dante's Peak (1997) Pierce Brosnan, Linda Hamilton. *Dir.* Roger Donaldson.

Darkman (1990) Liam Neeson (Peyton Westlake / Darkman). Scientist left for dead by thugs re-emerges as Darkman. *Dir.* Sam Raimi.

Darling (1965) Julie Christie, Dirk Bogarde, Laurence Harvey. *Dir.* John Schlesinger.

Dave (1993) Kevin Kline, Sigourney Weaver, Frank Langella, Ben Kingsley. US President suffers a stroke and a Baltimore businessman is hired to impersonate him. *Dir.* Ivan Reitman.

David Copperfield (1934) Freddie Bartholomew (young David), Frank Lawton (David as a man), WC Fields (Micawber). Charles Laughton was original choice for Micawber but resigned after 2 days. *Dir.* George Cukor.

Day at the Races, A (1937) First of the high-budget Marx Brothers films. *Dir.* Sam Wood.

Day of the Beast (1995) Alex Angulo, Armando de Razza, Santiago Segura. Priest attempts to track down the Anti-Christ who is to be born in Madrid. *Dir.* Alex de la Iglesia.

Day of the Jackal, The (1973) Edward Fox, Michael Lonsdale, Alan Badel, Eric Porter. *Dir.* Fred Zinnemann.

Day of the Triffids, The (1962) Howard Keel, Kieron Moore, Janette Scott, Nicole Maurey. *Dir.* Steve Sekely.

Daylight (1996) Sylvester Stallone, Amy Brenneman, Viggo Mortensen, Karen Young, Claire Bloom. Diverse group of people are trapped in Manhattan's Holland Tunnel. *Dir.* Rob Cohen.

Days of Thunder (1990) Tom Cruise (Cole Trickle), Robert Duvall (Harry Hogge), Nicole Kidman (Dr Claire Lewicki). *Dir.* Tony Scott.

Dead Again (1991) Kenneth Branagh (Roman Strauss / Mike), Andy Garcia (Gray Baker), Derek Jacobi (Franklyn Madson), Emma Thompson (Margaret Strauss / Grace). *Dir.* Kenneth Branagh.

Dead Calm (1989) Sam Neill (John Ingram), Nicole Kidman (Rae Ingram), Billy Zane (Hughie Warriner). *Dir.* Phillip Noyce.

Dead Man Walking (1995) Susan Sarandon (Sister Helen Prejean), Sean Penn (Matthew Poncelet). *Dir.* Tim Robbins.

Dead Men Don't Wear Plaid (1982) Steve Martin, Rachel Ward, Carl Reiner, Reni Santoni. Bogart,

Ladd, Bacall, Stanwyck also appear in film-clip editing. *Dir.* Carl Reiner.

Dead Poets Society (1989)   Robin Williams (John Keating), Robert Sean Leonard, Ethan Hawke, Josh Charles. Keating's motto: 'Carpe Diem (Seize the Day)'. *Dir.* Peter Weir.

Dead Pool, The (1988)   Clint Eastwood (Harry Callahan), Patricia Clarkson, Liam Neeson, Evan C Kim. Famous scene of a car chase involving a toy car. Jim Carrey has small part as a murder victim. *Dir.* Buddy van Horn.

Dead Ringers (1988)   Jeremy Irons (Beverly / Elliot Mantle), Geneviève Bujold (Claire Niveau). Concerns identical twins, gynaecologists. *Dir.* David Cronenberg.

Dealers (1989)   Paul McGann (Daniel Pasco), Rebecca DeMornay (Anna Schuman), Derrick O'Connor (Robby Barrell). TV series *Capital City* was a spin-off. *Dir.* Colin Bucksey.

Dear Diary (1994)   Jennifer Beals, Nanni Moretti, Alexandre Rockwell. *Dir.* Nanni Moretti.

Death in Venice (1971)   Dirk Bogarde, Bjorn Andresen, Silvana Mangano Gustav Mahler's music is memorable. *Dir.* Luchino Visconti.

Death of a Salesman (1985)   Dustin Hoffman (Willy Loman), Charles Durning (Charley), Kate Reid (Linda), Stephen Lang (Happy), John Malkovich. Screenplay: Arthur Miller. Film was made for cable TV. *Dir.* Volker Schlondorff.

Death on the Nile (1978)   Peter Ustinov, Bette Davis, Mia Farrow, David Niven, Maggie Smith. Agatha Christie novel with Hercule Poirot. *Dir.* John Guillermin.

Death Race 2000 (1975)   David Carradine, Simone Griffeth, Sylvester Stallone. *Dir.* Paul Bartel.

Death Wish (1974)   Charles Bronson, Hope Lange, Vincent Gardenia. Four follow-on films – 1981, 1985, 1987, 1993 – similar plots. *Dir.* Michael Winner.

Deathtrap (1982)   Michael Caine, Christopher Reeve, Dyan Cannon. From the play by Ira Levin. *Dir.* Sidney Lumet.

Deepstar Six (1989)   Taurean Blacque, Nancy Everhard, Greg Evigan. Underwater thriller. *Dir.* Sean Cunningham.

Deer Hunter, The (1978)   Robert De Niro, John Savage, Christopher Walken, Meryl Streep. Vietnam thriller that won 3 Oscars. *Dir.* Michael Cimino.

Defence of the Realm (1985)   Gabriel Byrne (Nick Mullen), Greta Scacchi (Nina Beckman), Denholm Elliott (Vernon Bayliss), Robbie Coltrane (Leo McAskey). *Dir.* David Drury.

Defiant Ones, The (1958)   Tony Curtis, Sidney Poitier, Theodore Bikel, Lon Chaney Jnr. Prison escape drama, with black and white prisoners chained together, that won 3 Oscars. *Dir.* Stanley Kramer.

Delinquents, The (1989)   Notable only for being Kylie Minogue's debut feature. *Dir.* Chris Thomson.

Deliverance (1972)   Burt Reynolds, Jon Voight, Ned Beatty. From James Dickey's novel. *Dir.* John Boorman.

Demolition Man (1993)   Sylvester Stallone (John Spartan), Wesley Snipes (Simon Phoenix), Lori Petty, Nigel Hawthorne, Melinda Dillon. Futuristic thriller with Stallone as former cop released from suspended animation. *Dir.* Marco Brambilla.

Dennis the Menace (1993)   Walter Matthau, Mason Gamble, Joan Plowright, Christopher Lloyd, Lea Thompson. Story of the 6-yr-old menace. *Dir.* Nick Castle.

Desert Fox, The (1951)   James Mason, Jessica Tandy, Cedric Hardwicke. Biography of Erwin Rommel. *Dir.* Henry Hathaway.

Desert Rats, The (1953)   James Mason (Rommel), Richard Burton, Robert Newton. *Dir.* Robert Wise.

Desperado (1995)   Antonio Banderas, Salma Hayek, Joaquin de Almeida, Cheech Marin, Quentin Tarantino. Man with guitar case full of weapons walks into a Mexican town and starts shooting. *Dir.* Robert Rodriguez.

Desperate Hours (1990)   Mickey Rourke (Michael Bosworth), Anthony Hopkins (Tim Cornell), Mimi Rogers (Nora). *Dir.* Michael Cimino.

Desperate Measures (1998)   Michael Keaton, Andy Garcia. Detective Frank Connor is forced to choose between his badge and his son. *Dir.* Barbet Schroeder.

Desperately Seeking Susan (1985)   Madonna, Aidan Quinn, Rosanna Arquette. Madonna's first starring role. *Dir.* Susan Seidelman.

Destiny Turns on the Radio (1995)   James LeGros, Dylan McDermott, Quentin Tarantino, James Belushi, Nancy Travis. Bank robber gets out of jail and travels to Las Vegas to reclaim his loot. *Dir.* Jack Baran.

Devil Rides Out, The (1968)   Christopher Lee, Charles Gray, Patrick Mower. From Dennis Wheatley's novel. *Dir.* Terence Fisher.

Devils, The (1970)   Vanessa Redgrave, Oliver Reed, Dudley Sutton, Gemma Jones. *Dir.* Ken Russell.

Devil's Own, The (1997)   Harrison Ford (Tom O'Meara), Brad Pitt (Frankie McGuire). *Dir.* Alan J Pakula.

Diabolique (1996)   Sharon Stone, Isabelle Adjani, Kathy Bates. Wife and mistress of unpleasant schoolmaster conspire to murder him. *Dir.* Jeremiah Chechnik.

Dial M for Murder (1954)   Ray Milland, Grace Kelly, Robert Cummings. Shot in 3D but never released in 3D form. *Dir.* Alfred Hitchcock.

Diamonds Are Forever (1971)   Sean Connery, Charles Gray (Blofeld), Jill St John (Tiffany Case), Lana Wood (Plenty O'Toole). Theme song sung by Shirley Bassey. *Dir.* Guy Hamilton.

Dick Tracy (1990)   Warren Beatty, Madonna (Breathless Mahoney), Dick Van Dyke, Al Pacino (Big Boy Caprice), Dustin Hoffman (Mumbles), Charlie Korsmo (Kid), Kathy Bates (Mrs Green), James Caan (Spaldini). Won 3 Oscars. *Dir.* Warren Beatty.

Die Another Day (2002)   Pierce Brosnan (James Bond), Halle Berry (Jinx), Rick Yune (Zao), Madonna (Verity), Judi Dench (M), John Cleese (Q), Rosamund Pike (Miranda Frost), Michael Madsen (Damian Falco), Toby Stephens (Gustav Graves), Samantha Bond (Moneypenny). Theme song sung by Madonna. *Dir.* Lee Tamahori.

Die Hard (1988)   Bruce Willis (John McClane), Bonnie Bedelia (Holly Gennaro McClane), Alan Rickman (Hans Gruber). 3 sequels followed. *Dir.* John McTiernan.

Diner (1982)   Steve Guttenberg (Eddie), Daniel Stern (Shrevie), Mickey Rourke (Boogie), Kevin Bacon (Fenwick), Ellen Barkin (Beth), Timothy Daly (Billy). Five men on verge of manhood hang out at Fells Point Diner. *Dir.* Barry Levinson.

Dirty Dancing (1987)   Patrick Swayze (Johnny Castle), Jennifer Grey (Baby Houseman). Variant on *Saturday Night Fever*. *Dir.* Emile Ardolino.

Dirty Dingus Magee (1970)   Frank Sinatra, George Kennedy. Western comedy. *Dir.* Burt Kennedy.

Dirty Dozen, The (1967)   Lee Marvin, Robert Ryan,

Charles Bronson, Telly Savalas, Ernest Borgnine, Jim Brown, John Cassavetes, George Kennedy, Richard Jaeckel, Trini Lopez, Ralph Meeker, Clint Walker, Donald Sutherland. *Dir.* Robert Aldrich.

Dirty Mary, Crazy Larry (1974)   Peter Fonda, Susan George, Roddy McDowall (uncredited). *Dir.* John Hough.

Dirty Rotten Scoundrels (1988)   Steve Martin (Freddie Benson), Michael Caine (Lawrence Jamieson). Remake of *Bedtime Story* (1964). *Dir.* Frank Oz.

Distinguished Gentleman, The (1992)   Eddie Murphy (Thomas Jefferson Johnson), Lane Smith (Dick Dodge), James Garner. *Dir.* Jonathan Lynn.

DOA (1950)   Edmond O'Brien, Pamela Britton, Neville Brand, Luther Adler. Title stands for 'Dead on Arrival' and concerns a professor, who has been poisoned by a slow-acting drug, in a race against time to track down his murderer. *Dir.* Rudolph Maté.

DOA (1988)   Dennis Quaid (Dexter Cornell), Meg Ryan (Sydney Fuller), Charlotte Rampling (Mrs Fitzwaring). Remake of the 1950 classic. *Dir.* Rocky Morton and Annabel Jankel.

Doc Hollywood (1991)   Michael J Fox (Dr Benjamin Stone), Julie Warner (Lou), Bridget Fonda (Nancy Lee), George Hamilton (Dr Halberstrom). Famous scene of Warner urinating to throw hunters off their prey's scent. *Dir.* Michael Caton-Jones.

Doctor and the Devils (1986)   Timothy Dalton (Dr Thomas Rock), Jonathan Pryce (Robert Fallon), Twiggy (Jenny Bailey), Beryl Reid, TP McKenna, Patrick Stewart. Screenplay by Dylan Thomas. *Dir.* Freddie Francis.

Dr Dolittle (1967)   Rex Harrison, Anthony Newley, Samantha Eggar, Richard Attenborough. Oscars for Best Song ('Talk to the Animals') and Special Effects. LB Abbott. *Dir.* Richard Fleischer.

Dr Dolittle (1998)   Eddie Murphy (Dr Dolittle), Ossie Davis, Oliver Platt, Peter Boyle. *Dir.* Betty Thomas.

Dr Dolittle 2 (2001)   Sequel to the 1998 film with similar cast. *Dir.* Steve Carr.

Doctor in the House (1954)   Dirk Bogarde, Kenneth More, Kay Kendall, Donald Sinden. First of many *Doctor* stories, followed by TV series. *Dir.* Ralph Thomas.

Doctor No (1962)   Sean Connery, Ursula Andress (Honeychile Rider), Joseph Wiseman (Dr No), Jack Lord. First of the James Bond stories to be filmed (James Bond theme by Monty Norman). *Dir.* Terence Young.

Dr Strangelove (1963)   Peter Sellers, George C Scott. Black comedy Peter Sellers plays 3 parts. *Dir.* Stanley Kubrick.

Dr Who and the Daleks (1965)   Peter Cushing, Roy Castle, Roberta Tovey, Jennie Linden. First *Dr Who* film; sequel in 1966. *Dir.* Gordon Flemyng.

Doctor Zhivago (1965)   Omar Sharif, Julie Christie, Rod Steiger, Alec Guinness, Rita Tushingham, Geraldine Chaplin, Tom Courtenay, Adrienne Corri. Oscars for Maurice Jarre (Music), Freddie Young (Photography), and Robert Bolt (Screenplay). *Dir.* David Lean.

Dog Day Afternoon (1975)   Al Pacino, John Cazale, Charles Durning, Chris Sarandon, Sully Boyar. *Dir.* Sidney Lumet.

Dog Soldiers (2002)   Sean Pertwee (Sgt Harry Wells), Kevin McKidd, Emma Cleasby. Story of an army patrol in the Highlands of Scotland besieged by werewolves. *Dir.* Neil Marshall.

Dolores Claiborne (1995)   Kathy Bates, Jennifer

Jason Leigh, Judy Parfitt, Christopher Plummer. Housekeeper acquitted of murder is then arrested for killing her boss. *Dir.* Taylor Hackford.

Donnie Brasco (1997)   Al Pacino (Ben 'Lefty' Ruggiero), Johnny Depp (Donnie Brasco / Joe Pistone), Michael Madsen (Sonny). *Dir.* Mike Newell.

Don't Look Now (1973)   Donald Sutherland, Julie Christie. Daphne du Maurier story, set in Venice. *Dir.* Nicolas Roeg.

Doors, The (1991)   Val Kilmer (Jim Morrison), Meg Ryan (Pamela Courson), Billy Idol (Cat). *Dir.* Oliver Stone.

Double Indemnity (1944)   Fred MacMurray, Barbara Stanwyck, Edward G Robinson, Tom Powers, Porter Hall, Jean Heather, Byron Barr. An insurance agent connives with the wife of a client to kill her husband and claim on the policy. Screenplay by Billy Wilder and Raymond Chandler based on the novel by James M Cain. *Dir.* Billy Wilder.

Down and Out in Beverly Hills (1986)   Nick Nolte (Jerry Baskin), Richard Dreyfuss (Davie Whiteman), Bette Midler (Barbara Whiteman), Little Richard (Orvis Goodnight). *Dir.* Paul Mazursky.

Downhill Racer (1969)   Robert Redford, Gene Hackman, Camilla Sparv. Plotless film about a skier. *Dir.* Michael Ritchie.

Dracula (1931)   Bela Lugosi, Helen Chandler, David Manners. Numerous follow-on films from this Bram Stoker novel. *Dir.* Tod Browning.

Dracula 2001 (2000)   Christopher Plummer (Van Helsing), Jonny Lee Miller, Justine Waddell, Gerard Butler (Dracula). US title: *Dracula 2000*. *Dir.* Patrick Lussier.

Dragnet (1987)   Dan Aykroyd (Joe Friday), Tom Hanks (Streebek), Christopher Plummer (Whirley), Harry Morgan (Bill Gannon). *Dir.* Tom Mankiewicz.

Dragon: The Bruce Lee Story (1993)   Jason Scott Lee, Robert Wagner, Michael Learned, Lauren Holly, Nancy Kwan. *Dir.* Rob Cohen.

Dragonheart (1996)   Dennis Quaid, David Thewlis, Pete Postlethwaite, voice of Sean Connery. *Dir.* Rob Cohen.

Dream Team, The (1989)   Michael Keaton (Billy Caulfield), Christopher Lloyd (Henry Sikorsky), Peter Boyle (Jack McDermott), Stephen Furst (Albert Ianuzzi). Four mental patients have to fend for themselves in Manhattan. *Dir.* Howard Zieff.

Dreamscape (1984)   Dennis Quaid (Alex), Max Von Sydow (Paul), Christopher Plummer (Bob), Kate Capshaw (Jane), George Wendt (Charlie). *Dir.* Joseph Ruben.

Dressed to Kill (1980)   Michael Caine, Angie Dickinson, Nancy Allen. Michael Caine plays a transvestite killer. *Dir.* Brian De Palma.

Dresser, The (1983)   Albert Finney (Sir), Tom Courtenay (Norman), Edward Fox (Oxenby). *Dir.* Peter Yates.

Driven (2001)   Sylvester Stallone (Joe Tanto), Burt Reynolds (Carl Henry), Kip Pardue (Jimmy Bly), Gina Gershon (Cathy Moreno), Stacy Edwards (Lucretia Clans). *Dir.* Renny Harlin.

Driving Miss Daisy (1989)   Jessica Tandy (Daisy Werthan), Morgan Freeman (Hoke Colburn), Dan Aykroyd (Boolie). Won 4 Oscars. *Dir.* Bruce Beresford.

Drugstore Cowboy (1989)   Matt Dillon (Bob Hughes), Kelly Lynch (Dianne Hughes), Heather Graham (Nadine), William S Burroughs (Tom the Priest). *Dir.* Gus Van Sant.

Dry White Season, A (1989)   Donald Sutherland

(Ben Du Toit), Janet Suzman (Susan), Susan Sarandon (Melanie Bruwer), Marlon Brando (Ian McKenzie). Set in apartheid South Africa. *Dir.* Euzhan Palcy.

Duck Soup (1933) The Marx Brothers, Margaret Dumont. According to *Time Out* the best Marx Bros film. *Dir.* Leo McCarey.

Duet for One (1986) Julie Andrews (Stephanie Anderson), Alan Bates (David Cornwallis), Max Von Sydow (Dr Louis Feldman), Liam Neeson (Totter). Famous violinist develops multiple sclerosis. *Dir.* Andrei Konchalovsky.

Duke Wore Jeans, The (1958) Tommy Steele, June Laverick, Michael Medwin. *Dir.* Gerald Thomas.

Dune (1984) Kyle MacLachlan (Paul Atreides), Francesca Annis (Lady Jessica), Sting (Feyd Rautha), Kenneth McMillan (Baron Harkonnen). Based on Frank Herbert's epic SF novel. *Dir.* David Lynch.

Dunkirk (1958) John Mills, Richard Attenborough, Bernard Lee. Directed by Barry Norman's father. Factual story. *Dir.* Leslie Norman.

Eagle Has Landed, The (1976) Michael Caine, Donald Sutherland, Jenny Agutter, Robert Duvall, Donald Pleasence (Himmler). Involves a Nazi plot to kill Churchill. *Dir.* John Sturges.

Earth Girls Are Easy (1988) Geena Davis (Valerie Dale), Jeff Goldblum (Mac), Jim Carrey (Wiploc), Julie Brown (Candy Pink). *Dir.* Julien Temple.

Earthquake (1974) Charlton Heston, Ava Gardner, Lorne Greene, George Kennedy. First film to use 'Sensurround'. Big box-office hit. *Dir.* Mark Robson.

East of Sudan (1964) Anthony Quayle, Sylvia Syms, Jenny Agutter. *Dir.* Nathan Juran.

Easter Parade (1948) Fred Astaire, Judy Garland, Ann Miller. Music by Irving Berlin. *Dir.* Charles Walters.

Easy Street (1917) Charles Chaplin, Edna Purviance, Albert Austin. Tramp is reformed by missionary and becomes a policeman. *Dir.* Charles Chaplin.

Eddie (1996) Whoopi Goldberg (Eddie), Frank Langella (Wild Bill Burgess), Dennis Farina (John Bailey). *Dir.* Steve Rash.

Educating Rita (1983) Michael Caine (Dr Frank Bryant), Julie Walters (Rita), Maureen Lipman (Trish), Michael Williams (Brian). From the play by Willie Russell; shot in Ireland for tax reasons. *Dir.* Lewis Gilbert.

Edward Scissorhands (1990) Johnny Depp, Winona Ryder (Kim Boggs), Dianne Wiest (Peg), Alan Arkin (Bill), Vincent Price (Inventor). *Dir.* Tim Burton.

Eiger Sanction, The (1975) Clint Eastwood, George Kennedy, Vonetta McGee. Art teacher returns to CIA post as an exterminator. *Dir.* Clint Eastwood.

8 Mile (2002) Eminem, Kim Basinger, Brittany Murphy, Mekhi Phifer. *Dir.* Curtis Hanson.

Eight and a Half (1963) Marcello Mastroianni, Claudia Cardinale, Anouk Aimée. Fellini self portrait. Best Foreign Film Oscar. (The 8 1/2 refers to the number of films Fellini had then made.) *Dir.* Federico Fellini.

18 Again! (1988) George Burns (Jack Watson), Charlie Schlatter (David Watson), Tony Roberts (Arnold). *Dir.* Paul Flaherty.

84 Charing Cross Road (1987) Anne Bancroft (Helene), Anthony Hopkins (Frank Doel), Judi Dench (Nora Doel). Based on a true story of the late Helene Hanff. *Dir.* David Jones.

Elephant Boy (1937) Sabu, Wilfrid Hyde-White. Based on a Kipling novel, made a star of Sabu. *Dir.* Robert Flaherty.

Elephant Man, The (1980) Anthony Hopkins, John Hurt (John Merrick), Anne Bancroft, John Gielgud. *Dir.* David Lynch.

Elmer Gantry (1960) Burt Lancaster, Jean Simmons, Arthur Kennedy, Shirley Jones. Oscars for Lancaster, Jones and Brooks (writer). *Dir.* Richard Brooks.

Emma (1996) Gwyneth Paltrow, Toni Collette, Ewan McGregor, Greta Scacchi, Sophie Thompson, Phyllida Law. Rachel Portman won Oscar for Music. *Dir.* Douglas McGrath.

Emmanuelle (1974) Sylvia Kristel, Marika Green, Daniel Sarky. Big soft-porn cinema hit, spawned 6 sequels. *Dir.* Just Jaeckin.

Empire of the Sun (1987) Christian Bale (Jim), John Malkovich (Basie), Miranda Richardson (Mrs Victor), Screenplay by Tom Stoppard, from JG Ballard's autobiographical novel. *Dir.* Steven Spielberg.

Empire Strikes Back, The (1980) Mark Hamill, Harrison Ford, Carrie Fisher. Second of the *Star Wars* films. *Dir.* Irvin Kershner.

Enchanted April (1991) Miranda Richardson (Rose Arbuthnot), Joan Plowright (Mrs Fisher), Alfred Molina (Mellersh Wilkins), Josie Lawrence (Lottie Wilkins). A quartet of Edwardian ladies go on holiday in an Italian villa. *Dir.* Mike Newell.

Endless Summer, The (1966) Study of surfing round the world. Documentary which has become a cult among surfers. *Dir.* Bruce Brown.

Enemy at the Gates (2001) Joseph Fiennes (Danilov), Jude Law (Vassili Zaitsev), Rachel Weisz, Bob Hoskins, Ed Harris. Setting of the Siege of Stalingrad. *Dir.* Jean-Jacques Annaud.

Enforcer, The (1976) Clint Eastwood, Tyne Daly, Bradford Dillman. Third of the *Dirty Harry* films. *Dir.* James Fargo.

English Patient (1996) Ralph Fiennes (Count Almasy), Kristin Scott-Thomas, Juliette Binoche, Willem Dafoe, Colin Firth. Dying Hungarian count recalls his doomed affair with the English wife of a colleague. Based on Michael Ondaatje's book. Won 9 Academy Awards. *Dir.* Anthony Minghella.

Entertainer, The (1960) Laurence Olivier, Joan Plowright, Alan Bates, Albert Finney. *Dir.* Tony Richardson.

Equinox (1992) Matthew Modine, Lara Flynn Boyle, Marisa Tomei, Fred Ward, Lori Singer. Timid garage mechanic discovers he has a killer brother. *Dir.* Alan Rudolph.

Eraser (1996) Arnold Schwarzenegger, James Caan, James Coburn, Vanessa Williams. Agent for the Federal Witness Protection Program discovers he can trust no one. *Dir.* Charles Russell.

Erik the Viking (1989) Tim Robbins (Erik), Mickey Rooney (Erik's grandfather), Eartha Kitt (Freya), Terry Jones (King Arnulf), John Cleese. *Dir.* Terry Jones.

Erin Brockovich (1999) Julia Roberts, Aaron Eckhart, Albert Finney, Marg Helgenberger, Cherry Jones, Peter Coyote, Veanne Cox. *Dir.* Steven Soderbergh. (The film was made in late 1999, too late for the 2000 Oscars.) True story of a twice-divorced single parent lawyer who took on the might of the Pacific Gas and Electric, accusing them of contaminating a town's water supply.

Escape from Alcatraz (1979) Clint Eastwood, Patrick McGoohan, Jack Thibeau. *Dir.* Don Siegel.

Escape from LA (1996)   Kurt Russell (Snake Plissken), Steve Buscemi. Set in year 2013. *Dir*. John Carpenter.

ET – The Extra Terrestrial (1982)   Dee Wallace (Mary), Henry Thomas (Elliott), Drew Barrymore (Gertie). ET was 3 million light years from home. *Dir*. Steven Spielberg.

Ethan Frome (1993)   Liam Neeson, Patricia Arquette, Joan Allen. Massachusetts community is setting for story of minister and his crippled driver. *Dir*. John Madden.

Eureka (1983)   Gene Hackman, Theresa Russell, Rutger Hauer, Jane Lapotaire, Mickey Rourke, Joe Pesci. Gold prospector strikes it rich, but at a price. *Dir*. Nicolas Roeg.

Every Which Way But Loose (1978)   Clint Eastwood, Sondra Locke, Ruth Gordon. The 1980 sequel *Any Which Way You Can* is the same story. *Dir*. James Fargo.

Everyone Says I Love You (1996)   Woody Allen, Julia Roberts, Drew Barrymore, Alan Alda, Goldie Hawn. *Dir*. Woody Allen.

Evil That Men Do, The (1984)   Charles Bronson (Holland), Theresa Saldana, José Ferrer. *Dir*. J Lee Thompson.

Evil under the Sun (1982)   Peter Ustinov, James Mason, Diana Rigg, Maggie Smith, Roddy McDowall. Agatha Christie novel starring Hercule Poirot. *Dir*. Guy Hamilton.

Evita (1996)   Madonna, Antonio Banderas, Jonathan Pryce, Jimmy Nail. Best Song Oscar: 'You Must Love Me' (Andrew Lloyd-Webber & Tim Rice). *Dir*. Alan Parker.

Evolution (2001)   David Duchovny, Julianne Moore, Orlando Jones, Seann William Scott, Ted Levine. *Dir*. Ivan Reitman.

Executive Suite (1954)   Fredric March, William Holden, June Allyson, Barbara Stanwyck, Walter Pidgeon, Shelley Winters. Boardroom battle. *Dir*. Robert Wise.

Exorcist, The (1973)   Ellen Burstyn, Max Von Sydow, Linda Blair, Lee J Cobb. *Dir*. William Friedkin.

Expresso Bongo (1959)   Cliff Richard, Laurence Harvey, Sylvia Syms, Gilbert Harding. *Dir*. Val Guest.

Eyes Wide Shut (1999)   Tom Cruise (Dr Bill Hayard), Nicole Kidman, Madison Eginton, Marie Richardson. *Dir*. Stanley Kubrick.

Fabulous Baker Boys, The (1989)   Jeff Bridges (Jack Baker), Beau Bridges (Frank), Michelle Pfeiffer (Susie Diamond). Pianist brothers ginger up their act by taking on a singer. *Dir*. Steve Kloves.

Face (1997)   Robert Carlyle, Ray Winstone, Damon Albarn. Five criminals undertake a robbery, one of them is a traitor. *Dir*. Antonia Bird.

Face Off (1997)   John Travolta, Nicolas Cage. *Dir*. John Woo.

Faithful (1996)   Cher, Chazz Palminteri, Ryan O'Neal, Paul Mazursky, Amber Smith. Hitman chats to his victim whilst waiting for the signal to kill. *Dir*. Paul Mazursky.

Falling Down (1993)   Michael Douglas (D-Fens), Robert Duvall (Prendergast), Barbara Hershey (Beth), Tuesday Weld (Mrs Prendergast). *Dir*. Joel Schumacher.

Fan, The (1996)   Robert De Niro (Gil Renard), Wesley Snipes (Bobby Rayburn), Ellen Barkin. Baseball fan kidnaps the son of a star player. *Dir*. Tony Scott.

Fantasia (1940)   Cartoon characters to music of Bach, Tchaikovsky, Dukas, Stravinsky, Beethoven, Ponchielli, Schubert and Mussorgsky. *Dir*. Ben Sharpsteen.

Fantastic Voyage (1966)   Stephen Boyd, Raquel Welch, Edmond O'Brien, Donald Pleasence, Arthur O'Connell, Arthur Kennedy. *Dir*. Richard Fleizcher.

Far from the Madding Crowd (1967)   Julie Christie, Peter Finch, Alan Bates, Terence Stamp (Sgt Troy). Set in Victorian Wessex. *Dir*. John Schlesinger.

Farewell My Lovely (1944)   Dick Powell, Claire Trevor, Anne Shirley, Mike Mazurki, Otto Kruger. Aka: *Murder My Sweet*. *Dir*. Edward Dmytryk.

Farewell My Lovely (1975)   Robert Mitchum, Charlotte Rampling, John Ireland, Sylvia Miles. Remake of the Raymond Chandler classic. *Dir*. Dick Richards.

Fargo (1996)   Frances McDormand, William H Macy, Steve Buscemi, Harve Presnell, Peter Stormare. Car salesman with money troubles hires criminals to kidnap his wife for ransom. Nothing goes to plan. *Dir*. Joel Coen.

Fast and the Furious, The (2001)   Paul Walker, Vin Diesel, Michelle Rodriguez, Rick Yune, Jordana Brewster. *Dir*. Rob Cohen.

Fatal Attraction (1987)   Michael Douglas (Dan Gallagher), Glenn Close (Alex Forrest), Anne Archer (Beth Gallagher), Fred Gwynne (Arthur). *Dir*. Adrian Lyne.

Father of the Bride (1950)   Spencer Tracy, Elizabeth Taylor, Leo G Carroll. *Dir*. Vincente Minnelli.

Father of the Bride (1991)   Steve Martin (George Banks), Diane Keaton (Nina Banks), Kimberly Williams (Annie Banks). Remake of the Spencer Tracy classic. *Dir*. Charles Shyer.

Father's Day (1997)   Robin Williams (Dale), Billy Crystal (Jack), Nastassja Kinski (Colette), Charlie Hofheimer (Scott), Mel Gibson. *Dir*. Ivan Reitman.

Fear (1996)   Reese Witherspoon, Mark Wahlberg. *Dir*. James Foley.

Ferris Bueller's Day Off (1986)   Matthew Broderick (Ferris Bueller), Alan Ruck (Cameron Frye), Mia Sara (Sloane Peterson). *Dir*. John Hughes.

Fever Pitch (1996)   Colin Firth, Ruth Gemmell, Neil Pearson. Obsession with Arsenal FC creates romantic problems for teacher. *Dir*. David Evans.

Few Good Men, A (1992)   Tom Cruise (Lt JG Kaffee), Jack Nicholson (Colonel Jessep), Demi Moore (Lt Cdr Galloway), Kevin Bacon (Capt Ross), Kiefer Sutherland (Lt Kendrick). *Dir*. Rob Reiner.

Fiddler on the Roof (1971)   Topol, Norma Crane, Molly Picon. Topol recreates his classic stage role. *Dir*. Norman Jewison.

Field, The (1990)   Richard Harris (Bull McCabe), Sean Bean (Tadgh McCabe), Frances Tomelty (Widow), Brenda Fricker (Maggie McCabe), John Hurt (Bird O'Donnell), Tom Berenger (The American). *Dir*. Jim Sheridan.

Field of Dreams (1989)   Kevin Costner (Ray Kinsella), Amy Madigan (Annie), James Earl Jones (Terence Mann), Burt Lancaster (Dr Moonlight Graham), Ray Liotta (Shoeless Joe Jackson). Famous line: 'If you build it, he will come'. *Dir*. Phil Alden Robinson.

Fierce Creatures (1997)   John Cleese, Jamie Lee Curtis, Kevin Kline, Michael Palin, Ronnie Corbett, Robert Lindsay. Unsuccessful follow-up to *A Fish Called Wanda*. Fred Schepisi replaced Young as director for three weeks whilst refilming the final scenes. *Dir*. Robert Young.

Fifth Element, The (1997) Gary Oldman (Zorg), Bruce Willis (Will Dallas), Milla Jovovich (Leeloo), Ian Holm (Cornelius). Costumes by Jean-Paul Gaultier. *Dir.* Luc Besson.

51st State, The (2001) Samuel L Jackson (Elmo McElroy), Meatloaf (The Lizard), Robert Carlyle (Felix DeSouza), Sean Pertwee (Detective Virgil Kane), Ricky Tomlinson (Leopold Durant), Emily Mortimer (Dakota Phillips), Steven Walters (Blowfish). American inventor of a new drug goes to Liverpool to sell the formula for $20 million to a local drug baron. *Dir.* Ronny Yu.

Fight Club (1999) Brad Pitt, Edward Norton, Helena Bonham Carter, Meatloaf. *Dir.* David Fincher.

Final Fantasy: The Spirits Within (2001) Voices of Ming-Na, Alec Baldwin, Ving Rhames, Steve Buscemi, Peri Gilpin, Donald Sutherland, James Woods, Jean Simmons. Animation film about a female scientist in 2065 and her battle to rid the world of powerful aliens known as phantoms. *Dir.* Hironobu Sakaguchi and Moto Sakakibara.

Finian's Rainbow (1968) Fred Astaire, Petula Clark, Tommy Steele. Tommy Steele plays a leprechaun. *Dir.* Francis Ford Coppola.

Firm, The (1993) Tom Cruise (Mitch Deere), Gene Hackman, Jeanne Tripplehorn. Cruise is the new boy at a Memphis law firm run, unknown to him, by the Mafia. Based on bestseller by John Grisham. *Dir.* Sydney Pollack.

First Blood (1982) Sylvester Stallone (John Rambo), Richard Crenna (Trautman), Brian Dennehy (Teasle). Q Moonblood on the writing credits is Stallone. *Dir.* Ted Kotcheff.

First Great Train Robbery, The (1978) Sean Connery, Donald Sutherland, Lesley-Anne Down. Wayne Sleep makes his first movie appearance. *Dir.* Michael Crichton.

First Knight (1995) Sean Connery, Richard Gere, Julia Ormond, Ben Cross, John Gielgud. King Arthur story that lost money at the box office. *Dir.* Jerry Zucker.

Fish Called Wanda, A (1988) John Cleese (Archie Leach), Jamie Lee Curtis (Wanda), Kevin Kline (Otto), Michael Palin (Ken). Big box office hit, Oscar for Kevin Kline. *Dir.* Charles Crichton.

Fisher King, The (1991) Robin Williams (Parry), Jeff Bridges (Jack Lucas), Amanda Plummer (Lydia), Ted Ross (Limo Bum), Tom Waits. *Dir.* Terry Gilliam.

Five Easy Pieces (1970) Jack Nicholson, Karen Black, Fannie Flagg. Jack Nicholson plays a pianist. *Dir.* Bob Rafelson.

Flash Gordon (1980) Topol, Max Von Sydow, Brian Blessed, Timothy Dalton. Music by Queen. *Dir.* Michael Hodges.

Flashdance (1983) Jennifer Beals (Alex Owens), Michael Nouri (Nick Hurley), Lilia Skala (Hanna Long). *Dir.* Adrian Lyne.

Flatliners (1990) Kiefer Sutherland (Nelson Wright), Julia Roberts (Rachel Mannus), Kevin Bacon (David Labraccio), William Baldwin (Joe Hurley). *Dir.* Joel Schumacher.

Fletch (1985) Chevy Chase (Fletch), Joe Don Baker (Chief Karlin). Sequel: *Fletch Lives* (1989). *Dir.* Michael Ritchie.

Flintstones, The (1994) John Goodman, Elisabeth Perkins, Rick Moranis, Rosie O'Donnell, Elizabeth Taylor. *Dir.* Brian Levant.

Fly, The (1958) David Hedison, Patricia Owens, Vincent Price, Herbert Marshall. Classic horror film. *Dir.* Kurt Neumann.

Fly, The (1986) Jeff Goldblum (Seth Brundle), Geena Davis (Veronica Quaife). David Cronenberg makes a cameo performance as the gynaecologist. *Dir.* David Cronenberg.

Fools Rush In (1997) Matthew Perry, Salma Hayek, Jon Tenney, Jill Clayburgh. *Dir.* Andy Tennant.

Footloose (1984) Kevin Bacon (Ren), Lori Singer (Ariel), John Lithgow (Reverend Shaw Moore). *Dir.* Herbert Ross.

For Me and My Gal (1942) Judy Garland, Gene Kelly, George Murphy. *Dir.* Busby Berkeley.

For the Boys (1991) Bette Midler (Dixie Leonard), James Caan (Eddie Sparks), George Segal (Art Silver). *Dir.* Mark Rydell.

For Your Eyes Only (1981) Roger Moore, Topol, Carole Bouquet (Melina), Julian Glover (Kristatos). Ian Fleming does not get credit of any kind for this film. (Theme song: Sheena Easton.) *Dir.* John Glen.

Forbidden Planet (1956) Walter Pidgeon, Anne Francis, Leslie Nielsen, Warren Stevens, Jack Kelly. Set in AD 2200 and follows the plot of Shakespeare's *The Tempest*. *Dir.* Fred M Wilcox.

Forever Amber (1947) Linda Darnell, Cornel Wilde, George Sanders (Charles II), Richard Greene, Jessica Tandy. Costume drama set in the reign of Charles II. *Dir.* Otto Preminger.

Forever Young (1992) Mel Gibson (Daniel), Jamie Lee Curtis (Claire), Elijah Wood (Nat), George Wendt (Harry). *Dir.* Steve Miner.

Forrest Gump (1994) Tom Hanks, Robin Wright, Gary Sinise, Sally Field, Hanna R Hall. Won 6 Oscars. *Dir.* Robert Zemeckis.

Fort Apache (1948) Henry Fonda, John Wayne, Shirley Temple, Victor McLaglen, Ward Bond. *Dir.* John Ford.

Fort Apache, the Bronx (1980) Paul Newman, Ed Asner, Ken Wahl, Danny Aiello. *Dir.* Daniel Petrie.

Fortune Cookie, The (1966) Walter Matthau, Jack Lemmon. GB title: *Meet Whiplash Willie*. *Dir.* Billy Wilder.

40 Days and 40 Nights (2002) Josh Hartnett (Matt), Shannyn Sossamon (Erica Sutton), Paulo Costanzo (Ryan), Adam Trese (John), Emmanuelle Vaugier, Vinessa Shaw. Computer whizz-kid gives up sex for Lent. *Dir.* Michael Lehmann.

48 Hrs (1982) Nick Nolte (Jack Cates), Eddie Murphy (Reggie Hammond), Annette O'Toole (Elaine). Sequel: *Another 48 Hrs* (1990). *Dir.* Walter Hill.

49th Parallel (1941) Eric Portman, Laurence Olivier, Leslie Howard, Raymond Massey, Glynis Johns. US title: *The Invaders*. *Dir.* Michael Powell.

Foul Play (1978) Goldie Hawn, Chevy Chase, Burgess Meredith, Rachel Roberts, Dudley Moore. Two innocents in San Francisco get involved in plot to assassinate the Pope. *Dir.* Colin Higgins.

Four for Texas (1963) Dean Martin, Frank Sinatra, Anita Ekberg, Ursula Andress, Charles Bronson, Victor Buono, 3 Stooges. *Dir.* Robert Aldrich.

Four Horsemen of the Apocalypse, The (1921) Rudolph Valentino, Alice Terry, Alan Hale, Wallace Beery. Young Argentinian fights for his father's country, France, in WWI. 1961 remake starred Glenn Ford. *Dir.* Rex Ingram.

Four Musketeers, The (Revenge of Milady), (1974) Michael York, Oliver Reed, Frank Finlay, Richard Chamberlain, Raquel Welch, Faye Dunaway, Charlton Heston. *Dir.* Richard Lester.

Four Weddings and a Funeral (1994) Hugh Grant,

Andie MacDowell, Kristin Scott Thomas, Simon Callow. *Dir.* Mike Newell.

1492: Conquest of Paradise (1992)   Gérard Depardieu (Columbus), Armand Assante (Sanchez), Sigourney Weaver (Queen Isabel). *Dir.* Ridley Scott.

Fourth Protocol, The (1987)   Michael Caine (John Preston), Pierce Brosnan (Petrofsky), Joanna Cassidy (Vassileva). Thriller by Frederick Forsyth. *Dir.* John Mackenzie.

Fox, The (1968)   Anne Heywood, Sandy Dennis, Keir Dullea. Based on DH Lawrence's novella. *Dir.* Mark Rydell.

Francis (1949)   Donald O'Connor, Patricia Medina, Chill Wills (as voice of Francis the Mule). Series of sequels followed. *Dir.* Arthur Lubin.

Frankenstein (1931)   Boris Karloff, Colin Clive, Mae Clarke, Edward Van Sloan. Series of sequels followed. *Dir.* James Whale.

Frankie and Johnny (1966)   Elvis Presley, Donna Douglas, Nancy Kovack. *Dir.* Frederick De Cordova.

Frankie and Johnny (1991)   Al Pacino (Johnny), Michelle Pfeiffer (Frankie). *Dir.* Garry Marshall.

Frantic (1988)   Harrison Ford (Richard Walker), Betty Buckley (Sondra Walker), Emmanuelle Seigner. American cardiologist searching for his kidnapped wife in Paris becomes embroiled with Arabs. *Dir.* Roman Polanski.

Freebie and the Bean (1974)   Alan Arkin, James Caan, Loretta Swit. *Dir.* Richard Rush.

French Connection, The (1971)   Gene Hackman (Popeye Doyle), Roy Scheider, Fernando Rey. Oscars for Best Picture, Best Director, Best Actor (Hackman) and Ernest Tidyman took Oscar for Best Adapted Screenplay. *Dir.* William Friedkin.

French Lieutenant's Woman (1981)   Meryl Streep, Jeremy Irons, Leo McKern, Peter Vaughan. Harold Pinter adaption of John Fowles's novel. *Dir.* Karel Reisz.

Frenzy (1972)   Barry Foster, Jon Finch, Alec McCowen, Vivien Merchant, Anna Massey, Billie Whitelaw. Anthony Shaffer adapted *Goodbye Piccadilly, Farewell Leicester Square* by Arthur La Bern. *Dir.* Alfred Hitchcock.

Freshman, The (1990)   Marlon Brando (Carmine Sabatini), Matthew Broderick (Clark Kellogg), Maximilian Schell (Larry London). *Dir.* Andrew Bergman.

Freud (1962)   Montgomery Clift, Larry Parks, Susannah York, David McCallum. *Dir.* John Huston.

Friday the 13th (1980)   Betsy Palmer, Adrienne King, Jeannine Taylor, Robbi Morgan. Others in series include part 4 *The Final Chapter* and the last (part 8), *Jason Takes Manhattan*. *Dir.* Sean S. Cunningham.

Fried Green Tomatoes at the Whistle Stop Cafe (1992)   Kathy Bates (Evelyn Couch), Jessica Tandy (Ninny Threadgoode). *Dir.* Jon Avnet.

Friendly Persuasion (1956)   Gary Cooper, Dorothy McGuire, Anthony Perkins. No script credit (the writer, Michael Wilson, was blacklisted). *Dir.* William Wyler.

Fright Night (1985)   Chris Sarandon (Jerry Dandridge), Roddy McDowall (Peter Vincent). William Ragsdale (Charley Brewster). Present-day vampires. McDowall's character named as tribute to Peter Cushing and Vincent Price. *Dir.* Tom Holland.

Fright Night Part 2 (1988)   Roddy McDowall, William Ragsdale. *Dir.* Tommy Lee Wallace.

Frisco Kid, The (1979)   Gene Wilder, Harrison Ford, Leo Fuchs. *Dir.* Robert Aldrich.

Fritz the Cat (1971)   First 'X'-rated cartoon, about the adventures of an alleycat in New York. *Dir.* Ralph Bakshi.

From Hell (2001)   Johnny Depp (Inspector Fred Abberline), Heather Graham (Mary Kelly), Ian Holm, Robbie Coltrane. Twist on the Jack the Ripper story. *Dir.* Albert Hughes and Allen Hughes.

From Here to Eternity (1953)   Burt Lancaster, Deborah Kerr, Frank Sinatra, Montgomery Clift. *Dir.* Fred Zinnemann.

From Russia with Love (1963)   Sean Connery, Robert Shaw (Red Grant), Daniela Bianchi (Tatiana Romanova), Lotte Lenya (Rosa Kleb), Bernard Lee, Lois Maxwell, Pedro Armendariz.Theme song sung by Matt Monro. *Dir.* Terence Young.

Front Page, The (1931) Adolph Merjon, Pat O'Brien, Mary Brian, Walter Catlett, Edward Everett Horton. *Dir.* Lewis Milestone.

Front Page, The (1974)   Walter Matthau, Jack Lemmon, Susan Sarandon, David Wayne, Vincent Gardenia. *Dir.* Billy Wilder.

Fugitive, The (1993)   Harrison Ford (Dr Richard Kimble), Tommy Lee Jones (Lt Gerard). *Dir.* Andrew Davis.

Full Metal Jacket (1987)   Matthew Modine (Private Joker), Adam Baldwin (Animal Mother), Dorian Harewood (Eightball), Vincent D'Onofrio (Private Pyle). *Dir.* Stanley Kubrick.

Full Monty, The (1997)   Robert Carlyle (Gaz), Mark Addy (Dave), Tom Wilkinson (Gerald), Hugo Speer (Guy), Paul Barber (Horse), Steve Huison (Lomper). Unemployed Sheffield welders decide to become male strippers. *Dir.* Peter Cattaneo.

Funeral, The (1996)   Christopher Walken, Isabelle Adjani, Chris Penn, Annabella Sciorra. *Dir.* Abel Ferrara.

Funeral in Berlin (1967)   Michael Caine (Harry Palmer), Oscar Homolka, Eva Renzi, Hugh Burden. *Dir.* Guy Hamilton.

Funny Girl (1968)   Barbra Streisand (Fanny Brice), Omar Sharif, Walter Pidgeon, Kay Medford. *Dir.* William Wyler.

Funny Lady (1975)   Barbra Streisand, James Caan, Ben Vereen, Omar Sharif, Roddy McDowall. *Dir.* Herbert Ross.

Funny Thing Happened on the Way to the Forum, A (1966)   Zero Mostel, Phil Silvers, Michael Crawford, Michael Hordern, Buster Keaton. *Dir.* Richard Lester.

Futureworld (1976)   Peter Fonda, Blythe Danner, Yul Brynner, Arthur Hill, Stuart Margolin. *Dir.* Richard T Heffron.

Game, The (1997)   Michael Douglas (Nicholas Van Orton), Sean Penn (Conrad Van Orton). *Dir.* David Fincher.

Games, The (1970)   Stanley Baker, Michael Crawford, Ryan O'Neal, Charles Aznavour. Four men take part in the Rome Olympics marathon. *Dir.* Michael Winner.

Gandhi (1982)   Ben Kingsley (Gandhi), Candice Bergen (Margaret Bourke-White), Edward Fox (General Dyer), Daniel Day Lewis (Colin). *Dir.* Richard Attenborough.

Gardens of Stone (1987)   James Caan (Clell Hazard), Anjelica Huston (Samantha Davis), James Earl Jones (Goody Nelson). Vietnam War from the perspective of soldiers guarding Arlington National Cemetery. *Dir.* Francis Ford Coppola.

Gaslight (1940)   Anton Walbrook, Diana Wynyard, Frank Pettingell, Robert Newton, Jimmy Hanley. Victorian schizophrenic tries to drive his wife insane because of his guilty past. *Dir*. Thorold Dickinson.

Gaslight (1944)   Charles Boyer, Ingrid Bergman, Joseph Cotten, Angela Lansbury. Remake of the 1940 film. *Dir*. George Cukor.

Genevieve (1953)   Dinah Sheridan, John Gregson, Kay Kendall, Kenneth More, Joyce Grenfell. Genevieve was a classic car (Darracq). *Dir*. Henry Cornelius.

Genghis Khan (1964)   Omar Sharif, Stephen Boyd, James Mason, Telly Savalas, Françoise Dorléac. *Dir*. Henry Levin.

Gentleman Jim (1942)   Errol Flynn, Alan Hale, Ward Bond. Based on the life of world heavyweight boxing champion Jim Corbett. *Dir*. Raoul Walsh.

Gentlemen Marry Brunettes (1955)   Jane Russell, Jeanne Crain, Alan Young, Rudy Vallee. Sequel to *Gentlemen Prefer Blondes*. *Dir*. Richard Sale.

Gentlemen Prefer Blondes (1953)   Jane Russell, Marilyn Monroe, Charles Coburn. Based on Anita Loos's novel. *Dir*. Howard Hawks.

Geordie (1955)   Bill Travers, Alastair Sim, Norah Gorsen, Stanley Baxter. Sickly Scottish boy becomes Olympic hammer thrower. *Dir*. Frank Launder.

George Raft Story, The (1961)   Ray Danton, Julie London, Jayne Mansfield, Frank Gorshin, Neville Brand (Al Capone). GB title: *Spin of a Coin*. *Dir*. Joseph M Newman.

Georgy Girl (1966)   James Mason, Lynn Redgrave, Charlotte Rampling, Alan Bates, Rachel Kempson. *Dir*. Silvio Narizzano.

Gerald McBoing Boing (1951)   Cartoon written by Dr Seuss (Theodore Geisel), which won an Oscar. *Dir*. Robert Cannon.

Get Carter (1971)   Michael Caine, John Osborne, Ian Hendry, Britt Ekland. Based on Ted Lewis's novel *Jack's Return Home*. *Dir*. Mike Hodges.

Get Shorty (1995)   John Travolta, Gene Hackman, Rene Russo, Danny De Vito. Miami debt collector for the Mob goes to Las Vegas and discovers a talent for film production. *Dir*. Barry Sonnenfeld.

Getaway, The (1972)   Steve McQueen, Ali MacGraw, Ben Johnson, Sally Struthers, Slim Pickens. *Dir*. Sam Peckinpah.

Getaway, The (1994)   Alec Baldwin, Kim Basinger, Michael Madsen, James Woods. *Dir*. Roger Donaldson.

Ghost (1990)   Patrick Swayze (Sam Wheat), Demi Moore (Molly Jensen), Whoopi Goldberg (Oda Mae Brown). *Dir*. Jerry Zucker.

Ghost in the Machine (1993)   Karen Allen, Chris Mulkey, Ted Marcoux, Nancy Fish. *Dir*. Rachel Talalay.

Ghost World (2001)   Thora Birch (Enid), Scarlett Johansson (Rebecca), Steve Buscemi (Seymour), Teri Garr (Maxine). Two teenagers leave high school and feel inadequate in the adult world. *Dir*. Terry Zwigoff.

Ghostbusters (1984)   Bill Murray (Dr Peter Venkman), Dan Aykroyd (Dr Raymond Stantz), Harold Ramis (Dr Egon Spengler), Sigourney Weaver (Dana Barrett), Rick Moranis (Louis Tully). *Ghostbusters II* (1989), was sequel. Ramis and Aykroyd also wrote the screenplay. *Dir*. Ivan Reitman.

Ghosts from the Past (1997)   Alec Baldwin (DeLaughter), Whoopi Goldberg (Myrlie), James Woods (Byron De La Beckwith). Original title: *Ghosts of Mississippi*. *Dir*. Rob Reiner.

GI Jane (1997)   Demi Moore (Lt Jordan O'Neill),

Anne Bancroft (Senator Lillian DeHaven). *Dir*. Ridley Scott.

Giant (1956)   Rock Hudson, Elizabeth Taylor, James Dean, Mercedes McCambridge, Carroll Baker, Chill Wills, Rod Taylor, Earl Holliman. *Dir*. George Stevens.

Gigi (1958)   Leslie Caron, Louis Jourdan, Maurice Chevalier, Hermione Gingold, Eva Gabor. *Dir*. Vincente Minnelli.

Gilda (1946)   Rita Hayworth, Glenn Ford, George Macready. *Dir*. Charles Vidor.

Girl 6 (1996)   Theresa Randle, Isaiah Washington, Spike Lee. Unsuccessful actress is employed as a sex chat operator. *Dir*. Spike Lee.

Girls Girls Girls (1962)   Elvis Presley, Stella Stevens, Laurel Goodwin. *Dir*. Norman Taurog.

Give My Regards to Broad Street (1984)   Paul McCartney, Bryan Brown, Ringo Starr, Barbara Bach, Tracey Ullman, Ralph Richardson. *Dir*. Peter Webb.

Gladiator (2000)   Russel Crowe (Maximus), Joaquin Phoenix (Commodus), Connie Nielson, Derek Jacobi, Richard Harris (Emperor Marcus Aurelius), Oliver Reed (Proximo). *Dir*. Ridley Scott.

Glass Menagerie, The (1950)   Gertrude Lawrence, Jane Wyman, Kirk Douglas, Arthur Kennedy. Shy, crippled girl seeks escape from her shabby life in St Louis. *Dir*. Irving Rapper.

Glass Menagerie, The (1987)   Joanne Woodward, John Malkovich, Karen Allen. Remake of earlier version of Tennessee Williams' play. *Dir*. Paul Newman.

Glass Mountain, The (1949)   Michael Denison, Dulcie Gray, Tito Gobbi. Nino Rota's music score is memorable and haunting. *Dir*. Henry Cass.

Gleaming the Cube (1988)   Christian Slater, Steven Bauer, Richard Herd. Skateboarding film. *Dir*. Graeme Clifford.

Glenn Miller Story, The (1954)   James Stewart, June Allyson, Harry Morgan, Charles Drake, Louis Armstrong, Gene Krupa. *Dir*. Anthony Mann.

Gloria (1980)   Gena Rowlands, John Adames, Buck Henry. *Dir*. John Cassavetes.

Glory (1989)   Matthew Broderick (Col Robert G Shaw), Denzel Washington (Private Trip), Cary Elwes (Maj Cabot Forbes), Morgan Freeman (Sgt Maj John Rawlins). *Dir*. Edward Zwick.

Go-Between, The (1970)   Alan Bates, Julie Christie, Michael Redgrave, Dominic Guard, Michael Gough, Margaret Leighton, Edward Fox. Harold Pinter adaptation of LP Hartley's novel. *Dir*. Joseph Losey.

Godfather, The (1972).   Marlon Brando, Al Pacino, James Caan, Robert Duvall, Diane Keaton, Richard Conte. *Dir*. Francis Ford Coppola.

Godfather Part II, The (1974)   Al Pacino, Robert De Niro, Diane Keaton, Robert Duvall, Lee Strasberg, Troy Donahue. The first sequel to win a Best Picture Oscar (and 5 others). *Dir*. Francis Ford Coppola.

Godfather Part III, The (1990)   Al Pacino, Diane Keaton, Talia Shire, Andy Garcia, Eli Wallach, Sofia Coppola. *Dir*. Francis Ford Coppola.

Godzilla (1955)   Raymond Burr, Takashi Shimura, Momoko Kochi. *Dir*. Inoshiro Honda.

Godzilla (1998)   Matthew Broderick, Jean Reno, Maria Pitillo, Hank Azaria, Kevin Dunn, Michael Lerner, Harry Shearer. As a result of French nuclear tests in the Pacific, a giant lizard invades Manhattan. Remake of the Japanese classic. *Dir*. Roland Emmerich.

Goin' South (1978)   Jack Nicholson, Mary Steenburgen, Christopher Lloyd, John Belushi. *Dir.* Jack Nicholson.

Going My Way (1944)   Bing Crosby (Father O'Malley), Barry Fitzgerald, Rise Stevens, Gene Lockhart. *Dir.* Leo McCarey.

Goldeneye (1995)   Pierce Brosnan, Sean Bean (Alec Trevelyan), Izabella Scorupco (Natalaya Simonova), Famke Janssen (Xenia Onatopp), Judi Dench (M), Desmond Llewelyn (Q), Samantha Bond (Miss Moneypenny), Joe Don Baker (Jack Wade), Robbie Coltrane (Valentin). Title song written by Bono and The Edge and performed by Tina Turner. *Dir.* Martin Campbell.

Goldfinger (1964)   Sean Connery, Honor Blackman (Pussy Galore), Gert Fröbe (Auric Goldfinger), Harold Sakatá (Oddjob), Bernard Lee, Lois Maxwell, Desmond Llewellyn, Shirley Eaton. Theme song sung by Shirley Bassey. *Dir.* Guy Hamilton.

Gone with the Wind (1939)   Clark Gable, Vivien Leigh, Olivia de Havilland, Leslie Howard, Thomas Mitchell, Hattie McDaniel, Butterfly McQueen. *Dir.* Victor Fleming (with George Cukor, Sam Wood, B Reeves Eason).

Good Earth, The (1937)   Paul Muni, Luise Rainer, Keye Luke. Chinese peasant grows rich but loses his wife. *Dir.* Sidney Franklin.

Good Morning, Vietnam (1987)   Robin Williams (Adrian Cronauer), Forest Whitaker (Edward Garlick). *Dir.* Barry Levinson.

Good Mother, The (1988)   Diane Keaton (Anna), Liam Neeson (Leo). *Dir.* Leonard Nimoy.

Good Son, The (1993)   Macaulay Culkin, Elijah Wood, Wendy Crewson, Quinn Culkin. Ten-year-old boy is a sadistic killer. *Dir.* Joseph Ruben.

Good, the Bad and the Ugly, The (1966)   Clint Eastwood, Eli Wallach, Lee Van Cleef. *Dir.* Sergio Leone.

Good Will Hunting (1997)   Robin Williams, Matt Damon (Will Hunting), Ben Affleck, Minnie Driver, Stellan Skarsgard. Janitor is spotted as a mathematical genius. *Dir.* Gus Van Sant.

Goodbye, Columbus (1969)   Richard Benjamin, Ali MacGraw, Jack Klugman. Jewish librarian has an affair with daughter of a nouveau riche family. *Dir.* Larry Peerce.

Goodbye Girl, The (1977)   Richard Dreyfuss, Marsha Mason, Quinn Cummings. Neil Simon story. *Dir.* Herbert Ross.

Goodbye, Mr Chips (1939)   Robert Donat, Greer Garson, Paul Henreid, John Mills. James Hilton's novel adapted by RC Sherriff, Claudine West & Eric Maschwitz. *Dir.* Sam Wood.

Goodbye, Mr Chips (1969)   Peter O'Toole, Petula Clark, Michael Redgrave, Sian Phillips. Musical remake of the 1939 classic. *Dir.* Herbert Ross.

Goodfellas (1990)   Robert De Niro (James Conway), Ray Liotta (Henry Hill), Joe Pesci (Tommy De Vito), Lorraine Bracco (Karen Hill), Catherine Scorsese (Tommy's mother). *Dir.* Martin Scorsese.

Goonies, The (1985)   Sean Astin (Mickey), Josh Brolin (Brand), Jeff Cohen (Chunk), Corey Feldman (Mouth). Screenplay by Chris Columbus, based on a Steven Spielberg story. *Dir.* Richard Donner.

Gorillas in the Mist (1988)   Sigourney Weaver (Diane Fossey), Bryan Brown (Bob Campbell). *Dir.* Michael Apted.

Gorky Park (1983)   William Hurt (Arkady Renko), Lee Marvin (Jack Osborne). Filmed mainly in Helsinki. *Dir.* Michael Apted.

Gosford Park (2001)   Maggie Smith (Constance, Countess of Trentham), Michael Gambon (Sir William McCordle), Kristin Scott Thomas (Lady Sylvia McCordle), Camilla Rutherford (Isobel McCordle), Eileen Atkins (Mrs Croft), Jeremy Northam (Ivor Novello), Clive Owen (Robert Parks), Alan Bates (Jennings), Helen Mirren (Mrs Wilson), Stephen Fry (Inspector Thompson), Sophie Thompson (Dorothy), Derek Jacobi (Probert), Richard E Grant (George). Set in a country house in the 1930s, the weekend guests fall under suspicion when the host is killed twice! Julian Fellowes won an Oscar for his script. *Dir.* Robert Altman.

Grace of My Heart (1996)   Illeana Douglas, John Turturro, Eric Stoltz, Patsy Kensit, Bridget Fonda, Matt Dillon. Based loosely on Carole King, with Illeana Douglas's voice dubbed by Kristen Vigard. *Dir.* Allison Anders.

Graduate, The (1967)   Dustin Hoffman (Benjamin Braddock), Anne Bancroft (Mrs Robinson), Katharine Ross, William Daniels. *Dir.* Mike Nichols.

Grand Canyon (1991)   Danny Glover, Kevin Kline, Steve Martin. Black truck driver and white lawyer form an unlikely friendship. *Dir.* Lawrence Kasdan.

Grand Hotel (1932)   Greta Garbo (Grusinskaya), John Barrymore, Lionel Barrymore, Joan Crawford. Famous Garbo line: 'I want to be alone'. *Dir.* Edmund Goulding.

Grand Prix (1966)   James Garner, Eva Marie Saint, Yves Montand. *Dir.* John Frankenheimer.

Grande Illusion, La (1937)   Pierre Fresnay, Erich Von Stroheim, Jean Gabin. Three captured French WWI pilots have uneasy relationship with their German commandant. *Dir.* Jean Renoir.

Grapes of Wrath, The (1940)   Henry Fonda, Jane Darwell, John Carradine, Grant Mitchell. From the John Steinbeck novel. Oklahoma farmers trek to California after dust bowl disaster of the Thirties. *Dir.* John Ford.

Grease (1978)   John Travolta, Olivia Newton-John, Stockard Channing, Frankie Avalon, Jeff Conaway, Sha Na Na, Eve Arden, Sid Caesar. School: Rydell High. *Dir.* Randal Kleiser.

Grease 2 (1982)   Maxwell Caulfield, Michelle Pfeiffer, Lorna Luft, Eve Arden, Sid Caesar. *Dir.* Patricia Birch.

Great Balls of Fire (1989)   Dennis Quaid (Jerry Lee Lewis), Winona Ryder (Myra Gale Lewis), John Doe (JW Brown). Peter Cook is 'First English Reporter'. *Dir.* Jim McBride.

Great Caruso, The (1951)   Mario Lanza, Ann Blyth, Jarmila Novotna, Alan Napier. *Dir.* Richard Thorpe.

Great Escape, The (1963)   James Garner, Steve McQueen, Richard Attenborough, Charles Bronson, Donald Pleasence, James Coburn, David McCallum, Gordon Jackson, John Leyton. *Dir.* John Sturges.

Great Expectations (1934)   Phillip Holmes (Pip), Jane Wyatt (Estella), Henry Hull (Magwitch), Alan Hale (Joe Gargery), Francis L Sullivan (Jaggers), Florence Reed (Miss Havisham). *Dir.* Stuart Walker.

Great Expectations (1946)   John Mills, Bernard Miles, Finlay Currie, Martita Hunt, Valerie Hobson, Jean Simmons, Alec Guinness, Francis L Sullivan. *Dir.* David Lean.

Great Gatsby, The (1949)   Alan Ladd, Macdonald Carey, Barry Sullivan. Based on novel by F Scott Fitzgerald. *Dir.* Elliott Nugent.

Great Gatsby, The (1974)   Robert Redford, Mia Farrow, Karen Black, Sam Waterston, Lois Chiles.

Screenplay by Francis Ford Coppola. Nelson Riddle gained Oscar for music. *Dir.* Jack Clayton.

Great Muppet Caper, The (1981)   Diana Rigg, Charles Grodin, John Cleese, Peter Ustinov, Robert Morley, Trevor Howard. Peter Falk has cameo as a tramp. *Dir.* Jim Henson.

Great St Trinian's Train Robbery, The (1966) Frankie Howerd, Dora Bryan, Reg Varney, George Cole. *Dir.* Frank Launder.

Great Santini, The (1979)   Robert Duvall, Michael O'Keefe, Blythe Danner, Julie Anne Haddock. *Dir.* Lewis John Carlino.

Great Scout and Cathouse Thursday, The (1976) Lee Marvin, Oliver Reed, Kay Lenz, Robert Culp, Elizabeth Ashley, Sylvia Miles, Strother Martin. *Dir.* Don Taylor.

Great Waldo Pepper, The (1975)   Robert Redford, Bo Svenson, Bo Brundin, Susan Sarandon. *Dir.* George Roy Hill.

Great Waltz, The (1938)   Fernand Gravet, Luise Rainer, Miliza Korjus. Biopic of Johann Strauss the Younger. *Dir.* Julien Duvivier.

Great White Hope, The (1970)   James Earl Jones, Jane Alexander, Lou Gilbert, Hal Holbrook. Jack Johnson story (he's called Jefferson in the film). *Dir.* Martin Ritt.

Great White Hype, The (1996)   Samuel L Jackson, Jeff Goldblum, John Rhys-Davies. *Dir.* Reginald Hudlin.

Great Ziegfeld, The (1936)   William Powell, Luise Rainer (Anna Held), Myrna Loy (Billie Burke), Frank Morgan, Ray Bolger, Fanny Brice. Biopic of impresario Florenz Ziegfeld. *Dir.* Robert Z Leonard.

Greatest, The (1977)   Muhammad Ali, Ernest Borgnine, Robert Duvall, Ben Johnson, James Earl Jones. *Dir.* Tom Gries.

Greatest Show on Earth, The (1952)   Betty Hutton, Cornel Wilde, Charlton Heston, James Stewart, Dorothy Lamour, John Ringling North. *Dir.* Cecil B de Mille.

Greatest Story Ever Told, The (1965)   Max Von Sydow, Dorothy McGuire, Claude Rains, José Ferrer, David McCallum, Charlton Heston, Sidney Poitier, John Wayne, Pat Boone, Telly Savalas, Angela Lansbury. Famous John Wayne line: 'Truly this man was the Son of God'. *Dir.* George Stevens.

Greed (1925)   Gibson Gowland, Zasu Pitts, Jean Hersholt. Ex-miner dentist kills his wife and later in Death Valley kills her lover but is bound to him by handcuffs. Re-edited by June Mathis, this film is memorable for its original length of nearly 9 hours. *Dir.* Erich Von Stroheim.

Green Berets, The (1968)   John Wayne, David Janssen, Jim Hutton, Aldo Ray, Patrick Wayne. Vietnam War film. *Dir.* John Wayne.

Gremlins (1984)   Zach Galligan (Billy), Hoyt Axton (Rand Peltzer), Phoebe Cates (Kate), Keye Luke (Grandfather), Judge Reinhold (Gerald). Don't get them wet and never feed them after midnight. Sequel: *Gremlins II (The New Batch)*. *Dir.* Joe Dante.

Greystoke: The Legend of Tarzan, Lord of the Apes (1984)   Christopher Lambert (John Clayton / Tarzan), Ralph Richardson (Lord Greystoke), Andie MacDowell (Jane Porter). *Dir.* Hugh Hudson.

Gridlock'd (1997)   Tim Roth (Stretch), Tupac Shakur (Spoon), Thandie Newton (Cookie). *Dir.* Vondie Curtis-Hall.

Grifters, The (1990)   Anjelica Huston (Lily Dillon),

John Cusack (Roy Dillon), Annette Bening (Myra Langtry). *Dir.* Stephen Frears.

Groundhog Day (1993)   Bill Murray (Phil), Andie MacDowell (Rita). Weatherman Murray is cursed to live the same day over and over. *Dir.* Harold Ramis.

Groundstar Conspiracy, The (1972)   George Peppard, Michael Sarrazin, James Olson. *Dir.* Lamont Johnson.

Group, The (1966)   Joanna Pettet, Candice Bergen, Jessica Walter, Joan Hackett, Elizabeth Hartman, Kathleen Widdoes, Larry Hagman, Hal Holbrook, Robert Emhardt. *Dir.* Sidney Lumet.

Guarding Tess (1994)   Shirley MacLaine, Nicolas Cage, Austin Pendleton, Richard Griffiths. Secret Service agent engages in battle of wills with a former First Lady. *Dir.* Hugh Wilson.

Guess Who's Coming to Dinner (1967)   Spencer Tracy, Katherine Hepburn, Sidney Poitier, Katharine Houghton. Katherine Houghton is the niece of Katharine Hepburn. *Dir.* Stanley Kramer.

Gunfight at the OK Corral (1957)   Burt Lancaster, Kirk Douglas, Jo Van Fleet, Rhonda Fleming, John Ireland. *Dir.* John Sturges.

Gunfighter, The (1950)   Gregory Peck, Helen Westcott, Karl Malden. *Dir.* Henry King.

Guns of Navarone (1961)   Gregory Peck, David Niven, Stanley Baker, Anthony Quinn, Anthony Quayle, James Darren, James Robertson Justice, Richard Harris. *Dir.* J Lee Thompson.

Guys and Dolls (1955)   Frank Sinatra, Marlon Brando, Jean Simmons, Vivian Blaine, Stubby Kaye. *Dir.* Joseph L Mankiewicz.

Gypsy (1962)   Rosalind Russell, Natalie Wood, Karl Malden. *Dir.* Mervyn Le Roy.

Hairspray (1988)   Sonny Bono (Franklin Von Tussle), Ruth Brown (Motormouth Maybell), Divine (Edna Turnblad / Arvin Hodgepile), Deborah Harry (Velma Von Tussle), Ricki Lake (Tracy Turnblad), Pia Zadora (Beatnik chick). *Dir.* John Waters.

Half Moon Street (1986)   Sigourney Weaver (Lauren Slaughter), Michael Caine (Lord Bullbeck). *Dir.* Bob Swaim.

Halloween (1978)   Jamie Lee Curtis, Donald Pleasence (Dr Loomis). *Dir.* John Carpenter.

Halloween 2 (1981)   Jamie Lee Curtis, Donald Pleasence (Dr Loomis). *Dir.* Rick Rosenthal.

Halloween 3: Season of the Witch (1983)   Tom Atkins, Stacey Nelkin, Dan O'Herlihy. *Dir.* Tommy Lee Wallace.

Halloween 4: The Return of Michael Myers (1988) Donald Pleasence, Ellie Cornell, Danielle Harris. *Dir.* Dwight H Little.

Halloween 5: The Revenge of Michael Myers (1989) Donald Pleasence, Danielle Harris, Wendy Kaplan, Ellie Cornell, Donald L Shanks, Jeffrey Landman, Beau Starr. *Dir.* Dominique Othenin-Girard.

Halloween H2O (1998)   Jamie Lee Curtis, Adam Arkin, Josh Harnett, Michelle Williams, Adam Hann-Byrd. *Dir.* Steve Miner.

Halloween: Resurrection (2002)   Jamie Lee Curtis, Brad Loree, Busta Rhymes, Tyra Banks, Luke Kirby. When a group of teenagers win a contest to spend a night in Michael Myers's childhood home to be broadcast live on the internet, they believe they are in for a little fun and some free publicity. But it all goes frightfully wrong and the game turns into a battle for survival. *Dir.* Rick Rosenthal.

Hamlet (1948)   Laurence Olivier, Eileen Herlie, Jean

CINEMA

Simmons, Peter Cushing, Patrick Troughton. *Dir.* Laurence Olivier.

Hamlet (1990)   Mel Gibson, Glenn Close, Alan Bates, Paul Scofield, Helena Bonham Carter, Ian Holm. *Dir.* Franco Zeffirelli.

Hand that Rocks the Cradle, The (1992)   Rebecca DeMornay (Peyton Flanders), Annabella Sciorra (Claire Bartel), Matt McCoy (Michael Bartel). *Dir.* Curtis Hanson.

Handful of Dust (1988)   James Wilby (Tony Last), Kristin Scott Thomas (Brenda Last), Anjelica Huston (Mrs Rattery), Stephen Fry (Reggie), Alec Guinness (Mr Todd), Judi Dench (Mrs Beaver). *Dir.* Charles Sturridge.

Hang 'em High (1967)   Clint Eastwood, Inger Stevens, Pat Hingle. *Dir.* Ted Post.

Hannah and Her Sisters (1986)   Woody Allen (Micky), Michael Caine (Elliot), Mia Farrow (Hannah), Carrie Fisher (April), Barbara Hershey (Lee), Maureen O'Sullivan (Hannah's mother). *Dir.* Woody Allen.

Hannibal Brooks (1968)   Oliver Reed, Michael J Pollard. *Dir.* Michael Winner.

Hanover Street (1979)   Harrison Ford, Lesley-Anne Down, Christopher Plummer, Alec McCowen, Max Wall. *Dir.* Peter Hyams.

Hans Christian Andersen (1952)   Danny Kaye, Zizi Jeanmaire, Farley Granger. *Dir.* Charles Vidor.

Happiest Days of Your Life, The (1950)   Alastair Sim, Margaret Rutherford, Joyce Grenfell, Richard Wattis. *Dir.* Frank Launder.

Happy Hooker, The (1975)   Lynn Redgrave (Xaviera Hollander). *Dir.* Nicholas Sgarro.

Hard Day's Night, A (1964)   Beatles, Wilfrid Brambell, John Junkin, Norman Rossington, Victor Spinetti, Brian Epstein. *Dir.* Richard Lester.

Hard Way, The (1991)   Michael J Fox (Nick Lang), James Woods (John Moss), Annabella Sciorra (Susan). *Dir.* John Badham.

Harder They Fall, The (1956)   Humphrey Bogart, Rod Steiger, Max Baer, Jan Sterling. Bogart's last film. *Dir.* Mark Robson.

Hardy Family (1936–58)   Mickey Rooney, Lewis Stone, Fay Holden, Cecilia Parker, Sara Haden, Spring Byington, Lionel Barrymore. Howard Koch directed the last of the series: *Andy Hardy Comes Home*. *Dir.* George B Seitz.

Harry and Tonto (1974)   Art Carney, Ellen Burstyn, Chief Dan George, Larry Hagman. Tonto was a cat. *Dir.* Paul Mazursky.

Harry Potter and the Chamber of Secrets (2002) Largely the same cast and characters as in *Philosopher's Stone* although new characters include Kenneth Branagh (Gilderoy Lockhart). *Dir.* Chris Columbus.

Harry Potter and the Philosopher's Stone (2001) Daniel Radcliffe (Harry Potter), Rupert Grint (Ron Weasley), Emma Watson (Hermione Granger), Robbie Coltrane (Hagrid), Richard Griffiths (Uncle Vernon Dursley), Richard Harris (Albus Dumbledore), Ian Hart (Professor Quirrell / Voldemort), John Hurt (Mr Ollivander), Alan Rickman (Professor Snape), Fiona Shaw (Aunt Petunia Dursley), Maggie Smith (Professor McGonagall), Julie Walters (Mrs Weasley), John Cleese (Nearly Headless Nick), Richard Bremner (He Who Must Not Be Named), Tom Felton (Draco Malfoy). US title: *Harry Potter and the Sorcerer's Stone. Dir.* Chris Columbus.

Harvey (1950)   James Stewart (Elwood P Dowd), Josephine Hull (Veta Louise), Victoria Horne. *Dir.* Henry Koster.

Hawk the Slayer (1980)   Jack Palance, John Terry, Bernard Bresslaw. *Dir.* Terry Marcel.

Head (1968)   Monkees, Victor Mature. Written by Jack Nicholson & Bob Rafelson. *Dir.* Bob Rafelson.

Hear My Song (1992)   Ned Beatty (Josef Locke: voice of Vernon Midgley), Adrian Dunbar (Mickey O'Neill), Shirley Anne Field (Cathleen Doyle), David McCallum (Jim Abbott). *Dir.* Peter Chelsom.

Heart Is a Lonely Hunter, The (1968)   Alan Arkin, Sondra Locke, Stacy Keach. Based on Carson McCullers's story of a deaf mute. *Dir.* Robert Ellis Miller.

Heartbreak Ridge (1986)   Clint Eastwood (Highway), Marsha Mason (Aggie). *Dir.* Clint Eastwood.

Heartburn (1986)   Meryl Streep (Rachel), Jack Nicholson (Mark), Jeff Daniels (Richard), Stockard Channing (Julie). *Dir.* Mike Nichols.

Heat (1995)   Al Pacino, Robert De Niro, Val Kilmer, Jon Voight. Based on TV movie: *L.A. Takedown*. First film in which the 2 stars actually filmed scenes together. *Dir.* Michael Mann.

Heathers (1989)   Winona Ryder (Veronica Sawyer), Christian Slater (JD), Shannen Doherty (Heather Duke), Lisanne Falk (Heather McNamara), Kim Walker (Heather Chandler). *Dir.* Michael Lehmann.

Heaven and Earth (1993)   Tommy Lee Jones, Joan Chen, Haing S Ngor, Debbie Reynolds. Vietnamese woman endures hardships and torments from both sides during the war. *Dir.* Oliver Stone.

Heaven Can Wait (1943)   Don Ameche, Gene Tierney, Laird Cregar, Charles Coburn. *Dir.* Ernst Lubitsch.

Heaven Can Wait (1978)   Warren Beatty, Julie Christie, James Mason (Mr Jordan), Dyan Cannon, Vincent Gardenia. Remake of *Here Comes Mr Jordan* (1941). *Dir.* Warren Beatty.

Heaven Knows, Mr Allison (1957)   Robert Mitchum, Deborah Kerr. Marine and nun marooned on Pacific island during WW2. *Dir.* John Huston.

Heavenly Creatures (1994)   Melanie Lynskey, Kate Winslet, Diane Kent. *Dir.* Peter Jackson.

Heavens Above (1963)   Peter Sellers, Isabel Jeans, Ian Carmichael, Irene Handl, Eric Sykes, Bernard Miles. *Dir.* John Boulting.

Heaven's Gate (1980)   Kris Kristofferson, Christopher Walken, John Hurt, Jeff Bridges. Famous Western, remembered as a box office disaster. *Dir.* Michael Cimino.

Hedda (1975)   Glenda Jackson, Peter Eyre, Jennie Linden, Patrick Stewart, Timothy West. *Dir.* Trevor Nunn.

Heidi (1937)   Shirley Temple, Jean Hersholt, Arthur Treacher. Based on Johanna Spyri's novel. *Dir.* Allan Dwan.

Heiress, The (1949)   Olivia de Havilland, Ralph Richardson, Montgomery Clift, Miriam Hopkins, Ray Collins. Based on Henry James's novel *Washington Square* and the play of the same name by Ruth and Augustus Goetz. *Dir.* William Wyler.

Helen Morgan Story, The (1957)   Ann Blyth, Paul Newman, Walter Woolf King (Ziegfeld). GB title: *Both Ends of the Candle. Dir.* Michael Curtiz.

Hellfire Club, The (1960)   Keith Michell, Peter Arne, Adrienne Corri, Peter Cushing, David Lodge. *Dir.* Robert S Baker and Monty Berman.

Hello Dolly (1969)   Barbra Streisand, Walter Matthau, Michael Crawford, Marianne McAndrew, Tommy Tune. Based on Thornton Wilder's play *The Matchmaker. Dir.* Gene Kelly.

Hell's Angels (1930)   Ben Lyon, James Hall, Jean Harlow. *Dir.* Howard Hughes.

Hellzapoppin (1942)   Ole Olsen, Chic Johnson, Hugh Herbert, Martha Raye, Mischa Auer. Montage of Mirth and Madness. *Dir.* HC Potter.

Help! (1965)   Beatles, Leo McKern, Eleanor Bron, Victor Spinetti. *Dir.* Dick Lester.

Henry and June (1990)   Fred Ward (Henry Miller), Uma Thurman (June Miller), Maria De Medeiros (Anaïs Nin). Censors created a new 'NC-17' rating to cover rude but artistically worthwhile films. *Dir.* Philip Kaufman.

Henry V (1944)   Laurence Olivier, Robert Newton, Leslie Banks, Esmond Knight, Renée Asherson. *Dir.* Laurence Olivier.

Henry V (1989)   Kenneth Branagh, Derek Jacobi, Brian Blessed, Ian Holm, Alec McCowen, Robbie Coltrane (Falstaff), Emma Thompson (Katherine). *Dir.* Kenneth Branagh.

Henry VIII and His Six Wives (1972)   Keith Michell, Frances Cuka (Aragon), Charlotte Rampling (Boleyn), Jane Asher (Seymour), Jenny Bos (Cleves), Lynne Frederick (Howard), Barbara Leigh-Hunt (Parr). *Dir.* Waris Hussein.

Hercules (1997)   Voices of: Tate Donovan (Hercules), Rip Torn (Zeus), James Woods (Hades), Danny De Vito (Philoctetes), Susan Egan (Meg). Cartoons by Gerald Scarfe. *Dir.* John Musker & Ron Clements.

Here Come the Huggetts (1948)   Jack Warner, Kathleen Harrison, Susan Shaw, Petula Clark, Jimmy Hanley, Diana Dors. Britain's answer to the Hardys. *Dir.* Ken Annakin.

Here Comes Mr Jordan (1941)   Robert Montgomery, Evelyn Keyes, Claude Rains. Much-copied plot about a prizefighter cum saxophonist arriving in heaven too early. *Dir.* Alexander Hall.

Heroes of Telemark, The (1965)   Kirk Douglas, Richard Harris, Ulla Jacobsson, Roy Dotrice, Michael Redgrave. *Dir.* Anthony Mann.

High Anxiety (1977)   Mel Brooks, Madeline Kahn, Cloris Leachman. Psychologist suspects his predecessor was murdered. *Dir.* Mel Brooks.

High Noon (1952)   Gary Cooper (Will Kane), Grace Kelly, Thomas Mitchell, Lloyd Bridges, Lon Chaney. Tex Ritter sang Dimitri Tiomkin's theme tune. Action takes place during the 85 minutes of running time. *Dir.* Fred Zinnemann.

High School High (1996)   Jon Lovitz (Mr Clark), Tia Carrere (Victoria). School is Marion Berry High. *Dir.* Hart Bochner.

Highlander (1986)   Christopher Lambert (Connor MacLeod), Roxanne Hart (Brenda Wyatt), Sean Connery (Ramirez). *Highlander II: The Quickening* was the 1990 sequel. *Dir.* Russell Mulcahy.

His Girl Friday (1940)   Cary Grant, Rosalind Russell, Ralph Bellamy, Gene Lockhart. Remake of *The Front Page* (1931). *Dir.* Howard Hawks.

History of Mr Polly, The (1949)   John Mills, Sally Ann Howes, Megs Jenkins, Finlay Currie. Based on HG Wells's novel. *Dir.* Anthony Pelissier.

Hit, The (1984)   John Hurt, Terence Stamp, Tim Roth, Laura Del Sol, Fernando Rey. *Dir.* Stephen Frears.

Hitler – The Last Ten Days (1973)   Alec Guinness, Simon Ward, Doris Kunstmann, Diane Cilento, Eric Porter, Joss Ackland. *Dir.* Ennio de Concini.

Hobson's Choice (1953)   Charles Laughton, Brenda de Banzie, John Mills, Helen Haye, Prunella Scales. Based on Harold Brighouse's play. *Dir.* David Lean.

Hoffa (1992)   Jack Nicholson, Danny De Vito, Armand Assante. *Dir.* Danny De Vito.

Holiday Inn (1942)   Bing Crosby, Fred Astaire, Walter Abel, Marjorie Reynolds. Won Oscar for the song 'White Christmas'. *Dir.* Mark Sandrich.

Hollywood or Bust (1956)   Dean Martin, Jerry Lewis, Pat Crowley, Anita Ekberg. Last of the Martin & Lewis films. *Dir.* Frank Tashlin.

Home Alone (1990)   Macaulay Culkin (Kevin McCallister), Joe Pesci (Harry), Daniel Stern (Marv), John Candy (Gus). *Dir.* Chris Columbus.

Home Alone 2: Lost in New York (1992)   Macaulay Culkin (Kevin McCallister), Joe Pesci (Harry), Daniel Stern (Marv), Brenda Fricker (Pigeon Lady). *Dir.* Chris Columbus.

Homeboy (1988)   Mickey Rourke (Johnny Walker), Christopher Walken (Wesley), Kevin Conway (Grazziano). *Dir.* Michael Seresin.

Honey, I Blew up the Kid (1992)   Rick Moranis (Wayne Szalinski), Lloyd Bridges (Clifford Sterling), Marcia Strassman (Diane). 'Blew up' in as much as the baby grows to 100 feet tall. *Dir.* Randal Kleiser.

Honey, I Shrunk the Kids (1989)   Rick Moranis (Wayne Szalinski), Matt Frewer (Big Russ Thompson), Marcia Strassman (Diane), Kristine Sutherland (Mae Thompson). *Dir.* Joe Johnston.

Honkytonk Man (1982)   Clint Eastwood (Red Stovall), Kyle Eastwood (Whit), John McIntire (Grandpa). *Dir.* Clint Eastwood.

Honorary Consul, The (1983)   Michael Caine (Charley Fortnum), Richard Gere (Dr Plarr), Bob Hoskins (Col Perez). US title: *Beyond the Limit*. *Dir.* John MacKenzie.

Hook (1991)   Dustin Hoffman (Capt Hook), Robin Williams (Peter Banning / Pan), Julia Roberts (Tinkerbell), Bob Hoskins (Smee). *Dir.* Steven Spielberg.

Hoop Dreams (1994)   William Gates, Arthur Agee, Emma Gates. *Dir.* Steve James.

Hooper (1978)   Burt Reynolds, Sally Field, Brian Keith, Jan Michael Vincent, Adam West. Ageing stuntman decides on one last sensational stunt. *Dir.* Hal Needham.

Hoosiers (1986)   Gene Hackman, Barbara Hershey, Dennis Hopper, Sheb Wooley. Triumphs of an Indiana high school basketball team. *Dir.* David Anspaugh.

Horse Feathers (1932)   Groucho (Wagstaff), Chico, Zeppo, Harpo Marx, Thelma Todd. College football team needs to win. *Dir.* Norman Z McLeod.

Hound of the Baskervilles (1939)   Basil Rathbone, Nigel Bruce, Richard Greene, John Carradine. *Dir.* Sidney Lanfield.

Hound of the Baskervilles (1959)   Peter Cushing, André Morell, Christopher Lee, John Le Mesurier. *Dir.* Terence Fisher.

Hound of the Baskervilles (1977)   Peter Cook (Sherlock Holmes), Dudley Moore (Watson), Denholm Elliott (Stapleton), Terry-Thomas (Mortimer), Max Wall, Spike Milligan, Penelope Keith. *Dir.* Paul Morrissey.

Houseboat (1958)   Cary Grant, Sophia Loren, Martha Hyer, Harry Guardino. *Dir.* Melville Shavelson.

Housesitter (1992)   Steve Martin (Davis), Goldie Hawn (Gwen). One-night stand turns into a comic fatal attraction. *Dir.* Frank Oz.

How Green Was My Valley (1941)   Walter Pidgeon, Maureen O'Hara, Roddy McDowall. Based on Richard Llewellyn's novel. *Dir.* John Ford.

How I Won the War (1967)   Michael Crawford, John Lennon, Roy Kinnear, Lee Montague, Michael Hordern. *Dir*. Richard Lester.

How the West Was Won (1962)   Debbie Reynolds, Carroll Baker, Lee J Cobb, Henry Fonda, James Stewart, Gregory Peck. Spencer Tracy was the narrator. *Dir*. Henry Hathaway, John Ford, George Marshall.

How to Marry a Millionaire (1953)   Lauren Bacall, Marilyn Monroe, Betty Grable, William Powell, Cameron Mitchell. *Dir*. Jean Negulesco.

Howard's End (1992)   Anthony Hopkins (Henry Wilcox), Vanessa Redgrave (Ruth), Helena Bonham Carter (Helen), Emma Thompson (Margaret Schlegel). The Howard's End of the title is a house. *Dir*. James Ivory.

Howling, The (1980)   Dee Wallace, Patrick Macnee, Kevin McCarthy. *Dir*. Joe Dante.

Howling II: Your Sister Is a Werewolf (1985)   Christopher Lee, Annie McEnroe, Reb Brown. Filmed in Czechoslavakia and not a sequel to *The Howling*. *Dir*. Philippe Mora.

Hud (1963)   Paul Newman, Patricia Neal, Melvyn Douglas, Brandon De Wilde. *Dir*. Martin Ritt.

Hue and Cry (1946)   Alastair Sim, Jack Warner, Harry Fowler. First of the Ealing comedies concerns crooks passing information in a boys' paper. *Dir*. Charles Crichton.

Hunchback of Notre Dame, The (1939)   Charles Laughton, Cedric Hardwicke, Maureen O'Hara, Edmond O'Brien, Thomas Mitchell. Remake of the Lon Chaney 1923 film. *Dir*. William Dieterle.

Hunchback of Notre Dame, The (1956)   Anthony Quinn, Gina Lollobrigida. French / Italian production of the classic story. *Dir*. Jean Delannoy.

Hunger, The (1983)   Catherine Deneuve (Miriam), David Bowie (John), Susan Sarandon (Sarah Roberts). *Dir*. Tony Scott.

Hunt for Red October, The (1990)   Sean Connery (Capt Marko Ramius), Alec Baldwin (Jack Ryan), Sam Neill (Capt Borodin). *Dir*. John McTiernan.

Hunter, The (1980)   Steve McQueen, Eli Wallach, Ben Johnson. McQueen's last film. *Dir*. Buzz Kulik.

Hurlyburly (1998)   Sean Penn (Eddie), Kevin Spacey (Mickey), Robin Wright Penn, Garry Shandling, Meg Ryan, Chazz Pálminteri, Anna Paquin. *Dir*. Anthony Drazan.

Husbands and Wives (1992)   Woody Allen (Gabe Roth), Judith Lewis (Rain), Blythe Danner (Rain's mother), Mia Farrow (Judy Roth), Judy Davis (Sally). *Dir*. Woody Allen.

Hustler, The (1961)   Paul Newman, Jackie Gleason, George C Scott, Piper Laurie. *Dir*. Robert Rossen.

Hustler White (1996)   Tony Ward, Bruce LaBruce, Kevin Kramer. *Dir*. Bruce LaBruce.

I Accuse (1958)   José Ferrer (Dreyfus), Anton Walbrook (Esterhazy), Emlyn Williams (Zola). Written by Gore Vidal. *Dir*. José Ferrer.

I Am a Camera (1955)   Julie Harris, Laurence Harvey, Shelley Winters, Anton Diffring. John Collier adaptation of Isherwood stories and the stage play by John Van Druten. *Dir*. Henry Cornelius.

I Am a Fugitive from a Chain Gang (1932)   Paul Muni, Glenda Farrell, Helen Vinson, Preston Foster. *Dir*. Mervyn Le Roy.

I Confess (1953)   Montgomery Clift, Anne Baxter, Brian Aherne, Karl Malden. Priest hears confession of a murderer and has a dilemma. *Dir*. Alfred Hitchcock.

I Married a Witch (1942)   Fredric March, Veronica Lake, Cecil Kellaway, Susan Hayward, Elizabeth Patterson. *Dir*. René Clair.

I Wanna Hold Your Hand (1978)   Nancy Allen, Bobby diCicco, Marc McClure. *Dir*. Robert Zemeckis.

I Want to Live (1958)   Susan Hayward, Simon Oakland, Virginia Vincent, Theodore Bikel. Based on the Barbara Graham story of a prostitute executed despite doubts as to her guilt. *Dir*. Robert Wise.

I Was a Male War Bride (1949)   Cary Grant, Ann Sheridan, Marion Marshall. *Dir*. Howard Hawks.

I Was Monty's Double (1958)   John Mills, Cecil Parker, ME Clifton-James. US title: *Hell, Heaven and Hoboken*. *Dir*. John Guillermin.

Ice-Age (2002)   Voices of Ray Romano (Manfred), John Leguizamo (Sid), Denis Leary (Diego), Goran Visnjic (Soto), Jack Black (Zeke), Tara Strong (Roshan). Animated sloth, mammoth and sabre-toothed tiger combine to return a lost child to his tribe during the ice-age. *Dir*. Carlos Saldanha and Chris Wedge.

Ice Cold in Alex (1958)   John Mills, Sylvia Syms, Anthony Quayle, Harry Andrews. *Dir*. J Lee Thompson.

Ice Station Zebra (1968)   Rock Hudson, Patrick McGoohan, Ernest Borgnine, Jim Brown. Based on the Alistair MacLean story. *Dir*. John Sturges.

Ideal Husband, An (1999)   Cate Blanchett, Minnie Driver, Rupert Everett, Peter Vaughan, Julianne Moore. *Dir*. Oliver Parker.

If (1968)   Malcolm McDowell, David Wood, Richard Warwick, Arthur Lowe. *Dir*. Lindsay Anderson.

If These Walls Could Talk (1996)   Demi Moore, Cher. TV movie. *Dir*. Nancy Savoka and Cher.

I'm All Right Jack (1959)   Ian Carmichael, Peter Sellers, Irene Handl, Richard Attenborough, Terry-Thomas, Dennis Price, Margaret Rutherford. *Dir*. John Boulting.

Importance of Being Earnest, The (1952)   Michael Redgrave, Michael Denison, Edith Evans, Margaret Rutherford, Dorothy Tutin. *Dir*. Anthony Asquith.

Importance of Being Earnest, The (2002)   Rupert Everett, Colin Firth, Frances O'Connor, Reese Witherspoon, Judi Dench. *Dir*. Oliver Parker.

In Search of the Castaways (1961)   Maurice Chevalier, Hayley Mills, George Sanders, Wilfrid Hyde-White, Wilfrid Brambell. *Dir*. Robert Stevenson.

In the Bleak Midwinter (1995)   Michael Maloney, Richard Briers, Julia Sawalha, Joan Collins, Jennifer Saunders. Story of a production of *Hamlet* in a village church. *Dir*. Kenneth Branagh.

In the Heat of the Night (1967)   Sidney Poitier, Rod Steiger, Warren Oates. *Dir*. Norman Jewison.

In Which We Serve (1942)   Noël Coward, Bernard Miles, John Mills, Richard Attenborough, Celia Johnson, Michael Wilding. Viewed as one of the best propaganda wartime films. *Dir*. Noël Coward and David Lean.

Inchon (1981)   Laurence Olivier (General MacArthur), Jacqueline Bisset, David Janssen, Ben Gazzara, Richard Roundtree. *Dir*. Terence Young.

Incredible Journey, The (1963)   Disney cartoon about 2 dogs and a cat and their 250-mile journey home after being separated from their owners. *Dir*. Fletcher Markle.

Incredible Shrinking Man, The (1957)   Grant Williams, Randy Stuart, April Kent. Radioactive mist is the cause of the shrinking. *Dir*. Jack Arnold.

Incredible Shrinking Woman, The (1981)   Lily

Tomlin, Charles Grodin, Ned Beatty, Henry Gibson. A new perfume causes the diminution in this case. *Dir.* Joel Schumacher.

Indecent Proposal (1993)   Robert Redford (John Gage), Demi Moore (Diana Murphy), Woody Harrelson (David Murphy), Billy Connolly (Auction MC). *Dir.* Adrian Lyne.

Independence Day (1996)   Will Smith (Capt Steve Hiller), Bill Pullman (President Whitmore), Jeff Goldblum, Judd Hirsch, Harry Connick Jnr, Brent Spiner. Pilot and computer expert battle an alien force. *Dir.* Roland Emmerich.

Indiana Jones and the Last Crusade (1989) Harrison Ford, Sean Connery (Professor Henry Jones), Denholm Elliott (Marcus Brody), John Rhys-Davies (Sallah), Julian Glover (Walter Donovan). *Dir.* Steven Spielberg.

Indiana Jones and the Temple of Doom (1984) Harrison Ford, Kate Capshaw (Willie Scott), Ke Huy Quan (Short Round). Prequel to *Raiders of the Lost Ark* (action takes place in 1935). *Dir.* Steven Spielberg.

Indiscreet (1958)   Cary Grant, Ingrid Bergman, Phyllis Calvert, Cecil Parker, David Kossoff, Megs Jenkins. Not very indiscreet as it happens, as the loving couple are both single. *Dir.* Stanley Donen.

Informer, The (1935)   Victor McLaglen, Heather Angel, Margot Grahame, Una O'Connor. Story of IRA allegiances. *Dir.* John Ford.

Inherit the Wind (1960)   Spencer Tracy, Fredric March, Dick York, Florence Eldridge, Gene Kelly. Fictionalised account of the Scopes Monkey Trial of 1925 when a teacher was accused of teaching Darwin's Theory of Evolution and, consequently, blasphemy. *Dir.* Stanley Kramer.

Inn of the Sixth Happiness, The (1958)   Ingrid Bergman, Curt Jurgens, Robert Donat. Biopic of the missionary Gladys Aylward and her work in China. *Dir.* Mark Robson.

Inner Circle, The (1991)   Tom Hulce (Ivan Sanshin), Lolita Davidovich (Anastasia), Bob Hoskins (Beria), Alexandre Zbruev (Stalin). Cinema projectionist goes to work for Stalin. *Dir.* Andrei Konchalovsky.

Innerspace (1987)   Dennis Quaid (Lt Tuck Pendleton), Martin Short (Jack Putter), Meg Ryan (Lydia Maxwell), Kevin McCarthy (Victor Scrimshaw). Version of *The Fantastic Voyage. Dir.* Joe Dante.

Insider, The (1999)   Al Pacino (Lowell Bergman), Russell Crowe (Jeffrey Wigand), Rip Torn (John Scanlon), Christopher Plummer (Mike Wallace), Diane Venora (Liare Wigand) Michael Gambon (Thomas Sandefor).   *Dir.* Michael Mann.

Insignificance (1985)   Gary Busey (The Ballplayer), Tony Curtis (The Senator), Michael Emil (The Professor), Theresa Russell (The Actress), Will Sampson (The Elevator Attendant). Four people resembling Monroe, Einstein, McCarthy & Di Maggio meet in New York hotel. *Dir.* Nicolas Roeg.

Insomnia (2002)   Al Pacino, Martin Donovan, Hilary Swank, Paul Dooley. Not to be confused with the 1997 Norwegian film of the same name. *Dir.* Christopher Nolan.

Inspector Calls, An (1954)   Alastair Sim, Jane Wenham, Bryan Forbes, Arthur Young. *Dir.* Guy Hamilton.

International Velvet (1978)   Nanette Newman, Tatum O'Neal, Anthony Hopkins, Christopher Plummer. *Dir.* Bryan Forbes.

Intersection (1994)   Sharon Stone, Richard Gere, Martin Landau. *Dir.* Mark Rydell.

Intermezzo (1939)   Leslie Howard, Ingrid Bergman, John Halliday, Edna Best, Cecil Kellaway. A virtuoso violinist has an affair with his musical protégée. *Dir.* Gregory Ratoff (William Wyler is thought to have assisted).

Intolerance (1916)   Mae Marsh, Lillian Gish, Constance Talmadge. Four stories depicting intolerance and persecution through the ages. *Dir.* DW Griffith.

Invasion of the Body Snatchers (1956)   Kevin McCarthy, Dana Wynter, Larry Gates, King Donovan, Carolyn Jones, Sam Peckinpah. Small American town is taken over by aliens. *Dir.* Don Siegel.

Invasion of the Body Snatchers (1978)   Donald Sutherland, Brooke Adams, Leonard Nimoy, Jeff Goldblum, Kevin McCarthy, Don Siegel. San Francisco becomes the venue for the remake of the 1956 classic. *Dir.* Philip Kaufman.

Invisible Man, The (1933)   Claude Rains (Dr Griffin), Gloria Stuart, Una O'Connor. *Dir.* James Whale.

Ipcress File, The (1965)   Michael Caine (Harry Palmer), Nigel Green, Sue Lloyd, Gordon Jackson. The Michael Caine character was never named in the novel by Len Deighton. *Dir.* Sidney J Furie.

IQ (1994)   Tim Robbins, Meg Ryan, Walter Matthau (Einstein), Stephen Fry, Keene Curtis (Eisenhower). *Dir.* Fred Schepisi.

Iris (2001)   Judi Dench (Iris Murdoch), Jim Broadbent (John Bayley), Kate Winslet (Young Iris), Hugh Bonneville (Young John), Penelope Wilton (Janet Stone), Juliet Aubrey (Young Janet), Eleanor Bron, Joan Bakewell. Jim Broadbent won Oscar as Best Supporting Actor. *Dir.* Richard Eyre.

Irma La Douce (1963)   Shirley MacLaine, Jack Lemmon, Lou Jacobi. Paris policeman falls for a prostitute and becomes her pimp. *Dir.* Billy Wilder.

Ishtar (1987)   Warren Beatty (Lyle Rogers), Dustin Hoffman (Chuck Clarke), Isabelle Adjani (Shirra Assel). Second biggest flop of all time. *Dir.* Elaine May.

Island of Dr Moreau (1977)   Burt Lancaster, Michael York, Nigel Davenport, Barbara Carrera. Story of shipwrecked sailors on a Pacific Island in 1911. *Dir.* Don Taylor.

It Happened One Night (1934)   Clark Gable, Claudette Colbert, Walter Connolly, Alan Hale, Ward Bond. Earned Oscars for both its stars. *Dir.* Frank Capra.

It Takes Two (1995)   Kirstie Alley, Steve Guttenberg, Mary-Kate and Ashley Olsen. *Dir.* Andy Tennant.

Italian Job, The (1969)   Michael Caine, Noël Coward, Benny Hill, Rossano Brazzi, Irene Handl, Fred Emney, John Le Mesurier, Simon Dee, Robert Powell. Crooks stage a traffic jam in Turin to pull off a robbery. *Dir.* Peter Collinson.

It's a Mad Mad Mad Mad World (1963)   Spencer Tracy, Jimmy Durante, Mickey Rooney, Phil Silvers, Terry-Thomas, Peter Falk, Buster Keaton, The 3 Stooges. Buried loot is the instigator of mayhem. *Dir.* Stanley Kramer.

It's a Wonderful Life (1946)   James Stewart, Henry Travers (Clarence), Donna Reed, Lionel Barrymore, Thomas Mitchell. James Stewart's favourite film and many believe Frank Capra's finest. *Dir.* Frank Capra.

It's a Wonderful World (1939)   James Stewart, Claudette Colbert, Frances Drake, Guy Kibbee. *Dir.* WS Van Dyke II.

Jack (1996)   Robin Williams, Diane Lane, Jennifer Lopez, Bill Cosby. *Dir.* Francis Ford Coppola.

Jack the Bear (1993)   Danny De Vito, Robert J

C
I
N
E
M
A

Steinmiller Jnr, Miko Hughes. *Dir*. Marshall Herskovitz.

Jackal, The (1997)   Bruce Willis (The Jackal), Richard Gere (Declan Mulqueen), Sidney Poitier (Preston), Diane Venora (Valentina Koslova), Mathilda May (Isabella). *Dir*. Michael Caton-Jones.

Jackie Brown (1998)   Pam Grier (Jackie Brown), Samuel L Jackson (Ordell Robbie), Robert Forster (Max Cherry), Michael Keaton, Michael Bowen, Robert De Niro (Louis Gara). Air stewardess smuggles cash into America for a gun-runner. *Dir*. Quentin Tarantino.

Jagged Edge (1985)   Jeff Bridges (Jack Forrester), Glenn Close (Teddy Barnes), Robert Loggia (Sam Ransom). *Dir*. Richard Marquand.

James and the Giant Peach (1996)   Paul Terry, Joanna Lumley, Pete Postlethwaite. *Dir*. Henry Selick.

Jason X (2002)   Kane Hodder (Jason), Lexa Doig (Rowan), Chuck Campbell (Tsunaron), Lisa Ryder (KAY-EM 14), Peter Mensah (Sgt Brodski), David Cronenberg (Dr Wimmer). Science fiction story set in the 25th century concerning students aboard a spaceship who revive a frozen serial killer. *Dir*. Jim Isaac.

Jaws (1975)   Robert Shaw, Roy Scheider, Richard Dreyfuss, Lorraine Gary. Long Island resort: Amity. *Dir*. Steven Spielberg.

Jaws 2 (1978)   Roy Scheider, Lorraine Gary. *Dir*. Jeannot Szwarc.

Jaws 3-D (1983)   Dennis Quaid (Mike), Bess Armstrong (Kathryn), Simon MacCorkindale (Philip), Louis Gossett Jr (Calvin). *Dir*. Joe Alves.

Jaws: the Revenge (1987)   Lorraine Gary (Ellen Brody), Lance Guest (Michael), Mario Van Peebles (Jake), Karen Young (Carla), Michael Caine (Hoagie). *Dir*. Joseph Sargent.

Jazz Singer, The (1927)   Al Jolson, May McAvoy, Warner Oland. Notable for being the first talkie. *Dir*. Alan Crosland.

Jean de Florette (1987)   Yves Montand (Cesar Soubeyran), Gérard Depardieu (Jean de Florette), Daniel Auteuil (Ugolin), Elisabeth Depardieu (Aimée), Ernestine Mazurowna (Manon). Sequel: *Manon des Sources*. *Dir*. Claude Berri.

Jennifer 8 (1992)   Andy Garcia (John Berlin), Uma Thurman (Helena Robertson). Serial killer preys on blind women. *Dir*. Bruce Robinson.

Jerry Maguire (1996)   Tom Cruise, Cuba Gooding Jnr. *Dir*. Phillip Noyce.

Jesus Christ Superstar (1973)   Ted Neeley, Carl Anderson, Yvonne Elliman. Melvyn Bragg wrote the screenplay with Jewison. *Dir*. Norman Jewison.

Jewel of the Nile (1985)   Michael Douglas (Jack), Kathleen Turner (Joan), Danny De Vito (Ralph). Film is dedicated to Diane Thomas, the writer of *Romancing the Stone*. *Dir*. Lewis Teague.

Jezebel (1938)   Bette Davis, Henry Fonda. US Civil War epic. *Dir*. William Wyler.

JFK (1991)   Kevin Costner (Jim Garrison), Sissy Spacek (Liz Garrison), Tommy Lee Jones (Clay Shaw), Joe Pesci (David Ferrie), Gary Oldman (Lee Harvey Oswald), Brian Doyle-Murray (Jack Ruby). *Dir*. Oliver Stone.

Jim Thorpe, All-American (1951)   Burt Lancaster (Thorpe), Charles Bickford, Phyllis Thaxter. Truish story of the Native American who became a star footballer. *Dir*. Michael Curtiz.

Jingle All the Way (1996)   Arnold Schwarzenegger (Howard Langston), Rita Wilson (Liz Langston), Jake Lloyd (Jamie Langston), Sinbad, James Belushi. *Dir*. Brian Levant.

Joan of Arc (1948)   Ingrid Bergman, José Ferrer, Francis L Sullivan. *Dir*. Victor Fleming.

John Paul Jones (1959)   Robert Stack, Charles Coburn (Benjamin Franklin), Bette Davis (Catherine the Great). Notable for its unending list of star cameos. *Dir*. John Farrow.

Johnny Belinda (1948)   Jane Wyman, Lew Ayres, Charles Bickford, Agnes Moorehead. Deaf mute is raped and the local doctor is suspected of being the father of the baby. *Dir*. Jean Negulesco.

Joker Is Wild, The (1957)   Frank Sinatra, Mitzi Gaynor, Eddie Albert, Jeanne Crain. The song 'All the Way' won an Academy Award. *Dir*. Charles Vidor.

Jokers, The (1967)   Michael Crawford, Oliver Reed, Harry Andrews, James Donald, Daniel Massey, Michael Hordern, Frank Finlay, Rachel Kempson. Two brothers decide to 'borrow' and replace the crown jewels. *Dir*. Michael Winner.

Jolson Story, The (1946)   Larry Parks (voice of Jolson), Evelyn Keyes. *Dir*. Alfred E Green.

Journey into Fear (1942)   Joseph Cotten, Dolores del Rio, Orson Welles. Munitions expert finds himself in danger from assassins in Istanbul. *Dir*. Norman Foster.

Journey to Shiloh (1967)   James Caan, Michael Sarrazin, Brenda Scott, Paul Petersen, Don Stroud, Harrison Ford. Seven young Texans leave home to fight in the Civil War. *Dir*. William Hale.

Journey to the Center of the Earth (1959)   James Mason, Arlene Dahl, Pat Boone, Diane Baker. Film ends with the team being catapulted out of Stromboli. *Dir*. Henry Levin.

Judge Dredd (1995)   Sylvester Stallone, Armand Assante, Diane Lane, Ian Dury, Max Von Sydow. Set in Mega City One in AD 2139. *Dir*. Danny Cannon.

Judgment at Nuremberg (1961)   Spencer Tracy, Marlene Dietrich, Burt Lancaster, Richard Widmark, Maximilian Schell, Judy Garland, Montgomery Clift, William Shatner. *Dir*. Stanley Kramer.

Judgment in Berlin (1988)   Martin Sheen (Herbert J Stern), Sam Wanamaker (Bernard Hellring). Director is Sean Penn's father. *Dir*. Leo Penn.

Juggernaut (1974)   Richard Harris, David Hemmings, Omar Sharif, Anthony Hopkins. Transatlantic liner is threatened by a mad bomber. *Dir*. Richard Lester.

Julia (1977)   Jane Fonda, Vanessa Redgrave, Jason Robards Jnr, Maximilian Schell, Hal Holbrook. Based on Lillian Hellman's book *Pentimento*. *Dir*. Fred Zinnemann.

Julius Caesar (1953)   John Gielgud, Marlon Brando, James Mason, Greer Garson, Deborah Kerr. *Dir*. Joseph L Mankiewicz.

Jumanji (1995)   Robin Williams, Bonnie Hunt, Kirsten Dunst. Two children play a mysterious board game that releases, after 25 years, a child and some ferocious animals. *Dir*. Joe Johnston.

Jumpin' Jack Flash (1986)   Whoopi Goldberg (Terry Doolittle), Tracey Ullman, James Belushi, Jonathan Pryce. *Dir*. Penny Marshall.

Jungle Fever (1991)   Wesley Snipes (Flipper Purify), Annabella Sciorra (Angela Tucci), Spike Lee (Cyrus), Anthony Quinn (Lou Carbone), Samuel L Jackson (Gator Purify). *Dir*. Spike Lee.

Jurassic Park (1993)   Richard Attenborough, Jeff Goldblum, Sam Neill, Laura Dern, Samuel L Jackson, Bob Peck. *Dir*. Steven Spielberg.

Jurassic Park III (2001)   Sam Neill (Dr Alan Grant), William H Macy, Tea Leoni, Laura Dern. *Dir*. Joe Johnston.

Just a Gigolo (1978)   David Bowie, Sydne Rome, Kim Novak, Marlene Dietrich, David Hemmings, Curt Jurgens. *Dir*. David Hemmings.

K-9 (1989) James Belushi (Thomas Dooley), Mel Harris (Tracy), Kevin Tighe (Lyman). Not the same K-9 as in *Dr Who*. *Dir*. Rod Daniel.

K-19: The Widowmaker (2002) Harrison Ford (Captain Alexi Vostrikov), Sam Spruell, Liam Neeson (Mikhail Polenin), Peter Sarsgaard (Vadim Ratchenko), George Anton (Konstantin Poliansky), Steve Cumyn, Steve Nicholson, Chris Redman, Tygh Runyan. Based on a true-life story which follows the fate of Captain Alexi Vostrikov who, at the height of the Cold War, is ordered to take over command of nuclear missile submarine K-19, pride of the Soviet Navy. His assignment: prepare the K-19 for sea and take her out on patrol – no matter what the cost. But problems with the K-19 arise that may lead to a core meltdown and explosion that will certainly kill all aboard, and possibly trigger nuclear war. In a daring act of heroism, Vostrikov must choose between his orders from the Kremlin and the lives of his men and his country. *Dir*. Kathryn Bigelow.

Kaleidoscope (1966) Warren Beatty, Susannah York, Clive Revill, Eric Porter. Playboy breaks into card factory to mark the cards and so enable him to clean up. *Dir*. Jack Smight.

Kansas City (1996) Jennifer Jason Leigh, Miranda Richardson, Harry Belafonte. Woman kidnaps a politician's drug addicted wife in a bid to get her husband released by the gangsters holding him. *Dir*. Robert Altman.

Karate Kid, The (1984) Ralph Macchio (Daniel), Pat Morita (Miyagi), Elisabeth Shue (Ali), Martin Kove (Kreese), William Zabka (Johnny). *Dir*. John G Avildsen.

Karate Kid Part II, The (1986) Ralph Macchio, Pat Morita, Nobu McCarthy (Yukie), Danny Kamekona (Sato). *Dir*. John G. Avildsen.

Karate Kid III, The (1989) Ralph Macchio, Pat Morita (Miyagi), Robyn Lively (Jessica Andrews). *Dir*. John G Avildsen.

Kate and Leopold (2001) Meg Ryan (Kate McKay), Hugh Jackman (Leopold), Liev Schreiber, Natasha Lyonne, Breckin Meyer. An English duke is transported from 1876 to the present day and falls in love. *Dir*. James Mangold.

Kelly's Heroes (1970) Clint Eastwood, Telly Savalas, Don Rickles, Donald Sutherland. *Dir*. Brian G Hutton.

Kentuckian, The (1955) Burt Lancaster, Dianne Foster, Walter Matthau, John McIntire. *Dir*. Burt Lancaster.

Kes (1969) David Bradley, Lynne Perrie, Colin Welland, Brian Glover. *Dir*. Ken Loach.

Key Largo (1948) Humphrey Bogart, Lauren Bacall, Claire Trevor, Edward G Robinson, Lionel Barrymore. *Dir*. John Huston.

Kickboxer (1989) Jean Claude Van Damme, Dennis Alexio, Tong Po (Michel Qissi). *Dir*. Mark DiSalle and David Worth.

Kid, The (1921) Charles Chaplin, Jackie Coogan, Edna Purviance. *Dir*. Charles Chaplin.

Kid for Two Farthings, A (1955) Celia Johnson, Diana Dors, David Kossoff, Primo Carnera, Sydney Tafler. *Dir*. Carol Reed.

Kid from Brooklyn, The (1946) Danny Kaye, Virginia Mayo, Eve Arden, Walter Abel. Timid milkman becomes a prizefighter. *Dir*. Norman Z McLeod.

Kid Galahad (1937) Edward G Robinson, Bette Davis, Humphrey Bogart, Harry Carey. *Dir*. Michael Curtiz.

Kid Galahad (1962) Elvis Presley, Lola Albright, Gig Young, Charles Bronson. *Dir*. Phil Karlson.

Kidnapped (1971) Michael Caine, Lawrence Douglas, Trevor Howard, Jack Hawkins, Donald Pleasence, Gordon Jackson. Other versions starred Warner Baxter and Freddie Bartholomew (1938), and Peter Finch and James MacArthur (1959). *Dir*. Delbert Mann.

Kids (1995) Lee Fitzpatrick, Sarah Henderson, Justin Pearce. Day in the life of teenagers includes sex and skateboarding. *Dir*. Larry Clark.

Killers, The (1946) Burt Lancaster, Edmond O'Brien, Ava Gardner. *Dir*. Robert Siodmak.

Killers, The (1964) John Cassavetes, Lee Marvin, Clu Gulager, Angie Dickinson, Ronald Reagan. Ronald Reagan's last film and the first in which he played a bad guy. *Dir*. Don Siegel.

Killer: A Journal of Murder (1996) James Woods (Carl Panzram), Robert Sean Leonard (Henry Lesser). True story set in Leavenworth Prison, Kansas. *Dir*. Tim Metcalfe.

Killing Fields, The (1984) Sam Waterston (Sydney Schanberg), Haing S Ngor (Dith Pran), John Malkovich (Al Rockoff). *Dir*. Roland Joffé.

Killing of Sister George, The (1969) Beryl Reid, Susannah York, Coral Browne, Patricia Medina, Roland Fraser. *Dir*. Robert Aldrich.

Kind Hearts and Coronets (1949) Dennis Price, Alec Guinness, Valerie Hobson, Joan Greenwood, Arthur Lowe. Alec Guinness plays the 8 members of the D'Ascoyne family. *Dir*. Robert Hamer.

Kind of Loving, A (1962) Alan Bates, June Ritchie, Thora Hird, Bert Palmer. Keith Waterhouse & Willis Hall adapted Stan Barstow's story. *Dir*. John Schlesinger.

Kindergarten Cop (1990) Arnold Schwarzenegger (John Kimble), Penelope Ann Miller (Joyce Paulmarie), Pamela Reed (Phoebe O'Hara), Linda Hunt (Miss Schlowski). *Dir*. Ivan Reitman.

King and I, The (1956) Yul Brynner, Deborah Kerr, Rita Moreno. *Dir*. Walter Lang.

King and I, The (1999) Voices of Miranda Richardson, Ian Richardson, Martin Vidnovic, Darrell Hammond. *Dir*. Richard Rich.

King David (1985) Richard Gere (David), Edward Woodward (Saul), Alice Krige (Bathsheba), Dennis Quilley (Samuel). *Dir*. Bruce Beresford.

King Kong (1933) Fay Wray, Robert Armstrong (Carl Denham), Bruce Cabot. *Dir*. Merian C Cooper & Ernest B Schoedsnack.

King Kong (1976) Jeff Bridges, Charles Grodin, Jessica Lange. This Dino de Laurentiis production was something of a spoof. *Dir*. John Guillermin.

King of Comedy, The (1983) Robert De Niro (Rupert Pupkin), Jerry Lewis (Jerry Langford), Diahnne Abbott (Rita). *Dir*. Martin Scorsese.

King of Kings (1961) Jeffrey Hunter, Robert Ryan, Siobhan McKenna. *Dir*. Nicholas Ray.

King Ralph (1991) John Goodman (Ralph Jones), Peter O'Toole (Sir Cedric Willingham), John Hurt (Lord Graves), Joely Richardson (Princess Anna), Leslie Phillips (Gordon), Julian Glover (King Gustav), Judy Parfitt (Queen Katherine). The whole of the Royal Family are wiped out, leaving a lounge pianist as King. *Dir*. David S Ward.

King Rat (1965) George Segal, Tom Courtenay, John Mills, James Fox, Leonard Rossiter. Based on James Clavell novel about collaboration in Changi POW camp during WW2. *Dir*. Bryan Forbes.

King Solomon's Mines (1950) Stewart Granger, Deborah Kerr, Richard Carlson. *Dir*. Compton Bennett.

King Solomon's Mines (1985) Richard Chamberlain, Sharon Stone, Herbert Lom, John Rhys-Davies. *Dir*. J Lee Thompson.

CINEMA

King's Row (1941)   Ann Sheridan, Robert Cummings, Ronald Reagan (Drake), Claude Rains. Reagan took the name of his autobiography from a line in this film. *Dir.* Sam Wood.

Kipps (1941)   Michael Redgrave, Phyllis Calvert, Diana Wynyard, Michael Wilding. Later turned into a musical as *Half a Sixpence. Dir.* Carol Reed.

Kismet (1955)   Howard Keel, Ann Blyth, Vic Damone, Sebastian Cabot. Musical based on Borodin. *Dir.* Vincente Minnelli.

Kiss Me Kate (1953)   Howard Keel, Kathryn Grayson, Ann Miller, Keenan Wynn. Musical version of *The Taming of the Shrew. Dir.* George Sidney.

Kiss of the Spider Woman (1985)   William Hurt (Molina), Raul Julia (Valentin), Sonia Braga (Leni Lamaison / Marta). Flamboyant gay shares South American prison cell with a radical activist. *Dir.* Hector Babenco.

Kissin' Cousins (1963)   Elvis Presley, Arthur O'Connell, Glenda Farrell, Jack Albertson. Presley plays 2 parts. *Dir.* Gene Nelson.

Kitty Foyle (1940)   Ginger Rogers, Dennis Morgan, James Craig, Eduardo Ciannelli. *Dir.* Sam Wood.

Klansman, The (1974)   Lee Marvin, Richard Burton, Cameron Mitchell, OJ Simpson, Linda Evans. *Dir.* Terence Young.

Klute (1971)   Jane Fonda, Donald Sutherland, Roy Scheider. *Dir.* Alan J Pakula.

Knack, The (1965)   Michael Crawford, Ray Brooks, Rita Tushingham. *Dir.* Richard Lester.

Knight's Tale, A (2001)   Heath Ledger, Rufus Sewell, Paul Bettany (Chaucer), Laura Fraser, Mark Addy. *Dir.* Brian Helgeland.

Kotch (1971)   Walter Matthau, Deborah Winter. *Dir.* Jack Lemmon.

Krakatoa, East of Java (1968)   Maximilian Schell, Diane Baker, Brian Keith, Rossano Brazzi, Sal Mineo. Krakatoa is actually west of Java. *Dir.* Bernard Kowalski.

Kramer versus Kramer (1979)   Dustin Hoffman, Justin Henry, Meryl Streep, Jane Alexander, Howard Duff. Based on an Avery Corman novel. *Dir.* Robert Benton.

Krays, The (1990)   Gary Kemp (Ronnie), Martin Kemp (Reggie), Billie Whitelaw (Violet), Susan Fleetwood (Rose), Jimmy Jewell (Cannonball Lee), Tom Bell (Jack 'The Hat' McVitie). *Dir.* Peter Medak.

L-Shaped Room, The (1962)   Leslie Caron, Tom Bell, Brock Peters, Cicely Courtneidge, Bernard Lee, Avis Bunnage, Pat Phoenix, Emlyn Williams. *Dir.* Bryan Forbes.

La Bamba (1987)   Lou Diamond Phillips (Ritchie Valens), Esai Morales (Bob Morales), Rosana De Soto (Connie Valenzuela). *Dir.* Luis Valdez.

LA Confidential (1997)   Danny De Vito (Sid Hudgens), Kim Basinger (Lynn Bracken), Kevin Spacey (Jack Vincennes), Russell Crowe (Bud White), Guy Pearce (Ed Exley). Hooker with a facial similarity to Veronica Lake gets mixed up in murder investigation. *Dir.* Curtis Hanson.

LA Story (1991)   Steve Martin (Harris K Telemacher), Victoria Tennant (Sara McDowel), Iman (Cynthia), Richard E Grant (Roland), Marilu Henner (Trudi), Patrick Stewart (Maître d' at L'Idiot). *Dir.* Mick Jackson.

Labyrinth (1986)   David Bowie (Jareth), Jennifer Connelly (Sarah), Toby Froud (Toby), Shelley Thompson (Stepmother). *Dir.* Jim Henson.

Lady Caroline Lamb (1972)   Sarah Miles, Jon Finch, Richard Chamberlain (Byron), Margaret Leighton, John Mills (Canning), Ralph Richardson (George III), Laurence Olivier (Wellington). *Dir.* Robert Bolt.

Lady Sings the Blues (1972)   Diana Ross (Billie Holliday), Billy Dee Williams, Richard Pryor. *Dir.* Sidney J Furie.

Lady Vanishes, The (1938)   Margaret Lockwood, Michael Redgrave, Dame May Whitty, Googie Withers. A 1979 remake starring Cybill Shepherd and Elliott Gould flopped. *Dir.* Alfred Hitchcock.

Lady with the Lamp, The (1951)   Anna Neagle, Michael Wilding. *Dir.* Herbert Wilcox.

Ladykillers, The (1955)   Alec Guinness, Katie Johnson, Peter Sellers, Herbert Lom, Frankie Howerd. *Dir.* Alexander Mackendrick.

Lamerica (1994)   Enrico Lo Verso, Michele Placido. *Dir.* Gianni Amelio.

Land and Freedom (1995)   Ian Hart, Rosana Pastor, Iciar Bollain. *Dir.* Ken Loach.

Lantana (2001)   Anthony LaPaglia, Geoffrey Rush, Barbara Hershey, Kerry Armstrong. *Dir.* Ray Lawrence.

Lara Croft: Tomb Raider (2001)   Angelina Jolie (Lara), Iain Glen, Noah Taylor, Leslie Philips, Chris Barrie, Daniel Craig. *Dir.* Simon West. Angelina Jolie's father Jon Voight is cast as her on-screen father in this film.

Lassie Come Home (1943)   Roddy McDowall, Elizabeth Taylor, Donald Crisp. Based on an Eric Knight story. *Dir.* Fred M Wilcox.

Last Action Hero, The (1993)   Arnold Schwarzenegger, Mercedes Ruehl, F Murray Abraham, Art Carney, Anthony Quinn. *Dir.* John McTiernan.

Last Boy Scout, The (1992)   Bruce Willis (Joe Hallenbeck), Damon Wayans (Jimmy Dix), Chelsea Field (Sarah Hallenbeck). *Dir.* Tony Scott.

Last Dance (1996)   Sharon Stone (Cindy Liggett), Rob Morrow (Rick Hayes). *Dir.* Bruce Beresford.

Last Detail, The (1973)   Jack Nicholson, Otis Young, Randy Quaid, Clifton James. *Dir.* Hal Ashby.

Last Emperor, The (1987)   John Lone (Pu Yi), Peter O'Toole (RJ), Joan Chen (Wan Jung). *Dir.* Bernardo Bertolucci.

Last Exit to Brooklyn (1990)   Stephen Lang (Harry Black), Jennifer Jason Leigh (Tralala), Burt Young (Big Joe), Peter Dobson (Vinnie). *Dir.* Uli Edel.

Last Hard Men, The (1976)   Charlton Heston, James Coburn, Barbara Hershey, Christopher Mitchum. *Dir.* Andrew V McLaglen.

Last Man Standing (1996)   Bruce Willis, Christopher Walken, Bruce Dern, Alexandra Powers. Set in Texas during the Depression of the 1930s, it concerns a gunman on the run and rival bootleggers. *Dir.* Walter Hill.

Last of the Dogmen (1995)   Tom Berenger, Barbara Hershey, Kuttwood Smith, Steve Reevis. Bounty hunter discovers a group of Cheyenne in Montana. *Dir.* Tab Murphy.

Last of the Mohicans, The (1992)   Daniel Day-Lewis (Hawkeye), Madeleine Stowe (Cora), Russell Means (Chingachgook), Eric Schweig (Uncas). *Dir.* Michael Mann.

Last Orders (2001)   Michael Caine (Jack), Bob Hoskins (Ray), Tom Courtenay (Vic), David Hemmings (Lenny), Ray Winstone (Vince), Helen Mirren (Amy). Three elderly Londoners reminisce on past lives and loves as they gather for a trip to the seaside to scatter the ashes of a mutual friend. Based on a novel by Graham Swift. *Dir.* Fred Schepisi.

Last Picture Show, The (1971)   Timothy Bottoms, Jeff Bridges, Cybill Shepherd, Ben Johnson, Cloris Leachman, Ellen Burstyn. *Dir.* Peter Bogdanovich.

Last Seduction, The (1994)   Linda Fiorentino, Peter Berg, Bill Nunn, Bill Pullman. Woman leaves her husband taking with her a million dollars he made from a drug deal. *Dir*. John Dahl.

Last Summer (1969)   Barbara Hershey, Richard Thomas, Bruce Davison, Cathy Burns, Ralph Waite. *Dir*. Frank Perry.

Last Tango in Paris (1972)   Marlon Brando, Maria Schneider. *Dir*. Bernardo Bertolucci.

Last Temptation of Christ, The (1988)   Willem Dafoe (Jesus), Harvey Keitel (Judas), Barbara Hershey (Mary Magdalene), David Bowie (Pontius Pilate). *Dir*. Martin Scorsese.

Last Tycoon, The (1976)   Robert De Niro, Robert Mitchum, Tony Curtis, Jeanne Moreau, Jack Nicholson, Donald Pleasence. *Dir*. Elia Kazan.

Lavender Hill Mob, The (1951)   Alec Guinness, Stanley Holloway, Sid James, Alfie Bass, Audrey Hepburn. Bank clerk masterminds bullion robbery by moulding Eiffel Towers in gold to be smuggled to France. *Dir*. Charles Crichton.

Lawrence of Arabia (1962)   Peter O'Toole, Omar Sharif, Arthur Kennedy, Jack Hawkins, Alec Guinness. Screenplay by Robert Bolt. *Dir*. David Lean.

League of Gentlemen, The (1960)   Jack Hawkins, Richard Attenborough, Roger Livesey, Bryan Forbes, Nigel Patrick, Nanette Newman. *Dir*. Basil Dearden.

Leaving Las Vegas (1995)   Nicolas Cage, Elisabeth Shue, Julian Sands, Richard Lewis. Alcoholic writer goes to Las Vegas to drink himself to death. *Dir*. Mike Figgis.

Left-Handed Gun, The (1958)   Paul Newman (Billy the Kid), John Dehner (Pat Garrett). *Dir*. Arthur Penn.

Legally Blonde (2001)   Reese Witherspoon, Luke Wilson, Selma Blair, Matthew Davis, Victor Garber. *Dir*. Robert Luketic.

Legend of the Lone Ranger, The (1981)   Klinton Spilsbury, Michael Horse, Christopher Lloyd, Matt Clark. *Dir*. William A Fraker.

Lemon Drop Kid, The (1951)   Bob Hope, Marilyn Maxwell, Lloyd Nolan. Based on a Damon Runyon story. *Dir*. Sidney Lanfield.

Lenny (1974)   Dustin Hoffman (Lennie Bruce), Valerie Perrine. *Dir*. Bob Fosse.

Les Misérables (1995)   Jean-Paul Belmondo, Michel Boujenah, Rufus. *Dir*. Claude Lelouch.

Lethal Weapon (1987)   Mel Gibson (Martin Riggs), Danny Glover (Roger Murtaugh), Gary Busey (Joshua). Vietnam veteran turned cop is unhinged by his wife's death and has a death wish. *Dir*. Richard Donner.

Lethal Weapon 2 (1989)   Mel Gibson, Danny Glover, Joe Pesci (Leo Getz), Patsy Kensit (Rika Van Den Haas), Joss Ackland. South African drug runners unfortunately meet Martin Riggs. *Dir*. Richard Donner.

Lethal Weapon 3 (1992)   Mel Gibson, Danny Glover, Joe Pesci, Rene Russo (Lorna Cole). *Dir*. Richard Donner.

Let's Make Love (1960)   Yves Montand, Marilyn Monroe, Tony Randall, Wilfrid Hyde-White, Frankie Vaughan, Bing Crosby, Gene Kelly. Multi-millionaire learns he is to be burlesqued, so joins the cast. *Dir*. George Cukor.

Letter to Brezhnev (1985)   Alfred Molina (Sergei), Peter Firth (Peter), Margi Clarke (Teresa), Tracy Lea (Tracy). Liverpool lass falls in love with a Russian sailor. *Dir*. Chris Bernard.

Liar Liar (1997)   Jim Carrey (Fletcher Reede), Amanda Donohoe, Justin Cooper, Jennifer Tilly. (Out-takes shown as end credits roll.) *Dir*. Tom Shadyac.

Licence to Kill (1989)   Timothy Dalton, Carey Lowell (Pam Bouvier), Anthony Zerbe (Milton Krest), Robert Davi (Frank Sanchez), Caroline Bliss (Moneypenny), Robert Brown (M), Talisa Soto (Lupe Lamora). Book title: *Licence Revoked*. Title song by Gladys Knight. *Dir*. John Glen.

Licensed to Kill (1965)   Tom Adams, Veronica Hurst, Karel Stepanek. US title: *The Second Best Secret Agent in the Whole Wide World*. *Dir*. Lindsay Shonteff.

Life at the Top (1965)   Laurence Harvey (Joe Lampton), Jean Simmons, Honor Blackman, Michael Craig, Margaret Johnston. *Dir*. Ted Kotcheff.

Life Is Beautiful (1997)   Roberto Benigni, Nicoletta Braschi, Giustino Durano, Horst Buchholz. *Dir*. Roberto Benigni

Lilo & Stitch (2002)   Voices of Daveigh Chase (Lilo), Chris Sanders (Stitch), Tia Carrere, Zoe Caldwell, Ving Rhames. Lilo is a young Hawaiian girl who adopts a 'dog' named Stitch who is actually an alien genetic experiment gone horribly awry. Stitch has crash-landed on Earth, where he immediately begins wreaking havoc. Through her generosity, Lilo teaches Stitch the one thing he wasn't designed to do: to care about others. *Dir*. Dean DeBlois and Chris Sanders.

Limelight (1952)   Charlie Chaplin, Claire Bloom, Buster Keaton, Sydney Chaplin. *Dir*. Charlie Chaplin.

Lion in Winter, The (1968)   Katharine Hepburn (Eleanor of Aquitaine), Peter O'Toole (Henry II), Anthony Hopkins. *Dir*. Anthony Harvey.

Lion King, The (1994)   Voices of Matthew Broderick, Rowan Atkinson, Whoopi Goldberg, Jeremy Irons, Robert Guillaume, James Earl Jones. Songs include: 'Can You Feel the Love Tonight', 'Circle of Life' & 'Hakuna Matata'. (Music by Elton John, lyrics by Tim Rice.) *Dir*. Roger Allers.

Liquidator, The (1965)   Rod Taylor, Trevor Howard, David Tomlinson, Wilfrid Hyde-White, Derek Nimmo. *Dir*. Jack Cardiff.

List of Adrian Messenger, The (1963)   George C Scott, Kirk Douglas, Clive Brook, Dana Wynter, Robert Mitchum, Frank Sinatra, Tony Curtis, Burt Lancaster. The cameos by the last 4 listed stars are debatable as they are unrecognisable. *Dir*. John Huston.

Lisztomania (1975)   Roger Daltrey, Sara Kestelman, Paul Nicholas, Fiona Lewis, Ringo Starr. *Dir*. Ken Russell.

Little Big Man (1970)   Dustin Hoffman, Martin Balsam, Faye Dunaway, Chief Dan George. *Dir*. Arthur Penn.

Little Caesar (1931)   Edward G Robinson, Douglas Fairbanks Jnr, Glenda Farrell. *Dir*. Mervyn Le Roy.

Little Dorrit (1987)   Derek Jacobi (Arthur Clennam), Alec Guinness (William Dorrit), Max Wall (Flintwinch). There are 211 people named on the cast list, which is a record for a British film. *Dir*. Christine Edzard.

Little Foxes, The (1941)   Bette Davis, Herbert Marshall, Teresa Wright, Dan Duryea. Based on a Lillian Hellman story. *Dir*. William Wyler.

Little Giants (1994)   Rick Moranis, Ed O'Neil, John Madden. Wimp decides to create a young football team full of misfits. *Dir*. Duwayne Dunham.

Little Shop of Horrors (1986)   Rick Moranis (Seymour Krelborn), Ellen Greene (Audrey), Vincent Gardenia (Mushnik), Steve Martin (Orin Scrivello, DDS). Voice of the plant (Audrey II): Levi Stubbs of the Four Tops. *Dir*. Frank Oz.

Little Women (1933)   Katharine Hepburn, Paul Lukas, Joan Bennett, Frances Dee, Spring Byington. *Dir*. George Cukor.

C
I
N
E
M
A

Little Women (1949) June Allyson, Elizabeth Taylor, Peter Lawford, Margaret O'Brien, Janet Leigh, Mary Astor. *Dir*. Mervyn Le Roy.

Little Women (1994) Winona Ryder, Gabriel Byrne, Trini Alvarado, Samantha Mathis, Susan Sarandon. *Dir*. Gillian Armstrong.

Live and Let Die (1973) Roger Moore, Yaphet Kotto (Dr Kananga), Jane Seymour (Solitaire). Paul McCartney wrote and performed theme song. *Dir*. Guy Hamilton.

Living Daylights (1987) Timothy Dalton, Maryam d'Abo (Kara Milovy), Jeroen Krabbe (Gen Georgi Koskov), Joe Don Baker (Brad Whitaker), John Rhys-Davies (Gen Leonid Pushkin), Robert Brown (M), Desmond Llewellyn (Q), Caroline Bliss (Moneypenny), John Terry (Felix Leiter). Theme Song by A-Ha. *Dir*. John Glen.

Local Hero (1983) Burt Lancaster (Happer), Peter Riegert (Mac), John Gordon Sinclair (Ricky). TV series *Northern Exposure* was strongly influenced by this film. *Dir*. Bill Forsyth.

Loch Ness (1995) Ted Danson, Joely Richardson, Ian Holm, John Savident. US scientist tries to debunk the monster myth. *Dir*. John Henderson.

Lock Up (1989) Sylvester Stallone (Frank Leone), Donald Sutherland (Warden Drumgoole). *Dir*. John Flynn.

Logan's Run (1976) Michael York, Richard Jordan, Jenny Agutter, Farrah Fawcett-Majors, Peter Ustinov. Based on SF novel by William F Nolan. *Dir*. Michael Anderson.

Lolita (1962) James Mason, Shelley Winters, Sue Lyon, Peter Sellers. Lolita is 14 years old. *Dir*. Stanley Kubrick.

London Kills Me (1991) Justin Chadwick, Steven Mackintosh, Emer McCourt, Roshan Seth, Fiona Shaw. Down on his luck drug pusher is told he can have a job as a waiter if he can acquire a decent pair of shoes. *Dir*. Hanif Kureishi.

Loneliness of the Long Distance Runner, The (1962) Tom Courtenay, Michael Redgrave, James Bolam, Avis Bunnage. *Dir*. Tony Richardson.

Lonely Are the Brave (1962) Kirk Douglas, Walter Matthau, Gena Rowlands, Carroll O'Connor. Modern technology is pitted against a last rebel cowboy. *Dir*. David Miller.

Long and the Short and the Tall, The (1960) Laurence Harvey, Richard Todd, David McCallum, Richard Harris. US title: *Jungle Fighters*. *Dir*. Leslie Norman.

Long Good Friday, The (1980) Bob Hoskins, Helen Mirren, Dave King, Bryan Marshall, Eddie Constantine, Stephen Davis. *Dir*. John Mackenzie.

Long Goodbye, The (1973) Elliott Gould, Nina Van Pallandt, Sterling Hayden, Mark Rydell, Henry Gibson. *Dir*. Robert Altman.

Long Kiss Goodnight, The (1996) Geena Davis, Samuel L Jackson, Patrick Malahide. *Dir*. Renny Harlin.

Long Riders, The (1980) Stacy Keach, James Keach, David Carradine, Keith Carradine, Robert Carradine, Dennis Quaid, Randy Quaid. Story of the Younger, Miller and James boys. *Dir*. Walter Hill.

Longest Day, The (1962) John Wayne, Robert Mitchum, Henry Fonda, Robert Ryan, Roddy McDowall, Robert Wagner, Paul Anka, Fabian, Jeffrey Hunter, Rod Steiger, Red Buttons, Richard Burton, Sean Connery. *Dir*. Andrew Marton.

Look Back in Anger (1959) Richard Burton, Mary Ure, Claire Bloom, Edith Evans, Donald Pleasence. *Dir*. Tony Richardson.

Look Who's Talking (1989) John Travolta (James), Kirstie Alley (Mollie), Olympia Dukakis (Rosie), George Segal (Albert). Bruce Willis was the voice of Mikey. *Dir*. Amy Heckerling.

Look Who's Talking Too (1990) John Travolta, Kirstie Alley, Olympia Dukakis, Roseanne Arnold (voice of Julie), Mel Brooks (voice of Mr Toilet Man), Bruce Willis (voice of Mikey). *Dir*. Amy Heckerling.

Loot (1970) Richard Attenborough, Lee Remick, Hywel Bennett, Milo O'Shea, Dick Emery. *Dir*. Silvio Narizzano.

Lord of the Flies (1963) James Aubrey, Tom Chapin, Hugh Edwards. Remake in 1990 was directed by Harry Hook. *Dir*. Peter Brook.

Lord of the Rings (1978) Cartoon version of Tolkien's book with voices of Christopher Guard and John Hurt. *Dir*. Ralph Bakshi.

Lord of the Rings: The Fellowship of the Ring, The (2001) Ian McKellen (Gandalf), Elijah Wood (Frodo Baggins), Viggo Mortensen (Aragorn), Sean Astin (Sam), Cate Blanchett (Galadriel), Sean Bean (Boromir), John Rhys-Davies (Gimli), Liv Tyler (Arwen), Billy Boyd (Pippin), Christopher Lee (Saruman), Ian Holm (Bilbo Baggins), Andy Serkis (Gollum), Dominic Monaghan (Merry), Orlando Bloom (Legolas). Multiple Oscar winner concerning a hobbit who inherits a magic ring that could enslave all the people of Middle Earth unless it is destroyed. *Dir*. Peter Jackson.

Lord of the Rings: The Two Towers, The (2002) The second chapter in the JRR Tolkien saga. The hobbits Frodo and Sam brave terrible dangers in an attempt to have the evil ring destroyed, while Aragorn, Legolas and their allies strive to rescue the abducted hobbits Pippin and Merry from the clutches of evil. The great wizard Gandalf also makes his miraculous return to aid in the struggle against the united towers of Saruman and Sauron (Sala Baker). *The Two Towers* has the same cast as *The Fellowship of the Ring* but new characters include Bernard Hill's Théoden, David Wenham's Faramir, Karl Urban's Éomer, and Brad Dourif as Grima Wormtongue. *Dir*. Peter Jackson.

Lost Highway (1997) Bill Pullman, Patricia Arquette, Balthazar Getty. *Dir*. David Lynch.

Lost Horizon (1937) Ronald Colman, HB Warner, Thomas Mitchell, Sam Jaffe. Remade in 1972 with Peter Finch in Colman role. *Dir*. Frank Capra.

Lost Weekend, The (1945) Ray Milland (Don Birnam), Jane Wyman, Howard da Silva. *Dir*. Billy Wilder.

Lost World, The: Jurassic Park (1997) Jeff Goldblum (Dr Ian Malcolm), Julianne Moore, Pete Postlethwaite, Richard Attenborough (John Hammond). *Dir*. Steven Spielberg.

Love Is a Many-Splendored Thing (1955) Jennifer Jones, William Holden, Torin Thatcher. Sammy Fain & Paul Francis Webster won an Academy Award for the title song. *Dir*. Henry King.

Love Me Tender (1956) Richard Egan, Debra Paget, Elvis Presley, Neville Brand, James Drury. *Dir*. Robert D Webb.

Love Me Tonight (1932) Maurice Chevalier, Jeanette MacDonald, Charles Butterworth, Myrna Loy. *Dir*. Rouben Mamoulian.

Love on the Dole (1941) Deborah Kerr, Clifford Evans, George Carney. Based on Walter Greenwood's novel. *Dir*. John Baxter.

Love Story (1970) Ali MacGraw, Ryan O'Neal (Oliver Barrett IV), Ray Milland. 1978 sequel: *Oliver's Story*. *Dir*. Arthur Hiller.

Lust for Life (1956) Kirk Douglas (Vincent Van Gogh), Anthony Quinn (Paul Gauguin). *Dir.* Vincente Minnelli.

Mad Dog and Glory (1992) Robert De Niro, Uma Thurman, Bill Murray. Timid cop is given a present of a beautiful girl for a week by a gangster. *Dir.* John McNaughton.

Mad Max (1979) Mel Gibson, Joanne Samuel. *Dir.* George Miller.

Mad Max 2 (1981) Mel Gibson, Bruce Spence, Vernon Wells. *Dir.* George Miller.

Mad Max beyond Thunderdome (1985) Mel Gibson, Tina Turner, Angelo Rossitto, Helen Buday. *Dir.* George Miller.

Madame Bovary (1949) Jennifer Jones, Van Heflin, James Mason, Louis Jourdan. A 1991 remake starring Isabelle Huppert kept to the original plot a little better. *Dir.* Vincente Minnelli.

Made in America (1993) Whoopi Goldberg, Ted Danson, Will Smith. Black teenager, born by artificial insemination, discovers her father is a white car salesman. *Dir.* Richard Benjamin.

Madness of King George, The (1994) Nigel Hawthorne, Helen Mirren, Ian Holm, Amanda Donohoe, Rupert Everett, Rupert Graves. *Dir.* Nicholas Hytner.

Magic Christian (1969) Peter Sellers, Ringo Starr, Richard Attenborough, Laurence Harvey, Spike Milligan, Raquel Welch, John Cleese. Yul Brynner cameo as a transvestite nightclub singer. *Dir.* Joseph McGrath.

Magnificent Seven, The (1960) Yul Brynner, Steve McQueen, Robert Vaughn, James Coburn, Charles Bronson, Brad Dexter, Horst Buchholz. *Dir.* John Sturges.

Malcolm X (1992) Denzil Washington, Angela Bassett, Albert Hall, Al Freeman Jnr, Spike Lee. Based on the book *Autobiography of Malcolm X as told to Alex Haley*. *Dir.* Spike Lee.

Mame (1974) Lucille Ball, Beatrice Arthur, Robert Preston, Bruce Davison. *Dir.* Gene Saks.

Man and a Woman, A (1966) Anouk Aimée, Jean-Louis Trintignant. Best Foreign Film Oscar. Concerns a racing driver and a script girl who fall in love. *Dir.* Claude Lelouch.

Man Called Horse, A (1970) Richard Harris, Judith Anderson, Jean Gascon, Manu Tupou. Sequels: *Return of a Man Called Horse* (1976), & *Triumphs of a Man Called Horse* (1984). *Dir.* Elliot Silverstein.

Man for All Seasons, A (1966) Paul Scofield, Wendy Hiller, Susannah York, Robert Shaw, Orson Welles, John Hurt, Corin Redgrave. Events leading to the execution of Sir Thomas More. *Dir.* Fred Zinnemann.

Man in the Iron Mask, The (1939) Louis Hayward, Warren William (D'Artagnan), Alan Hale, Bert Roach, Joseph Schildkraut. King Louis XIV keeps his twin brother prisoner. *Dir.* James Whale.

Man of the Year (1995) Dirk Shafer, Vivian Paxton, Deidra Shafer. Documentary about events surrounding the homosexual Dirk Shafer's awarding of the 1992 *Playgirl* magazine's Man of the Year. *Dir.* Dirk Shafer.

Man Who Came to Dinner, The (1941) Bette Davis, Monty Woolley, Ann Sheridan, Jimmy Durante (spoofing Harpo Marx). *Dir.* William Keighley.

Man Who Could Work Miracles, The (1936) Roland Young, Ralph Richardson, Ernest Thesiger, George Sanders. Based on the HG Wells story. *Dir.* Lothar Mendes.

Man Who Fell to Earth, The (1976) David Bowie, Rip Torn, Candy Clark. *Dir.* Nicolas Roeg.

Man Who Knew too Much, The (1934) Leslie Banks, Edna Best, Peter Lorre. *Dir.* Alfred Hitchcock.

Man Who Knew too Much, The (1956) James Stewart, Doris Day, Bernard Miles. Remake of the 1934 film. *Dir.* Alfred Hitchcock.

Man Who Shot Liberty Valance, The (1962) John Wayne, James Stewart, Lee Marvin, Vera Miles. John Wayne shot Liberty Valance. *Dir.* John Ford.

Man Who Wasn't There, The (2001) Billy Bob Thornton (Ed Crane), Frances McDormand (Doris Crane), Michael Badalucco, James Gandolfini. Set in the 1940s. *Dir.* Joel Coen.

Man Who Would Be King, The (1975) Sean Connery, Michael Caine, Christopher Plummer (Kipling), Shakira Caine, Saeed Jaffrey. Based on a Rudyard Kipling story. *Dir.* John Huston.

Man with the Golden Arm (1956) Frank Sinatra, Kim Novak, Eleanor Parker, Arnold Stang. Golden Arm refers to the card-dealing expertise of the lead character. *Dir.* Otto Preminger.

Man with the Golden Gun (1974) Roger Moore, Christopher Lee (Scaramanga), Britt Ekland (Mary Goodnight), Maud Adams (Andrea Anders), Hervé Villechaize, Clifton James, Richard Loo. Title song performed by Lulu. *Dir.* Guy Hamilton.

Man without a Face, The (1993) Mel Gibson, Margaret Whitton, Fay Masterson, Viva. Boy remembers how he was helped to enter a military academy by a disfigured former teacher. *Dir.* Mel Gibson.

Mandy (1952) Jack Hawkins, Terence Morgan, Phyllis Calvert, Mandy Miller. Little deaf girl is sent to a special school. *Dir.* Alexander Mackendrick.

Manhattan (1979) Woody Allen, Diane Keaton, Meryl Streep, Mariel Hemingway. *Dir.* Woody Allen.

Manhattan Murder Mystery (1993) Woody Allen, Alan Alda, Anjelica Huston, Diane Keaton. *Dir.* Woody Allen.

Marathon Man (1976) Dustin Hoffman, Laurence Olivier, Roy Scheider, William Devane. *Dir.* John Schlesinger.

Marnie (1964) Tippi Hedren, Sean Connery, Martin Gabel, Diane Baker. Rich man marries a kleptomaniac who sees red when she sees red! *Dir.* Alfred Hitchcock.

Mars Attacks! (1996) Jack Nicholson, Glenn Close, Annette Bening, Michael J Fox, Pierce Brosnan, Rod Steiger, Danny De Vito, Tom Jones. *Dir.* Tim Burton.

Marty (1955) Ernest Borgnine, Betsy Blair, Jerry Paris. *Dir.* Delbert Mann.

Mary of Scotland (1936) Katharine Hepburn, Fredric March, Donald Crisp. *Dir.* John Ford.

Mary Poppins (1964) Julie Andrews, Dick Van Dyke, Glynis Johns, David Tomlinson, Elsa Lanchester, Arthur Treacher. Among many other awards, the song 'Chim Chim Cheree' won the Oscar for Best Song. *Dir.* Robert Stevenson.

Mary Queen of Scots (1971) Vanessa Redgrave, Glenda Jackson, Trevor Howard, Patrick McGoohan, Nigel Davenport. *Dir.* Charles Jarrott.

M*A*S*H (1970) Donald Sutherland, Elliott Gould, Sally Kellerman, Robert Duvall, Gary Burghoff. *Dir.* Robert Altman.

Mask, The (1994) Jim Carrey, Amy Yasbeck, Peter Riegert. *Dir.* Charles Russell.

Matilda (1997) Danny De Vito, Mara Wilson (Matilda), Rhea Perlman, Pam Ferris. Based on Roald Dahl's bestseller. *Dir.* Danny De Vito.

Matter of Life and Death, A (1946) David Niven, Roger Livesey, Kim Hunter, Marius Goring, Raymond Massey, Abraham Sofaer. US title: *Stairway to Heaven*. *Dir.* Michael Powell.

C
I
N
E
M
A

Maverick (1994) Mel Gibson, Jodie Foster, James Garner, Graham Greene, James Coburn, Alfred Molina. *Dir.* Richard Donner.

Mean Streets (1973) Robert De Niro, Harvey Keitel, Amy Robinson. *Dir.* Martin Scorsese.

Meet Me in St Louis (1944) Judy Garland, Margaret O'Brien, Tom Drake, Mary Astor. *Dir.* Vincente Minnelli.

Men, The (1950) Marlon Brando, Teresa Wright, Everett Sloane, Jack Webb. Reissue title: *Battle Stripe. Dir.* Fred Zinnemann.

Men in Black II (2002) Tommy Lee Jones, Will Smith, Rip Torn. Sequel to *MIB (Men In Black). Dir.* Barry Sonnenfeld.

Men of Respect (1990) John Turturro, Katherine Borowitz, Dennis Farina, Peter Boyle, Rod Steiger. Gangster setting for Shakespeare's *Macbeth. Dir.* William Reilly.

Mercury Rising (1998) Bruce Willis, Alec Baldwin, Miko Hughes, Chi McBride, Kim Dickens, Robert Stanton, Carrie Preston, Bodhi Pine Elfman, LL Ginter, John Carroll Lynch, Peter Stormare. *Dir.* Harold Becker.

Mermaids (1990) Cher, Bob Hoskins, Winona Ryder. Daughter, torn between becoming a nun and her feelings for a handsome boy, resolves her difficulties with her flirtatious mother. *Dir.* Richard Benjamin.

Merry Christmas, Mr Lawrence (1982) David Bowie, Tom Conti, Ryuichi Sakamoto, Takeshi. *Dir.* Nagisa Oshima.

Metro (1997) Eddie Murphy (Scott Roper), Michael Rapaport, Kim Miyori. *Dir.* Thomas Carter.

Mexican, The (2001) Brad Pitt (Jerry Welbach), Julia Roberts (Samantha), James Gandolfini (Leroy). Incompetent crook is sent to Mexico to bring back a priceless pistol for his boss whilst his girlfriend is held as ransom. Gene Hackman as Arnold Margolese is uncredited. *Dir.* Gore Verbinski.

Miami Rhapsody (1995) Sarah Jessica Parker, Gil Bellows, Antonio Banderas, Mia Farrow, Paul Mazursky, Naomi Campbell. Woman contemplating marriage observes the marital errors being committed by her siblings and friends. *Dir.* David Frankel.

MIB (Men in Black), (1997) Tommy Lee Jones (K), Will Smith (J), Linda Fiorentino (Dr Weaver), Rip Torn (Zed). SF film in which Will Smith performs title track & Snoop Doggy Dogg the soundtrack album. *Dir.* Barry Sonnenfeld.

Michael Collins (1996) Liam Neeson (Michael Collins), Aidan Quinn (Harry Boland), Julia Roberts (Kitty Kiernan). *Dir.* Neil Jordan.

Microcosmos (1996) French documentary film revolving around stag beetles' attempts to gain control of a twig. *Dir.* Marie Perennau & Claude Nuridsany.

Midnight Cowboy (1969) Dustin Hoffman, Jon Voight, Brenda Vaccaro, Sylvia Miles. *Dir.* John Schlesinger.

Midnight Express (1978) John Hurt, Brad Davis, Randy Quaid, Bo Hopkins. *Dir.* Alan Parker.

Midsummer Night's Dream, A (1935) James Cagney, Dick Powell, Jean Muir, Mickey Rooney, Olivia de Havilland. *Dir.* Max Reinhardt.

Midsummer Night's Dream, A (1996) Lindsay Duncan, Alex Jennings, Alfred Burke. *Dir.* Adrian Noble.

Mighty, The (1998) Sharon Stone, Gena Rowlands Harry Dean Stanton, Gillian Anderson, Meatloaf. *Dir.* Peter Chelsom.

Mighty Aphrodite (1995) Woody Allen, Helena Bonham Carter, Mira Sorvino, F Murray Abraham, Olympia Dukakis, Peter Weller, Claire Bloom, Michael Rapaport. Sportswriter's attempt to rescue the mother of his adopted son from life as a prostitute. *Dir.* Woody Allen.

Mighty Ducks, The (1992) Emilio Estevez, Joss Ackland, Lane Smith, Heidi King. Lawyer on community service for drink-driving adopts a hockey team. GB title: *Champions. Dir.* Stephen Herek.

Mighty Quinn, The (1989) Denzel Washington, James Fox, Mimi Rogers, M Emmet Walsh, Norman Beaton. Caribbean police investigate the murder of an American. *Dir.* Carl Shenkel.

Mike Bassett: England Manager (2001) Ricky Tomlinson (Mike Bassett), Amanda Redman, Bradley Walsh, Philip Jackson, Phil Jupitus, Pele (as himself). *Dir.* Steve Barron.

Million Pound Note, The (1953) Gregory Peck, Jane Griffiths, Ronald Squire, Joyce Grenfell, Wilfrid Hyde-White. Based on a Mark Twain story. *Dir.* Ronald Neame.

Minority Report (2002) Tom Cruise, Colin Farrell, Samantha Morton, Max von Sydow, Lois Smith. *Dir.* Steven Spielberg.

Miracle on 34th Street (1994) Richard Attenborough, Elizabeth Perkins, Robert Prosky. Remake of the 1947 film starring Edmund Gwenn & Maureen O'Hara. *Dir.* Les Mayfield.

Miracle Worker, The (1962) Anne Bancroft, Patty Duke, Victor Jory. *Dir.* Arthur Penn.

Miranda (1947) Glynis Johns, Griffith Jones, Googie Withers, Margaret Rutherford, David Tomlinson. Sequel to this mermaid movie was *Mad About Men,* starring Johns and Donald Sinden. *Dir.* Ken Annakin.

Misery (1990) James Caan, Kathy Bates, Richard Farnsworth, Lauren Bacall. Disturbed fan kidnaps an injured novelist and forces him to write a novel. *Dir.* Rob Reiner.

Misfits, The (1961) Clark Gable, Marilyn Monroe, Montgomery Clift, Eli Wallach, Kevin McCarthy. Film about cowboys in the Nevada desert roping mustangs but more famous for its co-stars' imminent deaths. *Dir.* John Huston.

Mission, The (1986) Robert De Niro, Jeremy Irons, Ray McAnally, Liam Neeson, Cherie Lunghi. Music by Ennio Morricone. *Dir.* Roland Joffe.

Mission Impossible (1996) Tom Cruise, Jon Voight, Kristin Scott-Thomas, Vanessa Redgrave. *Dir.* Brian De Palma.

Missionary, The (1983) Michael Palin, Maggie Smith, Trevor Howard, Michael Hordern, Denholm Elliott. *Dir.* Richard Loncraine.

Mississippi Burning (1988) Gene Hackman, Willem Dafoe, Frances McDormand. *Dir.* Alan Parker.

Missouri Breaks (1976) Marlon Brando, Jack Nicholson, Randy Quaid, Kathleen Lloyd. *Dir.* Arthur Penn.

Moby Dick (1956) Gregory Peck, Richard Basehart, Orson Welles, James Robertson Justice. Based on Herman Melville's novel. *Dir.* John Huston.

Mommie Dearest (1981) Faye Dunaway, Diana Scarwid, Steve Forrest, Howard da Silva (Louis B Mayer). Joan Crawford life story. *Dir.* Frank Perry.

Mona Lisa (1986) Bob Hoskins, Cathy Tyson, Michael Caine, Robbie Coltrane. *Dir.* Neil Jordan.

Money Train (1995) Wesley Snipes, Woody Harrelson, Jennifer Lopez. *Dir.* Joseph Ruben.

Monty Python and the Holy Grail (1975) John Cleese, Graham Chapman, Terry Gilliam, Eric Idle, Michael Palin, Terry Jones. *Dir.* Terry Gilliam and Terry Jones.

Monty Python's Life of Brian (1979) John Cleese, Graham Chapman, Terry Gilliam, Eric Idle, Michael

Palin, Terry Jones. *Dir.* Terry Jones.

Monty Python's The Meaning of Life (1983)   John Cleese, Graham Chapman, Terry Gilliam, Eric Idle, Michael Palin, Terry Jones. *Dir.* Terry Jones.

Moon is Blue, The (1953)   Maggie McNamara, David Niven, William Holden, Tom Tully, Dawn Addams. *Dir.* Otto Preminger.

Moonlighting (1982)   Jeremy Irons, Eugene Lipinski, Jiri Stanislaw. Four Polish building workers arrive in London to renovate a house and hear of social unrest at home. *Dir.* Jerzy Skolimowski.

Moonraker (1979)   Roger Moore, Lois Chiles (Holly Goodhead), Michael Lonsdale (Hugo Drax). Title song performed by Shirley Bassey. *Dir.* Lewis Gilbert.

Moonstruck (1987)   Cher, Nicolas Cage, Vincent Gardenia, Olympia Dukakis, Danny Aiello. Young widow falls for the estranged brother of her husband-to-be. *Dir.* Norman Jewison.

Moonwalker (1988)   Michael Jackson, Joe Pesci, Sean Lennon. *Dir.* Colin Chilvers.

Moulin Rouge (2001)   Nicole Kidman, Ewan McGregor, Jim Broadbent, John Leguizamo (Toulouse-Lautrec), Matthew Whittet (Satie), Kylie Minogue (Green Fairy), Garry McDonald (The Doctor). *Dir.* Baz Luhrmann.

Mouse on the Moon, The (1963)   Margaret Rutherford, Ron Moody, Bernard Cribbins, David Kossoff, Terry-Thomas, Michael Crawford. Sequel to *The Mouse That Roared*; concerning home-made wine making excellent rocket-fuel. *Dir.* Richard Lester.

Mouse That Roared, The (1959)   Peter Sellers (three roles), Jean Seberg, David Kossoff, William Hartnell, Leo McKern. Tiny Duchy of Grand Fenwick is bankrupt, so decides to declare war on USA, be defeated, and then accept aid. *Dir.* Jack Arnold.

Move over Darling (1963)   Doris Day, James Garner, Polly Bergen, Chuck Connors. Wife returns home after shipwreck to find her husband remarried. *Dir.* Michael Gordon.

Mr and Mrs Bridge (1990)   Paul Newman, Joanne Woodward, Robert Sean Leonard, Blythe Danner, Simon Callow. Inhibited lawyer gradually erodes his wife's personality. *Dir.* James Ivory.

Mr Deeds Goes to Town (1936)   Gary Cooper, Jean Arthur, Raymond Walburn, Margaret Seddon. Small-town poet inherits fortune and sets New York on its heels with his honesty. *Dir.* Frank Capra.

Mr Jones (1993)   Richard Gere, Lena Olin, Anne Bancroft. Manic depressive begins an affair with his psychiatrist. *Dir.* Mike Figgis.

Mr Smith Goes to Washington (1939)   James Stewart, Claude Rains, Jean Arthur, Thomas Mitchell, Edward Arnold. Senator exposes corruption in high places. *Dir.* Frank Capra.

Mrs Brown (1997)   Billy Connolly (John Brown), Dame Judi Dench (Queen Victoria). *Dir.* John Madden.

Mrs Dalloway (1998)   Vanessa Redgrave, Rupert Graves, Natascha McElhone, Michael Kitchen. *Dir.* Marleen Gorris.

Mrs Doubtfire (1993)   Robin Williams, Sally Field, Pierce Brosnan, Robert Prosky. *Dir.* Chris Columbus.

Mrs Miniver (1942)   Greer Garson, Walter Pidgeon, Teresa Wright. Multi-award winning film. *Dir.* William Wyler.

Mrs Pollifax – Spy (1970)   Rosalind Russell, Darren McGavin. Written by CA McKnight, who was, in fact, Rosalind Russell. *Dir.* Leslie Martinson.

Much Ado about Nothing (1993)   Kenneth Branagh, Emma Thompson, Richard Briers, Michael Keaton, Denzel Washington. *Dir.* Kenneth Branagh.

Mudlark, The (1950)   Alec Guinness, Irene Dunne, Andrew Ray, Anthony Steel, Finlay Currie. Scruffy boy from the docks breaks into Windsor Castle to visit Queen Victoria. *Dir.* Jean Negulesco.

Mulholland Falls (1996)   Nick Nolte, Melanie Griffith, Treat Williams, John Malkovich, Bruce Dern. *Dir.* Lee Tamahori.

Multiplicity (1996)   Michael Keaton, Andie MacDowell, Ann Cusack. *Dir.* Harold Ramis.

Mummy, The (1932)   Boris Karloff, Zita Johann, David Manners, Arthur Byron, Edward Van Sloan. Boris Karloff was billed as 'Karloff the Uncanny'. *Dir.* Karl Freund.

Mummy Returns, The (2001)   Brendan Fraser, Rachel Weisz, John Hannah, Arnold Vosloo (The Mummy), Kevin O'Conner. *Dir.* Stephen Sommers. Acting debut of wrestling superstar 'The Rock' as The Scorpion King.

Mummy, The (1959)   Peter Cushing, Christopher Lee, Yvonne Furneaux, Eddie Byrne, Felix Aylmer, Raymond Huntley, John Stuart. *Dir.* Terence Fisher.

Mummy, The (1999)   Brendan Fraser, Rachel Weisz, John Hannah, Arnold Vosloo, Kevin O'Connor. *Dir.* Stephen Sommers.

Muppet Movie, The (1979)   Charles Durning, Edgar Bergen, Bob Hope, Milton Berle, Mel Brooks, James Coburn, Dom DeLuise, Elliott Gould, Cloris Leachman, Telly Savalas, Orson Welles. *Dir.* James Frawley.

Muppets Take Manhattan, The (1984)   Dabney Coleman, Art Carney, James Coco, Joan Rivers, Gregory Hines, Linda Lavin. *Dir.* Frank Oz.

Murder by Decree (1978)   Christopher Plummer, James Mason, Anthony Quayle, David Hemmings, Susan Clark, John Gielgud, Donald Sutherland, Frank Finlay, Geneviève Bujold. Sherlock Holmes investigates the murders of 'Jack the Ripper'. *Dir.* Bob Clark.

Murder Most Foul (1964)   Margaret Rutherford, Ron Moody, Charles Tingwell, Andrew Cruickshank, Megs Jenkins, Ralph Michael, James Bolam, Stringer Davis, Francesca Annis, Dennis Price, Terry Scott. Based on the Agatha Christie novel *Mrs McGinty's Dead*. *Dir.* George Pollock.

Murder on the Orient Express (1974) Albert Finney, Ingrid Bergman, Lauren Bacall, Wendy Hiller, Sean Connery, Vanessa Redgrave, Michael York, Martin Balsam, Richard Widmark, Jacqueline Bisset, Jean-Pierre Cassel, Rachel Roberts, George Coulouris, John Gielgud, Anthony Perkins, Colin Blakely, Jeremy Lloyd, Denis Quilley. Hercule Poirot solves this Agatha Christie story. *Dir.* Sidney Lumet.

Murders in the Rue Morgue (1932)   Bela Lugosi, Sidney Fox, Leon Ames, Bert Roach, Brandon Hurst. *Dir.* Robert Florey.

Murders in the Rue Morgue (1971)   Jason Robards Jnr, Herbert Lom, Lilli Palmer, Adolfo Celi, Michael Dunn, Christine Kaufmann. *Dir.* Gordon Hessler.

Muriel's Wedding (1994)   Toni Collette, Bill Hunter, Rachel Griffiths, Jeanie Drynan. *Dir.* PJ Hogan.

Murphy's Law (1986)   Charles Bronson, Carrie Snodgress, Kathleen Wilhoite, Robert F Lyons, Richard Romanus. *Dir.* J Lee Thompson.

Murphy's War (1971)   Peter O'Toole, Sian Phillips, Philippe Noiret, Horst Janson. *Dir.* Peter Yates.

Music Lovers, The (1970)   Richard Chamberlain, Glenda Jackson, Christopher Gable, Max Adrian, Isabelle Telezynska, Maureen Pryor, Andrew Faulds. Screenplay written by Melvyn Bragg. *Dir.* Ken Russell.

Music Man, The (1962)   Robert Preston, Shirley

Jones, Buddy Hackett, Hermione Gingold, Pert Kelton, Paul Ford. *Dir.* Morton da Costa.

Mutiny on the Bounty (1935)   Charles Laughton, Clark Gable, Franchot Tone, Movita, Dudley Digges. *Dir.* Frank Lloyd.

Mutiny on the Bounty (1962)   Trevor Howard, Marlon Brando, Richard Harris, Hugh Griffith, Tarita, Richard Haydn, Gordon Jackson. *Dir.* Lewis Milestone.

My Beautiful Laundrette (1985)   Saeed Jaffrey, Roshan Seth, Daniel Day-Lewis, Shirley Anne Field. Based on the Hanif Kureishi work. *Dir.* Stephen Frears.

My Big Fat Greek Wedding (2002)   Nia Vardalos, John Corbett, Michael Constantine, Andrea Martin. Low-budget, unlikely smash hit of the year. Apparently the wedding dress featured in the film was bought by a viewer for a pittance and sold following the film's success for an amount approaching the budget of the film!! *Dir.* Joel Zwick.

My Favourite Martian (1999)   Christopher Lloyd, Jeff Daniels, Elizabeth Hurley, Daryl Hannah, Ray Walston. *Dir.* Donald Petrie. Based on the TV series starring Ray Walston and Bill Bixby.

Mysterious Dr Fu Manchu, The (1929)   Warner Oland played the Sax Rohmer character in early films in the series. *Dir.* Various.

Naked (1993)   David Thewlis, Lesley Sharp, Katrin Cartlidge, Greg Cruttwell. *Dir.* Mike Leigh.

Naked Edge, The (1961)   Gary Cooper, Deborah Kerr, Peter Cushing, Michael Wilding, Diane Cilento. *Dir.* Michael Anderson.

Naked Gun, The: From the Files of Police Squad (1988)   Leslie Nielsen, Priscilla Presley, Ricardo Montalban, OJ Simpson, George Kennedy. *Dir.* David Zucker.

Naked Gun 2 1/2, The: The Smell of Fear (1991)   Leslie Nielsen, Priscilla Presley, Robert Goulet, OJ Simpson, George Kennedy. *Dir.* David Zucker.

Naked Gun 33 1/3, The: The Final Insult (1994)   Leslie Nielsen, Priscilla Presley, Fred Ward, OJ Simpson, George Kennedy, Anna Nicole Smith. *Dir.* Peter Segal.

Naked in New York (1993)   Eric Stoltz, Mary-Louise Parker, Ralph Macchio, Jill Clayburgh, Tony Curtis, Kathleen Turner, Timothy Dalton, Whoopi Goldberg, Quentin Crisp. *Dir.* Dan Algrant.

Naked Lunch (1991)   Peter Weller, Judy Davis, Ian Holm, Roy Scheider, Julian Sands. Drug-addicted writer emulates William Tell with fatal results. *Dir.* David Cronenberg.

Name of the Rose, The (1986)   Sean Connery (William of Baskerville), F Murray Abraham (Bernardo Gui), Christian Slater (Adso of Melk), Feodor Chaliapin (Jorge de Burgos), William Hickey (Ubertino de Casale). Based on Umberto Eco novel. *Dir.* Jean-Jacques Annaud.

Narrow Margin (1952)   Charles McGraw, Marie Windsor, Jacqueline White, Queenie Leonard. Police try to guard a witness on a train from Chicago to LA. The 1990 remake starred Gene Hackman and Anne Archer. *Dir.* Richard Fleischer.

National Lampoon's Animal House (1978)   John Belushi, Tim Matheson, Donald Sutherland, John Vernon. First of the series which continued with *Movie Madness* (1981), *Class Reunion* (1982), *Vacation* (1983), *European Vacation* (1985), *Christmas Vacation* (1989), *Loaded Weapon* (1993), and *Senior Trip* (1995). The Chevy Chase character in 3 of the films was Clark Griswold. *Dir.* John Landis.

National Velvet (1945)   Mickey Rooney, Elizabeth Taylor, Anne Revere, Donald Crisp, Angela Lansbury. *Dir.* Clarence Brown.

Natural, The (1984)   Robert Redford (Roy Hobbs), Robert Duvall (Max Mercy), Glenn Close (Iris), Kim Basinger (Memo Paris), Barbara Hershey (Harriet Bird), Robert Prosky (Judge), Joe Don Baker (The Whammer). Ups and downs of a baseball star. *Dir.* Barry Levinson.

Natural Born Killers (1994)   Woody Harrelson, Juliette Lewis, Robert Downey Jnr, Tommy Lee Jones. Young couple become mass murderers while winning the affection of the media. *Dir.* Oliver Stone.

Ned Kelly (1970)   Mick Jagger, Allen Bickford, Geoff Gilmour, Mark McManus. Story of the 19th-century Australian outlaw. *Dir.* Tony Richardson.

Nell (1994)   Jodie Foster, Liam Neeson, Natasha Richardson. Two doctors endeavour to talk to a young woman who speaks a solitary language. *Dir.* Michael Apted.

Net, The (1995)   Sandra Bullock, Jeremy Northam, Dennis Miller, Diane Baker. *Dir.* Irwin Winkler.

Network (1976)   Peter Finch (Howard Beale), William Holden (Max Schumacher), Faye Dunaway, Robert Duvall, Ned Beatty. Peter Finch was awarded a posthumous Academy Award. *Dir.* Sidney Lumet.

Nevada Smith (1966)   Steve McQueen, Karl Malden, Brian Keith, Suzanne Pleshette. Scenes from the early life of the *Carpetbaggers* character. *Dir.* Henry Hathaway.

Never Been Kissed (1998)   Drew Barrymore, David Arquette, Michael Vartan, Leelee Sobieski, Jeremy Jordan. *Dir.* Raja Gosnell.

Never on Sunday (1959)   Melina Mercouri, Jules Dassin. Original title: *Pote tin Kyriaki*. *Dir.* Jules Dassin.

Never Say Never Again (1983)   Sean Connery, Klaus Maria Brandauer (Largo), Max Von Sydow (Blofeld), Alec McCowen (Q), Kim Basinger (Domino), Edward Fox, Rowan Atkinson, Barbara Carrera (Fatima). Remake of *Thunderball*, so titled because Connery vowed he would never make another Bond movie after *Diamonds Are Forever*. *Dir.* Irvin Kershner.

New York, New York (1977)   Liza Minnelli, Robert De Niro, Lionel Stander, Barry Primus. *Dir.* Martin Scorsese.

New York Stories (1989)   *Life Lessons*: Nick Nolte, Patrick O'Neal, Rosanna Arquette, Steve Buscemi, Debbie Harry, Peter Gabriel. *Dir.* Martin Scorsese. *Life without Zoe*: Talia Shire, Giancarlo Giannini, Heather McComb, Carmine Coppola. *Dir.* Francis Ford Coppola. *Oedipus Wrecks*: Woody Allen, Mia Farrow, Julie Kavner, Mae Questel, Mayor Ed Koch. *Dir.* Woody Allen.   Teacher sets the 3 top boys an essay – topic: 'My Story about New York' and the 3 separately directed stories follow.

Next of Kin (1989)   Patrick Swayze (Truman Gates), Liam Neeson (Briar Gates), Adam Baldwin (Joey Rosselini). *Dir.* John Irvin.

Niagara (1952)   Joseph Cotten, Jean Peters, Marilyn Monroe. *Dir.* Henry Hathaway.

Nicholas and Alexandra (1971)   Michael Jayston, Janet Suzman, Laurence Olivier, Jack Hawkins, Tom Baker, Michael Redgrave. Life of Tsar Nicholas II from 1904 until the execution of his family in 1918. *Dir.* Franklin Schaffner.

Nickelodeon (1976)   Ryan O'Neal, Burt Reynolds, Tatum O'Neal, Brian Keith, Stella Stevens. Events leading up to the premiere of *The Birth of a Nation*. *Dir.* Peter Bogdanovich.

Night and Day (1946)   Cary Grant (Cole Porter), Alexis Smith, Monty Woolley, Mary Martin, Jane Wyman, Eve Arden. *Dir.* Michael Curtiz.

Night and the City (1992)   Robert De Niro (Harry Fabian), Jessica Lange (Helen Nasseros), Alan King (Boom Boom Grossman). Remake of the 1950 classic starring Richard Widmark and Gene Tierney. *Dir.* Irwin Winkler.

Night at the Opera, A (1935)   Groucho Marx, Chico Marx, Harpo Marx, Margaret Dumont. *Dir.* Sam Wood.

Night Crossing (1982)   John Hurt, Jane Alexander, Beau Bridges, Ian Bannen. East Germans escape to the West via air balloon. *Dir.* Delbert Mann.

Night Falls on Manhattan (1997)   Andy Garcia (Sean Casey), Ian Holm. *Dir.* Sidney Lumet.

Night in Casablanca, A (1946)   Groucho Marx (Kornblow), Chico Marx, Harpo Marx, Lisette Verea (Beatrice). *Dir.* Archie Mayo.

Night of the Hunter (1955)   Robert Mitchum, Shelley Winters, Lillian Gish, Peter Graves. Psychopathic preacher on the trail of hidden loot. *Dir.* Charles Laughton.

Night of the Iguana (1964)   Richard Burton, Deborah Kerr, Ava Gardner, Sue Lyon. Disbarred clergyman becomes a courier in Mexico and is chased by teenage nymphomaniac. *Dir.* John Huston.

Night on Earth (1992)   Winona Ryder (Corky), Gena Rowlands (Victoria Snelling), Giancarlo Esposito (Yo Yo). Five people take simultaneous taxi rides in 5 cities, i.e. LA, New York, Paris, Rome & Helsinki. *Dir.* Jim Jarmusch.

Night Porter, The (1973)   Dirk Bogarde, Charlotte Rampling. Wife of opera conductor recognises porter as a former SS officer. *Dir.* Liliana Cavani.

Night Shift (1982)   Henry Winkler, Michael Keaton, Shelley Long, Gina Hecht, Kevin Costner (Frat Boy). *Dir.* Ron Howard.

Night They Raided Minsky's, The (1968)   Jason Robards, Britt Ekland, Norman Wisdom, Bert Lahr. *Dir.* William Friedkin.

Night to Remember, A (1958)   Kenneth More, Honor Blackman, David McCallum. *Dir.* Roy Baker.

Nightmare Before Christmas, The (1993)   Voices of Danny Elfman, Chris Sarandon, William Hickey, Catherine O'Hara. Based on a Tim Burton story. *Dir.* Henry Selick.

Nightmare on Elm Street, A (1984)   John Saxon, Ronee Blakley, Robert Englund (Freddie). *Dir.* Wes Craven.

Nightmare on Elm Street, A, 2: Freddy's Revenge (1985)   Mark Patton, Clu Gulager, Hope Lange, Kim Myers, Robert Englund (Freddie). *Dir.* Jack Sholder.

Nightmare on Elm Street, A, 3: Dream Warriors (1987)   Heather Langenkamp, Patricia Arquette, Robert Englund (Freddie). *Dir.* Chuck Russell.

Nightmare on Elm Street, A, 4: The Dream Master (1988)   Rodney Eastman, Danny Hassel, Robert Englund (Freddie). *Dir.* Renny Harlin.

Nightmare on Elm Street, A: The Dream Child (1989)   Lisa Wilcox, Kelly Jo Minter, Danny Hassel, Robert Englund (Freddie). Last of the series called *Freddy's Dead: The Final Nightmare* (1991). *Dir.* Stephen Hopkins.

Nil by Mouth (1997)   Ray Winstone (Ray), Kathy Burke (Valerie). *Dir.* Gary Oldman.

Nine and a Half Weeks (1986)   Mickey Rourke, Kim Basinger. *Dir.* Adrian Lyne.

976–EVIL (1988)   Stephen Geoffreys (Hoax), Sandy Dennis (Aunt Lucy). The title refers to the Devil's freephone number. *Dir.* Robert Englund.

9/30/55 (1977)   Richard Thomas, Susan Tyrrell, Dennis Quaid. Title refers to the death of James Dean and the effect on an Arkansas student. *Dir.* James Bridges.

Nine to Five (1980)   Jane Fonda, Dolly Parton, Lily Tomlin, Dabney Coleman, Sterling Hayden. Three office women plot to get rid of their boss. *Dir.* Colin Higgins.

1984 (1984)   John Hurt (Winston Smith), Richard Burton (O'Brien), Suzanna Hamilton (Julia), Cyril Cusack (Carrington). A 1955 version starred Michael Redgrave and Edmond O'Brien. *Dir.* Michael Radford.

1941 (1979)   Dan Aykroyd, Ned Beatty, John Belushi, Christopher Lee, Robert Stack, Lorraine Gary. Farce concerning a stray Japanese submarine terrorising Hollywood after Pearl Harbor. *Dir.* Steven Spielberg.

Ninotchka (1939)   Greta Garbo, Melvyn Douglas, Bela Lugosi. *Dir.* Ernst Lubitsch.

Nixon (1995)   Anthony Hopkins (Nixon), Joan Allen (Pat Nixon), Powers Boothe (Alexander Haig), Ed Harris (E Howard Hunt), Paul Sorvino (Henry Kissinger). *Dir.* Oliver Stone.

Nobody's Fool (1994)   Paul Newman, Jessica Tandy, Bruce Willis, Melanie Griffith. A 60-yr-old handyman has a chance to make up for a disappointing life. *Dir.* Robert Benton.

Noises Off (1992)   Carol Burnett (Dotty Otley / Mrs Clackett), Michael Caine (Lloyd Fellowes), Denholm Elliott, Julie Hagerty, Marilu Henner, Christopher Reeve. Adaptation of Michael Frayn's farce about a second-rate touring company. *Dir.* Peter Bogdanovich.

No Place To Go (*Die Unberührbare*) (2001)   Hannelore Elsner (Hanna), Vadim Glowna, Tonio Arango, Michael Gwisdek, Bernd Stempel. *Dir.* Oskar Röhler.

North by Northwest (1959)   Cary Grant, Eva Marie Saint, James Mason. *Dir.* Alfred Hitchcock.

North Dallas Forty (1979)   Nick Nolte, Mac Davis, Charles Durning, Bo Svenson. Gruelling life of an American football player. *Dir.* Ted Kotcheff.

Notorious (1946)   Cary Grant, Ingrid Bergman, Claude Rains, Louis Calhern. Lady marries a Nazi in Rio to help the American government. *Dir.* Alfred Hitchcock.

Notting Hill (1999)   Julia Roberts, Hugh Grant, Hugh Bonneville, Emma Chambers, Alec Baldwin. *Dir.* Roger Michell.

Nuns on the Run (1990)   Eric Idle, Robbie Coltrane, Janet Suzman, Doris Hare. *Dir.* Jonathan Lynn.

Nun's Story, The (1959)   Audrey Hepburn, Peter Finch, Edith Evans, Peggy Ashcroft. Belgian girl joins a strict order of nuns. *Dir.* Fred Zinnemann.

Nurse Edith Cavell (1939)   Anna Neagle, George Sanders. Based on Reginald Berkeley's novel *Dawn*. *Dir.* Herbert Wilcox.

Nutty Professor, The (1996)   Eddie Murphy (plays 7 roles), James Coburn, Jada Pinkett. *Dir.* Tom Shadyac.

Object of Beauty, The (1991)   John Malkovich, Andie MacDowell, Joss Ackland, Bill Paterson, Jack Shepherd. *Dir.* Michael Lindsay-Hogg.

Objective Burma! (1945)   Errol Flynn, James Brown, William Prince. Exploits of a US platoon during the Burma campaign. The film caused a furore among the Burma Star Organisation and nearly created a diplomatic fallout by failing to mention the British contribution. *Dir.* Raoul Walsh.

Obsession (1976)   Cliff Robertson, Geneviève Bujold, John Lithgow. Widower meets the double of his dead wife. *Dir.* Brian De Palma.

Ocean's Eleven (1960)   Frank Sinatra, Peter Lawford, Sammy Davis Jnr, Dean Martin, Richard Conte, Ilka Chase, Cesar Romero, Joey Bishop,

Patrick Wymore, Akim Tamiroff, Henry Silva, Angie Dickinson. *Dir.* Lewis Milestone.

Ocean's Eleven (2001) George Clooney (Danny Ocean), Julia Roberts (Tess Ocean), Brad Pitt (Rusty Ryan), Matt Damon (Linus), Andy Garcia (Terry Benedict), Casey Affleck (Virgil Malloy), Scott Caan (Turk Malloy), Don Cheadle (Basher Tarr), Elliott Gould (Reuben Tishkoff), Carl Reiner (Saul Bloom). Remake of the 1960 film of the same name. *Dir.* Steven Soderbergh.

Octopussy (1983) Roger Moore, Maud Adams (Octopussy), Louis Jourdan (Prince Kamel Khan), Steven Berkoff (Orlov), Robert Brown (M), Desmond Llewelyn (Q). Tennis player Vijay Amritraj appeared in a cameo role. Title song performed by Rita Coolidge. *Dir.* John Glen.

Odd Couple, The (1968) Jack Lemmon (Felix Unger), Walter Matthau (Oscar Goldman). Written by Neil Simon. *Dir.* Gene Saks.

Odessa File, The (1974) Jon Voigt, Maria Schell, Maximilian Schell, Derek Jacobi. *Dir.* Ronald Neame.

Of Mice and Men (1939) Burgess Meredith, Lon Chaney Jnr, Betty Field, Charles Bickford. Itinerant worker looks after his immensely strong but mentally retarded cousin. The 1992 remake starred John Malkovich and Gary Sinise. *Dir.* Lewis Milestone.

Officer and a Gentleman, An (1982) Richard Gere (Zack Mayo), Debra Winger, Lou Gossett Jnr, David Keith, Lisa Blount. Oscars for Lou Gossett Jnr (Best Supporting), and song ('Up Where We Belong'). *Dir.* Taylor Hackford.

Oh What a Lovely War (1969) Ralph Richardson, Meriel Forbes, John Gielgud, Kenneth More, John Clements, Joe Melia, Paul Daneman, Jack Hawkins, Maggie Smith, John Mills, Michael Redgrave, Laurence Olivier, Susannah York, Dirk Bogarde, Phyllis Calvert, Vanessa Redgrave. Musical fantasia of World War I. *Dir.* Richard Attenborough.

O.H.M.S. (1936) John Mills, Wallace Ford, Anna Lee. British forces in China are joined by an American gangster on the run, who dies a hero. US title: *You're in the Army Now. Dir.* Raoul Walsh.

Oklahoma (1955) Gordon Macrae, Shirley Jones, Rod Steiger, Eddie Albert. *Dir.* Fred Zinnemann.

Oklahoma Kid, The (1939) James Cagney, Humphrey Bogart, Rosemary Lane, Donald Crisp, Ward Bond. *Dir.* Lloyd Bacon.

Old Gringo (1989) Jane Fonda (Harriet Winslow), Gregory Peck (Ambrose Bierce), Jimmy Smits (Tomas Arroyo). *Dir.* Luis Puenzo.

Old Man and the Sea, The (1958) Spencer Tracy, Felipe Pazos, Harry Bellaver. *Dir.* John Sturges.

Old Mother Riley (1935–52) Arthur Lucan (Old Mother Riley), Kitty McShane (his daughter). Series of films with Lucan and his real-life wife playing mother and daughter. *Stars on Parade* was the first of the series and *Mother Riley Meets the Vampire* the last. *Dir.* Maclean Rogers.

Oliver! (1968) Ron Moody, Oliver Reed, Harry Secombe, Mark Lester, Shani Wallis, Jack Wild. *Dir.* Carol Reed.

Oliver Twist (1948) Alec Guinness, Robert Newton, Francis L Sullivan, John Howard Davies, Anthony Newley, Diana Dors, Mary Clare, Kay Walsh. *Dir.* David Lean.

Oliver's Story (1978) Ryan O'Neal, Candice Bergen, Nicola Pagett, Ray Milland. *Dir.* John Korty.

Omega Man, The (1971) Charlton Heston, Rosalind Cash, Anthony Zerbe. Based on the novel *I am Legend* by Richard Matheson. Set in 1977 Los Angeles after a germ warfare plague has decimated the world's population. *Dir.* Boris Sagal.

Omen, The (1976) Gregory Peck, Lee Remick, David Warner, Billie Whitelaw, Leo McKern, Patrick Troughton. Three inferior sequels were made. *Dir.* Richard Donner.

On Deadly Ground (1994) Steven Seagal, Michael Caine, Joan Chen, Chief Irvin Brink. *Dir.* Steven Seagal.

On Golden Pond (1981) Henry Fonda, Katharine Hepburn, Jane Fonda, Dabney Coleman, Doug McKeon. *Dir.* Mark Rydell.

On Her Majesty's Secret Service (1969) George Lazenby, Diana Rigg (Tracy Vicenzo née Draco), Telly Savalas (Blofeld). *Avengers* fans note: not only does Diana Rigg become Mrs Bond but Joanna Lumley is one of the lovelies in the Swiss Alps and Honor Blackman is visible in a clip from *Goldfinger* in the opening titles. *Dir.* Peter Hunt. Theme song: 'We have all the time in the world' performed by Louis Armstrong.

On the Beach (1959) Gregory Peck, Ava Gardner, Fred Astaire, Anthony Perkins, Donna Anderson. Crew of serving American submarine wait for the devastation of atomic war to catch up with them in Australia. *Dir.* Stanley Kramer.

On the Buses (1971) Reg Varney, Doris Hare, Anna Karen, Michael Robbins, Stephen Lewis. Sequels: *Mutiny on the Buses* (1972), and *Holiday on the Buses* (1973). *Dir.* Harry Booth.

On the Double (1961) Danny Kaye, Dana Wynter, Wilfrid Hyde-White, Diana Dors, Margaret Rutherford, Allan Cuthbertson, Jesse White. American private is asked to impersonate a British Intelligence officer. *Dir.* Melville Shavelson.

On the Fiddle (1961) Alfred Lynch, Sean Connery, Wilfrid Hyde-White, Kathleen Harrison, Cecil Parker, Alan King, Eleanor Summerfield, Eric Barker, John Le Mesurier, Terence Longdon. US title: *Operation Snafu*. Wide boy and slow-witted gypsy's adventures in the RAF. *Dir.* Cyril Frankel.

On the Town (1949) Frank Sinatra, Gene Kelly, Jules Munshin, Ann Miller, Vera-Ellen, Betty Garrett. Gene Kelly directed the dance scenes. *Dir.* Stanley Donen.

On the Waterfront (1954) Marlon Brando, Eva Marie Saint, Rod Steiger, Lee J Cobb, Karl Malden. *Dir.* Elia Kazan.

Once a Jolly Swagman (1948) Dirk Bogarde, Renée Asherson, Bonar Colleano, Bill Owen. US title: *Maniacs on Wheels*. Factory worker becomes a speedway rider. *Dir.* Jack Lee.

Once Around (1991) Richard Dreyfuss, Holly Hunter, Danny Aiello, Gena Rowlands, Laura San Giacomo. *Dir.* Lasse Hallstrom.

Once Bitten (1985) Lauren Hutton, Jim Carrey, Karen Kopins, Cleavon Little. Teenage sex problems are complicated by a visiting vampiress. *Dir.* Howard Storm.

Once More with Feeling (1960) Yul Brynner, Kay Kendall, Geoffrey Toone, Maxwell Shaw, Mervyn Johns. Volatile private life of an orchestral conductor. *Dir.* Stanley Donen.

Once Upon a Crime (1992) John Candy, James Belushi, Cybill Shepherd, Sean Young, Joss Ackland. *Dir.* Eugene Levy.

Once Upon a Horse (1958) Dan Rowan, Dick Martin, Martha Hyer, Leif Erickson, Nita Talbot, James Gleason. Two cowboys steal a herd of cattle but can't afford to feed them. The two stars later went on to revolutionise TV comedy with their *Laugh-in* shows. *Dir.* Hal Kanter.

Once Upon a Time in America (1984) Robert De Niro (Noodles), James Woods (Max), Elizabeth

McGovern (Deborah), Treat Williams (Jimmy O'Donnell), Tuesday Weld (Carol), Joe Pesci (Frankie), Danny Aiello (Police Chief Aiello), William Forsythe (Cockeye). Story of four Jewish gangsters known as the 'Kosher Nostra', from 1922 to 1968. It is a 228-minute film which has a 147-minute version. *Dir.* Sergio Leone.

Once Upon a Time in the West (1969)   Henry Fonda, Claudia Cardinale, Jason Robards, Charles Bronson. Notable for its opening credits which last for the first 12 minutes of film time. *Dir.* Sergio Leone.

Once Were Warriors (1994)   Rena Owen, Temuera Morrison. This film is the top NZ film as regards box office takings. *Dir.* Lee Tamahori.

One-Eyed Jacks (1961)   Marlon Brando, Karl Malden, Pina Pellicer, Katy Jurado, Slim Pickens, Ben Johnson. Based on the novel *The Authentic Death of Hendry Jones* by Charles Neider. *Dir.* Marlon Brando.

One False Move (1992)   Bill Paxton (Dale 'Hurricane' Dixon), Cynda Williams (Fantasia / Lila), Michael Beach (Pluto), Billy Bob Thornton (Ray Malcolm), Jim Metzler (Dud Cole). Two killers on the run with their black girlfriend go to Alabama where the sheriff is waiting. Cynda Williams and Billy Bob Thornton fell in love on set and married soon after. *Dir.* Carl Franklin.

One Fine Day (1996)   Michelle Pfeiffer, George Clooney, Charles Durning, Mae Whitman. Two busy single parents fall in love. *Dir.* Michael Hoffman.

One from the Heart (1982)   Frederic Forrest (Hank), Teri Garr (Frannie), Raul Julia (Ray), Nastassja Kinski (Leila). Rebecca DeMornay's screen debut in the restaurant scene with the line: 'Excuse me, I think those are my waffles'. First film for Coppola's Zoetrope studios. *Dir.* Francis Ford Coppola.

187 (1997)   Samuel L Jackson (Trevor Garfield), Tony Plana. Title refers to the Californian penal code for murder. School: John Quincy Adams High. *Dir.* Kevin Reynolds.

101 Dalmatians (1996)   Glenn Close, Jeff Daniels, Joan Plowright, Joely Richardson, Hugh Laurie. Live-action remake of the 1961 animated film. *Dir.* Stephen Herek. The sequel *102 Dalmatians* was released in 2000.

One Hundred Men and a Girl (1937)   Deanna Durbin was the girl and the men were an orchestra. *Dir.* Henry Koster.

One Million Years BC (1966)   John Richardson, Raquel Welch, Robert Brown. *Dir.* Don Chaffey.

One Woman or Two (1985)   Gérard Depardieu (Julien Chayssac), Sigourney Weaver (Jessica Fitzgerald), Dr Ruth Westheimer (Mrs Heffner). Advertising woman uses an archaeologist as basis for a new campaign and falls in love. *Dir.* Daniel Vigne.

Onibaba (1964)   Nobuko Otowa, Jitsuko Yoshimura, Kei Sato. Mother and daughter live by preying on stray soldiers. Aka: *The Hole. Dir.* Kaneto Shindo.

Operation Crossbow (1965)   George Peppard, Tom Courtenay, John Mills, Sophia Loren, Lilli Palmer, Trevor Howard. *Dir.* Michael Anderson.

Ordinary People (1980)   Donald Sutherland, Mary Tyler Moore, Timothy Hutton, Judd Hirsch. Oscars for Hutton, Redford and Alvin Sargent (screenplay). *Dir.* Robert Redford.

Othello (1965)   Laurence Olivier, Frank Finlay, Maggie Smith, Derek Jacobi. The 1995 Oliver Parker film starred Laurence Fishburne and Ken Branagh (Iago). *Dir.* Stuart Burge.

Others, The (2001)   Nicole Kidman (Grace), Christopher Eccleston (Charles), Fionnula Flanagan (Mrs Mills), James Bentley (Nicholas), Eric Sykes (Mr Tuttle), Elaine Cassidy (Lydia). Set in the 1940s. *Dir.* Alejandro Amenabar.

Our Man Flint (1965)   James Coburn, Lee J Cobb. *Dir.* Daniel Mann.

Our Man in Havana (1965)   Alec Guinness, Noël Coward, Burl Ives, Maureen O'Hara, Ralph Richardson. *Dir.* Carol Reed.

Out of Africa (1985)   Robert Redford (Denys), Meryl Streep (Karen Blixen), Klaus Maria Brandauer, Michael Gough. *Dir.* Sydney Pollack.

Outbreak (1995)   Dustin Hoffman, Rene Russo, Morgan Freeman, Donald Sutherland, Kevin Spacey. *Dir.* Wolfgang Petersen.

Outland (1981)   Sean Connery, Peter Boyle, Kika Markham. *Dir.* Peter Hyams.

Outlaw Josey Wales, The (1976)   Clint Eastwood, Chief Dan George, Sondra Locke. *Dir.* Clint Eastwood.

Outrageous Fortune (1987)   Bette Midler (Sandy), Shelley Long (Lauren), Robert Prosky, Peter Coyote. *Dir.* Arthur Hiller.

Outsiders, The (1983)   Matt Dillon (Dallas Winston), Ralph Macchio (Johnny Cade), Patrick Swayze (Darrel Curtis), Robb Lowe (Sodapop Curtis), Emilio Estevez (Two-Bit Matthews), Tom Cruise (Steve Randle). *Dir.* Francis Ford Coppola.

Over the Top (1987)   Sylvester Stallone (Lincoln Hawk), Robert Loggia (Jason Cutler), Susan Blakely (Chris Hawk). *Dir.* Menahem Golan.

Overboard (1987)   Goldie Hawn (Joanna / Annie), Kurt Russell (Dean Proffitt), Roddy McDowall (Andrew). *Dir.* Garry Marshall.

Owl and the Pussycat, The (1970)   Barbra Streisand, George Segal, Robert Klein, Allen Garfield. *Dir.* Herbert Ross.

Paint Your Wagon (1969)   Lee Marvin, Clint Eastwood (Pardner), Jean Seberg, Harve Presnell, Ray Walston. *Dir.* Joshua Logan.

Pal Joey (1957)   Frank Sinatra, Rita Hayworth, Kim Novak. *Dir.* George Sidney.

Pale Rider (1985)   Clint Eastwood (Preacher), Michael Moriarty, Carrie Snodgrass, Chris Penn, Richard Kiel. *Dir.* Clint Eastwood.

Paleface, The (1948)   Bob Hope, Jane Russell, Robert Armstrong. Song 'Buttons and Bows' (music by J Livingston, lyrics by Ray Evans) won Oscar. Sequel was *Son of Paleface* and 1968 remake was *The Shakiest Gun in the West. Dir.* Norman Z Mcleod.

Pallbearer (1996)   David Schwimmer, Gwyneth Paltrow, Michael Rapaport, Barbara Hershey. *Dir.* Matt Reeves.

Palm Beach Story, The (1942)   Claudette Colbert, Joel McCrea, Rudy Vallee (Hackensacker), Robert Dudley (Weenie King). Engineer's wife travels to Florida with her sights set on a millionaire. *Dir.* Preston Sturges.

Palookaville (1996)   Adam Trese (Jerry), William Forsythe (Sid), Vincent Gallo (Russ), Frances McDormand. Story of 3 bungling would-be criminals. *Dir.* Alan Taylor.

Panic Room (2002)   Jodie Foster, Kristen Stewart, Forest Whitaker, Jared Leto, Dwight Yoakam. *Dir.* David Fincher.

Panther (1995)   Kadeem Hardison, Bokeem Woodbine, Joe Don Baker, Nefertiti. Black Vietnam vet recalls his role in the Black Panther movement. *Dir.* Mario Van Peebles.

Paper, The (1994)   Michael Keaton, Glenn Close, Marisa Tomei, Robert Duvall, Randy Quaid. *Dir.* Ron Howard.

Paper Chase, The (1973)   Timothy Bottoms, Lindsay

Wagner, John Houseman, Graham Bickel. Based on John Jay Osborn Jnr novel. Houseman won Oscar and film spawned a successful TV series of the same name. *Dir.* James Bridges.

Paper Moon (1973)   Ryan O'Neal, Tatum O'Neal, Madeline Kahn, John Hillerman. Tatum O'Neal won an Oscar. *Dir.* Peter Bogdanovich.

Paper Tiger (1975)   David Niven, Toshiro Mifune, Hardy Kruger, Ando, Ronald Fraser, Ivan Desny. Englishman becomes tutor to the son of a Japanese ambassador. *Dir.* Ken Annakin.

Papillon (1973)   Dustin Hoffman, Steve McQueen. *Dir.* Franklin Schaffner.

Paradise (1991)   Melanie Griffith (Lily Reed), Don Johnson (Ben Reed), Elijah Wood, Louise Latham. The first film that Griffith and Johnson starred in together. Remake of *Le Grand Chemin* directed in 1987 by Jean-Loup Hubert. *Dir.* Mary Agnes Donoghue.

Parallax View, The (1974)   Warren Beatty, Paula Prentiss, William Daniels. Witnesses to political assassination are systematically killed. *Dir.* Alan J Pakula.

Parenthood (1989)   Steve Martin (Gil), Mary Steenburgen (Karen), Dianne Wiest (Helen), Jason Robards (Frank), Rick Moranis (Nathan), Tom Hulce (Larry), Keanu Reeves (Tod), Leaf Phoenix (Gary). Four generations of a large family have different approaches to parenthood. *Dir.* Ron Howard.

Parole Officer, The (2001)   Steve Coogan (Simon Garden), Lena Headey, Om Puri, Steven Waddington, Ben Miller, Stephen Dillane, Jenny Agutter, Omar Sharif (Victor Bondarenko). *Dir.* John Duigan.

Passage to India, A (1984)   Judy Davis (Adela Quested), Victor Banerjee (Dr Aziz), Peggy Ashcroft (Mrs Moore), James Fox (Richard Fielding), Alec Guinness (Godbole), Nigel Havers, Art Malik Richard Wilson (Turton), Saeed Jaffrey, Clive Swift, Roshan Seth. David Lean's first film for 14 years. It was also his last. *Dir.* David Lean.

Passport to Pimlico (1949)   Stanley Holloway, Margaret Rutherford, Basil Radford, Sydney Tafler, Hermione Baddeley. Part of postwar London is discovered to belong to Burgundy and the residents find themselves free of rationing restrictions. Based on a real-life story whereby the Canadian government presented to Holland the room where Princess Juliana was to bear a child. *Dir.* Henry Cornelius.

Pat and Mike (1952)   Spencer Tracy, Katharine Hepburn, Aldo Ray. Small-time sports promoter takes on a female intellectual multi-champion. *Dir.* George Cukor.

Patriot Games (1992)   Harrison Ford (Jack Ryan), Anne Archer, Patrick Bergin, Sean Bean, Samuel L Jackson James Fox, Richard Harris, James Earl Jones, Thora Birch. *Dir.* Philip Noyce.

Patton (1969)   George C Scott, Karl Malden, Michael Bates. Famous for Scott's refusal to collect his Oscar. *Dir.* Franklin Schaffner.

Patty Hearst (1988)   Natasha Richardson, William Forsythe, Ving Rhames, Frances Fisher. *Dir.* Paul Schrader.

Peacemaker, The (1997)   Nicole Kidman (Dr Julia Kelly), George Clooney (Lt Col Thomas Devoe). First film from Steven Spielberg's Dreamworks Studio. *Dir.* Mimi Leder.

Pearl Harbor (2001)   Ben Affleck, Josh Hartnett, Kate Beckinsale, Cuba Gooding, Jon Voight, Dan Aykroyd, Alec Baldwin, James King, Tom Sizemore, *Dir.* Michael Bay.

Pearl of Death, The (1944)   Basil Rathbone (Holmes), Nigel Bruce (Watson), Dennis Hoey, Miles Mander, Rondo Hatton. Based on Conan Doyle's 'The Six Napoleons'. *Dir.* Roy William Neill.

Peggy Sue Got Married (1986)   Kathleen Turner (Peggy Sue), Nicolas Cage (Charlie Bodell), Jim Carrey (Walter Getz), Barry Miller, Catherine Hicks, Joan Allen, Helen Hunt (Beth Bodell). *Dir.* Francis Ford Coppola.

Pelican Brief, The (1993)   Julia Roberts, Denzel Washington, Sam Shepard, John Heard, Robert Culp. Law student is stalked by hitmen after she suspects their involvement in murder of 2 judges. *Dir.* Alan J Pakula.

People vs Larry Flint, The (1996)   Woody Harrelson (Larry Flynt, the self-styled King of Sleaze), Courteney Love, Edward Norton. Biopic of the publisher of soft porn mag *Hustler*. *Dir.* Milos Forman.

Perez Family, The (1995)   Marisa Tomei, Alfred Molina, Anjelica Huston. *Dir.* Mira Nair.

Perfect (1985)   John Travolta (Adam), Jamie Lee Curtis (Jessie), Anne De Salvo (Frankie). Journalist falls in love with aerobics teacher he is investigating. *Dir.* James Bridges.

Perfect Storm, The (1999)   George Clooney, Mark Wahlberg, Diane Lane, Mary Elizabeth Mastrantonio, Michael Ironside. Six Massachusetts fishermen encounter a raging storm in their boat 'Andrea Gail'. *Dir.* Wolfgang Peterson.

Perfect World, A (1993)   Clint Eastwood, Kevin Costner, Laura Dern. *Dir.* Clint Eastwood.

Performance (1970)   James Fox, Mick Jagger, Anita Pallenberg, Allan Cuthbertson. *Dir.* Nicolas Roeg & Donald Cammell.

Perils of Pauline, The (1934)   Betty Hutton, John Lund, Billy de Wolfe. The career of silent serial queen Pearl White. *Dir.* George Marshall.

Personal Services (1987)   Julie Walters (Christine Painter), Alec McCowen (Wing Commander Morton), Shirley Stellfox. Read 'Cynthia Payne' for Christine Painter. *Dir.* Terry Jones.

Peter's Friends (1992)   Kenneth Branagh (Andrew), Alphonsia Emmanuel (Sarah), Stephen Fry (Peter), Hugh Laurie (Roger), Phyllida Law (Vera), Rita Rudner (Carol), Emma Thompson (Maggie). *Dir.* Kenneth Branagh.

Phantom of the Opera (1925)   Lon Chaney, Mary Philbin, Norman Kerry. Remakes include 1943 version with Claude Rains, 1962 film with Herbert Lom and 1989 version with Robert Englund. *Dir.* Rupert Julian.

Phenomenon (1996)   John Travolta, Kyra Sedgwick, Robert Duvall, Forest Whitaker, Brent Spiner. Simpleton is struck by a strange light which raises his IQ and his sensitivity. *Dir.* James Cameron.

Philadelphia (1993)   Tom Hanks, Denzel Washington, Jason Robards, Mary Steenburgen, Antonio Banderas, Joanne Woodward, Robert Ridgely. Homosexual lawyer with AIDS sues his firm for unfair dismissal. *Dir.* Jonathan Demme.

Philadelphia Story, The (1940)   Katharine Hepburn, Cary Grant, James Stewart, Ruth Hussey. *Dir.* George Cukor.

Piano, The (1993)   Holly Hunter, Harvey Keitel, Sam Neill, Genevieve Lemon. *Dir.* Jane Campion.

Picnic (1955)   William Holden, Kim Novak, Rosalind Russell, Susan Strasberg. *Dir.* Joshua Logan.

Picnic at Hanging Rock (1975)   Rachel Roberts, Dominic Guard, Helen Morse, Vivian Gray. *Dir.* Peter Weir.

Picture of Dorian Gray, The (1945)   Hurd Hatfield

(Gray), George Sanders (Sir Henry), Donna Reed, Angela Lansbury. *Dir*. Albert Lewin.

Pillow Talk (1959)   Doris Day, Rock Hudson, Tony Randall, Thelma Ritter. First of the partnership films of Day and Hudson, this one concerning a party line love affair. *Dir*. Michael Gordon.

Pink Panther, The (1963)   David Niven, Peter Sellers, Capucine, Claudia Cardinale, Robert Wagner. The seven sequels were *A Shot in the Dark, Inspector Clouseau, Return of the Pink Panther, The Pink Panther Strikes Again, The Revenge of the Pink Panther, Trail of the Pink Panther* and *Son of the Pink Panther*. *Dir*. Blake Edwards.

Pit and the Pendulum, The (1961)   Vincent Price, Barbara Steele, John Kerr. *Dir*. Roger Corman.

Place in the Sun, A (1951)   Montgomery Clift, Elizabeth Taylor, Shelley Winters, Raymond Burr. Man is offered the chance of a rich wife, but allows himself to be convicted and executed for the accidental death of his former fiancée. *Dir*. George Stevens.

Planes, Trains and Automobiles (1987)   Steve Martin (Neal Page), John Candy (Del Griffith), Laila Robbins, Kevin Bacon. Yuppie attempts to get home to his family for a snowy Thanksgiving. *Dir*. John Hughes.

Planet of the Apes (1968)   Charlton Heston, Roddy McDowall, Kim Hunter, James Whitmore. John Chambers won Oscar for Make-up. Sequels included *Beneath the Planet of the Apes* (1969), *Escape from the Planet of the Apes* (1970), *Conquest of the Planet of the Apes* (1972), and *Battle for the Planet of the Apes* (1973). *Dir*. Franklin Schaffner.

Platoon (1986)   Tom Berenger (Sgt Barnes), Willem Dafoe (Sgt Elias), Charlie Sheen (Chris), Johnny Depp (Lerner), Forest Whitaker (Big Harold). *Dir*. Oliver Stone.

Play Misty for Me (1971)   Clint Eastwood, Jessica Walter, Donna Mills, John Larch. *Dir*. Clint Eastwood.

Player, The (1992)   Tim Robbins (Griffin Mill), Greta Scacchi (June Gudmundsdottir), Fred Ward (Walter Stuckel), Whoopi Goldberg (Det. Avery), Richard E Grant (Tom Oakley), Sydney Pollack (Dick Mellen). This satire on Hollywood also starred 65 other stars who accepted nominal fees, including, Steve Allen, Cher, James Coburn, Peter Falk, Teri Garr, Jeff Goldblum, Elliott Gould, Joel Groy, Anjolica Huston, Sally Kellerman, Jack Lemmon, Marlee Matlin, Nick Nolte, Malcolm McDowell, Burt Reynolds, Julia Roberts, Mimi Rogers, Annie Ross, Jill St John, Susan Sarandon, Rod Steiger, Lily Tomlin, Robert Wagner, Bruce Willis. *Dir*. Robert Altman.

Ploughman's Lunch, The (1983)   Jonathan Pryce (James Penfield), Tim Curry (Jeremy Hancock), Charlie Dore (Sue Barrington). British journalist furthers his career by rewriting history. *Dir*. Richard Eyre.

Pocahontas (1995)   Voices of Mel Gibson, Irene Bedard, David Ogden Stiers, Judy Kuhn, Billy Connolly. *Dir*. Mike Gabriel and Eric Goldberg.

Point Blank (1967)   Lee Marvin, Angie Dickinson, Keenan Wynn, Carroll O'Connor. Based on the novel *The Hunter* by Richard Stark. *Dir*. John Boorman.

Point Break (1991)   Patrick Swayze (Bodhi), Keanu Reeves (Johnny Utah), Gary Busey, Lori Petty. FBI man Reeves infiltrates a gang of surfers to investigate bank robberies. *Dir*. Kathryn Bigelow.

Pokemon: The First Movie (1999)   Animation based on the popular Japanese characters. To date two subsequent sequels have arisen – *Pokemon 2: The Power of One; Pokemon 3 the Movie: Spell of the Unknown*. *Dir*. Kunihiko Yuyama.

Police Academy (1984)   Steve Guttenberg (Carey), Kim Cattrall (Karen), Bubba Smith (Moses), GW Bailey (Lt. Harris), David Graf (Tackleberry), Donovan Scott (Leslie). Sequels include *2: Their First Assignment; 3: Back in Training; 4: Citizens on Patrol; 5: Assignment Miami Beach; 6: City under Siege*. *Dir*. Hugh Wilson.

Poltergeist (1982)   JoBeth Williams, Craig T Nelson, Beatrice Straight, Oliver Robbins, Dominique Dunne. Two inferior sequels were made. *Dir*. Tobe Hooper.

Pope Joan (1972)   Liv Ullmann, Trevor Howard, Olivia de Havilland, Franco Nero, Maximilian Schell. *Dir*. Michael Anderson.

Pope Must Die, The (1991)   Robbie Coltrane, Beverly D'Angelo, Herbert Lom, Alex Rocco, Annette Crosbie. *Dir*. Peter Richardson.

Popeye (1980)   Robin Williams, Shelley Duvall, Ray Walston. *Dir*. Robert Altman.

Postcards From the Edge (1990)   Meryl Streep, Shirley MacLaine, Dennis Quaid, Gene Hackman, Richard Dreyfuss, Annette Bening. *Dir*. Mike Nichols.

Postman Always Rings Twice, The (1981)   Jack Nicholson, Jessica Lange, Anjelica Huston. Remake of the 1946 film starring Lana Turner & John Garfield. *Dir*. Bob Rafelson.

Predator (1987)   Arnold Schwarzenegger (Dutch), Carl Weathers (Dillon), Kevin Peter Hall (The Predator). *Predator 2* starred Danny Glover and Gary Busey. *Dir*. John McTiernan.

Prêt-à-Porter (1994)   Anouk Aimée, Lauren Bacall, Kim Basinger, Sophia Loren, Marcello Mastroianni, Julia Roberts, Teri Garr, Tracey Ullman, Richard E Grant. Aka *Ready to Wear*. *Dir*. Robert Altman.

Pretty Woman (1990)   Richard Gere (Edward Lewis), Julia Roberts (Vivian Ward), Ralph Bellamy (James Morse). *Dir*. Garry Marshall.

Prick up Your Ears (1987)   Gary Oldman (Joe Orton), Alfred Molina (Kenneth Halliwell), Vanessa Redgrave (Peggy), Julie Walters (Elsie Orton), Lindsay Duncan (Anthea Lahr). *Dir*. Stephen Frears.

Prime of Miss Jean Brodie, The (1969)   Maggie Smith, Robert Stephens, Pamela Franklin, Celia Johnson, Gordon Jackson. *Dir*. Ronald Neame.

Prince and the Pauper (1937)   Errol Flynn, Claude Rains, Billy and Bobby Mauch, Montagu Love (Henry VIII). Edward VI changes place with a street urchin. *Dir*. William Keighley. The 1977 remake starred Mark Lester, Oliver Reed and Raquel Welch (*Dir*. Richard Fleischer).

Prince and the Showgirl (1957)   Laurence Olivier, Marilyn Monroe, Sybil Thorndike. *Dir*. Laurence Olivier.

Prince of Tides, The (1991)   Nick Nolte (Tom Wingo), Barbra Streisand (Susan Lowenstein), Blythe Danner, Kate Nelligan. *Dir*. Barbra Streisand.

Prisoner of Zenda (1952)   Stewart Granger, James Mason, Deborah Kerr, Louis Calhern. *Dir*. Richard Thorpe. Remake of the 1937 classic starring Ronald Colman and Douglas Fairbanks Jr (*Dir*. John Cromwell). A further remake of 1979 starred Peter Sellers and Lynne Frederick (*Dir*. Richard Thorpe).

Private Function, A (1984)   Michael Palin, Maggie Smith, Denholm Elliott, Richard Griffiths, Betty the Pig. *Dir*. Malcolm Mowbray.

Private Life of Henry VIII, The (1933)   Charles Laughton, Elsa Lanchester, Robert Donat, Merle Oberon. *Dir*. Alexander Korda.

Private Parts (1996)   Howard Stern (as himself), Mary McCormack (Alison). Screen biography of top US disc jockey. *Dir*. Betty Thomas.

Prizzi's Honor (1985)   Jack Nicholson, Kathleen Turner, Robert Loggia, Anjelica Huston. *Dir*. John Huston.

Producers, The (1968)   Zero Mostel, Gene Wilder, Kenneth Mars. The play within the film is *Springtime for Hitler. Dir.* Mel Brooks.

Prospero's Books (1991)   John Gielgud, Michael Clark, Tom Bell, Mark Rylance. *Dir.* Peter Greenaway.

Psycho (1960)   Anthony Perkins, Vera Miles, Janet Leigh, John Gavin, Martin Balsam. Shower stabbing scene was directed by Saul Bass. Two sequels also starring Perkins in 1983 and 1986. *Dir.* Alfred Hitchcock.

Pulp Fiction (1994)   John Travolta, Samuel L Jackson, Uma Thurman, Harvey Keitel, Tim Roth, Bruce Willis, Rosanna Arquette. *Dir.* Quentin Tarantino.

Punchline (1988)   Sally Field (Lilah Krytsick), Tom Hanks (Steven Gold), John Goodman (John Krytsick), Mark Rydell (Romeo), Kim Greist (Madeline Urie). As the title suggests the film examines the world of a stand-up comedian. *Dir.* David Seltzer.

Quadrophenia (1979)   Phil Daniels, Mark Wingett, Philip Davis, Sting, Leslie Ash, Toyah Wilcox. *Dir.* Frank Roddam.

Queen Christina (1933)   Greta Garbo, John Gilbert, Ian Keith, Lewis Stone, Reginald Owen. Queen of Sweden roams the country to escape a political marriage. *Dir.* Rouben Mamoulian.

Quick and the Dead, The (1995)   Sharon Stone, Gene Hackman, Leonard DiCaprio. *Dir.* Sam Raimi.

Quiet American, The (2002)   Michael Caine, Brendan Fraser, Do Thi Hai Yen, Rade Sherbedgia. Set in Vietnam in 1952 during the Vietnamese liberation war against French rule, this is the story of a romantic triangle that develops between a young CIA agent (Fraser), a beautiful young Vietnamese woman (Do Hai Yen) and a British reporter (Caine). Based on the Graham Greene novel. *Dir.* Phillip Noyce.

Quiet Man, The (1952)   John Wayne, Maureen O'Hara, Barry Fitzgerald, Victor McLaglen, Ward Bond. *Dir.* John Ford.

Quigley Down Under (1990)   Tom Selleck, Laura San Giacomo, Alan Rickman, Chris Haywood. In 1860s Australia, an American hired gun is outlawed. *Dir.* Simon Wincer.

Quiller Memorandum, The (1966)   George Segal, Max Von Sydow, Alec Guinness, Senta Berger, George Sanders. *Dir.* Michael Anderson.

Quiz Show (1994)   John Turturro, Ralph Fiennes, Rob Morrow, Paul Scofield, Martin Scorsese. *Dir.* Robert Redford.

Quo Vadis (1951)   Robert Taylor, Deborah Kerr, Peter Ustinov, Leo Genn. *Dir.* Mervyn Le Roy.

Radio Days (1987)   Woody Allen (Narrator), Mia Farrow (Sally White), Seth Green (Little Joe), Julie Kavner (Mother), Michael Tucker (Father), Diane Keaton (New Year's singer). *Dir.* Woody Allen.

Rage, The: Carrie 2 (1999)   Emily Bergl, Jason London, Dylan Bruno, Amy Irving, John Doe, Zachery Ty Bryan. *Dir.* Katt Shea.

Rage in Harlem, A (1991)   Forest Whitaker, Gregory Hines, Robin Givens, Danny Glover. *Dir.* Bill Duke.

Raging Bull (1980)   Robert De Niro, Cathy Moriarty, Joe Pesci. *Dir.* Martin Scorsese.

Raiders of the Lost Ark (1981)   Harrison Ford, Karen Allen, John Rhys-Davies, Denholm Elliott. *Dir.* Steven Spielberg.

Railway Children, The (1970)   Dinah Sheridan, William Mervyn, Jenny Agutter, Sally Thomsett, Bernard Cribbins. *Dir.* Lionel Jeffries.

Rain Man (1988)   Dustin Hoffman (Raymond

Babbitt), Tom Cruise (Charles Babbitt), Valerie Golino (Susanna). *Dir.* Barry Levinson.

Raising Arizona (1987)   Nicolas Cage (HI), Holly Hunter (Ed), Trey Wilson (Nathan Arizona Sr), John Goodman (Gale). *Dir.* Joel Coen.

Rambo: First Blood Part II (1985)   Sylvester Stallone, Richard Crenna, Steven Berkoff. Written by Sylvester Stallone & James Cameron. *Dir.* George Pan Cosmatos.

Rambo III (1988)   Sylvester Stallone, Richard Crenna, Marc de Jonge. Written by Sylvester Stallone and Sheldon Lettich. *Dir.* Peter MacDonald.

Ran (1985)   Tatsuya Nakadai, Satoshi Terao. Japanese version of *King Lear. Dir.* Akira Kurosawa.

Reach for the Sky (1956)   Kenneth More (Douglas Bader), Muriel Pavlow. *Dir.* Lewis Gilbert.

Rear Window (1954)   James Stewart, Grace Kelly, Raymond Burr. *Dir.* Alfred Hitchcock.

Rebecca (1940)   Laurence Olivier, Joan Fontaine, George Sanders. *Dir.* Alfred Hitchcock.

Rebel without a Cause (1955)   James Dean, Natalie Wood, Jim Backus, Sal Mineo, Dennis Hopper. *Dir.* Nicholas Ray.

Red Heat (1988)   Arnold Schwarzenegger (Ivan Danko), James Belushi (Art Ridzik), Peter Boyle (Lou Donnelly). *Dir.* Walter Hill.

Red Sonja (1985)   Arnold Schwarzenegger (Kalifor), Brigitte Nielsen (Red Sonja). *Dir.* Richard Fleischer.

Reds (1981)   Warren Beatty (John Reed), Diane Keaton, Edward Herrmann, Jerzy Kosinski, Jack Nicholson. *Dir.* Warren Beatty.

Relic, The (1997)   Tom Sizemore (D'Agosta), Penelope Ann Miller (Dr Margo Green). *Dir.* Peter Hyams.

Remains of the Day, The (1993)   Anthony Hopkins, Emma Thompson, James Fox, Christopher Reeve, Peter Vaughan, Hugh Grant. *Dir.* James Ivory.

Repulsion (1965)   Catherine Deneuve, Ian Hendry, John Fraser, Patrick Wymark. *Dir.* Roman Polanski.

Reservoir Dogs (1991)   Lawrence Tierney, Harvey Keitel (Mr White), Tim Roth (Mr Orange), Eddie Bunker (Mr Blue), Michael Madsen (Mr Blonde), Steve Buscemi (Mr Pink), Quentin Tarantino (Mr Brown). *Dir.* Quentin Tarantino.

Resident Evil (2002)   Milla Jovovich (Alice), Michelle Rodriguez (Rain), Eric Mabius (Matt), Michaela Dicker (Red Queen). Virus turns workers into flesh-eating zombies. *Dir.* Paul WS Anderson.

Return of the Swamp Thing (1989)   Louis Jourdan (Dr Anton Arcane), Heather Locklear (Abby Arcane), Dick Durock (Swamp Thing). *Dir.* Jim Wynorski.

Return of the Jedi (1983)   Mark Hamill, Harrison Ford, Carrie Fisher, Billy Dee Williams. *Dir.* Richard Marquand.

Revenge (1990)   Kevin Costner (Jay Cochran), Anthony Quinn (Tiburon), Madeleine Stowe (Miryea). *Dir.* Tony Scott.

Revenge of the Pink Panther (1978)   Peter Sellers, Herbert Lom, Dyan Cannon. *Dir.* Blake Edwards.

Reversal of Fortune (1990)   Jeremy Irons (Claus Von Bulow), Glenn Close (Sunny Von Bulow), Julie Hagerty (Alexandra). *Dir.* Barbet Schroeder.

Revolution (1985)   Al Pacino (Tom Dobb), Donald Sutherland (Sgt Major Peasy), Nastassja Kinski (Daisy). Notable for being the biggest flop of all time. *Dir.* Hugh Hudson.

Rhapsody in Blue (1945)   Robert Alda (George Gershwin), Joan Leslie, Alexis Smith. *Dir.* Irving Rapper.

Richard III (1995)   Ian McKellen, Annette Bening, Jim Broadbent, Robert Downey Jnr, Kristin Scott-

Thomas, Maggie Smith, Nigel Hawthorne. Ian McKellen wrote the screenplay. *Dir*. Richard Loncraine.

Rififi (1955)   Jean Servais, Carl Mohner, Jules Dassin. Famous for its 25 minutes of silence whilst robbery is taking place. *Dir*. Jules Dassin.

Right Stuff, The (1983)   Sam Shepard (Chuck Yeager), Barbara Hershey (Glennis), Scott Glenn (Alan Shepard), Ed Harris (John Glenn), Fred Ward (Gus Grissom), Dennis Quaid (Gordon Cooper). *Dir*. Philip Kaufman.

Rising Sun (1993)   Sean Connery, Harvey Keitel, Wesley Snipes, Mako. *Dir*. Philip Kaufman.

Road House (1989)   Patrick Swayze, Kelly Lynch, Sam Elliott, Ben Gazzara, Marshall Teague. *Dir*. Rowdy Herrington.

Road to Hong Kong (1962)   Bob Hope, Bing Crosby, Dorothy Lamour, Joan Collins, Peter Sellers, Frank Sinatra, Dean Martin, David Niven. Last of the seven *Road* films. *Dir*. Norman Panama.

Road to Perdition (2002)   Tom Hanks (Michael Sullivan), Paul Newman (John Rooney), Jude Law (Maguire), Jennifer Jason Leigh (Annie Sullivan), Tyler Hoechlin (Michael Sullivan Jr) *Dir*. Sam Mendes.

Road to Singapore (1940)   Bob Hope, Bing Crosby, Dorothy Lamour, Anthony Quinn. First of the seven *Road* films, destination followed by Zanzibar, Moscow, Utopia, Rio, Bali and Hong Kong. *Dir*. Victor Schertzinger.

Rob Roy (1995)   Liam Neeson, Jessica Lange, John Hurt, Tim Roth. *Dir*. Michael Caton-Jones.

Robe, The (1953)   Richard Burton, Jean Simmons, Michael Rennie, Victor Mature, Richard Boone. *Dir*. Henry Koster.

Robin Hood (1991)   Patrick Bergin, Uma Thurman, Edward Fox. *Dir*. John Irvin.

Robin Hood: Men in Tights (1993)   Cary Elwes, Richard Lewis, Roger Rees, Tracey Ullman, Mel Brooks, Isaac Hayes, Patrick Stewart. *Dir*. Mel Brooks.

Robin Hood: Prince of Thieves (1991)   Kevin Costner, Morgan Freeman, Christian Slater, Alan Rickman, Sean Connery (uncredited). Title song: 'Everything I Do I Do for You' by Bryan Adams. *Dir*. Kevin Reynolds.

Robocop (1987)   Peter Weller, Nancy Allen, Ronny Cox. *Dir*. Paul Verhoeven.

Rock, The (1996)   Sean Connery, Nicolas Cage, Ed Harris. *Dir*. Michael Bay.

Rocking Horse Winner, The (1949)   John Mills, Valerie Hobson, John Howard Davies, Cyril Smith. Based on a DH Lawrence short story. *Dir*. Anthony Pelissier.

Rocky (1976)   Sylvester Stallone, Burgess Meredith, Talia Shire, Carl Weathers. Written by Sylvester Stallone. *Dir*. John G Avildsen.

Rocky II (1979)   Stallone, Meredith, Shire, Weathers. Written and directed by Stallone.

Rocky III (1982)   Stallone, Meredith, Shire, Weathers, Mr T, Hulk Hogan. Written and directed by Stallone.

Rocky IV (1985)   Stallone, Dolph Lundgren, T Shire, Weathers, Brigitte Nielsen. Written and directed by Stallone.

Rocky V (1990)   Stallone, Meredith, Shire, Burt Young, Sage Stallone. Written by Stallone. *Dir*. John G Avildsen.

Rocky Horror Picture Show, The (1975)   Tim Curry, Susan Sarandon, Meat Loaf, Little Nell. *Dir*. Jim Sharman.

Roman Holiday (1953)   Gregory Peck, Audrey Hepburn, Eddie Albert, Hartley Power. *Dir*. William Wyler.

Roman Scandals (1933)   Eddie Cantor, Gloria Stuart, Ruth Etting, Edward Arnold. *Dir*. Frank Tuttle.

Romancing the Stone (1984)   Michael Douglas, Kathleen Turner, Danny De Vito, Zack Norman. *Dir*. Robert Zemeckis.

Rookie, The (1990)   Clint Eastwood (Nick Pulovski), Charlie Sheen (David Ackerman), Raul Julia (Strom). *Dir*. Clint Eastwood.

Rookie of the Year (1993)   Gary Busey, Thomas Ian Nicholas, Albert Hall, John Candy (uncredited). Young boy becomes pitcher for the Chicago Cubs after his arm is injured in an accident. *Dir*. Daniel Stern.

Room at the Top (1959)   Laurence Harvey, Simone Signoret, Heather Sears, Donald Wolfit. Based on John Braine's novel. *Dir*. Jack Clayton.

Room with a View, A (1986)   Maggie Smith (Charlotte Bartlett), Helena Bonham Carter (Lucy Honeychurch). Opens in Italy in 1907. *Dir*. James Ivory.

Rope (1948)   James Stewart, John Dall, Farley Granger, Joan Chandler. Two homosexuals murder a friend for the thrill of it and hide his body in a trunk from which they serve cocktails to a party. *Dir*. Alfred Hitchcock.

Rose, The (1979)   Bette Midler, Alan Bates, Frederic Forrest, Harry Dean Stanton. *Dir*. Mark Rydell.

Rosencrantz and Guildenstern Are Dead (1990)   Gary Oldman (Rosencrantz), Tim Roth (Guildenstern), Iain Glen (Prince Hamlet). *Dir*. Tom Stoppard.

Running Man, The (1987)   Arnold Schwarzenegger (Ben Richards), Maria Conchita Alonso (Amber Mendez), Yaphet Kotto (Laughlin), Jim Brown (Fireball). *Dir*. Paul Michael Glaser.

Rush Hour (1998)   Jackie Chan (Lee), Chris Tucker (Carter), Tom Wilkinson, Elizabeth Pena, Mark Rolston, Tzi Ma, Philip Baker Hall. Chinese detective joins a disgraced LA cop in bringing a master criminal to justice. *Dir*. Brett Ratner.

Rush Hour 2 (2001)   Jackie Chan (Lee), Chris Tucker (Carter), John Lone (Ricky Tan), Zhang Ziyi (Hui Li). Sequel set in Hong Kong. *Dir*. Brett Ratner.

Russia House, The (1990)   Sean Connery, Michelle Pfeiffer, Roy Scheider, James Fox. *Dir*. Fred Schepisi.

Ruthless People (1986)   Bette Midler, Danny De Vito, Judge Reinhold, Helen Slater. *Dir*. Jim Abrahams.

Ryan's Daughter (1970)   Robert Mitchum, Sarah Miles, John Mills, Trevor Howard. *Dir*. David Lean.

Saint, The (1997)   Val Kilmer (Simon Templar), Elisabeth Shue (Emma Russell). Roger Moore's voice heard on car radio. *Dir*. Phillip Noyce.

Santa Claus: The Movie (1985)   Dudley Moore (Patch), John Lithgow (BZ), David Huddleston (Claus), Burgess Meredith (Elf). *Dir*. Jeannot Szwarc.

Saturday Night and Sunday Morning (1960)   Albert Finney, Shirley Anne Field, Rachel Roberts. Nottingham factory worker is dissatisfied with his lot. *Dir*. Karel Reisz.

Saturday Night Fever (1977)   John Travolta, Karen Lynn Gorney, Barry Miller. *Dir*. John Badham.

Save the Last Dance (2001)   Julia Stiles (Sara), Sean Patrick Thomas (Derek), Kerry Washington (Chenille), Fredro Starr (Malakai). Young white ballerina moves to Chicago and falls in love with a black youth. *Dir*. Thomas Carter.

Saving Private Ryan (1998)   Tom Hanks, Edward Burns, Tom Sizemore, Matt Damon, Ted Danson, Harve Presnell. *Dir*. Steven Spielberg. (Author's Note: I believe this is the first work to be published which highlights a subtle continuity error. After losing one of the eight original platoon members all eight can be seen marching across a field, but fortunately become seven again on arrival at a radar station!)

Scandal (1989)   John Hurt (Stephen Ward), Joanne Whalley-Kilmer (Christine Keeler), Bridget Fonda (Mandy Rice-Davies), Ian McKellen (John Profumo), Leslie Phillips, Britt Ekland, Jean Alexander, Jeroen Krabb, Michael Ironside. *Dir.* Michael Caton-Jones.

Scanners (1981)   Stephen Lock, Jennifer O'Neill, Patrick McGoohan, Michael Ironside. *Dir.* David Cronenberg.

Scanners II: The New Order (1991)   David Hewlett, Yvan Ponton, Raoul Trujillo. *Dir.* Christian Duguay.

Scanners III: The Takeover (1992)   Liliana Komorowska, Valerie Valcis, Steve Parrish, Harry Hill. *Dir.* Christian Duguay.

Scarface (1983)   Al Pacino (Tony Montana), Steven Bauer (Manny Ray), Michelle Pfeiffer (Elvira), Mary Elizabeth Mastrantonio (Gina), Robert Loggia (Frank Lopez), F Murray Abraham (Omar). *Dir.* Brian De Palma.

Scarlet Letter, The (1995)   Demi Moore, Gary Oldman, Robert Duvall, Robert Prosky, Joan Plowright. Set in C17 Massachusetts; a settler's wife gives birth to an illegitimate daughter. Based on the Nathaniel Hawthorne novel, the scarlet letter is 'A' for adultery. *Dir.* Roland Joffé.

Scary Movie (2000)   Marlon Wayans (Shorty), Shawn Wayans (Ray), Anna Faris (Cindy), Shannon Elizabeth (Buffy), Cheri Oteri (Gail Hailstorm). A killer murders high-school children in this horror-movie spoof. *Dir.* Keenen Ivory Wayans.

Scary Movie 2 (2001)   Marlon Wayans (Shorty), Shawn Wayans (Ray), Anna Faris (Cindy), Regina Hall (Brenda), Chris Masterson (Buddy), Tim Curry (The Professor), Kathleen Robertson (Theo), James Woods (Father McFeely). Sequel concerning psychology professor who invites students to spend a weekend in a haunted house. *Dir.* Keenen Ivory Wayans.

Scenes from a Mall (1991)   Bette Midler, Woody Allen, Paul Mazursky. *Dir.* Paul Mazursky.

Scent of a Woman (1992)   Al Pacino, Chris O'Donnell, Gabrielle Anwar. Blind ex-officer takes young man under his wing. *Dir.* Martin Brest.

Schindler's List (1993)   Liam Neeson, Ben Kingsley, Ralph Fiennes. *Dir.* Steven Spielberg.

Scooby-Doo (2002)   Freddie Prinze Jr (Fred), Sarah Michelle Gellar (Daphne), Matthew Lillard (Shaggy), Linda Cardellini (Velma). Real-life version of the Hanna-Barbera cartoon. *Dir.* Raja Gosnell.

Scorpion King, The (2002)   Dwayne Johnson, Steven Brand, Michael Clarke Duncan, The Rock (Mathayus/The Scorpion King), Kelly Hu, Bernard Hill. Spin-off from *The Mummy Returns. Dir.* Chuck Russell.

Scream (1996)   David Arquette, Neve Campbell (Sidney), Courteney Cox (Gale Weathers), Drew Barrymore. *Dir.* Wes Craven.

Screamers (1996)   Peter Weller, Roy Dupuis, Jennifer Rubin, Ron White. Set in 2078 on the planet Sirius 6B where killer robots run amok. *Dir.* Christian Duguay.

Secret Garden, The (1949)   Margaret O'Brien, Herbert Marshall, Gladys Cooper, Elsa Lanchester, Dean Stockwell, Brian Roper. Adaptation of the novel by Frances Hodgson Burnett which was shot in black and white but the scenes in the garden were filmed in Technicolor. A 1993 remake starred Maggie Smith. *Dir.* Fred M Wilcox.

Sea of Love (1989)   Al Pacino (Frank Keller), Ellen Barkin (Helen Cruger), John Goodman (Sherman Touhy). Cop investigating murders of lonely hearts advertisers places an ad himself. *Dir.* Harold Becker.

Sebastiane (1976)   Leonardo Treviglio, Barney James, Neil Kennedy, Ken Hicks. Title character is banished by Emperor Diocletian and suffers further tragedy. Dialogue is in Latin with English subtitles. *Dir.* Derek Jarman and Paul Humfress.

Secrets and Lies (1995)   Timothy Spall, Phyllis Logan, Brenda Blethyn, Claire Rushbrook, Marianne Jean-Baptiste. *Dir.* Mike Leigh.

See No Evil, Hear No Evil (1989)   Gene Wilder (Dave Lyons), Richard Pryor (Wally Karew). Pryor is blind and Wilder is deaf. *Dir.* Arthur Hiller.

Seize the Day (1986)   Robin Williams, Joseph Wiseman. Based on a Saul Bellow novel. *Dir.* Fielder Cook.

Sense and Sensibility (1995)   Emma Thompson, Alan Rickman, Kate Winslet, Hugh Grant, Hugh Laurie, Gemma Jones. Emma Thompson wrote the screenplay. *Dir.* Ang Lee.

September (1987)   Denholm Elliott (Howard), Dianne Wiest (Stephanie), Mia Farrow (Lane), Elaine Stritch. *Dir.* Woody Allen.

Serendipity (2001)   John Cusack, Kate Beckinsale, Jeremy Piven, Molly Shannon. *Dir.* Peter Chelsom.

Sgt Bilko (1996)   Steve Martin, Dan Aykroyd. *Dir.* Jonathan Lynn.

Sgt Pepper's Lonely Hearts Club Band (1978)   Peter Frampton, Bee Gees, George Burns, Frankie Howerd, Donald Pleasence, Paul Nicholas, Alice Cooper, Steve Martin, Earth Wind & Fire, Sandy Farina. *Dir.* Michael Schultz.

Seven (1995)   Brad Pitt, Morgan Freeman, Richard Roundtree, Kevin Spacey. *Dir.* David Fincher.

Seven Brides for Seven Brothers (1954)   Howard Keel, Jane Powell, Jeff Richards, Russ Tamblyn. *Dir.* Stanley Donen.

Seven Year Itch, The (1955)   Tom Ewell, Marilyn Monroe, Sonny Tufts, Evelyn Keyes. *Dir.* Billy Wilder.

Seven Years in Tibet (1997)   Brad Pitt, David Thewlis, BD Wong. *Dir.* Jean-Jacques Annaud.

Shadow, The (1994)   Alec Baldwin, Penelope Ann Miller, Tim Curry. In the 1930s a former criminal battles against a descendant of Genghis Khan. *Dir.* Russell Mulcahy.

Shakespeare in Love (1998)   Gwyneth Paltrow, Joseph Fiennes, Geoffrey Rush, Colin Firth, Ben Affleck, Judi Dench, Rupert Everett, Simon Callow, Martin Clunes, Antony Sher, Imelda Staunton. *Dir.* John Madden. Judi Dench won Best Supporting Actor Oscar although only on screen for eight minutes. Daniel Day-Lewis and Julia Roberts turned down the lead roles.

Shadowlands (1993)   Anthony Hopkins, Debra Winger, John Wood. Biopic of CS Lewis and his love for an American woman. *Dir.* Richard Attenborough.

Shallow Hal (2001)   Gwyneth Paltrow, Jack Black (Hal), Jason Alexander, René Kirby. Man who judges women on superficial looks is hypnotised to see only their inner beauty and falls for a 300lb woman. *Dir.* Bobby Farrelly and Peter Farrelly.

Shawshank Redemption, The (1994)   Tim Robbins, Morgan Freeman, Bob Gunton, James Whitmore. *Dir.* Frank Darabont.

Sheena, Queen of the Jungle (1984)   Tanya Roberts, Ted Wass, Donovan Scott. *Dir.* John Guillermin.

Sheik, The (1921)   Rudolph Valentino, Agnes Ayres. English heiress falls for a desert chieftain. Notable for two reasons: it was the film that made a star of

Valentino; and it was based on the novel by EM Hull, often considered the first novel of the Romantic Fiction genre. *Dir.* George Melford.

Shine (1996)   Armin Mueller-Stahl, Geoffrey Rush, Noah Taylor, Lynn Redgrave, Googie Withers, John Gielgud. Based on the life of pianist David Helfgott. *Dir.* Scott Hicks.

Ship of Fools (1965)   Vivien Leigh, Simone Signoret, Oskar Werner, Lee Marvin. German line *Vera Cruz* leaves for Bremerhaven with a mixed bag of passengers. *Dir.* Stanley Kramer.

Shirley Valentine (1989)   Pauline Collins, Tom Conti, Julia McKenzie, Alison Steadman, Joanna Lumley, Bernard Hill. *Dir.* Lewis Gilbert.

Shooting Fish (1997)   Dan Futterman, Stuart Townsend, Kate Beckinsale, Annette Crosbie, Jane Lapotaire, Phyllis Logan. *Dir.* Stefan Schwartz.

Shooting Party, The (1984)   James Mason (Ralph Nettleby), Dorothy Tutin, Edward Fox, Cheryl Campbell, John Gielgud. *Dir.* Alan Bridges.

Shootist, The (1976)   John Wayne, Lauren Bacall, James Stewart, Ron Howard, Hugh O'Brian. *Dir.* Don Siegel.

Short Cuts (1993)   Andie MacDowell, Bruce Davison, Jack Lemmon, Robert Downey Jnr. Lives of 9 dysfunctional suburban couples intertwine. *Dir.* Robert Altman.

Shrek (2001)   Voices of Mike Myers (Shrek), Eddie Murphy (Donkey), Cameron Diaz (Princess Fiona), John Lithgow (Lord Farquaad), Vincent Cassel (Monsieur Hood). Animation in which an ugly green ogre agrees to rescue a princess in return for having his swamp vacated but falls in love with her. *Dir.* Andrew Adamson and Vicky Jenson.

Silence of the Lambs (1991)   Jodie Foster (Clarice Starling), Anthony Hopkins (Dr Hannibal Lecter), Scott Glen. *Dir.* Jonathan Demme.

Silkwood (1983)   Meryl Streep, Cher, Kurt Russell. Female worker in nuclear processing plant mysteriously dies before she denounces safety aspects of the plant. *Dir.* Mike Nichols.

Silverado (1985)   Scott Glen, Kevin Costner, John Cleese, Kevin Kline, Rosanna Arquette, Danny Glover. *Dir.* Lawrence Kasdan.

Single White Female (1992)   Bridget Fonda (Allison Jones), Jennifer Jason Leigh (Hedra Carlson), Steven Weber. *Dir.* Barbot Schroeder.

Sirens (1994)   Hugh Grant, Tara FitzGerald, Sam Neill, Elle MacPherson. *Dir.* John Duigen.

Sister Act (1992)   Whoopi Goldberg, Maggie Smith, Harvey Keitel. *Dir.* Emile Ardolino.

Sister Act 2: Back in the Habit (1993)   Whoopi Goldberg, Maggie Smith, James Coburn. *Dir.* Bill Duke.

Sixth Sense, The (1999)   Bruce Willis (Malcolm Crowe), Toni Collette, Haley Joel Osment (Cole). *Dir.* M. Night Shyamalan.

Sleeper (1973)   Woody Allen, Diane Keaton, John Beck. *Dir.* Woody Allen.

Sleeping with the Enemy (1990)   Julia Roberts, Patrick Bergin. *Dir.* Joseph Ruben.

Sleepless in Seattle (1993)   Tom Hanks, Meg Ryan, Ross Malinger. *Dir.* Nora Ephron.

Sleepy Hollow (1999)   Johny Depp (Ichabod Crane), Christina Ricci (Katrina Van Tassel), Michael Gambon (Bactus Van Tassel), Christopher Lee (Burgomaster), Christopher Walken (Hessian Horseman). *Dir.* Tim Burton.

Sliding Doors (1998)   Gwyneth Paltrow, John Hannah, John Lynch, Jeanne Tripplehorn, Virginia McKenna. *Dir.* Peter Howitt.

Sliver (1993)   Sharon Stone, William Baldwin, Tom Berenger, Martin Landau. Based on an Ira Levin novel. *Dir.* Philip Noyce.

Smilla's Feeling for Snow (1997)   Julia Ormond (Smilla), Gabriel Byrne, Richard Harris (Tork), Vanessa Redgrave, Bob Peck, Jim Broadbent, Robert Loggia. *Dir.* Bille August.

Sneakers (1992)   Robert Redford, Dan Aykroyd, Ben Kingsley, River Phoenix, Sidney Poitier. Experts hired to recover electronic device that can penetrate the government's most secure computer systems. *Dir.* Phil Alden Robinson.

Snow Dogs (2002)   Cuba Gooding Jr (Ted Brooks), James Coburn (Thunder Jack), Sisqo, Graham Greene, Michael Bolton (as himself). Dentist goes to Alaska to search for his roots. *Dir.* Brian Levant.

Snow White: A Tale of Terror (1997)   Monica Keena (Lilli), Sam Neill (Baron Hoffman), Sigourney Weaver (Claudia).

Somebody up There Likes Me (1956)   Paul Newman (Rocky Graziano), Pier Angeli, Sal Mineo, Steve McQueen. *Dir.* Robert Wise.

Some Like It Hot (1939)   Bob Hope, Shirley Ross, Una Merkel, Gene Krupa. Sideshow owner runs out of money. *Dir.* George Archainbaud.

Some Like It Hot (1959)   Tony Curtis, Jack Lemmon, Marilyn Monroe, Joe E Brown, George Raft. *Dir.* Billy Wilder.

Sommersby (1993)   Richard Gere, Jodie Foster. Remake of *The Return of Martin Guerre*. *Dir.* Jon Amiel.

Son of Lassie (1945)   Peter Lawford, Donald Crisp, Nigel Bruce. The first sequel to *Lassie Come Home*; many more followed. *Dir.* S Sylvan Simon.

Son of the Pink Panther (1993)   Robert Benigni, Herbert Lom, Claudia Cardinale, Burt Kwouk. *Dir.* Blake Edwards.

Song of Bernadette, The (1943)   Jennifer Jones, Charles Bickford, William Eythe. *Dir.* Henry King.

Song to Remember, A (1944)   Cornel Wilde, Merle Oberon, Paul Muni. Life and death of Chopin. *Dir.* Charles Vidor.

Sophie's Choice (1982)   Meryl Streep, Kevin Kline, Josh Mostel. *Dir.* Alan J Pakula.

Sound of Music, The (1965)   Julie Andrews, Christopher Plummer, Richard Haydn, Marni Nixon. *Dir.* Robert Wise.

Soylent Green (1973)   Charlton Heston, Edward G Robinson, Leigh Taylor-Young. Set in 2022, the Soylent Green of the title is synthetic food. *Dir.* Richard Fleischer.

Space Jam (1996)   Michael Jordan, Bugs Bunny, voice of Danny De Vito. *Dir.* Joe Pytka.

Space Truckers (1997)   Dennis Hopper, Stephen Dorff, Debi Mazar, Charles Dance. Set in 2196; BMW's Bio-Mechanical Warriors. *Dir.* Stuart Gordon.

Specialist, The (1994)   Sharon Stone, Sylvester Stallone, Rod Steiger, James Woods. *Dir.* Luis Llosa.

Speed (1994)   Sandra Bullock, Keanu Reeves, Dennis Hopper, Jeff Daniels. *Dir.* Jan de Bont.

Spiceworld (1997)   Spice Girls, Richard E Grant. Originally called: *Five*. *Dir.* Bob Spiers.

Spider-Man (2002)   Tobey Maguire (Peter Parker / Spider-Man), Willem Dafoe (Norman Osborn / The Green Goblin), Kirsten Dunst (Mary Jane Watson), James Franco (Harry Osborn), Cliff Robertson (Ben Parker), Rosemary Harris (May Parker). *Dir.* Sam Raimi.

Spitfire Grill, The (1996)   Ellen Burstyn, Marcia Gay Harden, Alison Elliott. *Dir.* Lee David Zlotoff.

Splash! (1984)   Tom Hanks (Allen Bauer), Daryl Hannah (Madison), John Candy, Eugene Levy. *Dir.* Ron Howard.

Splitting Heirs (1993) Rick Moranis (Henry), Eric Idle (Tommy Patel), Barbara Hershey, Catherine Zeta Jones, John Cleese (Raoul P Shadgrind), Stratford Johns, Eric Sykes. *Dir*. Robert Young.

Spy Hard (1996) Leslie Nielsen (Agent WD-40), Andy Griffith, Nicollette Sheridan. *Dir*. Rick Friedberg.

Spy Who Loved Me, The (1977) Roger Moore, Barbara Bach (Major Anya Amasova), Curt Jurgens (Stromberg). Theme song 'Nobody Does it Better' performed by Carly Simon. *Dir*. Lewis Gilbert.

Stagecoach (1939) John Wayne, Claire Trevor, Thomas Mitchell, Andy Devine. The 1966 remake starred Ann-Margret & Bing Crosby. *Dir*. John Ford.

Stalag 17 (1953) William Holden, Don Taylor, Otto Preminger, Peter Graves, Neville Brand. *Dir*. Billy Wilder.

Stanley and Iris (1990) Jane Fonda, Robert De Niro. *Dir*. Martin Ritt.

Stanza del Figlio, La (2001) Nanni Moretti (Giovanni), Laura Morante (Paola). Apparent family bliss falls apart when the young son dies in an accident. *Dir*. Nanni Moretti.

Star! (1968) Julie Andrews, Richard Crenna, Daniel Massey (Noël Coward), Bruce Forsyth, Beryl Reid. Biopic of Gertrude Lawrence. *Dir*. Robert Wise.

Star Is Born, A (1937) Janet Gaynor, Fredric March, Adolphe Menjou, Andy Devine. *Dir*. William A Wellman.

Star Is Born, A (1954) Judy Garland, James Mason, Charles Bickford. *Dir*. George Cukor.

Star Is Born, A (1976) Barbra Streisand, Kris Kristofferson, Gary Busey, Paul Mazursky. *Dir*. Frank Pierson.

Star Trek: First Contact (1996) Patrick Stewart, Jonathan Frakes, Brent Spiner, Michael Dorn, LeVar Burton. *Dir*. Jonathan Frakes.

Star Trek: Generations (1994) Patrick Stewart, William Shatner, Malcolm McDowell, Jonathan Frakes, Brent Spiner, Whoopi Goldberg. *Dir*. David Carson.

Star Trek: The Motion Picture (1979) William Shatner, Leonard Nimoy, DeForest Kelley, Persis Khambatta. *Dir*. Robert Wise.

Star Trek II: The Wrath of Khan (1982) William Shatner, Leonard Nimoy, DeForest Kelley, Ricardo Montalban. Sequel to TV episode 'Space Seed'. *Dir*. Nicholas Meyer.

Star Trek III: The Search for Spock (1984) William Shatner, Leonard Nimoy, DeForest Kelley, Robert Hooks. *Dir*. Leonard Nimoy.

Star Trek IV: The Voyage Home (1986) William Shatner, Leonard Nimoy, DeForest Kelley, Catherine Hicks, Jane Wyatt. *Dir*. Leonard Nimoy.

Star Trek V: The Final Frontier (1989) William Shatner, Leonard Nimoy, DeForest Kelley, David Warner. *Dir*. William Shatner.

Star Trek VI: The Undiscovered Country (1991) William Shatner, Leonard Nimoy, DeForest Kelley, David Warner, Christian Slater, Christopher Plummer. *Dir*. Nicholas Meyer.

Star Wars (1977) Mark Hamill, Harrison Ford, Alec Guinness, Carrie Fisher, Anthony Daniels (C3PO), Kenny Baker (R2D2), Dave Prowse. *Dir*. George Lucas.

Star Wars: Episode I – The Phantom Menace (1999) Liam Neeson, Ewan McGregor, Natalie Portman, Jake Lloyd, Frank Oz, Ray Park, Ian McDiarmid, Samuel L Jackson, Brian Blessed, Sofia Coppola, Pernilla August. *Dir*. George Lucas.

Star Wars: Episode II – Attack of the Clones (2002) Ewan McGregor (Obi-Wan Kenobi), Natalie Portman (Padme), Christopher Lee (Count Dooku), Hayden Christensen (Anakin Skywalker), Samuel L. Jackson (Mace Windu), Yoda (voice of Frank Oz), Kenny Baker (R2-D2), Anthony Daniels (C-3PO). *Dir*. George Lucas.

Starman (1984) Jeff Bridges, Karen Allen. Alien arrives in Wisconsin. *Dir*. John Carpenter.

Starship Troopers (1997) Casper van Dien, Dina Meyer, Denise Richards, Jake Busey, Michael Ironside. *Dir*. Paul Verhoeven.

Stay Hungry (1976) Jeff Bridges, Sally Field, Arnold Schwarzenegger, Robert Englund. *Dir*. Bob Rafelson.

Staying Alive (1983) John Travolta, Cynthia Rhodes, Finola Hughes, Steve Inwood. Sequel to *Saturday Night Fever*. Tony Manero becomes a Broadway dancer. *Dir*. Sylvester Stallone.

Steaming (1985) Vanessa Redgrave (Nancy), Sarah Miles (Sarah), Diana Dors (Violet), Patti Love, Brenda Bruce. *Dir*. Joseph Losey.

Steel Magnolias (1989) Sally Field, Dolly Parton, Shirley MacLaine, Daryl Hannah, Olympia Dukakis, Julia Roberts, Tom Skerritt. *Dir*. Herbert Ross.

Stepford Wives, The (1974) Katharine Ross, Paula Prentiss, Nanette Newman, Patrick O'Neal. *Dir*. Bryan Forbes.

Sting, The (1973) Paul Newman, Robert Redford, Robert Shaw. *Dir*. George Roy Hill.

Stormy Monday (1988) Melanie Griffith (Kate), Tommy Lee Jones (Cosmo), Sting (Finney), Sean Bean (Brendan). *Dir*. Mike Figgis.

Strange Days (1995) Ralph Fiennes (Lenny Nero), Angela Bassett, Juliette Lewis, Tom Sizemore, Michael Wincott. *Dir*. Kathryn Bigelow.

Strangers on a Train (1951) Farley Granger, Robert Walker, Ruth Roman, Patricia Hitchcock. *Dir*. Alfred Hitchcock.

Straw Dogs (1971) Dustin Hoffman, Susan George, Peter Vaughan, David Warner, TP McKenna. Based on Gordon M Williams novel *The Siege of Trencher's Farm*. *Dir*. Sam Peckinpah.

Striptease (1996) Demi Moore (Erin Grant), Burt Reynolds (David Dilbeck). Strip club name: The Eager Beaver. *Dir*. Andrew Bergman.

Stuart Little (1999) Geena Davis (Mrs Little), Hugh Laurie (Mr Little), Jonathan Lipnicki (George Little), Dabney Coleman (Dr Beechwood), voices of Michael J Fox (Stuart Little), Nathan Lane. *Dir*. Rob Minkoff.

Stuart Little 2 (2002) Geena Davis (Mrs Little), Hugh Laurie (Mr Little), voice of Michael J Fox (Stuart Little). *Dir*. Rob Minkoff

Substitute, The (1996) Tom Berenger, Ernie Hudson, Diane Venora. Commando-trained man takes over teaching position when his girlfriend is beaten up. *Dir*. Robert Mandel.

Sudden Impact (1983) Clint Eastwood (Callahan), Sondra Locke (Jennifer Spencer), Pat Hingle. *Dir*. Clint Eastwood.

Suddenly Last Summer (1959) Katharine Hepburn, Elizabeth Taylor, Mongomery Clift. *Dir*. Joseph L Mankiewicz.

Summer Holiday (1962) Cliff Richard, Lauri Peters, Melvyn Hayes, Una Stubbs. *Dir*. Peter Yates.

Summer of '42 (1971) Jennifer O'Neill, Gary Grimes, Jerry Houser. *Dir*. Robert Mulligan.

Sunday, Bloody Sunday (1971) Glenda Jackson, Peter Finch, Murray Head. *Dir*. John Schlesinger.

Sundowners, The (1960) Robert Mitchum, Deborah Kerr, Glynis Johns, Peter Ustinov. *Dir*. Fred Zinnemann.

Sunset (1988) Bruce Willis (Tom Mix), James Garner (Wyatt Earp), Malcolm McDowell. *Dir*. Blake Edwards.

Sunset Boulevard (1950)   William Holden, Gloria Swanson, Erich Von Stroheim, Cecil B de Mille, Buster Keaton, Hedda Hopper. *Dir.* Billy Wilder.

Super Mario Brothers (1993)   Bob Hoskins, Dennis Hopper, John Leguizamo. *Dir.* Rocky Morton and Annabel Jankel.

Supergirl (1984)   Faye Dunaway (Selena), Helen Slater (Supergirl / Linda Lee), Peter O'Toole (Zeitar), Peter Cook, Simon Ward, Brenda Vaccaro, Mia Farrow. *Dir.* Jeannot Szwarc.

Superman (1978)   Christopher Reeve, Marlon Brando, Susannah York, Margot Kidder, Glenn Ford, Gene Hackman, Trevor Howard. *Dir.* Richard Donner.

Superman 2 (1980)   Christopher Reeve, Susannah York, Margot Kidder, Gene Hackman, Ned Beatty, Terence Stamp. *Dir.* Richard Lester.

Superman 3 (1983)   Christopher Reeve, Richard Pryor, Jackie Cooper, Margot Kidder, Pamela Stephenson, Robert Vaughn. *Dir.* Richard Lester.

Superman 4: The Quest for Peace (1987) Christopher Reeve, Gene Hackman, Jackie Cooper, Margot Kidder. *Dir.* Sidney J Furie.

Surviving Picasso (1996)   Anthony Hopkins (Picasso), Natascha McElhone (Françoise). *Dir.* James Ivory.

Swallows and Amazons (1974)   Virginia McKenna, Ronald Fraser, Simon West, Sophie Neville. *Dir.* Claude Whatham.

Sweet Charity (1969)   Shirley MacLaine, Ricardo Montalban, Chita Rivera, Stubby Kaye, Sammy Davis Jnr. *Dir.* Bob Fosse.

Sweet Liberty (1986)   Alan Alda, Michael Caine, Michelle Pfeiffer, Lilian Gish, Bob Hoskins. College professor is alarmed as he watches the Hollywood filming of his historical novel. *Dir.* Alan Alda.

Swing Shift (1984)   Goldie Hawn, Kurt Russell, Fred Ward, Christine Lahti. *Dir.* Jonathan Demme.

Swiss Family Robinson, The (1960)   John Mills, Dorothy McGuire, James MacArthur, Janet Munro. *Dir.* Ken Annakin.

Sword of Sherwood Forest (1960)   Richard Greene, Peter Cushing, Richard Pasco, Niall MacGinnis, Oliver Reed. *Dir.* Terence Fisher.

Swordfish (2001)   John Travolta (Gabriel Shear), Hugh Jackman, Halle Berry (Ginger), Don Cheadle, Vinnie Jones (Marco). Computer hacker is hired by a secret agent and thief to steal government funds. *Dir.* Dominic Sena.

Taking of Pelham 123, The (1974)   Walter Matthau, Robert Shaw, Martin Balsam, Hector Elizondo. Four gunmen hold a New York subway train to ransom. *Dir.* Joseph Sargent.

Tale of Two Cities, A (1958)   Dirk Bogarde, Dorothy Tutin, Christopher Lee, Donald Pleasence, Alfie Bass. Remake of 1935 classic. *Dir.* Ralph Thomas.

Talented Mr Ripley, The (1999)   Matt Damon (Tom Ripley), Jude Law (Dickie Greenleaf), Gwyneth Paltrow (Marge Sherwood), Cate Blanchett (Meredith Logue), Philip Seymour Hoffman (Freddie Miles). *Dir.* Anthony Minghella. Anthony Minghella wrote the screen play based on Patricia Highsmith's novel.

Tales from the Darkside: The Movie (1991)   Debbie Harry is a cannibal waiting to eat a young boy once he has told her 3 stories. *The Wraparound Story*: Deborah Harry (Betty), Matthew Lawrence (Timmy). *Lot 249*: Christian Slater, Steve Buscemi, Robert Sedgwick, Julianne Moore. *Cat from Hell*: David Johansen, William Hickey. *Lover's Vow*: James Remar, Rae Dawn Chong, Robert Klein. *Dir.* John Harrison.

Talk Radio (1988)   Eric Bogosian (Barry Champlain), Ellen Greene, Leslie Hope, Alec Baldwin. *Dir.* Oliver Stone.

Tall Guy, The (1989)   Jeff Goldblum (Dexter King), Emma Thompson (Kate Lemon), Rowan Atkinson (Ron Anderson). *Dir.* Mel Smith.

Tango and Cash (1989)   Kurt Russell, Sylvester Stallone, Jack Palance, Teri Hatcher, Michael J Pollard. *Dir.* Andrei Konchalovsky.

Tank Girl (1994)   Lon Petty, Ice T, Naomi Watts, Malcolm McDowell. *Dir.* Rachel Talalay.

Tank Malling (1988)   Ray Winstone, Jason Connery, Amanda Donohoe, John Conteh, Terry Marsh, Nick Berry. *Dir.* James Marcus.

Tap (1989)   Gregory Hines, Suzanne Douglas, Sammy Davis Jnr (Little Mo). *Dir.* Nick Castle.

Taps (1981)   Timothy Hutton, George C Scott, Sean Penn, Tom Cruise. *Dir.* Harold Becker.

Taras Bulba (1962)   Yul Brynner, Tony Curtis, Christine Kaufmann, Sam Wanamaker. *Dir.* J Lee Thompson.

Tarzan the Apeman (1981)   Bo Derek, Miles O'Keeffe (Tarzan), Richard Harris, John Phillip Law, Wilfrid Hyde-White. *Dir.* John Derek.

Taste of Honey, A (1961)   Rita Tushingham, Dora Bryan, Murray Melvin. Based on Shelagh Delaney play. *Dir.* Tony Richardson.

Taxi Driver (1976)   Robert De Niro (Travis Bickle), Jodie Foster, Cybill Shepherd, Harvey Keitel. *Dir.* Martin Scorsese.

Teenage Mutant Ninja Turtles (1990)   Judith Hoag (April O'Neil), Elias Koteas (Casey Jones), Josh Pais (Raphael), Michelan Sisti (Michelangelo), Leif Tilden (Donatello), David Forman (Leonardo). Michael Pressman's 1991 sequel: *Teenage Mutant Ninja Turtles II: The Secret of the Ooze*. *Dir.* Steve Barron.

Ten Commandments, The (1956)   Charlton Heston (Moses), Yul Brynner, Edward G Robinson, Anne Baxter, Yvonne De Carlo. *Dir.* Cecil B de Mille.

Ten Little Indians (1965)   Wilfrid Hyde-White, Dennis Price, Stanley Holloway, Shirley Eaton, Hugh O'Brian, Daliah Lavi, Fabian, Mario Adorf. Based on Agatha Christie's novel. *Dir.* George Pollock.

Ten Rillington Place (1971)   Richard Attenborough, John Hurt, Judy Geeson. Account of the Christie murders of the 1940s. *Dir.* Richard Fleischer.

10 Things I Hate About You (1999)   Heath Ledger, Julia Stiles, Joseph-Gordon Levitt, Andrew Keegan, Susan May Pratt. *Dir.* Gil Junger. Teenage comedy loosely based on Shakespeare's *The Taming of the Shrew*.

10 to Midnight (1983)   Charles Bronson (Leo Kessler), Lisa Eilbacher (Laurie), Andrew Stevens, Gene Davis. *Dir.* J Lee Thompson.

Tender Mercies (1982)   Robert Duvall, Tess Harper, Betty Buckley. Robert Duvall sang the songs himself. *Dir.* Bruce Beresford.

Tequila Sunrise (1988)   Mel Gibson (McKussic), Michele Pfeiffer, Kurt Russell, Raul Julia. *Dir.* Robert Towne.

Terminator, The (1984)   Arnold Schwarzenegger, Linda Hamilton, Michael Biehn. *Dir.* James Cameron.

Terminator 2: Judgment Day (1991)   Arnold Schwarzenegger, Linda Hamilton, Edward Furlong. *Dir.* James Cameron.

Terms of Endearment (1983)   Shirley MacLaine, Jack Nicholson, Debra Winger, Danny De Vito. *Dir.* James L Brooks.

Texas Chainsaw Massacre, The (1974)   Marilyn Burns, Allen Danziger, Paul A Partain. *Dir.* Tobe Hooper.

Thelma and Louise (1991)   Susan Sarandon (Louise Sawyer), Geena Davis (Thelma Dickinson), Harvey Keitel, Brad Pitt. *Dir.* Ridley Scott.

There's No Business Like Show Business (1954) Ethel Merman, Dan Dailey, Marilyn Monroe, Donald

O'Connor, Johnny Ray, Mitzi Gaynor, Hugh O'Brian. *Dir.* Walter Lang.

They Died with Their Boots On (1941)   Errol Flynn, Olivia de Havilland, Arthur Kennedy, Anthony Quinn, Sidney Greenstreet. Biopic of General Custer. *Dir.* Raoul Walsh.

They Shoot Horses, Don't They? (1969)   Gig Young, Jane Fonda, Susannah York, Red Buttons. Tragedy during a six-day marathon dance contest in the 1930s. *Dir.* Sydney Pollack.

Thief of Baghdad (1940)   Conrad Veidt, John Justin (died in 2002), Sabu, June Duprez. The visual effects make this the best version of this oft-filmed story. The 1924 film starred Douglas Fairbanks, the 1960 film Steve Reeves, and the 1978 film Roddy McDowall, Frank Finlay, Terence Stamp and Peter Ustinov. The 1924 film won Oscars for photography and art direction. *Dir.* Michael Powell, Ludwig Berger and Tim Whelan.

Thin Man, The (1934)   William Powell, Myrna Loy, Maureen O'Sullivan. *Dir.* WS Van Dyke.

Thing, The (1951)   Robert Cornthwaite, Kenneth Tobey, James Arness (the Thing). GB title: *The Thing from Another World. Dir.* Christian Nyby.

Thing, The (1982)   Kurt Russell, A Wilford Brimley, TK Carter. Remake of the 1951 film, although this 'Thing' is a metamorphic creature that can now enter and take over the protagonists. *Dir.* John Carpenter.

Things To Do in Denver When You're Dead (1995) Andy Garcia (Jimmy the Saint), Christopher Walken, Christopher Lloyd. *Dir.* Gary Fleder.

Thinner (1987)   Robert John Burke (William Halleck). Stephen King wrote the novel under the pseudonym Richard Bachman. *Dir.* Tom Holland.

Third Man, The (1949)   Orson Welles (Harry Lime), Joseph Cotten, Trevor Howard, Alida Valli, Bernard Lee, Wilfrid Hyde-White. *Dir.* Carol Reed.

Thirty-Nine Steps, The (1935)   Robert Donat, Madeleine Carroll, Peggy Ashcroft. *Dir.* Alfred Hitchcock.

Thirty-Nine Steps, The (1959)   Kenneth More, Taina Elg, Barry Jones. *Dir.* Ralph Thomas.

Thirty-Nine Steps, The (1978)   Robert Powell, Karen Dotrice, John Mills. *Dir.* Don Sharp.

This Is Spinal Tap (1984)   Michael McKean (David St Hubbins), Christopher Guest (Nigel Tufnel), Harry Shearer (Derek Smalls), RJ Parnell (Mick Shrimpton), Rob Reiner (Marti DiBerti). Cameos by Anjelica Huston, Patrick Macnee and Billy Crystal. *Dir.* Rob Reiner.

This Sporting Life (1963)   Richard Harris, Rachel Roberts, Alan Badel, William Hartnell, Arthur Lowe, Colin Blakely. *Dir.* Lindsay Anderson.

Thomas Crown Affair, The (1968)   Steve McQueen, Faye Dunaway, Yaphet Kotto. *Dir.* Norman Jewison.

Thoroughly Modern Millie (1967)   Julie Andrews, Mary Tyler Moore, James Fox. *Dir.* George Roy Hill.

Three Amigos! (1986)   Chevy Chase (Dusty Bottoms), Steve Martin (Lucky Day), Martin Short (Ned Nederlander). *Dir.* John Landis.

Three Colours: Blue (1993)   Juliette Binoche, Benoît Régent, Florence Pernel. First part of trilogy based on the colours of the French tricolour. *Dir.* Krzysztof Kieslowski.

Three Colours: Red (1994)   Juliette Binoche, Irene Jacob, Jean-Louis Trintignant, Julie Delpy. Third part of trilogy based on the colours of the French tricolour. *Dir.* Krzysztof Kieslowski.

Three Colours: White (1993)   Zbigniew Zamachowski, Julie Delpy, Juliette Binoche, Florence Pernel. Second part of trilogy based on the colours of the French tricolour. *Dir.* Krzysztof Kieslowski.

Three Days of the Condor (1975)   Robert Redford, Faye Dunaway, Cliff Robertson, Max Von Sydow. *Dir.* Sydney Pollack.

Three Faces of Eve, The (1957)   Joanne Woodward, Lee J Cobb. Introduced by Alistair Cooke. *Dir.* Nunnally Johnson.

Three Fugitives (1989)   Nick Nolte (Dan Lucas), Martin Short (Ned Perry), Sarah Rowland Doroff, James Earl Jones. *Dir.* Francis Veber.

Three Kings (1999)   George Clooney (Major Archie Gates), Ice Cube (Chief Elgin), Mark Wahlberg (Sgt Barlow). *Dir.* David O. Russell.

Three Men and a Baby (1987)   Tom Selleck (Peter), Steve Guttenberg (Michael), Ted Danson (Jack), Nancy Travis. *Dir.* Leonard Nimoy.

Three Men and a Little Lady (1990)   Tom Selleck, Steve Guttenberg, Ted Danson, Nancy Travis, Sheila Hancock. *Dir.* Emilio Ardelino.

Three Men in a Boat (1956)   David Tomlinson, Jimmy Edwards, Laurence Harvey, Shirley Eaton, Jill Ireland. *Dir.* Ken Annakin.

Three Musketeers, The (1993)   Charlie Sheen, Kiefer Sutherland, Chris O'Donnell, Rebecca DeMornay. *Dir.* Stephen Herek.

Three Musketeers, The (The Queen's Diamonds), (1973)   Michael York, Oliver Reed, Richard Chamberlain, Frank Finlay, Raquel Welch, Geraldine Chaplin, Spike Milligan, Faye Dunaway, Charlton Heston, Christopher Lee. *Dir.* Richard Lester.

Throw Momma from the Train (1987)   Danny De Vito (Owen), Billy Crystal (Larry), Kim Greist (Beth), Anne Ramsey (Momma), Kate Mulgrew, Rob Reiner, Annie Ross, Oprah Winfrey (as herself). *Dir.* Danny De Vito.

Thunderball (1965)   Sean Connery, Adolfo Celi (Emilio Largo), Claudine Auger (Domino). Title song performed by Tom Jones. *Dir.* Terence Young.

Thunderbolt and Lightfoot (1974)   Clint Eastwood, Jeff Bridges, George Kennedy, Catherine Bach. *Dir.* Michael Cimino.

THX 1138 (1970)   Robert Duvall, Donald Pleasence. *Dir.* George Lucas.

Tiger Bay (1959)   Hayley Mills, John Mills, Horst Buchholz, Megs Jenkins. *Dir.* J Lee Thompson.

Tightrope (1984)   Clint Eastwood (Wes Block), Geneviève Bujold (Beryl Thibodeax), Alison Eastwood (Amanda). *Dir.* Richard Tuggle.

Time after Time (1980)   Malcolm McDowell, David Warner, Mary Steenburgen. Jack the Ripper in modern San Francisco via HG Wells's time machine. *Dir.* Nicholas Meyer.

Time Bandits (1981)   John Cleese (Robin Hood), Sean Connery (Agamemnon), Ian Holm (Napoleon), Ralph Richardson (God), David Warner (Satan). *Dir.* Terry Gilliam.

Time Machine, The (1960)   Rod Taylor, Yvette Mimieux, Alan Young, Sebastian Cabot. Victorian scientist builds a machine which transports him to the year 802701. *Dir.* George Pal.

Time of Your Life (1948)   James Cagney, William Bendix, Jeanne Cagney, Wayne Morris, Broderick Crawford, Ward Bond. Group of eccentrics meet in a San Francisco bar. *Dir.* HC Potter.

Time to Kill, A (1996)   Sandra Bullock, Matthew McConaughey, Samuel L Jackson, Donald & Kiefer Sutherland. Ku Klux Klan still has power in small Mississippi town. *Dir.* Joel Schumacher.

Tin Cup (1996)   Kevin Costner, Rene Russo, Don Johnson. *Dir.* Ron Shelton.

Tin Men (1987)   Richard Dreyfuss (Bill 'BB' Babowsky), Danny De Vito (Ernie Tilley), Barbara Hershey (Nora). *Dir.* Barry Levinson.

Titanic (1997)   Kate Winslet, Leonardo DiCaprio.

Equalled the record of Ben Hur by gaining 11 Oscars (14 nominations). *Dir.* James Cameron.

To Be or Not to Be (1983)   Mel Brooks (Frederick Bronski), Anne Bancroft (Anna), Tim Matheson (Lt Andre Sobinski), Charles Durning (Col Erhardt), José Ferrer (Prof Siletski), Christopher Lloyd (Capt Schultz). *Dir.* Alan Johnson.

To Catch a Thief (1955)   Cary Grant, Grace Kelly. *Dir.* Alfred Hitchcock.

To Die For (1995)   Nicole Kidman, Matt Dillon, Joaquin Phoenix, David Cronenberg, George Segal (uncredited). Fame-obsessed weather woman on local TV station describes how she murdered her husband. *Dir.* Gus Van Sant.

To Have and Have Not (1945)   Humphrey Bogart, Lauren Bacall, Walter Brennan, Hoagy Carmichael. US charter boat captain in Martinique gets involved with Nazis. *Dir.* Howard Hawks.

To Kill A Mockingbird (1962)   Gregory Peck (Atticus Finch), Mary Badham (Jean Louise 'Scout' Finch), Philip Alford (Jem Finch), John Megna (Dill Harris), Frank Overton (Sheriff Heck Tate), Brock Peters (Tom Robinson), Rosemary Murphy (Miss Maudie Atkinson), Robert Duvall (Arthur 'Boo' Radley). Kim Stanley was the narrator as the older Scout Finch. Screenplay by Horton Foote and based on Harper Lee novel about a black man, Tom Robinson, being falsely accused of rape and the attempt to defend him by Atticus Finch, the whole struggle seen through the eyes of his young daughter, Scout. Music by Elmer Bernstein. Won Oscars for Best Screenplay and Best Actor. *Dir.* Robert Mulligan.

To Sir with Love (1967)   Sidney Poitier, Judy Geeson, Suzy Kendall, Lulu. *Dir.* James Clavell.

Tom Brown's Schooldays (1940)   Freddie Bartholomew, Jimmy Lydon, Cedric Hardwicke, Billy Halop, Gale Storm. The 1951 remake starred Robert Newton and John Howard Davies (Tom). *Dir.* Robert Stevenson.

Tom Horn (1979)   Steve McQueen, Linda Evans, Slim Pickens. *Dir.* William Wiard.

Tombstone (1993)   Kurt Russell, Val Kilmer, Sam Elliott, Charlton Heston. Narrated by Robert Mitchum. *Dir.* George P Cosmatos.

Tomorrow Never Dies (1997)   Pierce Brosnan (James Bond), Michelle Yeoh (Wai Lin), Teri Hatcher (Paris Carver), Jonathan Pryce (Elliot Carver). Theme song sung by Sheryl Crow. *Dir.* Roger Spottiswoode.

Too Hot to Handle (1991)   Kim Basinger (Vicki Rosemary Anderson), Alec Baldwin (Charley Raymond Pearl), Robert Loggia, Elisabeth Shue, Armand Assante. *Dir.* Jerry Rees.

Tootsie (1982)   Dustin Hoffman (Michael Dorsey / Dorothy), Teri Garr, Dabney Coleman, Jessica Lange, Charles Durning, Bill Murray, Sydney Pollack, Geena Davis. *Dir.* Sydney Pollack.

Top Gun (1986)   Tom Cruise (Maverick), Kelly McGillis (Charlie), Val Kilmer (Ice), Tom Skerritt (Viper), Anthony Edwards (Goose), Michael Ironside (Jester), John Stockwell (Cougar), Meg Ryan (Carole), Tim Robbins (Merlin), Barry Tubb (Wolfman), Clarence Gilyard (Sundown). *Dir.* Tony Scott.

Top Hat (1935)   Fred Astaire, Ginger Rogers. *Dir.* Mark Sandrich.

Tora! Tora! Tora! (1970)   Martin Balsam, Joseph Cotten, Jason Robards. Events leading up to Pearl Harbor. *Dir.* Richard Fleischer.

Torn Curtain (1966)   Paul Newman, Julie Andrews. *Dir.* Alfred Hitchcock.

Total Eclipse (1995)   Leonardo DiCaprio (Arthur Rimbaud, the 19th-century poet), David Thewlis (Verlaine). *Dir.* Agnieszka Holand.

Total Recall (1990)   Sharon Stone, Arnold Schwarzenegger (Doug Quaid), Rachel Ticotin, Michael Ironside. *Dir.* Paul Verhoeven.

Tough Guys (1986)   Burt Lancaster (Harry Doyle), Kirk Douglas (Archie Long), Charles Durning, Eli Wallach. *Dir.* Jeff Kanew.

Towering Inferno, The (1974)   Paul Newman, Steve McQueen, William Holden, Faye Dunaway, Fred Astaire, OJ Simpson, Robert Wagner, Jennifer Jones, Robert Vaughn, Richard Chamberlain. *Dir.* John Guillermin.

A Town Like Alice (1956)   Virginia McKenna, Peter Finch, Takagi, Marie Lohr, Maureen Swanson, Jean Anderson. Life among women prisoners of the Japanese in Malaya. Based on Nevil Shute's novel. *Dir.* Jack Lee.

Toxic Avenger, The (1985)   Andree Maranda, Mitchell Cohen, Pat Ryan Jnr. Archetypal Troma trash-fest. Ron Fazio took over the role of the supercharged weakling in the sequels. *Dir.* Michael Herz.

Toy Story (1995)   Voices of Tom Hanks, Don Rickles, Jim Varney, Tim Allen. First full-length computer-animated feature film. Song: 'You've Got a Friend in Me' (music and lyrics by Randy Newman). *Dir.* John Lasseter.

Toy Story 2 (1999)   Voice of Woody (Tom Hanks), Tim Allen, Joan Cusack. *Dir.* Ash Brannan and John Lasseter.

Toys (1992)   Robin Williams, Michael Gambon, LL Cool J, Joan Cusack, Donald O'Connor. *Dir.* Barry Levinson.

Trading Places (1983)   Dan Aykroyd, Eddie Murphy, Ralph Bellamy, Don Ameche, Jamie Lee Curtis, Denholm Elliott. *Dir.* John Landis.

Trail of the Pink Panther (1982)   Peter Sellers, Joanna Lumley, Herbert Lom, David Niven. *Dir.* Blake Edwards.

Trainspotting (1996)   Ewan McGregor, Ewen Bremner, Jonny Lee Miller, Robert Carlyle, Kelly MacDonald. *Dir.* Danny Boyle.

Trapeze (1956)   Burt Lancaster, Tony Curtis, Gina Lollobrigida, Sid James. *Dir.* Carol Reed.

Treasure Island (1990)   Charlton Heston, Oliver Reed, Christian Bale, Christopher Lee, Richard Johnson. *Dir.* Raúl Ruiz. Earlier versions 1934 (*Dir.* Victor Fleming); 1950 (*Dir.* Byron Haskin).

Treasure of the Sierra Madre, The (1948)   Humphrey Bogart, Walter Huston, Tim Holt, John Huston. *Dir.* John Huston.

Trial, The (1962)   Orson Welles, Jeanne Moreau, Anthony Perkins. Joseph K is tried and condemned for an unspecified crime. *Dir.* Orson Welles. 1992 remake (*Dir.* David Jones) starred Anthony Hopkins & Kyle MacLachlan.

Trials of Oscar Wilde, The (1960)   Peter Finch, Yvonne Mitchell, John Fraser, James Mason. US title: *The Man with the Green Carnation. Dir.* Ken Hughes.

Trouble with Girls, The (1969)   Elvis Presley, Marlyn Mason, Vincent Price. Manager of an educational medicine show (a chautauqua) gets involved in a murder. *Dir.* Peter Tewksbury.

True Grit (1969)   John Wayne, Kim Darby, Glen Campbell, Robery Duvall, Dennis Hopper. *Dir.* Henry Hathaway.

True Lies (1994)   Arnold Schwarzenegger, Jamie Lee Curtis, Tom Arnold, Charlton Heston. US secret agent pretends to be a computer salesman to his wife. *Dir.* James Cameron.

True Romance (1993)   Christian Slater, Patricia Arquette, Dennis Hopper, Val Kilmer, Brad Pitt, Gary

Oldman, Christopher Walken. Quentin Tarantino story about a shop assistant and a callgirl who go on the run with a case full of cocaine. *Dir.* Tony Scott.

True Stories (1986)   David Byrne (Narrator), John Goodman (Louis Fyne), Annie McEnroe (Kay Culver). Famous for the club scene where a multitude of characters mime to Byrne's voice. *Dir.* David Byrne.

Truly, Madly, Deeply (1990)   Juliet Stevenson (Nina), Alan Rickman (Jamie), Bill Paterson, Michael Maloney. *Dir.* Anthony Minghella.

Truman Show, The (1998)   Jim Carrey, Laura Linney, Noah Emmerich, Ed Harris, Natascha McElhone. *Dir.* Peter Weir.

Tunes of Glory (1960)   Alec Guinness, John Mills, Susanna York, Dennis Price, Kay Walsh, Duncan Macrae. *Dir.* Ronald Neame.

Turbulence (1997)   Lauren Holly (Teri Halloran), Ray Liotta (Ryan Weaver), Brenda Gleeson (Stubbs). *Dir.* Robert Butler.

Turner & Hooch (1989)   Tom Hanks, Mare Winningham, John McIntire. Cop teams up with a dog to solve a murder. *Dir.* Roger Spottiswoode.

Turning Point, The (1977)   Anne Bancroft, Shirley MacLaine, Mikhail Baryshnikov, Tom Skerritt. *Dir.* Herbert Ross.

Twelfth Night (1996)   Helena Bonham Carter, Richard E Grant, Nigel Hawthorne, Mel Smith, Imogen Stubbs. *Dir.* Trevor Nunn.

Twelve Angry Men (1957)   Henry Fonda, Lee J Cobb, EG Marshall, Jack Warden, Ed Begley, George Voskovec, Jack Klugman, John Fiedler, Martin Balsam, Robert Webber, Edward Binns, Joseph Sweeney. *Dir.* Sidney Lumet.

Twelve Monkeys (1995)   Bruce Willis, Brad Pitt, Madeleine Stowe, Christopher Plummer. Set in 2035; a convict is sent back to 1996 to discover cause of pandemic disease. *Dir.* Terry Gilliam.

Twelve O'Clock High (1949)   Gregory Peck, Hugh Marlowe, Gary Merrill, Dean Jagger. *Dir.* Henry King.

28 Days (2000)   Sandra Bullock (Gwen Cummings), Viggo Mortensen (Eddie Boone), Dominic West (Jasper), Diane Ladd (Bobbie Jean), Elizabeth Perkins (Lily), Steve Buscemi (Cornell). An alcoholic woman is sent to a rehabilitation centre to dry out, hence the title. *Dir.* Betty Thomas.

28 Days Later ... (2002)   Cillian Murphy, Naomie Harris, Megan Burns, Brendan Gleeson, Noah Huntley. Not a sequel to *28 Days* but a science fiction drama concerning a deadly virus unleashed on the British public following a raid on a primate research centre. The virus causes a deadly rage. *Dir.* Danny Boyle.

Twenty Thousand Leagues under the Sea (1954) Kirk Douglas, James Mason, Paul Lukas, Peter Lorre. *Dir.* Richard Fleischer.

Twilight Zone: The Movie (1983)   Dan Aykroyd, Vic Morrow, Scatman Crothers, Kevin McCarthy. Four supernatural stories. *Dir.* John Landis, Steven Spielberg, Joe Dante, George Miller.

Twin Town (1997)   Rhys Ifans, Llyr Evans, Keith Allen. *Dir.* Kevin Allen.

Twinky (1969)   Charles Bronson, Susan George, Trevor Howard. 16-yr-old schoolgirl marries a dissolute 40-yr-old American author. *Dir.* Richard Donner.

Twins (1988)   Arnold Schwarzenegger (Julius Benedict), Danny De Vito (Vincent Benedict). *Dir.* Ivan Reitman.

Twister (1996)   Helen Hunt, Bill Paxton, Lois Smith. *Dir.* Jan de Bont.

Two Days in the Valley (1996)   Danny Aiello, James Spader, Jeff Daniels, Teri Hatcher, Louise Fletcher, Keith Carradine. *Dir.* John Herzfeld.

Two Much (1996)   Antonio Banderas, Melanie Griffith, Danny Aiello, Daryl Hannah. Art dealer, engaged to wealthy woman, invents a twin brother so that he can marry her sister. *Dir.* Fernando Trueba.

Two Mules for Sister Sara (1969)   Clint Eastwood, Shirley MacLaine. *Dir.* Don Siegel.

2001: A Space Odyssey (1968)   Keir Dullea, Gary Lockwood, Leonard Rossiter, Robert Beatty, Douglas Rain (voice of Hal). Film based on Arthur C Clarke story 'The Sentinel'. Computer: Hal 9000 stands for Holistic Algorithmic. Journeyed to moon of Jupiter, although it was to the rings of Saturn in the book. *Dir.* Stanley Kubrick.

2010 (1984)   Roy Scheider, Helen Mirren, John Lithgow, Keir Dullea. *Dir.* Peter Hyams.

Two-Way Stretch (1960)   Peter Sellers, Wilfrid Hyde-White, Lionel Jeffries, Bernard Cribbins, David Lodge, Beryl Reid, Irene Handl. Three convicts break out of jail to do a robbery. *Dir.* Robert Day.

Ultimate Warrior, The (1975)   Yul Brynner, Max Von Sydow, Joanna Miles. Set in New York AD 2012. *Dir.* Robert Clouse.

Unforgiven (1992)   Clint Eastwood, Gene Hackman, Morgan Freeman, Richard Harris. *Dir.* Clint Eastwood.

Unforgiven, The (1960)   Burt Lancaster, Audrey Hepburn, Audie Murphy. *Dir.* John Huston.

Universal Soldier (1992)   Jean-Claude Van Damme, Dolph Lundgren. *Dir.* Roland Emmerich.

Unsinkable Molly Brown, The (1964)   Debbie Reynolds, Harve Presnell, Ed Begley. *Dir.* Charles Walters.

Untouchables, The (1987)   Kevin Costner, Sean Connery (Jim Malone), Robert De Niro (Al Capone), Andy Garcia. *Dir.* Brian De Palma.

Uptown Saturday Night (1974)   Sidney Poitier, Bill Cosby, Harry Belafonte, Flip Wilson, Richard Pryor. Friends pursue crooks who have stolen a winning lottery ticket. *Dir.* Sidney Poitier.

Urban Cowboy (1980)   John Travolta, Debra Winger. *Dir.* James Bridges.

Used Cars (1980)   Kurt Russell, Gerrit Graham, Jack Russell. *Dir.* Robert Zemeckis.

Usual Suspects, The (1995)   Gabriel Byrne, Stephen Baldwin, Kevin Spacey, Pete Postlethwaite. *Dir.* Bryan Singer.

Valentino (1977)   Rudolf Nureyev, Leslie Caron, Michelle Phillips. *Dir.* Ken Russell.

Valley of the Dolls (1967)   Barbara Parkins, Patty Duke, Susan Hayward, Sharon Tate, Martin Milner. *Dir.* Mark Robson.

Vanilla Sky (2001)   Tom Cruise (David Aames), Penelope Cruz, Cameron Diaz, Kurt Russell, Jason Lee, Noah Taylor, Timothy Spall, Tilda Swinton. Accused of murder, a publishing tycoon explains to a prison psychiatrist how his life fell apart. *Dir.* Cameron Crowe.

Verdict, The (1982)   Paul Newman, James Mason, Charlotte Rampling. *Dir.* Sidney Lumet.

Vertigo (1958)   James Stewart (Detective John 'Scottie' Ferguson), Kim Novak (Madeleine Elster / Judy Barton), Barbara Bel Geddes (Marjorie 'Midge' Wood), Tom Helmore (Gavin Elster), Henry Jones (Coroner). A detective with a fear of heights is hired by old schoolfriend Gavin Elster to follow his wife Madeleine. Ferguson falls in love with her but she apparently falls to her death. Then he meets her double. *Dir.* Alfred Hitchcock.

Very Important Person (1961)   James Robertson Justice, Stanley Baxter, Leslie Phillips. *Dir.* Ken Annakin.

Vice Versa (1988)   Judge Reinhold, Fred Savage, Corinne Bohrer. *Dir.* Brian Gilbert.

Victor / Victoria (1982) James Garner, Julie Andrews, Robert Preston, John Rhys-Davies. *Dir.* Blake Edwards.

View to a Kill, A (1985) Roger Moore, Christopher Walken (Max Zorin), Grace Jones (May Day), Tanya Roberts (Stacey Sutton), Patrick MacNee, Fiona Fullerton, David Yip. Title song performed by Duran Duran. *Dir.* John Glen.

Vikings, The (1958) Kirk Douglas, Tony Curtis, Janet Leigh, Ernest Borgnine. Orson Welles was the narrator. *Dir.* Richard Fleischer.

Village of the Damned (1960) George Sanders, Barbara Shelley, Laurence Naismith. Village women simultaneously give birth to fair-haired, genius level, telepathic children with eerie results. *Dir.* Wolf Rilla.

Village of the Damned (1995) Christopher Reeve, Kirstie Alley, Linda Kozlowski, Mark Hamill. *Dir.* John Carpenter.

Villain (1971) Richard Burton, Ian McShane, Nigel Davenport, TP McKenna. *Dir.* Michael Tuchner.

VIPs, The (1963) Richard Burton, Elizabeth Taylor, Rod Taylor, Maggie Smith, Orson Welles, Louis Jourdan, Lance Percival. *Dir.* Anthony Asquith.

Virginian, The (1929) Gary Cooper, Walter Huston. 1946 remake starred Joel McCrea & Brian Donlevy. *Dir.* Victor Fleming.

Viva Las Vegas (1964) Elvis Presley, Ann-Margret. Presley plays a sports car racer. *Dir.* George Sidney.

Viva Zapata (1952) Marlon Brando, Anthony Quinn, Jean Peters, Joseph Wiseman. *Dir.* Elia Kazan.

Volcano (1997) Tommy Lee Jones (Mike Roark), Gaby Hoffmann, Don Cheadle, Anne Heche (Dr Amy Barnes). *Dir.* Mick Jackson.

Von Ryan's Express (1965) Frank Sinatra, Trevor Howard, Sergio Fantoni. *Dir.* Mark Robson.

Voyage to the Bottom of the Sea (1961) Walter Pidgeon, Robert Sterling, Joan Fontaine, Peter Lorre, Barbara Eden. Spawned a long-running TV series. *Dir.* Irwin Allen.

Wag the Dog (1998) Dustin Hoffman, Robert De Niro. *Dir.* Barry Levinson.

Wages of Fear, The (1953) Yves Montand, Folco Lulli, Peter Van Eyck, Charles Vanel. Nitro-glycerine is the substance transported over dangerous roads to put out oil well fire. *Dir.* Henri-Georges Clouzot.

Wait until Dark (1967) Audrey Hepburn, Alan Arkin, Richard Crenna, Efrem Zimbalist Jnr. *Dir.* Terence Young.

Walkabout (1970) Jenny Agutter, Lucien John, David Gulpilil. *Dir.* Nicolas Roeg.

War, The (1994) Kevin Costner, Elijah Wood, LaToya Chisholm. *Dir.* Jon Avnet.

War Games (1983) Matthew Broderick, Dabney Coleman, John Wood. *Dir.* John Badham.

War of the Roses, The (1989) Michael Douglas, Kathleen Turner, Danny De Vito. *Dir.* Danny De Vito.

Waterworld (1995) Kevin Costner, Dennis Hopper, Jeanne Tripplehorn. *Dir.* Kevin Reynolds.

Way We Were, The (1973) Robert Redford, Barbra Streisand, Patrick O'Neal. *Dir.* Sydney Pollack.

Wedding Banquet, The (1993) Mitchell Lichtenstein, Winston Chao, May Chin. *Dir.* Ang Lee.

Welcome II The Terrordome (1994) Suzette Llewellyn, Saffron Burrows. *Dir.* Ngozi Onwurah.

Welcome to the Dollhouse (1995) Heather Matarazzo, Victoria Davis. *Dir.* Todd Solondz.

We're No Angels (1954) Humphrey Bogart, Peter Ustinov, Aldo Ray, Basil Rathbone. *Dir.* Michael Curtiz.

We're No Angels (1989) Robert De Niro, Sean Penn, Demi Moore. Remake of the 1954 film. *Dir.* Neil Jordan.

West Side Story (1961) Natalie Wood, Richard Beymer, Russ Tamblyn, George Chakiris, Rita Moreno. *Dir.* Robert Wise.

Westerner, The (1940) Gary Cooper, Walter Brennan, Charlton Heston. *Dir.* William Wyler.

Westworld (1973) Yul Brynner, Richard Benjamin, James Brolin. *Dir.* Michael Crichton.

Whatever Happened to Baby Jane? (1962) Bette Davis, Joan Crawford, Victor Buono. *Dir.* Robert Aldrich.

What's New Pussycat? (1965) Peter O'Toole, Peter Sellers, Woody Allen, Ursula Andress, Capucine. *Dir.* Woody Allen.

What's Up Doc? (1972) Barbra Streisand, Ryan O'Neal. *Dir.* Peter Bogdanovich.

When Saturday Comes (1996) Sean Bean (Jimmy Muir), Emile Lloyd (Annie Doherty), Pete Postlethwaite. *Dir.* Maria Giese.

When We Were Kings (1996) Documentary of Muhammad Ali's defeat of George Foreman in Zaïre. *Dir.* Leon Gast.

Where Eagles Dare (1969) Richard Burton, Clint Eastwood, Mary Ure. Seven Allied agents land in Bavarian Alps to rescue officer from impregnable castle during World War II. *Dir.* Brian G Hutton.

Whistle down the Wind (1961) Hayley Mills, Bernard Lee, Alan Bates, Norman Bird. Three children think a murderer on the run is Jesus. *Dir.* Bryan Forbes.

White Christmas (1954) Bing Crosby, Danny Kaye, Rosemary Clooney, Dean Jagger. *Dir.* Michael Curtiz.

White Heat (1949) James Cagney, Edmond O'Brien, Margaret Wycherly, Virginia Mayo. *Dir.* Raoul Walsh.

White Hunter, Black Heart (1990) Clint Eastwood (John Wilson), Jeff Fahey (Pete Verrill), Marisa Berenson (Kay Gibson), Timothy Spall (Hodkins). Fictionalised account of John Huston during the shooting of *The African Queen. Dir.* Clint Eastwood.

White Men Can't Jump (1992) Wesley Snipes, Woody Harrelson, Rosie Perez. *Dir.* Ron Shelton.

White Mischief (1987) Charles Dance, Greta Scacchi, John Hurt, Sarah Miles, Trevor Howard. *Dir.* Michael Radford.

White Nights (1985) Mikhail Baryshnikov, Gregory Hines, Helen Mirren, Isabella Rossellini. Best Song Oscar for 'Say You, Say Me' by Lionel Richie. *Dir.* Taylor Hackford.

White Squall (1996) Jeff Bridges (Christopher 'Skipper' Sheldon). Boat: *The Albatross. Dir.* Ridley Scott.

Who Framed Roger Rabbit? (1988) Bob Hoskins (Eddie Valiant). Animation synchronised with live action. Christopher Lloyd (Judge Doom). Jessica Rabbit's speaking voice was Kathleen Turner and singing voice was Amy Irving. *Dir.* Robert Zemeckis.

Whoops Apocalypse (1986) Loretta Swit (President Adams), Peter Cook (Sir Mortimer Chris). *Dir.* Tom Bussmann.

Who's Afraid of Virginia Woolf? (1966) Richard Burton, Elizabeth Taylor, George Segal, Sandy Dennis. Based on Edward Albee's play. *Dir.* Mike Nichols.

Wicked Lady, The (1945) Margaret Lockwood, James Mason, Michael Rennie. The 1983 remake starred Faye Dunaway in the Lockwood role. *Dir.* Leslie Arliss.

Wild Bunch, The (1969) William Holden, Ernest Borgnine, Robert Ryan, Warren Oates, Edmond O'Brien. *Dir.* Sam Peckinpah.

Wild One, The (1954) Marlon Brando, Lee Marvin, Mary Murphy. The Garutso lens created the sharpness of photography. *Dir.* Laslo Benedek.

CINEMA

Willard (1971)   Bruce Davison, Elsa Lanchester, Ernest Borgnine, Sondra Locke. Shy, introverted man breeds and trains rats to kill his enemies. *Dir.* Daniel Mann.

William Shakespeare's Romeo and Juliet (1996) Leonardo DiCaprio, Claire Danes, Brian Dennehy, Pete Postlethwaite. *Dir.* Baz Luhrmann.

Wind in the Willows, The (1996)   Steve Coogan (Mole), Eric Idle (Rat), Terry Jones (Toad), Stephen Fry, Julia Sawalha. *Dir.* Terry Jones.

Winslow Boy, The (1948)   Robert Donat, Cedric Hardwicke, Margaret Leighton, Wilfrid Hyde-White, Kathleen Harrison. Father endeavours to prove the innocence of naval cadet son, expelled for stealing postal order. *Dir.* Anthony Asquith.

Wish You Were Here (1987)   Emily Lloyd, Tom Bell, Clare Clifford. *Dir.* David Leland.

Witches of Eastwick, The (1987)   Jack Nicholson, Cher, Susan Sarandon, Michelle Pfeiffer. *Dir.* George Miller.

Witness (1985)   Harrison Ford, Kelly McGillis, Lukas Haas, Alexander Godunov. *Dir.* Peter Weir.

Witness for the Prosecution (1957)   Charles Laughton, Tyrone Power, Marlene Dietrich, Elsa Lanchester. *Dir.* Billy Wilder.

Wiz, The (1978)   Diana Ross, Michael Jackson, Lena Horne, Richard Pryor. *Dir.* Sidney Lumet.

Wizard of Oz, The (1939)   Judy Garland, Frank Morgan, Bert Lahr (Lion), Jack Haley (Tin Man), Ray Bolger (Scarecrow). *Dir.* Victor Fleming.

Wolf (1994)   Jack Nicholson, Michelle Pfeiffer, James Spader, Kate Nelligan, Christopher Plummer. *Dir.* Mike Nichols.

Woman in a Dressing Gown (1957)   Yvonne Mitchell, Anthony Quayle, Sylvia Syms, Andrew Ray. *Dir.* J Lee Thompson.

Women in love (1969)   Glenda Jackson, Jennie Linden, Alan Bates, Oliver Reed. Famous for its nude wrestling scene between Bates and Reed. *Dir.* Ken Russell.

Working Girl (1988)   Harrison Ford, Sigourney Weaver, Melanie Griffith, Alec Baldwin, Olympia Dukakis. *Dir.* Mike Nichols.

Working Girls (1986)   Louise Smith, Ellen McElduff, Amanda Goodwin. *Dir.* Lizzie Borden.

World Is Not Enough, The (1999)   Pierce Brosnan, Robert Carlyle (Renard), Sophie Marceau (Elektra), Denise Richards (Christmas Jones), Judi Dench (M), Robbie Coltrane, John Cleese (R). Theme song performed by Shirley Manson of Garbage. *Dir.* Michael Apted.

World of Suzie Wong, The (1960)   William Holden, Nancy Kwan, Sylvia Syms, Michael Wilding, Jackie Chan. *Dir.* Richard Quine.

Wrong Box, The (1966)   Ralph Richardson, John Mills, Michael Caine, Peter Cook, Dudley Moore, Peter Sellers, Tony Hancock, Nanette Newman. Two Victorian brothers are last survivors of a tontine agreement and try to kill each other. *Dir.* Bryan Forbes.

Wrong Man, The (1957)   Henry Fonda, Vera Miles, Anthony Quayle. *Dir.* Alfred Hitchcock.

Wuthering Heights (1939)   Laurence Olivier, Merle Oberon, David Niven, Flora Robson. *Dir.* William Wyler.

Wuthering Heights (1970)   Timothy Dalton, Anna Calder-Marshall, Ian Ogilvy. *Dir.* Robert Fuest.

Wyatt Earp (1994)   Kevin Costner, Dennis Quaid, Gene Hackman, Mark Harmon, Isabella Rossellini. *Dir.* Lawrence Kasdan.

Xanadu (1980)   Olivia Newton-John, Gene Kelly, Michael Beck. *Dir.* Robert Greenwald.

xXx (2002)   Samuel L Jackson (Agent Gibbons), Vin Diesel (Xander Cage / Triple X), Marton Csokas (Yorgi), Asia Argento (Yelena). Spy thriller in which agents infiltrate a cult group, Anarchy 99, who have made a biological weapon named Silent Night. *Dir.* Rob Cohen.

Y Tu Mama También (2001)   Maribel Verdu (Luisa Cortes), Gael Garcia Bernal (Julio Zapata). Two Mexican youths learn about life and love from an older woman while travelling to find the perfect beach. *Dir.* Alfonso Cuaron.

Yankee Doodle Dandy (1942)   James Cagney, Walter Huston, Eddie Foy Jnr. Life story of dancer George M Cohan. *Dir.* Michael Curtiz.

Yanks (1979)   Vanessa Redgrave, Richard Gere, Rachel Roberts. *Dir.* John Schlesinger.

Year of the Dragon, The (1985)   Mickey Rourke, John Lone, Ariane. *Dir.* Michael Cimino.

Yearling, The (1946)   Gregory Peck, Jane Wyman. *Dir.* Clarence Brown.

Yellow Rolls Royce, The (1964)   Rex Harrison, Jeanne Moreau, Omar Sharif, Ingrid Bergman, Shirley MacLaine. Aristocrat, gangster and millionairess in turn own an expensive car. *Dir.* Anthony Asquith.

Yellowbeard (1983)   Graham Chapman, Peter Cook, Marty Feldman, Eric Idle, John Cleese, Spike Milligan, Beryl Reid, Susannah York. *Dir.* Mel Damski.

Yentl (1983)   Barbra Streisand, Mandy Patinkin, Amy Irving, Nehemiah Persoff. Barbra Streisand also co-wrote with Jack Rosenthal. *Dir.* Barbra Streisand.

You Only Live Twice (1967)   Sean Connery, Akiko Wakabayashi (Aki), Tetsuro Tamba, Charles Gray, Donald Pleasence (Blofeld), Bernard Lee, Mie Hama (Kissy Suzuki). Theme song sung by Nancy Sinatra. *Dir.* Lewis Gilbert.

Young Bess (1953)   Jean Simmons, Stewart Granger, Charles Laughton (Henry VIII), Kay Walsh, Deborah Kerr. *Dir.* George Sidney.

Young Frankenstein (1974)   Gene Wilder, Marty Feldman, Madeline Kahn, Gene Hackman. *Dir.* Mel Brooks.

Young Guns (1988)   Emilio Estevez, Kiefer Sutherland, Charlie Sheen, Terence Stamp, Jack Palance, Patrick Wayne. *Dir.* Christopher Cain.

Young Guns II (1990)   Emilio Estevez, Kiefer Sutherland, Lou Diamond Phillips, Christian Slater, James Coburn. *Dir.* Geoff Murphy.

Zardoz (1974)   Sean Connery, Charlotte Rampling, John Alderton. Set in the year 2293. *Dir.* John Boorman.

Ziegfeld Follies (1946)   Fred Astaire, Lucille Ball, Jimmy Durante, Fanny Brice, Lena Horne, Esther Williams, Judy Garland, Red Skelton, Gene Kelly. *Dir.* Vincente Minnelli.

Zorba the Greek (1964)   Anthony Quinn, Alan Bates, Lila Kedrova. *Dir.* Michael Cacoyannis.

Zorro the Gay Blade (1981)   George Hamilton, Lauren Hutton, Brenda Vaccaro, Ron Leibman, James Booth. *Dir.* Peter Medak.

Zulu (1964)   Stanley Baker, Jack Hawkins, Michael Caine, James Booth, Ivor Emmanuel. *Dir.* Cy Endfield.

Zulu Dawn (1979)   Burt Lancaster, Denholm Elliott, Peter O'Toole, John Mills. *Dir.* Douglas Hickox. Famous for being the last listed film in 'Halliwell's' Film Guide'.

NB: It is hoped that this is a fairly representative catalogue of cinematic history, but it is inevitable that some films of quality will not be listed.

Films: General Information

Abba hits featured   *Muriel's Wedding.*

Acromegaly: sufferer   Rondo Hatton (d.1946), often billed as 'The Brute Man' or 'The Creeper', suffered from this enlargement of the bones.

Archers: nickname   Film makers Michael Powell and Emeric Pressburger (and name of their film company).

Bafta President   Princess Anne, The Princess Royal.

Barons   Richard Attenborough (Richmond on Thames), Laurence Olivier (Brighton).

Benchley shorts   Popular one-reel shorts delivered by Robert Benchley, sitting behind a desk, pontificating on aspects of modern living.

Bond Cars   All four-wheeled transport driven by the six Bonds. *Dr No* (Sunbeam Alpine), *From Russia with Love* (Bentley Mark IV), *Goldfinger* (Aston Martin DB5), *Thunderball* (Aston Martin DB5), *Casino Royale* (black Bentley), *On Her Majesty's Secret Service* (Aston Martin DBS), *Diamonds Are Forever* (moon buggy and Ford Mustang Mach 1), *Live and Let Die* (double-decker bus and white Coronado), *The Man with the Golden Gun* (red AMC Hornet), *The Spy Who Loved Me* (white Lotus Esprit), *Moonraker* (MP Roadster), *For Your Eyes Only* (Lotus Esprit Turbo and Citroen 2CV), *Octopussy* (Mercedes 250SE), *Never Say Never Again* (black Bentley), *A View to a Kill* (Renault 11), *The Living Daylights* (Aston Martin DBS V8 Vantage as a coupé and as a soft-top Volante version, also drove an Audi 200 Quattro), *Licence to Kill* (Kenworth W900B Truck), *Goldeneye* (BMW Z3 Roadster and Aston Martin DB5), *Tomorrow Never Dies* (BMW 750iL and Aston Martin DB5), *The World Is Not Enough* (silver BMW Z8), *Die Another Day* (Aston Martin V12 Vanquish).

Bowery Boys   Leo Gorcey, Huntz Hall, Bob Jordan, Gabriel Dell, Bernard Gorcey, David Gorcey, Billy Benedict, Bennie Bartlett.

Carry On Cleo: US video title   *Caligula's Funniest Home Videos.*

Carry On films   *Carry On Sergeant* (1958), *Carry On Nurse* (1959), *Carry On Teacher*, (1959), *Carry On Constable* (1960), *Carry On Regardless* (1961), *Carry On Cruising* (1962), *Carry On Cabby* (1963), *Carry On Cleo* (1964), *Carry On Spying* (1964), *Carry On Jack* (US title: *Carry On Venus*) (1964), *Carry On Cowboy* (1965), *Carry On – Don't Lose Your Head* (1966), *Carry On – Follow that Camel* (1966), *Carry On Screaming* (1966), *Carry On Doctor* (1968), *Carry On Up the Khyber* (1968), *Carry On Again Doctor* (1969), *Carry On Camping* (1969), *Carry On Up the Jungle* (1970), *Carry On Loving* (1970), *Carry On Henry* (1971), *Carry On at Your Convenience* (1971), *Carry On Abroad* (1972), *Carry On Matron* (1972), *Carry On Girls* (1973), *Carry On Dick* (1974), *Carry On Behind* (1975), *Carry On England* (1976), *Carry On Emmanuelle* (1978), *Carry On Columbus* (1992).

Celluloid film: innovator   William Friese-Greene (1888).

Cinéma vérité   Film technique that utilises raw, natural sound, hand-held cameras and little rehearsal.

Cinemascope: first film   *The Robe* (1953).

Cinematic projections: early examples   Stroboscope, zoetrope, thaumatrope and praxinoscope.

Cinerama: invented   New York 1952.

Directors: film with 10   *Aria* (1988).

Documentary film: pioneer   John Grierson.

Dolby Stereo: invented   1980.

Film à clef   Film that appears to be a fictional work, but is in fact based on a true story.

Film festival: first   Venice, 1932.

Film: first British feature   *Oliver Twist* (Aug 1912).

Film: first before paying audience   *Young Griffo v Battling Charles Barnett* (New York, 20 May 1895).

Film: first over one hour long   *The Story of the Kelly Gang* (Melbourne, 24 Dec 1906).

Film: most expensive shot in Britain   *The Fifth Element* (1997).

Gulf War story   *Courage under Fire.*

Hitchcock cameos   *The Lodger* (1926) Seen seated at desk in a newsroom, and later he's one of the onlookers watching arrest of Ivor Novello. *Blackmail* (1929) Bothered by a young boy on the Underground as he is trying to read a book. *Murder!* (1930) He is a passer-by on the street. *The Thirty-Nine Steps* (1935) Again, he is a passer-by on the street. *Young and Innocent* (1937) Appears as a clumsy press photographer. *The Lady Vanishes* (1938) Appears in a London railway station. *Rebecca* (1940) Appears standing outside a telephone booth while George Sanders is making a call. *Foreign Correspondent* (1940) Reading newspaper on the street, before Joel McCrea meets Van Meer (Albert Basserman). *Mr & Mrs Smith* (1941) On the street, unaware of Robert Montgomery. *Saboteur* (1942) At the news-stand. *Shadow of a Doubt* (1943) Holding a full house whilst playing poker on a train. *Lifeboat* (1944) Pictured in a before-and-after weight reduction advertisement in paper read by William Bendix. *Spellbound* (1945) Getting out of a crowded hotel lift. *Notorious* (1946) Drinking champagne at a party. *The Paradine Case* (1948) Carrying a cello case. *Rope* (1948) Crossing the street during the opening credits. *Under Capricorn* (1949) Seen first at Governor's house and then on steps of Government House. *Stage Fright* (1950) Turning round in the street to look at Jane Wyman, who's talking to herself. *Strangers on a Train* (1951) Boarding a train carrying a bass violin. *I Confess* (1953) Crossing the screen at the top of a long staircase. *Dial M for Murder* (1954) In a class reunion photo. *Rear Window* (1954) Winding a clock in the musician's apartment. *To Catch a Thief* (1955) On a bus, next to Cary Grant. *The Trouble with Harry* (1955) At an outdoor exhibition. *The Man Who Knew Too Much* (1956) Watching Arab acrobats in Marrakesh marketplace. *Vertigo* (1958) Crossing the street. *North by Northwest* (1959) Running to catch a bus, with the door slamming in his face. *Psycho* (1960) Standing outside the real-estate office, wearing a ten gallon hat. *The Birds* (1963) Exiting a pet shop, with 2 Scottie dogs. *Marnie* (1964) Coming out of a hotel room. *Torn Curtain* (1966) In hotel lobby with baby on his lap (his theme tune playing softly). *Topaz* (1969) Wheelchair-bound being attended by a nurse (in an airport). *Frenzy* (1972) Spectator in a crowd scene. *Family Plot* (1976) In silhouette behind the door of the Office of Vital Statistics.

Hollywood studio: first   Centaur Film Company (Horsley).

Latin dialogue   *Sebastiane* (directed by Derek Jarman).

Marilyn Monroe: film shooting when died *Something's Gotta Give.*

Monarch acted in film Edward VIII (whilst Prince of Wales), *The Power of Right* & *The Warrior Strain* (1919). Prince Charles was the first member of the Royal Family to speak in a fiction film: *Grime Goes Green* (1990).

Movie camera: first patent William Friese-Greene (1888).

Nicolas Cage: famous relation Nephew of Francis Ford Coppola.

Oscar: first British Charles Laughton for *Private Life of Henry VIII* in 1934.

Oscar nominations: most without winning *The Color Purple* and *The Turning Point* each had 11 Oscar nominations but failed to win a single award.

Oscar nominations: records Meryl Streep was nominated for a record 13th time in 2003 while Jack Nicholson was nominated for a record 12th time in 2003, in the acting categories.

Oscar statuettes Designed by Cedric Gibbons and sculpted by George Stanley.

Oscars: film with most awards *Ben Hur* (1959) and *Titanic* (1997): 11.

Oscars: films with most nominations *All About Eve* (1950) and *Titanic* (1998), each nominated in 14 categories.

Pamela Stephenson: film sued for £3.5m *Hello, She Lied* (renamed *Miami Hustle*); replaced by Kathy Ireland.

Pearl and Dean: music called Asteroid.

Picasso painting in lieu of cash Robin Williams received a $7 million Picasso in lieu of earnings for *Aladdin.*

Road films: first in colour *Road to Bali* (1952).

Road films: order Singapore, Zanzibar, Morocco, Utopia, Rio, Bali, Hong Kong.

Ronald Reagan films: include *Accidents Will Happen* (1938), *Angels Wash their Faces* (1939), *Bedtime for Bonzo* (1951), *Hellcats of the Navy* (1957), *Cattle Queen of Montana* (1954), *The Killers* (1964).

Smell-O-Vision: first film *The Scent of Mystery* (1959).

Sound film: first *Jazz Singer* (1927).

Tarzan: actors played Johnny Weissmuller 1932–48, Lex Barker 1949–53, Gordon Scott 1955–60, Jock Mahoney 1962–3, Mike Henry 1966–8. Also Miles O'Keeffe, Buster Crabbe, Frank Merrill, Christopher Lambert.

Third Man: famous quote 'In Italy for 30 years under the Borgias they had warfare, terror, murder and bloodshed, but they produced Michelangelo, Leonardo da Vinci and the Renaissance. In Switzerland, they had brotherly love, they had 500 years of democracy and peace – and what did they produce? The cuckoo clock.'

Triangle Film Corporation Formed in 1915 by DW Griffiths, Thomas Ince and Mack Sennett.

United Artists Formed in 1919 by Mary Pickford, Douglas Fairbanks, Charlie Chaplin and DW Griffiths.

Videodrome: presenters Alex Cox, Mark Cousins.

Western film: first in USA *The Great Train Robbery* (directed by Edwin Porter, 1903).

First Films

Actor	Film	Actor	Film
Danny Aiello	*Bang the Drum Slowly* (1973)	Mary Astor	*Hope* (1922)
Claude Akins	*A Place in the Sun* (1951)		Short: *The Beggar Maid*
Alan Alda	*Gone Are the Days* (1963)		(1921)
Woody Allen	*What's New Pussycat* (1965)	Rowan Atkinson	*The Secret Policeman's Ball*
Kirstie Alley	*One More Chance* (1981)		(1979)
June Allyson	*All Girl Revue* (1937)	Richard Attenborough	*In Which We Serve* (1942)
Mädchen Amick	*The Borrower* (1989)	Gene Autry	*In Old Santa Fe* (1934)
Dana Andrews	*Lucky Cisco Kid* (1938)	Dan Aykroyd	*Love at First Sight* (1976)
Harry Andrews	*Red Beret, The* (1952)		Short and voice only: *The Gift*
Julie Andrews	*Mary Poppins* (1964)		*of Winter* (1974)
	As extra: *The Reluctant*	Lew Ayres	*The Sophomore* (1929)
	Debutante (1958) Voice only:	Charles Aznavour	*Les Disparus de Saint-Agil*
	Rose of Baghdad (1952)		(1938) US title: *Boys'*
Gabrielle Anwar	*Manifesto* (1988)		*School*
Anne Archer	*The All-American Boy* (1970;	Lauren Bacall	*To Have and Have Not*
	released 1973)		(1944)
Eve Arden	*Song of Love* (1929)	Kevin Bacon	*National Lampoon's Animal*
Alan Arkin	*Calypso Heat Wave* (1957)		*House* (1978)
George Arliss	*Devil, The* (1921)	Carroll Baker	*Easy to Love* (1953)
Edward Arnold	*The Heart of Virginia Keep*	Joe Don Baker	*Cool Hand Luke* (1967)
	(1916)	Stanley Baker	*Undercover* (1943)
	Short: *When the Man Speaks*	Alec Baldwin	*Forever Lulu* (1987)
	(1916)		TV film: *Sweet Revenge*
Rosanna Arquette	*More American Graffiti* (1979)		(1984)
	TV film: *Having Babies II* (1977)	William Baldwin	*Born on the Fourth of July*
Jean Arthur	*Cameo Kirby* (1923)		(1989)
	Short: *Somebody Lied* (1923)	Martin Balsam	*On the Waterfront* (1954)
Armand Assante	*The Lords of Flatbush* (1974)	Anne Bancroft	*Don't Bother to Knock* (1952)
Fred Astaire	*Dancing Lady* (1933)	Theda Bara	*A Fool There Was* (1914)
	Short: *Municipal Bandwagon*	Brigitte Bardot	*Le Trou Normand* (1952)
	(1932)	Ellen Barkin	*The Diner* (1982)

Actor	Film	Actor	Film
Drew Barrymore	Altered States (1980)	Leslie Caron	An American in Paris (1951)
Ethel Barrymore	The Nightingale (1914)	David Carradine	Taggart (1965)
John Barrymore	An American Citizen (1913)	Keith Carradine	A Gunfight (1970)
Lionel Barrymore	Men and Women (1914)	Jim Carrey	Introducing Janet (1982)
	Short: Friends (1969)		TV film: Rubberface (1981)
Kim Basinger	Hard Country (1981)	Richard Chamberlain	The Secret of the Purple Reef
Alan Bates	It's Never Too Late (1956)		(1960)
Kathy Bates	Taking Off (1971)	Lon Chaney	Storm and Sunshine (1910)
Anne Baxter	Twenty Mule Team (1940)	Charlie Chaplin	Charlie as a Piano Mover
Warren Beatty	Splendor in the Grass (1961)		(1910)
Bonny Bedelia	The Gypsy Moths (1969)	Cyd Charisse	Something to Shout About
Harry Belafonte	Bright Road (1953)		(1942).
Ralph Bellamy	The Secret Six (1931)		Short: Rhumba Serenade
William Bendix	Woman of the Year (1942)		(1941)
Tom Berenger	The Sentinel (1976)	Cher	Wild on the Beach (1965)
Candice Bergen	The Group (1966)	Maurice Chevalier	Le Mauvais Garçon (1921)
Ingrid Bergman	Munkbrogreven (1934)		Short: Trop Crédule (1908)
Juliette Binoche	Liberty Belle (1981)	Julie Christie	Crooks Anonymous (1962)
Jacqueline Bisset	The Knack (1964)	John Cleese	Interlude (1968)
Honor Blackman	Daughter of Darkness (1947)	Montgomery Clift	The Search (1948)
Claire Bloom	The Blind Goddess (1948)	George Clooney	Grizzly II – The Predator
Dirk Bogarde	Dancing With Crime (1947)		(1982)
	As extra: Come on	Glenn Close	The World According to Garp
	George (1939)		(1982)
Humphrey Bogart	A Devil with Women (1930).		TV film: Orphan Train (1979)
	As extra: The Dancing	James Coburn	Ride Lonesome (1959)
	Team (1928)	Claudette Colbert	For the Love of Mike (1927)
Ernest Borgnine	China Corsair (1951)	George Cole	Cottage to Let (1941)
Clara Bow	Beyond the Rainbow (1921)	Joan Collins	Lady Godiva Rides Again
Stephen Boyd	Lilacs in the Spring (1954) US		(1951)
	title: Let's Make Up	Ronald Colman	The Toilers (1919)
Charles Boyer	L'Homme du Large (1920)		Short: The Live Wire (1917)
Kenneth Branagh	High Season (1986)	Sean Connery	Lilacs in the Spring (1954)
Marlon Brando	The Men (1950)	Tom Conti	Flame (1974)
Walter Brennan	Watch Your Wife (1926)	Jackie Coogan	Skinner's Baby (1916)
Beau Bridges	No Minor Vices (1948)	Gary Cooper	Blind Justice (1923)
Jeff Bridges	The Company She Keeps	Harry H Corbett	Never Look Back (1952)
	(1950) (as baby)	Kevin Costner	Night Shift (1982) (Sizzle
Lloyd Bridges	They Dare Not Love (1941)		Beach, USA made in late
Charles Bronson	You're in the Navy Now		70s but not shown till 1986)
	(1951) Aka USS Teakettle	Joseph Cotten	Citizen Kane (1941)
	(as Charles Buchinski)		Unreleased: Too Much
Mel Brooks	Putney Swope (1969)		Johnson (1938)
	As narrator: The Critic (1963)	Tom Courtenay	Loneliness of the Long
Pierce Brosnan	The Long Good Friday (1980)		Distance Runner (1962)
	Short: Resting Rough (1979)	Noël Coward	Hearts of the World (1918)
Yul Brynner	Port of New York (1949)	Broderick Crawford	Woman Chases Man (1937)
Sandra Bullock	A Fool and His Money	Joan Crawford	Lady of the Night (1925)
	(1988)		Short: Miss MGM (1925)
George Burns	Lamb Chops (1929)	Michael Crawford	Soap Box Derby (1957)
Raymond Burr	San Quentin (1946)	Bing Crosby	King of Jazz (1930)
Richard Burton	The Last Days of Dolwyn		Short: Ripstitch the Tailor (1930)
	(1948)	Tom Cruise	My Bodyguard (1980)
Max Bygraves	Bless 'em All (1949)	Billy Crystal	Rabbit Test (1978)
Gabriel Byrne	The Outsider (1979)		TV film: Death Flight (1977)
	BFI 'Art' film: On a Paving	Macaulay Culkin	Rocket Gibraltar (1988)
	Stone Mounted (1978)	Jamie Lee Curtis	Halloween (1978)
James Caan	Irma La Douce (1963)		TV film: Operation Petticoat
Nicolas Cage	Fast Times at Ridgemont		(1977)
	High (1982).	Tony Curtis	Criss Cross (1948)
	TV film: The Best of Times	John Curtis	Class (1983)
	(1981) as Nicolas	Peter Cushing	The Man in the Iron Mask
	Coppola (both)		(1939)
James Cagney	Sinner's Holiday (1930)	Willem Dafoe	Heaven's Gate (1980)
Michael Caine	A Hill in Korea (1956)	Jim Dale	6.5 Special (1958)
Simon Callow	Amadeus (1984)	Timothy Dalton	The Lion in Winter (1968)
John Candy	Class of '44 (1973)	Charles Dance	The Spy Who Loved Me
Claudia Cardinale	Goha (1957)		(1977)
	Short: Chaines d'Or (1956)	Jeff Daniels	Ragtime (1981)
Ian Carmichael	Bond Street (1948)	Ted Danson	The Onion Field (1979)

C
I
N
E
M
A

Actor	Film
Kim Darby	*The Restless Ones* (1965)
	As extra: *Bye Bye Birdie* (1963)
Sammy Davis Jnr	*The Benny Goodman Story* (1956)
	Short: *Rufus Jones for President* (1933)
Bette Davis	*Bad Sister* (1931)
Geena Davis	*Tootsie* (1982)
Nancy Davis	*Shadow on the Wall* (1950)
Daniel Day-Lewis	*Sunday, Bloody Sunday* (1971)
Doris Day	*Romance on the High Seas* (1948) GB title: *It's Magic*
	Short: *My Lost Horizon* (1941)
Yvonne De Carlo	*Harvard Here I Come* (1941) GB title: *Here I Come*
	Short: *I Look at You* (1941)
Olivia De Havilland	*A Midsummer Night's Dream* (1935)
Rebecca DeMornay	*One From the Heart* (1982)
Robert De Niro	*Trois Chambres à Manhattan* (1966)
Danny De Vito	*Dreams of Glass* (1969)
James Dean	*Sailor Beware* (1951)
Judi Dench	*The Third Secret* (1964)
Catherine Deneuve	*Les Collégiennes* (1956)
Gérard Depardieu	*Le Beatnik et le Minet* (1965)
Johnny Depp	*A Nightmare on Elm Street* (1984)
Brad Dexter	*The Asphalt Jungle* (1950)
Leonardo DiCaprio	*Critters 3* (1991)
Marlene Dietrich	*So Sind die Männer* (1922) Aka *Der Kleine Napoleon*
Matt Dillon	*Over the Edge* (1979)
Robert Donat	*Men of Tomorrow* (1932)
Amanda Donohoe	*Foreign Body* (1986)
	Castaway (1986) released at the same time
Diana Dors	*The Shop at Sly Corner* (1946)
Kirk Douglas	*The Strange Love of Martha Ivers* (1946)
Michael Douglas	*Hail, Hero* (1969)
	TV film: *The Experiment* (1968)
Richard Dreyfuss	*The Graduate* (1967)
Faye Dunaway	*The Happening* (1967)
Deanna Durbin	*Three Smart Girls* (1936)
	Short: *Every Sunday* (1936)
Robert Duvall	*To Kill a Mockingbird* (1962)
	TV film: *John Brown's Raid* (1960)
Clint Eastwood	*Revenge of the Creature* (1955)
	Short: *A Day in a Hollywood Star Factory* (1955)
Michael Elphick	*Fraulein Doktor* (1968)
Eminem	*Da Hip Hop Witch* (2000)
Edith Evans	*A Honeymoon for Three* (1915)
Douglas Fairbanks	*The Lamb* (1915)
Douglas Fairbanks Jr	*Stephen Steps Out* (1923)
Peter Falk	*Wind across the Everglades* (1958)
Mia Farrow	*John Paul Jones* (1959)
Marty Feldman	*The Bed Sitting Room* (1969)
Sally Field	*Moon Pilot* (1962)
Gracie Fields	*Sally in Our Alley* (1931)
WC Fields	*Janice Meredith* (1924) GB title: *The Beautiful Rebel*
	Short: *Pool Sharks* (1915)
Ralph Fiennes	*Emily Brontë's Wuthering Heights* (1992)
	A Dangerous Man – Lawrence after Arabia (1991) was a TV

Actor	Film
	film never released in cinemas
Peter Finch	*Dad and Dave Come to Town* (1938)
	Unreleased: *Magic Shoes* (1935)
Albert Finney	*The Entertainer* (1960)
Errol Flynn	*Dr H. Erben's New Guinea Expedition* (1932)
Henry Fonda	*The Farmer Takes a Wife* (1935)
Jane Fonda	*Tall Story* (1960)
Joan Fontaine	*No More Ladies* (1935) (as Joan Burfield)
Glenn Ford	*Heaven With a Barbed Wire Fence* (1939)
	Short: *Night in Manhattan* (1937)
Harrison Ford	*Dead Heat on a Merry-Go-Round* (1966)
George Formby	*By the Shortest of Heads* (1915)
Jodie Foster	*Napoleon and Samantha* (1972)
Edward Fox	*The Mind Benders* (1962)
James Fox	*The Miniver Story* (1950) (as William Fox)
Michael J Fox	*Letters From Frank* (1979)
Tony Franciosa	*A Face in the Crowd* (1957)
Clark Gable	*Forbidden Paradise* (1924)
Greta Garbo	*Fortune Hunter* (1921)
	Short: *How Not to Dress* (1921)
Andy Garcia	*Blue Skies Again* (1983)
	TV film: *Hill Street Blues* (1980) Pilot for series
Ava Gardner	*HM Pulham Esq* (1941)
	Short: *Fancy Answers* (1941)
Judy Garland	*Pigskin Parade* (1936) GB title: *Harmony Parade.*
	Short: *The Meglin Kiddie Revue* (1929) (billed as a Gumm sister)
James Garner	*Toward the Unknown* (1956) GB title: *Brink of Hell*
Greer Garson	*Goodbye Mr Chips* (1939)
	As extra: *21 Days* (1937) US title: *21 Days Together*
Richard Gere	*Report to the Commissioner* (1974). GB title: *Operation Undercover*
Mel Gibson	*Summer City* (1977)
John Gielgud	*Who is the Man?* (1924)
Lillian Gish	*Judith of Bethulia* (1914)
	Short: *Oil and Water* (1912)
Whoopi Goldberg	*Citizen* (1982) (released 1983)
Jeff Goldblum	*Death Wish* (1974)
Elliott Gould	*The Confession* (1964) GB title: *Quick, Let's Get Married!*
Betty Grable	*Happy Days* (1929)
Stewart Granger	*A Southern Maid* (1933) As stand-in: *I Spy* (1933)
Cary Grant	*This Is the Night* (1932)
Hugh Grant	*Privileged* (1982)
Richard E Grant	*Withnail and I* (1986)
	TV film: *Honest, Decent and True* (1985)
Richard Greene	*Four Men and a Prayer* (1938)
Sydney Greenstreet	*The Maltese Falcon* (1941)
John Gregson	*Saraband for Dead Lovers* (1948)
Melanie Griffith	*Smith!* (1969)

Actor	Film	Actor	Film
Charles Grodin	*Rosemary's Baby* (1968)		(1978)
	TV film: *The Meanest Men in the West* (1962)	Anjelica Huston	*Sinful Davey* (1969)
		John Huston	*The Shakedown* (1928)
Alec Guinness	*Great Expectations* (1946)	Jeremy Irons	*Nijinsky* (1980)
	As extra: *Evensong* (1934)	Burl Ives	*Smoky* (1946)
Gene Hackman	*Mad Dog Coll* (1961)	Glenda Jackson	*The Extra Day* (1956)
Larry Hagman	*Ensign Pulver* (1964)	Gordon Jackson	*The Foreman Went to France* (1942)
	TV film: *The Member of the Wedding* (1958)	Derek Jacobi	*Othello* (1965)
Susan Hampshire	*The Woman in the Hall* (1947)	Sid James	*Black Memory* (1947)
Tony Hancock	*Orders Are Orders* (1954)	Martin Jarvis	*Secrets of a Windmill Girl* (1965)
Tom Hanks	*He Knows You're Alone* (1980)	Lionel Jeffries	*Stage Fright* (1950)
Daryl Hannah	*The Fury* (1978)	Celia Johnson	*Dirty Work* (1934)
Oliver Hardy	*Outwitting Dad* (1913)	Don Johnson	*Good Morning ... and Goodbye!* (1967)
Jean Harlow	*Moran of the Marines* (1928)		
Woody Harrelson	*Harper Valley PTA* (1978)		GB title: *The Lust Seekers* (Russ Meyer epic!)
Ed Harris	*Coma* (1977)	Al Jolson	*The Jazz Singer* (1927)
	TV film: *The Amazing Howard Hughes* (1977)		Short: *April Showers* (1926)
Richard Harris	*Alive and Kicking* (1958)	Tommy Lee Jones	*Love Story* (1970)
Rex Harrison	*The Great Game* (1930)	Louis Jourdan	*Le Corsaire* (1939)
Laurence Harvey	*House of Darkness* (1948)	Boris Karloff	*The Dumb Girl of Portici* (1916)
Rutger Hauer	*Repelstweltje* (1973)	Danny Kaye	*Up in Arms* (1944)
Jack Hawkins	*Birds of Prey* (1930)		Short: *Dime a Dance* (1937)
Goldie Hawn	*The One and Only Genuine Original Family Band* (1968)	Stacy Keach	*The Heart Is a Lonely Hunter* (1968)
Will Hay	*Those Were the Days* (1934)	Buster Keaton	*The Saphead* (1920)
	Short: *Know Your Apples* (1933)		Short: *A Reckless Romeo* (1917)
Susan Hayward	*Hollywood Hotel* (1937)	Diane Keaton	*Lovers and Other Strangers* (1970)
Rita Hayworth	*Cruz Diablo* (1934)		
	Short: *La Fiesta* (1926) (as Rita Cansino)	Michael Keaton	*Night Shift* (1982)
Van Heflin	*A Woman Rebels* (1936)	Howard Keel	*The Small Voice* (1948) (as Harold Keel)
David Hemmings	*Night and the City* (1950)		
Ian Hendry	*Simon and Laura* (1955)	Harvey Keitel	*Who's That Knocking at My Door* (1968)
Audrey Hepburn	*Nederlan in 7 Lessen* (1948)		Unreleased: *Bring on the Dancing Girls* (1965)
Katharine Hepburn	*A Bill of Divorcement* (1932)		
Barbara Hershey	*With Six You Get Egg Roll* (1968)	Gene Kelly	*For Me and My Gal* (1942)
Charlton Heston	*Peer Gynt* (1941)		GB title: *For Me and My Girl*
Wendy Hiller	*Lancashire Luck* (1937)	Grace Kelly	*Fourteen Hours* (1951)
Dustin Hoffman	*The Tiger Makes Out* (1967)	George Kennedy	*The Little Shepherd of Kingdom Come* (1961)
Paul Hogan	*Fatty Finn* (1980)		
William Holden	*Prison Farm* (1938)	Patsy Kensit	*For the Love of Ada* (1972)
Judy Holliday	*Greenwich Village* (1944)	Deborah Kerr	*Major Barbara* (1941)
	Unreleased: *Too Much Johnson* (1938)		*Contraband* (1940) first film but scene was cut
Stanley Holloway	*The Rotters* (1921)	Nicole Kidman	*Bush Christmas* (1982)
Ian Holm	*Girls at Sea* (1958)	Val Kilmer	*Top Secret!* (1984)
Bob Hope	*The Big Broadcast of 1938* (1938)	Ben Kingsley	*Fear Is the Key* (1972)
		Nastassja Kinski	*Falsche Bewegung* (1975)
	Short: *Paree, Paree* (1934)		GB title: *Wrong Movement*
Anthony Hopkins	*The Lion in Winter* (1968)	Eartha Kitt	*Casbah* (1948)
	Short: *Changes* (1963)	Kevin Kline	*Sophie's Choice* (1982)
Dennis Hopper	*Johnny Guitar* (1954)	Kris Kristofferson	*The Last Movie* (1971)
Bob Hoskins	*Up the Front* (1972)	Alan Ladd	*Once in a Lifetime* (1932)
Leslie Howard	*The Happy Warrior* (1917)	Veronica Lake	*All Women Have Secrets* (1939) (as Constance Keane)
	Short: *The Heroine of Mons* (1914)	Hedy Lamarr	*Geld auf der Strasse* (1930) (as Hedy Kiesler)
Trevor Howard	*Volga-Volga* (1944) (dubbed voice)		
		Christopher Lambert	*Le Bar du Téléphone* (1981)
Frankie Howerd	*The Runaway Bus* (1954)	Dorothy Lamour	*The Jungle Princess* (1936)
Rock Hudson	*Fighter Squadron* (1948)		Short: *The Stars Can't Be Wrong* (1936)
Holly Hunter	*The Burning* (1981)		
Jeffrey Hunter	*A Date with Judy* (1948)	Burt Lancaster	*The Killers* (1946)
Isabelle Huppert	*Faustine et le Bel Été* (1971)	Michael Landon	*I Was A Teenage Werewolf* (1957)
	GB title: *Faustine*		
John Hurt	*The Wild and the Willing* (1962)	Jessica Lange	*King Kong* (1976)
William Hurt	*Altered States* (1980)		Short: *Home Is Where the Heart Is* (1970)
	TV film: *Verna the USO Girl*		

C
I
N
E
M
A

Actor	Film
Angela Lansbury	Gaslight (1944). GB title: The Murder in Thornton Square
Mario Lanza	Winged Victory (1944)
Charles Laughton	Piccadilly (1929)
	Short: Bluebottles (1928)
Stan Laurel	Lucky Dog (1917)
Peter Lawford	Poor Old Bill (1930)
Bruce Lee	Golden Gate Girl / Tears of S. Francisco (1941, aged 3 months)
	The Birth of Mankind (1946, first professional role)
Christopher Lee	Corridor of Mirrors (1948)
Gypsy Rose Lee	You Can't Have Everything (1937) (as Louise Hovick)
Janet Leigh	The Romance of Rosy Ridge (1947)
Jennifer Jason Leigh	Eyes of a Stranger (1981)
Vivien Leigh	Things Are Looking Up (1934)
Jack Lemmon	It Should Happen to You (1953)
Jerry Lewis	My Friend Irma (1949)
Juliette Lewis	Any Which Way You Can (1980)
Emily Lloyd	Wish You Were Here (1987)
Harold Lloyd	Samson and Delilah (1913)
Margaret Lockwood	Lorna Doone (1934)
Gina Lollobrigida	L'Aguila Nera (1946)
Herbert Lom	Zena Pod Krizem (1937)
Carole Lombard	A Perfect Crime (1921) (as Jane Peters)
Sophia Loren	Cuori Sul Mare (1950) (as Sofia Scicolone)
Peter Lorre	Bomben auf Monte Carlo (1931)
Rob Lowe	The Outsiders (1983)
	TV film: Thursday's Child (1982)
Myrna Loy	Pretty Ladies (1925)
Bela Lugosi	Alarscobal (1917)
Dolph Lundgren	For Your Eyes Only (1981)
Ida Lupino	The Love Race (1932)
David McCallum	Ill Met By Moonlight (1956)
Jeanette MacDonald	The Love Parade (1929)
Roddy McDowall	Grime Doesn't Pay (1935)
Andie MacDowell	Greystoke: The Legend of Tarzan Lord of Apes (1984)
Malcolm McDowell	If (1968). Poor Cow (1967) first film but scene was cut
Kelly McGillis	Reuben, Reuben (1983)
Patrick McGoohan	The Dam Busters (1954)
Ali MacGraw	A Lovely Way to Die (1968) GB title: A Lovely Way to Go
Virginia McKenna	Father's Doing Fine (1952)
Leo McKern	Murder in the Cathedral (1952)
Kyle MacLachlan	Dune (1984)
Victor McLaglen	The Call of the Road (1920)
Shirley MacLaine	The Trouble with Harry (1955)
Fred MacMurray	Girls Gone Wild (1929)
Patrick MacNee	Sailors Three (1940)
Steve McQueen	Somebody up There Likes Me (1956)
Ian McShane	The Wild and the Willing (1962)
Madonna	A Certain Sacrifice (1978)
Anna Magnani	Scampolo (1927)
Lee Majors	Strait-Jacket (1964) (as Lee Yeary)
Karl Malden	They Knew What They Wanted (1940)
John Malkovich	Places in the Heat (1984)
	TV film: Word of Honor (1981)
Jayne Mansfield	Prehistoric Women (1950)
Fredric March	The Devil (1920)
Dean Martin	My Friend Irma (1949)

Actor	Film
Steve Martin	Sgt Pepper's Lonely Heart's Club Band (1978)
	Short: The Absent-Minded Waiter (1977)
Lee Marvin	Teresa (1950)
Marx Brothers	The Cocoanuts (1929)
	Limited release: Humorist (1926)
Harpo Marx	Too Many Kisses (1925)
James Mason	Late Extra (1935) (The name of his fan club's news letter)
Raymond Massey	The Crooked Billet (1929) Aka International Spy
Marcello Mastroianni	I Miserabili (1947)
	As extra: Marionette (1938)
Walter Matthau	The Kentuckian (1955)
Jessie Matthews	The Beloved Vagabond (1923)
Victor Mature	The Housekeeper's Daughter (1939)
Virginia Mayo	Stand by for Action (1942) GB title: Cargo of Innocents
Melina Mercouri	Stella (1954)
Ethel Merman	Follow the Leader (1930)
Bette Midler	Hawaii (1966)
Toshiro Mifune	Shin Baka Jidai (1946)
Sarah Miles	Term of Trial (1962)
Ray Milland	The Plaything (1929) (as Spike Milland)
Max Miller	The Good Companions (1933)
Spike Milligan	Penny Points to Paradise (1951)
Hayley Mills	Tiger Bay (1959)
John Mills	The Midshipmaid (1932)
	Limited release: Words and Music (1932)
Juliet Mills	In Which We Serve (1942) (as baby)
Liza Minnelli	Easter Parade (1948) (as baby)
Kylie Minogue	The Delinquents (1989)
Carmen Miranda	A Voz do Carnaval (1933)
Helen Mirren	Herostratus (1967)
Robert Mitchum	Hoppy Serves a Writ (1943)
Tom Mix	The Heart of Texas Ryan (1917).
	Short: On the Little Big Horn (1909)
Marilyn Monroe	The Shocking Miss Pilgrim (1946)
Yves Montand	Etoile sans Lumière (1945)
Demi Moore	Choices (1981)
Dudley Moore	The Wrong Box (1966)
	As narrator: The Hat (1964)
Roger Moore	Caesar and Cleopatra (1945)
Jeanne Moreau	Dernier Amour (1948)
Kenneth More	Look up and Laugh (1935)
Robert Morley	Marie Antoinette (1938)
Zero Mostel	DuBarry Was a Lady (1943)
Paul Muni	The Valiant (1929)
Eddie Murphy	48 Hrs (1982)
Audie Murphy	Beyond Glory (1948)
Bill Murray	Meatballs (1979)
	Short: The Hat Act (1976)
	Voice only: Jungle Burger (1975)
Anna Neagle	Those Who Love (1929) (as Marjorie Robertson)
Liam Neeson	Excalibur (1981)
Sam Neill	Ashes (1975)
Anthony Newley	The Little Ballerina (1947)
	Short: Dusty Bates (1947)

Actor	Film
Paul Newman	*The Silver Chalice* (1954)
Jack Nicholson	*The Cry Baby Killer* (1958)
Leslie Nielsen	*The Vagabond King* (1956)
David Niven	*There Goes the Bride* (1932)
Nick Nolte	*The Feather Farm* (1965)
Chuck Norris	*The Wrecking Crew* (1968)
Kim Novak	*The Veils of Baghdad* (1953)
Ivor Novello	*Call of the Blood* (1919)
Warren Oates	*Up Periscope!* (1958)
Merle Oberon	*The Three Passions* (1929)
Edmond O'Brien	*Prison Break* (1938)
Pat O'Brien	*Compliments of the Season* (1930)
Donald O'Connor	*Melody for Two* (1937)
Maureen O'Hara	*Kicking the Moon Around* (1938) as Maureen Fitzsimmons
Gary Oldman	*Remembrance* (1982)
Laurence Olivier	*Too Many Crooks* (1930)
Ryan O'Neal	*The Big Bounce* (1969) TV film: *This Rugged Land* (1962)
Tatum O'Neal	*Paper Moon* (1973)
Maureen O'Sullivan	*Song o' My Heart* (1930)
Richard O'Sullivan	*Dance Little Lady* (1954)
Peter O'Toole	*The Savage Innocents* (1959)
Al Pacino	*Me Natalie* (1969)
Jack Palance	*Panic in the Streets* (1950) (as Walter Palance)
Lilli Palmer	*Crime Unlimited* (1935)
Dolly Parton	*The Nashville Sound* (1970)
Gregory Peck	*Days of Glory* (1944)
Sean Penn	*Taps* (1981) TV film: *The Killing of Randy Webster* (1980)
George Peppard	*The Strange One* (1957) GB title: *End as a Man*
Anthony Perkins	*The Actress* (1953)
Joe Pesci	*Hey, Let's Twist* (1961) (as Joe Ritchie)
Michelle Pfeiffer	*Falling in Love Again* (1979)
Leslie Phillips	*A Lassie from Lancashire* (1935)
River Phoenix	*Explorers* (1985) TV film: *Surviving* (1985)
Mary Pickford	*Through the Breakers* (1909)
Walter Pidgeon	*Mannequin* (1925)
Brad Pitt	*Cutting Class* (1989) TV film: *A Stoning in Fulham County* (1988)
Donald Pleasence	*The Beachcomber* (1954)
Christopher Plummer	*Wind Across the Everglades* (1958)
Sidney Poitier	*From Whence Cometh My Help* (1949)
Eric Portman	*The Girl from Maxim's* (1933)
Dick Powell	*Street Scene* (1931)
Robert Powell	*Robbery* (1967)
William Powell	*When Knighthood Was In Flower* (1922)
Tyrone Power	*Tom Brown of Culver* (1932)
Stefanie Powers	*Tammy Tell Me True* (1961)
Elvis Presley	*Love Me Tender* (1956)
Robert Preston	*King of Alcatraz* (1938)
Dennis Price	*A Canterbury Tale* (1944) As extra: *No Parking* (1938)
Vincent Price	*Service de Luxe* (1938)
Richard Pryor	*The Busy Body* (1966)
Bill Pullman	*Ruthless People* (1986)
Dennis Quaid	*Crazy Mama* (1975)

Actor	Film
Anthony Quayle	*Moscow Nights* (1935)
Aidan Quinn	*Reckless* (1984)
Anthony Quinn	*The Milky Way* (1936)
George Raft	*Queen of the Night Clubs* (1929)
Luise Rainer	*Ja, der Himmel über Wien* (1930)
Claude Rains	*Build Thy House* (1920)
Charlotte Rampling	*The Knack and How to Get it* (1965)
Basil Rathbone	*Innocent* (1921)
Ronald Reagan	*Love Is on the Air* (1937) GB title: *The Radio Murder Mystery*
Robert Redford	*War Hunt* (1962). TV film: *In the Presence of Mine Enemies* (1960). (Charles Laughton played a rabbi in this film!)
Lynn Redgrave	*Tom Jones* (1963)
Michael Redgrave	*Secret Agent* (1936)
Vanessa Redgrave	*Behind the Mask* (1958)
Oliver Reed	*Value for Money* (1955)
Christopher Reeve	*Gray Lady Down* (1977)
Keanu Reeves	*The Prodigal* (1984). Video only: *Act of Vengeance* (1984)
Lee Remick	*A Face in the Crowd* (1957)
Burt Reynolds	*Angel Baby* (1961)
Debbie Reynolds	*June Bride* (1948)
Cliff Richard	*Serious Charge* (1959)
Joely Richardson	*The Charge of the Light Brigade* (1968)
Miranda Richardson	*Dance with a Stranger* (1984)
Natasha Richardson	*The Charge of the Light Brigade* (1968)
Ralph Richardson	*The Ghoul* (1933)
Brian Rix	*Reluctant Heroes* (1951)
Jason Robards Jnr	*The Journey* (1958)
Tim Robbins	*No Small Affair* (1984)
Julia Roberts	*Blood Red* (1988 but released 1990) *Baja Oklahoma* (shown in selected cinemas) 1988
Rachel Roberts	*Valley of Song* (1953)
Cliff Robertson	*Corvette K-225* (1943) GB title: *The Nelson Touch*
Dale Robertson	*The Boy with Green Hair* (1948)
Paul Robeson	*Body and Soul* (1924)
Edward G Robinson	*Arms and the Woman* (1916)
Flora Robson	*Gentleman of Paris* (1931)
Ginger Rogers	*Queen High* (1930) Short: *Campus Sweethearts* (1929)
Roy Rogers	*Way Up Thar* (1935) (as Dick Weston) Short: *Slightly Static* (1935) (as Leonard Slye)
Will Rogers	*Laughing Bill Hyde* (1918)
Gilbert Roland	*The Lady Who Lied* (1925)
Cesar Romero	*The Shadow Laughs* (1933)
Mickey Rooney	*Orchids and Ermine* (1927) Short: *Not to Be Trusted* (1926)
Katharine Ross	*Shenandoah* (1965)
Isabella Rossellini	*A Matter of Time* (1976)
Leonard Rossiter	*The Two-Headed Spy* (1958)
Tim Roth	*Meantime* (1983) TV film: *Made in Britain* (1983)

CINEMA

Actor	Film
Richard Roundtree	What Do You Say to a Naked Lady (1969)
Mickey Rourke	1941 (1979). TV film: Panic on Page One (1979) Aka City in Fear
Gena Rowlands	The High Cost of Loving (1958)
Jane Russell	The Outlaw (1943)
Kurt Russell	The Absent-Minded Professor (1961)
Rosalind Russell	Forsaking All Others (1934)
Theresa Russell	The Last Tycoon (1976)
Rene Russo	Major League (1989)
Margaret Rutherford	Talk of the Devil (1936)
Meg Ryan	Rich and Famous (1981)
Robert Ryan	The Ghost Breakers (1940)
Winona Ryder	Lucas (1986)
George Sanders	Love, Life and Laughter (1934)
Susan Sarandon	Joe (1970)
Telly Savalas	The Young Savages (1961)
John Saxon	It Should Happen to You (1953)
Greta Scacchi	Das Zweite Gesicht (1982) Short: Dead on Time (1981)
Roy Scheider	The Curse of the Living Corpse (1963) as Roy R Scheider
Maximilian Schell	Die Letzte Brücke (1954)
Romy Schneider	Wenn der Weisse Flieder Wieder Blüht (1953)
Arnie Schwarzenegger	Hercules Goes Bananas (1969) (as Arnold Strong)
Paul Scofield	That Lady (1955)
Kristin Scott-Thomas	Under the Cherry Moon (1986)
Randolph Scott	Sharp Shooters (1928)
George C Scott	The Hanging Tree (1959)
Steven Seagal	Above the Law (1988) GB title: Nico
Jean Seberg	Saint Joan (1957)
Harry Secombe	Hocus Pocus (1948)
George Segal	The Young Doctors (1961)
Tom Selleck	Myra Breckinridge (1970) Judd for the Defense: The Holy Ground (1969) was a made-for-TV film series
Peter Sellers	Penny Points to Paradise (1951) As extra: Oliver Twist (1948) Voice only: The Black Rose (1950)
Jane Seymour	Oh What a Lovely War (1969)
Omar Sharif	The Blazing Sun (1954) (as Omar el Cherif)
William Shatner	The Brothers Karamazov (1958) TV film: The Defenders (1957)
Robert Shaw	The Lavender Hill Mob (1951)
Norma Shearer	Way Down East (1920)
Charlie Sheen	Grizzly II: The Predator (1982) TV film: The Execution of Private Slovik (1974)
Martin Sheen	The Incident (1967)
Sam Shepard	Renaldo and Clara (1977) Voice only: Easy Rider (1969)
Cybill Shepherd	The Last Picture Show (1971)
Ann Sheridan	Search for Beauty (1934) (as Clara Lou Sheridan)
Dinah Sheridan	I Give My Heart (1934)
Brooke Shields	Communion / Alice Sweet Alice (1977)
Dinah Shore	Thank Your Lucky Stars (1943)
Simone Signoret	Le Prince Charmant (1942)

Actor	Film
Phil Silvers	Hit Parade of 1941 (1940) Short: Here's Your Hat (1937)
Alicia Silverstone	The Crush (1993) TV film: Scattered Dreams (1992)
Alastair Sim	Riverside Murder (1935)
Jean Simmons	Give Us the Moon (1944)
Frank Sinatra	Las Vegas Nights (1941) GB title: The Gray City Short: Major Bowes' Amateur Theatre of the Air (1935)
Donald Sinden	Portrait from Life (1948)
Christian Slater	The Legend of Billie Jean (1985). TV film. Living Proof: The Hank Williams Jr Story (1983)
Maggie Smith	Child in the House (1956)
Jimmy Smits	Running Scared (1986) TV film: Rockabye (1986)
Wesley Snipes	Wildcats (1986)
Elke Sommer	Das Totenschiff (1958)
Ann Sothern	Broadway Nights (1927)
Sissy Spacek	Prime Cut (1972) As extra: Trash (1970)
James Spader	Team-Mates (1978)
Robert Stack	First Love (1939)
Sylvester Stallone	Party at Kitty and Studs (1970) Re-released as: The Italian Stallion
Terence Stamp	Billy Budd (1962)
Barbara Stanwyck	Broadway Nights (1927)
Anthony Steel	Quartet (1948)
Tommy Steele	Kill Me Tomorrow (1957)
Mary Steenburgen	Goin' South (1978)
Rod Steiger	Teresa (1951)
Inger Stevens	Man on Fire (1957)
Stella Stevens	Say One for Me (1959)
James Stewart	The Murder Man (1935) Short: Important News (1935)
Sting	Quadrophenia (1979)
Eric Stoltz	Fast Times at Ridgemont High (1982) TV film: The Grass Is Always Greener over the Septic Tank (1978)
Sharon Stone	Stardust Memories (1980)
The 3 Stooges	Hollywood on Parade (1930)
Meryl Streep	Julia (1977) Voice only: Everybody Rides a Carousel (1976)
Barbra Streisand	Funny Girl (1968)
Donald Sutherland	The World Ten Times Over (1963)
Kiefer Sutherland	Max Dugan Returns (1983)
Gloria Swanson	Her Decision (1918) Short: The Romance of an American Duchess (1915)
Patrick Swayze	Skatetown USA (1979)
Eric Sykes	Orders Are Orders (1954)
Sylvia Syms	My Teenage Daughter (1955)
Russ Tamblyn	Boy with Green Hair (1948) (as Rusty Tamblyn)
Jacques Tati	Retour à la Terre (1938) Short: Oscar, Champion de Tennis (1932)
Elizabeth Taylor	One Born Every Minute (1942) Short: Man or Mouse (1942)
Robert Taylor	Handy Andy (1934)

Actor	Film
Rod Taylor	*The Sturt Expedition* (1951) (as Rodney Taylor)
Shirley Temple	*The Red-Haired Alibi* (1932) Short: *War Babies* (1932)
Terry Thomas	*It's Love Again* (1936)
Emma Thompson	*The Tall Guy* (1989)
Sybil Thorndike	*Moth and Rust* (1921)
Uma Thurman	*Kiss Daddy Good Night* (1987)
Gene Tierney	*The Return of Frank James* (1940)
Richard Todd	*For Them That Trespass* (1948)
Lily Tomlin	*Nashville* (1975)
David Tomlinson	*Garrison Follies* (1940) Short: *Name, Rank and Number* (1940)
Spencer Tracy	*Up the River* (1930) Short: *Taxi Talks* (1930)
Bill Travers	*Conspirator* (1950)
John Travolta	*The Devil's Rain* (1975)
Claire Trevor	*Life in the Raw* (1933)
Tommy Trinder	*Almost a Honeymoon* (1938)
Jean-Louis Trintignant	*Si Tous les Gars du Monde* (1955) GB title: *Race for Life* Short: *Pechinef* (1955)
Forrest Tucker	*The Westerner* (1940)
Kathleen Turner	*Body Heat* (1981)
Lana Turner	*A Star Is Born* (1937)
Rita Tushingham	*A Taste of Honey* (1961)
Twiggy	*The Boy Friend* (1971)
Liv Ullman	*Fjol til Fjells* (1957)
Robert Urich	*Magnum Force* (1973)
Peter Ustinov	*Hullo Fame!* (1940)
Rudolph Valentino	*My Official Wife* (1914)
Rudy Vallee	*Vagabond Lover* (1929) Short: *Radio Rhythm* (1929)
Lee Van Cleef	*The Showdown* (1950)
Jean-Claude Van Damme	*Rue Barbar* (1983) US title: *Street of the Damned*
Dick Van Dyke	*Bye Bye Birdie* (1963)
Frankie Vaughan	*Ramsbottom Rides Again* (1957) Singing commentary: *Escape in the Sun* (1956)
Robert Vaughn	*The Ten Commandments* (1956)
Conrad Veidt	*Der Spion* (1916)
Monica Vitti	*Ridere, Ridere, Ridere* (1955)
Jon Voight	*The Hour of the Gun* (1967)
Erich Von Stroheim	*Captain McLean* (1914)
Max Von Sydow	*Bara en Mor* (1949)
Robert Wagner	*The Happy Years* (1950)
Christopher Walken	*Me and My Brother* (1968)
Clint Walker	*Mighty Joe Young* (1949) (as Norman Walker)
Eli Wallach	*Baby Doll* (1956) TV film: *Danger* (1952)
Julie Walters	*Educating Rita* (1983) Short: *Occupy!* (1976)
Rachel Ward	*Night School* (1980) GB title: *Terror Eyes*
Simon Ward	*If* (1968)
David Warner	*Loneliness of the Long Distance Runner* (1962)
Jack Warner	*The Dummy Talks* (1943)
Denzel Washington	*Carbon Copy* (1981) TV film: *Wilma* (1977)
Dennis Waterman	*Night Train for Inverness* (1959)
John Wayne	*Brown of Harvard* (1926)
Dennis Weaver	*Riders of Vengeance* (1952)
Sigourney Weaver	*Annie Hall* (1977)
Clifton Webb	*Polly with a Past* (1920)
Johnny Weissmuller	*Glorifying the American Girl* (1929)
Raquel Welch	*Roustabout* (1964)
Tuesday Weld	*The Wrong Man* (1956)
Orson Welles	*Citizen Kane* (1941) Short: *The Hearts of Age* (1934) (Home-made) Unreleased: *Too Much Johnson* (1938). As narrator: *Swiss Family Robinson* (1940)
Mae West	*Night after Night* (1932) Short: unidentified 'Screen Snapshot' (1930)
Joanne Whalley-Kilmer	*The Wall* (1982)
Billie Whitelaw	*The Fake* (1953)
Pearl White	*The Life of Buffalo Bill* (1910)
Richard Widmark	*Kiss of Death* (1947)
Gene Wilder	*Bonnie and Clyde* (1967)
Cornel Wilde	*The Lady With Red Hair* (1940)
Michael Wilding	*Heads We Go* (1933) As extra: *Bitter Sweet* (1933)
Nicol Williamson	*Inadmissible Evidence* (1968) Short: *The Six-Sided Triangle* (1963)
Emlyn Williams	*The Frightened Lady* (1932)
Esther Williams	*Andy Hardy's Double Life* (1942)
Kenneth Williams	*Trent's Last Case* (1952)
Robin Williams	*Can I Do It 'til I Need Glasses* (1977)
Bruce Willis	*The First Deadly Sin* (1980) TV film: *Ziegfeld – The Man & His Women* (1978)
Barbara Windsor	*Belles of St Trinian's* (1954)
Oprah Winfrey	*The Color Purple* (1985)
Debra Winger	*Slumber Party '57* (1976)
Kate Winslet	*Heavenly Creatures* (1994)
Shelley Winters	*What a Woman!* (1943) GB title: *The Beautiful Cheat*
Norman Wisdom	*A Date with a Dream* (1948)
Googie Withers	*The Girl in the Crowd* (1934)
Sir Donald Wolfit	*Down River* (1931)
Natalie Wood	*Happy Land* (1943) (as Natasha Gurdin)
James Woods	*The Visitors* (1971)
Edward Woodward	*Where There's a Will* (1955)
Joanne Woodward	*Count Three and Pray* (1955)
Fay Wray	*What Price Goofy* (1925) Short: *Gasoline Love* (1923)
Teresa Wright	*The Little Foxes* (1941)
Jane Wyman	*The Kid from Spain* (1932) (as Sarah Jane Fulks)
Michael York	*The Mind Benders* (1962)
Susannah York	*Tunes of Glory* (1960)
Gig Young	*Misbehaving Husbands* (1940) (as Byron Barr)
Loretta Young	*The Only Way* (1917) (as Gretchen Young)
Robert Young	*The Black Camel* (1931)
Sean Young	*Stripes* (1981). TV film: *Jane Austen in Manhattan* (1980)
Pia Zadora	*Santa Claus Conquers the Martians* (1964)
Catherine Zeta-Jones	*Les Mille et Une Nuits* (1001 Nights) (1989)
Mai Zetterling	*Lasse-Maja* (1941)

CINEMA

NB: This is an area where many fine sources of information will inevitably differ, depending on the definition given of 'first film'. To give an example of the inherent dangers in answering questions on screen debuts, we can look at the early career of Orson Welles.

The 1941 classic, *Citizen Kane*, is often considered to be Welles's first film performance; but whilst it was certainly his first feature film, he did in fact do various film work before this. His potential was first spotted in his home-made film of 1934, *The Hearts of Age*, a film short that never went on general release. The unreleased film *Too Much Johnson* (1938) was shown to private audiences, although it was eventually lost to the world in a fire at Welles's Spanish home.

If narration is considered a film role, then the 1940 film *Swiss Family Robinson*, starring Thomas Mitchell and Freddie Bartholomew, could also be regarded as his big screen debut.

The approach taken in listing these is to cite an actor's debut in a film on general release and to mention prior work underneath. Many jobbing screen actors start their careers making 'film shorts', often shown before a main feature, but these films are rarely listed in cinema catalogues and are only included here if they predate a debut in a full-length feature. 'Made for television' films are treated in a similar vein.

Last Films

Actor	Film
Fred Astaire	*Ghost Story* (1981)
Mary Astor	*Hush, Hush, Sweet Charlotte* (1964)
Gene Autry	*It's Showtime* (1976)
Lew Ayres	*Letters from Frank* (1979)
	TV film: *Cast the First Stone* (1989)
Ingrid Bergman	*Autumn Sonata* (1978)
	TV film: *A Woman Called Golda* (1982)
Humphrey Bogart	*The Harder They Fall* (1956)
Stephen Boyd	*The Squeeze* (1977)
Charles Boyer	*A Matter of Time* (1976)
Yul Brynner	*Futureworld* (1976)
George Burns	*Radioland Murders* (1994)
Raymond Burr	*Delirious* (1991)
	TV film: *Perry Mason: The Case of the Killer Kiss* (1993)
Richard Burton	*1984* (1984)
	TV film: *Ellis Island* (1984)
James Cagney	*Ragtime* (1981)
	TV film: *Terrible Joe Moran* (1984)
John Candy	*Canadian Bacon* (1995)
Lon Chaney	*The Unholy Three* (1930)
Charlie Chaplin	*A Countess from Hong Kong* (1966)
Maurice Chevalier	*Monkeys Go Home* (1967)
	Voice only: *The Aristocats* (1970)
Montgomery Clift	*The Defector* (1966)
James Coburn	*Snow Dogs* (2002)
Claudette Colbert	*Parrish* (1961)
	TV film: *The Two Mrs Grenvilles* (1987)
Ronald Colman	*The Story of Mankind* (1957)
Jackie Coogan	*The Prey* (1983)
Gary Cooper	*The Naked Edge* (1961)
Harry H Corbett	*Silver Dream Racer* (1980)
Joseph Cotten	*Rambo Sfida la Citta* (1982)
Noël Coward	*The Italian Job* (1969)
Broderick Crawford	*Liar's Moon* (1981)
Joan Crawford	*Trog* (1970)
	TV film: *We're Going to Scare You to Death* (1975)
Bing Crosby	*That's Entertainment* (1974)
Peter Cushing	*Biggles* (1986)
Bette Davis	*Wicked Stepmother* (1989)
	Short: *Hairway to the Stars* (1989)
Sammy Davis Jnr	*Tap* (1988)

Actor	Film
	TV film: *The Kid Who Loved Christmas* (1990)
James Dean	*Giant* (1956)
Brad Dexter	*Secret Ingredient* (1990)
Marlene Dietrich	*Marlene* (1984)
Robert Donat	*The Inn of the Sixth Happiness* (1958)
Diana Dors	*Steaming* (1985)
Michael Elphick	TV film: *Ken Russell's Treasure Island* (1995)
Edith Evans	*Nasty Habits* (1976)
Douglas Fairbanks	*The Private Life of Don Juan* (1934)
Marty Feldman	*Yellowbeard* (1983)
Gracie Fields	*Madame Pimpernel* (1945)
WC Fields	*Sensations of 1945* (1944)
Peter Finch	*Network* (1976)
	TV film: *Raid on Entebbe* (1977)
Errol Flynn	*Cuban Rebel Girls* (1959)
Henry Fonda	*On Golden Pond* (1981)
	TV film: *Summer Solstice* (1981)
George Formby	*George in Civvy Street* (1946)
Clark Gable	*The Misfits* (1961)
Greta Garbo	*Two-Faced Woman* (1941)
Ava Gardner	*Roma Regina* (1982)
Judy Garland	*I Could Go on Singing* (1963)
Greer Garson	*Directed by William Wyler* (1986)
Lillian Gish	*The Whales of August* (1987)
Betty Grable	*How to Be Very Very Popular* (1955)
Stewart Granger	*Oro Fina (Fine Gold)* (1988)
	TV film: *Chameleons* (1989)
Cary Grant	*Elvis – That's the Way It Is* (1970)
Sydney Greenstreet	*Malaya* (1949)
	GB title: *East of the Rising Sun*
John Gregson	*The Tiger Lily* (1975)
Tony Hancock	*The Wrong Box* (1966)
Oliver Hardy	*Meet Bela Lugosi and Oliver Hardy* (1952)
Jean Harlow	*Saratoga* (1937)
Richard Harris	*Harry Potter and the Chamber of Secrets* (2002)
Rex Harrison	*A Time to Die* (1983). Aka *Seven Graves for Rogan*
Jack Hawkins	*The Last Lion* (1973)
	TV film: *QB VII* (1974)

Actor	Film
Susan Hayward	*The Revengers* (1972) TV film: *Say Goodbye,* *Maggie Cole* (1972)
Rita Hayworth	*Circle* (1976)
Will Hay	*My Learned Friend* (1943)
Van Heflin	*The Big Bounce* (1969) TV film: *The Last Child* (1971)
Audrey Hepburn	*Always* (1989)
William Holden	*S.O.B.* (1981) TV film: *Mysteries of the* *Sea* (1981) (as narrator)
Judy Holliday	*Bells Are Ringing* (1960)
Stanley Holloway	*Journey into Fear* (1976)
Leslie Howard	*The First of the Few* (1942)
Trevor Howard	*The Dawning* (1988) Died whilst filming *Stille* *Nacht,* about the author of the carol 'Silent Night'
Frankie Howerd	*Sgt Pepper's Lonely Hearts* *Club Band* (1978)
Rock Hudson	*The Ambassador* (1984) TV film: *The Vegas Strip* *Wars* (1985)
Jeffrey Hunter	*Mafia Mob* (1969)
John Huston	*John Huston and the* *Dubliners* (1987)
Burl Ives	*Two Moon Junction* (1988)
Gordon Jackson	*The Whistle Blower* (1986) TV film: *The Lady and the* *Highwayman* (1989)
Sid James	*Carry On Dick* (1974)
Celia Johnson	*The Prime of Miss Jean* *Brodie* (1968) TV film: *The Hostage Tower* (1980)
Al Jolson	*Rhapsody in Blue* (1945) Voice only: *Jolson Sings* *Again* (1949)
Boris Karloff	*The Incredible Invasion* (1969). Limited release: *House of* *Evil* (1972) Unseen footage: *Transylvania Twist* (1989)
Danny Kaye	*The Madwoman of Chaillot* (1969) Short: *Pied Piper* (1972) TV film: *Once They Marched* *through a Thousand Towns* (1981) US title: *Skokie*
Buster Keaton	*A Funny Thing Happened on* *the Way to the Forum* (1966) Short: *The Scribe* (1966)
Gene Kelly	*That's Entertainment III* (1994)
Grace Kelly	*Invitation to Monte Carlo* (1959) As narrator: *The Children of* *Theatre Street* (1978)
Alan Ladd	*The Carpetbaggers* (1964)
Veronica Lake	*Flesh Feast* (1970)
Dorothy Lamour	*Creepshow 2* (1987)
Burt Lancaster	*Field of Dreams* (1989) TV film: *Separate but Equal* (1991)
Mario Lanza	*For the First Time* (1959)
Charles Laughton	*Advise and Consent* (1962)
Stan Laurel	*Atoll K* (1951). GB title: *Robinson Crusoeland*
Peter Lawford	*Where Is Parsifal?* (1984)
Bruce Lee	*Game of Death* (1978, posthumously)

Actor	Film
Gypsy Rose Lee	*The Trouble with Angels* (1966) TV film: *The Over the Hill* *Gang* (1969)
Vivien Leigh	*Ship of Fools* (1965)
Harold Lloyd	*The Sins of Harold* *Diddlebock* (1947) GB title: *Mad Wednesday*
Margaret Lockwood	*The Slipper and the Rose* (1976)
Carole Lombard	*To Be or Not to Be* (1942)
Peter Lorre	*Muscle Beach Party* (1964)
Myrna Loy	*Just Tell Me What You Want* (1980). TV film: *Summer Solstice* (1981)
Bela Lugosi	*Plan 9 from Outer Space* (1957)
Ida Lupino,	*Deadhead Miles* (1982)
Jeanette MacDonald	*The Sun Comes Up* (1948) TV film: *Charley's Aunt* (1957)
Leo McKern	*Molokai – The Story of Father* *Damien* (1999)
Victor McLaglen	*The Italians Are Crazy* (1958)
Fred MacMurray	*The Swarm* (1978)
Anna Magnani	*Fellini's Roma* (1972)
Jayne Mansfield	*Mondo Hollywood* (1967)
Fredric March	*The Iceman Cometh* (1973)
Dean Martin	*Cannonball Run II* (1983) TV film: *Half Nelson* (1985)
Lee Marvin	*The Delta Force* (1986)
Marx Brothers	*Love Happy* (1950) Guest appearances in separate episodes of *The* *Story of Mankind* (1957) TV film: *The Incredible* *Jewel Robbery* (1960) Later films did not include all 3 main brothers
James Mason	*The Assisi Underground* (1984)
Raymond Massey	*MacKenna's Gold* (1969) TV film: *The President's* *Plane Is Missing* (1973)
Marcello Mastroianni	*Journey to the Beginning of* *the World* (1996)
Jessie Matthews	*Never Never Land* (1980)
Victor Mature	*Firepower* (1979) TV film: *Samson and Delilah* (1984)
Steve McQueen	*The Hunter* (1980)
Melina Mercouri	*Keine Zufallige Geschichte* (1983) US title: *Not by* *Coincidence*
Ethel Merman	*Airplane!* (1980)
Ray Milland	*The Sea Serpent* (1985)
Max Miller	*Asking for Trouble* (1943)
Carmen Miranda	*Scared Stiff* (1953)
Robert Mitchum	*Waiting for Sunset* (1997)
Tom Mix	*Rustlers' Roundup* (1933) Short film Series: *The* *Miracle Rider* (1935)
Marilyn Monroe	*The Misfits* (1961) (uncompleted) *Something's* *Got to Give*
Yves Montand	*IP5: L'Ile aux Pachydermes* (1992)
Kenneth More	*The Spaceman and King* *Arthur* (1979) TV film: *A Tale of Two Cities* (1981)
Robert Morley	*Istanbul* (1989) TV film: *The Lady and the*

CINEMA

Actor	Film
	Highwayman (1989)
Zero Mostel	*Best Boy* (1979)
Paul Muni	*The Last Angry Man* (1959)
Audie Murphy	*A Time for Dying* (1969)
Anna Neagle	*The Lady Is a Square* (1959)
David Niven	*Curse of the Pink Panther* (1983)
Ivor Novello	*Autumn Crocus* (1934)
Warren Oates	*Blue Thunder* (1983)
Merle Oberon	*Interval* (1973)
Edmond O'Brien	*Dream No Evil* (1976)
Pat O'Brien	*Ragtime* (1981)
Laurence Olivier	*War Requiem* (1988)
Lili Palmer	*The Holcroft Covenant* (1985) TV film: *Peter the Great* (1986)
George Peppard	*The Tigress* (1992)
Anthony Perkins	*The Mummy Lives* (1992) TV film: *In the Deep Woods* (1992)
River Phoenix	*The Thing Called Love* (1993) Uncompleted: *Dark Blood* (1994)
Mary Pickford	*Star Night at the Cocoanut Grove* (1935)
Walter Pidgeon	*Sextette* (1977)
Donald Pleasence	*Halloween 6: The Curse of Michael Myers* (1995) Uncompleted: *Fotogrammi Mortal* (1996) (aka *Fatal Frames*). After he died his role was played by an actor in his face mask (as was Rossano Brazzi's, who also died). David Warbeck (the 'Milk Tray' man) died soon after the release of the film
Eric Portman	*Deadfall* (1968)
Dick Powell	*Susan Slept Here* (1954)
William Powell	*Mister Roberts* (1955)
Tyrone Power	*Witness for the Prosecution* (1957)
Elvis Presley	*That's the Way It Is* (1970) TV film: *Elvis on Tour* (1972)
Robert Preston	*The Last Starfighter* (1984) TV film: *Outrage* (1986)
Dennis Price	*Theatre of Blood* (1973) Unreleased: *Son of Dracula* (1974) Aka *Count Downe* (also starred Ringo Starr)
Vincent Price	*Edward Scissorhands* (1990) TV film: *The Heart of Justice* (1992) Voice only: *The Thief and the Cobbler* (1995) Aka *Arabian Knight*
Anthony Quayle	*King of the Wind* (1989)
George Raft	*The Man with Bogart's Face* (1979)
Claude Rains	*The Greatest Story Ever Told* (1965)
Basil Rathbone	*Hillbillies in a Haunted House* (1968)
Ronald Reagan	*The Killers* (1964)
Michael Redgrave	*Nicholas and Alexandra* (1971) As narrator: *Roosevelt: The Power behind the Smile* (1975)
Lee Remick	*The Vision* (1987)

Actor	Film
Ralph Richardson	*Directed by William Wyler* (1986) (posthumously)
Rachel Roberts	*Charlie Chan and the Curse of the Dragon Queen* (1980) TV film: *The Hostage Tower* (1980)
Paul Robeson	*Paul Robeson: Tales of Manhattan* (1979)
Edward G Robinson	*Soylent Green* (1973)
Flora Robson	*Clash of the Titans* (1981)
Ginger Rogers	*The Confession* (1964) GB title: *Let's Get Married* TV film: *Harlow* (1964)
Will Rogers	*In Old Kentucky* (1935)
Gilbert Roland	*Barbarosa* (1982)
Cesar Romero	*The Player* (1992)
Rosalind Russell	*Mrs Pollifax – Spy* (1970) TV film: *The Crooked Hearts* (1972)
Margaret Rutherford	*Arabella* (1969)
Robert Ryan	*The Outfit* (1973)
George Sanders	*Psychomania* (1972)
Telly Savalas	*Backfire* (1994)
Romy Schneider	*La Passante du Sans-Souci* (1981)
Randolph Scott	*Ride the High Country* (1962). GB title: *Guns in the Afternoon*
Jean Seberg	*The Wild Duck* (1976)
Peter Sellers	*Trail of the Pink Panther* (1982) (posthumous)
Robert Shaw	*Avalanche Express* (1979) (posthumous)
Norma Shearer	*Her Cardboard Lover* (1942)
Ann Sheridan	*Triangle on Safari* (1957) TV film: *Without Incident* (1957)
Dinah Shore	*Health* (1979) TV film: *Death Car on the Freeway* (1979)
Simone Signoret	*L'Etoile du Nord* (1982): As narrator: *Des 'Terroristes' à la Retraite* (1983)
Phil Silvers	*Hollywood Blue* (1980) aka *The Happy Hooker Goes to Hollywood*
Alastair Sim	*Escape from the Dark* (1976)
Barbara Stanwyck	*The Night Walker* (1965) TV film: *The Thorn Birds* (1983)
Anthony Steel	*The Monster Club* (1981)
Rod Steiger	*Poolhall Junkies* (2002)
James Stewart	*A Tale of Africa* (1981) TV film: *North and South II* (1986) Voice only: *An American Tail 2: Fievel Goes West* (1991)
The 3 Stooges	*Dr Death – Seeker of Souls* (1973)
Gloria Swanson	*Airport 1975* (1974)
Jacques Tati	*Traffic* (1971) Limited release: *Parade* (1974)
Robert Taylor	*The Glass Sphinx* (1968)
Shirley Temple	*A Kiss for Corliss* (1949)
John Thaw	*Chaplin* (1992) TV film: *Buried Treasure* (2001)
Terry Thomas	*Happy Birthday Harry!* (1981)
Sybil Thorndike	*Uncle Vanya* (1963)
Gene Tierney	*The Pleasure Seekers* (1964) TV film: *Daughter of the Mind*

Actor	Film
	(1969)
Spencer Tracy	Guess Who's Coming to Dinner (1967)
Bill Travers	Christian the Lion (1973)
	TV film: Bloody Ivory (1979)
Tommy Trinder	Barry McKenzie Holds His Own (1974)
Lana Turner	Witches' Brew (1978; released 1985)
Robert Urich	Jock – A True Tale of Friendship (2001)
Rudolph Valentino	Son of the Sheik (1926)
Rudy Vallee	The Perfect Woman (1978)
Lee Van Cleef	Speed Zone (1989)
Conrad Veidt	Above Suspicion (1943)
Erich Von Stroheim	L'Homme Aux Cent Visages (1956).
	GB title: Man of a Thousand Faces
Jack Warner	Dominique (1978)
John Wayne	The Shootist (1976)
Clifton Webb	Satan Never Sleeps (1962)
Johnny Weissmuller	Devil Goddess (1955)
	Guest appearance: That's

Actor	Film
	Entertainment II (1976)
Orson Welles	Someone to Love (1987) (posthumous)
Mae West	Sextette (1977)
Pearl White	Perils of Paris (1925)
Cornel Wilde	Vultures in Paradise / Flesh and Bullets (1983)
Michael Wilding	Lady Caroline Lamb (1972)
	TV film: Frankenstein: The True Story (1973)
Emlyn Williams	The Walking Stick (1970)
	TV film: Past Caring (1985)
Kenneth Williams	Carry On Emmanuelle (1978)
Sir Donald Wolfit	The Charge of the Light Brigade (1968)
Natalie Wood	Brainstorm (1981; released posthumously, 1983)
Fay Wray	Summer Love (1957).
	TV film: Gideon's Trumpet (1980)
Gig Young	Game of Death (1978)
Mai Zetterling	Morfars Resa (1993)

CINEMA

Oscars (Academy Awards)

*Year	Best Film	Best Actor	Best Actress	Best Director
1929	Wings (1927)	Emil Jannings (The Way of All Flesh)	Janet Gaynor (Seventh Heaven)	Frank Borzage (Seventh Heaven)
				Lewis Milestone (Two Arabian Knights)†
1930	The Broadway Melody	Warner Baxter (In Old Arizona)	Mary Pickford (Coquette)	Frank Lloyd (The Divine Lady)
1931	All Quiet on the Western Front	George Arliss (Disraeli)	Norma Shearer (The Divorcee)	Lewis Milestone (All Quiet on the Western Front)
1932	Cimarron (1930)	Lionel Barrymore (A Free Soul)	Marie Dressler (Min and Bill)	Norman Taurog (Skippy)
1933	Grand Hotel	Fredric March (Dr Jekyll and Mr Hyde) / Wallace Beery (The Champ)	Helen Hayes (The Sin of Madelon Claudet)	Frank Borzage (Bad Girl)
1934	Cavalcade (1932)	Charles Laughton (Private Life of Henry VIII)	Katharine Hepburn (Morning Glory)	Frank Lloyd (Cavalcade)
1935	It Happened One Night	Clark Gable (It Happened One Night)	Claudette Colbert (It Happened One Night)	Frank Capra (It Happened One Night)
1936	Mutiny on the Bounty	Victor McLaglen (The Informer)	Bette Davis (Dangerous)	John Ford (The Informer)
1937	The Great Ziegfeld	Paul Muni (The Story of Louis Pasteur)	Luise Rainer (The Great Ziegfeld)	Frank Capra (Mr Deeds Goes to Town)
1938	The Life of Emile Zola	Spencer Tracy (Captains Courageous)	Luise Rainer (The Good Earth)	Leo McCarey (The Awful Truth)
1939	You Can't Take it with You	Spencer Tracy (Boys Town)	Bette Davis (Jezebel)	Frank Capra (You Can't Take It With You)
1940	Gone with the Wind	Robert Donat (Goodbye Mr Chips)	Vivien Leigh (Gone with the Wind)	Victor Fleming (Gone with the Wind)
1941	Rebecca	James Stewart (The Philadelphia Story)	Ginger Rogers (Kitty Foyle)	John Ford (The Grapes of Wrath)
1942	How Green Was My Valley	Gary Cooper (Sergeant York)	Joan Fontaine (Suspicion)	John Ford (How Green Was My Valley)
1943	Mrs Miniver	James Cagney (Yankee Doodle Dandy)	Greer Garson (Mrs Miniver)	William Wyler (Mrs Miniver)
1944	Casablanca (1942)	Paul Lukas (Watch on the Rhine)	Jennifer Jones (The Song of Bernadette)	Michael Curtiz (Casablanca)
1945	Going My Way	Bing Crosby (Going My Way)	Ingrid Bergman (Gaslight)	Leo McCarey (Going My Way)
1946	The Lost Weekend	Ray Milland (The Lost Weekend)	Joan Crawford (Mildred Pearce)	Billy Wilder (The Lost Weekend)
1947	The Best Years of Our Lives	Fredric March (The Best Years of Our Lives)	Olivia de Havilland (To Each His Own)	William Wyler (The Best Years of Our Lives)
1948	Gentleman's Agreement	Ronald Colman (A Double Life)	Loretta Young (The Farmer's Daughter)	Elia Kazan (Gentleman's Agreement)
1949	Hamlet	Laurence Olivier (Hamlet)	Jane Wyman (Johnny Belinda)	John Huston (The Treasure of the Sierra Madre)
1950	All the King's Men	Broderick Crawford (All the King's Men)	Olivia De Havilland (The Heiress)	Joseph L Mankiewicz (A Letter To Three Wives)
1951	All about Eve	José Ferrer (Cyrano de Bergerac)	Judy Holliday (Born Yesterday)	Joseph L Mankiewicz (All about Eve)
1952	An American In Paris	Humphrey Bogart (The African Queen)	Vivien Leigh (A Streetcar Named Desire)	George Stevens (A Place in the Sun)
1953	The Greatest Show on Earth	Gary Cooper (High Noon)	Shirley Booth (Come Back Little Sheba)	John Ford (The Quiet Man)
1954	From Here to Eternity	William Holden (Stalag 17)	Audrey Hepburn (Roman Holiday)	Fred Zinnemann (From Here to Eternity)
1955	On the Waterfront	Marlon Brando (On the Waterfront)	Grace Kelly (The Country Girl)	Elia Kazan (On the Waterfront)
1956	Marty	Ernest Borgnine (Marty)	Anna Magnani (The Rose Tattoo)	Delbert Mann (Marty)
1957	Around the World in Eighty Days	Yul Brynner (The King and I)	Ingrid Bergman (Anastasia)	George Stevens (Giant)
1958	The Bridge on the River Kwai	Alec Guinness (The Bridge on the River Kwai)	Joanne Woodward (The Three Faces of Eve)	David Lean (The Bridge on the River Kwai)
1959	Gigi	David Niven (Separate Tables)	Susan Hayward (I Want To Live)	Vincente Minnelli (Gigi)
1960	Ben Hur	Charlton Heston (Ben Hur)	Simone Signoret (Room at the Top)	William Wyler (Ben Hur)
1961	The Apartment	Burt Lancaster (Elmer Gantry)	Elizabeth Taylor (Butterfield 8)	Billy Wilder (The Apartment)
1962	West Side Story	Maximilian Schell (Judgment at Nuremberg)	Sophia Loren (Two Women)	Jerome Robbins & Robert Wise (West Side Story)

*Year	Best Film	Best Actor	Best Actress	Director
1963	Lawrence of Arabia	Gregory Peck (To Kill a Mockingbird)	Anne Bancroft (The Miracle Worker)	David Lean (Lawrence of Arabia)
1964	Tom Jones	Sidney Poitier (Lilies of the Field)	Patricia Neal (Hud)	Tony Richardson (Tom Jones)
1965	My Fair Lady	Rex Harrison (My Fair Lady)	Julie Andrews (Mary Poppins)	George Cukor (My Fair Lady)
1966	The Sound of Music	Lee Marvin (Cat Ballou)	Julie Christie (Darling)	Robert Wise (The Sound of Music)
1967	A Man for All Seasons	Paul Scofield (A Man for All Seasons)	Elizabeth Taylor (Who's Afraid of Virginia Woolf)	Fred Zinnemann (A Man for All Seasons)
1968	In the Heat of the Night	Rod Steiger (In the Heat of the Night)	Katharine Hepburn (Guess Who's Coming To Dinner)	Mike Nichols (The Graduate)
1969	Oliver!	Cliff Robertson (Charly)	Katherine Hepburn (The Lion in Winter) / Barbra Streisand (Funny Girl)†	Carol Reed (Oliver!)
1970	Midnight Cowboy	John Wayne (True Grit)	Maggie Smith (The Prime of Miss Jean Brodie)	John Schlesinger (Midnight Cowboy)
1971	Patton	George C Scott (Patton) refused Oscar	Glenda Jackson (Women in Love)	Franklin Schaffner (Patton)
1972	The French Connection	Gene Hackman (The French Connection)	Jane Fonda (Klute)	William Friedkin (The French Connection)
1973	The Godfather	Marlon Brando (The Godfather; refused Oscar)	Liza Minnelli (Cabaret)	Bob Fosse (Cabaret)
1974	The Sting	Jack Lemmon (Save the Tiger)	Glenda Jackson (A Touch of Class)	George Roy Hill (The Sting)
1975	The Godfather Part II	Art Carney (Harry and Tonto)	Ellen Burstyn (Alice Doesn't Live Here Any More)	Francis Ford Coppola (The Godfather Part II)
1976	One Flew over the Cuckoo's Nest	Jack Nicholson (One Flew over the Cuckoo's Nest)	Louise Fletcher (One Flew Over the Cuckoo's Nest)	Milos Forman (One Flew over the Cuckoo's Nest)
1977	Rocky	Peter Finch (Network: posthumously awarded)	Faye Dunaway (Network)	John G Avildsen (Rocky)
1978	Annie Hall	Richard Dreyfuss (The Goodbye Girl)	Diane Keaton (Annie Hall)	Woody Allen (Annie Hall)
1979	The Deer Hunter	Jon Voight (Coming Home)	Jane Fonda (Coming Home)	Michael Cimino (The Deer Hunter)
1980	Kramer versus Kramer	Dustin Hoffman (Kramer versus Kramer)	Sally Field (Norma Rae)	Robert Benton (Kramer versus Kramer)
1981	Ordinary People	Robert De Niro (Raging Bull)	Sissy Spacek (Coal Miner's Daughter)	Robert Redford (Ordinary People)
1982	Chariots of Fire	Henry Fonda (On Golden Pond)	Katharine Hepburn (On Golden Pond)	Warren Beatty (Reds)
1983	Gandhi	Ben Kingsley (Gandhi)	Meryl Streep (Sophie's Choice)	Richard Attenborough (Gandhi)
1984	Terms of Endearment	Robert Duvall (Tender Mercies)	Shirley MacLaine (Terms of Endearment)	James L Brooks (Terms of Endearment)
1985	Amadeus	F Murray Abraham (Amadeus)	Sally Field (Places in the Heart)	Milos Forman (Amadeus)
1986	Out of Africa	William Hurt (Kiss of the Spider Woman)	Geraldine Page (The Trip to Bountiful)	Sydney Pollack (Out of Africa)
1987	Platoon	Paul Newman (The Color of Money)	Marlee Matlin (Children of a Lesser God)	Oliver Stone (Platoon)
1988	The Last Emperor	Michael Douglas (Wall Street)	Cher (Moonstruck)	Bernardo Bertolucci (The Last Emperor)
1989	Rain Man	Dustin Hoffman (Rain Man)	Jodie Foster (The Accused)	Barry Levinson (Rain Man)
1990	Driving Miss Daisy	Daniel Day Lewis (My Left Foot)	Jessica Tandy (Driving Miss Daisy)	Oliver Stone (Born on the Fourth of July)
1991	Dances with Wolves	Jeremy Irons (Reversal of Fortune)	Kathy Bates (Misery)	Kevin Costner (Dances with Wolves)
1992	Silence of the Lambs	Anthony Hopkins (Silence of the Lambs)	Jodie Foster (Silence of the Lambs)	Jonathan Demme (Silence of the Lambs)
1993	Unforgiven	Al Pacino (Scent of a Woman)	Emma Thompson (Howard's End)	Clint Eastwood (Unforgiven)
1994	Schindler's List	Tom Hanks (Philadelphia)	Holly Hunter (The Piano)	Steven Spielberg (Schindler's List)
1995	Forrest Gump	Tom Hanks (Forrest Gump)	Jessica Lange (Blue Sky)	Robert Zemeckis (Forrest Gump)
1996	Braveheart	Nicolas Cage (Leaving Las Vegas)	Susan Sarandon (Dead Man Walking)	Mel Gibson (Braveheart)
1997	The English Patient	Geoffrey Rush (Shine)	Frances McDormand (Fargo)	Anthony Minghella (The English Patient)
1998	Titanic	Jack Nicholson (As Good As it Gets)	Helen Hunt (As Good As it Gets)	James Cameron (Titanic)
1999	Shakespeare in Love	Roberto Benigni (Life is Beautiful)	Gwyneth Paltrow (Shakespeare in Love)	Steven Spielberg (Saving Private Ryan)

CINEMA

*Year	Best Film	Best Actor	Best Actress	Director
2000	American Beauty	Kevin Spacey (American Beauty)	Hilary Swank (Boy's Don't Cry)	Sam Mendes (American Beauty)
2001	Gladiator	Russell Crowe (Gladiator)	Julia Roberts (Erin Brockovich)	Steven Soderbergh (Traffic)
2002	A Beautiful Mind	Denzel Washington (Training Day)	Halle Berry (Monsters Ball)	Ron Howard (A Beautiful Mind)
2003	Chicago	Adrien Brody (The Pianist)	Nicole Kidman (The Hours)	Roman Polanski (The Pianist)

* Probably the most frustrating question for any quiz player is in determining what a question setter means when asking a question about the Oscars. The confusion arises because the Oscars are awarded for films made the previous year, which means the question must be qualified – e.g. the 1997 Best Film Oscar was awarded to *The English Patient*, which was a 1996 film release. It must be said that the real confusion lies in the fact that, even when the question is qualified, bad research will cause a wrongly given answer by an unaware question setter. The suggested phraseology to use in such a question would be: 'At the 1996 Oscar ceremony, which film was awarded the Best Film Oscar?'. The answer is *Braveheart*. However, if the question was: 'Which 1996 film won the Oscar for Best Film?' then the answer would clearly be *The English Patient*. The problem with the question 'Which film won the Best Film Oscar in 1996?' is that although seemingly unambiguous, as clearly only one Oscar ceremony took place in 1996, many sources refer to the film release date, quite wrongly. I can only suggest that question setters take more care with such questions or that an appropriately qualified answer must be accepted. All of the above films were premiered in the year prior to the award unless the date is specifically given, since as on rare occasions a film has been released too late for consideration for a nomination, as in the case of *Casablanca*.
† Separate award for Comedy Director.

Oscars (Academy Awards) continued

Best Supporting Actor

Year	Actor	Film
1937	Walter Brennan	Come and Get It
1938	Joseph Schildkraut	The Life of Emile Zola
1939	Walter Brennan	Kentucky
1940	Thomas Mitchell	Stagecoach
1941	Walter Brennan	The Westerner
1942	Donald Crisp	How Green Was My Valley
1943	Van Heflin	Johnny Eager
1944	Charles Coburn	The More the Merrier
1945	Barry Fitzgerald	Going My Way
1946	James Dunn	A Tree Grows in Brooklyn
1947	Harold Russell	The Best Years of Our Lives
1948	Edmund Gwenn	Miracle on 34th Street
1949	Walter Huston	The Treasure of the Sierra Madre
1950	Dean Jagger	Twelve O'Clock High
1951	George Sanders	All about Eve
1952	Karl Malden	A Streetcar Named Desire
1953	Anthony Quinn	Viva Zapata!
1954	Frank Sinatra	From Here to Eternity
1955	Edmond O'Brien	The Barefoot Contessa
1956	Jack Lemmon	Mister Roberts
1957	Anthony Quinn	Lust for Life
1958	Red Buttons	Sayonara
1959	Burl Ives	The Big Country
1960	Hugh Griffith	Ben-Hur
1961	Peter Ustinov	Spartacus
1962	George Chakiris	West Side Story
1963	Ed Begley	Sweet Bird of Youth
1964	Melvyn Douglas	Hud
1965	Peter Ustinov	Topkapi
1966	Martin Balsam	A Thousand Clowns
1967	Walter Matthau	The Fortune Cookie
1968	George Kennedy	Cool Hand Luke
1969	Jack Albertson	The Subject Was Roses
1970	Gig Young	They Shoot Horses Don't They?
1971	John Mills	Ryan's Daughter
1972	Ben Johnson	The Last Picture Show
1973	Joel Grey	Cabaret
1974	John Houseman	The Paper Chase
1975	Robert De Niro	The Godfather Part II
1976	George Burns	The Sunshine Boys
1977	Jason Robards	All the President's Men
1978	Jason Robards	Julia
1979	Christopher Walken	The Deer Hunter
1980	Melvyn Douglas	Being There
1981	Timothy Hutton	Ordinary People
1982	John Gielgud	Arthur
1983	Louis Gossett Jr	An Officer and a Gentleman
1984	Jack Nicholson	Terms of Endearment
1985	Haing S Ngor	The Killing Fields
1986	Don Ameche	Cocoon
1987	Michael Caine	Hannah and Her Sisters
1988	Sean Connery	The Untouchables
1989	Kevin Kline	A Fish Called Wanda
1990	Denzel Washington	Glory
1991	Joe Pesci	Goodfellas
1992	Jack Palance	City Slickers
1993	Gene Hackman	Unforgiven
1994	Tommy Lee Jones	The Fugitive

Best Supporting Actress

Year	Actress	Film
1937	Gale Sondergaard	Anthony Adverse
1938	Alice Brady	In Old Chicago
1939	Fay Bainter	Jezebel
1940	Hattie McDaniel	Gone with the Wind
1941	Jane Darwell	The Grapes of Wrath
1942	Mary Astor	The Great Lie
1943	Teresa Wright	Mrs Miniver
1944	Katina Paxinou	For Whom the Bell Tolls
1945	Ethel Barrymore	None but the Lonely Heart
1946	Anne Revere	National Velvet
1947	Anne Baxter	The Razor's Edge
1948	Celeste Holm	Gentleman's Agreement
1949	Claire Trevor	Key Largo
1950	Mercedes McCambridge	All the King's Men
1951	Josephine Hull	Harvey
1952	Kim Hunter	A Streetcar Named Desire
1953	Gloria Grahame	The Bad and the Beautiful
1954	Donna Reed	From Here to Eternity
1955	Eva Marie Saint	On the Waterfront
1956	Jo Van Fleet	East of Eden
1957	Dorothy Malone	Written on the Wind
1958	Miyoshi Umeki	Sayonara
1959	Wendy Hiller	Separate Tables
1960	Shelley Winters	The Diary of Anne Frank
1961	Shirley Jones	Elmer Gantry
1962	Rita Moreno	West Side Story
1963	Patty Duke	The Miracle Worker
1964	Margaret Rutherford	The V.I.P.s
1965	Lila Kedrova	Zorba the Greek
1966	Shelley Winters	A Patch of Blue
1967	Sandy Dennis	Who's Afraid of Virginia Woolf?
1968	Estelle Parsons	Bonnie and Clyde
1969	Ruth Gordon	Rosemary's Baby
1970	Goldie Hawn	Cactus Flower
1971	Helen Hayes	Airport
1972	Cloris Leachman	The Last Picture Show
1973	Eileen Heckart	Butterflies Are Free
1974	Tatum O'Neal	Paper Moon
1975	Ingrid Bergman	Murder on the Orient Express
1976	Lee Grant	Shampoo
1977	Beatrice Straight	Network
1978	Vanessa Redgrave	Julia
1979	Maggie Smith	California Suite
1980	Meryl Streep	Kramer vs. Kramer
1981	Mary Steenburgen	Melvin and Howard
1982	Maureen Stapleton	Reds
1983	Jessica Lange	Tootsie
1984	Linda Hunt	The Year of Living Dangerously
1985	Peggy Ashcroft	A Passage to India
1986	Anjelica Huston	Prizzi's Honor
1987	Dianne Wiest	Hannah and Her Sisters
1988	Olympia Dukakis	Moonstruck
1989	Geena Davis	The Accidental Tourist
1990	Brenda Fricker	My Left Foot
1991	Whoopi Goldberg	Ghost
1992	Mercedes Ruehl	The Fisher King
1993	Marisa Tomei	My Cousin Vinny
1994	Anna Paquin	The Piano

CINEMA

Year	Actor	Film	Actress	Film
1995	Martin Landau	Ed Wood	Dianne Wiest	Bullets over Broadway
1996	Kevin Spacey	The Usual Suspects	Mira Sorvino	Mighty Aphrodite
1997	Cuba Gooding Jr	Jerry Maguire	Julliette Binoche	The English Patient
1998	Robin Williams	Good Will Hunting	Kim Basinger	L.A. Confidential
1999	James Coburn	Affliction	Judi Dench	Shakespeare in Love
2000	Michael Caine	The Cider House Rules	Angelina Jolie	Girl Interrupted
2001	Benicio Del Toro	Traffic	Marcia Gay Harden	Pollock
2002	Jim Broadbent	Iris	Jennifer Connelly	A Beautiful Mind
2003	Chris Cooper	Adaptation	Catherine Zeta-Jones	Chicago

Best Original Song

Year	Film	Artist	Song
1935	The Gay Divorcee	Con Conrad (composer), Herb Magidson (lyricist)	The Continental
1936	Gold Diggers	Harry Warren (composer), Al Dunin (lyricist)	Lullaby of Broadway
1937	Swing Time	Jerome Kern (composer), Dorothy Fields (lyricist)	The Way You Look Tonight
1938	Waikiki Wedding	Harry Owens	Sweet Leilani
1939	The Big Broadcast	Ralph Rainger (composer), Leo Robin (lyricist)	Thanks for the Memory
1940	The Wizard of Oz	Harold Arlen (composer), EY Harburg (lyricist)	Over the Rainbow
1941	Pinocchio	Leigh Harline (composer), Ned Washington (lyricist)	When You Wish upon a Star
1942	Lady Be Good	Jerome Kern (composer), Oscar Hammerstein II (lyricist)	The Last Time I Saw Paris
1943	Holiday Inn	Irving Berlin	White Christmas
1944	Hello, Frisco, Hello	Harry Warren (composer), Mack Gordon (lyricist)	You'll Never Know
1945	Going My Way	James Van Heusen (composer), Johnny Burke (lyricist)	Swinging on a Star
1946	State Fair	Richard Rodgers (composer), Oscar Hammerstein II (lyricist)	It Might As Well Be Spring
1947	The Harvey Girls	Harry Warren (composer), Johnny Mercer (lyricist)	On the Atchison, Topeka and the Santa Fe
1948	Song of the South	Allie Wrubel (composer), Ray Gilbert (lyricist)	Zip-A-Dee-Doo-Dah
1949	The Paleface	Jay Livingston (composer), Ray Evans (lyricist)	Buttons and Bows
1950	Neptune's Daughter	Frank Loesser	Baby, It's Cold Outside
1951	Captain Carey U.S.A.	Jay Livingston (composer), Ray Evans (lyricist)	Mona Lisa
1952	Here Comes the Groom	Hoagy Carmichael (composer), Johnny Mercer (lyricist)	In the Cool, Cool, Cool of the Evening
1953	High Noon	Dimitri Tiomkin (composer), Ned Washington (lyricist)	High Noon (Do Not Forsake Me, Oh My Darlin')
1954	Calamity Jane	Sammy Fain (composer), Paul Francis Webster (lyricist)	Secret Love
1955	Three Coins in the Fountain	Jule Styne (composer), Sammy Cahn (lyricist)	Three Coins in the Fountain
1956	Love is a Many-Splendored Thing	Sammy Fain (composer), Paul Francis Webster (lyricist)	Love is a Many-Splendored Thing
1957	The Man Who Knew Too Much	Jay Livingston (composer), Ray Evans (lyricist)	Whatever Will Be, Will Be (Que Sera, Sera)
1958	The Joker Is Wild	James Van Heusen (composer), Sammy Cahn (lyricist)	All The Way
1959	Gigi	Frederick Loewe (composer), Allan Jay Lerner (lyricist)	Gigi
1960	A Hole in the Head	James Van Heusen (composer), Sammy Cahn (lyricist)	High Hopes
1961	Never on Sunday	Manos Hadjidakis	Never On Sunday
1962	Breakfast at Tiffany's	Henry Mancini (composer), Johnny Mercer (lyricist)	Moon River
1963	Days of Wine and Roses	Henry Mancini (composer), Johnny Mercer (lyricist)	Days of Wine and Roses

Year	Film	Artist	Song
1964	*Papa's Delicate Condition*	James Van Heusen (composer), Sammy Cahn (lyricist)	Call Me Irresponsible
1965	*Mary Poppins*	Richard M Sherman (composer), Robert B Sherman (lyricist)	Chim Chim Cher-ee
1966	*The Sandpiper*	Johnny Mandel (composer), Paul Francis Webster (lyricist)	The Shadow of Your Smile
1967	*Born Free*	John Barry (composer), Don Black (lyricist)	Born Free
1968	*Doctor Dolittle*	Leslie Bricusse	Talk to the Animals
1969	*The Thomas Crown Affair*	Michel Legrand, Alan Bergman, Marilyn Bergman	The Windmills of Your Mind
1970	*Butch Cassidy and the Sundance Kid*	Burt Bacharach (composer), Hal David (lyricist)	Raindrops Keep Fallin' On My Head
1971	*Lovers and Other Strangers*	Fred Karlin, Robb Royer [aka Robb Wilson] James Griffin [aka Arthur James]	For All We Know
1972	*Shaft*	Isaac Hayes	Theme from Shaft
1973	*The Poseidon Adventure*	Al Kasha (composer), Joel Hirschhorn (lyricist)	The Morning After
1974	*The Way We Were*	Marvin Hamlisch, Alan Bergman, Marilyn Bergman	The Way We Were
1975	*The Towering Inferno*	Al Kasha (composer), Joel Hirschhorn (lyricist)	We May Never Love Like This Again
1976	*Nashville*	Keith Carradine	I'm Easy
1977	*A Star is Born*	Barbara Streisand (composer), Paul Williams (lyricist)	Evergreen (Love Theme from A Star is Born)
1978	*You Light Up My Life*	Joseph Brooks	You Light Up My Life
1979	*Thank God It's Friday*	Paul Jabara	Last Dance
1980	*Norma Rae*	David Shire (composer), Norman Gimbel (lyricist)	It Goes Like It Goes
1981	*Fame*	Michael Gore (composer), Dean Pitchford (lyricist)	Fame
1982	*Arthur*	Burt Bacharach, Carole Bayer Sager, Christopher Cross, Peter Allen	Arthur's Theme (Best That You Can Do)
1983	*An Officer and a Gentleman*	Jack Nitzsche, Buffy Saint-Marie, Will Jennings	Up Where We Belong
1984	*Flashdance*	Giorgio Moroder, Keith Forsey, Irene Cara	Flashdance . . . What a Feeling
1985	*The Woman in Red*	Stevie Wonder	I Just Called to Say I Love You
1986	*White Nights*	Lionel Richie	Say You, Say Me
1987	*Top Gun*	Giorgio Moroder (composer), Tom Whitlock (lyricist)	Take My Breath Away
1988	*Dirty Dancing*	Franke Previte, John DeNicola, Donald Markowitz	(I've Had) The Time of My Life
1989	*Working Girl*	Carly Simon	Let the River Run
1990	*The Little Mermaid*	Alan Menken (composer), Howard Ashman (lyricist)	Under the Sea
1991	*Dick Tracy*	Stephen Sondheim	Sooner Or Later (I Always Get My Man)
1992	*Beauty and the Beast*	Alan Menken (composer), Howard Ashman (lyricist)	Beauty and the Beast
1993	*Aladdin*	Alan Menken (composer), Tim Rice (lyricist)	A Whole New World
1994	*Philadelphia*	Bruce Springsteen	Streets of Philadelphia
1995	*The Lion King*	Elton John (composer), Tim Rice (lyricist)	Can You Feel the Love Tonight
1996	*Pocahontas*	Alan Menken (composer), Stephen Schwartz (lyricist)	Colors of the Wind
1997	*Evita*	Andrew Lloyd Webber (composer), Tim Rice (lyricist)	You Must Love Me
1998	*Titanic (1997)*	James Horner (composer), Will Jennings (lyricist)	My Heart Will Go On
1999	*The Prince of Egypt*	Stephen Schwartz	When You Believe
2000	*Tarzan*	Phil Collins	You'll Be In My Heart
2001	*Wonderboys*	Bob Dylan	Things Have Changed
2002	*Monsters Inc*	Randy Newman	If I Didn't Have You
2003	*8 Mile*	Eminem	Lose Yourself

C
I
N
E
M
A

COMPUTERS

Common Terms

Artificial Intelligence A word coined in the USA in 1956 as the ultimate aim for electronic processing ability. Although great strides have been made towards a device that would stimulate human thought processes, as yet, no such device exists and the term is used to describe advanced programs such as PROLOG which allows empirical evidence to guide future decisions.

ASCII American Standard Code for Information Interchange (computer code for representing alphanumeric characters.

bit (binary digit) Smallest unit of data manageable by a computer.

bootstrap Technique for loading the first few program instructions into a computer main store to enable the rest of the program to be introduced from an input device.

busbar Group of electrical conductors maintained at low voltage, used for carrying data in binary form between the various parts of a computer or its peripherals.

byte Equivalent of eight bits (generally makes up a character of information). It is possible to have a six-bit byte.

computer: definition A machine that carries out a programmed sequence of instructions by translation of coded data. Digital computers use binary code which is represented by eletrical current being turned off and on. Analogue computers use continuous variables as opposed to the discreet data of digital machines. A simple example of an analogue computer would be a set of scales.

computer generations The developement of computers is sometimes viewed as falling into several phases or generations. First generation began with the ENIAC (electronic numerical integrator and calculator) modern computers designed by J. Presper Eckert and John W Mauchly, both of the University of Pennsylvania. Completed in 1946, this was first all-purpose, all-electronic digital computer. A special-purpose, all-electronic computing machine called Colossus had earlier been developed at Bletchley Park, in England, and was in operation by December 1943. The Colossus was designed (by the computer genius Alan Turing) to decipher codes generated by the German electromechanical enciphering devices known as Enigma machines. The successor to ENIAC was EDVAC (Electronic Discrete Variable Automatic Computer).

The 'second generation' of modern computers began in 1959, when machines employing semiconductor devices known as transistors became commercially available.

The 'third generation' of modern computers began in the late 1960s, when integrated circuits were imprinted on silicon chips. This permitted the construction of large 'mainframe' computers with much higher operating speeds.

The 'fourth generation' of modern computers began in the 1980s. This and subsequent generations have continued to develop very large-scale integration (VLSI) and have promoted the advancement of virtual reality (VR) and computer aided design (CAD).

The 'fifth generation' of modern computers is an ongoing general development of recent technological advances. Using recent engineering advances for example, computers are able to accept spoken word instructions (voice recognition) and imitate human reasoning. The ability to translate a foreign language is now commonplace.

Computer Programming languages (high-level)

ADA Designed for dealing with real-time processing problems and used for military and other systems. It was named after Augusta Ada Byron, Lady Lovelace (assistant to Charles Babbage), and developed in the late 1970s by the US Defense Department.

AED Algol Extended for Design.

ALGOL ALGorithmic Orientated Language, principally used for scientific and mathematical problems (types: ALGOL 60 and ALGOL 68).

APL A Programming Language.

APT Automatically Programmed Tools.

BASIC Beginners All-purpose Symbolic Instruction Code.

BCPL Basic Computer Programming Language.

C Introduced at Bell Laboratories in 1974 and originally developed for use in the UNIX operating system.

COBOL COmmon Business-Oriented Language (developed in 1959).

COGO CO-ordinate GeOmetry.

COMAL COMmon Algorithmic Language.

CORAL Computer On-line ReAL time.

FORTH Name derives from an intention to provide a language for fourth-generation computers. It uses a notation called reverse polish, in which an operator is always preceded by its arguments. FORTH is popularly used for writing video game programs.

FORTRAN FORmula TRANslation (Invented in 1956).

GPSS General Purpose Systems Simulation.

LISP LISt Processor (introduced in 1960). Its basic entity is an s-expression (symbolic expression) which is either an atomic symbol or a list structure.

LOGO A simple, interactive language which is compact enough to run on most microcomputers but also embodies powerful programming facilities. It is used extensively for teaching programming to children.

ML Meta Language.

PASCAL ALGOL-related language named after the scientist-philosopher Blaise Pascal (1623–62). Pascal is a teaching language developed in the late 1960s.

PL/1 Programming Language 1, a multipurpose programming language designed for solving both business and scientific problems.

PL/M Programming Language for Micro Computers.

PROLOG PROgramming in LOGic. There the emphasis is on description rather than on action, eg to find the greater of two input numbers, one would describe what 'greater of' meant and then query it with the given numbers as data.

SIMULA SIMUlation LAnguage.

SNOBOL StriNg-Oriented symBOlic Language, provides facilities for the manipulation of strings of characters by pattern-matching expressions. SNOBOL is particularly applicable for text editing, linguistics and the compiling and symbolic manipulation of algebraic expressions.

SQL Structured Query Language.

computer: makes and models: Commodore: Amiga and PET; Apple: Macintosh; Sinclair: Spectrum and ZX80 / 1; Packard Bell: Legend; DEC: Vax; IBM: PS/2; Acorn: BBC Micro; Digital: Equipment Corporation-PDP Series.

computer: mechanical pioneers Charles Babbage (1791–1871) designed computing machines that he called the 'Difference Engine' and 'Analytical Engine' in the 1820s and 30s. They were never built but the first practical programmed computer built by Georg Scheutz of Stockholm and exhibited at the Paris Exposition of 1855 was based on Babbage's Difference Engine. The mechanical adding machine developed by Blaise Pascal in 1642 which used a 10:1 gearing ratio to represent decimal columns, can be regarded as the ancestor of the computer.

computer programmer: first Ada Byron, Countess Lovelace, assistant to Charles Babbage (see computer mechanical pioneers), is generally recognised as the first 'computer programmer'. The first proposal for a computer language, however, was by German philosopher Gottfried Leibniz (1646–1716), who devised a system allowing logic statements to be dealt with mathematically, using the digit 0 for false and 1 for true.)

computer: types Micro, mini, mainframe (computers can also be categorised as digital and analog).

CPU Central Processing Unit; the electronic decision making device within a computer.

DTP Desktop Publishing; the production of high-quality printed matter using a desktop computer and a laser printer. Some examples of packages are Pagemaker and QuarkXpress, Adobe Illustrator, Microsoft Publisher, Corel Draw, GST and Serif.

exabyte one billion billion characters of information.

gigabyte one billion characters of information.

GIGO Garbage In, Garbage Out. Computer user's proverb meaning if you use unreliable data you will get unreliable results.

Hardware The electronic and mechanical components of a computer are called the hardware; this includes the processing unit.

high-level language Computer programming language that is closer to human language or mathematical notation than to machine language.

home computer: first Apple-1; created by Steve Wozniak and Steve Jobs in 1977.

k Kilobyte (1,024 bytes).

Internet An international computer network linking computers from educational institutions, government agencies, and industry.

Lara Croft Heroine of the video game 'Tomb Raider'.

Laptops: first Became prevalent in 1987, although the first laptop machine with a full colour screen was developed in 1990.

Laser printer developed in 1987 using the principle of the Xerox copier.

LCD Liquid Crystal Display.

low-level language Computer-programming. language that is closer to machine language than to human language.

m Megabyte (1,024 kilobytes).

microprocessor: first Intel 4004.

modem Acronym for MOdulator DEModulator, a device used to enable computers to communicate with one another via telephone lines.

motherboard Printed circuit board through which all hardware and software devise send electronic to talk to each other.

MS-DOS MicroSoft Disc Operating System.

network Group of computers connected in order to share and exchange information.

nibble Equivalent of four bits.

OS Operating System: a program that controls the overall operation of a computer system, typically by performing such tasks as memory allocation, job scheduling and input/output control.

pixel Picture element: one of the number of very small dots that make up the picture on a visual display unit.

port Socket used to connect a computer to other devices.

punched card: inventor The American Dr Herman Hollerith (1860–1929) invented the punched-card system in 1890; his company, the Tabulating Machine Co. became IBM in 1924. Hollerith's device enabled a census to be taken in six weeks rather than the six years required by manual analysis. Mechanical punched cards had been suggested earlier by Charles Babbage; and the 'Jacquard Loom' of 1801 is an even earlier example of punched card principles but Hollerith patented the system and was the first to use electrical contacts.

RAM Random Access Memory; temporary storage space that is lost when the computer is switched off.

ROM Read-Only Memory; permanent storage device that holds data that cannot be altered by the user.

software the programs and operating information used by a computer.

spreadsheets: first The first spreadsheet program Visicalc was developed on the Apple-2 in 1979.

terabyte Approximately a thousand billion characters of information.

Turing Test Test for successful artificial intelligence that depends on a human not being able to tell that he or she is communicating with a computer. No computer has ever passed the Turing Test.

VGA Video Graphics Array (Super VGA is the advanced array).

video games: 1st Pong (established in Italy in the early 1970s).

Video games: famous Super Mario Brothers by Nintendo, Sonic the Hedgehog by Sega, Donkey Kong by Atari, Tomb Raider by Eios, Duke Nukem by 3D Realms, and Doom by Idoh.

Windows User-friendly operating system created by Microsoft.

NB: Many computer acronyms (eg AI, DOS, WYSIWYG, VDU, and MIPS) can be found listed in the Abbreviations section.

Internet Chat Abbreviations

Abbreviation	Meaning
AAMOF	as a matter of fact
AFAIK	as far as I know
AFK	away from keyboard
AIM	AOL instant messenger
ASAP	as soon as possible
ASL?	age, sex, location?
ATK	at the keyboard
B4	before
BBIAB	be back in a bit
BB4N	bye bye for now
BBFN	bye bye for now
BBL	be back later
BBS	be back soon
BEG	big evil grin
BF	boyfriend
BFN	bye for now
BION	believe it or not
BOT	back on topic
BRB	be right back
BRB NC	be right back, nature calls
BRS	big red switch
BTW	by the way
BWL	bursting with laughter
CID	crying in disgrace
CRBT	crying real big tears
CSG	chuckle, snigger, grin
C U L8ER	see you later
C U L8TER	see you later
C YA	see ya (you)
DC'D	disconnected
DIKU	do I know you
EG	evil grin
FAQ	frequently asked questions
FCOL	for crying out loud
FFS	for fuck sake
FOAF	friend of a friend
FTF	face to face
F2F	face to face
FUBAR	fucked up beyond all recognition
FUD	fear, uncertainty and doubt
FWIW	for what it's worth
FYI	for your information
GF	girlfriend
GG	good game
GMTA	great minds think alike
GR8	great
GL	good luck
GTG	got to go
H&K	hugs and kisses
HAGN	have a good night
HAND	have a nice day
HB	hurry back
HLOL	hysterically laughing out loud
HTH	hope that helps
IAAA	I am an accountant
IAAL	I am a lawyer
IANALB	I am not a lawyer . . . but
IC	I see
IJWTS	I just want to say
ILU	I love you
ILY	I love you
IMHO	in my humble opinion
IMY	I miss you
INPO	in no particular order
IOW	in other words
IRL	in real life
ISRN	I'll stop rambling now

Abbreviation	Meaning
ITA	I totally agree
ITFA	in the final analysis
IWALU	I will always love you
IWALY	I will always love you
J/K	just kidding
JK	joke
JMO	just my opinion
K	okay
KISS	keep it simple, stupid
KOL	kiss on lips
L8R	later
L8R G8R	later 'gator
LJBF	let's just be friends
LMAO	laughing my arse off
LOL	laughing out loud
LOLOL	laughing out loud online
LTNS	long time no see
LTNT	long time no type
LUVYA	love ya (you)
LY4E	love you for ever
M/F	male or female?
MOTD	message of the day
MSG	message
MYOB	mind your own business
NBD	no big deal
N1	nice one
NM	never mind
NP	no problem
NQA	no questions asked
NRN	no reply necessary
OAUS	on an unrelated subject
OMG	oh my god
OIC	oh I see
OTOH	on the other hand
12345	talk about school
PDS	please don't shout
PM	private message
PMBI	pardon my butting in
PML	pissing myself laughing
POV	point of view
PTMM	please tell me more
RHIP	rank has its privileges
ROFL	rolling on floor laughing
ROTF	rolling on the floor
ROTFL	rolling on the floor laughing
ROTFLMAO	rolling on the floor laughing my arse off
RTBM	read the bloody manual
RTFM	read the fucking manual
RTM	read the manual
RTSM	read the stupid manual
RYS	read your screen
SICS	sitting in chair sniggering
SLM	see last mail
SO	significant other
SS	so sorry
SUAKM	shut up and kiss me
SWIM	see what I mean
SWL	screaming with laughter
SYT	sweet young thing
TANJ	there ain't no justice
TCOB	taking care of business
TOBAL	there oughta be a law
TPTB	the powers that be
TSR	totally stupid rules
TTFN	ta ta for now
TTYL	talk to you later
TY	thank you

TYCLO	turn your caps lock off	:-)	smiling
TYVM	thank you very much	:-0	shock
VG	very good	:'-(	crying
VN	very nice	X=	fingers crossed
WAEF	when all else fails	:-w	a liar – speaks with forked tongue
WB	welcome back	:=)	little Hitler
WG	wicked grin	:*	kissing
WTF	what the fuck	:-X	kissing
WTG	way to go	$-)	greedy
WTGP	want to go private?	:-L~~	drooling
WTH	what/who the hell	}:	devil
YGLT	you're gonna love this	<:-)	idiot
YMMV	your mileage may vary	:-S	confused
YW	you're welcome	:-(	sad

COMPUTERS

CURRENT AFFAIRS

Daily Record 2001

January

1 Fiona Reynolds, 42, former head of the Council for the Protection of Rural England, became director general of the National Trust, as replacement for Martin Drury.

4 A seven-year-old British girl, Bethany Park, fell to her death over the Lisbon Falls in Mpumalanga Province, South Africa.

6 Prince Charles broke a bone in his shoulder following a fall from his horse whilst riding with the Meynell Hunt in Derbyshire.

8 Judge Ann Goddard, 64, was attacked in court by a defendant who leapt from the dock and punched her repeatedly.

10 Vincent Bethell was cleared of causing a public nuisance by his refusal to wear clothes in public. After five months in Brixton prison awaiting trial a jury unanimously found him innocent. The biting winds outside Southwark Crown Court forced Mr Bethell to don the prison-issue tracksuit, the first time he had worn any clothing since 13 August 2000.

11 Writer Lorna Sage died a week after her latest book *Bad Blood* won the Whitbread Biography of the Year award.

12 Johnny Vaughan and Denise Van Outen bowed out as presenters of Channel 4's *The Big Breakfast*.

16 President Kabila of the Democratic Republic of Congo was shot dead by a member of his personal bodyguard.

21 The Archbishop of Westminster, the Most Reverend Cormac Murphy-O'Connor, was among 37 new cardinals elevated by the Pope.

24 Peter Mandelson, the Northern Ireland Secretary, resigned from the Cabinet and was succeeded by John Reid.

28 British Telecom announced that the traditional red phone box, as designed by Sir Giles Gilbert Scott in 1936 and known as K6, is now almost extinct, and the steel and glass versions which replaced them in the 1980s are also endangered species, as the increase in mobile phone use has reduced their viability.

31 Abdul Baset Ali al-Megrahi, a Libyan intelligence agent, was jailed for a minimum of 20 years for killing the 270 victims of the Lockerbie bombing. The Scottish court sitting in the Netherlands acquitted Al-Amin Khalifa Fhimah.

February

6 Ariel Sharon, 72, won a landslide victory over Ehud Barak to become the new Israeli Prime Minister.

14 Rober Earl, owner of the Planet Hollywood chain, bought the bikini worn by Ursula Andress in the film *Dr No* for £41,125 at Christie's auction house in South Kensington.

16 The United States and Great Britain launched the biggest air raid on targets around Baghdad since Operation Desert Fox in December 1998.

20 Alexander McQueen was named as British Designer of the Year at the British Fashion Awards. Other award winners included Kate Moss as British Model of the Year and Jemima Khan as Best-Dressed Celebrity.

22 At the 43rd Grammy Awards ceremony at the Staples Centre in Los Angeles, Steely Dan won the top honour of Best Album with *Two Against Nature*, their first album in 20 years.

23 The 25th Laurence Olivier Awards were hosted by Clive Anderson. The Best Actress category was won by Julie Walters for her portrayal of the loyal mother in *All My Sons* at the Royal National Theatre.

25 At the annual Bafta Awards in London, Jamie Bell won Best Actor for his title role in *Billy Elliot* and Julia Roberts won Best Actress for her part in *Erin Brockovich*.

26 The Brit Awards, hosted by Ant and Dec, the Geordie television presenters, were dominated by Robbie Williams, who won Best British Male Solo Artist, Best British Single and Best British Video. Craig David won a record six nominations but failed to win a single category, the biggest surprise being beaten by Fat Boy Slim as Best British Dance Act.

28 A Land-Rover careered into the path of a high-speed train near Selby, North Yorkshire, causing the express to collide with a coal train. Both train drivers were killed as well as at least eight passengers. The car driver, Gary Hart, 36, suffered minor injuries.

March

5 Centrica, the gas company which owns the Automobile Association, agreed to pay £20 million to Ordnance Survey in an out-of-court settlement for the plagiarising of their maps. OS proved their case by purposely including subtle errors in their cartography to protect themselves from plagiarists.

9 Jack Dee, Keith Duffy, Chris Eubank, Vanessa Feltz, Claire Sweeney and Anthea Turner began a week-long celebrity version of *Big Brother* in aid of Comic Relief.

12 At the annual Screen Actors' Guild awards in Los Angeles, the Best Male Leading Actor award was won by Benicio Del Toro for his role in *Traffic*. Best Female Leading Actor was Julia Roberts for *Erin Brockovich*.

13 The Princess Royal was fined £400 for driving her Bentley at 93mph on the A417 dual carriageway in August last year.

14 Julien Macdonald was named as the successor to Alexander McQueen as head designer at the House of Givenchy.

16 Comedian Jack Dee emerged triumphant from the *Celebrity Big Brother* house.

18 The television 'Popstars' band, Hear'Say, reached the Number One spot in the UK charts with their first single, 'Pure and Simple', which has become the best-selling debut single of all time.

20   Chanel, the French perfume-maker, dropped actress Carole Bouquet as its ambassador after 15 years.
22   The London Stock Market suffered its biggest one-day fall since Black Wednesday in October 1992. The FTSE 100 Index tumbled 4.1 per cent, shedding 225.90 points to 5,314.8
26   The Post Office changed its name to Consignia PLC but remained wholly owned by the UK government. Steve Martin hosted the 73rd Oscar Awards ceremony in Los Angeles.
28   A total of 153 million people listened to the World Service every week last year to secure its position as the world's most listened-to radio network.
29   British oarsman Jim Shekhdar, 54, became the first man to row across the Pacific Ocean non-stop and unaided. The 8,000-mile voyage took 274 days and ended with him being flung from his 23ft boat just off North Stradbroke Island, off the Queensland coast near Brisbane, forcing him to swim the final few hundred yards.
30   Stuart Lubbock, a 31-year-old father-of-two, was found dead in comedian Michael Barrymore's swimming pool.
31   Designer Stella McCartney signed a £15 million deal with Italian fashion giants Gucci to launch her designs worldwide.

April

1   An American spyplane collided with a Chinese fighter jet in international airspace and was forced to make an emergency landing. The Chinese plane was lost in the South China Sea. Former Tatton MP Neil Hamilton, was informed by the Law Lords that he could not appeal to the House of Lords over his libel action against Mohamed Al Fayed.
2   Slobodan Milosevic was arrested and taken from his home in Dedinje and detained in Belgrade's central jail.
5   Dutch lorry driver Perry Wacker, 33, was jailed for 14 years for his part in the killing of 58 illegal Chinese immigrants in June of last year, when he closed the air vent to the sealed container in which they were being transported from Zeebrugge to Dover.
6   Pakistan's Supreme Court set aside the corruption convictions of former Prime Minister Benazir Bhutto.
8   Kevin Olmstead, a 42-year-old engineer, won a record £1.5million on the US version of *Who Wants to Be a Millionaire*.
9   David Edwards, a physics teacher from Staffordshire, became the second jackpot winner of *Who Wants to Be a Millionaire*.
10   The Dutch parliament approved a law that made The Netherlands the first country to decriminalise euthanasia.
11   Sir Elton John lost a High Court action to recover touring expenses from representatives of his previous manager John Reid. The three-month hearing is expected to cost the musician in excess of £8 million.
12   The 24 aircrew of the spyplane held by the Chinese authorities since 1 April returned safely to the United States.
16   An American version of *The Weakest Link* was broadcast, with presenter Anne Robinson receiving enormous criticism from *The Washington Post* and *The New York Times*.
18   *Woman's Realm*, the 43-year-old ladies' magazine, was closed by its publisher IPC Media.
19   Berkeley Square, London, was sold to the Saudi Arabian royal family for £335 million.
20   Conductor Giuseppe Sinopoli collapsed and died during Act III of Verdi's *Aida* at the Deutsche Oper in Berlin.
26   The first 15 'people's peers' were appointed, and included Sir Paul Condon, the former Metropolitan Police Commissioner, Lady Howe of Aberavon, and Professor Susan Greenfield, director of the Royal Institution of Great Britain and author of several books on the brain.
30   Lenny Henry's one-off BBC1 sketch show *In Pieces* won the Golden Rose of Montreux at the annual awards in Switzerland.

May

1   BBC chairman Sir Christopher Bland became chairman of British Telecom.
3   Anne Owers, 53, was announced as the replacement for the retiring Sir David Ramsbotham as chief inspector of the 137 jails in England and Wales. Ms Owens will take up her post in August.
6   American Dennis Tito, 60, the world's first space tourist, who paid an estimated $20 million for his six-day space voyage, arrived back on Earth in the Soyuz capsule 50 miles northeast of Arkalyk on the Kazakh steppe.
7   Ronnie Biggs, the escaped Great Train Robber, attended West London Magistrates' Court and, after identification, was sent to Belmarsh Prison to finish his sentence. Biggs was flown to Britain from Brazil courtesy of the *Sun* newspaper.
8   *The Wicker Man*, southwest England's answer to the *Angel of the North*, was destroyed by arsonists. The 40ft willow sculpture, created by Serena de la Hey eight months ago, dominated the skyline beside the M5 in the Somerset Levels.
9   Edward Heath, the retiring Father of the House, made his final speech in the House of Commons.
14   Classical cellist Julian Lloyd Webber became the first official busker on London's Tube network following a by-law change allowing buskers to perform if they have permission. Webber played a selection of music, composed by his brother, at Westminster Underground station, in aid of The Prince's Trust. Tom Green, a Mormon with five wives and 29 children, became the first man in half a century to stand trial for bigamy in Utah, although it is believed there are tens of thousands of polygamists in the Mormon capital of the world.
15   Tony Blair's Cabinet reshuffle included David Blunkett being named as Home Secretary as replacement for Jack Straw, who in turn replaces John Prescott at the Department of Environment, Transport and the Regions.
16   Deputy Prime Minister John Prescott threw a punch at an egg-throwing protester, Craig Evans, at a Labour rally in Rhyl, North Wales.

CURRENT AFFAIRS

17   Polly Vacher, 57, from Drayton, near Abingdon, Oxfordshire, became the first woman to fly solo round the world in a single-engined plane via Australia and the Pacific when she touched down at Birmingham airport four months after setting out. The 47-stage journey amounted to 950 flying hours.

18   Sir Ludovic Kennedy, president of the Voluntary Euthanasia Society, announced he is abandoning the Liberal Democrats after 45 years because Charles Kennedy, the Lib Dem leader, will not promote voluntary euthanasia.

23   Actor Jeremy Irons caused controversy when he covered his 15th-century home, Kilcoe Castle, in limestone wash that has turned a peach-pink colour. The castle situated in Skibbereen, west Cork, was built in 1450 for the McCarthy clan.

27   A French train covered the 672 miles between Calais and Marseilles in a world-record 3hr 29min, reaching 229mph.

30   Former French Foreign Minister Roland Dumas was sentenced to six months in jail for accepting thousands of pounds of gifts from his mistress, all financed by the Elf-Aquitaine oil corporation.

31   The Classical Brits at the Royal Albert Hall were dominated by the Mancunian tenor Russell Watson, who won Album of the Year and Best-Selling Classical Debut Album. Kennedy (i.e. Nigel, the violinist, who at that time had dispensed with his first name) won Male Artist of the Year and Angela Gheorghiu won Female Artist of the Year whilst Sir Simon Rattle won the Outstanding Contribution Award.

June

4   Nepal is under curfew as its third king in four days dons the symbolic bird-of-paradise crown. The new King Gyanendra is the uncle of the deceased Crown Prince Dipendra, who is reported to have shot his father King Birendra before unsuccessfully attempting to take his own life (although he died of his wounds on 6 June). There remains a mystery surrounding the deaths of Dipendra and his parents. Many believe it may have been a series of political assassinations, whilst others believe that an automatic weapon owned by Dipendra went off by mistake killing several people on 1 June.

5   The billionaire philanthropist Sir Paul Getty made a £5 million donation to the Conservative Party. The Duke of York announced he would become patron of the English National Ballet.

6   A jury in Washington awarded lifelong smoker Richard Boeken, 56, $3 billion after deciding that the tobacco giant Philip Morris was responsible for his cancer. The Home and Leisure Accident Surveillance System issued a report listing household injuries in Great Britain for 1999. Tea cosies (37), talcum powder (73), bread bins (91), dustpans (146), toilet-roll holders (329), clogs (633), false teeth (933), trouser accidents (5,945), socks and tights (10,773) and vegetable incidents (13,132), were some of the more surprising causes of hospitalisations during the year.

7   Tony Blair headed back to Downing Street to form a new government following Labour's landslide victory in the General Election.

8   Lisa Ellis (Penny) was the first evacuee from the new series of the Channel 4 game show *Big Brother*.

11   Timothy McVeigh, the man who detonated a lorry packed with a 7,000lb fertiliser bomb in front of the Alfred P. Murrah Federal Building in Oklahoma City, killing 168 people, was executed by lethal injection.

16   The Queen's Birthday Honours List included knighthoods for racing driver Jackie Stewart and flautist James Galway.

17   Marius Brenciu, a 27-year-old teaching assistant from Romania, won both major prizes at the Cardiff Singer of the World.

22   The Parole Board announced that Robert Thompson and Jon Venables, the convicted killers of James Bulger, were released on life licence.

24   Foster the vulture was caught by 21-year-old falconer, Jo Lobb, in the garden of a Suffolk rectory and returned to his aviary at Banham Zoo, near Diss in Norfolk, after escaping a week ago during a flying display.

28   Former president of the Federal Republic of Yugoslavia Slobodan Milosevic was flown to The Hague to stand before the International War Crimes Tribunal to be formally charged with crimes against humanity, including the mass murder and deportation of Kosovo Albanians, and responsibility for specific village massacres. His trial is not expected to begin until next year.

29   The latest evictee from the Channel 4 *Big Brother* house was Paul Ferguson, alias Bubble.

July

2   Barry George was found guilty by a 10–1 majority verdict of murdering broadcaster Jill Dando outside her London home.
      Speke airport in Liverpool was renamed in honour of Beatle John Lennon.

6   Amma the lap dancer became the fifth *Big Brother* evacuee.

12   Richard Madeley and Judy Finnegan ended their 13-year stint as presenters of *This Morning*.

15   Yasemin Dalkilic, a 22-year-old diver from Turkey, broke the world record for freediving when she plunged 105 metres into the Red Sea before surfacing two and a half minutes later.

19   Jeffrey Archer began a four-year prison term at Belmarsh Jail after being found guilty of rigging the 1987 libel action that won him £500,000.

20   An anti-capitalist protester, Carlo Giuliani, was shot dead by Italian Carabinieri at the G8 summit in Genoa. Paul Clarke was evicted from the *Big Brother* House, thereby ending the televised romance with Helen Adams.

23   Michael Jackson, chief executive of Channel 4, announced he was quitting to become chief executive of USA Entertainment.

25   Charlotte Hoborough, a 24-year-old detective constable from South Wales, won the £1 million prize in the ITV series *Survivor*. Jackie Carey, a 31-year-old airline industry executive, was the runner-up.

26   Sir Paul McCartney announced his engagement to the anti-landmine campaigner Heather Mills.

27   Sir David Ramsbotham, the Chief Inspector of Prisons, retired.

August

2   Radislav Krstic, the commander of the Drina Wolves unit of the Bosnian Serb army, was jailed for 46 years for his part in the mass executions of Muslims; he became the first man convicted of genocide by The Hague War Crimes Tribunal.

22   Robertsons announces it is to replace its Golly logo with drawings of Roald Dahl characters drawn by Quentin Blake.

28   PC Karl Bluestone, 36, from Gravesend in Kent, fatally wounded his wife and two of his children with a claw hammer before hanging himself in his garage. His two other children, Jack and Jessica, survived the attack. Neil and Christine Hamilton were cleared of taking part in a serious sexual assault on Nadine Milroy-Sloan, 28.

31   Diane Pretty, terminally ill with Motor Neurone Disease, was given leave to challenge the law against assisted suicide.

September

6   American model Carolyn Murphy was announced as the replacement for Elizabeth Hurley as the face of Estée Lauder.

11   North America was subjected to a devastating series of terrorist attacks. American Airlines flight AA11, a Boeing 767 from Boston, was hijacked en route to Los Angeles and crashed into the World Trade Center North Tower at 8.58am (1.58pm BST), killing all 92 on board. United Airlines flight UA175, a Boeing 767 from Boston, was also hijacked en route to Los Angeles and crashed into the World Trade Center South Tower at 9.16am (2.16pm BST), killing all 65 on board. American Airlines flight AA77, a Boeing 757, was hijacked en route from Washington to Los Angeles and crashed into the Pentagon at 9.43am (2.43pm BST), killing 64 on board. United Airlines flight UA93, a Boeing 757, from Newark to San Francisco, targeted for Camp David, crashed at 10.30am (3.30pm BST), 80 miles south-east of Pittsburgh, killing 45 on board. Thousands more were killed in the buildings and on the streets below. None of the known enemies of America admitted to the attacks, but the number one suspect was Osama bin Laden, the millionaire Saudi terrorist, thought to be hiding out in Afghanistan.

12   Iain Duncan Smith gained 61 per cent of the party vote to become the new leader of the Conservative Party.

13   The 19 suicide hijackers were named by the FBI; many were of Middle East descent and were based in Florida.

14   Iain Duncan Smith's Shadow Cabinet was announced as Michael Howard (Shadow Chancellor), David Davis (Chairman), Michael Ancram (Shadow Foreign Secretary), David Willetts (Work and Pensions), Tim Yeo (Shadow Culture Secretary), Bernard Jenkin (Shadow Defence Secretary), David Maclean (Chief Whip), John Bercow (Chief Secretary to the Treasury), Liam Fox (Shadow Health Secretary), Caroline Spelman (Shadow International Development Secretary), Oliver Letwin (Shadow Home Secretary), Quentin Davies (Shadow Northern Ireland Secretary), Damian Green (Education Secretary), Lord Strathclyde (Shadow Leader of the Lords), Eric Pickles (Shadow Transport Minister), Peter Ainsworth (Shadow Secretary of State for Environment, Food and Rural Affairs), John Whittingdale (Shadow Trade and Industry), Theresa May (Local Government and the Regions), Tim Collins (Cabinet Office), Lord Cope of Berkeley (Opposition Chief Whip in the Lords), Jacqui Lait (Shadow Scottish Secretary), Nigel Evans (Shadow Welsh Secretary), and Eric Forth (Shadow Leader of the Commons).

18   Gavyn Davies was confirmed as the new chairman of the BBC in succession to Sir Christopher Bland.

19   Operation Noble Eagle was launched when the aircraft carrier USS *Theodore Roosevelt* set sail from the United States. Its task is to eliminate terrorist networks around the world.

21   Television presenter Nick Hancock paid £23,500 at Sotheby's auction for Sir Stanley Matthews' FA Cup Final winner's medal from 1953.

23   Prince William arrives in St Andrews to begin his four years as an undergraduate. He will be known as William Wales.

24   The Liberal Democratic Party Conference opened in Bournemouth.

30   Mullah Zaeef, the Taliban ambassador to Pakistan, admitted for the first time that Osama bin Laden was being hidden in Afghanistan.

October

1   The Labour Party Conference opened in Brighton.

2   Tony Blair addressed the Labour Party Conference with a stirring anti-terrorism speech. Swissair was forced to ground all of its aircraft when it ran out of cash to pay for fuel.

3   The BBC poll to celebrate tomorrow's National Poetry Day was won by Edward Lear's *The Owl and the Pussy Cat*.

4   At Nottingham Crown Court Michael Stone was convicted for the second time of the 1996 murders of Dr Lin Russell and her daughter Megan, 6, and for the attempted murder of Josie Russell, 9. He continues his three life sentences.

5   The Supreme Court of Georgia ruled that the electric chair was no longer an acceptable form of capital punishment. Only Nebraska and Alabama continue to use the chair as their sole method of carrying out the death penalty.

8   The Conservative Party Conference opened in Blackpool.

15   Jeffrey Archer was moved from Wayland Jail in Norfolk to North Sea Camp Prison in Boston, Lincolnshire.

17   Australian novelist Peter Carey won the Booker Prize with his *True History of the Kelly Gang*.

23   Home Secretary David Blunkett announced that possessing cannabis will no longer be an arrestable offence. The drug is to be recategorised from a Class B to a Class C drug, putting it on par with anabolic steroids and tranquillisers. Possession will still be illegal, but most users will escape with a warning from the police.

29   Steffi Graf gives birth to a 5lb 7oz baby boy, Jaden Gil, at a private hospital in Las Vegas. André Agassi is the father.

CURRENT AFFAIRS

31   Baroness (Shirley) Williams of Crosby was elected leader of the Liberal Democrats in the House of Lords in succession to Lord Rogers of Quarry Bank.

November
1   Viscount Cranborne, the former leader of the Lords, announced his intention to leave the Upper House because of its new rules about declaration of interests.
2   It was announced that Joanna Riding would replace Martine McCutcheon as Eliza Doolittle in the West End production of *My Fair Lady*.
5   The new 20 million lira note, worth about £8.50, became legal tender in Turkey.
6   Michael Bloomberg, 59, defeated his Democratic Party rival Mark Green to secure the mayoralty of New York, the first time a Republican candidate has won consecutive elections. The present incumbent, Rudolph Giuliani, had served the maximum two terms allowed under New York state laws. Ulster Unionist leader David Trimble was re-elected as First Minister for Northern Ireland amid angry scenes inside the parliament buildings at Stormont. SDLP leader-elect Mark Durkan was elected Deputy First Minister.
7   Air France and British Airways Concordes resumed passenger flights following structural modifications made as a result of the Air France Concorde crash near Paris on 25 July 2000.
8   Henry McLeish resigned as Scotland's First Minister after a row over the sub-letting of his constituency office.
10   John Howard, the Liberal Party leader, began his third term as Australian Prime Minister.
12   American Airlines Airbus A300-600 (Flight 587) crashed soon after take-off from New York's JFK Airport killing all 255 passengers and crew as well as five people on the ground. The plane, bound for the Dominican Republic, came down in the Queens area of New York.
16   Ramadan, the Muslim month of fasting, began in Saudi Arabia, although the crescent moon was not sighted in Oman where the lunar month will begin tomorrow.
19   Stephen Byers, the Secretary of State for Transport, Local Government and the Regions, gave the go-ahead for a fifth terminal at Heathrow Airport, London, although the volume of traffic is to be capped at 480,000 per year, a rise of 20,000 on its present annual figures.
20   35 Western members of the banned Falun Gong sect were expelled from China following a protest in Tiananmen Square, Beijing. The protesters, including seven from Sweden and six from the United States of America, unfurled a yellow banner with their motto of 'Truthfulness, Compassion and Forbearance' before being arrested.
21   Jonathan King, the self-styled King of Hits, was sentenced to seven years' imprisonment for sex offences against schoolboys.
22   Jack McConnell (Labour) was elected First Minister of Scotland as replacement to Henry McLeish. In the first parliamentary by-election since the General Election, the Ipswich seat vacated by the deceased Jamie Cann was won by another Labour candidate, Christopher Mole.
28   The last remaining FMD notice was withdrawn from the 1,500 farms in Cumbria, North Yorkshire and County Durham at midnight, which officially brought the foot-and-mouth epidemic under control.
29   George Harrison, the youngest of The Beatles, died of cancer in Los Angeles.

December
3   The Segway Human Transporter, a cross between a hand mower and a micro scooter, was unveiled in New York. Dean Kamen, its inventor, believes it will revolutionise commuter travel and eventually displace cars.
4   Desperate Dan, the oldest character in the world's oldest comic, is 64 today.
6   The Countess of Wessex was airlifted to the King Edward VII hospital in London, where she underwent an operation for an ectopic pregnancy.
9   The Turner Prize was won by Martin Creed for his *Work 227: The lights going on and off*.
11   The BBC television chief Mark Thompson announced he is to become the new chief executive of Channel 4.
12   Roy Whiting was sentenced to life imprisonment for the abduction and murder of eight-year-old Sarah Payne.
20   Argentina's President de la Rúa resigned amid a wave of violent protests against the country's economic crisis.
23   A passenger on American Airlines Flight 63, who was travelling on a false passport under the name of Richard Reid, was overwhelmed by passengers and crew members as he attempted to light the detonating fuse of a C4 plastic explosive device concealed in the heel of his shoe. Police later gave his real name as Tariq Raja, a naturalised Briton.
26   JK Rowling, author of the Harry Potter books, married Dr Neil Murray in a private ceremony in Aberfeldy, Perthshire.
27   Iain Duncan Smith became the first Conservative Party leader to refuse to join the Carlton Club because it bars women from becoming full members.
31   The New Year's Honours List included knighthoods for radio broadcaster Jimmy Young and actor Ben Kingsley.

Obituaries 2001

January

1   Arthur Rudolph, German rocket scientist, born 9 Nov 1906
        Ray Walston, actor, born 2 Dec 1914
2   George Carman, barrister, born 6 Oct 1929
        William Rogers, US Secretary of State 1968–73, born 23 June 1913
3   George H Brown, film producer, born 24 July 1913
4   Les Brown, big band leader, born 14 March 1912
5   Professor Elizabeth Anscombe, philosopher, born 18 March 1919
        Melja Hlavsa, Czech rock musician, born 6 March 1951
7   James Carr, soul singer, born 13 June 1942
        Catherine Storr, children's author, born 21 July 1913
8   Paul Winterton (Andrew Garve), crime writer, born 12 Feb 1908
9   Paul Vanden Boeynants, Belgian politician, born 22 May 1919
10   Allan Davis, theatre producer, born 30 Aug 1913
        Sarah Raphael, artist, born 10 Aug 1960
11   Sir Denys Lasdun, architect, born 8 Sept 1914
        Michael Williams, actor, born 9 July 1935
        Lorna Sage, writer, born in 1943
12   Adhemar Da Silva, athlete, born 29 Sept 1927
        Kyra Vayne, opera singer, born 29 Jan 1916
16   Auberon Waugh, author and journalist, born 17 Nov 1939
        Laurent Kabila, President of the Democratic Republic of Congo, born 27 Nov 1939
18   Lord (Reginald) Prentice, politician, born 16 July 1923
        Gregory Corso, poet, born 26 March 1930
21   Antony Brown, newscaster and author, born 4 April 1922
24   Betty Kenward, society columnist (Jennifer's Diary), born 14 July 1906
25   Alfred Cohen, artist, born 9 May 1920
        Peggie Scriven, tennis player, born 17 Aug 1912
26   Stan Smith, artist, born 3 April 1929
        Keith Latham, baritone, born 27 Jan 1954
27   Marie José, last Queen of Italy, born in Ostend, Belgium on 4 Aug 1906
30   Air Vice-Marshal James Edgar ('Johnnie') Johnson, fighter ace, born 9 March 1915
        David Heneker, composer and lyricist, born 31 March 1906
        John Prebble, author and historian, born 23 June 1915

February

1   Abigail McCarthy, writer and journalist, born 16 April 1915
2   Patti Chamoun, model and actress, born 7 Sept 1928
4   Sonia Arova, ballerina, born 20 June 1926
        Iannis Xenakis, composer, born 29 May 1922
        JJ Johnson, trombone player and composer, born 22 Jan 1924
5   Inna Zubkovskaya, ballerina, born 29 Nov 1923
6   Sir Richard Southern, historian, born 8 Feb 1912
7   Anne Morrow Lindbergh (wife of Charles Lindbergh), author, born 22 June 1906
        Dale Evans, actress and singer, born 31 Oct 1912
8   Leslie Edwards, ballet dancer, born 6 Aug 1916
9   Reginald Marsh, actor, born 17 Sept 1926
10   Buddy Tate, jazz tenor saxophonist and bandleader, born 22 Feb 1912
        Abraham D Beame, former mayor of New York, born in London on 20 March 1906
12   Tiberio Mitri, boxer, born 12 July 1926
13   Moses Molelekwa, jazz pianist and composer, born 17 April 1973
14   Alan Ross, author and editor of the *London Magazine*, born 6 May 1922
15   Burt Kennedy, film director and screenwriter, born 3 Sept 1922
        Dave Dick, jockey, born 8 March 1924
17   Barry Burman, painter, born 14 June 1943
18   Balthus, portrait painter, born 29 Feb 1908
19   Stanley Kramer, film director, born 29 Sept 1913
        Charles Trenet, poet and singer, born 18 May 1913
20   Ronnie Hilton, singer, born 26 Jan 1927
22   Christopher Mitchell, actor, born 21 May 1947
        Lord Cledwyn of Penrhos, politician, born 14 Sept 1916
23   Dame Ruth Railton, founder of the National Youth Orchestra of Great Britain, born 14 Dec 1915
        Robert Enrico, film director, born in 1931
24   Donald Garrow, former British skiing champion, born 25 Jan 1918
        Andrew Mulligan, rugby player, born 4 Feb 1936
25   Sir Donald Bradman, cricketer, born 27 Aug 1908
        AR Ammons, poet, born 18 Feb 1926
27   Stan Cullis, footballer and manager, born 25 Oct 1915

CURRENT AFFAIRS

March

1	Joseph Cyril Bamford, inventor of the JCB, born 21 June 1916
2	John Diamond, journalist and broadcaster, born 10 May 1953
4	Glenn Hughes, singer with The Village People, born 18 July 1950
6	Portia Nelson, actress and author, born in 1921
7	Frankie Carle, bandleader and songwriter, born 25 March 1903
8	Dame Ninette de Valois, founder and director of the Royal Ballet, born 6 June 1898
10	Professor Sir Michael Woodruff, pioneer of transplant surgery, born 3 April 1911
12	Robert Ludlum, author, born 25 May 1927
13	Norman Rodway, actor, born 9 Feb 1929
15	Ann Sothern, actress, born 22 Jan 1909
17	Ralph Thomas, film director, born 10 Aug 1915
	John Napper, artist, born 17 Sept 1916
18	John Phillips, singer and songwriter, born 30 Aug 1935
19	Norman Mitchell, actor, born 27 Aug 1918
	Gordon Brown, rugby player, born 1 Nov 1947
22	William Hanna, animator, born 14 July 1910
23	Muriel Young, television presenter and producer, born 19 June 1928
	Willie Horne, rugby league player, born 23 Jan 1922
24	Brian Trubshaw, first Concorde test pilot, born 29 Jan 1924
27	Irene Thomas, radio personality and former Brain of Britain, born 28 June 1920
28	Jimmy Miller, singer, pianist and bandleader, born 30 Dec 1916
29	John Lewis, jazz pianist and composer, born 3 May 1920
31	David Rocastle, footballer, born 2 May 1967

April

1	Jean Anderson, actress, born 12 Dec 1907
3	John Clinch, sculptor, born 23 Nov 1934
5	Lord Malcolm Newton Shepherd, Leader of the House of Lords 1974–6, born 27 Sept 1918
9	Graziella Sciutti, soprano and opera director, born 17 April 1932
	Shakoor Rana, cricket umpire, born 3 April 1936
10	Nyree Dawn Porter, actress, born 22 Jan 1940
11	Sir Harry Secombe, comedian and singer, born 8 Sept 1921
13	Sydney Foley, marine artist, born 11 Nov 1916
	Jimmy Logan, entertainer, born 4 April 1928
14	Jim Baxter, footballer, born 29 Sept 1939
15	Joey Ramone, punk singer, born 19 May 1951
16	Alec Stock, football manager, born 30 March 1917
17	Michael Ritchie, film and television director, born 28 Nov 1938
18	Billy Mitchell, jazz tenor saxophonist, born 11 March 1926
19	Robert Paparemborde, French rugby player, born 5 July 1948
20	Giuseppe Sinopoli, composer and conductor, born 2 Nov 1946
	Bert Sutcliffe, New Zealand cricketer, born 17 Nov 1923
21	The Duke of Argyll, born 28 Aug 1937
	David Nathan, writer and critic, born 9 Dec 1926
23	David Walker, astronaut, born 20 May 1944
25	Michele Alboreto, Italian racing driver, born 23 Dec 1956
26	Guy Butler, writer, born 21 Jan 1918
	Bryon Butler, BBC Radio football correspondent, born 5 June 1934
27	John Winton, author, born 3 May 1931
28	Ken Hughes, film director, born 19 Jan 1922
	Paul Daneman, actor, born 26 Oct 1925
29	Rita Hunter, soprano, born 15 Aug 1933
	Hugh Macpherson, poet and diplomat, born 17 Feb 1953

May

2	Ted Rogers, comedian, born 20 July 1935
4	Billy Higgins, jazz drummer, born 11 Oct 1936
5	Boozoo Chavis, zydeco singer and accordionist, born 23 Oct 1930
9	Leslie Sands, actor and writer, born 19 May 1921
11	Douglas Adams, author, born 11 March 1952
12	Perry Como, singer, born 18 May 1913
	Didi, Brazilian footballer, born 8 Nov 1928
	Alexei Tupolev, aircraft designer of the Russian Concorde, born 20 May 1925
	Simon Raven, author, critic and dramatist, born 28 Dec 1927
13	RK Narayan, author, born 10 Oct 1906
14	Gil Langley, Australian wicketkeeper and batsman, born 14 Sept 1919
15	Bobby Murdoch, footballer, born 17 Aug 1944
17	Joe Baker, comic actor, born in 1928
19	Susannah McCorkle, US jazz singer, born 4 Jan 1946
20	Willie Foster, blues harmonica player, born 19 Sept 1921
22	Jack Watling, actor, born 13 Jan 1923

23	Jeno Fock, Hungarian politician, born 17 May 1916
25	Alberto Korda, photographer, born 14 Sept 1928
27	Victor Kiam, entrepreneur, born 7 Dec 1926
	Ralph Nichols, last British player to win the men's singles at the All England Badminton Championships, born 12 Aug 1910
29	John Fleming, writer on art, born 12 June 1919
30	Laurence Sterne, aeronautical engineer, born 2 July 1916
	Tony Long, sculptor, born 30 Aug 1942

June

1	King Birendra and Queen Aiswarya of Nepal, born 28 Dec 1945 and 7 Nov 1949 respectively
2	Joey Maxim, world light-heavyweight boxing champion 1950-52, born 28 March 1922
3	Anthony Quinn, actor, born 21 April 1915
4	King Dipendra of Nepal, born 27 June 1971
8	Rosemary Rapaport, violinist, born 29 March 1918
9	Malcolm Cooper, rifle shooter, born Dec 1947
	Ronnie Allen, footballer and manager, born 15 Jan 1929
	Yaltah Menuhin, pianist, born 7 Oct 1921
12	Joseph Brady, actor, born 9 Oct 1928
13	Sir David Spedding, chief of the Secret Intelligence Service 1994–9, born 7 March 1943
17	Cardinal Thomas Winning, Roman Catholic Archbishop of Glasgow 1974–2001, born 3 June 1925
	Professor Donald Cram, chemist, born 22 April 1919
18	Nan Kenway, comedienne and pianist, born 23 March 1905
19	David Sylvester, art critic, born 21 Sept 1924
20	Wallace Reyburn, author, born 3 July 1913
	Angela Browne, actress, born 14 June 1938
	Nancy Spender, painter, born 29 Oct 1909
21	John Lee Hooker, blues guitarist, born 22 Aug 1920
	Carroll O'Connor, actor, born 2 Aug 1924
	Soaad Husni (the Arab Cinderella), Egyptian actress, born 16 Dec 1943
26	Gina Cigna, opera singer, born 6 March 1900
27	Jack Lemmon, actor, born 8 Feb 1925
	Tove Jansson, Finnish artist and writer (creator of the Moomins), born 9 Aug 1914
28	Joan Sims, actress, born 9 May 1930
29	Mary Barnes, artist and writer, born 4 Feb 1923
30	Joe Henderson, jazz saxophonist, born 24 April 1937
	Chet Atkins, guitarist and record producer, born 20 June 1924
	Joe Fagan, football manager, born 12 March 1921

July

1	Halina Czerny-Stefanska, Polish pianist, born 31 Dec 1922
3	Billy Liddell, footballer, born 10 Jan 1922
	Mordecai Richler, author, born 27 Jan 1931
	Delia Derbyshire, composer of the *Dr Who* theme tune, born 5 May 1937
4	Arthur Concello, trapeze artist, born 26 March 1912
5	Ernie K-Doe, rhythm and blues singer, born 22 Feb 1936
7	Fred Neil, composer of 'Everybody's Talkin' ', born 1 Jan 1937
12	James Bernard, composer (of Hammer horror films) and screenwriter, born 20 Sept 1925
14	Arthur Worsley, ventriloquist, born 16 Oct 1920
16	Maurice de Bévère (Morris), Belgian cartoonist (creator of cowboy Lucky Luke), born 1 Dec 1923
17	Katharine Graham, publisher of *The Washington Post*, born 16 June 1917
18	Mimi Farina, singer, born 30 April 1945
	Jules Buck, film producer, born 30 July 1917
	Roy Gilchrist, West Indian cricketer, born 28 June 1934
19	Judy Clay, soul singer, born 12 Sept 1938
23	Eudora Welty, author, born 13 April 1909
24	Prince Fahd Salman, race-horse owner, born in 1955
25	Phoolan Devi (aka the Bandit Queen), Indian politician, born 10 Aug 1963
26	Josef Klaus, Austrian Chancellor 1964–70, born 15 Aug 1910
30	John Walters, musician and broadcaster, born 16 May 1938
31	Marshal Francisco da Costa Gomes, former President of Portugal, born 30 June 1914
	Bert Foord, BBC television weatherman, born 22 Dec 1930

August

1	Joe Lynch, actor, born 16 July 1925
3	Francis Aungier Pakenham, 7th Earl of Longford, social reformer, born 5 Dec 1905
	Gina Ware, actress and owner of the Gateways Club, the first openly lesbian club in England, born 18 March 1922
4	Binkie Stuart (real name Elisabeth Alison Fraser), child actress, born 11 March 1932
	Joseph Cooper, pianist and broadcaster, born 7 Oct 1912
5	Kenneth MacDonald, actor, born 20 Nov 1950
6	Dorothy Tutin, actress, born 8 April 1931

CURRENT AFFAIRS

7	Larry Adler, harmonica player, born 10 Feb 1914
8	George Mann, cricketer and war hero, born 6 Sept 1917
11	Percy Stallard, founder of modern-day road cycle racing, born 19 July 1909
13	Jimmy Knapp, general secretary, National Union of Railwaymen 1983–90 and RMT since 1990, born 29 Sept 1940
14	Nicolas Orloff, dancer, born in 1914
17	Anthony Earnshaw, artist and writer, born 9 Oct 1924
19	Donald Woods, anti-apartheid campaigner, born 15 Dec 1933
	Les Sealey, goalkeeper, born 29 Sept 1957
20	Sir Frederick Hoyle, astronomer and writer, born 24 June 1915
	Kim Stanley, actress, born 11 Feb 1925
22	Bernard Heuvelmans, cryptozoologist, born 10 Oct 1916
23	Kathleen Freeman, actress, born 17 Feb 1919
24	Jane Greer, actress, born 9 Sept 1924
25	Ken Tyrrell, Formula One team owner, born 3 May 1924
	Aaliyah (Haughton), singer and actress, born 16 Jan 1979
28	Juan Munoz, sculptor, born 17 June 1953
30	Govan Mbeki, writer, politician and former political prisoner, born 9 July 1910
31	Lord Hamlyn, publisher and philanthropist, born 12 Feb 1926

September

1	Brian Moore, football commentator, born 28 Feb 1932
	Bobby Evans, footballer, born 16 April 1927
2	Christiaan Barnard, heart surgeon, born 8 Nov 1922
	Troy Donahue, actor, born 27 Jan 1936
3	Pauline Kael, film critic, born 19 June 1919
5	Terry Gilbert, dancer and choreographer, born 11 Sept 1932
9	Lord Sefton of Garston, former chairman of Merseyside County Council, born 5 Aug 1915
11	Barbara Olson, lawyer and biographer of Hillary Clinton, died on American Airlines flight 77, born in 1956
	David Angell, executive producer of Frasier, died on American Airlines flight 11, born in 1947
	Berry Berenson, photographer and actress, former wife of Anthony Perkins, died on American Airlines flight 11, born in 1948
	Henry George Reginald Molyneux Herbert, 7th Earl of Carnarvon, born 19 Jan 1924
12	Alex Scott, footballer, born 22 Nov 1936
13	Jaroslav Drobny, tennis player, born 12 Oct 1921
	Dorothy McGuire, actress, born 14 June 1918
14	Stelios Kazantzidis, singer, born 29 Aug 1931
15	Ahmad Shah Masood, Mujahedin leader (aka Lion of Panjshir), born in 1953
16	Sam Arkoff, film producer, born 12 June 1918
17	Thomas 'Dickie' Dodds, cricketer, born 29 May 1919
	Sandy Saddler, former world featherweight boxing champion, born 23 June 1926
19	Jane Dudley, dancer and choreographer, born 3 April 1912
20	Marcos Pérez Jiménez, former President of Venezuela 1952–8, born in 1914
22	Isaac Stern, violinist, born 21 July 1920
24	Lord Shore of Stepney, former Labour MP, born 24 May 1924
27	Helen Cherry, actress, born 24 Nov 1915
28	Irina von Meyendorff, actress, born 6 June 1916
29	Nguyen Van Thieu, President of South Vietnam 1967–75, born 5 April 1923
	Gellu Naum, poet, born 1 Aug 1915

October

2	Manny Albam, jazz composer, born 22 June 1922
3	Tatiana Menotti, soprano, born 24 June 1909
	Charles Stewart, children's book illustrator and authority on costume, born 18 Nov 1915
4	Patsy Burt, racing driver, born 10 July 1928
	Gerd Larsen, ballet dancer, born 19 Feb 1921
5	Emilie Schindler, wartime industrialist, born 22 Oct 1907
	Peter Burge, Australian cricketer and first match referee to suspend a player, born 17 May 1932
7	Reg Matthews, former Coventry and England footballer, born 20 Dec 1932
	Alf Gover, cricketer, born 29 Feb 1908
8	Laurie MacMillan, BBC Radio newsreader, born 10 May 1947
9	Herbert Ross, film director and choreographer, born 13 May 1927
10	Eddie Futch, boxing trainer, born 9 Aug 1911
12	Lord Hailsham of Saint Marylebone, Lord Chancellor 1970–4 and 1979–87, born 9 Oct 1907
15	Anne Ridler, poet and translator of opera libretti, born 30 July 1912
17	Jay Livingston, songwriter, born 28 March 1915
20	Roy Ullyett, sports cartoonist, born 16 March 1914
21	Professor Sir John Plumb, historian, born 20 Aug 1911
	Bertie Mee, double-winning Arsenal FC manager, born 25 Dec 1918
25	Daniel Wildenstein, racehorse breeder and owner, born 11 Sept 1917
	Princess Soraya Esfandiari Bakhtiari, former Iranian royal consort, born 22 June 1932
26	Richard Seifert, architect, born 25 Nov 1910

29   Colin Deveraux, female impersonator (Dockyard Doris), born 8 Feb 1951
        Spike Robinson, jazz saxophonist, born 16 Jan 1930
31   Jenny Laird, actress, born 13 Feb 1912

November
2   Julian Holland, journalist and author, born 22 Dec 1907
3   Professor Sir Ernst Gombrich, art historian, born 30 March 1909
4   Michael Ivens, poet and journalist, born 15 March 1924
5   Roy Boulting, film producer and director, born 21 Nov 1913
6   Anthony Shaffer, playwright and screenwriter, born 15 May 1926
7   Ronald Townsend (Smokey the Clown), born 18 April 1925
9   Nancye Bolton, tennis player, born 10 June 1917
        Denis Atkinson, cricketer, born 9 Aug 1926
10   Ken Kesey, author, born 17 Sept 1935
11   Sir Denis Spotswood, Marshal of the Royal Air Force and Chief of the Air Staff 1971–4, born 26 Sept 1916
12   Tony Miles, Britain's first chess grandmaster, born 23 April 1955
13   Peggy Mount, actress, born 2 May 1916
        Cornelius Warmerdam, pole-vaulter (first to clear 15 feet), born 22 June 1915
14   Allan Leat, musician and discographer, born 23 Nov 1916
        Charlotte Coleman, actress, born 3 April 1968
15   Darrell Viner, installation artist, born 12 Dec 1946
16   Tommy Flanagan, jazz pianist, born 16 March 1930
17   Michael Karoli, guitarist with German band Can, born 29 April 1948
18   Katharine Moore, writer, born 25 April 1898
21   Sultan Salahuddin Abdul Aziz Shah, 11th King of Malaysia, born 8 March 1926
        Seymour Reit, writer and illustrator (Casper the Friendly Ghost), born 11 Nov 1918
23   Mary Whitehouse, television campaigner against sex and violence, born 13 June 1910
        Gerhard Stoltenberg, German Minister of Defence 1989–92, born 29 Sept 1928
24   Rachel Gurney, actress, born 2 March 1920
        Melanie Thornton, singer with La Bouche, born 13 May 1967
25   David Gascoyne, poet, born 10 Oct 1916
28   Norman Lumsden, opera singer and actor (JR Hartley), born 16 Sept 1906
        Sir Richard Trehane, chairman of the Milk Marketing Board 1958–77, born 13 July 1913
29   George Harrison, guitarist, singer and composer, born 25 Feb 1943
        John Knowles, novelist, born 16 Sept 1926
        Budd Boetticher, film director, born 29 July 1916
        Maurice Cullen, boxer, born 30 Dec 1937

December
2   Carlos Sancha, portrait painter, born 27 April 1920
3   Gerhart Riegner, Secretary-General of the World Jewish Congress 1965–83, born 12 Sept 1911
        Viktor Fedotov, conductor, born 8 July 1933
6   Sir Peter Blake, yachtsman, born 1 Oct 1948
        David Astor, editor of *The Observer* 1948–75, born 5 March 1912
9   Field Marshal Lord Carver, Chief of the Defence Staff, 1973–6, born 24 April 1915
11   John Mitchum, actor, born 6 Sept 1919
12   Professor Ardito Desio, geologist and leader of the first expedition to climb K2, born 18 April 1897
14   WG Sebald, German author and scholar, born 18 May 1944
        Conte Candoli, jazz trumpeter, born 12 July 1927
        Olive Norton, ballerina and teacher, born 25 Nov 1918
16   Martha Mödl, opera singer, born 22 March 1912
        Stuart Adamson, rock singer with Big Country, born 11 April 1958
18   Clifford T Ward, singer and songwriter, born 10 Feb 1946
20   Leopold Senghor, President of Senegal 1960–80, born 9 Oct 1906
26   Sir Nigel Hawthorne, actor, born 5 April 1929
27   Paul Hogarth, artist, born 4 Oct 1917
        Ian Hamilton, poet and biographer, born 24 March 1938
29   Takashi Asahina, conductor, born in 1908
30   Ralph Sutton, jazz pianist, born 4 Nov 1922
31   John Grigg, writer and historian, born 15 April 1924

CURRENT AFFAIRS

Sporting Record 2001

January
3   Phil Taylor won his ninth world darts championship when he defeated John Part of Canada 7–0 in the Skol-sponsored version of the championship, at the Circus Tavern, Purfleet, Essex.

Daryll Cullinan of South Africa scored his fourth consecutive century in Test innings, at Newlands, Cape Town.

7   Ted Hankey, the reigning Embassy world darts champion, won his first round match against Shaun Greatbatch despite a 20-minute interruption for a female streaker.

9   Jacques Kallis of South Africa scored his first one-day international century in 53 matches during his side's eight-wicket win over Sri Lanka at Paarl.

11   Trina Gulliver defeated her fellow Briton Mandy Solomons 2–1 to win the Embassy Women's World Darts Championship at the Lakeside Country Club, Frimley Green.

14   John Walton defeated Ted Hankey 6–2 in the Embassy World Darts Championship final at Frimley Green, Surrey.

17   Mark Foster of Great Britain set a world 50 metres butterfly short-course record of 22.87sec in Sheffield.

21   Mark Foster of Great Britain set a European 50 metres freestyle short-course record of 21.24sec in Berlin.

24   The Linda McCartney–Jacobs Creek cycling team, led by Max Sciandri of Great Britain, was disbanded.

25   Andrew Magee of the USA scored a hole in one on the par four 333-yard 17th hole at the Tournament Players Course at Scotsdale, during the first round of the Phoenix Open. This feat has only ever been equalled once before, in 1971 when little-known tournament pro John Hudson holed out on the 314-yard 12th hole in the Martini International at Royal Norwich.

26   After 52 rounds of par or better in US PGA Tour events Tiger Woods shot a two-over-par 73 in the second round of the Phoenix Open.

28   Mark Foster of Great Britain set a world 50 metres freestyle short-course record of 21.13sec in Paris.

Mark Calcavecchia of the United States won the Phoenix Open with a 28-under-par 256.

29   The Baltimore Ravens beat the New York Giants 34–7 in Super Bowl XXXV at the Raymond James Stadium, Florida.

The International Paralympic Committee suspended all intellectually disabled athletes, pending a review following criticism that most of Spain's victorious basketball team were found to have no mental disability.

30   Neil Smith, the former world champion, won the St James's Place British professional rackets title.

February
2   Martina Ertl of Germany won the women's combined gold medal at the world skiing championships in St Anton, Austria.

3   In the Six Nations Rugby Union Championship England beat Wales 44–15 and Ireland beat Italy 41–22.

4   France beat Scotland 16–6 In the Six Nations Rugby Union Championship at the Stade de France.

6   Michaela Dormeister of Austria won the gold medal in the women's downhill at the world skiing championships.

Kjetil Andre Aamodt of Norway won the men's combined gold medal at the world championships in St Anton, Austria.

7   Hannes Trinkl of Austria won the men's downhill gold medal at the world skiing championships in St Anton, Austria.

Anja Paerson of Sweden won the women's slalom gold medal as World Cup slalom leader Janica Kostelic, of Croatia, failed to win a medal.

8   Michael von Grünigen of Switzerland won the men's giant slalom gold at the world championships in St Anton, Austria.

11   Ellen MacArthur, 24, became the fastest woman and youngest person to circumnavigate the world in a single-handed race when she finished second in the 24,000-mile Vendée Globe race in her 60ft yacht *Kingfisher Challenge*.

Wang Liqin of China, the world No. 1 table tennis player, won the Sportingbet English Open with a 21–18, 21–10, 21–19, win over Christophe Legout, of France.

Paul Hunter beat Fergal O'Brien 10–9 in the final of the Benson and Hedges Masters at Wembley Conference Centre.

14   Scott Allison, the Sheffield Steelers forward, was suspended for a record 14 matches for his part in a brawl with Nottingham Panthers' players during an ice hockey match on 9 February.

15   Jason Queally, the 1,000 metres individual sprint gold medal winner at the Sydney Olympics, was hospitalised in Florida following a fall from his bike whilst training with the British squad.

17   In the Six Nations Rugby Union Championship England beat Italy 80–23. In other matches Ireland beat France 22–15 and Scotland and Wales drew 28–28.

18   Tim Henman beat Andreas Vinciguerra 6–3, 6–4, to claim the Copenhagen Open tennis title.

Colin Montgomerie of Scotland won the Australian Masters golf title.

Alexandra Coomber of Great Britain won her second consecutive World Cup skeleton bob title in Park City, Utah.

19   American racing driver Dale Earnhardt was killed in a crash on the last lap of the Daytona 500.

24   Roy Jones Jr beat Derrick Harmon, who failed to start the 11th round of their WBA, WBC and IBF light-heavyweight title fight, in Tampa, Florida.

25   City of Ely beat White Knights 82–75 in the Canada Life National Inter-Club Bowls Championships for the Denny Cup.

26   Sri Lanka defeated England by an innings and 28 runs in the first Test match, at the Esplanade Ground, Galle, Sri Lanka.
27   Horse racing was suspended due to the foot-and-mouth crisis.

March
3   In the Six Nations Rugby Union Championship England beat Scotland 43–3 and France defeated Italy 30–19.
      The Wales versus Ireland game at the Millennium Stadium was postponed due to the threat of spreading foot-and-mouth.
4   Michael Schumacher won the Australian Formula One Grand Prix on the Alber Park circuit in Melbourne, but the race was marred by the death of a marshal.
      Hermann Maier of Austria won his fourth World Cup giant-slalom title after winning at Kvitfjell, Norway.
      Peter Scantlebury became the leading scorer in British basketball history in Sheffield Sharks' 93–88 victory over Newcastle Eagles. His 16-point tally gave him a total of 8,961 to overhaul the record of Russ Saunders.
9   The first gold medal of the eighth World Indoor Athletics Championships was won by Paolo Camossi of Italy who jumped 17.32 metres to narrowly beat Jonathan Edwards in the triple jump.
      Former Prime Minister John Major was elected to the committee of the MCC.
11   England beat Sri Lanka by three wickets in the second Test at the Asgiriya Stadium, Kandy, to level the series 1–1.
      Daniel Caines of Great Britain won the 400 metres gold medal at the World Indoor Athletics Championships in Lisbon.
15   India won an unlikely victory over Australia by 171 runs at Eden Gardens, Calcutta. Following on 274 runs behind the Australian first innings total they amassed a second innings 657 for 7 before bowling out the Aussies for 212.
      Liverpool beat FC Porto 2–0 (2–0 on agg) to reach the semi-finals of the Uefa Cup.
16   Annika Sorenstam of Sweden became the first woman golfer to shoot a sub-60 round in a bona fide tour event when she scored a 59 in the Standard Register Ping tournament in Phoenix, Arizona.
      George Graham was dismissed as Tottenham Hotspur FC manager.
17   England beat Sri Lanka by four wickets in the third Test in Colombo, to win the three-match series 2–1.
      Leicester won their third rugby union Zurich Premiership in succession following a 51–7 trouncing of Newcastle.
      In the Six Nations Rugby Union Championship Scotland beat Italy 23–19 and Wales defeated France 43–35.
18   Michael Schumacher won the Malaysian Formula One Grand Prix on the Sepang circuit, Kuala Lumpur.
      Des Smyth at 48 years and 34 days became the oldest winner in the history of the European golf tour when he won the Madeira Island Open. Neil Coles was the previous oldest when he won the Sanyo Open in 1982, albeit 22 days younger.
      Oxford beat Hatfield 4–1 to win the Pol Roger National Inter-Club real tennis championship at Moreton Morrell.
      Dario Frigo of Italy, riding for Fasso Bortolo, won the Paris–Nice seven-stage cycle race.
19   West Indian pace bowler Courtney Walsh captured his 500th Test wicket when he dismissed Jacques Kallis in the second Test against South Africa in Port of Spain.
20   Alain Baxter and Emma Carrick-Anderson won the men's and women's British Land National Championships giant slalom titles, in Saalbach-Hinterglemm, Austria.
21   Peter Nicol, the world squash champion, signed to represent England rather than his native Scotland, as England's lottery-funded World Class Performance Programme was deemed more beneficial for his professional future.
23   Emma Carrick-Anderson won the British Land National Championships slalom title, in Saalbach-Hinterglemm, Austria.
24   Cambridge beat Oxford by two and a half lengths in the 147th Boat Race, notable for its first-ever restart after 23 strokes as the crews locked oars. Goldie (Cambridge) beat Isis (Oxford) by six lengths in the reserve race.
      Paula Radcliffe won the World Cross Country Championship long-course race in Ostend, Belgium.
      Ice-skater Michelle Kwan of the United States retained her women's title in the World Championships in Vancouver.
25   England defeated Finland 2–1 at Anfield to reach second place in World Cup qualifying Group nine. Ireland defeated Cyprus 4–0 in Group two to remain in second place and Scotland drew 2–2 with Belgium to maintain second spot in Group six. Wales only managed a 2–2 draw with Armenia in Group five and Northern Ireland were beaten 1–0 by the Czech Republic in Group three and both were struggling in fourth place in their groups.
26   Tiger Woods won the Players Championship in Ponte Vedra Beach, Florida, by a stroke from Vijay Singh of Fiji.
29   Horse racing resumed after the foot-and-mouth crisis with meetings at Exeter and Musselburgh.

April
1   Ronnie O'Sullivan beat Stephen Hendry 9–8 to win the Irish Masters snooker title at the City-West Hotel, Dublin.
      McLaren's David Coulthard won the Brazilian formula One Grand Prix on the Interlagos circuit, São Paulo, Brazil. His success ended Michael Schumacher's run of six consecutive Grand Prix wins.
4   Dubravko Rajcevic, 46, was found guilty by a Miami jury of stalking Swiss tennis player Martina Hingis.
7   Marco Antonio Barrera defeated Naseem Hamed on a unanimous points count in Las Vegas to win the

vacant IBO World Featherweight Championship whilst Luton-based Billy Schwer won a points decision over Newton Villareal at the Wembley Conference Centre, London, to win the IBO Light-Welterweight Championship.

England defeated France 48–19 in the Six-Nations Rugby Union Championship whilst Wales beat Italy 33–23 in Rome.

Red Marauder won the Grand National from Smarty with the other 38 runners all failing to complete the course, however Blowing Wind and Papillon were remounted to finish third and fourth.

8	Tiger Woods won the US Masters from David Duval and Phil Mickelson.
11	Nick Faldo and his former caddie Fanny Sunesson reunited for a golf tournament on Hilton Head Island, South Carolina.
14	Sir Alex Ferguson became the most successful manager in English football as Manchester United clinched their seventh Premiership crown in nine years.
15	Ralf Schumacher won the San Marino Formula One Grand Prix at Imola.
16	Fulham gained a 1–1 draw with Sheffield Wednesday to become champions of the Nationwide League first division.

Markus Fuchs of Switzerland on Tinka's Boy claimed his first showjumping World Cup, thwarting a fourth successive win by Rodrigo Pessoa, the world champion from Brazil.

Bong-Ju Lee of South Korea won the 105th Boston Marathon in a time of 2hr 9min 43sec, ending a 10-year winning streak by Kenyan runners in the world's oldest continuing marathon.

17	Valencia beat Arsenal 1–0 (2–2 on agg) and proceed to the semi-finals of the European Cup on the away goals rule.

Leeds beat Deportivo La Coruña 3–2 on aggregate and proceed to the semi-finals of the European Cup despite losing the second leg 2–0.

18	Bayern Munich beat Manchester United 2–1 (3–1 on agg) in the quarter-finals of the European Cup.
22	Moroccan Abdelkader El Mouaziz and Ethiopian Derartu Tulu won the men's and women's Flora London Marathon. Tanni Grey-Thompson gained her fifth London victory in the women's wheelchair race.

Lennox Lewis was knocked out by American Hasim Rahman in the fifth round of their undisputed heavyweight title fight in Carnival City, Johannesburg.

23	Courtney Walsh, the West Indian fast bowler, retired from Test cricket following his team's 130-run victory over South Africa at Sabina Park. Walsh's final record tally of wickets stood at 519.

Ruud van Nistelroy became the most expensive player in British football when Manchester United paid PSV Eindhoven £19 million for his services.

24	The annual Isle of Man TT motor-cycle races were cancelled for the first time other than during the world wars as the foot-and-mouth crisis reached epidemic proportions.
28	Tony McCoy won the National Hunt Jockey's Championship with a final total of 191 wins.

Joe Calzaghe stopped Mario Veit in the first round to retain his World Boxing Organisation super-middleweight title.

29	Michael Schumacher won the Spanish Formula One Grand Prix in Barcelona.

May

5	Golan, ridden by Keiren Fallon and trained by Michael Stoute, won the Sagitta 2,000 Guineas at Newmarket.
6	Colin McRae won Rally Argentina from his arch-rival Richard Burns.

Ameerat, ridden by Philip Robinson and trained by Michael Jarvis, won the Sagitta 1,000 Guineas at Newmarket.

7	Ronnie O'Sullivan beat John Higgins 18–14 in the Embassy World Snooker Championship final at the Crucible, Sheffield.
8	Valencia beat Leeds United 3–0 (3–0 on agg) in the semi-final, second leg, of the European Cup.
9	Bayern Munich defeated Real Madrid 2–1 (3–1 on agg) to reach the European Cup final.
12	Liverpool defeated Arsenal 2–1 to win the first FA Cup final held at the Millennium Stadium, Cardiff.

Felix Trinidad, the unbeaten Puerto Rican boxer, knocked out American William Joppy to win the WBA middleweight championship in Madison Square Garden, New York.

13	Ronnie O'Sullivan defeated Stephen Hendry 9–7 in the Sportingbet.co.uk Premier League snooker final.
18	West Indies star batsman Brian Lara turned out for Lashings, a Maidstone pub side, against the University of Kent and scored 77 off 58 balls before being caught and bowled by Vishal Agarwal, 20, a second-year student of actuarial science. Lashings, who also numbered television presenter Jamie Theakston among their eleven, won the match by 115 runs.
19	England cricket captain Nasser Hussain had his right thumb broken by a delivery from Shoaib Akhtar during the first npower Test against Pakistan.

Audley Harrison, the Olympic super-heavyweight boxing champion, made a successful professional debut by stopping American Mike Middleton in the first round at the Wembley Arena, London.

21	George Burley, the manager of Ipswich Town, was named manager of the year for steering his team to fifth in the FA Carling Premiership and qualifying for the Uefa Cup.
22	Althea Storm, a four-year-old greyhound, beat Speckled Jim, a five-year-old pigeon, in a special race at Wimbledon Greyhound Stadium.
24	Former England manager Kevin Keegan returned to football as manager of Manchester City.
25	England defeated Mexico 4–0 in an international football friendly at Pride Park.
26	Black Minnaloushe, ridden by Johnny Murtagh, won the Irish 2,000 Guineas and Aiden O'Brien trained the first three home.
27	Michael Schumacher won the Monaco Formula One Grand Prix to extend his lead in the world drivers championship.

Imagine, ridden by Seamus Heffernan and trained by Aiden O'Brien, won the Entenmann's Irish 1,000 Guineas.

June
2   Despite Vinnie Jones, the actor, having two dogs in the final, Rapid Ranger won the Greyhound Derby at Wimbledon.
4   Pakistan beat England by 108 runs in the second npower Test match at Old Trafford to level the two-match series.
6   England beat Greece 2–0 in Athens to close the gap to six points on Germany in Group Nine of the World Cup qualifiers.
8   Imagine, ridden by Mick Kinane and trained by Aiden O'Brien, won the Vodafone Oaks at Epsom.
9   Galileo, ridden by Mick Kinane and trained by Aiden O'Brien, won the Vodafone Derby at Epsom.
10 Ralf Schumacher won the Canadian Formula One Grand Prix in Montreal, beating his brother Michael into second.
    Point Given, ridden by Gary Stevens, won the Belmont Stakes by over 12 lengths in New York.
17 Colin McRae and his co-driver Nick Grist won the Acropolis Rally.
24 Michael Schumacher won the European Formula One Grand Prix at the Nürburgring from Colombian Juan Pablo Montoya.
27 Barry Cowan from Ormskirk was narrowly beaten by Pete Sampras 6–3, 6–2, 6–7, 4–6, 6–3, in the 2nd round at Wimbledon.
29 Pete Sampras equalled Rod Laver's record of 31 consecutive wins at Wimbledon when he defeated Armenian Sargis Sargsian in the third round.

July
1   Michael Schumacher won the French Formula One Grand Prix at Magny Cours, beating his brother Ralf into second.
2   Pete Sampras was beaten by Roger Federer in the fourth round of the Wimbledon Championships.
6   Pat Rafter defeated André Agassi in the semi-finals of the Wimbledon Men's Singles Championship.
7   The Lions rugby union team were beaten 35–14 by Australia.
8   Goran Ivanisevic defeated Tim Henman in the semi-finals of the Wimbledon Men's Singles Championship.
    Australia defeated England by an innings in the first Ashes Test after the last seven wickets fell for 22 runs.
    Zinedine Zidane, the French midfielder, moved from Juventus to Real Madrid for an estimated £45.62 million.
9   Goran Ivanisevic, world-ranked 125, defeated Pat Rafter 6–3, 3–6, 6–3, 2–6, 9–7 to become the first wild card entry to win a grand slam tennis event, the Wimbledon Men's Singles Championship.
10 Katie Summers, 16, from Gloucester, qualified as Britain's youngest female football referee.
11 Goran Ivanisevic rose 73 places to 52 in the latest ATP Champions Race rankings; André Agassi remains number one.
13 The 122-member International Olympic Committee voted Beijing as the venue for the 2008 Olympic Games.
14 Martin Lee of Great Britain was defeated 6–1, 6–4 by Neville Godwin of South Africa in his first ATP Tour final in Newport, Rhode Island, but rose to 95 in the ATP Champions Race.
    Dwain Chambers ran 10.01sec for 100 metres at the Norwich Union World Championships trials in Birmingham, the fastest-ever run by a Briton on home soil.
15 Mika Hakkinen won the British Formula One Grand Prix at Silverstone.
16 Jacques Rogge, a 59-year-old Belgian orthopaedic surgeon, was elected President of the International Olympic Committee (IOC) as replacement for Juan Antonio Samaranch.
20 Tim Henman announced that Larry Stefanki would be his new tennis coach as replacement for David Felgate.
22 Ian Woosnam was penalised two strokes in the final round of the British Open for having 15 clubs in his bag. His caddie Miles Byrne took full responsibility for failing to notice the additional club.

August
4   Guinea Hunter, ridden by Jamie Spencer, won the Vodafone Stewards' Cup at Goodwood.
12 Olga Yegorova of Russia won the gold medal for 5,000 metres at the World Athletic Championships despite failing a drug test for erythropoietin (EPO). The testers failed to back up the urine sample with a blood test, thereby nullifying the test.
13 Britain managed only one gold medal at the World Athletic Championships in Edmonton by way of Jonathan Edwards in the Triple Jump.
15 Holland defeated England 2–0 in a friendly football International at White Hart Lane.
    Michael Schumacher won the Hungarian GP in Budapest to gain his fourth Formula One drivers' championship.
20 England beat Australia by six wickets in the fourth Test match at Headingley.
24 Liverpool beat Bayern Munich 3–2 in Monaco to win the European Super Cup.
25 Matthew Pinsent and James Cracknell won a gold medal in the coxed pairs at the World Rowing Championships and two hours later won a second gold in the coxless pairs.
    Manchester United FC sold Dutch defender Jaap Stam to Lazio for £18 million.
    Australia defeated England by an innings and 25 runs in the fifth and final Test at the Oval to win the series 4–1.
28 Former England cricket captain Mike Atherton announced his retirement from first-class cricket.
31 American wonder-horse Point Given, winner of the Preakness and Belmont Stakes, was retired following an injury.

September
1   England defeated Germany 5–1 in Berlin to keep their hopes of automatic World Cup qualifying alive. In other qualifying groups the Republic of Ireland defeated Holland, Scotland drew with Croatia and Wales drew with Armenia.
    Somerset defeated Leicester by 41 runs to become the first holders of the C&G Trophy, the former Gillette Cup.

2   Sam Torrance named the wild card entries for the European Ryder Cup team as Sergio Garcia and Jesper Parnevik. The two American wild card entries were announced as Paul Azinger and Scott Verplank.
      World Formula One world champion Michael Schumacher won the Belgian GP to exceed the 52 wins of Alain Prost.

5   England defeated Albania 2–0 at St James' Park to top World Cup qualifying group nine. In other qualifying games Belgium beat Scotland 2–0, Norway defeated Wales 3–2, and Northern Ireland beat Iceland 3–0.
      Dwain Chambers secured a gold medal for Britain in the 100 metres at the Goodwill Games in Brisbane.

8   The Godolphin team's Fantastic Light, ridden by Frankie Dettori, defeated the unbeaten Galileo in the Irish Champion Stakes at Leopardstown.

15   CART driver Alex Zanardi lost both his legs in a high-speed crash in Germany.
      The Rothmans Royals St Leger was won by Milan, ridden by Michael Kinane and trained by AP O'Brien.
      The Jefferson Smurfit Memorial Irish St Leger was won by Vinnie Roe, ridden by Pat Smullen and trained by DK Weld

16   The Ryder Cup was postponed for one year following the terrorist attacks on North America. It was agreed that next year's event will be played with the same teams chosen for the 2001 event irrespective of current form.
      Juan Pablo Montoya of Colombia won the Italian Formula One Grand Prix at Monza.
      Jason Bohn from North America scored the lowest-ever score in a professional golf tournament, 58, when winning the Bayer Classic on the Canadian Tour.

17   Pittsburgh Pirates played New York Mets in the first baseball match since the atrocities of 11 September.
      Tony McCoy broke the record for the fastest 100 winners of the National Hunt season by seven weeks.

22   British Olympic boxing champion Audley Harrison won his second professional bout with a hard-fought points win over Derek McCafferty at the TeleWest Arena in Newcastle.

23   Great Britain beat Ecuador 4–1 in the Davis Cup to regain their position in the world elite.

29   Bernard Hopkins of the USA stopped the previously unbeaten Felix Trinidad of Puerto Rica in the 12th round of their unification fight to become the first undisputed World Middleweight boxing champion since Sugar Ray Leonard in 1987.

30   Tony Rickardsson of Sweden became World Speedway Champion, although Jason Crump won the final GP in Sweden.
      Troy Bayliss of Australia became World Superbike Champion at Imola.
      Mika Hakkinen won the US Grand Prix in Indianapolis.

October

2   Olga Yegorova of Russia, who won the gold medal for 5,000 metres at the World Athletic Championships despite failing a drug test, had her doping case dropped by French authorities.

6   David Beckham scored a late equaliser in the 2–2 draw with Greece at Old Trafford to ensure World Cup qualification.

7   Sakhee, trained by Saeed bin Suroor and ridden by Frankie Dettori, won the Prix de' l'Arc de Triomphe at Longchamp.
      Paula Radcliffe retained her world half-marathon title in Bristol.

9   Nicola Cooke of Great Britain won the gold medal in the junior women's cycling time trial at the World Championships in Lisbon.

13   Joe Calzaghe completed his ninth successful defence of his WBO super-middleweight title when he defeated Will McIntyre in the fourth round. Mike Tyson beat Brian Nielsen in the seventh round on the same Danish bill.
      Gérard Houllier underwent heart surgery after suffering chest pains during Liverpool's 1–1 draw against Leeds at Anfield.

14   Ian Woosnam beat Padraig Harrington in the final of the Cisco World Matchplay Championship at Wentworth.
      Pippa Funnell, riding Supreme Rock, gained her second successive European three-day event title in Pau, France.
      Michael Schumacher won the Japanese Grand Prix to gain his ninth Formula One win of the season.

17   England defeated Romania 134–0 at Twickenham, a world record rugby union Test score, with Charlie Hodgson scoring an England individual record of 44 points.

20   Audley Harrison knocked out Piotr Jurczyk in the second round at Glasgow's Kelvin Hall to gain his third straight win.

21   Snooker player Stephen Lee defeated Peter Ebdon 9-4 in the final of the LG Cup in Preston.

27   Ricky 'Hitman' Hatton stopped Freddie Pendleton in the second round to retain his WBU light-welterweight boxing title.

28   Tim Henman defeated Roger Federer 6–3, 6–4, 6–2, in the Davidoff Swiss Indoors final in Basle.

30   Michael Jordan made his second return to professional basketball playing for Washington Wizards.

November

10   England drew 1–1 with Sweden in a friendly football international.

11   Following seven runner-up positions on the European Golf Tour, Padraig Harrington won the Volvo Masters in Jerez, Spain, by one stroke from Paul McGinley.

15   Ireland were beaten 1–0 by Iran but go through to the football World Cup finals 2–1 on aggregate.

17   Lennox Lewis regained the WBC and IBF world heavyweight boxing titles after knocking out Hasim Rahman in the fourth round of their scheduled 12-round contest in Las Vegas.

18   Ernie Els and Retief Goosen of South Africa won golf's EMC World Cup in Taiheiyo, Japan.

22   Tiger Woods won the Grand Slam of Golf title, for the four major winners, for the fourth consecutive year.

23	Colin McRae, the leader of the rally drivers' championship, crashed out of the Network Q Rally of Great Britain.
24	Dario Gradi celebrated his 1,000th game as a football manager when his Crewe team drew 2–2 with Norwich.
25	Richard Burns became England's first world rally champion, and Britain's first since Colin McRae in 1995, when he took third place in the Network Q Rally of Great Britain.
30	Adrian Maguire became the seventh National Hunt jockey to ride 1,000 winners when Fiori won at Carlisle.

December

1	The England football team was drawn with Argentina, Nigeria and Sweden in Group F for the 2002 World Cup finals.
	What's Up Boys, trained by Philip Hobbs and ridden by Paul Flynn, won the Hennessy Gold Cup at Newbury.
2	France defeated Australia 3–2 to win the Davis Cup in Melbourne.
5	Tim Foster, 31, a member of the gold-medal winning British coxless four at the Sydney Olympics, announced his retirement from international competition in order to concentrate on coaching.
6	Indian cricketers defeated England by 10 wkts in the first Test match in Mohali.
8	Zimbabwe were dismissed by Sri Lanka for 38 runs in Colombo, the lowest-ever International one-day score.
	Geoff Huegill of Australia broke the men's 50m butterfly short-course world record with a time of 22.84sec in Melbourne.
	Zoe Jones and Matthew Davies won the ladies' and men's British figure-skating championships at Basingstoke.
11	Oxford defeated Cambridge 9–6 in the annual Rugby Union university match for the inaugural MMC trophy.
12	Craig White scored his maiden Test century during the second Test match in Ahmedabad.
15	The second Test match in Ahmedabad, between England and India, was drawn.
	Britain's James Hickman regained the 200m butterfly crown at the European short-course championship in Antwerp.
	Ricky Hatton stopped Justin Rowsell in the second round to retain his WBU light-welterweight boxing title at Wembley.
16	Ronnie O'Sullivan overwhelmed Ken Doherty 10-1 to win the UK Championship snooker title in York.
17	Michael Owen was named European Footballer of the Year as David Beckham narrowly missed out to Luis Figo as World Footballer of the Year.
20	Anil Kumble of India became the fourth spin bowler to reach 300 Test wickets when Matthew Hoggard was given out lbw.
21	Ray Reardon and Rex Williams were expelled from the World Professional Billiards and Snooker Association.
22	The USA defeated the European team 12–1 to win the Mosconi Cup pool tournament a day early.
23	The third Test ended in a draw in Bangalore, giving India a 2–1 series win against England.
26	Florida Pearl, ridden by Adrian Maguire, won the King George VI steeplechase at Kempton.

CURRENT AFFAIRS

Daily Record 2002

January

1	All EEC countries except Sweden, Denmark and the United Kingdom introduced the euro, made up of 100 cents, as their main unit of currency. The euro notes will have face values of 5, 10, 20, 50, 100, 200 and 500 euros. Coins will be 1, 2, 5, 10, 20, and 50 cents and 1 and 2 euros. The euro is currently worth 61p.
2	Eduardo Duhalde was sworn in as the new President of Argentina, replacing the disgraced President de la Rúa.
7	Gordon and Sarah Brown's 10-day-old daughter Jennifer Jane died three days after suffering a brain haemorrhage.
	Yves Saint Laurent announced his retirement from the world of haute couture.
9	Dave Gilmour, the Pink Floyd rock star, donated the £4.5 million receipts from the sale of his London home to the homeless charity Crisis.
11	Gary Hart, 37, was jailed for five years for causing the deaths of ten people in the Selby rail disaster after falling asleep at the wheel of his Land Rover.
12	Andrew Lloyd Webber's long-running musical *Starlight Express* closed after 17 years and 10 months and 7,406 performances at the Victoria Apollo Theatre.
18	A volcanic eruption of Mount Nyiragongo in the Democratic Republic of the Congo devastated thousands.
21	British actor Jim Broadbent won a Golden Globe award for Best Supporting Actor for his portrayal of John Bayley in *Iris*.
23	American singer Mariah Carey was dumped by Virgin Records but given a $28 million pay-off.
27	Donald Rumsfeld, the US Secretary of Defence, announced that the 158 Muslim extremists detained at the Camp X-Ray military camp at Guantanamo Bay, Cuba, would not be classified as prisoners of war.
31	Afghan leader Hamid Karzai addressed a press conference at Downing Street to thank Britain for freeing his country.

February

2   Crown Prince Willem Alexander of the Netherlands married Maxima Zorreguieta, a 30-year-old Argentinian. Darius Danesh became the last person to be voted off the ITV *Pop Idol* show despite polling 1.2 million votes.

4   Amy Gehring, 26, a biology teacher, was cleared at Guildford Crown Court of having sex with under-age boys.

9   HRH Princess Margaret died peacefully in her sleep at 6.30 am in the King Edward VII Hospital, London. Will Young defeated Gareth Gates in the final of the ITV *Pop Idol* series, receiving almost five million votes on the night.

12   Slobodan Milosevic began his trial in The Hague for genocide, crimes against humanity, and war crimes.

15   Princess Margaret was cremated at Slough Crematorium and a funeral service was held at St George's Chapel, Windsor.

16   Martine McCutcheon was named Best Actress in a Musical at the Laurence Olivier Awards, for her performance as the Cockney flower-girl Eliza Doolittle in *My Fair Lady*.

17   Actress Joan Collins married her fifth husband Percy Gibson at Claridge's in London.

18   Five market traders who wanted to continue weighing goods in pounds and ounces lost their appeals in the High Court.
The four men who planned the abortive diamond robbery at the Millennium Dome in November 2000 were jailed for a total of 66 years. A fifth man was cleared of robbery but given five years for theft.

19   The world's tallest man at 7ft 9in was named as Hussain Bisad, 27, a Somalian currently residing in Neasden, North London.

24   The fantasy epic *The Lord of the Rings* won five awards at the Bafta Award Ceremony, including Best Film and Director.

28   In the 'Forbes Global' list of the world's super-rich, Bill Gates, the Microsoft supremo, remains in first position whilst the Duke of Westminster's property holdings in London's West End keeps him atop of the British contingent in the list.

March

3   In a National Referendum Switzerland voted to join the United Nations, the application is to be made on 10 September.

5   Pamela Stephenson's biography of her husband Billy Connolly won the British Book Awards 'Book of the Year'.

6   Booker Prize-winning author Arundhati Roy was sentenced to a day in prison for criminal contempt of court by the Supreme Court of India as a result of her demonstration against the increase in height of the Sarda Sarovar Dam.

10   King, a three-year-old standard poodle with undocked tail, became Crufts' Supreme Champion.

15   Yoko Ono unveiled a seven foot bronze statue of John Lennon, sculpted by Tom Murphy, at the airport in Liverpool named in his honour.

19   Zimbabwe's membership of the Commonwealth was suspended for one year because of the political violence during the recent presidential election.

24   Halle Berry made Oscar history by becoming the first black woman to win the Best Actress award. Denzel Washington won the Best Actor award. Jim Broadbent won Best Supporting Actor for his performance in *Iris*. Rap star Ashley Walters, a member of garage band So Solid Crew, was sentenced to 18 months for carrying a loaded revolver in his car.

25   The postal group Consignia announced 15,000 job cuts as part of a long-term reorganisation to improve the service.

26   The BBC announced it is to drop its globe logo for a series of 'multicultural' logos featuring ethnically diverse, and some disabled, dancers.

27   Supermodel Naomi Campbell was awarded £3,500 in damages against the *Mirror* for breach of her privacy. Administrators were appointed to take control of ITV Digital, jointly owned by Carlton Communications and Granada.

28   The Queen performed the ceremony of the Royal Maundy at Canterbury Cathedral. Since she is 76, 76 men and 76 women received a small white bag containing 76p worth of specially minted, but legally spendable, silver coins with values of one, two, three, and four pence each. The specially chosen band, whose Christian works qualified them for the handout, also received a red bag containing a £5 coin and a 50p piece, coined to mark the Golden Jubilee.

29   The C4 morning show *The Big Breakfast*, first broadcast on September 28, 1992, ended today.

30   Her Majesty Queen Elizabeth the Queen Mother died peacefully in her sleep aged 101.

April

5   Her Majesty Queen Elizabeth the Queen Mother lay in state at Westminster Hall, London.
Peter Buck, the 45-year-old guitarist with REM, was cleared of ransacking a first-class cabin during a drunken rampage aboard a British Airways flight from Seattle to London last April. The Crown Court in Isleworth, which heard testimony from Bono of U2 and Michael Stipe, accepted his explanation that a pre-take-off sleeping pill mixed with five glasses of wine had caused him to act out of character.

9   Her Majesty Queen Elizabeth the Queen Mother's funeral took place at Westminster Abbey.

11   Vlajko Stojiljkovic, the former interior minister during the Slobodan Milosevic regime in Kosovo, shot himself on the steps of the parliament building after seeing parliament pass a law allowing for his extradition to the United Nations war crimes tribunal in The Hague.

12   Freemasons, who have worn black ties at lodge meetings since 1918 as a mark of respect for those who died in the Great War, announced they would dispense with the tradition and will throw the design open to competition.

17   The Chancellor of the Exchequer Gordon Brown raised the National Insurance Rate from 10 to 11 per cent.
         Camelot announced that Billy Connolly, the Scottish comedian, was to appear in a series of television
         commercials as part of a marketing campaign to reverse flagging interest.

18   A light aircraft crashed into the 417-feet-high Pirelli Tower, Milan, killing five people including the pilot.
         Zahir Shah, the former king of Afghanistan, returned home after 29 years in exile in Rome.

19   Edexcel, the examining board that has been criticised for a series of errors, announced they would use
         student teachers to mark this year's GCSE exams.

20   Sheila Hancock accepted a Bafta award on behalf of her late husband John Thaw. The Lew Grade award,
         chosen by television viewers, was for his portrayal of a tough businessman in the ITV drama *Buried*
         Treasure.

21   Jean-Marie Le Pen, the leader of France's extreme right-wing National Front, scored an unexpected victory
         over Lionel Jospin, the socialist prime minister, in the first round of the presidential elections to set up a
         battle with Jacques Chirac.

22   Prince William passed his full motorcycle test, enabling him to ride any bike restricted to 33 brake horse
         power until his 21st birthday.

23   For the first time since Lois Wilkinson and Andrea Simpson (The Caravelles) hit the US charts with 'You
         Don't Have to Be a Baby to Cry' on 26 October 1963, there was no British entry in the American Billboard
         Top 100 singles.

24   Adrian Noble announced he would not be renewing his contract as artistic director of the Royal
         Shakespeare Company. The chief executive's annual contract terminates next March.

25   Two teenage brothers, referred to as Child A and Child B, were acquitted at the Old Bailey of the murder of
         Damilola Taylor.

26   A 19-year-old German student, Robert Steinhäuser, ran amok in the Johann Gutenberg secondary school
         in Erfurt, eastern Germany, killing 12 teachers, two pupils, a school secretary, and a policeman, before
         turning the gun on himself.
         Six British plane-spotters were sentenced to three years in jail in Kalamata, southern Greece, accused of
         spying.
         Mark Shuttleworth, a South African Internet millionaire, began the ten-day space trip that he undertook at a
         cost of £14 million. The launch from Baikonur Cosmodrome, Kazakhstan, made him the second amateur to
         pay his way into orbit following Dennis Tito's trip last year.

27   Stewart Duff, an Elvis Presley impersonator, won the latest series of the ITV1 music show *Stars in their*
         Eyes.

28   Diane Pretty and her husband Brian lost their court battle for her right to die with his help before the
         'distressing and undignified' terminal stages of motor neurone disease.

30   Administrators switched off ITV Digital pay television channels after failing to find a buyer.

May

2   The Conservatives made modest gains in the English local elections on a disappointing night for Iain
         Duncan Smith.

4   Mark Collinson, who was sentenced to six months imprisonment last week for collecting abandoned golf
         balls at Whetstone Golf Course, near Leicester, was freed after serving just 10 days of his sentence.

5   Jacques Chirac swept to a landslide victory in the French presidential election, winning more than 80 per
         cent of the poll.
         Jean-Pierre Raffarin was announced as the French interim Prime Minister until the elections on 16 June.
         Ann Winterton, the Shadow Rural Affairs Minister, was sacked from the Shadow Cabinet over a racist joke
         told at a rugby club dinner. Mark Shuttleworth safely landed at Arkalyk, Kazakhstan, after his 10-day space
         trip orbiting the earth 16 times a day.

6   Pim Fortuyn was assassinated in Hilversum whilst walking to his car. The 54-year-old Dutch politician was
         shot six times.
         The matador Manuel Benitez, 'El Cordobés', announced on his 66th birthday that he is to retire on 1 June.
         El Cordobés had been at the top of his profession for more than four decades and chose his son to cut off
         his pigtail (*coleta*) to signify that he is finally stepping down.

8   In a poll carried out by Guinness World Records, the most popular single of all time was Queen's 'Bohemian
         Rhapsody'.

10   The fifth disaster on Britain's railways in as many years left eight dead and six critically injured. The 12.45
         from King's Cross to King's Lynn, which was carrying 151 passengers, derailed approaching Potters Bar
         station in North London.

11   Diane Pretty, who lost a legal battle two weeks ago for her husband to be allowed to help her to commit
         suicide, died following breathing difficulties, a frequent final complication of motor neurone disease.

15   Woody Allen opened the 55th Cannes Film Festival.

17   It was announced that Eliza Manningham-Buller would replace Stephen Lander as Director-General of MI5
         on 8 October.

23   Sir Cliff Richard launched a new red wine from grapes on his estate near Albufeira, Portugal. The wine,
         named Vida Nova (New Life), will go on sale at Waitrose in July for £8.99 a bottle.

24   C4's *Big Brother* began; the 12 inmates entering the house were Lee Davey, Sunita Sharma, Jonny Regan,
         PJ Ellis, Adele Roberts, Kate Lawler, Spencer Smith, Alison Hammond, Alex Sibley, Jade Goody, Sandy
         Cumming and Lynne Moncrief.
         Madonna made her West End debut in David Williamson's play *Up for Grabs* at the Wyndham's Theatre.

25   A China Airlines Boeing 747-200 crashed on a flight from Hong Kong to Taiwan killing all 225 passengers
         and crew.
         A train crash in Mozambique was reported to have caused the death of over 200 passengers and injured
         400 more.

CURRENT AFFAIRS

The Eurovision Song Contest in Tallinn, Estonia, was won by Latvia. Jessica Garlick, the UK representative came 4th.

| 28 | Stephen Byers resigned his position of Transport Secretary in a statement made from 10 Downing Street. |
| 29 | Alistair Darling was announced as Britain's new Transport Minister as replacement for Stephen Byers. |

Sunita Sharma decided to leave the *Big Brother* house of her own volition.

| 31 | Lynne Moncrief became the first person evacuated from the *Big Brother* house. |

June

1 Michael Parkinson introduced the Promenade Concert from Buckingham Palace, organised by the BBC. Highlights included the 13-year-old clarinettist Julian Bliss's performance of Messager's *Solo de Concours*.

2 A fire broke out in a roof void in the East Gallery of Buckingham Palace but was soon brought under control.

3 An estimated 200 million people in 60 countries witnessed the pop concert at Buckingham Palace to celebrate the Queen's Golden Jubilee. Sir Paul McCartney closed the proceedings with a rousing rendition of 'Hey Jude'.

7 Alison Hammond became the second evacuee of the *Big Brother* house.

9 PricewaterhouseCoopers announced it is to rename its PwC Consulting offshoot 'Monday'.

11 Former Beatle Sir Paul McCartney married Heather Mills in the grounds of Castle Leslie, County Monaghan. Dr John Sentamu, suffragan Bishop of Stepney, was appointed as the new diocesan Bishop of Birmingham, replacing Dr Mark Santer who retired in May. Dr Sentamu becomes Britain's first senior black bishop.

12 Rolling Stones' singer Mick Jagger was awarded a knighthood in the Golden Jubilee Birthday Honours List. Sandy Cumming escaped from the *Big Brother* house by climbing over the roof.

13 Many local authorities throughout the UK allowed young children into cinemas to watch the new *Spider-Man* film, despite the British Board of Film Classification giving it a 12 certificate. The 1909 Cinema Act facillitates this discretion, first used eight years ago when *Mrs Doubtfire* was deemed a PG by local councils rather than the 12 issued by the BBFC. In that instance the BBFC relented and changed the certificate to PG.

14 Lee Davey was voted out of the *Big Brother* house by an overwhelming majority.

16 Jean-Pierre Raffarin was confirmed as the French Prime Minister following M. Chirac's Union for the Presidential Majority party winning 399 of the 577 seats. Timothy Culley entered the *Big Brother* house as replacement for Sandy Cumming.

21 Spencer Smith, the favourite for the *Big Brother* title, was evicted in a close battle with Alex Sibley.

23 A little-known Elvis Presley recording 'A Little Less Conversation' from his 1968 film *Live a Little, Love a Little*, reached the top of the UK charts to give him a record 18th chart-topper.

26 Russia was granted full membership of the former G7 alliance and it will now officially be known as the G8. The Queen appointed the Prince of Wales a member of the Order of Merit

28 Sophie Pritchard, who replaced Sunita Sharma in the *Big Brother* house, was evicted by the public vote.

July

2 Steve Fossett, 58, on his sixth attempt, became the first man to fly a balloon solo and non-stop around the world.

3 A marble statue of Baroness Thatcher in the Guildhall art gallery, London, was decapitated by a man wielding an iron bar.

5 The world's largest maze was opened at Christchurch, Dorset. The 16-acre attraction was designed in the shape of a deer.
Adele Roberts became the latest evictee from the *Big Brother* house after a four-way nomination.

7 A Royal Navy destroyer, HMS *Nottingham*, was badly damaged when it ran into rocks near Lord Howe Island in the Tasman Sea.

8 John Taylor, 46, was sentenced to life imprisonment after pleading guilty at Leeds Crown Court to the kidnap and murder of 16-year-old Leanne Tiernan.

11 The European Court of Human Rights in Strasbourg ruled that Christine Goodwin, 65, could legally marry a man although born a man herself. The judgement is expected to create civil recognition for Britain's estimated 5,000 transsexuals.
Nicholas Payne, the director of English National Opera, stood down after four years in the post.

12 Terry Pratchett won the Carnegie Medal for his book *The Amazing Maurice and His Educated Rodents*. PJ Ellis became the latest evictee from the *Big Brother* house.

14 Maxime Brunerie, 25, a neo-Nazi, attempted to shoot President Chirac as he passed the Arc de Triomphe during the military celebrations in Paris for Bastille Day.

15 World markets suffered a new Black Monday as the dollar and share prices plummeted.

16 Jim Moir, controller of Radio 2, announced he will stand down as soon as a suitable replacement is found.

19 Timothy Culley became the final nominated evictee from the *Big Brother* house.

23 Dr Rowan Williams, Archbishop of Wales, was announced as the successor to Dr George Carey as Archbishop of Canterbury, the position to be taken up later in the year.

26 Kate Lawler won the *Big Brother 3* title from Jonny Regan, Alex Sibley and Jade Goody.

28 Alan Duncan, the front bench spokesman on foreign affairs, became the first Conservative MP to openly declare his homosexuality.

30 Writer William Trevor became the third Irishman to be made an honorary knight following Bob Geldof and Tony O'Reilly.
The University of Queensland's Hyshot scramjet project successfully launched a Terrier Orion Mk70 rocket fitted with a ramjet engine at Woomera Airbase. The 10-minute flight was to an altitude of 200 miles and the scramjet engine fell back to earth and scooped up and compressed oxygen from the air, thereby enabling a hypersonic speed of Mach 7.6. The consequences of the hypersonic ignition could mean long-haul flight times could be dramatically reduced.

August

1   Sir Quentin Thomas, 58, was announced as the successor to Andreas Whittam Smith as president of the British Board of Film Classification.
2   An outbreak of Legionnaire's disease was traced to an air-conditioning system at an arts centre called Forum 28 in Barrow-in-Furness.
4   Helen Boaden, the controller of Radio 4, announced that Jeremy Paxman is to step down as presenter of *Start the Week* after five years. Andrew Marr, the BBC's political editor, takes over when it returns in November.
6   Cherie Blair, 47, wife of the Prime Minister, suffered a miscarriage and was forced to have an emergency operation.
7   A Rubens masterpiece, *Head of a Man*, which was stolen in 1986 by the infamous art thief Martin 'The General' Cahill, was recovered at an address in North Dublin.
8   Sapamurad Niyazov, aka Turkmenbashi the Great, was made President for Life of the former Soviet republic of Turkmenistan. He immediately renamed the days of the week and the months of the year.
13   The worst floods in Europe for a century caused the Danube to break several banks and dams, resulting in extreme flooding in Vienna and other towns and cities across southern Austria and Germany. In Prague, hundreds of patients had to be evacuated from hospitals and art treasures and museum pieces had to be removed to safe havens.
14   The pass rate in this year's A level examinations reached 94.3 per cent, with one in five attaining A grades.
16   The state premier of South Australia, Mike Rann, officially declared the Second World War over after his government stumbled upon a piece of wartime legislation, the Emergency Powers Act of 1941, which had never been repealed.
17   The bodies of missing 10-year-olds Holly Wells and Jessica Chapman were found in Thetford Forest, near the RAF Lakenheath base, between the village of Brandon and Mildenhall, Suffolk.
18   Palestinian terrorist Abu Nidal was reportedly found shot dead in his flat.
19   Sidney Sussex College, Cambridge, captained by David Lidington, the Conservative MP for Aylesbury, won the BBC 2 *University Challenge Revisited* series, beating Keele University in the final.
20   Ian Huntley, a school caretaker from Soham, Cambridgeshire, was charged with the murder of Holly Wells and Jessica Chapman, the two 10-year-old girls missing from Soham since August 4.
25   A new Granada television show, *I'm a Celebrity Get Me Out of Here*, began. Eight celebrities – Nigel Benn, Tony Blackburn, Rhona Cameron, Darren Day, Uri Geller, Christine Hamilton, Nell McAndrew and Tara Palmer-Tomkinson – were left to fend for themselves in the jungle outback of Queensland, Australia, and after being nominated by the public to do a series of tests concerning live insects and reptiles, would be nominated off one by one.
26   The Earth Summit in Johannesburg began.
30   Benazir Bhutto, the London-based exiled former Pakistan Prime Minister, was prevented from standing in her country's parliamentary elections by the military government.

September

1   Victoria Beckham gave birth to a 7lb 4oz baby boy, named Romeo, by Caesarean section.
5   President Karzai of Afghanistan survived an assassination attempt when a man opened fire on his car as it travelled through the centre of Kabul. The man was killed by security guards and the President escaped unharmed.
7   Sir Simon Rattle made his debut as maestro of the Berlin Philharmonic in its home city with a techno-inspired piece called *Asyla*, by the young English composer Thomas Adès.
14   Linda, a 28-year-old hippopotamus, died after swallowing a tennis ball thrown into her enclosure at Dublin Zoo. Hoovie the hippo and his father, Henry, began to receive goodwill messages and gifts from children throughout Ireland.
17   Richard Van Pham, from Long Beach, California, was found on his wrecked sailing boat by the frigate USS *McClusky* after being lost in the Pacific Ocean for over three months. Mr Van Pham's 26ft boat, *Sea Breeze*, was caught in a storm which damaged his mast, outboard motor and radio. The 62-year-old Vietnamese immigrant was heading for Santa Catalina Island 25 miles off the west coast of America, but he was eventually found 300 miles southwest of Costa Rica.
     Niomi McLean-Daley, aka Ms Dynamite, became the first black female artist to win the prestigious Mercury Music Prize, for her debut album *A Little Deeper*.
20   The remains of the 13-year-old schoolgirl Milly Dowler, missing for nearly six months, were found by two Polish mushroom pickers on the edge of a Hampshire wood. A record 5.3 billion shares were traded on the busiest day in the 201-year history of the Stock Exchange.
21   Dawn Airey, 41, the head of Channel 5 (now known as Five), was appointed as managing director of Sky Networks.
22   The Countryside Alliance organised the Liberty and Livelihood march through the streets of London in protest against the government's proposed ban on hunting. Over 400,000 people supported the protest.
23   An earthquake measuring 4.8 on the Richter scale had its epicentre six miles below the Midlands town of Dudley.
24   The five judges of the 2002 Booker Prize, which included comedian David Baddiel, announced their shortlist of six novels. The shorlisted books were *Life of Pi* by Yann Martel, *Family Matters* by Rohinton Mistry, *Unless* by Carol Shields, *The Story of Lucy Gault* by William Trevor, *Fingersmith* by Sarah Waters, and *Dirt Music* by Tim Winton. 26-year-old Zadie Smith, whose debut novel *White Teeth* sold 800,000 copies but failed to make the shortlist, was disappointed once again when her new novel *The Autograph Man* also failed to make the final six. Hubert Bouchet, 48, who admitted breaking a fire alarm, was fined 60 euros (£38) by magistrates at Barry, South Wales, the first person to be fined in euros by a British court.
25   Ross Stretton, the director of the Royal Ballet, resigned his position after a turbulent year in the job.

CURRENT AFFAIRS

27   Sir William Stubbs, the guardian of the nation's education standards, was sacked by Estelle Morris, the
        Education Secretary, following an independent inquiry which found the government guilty of replacing A
        levels with AS/A2 levels that no one understood.
28   Former Cabinet Minister Edwina Currie disclosed details of a four-year affair with former Prime Minister
        John Major, in her diaries made public in a national newspaper.
30   Austin Mitchell, the Labour MP for Grimsby, changed his surname to Haddock by deed poll to promote the
        fishing industry which was once the mainstay of his Lincolnshire constituency.

October
1   Ms Dynamite, 21, was Britain's top female rap artist at the Mobo Awards (Music of Black Origin). She won
        UK Act of the Year, Best Newcomer and Single of the Year with It Takes More. Hear'Say, the band created by
        the talent show Popstars, split up following a decline in public support.
2   Pop singer Robbie Williams signed a contract worth up to £70 million with EMI, the largest ever in British
        music history, although way short of the estimated £623 million paid to Michael Jackson by Sony. Stuart
        Goddard, aka Adam Ant, the 1980s pop star, was given a 12-month community rehabilitation order following
        an incident in the Prince of Wales, Kentish Town, North London, when locals began whistling the theme
        from The Good, the Bad and the Ugly as he entered the pub in cowboy hat. Goddard threw an alternator
        through a window and hit a guitarist, Plato Contostavlos, before threatening to shoot drinkers with an
        imitation pistol.
3   Jeffrey Archer paid the Daily Star almost £2 million in an out-of-court settlement covering the £500,000 libel
        damages awarded against Express Newspapers in 1987 in a case in which Archer had lied, plus legal costs
        and interest.
4   King Gyanendra of Nepal sacked his prime minister Sher Bahadur Deuba, the first time since the
        absolute monarchy was abolished in 1990 that the king has assumed power in Nepal. Betty Bullock of
        Newport Beach, California, a terminally ill cancer patient, was awarded $28 billion (£18 million) punitive
        damages against the Philip Morris tobacco company for hiding evidence about the link between smoking
        and cancer.
5   Two British scientists, Sir John Sulston and Sydney Brenner, won the Nobel Prize for Medicine for their
        genetic discoveries. American Robert Horvitz, who worked with the British scientists in the 1970s and
        1980s, shared the award.
6   A French-owned 158,000-tonne supertanker, Limberg, chartered to the Malaysian oil firm Petronas, was
        holed by a small boat, thought to be carrying explosives, as it approached the Yemeni port of Mina al-
        Dabah. The German-born Prince Claus of the Netherlands, husband of Queen Beatrix, died, aged 76.
7   A 13-year-old boy became the eighth victim of the Washington suburban sniper, known as 'the beltway
        killer'. The killing spree, which began on 2 October, had been confined to adults, only one of whom survived
        and who all lived in either Prince George's County or Montgomery County, the two Maryland counties that
        border Washington. The teenage boy was seriously injured but alive.
8   A service was held in honour and remembrance of Milly Dowler at Guildford Cathedral. Two Americans,
        Daniel Kahneman and Vernon Smith, were awarded the Nobel Prize for Economics for their study of how
        the consumer makes choices both financial and psychological before spending.
9   One of the world's biggest sculptures was unveiled at the Tate Modern in London. At 500 ft long and 10
        storeys high, Marsyas, an immense flute-shaped structure by Anish Kapoor, filled the entire space of the
        Tate's Turbine Hall.
10   Iain Duncan Smith closed the Conservative Party Conference in Bournemouth with a speech imploring
        critics 'Do not underestimate the determination of a quiet man.' Imre Kertész, 72, became the first
        Hungarian to win the Nobel Prize for Literature.
11   Former US President Jimmy Carter was awarded the Nobel Peace Prize for his globetrotting efforts to end
        wars and defend human rights. King Gyanendra of Nepal named Lokendra Bahadur Chand as his new
        Prime Minister.
12   Madonna's new film Swept Away, directed by her husband Guy Ritchie, opened to the worst reviews of her
        career.
13   A car-bomb explosion caused devastation in a nightclub in Bali, Indonesia. Up to 200 people were feared
        dead in the blast at the Sari Club in Kuta Beach, Bali, many of whom were Australians and local people,
        although several Britons also died.
14   Athlete Paula Radcliffe won the annual Women of the Year Outstanding Achievement Award. Master of the
        Rolls Lord Phillips, sitting with Lords Justices Chadwick and Keene, overturned the original decision in
        favour of supermodel Naomi Campbell concerning an article in the Mirror last year that was deemed to have
        breached her right to confidentiality when it published details of her attendance at a Narcotics Anonymous
        meeting in London.
15   At the annual National TV Awards BBC1's Auf Wiedersehen Pet won the most popular drama award and
        Who Wants to Be a Millionaire won most popular quiz show for the fourth year running, but the most
        successful winners were David Jason (most popular comedy performer and most popular actor) and Ant &
        Dec, who won three awards including a special recognition award.
16   Nigel Pickard was appointed ITV's director of programmes on the day that Carlton and Granada, the two
        biggest ITV companies, confirmed that they had agreed to merge.
19   World chess champion Vladimir Kramnik was held to a 4-4 draw by the Deep Fritz computer in a challenge
        match billed as the 'Brains in Bahrain' match. The sniper who had been terrorising the Washington suburbs
        since October 2 claimed his 12th victim and 10th fatality.
22   Canadian Yann Martel won the £50,000 Man Booker Prize, fiction's most coveted award, with his second
        novel Life of Pi.
23   Estelle Morris resigned as Secretary of State for Education and Skills. Chechen rebels took over a packed
        Moscow theatre and demanded a complete Russian withdrawal from the separatist Muslim republic of

Chechnya. Alastair Irvine, the 25-year-old son of the Lord Chancellor, was jailed for 16 months in California for various offences arising out of a fixation for a female student.

24 Charles Clarke was appointed as successor to Estelle Morris as Education Secretary. Other Cabinet movements included John Reid from Northern Ireland to Labour Chairman and Paul Murphy from Welsh Secretary to Ulster. Peter Hain was brought into the Cabinet as Secretary of State for Wales.
Two hundred prisoners were moved from Lincoln prison following a riot thought to be triggered by overcrowding.
Police arrested two men in connection with the sniper killings that had terrorised the Washington suburbs since 2 October, claiming 13 victims, 10 of whom died,

26 Russian forces ended the three-night siege of the Moscow theatre, killing most of the 50 Chechen rebels although three terrorists survived. 115 hostages were killed during the assault, which was forced upon the authorities by the rebels beginning to carry out their threat to execute some of the 800 theatregoers. Only two died by the hands of the terrorists.

27 The Archbishop of Canterbury, George Carey, delivered his valedictory sermon in the parish church, Dagenham, Essex.

29 Broadcaster Angus Deayton was sacked as chairman of the BBC's *Have I Got News For You* programme following revelations of his private life.

30 Sotheby's auction house was fined almost £13m by the European Commission for operating a price-fixing cartel with its arch rival Christie's for most of the 1990s. John Leslie, the television presenter, was sacked from the ITV show *This Morning* after he failed to respond to allegations about his personal life. The new BBC-backed digital television service, Freeview, was launched.

November

5 Former MI5 officer David Shayler was jailed for six months at the Old Bailey for disclosing top-secret documents to the *Mail on Sunday*.

6 Six British plane-spotters who were sentenced for spying on 26 April were acquitted in an appeal court in Kalamata, Greece.

7 Peter Shaw, a British banker held hostage for five months chained inside a hole in the mountains of Georgia, returned to Britain after escaping his captors two days ago.

10 James Kilgore, the founder of the Symbionese Liberation Army that kidnapped heiress Paty Hearst, was arrested in Cape Town after a 27-year manhunt.

13 Robert Brown, 44, was freed from prison after serving 25 years for murder when his conviction was quashed because of police corruption that made the verdict unsafe.

14 Celebrity chef Jamie Oliver opened a restaurant in Shoreditch, London, staffed by unemployed youngsters with no catering qualifications. The restaurant, Fifteen, is featured in a Channel 4 series, *Jamie's Kitchen*.

15 Myra Hindley, the Moors murderer, died at West Suffolk Hospital in Bury St Edmunds after being moved from Highpoint jail. She is to be cremated at Cambridge Crematorium on 20 November.

18 *Die Another Day*, the 20th James Bond film, was premiered at the Royal Albert Hall, London.

19 *Prestige*, a tanker carrying 70,000 tons of fuel, broke up and sank off Spain's north-west coast, causing massive environmental damage.

20 Mark Owen, Les Dennis, Goldie, Sue Perkins, Anne Diamond and Melinda Messenger began C4's *Celebrity Big Brother*.
Professor Gunther von Hagens performed the first public autopsy in Britain for 170 years. The dissection of a 72-year-old German man was carried out in front of a paying audience in the Atlantis art gallery, Brick Lane, London.

21 The Fire Brigades Union failed to accept new working practices tied to a 16 per cent pay rise and army firefighters were on standby for the next eight days as firemen decided to strike. The Princess Royal was fined £500 for failing to control her English bull terrier, Dotty, which bit two young boys in Windsor Great Park. The judge sitting at East Berkshire Magistrates' Court warned that the three-year-old dog would be put down if there was a further offence.

22 The Miss World contest was postponed following fears over the safety of contestants as protesters tried to storm their hotels. The contest will now be moved from Abuja, Nigeria, to London, England, on 7 December.

23 The five-man group managed by Pete Waterman and named 'One True Voice' was chosen by the viewers of the ITV show *Popstars: The Rivals* and included Jamie Shaw, Keith Semple, Anton Gordon, Daniel Pearce and Matt Johnson. The unlucky person to miss out on the final line-up was Chris Park.

24 Naturalist David McRae died after being bitten by a bat and contracting rabies, the first such case for 100 years in Britain.
Winston Churchill was voted the greatest Briton of all time in a nationwide poll, beating Isambard Kingdom Brunel and Diana, Princess of Wales, into second and third places respectively. The other final places were Charles Darwin (4), William Shakespeare (5), Isaac Newton (6), Elizabeth I (7), John Lennon (8), Horatio Nelson (9), Oliver Cromwell (10). Goldie became the first celebrity to be evicted from the *Big Brother* house in the 2002 series on Channel 4.

26 Anne Diamond became the second celebrity to be evicted from the *Big Brother* house in the 2002 series on Channel 4.

28 MyTravel, the tour operator formerly known as Airtours, announced annual losses of £72.8 million. Sue Perkins became the third celebrity to be evicted from the *Big Brother* house in the 2002 series on Channel 4.

29 Former 'Take That' star Mark Owen won the 2002 *Celebrity Big Brother* television show. Les Dennis was placed second and Melinda Messenger third.

30 Javine Hylton was the final person to be voted off the ITV show, *Popstars: The Rivals*. The winners, whose band is named 'Girls Aloud', include Kimberley Walsh, Nadine Coyle, Nicola Roberts, Cheryl Tweedy and Sarah Harding.

CURRENT AFFAIRS

December
1   Liam Gallagher, lead singer of the rock band Oasis, had two front teeth knocked out in a bar-room brawl in
     Munich.
2   Dr Rowan Williams was ceremonially confirmed as the successor to Dr George Carey as 104th Archbishop
     of Canterbury.
3   The case against Harold Brown, the second royal butler accused of stealing from Diana, Princess of Wales,
     was thrown out by the Director of Public Prosecutions, Sir David Calvert-Smith. Mr Brown was accused of
     stealing a jewel-encrusted model of a dhow, and a diamond and emerald bracelet with matching earrings
     and a daffodil motif.
5   A media furore blew up over a property deal involving Cherie Blair, the Prime Minister's wife. Mrs Blair asked
     her friend Carole Caplin to look at a property in Bristol with a view to buying it for her son, who was to
     attend Bristol University, and the deal was finalised by Peter Foster, a convicted criminal and boyfriend of
     Miss Caplin. The *Daily Mail* suggested some impropriety on Cherie Blair's behalf, although all such
     accusations were strenuously denied and remained unproven.
     The US Senate held its first-ever 100th birthday party for a sitting member when Strom Thurmond reached
     that landmark today. His home state of South Carolina declared 'Strom Thurmond Day' and held a party
     around his statue in Edgefield.
6   Britain's two million Muslims celebrated Eid-ul-Fitr (celebration of charity), the end of the fasting month of
     Ramadan.
     Actress Winona Ryder was put on probation for three years, fined $10,000 (£6,500) and ordered to do 480
     hours of community service as a result of her conviction for a shoplifting spree in Beverly Hills last
     Christmas.
7   Azra Akin, Miss Turkey, won the Miss World contest at Alexandra Palace, London.
8   The £20,000 Turner Prize was won by Keith Tyson, a 33-year-old Cumbrian artist, who submitted a black
     plastic column, purportedly packed with computers which are set to operate for 33,000 years, and called
     The Thinker (after Rodin), an LED display counting the seconds up to 76.5 years (the average human
     lifespan), and 39 quasi-scientific paintings and drawings
13   David Sneddon, 24, won the BBC's *Fame Academy* competition and with it a millionaire's lifestyle for a year.
     Runner-up in the competition was Sinead Quinn, 22, and Lemar Obika, 24, was placed third.
14   A fleet of nearly 2,900 luxury cars was lost aboard the Norwegian cargo vessel *Tricolor* when it sank after
     colliding with the Bahamas-registered cargo vessel *Kariba* in the English Channel 30 miles from Ramsgate.
20   Veteran broadcaster Jimmy Young hosted his last radio show after 29 years in the morning slot. The 81-
     year-old disc jockey and former singer was axed by Jim Moir, the Controller of Radio 2.
22   The Christmas Number One was 'Sound of the Underground' by Girls Aloud, beating their *Pop Stars: The
     Rivals* opponents One True Voice into second spot.
23   Iraqi jet fighters shot down an unmanned American surveillance plane after breaching the country's
     southern no-fly zone.
26   Andrew 'Jack' Whittaker, a 55-year-old construction boss, won $314.9 million (£196.8 million) on the
     American National Lottery, making him the biggest-ever single winner of a lottery.
27   BBC 1's *Only Fools and Horses*, with 16.3 million viewers, was the top Christmas programme.
30   The New Year's Honours List included knighthoods for actor Alan Bates and film director Ridley Scott.

Obituaries 2002

January
1   Julia Phillips, film producer, born 7 April 1944
2   Charlie Mitten, footballer, born in Rangoon 17 Jan 1921
3   Mickey Dora, surfer, born 11 Aug 1934
12   Cyrus Vance, US Secretary of State, 1977–80, born 27 March 1917
     Moss Evans, general secretary of the Transport and General Workers' Union 1978–85, born 13 July 1925
     Lady Violet Powell, author, born 13 March 1912
     Stanley Unwin, entertainer, born 7 June 1911
13   Ted Demme, film and television director, born 26 Oct 1963
14   Lord Young of Darlington, sociologist, born 9 Aug 1915
15   Michel Poniatowski, French Minister of the Interior 1974–7, born 16 May 1922
16   Ivan Foxwell, film producer, born 22 Feb 1914
     Carl 'Bobo' Olson, world middleweight boxing champion, born 11 July 1928
17   Peter Adamson, actor, born 16 Feb 1930
     Bill Mason, film-maker, born 9 Nov 1915
19   Vava (Edvaldo Izidio Neto), Brazilian footballer, born 12 Nov 1934
20   Jeff Astle, footballer, born 13 May 1942
     John Jackson, blues guitarist, born 25 Feb 1924
21   Peggy Lee, singer and songwriter, born 26 May 1920
22   Kenneth Armitage, sculptor, born 18 July 1916
     Brendan O'Dowda, tenor, born 1 Oct 1925
     John McGrath, writer and theatre director, born 1 June 1935
23   Professor Robert Nozick, political philosopher, born 16 Nov 1938
24   Dick Saunders, jockey, born 28 July 1933
25   Will Camp, publicist (coined the phrase 'high speed gas'), born 12 May 1926

28   Astrid Lindgren, children's author, born 14 Nov 1907
29   Stratford Johns, actor, born 22 Sept 1925
30   Inge Morath, photographer, born 27 May 1923

February
1   Hildegard Knef, actress, born 28 Dec 1925
4   Agatha Barbara, President of Malta 1982–7, born 11 March 1923
    John Bromley, former head of ITV Sport, born 12 Jan 1934
5   Angela Du Maurier, writer, born 1 March 1904
6   Professor Max Perutz, scientist, born 19 May 1914
    Lady Viola Tait, opera singer and author, born 1 Nov 1911
7   Zizinho (Thomaz Soares da Silva), Brazilian footballer, born 14 Sept 1921
    Jack Fairman, racing driver, born 15 March 1913
8   Bob Wooler, disc jockey, born 19 Jan 1926
9   Princess Margaret, Countess of Snowdon, born 21 Aug 1930
    Roy Noakes, sculptor, born 10 June 1936
10   Dave Van Ronk, blues and folksinger, born 30 June 1936
11   Barry Foster, actor, born 21 Aug 1927
13   Waylon Jennings, country singer, born 15 June 1937
14   Nandor Hidegkuti, Hungarian footballer, born in 1922
    Günter Wand, conductor, born 7 Jan 1912
    Mick Tucker, drummer with the Sweet, born 17 July 1948
15   Huw Evans, economist, born 21 Aug 1941
16   Sir Walter Winterbottom, England football manager, born 31 Jan 1913
17   Anthony Benjamin, artist, born 29 March 1931
21   John Thaw, actor, born 3 Jan 1942
22   Chuck Jones, animator and director, born 12 Sept 1912
23   Alice Wallace, actress, born 11 April 1925
24   Leo Ornstein, composer and pianist, born 2 Dec 1892
26   Lawrence Tierney, actor, born 15 March 1919
27   Spike Milligan, comedian, actor, musician and writer, born 16 April 1918

March
1   Richard Moore, cricketer, born 14 Nov 1913
2   Geoff Pymar, speedway rider and golf caddie, born 14 Feb 1912
3   Harlan Howard, songwriter, born 8 Sept 1927
5   Harry Wingfield, illustrator of Ladybird's Peter and Jane series, born 4 Dec 1910
6   Alice Bauer, professional golfer, born 6 Oct 1927
9   Irene Worth, actress, born 23 June 1916
10   Shirley Scott, jazz organist, born 14 March 1934
11   Professor James Tobin, Nobel-prizewinning economist, born 5 March 1918
12   Spyros Kyprianou, President of the Republic of Cyprus 1977–89, born 28 Oct 1932
    Jean-Paul Riopelle, painter and sculptor, born 7 Oct 1923
14   Hans-Georg Gadamer, German philosopher, born 11 Feb 1900
16   Sir Marcus Fox, former chairman of the 1922 Committee, born 11 June 1927
17   Gösta Winbergh, Swedish tenor, born 30 Dec 1943
18   Harry Hayes, jazz saxophonist, born 23 March 1909
20   Emiliano Váldez, boxer, born 24 March 1973
21   Eileen Farrell, soprano, born 13 Feb 1920
    John May, creator of the slogan 'You're never alone with a Strand', born 8 Sept 1926
    Harry Wingfield, Ladybird book illustrator, born 4 Dec 1910
22   James F Blake, bus driver in the Rosa Parks controversy (see USA general information), born in 1913
23   Ben Hollioake, cricketer, born in Melbourne 11 Nov 1977
24   Michael Finn, artist, born 7 July 1921
25   Kenneth Wolstenholme, football commentator, born 17 July 1920
27   Dudley Moore, comedian, actor, composer, and pianist, born 18 April 1935
    Milton Berle, comedian, born 12 July 1908
    Billy Wilder, film director, born 22 June 1906
29   John 'Speedy' Keen, singer, drummer, composer ('Something in the Air'), born 29 March 1945
30   Her Majesty Queen Elizabeth the Queen Mother, born 4 Aug 1900
31   Barry Took, comedian and writer, born 19 June 1928

April
1   Hans-Georg Gadamer, German philosopher, born 11 Feb 1900
    Elizabeth Cadbury-Brown, architect, born 28 March 1922
    John Cameron, baritone, born 20 March 1918
    Lawrence Toynbee, artist (son of historian Arnold Toynbee), born 22 Dec 1922
3   Frank Tovey aka Fad Gadget, singer and electronic musician, born 8 Sept 1956
7   David Sweetman, poet, novelist and film-maker, born 16 March 1943
8   George Francis, boxing trainer, born 28 June 1928
9   Maria Felix, Mexican film star, born 8 April 1914
13   Ian Gillies (aka Mycroft), quiz champion and compiler, born 7 Dec 1927

14   Mark Ermler, conductor, born 4 May 1932
15   Amelia Batchelor, actress (the torch-bearing symbol of Columbia Pictures), born 2 Feb 1908
        William Reed, composer, born 16 Oct 1910
16   Robert Urich, actor, born 16 Dec 1946
        Ramiro de León Carpio, President of Guatemala 1993–6, born 12 Jan 1942
18   Thor Heyerdahl, Norwegian anthropologist and explorer, born 6 Oct 1914
20   Alan Dale, singer, born 9 July 1925
        Francis Lemarque (born Nathan Korb), French singer, born 25 Nov 1917
        Will Spencer, cartoonist, born 23 April 1921
23   Linda Boreman (aka Linda Lovelace), actress, born 10 Jan 1949
        Christopher Price, broadcaster, born 21 Sept 1967
25   Michael Bryant, actor, born 5 April 1928
26   Lisa 'Left Eye' Lopes (member of pop group TLC), born 27 May 1971
27   Stan Lynn, footballer, born 18 June 1928
        Guila Bustabo, violinist, born 25 Feb 1916
28   Sir Peter Parker, head of British Rail 1976–83, born 30 Aug 1924
        Aleksandr Lebed, Russian politician, born 20 April 1950
29   John Middleton Murry, writer, born 9 May 1926

May
2   John Nathan-Turner, television and theatre producer, born 12 Aug 1947
3   Baroness Castle of Blackburn, politician, born 6 Oct 1910
4   Barbara Newman, variety artiste (Priscilla the goose), born 11 April 1914
        John Kohn, film producer and writer, born 27 Nov 1925
5   George Sidney, film director, born 4 Oct 1916
        Hugo Bánzer Suárez, former President of Bolivia, born 10 May 1926
        Michael Todd Jr, film producer (pioneer of Smell-o-Vision in *Scent of Mystery* 1960), born 8 Oct 1929
6   Otis Blackwell, songwriter, born in 1931
        Pim Fortuyn, Dutch politician, born 19 Feb 1948
7   Monica Sinclair, contralto, born 23 March 1925
9   Joan Floyd, artist, born 17 May 1913
10   Yves Robert, actor and director, born 19 June 1920
11   Patrick Fyffe, drag artiste (Dame Hilda Bracket), born 23 Jan 1942
        Bill Peet, cartoonist and author, born 29 Jan 1915
13   Ruth Cracknell, actress, born 6 July 1926
15   Nellie Shabalala, singer and pastor, born 23 Sept 1952
        Bryan Pringle, actor, born 19 Jan 1935
16   Charles Simon, actor, born 4 Feb 1909
17   Lord Moyola (James Chichester-Clark), Prime Minister of Northern Ireland 1969–71, born 12 Feb 1923
        Norman Vaughan, comedian, born 10 April 1927
        Sharon Seeley, songwriter, born 4 April 1940
        Little Johnny Taylor, blues singer, born 11 Feb 1943
18   Dave Boy Smith, professional wrestler, born 27 Nov 1962
19   Sir John Gorton, Prime Minister of Australia 1968–71, born 9 Sept 1911
20   Sandor Konya, Hungarian operatic tenor, born 23 Sept 1923
21   Niki de Saint Phalle, artist, born 29 Oct 1930
        Elisabeth Vellacott, artist, born 28 Jan 1905
22   Major Dick Hern, horseracing trainer, born 20 Jan 1921
23   Sam Snead, golfer, born 27 May 1912
24   Thelma Litster, ballet dancer and teacher, born 22 June 1935
        Wallace Markfield, author, born 12 Aug 1926
25   Sir Arthur Gold, former chairman of the British Olympic Association, born 10 Jan 1917
        Pat Coombs, actress, born 27 Aug 1926
26   Mamo Wolde, Ethiopian athlete, born 12 June 1932
28   Mildred Wirt Benson, author, born 10 July 1905
29   Charles Ede, founder of the Folio Society, born 22 Oct 1921
30   John B Keane, Irish playwright and novelist, born 21 July 1928
31   SP Gupte, Indian cricketer, born 11 Dec 1929

June
1   Hansie Cronje, cricketer, born 25 Sept 1969
3   Lew Wasserman, film mogul, born 15 March 1913
4   Fernando Belaúnde Terry, former President of Peru, born 7 Oct 1913
5   Truck Parham, jazz double bassist, born 25 Jan 1911
6   Dee Dee Ramone, punk musician, born 18 Sept 1952
        Jimmie Lee Robinson, blues musician, born 30 April 1931
7   Signe Hasso, Swedish actress, born 15 Aug 1910
11   Maurits Sillem, conductor and pianist, born 26 July 1929
12   Bill Blass, fashion designer, born 22 June 1922
13   Ralph Shapey, composer and conductor, born 12 March 1921
14   José Bonilla, former world flyweight boxing champion, born 19 Nov 1967
        Olive Blackham, puppeteer, born 15 Feb 1899

15	Said Belqola, football referee (first African to take charge of a World Cup final), born in 1956
	Colin Busby, trombonist, born 23 July 1930
17	Fritz Walter, captain of the 1954 World Cup-winning German team, born 31 Oct 1920
	Willie Davenport, athlete, born 8 June 1943
	Walter Villa, Italian motorcycle racing champion, born 13 Aug 1943
19	James Lucas, author and historian, born 4 Dec 1923
22	Ann Landers, agony aunt, born 4 July 1918
24	The 17th Duke of Norfolk, Miles Francis Stapleton Fitzalan-Howard, Earl Marshal of England, born 21 July 1915
	Ian Niall (Andrew McNeillie), author, born 7 Nov 1916
26	Dolores Gray, singer and actress, born 7 June 1924
	Dermot Walsh, actor, born 10 Sept 1924
27	John Entwistle, bass-player with The Who, born 9 Oct 1944
29	Rosemary Clooney, singer, born 23 May 1928
	Margaret Johnston, actress, born 10 Aug 1918

July

1	Sid Avery, photographer, born 12 Oct 1918
	Maritta Wolff, novelist, born 25 Dec 1918
2	Ray Brown, jazz double bassist, born 13 Oct 1926
	Earle Brown, composer, born 26 Dec 1926
4	Mikhail Alexandrovitch, tenor, born 23 July 1914
5	Ted Williams, American baseball player, born 30 Aug 1918
	Katy Jurado, actress, born 16 Jan 1924
6	John Frankenheimer, film director, born 19 Feb 1930
	Kenneth Koch, poet, born 27 Feb 1925
7	Ray Wood, goalkeeper who survived the Manchester United air disaster, born 11 June 1931
9	Rod Steiger, actor, born 14 April 1924
	Gerald Campion, actor (famous for playing Billy Bunter on television), born 23 April 1921
10	Alan Shulman, composer and cellist, born 4 June 1915
11	Rosco Gordon, blues singer and songwriter, born 10 April 1928
12	Margaret Elliott, Airfix heiress and artist, born 13 Oct 1922
13	Yousuf Karsh, portrait photographer, born in Mardin, Armenia, 23 Dec 1908
	Carey Blyton (nephew of Enid), composer and editor, born 14 March 1932
14	Joaquin Balaguer, former President of the Dominican Republic, born 1 Sept 1907
	Shirley Nolan, founder of the Anthony Nolan Trust (bone marrow register), born in 1942
15	Monty Berman, costumier, born 16 Feb 1912
17	Dr Joseph Luns, Secretary-General of Nato 1971–84, born 28 Aug 1911
19	Frank Taylor, sports journalist, born 7 Dec 1920
	Jimmy King, blues guitarist, born 4 Dec 1964
21	Gus Dudgeon, record producer, born 30 Sept 1942
22	Marian Montgomery, jazz and cabaret singer, born 17 Nov 1934
	Prince Ahmed bin Salman bin Abdul Aziz, businessman and racehorse owner, born 17 Nov 1958
23	Leo McKern, Australian actor, born 16 March 1920
	Chaim Potok, author, born 17 Feb 1929
	Lord Weinstock, managing director of GEC 1963–96, born 29 July 1924
	John Miller, artist, born 30 July 1931
24	Maurice Denham, actor, born 23 Dec 1909
25	Angus Montagu, 12th Duke of Manchester, born 9 Oct 1938
	George Bruce, poet and broadcaster, born 10 March 1909
	Idrees Sulieman, jazz trumpeter, born 7 Aug 1923
26	Tony Anholt, actor, born 19 Jan 1941
	Dirk Sanders, choreographer and film-maker, born in 1933
	Pat Douthwaite, artist, born 28 July 1939
27	Alexander Sinclair, golfer, born 6 July 1920
	Peggy Sager, ballerina, born 6 Jan 1924
28	Jack Karnhem, billiards player and snooker commentator, born 18 June 2002
29	Peter Bayliss, actor, born 27 June 1922
30	Gale Law, dancer, born 29 Oct 1934

August

2	Joe Allison, country music songwriter and disc jockey, born 3 Oct 1924
	Roy Kral, jazz singer and pianist, born 10 Oct 1921
3	Carmen Silvera, actress, born 2 June 1922
5	Chick Hearn, basketball commentator, born 27 Nov 1916
	Daniel Kelly, impresario, born in 1930
7	Lord Oranmore and Browne, born 21 Oct 1901
8	Ronnie Stephenson, jazz drummer, born 25 Jan 1937
10	Michael Houser, guitarist and singer with American rock band Widespread Panic, born 6 Jan 1962
	Doris Wishman, film director, born 23 April 1920
11	Jiri Kolar, Czech writer and artist, born 24 Sept 1914
	Russell Lucas, author, born 11 Feb 1930

CURRENT AFFAIRS

12	Michael De-La-Noy, writer, born 3 April 1934
13	Norman Jolley, actor and writer, born 21 Feb 1916
	Galen Rowell, photographer, born 23 Aug 1940
14	Anneline Malebo, singer, born in 1953
	Susan MacFarlane, artist, born 17 June 1938
16	Jeff Corey, actor, born 10 Aug 1914
18	Dean Riesner, screenwriter, born 3 Nov 1918
19	Eduardo Chillida, sculptor, born 10 Jan 1924
22	Val McCalla, founder and publisher of *The Voice*, born 3 Oct 1943
23	Lawrence Batley, creator of the Cash-and-Carry, born 15 Feb 1911
25	William Warfield, baritone, born 22 Jan 1920
	Daphne Ibbott, pianist, born 29 April 1918
	Dorothy Hewett, poet and playwright, born 21 May 1923
27	George Mitchell, musical arranger and conductor, born 27 Feb 1917
28	Stuart Morgan, art critic, born 25 Jan 1948
	Fred Darrington, sand sculptor, born 28 Aug 1910
29	Lance Macklin, racing driver, born 2 Sept 1919
30	J Lee-Thompson, film director, born 1 Aug 1914
	Prince Zeid bin Shaker, former Prime Minister of Jordan, born 4 Sept 1934
31	Lionel Hampton, jazz vibraphonist and bandleader, born 20 April 1908
	Lord Porter of Luddenham, scientist and Nobel Laureate, born 6 Dec 1920

September

1	Turk Van Lake, jazz guitarist, born 15 June 1918
	Bob Helm, jazz clarinettist, born 18 July 1914
2	Richard (Bob) Walton, trumpeter, born 23 Feb 1913
	Sir Robert Wilson, astrophysicist, born 16 April 1927
3	Peter Turner, author and rower, born 13 Sept 1928
	Len Wilkinson, cricketer, born 5 Nov 1914
4	Vlado Perlemuter, pianist, born 26 May 1904
5	William Cooper (real name Harry Hoff), author, born 4 Aug 1910
6	John CP Constable (great-great-grandson of John Constable), born 28 Sept 1928
	Baroness (Janet) Young, politician, born 23 Oct 1926
7	Michael Elphick, actor, born 19 Sept 1946
	Katrin Cartlidge, actress, born 15 May 1961
	Lt-Colonel Uziel Gal, inventor of the Uzi sub-machinegun, born in Germany on 15 Dec 1923
8	Henri Rol-Tanguy, French Resistance leader, born 12 June 1908
	Ken Ashton, former general secretary of the National Union of Journalists, born 9 Nov 1925
11	Kim Hunter, actress, born 12 Nov 1922
	Johnny Unitas, American football quarterback, born 7 May 1933
12	Pat Marriott, artist and illustrator, born 16 May 1920
14	Paul Williams, saxophonist and band leader, born 13 July 1915
15	Hilda Brabban, creator of Bill and Ben the Flowerpot Men, born 29 April 1914
	Dwight Whylie, Britain's first black radio announcer, born 7 June 1936
	James Mitchell, television writer and novelist, born 12 March 1926
16	Doreen Casey, dancer, born 3 July 1929
17	Michael (Dodo) Marmarosa, jazz pianist, born 12 Dec 1925
	Denys Fisher, inventor of the Spirograph, born 11 May 1918
18	Bob Hayes, athlete and American footballer, born 20 Dec 1942
	Alexander Mackenzie, artist and teacher, born 9 April 1923
	Mauro Ramos De Oliveira, footballer, born 30 Aug 1930
19	Ian Hutchinson, footballer, born 4 Aug 1948
20	Joan Littlewood, theatre director, born 6 Oct 1914
	William Rosenberg, founder of Dunkin' Donuts, born in 1919
	Nils Stevenson, manager of the Sex Pistols and Siouxsie and the Banshees, born 25 Feb 1953
	Pat Saward, footballer, born 17 Aug 1928
21	Peter Kowald, jazz double bass player, born 21 April 1944
	Julio 'crazy legs' Pérez, Uruguayan footballer, born 19 June 1926
22	Anthony Milner, composer, born 13 May 1925
	Joseph Nathan Kane, writer and fact collector, born 23 Jan 1899
24	Tim Rose, singer and songwriter, born 23 Sept 1940
26	Captain Kathleen McGrath, first woman to command an American warship (in 1998), born 4 June 1952
27	Ivan Jelinek, Czech poet and broadcaster, born 6 June 1909
	Charles Henri Ford, author, born 10 Feb 1908
29	Milton 'Mickey' Newbury, singer and songwriter, born 19 May 1940
	Bob Cobbing, poet and publisher, born 30 July 1920
30	Ellis Larkins, jazz pianist, born 15 May 1923

October

2	Bruce Paltrow, producer and director (husband of actress Blythe Danner), born 26 Nov 1943
3	John Weitz, fashion designer, born 25 May 1923
4	Marcus Palliser, author, born 8 Jan 1949

André Delvaux, film-maker, born 21 March 1926
5   Mia Slavenska, ballerina, born in 1914
     Morag Hood, actress, born 13 Dec 1942
6   Prince Claus of the Netherlands, born 26 Sept 1926
7   Helen Gaskell, oboist, born 14 Jan 1906
8   Phyllis Calvert, actress, born 18 Feb 1915
9   Arnie Boehm, boxing trainer, born in 1933
     Charles Guggenheim, film-maker, born 31 March 1924
10   Zara Nelsova, cellist, born 24 Dec 1917
11   Ron Gray, football manager, born 25 June 1920
12   Ray Conniff, trombonist and band leader, born 6 Nov 1916
     Sidney Pink, film producer and director, born in 1916
     Audrey Mestre, world champion freediver, born 11 Aug 1974
13   Sir Garfield Todd, Prime Minister of Southern Rhodesia 1953–8, born in New Zealand 13 July 1908
     Stephen Ambrose, author and historian, born 10 Jan 1936
14   Norbert Schultze, composer of 'Lili Marleen', born 6 Jan 1911
     Wilfred Greatorex, writer and television script editor, born 27 May 1922
     Irving Davies, dancer and choreographer, born 26 April 1926
     Meriel Tufnell, first woman jockey to ride a winner in England, born 12 Dec 1948
15   Jack Lee, film director, born 27 Jan 1913
17   Pattie Coldwell, broadcaster, born 14 May 1952
     Henri Renaud, jazz pianist, born 20 April 1925
     Derek Bell, harpist (member of the Chieftains), born 21 Oct 1935
18   Roman Tam (born Tam Pak-sin), Chinese entertainer, born in 1949
19   Mehli Mehta, violinist, conductor, and founder of the Bombay Symphony Orchestra, born 25 Sept 1908
     Nikolai Rukavishnikov, cosmonaut, born 18 Sept 1932
20   Bernard Fresson, actor, born 27 May 1931
21   Baroness (Beatrice) Serota, born 15 Oct 1919
     Gina Lee, jazz double bassist, born 10 Feb 1943
     Manfred Ewald, sports administrator responsible for the East German athletics drugs scandal, born 17 May 1926
22   Queen Geraldine of Albania, Queen Consort to King Zog, born in Budapest, 6 Aug 1915
     Richard Helms, former Director of the CIA, born 30 March 1913
23   Elizabeth, Countess of Longford, author, born 30 Aug 1906
     János Nyiri, playwright and novelist, born 9 Nov 1932
     Adolph Green, lyricist, screenwriter and actor, born 2 Dec 1914
24   Charmian May, actress, born 16 June 1937
25   Richard Harris, actor, born 1 Oct 1930
     Peggy Moran, actress, born 23 Oct 1918
     John Robert Russell, 13th Duke of Bedford, born 24 May 1917
27   André De Toth, film director, born 15 May 1913
28   Raymond Savignac, poster artist, born 6 Nov 1907
     Jack Barton, television producer, born 22 Oct 1916
     Zeph Gladstone (Vera Downend in *Crossroads*), actress, born 20 Sept 1937
30   Jam Master Jay (born Jason Mizell), member of Run DMC, born 21 Jan 1965
     Juan Antonio Bardem, film-maker, born 2 June 1922
31   Raf Vallone, actor, born 17 Feb 1916

November
1   John Roberts, sculptor, born 18 March 1946
2   Brian Behan (brother of Brendan), author, born 10 Nov 1926
     Lord (Robert) Haslam, former chairman of British Coal and of British Steel, born 4 Feb 1923
3   Jimmy Pike (traditional name Kurnti Kurjarra), Aboriginal artist, born in 1940
     Lonnie Donegan, skiffle musician, born 29 April 1931
5   Billy Guy, baritone, born 20 June 1936
     Billy Mitchell, singer, born in 1931
7   Dilys Hamlett, actress, born 31 March 1928
9   Iris Portal, biographer, born 15 June 1905
     Willam Schutz, writer, born 19 Dec 1925
13   Juan Schiaffino (aka Pepe), footballer, born 28 July 1925
     Bill Berry, jazz cornettist, born 14 Sept 1930
14   Eddie Bracken, actor, born 7 Feb 1920
17   Abba Eban, Israeli politician, born in Cape Town 2 Feb 1915
18   James Coburn, actor, born 31 Aug 1928
19   Max Reinhardt, publisher, born 30 Nov 1915
     John Bunting, sculptor, born 3 Aug 1927
20   Lord Emslie, judge, born 6 Dec 1919
21   Hadda Brooks, pianist and singer, born 29 Oct 1916
22   Adele Jergens, film actress, born 26 Nov 1917
23   Roberto Matta, painter, born 11 Nov 1911
24   Noel Davis, film and television director, born 1 March 1927
     Peter Whitaker, actor, born 12 Feb 1921
     Harriet Doerr, author, born 8 April 1910

25   Karel Reisz, film and theatre director, born 21 July 1926
26   Stanley Black, pianist, composer and conductor, born 14 June 1913
        Dorothy Lightfoot, artist, born 5 Aug 1909
29   John Justin, actor, born 24 Nov 1917
30   Alan Ashman, football manager, born 30 May 1928

December
1   Boris Schapiro, bridge player, born 22 Aug 1909
        Abu Abraham, cartoonist, born 11 June 1924
2   Mal Waldron, jazz pianist and composer, born 16 Aug 1925
3   Klaus Löwitsch, actor, born 8 April 1936
        Sidney Sager, composer and conductor, born 17 May 1917
5   General Ne Win, dictator of Burma 1962–88, born 14 May 1911
        Bob Berg, jazz saxophonist, born 7 April 1951
        Arvell Shaw, jazz double bass player, born 15 Sept 1923
9   Mary Hansen, singer (with Stereolab), born 1 Nov 1966
        To Huu, Vietnamese politician and poet, born in 1920
10   Ian MacNaughton, actor and television director, born 30 Dec 1925
11   Arthur Metcalfe, racing cyclist, born 27 Sept 1938
12   Brad Dexter, actor and producer, born 9 April 1917
        Dee Brown, author and librarian, born 29 Feb 1908
13   Jim Russell, artist, born 30 June 1933
15   Sidney Glazier, film producer, born 29 May 1916
16   Don Vesco, world wheel-driven land speed record holder, born 3 April 1939
17   Colin Clark, film producer and writer, born 9 Oct 1932
        Frederick Knott, dramatist and scriptwriter, born 28 Aug 1916
18   Sir Bert Millichip, chairman of the Football Association 1981–96, born 5 Aug 1914
        Arthur Rowley, footballer, born 21 April 1926
        James Hazeldine, actor and director, born 4 April 1947
19   Barbara Lott, actress, born 15 May 1920
20   Grote Reber, inventor of the radio telescope, born 22 Dec 1911
21   Rayne Kruger, writer and businessman, born 29 Jan 1922
22   Joe Strummer (John Mellor), rock singer, born 21 Aug 1952
24   James Ferman, chairman of the British Board of Film Classification 1975–99, born 11 April 1930
        Jake Thackray, singer and songwriter, born 22 Feb 1938
26   Herb Ritts, photographer, born in 1952
27   George Roy Hill, film director, born 20 Dec 1921
        Wentworth Hubert Charles Beaumont, 3rd Viscount Allendale, born 12 Sept 1922
29   Don Clarke, rugby player, born 10 Nov 1933
        Vivien Neves, model, born 20 Nov 1947
30   Mary Wesley, author, born 24 June 1912
31   DJ Enright, poet, teacher and man of letters, born 11 March 1920

Sporting Record 2002

January
1   Leeds United topped the FA Barclaycard Premiership following a 3-0 win over West Ham United.
4   Tim Henman beat Greg Rusedski 6–4, 6–4, in the quarter-finals of the Australian Hardcourt Championships
        in Adelaide.
        Zoe Baker of Great Britain broke the shortcourse world record for the 50 metres breaststroke in Durban in a
        time of 30.53sec.
5   Phil Taylor won his 10th world darts championship when he beat Peter Manley 7–0 in the PDC version in
        Purfleet.
6   Tim Henman defeated Mark Philippoussis in three sets to win the Australian Hardcourt Championships in
        Adelaide.
9   London Broncos rugby league team announced they would be moving to Brentford FC for the new Tetley's
        Super League season, their seventh change of home venue since 1980.
10   Greg Rusedski beat Goran Ivanisevic 6–2, 0–6, 6–3 in the quarter-finals of the Heineken Open in Auckland,
        the first time he had beaten the Croatian in ten meetings.
11   Tony McCoy reached the fastest-ever 200 wins in a National Hunt season when Native Man won at
        Huntingdon.
12   Greg Rusedski defeated J Golmard of France in the final of the Heineken Open in Auckland.
13   Tony David of Australia defeated Mervyn King of England 6–4 in the final of the Embassy Darts World
        Championship.
        Chester Jets defeated Birmingham Bullets 112-105 in the National Basketball Cup Final at Sheffield Arena.
15   Sri Lankan spin bowler Muttiah Muralitharan, 29, became the youngest man to take 400 Test wickets.
18   Tim Henman beat Greg Rusedski 6–4, 6–3, 1–6, 6–3, in the third round of the Australian Open at
        Melbourne Park.
20   Tim Henman was defeated by Jonas Bjorkman in straight sets in the Australian Open.
        Justin Rose won the Dunhill Championship golf tournament at Houghton Golf Club, Johannesburg.

Tony Allcock defeated Richard Corsie 8–3, 9–4, in the final of the world indoor singles championship.
Ruud van Nistelroy became the first man to score in eight successive Premiership games when he scored a penalty during Manchester United's 2–1 win over Blackburn Rovers.

23   Tony McCoy won a steeplechase at Southwell after remounting following a fall, as all the other six runners failed to finish.
Ed Moses of the United States broke his own short-course 100 metres breaststroke world record with a time of 57.47sec on the second day of the World Cup meeting in Stockholm.

24   Tommi Makinen of Finland was awarded the Monte Carlo Rally after Citroën, for whom Sebastien Loeb won the race, withdrew their appeal against a time penalty.

25   Jennifer Capriati saved four match points to beat Martina Hingis in the final of the Australian Open in Melbourne.

26   Thomas Johansson defeated Marat Safin in the final of the Australian Open tennis championships in Melbourne.

27   Hugh Duff and Paul Foster teamed up to win the World Indoor Bowls Championship at Potters Leisure Resort, Hopton-on-Sea, defeating Graham Robertson and Greg Harlow 5–8, 10–8, 2–1 in the final.
Zoe Baker of Great Britain broke the 50 metres breaststroke short-course world record in Berlin with a time of 30.31sec.

February

2   In the Six Nations Rugby Union Championship, England defeated Scotland 29–3, and France defeated Italy 33–12.

3   In the Six Nations Rugby Union Championship, Ireland defeated Wales 54–10 at Lansdowne Road.
England beat India by 5 runs at the Wankhede Stadium, Bombay (Mumbai), to draw the International cricket series 3–3.
New England Patriots gained a shock 20–17 triumph over St Louis Rams in Superbowl XXXVI in New Orleans.

6   New Zealander Graham Henry was replaced as Welsh Rugby Union head coach by Steve Hansen.

9   Ricky Hatton stopped Mikhail Krivolapov of Russia in the 9th round to retain his WBU light-welterweight boxing title.

10   Sweden defeated Great Britain 3–2 in the Davis Cup to reach the quarter-finals stage.
Paul Hunter defeated Mark Williams 10–9 to retain the Benson and Hedges Masters snooker tournament at Wembley.
Fritz Strobl of Austria won the gold medal in the men's downhill skiing competition at the Winter Olympics in Salt Lake City.

12   Jamie Salé and David Pelletier of Canada were controversially denied the gold medal for the figure skating pairs by the Russian pair Elena Berezhnaya and Anton Sikharulidze although appearing to many to have skated a superior routine. The 5–4 awarding of first places to the Russians included an alleged collusion by the French and Russian judges.

13   Mike Tyson was granted a licence to fight in the state of Georgia despite controversy over new criminal charges.

14   Lennox Lewis was awarded $8 million (£5.6 million) after a New York court found in his favour against Panos Eliades, his former promoter. Eliades brought the original action for breach of contract but was counter-sued by Lewis.

15   The International Olympic Committee decided to award Jamie Salé and David Pelletier a gold medal after finding evidence that the French judge Marie-Reine Le Gougne had 'submitted to a certain pressure' before casting her vote.

16   In the Six Nations Rugby Union Championship, England defeated Ireland 45–11 at Twickenham. In other matches France defeated Wales 37–33 In Cardiff, and Scotland defeated Italy 29–12 in Rome.

17   Janine Whitlock broke the British indoor pole vault record with a leap of 4.44 metres.

20   Alex Coomber, 28, an RAF intelligence officer, won a bronze medal for Great Britain in the skeleton bobsleigh at the Winter Olympic Games in Salt Lake City, Utah.

21   Rhona Martin the Great Britain skip delivered a perfect final stone to win the first gold medal for Britain since 1984, beating Switzerland 4–3 in the ladies curling final.

23   Alain Baxter won a bronze medal in the men's slalom, the first-ever British Winter Olympic skiing medal.

24   Blackburn Rovers defeated Tottenham Hotspurs 2–1 in the Worthington Cup final in Cardiff.

25   The Accenture World Matchplay golf tournament in California was won by Kevin Sutherland.

26   New Zealand defeated England 3–2 in a men's One-Day International cricket series.

March

2   In the Six Nations Rugby Union Championship, France defeated England 20–15 at the Stade de France. In other matches Wales defeated Italy 44–20 and Ireland defeated Scotland 43–22.
Colin Jackson claimed the 110 metres hurdles title at the European Indoor Athletics Championships in Vienna.

3   At the European Indoor Athletics Championships the Poles Plawgo (400 metres) and Czepiewski (800 metres) won their respective titles wearing the same pair of spikes! Jason Gardener of Great Britain won the 60 metres title in 6.49sec.
Michael Schumacher won the Australian Formula One Grand Prix on the Albert Park circuit in Melbourne.

5   Alain Baxter, the Scottish skier who won a bronze medal in the men's slalom at the Winter Olympics in Utah, tested positive for the stimulant methamphetamine.

8   Cambridge defeated Oxford 8–1 in the varsity boxing match at Oxford Town Hall.

12   The Cheltenham Festival got off to a sad start when reigning champion hurdler Istabraq was pulled up after jumping the second flight and the Martin Pipe trained Valiramix was destroyed after collapsing when looking likely to win the race.

14   Best Mate, ridden by Jim Culloty and trained by Henrietta Knight, won the Cheltenham Gold Cup.
16   England defeated New Zealand in the first Test match of the three-Test series in Christchurch. Graham
        Thorpe scored the third-fastest Test double-century in England's second innings only to have it demoted to
        fourth following Nathan Astle's 153-ball double-century, the fastest ever in a Test match. England eventually
        won the match by 98 runs.
        A first division football match between Sheffield United and West Bromwich Albion was abandoned in the
        82nd minute by referee Eddie Wolstenholme after United were reduced to six men through sendings off and
        injuries.
17   Ralf Schumacher won the Malaysian Formula One Grand Prix from Juan Pablo Montoya and Michael
        Schumacher.
21   Alain Baxter, the Scottish skier, was stripped of his bronze medal gained in the men's slalom at the Winter
        Olympics.
22   Zucchero, ridden by Simon Whitworth and trained by David Arbuthnot, won the Random.bet.com Lincoln at
        Doncaster.
23   In the Six Nations Rugby Union Championship, England defeated Wales 50–10 at Twickenham. In other
        matches France defeated Scotland 22–10 and Ireland defeated Italy 32–17.
24   Oxford won the Women's Boat Race, helping Jessica Wilson to become the first president to win the race for
        both Oxford and Cambridge.
27   England were beaten 2–1 by Italy in a friendly International football match at Elland Road.
        The No. 10 shirt worn by Pele during the 1970 World Cup final fetched a record £157,750 at auction at
        Christie's.
30   Oxford won the 148th University Boat Race. The Oxford Isis crew beat Goldie in the reserve match.
31   Michael Schumacher won the Brazilian Formula One Grand Prix on the Interlagos circuit in São Paulo.
        André Agassi won his 700th international title when he defeated Roger Federer in the final of the Nasdaq
        Open.

April
1   Sussex cricket all-rounder Umer Rashid, 26, died alongside his brother Burhan, in a drowning accident in
        Grenada.
2   Tony McCoy surpassed Sir Gordon Richards's tally of the most winners in a horse-racing season when
        Valfonic won the 4.10 at Warwick to give him his 270th win.
3   New Zealand defeated England by 78 runs in the third Test in Auckland to draw the three-match series 1–1.
6   Bill McLaren, the voice of rugby, retired from broadcasting after commentating on the 27–22 Scottish defeat
        of Wales. In other Six Nations Rugby Union Championship matches, France defeated Ireland 44–5 to
        secure the Grand Slam.
        The Aintree Grand National was won by Bindaree, ridden by Jim Culloty and trained by Nigel Twiston-
        Davies.
7   In the Six Nations Rugby Union Championship, England defeated Italy 45–9.
        James Hickman won the 200 metres Butterfly at the world short-course swimming championships in Moscow.
        Georgina Harland won the opening Modern Pentathlon World Cup event in Madrid and the British squad
        won the team event.
9   Liverpool were beaten 4–2 by Bayer Leverkusen in the 2nd leg of the UEFA Champions League Qtr-finals to
        lose 4–3 on agg.
10   David Beckham broke a bone in his left foot following a tackle by Argentinian Pedro Duscher of Deportivo La
        Coruna.
13   Chris Tomlinson leapt 8.27 metres at a minor meeting in Tallahassee, Florida, to eclipse the oldest British
        record in the books, that of Lynn Davies, who long-jumped 8.23 metres in 1968: a record that stood for 34
        years.
        Leicester defeated Newcastle 20–12 to win the rugby union Zurich Premiership.
        Arnold Palmer played his final round of the US Masters following 48 starts, four wins and 12 top-10 finishes.
14   Paula Radcliffe won the Flora London Marathon in a record time of 2hr 18min 56sec. The men's race was
        won by Khalid Khannouchi of Morocco, who broke his own world-best time in 2hr 5min 38sec. Haile
        Gebrselassie was third on his debut.
        Michael Schumacher won the San Marino Formula One Grand Prix at Imola, from team-mate Rubens
        Barichello.
        Arsenal beat Middlesbrough 1–0 and Chelsea defeated Fulham by the same score in the FA Cup semi-
        finals.
        Tiger Woods won the US Masters Golf Championship, from Retief Goosen, with rounds of 70–69–66–71.
15   Peter Nicol, formerly of Scotland and now English, beat John White 15–9, 15–8, 15–8 in the final of the
        British Open Squash Championships. Sarah Fitz-Gerald of Australia beat Tanya Bailey of England 9–3, 9–0,
        9–0 in the women's final.
17   Michael Owen, making his debut as the England football captain, scored the first goal in the 4–0 defeat of
        Paraguay in a soccer friendly at Anfield.
18   Tim Henman defeated Thomas Johansson 2–6, 6–4, 7–6, to reach the semi-finals of the Monte Carlo
        Masters, the first time the British No. 1 had got past the quarter-finals of a clay court tournament.
19   Lloyd Scott, a 40-year-old leukemia sufferer with an artificial hip, took five days, eight hours, 29 minutes and
        46 seconds to complete this year's London Marathon to finish in 32,875th and last place, having competed
        wearing a 120lb diver's suit.
20   Joe Calzaghe made a tenth successful defence of his WBO super-middleweight title when he scored a
        unanimous points victory over former IBF champion Charles Brewer, in Cardiff. Audley Harrison, the
        Olympic super-heavyweight gold medallist, continued his progress by stopping Julius Long of the United
        States in the second round.

21	Great Britain and Ireland defeated Continental Europe in the Seve Trophy at Druids Glen Golf Course, County Wicklow.
23	India defeated the West Indies in the second Test match in Port of Spain, their first Test win in the Caribbean since 1976.
27	Bounce Back, ridden by Tony McCoy and trained by Martin Pipe, won the Attheraces Gold Cup, the former Whitbread Gold Cup, to set a jockeys' record of 289 winners at the end of the National Hunt season which starts again in two day's time.
28	Michael Schumacher won the Spanish Formula One Grand Prix at the Circuit de Catalunya, Barcelona.
30	Bayer Leverkusen drew 1–1 with Manchester United at home to reach the final of the Uefa Champions League on the away-goals rule following a 3–3 aggregate score.

May

1	Real Madrid drew with Barcelona 1–1 in Madrid to gain a place in the Champions League final 3–1 on aggregate.
2	Inzamam-ul-Haq scored 329 on the second day of the first Test to help Pakistan make a record 643 against New Zealand.
4	Arsenal, with goals from Ray Parlour and Freddie Ljungberg, defeated Chelsea 2–0 to win the FA Cup final in Cardiff.
	A last-minute goal by Peter LovenKrands gave Rangers a 3–2 Scottish Cup final win over Celtic at Hampden Park.
	Rock of Gibraltar, owned by Manchester United manager Alex Ferguson, won the Sagitta 2,000 Guineas at Newmarket.
	War Emblem, trained by Bob Baffert, won the Kentucky Derby at Churchill Downs.
5	Kazzia, ridden by Frankie Dettori and trained by Saeed Bin Suroor, won the Sagitta 1,000 Guineas at Newmarket.
	Berhane Adere of Ethiopia won the women's World Half Marathon Championship in Brussels.
6	Peter Ebdon defeated Stephen Hendry 18–17 to win the World Professional Snooker Championship in Sheffield. Ebdon moves up to number three in the rankings for next year but Ronnie O'Sullivan becomes the world number one.
8	Arsenal did the double when they beat Manchester United 1–0 at Old Trafford to win the Premiership with a game to go.
12	Birmingham City FC beat Norwich City 4–2 in a penalty shoot-out following a drawn Nationwide League first division play-off final in Cardiff. Birmingham rejoin the Premiership after an absence of 16 years.
15	Real Madrid defeated Bayer Leverkusen 2–1 in the European Champions League final at Hampden Park, Scotland.
16	Centuries by Atapattu and Jayawardena gave Sri Lanka a good start on day one of the first Test against England at Lords.
18	Naseem Hamed defeated Manuel Calvo to win the vacant IBO Featherweight Championship at the London Arena. Also on the card Michael Brodie won a hard-fought battle against Argentinian Pastor Maurin for the vacant WBF featherweight title and Colin Dunne retained his WBU lightweight belt with a points victory over Wayne Rigby.
	Indonesia secured a fifth successive Thomas Cup title after beating the Malaysian badminton team 3–2 in China.
19	Simon Lessing and Jodie Swallow won the men's and women's British Triathlon Championships at Teeside.
20	Centuries by Mark Butcher and Michael Vaughan ensured the first Test against Sri Lanka ended in a draw.
	Tiger Woods defeated Colin Montgomerie in a play-off to win the Deutsche Bank-SAP Open in Heidelberg.
23	The Republic of Ireland's football captain Roy Keane was sent home from the World Cup by manager Mick McCarthy.
25	Sir Alex Ferguson's 2,000 Guineas winner Rock of Gibraltar won the Irish equivalent at the Curragh.
26	David Coulthard won the Monaco Formula One Grand Prix at the Monte Carlo circuit.
	Anders Hansen of Denmark won the Volvo PGA Championship at Wentworth by five strokes from Colin Montgomerie.
31	Senegal defeated France 1–0 in the opening game of the Fifa World Cup.

June

1	South African cricketer Hansie Cronje was killed in a plane crash near his home town of George in the Outeniqua mountains.
	Ricky Hatton defeated Eamonn Magee on points to retain his WBU Light-welterweight Championship in Manchester.
2	England defeated Sri Lanka by an innings and 111 runs in the second Test match at Edgbaston.
	England drew 1–1 with Sweden in their opening game of the football World Cup.
5	The Republic of Ireland drew 1–1 with Germany to increase their chances of qualifying for the knockout stages of the World Cup.
7	A 44th-minute penalty by David Beckham gave England a 1–0 win over Argentina in Group F of the World Cup.
	Kazzia, ridden by Frankie Dettori and trained by Saeed bin Suroor, won the Vodafone Oaks at Epsom.
8	High Chaparral, ridden by Johnny Murtagh and trained by Aiden O'Brien, won the Vodafone Derby at Epsom.
	Lennox Lewis knocked out Mike Tyson in the 8th round of their world heavyweight title fight in Memphis, Tennessee.
	Ryan Sullivan of Australia won the British Speedway Grand Prix at the Millennium Stadium, Cardiff.
	Serena Williams defeated her sister Venus 7–5, 6–3, in the final of the French Open Tennis Championships

CURRENT AFFAIRS

9   The first Volvo Ocean Race, ending its 32,700 nautical miles in Kiel, Germany, was won by John Kostecki's Illbruck Challenge.
     Michael Schumacher won the Canadian Formula One Grand Prix in Montreal.
     Albert Costa defeated Juan Carlos Ferrero 6–1, 6–0, 4–6, 8–3, in an all-Spanish final of the French Open Tennis Championships.
     Darren Clarke won the Compass Group English Open Golf Championship at the Forest of Arden Course.
11   Ireland qualified for the last 16 of the World Cup following a 3–0 win over Saudi Arabia in Yokohama.
12   England qualified for the last 16 of the World Cup following a 0–0 draw with Nigeria in their last group match.
13   The Los Angeles Lakers beat New Jersey Nets 4–0 in the NBA Basketball Finals Series.
14   Former England football manager Bobby Robson was awarded a knighthood in the Golden Jubilee Birthday Honours List.
15   England beat Denmark 3–0 to reach the quarter-finals of the World Cup.
16   Tiger Woods won the US Open golf championship at Farmingdale, New York.
     Ireland were beaten in a penalty shoot-out after drawing with Spain in the last 16 of the World Cup.
17   England beat Sri Lanka by ten wickets, with an over to spare, in the third Test match at Old Trafford.
19   The Cheltenham & Gloucester Trophy match between Surrey and Glamorgan at the Oval produced several records. Surrey batsman Alistair Brown scored 268 off 160 balls, the highest one-day score. Surrey's winning score of 438 was the highest one-day team score and the match aggregate of 867 runs scored was also a record.
20   Royal Rebel, ridden by Johnny Murtagh and trained by Mark Johnston, retained the Ascot Gold Cup.
21   England were beaten 2–1 by Brazil in the quarter-finals of the World Cup.
22   Warwickshire defeated Essex by five wickets to win the last-ever Benson & Hedges Cup Final at Lords.
     Marco Antonio Barrera defeated Erik Morales on points to become the WBC World Featherweight Boxing Champion.
23   Rubens Barrichello won the European Formula One Grand Prix at the Nürburgring.
     The Great Britain men's athletics team won the European Cup in Annecy, France.
25   Germany defeated South Korea 1–0 in the World Cup semi-finals.
26   Brazil defeated Turkey 1–0 in the second World Cup semi-final match.
     In a day of shocks at Wimbledon, Pete Sampras was beaten by George Bastl of Switzerland, André Agassi by Paradorn Srichaphan, and Marat Safin by Belgian Olivier Rochus.
30   Brazil defeated Germany 2–0 to win the football World Cup. Ronaldo scored both goals.
     High Chaparral, ridden by Mick Kinane and trained by Aiden O'Brien, won the Budweiser Irish Derby at the Curragh.
     Soren Hansen of Denmark won the last Murphy's Irish Open to be played at the Fota Island golf club.
     Dwain Chambers of Great Britain defeated world number one sprinter Maurice Greene for the second time in three days.

July
2   Greg Rusedski was beaten in five sets by Xavier Malisse of Belgium in the fourth round at Wimbledon.
5   Tim Henman was beaten 7–5, 6–1, 7–5, by Lleyton Hewitt of Australia in the Wimbledon semi-finals.
6   Serena Williams defeated her sister Venus 7–6, 6–3, to win the ladies' singles final at Wimbledon.
     Lance Armstrong won the prologue seven-kilometre time trial on the opening day of the Tour de France cycle race.
     Hawk Wing, ridden by Mick Kinane and trained by Aiden O'Brien, won the Coral Eurobet Eclipse at Sandown Park.
7   Lleyton Hewitt defeated David Nalbandian of Argentina 6–1, 6–3, 6–2, to win the men's singles final at Wimbledon.
     Michael Schumacher won the British Formula One Grand Prix at Silverstone.
     Phil Taylor defeated Ronnie Baxter 3–0 to win the Las Vegas Desert Classic darts tournament.
8   Terry Venables was announced as the new manager of Leeds United FC.
10   British heavyweight boxer Audley Harrison won a points decision over Dominic Negus at Wembley Conference Centre.
13   India defeated England in the final of the NatWest Series at Lord's in a dramatic finale. Marcus Trescothick and Nasser Hussain both scored centuries in England's huge 325 for five wickets but India scraped home with three balls to spare.
14   Colin McRae won the Safari Rally for the third time to gain his 25th career win in world rally events.
19   Aussie left-hander Mike Hussey became the first batsman to reach 1,000 first-class runs this season when he hit 163 not out for Northants at Worcester.
20   Rio Ferdinand was transferred from Leeds to Manchester United for a British record £30 million.
     Tiger Woods shot his worst-ever round as a professional when he scored 81 in the third round of the Open.
     Colin Montgomerie equalled the tour record for the greatest disparity in rounds when he followed a 64 with an 84 in the Open.
21   Michael Schumacher won the French Formula One Grand Prix at Magny-Cours and with it the World Drivers' Championship.
     Ernie Els won the Open Championship at Muirfield following a four-way play-off with Stuart Appleby, Steve Elkington and Thomas Levet. The two Australians were eliminated, leaving Els to beat the Frenchman Levet in a sudden-death play-off.
     Earl 'the Pearl' Strickland beat Francisco 'Django' Bustamente of the Philippines 17–15 to win the world 9-ball pool title.
27   Former heavyweight boxing champion of the world Larry Holmes defeated Eric 'Butterbean' Esch on points in Virginia.

28   Lance Armstrong won the Tour de France cycle race.
29   England defeated India by 170 runs in the first npower Test at Lord's.
31   Zoe Baker of England won the gold medal for the 50 metres breaststroke in the Commonwealth Games in Manchester in 30.60sec following her world record swim of 30.57sec in the semi-finals.

August
2   Natalie du Toit of South Africa made history when she made the final of both the disabled and able-bodied swimming finals at the Commonwealth Games in Manchester.
3   Bond Boy, ridden by Chris Catlin and trained by Bryan Smart, won the Vodafone Stewards' Cup at Goodwood.
4   The Commonwealth Games ended with Australia heading the medals table with 82 golds, the England team securing second spot with 54 golds, and India edging out Canada with a final gold medal tally of 32.
6   Paula Radcliffe of Great Britain won the 10,000 metres at the European Championships in Munich in 30min 01.09sec.
7   Dwaine Chambers won the 100 metres gold medal at the European Championships in a time of 9.96 seconds.
8   Jonathan Edwards won the bronze medal behind Christian Olsson from Sweden in the European Championship triple jump final in Munich.
9   Steve Backley won his fourth successive javelin gold medal at the European Championships.
      Australia called off its three-Test cricket tour of Pakistan this autumn amid fears for the players' safety.
10   Ashia Hansen won the women's triple jump gold medal at the European Championships with her winning leap coming in the final round, just as she did in the Commonwealth Games competition.
      Colin Jackson won the 110 metres hurdles gold medal at the European Championships in Munich.
      Former England cricket captain Mike Atherton won £68,612 on the Scoop6, a popular Saturday afternoon horseracing bet.
11   A 68th-minute goal by Gilberto Silva gave Arsenal a 1–0 win over Liverpool in the FA Community Shield (the former FA Charity Shield) at the Millennium Stadium, Cardiff.
16   Greg Rusedski beat Lleyton Hewitt 7–6, 6–4, in the third round of the RCA Championships. With his win over Marat Safin the previous week in Cincinnati he had defeated the top two players in the world within the last seven days.
      Dwaine Chambers ran a time of 9.94sec in the semi-final of the 100 metres in Zurich, although only placing third in 10.05sec in the final behind Tim Montgomery.
17   The Premiership football season began with the Big Three of Arsenal, Manchester United and Liverpool all winning.
      Joe Calzaghe retained his WBO super-middleweight title when he beat Puerto Rican Miguel Jiminez on a unanimous points decision in Cardiff. The victory was Calzaghe's 11th successful defence.
18   Rich Beem of the USA won the US PGA Championship by one stroke from Tiger Woods, in Minnesota.
      Rubens Barrichello won the Hungarian Formula One Grand Prix in Budapest.
      Laila Ali, the daughter of Muhammad Ali, former heavyweight boxing champ, stopped Suzy Taylor in the second round to claim the IBA super-middleweight title.
21   Neil Lennon, the Celtic player who was to captain Northern Ireland in a friendly against Cyprus, withdrew following a death threat from a loyalist paramilitary organisation.
22   John Terry, the Chelsea footballer, was cleared on a charge of attacking a bouncer with a bottle outside a London nightclub.
26   India beat England by an innings and 46 runs at Headingley, to level the Test series 1–1 with one to play.
27   Tony McCoy became the winning-most National Hunt jockey of all time when Mighty Montefalco won the 2.50 race at Uttoxeter to give him his 1,700th winner, beating the record 1,699 of Richard Dunwoody.
      Manchester United defeated the Hungarians of Zalaegerszeg 5–0 (5–1 on aggregate) to secure a place in the first group stage of the Champions League.
30   34-year-old German Albrecht Stromeyer was charged with stalking world No. 1 women's tennis player Serena Williams.
31   Yorkshire beat Somerset in the Cheltenham & Gloucester Cup final at Lord's with Matthew Elliott scoring 128 not out.

September
1   Michael Schumacher won the Belgian Formula One Grand Prix at Francorchamps, his 10th of the season, to break the record nine wins achieved jointly by Nigel Mansell and himself.
      Sonia O'Sullivan won the Flora Light Challenge 5K in Hyde Park, London, in a record time of 14min 56sec.
      William Fox-Pitt riding Highland Lad won the Burghley Masterfoods Horse Trials.
7   Serena Williams defeated her sister Venus in straight sets in the ladies' final of the US Open tennis championships at Flushing Meadows.
      Surrey won the Frizzell County Cricket Championship for the third time in four years.
8   Pete Sampras beat André Agassi 6–3, 6–4, 5–7, 6–4, in the final of the US Open tennis championships at Flushing Meadows.
      Rock of Gibraltar, owned by Sir Alex Ferguson, won his seventh consecutive Group One race, beating the modern-day record of the great Mill Reef. The latest win came in the Netjets Prix Du Moulin at Longchamp.
14   Tim Montgomery of the USA broke the world record for the 100 metres in Paris with a time of 9.78sec. In the same race Dwaine Chambers of Great Britain equalled Linford Christie's British and European record of 9.87sec.
      Oscar De La Hoya defeated Fernando Vargas in the 11th round at the Mandalay Bay hotel in Las Vegas, to add the WBA belt to his own WBC light-middleweight crown.

15   Rubens Barrichello won the Italian Formula One Grand Prix at Monza.
        Jeanette Brakewell riding Over to You won the individual silver medal behind Jean Teulère, the first
        Frenchman to win the world three-day-event title. The Great Britain team won the bronze medal behind the
        Mark Phillips-trained US team.

16   Bill Waugh, who led the England hockey team to a bronze medal in the 1998 Commonwealth Games,
        retired, aged 29.

18   Australian spin-bowling legend Shane Warne signed a two-year contract with Hampshire for next cricket
        season.

21   James Cracknell and Matthew Pinsent retained their coxless pairs world title in Seville, Spain.
        Triple jumper Jonathan Edwards was the only Briton to win a World Cup title in Madrid. Africa retained the
        men's cup and Russia won the women's cup.

22   Great Britain defeated Thailand 3–2 to secure its place in the 16-nation World Group of the Davis Cup next
        year.
        The United States lady golfers regained the Solheim Cup 15½–12½ in Edina, Minnesota.
        Zara Phillips won the silver medal in the European Young Riders three-day-event championship in Austria.
        James Thompson won the British Touring Car Championship after his main rival retired from the final round
        at Donington Park.
        Dermott Lennon from Co. Down became Ireland's first world showjumping champion.

23   Surrey batsman Graham Thorpe withdrew from the England team to tour Australia this winter.
        Julie Mann, the English national badminton champion, won the US Open in Los Angeles.
        Former world champion Jansher Khan resumed his squash career with a 3-0 win over Arshad Iqbal Burki in
        the CNS Open in Karachi, after three years out with knee problems.

24   Michael Olowokandi, the NBA basketball player from London, signed a one-year contract with the Los
        Angeles Clippers worth $6.1 million (about £4 million), to become one of Britain's wealthiest sportsmen.
        The football used for the 1888 FA Cup Final in which West Bromwich Albion defeated Preston North End
        2–1 was sold for £32,900 at a memorabilia auction at Christie's, South Kensington.

25   Australian cyclist Bradley McGee won the four-kilometre individual pursuit, the first event of the world track
        championships in Copenhagen.

26   Chris Hoy of Great Britain won the gold medal in the men's kilometre time-trial at the world track
        championships in Copenhagen.
        Pole-vaulter Janine Whitlock was found guilty of a doping offence by UK Athletics and banned from
        competing until July 2004.
        Former world rally champion Colin McRae signed a reported £5 million contract to join Citroën for next
        season.

27   The three-man team of Chris Hoy, Jamie Staff and Craig MacLean won the team sprint gold medal at the
        World Track Championships in Copenhagen.

28   Chris Newton of Great Britain won the gold medal in the points race at the World Track Championships in
        Copenhagen.

29   Europe won the Ryder Cup by 15½pts to 11½pts with Paul McGinley holing the winning putt at the Belfry.
        Rubens Barrichello won the US Formula One Grand Prix at Indianapolis in controversial style as his team-
        mate and world champion Michael Schumacher eased up before the line with the apparent intention of
        crossing the line together but miscalculated and Barrichello was given the race win by the smallest of
        margins.
        Spain's Aitor Gonzales won the Tour of Spain after winning the 21st and final stage, a 41.2km time trial
        ending in Madrid.
        Colin Edwards, known as the Texan Tornado, won the World Superbike Championship from Australian Troy
        Bayliss.
        Ronnie O'Sullivan beat John Higgins 9–4 in the final of the Regal Masters in Glasgow, the first event of the
        new season.

30   Stephen Smith was disqualified during the WBU light-welterweight title fight with holder Ricky Hatton after
        Smith's father Darkie Smith entered the ring and pushed referee Mickey Vann.
        Darren Hall, the winner of the English national badminton title a record 10 times, officially retired from the sport.

October

2   Wolverhampton beat Eastbourne 93–87 (49–41, 44–46) over two legs to win the first Elite League
        speedway grand final.

3   Viking Stavanger beat Chelsea 4–2 (5–4 on agg) in the UEFA Cup first round, however Leeds qualified for
        the second round after a 1–1 draw (2–1 on agg) with the Ukrainian side Metalurg Zaporizhzhya. Other
        results included a 2–0 win for Celtic (10–1 on agg) over FK Suduva, a 3–3 draw between CSKA Sofia and
        Blackburn Rovers (4–4 on agg but Blackburn went through on away goals), a 2–2 draw between Fulham
        and Hajduk Split (3–2 to Fulham on agg), a 1–0 win for Ipswich over FK Sartid (2–1 to Ipswich on agg) and
        a 4–3 win for Livingston over Sturm Graz (Sturm Graz won 8–6 on agg). The biggest shock of the round was
        the defeat of Rangers by Czech minnows Viktoria Zizkov on the away goals rule after winning the second
        leg 3–1 but losing the first leg 2–0.
        Great Britain were drawn away against Australia in the Davis Cup World Group, the tie to be played next
        February.
        Alex Coomber, 27, Britain's bronze medallist in the skeleton bob at this year's Winter Olympics, retired from
        the sport.
        Lynne Taylor, from Wallsall, broke the 840 miles Land's End to John O'Groats cycling record with a time of
        two days, four hours, 45 minutes, 11 seconds.

4   David Morgan was confirmed as the new chairman of the England and Wales Cricket Board as replacement
        for Lord MacLaurin from 1 January 2003.

5   Beauchamp Pilot, ridden by Eddie Ahern and trained by Gerard Butler, won the Tote Cambridgeshire at Newmarket.

Audley Harrison continued his unbeaten professional boxing record with a two-round stoppage of American Wade Lewis.

6   Europe's richest race, the Prix de l'Arc de Triomphe-Lucien Barrière, was won by Marienbard, ridden by Frankie Dettori and trained by Saeed Bin Suroor at the Godolphin set-up in Dubai.

Arsenal defeated Sunderland 3–1 to extend their unbeaten Premiership record to 30 matches.

Sonia O'Sullivan and Paul Kosgei won the elite races in the Great North Run, Kosgei running 59min 58sec.

7   Bob Murray, the Sunderland chairman, sacked his manager Peter Reid after seven years at the club. Martin Hinshelwood was replaced as manager of Brighton and Hove Albion by Steve Coppell after ten consecutive defeats.

8   Julian White, the Bristol prop, was banned for 10 weeks for butting the Leicester loose-head Graham Rowntree.

9   Following a BBC television *Panorama* exposé of corruption in horse racing, Jeremy Phipps, the Jockey Club's head of security, resigned amid allegations of double standards.

South Africa beat Bangladesh in the third and final one-day international in Kimberley, South Africa, to create a new world record of 23 consecutive one-day international losses stretching back to when they beat Pakistan in the 1999 World Cup.

10   Santiago Botero of Colombia won the World Road Championships men's elite time-trial on the Zolder motor-racing track in Belgium. David Millar and Stuart Dangerfield of Great Britain finished in sixth and 26th place respectively.

Charlotte Cornwallis, the British world champion, won the French Open real tennis championship in Paris.

12   Despite a weather-battered pitch England beat Slovakia 2–1 at the Slovan stadium in Group Seven of the European Nations football championship. In other European Championship qualifiers Spain beat Northern Ireland 3–0 in Group Six and Scotland defeated Iceland 2-0 in Group Five.

Pakistan were bowled out by Australia for 59 and 53 to lose the second Test in Sharjah by an innings and 198 runs.

Scott Nicholls of Ipswich won the British Championship speedway final in Coventry after defending champion Mark Loram was stretchered off after crashing.

13   Five-times world champion Michael Schumacher won the Japanese Formula One Grand Prix at Suzuka, to claim his 11th victory of the season. It was also Schumacher's 50th pole position on the grid, and other records include becoming the first driver to finish on the podium in every race of a Formula One season and a record 68-point winning margin.

Paula Radcliffe of Great Britain ran a world-best time in the Chicago Marathon, her 2hr 17min 18sec beating the previous record by 90sec. Khalid Khannouchi, born in Morocco but competing for the United States, won the men's race.

Snooker player Chris Small, from Edinburgh, beat Glaswegian Alan McManus 9–5 in the final of the LG Cup at Preston.

15   Manchester United & Ireland footballer Roy Keane was given a five-match ban, starting on 4 November, and handed a record fine of £150,000, for comments made about a premeditated tackle on Alf Inge Haaland, in his autobiography co-written with Eamon Dunphy.

16   England were held to a 2–2 draw by Macedonia at St Mary's Stadium, Southampton, in the European Nations football championship. In other matches Ireland lost to Switzerland 1–2 and Northern Ireland drew with Ukraine 0–0, but Wales, under new manager Mark Hughes, defeated Italy 2–1 in front of 70,000 spectators at the Millennium Stadium, Cardiff.

18   Michael Campbell defeated Nick Faldo at the 43rd hole in the first round of the Cisco World Matchplay Championship, in a match carried over from the previous evening, the longest in the history of the event.

19   Scottish featherweight Scott Harrison gained a unanimous points decision over Argentinian Julio Pablo Chacon in Glasgow, to win the WBO title once held by Prince Naseem Hamed.

Arsenal lost their record 30-match unbeaten Premiership record when beaten 2–1 by Everton at Goodison Park. Wayne Rooney, of Everton, at 16 years and 360 days became the Premiership's youngest-ever scorer.

St Helens defeated Bradford 19–18 in the Tetley's Super League Grand Final, the winning point being scored in the last minute by a Sean Long drop-kick.

20   Ernie Els of South Africa won the Cisco World Matchplay Championship at Wentworth, defeating Sergio Garcia 2&1.

Australia defeated England 2–1 in the final of the Women's World Team Squash Championship in Odense, Denmark.

21   Tim Don, of Great Britain, won the world duathlon title in Georgia, beating Greg Bennett, of Australia, by one second.

24   German tennis player Boris Becker was given a two-year prison sentence, suspended for three years, for tax evasion.

25   Defeat for Tim Henman at the hands of David Nalbandian meant that he was denied a top-eight spot for inclusion in the Tennis Masters Cup in Shanghai in November. Henman, who was the defending champion, lost 3–6, 7–6, 6–2, in the quarter-finals of the Davidoff Swiss Indoors Championship.

26   Horse-racing trainer Ian Balding bowed out of the game with a 14–1 winner.

27   Phil Taylor beat John Part 7–3 in the final of the Paddy Power World Grand Prix of darts.

Mark Waugh was dropped from the Australian team in favour of Darren Lehmann and immediately retired from Test cricket.

28   Anaheim beat San Francisco 4–3 to win baseball's World Series.

Team Bath became the first university side to reach the FA Cup first round proper in 122 years following their defeat of Horsham in a penalty shoot-out.

CURRENT AFFAIRS

Tony Drago of Malta compiled his first-ever maximum 147 break in competition during a 5–3 defeat by Stuart Bingham in the fifth round of the Benson and Hedges Championship in Mansfield.

31 Adam Crozier, chief executive of the Football Association, resigned his position.

November

2 AS Adema beat Stade Olympique L'Emyrne 149–0, a world record for the number of goals scored in any one football match. The match, played in Madagascar, was marred by a protest against poor refereeing which caused Stade to repeatedly knock the ball in their own net.

3 Englishman Ian Poulter won the Italian Open Golf Championship on the Olgiata course, Rome.
Steve Mifsud of Australia beat Tim English of Wales 11–6 in the final of the IBSF World Amateur Snooker Championship.

5 Worcestershire County Cricket Club announced that Graeme Hick would not be their captain for next season.
Mick McCarthy resigned as manager of the Republic of Ireland's football team.
Darkie Smith, father of Stephen Smith, had his licence withdrawn by the British Boxing Board of Control following the incident that caused his son to be disqualified from his world title fight against Ricky Hatton on 30 September.

9 Jonny Wilkinson scored 21 points for the England rugby union team during their 31–28 victory over the New Zealand All Blacks at Twickenham. In other matches Ireland beat Australia 18–9 at Lansdowne Road and Wales beat Fiji 58–14 at the Millennium Stadium, Cardiff.
New Zealand defeated Great Britain 30–16 in a rugby league international at Ewood Park.

10 Matthew Hayden became only the seventh man to score centuries in each innings of an Ashes Test during the 384-run defeat of England in the first Test at The Gabba, Brisbane. The other six batsmen were Bardsley, Sutcliffe, Hammond, Compton, Morris and Steve Waugh.
Leanda Cave of Great Britain won the senior women's title at the World Triathlon Championships in Cancun, Mexico.

11 A coroner ruled that former England footballer Jeff Astle died from dementia brought on by repeatedly heading the heavy leather ball of his day.

12 Liverpool were knocked out of the Champions League following a 3–3 draw with FC Basle.

13 Newcastle United beat Feyenoord 3–2 in Rotterdam to become the first side to qualify for the second phase of the Champions League after starting with three defeats.

16 England beat Australia 32–31 in a rugby union international at Twickenham. In other matches Scotland beat South Africa 21–6 at Murrayfield and Wales beat Canada 32–21 at The Millennium Stadium, Cardiff.

17 Paul Hunter defeated Ian McCulloch 9–4 in the final of the British Open Snooker Championship at Telford.
Lleyton Hewitt of Australia, the world number one tennis player, retained the Tennis Masters Cup in Shanghai, when he beat Juan Carlos Ferrero 7–5, 7–5, 2–6, 2–6, 6–4 in the final.
Paula Radcliffe, the British distance runner, was announced as the IAAF world woman athlete of the year in Monte Carlo.
Jamie Schroeder of the United States won the men's British Indoor Rowing Championship at Birmingham in 5min 47.6sec.

21 Disgraced former jockey Dermot Browne was warned off for 20 years by the Jockey Club following his admission that he had 'stopped' 23 horses over a six-week spell.

23 England defeated South Africa 53–3 in a rugby union international match at Twickenham. In other matches New Zealand beat Wales 43-17 and Ireland defeated Argentina 16–7.
Great Britain defeated New Zealand 16–10 in a rugby league international at the JJB Stadium.
Ellen MacArthur of Great Britain, in her 60ft yacht *Kingfisher*, won the 3,450-mile Route du Rhum from St Malo to Guadeloupe.

24 Australia defeated England by an innings and 51 runs in the second Test match in Adelaide.

25 Audley Harrison maintained his unbeaten professional boxing record with a first-round knockout of American Shawn Robinson in Atlantic City, New Jersey.
Donald McRae became the first author to win the William Hill Sports Book of the Year for the second time with *In Black and White: The Untold Story of Joe Louis and Jesse Owens*.

26 Former World Formula One Champion Niki Lauda was sacked by Jaguar as team principal for lacking 'technical depth'.
Iranian Olympic champion Hossein Rezazadeh broke the world record for the clean and jerk with a lift of 263kg in the super-heavyweight (over 195kg) category of the World Championships in Warsaw, Poland.

28 Lo Shih-Kal, of Taiwan, became the youngest player to take part in a European tour event when the 13-year-old amateur shot a four-over-par 73 in the Hong Kong Open at Fanling.

December

1 Australia defeated England by an innings and 48 runs in the third Test at the WACA in Perth to retain the Ashes.

2 The Arrows Formula One team had their application to take part in the 2003 championship turned down by the FIA.

3 Australian Rob Fahey, the defending champion, won the Real Tennis World Championship at Hampton Court Palace, beating Tim Chisholm of the USA seven sets to six, the first time the thirteenth set has been required in the competition, which dates back to 1740, making it the oldest in international sport.

4 David Byas, the only man to have been capped and to have scored a century for both Lancashire and Yorkshire, retired from first-class cricket for the second time. Byas originally retired from Yorkshire last year but was tempted back for a season with Lancashire.

6 David Gourlay, the world's top-ranked bowler, won the HJ Hall Scottish Masters, beating Darren Burnett in the final.

8	Paula Radcliffe was voted BBC Sports Personality of the Year.
12	American sprinter Marion Jones parted from her long-time coach, Trevor Graham, and will work with Canadian Derek Hansen in future.
13	Warwickshire left-arm spinner Ashley Giles was ruled out of the Ashes series in Australia following slow recovery from a broken wrist. Defending champion Peter Nicol was beaten in the semi-finals of the World Squash Open by John White. Ironically, White is an Australian who now represents Scotland, whilst Nicol is a Scot who now represents England. In the other semi-final Jonathon Power was forced to retire when leading 15–3, 10–10, after being struck by the racket of his opponent, David Palmer, of Australia. Sheffield Sharks moved six points clear at the top of the British Basketball League following their 105–72 win over Newcastle Eagles.
14	David Palmer of Australia defeated John White, 13–15, 12–15, 15–6, 15–14, 15–11 in the final of the World Squash Open.
15	Mark Williams defeated Ken Doherty 10-9 in the final of the PowerhouseUK Snooker championship at the Barbican Centre in York.
16	Patrice Hagelauer, the Frenchman who is the current Lawn Tennis Association director of performance, announced he would be standing down from the job in the new year. Ronaldo, the Brazilian striker, was named the European Footballer of the Year.
17	England beat Sri Lanka by 43 runs at the Gabba in Perth to end their 13-match spell without a win. Ronaldo was named the World Footballer of the Year.
18	The Romanian Gymnastic Federation banned Lavinia Milosovici, 26, Claudia Presecan, 23, and Corina Ungureanu, 22, from coaching and refereeing in official competitions for five years after they appeared nude in a Japanese DVD film.
19	Tony Lewis, the former England cricket captain, was appointed non-executive chairman of World Snooker Ltd (WSL), which manages the assets and organises the professional tour for the WPBSA, the sport's governing body.
20	England beat Sri Lanka by 95 runs at the Gabba in Perth to record their second One-Day International win in the VB Series against Australia and Sri Lanka. Vincenzo Polli, of Italy, was killed in a crash during the final round of the UIM Formula One World Powerboat Championship in Abu Dhabi.
22	Europe beat the USA 12-9 in the annual Mosconi Cup pool competition, Steve Davis sinking the winning pot at York Hall, Bethnal Green.
26	Best Mate, ridden by Tony McCoy and trained by Henrietta Knight, won the Pertemps King George VI Chase at Kempton. Tony McCoy beat his own record of the fastest 200 winners in a season when Lord Sam won the novices hurdle at Kempton. Two records were broken in the Barclaycard Premiership: Wayne Rooney, 17, of Everton became the youngest player to be sent off and James Milner, of Leeds United, became the league's youngest-ever scorer at 16 years and 357 days.
27	Mini Sensation, ridden by Tony Dobbin and trained by Jonjo O'Neill, won the Welsh Grand National at Chepstow.
29	Michael Vaughan's 145 during the fourth Test in Melbourne made him the highest run-scorer in Test cricket in 2002.
30	Australia beat England by five wickets in the fourth Test to take a 4–0 lead in the Ashes series.
31	Jonny Wilkinson, the 23-year-old England fly half, became the youngest rugby union player to receive a New Year's Honour when he was awarded an MBE.

CURRENT AFFAIRS

Birthdays 2002

January

1	JD Salinger, author, 83, John Fuller, poet, 66, Baroness Miller of Chilthorne Domer, 48
2	David Bailey, photographer, 64, Sir Richard Bayliss, physician to the Queen 1970–85, 85
3	Michael Schumacher, racing driver, 33, Mel Gibson, actor, 46, Sir George Martin, record producer, 76
4	Grace Bumbry, opera singer, 65, Iain Cuthbertson, actor, 72, Margaret Marshall, opera singer, 53
5	Diane Keaton, actress, 56, General Sir Michael Rose, soldier, 62, Maurizio Pollini, pianist, 60
6	Rowan Atkinson, comedian, 47, Kapil Dev, cricketer, 43, Angus Deayton, broadcaster and writer, 46, Terry Venables, football manager and writer, 59, Barry John, rugby player, 57
7	Ian Le Frenais, screenwriter, 65, Nicolas Cage, actor, 38, Ross Norman, squash player, 43
8	David Bowie, singer, 55, Shirley Bassey, singer, 65, Stephen Hawking, physicist, 60, Ron Moody, actor, 78
9	Joan Baez, singer, 61, Joely Richardson, actress, 37, Clive Dunn, actor, 80, Susannah York, actress, 60
10	Rod Stewart, singer, 57, Derek Hammond-Stroud, operatic baritone, 76
11	Henry Cecil, racehorse trainer, 59, Bryan Robson, football manager, 45, Arthur Scargill, trade unionist, 64
12	Michael Aspel, broadcaster, 69, PW Botha, former President of South Africa, 86, Kirstie Alley, actress, 47, Joe Frazier, heavyweight boxer, 58, Des O'Connor, entertainer, 70, Brendan Foster, athlete, 54
13	Stephen Hendry, snooker player, 33, Michael Bond, author, 76, Ronan Rafferty, golfer, 38
14	Faye Dunaway, actress, 61, Trevor Nunn, theatre director, 62, Warren Mitchell, actor, 76, Peter Barkworth, actor, 73, Richard Briers, actor, 68, Maina Gielgud, ballerina, 57
15	Princess Michael of Kent, 57, Margaret Beckett, politician, 59, Chuck Berry, singer, 76, Frank Bough, broadcaster, 69
16	Christine Truman, tennis player, 61, Cliff Thorburn, snooker player, 54, Kate Moss, model, 28, Susan Sontag, writer, 69

17	Muhammad Ali, heavyweight boxer, 55, Vidal Sassoon, hair stylist, 74, Jim Carrey, actor, 40, Moira Shearer, ballerina, 76
18	Kevin Costner, actor, 47, Paul Keating, former Australian Prime Minister, 58, John Boorman, film director, 69, Chief Emeka Anyaoku, Commonwealth Secretary-General 1999–2000, 69, Raymond Briggs, illustrator, 68, David Bellamy, botanist and broadcaster, 69, Peter Beardsley, footballer, 41, Mark Rylance, theatre director, 42
19	Stefan Edberg, tennis player, 36, Dolly Parton, singer, 56, Simon Rattle, conductor, 47, Richard Dunwoody, jockey, 38, Michael Crawford, actor, 60, Richard Lester, film director, 70, Phil Everly, singer, 63, Robert Palmer, singer, 53
20	Buzz Aldrin, astronaut, 72, Tom Baker, actor, 66, Liza Goddard, actress, 52, David Lynch, film producer, 56
21	Placido Domingo, operatic tenor, 61, Jack Nicklaus, golfer, 62, Paul Scofield, actor, 80, John Kentish, tenor, 92
22	Nigel Benn, boxer, 38, George Foreman, boxer and actor, 54, John Hurt, actor, 62, Claire Rayner, agony aunt, 71, Mary Hayley Bell, playwright, 91
23	Jeanne Moreau, actress, 74, Lord Strathcarron, 78, Lord Sutherland, 70
24	Neil Diamond, singer, 61, Bamber Gascoigne, author, 67, Desmond Morris, zoologist, 74, Nastassia Kinski, actress, 41
25	Cory Aquino, former President of the Philippines, 69, Raymond Baxter, broadcaster, 80, Angela Thorne, actress, 63, David Ginola, footballer, 35, Emma Freud, broadcaster, 40
26	Paul Newman, actor, 77, Ronald Allison, author, 70, Christopher Hampton, playwright, 56, Eartha Kitt, singer, 74
27	Lord Rix, actor and president of Mencap, 78, Nina Milkina, pianist, 83, Jack Brymer, clarinettist, 87
28	Mikhail Baryshnikov, ballet dancer, 54, Alan Alda, actor, 66, Sir John Tavener, composer, 58
29	Germaine Greer, writer and broadcaster, 63, Tom Selleck, actor, 57, John Junkin, actor and writer, 72, Leslie Bricusse, composer and lyricist, 71, Peter Byrne, actor, 74, Andy Roberts, cricketer, 51, Raman Subba Row, cricketer, 70, Oprah Winfrey, actress and talk show host, 48
30	Phil Collins, rock singer, 51, Gene Hackman, actor, 72, Vanessa Redgrave, actress, 65, John Profumo, politician, 87
31	Queen Beatrix of the Netherlands, 64, Minnie Driver, actress, 31, Norman Mailer, author, 79, Jean Simmons, actress, 73

February

1	Boris Yeltsin, Russian President 1991–9, 71, Josceline Dimbleby, cookery writer, 59, Don Everly, vocalist, 65, Peter Sallis, actor, 81, Dame Muriel Spark, writer, 84, Renata Tebaldi, soprano, 80
2	Andrew Davis, conductor, 58, David Jason, actor, 62, Valéry Giscard d'Estaing, President of France 1974–81, 76, Elaine Stritch, actress, 75, Libby Purves, broadcaster and columnist, 52
3	Val Doonican, singer, 73, Gillian Ayres, painter, 72, Kirsty Wark, television presenter, 47
4	Norman Wisdom, actor and comedian, 87, Russell Hoban, writer, 77, Matthew Yates, athlete, 33
5	Douglas Hogg, politician, 57, Charlotte Rampling, actress, 56, Susan Hill, playwright and novelist, 60
6	Patrick MacNee, actor, 80, Ronald Reagan, US President, 91, Keith Waterhouse, writer, 73, Kevin Whately, actor, 51, Jimmy Tarbuck, comedian, 62, Fred Trueman, cricketer, 71, Denis Norden, broadcaster, 80, Gayle Hunnicutt, actress, 59
7	Peter Jay, broadcaster, 65, Dora Bryan, actress, 78, Eddie Izzard, comedian, 40, David Park, author, 49
8	John Williams, composer, 70, John Grisham, author, 47, Osian Ellis, harpist, 74, Rachel Cusk, author, 35
9	Mia Farrow, actress, 57, Sandy Lyle, golfer, 44, Ben E King, singer, 60, Janet Suzman, actress, 63, Brian Bennett, drummer, 62, Dr Garret Fitzgerald, Prime Minister of the Republic of Ireland 1981–2 and 1982–7, 76
10	Greg Norman, golfer, 47, Mark Spitz, swimmer, 52, Michael Apted, film director, 61, Nicholas Owen, broadcaster, 55
11	Dennis Skinner, politician, 70, Leslie Nielsen, actor, 76, John Surtees, motor-racing champion, 68
12	Steve Backley, javelin thrower, 33, Franco Zeffirelli, film director, 79, Simon MacCorkindale, actor, 50
13	Liam Brady, footballer, 46, Kim Novak, actress, 69, Robbie Williams, singer, 28, George Segal, actor, 68
14	Kevin Keegan, football manager, 51, Alan Parker, film director, 58, Michael Rudman, theatre producer, 63
15	Claire Bloom, actress, 71, Jane Seymour, actress, 51, Clare Short, politician, 56, John Adams, composer, 52
16	Anthony Dowell, ballet dancer, 59, John McEnroe, tennis player, 43, John Schlesinger, film director, 76, Iain Banks, author, 48, Paul Bailey, novelist, 65, FGR Cuming, painter, 72, David Griffiths, portrait painter, 63
17	Alan Bates, actor, 68, Barry Humphries, entertainer and writer, 68, Baroness Rendell of Babergh, author, 72, Patricia Routledge, actress, 68, Julia McKenzie, actress and singer, 61, Norman Pace, comedian, 49
18	Bobby Robson, football manager, 69, Prue Leith, writer, 52, Milos Forman, film director, 70, Gary Neville, footballer, 27, Len Deighton, author, 73, Graeme Garden, actor, 59, Colin Jackson, athlete, 35, Ned Sherrin, writer and broadcaster, 71
19	HRH The Duke of York, 42, Hana Mandlikova, tennis player, 40, Smokey Robinson, singer, 62, Gwen Taylor, actress, 63
20	Robert Altman, film director, 77, Jimmy Greaves, footballer, 62, Mike Leigh, dramatist, 59, Sidney Poitier, actor, 75
21	Harald V, King of Norway, 65, Jilly Cooper, author, 65, Alan Rickman, actor, 56, Peter McEnery, actor, 62
22	Bruce Forsyth, entertainer, 74, Sir John Mills, actor, 94, Nigel Planer, actor, 49, Sheila Hancock, actress, 69, Julie Walters, actress, 52, Niki Lauda, racing driver, 53
23	Helena Sukova, tennis player, 37, Sylvie Guillem, ballet dancer, 37, Anton Mosimann, chef, 55
24	Brian Close, cricketer, 71, Denis Law, footballer, 62, Richard Hamilton, painter, 80, Paul Jones, singer and actor, 60, Denis Waterman, actor, 54, Peter Terson, dramatist, 70, Derek Randall, cricketer, 51
25	Elkie Brooks, singer, 57, Sir Tom Courtenay, actor, 65, Lord Puttnam, film producer, 61

26   Johnny Cash, singer, 70, Sir Everton Weekes, cricketer, 77, Emma Kirkby, soprano, 53, Tony Selby, actor, 64

27   Paddy Ashdown, Leader of Liberal Democrats 1988–99, 61, Elizabeth Taylor, actress, 70, Timothy Spall, actor, 45, Dame Antoinette Sibley, prima ballerina, 63, Rabbi Julia Neuberger, 52, Ralph Nader, consumer protection pioneer, 68

28   Peter Alliss, golfer, 71, Barry McGuigan, boxer, 41, Stephanie Beacham, actress, 53, Alfred Burke, actor, 84

29   Joss Ackland, actor, 74, Mario Andretti, racing driver, 62

March

1   Harry Belafonte, singer, 75, David Broome, showjumper, 62, Roger Daltrey, singer and actor, 58

2   John Gardner, composer, 85, Mikhail Gorbachev, Russian politician, 71, Ian Woosnam, golfer, 44, Dame Naomi James, yachtswoman and author, 53, Lou Reed, rock singer, 59, JPR Williams, rugby player, 53

3   Miranda Richardson, actress, 44, Fatima Whitbread, athlete, 41, Ronald Searle, artist and cartoonist, 82

4   Kenny Dalglish, footballer, 51, Patrick Moore, astronomer and presenter, 79, Bernard Haitink, conductor, 73, Alan Sillitoe, writer, 74, Peter Skellern, composer and singer, 55, Ralph Kirshbaum, cellist, 56

5   Elaine Page, singer, 54, Richard Hickox, conductor, 54, Barry Tuckwell, horn player and conductor, 71

6   Valentina Tereshkova, first woman in space, 65, Dame Kiri Te Kanawa, opera singer, 58, Lord Sheppard of Liverpool, 73

7   Viv Richards, cricketer, 50, Sir Ranulph Fiennes, explorer and author, 58, Ivan Lendl, tennis player, 42, Earl of Snowdon, photographer, 72, Piers Paul Read, author, 61, Sir Eduardo Paolozzi, sculptor, 78

8   Lynn Redgrave, actress, 59, Phil Edmonds, cricketer, 51, Gyles Brandreth, broadcaster and author, 49, Lord Hurd of Westwell, 72, Sir Anthony Caro, sculptor, 78, Lynn Seymour, ballerina, 63, David Wilkie, swimmer, 48

9   Bill Beaumont, rugby player, 50, Juliette Binoche, actress, 38, Bobby Fischer, chess player, 59

10   Prince Edward, Earl of Wessex, 38, Fou Ts'ong, concert pianist, 68, Andrew Parrott, conductor, 55

11   Lord Lawson of Blaby, 70, Rupert Murdoch, chairman of the News Corporation, 71, Louis Brough, tennis player, 79

12   Liza Minnelli, actress and singer, 56, David Mellor, broadcaster, 53, Edward Albee, dramatist, 74, Norbert Brainin, violinist, 79, Anish Kapoor, artist and sculptor, 48, Googie Withers, actress, 85

13   Neil Sedaka, singer and composer, 63, Sir Robert Mark, former Police Commissioner, 85, David Nobbs, writer, 67

14   Michael Caine, actor, 69, Pam Ayres, poet, 55, Sir Colin St John Wilson, architect, 80, Jasper Carrott, comedian, 57, Tessa Sanderson, athlete, 46, Rita Tushingham, actress, 60

15   Ben Okri, author, 43, Mike Love, singer with the Beach Boys, 58, Robert Nye, author and poet, 63

16   Bernardo Bertolucci, film director, 61, Leo McKern, actor, 82, Teresa Berganza, singer, 67, Kate Nelligan, actress, 51

17   Sir Robin Knox-Johnston, yachtsman, 63, Kurt Russell, actor, 51, Penelope Lively, writer, 69, Galina Samsova, ballerina, 65, Michael Whitaker, showjumper, 42, Alexander McQueen, fashion designer, 33

18   Ron Atkinson, football manager, 63, Alex Higgins, snooker player, 53, Pat Eddery, jockey, 50, Courtney Pine, saxophonist, 38, John Updike, author, 70

19   Glenn Close, actress, 55, Patrick McGoohan, actor, 74, Bruce Willis, actor, 47, Philip Roth, author, 69

20   William Hurt, actor, 52, Dame Vera Lynn, singer, 85, Brian Mulroney, politician, 63, Spike Lee, actor and director, 45

21   Brian Clough, football manager, 67, Timothy Dalton, actor, 56, Ann Mackay, soprano, 46, Ieuan Evans, rugby player, 38, Lord Oaksey, jockey and racing pundit, 73, Lord Heseltine, politician, 69, Michael Foreman, writer and illustrator, 64

22   George Benson, jazz guitarist and singer, 59, Lord Lloyd Webber, composer, 54, Marcel Marceau, mime artist, 79, Stephen Sondheim, composer, 72, William Shatner, actor, 71, Leslie Thomas, author, 71

23   Princess Eugenie of York, 12, Mike Atherton, cricketer, 34, Norman Bailey, baritone, 69, Wasim Bari, cricketer, 54, Roger Bannister, athlete, 73, Sir Steven Redgrave, rower, 40, Sir David McNee, policeman, 77

24   Sir Alan Sugar, Amstrad chairman, 55, Benjamin Luxon, baritone, 65, Dario Fo, playwright and actor, 76

25   Aretha Franklin, singer, 60, Richard O'Brien, actor and writer, 60, Sir Elton John, composer and singer, 55

26   Pierre Boulez, composer and conductor, 77, Leonard Nimoy, actor and producer, 71, Diana Ross, singer, 58, Kyung-Wha Chung, violinist, 54, William Hague, politician, 41, Elizabeth Jane Howard, novelist, 79

27   Lord Callaghan of Cardiff, 90, Mstislav Rostropovich, conductor and cellist, 75, Michael York, actor, 60, Quentin Tarantino, film director, 39, Julian Glover, actor, 67, Maria Ewing, opera singer, 52

28   Richard Eyre, theatre director, 59, Neil Kinnock, politician, 60, Michael Parkinson, broadcaster, 67, Richard Stilgoe, lyricist and entertainer, 59, Rosemary Ashe, soprano, 49, Nasser Hussain, cricketer, 34

29   Lord Tebbit, politician, 71, Eric Idle, comedic actor, 59, Sir Richard Rodney Bennett, composer, 66, John Major, politician, 59, Jennifer Capriati, tennis player, 26, John Suchet, television journalist, 58

30   Warren Beatty, actor, 65, Eric Clapton, rock musician, 57, Tom Sharpe, novelist, 74, Rolf Harris, singer and artist, 72, Sue Cook, broadcaster, 53, Lord MacLaurin of Knebworth, 65

31   Richard Chamberlain, actor, 67, Robbie Coltrane, actor and comedian, 52, Al Gore, Vice-President of the United States, 54, John Fowles, writer, 76, Lord Steel of Aikwood, politician, 64, Roger Black, athlete, 36, Ewan McGregor, actor, 31

April

1   David Gower, cricketer 45, Steve Race, musician, 81, Stephen Fleming, New Zealand cricketer, 29

2   Linford Christie, athlete, 42, Penelope Keith, actress, 62, Sue Townsend, writer, 56, Jack Brabham, racing driver, 76, Catherine Gaskin, author, 73, Dermot Reeve, cricketer, 39, Barry Hills, racehorse trainer, 65

3   Alec Baldwin, actor, 44, Tony Benn, politician, 77, Doris Day, actress and singer, 78, Jonathan Lynn,

CURRENT AFFAIRS

director, 59, Marlon Brando, actor, 78, Eddie Murphy, actor, 41, John Virgo, snooker player and presenter, 56

4   Margaret Dupont, tennis player, 84, Maya Angelou, author, 74, Trevor Griffiths, playwright, 67

5   Jane Asher, actress, 56, Gregory Peck, actor, 86, Arthur Hailey, author, 82, Colin Powell, US Secretary of State, 65

6   Felicity Palmer, opera singer, 58, Roger Cook, broadcaster, 59, Paul Daniels, magician, 64, André Previn, musician, 73, Rory Bremner, impressionist, 41, Joan Carlyle, soprano, 71, Willis Hall, writer, 73, Lord Frederick Windsor, 23

7   Francis Ford Coppola, director, 63, Sir David Frost, broadcaster, 63, Ian Richardson, actor, 68, Russell Crowe, actor, 38, James Garner, actor, 74, Gerry Cottle, circus proprietor, 57, Ravi Shankar, sitar player, 82, Cliff Morgan, broadcaster, 72

8   Ian Smith, Rhodesian politician, 83, Alec Stewart, cricketer, 39, Tony Banks, politician, 59, Hywel Bennett, actor, 58, Kofi Annan, Secretary-General of the UN, 64, Julian Lennon, musician, 39, Vivienne Westwood, fashion designer, 61

9   Seve Ballesteros, golfer, 45, Hannah Gordon, actress, 61, Alan Knott, cricketer, 56, Valerie Singleton, broadcaster, 65, Vincent O'Brien, racehorse trainer, 85, Ian Duncan Smith, politician, 48, Jacques Villeneuve, racing driver, 31

10   Gloria Hunniford, broadcaster, 62, Omar Sharif, actor, 70, Dave Moorcroft, athlete, 49, Paul Theroux, writer, 61, Lesley Garrett, soprano, 47, Stan Mellor, jockey and racehorse trainer, 65

11   Gervase de Peyer, clarinettist, 76, Clive Exton, scriptwriter and playwright, 72

12   Sir Alan Ayckbourn, playwright, 63, Montserrat Caballé, opera and concert singer, 69, Bryan Magee, writer, 72, Jeremy Beadle, television presenter and charity fundraiser, 54

13   Davis Love III, golfer, 38, Edward Fox, actor, 65, Seamus Heaney, poet, 63, Jonjo O'Neill, jockey and trainer, 50, Gary Kasparov, chess player, 39, Howard Keel, singer and actor, 83, Peter Davison, actor, 51

14   Julie Christie, actress, 62, Rod Steiger, actor, 77, Julian Lloyd Webber, cellist, 51, Paddy Hopkirk, rally driver, 69, David Hope, Archbishop of York and former Archbishop of London, 62

15   Lord Archer of Weston-super-Mare, author and politician, 62, Claudia Cardinale, actress and photographer, 64, Sir Neville Mariner, conductor, 78, Emma Thompson, actress, 43, Alan Plater, scriptwriter, 67

16   Joan Bakewell, broadcaster, writer and chairman of the British Film Institute, 69, Conchita Martinez, tennis player, 30, Sir Peter Ustinov, actor, dramatist and film director, 81, Merce Cunningham, choreographer, 83, Lynne Franks, writer, 54

17   Dr Michael Stroud, explorer, 47, Clare Francis, yachtswoman and writer, 56, Chris Barber, jazz trombonist, 72, Bella Freud, fashion designer, 41, Nick Hornby, writer, 45, Ricardo Patrese, racing driver, 48, Victoria Adams, singer, 28, Sean Bean, actor, 43, Olivia Hussey, actress, 51, James Last, bandleader, 73, Henry Kelly, broadcaster, 56

18   Hayley Mills, actress, 56, Teddy Taylor, politician, 65, Nick Farr-Jones, Australian rugby player, 40

19   Sue Barker, television presenter and former tennis player, 46, Ruby Wax, comedian and actress, 49, Michel Roux, chef, 61, Dickie Bird, cricket umpire, 69, Trevor Francis, footballer, 48, Murray Perahia, pianist, 55

20   Nicholas Lyndhurst, actor, 41, Ray Brooks, actor, 63, Jessica Lange, actress, 53, Sebastian Faulks, author, 49, Gro Harlem Brundtland, Director-General of the World Health Organisation, 63, Ryan O'Neal, actor, 61, Rachel Whiteread, sculptor, 39, Luther Vandross, singer, 51, Peter Snow, broadcaster, 64, Leslie Phillips, actor, 78

21   John Mortimer, QC, barrister and author, 79, Angela Barrett, tennis player, 70, Andie MacDowell, actress, 44

22   George Cole, actor, 77, Jack Nicholson, actor, 65, Charles Sisson, poet, 88, Glen Campbell, singer, 64

23   Lady Gabriella Windsor, daughter of Prince and Princess Michael of Kent, 21, Shirley Temple Black, actress, 74, JP Donleavy, author, 76, Professor George Stainer, author, 73, Lady Victoria Glendinning, author, 65

24   Jean-Paul Gaultier, fashion designer, 50, Barbra Streisand, actress and singer, 60, Bridget Riley, artist, 71, Shirley Maclaine, actress, 68, Clement Freud, writer, 78, Johan Cruyff, footballer, 55, John Williams, guitarist, 61

25   Al Pacino, actor, 62, Earl of Lichfield, photographer, 63, Eric Bristow, darts player, 45, David Shepherd, artist, 71

26   David Coleman, sports commentator, 76, Peter Schaufuss, ballet dancer, 52, Marquess of Bute, racing driver, 44

27   Darcey Bussell, ballerina, 33, Igor Oistrakh, violinist, 71, Michael Fish, meteorologist, 58, John Daly, golfer, 36, Lady Helen Taylor, daughter of the Duke and Duchess of Kent, 38, Dr Jeffrey Tate, conductor, 59

28   Kenneth Kaunda, Zambian politician, 78, Nicola LeFanu, composer, 55, Mike Brearley, cricketer, 60, Ian Rankin, author, 42

29   André Agassi, tennis player, 32, Zubin Mehta, conductor, 66, Zizi Jeanmaire, dancer, 78, Michelle Pfeiffer, actress, 45, Daniel Day-Lewis, actor, 45, Johnny Miller, golfer, 55, Jonah Barrington, squash player, 61, Jeremy Thorpe, politician, 73

30   Leslie Grantham, actor, 56, Dickie Davies, sports commentator, 69, Bobby Vee, singer, 59, Jill Clayburgh, actress, 58, Wilie Nelson, singer and actor, 71, Tony Harrison, poet, 65, Percy Heath, jazz musician, 79, Cloris Leachman, actress, 76

May

1   Lady Sarah Chatto, 38, Steve Cauthen, jockey, 42, Joanna Lumley, actress, 56, Gordon Greenidge, cricketer, 51

2   Brian Lara, cricketer, 33, Jimmy White, snooker player, 40, David Beckham, footballer, 27, David Suchet, actor, 56, John Neville, actor, 77, Alan Titchmarsh, horticulturalist, writer and broadcaster, 53

3 James Brown, soul singer, 69, Henry Cooper, 68, Allan Wells, athlete, 50, Norman Thelwell, artist, 79, Sandi Toksvig, writer and comedienne, 44, Ben Elton, writer and comedian, 43

4 Michael Barrymore, comedian and actor, 50, Eric Sykes, writer and comedian, 79, Marisa Robles, harpist, 65

5 Michael Palin, actor and television presenter, 59, Tammy Wynette, country singer, 60

6 Alexander George Thynne, 7th Marquess of Bath, 70, Tony Blair, politician, 49, Graham Souness, football manager, 49

7 Scobie Breasley, jockey, 87, Peter Carey, novelist, 59, Richard O'Sullivan, actor, 58, Elisabeth Söderström, soprano, 75

8 David Attenborough, broadcaster and naturalist, 76, Jack Charlton, footballer, 67, Lord Lamont of Lerwick, 60, Viviana Durante, ballerina, 35, Heather Harper, soprano, 72, Dame Felicity Lott, soprano, 55

9 Richard Adams, author, 82, Alan Bennett, dramatist 68, Candice Bergen, actress, 56, Terry Downes, boxer, 66, Albert Finney, actor, 66, Glenda Jackson, actress and politician, 66, Billy Joel, singer, 53, Geraldine McEwan, actress, 70

10 Maureen Lipman, actress, 56, Denis Thatcher, businessman, 87, Michael Shea, former press secretary to the Queen, 64, Bono, lead singer with U2, 41, Barbara Taylor Bradford, writer, 69

11 John Parrott, snooker player and television personality, 38, Jeremy Paxman, broadcaster, 52, Judith Weir, composer, 48, Sir Rhodes Boyson, politician, 77, Lady Rachel Billington, writer, 60, Natasha Richardson, actress, 39

12 Burt Bacharach, composer, 73, Alan Ball, footballer, 57, Michael Ignatieff, writer, 55, Jenny Murray, broadcaster, 52, Susan Hampshire, actress, 60, Steve Winwood, rock musician, 54, Dr Miriam Stoppard, writer and broadcaster, 65

13 Peter Gabriel, musician, 52, Richard Madeley, broadcaster, 46, Stevie Wonder, musician, 52, Bea Arthur, actress, 77, Zoë Wanamaker, actress, 53, Helen Sharman, astronaut, 39, Selina Scott, broadcaster, 51, Tim Pigott-Smith, actor, 56

14 George Lucas, film director, 58, Francesca Annis, actress, 57, Sir Chay Blyth, yachtsman, 62, Sian Phillips, actress, 68

15 Zara Phillips, daughter of Princess Anne and Mark Phillips, 21, Ted Dexter, cricketer, 67, Anthony and Peter Shaffer, playwrights, 76, Mike Oldfield, composer, 49

16 Judy Finnegan, broadcaster, 54, Roy Hudd, comedian and actor, 66, Gabriella Sabatini, tennis player, 32

17 Sir Michael Beetham, Marshal of the RAF, 79, Sugar Ray Leonard, boxer, 46, Birgit Nilsson, soprano, 84

18 Pope John Paul II, 82, Toyah Wilcox, singer and actress, 44, Nobby Stiles, footballer, 60, John Bruton, politician, 55

19 Candice Bergen, actress, 56, David Jacobs, broadcaster, 76, Edward de Bono, lateral thinker, 69, James Fox, actor, 63, Victoria Wood, comedienne, 49, Sandy Wilson, composer, 78, Stephen Varcoe, baritone, 53, Pete Townshend, guitarist, 57

20 Lynn Davies, athlete, 60, Cher, singer and actress, 56, Earl Spencer, 38, Keith Fletcher, cricketer, 58

21 Mary Robinson, President of Ireland 1990–97 and United Nations High Commissioner for Human Rights, 58, Malcolm Fraser, Prime Minister of Australia 1975–83, 72, Rosalind Plowright, soprano, 53

22 Cheryl Campbell, actress, 53, Kenny Ball, trumpeter, 71, George Best, footballer, 56, Anthony Holden, writer, 55

23 Anatoly Karpov, chess player, 51, Nigel Davenport, actor, 74, Humphrey Lyttelton, broadcaster and jazz writer, 81, Joan Collins, actress, 69, Graeme Hick, cricketer, 36, Artie Shaw, bandleader, 92, John Newcombe, tennis player, 58

24 Liz McColgan, athlete, 38, Bob Dylan, songwriter, 61, Arnold Wesker, playwright, 70, Stanley Baxter, comedian, 76, Adrian Moorhouse, swimmer, 38, William Trevor, writer, 74, Eric Cantona, footballer, 36

25 Julian Clary, comedian, 43, Sir Ian McKellen, actor, 63, Beverly Sills, soprano, 73, David Wynne, sculptor, 76

26 Helena Bonham-Carter, actress, 36, Zola Budd, athlete, 36, Roy Dotrice, actor, 77, Philip Treacy, fashion designer, 35

27 Pat Cash, tennis player, 37, Henry Kissinger, US Secretary of State 1973–7, 79, Paul Gascoigne, footballer, 35, Thea Musgrave, composer, 74, Christopher Lee, actor, 80, Duncan Goodhew, swimmer, 45, Lewis Collins, actor, 56

28 Faith Brown, impressionist, 55, Rachel Kempson, actress, 92, Dame Thora Hird, actress, 91, Julian Slade, composer, 72

29 Nanette Newman, actress, 63, Martin Pipe, racehorse trainer, 57, Bob Hope, entertainer, 99, Francis Rossi, musician, 53

30 Harry Enfield, comedian, 41, Bob Willis, cricketer, 53, Ray Cooney, theatre producer, 70, Andrew Farrell, rugby player, 27

31 John Prescott, politician, 64, Terry Waite, former special envoy for the Archbishop of Canterbury, 63, Clint Eastwood, actor, 72, Lynda Bellingham, actress, 54, Ben de Lisi, fashion designer, 47, Peter Winterbottom, rugby player, 42

June

1 Lord Foster of Thames Bank, architect, 67, Robert Powell, actor, 58, Gerald Scarfe, artist, 66, Edward Woodward, actor, 72, Lord Deedes, *Daily Telegraph* editor 1974–86, 89, Bob Monkhouse, entertainer, 74, Paco Peña, guitarist, 60

2 King Constantine of the Hellenes, 62, Charlie Watts, drummer, 61, Marvin Hamlisch, composer, 58, Robin Orr, composer, 93

3 Penelope Wilton, actress, 56, Sir Wilfred Thesiger, explorer, 92, Tony Curtis, actor, 72, Alain Resnais, film director, 80

4 Geoffrey Palmer, actor, 75, Bob Champion, jockey and trainer, 54, Andrea Jaeger, tennis player, 37

5   Moira Anderson, singer, 62, Sheila Sim, actress, 80, Margaret Drabble, author, 63, David Hare, playwright, 55

6   David Blunkett, politician, 55, Bjorn Borg, tennis player, 46, Mike Gatting, cricketer, 45, Frank Tyson, cricketer, 72, Giacomo Aragall, tenor, 64, Sara Banerji, writer, 70, Paul Esswood, counter-tenor, 60, Willie-John McBride, rugby player, 62

7   Virginia McKenna, actress, 71, Curtis Robb, athlete, 30, James Ivory, film director, 74, Ronald Pickup, actor, 62, Liam Neeson, actor, 50, Michael Pennington, actor, 59, Tom Jones, singer, 62, Neal Radford, cricketer, 45

8   Professor Francis Crick, biologist, 86, Norma Shaw, bowler, 65, Ray Illingworth, cricketer, 70, Derek Underwood, cricketer, 57

9   Tony Britton, actor, 78, Charles Saatchi, advertising executive, 59, Michael J Fox, actor, 41, Lady Anita Burgh, novelist, 65

10   HRH Prince Philip, Duke of Edinburgh, 81, Gordon Burns, television presenter, 60, David Platt, footballer, 36, Anthony Rooley, lutenist, 58, Saul Bellow, writer, 87, Elizabeth Hurley, actress, 37, Lionel Jeffries, actor, 76

11   Gene Wilder, actor, 67, Jackie Stewart, racing driver, 63, Jean Alesi, racing driver, 38, Tony Allcock, bowler, 47, Diana Armfield, painter, 82, Michael Cacoyannis, film director, 80, Gemma Craven, actress, 52, Hugh Laurie, actor, 43

12   Vic Damone, singer, 74, George Bush, US President, 78, Pat Jennings, footballer, 57, Oliver Knussen, composer, 50

13   Peter Scudamore, National Hunt jockey, 44, Gwynne Howell, opera singer, 64, Malcolm McDowell, actor, 59

14   Anthony Sher, actor and writer, 53, Paul Boateng, politician, 51, Steffi Graf, tennis player, 33, Mike Yarwood, entertainer, 61

15   Johnny Herbert, racing driver, 38, Mary Ellis, actress, 105, Richard Baker, broadcaster, 77, Simon Callow, actor, 53

16   Dame Eileen Atkins, actress, 68, Professor Erich Segal, writer, 65, James Bolam, actor, 64, Simon Williams, actor, 56

17   Professor Sir Alan Walters, economist, 76, Ken Livingstone, Mayor of London, 57, Ken Loach, television and film director, 66, Barry Manilow, singer and composer, 56, Sir Edward Downes, conductor, 78

18   Isabella Rossellini, actress, 50, Michael Blakemore, film and theatre director, 74, Sir Paul McCartney, musician, 60, Ian Carmichael, actor, 82, Peter Donohoe, pianist, 49, Delia Smith, cookery writer and broadcaster, 61

19   Aung San Suu Kyi, Nobel Laureate, 57, Gilbert Edward George Lariston Elliot-Murray-Kynynnand, 6th Earl of Minto, 74, Charlie Drake, comedian, 77, Salman Rushdie, writer, 55, Kathleen Turner, actress, 48, Rory Underwood, rugby player, 39, Barry Hearn, businessman, 54

20   Anthony Buckeridge, author, 90, Wendy Craig, actress, 68, Stafford Dean, opera singer, 65, Allan Lamb, cricketer, 48, Stephen Frears, film director, 61, Duchess of Gloucester, 56, Nicole Kidman, actress, 35, Vikram Seth, novelist, 50, Lionel Richie, singer and songwriter, 53, Brian Wilson, singer and songwriter, 60

21   Prince William of Wales, 20, Ray Davies, singer and songwriter, 58, Don Black, lyricist, 64, John Edrich, cricketer, 65, Benazir Bhutto, Prime Minister of Pakistan 1988–90 and 1993–6, 49, Ian McEwan, author, 54, Jane Russell, actress, 81

22   RJ Montague, founder of Tiphook, 54, Dame Cicely Saunders, founder of St Christopher's Hospice, Sydenham, 84, Prunella Scales, actress, 70, Esther Rantzen, broadcaster, 62, Alastair Stewart, broadcaster, 50

23   Lord Irvine of Lairg, Lord Chancellor, 62, Kim Begley, tenor, 50, Julian Hipwood, polo player, 56, Miriam Karlin, actress, 77

24   Anita Desai, novelist, 65, Betty Jackson, fashion designer, 53, Mary Wesley, author, 90, Jeff Beck, guitarist, 58, Mick Fleetwood, drummer, 60, Ian Christie, clarinettist and film critic, 75

25   George Michael, singer, 39, Peter Blake, artist, 70, Cyril Fletcher, broadcaster, 89, Sidney Lumet, film director, 78, Vladimir Kramnik, world chess champion, 27

26   Claudio Abbado, conductor, 69, Colin Wilson, author, 71, Georgie Fame, singer and songwriter, 59, Greg LeMond, cyclist, 41

27   Hugh Wood, composer, 70, Alan Coren, writer and broadcaster, 64, Mary McAleese, Irish politician, 51

28   Kathy Bates, actress, 54, Harold Evans, former editor of the Times and Sunday Times, 74, Stan Barstow, writer, 74, Howard Barker, playwright and poet, 56, Correlli Barnett, author, 75, Mel Brooks, actor and film director, 76

29   Charlotte Bingham, playwright, 60, Sir Rex Hunt, Governor and Commander-in-Chief, Falkland Islands, 1980–82, 76

30   Lena Horne, singer, 85, John Fortune, actor and scriptwriter, 63, Christopher Lloyd, Surveyor of the Queen's Pictures, 52, Ralf Schumacher, racing driver, 27, MJK Smith, cricketer, 69

July

1   Leslie Caron, actress, 71, Garry Schofield, rugby league player, 37, Carl Lewis, athlete, 41, Dan Aykroyd, actor, 50, Olivia de Havilland, actress, 86, Hans Werner Henze, composer, 76, Trevor Eve, actor, 51

2   John Timpson, broadcaster, 74, Eva Lambert, artist, 67, Mary Craig, writer and broadcaster, 74, Jerry Hall, model, 46

3   Tom Stoppard, playwright, 65, Julie Burchill, writer, 43, Tom Cruise, actor, 40, Brigitte Fassbaender, mezzo-soprano, 63, Sir Richard Hadlee, cricketer, 51, Carlos Kleiber, conductor, 72, Ken Russell, film director, 75, Susan Penhaligon, actress, 53

4   Alec and Eric Bedser, cricketers, 84, Colin Welland, actor and playwright, 68, René Arnoux, racing driver, 54, Henri Leconte, tennis player, 39, Gina Lollobrigida, actress, 75, Neil Simon, playwright, 75

5   Gianfranco Zola, footballer, 36, John Wright, cricketer, 48, Elizabeth Emanuel, fashion designer, 49, Mark
     Cox, tennis coach, 59
6   Geraldine James, actress, 52, George W Bush, US President, 56, The Dalai Lama, 67, Dave Allen,
     comedian, 66, Vladimir Ashkenazy, pianist and conductor, 65, Dame Mary Peters, athlete, 63, Jonathan
     Porritt, environmentalist, 52, Geoffrey Rush, actor, 51, Jennifer Saunders, comedienne, 44, Tony Lewis,
     cricketer, 64, Sylvester Stallone, actor, 56
7   Gian Carlo Menotti, composer, 91, Pierre Cardin, fashion designer, 80, Ringo Starr, drummer, 62, Bill Oddie,
     actor, 61, Tony Jacklin, golfer, 58, Michael Howard, politician, 61, Michael Ancram, politician, 57, Jeremy
     Guscott, rugby player, 37
8   Keith Fielding, rugby league player, 53, Mal Meninga, rugby league player, 42, Pauline Quirke, actress, 43,
     Brian Walden, broadcaster and Labour MP for Birmingham, All Saints, 1964–74, 70
9   Richard Wilson, actor, 66, Tom Hanks, actor, 46, David Hockney, artist, 65, Professor Richard Demarco,
     watercolourist, 72
10   Ian Wallace, actor and broadcaster, 83, Sunil Gavaskar, cricketer, 53, Virginia Wade, tennis player, 57, John
     Dunlop, racehorse trainer, 63, Josephine Veasey, opera singer, 72, James Aldridge, author, 84
11   Gough Whitlam, former Australian PM, 86, Richard Chartres, Bishop of London, 55, Giorgio Armani, fashion
     designer, 68
12   Jennifer Saunders, comedienne, 44, Gareth Edwards, rugby player, 55, Sir Alastair Burnet, newsreader, 74
13   Ian Hislop, editor of *Private Eye*, 42, Patrick Stewart, actor, 64, Harrison Ford, actor, 60, David Storey,
     playwright, 69
14   Bruce Oldfield, designer, 52, Gerald Ford, US President 1974–7, 89, Sue Lawley, broadcaster, 56, Ingmar
     Bergman, director, 84
15   Julian Bream, guitarist and lutenist, 69, Carmen Callil, founder of Virago publishing house, 64, Linda
     Ronstadt, singer, 56, Sir Harrison Birtwistle, composer, 68, Robert Conquest, writer, 85, Ann Jellicoe,
     playwright and theatre director, 75, Professor Jocelyn Bell Burnell, astronomer, 59, Geoffrey Burgon,
     composer, 61, Juliet Pannett, portrait painter, 91
16   Pinchas Zukerman, violinist, 54, Margaret Court, tennis player, 60, Dr Anita Brookner, author and art
     historian, 74, Shirley Hughes, author and illustrator, 75, Joanna MacGregor, pianist, 43, James Macmillan,
     composer, 43
17   Hardy Amies, dressmaker, 93, Marques de Samaranch, President of International Olympic Committee
     1980–2001, 82, Wayne Sleep, dancer and choreographer, 54, Donald Sutherland, actor, 67, Tim Brooke-
     Taylor, actor, 62
18   Richard Branson, founder and chairman of the Virgin Group, 52, Nick Faldo, golfer, 45, Senator John Glenn,
     astronaut, 81, Nelson Mandela, statesman, 84, Yevgeny Yevtushenko, poet, 69, Jim Watt, boxer, 54, Dennis
     Lillee, cricketer, 54, David Hemery, athlete, 58, Richard Pasco, actor, 76
19   Brian May, guitarist, 55, Ilie Nastase, tennis player, 56, Evelyn Glennie, percussionist, 37, Adrian Noble,
     theatre director, 52
20   Diana Rigg, actress, 64, Charlie Magri, boxer, 46, Jacques Delors, former President of Commission of the
     EEC, 77, Sir Edmund Hillary, first man to reach the summit of Mount Everest, 83
21   Norman Jewison, film director, 76, Karel Reisz, film director, 76, Dr Sir Jonathan Miller, opera and theatre
     director, 68, Bill Pertwee, actor, 76, Julian Pettifer, broadcaster, 67
22   Bryan Forbes, film producer, 76, Jimmy Hill, broadcaster, 74, Danny Glover, actor, 55, Helen Lawrence,
     mezzo-soprano, 60, Willem Dafoe, actor, 47, Bonnie Langford, actress, 38, Terence Stamp, actor, 64
23   David Essex, singer and actor, 55, Danny La Rue, entertainer, 75, Lord Rogers of Riverside, architect, 69,
     Graham Gooch, cricketer, 49, Clive Rice, South African and Notts cricketer, 53, Michael Foot, politician, 89
24   Peter Yates, film director and producer, 73, Quinlan Terry, architect, 65, Martin Keown, footballer, 36
25   Lord Nicholas Windsor, 32, Right Rev Barry Rogerson, Bishop of Bristol, 66, Iman, supermodel, 47, James
     Butler, sculptor, 71
26   Sir Michael Jagger, singer, 59, Blake Edwards, film-maker, 80, Helen Mirren, actress, 57, Lance Percival,
     actor and singer, 69, Pauline Clare, Chief Constable of Lancashire, 55, Dr Brian Mawhinney, politician, 62,
     Barbara Jefford, actress, 72
27   Michael Ball, singer, 40, Allan Border, cricketer, 47, Jack Higgins, novelist, 73, Baroness Williams of Crosby,
     politician, 72, Christopher Dean, ice skater, 44, Joe Durie, tennis player, 42, Lord Jenkins of Putney,
     politician, 94
28   Ian McCaskill, meteorologist, 64, Sir Garfield Sobers, cricketer, 66, Riccardo Muti, conductor, 61
29   Sally Gunnell, athlete, 36, Lord Scarman, 91, Joe Johnson, snooker player, 50, Max Faulkner, golfer, 86
30   Peter Bogdanovich, film director, 64, Kate Bush, singer, 44, Arnold Schwarzenegger, actor, 55, Stan
     Stennett, actor, 75, Teresa Cahill, opera singer, 58, Richard Johnson, actor, 75, Daley Thompson, athlete,
     44, Sir Clive Sinclair, inventor, 62
31   Evonne Cawley, tennis player, 51, Jonathan Dimbleby, broadcaster, 58, Peter Nichols, playwright, 75, Milton
     Friedman, economist, 90, JK Rowling, author, 37

August
1   Yves St Laurent, fashion designer, 66, Sam Mendes, film and theatre director, 37, Frank Hauser, theatre
     director, 80
2   Peter O'Toole, actor, 70, Alan Whicker, broadcaster, 81, Rose Tremain, novelist and playwright, 59, Karl
     Miller, writer, 71
3   Terry Wogan, broadcaster, 64, Tony Bennett, singer, 76, Jack Straw, politician, 56, Martin Sheen, actor, 62,
     Steven Berkoff, actor, director and writer, 65, Baroness James of Holland Park, writer, 82
4   William Cooper, novelist, 92, Georgina Hale, actress, 59, Martin Jarvis, actor, 61, Dr Jack Cunningham,
     politician, 60
5   Neil Armstrong, astronaut, 72, John Whittaker, show jumper, 47, Barbara Flynn, actress, 54, Alan Howard,

actor, 65, Carla Lane, writer, 65, Jimmy Webb, songwriter, 56, Oleg Luzhny, footballer, 34, Billy Bingham, football manager, 71

6   Dom Mintoff, Prime Minister of Malta 1971–84, 86, Chris Bonington, mountaineer, 68, Jack Parnell, drummer, 79, Frank Finlay, actor, 76, Freddie Laker, entrepreneur, 80, Barbara Windsor, actress, 65, Charles Wood, writer, 70, Billy Boston, rugby union player, 68, Michael Deeley, film producer, 70, Sir Howard Hodgkin, painter, 70

7   Greg Chappell, cricketer, 54, Alexei Sayle, comedian, 50, Walter Swinburn, jockey, 41, Nick Ross, broadcaster, 55, Kenneth Kendall, broadcaster, 78, Philip Snow, author, 87, Dominic Cork, cricketer, 31

8   Princess Beatrice of York, 14, Nigel Mansell, racing driver, 49, Dustin Hoffman, actor, 65, Keith Barron, actor, 58

9   Melanie Griffith, actress, 45, Whitney Houston, singer, 39, Rod Laver, tennis player, 64, Posy Simmonds, cartoonist, 57, James Naughtie, broadcaster and journalist, 51

10   Roy Keane, footballer, 31, Kate O'Mara, actress, 63, Rosanna Arquette, actress, 43, John Alldis, conductor, 73, Barry Unsworth, author, 72, Lawrence Dallaglio, rugby union player, 30, Paul Newlove, rugby league player, 31

11   Anna Massey, actress, 65, Tamás Vásáry, pianist and conductor, 69, Raymond Leppard, conductor, 75, Don Boyd, film director, 54, Professor Alun Hoddinott, composer, 73

12   Mark Knopfler, guitarist, 53, Norris McWhirter, writer and broadcaster, 77, Pete Sampras, tennis player, 31, Peter West, sports commentator and Come Dancing host, 82, Les Ferdinand, footballer, 36, Suzanne Vega, singer, 43

13   President Fidel Castro of Cuba, 75, Alan Shearer, footballer, 32, Marie Helvin, model, 50, Tony Jarrett, athlete, 34, Sheila Armstrong, soprano, 60, George Shearing, jazz pianist, 83

14   Sarah Brightman, singer, 41, Buddy Greco, singer, 76, Steve Martin, actor, 57, Frederick Raphael, author, 71

15   The Princess Royal, 52, Oscar Peterson, jazz pianist, 77, Lord Waldegrave of North Hill, politician, 56, Tony Robinson, actor and writer, 56, Dame Wendy Hiller, actress, 90

16   Helen Storey, fashion designer, 43, Trevor McDonald, broadcaster, 63, Madonna, singer, 44, Jeff Thomson, cricketer, 52, Sean Brady, Archbishop of Armagh and Primate of All Ireland, 63, Katherine Hamnett, fashion designer, 55

17   Robert de Niro, actor, 59, Nelson Piquet, racing driver, 50, Sir Vidia Naipaul, author and Nobel Laureate, 70, George Melly, jazz singer, 76, Alan Minter, boxer, 51, Robin Cousins, ice skater, 45, Guillermo Vilas, tennis player, 50

18   Brian Aldiss, writer, 77, Caspar Weinberger, US Secretary of Defence 1981–7, 85, Patrick Swayze, actor, 50, Robert Redford, actor and director, 65, Roman Polanski, film director, 69

19   Bill Clinton, President of the United States of America 1993–2001, 56, Willie Shoemaker, jockey, 71, David Lodge, actor, 81, Richard Ingrams, editor of The Oldie, 65

20   Finlay Calder, rugby player, 45, John Emburey, cricketer, 50, Robert Plant, rock singer, 54, Dame Anne Evans, soprano, 61

21   Barry Norman, broadcaster and journalist, 69, Kenny Rogers, country music singer, 64, Donald Dewar, politician, 64, Dame Janet Baker, mezzo-soprano, 69, Christopher Brasher, athlete and founder of the London Marathon, 74

22   Ray Bradbury, author, 82, Steve Davis, snooker player, 45, Mats Wilander, tennis player, 38, Henri Cartier-Bresson, photographer, 94, Honor Blackman, actress, 76, Karlheinz Stockhausen, composer, 74, General Norman Schwarzkopf, Commander US Central Command 1988–91, 68

23   Geoff Capes, shot-putter and strongman, 53, Peter Lilley, politician, 59, Willy Russell, author and dramatist, 55

24   Stephen Fry, actor and writer, 45, Sam Torrance, golfer, 49, Dame Antonia Byatt, writer, 66, Charles Causley, poet, 85, Paul Barker, writer and broadcaster, 67, Carlo Curley, organist, 50, Tommy Docherty, football manager, 74, Jean-Michel Jarre, musician, 54, Cardinal Cormac Murphy O'Connor, Archbishop of Westminster, 70

25   Sean Connery, actor, 72, Martin Amis, writer, 53, Frederick Forsyth, author, 64, Anne Archer, actress, 55

26   The Duke of Gloucester, 58, Alison Steadman, actress, 56, Chris Boardman, cyclist, 34

27   Lady Antonia Fraser, writer, 70, Gerhard Berger, racing driver, 43, Bernard Langer, golfer, 45, Derek Warwick, racing driver, 48, John Lloyd, tennis player, 48, Michael Holroyd, author, 67, Jeanette Winterson, writer, 43

28   Emlyn Hughes, footballer, 55, Sir Godfrey Hounsfield, EMI Scanner inventor, 83, Imogen Cooper, concert pianist, 53

29   William Friedkin, film director, 63, Elliot Gould, actor, 64, Michael Jackson, singer, 44, Lenny Henry, comedian, 44, Lord (Richard) Attenborough, actor, 79, Dame Mary Donaldson, former Lord Mayor of London, 81, Thom Gunn, poet, 73, Lord (Marmaduke) Hussey, former chairman of the BBC, 79, Rebecca De Mornay, actress, 40

30   John Peel, broadcaster, 63, Lord Healey, politician, 85

31   Richard Gere, actor, 53, Van Morrison, singer, 57, Clive Lloyd, cricketer, 58, Liz Forgan, writer and broadcaster, 58, Ed Moses, athlete, 47, Itzhak Perlman, violinist, 57, Professor Sir Bernard Lovell, founder of Jodrell Bank, 89

September

1   Gloria Estefan, singer, 45, Ruud Gullit, footballer, 40, Barry Gibb, singer, 59, Milton Shulman, film and theatre critic, 84, Lord Parkinson, politician, 71, Margaret Ewing, politician, 57, Marquess of Exeter, writer, 67

2   Jimmy Connors, tennis player, 50, Victor Spinetti, actor, 69, Michael Hastings, playwright, 64

3   Pauline Collins, actress, 62, Raquel Welch, actress, 62, Geoff Arnold, cricketer, 58, Al Jardine, singer, 60, Charlie Sheen, actor, 37, Susan Milan, flautist, 55, Gareth Southgate, footballer, 32

4 Tom Watson, golfer, 53, Air Marshal Sir John Cheshire, 60, Bill Kenwright, actor and theatrical impresario, 57, Joan Aiken, author, 78, Dinsdale Landen, actor, 70

5 Tracy Edwards, yachtswoman, 40, Dick Clement, scriptwriter, 65, GW Tremlett, author and broadcaster, 63

6 Roger Knight, Secretary of the MCC, 56, Greg Rusedski, tennis player, 29, Tim Henman, tennis player, 28, John Young, rugby player and chairman of Lloyd's Regulatory Board, 65, Roger Law, puppeteer and satirist, 61

7 Elia Kazan, film director, 93, Kevin Curran, cricketer, 43, George Ellis, athlete, 70, Peter Gill, stage director, 63

8 Anne Diamond, presenter, 48, Jeannette Altwegg, ice skater, 72, Michael Frayn, novelist and playwright, 69, Geoff Miller, cricketer, 50, Sir Peter Maxwell Davies, composer and conductor, 68

9 Michael Keaton, actor, 51, Chaim Topol, actor, 67, Dave Stewart, musician, 50, Raine Countess Spencer, 73, Hugh Grant, actor, 42, Neil Holmes, powerboat racer, 43, Julia Sawalha, actress, 34, Margaret Tyzack, actress, 71

10 Arnold Palmer, golfer, 73, Beryl Cook, painter, 76, Sir Thomas Allen, opera singer, 58, Colin Firth, actor, 42, Bill Rodgers, golfer, 51, Norman Morrice, choreographer, 71, Michael Barry, food journalist and broadcaster, 61

11 Franz Beckenbauer, footballer, 57, Anthony Browne, book illustrator, 56, Eddie George, governor, Bank of England, 64, Herbert Lom, actor, 85, Judith Howarth, soprano, 40, Brian de Palma, film director, 58

12 Sir Ian Holm, actor, 71, Maria Aitken, actress, 57, Bertie Ahern, Prime Minister of the Republic of Ireland, 51

13 Jacqueline Bisset, actress, 58, Goran Ivanisevic, tennis player, 31, Lord (Colin) Moynihan, 47, Shane Warne, cricketer, 33

14 Ray Wilkins, footballer, 46, Nicol Williamson, actor, 64, Sandra Blow, painter, 77, Martyn Hill, tenor, 58

15 Prince Henry of Wales, 18, Oliver Stone, film director, 56, Richard Gordon, author, 81, Tommy Lee Jones, actor, 56, Graham Taylor, football manager, 58, Jessye Norman, soprano, 57

16 Lauren Bacall, actress, 78, BB King, guitarist and singer, 77, Charles Haughey, former Irish Prime Minister, 77, Lee Kuan Yew, former Prime Minister of Singapore, 79, Lloyd Grossman, broadcaster, 52, Andy Irvine, rugby player, 51

17 Damon Hill, racing driver, 42, Sir Stirling Moss, racing driver, 73, Des Lynam, broadcaster, 60, Mary Stewart, novelist, 86, Tessa Jowell, politician, 55, Karen Straker-Dixon, showjumper, 38, Anne Bancroft, actress, 71

18 Peter Shilton, goalkeeper, 53, Marjorie Mowlam, politician, 53, Jack Cardiff, film director, 88, Russ Abbot, entertainer, 55, Ray Alan, ventriloquist, 72, Sol Campbell, footballer, 28, Darren Gough, cricketer, 32, Siobhan Davies, choreographer, 52

19 Kate Adie, broadcaster, 57, Jeremy Irons, actor, 54, Zandra Rhodes, fashion designer, 62, Captain Jim Fox, athlete, 61, Twiggy, actress, 53, Pete Murray, broadcaster, 74, Rosemary Harris, actress, 72, Ray Cooper, percussionist, 60, David Seaman, goalkeeper, 39, Arthur Willis, composer, 76, Kurt Sanderling, conductor, 90

20 John Dankworth, jazz musician, 75, Sophia Loren, actress, 68, Fred Winter, equestrian, 76, Jane Manning, soprano, 64

21 Larry Hagman, actor, 71, Jimmy Young, broadcaster, 79, Shirley Conran, writer, 70, Leonard Cohen, singer and poet, 68, Curtley Ambrose, cricketer, 39, Simon Mayo, broadcaster, 44, Bill Murray, actor, 52

22 Captain Mark Phillips, equestrian, 54, Fay Weldon, writer, 71, Gina Fratini, fashion designer, 71, Dannie Abse, writer, 79, Ronaldo Luiz Nazario de Lima, Brazilian footballer, 26, Maria Charles, actress, 73

23 Ray Charles, singer and pianist, 72, Mickey Rooney, actor, 82, Bruce Springsteen, rock singer, 53, Cherie Booth, QC, 48, Julio Iglesias, singer, 59, Norma Winstone, singer, 61, Nicholas Witchell, broadcaster, 49, Frank Foster, saxophonist, 74

24 John Rutter, composer and conductor, 57, Jack Dee, comedian, 41, Brian Glanville, author and journalist, 71

25 Felicity Kendal, actress, 56, Lord (Leon) Brittan of Spennithorne, politician, 63, Christopher Reeve, actor, 50, Ronnie Barker, actor, 73, Colin Davis, conductor, 75, Michael Douglas, actor, 58, Catherine Zeta-Jones, actress, 33, Will Smith, actor and singer, 34, Timothy Severin, author and explorer, 62, Barbara Walters, US television presenter, 71

26 Ian Chappell, cricketer, 59, Bryan Ferry, singer, 57, Lucette Aldous, ballerina, 64, Anne Robinson, broadcaster, 58, Serena Williams, tennis player, 21, Olivia Newton-John, singer, 54

27 Diane Abbott, politician, 49, Josephine Barstow, opera singer, 62, Barbara Dickson, singer and actress, 54, Meatloaf, rock singer, 55, Denis Lawson, actor, 55, Gordon Honeycombe, author and broadcaster, 66

28 Brigitte Bardot, actress, 68, Jon Snow, television journalist, 55, Mika Hakkinen, racing driver, 34, Peter Egan, actor, 56, Gwyneth Paltrow, actress, 30, John Scott, former England rugby captain, 48

29 Lord (Sebastian) Coe, athlete and politician, 46, Lech Walesa, former President of Poland and Nobel Laureate, 59, Michelangelo Antonioni, film director, 90, Richard Bonynge, opera conductor, 72, Colin Dexter, author, 72, Patricia Hodge, actress, 56, Gareth Davies, former rugby captain of Wales, 46

30 Viscount Cranborne, politician, 56, Deborah Kerr, actress, 81, Angie Dickinson, actress, 71, Anthony Green, painter, 63, Johnny Mathis, singer, 64, Ian Ogilvy, actor, 60, Victoria Tennant, actress, 52, Rula Lenska, actress, 55

October

1 Julie Andrews, actress, 67, Richard Harris, actor, 69, Phil de Glanville, rugby player, 34, Sandy Gall, broadcaster, 75, Jimmy Carter, President of the USA 1977–81, 78, Cardinal Cahal Daly, former Primate of All Ireland, 85, Harry Hill, comedian, 38

C
U
R
R
E
N
T

A
F
F
A
I
R
S

2   Trevor Brooking, footballer, 54, Sting (Gordon Sumner), singer, 51, Jan Morris, writer, 76, Wade Dooley, rugby player, 45, Jana Novotna, tennis player, 34, Jon Speelman, chess player, 46, Anna Ford, broadcaster, 59, Peter Frankl, pianist, 67

3   Shridath (Sonny) Ramphal, former secretary-general of the Commonwealth, 74, Kevin Richardson, vocalist, 30, Gore Vidal, author, 77, Zeinab Badawi, broadcaster, 43, Christopher Bruce, dancer, 57, Chubby Checker, singer, 61, Lindsey Buckingham, rock guitarist, 55, Fred Couples, golfer, 43, Ruggero Raimondi, operatic bass, 61

4   Jackie Collins, novelist, 65, Basil D'Oliveira, cricketer, 71, Charlton Heston, actor, 78, Ray Floyd, golfer, 60, Susan Sarandon, actress, 56, Sir Terence Conran, restaurateur and designer, 71, Anneka Rice, broadcaster, 44

5   Bob Geldof, singer and founder of Band Aid, 48, Vaclav Havel, President of Czech Republic, 66, Glynis Johns, actress, 79, Laura Davies, golfer, 39, Ray Clemence, footballer, 54, Robert Kee, author and broadcaster, 83

6   Lord (Melvyn) Bragg, broadcaster, 63, Tony Greig, cricketer, 56, Richie Benaud, cricketer, 72

7   Jayne Torvill, ice skater, 45, Desmond Tutu, former Archbishop of Cape Town, 71, Clive James, broadcaster, 63, Yo Yo Ma, cellist, 47, Thomas Keneally, author, 67, Miss Yaltah Menuhin, pianist, 81, Sir Timothy Ackroyd, actor, 44, June Allyson, actress, 85, Christopher Booker, journalist and author, 65, Professor Harold Dexter, organist, 82

8   Betty Boothroyd, politician, 73, Chevy Chase, actor, 59, Sigourney Weaver, actress, 53, Maurice Cockrill, artist, 66, Bel Mooney, writer and broadcaster, 56, Albert Roux, chef and restaurateur, 67, Ray Reardon, snooker player, 70

9   The Duke of Kent, 67, Joe Ashton, politician, 69, Steve Ovett, athlete, 47, John Doubleday, sculptor, 55, Bill Tidy, cartoonist, 69, Donald Sinden, actor, 79, Brian Blessed, actor, 66, Sir Nicholas Grimshaw, architect, 63, Annika Sorenstam, golfer, 32, Andy Platt, rugby league player, 39, Sally Burgess, singer, 49, Peter Elliott, athlete, 40

10   Charles Dance, actor, 56, Harold Pinter, playwright, 72, Chris Tarrant, broadcaster, 56, Tony Adams, footballer, 36, Nicholas Parsons, broadcaster, 74, Midge Ure, singer, 49, Ben Vereen, actor, 56, Willard White, singer and actor, 56, Matthew Pinsent, rower, 32, David Hempleman-Adams, explorer, 46, Lance Cairns, cricketer, 53

11   Sir Bobby Charlton, footballer, 65, Dawn French, actress, 45, Maria Bueno, tennis player, 63, David Rendall, tenor, 54

12   Magnus Magnusson, broadcaster, 73, Luciano Pavarotti, tenor, 67, Rick Parfitt, rock star, 54, David Threlfall, actor, 49, Angela Rippon, broadcaster and chairman of the English National Ballet, 58, Kenneth Griffith, actor and writer, 81

13   Baroness Thatcher, politician, 77, Edwina Currie, politician, 56, John Snow, cricketer, 61, Sir Terry Frost, artist, 87, John Regis, athlete, 36, Paul Simon, musician, 61, Michael Heath, cartoonist, 67

14   Steve Cram, athlete, 42, Roger Moore, actor, 75, Sir Cliff Richard, vocalist, 62, Roger Taylor, tennis player, 61, Christopher Timothy, actor, 62, Justin Hayward, singer, 56

15   The Duchess of York, 43, David Trimble, Northern Ireland's First Minister, 58, Chris De Burgh, singer, 54, Professor JK Galbraith, economist, 94, Craig Chalmers, rugby player, 34

16   Max Bygraves, entertainer, 80, Terry Griffiths, snooker player, 55, Baroness Nicholson of Winterbourne, politician, 61, Peter Bowles, actor, 66, Dr Stefan Buczacki, biologist, 57, Günter Grass, writer, 75, Angela Lansbury, actress, 77

17   Harry Carpenter, broadcaster, 77, Margot Kidder, actress, 54, Ann Jones, tennis player, 64, Arthur Miller, playwright, 87, Stephen Kovacevich, pianist, 62, Graham Le Saux, footballer, 34, Sir Cameron Mackintosh, musical producer, 56, Ernie Els, golfer, 33

18   Michael Stich, tennis player, 34, Martina Navratilova, tennis player, 46, Mary Symes, the first woman coroner, 90, Chuck Berry, rock 'n' roll singer, 76, Jean-Claude Van Damme, actor, 42, Paul Palmer, swimmer, 28

19   John Le Carré, author, 71, Admiral of the Fleet Sir Michael Pollock, 86, Sir Michael Gambon, actor, 62, Evander Holyfield, boxer, 40, Phil Davies, rugby player, 39, Bernard Hepton, actor, 77

20   Chris Cowdrey, cricketer, 45, Lord Montagu of Beaulieu, 76, Eddie Macken, showjumper, 53, Allan Donald, cricketer, 36, Emma Tennant, writer, 65, Ian Rush, footballer, 41, Timothy West, actor, 68

21   Sir Malcolm Arnold, composer, 81, Geoff Boycott, cricketer, 62, Peter Mandelson, politician, 49, Simon Gray, playwright, 66, David Campese, rugby player, 40, Natalia Makarova, ballerina, 62, Paul Ince, footballer, 35, Manfred Mann, musician, 62, Sir William Whitfield, architect, 82, Nadia Nerina, ballerina, 75

22   Derek Jacobi, actor, 64, Joan Fontaine, actress, 85, Catherine Deneuve, actress, 59, Sir Michael Stoute, racehorse trainer, 57, Jeff Goldblum, actor, 50, Doris Lessing, author, 83, Christopher Lloyd, actor, 64, John Blashford-Snell, explorer, 66

23   Pele, footballer, 62, Johnny Carson, broadcaster, 77, Anita Roddick, businesswoman, 60, Maggi Hambling, artist, 57, George Cohen, footballer, 63

24   Jonathan Davies, rugby player, 40, Bill Wyman, guitarist, 66, Sir Mark Tully, journalist and broadcaster, 67, Kevin Kline, actor, 55, Robert Edward Peter Gascoyne-Cecil, 6th Marquess of Salisbury, 86, Luciano Berio, composer, 77, Frank Delaney, writer, 60

25   Galina Vishnevskaya, soprano, 76, Joe Mercer, jockey, 68, Imran Khan, cricketer, 50, Michael Lynagh, rugby player, 39

26   Bob Hoskins, actor, 60, Gyorgy Pauk, violinist, 66, John Arden, playwright, 72, Adam Mars-Jones, writer, 48, Hillary Clinton, New York Senator, 55, Andrew Motion, Poet Laureate, 50, Audley Harrison, boxer, 31

27   David Bryant, flat green bowler, 71, John Cleese, actor, 63, Leonard Rosoman, painter, 89, Mark Taylor, cricketer, 38, Glenn Hoddle, footballer and manager, 45, AN Wilson, author, 52, Roberto Benigni, actor, 50, Simon Le Bon, singer, 44

28   Carl Davis, composer and conductor, 66, Julia Roberts, actress, 35, Bill Gates, chairman of Microsoft, 47,

David Dimbleby, broadcaster, 64, Dame Cleo Laine, singer, 75, Hank Marvin, guitarist, 61, Michael Noakes, painter, 69, Joan Plowright (Lady Olivier), actress, 73, Geoff Reeve, film producer, 70, Miyako Yoshida, ballerina, 37

29   Richard Dreyfuss, actor, 55, Robert Hardy, actor, 77, Jack Shepherd, actor, 62, Jon Vickers, tenor, 76, Frank Sedgman, tennis player, 75, Michael Jayston, actor, 67, Michael Vaughan, cricketer, 28

30   Michael Winner, film director, 67, Juliet Stevenson, actress, 46, Richard Alston, choreographer, 54

31   Sir James Savile, broadcaster, 76, Dick Francis, author, 82, Michael Collins, astronaut, 72, Barrie Keeffe, dramatist, 57, Barbara Bel Geddes, actress, 80, Eddie Charlton, snooker player, 73, Charles Moore, *Daily Telegraph* editor, 46

November

1   Gary Player, golfer, 67, Victoria de los Angeles, singer, 79, Nick Owen, broadcaster, 55, Gerald Ratner, businessman, 53

2   Ken Rosewall, tennis player, 68, Alan Jones, racing driver, 56, Bruce Welch, guitarist, 61, Paul Johnson, writer, 74

3   Viscount Linley, designer, 41, Roseanne Arnold, actress, 50, Charles Bronson, actor, 80, Roy Emerson, tennis player, 66, Lulu, singer, 54, Ian Wright, footballer, 39, Albert Reynolds, former PM of Eire, 70, Ludovic Kennedy, broadcaster, 83, Violetta Elvin, ballerina, 77, Larry Holmes, boxer, 53, Vanni Treves, chairman of Channel 4 Television, 62

4   Walter Cronkite, broadcaster, 86, Michael Meacher, politician, 63, Malandra Burrows, actress, 37, Art Carney, actor, 84, Sean 'P Diddy' Combs, rap artist, 32, Rodney Marsh, cricketer, 55, Loretta Swit, actress, 58, Joan Rodgers, soprano, 46

5   Bryan Adams, singer, 43, Art Garfunkel, musician, 61, Lester Piggott, jockey, 67, Dennis Andries, boxer, 51, Sam Shepard, playwright and actor, 59, Jim Moir, Controller, BBC Radio 2, 61

6   Sally Field, actress, 56, Frank Carson, comedian, 76, Mike Nichols, film director, 71, Nigel Havers, actor, 51, PJ Proby, vocalist, 64, Bernat Klein, designer, 80, Daniele Gatti, conductor, 41

7   John Barnes, footballer, 39, Dame Gwyneth Jones, soprano, 66, Billy Graham, evangelist, 84, Helen Suzman, politician, 85, Jonathan Palmer, racing driver, 46, Su Pollard, actress, 53, Dame Joan Sutherland, soprano, 76

8   Ken Dodd, entertainer, 71, Rifat Ozbek, fashion designer, 49, Martin Peters, footballer, 59, Rupert Allason, author, 51, Alain Delon, actor, 67, Kazuo Ishiguro, author, 48, Gordon Ramsay, restaurateur, 36, Richard Stoker, composer, 64

9   Tom Weiskopf, golfer, 60, Ronald Harwood, writer, 68, Alistair Horne, author, 77, Hugh Leonard, playwright, 76, Tony Slattery, writer and actor, 43, Marina Warner, writer and critic, 56, David Duval, golfer, 31, Roger McGough, poet, 65

10   Tim Rice, lyricist and broadcaster, 58, Robert Carrier, cookery writer, 79, Roy Scheider, actor, 67

11   Ron Greenwood, football manager, 82, Demi Moore, actress, 40, June Whitfield, actress, 77, Rodney Marsh, cricketer, 55

12   Chad Varah, founder of the Samaritans, 91, Nadia Comaneci, gymnast, 41, Dame Peggy Fenner, politician, 80

13   Rt Rev Lord (George) Carey of Clifton, former Archbishop of Canterbury, 67, Alexandra Shulman, editor of *Vogue*, 45, Whoopi Goldberg, actress, 47, Lord Jacobs, chairman of the British School of Motoring 1973–90, 71

14   Prince of Wales, 54, Steffano Gabbana, fashion designer, 40, Mark Le Fanu, general secretary of the Society of Authors, 56, Dr Boutros Boutros-Ghali, former Secretary General of the United Nations, 80, Koji Tatsuno, fashion designer, 40

15   Peter Phillips, son of the Princess Royal, 25, JG Ballard, writer, 72, Daniel Barenboim, musician, 60, Petula Clark, singer, 70

16   Frank Bruno, boxer, 41, Willie Carson, jockey, 60, Griff Rhys Jones, actor and writer, 49, Waqar Younis, cricketer, 31, Sir Magdi Yacoub, cardiothoracic surgeon, 67, Lorraine Heggessey, Controller, BBC1, 46, Paul Scholes, footballer, 28

17   Martin Scorsese, film director, 60, Danny De Vito, actor and film director, 58, Jonathan Ross, broadcaster, 42, Michael Adams, chessplayer, 31, Sir Charles Mackerras, conductor, 77, Fenella Fielding, actress, 68

18   David Hemmings, actor, 61, Admiral of the Fleet, Sir Henry Leach, 79, Baroness Jay of Paddington, politician, 63

19   Jodie Foster, actress, 40, Lady Davina Windsor, 25, Meg Ryan, actress, 41, David Lloyd-Jones, conductor, 68, Calvin Klein, fashion designer, 60

20   Alistair Cooke, broadcaster, 94, Dulcie Gray, actress, 82, Gareth Chilcott, rugby player, 46, Nadine Gordimer, author, 79

21   Goldie Hawn, actress, 57, Malcolm Williamson, Master of the Queen's Music, 71, Natalia Makarova, ballerina, 62, Dame Beryl Bainbridge, writer, 68, Georgina Battiscombe, author, 97

22   Boris Becker, tennis player, 35, Jamie Lee Curtis (Lady Haden-Guest), actress, 44, Billie Jean King, tennis player, 59, Tom Conti, actor, 60, Terry Gilliam, film animator, 62, Sir Peter Hall, drama director, 72, John Bird, actor and writer, 66

23   Most Reverend Patrick Kelly, Archbishop of Liverpool, 64, Alan Mullery, footballer, 61, Michael Gough, actor, 86, Krzysztof Penderecki, composer, 69, Diana Quick, actress, 56, Christopher Logue, poet, 76

24   Ian Botham, cricketer, 47, Billy Connolly, comedian, 60, Lynn Chadwick, sculptor, 88, Paul Thorburn, rugby player, 40, David Kossoff, actor and author, 83, Charles Osborne, author, 75, Vivien Saunders, golfer, 56

25   Francis Durbridge, playwright, 85, Imran Khan, cricketer, 50, Charles Kennedy, politician, 43, Yvonne Kenny, opera singer, 52

26   John Gummer, politician, 63, Tina Turner, singer, 64, Charles Forte, businessman, 94

27   John Alderton, actor, 62, Rodney Bewes, actor, 65, Sir John Maddox, writer and broadcaster, 77, Viktoria Mullova, violinist, 43, Verity Lambert, film and television producer, 65, Alan Simpson, writer, 73

CURRENT AFFAIRS

28 Kriss Akabusi, athlete, 44, Keith Miller, cricketer, 83, Dervla Murphy, author, 71, Stephen Roche, cyclist, 43, Manolo Blahnik, fashion-shoe designer, 60, Fiona Armstrong, broadcaster, 46

29 Jacques Chirac, French President, 70, Ryan Giggs, footballer, 29, Derek Jameson, journalist and broadcaster, 73, John Mayall, blues musician, 69, Louise Winter, mezzo-soprano, 43, Geoffrey Moorhouse, writer, 71

30 Gary Lineker, footballer, 42, Marguerite Porter, ballerina, 54, David Mamet, writer, stage and film director, 55, George Graham, footballer, 58, Radu Lupu, pianist, 57, Laurent Jalabert, cyclist, 34, Ridley Scott, film director, 65

December

1 Woody Allen, actor and director, 67, Dame Alicia Markova, ballerina, 92, Bette Midler, actor and singer, 57, Andy Ripley, rugby player and rower, 55, Stephen Poliakoff, playwright, 50, Lee Trevino, golfer, 63, Keith Michell, actor, 74, Arjuna Ranatunga, Sri Lankan cricketer, 39, Sarfraz Nawaz, Pakistani cricketer, 54, Mike Denness, England cricketer, 62

2 Alexander Haig, former US Secretary of State, 78, Peter Harding, Marshal of the RAF, 69, Monica Seles, tennis player, 29

3 Trevor Bailey, cricketer, 79, Jean-Luc Godard, film director, 72, Mel Smith, comedian, 50, Daryl Hannah, actress, 42, Franz Klammer, skier, 49, Andy Williams, singer, 72, Paul Nicholas, actor, 52, Craig Raine, poet, 58

4 Jeff Bridges, actor, 53, Ronnie Corbett, comedian, 72, Pamela Stephenson, actress and writer, 52, Yvonne Minton, mezzo-soprano, 64, Gemma Jones, actress, 60, Constantino Rocca, golfer, 46, Deanna Durbin, actress and singer, 81, Anke Huber, tennis player, 28

5 Lord Chalfont, chairman of the Radio Authority 1991–4, 83, Little Richard, entertainer, 67, José Carreras, tenor, 56, Hanif Kureishi, author, 48, Sheridan Morley, author and broadcaster, 61, Jeremy Sandford, writer and musician, 68, Ronnie O'Sullivan, snooker player, 27, Lanny Wadkins, golfer, 53, Paddy McMahon, showjumper, 69

6 Dave Brubeck, jazz musician, 82, Gerry Francis, footballer, 51, Eric Newby, writer, 83, Peter Willey, cricketer, 53, Charles Vance, actor and producer, 73, Keke Rosberg, Formula One champion, 54, Nick Park, animator, 43, Richard Krajicek, tennis player, 31, Per-Ulrik Johansson, golfer, 36, Helen Liddell, politician, 52, Geoff Hoon, politician, 49

7 Sir Sidney Samuelson, British Film Commissioner, 1991–7, 77, Eli Wallach, actor, 87, Helen Watts, opera singer, 75, Nicole Appleton, singer, 28, Sue Johnston, actress, 59, Chris Joynt, rugby league player, 31

8 Kim Basinger, actress, 49, Lucien Freud, artist, 80, Sir James Galway, flautist, 63, Sir Geoff Hurst, footballer, 61, Les Ferdinand, footballer, 36, Sir David Hay, cardiologist and twin brother of Sir Hamish Hay, NZ politician, 75

9 Kirk Douglas, actor, 86, Bob Hawke, Australian politician, 73, Joan Armatrading, singer, 52, John Malkovich, actor, 49, Dame Elisabeth Legge-Schwarzkopf, opera singer, 87, Dame Judi Dench, actress, 68, Joanna Trollope, writer, 59, Susan Bullock, soprano, 44, Mervyn Davies, rugby player, 56, Ian McIntyre, writer and broadcaster, 71

10 Lord (John) Birt, Director-General of the BBC 1992–2000, 58, Kenneth Branagh, actor, 42, Nicolas Kynaston, organist, 61, Raphael Maklouf, sculptor, 65, Jahangir Khan, squash player, 39

11 Carlo Ponti, film director, 89, Alexander Solzhenitsyn, author, 84, Cliff Michelmore, broadcaster, 83, Anna Carteret, actress, 60, Vishy Anand, chess player, 33

12 Will Carling, rugby union player, 37, Dionne Warwick, singer, 61, Emerson Fittipaldi, racing driver, 56, Lionel Blair, dancer, 71, Jasper Conran, fashion designer, 43, Connie Francis, singer, 64, Cliff Holden, painter, 83, Denise Coffey, actress, 66, Tracy Austin, tennis player, 42, Anne Coates, film producer and editor, 77

13 The Aga Khan, 66, John Francome, jump jockey, 50, George Shultz, US politician, 82, Dick Van Dyke, actor, 77, Anouska Hempel (Lady Weinberg), hotelier and designer, 61, Robert Lindsay, actor, 53, Christopher Plummer, actor, 73

14 Stan Smith, tennis player, 56, Michael Owen, footballer, 23, Rosalyn Tureck, conductor, 88, Barbara Leigh-Hunt, actress, 67

15 Lanfranco Dettori, jockey, 32, Edna O'Brien, author, 66, Ida Haendel, violinist, 78, Michael Bogdanov, theatre director, 64, Don Johnson, actor, 53, Joe Jordan, footballer, 51, Oscar Niemeyer, architect, 95, Henrietta Knight, racehorse trainer, 56

16 Arthur C Clarke, science fiction writer, 85, Liv Ullmann, actress, 64, Joel Garner, cricketer, 50, Peter Dickinson, author, 75, Richard Cockerill, rugby union player, 32, Trevor Pinnock, harpsichordist and conductor, 56

17 Kerry Packer, businessman, 65, Robert Robinson, broadcaster, 75, Tommy Steele, entertainer, 66, Bernard Hill, actor, 58, Christopher Cazenove, actor, 57, Dominic Lawson, editor of the *Sunday Telegraph*, 46, Baroness Strange, writer, 74

18 Keith Richard, guitarist, 59, Steven Spielberg, film-maker, 55, Arantxa Sanchez Vicario, tennis player, 31

19 David Harrington Angus Douglas, 12th Marquess of Queensberry, 73, Upamanyu Chatterjee, novelist, 43, Tim Parks, novelist, 48, Steven Isserlis, cellist, 44

20 Jenny Agutter, actress, 50, Uri Geller, showman and spoon-bender, 56, Michael Beaumont, Seigneur of Sark, 75

21 Jane Fonda, actress, 65, Chris Evert, tennis player, 48, Kurt Waldheim, Austrian politician, 84, Greville Starkey, jockey, 63, Michael Tilson Thomas, conductor, 58, Geoff Lewis, jockey and trainer, 67

22 Maurice and Robin Gibb, singers, 53, Duke of Westminster, 51, James Burke, broadcaster, 66, Ken Whitmore, playwright, 63

23 Helmut Schmidt, former German Chancellor, 84, Emperor Akihito of Japan, 69, Christopher Lawrence, goldsmith, 66, Belinda Lang, actress, 49, Graham Kelly, chief executive of the Football Association, 57

24 Carol Vorderman, television presenter, 42, Professor Anthony Clare, psychiatrist, 60, Philip Ziegler, author, 73

25 Annie Lennox, singer, 48, Ismael Merchant, film producer, 66, Princess Alice, Duchess of Gloucester, 101, Princess Alexandra, 66, Jim Bolger, racehorse trainer, 61, Nigel Starmer-Smith, sports commentator, 58

26 Jane Lapotaire, actress, 58, Dame Thea King, clarinettist, 77, Denis Quilley, actor, 75, Harry Christophers, conductor, 49, Dermot Murnaghan, broadcaster, 45, Anna Scher, founder of the Anna Scher Theatre, 58

27 Gérard Depardieu, actor, 54, Janet Street-Porter, 56, Polly Toynbee, journalist, 56, Pat Moss, rally driver, 68

28 Nigel Kennedy, violinist, 46, Dame Maggie Smith, actress, 68, Denzel Washington, actor, 48, Sir Max Hastings, former editor of the *Daily Telegraph* and *Evening Standard*, 57, Lord Hattersley, politician, 70

29 Ted Danson, actor, 55, Martin Offiah, rugby league player, 36, Harvey Smith, showjumper, 64, John Voight, actor, 64, Bernard Cribbins, actor, 74, Mary Tyler Moore, actress and television executive, 66, Alan Rusbridger, editor of the *Guardian*, 49

30 Gordon Banks, goalkeeper, 65, Bo Diddley, guitarist and singer, 74, Timothy Mo, writer, 52

31 Anthony Hopkins, actor, 65, Ben Kingsley, actor, 59, Alex Salmond, politician, 48, Sir Alex Ferguson, football manager, 61, Michael Bonallack, golfer, 68, Stephen Cleobury, conductor, 54, Tess Jaray, artist, 65, Jean-Pierre Rives, rugby player, 50

CURRENT AFFAIRS

EDUCATION

Public Schools	Founded
King's School, Canterbury, Kent	600
King's School, Rochester, Kent	604
St Peter's School, York	627
Sherborne School, Dorset*	705
St Alban's	948
King's School, Ely	973
Winchester	1382
Eton	1440
City of London	1442
Loughborough	1495
St Paul's	1509
Giggleswick School, N. Yorks	1512
Manchester Grammar	1515
Sedbergh School, Cumbria	1525
Bristol Grammar	1532
Berkhamsted, Herts	1541
Christ College, Brecon	1541
King's Worcester	1541
Bristol Cathedral	1542
Bradford Grammar School, West Yorkshire	1548
Bedford	1552
Leeds Grammar School	1552
Christ's Hospital, Horsham	1553
Tonbridge	1553
Shrewsbury	1552
Gresham's School, Holt, Norfolk	1555
Oundle, Northants	1556
Repton, Derby	1557
Merchant Taylors', Northwood	1560
Westminster	1560
Kingston	1561
Felsted, Dunmow, Essex	1564
Highgate	1565
Rugby	1567
Harrow	1571
Uppingham, Oakham	1584
Stonyhurst, RC, Clitheroe	1593
Wellingborough, Northants	1595
Trinity School, Croydon	1596
Whitgift School, Croydon	1596
Blundell's, Tiverton	1604
Downside, RC, Somerset	1607
Charterhouse, Godalming	1611
Douai, RC	1615
Dulwich College	1619
Merchant Taylors', Liverpool	1620
Haberdashers' Aske's, Herts	1690

Public Schools	Founded
Dame Allan's Boys', Newcastle upon Tyne	1705
Churcher's College, Petersfield	1722
Robert Gordon, Aberdeen	1729
James Allen's Girls' School	1741
Ampleforth, RC, North Yorkshire	1802
Wellington School, Somerset	1837
Cheltenham	1841
Marlborough College, Wiltshire	1843
Brighton College	1845
Radley College, Abingdon	1847
Lancing	1848
Hurstpierpoint, West Sussex	1849
Bradfield, Reading	1850
City of London Freemen's, Ashtead	1854
Cheadle Hulme, Cheshire	1855
Ardingly, West Sussex	1858
Oratory School, RC, Woodcote, Berks	1859
Wellington College, Crowthorne, Berks	1856
King's, Tynemouth	1860
Clifton, Bristol	1862
Haileybury, Hertford	1862
Cranleigh	1863
Fettes, Edinburgh	1870
Leys, Cambridge	1875
John Lyon, Harrow, Middlesex	1876
Alleyn's School	1882
Roedean	1885
Merchant Taylors' Girls, Liverpool	1888
Bedales, Petersfield	1893
Benenden, Cranbrook, Kent	1923
Cranford, Wimbourne	1923
Stowe, Buckinghamshire	1923
Gordonstoun, Elgin	1934
Millfield, Street, Somerset	1935

British Universities Founded

	Founded
Oxford	1249
Cambridge	1284
St Andrew's	1411
Glasgow	1451
Aberdeen	1495

British Universities	Founded
Edinburgh	1583
UMIST	1824
Durham	1832
London	1836
Manchester	1851
Newcastle Upon Tyne	1852
Wales, Cardiff	1893
Birmingham	1900
Liverpool	1903
Leeds	1904
Sheffield	1905
Queen's, Belfast	1908
Bristol	1909
Reading	1926
Nottingham	1948
Southampton	1952
Hull	1954
Exeter	1955
Leicester	1957
Sussex	1961
Keele	1962
East Anglia	1963
York	1963
Lancaster	1964
Essex	1964
Strathclyde, Glasgow	1964
Warwick, Coventry	1965
Kent	1965
Ulster	1965
Loughborough	1966
Heriot-Watt, Edinburgh	1966
Surrey, Guildford	1966
Bradford	1966
Bath	1966
Brunel, Uxbridge	1966
City	1966
Aston, Birmingham	1966
Stirling	1967
Dundee	1967
Salford	1967
Open	1969
Cranfield	1969
Buckingham	1976

British Universities: Former Polytechnics

	Founded
Leeds Metropolitan	1992
Kingston	1992
Huddersfield	1992
Hertfordshire	1992
Greenwich	1992

NB: There are currently over 1,000 Independent Schools (Public Schools). The list here is not comprehensive, rather a cross-section of the better-known ones.

*Education at Sherborne was started by St Aldhelm when he became the first bishop of Sherborne in 705. However the school was linked with the Benedictine Abbey. The earliest known Master was Thomas Copeland in 1437. Edward VI refounded the school in 1550 on its present site.

British Universities: Former Polytechnics	Founded
North London	1992
Wolverhampton	1992
Glamorgan	1992
Westminster	1992
West of England (Bristol)	1992
Paisley	1992
Plymouth	1992
Portsmouth	1992
Robert Gordon (Aberdeen)	1992
Sheffield Hallam	1992
South Bank	1992
Staffordshire	1992
Sunderland	1992
Teesside	1992
Thames Valley	1992
Northumbria at Newcastle	1992
Nottingham Trent	1992
Liverpool John Moores	1992
Manchester Metropolitan	1992
Middlesex	1992
Napier (Edinburgh)	1992
De Montfort (Leicester)	1992
Anglia Polytechnic (Chelmsford)	1992
Bournemouth	1992
Brighton	1992
Coventry	1992
Central England (Perry Barr)	1992
Central Lancashire (Preston)	1992
London Guildhall	1993
Luton	1993
Oxford Brookes	1993
Derby	1993
Glasgow Caledonian	1993
East London	1993
Abertay Dundee	1994
Lincoln and Humberside	1996

University of Cambridge

College	Founded
Peterhouse	1284
Clare	1326
Pembroke	1347

University of Cambridge College	Founded
Gonville and Caius	1348
Trinity Hall	1350
Corpus Christi	1352
King's	1441
Queens'	1448
St Catharine's	1473
Jesus	1496
Christ's	1505
St John's	1511
Magdalene	1542
Trinity	1546
Emmanuel	1584
Sidney Sussex	1596
Downing	1800
Homerton	1824
Girton	1869
Newnham	1871
Selwyn	1882
Hughes Hall	1885
St Edmund's	1896
New Hall	1954
Churchill	1960
Darwin	1964
Lucy Cavendish	1965
Wolfson	1965
Clare Hall	1966
Fitzwilliam	1966
Robinson	1977

University of Oxford

College	Founded
University	1249
Balliol	1263
Merton	1264
St Edmund Hall	1278
Exeter	1314
Oriel	1326
The Queen's	1340
New College	1379
Lincoln	1427
All Souls	1438
Magdalen	1458
Brasenose	1509
Corpus Christi	1517
Christ Church	1546

University of Oxford College	Founded
Trinity	1554
St John's	1555
Jesus	1571
Wadham	1612
Pembroke	1624
Worcester	1714
Harris Manchester	1786
Regent's Park*	1810
Keble	1868
Hertford	1874
Wycliffe Hall*	1877
Lady Margaret Hall	1878
Somerville	1879
St Hugh's	1886
Mansfield	1886
Campion Hall*	1896
St Benet's Hall*	1897
Greyfriars*	1910
Blackfriars*	1921
St Peter's	1929
Nuffield	1937
St Hilda's	1938
St Antony's	1950
St Anne's	1952
Linacre	1962
St Catherine's	1962
St Cross	1965
Templeton	1965
Wolfson	1966
Green	1979
Kellogg**	1990

*classified as Permanent Private Halls
**from 1990 to 1994 called Rewley House

University of London
College
Birkbeck College
Charing Cross and Westminster Medical
Goldsmith's College
Heythrop College
Imperial College of Science
King's College London
London Business School
London Hospital Medical College
London School of Economics and Political Science
London School of Hygiene and Tropical Medicine
London School of Jewish Studies
Queen Mary and Westfeld College
Royal Free Hospital School of Medicine
Royal Holloway
Royal Postgraduate Medical School
Royal Veterinary College
School of Oriental and African Studies
School of Pharmacy
St Bartholomew's and the Royal London School
    of Medicine and Dentistry
St George's Hospital Medical School
United Medical and Dental Schools of Guy's and
    St Thomas' Hospitals
University College London
Wye College

University of Durham
College
Collingwood
Graduate Society
Grey
Hatfield
Neville's Cross
St Aidan's
St Chad's
St Cuthbert's
St Hild & St Bede
St John's
St Mary's
Trevelyan
University (Durham)
University (Stockton)
Ushaw
Van Mildert

Miscellaneous Information

Baker Days	Part of the controversial education reform bill, during Kenneth Baker's tenancy as Education Minister 1986–89. His legislation on the in-service training days for teachers came to be known as Baker Days.
City Technology Colleges	Set up in the 1980s in an attempt to widen the choices of secondary education in disadvantaged urban areas. There are seven CTCs at present and they are state-aided.
Dulwich College	Founded by the English actor Edward Alleyn in 1619 but a distinct school from Alleyn's School, founded in 1882. Old Boys of Dulwich College are however known as Old Alleynians.
GCSE	General Certificate of Secondary Education.
GNVQ	General National Vocation Qualification (Further Education).
Gordonstoun	Founded by Kurt Hahn in 1934.
Grant-Maintained Schools	Came into being as a result of the 1988 Education Act which permits schools with more than 300 pupils to opt out of local authority control if the majority of parents wish to do so. These schools are funded by central government.
Independent Schools	Receive no grants from Public Funds and are funded by fees and contributions, and run by trusts.
Lyceum school	Founded by Aristotle.
Mottoes	Eton – Floreat Etona (May Eton Flourish), Rugby – Orando Laborando (By Praying and by Working), Winchester – Manners Makyth Man, Ampleforth College – Dieu le Ward (God Protect Him), The Ridings, Calderdale – Together We Make the Difference.
National Curriculum	Under the 1988 Education Act the National Curriculum was set out in four Key Stages of a child's development. Key Stage 1 and 2 concerned 5–11-year-olds and stated that Core Subjects would include English, (Welsh in Welsh-speaking schools) Maths and Science; and the Foundation Subjects would be Design & Technology, Information Technology, History, Geography, Art, Music and PE. Key Stage 3 caters for 11–14-year-olds and states that a Modern Foreign Language must be included. Key Stage 4 concerns 14–16-year-olds. The Act states that the child must be tested at the end of each Key Stage i.e. 7, 11, and 14-years-old. 16-year-olds only require testing if staying in education.
Newnham College: 1st Male Fellow	Dr Rachel Padman (who had a sex change operation in 1982).
Parents Charter	Booklet informing parents about the education system.
Public Schools: Famous Founders	John Lyon (Harrow), Elizabeth I (Westminster), William of Wykeham (Winchester), Henry VI (Eton), Thomas Sutton (Charterhouse), Edward Alleyne (Dulwich College), Lawrence Sheriff (Rugby), John Colet (St Paul's), Edward VI (Shrewsbury).

Public Schools: Meaning	In recent years the term 'Public School' applies to those Independent Schools in membership of the Headmasters' and Headmistresses' Conference, the Governing Bodies Association or the Governing Bodies of Girl's Schools Association. Historically Public Schools were fee-paying private boarding schools, for pupils aged 13 years and above, which gained sufficient reputation to attract pupils from backgrounds of social worthiness. Public schools were contrasted with 'Private Schools' which were run for the profit of their proprietors. In Scotland, the term Public School refers to a free state school, open to all.
School Age Limits	In Great Britain schooling is compulsory between the ages of 5 and 16 (4 and 16 in Northern Ireland).
Scotvec	Scottish Vocational Education Council (Further Education).
St Andrews: Colleges	United College of St Salvator & St Leonard, College of St Mary.
Subfusc	Formal academic dress, especially at Oxford University.
UCAS	The Universities and Colleges Admissions Service acts as a clearing-house for those applying for admission to full-time first degree and first diploma courses at universities and other higher education institutions in the UK. UCAS was established in 1993 from the merger of the former Universities Central Council on Admissions (UCCA), the Polytechnics Central Admissions System (PCAS) and the Standing Conference on University Entrance (SCUE).
University: Most Students	Open University has the most registered students although London University has most on campus.

EDUCATION

FAMOUS PEOPLE

Occupations: Former and Alternative

Joseph Addison (essayist)   MP for Malmesbury (1708–19)

Aesop (fable writer)   Phrygian slave

Prince Albert (husband of Queen Victoria)   musician

Woody Allen (comic actor and director)   jazz clarinet player

Idi Amin (Ugandan politician)   British army sergeant

Kingsley Amis (writer)   English lecturer at Swansea University

Clive Anderson (comedian and broadcaster)   barrister

Andrew, St (Apostle)   fisherman

John Arlott (cricket commentator)   policeman

Henry Armstrong (American boxer)   Baptist minister

Paddy Ashdown (politician)   Royal Marine

Isaac Asimov (science fiction writer)   biochemist

Clement Attlee (British prime minister)   lawyer and social worker

WH Auden (poet and essayist)   stretcher bearer (Spanish Civil War)

Alfred Austin (poet)   lawyer

Alan Ayckbourn (playwright)   BBC Radio drama producer

Francis Bacon (philosopher)   Lord Chancellor

Mily Balakirev (composer)   railway official

Hastings Banda (Malawian politician)   physician

Roger Bannister (athlete)   doctor

Brendan Behan (author)   painter & decorator and IRA member

Hilaire Belloc (poet and writer)   Liberal MP

Alexander Graham Bell (inventor)   speech therapist to the deaf

Arnold Bennett (novelist)   solicitor's clerk

Cilla Black (entertainer)   coat checker-In (Cavern Club, Liverpool)

RD Blackmore (novelist)   lawyer

Alexander Borodin (composer)   professor of chemistry

Jim Bowen (comedian)   teacher

John Buchan (novelist)   lawyer, publisher and MP for Scottish Universities (1927–35)

Robert Burns (poet)   excise officer and farmer

Michael Caine (actor)   Billingsgate fish porter

James Callaghan (British prime minister)   civil servant (tax officer)

Geoff Capes (athlete)   policeman

Lewis Carroll (writer)   mathematics lecturer

Jimmy Carter (US president)   peanut farmer

Joyce Cary (novelist)   civil servant in Nigeria

Giacomo Casanova (Italian adventurer)   librarian, spy and lottery director

Fidel Castro (Cuban President)   film extra

Miguel Cervantes (novelist)   professional soldier

Geoffrey Chaucer (poet)   customs officer, MP and soldier

Claude Lorraine (artist)   pastry cook

William Cobbett (writer)   soldier and MP for Oldham (1832–5)

Edward Coke (lawyer)   MP for Aldeburgh (1589)

Perry Como (singer)   barber

Sean Connery (actor)   coffin polisher and Royal Navy sailor

Billy Connolly (comedian and actor)   shipyard worker

Gary Cooper (actor)   photographer and stuntman

Tommy Cooper (comic magician)   guardsman

Andres Courrèges (fashion designer)   civil engineer

AJ Cronin (novelist)   inspector of mines

César Cui (Russian composer)   military engineer

Dante Alighieri (Italian poet)   embassy official

Walter De La Mare (poet and novelist)   oil company worker

Christopher Dean (figure skater)   policeman

Dave Dee (pop singer)   policeman

Daniel Defoe (writer)   brickmaker and shopkeeper

Charles Dickens (writer)   court stenographer and factory shoe black

Benjamin Disraeli (British prime minister)   novelist

John Donne (poet)   dean of St Paul's Cathedral (1621–31)

Sir Arthur Conan Doyle (writer)   doctor (ophthalmologist)

John Boyd Dunlop (inventor)   veterinary surgeon

Albrecht Dürer (painter and engraver)   draughtsman

John Dyer (poet and painter)   lawyer

Clint Eastwood (actor)   swimming instructor

Thomas Alva Edison (inventor)   telegraph operator and newsboy

Albert Einstein (physicist)   Patent Office clerk

TS Eliot (poet and dramatist)   clerk with Lloyd's Bank

Juan Fangio (racing driver)   bus driver

Michael Faraday (physicist)   bookseller and laboratory technician

William Faulkner (novelist)   postmaster

Kathleen Ferrier (contralto)   telephone operator

Frank Finlay (actor)   butcher

F Scott Fitzgerald (novelist)   Hollywood scriptwriter

Ian Fleming (novelist)   intelligence officer and journalist

Errol Flynn (actor)   policeman (Tasmania)

Gerald Ford (US President)   male model

George Foreman (boxer)   minister

George Formby (entertainer)   jockey

Benjamin Franklin (US statesman)   printer and scientist

Frederick I I, the Great (king of Prussia)   musician

Billy Fury (singer)   tugboat worker

Clark Gable (actor)   lumberjack

Galileo Galilei (astronomer)   doctor, mathematician and natural philosopher

Greta Garbo (actress)   milliner's model

Graeme Garden (comic actor)   doctor

Giuseppe Garibaldi (Italian patriot)   candlemaker and privateer

James Garner (actor)   swimsuit model

David Garrick (actor)   wine merchant

Richard Gatling (US inventor)   doctor

Paul Gauguin (artist)   stockbroker and labourer on Panama Canal

Jean Genet (author)   professional criminal and male prostitute

Edward Gibbon (historian)   MP for Liskeard (1774–80)

William S Gilbert (librettist)   barrister and cartoonist

Joseph Goebbels   newspaper editor

Johann Goethe (poet and dramatist)   fire chief, newspaper critic and Court Official

Sam Goldwyn (film producer)   glove salesman

WG Grace (cricketer)   doctor

Kenneth Grahame (writer)   secretary to Bank of England

Cary Grant (actor)   acrobat

Robert Graves (poet and novelist)   professor of English (Cairo University)

Fulke Greville (poet)   MP for Warwickshire

Zane Grey (writer)   dentist

Terry Griffiths (snooker player)   postman

Che Guevara (revolutionary leader)   doctor

Gareth Hale (comedian)   PE teacher

Thomas Hardy (writer)   architect

Bob Harris (broadcaster)   policeman

Russell Harty (broadcaster)   teacher

Alex Harvey (musician)   lion tamer

Nathaniel Hawthorne (writer)   American consul in Liverpool (1853–7)

AP Herbert (writer)   MP for Oxford University (1935–50)

William Herschel (astronomer)   music teacher

Benny Hill (comedian)   milkman

Harry Hill (comedian)   doctor

Adolf Hitler (dictator)   painter of postcards

Ho Chi Minh (Vietnamese politician)   hotel worker and pastry cook

Bob Hope (comedian)   boxer

Gerard Manley Hopkins (poet)   classics professor (University College Dublin)

Bob Hoskins (actor)   market porter, fire-eater, steeplejack and seaman

AE Housman (poet)   classics teacher

Rod Hull (comedian)   electrician

Gareth Hunt (actor)   merchant seaman

Henryk Ibsen (dramatist)   pharmacist

Julio Iglesias (vocalist)   goalkeeper

Charles Ives (composer)   insurance executive

David Jason (actor)   electrician

Andrew Johnson (US president)   tailor

James Prescott Joule (physicist)   brewer

James Robertson Justice (actor)   naturalist

Wassily Kandinsky (artist)   lawyer

Harvey Keitel (actor)   US marine

Charles Kingsley (author)   Cambridge history professor

Alphonse de Lamartine (poet and historian)   French foreign minister (1848)

Burt Lancaster (actor)   circus acrobat

Eddie Large (comedian)   electrician

Philip Larkin (poet)   librarian (of Hull University)

Antoine Lavoisier (chemist)   tax collector

Lee Kuan Yew (Singapore politician)   barrister

Vladimir Lenin (Russian revolutionary)   lawyer

Leopold I of Habsburg (Holy Roman Emperor)   musician

Franz Liszt (musician)   priest

Little Richard (musician)   minister

Syd Little (comedian)   decorator

Henry Wadsworth Longfellow (poet)   Harvard lecturer

St Luke (New Testament evangelist)   painter and physician

John Lydgate (poet)   monk

Thomas Macaulay (author)   lawyer and MP for Calne, Leeds, and Edinburgh

Harold MacMillan (British prime minister)   publisher

Norman Mailer (writer)   candidate for NY mayor (4th of 5)

André Malraux (writer)   archaeologist and pilot in the Spanish civil war

Thomas Malthus (economist)   clergyman

Nelson Mandela (South African statesman)   lawyer

Walter de la Mare (poet and novelist)   Standard Oil Company employee

John Marston (dramatic poet)   lawyer

Andrew Marvell (poet)   MP for Hull (1659–78)

Karl Marx (political and economic theorist)   journalist and editor

Marcello Mastroianni (actor)   draughtsman and cashier

Quentin Matsys (Massys) (Flemish painter)   blacksmith

St Matthew (apostle)   tax collector

William Somerset Maugham (writer)   surgeon and wartime secret agent

Herman Melville (writer)   customs officer, bank clerk and adventurer

Gregor Mendel (biologist and botanist)   monk

Jonathan Miller (stage director and author)   doctor

John Mills (actor)   toilet paper salesman

Robert Mitchum (actor)   miner and professional boxer

Matt Monro (singer)   bus driver

Roger Moore (actor)   male model

Samuel Morse (inventor)   artist

Arthur Mullard (actor)   professional boxer

Modest Mussorgsky (composer)   civil servant

Dame Anna Neagle (actress)   dance instructor

Jawaharlal Nehru (Indian statesman)   lawyer

Thomas Newcomen (inventor)   blacksmith

Bob Newhart (comedian)   accountant

Paul Newman (actor)   motor racing driver

Isaac Newton (scientist)   warden of the Mint and MP

Harold Nicolson (author and critic)   MP for West Leicester (1935–45)

David Niven (actor)   army officer

Julius Nyerere (Tanzanian politician)   teacher

Milton Obote (Ugandan politician)   labourer, clerk and salesman

Sean O'Casey (playwright)   building labourer

Tom O'Connor (comedian)   teacher

Bruce Oldfield (musician)   art teacher

George Orwell (novelist)   policeman (Burma)

David Owen (politician)   doctor

Norman Pace (comedian)   PE teacher

Thomas Love Peacock (novelist and poet)   chief examiner of East India Company

Peter I, the Great (Russian tsar)   shipwright

St Peter (apostle)   fisherman

François André Philidor (composer)   chess master

Enoch Powell (politician)   professor of Greek

Magnus Pyke (science broadcaster)   nutritionist

Salvatore Quasimodo (poet)   engineer

Edgar Quinet (writer)   politician

François Rabelais (satirist)   doctor and monk

FAMOUS PEOPLE

Sir Walter Raleigh (explorer and navigator)   MP for Devon (1585)

Charles Reade (writer)   lawyer

Ray Reardon (snooker player)   policeman and miner

Paul Revere (American patriot)   silversmith

Arthur Rimbaud (poet)   gun runner and merchant

Joan Rivers (comedian)   fashion co-ordinator for Bond Stores

Auguste Rodin (sculptor)   ornamental mason

Peter Roget (thesaurus writer)   doctor

Leonard Rossiter (actor)   insurance agent

Henri Rousseau (painter)   customs officer

Salman Rushdie (writer)   actor and advertising copywriter

Willie Rushton (satirist)   cartoonist

Sir Walter Scott (novelist and poet)   lawyer

William Shakespeare (writer)   actor

Richard Brinsley Sheridan (dramatist)   MP for Stafford and Ilchester

Nevil Shute (writer)   engineer (worked on R100)

Sir Philip Sidney (poet)   professional soldier

Norodom Sihanouk (Cambodian politician)   musician

Delia Smith (cookery writer)   hairdresser and Norwich City FC director

CP Snow (novelist)   parliamentary sec (Ministry of technology) and physicist

Benjamin Spock (paediatrician)   Naval officer and olympic oarsman

Jerry Springer (talk-show host)   lawyer

Joseph Stalin (Soviet leader)   trainee monk

Freddie Starr (comedian)   bricklayer

Sir Richard Steele (essayist)   MP for Stockbridge (1713)

Tommy Steele (entertainer)   merchant seaman

Laurence Sterne (novelist)   clergyman

Wallace Stevens (poet)   insurance company executive

Rod Stewart (singer)   footballer (Brentford) and gravedigger

David Storey (writer)   Rugby League professional

Jonathan Swift (writer)   clergyman

Charles Talleyrand-Périgord (statesman)   abbot

Jimmy Tarbuck (comedian)   milkman

Pyotr Tchaikovsky (composer)   civil servant

Shirley Temple (actress)   US ambassador to Ghana

Valentina Tereshkova (astronaut)   cotton mill worker

Margaret Thatcher (British prime minister)   research chemist and barrister

John Thaw (actor)   market porter

JRR Tolkien (writer)   Oxford English professor

Leo Tolstoy (writer)   army officer

Anthony Trollope (writer)   Post Office worker

Harry S Truman (US president)   haberdasher

Desmond Tutu (archbishop of Cape Town)   schoolteacher

Liv Ullmann (actress)   UNICEF ambassador

John Vanbrugh (playwright)   architect

Vincent Van Gogh (artist)   trainee priest

Jules Verne (writer)   librettist

King Vidor (film director)   cinema projectionist and cameraman

Kurt Vonnegut (writer)   soldier

Lech Walesa (Polish politician)   electrician

Lew Wallace (author)   soldier

Bradley Walsh (comedian)   footballer (Brentford)

George Washington (US president)   British army colonel

Noah Webster (lexicographer)   lawyer and teacher

Chaim Weizmann (Israeli statesman)   biochemist

Orson Welles (actor and director)   picador

HG Wells (writer)   draper's assistant and teacher

Walt Whitman (poet)   teacher and printer

William Wilberforce (philanthropist)   MP for Hull and Yorkshire

Billy Wilder (film director)   journalist and crime reporter

Tennessee Williams (playwright)   poet-waiter and cinema usher

Ludwig Wittgenstein (philosopher)   teacher, porter, gardener and engineer

Terry Wogan (broadcaster)   bank clerk

Ermanno Wolf-Ferrari (composer)   artist

William Wordsworth (poet)   stamp distributor

Harry Worth (comic actor)   miner

Sir Christopher Wren (architect)   professor of astronomy

Tammy Wynette (singer)   beautician

JR Wyss (writer and philosopher)   Swiss national anthem writer

Yohji Yamamoto (fashion designer)   lawyer

Boris Yeltsin (Russian president)   construction company director

Andrew John Young (poet)   clergyman

Brigham Young (Mormon leader)   carpenter, painter and glazier

Lazarus Zamenhof (language inventor)   oculist and philologist

Franco Zeffirelli (film director)   actor and costume designer

Count Von Zeppelin (airship inventor)   US Civil War soldier

Emile Zola (novelist)   clerk in publishing house

Assassinations

681BC	*Sennacherib of Assyria* Murdered by his two sons.
514BC	*Hipparchus of Athens* Killed by Harmodius and Aristogeiton, two Athenians.
465BC	*Xerxes I of Persia* Killed by members of his court, led by Artabanus.
336BC	*Philip II of Macedon* Killed by Pausanias, a Spartan regent and general.
330BC	*Darius III (Codomannus) of Persia* Slain by a satrap, Arterxes (Ardashir), whilst fleeing Alexander the Great.
44BC	*Julius Caesar (Roman dictator)* Stabbed by Brutus, Cassius and others in the Senate.
41	*Caligula (Roman emperor)* Murdered by Cassius Chaerea, an officer of his guard.
54	*Claudius I (Roman Emperor)* Ate poisoned mushrooms served by his wife, Agrippina the Younger.
96	*Domitian (Roman dictator)* Stabbed in his bedroom by Stephanus, a freed slave.
192	*Commodus (Roman Emperor)* Strangled by wrestler Narcissus, at the behest of his mistress, Marcia.
978	*Edward the Martyr (King of England)* Murdered at Corfe Castle by his younger half-brother Ethelred's household, led by Elfthryth.
1057	*Macbeth (King of Scotland)* Killed by Malcolm III, Canmore, at Lumphanan (15 August).
1170	*Thomas à Becket* Killed by four knights, Fitzurse, Tracy, De Merville and Le Breton in Canterbury Cathedral.
1192	*Conrad, King of Jerusalem* Killed by members of the militant Islamic sect, the Assassins, who gave assassination their name.
1327	*Edward II of England* Murdered in Berkeley Castle possibly with a red-hot poker at the instigation of his wife, Isabella, and her lover Roger de Mortimer; possible perpetrators were De Gournay and Maltravers.
1437	*James I of Scotland* Murdered in court residence, a Dominican monastery, by assassins led by Sir Robert Graham.
1471	*Henry VI of England* Murdered in the Tower of London, possibly by Richard of Gloucester, the future Richard III.
1488	*James III of Scotland* Murdered following defeat of royal army at Sauchieburn by unknown.
1533	*Atahualpa (Last Inca ruler)* Strangled by Spanish forces under Francisco Pizarro.
1541	*Francisco Pizarro* Murdered at his home in Lima, possibly by Juan de Rada at the instigation of Diego de Almagro.
1567	*Henry, Lord Darnley (husband of Mary, Queen of Scots)* Strangled by Scottish nobles after explosion at Kirk O' Field.
1584	*William the Silent (aka William of Orange)* Shot at Delft by Balthasar Gerard.
1589	*Henry III of France* Stabbed by Jacques Clément, a fanatical Dominican.
1610	*Henry IV of France* Murdered by François Ravaillac, a Catholic fanatic.
1628	*Duke of Buckingham* Stabbed at Portsmouth en route for La Rochelle by John Felton, a discontented subaltern.
1634	*Prince Wallenstein (German general)* Killed by Devereux.
1762	*Peter III, Tsar of Russia* Strangled in captivity by Count Aleksei Orlov, the lover of his wife and future empress, Catherine.
1793	*Jean Paul Marat (French Revolutionary)* Stabbed in his bath by Charlotte Corday.
1801	*Paul I of Russia* Strangled by army officers who had conspired to force his abdication.
1812	*Spencer Perceval (PM)* Shot while entering lobby of the House of Commons by John Bellingham, a bankrupt Liverpool broker.
1865	*Abraham Lincoln* Shot by actor John Wilkes Booth in Ford's Theater, Washington, while watching *Our American Cousin*.
1872	*Richard Burke, Earl of Mayo* Stabbed to death by Shere Ali, a convict, while inspecting the settlement at Port Blair on the Andaman Islands.
1881	*James A Garfield (US President)* Shot in a station by Charles Guiteau, a disappointed office-seeker.
	Alexander II of Russia Died from injuries after a bomb was thrown near his palace by Nihilists, led by Sophia Perovskaya.
1882	*Lord Frederick Cavendish (Chief Secretary for Ireland)* Murdered by 'Irish invincibles' in Phoenix Park, Dublin.
1894	*Marie François Carnot (French President)* Stabbed by anarchist Cesare Giovanni Santo Caserio.
1897	*Antonio Cánovas del Castillo (Spanish Premier)* Shot by Italian anarchist Angiolillo at the bath of Santa Agueda, Vitoria.
1900	*Umberto I of Italy* Murdered by anarchist G Bresci in Monza.
1901	*William McKinley (US President)* Shot by anarchist Leon Czolgosz in Buffalo, NY.
1903	*Alexander Obrenovich (King of Serbia)* Murdered by military conspirators, along with his wife, Draga.
1913	*George I of Greece* Murdered by a Greek, Schinas, in Salonika.
1914	*Archduke Franz Ferdinand* Shot in a car by Gavrilo Princip in Sarajevo (28 June); the assassination helped to precipitate World War I.
	Jean Jaurès (French Socialist) Shot by nationalist Raoul Villain in café.
1916	*Rasputin (Russian monk)* Killed and dumped in River Neva by group of nobles led by Prince Feliks Yusupov and Grand Duke Dimitry Pavlovich, revenging his influence over Tsarina Alexandra.
1922	*Michael Collins (Sinn Fein leader)* Killed in an ambush between Bandon and Macroom in the Irish Free State.
1923	*Pancho Villa (Mexican Revolutionary)* Assassinated on his ranch at Parral, Mexico (20 June).

FAMOUS PEOPLE

1934   *Dr Engelbert Dollfuss* *(Austrian Chancellor)* Shot by Nazis in the Chancellery.
        Sergey Mironovich Kirov *(Russian Communist)* Shot by Leonid Nikolayev at the Communist Party HQ (1 December); Stalin subsequently purged Leningrad of all suspected anti-Stalinists.
        Alexander I of Yugoslavia *(King of the Serbs, Croats and Slovenes)* Murdered in Marseilles by a Macedonian terrorist.
1935   *Huey Long* *(US politician)* Murdered by Dr Carl Austin Weiss.
1940   *Leon Trotsky* *(exiled Russian leader)* Killed with an ice pick in Mexico by Ramón Mercader.
1942   *Reinhard Heydrich* *(second-in-command in the Nazi Secret Police)* Murdered by Czech resistance fighters.
1943   *Isoruku Yamamoto (Japanese Admiral)* Plane intercepted and shot down by US P-38 fighter squad after Japanese naval code was broken.
1948   *Mohandas Gandhi* *(Indian leader)* Shot by Hindu fanatic Nathuran Godse at Birla House, New Delhi.
        Count Folke Bernadotte *(Swedish diplomat)* Murdered by Jewish extremists in ambush in Jerusalem.
1951   *Abdullah I of Jordan* Murdered by member of Jihad faction.
        Liaquat Ali Khan *(Pakistani PM)* Murdered in Rawalpindi by fanatics advocating war with India.
1958   *Faisal II of Iraq* Murdered with his entire household during a military coup.
1959   *Solomon Bandaranaike* *(Sri Lankan statesman)* Murdered by Buddhist monk Talduwe Somarama.
        Rafael Trujillo Molina *(Dominican Republic dictator)* Machine-gunned in car by assassins including General JT Diaz.
1963   *John F Kennedy* *(US President)* Shot while riding in open Lincoln Continental in Dallas, Texas, by rifleman Lee Harvey Oswald (22 Nov).
1965   *Malcolm X* *(Black Muslim leader)* Shot at political rally.
1966   *Hendrik Verwoerd* *(South African Premier)* Stabbed by parliamentary messenger Dimitri Tsafendas.
1968   *Martin Luther King* *(civil rights leader)* Shot on hotel balcony by James Earl Ray in Memphis, Tennessee.
        Robert F Kennedy *(US Senator)* Shot by Jordanian Arab immigrant Sirhan Bishara Sirhan in the Hotel Ambassador, Los Angeles.
1975   *King Faisal of Saudi Arabia* Murdered by his nephew, Prince Faisal.
1976   *Christopher Ewart-Biggs* *(British Ambassador to Eire)* Car blown up by IRA landmine.
        Georgi Markov (Bulgarian dissident) Infected with poisoned pellet on Westminster Bridge by Bulgarian agent.
1978   *Aldo Moro, former Italian PM* Kidnapped by Red Brigade and later found dead.
        Wafizulah Amin (President of Afghanistan) Killed with his mistress in the presidential palace, Kabul, by KGB commandos.
1979   *Airey Neave, MP* Killed by IRA bomb in House of Commons car park.
        Lord Mountbatten Killed by IRA bomb in sailing boat while fishing off County Sligo, Ireland.
        Park Chung Hee *(South Korean President)* Shot in restaurant by chief of Korean Central Intelligence Agency.
1980   *John Lennon* *(former Beatle)* Shot by Mark Chapman outside his apartment in New York.
        Oscar Romero *(Salvadorean RC Prelate)* Murdered by government troops.
1981   *Anwar Sadat* *(Egyptian President)* Shot by rebel soldier Khalid Ahmed Shawki and others while reviewing military parade.
        Zia ur-Rahman *(Bangladeshi President)* Shot by military and replaced as President by Abdus Sattar.
1983   *Benigno Aquino* *(Filipino politician)* Shot in the head at Manila airport by a government-backed assassin.
1984   *Indira Gandhi* *(Indian PM)* Murdered by members of her Sikh bodyguard (Satwant and Beant Singh).
1986   *Olof Palme* *(Swedish PM)* Shot in Stockholm as he walked home from cinema by unknown hand.
1988   *General Zia ul-Haq* *(Pakistani leader)* Killed in air crash owing to sabotage.
1991   *Rajiv Gandhi* *(Former Indian PM)* Blown up during an election campaign by Thanu.
1992   *Muhammad Boudiaf* *(President of Algeria's High State Council)* Murdered during a speech.
1995   *Yitzhak Rabin* *(Israeli PM)* Murdered by Yigal Amir.
2002   *Pim Fortuyn (Dutch Politician)* Shot six times whilst walking to his car in Hilversum. Six months after the shooting Volkert Van de Graaf confessed to the murder.

Attempted Assassinations

Count Otto von Bismarck Attempts by Kulimann (1874) and Blind (1866).

Cassius Marcellus Clay (US Emancipationist and Senator) Shot point-blank during a speech in 1843 and used a Bowie knife to cut off the attacker's ear and nose and also cut out one of his eyes! Not to be confused with his illustrious namesake, who presumably would have dispatched the assailant with a swift left hook.

Queen Elizabeth I Numerous plots to replace Elizabeth on the throne by Mary Queen of Scots, notably the Ridolfi and Babington plots, but the only person to be put to death for an alleged direct attempt was Dr Lopez, her physician, in 1594.

Gerald Ford Assassination attempt by Lynette 'Squeaky' Fromme, member of Charles Manson's 'family' (1975).

Henry Frick Steel magnate who was shot and stabbed by anarchist Alexander Berkman (1892).

George III James Hadfield attempted assassination in 1800 but was acquitted due to insanity.

Hitler Bomb planted by Colonel Von Stauffenberg at his Wolf's Lair HQ in E Prussia in 1944 exploded but failed to kill him.

John Paul II Shot by Mehmet Ali Agca in 1981.

Lenin Assassination attempt by Fanny Kaplan in 1918 caused his health to go into steady decline.

Leopold II Gennaro Rubino made an attempt on the life of the Belgian king in 1902.

Napoleon III Felice Orsini attempted his assassination, but Napoleon eventually died of a gall bladder infection.

Prince of Wales Jean Baptiste Sipido made an attempt on the life of the future King Edward VII (1900).

Ronald Reagan Shot by John Hinckley in 1981.

Franklin Delano Roosevelt In 1933 he and Chicago mayor Anton Cermak were shot at by Giuseppe Zangara. Cermak was mortally wounded, whilst Roosevelt became President.

Theodore Roosevelt Attempt on life by John F Schrank, 14 October 1912. Despite being shot in the chest at a political rally managed to continue his speech for 90 minutes before seeking medical assistance.

William Henry Seward (US Senator) Survived an assassination attempt on 14 April 1865 (the same night Abraham Lincoln was shot) when Lewis Payne, an associate of John Wilkes Booth, broke into his bedroom and stabbed him repeatedly.

Shah of Persia Francois Salsou made an attempt on the life of the Shah in 1900.

Margaret Thatcher The IRA Grand Hotel bombing in Brighton (Oct 1984) was an attempt on her life.

Queen Victoria Attempts by Edward Oxford (1840), John William Bean (1842), John Francis (1842), William Hamilton (1849), Robert Pate (1850), Arthur O'Connor (1872) and Roderick Maclean (1882).

George Wallace Left paralysed after being shot by Arthur Bremer in 1972.

Andy Warhol Shot by Valerie Solanis, one of his starlets, in 1968.

Catchphrases and Slogans

NB: The list below shows a phrase and the most identifiable body to that phrase. In most cases the details are self-explanatory and where the phrase has actually been coined by a person then his information is given. Many phrases will be of doubtful origin and no attempt has been made to authenticate entries as original spoutings. To give Robert Walpole as an example from my list: the phrase 'every man has his price' is identified with the prime minister but the phrase was almost certainly used as a maxim centuries earlier, although impossible to research. Many more catchphrases associated with household products will be found in the TV Advert section.

a good idea . . . son Max Bygraves (as Archie Andrew's tutor in *Educating Archie*)

all human life is there News of the World (advertising slogan from a Henry James novel)

all done in the best possible taste Kenny Everett (in the guise of the leggy Miss Cupid Stunt)

a man of my cal-aye-ber Tony Hancock (originally coined in *Hancock's Half-Hour*)

and now for something completely different John Cleese (in *Monty Python*)

and that's the way it is Walter Cronkite (in concluding his CBS TV *Evening News* programme)

and the next Tonight will be tomorrow night Cliff Michelmore (at the end of the nightly BBC magazine programme)

are you looking for a punch up the bracket? Tony Hancock (originally coined in *Hancock's Half-Hour*)

are you sitting comfortably ? Julia Lang (on BBC radio's *Listen with Mother*)

as it happens Jimmy Savile

ask the audience Chris Tarrant (in *Who Wants to be a Millionaire*)

as the art mistress said to the gardener Monica (Beryl Reid) as Archie Andrew's posh friend in *Educating Archie*

aw don't embarrass me Lenny the Lion (ventriloquist Terry Hall's creation)

awight at the back (sic) Michael Barrymore (at the start of many of his shows)

beam me up, Scotty Attributed to Captain Kirk (William Shatner) in *Star Trek*

because it is there George Leigh Mallory (on being asked why he wanted to climb Mt Everest)

before you can say Jack Robinson Richard Brinsley Sheridan (in the Commons to avoid using a fellow MP's name)

before your very eyes Arthur Askey (from the name of his first television series as a proof of live TV)

be like dad, keep mum 1941 propaganda slogan advising civilians to not talk about war-related issues)

be prepared Pears' Soap usurped the slogan from the motto of the Boy Scout movement

Bernie, the bolt Bob Monkhouse (in the *Golden Shot*). Bernie's real name was Derek Young

better red than dead Bertrand Russell (in a 1958 article stating Communism was preferable over death)

bet you can't eat three Ian Botham (used in an advertising campaign for Shredded Wheat)

Beulah, peel me a grape Mae West (first said by the actress to a black maid in the film *I'm No Angel*)

Big Bang, the Nickname for the London Stock Exchange deregulation of 27 October 1986

Big Brother is watching you George Orwell in his novel *Nineteen Eighty-Four* first coined this cry for democracy

big-hearted Arthur, that's me Arthur Askey (introducing himself on radio's *Band Wagon*)

black is beautiful Stokely Carmichael (at a civil rights rally in Memphis in 1966)

black power Usually attributed to Stokely Carmichael after shooting of James Meredith in 1966

blonde bombshell Jean Harlow (not so much a catchphrase more a description and nickname)

book 'em Danno Steve McGarrett (Jack Lord) to Detective 'Danno' Williams in *Hawaii Five O*

boom, boom Billy Bennett (the comedian coined the phrase to underline the punchline of a gag). Basil Brush and Eric Morecambe usurped Billy Bennett's catchphrase in their acts

booyakasha! Sacha Baron Cohen in the guise of rapper Ali G.

FAMOUS PEOPLE

born 1820, still going strong   Johnnie Walker whisky slogan first used in 1908

British are coming, the   Colin Welland (after collecting an Oscar for the film *Chariots of Fire*)

buck stops here, the   Harry S Truman (from a sign on his desk in the Oval Office)

bumper bundle   Coined by Jean Metcalfe whilst introducing *Two-Way Family Favourites*. The phrase denotes a large number of requests for the same record

can I do you now sir?   Mrs Mopp (Dorothy Summers) in *ITMA* i.e. *It's That Man Again*

can we talk?   Joan Rivers (interjection used by the comedienne to link her jokes)

can you hear me, mother ?   Sandy Powell (coined in 1932, probably the first radio catchphrase that caught on)

carry on London   Freddie Grisewood (at the end of BBC radio's *In Town Tonight*)

clap hands, here comes Charley   Charlie Kunz (became the signature tune of the *American pianist*)

clunk, click, every trip   Jimmy Savile (from a seat-belt campaign launched in 1971)

come on down   *The Price is Right* (originated in America when the popular show began in 1957)

come up and see me sometime   Mae West (originally said as 'Why don't you come up sometime and see me)

come with me to the Casbah   Charles Boyer (attributed to the 1938 film *Algiers* although not in the final cut)

customer is always right, the   H Gordon Selfridge (the American pioneer of the large department store)

daft as a brush   Ken Platt (comedian who corrupted the northern phrase 'soft as a brush')

day war broke out, the   Robb Wilton (after WWII the comedian substituted 'peace' for 'war')

dead as a door-nail   From Langland's *Piers Plowman* (door-nail was a knob on which a knocker struck)

did you spot this week's deliberate mistake?   Lionel Gamlin (from his BBC radio series *Monday Night at Seven*)

didn't he do well?   Bruce Forsyth (at the end of the conveyor belt finale of the *Generation Game*)

dig for victory   Sir Reginald Dorman Smith (slogan asking people to grow food during WWII)

disgusted . . . Tunbridge Wells   Stock phrase used when the writer does not want to give their name

dodgy   Norman Vaughan (the phrase was accompanied by a thumbs-down gesture)

doesn't it make you want to spit?   Arthur Askey (from the radio show *Band Wagon*)

don't forget the fruit gums mum   Roger Musgrave (the copywriter coined the phrase for Rowntree's Fruit Gums)

don't spit, remember the Johnstown flood   US admonition against spitting (citing the 1889 flood caused by a dam bursting)

don't touch me   Julian Clary (said by the comedian when any contact is made on his person)

don't worry, be happy   George Bush (unofficial campaign slogan used in the 1988 presidential election)

do you know the Bishop of Norwich?   An allusion to a port drinker who is holding on to the bottle and not passing it round

Drinka Pinta Milka Day   Bertrand Whitehead (the Executive Officer of the National Milk Publicity Council)

eat my shorts   Bart Simpson in the cartoon series *The Simpsons*

economical with the truth   Sir Robert Armstrong (whilst being cross-examined in 1986 regarding MI5 secrets)

elementary, my dear Watson   Sherlock Holmes (attributed to him but not to be seen in Conan Doyle's writings)

eleventh commandment, the   George Whyte-Melville (cites 'thou shalt not be found out' in his book *Holmby House*)

'er indoors   Arthur Daley (George Cole) in the ITV series *Minder*

evening all   George Dixon (Jack Warner) in *Dixon of Dock Green*

ever-open door, the   Dr Barnardo's Homes (slogan used to describe the homes in the 1950s)

everybody out   Paddy (Miriam Karlin) as the shop steward in the BBC's *The Rag Trade*

everybody wants to get into the act   Jimmy Durante (subsequently changed to everybody wants to get in on the act)

every man has his price   Often attributed to Robert Walpole

every picture tells a story   Appears to originate in 1904 as a slogan for Doan's Backache and Kidney Pills. The slogan was accompanied by a picture of a person bent over with back pain

everything in the garden's lovely   Marie Lloyd (from the title of one of her popular songs)

expletive deleted   Made famous by the Watergate transcripts but a general US term in documents

exterminate . . . exterminate   Daleks (in the BBC television series *Dr Who*)

eyes and ears of the world, the   Slogan promoting the cinema newsreel, *Paramount News* 1927–57

fifty fifty   Chris Tarrant (in *Who Wants to be a Millionaire*)

fleet's lit up, the   Cdr Tommy Woodrooffe (the BBC radio commentator coined the phrase in 1937)

flippin' kids   Tony Hancock (as Archie Andrew's tutor in *Educating Archie*)

Flying Fickle Finger of Fate Award, the   Prize in a mock talent contest in Rowan and Martin's *Laugh In*

F. T. A. (Fuck The Army)   Popular American graffiti used since 1960 among US Army recruits to express a dislike for orders especially in the Vietnam conflict. Protestants use F. T. P. to express their dislike for the Pope and N. Irish patriots use F. T. Q. for the Queen

fully paid-up member of the human race   Kenneth Clarke (described as such by the *Observer* on 31 July 1988)

get out of that   Eric Morecambe (whilst pressing his down-turned palm under Ernie Wise's chin)

gis a job   Yosser Hughes (Bernard Hill) in *Boys from the Blackstuff*

give 'em the money Barney   Wilfred Pickles (*Have a Go*) to Barney Colehan

give 'em the money Mabel   Wilfred Pickles (to his wife Mabel in radio's *Have a Go*)

go ahead, make my day   Harry Callahan (Clint Eastwood) originally in the 1983 film *Sudden Impact*. Ronald Reagan (in an address to the 1985 American Business Conference)

Godfrey Daniel   WC Fields (used in place of 'God, damn you' to comply with the strict Hay's Code)

gone for a Burton   RAF expression of WWII denoting a presumed dead person had gone for a drink *good game, good game*   Bruce Forsyth (at the end of each round of the *Generation Game*)

good morning sir; was there something?   Sam Costa (in the radio programme *Much Binding in the Marsh*)

goodnight children everywhere   Uncle Mac (Derek McCulloch) in BBC radio's *Children's Hour*

goodnight, Mrs Calabash . . . wherever you are   Jimmy Durante (when ending his radio and television appearances)

goody, goody gumdrops   Humphrey Lestocq (presenter of BBC television's *Whirligig* in the 1950s)

greatest show on earth, the   PT Barnum (describing the merger of his circus with Bailey's in 1881)

happy as a sandboy   The phrase alludes to the happiness of the door-to-door sellers of sand during the nineteenth century. Sand was bought as an absorber of liquids and scourer

happy as Larry   An Australian expression of delight referring to the boxer Larry Foley 1847–1917

hat-trick   Originating in cricket parlance when the taker of 3 successive wickets would be awarded a new hat for his feat. The term is now used for any triple success

have a gorilla   Neddie Seagoon (Harry Secombe) offering a cigarette in the *Goon Show*

haves and the have-nots   Sancho Panza (in Miguel Cervantes' *Don Quixote*)

he can't fart and chew gum at the same time   President Lyndon Johnson's insulting description of President Gerald Ford

he can't walk and chew gum at the same time   Revision of Lyndon Johnson's words when Ford became President in 1974

Heinz the Bolt   Jackie Rae (in television's the *Golden Shot*). Heinz later became Bernie the Bolt

hello folks   Tommy Handley (eponymous hero of *It's That Man Again*)

hello folks and world   Neddie Seagoon (Harry Secombe) in the *Goon Show*

hello, good evening, and welcome   David Frost (coined in the *Frost Programme* but has become his stock greeting)

hello, it's me, Twinkletoes   Bernard Bresslaw (as Archie Andrews' tutor in *Educating Archie*)

hello my darlings   Charlie Drake (usual opening greeting of the diminutive funny man)

hello peeps   Stavros (Harry Enfield)

hello playmates   Arthur Askey (introducing himself on radio's *Band Waggon*)

hello possums   Dame Edna Everage (Barry Humphries)

hello sailor   Minnie Bannister (Spike Milligan) in the classic Goon's script *Tales of Men's Shirts*. The phrase has entered the language as a camp double-entendre

here and now, before your very eyes   Arthur Askey (original catchphrase from the series *Before Your Very Eyes*)

here's another fine mess you've gotten me into   Oliver Hardy (invariably to his long-suffering partner Stan Laurel)

here's a pretty kettle of fish   Queen Mary (to Stanley Baldwin referring to the abdication crisis of 1936)

here's Johnny   Ed McMahon (introduction to Johnny Carson on NBC's *Tonight show*)

here's looking at you kid   Rick Blaine (Humphrey Bogart) in *Casablanca*. The phrase is used four times

here we are again   Joey the Clown (Joseph Grimaldi)

one of the oldest attributable catchphrases

he's fallen in the water   Little Jim (Spike Milligan) in the *Goon Show*

he's loo-vely, Mrs Hoskins . . . . he's loo-oo-vely   Ivy (Ted Ray) in the comedian's hit radio programme *Ray's a Laugh*

hi there pop pickers   Alan Freeman (Australian disc-jockey) whilst presenting *Pick of the Pops*

how's about that then, guys and gals   Jimmy Savile (phrase used by the disc-jockey after a particularly good record)

how tickled I am   Ken Dodd (whilst usually shoving a tickling stick between his legs from behind)

I am the greatest   Muhammad Ali (Cassius Clay) usurped the phrase from wrestler Gorgeous George

I could do that   Yosser Hughes (Bernard Hill) in *Boys from the Blackstuff*

I didn't get where I am today . . .   CJ (John Barron) in *The Fall and Rise of Reginald Perrin*

I do not like this game   Bluebottle (Peter Sellers) in the *Goon Show*

I don't mind if I do   Colonel Chinstrap (Jack Train) in *ITMA* whenever a drink was offered him

if it ain't broke, why fix it?   Bert Lance (President Carter's Director of the Office of Management and Budget) speaking on the subject of governmental reorganisation

If it's up there I'll give you the money myself   Les Dennis (in *Family Fortunes*)

If you can't stand the heat, get out of the kitchen   Harry S Truman (when he gave his reason for not standing in the 1952 elections). Truman himself was quoting Major-General Harry Vaughan

I got a horse   Ras Prince Monolulu (Peter Carl McKay) racing pundit of the 1930s to the 1950s

I'll be leaving you now, sir   Claud Snudge (Bill Fraser) in Granada Television's *Bootsie and Snudge*

illegitimi non carborundum   General 'Vinegar Joe' Stilwell used this motto during WWII under the pretence that it meant 'don't let the bastards grind you down'

I'll give it foive   Janice Nicholls; a member of the public who took part in *Thank Your Lucky Stars* Spin-a-Disc panel and became famous when she gave a maximum five

I'll give you the results in reverse order   Eric Morley (giving *Miss World* results)

I'm a little worried about Jim   Mrs Dale (in *Mrs Dale's Diary*)

I mean that most sincerely, friends   Hughie Green (phrase usually accompanied by a clenched fist gesture)

I'm afraid that I was very, very drunk   Rowley Birkin QC (Paul Whitehouse) in the BBC television comedy, *The Fast Show*

I'm a little bit werrrr, a little bit weyyyy!   Chris Jackson (the geezer who'd nick anything) as played by Paul Whitehouse in the BBC comedy *The Fast Show*

I'm in charge   Bruce Forsyth (whilst introducing the Beat the Clock section at the Palladium)

I'm not a number, I'm a free man   The Prisoner (Patrick McGoohan) spoken in defiance of his number 6 nomenclature

I'm smarter than the average bear   Yogi Bear (whilst constantly outwitting ranger John Smith in Jellystone Park)

in like Flynn   Errol Flynn (alluding to his legendary bedroom prowess)

I only arsked (sic)   Popeye Popplewell (Bernard Bresslaw) in *The Army Game*

I say, I say, I say   Murray and Mooney; a famous double act of the 1930s in which Harry Mooney would utter the immortal words and Harry Murray would invariably reply with 'I don't wish to know that, kindly leave the stage'

I say, what a smasher   Charlie Chester (from the BBC radio programme *Stand Easy*)

is she a friend of Dorothy ?   An allusion to a homosexual (from Judy Garland's character in *The Wizard of Oz*). The phrase arose from Judy Garland's friendships within male homosexual circles

I thang you (sic)   Arthur Askey (from the radio show *Band Waggon*)

I think the answer lies in the soil   Arthur Fallowfield (Kenneth Williams) in *Beyond Our Ken*

I think we should be told   Attributed to John Junor by *Private Eye* in a parody of his opinion column in the *Sunday Express*. Although the column invariably used the phrase it is doubtful whether Junor ever actually used the phrase himself

it'll play in Peoria   Coined by John Ehrlichman during the Nixon election campaign of 1969. The phrase was an allusion to whether policies would appeal to 'Middle America'. Peoria is in Illinois and was chosen as it had four syllables and scanned well

it never rains, but it pours   John Arbuthnot (the inventor of 'John Bull' coined this phrase in 1726)

it's goodnight from me . . . and it's goodnight from him   Ronnie Barker and Ronnie Corbett (*The Two Ronnies*)

it's only a bloody game   Magnus Magnusson would invariably say this to settle the nerves of contenders of *Mastermind*; of course, this ice-breaker was only for the ears of the audience and participants

it's the way I tell 'em   Frank Carson (full phrase is 'you've heard them all before but it's the way I tell 'em')

it's turned out nice again   George Formby (invariably opened his act with this phrase)

I've arrived, and to prove it, I'm here   Max Bygraves (as Archie Andrews' tutor in *Educating Archie*)

I've found it, I've found the lost chord   Jimmy Durante (whilst playing the piano he would feign this new discovery)

I've got a million of 'em   Jimmy Durante (after telling a joke) Max Miller later used this phrase

I've got his pecker in my pocket   Lyndon B Johnson (dates from his time as Senate Majority leader in Washington)

I've started so I'll finish   Magnus Magnusson would say this if he had started asking a question on the BBC's *Mastermind* programme but the time had elapsed and the hooter sounded

I wanna tell you a story   Max Bygraves (as Archie Andrew's tutor in *Educating Archie*)

I want me tea   Grandma Grove (Nancy Roberts) who often made this demand in the *Grove Family*

I want to be alone   Greta Garbo never actually spoke these words off-set although she was very reclusive. The most often quoted origin of these words on screen is in the 1932 film *Grand Hotel*, however she utters the immortal words in the earlier 1929 film *The Single Standard* but as it was a silent film it was subtitled

I won't take me coat off; I'm not stopping   Ken Platt, the northern comedian's catchphrase was coined by Ronnie Taylor, producer of radio's *Variety Fanfare*, in 1951

jolly hockey sticks   Monica (Beryl Reid) as Archie Andrews' posh friend in *Educating Archie*

just give me the facts, ma'am   Joe Friday (Jack Webb) in *Dragnet*

just like that   Tommy Cooper (sometimes the master comedian would say 'not like that, like that')

K-E-Y-N-S-H-A-M   Horace Batchelor, the football pools export on Radio Luxembourg would always end his advert by spelling out his address in Bristol

Kilroy was here   Phrase used in WWII to allude to the US Air Transport Command. The phrase is of doubtful origin but it is beloved of graffiti writers

kiss of death, the   Stock phrase deriving from the kiss of betrayal given by Judas to Christ

lady bountiful   George Farquhar coined the phrase from the name of a character in his 1707 work *The Beaux Stratagem* but phrase is now applied to a woman who is conspicuously generous to others less fortunate than herself

laugh and the world laughs with you   From Ella Wheeler Wilcox poem 'Solitude', it continues 'weep and you weep alone'

left hand down a bit   Leslie Phillips (in *The Navy Lark*) Jon Pertwee would reply 'left hand down it is, sir'

let's get outta here   In a survey of stock film phrases this is the most often said in film history

life begins at forty   William B Pitkin (Professor of Journalism at Columbia University in a 1932 book)

listening bank, the   Midland Bank (advertising slogan used from 1980 onwards)

little of what you fancy does you good, a   Marie Lloyd popularised the phrase in a song written by Fred W Leigh and George Arthurs. The phrase was invariably accompanied by a suggestive wink

Lloyd George knew my father   Tommy Rhys Roberts, whose father did indeed know Lloyd George, popularised the phrase, which became a Welsh standard song, sung to the tune of 'Onward Christian Soldiers'

loadsamoney   Harry Enfield character (first seen in *Friday Night Live*) who was a plasterer by trade

loook   Alf Garnett (Warren Mitchell) in *Till Death Us Do Part*

love me, love my dog   St Bernard of Clairvaux first espoused this philosophical metaphor, which meant in effect, you must love me warts and all. Incidentally St Bernard of Clairvaux is not the St Bernard (of Menthon) after whom the breed of Alpine dog is named

love you madly   Duke Ellington often said 'We'd like you to know that the boys in the band all . . .'

man for all seasons, a   Robert Bolt's title for his 1960 play about Sir Thomas More has entered the language to describe an adaptable, all-round accomplished person

man on the Clapham omnibus, the   Lord Bowen first coined this phrase in 1903 when summing up a case. The phrase has entered the modern idiom to represent the ordinary man in the street

man they couldn't gag, the   Peter Wilson (nickname of the *Daily Mirror* sports columnist)

man you love to hate, the   Erich von Stroheim (epithet rather than catchphrase)

Martini . . . shaken not stirred   James Bond (The line is first spoken in *Goldfinger* but does not appear in the books)

mean! moody! magnificent   Jane Russell (epithet rather than catchphrase) first used as slogan for *The Outlaw mind how you go* George Dixon (Jack Warner) in *Dixon of Dock Green*

mind my bike Jack Warner popularised this unlikely hit phrase on radio

moment of truth, the The phrase derives from a Spanish bullfighting term 'El momento de la verdad' in which the final sword thrust kills the animal

Mounties always get their man, the Unofficial motto of the Royal Canadian Mounted Police first coined by John J Healy, although the official motto since 1873 is 'Maintain the Right'

Mr Big Ian Fleming coined the phrase in his second novel *Live and Let Die* (1954). The character's name was Buonaparte Ignace Gallia, hence Mr Big. The phrase has come to mean any top man in an organisation

Mr Clean James Baker the American Secretary of State was given this epithet

Much Binding in the Marsh Not so much a catchphrase but this popular radio programme, that grew out of an edition of *Merry-Go-Round* and starred Kenneth Horne and Richard Murdoch, became the instigator of many catchphrases and a song of the same title

mum, mum, they're laughing at me Arthur English (whilst playing his cockney spiv character and unfurling his kipper tie)

my flabber has never been so gasted Frankie Howerd coined this ridiculous phrase that became an essential part of his act. He would say 'I'm flabbergasted, in fact my flabber has never been so gasted'

my name's Monica Beryl Reid (as Archie Andrew's posh friend in *Educating Archie*)

nah . . . Luton airport Lorraine Chase (in a famous advert for Campari)

never change / swap horses in midstream Abraham Lincoln is identified with the phrase in a citation of 1864

never knowingly undersold John Lewis Partnership (slogan) devised by John Spedan Lewis in 1920

nice 'ere innit Lorraine Chase (in a famous advert for Campari)

nice to see you, to see you nice Bruce Forsyth (originally from the *Generation Game* but often used in other shows)

night of the long knives, the Originally referred to the night of 2 July 1934 when Hitler, aided by Himmler's black-shirted SS, liquidated the leadership of the brown-shirted SA. The phrase has entered modern vernacular to mean a surprise bloodless purge, for example Harold Macmillan's wholesale reorganisation of his cabinet in 1962

nine days' wonder Possibly traced back to Geoffrey Chaucer and more recently alluding to the fact that a puppy is blind for the first nine days of its life. The phrase has come to mean anything of short-lived appeal

no such thing as a free lunch The Nobel Prize-winning economist Milton Friedman is identified with the saying and he wrote a book of this name, but the phrase dates back to the 19th century

not a lot Paul Daniels (usually before doing a trick he would say 'you're going to like this . . .')

not 'arf Alan Freeman would say this phrase out of context, which perhaps gave it appeal

not tonight, Josephine Napoleon I (attributed but never actually said)

now that's magic Paul Daniels (after successfully performing a slick trick)

nudge nudge, wink wink, say no more squire Eric Idle (in *Monty Python*) showing suspect pictures to Terry Jones

often a bridesmaid, but never a bride Milton Feasley wrote this slogan for Listerine mouthwash in 1923

oh hello, I'm Julian, and this is my friend Sandy Hugh Paddick (referring to Kenneth Williams in *Round the Horne*)

old soldiers never die, they simply fade away General Douglas MacArthur whilst addressing congress on 19 April 1951 after being dismissed by President Truman. The phrase originated much earlier

one foot in the grave Jonathan Swift in *Gulliver's Travels* (1726) made the phrase popular in connection with the Struldbruggs of Laputa

one small step for man Neil Armstrong's exact words when walking on the moon were 'That's one small step for a man, one giant leap for mankind'

only the names have been changed Narrator of the detective series *Dragnet* would continue . . . .'to protect the innocent'

on with the motley (vesti la giubba) From Leoncavallo's opera *I Pagliacci* relating to the fact that the clown must carry on despite a broken heart

on your bike Norman Tebbit, addressing the Conservative Party conference on 15 Oct 1981. He related how his father was brought up with unemployment but instead of rioting got on his bike and looked for work

ooh Betty Frank Spencer (Michael Crawford) in *Some Mothers do 'ave 'em*

ooh you are awful, but I like you Mandy (Dick Emery) accompanied by a slap on the interviewer's shoulder

oooo arr, me ol' pal, me ol' beauty Walter Gabriel (Chris Gittins) in the *Archers*

orft we jolly well go Jimmy Young (after finishing the link with Terry Wogan would utter these words)

pass The stock reply of contenders on the BBC's *Mastermind* programme to save time if the answer did not immediately spring to mind

pass the sick-bag, Alice John Junor (used in his *Sunday Express* column and parodied by *Private Eye*)

phone a friend Chris Tarrant (in *Who Wants to Be a Millionaire*)

pile it high, sell it cheap Sir John Cohen, founder of Tesco supermarkets, coined this phrase

play it again Sam attributed to Humphrey Bogart as Rick Blaine in *Casablanca*, although he never actually said these words

pop goes the weasel W R Mandale wrote the rhyme 'Up and down the City Road, In and out the Eagle, That's the way the money goes, Pop goes the weasel'. The meaning of the rhyme is uncertain but 'Pop' means to pawn

probably the best lager in the world Carlsberg (1973 advertising slogan voiced by Orson Welles)

public enemy No. 1 John Dillinger (Attorney General Homer Cummings gave this name to the murderer)

Queen Anne's dead Phrase of uncertain origin but used to put down someone who delights in telling you some very old news or what you knew already

quick and the dead, the from the New Testament 2 Timothy 4:1. The quick in this context meant the living

FAMOUS PEOPLE

read my lips   George Bush popularised this phrase in his acceptance speech for the Republican nomination on 19 August 1988. The rest of the line was 'no new taxes'

real thing, it's the   Coca-Cola (advertising slogan dating from 1942)

refreshes the parts other beers cannot
reach   Heineken (advertising slogan for the lager)

respec'   Sacha Baron Cohen in the guise of rapper Ali G

right monkey   Al Read (the popular northern comedian also used 'cheeky monkey' in his act)

rock on, Tommy   Bobby Ball (the comedian would often tug his braces at the same time)

Rodney, you plonker   Del Boy (David Jason) to his younger brother in Only Fools and Horses

roses grow on you   Norman Vaughan (advertising campaign for Roses Chocolates)

say goodnight Dick   Dan Rowan (in Rowan and Martin's Laugh In) to his co-star Dick Martin

say goodnight Gracie   George Burns (to his wife and co-star Gracie Allen)

say it with flowers   Patrick O' Keefe an advertising agent coined the phrase in 1917

shame, shame   Bruce Forsyth (usually accompanied by a cuddle from him)

she who must be obeyed   Horace Rumpole (Leo McKern) referring to his wife in John Mortimer's Rumpole of the Bailey. The original expression came from Henry Rider Haggard's novel She and referred to the all-powerful Ayesha

short, fat, hairy legs   Eric Morecambe (referring to Ernie Wise)

shut that door   Larry Grayson (turning towards the wings and intimating a draught)

silly old moo   Alf Garnett (Warren Mitchell) referring to Elsie, his wife, in Till Death Us Do Part

sit (sssit)   Barbara Woodhouse (whilst demonstrating her methods of training dogs)

slow, slow, quick, quick, slow   Victor Sylvester popularised this quickstep tempo in his radio and television series

smile, you're on . . .   Candid Camera (first coined by Allen Funt in the original American version)

sock it to me   Judy Carne (in Rowan and Martin's Laugh In)

somebody up there likes me   Rocky Graziano (world champion boxer had a film and book about him with this title)

some mothers do 'ave 'em   Jimmy Clitheroe (corruption of the phrase 'don't some mothers have 'em')

somewhere to the right of Genghis Khan   Arthur Scargill relating a political standpoint to John Mortimer

speak as you find, that's my motto   Nola Purvis (Pat Coombs) in the radio series Hello Playmates

spend, spend, spend, I'm going to   Viv Nicholson (after winning £152,000 on Littlewoods football pools in 1961)

stone me   Tony Hancock (originally coined in Hancock's Half-Hour)

stop me and buy one   Lionel and Charles Rodd came up with this slogan for Wall's ice-cream in 1923 although in those days it was for ice-cream tricycles rather than vans

stop messin' abaht (sic)   Kenneth Williams (originally coined by Williams in Hancock's Half-Hour)

suck it and see   Charlie Naughton of the Crazy Gang coined this phrase, which meant 'try it'

suit you sir!   Ken and Kenneth the tailors in the BBC comedy series The Fast Show

sweet Fanny Adams   The phrase originates from the murder of an eight-year-old child in 1867. Fanny Adams was the victim of Frederick Booth, a solicitor's clerk, who grotesquely mutilated her body. As these things tend to go, at around the same time, the Royal Navy issued tinned meat which sailors flippantly said probably contained the remains of the little girl. Fanny Adams became slang for mutton or stew and later any worthless item. In modern day vernacular 'Sweet F. A.' can also mean sweet fuck-all

swinging   Norman Vaughan (the phrase was accompanied by a thumbs-up gesture)

ten, four   Dan Matthews (Broderick Crawford) in the American detective series Highway Patrol. The phrase signified agreement and was always being bellowed into the radio

thank you music lovers   Spike Jones, the American musician, would murder a classic piece of music along the same lines as Les Dawson or Eric Morecambe and then proceed to say . . .

that'll do nicely, sir   American Express (advertising slogan originating in the late 1970s)

that's all folks   Merry Melodies (Warner Brothers cartoons) written at the end of their cartoons

that's magic   Paul Daniels (after completion of a successful trick or illusion)

the ranger ain't gonna like it Yogi   Booboo bear (when Yogi bear had inventive ideas for stealing picker-nick baskets)

there's more   Jimmy Cricket (whilst telling a joke in his act)

there's no answer to that   Eric Morecambe (cleverly used if the quick-witted comedian was stuck for words)

thinking man's crumpet, the   Frank Muir coined this phrase about television presenter Joan Bakewell

this is Funf speaking   Funf the spy (in ITMA, i.e. It's That Man Again)

today is the first day of the rest of your life   Charles Dederich (founder of anti-heroin centres in the USA)

too little, too late   Professor Allan Nevins wrote this in an article in Current History (1935), referring to the Nazi menace in Germany and the lack of remedial action

T. T. F. N. (ta-ta for now)   Mrs Mopp (Dorothy Summers) in ITMA. Jimmy Young adopted this phrase in his popular Radio Two morning show

turn on, tune in, drop out   Dr Timothy Leary coined this pro drug phrase in 1967, although he himself suggests that he stole the phrase from Marshall McLuhan

unacceptable face of capitalism   Edward Heath coined this phrase in 1973 when replying to a question from Jo Grimond in the House of Commons

up and under   Eddie Waring (the much imitated rugby commentator was synonymous with the phrase)

very interesting, but stupid   Arte Johnson (in Rowan and Martin's Laugh In) dressed as a German soldier and smoking a cigarette in a holder

wakey, wakey   Billy Cotton (a fanfare of Somebody Stole My Gal would follow this cry)

walkies   Barbara Woodhouse (whilst demonstrating her methods of training dogs) weekend starts here, the   Ready Steady Go (the Friday night pop show was always preceded by these words)

week is a long time in politics, a   Harold Wilson (also deliberated that 48 hours was a long time in politics)

well, he would, wouldn't he?   Mandy Rice-Davies (referring to Lord Astor's denial of involvement with her)

were you truly wafted here from paradise?   Terry Howard wrote this Campari advert, which made Lorraine Chase a star

what do you think of it so far?   Eric Morecambe would rhetorically ask this question whilst either performing one of Ernie's plays or during a lull between sketches. The stock reply by Eric himself was 'rubbish', which was often said through an inanimate object by way of him throwing his voice or saying it between clenched teeth

what's new pussycat ?   Warren Beatty (coined the phrase and had the film originally written for him)

what's on the table Mabel ?   Wilfred Pickles (to his wife Mabel in radio's Have a Go)

what's up, doc ?   Bugs Bunny originally said these words to his adversary Elmer J Fudd, a doctor, but eventually would say this as a form of greeting to almost everyone. The full phrase was 'er, what's up doc?' followed by a crunch on a carrot

when the going gets tough, the tough get going   Joseph P Kennedy, the father of John F Kennedy, used this phrase in the bringing up of his sons, in an effort to help them through adversity

who dares wins, Rodney   Del Boy (David Jason) in Only Fools and Horses

who loves ya, baby?   Theo Kojak (Telly Savalas) in the popular American detective series, Kojak

wind of change, the   Harold Macmillan used this phrase, written by Sir David Hunt, in describing the change of political standing in Africa in 1960

winter of discontent, the   The phrase originates in the opening line of the eponymous Richard of Gloucester in Shakespeare's Richard III, however the term is now used as a description of the winter of 1978/79 when industrial action became rife due to the Labour Government's endeavours to curb pay rises

without hesitation, deviation or repetition   Just a Minute (the popular radio panel game meant guests had to speak for a minute)

world's favourite airline, the   British Airways slogan

wot, no Chad   The phrase was very common in Britain during WWII and was accompanied by a depiction of a bald-headed man appearing over a wall and inquiring 'wot, no . . .' the blank being filled in by any commodity in short supply. Its origin is uncertain

yaroooo   Billy Bunter (created by Frank Richards)

you ain't heard nothin' yet   Al Jolson (the most often misquoted catchphrase of all. The line is from The Jazz Singer)

you ain't seen nothin' yet   President Ronald Reagan used this phrase as a slogan during his 1984 re-election bid

you bet your sweet bippy   Dick Martin (in Rowan and Martin's Laugh In) popular 1960s US comedy show

you cannot be serious   John McEnroe (much caricatured phrase that the tennis player often said on court)

you can run but you can't hide   Joe Louis (said of Billy Conn, a nifty heavyweight of the day who Louis knocked out)

you can't see the join   Eric Morecambe (talking about Ernie Wise's fictitious wig)

you dirty old man   Harold Steptoe (Harry H Corbett) addressing his father in Steptoe and Son

you dirty rat   Cagney, James (dirty double-crossing rat were actual words in Blonde Crazy 1931)

you dirty rotten swine, you   Bluebottle (Peter Sellers) in the Goon Show

you lucky people   Tommy Trinder used this phrase whilst compering the Sunday Night at the London Palladium shows and it became his stock phrase identified with him

your starter for ten   Bamber Gascoigne (an on the buzzer question to teams in University Challenge)

you too can have a body like mine   Charles Atlas (slogan used for his mail-order body-building lessons)

you've never had it so good   Harold MacMillan (actually said 'most of our people have never had it so good')

FAMOUS PEOPLE

Causes of Death

Ace, Johnny   Rhythm and blues act, died playing Russian roulette (1954).

Alexander the Great   Died aged 32 after a prolonged banquet and drinking bout (323 BC).

Alkan, Charles-Henri Valentin   French pianist and composer who died when bookshelf collapsed on him whilst reaching for the Talmud (1888).

Antony, Mark   Roman triumvir, committed suicide by running onto his sword in 31 BC (misled by a false report of Cleopatra's death).

Archer, Fred   English champion jockey, shot himself during an attack of typhoid (1886).

Astor, John Jacob   American financier, went down in the Titanic in 1912.

Bach, Johann Sebastian   German composer, suffered stroke following unsuccessful eye operation (1750).

Ballard, Florence   Supremes vocalist, died of a heart attack aged 32 yrs 7 mths.

Barnett, Lady Isobel   Committed suicide in her bathroom on 20 October 1980, one week after being found guilty of shoplifting.

Bartók, Bela   Hungarian composer, died of leukaemia (1945).

Beethoven, Ludwig van   German compuser, died of cirrhosis of the liver (lupus erythematosus is sometimes considered an alternative cause) (1827).

Belushi, John   American actor, died of drug-related illness, aged 33 yrs 1 mth (1982).

Berg, Alban   Austrian composer, died from infection from a septic insect bite (1935).

Berlioz, Hector   French composer, died following brain haemorrhage (1869).

Billy the Kid   Pseudonym of Henry McCarty, aka William H Bonney, American bandit, shot by sheriff Pat Garrett in 1881.

Bizet, Georges   French composer, died of angina pectoris complicated by rheumatoid arthritis (1875).

Bolan, Marc   T Rex singer, died in car crash aged 30 yrs 2 mths (1977).

Bonham, John   Led Zeppelin member, died of alcohol poisoning, aged 32 yrs 3 mths (1980).

Brahms, Johannes   German composer, died of liver cancer (1897).

Brooke, Rupert   English poet, died of septicaemia, aged 27 yrs (1915).

Brown, Grace   Murdered by Chester Gillett in 1906; formed basis for Theodore Dreiser's book *An American Tragedy*.

Calmette, Gaston   Editor of *Le Figaro*, shot by Madame Caillaux, wife of the French Finance Minister, accusing her husband of fraud; she was later acquitted (1914).

Calvi, Roberto   Italian banker, found hanging from scaffolding under Blackfriars Bridge (18 June 1982).

Carpenter, Karen   American vocalist and drummer, died aged 32 yrs 11 mths from heart attack caused by anorexia nervosa (1983).

Castlereagh, Viscount   British statesman, stabbed himself with a penknife (1822).

Chausson, Ernest   French composer, died in a bicycle accident (1899).

Childers, Erskine   Irish nationalist, was executed in 1922 by the Irish Free State authorities.

Chopin, Fryderyk   Polish composer, died of pulmonary tuberculosis (1849).

Clarke, Ossie   Fashion designer, murdered by his flatmate Diego Cogolato (7 August 1996).

Cleopatra   Queen of Egypt, allegedly committed suicide by allowing an asp to bite her breast (30 BC).

Cline, Patsy   Top American country singer, died in a plane crash aged 30 yrs 5 mths (1963).

Clive, Robert (of Plassey)   English soldier, committed suicide (after several attempts) by shooting himself (1774).

Kurt Cobain   Lead singer of Nirvana, shot himself dead aged 27 yrs 1 mth (1994).

Cogan, Alma   English singer, died of cancer aged 34 yrs 5 mths (1966).

Cooke, Sam   American soul singer, shot dead aged 33 yrs 9 mths (1964).

Crane, Harold Hart   American poet, committed suicide by leaping from a steamboat into the Caribbean (1932).

Davison, Emily   Suffragette, threw herself under the King's horse in the 1913 Epsom Derby.

Dean, James   American actor, died in a car crash in 1955, aged 24.

Debussy, Claude   French composer, died of cancer of the rectum (1918).

Delius, Frederick   English composer, died of syphilis in 1934.

Diana, Princess of Wales   Died in Paris car crash (31 Aug 1997).

Dvořák, Antonín   Czech composer, died of a brain haemorrhage (1904).

Eastman, George   American inventor of the Kodak camera, shot himself in 1932.

Elgar, Edward   English composer, died of a brain tumour in 1934.

Elliot, 'Mama' Cass   American singer, died of a heart attack, aged 32 yrs 10 mths (1974).

Epstein, Brian   Manager of the Beatles, died of a drugs overdose in 1967.

Fayed, Dodi   Son of Harrods director, died in Paris car crash (31 Aug 1997).

Freud, Sigmund   Austrian neurologist and founder of psychoanalysis, died of cancer in 1939.

Garland, Judy   American entertainer, died of a drugs overdose in 1969.

Genovese, Kitty   Famous New York murder; nobody answered her calls for help.

Gershwin, George   American composer, died of a brain tumour (1937).

Gibb, Andy   Brother of the Bee Gees, died aged 30 of drug-related illness (1988).

Gibb, Maurice   Member of the BeeGees, died of a heart attack following an operation to clear an intestinal blockage. Maurice was born 22 December 1949 and died 12 January 2003.

Granados, Enrique   Spanish composer, died when his ship SS *Sussex* was torpedoed by a German sub in the English Channel (1916).

Grieg, Edvard   Norwegian composer, died from coronary artery disease with angina pectoris (1907).

Hamm, Pete   Badfinger member and co-writer of 'Without You', committed suicide after depression brought on possibly by royalty problems (1975).

Hancock, Tony   Birmingham-born comedian, took a drug overdose in a Sydney hotel room in 1968.

Hannibal   Carthaginian soldier, committed suicide by poison when the Romans demanded his surrender (182 BC).

Haydn, Franz Joseph   Austrian composer, died of arteriosclerosis (1809).

Hemingway, Ernest   American novelist, shot himself in the mouth in Ketchum, Idaho (1961).

Hendrix, Jimi   American guitarist, suffocated in his own vomit after mixing drugs and alcohol aged 27 yrs 9 mths (1970).

Hickok, Wild Bill   American gunfighter, shot from behind by Jack McCall whilst playing poker in 1876. Hickok's hand was a queen and 2 pair aces over eights (Dead man's hand).

Himmler, Heinrich   German Nazi leader committed suicide with a cyanide phial concealed in his mouth (1945).

Holly, Buddy   Rock and roll pioneer, died aged 22 yrs 5 months in a plane crash (with Ritchie Valens, 17 yrs 9 mths, and the Big Bopper, 29 yrs 4 mths) in 1959.

Hutchence, Michael   Lead singer with INXS, found hanging in a Sydney hotel room (21 Nov 1997).

Iliffe, Marc   (Britain's Strongest Man 2002) Hanged himself in his gym in February 2003.

Ingram, Herbert   English journalist, founder of the *Illustrated London News* and MP for Boston from 1856, drowned in a boat collision on Lake Michigan in 1860.

Ireton, Henry   English Parliamentarian soldier, died of the plague in 1651.

Irving, Laurence   Novelist son of actor Sir Henry Irving, drowned in the *Empress of Ireland* disaster in 1914.

James, Jesse   Wild West robber, shot in the back of the head by Bob Ford (1882).

Jones, Brian   Member of the Rolling Stones, drowned in a swimming pool (aged 27 yrs 4 mths) soon after leaving the group in 1969.

Joplin, Janis   American folk singer, died aged 27 yrs 8 mths of heroin overdose (1970).

Klee, Paul   Swiss artist, died of a heart attack (1940).

Koestler, Arthur and Cynthia   Hungarian-born British author and his wife, committed suicide together in 1983 when he became terminally ill.

Leclair, Jean Marie French composer, stabbed in his own home, possibly by his wife (1764).

Liszt, Franz Hungarian composer, died of pneumonia (1886).

London, Jack American novelist, committed suicide by taking poison in 1916.

Lully, Jean-Baptiste French composer, died of gangrene and blood poisoning after he struck himself in the foot whilst conducting with a pointed cane (1687).

Lynott, Phil Thin Lizzy vocalist and guitarist, died of drug-related illness aged 34 yrs 4 mths (1986).

Markov, Georgi Bulgarian defector, famously murdered by the poison 'ricin' dispensed from the tip of an umbrella (1978).

Marten, Maria Mole-catcher's daughter, murdered by William Corder in May 1827 at the Red Barn at Polstead nr Ipswich.

Mendelssohn, Felix German composer, died of brain haemorrage (1847).

Milk, Harvey US gay rights activist and politician, killed alongside San Francisco Mayor, George Moscone, by ex-city employee Dan White (1978).

Mishima, Yukio Japanese writer, born Hiraoka Kimitake, committed Seppuku in 1970.

Monroe, Marilyn American model and actress, died from an overdose of sleeping pills in 1962.

Moon, Keith Who drummer, died of alcoholic poisoning aged 32 (in the same flat that Mama Cass died, owned by Harry Nilsson) in 1978.

Morrison, Jim Doors vocalist, died of drug related illness in 1971 (aged 27 yrs 6 mths); buried in Paris.

Mozart, Wolfgang Austrian composer died of heated military fever (nowadays usually considered to be Bright's Disease) (1791).

Murrell, Hilda Famous botanist (rose grower) and peace campaigner, found stabbed in a wood (1984) in suspicious circumstances as she was linked with documents about the sinking of the *General Belgrano*.

Niven, David English actor, died of motor neurone disease (1983).

Orton, Joe English dramatist, struck by hammer wielded by lover Kenneth Halliwell (1967), who subsequently committed suicide.

Owen, Wilfred English poet, killed on the bank of the Oise-Sambre Canal, nr Ors, one week before the armistice was signed in 1918.

Palach, Jan Czech philosophy student, set fire to himself in Jan 1969 in protest at the Russian invasion of Czechoslovakia the previous year.

Pasolini, Pier Paolo Italian writer and director, murdered, possibly as a result of a homosexual encounter, by Giuseppe Pelosi (1975).

Plath, Sylvia Poet wife of Ted Hughes, committed suicide by gassing herself (1963).

Pliny the Elder Roman writer, died in Stabiae (Castellamare) in AD 79 overcome by fumes from Vesuvius.

Presley, Elvis American singer, died of drug-related illnesses in 1977.

Prokofiev, Sergei Russian composer, died of brain haemorrage (1953).

Puccini, Giacomo Italian composer, died of throat cancer (1924).

Quisling, Vidkun Norwegian Fascist leader and puppet PM in occupied Norway, executed in May 1945.

Rachmaninov, Sergei Russian composer and pianist, died of malignant melanoma (1943).

Ravel, Maurice French composer, died of brain tumour (1937).

Redding, Otis Soul singer, died aged 26 yrs 3 mths in a plane crash (1967).

Relf, Keith Yardbirds musician, electrocuted himself, aged 33 yrs 1 mth (1976).

Rimsky-Korsakov, Nikolai Russian composer, died of coronary artery disease with angina pectoris (1908).

Riperton, Minnie American singer, died of cancer aged 31 yrs 8 mths (1979).

Rivett, Sandra Children's nanny, probably murdered by Lord Lucan in 1974 (convicted in absentia 19 June 1975).

Rizzio, David Italian courtier to Mary Queen of Scots, murdered by Scottish noblemen including the Earls of Morton and Lindsay, at the instigation of Lord Darnley (1566).

Robsart, Amy Wife of the Earl of Leicester (favourite of Elizabeth I), found dead at the bottom of a flight of stairs at Cumnor Place, Berkshire (1560).

Rossini, Gioacchino Italian composer, died of cancer of the rectum (1868).

Rothko, Mark Latvian-born American painter, committed suicide by slashing his wrists (1970).

Schubert, Franz Austrian composer, died of typhoid fever (1828).

Scriabin, Alexander Russian composer, died of an infection of a facial carbuncle (1915).

Shannon, Del American pop singer, shot himself whilst depressed (1990).

Siddall, Elizabeth Wife of Dante Gabriel Rossetti, took overdose of laudanum (1862).

Silkwood, Karen US nuclear activist, died in a car crash; her car was suspected to have been forced off the road (1973).

Stradella, Alessandro Italian composer, murdered by persons unknown (1682).

Tchaikovsky, Piotr Russian composer, died of cholera in 1893.

Tone, Wolfe Irish nationalist, cut his throat with a penknife whilst awaiting hanging in Dublin (1798).

Tyler, Wat Leader of the Peasants' Revolt of 1381, wounded by William Walworth, Mayor of London and subsequently dragged from his hospital bed (St Bartholomew's) and beheaded.

Van Gogh, Vincent Dutch painter, shot himself whilst depressed (1890).

Versace, Gianni Murdered outside his Miami home (15 July 1997) by serial killer Andrew Cunanan, who committed suicide shortly afterwards.

Wagner, Richard German composer, died of coronary artery disease with angina pectoris (1883).

Wallace, William Scottish patriot, famously depicted in the film *Braveheart*. After being hanged, drawn and quartered by the British, his quarters were sent to Newcastle, Berwick, Stirling and Perth, as a reminder of his insurrection (1305).

Weber, Carl German composer, died of pulmonary tuberculosis and ulcerated larynx (1826).

Webern, Anton von Austrian composer, shot and killed by an American military policeman whilst out after curfew (1945).

Westbrook, Harriet First wife of the poet PB Shelley, committed suicide by drowning herself in the Serpentine, Hyde Park (1816).

Woolf, Virginia English novelist, drowned herself in the River Ouse, near her home at Rodmell in Sussex (1941).

FAMOUS PEOPLE

Yamamoto, Isoruku   Japanese admiral who directed the attack on Pearl Harbor; his plane was shot down over the Solomon Islands in 1943.

Zweig, Stefan   Austrian-born British writer, committed suicide with his second wife in 1942.

NB: This section gives only a selective list; further death details may be found in other sections, eg Assassinations and Monarchs.

Countries of Birth

John Dalberg, 1st Baron Acton   (Italy)   English Historian

Joy Adamson   (Austria)   British Naturalist

Shmuel Yosef Agnon   (Poland)   Israeli Writer

Viscount Alanbrooke   (France)   British Soldier

Josef Albers   (Germany)   American Painter

Alexander Alekhine   (Russia)   French Chess master

Gubby Allen   (Australia)   English Cricketer

Peter Alliss   (Germany)   British Golfer

Jeanette Altwegg   (India)   British Skating Gold Medallist

Lawrence Alma-Tadema   (Holland)   British Painter

Leopold Amery   (India)   English Tory Politician

Lindsay Anderson   (India)   British Film Director

Mario Andretti   (Italy)   US Racing Driver

Edward Ardizzone   (Vietnam)   British Illustrator

Michael Arlen   (Bulgaria)   British Novelist

Pamela Armstrong   (Borneo)   British Newscaster

Paddy Ashdown   (India)   English Politician

Vladimir Ashkenazy   (Russia)   Icelandic Pianist

Frederick Ashton   (Ecuador)   English Choreographer

John Jacob Astor   (Germany)   American Financier

Nancy Astor   (USA)   British Politician

WH Auden   (England)   American Writer

John Audubon   (Haiti)   American Ornithologist

Frank Auerbach   (Germany)   British Artist

Charles Aznavour   (Armenia)   French Singer

Leo Baekland   (Belgium)   American Chemist

Bruce Bairnsfather   (India)   British Cartoonist

George Baker   (Bulgaria)   British Actor

JG Ballard   (China)   British Writer

Daniel Barenboim   (Argentina)   Israeli Pianist

Victor Barna   (Hungary)   British Table-Tennis Champion

John Barnes   (Jamaica)   English Footballer

Raymond Barre   (Réunion)   French Politician

Lord Beaverbrook   (Canada)   British Newspaper Magnate

Bee Gees   (Isle of Man)   Australian Pop Group

Menachem Begin   (Poland [now Russia])   Israeli Statesman

Georg von Bekesy   (Hungary)   US Physiologist

Hilaire Belloc   (France)   British Writer

Saul Bellow   (Canada)   US Writer

Baruj Benacerraf   (Venezuela)   US Immunologist

Floella Benjamin   (Trinidad)   British TV Presenter

Jill Bennett   (Straits Settlement, now Malaysia)   British Actress

Irving Berlin   (Russia)   US Composer

Isaiah Berlin   (Latvia)   British Philosopher

Pete Best   (India)   British Musician

Hans A Bethe   (Germany [Strasbourg, now France])   US Physicist

Lord Beveridge   (India)   British Economist

Zulfikar Ali Bhutto   (India)   Pakistani Statesman

Isla Blair   (India)   British Actress

George Blake   (Netherlands)   British Spy (for Soviet Union)

Nicolas Bloembergen   (Netherlands)   US Physicist

Paul Boateng   (Ghana)   British Politician

Andrew Bonar Law   (Canada)   English Prime Minister

Alan Bond   (England)   Australian Businessman

Daniel Bovet   (Switzerland)   Italian Pharmacologist

Anne Bradstreet   (England)   US Poet

Gyles Brandreth   (West Germany)   British Author and Politician

Frank Brangwyn   (Belgium)   Welsh Painter

Chris Brasher   (British Guiana)   British Athlete

Walter Houser Brattain   (China)   US Physicist

Fenner Brockway   (India)   English Politician

Joseph Brodsky   (Russia)   US Poet

Ford Madox Brown   (France)   English Painter

Herbert C Brown   (England)   US Chemist

Yul Brynner   (Russia)   US Actor

Frances Hodgson Burnett   (England)   US Novelist

Terry Butcher   (Singapore)   English Footballer

Andrew Caddick   (New Zealand)   English Cricketer

Maria Callas   (United States)   Greek Soprano

Albert Camus   (Algeria)   French Writer

Jacques Canetti   (Bulgaria)   French Record Producer

Frank Capra   (Sicily)   US Film Director

Claudia Cardinale   (Tunisia)   Italian Actress

Barbara Carrera   (Nicaragua)   US Actress

Anna Carteret   (India)   British Actress

Gian Domenico Cassini   (Genoa)   French Astronomer

Marc Chagall   (Russia)   French Artist

Ernst Boris Chain   (Germany)   British Biochemist

William Chambers   (Sweden)   Scottish Architect

Philippe de Champaigne   (Belgium)   French Painter

Subrahmanyan Chandrasekhar   (India [Lahore, now Pakistan])   US Astrophysicist

Louis Chevrolet   (Switzerland)   US Automobile Engineer

Erskine Childers   (England)   Irish Writer and Nationalist

Glynn Christian   (New Zealand)   British TV Broadcaster

Julie Christie   (India)   English Actress

Linford Christie   (Jamaica)   British Olympic Gold Medallist

Christo   (Bulgaria)   American Artist

Elizabeth Connell   (South Africa)   Irish Soprano

Joseph Conrad   (Poland)   English Novelist

Alistair Cooke   (UK)   American Journalist and Broadcaster

Harry H Corbett   (Burma)   English Actor
Carl Ferdinand Cori   (Czechoslovakia)   US Biochemist
Allan Cormack   (South Africa)   US Physicist
John Cornforth   (Australia)   British Chemist
Sir Michael Costa   (Italy)   British Conductor
André Frédéric Cournand   (France)   US Physicist
Cicely Courtneidge   (Australia)   English Actress
Colin Cowdrey   (India)   English Cricketer
Frederic Cowen   (Jamaica)   English Composer
Kid Creole   (Canada)   US Singer
Cyril Cusack   (South Africa)   Irish Actor
György Cziffra   (Hungary)   French Pianist
Frank Damrosch   (Germany)   US Conductor
Walter Damrosch   (Germany)   US Conductor
Dana (Rosemary Scallon)   (England)   Irish Singer
Edward Dannreuther   (Alsace)   English Pianist
Nyree Dawn Porter   (New Zealand)   British Actress
Edward De Bono   (Malta)   British Psychologist
Chris De Burgh   (Argentina)   British Singer
Christian R De Duve   (England)   Belgian Biochemist
Hans Dehmelt   (Germany)   US Physicist
Max Delbruck   (Germany)   US Biophysicist
Eamon De Valera   (USA)   Irish Politician
Ted Dexter   (Italy)   English Cricketer
Thomas Dolby   (Egypt)   British Musician
Gabrielle Drake   (Pakistan)   British Actress
Marcel Duchamp   (France)   American artist
Renato Dulbecco   (Italy)   American Biologist
George Du Maurier   (France)   English Writer
Lawrence and Gerald Durrell   (India)   English Writers
Sophie-Carmen Eckhardt-Gramatté   (Russia)   Canadian Composer
Glynn Edwards   (Malaya)   British Actor
Albert Einstein   (Germany)   Swiss physicist
Brian Elias   (India)   English Composer
Iso Elinson   (Russia)   British Pianist
TS Eliot   (USA)   British Poet
Mary Ellis   (USA)   English Soprano
Gloria Estefan   (Cuba)   American Singer
Eusebio   (Mozambique)   Portuguese Footballer
Enrico Fermi   (Italy)   US Nuclear Physicist
Edmond H Fischer   (China)   US Chemist
Bob Fitzsimmons   (England)   American Boxer
Errol Flynn   (Tasmania)   American Actor
CS Forester   (Egypt)   British Writer
Malcolm Forsyth   (South Africa)   Canadian Composer
Harry Freedman   (Poland)   Canadian Composer
Lucien Freud   (Germany)   British Artist
Marya Freund   (Poland)   French Soprano
Géza Frid   (Hungary)   Dutch Composer
Oskar Fried   (Germany)   Russian Conductor
Fiona Fullerton   (Nigeria)   British Actress
Henry Fuseli   (Switzerland)   British Painter
Dennis Gabor   (Hungary)   British Physicist
Ivan Galamian   (Iran)   US Violinist
Sandy Gall   (Malaya)   British Newsreader
Lamberto Gardelli   (Italy)   Swedish Conductor
Baron Francois Gérard   (Italy)   French Painter
Ivar Giaever   (Norway)   US Physicist
Mel Gibson   (USA)   Australian Actor

Werner Wolf Glaser   (Germany)   Swedish Composer
Vinko Globokar   (France)   Yugoslav Trombonist
Alma Gluck   (Romania)   American Soprano
Maria Goeppert-Mayer   (Germany [Katowice, now Poland])   US Physicist
James Goldsmith   (France)   British Tycoon
Adam Lindsay Gordon   (Azores)   Australian Poet
Arshile Gorky   (Armenia)   US Painter
Bryan Gould   (New Zealand)   British Politician
Ragnar Granit   (Finland)   Swedish Physiologist
Bernie Grant   (British Guiana)   English Politician
Cary Grant   (England)   US Actor
El Greco   (Crete (Candia))   Spanish Painter
Silvia Greenberg   (Romania)   Israeli Soprano
Tony Greig   (South Africa)   English Cricketer
André Grétry   (Belgium)   French Composer
Dulcie Grey   (Malaya)   British Actress
Frederick Grinke   (Canada)   British Violinist
Walter Gropius   (Germany)   US Architect
Georg Grosz   (Germany)   US Painter
Giovanni Guardi   (Austria)   Venetian Painter
Roger Guillemin   (France)   US Physiologist
Richard Hageman   (Holland)   US Composer
Thomas Duffus Hardy   (Jamaica)   English Archivist
Friedrich von Hayek   (Austria)   British Economist
Jascha Heifetz   (Lithuania)   US Violinist
László Heltay   (Hungary)   British Conductor
Victor Hely-Hutchinson   (South Africa)   English Composer
Audrey Hepburn   (Belgium)   American Actress
William Herschel   (Germany)   British Astronomer
Gerhard Herzberg   (Germany)   Canadian Physical Chemist
Rudolf Hess   (Egypt)   German Politician
Victor Hess   (Austria)   US Physicist
Hermann Hesse   (Germany)   Swiss Novelist
Dorothy Hodgkin   (Egypt)   English Chemist
Roald Hoffmann   (Poland)   US Chemist
Adam Hollioake   (Australia)   English Cricketer
Ben Hollioake   (Australia)   England Cricketer
Bob Holness   (South Africa)   British Presenter
Gordon Honeycombe   (India [now Pakistan])   British TV Presenter
Bob Hope   (England)   US Comedian
Harry Houdini   (Hungary)   US Escapologist
John Houseman   (Hungary)   US Actor / Director
Charles B Huggins   (Canada)   American Surgeon
William Morris Hughes   (Wales)   Australian Statesman
Olivia Hussey   (Argentina)   British Actress
Anjelica Huston   (Ireland)   American Actress
Alec Issigonis   (Turkey)   British Automobile Designer
Eddie Izzard   (Yemen)   English Comedian
Sid James   (South Africa)   British Actor
Karl Jaspers   (Germany)   Swiss Philosopher
Niels K Jerne   (England)   Danish Immunologist
Ruth Prawer Jhabvala   (Germany)   British Novelist
Alexander Johnson   (England)   American Philosopher
Dom Joly   (Lebanon)   British Comedian
Vasily Kandinsky   (Russia)   French Painter
Anna Karen   (South Africa)   British Actress
Boris Karloff   (England)   US Actor

FAMOUS PEOPLE

Yousef Karsh (Turkey) Canadian Photographer
Kenneth Kendall (India) British TV Presenter
Har Gobind Khorana (India [Raipur, now Pakistan]) US Molecular Chemist
Nicole Kidman (Honolulu, Hawaii, USA) Australian Actress
Wilson Kipketer (Kenya) Danish Athlete
Rudyard Kipling (India) English Writer
Henry Kissinger (Germany) US Politician
Aaron Klug (Lithuania) British Biophysicist
Godfrey Kneller (Germany) British Artist
Arthur Koestler (Hungary) British Author
Oskar Kokoschka (Austria) British Artist
Tjalling Koopmans (Netherlands) US Economist
Alexander Korda (Hungary) British Film Producer
Alexis Korner (France) British Musician
Hans Adolf Krebs (Germany) British Biochemist
Polykarp Kusch (Germany) US Physicist
Simon Kuznets (Russia) US Economist
John Lang (Scotland) Australian Clergyman
Angela Lansbury (England) US Actress
Danny La Rue (Ireland) British Entertainer
Charles Laughton (England) US Actor
Stan Laurel (England) US Actor / Comedian
Sir Austen Layard (France) English Archaeologist
Bernard Leach (Hong Kong) English Potter
Vivien Leigh (India) British Actress
Peter Lely (Netherlands) British Painter
Philipp EA Lenard (Hungary) German Physicist
Wassily Leontief (Russia) US Economist
Doris Lessing (Persia [now Iran]) British Writer
W Arthur Lewis (St Lucia) British Economist
Wyndham Lewis (Canada) English Novelist / Painter
Eric Liddell (China) Scottish Athlete
Basil Liddell Hart (France) English Historian
Fritz A Lipmann (Germany) US Biochemist
David Lloyd George (England) Welsh Politician
Margaret Lockwood (India) British Actress
Frederick Loewe (Austria) US Composer
Peter Lorre (Hungary) US Actor
David Low (New Zealand) British Political Cartoonist
Henry Luce (China) US Magazine Publisher
Bela Lugosi (Lugos Hungary [Lugos, now Romania]) US Actor
Jean-Baptiste Lully (Italy) French Composer
Joanna Lumley (Kashmir) British Actress
Salvador Luria (Italy) US Biologist
Rosa Luxemburg (Poland) German Revolutionary
Roddy McDowall (England) US Actor
John McEnroe (West Germany) US Tennis Player
Thomas McGee (Ireland) Canadian Writer
Patrick McGoohan (USA) British Actor
Shane MacGowan (England) Irish Musician
Donald McIntyre (New Zealand) English Bass-Baritone
Leo McKern (Australia) British Actor
Jean-Paul Marat (Switzerland) French Revolutionary
Ann-Margret (Sweden) US Actress
Raymond Massey (Canada) US Actor
William Somerset Maugham (France) British Writer
Robert Maxwell (Czechoslovakia) British Businesman

Jules Mazarin (Italy) French Prelate
Peter B Medawar (Brazil) British Zoologist
Golda Meir (Ukraine) Israeli Politician
Gian-Carlo Menotti (Italy) US Composer
Freddie Mercury (Zanzibar) British Singer
William Mervyn (Kenya) British Actor
Albert Michelson (Germany) US Physicist
Bette Midler (Hawaii [now US State]) US Singer
Ludwig Mies Van Der Rohe (Germany) USA Architect
Spike Milligan (India) British Comedian
Guy Mitchell (Yugoslavia) US Singer
Franco Modigliani (Italy) US Economist
Yves Montand (Italy) French Actor and Singer
Lola Montez (Eire) US Dancer
Benjamin Mottelson (USA) Danish Physicist
Vladimir Nabokov (Russia) US Novelist
Sam Neill (New Zealand) Australian Actor
Olivia Newton-John (UK) Australian Actress
Mike Nichols (Germany) US Film Director
Harold Nicolson (Persia [now Iran]) British Diplomat
Merle Oberon (India) British Actress
Severo Ochoa (Spain) US Biochemist
Jacques Offenbach (Germany) French Composer
Claes Oldenburg (Sweden) US Sculptor
Isaac Oliver (France) English Painter
Charles Chadwick Oman (India) English Historian
Lars Onsager (Norway) US Physical Chemist
Eugene Ormandy (Hungary) US Conductor
George Orwell (India) British Novelist
Thomas Paine (England) US Writer and Revolutionary
George Palade (Romania) US Biologist
Lili Palmer (Austria) French Actress
Adelina Patti (Spain) Italian Soprano
IM Pei (China) US Architect
Susan Penhaligon (Philippines) British Actress
Arno Penzias (Germany) US Astrophysicist
Max F Perutz (Austria) British Biochemist
Antoine Pevsner (Russia) French Painter
Harry Philby (Ceylon [Sri Lanka]) English Arabist and Explorer
Kim Philby (India) British Spy (for Soviet Union)
HRH Prince Philip (Greece) British Duke and Consort to the Queen
Camille Pissarro (West Indies [St Thomas]) French Painter
Sidney Poitier (Bahamas) US Actor
Roman Polanski (France) Polish Film Maker
Vladimir Prelog (Bosnia) Swiss Chemist
Emeric Pressburger (Hungary) British Film Writer
Ilya Prigogine (Russia) Belgian Chemist
Victoria Principal (Japan) US Actress
Juliet Prowse (South Africa) US Dancer
Anthony Quinn (Mexico) US Actor
Peter Rachman (Poland) British Property Developer
Stamford Raffles (Jamaica [at sea]) English Colonial Administrator
Basil Rathbone (South Africa) British Actor
Cyril Regis (French Guiana) English Footballer
Elisabeth Rethberg (Germany) US Soprano
Cliff Richard (India) British Vocalist
Frederick Sleigh Roberts (India) English Soldier

Edward G Robinson (Romania) US Actor
Richard Rogers (Italy) English Architect
Ronald Ross (India) British Physician
Mark Rothko (Latvia) US Painter
Eero Saarinen (Finland) US Architect
Albert Sabin (Poland) American Physician
Andrew Sachs (Germany) British Actor
Nelly Leonie Sachs (Germany) Swedish Poet and
  Playwright
Yves Saint Laurent (Algeria) French Fashion
  Designer
Pamela Salem (India) British Actress
George Sanders (Russia) British Actor
Tessa Sanderson (Jamaica) British Olympic Gold
  Medallist
John Singer Sargent (Italy) US Painter
Andrew Schally (Poland) US Biochemist
Elsa Schiaparelli (Italy) French Fashion Designer
Shaun Scott (Canada) British Actor
Emilio Segre (Italy) US Physicist
Harry Selfridge (USA) British Merchant
Aloys Senefelder (Czechoslovakia) German
  Printer and Inventor
Robert Service (England) Canadian Poet
Yitzhak Shamir (Poland) Israeli Politician
William Bradford Shockley (England) US
  Physicist
Walter Sickert (Germany) English Artist
Claude Simon (Madagascar) French Novelist
Isaac Bashevis Singer (Poland) US Writer
Israel Singer (Poland) US Writer
Elaine Smith (Scotland) Australian Actress
Sydney Smith (New Zealand) British Poet
George Solti (Hungary) British Conductor
Basil Spence (India) Scottish Architect
Sheila Steafel (South Africa) British Actress
Brian Stein (South Africa) English Footballer
Max Steiner (Austria) US Composer
Edward Stourton (Nigeria) UK TV Presenter
Robert Swinhoe (India) English Naturalist

Yves Tanguy (France) US Painter
WM Thackeray (India) British Author
Mother Teresa (Yugoslavia) Indian Roman
  Catholic Nun
Roy Thomson (Canada) British Newspaper
  Magnate
Angela Thorne (India [now Pakistan]) British
  Actress
Debbie Thrower (Kenya) British TV Presenter
Dmitri Tiomkin (Russia) US Composer
Richard Todd (Ireland) English Actor
JRR Tolkien (South Africa) English Novelist
Walter Trog (Canada) British Cartoonist
Liv Ullmann (Japan) Norwegian Actress
Rudolph Valentino (Italy) American Actor
Victor Vasarely (Hungary) French Painter
Hendrik Verwoerd (Holland) South African
  Politician
Colin Viljoen (South Africa) English Footballer
Selman A Waksman (Russia) US Biochemist
Hugh Walpole (New Zealand) British Novelist
Max Weber (Russia) US Painter
Vanessa-Mae (Singapore) British Violinist
Victor Weisz (Germany) British Political Cartoonist
Benjamin West (USA) English Painter
Alan Whicker (Egypt) British Broadcaster
Joseph Blanco White (Spain) English Poet
Patrick White (England) Australian Author
Terence Hanbury White (India) British Novelist
Roger Whitaker (Kenya) South African Singer
Eugene Paul Wigner (Hungary) US Physicist
Billy Wilder (Austria) US Film Maker
David Wilkie (Sri Lanka) Scottish Swimmer
John Williams (Australia) British Guitarist
Malcolm Williamson (Australia) British Composer
Bruce Willis (Germany) US Actor
Orde Wingate (India) British Soldier
William Wyler (Germany [Mulhausen, now France])
  US Film Maker

Dying Words

Independence for ever **John Adams** *US President*
It is the last of Earth, I am content **John Quincy Adams** *US President*
See in what peace a Christian can die **Joseph Addison** *Essayist*
Kurt **Alfred Adler** *Psychologist*
If I feel in good form I shall take the difficult way up. If I do not, I shall take the easy one. I shall join you in an hour **Albert I** *King of Belgium*
I have had wealth, rank and power, but if these were all I had, how wretched I would be **Prince Albert** *Queen Victoria's Consort*
I have such sweet thoughts **Prince Albert** *Queen Victoria's Consort*
Is it not meningitis? **Louisa M Alcott** *American writer*
I am sweeping through the gates, washed in the blood of the lamb **Alexander II** *Russian Tsar*
Clasp my hand dear friend, I am dying **Vittorio Alfieri** *Italian Poet*
Haircut! **Albert Anastasia** *US gangster*

Give the boys a holiday **Anaxagoras** *Philosopher*
Monsieur, I beg your pardon. I did not do it on purpose **Marie Antoinette** *French Queen*
I see my God He calls me to Him **Antony of Padua** *Monk*
Wait till I have finished my problem **Archimedes** *Greek Mathematician*
May God forgive me for putting on any other **Benedict Arnold** *American Traitor*
I desire to die and be with Christ **Roger Ascham** *Elizabeth I's tutor*
Am I dying, or is this my birthday? **Nancy Astor** *British Politician*
Do you think I have played my part pretty well through the farce of life? **Augustus** *Roman Emperor*
The murder of the Queen has been represented to me as a deed; lawful and meritorious, I die a firm Catholic **Anthony Babington** *Plotter against Elizabeth I*
My name and memory I leave to men's charitable speeches, to foreign nations and to the next age **Francis Bacon** *Statesman and philosopher*

Oh God, here I go ... **Max Baer** *Heavyweight Boxer*

Let me have my own fidgets **Walter Bagehot** *Economist*

I can't sleep **JM Barrie** *Scottish Author*

I am a priest, fie, fie! All is gone **Cardinal Beaton** *Scottish prelate*

I am prepared to die for Christ and his Church **Thomas à Becket** *Archbishop of Canterbury*

Gloria Patri et Filio et Spiritu Sancto **Venerable St Bede** *Theologian and historian*

It is well, you have said the truth, it is indeed **Venerable St Bede** *Theologian and historian*

Now comes the mystery **Henry Ward Beecher** *US Clergyman*

Too bad, too bad! It's too late **Ludwig Van Beethoven** *Composer*

I shall hear in heaven **Ludwig van Beethoven** *Composer*

I thank God for having enabled me to meet my fate with so much fortitude and resignation **John Bellingham** *Assassin of Spencer Perceval*

One thousand greetings to Balakirev **Hector Berlioz** *Composer*

I want to live because there are a few things I want to do **Aneurin Bevan** *British Politician*

Who's there? **Billy the Kid** *American Outlaw*

I do not fear death **Thomas Blood** *Irish Adventurer*

My belief is rooted in hope **Léon Blum** *French Prime Minister*

I should never have switched from scotch to Martinis **Humphrey Bogart** *Film Actor*

It is a great consolation to a poet on the point of death that he has never written a line injurious to good morals **Nicolas Boileau** *French Poet*

The executioner is, I believe, very expert; and my neck is very slender **Anne Boleyn** *Queen Consort*

Take my baggage on board the frigate **Simon Bolivar** *Venezuelan Revolutionary*

Goodbye and God bless you, I'll see you again, tomorrow **Horatio Bottomley** *British Politician*

At least one knows that death will be easy **Bertold Brecht** *German Playwright*

puddle it, puddle it and puddle it again **James Brindley** *Engineer*

'tis enough – I shall need no more **James Brindley** *Engineer (according to Josiah Wedgwood)*

Take courage Charlotte, take courage **Anne Brontë** *Author*

If you will send for the doctor I will see him now **Emily Brontë** *Author*

Decay is inherent in all component things **Buddha (Prince Gautama Siddhartha)** *Founder of Buddhism*

I wish Johnny would come **Buffalo Bill** *American Frontiersman*

Well I think it is about time to go to bed now **Sir Redvers Buller** *Colonial Administrator*

World without end **John Bunyan** *Religious Writer*

With the best that was in me I have tried to write more happiness into the world **Frances Hodgson Burnett** *American Novelist*

Don't let the awkward squad fire over my grave **Robert Burns** *Scottish Poet*

I must sleep now **Lord George Byron** *English Poet*

Now I shall go to sleep **Lord George Byron** *English Poet*

Et tu, Brute **Julius Caesar** *Roman Statesman*

I am still alive! **Caligula** *Roman Emperor*

Spain and Portugal **George Canning** *British Prime Minister*

So this is death, well ... **Thomas Carlyle** *Historian and essayist*

Take away those pillows, I shall need them no more **Lewis Carroll** *Author*

Bankhead, let me fall into your arms. It is all over **Viscount Robert Castlereagh** *British statesman*

Stand by me, Tom, and we will die together **Robert Catesby** *Gunpowder Plotter*

Lord, into thy hands I commend my spirit **Catherine of Aragon** *Henry VIII's first wife*

Now I am master of myself **Marcus Porcius Cato (The Younger)** *Roman statesman*

Patriotism is not enough. I must have no hatred or bitterness towards anyone **Edith Cavell** *Nurse*

Italy is made – all is safe **Camillo Cavour** *Italian Patriot*

Pontier! Pontier! **Paul Cézanne** *French artist*

Approaching dissolution brings relief **Neville Chamberlain** *British Prime Minister*

Lord, into thy hands I commend my spirit **Charlemagne** *King of the Franks*

Remember **Charles I** *British King*

I have been a most unconscionable time a-dying, but I hope you will excuse it **Charles II** *English King*

Do not, do not let poor Nelly starve **Charles II** *English King*

Nurse, Nurse, what murder, what blood! Oh! I have done wrong, God pardon me **Charles IX** *French King*

I hope never again to commit a mortal sin, nor even a venial one, if I can help it **Charles VIII** *French King*

Give Dayrolles a chair **Philip Dormer Chesterfield** *English Statesman*

The issue now is clear, it is between light and darkness and everyone must choose his side **GK Chesterton** *British Essayist*

Glory to God for all things **St John Chrysostom** *Syrian Churchman*

Oh I'm so bored with it all **Winston Churchill** *British Prime Minister*

Strike **Marcus Tullius Cicero** *Roman Statesman*

Doctor, do you think it could have been the sausage? **Paul Claudel** *French writer*

I wish to be buried standing – facing Germany **Georges Clemenceau** *French Premier*

Thy kingdom come, thy will be done **Edward Coke** *English Jurist*

Honour these grey hairs young man **Admiral Gaspard Coligny** *French Huguenot Leader*

I am signing my death warrant **Michael Collins** *Irish Patriot*

Lord, into thy hands I commend my spirit **Christopher Columbus** *Italian Explorer*

What an irreparable loss **Auguste Comte** *French Philosopher*

My time has come to die **Confucius** *Chinese Philosopher*

You, Jess, I am better this morning. I can always get a rise out of you **Joseph Conrad** *British Author*

Now, O Lord, set thy servant free **Nicolas Copernicus** *Polish Astronomer*

That was the best ice-cream soda I ever tasted **Lou Costello** *American Comedian*

Goodnight my darlings, I'll see you tomorrow **Noël Coward** *British Playwright*

That unworthy hand! **Thomas Cranmer** *Archbishop of Canterbury*

My design is to make what haste I can to be gone **Oliver Cromwell** *Lord Protector of England*

That was a great game of golf, fellers **Bing Crosby** *American Singer*

Benteen – come on – big village – be quick – bring packs **George Custer** *US soldier*

Nurse, it was I that discovered that leeches had red blood **Georges Cuvier** *French naturalist*

Be sure you show the mob my head, it will be a long time before they see its like **Georges Danton** *French Revolutionary Leader*

I am not in the least afraid to die **Charles Darwin** *English Naturalist*

My fun days are over **James Dean** *American Film Star*

Lord, into thy hands I commend my spirit **Robert Devereux** *Earl of Essex*

The bullet hasn't been made that can kill me **Legs Diamond** *Gangster*

On the ground! **Charles Dickens** *Author*

The first step towards philosophy is incredulity **Denis Diderot** *French man of letters*

Dammit! put them back on. This is funny **Doc Holliday** *Gambler and gunfighter*

I have deserved a thousand deaths **John Dudley** *Duke of Northumberland*

Adieu my friends, I go on to glory **Isadora Duncan** *Dancer*

It is very beautiful over there **Thomas Alva Edison** *American Inventor*

Carry my bones before you on your march, for the rebels will not be able to endure the sight of me **Edward I** *King of England*

Trust in God and you need not fear **Jonathan Edwards** *American Philosopher*

All my possessions for a moment of time **Elizabeth I** *Queen of England*

I die for my king and for France **Louis Duke of Enghien** *French soldier*

Dear God! **Desiderius Erasmus** *Dutch Humanist*

Channel 5 is shit! **Adam Faith** *Singer and Actor*

Now I'll have eine kleine pause **Kathleen Ferrier** *Opera Singer*

On the whole, I'd rather be in Philadelphia **WC Fields** *American Comedian*

The nourishment is palatable **Millard Fillmore** *US President*

I've had a hell of a lot of fun and I've enjoyed every minute of it **Errol Flynn** *Actor*

I am a dead man, Lord have mercy upon me **Gaston de Foix** *French Soldier*

I suffer nothing, but I feel a sort of difficulty in living longer **Bernard Fontenelle** *French Author*

It don't signify, my dearest, dearest Liz **Charles James Fox** *English Statesman*

Never heed! The Lord's power is over all weakness and death **George Fox** *English Religious Leader*

We are all going to Heaven and Van Dyke is of the company **Thomas Gainsborough** *English landscape painter*

Yet it still moves **Galileo Galilei** *Astronomer*

Feed them when I am gone **Giuseppe Garibaldi** *Italian Patriot*

Wally, what is this? It is death, my boy. They have

deceived me **George IV** *British King*

Bugger Bognor **George V** *British King*

How is the Empire? **George V** *British King*

Put your hands on my shoulders and don't struggle **WS Gilbert** *Librettist*

Let's do it **Gary Gilmore** *American Murderer*

Light, more light **Johann Wolfgang Goethe** *German poet and dramatist*

Where is the Mahdi ? **Charles Gordon** *British general*

I want nobody distressed on my account **Ulysses S Grant** *American Soldier and Statesman*

It is done **Horace Greeley** *American Politician*

Lord, into thy hands I commend my spirit **Lady Jane Grey** *English Queen*

Well if it must be so **Edvard Grieg** *Composer*

I hope to see you on Tuesday at 10.30 am **Earl Douglas Haig** *British General*

I regret that I have but one life to give for my country **Nathan Hale** *American Soldier*

Remember, my Eliza, you are a Christian **Alexander Hamilton** *American Politician*

The rest is silence **Hamlet** *Shakespearean Character*

Let us now relieve the Romans of their fears by the death of a feeble old man **Hannibal** *Carthaginian Soldier*

That's good. Go on, read some more **Warren Harding** *US President*

Four sixes to beat **John Wesley Hardin** *American Outlaw*

I am about the extent of a tenth of a gnat's eyebrow better **Joel Chandler Harris** *American Author*

Cheer up, children, I'm all right **Franz Joseph Haydn** *Composer*

I know I'm going where Lucy is **Rutherford B Hayes** *US President*

Monks! Monks! Monks! **Henry VIII** *King of England*

One more summer and another winter **Hermann Hesse** *German Novelist*

Moderately, I am continuing to orbit **Richard Hillary** *English fighter pilot and writer*

And I wish myself the joy of your fellowship at Whitsuntide **Gustav Holst** *Composer*

I am tired of fighting. I guess this thing is going to get me **Harry Houdini** *Escapologist*

I'll tell that story on the golden floor **AE Housman** *Poet*

Texas, Texas, Margaret **Sam Houston** *Texan patriot*

I die a Queen, but I would rather die the wife of Culpepper. **Catherine Howard** *Henry VIII's Fifth Wife*

God have mercy on my soul. Good people, I beg you pray for me. I see the black light **Victor Hugo** *French Poet*

Truth, truth **Anne Hyde** *Duchess of York*

Let us cross over the river and sit in the shade of the trees **Thomas Jackson** *US Civil War General*

It came with a lass and it will go with a lass **James V** *King of Scotland*

Do not hack me as you did my Lord Russell **James, Duke of Monmouth** *Charles II's illegitimate son*

That picture is crooked **Jesse James** *Train Robber*

Jesus Jesus Jesus, blessed be God **Joan of Arc** *French Patriot*

I commit my soul to God and my body to Saint Alstane **John** *King of England*

This is it, I'm going, I'm going **Al Jolson** *Singer*

Napoleon! Elba! Marie Louise! **Josephine** *French Empress*

Give me another horse, Howard! **Edmund Kean** *British Actor*

Such is life **Ned Kelly** *Australian Outlaw*

I wish to God you had heard them as I have heard them, and I praise God of that heavenly sound **John Knox** *Scottish Church Reformer*

Ah well, it is not the first time an innocent man has been condemned **Henri Landru** *French Murderer*

We shall this day light such a candle, by God's grace, in England, as I trust shall never be put out **Hugh Latimer** *Protestant Martyr*

I think it is time for morphine **DH Lawrence** *British Author*

Strike the tent **Robert E Lee** *Confederate General*

Now I have finished with all earthly business, and high time too **Franz Lehar** *Hungarian Composer*

Yes, yes, my dear child, now comes death. They won't think anything about it **Abraham Lincoln** *US President*

Tristan! **Franz Liszt** *Composer*

Jerusalem, Jerusalem **Louis IX** *French King*

Why weep you? Did you think I would live for ever? I thought dying was harder **Louis XIV** *French King*

Repeat those words, Monsieur Almoner, repeat them **Louis XV** *French King*

Frenchmen I Die guiltless of the crimes imputed to me. Pray God my blood falls not on France **Louis XVI** *French King*

I shall drink the cup to the last dregs **Louis XVI** *French King*

A king should die standing up **Louis XVIII** *French King*

Marty **Lucky Luciano** *US gangster*

Keep Paddy behind the big mixer **Alfred MacAlpine** *British building tycoon*

Lay on Macduff, and damned be him that first cries 'hold enough' **Macbeth** *Shakespearean Character*

Now all is over, let the piper play 'Return no More' **Rob Roy MacGregor** *Scottish Outlaw*

I love my country more than my soul **Niccolo Machiavelli** *Italian Statesman*

We are all going, we are all going ... oh dear! **William McKinley** *US President*

Mozart! **Gustav Mahler** *Composer*

Let's cool it, brothers **Malcolm X** *Black Muslim Leader*

I love the rain, I want the feeling of it on my face **Katherine Mansfield** *Writer*

Act in accordance with past principles **Mao Zedong** *Chinese Ruler*

Last words are for fools who haven't said enough **Karl Marx** *Philosopher*

My Lord, why do you not go on? I am not afraid to die **Mary II** *English Queen*

When I am dead and opened, you shall find Calais lying in my heart **Mary Tudor** *English Queen*

Thank you, Monsieur **Mata Hari** *Dutch Spy*

Dying is a very dull, dreary affair. My advice to you is to have nothing whatever to do with it **William Somerset Maugham** *British Writer*

Lotte! **Ferdinand-Joseph Maximilian** *Mexican Emperor*

I am crossing a beautiful wide river and the opposite shore is coming nearer and nearer **George Meade** *US Civil War General*

Ah, my God, I am dead **Catherine de Medici** *Florentine Ruler*

God bless Captain Vere **Herman Melville** *US Author*

Forgive some sinner and wink your eye at some homely girl **HL Mencken** *American Essayist*

Weary, very weary **Felix Mendelssohn** *Composer*

My soul I resign to God, my body to the Earth, My worldly goods to my next of kin **Michelangelo** *Italian sculptor and painter*

O Allah! Pardon my sins. Yes I come **Muhammad** *Founder of Islam*

For all my misfortunes, Malinche, I bear you no ill will **Montezuma II** *Aztec Emperor*

Commend your souls to God, for our bodies are the foe's **Simon de Montfort** *British Aristocrat*

See me safe up; for my coming down let me shift for myself **Thomas More** *English Statesman*

Did I not tell you I was writing this for myself **Wolfgang Amadeus Mozart** *Composer*

Put that bloody cigarette out **HH Munro** *British Author*

But, but, Mr Colonel ... **Benito Mussolini** *Italian Dictator*

France! Army! Head of the army! Josephine! **Napoleon 1** *French Emperor*

I don't need anything more ... Poultices **Napoleon II** *Duke of Reichstadt*

Were you at Sedan? **Napoleon III** *French Emperor*

Thank God I have done my duty, kiss me, Hardy **Horatio Nelson** *British Naval commander*

What an artist the world is losing in me **Nero** *Roman Emperor*

I seem to have been only a boy playing on the seashore and diverting myself in now and then finding a smoother pebble or prettier shell than the ordinary whilst the great ocean of truth lay all undiscovered before me **Isaac Newton** *Scientist*

I am just going outside and I may be some time **Captain Lawrence Oates** *Explorer*

Die, my dear doctor, that's the last thing I shall do **Viscount Palmerston** *British Prime Minister*

Get my swan costume ready **Anna Pavlova** *Ballerina*

What is the scaffold? A short cut to Heaven **Charles Peace** *Murderer*

To be like Christ is to be a Christian **William Penn** *English Quaker*

Murder! **Spencer Perceval** *British Prime Minister*

Do not weep, do not grieve **Henri Pétain** *French Soldier*

Drink to me **Pablo Picasso** *Spanish Artist*

The hearse, the horse, the driver and – enough **Luigi Pirandello** *Italian Dramatist*

I think I could eat one of Bellamy's veal pies **William Pitt (the younger)** *British Prime Minister*

Oh my country, how I leave thee **William Pitt (the younger)** *British Prime Minister*

Lord help my soul **Edgar Allan Poe** *Writer*

I am dying, sir, of a hundred good symptoms **Alexander Pope** *Poet*

Turn up the lights, I don't want to go home in the dark **William Porter (O'Henry)** *US Short Story Writer*

I am going to sleep like you, but we shall all awake together and, I trust to everlasting happiness **Joseph Priestley** *Chemist*

My poor Elvira, my poor wife **Giacomo Puccini** *Composer*

Sister, sister, sister **Thomas de Quincey** *British Writer*

I could wish this tragic scene were over, but I hope to go through it with becoming dignity **James Quin** *Irish Actor*

Let down the curtain, the farce is over **François Rabelais** *French writer*

I am going to seek the great, perhaps **François Rabelais** *French writer*

It matters little how the head lies, so the heart be right **Walter Raleigh** *English Explorer and Statesman*

I look like a Moor **Maurice Ravel** *French Composer*

I know that all things on earth must have an end, and now I am come to mine **Joshua Reynolds** *English Artist*

Turn me over, Jack **Cecil Rhodes** *South African Statesman*

So little done, so much to do **Cecil Rhodes** *South African Statesman*

Take off his chains, give him a hundred shillings, and let him go **Richard I** *King of England*

Treason, treason! **Richard III** *King of England*

I have no enemies save those of the state **Cardinal Richelieu** *French Statesman*

Don't you think I'll be back? **Manfred von Richthofen** *German Air Ace*

O Liberty! What crimes are committed in thy name **Madame Marie Roland** *French Revolutionary*

I have a terrific headache **FD Roosevelt** *US President*

We are the first victims of American fascism **Ethel Rosenberg** *Alleged Atom Spy*

There is God! Yes, God Himself, who is opening his arms and inviting me to taste at last that eternal and unchanging joy that I had so long desired **Jean-Jacques Rousseau** *French Political Theorist*

You can keep the things of bronze and stone and give me one man to remember me just once a year **Damon Runyon** *American Writer*

The bitterness of death is now past **Lord William Russell** *English Whig Statesman*

Of all his victories, realms and riches, nothing remains to him but this **Saladin** *Sultan of Egypt and Syria*

I am leaving you with your worries, good luck **George Sanders** *British Film Star*

Ah, my children, you cannot cry for me so much as I have made you laugh **Paul Scarron** *French Writer*

Many things are growing plain and clear to my understanding. One look at the sun **Johann Von Schiller** *German Dramatist*

Here, here is my end **Franz Schubert** *Composer*

French Canadian bean soup. I want to pay. Let them leave me alone **Dutch Schultz** *New York Gangster*

God bless you all, I feel myself again **Sir Walter Scott** *British Novelist*

I can't live any longer with my nerves **Jean Seberg** *US Film Star*

They couldn't hit an elephant at this dist ... **John Sedgwick** *US General*

I am absolutely undone **Richard Brinsley Sheridan** *Irish Writer and Statesman*

I believe we must adjourn the meeting to some other place **Adam Smith** *Economist*

Let me go **Capt EJ Smith** *Captain of SS Titanic*

That's right Brother Taylor, parry them off as well as you can **Joseph Smith** *Mormon Martyr*

Crito, we owe a cock to Aesculapius; pay it and do not let it pass **Socrates** *Greek Philosopher*

Beautifully done **(Sir) Stanley Spencer** *British Artist*

Four o'clock. How strange, so that is time. Strange, enough! **Sir Henry Stanley** *Explorer*

I feel faint **Adlai Stevenson** *American Politician*

If this is dying, I don't think much of it **Lytton Strachey** *Biographer*

Put not your trust in princes **Thomas Strafford** *English Statesman*

Thy necessity is yet greater than mine **Philip Sydney** *British Soldier and Poet*

Lord, into thy hands I commend my spirit **Torquato Tasso** *Italian Poet*

How sweet it is to rest **John Taylor** *English Poet*

I have tried to do my duty, and am not afraid to die. I am ready **Zachary Taylor** *US President*

Brother warriors, we are about to enter an engagement from which I will not return. My body will remain on the field of battle **Tecumseh** *Indian Chief*

I have opened it **Lord Alfred Tennyson** *Poet*

Gentlemen of the jury, you may retire **Charles Tenterden** *Lord Chief Justice*

And my heart throbbed with an exquisite bliss **William Thackeray** *British Novelist*

To the health of the fair Critias **Theramenes** *Athenian Statesman*

I shall soon know the grand secret **Arthur Thistlewood** *English Conspirator*

I've had 18 straight whiskies, I think that's a record ... after 39 yrs this is all I've done **Dylan Thomas** *Poet*

I leave this world without a regret **Henry Thoreau** *American Essayist*

God bless ... God damn **James Thurber** *American humorist*

I'll be shot if I don't believe I'm dying **Edward Thurlow** *English Politician*

Oh look, see how the cherry blossoms fall mutely **Hideki Tojo** *Japanese Politician and Soldier*

The enemy have demanded a surrender and I have answered the summons with a cannon shot and our flag still waves proudly from the walls **W Barrett Travis** *Commander of the Alamo*

Now I stretch out my hand, and from the further shore I bid adieu to all who have cared to read any among the many words I have written **Anthony Trollope** *British Novelist*

I feel here that this time they have succeeded **Leon Trotsky** *Russian Leader*

The sun is God **JMW Turner** *British Artist*

Death, the only immortal, who treats us all alike, whose peace and whose refuge are for all, the soiled and the pure, the rich and the poor, the loved and unloved **Mark Twain** *American Novelist*

Lord forgive my sins. Especially my sins of omission **James Ussher** *Archbishop of Armagh*

I want the sunlight to greet me **Rudolph Valentino** *Film star*

I shall never get rid of this depression **Vincent Van Gogh** *Artist*

I suppose I am now becoming a God **Vespasian** *Roman Emperor*

Oh that peace may come **Victoria** *British Queen*

Do let me die in peace **Voltaire** *French Author and Philosopher*

I am fond of them, of the inferior beings of the abyss, of those who are full of longing **Richard Wagner,** *Composer*

It is well, I die hard, but am not afraid to go **George Washington** *US President*

A last interview ... **Ethel Waters** *US Blues Singer*

Life, life, death, death, how curious it is **Daniel Webster** *American Statesman*

Go away, I'm all right **HG Wells** *Author*

I shall be satisfied with thy likeness – satisfied **Charles Wesley** *English Hymn Writer*

I am dying as I have lived: beyond my means **Oscar Wilde** *Dramatist*

Either this wallpaper goes or I do **Oscar Wilde** *Dramatist*

O my God, have mercy upon this poor people **William the Silent** *Stadholder of the Netherlands*

Edith **Woodrow Wilson** *US President*

I fear not this fire **George Wishart** *Scottish Reformer*

Give me back my youth **John Wolcot** *English Satirist*

What! do they run already? Then I die happy **James Wolfe** *English General*

Had I but served God as diligently as I have served the King, He would not have given me over in my grey hairs **Thomas Wolsey** *English Prelate*

Is that you Dora? **William Wordsworth** *Poet*

Mind your own business **Percy Wyndham-Lewis** *British artist*

Better fighting death than a slave's life **Emiliano Zapata** *Mexican Revolutionary*

Make my skin into drumheads for the Bohemian cause **John Ziska** *Bohemian Hussite Leader*

NB: This is an area of uncertainty and vagueness and cannot be said to be a true and exact glossary of last words. That is because quite often there would be some controversy over the reported words uttered before death by a solitary witness, and even when witnessed by many people there would often be a conflict of opinion, hence the need for double entries for various persons. It is thought, perhaps, that some of the more witty sayings were possibly the sort of thing that a particular person would have said and it is in the way of a tribute to a person that not too many questions would be asked. The point to remember about these last utterances is not so much the truth of the speech *per se*, but rather the fact that the words are universally identifiable with these people. Several persons have more than one entry for the reasons stated above.

First names
(of people better known by other names)

Alvar Aalto – Hugo *Finnish Architect*

Patrick Abercrombie – Leslie *English Architect*

Pepper Anderson – Suzanne *TV character (Police Woman)*

Antonioni – Michelangelo *Film Director*

Corazon Aquino – Maria *Filipino President*

Yasser Arafat – Mohammed *Palestinian Resistance Leader*

Louis Armstrong – Daniel *Jazz Musician*

Cash Asmussen – Brian Keith *US Jockey*

Avon – Kerr *Blake 7 character*

Balakirev – Mily *Russian Composer*

Balzac – Honoré de *French Writer*

Banacek – Thomas *TV Character*

Batista – Fulgencio *Cuban President*

Max Beerbohm – Henry *English Writer and Caricaturist*

Bix Beidebecke – Leon *Jazz Cornet Player*

Hilaire Belloc – Joseph *French-born Writer*

Arnold Bennett – Enoch *English Novelist*

Ingmar Bergman – Ernst *Film Director*

Busby Berkeley – William *Choreographer and Director*

Hector Berlioz – Louis *French Composer*

Ali Bhutto – Zulfikar *Pakistani Statesman*

John Biffen – William *English Politician*

Laurence Binyon – Robert *Poet*

Bizet – Georges Alexandre Césare Léopold *French Composer*

Blake – Roj *'Blake's 7' Character*

Boccaccio – Giovanni *Italian Writer*

Bodie and Doyle – William and Ray *TV Characters ('The Professionals')*

Bootsie (Pte 'excused boots' Bisley) – Montague *TV Character ('The Army Game')*

Lord Byron – George *English Poet*

Calamity Jane – Martha *Wild West Heroine*

James Callaghan – Leonard *British Politician*

Callan – David *TV Character*

Hoss Cartwright – Eric *TV Western Hero ('Bonanza')*

Casanova – Giovanni Jacopo *Poet and Libertine*

Casey Jones – John Luther *TV Character based on Ballad*

Emmanuel Chabrier – Alexis *French Composer*

Paddy Chayevsky – Sidney *Playwright*

Chekov – Pavel *Star Trek Character*

Erskine Childers – Robert *Anglo-Irish Writer*

Colette – Sidonie *French Novelist*

Colin Cowdrey – Michael *English Cricketer*

Crane – Richard *TV Character*

Sonny Crockett – James *Miami Vice Character*

Cui – César *Russian Composer*

Robert Cummings – Charles *US Actor*

Bette Davis – Ruth *US Actress*

Debussy – Achille-Claude *French Composer*

Edgar Degas – Hilaire-Germain *French Artist*

Paul Delaroche – Hippolyte *French Painter*

Delibes – Léo *French Composer*

Delius – Frederick *English Composer*

Legs Diamond – Jack *Gangster*

Fats Domino – Antoine *US Vocalist*

Lonnie Donegan – Anthony *Skiffle Musician*

Donizetti – Gaetano *Italian Composer*
Faye Dunaway – Dorothy *US Actress*
Dvorak – Antonin *Czech Composer*
Eddie 'the eagle' Edwards – Michael *British Skijumper*
Samantha Eggar – Victoria *US Actress*
Erasmus – Desiderius *Dutch Humanist*
Escoffier – Auguste *French Chef*
Private Fender – Sam *TV Character ('Bilko')*
Figgis – Roy *TV Character ('Only When I Laugh')*
Finlay, Dr – Alan (Bill Simpson) *TV Character*
Finlay, Dr – John (David Rintoul) *TV Character*
Private Fraser – James *'Dad's Army' Character*
Paul Gaughin – Eugène *French Post-Impressionist*
Gigli – Beniamino *Italian Tenor*
Gill, Eric – Arthur *English Sculptor*
Glinka – Mikhail *Russian Composer*
Glover – Archie *TV Character ('Only When I Laugh')*
Gluck – Christoph *German Composer*
Private Godfrey – Charles *'Dad's Army' Character*
Joseph Goebbels – Paul *Nazi Leader*
Pancho Gonzales – Richard *US Tennis Player*
Gounod – Charles *French Composer*
Goya – Francisco *Spanish Painter*
Ulysses S Grant – Hiram *US President*
Graham Greene – Henry *British Novelist*
Florence Griffith-Joyner – Delorez *US Athlete*
Brothers Grimm – Jacob and Wilhelm *Folktale collectors*
Che Guevara – Ernesto *Argentinian Revolutionary Leader*
Colonel Hall – John *TV Character ('Bilko')*
Mrs Hall – Nell *TV Character ('Bilko')*
Dashiell Hammett – Samuel *US Novelist*
Learned Hand – Billings *American Jurist*
Patsy Hendren – Elias *England Cricketer*
Barbara Hepworth – Jocelyn *English Sculptor*
William Herschel – Frederick *British Astronomer*
Rudolf Hess – Richard *Nazi Leader*
Patricia Highsmith – Mary *US Novelist*
Hinge and Bracket – Dr Evadne and Dame Hilda *comic duo*
Doc Holliday – John *Western gunfighter*
Holman Hunt – William *English Painter*
Honegger – Arthur *Swiss Composer*
Ron L Hubbard – Lafayette *SF Writer and Scientology Founder*
John Humphreys – Desmond *TV and Radio Presenter*
Lauren Hutton – Mary *US Actress*
Ivanhoe – Wilfred *Literary Character*
Jacuzzi – Candido *Inventor of luxury bath*
Storm Jameson – Margaret *British Novelist*
Janáček – Leoš *Czech Composer*
Jeeves – Reginald *PG Wodehouse character (named after Warwickshire Cricketer)*
Corporal Jones – Jack *'Dad's Army' Character*
Miss Jones – Ruth *TV Character ('Rising Damp')*
Khachaturian – Aram *Armenian Composer*
Kookie – Gerald (Lloyd Kookson III) *TV Character ('77 Sunset Strip')*
Lucky Luciano – Charles *Gangster*
Lugg – Magersfontein *Literary Character: Campion's Manservant*
Lytton Strachey – Giles *Biographer*

Harold Macmillan – Maurice *British Prime Minister*
Magnificent Evans – Plantagenet *TV Character*
Mr Magoo – Quincy *Cartoon Character*
Captain Mainwaring – George *Dad's Army Character*
Paul McCartney – James *Beatle*
Campbell Menzies – Walter *MP and Former Athlete*
Mrs Merton – Dorothy *TV Character*
Miles Van Der Rohe – Ludwig *Architect*
Milhaud – Darius *French Composer*
Glen Miller – Alton *Bandleader*
Monteverdi – Claudio *Italian Composer*
Morse – Endeavour *Fictional detective*
Angela Mortimer – Florence *British Wimbledon Champion*
Mulder and Scully – Fox and Dana *TV Characters ('X Files')*
Brian Mulroney – Martin *Canadian Politician*
Murillo – Bartolomé *Spanish Painter*
Mussorgsky – Modest *Russian Composer*
Ogden Nash – Frederic *American Poet*
Birgit Nilsson – Märta *Swedish Soprano*
Captain Oates – Lawrence *Explorer*
Milton Obote – Apollo *Ugandan Politician*
Offenbach – Jacques *French Composer*
King Oliver – Joseph *American Cornet-player*
Palestrina – Giovanni *Italian Composer*
Captain Peacock – Stephen *TV Character*
Petrocelli – Tony *TV Character*
Brad Pitt – William *US Actor*
Graeme Pollock – Robert *South African Cricketer*
Jackson Pollock – Paul *American Action Painter*
Ponchielli – Amilcare *Italian Composer*
Potsie Weber – Warren *TV Character (Happy Days)*
Beatrix Potter – Helen *English Children's Writer*
Enoch Powell – John *British Politician*
Pressburger and Powell – Emeric and Michael *Film Makers*
Princip – Gavrilo *Assassin*
Prokofiev – Sergey *Russian Composer*
Puccini – Giacomo *Italian Composer*
Captain Pugwash – Horatio *TV Character*
Professor Quatermass – Bernard *TV Character*
Dan Quayle – James *US Vice-President*
Rachmaninoff – Sergey *Russian Composer*
Sonny Ramphal – Shridath *Secretary-General of the Commonwealth*
Ravel – Maurice *French Composer*
Django Reinhardt – Jean Baptiste *Belgian Guitarist*
Viv Richards – Isaac *West Indian Cricketer*
Cardinal Richelieu – Armand *French politician-prelate*
Rigsby – Rupert *TV Character ('Rising Damp')*
Rimsky-Korsakov – Nikolay *Russian Composer*
Sergeant Ritzik – Rupert *TV Character ('Bilko')*
Auguste Rodin – René-François *French Sculptor*
Rossini – Gioachino *Italian Composer*
Rostropovich – Mstislav *Russian Musician*
Mr Rumbold – Cuthbert *TV Character*
Salman Rushdie – Ahmed *British Novelist*
Anwar Sadat – Mohamed *Egyptian President*
Saint-Saens – Charles Camille *French Composer*
Vicario Sanchez – Arantxa *Tennis Player*
Savonarola – Girolamo *Italian Religious Reformer*
Schubert – Franz Peter *Austrian Composer*
Schumann – Robert *German Composer*

F
A
M
O
U
S

P
E
O
P
L
E

Paul Scofield – David   *English Actor*
Scottie – Montgomery   *'Star Trek' Character*
Norman Shaw – Richard   *English Architect*
Shelley – James   *TV Character*
Phones (Sheridan) – George   *TV Character*
('Stingray')
Shostakovich – Dmitry   *Russian Composer*
Sibelius – Jean   *Finnish Composer*
Mrs Slocombe – Betty   *TV Character*
Smetana – Bedrich   *Czech Composer*
Colonel Hannibal Smith – John   *TV Character*
Snudge – Claude   *TV Character ('Army Game')*
Leland Stanford – Amasa   *US Railway Magnate*
Starsky and Hutch – David and Ken   *TV policemen*
Nobbie Stiles – Norbert   *Footballer*
Stockhausen – Karlheinz   *German Composer*
August Strindberg – Johann   *Swedish Playwright*
Sulu – Hikaru   *'Star Trek' character*
Booth Tarkington – Newton   *US Author*
Tchaikovsky – Pyotr   *Russian Composer*
Tinker – Edward Sexton   *Blake's Assistant*

Daley Thompson – Francis   *Athlete*
Wolfe Tone – Theobald   *Irish Nationalist*
Topol – Chaim   *Israeli Actor*
Uccello – Paolo   *Florentine Painter*
Verdi – Giuseppe   *Italian Composer*
Vivaldi – Antonio   *Italian Composer*
Richard Wagner – Wilhelm   *German Composer*
Private Walker – James   *'Dad's Army' Character*
Dionne Warwick – Marie   *US Singer*
Dr Watson – John   *Literary Character*
Weber – Carl   *German Composer*
Webern – Anton   *Austrian Composer*
Orson Welles – George   *Film Maker and Actor*
Andy Williams – Howard   *US Singer*
Harold Wilson – James   *British Prime Minister*
Debra Winger – Marie   *US Actress*
Terry Wogan – Michael   *Broadcaster*
Wolf-Ferrari – Ermanno   *Italian Composer*
Roy Wood – Ulysses   *Pop Musician*
Virginia Woolf – Adeline   *English Novelist*

Firsts

Air Hostess Ellen Church	1930
Airmail (GB) 9 Sept	1911
Airmail Stickers 17 Aug	1918
Appendix Operation	
George Thomas Morton	1887
Athlete to use Crouch Start	
Charles Sherrill	1888
Atom Bomb	
Alamogordo Air Base, New Mexico (16 July)	1945
Atom Bomb (UK)	
Monte Bello Islands off West Australia	1952
Atomic Power Station (large-scale)	
Calder Hall, Cumbria	1956
Atomic Research Centre (UK)	
Harwell in Berkshire	1946
Baronet Nicholas Bacon of Redgrove	1611
Bikini 24 June	1950
Blood transfusion	
Montpellier University, France	1667
Boy Scout Movement	
Brownsea Island, Poole, Dorset	1907
Breakfast Cereal (ready to eat)	
Shredded Wheat	1893
Bus Conductress Kate Barton	1909
Bus Service (scheduled) Shillibeer's	
Marylebone to Euston Rd Service	1829
Capital Gains Tax 6 April	1965
Car Tax Discs	
On windowscreen from 1 Jan	1921
Casino (UK) Metropole in Brighton	1962
Catamaran	
Experiment, built for Sir William Petty:	
adaptation from traditional Polynesian	
design	1662
Channel Swim: both ways (UK)	
Kevin Murphy (non-stop) in 35 hrs 10 mins	1970
Chelsea Flower Show	
20–22 May by Royal Horticultural Society	1913
Christmas Card John Calcott Horsley	
designed for Henry Cole	1843

Christmas Speech of Sovereign	
Elizabeth II	1957
Christmas Tree From German idea	1605
Circumnavigation of Earth	
Juan Sebastian Del Cano in *Victoria*	
(Magellan killed en route)	1522
Circumnavigation of Earth: Non-stop Solo	
Robin Knox-Johnston in *Suhaili*	1969
Club Colours	
Black, Red, Gold of I Zingari Cricket Club	1845
Coeducational School	
Henry Morley opened Marine Terrace,	
Cheshire	1849
Comic *Comic Cuts* an 8-page weekly	1890
Comic Strip in Newspaper	
Richard Outcault's 'Yellow Kid'	1897
Credit Card Diners Club, New York	1950
Cremation (UK)	
Honoretta Pratt	1769
Cub Scouts	
Robertsbridge, Sussex (2 Feb)	1914
Daylight Saving (UK) Clocks put forward	
I hour	1916
Detective Story Edgar Allan Poe's	
The Murders in the Rue Morgue	1841
Diet (scientifically planned)	
Dr Harvey for undertaker William Banting	1862
Dinner Jacket	
Worn by G Lorillard, Tuxedo Park Country	
Club, NY	1886
Dresswear hire firm (UK)	
Moss Bros of Covent Garden	1860
Driving tests (UK) Leslie Hore-Belisha	
instigated voluntary tests	1935
Duke (UK)	
Edward, Duke of Cornwall	1337
Electric lamp J Lindsay developed	
but did not patent lamp	1835
Electric oven Installed Hotel Bernina,	
Samaden, Switzerland	1889

Electric power station
Central Power Station, Godalming, Surrey   1881
Escalator (UK)
Harrods Department Store   1898
Family allowance   15 June (5s per child)   1945
Film festival   Hotel Excelsior Venice, Italy   1932
Fire brigade (UK)
Nicholas Barbon established in London   1684
Fixed penalty parking ticket (UK)
19 Sept   1961
Football: televised live (UK)
Wembley Cup Final   1938
Four-minute mile
Roger Bannister in 3: 59.4 (Oxford)   1954
Fruit machine
Liberty Bell designed by Charles Frey   1889
GCE 'O' and 'A' Levels
Introduced to replace School Certificate   1950
GCSE   Introduced to replace CGE 'O' Level   1988
Girl Guide   Allison Cargill   1908
Gold disc
Glen Miller's 'Chattanooga Choo Choo'   1941
Greetings card   Designer W Harvey
engraved by J Thompson   1829
Heart Transplant
Christiaan Barnard, Groote Schuur Hospital   1967
Helicopter (free flight)   Twin-rotor machine
designed by Paul Cornu   1907
Hydrofoil (UK)
'Miranda III' by John Thornycroft   1909
Hydrogen bomb   Detonated by USA
at Eniwetok, Marshall Isles   1952
Indianapolis 500   Won by Ray Harroun
(30 May)   1911
In-flight movie   Conan Doyle's
The Lost World   1925
Isle of Man TT Races
Won by Charles Collier on a Matchless   1907
Jazz band   Led by Buddy Bolden,
New Orleans   1900
Jukebox   Installed at Palais Royal Saloon,
San Francisco   1889
Life insurance policy   Taken out by London
Alderman Richard Martin   1583
Lighthouse (UK)   Spurn Point, Yorkshire   1427
Lord Mayor's Show   Instigated by
Sir John Norman   1453
Loudspeaker
Auxetophone by Horace Short   1900
Luncheon Vouchers (UK)   1 Jan   1955
Meteorological satellite   Tiros I   1960
Miss World Contest   19 April   1951
Monarch to Abdicate: English   Richard II   1399
MOT test   12 Sept   1960
Motorway   Avus Autobahn, Germany   1921
Moving staircase (UK)   Earls Court Station   1911
National park   Yellowstone, Wyoming   1872
National park: GB   Peak District   1950
National Savings stamps
On sale from 8 July   1918
Newspaper colour supplement (UK)
Sunday Times   1962
North Sea gas   Piped ashore by BP   1967
Nuclear merchant vessel
Savannah (launched in New Jersey)   1962
Old age pensions
Bismarck introduced in Germany   1889

Old age pensions (UK)
Introduced on 1 Jan   1909
Old school tie   Old Etonian, of narrow
blue and broad black stripes   1900
Opera
Jacopo Peri's *Dafne*, libretto by Rinuccini   1597
Oral contraceptive (UK)
Marketed on 18 Aug (invented 1954)   1960
Parachute jump (aeroplane)
Albert Berry from a height of 1,500 feet   1912
Parachute jump (balloon)   André-Jacques
Garnerin from a height of 2,230 feet   1797
Parcel post   Introduced on 1 Aug   1883
Parking meter (UK)
(America had them from 1935)   1958
Parking ticket (UK)
Dr Thomas Creighton was first victim   1960
Pedestrian crossing (UK)
Parliament Square, London   1926
Photo finish: horse race
Introduced by Ernest Marks, New Jersey   1888
Photographic process
Louis Daguerre first commercial success   1839
Pneumatic motor car tyres
Michelin fitted first tyre to a 4hp Daimler   1895
Policewoman
Mrs Alice Stebbins Wells of the LAPD   1910
Policewoman (UK)   27 Nov   1914
Postage stamp (adhesive)
James Chalmers of Dundee printed first   1834
Postage stamp (perforations)
Penny Red, issued in Feb   1854
Postal orders (UK)
Introduced on 1 Jan   1881
Postcard (UK)   Introduced on 1 Oct   1870
Premium Bonds
On sale from 1 Nov   1956
Prince of Wales: English
Edward of Caernarvon, later Edward II   1301
Prisoner of War camp
Norman X Depot, Stilton, for French PoWs   1797
Public library (UK)
Jerrom Goodwyn Library, Norwich   1608
Recorded delivery   1 Feb   1961
Registered letters
Introduced by GPO on 1 Jan   1878
Row across the Atlantic
Capt John Ridgway and Sgt Chay Blyth   1966
Row across the Atlantic (solo)
Tom McLean in 20 ft dory *Super Silver*   1969
Sex Change Operation   George/Christine
Jorgensen by Dr K Hamburger   1952
Space Flight (manned)
Vostok I, piloted by Yuri Gagarin   1961
Space flight (by woman)
Vostok VI, piloted by Valentina Tereshkova   1963
Space walk
Aleksey Leonov, from *Voshkod II*   1965
Spacecraft on the Moon   *Luna II*   1959
Spiritualist mediums
Margaretta and Kate Fox from New York   1848
Starting stalls: horse race (UK)
Newmarket on 8 July   1965
Tape recorder
Telagraphone by Valdemar Poulsen   1898
Telegrams (UK)
I shilling for 20 words (1st worldwide in 1843)   1870

FAMOUS PEOPLE

Telephone directory (UK)			**Vending machine (automatic)**	
Published by London Telephone Co	1880		Patented by Carl Ade in Germany	1867
Telephone speaking clock (UK)			**Victoria Cross** Mate Charles Lucas, for	
Aka TIM was voice of Ethel Cain for 20 yrs	1936		action aboard HMS *Hecla*	1854
Television announcer (UK) Leslie Mitchell	1936		**Voting rights for women**	
Television commercial, black and white (UK)			New Zealand was 1st country to allow	1893
Gibbs SR Toothpaste	1955		Finland 1st in Europe 1906	
Television commercial, colour (UK)			**Windscreen wipers (mechanical)**	
Birds Eye Peas	1969		Introduced in the USA	1916
Television licence (UK) Cost of £2	1946		**Windscreen wipers (electrical)**	
Television communications satellite			The 'Berkshire', produced in the USA	1923
Bell Telephone 'Telstar'	1962		**Woman cabinet minister (UK)**	
Traffic lights Parliament Square, London	1868		Margaret Bondfield, Minister of Labour	1929
Traffic lights: electric (UK) July	1926		**Woman doctor (US)** Elizabeth Blackwell	1849
Traffic lights: automatic (UK) 5 Nov	1927		**Woman doctor (UK)**	
Traffic wardens (UK)			Elizabeth Garrett Anderson	1859
15 Sept in London	1960		**Woman MP (UK)** Constance, Countess	
Train accident fatality			Markievicz, Sinn Fein MP	1918
William Huskisson MP, run down by *Rocket*	1830		**Woman MP (to take seat)**	
Traveller's cheques			Nancy Astor for Plymouth Sutton	1919
Introduced on 1 Jan	1772		**Woman novelist**	
Underground railway (UK)			Lady Murasaki, Japan	c1004
Metropolitan Line Paddington to Farringdon	1863		**Woman novelist (UK)** Aphra Behn	1687
Underground railway (electric)			**Woman pilot** Baronne Elise de la Roche	1909
City branch of the Northern line	1890		**Woman prime minister**	
Undergound map			Mrs Sirimavo Bandaranaike of Ceylon	1960
Albert Stanley, Lord Ashfield instigated	1908		**Women's Institute**	
Underground (Tube) train (automatic)			Stoneycreek, Ontario, Canada	1897
Central Line Woodford to Hainault	1964		**Yellow lines restricting parking** Laid in	
Vending machine			Slough	1956
So-called 'Honesty' tobacco boxes,			**Zebra crossing** 31 Oct	1951
1d a go	1615			

NB: Although this topic of 'firsts' has been listed in the Famous People section, many of the entries relate to inanimate objects. This is purely a matter of expediency and is not an oversight on the part of the author.

Initials: Known by

WH Auden Wystan Hugh
British poet

AJ Ayer Alfred Jules
English philosopher

CPE Bach Carl Philipp Emanuel
German composer

JC Bach Johann Christian
German composer

JS Bach Johann Sebastian
German composer

RM Ballantyne, Robert Michael
Scottish author

JG Ballard James Graham
British writer

JC Bamford Joseph Cyril
Founder of JCB Company

BA Baracus Bad Attitude
Fictional TV character ('A Team')

PT Barnum Phineas Taylor
US showman

JM Barrie James Matthew
Scottish novelist

HE Bates Herbert Ernest
English novelist

CC Beck Clarence
US graphic artist

AC Benson Arthur Christopher
English author and poet

EF Benson Edward Frederic
English author

EC Bentley Edmund Clerihew
English journalist and novelist

RD Blackmore Richard
Doddridge *English novelist*

PW Botha Pieter Willem
South African politician

RA Butler Richard Austen
British politician

AS Byatt Antonia Susan
English novelist and critic

GK Chesterton Gilbert Keith
English novelist

JM Coetzee John Michael
South African novelist

GDH Cole George Douglas
Howard *British economist*

AE Coppard Alfred Edgar
English poet and writer

AJ Cronin Archibald Joseph
Scottish novelist

ee cummings Edward Estlin
American writer and painter

WH Davies William Henry
British poet

JW De Forest John William *US*
novelist and historian

FW De Klerk, Frederik Willem
South African politician

RF Delderfield Ronald Frederick
English playwright

EL Doctorow Edgar Lawrence
US novelist

JP Donleavy James Patrick
Irish novelist

TS Eliot Thomas Stearns
poet and dramatist

JK Ewers John Keith *Australian
writer*

JR Ewing John Ross
Fictional TV character ('Dallas')

UA Fanthorpe Ursula Askham
British poet

JG Farrell James Gordon
English novelist

EH Fellowes Edmund Horace
English musicologist

WC Fields William Claude
American comedy actor

CS Forester Cecil Scott
British writer

EM Forster Edward Morgan
English novelist

AJ Foyt Anthony Joseph
US racing driver

EA Freeman   Edward Augustus
British historian

CB Fry   Charles Burgess
English sportsman

JK Galbraith   John Kenneth
economist

TS Garp   Technical Sergeant
John Irving character

WS Gilbert   William Schwenck
English operetta librettist

KC Gillette   King Camp
American inventor

WE Gladstone   William Ewart
British politician

EW Godwin   Edward William
English architect and designer

HL Gold   Horace Leonard
science fiction writer

WG Grace   William Gilbert
English cricketer

DW Griffith   David Wark
American film director

AB Guthrie   Alfred Bertram
US writer

MC Hammer   Master of
Ceremonies   *US rap artist*

WC Handy   William Christopher
US Blues composer

LP Hartley   Leslie Poles
English author

HJ Heinz   Henry John
US food manufacturer

WE Henley   William Ernest
English poet and critic

GA Henty   George Alfred
English novelist

AP Herbert   Alan Patrick
English writer

AD Hope   Alec Derwent
Australian poet

EW Hornung   Ernest William
English writer

AE Housman   Alfred Edward
English poet

EM Hull   Edith Maude   *British
writer*

TE Hulme   Thomas Ernest
British essayist and poet

CLR James   Cyril Lionel Robert
Trinidadian writer

MR James   Montague Rhodes
ghost story writer

PD James   Phyllis Dorothy
English writer

WE Johns   William Earl
English writer and aviator

MM Kaye   Mary Margaret
British writer

HRF Keating   Henry Raymond
Fitzwalter   *UK detective
story writer*

AL Kennedy   Alison Louise
British writer

BB King   Blues Boy
singer/guitarist

WP Kinsella   William Patrick

Canadian writer

RB Kitaj   Ronald Brooks
American painter

LC Knight   Lionel Charles
British critic and author

RD Laing   Ronald David
Scottish psychiatrist

CJ Lamb   Cara Jean
fictional TV character (LA Law)

kd lang   Kathryn Dawn
Canadian singer

DH Lawrence   David Herbert
English novelist

TE Lawrence   Thomas Edward
British soldier and writer

FR Leavis   Frank Raymond
English literary critic

GH Lewes   George Henry
British writer

CS Lewis   Clive Staples *Irish writer*

HP Lovecraft   Howard Phillips
US science fiction writer

LS Lowry   Laurence Stephen
English artist

HL Mencken   Henry Louis
US journalist

AA Michelson   Albert Abraham
US physicist

AA Milne   Alan Alexander
children's writer

LM Montgomery   Lucy Maud
Canadian novelist

CL Moore   Catherine Lucille   *US
science fiction writer*

JP Morgan   John Pierpont
US financier

JB Morton   John Bingham
British journalist (Beachcomber)

HH Munro   Hector Hugh
English writer (Saki)

VS Naipaul   Vidiadhar
Surajprasad   *Trinidadian
novelist*

RK Narayan   Rasipuram
Kirshnaswamy   *Indian novelist*

PH Newby   Percy Howard
British novelist

TV Olsen   Theodore Victor
US Westerns writer

PJ O'Rourke   Patrick John
US journalist

CJ Parker   Casey Jean
*Fictional TV character
('Baywatch')*

SJ Perelman   Sydney Joseph
US writer

TF Powys   Theodore Francis
British writer

JB Priestley   John Boynton
English novelist

VS Pritchett   Victor Sawdon
English writer

JD Rockefeller   John Davison
US businessman

AV Roe   Alliot Verdon
English aviation pioneer

JK Rowling   Joanne Kathleen
English children's writer

JD Salinger   Jerome David
US novelist

EH Shepard   Ernest Howard
English illustrator

RC Sherriff   Robert Cedric
English novelist

NF Simpson   Norman Frederick
British playwright

OJ Simpson   Orenthal James
US sportsman

VP Singh   Vishwanath Pratap
Indian politician

CH Sisson   Charles Hubert
British poet

BF Skinner   Burrhus Fredric
US psychologist

EE 'Doc' Smith   Edward Elmer
US science fiction writer

WH Smith   William Henry
English newsagent

CP Snow   Charles Percy
English novelist

HM Stanley   Henry Morton
journalist and explorer

JIM Stewart   John Innes
Mackintosh   *English writer*

JEB Stuart   James Ewell Brown
Confederate general

JM Synge   John Millington   *Irish
dramatist*

AJP Taylor   Alan John Percivale
English historian

DM Thomas   Donald Michael
English writer

EP Thompson   Edward Palmer
British historian

EMW Tillyard   Eustace Mandeville
Wetenhall   *British scholar and
critic*

JRR Tolkien   John Ronald Reuel
philologist and author

PL Travers   Pamela Lyndon
author of Mary Poppins

AE Van Vogt   Alfred Elton
science fiction writer

HG Wells   Herbert George
English novelist

EB White   Elwyn Brooks
US essayist and novelist

TH White   Terence Hanbury
English novelist

JPR Williams   John Peter Rhys
Welsh rugby player

WD and HO Wills   William Day
and Henry Overton
tobacco manufacturers

PG Wodehouse   Pelham Grenville
English novelist

FW Woolworth   Frank Winfield
US businessman

PC Wren   Percy Christopher
English novelist

WB Yeats   William Butler
Irish poet

Inventions and Discoveries

Adding machine *Blaise Pascal*	1642	
Aeroplane (steam powered) *Clement Ader*	1886	
Aeroplane *Wright Brothers*	1903	
Aerosol *Erik Rotheim*	1926	
Air Pump *Otto Von Guericke*	1654	
Airship (non-rigid) *Henri Giffard*	1852	
Airship (rigid) *Ferdinand Von Zeppelin*	1900	
Ambulance *Baron Dominique Jean Larrey*	1792	
Anaesthesia *William Morton*	1846	
Antiseptic surgery *Joseph Lister*	1867	
Aqualung *Cousteau and Gagnan*	1943	
Aspirin (synthesization) *Kolbe, Heinrich*	1859	
Aspirin (intro into medicine) *H Dresser of Bayer AG*	1899	
Assembly line *Samuel Colt*	1855	
Atom bomb *Frisch, Bohr, Peierls*	1939	
Baby incubator *Dr Alexandre Lion*	1891	
Bakelite *Leo H Baekeland*	1907	
Balloon *Montgolfier Brothers*	1783	
Balloons: rubber *Michael Faraday*	1824	
Balloons: toy *JG Ingram*	1847	
Ball-point pen *John T Loud*	1888	
Ball-point pen (mass-produced) *László Biro*	1938	
Barbed wire (manufacture) *Joseph Glidden*	1874	
Barbed wire (patent) *Lucien B Smith*	1867	
Barometer *Evangelista Torricelli*	1643	
Battery (electric) *Alessandro Volta*	1800	
Bell (electric) *Joseph Henry*	1831	
Betatron *Donald Kerst*	1940	
Bicycle *Kirkpatrick MacMillan*	1839	
Bicycle (spoked wheels) *James Starley*	1870	
Bifocal Lens *Benjamin Franklin*	1780	
Bikini *Louis Reard*	1946	
Boy Scout movement *Sir Robert Baden-Powell*	1907	
Bra (cantilevered) *Robard Howard Hughes*	1943	
Breakfast cereal (ready to eat) *Henry D Perky*	1893	
Bunsen burner *Robert Wilhelm Bunsen*	1855	
Burglar alarm *Edwin T Holmes*	1858	
Cable-car *W Ritter*	1866	
Calculating clock *Wilhelm Schickard*	1623	
Calculus *Leibniz and Newton*	1684	
Canning *Nicholas Appert*	1795	
Car (3 process wheel steam tractor) *Nicolas Cugnot*	1769	
Car (petrol) *Karl Benz*	1888	
Car speedometer *Thorpe and Salter*	1902	
Carbon fibres *Courtaulds*	1964	
Carbon paper *Ralph Wedgewood*	1806	
Carburettor *Gottlieb Daimler*	1876	
Carpet sweeper *Melville R Bissell*	1876	
Cash register *James Ritty*	1879	
Cats' eyes *Percy Shaw*	1933	
Cellophane *Dr Jacques Brandenberger*	1908	
Celluloid *Alexander Parkes*	1861	
Cement (Portland) *Joseph Aspdin*	1824	
Centigrade thermometer *Anders Celsius*	1742	
Chewing gum (commercial) *John Curtis*	1848	
Chocolate (solid) *François-Louis Cailler*	1819	
Christmas card *Sir Henry Cole*	1843	
Chronometer *John Harrison*	1735	

Cinematography *Lumière brothers*	1895	
Circulation of the blood *William Harvey*	1628	
Clock (mechanical) *I-Hsing and Liang-Tsan*	725	
Clock (quartz) *Warren Alvin Marrison*	1929	
Cloud chamber *Charles Thomson Rees Wilson*	1927	
Cluedo *Anthony Pratt*	1948	
Coca-Cola *Dr John Pemberton*	1886	
Coffee (instant) *Nestles*	1937	
Compact disc *Philips and Sony*	1979	
Computer *Charles Babbage*	1835	
Computer (electronic) *Eckert and Mauchly*	1946	
Concrete (reinforced) *François Hennebique*	1892	
Condensed milk *Gail Borden*	1858	
Condom *Gabriel Fallopius*	1560	
Contact lens *Adolph E Fick*	1887	
Contraceptive pill *Dr Gregory Pincus*	1950	
Cordite *Dewar and Abel*	1905	
Corrugated iron *Pierre Carpentier*	1853	
Credit card *Ralph Scheider*	1950	
Crossword puzzle *Arthur Wynne*	1913	
Cyclotron *James Chadwick*	1935	
DDT *Paul Muller*	1939	
Decompression chamber *Robert H Davis*	1929	
Disc brake *Dr F Lanchester*	1902	
Diving suit *Andrew Becker*	1715	
DNA structure *Francis Crick and James Watson*	1953	
Dome (geodesic) *Richard Buckminster Fuller*	1945	
Double-entry bookkeeping *Lucas Paciolus*	1495	
Doughnut (with hole) *Hanson Gregory*	1847	
Drill (electric) *Wilhelm Fein*	1895	
Drill (pneumatic) *Germain Sommelier*	1861	
Dry-cleaning *M Jolly-Bellin*	1849	
Dynamite *Alfred Nobel*	1863	
Dynamo *Hippolyte Pixii*	1832	
Elastic bands *Stephen Perry*	1845	
Electric chair *Harold Brown and EA Kenneally*	1890	
Electric fan *Dr Schuyler Skaats*	1882	
Electric flat iron *HW Seeley*	1882	
Electric generator *Michael Faraday*	1831	
Electric guitar *Rickenbacker, Barth and Beauchamp*	1931	
Electric heating system *Dr W Leigh Burton*	1887	
Electric lamp *Independently invented by Joseph, Swan and Thomas Alva Edison*	1879	
Electric motor (AC) *Nikola Tesla*	1888	
Electric motor (DC) *Zenobe Gramme*	1873	
Electrocardiography *Willem Einthoven*	1903	
Electromagnet *William Sturgeon*	1824	
Electron *JJ Thomas*	1897	
Electronic computer (dedicated) *Alan Turing*	1943	
Electronic computer (general purpose) *Eckert and John Mauchly*	1946	
Electronic computer (commercially available) *Eckert and Mauchly*	1951	
Endoscope *Pierre Segalas*	1827	

Equals sign (mathematics) *Robert Record* 1557
Escalator *Jesse W Reno* 1892
Esperanto *Dr Ludovic Zamenhof* 1887
Exclamation mark *J Day* 1553
Facsimile machine (Fax) *Arthur Korn* 1907
Ferrofluids *Ronald Rosensweig* 1968
Film (Moving outlines) *Louis Le Prince* 1885
Film (Talking) *Engl, Mussolle and Vogt* 1922
Film (Musical sound) *Lee De Forest* 1923
Fingerprint classification *Francis Galton* 1891
Fire extinguisher *M Fuches* 1734
Flying doctor service *KH Vincent Welsh* 1928
Foam rubber *John Boyd Dunlop* 1929
Food processor *Kenneth Wood* 1947
Fountain pen *Lewis Edson Waterman* 1884
Frozen food *Clarence Birdseye* 1930
Galvanometer *André-Marie Ampère* 1834
Gas fire *Philippe Lebon* 1799
Gas lighting *William Murdock* 1792
Gas meter *William Clegg* 1815
Gearbox (automatic) *Hermann Fottinger* 1910
Genetics *Gregor Mendel* 1865
Geodesic dome *Richard Buckminster Fuller* 1945
Gift coupons *Benjamin Talbert Babbit* 1865
Girl Guides *Robert and Agnes Baden-Powell* 1910
Glider *Sir George Cayley* 1853
Golliwog *Florence K Upton* 1895
Gramophone *Thomas Alva Edison* 1878
Gravitation, laws of *Isaac Newton* 1684
Gun cotton *Christian Friedrich Schönbein* 1845
Gyro-compass *Elmer Sperry* 1911
Gyroscope *Leon Foucault* 1852
Half-tone process *Carl Gustaf Wilhelm Carleman* 1871
Hearing aid (electric) *Miller Reese Hutchinson* 1901
Heart (artificial) *Vladimir Demikhov* 1937
Helicopter *Louis and Jacques Breguet* 1907
Holography *Dennis Gabor* 1947
Hovercraft *Christopher Cockerell* 1955
Hydrofoil *Comte de Lambert* 1897
Ice-cream cones *Italo Marcioni* 1896
Identikit *Hugh McDonald* 1959
Insulin *Frederick Grant Banting and Charles Herbert Best* 1921
Intelligence test (IQ) *Alfred Binet* 1896
Iron Lung *Philip Drinker* 1927
Jeans *Levi Strauss* 1850
Jet engine *Sir Frank Whittle* 1937
Jigsaw puzzle *John Spilsbury* 1767
Jukebox (pre-selective) *John C Dunton* 1905
Kaleidoscope *Sir David Brewster* 1816
Knitting machine *William Lee* 1589
Laser *Theodore Maiman* 1960
Lathe, screw-cutting *Henry Maudslay* 1800
Launderette *JF Cantrell* 1934
Lawn mower *Edwin Budding and John Ferrabee* 1830
Lie detector *John Larson* 1928
Lift (mechanical) *Elisha G Otis* 1852
Lightning conductor *Benjamin Franklin* 1752
Linoleum *Frederick Walton* 1860
Lithography *Aloys Senefelder* 1796
Locomotive *Richard Trevithick* 1804
Logarithms *John Napier* 1614

Loom, power *Edmund Cartwright* 1785
Loudspeaker *Horace Short* 1898
Loudspeaker (electric) *Miller Reece Hutchinson* 1906
Machine gun *James Puckle* 1718
Margarine *Hippolyte Mège-Mouriés* 1869
Maser *Charles H Townes* 1953
Match *Robert Boyle* 1680
Match (friction) *John Walker* 1826
Match (safety) *JE Lundstrom* 1855
Metronome *Dietrich Nikolaus Winkel* c1800
Microchip *Jack Saint Clair Kilby* 1958
Microphone *Alexander Graham Bell* 1876
Micro-processor *Moore and Hoff Noyce* 1971
Microscope *Zacharias Janssen* 1590
Microscope (electron) *EAF Ruska* 1933
Microwave oven *Percy Spencer* 1945
Miner's safety lamp *Sir Humphry Davy* 1816
Missile (air-to-air) *Herbert Wagner* 1943
Monopoly *Charles Darrow* 1931
Motor cycle *Gottlieb Daimler* 1885
Neon lamp *Georges Claude* 1910
Neptune (planet) *Johann Gottfried Galle* 1846
Neutron *James Chadwick* 1935
Non-stick pan *Marc Gregoir* 1954
Nylon *Wallace Carothers* 1937
Optical fibres *Navinder Kapany* 1955
Oven (electric) *Bernina Hotel, Switzerland* 1889
Ozone *Christian Friedrich Schönbein* 1840
Pacemaker (implantable) *Wilson Greatbach* 1956
Paint (acrylic) *Reeves Ltd* 1964
Paint (fluorescent) *Joe and Bob Switzer* 1933
Paper *Tsai Lun* 105
Paper (from wood pulp) *Gottlob Keller* 1844
Paper clip *Johann Vaaler* 1900
Parachute *Jean-Pierre Blanchard* 1785
Parachute (patent) *André-Jacques Garnerin* 1802
Parking meter *Carlton Magee* 1935
Pasteurisation *Louis Pasteur* 1863
Pen (ball-point) *Laszlo Biro* 1938
Pen (fountain) *Lewis Waterman* 1884
Pencil (using pulverised graphite lead) *Nicolas Jacques Conté* 1795
Pendulum clock *Christiaan Huygens* 1656
Penicillin *Sir Alexander Fleming* 1928
Periodic table *Dmitri Mendelev* 1866
Photoelectric cell *Johann Phillip Elster and Hans F Geitel* 1896
Photographic lens *William H Wollaston* 1812
Photography (on pewter plate) *Joseph Nicéphore Niepce* 1826
Photography (on paper) *William Henry Fox Talbot* 1835
Photography (colour) *James Clerk Maxwell* 1861
Photography (on film) *John Carbutt* 1888
Pianoforte *Bartolomeo Cristofori* 1709
Pillar box (UK) *Anthony Trollope* 1851
Plastics *Alexander Parkes* 1852
Pluto (planet) *Clyde Tombaugh* 1930
Plutonium *GT Seaborg, JW Kennedy and AC Wahl* 1940
Pneumatic bicycle tyres *John Boyd Dunlop* 1887
Pneumatic tyres *RW Thompson.* 1845
Pocket calculator *Kilby, Tassell and Merryman* 1972
Polio vaccine (injection) *Jonas Salk* 1952

FAMOUS PEOPLE

Polio vaccine (oral)	Albert Sabin	1957	Stereotype	William Ged	1725
Polythene	RO Gibson	1933	Stethoscope	René Laennec	1816
Potato crisps	George Crum	1853	Stopwatch	Jean Moyse	1776
Pressure cooker	Denis Papin	1679	Submarine	Cornelius Jacobszoon Drebbel	1624
Printing press (wooden)	Johann Gutenberg	1455	Sun-tan cream	Eugene Schueller	1936
Printing (rotary)	Richard Hoe	1846	Syringe (hypodermic)	Charles Gabriel Pravaz	1835
Propeller (boat, hand-operated)	David Bushnell	1775	Table tennis	James Gibb	1890
Propeller (ship)	Francis Smith	1837	Tampon	Earl Hass	1830
Propeller (ship), patent	Isambard Kingdom Brunel	1844	Tank	Ernest Swinton	1914
Proton	Ernest Rutherford	1920	Tape Recorder	Louis Blattner	1929
Pyramid	Imhotep	2650BC	Telegraph (electric)	George Louis Lesage	1774
Radar (application)	Taylor and Young	1930	Telegraph	M Lammond	1787
Radar (theory)	Nikola Tesla	1900	Telegraph code	Samuel Morse	1837
Radar (UK)	Robert Watson-Watt	1935	Telephone	Antonio Meucci	1849
Radio telegraphy	Mahlon Loomis	1864	Telephone (patent)	Alexander Graham Bell	1876
Radio telegraphy (transatlantic)	Guglielmo Marconi	1901	Telephone switchboard	Almon B Strowger	1889
Radioactivity	Henri Becquerel	1896	Telescope (refractor)	Hans Lippershey	1608
Rails (iron)	Abraham Darby	1738	Television (mechanical)	John Logie Baird	1926
Railway airbrake	George Westinghouse	1863	Tennis	Walter G Wingfield	1873
Railway (electric)	Ernst Siemens	1878	Terylene	JR Whinfield and JT Dickson	1941
Railway (underground)	Charles Pearson	1843	Thermometer	Galileo Galilei	1593
Rayon	Joseph Swan	1883	Thermometer (mercury)	Gabriel Fahrenheit	1714
Razor (safety)	King Camp Gillette	1895	Thimble	Nicolas Van Benschoten	1684
Razor (electric)	Jacob Schick	1931	Toothbrush	William Addis	1649
Record (flat disc)	Emil Berliner	1888	Top hat	John Hetherington	1797
Record (LP)	Peter Goldmark	1948	Torpedo (UK)	Robert Whitehead	1866
Refrigerator	James Harrison and Alexander Catlin Twinning	1850	Traffic lights	JP Knight	1868
Revolver	Samuel Colt	1835	Traffic lights (automatic)	Alfred Benesch	1914
Rickshaw	Jonathan Scobie	1869	Transformer	Michael Faraday	1831
Roller Skates	Joseph Merlin	1760	Transistor	John Bardeen, William Bradley Shockley and Walter Brattain	1948
Roulette Wheel	Blaise Pascal	1647	Travel agency	Thomas Cook	1841
Rubber (latex foam)	Dunlop Rubber Co	1928	Travellers cheques	Robert Herries	1772
Rubber (tyres)	Thomas Hancock	1846	Travellers cheques (commercial) American Express		1891
Rubber (vulcanised)	Charles Goodyear	1841	Tubercle bacillus	Robert Koch	1882
Rubber (waterproof)	Charles Macintosh	1823	Tuning fork	John Shore	1711
Rubik cube	Erno Rubik	1975	Turbojet	Frank Whittle	1928
Safety pin	Walter Hunt	1849	Typewriter	Pellegrine Tarri	1808
Scooter	Walter Lines	1897	Typewriter (patent)	William Burt	1829
Scotch tape	Richard Drew	1930	Typewriter (mass production)	Christopher Sholes	1874
Scrabble	James Brunot	1950	Ultrasonography (obstetric)	Ian Donald	1979
Sealing wax	Gerard Hermann	1554	Uranus	William Herschel	1781
Seismographic scale	Charles Francis Richter	1935	Vaccination	Edward Jenner	1770
Self-starter motor (UK)	Charles F Kettering	1911	Vacuum cleaner (electric)	Hubert Cecil Booth	1901
Sewing machine	Thomas Saint	1790	Vacuum cleaner (steam)	Ives McGaffrey	1871
Shorthand	Marcus Tullius Tiro	63BC	Vacuum flask	James Dewar	1892
Shorthand (modern world)	Timothy Bright	1588	Vending machine	Percival Everitt	1883
Skyscraper	William Le Baron Jenny	1882	Ventilator	Théophile Guibal	1858
Slide rule	William Oughtred	1621	Video recorder	Ampex Co	1956
Snooker	Sir Neville Chamberlain	1875	Videophone	American Telegraph and Telephone Co	1927
Spectacles	Salvino degli Armati and Alessandro delle Spina	c1280	Vulcanised rubber	Charles Goodyear	1839
Spinning frame	Richard Arkwright	1769	Washing machine (electric)	Hurley Machine Co	1907
Spinning jenny	James Hargreaves	1764	Watch	Bartholomew Manfredi	1462
Spinning mule	Samuel Crompton	1779	Watch (waterproof)	Rolex	1927
Spirit level	JM Thévenot	1666	Water closet	Sir John Harington	1589
Stamp (perforations)	Henry Archer	1854	Welder (electric)	Elisha Thomson	1877
Stapler	Charles Henry Gould	1868	Wheel	Mesopotamians	c3500BC
Steam engine	Thomas Savery	1698	White road markings	Edward Norris Hines	1911
Steam engine (condenser)	James Watt	1765	Wire recorder (mechanical)	Valdemar Poulsen	1898
Steam engine (piston)	Thomas Newcomen	1712	Xerox copier	Chester Carlson	1938
Steamship	JC Perier	1775	X-ray	Wilhelm Konrad Röntgen	1895
Steamturbine (ship's)	Charles Parsons	1894	Zip fastener	Whitcomb L Judson	1891
Steel production	Henry Bessemer	1855			
Steel (stainless)	Harry Brearley	1913			

Marriages: By Female Spouse

Diahnne Abbott	Actress	Robert De Niro	Actor
Paula Abdul (2)	Singer	Emilio Estevez	Actor
Victoria Adams	Spice girl	David Beckham	Footballer
Princess Adelaide of Saxe-Coburg Meiningen	German noblewoman	William IV	British king
Agrippina	Roman noblewomen	Claudius	Roman emperor
Pauline de Ahna	Soprano	Richard Strauss	Composer
Anouk Aimée (2)	Actress	Albert Finney (5)	Actor
Aisha	Muhammad's favourite wife	Muhammad	Founder of Islam
Maria Aitken	Actress	Nigel Davenport	Actor
Nadiya Aja (2)	Saudi tycoon's daughter	Omar Sharif	Actor and bridge player
Kitty Aldridge	Actress	Mark Knopfler	Musician
Princess Alexandra of Schlesung-Holstein-Sorderburg	Danish princess	Edward VII	British king
Princess Alexandra	British princess	Angus Ogilvy	Businessman
Alison Allen	TV producer	Keith Allen	Actor
Catherine Allen	Secretary	Frankie Dettori	Jockey
Gracie Allen	Comedienne	George Burns	Comedian and actor
Lorraine Allen (2)	Singer	Xavier Cugat	Band leader
June Allyson (2)	Actress	Dick Powell	Actor
Amphitrite	Greek mythical sea nymph	Poseidon	Greek god of the Sea
Debra Anderson (1)	Childhood sweetheart	Sean Bean	Actor
Loni Anderson (2)	Actress	Burt Reynolds (3)	Actor
Pamela Anderson (3)	Actress	Tommy Lee	Singer
Nina Andreevskaya	Moscow socialite	Wassily Kandinsky	Russian artist
Ursula Andress (1)	Actress	John Derek	Actor and director
Julie Andrews	Actress/singer	Blake Edwards (2)	Film director
Marie Angel	Australian soprano	David Freeman	Opera director
Jennifer Aniston	Actress	Brad Pitt	Actor
Princess Anne	British princess	Mark Phillips (1)	Equestrian rider
		Tim Laurence (2)	Naval Officer
Princess Anne	Danish princess	James I	British king
Anne of Bohemia (1)	Emperor Charles IV's daughter	Richard II	English king
Queen Anne	British queen	George of Denmark	Danish Prince
Marie Antoinette	French princess	Louis XVI	King of France
Aphrodite	Greek goddess of Love	Hephaestus	Greek god of fire
Frances Appleton	Socialite	Henry W Longfellow	US poet
Natalie Appleton	Pop singer	Liam Howlett	Musician
Ariadne	Mythical daughter of King Minos of Crete	Dionysus	Greek god of wine
Jean Armour	Socialite	Robert Burns	Poet
Patricia Arquette	Actress	Nicholas Cage	Actor
Debbie Ash (1)	Actress	Eddie Kidd	Stunt motorcyclist
Leslie Ash	Actress	Lee Chapman	Footballer
Jane Asher	Cook	Gerald Scarfe	Cartoonist
Edwina Ashley	Heiress and charity worker	Louis Mountbatten	Naval commander
Elizabeth Ashley	Actress	James Farentino (1)	Actor
		George Peppard (2)	Actor
Atalanta	Mythical Greek huntress	Milanion	Mythical Greek athlete
Rosalind Ayres	Actress	Martin Jarvis	Actor
Lauren Bacall	Actress	Humphrey Bogart (1)	Actor
		Jason Robards (2)	Actor
Barbara Bach (2)	Actress	Ringo Starr	Musician
Maria Barbara Bach (1)	Cousin of JS Bach	JS Bach	Composer
Enid Bagnold	Author	Sir G Roderick Jones	MD of Reuters
Lilian Bailey	American soprano	George Henschel	Baritone
Barbara Bain	Actress	Martin Landau	Actor
Shakira Baksh (2)	Actress and model	Sir Michael Caine	Actor
Jill Balcon	Actress	Cecil Day-Lewis	Poet
Caroline Balestier	Publishing heiress	Rudyard Kipling	Novelist and poet
Lucille Ball	Comedienne and actress	Desi Arnaz	Musician and actor
Zoe Ball	TV presenter	Norman Cook	Musician
Rose Bampton	Soprano	Wilfred Pelletier	Conductor
Anne Bancroft	Actress	Mel Brooks	Actor/producer
Glynis Barber	Actress	Michael Brandon (2)	Actor
Emma Bardac (2)	Socialite	Claude Debussy	Composer

Brigitte Bardot (1)	Actress	Roger Vadim	Film director
Margherita Barezzi (1)	Daughter of Verdi's sponsor	Giuseppe Verdi	Composer
Ellen Barkin	Actress	Gabriel Byrne	Actor
Nora Barnacle	Socialite	James Joyce	Irish writer
Pinkie Barnes	Table tennis international	Sam Kydd	Actor
Roseanne Barr	Actress	Tom Arnold (2)	Actor
	Actress	Ben Thomas (3)	Actor
Elizabeth Barrett	Poet	Robert Browning	Poet
Kim Basinger	Actress	Alec Baldwin (2)	Actor
Elizabeth Batts	Captain's wife	James Cook	Seaman and explorer
Stephanie Beacham	Actress	John McEnery	Actor
Priscilla Beaulieu	Actress	Elvis Presley	Singer
Mary Hayley Bell	Playwright	John Mills	Actor
Annette Bening	Actress	Warren Beatty	Actor
Jill Bennett	Actress	John Osborne (1)	Playwright
		Willis Hall (2)	
Veronica Bennett	Singer	Phil Spector	Record producer
Berengaria	Princess of Navarre	Richard 1	English king
Candice Bergen (3)	Actress	Louis Malle	Director
Ingrid Bergman (2)	Actress	Roberto Rossellini (2)	Director
Joy Beverley	Singer	Billy Wright	Footballer
Anne Birley (3)	Lady Annabel Vane-Tempest Stewart	James Goldsmith	Tycoon
Blanche of Lancaster (1)	English noblewoman	John of Gaunt	English prince
Melanie Blatt	Pop singer	Stuart Zender	Musician
Renate Blauel	Actress	Elton John	Vocalist and composer
Joan Blondell	Actress	Dick Powell (1)	Actor
		Mike Todd (2)	Showman and film producer
Claire Bloom	Actress	Rod Steiger (1)	Actor
		Philip Roth (3)	Novelist
Maureen Blott (2)	Actress	Harry H Corbett	Actor
Jean Boht	Actress	Carl Davis	Composer
Cherie Booth	Barrister	Tony Blair	Politician
Connie Booth	Actress	John Cleese	Actor
Catherine Boucher	Illiterate pauper	William Blake	Poet and painter
Boudicca	Queen of Iceni	Prasutagus	King of Iceni
Margaret Bourke-White	Photo-journalist	Erskine Caldwell	US author
Jacqueline Bouvier	Socialite	John F Kennedy (1)	US president
Elizabeth Bowen	Irish novelist	Alan Charles Cameron	Businessman
Marjory Bowes (1)	John Knox's 1st wife	John Knox	Religious reformer
Patti Boyd	Model	George Harrison (1)	Musician
		Eric Clapton (2)	Musician
Elizabeth Boyle	Socialite	Edmund Spenser	English poet
Philippa Braithewaite (2)	TV Producer	Martin Clunes	Actor
Sarah Brightman (2)	Singer	Andrew Lloyd Webber (2)	Composer
Cosima Von Bülow	Franz Liszt's daughter	Hans von Bülow (1)	Conductor
Christie Brinkley (2)	Model	Billy Joel (2)	Singer
May Britt	Actress	Sammy Davis Jnr	Entertainer
Vera May Brittain	Writer	George Catlin	Professor of politics
Charlotte Brontë	Writer	Arthur Bell Nicholls	Curate
Janet Brown	Impressionist	Peter Butterworth	Actor
Melanie Brown	Spice girl	Jimmy Gulzar	Musician
Coral Browne	Actress	Vincent Price	Actor
Jill Browne	Actress	John Alderton (1)	Actor
		Brian Wolfe (2)	Theatre producer
Anna Brueghel	Daughter of Jan Brueghel	David Teniers the Younger	Flemish painter
Sheila Buckley	Secretary	John Stonehouse	Politician
Cosima von Bülow (2)	Franz Liszt's daughter	Richard Wagner	Composer
Fanny Burney	English novelist	General D'Arblay	French émigré
Margaret Burr	Daughter of 4th Duke of Beaufort	Thomas Gainsborough	English painter
Irene Busch	Musician	Rudolf Serkin	Pianist
Penny Calvert	Dancer	Bruce Forsyth (1)	Entertainer
		Peter Murray Hill (2)	Actor and bookseller
Dyan Cannon (4)	Actress	Cary Grant	Actor
Sarah Caplin	TV executive	Nick Ross	Broadcaster
Kate Capshaw (2)	Actress	Steven Spielberg (2)	Director
Mariah Carey	Singer	Tommy Mottola	President of Sony Music
Judy Carne	Actress	Burt Reynolds	Actor
Caroline of Ansbach	German noblewoman	George II	British king
Caroline of Brunswick	German noblewoman	George IV	British king

Caroline of Monaco	Princess	*Pierre Junot (1)*	*Businessman*
		Stefano Casiraghi (2)	*Businessman*
		Prince Ernst August (3)	*Hanoverian Prince*
Leslie Caron	Actress	*Peter Hall*	*Theatre director*
Theresa Carreño (1)	Pianist	*Eugène D'Albert*	*Composer and pianist*
June Carter	Singer	*Johnny Cash*	*Singer*
Martita Casals	Pablo Casals' widow	*Eugene Istomin*	*Pianist*
Carmen Castillo (1)	Singer	*Xavier Cugat*	*Bandleader*
Phoebe Cates	Actress	*Kevin Kline*	*Actor*
Princess Catherine	Valois princess	*Owen Tudor (1)*	*Grandfather of Henry V11*
Catherine I	Russian empress	*Peter the Great (2)*	*Russian Tsar*
Catherine II (the Great)	Russian empress	*Peter III*	*Russian Tsar*
Catherine de-Medici	Queen of France	*Henry II*	*French king*
Catherine of Braganza	Portuguese princess	*Charles II*	*English king*
Catherine of Valois	French princess	*Henry V (2)*	*English king*
Anna Cermakova	Socialite	*Antonin Dvorák*	*Composer*
Alice Charigot	Socialite	*Pierre-Auguste Renoir*	*French painter*
Charlotte Sophia	German noblewoman	*George III*	*British king*
Charlotte Charpentier	Daughter of French émigré	*Walter Scott*	*Scottish novelist*
Cher	Actress/Singer	*Sonny Bono (1)*	*Actor and politician*
		Greg Allmann (2)	*Musician*
Helen Cherry	Actress	*Trevor Howard*	*Actor*
Chiang Ching (3)	Actress	*Mao Zedong*	*Chinese leader*
Agatha Christie	Writer	*Max Mallowan*	*Archaeologist*
Diane Cilento (1)	Actress	*Sean Connery*	*Actor*
Cleopatra VII	Queen of Egypt	*Ptolemy XIII (1)*	*Egyptian Ruler*
		Mark Antony (2) ?	*Roman General*
Rosemary Clooney	Singer	*José Ferrer*	*Actor*
Clotilda	Queen of the Franks	*Clovis I*	*King of the Franks*
Clytemnestra	Mythical Queen of Mycenae	*Agamemnon*	*Mythical King of Mycenae*
Isabella Colbran (1)	Spanish soprano	*Gioacchino Rossini*	*Composer*
Venetia Collett-Barrett (1)	Actress	*Edward Woodward*	*Actor*
Joan Collins (1)	Actress	*Anthony Newley (1)*	*Actor and singer*
Pauline Collins (2)	Actress	*John Alderton*	*Actor*
Jane Colt (1)	Farmer's daughter	*Thomas More*	*Chancellor of England*
Shirley Conran	Authoress	*Terence Conran*	*Businessman*
Constance of Castile (2)	Castilian princess	*John of Gaunt*	*English prince*
Sarah Cook	Schoolgirl (13 when married)	*Musa Komeagac*	*Turkish waiter*
Rita Coolidge (2)	Singer	*Kris Kristofferson*	*Actor*
Dolores Costello	Actress	*John Barrymore*	*Actor*
Cicely Courtneidge	Actress	*Jack Hulbert*	*Actor*
Courtney Cox	Actress	*David Arquette*	*Actor*
Maureen Cox (1)	Childhood sweetheart	*Ringo Starr*	*Musician*
Charlotte Mary Craddock (1)	Socialite	*Henry Fielding*	*English novelist*
Jill Craigie	TV scriptwriter and author	*Michael Foot*	*Politician*
Gemma Craven (1)	Actress	*Frazer Hines*	*Actor*
Cindy Crawford	Supermodel	*Richard Gere*	*Actor*
Joan Crawford	Actress	*Douglas Fairbanks Jnr (2)*	*Actor*
Creusa	Mythical Roman character	*Aeneas*	*Mythical Trojan prince*
Cristina	Spanish Infanta	*Inaki Vrdangarin*	*Handball player*
Abigail Cruttenden (3)	Actress	*Sean Bean*	*Actor*
Cynthia Curzon (1)	English noblewoman	*Oswald Mosley*	*Politician*
Sinead Cusack	Actress	*Jeremy Irons*	*Actor*
Martha Custis	Socialite	*George Washington*	*President of USA*
Sasha Czack (1)	Theatre usher	*Sylvester Stallone*	*Actor*
Lili Damita (1)	Socialite	*Errol Flynn*	*Actor*
Bebe Daniels	Radio comedienne	*Ben Lyon*	*Radio comedian*
Mary Daniel (2)	Maid	*Henry Fielding*	*English novelist*
Blythe Danner	Actress	*Bruce Paltrow*	*Director*
Joy Davidman	Poet	*CS Lewis*	*Author*
Geena Davis	Actress	*Renny Harlin (1)*	*Film director*
		Jeff Goldblum (2)	*Actor*
Nancy Davis (2)	Actress	*Ronald Reagan*	*US president*
Sharron Davis	Swimmer	*Derek Redmond*	*Athlete*
Isabel Dean	Actress	*William Fairchild*	*Playwright*
Sandra Dee	Actress	*Bobby Darin*	*Singer*
Judi Dench	Actress	*Michael Williams*	*Actor*
Catherine Deneuve (2)	Actress	*David Bailey*	*Photographer*
Bo Derek (3)	Actress	*John Derek*	*Actor and director*
Donna D'Errico	'Baywatch' actress	*Nikki Sixx*	*Motley Crue guitarist*
Félicité Desmousseaux	Actress	*César Franck*	*Composer*

Colleen Dewhurst	Socialite	*George C Scott*	*Actor*
Angie Dickinson (2)	Actress	*Burt Bacharach (2)*	*Composer*
Sandra Dickinson	Actress	*Peter Davison*	*Actor*
Marlene Dietrich	Actress	*Rudolf Seiber (1)*	*Production assistant*
Kitty Dobbs	Niece of Beatrice Webb	*Malcolm Muggeridge*	*Journalist*
Hilda Doolittle	US poet	*Richard Aldington*	*Poet and novelist*
Diana Dors	Actress	*Alan Lake (3)*	*Actor*
		Dickie Dawson (2)	*US comedian*
Michele Dotrice (2)	Actress	*Edward Woodward*	*Actor*
Angela Douglas	Irish actress	*Kenneth More*	*Actor*
Lesley-Anne Down (2)	Actress	*William Friedkin (1)*	*Film director*
Margaret Drabble	Novelist	*Clive Swift (1)*	*Author*
		Michael Holroyd (2)	*Biographer*
Isadora Duncan (1)	Dancer	*Sergei Yessenin*	*Poet*
Jacqueline Du Pré	Cellist	*Daniel Barenboim*	*Pianist*
Otilie Dvorák	Daughter of Antonin Dvorák	*Josef Suk*	*Violinist*
Linda Eastman	Photographer	*Paul McCartney (2)*	*Musician*
Nora Eddington (3)	Actress	*Errol Flynn*	*Actor*
Martha Eggerth	Soprano	*Jan Kiepura*	*Tenor*
Anita Ekberg	Actress	*Anthony Steele*	*Actor*
Britt Ekland	Actress	*Peter Sellers (1)*	*Actor*
		Slim Jim Phantom McDonnell (2)	*Musician*
Eleanor of Aquitaine	French noblewoman	*Louis VII (1)*	*French king*
		Henry II	*English king*
Eleanor of Castile	Castilian princess	*Edward I*	*English king*
Eleanor of Provence	French noblewoman	*Henry III*	*English king*
George Eliot	Authoress	*John Walter Cross*	*Banker*
Elizabeth Bowes-Lyon	Earl of Strathmore's daughter	*George VI*	*British king*
Elizabeth of York	English princess	*Henry VII*	*English King*
Elizabeth Woodville	English noblewoman	*Edward IV*	*English King*
Jill Esmond (1)	Actress	*Laurence Olivier*	*Actor*
Eudoxia	Russian noblewoman	*Peter the Great (1)*	*Russian Tsar*
Dale Evans	Actress and singer	*Roy Rogers*	*Actor and singer*
Linda Evans (2)	Actress	*John Derek*	*Actor and director*
Chris Evert	Tennis player	*John Lloyd (1)*	*Tennis player*
Siobhan Fahey	Singer	*Dave Stewart*	*Musician*
Mia Farrow	Actress	*Frank Sinatra (1)*	*Singer*
		André Previn (2)	*Conductor*
Farrah Fawcett (2)	Actress	*Lee Majors (1)*	*Actor*
		Ryan O'Neal (2)	*Actor*
Gracie Fields	Singer	*Monty Banks*	*Film director*
Judy Finnegan	TV presenter	*Richard Madeley*	*TV presenter*
Carina Fitzalan-Howard (2)	Noblewoman	*David Frost*	*Broadcaster*
Carrie Fisher (2)	Actress	*Paul Simon*	*Singer and composer*
Jennifer Flavin (3)	Model	*Sylvester Stallone*	*Actor*
Jane Fonda	Actress	*Roger Vadim (1)*	*Film director*
		Tom Hayden (2)	*Politician*
	Politician	*Ted Turner (3)*	*Media Mogul*
Anna Ford	Broadcaster	*Mark Boxer*	*Cartoonist and journalist*
Margaret Forster	Author	*Hunter Davies*	*Author*
Helen Frankenthaler	US artist	*Robert Motherwell*	*US artist*
Lady Antonia Fraser (2)	Authoress	*Harold Pinter*	*Playwright*
Lynne Frederick	Actress	*Peter Sellers (1)*	*Actor*
		David Frost (2)	*Broadcaster*
Dido Freire (2)	Brazilian film-maker's daughter	*Jean Renoir*	*Film director*
Dawn French	Comedienne	*Lenny Henry*	*Comedian*
Valerie French	Actress	*Michael Pertwee*	*Actor*
Agnes Frey	Merchant's daughter	*Albrecht Dürer*	*German painter*
Edith Fricker	Socialite	*Robert Southey*	*Poet*
Sarah Fricker	Socialite	*Samuel Taylor Coleridge*	*Poet*
Sadie Frost	Actress	*Gary Kemp (1)*	*Actor and musician*
		Jude Law (2)	*Actor*
Fiona Fullerton (1)	Actress	*Simon MacCorkindale*	*Actor*
Magda Gabor (4)	Actress	*George Sanders (3)*	*Actor*
Zsa Zsa Gabor	Actress	*Conrad Hilton (2)*	*Businessman*
		George Sanders (3)	*Actor*
Myte Garcia	Belly dancer	*Prince (Symbol)*	*Singer*
Ava Gardner (2)	Actress	*Mickey Rooney (1)*	*Actor*
		Artie Shaw (2)	*Bandleader*
		Frank Sinatra (3)	*Singer*

Judy Garland	Actress	Vincente Minnelli (2)	Film director
		Sid Luft (3)	Entertainer
Jill Gascoigne (1)	Actress	Alfred Molina (2)	Actor
Sarah Michelle Gellar	Actress	Freddie Prinze Jnr	Actor
Elvira Gemignani	Socialite	Giacomo Puccini	Composer
Susan George (2)	Actress	Simon MacCorkindale	Actor
Robin Givens (1)	Actress	Mike Tyson (2)	Boxer
Alma Gluck	Soprano	Efrem Zimbalist	Violinist
Liza Goddard	Actress	Colin Baker (1)	Actor
		Alvin Stardust (3)	Pop singer
Paulette Goddard (3)	Actress	Charlie Chaplin (2)	Actor
		Burgess Meredith (3)	Actor
		Erich Maria Remarque (4)	Author
Lady Godiva	Countess of Mercia	Leofric	Earl of Mercia
Beatrix Godwin	Widow of EW Godwin (architect)	James McNeill Whistler	Artist
Mary Godwin	Writer	Percy Bysshe Shelley	Poet
Jane Goldman	Writer	Jonathan Ross	TV presenter
Stephanie Goldner	Harpist	Eugene Ormandy	Conductor
Jemima Goldsmith	Heiress	Imran Khan	Cricketer
Betty Grable	Actress	Jackie Coogan (1)	Actor
		Harry James (2)	Musician
Dulcie Gray	Actress	Michael Denison	Actor
Effie Gray	Artist	John Ruskin (1)	Art Critic
		John Everett Millais (2)	Artist
Elspet Gray	Actress	Brian Rix	Actor
Alex Greaves	Jockey	David Nicholls	Horseracing trainer
Sarah Greene	TV presenter	Mike Smith	TV presenter
Debbie Greenwood	TV presenter (former Miss UK)	Paul Coia	TV presenter
Lady Jane Grey	English noblewoman	Lord Guildford Dudley	English nobleman
Lita Grey (2)	Actress	Charlie Chaplin	Actor
Melanie Griffith	Actress	Don Johnson (1) + (3)	Actor
		Antonio Banderas (4)	Actor
Tammie Grimes	Actress	Christopher Plummer	Actor
Diana Guinness (2)	Nancy Mitford's sister	Oswald Mosley	Politician
Nina Hagerup	Singer (Grieg's Cousin)	Edvard Grieg	Composer
Geneviève Halévy	Composer's daughter	Georges Bizet	Composer
Faten Hamama (1)	Actress	Omar Sharif	Actor and bridge player
Alana Hamilton (1)	Model	Rod Stewart (2)	Singer
Sheila Hancock	Actress	John Thaw (2)	Actor
Sue Hanson	Actress	Carl Wayne	Actor and Singer
Harriet Harman	British politician	Jack Dromey	Trade unionist
Harmonia	Mythical daughter of Ares and Aphrodite	Cadmus	Mythical founder of Thebes
Mildred Harris (1)	Actress	Charlie Chaplin	Actor
Deborah Harry (common law)	Singer	Chris Stein (common law)	Guitarist
Teri Hatcher	Actress	Jon Tenney	Actor
Ann Hathaway	Farmer's daughter	William Shakespeare	Playwright
June Haver	Actress	Fred MacMurray	Actor
Jacquetta Hawkes	Archaeologist	JB Priestley	Author
Goldie Hawn	Actress	Kurt Russell	Actor
Anne Hayes (1)	Housewife	Peter Sellers	Actor
Rita Hayworth	Actress	Orson Welles (2)	Actor and director
		Aly Khan (3)	Middle Eastern prince
Patty Hearst	Heiress	Bernard Shaw	Bodyguard
Lillian Hellman	Playwright	Dashiell Hammett	Author
Heloise	Abelard's wife	Peter Abelard	French philosopher
Marie Helvin (3)	Model	David Bailey	Photographer
Anouska Hempel	Actress	Mark Weinberg	Businessman
Henrietta Maria	French princess	Charles I	British king
Audrey Hepburn	Actress	Mel Ferrer	Actor
Barbara Hepworth	Sculptor	John Skeaping (1)	Sculptor
		Ben Nicholson (2)	Artist
Hera (3)	Sister of Zeus	Zeus	Greek supreme god
Lady Herries	Racehorse trainer	Colin Cowdrey	Cricketer
Irene Hervey	Actress	Allan Jones	Singer and actor
Eva Herzigova	Model	Tico Torres	Pop musician (Bon Jovi)
Andrée Heurschling (1)	Artist's model	Jean Renoir	Film director
Hildegarde	Queen of the Franks	Charlemagne	King of the Franks
Faith Hill	Country singer	Tim McGraw	Country singer

Melanie Hill (2)	Actress ('Bread')	Sean Bean	Actor
Tracy Hilton	Housewife	Jim Davidson	Comedian
Gill Hinchcliffe	TV Production assistant	David Jason	Actor
Liz Hobbs (2)	Waterskier	Frazer Hines	Actor
Valerie Hobson	Actress and dancer	John Profumo (2)	Politician
Chaatal Hochuli (1)	Swiss Heiress	Ernst August	Prince of Hanover
Catherine Hogarth	Newspaper magnate's daughter	Charles Dickens	Author
Alison Holloway	Presenter	Jim Davidson	Comedian
Lauren Holly	Actress	Jim Carrey	Actor
Marilyn Horne	Mezzo-soprano	Henry Lewis	Conductor
Whitney Houston	Singer	Bobby Brown	Singer
Elizabeth Jane Howard	Novelist	Kingsley Amis	Novelist and poet
Clementine Hozier	Charity worker	Winston Churchill	Politician
Mabel Hubbard	Deaf student	Alexander Graham Bell	Inventor
Benita Hume	Actress	Ronald Culman (1)	Actor
		George Sanders (2)	Actor
Kirsty Hume	Model	Donovan Leitch	Actor
Gayle Hunnicut	Actress	David Hemmings	Actor
Rachel Hunter (2)	Model	Rod Stewart	Singer
Anjelica Huston	Actress and director	Robert Graham	Sculptor
Mary Hutchinson	Socialite	William Wordsworth	Poet
Barbara Hutton (2)	Actress	Cary Grant	Actor
Judy Huxtable (2)	Actress	Peter Cook	Comedian and writer
Anne Hyde (1)	Daughter of Earl of Clarendon	James II	English King
Georgie Hyde-Lees	Socialite	WB Yeats	Poet
Ildico	Consort of Attila	Attila the Hun	Hunnish ruler
Iman	Model	David Bowie (2)	Singer/composer
Jill Ireland	Actress	David McCallum (1)	Actor
		Charles Bronson (2)	Actor
Isabella	Daughter of Philip IV of France	Edward II	English king
Isabella of Angoulême (2)	French noblewoman	John	King of England
Isabelle (2)	Daughter of Charles VI of France	Richard II	English king
Hattie Jacques	Actress	John Le Mesurier	Actor
Storm Jameson	Novelist	Guy Chapman (2)	Historian
Susan Jameson	Actress	James Bolam	Actor
Samantha Janus	Actress	Mauro Mantovani	Actor
Aino Järnefelt	General's daughter	Jean Sibelius	Composer
Zizi Jeanmaire	Dancer	Roland Petit	Choreographer
Cécile Jeanrenaud	Clergyman's daughter	Felix Mendelssohn	Composer
Ffion Jenkins	Ex-civil servant	William Hague	Politician
Jenny Jerome	Daughter of NY businessman	Lord Randolph Churchill	Politician
Jezebel	Queen of Israel	Ahab	King of Israel
Amy Johnson	Aviator	Jim Mollison	Aviator
Angelina Jolie	Actress	Johnny Lee Miller (1)	Actor
		Billy Bob Thornton (2)	Actor
Jennifer Jones	Actress	Robert Walker (1)	Actor
		David O'Selznick (2)	Director
Joséphine de Beauharnais	French noblewoman	Napoleon I	French emperor
Yootha Joyce	Actress	Glyn Edwards	Actor
Angelica Kauffmann	Swiss painter	Antonio Zucchi	Venetian painter
Ruby Keeler	Actress	Al Jolson	Entertainer
Maria Anna Keller	Hairdresser's daughter	Franz Joseph Haydn	Composer
Barbara Kelly	Actress and presenter	Bernard Braden	Actor and presenter
Margaret Kempson (1)	Housewife	Denis Thatcher	Businessman
Rachel Kempson	Actress	Michael Redgrave	Actor
Kay Kendall (3)	Actress	Rex Harrison	Actor
Suzy Kendall (1)	Actress	Dudley Moore	Entertainer
Cherly Kennedy	Actress	Tom Courtenay	Actor
Jacqueline Kennedy	Socialite	Aristotle Onassis (2)	Businessman
Patsy Kensit	Actress	Jim Kerr (2)	Musician
		Liam Gallagher (3)	Pop musician
Nicole Kidman (2)	Actress	Tom Cruise	Actor
Carole King	Singer/composer	Gerry Goffin	Composer
Henrietta Knight	Racehorse trainer	Terry Biddlecombe	Jockey
Vivienne Knight (3)	Scriptwriter	Patrick Campbell	Irish writer and wit
Gertrud Kolisch (2)	Musician	Arnold Schoenberg	Composer
Cleo Laine	Jazz singer	John Dankworth (2)	Jazz musician

Elsa Lanchester	Actress	*Charles Laughton*	*Actor*
Abbe Lane (3)	Singer	*Xavier Cugat*	*Bandleader*
Brogan Lane (3)	Actress	*Dudley Moore*	*Entertainer*
Hope Lange	Actress	*Alan J Pakula (2)*	*Film director*
Louise Lasser (2)	Actress	*Woody Allen*	*Actor/director*
Sue Lawley	Broadcaster	*Hugh Williams*	*TV magnate*
Evelyn Lear	Soprano	*Thomas Stewart*	*Baritone*
Kelly Le Brock	Actress	*Steven Seagal (2)*	*Actor*
Michelle Lee (2)	Actress and singer	*James Farentino*	*Actor*
Jane Leeves	Actress	*Marshall Coben*	*US television executive*
Janet Leigh	Actress	*Tony Curtis (3)*	*Actor*
Vivien Leigh (2)	Actress	*Laurence Olivier (2)*	*Actor*
Margaret Leighton	Actress	*Laurence Harvey (2)*	*Actor*
		Michael Wilding (3)	*Actor*
Rula Lenska (3)	Actress	*Dennis Waterman (2)*	*Actor*
Lotte Lenya	Actress/singer	*Kurt Weill (1)*	*Composer*
Kay Lenz	Actress	*David Cassidy*	*singer*
Tea Leoni	Actress	*David Duchovny (2)*	*Actor*
Lyubov Leonidovna (2)	Russian ballerina	*Marius Petipa*	*French choreographer*
Ginette Lery (2)	Secretary	*JamesGoldsmith*	*Tycoon*
Astriel Lindstrom (2)	Model	*Bill Wyman*	*Musician*
Muriel Ling (1)	Model	*Harold Robbins*	*Writer*
Elizabeth Linley	Composer's daughter	*Richard Brinsley Sheridan*	*Irish dramatist*
Maureen Lipman	Actress	*Jack Rosenthal*	*Playwright*
Constance Lloyd	Socialite	*Oscar Wilde*	*Playwright/novelist*
Sue Lloyd	Actress	*Ronald Allen*	*Actor*
Lina Llubera	Spanish singer	*Sergei Prokofiev*	*Composer*
Heather Locklear (2)	Actress	*Tommy Lee*	*Singer*
Victoria Lockwood	Model	*Earl Charles Spencer*	*English nobleman*
Carole Lombard (1)	Actress	*William Powell (1)*	*Actor*
		Clark Gable (2)	*Actor*
Claudine Longet	Actress	*Andy Williams*	*Singer*
Anita Lonsborough	Swimmer	*Hugh Porter*	*Cyclist*
Lydia Lopokova	Ballerina	*John Maynard Keynes*	*Economist*
Sophia Loren	Actress	*Carlo Ponti*	*Film producer*
Courtney Love	Actress/singer	*Kurt Cobain (2)*	*Musician (Nirvana)*
Sarah Lowndes	Poet	*Bob Dylan*	*Musician*
Lorna Luft	Singer	*Colin Freeman*	*Musical director*
Linda Lusardi	Actress and model	*Sam Kane*	*Actor*
Emma Lyon	Blacksmith's daughter	*William Hamilton*	*Scottish diplomat*
Lulu	Singer	*Maurice Gibb*	*Singer*
Carol McGiffin	Radio DJ	*Chris Evans*	*Television presenter*
Cathy McGowan	Broadcaster	*Hywel Bennett*	*Actor*
Ali MacGraw	Actress	*Steve McQueen (2)*	*Actor*
Heather McIntyre	Actress and playwright	*William Hartnell*	*Actor*
Virginia McKenna	Actress	*Denholm Elliott (1)*	*Actor*
		Bill Travers (2)	*Actor*
Alison McNair	Doctor's daughter	*Donald Dewar (1)*	*British politician*
		Alexander AM Irvine (2)	*Lord Chancellor*
Kitty McShane	Music-hall artist	*Arthur Lucan*	*Music-hall artist*
Madonna	Singer and actress	*Sean Penn (1)*	*Actor*
		Guy Ritchie (2)	*Film director*
Justine Mahler	Sister of Gustav Mahler	*Arnold Rosé*	*Austrian violinist*
Madame de Maintenon	Louis XIV's 2nd wife	*Louis XIV*	*King of France*
Maria Malibran	Contralto	*Charles de Bériot*	*Violinist and composer*
Erika Mann	Writer	*WH Auden*	*Poet and essayist*
Jayne Mansfield	Actress	*Mickey Hargitay*	*Body-builder*
Katherine Mansfield	NZ writer	*George Bowden (1)*	*Businessman*
		John Middleton Murry	*Writer and critic*
Leslie Manville (1)	Actress	*Gary Oldman*	*Actor*
Margaret of Anjou	French noblewoman	*Henry VI*	*English king*
Princess Margaret	Elizabeth II's sister	*Anthony Armstrong Jones*	*Photographer*
Maria Theresa	Spanish princess	*Louis XIV*	*King of France*
Marie Louise	Austrian archduchess	*Napoleon I*	*French emperor*
Jean Marsh (1)	Actress	*Jon Pertwee*	*Actor*
Marion Marshall (2)	Actress	*Robert Wagner*	*Actor*
Barbara Marx (4)	Actress	*Frank Sinatra*	*Singer*
Mary II	British queen	*William III*	*British king*
Mary of Guise	French noblewoman	*James V*	*King of Scotland*
Mary of Modena (2)	Italian noblewoman	*James II*	*British king*

FAMOUS PEOPLE

Mary of Teck	German noblewoman	George V	British king
Mary Stewart	Queen of Scots	Francis II (1)	French Dauphin then king
		Henry Darnley (2)	English nobleman
		Earl of Bothwell (3)	Scottish nobleman
Anna Massey	Actress	Jeremy Brett	Actor
Meg Matthews	Record company secretary	Noel Gallagher	Pop musician
Luisa Mattioli (2)	Housewife	Roger Moore	Actor
Sharon Maughan	Actress	Trevor Eve	Actor
Patricia Maynard (2)	Actress	Dennis Waterman	Actor
Patricia Medina	Actress	Richard Greene	Actor
Wilnelia Merced (3)	Beauty queen	Bruce Forsyth	Entertainer
Vivien Merchant (1)	Actress	Harold Pinter	Playwright
Melina Mercouri	Actress	Jules Dassin	Film director
Ethel Merman	Singer	Ernest Borgnine (3)	Actor
Messalina (3)	Roman noblewoman	Nero	Roman emperor
Jean Metcalfe	Broadcaster	Cliff Michelmore	Broadcaster
Metis (1)	Greek sea nymph	Zeus	Greek supreme god
Alice Middleton (2)	Widow of London mercer	Thomas More	Chancellor of England
Annabella Milbanke	Heiress	Lord Byron	Poet
Sarah Miles	Actress	Robert Bolt	Playwright
Antonina Miliukova	Pupil of Tchaikovsky	Pyotr Tchaikovsky	Composer
Rebecca Miller	Actress (Arthur Miller's daughter)	Daniel Day-Lewis	Actor
Elizabeth Minshull (3)	Milton's 3rd wife	John Milton	Poet
Marilyn Monroe	Actress	Jim Dougherty (1)	Policeman
		Joe Di Maggio (2)	Baseball player
		Arthur Miller (3)	Playwright
Margaret Montgomerie	Socialite	James Boswell	Biographer
Elizabeth Montgomery (3)	Actress	Gig Young	Actor
LM Montgomery	Canadian novelist	Ewan Macdonald	Presbyterian minister
Fanny Moody	English soprano	Charles Manners	Irish bass and impresario
Bel Mooney	Writer and broadcaster	Jonathan Dimbleby	Broadcaster
Demi Moore	Actress	Bruce Willis	Actor
Jeanne Moreau (1)	Actress	William Friedkin (3)	Film director
Anne Morrow	Writer	Charles Lindbergh	Aviator
Angela Mortimer	British Wimbledon champion	John Barrett	Tennis commentator
Iris Murdoch	Writer	John Bayley	Professor of literature
Patricia Neal	Actress	Roald Dahl	Writer
Nefertiti	Egyptian queen	Akhenaton	Egyptian king
Hildegarde Neil (2)	Actress	Brian Blessed	Actor
Wendy Neuss	Producer ('Star Trek')	Patrick Stewart	Actor (StarTrek)
Anne Nevill	English Noblewoman	Richard III	English king
Nanette Newman	Actress	Bryan Forbes	Actor and director
Sue Nicholls	Actress	Mark Eden	Actor
Mary Ellen Nicolls (1)	Daughter of Thomas Love Peacock	George Meredith	English novelist
Brigitte Nielsen (2)	Actress	Sylvester Stallone	Actor
Frances Nisbet	Doctor's widow	Horatio Nelson	English naval hero
Catherine Nossenko (1)	Stravinsky's cousin	Igor Stravinsky	Composer
Kim Novak	Actress	Richard Johnson (1)	Actor
Jane Nugent	Secretary	Edmund Burke	British statesman
Louise Nurding	Pop singer	Jamie Redknapp	Footballer
Merle Oberon (2)	Actress	Alexander Korda	Film director
Octavia (1)	Roman noblewoman	Nero	Roman emperor
Octavia (1)	Emperor Augustus' sister	Marc Antony	Roman general
Georgia O'Keefe	US painter	Alfred Stieglitz	US photographer
Tamsin Olivier	Pub owner	Simon Dutton	Actor
Julia Trevelyan Oman	Designer	Roy Strong	Writer and historian
Tatum O'Neal	Actress	John McEnroe	Tennis player
Oona O'Neill (4)	Playwright's daughter	Charlie Chaplin	Actor
Yoko Ono (2)	Artist	John Lennon (2)	Musician
Dorothy Osborne	Daughter of governor of Guernsey	William Temple	Diplomat and essayist
Fanny Osbourne	Actress	Robert Louis Stevenson	Author
Ann Packer	Athlete	Robbie Brightwell	Athlete
Wendy Padbury	Actress	Melvyn Hayes	Actor
Geraldine Page	Actress	Rip Torn	Actor
Grace Palermo (5)	Socialite	Harold Robbins	Writer
Lilli Palmer (2)	Actress	Rex Harrison (1)	Actor
Pandora	First woman of Greek myth	Epimetheus	Titan

May Pang	Authoress	*Tony Visconti*	*Record producer*
Vanessa Paradis	Singer	*Johnny Depp*	*Actor*
Euphrosyne Parepa	Soprano	*Karl Rosa*	*German conductor*
Mary Parker	Actress	*Harold French*	*Actor and theatre director*
Sarah Jessica Parker	Actress	*Matthew Broderick*	*Actor*
Isabel Patiño (1)	Bolivian tin magnate's daughter	*James Goldsmith*	*Tycoon*
Charlotte Payne-Townshend	Heiress	*George Bernard Shaw*	*Dramatist*
Rhea Perlman	Actress	*Danny DeVito*	*Actor*
Olympie Pélissier (2)	Parisian hostess	*Gioacchino Rossini*	*Composer*
Penelope	Daughter of King Icarius of Sparta	*Odysseus*	*Mythical king of Ithaca*
Christine Perfect	Singer	*John McVie*	*Musician*
Jean Peters	Actress	*Howard Hughes*	*Businessman*
Sandy Pflueger (2)	Equestrian rider	*Mark Phillips*	*Equestrian rider*
Maggie Philbin	TV presenter	*Keith Chegwin*	*TV presenter*
Philippa Hainault	Dutch noblewoman	*Edward III*	*English king*
Fiona Phillips	GMTV presenter	*Martin Frizell*	*GMTV presenter*
Michelle Phillips	Actress and singer	*Dennis Hopper*	*Actor*
Siân Phillips	Actress	*Peter O'Toole (2)*	*Actor*
Pat Phoenix (2)	Actress	*Anthony Booth (3)*	*Actor*
Paloma Picasso	Beautician and businesswoman	*Rafael Lopez-Cambil*	*Argentinian playwright*
Evelyn Pickering	Pre-Raphaelite artist	*William Frend De Morgan*	*Pre-Raphaelite artist*
Mary Pickford (2)	Actress	*Douglas Fairbanks Snr*	*Actor*
Billie Piper	Pop singer	*Chris Evans*	*Disc Jockey*
Valerie Pitts	TV presenter	*Georg Solti*	*Conductor*
Minna Planer (1)	Opera singer and actress	*Richard Wagner (1)*	*Composer*
Sylvia Plath	Poet	*Ted Hughes*	*Poet*
Suzanne Pleshette	Actress	*Troy Donahue*	*Actor*
Joan Plowright (3)	Actress	*Laurence Olivier*	*Actor*
Pocahontas	Princess	*John Rolfe*	*English colonist*
Lily Pons	Soprano	*André Kostelanetz*	*Conductor*
Poppaea (2)	Roman noblewoman	*Nero*	*Roman emperor*
Elizabeth Porter	Schoolteacher	*Samuel Johnson*	*Writer and lexicographer*
Beatrix Potter	Author and illustrator	*William Heelis*	*Solicitor*
Eleanor Powell (3)	Actress	*Glenn Ford*	*Actor*
Mary Powell (1)	Royalist sympathiser	*John Milton*	*Poet*
Stefanie Powers	Actress	*Gary Lockwood*	*Actor*
Lisa-Marie Presley	Actress	*Danny Keough (1)*	*Rock musician*
		Michael Jackson (2)	*Entertainer*
		Nicolas Cage (3)	*Actor*
Kelly Preston	Actress	*John Travolta*	*Actor*
Soon-Yi Previn (3)	Personal assistant	*Woody Allen*	*Actor/director*
Libby Purves	Broadcaster	*Paul Heiney*	*Broadcaster*
Pyrrha	Daughter of Epimetheus and Pandora	*Deucalion*	*Son of Prometheus*
Miranda Quarry (3)	Actress	*Peter Sellers*	*Actor*
Gilda Radner	Psychotherapist	*Gene Wilder*	*Actor*
Anna Raeburn	Agony Aunt	*Nick Lilley*	*Businessman*
Gillian Raine (2)	Actress	*Leonard Rossiter*	*Actor*
Charlotte Rampling	Actress	*Jean-Michel Jarre*	*Musician*
Esther Rantzen	Broadcaster	*Desmond Wilcox*	*Producer*
Anthea Redfern (2)	Presenter	*Bruce Forsyth*	*Entertainer*
Vanessa Redgrave	Actress	*Franco Nero (1)*	*Actor*
		Tony Richardson (2)	*Film producer*
Alma Reville	Actress	*Alfred Hitchcock*	*Film director*
Debbie Reynolds (2)	Actress	*Eddie Fisher*	*Singer*
Ingeborg Rhosea (2)	Novelist	*Jon Pertwee*	*Actor*
Anneka Rice	TV presenter	*Nick Allott*	*Theatre producer*
Frieda von Richthofen	Socialite	*DH Lawrence*	*Writer*
Rachel Robards	Colonel's daughter	*Andrew Jackson*	*US president*
Amy Robbins	Student	*HG Wells*	*Author*
Margaret Roberts (2)	Politician	*Dennis Thatcher*	*Businessman*
Rachel Roberts (4)	Actress	*Rex Harrison*	*Actor*
Amy Robsart	Socialite	*Robert Dudley*	*Earl of Leicester*
Julie Rogers	Singer	*Michael Black*	*Theatrical agent*
Mimi Rogers (1)	Actress	*Tom Cruise*	*Actor*
Wenda Rogerson	Fashion model	*Norman Parkinson*	*Photographer*
Primula Rollo	Cipher clerk	*David Niven*	*Actor*

FAMOUS PEOPLE

Micheline Roquebrune (2)	Artist	*Sean Connery*	*Actor*
Isabella Rossellini (4)	Actress	*David Lynch (1)*	*Actor*
		Martin Scorsese (2)	*Director*
Jelka Rosen	Singer	*Frederick Delius*	*Composer*
Hannah Rothschild	Heiress	*Lord Rosebery*	*Scottish statesman*
Nicole Rothschild (4th)	Actress	*Dudley Moore*	*Entertainer*
Debbie Rowe (2)	Nurse	*Michael Jackson*	*Entertainer*
Gena Rowlands	Actress	*John Cassavetes*	*Actor*
Roxana	Queen of Macedon	*Alexander the Great*	*King of Macedon*
Meg Ryan (2)	Actress	*Dennis Quaid*	*Actor*
Sue Ryder	Philanthropist	*Leonard Cheshire*	*Philanthropist*
Vita Sackville-West	Poet and novelist	*Harold Nicolson*	*Diplomat*
Carol Bayer Sager (3)	Singer	*Burt Bacharach*	*Composer*
Jill St John	Actress	*Jack Jones (1)*	*Singer*
		Robert Wagner (2)	*Actor*
Beatrice Salkeld	Illustrator	*Brendan Behan*	*Irish writer*
Olga Samaroff (1)	Pianist	*Leopold Stokowski*	*Conductor*
Susan Sarandon	Actress	*Tim Robbins*	*Actor*
(common law)		*(common law)*	
Maria Elena Santiago	Secretary	*Buddy Holly*	*Musician*
Jennifer Saunders	Comedienne	*Ade Edmondson*	*Comedian*
Zelda Sayre	Socialite	*Francis Scott Fitzgerald*	*Novelist*
Prunella Scales	Actress	*Timothy West*	*Actor*
Alma Maria Schindler	Artist and musician	*Gustav Mahler (1)*	*Composer*
		Walter Gropius (2)	*Architect*
		Franz Werfel (3)	*Writer*
Elizabeth Schumann	German soprano	*Carl Alwin*	*German pianist/ conductor*
Coretta Scott	Music graduate	*Martin Luther King*	*Civil rights leader*
Janette Scott (3)	Actress	*Mel Tormé (1)*	*Singer*
		Jackie Rae (3)	*TV presenter*
Kyra Sedgwick	Actress	*Kevin Bacon*	*Actor*
Phyllis Sellick	Pianist	*Cyril Smith*	*Pianist*
Sandie Shaw	Singer	*Jeff Banks*	*Fashion designer*
Moira Shearer	Ballet dancer	*Ludovic Kennedy*	*Broadcaster*
Evgenia Shelepin (2)	Trotsky's secretary	*Arthur Ransome*	*Writer*
Dinah Sheridan	Actress	*Jimmy Hanley (2)*	*Entertainer*
		Sir John Davis (2)	*Rank chairman*
Brooke Shields	Actress	*André Agassi*	*Tennis player*
Elizabeth Siddal	Model	*Dante Gabriel Rossetti*	*Poet and painter*
Simone Signoret	Actress	*Yves Montand (2)*	*Actor*
Sheila Sim	Actress	*Richard Attenborough*	*Actor*
Jean Simmons	Actress	*Stewart Granger*	*Actor*
Carly Simon	Singer	*James Taylor*	*Composer*
Carole Smillie	TV presenter	*Alex Knight*	*Restaurateur*
Anna Nicole Smith	Actress	*J Howard Marshall II*	*Oil Tycoon*
Delia Smith	Cookery writer	*Michael Wynn Jones*	*Publisher*
Maggie Smith	Actress	*Robert Stephens*	*Actor*
Mandy Smith (3)	Model	*Bill Wyman*	*Rolling Stone*
Michelle Smith	Irish swimmer	*Erik De Bruin*	*Dutch discus thrower*
Harriet Smithson	Irish actress	*Hector Berlioz*	*Composer*
Wendy Snowden	Actress	*Peter Cook*	*Comedian and writer*
Sophia Dorothea	German noblewoman	*George I*	*British king*
Dorothy Squires (1)	Singer	*Roger Moore (2)*	*Actor*
Barbara Stanwick	Actress	*Robert Taylor*	*Actor*
Jann Stapp (6)	Businesswoman	*Harold Robbins*	*Writer*
Alison Steadman	Actress	*Mike Leigh*	*Dramatist*
Sheila Steafel (1)	Actress	*Harry H Corbett*	*Actor*
Marion Stein	Musician	*7th Earl of Harewood (1)*	*English nobleman*
		Jeremy Thorpe (2)	*Politician*
Pamela Stephenson	Actress and comedienne	*Nicholas Ball (1)*	*Actor*
		Billy Connolly (2)	*Scottish comedian*
Virginia Stephen	Novelist	*Leonard Woolf*	*Publisher and writer*
Margaret Stewart (2)	Lord Ochiltree's daughter	*John Knox*	*Religious reformer*
Miriam Stoppard	TV presenter and journalist	*Christopher Hogg (2)*	*Industrialist*
Susan Stranks	Presenter	*Robin Ray*	*Broadcaster*
Barbra Streisand	Singer and actress	*Elliot Gould (1)*	*Actor*
		James Brolin (2)	*Actor*
Giuseppina Strepponi (2)	Soprano	*Giuseppe Verdi*	*Composer*
Imogen Stubbs (3)	Actress	*Trevor Nunn*	*Artistic director*
Una Stubbs	Actress	*Peter Gilmore (1)*	*Actor*

		Nicky Henson (2)	Entertainer
Trudie Styler (2)	Actress	Sting	Singer
Vera de Bosset Sudekeine (2)	Ballet dancer	Igor Stravinsky	Composer
Margaret Sullavan	Actress	William Wyler	Film director
Anna Beth Sully (1)	Actress	Douglas Fairbanks Snr	Actor
Mariya Surovshchikova (1)	Russian ballerina	Marius Petipa	French choreographer
Joan Sutherland	Soprano	Richard Bonynge	Conductor
Janet Suzman (1)	Actress	Trevor Nunn	Artistic director
Gloria Swanson	Actress	Wallace Beery	Actor
Catherine Swynford (3)	Former mistress	John of Gaunt	English Prince
Jessica Tandy	Actress	Jack Hawkins (1)	Actor
		Hume Cronyn (2)	Actor
Sharon Tate (2)	Actress	Roman Polanski	Director
Christine Taylor	Actress	Ben Stiller	Actor
Elizabeth Taylor	Actress	Nicky Hilton (1)	Hotelier
		Michael Wilding (2)	Actor
		Mike Todd (3)	Film producer
		Eddie Fisher (4)	Singer
		Richard Burton(5 and 6)	Actor
		John Warner (7)	Senator
		Larry Fortensky (8)	Builder
Kiri Te Kanawa	Opera singer	Desmond Park	Mining engineer
Victoria Tennant	English actress	Steve Martin	US actor
Ellen Terry	English actress	George Frederick Watts (1)	English painter
		James Carew (2)	US actor
		Charlie Kelly (3)	Actor
Josephine Tewson (1)	Actress	Leonard Rossiter	Actor
Rosalie Texier (1)	Dressmaker	Claude Debussy	Composer
Themis (2)	Daughter of Gaia and Uranus	Zeus	Greek supreme god
Theodora	Actress	Justinian	East Roman emperor
Thetis	Mythical sea nymph (Nereid)	Peleus	Mythical King of Phthia
Emma Thompson	Actress	Kenneth Branagh	Actor
Elspeth Thomson	Socialite	Kenneth Grahame	Children's writer
Sybil Thorndike	Actress	Lewis Casson	Actor and manager
Hester Thrale	Writer	Gabriel Piozzi	Musician
Julia Thuillier	Socialite	Walter Savage Landor	Writer
Uma Thurman	Actress	Gary Oldman (1)	Actor
		Ethan Hawke (2)	Actor
Pauline Tiltson	Businesswoman	John Prescott	British politician
Ann Todd	Actress	David Lean	Film director
Mary Todd	Socialite	Abraham Lincoln	US president
Frances Tomelty (1)	Actress	Sting	Singer
Wanda Toscanini	Musician	Vladimir Horowitz	Pianist
Ludmilla Tourischeva	Gymnast	Valeri Borzov	Athlete
Marie Truffot	Socialite	Camille Saint-Saëns	Composer
Ivana Trump	Former wife of Donald Trump	Ricardo Mazzucchelli (2)	Italian businessman
Anthea Turner	TV presenter	Peter Powell (1)	Disc jockey and producer
		Grant Bovey (2)	Businessman
Cora Turner	Opera singer	Hawley Crippen	Murderer
Lana Turner	Actress	Lex Barker (5)	Actor
		Artie Shaw (1)	Bandleader
Martha Turner	Farmer's daughter	John Clare	Poet
Monica Turner (2)	Actress	Mike Tyson (1)	Boxer
Twiggy	Model and actress	Leigh Lawson (2)	Actor
Cathy Tyson	Actress	Craig Charles	Actor
Mary Ure	Actress	John Osborne (1)	Playwright
		Robert Shaw (2)	Actor
Saskia Uylenburgh	Burgomaster's daughter	Rembrandt Van Rijn	Dutch painter
Joanna Van Gyseghem (1)	Actress	Ralph Bates	Actor
Eva Marie Violetti	Viennese dancer	David Garrick	Actor
Galina Vishnevskaya	Soprano	Mstislav Rostropovich	Cellist and conductor
Carol Vorderman	TV presenter	Paddy King	Businessman
Marie Vulliamy (2)	Socialite	George Meredith	English novelist
Lindsay Wagner	Actress	Alan Rider (1)	Music publisher
		Michael Brandon (2)	Actor
		Henry Kingi (3)	Stuntman
		Lawrence Mortoff (4)	Producer

FAMOUS PEOPLE

Lillias Walker (2)	Actress	*Peter Vaughan*	*Actor*
Lalla Ward (2)	Actress	*Tom Baker*	*Actor*
Rachel Ward	Actress	*Bryan Brown*	*Australian actor*
Sophie Ward	Actress	*Paul Hobson*	*Vet*
Sandra Warfield	Soprano	*James McCracken*	*Tenor*
Wallis Simpson	American socialite	*Edward VIII*	*British king*
Lavinia Warren	Circus performer	*Tom Thumb*	*Circus performer*
Jan Waters (2)	Actress	*Peter Gilmore (1)*	*Actor*
Ruby Wax	Comedienne	*Edward Bye*	*Producer*
Constance Weber	Singer	*Wolfgang Amadeus Mozart*	*Composer*
Denise Welch	Actress	*Tim Healy*	*Actor*
Tuesday Weld (2)	Actress	*Dudley Moore (2)*	*Entertainer*
Jane Baillie Welsh	Doctor's daughter	*Thomas Carlyle*	*Essayist*
Joanne Whalley	Actress	*Val Kilmer*	*Actor*
Billie Whitelaw (1)	Actress	*Peter Vaughan*	*Actor*
Clara Wieck	Pianist	*Robert Schumann*	*Composer*
Cynda Williams	Actress	*Billy Bob Thornton*	*Actor*
Esther Williams (4)	Actress	*Fernando Lamas (4)*	*Actor*
Penelope Wilton (4)	Actress	*Ian Holm*	*Actor*
Shelley Winters	Actress	*Tony Franciosa (2)*	*Actor*
Reese Witherspoon	Actress	*Ryan Phillippe*	*Actor*
Natalie Wood	Actress	*Robert Wagner*	*Actor*
Victoria Wood	Comedienne	*Geoffrey Durham*	*Comedian*
Catherine Woodcock (2)	Commoner	*John Milton*	*Poet*
Catherine Woodville	Sister-in-law of Edward IV	*Henry Stafford*	*2nd Duke of Buckingham*
Joanne Woodward	Actress	*Paul Newman*	*Actor*
Helen Worth	Actress	*Michael Angelis*	*Actor*
Syreeta Wright	Singer	*Stevie Wonder*	*Musician*
Anna Magdalena Wülken (2)	Soprano	*JS Bach*	*Composer*
Tessa Wyatt	Actress	*Tony Blackburn*	*Disc jockey*
Jane Wyman (1)	Actress	*Ronald Reagan (3)*	*US president*
Patrice Wymore (2)	Actress	*Errol Flynn*	*Actor*
Xanthippe	Athenian	*Socrates*	*Philosopher*
Paula Yates	Broadcaster	*Bob Geldof*	*Singer*
Cecilia Young	Singer	*Thomas Arne*	*Composer*
Mathilde von Zemlinsky (1)	Musician	*Arnold Schoenberg*	*Composer*
Catherine Zeta Jones (2)	Actress	*Michael Douglas*	*Actor*
Marta Ziegler	Socialite	*Béla Bartók*	*Composer*
Anna Zimmerman	Housewife	*Charles Gounod*	*Composer*

Marriages: By Male Spouse

Peter Abelard	French philosopher	*Héloïse*	*Abelard's Roman wife*
Aeneas	Mythical Trojan prince	*Creusa*	*Mythical character*
Agamemnon	Mythical king of Mycenae	*Clytemnestra*	*Mythical queen of Mycenae*
André Agassi	Tennis player	*Brooke Shields*	*Actress*
Ahab	King of Israel	*Jezebel*	*Queen of Israel*
Akhenaton	Egyptian king	*Nefertiti*	*Egyptian queen*
John Alderton	Actor	*Jill Browne (1)*	*Actress*
		Pauline Collins (2)	*Actress*
Richard Aldington	Poet/novelist	*Hilda Doolittle*	*US poet*
Alexander the Great	King of Macedon	*Roxana*	*Queen of Macedon*
Keith Allen	Actor	*Alison Allen*	*Television producer*
Ronald Allen	Actor	*Sue Lloyd*	*Actress*
Woody Allen	Actor and director	*Louise Lasser (2)*	*Actress*
		Soon-Yi Previn (3)	*Personal assistant*
Greg Allmann (2)	Musician	*Cher*	*Actress and singer*
Nick Allott	Theatre producer	*Anneka Rice*	*TV presenter*
Carl Alwin	German pianist and conductor	*Elizabeth Schumann*	*German soprano*
Kingsley Amis	Novelist and poet	*Elizabeth Jane Howard*	*Novelist*
Michael Angelis	Actor	*Helen Worth*	*Actress*
Marc Antony	Roman general	*Octavia (1)*	*Emperor Augustus' sister*
		Cleopatra VII	*Queen of Egypt*
Thomas Arne	Composer	*Cecilia Young*	*Singer*

Desi Arnaz	Musician and actor	Lucille Ball	Comedienne and actress
Tom Arnold (2)	Actor	Roseanne Barr	Actress
David Arquette	Actor	Courtney Cox	Actress
Richard Attenborough	Actor	Sheila Sim	Actress
Attila the Hun	Hunnish ruler	Ildico	Consort of Attila
WH Auden	Poet and essayist	Erika Mann	Writer
JS Bach	Composer	Maria Barbara Bach (1)	Cousin of JS Bach
		Anna Magdalena Wülken (2)	Soprano
Burt Bacharach	Composer	Angie Dickinson	Actress
		Carol Bayer Sager (3)	Singer
Kevin Bacon	Actor	Kyra Sedgwick	Actress
David Bailey	Photographer	Marie Helvin (3)	Model
		Catherine Deneuve (2)	Actress
Colin Baker (1)	Actor	Liza Goddard (1)	Actress
Tom Baker	Actor	Lalla Ward (2)	Actress
Alec Baldwin (2)	Actor	Kim Basinger	Actress
Nicholas Ball (1)	Actor	Pamela Stephenson	Actress and comedienne
Antonio Banderas (4)	Actor	Melanie Griffith (2)	Actress
Jeff Banks	Fashion designer	Sandie Shaw	Singer
Monty Banks	Film director	Gracie Fields	Singer
Daniel Barenboim	Pianist	Jacqueline Du Pré	Cellist
Lex Barker (5)	Actor	Lana Turner (3)	Actress
John Barrett	Tennis commentator	Angela Mortimer	British Wimbledon champion
John Barrymore	Actor	Dolores Costello	Actress
Béla Bartók	Composer	Marta Ziegler	Socialite
Ralph Bates	Actor	Joanna Van Gyseghem (1)	Actress
John Bayley	Professor of literature	Iris Murdoch	Writer
Sean Bean	Actor	Debra Anderson (1)	Childhood sweetheart
		Melanie Hill (2)	Actress ('Bread')
		Abigail Cruttenden (3)	Actress ('Sharpe')
Warren Beatty	Actor	Annette Bening	Actress
David Beckham	Footballer	Victoria Adams	Spice Girl
Wallace Beery	Actor	Gloria Swanson	Actress
Brendan Behan	Irish writer	Beatrice Salkeld	Illustrator
Alexander Graham Bell	Inventor	Mabel Hubbard	Deaf student
Hywel Bennett	Actor	Cathy McGowan	Broadcaster
Charles de Beriot	Violinist	Maria Malibran	Contralto
Hector Berlioz	Composer	Harriet Smithson	Irish actress
Terry Biddlecombe	Jockey	Henrietta Knight	Racehorse trainer
Georges Bizet	Composer	Geneviève Halévy	Composer's daughter
Michael Black	Theatrical agent	Julie Rogers	Singer
Tony Blackburn	Disc jockey	Tessa Wyatt	Actress
Tony Blair	Politician	Cherie Booth	Barrister
William Blake	English poet and painter	Catherine Boucher	Illiterate pauper
Brian Blessed	Actor	Hildegarde Neil (2)	Actress
Humphrey Bogart (1)	Actor	Lauren Bacall (4)	Actress
James Bolam	Actor	Susan Jameson	Actress
Robert Bolt	Playwright	Sarah Miles	Actress
Sonny Bono (1)	Actor and politician	Cher (2)	Actress and singer
Richard Bonynge	Conductor	Joan Sutherland	Soprano
Anthony Booth (3)	Actor	Pat Phoenix (2)	Actress
Ernst Borgnine (3)	Actor	Ethel Merman (3)	Singer
Valeri Borzov	Athlete	Ludmilla Tourischeva	Gymnast
James Boswell	Biographer	Margaret Montgomerie	Socialite
Earl of Bothwell (3)	Scottish nobleman	Mary Stewart	Queen of Scots
Grant Bovey (2)	Businessman	Anthea Turner	TV presenter
George Bowden (1)	Businessman	Katherine Mansfield	NZ writer
David Bowie (2)	Singer and composer	Iman	Model
Mark Boxer	Cartoonist	Anna Ford	Broadcaster
Bernard Braden	Actor and presenter	Barbara Kelly	Actress and presenter
Kenneth Branagh	Actor	Emma Thompson	Actress
Michael Brandon (2)	Actor	Glynis Barber	Actress
		Lindsay Wagner	Actress
Jeremy Brett	Actor	Anna Massey	Actress
Robbie Brightwell	Athlete	Ann Packer	Athlete
Matthew Broderick	Actor	Sarah Jessica Parker	Actress
James Brolin (2)	Actor	Barbara Streisand (3)	Singer and actress
Charles Bronson (2)	Actor	Jill Ireland (2)	Actress
Mel Brooks	Actor and producer	Anne Bancroft	Actress

Robert Browning	Poet	*Elizabeth Barrett*	*Poet*
Bobby Brown	Singer	*Whitney Houston*	*Singer*
Bryan Brown	Australian actor	*Rachel Ward*	*Actress*
Hans von Bülow (1)	Conductor	*Cosima von Bülow*	*Franz Liszt's daughter*
Edmund Burke	British statesman	*Jane Nugent*	*Secretary*
George Burns	Comedian and actor	*Gracie Allen*	*Comedienne*
Robert Burns	Poet	*Jean Armour*	*Socialite*
Richard Burton (5 and 6)	Actor	*Elizabeth Taylor*	*Actress*
Peter Butterworth	Actor	*Janet Brown*	*Impressionist*
Edward Bye	Producer	*Ruby Wax*	*Comedienne*
Gabriel Byrne	Actor	*Ellen Barkin*	*Actress*
Lord Byron	Poet	*Annabella Milbanke*	*Heiress*
Cadmus	Mythical founder of Thebes	*Harmonia*	*Daughter of Ares and Aphrodite*
Nicolas Cage	Actor	*Patricia Arquette (1)*	*Actress*
		Lisa-Marie Presley (2)	*Singer and actress*
Michael Caine	Actor	*Shakira Baksh (2)*	*Actress and model*
Erskine Caldwell	American author	*Margaret Bourke-White*	*Photo-journalist*
Alan Charles Cameron	Businessman	*Elizabeth Bowen*	*Irish novelist*
Patrick Campbell	Irish writer and wit	*Vivienne Knight (3)*	*Scriptwriter*
James Carew (2)	US actor	*Ellen Terry*	*English actress*
Thomas Carlyle	Essayist	*Jane Baillie Welsh*	*Doctor's daughter*
Jim Carrey	Actor	*Lauren Holly*	*Actress*
Johnny Cash	Singer	*June Carter*	*Singer*
Stefano Casiraghi (2)	Businessman	*Caroline of Monaco*	*Princess*
John Cassavetes	Actor	*Gena Rowlands*	*Actress*
David Cassidy	Singer	*Kay Lenz*	*Actress*
Lewis Casson	Actor and manager	*Sybil Thorndike*	*Actress*
George Catlin	Professor of politics	*Vera May Brittain*	*Writer*
Charlie Chaplin	Actor	*Mildred Harris (1)*	*Actress*
		Lita Grey (2)	*Actress*
		Paulette Goddard (3)	*Actress*
		Oona O'Neil (4)	*Playwright's daughter*
Guy Chapman (2)	Historian	*Storm Jameson*	*Novelist*
Lee Chapman	Footballer	*Leslie Ash*	*Actress*
Charlemagne	King of the Franks	*Hildegarde*	*Queen of the Franks*
Charles I	British king	*Henrietta Maria*	*French princess*
Charles II	British king	*Catherine of Braganza*	*Portuguese princess*
Craig Charles	Actor	*Cathy Tyson*	*Actress*
Keith Chegwin	TV presenter	*Maggie Philbin*	*TV presenter*
Leonard Cheshire	Philanthropist	*Baroness Sue Ryder*	*Philanthropist*
Lord Randolph Churchill	Politician	*Jenny Jerome*	*Daughter of NY businessman*
Winston Churchill	Politician	*Clementine Hozier*	*Charity worker*
Eric Clapton (2)	Musician	*Patti Boyd (1)*	*Model*
John Clare	Poet	*Martha Turner*	*Farmer's daughter*
Claudius	Roman emperor	*Agrippina*	*Roman noblewomen*
John Cleese	Actor	*Connie Booth*	*Actress*
Clovis I	King of the Franks	*Clotilda*	*Queen of the Franks*
Martin Clunes	Actor	*Philippa Braithewaite (2)*	*TV producer*
Kurt Cobain (2)	Musician (Nirvana)	*Courtney Love*	*Actress and singer*
Marshall Coben	US television executive	*Jane Leeves*	*Actress*
Paul Coia	TV presenter	*Debbie Greenwood*	*TV presenter (former Miss UK)*
Samuel Taylor Coleridge	Poet	*Sarah Fricker*	*Socialite*
Ronald Colman	Actor	*Benita Hume (2)*	*Actress*
Sean Connery	Actor	*Diane Cilento (1)*	*Actress*
		Micheline Roquebrune (2)	*Artist*
Billy Connolly (2)	Scottish comedian	*Pamela Stephenson*	*Actress and comedienne*
Terence Conran	Businessman	*Shirley Conran*	*Authoress*
Jackie Coogan (1)	Actor	*Betty Grable*	*Actress*
James Cook	British seaman and explorer	*Elizabeth Batts*	*Captain's wife*
Norman Cook	Musician	*Zoe Ball*	*TV presenter*
Peter Cook	Comedian and writer	*Wendy Snowden (1)*	*Actress*
		Judy Huxtable (2)	*Actress*
Harry H Corbett	Actor	*Sheila Steafel (1)*	*Actress*
		Maureen Blott (2)	*Actress*
Tom Courtenay	Actor	*Cheryl Kennedy*	*Actress*
Colin Cowdrey	Cricketer	*Lady Herries*	*Racehorse trainer*
Hawley Crippen	Murderer	*Cora Turner*	*Opera singer*
Hume Cronyn (2)	Actor	*Jessica Tandy*	*Actress*
John Walter Cross	Banker	*George Eliot*	*Authoress*

Tom Cruise	Actor	Mimi Rogers (1)	Actress
		Nicole Kidman (2)	Actress
Xavier Cugat	Bandleader	Carmen Castillo (1)	Singer
		Lorraine Allen (2)	Singer
		Abbe Lane (3)	Singer
Tony Curtis (3)	Actor	Janet Leigh	Actress
Roald Dahl	Writer	Patricia Neal	Actress
Eugène D'Albert	Composer and pianist	Theresa Carreño (1)	Pianist
John Dankworth (2)	Jazz musician	Cleo Laine	Jazz singer
General D'Arblay	French émigré	Fanny Burney	English novelist
Bobby Darin	Singer	Sandra Dee	Actress
Henry Darnley (2)	English nobleman	Mary Stewart	Queen of Scots
Jules Dassin	Film director	Melina Mercouri	Actress
Nigel Davenport	Actor	Maria Aitken	Actress
Jim Davidson	Comedian	Tracy Hilton	Housewife
		Alison Holloway	TV presenter
Hunter Davies	Author	Margaret Forster	Author
Carl Davis	Composer	Jean Boht	Actress
Sir John Davis (2)	Rank chairman	Dinah Sheridan	Actress
Sammy Davis Jnr	Entertainer	May Britt	Actress
Peter Davison	Actor	Sandra Dickinson	Actress
Dickie Dawson (2)	US comedian	Diana Dors	Actress
Cecil Day-Lewis	Poet	Jill Balcon	Actress
Daniel Day-Lewis	Actor	Rebecca Miller	Actress (Arthur Miller's daughter)
Erik De Bruin	Dutch discus thrower	Michelle Smith	Irish swimmer
William Frend De Morgan	Pre-Raphaelite artist	Evelyn Pickering	Pre-Raphaelite artist
Robert De Niro	Actor	Diahnne Abbott	Actress
Claude Debussy	Composer	Rosalie Texier (1)	Dressmaker
		Emma Bardac (2)	Socialite
Frederick Delius	Composer	Jelka Rosen	Singer
Michael Denison	Actor	Dulcie Gray	Actress
Johnny Depp	Actor	Vanessa Paradis	Singer
John Derek	Actor and director	Ursula Andress (1)	Actress
		Linda Evans (2)	Actress
		Bo Derek (3)	Actress
Frankie Dettori	Jockey	Catherine Allen	Secretary
Deucalion	Son of Prometheus	Pyrrha	Daughter of Epimetheus and Pandora
Danny DeVito	Actor	Rhea Perlman	Actress
Donald Dewar (1)	British politician	Alison McNair	Doctor's daughter
Joe Di Maggio (2)	Baseball player	Marilyn Monroe (2)	Actress
Charles Dickens	Author	Catherine Hogarth	Newspaper magnate's daughter
Jonathan Dimbleby	Broadcaster	Bel Mooney	Writer and broadcaster
Dionysus	Greek god of wine	Ariadne	Mythical daughter of King Minos of Crete
Troy Donahue	Actor	Suzanne Pleshette	Actress
Jim Dougherty (1)	Policeman	Marilyn Monroe	Actress
Michael Douglas	Actor	Catherine Zeta Jones (2)	Actress
Jack Dromey	Trade unionist	Harriet Harman	British politician
David Duchovny (2)	Actor	Tea Leoni	Actress
Lord Guilford Dudley	English nobleman	Lady Jane Grey	English noblewoman
Robert Dudley	Earl of Leicester	Amy Robsart	Socialite
Albrecht Dürer	German painter	Agnes Frey	Merchant's daughter
Geoffrey Durham	Comedian	Victoria Wood	Comedienne
Simon Dutton	Actor	Tamsin Olivier	Pub owner
Antonin Dvořák	Composer	Anna Cermakova	Socialite
Bob Dylan	Musician	Sarah Lowndes	Poet
Mark Eden	Actor	Sue Nicholls	Actress
Ade Edmondson	Comedian	Jennifer Saunders	Comedienne
Edward I	English king	Eleanor	Castilian princess
Edward II	English king	Isabella	Daughter of Philip IV of France
Edward III	English king	Philippa Hainault	Dutch noblewoman
Edward IV	English king	Elizabeth Woodville	English noblewoman
Edward VII	British king	Alexandra	Danish princess
Edward VIII	British king	Wallis Simpson	American socialite
Blake Edwards (2)	Film director	Julie Andrews	Actress and singer
Glyn Edwards	Actor	Yootha Joyce	Actress
Denholm Elliott (1)	Actor	Virginia McKenna	Actress
Epimetheus	Greek Titan	Pandora	First woman of Greek myth

Ernst August of Hanover (3)	Hanoverian prince	*Chantal Hochuli (1)*	*Swiss Heiress*
		Caroline of Monaco (2)	*Princess*
Emilio Estevez	Actor	*Paula Abdul (2)*	*Singer*
Chris Evans	Disc jockey	*Carol McGiffin (1)*	*Radio DJ*
		Billie Piper (2)	*Pop singer*
Trevor Eve	Actor	*Sharon Maughan*	*Actress*
Douglas Fairbanks Jnr (2)	Actor	*Joan Crawford*	*Actress*
Douglas Fairbanks Snr	Actor	*Anna Beth Sully (1)*	*Actress*
Douglas Fairbanks Snr (2)	Actor	*Mary Pickford (2)*	*Actress*
William Fairchild	Playwright	*Isabel Dean*	*Actress*
James Farentino	Actor	*Elizabeth Ashley (1)*	*Actress*
		Michele Lee (2)	*Actress and singer*
José Ferrer	Actor	*Rosemary Clooney*	*Singer*
Mel Ferrer	Actor	*Audrey Hepburn*	*Actress*
Henry Fielding	English novelist	*Charlotte Mary Craddock (1)*	*Socialite*
		Mary Daniel (2)	*Maid*
Albert Finney (5)	Actor	*Anouk Aimée (2)*	*Actress*
Eddie Fisher (1)	Singer	*Debbie Reynolds (2)*	*Actress*
		Elizabeth Taylor (3)	*Actress*
		Connie Stevens (4)	*Actress*
Francis Scott Fitzgerald	Novelist	*Zelda Sayre*	*Socialite*
Errol Flynn	Actor	*Patrice Wymore (2)*	*Actress*
		Lili Damita (1)	*Socialite*
Michael Foot	Politician	*Jill Craigie*	*TV scriptwriter and author*
Bryan Forbes	Actor and director	*Nanette Newman*	*Actress*
Glenn Ford	Actor	*Eleanor Powell (3)*	*Actress*
Bruce Forsyth	Entertainer	*Wilnelia Merced (3)*	*Beauty queen*
		Penny Calvert (1)	*Dancer*
		Anthea Redfern (2)	*Presenter*
Larry Fortensky (8)	Builder	*Elizabeth Taylor*	*Actress*
Tony Franciosa (2)	Actor	*Shelley Winters*	*Actress*
Francis II (1)	French Dauphin then king	*Mary Stewart*	*Queen of Scots*
César Franck	Composer	*Félicité Desmousseaux*	*Actress*
Colin Freeman	Musical director	*Lorna Luft*	*Singer*
David Freeman	Operatic director	*Marie Angel*	*Australian soprano*
Harold French	Actor and theatre director	*Mary Parker*	*Actress*
William Friedkin	Film director	*Lesley-Anne Down (2)*	*Actress*
		Jeanne Moreau (1)	*Actress*
Martin Frizell	GMTV presenter	*Fiona Phillips*	*GMTV presenter*
David Frost	Broadcaster	*Lynne Frederick (1)*	*Actress*
		Carina Fitzalan Howard (2)	*Noblewoman*
Clark Gable (2)	Actor	*Carole Lombard (3)*	*Actress*
Thomas Gainsborough	English painter	*Margaret Burr*	*Daughter of 4th Duke of Beaufort*
Liam Gallagher (3)	Pop musician	*Patsy Kensit*	*Actress and singer*
Noel Gallagher	Pop artist	*Meg Matthews*	*Record company secretary (Creation)*
David Garrick	Actor	*Eva Marie Violetti*	*Viennese dancer*
Bob Geldof	Singer	*Paula Yates*	*Broadcaster*
George I	British king	*Dorothea Sophia*	*German noblewoman*
George II	British king	*Caroline of Ansbach*	*German noblewoman*
George III	British king	*Charlotte Sophia*	*German noblewoman*
George IV	British king	*Caroline of Brunswick*	*German noblewoman*
George V	British king	*Mary of Teck*	*German noblewoman*
George VI	British king	*Elizabeth Bowes-Lyon*	*Earl of Strathmore's daughter*
George of Denmark	Danish Prince	*Queen Anne*	*British queen*
Richard Gere	Actor	*Cindy Crawford*	*Supermodel*
Maurice Gibb	Musician	*Lulu*	*Singer*
Peter Gilmore (1)	Actor	*Jan Waters (2)*	*Actress*
		Una Stubbs (1)	*Actress*
Gerry Goffin	Composer	*Carole King*	*Singer and composer*
Jeff Goldblum (2)	Actor	*Geena Davis*	*Actress*
James Goldsmith	Tycoon	*Ginette Lery (2)*	*Secretary*
		Isabel Patiño (1)	*Bolivian tin magnate's daughter*
		Anne Birley (3)	*Lady Annabel Vane-Tempest Stewart*
Elliot Gould (1)	Actor	*Barbra Streisand*	*Singer and actress*
Charles Gounod	Composer	*Anna Zimmerman*	*Housewife*
Kenneth Grahame	Children's writer	*Elspeth Thomson*	*Socialite*

Robert Graham	Sculptor	*Anjelica Huston*	*Actress and director*
Stewart Granger	Actor	*Jean Simmons*	*Actress*
Cary Grant	Actor	*Barbara Hutton (2)*	*Actress*
		Dyan Cannon (4)	*Actress*
Richard Greene	Actor	*Patricia Medina*	*Actress*
Edvard Grieg	Composer	*Nina Hagerup*	*Singer (Grieg's cousin)*
Walter Gropius (2)	Architect	*Alma Maria Schindler (1)*	*Musician*
Jimmy Gulzar	Musician	*Melanie Brown*	*Spice Girl*
William Hague	Politician	*Ffion Jenkins*	*Ex Civil Servant*
Peter Hall	Theatre director	*Leslie Caron*	*Actress*
Willis Hall	Writer	*Jill Bennett (2)*	*Actress*
William Hamilton	Scottish diplomat	*Emma Lyon*	*Blacksmith's daughter*
Dashiell Hammett	Author	*Lillian Hellman*	*Playwright*
Jimmy Hanley	Entertainer	*Dinah Sheridan (1)*	*Actress*
7th Earl of Harewood (1)	English nobleman	*Marion Stein*	*Musician*
Hargitay (2)	Body-builder	*Jayne Mansfield*	*Actress*
Renny Harlin (1)	Film director	*Gena Davis*	*Actress*
George Harrison (1)	Musician	*Patti Boyd (1)*	*Model*
Rex Harrison	Actor	*Lilli Palmer (2)*	*Actress*
		Kay Kendall (3)	*Actress*
		Rachel Roberts (4)	*Actress*
William Hartnell	Actor	*Heather McIntyre*	*Actress and playwright*
Laurence Harvey (2)	Actor	*Margaret Leighton*	*Actress*
Ethan Hawke (2)	Actor	*Uma Thurman*	*Actress*
Jack Hawkins (1)	Actor	*Jessica Tandy*	*Actress*
Tom Hayden (2)	Politician	*Jane Fonda*	*Actress*
Franz Joseph Haydn	Composer	*Maria Anna Keller*	*Hairdresser's daughter*
Melvyn Hayes	Actor	*Wendy Padbury*	*Actress*
Tim Healy	Actor	*Denise Welch*	*Actress*
William Heelis	Solicitor	*Beatrix Potter*	*Author and illustrator*
Paul Heiney	Broadcaster	*Libby Purves*	*Broadcaster*
David Hemmings	Actor	*Gayle Hunnicutt*	*Actress*
Henry II	French king	*Catherine de Medici*	*Queen of France*
Henry II (2)	English king	*Eleanor of Aquitaine*	*French noblewoman*
Henry III	English king	*Eleanor of Provence*	*French noblewoman*
Henry V (2)	English king	*Catherine of Valois*	*French princess*
Henry VI	English king	*Margaret of Anjou*	*French noblewoman*
Henry VII	English king	*Elizabeth of York*	*English princess*
Lenny Henry	Comedian	*Dawn French*	*Comedienne*
George Henschel	Baritone	*Lilian Bailey*	*American soprano*
Nicky Henson (2)	Entertainer	*Una Stubbs*	*Actress*
Hephaestus	Greek god of fire	*Aphrodite*	*Greek goddess of Love*
Peter Murray Hill	Actor and bookseller	*Phyllis Calvert*	*Actress*
Conrad Hilton (2)	Hotelier	*Zsa Zsa Gabor*	*Actress*
Nicky Hilton Jnr	Hotelier	*Elizabeth Taylor*	*Actress*
Frazer Hines	Actor	*Gemma Craven (1)*	*Actress*
		Liz Hobbs (2)	*Waterskier*
Alfred Hitchcock	Film director	*Alma Reville*	*Actress*
Paul Hobson	Vet	*Sophie Ward*	*Actress*
Christopher Hogg (2)	Industrialist	*Miriam Stoppard*	*TV presenter and journalist*
Buddy Holly	Musician	*Maria Elena Santiago*	*Secretary*
Ian Holm	Actor	*Penelope Wilton (4)*	*Actress*
Michael Holroyd (2)	Biographer	*Margaret Drabble*	*Novelist*
Dennis Hopper	Actor	*Michelle Phillips*	*Actress and singer*
Vladimir Horowitz	Pianist	*Wanda Toscanini*	*Musician*
Trevor Howard	Actor	*Helen Cherry*	*Actress*
Liam Howlett	Musician	*Natalie Appleton*	*Pop singer*
Howard Hughes	Businessman	*Jean Peters*	*Actress*
Ted Hughes	Poet	*Sylvia Plath*	*Poet*
Jack Hulbert	Actor	*Cicely Courtneidge*	*Actress*
Timothy Hutton	Actor	*Debra Winger*	*Actress*
Jeremy Irons	Actor	*Sinead Cusack*	*Actress*
Alexander Irvine (2)	Irvine of Lairg	*Alison McNair*	*Doctor's daughter*
Eugene Istomin	Pianist	*Martita Casals*	*Pablo Casals' widow*
Andrew Jackson	US president	*Rachel Robards*	*Colonel's daughter*
Michael Jackson	Entertainer	*Lisa-Marie Presley (1)*	*Singer and actress*
		Debbie Rowe (2)	*Nurse*
James I	English king	*Anne*	*Danish princess*
James II	English king	*Anne Hyde (1)*	*Daughter of the Earl of Clarendon*
		Mary of Modena (2)	*Italian noblewoman*
James V	King of Scotland	*Mary of Guise*	*French noblewoman*

FAMOUS PEOPLE

Harry James	Musician	*Betty Grable*	*Actress*
Jean-Michel Jarre	Musician	*Charlotte Rampling*	*Actress*
Martin Jarvis	Actor	*Rosalind Ayres*	*Actress*
David Jason	Actor	*Gill Hinchcliffe*	*TV production assistant*
Billy Joel (2)	Singer	*Christie Brinkley (2)*	*Model*
John	King of England	*Isabella of Angoulême (2)*	*French noblewoman*
John of Gaunt	English prince	*Blanche of Lancaster (1)*	*English noblewoman*
		Constance of Castile (2)	*Castilian princess*
		Catherine Swynford (3)	*Former mistress*
Elton John	Vocalist and composer	*Renate Blauel*	*Actress*
Don Johnson (1) & (3)	Actor	*Melanie Griffith*	*Actress*
Richard Johnson (1)	Actor	*Kim Novak*	*Actress*
Samuel Johnson	Writer and lexicographer	*Elizabeth Porter*	*Schoolteacher*
Al Jolson	Entertainer	*Ruby Keeler*	*Actress*
Allan Jones	Singer and actor	*Irene Hervey*	*Actress*
Anthony Armstrong Jones	Photographer	*Princess Margaret*	*Elizabeth II's sister*
Sir G Roderick Jones	MD of Reuters	*Enid Bagnold*	*Authoress*
Jack Jones (2)	Singer	*Jill St John (2)*	*Actress*
James Joyce	Irish writer	*Nora Barnacle*	*Socialite*
Pierre Junot	Businessman	*Caroline of Monaco*	*Princess*
Justinian	East Roman emperor	*Theodora*	*Actress*
Wassily Kandinsky	Russian artist	*Nina Andreevskaya*	*Moscow socialite*
Sam Kane	Actor	*Linda Lusardi*	*Actress and model*
Charles Kelly (2)	Actor	*Ellen Terry*	*Actress*
Gary Kemp (1)	Actor and musician	*Sadie Frost*	*Actress*
John F Kennedy (1)	US president	*Jacqueline Bouvier*	*Socialite*
Ludovic Kennedy	Broadcaster	*Moira Shearer*	*Ballet dancer*
Danny Keough (1)	Rock musician	*Lisa-Marie Presley*	*Singer and actress*
Jim Kerr (2)	Musician	*Patsy Kensit*	*Actress*
John Maynard Keynes	Economist	*Lydia Lopokova*	*Ballerina*
Aly Khan (3)	Middle Eastern prince	*Rita Hayworth (1)*	*Actress*
Imran Khan	Cricketer	*Jemima Goldsmith*	*Heiress*
Eddie Kidd	Stunt motorcyclist	*Debbie Ash (1)*	*Actress*
Jan Kiepura	Tenor	*Martha Eggerth*	*Soprano*
Val Kilmer	Actor	*Joanne Whalley*	*Actress*
Martin Luther King	Civil rights leader	*Coretta Scott*	*Music graduate*
Paddy King	Businessman	*Carol Vorderman*	*TV presenter*
Henry Kingi (3)	Stuntman	*Lindsay Wagner*	*Actress*
Rudyard Kipling	Novelist and poet	*Caroline Balestier*	*Publishing heiress*
Kevin Kline	Actor	*Phoebe Cates*	*Actress*
Alex Knight	Restaurateur	*Carole Smillie*	*TV presenter*
Mark Knopfler	Musician	*Kitty Aldridge*	*Actress*
John Knox	Religious reformer	*Marjory Bowes (1)*	*John Knox's 1st wife*
		Margaret Stewart (2)	*Lord Ochiltree's daughter*
Musa Komeagac	Turkish waiter	*Sarah Cook*	*Schoolgirl*
			(13 when married)
Alexander Korda	Film director	*Merle Oberon (2)*	*Actress*
André Kostelanetz	Conductor	*Lily Pons*	*Soprano*
Kris Kristofferson	Actor	*Rita Coolidge (2)*	*Singer*
Sam Kydd	Actor	*Pinkie Barnes*	*Table tennis international*
Alan Lake (3)	Actor	*Diana Dors*	*Actress*
Fernando Lamas (4)	Actor	*Esther Williams (4)*	*Actress*
Martin Landau	Actor	*Barbara Bain*	*Actress*
Walter Savage Landor	Writer	*Julia Thuillier*	*Socialite*
Charles Laughton	Actor	*Elsa Lanchester*	*Actress*
Tim Laurence (2)	Naval officer	*Princess Anne*	*British princess*
Jude Law (2)	Actor	*Sadie Frost*	*Actress*
DH Lawrence	Writer	*Frieda von Richthofen*	*Socialite*
Leigh Lawson (2)	Actor	*Twiggy*	*Model and actress*
David Lean	Film director	*Ann Todd*	*Actress*
John Le Mesurier	Actor	*Hattie Jacques*	*Actress*
Tommy Lee	Singer	*Heather Locklear (2)*	*Actress*
		Pamela Anderson (3)	*Actress*
Mike Leigh	Dramatist	*Alison Steadman*	*Actress*
Donovan Leitch	Actor	*Kirsty Hume*	*Model*
John Lennon (2)	Musician	*Yoko Ono (2)*	*Artist*
Leofric	Earl of Mercia	*Lady Godiva*	*Countess of Mercia*
CS Lewis	Author	*Joy Davidman*	*Poet*
Henry Lewis	Conductor	*Marilyn Horne*	*Mezzo-soprano*
Nick Lilley	Businessman	*Anna Raeburn*	*Agony aunt*
Abraham Lincoln	US president	*Mary Todd*	*Socialite*
Charles Lindbergh	Aviator	*Anne Morrow*	*Writer*

John Lloyd (1)	Tennis player	*Chris Evert*	*Tennis player*
Andrew Lloyd Webber (2)	Composer	*Sarah Brightman (2)*	*Singer*
Gary Lockwood	Actor	*Stefanie Powers*	*Actress*
Henry W Longfellow	US poet	*Frances Appleton*	*Socialite*
Rafael Lopez-Cambil	Argentinian playwright	*Paloma Picasso*	*Beautician and businesswoman*
Louis VII (1)	King of France	*Eleanor of Aquitaine*	*French noblewoman*
Louis XIV	King of France	*Maria Theresa (1)*	*Spanish princess*
		Madame de Maintenon (2)	*Louis X1V's 2nd wife*
Louis XVI	King of France	*Marie Antoinette*	*French princess*
Arthur Lucan	Music-hall artist	*Kitty McShane*	*Music-hall artist*
Sid Luft (3)	Entertainer	*Judy Garland*	*Actress*
David Lynch	Director	*Isabella Rossellini (3)*	*Actress*
Ben Lyon	Radio comedian	*Bebe Daniels*	*Radio comedienne*
Simon MacCorkindale	Actor	*Fiona Fullerton (1)*	*Actress*
		Susan George (2)	*Actress*
Ewan Macdonald	Presbyterian minister	*LM Montgomery*	*Canadian novelist*
Fred MacMurray	Actor	*June Haver*	*Actress*
Richard Madeley	TV presenter	*Judy Finnegan*	*TV presenter*
Gustav Mahler	Composer	*Alma Maria Schindler (1)*	*Musician*
Lee Majors	Actor	*Farrah Fawcett (2)*	*Actress*
Louis Malle	Director	*Candice Bergen (3)*	*Actress*
Max Mallowan	Archaeologist	*Agatha Christie*	*Writer*
Charles Manners	Irish bass and impresario	*Fanny Moody*	*English soprano*
Mauro Mantovani	Actor	*Samantha Janus*	*Actress*
Mao Zedong	Chinese leader	*Chiang Ching*	*Actress*
J Howard Marshall II	Oil tycoon	*Anna Nicole Smith*	*Actress*
Steve Martin	Actor	*Victoria Tennant*	*Actress*
Ricardo Mazzucchelli (2)	Italian businessman	*Ivana Trump*	*Former wife of Donald Trump*
David McCallum (1)	Actor	*Jill Ireland*	*Actress*
Paul McCartney (2)	Musician	*Linda Eastman*	*Photographer*
James McCracken	Tenor	*Sandra Warfield*	*Soprano*
Slim Jim Phantom McDonnell	Musician	*Britt Ekland (1)*	*Actress*
John McEnery	Actor	*Stephanie Beacham*	*Actress*
John McEnroe	Tennis player	*Tatum O'Neal*	*Actress*
Tim McGraw	Country singer	*Faith Hill*	*Country singer*
Steve McQueen (2)	Actor	*Ali MacGraw*	*Actress*
John McVie	Musician	*Christine Perfect*	*Singer*
Felix Mendelssohn	Composer	*Cécile Jeanrenaud*	*Clergyman's daughter*
Burgess Meredith (3)	Actor	*Paulette Goddard*	*Actress*
George Meredith	English novelist	*Mary Ellen Nicolls (1)*	*Daughter of Thomas Love Peacock*
		Marie Vulliamy (2)	*Socialite*
Cliff Michelmore	Broadcaster	*Jean Metcalfe*	*Broadcaster*
Milanion	Mythical Greek athlete	*Atalanta*	*Mythical Greek huntress*
John Everett Millais (2)	Artist	*Effie Gray*	*Artist*
Arthur Miller (3)	Playwright	*Marilyn Monroe*	*Actress*
Johnny Lee Miller (1)	Actor	*Angelina Jolie*	*Actress*
John Mills	Actor	*Mary Hayley Bell*	*Playwright*
John Milton	Poet	*Mary Powell (1)*	*Royalist sympathiser*
		Catherine Woodcock (2)	*Second wife*
		Elizabeth Minshull (3)	*Third wife*
Vincente Minnelli (2)	Film director	*Judy Garland*	*Actress*
Alfred Molina (2)	Actor	*Jill Gascoigne (1)*	*Actress*
Jim Mollison	Aviator	*Amy Johnson*	*Aviator*
Yves Montand (2)	Actor	*Simone Signoret*	*Actress*
Dudley Moore	Entertainer	*Suzy Kendall (1)*	*Actress*
		Tuesday Weld (2)	*Actress*
		Brogan Lane (3)	*Actress*
		Nicole Rothschild (4th)	*Actress*
Roger Moore	Actor	*Dorothy Squires (1)*	*Singer*
		Luisa Mattioli (2)	*Housewife*
Kenneth More	Actor	*Angela Douglas*	*Irish actress*
Thomas More	Chancellor of England	*Jane Colt (1)*	*Farmer's daughter*
		Alice Middleton (2)	*Widow of London mercer*
Lawrence Mortoff (4)	Producer	*Lindsay Wagner*	*Actress*
Oswald Mosley	Politician	*Cynthia Curzon (1)*	*English noblewoman*
		Diana Guinness (2)	*(Nancy Mitford's sister)*
Robert Motherwell	US artist	*Helen Frankenthaler*	*US artist*

F
A
M
O
U
S

P
E
O
P
L
E

Tommy Mottola	President of Sony Music	Mariah Carey	Singer
Louis Mountbatten	Naval commander	Edwina Ashley	Heiress and charity worker
Wolfgang Amadeus Mozart	Composer	Constance Weber	Singer
Malcolm Muggeridge	Journalist	Kitty Dobbs	Niece of Beatrice Webb
Muhammad	Founder of Islam	Aisha	Muhammad's favourite wife
John Middleton Murry (2)	Writer and critic	Katherine Mansfield	NZ short story writer
Napoleon I	French emperor	Josephine de Beauharnais (1)	French empress
		Marie Louise (2)	Austrian archduchess
Liam Neeson (2)	Actor	Natasha Richardson	
Horatio Nelson	English naval hero	Frances Nisbet	Doctor's widow
Nero	Roman emperor	Octavia (1)	Roman noblewoman
		Poppaea (2)	Roman noblewoman
		Messalina (3)	Roman noblewoman
Franco Nero (1)	Actor	Vanessa Redgrave	Actress
Anthony Newley (1)	Actor and singer	Joan Collins (1)	Actress
Paul Newman	Actor	Joanne Woodward	Actress
Arthur Bell Nicholls	Curate	Charlotte Brontë	Writer
David Nicholls	Horseracing trainer	Alex Greaves	Jockey
Ben Nicholson (2)	Artist	Barbara Hepworth	Sculptor
Harold Nicolson	Diplomat	Vita Sackville-West	Poet and novelist
David Niven	Actor	Primula Rollo	Cipher Clerk
Trevor Nunn	Artistic director	Janet Suzman (1)	Actress
		Imogen Stubbs (3)	Actress
Odysseus	Mythical king of Ithaca	Penelope	Daughter of King Icarius of Sparta
Angus Ogilvy	Businessman	Princess Alexandra	British princess
Gary Oldman	Actor	Leslie Manville (1)	Actress
		Uma Thurman (2)	Actress
Laurence Olivier	Actor	Jill Esmond (1)	Actress
		Vivien Leigh (2)	Actress
		Joan Plowright (3)	Actress
Aristotle Onassis (2)	Businessman	Jacqueline Kennedy	Socialite
Ryan O'Neal (2)	Actor	Farrah Fawcett	Actress
Eugene Ormandy	Conductor	Stephanie Goldner	Harpist
John Osborne	Playwright	Mary Ure (2)	Actress
		Jill Bennett (4)	Actress
Peter O'Toole (2)	Actor	Sian Phillips	Actress
Alan J Pakula (2)	Film director	Hope Lange	Actress
Bruce Paltrow	Television director	Blythe Danner	Actress
Desmond Park	Mining engineer	Kiri Te Kanawa	Opera singer
Norman Parkinson	Photographer	Wenda Rogerson	Model
Peleus	Mythical king of Phthia	Thetis	Mythical sea nymph (Nereid)
Wilfred Pelletier	Conductor	Rose Bampton	Soprano
Sean Penn (1)	Actor	Madonna	Singer and actress
George Peppard (2)	Actor	Elizabeth Ashley	Actress
Jon Pertwee	Actor	Jean Marsh (1)	Actress
	Actor	Ingeborg Rhosea (2)	Novelist
Michael Pertwee	Actor	Valerie French	Actress
Peter the Great (1)	Russian tsar	Catherine I	Russian empress
		Eudoxia	Russian noblewoman
Peter III	Russian tsar	Catherine II (the Great)	Russian empress
Marius Petipa	French choreographer	Mariya Surovshchikova (1)	Russian ballerina
		Lyubov Leonidovna (2)	Russian ballerina
Roland Petit	Choreographer	Zizi Jeanmaire	Dancer
Ryan Phillippe	Actor	Reese Witherspoon	Actress
Mark Phillips	Equestrian rider	Sandy Pflueger (2)	Equestrian rider
		Princess Anne (1)	British princess
Harold Pinter	Playwright	Vivien Merchant (1)	Actress
		Lady Antonia Fraser (2)	Authoress
Gabriel Piozzi	Musician	Hester Thrale	Writer
Brad Pitt	Actor	Jennifer Aniston	Actress
Christopher Plummer	Actor	Tammie Grimes	Actress
Roman Polanski	Director	Sharon Tate (2)	Actress
Carlo Ponti	Film producer	Sophia Loren	Actress
Hugh Porter	Cyclist	Anita Lonsborough	Swimmer
Poseidon	Greek god of the sea	Amphitrite	Mythical Greek sea nymph
Dick Powell	Actor	Joan Blondell (1)	Actress
		June Allyson (2)	Actress

Peter Powell (1)	Disc jockey and producer	Anthea Turner	TV presenter
William Powell	Actor	Carole Lombard	Actress
Prasutagus	King of Iceni	Boudicca	Queen of Iceni
John Prescott	British politician	Pauline Tiltson	Businesswoman
Elvis Presley	Singer	Priscilla Beaulieu	Actress
André Previn (2)	Conductor	Mia Farrow (3)	Actress
Vincent Price	Actor	Coral Browne	Actress
JB Priestley	Author	Jacquetta Hawkes	Archaeologist
Prince (Symbol)	Singer	Myte Garcia	Belly dancer
Freddie Prinze Jnr	Actor	Sarah Michelle Gellar	Actress
John Profumo	Politician	Valerie Hobson	Actress and dancer
Sergei Prokofiev	Composer	Lina Llubera	Spanish singer
Ptolemy XII	Egyptian ruler	Cleopatra III	Queen of Egypt
Ptolemy XIII (1)	Egyptian Ruler	Cleopatra VII	Queen of Egypt
Giacomo Puccini	Composer	Elvira Gemignani	Socialite
Dennis Quaid	Actor	Meg Ryan (2)	Actress
Jackie Rae (3)	TV presenter	Janette Scott	Actress
Arthur Ransome	Writer	Evgenia Shelepin (2)	Trotsky's secretary
Robin Ray	Broadcaster	Susan Stranks	TV presenter
Ronald Reagan	US president	Jane Wyman (1)	Actress
		Nancy Davis (2)	Actress
Michael Redgrave	Actor	Rachel Kempson	Actress
Jamie Redknapp	Footballer	Louise Nurding	Pop singer
Derek Redmond	Athlete	Sharron Davis	Swimmer
Erich Maria Remarque (4)	Author	Paulette Goddard	Actress
Rembrandt Van Rijn	Dutch painter	Saskia Uylenburgh	Burgomaster's daughter
Jean Renoir	Film director	Andrée Heurschling (1)	Artist's model
		Dido Freire (2)	Brazilian film-maker's daughter
Pierre-Auguste Renoir	French painter	Alice Charigot	Socialite
Burt Reynolds	Actor	Judy Carne (1)	Actress
		Loni Anderson (2)	Actress
Richard I	English king	Berengaria	Princess of Navarre
Richard II	English king	Anne of Bohemia (1)	Emperor Charles 1V's daughter
		Isabelle (2)	Daughter of Charles VI of France
Richard III	English king	Anne Nevill	English noblewoman
Tony Richardson (2)	Film producer	Vanessa Redgrave	Actress
Shane Richie	Comedian	Coleen Nulan	Singer
Guy Ritchie (2)	Film director	Madonna	Singer and Actress
Allan Rider (1)	Music publisher	Lindsay Wagner	Actress
Brian Rix	Actor	Elspet Gray	Actress
Jason Robards (2)	Actor	Lauren Bacall (3)	Actress
Harold Robbins	Writer	Muriel Ling (1)	Model
		Grace Palermo (5)	Socialite
		Jann Stapp (6)	Businesswoman
Tim Robbins (common law)	Actor (common law)	Susan Sarandon (common law)	Actress
Roy Rogers	Actor and singer	Dale Evans	Actress and singer
John Rolfe	English Colonist	Pocahontas	Indian princess
Mickey Rooney	Actor	Ava Gardner	Actress
Karl Rosa	German conductor	Euphrosyne Parepa	Soprano
Arnold Rosé	Violinist	Justine Mahler	Sister of Gustav Mahler
Lord (Primrose) Rosebery	Scottish statesman	Hannah Rothschild	Heiress
Jack Rosenthal	Playwright	Maureen Lipman	Actress
Jonathan Ross	TV presenter	Jane Goldman	Writer
Nick Ross	Presenter	Sarah Caplin	TV executive
Roberto Rossellini (2)	Director	Ingrid Bergman (2)	Actress
Dante Gabriel Rossetti	Poet and painter	Elizabeth Siddal	Model
Gioacchino Rossini	Composer	Isabella Colbran (1)	Spanish soprano
		Olympie Pélissier (2)	Parisian hostess
Leonard Rossiter	Actor	Josephine Tewson (1)	Actress
		Gillian Raine (2)	Actress
Mstislav Rostropovich	Cellist and conductor	Galina Vishnevskaya	Soprano
Philip Roth	Novelist	Claire Bloom	Actress
John Ruskin (1)	Art Critic	Effie Gray	Artist
Kurt Russell	Actor	Goldie Hawn	Actress
Camille Saint-Saëns	Composer	Marie Truffot	Socialite
George Sanders	Actor	Zsa Zsa Gabor (2)	Actress
		Benita Hume (3)	Actress
		Magda Gabor (4)	Actress

Name	Role	Name	Role
Gerald Scarfe	Cartoonist	Jane Asher	Actress and cook
Arnold Schoenberg	Composer	Mathilde von Zemlinsky (1)	Musician
		Gertrud Kolisch (2)	Musician
Robert Schumann	Composer	Clara Wieck	Pianist
Martin Scorsese	Director	Isabella Rossellini (4)	Actress
George C Scott	Actor	Colleen Dewhurst	Socialite
Walter Scott	Scottish novelist	Charlotte Charpentier	Daughter of French émigré
Steven Seagal (2)	Actor	Kelly Le Brock	Actress
Rudolf Seiber (1)	Production assistant	Marlene Dietrich	Actress
Peter Sellers	Actor	Anne Hayes (1)	Housewife
		Britt Ekland (2)	Actress
		Miranda Quarry (3)	Actress
		Lynne Frederick (4)	Actress
David O Selznick (2)	Director	Jennifer Jones (2)	Actress
Rudolf Serkin	Pianist	Irene Busch	Musician
William Shakespeare	Playwright	Ann Hathaway	Farmer's daughter
Omar Sharif	Actor and bridge player	Faten Hamama (1)	Actress
		Nadiya Aja (2)	Saudi tycoon's daughter
Artie Shaw	Bandleader	Lana Turner (1)	Actress
		Ava Gardner (2)	Actress
Bernard Shaw	Bodyguard	Patty Hearst	Heiress
George Bernard Shaw	Dramatist	Charlotte Payne-Townshend	Heiress
Robert Shaw (2)	Actor	Mary Ure	Actress
Percy Bysshe Shelley	Poet	Mary Godwin	Writer
Richard Brinsley Sheridan	Irish dramatist	Elizabeth Linley	Composer's daughter
Jean Sibelius	Composer	Aino Järnefelt	General's daughter
Paul Simon	Singer and composer	Carrie Fisher (2)	Actress
Frank Sinatra	Singer	Ava Gardner (2)	Actress
		Mia Farrow (3)	Actress
		Barbara Marx (4)	Actress
Nikki Sixx	Motley Crue guitarist	Donna D'Errico	'Baywatch' actress
John Skeaping (1)	Sculptor	Barbara Hepworth	Sculptor
Cyril Smith	Pianist	Phyllis Sellick	Pianist
Mike Smith	TV presenter	Sarah Greene	TV presenter
Socrates	Philosopher	Xanthippe	Athenian
David Solkin	Businessman	Janet Street-Porter	TV presenter
Georg Solti	Conductor	Valerie Pitts	TV presenter
Robert Southey	Poet	Edith Fricker	Socialite
Phil Spector	Record producer	Veronica Bennett	Singer
Earl Charles Spencer	English nobleman	Victoria Lockwood	Model
Edmund Spenser	English poet	Elizabeth Boyle	Socialite
Steven Spielberg (2)	Director	Kate Capshaw (2)	Actress
		Amy Irving (1)	Actress
Henry Stafford	2nd Duke of Buckingham	Catherine Woodville	Sister-In-law of Edward 1V
Sylvester Stallone	Actor	Sasha Czatv (1)	Theatre usher
		Brigitte Nielsen (2)	Actress
		Jennifer Flavin (3)	Model
Alvin Stardust (3)	Pop singer	Liza Goddard	Actress
Ringo Starr	Musician	Maureen Cox (1)	Childhood sweetheart
		Barbara Bach (2)	Actress
Anthony Steele	Actor	Anita Ekberg	Actress
Rod Steiger (1)	Actor	Claire Bloom	Actress
Chris Stein (common law)	Guitarist	Deborah Harry (common law)	Singer
Robert Stephens	Actor	Maggie Smith	Actress
Robert Louis Stevenson	Author	Fanny Osbourne	Actress
Dave Stewart	Musician	Siobhan Fahey	Singer
Patrick Stewart	Actor ('Startrek')	Wendy Neuss	Producer ('Startrek')
Rod Stewart	Singer	Alana Hamilton (1)	Model
		Rachel Hunter (2)	Model
Thomas Stewart	Baritone	Evelyn Lear	Soprano
Alfred Stieglitz	US photographer	Georgia O' Keeffe	US painter
Ben Stiller	Actor	Christine Taylor	Actress
Sting	Singer	Frances Tomelty (1)	Actress
		Trudi Styler (2)	Actress
Leopold Stokowski	Conductor	Olga Samaroff (1)	Pianist
John Stonehouse	Politician	Sheila Buckley	Secretary
Richard Strauss	Composer	Pauline de Ahna	Soprano
Igor Stravinsky	Composer	Catherine Nossenko (1)	Stravinsky's cousin
		Vera de Bosset Sudekeine (2)	Ballet dancer

Roy Strong	Writer and historian	Julia Trevelyan Oman	Designer
Josef Suk	Violinist	Otilie Dvořák	Daughter of Antonin Dvořák
Clive Swift (1)	Author	Margaret Drabble	Novelist
James Taylor	Composer	Carly Simon	Singer
Robert Taylor	Actor	Barbara Stanwyck	Actress
Pyotr Tchaikovsky	Composer	Antonina Miliukova	Pupil of Tchaikovsky
William Temple	Diplomat and essayist	Dorothy Osborne	Daughter of governor of Guernsey
David Teniers the Younger	Flemish painter	Anna Brueghel	Daughter of Jan Brueghel
Jon Tenney	Actor	Teri Hatcher	Actress
Denis Thatcher	Businessman	Margaret Kempson (1)	Housewife
		Margaret Roberts (2)	Politician
John Thaw (2)	Actor	Sheila Hancock	Actress
Ben Thomas (2)	Actor	Roseanne Barr	Actress
Billy Bob Thornton	Actor	Cynda Williams (1)	Actress
		Angelina Jolie (2)	Actress
Jeremy Thorpe (2)	Politician	Marion Stein	Musician
Tom Thumb	Circus performer	Lavinia Warren	Circus performer
Mike Todd	Showman	Elizabeth Taylor (3)	Actress
		Joan Blondell (2)	Actress
Mel Tormé (1)	Singer	Janette Scott (3)	
Rip Torn	Actor	Geraldine Page	Actress
Tico Torres	Pop musician (Bon Jovi)	Eva Herzigova	Model
Bill Travers	Actor	Virginia McKenna (2)	Actress
John Travolta	Actor	Kelly Preston	Actress
Owen Tudor (1)	Grandfather of Henry VII	Catherine	Valois princess
Ted Turner (3)	Media mogul	Jane Fonda	Actress
Mike Tyson	Boxer	Robin Givens (1)	Actress
		Monica Turner (2)	Actress
Inaki Urdangarin	Handball player	Christina	Spanish Infanta
Roger Vadim	Film director	Brigitte Bardot (1)	Actress
		Jane Fonda (2)	Actress
Peter Vaughan	Actor	Billie Whitelaw (1)	Actress
		Lillias Walker (2)	Actress
Giuseppe Verdi	Composer	Margherita Barezzi (1)	Daughter of Verdi's sponsor
		Giuseppina Strepponi (2)	Soprano
Tony Visconti	Record producer	May Pang	Author
Richard Wagner	Composer	Minna Planer (1)	Opera singer and actress
		Cosima Von Bülow (2)	Franz Liszt's daughter
Robert Wagner	Actor	Natalie Wood (1) and (3)	Actress
		Marion Marshall (2)	Actress
		Jill St John (4)	Actress
Robert Walker (1)	Actor	Jennifer Jones	Actress
John Warner (7)	Senator	Elizabeth Taylor	Actress
George Washington	US president	Martha Custis	Socialite
Dennis Waterman	Actor	Patricia Maynard (2)	Actress
		Rula Lenska (3)	Actress
George Frederick Watts (1)	English painter	Ellen Terry	English actress
Carl Wayne	Actor and singer	Sue Hanson	Actress
Kurt Weill	Composer	Lotte Lenya	Actress and singer
Mark Weinberg	Businessman	Anouska Hempel	Actress
Orson Welles (2)	Actor and director	Rita Hayworth (2)	Actress
HG Wells	Author	Amy Robbins	Student
Franz Werfel (3)	Writer	Alma Maria Schindler	Musician
Timothy West	Actor	Prunella Scales	Actress
James McNeill Whistler	Artist	Beatrix Godwin	Widow of EW Godwin (architect)
Desmond Wilcox	Producer	Esther Rantzen	Broadcaster
Herbert Wilcox	Film director	Anna Neagle	Actress
Oscar Wilde	Playwright and novelist	Constance Lloyd	Socialite
Gene Wilder	Actor	Gilda Radner	Psychotherapist
Michael Wilding	Actor	Elizabeth Taylor (2)	Actress
		Margaret Leighton (4)	Actress
William III	British king	Mary II	British queen
William IV	British king	Adelaide	German noblewoman
Andy Williams	Singer	Claudine Longet	Actress
Hugh Williams	TV magnate	Sue Lawley	Broadcaster
Michael Williams	Actor	Judi Dench	Actress
Bruce Willis	Actor	Demi Moore	Actress
Brian Wolfe (2)	Theatre producer	Jill Browne	Actress
Stevie Wonder	Musician	Syreeta Wright	Singer

Edward Woodward	Actor	*Venetia Barrett (1)*	*Actress*
		Michelle Dotrice (2)	*Actress*
Leonard Woolf	Publisher and writer	*Virginia Stephen*	*Novelist*
William Wordsworth	Poet	*Mary Hutchinson*	*Socialite*
Billy Wright	Footballer	*Joy Beverley*	*Singer*
William Wyler	Film director	*Margaret Sullavan*	*Actress*
Bill Wyman	Rolling Stone	*Astrid Lundstrom (2)*	*Model*
		Mandy Smith (3)	*Model*
Michael Wynn Jones	Publisher	*Delia Smith*	*Cookery writer*
WB Yeats	Poet	*Georgie Hyde-Lees*	*Socialite*
Sergei Yessenin	Poet	*Isadora Duncan (1)*	*Dancer*
Gig Young	Actor	*Elizabeth Montgomery (3)*	*Actress*
Stuart Zender	Musician	*Melanie Blatt*	*Pop singer*
Zeus	Greek supreme god	*Metis (1)*	*Greek sea nymph*
		Themis (2)	*Daughter of Gaia and Uranus*
		Hera (3)	*Sister of Zeus*
Efrem Zimbalist	Violinist	*Alma Gluck*	*Soprano*
Antonio Zucchi	Venetian painter	*Angelica Kaufmann*	*Swiss painter*

Middle Names: Ordered by Middle Name

First Name	Middle Name(s)	Surname	
Søren	**Aabye**	KIERKEGAARD	Danish philosopher
Herbert	**Aaron**	HAUPTMAN	US physicist
Elvis	**Aaron**	PRESLEY	US singer
Selman	**Abraham**	WAKSMAN	US biochemist
James	**Abram**	GARFIELD	US president
Claude	**Achille**	DEBUSSY	Composer
John	**Addington**	SYMONDS	Author
Hans	**Adolph**	KREBS	British biochemist
Walter	**Adolf**	GROPIUS	Architect
Henry	**Agard**	WALLACE	US vice-president
Robin	**Airling**	HANBURY-TENISON	Explorer
Chester	**Alan**	ARTHUR	US president
Bob	**Alan**	DYLAN	Singer and composer
Graham	**Alan**	GOOCH	Cricketer
James	**Albert**	MICHENER	Author
Francis (Frank)	**Albert**	SINATRA	Singer
Hans	**Albrecht**	BETHE	US physicist
John	**Alden**	CARPENTER	Musician and businessman
Gene	**Alden**	HACKMAN	Actor
Nelson	**Aldrich**	ROCKEFELLER	US vice-president
Nicholas	**Alexander**	FALDO	Golfer
Alan	**Alexander**	MILNE	Author
Robert	**Alexander**	RUNCIE	Archbishop of Canterbury
Peter	**Alexander**	USTINOV	Actor and writer
Henry	**Alfred**	KISSINGER	US statesman
Marcus	**Algernon**	ADAMS	Photographer
Enid	**Algerine**	BAGNOLD	Author
Ellen	**Alice**	TERRY	Actress
Charles	**Allston**	COLLINS	Artist
Tony	**Aloysius**	HANCOCK	TV character
James	**Aloysius**	HANSOM	Designer
Thomas	**Alva**	EDISON	Inventor
Pedro	**Alvarez**	CABRAL	Navigator
Elmer	**Ambrose**	SPERRY	US inventor
Billy	**Ambrose**	WRIGHT	Footballer
Meyer	**Amschel**	ROTHSCHILD	German financier
Nikolai	**Andreievich**	RIMSKY-KORSAKOV	Composer
Michael J	**Andrew**	FOX	Actor
Miguel	**Angel**	ASTURIAS	Guatemalan poet
George	**Anthony**	NEWLEY	Actor and singer
Giacomo	**Antonio**	PUCCINI	Composer
Hendrik	**Antoon**	LORENTZ	Dutch physicist
Benjamin	**Apthorp**	GOULD	US astronomer
Spangler	**Arlington**	BROUGH	Actor
Enoch	**Arnold**	BENNETT	Author
Philip	**Arnold**	HESELTINE	Composer

First Name	Middle Name(s)	Surname	
Eric	**Arthur**	BLAIR	Author
Kenneth	**Arthur**	DODD	Comedian
Cliff	**Arthur**	MICHELMORE	Broadcaster
Robert	**Arthur Talbot**	CECIL	British prime minister
Pierre	**Athanase**	LAROUSSE	French publisher
George	**Augustus**	ARLISS	Actor
Charles	**Augustus**	LINDBERGH	US aviator
Francis	**Aungier**	LONGFORD	Prison reformer
Richard	**Austen**	BUTLER	Politician
Henry	**Austin**	DOBSON	Poet
Erik	**Axel**	KARLFELDT	Swedish poet
Julia	**Babette Sarah**	NEUBERGER	Rabbi
Thomas	**Babington**	MACAULAY	Author
Brian	**Baden**	MOORE	Football commentator
Thomas	**Bailey**	ALDRICH	Author
Jane	**Baillie**	CARLYLE	Wife of Thomas Carlyle
Lyndon	**Baines**	JOHNSON	US president
Ronnie	**Balfour**	CORBETT	Comedian
Robert	**Banks**	JENKINSON	British prime minister
Robert	**Bannatyne**	FINLAY	Politician
Jocelyn	**Barbara**	HEPWORTH	Sculptor
Ruth	**Barbara**	RENDELL	Crime novellist
Peter	**Barker Howard**	MAY	Cricketer
John	**Barry**	HUMPHRIES	Comedian and writer
Isaac	**Bashevis**	SINGER	Writer
George	**Basil**	HUME	Cardinal
Upton	**Beall**	SINCLAIR	US novelist
Claire	**Berenice**	RAYNER	Broadcaster
Alan	**Beresford**	B' STARD	TV character ('New Statesman')
Norman	**Beresford**	TEBBIT	Politician
Colin	**Berkeley**	MOYNIHAN	Politician
Henry	**Bernard**	LEVIN	Journalist and author
George	**Bernard**	SHAW	Author
John (Jack)	**Berry**	HOBBS	English cricketer
George	**Biddell**	AIRY	Astronomer
Rutherford	**Birchard**	HAYES	US president
John	**Bird**	SUMNER	Archbishop of Canterbury
John ('Dizzy')	**Birks**	GILLESPIE	Jazz trumpeter
Bill	**Blackledge**	BEAUMONT	Rugby union player
Joseph	**Blanco**	WHITE	English poet
Cecil	**Blount**	DE MILLE	Film director
John	**Bodkin**	ADAMS	Doctor and murder suspect
Christian	**Boehmer**	ANFINSEN	US biochemist
Wilson	**Boit**	KIPKETER	Kenyan s/chase WR 13/8/97
Ulrich	**Bonnell**	PHILLIPS	US historian
Ernst	**Borls**	CHAIN	German biochemist
Arthur	**Bowden**	ASKEY	Comedian
Richard	**Bowdler**	SHARPE	Ornithologist
Lester	**Bowles**	PEARSON	Canadian politician
Leslie	**Bowyer**	CHARTERIS	Author
John	**Boyd**	DUNLOP	Inventor
John	**Boynton**	PRIESTLEY	Author
William	**Bradford**	SHOCKLEY	American physicist
James	**Branch**	CABELL	Novelist
Charles	**Brenton**	HUGGINS	American surgeon
William	**Bridges**	ADAMS	Engineer
George	**Brinton**	McCLELLAN	US soldier
Roy	**Broadbent**	FULLER	Poet
Amos	**Bronson**	ALCOTT	Transcendentalist
Susan	**Brownell**	ANTHONY	Suffragette
Marshall	**Bruce**	MATHERS III	Rap artist (aka Eminem)
Lawrence	**Bruno Nero**	DALLAGLIO	Rugby player
Lee	**Buck**	TREVINO	American golfer
Matthew	**Bunker**	RIDGWAY	US soldier
Charles	**Burgess**	FRY	Sportsman
Walter	**Burley**	GRIFFIN	US architect
Lawrence	**Burnett**	GOWING	Painter
Robert	**Burns**	WOODWARD	American chemist
Stephen	**Burton**	LANCASTER	Actor
Paul	**Bustill Le Roy**	ROBESON	Actor

First Name	Middle Name(s)	Surname	
William	**Butler**	YEATS	Author
James	**Byron**	DEAN	Actor
Percy	**Bysshe**	SHELLEY	Poet
John	**Cabell**	BRECKINRIDGE	US vice-president
Henry	**Cabot**	LODGE	US senator
Ben	**Caine**	HOLLIOAKE	English cricketer
John	**Caldwell**	CALHOUN	US vice-president
Hugh	**Callum**	LAURIE	Actor and comedian
John	**Calvin**	COOLIDGE	US president
Edward	**Calvin**	KENDALL	American chemist
John	**Cameron**	MORTON	Journalist
King	**Camp**	GILLETTE	Inventor
Donald	**Campbell**	DEWAR	British politician
Patricia	**Campbell**	HEARST	Heiress
Archibald	**Campbell**	TAIT	Archbishop of Canterbury
Christopher	**Carandini**	LEE	Actor
John	**Carew**	ECCLES	Australian neurophysiologist
Peter	**Carl**	FABERGÉ	Russian goldsmith
Peter	**Carl**	GOLDMARK	Inventor
Wilhelm	**Carl**	GRIMM	Folklorist
Linus	**Carl**	PAULING	Scientist
Daniel	**Carleton**	GAJDUSEK	US virologist
Hugh	**Carleton**	GREENE	Journalist and broadcaster
Percy	**Carlyle**	GILCHRIST	Metallurgist
Gertrude	**Caroline**	EDERLE	US swimmer
Hugh	**Caswell Tremenheere**	DOWDING	RAF chief
Maureen	**Catherine**	CONNOLLY	Tennis pro
George	**Catlett**	MARSHALL	US soldier and statesman
Lawrence (Larry)	**Cecil**	ADLER	Musician
James	**Cellan**	JONES	Film director
Thomas	**Chandler**	HALIBURTON	Canadian writer
Joel	**Chandler**	HARRIS	Author
Samuel	**Chao Chung**	TING	US physicist
Frederick	**Chapman**	ROBBINS	US physiologist
Kenneth	**Charles**	BRANAGH	Actor
Tjalling	**Charles**	KOOPMANS	US economist
Anthony	**Charles Lynton**	BLAIR	Politician
Richard	**Charles Nicholas**	BRANSON	Entrepreneur
Denis	**Charles Scott**	COMPTON	Cricketer
Rodney	**Charlton**	TROTTER	'Fools and Horses' character
Walter	**Chauncy**	CAMP	American footballer
Rupert	**Chawner**	BROOKE	Poet
Johann	**Christian**	BACH	Composer
Patrick	**Christopher**	STEPTOE	Gynaecologist
Dennis	**Christopher George**	POTTER	Playwright
Chris	**Clairmonte**	LEWIS	Cricketer
Herbert	**Clark**	HOOVER	US president
William	**Claude**	FIELDS	Comedian and actor
Roy	**Claxton**	ACUFF	Country musician
Harold	**Clayton**	LLOYD	US film comedian
Thomas	**Clayton**	WOLFE	Novelist
Elizabeth	**Cleghorn**	GASKELL	Writer
Edmund	**Clerihew**	BENTLEY	Writer
Marcus	**Cocceius**	NERVA	Roman emperor
John	**Cody Fiddler**	SIMPSON	News reporter
Michael	**Colin**	COWDREY	Cricketer
Norman	**Colin**	DEXTER	Author
Stephen	**Collins**	FOSTER	US songwriter
Mel	**Columcille**	GIBSON	Actor
Louis	**Comfort**	TIFFANY	Glassmaker
Milner	**Connorton**	GRAY	Graphic designer
George	**Corley**	WALLACE	Governor of Alabama
Gianfranco	**Corsi**	ZEFFIRELLI	Film director
Alfred	**Cort**	HADDON	Anthropologist
Ingvar	**Costa**	CARLSSON	Swedish politician
Reginald	**Cotterell**	BUTLER	Sculptor
John	**Couch**	ADAMS	Astronomer
Ludovic	**Coverley**	KENNEDY	Broadcaster
John	**Cowdery**	KENDREW	English biochemist
Cornelius	**Crane**	CHASE	Actor

First Name	Middle Name(s)	Surname	
Elzie	**Crisler**	SEGAR	US strip cartoonist
Betsy	**Cromer**	BYARS	Novelist
John	**Crowe**	RANSOM	US poet and critic
Dorothy	**Crowfoot**	HODGKIN	Scientist
William	**Cullen**	BRYANT	Poet
Gene	**Curran**	KELLY	Dancer
Gordon	**Cuthbert**	GREENIDGE	Cricketer
Len	**Cyril**	DEIGHTON	Novelist
Herman	**Cyril**	McNEILE	Author
Austin	**Danger**	POWERS	Film character
Gabriel	**Daniel**	FAHRENHEIT	Physicist
Arnold	**Daniel**	PALMER	Golfer
Dwight	**David**	EISENHOWER	US president
Benny	**David**	GOODMAN	US jazz clarinetist
Jerome	**David**	SALINGER	Author
Joan	**Dawson**	BAKEWELL	Broadcaster
Alfred	**Day**	HERSHEY	US biologist
Humphrey	**De Forest**	BOGART	Actor
Everton	**Decourcey**	WEEKES	West Indian cricketer
Franklin	**Delano**	ROOSEVELT	US president
William	**Denby**	HANNA	US animated cartoonist
Danny	**Dennio**	BLANCHFLOWER	Footballer
Michael	**Denzil Xavier**	PORTILLO	Politician
Earl	**Derr**	BIGGERS	US novelist
Henri	**Desire**	LANDRU	French murderer
Andrew	**Dewar**	GIBB	Scottish jurist
Miles	**Dewey**	DAVIS	Jazz musician
James	**Dewey**	WATSON	US biologist
Maureen	**Diane**	LIPMAN	Actress
Michael	**Dibdin**	HESELTINE	Politician
John	**Dickson**	CARR	US detective writer
Richard	**Doddridge**	BLACKMORE	Author
Juan	**Domingo**	PERÓN	Argentinian president
Frederick	**Donald**	COGGAN	Archbishop of Canterbury
Harry	**Donald**	SECOMBE	Comedian and singer
Alan	**Donald**	WHICKER	Broadcaster
Stella	**Dorothea**	GIBBONS	Writer
Phyllis	**Dorothy**	JAMES	Authoress
Heber	**Doust**	CURTIS	US astronomer
Henry	**Drysdale**	DAKIN	Chemist
Donald	**Duart**	MACLEAN	English traitor
Thomas	**Duffus**	HARDY	Archivist
Charlie	**Dunbar**	BROAD	Philosopher
John	**Dunmore**	LANG	Clergyman
Bob	**Dylan**	WILLIS	Cricketer
Anthony	**Dymoke**	POWELL	English novelist
James	**Earl**	CARTER	US president
Alfred	**Edgar**	COPPARD	Writer
John	**Edgar**	HOOVER	FBI director
Billy	**Edmund**	BUTLIN	Businessman
Ferdinand	**Edralin**	MARCOS	Filipino president
Lewis	**Edson**	WATERMAN	Inventor
Alfred	**Edward**	HOUSMAN	Author
Thomas	**Edward**	LAWRENCE	Author and soldier
Jonas	**Edward**	SALK	Biologist
Joseph	**Eggleston**	JOHNSTON	US soldier
Michael	**Elias**	BALCON	Film producer
Walt	**Elias**	DISNEY	Film producer
Gottlieb	**Eliel**	SAARINEN	Finnish/US architect
Mary	**Elizabeth**	PETERS	Pentathlete
Mai	**Elizabeth**	ZETTERLING	Actress and director
James	**Elroy**	FLECKER	Poet
Douglas	**Elton**	FAIRBANKS (Snr)	Actor
Charles	**Elwood**	YEAGER	US test pilot
George	**Emil**	PALADE	US biologist
Angelina	**Emily**	GRIMKE	US feminist
Barry	**Emmanuel**	TUCKWELL	Australian musician
John	**Enoch**	POWELL	British politician
George	**Eric**	NEWBY	Author
Oswald	**Ernald**	MOSLEY	British politician

First Name	Middle Name(s)	Surname	
Herbert	**Ernest**	BATES	Author
John	**Ernest**	STEINBECK	US novelist
Nigel	**Ernest James**	MANSELL	Racing driver
Robert	**Erskine**	CHILDERS	Writer
Richard	**Erskine Frere**	LEAKEY	Palaeontologist and naturalist
Bartolomé	**Estebàn**	MURILLO	Spanish painter
Maria	**Esther**	BUENO	Tennis player
Linda	**Esther**	GRAY	Scottish soprano
Willis	**Eugene**	LAMB	American physicist
Richard	**Evelyn**	BYRD	Explorer
Norman	**Everard**	BROOKES	Tennis player
William	**Ewart**	GLADSTONE	British prime minister
Adlai	**Ewing**	STEVENSON	US politician
Charles	**Farrar**	BROWNE	Humorist and writer
Pearl	**Fay**	WHITE	US actress
Igor	**Fedorovich**	STRAVINSKY	Composer
Isidor	**Feinstein**	STONE	US journalist
David	**Feodorovich**	OISTRAKH	Violinist
Carl	**Ferdinand**	CORI	American biochemist
Max	**Ferdinand**	PERUTZ	British biochemist
Ana	**Fidelia**	QUIROT	Cuban athlete
Dwight	**Filley**	DAVIS	Founder of Davis Cup
Oscar	**Fingal O'Flahertie Wills**	WILDE	Writer
Robin	**Finlayson**	COOK	Politician
Samuel	**Finley Breese**	MORSE	US inventor
Harlan	**Fiske**	STONE	US judge
John	**Fitzgerald**	KENNEDY	US president
Harry	**Flood**	BYRD	Politician
Lillian	**Florence**	HELLMAN	US playwright
Sarah	**Flower**	ADAMS	English poet
Chester	**Floyd**	CARLSON	US inventor
Sade	**Folasade**	ADU	Singer
Leopoldo	**Fortunato**	GALTIERI	Argentinian politician
Norman	**Foster**	RAMSEY	US physicist
Geoffrey	**Francis**	FISHER	Archbishop of Canterbury
Robert	**Francis**	KENNEDY	US politician
Donald	**Francis**	TOVEY	Pianist and composer
Daley	**Francis Morgan**	THOMPSON	Athlete
James	**Franciscus**	DURANTE	Entertainer
Charles	**François**	GOUNOD	Composer
Anatole	**François**	THIBAULT	Author
John	**Franklin**	CANDY	Actor
Samuel	**Franklin**	CODY	Aviator
John	**Franklin**	ENDERS	US bacteriologist
Billy	**Franklin**	GRAHAM	US evangelist
Robert	**Franklin**	STROUD	Birdman of Alcatraz
William	**Frederick**	CODY	Showman
Ronald	**Frederick**	DELDERFIELD	Author
Alexander	**Frederick**	DOUGLAS-HOME	British prime minister
Spencer	**Frederick**	GORE	Painter
George	**Frederick**	HANDEL	Composer
Walter	**Frederick (Fritz)**	MONDALE	US vice-president
Thomas	**Frognall**	DIBDIN	Librarian
Robert	**Gabriel**	MUGABE	Zimbabwean president
Mario	**Gabriele**	ANDRETTI	Racing driver
Sidonie	**Gabrielle**	COLETTE	Author
Matthew	**Galbraith**	PERRY	US naval officer
Warren	**Gamaliel**	HARDING	US president
Gabriel	**Garcia**	MARQUEZ	Columbian author
Jan	**Garrigue**	MASARYK	Czech statesman
Charles	**Gates**	DAWES	US vice-president
Johannes	**Gensfleisch**	GUTENBERG	German printer
Billy	**George**	BUNTER	Fictional character
Lawrence	**George**	DURRELL	Novelist
Rodney	**George**	LAVER	Tennis player
Roger	**George**	MOORE	Actor
Andre	**George**	PREVIN	Conductor
William	**Gerald**	GOLDING	Novelist
John	**Gerard**	BRAINE	Novelist
William	**Gershom**	COLLINGWOOD	Artist

First Name	Middle Name(s)	Surname	
Roger	**Gilbert**	BANNISTER	Athlete
William	**Gilbert**	GRACE	Cricketer
Ian	**Gillett**	CARMICHAEL	Actor
Eugene	**Gladstone**	O'NEILL	US playwright
William	**Gladstone**	STEWART	TV broadcaster/producer
Alton	**Glenn**	MILLER	Band leader
Charles	**Glover**	BARKLA	English physicist
Robson	**Golightly**	GREEN	Actor
Dean	**Gooderham**	ACHESON	US statesman
Sydney	**Goodsir**	SMITH	Poet
James	**Gordon**	BROWN	Politician
George	**Gordon**	BYRON	Poet
Neil	**Gordon**	KINNOCK	Politician
Harry	**Gordon**	SELFRIDGE	British merchant
Robert	**Graeme**	POLLOCK	Cricketer
Norman	**Graham**	HILL	Racing driver
James	**Graham**	BALLARD	Author
Frederick	**Grant**	BANTING	Physiologist
Lewis	**Grassic**	GIBBON	Novelist
Elisha	**Graves**	OTIS	Inventor
Charles	**Greely**	ABBOT	Astrophysicist
Emily	**Greene**	BALCH	US social reformer
Eldred	**Gregory**	PECK	Actor
Pelham	**Grenville**	WODEHOUSE	Author
Jack	**Griffith**	LONDON	US novelist
Thomas	**Griffiths**	WAINEWRIGHT	Art critic and murderer
Samuel	**Griswold**	GOODRICH	US publisher
Stephen	**Grover**	CLEVELAND	US president
James	**Grover**	THURBER	Humorist
Carl	**Gustav**	JUNG	Swiss psychiatrist
Magdi	**Habib**	YACOUB	Surgeon
Edvard	**Hagerup**	GRIEG	Norwegian composer
William	**Hale**	WHITE	Writer
Barbara	**Hamilton**	CARTLAND	Writer
George	**Hamilton**	GORDON	British prime minister
Charles	**Hamilton**	SORLEY	Poet
Glen	**Hammond**	CURTISS	US air pioneer
Terence	**Hanbury**	WHITE	Novelist
Fred	**Handel**	ELLIOTT	'Coronation Street' character
John	**Hanning**	SPEKE	Explorer
Martin	**Harcourt**	CHIVERS	Footballer
Charles	**Hard**	TOWNES	American physicist
Terence (Terry)	**Hardy**	WAITE	Religious adviser
Maurice	**Harold**	MACMILLAN	British prime minister
James	**Harold**	WILSON	British prime minister
Emma	**Harriet**	NICHOLSON	Politician
Roy	**Harris**	JENKINS	Politician
Kenneth	**Harry**	CLARKE	Politician
Francis	**Harry Compton**	CRICK	Biologist
Hawley	**Harvey**	CRIPPEN	Murderer
John	**Harvey**	KELLOGG	Inventor
Willis	**Haviland**	CARRIER	US inventor
Alfred	**Hawthorne**	HILL	Comedian
Mary	**Hayley**	BELL	Playwright
David	**Hayward**	BOWIE	Musician
Oliver	**Hazard**	PERRY	US naval officer
Publius	**Helvius**	PERTINAX	Roman emperor
Joan	**Henrietta**	COLLINS	Actress
Herbert	**Henry**	ASQUITH	British prime minister
William	**Henry**	CAVENDISH-BENTINCK	British prime minister
Augustus	**Henry**	FITZROY	British prime minister
William	**Henry**	HARRISON	US president
Fiorello	**Henry**	LA GUARDIA	US politician
Richard	**Henry Simpson**	STILGOE	Songwriter and broadcaster
Robert	**Hepler**	LOWE	Actor
Horatio	**Herbert**	KITCHENER	Irish soldier and statesman
David	**Herbert**	LAWRENCE	Author
George	**Herbert Walker**	BUSH	US president
Elton	**Hercules**	JOHN	Singer and composer
John	**Herschel**	GLENN	US astronaut and politician

First Name	Middle Name(s)	Surname	
Cyrus	**Herzl**	GORDON	US Hebrew scholar
Margaret	**Hilda**	THATCHER	British prime minister
Virginia	**Hilda Brunette Maxwell**	BOTTOMLEY	Politician
Henry	**Hinchcliffe**	AINLEY	Actor
Dag	**Hjalmar Agne Carl**	HAMMARSKJÖLD	Swedish statesman
Arthur	**Holly**	COMPTON	Physicist
Eric	**Honeywood**	PARTRIDGE	Lexicographer
James	**Hopwood**	JEANS	Physicist and astronomer
Hubert	**Horatio**	HUMPHREY	US vice-president
Walter	**Houser**	BRATTAIN	American physicist
Jeffrey	**Howard**	ARCHER	Author
Tasker	**Howard**	BLISS	Soldier and statesman
William	**Howard**	STEIN	US biochemist
William	**Howard**	TAFT	US president
Bernard	**Howell**	LEACH	English potter
William	**Howson**	TAYLOR	Potter
George	**Hoy**	FORMBY	Singer and musician
John	**Hoyer**	UPDIKE	Author
Elinor	**Hoyt**	WYLIE	US author
Thomas	**Huckle**	WELLER	US physiologist
Wystan	**Hugh**	AUDEN	Poet
Michael	**Hugh**	MEACHER	Politician
Hector	**Hugh**	MUNRO	Author
Mark	**Hume**	McCORMACK	Promoter
David	**Hunter**	HUBEL	US neurophysiologist
William	**Hunter Fisher**	CARSON	Jockey
Robert	**Hutchings**	GODDARD	US rocket pioneer
Leonid	**Ilich**	BREZHNEV	USSR president
Vladimir	**Ilyich**	LENIN	Russian revolutionary
Pyotr	**Ilyich**	TCHAIKOVSKY	Composer
Reginald	**Iolanthe**	PERRIN	TV character
Alexander	**Isaevich**	SOLZHENITSYN	Author
Jeremy	**Israel**	ISAACS	Arts mogul
George	**Ivan**	MORRISON	Singer and composer
James	**Jackson**	JEFFRIES	Boxing champion
Paul	**Jackson**	POLLOCK	US artist
Samuel	**Jackson**	SNEAD	Golfer
Lucinda	**Jane**	GREEN	Three-day eventer
Kiri	**Janette**	TE KANAWA	Opera singer
Abel	**Janszoon**	TASMAN	Navigator
Stanley	**Jasspon**	KUNITZ	US poet
William	**Jefferson**	HAGUE	Politician
William	**Jefferson Blyth**	CLINTON	US president
Michael	**Jeffrey**	JORDAN	US basketball player
Ada	**Jemima**	CROSSLEY	Australian contralto
John	**Jeremy**	THORPE	Politician
Gary	**Jim**	PLAYER	Golfer
Barbra	**Joan**	STREISAND	Singer
Liv	**Johanne**	ULLMANN	Norwegian actress
Stephen	**John**	FRY	Actor and author
Tony	**John**	HANCOCK	Comedy actor
Arthur	**John**	GIELGUD	Actor
Frederick	**John**	ROBINSON	British prime minister
Henry	**John**	TEMPLE	British prime minister
Jeremy	**John Durham**	ASHDOWN	Politician
Charles	**John Huffam**	DICKENS	Author
Ralph	**Johnson**	BUNCHE	American economist
Angelina	**Jolie**	VOIGHT	Actress
Irene	**Joliot**	CURIE	Nuclear physicist
Anders	**Jonas**	ANGSTROM	Physicist
Samuel	**Jones**	TILDEN	US politician
Richard	**Jordan**	GATLING	Inventor
Michael	**Joseph**	CAINE	Actor
Archibald	**Joseph**	CRONIN	Author
Bruce	**Joseph**	FORSYTH	Entertainer
Israel	**Joshua**	SINGER	Writer
Stephen	**Joshua**	SONDHEIM	Composer and lyricist
River	**Jude**	PHOENIX	Actor
Diane	**Julie**	ABBOT	Politician
Ferdinand	**Julius**	COHN	Botanist

First Name	Middle Name(s)	Surname	
Annie	Jump	CANNON	US astronomer
Seamus	Justin	HEANEY	Poet
Aimo	Kaarlo	CAJANDER	Finnish politician
Niels	Kai	JERNE	Danish immunologist
Julius	Kambarage	NYERERE	Tanzanian president
Hastings	Kamuzu	BANDA	Malawi politician
Mohandas	Karamchand	GANDHI	Indian leader
Uma	Karuna	THURMAN	Actress
Haldan	Keffer	HARTLINE	US physiologist
Gilbert	Keith	CHESTERTON	Author
Will	Keith	KELLOGG	Inventor
Dennis	Keith	LILLEE	Australian cricketer
Lester	Keith	PIGGOTT	Jockey
Michael	Kemp	TIPPETT	Composer
Edward ('Duke')	Kennedy	ELLINGTON	Composer and pianist
Tom	Kennerley	WOLFE	Novelist
Laurence	Kerr	OLIVIER	Actor
Philip	Kindred	DICK	US writer
Henry	Kirke	BROWN	Sculptor
Ragnar	Kittil	FRISCH	Norwegian economist
Jerome	Klapka	JEROME	Author
Hablot	Knight	BROWNE	Illustrator
James	Knox	POLK	US president
Sally	Kristen	RIDE	US astronaut
Ian	Lancaster	FLEMING	English novelist
Raymond	Landry	POINCARÉ	French statesman
Edwin	Landseer	LUTYENS	English architect
Samuel	Langhorne	CLEMENS	Author
Mervyn	Laurence	PEAKE	Author and artist
Bernard	Law	MONTGOMERY	Field marshal
Edward	Lawrie	TATUM	US biochemist
James	Leathes	PRIOR	Politician
George	Ledyard	STEBBINS	US botanist
Sheldon	Lee	GLASHOW	US physicist
Dustin	Lee	HOFFMAN	Actor
Arthur	Lehman	GOODHART	US jurist
Walter	Leland	CRONKITE	US broadcaster
James	Leonard	CALLAGHAN	British prime minister
George	Leonard	CAREY	Archbishop
Geoffrey	Leonard	CHESHIRE	Philanthropist
Aldous	Leonard	HUXLEY	Novelist
Winston	Leonard Spencer	CHURCHILL	British prime minister
Nelly	Leonie	SACHS	Swedish poet and playwright
Mstislav	Leopoldovich	ROSTROPOVICH	Cellist
John	Leslie	PRESCOTT	Politician
Bob	Leslie Townes	HOPE	Comedian
Basil	Lewis	D'OLIVEIRA	Cricketer
David	Lewis	JACOBS	Broadcaster
Harry (Bing)	Lillis	CROSBY	Vocalist and actor
Adam	Lindsay	GORDON	Australian poet
John	Liptrot	HATTON	Composer
Chris	Livingstone	EUBANK	Boxer
Adam	Llewellyn De Vere	ADAMANT	Fictional TV character
James	Logie	ROBERTSON	Poet
Val	Logsdon	FITCH	US physicist
Hugh	Longbourne	CALLENDAR	Physicist
Ezra	Loomis	POUND	Poet
Siegfried	Lorraine	SASSOON	Poet
Carl	Lotus	BECKER	US historian
John	Loughborough	PEARSON	Architect
Esther	Louise	RANTZEN	TV presenter
Thomas	Love	PEACOCK	Novelist and poet
Thomas	Lovell	BEDDOES	Poet and physiologist
Verney	Lovett	CAMERON	Explorer
Anita	Lucia	RODDICK	Businesswoman
Jacques	Lucien Jean	DELORS	European politician
Caroline	Lucretia	HERSCHEL	Astronomer
Lazarus	Ludwig	ZAMENHOF	Inventor of Esperanto
Jacob	Ludwig Carl	GRIMM	Folklorist
Maria	Lurdes	MUTOLA	Mozambican athlete

FAMOUS PEOPLE

First Name	Middle Name(s)	Surname	
Jean	**Lyndsey Torren**	MARSH	Actress
Kenneth	**Mackenzie**	CLARK	Art historian
Michael	**Mackintosh**	FOOT	Politician
William	**Maddock**	BAYLISS	Physiologist
Eartha	**Mae**	KITT	Singer
William	**Makepeace**	THACKERAY	Author
onald	**Malcolm**	CAMPBELL	Car and boat racer
Gerald	**Malcolm**	DURRELL	Writer and naturalist
James	**Mallahan**	CAIN	Writer
Alice	**Malsenior**	WALKER	US novelist
Gerard	**Manley**	HOPKINS	Poet
Vosdanig	**Manoog**	ADOIAN	Painter
Cassius	**Marcellus**	CLAY	Boxer
Leon	**Marcus**	URIS	US author
William	**Marcy**	TWEED	US politician and criminal
Penelope	**Margaret**	LIVELY	Writer
Erich	**Maria**	REMARQUE	Author
Victor	**Marie**	HUGO	French writer
Dylan	**Marlais**	THOMAS	Poet
John	**Marlan**	POINDEXTER	US naval officer
David	**Martin Scott**	STEEL	Politician
John	**Marwood**	CLEESE	Actor
Meryl	**Mary Louise**	STREEP	Actress
Thomas	**Massa**	ALSAGER	Newspaper manager
Thomas	**Masterman**	HARDY	Naval officer
Kenneth	**Mathieson**	DALGLISH	Footballer
Alan	**Mathison**	TURING	Mathematician
James	**Matthew**	BARRIE	Author
Gerald	**Maurice**	EDELMAN	US biochemist
Hugh	**Maxwell**	CASSON	Architect
Liza	**May**	MINNELLI	Singer
Quintin	**McGarel**	HOGG	Politician
James	**McGill**	BUCHANAN	American economist
Edwin	**McMasters**	STANTON	US statesman
Frank	**Meadow**	SUTCLIFFE	Photographer
Alexander	**Meigs**	HAIG	US soldier
Friedrich	**Melchior**	GRIMM	Journalist
Maria	**Meneghini**	CALLAS	Operatic soprano
Richard	**Mentor**	JOHNSON	US vice-president
Isaac	**Merritt**	SINGER	US inventor
Robert	**Merton**	SOLOW	American economist
William	**Mervyn**	PICKWOAD	Actor
Ian	**Michael**	CHAPPELL	Cricketer
Arthur	**Michael**	RAMSEY	Archbishop of Canterbury
Arthur	**Michell**	RANSOME	Author
Frank	**Michler**	CHAPMAN	Ornithologist
John	**Middleton**	MURRY	Writer and critic
George	**Mifflin**	DALLAS	US vice-president
Richard	**Milhous**	NIXON	US president
Ernest	**Millar**	HEMINGWAY	American novelist
Dorothy	**Miller**	RICHARDSON	English novelist
John	**Millington**	SYNGE	Author
Thomas	**Milner**	GIBSON	Politician
Philip	**Milton**	ROTH	Novelist
Samora	**Moises**	MACHEL	Mozambique president
Charles	**Monroe**	SCHULZ	US cartoonist
Augustus	**Montague**	TOPLADY	Clergyman and hymnist
Edward	**Montgomery**	CLIFF	Actor
Sarah	**Moore**	GRIMKE	US feminist
Edward	**Moore**	KENNEDY	US politician
Edward	**Morgan**	FORSTER	Author
Barry	**Morris**	GOLDWATER	US politician
Bill	**Morris**	LAWRY	Australian cricketer
Jack	**Morris**	ROSENTHAL	Playwright
Frank	**Mortimer Magilinne**	WORRELL	Cricketer
Henry	**Morton**	STANLEY	Explorer and journalist
John	**Moses**	BROWNING	Gunsmith and inventor
Stephen	**Moulton**	BABCOCK	US agricultural chemist
Kenesaw	**Mountain**	LANDIS	Baseball commissioner
Desmond	**Mpilo**	TUTU	South African prelate

First Name	Middle Name(s)	Surname	
Joshua	**Mqabuko Nyongolo**	NKOMO	Zimbabwean politician
Nicholas	**Murray**	BUTLER	US educationist
Christopher	**Murray**	GRIEVE	Poet
Michael	**Murray**	HORDERN	Actor
John	**Nance**	GARNER	US vice-president
Maggie	**Natalie**	SMITH	Actress
Christian	**Neethling**	BARNARD	Surgeon
Pablo	**Neftali Reyes**	NERUDA	Poet
Leon	**Neil**	COOPER	US physicist
Omar	**Nelson**	BRADLEY	US soldier
Johann	**Nepomuk**	HUMMEL	Austrian pianist
Johann	**Nepomuk**	MAELZEL	German inventor
Bob	**Nesta**	MARLEY	Musician
Arthur	**Neville**	CHAMBERLAIN	Politician
Sebastian	**Newbold**	COE	Athlete and politician
Godfrey	**Newbold**	HOUNSFIELD	English electrical engineer
Edith	**Newbold**	WHARTON	Author
Joseph	**Nicéphore**	NIEPCE	Inventor
Conrad	**Nicholson**	HILTON	Businessman
Louis	**Nicolas**	VAUQUELIN	Chemist
Herbert	**Nigel**	GRESLEY	Locomotive engineer
Florence	**Nightingale**	GRAHAM	Beautician
Boris	**Nikolayevich**	YELTSIN	Russian president
Dirk	**Niven**	BOGARDE	Actor
Alfred	**North**	WHITEHEAD	Philosopher and mathematician
Cyril	**Northcote**	PARKINSON	Political scientist
Oliver	**Norville**	HARDY	Actor
William	**Nunn**	LIPSCOMB	US chemist
Thomas	**Octave Murdoch**	SOPWITH	Aircraft designer
Frederick	**Ogden**	NASH	Poet
Donald	**Olding**	HEBB	Canadian psychologist
Robert	**Oliver**	REED	British actor
David	**Oliver**	SELZNICK	US cinema mogul
Donald	**Oliver**	SOPER	Methodist minister
Judi	**Olivia**	DENCH	Actress
Henri	**Omer**	PÉTAIN	French statesman
James	**Orchard**	HALLIWELL-PHILLIPPS	Shakespearean scholar
Ronald	**Ossary**	DUNLOP	Irish painter
Hamilton	**Othanel**	SMITH	US molecular biologist
Selma	**Ottiliana Lovisa**	LAGERLOF	Swedish novelist
George	**Paget**	THOMSON	English physicist
Richard	**Palethorpe**	TODD	Actor
Publius	**Papinius**	STATIUS	Roman poet
David	**Paradine**	FROST	Interviewer and presenter
Clifton	**Parmelee**	WEBB	Actor
Levi	**Parsons**	MORTON	US vice-president
James	**Patrick**	DONLEAVY	Author
Nigel	**Paul**	KENNEDY	Violinist
James	**Paul**	MCCARTNEY	Musician and composer
Anton	**Pavlovich**	CHEKHOV	Russian author
George	**Peabody**	GOOCH	Politician
Walter	**Percy**	CHRYSLER	Automobile manufacturer
Charles	**Percy**	SNOW	Author
Vladimir	**Petrovich**	KUTS	Russian athlete
Francis	**Peyton**	ROUS	American pathologist
Anthony	**Philip**	HOPKINS	Actor
Archibald	**Philip**	PRIMROSE	British prime minister
Georg	**Philipp**	TELEMANN	Composer
Harry	**Philmore**	LANGDON	US comedian
Noël	**Pierce**	COWARD	Actor and dramatist
Samuel	**Pierpont**	LANGLEY	US aeronautic pioneer
Hilaire	**Pierre**	BELLOC	Writer
Lionel	**Pigot**	JOHNSON	Poet
Leslie	**Poles**	HARTLEY	Author
Klas	**Pontus**	ARNOLDSON	Swedish politician
James	**Prescott**	JOULE	Physicist
John	**Presper**	ECKERT	American inventor
Bob	**Primrose**	WILSON	Goalkeeper and broadcaster
Bob	**Prometheus**	FITZSIMMONS	Boxer
Arthur	**Quiller**	COUCH	Man of letters

FAMOUS PEOPLE

First Name	Middle Name(s)	Surname	
John	**Quincy**	ADAMS	US president
Edward (Ted)	**Ralph**	DEXTER	Cricketer
James	**Ramsay**	MACDONALD	British prime minister
William	**Randal**	CREMER	Nobel laureate
Leroy	**Randle**	GRUMMAN	US aircraft pioneer
Joseph	**Randolf**	ACKERLEY	Author
Philip	**Ranulph**	DE GLANVILLE	Rugby Union player
Clement	**Raphael**	FREUD	Liberal politician
Michael	**Ray Dibdin**	HESELTINE	Politician
Tyrus	**Raymond**	COBB	Baseball player
Anna	**Raymond**	MASSEY	Actress
Daniel	**Raymond**	MASSEY	Actor
Brian	**Rayner**	COOK	English baritone
Miller	**Reece**	HUTCHINSON	Inventor
Edward	**Regan**	MURPHY	US comedian
Georges	**Remi**	HERGÉ	Belgian cartoonist
Jaques	**René**	CHIRAC	Prime minister
Christian	**René**	DE DUVE	Belgian biochemist
John	**Richard**	SCHLESINGER	Film director
Humphrey	**Richard Adeane**	LYTTELTON	Musician
Nigel	**Richard Patton**	DEMPSTER	Gossip columnist
Henry	**Rider**	HAGGARD	Novelist
Howard	**Robard**	HUGHES	Businessman
Ian	**Robert**	MAXWELL	Businessman
Sheridan	**Robert**	MORLEY	Author and broadcaster
Trevor	**Robert**	NUNN	Theatre director
Christopher	**Robert**	SMITH	British politician
Henry	**Robinson**	LUCE	US magazine publisher
Joseph	**Roland**	BARBERA	US animated cartoonist
Nelson	**Rolihlahla**	MANDELA	South African president
Kenneth	**Ronald**	ROSEWALL	Tennis player
John	**Ronald Reuel**	TOLKIEN	Author
Elizabeth	**Rosemond**	TAYLOR	Actress
Henry	**Rowley**	BISHOP	Composer
John	**Roy**	MAJOR	British prime minister
Benjamin	**Roy**	MOTTELSON	Danish physicist
Johann	**Rudolf**	WYSS	Swiss writer
Gerald	**Rudolph**	FORD	US president
William	**Rufus de Vane**	KING	US vice-president
Keith	**Rupert**	MURDOCH	Businessman
John	**Rushworth**	JELLICOE	Naval commander
David	**Russell**	LANGE	New Zealand politician
Steve	**Russell**	RACE	Broadcaster
Carlos	**Saavedra**	LAMAS	Argentinian jurist
Garfield	**St Aubrun**	SOBERS	Cricketer
Ahmed	**Salman**	RUSHDIE	Author
Richard	**Samuel**	ATTENBOROUGH	Actor
Baruch	**Samuel**	BLUMBERG	US biochemist
Robert	**Sanderson**	MULLIKEN	American chemist
Cherilyn (Cher)	**Sarkisian**	LAPIERRE	Singer
Arthur	**Sarsfield**	WARD	Author
Carlos	**Saul**	MENEM	Argentinian politician
Walter	**Savage**	LANDOR	Writer
Victor	**Sawdon**	PRITCHETT	Writer and critic
Wilfrid	**Scawen**	BLUNT	Poet
James	**Schoolcraft**	SHERMAN	US vice-president
William	**Schwenck**	GILBERT	Librettist
Jimmy	**Scott**	CONNORS	Tennis player
Cecil	**Scott**	FORESTER	Author
Michael	**Scudamore**	REDGRAVE	Actor
Peter	**Seamus**	O'TOOLE	Irish actor
Johann	**Sebastian**	BACH	Composer
John	**Selwyn**	GUMMER	Politician
Tiberius	**Sempronius**	GRACCHUS	Roman statesman
Sergei	**Sergeyevich**	PROKOFIEV	Composer
William	**Seward**	BURROUGHS	Author
Clarence	**Seward**	DARROW	US lawyer
Frederick (Freddy)	**Sewards**	TRUEMAN	Cricketer
Robert	**Seymour**	BRIDGES	Poet
Jane	**Seymour**	FONDA	Actress

First Name	Middle Name(s)	Surname	
Arthur	**Seymour**	SULLIVAN	Composer
Hugh	**Seymour**	WALPOLE	Novelist
Edward	**Sheriff**	CURTIS	US photographer
Charles	**Sherwood**	STRATTON	Circus performer
Philip	**Showalter**	HENCH	American physician
Ulysses	**Simpson**	GRANT	US president
Harry	**Sinclair**	LEWIS	US novelist
Frederick	**Sleigh**	ROBERTS	British soldier
Simon	**Smith**	KUZNETS	US economist
Aristotle	**Socrates**	ONASSIS	Shipping magnate
Canaan	**Sodindo**	BANANA	Zimbabwe president
William	**Somerset**	MAUGHAM	Author
Richard	**Southwell**	BOURKE	Earl of Mayo
John	**Spedan**	LEWIS	Businessman
Charlie	**Spencer**	CHAPLIN	Comedy actor
Herbert	**Spencer**	GASSER	US physiologist
Henry	**Spencer**	MOORE	Sculptor
Elizabeth	**Sprague**	COOLIDGE	American pianist
Stavros	**Spyros**	NIARCHOS	Greek ship owner
Richard	**Stafford**	CRIPPS	Politician
Thomas	**Stamford**	RAFFLES	Colonial administrator
Clive	**Staples**	LEWIS	Author
Thomas	**Stearns**	ELIOT	Poet
Gavin	**Steel**	STRANG	Politician
Greg	**Stephen**	CHAPPELL	Cricketer
Laurence	**Stephen**	LOWRY	Artist
Robert	**Strange**	McNAMARA	Businessman
John	**Stuart**	BLACKIE	Scholar
Jenny	**Susan**	PITMAN	Racehorse trainer
Henrietta	**Swan**	LEAVITT	US astronomer
Pearl	**Sydenstricker**	BUCK	Author
William	**Sydney**	PORTER	Author
John	**Taliaferro**	THOMPSON	US soldier and inventor
Booker	**Taliaferro**	WASHINGTON	US educationalist
William	**Tatem**	TILDEN	US tennis player
Phineas	**Taylor**	BARNUM	Showman
Barbara	**Taylor**	BRADFORD	Novelist
Samuel	**Taylor**	COLERIDGE	Poet
Charles	**Taze**	RUSSELL	Religious leader
William	**Tecumseh**	SHERMAN	General
Joseph	**Teodor**	CONRAD	Author
Ernesto	**Teodoro**	MONETA	Italian journalist
Michael	**Terence**	ASPEL	Broadcaster
Ian	**Terence**	BOTHAM	Cricketer
Michael	**Terence**	WOGAN	Broadcaster
Spiro	**Theodore**	AGNEW	US vice-president
René	**Théophile Hyacinthe**	LAENNEC	French physician
Randall	**Thomas**	DAVIDSON	Archbishop of Canterbury
Alfred	**Thompson**	DENNING	Law lord
Wednesday	**Thursday**	ADDAMS	'Addams Family' character
James	**Tiberius**	KIRK	Starship captain ('Star Trek')
Hugh	**Todd Naylor**	GAITSKELL	Politician
Rex	**Todhunter**	STOUT	US detective writer
Roger	**Tory**	PETERSON	US ornithologist
Marcus	**Tullius**	TIRO	Inventor
William	**Turner**	WALTON	Composer
Ranulph	**Twistleton-Wykeham**	FIENNES	Explorer
Bobby	**Tyre**	JONES	US golfer
Gabriel	**Urbain**	FAURE	Composer
Basil	**Urwin**	SPENCE	Architect
Comer	**Vann**	WOODWARD	US historian
Sergey	**Vasilyevich**	RACHMANINOV	Composer
Ralph	**Vaughan**	WILLIAMS	Composer
Nicholas	**Verity**	KNIGHT	Cricketer
Eddie	**Vernon**	RICKENBACKER	Fighter pilot
Eugene	**Victor**	DEBS	US politician
Mia	**Villiers**	FARROW	Actress
Michael	**Vincent**	O'BRIEN	Racehorse trainer
Sarah	**Virginia**	WADE	Tennis player
Adeline	**Virginia**	WOOLF	Novelist

First Name	Middle Name(s)	Surname	
Henry	**Wager**	HALLECK	US soldier
Ralph	**Waldo**	EMERSON	US poet
King	**Wallis**	VIDOR	Film director
Luis	**Walter**	ALVAREZ	US physicist
John	**Warcup**	CORNFORTH	British chemist
David	**Wark**	GRIFFITH	Film director
Henry	**Warren**	BEATY	Actor
Dave	**Warren**	BRUBECK	Jazz musician
Charles	**Warren**	FAIRBANKS	US vice-president
Marshall	**Warren**	NIRENBERG	US biochemist
Jimmy	**Warren**	WHITE	Snooker player
George	**Washington**	CABLE	Novelist
Norman	**Washington**	MANLEY	Jamaican politician
James	**Watson**	CRONIN	US physicist
Charles	**Watson**	WENTWORTH	British prime minister
Richard	**Wayne**	PENNIMAN	Musician
George	**Wells**	BEADLE	US biochemical geneticist
Rainer	**Werner**	FASSBINDER	Film director
Marthinus	**Wessels**	PRETORIUS	South African general
William	**Wetmore**	STORY	Poet and sculptor
Edward	**Wheewall**	HOLDEN	Motor pioneer
Alan	**Whipper**	WELLS	Athlete
Jack	**Whitaker**	STRAW	Politician
Edward	**White**	BENSON	Archbishop of Canterbury
Arnold	**Whittaker**	WOLFENDALE	Astronomer
Caryl	**Whittier**	CHESSMAN	Convict and author
Bertie	**Wilberforce**	WOOSTER	Fictional character
Robert	**Wilhelm**	BUNSEN	Physicist
William	**Wilkie**	COLLINS	Novelist
Caspar	**Willard**	WEINBERGER	US politician
Johnnie	**William**	CARSON	US TV personality
Emile	**William Ivanhoe**	HESKEY	Footballer
Jack	**William**	NICKLAUS	Golfer
Brian	**Wilson**	ALDISS	Science fiction writer
Woodrow (Woodie)	**Wilson**	GUTHRIE	US folk singer
Ronald	**Wilson**	REAGAN	US president
Joseph	**Wilson**	SWAN	Physicist
James (Jimmy)	**Wilson Vincent**	SAVILE	Broadcaster
Frank	**Winfield**	WOOLWORTH	US businessman
Arthur	**Wing**	PINERO	Playwright
Gary	**Winston**	LINEKER	Footballer
John	**Winston (then Ono)**	LENNON	Musician and composer
Wells	**Wintemute**	COATES	Architect
John	**Winthrop**	HACKETT	Soldier and academic
Victor	**Witter**	TURNER	Anthropologist
Roger	**Wolcott**	SPERRY	US neuroscientist
Jonathan	**Wolfe**	MILLER	Broadcaster
Theobald	**Wolfe**	TONE	Irish nationalist
Robert	**Woodrow**	WILSON	US physicist
Thomas	**Woodrow**	WILSON	US president
Dickinson	**Woodruff**	RICHARDS	American physician
Ronald	**Wreyford**	NORRISH	English chemist
William	**Wymark**	JACOBS	Short story writer
William	**Wyndham**	GRENVILLE	British prime minister
Franz	**Xaver**	HABERL	German musicologist
Denis	**Yates**	WHEATLEY	Novelist
Paul	**Yaw**	BOATENG	Politician
Susannah	**Yolande**	YORK	Actress
Shmuel	**Yosef**	AGNON	Israeli novelist
Konrad	**Zacharias**	LORENZ	Austrian zoologist

Middle Names: Ordered by Surname

First Name	Middle Name(s)	Surname	
Charles	**Greely**	ABBOT	Astrophysicist
Diane	**Julie**	ABBOT	Politician
Dean	**Gooderham**	ACHESON	American statesman
Joseph	**Randolf**	ACKERLEY	Author

First Name	Middle Name(s)	Surname	
Roy	Claxton	ACUFF	Country musician
Adam	Llewellyn De Vere	ADAMANT	Fictional TV character
John	Bodkin	ADAMS	Doctor and murder suspect
John	Couch	ADAMS	Astronomer
John	Quincy	ADAMS	US president
Marcus	Algernon	ADAMS	Photographer
Sarah	Flower	ADAMS	English poet
William	Bridges	ADAMS	Engineer
Wednesday	Thursday	ADDAMS	'Addams Family' character
Lawrence (Larry)	Cecil	ADLER	Musician
Vosdanig	Manoog	ADOIAN	Painter
Sade	Folasade	ADU	Singer
Spiro	Theodore	AGNEW	US vice-president
Shmuel	Yosef	AGNON	Israeli novelist
Henry	Hinchcliffe	AINLEY	Actor
George	Biddell	AIRY	Astronomer
Amos	Bronson	ALCOTT	Transcendentalist
Brian	Wilson	ALDISS	Science fiction writer
Thomas	Bailey	ALDRICH	Author
Thomas	Massa	ALSAGER	Newspaper manager
Luis	Walter	ALVAREZ	US physicist
Mario	Gabriele	ANDRETTI	Racing driver
Christian	Boehmer	ANFINSEN	US biochemist
Anders	Jonas	ANGSTROM	Physicist
Susan	Brownell	ANTHONY	Suffragette
Jeffrey	Howard	ARCHER	Author
George	Augustus	ARLISS	Actor
Klas	Pontus	ARNOLDSON	Swedish politician
Chester	Alan	ARTHUR	US president
Jeremy	John Durham	ASHDOWN	Politician
Arthur	Bowden	ASKEY	Comedian
Michael	Terence	ASPEL	Broadcaster
Herbert	Henry	ASQUITH	British prime minister
Miguel	Angel	ASTURIAS	Guatemalan poet
Richard	Samuel	ATTENBOROUGH	Actor
Wystan	Hugh	AUDEN	Poet
Alan	Beresford	B'STARD	TV character ('New Statesman')
Stephen	Moulton	BABCOCK	US agricultural chemist
Johann	Christian	BACH	Composer
Johann	Sebastian	BACH	Composer
Enid	Algerine	BAGNOLD	Author
Joan	Dawson	BAKEWELL	Broadcaster
Emily	Greene	BALCH	US social reformer
Michael	Elias	BALCON	Film producer
James	Graham	BALLARD	Author
Canaan	Sodindo	BANANA	Zimbabwean president
Hastings	Kamuzu	BANDA	Malawi politician
Roger	Gilbert	BANNISTER	Athlete
Frederick	Grant	BANTING	Physiologist
Joseph	Roland	BARBERA	US animated cartoonist
Charles	Glover	BARKLA	English physicist
Christian	Neethling	BARNARD	Surgeon
Phineas	Taylor	BARNUM	Showman
James	Matthew	BARRIE	Author
Herbert	Ernest	BATES	Author
William	Maddock	BAYLISS	Physiologist
George	Wells	BEADLE	US biochemical geneticist
Henry	Warren	BEATY	Actor
Bill	Blackledge	BEAUMONT	Rugby Union player
Carl	Lotus	BECKER	US historian
Thomas	Lovell	BEDDOES	Poet and physiologist
Mary	Hayley	BELL	Playwright
Hilaire	Pierre	BELLOC	Writer
Enoch	Arnold	BENNETT	Author
Edward	White	BENSON	Archbishop of Canterbury
Edmund	Clerihew	BENTLEY	Writer
Ernst	Ingmar	BERGMAN	Film producer
Hans	Albrecht	BETHE	US physicist
Earl	Derr	BIGGERS	US novelist
Henry	Rowley	BISHOP	Composer

FAMOUS PEOPLE

First Name	Middle Name(s)	Surname	
John	**Stuart**	BLACKIE	Scholar
Richard	**Doddridge**	BLACKMORE	Author
Anthony	**Charles Lynton**	BLAIR	Politician
Eric	**Arthur**	BLAIR	Author
Danny	**Dennio**	BLANCHFLOWER	Footballer
Tasker	**Howard**	BLISS	Soldier and statesman
Baruch	**Samuel**	BLUMBERG	US biochemist
Wilfrid	**Scawen**	BLUNT	Poet
Paul	**Yaw**	BOATENG	Politician
Dirk	**Niven**	BOGARDE	Actor
Humphrey	**De Forest**	BOGART	Actor
Ian	**Terence**	BOTHAM	Cricketer
Virginia	**Hilda Brunette Maxwell**	BOTTOMLEY	Politician
Richard	**Southwell**	BOURKE	Earl of Mayo
David	**Hayward**	BOWIE	Musician and singer
Barbara	**Taylor**	BRADFORD	Novelist
Omar	**Nelson**	BRADLEY	US soldier
John	**Gerard**	BRAINE	Novelist
Kenneth	**Charles**	BRANAGH	Actor
Richard	**Charles Nicholas**	BRANSON	Entrepreneur
Walter	**Houser**	BRATTAIN	US physicist
John	**Cabell**	BRECKINRIDGE	US vice-president
Leonid	**Ilich**	BREZHNEV	USSR president
Robert	**Seymour**	BRIDGES	Poet
Charlie	**Dunbar**	BROAD	Philosopher
Rupert	**Chawner**	BROOKE	Poet
Norman	**Everard**	BROOKES	Tennis player
Spangler	**Arlington**	BROUGH	Actor
Henry	**Kirke**	BROWN	Sculptor
James	**Gordon**	BROWN	Politician
Charles	**Farrar**	BROWNE	Humorist and writer
Hablot	**Knight**	BROWNE	Illustrator
John	**Moses**	BROWNING	Gunsmith and inventor
Dave	**Warren**	BRUBECK	Jazz musician
William	**Cullen**	BRYANT	Poet
James	**McGill**	BUCHANAN	American economist
Pearl	**Sydenstricker**	BUCK	Author
Maria	**Esther**	BUENO	Tennis player
Ralph	**Johnson**	BUNCHE	American economist
Robert	**Wilhelm**	BUNSEN	Physicist
Billy	**George**	BUNTER	Fictional character
William	**Seward**	BURROUGHS	Author
George	**Herbert Walker**	BUSH	US president
Nicholas	**Murray**	BUTLER	US educationist
Reginald	**Cotterell**	BUTLER	Sculptor
Richard	**Austen**	BUTLER	Politician
Billy	**Edmund**	BUTLIN	Businessman
Betsy	**Cromer**	BYARS	Novelist
Richard	**Evelyn**	BYRD	Explorer
Harry	**Flood**	BYRD	Politician
George	**Gordon**	BYRON	Poet
James	**Branch**	CABELL	Novelist
George	**Washington**	CABLE	Novelist
Pedro	**Alvarez**	CABRAL	Navigator
James	**Mallahan**	CAIN	Writer
Michael	**Joseph**	CAINE	Actor
Aimo	**Kaario**	CAJANDER	Finnish politician
John	**Caldwell**	CALHOUN	US vice-president
James	**Leonard**	CALLAGHAN	British prime minister
Maria	**Meneghini**	CALLAS	Operatic soprano
Hugh	**Longbourne**	CALLENDAR	Physicist
Verney	**Lovett**	CAMERON	Explorer
Walter	**Chauncy**	CAMP	American footballer
Donald	**Malcolm**	CAMPBELL	Car and boat racer
John	**Franklin**	CANDY	Actor
Annie	**Jump**	CANNON	US astronomer
George	**Leonard**	CAREY	Archbishop
Chester	**Floyd**	CARLSON	US inventor
Ingvar	**Costa**	CARLSSON	Swedish politician
Jane	**Baillie**	CARLYLE	Wife of Thomas Carlyle

First Name	Middle Name(s)	Surname	
Ian	Gillett	CARMICHAEL	Actor
John	Alden	CARPENTER	Musician and businessman
John	Dickson	CARR	US detective writer
Willis	Haviland	CARRIER	US inventor
Johnnie	William	CARSON	US TV personality
William	Hunter Fisher	CARSON	Jockey
James	Earl	CARTER	US president
Barbara	Hamilton	CARTLAND	Writer
Hugh	Maxwell	CASSON	Architect
William	Henry	CAVENDISH-BENTINCK	British prime minister
Robert	Arthur Talbot	CECIL	British prime minister
Ernst	Boris	CHAIN	German biochemist
Arthur	Neville	CHAMBERLAIN	Politician
Charlie	Spencer	CHAPLIN	Comedy actor
Frank	Michler	CHAPMAN	Ornithologist
Greg	Stephen	CHAPPELL	Cricketer
Ian	Michael	CHAPPELL	Cricketer
Leslie	Bowyer	CHARTERIS	Author
Cornelius	Crane	CHASE	Actor
Anton	Pavlovich	CHEKHOV	Russian author
Geoffrey	Leonard	CHESHIRE	Philanthropist
Caryl	Whittier	CHESSMAN	Convict and author
Gilbert	Keith	CHESTERTON	Author
Robert	Erskine	CHILDERS	Writer
Jaques	René	CHIRAC	French prime minister
Martin	Harcourt	CHIVERS	Footballer
Walter	Percy	CHRYSLER	Automobile manufacturer
Winston	Leonard Spencer	CHURCHILL	British prime minister
Kenneth	Mackenzie	CLARK	Art historian
Kenneth	Harry	CLARKE	Politician
Cassius	Marcellus	CLAY	Boxer
John	Marwood	CLEESE	Actor
Samuel	Langhorne	CLEMENS	Author
Stephen	Grover	CLEVELAND	US president
Edward	Montgomery	CLIFT	Actor
William	Jefferson Blyth	CLINTON	US president
Wells	Wintemute	COATES	Architect
Tyrus	Raymond	COBB	Baseball player
Samuel	Franklin	CODY	Aviator
William	Frederick	CODY	Showman
Sebastian	Newbold	COE	Athlete and politician
Frederick	Donald	COGGAN	Archbishop of Canterbury
Ferdinand	Julius	COHN	Botanist
Samuel	Taylor	COLERIDGE	Poet
Sidonie	Gabrielle	COLETTE	Author
William	Gershom	COLLINGWOOD	Artist
Charles	Allston	COLLINS	Artist
Joan	Henrietta	COLLINS	Actress
William	Wilkie	COLLINS	Novelist
Arthur	Holly	COMPTON	Physicist
Denis	Charles Scott	COMPTON	Cricketer
Maureen	Catherine	CONNOLLY	Tennis player
Jimmy	Scott	CONNORS	Tennis player
Joseph	Teodor	CONRAD	Author
Brian	Rayner	COOK	English baritone
Robin	Finlayson	COOK	Politician
Elizabeth	Sprague	COOLIDGE	American pianist
John	Calvin	COOLIDGE	US president
Leon	Neil	COOPER	US physicist
Alfred	Edgar	COPPARD	Writer
Ronnie	Balfour	CORBETT	Comedian
Carl	Ferdinand	CORI	American biochemist
John	Warcup	CORNFORTH	British chemist
Arthur	Quiller	COUCH	Man of letters
Noel	Pierce	COWARD	Actor and dramatist
Michael	Colin	COWDREY	Cricketer
William	Randal	CREMER	Nobel Laureate
Francis	Harry Compton	CRICK	Biologist
Hawley	Harvey	CRIPPEN	Murderer
Richard	Stafford	CRIPPS	Politician

First Name	Middle Name(s)	Surname	
Archibald	**Joseph**	CRONIN	Author
James	**Watson**	CRONIN	US physicist
Walter	**Leland**	CRONKITE	US broadcaster
Harry (Bing)	**Lillis**	CROSBY	Singer and actor
Ada	**Jemima**	CROSSLEY	Australian contralto
Irene	**Joliot**	CURIE	Nuclear physicist
Heber	**Doust**	CURTIS	US astronomer
Edward	**Sheriff**	CURTIS	US photographer
Glen	**Hammond**	CURTISS	US air pioneer
Henry	**Drysdale**	DAKIN	Chemist
Kenneth	**Mathieson**	DALGLISH	Footballer
Lawrence	**Bruno Nero**	DALLAGLIO	Rugby player
George	**Mifflin**	DALLAS	US vice-president
Clarence	**Seward**	DARROW	US Lawyer
Randall	**Thomas**	DAVIDSON	Archbishop of Canterbury
Dwight	**Filley**	DAVIS	Founder of Davis Cup
Miles	**Dewey**	DAVIS	Jazz musician
Charles	**Gates**	DAWES	US vice-president
Christian	**René**	DE DUVE	Belgian biochemist
Philip	**Ranulph**	DE GLANVILLE	Rugby Union player
Cecil	**Blount**	DE MILLE	Film director
James	**Byron**	DEAN	Actor
Eugene	**Victor**	DEBS	US politician
Claude	**Achille**	DEBUSSY	Composer
Len	**Cyril**	DEIGHTON	Novelist
Ronald	**Frederick**	DELDERFIELD	Author
Jacques	**Lucien Jean**	DELORS	European politician
Nigel	**Richard Patton**	DEMPSTER	Gossip columnist
Judi	**Olivia**	DENCH	Actress
Alfred	**Thompson**	DENNING	Law lord
Donald	**Campbell**	DEWAR	British politician
Norman	**Colin**	DEXTER	Author
Edward (Ted)	**Ralph**	DEXTER	Cricketer
Thomas	**Frognall**	DIBDIN	Librarian
Philip	**Kindred**	DICK	US writer
Philip	**Kindred**	DICK	US science fiction writer
Charles	**John Huffam**	DICKENS	Author
Walt	**Elias**	DISNEY	Film producer
Henry	**Austin**	DOBSON	Poet
Kenneth	**Arthur**	DODD	Comedian
Basil	**Lewis**	D'OLIVEIRA	Cricketer
James	**Patrick**	DONLEAVY	Author
Alexander	**Frederick**	DOUGLAS-HOME	British prime minister
Hugh	**Caswell Tremenheere**	DOWDING	RAF chief
John	**Boyd**	DUNLOP	Inventor
Ronald	**Ossary**	DUNLOP	Irish painter
James	**Franciscus**	DURANTE	Entertainer
Gerald	**Malcolm**	DURRELL	Writer and naturalist
Lawrence	**George**	DURRELL	Novelist
Bob	**Alan**	DYLAN	Singer and composer
John	**Carew**	ECCLES	Australian neurophysiologist
John	**Presper**	ECKERT	American inventor
Gerald	**Maurice**	EDELMAN	US biochemist
Gertrude	**Caroline**	EDERLE	US swimmer
Thomas	**Alva**	EDISON	Inventor
Dwight	**David**	EISENHOWER	US president
Thomas	**Stearns**	ELIOT	Author
Edward ('Duke')	**Kennedy**	ELLINGTON	Pianist
Fred	**Handel**	ELLIOTT	'Coronation Street' character
Ralph	**Waldo**	EMERSON	US poet
John	**Franklin**	ENDERS	US bacteriologist
Chris	**Livingstone**	EUBANK	Boxer
Peter	**Carl**	FABERGÉ	Russian goldsmith
Gabriel	**Daniel**	FAHRENHEIT	Physicist
Charles	**Warren**	FAIRBANKS	US vice-president
Douglas	**Elton**	FAIRBANKS (Snr)	Actor
Nicholas	**Alexander**	FALDO	Golfer
Mia	**Villiers**	FARROW	Actress
Rainer	**Werner**	FASSBINDER	Film director
Gabriel	**Urbain**	FAURÉ	Composer

First Name	Middle Name(s)	Surname	
William	Claude	FIELDS	Comedian and actor
Ranulph	Twistleton-Wykeham	FIENNES	Explorer
Robert	Bannatyne	FINLAY	Politician
Geoffrey	Francis	FISHER	Archbishop of Canterbury
Val	Logsdon	FITCH	US physicist
Augustus	Henry	FITZROY	British prime minister
Bob	Prometheus	FITZSIMMONS	Boxer
James	Elroy	FLECKER	Poet
Ian	Lancaster	FLEMING	English novelist
Jane	Seymour	FONDA	Actress
Michael	Mackintosh	FOOT	Politician
Gerald	Rudolph	FORD	US president
Cecil	Scott	FORESTER	Author
George	Hoy	FORMBY	Vocalist and musician
Edward	Morgan	FORSTER	Author
Bruce	Joseph	FORSYTH	Entertainer
Stephen	Collins	FOSTER	US songwriter
Michael J	Andrew	FOX	Actor
Clement	Raphael	FREUD	Liberal politician
Ragnar	Kittil	FRISCH	Norwegian economist
Kermit	The	FROG	Muppet
David	Paradine	FROST	Interviewer and presenter
Charles	Burgess	FRY	Sportsman
Stephen	John	FRY	Actor and author
Roy	Broadbent	FULLER	Poet
Hugh	Todd Naylor	GAITSKELL	Politician
Daniel	Carleton	GAJDUSEK	US virologist
Leopoldo	Fortunato	GALTIERI	Argentinian politician
Mohandas	Karamchand	GANDHI	Indian leader
James	Abram	GARFIELD	US president
John	Nance	GARNER	US vice-president
Elizabeth	Cleghorn	GASKELL	Writer
Herbert	Spencer	GASSER	US physiologist
Richard	Jordan	GATLING	Inventor
Andrew	Dewar	GIBB	Scottish jurist
Lewis	Grassic	GIBBON	Novelist
Stella	Dorothea	GIBBONS	Writer
Mel	Columcille	GIBSON	Actor
Thomas	Milner	GIBSON	Politician
Arthur	John	GIELGUD	Actor
William	Schwenck	GILBERT	Librettist
Percy	Carlyle	GILCHRIST	Metallurgist
John	Birks	GILLESPIE	Jazz trumpeter
King	Camp	GILLETTE	Inventor
William	Ewart	GLADSTONE	British prime minister
Sheldon	Lee	GLASHOW	US physicist
John	Herschel	GLENN	US astronaut and politician
Robert	Hutchings	GODDARD	US rocket pioneer
William	Gerald	GOLDING	Novelist
Peter	Carl	GOLDMARK	Inventor
Barry	Morris	GOLDWATER	US politician
George	Peabody	GOOCH	Politician
Graham	Alan	GOOCH	Cricketer
Arthur	Lehman	GOODHART	US jurist
Benny	David	GOODMAN	US jazz clarinetist
Samuel	Griswold	GOODRICH	US publisher
Adam	Lindsay	GORDON	Australian poet
Cyrus	Herzl	GORDON	US Hebrew scholar
George	Hamilton	GORDON	British prime minister
Spencer	Frederick	GORE	Painter
Benjamin	Apthorp	GOULD	US astronomer
Charles	François	GOUNOD	Composer
Lawrence	Burnett	GOWING	Painter
Tiberius	Sempronius	GRACCHUS	Roman statesman
William	Gilbert	GRACE	Cricketer
Billy	Franklin	GRAHAM	US evangelist
Florence	Nightingale	GRAHAM	Beautician
Ulysses	Simpson	GRANT	US president
Milner	Connorton	GRAY	Graphic designer
Linda	Esther	GRAY	Scottish soprano

FAMOUS PEOPLE

First Name	Middle Name(s)	Surname	
Lucinda	Jane	GREEN	Three-day eventer
Robson	Golightly	GREEN	Actor
Hugh	Carleton	GREENE	Journalist and broadcaster
Gordon	Cuthbert	GREENIDGE	Cricketer
William	Wyndham	GRENVILLE	British prime minister
Herbert	Nigel	GRESLEY	Locomotive engineer
Edvard	Hagerup	GRIEG	Norwegian composer
Christopher	Murray	GRIEVE	Poet
Walter	Burley	GRIFFIN	US architect
David	Wark	GRIFFITH	Film director
Angelina	Emily	GRIMKE	US feminist
Sarah	Moore	GRIMKE	US feminist
Friedrich	Melchior	GRIMM	Journalist
Jacob	Ludwig Carl	GRIMM	Folklorist
Wilhelm	Carl	GRIMM	Folklorist
Walter	Adolph	GROPIUS	Architect
Leroy	Randle	GRUMMAN	US aircraft pioneer
John	Selwyn	GUMMER	Politician
Johannes	Gensfleisch	GUTENBERG	German printer
Woodrow	Wilson	GUTHRIE	US folk singer
Franz	Xaver	HABERL	German musicologist
John	Winthrop	HACKETT	Soldier and academic
Gene	Alden	HACKMAN	Actor
Alfred	Cort	HADDON	Anthropologist
Henry	Rider	HAGGARD	Novelist
William	Jefferson	HAGUE	Politician
Alexander	Meigs	HAIG	US soldier
Thomas	Chandler	HALIBURTON	Canadian writer
Henry	Wager	HALLECK	US soldier
James	Orchard	HALLIWELL-PHILLIPPS	Shakespearean scholar
Dag	Hjalmar Agne Carl	HAMMARSKJÖLD	Swedish statesman
Robin	Airling	HANBURY-TENISON	Explorer
Tony	Aloysius	HANCOCK	TV character
Tony	John	HANCOCK	Comedy actor
George	Frederick	HANDEL	Composer
William	Denby	HANNA	US animated cartoonist
James	Aloysius	HANSOM	Designer
Warren	Gamaliel	HARDING	US president
Oliver	Norville	HARDY	Comedy actor
Thomas	Duffus	HARDY	Archivist
Thomas	Masterman	HARDY	Naval officer
Joel	Chandler	HARRIS	Author
William	Henry	HARRISON	US president
Leslie	Poles	HARTLEY	Author
Haldan	Keffer	HARTLINE	US physiologist
John	Liptrot	HATTON	Composer
Herbert	Aaron	HAUPTMAN	US physicist
Rutherford	Birchard	HAYES	US president
Seamus	Justin	HEANEY	Poet
Patricia	Campbell	HEARST	Heiress
Donald	Olding	HEBB	Canadian psychologist
Lillian	Florence	HELLMAN	US playwright
Ernest	Millar	HEMINGWAY	US novelist
Philip	Showalter	HENCH	US physician
Jocelyn	Barbara	HEPWORTH	Sculptor
Georges	Remi	HERGÉ	Belgian cartoonist
Caroline	Lucretia	HERSCHEL	Astronomer
Alfred	Day	HERSHEY	US biologist
Michael	Ray Dibdin	HESELTINE	Politician
Philip	Arnold	HESELTINE	Composer
Emile	William Ivanhoe	HESKEY	Footballer
Alfred	Hawthorne	HILL	Comedian
Norman	Graham	HILL	Racing driver
Conrad	Nicholson	HILTON	Businessman
John (Jack)	Berry	HOBBS	English cricketer
Dorothy	Crowfoot	HODGKIN	Scientist
Dustin	Lee	HOFFMAN	Actor
Quintin	McGarel	HOGG	Politician
Edward	Wheewall	HOLDEN	Motor pioneer
Ben	Caine	HOLLIOAKE	English cricketer

First Name	Middle Name(s)	Surname	
Herbert	**Clark**	HOOVER	US president
John	**Edgar**	HOOVER	FBI director
Bob	**Leslie Townes**	HOPE	Comedian
Gerard	**Manley**	HOPKINS	Poet
Anthony	**Philip**	HOPKINS	Actor
Michael	**Murray**	HORDERN	Actor
Godfrey	**Newbold**	HOUNSFIELD	English electrical engineer
Alfred	**Edward**	HOUSMAN	Author
David	**Hunter**	HUBEL	US neurophysiologist
Charles	**Brenton**	HUGGINS	US surgeon
Howard	**Robard**	HUGHES	Businessman
Victor	**Marie**	HUGO	French writer
George	**Basil**	HUME	Cardinal
Johann	**Nepomuk**	HUMMEL	Austrian pianist
Hubert	**Horatio**	HUMPHREY	US vice-president
John	**Barry**	HUMPHRIES	Comedian and writer
Miller	**Reece**	HUTCHINSON	Inventor
Aldous	**Leonard**	HUXLEY	Novelist
Jeremy	**Israel**	ISAACS	Arts mogul
David	**Lewis**	JACOBS	Broadcaster
William	**Wymark**	JACOBS	Short story writer
Phyllis	**Dorothy**	JAMES	Authoress
James	**Hopwood**	JEANS	Physicist and astronomer
James	**Jackson**	JEFFRIES	Boxing champion
John	**Rushworth**	JELLICOE	Naval commander
Roy	**Harris**	JENKINS	Politician
Robert	**Banks**	JENKINSON	British prime minister
Niels	**Kai**	JERNE	Danish immunologist
Jerome	**Klapka**	JEROME	Author
Elton	**Hercules**	JOHN	Vocalist and composer
Lyndon	**Baines**	JOHNSON	US president
Lionel	**Pigot**	JOHNSON	Poet
Richard	**Mentor**	JOHNSON	US vice-president
Joseph	**Eggleston**	JOHNSTON	US soldier
James	**Cellan**	JONES	Film director
Bobby	**Tyre**	JONES	US golfer
Michael	**Jeffrey**	JORDAN	US basketball player
James	**Prescott**	JOULE	Physicist
Carl	**Gustav**	JUNG	Swiss psychiatrist
Erik	**Axel**	KARLFELDT	Swedish poet
John	**Harvey**	KELLOGG	Inventor
Will	**Keith**	KELLOGG	Inventor
Gene	**Curran**	KELLY	Dancer
Edward	**Calvin**	KENDALL	US chemist
John	**Cowdery**	KENDREW	English biochemist
Edward	**Moore**	KENNEDY	US politician
John	**Fitzgerald**	KENNEDY	US president
Ludovic	**Coverley**	KENNEDY	Broadcaster
Nigel	**Paul**	KENNEDY	Violinist
Robert	**Francis**	KENNEDY	US politician
Søren	**Aabye**	KIERKEGAARD	Danish philosopher
William	**Rufus de Vane**	KING	US vice-president
Neil	**Gordon**	KINNOCK	Politician
Wilson	**Boit**	KIPKETER	Athlete
James	**Tiberius**	KIRK	Starship captain ('Star Trek')
Henry	**Alfred**	KISSINGER	USA statesman
Horatio	**Herbert**	KITCHENER	Irish soldier and statesman
Eartha	**Mae**	KITT	Singer
Nicholas	**Verity**	KNIGHT	Cricketer
Tjalling	**Charles**	KOOPMANS	US economist
Hans	**Adolf**	KREBS	British biochemist
Stanley	**Jasspon**	KUNITZ	US poet
Vladimir	**Petrovich**	KUTS	Russian athlete
Simon	**Smith**	KUZNETS	US economist
Fiorello	**Henry**	LA GUARDIA	US politician
René	**Théophile Hyacinthe**	LAENNEC	French physician
Selma	**Ottiliana Lovisa**	LAGERLOF	Swedish novelist
Carlos	**Saavedra**	LAMAS	Argentinian jurist
Willis	**Eugene**	LAMB	US physicist
Stephen	**Burton**	LANCASTER	Actor

FAMOUS PEOPLE

First Name	Middle Name(s)	Surname	
Kenesaw	**Mountain**	LANDIS	Baseball commissioner
Walter	**Savage**	LANDOR	Writer
Henri	**Désiré**	LANDRU	French murderer
John	**Dunmore**	LANG	Clergyman
Harry	**Philmore**	LANGDON	US comedian
David	**Russell**	LANGE	New Zealand politician
Samuel	**Pierpont**	LANGLEY	US aeronautic pioneer
Cherilyn (Cher)	**Sarkisian**	LAPIERRE	Singer
Pierre	**Athanase**	LAROUSSE	French publisher
Hugh	**Callum**	LAURIE	Actor and comedian
Rodney	**George**	LAVER	Tennis player
Thomas	**Edward**	LAWRENCE	Author and soldier
David	**Herbert**	LAWRENCE	Author
Bill	**Morris**	LAWRY	Australian cricketer
Bernard	**Howell**	LEACH	English potter
Richard	**Erskine Frere**	LEAKEY	Palaeontologist and naturalist
Henrietta	**Swan**	LEAVITT	US astronomer
Christopher	**Carandini**	LEE	Actor
Vladimir	**Ilyich**	LENIN	Russian revolutionary
John	**Winston (then Ono)**	LENNON	Musician and composer
Henry	**Bernard**	LEVIN	Journalist and author
Harry	**Sinclair**	LEWIS	US novelist
Chris	**Clairmonte**	LEWIS	Cricketer
Clive	**Staples**	LEWIS	Author
John	**Spedan**	LEWIS	Businessman
Dennis	**Keith**	LILLEE	Australian cricketer
Charles	**Augustus**	LINDBERGH	US aviator
Gary	**Winston**	LINEKER	Footballer
Maureen	**Diane**	LIPMAN	Actress
William	**Nunn**	LIPSCOMB	US chemist
Penelope	**Margaret**	LIVELY	Writer
Harold	**Clayton**	LLOYD	US film comedian
Henry	**Cabot**	LODGE	US senator
Jack	**Griffith**	LONDON	US novelist
Francis	**Aungier**	LONGFORD	Prison reformer
Hendrik	**Antoon**	LORENTZ	Dutch physicist
Konrad	**Zacharias**	LORENZ	Austrian zoologist
Robert	**Hepler**	LOWE	Actor
Laurence	**Stephen**	LOWRY	Artist
Henry	**Robinson**	LUCE	US magazine publisher
Edwin	**Landseer**	LUTYENS	English architect
Humphrey	**Richard Adeane**	LYTTELTON	Musician
Thomas	**Babington**	MACAULAY	Author
George	**Brinton**	McCLELLAN	US soldier
Mark	**Hume**	McCORMACK	Promoter
James	**Ramsay**	MACDONALD	British prime minister
Samora	**Moises**	MACHEL	Mozambican president
Donald	**Duart**	MACLEAN	English traitor
James	**Paul**	McCARTNEY	Musician and composer
Maurice	**Harold**	MACMILLAN	British prime minister
Robert	**Strange**	McNAMARA	Businessman and politician
Herman	**Cyril**	McNEILE	Author
Johann	**Nepomuk**	MAELZEL	German inventor
John	**Roy**	MAJOR	British prime minister
Nelson	**Rolihlahla**	MANDELA	South African president
Norman	**Washington**	MANLEY	Jamaican prime minister
Nigel	**Ernest James**	MANSELL	Racing driver
Ferdinand	**Edralin**	MARCOS	Filipino president
Bob	**Nesta**	MARLEY	Musician
Gabriel	**Garcia**	MARQUEZ	Columbian author
Jean	**Lyndsey Torren**	MARSH	Actress
George	**Catlett**	MARSHALL	American soldier and statesman
Jan	**Garrigue**	MASARYK	Czech statesman
Anna	**Raymond**	MASSEY	Actress
Daniel	**Raymond**	MASSEY	Actor
Marshall	**Bruce**	MATHERS III	Rep artist (aka Eminem)
William	**Somerset**	MAUGHAM	Author
Ian	**Robert**	MAXWELL	Businessman
Peter	**Barker Howard**	MAY	Cricketer
Michael	**Hugh**	MEACHER	Politician

First Name	Middle Name(s)	Surname	
Carlos	**Saul**	MENEM	Argentinian politician
Cliff	**Arthur**	MICHELMORE	Broadcaster
James	**Albert**	MICHENER	Author
Alton	**Glenn**	MILLER	Bandleader
Jonathan	**Wolfe**	MILLER	Broadcaster
Alan	**Alexander**	MILNE	Author
Liza	**May**	MINNELLI	Singer
Walter	**Frederick (Fritz)**	MONDALE	US vice-president
Ernesto	**Teodoro**	MONETA	Italian journalist
Bernard	**Law**	MONTGOMERY	Field marshal
Brian	**Baden**	MOORE	Football commentator
Henry	**Spencer**	MOORE	Sculptor
Roger	**George**	MOORE	Actor
Sheridan	**Robert**	MORLEY	Author and broadcaster
George	**Ivan (Van)**	MORRISON	Singer and composer
Samuel	**Finley Breese**	MORSE	US inventor
John	**Cameron**	MORTON	Journalist
Levi	**Parsons**	MORTON	US vice-president
Oswald	**Ernald**	MOSLEY	British politician
Benjamin	**Roy**	MOTTELSON	Danish physicist
Colin	**Berkeley**	MOYNIHAN	Politician
Robert	**Gabriel**	MUGABE	Zimbabwean president
Robert	**Sanderson**	MULLIKEN	American chemist
Hector	**Hugh**	MUNRO	Author
Keith	**Rupert**	MURDOCH	Businessman
Bartolomé	**Estebán**	MURILLO	Spanish painter
Edward	**Regan**	MURPHY	US comedian
John	**Middleton**	MURRY	Writer and critic
Maria	**Lurdes**	MUTOLA	Mozambique athlete
Frederic	**Ogden**	NASH	Poet
Pablo	**Neftali Reyes**	NERUDA	Poet
Marcus	**Cocceius**	NERVA	Roman emperor
Julia	**Babette Sarah**	NEUBERGER	Rabbi
George	**Eric**	NEWBY	Author
George	**Anthony**	NEWLEY	Actor and singer
Stavros	**Spyros**	NIARCHOS	Greek shipowner
Emma	**Harriet**	NICHOLSON	Politician
Jack	**William**	NICKLAUS	Golfer
Joseph	**Nicéphore**	NIEPCE	Inventor
Marshall	**Warren**	NIRENBERG	US biochemist
Richard	**Milhous**	NIXON	US president
Joshua	**Mqabuko Nyongolo**	NKOMO	Zimbabwean politician
Ronald	**Wreyford**	NORRISH	English chemist
Trevor	**Robert**	NUNN	Theatre director
Julius	**Kambarage**	NYERERE	Tanzanian president
Michael	**Vincent**	O'BRIEN	Racehorse trainer
David	**Feodorovich**	OISTRAKH	Violinist
Laurence	**Kerr**	OLIVIER	Actor
Aristotle	**Socrates**	ONASSIS	Shipping magnate
Eugene	**Gladstone**	O'NEILL	US playwright
Elisha	**Graves**	OTIS	Inventor
Peter	**Seamus**	O'TOOLE	Irish actor
George	**Emil**	PALADE	US biologist
Arnold	**Daniel**	PALMER	Golfer
Cyril	**Northcote**	PARKINSON	Political scientist
Eric	**Honeywood**	PARTRIDGE	Lexicographer
Linus	**Carl**	PAULING	Scientist
Thomas	**Love**	PEACOCK	Novelist and poet
Mervyn	**Laurence**	PEAKE	Author and artist
John	**Loughborough**	PEARSON	Architect
Lester	**Bowles**	PEARSON	Canadian politician
Eldred	**Gregory**	PECK	Actor
Richard	**Wayne**	PENNIMAN	Musician
Juan	**Domingo**	PERÓN	Argentinian president
Reginald	**Iolanthe**	PERRIN	TV character
Matthew	**Galbraith**	PERRY	US naval officer
Oliver	**Hazard**	PERRY	US naval officer
Publius	**Helvius**	PERTINAX	Roman emperor
Max	**Ferdinand**	PERUTZ	British biochemist
Henri	**Omer**	PÉTAIN	French statesman

First Name	Middle Name(s)	Surname	
Mary	Elizabeth	PETERS	Pentathlete
Roger	Tory	PETERSON	US ornithologist
Ulrich	Bonnell	PHILLIPS	US historian
River	Jude	PHOENIX	Actor
William	Mervyn	PICKWOAD	Actor
Lester	Keith	PIGGOTT	Jockey
Arthur	Wing	PINERO	Playwright
Jenny	Susan	PITMAN	Racehorse trainer
Gary	Jim	PLAYER	Golfer
Raymond	Landry	POINCARÉ	French statesman
John	Marlan	POINDEXTER	US naval officer
James	Knox	POLK	US president
Robert	Graeme	POLLOCK	Cricketer
Paul	Jackson	POLLOCK	US artist
William	Sydney	PORTER	Author
Michael	Denzil Xavier	PORTILLO	Politician
Dennis	Christopher George	POTTER	Playwright
Ezra	Loomis	POUND	Poet
Anthony	Dymoke	POWELL	English novelist
John	Enoch	POWELL	British politician
Austin	Danger	POWERS	Film character
John	Leslie	PRESCOTT	Politician
Elvis	Aaron	PRESLEY	American singer
Marthinus	Wessels	PRETORIUS	South African general
André	George	PREVIN	Conductor
John	Boynton	PRIESTLEY	Author
Archibald	Philip	PRIMROSE	British prime minister
James	Leathes	PRIOR	Politician
Victor	Sawdon	PRITCHETT	Writer and critic
Sergei	Sergeyevich	PROKOFIEV	Composer
Giacomo	Antonio	PUCCINI	Composer
Ana	Fidelia	QUIROT	Cuban athlete
Steve	Russell	RACE	Broadcaster
Sergey	Vasilyevich	RACHMANINOV	Composer
Thomas	Stamford	RAFFLES	Colonial administrator
Arthur	Michael	RAMSEY	Archbishop of Canterbury
Norman	Foster	RAMSEY	US physicist
John	Crowe	RANSOM	US poet and critic
Arthur	Michell	RANSOME	Author
Esther	Louise	RANTZEN	TV presenter
Claire	Berenice	RAYNER	Broadcaster
Ronald	Wilson	REAGAN	US president
Michael	Scudamore	REDGRAVE	Actor
Robert	Oliver	REED	British actor
Erich	Maria	REMARQUE	Author
Ruth	Barbara	RENDELL	Crime novelist
Dickinson	Woodruff	RICHARDS	US physician
Dorothy	Miller	RICHARDSON	English novelist
Eddie	Vernon	RICKENBACKER	Fighter pilot
Sally	Kristen	RIDE	US astronaut
Matthew	Bunker	RIDGWAY	US soldier
Nikolai	Andreievich	RIMSKY-KORSAKOV	Composer
Frederick	Chapman	ROBBINS	US physiologist
Frederick	Sleigh	ROBERTS	British soldier
James	Logie	ROBERTSON	Poet
Paul	Bustill Le Roy	ROBESON	Actor
Frederick	John	ROBINSON	British prime minister
Nelson	Aldrich	ROCKEFELLER	US vice-president
Anita	Lucia	RODDICK	Businesswoman
Franklin	Delano	ROOSEVELT	US president
Jack	Morris	ROSENTHAL	Playwright
Kenneth	Ronald	ROSEWALL	Tennis player
Mstislav	Leopoldovich	ROSTROPOVICH	Cellist
Philip	Milton	ROTH	Novelist
Meyer	Amschel	ROTHSCHILD	German financier
Francis	Peyton	ROUS	American pathologist
Robert	Alexander	RUNCIE	Archbishop of Canterbury
Ahmed	Salman	RUSHDIE	Author
Charles	Taze	RUSSELL	Religious leader
Gottlieb	Eliel	SAARINEN	Finnish–US architect

First Name	Middle Name(s)	Surname	
Nelly	**Leonie**	SACHS	Swedish poet and playwright
Jerome	**David**	SALINGER	Author
Jonas	**Edward**	SALK	Biologist
Seigfried	**Lorraine**	SASSOON	Poet
James	**Wilson Vincent**	SAVILE	Broadcaster
John	**Richard**	SCHLESINGER	Film director
Charles	**Monroe**	SCHULZ	US strip cartoonist
Harry	**Donald**	SECOMBE	Comedian and singer
Elzie	**Crisler**	SEGAR	US strip cartoonist
Harry	**Gordon**	SELFRIDGE	British merchant
David	**Oliver**	SELZNICK	US cinema mogul
Richard	**Bowdler**	SHARPE	Ornithologist
George	**Bernard**	SHAW	Author
Percy	**Bysshe**	SHELLEY	Poet
James	**Schoolcraft**	SHERMAN	US vice-president
William	**Tecumseh**	SHERMAN	General
William	**Bradford**	SHOCKLEY	US physicist
John	**Cody Fiddler**	SIMPSON	News reporter
Francis (Frank)	**Albert**	SINATRA	Singer
Upton	**Beall**	SINCLAIR	US novelist
Isaac	**Bashevis**	SINGER	Writer
Israel	**Joshua**	SINGER	Writer
Isaac	**Merritt**	SINGER	US inventor
Christopher	**Robert**	SMITH	British politician
Hamilton	**Othanel**	SMITH	US molecular biologist
Maggie	**Natalie**	SMITH	Actress
Sydney	**Goodsir**	SMITH	Poet
Samuel	**Jackson**	SNEAD	Golfer
Charles	**Percy**	SNOW	Author
Garfield	**St Auburn**	SOBERS	Cricketer
Robert	**Merton**	SOLOW	American economist
Aleksandr	**Isaevich**	SOLZHENITSYN	Author
Stephen	**Joshua**	SONDHEIM	Composer and lyricist
Donald	**Oliver**	SOPER	Methodist minister
Thomas	**Octave Murdoch**	SOPWITH	Aircraft designer
Charles	**Hamilton**	SORLEY	Poet
John	**Hanning**	SPEKE	Explorer
Basil	**Urwin**	SPENCE	Architect
Elmer	**Ambrose**	SPERRY	US inventor
Roger	**Wolcott**	SPERRY	US neuroscientist
Henry	**Morton**	STANLEY	Explorer and journalist
Edwin	**McMasters**	STANTON	US statesman
Publius	**Papinius**	STATIUS	Roman poet
George	**Ledyard**	STEBBINS	US botanist
David	**Martin Scott**	STEEL	Politician
William	**Howard**	STEIN	US biochemist
John	**Ernest**	STEINBECK	US novelist
Patrick	**Christopher**	STEPTOE	Gynaecologist
Adlai	**Ewing**	STEVENSON	US politician
William	**Gladstone**	STEWART	TV broadcaster and producer
Richard	**Henry Simpson**	STILGOE	Songwriter and broadcaster
Isidor	**Feinstein**	STONE	US journalist
Harlan	**Fiske**	STONE	US judge
William	**Wetmore**	STORY	Poet and sculptor
Rex	**Todhunter**	STOUT	US detective writer
Gavin	**Steel**	STRANG	Politician
Charles	**Sherwood**	STRATTON	Circus performer
Igor	**Fedorovich**	STRAVINSKY	Composer
Jack	**Whitaker**	STRAW	Politician
Meryl	**Mary Louise**	STREEP	Actress
Barbra	**Joan**	STREISAND	Singer
Arthur	**Seymour**	SULLIVAN	Composer
John	**Bird**	SUMNER	Archbishop of Canterbury
Frank	**Meadow**	SUTCLIFFE	Photographer
Joseph	**Wilson**	SWAN	Physicist
John	**Addington**	SYMONDS	Author
John	**Millington**	SYNGE	Author
William	**Howard**	TAFT	US president
Archibald	**Campbell**	TAIT	Archbishop of Canterbury
Abel	**Janszoon**	TASMAN	Navigator

FAMOUS PEOPLE

First Name	Middle Name(s)	Surname	
Elizabeth	**Rosemond**	TAYLOR	Actress
Edward	**Lawrie**	TATUM	US biochemist
William	**Howson**	TAYLOR	Potter
Pyotr	**Ilyich**	TCHAIKOVSKY	Composer
Kiri	**Janette**	TE KANAWA	Opera Singer
Norman	**Beresford**	TEBBIT	Politician
George	**Philipp**	TELEMANN	Composer
Henry	**John**	TEMPLE	British prime minister
Ellen	**Alice**	TERRY	Actress
William	**Makepeace**	THACKERAY	Author
Margaret	**Hilda**	THATCHER	British prime minister
Anatole	**François**	THIBAULT	Author
Dylan	**Marlais**	THOMAS	Poet
Daley	**Francis Morgan**	THOMPSON	Athlete
John	**Taliaferro**	THOMPSON	US soldier and inventor
George	**Paget**	THOMSON	English physicist
John	**Jeremy**	THORPE	Politician
James	**Grover**	THURBER	Humorist
Uma	**Karuna**	THURMAN	Actress
Louis	**Comfort**	TIFFANY	Glassmaker
Samuel	**Jones**	TILDEN	US politician
William	**Tatem**	TILDEN	US tennis player
Samuel	**Chao Chung**	TING	US physicist
Michael	**Kemp**	TIPPETT	Composer
Marcus	**Tullius**	TIRO	Inventor
Richard	**Palethorpe**	TODD	Actor
John	**Ronald Reuel**	TOLKIEN	Author
Theobald	**Wolfe**	TONE	Irish nationalist
Augustus	**Montague**	TOPLADY	Clergyman and hymnist
Donald	**Francis**	TOVEY	Pianist and composer
Charles	**Hard**	TOWNES	American physicist
Lee	**Buck**	TREVINO	American golfer
Rodney	**Charlton**	TROTTER	'Fools and Horses' character
Frederick (Freddy)	**Sewards**	TRUEMAN	Cricketer
Barry	**Emmanuel**	TUCKWELL	Australian musician
Alan	**Mathison**	TURING	Mathematician
Victor	**Witter**	TURNER	Anthropologist
Desmond	**Mpilo**	TUTU	South African prelate
William	**Marcy**	TWEED	US politician and criminal
Liv	**Johanne**	ULLMANN	Norwegian actress
John	**Hoyer**	UPDIKE	Author
Leon	**Marcus**	URIS	US author
Peter	**Alexander**	USTINOV	Actor and writer
Louis	**Nicolas**	VAUQUELIN	Chemist
King	**Wallis**	VIDOR	Film director
Angelina	**Jolie**	VOIGHT	Actress
Sarah	**Virginia**	WADE	Tennis player
Thomas	**Griffiths**	WAINEWRIGHT	Art critic and murderer
Terence (Terry)	**Hardy**	WAITE	Religious adviser
Selman	**Abraham**	WAKSMAN	US biochemist
Alice	**Malsenior**	WALKER	US novelist
George	**Corley**	WALLACE	Governor of Alabama
Henry	**Agard**	WALLACE	US vice-president
Hugh	**Seymour**	WALPOLE	Novelist
William	**Turner**	WALTON	Composer
Arthur	**Sarsfield**	WARD	Author
Booker	**Taliaferro**	WASHINGTON	US educationist
Lewis	**Edson**	WATERMAN	Inventor
James	**Dewey**	WATSON	US biologist
Clifton	**Parmelee**	WEBB	Actor
Everton	**Decourcey**	WEEKES	West Indian cricketer
Caspar	**Willard**	WEINBERGER	US politician
Thomas	**Huckle**	WELLER	US physiologist
Alan	**Whipper**	WELLS	Athlete
Charles	**Watson**	WENTWORTH	British prime minister
Edith	**Newbold**	WHARTON	Author
Denis	**Yates**	WHEATLEY	Novelist
Alan	**Donald**	WHICKER	Broadcaster
Jimmy	**Warren**	WHITE	Snooker player
Joseph	**Blanco**	WHITE	English poet
Pearl	**Fay**	WHITE	US actress

First Name	Middle Name(s)	Surname	
Terence	**Hanbury**	WHITE	Novelist
William	**Hale**	WHITE	Writer
Alfred	**North**	WHITEHEAD	Philosopher and mathematician
Oscar	**Fingal O'Flahertie Wills**	WILDE	Playwright and novelist
Ralph	**Vaughan**	WILLIAMS	Composer
Bob	**Dylan**	WILLIS	Cricketer
Bob	**Primrose**	WILSON	Goalkeeper and broadcaster
James	**Harold**	WILSON	British prime minister
Robert	**Woodrow**	WILSON	US physicist
Thomas	**Woodrow**	WILSON	US president
Pelham	**Grenville**	WODEHOUSE	Author
Michael	**Terence**	WOGAN	Broadcaster
Thomas	**Clayton**	WOLFE	Novelist
Tom	**Kennerley**	WOLFE	Novelist
Arnold	**Whittaker**	WOLFENDALE	Astronomer
Comer	**Vann**	WOODWARD	US historian
Robert	**Burns**	WOODWARD	American chemist
Adeline	**Virginia**	WOOLF	Novelist
Frank	**Winfield**	WOOLWORTH	US businessman
Bertie	**Wilberforce**	WOOSTER	Fictional character
Frank	**Mortimer Magilinne**	WORRELL	Cricketer
Billy	**Ambrose**	WRIGHT	Footballer
Elinor	**Hoyt**	WYLIE	US author
Johann	**Rudolf**	WYSS	Swiss writer
Magdi	**Habib**	YACOUB	Surgeon
Charles	**Elwood**	YEAGER	US test pilot
William	**Butler**	YEATS	Author
Boris	**Nikolayevich**	YELTSIN	Russian president
Susannah	**Yolande**	YORK	Actress
Lazarus	**Ludwig**	ZAMENHOF	Inventor of Esperanto
Gianfranco	**Corsi**	ZEFFIRELLI	Film director
Mai	**Elizabeth**	ZETTERLING	Actress and director

Nicknames

Joseph Addison **Atticus**

Aeschylus **Father of Greek Tragedy**

Muhammed Ali **Louisville Lip**

Queen Anne **Brandy Nan**

Anne of Cleves **Flanders Mare**

Lord George Anson **Father of the Royal Navy**

Thomas Aquinas **Angelic Doctor**

Aristophanes **Father of Comedy**

Richard Arkwright **Father of the Factory System**

Henry Armstrong **Homicide Hank**

Louis Armstrong **Satchmo (Satchel Mouth)**

Charles Atlas **World's Most Perfectly Developed Man**

Attila the Hun **Scourge of God**

Aurelian (Roman emperor) **Restorer of the World**

Stephen Babcock **Father of Scientific Dairying**

Francis Bacon **Father of Inductive Philosophy**

Roger Bacon **Father of Philosophy, Admirable Doctor (Doctor Mirabilis)**

John Logie Baird **Father of Television**

Joan Bakewell **Thinking Man's Crumpet** (by Frank Muir)

Theda Bara **Vamp**

John Barbour **Father of Scottish Poetry**

Sir John Barnard **Father of London**

John Barrymore **Great Profile**

Sir Edmund Barton **Father of Australia**

Elyesa Bazna (spy) **Cicero**

Bill Beaumont **Amiable Geronimo**

Alexander Graham Bell **Father of the Telephone**

Aphra Behn **Divine Astraea**

John Bell **Father of Sunday Newspapers**

Jeremy Bentham **Father of Utilitarianism**

Lavrenti Beria **Himmler of Russia**

David Berkowitz **Son of Sam**

Irving Berlin **Father of Published Ragtime**

Sarah Bernhard **Divine Sarah**

John Biddle **Father of English Unitarianism**

Clarence Birdseye **Father of Frozen Food**

Bismarck **Iron Chancellor**

Dr Greene Valadiman Black **Father of Modern Dentistry**

Simon Bolivar **Liberator**

Peter Bonetti **Cat**

Bononcini and Handel **Tweedle Dee and Tweedle Dum**

Jean Borotra **Bounding Basque**

James Boswell **Will O' the Wisp**

Clara Bow **It Girl**

Robert Boyle **Father of Chemistry**

Bessie Braddock **Workers' Champion**

William Bradford **Father of American History**

James Brindley **Father of Britain's Canals**

William Hill Brown **Father of the American Novel**

William Cullen Bryant **Father of American Poetry**

Martha Jane Burke **Calamity Jane**

Robert Burns **Bard of Ayrshire**

Richard Burton **The Voice**

George Bush **Wimp**

Francis X Bushman **Handsomest Man in the World**

David Bushnell **Father of the Submarine**

Caedmon **Father of English Song**

Cab Calloway   **King of Hi de Ho**
Walter Chauncey Camp   **Father of American Football**
Martha Jane Canary (Burke)   **Calamity Jane**
Thomas Carlyle   **Sage of Chelsea**
Primo Carnera   **Ambling Alp**
Judy Carne   **Sock-it-to-me-girl**
Georges Carpentier   **Orchid Kid**
Jacques Cartier   **Father of Canada**
John Cartwright   **Father of Reform**
Johnny Cash   **Man in Black**
Nicholas Catinat   **Father Thoughtful**
William Caxton   **Father of English Printing**
Sir George Cayley   **Father of Aviation**
Craig Chalmers   **Sponge**
Wilton Chamberlain   **Wilt the Stilt**
Lon Chaney Snr   **Man of a thousand Faces**
Charles I   **Martyr King, Ahab of the Nation,
  Britain's Josiah, White King**
Charles II   **Blackbird, Old Rowley, Merry Monarch**
Eddie Charlton   **Steady Eddie**
Henri Charrière   **Papillon**
Chris Chataway   **Red Fox**
Geoffrey Chaucer   **Father of English Poetry**
Cicero   **Father of his Country**
Cassius Clay   **Louisville Lip**
Georges Clemenceau   **Tiger**
Daniel Cohn-Bendit   **Danny the Red**
Mary Collier   **The Washer-woman (Poet)**
Peter Cook   **Cambridge Rapist**
John Calvin Coolidge   **Silent Cal**
Jim Corbett   **Gentleman Jim**
Paul Cotton   **Poco**
Noël Coward   **The Master**
Colin Cowdrey   **Kipper**
Alexander Cozens   **Father of English Watercolour**
Brigadier-General Alfred Critchley   **Father of
  Greyhound Racing**
Oliver Cromwell   **Old Noll, Nose Almighty, Old
  Ironsides**
Richard Cromwell   **Tumbledown Dick**
Aleister Crowley   **Wickedest Man in the World**
Duke of Cumberland   **Butcher**
Laurie Cunningham   **Black Pearl**
Edwina Currie   **Vindaloo**
Clarence Darrow   **Attorney for the Damned**
Freddie Davies (comedian)   **Parrot Face**
William Henry Davies   **Supertramp**
Steve Davis   **Interesting**
William Morris Davis   **Father of Geomorphology**
Eamon De Valera   **Father of the Irish Republic**
Rodrigo de Vivar   **El Cid**
Daniel Defoe   **Father of Modern Prose Fiction**
Jack Dempsey (heavyweight)   **Manassa Mauler,
  Nonpareil**
Joe Di Maggio   **Yankee Clipper**
Mildred Didrikson   **Babe**
Graham Dilley (cricketer)   **Picca**
Tommy Docherty   **Doc**
Antoine Domino   **Fats**
General Abner Doubleday   **Father of Baseball**
Antony Dowell and Antoinette Sibley   **Golden Pair**
Jimmy Durante   **Schnozzle**
Valentine Dyall   **Man in Black**
Nelson Eddy and Jeanette MacDonald   **America's
  Sweethearts**

Thomas Alva Edison   **Wizard of Menlo Park**
Edmund II   **Ironside**
Edward I   **Longshanks**
Edward III   **Father of English Commerce**
Edward V and brother Richard   **Princes in the Tower**
Edward (son of Edward III)   **Black Prince**
Eddie Edwards   **Eagle**
George Edwards   **Father of Ornithologists**
Elizabeth I   **Virgin Queen**
Elizabeth II   **Brenda** (by *Private Eye*)
Elizabeth Stuart (of Bohemia)   **Winter Queen**
Eminem   **The Real Slim Shady**
Empress Tzu Hsi   **Old Buddha**
Arthur English   **Prince of the Wide Boys**
Ethelred II   **Unready**
Eusebio   **Black Panther**
Eusebius of Caesarea   **Father of Ecclesiastical
  History**
Derrick Evans   **Mr Motivator**
Henry Fielding   **Father of the English Novel**
Tom Finney   **White Ghost**
Bob Fitzsimmons   **Cornishman, Antipodean**
George Formby Snr   **Wigan Nightingale**
Tregonwell Frampton   **Father of the English Turf**
Francis I of France   **Father of Letters**
John Francome   **Greatest Jockey** (by John
  McCririck)
Frederick I   **Barbarossa**
Frederick II   **Wonder of the World**
William Frederick   **Great Elector (of Brandenburg)**
Alan Freeman   **Fluff**
Tony Galento   **Two Ton**
Gandhi   **Mahatma ('Great Soul')**
Joel Garner   **Big Bird**
George III   **Farmer George**
George IV   **Adonis of Fifty**
Cass Gilbert   **Father of the Skyscraper**
Ian Gillis   **Mycroft**
Bernard Gilpin   **Father of the Poor**
Giotto Di Bondone   **Father of Modern Art**
Thomas Girtin   **Father of Modern Watercolour**
William Gladstone   **Grand Old Man (GOM)**
Captain Sir John Hawley Glover   **Father of the
  Hausas**
Major General Sir John Bagot Glubb   **Father of the
  Chin, Glubb Pasha**
Sir James Goldsmith   **Goldenballs** (by *Private Eye*)
Barry Goldwater   **AuH2O**
Graham Gooch   **Zap**
Benny Goodman   **King of Swing**
Charles Goodnight   **Father of the Cowboys**
Betty Grable   **Million Dollar Legs**
Ulysses Simpson Grant   **Uncle Sam**
Zachary Grey   **Father of Modern Commentators**
Florence Griffith-Joyner   **Flo Jo**
Grock   **King of Clowns**
Marvin Hagler   **Marvellous (later became first name)**
Archie Hahn   **Milwaukee Meteor**
John George Haigh   **Acid Bath Murderer, Vampire
  Killer**
Handel and Bononcini   **Tweedle Dum and Tweedle
  Dee**
WC Handy   **Father of the Blues**
Harold I   **Harefoot**
Russell Harty   **Sooty**

Mark Hateley (footballer)   **Attila**
Sir Christopher Hatton   **Mutton, the Dancing Chancellor**
Franz Josef Haydn   **Father of the Symphony**
Edward Heath   **Grocer**
Henry I of England   **Beauclerc**
Henry IV of France   **Father of the People**
Henry V   **Bluff Prince Hal**
Herodotus   **Father of History**
Michael Heseltine   **Tarzan, Veronica Lake, Action Man, Goldilocks**
Alex Higgins   **Hurricane**
Jimmy Hill   **Rabbi**
Bernard Hinault (cyclist)   **Badger**
Hippocrates   **Father of Medicine**
Bob Hite (Canned Heat)   **Bear**
James Hogg   **Ettrick Shepherd**
John Philip Holland   **Father of the Military Submarine**
Billie Holliday   **Lady Day**
Homer   **Father of Epic Poetry**
Thomas Hooker   **Father of American Democracy**
Matthew Hopkins   **Witchfinder General**
Lesley Hornby   **Twiggy**
Geoffrey Howe   **Mogadon Man**
Edmond Hoyle   **Father of the Game of Whist**
George Hudson   **Railway King**
Cordell Hull   **Father of the United Nations**
Barbara Hutton   **Poor Little Rich Girl**
Hypatia   **Divine Pagan**
Thomas Ince   **Father of Westerns**
Andrew Jackson   **Old Hickory**
General Thomas Jackson   **Stonewall (Battle of Bull Run)**
Joseph Holson Jagger   **Man Who Broke the Bank at Monte Carlo**
James I   **Wisest Fool in Christendom** (by Henry IV of France)
James II   **King over the Water**
Thomas Jefferson   **Moonshine Philosopher**
James J Jeffries   **Boilermaker**
Edward Jenner   **Father of Immunology**
William Le Baron Jenney   **Father of the Skyscraper**
Gilbert Jessop (cricketer)   **The Croucher**
Joan of Arc   **Maid of Orleans**
Samuel Johnson   **Great Cham**
Sir John Harvey Jones   **Admiral**
Ben Jonson   **Father of Poets**
Janis Joplin   **Pearl**
Scott Joplin   **Father of Ragtime**
William Joyce   **Lord Haw Haw**
Alberto Juantorena   **White Lightning**
Helen Kane   **Boop a Doop Girl**
Nora Kaye   **Duse of the Dance**
Buster Keaton   **The Great Stone Face**
Joseph Keaton   **Buster** (coined by Houdini)
Fanny Kemble   **Anne of Swansea**
Rev Geoffrey Kennedy   **Woodbine Willie**
Ludovic Kennedy   **Uckers**
Admiral Sir Henry Keppel   **Father of the Fleet**
Graham Kerr   **Galloping Gourmet**
King John   **Lackland**
Peter Kurten   **Monster of Düsseldorf**
Henri Landru   **Bluebeard**
Allen Lane   **Father of Penguin Paperbacks**
Niki Lauda   **Clockwork Mouse**
Rod Laver   **Rockhampton Rocket**

Antoine Lavoisier   **Father of Modern Chemistry**
Florence Lawrence   **Biograph Girl**
Frances Lawrence (novelist)   **Gidget**
John Lawrence   **Noble Lord** (by John McCririck)
Major General Stringer Lawrence   **Father of the Indian Army**
TE Lawrence   **Lawrence of Arabia**
Jean-Baptiste Le Moyne   **Father of Louisiana**
Jerry Lee Lewis   **Killer**
Eric Liddell   **Flying Scotsman**
Fred Lillywhite (cricketer)   **Nonpareil Bowler**
Jenny Lind   **Swedish Nightingale**
Charles Lindbergh   **Lone Eagle**
David Lloyd George   **Welsh Wizard**
Harry Longbaugh   **Sundance Kid**
Lord Longford   **Lord Porn**
Konrad Lorenz   **Father of Ethology**
Lorenzo de' Medici   **Father of Letters, The Magnificent**
Louis XII   **Father of the People**
Louis XIV   **Sun King**
Joe Louis   **Brown Bomber**
Lord Lucan   **Lucky**
Vera Lynn   **Forces Sweetheart**
Ma Rainey   **Mother of the Blues**
Mary McCauley   **Molly Pitcher**
Derek McCulloch   **Uncle Mac**
John McEnroe   **Superbrat**
Barry McGuigan   **Clones Cyclone**
Harold Macmillan   **Supermac**
McPartlin and Donnelly   **Ant and Dec**
James Madison   **Father of the Constitution**
Mary Mallon   **Typhoid Mary**
Rocky Marciano   **Brockton Blockbuster**
Frances Marion   **Swamp Fox**
Duchess of Marlborough   **Mrs Freeman**
Duke of Marlborough (1st)   **Anne's Great Captain**
Major William Martin (WW2 decoy)   **Man Who Never Was**
Mary I   **Bloody Mary**
Matilda   **Empress Maud**
Stanley Matthews   **Wizard of Dribble**
Colin Meads   **Pine Tree**
Bette Midler   **Divine Miss M**
Henry Miller   **Father of the Four Letter Word**
Joseph Miller   **Father of Jests**
Max Miller   **Cheekie Chappie**
Carmen Miranda   **Brazilian Bombshell**
Thelonius Monk   **High Priest of Bop**
Duke of Monmouth (James Scott)   **Absalom**
Jean Monnet   **Father of the Common Market**
Lady Mary Wortley Montague   **Sappho**
Helen Wills Moody   **Little Miss Poker Face**
Lewis Henry Morgan   **Father of American Anthropology**
Jedediah Morse   **Father of American Geography**
Charles Morton   **Father of Variety, Champagne, Father of the Halls**
Lord Louis Mountbatten   **Dickie**
Richard Murdoch   **Stinker**
Lindley Murray   **Father of English Grammar**
James Naismith   **Father of Basketball**
Renaldo Nehemiah (athlete)   **Skeets**
Jawaharlal Nehru   **Pandit ('Wise Man')**
Donald Neilson (Nappey)   **Black Panther**

Richard Neville (Earl of Warwick)   **Kingmaker**
Marshal Ney   **Bravest of the Brave**
Jack Nicklaus   **Golden Bear**
Florence Nightingale   **Lady with the Lamp**
Richard Nixon   **Tricky Dicky**
Kwame Nkrumah   **Showboy**
Greg Norman   **Great White Shark**
Senator George Norris   **Father of the
20th Amendment**
Paavo Nurmi   **Flying Finn**
Lord John Oaksey   **Noble Lord** (by John McCririck)
Ronald O'Bryan   **Candy Man Killer**
Chris Old (cricketer)   **Chilly**
Sir Henry Oliver   **Father of Modern Navigation**
Christina Onassis   **Thunderthighs**
Dr Robert Oppenheimer   **Father of the Atom Bomb**
Count D'Orsay   **Last of the Dandies**
Tessie O'Shea   **Two-Ton Tessie**
Richard Fellow Outcault   **Father of the Comic Strip**
Robert Owen   **Father of British Socialism**
Jesse Owens   **Ebony Antelope**
Lord Palmerston   **Pam**
Bonnie Parker   **Suicide Sal**
Charlie Parker   **Bird**
Archbishop Matthew Parker   **Nosey Parker**
General George Patton   **Old Blood and Guts**
Cynthia Payne   **Madame Sin**
Pele   **Black Pearl**
Vladimir Peniakoff (Belgian soldier)   **Popski**
Sir Henry Percy   **Hotspur**
Joseph Père   **Grey Eminence**
William Perry   **Refrigerator**
John Joseph Pershing   **Black Jack**
Marius Petipa   **Father of Classical Ballet**
Louis Philippe   **Citizen King**
Edith Piaf   **Little Sparrow**
Mary Pickford   **America's Sweetheart**
William Pitt   **Aeolus**
William Pitt the Elder   **Great Commoner**
Gary Player   **Man in Black**
John Playford   **Father of British Music Publishing**
Edgar Allan Poe   **Father of the Detective Story**
Alexander Pope   **Wasp of Twickenham**
Elvis Presley   **The Pelvis, The King**
Princess Michael of Kent   **Princess Pushy**
Ferenc Puskas   **Galloping Major**
Rufus Putnam   **Father of Ohio**
Max Quartermann   **Superhod**
Fabius Quintus   **Cunctator (Delayer)**
Rabelais   **Father of Ridicule**
Luise Rainer   **Viennese Teardrop**
Sonny Ramadhin   **Spin King**
Derek Randall (cricketer)   **Arkle**
Maharajah Ranjit Singh   **Lion of the Punjab**
Ranulf de Glanvill   **Father of Jurisprudence**
John Ray   **Father of English Natural History**
Johnny Ray   **Prince of Wails**
Nancy Reagan   **Smiling Mamba**
Ronald Reagan   **Teflon President**
Ray Reardon   **Dracula**
John Redwood   **Vulcan**
John Reid   **Father of American Golf**
John Rich   **Father of Harlequins, Father of English
Pantomime**
Richard I   **Lionheart, Yea and Nay**

Richard de Beauchamp   **Father of Courtesy**
Richard de Clare (2nd Earl of Pembroke)
Strongbow
Richard Duke of York and Edward V   **Princes in the
Tower**
Samuel Richardson   **Father of the English Novel**
Cardinal Richelieu   **Red Eminence**
Manfred von Richthofen   **Red Baron**
Eddie Rickenbacker   **Ace of Aces**
Robespierre   **Sea-Green Incorruptible**
George Robey   **Prime Minister of Mirth**
Derek Robinson   **Red Robbo**
Jimmie Charles Rodgers   **Father of Country Music**
Steve Rogers   **Captain America**
Erwin Rommel   **Desert Fox**
Ken Rosewall   **Muscles**
Stanley Rous   **Father of English Football**
William Hepburn Russell   **Father of the Pony Express**
Babe Ruth   **Sultan of Swat**
Ernest Rutherford   **Father of Nuclear Physics**
William Sacheverell   **First Whig**
St Anthony   **Father of Christian Monasticism**
St Ethelwold   **Father of Monks**
St Thomas Aquinas   **Father of Moral Philosophy**
Albert de Salvo   **Boston Strangler**
Sir Malcolm Sargent   **Flash Harry**
Sir Walter Scott   **Wizard of the North, Great
Unknown, Ariosto of the North, Old Peveril**
William Shakespeare   **Swan of Avon, Bard of Avon**
Percy Bysshe Shelley   **Ariel**
Ann Sheridan   **Oomph Girl**
Manny Shinwell   **Sinbad the Tailor**
Willie Shoemaker (jockey)   **Shoe**
Antoinette Sibley and Anthony Dowell   **Golden
Pair**
Igor Sikorsky   **Father of the Helicopter**
OJ Simpson   **The Juice**
Frank Sinatra   **The Voice**
Dennis Skinner   **Beast of Bolsover**
Adam Smith   **Father of Economics**
Bob Smith   **Wolfman Jack**
William Smith   **Father of English Geology**
Soeur Sourire   **Singing Nun**
John Philip Sousa   **March King**
Ursula Southiel   **Old Mother Shipton**
Countess Spencer   **Acid Raine**
John Spencer   **Sniffer**
Bruce Springsteen   **The Boss**
Craig Stadler (golfer)   **Walrus**
Sylvester Stallone   **Italian Stallion**
George Stephenson   **Father of Railways**
Sir Rowland Stephenson   **Father of Indian Railways**
Robert Franklin Stroud   **Birdman of Alcatraz**
Charles Edward Stuart   **Bonnie Prince Charlie,
Young Pretender, Young Chevalier**
James Edward Stuart   **Old Pretender, Old Chevalier**
Louis Sullivan (architect)   **Father of Modernism**
Peter Sutcliffe   **Yorkshire Ripper**
Thomas Tallis   **Father of English Church Music**
James T Tanner   **Father of Musical Comedy**
Dennis Taylor (snooker player)   **Silver Fox**
John Taylor   **Water Poet**
Edward Teach   **Blackbeard**
Norman Tebbit   **Chingford Skinhead**
Temujin   **Genghis Khan**
Alfred Lord Tennyson   **Merlin**

Margaret Thatcher   **Iron Lady, The Milk Snatcher, Attila the Hen**
Cliff Thorburn (snooker player)   **Grinder**
William Tilden   **Big Bill**
Timon (Athenian nobleman)   **Misanthrope of Athens**
Thomas Tompion   **Father of English Clockmaking**
Mel Tormé   **Velvet Fog**
Charles Townshend   **Turnip**
Hugh Montague Trenchard   **Father of the RAF**
Lee Trevino   **Super-Mex**
Richard Trevilthick   **Father of the Locomotive**
Freddie Trueman   **Fiery Fred**
Lyman Trumbell   **Father of the 13th Amendment**
Sophie Tucker   **Last of the Red Hot Mamas**
JMW Turner   **Admiral Pugsy Booth, Blackbirdy**
Lana Turner   **Sweater Girl**
William Turner (Dean of Wells)   **Father of English Botany**
Christopher Tye   **Father of the Anthem**
Frank Tyson (cricketer)   **Typhoon**
Mike Tyson   **Catskill Thunder**
Uganda   **Pearl of Africa**
US Defense Dept   **Foggy Bottom**
Rudolph Valentino   **Pink Powder Puff**
Rudy Vallee   **Vagabond Lover**
Venerable Bede   **Father of English History**
Queen Victoria   **Widow of Windsor**

Horace Walpole   **Autocrat of Strawberry Hill**
Rosalind P Walter   **Rosie the Riveter**
Izaak Walton   **Father of Angling**
George Washington   **Father of his Country**
Isaac Watts   **Father of English Hymnody**
James Watt   **Father of Steam**
John Wayne   **Duke**
Josiah Wedgwood   **Father of English Pottery**
Duke of Wellington   **Iron Duke, Old Nosey, Achilles of England**
Jimmy White   **Whirlwind**
William White (US writer)   **Sage of Emporia**
Ann Widdecombe   **Doris Karloff**
Bishop Samuel Wilberforce   **Soapy Sam**
William Willett   **Father of Daylight Saving**
William I   **Conqueror**
William I of Orange   **Silent**
William II   **Rufus**
William IV   **Silly Billy**
Esther Williams   **Hollywood's Mermaid**
Walter Winchell   **Father of the Gossip Column**
Orde Wingate   **Robin Hood**
Sir Henry Wood   **Old Timber**
Harry Wragg (jockey)   **The Head Waiter**
Philemon Wright   **Father of Ottawa**
Francis Xavier   **Apostle of the Indies**

Traditional Occupations and Hobbies

This list of definitions includes some now-defunct traditional occupations alongside hobbies, pastimes, and colloquial names for certain types of worker. It also lists some lesser-known meanings for familiar professions.

Actuary   Person employed to assess risks for insurance companies, a statistician
Alderman   Senior member of a local council (until 1974)
Ale conner   Inspector of beer and bread
Almoner   Hospital social worker
Amanuensis   Secretary employed to take dictation or copy manuscripts
Artificer   Serviceman trained in mechanics
Bhishti (bheesty)   Formerly a water carrier, in India
Bibliophile   Collector of books
Bibliopole   Dealer in rare books
Boatswain/bosun   Petty officer on a merchant ship or warrant officer on a warship, responsible for maintenance
Bowyer   Person who makes or sells archery bows
Broderer   Person who embroiders
Bumbailiff   Formerly, an officer employed to collect debts and arrest non-payers
Bursar   Official in charge of finance in educational institutions
Campanologist   Bell ringer
Cartographer   Person who draws maps
Cartomancer   Person who tells fortunes by use of playing cards
Cartophilist   Collector of cigarette cards
Cartwright   Maker of carts
Chandler   Maker or seller of candles; grocer
Charcutier   Pork butcher
Cobbler   Shoemaker
Colporteur   Hawker of books, especially bibles

Conchologist   Collector of shells
Cooper   Maker of barrels
Cordwainer   Shoemaker, leather worker
Costermonger   Fruit and vegetable salesman (formerly an apple vendor)
Couturier   Person who designs, makes and sells fashion clothes for women
Coxswain   Helmsman of a boat
Curator   Person in charge of a collection, e.g. in a museum or library
Currier   Person who grooms horses or curries leather
Deltiologist   Picture-postcard collector
Didactics   The art or science of teaching
Draper   Person who sells cloth and cloth goods
Ecdysiast   Striptease artist
Equerry   Formerly, an officer in the royal household responsible for the horses
Farrier   Person who shoes horses
Fletcher   Maker of arrows
Founder   Maker of bells and castings
Franklin   Substantial landowner of free but not noble birth (Middle Ages)
Fromologist   Person who collects cheese labels
Funambulist   Tightrope walker
Gatherer   Glass blower, and formerly a bookbinder
Glazier   Person who fits windows, doors etc, with glass
Goliard   Wandering scholar of 12th and 13th centuries, famed for riotous behaviour
Gombeen man   An Irish moneylender

Gricer   Person who seeks out and photographs unusual trains

Groom   Person employed to clean and generally look after horses

Haberdasher   Seller of sewing articles, e.g. buttons, needles, zips and ribbons

Haberdasher (USA)   Men's clothes outfitter

Hack   Run of the mill journalist

Hard hat   Construction worker

Horner   Person who made objects such as spoons and combs out of horn

Hosier   Person who sells stockings

Houseman   Junior doctor who is a member of the medical staff attached to a hospital

Ikebanist   Practitioner of the Japanese decorative art of flower arranging

Intern   North American equivalent to a houseman; it is also a US term for a student teacher

Ironmonger   Dealer in hardware, eg nuts, bolts and locks, etc

Jobber   Dealer in stocks and shares

Joiner   Person skilled in making finished woodwork, eg windows, doors and stairs

Kamikaze   Japanese pilot who performed suicide missions in World War II

Lepidopterist   Butterfly and moth collector

Locum tenens   Person who deputises for another in the same profession

Longshoreman   American equivalent of a docker or stevedore

Lorimer/loriner   Person who makes bits, spurs and other small metal objects

Matador   Principal bullfighter

Mercer   Textile dealer

Milliner   Person who makes or sells women's hats

Millwright   Engineer who designs, builds or repairs grain mills or mill machinery

Modiste   Fashionable dressmaker or milliner

Navvy   Labourer on a building site

Notary public   Solicitor licensed to prepare legal documents

Numismatist   Collector of coins and medals

Obstetrician   Physician who specialises in childbirth

Ocularist   Person who makes artificial eyes

Optometrist   Person qualified to examine the eyes and prescribe lenses; also called optician or ophthalmologist

Origamist   Person who folds paper into ornate figures and decorations

Paediatrician   Physician who specialises in children and their diseases

Paramedic   Person such as a laboratory technician who supplements the work of the medical profession

Pedagogue   A teacher or educator

Pedant   Archaic term for a teacher

Philatelist   Stamp collector

Phillumenist   Person who collects matchbox labels

Picador   In bullfighting or horseman who lances the bull in early stages in order to weaken it

Pilot   Person qualified to steer or guide a ship into or out of port

Potholer   Cave and underground passage explorer

Prestidigitator   Magician, especially one skilled in close sleight of hand

Publican   In Roman times, a tax collector

Purser   On a ship or plane, officer who keeps the accounts and attends to passenger welfare

Quantity surveyor   Person who estimates the cost of the materials and labour necessary for a construction job

Radiographer/radiologist   Person who takes X-rays

Recorder   Barrister or solicitor of at least ten years, standing appointed to sit as a judge in the Crown Court

Registrar   Hospital doctor, senior to a houseman but junior to a consultant

Roughneck   Worker in an oil-drilling operation

Saddler   Person who makes saddles, harnesses and other leather equipment for horses

Sandhog   North American term for person who works in underground or underwater construction projects

Scrivener   Formerly, a person who wrote out legal documents, a notary

Sempstress/seamstress   Woman who sews and makes clothes

Sensei   Japanese teacher of martial and other arts

Sexton   Church helper responsible for church upkeep

Shaman   Medicine man or witch doctor

Shipwright   Artisan skilled in shipbuilding

Spelunker   Cave explorer

Spodomancer   Person who makes prophecies by divination of ashes

Stationer   Person who sells stationery; formerly a publisher or bookseller

Steeplejack   Person skilled in construction and felling of steeples, spires, chimneys and towers

Stenographer   North American name for a shorthand typist

Stevedore   Person employed to load or unload a ship

Stoker   Person employed to tend a furnace, as on a steamship

Subaltern   Army officer below the rank of captain, usually a second lieutenant

Tanner   Person who tans skins and hides into leather

Timbrologist   Stamp collector

Topiarist   Person who shapes hedges into ornate shapes

Toreador   Rank-and-file bullfighter

Turner   Lathe operator

Upholsterer   Person who upholsters furniture

Vexillologist   Person who studies and collects information about flags

Vintner   Wine merchant

Vulcanologist   Person who studies volcanoes

Wainwright   Maker of wagons, wains and carts

Wheelwright/wheeler   Maker of wheels

Philosophers and Political Thinkers

Thales (c624–c545 BC) Greek natural philosopher and astronomer, born in Miletus, traditionally seen as the founder of European philosophy. Thales identified water as the basis of the universe and also predicted the solar eclipse that took place in 585 BC. He was included in the traditional canon of 'Seven Wise Men' and was the original 'absent-minded professor', having allegedly fallen into a well whilst looking at the stars.

Anaximander (c611–546 BC) Greek natural philosopher and astronomer, born in Miletus, and possibly a pupil of Thales. Anaximander is credited with producing the first maps. He was the second of the three great Milesian thinkers (the third was Anaximenes).

Pythagoras (c580– c500 BC) Greek philosopher and mathematician, born in Samos, Ionia. He established his ethico-political academy at Croton (now Crotona) in southern Italy. Famous for his theorem concerning properties of right-angled triangles.

Heraclitus (554–483 BC) Greek philosopher, born in Ephesus and nicknamed at various times 'the obscure' and 'the riddler'. Most famous doctrine is that everything is in a state of flux and that fire is the ultimate constituent of the world.

Confucius (551–479 BC) Chinese philosopher, born in what is now Shantung province. His birthday is celebrated on 28 September and is an official holiday in Taiwan ('Teacher's Day'). Although Confucius was not greatly revered in his lifetime, Confucianism, as expressed in his *Analects*, subsequently dominated Chinese life as both a religious and philosophical way of life.

Parmenides of Elea (510–483 BC) Greek philosopher from southern Italy and founder of the Eleatic school, which included his pupils Zeno and Melissus. His great work *On Nature* was written in hexameter verse.

Empedocles (c490–c430 BC) Greek philosopher, poet, statesman, religious teacher and physiologist, born in Acragas in Sicily. Empedocles held that the world is composed of four elements – air, fire, earth and water – which are governed by the opposing forces of love and discord. Heralded by his followers as a god, he allegedly died by leaping into the volcanic crater of Mount Etna whilst attempting to prove his divinity.

Socrates (469–399 BC) Athenian philosopher, held in such esteem that all earlier Greek philosophy is known as pre-Socratic. Little is known about him other than that he had an apparently shrewish wife, Xanthippe, and took part in military campaigns at Potidaea, Delium and Amphipolis. Socrates wrote nothing but was eulogised in the 'Dialogues' of his pupil, Plato. Socrates' approach was to question everything. He chose to pick holes in the deliberations of others and asked people to think for themselves. He was eventually charged with 'Impiety' and 'Corrupting the youth of Athens' and forced to die by drinking hemlock.

Democritus (c460–c370 BC) Greek philosopher, born in Abdera in Thrace and known as the 'laughing philosopher' because of his wry amusement at human foibles. A prolific writer, he is best known for the atomistic theory he developed from Leucippus.

Plato (c428–348 BC) Athenian philosopher who related the story of Socrates' trial in three of his *Dialogues*: the *Apology*, the *Crito* and the *Phaedo*. In c387 BC he founded the Academy, which became a famous establishment for philosophical, mathematical and scientific research. His writings comprise around 30 dialogues and a series of letters (only the seventh and eighth are likely to be genuine). The dialogue *Symposium* is an allegory of the search for love, and the *Republic* is an allegory of the search for justice. Plato was the teacher of Aristotle.

Aristotle (384–322 BC) Greek philosopher and scientist, born in Stagira, son of the court physician to the King of Macedon. Aristotle is one of the two most important philosophers of the ancient world, and one of the four or five most important of any time or place. For twenty years he was a member of Plato's Academy. When Plato died, Speusippus became head of the academy and Aristotle left Athens and became tutor to Alexander the Great (then aged 13). He returned to Athens in 335 BC and founded his 'Lyceum', so called from its proximity to the temple of Apollo Lyceius. The 'Aristotelian corpus' (1,462 pages of Greek text, including some spurious works) is probably derived from the lectures he gave in the Lyceum. Aristotle's followers became known as peripatetics (from his habit of walking around whilst lecturing). There is no doubt that many of the sub-categories of modern philosophy were formulated by Aristotle. He argued that although philosophy encompassed all areas of intellectual enquiry, there were distinct disciplines within this structure. Some areas in which Aristotle made a fundamental contribution in the expansion of philosophy as a science include logic, the study of nature, metaphysics, philosophy of mind, ethics and politics, and literary criticism and rhetorical theory. His works include the *Nicomachean Ethics*, *De Anima*, *Politics*, *Poetics*, *Metaphysics*, and the *Organon* (treatises on logic).

Epicurus (341–270 BC) Greek philosopher, born in Samos. His ethical philosophy was based on simple pleasures, friendship, and reflection. When Epicurus came to Athens in 306 BC he bought a house and established a school in the garden which became known as Ho Kepos (The Garden), where men and women of any background could attend. Like many of his predecessors he wrote treatises 'On Nature' but his best works were his ethical and theological dialogues, which made him a revered figure long after his death.

Lucretius (c99–55 BC) Roman philosopher and poet whose great works are his hexameter poem *De rerum natura* and his treatises attempting to separate philosophy from religion, which he denounced as the one great source of man's wickedness and misery. He was said to have died mad from the effects of a love potion administered by his wife, Lucilia.

Plotinus (c205–70) Born in Egypt of Roman parentage. His prolific writings were posthumously edited and arranged by his pupil, Porphyry, into six 'groups of nine books' or *Enneads*. These established the foundations of Neoplatonism, which combined Platonic with Pythagorean, Aristotelian and Stoic doctrines.

St Augustine of Hippo (354–430) Born in Tagaste in Numidia (modern Tunisia) of Roman descent, he was converted to Christianity in 386 and described his conversion in his most famous work *Confessions*. His other masterpiece was *The City of God*.

Roger Bacon (c1214–92)   English philosopher and scientist, probably born near Ilchester, Somerset. His soubriquet 'Doctor Mirabilis' was gained because of his learning in magic and alchemy and he was the first European to describe the process for making gunpowder. Bacon held radical philosophical views and was imprisoned by the Franciscans for some time because of his suspected heretical teachings.

St Thomas Aquinas (c1225–74)   Italian Dominican philosopher and theologian, born in the castle of Roccasecca, near Aquino, Sicily. His early education was at the monastery of Monte Cassino and then the University of Naples. He was a pupil of the Dominican scholar, Albertus Magnus, at the University of Paris and from 1256 began teaching there himself. In 1259 he was appointed theological adviser to the papal Curia. His two major works are *Summa theologica* and *Summa contra gentiles*. Thomas was known as 'Doctor Angelicus' and canonised a saint in 1323 by Pope John XXII. Thomism was the standard teaching of the Dominican order and has recently had a revival.

John Duns Scotus (c1265–1308)   Scottish scholastic philiosopher who became a Franciscan and was ordained a priest in St Andrew's Church, Northampton in 1291. He taught at Cologne, where he died and was buried. Duns Scotus was known by contemporaries as 'Doctor Subtilis' because of his extremely nuanced and technical resoning, but in the Renaissance the Scotists were dubbed 'Dunses' (hence the word 'dunce'). His important works include the *Opus Pariense* (Parisian Lectures), *Opus Oxiense* (Oxford Lectures, also known as the *Ordinatio*), *Tractatus de Primo Principio* and *Quaestiones Quodlibetales*.

William of Ockham (c1285–c1349)   English philosopher, theologian and political writer, born in Ockham, Surrey. William entered the Franciscan order after studying theology at Oxford, although he failed to graduate hence his nickname, 'the Venerable Inceptor'. He was excommunicated by John XXII and fled to Bavaria where he died of the Black Death. His works greatly upset the papacy and included *Summa Logicae, Quodlibeta Septem* and commentaries on the sentences of Peter Lombard and Aristotle His greatest philosophical contribution is 'Ockham's razor' or the 'Law of Parsimony', which states that entities are not to be multiplied beyond necessity. The principle was invoked previously by Durand de Saint-Pourçain but Ockham's frequent and sharp employment of the doctrine ensured that his name would be identified with the principle.

Nicholas of Cusa (1401–64)   German philosopher, scientist and churchman, born in Cues, Trier. He studied at Heidelberg and Padua, was ordained in 1430 and subsequently became a papal diplomat and Cardinal. Nicholas stressed the incomplete nature of man's knowledge of God and the universe. His main philosophical work is *De Docta Ignorantia* (1440) but he was the precursor of Copernicus as regards his non-geocentric theories.

Niccolò Machiavelli (1469–1527)   Italian political philosopher, statesman and writer, born in Florence. He rose to prominence after the demise of Savonarola's regime in 1498. He had a controversial career and was in and out of favour dependent on the political climate. His masterpiece, *The Prince*, was dedicated to Lorenzo de Medici and published 1532. This work epitomised his ethic of evil sometimes being necessary in order for good to prevail. Other works include *The Art of War*, and *Mandragola*, a comic play about seduction, as well as a discourse on Livy. He is buried in Santa Croce, Florence.

Giordano Bruno (1548–1600)   Italian philosopher, born in Nola, near Naples. He became a Dominican but came into conflict with the Inquisition due to his championing of Copernicus' heliocentricity theory, and his pantheistic views. He was eventually burned at the stake in Rome.

Sir Francis Bacon (1561–1626)   English philosopher and statesman who became Viscount St Albans. He was a leading proponent of Empiricism and rejected Aristotelian deductive logic. His works include *The Advancement of Learning, Novum Organum* and *The New Atlantis*. Bacon was also a leading parliamentarian and his methodical and logical approach was not trusted by his uncle, Lord Burghley. An example of his political expediency was to try to convict his former friend, the Earl of Essex. He apparently died from hypothermia caused while carrying out food preservation experiments on chickens.

Thomas Hobbes (1588–1679)   English political philosopher, born in Malmesbury (apparently prematurely, after his mother heard news of the approaching Spanish Armada). His first published work was a translation of Thucydides' *History* (1629); other works include *Elements of Law Natural and Politic* and his masterpiece 'Leviathan' (1651), in which he argues that absolutist government is needed to ensure law and order. His later works were published in Holland, the most famous being *Behemoth: a History of the causes of the Civil Wars of England*.

René Descartes (1596–1650)   French philosopher and mathematician, born near Tours in a town now called La-Haye, later renamed Descartes in his honour. He is often called the father of modern philosophy. Descartes was in Germany with the army of the Duke of Bavaria in 1619 when, on November 10th, he had a visionary dream in a stove-heated room, which revealed a scientific postulate that would link all possible human knowledge together into an all-embracing wisdom. Most of his major works were published shortly after the death of his illegitimate daughter, Francine, in 1640, the most famous being the *Discourse on Method* which framed the basis for Cartesian philosophy, the phrase '*Cogito ergo sum*' (I think therefore I am) encapsulating his rational methodology. He died of pneumonia and his last words were supposedly 'So my soul a time for parting'. He was buried in Stockholm but was later moved to Saint-Germain-des-Prés, Paris.

Baruch Spinoza (1632–77)   Dutch philosopher, born in Amsterdam. He was expelled from his Jewish community for heresy in 1656 and made a living grinding and polishing lenses (the glass dust was to cause his untimely death from consumption). His *Principia Philosophiae* was the only book published in his lifetime with his name on it. His main work, *Ethics*, was published posthumously. Spinoza is also known for his contributions to the development of an historical approach to the Bible.

John Locke (1632–74)   English empiricist philosopher, born in Wrington, Somerset. Locke's

Essay Concerning Human Understanding was the basis for the resurgence of Empiricism as an alternative to Cartesianism. He believed the mind at birth was a *tabula rasa*, as opposed to the Cartesian view that knowledge is derived from first principles.

Gottfried Wilhelm von Leibniz (1646–1716) German philosopher and mathematician, born in Leipzig. His optimism and faith in enlightenment and reason was satirised by Voltaire in *Candide* ('all is for the best in the best of all possible worlds'). His most famous work is the *Monadology*, in which he argues that the world is made up of an infinite number of units (monads), the highest of which is God. Apart from his philosophical essays, Leibniz also invented differential calculus, although the Royal Society formally declared Newton as its inventor in 1711 (nowadays both are credited).

Giovanni Vico (1668–1744) Italian philosopher, born in Naples. His major work, *Scienza Nuova* (The New Science), is concerned with the differences between scientific and historical explanation.

George Berkeley (1685–1753) Irish Anglican bishop and philosopher, born at Dysert Castle, Kilkenny. Bishop Berkeley was Dean of Derry and then Bishop of Cloyne; in between he tried to establish a college in the Bermudas but only got as far as Rhode Island. His celebrated claim that 'to be is to be perceived', whereby the contents of the material world are 'ideas' that only exist when they are perceived by a mind, is set out in his *Essay Towards a New Theory of Vision* and *A Treatise Concerning the Principles of Human Knowledge*. His other major work is *Three Dialogues Between Hylas and Philanous*.

David Hume (1711–76) Scottish philosopher and historian, born in Edinburgh. Hume's life was dogged in its early stages with fits of depression which he came to terms with whilst tutoring the insane nobleman, the Marquis of Annandale. His major works, *A Treatise of Human Nature* and *Dialogues Concerning Natural Religion* had a profound effect on Immanuel Kant and provoked the Idealists to counter Hume's scepticism. Hume was a friend of Rousseau but became embroiled in a famously bitter quarrel with him.

Jean-Jacques Rousseau (1712–78) French political philosopher, born in Geneva (his mother died in childbirth). He worked as a secretary and music copier in his early life. After a brief affair with Mme Louise de Warens he formed a lifelong liaison with Thérèse le Vasseur, with whom he had five children and eventually married in 1768. In 1762 he published his masterpiece *The Social Contract* which begins, 'Man is born free; and everywhere he is in chains.' His text, with its slogan 'Liberty, Equality, Fraternity', became the Bible of the French Revolution. At the invitation of David Hume, he lived at Wootton Hall near Ashbourne in Derbyshire. Here he began his *Confessions* but became increasingly paranoiac and returned to Paris where he completed the work. He became seriously insane and died in Ermenonville. His remains were placed alongside Voltaire's in the Panthéon in Paris.

Denis Diderot (1713–84) French philosopher and man of letters, born in Langres in Champagne, the son of a master cutler. He was a precursor of the Romanticists and was patronised by Catherine II, (the Great) of Russia. In 1743 he married Antoinette Champion, daughter of a linendraper, although his father disapproved. Diderot set out a philosophy of the arts and sciences which took the progress of civilisation to be a measure of mankind's moral improvement and perceived the Christian religion as morally harmful. From 1745 to 1772 Diderot served as chief editor of the *Encyclopédie*, one of the principal works of the Age of Enlightenment.

Immanuel Kant (1724–1804) German philosopher, born in Königsberg in Prussia (now Kaliningrad), the son of a saddler. He taught at the university and was known for his ordered way of life (locals allegedly set their watches by the time of his daily walks). Kant was a keen astronomer who predicted the existence of the planet Uranus before Herschel's discovery in 1781. Kant's most famous works, such as *Critique of Pure Reason* (1781), *Critique of Practical Reason* (1788) and *Critique of Judgement* (1790) were all pubished late in his life. Kant described his philosophy as 'transcendental' or 'critical' idealism.

Edmund Burke (1729–97) Irish philosopher and statesman, born in Dublin, and educated at a Quaker school and Trinity College. Burke's *Thoughts on the Present Discontents* and *Reflections on the French Revolution* were his masterpieces. Although a Whig all his life, Burke's political thought became, with Disraeli's, the philosophy of modern Conservatism.

Thomas Paine (1737–1809) English-born, American revolutionary philosopher and writer, born in Thetford, Norfolk, the son of a Quaker. He followed his father's trade as a corset maker before becoming, firstly as a sailor, then a schoolmaster and ultimately an exciseman. It was during this period that he first showed his tendency to speak out against what he felt were injustices and was dismissed for disturbing the status quo by deriding the lack of pay increases. Benjamin Franklin helped him emigrate to America, where he settled in Philadelphia and became a radical journalist. He published a pamphlet *Common Sense* following the outbreak of the American Revolutionary War urging an immediate declaration of independence. He returned to England, after visiting France, and published *The Rights of Man* (1792) a reply to Burke's *Reflections on the French Revolution*. He was indicted for treason but fled to France whereupon he fell foul of Robespierre and was imprisoned but later freed on the grounds of his American citizenship (1795). His book *The Age of Reason* (1796) mostly written in prison, upset many of his American friends, including George Washington. He died alone and in poverty on his farm in New Rochelle, New York.

Jeremy Bentham (1748–1832) English philosopher, jurist and social reformer, born in London. Bentham is best known as a proponent of Utilitarianism, as seen in his pioneering works *A Fragment on Government* (1776) and *Introduction to the Principles of Morals and Legislation* (1789), in which he argued that the proper objective of all conduct and legislation is 'the greatest happiness of the greatest number'. He developed 'hedonic calculus' to estimate the effects of different actions. Bentham became an honorary French citizen in 1792 and published treatises on social and penal reform. He also planned a special prison (Panopticon) and school (Chrestomathia), helped start the *Westminster Review* (1823) and founded University College, where his clothed skeleton is preserved.

Johann Fichte (1762–1814) German philosopher, born in Rammenau, Saxony, the son of a ribbon weaver. In 1793 Fichte married Johanna Maria Rahn and in the same year published two anonymous works, the most important being *Contribution to the Correction of the Public's Judgments Regarding the*

FAMOUS PEOPLE

French Revolution. He developed Kant's critical philosophy into a system of his own, which he named 'Theory of Science' (*Wissenschaftslehre*).

Georg Hegel (1770–1831) German Idealist philosopher, born in Stuttgart. After studying theology he became a lecturer at Jena but Napoleon's victory there in 1806 interrupted his career. Hegel worked temporarily as a newspaper editor at Bamberg and then headmaster of the gymnasium at Nuremberg. Hegel's first great work was *The Phenomenology of Mind* (1807), which describes the human mind's progression from mere consciousness through self-consciousness, reason, spirit and religion, to absolute knowledge. His second great work was *The Science of Logic* which gained him the chair at Heidelberg in 1816. Hegel's dialectic method of reasoning involved a sequence of thesis, antithesis and synthesis, and his doctrines influenced Karl Marx and contributed to the development of 'Modern Totalitarianism'. In 1818 he succeeded Fichte as professor in Berlin and remained there until his death from cholera.

Charles Fourier (1772–1837) French philosopher and social theorist, born in Besançon. He published a number of utopian socialist works including *The Social Destiny of Man; or, Theory of the Four Movements* (1857). Fourier argued for the existence of a natural social order corresponding to Newton's ordering of the physical universe, claiming that both evolved in eight ascending periods. In Harmony, the highest stage, human emotions would be freely expressed. Fournier declared that this stage could be attained by dividing society into phalanges, each comprising a commune approximately 1,800 people within which all property would be collectively owned. His other works include *Treatise on Domestic Agricultural Association* and *The New Industrial World.*

Friedrich Schelling (1775–1854) German idealist philosopher, born in Leonberg in Württemberg. His early work was influenced by Kant and Fichte, and included *On the Possibility and Form of Philosophy in General* and *Of the Ego as Principle of Philosophy* in which he discusses the theological concept of the 'Absolute'. Schelling's major work *System of Transcendental Idealism* was an attempt to unite his concept of nature having a spiritual separateness from man, with Fichte's philosophy that nature is merely a tool of man. Schelling spent time in Jena, where he replaced Fichte in his teaching post, and in 1803, married Caroline Schlegel, a leading German Romanticist. A disagreement with Hegel concerning the dispute with Fichte caused him to retreat to Munich. After the death of Caroline, he married her friend, Pauline Gotter.

Arthur Schopenhauer (1788–1860) German philosopher, born in Danzig, and whose metaphysical doctrines of the will were in contrast to Hegelian idealism. He was strongly influenced firstly by Plato, and then by Immanuel Kant, and also became friendly with the playwright and poet Goethe, who invited his assistance with some problems concerning his 'Farbenlehre' (theory of colours). After finishing *On Vision and Colours*, Schopenhauer began his masterpiece, *The World as Will and Idea*, which expounds his pessimismistic and atheistic views. The premise being that man's nature as willing beings inevitably leads to suffering and such a life is worse than non-existence.

Auguste Comte (1798–1857) French philosopher and social theorist, born in Montpellier, and usually considered the founder of modern sociology and Positivism. Comte was nicknamed the 'Thinker' and was rebellious by nature. He was the first thinker to advocate the use of scientific procedures in the study of economics and politics. In a typical non conformist act he married a prostitute, Caroline Massin, in 1821. He then became increasingly depressed and mentally disturbed culminating in a suicide attempt in the Seine which seemed to bring him to his senses. His wife, however, resorted to her previous occupation and Comte formed an alliance with Clotilde de Vaux which lasted for two years until her death in 1846. Comte's major work was *The Positive Philosophy of Auguste Comte*, which became the bible for students of Positivism.

John Stuart Mill (1806–73) English philosopher and social reformer, born in London, the son of Scottish philosopher James Mill. He began publishing in *The Traveller* in 1822 and helped form the Utilitarian Society, which met in Jeremy Bentham's house, and he ultimately modified some of Bentham's doctrines. As with many philosophers, both before and after, Mill endured a phase of severe depression but in 1830 met and eventually married the bluestocking, Harriet Taylor, who influenced his future works. Mill's works include *System of Logic, On Liberty, Principles of Political Economy, Utilitarianism*, as well as a celebrated autobiography.

Søren Kierkegaard (1813–55) Danish philosopher, born in Copenhagen, the son of a Jewish merchant. Kierkegaard is considered the founder of Existentialism. His most famous work is probably *Either-Or*, in which he opposes Hegel by arguing the importance of individual choice. He was a convert to Christianity, although he fought against the formal structure of religion and believed that God and some special disciples were above moral laws as we know them. His other works include *The Concept of Irony, Christian Discourses, Fear of Trembling*, and *The Sickness Unto Death.*

Karl Marx (1818–1883) German social, political and economic theorist, born in Trier. His Jewish parents converted to Protestantism out of political expediency. Marx became the inspiration for international Communism. He studied at Bonn and then Berlin University, where he met the 'young Hegelians' who were chiefly concerned with the critique of religion. His doctoral dissertation was on 'The Difference between the Philosophies of Nature in Democritus and Epicurus'. Marx worked firstly as a journalist and then editor of the liberal Cologne paper *Rheinische Zeitung* but after the paper was suppressed by the government, Marx emigrated to Paris and became a communist. It was here that he first stated his belief that the proletariat must itself be the agent of revolutionary change in society, and wrote his first critique of capitalism, 'Economic and Philosophical Manuscripts of 1844' (not published until 1932). Marx had by now become friendly with Friedrich Engels and under political pressure they moved to Brussels, where they wrote *German Ideology* and the famous *Communist Manifesto* (1848) which ends with the Communist rallying cry: 'The workers have nothing to lose but their chains. They have a world to win. Workers of all lands, unite!' Marx moved to London in 1849 and wrote the first volume of his most famous work, *Das Kapital*, in 1867 (future volumes followed in 1884 and 1894) where he forecast the classless society. Marx is buried in Highgate cemetery, London.

Wilhelm Dilthey (1833–1911) German philosopher,

born in Biebrich, Hesse. His central theme was the radical distinction between the natural sciences (*Naturwissenshaften*) and human sciences (*Geisteswissenschaften*). He also developed a theory of hermeneutics for the interpretation of historical texts and wrote biographies of Hegel, Lessing, Schleiermacher, and Goethe.

Friedrich Wilhelm Nietzsche (1844–1900)
German philosopher, scholar and writer, born in Röcken, Saxony, son of a Lutheran pastor. He was seen by Nazi ideologists as a precursor of Nazism due to his doctrine of the superman (*Übermensch*) expounded in *Thus Spake Zarathustra* and *Beyond Good and Evil*. Nietzsche rejected Christianity by arguing that 'God is Dead'. His first work was *The Birth of Tragedy*, which compared Dionysian and Apollonian values, and was dedicated to Richard Wagner, whose operas he regarded as the true successors to Greek tragedy. Other works include *On the Genealogy of Morals*, *Beyond Good and Evil*, *Untimely Meditations* and his autobiography *Ecce Homo* (published posthumously in 1908).

Henri Bergson (1859–1941) French philosopher, born in Paris, son of a Polish Jewish musician and an English mother. Bergson claimed that time (which he calls duration), cannot be analysed as a set of moments, but is unitary. He claimed the same distribution between movement and the trajectory it covers. This became known as 'process philosophy'. He won the Nobel Prize for Literature in 1927. His major works include *Time and Freewill*, *Matter and Memory* and *Creative Evolution*.

Edmund Husserl (1859–1938) German philosopher, born in Prossnitz in the Austrian empire, of Jewish parentage. He studied mathematics at Berlin and psychology at Vienna, under Franz Brentano, a leading Aristotelian scholar. Husserl taught at Halle, Göttingen and Freiburg. He was the founder of the philosophical school of phenomenology which gave rise to Gestalt psychology. Works include *On the Goals and Problems of Metaphysics*, *Logical Investigations* (in which Husserl employed his Phenomenological methods) and *Ideas: General Introduction to Pure Phenomenology*.

Nishida Kitarō (1870–1945) Japanese philosopher, born near Kanazawa, Ishikawa, son of a school teacher. Nishida is considered Japan's first original modern philosopher and his work typifies Japanese attempts to absorb Western philosophy into the oriental spiritual tradition. His memoirs, entitled *A Certain Professor's Statement upon Retirement from Kyoto Imperial University, December 1928*, became a Japanese best-seller.

Bertrand Russell (1872–1970) Welsh philosopher, mathematician and author, born in Trelleck, Gwent, and brought up by his grandmother (the widow of the Liberal PM) following the death of both his parents in his youth. Russell was educated at Trinity College, Cambridge and became British Embassy attaché in Paris. He married Alys Pearsall Smith in 1895 and wrote his first book, *German Social Democracy*, soon after. Russell's first major philosophical work was *The Problems of Philosophy* (1912), which is often heralded as the perfect introduction for students of the subject. His pacifism caused the loss of his Trinity fellowship in 1916 and his imprisonment in 1918, after which he visited the Soviet Union and met Lenin, Trotsky and Gorky. He subsequently wrote *Theory and Practice of Bolshevism*. Russell's philosophy was now based on the premise that scientific knowledge was the only factual knowledge. His other major philosophical work was *A History of Western Philosophy*. Russell was also the co-author (with AN Whitehead) of *Principia Mathematica*.

Otto Neurath (1882–1945) Austrian socialist philosopher, economist and historian. Neurath was famous for creating the Isotype language for visual education. He was a founder member of the Vienna Circle.

György Lukács (1885–1971) Hungarian Marxist philosopher and critic, born in Budapest, of a wealthy Jewish family. Early works include *Soul and Form*, and *Theory of the Novel*. He joined the Hungarian Communist Party in 1918 but after the defeat of the uprising in 1919 travelled to Vienna and then Moscow. His major work on Marxism, *History and Class Consciousness* (1923), was condemned by the Russian Communist party as heretical.

Ludwig Wittgenstein (1889–1951) Austrian-born British philosopher, born in Vienna, son of an industrialist. Wittgenstein studied mechanical engineering at Berlin but became increasingly interested in mathematics and went to Cambridge to study under Bertrand Russell. He served in the Austrian army in WWI and was captured and held as a POW near Monte Cassino. Here he wrote *Tractatus Logico Philosophicus*, which expounded his 'picture theory' and the nature and limits of language whereby the deep truths of the nature of reality and representation cannot properly be said but can only be shown. Wittgenstein became a naturalised British citizen in 1938 and spent much of his time in Cambridge, although he worked as a porter in Guy's Hospital during World War II. Wittgenstein is undoubtedly one of the pre-eminent philosophers of the twentieth century.

Martin Heidegger (1889–1976) German philosopher, born in Messkirch in Baden, son of a Catholic sexton. Heidegger was appointed rector at Freiburg in 1933 and pledged support for Hitler in his inaugural address. His writings concern the nature and predicament of human existence, the search for 'authenticity' and the distractions of Angst (anxiety). His major work, *Being and Time* (1927), although considered a masterpiece, is often misunderstood in philosophical circles due to its complexity. The essence of the work as a description of a fundamental ontology where he names the human entity 'Dasein' (the being) and argues that Dasein's own being is intrinsically temporal in as existential sense.

Rudolf Carnap (1891–1970) German-born American philosopher of Logical Positivism. He was a prominent member of the Vienna Circle and made significant contributions to logic, the philosophy of science, model theory and probability. He was viewed as an 'enfant terrible' in his early career but became one of the most respected philosophers of the twentieth century. Carnap was a great advocate of international languages (e.g. Esperanto).

Hans-Georg Gadamer (1900–2002) German philosopher, born in Marburg, Hesse. A pupil of Heidegger, his major work, *Truth and Method*, expounds his hermeneutic beliefs.

Karl Raimund Popper (1902–1994) Austrian-born British philosopher. Popper's greatest contributions are in philosophy of sciences and in political and social philosophy. His 'falsificationism' reverses the usual view that accumulated experience leads to scientific hypotheses. He was a member of the Vienna Circle.

Jean-Paul Sartre (1905–80)   French philosopher, dramatist and novelist, born in Paris. He studied at the Sorbonne with Simone de Beauvoir, with whom he had a lifelong relationship. He taught philosophy at Le Havre, Paris and Berlin but joined the French army in 1939 and became a POW in 1941. On his release he became a key member of the French Resistance. In 1946, Sartre and De Beauvoir founded the avant-garde monthly *Les Temps Modernes* and Sartre began to develop his Existentialist doctrines. He declined the 1964 Nobel Prize for Literature and campaigned against American involvement in Vietnam. Sartre's major works were *Being and Nothingness* and his semi-autobiographical work *Nausea*, and a later more detailed autobiography, *Words* (*Les Mots*).

Maurice Merleau-Ponty (1908–61)   French philosopher, born in Rochefort-sur-Mer, Charente-Maritime. Although, he was closely associated with Sartre and helped him and De Beauvoir found *Les Temps Modernes* in 1945 his philosophy was more akin to that of the German phenomenononologists Husserl and Heidegger. His major work was *The Phenomenology of Perception*.

Willard Quine (1908–2000)   American philosopher, born in Akron, Ohio. He was professor of philosophy at Harvard from 1948 to 1978 and was much influenced by Carnap, the Vienna Circle and Empiricism. His major works include *Two Dogmas of Empiricism*, *Word and Object* and *The Roots of Reference*.

Sir Alfred Jules Ayer (1910–89)   English philosopher, born in London. Ayer was educated at Eton and Oxford and served in the Welsh Guards in World War II before becoming a professor at University College London in 1947 and professor at Oxford in 1947. His major work, which was also his first, was *Language, Truth & Logic* (1936), which reflected the views of the Vienna Circle and established him a the leading English representative of logical positivism. It was dubbed 'The Young Man's book'. Ayer was knighted in 1970. His other major work was *The Problem of Knowledge*.

Albert Camus (1913–60)   French writer, born in Mondovi, Algeria, son of a farm labourer. After studying philosophy at Algiers, Camus became an actor, schoolmaster, playwright and journalist before World War II, and subsequently became a French Resistance activist. He then became co-editor of the left-wing newspaper *Combat* and wrote his Existentialist novel *The Stranger,* after which he became identified with 'the absurd'. His other great work was *The Plague*, in which a plague-stricken city, Oran, symbolises man's isolation. He was awarded the 1957 Nobel Prize for Literature for having 'illuminated the problems of the human conscience in our times.' He died in a car accident.

Michel Foucault (1926–84)   French philosopher, born in Poitiers. Foucault argued that social attitudes are manipulated by those in power, so that areas such as criminality, illness, sexuality and insanity have changing levels of acceptability dependent on the aims of government and others in positions of influence. His major works are *Madness and Civilization*, *The Order of Things*, and *The History of Sexuality*.

NB: The list above does not contain religious reformers such as John Calvin, or writers such as Voltaire. The people cited above have all made some contribution to the furtherance of philosophical theory. Although some writers are known for their philosophical utterances – e.g. Proudhon's 'property is theft' or Voltaire's 'if God did not exist it would be necessary to invent him' – this alone is not enough to warrant inclusion in this section. Karl Marx is a notable exception to this rule of thumb. It is true that he was not a philosopher by design but his words and deeds enhanced and expanded political and philosophical thought to such an extent that it would be crass to omit him. It should also be noted that many of the works listed above are English translations of foreign titles and as such are open to slight variations in interpretations.

An explanation of some philosophical terms

Dialectics	The philosophy of metaphysical contradictions and their solutions.
Empiricism	The belief that all knowledge derives from experience and that the mind cannot postulate in advance.
Existentialism	Modern philosophical movement that stresses the importance of personal experience and responsibility and the demands that they make on the individual, who is seen as a free agent in a deterministic and seemingly meaningless universe. Although Jean-Paul Sartre is often accredited as being the first person to name himself an existentialist, the works of Søren Kiekegaard have retrospectively been attributed as existential.
Hermeneutics	The art of interpretation of human behaviour and social institutions. Hermeneutics was originally the theory and method of interpreting the Bible and other theological texts but Wilhelm Dilthey extended it to the interpretation of all human acts and products.
Marxism	Marxism is a broad term that covers many different philosophical doctrines but ultimately relates to the various schools of thought that have flourished since the death of Karl Marx in 1883. Western Marxism usually includes those thinkers that were influenced by the Hegelian idea of dialectics and who focused their attention on the cultural as opposed to the economic aspects of capitalism.
Metaphysics	The branch of philosophy concerning first principles, especially of being and knowing. It is the study of the nature of reality and deals with such questions as the existence of God and the external world.
Nihilism	Philosophy of negation, rejection, or denial of some or all aspects of thought or life. An example would be moral nihilism, whereby any possibility of justifying or criticising moral judgements is rejected because morality is a cloak for egoistic self-seeking and therefore a sham. Nihilism is an extreme form of scepticism.
Ontology	The branch of metaphysics that deals with the nature of being.
Pascal's Wager	The postulate that it is better to wager that God does exist rather than on his non-existence.
Phenomenology	Movement founded by Husserl that concentrates on the detailed description of conscious experience without recourse to explanation, metaphysical assumptions or traditional philosophical questions.
Positivism	Extreme form of empiricism that rejects metaphysics and theology as seeking knowledge beyond the scope of experience and holds that experimental investigation and observation are the only sources of knowledge.
Scepticism	The view that we fail to know anything and the rejection of the postulate that some term of positive epistemic appraisal applies to our beliefs.
Solipsism	The extreme form of scepticism which denies the possibility of any knowledge other than of one's own existence.
Sophist	Pre-Socratic itinerant teacher of oratory and argument who was prepared to debate any matter however specious.
Stoicism	Greek philosophical system founded by Zeno of Citium (334–262 BC) in Athens c3000 BC. It views the world as permeated by rationality and divinely planned as the best possible organisation of matter. Moral goodness and happiness are achieved by replicating a perfect rationality in oneself, and by enacting one's own assigned role in the cosmic scheme of things.
Thomism	The name derives from Thomas Aquinas and relates to a body of philosophical and theological ideas that seek to articulate the intellectual content of Catholic Christianity.
Totalitarianism	Term adopted in the 1920s by the Italian Giovanni Gentile to describe the ideal fascist state. Totalitarianism has attracted the attention of philosophers because a number of classical philosophical systems have been suspected of harbouring totalitarian aspirations.
Vienna Circle	Group of about thirty to forty thinkers drawn from the social and natural sciences, logic and mathematics who met regularly in Vienna between the two world wars to discuss philosophy. Its manifesto was published in 1929 *The Scientific Conception of the World: The Vienna Circle* by Carnap, Hahn and Neurath. The inner sanctum of the group called the 'Schlick Circle', organised by the physics professor Moritz Schlick in 1924. Its members included Carnap, Neurath, Philip Frank, Kurt Gödel, and Edgar Zilsel. Other eminent philosophers such as Ludwig Wittgenstein and Karl Popper often joined discussion groups. The public profile of the circle was provided by the Ernst Mach Society, but in 1934 the society was suspended for political reasons, and in 1936 Moritz Schlick was murdered. The circle gradually disintegrated when many of its members were forced to leave Austria for racial and political reasons.

FAMOUS PEOPLE

Real Names: By Original Name

NB: This is not intended to be a comprehensive listing of pseudonyms but a selection of some of the best-known and most intriguing examples. It is an area that is surrounded with much uncertainty and potential for error. Generally the 'Assumed Name' is the more familiar, but not always (for instance when authors adopt a pen-name for a particular kind of writing). For people who have acquired titles, the title is given as the 'Assumed Name', although in such cases the 'Original Name' is of course equally valid. There is necessarily some overlap between this section and that on Nicknames.

Original Name		Assumed Name		
Abbott	Janet	*Baker*	Janet	*Mezzo-Soprano*
Abelsohn	Frank	*Vaughan*	Frankie	*Vocalist*
Abruza	Sophie	*Tucker*	Sophie	*Music Hall Singer*
Adair	William Penn	*Rogers*	Will	*US Actor*
Adams	Nathaniel	*Cole*	Nat King	*Vocalist*
Aday	Marvin Lee	*Meatloaf*		*Vocalist*
Addington	Henry	*Sidmouth*	Viscount	*Prime Minister of Great Britain*
Addison	Joseph	*Atticus*	(satirised by Pope)	*Essayist and Politician*
Adoian	Vosdanig Manoog	*Gorky*	Arshile	*US Painter*
Adu	Helen Folasade	*Sade*		*Vocalist*
Ahenobarbus	Lucius Domitius	*Nero*		*Roman Emperor*
Aherne	Michael	*Warrior*		*Gladiator*
Aken	Jerome van	*Bosch*	Hieronymus	*Dutch Painter*
Albert	Harold	*Cathcart*	Helen	*Royal Biographer*
Alepoudelis	Odysseus	*Elytis*	Odysseus	*Greek Poet*
Alexeyev	Konstantin Sergeivitch	*Stanislavsky*		*Actor*
Allason	Rupert	*West*	Nigel	*MP and Author*
Allegri	Antonio	*Correggio*		*Artist*
Amey	Ian	*Tich*		*Guitarist*
Amis	Kingsley	*Markham*	Robert	*Novelist*
Anderson	Roberta Joan	*Mitchell*	Joni	*Vocalist/Composer*
Andrews	Augustus George	*Arliss*	George	*Actor*
Andrews	William Forrest	*Forrest*	Steve	*US Actor*
Anson	Thomas Patrick John	*Lichfield*	Lord	*Photographer*
Arango	Dovoteo	*Villa*	Pancho	*Mexican Patriot*
Arbuckle	Penelope	*Dripping*	Lizzie	*Literary Character*
Arbuckle	Roscoe (Fatty)	*Goodrich*	William B	*Actor*
Arcelos	Raul Rafael Y	*Julia*	Raul	*Actor*
Arenson	Max	*Anderson*	Bronco Billy	*Entertainer*
Armstrong née Mitchell	Helen Porter	*Melba*	Dame Nellie	*Opera Singer*
Armstrong-Jones	David Albert Charles	*Linley*	Viscount	*Furniture Maker*
Arouet	François Marie	*Voltaire*		*Philosopher*
Ashdown	Jeremy	*Ashdown*	Paddy	*Politician*
Ashton	Winifred	*Dane*	Clemence	*English Dramatist*
Ashurst	Anne	*Craven*	Sara	*Novelist and 'Mastermind' Winner*
Asquith	Herbert	*Oxford*	Earl of	*Prime Minister of Great Britain*
Aurness	James	*Arness*	James	*US Actor*
Austerlitz	Frederick	*Astaire*	Fred	*Dancer and Actor*
Aznavurjal	Shahnovr	*Aznavour*	Charles	*Singer and Actor*
Bailey	William	*Rose*	Axl	*Pop Singer*
Baker	George	*Divine*	Father	*Religious Leader*
Baker	Tammy Marie	*Fox*		*TV Gladiator*
Baker	Norma Jean	*Monroe*	Marilyn	*Actress*
Balanchivadze	Georgi Melitonivich	*Balanchine*	George	*Choreographer*
Baldwin	Stanley	*Bewdley*	Earl of	*Prime Minister of Great Britain*
Baline	Israel	*Berlin*	Irving	*Composer*
Balsame	Guiseppe	*Cagliostro*	'Count'	*Italian Adventurer*
Barbarelli	Giorgio	*Giorgione*		*Artist*
Barbella	Rocco	*Graziano*	Rocky	*Boxer*
Barbieri	Gian-Francesco	*Guercino*		*Italian Painter*
Barker	Ronnie	*Wylie*	Gerald	*Writer*
Barr	Byron	*Young*	Gig	*Actor*
Barratt	Michael	*Stevens*	Shaking	*Vocalist*
Barrow	Joseph	*Louis*	Joe	*Boxer*

Original Name		Assumed Name		
Bartholomew	John Eric	**Morecambe**	Eric	*Comedian*
Basie	William	**Basie**	Count	*Musician*
Bates	Ellas	**Diddley**	Bo	*Vocalist*
Batson	Billy	**Marvel**	Captain	*Comic Book Hero*
Baumgartner	James	**Garner**	James	*Actor*
Bean	Frederick	**Avery**	Tex	*Cartoonist*
Beaty	Warren	**Beatty**	Warren	*Actor*
Beaty	Shirley	**Maclaine**	Shirley	*Actress*
Beauchamp	Katherine	**Mansfield**	Katherine	*NZ Writer*
Beedle	William	**Holden**	William	*Actor*
Begleiter	Lionel	**Bart**	Lionel	*Composer*
Benevetto	Anthony Dominic	**Bennett**	Tony	*Vocalist*
Bernardone	Giovanni de	**Francis of Assisi**	Saint	*Religious Leader*
Bernstein	Morris	**Louis**	Morris	*US Painter*
Berra	Lawrence Peter	**Berra**	Yogi	*Baseball Player*
Berry	Mike	**Bennett**	Lennie	*Comedian*
Beyle	Marie-Henri	**Stendhal**		*Author*
Bickel	Frederick	**March**	Fredric	*Actor*
Biden	Edmund	**Sturges**	Preston	*Writer and Director*
Bingham	Richard John	**Lucan**	Lord	*Suspected Murderer*
Bingzhi	Jiang	**Ding Ling**		*Chinese Novelist*
Birkinshaw	Franklin	**Weldon**	Fay	*Writer*
Birnbaum	Nathan	**Burns**	George	*Comedian*
Blair	Eric Arthur	**Orwell**	George	*Author*
Blamauer	Karoline Wilhelmine	**Lenya**	Lotte	*Austrian Actress*
Blau	Jenö	**Ormandy**	Eugene	*Musician*
Blixen	Karen	**Dinesen**	Isak	*Authoress*
Blythe	Lionel	**Barrymore**	Lionel	*Actor*
Blythe	Ethel	**Barrymore**	Ethel	*Actress*
Blythe	John	**Barrymore**	John	*Actor*
Bogaerde	Derek van den	**Bogarde**	Dirk	*Actor*
Bojaxhiu	Agnes Gonxha	**Theresa**	Mother	*Roman Catholic Nun*
Bollea	Terry	**Hogan**	Hulk	*Professional Wrestler and Actor*
Bookbinder	Elaine	**Brooks**	Elkie	*Vocalist*
Booth	George Hoy	**Formby Jnr**	George	*Music Hall Entertainer*
Booth	James	**Formby Snr**	George	*Music Hall Entertainer*
Bottom	Charles	**Bart**	Black	*Outlaw*
Bourgeois	Jeanne Marie	**Mistinguett**		*French Dancer*
Breitenberger	Edward	**Byrnes**	Edd	*Actor*
Bright	Gerald	**Geraldo**		*Musician*
Broadbent	Shirley Ann	**Barrie**	Amanda	*Actress*
Broadbent	Dora	**Bryan**	Dora	*Actress and Comedienne*
Brodribb	John Henry	**Irving**	Henry	*Actor*
Bronstein	Lev Davidovitch	**Trotsky**	Leon	*Russian Revolutionary*
Bronte	Anne	**Bell**	Acton	*Author*
Bronte	Emily	**Bell**	Ellis	*Author*
Bronte	Charlotte	**Bell**	Currer	*Author*
Brophy	Brigid Antonia	**Levey**	Lady	*Author and Playwright*
Brough	Spangler	**Taylor**	Robert	*Actor*
Brown	Rosemary	**Dana**		*Singer and Politician*
Brown	Angeline	**Dickinson**	Angie	*Actress*
Browne	Hablot Knight	**Phiz**		*Illustrator*
Browne	Charles Farrar	**Ward**	Artemus	*Humorist and Writer*
Broz	Josip	**Tito**	Marshal	*Yugoslav Leader*
Buchinski	Charles	**Bronson**	Charles	*Actor*
Bukht	Michael	**Barry**	Michael	*Food Journalist*
Bullock	Annie Mae	**Turner**	Tina	*Vocalist*
Bulsara	Frederick	**Mercury**	Freddie	*Vocalist*
Burgess	George	**Meredith**	Burgess	*Actor*
Burke	Martha Jane	**Jane**	Calamity	*Frontierswoman*
Burnett	Chester Arthur	**Wolf**	Howling	*Vocalist and Composer*
Burns	Ray	**Sensible**	Captain	*Vocalist*
Burrell	Orville Richard	**Shaggy**		*Pop Singer*
Burrell	Stanley Kirk	**Hammer**	MC	*Rapper*
Butterfield	Sylvia	**Dawn**	Elizabeth	*Actress*
Bygraves	Walter	**Bygraves**	Max	*Entertainer*
Byron	James	**Dean**	James	*Actor*
Caliari	Paolo	**Veronese**	Paolo	*Venetian Painter*
Calloway	Mark	**Undertaker**		*Wrestler*

FAMOUS PEOPLE

Original Name		Assumed Name		
Calvin	George	Leno	Dan	English Comedian
Campbell	Patrick	Glenavy	Baron	Irish Writer and Wit
Canale	Giovanni Antonio	Canaletto		Artist
Cansino	Marguerita	Hayworth	Rita	Actress
Caplin	Alfred Gerald	Capp	Al	Cartoonist
Carpentier	Harlean	Harlow	Jean	Actress
Carr	John Dickson	Dickson	Carter	US Detective Writer
Carroll	Daniel	La Rue	Danny	Female Impersonator
Carter	Charlton	Heston	Charlton	Actor
Cassavitis	Michael	Orlando	Tony	Vocalist
Cassotto	Robert Walden	Darin	Bobby	Vocalist
Castellucio	Frank	Valli	Frankie	Vocalist
Cavendish	William	Devonshire	Duke of	Prime Minister of Great Britain
Cavendish-Bentinck	William Henry	Portland	Duke of	Prime Minister of Great Britain
Cecil	Robert Arthur Talbot	Salisbury	Marquis of	Prime Minister of Great Britain
Cernick	Al	Mitchell	Guy	Vocalist
Chalupek	Appolonia	Negri	Pola	Actress
Chambers	James	Cliff	Jimmy	Vocalist
Chapman	John	Appleseed	Johnny	Missionary and Nurseryman
Chauchoin	Lily	Colbert	Claudette	Actress
Chauvin/Cauvin	Jean	Calvin	Jean	French Theologian
Chavarri	Emperatriz	Sumac	Yma	Musician
Cheeseman	Patrick	Wymark	Patrick	Actor
Chomette	Rene Lucien	Clair	Rene	Film Director
Christie	Agatha	Westmacott	Mary	Authoress
Ciccone	Madonna Louise	Madonna		Vocalist and Actress
Clapp	Eric	Clapton	Eric	Guitarist/Singer
Clary	Julian	Joan Collins' Fan Club		Entertainer
Clay	Cassius Marcellus	Ali	Muhammed	Boxer
Clemens	Samuel Langhorne	Twain	Mark	Author
Cobbett	William	Porcupine	Peter	Writer
Cobblepot	Oswald	Penguin		Batman Character
Cochrane	Elizabeth	Bly	Nellie	Aviatrix
Cocozza	Alfredo	Lanza	Mario	Opera Singer
Cody	William	Bill	Buffalo	Showman
Cohen	Sacha Baron	Ali G		Comedian
Cole	Maurice	Everett	Kenny	Disc Jockey and Comedian
Coles	Elizabeth	Taylor	Elizabeth	Novelist
Collins	Cathleen	Derek	Bo	Actress
Collins	Chris	Skinner	Frank	Comedian
Colon	Cristobel	Columbus	Christopher	Explorer
Compton	Spencer	Wilmington	Earl of	Prime Minister of Great Britain
Connery	Thomas	Connery	Sean	Actor
Connor	William	Cassandra	(Daily Mirror column)	Journalist
Cook	David	Essex	David	Vocalist and Actor
Cooper	Francis	Cooper	Gary	Actor
Coppola	Nicholas	Cage	Nicolas	US Actor
Cornwell	David	Le Carré	John	Author
Crabtree	Shirley	Daddy	Big	Wrestler
Craddock	Eugene Vincent	Vincent	Gene	Vocalist
Crane	Randolph	Scott	Randolph	Actor
Cripps	Bruce	Welch	Bruce	Guitarist
Cristillo	Louis	Costello	Lou	Comedian
Crocetti	Dino	Martin	Dean	Actor
Cromwell	Richard	Clark	John	Lord Protector of England
Crosby	Harry Lillis	Crosby	Bing	Vocalist and Actor
Crossley	James	Hunter		Gladiator
Culkin	Bonnie	Bedelia	Bonnie	TV Actress
Czaczkes	Shmuel Josef	Agnon	Shmuel Yosef	Israeli Novelist
Da Ponte	Giacomo	Bassano	Jacopo	Italian Painter
D'Abruzzo	Alfonso	Alda	Alan	Actor
Dallion	Susan	Sioux	Siouxsie	Vocalist

Original Name		Assumed Name		
Daly	Sandra	*Khashoggi*	Soraya	*Millionairess*
Dannay	Frederick	*Queen*	Ellery	*Author*
		Ross	Barnaby	*Author*
D'Antonguolla	Rudolpho	*Valentino*	Rudolph	*Actor*
Darnell Browder	Thomas August	*Creole*	Kid	*Vocalist*
Davies	Sharron	*Amazon*		*TV Gladiator and Swimmer*
Davies	Robert	*Carrott*	Jasper	*Comedian*
Davies	David Ivor	*Novello*	Ivor	*Composer*
Davies	Nigel	*Villeneuve*	Justin de	*Hair Stylist*
Davies	Trevor	*Dozy*		*Bass Player*
De Havilland	Joan	*Fontaine*	Joan	*Actress*
Deeks	Barbara	*Windsor*	Barbara	*Actress*
Demsky	Issar Danielovitch	*Douglas*	Kirk	*Actor*
Dénes	Gábor	*Gabor*	Dennis	*Physicist*
Denning	Alfred Thompson	*Whitchurch*	Baron of	*Law Lord*
Derbyshire	Tommy	*Cannon*	Tommy	*Comedy Straight Man*
Deutschendorf Jnr	Henry John	*Denver*	John	*Vocalist and Composer*
Dibley	Dwayne	*Cat*		*TV Character 'Red Dwarf'*
Dick	Derek	*Fish*		*Vocalist*
Dickens	Charles	*Boz*	(Monthly Magazine)	*Author*
Dinh Khai	Phan	*Le Duc Tho*		*Vietnamese Politician*
Disraeli	Benjamin	*Beaconsfield*	Earl of	*Prime Minister of Great Britain*
Dodgson	Charles Lutwidge	*Carroll*	Lewis	*Author*
Donaghue	Patrick	*Magenta*	Captain	*TV Fictional Character*
Doolittle	Hilda	*HD*		*Author*
Dorléac	Catherine	*Deneuve*	Catherine	*Actress*
Dorsey	Arnold	*Dorsey*	Gerry	*Vocalist*
		Humperdinck	Englebert	*Vocalist*
Douglas	Michael	*Keaton*	Michael	*Actor*
Douglas-Home	Alec	*Hirsel*	Lord Home of the	*Prime Minister of Great Britain*
Dudevant	Amandine Lucie Dupin	*Sand*	George	*Author*
Dukenfield	William Claude	*Fields*	WC	*Comedian and Actor*
		Kane Jeeves	Mahatma	*Comedian and Actor*
Dumble-Smith	Michael	*Crawford*	Michael	*Actor and Singer*
Dutt	Narendranath	*Vivekananda*	Swami	*Hindu Missionary*
Dwight	Reginald Kenneth	*John*	Elton Hercules	*Vocalist and Composer*
Dymond	John	*Beaky*		*Guitarist*
Dzhugashvili	Iosif Vissarionovich	*Stalin*	Joseph	*Russian Leader*
Eberst	Jakob	*Offenbach*	Jacques	*Composer*
Eden	Anthony	*Avon*	Earl of	*Prime Minister of Great Britain*
Edwards	Eileen Regina	*Twain*	Shania	*Pop Singer*
Egstrom	Norma	*Lee*	Peggy	*Vocalist*
Eichelbaum	Jack Leonard	*Warner*	Jack Leonard	*Film Mogul*
Einstein	Albert	*Brooks*	Albert	*Actor*
Elizabeth	of Romania	*Sylva*	Carmen	*Queen of Romania*
Elliot	Marion	*Styrene*	Poly	*Punk-Rock Singer*
Enos	William	*Berkeley*	Busby	*Choreographer*
Ercolani	James	*Darren*	James	*US Actor*
Estevez	Ramon	*Sheen*	Martin	*Actor*
Evans	Ernest	*Checker*	Chubby	*Vocalist*
Evans	Dave	*Edge*	The	*Musician*
Evans	Mary Ann	*Eliot*	George	*Author*
Fagan	Eleanora	*Holiday*	Billie	*Vocalist*
Fairfield	Cicely Isabel	*West*	Rebecca	*Author*
Fawkes	Ernest	*Trog*	Walter	*Cartoonist*
Federkiewicz	Stefania	*Powers*	Stefanie	*Actress*
Feld	Marc	*Bolan*	Marc	*Vocalist and Musician*
Fellows	Graham	*John*	Jilted	*Pop Singer Creation*
		Shuttleworth	John	
Fiersohn	Reba	*Gluck*	Alma	*American Soprano*
Filipepi	Alessandro	*Botticelli*	Sandro	*Artist*
Finklea	Tula Ellice	*Charisse*	Cyd	*Dancer*
Firbank	Louis	*Reed*	Lou	*Vocalist and Composer*
Fischman	Harve	*Bennett*	Harve	*US TV Producer*
Fitzroy	Augustus Henry	*Grafton*	Duke of	*Prime Minister of Great Britain*

Original Name		Assumed Name		
Fitzsimmons	Maureen	O'Hara	Maureen	Actress
Flaccus	Quintus Horatius	Horace		Poet
Flegenheimer	Arthur	Schultz	Dutch	Gangster
Fletcher	Susannah	York	Susannah	Actress
Foe	Daniel	Defoe	Daniel	Author
Forte	Fabiano	Fabian		Vocalist
Fowles	Gloria	Gaynor	Gloria	Vocalist
Frahm	Karl Herbert	Brandt	Willy	German Chancellor
Francabilla	Marchesa Caterina de	Boyle	Katie	TV Presenter
Franconers	Concetta	Francis	Connie	Vocalist
Frankel	Bernice	Arthur	Beatrice	US Actress
Frankenberg	Joyce	Seymour	Jane	Actress
Frazier	Richard	Ochre	Captain	TV Fictional Character
Frece	Lady De	Tilley	Vesta	Comedian
Frewer	Matt	Headroom	Max	TV Fictional Character
Fries	Victor	Freeze	Mr	Fictional Super-Villain
Frith	Mary	Cutpurse	Moll	Pick Pocket and Robber
Fucini	Renato	Tanfucio	Neri	Italian Writer
Fuertes	Dolores Adios	Menken	Adah Isaacs	US Actress & Poet
Fuhrhop	Roland	Rowland	Tiny	Businessman
Fulks	Sarah Jane	Wyman	Jane	Actress
Furnier	Vincent	Cooper	Alice	Vocalist
Fyffe	Patrick	Bracket	Hilda	TV Transvestite
Gadd	Paul	Glitter	Gary	Vocalist
Gaines	Donna Andrea	Summers	Donna	Vocalist
Garfunkel	Art	Graph	Tom	Half of 'Tom & Jerry' Duo
Gassion	Edith	Piaf	Edith	Vocalist
Gazzimos	Brenda Gail	Gayle	Crystal	Vocalist
Geisel	Theodore Seuss	Seuss	Dr	Author
Gelee	Claude	Lorrain	Claude	Landscape Painter
Gellen	Arthur	Hunter	Tab	Singer and Actor
Gendre	Louis	Jordan	Louis	Actor
George III	(in gardening periodicals)	Robinson	Ralph	British King
Georgiou	Stephen	Stevens	Cat	Vocalist
Gheraerd	Gheraerd	Erasmus	Desiderius	Scholar
Gilbert	Maria Eliza (Délores)	Montez	Lola	American Dancer
Gilhooly	Brenda	Tuesday	Gayle	Comedienne
Gillis	Ian	Mycroft		Brain of Britain
Gillis	Lester	Nelson	Baby Face	Gangster
Gillorly	Edna	Burstyn	Ellen	Actress
Glover	Brian	Arras	Leon	Professional Wrestler
Goddard	Stuart	Ant	Adam	Vocalist
Godfree	Edward	Aldington	Richard	English Poet
Goffage	John	Rafferty	Chips	Entertainer
Gold	Jacqueline	Summers	Ann	Businesswoman
Goldbert	Cyril Louis	Wyngarde	Peter	Actor
Goldenberg	Emmanuel	Robinson	Edward G	Actor
Goldenburger	Avron	Todd	Mike	Producer
Goldfish	Sam	Goldwyn	Sam	Film Producer
Goldstein	Elliott	Gould	Elliot	Actor
Gonne	Maud	MacBride	Maud	Irish Nationalist
Gonzalez	José Victoriano	Gris	Juan	Spanish Cubist Painter
Goodman	Theodosia	Bara	Theda	Vamp Actress
Goodrich	Samuel	Parley	Peter	US Publisher
Goodrich	Sandra	Shaw	Sandie	Vocalist
Gordon	George Hamilton	Aberdeen	Earl of	Prime Minister of Great Britain
Gorowicz	Vladimir	Horowitz	Vladimir	Russian Pianist
Gossart	Jan	Mabuse	Jan	Flemish Painter
Gothardt	Mathis	Grünewald	Mathias	German Painter
Gough	Damon	Badly Drawn Boy		Singer and Songwriter
Goyathlay		Geronimo		Apache Indian Chief
Graham	Florence Nightingale	Arden	Elizabeth	Beautician
Grasemann	Ruth	Rendell	Ruth	Crime Novelist
Gravelet	Jean François	Blondin	Charles	French Acrobat
Gray	Charles	White	Colonel	TV Fictional Character
Grayson	Dick	Robin		Fictional Super Hero

Original Name		Assumed Name		
Original Name		*Assumed Name*		
Green	David	**Ben-Gurion**	David	*Israeli Statesman*
Greenbaum	Peter	**Green**	Peter	*Musician*
Greene	Gladys	**Arthur**	Jean	*Actress*
Gregson	Michael	**Craig**	Michael	*Actor*
Gretzky	Wayne	**Great One**	The	*Ice Hockey Player*
Grieve	Christopher Murray	**MacDiarmid**	Hugh	*Poet*
Griffith	John	**London**	Jack	*Author*
Griffiths	Seymour	**Green**	LT	*TV Fictional Character*
Grossell	Ira	**Chandler**	Jeff	*Actor*
Gudjonsson	Halldór	**Laxness**	Halldor	*Icelandic Novelist*
Guiche	Lilian	**Gish**	Lilian	*Actress*
Guidi, Di Simone	Tommaso Di Giovanni	**Masaccio**		*Florentine Painter*
Guillerm	Nelly	**Verdy**	Violette	*French Dancer*
Gumm	Frances	**Garland**	Judy	*Actress and Singer*
Gurdin	Natasha	**Wood**	Natalie	*Actress*
Gustaffson	Greta	**Garbo**	Greta	*Actress*
Gutteridge	John	**Pallo**	Jackie	*Wrestler*
Guttoveggio	Joseph	**Creston**	Paul	*Musician*
Guynes	Demi	**Moore**	Demi	*Actress*
Hackenbacker	Hiram J	**Brains**	(Thunderbirds)	*Scientist*
Hall	Diane	**Keaton**	Diane	*Actress*
Halliley	John Elton	**Le Mesurier**	John	*Actor*
Hamill	Christopher	**Limahl**	(Kajagoogoo)	*Vocalist*
Hamilton	Charles	**Conquest**	Owen	*Author*
		Richards	Frank	*Author*
Hansen	Emil	**Nolde**	Emil	*German Painter*
Hardin	Charles	**Holly**	Buddy	*Vocalist*
Haris	Derek	**Derek**	John	*Actor*
Harmon	David	**Dee**	Dave	*Vocalist*
Harmsworth	Harold Sydney	**Rothermere**	Viscount	*Newspaper Magnate*
Harper	Robert	**Ball**	Bobby	*Comedian*
Harris	Joel Chandler	**Remus**	Uncle	*Author*
Harrison	Gerald	**Gee**	Dustin	*Impressionist*
Hartley	Vivien	**Leigh**	Vivien	*Actress*
Hartree	George	**Hawtrey**	Charles	*Actor*
Hatcher	Charles	**Starr**	Edwin	*Vocalist*
Haussman	Jacques	**Houseman**	John	*Actor*
Hawkins	Jack	**Hedley**	Jack	*Actor*
Hawkins	Anthony	**Hope**	Anthony	*Author*
Hawkins	Christian	**Slater**	Christian	*Actor*
Haynes	Brian	**Laine**	Denny	*Guitarist*
Haynes Jr	Cornell	**Nelly**		*Rapper*
Healey-Kay	Patrick	**Dolin**	Anton	*Choreographer*
Hearne	Richard	**Pastry**	Mr	*Actor*
Heemstra	Edda Hepburn Van	**Hepburn**	Audrey	*Actress*
Heimberger	Eddie	**Albert**	Eddie	*US Actor*
Hensley	Virginia	**Kline**	Patsy	*Vocalist*
Herzstein	Barbara	**Hershey**	Barbara	*Actress*
Heseltine	Les	**Dennis**	Les	*Comedian*
Heseltine	Philip Arnold	**Warlock**	Peter	*Composer*
Hesketh-Harvey	Kit	**Kit**		*Musical act 'Kit and the Widow'*
Heurschling	Andrée	**Hessling**	Catherine	*Jean Renoir's Wife (actress)*
Hewson	Paul	**Bono**		*Vocalist*
Hickenlooper	Lucie	**Samaroff**	Olga	*Musician*
Hicks	Thomas	**Steele**	Tommy	*Entertainer*
Hieronymus	Eusebius Sophronius	**Jerome**	St	*Italian Scholar*
Higginbottom	Minnie	**Staff**	Kathy	*Actress*
Hill	Alfred Hawthorne	**Hill**	Benny	*Comedian*
Hinault	Bernard	**Badger (Le Blaireau)**		*Cyclist*
Hoch	Jan Ludvik	**Maxwell**	Robert	*Businessman*
Hogg	James	**Ettrick Shepherd**		*Poet*
Hogg	Quintin	**Hailsham of Marylebone**	Baron	*Politician*
Holden	Bradley	**Grey**	Captain	*TV Fictional Character*
Hollenbeck	Webb Parmelee	**Webb**	Clifton	*Actor*
Hook/Aherne	Caroline	**Merton**	Mrs	*Comedian*

Original Name		Assumed Name		
Hookham	Margaret	*Fonteyn*	Margot	*Ballerina*
Hopkins	Gaynor	*Tyler*	Bonnie	*Vocalist*
Hornby	Leslie	*Twiggy*		*Actress*
Horowitz	Winona	*Ryder*	Winona	*Actress*
Hovick	Rose Louise	*Rose Lee*	Gypsy	*Entertainer*
Howell	Vernon	*Koresh*	David	*Branch Davidian cult Leader*
Huffman	Barbara	*Eden*	Barbara	*US Actress*
Huggins	Peter Jeremy	*Brett*	Jeremy	*Actor*
Humphries	Barry	*Everage*	Dame Edna	*Comedian*
Humphries	Barry	*Patterson*	Sir Les	*Comedian*
Hunter	Evan	*McBain*	Ed	*Writer*
Hyde	Edward	*Clarendon*	Earl of	*Statesman*
Illingworth	Harry	*Worth*	Harry	*Comedian*
Ingolia	Concetta	*Stevens*	Connie	*Actress*
Irving	Washington	*Knickerbocker*	Diedrich	*Author*
Iskowitz	Edward	*Cantor*	Eddie	*Comedian*
Isley	Pamela	*Ivy*	Poison	*Fictional Super-Villain*
Italiano	Anna Maria	*Bancroft*	Anne	*Actress*
Ivanhoe	Burl	*Ives*	Burl	*Actor and Singer*
Iyotake	Tatanka	*Sitting Bull*		*Sioux Indian Chief*
Jackson	O'Shea	*Ice Cube*		*Rapper and Actor*
Jacob	Lee	*Cobb*	Lee J	*Actor*
Jacobs	Rosetta	*Laurie*	Piper	*US Actress*
James	Michael	*Jayston*	Michael	*Actor*
Javal	Camille	*Bardot*	Brigitte	*Actress*
Jeanneret	Charles Edouard	*Corbusier*	Le	*Architect*
Jefferson	Arthur Stanley	*Laurel*	Stan	*Comedy Actor*
Jeffries	James Jackson	*Boilermaker*		*Boxing Champion*
Jenkins	Richard	*Burton*	Richard	*Actor*
Jenkins	Harold Lloyd	*Twitty*	Conway	*Vocalist*
Jenkinson	Robert Banks	*Liverpool*	Earl of	*Prime Minister of Great Britain*
Jensen	Anita	*Genée*	Adeline	*Ballerina*
Jewry	Bernard	*Fenton*	Shane	*Vocalist*
		Stardust	Alvin	*Vocalist*
Johnson	Carol Diahann	*Carroll*	Diahann	*Actress*
Johnson	Bruce	*Forsyth*	Bruce	*Entertainer*
Johnson	Caryn	*Goldberg*	Whoopi	*US Actress*
Johnson	Dwayne	*Rock*		*Actor and Wrestler*
Johnson	Lawrence	*Naismith*	Laurence	*Actor*
Johnson	William Eugene	*Pussyfoot*		*US Reformer*
Johnson	Hewlett	*Red Dean*		*English Prelate*
Johnson	Mike	*York*	Michael	*Actor*
Jones	Magnolia	*Angel*	Melody	*'Captain Scarlet' Character*
Jones	David	*Bowie*	David	*Vocalist and Composer*
Jones	Edward	*German*	Edward	*English Composer*
Jones	Edith	*Wharton*	Edith	*Author*
Judkins	Steveland	*Wonder*	Stevie	*Vocalist and Composer*
Judson	Edward Zane	*Buntline*	Ned	*Inventor*
Kalageropoulos	Cecilia	*Callas*	Maria	*Operatic Soprano*
Kam	Lee Yuen	*Lee*	Bruce	*Actor and Martial Artist*
Kaminker	Henriette Charlotte	*Signoret*	Simone	*Actress*
Kaminsky	Melvin	*Brooks*	Mel	*Actor*
Kaminsky	Noah	*Diamond*	Neil	*Vocalist and Composer*
Kaminsky	David Daniel	*Kaye*	Danny	*Entertainer*
Kappelhoff	Doris Von	*Day*	Doris	*Actress and Singer*
Katz	Phoebe	*Cates*	Phoebe	*Actress*
Kaumeyer	Dorothy Mary	*Lamour*	Dorothy	*Actress*
Kaye	Paul	*Pennis*	Dennis	*Actor and Comedian*
Kazanjoglou	Elia	*Kazan*	Elia	*Film Director*
Keane	Molly	*Farrell*	MJ	*Irish Novelist*
Kemal	Mustafa	*Ataturk*	Kemal	*Turkish Statesman*
Khan Jnr	Taidje	*Brynner*	Yul	*Actor*
Khaury	Herbert	*Tim*	Tiny	*Vocalist*
Kiesler	Hedwig	*Lamarr*	Hedy	*Actress*
Kilinster	Ian	*Lemmy*	(Motorhead)	*Vocalist*
King	Leslie	*Ford*	Gerald	*President USA*
King	Jefferson	*Shadow*		*TV Gladiator*
Kingsley	Charles	*Lot*	Parson	*Author*

Original Name		Assumed Name		
Klass	Eugene	Barry	Gene	US Actor
Klein	Carole	King	Carol	Vocalist
Konigsberg	Allen	Allen	Woody	Actor
Koreff	Nora	Kaye	Nora	American Ballerina
Korzeniowski	Jozef Teodor Konrad	Conrad	Joseph	Author
Kostrowitzky	Apollinaris	Apollinaire	Guillaume	French Poet
Kouyoumdjian	Dikran	Arlen	Michael	British Novelist
Kramer	Erich Maria	Remarque	Erich Maria	Author
Krampke	Hugh	O'Brien	Hugh	Actor
Kubelsky	Benjamin	Benny	Jack	Comedian
Kwan	Chan	Angel	Harmony	'Captain Scarlet' Character
Lake	Margaret	Meg	Mystic	TV Personality
Lamb	Charles	Elia		Essayist
Lamb	William	Melbourne	Viscount	Prime Minister of Great Britain
Lamburn	Richmal	Crompton	Richmal	Author
Landru	Henri	Bluebeard		French Murderer
Lange	Cedric	Hawk	Jeremy	Actor and TV Presenter
Langemanke	Lucille	Astor	Mary	Actress
Lawrence	Thomas Edward	Ross	Aircraftsman John Hume	Soldier and Author
		Shaw	T E (Royal Tank Corps)	Soldier and Author
Lawrie	Marie McLaughlin	Lulu		Vocalist
Lawson	Nigel	Blaby	Lord Lawson of	Politician
Leach	Archibald	Grant	Cary	Actor
Lee	Manfred B	Queen	Ellery	Author
		Ross	Barnaby	Author
Léger	Alexis Saint-Léger	Saint-John Perse		French Poet
Leitch	Donovan	Donovan		Vocalist
Letz	George	Montgomery	George	Actor
Levesque	Paul Michael	HHH		Wrestler
Levitch	Joseph	Lewis	Jerry	Actor and Comedian
Levy	Marion	Goddard	Paulette	Actress
Levy	Ivo	Montand	Yves	Actor
Lewis	Cecil Day	Blake	Nicholas	Detective Writer
Lewis	CS	Hamilton	Clive	Irish Writer
Lewis	Mike	Saracen		TV Gladiator
Liddell	Eric	Flying Scotsman		Athlete
Little	Malcolm	X	Malcolm	Civil Rights Leader
Lloyd George	David	Gwynedd of Dwyfor	Viscount	Prime Minister of Great Britain
Loewenstein	Laszlo	Lorre	Peter	Actor
Logan	George	Hinge	Dr Evadne	TV Transvestite
Longbaugh	Henry	Sundance Kid		Outlaw
Lorimer	Maxwell George	Wall	Max	Actor and Comedian
Loughran	Angus	Statto		TV Soccer Pundit
Louis	Joe	Brown Bomber		Boxer
Louis	Marilyn	Fleming	Rhonda	Actress
Lubbertszoon	Meyndert	Hobbema	Meindert	Dutch Painter
Lubowitz	Michael	Mann	Manfred	Musician
Lucas	Matt	Dawes (He's a baby)	George	Comedian
Luta	Mahpiua	Red Cloud	Oglala Teton Dakota	(Sioux) Chief
Lydon	John	Rotten	Johnny	Vocalist
Lyon	Emma (Amy)	Hamilton	Emma	Lady
Lytle	Donald Eugene	Paycheck	Johnny	Country Singer
Mabovitch	Golda	Meir	Golda	Israeli PM
McDaniel	Ellas	Diddley	Bo	Vocalist
McCarthy	Henry	Bonney	William	Billy the Kid
McGillicuddy	Cornelius	Mack	Connie	Baseball Player
McGregor	Robert	Roy	Rob	Scottish Freebooter
McGuinness	Eddie	Large	Eddie	Comedian
McGurran	Aidan	Lottery	Lenny	National Lottery Expert
Mackay	Mary	Corelli	Marie	English Novelist
McLoughlin	Mark	Pellow	Marti	Vocalist
McManus	Declan	Costello	Elvis	Vocalist and Composer
McMasters	Luke	Haystacks	Giant	Wrestler
McMath	Virginia	Rogers	Ginger	Actress and Dancer
Macmillan	Harold	Stockton	Earl of	Prime Minister of

Original Name   *Assumed Name*

				Great Britain
McMillan	Anthony Robert	*Coltrane*	Robbie	*Actor and Comedian*
McMurray	Barbara	*Flynn*	Barbara	*Actress*
McNeile	HC	*Sapper*		*Author*
McPherson	Graham	*Suggs*		*Vocalist*
Maddox	No-Name	*Manson*	Charles	*Cult Leader*
Mainwaring	Edward Stewart	*Stewart*	Ed	*Disc Jockey*
Makonnen	Ras Tafari	*Selassie*	Hailie	*Ethiopian Emperor*
Mapother	Tom Cruise	*Cruise*	Tom	*Actor*
Mariano	Agnolo di Cosimo	*Bronzino*	Il	*Painter*
Marks	Lilian Alice	*Markova*	Alicia	*Ballerina*
Maro	Publius Vergilius	*Virgil*		*Poet*
Marrow	Tracy	*Ice-T*		*Rapper and Actor*
Martin	Paul	*Merton*	Paul	*Comedian*
Marx	Julius	*Marx*	Groucho	*Actor*
Marx	Herbert	*Marx*	Zeppo	*Actor*
Marx	Adolph	*Marx*	Harpo	*Actor*
Marx	Milton	*Marx*	Gummo	*Actor*
Marx	Leonard	*Marx*	Chico	*Actor*
Massaccesi	Aristide	*D'Amato*	Joe	*Film Director*
Mathers III	Marshall	*Eminem*		*Rapper and Actor*
Mathieu	Henri Donat	*Saint-Laurent*	Yves	*French Designer*
Matthews	Pauline	*Dee*	Kiki	*Vocalist*
Matuschanskavasky	Walter	*Matthau*	Walter	*Actor*
Mavor	Osborne Henry	*Bridie*	James	*Dramatist*
		Henderson	Mary	*Dramatist*
Mayer	David	*Janssen*	David	*Actor*
Mayson	Isabella	*Beeton*	Mrs Isabella	*Cookery Writer*
Mazzola	Girolamo Francesco M	*Parmigiano*		*Italian Painter*
Mead	Cyril	*Little*	Syd	*Comedian*
Mellencamp	John	*Cougar*	John	*Vocalist*
Mellor	John	*Strummer*	Joe	*Rock Star*
Mendelssohn-Bartholdy	Felix	*Mendelssohn*	Felix	*Composer*
Menendez	Andres Arturo Garcia	*Garcia*	Andy	*Actor*
Mennini	Peter	*Mennin*	Peter	*Musician*
Mercer	Cecil William	*Yates*	Dornford	*Novelist*
Merisi	Michelangelo	*Caravaggio*		*Artist*
Meservey	Robert	*Preston*	Robert	*Actor*
Metcalfe	Paul	*Scarlet*	Captain	*TV Animation Character*
Micklewhite	Maurice	*Caine*	Michael	*Actor*
Middleton	Roger	*Colbourne*	Maurice	*Actor*
Middleton	Peggy	*De Carlo*	Yvonne	*Actress*
Mikhailovich	Sergius	*Stepnyak*		*Russian Revolutionary*
Millar	William	*Boyd*	Stephen	*Actor*
Miller	James	*MacColl*	Ewan	*Folk Singer*
Millet	Jean-François	*Francisque*		*Belgian Painter*
Milligan	Terence Alan	*Milligan*	Spike	*Comedian and Writer*
Mitchell	Ian	*Finch*	Peter	*Actor*
Mitchell	James Leslie	*Gibbon*	Lewis	*Novelist*
Mizell	George	*Mitchell*	Cameron	*Actor*
Modini	Robert	*Stack*	Robert	*Actor*
Moir	Jim	*Reeves*	Vic	*Comedian*
Molinsky	Joan	*Rivers*	Joan	*Comedienne*
Monro	Hector Hugh	*Saki*		*Author*
Montagu	John	*Sandwich*	Earl of	*Inventor of Sandwich*
Montgomery	Edward	*Clift*	Montgomery	*Actor*
Moodnick	Ronald	*Moody*	Ron	*Actor*
Moore	Alicia	*Pink*		*Actress and Singer*
Morganfield	McKinley	*Waters*	Muddy	*Vocalist*
Morhange	Charles-Valentin	*Alkan*	Charles-Valentin	*French Musician*
Morrison	Jeanette	*Leigh*	Janet	*Actress*
Morrison	George Ivan	*Morrison*	Van	*Vocalist and Composer*
Morrison	Marion	*Wayne*	John	*Actor*
Morrow	Jennifer Lee	*Leigh*	Jennifer Jason	*Actress*
Morton	John Cameron	*Beachcomber*	(*Daily Express* column)	*Journalist*
Mostel	Samuel Joel	*Mostel*	Zero	*Actor*
Mozee	Phoebe	*Oakley*	Annie	*Frontierswoman*

Original Name		Assumed Name		
Mulgrew	Jimmy	Cricket	Jimmy	Comedian
Müller	Lucas	Cranach	Lucas	German Painter
Müller	Johannes	Regiomontanus		German Mathematician
Munker	Ariane	Foster	Jodie	US Actress
Nakszynski	Nastassja	Kinski	Nastassia	Actress
Nankeville	Robert	Davro	Bobby	Comic Impressionist
Nascimento	Edson Arantes Do	Pele		Footballer
Needham	Yootha	Joyce	Yootha	Actress
Nelhams	Terry	Faith	Adam	Vocalist
Nelson	Benjamin	King	Ben E	Vocalist
Nelson	Prince Rogers	Prince (formerly)		Vocalist and Composer
Nice	Stephen	Harley	Steve	Pop Singer
Niewoehner	Dirk	Benedict	Dirk	US Actor
Norway	Neville	Shute	Neville	Author
Oaxaca	Rudolph	Quinn	Anthony	US Actor
O'Brien	Mary	Springfield	Dusty	Vocalist
O'Day	Dawn	Shirley	Anne	Actress
O'Donovan	Michael	O'Connor	Frank	Irish Writer
O'Dowd	George	George	Boy	Vocalist
O'Fearna	Sean	Ford	John	Film Director
O'Flaherty	Katherine	Chopin	Kate	Author and Feminist
O'Grady	Paul	Savage	Lily	Female Impersonator
Ohm	Peter	Vaughan	Peter	Actor
Olden	Charles	Ray	Ted	Comedian
Olsson	Ann-Margret	Margret	Ann	Actress
O'Mahoney	Tynian	Allen	Dave	Comedian
O'Nolan	Brian	O'Brien	Flann	Irish Writer
Ord	Irene	Larrigan	Tex	Author of Westerns
Orowitz	Eugene Maurice	Landon	Michael	US Actor
Orrico	Carmen	Saxon	John	Actor
Orton	Joe	Wellthorpe	Edna	Fictional Letter Writer
Osterberg	James Jewel	Pop	Iggy	Vocalist
Ostlere	Gordon	Gordon	Richard	Doctor and Author
O'Sullivan	Raymond	O'Sullivan	Gilbert	Vocalist
Pakenham	Francis Aungier	Longford	Lord	Prison Reformer
Pal (Female)		Lassie (Male)		Dog
Palaniuk	Walter	Palance	Jack	Actor
Palmer	Keith	Reality	Maxim	MC
Palmer	Vera Jane	Mansfield	Jayne	Actress
Panayiotou	Georgios	Michael	George	Vocalist and Composer
Papaceo	Anthony	Franciosa	Tony	Actor
Parker	Peter	Spiderman		Fictional Hero
Parker	Robert LeRoy	Cassidy	Butch	Outlaw Leader
Paton	Alison	Siren		TV Gladiator
Patterson	Henry	Higgins	Jack	Author
Paul	Maury	Knickerbocker	Cholly	NY Gossip Columnist
Paup	Theresa	Russell	Theresa	Actress
Peiser	Lilli	Palmer	Lilli	Actress
Pelham-Holles	Thomas	Newcastle	Duke of	Prime Minister of Great Britain
Penniman	Richard Wayne	Richard	Little	Vocalist and Musician
Pennington	Michael	Vegas	Johnny	Comedian
Penrose	Elizabeth	Markham	Elizabeth	Writer for Children
Perelmuth	Jacob Pincus	Peerce	Jan	Musician
Perez	Manuel Benitez	Cordobes	El	Matador
Perido	Nick	Como	Perry	Vocalist
Perks	William	Wyman	Bill	Musician
Perry	William	Refrigerator		American Footballer
Perske	Betty Joan	Bacall	Lauren	Actress
Peschkowsky	Michael	Nichols	Mike	US Film Director
Peshkov	Max	Gorky	Maxim	Author
Peters	Jane	Lombard	Carole	Actress
Petty-Fitzmaurice	William	Shelburne	Earl of	Prime Minister of Great Britain
Pickwoad	William	Mervyn	William	Actor
Pierre	Cherilyn Sarkisian La	Cher		Vocalist and Actress
Pietro/Fiesoli	Guido di	Angelico	Fra	Artist
Pisperikos	Elizabeth	Perkins	Elizabeth	Actress
Plemiannkov	Roger	Vadim	Roger	Film Director
Pointon	Juliette	Angel	Destiny	'Captain Scarlet'

Original Name		Assumed Name		Character
Poire	Emmanuel	D'Ache	Caran	French Illustrator
Poliakov	Nikolai	Coco		Clown
Popley	Bernard	Youens	Bernard	Actor
Poquelin	Jean-Baptiste	Molière		Playwright
Porter	William Sydney	O'Henry		Author
Pound	Ezra Loomis	Atheling	William	Poet
Powell	Clive	Fame	Georgie	Vocalist and Musician
Powles	Matilda Alice	Tilley	Vesta	Comedian
Pratt	Denis	Crisp	Quentin	Writer
Pratt	William Henry	Karloff	Boris	Actor
Prendergast	John Barry	Barry	John	Musician
Price	Ellen	Wood	Mrs Henry	English Novelist
Priestley	John Boynton	Goldsmith	Peter	Author
Primrose-Pechey	Phyllis	Craddock	Fanny	Television Cook
Prior-Palmer	Lucinda	Green	Lucinda	Three-Day Eventer
Pugh	Wynette	Wynette	Tammy	Vocalist
Quedens	Eunice	Arden	Eve	Actress
Quiller-Couch	Arthur	Q		Author
Quincey	Thomas	De Quincey	Thomas	Essayist
Quoirez	Françoise	Sagan	Françoise	Author
Rajan	John	Lord	Jack	Actor
Ramée, de la	Marie Louise	Ouida		English Novelist
Ranft	George	Raft	George	Actor
Rankin	Brian	Marvin	Hank	Guitarist
Ravenscroft	John	Peel	John	Disc Jockey
Reibnitz	Marie von	Michael of Kent	Princess	Austrian Princess
Relph	Harry	Tich	Little	Comedian
Relyea	Walter	Hayden	Sterling	Actor
Rendell	Ruth	Vine	Barbara	Crime Novelist
Richards	Pauline	Rocket		TV Gladiator
Richardson	Jiles Perry (JP)	Bopper	The Big	Vocalist
Riddle	James	Hoffa	Jimmy	US Union Leader
Riley	Helena	Panther		TV Gladiator
Ritchie	John	Vicious	Sid	Vocalist
Ritchie	Robert	Kid Rock		Rock Star
Robbins	Anne Frances	Davis	Nancy	Actress
Roberts	Russ	Abbot	Russ	Comedian
Robertson	James Logie	Haliburton	Hugh	Poet
Robertson	Anna Mary	Moses	Grandma	Artist
Robertson	Marjorie	Neagle	Anna	Actress
Robinson	Ray Charles	Charles	Ray	Vocalist
Robinson	Frederick John	Goderich	Viscount	Prime Minister of Great Britain
Robusti	Jacopo	Tintoretto		Artist
Rolfe	Frederick William	Corvo	Baron	Novelist
Rosenbaum	Borge	Borge	Victor	Comic Musician
Rosenberg	Leonard	Randall	Tony	Actor
Rose-Price	Dennistoun Franklyn	Price	Dennis	Actor
Rothschild	Dorothy	Parker	Dorothy	Author
Rowlands	John	Stanley	Henry Morton	Explorer
Ruane	Martin	McMasters	Luke	Wrestler
Rubin	Lynsey	De Paul	Lynsey	Vocalist
Rubin	Harold	Robbins	Harold	Author
Ruiz	Pablo	Picasso	Pablo	Artist
Russell	George William	AE		Irish Poet
Ruston	Audrey	Hepburn	Audrey	Actress
Saillot	Félicité	Desmousseaux	Félicité	Actress
Samaniegos	Ramon	Novarra	Ramon	Actor
Samuel	Henry	Seal		Vocalist
Samuels	Miriam	Karlin	Miriam	Actress
Sánchez	Illich Ramirez	Carlos the Jackal		Guerrilla
Sandeman	Mary	Aneka		Pop Singer
Santi/Sanzio	Raffaello	Raphael		Artist
Sarstedt	Richard	Kane	Eden	Vocalist
Sättler	Elisabeth	Rethberg	Elisabeth	Musician
Scallon (née Brown)	Rosemary	Dana		Singer and Politician
Scherer Jnr	Roy	Hudson	Rock	Actor
Schicklgrüber	Adolf	Hitler	Adolf	Dictator
Schipani	Pia	Zadora	Pia	Actress

Original Name		Assumed Name		
Schneider	Guenther	Arnold	Edward	Actor
Schrift	Shirley	Winters	Shelley	Actress
Schwabe	Cecil	Parker	Cecil	Actor
Schwartz	Bernard	Curtis	Tony	Actor
Schwatt	Aaron	Buttons	Red	Actor
Schweider	Alfred	Bruce	Lenny	Comedian
Scicolone	Sofia	Loren	Sophia	Actress
Scudéry	Madeleine de	Sappho		French Novelist
Seagull	Barbara	Hershey	Barbara	US Actress
Sekolovich	Mladen	Malden	Karl	Actor
Shalhoub	Michael	Sharif	Omar	Actor
Sharpe	Alexander John	Ellis	Alexander John	English Philologist
Shaw	George Bernard	Corno Di Bassetto	(Music critic for Star)	Author
Siciliano	Angelo	Atlas	Charles	Athlete
Siddhartha	Gautama	Buddha		Buddhism Founder
Sieffert	Ernst	Tauber	Richard	Austrian Tenor
Sigursteinnson	Magnus	Magnusson	Magnus	Broadcaster
Silberman	Jerome	Wilder	Gene	Actor
Silverman	Belle	Sills	Beverly	Musician
Simon	Paul	Landis	Jerry	Half of 'Tom & Jerry' Duo
Sims	Diane	Angel	Rhapsody	'Captain Scarlet' Character
Sinnott	Michael	Sennett	Mack	Film Producer
Sisson	Richard	Widow		Musical act 'Kit and the Widow'
Skikne	Larushka Mischa	Harvey	Laurence	Actor
Sklodowska	Manya	Curie	Marie	Physicist
Skryabin	Vyacheslav Mikhaylovich	Molotov	Vyacheslav Mikhaylovich	Russian Statesman
Skurnick	Estelle	Nicole		Renault Clio Advert
Slye	Leonard	Rogers	Roy	Actor
Smith	Robert	Jack	Wolfman	Disc Jockey
Smith	Gladys Mary	Pickford	Mary	Actress
Smith	James Marcus	Proby	PJ	Vocalist
Smith	James Todd	Cool James	Ladies Love (LL Cool J)	Rapper
Smith	Walker	Robinson	Sugar Ray	Boxer
Smith	Harold J	Silverheels	Jay	Actor
Smith	Reginald	Wilde	Marty	Vocalist
Smith	Kim	Wilde	Kim	Vocalist
Solberg	David	Soul	David	Actor
Sorya	Françoise	Aimée	Anouk	Actress
Southill	Ursula	Mother Shipton		Witch and Prophet
Spartanero	Franco	Nero	Franco	Actor
Springall	Charles	Drake	Charlie	Comedian
Stainer	Leslie	Howard	Leslie	Actor
Stanley	Edward	Derby	Earl of	Prime Minister of Great Britain
Stanley	Henry Morton	Rowlands	John	Explorer and Journalist
Stansfield	Grace	Fields	Gracie	Actress and Singer
Starkey	Richard	Starr	Ringo	Drummer and Composer
Steele	Richard	Bickerstaffe	Isaac	Author
Stengland	Inger	Stevens	Inger	Actress
Stephens	Yvette Marie	Khan	Chaka	Vocalist
Stern	Miriam	Stoppard	Miriam	Broadcaster
Stevens	Cat	Islam	Yusuf	Vocalist and Composer
Stevens	Shaking	Kent	Clark	Vocalist
Stevens	Ruby	Stanwyck	Barbara	Actress
Stevens	Terry	Thomas	Terry	Comedy Actor
Stevenson	Elizabeth	Gaskell	Elizabeth	Writer
Stewart	Charles Edward	Burke	Betty	Scottish Pretender
Stewart	James	Granger	Stewart	Actor
Stewart	John	Innes	Michael	Author
Stoppelmoor	Cheryl	Ladd	Cheryl	Actress
Stoute	Jenny	Rebel		TV Gladiator
Stovenour	June	Haver	June	Actress
Strataki	Anastasia	Stratas	Teresa	Soprano
Stratemeyer	Edward	Dixon	Franklin W	Author
Stratemeyer	Edward	Hope	Laura Lee	Author
Stratemeyer	Edward	Keene	Carolyn	Author
Stratton	Charles	Thumb	Tom	Circus Performer
Straussler	Thomas	Stoppard	Tom	Dramatist

Original Name		Assumed Name		
Stringer	Lynne	Caine	Marti	Comedienne and Singer
Stuart	Charles Edward	Burke	Betty	Bonnie Prince Charlie
Stuart	John	Bute	Earl of	Prime Minister of Great Britain
Sueur	Lucille le	Crawford	Joan	Actress
Sullivan (née Hopkins)	Gaynor	Tyler	Bonnie	Vocalist
Sumner	Gordon	Sting		Vocalist and Musician
Svenson	Adam	Blue	Captain	TV Fictional Character
Svenson	Beryl	Grey	Beryl	Ballerina
Svensson	Gloria	Swanson	Gloria	Actress
Swift	Jonathan	Bickerstaffe	Isaac	Author
Sykes	Norma	Sabrina		Model
Tarpley	Brenda	Lee	Brenda	Vocalist
Tatischeff	Jacques	Tati	Jacques	Actor
Teach	Edward	Blackbeard		Pirate
Tejada	Raquel	Welch	Raquel	Actress
Temple	Henry John	Palmerston	Viscount	Prime Minister of Great Britain
Tennenbaum	Irving	Stone	Irving	US Novelist
Tennyson	Alfred Lord	Merlin		Poet
Terzi	Orhan	DJ Quicksilver		Turkish Pop Star
Thackeray	William Makepeace	Titmarsh	Michael Angelo	Author
Thann	Nguyen Van	Chi-Minh	Ho	Vietnamese Politician
Thatcher	Margaret	Kesteven	Baroness Thatcher of	Prime Minister of Great Britain
Theotocopoulos	Domenico	Greco	El	Artist
Thibault	Anatole François	France	Anatole	Author
Thomas	George	Tonypandy	Viscount	Speaker of Commons
Thompson	Estelle	Oberon	Merle	Actress
Thornburg	Betty June	Hutton	Betty	US Comedy Actress
Thornley	Peter	Nagasaki	Kendo	Professional Wrestler
Ticker	Reuben	Tucker	Richard	Singer
Tidbury	Eldred	Gray	Donald	South African Actor
Titta	Ruffo	Ruffo	Titta	Baritone
Tomaling	Susan	Sarandon	Susan	Actress
Touchinsky	Alfred	Marks	Alfred	Actor/Comedian
Trendle	Doug	Bloodvessel	Buster	Vocalist
Trevorrow	Mark	Downe	Bob	Australian Comedian
Trimmler	Deborah	Kerr	Deborah	Actress
Truscott-Jones	Reginald	Milland	Ray	Actor
Tsering	Lhamo Thondup	Tenzin Gyatso		14th Dalai Lama
Tullius	Marcus	Cicero (from wart on nose)		Roman Statesman
Tureaud	Lawrence	T	Mr	Actor
Turner	Conrad	Black	Captain	'Captain Scarlet' Character
Ullman	Douglas	Fairbanks	Douglas	Actor
Ulyanov	Vladimir Ilyich	Lenin	Vladimir Ilyich	Russian revolutionary
Upchurch	Lou	Phillips	Lou Diamond	Actor
Uttini	Giuseppe	Verdi		Vocalist
Valentino	Wladziu	Liberace		Pianist
Valenzuela	Ritchie	Valens	Ritchie	Vocalist
Van Aken	Jerome	Bosch	Hieronymus	Dutch Painter
Van Den Bogaerde	Derek Niven	Bogarde	Dirk	Actor
Van der Faes	Pieter	Lely	Peter	British Painter
Van Varenberg	Jean-Claude	Van Damme	Jean-Claude	Actor
Vander Walt	Lize	Gold		TV Gladiator
Vecchio	Frank Lo	Laine	Frankie	Vocalist
Vecellio	Tiziano	Titian		Artist
Velline	Robert Thomas	Vee	Bobby	Vocalist
Vincent	Mark	Diesel	Vin	Actor
Vivar	Rodrigo diaz de	Cid	El	Spanish Warrior
Vliet	Don Van	Beefheart	Captain	Vocalist
Wainewright	Thomas Griffiths	Weathercock	Janus	Art Critic and Murderer
Wainwright	Karen	Angel	Symphony	'Captain Scarlet' Character
Walker	Edmund	Kemp	Jeremy	Actor
Wallace	Christopher	B.I.G.	Notorious	Pop Singer
Waller	Thomas Wright	Waller	Fats	Jazz Pianist
Walpole	Robert	Orford	Earl of	Prime Minister of Great Britain
Walters	Mrs Daryl	Blyton	Enid	Author

Original Name   *Assumed Name*

Original Name		Assumed Name		
Ward	Arthur Sarsfield	Rohmer	Sax	Author
Warner	Brian	Manson	Marilyn	Pop Star
Waters	Jack	Warner	Jack	Actor
Watkins	Ian	H		Pop Singer
Wayman	Eunice	Simone	Nina	Vocalist
Wayne	Bruce	Batman		Fictional Super Hero
Webb	Gary	Numan	Gary	Vocalist and Composer
Webb	Harold	Richard	Cliff	Singer
Weinstein	Bernie	Winters	Bernie	Comedian
Weiss	Ehrich	Houdini	Harry	Illusionist
Welch	Vera	Lynn	Vera	Singer
Wellesley	Arthur	Wellington	Duke of	Prime Minister of Great Britain
Wells	Julia	Andrews	Julie	Actress and Singer
Wentworth	Charles Watson	Rockingham	Marquis of	Prime Minister of Great Britain
Wesley	Arthur	Wellesley	Arthur	Prime Minister of Great Britain
Westcott	Fred	Karno	Fred	Impresario
Westover	Charles	Shannon	Del	Singer
Wettach	Adrien	Grock		Clown
White	Priscilla	Black	Cilla	Vocalist and Presenter
White	William	Grayson	Larry	Comedian
		Breen	Billy	
White	PD	James	PD	Author
White	David	Jason	David	Actor
White	William Hale	Rutherford	Mark	Writer
Whittaker	James	Bowen	Jim	Comedian
Wight	James	Herriot	James	Vet and Author
Wilde	Oscar	Melmoth	Sebastian	Author
Wilfred	Sir	Ivanhoe		Literary Character
Wilkens	Maybritt	Britt	May	Actress
Wilkie	Edward	Fawn	Doctor	'Captain Scarlet' Character
William	Walter	Maynard	Bill	Actor
Williams	Kim	Lightning		Gladiator
Wilson	Barbara	Batgirl		Fictional Film Hero
Wilson	Anthony	Burgess	Anthony	Writer
Wilson	Harold	Rievaulx	Lord	Prime Minister of Great Britain
Windsor	Albert	George VI	King	Sovereign
Winkle	Robert Van	Vanilla Ice		Rapper and Actor
Winogradsky	Boris	Delfont	Bernard	Impresario
Winogradsky	Louis	Grade	Lew	Impresario
Winter	Richard	Warwick	Richard	Actor
Wiseman	Ernest	Wise	Ernie	Comedian
Witko	Tasunko	Crazy Horse		Sioux Indian Chief
Wojtyla	Karol	John Paul II	Pope	Bishop of Rome
Wolcot	John	Pindar	Peter	Satirist
Wood	Henry	Klenovsky	Paul	English Conductor
Wood	Mathilda	LLoyd	Marie	Actress
Woodward	Thomas	Jones	Tom	Vocalist
Worrell	Charles	I Spy	Big Chief	Author
Wright	Archibald	Moore	Archibald	Boxer
Wunderman	Leslie	Carlisle	Belinda	Vocalist
Wupperman	Frank	Morgan	Frank	Actor
Wycherly	Ronald	Fury	Billy	Vocalist
Yanks	Byron	Janis	Byron	Musician
Yeary	Harvey Lee	Majors	Lee	Actor
Yin	Leslie Charles Bowyer	Charteris	Leslie	Author
Youdale	Diane	Jet		TV Gladiator
Young	Leslie Ronald	Young	Jimmy	Broadcaster
Young	Sandy	Phoenix		Gladiator
Young	Sarah	Carr	Sally	Vocalist
Yule Jnr	Joseph	Rooney	Mickey	Actor
Ze Schluderpacheru	Herbert	Lom	Herbert	Actor
Zerby	Deborah	Darby	Kim	Actress
Zimmerman	Robert Alan	Dylan	Bob	Vocalist and Composer
Zogu	Ahmed Bey	Zog	King	Albanian King
Zoine	Vincento	Edwards	Vince	US Actor
Zwinge	James Randall	Randi	Amazing	Magician

Real Names: By Assumed Name

Assumed Name		Original Name		
Abbot	Russ	Roberts	Russ	Comedian
Aberdeen	Earl of	Gordon	George Hamilton	British Prime Minister
AE		Russell	George William	Irish Poet
Agnon	Shmuel Yosef	Czaczkes	Shmuel Josef	Israeli Novelist
Aimée	Anouk	Sorya	Françoise	Actress
Albert	Eddie	Heimberger	Eddie	US Actor
Alda	Alan	D'Abruzzo	Alfonso	Actor
Aldington	Richard	Godfree	Edward	English Poet
Ali	Muhammad	Clay	Cassius Marcellus	Boxer
Ali G	–	Cohen	Sacha Baron	Comedian
Alkan	Charles-Valentin	Morhange	Charles-Valentin	French Musician
Allen	Dave	O'Mahoney	Tynian	Comedian
Allen	Woody	Konigsberg	Allen	Actor and Director
Amazon		Davies	Sharron	Swimmer and TV Gladiator
Anderson	Bronco Billy	Arenson	Max	Entertainer
Andrews	Julie	Wells	Julia	Actress and Singer
Aneka		Sandeman	Mary	Pop singer
Angel	Destiny	Pointon	Juliette	'Captain Scarlet' Character
Angel	Harmony	Kwan	Chan	'Captain Scarlet' Character
Angel	Melody	Jones	Magnolia	'Captain Scarlet' Character
Angel	Rhapsody	Sims	Diane	'Captain Scarlet' Character
Angel	Symphony	Wainwright	Karen	'Captain Scarlet' Character
Angelico	Fra	di Pietro	Guido di	Artist
Ant	Adam	Goddard	Stuart	Singer
Apollinaire	Guillaume	de Kostrowitzky	Wilhelm Apollinaris	French Poet
Appleseed	Johnny	Chapman	John	Missionary Nurseryman
Arden	Elizabeth	Graham	Florence Nightingale	Beautician
Arden	Eve	Quedens	Eunice	Actress
Arlen	Michael	Kouyoumdjian	Dikran	British Novelist
Arliss	George	Andrews	Augustus George	Actor
Arness	James	Aurness	James	US Actor
Arnold	Edward	Schneider	Guenther	Actor
Arras	Leon	Glover	Brian	Professional Wrestler
Arthur	Beatrice	Frankel	Bernice	US Actress
Arthur	Jean	Greene	Gladys	Actress
Astaire	Fred	Austerlitz	Frederick	Dancer and Actor
Astor	Mary	Langemanke	Lucille	Actress
Ataturk	Kemal	Kemal	Mustafa	Turkish Statesman
Atheling	William	Pound	Ezra Loomis	Poet
Atlas	Charles	Siciliano	Angelo	Athlete
Atticus		Addison	Joseph	Essayist and Politician
Avery	Tex	Bean	Frederick	Cartoonist
Aznavour	Charles	Aznavurjal	Shahnovr	Singer and Actor
Bacall	Lauren	Perske	Betty Joan	Actress
Badger (Le Blaireau)		Hinault	Bernard	Cyclist
Badly Drawn Boy	–	Gough	Damon	Singer and Songwriter
Baker	Janet	Abbott	Janet	Mezzo-soprano
Balanchine	George	Balanchivadze	Georgi Melitonivich	Choreographer
Bancroft	Anne	Italiano	Anna Maria	Actress
Bara	Theda	Goodman	Theodosia	Actress
Bardot	Brigitte	Javal	Camille	Actress
Barrie	Amanda	Broadbent	Shirley Ann	Actress
Barry	Gene	Klass	Eugene	US Actor
Barry	John	Prendergast	John Barry	Musician
Barry	Michael	Bukht	Michael	Food Journalist
Barrymore	Ethel	Blythe	Ethel	Actress
Barrymore	John	Blythe	John	Actor
Barrymore	Lionel	Blythe	Lionel	Actor
Bart	Lionel	Begleiter	Lionel	Composer

Assumed Name		Original Name		
Assumed Name		*Original Name*		
Bart	Black	**Bottom**	Charles	*Outlaw*
Basie	Count	**Basie**	William	*Musician*
Bassano	Jacopo	**Da Ponte**	Giacomo	*Italian Painter*
Batgirl		**Wilson**	Barbara	*Comic and*
				Film Heroine
Batman		**Wayne**	Bruce	*Comic and Film Hero*
Beachcomber	John	**Morton**	Cameron	*Newspaper Columnist*
Beaky		**Dymond**	John	*Guitarist*
Beatty	Warren	**Beaty**	Warren	*Actor*
Bedelia	Bonnie	**Culkin**	Bonnie	*Actress*
Beefheart	Captain	**Van Vliet**	Don	*Musician*
Beeton	Mrs	**Mayson**	Isabella	*Cookery Writer*
Bell	Acton	**Brontë**	Anne	*Novelist*
Bell	Currer	**Brontë**	Charlotte	*Novelist*
Bell	Ellis	**Brontë**	Emily	*Novelist*
Benedict	Dirk	**Niewoehner**	Dirk	*US Actor*
Ben-Gurion	David	**Green**	David	*Israeli Statesman*
Bennett	Harve	**Fischman**	Harve	*US TV Producer*
Bennett	Lennie	**Berry**	Mike	*Comedian*
Bennett	Tony	**Benevetto**	Anthony Dominic	*Vocalist*
Benny	Jack	**Kubelsky**	Benjamin	*Comedian*
Berkeley	Busby	**Enos**	William	*Choreographer*
Berlin	Irving	**Baline**	Israel	*Composer*
Bernhardt	Sarah	**Bernard**	Rosine	*Actress*
Berra	Yogi	**Berra**	Lawrence Peter	*Baseball Player*
Bickerstaffe	Isaac	**Steele**	Richard	*Author (shared pen-name)*
Bickerstaffe	Isaac	**Swift**	Jonathan	*Author (shared pen-name)*
B.I.G.	Notorious	**Wallace**	Christopher	*Pop Singer*
Bill	Buffalo	**Cody**	William	*Showman*
Billy the kid		**McCarty**	Henry	*Outlaw*
Blaby	Lord Lawson of	**Lawson**	Nigel	*Politician*
Captain Black		**Turner**	Conrad	*'Captain Scarlet'*
				Character
Black	Cilla	**White**	Priscilla	*Singer and TV Presenter*
Blackbeard		**Teach**	Edward	*Pirate*
Blake	Nicholas	**Day-Lewis**	Cecil	*Detective Writer*
Blondin	Charles	**Gravelet**	Jean François	*French Acrobat*
Bloodvessel	Buster	**Trendle**	Doug	*Singer*
Blue	Captain	**Svenson**	Adam	*TV Fictional Character*
Bluebeard		**Landru**	Henri	*French Murderer*
Bly	Nellie	**Cochrane**	Elizabeth	*Aviator*
Blyton	Enid	**Walters**	Mrs Daryl	*Author*
Bogarde	Dirk	**Van Den Bogaerde**	Derek	*Actor*
Boilermaker		**Jeffries**	James Jackson	*Boxing Champion*
Bolan	Marc	**Feld**	Marc	*Musician*
Bono		**Hewson**	Paul	*Musician*
Big Bopper		**Richardson**	Jiles Perry (JP)	*Musician*
Bonney	William	**McCarthy**	Henry	*Outlaw Billy the Kid*
Borge	Victor	**Rosenbaum**	Borge	*Comic and Musician*
Bosch	Hieronymus	**Van Aken**	Jerome	*Dutch Painter*
Botticelli	Sandro	**Filipepi**	Alessandro	*Artist*
Bowen	Jim	**Whittaker**	James	*Comedian*
Bowie	David	**Jones**	David	*Musician*
Boyd	Stephen	**Millar**	William	*Actor*
Boyle	Katie	**Francabilla**	Marchesa	*TV Presenter*
			Caterina de	
Boz		**Dickens**	Charles	*Author (occasional*
				pen-name)
Bracket	Hilda	**Fyffe**	Patrick	*Entertainer*
Brains		**Hackenbacker**	Hiram J	*'Thunderbirds' Character*
Brandt	Willy	**Frahm**	Karl Herbert	*German Chancellor*
Breen	Billy	**White**	William	*Comedian*
Brett	Jeremy	**Huggins**	Peter Jeremy	*Actor*
Bridie	James	**Mavor**	Osborne Henry	*Dramatist*
Britt	May	**Wilkens**	Maybritt	*Actress*
Bronson	Charles	**Buchinski**	Charles	*Actor*
Bronzino	il	**Mariano**	Agnolo di Cosimo	*Painter*
Brooks	Albert	**Einstein**	Albert	*Actor*
Brooks	Elkie	**Bookbinder**	Elaine	*Singer*
Brooks	Mel	**Kaminsky**	Melvin	*Actor and Director*

FAMOUS PEOPLE

Assumed Name		Original Name		
Brown Bomber		Louis	Joe	Boxer
Bruce	Lenny	Schweider	Alfred	Comedian
Bryan	Dora	Broadbent	Dora	Actress and Comedienne
Brynner	Yul	Khan Jnr	Taidje	Actor
Buddha		Siddhartha	Gautama	Founder of Buddhism
Buntline	Ned	Judson	Edward Zane	Inventor
Burgess	Anthony	Wilson	Anthony	Writer
Burke	Betty	Stuart	Charles Edward	Bonnie Prince Charlie
Burns	George	Birnbaum	Nathan	Comedian
Burstyn	Ellen	Gillorly	Edna	Actress
Burton	Richard	Jenkins	Richard	Actor
Buttons	Red	Schwatt	Aaron	Actor
Bygraves	Max	Bygraves	Walter	Entertainer
Byrnes	Edd	Breitenberger	Edward	Actor
Cage	Nicolas	Coppola	Nicholas	US Actor
Cagliostro	Count	Balsame	Giuseppe	Italian Adventurer
Caine	Michael	Micklewhite	Maurice	Actor
Caine	Marti	Stringer	Lynne	Comedienne and Singer
Callas	Maria	Kalageropoulos	Cecilia	Operatic Soprano
Calvin	Jean	Chauvin/Cauvin	Jean	French Theologian
Canaletto		Canale	Giovanni Antonio	Artist
Cannon	Tommy	Derbyshire	Tommy	Comedy Straight Man
Cantor	Eddie	Iskowitz	Edward	Comedian
Capp	Al	Caplin	Alfred Gerald	Cartoonist
Caravaggio		Merisi	Michelangelo	Artist
Carlisle	Belinda	Wunderman	Leslie	Vocalist
Carlos 'the Jackal'		Sánchez	Illich Ramirez	Revolutionary and Assassin
Carr	Sally	Young	Sara	Vocalist
Carroll	Diahann	Johnson	Carol Diahann	Actress
Carroll	Lewis	Dodgson	Charles Lutwidge	Author
Carrott	Jasper	Davies	Robert	Comedian
Cassandra		Connor	William	Journalist
Cassidy	Butch	Parker	Robert LeRoy	Outlaw Leader
Cat		Dibley	Dwayne	TV Character ('Red Dwarf')
Cates	Phoebe	Katz	Phoebe	Actress
Cathcart	Helen	Albert	Harold	Royal Biographer
Chandler	Jeff	Grossell	Ira	Actor
Charisse	Cyd	Finklea	Tula Ellice	Dancer
Charles	Ray	Robinson	Ray Charles	Singer
Charteris	Leslie	Yin	Leslie Charles Bowyer	Author
Checker	Chubby	Evans	Ernest	Singer
Cher		La Pierre	Cherilyn Sarkisian	Singer and Actress
Chi-Minh	Ho	Thann	Nguyen Van	Vietnamese Politician
Chopin	Kate	O'Flaherty	Katherine	Author
Cicero		Tullius	Marcus	Roman Statesman
Cid	El	Vivár	Rodrigo Díaz de	Spanish Warrior
Clair	René	Chomette	René Lucien	Film Director
Clapton	Eric	Clapp	Eric	Guitarist and Singer
Clarke	John	Cromwell	Richard	Son of Oliver Cromwell
Cliff	Jimmy	Chambers	James	Singer
Clift	Montgomery	Montgomery	Edward	Actor
Cobb	Lee J	Jacob	Lee	Actor
Coco		Poliakov	Nikolai	Clown
Colbert	Claudette	Chauchoin	Lily	Actress
Colbourne	Maurice	Middleton	Roger	Actor
Cole	Nat King	Adams	Nathaniel	Singer
Coltrane	Robbie	McMillan	Anthony Robert	Actor and Comedian
Como	Perry	Perido	Nick	Singer
Connery	Sean	Connery	Thomas	Actor
Conquest	Owen	Hamilton	Charles	Author
Conrad	Joseph	Korzeniowski	Jozef Teodor Konrad	Author
Cool James	Ladies Love	Smith	James Todd	Rap Singer
Cooper	Alice	Furnier	Vincent	Singer
Cooper	Gary	Cooper	Francis	Actor
Le Corbusier		Jeanneret	Charles Edouard	Architect

Assumed Name		Original Name		
El Cordobes		**Perez**	Manuel Benitez	*Matador*
Corelli	Marie	**Mackay**	Mary	*English Novelist*
Corno di Bassetto		**Shaw**	George Bernard	*Author (as music critic)*
Correggio		**Allegri**	Antonio	*Artist*
Corvo	Baron	**Rolfe**	Frederick William	*Novelist*
Costello	Elvis	**McManus**	Declan	*Singer and Composer*
Costello	Lou	**Cristillo**	Louis	*Comedian*
Cougar	John	**Mellencamp**	John	*Vocalist*
Craddock	Fanny	**Primrose-Pechey**	Phyllis	*Television Cook*
Craig	Michael	**Gregson**	Michael	*Actor*
Cranach	Lucas	**Müller**	Lucas	*German Painter*
Craven	Sara	**Ashurst**	Anne	*Novelist*
Crawford	Joan	**Le Sueur**	Lucille	*Actress*
Crawford	Michael	**Dumble-Smith**	Michael	*Actor and Singer*
Crazy Horse		**Witko**	Tasunko	*Sioux Indian Chief*
Creole	Kid	**Darnell Browder**	Thomas August	*Singer*
Creston	Paul	**Guttoveggio**	Joseph	*Musician*
Cricket	Jimmy	**Mulgrew**	James	*Comedian*
Crisp	Quentin	**Pratt**	Denis	*Writer*
Crompton	Richmal	**Lamburn**	Richmal	*Author*
Crosby	Bing	**Crosby**	Harry Lillis	*Singer and Actor*
Cruise	Tom	**Mapother**	Tom Cruise	*Actor*
Curie	Marie	**Sklodowska**	Manya	*Physicist*
Curtis	Tony	**Schwartz**	Bernard	*Actor*
Cutpurse	Moll	**Frith**	Mary	*Pickpocket and Robber*
D'Ache	Caran	**Poire**	Emmanuel	*French Illustrator*
Daddy	Big	**Crabtree**	Shirley	*Wrestler*
D'Amato	Joe	**Massaccesi**	Aristide	*Film Director*
Dana		**Scallon**	Rosemary	*Singer and Politician*
		(née Brown)		
Dane	Clemence	**Ashton**	Winifred	*English Dramatist*
Darby	Kim	**Zerby**	Deborah	*Actress*
Darin	Bobby	**Cassotto**	Robert Walden	*Singer*
Darren	James	**Ercolani**	James	*US Actor*
Davis	Nancy	**Robbins**	Anne Frances	*Actress*
Davro	Bobby	**Nankeville**	Robert	*Comic Impressionist*
Dawes (He's a baby)	George	**Lucas**	Matt	*Comedian*
Dawn	Elizabeth	**Butterfield**	Sylvia	*Actress*
Day	Doris	**Kappelhoff**	Doris Von	*Actress and Singer*
De Carlo	Yvonne	**Middleton**	Peggy	*Actress*
De Paul	Lynsey	**Rubin**	Lynsey	*Singer*
De Quincey	Thomas	**Quincey**	Thomas	*Essayist*
Dean	James	**Byron**	James	*Actor*
Dee	Dave	**Harman**	David	*Vocalist*
Dee	Kiki	**Matthews**	Pauline	*Singer*
Defoe	Daniel	**Foe**	Daniel	*Author*
Delfont	Bernard	**Winogradsky**	Boris	*Impresario*
Deneuve	Catherine	**Dorléac**	Catherine	*Actress*
Dennis	Les	**Heseltine**	Les	*Comedian*
Denver	John	**Deutschendorf Jnr**	Henry John	*Singer and Composer*
Derek	Bo	**Collins**	Cathleen	*Actress*
Derek	John	**Harris**	Derek	*Actor*
Desmousseaux	Félicité	**Saillot**	Félicité	*Actress*
Diamond	Neil	**Kaminsky**	Noah	*Singer and Composer*
Dickinson	Angie	**Brown**	Angeline	*Actress*
Dickson	Carter	**Carr**	John Dickson	*US Detective Writer*
Diddley	Bo	**Bates**	Otha Ellas	*Singer*
Diesel	Vin	**Vincent**	Mark	*Actor*
Dinesen	Isak	**Blixen**	Karen	*Writer*
Ding Ling		**Bingzhi**	Jiang	*Chinese Novelist*
Divine	Father	**Baker**	George	*Religious Leader*
Dixon	Franklin W	**Stratemeyer**	Edward	*Author*
DJ Quicksilver		**Terzi**	Orhan	*Turkish Pop Star*
Dolin	Anton	**Healey-Kay**	Patrick	*Choreographer*
Donovan		**Leitch**	Donovan	*Singer*
Dorsey	Gerry	**Dorsey**	Arnold	*Singer*
Douglas	Kirk	**Demsky**	Issur Danielovitch	*Actor*
Downe	Bob	**Trevorrow**	Mark	*Australian Comedian*
Dozy		**Davies**	Trevor	*Bass Player*
Drake	Charlie	**Springall**	Charles	*Comedian*

Assumed Name		Original Name		
Dylan	Bob	*Zimmerman*	Robert Alan	*Singer and Composer*
Eden	Barbara	*Huffman*	Barbara	*US Actress*
Edge	The	*Evans*	Dave	*Musician*
Edwards	Vince	*Zoine*	Vincento	*US Actor*
Elia		*Lamb*	Charles	*Essayist*
Eliot	George	*Evans*	Mary Ann	*Novelist*
Ellis	Alexander John	*Sharpe*	Alexander John	*English Philologist*
Elytis	Odysseus	*Alepoudelis*	Odysseus	*Greek Poet*
Eminem		*Mathers III*	Marshall	*Rapper and Actor*
Erasmus	Desiderius	*Gheraerd*	Gheraerd	*Scholar*
Essex	David	*Cook*	David	*Singer and Actor*
Everage	Dame Edna	*Humphries*	Barry	*Comedian*
Everett	Kenny	*Cole*	Maurice	*Disc Jockey and Comedian*
Fabian		*Forte*	Fabiano	*Singer*
Fairbanks	Douglas	*Ullman*	Douglas	*Actor*
Faith	Adam	*Nelhams*	Terry	*Singer*
Fame	Georgie	*Powell*	Clive	*Musician*
Farrell	MJ	*Keane*	Molly	*Irish Novelist*
Fawn	Doctor	*Wilkie*	Edward	*'Captain Scarlet' Character*
Fenton	Shane	*Jewry*	Bernard	*Singer*
Fields	WC	*Dukenfield*	William Claude	*Comedian and Actor*
Fields	Gracie	*Stansfield*	Grace	*Actress and Singer*
Finch	Peter	*Mitchell*	Ian	*Actor*
Fish		*Dick*	Derek	*Vocalist*
Fleming	Rhonda	*Louis*	Marilyn	*Actress*
Flying Scotsman		*Liddell*	Eric	*Athlete*
Flynn	Barbara	*McMurray*	Barbara	*Actress*
Fontaine	Joan	*De Havilland*	Joan	*Actress*
Fonteyn	Margot	*Hookham*	Margaret	*Ballerina*
Ford	Gerald	*King*	Leslie	*US President*
Ford	John	*O'Fearna*	Sean	*Film Director*
Formby Jnr	George	*Booth*	George Hoy	*Music Hall Entertainer*
Formby Snr	George	*Booth*	James	*Music Hall Entertainer*
Forrest	Steve	*Andrews*	William Forrest	*US Actor*
Forsyth	Bruce	*Johnson*	Bruce	*Entertainer*
Foster	Jodie	*Munker*	Ariane	*US Actress*
Fox		*Baker*	Tammy Marie	*TV Gladiator*
France	Anatole	*Thibault*	Anatole François	*Author*
Franciosa	Tony	*Papaceo*	Anthony	*Actor*
Francis	Connie	*Franconers*	Concetta	*Singer*
Francis of Assisi	Saint	*de Bernardone*	Giovanni	*Religious Leader*
Francisque		*Millet*	Jean-François	*Belgian Painter*
Freeze	Mr	*Fries*	Victor	*Fictional Super-Villain*
Fury	Billy	*Wycherly*	Ronald	*Vocalist*
Gabor	Dennis	*Dénes*	Gábor	*Physicist*
Garbo	Greta	*Gustaffsson*	Greta Louisa	*Actress*
Garcia	Andy	*Menendez*	Andres Arturo Garcia	*Actor*
Garfunkel	Art	*Graph*	Tom	*Half of 50s Singing Duo 'Tom & Jerry'*
Garland	Judy	*Gumm*	Frances	*Actress and Singer*
Garner	James	*Baumgartner*	James	*Actor*
Gaskell	Elizabeth	*Stevenson*	Elizabeth	*Writer*
Gayle	Crystal	*Gazzimos*	Brenda Gail	*Singer*
Gaynor	Gloria	*Fowles*	Gloria	*Singer*
Gee	Dustin	*Harrison*	Gerald	*Impressionist*
Genée	Adeline	*Jensen*	Anita	*Ballerina*
George	Boy	*O'Dowd*	George	*Singer*
Geraldo		*Bright*	Gerald	*Musician*
German	Edward	*Jones*	Edward	*English Composer*
Geronimo		*Goyathlay*		*Apache Indian Chief*
Giant Haystacks		*McMasters*	Luke	*Wrestler*
Gibbon	Lewis	*Mitchell*	James Leslie	*Novelist*
Giorgione		*Barbarelli*	Giorgio	*Artist*
Gish	Lillian	*Guiche*	Lilian	*Actress*
Glitter	Gary	*Gadd*	Paul	*Singer*
Gluck	Alma	*Fiersohn*	Reba	*American Soprano*
Goddard	Paulette	*Levy*	Marion	*Actress*
Gold		*Vander Walt*	Lize	*TV Gladiator*

Assumed Name		Original Name		
Goldberg	Whoopi	*Johnson*	Caryn	*US Actress*
Goldsmith	Peter	*Priestley*	John Boynton	*Author*
Goldwyn	Sam	*Gelbfisz*	Samuel	*Film Producer*
Goodrich	William B	*Arbuckle*	Roscoe Conkling (Fatty)	*Actor*
Gordon	Richard	*Ostlere*	Gordon	*Doctor and Author*
Gorky	Arshile	*Adoian*	Vosdanig Manoog	*US Painter*
Gorky	Maxim	*Peshkov*	Max	*Author*
Gould	Elliott	*Goldstein*	Elliott	*Actor*
Grade	Lew	*Winogradsky*	Louis	*Impresario*
Granger	Stewart	*Stewart*	James	*Actor*
Grant	Cary	*Leach*	Archibald	*Actor*
Gray	Donald	*Tidbury*	Eldred	*South African Actor*
Grayson	Larry	*White*	William	*Comedian*
Graziano	Rocky	*Barbella*	Rocco	*Boxer*
El Greco		*Theotocopoulos*	Domenico	*Artist*
L T Green		*Griffiths*	Seymour	*TV Fictional Character*
Green	Lucinda	*Prior-Palmer*	Lucinda	*Three-Day Eventer*
Green	Peter	*Greenbaum*	Peter	*Musician*
Grey	Captain	*Holden*	Bradley	*TV Fictional Character*
Grey	Beryl	*Svenson*	Beryl	*Ballerina*
Gris	Juan	*González*	Juan Victoriano	*Cubist Painter*
Grock		*Wettach*	Adrien	*Clown*
Grünewald	Matthias	*Gothardt*	Mathis	*German Painter*
Guercino		*Barbieri*	Gian-Francesco	*Italian Painter*
H		*Watkins*	Ian	*Pop Singer*
Haliburton	Hugh	*Robertson*	James Logie	*Poet*
Hamilton	Clive	*Lewis*	CS	*British Writer*
Hamilton	Emma	*Lyon*	Emma	*Lord Nelson's Mistress*
Hammer	MC	*Burrell*	Stanley Kirk	*Rapper*
Harley	Steve	*Nice*	Stephen	*Pop Singer*
Harlow	Jean	*Carpentier*	Harlean	*Actress*
Hart	Emma	*Lyon*	Emma (Amy)	*Blacksmith's Daughter*
Harvey	Laurence	*Skikne*	Larushka Mischa	*Actor*
Haver	June	*Stovenour*	June	*Actress*
Hawk	Jeremy	*Lange*	Cedric	*Actor and TV Presenter*
Hawtrey	Charles	*Hartree*	George	*Actor*
Hayden	Sterling	*Relyea*	Walter	*Actor*
Hayworth	Rita	*Cansino*	Marguerita	*Actress*
HD		*Doolittle*	Hilda	*Writer*
Headroom	Max	*Frewer*	Matt	*Fictional TV Character*
Hedley	Jack	*Hawkins*	Jack	*Actor*
Henderson	Mary	*Mavor*	Osborne Henry	*Dramatist*
Hepburn	Audrey	*Van Heemstra*	Edda Hepburn	*Actress*
Hepburn	Audrey	*Ruston*	Audrey	*Actress*
Herriot	James	*Wight*	James	*Vet and Author*
Hershey	Barbara	*Herzstein*	Barbara	*Actress*
Hershey	Barbara	*Seagull*	Barbara	*US Actress*
Hessling	Catherine	*Heurschling*	Andrée	*Jean Renoir's Wife (Actress)*
Heston	Charlton	*Carter*	Charlton	*Actor*
HHH (Triple H)		*Levesque*	Paul Michael	*Wrestler*
Higgins	Jack	*Patterson*	Henry	*Author*
Hill	Benny	*Hill*	Alfred Hawthorne	*Comedian*
Hinge	Evadne	*Logan*	George	*Entertainer*
Hirsel	Lord Home of the	*Douglas-Home*	Alec	*Prime Minister of Great Britain*
Hitler	Adolf	*Schicklgrüber*	Adolf	*Dictator*
Hobbema	Meindert	*Lubbertszoon*	Meyndert	*Dutch Painter*
Hoffa	Jimmy	*Riddle*	James	*US Union Leader*
Hogan	Hulk	*Bollea*	Terry	*Professional Wrestler and Actor*
Holden	William	*Beedle*	William	*Actor*
Holiday	Billie	*Fagan*	Eleanora	*Singer*
Holly	Buddy	*Hardin*	Charles	*Singer*
Hope	Anthony	*Hawkins*	Anthony	*Author*
Hope	Laura Lee	*Stratemeyer*	Edward	*Author*
Horowitz	Vladimir	*Gorowicz*	Vladimir	*Russian Pianist*
Houdini	Harry	*Weiss*	Ehrich	*Illusionist*
Houseman	John	*Haussman*	Jacques	*Actor*

F
A
M
O
U
S

P
E
O
P
L
E

Assumed Name		Original Name		
Howard	Leslie	*Stainer*	Leslie	*Actor*
Hudson	Rock	*Scherer Jnr*	Roy	*Actor*
Humperdinck	Engelbert	*Dorsey*	Arnold	*Singer*
Hunter		*Crossley*	James	*Gladiator*
Hunter	Tab	*Gellen*	Arthur	*Singer and Actor*
Hutton	Betty	*Thornburg*	Betty June	*US Comedy Actress*
I Spy	Big Chief	*Worrell*	Charles	*Author*
Ice Cube		*Jackson*	O'Shea	*Rapper and Actor*
Ice-T		*Marrow*	Tracy	*Rapper and Actor*
Innes	Michael	*Stewart*	John	*Author*
Irving	Henry	*Brodribb*	John Henry	*Actor*
Islam	Yusuf	*Stevens*	Cat	*Singer and Composer*
Ives	Burl	*Ivanhoe*	Burl	*Actor and Singer*
Ivy	Poison	*Isley*	Pamela	*Fictional Super-Villain*
Jack	Wolfman	*Smith*	Robert	*Disc Jockey*
James	PD	*White*	PD	*Writer*
Jane	Calamity	*Canary*	Martha Jane	*Frontierswoman*
Janis	Byron	*Yanks*	Byron	*Musician*
Janssen	David	*Mayer*	David	*Actor*
Jason	David	*White*	David	*Actor*
Jayston	Michael	*James*	Michael	*Actor*
Jet		*Youdale*	Diane	*TV Gladiator*
Joan Collins' Fan Club		*Clary*	Julian	*Entertainer*
John	Elton Hercules	*Dwight*	Reginald Kenneth	*Singer and Composer*
John	Jilted	*Fellows*	Graham	*Pop Singer*
John Paul II	Pope	*Wojtyla*	Karol	*Pope*
Jolie	Angelina	*Voight*	Angelina	*Actress*
Jones	Tom	*Woodward*	Thomas	*Singer*
Jordan	Louis	*Gendre*	Louis	*Actor*
Joyce	Yootha	*Needham*	Yootha	*Actress*
Julia	Raul	*Rafael Y Arcelos*	Raul	*Actor*
Kane	Eden	*Sarstedt*	Richard	*Singer*
Kane Jeeves	Mahatma	*Dukenfield*	William Claude	*Comedian and Actor*
Karlin	Miriam	*Samuels*	Miriam	*Actress*
Karloff	Boris	*Pratt*	William Henry	*Actor*
Karno	Fred	*Westcott*	Fred	*Impresario*
Kaye	Danny	*Kaminsky*	David Daniel	*Entertainer*
Kaye	Nora	*Koreff*	Nora	*Ballerina*
Kazan	Elia	*Kazanjoglou*	Elia	*Film Director*
Keaton	Diane	*Hall*	Diane	*Actress*
Keaton	Michael	*Douglas*	Michael	*Actor (Batman Actor)*
Keene	Carolyn	*Stratemeyer*	Edward	*Author*
Kemp	Jeremy	*Walker*	Edmund	*Actor*
Kerr	Deborah	*Trimmler*	Deborah	*Actress*
Kesteven	Baroness Thatcher of	*Thatcher*	Margaret	*Prime Minister of Great Britain*
Khan	Chaka	*Stephens*	Yvette Marie	*Singer*
Khashoggi	Soraya	*Daly*	Sandra	*Millionairess*
Kid Rock		*Ritchie*	Robert	*Rock Star*
King	Ben E	*Nelson*	Benjamin	*Singer*
King	Carol	*Klein*	Carole	*Singer*
Kinski	Nastassia	*Nakszynski*	Nastassja	*Actress*
Kit		*Hesketh-Harvey*	Kit	*Musical act 'Kit and the Widow'*
Klenovsky	Paul	*Wood*	Henry	*English Conductor*
Kline	Patsy	*Hensley*	Virginia	*Singer*
Knickerbocker	Cholly	*Paul*	Maury	*NY Gossip Columnist*
Knickerbocker	Diedrich	*Irving*	Washington	*Author*
Koresh	David	*Howell*	Vernon	*Branch Davidian Cult Leader*
La Rue	Danny	*Carroll*	Daniel	*Female Impersonator*
Ladd	Cheryl	*Stoppelmoor*	Cheryl	*Actress*
Laine	Denny	*Haynes*	Brian	*Guitarist*
Laine	Frankie	*Vecchio*	Frank Lo	*Vocalist*
Lamarr	Hedy	*Kiesler*	Hedwig	*Actress*
Lamour	Dorothy	*Kaumeyer*	Dorothy Mary	*Actress*
Landis	Jerry	*Simon*	Paul	*Half of 50s Singing Duo 'Tom & Jerry'*
Landon	Michael	*Orowitz*	Eugene Maurice	*US Actor*

Assumed Name		Original Name		
Lanza	Mario	Cocozza	Alfredo	Opera Singer
Large	Eddie	McGuinness	Eddie	Comedian
Larrigan	Tex	Ord	Irene	Author of Westerns
Lassie (male)		Pal (female)		Film Dog
Laurel	Stan	Jefferson	Arthur Stanley	Comedy Actor
Laurie	Piper	Jacobs	Rosetta	US Actress
Laxness	Halldór	Gudjonsson	Halldór	Icelandic Novelist
Le Carré	John	Cornwell	David	Author
Le Duc Tho		Dinh Khai	Phan	Vietnamese Politician
Le Mesurier	John	Halliley	John Elton	Actor
Lee	Brenda	Tarpley	Brenda	Vocalist
Lee	Bruce	Kam	Lee Yuen	Actor and Martial Artist
Lee	Peggy	Egstrom	Norma	Vocalist
Leigh	Janet	Morrison	Jeanette	Actress
Leigh	Jennifer Jason	Morrow	Jennifer Lee	Actress
Leigh	Vivien	Hartley	Vivien	Actress
Lely	Peter	Van der Faes	Pieter	Artist
Lemmy		Kilinster	Ian	Singer (Motorhead)
Lenin	Vladimir Ilich	Ulyanov	Vladimir Ilich	Russian Revolutionary
Leno	Dan	Calvin	George	English Comedian
Lenya	Lotte	Blamauer	Karoline Wilhelmine	Austrian Actress
Lewis	Jerry	Levitch	Joseph	Actor and Comedian
Liberace		Valentino	Wladziu	Pianist and Entertainer
Lightning		Williams	Kim	TV Gladiator
Limahl		Hamill	Christopher	Singer (Kajagoogoo)
Little	Syd	Mead	Cyril	Comedian
Lloyd	Marie	Wood	Mathilda	Actress
Lom	Herbert	Ze Schluderpacheru	Herbert	Actor
Lombard	Carole	Peters	Jane	Actress
London	Jack	Griffith	John	Author
Lord	Jack	Ryan	John Joseph	Actor
Loren	Sophia	Scicolone	Sofia	Actress
Lorraine	Claude	Gelée	Claude	Landscape Painter
Lorre	Peter	Loewenstein	Laszlo	Actor
Lot	Parson	Kingsley	Charles	Author
Lottery	Lenny	McGurran	Aidan	National Lottery Expert
Louis	Joe	Barrow	Joseph	Boxer
Louis	Morris	Bernstein	Morris	US Painter
Lulu		Lawrie	Marie McLaughlin	Singer
Lynn	Vera	Welch	Vera	Singer
Mabuse	Jan	Gossart	Jan	Flemish Painter
MacBride	Maud	Gonne	Maud	Irish Nationalist
MacColl	Ewan	Miller	James	Folk Singer
MacDiarmid	Hugh	Grieve	Christopher Murray	Poet
Mack	Connie	McGillicuddy	Cornelius	Baseball Player
Maclaine	Shirley	Beaty	Shirley	Actress
Madonna		Ciccone	Madonna Louise	Singer
Magenta	Captain	Donaghue	Patrick	Fictional TV Character
Magnusson	Magnus	Sigursteinnson	Magnus	Broadcaster
Majors	Lee	Yeary	Harvey Lee	Actor
Malden	Karl	Sekolovich	Mladen	Actor
Mann	Manfred	Lubowitz	Michael	Musician
Mansfield	Jayne	Palmer	Vera Jane	Actress
Mansfield	Katherine	Beauchamp	Kathleen	NZ Writer
Manson	Charles	Maddox	No-Name	Cult Leader
Manson	Marilyn	Warner	Brian	Pop Star
March	Fredric	Bickel	Frederick	Actor
Margret	Ann	Olsson	Ann-Margret	Actress
Markham	Elizabeth	Penrose	Elizabeth	Writer for Children
Markham	Robert	Amis	Kingsley	Novelist
Markova	Alicia	Marks	Lilian Alice	Ballerina
Marks	Alfred	Touchinsky	Alfred	Actor and Comedian
Martin	Dean	Crocetti	Dino	Actor
Marvel	Captain	Batson	Billy	Comics Hero
Marvin	Hank	Rankin	Brian	Guitarist
Marx	Chico	Marx	Leonard	Actor
Marx	Groucho	Marx	Julius	Actor
Marx	Gummo	Marx	Milton	Actor
Marx	Harpo	Marx	Adolph	Actor
Marx	Zeppo	Marx	Herbert	Actor

Assumed Name		Original Name		
Masaccio	di Simone Guidi	*de Giovanni*	Tommaso	*Florentine Painter*
Matthau	Walter	*Matuschanskavasky*	Walter	*Actor*
Maxwell	Robert	*Hoch*	Jan Ludvik	*Businessman*
Maynard	Bill	*William*	Walter	*Actor*
McBain	Ed	*Hunter*	Evan	*Writer*
McMasters	Luke	*Ruane*	Martin	*Wrestler*
Meatloaf		*Aday*	Marvin Lee	*Singer*
Meg	Mystic	*Lake*	Margaret	*TV Personality*
Meir	Golda	*Mabovitch*	Golda	*Israeli PM*
Melba	Dame Nellie	*Armstrong, née Mitchell*	Helen Porter	*Opera Singer*
Melbourne	Viscount	*Lamb*	William	*British Prime Minister*
Melmoth	Sebastian	*Wilde*	Oscar	*Author*
Mendelssohn	Felix	*Mendelssohn -Bartholdy*	Felix	*Composer*
Menken	Adah Isaacs	*Fuertes*	Dolores Adios	*American Actress and Poet*
Mennin	Peter	*Mennini*	Peter	*Musician*
Mercury	Freddie	*Bulsara*	Frederick	*Singer*
Meredith	Burgess	*Burgess*	George	*Actor*
Merlin		*Tennyson*	Alfred Lord	*Poet*
Merton	Mrs	*Hook/Aherne*	Caroline	*Comedienne*
Merton	Paul	*Martin*	Paul	*Comedian*
Mervyn	William	*Pickwoad*	William	*Actor*
Michael	George	*Panayiotou*	Georgios	*Vocalist and Composer*
Michael of Kent	Princess	*von Reibnitz*	Marie	*Princess*
Milland	Ray	*Truscott-Jones*	Reginald	*Actor*
Milligan	Spike	*Milligan*	Terence Alan	*Comedian and Writer*
Mistinguett		*Bourgeois*	Jeanne Marie	*French Dancer*
Mitchell	Cameron	*Mizell*	George	*Actor*
Mitchell	Guy	*Cernick*	Al	*Singer*
Mitchell	Joni	*Anderson*	Roberta Joan	*Singer and Composer*
Molière		*Poquelin*	Jean-Baptiste	*Playwright*
Molotov	Vyacheslav Mikhaylovich	*Skryabin*	Vyacheslav Mikhaylovich	*Russian Statesman*
Monroe	Marilyn	*Baker*	Norma Jean	*Actress*
Montand	Yves	*Levy*	Ivo	*Actor*
Montez	Lola	*Gilbert*	Maria Eliza (Délores)	*American Dancer*
Montgomery	George	*Letz*	George	*Actor*
Moody	Ron	*Moodnick*	Ronald	*Actor*
Moore	Archibald	*Wright*	Archibald	*Boxer*
Moore	Demi	*Guynes*	Demi	*Actress*
Morecambe	Eric	*Bartholomew*	John Eric	*Comedian*
Morgan	Frank	*Wupperman*	Frank	*Actor*
Morrison	Van	*Morrison*	George Ivan	*Singer and Composer*
Moses	Grandma	*Robertson*	Anna Mary	*Artist*
Mostel	Zero	*Mostel*	Samuel Joel	*Actor*
Mycroft		*Gillis*	Ian	*'Brain of Britain'*
Nagasaki	Kendo	*Thornley*	Peter	*Professional Wrestler*
Naismith	Laurence	*Johnson*	Lawrence	*Actor*
Neagle	Anna	*Robertson*	Marjorie	*Actress*
Negri	Pola	*Chalupek*	Appolonia	*Actress*
Nelly		*Haynes Jr*	Cornell	*Rapper*
Nelson	Baby Face	*Gillis*	Lester	*Gangster*
Nero		*Ahenobarbus*	Lucius Domitius	*Roman Emperor*
Nero	Franco	*Spartanero*	Franco	*Actor*
Newcastle	Duke of	*Pelham-Holles*	Thomas	*British Prime Minister*
Nichols	Mike	*Peschkowsky*	Michael	*American Film Director*
Nicole		*Skurnick*	Estelle	*'Renault Clio' Star of Advert*
Nolde	Emil	*Hansen*	Emil	*German Painter*
Novarra	Ramon	*Samaniegos*	Ramon	*Actor*
Novello	Ivor	*Davies*	David Ivor	*Composer*
Numan	Gary	*Webb*	Gary	*Vocalist and Composer*
Oakley	Annie	*Mozee*	Phoebe	*Frontierswoman*
Oberon	Merle	*Thompson*	Estelle	*Actress*
O'Brien	Flann	*O'Nolan*	Brian	*Irish Writer*
O'Brien	Hugh	*Krampke*	Hugh	*Actor*
Ochre	Captain	*Frazier*	Richard	*Fictional TV Character*
O'Connor	Frank	*O'Donovan*	Michael	*Irish Writer*
Offenbach	Jacques	*Eberst*	Jakob	*Composer*

Assumed Name		Original Name		
O'Hara	Maureen	Fitzsimmons	Maureen	Actress
O'Henry		Porter	William Sydney	Author
Orlando	Tony	Cassavitis	Michael	Vocalist
Ormandy	Eugene	Blau	Jenö	Musician
Orwell	George	Blair	Eric Arthur	Author
O'Sullivan	Gilbert	O'Sullivan	Raymond	Singer
Ouida		Ramée, de la	Marie Louise	English Author
Palance	Jack	Palaniuk	Walter	Actor
Pallo	Jackie	Gutteridge	John	Wrestler
Palmer	Lilli	Peiser	Lilli	Actress
Panther		Riley	Helena	TV Gladiator
Parker	Dorothy	Rothschild	Dorothy	Author
Parker	Cecil	Schwabe	Cecil	Actor
Parley	Peter	Goodrich	Samuel	US Publisher
Parmigianino	Il	Mazzola	Girolamo Francesco Maria	Italian Painter
Pastry	Mr	Hearne	Richard	Actor
Patterson	Sir Les	Humphries	Barry	Comedian
Paycheck	Johnny	Lytle	Donald Eugene	Country Singer
Peel	John	Ravenscroft	John	Disc Jockey
Peerce	Jan	Perelmuth	Jacob Pincus	Musician
Pele		do Nascimento	Edson Arantes Do	Footballer
Pellow	Marti	McLoughlin	Mark	Singer
Penguin		Cobblepot	Oswald	Batman Character
Pennis	Dennis	Kaye	Paul	Actor and Comedian
Perkins	Elizabeth	Pisperikos	Elizabeth	Actress
Phillips	Lou Diamond	Upchurch	Lou	Actor
Phiz		Browne	Hablot Knight	Illustrator
Phoenix		Young	Sandy	Gladiator
Piaf	Edith	Gassion	Edith	Singer
Pickford	Mary	Smith	Gladys Mary	Actress
Pindar	Peter	Wolcot	John	Satirist
Pink		Moore	Alicia	Actress and Singer
Pop	Iggy	Osterberg	James Jewel	Singer
Porcupine	Peter	Cobbett	William	Writer
Powers	Stefanie	Federkiewicz	Stefania	Actress
Preston	Robert	Meservey	Robert	Actor
Price	Dennis	Rose-Price	Dennistoun Franklyn	Actor
Prince		Nelson	Prince Rogers	Singer and Composer
Proby	PJ	Smith	James Marcus	Singer
Pussyfoot		Johnson	William Eugene	US Reformer
Q		Quiller-Couch	Arthur	Author and Anthologist
Queen	Ellery	Dannay	Frederick	Joint Authors
		Lee	Manfred B	
Quinn	Anthony	Oaxaca	Rudolph	US Actor
Rafferty	Chips	Goffage	John	Entertainer
Raft	George	Ranft	George	Actor
Randall	Tony	Rosenberg	Leonard	Actor
Randi	Amazing	Zwinge	James Randall	Magician
Raven	Paul	Gadd	Paul	Vocalist
Ray	Ted	Olden	Charles	Comedian
Reality	Maxim	Palmer	Keith	MC
Rebel		Stoute	Jenny	TV Gladiator
Red Cloud		Iuta	Mahpiua	(Sioux) Chief
Reed	Lou	Firbank	Louis	Singer and Composer
Reeves	Vic	Moir	Jim	Comedian
Regiomontanus		Müller	Johannes	German Mathematician
Remarque	Erich Maria	Kramer	Erich Maria	Author
Rendell	Ruth	Grasemann	Ruth	Crime Novelist
Rethberg	Elisabeth	Sättler	Elisabeth	Musician
Richard	Cliff	Webb	Harold	Singer
Richard	Little	Penniman	Richard Wayne	Singer
Richards	Frank	Hamilton	Charles	Author
Rivers	Joan	Molinsky	Joan	Comedienne
Robbins	Harold	Rubin	Harold	Author
Robin		Grayson	Dick	Comics Character
Robinson	Edward G	Goldenberg	Emmanuel	Actor
Robinson	Ralph	George III		British King (in Garden Periodicals)
Robinson	Sugar Ray	Smith	Walker	Boxer

FAMOUS PEOPLE

Assumed Name		Original Name		
Rock		*Johnson*	Dwayne	*Actor and Wrestler*
Rocket		*Richards*	Pauline	*TV Gladiator*
Rogers	Ginger	*McMath*	Virginia	*Actress and Dancer*
Rogers	Roy	*Slye*	Leonard	*Actor*
Rogers	Will	*Adair*	William Penn	*US Actor*
Rohmer	Sax	*Ward*	Arthur Sarsfield	*Author*
Rooney	Mickey	*Yule Jnr*	Joseph	*Actor*
Rose	Axl	*Bailey*	William	*Singer*
Rose Lee	Gypsy	*Hovick*	Rose Louise	*Entertainer*
Ross	Aircraftsman John Hume	*Lawrence*	Thomas Edward	*Soldier and Author*
Ross	Barnaby	*Dannay*	Frederick	*Joint Authors*
		Lee	Manfred B	
Rotten	Johnny	*Lydon*	John	*Singer*
Rowland	Tiny	*Fuhrhop*	Roland	*Businessman*
Rowlands	John	*Stanley*	Henry Morton	*Explorer/Journalist*
Roy	Rob	*McGregor*	Robert	*Scottish Outlaw*
Ruffo	Titta	*Titta*	Ruffo	*Baritone*
Russell	Theresa	*Paup*	Theresa	*Actress*
Rutherford	Mark	*White*	William Hale	*Writer*
Ryder	Winona	*Horowitz*	Winona	*Actress*
Sabrina		*Sykes*	Norma	*Model*
Sade		*Adu*	Helen Folasade	*Singer*
Sagan	Françoise	*Quoirez*	Françoise	*Novelist*
Saint-John Perse		*Léger*	Alexis Saint-Léger	*French Poet*
Saint-Laurent	Yves	*Mathieu*	Henri Donat	*French Designer*
Saki		*Monro*	Hector Hugh	*Writer*
Samaroff	Olga	*Hickenlooper*	Lucie	*Musician*
Sand	George	*Dudevant*	Amondine Lucie Dupin	*Writer*
Sapper		*McNeile*	Herman Cyril	*Author*
Sappho		*de Scudéry*	Madeleine	*French Novelist*
Saracen		*Lewis*	Mike	*TV Gladiator*
Sarandon	Susan	*Tomaling*	Susan	*Actress*
Savage	Lily	*O'Grady*	Paul	*Entertainer*
Saxon	John	*Orrico*	Carmen	*Actor*
Scarlet	Captain	*Metcalfe*	Paul	*Animated TV Character*
Schultz	Dutch	*Flegenheimer*	Arthur	*Gangster*
Scott	Randolph	*Crane*	Randolph	*Actor*
Seal		*Samuel*	Henry	*Singer*
Selassie	Hailie	*Makonnen*	Ras Tafari	*Ethiopian Emperor*
Sennett	Mack	*Sinnott*	Michael	*Film Producer*
Sensible	Captain	*Burns*	Ray	*Singer*
Dr Seuss		*Geisel*	Theodore Seuss	*Author*
Seymour	Jane	*Frankenberg*	Joyce	*Actress*
Shadow		*King*	Jefferson	*TV Gladiator*
Shaggy		*Burrell*	Orville Richard	*Pop Singer*
Shannon	Del	*Westover*	Charles	*Singer*
Sharif	Omar	*Shalhoub*	Michael	*Actor*
Shaw	Sandie	*Goodrich*	Sandra	*Singer*
Shaw	TE	*Lawrence*	Thomas Edward	*Soldier and Author (in Royal Tank Corps)*
Sheen	Martin	*Estevez*	Ramon	*Actor*
Shipton	Mother	*Southill/Southiel*	Ursula	*Prophetess*
Shirley	Anne	*O'Day*	Dawn	*Actress*
Shute	Neville	*Norway*	Neville	*Author*
Shuttleworth	John	*Fellows*	Graham	*Singer and Songwriter*
Signoret	Simone	*Kaminker*	Henriette Charlotte	*Actress*
Sills	Beverly	*Silverman*	Belle	*Musician*
Silverheels	Jay	*Smith*	Harold J	*Actor*
Simone	Nina	*Wayman*	Eunice	*Singer*
Sioux	Siouxsie	*Dallion*	Susan	*Singer*
Siren		*Paton*	Alison	*TV Gladiator*
Sitting Bull		*Iyotanka*	Tatanka	*Sioux Hunkpapa Chief*
Skinner	Frank	*Collins*	Chris	*Comedian*
Slater	Christian	*Hawkins*	Christian	*Actor*
Soul	David	*Solberg*	David	*Actor*
Spiderman		*Parker*	Peter	*Fictional Superhero*
Springfield	Dusty	*O'Brien*	Mary	*Singer*
Stack	Robert	*Modini*	Robert	*Actor*

Assumed Name		Original Name		
Staff	Kathy	Higginbottom	Minnie	Actress
Stalin	Joseph	Dzhugashvili	Iosif Vissarionovich	Russian Leader
Stanislavsky		Alexeyev Sergeivitch	Konstantin	Actor
Stanley	Henry Morton	Rowlands	John	Explorer
Stanwyck	Barbara	Stevens	Ruby	Actress
Stardust	Alvin	Jewry	Bernard	Singer
Starr	Edwin	Hatcher	Charles	Singer
Starr	Ringo	Starkey	Richard	Drummer and Composer
Statto		Loughran	Angus	TV Soccer Pundit
Steele	Tommy	Hicks	Thomas	Entertainer
Stendhal		Beyle	Marie-Henri	Author
Stepniak		Kravchinski	Sergei Mikhailovich	Russian Revolutionary
Stevens	Cat	Georgiou	Stephen	Singer
Stevens	Connie	Ingolia	Concetta	Actress
Stevens	Inger	Stengland	Inger	Actress
Stevens	Shakin'	Barrett	Michael	Singer
Stewart	Ed	Mainwaring	Edward Stewart	Disc Jockey
Sting		Sumner	Gordon	Vocalist and Musician
Stone	Irving	Tennenbaum	Irving	US Novelist
Stoppard	Miriam	Stern	Miriam	Broadcaster
Stoppard	Tom	Straussler	Thomas	Dramatist
Stratas	Teresa	Strataki	Anastasia	Soprano
Strummer	Joe	Mellor	John	Rock Star
Sturges	Preston	Biden	Edmund Preston	Writer and Director
Styrene	Poly	Elliot	Marion	Punk-Rock Singer
Suggs		McPherson	Graham	Singer (Madness)
Sumac	Yma	Chavarri	Emperatriz	Musician
Summer	Donna	Gaines	Donna Andrea	Singer
Summers	Ann	Gold	Jacqueline	Businesswoman
Sundance Kid		Longabaugh	Henry	Outlaw
Swanson	Gloria	Svensson	Gloria	Actress
Sylva	Carmen	Elizabeth	of Romania	Queen of Romania
T	T	Tureaud	Lawrence	Actor
Tanfucio	Neri	Fucini	Renato	Italian Writer
Tati	Jacques	Tatischeff	Jacques	Actor
Tauber	Richard	Seiffert	Ernst	Austrian Tenor
Taylor	Elizabeth	Coles	Elizabeth	Novelist
Taylor	Robert	Brough	Spangler	Actor
Tenzin Gyatso		Tsering	Lhamo Thondup	14th Dalai Lama
Theresa	Mother	Bojaxhiu	Agnes Gonxha	Roman Catholic Nun
Thomas	Terry	Stevens	Terry	Comedy Actor
Thumb	Tom	Stratton	Charles	Circus Performer
Tich		Amey	Ian	Guitarist
Tich	Little	Relph	Harry	Comedian
Tilley	Vesta	Powles	Matilda Alice	Male Impersonator
Tim	Tiny	Khaury	Herbert	Singer
Tintoretto		Robusti	Jacopo	Artist
Titmarsh	Michael Angelo	Thackeray	William Makepeace	Author
Tito		Broz	Josip	Yugoslav Leader
Todd	Mike	Goldenburger	Avron	Producer
Trog		Fawkes	Walter Ernest	Cartoonist and Clarinettist
Trotsky	Leon	Bronstein	Lev Davidovitch	Russian Revolutionary
Tucker	Richard	Ticker	Reuben	Singer
Tucker	Sophie	Abruza	Sophie	Music Hall Singer
Tuesday	Gayle	Gilhooly	Brenda	Comedienne
Turner	Tina	Bullock	Annie Mae	Singer
Twain	Mark	Clemens	Samuel Langhorne	Author
Twain	Shania	Edwards	Eileen Regina	Pop Singer
Twiggy		Hornby	Leslie	Model and Actress
Twitty	Conway	Jenkins	Harold Lloyd	Singer
Tyler	Bonnie	Sullivan (née Hopkins)	Gaynor	Singer
Uncle Remus		Harris	Joel Chandler	Author
Undertaker		Calloway	Mark	Wrestler
Vadim	Roger	Plemiannikov	Roger Vadim	Film Director
Valens	Ritchie	Valenzuela	Ritchie	Singer
Valentino	Rudolph	D'Antonguolla	Rudolpho	Actor
Valli	Frankie	Castellucio	Frank	Singer
Van Damme	Jean-Claude	Van Varenberg	Jean-Claude	Actor

Vanilla Ice		*Winkle*	Robert van	*Rapper and Actor*
Vaughan	Frankie	*Abelsohn*	Frank	*Singer*
Vaughan	Peter	*Ohm*	Peter	*Actor*
Vee	Bobby	*Velline*	Robert Thomas	*Singer*
Vegas	Johnny	*Pennington*	Michael	*Comedian*
Verdy	Violette	*Guillerm*	Nelly	*French Dancer*
Veronese	Paolo	*Caliari*	Paolo	*Venetian Painter*
Vicious	Sid	*Ritchie*	John	*Singer*
Villa	Pancho	*Arango*	Doroteo	*Mexican Patriot*
Villeneuve	Justin	*Davies*	Nigel	*Hair Stylist*
Vincent	Gene	*Craddock*	Eugene Vincent	*Singer*
Vine	Barbara	*Rendell*	Ruth	*Novelist*
Vivekananda	Swami	*Dutt*	Narendranath	*Hindu Missionary*
Voltaire		*Arouet*	François-Marie	*Philosopher*
Wall	Max	*Lorimer*	Maxwell George	*Actor and Comedian*
Ward	Artemus	*Browne*	Charles Farrar	*Writer and Humorist*
Warlock	Peter	*Heseltine*	Philip Arnold	*Composer*
Warner	Jack	*Waters*	Jack	*Actor*
Warner	Jack Leonard	*Eichelbaum*	Jack Leonard	*Film Mogul*
Warrior		*Aherne*	Michael	*TV Gladiator*
Warwick	Richard	*Winter*	Richard	*Actor*
Waters	Muddy	*Morganfield*	McKinley	*Singer*
Wayne	John	*Morrison*	Marion	*Actor*
Weathercock	Janus	*Wainewright*	Thomas Griffiths	*Art Critic and Murderer*
Webb	Clifton	*Hollenbeck*	Webb Parmalee	*Actor*
Welch	Bruce	*Cripps*	Bruce	*Guitarist*
Welch	Raquel	*Tejada*	Raquel	*Actress*
Weldon	Fay	*Birkinshaw*	Franklin	*Writer*
Wellthorpe	Edna	*Orton*	Joe	*Dramatist (as Fictional Letter Writer)*
West	Nigel	*Allason*	Rupert	*MP and Author*
West	Rebecca	*Fairfield*	Cicely Isabel	*Author*
Westmacott	Mary	*Christie*	Agatha	*Author (as Romantic Novelist)*
Wharton	Edith	*Jones*	Edith	*Author*
White	Colonel	*Gray*	Charles	*Fictional TV Character*
Widow		*Sisson*	Richard	*Musical act 'Kit and the Widow'*
Wilde	Kim	*Smith*	Kim	*Singer*
Wilde	Marty	*Smith*	Reginald	*Singer*
Wilder	Gene	*Silberman*	Jerome	*Actor*
Windsor	Barbara	*Deeks*	Barbara	*Actress*
Winters	Bernie	*Weinstein*	Bernie	*Comedian*
Winters	Shelley	*Schrift*	Shirley	*Actress*
Wise	Ernie	*Wiseman*	Ernest	*Comedian*
Wolf	Howling	*Burnett*	Chester Arthur	*Singer and Composer*
Wonder	Stevie	*Judkins*	Steveland	*Singer and Composer*
Wood	Mrs Henry	*Price*	Ellen	*English Novelist*
Wood	Natalie	*Gurdin*	Natasha	*Actress*
Worth	Harry	*Illingworth*	Harry	*Comedian*
Wylie	Gerald	*Barker*	Ronnie	*Writer*
Wyman	Bill	*Perks*	William	*Musician*
Wyman	Jane	*Faulks*	Sarah Jane	*Actress*
Wymark	Patrick	*Cheeseman*	Patrick	*Actor*
Wynette	Tammy	*Pugh*	Wynette	*Singer*
Wyngarde	Peter	*Goldbert*	Cyril Louis	*Actor*
X	Malcolm	*Little*	Malcolm	*Civil Rights Leader*
Yates	Dornford	*Mercer*	Cecil William	*Novelist*
York	Michael	*Johnson*	Mike	*Actor*
York	Susannah	*Fletcher*	Susannah	*Actress*
Youens	Bernard	*Popley*	Bernard	*Actor*
Young	Gig	*Barr*	Byron	*Actor*
Young	Jimmy	*Young*	Leslie Ronald	*Broadcaster*
Zadora	Pia	*Schipani*	Pia	*Actress*

NB: The area of pseudonyms is a veritable minefield for misinformation and errors, and although an attempt has been made to verify as many entries as possible it is inevitable that there will be doubt relating to some entries. To give an example of the intricacies that make an infallible list almost impossible to compile, many sources refer to Marlene Dietrich's original name as Von Losch, this is only partly true, as in fact her original name was Dietrich and only changed to von Losch when her mother remarried after the death of her father.

Where a person has more than one pseudonym an attempt has been made to place them in order of usage, for example, the wrestler Giant Haystacks was born Martin Ruane but initially fought under the name Luke McMasters and indeed is credited in the 1984 film, *Give My Regards to Broad Street*, under that name.

The format of the tables are basically surnames followed by Christian names, but where the person is titled or is known by just a single name, then the familiar name is in the left-hand box. This is not meant to be a fully comprehensive listing, as it would be possible to fill this whole book with pseudonyms and pen-names, but it is hoped that all the more common ones and a few less known but interesting ones are present. There is a small overlap between this section and the nicknames section as some of the entries warrant inclusion in both, because a nickname is sometimes adopted as the most famous title of a person.

Relationships

NB: Relations appear in alphabetical order within each category.
The relationship given is that of the second column to the first.

Arthur Conan Doyle	EW Hornung	*Brother-in-law*
Stanley Baldwin	Rudyard Kipling	*Cousin*
Richard Briers	Terry-Thomas	*Cousin*
George Clooney	Miguel Ferrer	*Cousin*
Elizabeth I	Mary Queen of Scots	*Cousin*
King George V	Kaiser Wilhelm II	*Cousin*
Christopher Lee	Ian Fleming	*Cousin*
Patrick McNee	David Niven	*Cousin*
Kate Robbins	Paul McCartney	*Cousin*
Ginger Rogers	Rita Hayworth	*Cousin*
Franklin D Roosevelt	Theodore Roosevelt	*5th cousin*
Herbert H Asquith	Violet Bonham-Carter	*Daughter*
Ingrid Bergman	Isabella Rossellini	*Daughter*
Vera Brittain	Shirley Williams	*Daughter*
William Jennings Bryan	Ruth Rohde	*Daughter*
Blythe Danner	Gwyneth Paltrow	*Daughter*
Debbie Reynolds and Eddie Fisher	Carrie Fisher	*Daughter*
Judy Garland	Lorna Luft	*Daughter*
	Liza Minnelli	*Daughter*
Jeremy Hawk	Belinda Lang	*Daughter*
Tippi Hedren	Melanie Griffith	*Daughter*
Helios & Perse	Circe	*Daughter*
Roger Kemble	Sarah Siddons	*Daughter*
King Agenor and Queen Telephassa	Europa	*Daughter*
King Cepheus and Queen Cassiopeia	Andromeda	*Daughter*
King Priam and Queen Hecuba	Cassandra	*Daughter*
Phyllida Law	Sophie Thompson	*Daughter*
	Emma Thompson	*Daughter*
Lord Longford	Lady Antonia Fraser	*Daughter*
Mary of Guise and James V	Mary Queen of Scots	*Daughter*
Arthur Miller	Rebecca Miller	*Daughter*
Thomas Moore	Margaret Roper	*Daughter*
Muhammad	Fatima	*Daughter*
Jawaharlal Nehru	Indira Gandhi	*Daughter*
Nanette Newman	Emma Forbes	*Daughter*
Tsar Nicholas II	Anastasia	*Daughter*
Oedipus and Jocasta	Antigone	*Daughter*
Ravi Shankar	Norah Jones	*Daughter*
Maureen O'Sullivan	Mia Farrow	*Daughter*
Jon Voight	Angelina Jolie	*Daughter*
Zeus and Leda	Helen and Clytemnestra	*Daughters*
Zeus and Metis	Athene	*Daughter*
Zeus and Themis	Clotho (one of the 3 Fates)	*Daughter*
Emmeline Pankhurst	Christabel and Sylvia	*Daughters*
Sigmund Freud	Clement and Lucian	*Grandsons*
Genghis Khan	Kublai Khan	*Grandson*
Herbert Beerbohm Tree	Oliver Reed	*Grandson*
Josiah Wedgwood	Charles Darwin	*Grandson*
Queen Victoria	Queen Elizabeth II	*Great-great-grand-daughter*
Queen Victoria	Duke of Edinburgh	*Great-great-grandson*
Bonnie Bedelia	Macaulay Culkin	*Nephew*
Rosemary Clooney	George Clooney	*Nephew*
Francis Ford Coppola	Nicolas Cage	*Nephew*
Lord Salisbury	Arthur Balfour	*Nephew*
Carol Reed	Oliver Reed	*Nephew*

FAMOUS PEOPLE

Ellen Terry	John Gielgud	*Nephew*
Circe	Medea	*Niece*
Sarah Siddons	Fanny Kemble	*Niece*
Echidna and Typhon	Cerberus, Chimaera, Hydra	*Offspring*
Poseidon and Medusa	Pegasus	*Offspring*
Dana Andrews	Steve Forrest	*Sibling*
Thomas Arne	Susanna Cibber	*Sibling*
Balarama	Krishna	*Sibling*
Warren Beatty	Shirley Maclaine	*Sibling*
David Broome	Liz Edgar	*Sibling*
Duggie Brown	Lynn Perrie	*Sibling*
Keith Chegwin	Janice Long	*Sibling*
Catherine Deneuve	Françoise Dorléac	*Sibling*
Margaret Drabble	AS Byatt	*Sibling*
Adila Fachiri (violinist)	Jelly Arányi (violinist)	*Sibling*
Marty Feldman	Fenella Fielding	*Sibling*
Joan Fontaine	Olivia de Havilland	*Sibling*
Lady Antonia Fraser	Rachel Billington	*Sibling*
Crystal Gayle	Loretta Lynn	*Sibling*
Graham Greene	Hugh Carleton Greene	*Sibling*
Michael Hamburger (poet)	Paul Hamlyn (publisher)	*Sibling*
Hannibal	Hasdrubal	*Sibling*
Eden Kane	Peter and Robin Sarstedt	*Siblings*
John Kemble	Sarah Siddons	*Sibling*
Jimmy Logan	Annie Ross	*Sibling*
Lord Rothermere	Lord Northcliffe	*Sibling*
Paul McCartney	Mike McGear	*Sibling*
John Mills	Annette Mills	*Sibling*
Liza Minnelli	Lorna Luft	*Sibling*
Gary Oldman	Laila Morse	*Sibling*
River Phoenix	Leaf, Rainbow, Summer, Liberty	*Siblings*
Brian Rix	Sheila Mercier	*Sibling*
Kate Robbins	Ted Robbins	*Sibling*
Eric Roberts	Julia Roberts	*Sibling*
Georhe Sanders	Tom Conway	*Sibling*
Julia Sawalha	Nadia Sawalha	*Sibling*
Talia Shire	Francis Ford Coppola	*Sibling*
Tanita Tikaram	Ramon Tikaram	*Sibling*
Jack Warner	Ethel and Doris Waters	*Siblings*
Virginia Woolf	Vanessa Bell	*Sibling*
Aeacus and Endeis	Peleus	*Son*
Anu and Ki	Enki and Enlil	*Sons*
Ares and Aphrodite	Eros	*Son*
Atreus and Aerope	Agamemnon	*Son*
David Carradine and Barbara Hershey	Free (changed to Tom)	*Son*
Charles Martel	Pepin the Short	*Son*
Cleopatra and Julius Caesar	Caesarion (Ptolemy XV)	*Son*
Cecil Day-Lewis and Jill Balcon	Daniel Day-Lewis	*Son*
Elizabeth and Zacharias	John the Baptist	*Son*
Erebos and Nyx	Charon	*Son*
Eric the Red	Leif Eriksson	*Son*
Indira Gandhi	Rajiv Gandhi	*Son*
Hamilcar	Hannibal	*Son*
Helios and Clymene	Phaethon	*Son*
Iapetus and Clymene	Prometheus, Atlas, Epimetheus, Menoetius	*Sons*
Jenny Jerome	Winston Churchill	*Son*
Jupiter and Latona	Apollo	*Son*
Rosa Kaufman (pianist)	Boris Pasternak	*Son*
King Agenor and Queen Telephassa	Cadmus	*Son*
King Glaucus and Queen Eurynome	Bellerophon	*Son*
King Laius and Queen Jocasta	Oedipus	*Son*
Mary Martin	Larry Hagman	*Son*
Mary Queen of Scots	James VI (Scotland) I (England)	*Son*
Osiris and Nephthys	Anubis	*Son*
Norrie Paramour	John Paramour (golf director)	*Son*
Peleus and Thetis	Achilles	*Son*
Pepin the Short	Charlemagne	*Son*
Priam and Hecuba of Troy	Paris	*Son*
Martin Sheen	Emilio Estevez and Charlie Sheen	*Sons*

Ellen Terry and EW Godwin	Edward Gordon Craig	*Son*
Suzanne Valadon	Maurice Utrillo	*Son*
Zebedee	St John	*Son*
Zeus and Danaë	Perseus	*Son*
Zeus and Leda	Castor, Polydeuces	*Sons*
Zeus and Leto	Apollo	*Son*
De Mille, Cecil B	Anthony Quinn	*Son-in-law*
Franz Liszt	Richard Wagner	*Son-in-law*
Thomas Mann	WH Auden	*Son-in-law*
Arthur Miller	Daniel Day Lewis	*Son-in-law*
Eugene O'Neill	Charlie Chaplin	*Son-in-law*
Peter Vaughan	Gregor Fisher	*Son-in-law*

Crime and Punishment

Dr John Bodkin Adams (1899–1983)   Physician who was tried in 1957 after one of his patients, Edith Morrell, died suspiciously. Like other elderly patients before her, Edith had made Adams a beneficiary of her will before dying by morphine overdose. On acquittal Adams was struck off but continued to treat private patients and was in fact reinstated by the General Medical Council in 1961. Whether he merely practised euthanasia or killed for personal gain will never be proven and the secret died with him.

Susan Barber (1956–)   In May 1981 Susan Barber placed half a teaspoonful of weedkiller in her husband Michael's steak-and-kidney pie after he caught her in bed with her lover and threw him out of the window. Michael Barber was diagnosed with Goodpasture's syndrome, a rare nervous condition, but died shortly after. The cause of death was recorded as pneumonia and kidney failure. His wife gained £15,000 from her husband's pension fund and set up home with her defenestrated lover, Richard Collins. David Evans, the pathologist who conducted the post mortem, began to have a few doubts and sent organs from Barber's body to ICI, the manufacturers of the weedkiller Gramoxone, and sure enough, traces of the poison were detected. Barber and Collins were arrested in April 1982 and he was sentenced to two years imprisonment for conspiracy while Susan Barber was jailed for life.

Anne Bonny (1692–?)   Irish pirate who lived in the early 18th century. Anne showed her fiery temper at an early age and is thought to have killed a servant girl with a case-knife. She was disinherited by her lawyer father and sailed to the Bahamas with her husband, the cause of the disinheritance. Bonny fell in with Captain John Rackham, the notorious Calico Jack, and sailed with him disguised as a man. Bizarrely enough another member of Jack's crew was Mary Read, who was also sailing under the guise of a man, and an amusing incident whereby Read tried to seduce Bonny proved to be the unveiling of both. In October 1720 Calico Jack's ship, *The Revenge*, was captured by a sloop on the orders of the governor of Jamaica and Jack was hung and Read and Bonny imprisoned. Mary Read died of a fever but Bonny managed to escape and her whereabouts remained a mystery.

Charles Bronson (1952–)   Born Michael Gordon Peterson and first imprisoned in 1974 for robbing a jeweller of £35, but his aggressive behaviour has added an extra 25 years to his sentences and he has experienced only a total of 69 days of freedom since then. Bronson has shown some ability as a cartoonist and poet. He married Miss Saira Rehman in June 2001 at Woodhill Prison and Lord Longford was best man.

Burke and Hare   William Burke (1792–1829) and William Hare (1790–c1860) met at Logue's lodging house, Edinburgh, in 1818. Sharing the same building was an army pensioner known as Old Donald, who died in 1827 owing Hare £4. Burke and Hare opened his coffin and substituted a sack of bark for his body and sold it for £7 10/- to Dr Robert Knox of Edinburgh's Anatomy School. Over the next 10 months Dr Knox became a regular customer of the pair, who at first produced a legitimate supply of corpses, but then began to create their own by foul means. Burke's common-law wife, Helen McDougal, or Hare's, Maggie Laird, would lure a victim back to the lodgings and then ply them with drink, Burke would then kneel on their chest, while stopping their breathing by placing his hands over their nose and mouth. This method became known as 'burking'. Victims included Mary Paterson, a local prostitute, and a local idiot called Daft Jamie, both of whose murders were suspected by Knox, who remained quiet. Eventually they slipped up by leaving the body of Margaret Docherty where other lodgers could find it. Hare and Laird escaped prosecution by turning King's evidence and the case against McDougal was unproven, but Burke was publicly hanged on 28 January 1829.

Capital punishment   Relevant dates in the history of capital punishment in Britain are as follows: In 1868 public execution was abolished, Michael Barrett (26 May) being the last victim. On 13 July 1955 Ruth Ellis was the last woman to be hanged in Britain. On 13 August 1964 Peter Anthony Allen and Gwynne Owen Evans were the last victims of a British hanging. On 9 November 1965 the death penalty was suspended for a trial period of five years, but in December 1969 Parliament confirmed the permanent abolition.

Mary Ann Cotton (1832–73)   District nurse from West Auckland, County Durham, who killed at least five people including her second husband Frederick, his two stepsons, and two lovers, a local excise officer named Quick-Manning and her lodger Joseph Natrass. She was suspected of killing many more, possibly 30. Her motive was invariably either to collect insurance money or to pave the way for a new liaison. Her chosen method of disposal was arsenic. She was eventually tried and sentenced to death in 1873. The hangman bungled the execution, causing her to take three and a half minutes to stop convulsing before dying at the rope's end.

Dr Hawley Harvey Crippen (1862–1910)   Crippen, a patent medicine salesman and physician, poisoned his second wife, Cora Turner, a would-be music-hall artiste working under the name of Belle Elmore, after becoming infatuated with his young secretary Ethel Le Neve. After the murder at their home at 39 Hilltop Crescent, Islington, North London, Ethel, who was privy to the murder, became anxious of its detection so the couple fled to Canada aboard the SS *Montrose* under the names of Mr Robinson and his son (Ethel). The ship's captain became suspicious and contacted Scotland Yard by radio telegraphy and the couple were arrested. The case was famous for being the first example of a successful conviction by use of radio. Crippen was tried for murder at the Old Bailey on 18 October 1910, found guilty and hanged at Pentonville on 23 November. Neve was tried separately but ably defended by FE Smith and acquitted. She lived till 1967.

DNA   DNA provides the building blocks of life – the unique gene code that makes us what we are. In 1985, Sir Alec Jeffreys developed the system, first discovered by Crick and Watson in 1953, so that police could take an individual's genetic 'fingerprint' to establish guilt. Colin Pitchfork was the first person to be convicted using DNA evidence when he was jailed for life in 1988 for murdering two schoolgirls. Pitchfork murdered 15-year-old Lynda Mann in 1983 in Narborough, Leicestershire. Three years later he killed Dawn Ashworth, also 15. A 17-year-old confessed to killing Dawn, but a DNA test proved his innocence, and the screening of 5,000 locals showed Pitchfork to be the culprit. DNA has also been used retrospectively, and James Hanratty, hanged for murdering civil servant Michael Gregston and raping and maiming his mistress, is the most famous example. Hanratty hijacked the couple in their car off the A6 in Berkshire, then attacked them near Bedford. He denied the crime, and family members battled for 40 years to prove his innocence, but his body was exhumed in 2001 and DNA tests proved his guilt.

Ruth Ellis (1927–55)   Model and nightclub manageress, Ellis shot and killed her lover, racing driver David Blakely, outside the Magdala public house in Hampstead on Good Friday 1955. She was tried and convicted at the Old Bailey in June and hanged at Holloway prison on 13 July 1955, the last woman to be hanged in England.

John George Haigh (1910–49)   Whilst living in a small hotel in Kensington, Haigh became friendly with Olive Durand-Deacon, a wealthy 69-year-old widow, who told him of her ideas for the marketing of cosmetics. Haigh invited her to his factory in Crawley, West Sussex, where she was shot and her body disposed of in a vat of sulphuric acid. On 20 February 1949 he then presented himself at Chelsea police station and reported her missing. Police became suspicious and checked his factory where they found the murder weapon and Mrs Durand-Dickson's plastic dentures. Haigh made a statement admitting to eight other murders, including three members of a family called McSwann, a Dr and Mrs Henderson and three other people whose identities he had never established. He was tried at Lewes Crown Court in July 1949 and was executed at Wandsworth Prison on 10 August 1949.

Hangmen   The most famous British public executioner was probably Albert Pierrepoint, who notched up 700 victims before his retirement. Albert died in 1982, leaving Syd Dernley as the last hangman to die since hanging was abolished.

Dernley aided in the execution of 20 criminals between 1949 and 1953 but was removed from the register in 1954. He died in 1994. William Calcraft (1800–79) was the last to perform in public as hangings were held in prisons after 1868. James Berry (1852–1913) is probably the second most famous hangman after Albert Pierrepoint, although John Ellis became a celebrity after becoming the executioner of Dr Crippen and Sir Roger Casement. Ellis (1874–1926) was haunted by the aftermath of his career and eventually cut his own throat with a barber's razor. Other famous hangmen include Richard Arnett (1674–1728), Edward Dennis (1717–86), Jack Ketch, byname of John Ketch (d.1686), the Billington family, James (1847–1901), Thomas (1872–1902), William (1873–1934) and John (1880–1905), William Marwood (1820–83), George Smith (1805–74), Henry Pierrepoint (1874–1922) and Thomas Pierrepoint (1870–1954).

Jack the Ripper   Unknown murderer of five prostitutes between August and November 1888 in Whitechapel, London. The five unfortunate victims were Mary Ann 'Polly' Nichols (42), Dark Annie Chapman (47), Elizabeth 'Long Liz' Stride (45), Catharine 'Kate Kelly' Eddowes (43) and Mary Jane Kelly (25). The inspector who initially investigated the murders was George Frederick Abberline (1843–1929).

William Kidd (1645–1701)   Originally a respected sea captain in New York when hired by a Whig syndicate in 1695 as a government- commissioned privateer authorised to seize pirates, freebooters and sea-rovers in the name of the British government, Kidd decided to turn pirate himself. During an angry exchange with a crew member in 1697 he shot and killed his gunner, William Moore. On 9 May 1701 Kidd was found guilty of the murder of Moore and on five indictments of piracy. He was hanged immediately at Execution Dock, Wapping. Unfortunately for Kidd the rope broke the first time, he fell to the ground in his drunken state, and had to be strung up a a second time.

Kray Twins   Reggie Kray (1933–2000) and his twin brother Ronnie (1933–95) established a grip on the criminal underworld in the 1960s through their protection rackets and frauds. They opened a club, the Double R, in Bow Road, east London, which soon became popular with a showbiz clientele. Ronnie, a closet homosexual, was the dominant twin, and earned the nickname 'The Colonel', Reggie had more of a business brain. In 1965 Reggie married Frances Shea, but she committed suicide in 1967. The Firm, as they became known, became increasingly involved in hostilities with Charlie Richardson's south London gang, and they arranged the escape from Dartmoor of Frank Mitchell, the so-called Mad Axeman, whose murder they subsequently ordered. On 8 March 1966 Ronnie Kray shot dead George Cornell, a Richardson henchman, in the Blind Beggar public house on the Mile End Road. Cornell's offence had been to call Ronnie 'a fat poof'. In October 1966 Reggie Kray fatally stabbed a small-time thief called Jack 'the Hat' McVitie in a borrowed flat in Stoke Newington. Jack's crime had apparently been to show disrespect to the boys by wearing Bermuda shorts in one of their clubs. Detective Superintendent Leonard 'Nipper' Read eventually established a case against the twins and they were brought to trial at the Old Bailey in January 1969, after a member of the 'Firm', Albert Donaghue, had turned Queen's evidence. They were acquitted of the

Mitchell murder but were convicted of murdering Cornell and McVitie.

Lord Lucan (1934–?)   John Bingham, the 7th Earl of Lucan, an inveterate gambler and merchant banker, inherited a quarter of a million pounds on the death of his father. By 1974 he was almost bankrupt. On the night of 7 November 1974 he killed Sandra Rivett, the nanny of his two children, in his house in Lower Belgrave Street, London, in mistake for his wife Veronica. After attacking his wife too, but failing to kill her, he drove to the house of his friend, Susan Maxwell-Scott, at Uckfield in Sussex. His car was discovered at Newhaven but he was never seen again.

Donald Merrett (1910–54)   At the age of 17 Merrett murdered his mother for the price of a motor bicycle. Twenty-five years later, and now calling himself Ronald Chesney, he murdered his wife and her mother. The first murder was in 1927, and although he claimed she shot herself in the neck, it became apparent over the course of her surviving 15 days that he murdered her for money, as he repeatedly forged her cheques during this period. He was charged with murder and forgery after her death, but due to the defence testimony of the eminent pathologist Bernard Spilsbury, who was appearing for the only time as a defence witness, was acquitted and served only twelve months on the forgery charge. On his release Merrett changed his name to Ronald Chesney and lived a life of petty crime until in 1954 he called on his wife, whom he had married when first released from prison, and knocked her out with drink before drowning her in the bath. He also killed her mother, who had intercepted him on leaving the house. He flew back to Germany but had been seen at the scene of the crime, an old people's home in Ealing, and before Interpol could arrest him he shot himself in the head in a wood near Cologne. Before he died he confessed to his German girlfriend that his real name was Donald Merrett and that when he was 17 he had killed his mother.

Moors Murderers   On 28 October 1965, Ian Brady, a 27-year-old stock-clerk, and Myra Hindley, a 23-year-old typist, were charged with the murder of ten-year-old Lesley Ann Downey at Chester Assizes. Lesley's body was found on Saddleworth Moor 13 days earlier. Police were subsequently alerted by a call from Hindley's brother-in-law, David Smith, who had witnessed the killing of 17-year-old Edward Evans with an axe. Police searched Brady's house and found Evans's body in a blanket. The police subsequently found a left-luggage ticket in Hindley's prayer book which led them to a suitcase containing tapes and pornographic photographs, one of which showed Hindley posing with a dog at what turned out to be the grave of a third murdered child, John Kilbride, aged 12. On 6 May, 1966, Brady was sentenced to three concurrent terms of life imprisonment for the murders of all three children while Hindley received two concurrent life sentences for the murders of Edward Evans and Lesley Ann Downey. Hindley died of lung cancer on 15 November 2002.

Charles Peace (1832–79)   Born in Manchester, the son of an animal trainer, Peace suffered an accident in childhood that left him crippled. To hide the loss of one finger he wore a false arm made of gutta-percha with a steel plate and a hook at the end of it. In 1876 he shot and killed a policeman whilst burgling a house. Two brothers were arrested for the murder and Peace attended the trial at which one of them,

William Habron, was sentenced to death. Peace's next victim was a Mr Dyson, whose wife had formed a loose liaison with Peace, although it was to soon become a stalking situation. As a result of this murder, Peace became a wanted man and moved to London, where he rented a villa in Peckham. He now changed his name to John Ward and lived with his wife and his mistress, Susan Thompson, maintaining his lifestyle by a series of burglaries that he would attend in his pony and trap, carrying his tools in a violin case. He was eventually caught after wounding a policeman in Blackheath. He was sentenced to life imprisonment for wounding the policeman and then taken to Sheffield to stand trial for the murder of Arthur Dyson. On the way to Sheffield he managed to escape from the train, but was injured in the fall and was soon recaptured. He was tried for murder at Leeds assizes, found guilty and hanged by William Marwood after being refused a last drink. William Habron was released with a full pardon and awarded £1,000 compensation.

Peter Reyn-Bardt (1919–93)   In May 1983 two peat-cutters working at Lindow Moss, near Wilmslow, Cheshire, dug up the skull of a middle-aged woman. Police reported the find to Peter Reyn-Bardt, a former executive with BOAC, whose wife Malika had disappeared in 1960, and under interrogation he confessed to her murder. He had strangled his wife, chopped up her body and buried the remains in the peat bog. He was tried and found guilty at Chester Crown Court and sentenced to life imprisonment. Subsequently the skull was sent to Oxford University for radiocarbon dating and was found to be dated *circa* 410 AD. The following year another skeleton was found in the bog with more obvious evidence of a violent death. However, this one turned out to be the remains of a man who had been killed in a ritualistic death circa 300 BC. The whereabouts of Mrs Reyn-Bardt's body remain a mystery.

Harold Shipman   Harold Frederick Shipman studied at Leeds University medical school and eventually achieved a mediocre degree. His mother had died of lung cancer in June 1963 and it is believed it was seeing her daily morphine administered by the local GP that led to his compulsion to set himself up as an angel of mercy, albeit in some cases for personal gain. Shipman married his fiancée Primrose and took up his first practice in 1974 at the age of 28 in the small Yorkshire town of Todmorden. In 1975 a suspicious receptionist, Marjorie Walker, noticed some peculiar entries in the controlled substances ledger of a local pharmacist whereby large quantities of pethidine, a morphine-based painkiller had been ordered by Dr Shipman. His explanation was that he was injecting the drug himself and he was fined £600 and booked into a drug rehabilitation centre without being struck off. In 1977 Shipman began working at the Donneybrook Medical Centre in Hyde, Manchester, and proceeded to rebuild his career. Despite doubts by several people over the years it was not until the death of Mrs Grundy, an 81-year-old former mayor of Hyde, on 24 June 1998, that questions were asked by Mrs Grundy's daughter Angela Woodruff, a solicitor by profession. Mrs Grundy had made a will in 1986 and lodged it with her daughter's law firm but now she was asked to believe that her mother had made another one without her knowledge and left £386,000 to Dr Shipman. Detective Superintendent Bernard Postles investigated and on reviewing the will came to the conclusion that Kathleen Grundy's signature had been forged and began to build a solid case against

Shipman with the help of several interested parties who now came forward and expressed their own doubts about him. His trial began in October 1999 at Preston Crown Court and on 31 January 2000 Shipman was found guilty of 15 counts of murder. The Department of Health estimates that Shipman may have killed 236 patients between 1974 and 1998.

George Joseph Smith (1872–1915)   Perpetrator of the Brides in the Bath Murders. In 1898 Smith married 19-year-old Beatrice Thornhill, his only legal wife. In 1910 he met and bigamously married Bessie Mundy in Weymouth calling himself Henry Williams. He eventually murdered Bessie by drowning her in a tin bath and attesting that she had a fit and drowned by misadventure. Smith subsequently gained from a trust fund set up in Bessie's name. He then bigamously married Alice Burnham in Southsea in November 1913 and then 'married' Margaret Lofty, a clergyman's daughter at Bath in 1914. In both cases he took his wives to the doctors before dispatching them, to show that they suffered from fits. A newspaper report of Margaret Lofty's death was seen by Alice Burnham's father, who alerted the police. The police soon realised that Smith was a murderer, and with the help of Bernard Spilsbury he was tried and found guilty, sentenced to death and hanged at Maidstone Prison on Friday 13 August 1915.

Peter Sutcliffe   Between 1975 and 1980 Sutcliffe murdered 13 women in the north of England. Many of his victims were prostitutes and were invariably banged over the head with a ball-pein hammer before being stabbed and mutilated. He was eventually caught during a routine check when he was found in a car with a prostitute. He asked the police if he could relieve himself and unknown to them at the time he hid his murder weapons behind an oil storage tank. The police ran a routine check on his car and found it had false plates. Sutcliffe was arrested and while in custody was found to be on the list of possible suspects. Sutcliffe, now nicknamed the Yorkshire Ripper, made a full confession and on 22 May 1981 was sentenced to life imprisonment. He began his sentence at Parkhurst but after being attacked was transferred to Broadmoor High Security Mental Institution, where he resides today.

FASHION AND DRESS

General Information

aba Loose gown worn in the Muslim world.

agal fillet of two or three cords used to fasten a keffiyeh on the head.

Agnès B Born Agnès Troublé in Versailles, France, 1941, she worked as a junior editor on *Elle* magazine before opening her first boutique. Her style is characterised by precise tailoring, simple subdued colours, usually black, natural materials and casual looks. In 1987 she launched her 'Le B' perfume range and a maternity collection.

aigrette Spray of gems worn on the head.

Alaia, Azzedine Tunisian designer who was a leading light throughout the 1980s but is experiencing a revival with his merger with Prada.

alb Long, white linen vestment with sleeves, usually worn by priests.

alpargata Light canvas shoe with a plaited fibre sole; an espadrille.

amice Rectangular piece of white linen worn by priests around the neck and shoulders under the alb, or formerly, on the head. Also a furred hood with long ends hanging down in front.

Amies, Sir Hardy (1909–2003) Queen's dressmaker for 50 years. Amies showed his first collection in 1946 and remained at the top of his profession until his death.

Armani, Giorgio Italian fashion designer based in Milan and New York. Armani opened his first fashion house in 1974 and, although well respected within his industry, rose to fame after dressing Richard Gere in the 1980 film *American Gigolo.*

Ashley, Laura Born in Merthyr Tydfil, South Wales (1925–85) as Laura Mountney. Married Bernard Ashley in 1949 and started a business manufacturing furnishing materials and wallpaper with patterns based upon document sources mainly from the 19th century. After giving up work to start a family she experimented with designing and making clothes, and this transformed the business into an international chain of boutiques, selling clothes, furnishing fabrics and wallpapers.

astrakhan wool Obtained from the Karakul breed of sheep.

babouche Turkish or oriental heelless slipper.

babushka Headscarf tied under the chin and worn by Russian peasant women.

Badgley Mischka American designers Mark Badgley and James Mischka. The duo are best known for their stellar beaded creations and 'aged look'. Their material is made in Italy and embroidered in Bombay, India.

balbriggan Knitted, unbleached cotton fabric, from which underwear is often made.

baldric Wide silk sash or leather belt worn over the opposite shoulder to the hip, for carrying a sword.

Balenciaga, Cristobal Spanish fashion designer (1895–1972) opened the House of Balenciaga in Paris, 1937, and retired in 1968.

Balmain, Pierre French fashion designer (1914–82) famous for his elegant simplicity. Immortalised by Peter Sarstedt in 'Where do you go to my lovely'.

Balmoral Can be a laced walking shoe, a woollen petticoat, a Scottish brimless hat, traditionally made of dark blue wool with a cockade and plume, a cloak, a jacket or mantle – all these styles set by Queen Victoria and Prince Albert in the 1850s and 60s.

bandanna Square of silk or cotton with spotted pattern, tied round the head or neck.

Banks, Jeff Born in Wales, 1943, became widely known in the mid 70s when he launched the 'Warehouse' chain. Presenter of the first dedicated television fashion programme, *The Clothes Show.*

banyan Loose-fitting shirt or jacket originally worn in India.

batiste Fine plain-weave cotton or linen fabric, used for shirts and dresses.

batwing sleeve Sleeve of a garment with a deep armhole and tight wrist.

bauchle General term for an old, worn shoe.

Bebe Top international brand name for designer shoes as in the name of their stores.

Benetton Fashion empire based in Treviso, Italy and identified with its sponsorship of rugby, basketball and volleyball but especially Formula One racing team.

Biba founder Barbara Hulanicki.

biggin Plain, close-fitting cap, often tied under the chin, popular in 16th and 17th centuries based on coif-like caps worn by the Béguines lay sisters.

bijouterie Costume jewellery or trinkets, particularly finger-rings, from which the name derives.

bikini designer Louis Réard.

Bikkembergs, Dirk Born in Cologne, Germany, 1959, of Belgian extraction, first came to prominence as a shoe designer before establishing himself as a top ready-to-wear designer. Along with Ann Demeulemeester, Dirk Van Saene, Walter Van Beirendonck, Dries Van Noten, and Martin Margiela, one of the so-called Anvers 'Group of Six'.

billycock Any of several round-crowned brimmed hats of felt, named after William Coke, for whom it was first made in the 19th century.

biretta Stiff clerical cap with either three or four upright pieces projecting outwards from the centre to the edge, coloured black for priests, purple for bishops, red for cardinals and white for certain members of religious orders.

Blahnik, Manolo Born in the Canary Islands of a Spanish mother and Czech father, Blahnik is a British-based designer of fashion shoes.

Bloomers Named after, and designed by Amelia Jenks Bloomer (1818–94), a New York campaigner for temperance and women's rights. Bloomers were originally the full-length Turkish trousers worn under a skirt in the 1850s, but evolved firstly into a knickerbock style, and made popular by lady cyclists in the 1890s, and subsequently into any loose-fitting ladies baggy undergarments.

boa Woman's long round scarf, usually of feathers or fur.

bodkin Blunt, large-eyed needle used for drawing tape through openwork, also a pin used in ancient times to fasten women's hair.

Body Shop founder Anita Roddick.

bolero Short jacket, just reaching the waist, as worn

by men in Spain; also a woman's short, open jacket, with or without sleeves.

bonnet rouge   Red cap worn by ardent supporters of the French Revolution.

bowler   Hard felt hat with a rounded crown and a narrow curled brim, named after William Bowler in the US who designed it in 1850; in the US, a derby.

breeks   Scottish name for breeches.

British warm   Army officer's full-length, thick overcoat.

brogue (1)   Rough shoe of untanned hide, formerly worn in Ireland but now having ornamental perforated bands and worn throughout the world.

brogue (2)   Waterproof leggings with feet, used by anglers.

buckram   Originally a fine cotton or linen fabric stiffened with size, later used in lining or stiffening clothes as well as bookbinding.

Bui, Barbara   French fashion designer best known for her clean lines and offbeat femininity that combines various cultural and ethnic influences. Daughter of a French mother and Vietnamese father, Bui first came to prominence when opening her 'Kabuki' boutique in the 1980s with her actor husband William Halimi. In 1998 she started her 'BB Initials' line and more recently has started a line in designer shoes.

buibui   Piece of black cloth worn as a shawl by Muslim women, especially on the North African coast.

bumfreezer   Short jacket ; also a slang name for an Eton jacket.

Burberry   Drapery business opened in Basingstoke, Hampshire, England, in 1865 by 21-year old Thomas Burberry, producing waterproof garbardine raincoats. Since 1988 has enjoyed success with its youthful collections.

burlap   Coarse fabric woven from jute or hemp.

burnous   Arab or Moorish hooded cloak, now worn as a fashion accessory in the Western world.

busby   Tall, fur helmet with a bag hanging from the top to the right side as worn by certain soldiers, usually hussars; it is also another name for a bearskin.

buskin   Originally, a thick-soled boot worn by tragic actors in ancient Athenian theatre; now a half-boot.

bustle   Pad or frame worn to puff out the top of a woman's skirt at the back.

Busuuti   Long garment with short sleeves and square neckline, as worn by Ugandan women.

cagoule   Thin-hooded outer jacket, especially one that is windproof and waterproof, and worn by mountaineers and others following outdoor pursuits.

calash (also calèche)   Woman's folding, hooped hood, worn in 18th century.

calico   White or unbleached cotton fabric with no printed design (originally from 'Calicut, on the Malabar coast,' a town in India).

calotte   Skullcap worn by Roman Catholic clergy.

cambric   Originally a fine white linen fabric of the late Tudor and early Stuart period and imported from the French town of Cambrai. The lightness of the material made it popular as a decorative accompaniment to dress as ruffs, cuffs, bands and handkerchiefs. Modern cambric is made from high-quality American or Egyptian cotton and is identified with good-quality underwear.

camisole   Woman's under-bodice with shoulder straps, originally designed as a cover for a corset.

capote   Long cloak or soldier's coat, usually with a hood; also a kind of 19th-century bonnet.

capuchin   Woman's cloak and hood resembling the dress of a Capuchin friar.

casque   Piece of armour to cover the head; a helmet.

castor   Hat made of beaver fur.

Cerruti   Founded in 1881 in Biella, Milan, by Antonio Cerruti as a fabric mill company, Cerruti became fashionable when Nino Cerruti, grandson of the founder developed the business into a ready-to-wear fashion house in 1957 when he opened 'Hitman' in Milan. In 1967 Nino opened 'Cerruti 1881', a men's couture house in the centre of Paris and soon established an international reputation. In 1976 Cerruti developed a women's ready-to-wear market and is now established in all aspects of haute couture.

cestus (1)   Pugilist's gauntlet of bull's hide loaded or studded with metal.

cestus (2)   Girdle, named after the girdle of Aphrodite.

chador/chuddar   Large shawl or veil worn by Muslim or Hindu women that covers them from head to foot.

Chanel, Coco   French fashion designer (1883–1971), worked as a milliner until 1912 and following service as a nurse during World War I, opened a couture house in Paris. She revolutionised women's fashions during the 1920s, her designs including the 'chemise' dress, the collarless cardigan jacket, and the 'little black dress'. Her designer perfume Chanel No. 5 became the ultimate status symbol. Chanel retired in 1938 but made a successful comeback in 1954 and her innovations such as the vogue for costume jewellery and the evening scarf have maintained their popularity.

Ch'ao-fu   Pre-modern Chinese man's robe with kimono-style upper body with long, close-fitting sleeves that terminated in the horse-hoof cuff introduced by the Manchus, and a closely-fitted neckband over which was worn a detached collar with wing-like tips that extended over the shoulders. The lower body consisted of a full, pleated skirt with a banded waist. Colours were dependent on rank.

chaplet   Ornamental wreath of flowers or beads worn on the head. Also a precious metal circlet, possibly set with gems.

chaps   protective leather trousers worn by American cowboys. The name comes from the Mexican 'chaparejos'.

chasuble   Long, sleeveless outer vestment worn by a priest when celebrating Mass.

chemise   Woman's loose-fitting undergarment or dress hanging straight from the shoulders.

cheongsam   Woman's garment with high neck and slit skirt, worn in China.

chiffon (1)   Light, diaphanous, plain-woven fabric of silk or nylon.

chiffon (2)   Trimmings or other adornments on a woman's dress.

chi-fu   Straight, kimono-sleeved robe, alternatively called lung-p'ao 'dragon robes', worn formally by both sexes in China under the Manchu empire.

chignon   Arrangement of long hair in a roll or knot at the back of the head.

ch'ima   Korean pleated skirt, as worn by women from the 15th century onward.

chintz   Brightly patterned cotton fabric with glazed finish (from a Hindi word that indicates a spatter or stain).

chiton Long tunic worn in ancient Greece made of wool, linen or cotton.

chlamys Short woollen cloak worn mostly by men in Ancient Greece.

choga Loose Afghan garment with long sleeves.

chōgori Traditional Korean jacket.

choli Short-sleeved blouse worn under a sari.

clinquant Imitation gold leaf worn as a fashion accessory.

cloche Woman's close-fitting bell-shaped hat.

Clothes Show BBC television programme that ran from 1985–8. Its presenters included Jeff Banks, Brenda Emmanus, Caryn Franklin, Tim Vincent and Margherita Taylor.

Coach Leading brand name in the field of luxury customised handbags for all occasions.

codpiece Bagged appendage to the fork of a man's breeches or close-fitting hose.

coif Close-fitting cap, worn under a veil in the Middle Ages or under a chainmail hood and tied under the chin with strings, now worn only by nuns.

coiffeur Professional hair-stylist.

coli Short-sleeved breast-length jacket, usually worn by Muslim women over a ghaghra.

Cook, Emma British designer who graduated in St Martins and like her classmates Stella McCartney and Alexander McQueen has become a leading light of the fashion industry. Formerly a consultant with Ghost, she is now freelance.

combinations One-piece woollen undergarment with long sleeves and legs; known in the USA as a union suit.

cote hardie Medieval close-fitting sleeved tunic, when worn by men long enough to cover the buttocks and belted around the hips; when worn by women, full-length and often unbelted..

cowl A cap or hood especially on a monk's habit.

Cox, Patrick Born in Canada, 1963, as a student he designed shoes for Vivian Westwood, Body Map and later for John Galliano. Cox introduced his own label 1987 and his fleurs-de-lys-logo is a sign of elegant fashion and quirky design.

cracowe Long pointed shoe named after the Polish city of Cracow (Kraków). It is thought that the marriage of Richard II of England to Anne of Bohemia in 1382 was responsible for the fashion in England.

cravat A scarf of silk or fine wool, worn round the neck, especially by men. Cravats were popularised by Croats in the French army during the Thirty Years' War and the name is a corruption of Croat.

crinoline In the 1830s a stiff fabric made of horsehair and cotton or linen thread, used for linings, hats and skirts. Later a petticoat with steel hoops worn under a skirt to make it stand out from the body in a bell-shape.

cuisse Piece of armour for the front of the thigh.

culottes Woman's breeches that hang like a skirt but have separate legs.

cymar (also simar, cimarra) Woman's loose gown, popular in the 17th and 18th centuries.

dalmatica Wide-sleeved, tunic-like vestment, open at the sides, worn by deacons and bishops. Originally worn by Roman noblemen from the 2nd century on and made of white Dalmatian wool.

damask Richly figured woven material, originally of silk, with a pattern visible on either side. It originated in Damascus in Syria.

dashiki Loose brightly coloured shirt worn in West Africa and also in the USA.

décolleté Low-cut neckline.

deerstalker Cloth cap, peaked in front and behind, with earflaps that are usually tied up on the top.

De La Renta, Oscar Born in the Dominican Republic, 1932, but became a naturalised American in the 1960s. He started his own company in 1965 with a reputation for opulent, ornately trimmed clothes, particularly evening dresses. In 1993 he became the first American to design for a French couture house, Pierre Balmain.

denim Originally serge de Nîmes (named from Nîmes, in France), now a twilled, hard-wearing, cotton fabric used for jeans.

dernier cri Latest fashion ('last cry').

dhoti Loincloth worn by male Hindus. The ends are passed between the legs and tucked in at the waist.

Dinnigan, Collette Born in South Africa to an Irish father and South African mother, she was brought up in New Zealand and after completing her education, emigrated to Australia. She started her own label in 1990 and in 1995 became the first Australian to have a full-scale ready-to-wear parade in Paris.

Dior, Christian French fashion designer (1905–57). Founded his fashion house in 1945 and achieved worldwide fame with his long-skirted 'New Look' of 1947. His later designs included the 'H' line and the 'A' line.

dirndl Dress in the style of an Alpine female peasant costume, with close-fitting bodice and full skirt.

Dolce & Gabbana Founded in Milan in 1982 by Domenico Dolce, a shy bearded Sicilian, and the Venetian Stefano Gabbana. Throughout the 1990s they have expanded their operations into menswear and a popular youth line. A further division of their operations has created a White Line for day-to-day basics, and a Black Line for fantasy goods.

Dolly Varden Woman's large hat, named after a Dickens' character in *Barnaby Rudge*; also a flowered dress.

dolman (1) Long Turkish robe, open in the front and with narrow sleeves.

dolman (2) Hussar's jacket worn with the sleeves hanging loose.

dolman (3) Woman's mantle with dolman sleeves.

dolman sleeve Loose sleeve made in one piece with the body of a coat; it has a wide armhole but a tight wrist.

domino (1) Large, hooded cloak, worn with an eye mask at a masquerade.

domino (2) The eye mask worn at masquerades.

Donna Karan Born in New York as Donna Faske in 1948, she began her career as a designer for Anne Klein and subsequently took control on her death in 1974. Karan eventually began her own company with second husband Stephen Weis.

doublet Close-fitting body garment with or without sleeves and a short skir, worn by men from the medieval times to the 17th century.

duchesse Soft, heavy kind of satin; also a type of chaise longue.

dundreary Long sidewhiskers worn without a beard, named after Lord Dundreary, a character in Tom Taylor's comedy (1858).

dungaree Coarse cotton fabric used chiefly for work clothes from a Hindi word.

durzi An Indian tailor.

Emanuels David, born 1952, and Elizabeth, born 1953, launched their label in 1975 but split up in the

FASHION AND DRESS

1990s. Their most famous creation was the wedding dress of Diana, Princess of Wales. Co-authors of *Style for all Seasons*.

Erotokritos Cyprus-born, Paris-based fashion designer who launched his own label in 1994 and since his first Paris show in 1996 has built a reputation for chic yet casual clothing.

Eton jacket Waist-length jacket with a V-shaped back, open in the front, formerly worn by pupils of Eton College.

Etro Italian company that specialises in selling extraordinary crafted, brightly coloured paisley (Etro's hallmark), foulard and brocade ties and vests, as well as finely tailored suits. Gimno Etro is the head of the empire and his three sons, Ippolito, Jacopo and Kean, are directors.

Farhi, Nicole French-born Algerian designer known for her luxurious and sensual woman's collections. She opened her first store in 1983 as part of a Harvey Nichols and in 1984 opened a boutique in New York. Farhi's home shop is in Clifford Street London.

farji Long, gown-like coat with short sleeves, made of wool or cotton (silk is forbidden to men by the Koran), as worn by Muslim priests or high officials.

farthingale Framework of hoops, or a hooped petticoat, used the 15th to 17th century to extend the skirts of a woman's dress.

Fendi Established in Rome, 1918, as a leather and fur workshop by Adele Casagrande (d. 1978). The named changed in 1925 when Adele married Edoardo Fendi. Since the death of Edoardo in 1954 the company has being run by his five daughters, Alda, Anna, Carla, Franca and Paola, although a controlling interest is now shared by Prada and Louis Vuitton. Karl Lagerfeld has designed the Fendi fur collection since 1962.

Ferré, Gianfranco Born in Legnano, Italy, 1944, he formed the Gianfranco Ferré company in 1978 with business partner Franco Mattioli. Unusually, Ferré has maintained a popularity in all aspects of the fashion industry, having had successful women's, men's and children's clothing lines and fragrances.

fez rimless felt or woollen cap, cylindrical in shape, usually red and with a tassel, usually worn by men in Muslim coutries and formerly the national head-dress of Turkey.

fichu Woman's small triangular shawl of lace for the shoulders and neck. Late 18th to late 19th century.

filibeg / philibeg Kilt worn by Scottish Highlanders.

finnesko Boot of reindeer skin with the hair on the outside.

forage cap Soldier's undress cap.

Ford, Tom Born in Texas 1962, he rose to prominence when taken on as Creative Director of Gucci and immmediately made an impact. Ford is sometimes known as the 'It' Boy of the fashion world, or more recently the 'King of Cool'. He has often been targeted by animal rights activists for his refusal to stop using fur in his designs.

Franz Josef Long sidewhiskers, merging into a moustache, named in honour of the emperor of Austria.

frippery Originally old or second-hand clothes or tawdry adornment in dress; now means showy.

frog Decorative braided coat-fastening, originally forming part of military dress, consisting of a spindle-shaped button and a loop and a braided loop that retains it.

furisode Long-sleeved outer kimono traditionally worn by young, unmarried Japanese girls (married women wearing the short-sleeved kimono known as a kosode).

gabardine Raincoat made from a smooth, durable, twill-woven cloth of worsted or cotton; also a long loose cloak.

gaberdine Twill-weave worsted, cotton, or spun-rayon fabric.

Galliano, John British fashion designer currently head of the Dior fashion empire.

galligaskins Loose, wide breeches or hose, especially as worn by men in the 16th and 17th centuries; also the leather leggings worn in the 19th century.

gallus Trouser braces of a type worn in the USA, where braces are called suspenders.

galosh Originally a clog, or wooden sole attached to a shoe, but now an overshoe, usually made of rubber or plastic.

Garroudi, Pierre Born in Tehran, Iran, 1959, and educated in Paris. He moved to New York in 1986 and opened his own fashion house in 1993. His designs are daring and innovative and his shows are erotic, witty and provocative.

georgette Thin silk or crêpe dress material, named after Georgette de la Plante, a French dressmaker.

gewgaw Worthless piece of frippery worn to be showy.

ghāghrā Open-fronted pleated skirt, as worn by Muslim women.

Ghost Tanya Sarne's 'Ghost' is well know for its trademark garment-dyed vintage-look viscose and ultra feminine garments. Its clothes are created by women for women.

Gibbs, Bill Scottish fashion designer (1943–88), launched his own label in 1971 in partnership with Kate Franklin. Inspired by the vast diversity and volume of ethnic costume as well as Scottish Highland dress. His signature motif was the bee (B for Bill).

Gibson girl Young woman typifying the fashionable ideal of around 1900, as represented in the work of Charles Dana Gibson (1867–1944) US artist.

gilet Waist-length, sleeveless garment, usually quilted and fastened up the front, designed to be worn over a blouse and often worn as part of a ballet dancer's costume. Gilet literally means waistcoat in French.

gingham Plain-woven cotton cloth, especially striped or checked (literally means 'striped' in Malay).

gipon Close-fitting padded tunic, buttoned down the front, the sleeves long enough to cover the knuckles, the neck round and low. Originally worn under medieval body armour.

Givenchy, Hubert Born in Beauvais, France, 1927, Hubert Givenchy opened his own house in 1952, producing ready-to-wear clothes under his Nouvelle Boutique label.

Gladstone bag A light portmanteau opening into two equal compartments and named after the British Prime Minister who carried such a bag.

Glengarry Brimless Scottish hat with a cleft down the centre and two ribbons hanging down the back, chiefly worn as part of Highland dress.

gorget (1) Collar-like piece of armour worn to protect the throat.

gorget (2) Part of a wimple worn by women to cover

the neck and shoulders, especially in the late Middle Ages.

greave   Piece of armour protecting the leg below the knee.

Gucci, Guccio   Italian fashion designer (1881–1953) born in Florence. He opened his first shop in Florence, 1920, and became known for his leather craftsmanship and accessories. His four sons joined the firm and in 1953 the first overseas shop opened in New York. The empire has had several corporate identities and after Gucci's grandson Maurizio's (1949–95) presidency from 1989 to 1993, the company was sold to the multinational Investcorp.

habergeon   Sleeveless coat of mail.

haik   Large cloak, usually white, worn by both sexes in North Africa.

hakama   Very full men's trousers, as worn in Japan from the 7th century onwards.

Hartnell, Sir Norman (1901–78)   Born in London and educated at Magdalene College, Cambridge. Started his own couturier business in 1923 and received the Royal Warrant in 1940. He was president of the Incorporated Society of London Fashion Designers (1946–56) and became famous for designing costumes for leading actresses of the day and Princess Elizabeth's Wedding and Coronation gowns.

hauberk   Piece of defensive armour, for neck and shoulders at first, but soon developed into a long mail shirt or military tunic.

haute couture   High fashion, literally 'high dressmaking'; collectively the leading dressmakers and fashion houses or their products.

Hermès   Founded in 1837 by Thierry Hermès, the world-famous fashion house began life as a manufacturer of equestrian accessories such as saddles, riding boots and bridles. The present regime is headed by Jean-Louis Dumas, the fifth family successor to the Hermès empire. The current head designer is Martin Margiela, who has expanded the repertoire into his trademark camel coats and grunge apparel but the reputation of Hermès is built upon the success of their silk scarf and handbag market. The 'Kelly' bag, as popularised by Grace Kelly, is still a bestseller.

himation   Outer garment worn over the left shoulder, and under the right, in ancient Greece.

hitatare   The formal court dress of a Samurai.

hobble skirt   Skirt so narrow at the hem as to impede walking; introduced before World War I

Holland   Smooth hard-wearing linen fabric.

Homburg   Man's felt hat with a narrow curled brim and a lengthwise dent in the crown.

houppelande   Medieval tunic or gown worn by both sexes, with full sleeves and long train, belted at the waist. The collar was high, often with a dagged edge.

imperial   Pointed tuft of whiskers on the chin, named in honour of Napoleon III (Emperor of France 1852–70).

isar   Wide trousers, usually worn by Muslim men under the jāmah.

Jacobs, Marc   Artistic director at Louis Vuitton since 1987 and now known as a leading designer in his own right. His colourful mat finishes in a 1960s style have become popular with celebrities and actress Winona Ryder was accused of shoplifting for Marc Jacob's designs.

Jacquard   Method of weaving a design directly into the fabric instead of being printed or dyed on. The piece of apparatus used for this type of weave is called a Jacquard loom, after its French inventor Joseph M Jacquard (1752–1834).

jāmah   Long-sleeved coat that reaches to, or below, the knees and has a belted waist; as worn by Muslim men.

jeans inventor   Levi Strauss.

Jimmy Choo   Born in 1961, his label was founded in 1996 in partnership with Tamara Yeardye and Sandra Choi, who is the Creative Director and designer of their popular fashion shoes which are affectionately known as 'Jimmys'.

Joseph   Founded by Joseph Ettedgui, born 1935, a highly influential retailer who provides a showcase for top designers

Jon, Anand   Indian fashion designer whose 'functional luxury' style is currently en vogue.

Juliet cap   Small net ornamental cap worn by brides etc.

Jungle Jap shops   Opened by Kenzo Takada in 1970.

juni hitoe   Japanese noblewoman's full court costume meaning 'twelve layer' but possibly with more.

karaginu   Outermost garment of the juni hitoe, consisting of a wide-sleeved jacket reaching only to the waist.

keffiyeh   Bedouin Arab's kerchief or larger square of wool cotton or linen worn as a headdress and held in place by an agal.

kebaya (1)   Light loose tunic of a type worn in SE Asia by both sexes.

kebaya (2)   Short tight-fitting long-sleeved jacket, together with a sarong the traditional dress of Malay and Indonesian women.

Kenzo   Popular name of Kenzo Takada, Japanese fashion designer, born in Kyoto. He had small success in his home country before moving to Paris and producing freelance collections in 1964. His Jungle Jap shop built his reputation as an innovator and his creations blend Oriental and Western influences with traditional designs. Kenzo is also a trendsetter in the field of knitwear.

képi   French military cap with a circular top and a horizontal peak.

kimono   A Japanese loose sashed ankle-length garment with wide sleeves. Literally means wear thing.

kirtle   Old English name for a woman's skirt or dress; also the name of a man's tunic or coat, usually reaching to the knees.

Klein, Anne   Native New Yorker Anne Klein made her name when setting up her company in 1968 and introducing a sporty element into US fashion. Following her death in 1974, Donna Karan and Louis Dell'Olio continued as co-designers and Dell'Olio remains the head designer and the overseer of the company's latest manifestation, Anne Klein II.

Klein, Calvin   Born in New York, USA, in 1942. Opened his first store in 1968 in partnership with long-time friend and businessman Barry Schwartz. The simple but sophisticated style of his clothes soon gained him recognition and this became universal when actress Brooke Shields modelled his designer jeans in the late 1970s. Klein popularised designer men's underwear in 1982 and following the success of his fragrances, Obsession, Eternity and Escape, his CK One became the first of the unisex fragrances.

F
A
S
H
I
O
N

A
N
D

D
R
E
S
S

knickerbockers Short, loose-fitting trousers gathered in at the knee or calf. Named after Diedrich Knickerbocker, fictitious author of a *History of New York* actually written by Washington Irving (1783–1859).

Lacroix, Christian Born in 1951, the French fashion designer opened the House of Lacroix in Paris, 1987, and specialises in ornate and frivolous designs.

Lagerfeld, Karl Born in 1939, Lagerfeld has been head of Chanel since 1983 and was previously chief designer of Chloe from 1963–84.

Lang, Helmut Born in Vienna, Austria, 1956, Lang has become a pioneer in many areas of the fashion industry. He is known for his use of techno fabrics, minimalism and deconstructionism.

La Perla Founded by Ada Masotti in Italy, 1954, and known for high-quality and luxurious, intimate apparel. Pioneered the wearing of bodysuits as outerwear, and sleepwear as casual clothes.

Laroche, Guy French fashion designer (1923–89), born in La Rochelle. He worked in millinery, first in Paris, then New York, before returning to Paris to start his own company. By 1961 he was producing both couture and ready-to-wear clothes. From 1966 his designs included menswear.

leghorn Hat made of fine plaited straw.

leg-of-mutton sleeve Sleeve which is full and loose on the upper arm but close-fitting on the forearm.

lei Polynesian garland made of flowers, feathers or shells; often given as a symbol of affection.

leotard Close-fitting one-piece garment named after Jules Léotard, a French trapeze artist (1830–70).

Levi's Proprietary name for a type of blue denim jeans, produced by Levi Strauss as working clothes in the 1860s.

Liripipe / Liripoop In medieval times, the extended tail of a hood which could be as much as five or six feet long; also a medieval slang name for a shoelace.

Louis Vuitton Founded in 1854 by luggage manufacturer Louis Vuitton Malletier, the label has become the most imitated of all top fashion houses. The reputation was founded on their luxurious leather bags, often using exotic leathers such as alligator, ostrich and lizard. In March 1987 Marc Jacobs became the artistic director.

mantelet / mantlet Women's short, loose, sleeveless cloak.

mantilla Light scarf, often made from black lace, worn over the head and shoulders, especially by Spanish women.

mantua Woman's loose gown of the 17th and 18th centuries. So spelled after an Italian city but originally from French manteau.

Marocain Dress fabric of ribbed crêpe.

McCartney, Stella Born in 1971, the daughter of Sir Paul McCartney, currently chief designer of the Chloe fashion house.

McQueen, Alexander Chief designer of the Givenchy fashion house and a contemporary of Emma Cook and Stella McCartney.

mignonette Light, fine, narrow lace used for trimming.

Missoni Founded in Gallarate, Varese, Italy, 1953, by Ottavio Missoni and his wife Rosita (née Jelmeni). The Missoni label, created in 1958, is known for its fluidity and colour of its creations, which have an affinity to art.

mitra / mitre (1) Headband worn by women in ancient Greece.

mitra / mitre (2) Tall Asian head-dress, regarded by the Romans as effeminate when worn by men; the ceremonial turban of a high priest. Also the deeply-cleft head-dress worn in the Christian Church by a bishop or abbot, especially as a symbol of episcopal office, forming in outline the shape of a pointed arch, and often made of embroidered white linen or satin.

Miyake, Issey Japanese fashion designer born in Hiroshima in 1938. His distinctive style combines Eastern and Western influences in his loose-fitting garments which have a theatrical quality to them by the use of dramatic asymmetric outline and varied textures.

mo Women's pleated train, part of the formal court costume established in Japan by the time of the 8th century.

mob cap Large indoor cap covering all the hair, worn by women in 18th and 19th centuries.

moccasin Soft leather shoe, originally worn by Native Americans.

Monmouth Flat, round cap formerly worn by soldiers and sailors.

Montana, Claude Began his career in London with the Carnaby Street movement, where he designed jewellery made from large coloured stones embedded in papier mâché. On his return to Paris he became popular for his designer leather outfits and his 1976 show at the Angelina tea rooms in Paris caught the imagination of the fashion industry.

Montera / montero Spanish peaked travelling cap with a spherical crown and flaps for lowering over the ears;also the black hat worn by bullfighters.

muff Soft insulated covering, cylindrical, into which both hands may be thrusted at opposite ends to keep warm.

mutch Woman's or child's linen cap.

mutton chops Sidewhiskers narrow at the top and broad and rounded at the bottom.

muu-muu Woman's loose, brightly coloured dress from Hawaii.

Naga-Bakama Japanese formal undergarment made of a stiff red cloth and fastened high up under the breast and covering the feet at the front but extending out to a train at the back.

napery Household linen, especially table linen.

New Look Christian Dior's 1947 creation of women's dress with narrow shoulders and long, full skirts.

Norfolk jacket Man's loose belted sporting jacket with box pleats.

Nutter, Tommy Welsh fashion designer (1943–92), revolutionised menswear by introducing high fashion to Savile Row in 1969, funded by pop singer Cilla Black.

nylons Stockings or tights made from a synthetic polymeric amid. The process was invented by Wallace Carothers in the 1930s and named after New York and London.

Oldfield, Bruce Born in 1950, launched his own label in 1975. Famous for his pretty and glamorous evening wear.

Oxfords Can be a type of shoe, shirt, or trousers (Oxford bags).

Ozbek, Rifat Turkish-born, 1953, British fashion designer who bizarrely first came to prominence for his extraordinary resemblance to Diana Vreeland. His transposing of ethnically inspired clothes into a modern context such as Indonesian Ikat patterns printed on slinky lycra tube skirts, and his opulent Oriental brocades woven into the English gentleman's tailcoats are trademark Ozbek creations.

paji   Traditional Korean trousers.

palisado   During the reign of Elizabeth, women wore their hair turned back from the forehead over a pad or a wire known as a palisado.

palla   Loose outer garment or outdoor wrap, usually worn by women in ancient Rome and Byzantium.

pallium (1)   Man's large rectangular outdoor cloak worn in ancient Rome.

pallium (2)   Woollen vestment conferred by the Pope on an archbishop, consisting of a narrow circular band worn round the shoulders with a short flap hanging from front and back.

Panama   Hat made originally from the plaited leaves of the jipijapa plant of Ecuador.

pannier   Framework, used to extend and support the skirt of a woman's dress in the late 17th and 18th centuries, and usually made from osier reeds or whalebone.

parure   Matching set of jewels designed to be worn together.

pashmina   A cashmere shawl made from pashm, the underfur of various Tibetan animals, but especially the goat.

patten   Shoe or clog with a raised sole, or set on an iron ring, for walking over mud or on uneven ground.

pauldron   Piece of shoulder armour.

pea-jacket   Sailor's short, double-breasted overcoat of coarse dark blue cloth, also pilot or reefer jacket.

pelerine   Woman's narrow cape with long, pointed ends in front (literally means 'pilgrim'); 18th and 19th century.

peplos   Half- or full-length loose outer robe often two lengths of fabric pinned at the shoulders worn by women in ancient Greece.

perizoma   Short pants worn by athletes in ancient Greece.

Perrin, Christina   New York-based designer of Swedish extraction. Popular in the late 1990s for her silhouettes in distinctive fabrications, avant-garde use of leather and fur, and her unusual tailoring and richness of colour.

Persian lamb   Silky, tightly curled fur of a breed of lamb called a Karakul, used in clothing.

peruke   Kind of wig worn in Europe from 1660 to 1800. A skullcap covered with hair at first imitating the natural hair of the head, later often much more elaborate and imposing (also periwig, perruque).

petasos   Low-crowned, wide-brimmed hat of ancient Greece, often with a cord which allowed it to be slung over the wearer's back when the weather permitted.

Petersham (1)   Thick, corded, silk ribbon used for stiffening in dressmaking.

Petersham (2)   A heavy overcoat or the rough cloth (usually dark blue) from which it was made.

petticoat   Woman's undergarment, but also, in Elizabethan times, a small coat worn by men under the doublet.

Piccadilly Weepers   Long sidewhiskers, worn without a beard.

pickelhaube   German soldier's spiked helmet.

pileus   Brimless, close-fitting felt cap, worn in ancient Greece; a similar cap was called a pilos.

pillbox   A small cylindrical hat worn at the back of the head and popularised by Jacqueline Kennedy in the 1960s.

pinking shears   Dressmaker's serrated shears for cutting a zigzag edge.

pith helmet   Light sun-helmet made of the dried pith of the sola plant.

plus-fours   Men's baggy knickerbockers reaching below the knee, now only worn for hunting or golf.

Poiret, Paul   French couturier (1879–1944), the most fashionable dress designer of pre-war Paris, and designer of the hobble skirt.

poleyn   Piece of armour for the knee.

poor boy   Type of pullover.

Prada   Since the mid 1990s there have been few status symbols as potent as the Prada-embossed silver triangle. Prada began life as a family-run leather goods business in Milan but enjoyed the patronage of a growing number of celebrities. The Prada empire has been run since 1978 by Patrizio Bertelli and his wife Miuccia Prada, the grand-daughter of the founder. In 1992 a youth-targeted 'Miu Miu' line was introduced as well as a 'Granello' and 'Prada Sport' range. Miuccia Prada has won critical praise for her innovative experiments in both fabric design and use of colour and her businessman husband equal praise for his shrewd purchasing of large share-holdings of rival operations such as Gucci, Lang, Alaia and Sander.

praetexta   Toga with purple edge, worn by some Roman magistrates and pre-adult boys.

p'u-fu   Three-quarter-length coat worn by men and women in China over their ch'ao-fu or chi-fu.

puggaree (also pagari)   Indian word for a full turban; also a pleated scarf around the crown of some hats, especially sun hats.

puttee (1)   A strip of cloth wound round the leg from ankle to knee as a legging.

puttee (2)   Leather-legging.

Quant, Mary   Born in London, 1934, opened her first boutique in Chelsea in 1955, and married one of her partners, Alexander Plunket Greene. She was the inventor of the mini skirt in the 1960s and hot pants in the early 1970s.

Rabanne, Paco   Born in the Basque area of Spain in 1934, Rabanne's first collection in 1966 entitled 'Twelve Unwearable Dresses' set the scene for his unconventional career. He has designed in plastic, chain metal, fluorescent leather, ostrich feathers, aluminium, paper, laser discs, fibre optic wire, socks and doorknobs.

Ralph Lauren   Born in the Bronx, NY in 1939 as Ralph Lifshitz, Lauren introduced the Polo label in 1967 and became popular following the 1974 film *The Great Gatsby* after many of his designs were worn.

reefer   An overcoat, as worn in North America, often called a gaitor or reefer jacket.

rerebrace   Piece of armour developed to cover the upper arm but later protecting to the shoulder and elbow.

Rhinegraves   Late 17th-century breeches, loose at the knee and wide like shorts, often with frilly embellishments.

Rhodes, Zandra   Born in 1940, first came to prominence when she opened the Fulham Road Clothes Shop in 1967. She is noted for her distinctive exotic designs in floating chiffons and silks.

roquelaure   Man's knee-length cloak with a cape collar, fashionable in the 18th century.

ruff   Decorative frill encircling the neck developed in mid-16th-century Spain and fashionable in Europe, in Jacobean and Elizabethan times. Also a frill around the sleeve of a garment.

sabaton   Piece of armour for the foot.

sabot   Shoe made from a single block of wood; a clog or, in Holland, a klomp.

Saint-Laurent, Yves   Born in Oran, Algeria, 1936, he studied in Paris and joined the House of Dior in 1955 after winning a Wool Secretariat design competition. On Dior's death in 1957 he took over the house. In 1962 he opened his own house and launched the first of his 160 Rive Gauche boutiques in 1966, selling ready-to-wear clothes, a trend that was soon copied by other fashion houses. Saint-Laurent also creates costumes for theatre, ballet, and films, and in 1985 was awarded a Best Fashion Design Oscar.

Sander, Jill   Born in Wesselburen, Germany, 1943, Sander is best known for her long, lean silhouettes. She has brought minimalism in fashion to an art form and superfluous buttons and zips have been banished. The Prada corporation presently own a large shareholding in the Sander fashion empire.

sand-shoe   Light canvas shoe with a rubber sole; a plimsoll.

sari   Traditional garment of Indian women, worn over a choli and an underskirt, consisting of a length of cotton, silk, or other cloth wrapped around the waist and draped over one shoulder.

sarong   Traditional skirtlike garment of the Malay archipelago, Java, and some Pacific islands, consisting of a long strip of cloth worn tucked round the waist or under the armpits by both sexes. Popularised by actress Dorothy Lamour in the 'Road' series of films.

sarong kebaya   Traditional dress of Malay and Indonesian women, consisting of a sarong and a kebaya.

Schiaparelli, Elsa   Italian fashion designer (1896–1973) born in Rome. After studying philosophy she worked as a film scriptwriter in America before venturing to Paris in 1920 and receiving her first order for a black sweater knitted with a white bow, ironically from an American store. Her following designs were innovative and sensational, and she was noted for her use of colour, including 'shocking pink', and also for her outrageous hats and use of zippers and buttons.

seersucker   Material of linen or cotton with a puckered surface.

semmit   An undervest, as worn in Scotland.

serge   Durable woollen or worsted fabric.

shako   Tall, cylindrical, military peaked cap worn with a plume or pompom.

Shilling, David   Born in 1953, from the age of 12 he designed the extravagant headwear made famous by his mother Gertrude at Royal Ascot. Launched his own label in 1975. Author of *Thinking Rich – A Personal Guide to Luxury Living*.

shitagasane   Kimono of white damask, worn under the ho, with an elongated train of up to 12 feet long.

sideburns   Short sidewhiskers, originally called Burnsides, after US Union General Ambrose Everett Burnside (1824–81) who wore them.

Siemens, Crystal   Canadian fashion designer who uses combinations of materials and colour to give an effect of light playing off the fabric.

Simons, Raf   Born in Belgium, 1968, his first show was in Milan in 1995. Subsequent shows in Paris and New York have highlighted his influence by pop culture, particularly David Bowie, and are described by himself as fashion, youth culture, music and performance parades.

skinny rib   Type of pullover.

smock-frock   Loose protective garment of coarse homepin linen or cotton reaching below the knees, traditionally worn by farm labourers before the machine age.

snood (1)   Pouchlike hat, often of net, loosely holding a woman's hair at the back.

snood (2)   Headband, formerly worn by young unmarried women in Scotland.

sokutai   Japanese court costume, exclusively worn by the emperor, with a yellow outer robe (ho) patterned with hō-ō birds and kilin, and baggy white damask trousers (ue-no-hakama).

soup and fish   Men's evening dress.

sou'wester   Waterproof hat with a very broad rim behind, worn especially by seamen.

spat   A short gaiter worn over the instep and reaching a little way above the ankle, worn to keep trousers or stockings clean, especially when riding. Spat is an abbreviation for Spatterdash, although nowadays a distinction is drawn between the fashion accessories.

spatterdash   Long gaiter or legging of leather or cloth, worn to keep trousers or stockings clean.

Stetson   Man's felt slouch hat with a broad brim and high crown, named after John Stetson (1830–1906), the hatter who designed it.

stock   Long white scarf worn with formal riding dress.

stomacher   Originally an ornamental 'V' or 'U' shaped piece of stiff material worn under a man's doublet to cover the chest and stomach. Later, an ornamental triangular panel filling the open front of a woman's dress, covering the breast and stomach, and often jewelled or embroidered.

suberakashi   The elaborate coiffure worn as part of the juni-hitoe, consisting of a lacquered, gold-sprinkled comb surmounted by a gold-lacquered chrysanthemum crest.

Sui, Anna   Born in Detroit, Michigan, USA, 1955, of Chinese extraction. Her baby-doll dresses of the early 1990s became in vogue with the inception of the grunge movement. Her designs are popular with pop musicians and models.

surplice   Loose, white linen vestment with wide sleeves, reaching to the knees or feet and worn over a cassock by clergy and choristers at church services.

surtout   Can be either a man's overcoat or a woman's hooded mantle.

tabard (1)   Coarse outer garment formerly worn by the peasantry or by monks and foot-soldiers.

tabard (2)   Short, open surcoat worn by a knight over his armour and emblazoned with armorial bearings.

taffeta   Fine, lustrous silk with a crisp texture, used for making formal dresses.

tallith   A shawl with fringed corners, traditionally worn by male jews whilst at prayer.

tam-o'-Shanter   Scottish, brimless woollen cap, with a bobble in the centre, usually worn pulled down at one side.

tammy   Glazed woollen or mixed fabric, used for linings or undergarments.

tarboosh   Cap, similar to a fez, usually of red felt with a tassel at the top, worn by Muslim men either alone or as part of a turban.

tasset   Piece of armour for the upper thigh.

tebenna   Forerunner of the Roman toga, as worn in ancient Greece.

tika dot   Mark on the forehead of Hindu women, indicating caste, or worn by both sexes as an ornament.

tiki   An amulet or figurine in the form of a carved representation of an ancestor, worn in some Polynesian cultures.

tippet (1)   In Elizabethan times, a long streamer-like part to a sleeve or hood. Also a woman's fur cape for the shoulders, often consisting of the whole fur of a fox or marten.

tippet (2)   The long stole worn by Anglican clergy during a service.

toga   Loose, flowing outer garment worn by Roman citizens and made of a single piece of cloth covering the whole body except the right arm.

toga virilis   White toga donned as a sign of manhood at the age of 14.

topi   Hat, originally Indian but now a type of pith helmet.

toque (1)   Woman's small, round, brimless hat, popular in Edwardian times.

toque (2)   Hat with a small brim and pouched crown, popular in the 16th century.

toque (3)   Canadian, close-fitting knitted hat, often with a tassel or pompom.

torchon   Coarse bobbin lace with geometrical designs.

toreador pants   Women's close-fitting, calf-length trousers.

trabea   Roman toga ornamented with horizontal purple stripes, worn as a state robe by kings, consuls and other men of rank in ancient Rome.

tricorn   Hat with the brim turned up on three sides.

trilby   Soft felt hat with a narrow brim and indented crown, resembling that worn in the stage version of *Trilby* by the eponymous heroine of George Du Maurier's novel of 1894.

trousseau   Clothes collected by a bride in preparation for her marriage.

turumagi   Traditional Korean overcoat.

Tuscan straw   Fine yellow wheat straw used for hats.

tutu   Ballet dancer's skirt made up of layers of stiffened frills, very short and standing out from the legs.

tutulus   Head-dress formed by plaiting the hair in a cone above the forehead, worn especially by a flamen and his wife.

tuxedo   Dinner jacket, named after Tuxedo Park in New York, site of a country club where the garment was first worn.

tweed   Rough-surfaced woollen cloth of varying texture, usually of mixed flecked colours, originally made in Scotland.

uchikake   Outer kimono, fashionable in the Muromachi period (14th–16th centuries), sometimes with a short-sleeved kimono (kosode), but later (18th century) with a coloured sash (obi) around the waist and bunched at the back.

uwagi   Outer kimono, of rich brocade, under which it is usual to wear a plain purple kimono and generally a third kimono-type robe known as itsutsu-ginu (usually having five bands of coloured silks attached at the sleeves, neckline and hem).

Valentino   Popular name of Valentino Garavani, Italian fashion designer, born in Rome, 1933. He opened his first house in 1959 and achieved universal recognition following his Florence show in 1962.

vambrace   Piece of armour for the arm, especially the forearm.

Van Dyke   Broad, lace or linen collar or neckerchief, with an edge deeply cut into large points, and

fashionable after the life of the painter (d. 1641) until the mid 18th century.

veldskoen   Strong suede or leather shoe or boot of South African origin.

vent   Opening or slit in a garment, especially in the lower edge of the back of a coat or skirt.

Versace, Donatella   Took over as head of the Versace empire following the murder of her brother in 1997. Under the terms of Gianni Versace's will Donatella was left a 20% shareholding, her brother Santo having a 35% shareholding and her daughter Allegra a 45% holding.

Versace, Gianni   Designer shot dead outside his Miami mansion by Andrew Cunanan (15 July 1997).

viyella   Fabric made from a twilled mixture of cotton and wool, named from Via Gellia, a valley in Derbyshire where it was first made.

Vreeland, Diana   Legendary fashion editor (1903–1989) of *Harper's Bazaar* and editor-in-chief of *Vogue*. Much parodied as the epitome of a fashion icon.

Watteau gown   Loose gown, worn over a tight bodice, with long, vertical pleats falling from the shoulders to the ground, popular in the early 18th century and named after costumes depicted by the French artist.

Westwood, Vivienne   Born in 1941, and first came to prominence in 1971 when she began a 13-year collaboration with Malcolm McLaren. She became the first British designer to show in Paris since Mary Quant when her 'Bufalo Collection', based on Peruvian women's fashion, caught the imagination in 1982. She was active in the punk rock fashion of the 1970s and the pioneer of the 'New Romantic' style of the early 1980s. Her designs have included leather bondage gear, latex lounge dresses, flesh-coloured body suits, slashed t-shirts and mink g-strings.

wide-awake   Soft felt hat with a low crown and wide brim.

Williamson, Matthew   Born and educated in London and known for his unique colour sense and exquisite embroidery and beading. His debut collection was in 1997 and his name is synonymous with 'The Karma Kit', a white leather clutch bag complete with leather flower, jasmine flower mist, a peppermint pulse-point balm, incense perfume and a pink travel candle

wimple   Piece of cloth draped around the head to frame the face, worn by women in the Middle Ages and still a part of the habit of some nuns.

winceyette   Lightweight napped flannelette used for nightclothes.

windcheater   Warm jacket, usually with a close-fitting knitted neck, cuffs and waistband.

Wong, Farida   Dress designer who has carved a niche as a high-quality designer of ballroom gowns for both amateurs and professionals.

Xuly Bët   Popular name of Kouyaté Lamine Badian, born in Bamako, Mali, 1962. His Xuly Bët (name means voyeur in his native Wolof dialect) label is identified with cheap and cheerful but quality goods, often recycled but always with an aesthetic quality. Very popular with the French youth culture.

Yamamoto, Yohji   Born in Tokyo, 1943, he is the only Japanese fashion designer to be awarded the French Chevalier de l'Ordre des Arts et Lettres. Apart from his very successful clothing creations he also designs opera costumes and ballet sets.

yarmulka   Skullcap worn by Jewish men.

yashmak   Veil concealing the face, except the eyes, worn by some Muslim women when in public.

FASHION AND DRESS

yukata Cotton kimono, worn by both men and women, formerly after bathing but now as outdoor wear on hot summer evenings.

Zoller, Amy Chicago-based fashion designer originally known for her minimalist silhouettes. Her reputation increased throughout the 1990s and she now has two shows a year in Chicago, Houston, New York and Los Angeles.

zucchetto Skullcap worn by Roman Catholic ecclesiastics: black for priests, purple for bishops, red for cardinals, and white for the Pope.

NB: This section is simply an A–Z of historical costume and dress, plus a few interesting snippets of additional information relating to designers and materials.

Miss World Winners

1951	Kiki Haakonson, Sweden
1952	May Louise Flodin, Sweden
1953	Denise Perrier, France
1954	Antigone Costanda, Egypt
1955	Carmen Zubillaga, Venezuela
1956	Petra Schurmann, Germany
1957	Marita Lindahl, Finland
1958	Penelope Coelen, South Africa
1959	Corine Rottschafer, Holland
1960	Norma Cappagli, Argentina
1961	Rosemarie Frankland, United Kingdom
1962	Catharine Lodders, Holland
1963	Carole Crawford, Jamaica
1964	Ann Sidney, United Kingdom
1965	Lesley Langley, United Kingdom
1966	Reita Faria, India
1967	Madeiline Hartog Bel, Peru
1968	Penelope Plummer, Australia
1969	Eva Reuber Staier, Austria
1970	Jennifer Hosten, Grenada
1971	Lucia Petterle, Brazil
1972	Belinda Green, Australia
1973	Marjorie Wallace, USA
1974	Anneline Kriel, South Africa (Helen Morgan the original winner was disqualified for being a wife and having an illegitimate child.)
1975	Winelia Merced, Puerto Rico
1976	Cindy Breakspeare, Jamaica
1977	Mary Stavin, Sweden
1978	Silvana Suarez, Argentina
1979	Gina Swainson, Bermuda
1980	Kimberly Santos, Guam
1981	Pilin Leon, Venezuela
1982	Mariasela Lebron, Dominican Republic
1983	Sarah Jane Hutt, United Kingdom
1984	Astrid Herrera, Venezuela
1985	Hofi Karlsdottir, Iceland
1986	Giselle Laronde, Trinidad
1987	Ulla Weigerstorfer, Austria
1988	Linda Petursdottir, Iceland
1989	Andeta Kreglicka, Poland
1990	Gina Marie Tolleson, USA
1991	Ninebeth Jiminez, Venezuela
1992	Julia Kourotchkina, Russia
1993	Lisa Hanna, Jamaica
1994	Aishwariya Rai, India
1995	Jacqueline Aquilera, Venezuela
1996	Irene Skliva, Greece
1997	Diana Hayden, India
1998	Linor Abargil, Israel
1999	Yukta Mookhey, India
2000	Priyanka Chopra, India
2001	Agbani Darego, Nigeria
2002	Azra Akin, Turkey

British Hairdressers of the Year

1985	Trevor Sorbie
1986	Trevor Sorbie
1987	Irvine & Rita Rusk
1988	Anthony Mascolo
1989	John Frieda
1990	Anthony Mascolo
1991	Trevor Sorbie
1992	Trevor Sorbie
1993	Andrew Collinge
1994	Nicky Clarke
1995	Anthony Mascolo
1996	Charles Worthington
1997	Andrew Collinge
1998	Charles Worthington
1999	Umberto Giannini
2000	Mark Hill
2001	Beverly Cobella
2002	Beverly Cobella

FOOD AND DRINK

Dishes, Ingredients and Terms

Aemono   Japanes term for a salad; 'dressed things'. A dress aemono may include fish, shellfish and seaweeds, poultry and cooked vegetables or may be made of only one ingredient

Agemono   Japanese culinary term for something deep-fried

Aïoli   Provençal sauce, mayonnaise, seasoned with garlic

Alboni sauce   brown sauce with pine kernels and redcurrants, served with venison

Allumettes   French, vegetables cut into matchstick-sized strips

Armoricaine   in the Breton fashion, with wine, brandy and tomato sauce

Angels on horseback   oysters wrapped in bacon

Antipasto   Italian term meaning 'before the meal', comparable to the French hors d'oeuvres

Artsoppa   Swedish, dried pea soup with ham

Avgolemono   Greek, sauce made with egg and lemon

Babka   Polish bread similar to a fruit cake

Bagna cauda   Italian sauce of garlic, anchovy and olive oil

Baklava   Turkish/Greek filo (Phyllo) pastry filled with nuts (usually walnuts and almonds), honey flavoured

Bannock   Scottish dish of oatmeal, soda and salt usually served with butter, honey or jam

Barquettes   boat-shaped pastry moulds served with assorted fillings (lit. little boats)

Béarnaise   French, egg yolk and butter sauce

Béchamel   French, white sauce flavoured with onion

Beurre, au   French, cooked in butter

Bigarade   French, orange-flavoured sauce served with duck

Biltong   South African, dried meat

Bird's nest soup   Chinese soup, contains saliva of swiftlet

Biryani   Indian dish of pilau rice and meat or fish in spiced gravy

Bisque   creamy soup usually made with sea food and enriched with cream or egg yolks

Black pudding   sausage made of pig's blood and fat with oatmeal and seasoning

Blanquette   French, meat stew made with white sauce

Blini   Russian, stuffed pancake made with buckwheat flour and classically topped with sour cream and caviar

Blintz   Jewish, pancakes stuffed with various sweet or savoury fillings, then fried

Bloater   herring or sometimes a mackerel, that has been salted, smoked and cured (kipper is slit open, a bloater is not)

Blutwurst   German, blood sausage

Boeuf bourguignon   French beef dish in red wine sauce

Bombe   spherical dessert dish consisting of an outer layer of ice cream or sherbet and a softer, inner layer of custard or mousse

Bonne femme   French, in country style, or housewife style, homely, also sole poached in fish stock

Bordelaise   Sauce of red wine, artichokes or shallots and marrow fat

Börek   Turkish savoury pastry filled with spinach, eggs, pumpkin, cheese, meat or fruit

Borsch (1) borsht   Russian, beetroot soup served with a sour cream garnish

Bouillabaisse   French fish stew cooked in a highly flavoured stock with oil, spices and herbs

Bouillon   French broth made by simmering meat, chicken, fish or vegetables in water (derives from 'to boil')

Bourride   Provençal fish stew with aïoli sauce

Bratwurst   German, fried sausage, usually pork

Bretonne, à la   French, garnished with beans

Brochette, en   French, on a skewer

Brouillé   French, scrambled

Bruxelloise   garnish for meat, composed of Brussel sprouts and pommes château, i.e. barrel-shaped potatoes, cooked in butter to a golden brown colour

Bubble and squeak   Originally meat, cabbage and potatoes fried up as leftovers

Calamares   Spanish fried squid or cuttlefish

Cannelloni   Italian pasta stuffed with meat or cheese in cheese sauce

Carpetbag steak   Australian, thick cut of steak stuffed with oysters

Cassata   Italian, ice cream dish of two types, cassata gelata and cassata siciliana. The siciliana is filled with ricotta cheese, the gelate with chopped nuts or candied fruit

Cassoulet   French casserole with haricot beans, meat and vegetables

Ceviche   South American dish of marinated raw fish

Chapatti   Indian, bread pancake

Charlotte russe   cold dessert made in a mould with sponge fingers enclosing a mash of whipped cream, lemon jelly and glacé cherries (literal meaning 'Russian Charlotte)

Charlotte: apple   hot dessert of bread pudding with an apple filling

Charlotte: strawberry   cold dessert similar to a Charlotte Russe but with a strawberry base

Chasseur   French sauce of white wine, mushrooms and onions

Châteaubriand   thick fillet steak

Chawan-mushi   the most popular example of mushimono. Small pieces of poultry, fish or vegetables mixed with beaten eggs and dashi are steamed in a cup. Chawan-mushi literally means 'teacup steamed' and is the only Japanese dish to be eaten with a spoon

Chicken Kiev   boned and flattened chicken breast wrapped around chilled butter lightly flavoured with chives, dipped in egg and breadcrumbs and fried

Chicken Marengo   Italian fried chicken in a sauce of garlic, tomatoes and white wine supposedly named after Napoleonic battle when the owner of an inn was forced to use any food available to make a dish

Chicken Maryland   Fried chicken served cold, iced or chilled

Chilli con carne   Mexican minced beef with chilli and beans

Chop suey   Originally a Cantonese dish that literally means 'bits and pieces' a way of dealing with leftovers by stir-frying; widely adopted in the USA under this Americanised name

Chorizo   Spanish, spiced pork sausage

Chow mein   Chinese-American fried noodles served with diced chicken, pork or seafood

Chowder   fish or seafood thick soup or stew

Churro   Spanish choux pastry fritter usually, served with a mug of chocolate

Ciabatta   moist aerated Italian bread made from olive oil. Ciabatta literally means slipper (from the shape of the loaf)

Cocido   Spanish, meat and vegetable stew

Cock-a-leekie   Scottish, leek served onions and sometimes with prunes and chicken stew

Colbert   French with lemon sauce, parsley and madeira

Colcannon   Irish, potato and cabbage dish

Coleslaw   Dutch and then American, shredded cabbage salad

Compôte   dish of fruit cooked in a light sugar syrup and served hot or cold

Consommé   French, clear soup

Coquilles Saint-Jacques   French scallops

Coulibiac   Russian, fish pie with buckwheat and chopped up hard-boiled eggs

Coulis   French term meaning 'to strain' and often referring to a thin vegetable or fuit pureé

Couscous   North African, steamed wheat mixed with semolina to form pasta-like pellets

Crécy, a la   French, garnished with carrots

Crêpe suzette   French, pancake with orange syrup and liqueur (Curacao)

Croque-monsieur   French, toasted cheese sandwich with ham

Croûte, en   French, in pastry

Cullen skink   Scottish, traditional soup made from finnan haddock and potatoes. Cullen is the village on the coast of the Moray Firth where the recipe originated and skink refers to the stock or broth, usually fish stock, but water or milk is occasionally used. An onion is often added for enhancement of flavour and the soup is garnished with parsley

Cumberland sauce   redcurrant-based sauce

Dashi   the basic Japanese soup stock consisting of dried bonito (Katsuobushi) and giant kelp (Kombu)

Daube, en   French, braised with vegetables in red wine and stock

Déglacer   French, deglaze, to add wine, cream or stock to juices in a pan, thereby making a gravy

Dente al   Italian, firm to the teeth

Devils on horseback   stuffed prunes wrapped in bacon

Dhall   general name for a variety of beans, peas and lentils used a staple in Indian cookery

Diablé   French, devilled

Dolmades   Greek/Turkish, vine leaves stuffed with meat and rice

Doner kebab   Middle Eastern, a block of seasoned, sliced lamb roasted on a spit

Doré   French, brushed with egg yolk

Duchesse   potatoes mashed in butter and egg shaped and then baked

Enchiladas   Mexican, fried, stuffed pancakes cooked with chilli-flavoured sauce

Entrecôte   steak cut from between two ribs

Espagnole   French, brown sauce (fat and flour cooked in oven to light brown colour with stock added)

Falafel   Middle Eastern, chickpea patties

Farci   French, stuffed

Fettucine   Italian, ribbon-shaped pasta

Filet mignon Henri IV   French, steak dish served with potatoes, artichoke hearts and Béarnaise sauce

Financière   French sauce made with Madeira and truffles

Florentine   French, with spinach

Focaccia   a flat savoury Italian bread made with and usually seasoned with herbs

Fondue   Swiss, melted cheese in white wine eaten with bread dips

Forestière   French, with bacon, mushrooms and potatoes

Forno, à la   from the oven

Fricassée   French meat stew in white sauce

Frikadelle   Swedish boiled meat ball

Fritto misto   Italian, seafood fried in batter

Gado gado   Indonesian, dish of vegetables in white sauce

Galantine   chopped meat in calves-head jelly

Garni   French, garnished

Gaspacho   Spanish, cold vegetable soup

Glaze   French, glossy finish produced by brushing food with beaten egg, milk, jelly or sugar syrup

Gnocchi   Italian, savoury dumplings

Goulash   Hungarian, paprika-flavoured meat stew

Granita   Italian, water ice

Gratin, au   French, browned with cheese and breadcrumbs

Gravlax   Scandinavian, raw pickled salmon with mustard and dill sauce

Grecque, à la   French, means ('Greek style'), cooked in oil and lemon juice (also an hors d'oeuvre with rice)

Guacamole   Mexican, avocado dip

Gumbo   stew with okra and rice

Haggis   Scottish, sheep's stomach filled with offal, oatmeal, suet and seasoning

Halva   Middle Eastern sesame seed, honey and almond sweet

Hoisin sauce   sauce made from soya beans

Hollandaise   French, sauce with egg yolk, vinegar, lemon juice and butter

Hot dog   Frankfurter in bun

Hummus   chickpea, garlic and sesame purée

Indienne, à la   French, curried

Jardinière   French, with garnish of fresh vegetables cut in julienne method

Julienne   French, vegetables cut in fine strips

Kebab   Turkish, lamb or mutton cooked on skewers (lit. on skewers)

Kedgeree   Originally Indian, rice and bean dish adapted as breakfast dish by the British with flaked fish and hard-boiled eggs

Korma   An Indian cooking instruction meaning 'to braise'

Kulfi   Indian ice cream made with reduced milk and nuts

Larding   threading strips of lard through lean meat to prevent dryness during roasting

Lasagne   flat pasta dish with minced meat, tomatoes and white cheese sauce

Laulau Hawaiian, steamed pork and fish cooked in leaves

Liaison French, binding agent such as egg yolk or cream

Lobscouse fisherman's stew associated with Liverpool but similar dishes with similar names come from Denmark, Germany and Norway

Lyonnaise sauce with white wine and onions fried in butter

Macédoine French, mixture of fruit or vegetables cut into small pieces

Madeleine small sponge cake

Maître d'hotel French, sauce with butter, parsley, lemon and cayenne pepper (lit. headwaiter)

Marrons glacés French candied chestnuts

Melba sauce sauce made with fresh raspberries and served with peach melba

Melba toast thin toast named after opera singer Dame Nellie Melba by French chef Auguste Escoffier

Meringue baked pudding made with egg white and sugar

Meunière French, floured and cooked in butter with salt, pepper and lemon juice and garnished with parsley

Mez(z)e Selection of hot and cold dishes served as an hors d'oeuvres in Eastern Mediterranean regions

Miso a paste made from fermented soya beans and barley or rice malt, used in Japanese cookery

Mocha Arabian, a kind of coffee flavouring, often with chocolate

Mornay French, béchamel sauce with grated Parmesan cheese

Mortadella Italian, sausage from Bologna

Moussaka Greek, minced lamb, aubergine and tomato dish topped with cheese

Mulligatawny Indian, curried soup (means 'pepper water')

Mushimono Japanese culinary term for steamed dishes such as chicken, fish or vegetables, often treated with saké

Nabemono Japanese culinary term for one-pot dishes usually cooked at the table by the diners. Sukiyaki is a typical example of nabemono

Nan Wheatflour leavened bread cooked in a clay tandoor

Nasi goreng Indonesian, meat and fried rice dish

Neige, à la French, white of egg beaten stiffly (literally means 'snow')

Nimono Japanese culinary term meaning 'to simmer'

Nougat French, sweet made from almonds and honey

Okashi Japanese culinary term for accompaniments to tea. Okashi can be made from various ingredients but usually based on sweet bean paste made with azuki bean

Osso bucco Italian, braised knuckle of veal dish cooked with wine and tomatoes

Paella Spanish, baked saffron rice with chicken, seafood and vegetables

Pancetta Italian cured belly of pork often used in pasta dressings. The name pancetta derives from the Italian for 'belly'

Papillote, en French, cooked in a greased paper bag

Parata Indian flaky unleavened bread smeared with ghee and rolled and stuffed before frying

Parisienne French, with round, ball artichoke hearts or other vegetables, shaped potatoes and leeks

Parmentier potato, diced and fried in butter (named from Baron Parmentier, who first introduced potatoes into France)

Pâté de foie gras French goose liver pâté

Paupiette French, thin slice of meat, or fillet of fish, rolled around a savoury filling

Pavlova fruit, cream and meringue dessert (named after ballerina Anna Pavlova)

Paysanne, à la French, in peasant style

Peach melba dessert made of halved peaches and vanilla ice cream and topped with raspberry purée – named after opera singer Dame Nellie Melba by French chef Auguste Escoffier

Périgueux sauce made with Madeira and truffles

Pesto Italian, sauce of basil, garlic, pine nuts and cheese.

Petit four French small cakes or crystallised fruit or sweets (literally means 'little oven').

Pilau/pilaf The cleaning of surface starch by means of simmering and steaming of rice to ensure separate grains

Piperade Basque tomatoes and peppers with egg beaten to a fluffy consistency

Pirozhki Russian, small pies with filling

Pissaladière French, pastry flan with onion, anchovy and black olives

Pizza Italian, flat-baked dough with various coverings (lit. pie)

Plat du jour French, dish of the day

Polenta Italian dish of maize, flour and water

Poivre, au French, with pepper

Profiteroles choux pastry puffs, covered with chocolate, usually with cream filling

Prosciutto Italian, smoked ham

Provençale French, prepared with garlic, oil and often, tomatoes

Pumpernickel German, malted rye bread

Quiche lorraine French, savoury flan with egg, bacon and cheese filling

Ragoût meat and vegetable stew

Raita Indian yoghurt-based cucumber salad

Ratatouille French, dish of aubergine, courgette, onions, peppers and tomatoes stewed in oil

Ravioli Italian, small pasta casings with stuffing

Red cooked braised in soy sauce and wine

Rijstafel Indonesian, a selection of dishes served with rice

Risotto Italian, rice dish cooked with stock

Rissole fried minced meat ball

Rogan josh Kashmiri, lamb curry with yoghurt

Rollmop German, raw herring with onion or gherkin pickled

Roux butter and flour cooked and constantly stirred until blended

Rum baba small sponge cake soaked in rum and syrup (invented by a Polish king: Stanislaus)

Sachertorte Austrian, chocolate sponge cake named after Sacher Hotel in Vienna

Salade niçoise tuna and anchovies

Saignant French, rare or underdone

Salmagundi English dish popular in 18th century and consisting of mixed salad items possibly with meat, eggs anchovies and onions

Salsa A spicy sauce especially served with Mexican food

Saltimbocca Italian, veal and ham dish

F
O
O
D

A
N
D

D
R
I
N
K

Sambal   Indonesian spiced pickle

Samosa   In Indian cuisine, small, crisp, flaky pastries, usually fried but may be baked. Samosas are stuffed with a variety of fillings such as cheese, egg, spiced minced meat, vegetables or sweets

Sashimi   Japanese, raw fish

Satay   Malaysian, grilled skewers of meat

Sauerkraut   German, pickled cabbage

Scotch broth: cereal used   barley

Scotch woodcock   anchovies and eggs on toast

Searing   browning meat rapidly with fierce heat to seal in the juices

Shiromono   Generic Japanese culinary term describing all soups but thick soups in particular

Shish kebab   Turkish, skewered meat pieces

Smörgasbord   Swedish buffet including herring, seafood, cheese and crispbread

Smørrebrød   Danish, open sandwich

Solyanka   Russian, cucumber soup

Sorbet   water ice, used to cleanse palate between courses

Soubise   white sauce with onion or purée of onions and rice to accompany some cuts of meat

Soufflé   French, dish of eggs whisked and baked

Soufflé cheese   Parmesan and Gruyère are the two cheeses used traditionally

Steak à la tartare   raw minced beef bound with egg into rissoles

Stollen   German, fruit loaf

Stroganoff   Russian, dish of thin strips of fillet of beef cooked in butter with sour cream and shallots

Strudel   German, thin sheet of filled dough rolled up and baked (literally meaning 'eddy' or 'whirlpool')

Suimono   Generic Japanese culinary term describing all clear soups

Sukiyaki   Japanese dish of beef and vegetables in soy sauce

Sunomono   Japanese culinary term meaning 'vinegared things' and referring to salad items given a vinegar dressing

Sushi   Japanese, vinegared rice with fresh fish or other seafood

Syllabub   dish dates from Elizabethan times. One definition claims that a favourite white wine in those days came from 'Sillery' in the Champagne region of France; the slang term for a bubbly drink was 'bub'; therefore the mixture of still wine and frothy cream became known as a 'syllabub'

Tabouli   cracked wheat with lemon, parsley, tomato and mint

Taco   Mexican, stuffed fried pancake

Tagliatelle   Italian, ribbon-shaped pasta

Tandoori   dish in a clay oven

Tapas   Spanish small appetisers served in bars and varied according to season and locality

Taramasalata   Greek, grey mullet smoked cod roe dip.

Tartare   mayonnaise sauce mixed with hard-boiled egg yolks, onions or chives or herbs, capers and gherkins

Tempura   Japanese, fish or vegetables deep-fried in butter

Teriyaki   Japanese culinary term referring to a special glaze of soy sauce, saké, and mirin, applied to fish, meat or poultry when partly grilled

Terrine, en   French, potted

Tikka   Indian term referring to meat or poultry cooked on skewers

Tiramisu   Italian dessert consisting of layers of sponge cake soaked in coffee and brandy or liqueur with powdered chocolate and mascarpone cheese. Tiramisu literally means 'pick-me-up'

Toad in the hole   English sausage in batter

Tortillas   Mexican, pancakes cooked on a griddle

Tournedos Rossini   named after the composer by French chef Auguste Escoffier; thick round slices of fillet steak garnished with sliced sautéed truffles and foie gras

Tourtière   Pie dish, for small pies

Tsukemono   Japanese culinary term referring to various pickled vegetables and also for pickled umeboshi, a plum-like fruit

Tzatziki   Greek, cucumber in yoghurt

Veal escalope   veal fried in breadcrumbs

Velouté   French, smooth white sauce with added white meat or fish stock

Vichyssoise   potato and leek soup, usually cold

Vindaloo   Indian, hot vinegary pork curry

Vol au vent   puff pastry shell with a variety of filling

Waffle   crisp golden brown pancake with deep indentations caused by the waffle-iron it is cooked in, often served with maple syrup

Waldorf salad   American, celery, apples, mayonnaise and walnuts named after the Waldorf Astoria Hotel in New York City

Wellington   English or Irish beef (or often any meat or fish) cooked in pastry

Welsh rarebit   cheese on toast sometimes melted with mustard and with beer added

White sauce   a roux with added milk used as a base for numerous sauces

Wiener schnitzel   Austrian, breaded veal cutlet

Wonton   Chinese, meat-filled dumplings

Yakimono   Japanese culinary term for something grilled

Zensai   Japanese culinary term for appetisers comparable to the French hors d'oeuvres

Zabaglione   Italian dessert made from egg yolks with marsala and sugar

Fruit and Vegetable Varieties

Apple   Allington pippin, Api, Blanche d'hiver, Blenheim, Bramley, Braeburn Calville, Cortland, Costard, Cox's Orange Pippin, Discovery, Ellison's Orange, Faro, Flower of Kent, Gillyflower, Gladstone, Golden Delicious, Granny Smith, Gravenstein, Idared, James Grieve, Jonathans, Laxton's Superb, McIntosh, Macoun, Mutsu, Newtown Pippin, Northern Spy, Pearmain Pippin, Reinette, Ribston Pippin, Rome Beauty, Russet, Star Kings, Wealthy, White Joaneting, White Transparent, Winesnap, Worcester, York Imperial.

Beetroot   Cheltenham Green Top, Crimson Globe, Nutting's Red Globe.

Broad bean   Bonny Lad, Bunyard's Exhibition, Express, Green Windsor, Red Epicure, Sutton, White Windsor.

Brussel sprouts Bedford-Fillbasket, Bedford Winter Harvest, Cambridge No 5, Early Half Tall, Fortress, Huizer's Late, Peer Gynt, Predora, Welland, Wellington, Widgen.

Cabbage April, Christmas Drumhead, Derby Day, Durham Early, Golden Acre, Greyhound, Hargenger, Hispy, January King, June Star, Ormskirk, Quickstep, Rear Guard, Spivoy, Spring Hero, Velocity, Winnigstadt, Wivoy.

Carrot Autumn King, Early Giant, Favourite, Figaro, Regulus Imperial, St Valery.

Cauliflower Alpha, Canberra, Dominant, Nevada, Snow Cap, Snow Crown.

Cherry Amarelle, Bigarreau, Bing, Black Tartarian, Bradbourne Black, Cherokee, Coe's Transparent, Early Rivers, Griotte, Guigne, May Duke, Montmorency, Morello, Napoleon, Rainier, Stella, Van.

Cucumber Bushcrop, Conqueror, King of the Ridge, Pacer, Pepita, Stockwood Ridge, Telegraph, Tokyo Slicer.

Dates Asharasi, Barhi, Deglet Noor, Fardh, Gundila, Halawi, Hilali, Khadrawi, Khalas, Khustawi, Khidri, Medjool, Mactoum, Naghal, Yatimeh, Zahidi.

French bean Cordon, Loch Ness, Long Bow, Masterpiece, Remus, Sprite, Tendergreen.

Gooseberry Admiral Beattie, Alma, Aston Red, Australia, Bellona, Blucher, Broom Girl, Careless, Clayton, Cousin's Seedling, Criterion, Crown Bob, Dan's Mistake, Early Sulphur, Firbob, Freedom, Green Gem, Green Ocean, Guido, Gunner, Heart of Oak, Hero of the Nile, Howard's Lancer, Ironmonger, Jubilee, Keepsake, King of Trumps, Lancashire Lad, Leveller, London, Lord Derby, Lord Kitchener, Macherauch's Seedling, Marigold, Matchless, May Duke, Peru, Plunder, Queen of Hearts, Queen of Trumps, Sir George Brown, Speedwell, Sultan Juror, Surprise, Suter Johnny, Talford, Trumpeter, Whinham's Industry, White Eagle, White Lion, Whitesmith, Woodpecker, Yellow Champagne.

Grape Alicante, Almeria, Barbera, Baresana, Barlinka, Cabernet Franc, Cabernet Sauvignon, Cardinal, Cassidy, Catawba, Chasselas, Cinsaut, Chardonnay, Concord, Delaware, Emporer, Gamay, Hermitage, Gewürztraminer, Grenache, Hanepoot, Irikara, Italia, Kiehmishi, Madeleine Royale, Malaga, Malvasia, Merlot, Montefiascone, Muscat, Nebbiolo, Niagara, Palamino, Perlette, Pinot Blanc, Pinot Gris, Pinot Noir, Portugieser, Red Emporer, Regina, Ribier, Riesling, Sangiovese, Sémillon, Shiraz, Simone, Sultanina, Syrah, Thompson's Seedless, Tokay, Ugni Blanc, Viognier, Waltham Cross, Zinfandel.

Grapefruit Duncan, Marsh.

Leek Catalina, Early Market, Giant Winter-Wila, Lyon

Prizetaker, Musselburgh, Royal Favourite, Walton Mammouth.

Lettuce Arctic King, Cos, Density, Fortune, Iceberg, Lakeland, Little Gem, Lobjoit's Green, Sabin, Saladin, Sigmaball, Stanstead Park, Paris White, Tom Thumb, Unrivalled, Webb's Wonder White.

Nut Acorn, Almond, Beech, Brazil, Breadnut, Calumpang, Candlenut, Chestnut, Cobnut, Coco de Mer, Coconut, Dika, Filbert, Gabon, Gingko, Gnetum, Groundnut, Hazelnut, Hickory, Illipe, Java Olive, Jojoba, Karaka, Kedrouvie, Kepayang, Kubuli, Macadamia, Madia, Manketti, Naras, Ngapi, Niger Seed, Okari, Olive, Oyster, Palm, Pecan, Pignut, Pili, Pine, Pistachio, Safflower, Sandalwood, Sapucaya, Sesame, Shea Butter, Souari, Sunflower, Walnut, Yeheb.

Onion Ailsa Craig, Autumn Queen, Bedfordshire Champion, Blood Red, Brunswick, Dobies Allrounder, Lancastrian, Marshall's Giant Fenglobe, North Holland Blood Red, Pearl Pickler, Ricardo, Southport Red Globe, Stuttgarter Giant, Sturon, Turbo.

Parsnip Improved Hollow Crown, The Student, Tender and True, White Gem.

Pea Feltham First, Histon Mini, Hurst Beagle, Hurst Green, Kelvedon Wonder, Little Marvel, Meteor, Onward, Semitar, Shaft.

Pear Abbé, Anjou, Bartlett, Beurré, Clapp Favourite, Conference, Doyenne du Comice, Glou Morceau, Jargonelle, Josephine de Malines, Kaiser, Louise Bonne der Jersey, Olivier de Serres, Passe Crasanne, Seckel, Wardens, Williams Bon Chrétien, Winter Nelis.

Plum Ambarella, Bokhara, Brazil, Burbank, Chrétien, Chickasaw, Czar, Davidson's, Denniston's Superb, Early Rivers, El Dorado, Greengage, Hog, Imperial Gage, Jew, Laxton's Cropper, Pershore, President, Prince's Gage, Red Gage, Santa Rosa, Victoria, Warwickshire Drooper, Washington.

Potato Arran Pilot, Arran Victory, Blue, Catriona, Craig's Royal, Desiree, Edgecote Purple, Esteema, King Edward, Majestic, Maris Piper, May Queen, Pink Fir Apple, Romano, Vanessa, Whites, Wilja.

Raspberry Lloyd George, Newburgh, Norfolk Giant.

Rhubarb Brandy Carr Scarlet, Cawood Delight, Royal Albert, Stock Bridge Arrow.

Runner bean Butler, Kelvedon Marvel, Mergoles.

Strawberry Baron Solemacher, Cambridge Vigour, Florence, Grandee, Hapil, Pegasus, Red Gauntlet.

Tomato Ailsa Craig, Alfresco, Alicante, Big Boy, Dombito, Early Girl, Eurocross, Golden Boy, Herald, Marmande, Minibel, Moneymaker, Piranto, Red Alert, Shirley, Tiny Tim, Supersonic.

Turnip Golden Ball, Green Globe, Model White, Veitch's Red Globe.

F
O
O
D

A
N
D

D
R
I
N
K

Fruit: Latin Names and Origin

English Name	Species	Origin
Apple	*Malus sylvestris*	Temperate regions
Apricot	*Prunus armeniaca*	Asia
Avocado	*Persea americana*	Central America
Banana	*Musa various species*	India/Asia
Bilberry	*Vaccinium myrtillus*	Europe/Asia
Blackberry	*Rubus fruticosus and other species*	Europe/Asia
Blackcurrant	*Ribes nigrum*	Europe/Asia/Africa
Blueberry	*Vaccinium various species*	Europe/USA

English Name	Species	Origin
Breadfruit	*Artocarpus atilis*	Malaysia
Carambola	*Averrhoa carambola*	Asia
Cherry (sour)	*Prunus cerasus*	Temperate regions
Cherry (sweet)	*Prunus avium*	Temperate regions
Clementine	*Citrus reticulata*	Mediterranean
Coconut	*Cocos nucifera*	Pacific
Cranberry	*Oxycoccus macrocarpus*	North America
Damson	*Prunus instititia*	Temperate regions
Date	*Phoenix dactylifera*	Persian Gulf
Fig	*Ficus carica*	Asia
Gooseberry	*Ribes grossularia*	Europe
Grape	*Vitis vinifera*	Asia
Grapefruit	*Citrus paradisi*	West Indies
Greengage	*Prunus domestica*	Temperate regions
Kiwi fruit	*Actinidia deliciosa*	China
Kumquat	*Fortunella margarita*	China
Lemon	*Citrus limon*	Asia
Lime	*Citrus aurantifolia*	Asia
Loganberry	*Rubus loganobaccus*	America
Loquat	*Eriobotrya japorica*	China/Japan
Mandarin	*Citrus reticulata*	China
Mango	*Mangifera indica*	Asia
Medlar	*Mespilus germanica*	Europe/Asia
Mulberry	*Morus nigra*	Asia
Nectarine	*Prunus persica*	China
Olive	*Olea europaea*	East Mediterranean
Orange	*Citrus sinensis*	China
Passion fruit	*Passiflora edulis*	South America
Peach	*Prunus persica*	China
Pear	*Pyrus cummunis*	Middle East/Europe
Persimmon	*Diospyros kaki*	Far East
Pineapple	*Ananas comosus*	South America
Plum	*Prunus domestica*	Temperate regions
Pomegranate	*Punica granatum*	Persia
Pomelo	*Citrus grandis*	Asia
Quince	*Cydonia oblonga*	Persia
Raspberry	*Rubus idaeus*	Northern hemisphere
Redcurrant	*Ribes rubrum*	Worldwide
Rhubarb	*Rheum rharbararum*	Asia
Satsuma	*Citrus nobilis*	Japan
Strawberry	*Fragaria x ananassa*	Europe/Asia
Ugli fruit	*Citrus reticulata*	Jamaica
Watermelon	*Citrullus lanatus*	Africa
Whitecurrant	*Ribes rubrum*	Europe

Vegetables: Latin Names and Origin

English Name	Species	Origin
Artichoke, Chinese	*Stachys affinis*	China
Artichoke, globe	*Cynara scolymus*	Mediterranean
Artichoke, Jerusalem	*Helianthus tuberosus*	North America
Aubergine	*Solanum melongena*	Asia/Africa
Avocado	*Persea americana*	Central America
Bean sprout	*Vigna radiata Glycirve maximus*	China
Broad bean	*Vicia faba*	Africa/Europe
Kidney bean	*Phaseolus vulgaris*	America
Runner bean	*Phaseolus coccineus*	America
Soya bean	*Glycine soja*	East Asia
Beetroot	*Beta vulgaris*	Mediterranean
Broccoli	*Brassica oleracea*	Europe
Brussel sprout	*Brassica oleracea*	North Europe
Cabbage	*Brassica oleracea*	Europe/Asia
Celery	*Apium graveolens*	Europe/Africa/USA
Chick-pea	*Cicer arietinum*	West Asia
Chives	*Allium schoenoprasum*	Europe/USA
Courgette	*Cucurbita pepo*	Africa/S. America
Cucumber	*Cucumis sativus*	Uncertain

English Name	Species	Origin
Fennel	Foeniculum vulgare	Italy
Garlic	Allium sativum	Uncertain
Gherkin	Cucumis anguria	Northern India
Kale	Brassica oleracea acephala	East Mediterranean
Kohlrabi	Brassica oleracea caulorapa	Asia
Leek	Allium porrum	Africa/Europe
Lettuce	Lactuca sativa	Middle East
Lettuce: lamb's tongue	Valerianella locusta	Europe
Mange-tout	Pisum sativum saccharatum	Near East
Mushroom	Agaricus campestris	Worldwide
Okra	Hibiscus esculentus	Africa
Onion	Allium cepa	Central Asia
Parsley	Petroselinum crispum	East Mediterranean
Parsnip	Pastinaca sativa	Europe
Pea	Pisum sativum	Asia/Europe
Pepper	Capsicum annuum	South America
Potato	Solanum tuberosum	South America
Pumpkin	Cucurbita pepo	South America
Radish	Raphanus sativus	China/Japan
Salsify	Tragopogon porrifolius	Europe
Sorrel	Rumex acetosa	Europe
Spinach	Spinacia oleracea	Persia
Squash, summer	Cucurbita pepo	America
Squash, winter	Cucurbita maxima	America
Swede	Brassica napus	Europe
Sweetcorn	Zea mays	Central & South America
Sweet potato	Ipomaea batatas	Central America
Tomato	Lycopersicon esculentum	South America
Turnip	Brassica rapa	Middle East
Water chestnut, Chinese	Eleocharis dulcis	China
Watercress	Nasturtium officinale	Europe/Asia
White cabbage	Brassica oleracea capitata	East Mediterranean
Yam	Dioscorea various species	Tropics

Spices: Latin names and Origin

English Name	Species	Origin
Acitrón	Echinocactus grandis	Mexico
Agar wood	Aquillaria agallocha	Asia
Ajmud	Trachyspermum roxburghianum	Asia
Ajowan	Trachyspermum ammi	Asia
Alexanders	Smyrnium olusatrum	Mediterranean
Allspice	Pimenta dioica	West Indies
Angelica	Angelica archangelica	Europe
Anise	Pimpinella anisum	Mediterranean
Annatto	Bixa orellana	West Indies
Asafoetida	Ferula assafoetida	Asia
Ashanti pepper	Piper guineense	West Africa
Balm	Melissa officinalis	Mediterranean
Balsam	Myroxylon balsamum	Asia
Basil	Ocimum basilicum	Asia
Bay	Laurus nobilis	Mediterranean
Bergamot	Monarda fistulosa	Mexico
Bistort	Polygonum bistorta	Europe
Bitter berries	Solanum aethiopicum	North Africa
Black cumin	Nigella sativa	Asia
Borage	Borago officinalis	Mediterranean
Burnet	Sanguisorba officinalis	Europe
Calamint	Calamintha sylvatica	Europe
Caper	Capparis spinosa	Mediterranean
Caraway	Carum carvi	Europe/Asia
Cardamom	Ellataria cardamomum	Asia
Cassia	Cinnamonum cassia	Asia
Cayenne	Capsicum frutescens	America/Africa
Cherry laurel	Laurocerasus officinalis	Mediterranean
Chervil	Anthriscus cerefolium	Asia
Chinese keys	Boesenbergia pandurata	Asia

F
O
O
D

A
N
D

D
R
I
N
K

English Name	Species	Origin
Cinnamon	*Cinnamomum zeylanicum*	Asia
Clary	*Salvia sclarea*	Europe
Cleavers	*Galium aparine*	Europe
Chilli pepper	*Capsicum annuum*	America
Cloves	*Syzygium aromaticum*	Moluccas
Coltsfoot (common)	*Tussilago farfara*	Europe
Coltsfoot (sweet)	*Petasites japonicus*	Japan
Comfrey	*Symphytum officinalis*	Europe
Coriander	*Coriandrum sativum*	Mediterranean
Corkwing	*Glehnia littoralis*	Asia
Costmary	*Tanacetum balsamita*	Asia
Costus	*Saussurea lappa*	Asia
Cowslip	*Primula veris*	Eurasia
Cubeb	*Piper cubeba*	Indonesia
Cumin seed	*Cuminum cyminum*	Mediterranean
Curry leaf	*Murraya koenigii*	India
Daun salam	*Syzygium polyanthum*	Indonesia
Dill	*Anethum graveolens*	Asia
Elecampane	*Inula helenium*	Europe
Epazote	*Chenopodium ambrosioides*	Mexico
Fennel	*Foeniculum vulgare*	Europe
Fenugreek	*Trigonella foenum-graecum*	India/Europe
Galingale/Galangal	*Alpinia galanga*	Asia
Garden mace	*Archillea decolorans*	Europe
Ginger	*Zingiber officinale*	Asia
Golden needles	*Hemerocallis fulva*	Asia
Grains of selim	*Xylopia aethiopica*	Africa
Ground Elder	*Aegopodium podagraria*	Europe
Guascas/huascas	*Galinsoga parviflora*	South America
Hedge garlic	*Alliaria petiolata*	Europe
Hogweed	*Heracleum sphondylium*	Eurasia
Horehound	*Marrubium vulgare*	Eurasia
Horseradish	*Armoracia rusticana*	Europe
Khus khus	*Vetiveria zizanioides*	Asia
Lemon grass	*Cymbopogon citratus*	Asia
Lemon verbena	*Lippia triphyllos*	Europe
Lime flowers	*Tilia platyphyllos*	Europe
Lovage	*Levisticum officinalis*	Europe
Mace	*Myristica fragrans*	Moluccas
Marjoram (sweet)	*Origanum majorana*	Mediterranean
Marjoram (wild)	*Origanum vulgare*	Europe
Mastic	*Pistacia lentiscus*	Mediterranean
Meadowsweet	*Filipendula ulmaria*	Northern Hemisphere
Melegueta pepper	*Aframomum melegueta*	Africa
Mint (water)	*Mentha aquatica*	Worldwide
Mint (wild)	*Mentha arvensis*	Asia
Mitsuba	*Cryptotaenia japonica*	Japan
Mugwort	*Artemisa vulgaris*	Northern Hemisphere
Mustard, black	*Brassica nigrar*	Worldwide
Mustard, white	*Sinapis aba*	Europe/Asia
Nasturtium	*Tropaeolum majus*	South America
Nutmeg	*Myristica fragrans*	Moluccas
Palilo	*Escobedia scabrifolio*	Peru
Paprika	*Capsicum annuum*	South America
Parsley	*Petroselenum crispum*	Mediterranean
Pennyroyal	*Mentha pulegium*	Asia
Pepper	*Piper nigrum*	India
Rau ram	*Polygonum odoratum*	Brazil
Rosemary	*Rosmarinus officinalis*	Mediterranean
Rue	*Ruta graveolens*	Mediterranean
Saffron	*Crocus sativus*	Eurasia
Sage	*Salvia officinalis*	Eurasia
Samphire (marsh)	*Salicornia europaea*	Europe
Samphire (rock)	*Crithmum maritmum*	Mediterranean
Sandalwood	*Santalum album*	India/Australia
Sansho	*Zanthoxylum piperitum*	Asia
Sarsaparilla	*Smilax officinalis*	America
Savory (summer)	*Satureja hortensis*	Mediterranean
Savory (winter)	*Satureja montana*	Mediterranean
Shado béni	*Eryngium foetidum*	Carribean

English Name	Species	Origin
Shiso	*Perilla frutescens*	Japan
Sichuan pepper	*Zanthoxylum silulans*	China
Smartweed	*Persicaria hydropiper*	Eurasia
Southernwood	*Artemisia abrotanum*	Europe
Spanish needles	*Bidens pilosa*	Worldwide
Spanish thyme	*Plectranthus amboinicus*	Uncertain
Spearmint	*Mentha spicata*	Mediterranean
Star anise	*Illicium verum*	China
Sweet cicely	*Myrrhis odorata*	Europe
Tansy	*Tanacetum vulgare*	Northern Hemisphere
Tarragon	*Artemisia dracunculus*	Eurasia
Thyme	*Thymus vulgaris*	Mediterranean
Turmeric	*Curcuma longa*	Asia
Vanilla	*Vanilla planifolia*	Central America
Vervain	*Verbena officinalis*	Europe
Wasabi	*Eutrema wasabi*	Japan
Water dropwort	*Oenanthe javanica*	Asia
Wintergreen	*Gaultheria procumbens*	North America
Woodruff	*Galium odoratum*	Eurasia
Wormwood (common)	*Artemisia absinthium*	Eurasia
Wormwood (Roman)	*Artemisia pontica*	Eurasia
Ylang-ylang	*Cananga odorata*	Asia
Zedoary	*Curcuma zedoaria*	Asia

Miscellaneous information

Abalone	shellfish
Aga: stoves from	Sweden (full name: Aktienbolagetgasackumalator)
Agurketid (Danish silly season)	literally means 'cucumber time': the season when they are served
Allspice: other name	pimento, Jamaican pepper
Associated with a place:	
Aberdeen	rowies (rolls) sausage
Arbroath	smokies
Bakewell	tart
Banbury	cake
Bath	bun, Oliver (biscuits)
Battenberg	cake
Berwick	cockles
Black Forest	gateau
Bologna	Bolognese sauce
Boston	baked beans, brown bread
Brussels	sprouts
Cayenne	pepper
Chelsea	bun
Cornish	pasty
Coventry	Godcakes
Cumberland	sausage, sauce
Denmark	pastries
Dublin	prawn
Dundee	cake
Eccles	cake
Frankfurt	sausage
Geneva	pudding
Genoa	fruit cake
Hamburg	hamburger
Hungary	goulash
Ireland	stew
Kendal	mint cake
Kiev	chicken
Lancashire	hot-pot
Lima	bean
Lorraine	quiche
Madeira	cake
Manchester	pudding
Maryland	chicken
Melton Mowbray	pork pie

F
O
O
D

A
N
D

D
R
I
N
K

Norway	lobster
Pontefract	liquorice cake
Seville	orange
Siena	cake
Switzerland (Swiss)	roll
Tabasco	sauce
Vichy	Vichyssoise soup
Vienna	loaf
Wales (Welsh)	(rabbit) rarebit
Whitstable	oysters
Windsor	bean
Worcester	sauce
Yorkshire	pudding
Bagel	doughnut-shaped roll cooked in water, then baked
Bain-Marie	large pan of boiling water in which a smaller pan is placed to help the cooking process
Baking powder	bicarbonate of soda, cream of tartar and starch
Banana: cooking variety	plantain
Bombay duck	fish
Bouquet garni	parsley, thyme, bay leaf, used as flavouring in stews etc.
Brawn	pig's head (occasionally sheep or cow's head)
Brisling	small herring-like fish
Caboc cheese	soft, Scottish cheese rolled in toasted oatmeal
Caviar	roe of sturgeon
Cendrés cheeses	coated with ashes originally from vine roots, later from industrial charcoal
Champignon	French name for mushrooms, but usually refers to button mushrooms
Charcuterie	French name for pork products (and for a shop that sells these)
Chayote	Mexican vegetable related to the gourd family also called choko, christifine, custard marrow, militon
Cheeses: blue veined	Gorgonzola, bleu d' Auvergnes, bleu de Bresse, Roquefort, Stilton
Cheese: holes formed by	carbon dioxide gas produced by bacteria in the milk sugar
Cheese: agent used to curdle milk for	rennet (from calf's stomach)
Cheese: largest producer	USA
Cheese: unusual types	
Emmental	Swiss, cheese with bigger holes than Gruyère
Feta	Greek, salted, based on sheep or goat's milk.
Gorgonzola	made from ewe's milk with blue veins (named after village near Milan)
Mozzarella	originally made from buffalo milk
Parmesan	made from skimmed milk
Ricotta	sweet cottage cheese
Roquefort	made from ewe's milk
Stilton	adds cream of one day to milk of next
Chef: 'Architect of French Cuisine'	Antonin Carême
Chewing gum: original base	chicle, the latex of the sapodilla tree
Cinnamon: from	bark of tree
Clementine: cross between	orange and tangerine
Coffee: source	pips of fruit (not beans)
Condensed milk: inventor	Gail Borden, US patent granted in 1856
Consumption: beer, most	Germany
Consumption: tea, most	Ireland
Consumption: wine, most	France consumes most wine overall but Portugal most per capita
Crab: how to tell if fresh	it should feel heavy but have no sound of water in it
Croissant	French, crescent-shaped roll
Croutons	toast pieces, fried in butter
Cuts of meat: beef neck	aka clod or sticking, it is usually used for stewing
beef sirloin	behind the neck (best beef for roasting)
beef topside	top of hind quarters of steer
Dariole (mould)	small and narrow with sloping sides used for setting creams and jellies or for steaming puddings
Denby Dale pie: created for	George III's recovery from an illness in 1788
Devon Garland cheese	layer of herbs pressed into the middle
Dredging	sprinkling with flour or icing sugar
E (European) numbers	code numbers used on food packaging which represent substances deemed safe by the EU
Edible grain crops: 9	wheat, barley, maize, oats, buckwheat, millet, rye, sorghum and rice
Eggs: brown or white more nutritious	no difference
Endive: English word for	chicory

Escargots	French, snails
Filbert: fruit of	hazel tree
Fines herbes	French, fresh chopped chives, chervil, parsley and tarragon but other fresh herbs may be added
Five-spice powder	Chinese, anise, pepper, cinnamon, cloves, fennel
Flageolet	a kind of haricot bean
Foodstuff: most extensively grown and eaten most generally by people	wheat (also used as animal fodder), rice
Fruit: nutrition	avocado is the most nutritious and cucumber the least
Gammon: part of pig from	thigh of legs (when salted and cured, this is ham)
Garam masala	mixed spices used in curry
Gas marks	Mark 1 – 250°F, Mark 2 – 275°F, Mark 3 – 300°F, Mark 4 – 325°F, Mark 5 – 350°F
Ghee	Indian clarified butter
Gohan	steamed rice
Grenadilla: aka	passion fruit
Grilling: Americans call	Broiling
Guinea pig: where eaten	Peru
Honey: nectar for 1 lb	from 2 million flowers
Indian bread	poori, chapati, naan
Indian cinnamon tea	masala chai
Indian prawn dish	jhinga
Indian rice: most often used	Basmati (grown in the Himalayan foothills)
Indian-style chicken	murghi
Insect: most eaten	grasshopper
Instant potato: invented	Edward Asselberg (1941)
Kipper	split smoked herring
Langouste	crayfish
Larousse Gastronomique:	
original author	Prosper Montagné
Licence: chefs require to prepare	fugu (puffer fish) in Japan, lethal if toxic parts are not completely removed
Loganberry	cross between a raspberry and a blackberry
Loquat: aka	Japanese medlar
Margarine: 1st ingredients	chopped sheep intestine, cow's udder, beef suet
Meat: cholesterol-free	kangaroo, possum
Milk: most protein	reindeer's milk contains three times as much protein as cow's milk
Milk: UHT; stands for	Ultra High Temperature
Miso	Japanese fermented soya bean paste
Mooli	long, parsnip-shaped vegetable, which tastes like radish
MSG	monosodium glutamate (used to intensify flavour)
Naan	Indian flat bread
Noisette	hazelnut (French)
Okra: called in Indian supermarkets	bhindi (aka ladies' fingers)
Omelette and a glass of wine, An	Elizabeth David book of the 1960s which challenged British eating habits
Onion family: smallest plant in	chive
Oranges: best for marmalade	Seville
Oysters: when to eat; saying	When there is an 'r' in the month
Palm trees: two fruits that grow on	coconuts and dates
Parboil	derived from old French for 'boiling thoroughly'; now means 'boiling preliminary to further cooking'
Pasteurisation: temperature	approx 63° C
Petits pois	small French green peas
Pitta	Middle Eastern flat bread
Potato: poisonous parts	leaves and fruit (tubers eaten)
Prosciutto	Italian smoked ham
Prunes: made from	dried plums
Quargel cheese: from	Austria (sharp cheese, caraway-flavoured)
Quotations:	
Clement Attlee	The House of Lords is like a glass of champagne that has stood for 5 days.
James Beard	A gourmet who thinks of calories is like a tart who looks at her watch.
Paul Bocuse	Cuisine is like fireworks display, nothing remains. It is *une fête*, rapid, ephemeral.
Michel Bourdin	Cooking is a way of giving and making yourself desirable.

FOOD AND DRINK

Mel Brooks	Where you eat is sacred.
George Burns	Actually, it only takes one drink to get me loaded. Trouble is, I can't remember if it's the thirteenth or the fourteenth.
Robert Byrne	Anybody who believes that the way to man's heart is through his stomach flunked geography.
Lord Byron	Let us have wine and women, mirth and laughter, Sermons and soda water the day after.
Titus Lucretius Carus	What is food to one man is bitter poison to others.
Malcolm de Chazal	Women eat when they talk, men talk when they eat.
Winston Churchill	[of champagne] In victory you deserve it, in defeat you need it.
Shirley Conran	Life is too short to stuff a mushroom.
Alexandre Dumas (Père)	Le Montrachet [a top Burgundy] should be drunk on the knees with head bared.
Edward VII	One not only drinks wine, one smells it, observes it, tastes it, sips it and – one talks about it.
William M Evarts	It was a brilliant affair – water flowed like champagne. (Description of a dinner given by teetotal President Rutherford B Hayes.)
Clifton Fadiman	Cheese – milk's leap towards immortality.
Sir Alexander Fleming	If penicillin can cure those who are ill, Spanish sherry can bring the dead back to life.
Clement Freud	If a bird says, 'Cluk bik bik bik bik' and 'Caw' you may kill it, eat it or ask Fortnums to pickle it in Napoleon brandy with wild strawberries. If it says, 'tweet' it is a dear and precious friend and you'd better lay off it if you want to remain a member of the Boodles.
Gail Greene	Great food is like great sex, the more you have the more you want.
Galileo	Wine is sunlight, held together by water.
Nubar Gulbenkian	The best number for a dinner party is two – myself and a damn good head waiter.
Philip W Haberman Jr	A gourmet is just a glutton with brains.
Ernest Hemingway	Wine is the most civilised thing in the world.
Horace	Wine is Life.
Jerome K Jerome	We drink one another's health and spoil our own.
Dr Johnson	Claret is the liquor for boys; port for men; but he who aspires to be a hero must drink brandy.
John Keats	Wine is only sweet to happy men.
Prue Leith	When you get to fifty-two food becomes more important than sex.
Joe E Lewis	A man is never drunk if he can lie on the floor without holding on.
Arnold Lobel	All's well that ends with a good meal.
Martin Luther	Who loves not women, wine and song, remains a fool his whole life long.
W Somerset Maugham	At a dinner party one should eat wisely but not too well, and talk well, but not too wisely.
George Mikes	On the Continent people have good food, in England people have good table manners.
Robert Morley	No man is lonely while eating spaghetti.
Napoleon	Champagne banishes etiquette.
Ogden Nash	Celery raw, develops the jaw; But celery stewed, Is more easily chewed.
Louis Pasteur	Wine is the most healthful and most hygienic of beverages. A meal without wine is like a day without sunshine.
St Paul	Use a little wine for thy stomach's sake.
Madame de Pompadour	Champagne is the only wine that leaves a woman beautiful after drinking it.
Anthony Powell	Dinner at Huntercombes' possessed only two dramatic features – the wine was a farce and the food a tragedy.
William Shakespeare	The food that to him now is as luscious as locusts, shall be to him shortly as bitter as coloquintida.
Robert Louis Stevenson	Wine is bottled poetry.
Jonathan Swift	I have been assured by a very knowing American of my acquaintance in London, that a young healthy child well nursed is at a year old a most delicious, nourishing and wholesome food, whether stewed, roasted, baked or boiled and I make no doubt that it will equally serve in a fricassee, or a ragout.
Raclette	Swiss mild cheese; also a dish made from it with potatoes, pickled onions and gherkins
Raisins: made from	dried grapes
Rambutan: aka	hairy lychee
Ramekin	small casserole dish
Ratafia	1. type of macaroon, small biscuit, 2. liqueur made from fruit juice and brandy, or essence of bitter almond
Restaurant guide: first European	Michelin 1900
Restaurant: first	Boulanger's, Paris (1765)
Sago	starch from the pith of a palm

Salami	Italian sausage flavoured with garlic (Latin for salted)
Sally Lunn: cake named after	legendary lady from Bath
Singin' hinny	Northumberland fruit loaf; it gets its name from the sound it makes as it cooks
Spam: name from	spiced ham
Spice: from same plant	nutmeg, mace
Spice: most expensive by weight	saffron
Stilton cheese	made in Leicester but became famous in the early 18th century, when it was sold in the Bell Inn, a coaching house on the Great North Road, at Stilton, Cambridgeshire
Sweetbread from	pancreas
Tabasco: name from	Mexican state
Tapioca: source	root of cassava (manioc)
Tartrazine	azo dye that produces a yellow colour (E102)
Tava	concave cast-iron plate used for cooking bread
Tea: the Champagne of Tea	Darjeeling
Tea: country that produces most	India produces 30% of the world's tea crop annually
Tea: originally dried over burning ropes	lapsang souchong
Tea: spoon used for extracting floating tea leaves	mote spoon
Tea: weekly ration during WW2	2 oz per week
Terrine	pot used for pâté or savoury mixtures
Tofu	Japanese soya bean curd
Tripe	cow's, sheep's or other animal's stomach lining
Truffles: how found	detected by trained pigs in France; by dogs in N/W Italy
Turmeric: obtained from	rhizomes of curcuma plant
Ugli: fruit cross between	grapefruit, tangerine and orange
Vegetable: oldest known	broad bean (also called fava)
Wok	hemispherical pan used in Chinese stir-fry cookery
Worcester Sauce: origin	India
Yarg	Cornish cheese that is wrapped in nettles

F O O D   A N D   D R I N K

Cocktails

Adonis dry sherry (2 parts), red vermouth (1 part), dash of orange bitters, twist of orange peel

Affinity scotch whisky (2 parts), dry vermouth (1 part), 2 dashes Angostura bitters

Afrodizzy white rum, banana liqueur, passion fruit juice, lemonade

Alaska gin (3 parts), yellow Chartreuse (1 part)

Alexander cognac (3 parts), crème de caçao (1 part) & cream (1 part)

Angel Face dry gin (1/3), apricot brandy (1/3), calvados (1/3)

Angel's Kiss sloe gin, dark crème de caçao, prunelle liqueur, whipping cream

Atta Boy gin, dry vermouth, grenadine

Bacardi white rum (2 parts), lemon juice (1 part), a dash of grenadine

Bamboo dry sherry (1/2), dry vermouth (1/2), a dash of orange bitters

Bellini champagne, peach juice

Bentley calvados (1/2), Dubonnet (1/2)

Between the Sheets Cointreau, brandy, rum, lemon juice

Black Russian vodka, Kahlúa, cola

Black Velvet champagne, stout (equal measures)

Black Widow white rum, Kahlúa

Block and Fall cognac (2 parts), Cointreau (2 parts), calvados (1 part), anisette (1 part)

Bloody Mary vodka, tomato juice, lemon juice, Worcester sauce, salt and pepper

Blue Star gin, dry vermouth, blue curaçao, orange juice

Bobby Burns whisky, sweet vermouth, Benedictine

Bombay brandy (2 parts), dry vermouth (1 part), red vermouth (1 part), dash of pastis, 2 dashes curaçao

Boomerang Canadian Club whiskey, Swedish punch, dry vermouth, lemon, Angostura

Bosom Caresser brandy, orange curaçao, grenadine, egg yolk

Bronx gin, sweet vermouth, dry vermouth, orange juice

Brooklyn rye whiskey (2 parts), red vermouth (1 part), 1 dash of maraschino, 1 dash of Amer Picon

Bucks Fizz champagne, orange juice, grenadine (optional)

Butt Wobbler gin, calvados, dry vermouth, Pernod, lemonade

Buttock Clencher tequila, gin, melon liqueur, pineapple juice, lemonade

Caruso gin, dry vermouth, green crème de menthe

Casino dry gin (9 parts), maraschino (1 part), lemon juice (1 part), orange bitters (1)

Champagne Cocktail champagne, brandy

Champs-Elysées brandy, Chartreuse, lemon juice, Angostura

Cinderella pineapple juice, orange juice, lemon juice, soda water, sugar

Claridge dry gin (2 parts), dry vermouth (2 parts), apricot brandy (1 part), Cointreau (1)

Clover Club   gin, grenadine, lime juice, egg white
Corcovado   tequila, Drambuie, blue curaçao, Lemonade
Corpse Reviver   brandy, sweet vermouth, calvados
Crème Puff   crème de menthe, milk, soda water
Cuba Libre   rum, lime juice, cola.
Czarina   vodka (2 parts), dry vermouth (1 part), apricot brandy (1 part), dash of Angostura bitters
Daiquiri   rum (4 parts), lemon juice (1 part), or lime juice, sugar
Dempsey   calvados, gin, Pernod, grenadine
Depth Charge   brandy, calvados, grenadine, lemon juice
Derby   dry gin (55ml, 2oz), 2 dashes of peach bitters, 2 sprigs of fresh mint
Diki-Diki   calvados (4 parts), Swedish punch (1 part), grapefruit juice (1 part)
Double or Drop   tequila, brandy, lime juice, honey
Dry Martini   gin (4 parts), vermouth (1 part)
Duchess   red vermouth (1 part), dry vermouth (1 part), pastis (1 part)
Earthquake   whisky, gin, and Pernod
East-India   brandy (6 parts), curaçao (1 part), orange juice (1 part)
Eclipse   sloe gin, grenadine, gin, a cherry
Fair and Warmer   white rum, sweet vermouth, orange curaçao
Fallen Angel   gin, lime juice, white crème de menthe, Angostura, lemonade
Floppy Dick   brandy, dry vermouth, sweet vermouth, triple sec, vermouth
Flu   Canadian Club whiskey, lemon juice, rock candy syrup, ginger brandy, Jamaican ginger
Fluffy Navel   brandy, dry vermouth, sweet vermouth, triple sec, Pernod
Fourth Degree   gin, sweet vermouth, dry vermouth, Pernod
Gibson   gin (4 parts), vermouth (1 part), served with a cocktail onion
Gimlet   gin, lime juice
Gin Fizz   gin (4parts), lemon juice (2parts), sugar, soda water
Gin Sling   gin, lemon juice, sugar (aka Pimm's No 1)
Gin Swizzle   gin, soda water, lime juice, sugar syrup, Angostura
Glad Eye   Pernod, crème de menthe
Grand Slam   Swedish punch, sweet vermouth, dry vermouth
Grasshopper   green crème de menthe, white crème de caçao, whipping cream
Green Dragon   champagne, Midori
Harvey Wallbanger   vodka (1 part), orange juice (2 parts), 2 teaspoons of Galliano (named after surfer, Tom Harvey)
Highball   whisky, Angostura bitters, ginger ale
Hoopla   brandy, Cointreau, dry vermouth, lemon juice
Hoots Mon   whisky, sweet vermouth, dry vermouth
Horse's Neck   brandy, Angostura, dry ginger ale
Hula Hula   gin, orange juice, Cointreau
Hurricane   rum, lime juice, passion fruit juice, orange juice, pineapple juice
John Collins   gin, lemon juice, spoonful of sugar, soda water
Jungle Juice   Pisang Ambon, Mandarine Napoléon, gin, orange juice, sugar
Kicker   Bacardi rum, calvados, sweet vermouth

Kir   glass of white wine with a teaspoon of crème de cassis stirred in
Kir Royale   glass of champagne with a teaspoon of crème de cassis stirred in
Knickerbocker   gin, dry vermouth, sweet vermouth
Knock Out Punch   gin, cider, Bénédictine, brandy, peach brandy, lemonade
Leap Year   gin, Grand Marnier, sweet vermouth, lemon juice
Macaroni   Pernod, sweet vermouth
Manhattan   rye whiskey (2 parts), sweet vermouth (1 part), bitters, maraschino cherry
   Named after a NY club and invented by Jenny Jerome (Winston Churchill's mother)
Margarita   tequila (2 parts), lemon juice (1 part), curaçao (1 part), glass is salted
Mary Pickford   white rum (1/2), natural pineapple juice (1/2), teaspoon grenadine, 6 dashes maraschino
Merry Widow   gin, dry vermouth, Bénédictine, Pernod, Angostura
Mikado   brandy (40 ml, 1 1/2oz), 2 drops curaçao, 2 drops crème de noyaux, 2 drops orange curaçao, 2 drops Orgeat, 2 drops Angostura bitters
Mint Julep   bourbon, sugar syrup, sprigs of mint
Monkey Gland   gin, orange juice, grenadine, 2 dashes of pastis
Monkey Wrench   white rum, grapefruit juice, lemon juice
Morning Glory   whisky, lemon juice, soda water, Angostura, sugar, egg white
Moscow Mule   Smirnoff vodka, lime juice, dry ginger ale
Negroni   red vermouth (1/3), Campari (1/3), dry gin (1/3)
Oh! Henry!   whisky, Bénédictine, ginger ale
Old Fashioned   bourbon, sugar cube, Angostura, 1/2 slice lemon, 1/2 slice orange, dash of soda water
Old Pal   rye whiskey (1/3), dry vermouth (1/3), Campari (1/3)
Orange Blossom   gin, orange juice, grenadine, orange bitters
Oriental   rye whiskey (1/2), red vermouth (1/4), white curaçao (1/4), 2 teaspoons fresh lemon juice
Paradise   gin, apricot brandy, orange juice
Parisian   dry gin (2 parts), dry vermouth (2 parts), créme de cassis (1 part)
Parisian Blonde   dark rum, triple sec, double cream, sugar syrup
Pimms 1–6   long drink with spirit base and fruit flavouring, bases as follows:
   (1) gin (2) whisky (3) brandy (4) rum (5) rye whisky (6) vodka
Pina Colada   rum, pineapple juice, coconut milk, whipping cream, sugar
Pink Elephant   bourbon, lemon juice, grenadine, egg white
Pink Lady   gin, grenadine, egg white
Planter's Punch   lime juice (1 part), sugar syrup (2 parts), rum (3 parts), Ice (4 parts), 2 dashes Angostura
Planter's Punch Rhyme   one of sour, two of sweet, three of strong, four of weak
Presto   brandy, sweet vermouth, orange juice, Pernod
Princeton   dry gin (2 parts), port (1 part), dash orange bitters, twist lemon peel
Prohibition   dry vermouth, gin, apricot brandy, orange juice

Purple Cactus   tequila, passion fruit juice, sweet sherry, grenadine

Rob Roy   Scotch whisky, vermouth, Angostura bitters

Rolls Royce   brandy, Cointreau, orange juice, egg white

Rose   dry vermouth (2 parts), Kirsch (1 part), dash strawberry syrup

Rusty Nail   whisky, Drambuie

Screwdriver   vodka orange juice

Sensation   gin, lemon juice, Maraschino, sprigs of mint

Sidecar   brandy, Cointreau, lemon juice

Singapore Sling   gin, Angostura bitters, lemon juice

Slow Comfortable Screw   vodka, Southern Comfort, sloe gin, orange juice

Snowball   Advocaat, lime juice, lemonade

Sporran Free   Drambuie, whisky, lemon juice, Angostura, soda water

Starboard Light   crème de menthe (9 parts), brandy (1 part)

Stinger   brandy, white crème de menthe

Tackety Boot   whisky, Drambuie, sweet vermouth, dry vermouth, lemonade

Tequila Sunrise   tequila, orange juice, grenadine

Third Degree   gin, dry vermouth, Pernod

Third Rail   white rum, brandy, calvados, Pernod

TNT   tequila, Tia Maria, Mandarine Napoléon

Tom and Jerry   rum, eggs, cinammon, sugar, cloves, allspice, soda, brandy, milk, nutmeg

Tom Collins   gin (1 part), lemon juice (1 part), sugar syrup (1 teaspoon), soda water

Tonsil Teaser   Grand Marnier, crème de banane, coffee liqueur, cream

Torpedo   brandy, coffee liqueur, egg white

Triple Testosterone   dark rum, white rum, triple sec, lime juice, Grenadine

Trouser Rouser   whisky, mango juice, pineapple, lime juice, crème de banane, egg white

Wembley   whiskey, dry vermouth, pineapple juice

Whisky Mac   whisky, green ginger wine

White Lady   gin, Cointreau, lemon juice

Whizz Bang   whisky, dry vermouth, orange bitters, Absinthe, Grenadine

Za-Za   Dubonnet (1/2), dry gin (1/2), dash Angostura bitters

Zombie   white rum, dark rum, pineapple juice, sugar

Flavouring

Absinthe   green alcoholic drink, technically a gin, originally having high wormwood content

Aki   plum-flavoured alcoholic drink

Akvavit   Scandinavian spirit made from potatoes and flavoured with caraway

Amaretto   almond-flavoured alcoholic drink

Angostura bitters   bitter aromatic tonic made from gentian and various spices, the true angostura bitters being obtained from the angostura bark

Arrack   rice-based spirit with a coconut flavour from Eastern countries

Aurum   orange-flavoured alcoholic drink (literal meaning 'gold'), based on Italian brandy

Ava   Polynesian drink made from peppers

B & B   Brandy and Bénédictine based liqueur

Beer   barley, flavoured with hops and fermented with yeast

Brandy   spirit distilled from the grape (literal meaning 'burnt wine'), Dutch 'brandewijn'

Calvados   spirit distilled from apples grown in the Basse-Normandie region

Cassis   blackcurrant-flavoured spirit

Chartreuse   either of two liqueurs, green or yellow, with an orange flavour

Cider   alcoholic drink made from the fermented juice of apples

Cointreau   colourless liqueur with orange flavouring

Curaçao   orange-flavoured liqueur originally made on the Caribbean island of that name

Drambuie   Scottish liqueur made from whisky and heather honey (secret recipe given by Bonnie Prince Charlie to MacKinnon family in 1746)

Gin   distilled grain flavoured with juniper berries

Grand Marnier   French cognac-based liqueur with an orange flavour

Izarra   Basque herb liqueur on an armagnac base that may be green or yellow (basque word for 'star')

Kahlúa   Mexican coffee-flavoured liqueur

Kirsch   brandy distilled from cherries, made principally in the Black Forest

Kriek-Lambic   cherry-flavoured Belgian beer

Kumiss/Koumiss   fermented mare's milk

Kümmel   Dutch grain liqueur flavoured with cumin and aniseed

Kvass   barley-flavoured East European drink distilled from stale bread

Lassi   yoghurt-based drink served with either salt or sugar

Maraschino   liqueur-flavoured with kernels of the marasca cherry and tasting of bitter almonds

Mastic   aniseed-flavoured liquor which has additional flavour from mastic gum resin

Mead   wine made by fermenting a solution of honey

Mirabelle   plum-flavoured alcoholic drink

Ouzo   Greek spirit with a strong aniseed flavour

Pastis   aniseed-flavoured apéritif from France

Pernod   aniseed-flavoured apéritif from France

Perry   alcoholic drink made from the fermented juice of pears

Port   sweet fortified dessert wine distilled from grapes

Pulque   Mexican drink made from the juice of the maguey, a kind of agave plant, literal meaning 'decomposed', since it will only keep for a day

Raki/Rakee   strong spirit distilled in Turkey and Yugoslavia and flavoured with aniseed

Retsina   Greek wine flavoured with pine wood resin

Ricard   aniseed-flavoured alcoholic drink

Rum   spirit made from sugar cane and flavoured with molasses

Sake/Saki   Japanese alcoholic drink made from fermented rice

Samshu   Chinese alcoholic drink made from fermented rice

Sangria   orange-flavoured Spanish red wine with cinnamon and cloves (literal meaning 'a bleeding')

Sherry   fortified wine made from grapes, originally only made in Jerez and San Lucar, Spain

FOOD AND DRINK

Shochu alcoholic drink flavoured by sweet potatoes

Slivovitz plum brandy from Eastern Europe, particularly Southern Slav regions

Southern Comfort peach and orange-flavoured liqueur with Bourbon base

Tequila Mexican drink made from the juice of the agave plant

Tia Maria coffee-flavoured liqueur from the West Indies

Tisane herbal infusion commonly with mint vervair or camomile. Literal meaning 'barley water'

Van der Hum South African Cape brandy liqueur

with tangerine and a touch of rum. Literal meaning 'What's his name' or 'So and So'

Vodka alcoholic drink originating in Russia and distilled from either potato or grain

Whiskey Irish whiskey (spelt with an 'e' in Ireland); the same spelling is always used in the USA

Whisky (grain) spirit made by distilling various kinds of grain. Literal meaning 'water of life'

Whisky (malt) spirit made by distilling barley. Literal meaning 'water of life'

Wine alcoholic drink produced by fermenting grapes

General Information

Alcohol: coffee effect on	makes worse
Alcohol content of beers and wines	on average, beers contain between 3 and 7% alcohol, whilst wines contain between 8 and 15%
Anjou rosé wine: from	Loire Valley
Asti Spumante: grape used	Muscat
Barbed wire	Australian term for lager, especially Castlemaine XXXX
Beer: highest alcohol content	barley wine
Bénédictine liqueur: distilled	Fécamp in Normandy (it is also distilled in the UK, where the most popular distillery is in Blackburn because a Lancashire regiment was stationed at Fécamp during the First World War)
Bottle sizes: Bordeaux	Magnum (2 bottles)
	Marie-Jeanne (3)
	Double Magnum (4)
	Jéroboam (6)
	Impériale (8)
Bottle sizes:other wines	Magnum (2)
	Jeroboam (4)
	Rehoboam (6)
	Methuselah (8)
	Salmanazar (12)
	Balthazar (16)
	Nebuchadnezzar (20)
Breweries, British: headquarters	Adnams – Suffolk; Badger – Dorset; Belhaven – Dunbar; Burtonwood – Warrington; Felinfoel – Llanelli; Greene King – Bury St Edmunds; Jennings – Cockermouth; King & Barnes – Horsham in Sussex; Marston's – Burton on Trent; Moorhouse's – Burnley; Morland – Abingdon; Rectory – Sussex; Wyre Piddle – Evesham, Worcs
Brewery: oldest in the world	Weihenstephan Brewery in Freising near Munich (founded 1040)
Cap Bon wine: from	Tunisia
Champagne: designations	brut (very dry), demi-sec (sweet), extra-sec (medium dry), Sec (medium sweet)
Champagne making: remuage	process of tilting the bottle and tapping it to help the sediment fall to the cork for subsequent removal, previously a manual process but now mechanical
Coca-Cola: original constituent	cocaine (until 1903)
Coffee: types	Blue Mountain, Bourbon, Caturra, Maragogype, Mocha, Mysore and Teaberry
Cru: French wine term	refers to the product of a growth from a single vineyard
Drink: drinking once could cause excommunication	chocolate (Central America in the 18th century)
Firkin of beer	9 gallons
French wine: only region to name its wines after the grape used	Alsace, eg. Riesling, Gewürztraminer and Muscat
Gin: former names	geneva (From French for juniper); Hollands (because the Dutch were the first to distil it)
Halbtrocken	any medium-dry German wine
Huckle-my-buff	Sussex drink of beer, eggs and brandy
Iced tea: inventor	Richard Blechynden (St Louis World Fair, 1904)
Iskra sparkling wine: from	Bulgaria (Iskra, meaning 'spark', is also from Russia)
Johnnie Walker Red Label: malt whisky used in blending of	Talisker, a single malt whisky from the Isle of Skye

Kvass	traditional Russian drink similar to beer made from rye flour mixed with a little sprouted barley
Monbazillac wine: from	Bergerac region of France
Port: aka	'the Englishman's Wine', because it was originally produced by British traders settled there
Port: maturity	it can take 40 years for a vintage port to reach maturity
Port: name from	Oporto, Portugal
Prohibition in USA	Between 1920 and 1933
Pub name: most popular in England	King's Head
Pub name: most popular in UK	Red Lion
Real ales: names (examples)	Brewer's Droop, Double Dragon, How's Your Father, Nessie's Monster Mash, Old Horny, Old Speckled Hen, Piddle in the Snow, Rector's Revenge, St Andrew's Witches' Brew, Snecklifter, Spingo, Workie Ticket
Red Stripe lager: from	Jamaica
Rioja	Northern Spanish wine-producing region divided into Alta, Alavesa and Baja
Scotch whisky: matured in	oak casks (formerly in sherry butts, now in casks sprayed with sherry concentrate)
Sheeps dip: aka	single malt Scotch whisky
Sherry: name from	Jerez, Spain
Sherry: standard cask	butt (contains 108 gallons)
Sherry: standard glass	copita (Tulip shaped)
Sherry: types	fino (dry, pale, young wine); oloroso (darker, heavier and fuller); amontillado (fuller both in colour and body and made by ageing finos); Manzanilla (palest and driest of finos)
Solera system	tiered system of blending wines in the making of sherry
Sparkling wine: invented by	Dom Pérignon (1639–1715), a Benedictine monk from Hautvillers Abbey
Spätlese	German term for 'late picked' wine; the riper grapes make the wine sweeter
Spingo beer: from	Helston in Cornwall
Spirit: best selling in the world	Bacardi
Stirrup cup	sloe gin is the traditional drink to take before hunting
Strega: liqueur from	Italy (literal meaning 'witch')
Table wine: Americans call	jug wine
Tea: bergamot-flavoured	Earl Grey
categories	black (fermented); green (unfermented); oolong (semi-fermented)
Chinese word for	cha
grades	orange pekoe (highest), pekoe, pekoe souchong, congou, pekoe dust, dust
Japanese ceremony	chanoyu
Original use	medicine
Used as currency	Siberia
Tiger beer: from	Singapore and Malaysia
Trocken	drier style of German wine
Tulip : glasses	best glass for serving cognac as balloon glass loses bouquet
Ullage	air gap between the cork and the wine, often found in very old wine; also refers to the space created in a wine barrel by evaporation
Vermouth: types	French has come to mean 'dry white', whilst Italian is 'sweet red'
VSOP	Very Special/Superior Old Pale: not more than 5 years old
Whisky: bourbon and rye contrast	bourbon comes from Kentucky, whilst rye comes from the USA and Canada; bourbon is aged in cold warehouses whilst rye is aged in heated rooms
Whisky: Johnnie Walker Black Label matured for	twelve years
Whisky: largest malt whisky distillery in the world	Suntory distillery at Hakushu, Japan
Whisky: meaning	water of life
Whisky: world's best-selling single-malt Scottish whisky	Glenfiddich
White Horse whisky: malt whisky used in blending of	Lagavulin
Wine: some famous Bordeaux districts	Entre-Deux-Mers, Graves, Margaux, Sauternes, St Emilion, Médoc, Pomerol
Wine: difference between English and British	English wine is made from grapes grown in England, British wine is made in Britain from concentrated grape juice imported from abroad and reconstituted with British water

FOOD
AND
DRINK

Wine: difference between sweet & dry	sweet wine is taken from the vat before all the sugar is converted to alcohol by fermentation
Wine: grape colours	red and rosé wines are made with red grapes, but white wine may be made with red or white grapes
Wine labels: AC, control designation	Appellation Contrôlée (French quality-control designation)
Wine labels: Cava	found on best sparkling wines from Spain (not quite as good as champagne), mostly from Catalonia
Wine labels: DOC, control designation	Denominazione di Origine Controllata (Italian quality-control designation)
Wine: Lacrima Christi	made on the south slopes of Mt Vesuvius, near Naples
Wine: length of cork denotes	the longer the cork, the longer period of time the wine is intended to be laid down for
Wine: louse that attacks vine roots of Vitis vinifera	*Phylloxera vastatrix* accidentally imported into Europe from the USA in the 1860s
Wine making: chapeau (hat)	term that refers to the layer of grape skins which rise to the surface during red wine fermentation
Wine making terms: must	unfermented grape juice seeds and skins; first stage in wine-making process or crushed grapes
Wine making: difference between red and white	skins of red grapes must be left in contact with the crushed grapes during fermentation, whilst the skins are removed before fermentation in production of white wine
Wine: marc	spirit distilled from grape skins and stalks
Wine: minimum alcohol content under EC laws	7%
Wine: off licence scale of sweetness	from 1 to 9: sweetest is 9 and driest is 1
Wine: origins	somewhere between the Black and Caspian seas, around 4000 BC
Wine producer: world's largest	Italy, in 8 years out of every 10, on average; otherwise France
Wine: rosé	basically white wine made from red grapes that causes it to be given a little colour and flavour by being left a short time with the skins
Wine: Sauternes, most expensive	Château Yquem
Wine: sparkling	sparkling wine is a wine which undergoes a second fermentation effervesces when poured
Wine: sparkling: production methods	méthode champenoise (bottle fermentation – method for best wines); cuve close; transfer system; transversage
Wine stored horizontally: reason	to keep cork in contact with the wine so that it does not shrink and admit air to the bottle
Wine: study of	oenology
Wine: some tasting terms:	
beefy	red wines high in alcohol, big, solid and chunky
buttery	refers to the soft, rich vanilla flavour imparted by new oak barrels
chewy	plenty of of tannin and a strong flavour
clean	no chemical or bacterial faults, and a straightforward, simple flavour
fat	heavy, perhaps clumsy
grapy	most common with Muscat, Gewürztraminer, and Müller-Thurgau, it denotes the flavour of the grape itself
green	unripe or tart
hard	red wines that have too much tannin
length	length of time and the way the flavour of wine continues to develop in the mouth after swallowing
prickly	refers to a wine with some residual gas left in it
stony	rather dull, empty dryness in either a red or white
tough	too much tannin
Wines: types:	
Amontillado	sherry
Amoroso	sherry
Asti Spumante	sparkling Italian wine from Muscat grape
Bull's Blood	Hungarian wine from Eger region
Chianti	Italian red wine from Tuscany
Claret	red Bordeaux wine (traditional English name for)
Fino	dry, light sherry
Hock	German Rhine wine (from the village called Hochheim)
Liebfraumilch	type of hock (blended wine from Rhine area)
Manzanilla	sherry (dry)
Marsala	Sicilian fortified wine
Moselle	German white wine
Oloroso	dark sherry

Retsina	Greek wine
Soave	white Italian wine
Tokay	Hungarian wine
Vinho Verde	white wine from the north of Portugal
Wine: vintage & non-vintage	vintage wine comes from a single harvest, whilst non-vintage is a blend of wines of more than one year
Wine: what it is	fermented juice of the grape; fermentation being a bio-chemical reaction in which sugar in grape juice is converted into ethyl alcohol and carbon dioxide gas
Wine: world's best seller	Lambrusco (especially popular in USA)
Zymurgy	the art or practice of fermentation in wine-making, brewing and distilling

FOOD AND DRINK

Geography

British Dependent Territories

Anguilla
Bermuda (Somers Islands)
British Antarctic Territory
British Indian Ocean Territory
British Virgin Islands
Cayman Islands
Falkland Islands

Gibraltar
Montserrat
Pitcairn Islands
St Helena and Dependencies
  (Ascension and Tristan Da Cunha)
South Georgia and South Sandwich Islands
Turks and Caicos Islands

Capitals

Country, State, County or Area	Capital or Admin Centre	Country, State, County or Area	Capital or Admin Centre
A'āli an-Nil (Upper Nile) (Sudan)	Malakāi	Amambay (Paraguay)	Pedro Juan
Aargau (Swiss canton)	Aarau		Caballero
Abaco and Mores Island (Bahamas)	Marsh Harbour	Amapá (Brazil)	Macapá
Abalang (Kiribati)	Tuarabu	Amazonas (Brazil)	Manaus
Abemama (Kiribati)	Kariatebike	Amazonas (Colombia)	Leticia
Abkhaziya (CIS)	Sukhumi	Amazonas (Peru)	Chachapoyas
Abruzzi (Italy)	L'Aquila	Ambae/Maéwo (Vanuatu)	Longana
Abyān (Yemen)	Zinjibār	Ambrym (Vanuatu)	Eas
Acklins Island (Bahamas)	Pompey Bay	**American Samoa**	Pago Pago
Acre (Brazil)	Rio Branco	Amou (Togo)	Amiamé
Adamous (Cameroon)	Ngaoundéré	An Giang (Vietnam)	Long Xuyen
Ad-Dagahliyah (Egypt)	Al-Mansurah	Anambra (Nigeria)	Enugu
Adrar (Mauritania)	Atar	Ancash (Peru)	Huaraz
Adygeya (Russia)	Maikop	Andalucia (Spain)	Seville
Afghanistan	Kabul	Andaman and Nicobar Islands	Port Blair
Agin-Buryat (Russia)	Aginskoe	Andhra Pradesh (India)	Hyderabad
Aichi (Japan)	Nagoya	**Andorra**	Andorra La Vella
Ain (France)	Bourg-en-Bresse	Andros Island (Bahamas)	Kemps Bay
Aisén del Gen Carlos Ibáñez del		**Angola**	Luanda
Campo (Chile)	Coihaique	**Anguilla**	The Valley
Aisne (France)	Laon	Anhui (aka Anhwei) (China)	Hefei (aka Ho-fei)
Akwa Ibom (Nigeria)	Uyo	An-Nil al-Azraq (Blue Nile) (Sudan)	Ad-Damazin
Alabama (USA)	Montgomery	**Antigua and Barbuda**	St John's
Alagoas (Brazil)	Maceió	Antioquia (Colombia)	Medellín
Al-Anbār (Iraq)	Ar-Ramādi	Antofagasta (Chile)	Antofagasta
Alania (Russia)	Vladikavkaz	Antrim (NI)	Belfast
Alaska (USA)	Juneau	Anzoátegui (Venezuela)	Barcelona
Al-Bahr al-Ahmar (Egypt)	Al-Ghurdaqah	Aorangi (NZ)	Timaru
Albania	Tirana	Appenzell Ausser-Rhoden	
Alberta (Canada)	Edmonton	(Swiss canton)	Herisau
Al-Biqa (Lebanon)	Zahlah	Appenzell Inner-Rhoden	
Al-Buhayrah (Egypt)	Damanhur	(Swiss canton)	Appenzell
Alderney	St Annes	Apulia (Italy)	Bari
Algeria	Algiers	Apure (Venezuela)	San Fernando de
Al-Gharbiyah (Egypt)	Tanjā		Apure
Alifu (Maldives)	Mahibadhoo	Apurimac (Peru)	Abancay
Al-Janub (Lebanon)	Sidon/Saydā	Aqua Grande (São Tomé and	
Al-Lādhiqiyah (Syria)	Latakia	Principe)	São Tomé
Allier (France)	Moulins	Aquitaine (France)	Bordeaux
Al-Mahrah (Yemen)	Al-Ghaydah	Aragón (Spain)	Zaragoza
Al-Minufiyah (Egypt)	Shibin al-Kawm	Aragua (Venezuela)	Maracay
Alpes-de-Haute-Provence (France)	Digne	Arakan/Rakhine (Burma)	Sittwe (aka Akyab)
Alpes-Maritimes (France)	Nice	Aranuka (Kiribati)	Takaeang
Al-Qalyubiyah (Egypt)	Banhā	Araucanía (Chile)	Temuco
Alsace (France)	Strasbourg	Ardèche (France)	Privas
Altai (Russia)	Gorno	Ardennes (France)	Charleville-
Alta Verapaz (Guatemala)	Cobán		Mézières
Alto Paraguay (Paraguay)	Fuerte Olimpio	**Argentina**	Buenos Aires
Alto Paraná (Paraguay)	Ciudad del Este	Arges (Romania)	Pitesti
Älvsborg (Sweden)	Vänersborg	Arhangay (Mongolia)	Tsetserieg
Al-Wādi al-Jadid (Egypt)	Al-Kharijah	Ariège (France)	Foix

Country, State, County or Area	Capital or Admin Centre	Country, State, County or Area	Capital or Admin Centre
Arizona (USA)	Phoenix	Basque Country (Spain)	Vitoria
Arkansas (USA)	Little Rock	Bas-Rhin (France)	Strasbourg
Armagh (NI)	Armagh	Basse-Kotto (Cape Verde)	Mobaye
Armenia	Yerevan	Basse-Normandie (France)	Caen
Arorae (Kiribati)	Roreti	Bas-Zaïre (Dem Rep of Congo)	Matadi
Arsi (Ethiopia)	Asela	Batha (Chad)	Ati
Artibonite (Haiti)	Gonaives	Bavaria (Germany)	Munich
Arua (Uganda)	Olaki	Bay (Somalia)	Baidoa
Aruba	Oranjestad		(Baydhabo)
Arunāchal Pradesh (India)	Itānagar	Bay of Plenty (NZ)	Tauranga
Ascension	Georgetown	Bazéga (Burkina Faso)	Kombissiri
Ashanti (Ghana)	Kumasi	Bedfordshire (Eng)	Bedford
Ash-Shamāl (Lebanon)	Tripoli/Tarābulus	Belait (Brunei)	Kuala Belait
Ash-Sharqiyah (Egypt)	Az-Zaqāziq	**Belgium**	Brussels
Assam (India)	Dispur	**Belize**	Belmopan
Assoli (Togo)	Bafilo	**Belorussia**	Minsk
Asturias (Spain)	Oviedo	Bendel (Nigeria)	Benin City
Atacama (Chile)	Copiapó	Bengo (Angola)	Caxito
Atacora (Benin)	Natitingou	Beni (Bolivia)	Trinidad
Atlántico (Colombia)	Barranquilla	**Benin**	Porto Novo (*de*
Atlántida (Honduras)	La Ceiba		*facto* Cotonou)
Atlantique (Benin)	Cotonou	Benue (Nigeria)	Makurdi
Aube (France)	Troyes	Berea (Lesotho)	Teyateyaneng
Aude (France)	Carcassonne	Berkshire (Eng)	Reading
Aust-Agder (Norway)	Arendal	**Bermuda**	Hamilton
Australia	Canberra	Berry Island (Bahamas)	Nicolls Town
Australian Capital Territory	Canberra	Beru (Kiribati)	Taubukinberu
Austria	Vienna	**Bhutan (aka Druk-Yul)**	Thimphu
Austurland (Iceland)	Egilsstadhir	Bié (Angola)	Kuito
Auvergne (France)	Clermont-Ferrand	Bihar (India)	Patna
Aveyron (France)	Rodez	Bihor (Romania)	Oradea
Avon (Eng)	Bristol	Bimini Islands (Bahamas)	Alice Town
Azerbaijan	Baku	Binah (Togo)	Pagouda
Azores (Portugal)	Ponta Delgada	Binh Dinh (Vietnam)	Quy Nhon
Azuay (Ecuador)	Cuenca	Binh Duong (Vietnam)	Thu Dau Mot
Ba Ria (Vietnam)	Vung Tau	Binh Phuoc (Vietnam)	Dung Xoai
Baa (Maldives)	Eydhafushi	Binh Thuan (Vietnam)	Phan Thiet
Bābil (Iraq)	Al-Hillah	Bíobío (Chile)	Concepción
Bács-Kiskun (Hungary)	Kecskemét	Bioko (Equatorial Guinea)	Malabo
Baden-Württemberg (Germany)	Stuttgart	Biombo (Guinea-Bissau)	Bissau
Bahamas	Nassau	Blekinge (Sweden)	Karlskrona
Bahia (Brazil)	Salvador	Boavista (Cape Verde)	Sal Rei
Bahoruco (Dominican Republic)	Neiba	Bokeo (Laos)	Houayxay
Bahr al-Ghazāl (Sudan)	Wāu	Bolikhamxay (Laos)	Pakxan
Bahrain	Manama	Bolivar (Colombia)	Cartagena
Baja California Norte (Mexico)	Mexicali	Bolivar (Ecuador)	Guaranda
Baja California Sur (Mexico)	La Paz	Bolivar (Venezuela)	Ciudad Bolivar
Baja Verapaz (Guatemala)	Salamá	**Bolivia**	Sucre–judicial
Bakool (Somalia)	Oddur (Xuddur)		La Paz–
Bale (Ethiopia)	Goba		administrative
Balearic Islands (Spain)	Palma de	Bombali (Sierra Leone)	Makeni
	Mallorca	Bomi (Liberia)	Tubmanburg
Bali (Indonesia)	Denpassar	Bonaire (Netherland Antilles)	Kralendijk
Baluchistān (Pakistan)	Quetta	Bong (Liberia)	Gbarnga
Bam (Burkina Faso)	Kongoussi	Bophuthatswana (South Africa)	Mmabatho
Bamingui-Bangoran (Cape Verde)	Ndélé	Boquerón (Paraguay)	Dr Pedro P. Peña
Banaadir (Somalia)	Mogadishu	Bora-Bora (French Polynesia)	Vaitape
	(Muqdisho)	Borders (Scotland)	Newtown St
Banaba (Kiribati)	Anteeren		Boswells
Bangladesh	Dhaka	Borgou (Benin)	Parakou
Banks/Torres (Vanuatu)	Sola	Borkou-Ennedi-Tibesti (Chad)	Faya
Baranya (Hungary)	Pécs	Bornholm (Denmark)	Renne
Barbados	Bridgetown	Borno (Nigeria)	Maiduguri
Bari (Somalia)	Bender Cassim	Borsod-Abaúj-Zemplén (Hungary)	Miskolc
	(Boosaaso)	**Bosnia and Hercegovina**	Sarajevo
Barima/Waini (Guyana)	Mabaruma	**Botswana**	Gaborone
Basel-Landschaft (Swiss canton)	Liestal	Botswana (Central)	Serowe
Basel-Stadt (Swiss canton)	Basel	Botswana (North East)	Masunga
Bashkir (Russia)	Ufa	Botswana (South East)	Ramotswa
Basilicata (Italy)	Potenza	Bouches-du-Rhône (France)	Marseille

GEOGRAPHY

Country, State, County or Area	Capital or Admin Centre	Country, State, County or Area	Capital or Admin Centre
Bouenza (Congo)	Madingou	Central (Scotland)	Stirling
Bougouriba (Burkina Faso)	Diébougou	**Central African Republic**	Bangui
Boulgou (Burkina Faso)	Tenkodogo	Central District (Israel)	Ramla
Boulkiemde (Burkina Faso)	Koudougou	Central Islands (Solomon Isles)	Tulagi
Bourgogne/Burgundy (France)	Dijon	Central Nepal	Kāthmāndu
Boyacá (Colombia)	Tunja	Central Province (Fiji)	Suva
Brabant (Flemish)	Louvain (Leuven)	Central Province (Kenya)	Nyeri
Brabant (Walloon)	Wavre	Central Province (Zambia)	Kabwe
Brakna (Mauritania)	Aleg	Central Region (Ghana)	Cape Coast
Brandenburg (Germany)	Potsdam	Central Region (Paraguay)	Asunción
Brava (Cape Verde)	Nova Sintra	Centrale Region (Togo)	Sokodé
Brazil	Brasilia	Centre Département (Haiti)	Hinche
Bretagne/Brittany (France)	Rennes	Centre Province (Cameroon)	Yaoundé
British Columbia (Canada)	Victoria	Cerro Largo (Uruguay)	Melo
Brong-Ahafo (Ghana)	Sunyani	Cesar (Colombia)	Valledupar
Brunei	Bandar Seri Begawan	Chaco (Argentina)	Resistencia
Buckinghamshire (Eng)	Aylesbury	Chaco (Paraguay)	Mayor Pablo Lagerenza
Buenos Aires (Argentina)	La Plata	**Chad**	N'Djamena
Bulgaria (aka Narodna Republic)	Sofia	Chagang-do (North Korea)	Kanggye
Bumthang (Bhutan)	Jakar	Champagne-Ardenne (France)	Châlons-sur-Marne
Bundibugyo (Uganda)	Busaru	Champasak (Laos)	Pakxé
Burgenland (Austria)	Eisenstadt	Charente (France)	Angoulême
Burkina Faso	Ouagadougou	Charente-Maritime (France)	La Rochelle
Burundi	Bujumbura	Chari-Baguirmi (Chad)	N'Djaména
Buryat (Russia)	Ulan-Ude	**Chechnya**	Dzhohar
Bushenyi (Uganda)	Bumbaire	Cher (France)	Bourges
Buskerud (Norway)	Drammen	Cheshire (Eng)	Chester
Caaguazú (Paraguay)	Coronel Oviedo	Chiapas (Mexico)	Tuxtla Gutiérrez
Cabañas (El Salvador)	Sensuntepeque	**Chile**	Santiago
Cabo Delgado (Mozambique)	Pemba	Chimborazo (Ecuador)	Riobamba
Calabria (Italy)	Catanzaro	Chimbu (Papua New Guinea)	Kundiawa
Caldas (Colombia)	Manizales	Chin (Myanmar)	Hakha
California (USA)	Sacramento	**China**	Beijing (aka Peking)
Calvados (France)	Caen	Chirang (Bhutan)	Damphu
Cambodia	Phnom Penh	Chiriqui (Panama)	David
Cambridgeshire (Eng)	Cambridge	Chobe (Botswana)	Kasane
Cameroon	Yaoundé	Chocó (Colombia)	Quibdó
Campania (Italy)	Naples	Chŏlla-namdo (South Korea)	Kwangju
Canada	Ottawa	Chŏlla-pukto (South Korea)	Ch'ŏnju
Cañar (Ecuador)	Azoques	Christmas Island (Aus)	Flying Fish Cove
Canary Islands (Spain)	Santa Cruz de Tenerife	Christmas Island/Kiritimati Atoll (Kiribati)	London
Canendiyú (Paraguay)	Salto del Guairá	Chubut (Argentina)	Rawson
Cantabria (Spain)	Santander	Chukut (Russia)	Anadyr
Cantagaio (São Tomé and Principe)	Santana	Chuquisaca (Bolivia)	Sucre
Cantal (France)	Aurillac	Chuvashia (Russia)	Cheboksary
Canterbury (NZ)	Christchurch	Ciskei (South Africa)	Bisho
Cape Verde	Praia	Citta (San Marino)	San Marino
Caprivi (Namibia)	Katima Mulilo	Clare (Rep of Ireland)	Ennis
Caquetá (Colombia)	Florencia	Clarendon (Jamaica)	May Pen
Carabobo (Venezuela)	Valencia	Cleveland (Eng)	Middlesbrough
Caras-Severin (Romania)	Resita	Clwyd (Wales)	Mold
Carchi (Ecuador)	Tulcan	Coahuila (Mexico)	Saltillo
Carlow (Rep of Ireland)	Carlow	Coast Province (Kenya)	Mombasa
Caroni (Trinidad and Tobago)	Chaguanas	Coclé (Panama)	Penonomé
Casanare (Colombia)	Yopal	Cocos (aka Keeling Islands) (Aus)	West Island
Castilla-La Mancha (Spain)	Toledo	Cojedes (Venezuela)	San Carlos
Castilla-León (Spain)	Valladolid	**Colombia**	Bogotá
Cat Island (Bahamas)	Arthur's Town	Colón (Honduras)	Trujillo
Catalonia (Spain)	Barcelona	Colorado (USA)	Denver
Catamarca (Argentina)	San Fernando	Commewijne (Suriname)	Nieuw Amsterdam
Cauca (Colombia)	Popoyán	Comoé (Burkina Faso)	Banfora
Caué (São Tomé and Principe)	São João Angolares	**Comoros Islands**	Moroni
Cavan (Rep of Ireland)	Cavan	**Congo: Democratic Republic**	Kinshasa
Cayman Islands	George Town	**Congo: People's Republic**	Brazzaville
Cayo (Belize)	San Ignacio	Connecticut (USA)	Hartford
Ceará (Brazil)	Fortaleza		

Country, State, County or Area	Capital or Admin Centre	Country, State, County or Area	Capital or Admin Centre
Cook Islands (New Zealand)	Ararua	Dublin (Rep of Ireland)	Dublin
Copperbelt (Zambia)	Ndola	Dumfries and Galloway (Scotland)	Dumfries
Coquimbo (Chile)	La Serena	Dundgovi (Mongolia)	Mandalgov
Cordillera (Paraguay)	Caacupé	Durham (Eng)	Durham
Córdoba (Colombia)	Montería	Dyfed (Wales)	Carmarthen
Corfu	Kerkira	Dzavhan (Mongolia)	Uliastay
Cork (Rep of Ireland)	Cork	East Berbice/Corentyne (Guyana)	New Amsterdam
Cornwall (Eng)	Truro	East Cape (NZ)	Gisborne
Coronie (Suriname)	Totness	East Flanders (Belgium)	Ghent
Corrèze (France)	Tulle	East New Britain (Papua	
Corse-du-Sud (France)	Ajaccio	New Guinea)	Rabaul
Corsica (France)	Ajaccio	East Sepik (Papua New Guinea)	Wewak
Cortés (Honduras)	San Pedro Sula	East Sussex (Eng)	Lewes
Costa Rica	San José	**East Timor**	Dili
Côte-d'Or (France)	Dijon	Easter Island	Hanga Roa
Côtes-du-Nord (France)	Saint-Brieuc	Eastern Equatoria (Sudan)	Jubã
Cotopaxi (Ecuador)	Latacunga	Eastern Highlands (Papua	
Covasna (Romania)	Sfintu Gheorghe	New Guinea)	Goroka
Crete	Khania	Eastern Nepal	Dhankutã
Creuse (France)	Guéret	Eastern Province (Fiji)	Levuka
Croatia	Zagreb	Eastern Province (Kenya)	Embu
Crooked Island (Bahamas)	Colonel Hill	Eastern Province (Sierra Leone)	Kenema
Cross River (Nigeria)	Calabar	Eastern Province (Zambia)	Chipata
Csongrád (Hungary)	Szeged	Eastern Region (Ghana)	Koforidua
Cuba	Havana	Eastern Timor (Pacific)	Dili
Cumbria (Eng)	Carlisle	**Ecuador**	Quito
Cundinamarca (Colombia)	Bogotá	Efaté (Vanuatu)	Vila
Cunene (Angola)	N'Giva	**Egypt**	Cairo
Curaçao (Netherland Antilles)	Willemstad	Ehime (Japan)	Matsuyama
Cuscatlán (El Salvador)	Cojutepeque	El Oro (Ecuador)	Machala
Cuvette (Congo)	Owando	El Paraiso (Honduras)	Yuscarán
Cuzco (Peru)	Cuzco	**El Salvador**	San Salvador
Cyprus	Nicosia	El-Acâba (Mauritania)	Kiffa
Czech Republic	Prague	Emilia-Romagna (Italy)	Bologna
Dac Lac (Vietnam)	Buon Ma Thuot	Enga (Papua New Guinea)	Wabag
Dadra and Nagar Haveli (India)	Silvassa	**England**	London
Dagestan (Russia)	Makhachkala	Entre Rios (Argentina)	Paraná
Dãrfur (Sudan)	Al-Fãshir	Epi (Vanuatu)	Ringdove
Darién (Panama)	La Palma	Equateur (Dem Rep of Congo)	Mbandaka
Delaware (USA)	Dover	**Equatorial Guinea**	Malabo
Demerara/Mahaica (Guyana)	Paradise	**Eritrea**	Asmara
Denmark	Copenhagen	Erongo (Namibia)	Swakopmund
Derbyshire (Eng)	Matlock	Espaillat (Dom Republic)	Moca
Des Plateaux (Togo)	Atakpamé	Espirito Santo (Brazil)	Vitória
Des Savanes (Togo)	Dapaong	Essequibo Islands (Guyana)	Vreed-en-Hoop
Deux-Sèvres (France)	Niort	Essex (Eng)	Chelmsford
Devon (Eng)	Exeter	Essonne (France)	Évry
Dhaalu (Maldives)	Kudahuvadhoo	Est (Cameroon)	Bertoua
Dhi Qãr (Iraq)	An-Nãsiriyah	**Estonia**	Tallinn
Dibër (Albania)	Peshkopi	Estuaire (Gabon)	Libreville
Dimashq (Syria)	Damascus	**Ethiopia**	Addis Ababa
Dimbovita (Romania)	Tirgoviste	Eua (Tonga)	Ohonua
Djibouti	Djibouti	Eure (France)	Évreux
Dolj (Romania)	Craiova	Eure-et-Loire (France)	Chartres
Dominica	Roseau	Evenki (Russia)	Tura
Dominican Republic	Santo Domingo	Extremadura (Spain)	Mérida
Donegal (Rep of Ireland)	Lifford	Extrême-Nord (Cameroon)	Maroua
Dong Nai (Vietnam)	Bien Hoa	Faafu (Maldives)	Magoodhoo
Dong Thap (Vietnam)	Sa Dec	**Faeroe Islands**	Thorshavn
Dordogne (France)	Périgueux	Falcón (Venezuela)	Coro
Dornod (Mongolia)	Choybaisan	**Falkland Islands**	Stanley
Dornogovi (Mongolia)	Saynshand	Fanning/Tabuaeran (Kiribati)	Paelau
Dorset (Eng)	Dorchester	Fãrs (Iran)	Shirãz
Doubs (France)	Besançon	Far-Western Nepal	Dipãyal
Doufelgou (Togo)	Niamtougou	Fejér (Hungary)	Székesfehérvár
Down (NI)	Downpatrick	Fermanagh (NI)	Enniskillen
Drenthe (Netherlands)	Assen	Fife (Scotland)	Glenrothes
Drôme (France)	Valence	**Fiji**	Suva
Duarte (Dominican Republic)	San Francisco de Macoris	Finistère (France)	Quimper
		Finland	Helsinki

GEOGRAPHY

Country, State, County or Area	Capital or Admin Centre	Country, State, County or Area	Capital or Admin Centre
Finnmark (Norway)	Vardø	Greater Manchester (Eng)	Manchester
Flevoland (Netherlands)	Lelystad	**Greece**	Athens
Flores (Uruguay)	Trinidad	**Greenland** (aka Kalaallit Nunaat)	Godthaab
Florida (USA)	Tallahassee		(aka Nuuk)
Fogo (Cape Verde)	São Filipe	**Grenada**	St George's
France	Paris	Gribingui-Economique (CA Rep)	Kaga-Bandoro
Francisco Morazán (Honduras)	Tegucigalpa	Guadalcanal (Solomon Isles)	Honiara
Frederiksborg (Denmark)	Hillerod	**Guadeloupe**	Basse-Terre
French Guiana	Cayenne	Guainia (Colombia)	Puerto Inirida
French Polynesia	Papeete	Guairá (Paraguay)	Villarica
Friesland (Netherlands)	Leeuwarden	**Guam**	Agana
Friuli-Venezia Giulia (Italy)	Trieste	Guanacaste (Costa Rica)	Liberia
Fujian (aka Fukien) (China)	Fuzhou (aka Foochow)	Guangdong (aka Kwangtung) (China)	Guangzhou (aka Canton)
Fyn (Denmark)	Odense	Guangxi Zhuang (aka Kwangsi Chuang) (China)	Nanning
Gaafu-Alifu (Maldives)	Vilgili		
Gaafu-Dhaalu (Maldives)	Thinadhoo	Guárico (Venezuela)	San Juan de Los Morros
Gabon	Libreville		
Galguduud (Somalia)	Dusa Marreb (Dhuusamarreeb)	**Guatemala**	Guatemala City
		Guayas (Ecuador)	Guayaquil
Galicia (Spain)	Santiago de Compostela	Guéra (Chad)	Mongo
		Guernsey	St Peter Port
Galway (Rep of Ireland)	Galway	Guerrero (Mexico)	Chilpancingo
Gambia	Banjul	Guidimaka (Mauritania)	Sélibaby
Gambier Islands (French Polynesia)	Rikitea	**Guinea**	Conakry
		Guinea-Bissau	Bissau
Gansu (aka Kansu) (China)	Lanzhou (aka Lan-chou)	Guizhou (aka Kweichow) (China)	Guiyang (aka Kuei-yang)
Ganzourgou (Burkina Faso)	Zorgho	Gujarāt (India)	Gāndhinagar
Gard (France)	Nîmes	Gulf (Papua New Guinea)	Kerema
Gaza (Mozambique)	Xai-Xai	Gulu (Uganda)	Bungatira
Gazankulu (South Africa)	Giyani	Gumma (Japan)	Maebashi
Gedo (Somalia)	Garbahaarrey	**Guyana**	Georgetown
Gelderland (Netherlands)	Arnhem	Gwent (Wales)	Cwmbran
Gemu Gofa (Ethiopia)	Arba Minch	Gwynedd (Wales)	Caernarfon
Georgia	Tbilisi	Ha Nan (Vietnam)	Phu Ly
Georgia (USA)	Atlanta	Ha Tay (Vietnam)	Ha Dong
Germany	Berlin	Haa-Alifu (Maldives)	Dhidhdhoo
Gers (France)	Auch	Haa-Dhaalu (Maldives)	Nolhivaranfaru
Ghana	Accra	Ha'apai (Tonga)	Pangai
Gia Lai (Vietnam)	Plei Ku	Hadramawt (Yemen)	Al-Mukallā
Gilãn (Iran)	Rasht	Haho (Togo)	Notsé
Gilbert Isles (Kiribati)	Bairiki	Hainan (China)	Haikou
Gironde (Aquitaine, France)	Bordeaux	Hainaut (Belgium)	Mons
Gloucestershire (Eng)	Gloucester	**Haiti**	Port-au-Prince
Gnagna (Burkina Faso)	Bogandé	Hajdú-Bihar (Hungary)	Debrecen
Gnyaviyani (Maldives)	Foah Mulah	Halab (Syria)	Aleppo
Goa (India)	Panaji	Halland (Sweden)	Halmstad
Goiás (Brazil)	Goiânia	Häme (Finland)	Hämeenlinna
Gojam (Ethiopia)	Debre Markos	Hamgyong-namdo (North Korea)	Hamhung
Golfe (Togo)	Lomé	Hamgyong-pukto (North Korea)	Ch'öngjin
Gongola (Nigeria)	Yola	Hampshire (Eng)	Winchester
Gorgol (Mauritania)	Kaédi	Hanover (Jamaica)	Lucea
Gorj (Romania)	Tirgu Jiu	Hararge (Ethiopia)	Harer
Gotland (Sweden)	Visby	Hardap (Namibia)	Mariental
Gourma (Burkina Faso)	Fada N'Gourma	Harghita (Romania)	Miercurea-Ciuc
Gozo (Malta)	Victoria	Haryana (India)	Chandigarh
Gracias a Dios (Honduras)	Puerto Lempira	Hau Giang (Vietnam)	Can Tho
Grampian (Scotland)	Aberdeen	Haute-Corse (France)	Bastia
Gran Canaria	Las Palmas	Haute-Garonne (France)	Toulouse
Grand Bahama	Freeport	Haute-Kotto (CA Rep)	Bria
Grand Bassa (Liberia)	Buchanan	Haute-Loire (France)	Le Puy
Grand Cape Mount (Liberia)	Robertsport	Haute-Marne (France)	Chaumont
Grand Gedeh (Liberia)	Zwedru	Haute-Normandie (France)	Rouen
Grand Kru (Liberia)	Barclayville	Hautes-Alpes (France)	Gap
Grande Anse (Haiti)	Jérémie	Haute-Sangha (CA Rep)	Berbérati
Granma (Cuba)	Bayamo	Haute-Saône (France)	Vesoul
Graubunden (Swiss canton)	Chur	Haute-Savoie (France)	Annecy
Greater Accra (Ghana)	Accra	Hautes-Pyrénées (France)	Tarbes
Greater London (Eng)	London	Haute-Vienne (France)	Limoges

Country, State, County or Area	Capital or Admin Centre	Country, State, County or Area	Capital or Admin Centre
Haute-Zaïre (Dem Rep of Congo)	Kisangani	Indre (France)	Châteauroux
Haut-Mbomou (CA Rep)	Obo	Indre-et-Loire (France)	Tours
Haut-Ogooué (Gabon)	Masuku	Ingushetia (Russia)	Nazran
Haut-Rhin (France)	Colmar	Inner Mongolia (aka Nei Monggol)	Hu-ho-hao-t'e (aka Hohhot)
Hauts-de-Seine (France)	Nanterre		
Hawaii (USA)	Honolulu	Intibucá (Honduras)	La Esperanza
Hawke's Bay (NZ)	Napier	Iowa (USA)	Des Moines
Hebei (China)	Shijazhuang	**Iran**	Tehran
Hedmark (Norway)	Hamar	**Iraq**	Baghdad
Heilongjiang (China)	Harbin	**Ireland, Republic of**	Dublin
Henan (China)	Zhengzhou	Irian Jaya (Indonesia)	Jayapura
Hentiy (Mongolia)	Öndörhaan	Isabel (Solomon Isles)	Buala
Hérault (France)	Montpellier	Isère (France)	Grenoble
Hercegovina	Mostar	Ishikawa (Japan)	Kanazawa
Hereford and Worcester (Eng)	Worcester	Islas de la Bahia (Honduras)	Roatán
Herrera (Panama)	Chitré	Isle of Man	Douglas
Hertfordshire (Eng)	Hertford	Isle of Wight	Newport
Hessen (Germany)	Wiesbaden	**Israel**	Jerusalem
Heves (Hungary)	Eger	**Italy**	Rome
Hhohho (Swaziland)	Mbabane	Itapúa (Paraguay)	Encarnación
Hidalgo (Mexico)	Pachuca	**Ivory Coast**	Yamoussoukro– admin
Highland (Scotland)	Inverness		Abidjan– legislative
Hiiraan (Somalia)	Beledweyne		
Himãchal Pradesh (India)	Shimla		
Hims (Syria)	Homs	Iwate (Japan)	Morioka
Hodh-ech-Chargui (Mauritania)	Néma	Izabal (Guatemala)	Puerto Barrios
Hodh-el-Gharbi (Mauritania)	Ayoûn el-Atroûs	Jakarta Raya (Indonesia)	Jakarta
Höfudhborgarsvaedhi (Iceland)	Reykjavik	Jalisco (Mexico)	Guadalajara
Hokkaidō (Japan)	Sapporo	**Jamaica**	Kingston
Honduras	Tegucigalpa	Jammu and Kashmir (India)	Srinagar (in summer)
Hong Kong (aka Hsiang Kang)	Victoria (on Hong Kong Isle)		Jammu (in winter)
Hordaland (Norway)	Bergen		
Horowhenua (NZ)	Levin	Jämtland (Sweden)	Östersund
Houaphan (Laos)	Xam Nua	**Japan**	Tokyo
Houet (Burkina Faso)	Bobo-Dioulasso	Jawar Barat (Indonesia)	Bandung
Hövsgöl (Mongolia)	Mörön	Jawar Tengah (Indonesia)	Semarang
Hubei (China)	Wuhan	Jawar Timur (Indonesia)	Surabaya
Huila (Colombia)	Neiva	Jersey	St Helier
Huíta (Angola)	Lubango	Jiangsu (aka Kiangsu) (China)	Nanjing (aka Nanking)
Humberside (Eng)	Beverley		
Hunan (China)	Changsha	Jiangxi (aka Kiangsi) (China)	Nanchang
Hunedoara (Romania)	Deva	Jilin (aka Kirin) (China)	Changchun
Hungary	Budapest	Johor (Malaysia)	Johor Baharu
Hwanghae-namdo (North Korea)	Haeju	**Jordan**	Amman
Hwanghae-pukto (North Korea)	Sariwŏn	Jubbada Dhexe (Somalia)	Bu'aale
Hyōgo (Japan)	Kōbe	Jubbada Hoose (Somalia)	Chisimayu (Kismaayo)
Ialomita (Romania)	Siobozia		
Ibaraki (Japan)	Mito	Jujuy (Argentina)	San Salvador
Iceland	Reykjavik	Junin (Peru)	Huancayo
Idaho (USA)	Boise	Junquli (Jongley) (Sudan)	Bor
Iganga (Uganda)	Bulamogi	Jura (France)	Lons-le-Saunier
Île-de-France (France)	Paris	Jura (Swiss canton)	Delémont
Îles Australes (French Polynesia)	Mataura	Kaafu (Maldives)	Male
Îles du Vent (French Polynesia)	Papeete	Kabale (Uganda)	Rubale
Îles Marquises (French Polynesia)	Taiohae	Kabardino-Balkaria (Russia)	Nalchik
Îles sous le Vent (French Polynesia)	Uturoa	Kabarole (Uganda)	Karambe
Îles Tuamotu et Gambier (French Polynesia)	Papeete	Kachin (Myanmar)	Myitkyinä
		Kadiogo (Burkina Faso)	Ouagadougou
Ille-et-Vilaine (France)	Rennes	Kagawa (Japan)	Takamatsu
Illinois (USA)	Springfield	Kalimantan Barat (Indonesia)	Pontianak
Ilubabor (Ethiopia)	Metu	Kalimantan Selatan (Indonesia)	Banjarmasin
Imbabura (Ecuador)	Ibarra	Kalimantan Tengah (Indonesia)	Palangkaraya
Imo (Nigeria)	Owerri	Kalmuck (Russia)	Elista
Inagua, Great and Little	Matthew Town	Kamuli (Uganda)	Namendwa
Inchiri (Mauritania)	Akjoujt	Kanagawa (Japan)	Yokohama
Independencia (Dominican Republic)	Jimani	Kanem (Chad)	Mao
		KaNgwane (South Africa)	Louieville
India (aka Bharat)	New Delhi	Kangwŏn-do (North Korea)	Wŏnson
Indonesia	Jakarta	Kangwŏn-do (South Korea)	Ch'unch'ŏn

GEOGRAPHY

Country, State, County or Area	Capital or Admin Centre	Country, State, County or Area	Capital or Admin Centre
Kansas (USA)	Topeka	Kyŏngsang-namdo (South Korea)	Masan
Kao-hsiung (Taiwan)	Feng-shan	Kyŏngsang-pukto (South Korea)	Taegu
Kapchorwa (Uganda)	Rukoki	**Kyrgyzstan**	Bishkek
Karachai-Cherkessia (Russia)	Cherkesst	La Altagracia (Dominican Republic)	Higüey
Kara-Kalpak (Russia)	Nukus	La Estrelleta (Dominican Republic)	Elias Piña
Karas (Namibia)	Keetmanshoop	La Guajira (Colombia)	Riohacha
Karelian (Russia)	Petrozavodsk	La Habana (Cuba)	Havana
Karen (Myanmar)	Pa-an	La Libertad (El Salvador)	Nueva San
Karnataka (India)	Bangalore		Salvador
Kärnten (Austria)	Klagenfurt	La Libertad (Peru)	Trujillo
Kasai-Occidental (Dem		La Pampa (Argentina)	Santa Rosa
Rep of Congo)	Kananga	La Paz (El Salvador)	Zacatecoluca
Kasai-Oriental (Dem		La Rioja (Spain)	Logrono
Rep of Congo)	Mbuji-Mayi	Laamu (Maldives)	Hithadhoo
Kayah (Myanmar)	Loi-kaw	Lac (Chad)	Bol
Kazakhstan	Astana	Lacs (Togo)	Aného
Kedah (Malaysia)	Alor Setar	Lagos (Nigeria)	Lkeja
Kefa (Ethiopia)	Jima	Lai Chau (Vietnam)	Dien Bien
Kelantan (Malaysia)	Kota Bharu	Lakshadweep Islands (India)	Kavaratti Island
Kemo-Gribingui (CA Rep)	Sibut	Lam Dong (Vietnam)	Da Lat
Kénédougou (Burkina Faso)	Orodara	Lambayeque (Peru)	Chiclayo
Kent (Eng)	Maidstone	Lampung (Indonesia)	Tanjung Karang
Kentucky (USA)	Frankfort	Lancashire (Eng)	Preston
Kenya	Nairobi	Landes (France)	Mont-de-Marsan
Kerala (India)	Trivandrum	Languedoc-Roussillon (France)	Montpellier
Kéran (Togo)	Kandé	Laois/Leix (Rep of Ireland)	Portlaoise
Kerry (Rep of Ireland)	Tralee	**Laos**	Vientiane
Keski-Suomi (Finland)	Jyväskylä	Lappi (Finland)	Rovaniemi
Kgalagadi (Botswana)	Tsabong	Lara (Venezuela)	Barquisimeto
Kgatleng (Botswana)	Mochudi	**Latvia**	Riga
Khakassia (Russia)	Abakan	Lavalleja (Uruguay)	Minas
Khammouan (Laos)	Thakhek	Lazio (Italy)	Rome
Khanh Hoa (Vietnam)	Nha Trang	**Lebanon**	Beirut
Khanty-Mansi (Russia)	Khanty-Mansüsk	Lebowa (South Africa)	Lebowakgomo
Khomas (Namibia)	Windhoek	Leicestershire (Eng)	Leicester
Kien Giang (Vietnam)	Rach Gia	Leitrim (Rep of Ireland)	Carrick-on-
Kildare (Rep of Ireland)	Naas		Shannon
Kilimanjaro (Tanzania)	Moshi	Lékoumou (Congo)	Sibiti
Kilkenny (Rep of Ireland)	Kilkenny	Lemba (São Tomé and Principe)	Neves
Kiribati	Bairiki on Tarawa Island	Lempira (Honduras)	Gracias
		Leribe (Lesotho)	Hiotse
Kitgum (Uganda)	Labongo	**Lesotho**	Maseru
Kloto (Togo)	Kpalimé	Lhaviyani (Maldives)	Naifaru
Koinaduga (Sierra Leone)	Kabala	Liaoning (China)	Shenyang
Kolonjë (Albania)	Ersekë	**Liberia**	Monrovia
Komárom (Hungary)	Tatabánya	Libertador Gen Bernardo	
Kombo St Mary (Gambia)	Kanifing	O'Higgins (Chile)	Rancagua
Komi (Russia)	Syktyv-Kar	**Libya**	Tripoli
Komy Permyak (Russia)	Kudymkar	**Liechtenstein**	Vaduz
Kono (Sierra Leone)	Sefadu	Liguria (Italy)	Genoa
Kopparberg (Sweden)	Falun	Likouala (Congo)	Impfondo
Koryak (Russia)	Palana	Limburg (Belgium)	Hasselt
Kosovo (Yugoslavia)	Pristina	Limburg (Netherlands)	Maastricht
Kossi (Burkina Fasso)	Nouna	Limerick (Rep of Ireland)	Limerick
Kouilou (Congo)	Pointe-Noire	Limousin (France)	Limoges
Kouritenga (Burkina Faso)	Koupéla	Lincolnshire (Eng)	Lincoln
Kozah (Togo)	Kara	Line Isles (Kiribati)	Kiritimati
Kronoberg (Sweden)	Växjö	**Lithuania**	Vilnius
Kuando Kubango (Angola)	Menongue	Littoral (Cameroon)	Douala
Kuanza Norte (Angola)	N'Dalatando	Lobata (São Tomé and Principe)	Guadalupe
Kuanza Sul (Angola)	Sumbe	Lobaye (CA Rep)	Mbaiki
Kunene (Namibia)	Opuwo	Lofa (Liberia)	Voinjama
Kuria (Kiribati)	Tabontebike	Logone Occidental (Chad)	Moundou
Kuwait	Kuwait	Logone Oriental (Chad)	Doba
KwaNdebele (South Africa)	Siyabuswa	Loire (France)	Saint-Etienne
Kwara (Nigeria)	Llorin	Loire-Atlantique (France)	Nantes
KwaZulu (South Africa)	Ulundi	Loiret (France)	Orléans
Kweneng (Botswana)	Molepolole	Loir-et-Cher (France)	Blois
Kymi (Finland)	Kouvola	Lombardy (Italy)	Milan
Kyŏnggi-do (South Korea)	Suwŏn	Londonderry (NI)	Londonderry

Country, State, County or Area	Capital or Admin Centre	Country, State, County or Area	Capital or Admin Centre
Long An (Vietnam)	Tan An	Maritime Region (Togo)	Lomé
Long Island (Bahamas)	Clarence Town	Markazi (Iran)	Arāk
Longford (Rep of Ireland)	Longford	Marlborough (NZ)	Blenheim
Loreto (Peru)	Iquitos	Marne (France)	Châlons-sur-Marne
Lorraine (France)	Metz		
Los Lagos (Chile)	Puerto Montt	Marowijne (Suriname)	Albina
Los Rios (Ecuador)	Babahoyo	**Marshall Islands**	Dalap-Uliga-Darrit
Los Santos (Panama)	Las Tablas	Martinique (France)	Fort-de-France
Lot (France)	Cahors	Maryland (Liberia)	Harper
Lot-et-Garonne (France)	Agen	Maryland (USA)	Annapolis
Lothian (Scotland)	Edinburgh	Masaka (Uganda)	Kaswa Bukoto
Louisiana (USA)	Baton Rouge	Mashonaland Central (Zimbabwe)	Bindura
Louth (Rep of Ireland)	Dundalk	Mashonaland East (Zimbabwe)	Marondera
Lower River (Gambia)	Mansakonko	Mashonaland West (Zimbabwe)	Chinhoyi
Lower Saxony (Germany)	Hanover	Masindi (Uganda)	Nyangeya
Lozère (France)	Mende	Massachusetts (USA)	Boston
Luapula (Zambia)	Mansa	Mat (Albania)	Burrel
Lubombo (Swaziland)	Siteki	Matabeleland North (Zimbabwe)	Bulawayo
Lunda Norte (Angola)	Lucapa	Matabeleland South (Zimbabwe)	Gwanda
Lunda Sol (Angola)	Saurimo	Mato Grosso (Brazil)	Cuiabá
Luxembourg	Luxembourg	Mato Grosso do Sul (Brazil)	Campo Grande
Luxembourg (Belgium)	Arlon	Matruh (Egypt)	Marsā Matruh
Macao (Portugal)	Macao	Maule (Chile)	Talca
MacCarthy Island (Gambia)	Kuntaur/ Georgetown	**Mauritania**	Nouakchott
		Mauritius	Port Louis
Macedonia	Skopje	Mayaguana (Bahamas)	Abraham's Bay
Macedonia (Greece)	Thessaloniki	Mayenne (France)	Laval
Madagascar	Antananarivo	Mayo (Rep of Ireland)	Castlebar
Madeira (Portugal)	Funchal	Mayo-Kebbi (Chad)	Bongor
Madhya Pradesh (India)	Bhopal	Mayotte (France)	Mamoudzou
Madre de Dios (Peru)	Puerto Maldonado	Maysān (Iraq)	Al-Amārah
		Māzandarān (Iran)	Sari
Magallanes y de la Antártica Chilena (Chile)	Punta Arenas	Mbale (Uganda)	Bunkoko
		Mbarara (Uganda)	Kakika
Magdalena (Colombia)	Santander	Mbomou (CA Rep)	Bangassou
Mahaica/Berbice (Guyana)	Fort Wellington	Meath (Rep of Ireland)	Trim
Maharashtra (India)	Bombay	Mecklenburg-West Pomerania (Germany)	Schwerin
Mahé (Seychelles)	Victoria		
Maiana (Kiribati)	Tebangetua	Meemu (Maldives)	Muli
Maine (USA)	Augusta	Meghālaya (India)	Shillong
Maine-et Loire (France)	Angers	Mehedinti (Romania)	Drobeta-Turnu-Severin
Maio (Cape Verde)	Porto Inglês		
Makira (Solomon Isles)	Kira Kira	Melaka (Malaysia)	Melaka
Malaita (Solomon Isles)	Auki	Merseyside (Eng)	Liverpool
Malawi	Lilongwe	Meta (Colombia)	Villavicencio
Malaysia	Kuala Lumpur	Metropolitan (Chile)	Santiago
Maldives	Malé	Meurthe-et-Moselle (France)	Nancy
Malekula (Vanuatu)	Lakatoro	Meuse (France)	Bar-le-Duc
Mali	Bamako	**Mexico**	Mexico City
Malta	Valletta	México (Mexican state)	Toluca
Maluku (Indonesia)	Ambon	Mé-zóchi (São Tomé and Principe)	Trinidade
Manabi (Ecuador)	Portoviejo		
Manawatu (NZ)	Palmerston North	Michigan (USA)	Lansing
Manche (France)	Saint-Lô	Michoacán (Mexico)	Morelia
Manchester (Jamaica)	Mandeville	**Micronesia**	Kolonia/Palikir
Manica (Mozambique)	Chimolo	Mid-Glamorgan (Wales)	Cardiff
Manicaland (Zimbabwe)	Mutare	Midi-Pyrénées (France)	Toulouse
Maniema (Dem Rep of Congo)	Kindu	Midland Province (Zimbabwe)	Gweru
Manipur (India)	Imphāl	Mid-Western Nepal	Surkhet
Manitoba (Canada)	Winnipeg	Mie (Japan)	Tsu
Manus (Papua New Guinea)	Lorengau	Milne Bay (Papua New Guinea)	Samarai
Mara (Tanzania)	Musoma	Minas Gerais (Brazil)	Belo Horizonte
Marakei (Kiribati)	Rawannawi	Minnesota (USA)	St Paul
Maramures (Romania)	Baia Mare	Minorca (Spain)	Mahon
Maranhão (Brazil)	São Luis	Miranda (Venezuela)	Los Teques
Marche (Italy)	Ancona	Mirditë (Albania)	Rrëshen
Margibi (Liberia)	Kakata	Misiones (Argentina)	Posadas
Maria Trinidad Sánchez (Dominican Republic)	Nagua	Misiones (Paraguay)	San Juan Bautista
Mari-El (Russia)	Yoshkar-Ola	Mississippi (USA)	Jackson

GEOGRAPHY

Country, State, County or Area	Capital or Admin Centre	Country, State, County or Area	Capital or Admin Centre
Missouri (USA)	Jefferson City	New Hampshire (USA)	Concorde
Miyagi (Japan)	Sendai	New Ireland (Papua New Guinea)	Kavieng
Mizorăm (India)	Ālzawi	New Jersey (USA)	Trenton
Moili (Comoros)	Fomboni	New Mexico (USA)	Santa Fe
Moldavia	Kishinev	New Providence (Bahamas)	Nassau
Moluccas (Indonesia)	Amboina	New South Wales	Sydney
Mon (Myanmar)	Moulmein	New York (USA)	Albany
Monaco	Monaco-Ville	**New Zealand**	Wellington
Monagas (Venezuela)	Maturin	Newfoundland (Canada)	St Johns
Monaghan (Rep of Ireland)	Monaghan	Ngamiland (Botswana)	Maun
Mongolia	Ulan Bator	Ngazidja (Comoros)	Moroni
Mono (Benin)	Lokossa	Nghe Tinh (Vietnam)	Vinh
Monseñor Nouel (Dominican Republic)	Bonao	Ngounié (Gabon)	Mouila
		Ngwaketse (Botswana)	Kanye
Montana (USA)	Helena	Niari (Congo)	Loubomo
Montenegro	Podgorica	Niassa (Mozambique)	Lichinga
Montserrado (Liberia)	Bensonville	**Nicaragua**	Managua
Montserrat	Plymouth	Nickerie (Suriname)	Nieuw Nickerie
Morazán (El Salvador)	San Francisco (Gotera)	Nicobar Islands (India)	Car Nicobar
		Nidwalden (Swiss canton)	Stans
Morbihan (France)	Vannes	Niederösterreich (Austria)	Sankt Pölten
Mordovia (Russia)	Saransk	Nièvre (France)	Nevers
Møre og Romsdal (Norway)	Molde	**Niger**	Niamey
Morelos (Mexico)	Cuernavaca	Niger (Nigeria)	Minna
Morobe (Papua New Guinea)	Lae	**Nigeria**	Abuja
Morocco	Rabat	Nikunau (Kiribati)	Rungata
Morona-Santiago (Ecuador)	Macas	Nimba (Liberia)	Sanniquellie
Moroto (Uganda)	Katikekile	Ninawă (Iraq)	Mosul
Moselle (France)	Metz	Ningxia Hui (China)	Yinchuan
Mouhoun (Burkina Faso)	Dédougou	Ninh Thuan (Vietnam)	Phan Rang
Moxico (Angola)	Lwena	Niuas (Tonga)	Hihifo
Moyen-Chari (Chad)	Sarh	Niue (New Zealand)	Alofi
Moyen-Ogooué (Gabon)	Lambaréné	Nógrád (Hungary)	Salgótarján
Mozambique	Maputo	Nonouti (Kiribati)	Teuabu
Mubende (Uganda)	Bageza	Noonu (Maldives)	Manadhoo
Mudug (Somalia)	Galcaio (Gaalkacyo)	Noord-Brabant (Netherlands)	s-Hertogenbosch
		Noord-Holland (Netherlands)	Haarlem
Mures (Romania)	Tirgu Mures	Nord (Cameroon)	Garoua
Musandam (Oman)	Khasab	Nord (France)	Lille
Myanmar (formerly Burma)	Yangon (Rangoon)	Nord (Haiti)	Cap-Haitien
		Nord-Est (Haiti)	Fort-Liberté
Nāgāland (India)	Kohima	Nordhurland eystra (Iceland)	Akureyri
Nahouri (Burkina Faso)	Pô	Nordhurland vestra (Iceland)	Saudhárkrókur
Namentenga (Burkina Faso)	Boulsa	Nordjylland (Denmark)	Alborg
Namibia	Windhoek	Nord-Kivu (Dem Rep of Congo)	Goma
Nana-Mambere (CA Rep)	Bouar	Nordland (Norway)	Bode
Napo (Ecuador)	Tena	Nord-Ouest (Cameroon)	Bamenda
Nariño (Colombia)	Pasto	Nord-Ouest (Haiti)	Port-de-Paix
Nariva/Mayaro (Trinidad and Tobago)	Rio Claro	Nord-Pas-de-Calais (France)	Lille
		Nord-Trønelag (Norway)	Steinkjer
Natal (South Africa)	Pietermaritsburg	Norfolk (Eng)	Norwich
National Capital District (Papua New Guinea)	Port Moresby	Norfolk Island (Aus)	Kingston
		Norrbotten (Sweden)	Luleá
Nauru	Yaren	Norte de Santander (Colombia)	Cúcuta
Navarre (Spain)	Pamplona	North Bank (Gambia)	Kerewan
Nayarit (Mexico)	Tepic	North Carolina (USA)	Raleigh
Ndzouani (Comoros)	Mutsamudu	North Dakota (USA)	Bismarck
Neamt (Romania)	Piatra Neamt	North Eastern Province (Kenya)	Garissa
Nebraska (USA)	Lincoln	**North Korea (aka Choson)**	Pyongyang
Ñeembucu (Paraguay)	Pilar	North Otago (NZ)	Dunedin
Negeri Sembilan (Malaysia)	Seremban	North Rhine–Westphalia (Germany)	Düsseldorf
Nelson Bays (NZ)	Nelson		
Nenets (Russia)	Naryan-Mar	North Solomons (Papua New Guinea)	Buka
Nepal	Kāthmāndu		
Netherlands Antilles	Willemstad	North West Frontier (Pakistan)	Peshāwar
Netherlands	Amsterdam	North Yorkshire (Eng)	Northallerton
Nevada (USA)	Carson City	Northamptonshire (Eng)	Northampton
Nevis (St Kitts and Nevis)	Charlestown	Northern District (Israel)	Tiberias
New Brunswick (Canada)	Fredericton	**Northern Ireland**	Belfast
New Caledonia (France)	Nouméa	Northern Mariana Islands (USA)	Chalan Kanoa

Country, State, County or Area	Capital or Admin Centre	Country, State, County or Area	Capital or Admin Centre
Northern Province (Fiji)	Labasa	Ouham-Pendé (CA Rep)	Bozoum
Northern Province (Papua		Overijssel (Netherlands)	Zwolle
New Guinea)	Popondetta	Övörhangay (Mongolia)	Arvayheer
Northern Province (Sierra Leone)	Makeni	Oxfordshire (Eng)	Oxford
Northern Province (Zambia)	Kasama	Oyo (Nigeria)	Ibadan
Northern Region (Ghana)	Tamale	Paama (Vanuatu)	Liro
Northern Territory (Aus)	Darwin	Paguê (São Tomé and Principe)	Principe
Northland (NZ)	Whangarei	**Pakistan**	Islamabad
Northumberland (Eng)	Morpeth	**Palau**	Koror Island
Northwest Territories (Canada)	Yellowknife	**Panama**	Panama City
North-Western Province (Zambia)	Solwezi	Panama Canal Zone	Balboa Heights
Norway	Oslo	Pando (Bolivia)	Cobija
Nottinghamshire (Eng)	Nottingham	**Papua New Guinea**	Port Moresby
Nova Scotia (Canada)	Halifax	Pará (Brazil)	Belém
Nueva Asunción (Paraguay)	General Eugenio	Para (Suriname)	Onverwacht
	A. Garay	**Paraguay**	Asunción
Nueva Esparta (Venezuela)	La Asunción	Paraíba (Brazil)	João Pessoa
Nuevo León (Mexico)	Monterrey	Paraná (Brazil)	Curitiba
Nugaal (Somalia)	Garoowe	Pas-de-Calais (France)	Arras
Nunavut (Canada)	Iqaluit	Passoré (Burkina Faso)	Yako
Nusa Tenggara Barat (Indonesia)	Mataram	Pastaza (Ecuador)	Puyo
Nusa Tenggara Timur (Indonesia)	Kupang	Paúl (Cape Verde)	Pombas
Nyanga (Gabon)	Tchibanga	Pays de la Loire (France)	Nantes
Nyanza (Kenya)	Kisumu	Pemba North (Tanzania)	Wete
Oberösterreich (Austria)	Linz	Pemba South (Tanzania)	Chake Chake
Obwalden (Swiss canton)	Sarnen	Penang/Pinang (Malaysia)	George Town
Offaly (Rep of Ireland)	Tullamore	P'eng-hu (Taiwan)	Ma-kung
Ogooué-Ivindo (Gabon)	Makokou	Pennsylvania (USA)	Harrisburg
Ogooué-Lolo (Gabon)	Koulamoutou	Pentecost (Vanuatu)	Loltong
Ogooué-Maritime (Gabon)	Port-Gentil	Peravia (Dominican Republic)	Bani
Ogou (Togo)	Atakpamé	Pernambuco (Brazil)	Recife
Ogun (Nigeria)	Abeokuta	**Peru**	Lima
Ohangwena (Namibia)	Oshikango	Pest (Hungary)	Budapest
Ohio (USA)	Columbus	Petén (Guatemala)	Ciudad Flores
Oio (Guinea-Bissau)	Farim	**Philippines**	Manila
Oise (France)	Beauvais	Phoenix Isles (Kiribati)	Kanton
Okavango (Namibia)	Rundu	Phu Khanh (Vietnam)	Nha Trang
Okinawa (Japan)	Naha City	Phu Tho (Vietnam)	Viet Tri
Oklahoma (USA)	Oklahoma City	Phu Yen (Vietnam)	Tuy Hoa
Olancho (Honduras)	Juticalpa	Piauí (Brazil)	Teresina
Olt (Romania)	Slatina	Picardie (France)	Amiens
Omaheke (Namibia)	Gobabis	Pichincha (Ecuador)	Quito
Oman	Muscat	Piedmont (Italy)	Turin
Ombella-Mpoko (CA Rep)	Bimbo	Pitcairn Islands	Adamstown
Ömnögovi (Mongolia)	Dalandzadgad	Plateau (Nigeria)	Jos
Omusati (Namibia)	Outapi	Plateaux (Congo)	Djambala
Ondo (Nigeria)	Akure	Pohjois-Karjala (Finland)	Joensuu
Onotoa (Kiribati)	Buariki	Poitou-Charentes (France)	Poitiers
Ontario (Canada)	Toronto	**Poland**	Warsaw
Oppland (Norway)	Lillehammer	Pomeroon/Supenaam (Guyana)	Anna Regina
Orange Free State (South Africa)	Bloemfontein	Poni (Burkina Faso)	Gaoua
Oregon (USA)	Salem	Pool (Congo)	Kinkala
Orissa (India)	Bhubaneswar	Portland (Jamaica)	Port Antonio
Orkney Islands	Kirkwall	**Portugal**	Lisbon
Orne (France)	Alen	Portuguesa (Venezuela)	Guanare
Oshana (Namibia)	Oshakati	Powys (Wales)	Llandrindod Wells
Oshikoto (Namibia)	Tsumeb	Prahova (Romania)	Ploiesti
Östergötland (Sweden)	Linköping	President Hayes (Paraguay)	Pozo Colorado
Østfold (Norway)	Moss	Prince Edward Island (Canada)	Charlottetown
Oti (Togo)	Sansanné-Mango	Principe (São Tomé and Principe)	São António
Otjozondjupa (Namibia)	Grootfontein	Provence-Alpes-Côte d'Azur	Marseille
Ouaddai (Chad)	Abéché	**Puerto Rico (USA)**	San Juan
Ouaka (CA Rep)	Bambari	Puglia (Italy)	Bari
Oubritenga (Burkina Faso)	Ziniaré	Punjab (India)	Chandigarh
Oudalan (Burkina Faso)	Gorom Gorom	Punjab (Pakistan)	Lahore
Oudomxay (Laos)	Xay	Putumayo (Colombia)	Mocoa
Ouémé (Benin)	Porto-Novo	Puy-de-Dôme (France)	Clermont-Ferrand
Ouest (Cameroon)	Bafoussam	Pwani (Tanzania)	Dar es Salaam
Ouest (Haiti)	Port-au-Prince	P'yongan-namdo (North Korea)	P'yŏngsan
Ouham (CA Rep)	Bossangoa	P'yongan-pukto (North Korea)	Sinujiu

GEOGRAPHY

Country, State, County or Area	Capital or Admin Centre	Country, State, County or Area	Capital or Admin Centre
Pyrénées-Atlantiques (France)	Pau	St Elizabeth (Jamaica)	Black River
Pyrénées-Orientales (France)	Perpignan	St Eustatius (Netherland Antilles)	Oranjestad
Qatar	Doha	St Helena	Jamestown
Qinghai (aka Tsinghai) (China)	Xining (aka Hsi-ning)	St James (Jamaica)	Montego Bay
		St Kitts (St Kitts and Nevis)	Basseterre
Quang Binh (Vietnam)	Dong Hoi	**St Kitts and Nevis**	Basseterre
Quang Nam (Vietnam)	Hoi An	**St Lucia**	Castries
Quang Nam-Hoi An (Vietnam)	Ha Long City	St Maarten (Netherland Antilles)	Philipsburg
Quang Ninh (Vietnam)	Ha Long City	St Martin and St Barthélemy	
Quang Tri (Vietnam)	Dong Ha	(Guadeloupe)	Marigot
Quebec (Canada)	Quebec	St Mary (Jamaica)	Port Maria
Queensland (Aus)	Brisbane	St Patrick (Trinidad and Tobago)	Siparia
Quiché (Guatemala)	Santa Cruz	St Thomas (Jamaica)	Morant Bay
Quinara (Guinea-Bissau)	Fulacunda	St Thomas and St John (US Virgins)	Charlotte Amalie
Quindio (Colombia)	Armenia	**St Vincent and Grenadines**	Kingstown
Quintana Roo (Mexico)	Chetumal	St-Pierre and Miquelon (France)	St-Pierre
Qwaqwa (South Africa)	Phuthaditjhaba	Saipan	Chalan Kanoa
Raa (Maldives)	Ugoofaaru	Saitama (Japan)	Urawa
Ragged Island (Bahamas)	Duncan Town	Sakha (Russia)	Yakutsk
Raiatea (French Polynesia)	Uturoa	Sakhalin Island	Yuzhno-Sakhalinsk
Rajasthan (India)	Jaipur		
Rakai (Uganda)	Byakabanda	Sal (Cape Verde)	Santa Maria
Región Autónoma del Atlántico		Salaj (Romania)	Zalău
Norte (Nicaragua)	Rosita	Salamat (Chad)	Am Timan
Región Autónoma del Atlántico		San Andrés y Providencia	San Andrés
Sur (Nicaragua)	Bluefields	**San Marino (Most Serene**	
Región I (Nicaragua)	Esteli	**Republic)**	San Marino
Región II (Nicaragua)	León	San Martín (Peru)	Moyobamba
Región III (Nicaragua)	Managua	San Salvador and Rum Cay	Cockburn Town
Región IV (Nicaragua)	Jinotepe	(Bahamas)	
Región V (Nicaragua)	Juigalpa	Sanaag (Somalia)	Erigavo
Región VI (Nicaragua)	Matagalpa		(Ceerigaabo)
Réunion (France)	Saint-Denis	Sánchez Ramirez (Dominican	Cotui
Rhineland Palatinate (Germany)	Mainz	Republic)	
Rhode Island (USA)	Providence	Sangha (Congo)	Ouesso
Rhodes (Greece)	Rhodes	Sangha-Économique (CA Rep)	Nola
Rhône (France)	Lyon	Sanguie (Burkina Faso)	Réo
Rhône-Alpes (France)	Lyon	Sanmatenga (Burkina Faso)	Kaya
Riau (Indonesia)	Pakanbaru	Santa Catarina (Brazil)	Florianópolis
Ribeira Grande (Cape Verde)	Ponta do Sol	Santa Catarina (Cape Verde)	Assomada
Rift Valley (Kenya)	Nakuru	Santa Cruz (Argentina)	Rio Gallegos
Rio Grande do Norte (Brazil)	Natal	Santa Cruz (Cape Verde)	Pedra Badejo
Rio Grande do Sul (Brazil)	Pôrto Alegre	Santa Rosa (Guatemala)	Cuilapa
Rio Muni (Equatorial Guinea)	Bata	Santander (Colombia)	Bucaramanga
Rio Negro (Argentina)	Viedma	Santiago (Dominican Republic)	Santiago de los Caballeros
Rio Negro (Uruguay)	Fray Bentos		
Risaraldo (Colombia)	Pereira	Santo/Maio (Vanuatu)	Luganville
Rivercess (Liberia)	Rivercess City	São Nicolau (Cape Verde)	Ribeira Brava
Rivers (Nigeria)	Port-Harcourt	**São Tomé and Príncipe**	São Tomé
Rogaland (Norway)	Stavanger	São Vicente (Cape Verde)	Mindelo
Romania	Bucharest	Saône-et-Loire (France)	Mâcon
Rondônia (Brazil)	Pôrto Velho	Saramacca (Suriname)	Groningen
Roraima (Brazil)	Boa Vista	Sarawak (Malaysia)	Kuching
Roscommon (Rep of Ireland)	Roscommon	**Sardinia (Italy)**	Cagliari
Rukungiri (Uganda)	Kagunga	Sarthe (France)	Le Mans
Rukwa (Tanzania)	Sumbawanga	Saskatchewan (Canada)	Regina
Russia	Moscow	**Saudi Arabia**	Riyadh
Ruvuma (Tanzania)	Songea	Savoie (France)	Chambéry
Rwanda	Kigali	Saxony (Germany)	Dresden
Ryukyu Islands (Japan)	Naha City (on Okinawa)	Saxony-Anhalt (Germany)	Magdeburg
		Schleswig-Holstein (Germany)	Kiel
Saarland (Germany)	Saarbrücken	Scilly Isles	Hugh Town
Saba (Netherland Antilles)	The Bottom	**Scotland**	Edinburgh
Sabah (Malaysia)	Kota Kinabalu	Seenu (Maldives)	Hithadoo
Sacatepéquez (Guatemala)	Antigua Guatemala	Seine-et-Marne (France)	Melun
		Seine-Maritime (France)	Rouen
St Andrew and St David (Trinidad and Tobago)	Sangre Grande	Seine-Saint-Denis (France)	Bobigny
		Selenge (Mongolia)	Sühbaatar
St Catherine (Jamaica)	Spanish Town	**Senegal**	Dakar
St Croix (US Virgins)	Christiansted	Sèno (Burkina Faso)	Dori

Country, State, County or Area	Capital or Admin Centre	Country, State, County or Area	Capital or Admin Centre
Serbia	Belgrade	Southern Province (Sierra Leone)	Bo
Sergipe (Brazil)	Aracaju	Southern Province (Zambia)	Livingstone
Seychelles	Victoria	Southland (NZ)	Invercargill
Shaanxi (aka Shensi)	Xi'an (aka Sian)	**Spain**	Madrid
Shaba (Dem Rep of Congo)	Lubumbashi	**Sri Lanka**	Colombo
Shabeellaha Dhexe (Somalia)	Giohar (Jawhar)	Staffordshire (Eng)	Stafford
Shabeellaha Hoose (Somalia)	Merca (Marka)	Stann Creek (Belize)	Dangriga
Shabwah (Yemen)	Atāq	Steiermark (Austria)	Graz
Shan (Myanmar)	Taunggyi	Storstrom (Denmark)	Nykebing
Shandong (aka Shantung) (China)	Jinan (aka Tsinan)	Strathclyde (Scotland)	Glasgow
		Suchitepéquez (Guatemala)	Mazatenango
Shanxi (China)	Taiyuan	Sucre (Colombia)	Sincelejo
Shaviyani (Maldives)	Farukolhu	Sucre (Venezuela)	Cumaná
	Funadhoo	Sud (Cameroon)	Ebolowa
Shepherd (Vanuatu)	Morua	Sud (Haiti)	Les Cayes
Shetland Islands	Lerwick	**Sudan**	Khartoum
Shewa (Ethiopia)	Addis Ababa	Sud-Est (Haiti)	Jacmel
Shiga (Japan)	Ōtsu	Sudhurland (Iceland)	Selfoss
Shimane (Japan)	Matsue	Sudhurnes (Iceland)	Keflavik
Shiselweni (Swaziland)	Nhlangano	Sud-Kivu (Dem Rep of Congo)	Bukavu
Shropshire (Eng)	Shrewsbury	Sud-Ouest (Cameroon)	Buea
Sichuan (China)	Chengdu	Suffolk (Eng)	Ipswich
Sicily (Italy)	Palermo	Sühbaatar (Mongolia)	Baruun-urt
Sidamo (Ethiopia)	Awasa	Sulawesi Selatan (Indonesia)	Ujung Pandang
Sierra Leone	Freetown	Sulawesi Tengah (Indonesia)	Palu
Sikkim (India)	Gangtok	Sulawesi Tenggara (Indonesia)	Kendari
Sinā' al-Janubiyah (Egypt)	At-Tur	Sulawesi Utara (Indonesia)	Menado
Sinā' ash-Shamāliyah (Egypt)	Al-'Arish	Sumatera Barat (Indonesia)	Padang
Sinaloa (Mexico)	Culiacán	Sumatera Utara (Indonesia)	Medan
Sind (Pakistan)	Karāchi	**Suriname**	Paramaribo
Singapore	Singapore	Surrey (Eng)	Kingston-upon-Thames
Sinoe (Liberia)	Greenville		
Sissilli (Burkina Faso)	Léo	**Swaziland**	Mbabane
Sistān va Baluchestān (Iran)	Zāhedān	**Sweden**	Stockholm
Skaraborg (Sweden)	Mariestad	**Switzerland**	Berne
Skrapar (Albania)	Corovoda	**Syria**	Damascus
Sligo (Rep of Ireland)	Sligo	Szabics-Szatmár (Hungary)	Nyiregyháza
Slovakia	Bratislava	Tabasco (Mexico)	Villahermosa
Slovenia	Llubljana	Tabiteuea North (Kiribati)	Utiroa
Society Islands	Papeete	Tabiteuea South (Kiribati)	Buariki
Socotra (Yemen)	Tamrida	Táchira (Venezuela)	San Cristóbal
Södermanland (Sweden)	Nyköping	Taféa (Vanuatu)	Isangei
Sofala (Mozambique)	Beira	Tagant (Mauritania)	Tidjikdja
Sogn og Fjordane (Norway)	Leikanger	**Tahiti (France)**	Papeete
Solomon Islands	Honiara	T'al-chung (Taiwan)	Feng-yuan
Somalia	Mogadishu	Taimyr (Russia)	Dudinka
Somaliland	Berbera	Tai-nan (Taiwan)	Hsin-ying
Somerset (Eng)	Taunton	Tai-pei (Taiwan)	Pan-ch'iao
Somme (France)	Amiens	**Taiwan**	Taipei
Somogy (Hungary)	Kaposvár	**Tajikistan**	Dushanbe
Sonderjylland (Denmark)	Abenra	Tamana (Kiribati)	Bakaka
Sonora (Mexico)	Hermosillo	Tamaulipas (Mexico)	Ciudad Victoria
Soriano (Uruguay)	Mercedes	Tamil Nadu (India)	Madras
Sor-Trøndelag (Norway)	Trondheim	Tandjilé (Chad)	Lai
Soum (Burkina Faso)	Djibo	**Tanzania**	Dodoma
Sourou (Burkina Faso)	Tougan	Tapoa (Burkina Faso)	Diapaga
South Africa	Pretoria–admin	Taranaki (NZ)	New Plymouth
	Capetown–legislative	Tarapacá (Chile)	Iquique
	Bloemfontein–judicial	Tarawa North (Kiribati)	Abaokoro
		Tarawa South (Kiribati)	Bairiki
South Australia	Adelaide	Tarn (France)	Albi
South Carolina (USA)	Columbia	Tarn-et-Garonne (France)	Montauban
South Dakota (USA)	Pierre	Tasmania (Aus)	Hobart
South Glamorgan (Wales)	Cardiff	Tatarstan (Russia)	Kazan
South Korea	Seoul	Tayside (Scotland)	Dundee
South Yorkshire (Eng)	Barnsley	Tchaoudjo (Togo)	Sokodé
Southern District (Israel)	Beersheba	Telemark (Norway)	Skien
Southern Highlands (Papua New Guinea)	Mende	Teleorman (Romania)	Alexandria
		Temburong (Brunei)	Bangar
		Temotu (Solomon Isles)	Santa Cruz

GEOGRAPHY

Country, State, County or Area	Capital or Admin Centre	Country, State, County or Area	Capital or Admin Centre
Tennessee (USA)	Nashville	Upper River (Gambia)	Basse
Territoire de Belfort (France)	Belfort	Upper West (Ghana)	Wa
Texas (USA)	Austin	Uri (Swiss canton)	Altdorf
Thaa (Maldives)	Veymandhoo	**Uruguay**	Montevideo
Thailand	Bangkok	Ust-Ordyn-Buryat (Russia)	Ust-Ordynsk
Thames Valley (NZ)	Thames-Coromandel	Utah (USA)	Salt Lake City
		Uttar Pradesh (India)	Lucknow
Thua Thien (Vietnam)	Hue	Uusimaa (Finland)	Helsinki
Thurgau (Swiss canton)	Frauenfeld	Uvs (Mongolia)	Ulaangom
Thuringia (Germany)	Erfurt	**Uzbekistan**	Tashkent
Tibet (aka Xizang) (China)	Lhasa	Vaavu (Maldives)	Felidhoo
Ticino (Swiss canton)	Bellinzona	Vakaga (CA Rep)	Birao
Tien Giang (Vietnam)	My Tho	Valais (Swiss canton)	Sion
Tierra Del Fuego (Argentina)	Ushuaia	Val-de-Marne (France)	Créteil
Tigray (Ethiopia)	Mekele	Val-d'Oise (France)	Pontoise
Timis (Romania)	Timisoara	Valle (Honduras)	Nacaome
Timor Timur (Indonesia)	Dili	Valparaíso (Chile)	Valparaiso
Tipperary (Rep of Ireland)	Clonmel	Valverde (Dominican Republic)	Mao
Tiris Zemmour (Mauritania)	Fdérik	**Vanuatu**	Vila
Tirol (Austria)	Innsbruck	Var (France)	Toulon
Tobago (Trinidad and Tobago)	Scarborough	Värmland (Sweden)	Karlstad
Tocantins (Brazil)	Miracema do Tocantins	Vas (Hungary)	Szombathely
		Västerbotten (Sweden)	Umea
Tochigi (Japan)	Utsunomiya	Västernorrland (Sweden)	Härnösand
Togdheer (Somalia)	Burao (Burco)	Västmanland (Sweden)	Västerås
Togo	Lome	Vaucluse (France)	Avignon
Toledo (Belize)	Punta Gorda	Vaud (Swiss canton)	Lausanne
Tolima (Colombia)	Cali	Vaupés (Colombia)	Mitú
Tolna (Hungary)	Szekszárd	Vava'u (Tonga)	Neiafu
Tombali (Guinea-Bissau)	Catió	Venda (South Africa)	Thohoyandou
Tône (Togo)	Dapaong	Vendée (France)	La Roche-sur-Yon
Tonga	Nuku'alofa	**Venezuela**	Caracas
Tongariro (NZ)	Taupo	Veracruz (Mexico)	Jalapa
Tongatapu (Tonga)	Nuku'alofa	Veraguas (Panama)	Santiago
Tonkolili (Sierra Leone)	Magburaka	Vermont (USA)	Montpelier
Tororo (Uganda)	Sukulu	Vest-Agder (Norway)	Kristiansand
Töv (Mongolia)	Dzuunmod	Vestfirdhir (Iceland)	Isafjördhur
Transkei (South Africa)	Umtata	Vestfold (Norway)	Tønsberg
Transvaal (South Africa)	Pretoria	Vestjaelland (Denmark)	Sore
Trarza (Mauritania)	Rosso	Vesturland (Iceland)	Borgarnes
Trelawny (Jamaica)	Falmouth	Vichada (Colombia)	Puerto Carreño
Trinidad and Tobago	Port of Spain	Victoria (Aus)	Melbourne
Tripura (India)	Agartala	Victoria (Trinidad and Tobago)	Princes Town
Tristan da Cunha	Edinburgh	Vienne (France)	Poitiers
Tropojë (Albania)	Bajram	**Vietnam**	Hanoi
Trujillo (Venezuela)	Trujillo	Villa Clara (Cuba)	Santa Clara
Tucumán (Argentina)	San Miguel	Vinh Phuc (Vietnam)	Vinh Yen
Tungurahua (Ecuador)	Ambato	**Virgin Islands (British)**	Road Town
Tunisia	Tunis	**Virgin Islands (USA)**	Charlotte Amalie
Turkey	Ankara	Virginia (USA)	Richmond
Turkmenistan	Ashkhabad	Vo (Togo)	Vogan
Turks and Caicos Islands	Grand Turk	Vojvodina (Yugoslavia)	Novi Sad
Turku ja Pori (Finland)	Turku	Volta (Ghana)	Ho
Tuscany (Italy)	Florence	Vorarlberg (Austria)	Bregenz
Tuva (Russia)	Kyzyl	Vosges (France)	Épinal
Tuvalu	Fongafale (on Funafuti Isle)	Vrancea (Romania)	Focsani
		Waikato (NZ)	Hamilton
Tyne and Wear (Eng)	Newcastle-upon-Tyne	Wairarapa (NZ)	Masterton
		Wales	Cardiff
Tyrone (NI)	Omagh	Wallis and Futuna Islands (France)	Mata-Utu
Ucayali (Peru)	Pucallpa	Warwickshire (Eng)	Warwick
Udmurtia (Russia)	Izhevsk	Washington (USA)	Olympia
Uganda	Kampala	Wasit (Iraq)	Al-Kut
Ukraine	Kiev	Waterford (Rep of Ireland)	Waterford
Umbria (Italy)	Perugia	Wawa (Togo)	Badou
United Arab Emirates	Abu Dhabi	Welega (Ethiopia)	Nekemte
United Kingdom	London	Welo (Ethiopia)	Dese
United States of America	Washington DC	West Bengal (India)	Calcutta
Upper Demerara/Berbice (Guyana)	Linden	West Coast (NZ)	Greymouth
Upper East (Ghana)	Bolgatanga	West Flanders (Belgium)	Bruges

Country, State, County or Area	Capital or Admin Centre	Country, State, County or Area	Capital or Admin Centre
West Glamorgan (Wales)	Swansea	Xékong (Laos)	Thong
West Midlands (Eng)	Birmingham	Xianghoang (Laos)	Phônsavan
West New Britain (Papua		Xinjiang Uighur (China)	Urumqi
New Guinea)	Kimbe	Yamalo-Nenets (Russia)	Salekhard
West Sepik (Papua New Guinea)	Vanimo	Yamanashi (Japan)	Kōfu
West Sussex (Eng)	Chichester	Yanggang-do (North Korea)	Hyesan
West Virginia (USA)	Charleston	Yaracuy (Venezuela)	San Felipe
West Yorkshire (Eng)	Wakefield	Yatenga (Burkina Faso)	Ouahigouya
Western Area (Sierra Leone)	Freetown	**Yemen**	Sana'a
Western Australia	Perth	Yogyakarta (Indonesia)	Yogyakarta
Western Division (Gambia)	Brikama	Yonne (France)	Auxerre
Western Equatoria (Sudan)	Yambio	Yoto (Togo)	Tabligbo
Western Highlands (Papua		Yucatán (Mexico)	Mérida
New Guinea)	Mount Hagen	**Yugoslavia**	Belgrade
Western Isles (Scotland)	Stornoway	Yukon Territory (Canada)	Whitehorse
	(Lewis)	Yün-lin (Taiwan)	Tou-liu
Western Nepal	Pokharā	Yunnan (China)	Kunming
Western Province (Fiji)	Lautoka	Yvelines (France)	Versailles
Western Province (Kenya)	Kakamega	Zaïre (Angola)	M'Banza Kongo
Western Province (Papua		Zambézia (Mozambique)	Quelimane
New Guinea)	Daru	**Zambia**	Lusaka
Western Province (Solomon Isles)	Gizo	Zamora-Chinchipe (Ecuador)	Zamora
Western Province (Zambia)	Mongu	Zanzibar North (Tanzania)	Mkokotoni
Western Region (Ghana)	Sekondi-Takoradi	Zanzibar South and Central	
Western Sahara	Laâyoune	(Tanzania)	Koani
	(El Aaiún)	Zanzibar West (Tanzania)	Zanzibar
Western Samoa	Apia	Zeeland (Netherlands)	Middleburg
Westmeath (Rep of Ireland)	Mullingar	Zhejiang (aka Chekiang) (China)	Hangzhou (aka
Westmoreland (Jamaica)	Savanna-la-Mar		Hangchow)
Wexford (Rep of Ireland)	Wexford	**Zimbabwe**	Harare
Wicklow (Rep of Ireland)	Wicklow	Zio (Togo)	Tsévié
Wiltshire (Eng)	Trowbridge	Zona Especial III (Nicaragua)	San Carlos
Wisconsin (USA)	Madison	Zou (Benin)	Abomey
Woleu-Ntem (Gabon)	Oyem	Zoundwéogo (Burkina Faso)	Manga
Woqooyi Galbeed (Somalia)	Hargeysa	Zuid-Holland (Netherlands)	Hague
Wyoming (USA)	Cheyenne	Zulia (Venezuela)	Maracaibo

GEOGRAPHY

Capitals

Capital or Admin Centre	Country, State, County or Area	Capital or Admin Centre	Country, State, County or Area
Aarau	Aargau (Swiss Canton)	Akjoujt	Inchiri (Mauritania)
Abancay	Apurimac (Peru)	**Akmola**	**Kazakhstan**
Abaokoro	Tarawa North (Kiribati)	Akure	Ondo (Nigeria)
Abéché	Ouaddai (Chad)	Akureyri	Nordhurland eystra
Abenra	Sonderjylland (Denmark)		(Iceland)
Abeokuta	Ogun (Nigeria)	Al-Amārah	Maysān (Iraq)
Aberdeen	Grampian (Scotland)	Al-'Arish	Sinā' ash-Shamāliyah
Abidjan-legislative	**Ivory Coast**		(Egypt)
Abomey	Zou (Benin)	Albany	New York (USA)
Abraham's Bay	Mayaguana (Bahamas)	Albi	Tarn (France)
Abu Dhabi	United Arab Emirates	Albina	Marowijne (Suriname)
Abuja	**Nigeria**	Alborg	Nordjylland (Denmark)
Accra	**Ghana**	Aleg	Brakna (Mauritania)
	Greater Accra (Ghana)	Alen	Orne (France)
Adamstown	Pitcairn Islands	Aleppo	Halab (Syria)
Ad-Damazin	An-Nil al-Azraq (Blue Nile)	Alexandria	Teleorman (Romania)
	(Sudan)	Al-Fāshir	Dārfur (Sudan)
Addis Ababa	**Ethiopia**	Al-Ghaydah	Al-Mahrah (Yemen)
	Shewa (Ethiopia)	Al-Ghurdaqah	Al-Bahr al-Ahmar (Egypt)
Adelaide	South Australia	**Algiers**	**Algeria**
Agana	**Guam**	Al-Hillah	Bābil (Iraq)
Agartala	Tripura (India)	Alice Town	Bimini Islands (Bahamas)
Agen	Lot-et-Garonne (France)	Al-Kharijah	Al-Wādi al-Jadid (Egypt)
Aginskoe	Agin-Buryat (Russia)	Al-Kut	Wasit (Iraq)
Ajaccio	**Corsica (France)**	Al-Mansurah	Ad-Dagahliyah (Egypt)
	Corse-du-Sud (France)	Al-Mukallā	Hadramawt (Yemen)

Capital or Admin Centre	Country, State, County or Area	Capital or Admin Centre	Country, State, County or Area
Alofi	Niue (Pacific)	Avignon	Vaucluse (France)
Alor Setar	Kedah (Malaysia)	Awasa	Sidamo (Ethiopia)
Altdorf	Uri (Swiss Canton)	Aylesbury	Buckinghamshire (Eng)
Älzawi	Mizorăm (India)	Ayoûn el-Atroûs	Hodh-el-Gharbi
Am Timan	Salamat (Chad)		(Mauritania)
Ambato	Tungurahua (Ecuador)	Azoques	Cañar (Ecuador)
Amboina	Moluccas (Indonesia)	Az-Zaqāziq	Ash-Sharqiyah (Egypt)
Ambon	Maluku (Indonesia)	Babahoyo	Los Rios (Ecuador)
Amiamé	Amou (Togo)	Bac Giang	Ha Bac (Vietnam)
Amiens	Picardie (French Region)	Bac Lieu	Minh Hai (Vietnam)
	Somme (French	Badou	Wawa (Togo)
	Department)	Bafilo	Assoli (Togo)
Amman	**Jordan**	Bafoussam	Ouest (Cameroon)
Amsterdam	**Netherlands**	Bageza	Mubende (Uganda)
Anadyr	Chukut (Russia)	**Baghdad**	**Iraq**
Ancona	Marche (Italy)	Baia Mare	Maramures (Romania)
Andalucia	Seville (Spain)	Baidoa (Baydhabo)	Bay (Somalia)
Andorra La Vella	Andorra	**Bairiki on Tarawa Island**	**Kiribati**
Aného	Lacs (Togo)		Tarawa South (Kiribati)
Angers	Maine-et Loire (France)	Bairiki Islet	Gilbert Isles (Kiribati)
Angoulême	Charente (France)	Bajram	Tropojë (Albania)
Ankara	**Turkey**	Bakaka	Tamana (Kiribati)
Anna Regina	Pomeroon/Supenaam	**Baku**	**Azerbaijan**
	(Guyana)	Balboa Heights	Panama Canal Zone
Annapolis	Maryland (USA)	**Bamako**	**Mali**
An-Năsiriyah	Dhi Qār (Iraq)	Bambari	Ouaka (C. A. Rep)
Annecy	Haute-Savoie (France)	Bamenda	Nord-Ouest (Cameroon)
Antananarivo	**Madagascar**	**Bandar Seri Begawan**	**Brunei**
Anteeren	Banaba (Kiribati)	Bandung	Jawar Barat (Indonesia)
Antigua Guatemala	Sacatepéquez (Guatemala)	Banfora	Comoé (Burkina Faso)
Apia	**Samoa**	Bangalore	Karnataka (India)
Appenzell	Appenzell Inner-Rhoden	Bangar	Temburong (Brunei)
	(Swiss Canton)	Bangassou	Mbomou (C. A. Rep)
Aracaju	Sergipe (Brazil)	**Bangkok**	**Thailand**
Arāk	Markazi (Iran)	**Bangui**	**Central African Republic**
Ararua	Cook Islands	Banhã	Al-Qalyubiyah (Egypt)
	(New Zealand)	Bani	Peravia (Dom Republic)
Arba Minch	Gemu Gofa (Ethiopia)	Banjarmasin	Kalimantan Selatan
Arendal	Aust-Agder (Norway)		(Indonesia)
Arlon	Luxembourg (Belgium)	**Banjul**	**Gambia**
Armagh	Armagh (N.I.)	Barcelona	Anzoátegui (Venezuela)
Armenia	Quindio (Colombia)	Barcelona	Catalonia (Spain)
Arnhem	Gelderland (Netherlands)	Barclayville	Grand Kru (Liberia)
Ar-Ramādi	Al-Anbār (Iraq)	Bari	Apulia a.k.a. Puglia (Italy)
Arras	Pas-de-Calais (France)	Bar-le-Duc	Meuse (France)
Arthur's Town	Cat Island (Bahamas)	Barnsley	South Yorkshire (Eng)
Arvayheer	Övörhangay (Mongolia)	Barquisimeto	Lara (Venezuela)
Asela	Arsi (Ethiopia)	Barranquilla	Atlántico (Colombia)
Ashkhabad	Turkmenistan	Baruun-urt	Sühbaatar (Mongolia)
Asmara	Eritrea	Basel	Basel-Stadt (Swiss Canton)
Assen	Drenthe (Netherlands)	Basse	Upper River (Gambia)
Assomada	Santa Catarina	**Basse-Terre**	**Guadeloupe**
	(Cape Verde)	Basseterre	St Kitts and Nevis
Asunción	**Paraguay**		St Kitts (St Kitts and
	Central Region (Paraguay)		Nevis)
Atakpamé	Des Plateaux (Togolese	Bastia	Haute-Corse (France)
	Region)	Bata	Rio Muni (Equatorial
	Ogou (Togolese Prefecture)		Guinea)
Atāq	Shabwah (Yemen)	Baton Rouge	Louisiana (USA)
Atar	Adrar (Mauritania)	Bayamo	Granma (Cuba)
Athens	**Greece**	Beauvais	Oise (France)
Ati	Batha (Chad)	Bedford	Bedfordshire (Eng)
Atlanta	Georgia (USA)	Beersheba	Southern District (Israel)
At-Tur	Sină' al-Janubiyah (Egypt)	**Beijing (a.k.a. Peking)**	**China**
Auch	Gers (France)	Beira	Sofala (Mozambique)
Augusta	Maine (USA)	**Beirut**	**Lebanon**
Auki	Malaita (Solomon Isles)	Beledweyne	Hiiraan (Somalia)
Aurillac	Cantal (France)	Belém	Pará (Brazil)
Austin	Texas (USA)	**Belfast**	**Northern Ireland**
Auxerre	Yonne (France)		Antrim (N.I.)

Capital or Admin Centre	Country, State, County or Area	Capital or Admin Centre	Country, State, County or Area
Belfort	Territoire de Belfort (France)	Bozoum	Ouham-Pendé (CA Rep)
Belgrade	**Yugoslavia**	**Brasilia**	**Brazil**
	Serbia	**Bratislava**	**Slovakia**
Bellinzona	Ticino (Swiss Canton)	**Brazzaville**	**Congo: People's Republic**
Belmopan	**Belize**	Bregenz	Vorarlberg (Austria)
Belo Horizonte	Minas Gerais (Brazil)	Bria	Haute-Kotto (CA Rep)
Bender Cassim		Bridgetown	**Barbados**
(Boosaaso)	Bari (Somalia)	Brikama	Western Division (Gambia)
Benin City	Bendel (Nigeria)	Brisbane	Queensland (Aus)
Bensonville	Montserrado (Liberia)	Bristol	Avon (Eng)
Berbera	Somaliland	Bruge	West Flanders (Belgium)
Berbérati	Haute-Sangha (C. A. Rep)	**Brussels**	**Belgium**
Bergen	Hordaland (Norway)		Brabant (Belgium)
Berlin	**Germany**	Bu'aale	Jubbada Dhexe (Somalia)
Berne	**Switzerland**	Buala	Isabel (Solomon Isles)
Bertoua	Est (Cameroon)	Buariki	Onotoa (Kiribati)
Besancon	Doubs (France)		Tabiteuea South (Kiribati)
Beverley	Humberside (Eng)	Bucaramanga	Santander (Colombia)
Bhopal	Madhya Pradesh (India)	Buchanan	Grand Bassa (Liberia)
Bhubaneswar	Orissa (India)	**Bucharest**	**Romania**
Bien Hoa	Dong Nai (Vietnam)	**Budapest**	**Hungary**
Bimbo	Ombella-Mpoko (C. A. Rep)		Pest (Hungary)
Bindura	Mashonaland Central (Zimbabwe)	Buea	Sud-Ouest (Cameroon)
		Buenos Aires	**Argentina**
Birao	Vakaga (C. A. Rep)	**Bujumbura**	**Burundi**
Birmingham	West Midlands (Eng)	Buka	North Solomons (Papua New Guinea)
Bishkek	**Kyrgyzstan**		
Bisho	Ciskei (South Africa)	Bukavu	Sud-Kivu (Dem Rep of Congo)
Bismarck	North Dakota (USA)		
Bissau	**Guinea-Bissau**	Bulamogi	Iganga (Uganda)
	Biombo (Guinea-Bissau)	Bulawayo	Matabeleland North (Zimbabwe)
Black River	St Elizabeth (Jamaica)		
Blenheim	Marlborough (NZ)	Bumbaire	Bushenyi (Uganda)
Bloemfontein-judicial	**South Africa**	Bungatira	Gulu (Uganda)
	Orange Free State (South Africa)	Bunkoko	Mbale (Uganda)
		Buon Me Thoat	Dac Lac (Vietnam)
Blois	Loir-et-Cher (France)	Burao (Burco)	Togdheer (Somalia)
Bluefields	Región Autónoma del Atlántico Sur (Nic)	Burrel	Mat (Albania)
		Busaru	Bundibugyo (Uganda)
Bo	Southern Province (Sierra Leone)	Byakabanda	Rakai (Uganda)
		Caacupé	Cordillera (Paraguay)
Boa Vista	Roraima (Brazil)	Caen	Basse Normandie (French Region)
Bobigny	Seine-Saint-Denis (France)		Calvados (French Department)
Bobo-Dioulasso	Houet (Burkina Faso)		
Bode	Nordland (Norway)	Caernarfon	Gwynedd (Wales)
Bogandé	Gnagna (Burkina Faso)	**Cagliari**	**Sardinia (Italy)**
Bogotá	**Colombia**	Cahors	Lot (France)
	Cundinamarca (Colombia)	**Cairo**	**Egypt**
		Calabar	Cross River (Nigeria)
Boise	Idaho (USA)	Calcutta	West Bengal (India)
Bol	Lac (Chad)	Cali	Tolima (Colombia)
Bolgatanga	Upper East (Ghana)	Cambridge	Cambridgeshire (Eng)
Bologna	Emilia-Romagna (Italy)	Campo Grande	Mato Grosso do Sul (Brazil)
Bombay (Mumbai)	Maharashtra (India)		
Bonao	Monseñor Nouel (Dom Republic)	Can Tho	Hau Giang (Vietnam)
		Canberra	**Australia**
Bongor	Mayo-Kebbi (Chad)		Australian Capital Territory
Bor	Junquli (Jongley) (Sudan)		
Bordeaux	Aquitaine (French Region)	Cape Coast	Central Region (Ghana)
	Gironde (French Department)	**Capetown-legislative**	**South Africa**
		Cap-Haitien	Nord (Haiti)
Borgarnes	Vesturland (Iceland)	Car Nicobar	Nicobar Islands
Bossangoa	Ouham (C. A. Rep)	**Caracas**	**Venezuela**
Boston	Massachusetts (USA)	Carcassonne	Aude (France)
Bouar	Nana-Mambere (C. A. Rep)	**Cardiff**	**Wales**
Boulsa	Namentenga (Burkina Faso)		Mid-Glamorgan (Wales)
			South Glamorgan (Wales)
Bourg-en-Bresse	Ain (France)	Carlisle	Cumbria (Eng)
Bourges	Cher (France)	Carlow	Carlow (Eire)

GEOGRAPHY

Capital or Admin Centre	Country, State, County or Area	Capital or Admin Centre	Country, State, County or Area
Carmarthen	Dyfed (Wales)	Clonmel	Tipperary (Eire)
Carrick-on-Shannon	Leitrim (Eire)	Cobán	Alta Verapaz (Guatemala)
Carson City	Nevada (USA)	Cobija	Pando (Bolivia)
Cartagena	Bolivar (Colombia)	Cockburn Town	San Salvador & Rum Cay
Castlebar	Mayo (Eire)	Cojutepeque	Cuscatián (El Salvador)
Castries	**Saint Lucia**	Colhaique (Chile)	Aisén del Gen Carlos
Catanzaro	Calabria (Italy)		Ibáñez del Campo
Catió	Tombali (Guinea-Bissau)	Colmar	Haut-Rhin (France)
Cavan	Cavan (Eire)	**Colombo**	**Sri Lanka**
Caxito	Bengo (Angola)	Colonel Hill	Crooked Island
Cayenne	**French Guiana**		(Bahamas)
Chachapoyas	Amazonas (Peru)	Columbia	South Carolina (USA)
Chaguanas	Caroni (Trinidad & Tobago)	Columbus	Ohio (USA)
Chake Chake	Pemba South (Tanzania)	**Conakry**	**Guinea**
Chalan Kanoa	Northern Mariana Islands	Conceptión	Bio-Bio (Chile)
	(Pacific)	Concorde	New Hampshire (USA)
Chalan Kanoa	Saipan	**Copenhagen**	**Denmark**
Châlons-sur-Marne	Champagne-Ardenne	Copiapó	Atacama (Chile)
	(French Region)	Cork	Cork (Eire)
	Marne (French	Coro	Falcón (Venezuela)
	Department)	Coronel Oviedo	Caaguazú (Paraguay)
Chambéry	Savoie (France)	Corovoda	Skrapar (Albania)
Chandigar	Haryana (India)	Cotonou	Atlantique (Benin)
Chandigar	Punjab (India)	Cotui	Sánchez Ramirez
Changchun	Jilin (aka Kirin)		(Dom Republic)
Changsha	Hunan (China)	Craiova	Dolj (Romania)
Charleston	West Virginia (USA)	Créteil	Val-de-Marne (France)
Charlestown	Nevis (St Kitts and Nevis)	Cúcuta	Norte de Santander
Charleville-Mézières	Ardennes (France)		(Colombia)
Charlotte Amalie	**Virgin Islands (U.S.A.)**	Cuenca	Azuay (Ecuador)
	St Thomas & St John	Cuernavaca	Morelos (Mexico)
	(US Virgins)	Cuiabá	Mato Grosso (Brazil)
Charlottetown	Prince Edward Island	Cuilapa	Santa Rosa (Guatemala)
	(Canada)	Culiacán	Sinaloa (Mexico)
Chartres	Eure-et-Loire (France)	Cumaná	Sucre (Venezuela)
Châteauroux	Indre (France)	Curitiba	Paraná (Brazil)
Chaumont	Haute-Marne (France)	Cuzco	Cuzco (Peru)
Cheboksary	Chuvasia (Russia)	Cwmbran	Gwent (Wales)
Chelmsford	Essex (Eng)	Da Lat	Lam Dong (Vietnam)
Chengdu	Sichuan (China)	**Dakar**	**Senegal**
Cherkesst	Karachai-Cherkessia	Dalandzadgad	Ömnögovi (Mongolia)
	(Russia)	Damanhur	Al-Buhayrah (Egypt)
Chester	Cheshire (Eng)	**Damascus**	**Syria**
Chetumal	Quintana Roo (Mexico)		Dimashq (Syria)
Cheyenne	Wyoming (USA)	Damphu (Bhutan)	Chirang
Chichester	West Sussex (Eng)	Dangriga	Stann Creek (Belize)
Chiclayo	Lambayeque (Peru)	Dapaong	Des Savanes (Togolese
Chilpancingo	Guerrero (Mexico)		Region)
Chimolo	Manica (Mozambique)		Tône (Togolese
Chinhoyi	Mashonaland West		Prefecture)
	(Zimbabwe)	Dar es Salaam	Pwani (Tanzania)
Chipata	Eastern Province (Zambia)	Darrit-Uliga-Dalap	
Chisimayu (Kismaayo)	Jubbada Hoose (Somalia)	(on Majuro isle)	Marshall Islands
Chitré	Herrera (Panama)	Daru	Western Province
Ch'ŏngjin	Hamgyong-pukto (North		(Papua New Guinea)
	Korea)	Darwin	Northern Territory (Aus)
Ch'ŏnju	Chŏlla-pukto (South Korea)	David	Chiriqui (Panama)
Choybaisan	Dornod (Mongolia)	Debre Markos	Gojam (Ethiopia)
Christchurch	Canterbury (NZ)	Debrecen	Hajdú-Bihar (Hungary)
Christiansted	St Croix (US Virgins)	Dédougou	Mouhoun (Burkina Faso)
Ch'unch'ŏn	Kangwŏn-do (South Korea)	Delémont	Jura (Swiss Canton)
Chur	Graubunden (Swiss	**Denpassar**	**Bali (Indonesia)**
	Canton)	Denver	Colorado (USA)
Ciudad Bolivar	Bolivar (Venezuela)	Des Moines	Iowa (USA)
Ciudad del Este	Alto Paraná (Paraguay)	Dese	Welo (Ethiopia)
Ciudad Flores	Petén (Guatemala)	Deva	Hunedoara (Romania)
Ciudad Victoria	Tamaulipas (Mexico)	**Dhaka**	**Bangladesh**
Clarence Town	Long Island (Bahamas)	Dhankutā	Eastern Nepal
Clermont-Ferrand	Auvergne (Frech Region)	Dhidhdhoo	Haa-Alifu (Maldives)
Puy-de-Dôme	(French Department)	Diapaga	Tapoa (Burkina Faso)

Capital or Admin Centre	Country, State, County or Area	Capital or Admin Centre	Country, State, County or Area
Diébougou	Bougouriba (Burkina Faso)	Évreux	Eure (France)
Dien Bien	Lai Chau (Vietnam)	Évry	Essonne (France)
Digne	Alpes-de-Haute-Provence (France)	Exeter	Devon (Eng)
		Eydhafushi	Baa (Maldives)
Dijon	Bourgogne/Burgundy (French Region)	Fada N'Gourma	Gourma (Burkina Faso)
		Falmouth	Trelawny (Jamaica)
	Cote-d'Or (French Department)	Falun	Kopparberg (Sweden)
		Farim	Oio (Guinea-Bissau)
Dili	**Eastern Timor (Pacific)**	Farukolhu Funadhoo	Shaviyani (Maldives)
Dili	Timor Timur (Indonesia)	Faya	Borkou-Ennedi-Tibesti (Chad)
Dipāyal	Far-Western Nepal		
Dispur	Assam (India)	Fdérik	Tiris Zemmour (Mauritania)
Djambala	Plateaux (Congo)	Felidhoo	Vaavu (Maldives)
Djibo	Soum (Burkina Faso)	Feng-shan	Kao-hsiung (Taiwan)
Djibouti	**Djibouti**	Feng-yuan	T'ai-chung (Taiwan)
Doba	Logone Oriental (Chad)	Florence	Tuscany (Italy)
Dodoma	**Tanzania**	Florencia	Caquetá (Colombia)
Doha	**Qatar**	Florianópolis	Santa Catarina (Brazil)
Dong Ha	Quang Tri (Vietnam)	Flying Fish Cove	Christmas Island (Aus)
Dong Hoi	Quang Binh (Vietnam)	Foah Mulah	Gnyaviyani (Maldives)
Dorchester	Dorset (Eng)	Focsani	Vrancea (Romania)
Dori	Sèno (Burkina Faso)	Foix	Ariège (France)
Douala	Littoral (Cameroon)	Fomboni	Moili (Comoros)
Douglas	Isle of Man	**Fongafale**	
Dover	Delaware (USA)	**(on Funafuti atoll)**	**Tuvalu**
Downpatrick	Down (N.I.)	Fort Wellington	Mahaica/Berbice (Guyana)
Dr Pedro P. Peña	Boquerón (Paraguay)	Fortaleza	Ceará (Brazil)
Drammen	Buskerud (Norway)	**Fort-de-France**	**Martinique (France)**
Dresden	Saxony (Germany)	Fort-Liberté	Nord-Est (Haiti)
Drobeta-Turnu-Severin	Mehedinti (Romania)	Franceville	Haut-Ogooué (Gabon)
Dublin	**Republic of Ireland**	Frankfort	Kentucky (USA)
	Dublin (rep of Ireland)	Frauenfeld	Thurgau (Swiss Canton)
Dudinka	Taimyr (Russia)	Fray Bentos	Rio Negro (Uruguay)
Dumfries	Dumfries and Galloway (Scotland)	Fredericton	New Brunswick (Canada)
		Freeport	Grand Bahama
Duncan Town	Ragged Island (Bahamas)	**Freetown**	**Sierra Leone**
Dundalk	Louth (Eire)		Western Area (Sierra Leone)
Dundee	Tayside (Scotland)		
Dunedin	North Otago (NZ)	Fuerte Olimpio	Alto Paraguay (Paraguay)
Dungxoai	Binh Phuoc (Vietnam)	Fulacunda	Quinara (Guinea-Bissau)
Durham	Durham (Eng)	**Funchal**	**Madeira**
Dusa Marreb		Fuzhou (aka Foochow)	Fujian (aka Fukien)
(Dhuusamarreeb)	Galguduud (Somalia)	**Gaborone**	**Botswana**
Dushanbe	**Tadzhikstan**	Galcaio (Gaalkacyo)	Mudug (Somalia)
Düsseldorf	Nordrhein-Westfalen (Germany)	Galway	Galway (Eire)
		Gāndhinagar	Gujarāt (India)
Dzhohar	Chechnya	**Gangtok**	**Sikkim (India)**
Dzuunmod	Töv (Mongolia)	Gaoua	Poni (Burkina Faso)
Eas	Ambrym (Vanuatu)	Gap	Haute-Alpes (France)
Ebolowa	Sud (Cameroon)	Garbahaarrey	Gedo (Somalia)
Edinburgh	**Scotland**	Garissa	North Eastern Province (Kenya)
	Lothian (Scotland)		
Edinburgh	Tristan da Cunha	Garoowe	Nugaal (Somalia)
Edmonton	Alberta (Canada)	Garoua	Nord (Cameroon)
Eger	Heves (Hungary)	Gbarnga	Bong (Liberia)
Egilsstadhir	Austurland (Iceland)	General Eugenio A. Garay	Nueva Asunción (Paraguay)
Eisenstadt	Burgenland (Austria)	Genoa	Liguria (Italy)
Elias Piña	La Estrelleta (Dom Republic)	George Town	Penang/Pinang (Malaysia)
		Georgetown	Ascension
Elista	Kalmuck (CIS)	**Georgetown**	**Cayman Islands**
Embu	Eastern Province (Kenya)	**Georgetown**	**Guyana**
Encarnación	Itapúa (Paraguay)	Ghent	East Flanders (Belgium)
Ennis	Clare (Eire)	Gibeon	Namaland (Namibia)
Enniskillen	Fermanagh (N.I.)	Giohar Jawhar	Shabeellaha Dhexe (Somalia)
Enugu	Anambra (Nigeria)		
Épinal	Vosges (France)	Gibeon	Namaland (Namibia)
Erfurt	Thuringia (Germany)	Giohar (Jawhar)	Shabeellaha Dhexe (Somalia)
Erigavo (Ceerigaabo)	Sanaag (Somalia)		
Ersekë	Kolonjë (Albania)	Gisborne	East Cape (NZ)
Esteli	Región 1 (Nicaragua)	Giyani	Gazankulu (South Africa)

GEOGRAPHY

Capital or Admin Centre	Country, State, County or Area	Capital or Admin Centre	Country, State, County or Area
Gizo	Western Province (Solomon Isles)	Harper	Maryland (Liberia)
		Harrisburg	Pennsylvania (USA)
Glasgow	Strathclyde (Scotland)	Hartford	Connecticut (USA)
Glenrothes	Fife (Scotland)	Hasselt	Limburg (Belgium)
Gloucester	Gloucestershire (Eng)	**Havana**	**Cuba**
Goba	Bale (Ethiopia)		La Habana (Cuba)
Gobabis	Omaheke (Namibia)	Hefei (aka Ho-fei)	Anhui (aka Anhwei)
Godthaab (a.k.a.Nuuk)	**Greenland**	Helena	Montana (USA)
	(aka Kalaallit Nunaat)	**Helsinki**	**Finland**
Goiânia	Goiás (Brazil)		Uusimaa (Finland)
Goma	Nord-Kivu (Dem Rep of Congo)	Herisau	Appenzell Ausser-Rhoden (Swiss Canton)
Gonaives	Artibonite (Haiti)	Hermosillo	Sonora (Mexico)
Goroka	Eastern Highlands (Papua New Guinea)	Hertford	Hertfordshire (Eng)
		Higüey	La Altagracia (Dom Republic)
Gorom Gorom	Oudalan (Burkina Faso)		
Gracias	Lempira (Honduras)	Hihifo	Niuas (Tonga)
Grand Turk	**Turks and Caicos Islands**	Hillerod	Frederiksborg (Denmark)
Graz	Steiermark (Austria)	Hinche	Centre Departement (Haiti)
Greenville	Sinoe (Liberia)	Hiotse	Leribe (Lesotho)
Grenoble	Isère (France)	Hithadhoo	Laamu (Maldives)
Greymouth	West Coast (NZ)	Hithadoo	Seenu (Maldives)
Groningen	Saramacca (Suriname)	Ho	Volta (Ghana)
Grootfontein	Otjozondjupa (Nambia)	Hobart	Tasmania
Guadalajara	Jalisco (Mexico)	Hoi An	Quang Nam (Vietnam)
Guadalupe	Lobata (São Tomé & Principe)	Homs	Hims (Syria)
		Honiara	**Solomon Islands**
Guanare	Portuguesa (Venezuela)		Guadalcanal (Solomon Isles)
Guangzhou (aka Canton)	Guangdong (aka Kwangtung)	Honolulu	Hawaii (USA)
Guaranda	Bolivar (Ecuador)	Houayxay	Bokeo (Laos)
Guatemala City	**Guatemala**	Hsin-ying	Tai-nan (Taiwan)
Guayaquil	Guayas (Ecuador)	Huancayo	Junin (Peru)
Guéret	Creuse (France)	Huaraz	Ancash (Peru)
Guiyang (aka Kuei-yang)	Guizhou (aka Kweichow)	Hue	Bin Tri Thien (Vietnam)
Gwanda	Matabeleland South (Zimbabwe)	Hugh Town	Scilly Isles
		Hu-ho-hao-t'e (aka Hohhot)	Inner Mongolia (aka Nei Monggol)
Gweru	Midland Province (Zimbabwe)	Hyderabad	Andhra Pradesh (India)
Ha Dong	Ha Tay (Vietnam)	Hyesan	Yanggang-do (North Korea)
Ha Giang	Ha Tuyen (Vietnam)	Ibadan	Oyo (Nigeria)
Ha Long City	Quang Nam-Hoi An (Vietman)	Ibarra	Imbabura (Ecuador)
		Impfondo	Likouala (Congo)
Ha Long City	Quang Ninh (Vietman)	Imphāl	Manipur (India)
Haarlem	Noord-Holland (Netherlands)	Innsbruck	Tirol (Austria)
		Invercargill	Southland (NZ)
Haeju	Hwanghae-namdo (North Korea)	Inverness	Highland (Scotland)
		Ipswich	Suffolk (Eng)
Hague	Zuid-Holland (Netherlands)	Iqaluit	Nunavut (Canada)
Haikou	Hainan (China)	Iquique	Tarapacá (Chile)
Hakha	Chin (Myanmar)	Iquitos	Loreto (Peru)
Halifax	Nova Scotia (Canada)	Isafjördhur	Vestfirdhir (Iceland)
Halmstad	Halland (Sweden)	Isangei	Taféa (Vanuatu)
Hamar	Hedmark (Norway)	**Islamabad**	**Pakistan**
Hämeenlinna	Häme (Finland)	Itānagar	Arunāchal Pradesh (India)
Hamhung	Hamgyong-namdo (North Korea)	Izhevsk	Udmurtia (Russia)
		Jackson	Mississippi (USA)
Hamilton	**Bermuda**	Jacmel	Sud-Est (Haiti)
Hamilton	Waikato (NZ)	Jaipur	Rajasthan (India)
Hanga Roa	Easter Island	Jakar	Bumthang (Bhutan)
Hangzhou (aka Hangchow)	Zhejiang (aka Chekiang)	**Jakarta**	**Indonesia**
			Jakarta Raya (Indonesia)
Hanoi	**Vietnam**	Jalapa	Veracruz (Mexico)
Hanover	Niedersachsen (Germany)	Jamestown	St Helena
Harare	**Zimbabwe**	**Jayapura**	**Irian Jaya (Indonesia)**
Harbin	Heilongjiang (China)	Jefferson City	Missouri (USA)
Harer	Hararge (Ethiopia)	Jérémie	Grande Anse (Haiti)
Hargeysa	Woqooyi Galbeed (Somalia)	**Jerusalem**	**Israel**
		Jima	Kefa (Ethiopia)
Härnösand	Västernorrland (Sweden)	Jimani	Independencia (Dom

Capital or Admin Centre	Country, State, County or Area	Capital or Admin Centre	Country, State, County or Area
	Republic)	**Kiev**	**Ukraine**
Jinan (aka Tsinan)	Shandong (aka Shantung)	Kiffa	El-Acâba (Mauritania)
Jinotepe	Región IV (Nicaragua)	**Kigali**	**Rwanda**
João Pessoa	Paraíba (Brazil)	Kilkenny	Kilkenny (Eire)
Joensuu	Pohjois-Karjala (Finland)	Kimbe	West New Britain (Papua New Guinea)
Johor Baharu	Johor (Malaysia)		
Jos	Plateau (Nigeria)	Kindu	Maniema (Dem Rep of Congo)
Jubã	Eastern Equatoria (Sudan)		
Juigalpa	Región V (Nicaragua)	**Kingston**	**Jamaica**
Juneau	Alaska (USA)	Kingston	Norfolk Island
Juticalpa	Olancho (Honduras)	Kingston-upon-Thames	Surrey (Eng)
Jyväskylä	Keski-Suomi (Finland)	Kingstown	St Vincent and Grenadines
Kabala	Koinaduga (Sierra Leone)	Kinkala	Pool (Congo)
Kabul	**Afghanistan**	**Kinshasa**	**Congo: Democratic Republic**
Kabwe	Central Province (Zambia)		
Kaédi	Gorgol (Mauritania)	Kira Kira	Makira (Solomon Isles)
Kaga-Bandoro	Gribingui-Economique (CA Rep)	Kiritimati	Line Isles (Kiribati)
		Kirkwall	Orkney Islands
Kagunga	Rukungiri (Uganda)	Kisangani	Haute-Zaïre (Dem Rep of Congo)
Kakamega	Western Province (Kenya)		
Kakata	Margibi (Liberia)	**Kishinev**	**Moldavia**
Kakika	Mbarara (Uganda)	Kisumu	Nyanza (Kenya)
Kampala	**Uganda**	Kizyl	Tuva (CIS)
Kananga	Kasai-Occidental (Dem Rep of Congo)	Klagenfurt	Karnten (Austria)
		Koani	Zanzibar South & Central (Tanzania)
Kanazawa	Ishikawa (Japan)		
Kandé	Kéran (Togo)	Kōbe	Hyōgo (Japan)
Kanggye	Chagang-do (North Korea)	Koforidua	Eastern Region (Ghana)
Kanifing	Kombo St. Mary (Gambia)	Kōfu	Yamanashi (Japan)
Kanton	Phoenix Isles (Kiribati)	Kohima	Nāgāland (India)
Kanye	Ngwaketse (Botswana)	Kolonia/Palikir	Micronesia (Pacific)
Kaposvár	Somogy (Hungary)	Kombissiri	Bazéga (Burkina Faso)
Kara	Kozah (Togo)	Kongoussi	Bam (Burkina Faso)
Karāchi	Sind (Pakistan)	Koror Island	Palau (Pacific)
Karambe	Kabarole (Uganda)	Kota Bharu	Kelantan (Malaysia)
Kariatebike	Abemama (Kiribati)	Kota Kinabalu	Sabah (Malaysia)
Karlskrona	Blekinge (Sweden)	Koudougou	Boulkiemde (Burkina Faso)
Karlstad	Värmland (Sweden)	Koulamoutou	Ogooué-Lolo (Gabon)
Kasama	Northern Province (Zambia)	Koupéla	Kouritenga (Burkina Faso)
Kasane	Chobe (Botswana	Kouvola	Kymi (Finland)
Kaswa Bukoto	Masaka (Uganda)	Kpalimé	Kloto (Togo)
Kāthmāndu	**Nepal** Central Nepal	Kralendijk	Bonaire (Netherland Antilles)
Katikekile	Moroto (Uganda)	Kristiansand	Vest-Agder (Norway)
Katima Mulilo	Caprivi Oos (Namibia)	Kuala Belait	Belait (Brunei)
Kavaratti Island	Lakshadweep Islands (India)	**Kuala Lumpur**	**Malaysia**
		Kuching	**Sarawak (Malaysia)**
Kavieng	New Ireland (Papua New Guinea)	Kudahuvadhoo	Dhaalu (Maldives)
		Kudymkar	Komy Permyak (Russia)
Kaya	Sanmatenga (Burkina Faso)	Kuito	Bié (Angola)
		Kumasi	Ashanti (Ghana)
Kazan	Tatarstan	Kundiawa	Chimbu (Papua New Guinea)
Kecskemét	Bács-Kiskun (Hungary)		
Keetmanshoop	Karas (Namibia)	Kunming	Yunnan (China)
Keflavik	Sudhurnes (Iceland)	Kuntaur/Georgetown	MacCarthy Island (Gambia)
Kemps Bay	Andros Island (Bahamas)	Kupang	Nusa Tenggara Timur (Indonesia)
Kendari	Sulawesi Tenggara (Indonesia)		
		Kuwait	**Kuwait**
Kenema	Eastern Province (Sierra Leone)	Kwangju	Chōlla-namdo (South Korea)
Kerema	Gulf (Papua New Guinea)	La Asunción	Nueva Esparta (Venezuela)
Kerewan	North Bank (Gambia)	La Ceiba	Atlántida (Honduras)
Kerkira	**Corfu**	La Esperanza	Intibucá (Honduras)
Khania	**Crete**	La Palma	Darién (Panama)
Khartoum	**Sudan**	La Paz	Baja California Sur (Mexico)
Khanty-Mansūsk	Kharty-Mansi (Russia)	**La Paz-admin**	**Bolivia**
Khasab	Musandam (Oman)	La Plata	Buenos Aires
Khorixas	Damaraland (Namibia)	La Rochelle	Charente-Maritime (France)
Kiel	Schleswig-Holstein (Germany)	La Roche-sur-Yon	Vendée (France)
		La Serena	Coquimbo (Chile)

GEOGRAPHY

Capital or Admin Centre	Country, State, County or Area	Capital or Admin Centre	Country, State, County or Area
Laâyone (El Aaiún)	Western Sahara	Lokossa	Mono (Benin)
Labasa	Northern Province (Fiji)	Loltong	Pentecost (Vanuatu)
Labongo	Kitgum (Uganda)	**Lomé**	**Togo**
Lae	Morobe (Papua New Guinea)		Golfe (Togolese Prefecture)
Lahore	Punjab (Pakistan)		Maritime Region (Togo)
Lai	Tandjilé (Chad)	London	Christmas Island/Kiritimati
Lakatoro	Malekula (Vanuatu)		Atoll (Kiribati)
Lambaréné	Moyen-Ogooué (Gabon)	**London**	**England**
Lansing	Michigan (USA)		Greater London (Eng)
Lanzhou (aka Lan-chou)	Gansui (aka Kansu)		United Kingdom
Laon	Aisne (France)	Londonderry	Londonderry (N.I.)
L'Aquila	Abruzzi (Italy)	Long Xuyen	An Giang (Vietnam)
Las Palmas	Gran Canaria	Longana	Ambae/Maéwo (Vanuatu)
Las Tablas	Los Santos (Panama)	Longford	Longford (Eire)
Latacunga	Cotopaxi (Ecuador)	Lons-le-Saunier	Jura (France)
Latakia	Al-Lādhiqiyah (Syria)	Lorengau	Manus (Papua New Guinea)
Lausanne	Vaud (Swiss Canton)		
Lautoka	Western Province (Fiji)	Los Teques	Miranda (Venezuela)
Laval	Mayenne (France)	Loubomo	Niari (Congo)
Le Mans	Sarthe (France)	Louieville	KaNgwane (South Africa)
Le Puy	Haute-Loire (France)	Louvain (Leuven)	Brabant (Flemish)
Lebowakgomo	Lebowa (South Africa)	**Luanda**	**Angola**
Leeuwarden	Friesland (Netherlands)	Lubango	Huita (Angola)
Leicester	Leicestershire (Eng)	Lubumbashi	Shaba (Dem Rep of Congo)
Leikanger	Sogn og Fjordane (Norway)	Lucapa	Lunda Norte (Angola)
Lelystad	Flevoland (Netherlands)	Lucea	Hanover (Jamaica)
Léo	Sissilli (Burkina Faso)	Lucknow	Uttar Pradesh (India)
León	Región II (Nicaragua)	Luganville	Santo/Maio (Vanuatu)
Lerwick	Shetland Islands	Luleá	Norrbotten (Sweden)
Les Cayes	Sud (Haiti)	**Lusaka**	**Zambia**
Leticia	Amazonas (Colombia)	**Luxembourg**	**Luxembourg**
Levin	Horowhenua (NZ)	Lwena	Moxico (Angola)
Levuka	Eastern Province (Fiji)	Lyon	Rhône (France)
Lewes	East Sussex (Eng)	Lyon	Rhône-Alpes (France)
Lhasa (China)	**Tibet (aka Xizang)**	Maastricht	Limburg (Netherlands)
Liberia	Guanacaste (Costa Rica)	Mabaruma	Barima/Waini (Guyana)
Libreville	**Gabon**	Macao	Macao (Portugal)
	Estuaire (Gabon)	Macapá	Amapá (Brazil)
Lichinga	Niassa (Mozambique)	Macas	Morona-Santiago (Ecuador)
Liestal	Basel-Landschaft (Swiss Canton)	Maceió	Alagoas (Brazil)
		Machala	El Oro (Ecuador)
Lifford	Donegal (Eire)	Mâcon	Saône-et-Loire (France)
Lille	Nord (France)	Madingou	Bouenza (Congo)
Lille	Nord-Pas-de-Calais (France)	Madison	Wisconsin (USA)
Lillehammer	Oppland (Norway)	Madras	Tamil Nadu (India)
Lilongwe	**Malawi**	**Madrid**	**Spain**
Lima	**Peru**	Maebashi	Gumma (Japan)
Limerick	Limerick (Eire)	Magburaka	Tonkolili (Sierra Leone)
Limoges	Haute-Vienne (French Department)	Magdeburg	Saxony-Anhalt (Germany)
		Magoodhoo	Faafu (Maldives)
	Limousin (French Region)	Mahibadhoo	Alifu (Maldives)
Lincoln	Lincolnshire (Eng)	Mahon	Minorca
Lincoln	Nebraska (USA)	Maidstone	Kent (Eng)
Linden	Upper Demerara/Berbice (Guyana)	Mainz	Rheinland-Pfalz (Germany)
		Makeni	Bombali (Sierra Leone)
Linköping	Östergötland (Sweden)		Northern Province (Sierra Leone)
Linz	Oberosterreich (Austria)		
Liro	Paama (Vanuatu)	Makhachkala	Dagestan (CIS)
Lisbon	**Portugal**	Makokou	Ogooué-Ivindo (Gabon)
Little Rock	Arkansas (USA)	Ma-kung	P'eng-hu (Taiwan)
Liverpool	Merseyside (Eng)	Makurdi	Benue (Nigeria)
Livingstone	Southern Province (Zambia)	**Malabo**	**Equatorial Guinea**
			Bioko (Equatorial Guinea)
Ljubljana	**Slovenia**		
Lkeja	Lagos (Nigeria)	Malakāi	A'āli an-Nil (Upper Nile) (Sudan)
Llandrindod Wells	Powys (Wales)		
Llorin	Kwara (Nigeria)	Malduguri	Borno (Nigeria)
Logrono	La Rioja (Spain)	**Male**	**Maldives**
Loi-kaw	Kayah (Myanmar)		Kaafu (Maldives)

Capital or Admin Centre	Country, State, County or Area	Capital or Admin Centre	Country, State, County or Area
Mamoudzou	**Mayotte**	Menado	Sulawesi Utara (Indonesia)
Manadhoo	Noonu (Maldives)	Mende	Lozère (France)
Managua	**Nicaragua**	Mende	Southern Highlands (Papua New Guinea)
Managua	Región III (Nicaragua)		
Manama	**Bahrain**	Menongue	Kuando Kubango (Angola)
Manaus	Amazonas (Brazil)	Merca (Marka)	Shabeellaha Hoose (Somalia)
Manchester	Greater Manchester (Eng)		
Mandalgov	Dundgovi (Mongolia)	Mercedes	Soriano (Uruguay)
Mandeville	Manchester (Jamaica)	Merida	Extremadura (Spain)
Manga	Zoundwéogo (Burkina Faso)	Mérida	Yucatán (Mexico)
		Metu	Ilubabor (Ethiopia)
Manila	**Philippines**	Metz	Lorraine (French Region)
Manizales	Caldas (Colombia)	Metz	Moselle (French Department)
Mansa	Luapula (Zambia)		
Mansakonko	Lower River (Gambia)	Mexicali	Baja California Norte (Mexico)
Mao	Kanem (Chad)		
Mao	Valverde (Dom Republic)	**Mexico City**	**Mexico**
Maputo	**Mozambique**	Middleburg	Zeeland (Netherlands)
Maracaibo	Zulia (Venezuela)	Middlesbrough	Cleveland (Eng)
Maracay	Aragua (Venezuela)	Miercurea-Ciuc	Harghita (Romania)
Mariestad	Skaraborg (Sweden)	Milan	Lombardy (Italy)
Marigot	St-Martin & St Barthelemy (Guadeloupe)	Minas	Lavalleja (Uruguay)
		Mindelo	São Vicente (Cape Verde)
Marondera	Mashonaland East (Zimbabwe)	Minna	Niger (Nigeria)
		Minsk	**Bellorussia**
Maroua	Extrême-Nord (Cameroon)	Miracema do Tocantins	Tocantins (Brazil)
Marsã Matruh	Matruh (Egypt)	Miskolc	Borsod-Abaúj-Zemplén (Hungary)
Marseille	Bouches-du-Rhône (French Department) Provence-Alpes-Côte d'Azur (Region)	Mito	Ibaraki (Japan)
		Mitú	Vaupés (Colombia)
		Mkokotoni	Zanzibar North (Tanzania)
Marsh Harbour	Abaco & Mores Island	Mmabatho	Bophuthatswana (South Africa)
Masan	Kyŏngsang-namdo (South Korea)	Mobaye	Basse-Kotto (Cape Verde)
Maseru	**Lesotho**	Moca	Espaillat (Dom Republic)
Masterton	Wairarapa (NZ)	Mochudi	Kgatleng (Botswana)
Masunga	Botswana (North East)	Mocoa	Putumayo (Colombia)
Matadi	Bas-Zaïre (Dem Rep of Congo)	**Mogadishu (Muqdisho)**	**Somalia** Banaadir (Somalia)
Matagalpa	Región VI (Nicaragua)	Mold	Clwyd (Wales)
Mataram	Nusa Tenggara Barat (Indonesia)	Molde	Møre og Romsdal (Norway)
		Molepolole	Kweneng (Botswana)
Mataura	Îles Australes (French Polynesia)	Mombasa	Coast Province (Kenya)
		Monaco-Ville	
Mata-Utu	Wallis and Futuna Islands	**(aka Monaco)**	**Monaco**
Matlock	Derbyshire (Eng)	Monaghan	Monaghan (Eire)
Matsue	Shimane (Japan)	Mongo	Guéra (Chad)
Matsuyama	Ehime (Japan)	Mongu	Western Province (Zambia)
Matthew Town	Inagua, Great & Little		
Maturin	Monagas (Venezuela)	**Monrovia**	**Liberia**
Maun	Ngamiland (Botswana)	Mons	Hainaut (Belgium)
May Pen	Clarendon (Jamaica)	Montauban	Tarn-et-Garonne (France)
Mayor Pablo Lagerenza	Chaco (Paraguay)	Mont-de-Marsan	Landes (France)
Mazatenango	Suchitepéquez (Guatemala)	Montego Bay	St James (Jamaica)
		Montería	Córdoba (Colombia)
Mbabane	**Swaziland**	Monterrey	Nuevo León (Mexico)
	Hhohho (Swaziland)	**Montevideo**	**Uruguay**
Mbaiki	Lobaye (CA Rep)	Montgomery	Alabama (USA)
Mbandaka	Equateur (Dem Rep of Congo)	Montpelier	Vermont (USA)
		Montpellier	Hérault (French Department)
M'Banza Kongo	Zaïre (Angola)		Languedoc-Roussillon (French Region)
Mbuji-Mayi	Kasai-Oriental (Dem Rep of Congo)		
		Morant Bay	St Thomas (Jamaica)
Medan	Sumatera Utara (Indonesia)	Morelia	Michoacán (Mexico)
Medelin	Antioquia (Colombia)	Morioka	Iwate (Japan)
Mekele	Tigray (Ethiopia)	Mörön	Hövsgöl (Mongolia)
Melaka	Melaka (Malaysia)	**Moroni**	**Comoros Island**
Melbourne	Victoria (Aus)		Ngazidja (Comoros)
Melo	Cerro Largo (Uruguay)	Morpeth	Northumberland (Eng)
Melun	Seine-et-Marne (France)		

Capital or Admin Centre	Country, State, County or Area
Morua	Shepherd (Vanuatu)
Moscow	**Russia**
Moshi	Kilimanjaro (Tanzania)
Moss	Østfold (Norway)
Mostar	**Hercegovina**
Mosul	Ninawā (Iraq)
Mouila	Ngounié (Gabon)
Moulins	Allier (France)
Moulmein	Mon (Myanmar)
Moundou	Logone Occidental (Chad)
Mount Hagen	Western Highlands (Papua New Guinea)
Moyobamba	San Martin (Peru)
Muli	Meemu (Maldives)
Mullingar	Westmeath (Eire)
Munich	Bavaria (Germany)
Muscat	**Oman**
Musoma	Mara (Tanzania)
Mutare	Manicaland (Zimbabwe)
Mutsamudu	Ndzouani (Comoros)
My Tho	Tien Giang (Vietnam)
Myitkyinā	Kachin (Myanmar)
Naas	Kildare (Eire)
Nacaome	Valle (Honduras)
Nagoya	Aichi (Japan)
Nagua	Maria Trinidad Sánchez (Dom Republic)
Naha City	Okinawa (Japan) Ryukyu Islands (Japan)
Naifaru	Lhaviyani (Maldives)
Nairobi	**Kenya**
Nakuru	Rift Valley (Kenya)
Nalchik	Kabardino-Balkar (CIS)
Namendwa	Kamuli (Uganda)
Nanchang	Jiangxi (aka Kiangsi)
Nancy	Meurthe-et-Moselle (France)
Nanjing (aka Nanking)	Jiangsu (aka Kiangsu)
Nanning (China)	Kwangsi Chuang (aka Guangxi Zhuang)
Nanterre	Hauts-de-Seine (France)
Nantes	Loire-Atlantique (French Department) Pays de la Loire (French Region)
Napier	Hawke's Bay (NZ)
Naples	Campania (Italy)
Naryan-Mar	Nennets (Russia)
Nashville	Tennessee (USA)
Nassau	**Bahamas** New Providence (Bahamas)
Natal	Rio Grande do Norte (Brazil)
Natitingou	Atacora (Benin)
N'Dalatando	Kuanza Norte (Angola)
Ndélé	Bamingui-Bangoran (Cape Verde)
N'Djamena	**Chad** Chari-Baguirmi (Chad Prefecture)
Ndola	Copperbelt (Zambia)
Neiafu	Vava'u (Tonga)
Neiba	Bahoruco (Dom Repulic)
Neiva	Huila (Colombia)
Nekemte	Welega (Ethiopia)
Nelson	Nelson Bays (NZ)
Néma	Hodh-ech-Chargui (Mauritania)
Nevers	Nièvre (France)

Capital or Admin Centre	Country, State, County or Area
Neves	Lemba (São Tomé & Principe)
New Amsterdam	East Berbice/Corentyne (Guyana)
New Delhi	**India (aka Bharat)**
New Plymouth	Taranaki (NZ)
Newcastle-upon-Tyne	Tyne and Wear (Eng)
Newport	Isle of Wight
Newtown St Boswells	Borders (Scotland)
Ngaoundéré	Adamous (Cameroon)
N'Giva	Cunene (Angola)
Nha Trang	Khanh Hoa (Vietnam)
Nha Trang	Phu Khanh (Vietnam)
Nhlangano	Shiselweni (Swaziland)
Niamey	**Niger**
Niamtougou	Doufelgou (Togo)
Nice	Alpes-Maritimes (France)
Nicolls Town	Berry Island (Bahamas)
Nicosia	**Cyprus**
Nieuw Amsterdam	Commewijne (Suriname)
Nieuw Nickerie	Nickerie (Suriname)
Nîmes	Gard (France)
Niort	Deux-Sèvres (France)
Nola	Sangha-Économique (CA Rep)
Nolhivaranfaru	Haa-Dhaalu (Maldives)
Northallerton	North Yorkshire (Eng)
Northampton	Northamptonshire (Eng)
Norwich	Norfolk (Eng)
Notsé	Haho (Togo)
Nottingham	Nottinghamshire (Eng)
Nouakchott	**Mauritania**
Nouméa	New Caledonia (France)
Nouna	Kossi (Burkina Fasso)
Nova Sintra	Brava (Cape Verde)
Novi Sad	Vojvodina (Yugoslavia)
Nueva San Salvador	La Libertad (El Salvador)
Nuku'alofa	**Tonga** Tongatapu (Tonga)
Nukus	Kara-Kalpak (CIS)
Nyangeya	Masindi (Uganda)
Nyeri	Central Province (Kenya)
Nyiregyháza	Szabics-Szatmár (Hungary)
Nykebing	Storstrom (Denmark)
Nyköping	Södermanland (Sweden)
Obo	Haut-Mbomou (CA Rep)
Oddur (Xuddur)	Bakool (Somalia)
Odense	Fyn (Denmark)
Ohonua	Eua (Tonga)
Okakarara	Hereroland-Wes (Namibia)
Oklahoma City	Oklahoma (USA)
Olaki	Arua (Uganda)
Olympia	Washington (USA)
Omagh	Tyrone (N.I.)
Öndörhaan	Hentiy (Mongolia)
Onverwacht	Para (Suriname)
Opuwo	Kaokoland (Namibia)
Oradea	Bihor (Romania)
Oranjestad	**Aruba**
Oranjestad	St Eustatius (Netherland Antilles)
Orléans	Loiret (France)
Orodara	Kénédougou (Burkina Faso)
Oshakati	Oshana (Nambia)
Oshikango	Ohangwena (Nambia)
Oslo	**Norway**
Östersund	Jämtland (Sweden)
Ōtsu	Shiga (Japan)
Ottawa	**Canada**
Ouagadougou	**Burkina Faso**

Capital or Admin Centre	Country, State, County or Area	Capital or Admin Centre	Country, State, County or Area
Ouagadougou	Kadiogo (Burkina Faso)	**Phnom Penh**	**Cambodia**
Ouahigouya	Yatenga (Burkina Faso)	Phoenix	Arizona (USA)
Ouesso	Sangha (Congo)	Phônsavan	Xianghoang (Laos)
Outapi	Omusati (Namibia)	Phu Ly	Ha Nan (Vietnam)
Oviedo	Asturias (Spain)	Phuthaditjhaba	Qwaqwa (South Africa)
Owando	Cuvette (Congo)	Piatra Neamt	Neamt (Romania)
Owerri	Imo (Nigeria)	Pierre	South Dakota (USA)
Oxford	Oxfordshire (Eng)	Pietermaritsburg	Natal (South Africa)
Oyem	Woleu-Ntem (Gabon)	Pilar	Ñeembucu (Paraguay)
Pa-an	Karen (Myanmar)	Pitesti	Arges (Romania)
Pachuca	Hidalgo (Mexico)	Plei Ku	Gia Lai (Vietnam)
Padang	Sumatera Barat (Indonesia)	Ploiesti	Prahova (Romania)
Paelau	Fanning/Tabuaeran (Kiribati)	**Plymouth**	**Montserrat**
		Pô	Nahouri (Burkina Faso)
Pago Pago	American Samoa	Pointe-Noire	Kouilou (Congo)
Pagouda	Binah (Togo)	Poitiers	Poitou-Charentes
Pakanbaru	Riau (Indonesia)	Poitiers	Vienne (France)
Pakxan	Bolikhamxay (Laos)	Pokharã	Western Nepal
Pakxé	Champasak (Laos)	Pombas	Paúl (Cape Verde)
Palana	Koryak (Russia)	Pompey Bay	Acklins Island (Bahamas)
Palangkaraya	Kalimantan Tengah (Indonesia)	Ponta Delgada	Azores
		Ponta do Sol	Ribeira Grande (Cape Verde)
Palermo	**Sicily (Italy)**		
Palma de Mallorca	Balearic Islands (Spain)	Pontianak	Kalimantan Barat (Indonesia)
Palmerston North	Manawatu (NZ)		
Palu	Sulawesi Tengah (Indonesia)	Pontoise	Val-d'Oise (France)
		Popondetta	Northern Province (Papua New Guinea)
Pamplona	Navarre (Spain)		
Panaji	Goa (India)	Popoyán	Cauca (Colombia)
Panama City	**Panama**	Port Antonio	Portland (Jamaica)
Pan-ch'iao	Tai-pei (Taiwan)	Port Blair	Andaman and Nicobar Islands
Pangai	Ha'apai (Tonga)		
Papeete	**French Polynesia**	**Port Louis**	**Mauritius**
	Society Islands	Port Maria	St Mary (Jamaica)
	Tahiti	**Port Moresby**	**Papua New Guinea**
	Îles Tuamotu et Gambier (French Polynesia)		National Capital District (PNG)
	Îles du Vent (French Polynesia)	**Port of Spain**	**Trinidad and Tobago**
Paradise	Demerara/Mahaica (Guyana)	**Port-au-Prince**	**Haiti**
			Ouest (Haiti)
Parakou	Borgou (Benin)	Port-de-Paix	Nord-Ouest (Haiti)
Paramaribo	**Suriname**	Port-Genttil	Ogooué-Maritime (Gabon)
Paraná	Entre Rios (Argentina)	Port-Harcourt	Rivers (Nigeria)
Paris	**France**	Portlaoise	Laois/Leix (Eire)
	Île-de-France (France)	Pôrto Alegre	Rio Grande do Sul (Brazil)
Pasto	Nariño (Colombia)	Porto Inglês	Maio (Cape Verde)
Patna	Bihar (India)	**Porto Novo**	
Pau	Pyrénées-Atlantiques (France)	**(de facto Cotonou)**	**Benin**
		Pôrto Velho	Rondônia (Brazil)
Pécs	Baranya (Hungary)	Porto-Novo	Ouémé (Benin)
Pedra Badejo	Santa Cruz (Cape Verde)	Portoviejo	Manabi (Ecuador)
Pedro Juan Caballero	Amambay (Paraguay)	Posadas	Misiones (Argentina)
Pemba	Cabo Delgado (Mozambique)	Potenza	Basilicata (Italy)
		Potsdam	Brandenburg (Germany)
Penonomé	Coclé (Panama)	Pozo Colorado	President Hayes (Paraguay)
Pereira	Risaraldo (Colombia)		
Périgueux	Dordogne (France)	**Prague**	**Czech Republic**
Perpignan	Pyrénées-Orientales (France)	**Praia**	**Cape Verde**
		Preston	Lancashire (Eng)
Perth	Western Australia	Pretoria	Transvaal (South Africa)
Perugia	Umbria (Italy)	**Pretoria-admin**	**South Africa**
Peshãwar	North West Frontier (Pakistan)	Princes Town	Victoria (Trinidad & Tobago)
		Principe	Paguê (São Tomé & Principe)
Peshkopi	Dibër (Albania)		
Petrozavodsk	Karelian (CIS)	Pristina	Kosovo (Yugoslavia)
Phan Rang	Ninh Thuan (Vietnam)	Privas	Ardèche (France)
Phan Thiet	Thuan Hai (Vietnam)	Providence	Rhode Island (USA)
Philipsburg	St Maarten (Netherland Antilles)	Pucallpa	Ucayali (Peru)
		Puerto Barrios	Izabal (Guatemala)
		Puerto Carreño	Vichada (Colombia)

GEOGRAPHY

Capital or Admin Centre	Country, State, County or Area	Capital or Admin Centre	Country, State, County or Area
Puerto Inirida	Guainia (Colombia)	Roreti	Arorae (Kiribati)
Puerto Lempira	Gracias a Dios (Honduras)	Roscommon	Roscommon (Eire)
Puerto Maldonado	Madre de Dios (Peru)	**Roseau**	**Dominica**
Puerto Montt	Los Lagos (Chile)	Rosita	Región Autónoma del
Punta Arenas (Chile)	Magallanes y de la		Atlántico Norte (Nic)
	Antártica Chilena	Rosso	Trarza (Mauritania)
Punta Gorda	Toledo (Belize)	Rouen	Haute-Normandie (French
Puyo	Pastaza (Ecuador)		Region)
P'yŏngsan	P'yongan-namdo (North		Seine-Maritime (French
	Korea)		Department)
Pyongyang	**North Korea (aka**	Rovaniemi	Lappi (Finland)
	Choson)	Rrëshen	Mirditë (Albania)
Quebec	Quebec (Canada)	Rubale	Kabale (Uganda)
Quelimane	Zambézia (Mozambique)	Rukoki	Kapchorwa (Uganda)
Quetta	Baluchistān (Pakistan)	Rundu	Kavango (Namibia)
Qui Nhon	Nghia Binh (Vietnam)	Rungata	Nikunau (Kiribati)
Quibdó	Chocó (Colombia)	Saarbrücken	Saarland (Germany)
Quimper	Finistère (France)	Sacramento	California (USA)
Quito	**Ecuador**	Sa Dec	Dong Thap (Vietnam)
	Pichincha (Ecuador)	St Annes	Alderney
Quy Nhon	Binh Dinh (Vietnam)	Saint-Brieuc	Côtes-du-Nord (France)
Rabat	**Morocco**	**Saint-Denis**	**Réunion**
Rabaul	East New Britain (Papua	Saint-Etienne	Loire (France)
	New Guinea)	**St George's**	**Grenada**
Rach Gia	Kien Giang (Vietnam)	St Helier	Jersey
Raleigh	North Carolina (USA)	**St Johns**	**Antigua and Barbuda**
Ramla	Central District (Israel)	Saint-Lô	Manche (France)
Ramotswa	Botswana (South East)	St Paul	Minnesota (USA)
Rancagua (Chile)	Libertador Gen Bernardo	St Peter Port	Guernsey
	O'Higgins	Sal Rei	Boavista (Cape Verde)
Rangoon (Yangon)	**Burma (now Myanmar)**	Salamá	Baja Verapaz (Guatemala)
Rasht	Gilān (Iran)	Salem	Oregon (USA)
Rawannawi	Marakei (Kiribati)	Salgótarján	Nógrád (Hungary)
Rawson	Chubut (Argentina)	Salt Lake City	Utah (USA)
Reading	Berkshire (Eng)	Saltillo	Coahuila (Mexico)
Recife	Pernambuco (Brazil)	Salto del Guairá	Canendiyú (Paraguay)
Regina	Saskatchewan (Canada)	Salvador	Bahia (Brazil)
Renne	Bornholm (Denmark)	Samarai	Milne Bay (Papua New
Rennes	Bretagne/Brittany (French		Guinea)
	Region)	San Andrés	San Andrés y Providencia
	Ille-et-Vilaine (French	San Carlos	Cojedes (Venezuela)
	Department)	San Carlos	Zona Especial III
Réo	Sanguie (Burkina Faso)		(Nicaragua)
Resistencia	Chaco (Argentina)	San Cristóbal	Táchira (Venezuela)
Resita	Caras-Severin (Romania)	San Felipe	Yaracuy (Venezuela)
Reykavik	**Iceland**	San Fernando	Catamarca (Argentina)
	Höfudhborgarsvaedhi	San Fernando de Apure	Apure (Venezuela)
	(Iceland)	San Francisco de Macoris	Duarte (Dom Republic)
Rhodes	**Rhodes**	San Francisco (Gotera)	Morazán (El Salvador)
Ribeira Brava	São Nicolau (Cape Verde)	San Ignacio	Cayo (Belize)
Richmond	Virginia (USA)	**San José**	**Costa Rica**
Riga	**Latvia**	**San Juan**	**Puerto Rico**
Rikitea	Gambier Islands	San Juan Bautista	Misiones (Paraguay)
Ringdove	Epi (Vanuatu)	San Juan de Los Morros	Guárico (Venezuela)
Rio Branco	Acre (Brazil)	**San Marino**	**San Marino (Most Serene**
Rio Claro	Nariva/Mayaro (Trinidad &		**Republic)**
	Tobago)		Citta (San Marino)
Rio Gallegos	Santa Cruz (Argentina)	San Miguel	Tucumán (Argentina)
Riobamba	Chimborazo (Ecuador)	San Pedro Sula	Cortés (Honduras)
Riohacha	La Guajira (Colombia)	**San Salvador**	**El Salvador**
Rivercess City	Rivercess (Liberia)	San Salvador	Jujuy (Argentina)
Riyadh	**Saudi Arabia**	**Sana**	**Yemen Republic**
Road Town	**Virgin Islands (British)**	Sangre Grande	St Andrew & St David
Roatán	Islas de la Bahia		(Trinidad & Tobago)
	(Honduras)	Sankt Pölten	Niederösterreich (Austria)
Robertsport	Grand Cape Mount	Sanniquellie	Nimba (Liberia)
	(Liberia)	Sansanné-Mango	Oti (Togo)
Rodez	Aveyron (France)	Santa Clara	Villa Clara (Cuba)
Rome	**Italy**	Santa Cruz	Quiché (Guatemala)
	Lazio (Italy)	Santa Cruz	Temotu (Solomon Isles)

Capital or Admin Centre	Country, State, County or Area
Santa Cruz de Tenerife	Canary Islands (Spain)
Santa Fe	New Mexico (USA)
Santa Maria	Sal (Cape Verde)
Santa Rosa	La Pampa (Argentina)
Santana	Cantagaio (São Tomé & Principe)
Santander	Cantabria (Spain)
Santander	Magdalena (Colombia)
Santiago	**Chile**
Santiago	Metropolitan (Chile)
Santiago	Veraguas (Panama)
Santiago de Compostela	Galicia (Spain)
Santiago de los Caballeros	Santiago (Dom Republic)
Santo Domingo	**Dominican Republic**
São António	Principe (São Tomé & Principe)
São Filipe	Fogo (Cape Verde)
São João Angolares	Caué (São Tomé & Principe)
São Luis	Maranhão (Brazil)
São Tomé	**São Tomé and Príncipe**
	Aqua Grande (São Tomé & Principe)
Sapporo	Hokkaidō (Japan)
Saransk	Mordovia (Russia)
Sarajevo	**Bosnia and Hercegovina**
Sarh	Moyen-Chari (Chad)
Sari	Māzandarān (Iran)
Sariwŏn	Hwanghae-pukto (North Korea)
Sarnen	Obwalden (Swiss Canton)
Saudhárkrókur	Nordhurland vestra (Iceland)
Saurimo	Lunda Sol (Angola)
Savanna-la-Mar	Westmoreland (Jamaica)
Saynshand	Dornogovi (Mongolia)
Scarborough	Tobago
Sefadu	Kono (Sierra Leone)
Sekondi-Takoradi	Western Region (Ghana)
Selfoss	Sudhurland (Iceland)
Sélibaby	Guidimaka (Mauritania)
Semarang	Jawar Tengah (Indonesia)
Sendai	Miyagi (Japan)
Sensuntepeque	Cabañas (El Salvador)
Seoul	**South Korea**
Seremban	Negeri Sembilan (Malaysia)
Serowe	Botswana (Central)
Seville	Andalucia (Spain)
Sfintu Gheorghe	Covasna (Romania)
Shenyang	Liaoning (China)
s-Hertogenbosch	Noord-Brabant (Netherlands)
Shibin al-Kawm	Al-Minufiyah (Egypt)
Shijazhuang	Hebei (China)
Shillong	Meghālaya (India)
Shimla	Himāchal Pradesh (India)
Shirāz	Fārs (Iran)
Shrewsbury	Shropshire (Eng)
Sibiti	Lékoumou (Congo)
Sibut	Kemo-Gribingui (CA Rep)
Sidon/Saydā	Al-Janub (Lebanon)
Silvassa	Dadra and Nagar Haveli (India)
Sincelejo	Sucre (Colombia)
Singapore	**Singapore**
Sinujiu	P'yongan-pukto (North Korea)
Siobozia	Ialomita (Romania)
Sion	Valais (Swiss Canton)

Capital or Admin Centre	Country, State, County or Area
Siparia	St Patrick (Trinidad & Tobago)
Siteki	Lubombo (Swaziland)
Sittwe (aka Akyab)	Arakan/Rakhine (Burma)
Siyabuswa	KwaNdebele (South Africa)
Skien	Telemark (Norway)
Skopje	**Macedonia (Yugoslavia)**
Slatina	Olt (Romania)
Sligo	Sligo (Eire)
Sofia	**Bulgaria (aka Narodna Republic)**
Sokodé	Centrale Region (Togo) Tchaoudjo (Togolese Prefecture)
Sola	Banks/Torres (Vanuatu)
Solwezi	North-Western Province (Zambia)
Songea	Ruvuma (Tanzania)
Sore	Vestjaelland (Denmark)
Spanish Town	St Catherine (Jamaica)
Springfield	Illinois (USA)
Srinigar	Jammu and Kashmir (India)
Stafford	Staffordshire (Eng)
Stanley	**Falkland Islands**
Stans	Nidwalden (Swiss Canton)
Stavanger	Rogaland (Norway)
Steinkjer	Nord-Trønelag (Norway)
Stirling	Central (Scotland)
Stockholm	**Sweden**
Stornoway (Lewis)	Western Isles (Scotland)
St-Pierre	St-Pierre and Miquelon
Strasbourg	Alsace (French Region) Bas-Rhin (French Department)
Stuttgart	Baden-Württemberg (Germany)
St Johns	Newfoundland (Canada)
Sucre-judicial	**Bolivia** Chuquisaca (Bolivia)
Sühbaatar	Selenge (Mongolia)
Sukhumi	Abkhaziya (CIS)
Sukulu	Tororo (Uganda)
Sumbawanga	Rukwa (Tanzania)
Sumbe	Kuanza Sul (Angola)
Sunyani	Brong-Ahafo (Ghana)
Surabaya	Jawar Timur (Indonesia)
Surkhet	Mid-Western Nepal
Suva	Central Province (Fiji)
Suva	**Fiji**
Suwŏn	Kyŏnggi-do (South Korea)
Swakopmund	Erongo (Namibia)
Swansea	West Glamorgan (Wales)
Sydney	New South Wales
Syktyv-Kar	Komi (CIS)
Szeged	Csongrád (Hungary)
Székesfehérvár	Fejér (Hungary)
Szekszárd	Tolna (Hungary)
Szombathely	Vas (Hungary)
Tabligbo	Yoto (Togo)
Tabontebike	Kuria (Kiribati)
Taegu	Kyŏngsang-pukto (South Korea)
Taiohae	Îles Marquises (French Polynesia)
Taipei	**Taiwan**
Taiyuan	Shanxi (China)
Takaeang	Aranuka (Kiribati)
Takamatsu	Kagawa (Japan)
Talca	Maule (Chile)
Tallahassee	Florida (USA)

GEOGRAPHY

Capital or Admin Centre	Country, State, County or Area	Capital or Admin Centre	Country, State, County or Area
Tallinn	**Estonia**	**Tripoli**	**Libya**
Tamale	Northern Region (Ghana)	Tripoli/Tarābulus	Ash-Shamāl (Lebanon)
Tamrida	Socotra (Yemen)	Trivandrum	Kerala (India)
Tan An	Long An (Vietnam)	Trondheim	Sor-Trøndelag (Norway)
Tanjā	Al-Gharbiyah (Egypt)	Trowbridge	Wiltshire (Eng)
Tanjung Karang	Lampung (Indonesia)	Troyes	Aube (France)
Tarbes	Haute-Pyrénées (France)	Trujillo	Colón (Honduras)
Tashkent	**Uzbekistan**	Trujillo	La Libertad (Peru)
Tatabánya	Komárom (Hungary)	Trujillo	Trujillo (Venezuela)
Taubukinberu	Beru (Kiribati)	Truro	Cornwall (Eng)
Taunggyi	Shan (Myanmar)	Tsabong	Kgalagadi (Botswana)
Taunton	Somerset (Eng)	Tsetserieg	Arhangay (Mongolia)
Taupo	Tongariro (NZ)	Tsévié	Zio (Togo)
Tauranga	Bay of Plenty (NZ)	Tsu	Mie (Japan)
Tbilisi	**Georgia (CIS)**	Tsumeb	Oshikoto (Namibia)
Tchibanga	Nyanga (Gabon)	Tsumkwe	Boesmanland (Namibia)
Tebangetua	Maiana (Kiribati)	Tuarabu	Abalang (Kiribati)
Tegucigalpa	**Honduras**	Tubmanburg	Bomi (Liberia)
	Francisco Morazán (Honduras)	Tulagi	Central Islands (Solomon Isles)
Tehran	**Iran**	Tulcan	Carchi (Ecuador)
Temuco	Araucania (Chile)	Tullamore	Offaly (Eire)
Tena	Napo (Ecuador)	Tulle	Corrèze (France)
Tenkodogo	Boulgou (Burkina Faso)	**Tunis**	**Tunisia**
Tepic	Nayarit (Mexico)	Tunja	Boyacá (Colombia)
Teresina	Piauí (Brazil)	Tura	Evenki (Russia)
Teuabu	Nonouti (Kiribati)	Turin	Piedmont (Italy)
Teyateyaneng	Berea (Lesotho)	Turku	Turku ja Pori (Finland)
Thakhek	Khammouan (Laos)	Tuxtla Gutiérrez	Chiapas (Mexico)
Thames-Coromandel	Thames Valley (NZ)	Tuy Hoa	Phu Yen (Vietnam)
The Bottom	Saba (Netherland Antilles)	Ufa	Bashkir (CIS)
Thessalonika	**Macedonia (Greece)**	Ugoofaaru	Raa (Maldives)
Thimphu	**Bhutan (aka Druk-Yul)**	Ujung Pandang	Sulawesi Selatan (Indonesia)
Thinadhoo	Gaafu-Dhaalu (Maldives)		
Thohoyandou	Venda (South Africa)	Ulaangom	Uvs (Mongolia)
Thong	Xékong (Laos)	**Ulan Bator**	**Mongolia**
Thorshavn	**Faeroe Islands**	Ulan-Ude	Buryat (CIS)
Thu Dau Mot	Binh Duong (Vietnam)	Uliastay	Dzavhan (Mongolia)
Tiberias	Northern District (Israel)	Ulundi	KwaZulu (South Africa)
Tidjikdja	Tagant (Mauritania)	Umea	Västerbotten (Sweden)
Timaru	Aorangi (NZ)	Umtata	Transkei (South Africa)
Timisoara	Timis (Romania)	Urawa	Saitama (Japan)
Tirana	**Albania**	Urumchi (aka Urumqi)	Sinkiang Uighur (aka Xinjiang Uygur)
Tirgoviste	Dimbovita (Romania)		
Tirgu Jiu	Gorj (Romania)	Ushuaia	Tierra Del Fuego (Argentina)
Tirgu Mures	Mures (Romania)		
Titograd	**Montenegro**	Ust-Ordynsk	Ust-Ordyn-Buryat (Russia)
Tokyo	**Japan**	Utiroa	Tabiteuea North (Kiribati)
Toledo	Castilla-La-Mancha (Spain)	Utsunomiya	Tochigi (Japan)
Toluca	México (Mexican State)	Uturoa	Îles sous le Vent (French Polynesia)
Tønsberg	Vestfold (Norway)		Raiatea (French Polynesia)
Topeka	Kansas (USA)		
Toronto	Ontario (Canada)		
Totness	Coronie (Suriname)	Uyo	Akwa Ibom (Nigeria)
Tougan	Sourou (Burkina Faso)	**Vaduz**	**Liechtenstein**
Tou-liu	Yün-lin (Taiwan)	Vaitape	Bora-Bora
Toulon	Var (France)	Valence	Drôme (France)
Toulouse	Haute-Garonne (French Department)	Valencia	Carabobo (Venezuela)
	Midi-Pyrénées (French Region)	Valladolid	Castilla-León (Spain)
		Valledupar	Cesar (Colombia)
Tours	Indre-et-Loire (France)	**Valletta**	**Malta**
Tralee	Kerry (Eire)	**Valley, The**	**Anguilla**
Trenton	New Jersey (USA)	Valparaiso	Valparaiso (Chile)
Trieste	Friuli-Venezia Giulia (Italy)	Vänersborg	Älvsborg (Sweden)
Trim	Meath (Eire)	Vanimo	West Sepik (Papua New Guinea)
Trinidad	Flores (Uruguay)		
Trinidad	Beni (Bolivia)	Vannes	Morbihan (France)
Trinidade	Mé-zóchi (São Tomé & Principe)	Vardø	Finnmark (Norway)
		Västerás	Västmanland (Sweden)
		Växjö	Kronoberg (Sweden)

Capital or Admin Centre	Country, State, County or Area
Versailles	Yvelines (France)
Vesoul	Haute-Saône (France)
Veymandhoo	Thaa (Maldives)
Victoria	British Columbia (Canada)
Victoria	**Seychelles** Mahé (Seychelles)
Victoria (Guzo)	Malta
Victoria (on Hong Kong Island)	**Hong Kong (aka Hsiang Kang)**
Viedma	Rio Negro (Argentina)
Vienna	**Austria**
Vientiane	**Laos**
Viet Tri	Phu Tho (Vietnam)
Vila	**Vanuatu** Efaté (Vanuatu)
Vilgili	Gaafu-Alifu (Maldives)
Villahermosa	Tabasco (Mexico)
Villarica	Guairá (Paraguay)
Villavicencio	Meta (Colombia)
Vilnius	**Lithuania**
Vinh	Nghe Tinh (Vietnam)
Vinh Yen	Vinh Phuc (Vietnam)
Visby	Gotland (Sweden)
Vitoria	Basque Country (Spain)
Vitória	Espirito Santo (Brazil)
Vladikavkaz	Alania (Russia)
Vogan	Vo (Togo)
Voinjama	Lofa (Liberia)
Vreed-en-Hoop	Essequibo Islands (Guyana)
Wa	Upper West (Ghana)
Wabag	Enga (Papua New Guinea)
Wakefield	West Yorkshire (Eng)
Warsaw	**Poland**
Warwick	Warwickshire (Eng)
Washington DC	**United States of America**
Waterford	Waterford (Eire)
Wāu	Bahr al-Ghazāl (Sudan)
Wavre	Brabant (Walloon)
Wellington	**New Zealand**
West Island	Cocos (aka Keeling Islands) (Aus)
Wete	Pemba North (Tanzania)
Wewak	East Sepik (Papua New Guinea)
Wexford	Wexford (Eire)
Whangarei	Northland (NZ)
Whitehorse	Yukon Territory (Canada)
Wicklow	Wicklow (Eire)
Wiesbaden	Hessen (Germany)
Willemstad	**Netherland Antilles**

Capital or Admin Centre	Country, State, County or Area
	Curaçao (Netherland Antilles)
Winchester	Hampshire (Eng)
Windhoek	**Namibia**
Windhoek	Khomas (Namibia)
Winnipeg	Manitoba (Canada)
Wŏnson	Kangwŏn-do (North Korea)
Worcester	Hereford and Worcester (Eng)
Wuhan	Hubei (China)
Xai-Xai	Gaza (Mozambique)
Xam Nua	Houaphan (Laos)
Xay	Oudomxay (Laos)
Xi'an (aka Sian)	Shaanxi (aka Shensi)
Xining (aka Hsi-ning)	Qinghai (aka Tsinghai)
Yako	Passoré (Burkina Faso)
Yakutsk	Yakut (CIS)
Yambio	Western Equatoria (Sudan)
Yamoussoukro-admin	**Ivory Coast**
Yangon	**Myanmar**
Yaoundé	**Cameroon** Centre Province (Cameroon)
Yaren	**Nauru**
Yellowknife	Northwest Territories (Canada)
Yerevan	**Armenia**
Yinchuan	Ningxia Hui (China)
Yogyakarta	Yogyakarta (Indonesia)
Yokohama	Kanagawa (Japan)
Yola	Gongola (Nigeria)
Yopal	Casanare (Colombia)
Yushkar-Ola	Mari-El (Russia)
Yuscarán	El Paraiso (Honduras)
Yuzhno-Sakhalinsk	Sakhalin Island
Zacatecoluca	La Paz (El Salvador)
Zagreb	**Croatia**
Zāhedān	Sistān va Baluchestān (Iran)
Zahlah	Al-Biqa (Lebanon)
Zalāu	Salaj (Romania)
Zamora	Zamora-Chinchipe (Ecuador)
Zanzibar	Zanzibar West (Tanzania)
Zaragosa	Aragón (Spain)
Zhengzhou	Henan (China)
Ziniaré	Oubritenga (Burkina Faso)
Zinjibār	Abyān (Yemen)
Zorgho	Ganzourgou (Burkina Faso)
Zwedru	Grand Gedeh (Liberia)
Zwolle	Overijssel (Netherlands)

NB: This section is a fully comprehensive listing of all the world's capital cities, chief towns, and administrative centres. It can be assumed that where a capital is not included in this section it is because the State, County or Area has a capital with the same name. To simplify the process of researching the more obscure capitals, when the continent or country is perhaps unknown, all areas, be it Country, State, Island or City, which have a capital, admin centre or chief town, have been sorted alphabetically. Similarly, any area which is the capital, chief town, or administrative centre, of a larger area, has also been sorted alphabetically. This methodology ensures that, as long as you know one half of the equation, the other half can be found very quickly. All countries, and some of the more significant islands and states, have been printed in bold type.

GEOGRAPHY

Capitals: former

Aachen   Holy Roman Empire
Aarau (Switzerland)   Helvetic Republic
Abeokuta (Nigeria)   Egba State
Aden   South Yemen
Agra   India
Akmola   Kazakhstan
Alexandria   Egypt
Amarapura   Burma
Angkor Thom   Cambodia
Antigua Guatemala   Guatemala
Antioch   Ancient Syria
Anuradhapura   Ceylon
Arras   Artois Province
Ashur (Assur)   Assyria
Auch   Gascony
Auckland   New Zealand
Augusta   Georgia, USA
Ava   Burma
Ayutthaya (Ayuthia)   Thailand
Babylon   Babylonia
Baeza (Spain)   Moorish Kingdom
Bakhchisarai   Crimean Khans
Bamburgh   Northumbria
Bastia   Corsica
Belize   Belize
Bingerville   Ivory Coast
Bucharest   Wallachia
Calcutta   India
Chan Chan   Chimú Empire
Ctesiphon   Parthia
Cuzco   Inca Empire
Danzig   West Prussia
Dar Es Salaam   Tanzania
Dawson   Yukon
Entebbe   Uganda
Gondar   Ethiopia
Gordium   Phrygia
Grozny   Chechnya
Guthrie   Oklahoma (USA)
Hague, The   Netherlands
Hattusa   Hittite Empire
Hué   Annam
Jerusalem   Palestine
Karachi   Pakistan
Kaunas   Lithuania
Kracow   Poland
Kyoto   Japan

Kzyl-Orda   Kazakhstan
Lagos   Nigeria
Levuka   Fiji
Livingstone   Northern Rhodesia
Mandalay   Burma
Maribo   Lolland (Denmark)
Marrakesh   Morocco
Melbourne   Australia
Memphis   Ancient Egypt
Mocha   Yemen
M(o)ukden   Manchuria
Nanking   China
Nara (Heijo-Kyo)   Japan
New Orleans   Louisiana (USA)
Nineveh   Assyria
Olomouc   Moravia
Persepolis   Persia
Perth   Scotland
Philadelphia   USA
Quezon City   Philippines
Rawalpindi   Pakistan
Rio de Janeiro   Brazil
Rovigno   Istria
Saigon   South Vietnam
St George   Bermuda
St Mary's City   Maryland (USA)
St Petersburg   Russia
Sardis   Lydia
Scodra   Illyra
Sitka   Alaska
Stettin   Pomerania
Susa   Elam (Persian Empire)
Sydney   Australia
Tenochtitlán   Aztec Empire
Thebes   Ancient Egypt
Toledo   Spain
Toulouse   Languedoc
Trondheim   Norway
Trujillo   Honduras
Turku   Finland
Tyre   Phoenicia
Vathy   Ithaca
Winchester   England
Yasodharapura   Cambodia
Zanzibar   Oman
Zomba   Malawi

Continents

Continents	Area (Sq Miles)	% of Earth's Land	Lowest Point	Estimated population mid-1990
Asia	16,988,000	29.9	Dead Sea (-400 m)	3,317,800,000
Africa	11,506,000	20.3	Lake Assal (-156 m)	654,600,000
North America	9,365,000	16.5	Death Valley (-86 m)	435,800,000
South America	6,820,000	12.0	Valdés Peninsula (-40 m)	299,900,000
Antarctica	5,400,000	9.5	ice-covered (-2538 m)	No indigenous population
Europe	3,745,000	6.6	Caspian Sea (-28 m)	684,400,000
Australia	2,941,526	5.2	Lake Eyre (-16 m)	17,800,000

Deserts: World's Largest

#		Area (Sq Miles)	#		Area (Sq Miles)
1	Sahara	3,500,000	9	Thar	100,000
2	Australian	600,000	10	Somali	100,000
3	Gobi	500,000	11	Kyzyl Kum	100,000
4	Arabian	470,000	12	Atacama	70,000
5	Kalahari	225,000	13	Dasht-e Lut	20,000
6	Sonoran	120,000	14	Mojave	13,500
7	Kara Kum	120,000	15	Desierto de Sechura	10,000
8	Namib	110,000			

NB: The Gobi Desert includes the Takla Makan area, comprising 125,000 sq miles. The Kara Kum and the Kyzyl Kum are often considered as one large desert, the Turkestan.

Earth's Extremes

coldest place	Plateau Station, Antarctica: annual average temperature -56.7 deg C
deepest canyon	Colca River Canyon, Peru: 3,625 m
driest place	Atacama Desert, Chile: rainfall negligible
greatest tides	Bay of Fundy, Nova Scotia: 16 m
highest waterfall	Angel, Venezuela: 3,212′ (979 m)
hottest place	Dalol, Danakil Depression, Ethiopia: annual average temperature 35 deg C
largest canyon	Grand Canyon, Colorado River, Arizona: 466 km long and 183 m to 29 km wide, about 1.6 km deep
longest reef	Great Barrier Reef, Australia: 2,012 km
most predictable geyser	Old Faithful, Wyoming: annual average interval 69 to 78 minutes
wettest place	Mount Waialeale, Hawaii: annual average rainfall 16,800 mm

Major Earthquakes

	Richter scale	Estimated deaths	Year
Antioch, Turkey		250,000	526
Corinth, Greece		45,000	856
Shensi Province, China		830,000	1556
Catania, Italy		60,000	1693
Calcutta, India		300,000	1737
Lisbon, Portugal		60,000	1755
Calabria, Italy		50,000	1783
San Francisco	8.3	452	1906
Messina	7.5	83,000	1908
Avezzano, Italy	7.5	29,980	1915
Gansu, China	8.6	100,000	1920
Tokyo	8.3	140,000	1923
Nan-Shan, China	8.3	200,000	1927
Gansu, China	7.6	70,000	1932
Quetta, India	7.5	30,000	1935
Erzincan, Turkey	7.9	30,000	1939
Chillán, Chile	8.3	28,000	1939
Assam, India	8.7	1,526	1950
USSR	7.3	110,000	1948
Agadir, Morocco	5.8	12,000	1960
Anchorage, Alaska	9.2	131	1964
Northern Peru	7.7	66,794	1970
Managua, Nicaragua	6.5	7,000	1971
Guatemala City	7.5	23,000	1976
Tangshan, China	8.2	242,000	1976
NE Iran	7.7	25,000	1978
El Asnam, Algeria	7.3	20,000	1980
Mexico	8.1	25,000	1985
Armenia, USSR	6.9	25,000	1988
San Francisco	7.1	300	1989
Roudhon, NW Iran	7.7	50,000	1990

GEOGRAPHY

	Richter scale	Estimated deaths	Year	
Latur, India	6.5	9,748	1993	
Kobe, Japan	7.2	5,500	1995	
Neftegursk, Russia	7.5	1,989	1995	
Qayen, NE Iran	7.1	4,000	1997	
Ismit, Turkey	7.8	2,000+	1999	

NB: The estimated deaths caused by these earthquakes are listed purely to indicate the devastation. It is very hard to draw accurate conclusions, as government statistics are in some instances based on bodies recovered. To give Tokyo 1923 as an example, the official death toll was 99,330, but that figure does not take into account the deaths caused by fire, famine, pestilence, and shock in the aftermath or the persons missing presumed dead.

European Cities of Culture

1985	Athens
1986	Florence
1987	Amsterdam
1988	Berlin
1989	Paris
1990	Glasgow
1991	Dublin
1992	Madrid
1993	Antwerp
1994	Lisbon
1995	Luxemburg
1996	Copenhagen
1997	Thessaloniki
1998	Stockholm
1999	Weimar
2000	Avignon, Bergen, Bologna, Brussels, Helsinki, Krakow, Prague, Reykjavik, Santiago de Compostela (Spain)
2001	Rotterdam and Porto
2002	Bruges and Salamanca
2003	Graz

NB: In 1999 the European Cities of Culture were renamed Cultural Capitals of Europe.

General Information

anabranch   Stream that leaves a river and re-enters it lower down, especially in Australia.

Appalachian trail   Public footpath that runs for over 2,000 miles between Mount Springer in Georgia and Mount Katahdin in Maine.

arroyo   Dry channel in a semi-arid area that may be subject to flash flooding during seasonal downpours.

atmospheric layers   Troposphere is the lowest layer, 11 miles thick at the equator. Stratosphere lies above the troposphere, contains most of the ozone layer. Mesosphere lies above the stratosphere and is often considered part of it. Thermosphere lies between the mesosphere and the exosphere reaching altitudes of 250 miles. Ionosphere is the area charged by the Sun's radiation, between 40 and 600 miles, and has 4 main layers: the D-layer (40–60 miles), E-layer (60–95 miles), F1 and F2-layers (95–250 miles). Exosphere is the outermost layer of the Earth's atmosphere.

berg   Hot, dry north wind of Cape Province and Natal.

Bermuda: nine counties   Devonshire, Hamilton, Paget, Pembroke, Sandys, Smith's, Southampton, Warwick, St George's

bise   Cold, dry north wind prevalent in Switzerland and southern France.

bora   Strong northerly wind that blows in the northern Adriatic.

brickfielder   Hot, dry north wind of Australia.

bridge: longest by span   Akashi-Kaikyo, Shikoku, Japan (6,528′).

building: tallest inhabited   Chongqing Tower, China (1,499′). The 2nd tallest is the Petronas Towers, Kuala Lumpur (1,482′). The Sears Tower, Chicago, is the 3rd tallest (1,454′) but with the television mast is 1,707′. Canary Wharf Tower, designed by Cesar Pelli, is currently the tallest British building (800′).

building: tallest uninhabited   Warszawa Radio Mast, Konstantynow, Poland (2,120′), although under repair after collapsing in 1991. 2nd tallest structure is KTHI-TV Mast, N. Dakota (2,063′). 3rd is the CN Tower, Toronto (1,822′).

buran   Snowstorm accompanied by high winds, chiefly prevalent in the Russian Steppes.

cataract   A large, rushing waterfall, usually over a precipice.

chinook   Warm dry wind that blows in the Rocky Mountain region of North America.

clouds: classification   *High cloud:* Cirrus – detached clouds resembling feathers, named from the Latin for 'lock of hair'. Cirrocumulus – rounded small clouds appearing in the form of grains or ripples. Cirrostratus – white veil of smooth fibrous ice crystals, often forming a halo of light.
Middle cloud: Altocumulus – grey or white clouds having rounded shapes, sometimes touching.

Altostratus – flat, grey sheet cloud, often obscuring the Sun and often bringing drizzle. Nimbostratus – flat, shapeless clouds which are the main source of rain and snow. *Low Cloud:* Cumulus – detached clouds that vary from small fleeces to large cauliflower shapes. Cumulonimbus – often anvil-shaped and noted for its accompaniment of thunder. Stratus – shapeless thin, grey cloud, often starting as fog. Stratocumulus – round-shaped patchy cloud often formed as Cumulus but thinning out.

coastline: longest   Canada (152,100 miles).

coastline: shortest   Monaco (3.5 miles).

continental extremities   west–east–north–south
Africa – Cape Vert, Senegal; Ras Hafun, Somalia; Cape Blanc, Tunisia; Cape Agulhas, South Africa. *Asia* – Cape Baba, Turkey; Cape Dezneva, Russia; Cape Celjuskin, Russia; Cape Piai, Malaysia. *Australia* – Steep Point; Cape Byron; Cape York; South East Point, Tasmania. *Europe* – Cape Roca, Portugal; Kara River; North Cape, Norway; Point Tarifa, Spain. *North America* – Cape Prince of Wales, Alaska; Cape Charles, Newfd; Boothia peninsula, NWT; SW Panama. *South America* – Punta Pariña, Peru; Cape Branco, Brazil; Punta Gallinas, Colombia; Cape Horn.
It should be noted that some countries are included in different continents from the country that administers them, e.g. Greenland is administered by Denmark, although part of North America.

cordillera   System or group of parallel mountain ranges together with intervening plateaux, especially of the Andes and in Central America and Mexico.

dams: tallest   Rogun Dam in Tajikistan (1,098′) is the tallest, followed by Nurek Dam in Tajikistan (984′). The 3rd tallest dam is the Grande Dixence in Switzerland (935′).

depression: deepest   Dead Sea (1,296′ below sea level), Turfan Depression, China (505′), Qattara Depression, Egypt (436′).

desert: meaning   From the Latin word *desertus* meaning 'abandoned'.

dictionary of places   Gazetteer.

driest place on Earth   Calama in the Atacama Desert, Chile, has no recorded rainfall.

Earth: composition   The most abundant elements of the Earth's composition are iron (35.9%), oxygen (28.5%), magnesium and silicon (each about 15%). The most abundant elements of the Earth's crust are oxygen, silicon, and aluminium.

Earth: dimensions
Mass 5,974,000,000,000,000,000,000,000 metric tons.
Area 510,066,000 square Kilometres.
Land 148,429,000 square Kilometres (29.1%).
Water 361,637,000 square Kilometres (70.9%).
Population 5,420, 391,000 approximately.

Earth's layers   crust, mantle, core.

El Niño   Destructive climatic phenomenon involving a periodic change of direction in the prevailing trade winds and ocean currents flowing from the Americas to Asia across the southern Pacific.

Etesian   Dry north wind blowing over the Aegean and eastern Mediterranean during the summer months (aka Meltemi).

Fö(e)hn   Hot southerly wind on the northern slopes of the Alps.

footpaths   Dales Way – runs for 81 miles from Ilkley in West Yorkshire to Bowness-on-Windermere. Icknield Way – most ancient road in Britain, 105 miles from Ridgeway to Peddars Way. Mid Shires Way – opened in 1994 covering 225 miles from Buckinghamshire to Greater Manchester. North Downs Way – stretches 141 miles from south-west of London (Farnham) to the Dover coast. Offa's Dyke – follows the English/Welsh border for 168 miles via the Wye Valley. Peddars Way – 94-mile stretch from Thetford to Cromer. Pembrokeshire Coastal Path – 186-mile stretch from Amroth on Carmarten Bay to west of Cardigan. Pennine Way – follows course of the Pennines from Edale in Derbyshire to Kirk Yetholm in the Borders. Ridgeway – runs 85 miles from Avebury to Ivinghoe Beacon. South Downs Way – 106-mile walk from Beachy Head to Winchester. South-west Coastal Path – runs 600 miles from Minehead in Somerset to Poole Harbour. West Highland Way – 95-mile route from Milngavie, near Glasgow to north of Fort William.

fumarole   Opening in or near a volcano through which hot vapours emerge.

ghibli   Hot, dry southerly wind of Libya.

glacier types   continental, mountain, piedmont.

grasslands   Africa – savannah; Argentina/Paraguay – pampas; North America – prairies; Russia – Steppes.
In other South American countries the general term for a grassland is llanos. The Sahel of West Africa is a semi-arid transitional area between grassland and desert.

Great Lakes: mnemonic   HOMES Huron, Ontario, Michigan, Erie, Superior

Green Line   Boundary dividing Cyprus between Greek south and Turkish north since the 1974 Turkish invasion.

gregale   Strong north-east wind blowing in the Mediterranean.

Gutenberg discontinuity   The core–mantle boundary of the Earth.

haboob   Violent and oppressive seasonal wind blowing in Sudan and causing fierce sand storms.

harmattan   Parching dusty land-wind of the W African coast, blowing from the Sahara Desert.

helm   Violent wind of the Lake District of England which often culminates in the formation of a cloud hanging over the mountain tops.

hypsography   Description or mapping of the contours of the earth's surface.

isocheim   Line on a map connecting places having the same average temperature in winter.

isohyet   Line on a map connecting places having the same amount of rainfall in a given period.

Itaipu dam   Joint project by Brazil and Paraguay on the River Parana. Largest hydro-electric dam in the world.

jungle: meaning   From the Hindi *Jangal* meaning 'wilderness'.

Kanaks   Native Melanesian population of the French overseas territory of New Caledonia.

Kashmir   Territory in the north-west of the Indian subcontinent which has been the subject of rival claims by India and Pakistan and the cause of 2 wars between them in 1948 and 1965.

Kentish man   West of the Medway.

khamsin   Hot south or south-easterly wind occurring in Egypt for about 50 days in March, April and May.

Levant   Area of the Mediterranean bordering Syria and the Lebanon.

lithosphere   Rigid outer part of the earth consisting of the crust and upper mantle.

Maghreb   Region of North Africa bordering the Mediterranean and comprising Morocco, Algeria, Tunisia and Libya.

GEOGRAPHY

man of Kent   East of the Medway.

Mashriq   Geographical region including Egypt, Sudan, Saudi Arabia, Yemen, Oman, Kuwait, UAE, Jordan, Lebanon, Syria and Iraq.

Medway towns   Chatham, Gillingham, Rochester, Strood.

mistral   Cold northerly wind that blows down the Rhône valley and southern France into the Mediterranean.

mofette   Exhalation of vapour from a volcano. Sometimes used as an alternative name for the fumarole itself.

Moho   Abbreviation for the Mohorovicic discontinuity, the boundary separating the earth's crust and mantle.

monsoon   Seasonal wind of SW Asia and the Indian Ocean which brings heavy summer rain.

pampero   Strong cold SW wind in S. America blowing from the Andes towards the Atlantic.

peninsulas   Arabian is the largest (1,250,000 sq miles); second largest is the Southern Indian (800,000 sq miles).

permafrost   General term for ground that is permanently frozen (see tundra).

Pig Island   Australian and NZ slang word for New Zealand.

puna   Cold, dry wind of the Andes in Peru.

rock: types   Igneous, sedimentary, metamorphic.

Sargasso Sea   Area of the North Atlantic, named after the 'Sargassum' seaweed that floats on the surface. The Sargasso lies south of Bermuda and is noted for having no land borders.

simoom   Hot, suffocating wind of North Africa.

sirocco   Hot, dusty wind blowing from North Africa across southern Europe via the Mediterranean.

solano   Hot, dusty south-easterly wind of mainland Spain.

Sumatra   Violent wind in the Strait of Malacca and the Malay peninsula blowing from the direction of Sumatra.

taiga (cold forest)   Coniferous forests of sub-Arctic North America and Eurasia bordered by tundra and steppes.

tectonic plates   Regions of the Earth's crust that may be oceanic or continental, and relate to the activity within the Earth, creating new surface material, moving the plates against or underneath each other, changing their location over time, forming mountain ranges and causing earthquakes and volcanic activity.

temperature: highest recorded   Al' Aziziyah, Libya, at 136 degrees Fahrenheit (58°C).

temperature: lowest recorded   Vostock Station, Antarctica, at -129 degrees Fahrenheit (-89°C).

tombolo   Narrow sand or shingle bar linking a small island with mainland.

tramontana   Cold north wind in the Adriatic.

tundra   Area south of the North Pole where the layers of soil are permanently frozen.

tunnels: longest vehicular   Seikan Rail Tunnel, Japan (33.49 miles); Channel Tunnel, Cheriton, Kent – Sangatte, Calais (31.03 miles).

tunnels: longest non-vehicular   Delaware Aqueduct, NY State (105 miles).

twilight: types   Civil, nautical, astronomical (6, 12 and 18 degrees angle of the sun below the horizon).

typhoon   Tropical storm in the western Pacific.

volcanic eruptions: famous   Krakatoa (1883); Mont Pelée, Martinique (1902); Mount St Helens, Washington State (1980).

volcano: classifications   active, dormant, extinct.

volcano: highest   Cotopaxi in Ecuador is the highest continuously active volcano (19,347'), although Guallatiri in Chile at 19,882' is the highest dormant and Aconcagua at 22,834', and also in the Andes, is the highest extinct volcano (excluding underwater volcanoes).

Volcano Islands   Three small volcanic islands, San Alexander (Kita-Iō) Iwo Jima (Iō) San Augustino (Minami-Iō), of the West Pacific between the Bonin Islands and the Mariana Islands. Japan has claimed the islands since 1891, apart from a brief USA administration from 1951 to 1968.

volcano: types   Fissure and central.

williwaw   Sudden, strong cold wind originally describing the squall through the Strait of Magellan but now describing any sudden strong wind of Alaska and Canada.

Zanzibar   Principal islands are Zanzibar and Pemba islands. Joined with Tanganyika in 1964 to become Tanzania. Zanzibar's African population call themselves 'Shirazi' after the ancient Persian principality of Shîrâz, as traders from the Persian Gulf began to settle there after the 7th century.

zonda   Hot dusty north wind of Argentina.

Geological Ages

Era	Period	Epoch	Years ago (m)	Life forms
Cenozoic		Holocene	0.01	
	Quaternary	Pleistocene	1.64	humans appeared
		Pliocene	5.2	
		Miocene	23.5	
	Tertiary	Oligocene	35.5	
		Eocene	56.5	
		Palaeocene	65	mammals flourished
Mesozoic	Cretaceous		146	heyday of dinosaurs
	Jurassic		208	first birds
	Triassic		245	first mammals and dinosaurs
Palaeozoic	Permian		290	reptiles expanded
	Carboniferous		363	first reptiles
	Devonian		409	first amphibians
	Silurian		439	first land plants
	Ordovician		510	first fish
	Cambrian		570	first fossils
Precambrian	Proterozoic		3500	earliest living things
	Archaean		4600	

Ice Ages: years before present

Pleistocene	1.64m–10,000
Permo-Carboniferous	330–250m
Ordovician	440–430m
Varangian	615–570m
Sturtian	820–770m
Gnejsö	940–880m
Huronian	2700–1800m

Island Groups

Group	Administered by	Sea Area	Main Islands
Admiralty	Papua New Guinea	Pacific Ocean	Manus, Los Reyes, Rambutyo, Tong, Pak, Baluan. Lou Purdy Islands are a sub division of the Admiralty Islands.
Aeolian (aka Eolie)	Italy	Tyrrhenian Sea	Stromboli, Lipari, Vulcano, Salina, Filicudi, Panarea.
Åland	Finland	Gulf of Bothnia	Åland, Ahvenanmaa, Eckero, Lemland, Lumparland, Vardo.
Aleutian	Alaska, USA	Pacific Ocean	Andreanof, Adak, Amchitka, Atka, Attu, Fox, Kiska, Near, Rat, Seguam, Umnak, Unalaska, Unimak, Yunaska.
Alexander Archipelago	Alaska, USA	Gulf of Alaska	Baranof (chief city Sitka), Prince of Wales, Chichagof, Admiralty, Mitkof, Wrangell, Revillagigedo (chief city Ketchikan), Kupreanof, Zaremba, Kuiu, Kosciusko, Yakobi, Heceta.
Andaman (204 islands)	India	Bay of Bengal	North, Middle and South Andaman Islands (collectively known as Great Andaman).
Andreanof	Alaska, USA	Pacific Ocean	Kanaga, Great Sitkin, Amlia, Atka, Adak, Tanaga, Delarof. Andreanof Islands are a sub-division of the Aleutians.
Antilles, Greater	Various	Caribbean Sea	Cuba, Jamaica, Hispaniola, Puerto Rico.
Antilles, Lesser	Various	Caribbean Sea	Windward, Leeward, Netherlands Antilles.
Azores	Portugal	Atlantic Ocean	Flores, Corvo, Terceira, Graciosa, São Jorge, Faial, Pico, Santa Maria, Formigar, São Miguel.
Bahamas (700)	UK	Atlantic Ocean	Great Abaco, Acklins, Andros, Berry, Cay, New Providence, Grand Bahama, Inagua, Long, Mayaguana, Bimini, Cat, Exuma, Ragged, Crooked, Eleuthera. Nassau, the capital, is on New Providence and it was here that Columbus made his first landfall in the New World, 12 Oct 1492. Highest point: Mt Alvernia (formerly Como Hill), 206', on Cat Island.
Balearic	Spain	Mediterranean	Ibiza, Majorca, Minorca, Formentera, Cabrera.
Banks	Vanuatu	Pacific Ocean	Vanua Lava, Santa Maria (Gaua), Mota, Mota Lava (Saddle).
Bay Islands	Honduras	Caribbean Sea	Utila, Roatan, Guanja.
Bermuda (138) (aka Somers' Isles)	UK	Atlantic Ocean	Great Bermuda (aka Main), Boaz, Ireland, St David's, St George's, Somerset. All these inhabited islands are now joined by bridges.
Bismarck Archipelago	Papua New Guinea	Pacific Ocean	New Britain, New Ireland, Admiralty, Lavonga, New Hanover.
Bissagos	Guinea-Bissau	Atlantic Ocean	Orango, Formosa, Caravela, Roxa.
Canadian Arctic	Canada	Arctic Ocean	Baffin, Victoria, Queen Elizabeth, Banks.
Canaries	Spain	Atlantic Ocean	Tenerife, Gomera, Las Palmas, Lanzarote, Hierro, Fuerteventura, Gran Canaria.
Cape Verde Islands (10)	Cape Verde	Atlantic Ocean	Windward Islands: Barlavento, Santo Antão, São Vicente, São Nicolau, Boa Vista, Sal Sotavento, Santa Luzia. Leeward Islands: São Tiago, Maio Fogo, Brava.
Caroline (680)	USA	Pacific Ocean	Yap, Ponape (Ascension or Pohnpei), Truk, Kusac, Belau.
Chagos	UK	Indian Ocean	Diego Garcia, Peros, Banhos, Salomon.
Channel	UK	English Channel	Jersey, Guernsey, Alderney, Sark, Herm.
Channel (Santa Barbara)	USA	Pacific Ocean	San Miguel, Santa Rosa, Santa Cruz, Anacapa, Santa Barbara, San Nicolas, Santa Catalina, San Clemente.

GEOGRAPHY

Group	Administered by	Sea Area	Main Islands
Chonos Archipelago	Chile	Pacific Ocean	Chaffers, Benjamin, James, Melchior, Victoria, Luz.
Commander	Russia	Bering Sea	Bering, Medny.
Comoros	Comoros	Mozambique Channel	Grande Comore, Anjouan, Mohéli, Mayotte.
Cook	New Zealand	Pacific Ocean	Rarotonga, Palmerston, Mangaia, Aitutaki.
Crozet	France	Indian Ocean	Île de la Possession, Îles des Pingouins, Îles des Apôtres.
Cyclades (220)	Greece	Aegean Sea	Andros, Mikonos, Milos, Naxos, Paros, Kithnos, Serifos, Siros, Tinos.
Denmark	Denmark	Baltic Sea	Zealand, Fyn, Lolland, Falster, Sjael/Langeland, Bornholm.
Desolation	France	Indian Ocean	Kerguelen, Grande Terre.
Dodecanese	Greece	Aegean Sea	Kasos, Karpathos, Rhodes, Samos, Khalki, Tilos, Simi, Astipalaia, Kalimnos, Leros, Patmos, Kos.
Egadi (Aegadi)	Italy	Mediterranean	Favignana, Levanzo, Marettimo.
Ellice	Tuvalu	Pacific Ocean	Funafuti, Nukefetau, Nukulailai, Nanumea.
Falkland (200)	UK	Atlantic Ocean	West Falkland, East Falkland, South Georgia, South Sandwich.
Farne (Staple)	UK	North Sea	House, Long Stone (lighthouse was the home of Grace Darling). St Cuthbert died on House (Inner Farne) in 687. Nowadays the group is a bird sanctuary and home for grey seals.
Faroe (17 inhabited)	Denmark	Atlantic Ocean	Stromo (Streymoy), Ostero (Eysturoy), Vågø (Vágar), Sando (Sandoy), Bordo (Bordhoy), Sudero (Sudhuroy).
Fiji	Fiji	Pacific Ocean	Viti Levu, Vanua Levu.
Frisian, East	Germany and Denmark	North Sea	Borkum, Juist, Norderney, Langeoog, Spiekeroog, Wangerooge.
Frisian, North	Germany and Denmark	North Sea	Sylt, Fohr, Nordstrand, Pellworm, Amrum (German); Romo, Fano, Mando (Danish).
Frisian, West	Germany and Denmark	North Sea	Texel, Vlieland, Terschelling, Ameland, Schiermonnikoog.
Galapagos (19)	Ecuador	Pacific Ocean	San Cristobal, Santa Cruz, Isabela, Floreana, Santiago, San Salvador, Rabida, Darwin, Wolf, Pinta, Marchena, Genovesa, Española, Santa Maria, Santa Fe, Pinzon, Fernandina, Baltra. Isabela (Albemarle) is largest, Santa Cruz (Indefatigable) is 2nd. Highest point is Mt Azul.
Gilbert	Kiribati	Pacific Ocean	Tarawa, Makin, Abaiang, Abemama, Tabiteuea, Nonouti, Beru.
Gotland	Sweden	Baltic Sea	Gotland, Faro, Karlso.
Great Britain	United Kingdom	Atlantic Ocean	Isle of Wight, Orkneys, Shetlands, Hebrides, Scillies, Skomer, Ramsey, Skokholm, Caldey, Holy, Lundy, Brownsea, Rat, Sully, Flat Holm, Horsey, Osea, Skerries, Bardsey, Hilbre, Little Eye, Read's, Calf of Man, Ailsa Crag, Craigleith, Fidra, Bass Rock, May, St Serfs (in Loch Leven).
Greater Sunda	Indonesia	South China Sea	Sumatra, Java, Borneo, Celebes (Sulawesi), Belitung. North-west Borneo is not under Indonesian administration.
Greenland	Denmark	Atlantic/Arctic	Greenland, Disko.
Hawaiian	USA	Pacific Ocean	Hawaii, Oahu, Maui, Lanai, Kauai, Molokai, Kahoolawe, Niihau.
Heard and McDonald	Australia	Indian Ocean	Heard, McDonald, Shag.
Hebrides, Inner	UK	Atlantic Ocean	Skye (chief town is Portree; home of the Cuillin Hills; also famous as the refuge of the Young Pretender in 1746), Raasay, Mull (chief town is Tobermory; contains Ben More at 3,171'); Eigg, Coll, Tiree, Iona, Staffa, Jura, Islay, Rum, Muck, Arran (containing Goat Fell at 2,868'), Colonsay and Oronsay.
Hebrides, Outer	UK	Atlantic Ocean	Lewis with Harris, North and South Uist, Benbecula, Baleshare, Barra, Bernera, Berneray, Eriskay, Grimsay, Scalpay, Vatersay.
Indonesia (13,677)	Indonesia	Pacific Ocean	Java, Sumatra, Kalimantan, Celebes, Lesser Sundas, Moluccas, Rian-Lingga Archipelago, Irian Jaya.
Ionian	Greece	Aegean Sea	Kerkira, Kefallinia, Zakinthos, Levkas.

Group	Administered by	Sea Area	Main Islands
Japan	Japan	Pacific Ocean	Hokkaido, Honshu, Shikoku, Kyushu, Ryuku.
Juan Fernandez	Chile	Pacific Ocean	Mas a Tierra (Nearer Land Island, aka Robinson Crusoe Island), Mas Afuera (Farther Out Island, aka Alexander Selkirk Island).
Kermadec	New Zealand	South Pacific	Raoul (Sunday), Macauley, Curtis. Highest point is Mt Mumukai at 1723′ on Raoul Island.
Kuril (56)	Russia	Pacific Ocean	Shumsu, Iturup, Urup, Paramushir, Onekotan, Shiaskhotan, Kunashir, Shimushir, Shikotanto.
Lakshadweep	India	Arabian Sea	Amindivi, Laccadive, Minikoy (Maliku), Androth, Kavaratti.
Leeward Islands	Lesser Antilles	Caribbean Sea	Virgin Islands, Anguilla, Saint-Martin, St Christopher and Nevis, Antigua and Barbuda, Montserrat, Guadeloupe. Highest point is Mt Soufrière (on Guadeloupe) at 4813′.
Lesser Sunda	Indonesia/Timor	Indian Ocean	Bali, Lombok, Sumbawa, Sumba, Flores, Timor, Alor.
Line	Kiribati	Pacific Ocean	Christmas, Fanning, Washington.
Lipari	Italy	Tyrrhenian Sea	see Aeolian Islands.
Lofoten	Norway	Norwegian Sea	Hinney, Austvagey, Vestvagey, Moskenes.
Madeira	Portugal	Atlantic Ocean	Madeira, Ilha do Porto Santo, Ilhas Desertas, Ilhas Selvagens.
Malay Archipelago	Malaysia	Pacific/Indian	Borneo, Celebes, Java, Luzon, Mindanao, New Guinea, Sumatra.
Maldives (200 inhabited)	Maldives	Indian Ocean	The atolls of the Maldives are listed in the 'capitals'. The word 'atoll' is, in fact, a Maldive word.
Malta	Malta	Mediterranean	Malta, Gozo, Comino.
Mariana (14)	USA	Pacific Ocean	Saipan, Tinian, Rota, Pagan, Guguan.
Marquesas	France	Pacific Ocean	Nuku Hiva, Ua Pu, Ua Huka, Hiva Oa, Tahuata, Fatu Hiva, Eiao Hatutu.
Marshall	Marshall	Pacific Ocean	Bikini, Wotha, Kwajalein, Eniwetok, Maiura, Jalut, Rogelap.
Mascarenes	France/Mauritius	Indian Ocean	Réunion, Mauritius, Rodrigues.
Melanesia	Various	Pacific Ocean	Solomon Islands, Bismarck Archipelago, New Caledonia, Papua New Guinea, Fiji, Vanuatu.
Mentawai	Indonesia	Indian Ocean	Siberut, Sipura, Pagai, Utara (North Pagai), Pagai Selatan Utara and Pagai Selatan (South Pagai), aka Nassau Islands.
Micronesia	Various	Pacific Ocean	Caroline, Gilberts, Marianas, Marshalls, Guam, Kiribati, Nauru.
Moluccas (Maluku)	Indonesia	Pacific Ocean	Halmahera, Bacan, Sula, Obi, Moratai, Ternate.
Mussau	Papua New Guinea	Pacific Ocean	Mussau, Emira, Tench, Emira, Emananus, Tabalo.
Near	Alaska, USA	Pacific Ocean	Agattu, Semichi, Attu, Alaid, Nizki, Shemya. Near Islands are a sub division of the Aleutians.
New Hebrides	Vanuatu	Pacific Ocean	Espiritu Santo, Malekula, Efate, Ambrim, Eromanga, Tanna, Epi, Pentecost, Aurora.
New Siberian	Russia	Arctic Ocean	Kotelny, Faddeyevski.
Newfoundland	Canada	Atlantic Ocean	Prince Edward, Anticosti.
Nicobar (12)	India	Bay of Bengal	Great Nicobar, Camorta with Nancowry, Car Nicobar, Teressa, Little Nicobar. Usually considered with the Andamans as a joint group.
Ninigo Islands	Papua New Guinea	Pacific Ocean	Manu, Aua, Wuvulu, Heina, Kaniet Islands, Hermit Islands.
Northern Land	Russia	Arctic Ocean	Komsomolets, Bolshevik, October Revolution.
Norway	Vietnam	Gulf of Tonkin	aka Xuy Nong Chao.
Novaya Zemlya	Russia	Arctic Ocean	North and South Novaya Zemlya.
Orkney	UK	North Sea	Mainland, North and South Ronaldsay, Stronsay, Papa Westray, Hoy, Shapinsay, Rousay, Sanday, Burray, Eday, Flotta and Fara, Westray.
Parry	NWT Canada	Arctic Ocean	Bathurst, Melville, Cornwallis, Devon.
Pelagian	Italy	Mediterranean	Lampedusa, Linosa, Lampione.
Philippines (7100)	Philippines	Pacific Ocean	Luzon, Mindanao, Samar, Palawan, Mindoro, Panay, Negros, Leyte, Masbate, Bohol, Cebu.
Polynesia	Various	Pacific Ocean	New Zealand, French Polynesia, Phoenix Islands, Hawaii, Line, Pitcairn, Tokelau, Tonga, Society, Easter, Samoa, Kiribati, Ellice, Cook.

GEOGRAPHY

Group	Administered by	Sea Area	Main Islands
Pribilof (Fur Seal)	Alaska, USA	Bering Sea	St Paul, St George, Walrus, Otter.
Prince Edward	South Africa	Indian Ocean	Prince Edward, Marion.
Queen Charlotte (150)	Canada	Pacific Ocean	Prince Rupert, Graham, Moresby, Louise, Lyell, Kunghit.
Queen Elizabeth	NWT Canada	Arctic Ocean	Ellesmere, Mackenzie King, Parry Islands, Zverdrup Islands.
Rat	Alaska, USA	Pacific Ocean	Kiska, Amchitka, Semisopochnoi, Little Sitkin, Little Kiska. Rat Islands are a subdivision of the Aleutians.
Santa Barbara	USA	Pacific Ocean	see Channel Islands.
São Tomé and Principe	São Tomé	Atlantic Ocean	São Tomé, Principe.
Scilly (150)	UK	English Channel	St Mary's, St Martin's, Tresco, St Agnes, Bryher.
Seychelles (115)	Seychelles	Indian Ocean	Praslin, La Digue, Silhouette, Mahé, Bird.
Shetland (100)	UK	North Sea	Mainland, Unst, Yell, Fetlar, Whalsay, Bressay, Muckle Roe, Trondra, West Burra, Housay, Fair Isle, East Burra.
Society	France	Pacific Ocean	Windward and Leeward, Tahiti.
Solomon	Solomon	Pacific Ocean	Choiseul, Guadalcanal, Malaita, New Georgia, San Cristobal, Santa Isabel, Vella Lavella, Kolombangara. Highest point is Mt Makarakomburu.
South Orkney	UK	Atlantic Ocean	Coronation, Signy, Laurie, Inaccessible.
South Shetland	UK	Atlantic Ocean	King George, Elephant, Clarence, Gibbs, Nelson, Livingstone, Greenwich, Snow.
Sri Lanka	Sri Lanka	Indian Ocean	Mannar, Sri Lanka.
Taiwan	China	China Sea/Pacific	Taiwan, Lan Hsu, Lu Tao, Quemoy, Pescadores.
Tasmania	Australia	Tasman Sea	Tasmania, King, Flinders, Bruny.
Tierra Del Fuego	Arg/Chile	Pacific Ocean	Tierra Del Fuego, Isla de los Estados, Hoste, Navarino, Wollaston, Desolación, Santa Ines, Clarence, Dawson, Diego Ramirez.
Tres Marias	Mexico	Pacific Ocean	Maria Madre, Maria Magdalena, Maria Cleofas, San Juanito.
Tristan da Cunha	UK	Atlantic Ocean	Tristan da Cunha, Gough, Inaccessible, Nightingale.
Tuamotu Archipelago	France	Pacific Ocean	Makatea, Fakarava, Rangiroa, Anaa, Hao, Reao, Gambier, Duke of Gloucester.
Vesterålen	Norway	Norwegian Sea	Hinnoy, Langoya, Andoya, Hadseloy.
Virgin	USA	Caribbean Sea	St Croix, St Thomas, St John.
Virgin	UK	Caribbean Sea	Tortola, Virgin Gorda, Anegada, Jost Van Dyke.
Visayas (Bisayas)	Philippines	Philippine/ Sulu Sea	Bohol, Cebu, Leyte, Masbate, Negros, Panay, Samar.
Windward Islands	Lesser Antilles	Caribbean Sea	Dominica, Martinique, St Lucia, St Vincent, Grenada, Grenadines.
Zanzibar	Tanzania	Indian Ocean	Zanzibar, Tumbatu, Kwale.
Zemlya Frantsa-Iosifa	Russia	Arctic Ocean	Graham Bell, Wilczekland, Georgeland, Hooker, Zemlya Alexsandry, Ostrov Rudol'fa.

Islands

Island	Area	Administered by	Sq Miles
Adelaide	British Antarctic Territory	Great Britain	1,400
Admiralty	Alexander Archipelago	Alaska, USA	1,709
Alderney	English Channel	Great Britain	3
	Nearest of the Channel Islands to France		
Alexander I	British Antarctic Territory	Great Britain	16,700
	Largest island in Antarctica		
Andros	Atlantic Ocean	Bahamas	2,300
Andros	Aegean Sea	Greece	145
	The 2nd largest island of the Cyclades		
Anticosti	Gulf of St Lawrence	Quebec, Canada	3,066
Ascension (Pohnpei)	Pacific Ocean	Micronesia	129
	Highest peak is Mt Totolom at 2,595'		
Ascension	Atlantic Ocean	Great Britain	34
Bali	Indian Ocean	Indonesia	2,147
Bananal	Goiás State	Brazil	7,720
	World's largest inland island		
Banks	Beaufort Sea	NWT, Canada	27,038
Bathurst	Timor Sea	NT Australia	1,000

Island	Area	Administered by	Sq Miles
Bathurst	Arctic Ocean	NWT Canada	6,194
Bioko	Gulf of Guinea	Equatorial Guinea	779
Bolshevik	Arctic Ocean	Russia	4,368
Bougainville	Solomon Sea	Papua New Guinea	3,880
	Highest peaks Mt Balbi 9,000',		
	Mt Bagana 6,560', Mt Takuan 7,358'		
Bouvet	South Atlantic	France	23
Cape Breton	Nova Scotia	Canada	3,981
Cebu	Bohol Sea	Philippines	1,703
Chatham Island	South Pacific	New Zealand	348
	Chief town is Waitangi		
Chiloé	Pacific Ocean	Chile	3,241
	Chief town is Castro		
Christmas	Indian Ocean	Australia	52
	Highest point is Murry Hill at 1,184'		
Christmas (Kiritimati)	Pacific Ocean	Kiribati	150
	Largest island of purely coral formation in		
	the world		
Clipperton	Pacific Ocean	France	2
Coats	Northwest Territories	Canada	2,123
Cocos	Pacific Ocean	Costa Rica	9
Cornwallis	Northwest Territories	Canada	2,701
Corsica	Mediterranean	France	3,352
	Highest peak is Mont Cinto 8,890'		
Crete	Mediterranean	Greece	3,190
	Highest peak is Mt Ida 8,058'		
Cyprus	Mediterranean	Cyprus	3,572
Desolation Island	Indian Ocean	French Antarctica	2,239
	aka Kerguélen Island		
Devon	Northwest Territories	Canada	21,331
Disko	Davis Strait	Greenland	3,312
East Falkland	South Atlantic	Great Britain	2,550
	Highest peak is Mt Usborne, 2,312'		
Easter (Rapa Nui)	Pacific Ocean	Chile	63
	Famous for rongorongo hieroglyphs and		
	stone statues in human form		
Éfaté	Pacific Ocean	Vanuatu	353
	aka Vaté or Sandwich; highest peak is		
	Mt Macdonald, 2,123'		
Ellesmere	Northwest Territories	Canada	75,767
Euboea	Aegean Sea	Greece	1,412
	The 2nd largest island in Greece after Crete		
Flores	Indian Ocean	Indonesia	5,500
Flores	Azores	Portugal	55
	Highest peak is Morro Grande, 3,087'		
Fyn	Baltic Sea	Denmark	1,152
Gotland	Baltic	Sweden	1,212
Graham	British Columbia	Canada	2,456
Guernsey	English Channel	Great Britain	24
	The 2nd largest of the Channel Islands		
Hai-nan	Kwangtung	China	12,962
Halmahera	Moluccas	Indonesia	6,865
Heard	Indian Ocean	Australia	351
	Highest peak is Mt Mawson on Big Ben		
	Mountain at 9,005'		
Hispaniola	Caribbean	Haiti/Dominican Republic	29,418
	Offshore islands include Gonâve and		
	Tortuga Island		
Holy Island	North Sea	Great Britain	2
(Lindisfarne)	St Aidan established church and monastery		
	in 635 and the 7th-century Lindisfarne		
	Gospels are now housed in the British		
	Museum. Of the other Holy Islands, the most		
	notable is the one off the coast of Anglesey		
Hoste	Pacific Ocean	Chile	1,590
Ibiza	Mediterranean	Spain	221
	Highest point is La Atalaya at 1,558'		
Iturup	Sea of Okhotsk	Russia	2,596
Iwo Jima	West Pacific	Japan	8
	Famous photo of marines raising the US flag		
	over Mt Suribachi in Feb 1945		

GEOGRAPHY

Island	Area	Administered by	Sq Miles
Jan Mayen	Greenland Sea	Norway	144
	Home of the Beerenberg volcano, 7,470'		
Jersey	English Channel	Great Britain	44
	Largest and southernmost of the Channel Islands		
Kangaroo	South Australia	Australia	1,680
Kerguélen	Indian Ocean	French Antarctica	2,239
	aka Desolation Island		
Kiritimati	Pacific Ocean	Kiribati	see Christmas Islands
Kodiak	Gulf of Alaska	Alaska, USA	3,588
Kyushu	Pacific	Japan	16,274
	Kyushu means 'the nine provinces'		
Lanzarote	Atlantic Ocean	Spain	307
	Easternmost of the Canary Islands		
Leyte	Philippine Sea	Philippines	2,785
Lindisfarne	North Sea	Great Britain	see Holy Island
Long Island	New York	USA	1,723
Lundy	Bristol Channel	Great Britain	1
Mackenzie King	Northwest Territories	Canada	1,949
Mactan	Bohol Strait	Philippines	24
	Ferdinand Magellan was killed here by Chief Lapulapu on 27 Apr 1521		
Majorca	Mediterranean	Spain	1,405
Man	Irish Sea	Great Britain	221
Mansel	Northwest Territories	Canada	1,228
Marajó	Atlantic Ocean	Brazil	15,500
Martinique	Caribbean	France	417
	Site of the Carbet Mountains: highest peaks Lacroix, 3,924', Piquet, 3,806'; Dumauzé, 3,638'; Alma, 3,625'; Boucher, 3,510'		
Melville	Timor Sea	NT Australia	2,240
Milne Land	Arctic Ocean	Greenland	1,400
Minorca	Mediterranean	Spain	258
	The 2nd largest of the Balearics		
Náxos	Aegean Sea	Greece	165
	Largest island of the Cyclades, highest peak Mt Zeus at 3,377'		
Negros	Philippine Sea	Philippines	4,905
New Britain	Bismarck Archipelago	Papua New Guinea	14,100
New Caledonia	Coral Sea	Papua New Guinea	6,467
New Ireland	Bismarck Archipelago	Papua New Guinea	3,340
Norway	Beaufort Sea	NWT, Canada	13
Palawan	South China Sea	Philippines	4,550
Panay	Sulu Sea	Philippines	4,446
Pitcairn	Pacific Ocean	Great Britain	2
Pohnpei	Pacific Ocean	Micronesia	see Ascension
Prince Charles	Foxe Basin	NWT, Canada	3,676
Prince Edward	Gulf of St Lawrence	Canada	2,184
Prince of Wales	Alexander Archipelago	Alaska, USA	2,731
	Islands of the same name in Canada and Australia		
Puerto Rico	Caribbean	USA	3,435
Réunion	Indian Ocean	France	970
Riesco	Pacific Ocean	Chile	1,973
Roosevelt	East River	NY City, USA	1
Roosevelt	Ross Sea	NZ Antarctica	2,900
St Helena	South Atlantic	Great Britain	47
	Peaks include Mt Actaeon at 2,685' and Diana Peak at 2,700'		
St Lawrence	Bering Sea	Alaska, USA	1,780
Samar	Philippine Sea	Philippines	5,050
Santa Catalina	Pacific Ocean	USA	74
	One of the Channel Islands, highest peak Mt Orizaba at 2,130'		
Sardinia	Mediterranean	Italy	9,194
Sark	English Channel	Great Britain	2
	Sark's area includes Brechou		
Seram (Ceram)	West Pacific	Indonesia	6,621
	Highest point is Mt Binaiyi 9,905'		
Shikoku	Pacific Ocean	Japan	7,261
Sicily	Mediterranean	Italy	9,830

Island	Area	Administered by	Sq Miles
Socotra	Indian Ocean	Yemen	1,400
Somerset	Northwest Territories	Canada	9,570
South Georgia	Falklands Islands	Great Britain	1,450
Southampton	Hudson Bay	NWT, Canada	15,913
Spitsbergen	Barents Sea	Norway	15,075
Stewart Island	Pacific Ocean	New Zealand	674
	Third largest NZ island after North and South		
Sumbawa	Indian Ocean	Indonesia	5,965
Taiwan (Formosa)	Pacific Ocean	Taiwan (Formosa)	13,851
Tasmania	Indian Ocean	Australia	24,868
	Other islands in the Tasmanian state include Bruny, King, Flinders and Macquarie		
Tenerife	Atlantic Ocean	Spain	795
	Largest of the Canary Islands		
Timor	Indian Ocean	Indonesia/Timor	11,883
Traill	Greenland Sea	Greenland	1,300
Vancouver	Pacific Ocean	BC, Canada	12,079
Vanua Levu	Pacific Ocean	Fiji	2,137
Viti Levu	Pacific Ocean	Fiji	4,011
Wellington	Pacific Ocean	Chile	2,549
West Falkland	South Atlantic	Great Britain	1,750
Wight	English Channel	Great Britain	147
	Largest British island outside the mainland		
Wrangel	Chukchi Sea	Russia	2,800
Yap	Pacific Ocean	USA Micronesia	21
	Highest peak is Mt Tabiwol at 568'		
Zealand (Sjaelland)	Baltic Sea	Denmark	2,713
Zemlya Aleksandry	Franz Josef Land	Russia	1,080
Zemlya Georga	Franz Josef Land	Russia	1,120

Islands: world's largest

		Area (Sq Miles)	Location
1	Greenland	840,000	Arctic Ocean
2	New Guinea	306,000	Western Pacific
3	Borneo	280,100	Western Pacific
4	Madagascar	226,658	Indian Ocean
5	Baffin Island	195,928	Arctic Ocean
6	Sumatra	165,000	Indian Ocean
7	Honshu	87,805	North Pacific
8	Great Britain	84,186	North Atlantic
9	Victoria Island	83,897	Arctic Ocean
10	Ellesmere Island	75,767	Arctic Ocean
11	Celebes (Sulawesi)	69,000	Indian Ocean
12	South Island (NZ)	58,305	South Pacific
13	Java	48,900	Indian Ocean
14	Cuba	44,218	North Atlantic
15	North Island (NZ)	44,035	South Pacific
16	Newfoundland	42,030	North Atlantic
17	Luzon	40,880	West Pacific
18	Iceland	39,770	North Atlantic
19	Mindanao	36,775	West Pacific
20	Ireland	31,839	North Atlantic
21	Hokkaido	30,077	North Pacific
22	Hispaniola	29,418	North Atlantic
23	Sakhalin	28,597	North Pacific
24	Tasmania	26,383	South Pacific
25	Sri Lanka	25,332	Indian Ocean

GEOGRAPHY

NB: What is the largest island in the world? This is the subject of constant frustration to the more enlightened quiz player. In fact, the answer is very simple when one understands that the dictionary defines an island as a body of land, smaller than a continent, that is wholly surrounded by water. The dictionary defines Australia as the smallest continent and consequently, although it is surrounded by water, it clearly should not be included in geographical listings of islands. If an island was to be considered any area of land wholly surrounded by water then the whole of mainland Eurasia would in fact be far larger than Australia!

Lakes: world's largest

		Location	Area Sq Miles	Details
1	Caspian Sea	Russia, Kazakhstan, Turkmenistan, Azerbaijan, Iran	143,552	classed as a brackish lake; although salinity rises to 32% in the Kara-Bogaz-Gol Gulf, it is negligible around the Volga area
2	Superior	Canada, USA	31,795	often considered the largest freshwater lake in the world, although the Caspian Sea is freshwater in parts; the largest of the Great Lakes of North America
3	Victoria	Uganda, Tanzania, Kenya	26,834	aka Victoria Nyanza, the chief reservoir of the Nile
4	Huron	Canada, USA	23,011	one of the Great Lakes, often considered as a single entity with Lake Michigan
5	Michigan	USA	22,394	one of the Great Lakes, often considered as a single entity with Lake Huron
6	Aral Sea	Uzbekistan, Kazakhstan	15,444	the largest true salt lake in the world, although its area has been severely diminished
7	Tanganyika	Dem Rep of Congo, Tanzania, Zambia, Burundi	12,703	at 410 miles it is the longest true freshwater lake in the world, and at 4,710' the second deepest in the world
8	Great Bear	Northwest Territories (Canada)	12,279	lying astride the Arctic Circle, it is the largest lake wholly in Canada
9	Baikal	Russia	11,776	world's deepest lake at 5,314'
10	Malawi (Nyasa)	Malawi, Tanzania, Mozambique	11,429	aka Lake Nyasa (which means 'lake')
11	Great Slave	Northwest Territories (Canada)	11,031	links the Mackenzie River to the Slave River
12	Erie	Canada, USA	9,910	one of the 5 Great Lakes of North America
13	Winnipeg	Manitoba (Canada)	9,417	named from the Cree Indian words for 'muddy water'
14	Ontario	Canada, USA	7,550	smallest of the Great Lakes of North America
15	Balkhash	Kazakhstan	7,115	shallow salt lake whose area has varied considerably over the years
16	Chad	Cameroon, Chad, Niger, Nigeria	6,875	freshwater lake whose area varies from about 4,000 to 10,000 sq miles
17	Ladoga (Ladozhskoye)	Russia	6,835	largest lake in Europe, situated near the Gulf of Finland; there is also a small lake in Indiana, USA, of the same name
18	Maracaibo	Venezuela	5,150	large brackish inlet of the Caribbean Sea, lying in the Maracaibo Basin
19	Bangweulu	Zambia	3,800	Bangweulu is Bantu for 'large water'
20	Onega	Russia	3,753	second-largest lake in Europe, situated between Lake Ladoga and the White Sea
21	Eyre	South Australia	3,600	dry for most of the year
22	Volta	Ghana	3,283	artificial lake
23	Titicaca	Peru, Bolivia	3,200	highest navigable lake in the world at 12,500' above sea level
24	Nicaragua	Nicaragua	3,190	freshwater lake, the largest lake of Central America
25	Athabasca	Saskatchewan, Alberta (Canada)	3,064	explored by Samuel Hearne in 1771, who named it 'Lake of the Hills'
26	Reindeer	Saskatchewan, Manitoba (Canada)	2,568	the Reindeer River links the lake to the Churchill River
27	Tonle Sap	Cambodia	2,525	linked to the Mekong by the Tonle Sap River
28	Rudolf	Ethiopia, Kenya	2,473	known as Lake Turkana in Kenya
29	Issyk Kul	Kyrgyzstan	2,408	salt lake
30	Torrens	South Australia	2,230	dry for most of the year
31	Albert	Uganda, Dem Rep of Congo	2,160	aka Albert Nyanza and since 1973 Lake Mobuto Sese Seko
32	Vänern	Sweden	2,156	largest lake in Sweden and a major source of hydroelectric power
33	Urmia	Iran	2,150	salt lake
34	Netilling	Northwest Territories (Canada)	2,140	situated in Baffin Island
35	Winnipegosis	Manitoba (Canada)	2,075	situated north of Lake Manitoba and west of Lake Winnipeg
36	Kariba	Zambia, Zimbabwe	2,000	artificial lake formed by the damming of the Zambesi River
37	Mweru	Zambia, Dem Rep of Congo	1,900	Mweru is the Bantu word for 'lake'
38	Nipigon	Ontario (Canada)	1,872	Nipigon is the Indian word for 'deep, clear water'
39	Gairdner	South Australia	1,845	dry for most of the year
40	Manitoba	Manitoba (Canada)	1,799	lies south of lakes Winnipeg and Winnipegosis

		Location	Area Sq Miles	Details
41	Koko Nor	Tsinghai (China)	1,770	salt lake, aka Ch'ing Hai or Tsing Hai
42	Taymyr	Russia	1,760	freshwater lake
43	Kyoga	Uganda	1,710	freshwater lake
44	Great Salt	Utah (USA)	1,700	salt lake that has varied from about 2,400 sq miles in 1873 to 950 sq miles in 1963 depending on the level of evaporation and the flow of the surrounding rivers; largest salt lake in the Western Hemisphere
	Iso Saimaa	Finland	1,700	largest lake in Finland
46	Kharka (Hsing-K'ai)	Russia, China	1,690	freshwater lake
47	Lake of the Woods	Canada, USA	1,679	situated where the provinces of Ontario and Manitoba and the US State of Minnesota meet
48	Dubawnt	Northwest Territories (Canada)	1,480	freshwater lake
49	Van	Turkey	1,434	salt lake
50	Tana	Ethiopia	1,418	freshwater lake
51	Peipus	Estonia, Russia	1,400	freshwater lake
52	P'o-yang	Kiangsi (China)	1,383	freshwater lake
53	Uvs	Mongolia	1,300	salt lake
54	Amadjuak	Northwest Territories (Canada)	1,203	freshwater lake
55	Tung-t-'ing	Hunan (China)	1,089	freshwater lake
56	Kivu	Rwanda, Dem Rep of Congo	1,040	freshwater lake
57	Wollaston	Saskatchewan (Canada)	1,035	freshwater lake
58	Alakol	Kazakhstan	1,025	salt lake
59	Hövsgöl	Mongolia	1,012	freshwater lake
60	Illamna	Alaska (USA)	1,000	freshwater lake
	Poopó	Bolivia	1,000	salt lake
	Rukwa	Tanzania	1,000	salt lake
	Chilwa	Malawi, Mozambique	1,000	salt lake
64	Edward (Idi Amin Dada)	Uganda, Dem Rep of Congo	970	freshwater lake
65	Chany	Russia	960	salt lake
66	Tangra (T'ang-ku-la-yu-mu)	Tibet, China	950	salt lake
67	T'ai	Chekiang, Kiangsu (China)	936	freshwater lake
68	Mistassini	Quebec (Canada)	902	freshwater lake
69	Frome	South Australia	900	dry for most of the year
70	Hu-lun	Inner Mongolia	894	freshwater lake
71	Leopold II (Mai-Ndombe)	Dem Rep of Congo	890	freshwater lake
72	Nueltin	Northwest Territories, Manitoba (Canada)	880	freshwater lake
73	Southern Indian	Manitoba (Canada)	868	freshwater lake
74	Buenos Aires	Chile, Argentina	865	freshwater lake
75	Michikamau	Newfoundland (Canada)	784	freshwater lake
76	Lama	Russia	772	freshwater lake
77	Lop Nor (Lo-pu)	Sinkiang (China)	770	dry for most of the year
78	Hung-tse	Anhwei, Kiangsu (China)	757	freshwater lake
79	Hamar	Iraq	750	freshwater lake
80	Na-mu (Nam)	Tibet, China	741	salt lake
81	Vättern	Finland	738	freshwater lake
82	Baker	Northwest Territories (Canada)	729	freshwater lake
83	Ch'i-lin (Zilling)	Tibet, China	720	salt lake
84	Chiquita	Argentina	714	salt lake
85	Okeechobee	Florida (USA)	700	freshwater lake
86	Martre	Northwest Territories (Canada)	686	freshwater lake
87	Har Us	Mongolia	680	freshwater lake
88	Williston	British Columbia (Canada)	641	freshwater lake
89	Seul	Ontario (Canada)	640	freshwater lake
90	Pontchartrain	Louisiana (USA)	625	usually considered a tidal lagoon, as it is connected to the Gulf of Mexico by the Rigolets
91	Tengiz	Kazakhstan	614	salt lake
92	Tuz	Turkey	580	salt lake
	Po-ssu-t'eng (Baghrash)	Sinkiang (China)	580	freshwater lake
94	Yathkyed	Northwest Territories (Canada)	559	freshwater lake
95	Claire	Alberta (Canada)	555	freshwater lake
96	Cree	Saskatchewan (Canada)	554	freshwater lake

G
E
O
G
R
A
P
H
Y

	Location	Area Sq Miles	Details
97 Argentino	Argentina	546	freshwater lake
Ronge	Saskatchewan (Canada)	546	freshwater lake
99 Hyargas	Mongolia	543	salt lake
100 Eau Claire	Quebec (Canada)	534	freshwater lake
101 Moose	Manitoba (Canada)	528	freshwater lake
102 Sevan	Armenia	525	freshwater lake
103 Cedar	Manitoba (Canada)	522	freshwater lake
104 Kasba	Northwest Territories (Canada)	518	freshwater lake
105 Bienville	Quebec (Canada)	482	freshwater lake
106 Island	Manitoba (Canada)	472	freshwater lake
107 St Clair	Canada, USA	460	freshwater lake
108 Becharof	Alaska (USA)	458	freshwater lake
109 Lesser Slave	Alberta (Canada)	451	freshwater lake
Red	Minnesota (USA)	451	freshwater lake
111 Abaya	Ethiopia	448	freshwater lake
112 Gods	Manitoba (Canada)	444	freshwater lake
113 Toba	Sumatra (Indonesia)	440	freshwater lake
Mälaren	Sweden	440	freshwater lake
115 Champlain	Canada, USA	435	freshwater lake
116 Aberdeen	Northwest Territories (Canada)	425	freshwater lake
Stefanie	Ethiopia	425	salt lake
118 Päyänne	Finland	421	freshwater lake
119 Viedma	Argentina	420	freshwater lake
120 Chapala	Mexico	417	freshwater lake
Napaktulik	Northwest Territories (Canada)	417	freshwater lake
122 Mackay	Northwest Territories (Canada)	410	freshwater lake
123 Managua	Nicaragua	402	freshwater lake
124 Eyasi	Tanzania	400	salt lake
125 Dead Sea	Israel, Jordan	394	salt lake; the lowest body of water on Earth at 1,312' below sea level
126 San Martin (O'Higgins)	Argentina, Chile	391	freshwater lake
127 Saint-Jean	Quebec (Canada)	387	freshwater lake
128 Wei-shan	Kiangsu, Shantung (China)	386	freshwater lake
Ebi	Sinkiang (China)	386	salt lake
Inari	Finland	386	freshwater lake
131 Limen	Russia	379	freshwater lake
132 Pipmuacan	Quebec (Canada)	378	freshwater lake
133 Garry	Northwest Territories (Canada)	377	freshwater lake
134 Contwoyto	Northwest Territories (Canada)	370	freshwater lake
135 Abitibi	Ontario (Canada)	360	freshwater lake
Rainy	Canada, USA	360	freshwater lake
137 Bay	Luzon (Philippines)	356	salt lake
138 Hottah	Northwest Territories (Canada)	354	freshwater lake
139 Natron	Tanzania	350	salt lake
140 Oulu	Finland	348	freshwater lake
141 Salton Sea	California (USA)	340	salt lake
P'u-mo (Pomo)	Tibet, China	340	freshwater lake
Amadeus	Northern Territories (Australia)	340	dry for most of the year
144 Llanquihue	Chile	330	freshwater lake
145 Pielinen	Finland	328	freshwater lake
146 Aylmer	Northwest Territories (Canada)	327	freshwater lake
147 Eskimo North	Northwest Territories (Canada)	324	freshwater lake
148 Nipissing	Ontario (Canada)	321	freshwater lake
149 Teshekpuk	Alaska (USA)	315	freshwater lake
150 Imandra	Russia	314	freshwater lake
151 Terinam (Cha-jih-nan-mu)	Tibet, China	313	freshwater lake
152 Colhué Huapi	Argentina	310	freshwater lake
153 Yamdrok (Yang-cho-yung)	Tibet, China	309	freshwater lake
Ch'ao	Anhwei (China)	309	freshwater lake
155 Nonacho	Northwest Territories (Canada)	303	freshwater lake
156 Abe	Djibouti, Ethiopia	300	salt lake
Peter Pond	Saskatchewan (Canada)	300	freshwater lake
Seletyteniz	Kazakhstan	300	freshwater lake
159 Atlin	British Columbia, Yukon (Canada)	299	freshwater lake
160 Minto	Quebec (Canada)	294	freshwater lake
161 Cross	Manitoba (Canada)	292	freshwater lake

Other Notable Lakes	Location	Area Sq Miles	Details
Bala (Llyn Tegid)	Gwynedd, Wales	1.69	deepest lake in Wales (125′)
Balaton	Hungary	230.96	largest lake of central Europe
Bassenthwaite Water	Cumbria, England	2.06	Lake District lake
Bitter Lakes	Suez Canal	219.86	named for its high concentrations of sodium sulphate, as opposed to alkali lakes which contain sodium carbonate
Coniston	Cumbria, England	1.89	famous for the water speed exploits of both Malcolm and his son Donald Campbell
Constance (Bodensee)	Switzerland, Germany, Austria	209.69	forms part of the River Rhine; first flight of the Zeppelin (2 July 1900) was from a floating hangar on Lake Constance
Crater	Oregon (USA)	28.14	deepest lake in USA (1,932′)
Derwent Water	Cumbria, England	2.06	Lake District lake
Ellesmere	South Island (New Zealand)	69.76	brackish lake
Geneva (Lac Léman)	Switzerland, France	225.19	lake is formed by the Rhône River
Lomond	Strathclyde Region, Scotland	27.46	largest lake of mainland Britain
Mead	Arizona, Nevada	229.84	reservoir of Hoover Dam formed by the damming of the Colorado River, it forms, with Lake Powell, the extremities of the Grand Canyon National Park
Menteith	Central Region, Scotland	1.48	the only true Scottish lake, as all the others are lochs. The lake contains 3 islands including Inchmahome, the temporary hideaway of the young Mary, Queen of Scots after the Battle of Pinkie in 1547
Mono	California	87.62	devoid of any life due to its high alkalinity
Morar	Highlands, Scotland	10.33	deepest lake in Great Britain (1,017′)
Neagh	Northern Ireland	147.39	largest lake in the British Isles; it borders all the 6 counties bar Co Fermanagh
Ness	Highlands, Scotland	21.87	famous for its monster legend
Ohrid	Albania, Former Yugoslav Rep of Macedonia	134.49	deepest lake in the Balkans (938′)
Seneca	New York (USA)	67.44	largest and deepest (618′) of the Finger Lakes
Tahoe	California, Nevada (USA)	193.79	freshwater lake
Tiberias (Sea of Galilee)	Israel	64.34	Old Testament name 'Kinneret', later 'Gennesaret'
Ullswater	Cumbria, England	3.44	the 2nd largest lake in England
Vyrnwy	Powys, Wales	1.75	largest lake in Wales
Wastwater	Cumbria, England	1.12	deepest lake in England (260′)
Windermere	Cumbria, England	5.69	largest lake in England. Henry Segrave died on this lake in 1930 while attempting a water speed record
Zurich	Zurich (Switzerland)	34.11	freshwater lake

GEOGRAPHY

Mountains

10 Highest	Height (ft)	Height (m)	Range	First Climbed	By	Country
Everest	29,035	8,850	Himalaya	29 May 1953	Hillary (NZ) and Tenzing Norgay	Nepal/Tibet
K2 (Chogori)	28,250	8,610	Karakorum	31 July 1954	Compagnoni and Lacedelli (Italian)	Pakistan
Kanchenjunga	28,208	8,597	Himalaya	25 May 1955	Charles Evans (British)	Nepal/Sikkim
Lhotse	27,923	8,511	Himalaya	18 May 1956	Luchsinger and Reiss (Swiss)	Nepal/Tibet
Makalu 1	27,824	8,481	Himalaya	15 May 1955	Couzy and Terray (French)	Nepal/Tibet
Dhaulagiri 1	26,795	8,167	Himalaya	13 May 1960	Max Eiselin (Swiss)	Nepal
Manaslu 1 (Kutang)	26,760	8,156	Himalaya	9 May 1956	Japanese expeditions	Nepal
Cho Oyu	26,750	8,153	Himalaya	19 Oct 1954	Tichy and Jochler (Austrian)	Nepal/Tibet
Nanga Parbat (Diamir)	26,660	8,124	Himalaya	3 Jul 1953	Hermann Buhl (Austrian)	Pakistan
Annapurna 1	26,546	8,091	Himalaya	3 Jun 1950	Herzog and Lachenal (French)	Nepal

Highest subsidiary peaks	Height (ft)	Height (m)	Range	First Climbed
Everest South Summit	28,707	8,750	Himalaya	26 May 1953
Lhotse (Zemu gap peak)	27,591	8,410	Himalaya	unclimbed
Kanchenjunga West	27,894	8,502	Himalaya	14 May 1973
Kanchenjunga South Peak	27,848	8,488	Himalaya	19 May 1978
Kanchenjunga Middle Peak	27,806	8,475	Himalaya	22 May 1978
Lhotse Shar	27,504	8,383	Himalaya	12 May 1970

Highest Continental Peaks	Height (ft)	Height (m)	Range	General Info
Africa – Kilimanjaro (Kibo peak)	19,340	5,895	Monarch	dormant Tanzanian volcano 1st climbed by Meyer and Purtscheller 1889
Antarctica – Vinson Massif	16,864	5,140	Ellsworth	first climbed in 1966
Asia – Everest	29,035	8,856	Himalaya	29 May 1953 Hillary (NZ) and Tenzing Norgay
Europe, East – Elbrus	18,510	5,642	Caucasus	extinct volcano, first climbed in 1874
Europe, West – Mt Blanc	15,771	4,807	Alps	first climbed by Jacques Balmat in 1786
North America – Mt McKinley	20,320	6,194	Alaska Range	known to local Indians as Denali and 1st climbed on 7 June 1913 by Stuck and Karstens, although smaller North Peak was climbed by Taylor and Anderson in 1910
Mainland North America – Whitney	14,494	4,418	Sierra Nevada	first climbed by AH Johnson, CD Begole, J Lucas in 1873
South America – Aconcagua	22,834	6,960	Andes	first climbed by Matthias Zurbriggen in 1897
Australia – Kosciusko	7,316	2,228	Great Dividing Range	named by Paul Strzelecki in 1840 in honour of Polish patriot

Mountain Ranges: longest

	Miles	Kilometres	High Point	Height (ft)
Andes	4,500	7,240	Aconcagua (Arg)	22,834
Rockies (Western America)	3,000	4,827	Mt Elbert (US)	14,433
Himalaya–Karakorum–Hindu Kush	2,400	3,861	Everest (China/Nepal)	29,035
Great Dividing Range (Aus)	2,250	3,620	Kosciusko	7,316
Trans-Antarctic Mts	2,200	3,540	Vinson	16,863
Brazilian Atlantic Coast Range	1,900	3,057	Bandeira	9,482
West Sumatran–Javan Range	1,800	2,896	Kerintji	12,484
Aleutian Range (Alaska)	1,600	2,574	Shishaldin	9,387
Tien Shan (Kyrgyzstan/China)	1,400	2,252	Pik Pobeda	24,406
Central New Guinea Range	1,250	2,011	Jayakusumu (Ngga Pulu)	16,503
Altai Mountains (Russia/Mongolia)	1,250	2,011	Gora Belukha	14,783
Urals (Russia)	1,250	2,011	Gora Narodnaya	6,214
Kamchatka (Russia)	1,200	1,930	Klyuchevskaya Sopka	15,910
Atlas (North Africa)	1,200	1,930	Jebel Toubkal (Morocco)	13,665
Verkhoyansk (Russia)	1,000	1,609	Gora Mas Khaya	9,708
Western Ghats (India)	1,000	1,609	Anai Madi	8,841
Sierra Madre Oriental (Mexico)	950	1,528	Orizaba (Citlaltépetl)	18,406
Zagros (Iran)	950	1,528	Zard Kuh	14,921
Scandinavian Range (Nor/Swed)	950	1,528	Galdhopiggen (Nor)	8,098
Semien Mountains (Ethiopia)	900	1,448	Ras Dashen	15,158
Sierra Madre Occidental (Mexico)	900	1,448	Nevado de Colima	13,993
Malagasy Range (Madagascar)	850	1,367	Tsaratanana	9,465
Drakensberg (S Africa)	800	1,287	Thabana Ntlenyana	11,425
Chersky Range (Russia)	800	1,287	Gora Pobeda (Mt Victory)	10,325
Caucasus (Geor/Rus/Azer)	750	1,206	Elbrus, West Peak	18,510
Alaska Range	700	1,126	McKinley, South Peak	20,320
Assam–Burma Range	700	1,126	Hkakabo Razi	19,296
Cascades (USA/Canada)	700	1,126	Rainier (US)	14,410
Crocker Range (Borneo)	700	1,126	Kinabalu (Mal)	13,455
Apennines (Italy)	700	1,126	Corno Grande	9,617
Appalachians (Eastern USA)	700	1,126	Mt Mitchell	6,684
Alps	650	1,045	Mt Blanc (Fr)	15,771
Elburz Mountains (Iran)	560	900	Mt Damavand	18,386
Allegheny Mountains (USA)	500	800	Spruce Knob	4,862
Pyrenees (France/Spain)	270	434	Mt Aneto (Spa)	11,178
Jura (France/Switzerland)	225	360	Crêt de la Neige (Fr)	5,636

NB: A definition of a mountain is an upward projection of the Earth's surface with an altitude of at least 600 m (about 1,968′), often having a rocky surface.
Mountains that are not part of a designated range, e.g. Kilimanjaro, are known as monarchs.
The list of mountains and ranges that follows is a fair representation of the major peaks and systems in the world, but more information can be found in the World Geographical Gazetteer (see below).
The list also contains details of the major volcanic mountains. A few general terms are listed below.

Mountain Ranges: general

Name	Area	Details
Absaroka Range	USA	Situated in north-western Wyoming and southern Montana, highest point is Francs Peak
Adirondacks	USA	Situated in north-eastern New York state, highest peak being Mt Marcy
Aleutian Range	USA	Stretching across southern Alaska and north Pacific islands, highest peak being Shishaldin
Allegheny Mountains	USA	Part of the Appalachians extending south-southwestward for more than 500 miles from north-central Pennsylvania to south-western Virginia
Alps	Central Europe	Extending about 650 miles from the Gulf of Genoa in the south-west to Vienna in the north-east. Highest peak is Mont Blanc
Altai Mountains	Central Asia	Running in a southeast–northwest direction from the Gobi desert to the West Siberian Plain, through Chinese, Mongolian and Soviet territory. Highest peak is Belukha
Amambai Mountains	Brazil–Paraguay	Situated in western Mato Grosso do Sul state of Brazil, and eastern Paraguay
Andes	South America	Stretching the length of the South American continent from Lake Maracaibo in the north to the Tierra del Fuego archipelago in the south
Apennine Range	Italy	The backbone of peninsular Italy extending from the Colle di Cadibona, close to the maritime Alps in the north-west, as far as the Egadi Islands to the west of Sicily
Appalachians	USA	Extending from the Gaspé Peninsula in Quebec through eastern United States southward to central Alabama
Apuseni Range	Romania	Subgroup of the Western Carpathians, lying north of the Mures River in north-western Romania
Arávalli Range	India	Situated in northern India and running north-easterly for 350 miles through Rãjasthãn state. Highest point is Guru Sikhar on Mount Abu
Armorican Massif	France	Flattened erosional upland encompassing the western French départements of Finistère, Côtes-du-Nord, Morbihan, and Ille-et-Vilaine and parts of Manche, Orne, Mayenne, Maine-et-Loire, Loire-Atlantique, and Vendée. Highest mountain in the Massif is Avaloirs, in Orne at 1,368′
Atherton Tableland	Australia	Also called the Atherton Plateau, part of the Great Dividing Range
Athos Range	Antarctica	Located in West Antarctica, joining the Lambert Glacier
Atlas	North Africa	Running north-east to south-west through the three countries of the Maghrib i.e. Morocco, Algeria, and Tunisia, the highest point Jebel Toubkal being in Morocco
Australian Alps	Australia	Part of the Great Dividing Range, occupying the south-easternmost corner of Australia, in eastern Victoria and south-eastern New South Wales
Balkan Mountains	Bulgaria	Extending from the Timok Valley near the Yugoslav border and stretching eastward towards the Black Sea, highest point is Botev Peak
Baranya Mountains	Hungary	See Mecsek Mountains
Beartooth Range	USA	North-eastern spur of the Absarokas, highest point is Granite Peak
Berkshire Hills	USA	Segment of the Appalachians in western Massachusetts, Mt Greylock being the highest point in the state
Black Mountain Range	Bhutan	Southern spur of the Assam Himalayas
Black Mountains	Wales	Situated in east Dyfed and west Powys, highest peak being Carmarthen Van
Black Mountains	Wales	Situated in east Gwent, highest peak being Waun Fach
Black Mountains	USA	Situated in Yancey County in western North Carolina, extending from the Blue Ridge Mountains
Blue Ridge Mountains	USA	Part of the Appalachians extending south-west from Carlisle, Pennsylvania, through Maryland, Virginia, N. Carolina, South Carolina, to Mt Oglethorpe in Georgia
Brecon Beacons	Wales	Red sandstone mountains
Cader Idris	Wales	Situated in Gwynedd, highest point is Pen-y-Gader (Cader Idris means 'chair of Idris')
Caribou Mountains	Canada	Major subdivision of the Columbia Mountains in British Columbia, highest peak is Mt Sir Wilfrid Laurier

GEOGRAPHY

Name	Area	Details
Carpathians	East Europe	Crescent-shaped continuation of the Alps running through parts of The Czech Republic, Poland, Hungary, Romania, and the Ukraine, highest peak being Mt Gerlach (Gerlachovsky Stit)
Cascades	USA–Canada	Extending 700 miles from Lassen Peak in northern California, through Oregon and Washington to the Fraser River in southern British Columbia
Catskills	USA	Dissected segment of the Allegheny Plateau, and part of the Appalachians, lying mainly in Greene and Ulster counties of south-eastern New York. Highest point is Slide Mountain
Caucasus	East Europe	Situated between the Black Sea and the Caspian Sea on the border of Russia, Georgia and Azerbaijan, highest point being Mt Elbrus
Cheviots	England	Range of rounded hills, mainly in Northumberland, forming the border between England and Scotland, highest point is Cheviot Peak
Chilterns	England	Range of chalk hills stretching 40 miles north-east from the Thames near Reading, highest point is Coombe Hill
Columbia Mountains	Canada – USA	Major mountain group of British Columbia that includes the Selkirk, Monashee, Cariboo, and Purcell ranges.
Dângrêk Mountains	Asia	Situated between Thailand and Cambodia
Darling Range	Australia	Situated on the south-west coast of Western Australia, highest peaks are Mt Cooke, Mt Solus and Mt Dale
Dartmoor	England	Area of high moorland in Devon, highest peak being High Willhays
Dauphiné Alps	France	Western spur of the Cottian Alps in south-eastern France
Dolomites	Italy	Eastern section of the northern Italian Alps, named after the 18th-century French geologist, Dieudonné Dolomieu, highest peak being Marmolada
Dome Rock Mountains	USA	Situated in western Arizona in the Sonoran Desert region near the California border
Drakensberg	South Africa	Extends from north-eastern Transvaal, through Lesotho, to south-eastern Cape Province, highest peak being Mt Thabana Ntlenyana
Durack Range	Australia	Situated in northern Western Australia, forming the eastern edge of the Kimberley Plateau
Elburz Mountains	Iran	Situated in northern Iran, highest point Mt Damāvand
Exmoor	England	Area of high moorland on the border of Somerset and Devon, highest point being Dunkery Beacon
Fan Si Pan Mountains	Vietnam	Situated in northern Vietnam, the highest peak is Mt Fan Si Pan
Flinders Range	Australia	Situated in eastern South Australia between Lake Torrens and Lake Frome, highest peak is St Mary
Gawler Ranges	Australia	Situated in South Australia, the eastern sector is known as the Middleback Ranges; the highest peak is Mount Bluff
Ghāts	India	Two ranges, East and West, forming the eastern and western edges of the Deccan Plateau of peninsular India. Ghāts means 'river landing stairs'
Golan Heights	Middle East	Situated in south-western Syria, overlooking the upper Jordan Valley, occupied by Israel since 1967 and unilaterally annexed in 1981
Grampians	Scotland	Dividing the Highlands and Lowlands, and including Ben Nevis, highest peak in the UK, the Cairngorms & Schiehallion
Great Dividing Range	Australia	Parallels the coasts of Queensland, New South Wales, and Victoria
Great Smoky Mountains	USA	Western segment of the Appalachian Mountains between Asheville, North Carolina and Knoxville, Tennessee; they are sometimes considered part of the Unaka Mountains
Great Western Mountains	Australia	Situated in central Tasmania, highest peak is Ironstone Mountain
Hamersley Range	Australia	Situated in the Pilbara region, north-western Western Australia, highest peak Mt Bruce
Himalayas	Central Asia	Extends in a south-easterly arc from Nanga Parbat peak in Jammu and Kashmir, to Namcha Barwa peak in Tibet, it contains 9 of the 14 highest peaks in the world and touches India, China, Nepal, Sikkim, and Bhutan
Hindu Kush	Central Asia	Stretches 1000 miles from the Pakistan/Chinese border in the east to a south-westerly point in Afghanistan; highest point is Tirich Mir
Jura Mountains	Central Europe	Situated on the Franco-Swiss border from the Rhône River to the Rhine
Karakoram Range	Central Asia	Northern extension of the Himalayas stretching from easternmost Afghanistan south-eastward into Jammu and Kashmir, highest peak being K2
Kibara Mountains	Zaïre	Reaching heights of 6,070' and situated in the Upemba National Park
King Leopold Ranges	Australia	Situated in northern Western Australia, forming the south-western edge of the Kimberley Plateau, highest peak is Mt Ord at just over 3,000'
Kipengere Range	Tanzania	Situated north of Lake Malawi

Name	Area	Details
Kunlun Mountains	China	Extends from the Pamirs due east along the coast of Sinkiang to the Sino-Tibetan range of Tsinghai
Kwanto Range	Japan	Aka Kantō-sammyaku, situated on Honshu, the northern range is known as the Chichibu Mts
Kyrenia Mountains	Cyprus	Extending 100 miles east to west from Cape St Andreas to Cape Kormakiti, highest point being Mt Kyparissovouno
Lofty Range	Australia	Situated on the Tropic of Capricorn in Western Australia
MacDonnell Ranges	Australia	Situated in south central Northern Territory, west of Alice Springs; Mt Ziel being the highest peak
Malverns	England	Granite ridge of Hereford and Worcester, high point being Worcester Beacon
Mealy Mountains	Canada	Situated south of Lake Melville in the Labrador peninsula of Newfoundland
Mecsek Mountains	Hungary	Aka Baranya Mts, situated in Baranya (Megye) county, southern Hungary. Highest peak is at Zengö
Monashee	Canada	Major subdivision of the Columbia Mountains in British Columbia
Mount Lofty Ranges	Australia	Situated in South Australia as a continuation of the Flinders range, highest point is Mt Byron
North Yolla Bolly Mountains	USA	California mountain range
Ore Mountains	East Europe	Situated on the border of Czech Republic and Eastern Germany highest peak is Klinovec at 4080'
Ozark Mountains	USA	Extends south-westward from St Louis, Missouri to the Arkansas River, highest point being Taum Sauk Mountain
Pamirs	Tajikistan	Often called 'The Roof of the World', highest point Communism Peak
Pare Range	Tanzania	Situated near the border with Kenya
Parecis Range	Brazil	Situated near the border with Bolivia
Peak District	England	Hill area in Derbyshire, forming the southern end of the Pennines, highest peak being Kinder Scout
Pennines	England	Range of limestone hills with a footpath stretching from Edale in Derbyshire to Kirk Yetholm in the Borders, highest point is Cross Fell
Pisgah Range	Jordan	Situated north-east of the Dead Sea, the ridge includes Mt Nebo
Przhevalsky Range (Arkatag)	Central Asia	Extension of the Kunlun Mountains, highest peak being Wu-Lu-k'o-mu-shih Ling
Purcell Range	Canada – USA	Major subdivision of the Columbia Mountains extending from British Columbia into northern Idaho
Queen Alexandra Range	Antarctica	Situated in the Ross Dependency (NZ admin), highest point Mt Kirkpatrick
Queen Elizabeth Range	Antarctica	Situated in the Ross Dependency (NZ admin), highest point Mt Miller
Queen Maud Range	Antarctica	Situated in the Ross Dependency (NZ admin), the range is a subdivision of the Transarctic Mountains
Rhodope Mountains	Balkan Peninsula	Situated mainly in Bulgaria, but extends into Macedonia, Greece, and Turkey, highest point being Golyam Perelik
Ring of Fire	Pacific	Not a mountain range but a colloquial name for the band of volcanoes that circle the Pacific and erupt frequently
Rockies	USA – Canada	Extending from British Columbia to New Mexico, highest peak is Mt Elbert
Ruwenzori Range	Zaire – Uganda	Highest mountain in the range is Mt Stanley, the highest peak being Margherita
Salt Range	Pakistan	Situated between the valleys of the Indus and Jhelum rivers of the northern Punjab, highest point being Mt Sakesar
San Bernardino Mountains	USA	Segment of the Pacific coast Ranges of southern California extending from Cajon Pass to Gorgonio Pass, highest point being San Gorgonio
San Francisco Peaks	USA	Three summits, Humphreys, Agassiz, and Fremont, on the ridge of an eroded volcano, 10 miles north of Flagstaff in north central Arizona
San Gabriel Mountains	USA	Segment of the Pacific coast Ranges of southern California extending from Newhall Pass to Cajon Pass, highest point being Mt San Antonio
San Jacinto Mountains	USA	Segment of the Pacific Coast Ranges of southern California extending from Gorgonio Pass to Santa Rosa Mountains
Sangre de Cristo Mountains	USA	Segment of the southern Rockies, extending south-eastward for about 250 miles, from Poncha Pass in south Colorado to north central New Mexico, highest point being Blanca Peak
Santa Marta Mountains	Colombia	Part of the Andes of northern Colombia, highest point Pico Cristóbal Colón is also the highest peak in Colombia
Sarykol Range	Central Asia	Borders Tajikistan and China, highest point being Mt Lyavirdyr

GEOGRAPHY

Name	Area	Details
Sawatch Range	USA	Segment of the southern Rocky Mountains in central Colorado stretching from the Eagle River to Saguache, highest point being Mt Elbert
Selkirk Mountains	Canada – USA	Major subdivision of the Columbia Mountains extending for 200 miles from British Columbia into northern Idaho and Montana, highest peak is Mt Sir Stanford
Sentinel Range	Antarctica	Located in West Antarctica, joining the Heritage Range, making up the Ellsworth Mountain Range, contains the Continent's highest peak, Vinson Massif
Sierra Madre	Mexico	Includes the 3 ranges, Sierra Madre Occidental, Sierra Madre Oriental, and Sierra Madre del Sur (to the south)
Sierra Madre de Chiapas	Mexico	Aka Sierra de Soconusco, and extending to the south-east along the Pacific Coast from the Isthmus of Tehuantepec to the Guatemalan border
Sierra Nevada	Spain	Highest division of the Penibético Mountain System of south-eastern Spain, highest point being Cerro de Mulhacén
Sierra Nevada Range	USA	Extending for more than 250 miles along the eastern edge of California, from the Mojave Desert in the south to the Cascades in the north, highest peak is Mt Whitney
Southern Alps	New Zealand	Situated on South Island and extending from Haast Pass, north-eastwards to Arthur's Pass, highest point being Mt Cook
Sperrin Mountains	N. Ireland	Situated 20 miles south-east of Londonderry, major peaks include, Mullaclogher, Sawel, and Mullaghaneany
St Elias Range	Canada	Situated in south-western Yukon Territory near the Pacific coast, highest peak is Mt Logan
Tatras	East Europe	Situated along the Slovak – Polish border, it is the highest range of the Central Carpathians, high point being Mt Gerlach
Transylvanian Alps	Romania	Aka Southern Carpathians, the section of the Carpathians between the Prahova River Valley and the gap between the Timis and Cerna rivers, highest point Mt Moldoveanu
Uinta Mountains	USA	Mountain range in N.E. Utah, part of the Rocky Mountains, the highest point being Kings Peak
Unaka Mountains	USA	Extending from south-west Virginia, along the Tennessee-North Carolina border, into northern Georgia. Unaka means 'white' in Cherokee
Urals	Russia	Extending from the Arctic Ocean to northern Kazakhstan, forming part of the boundary between Europe and Asia, highest peak Mt Narodnaya
Velikonda Range	India	Situated in Andhra Pradesh state of southern India
Virunga Range	Central Africa	Also spelled Birunga, and also called M'Fumbiro Mountains. The range straddles Zaire, Rwanda and Uganda, although, the highest peak, Karisimbi, borders Zaire & Rwanda
Vosges Mountains	France	Extending west of the Rhine River Valley in the Haut-Rhin, Bas-Rhin, and Vosges départements of eastern France; highest point Ballon de Guebwiller
White Mountains	USA	Segment of the Appalachians extending across New Hampshire and into western Maine, highest point is Mt Washington
Wilhelmina Gebergte	Suriname	Forming part of South America's granitic Precambrian Guiana Shield, highest point being Juliana Top
Wilson's Promontory	Australia	Not a range of mountains as such but the southernmost point of the Australian mainland, in Victoria; it is a mountainous area, highest point being Mt Latrobe
Wind River Range	USA	Situated in the central Rocky Mountains, west central Wyoming, the highest peak being Gannett Peak
Wrangell Mountains	USA	Segment of the Pacific Coast Range, extending southward in south-eastern Alaska for about 100 miles from the Copper River to the St Elias Mountains near the Yukon border; the highest point is Mt Blackburn
Yablonovy Range	Russia	Situated in the Transbaikalia region of Chita and Buryat, highest point being Mt Kusotuy
Zagros Mountains	Iran	Situated in south-west Iran, extending north-west to south-east from the Sirvān (Diyala) river to Shirāz, the highest peak being Zard Kuh
Zambales Mountains	Philippines	Situated in the south-western part of northern Luzon, from Lingayen Gulf in the north to the entrance to Manila Bay in the south, highest point being High Peak
Zeravshan Range	Tadzhik – Uzbek	Extends 230 miles as an east-west parallel to the Turkistan Range, highest point being Chimtorga

Mountain Passes, Valleys and Gorges

Arthur's	the lowest pass (3,038') of the Southern Alps, west-central South Island, New Zealand, the Otira Tunnel crosses the Alps at this point
Berthoud	situated in the Front Range of the central Rocky Mountains at an altitude of 11,315'
Bran	situated to the west of Predeal Pass and linking Brasov to Cimpulung between the Bucegi Massif and the Fagaras Mountains, Romania
Brenner	lying on the Italian–Austrian border and at 4,498' one of the lowest Alpine passes
Cameron	situated in the extreme southerly end of the Medicine Bow Mountains in Colorado at an altitude of 10,285'
Great Saint Bernard	lying on the Italian–Swiss border and at 8,100' one of the highest Alpine passes
Gumal	situated between the Khyber pass and Bolān pass and connects Ghazni in eastern Afghanistan with Tānk and Dera Ismāil Khān in Pakistan
Iron Gate	last gorge of the Djerdap gorge system on the Danube River, dividing the Carpathian and Balkan mountains and forming part of the boundary between Yugoslavia and Romania. The gorge is two miles long and 530' wide
Katára (Métsovo in Albania)	situated in the Pindus Mountains of northern Greece and southern Albania at an altitude of 5,593'
Khyber	Connecting Kābul, Afghanistan, with Peshāwar, Pakistan. The pass is extremely undulating and reaches 3,518' at its highest point
Kicking Horse	situated on the Alberta–British Columbia border, the highest point on the Canadian Pacific Railway at 5,338'
Little Saint Bernard	at 7,178' one of the highest passes of the French Alps. The road across the pass links France and Italy
Lolo	situated in the Bitterroot Range along the Idaho–Montana border at an altitude of 5,236'
Loveland	situated in the Front Range of the central Rocky Mountains at an altitude of 11,990 feet.
Marias	situated in the Lewis Range of the northern Rockies at an elevation of 5,216'
Métsovo (Katára in Greece)	situated in the Pindus Mountains of northern Greece and southern Albania at an altitude of 5,593'
Pajares	railway pass through the Cantabrian Mountains of northern Spain linking Oviedo and León at an altitude of 4,524'
Pele	cuts through the Black Mountain Range of the Assam Himalayas at an altitude of 11,055'
Plöcken (Passo di Monte Croce) Predeal	situated at an elevation of 4,462' in the Carnic Alps on the Austrian–Italian border links the city of Brasov and the Birsei Depression to the north with the city of Ploiesti and the Danube Plain to the south, across the Transylvanian Alps (Southern Carpathians)
Predel	separates the Julian Alps at the Italian–Slovenian border at an altitude of 3,793'
Radstädter Tauern	situated in the Niedere Tauern Range at an elevation of 5,705'
Saint Gothard	a 16-mile-long pass situated in the Lepontine Alps of southern Switzerland. The pass has an altitude of 6,916'; the nine-mile-long St Gothard railway tunnel underneath the pass links Italy and Switzerland via Milan and Luzern; the ten-mile long St Gothard road tunnel links Göschenen and Airolo
Simplon	situated in the southern Swiss Alps at an altitude of 6,581'; the Simplon railway tunnel cuts through beneath the pass and connects Brig, Switzerland and Iselle, Italy
Uspallata	situated in the Andes, at 12,500', connecting Mendoza, Argentina and Santiago, Chile

GEOGRAPHY

Mountains (General)

Name	Area	Height (ft)	Details
Abu (Guru Sikhar)	India	5,650	highest mountain in the Arāvalli range of northern India
Aconcagua	Argentina	22,834	highest peak in the Andes and in the Western Hemisphere, first climbed in 1897
Adam's Peak	Sri Lanka	7,360	situated in south-western Sri Lanka, 11 miles north-east of Ratnapura; famous for its footprint (5'4" x 2'6") revered as the Buddha's, Adam's or Siva's, dependent on faith
Alverstone	North America	14,565	situated in the St Elias Mountains, on the Yukon/Alaska border, and first climbed in 1951
Ampato	Peru	20,702	situated in the Andes, first climbed in 1972
Anai Mudi	India	8,842	situated in Kottayam district, eastern Kerala state, SW India, in the Western Ghāts, highest point of peninsular India
Annapurna	Nepal	26,546	first peak above 26,000' to be climbed to the summit, on 3 June 1950, by Maurice Herzog and Louis Lachenal
Apo	Philippines	9,690	volcanic mountain, the highest point of the Philippines, part of the Cordillera Central
Aragats	Armenia	13,418	highest point in both Armenia, and the Little Caucasus range
Ararat (Agri Dagi)	Turkey	17,011	extinct volcano, highest peak in Turkey. Little Ararat (Kucuk Agri Dagi) rises to 12,782'
Aspiring	New Zealand	9,932	situated in the Southern Alps of west central South Island, first climbed in 1909 by Major Bernard Head

Name	Area	Height (ft)	Details
Athos	Greece	6,670	situated in northern Greece, it is also the site of a semi-autonomous republic of Greek Orthodox monks
Backbone	USA	3,360	highest point in Maryland
Baden-Powell	USA	9,389	twin peak, with North Baldy, and situated in the San Gabriel Mountains
Baker	USA	10,778	volcano situated in the Cascade range in Washington
Ballon de Guebwiller	France	4,672	highest peak of the Vosges Mountains
Bandeira	Brazil	9,482	situated on the border of Espirito Santo and Minas Gerais states, eastern Brazil; until Neblina peak was discovered in 1962 Bandeira was the highest known peak in Brazil
Batu	Ethiopia	14,130	situated in the Eastern Highlands between the Genale and Shebele rivers
Bear	USA	14,831	situated in the Wrangell Mountains, first climbed in 1951
Belukha	Russia	14,783	highest peak in the Altai Mountain range
Ben Macdui	Scotland	4,296	highest peak of the Cairngorm Mountains and the second highest mountain in the British Isles
Ben Nevis	Scotland	4,406	highest mountain of the British Isles
Betling Sib	India	3,280	highest peak of the Tripura Hills of north-eastern India
Big Black Mountain	USA	4,150	highest peak of Kentucky
Blackburn	USA	16,523	highest point in Alaska's Wrangell Mountains, first climbed in 1912
Blanc	France/Italy	15,771	highest peak in the Alps
Blanca Peak	USA	14,345	highest peak in the Sangre de Cristo Mountains of Colorado/New Mexico
Blue Mountain Peak	Jamaica	7,402	highest peak of the Blue Mountains in eastern Jamaica
Bluff	Australia	1,550	highest peak of the Gawler ranges of South Australia
Bolivar	Venezuela	16,427	situated in the Sierra Nevada National Park of Mérida and Barinas states, north-western Venezuela; Pico Bolivar (Columna) is marginally higher than Humboldt and Bonpland and is the highest peak in Venezuela: the cable-car running from Mérida to nearby Pico Espejo (Mirror Peak), 15,600', is thought to be the highest in the world
Bona	USA	16,421	situated in the Wrangell Mountains, first climbed in 1930
Botev Peak	Bulgaria	7,795	highest point in the Balkan Mountain range
Boundary Peak	USA	13,140	highest point in Nevada
Brasstown Bald	USA	4,784	highest point in Georgia, part of the Unaka range of the Blue Ridge
Brown	USA	14,530	situated in the Alaska range
Bruce	Australia	4,056	highest peak in the Hamersley range, and the highest in Western Australia
Bukit Maxwell	Malaysia	3,399	situated in Taiping, West Malaysia, and formerly called Mazwells Hill
Byron	Australia	3,058	highest point of the Mount Lofty ranges of South Australia
Carrantuohill	Ireland	3,414	highest point of Macgillicuddy's Reeks in County Kerry and highest mountain in Ireland
Carmarthen Van	Wales	2,632	highest peak of the Black Mountains of east Dyfed
Carn Mairg	Scotland	3,087	highest peak of the Monadhliath Mountains in the Highlands between Loch Ness and the River Spey; aka Grey Hills
Chances Peak	Montserrat	3,002	situated east of the capital Plymouth in the Soufrière Hills
Cheaha	USA	2,407	highest point in Alabama
Cheviot Peak	England	2,676	highest point of the Cheviots of northern England
Chimborazo	Ecuador	20,561	extinct volcano in the Andes of central Ecuador
Chimtorga	Tajik/Uzbek	18,009	highest point of the Zeravshan range
Churchill	USA	15,638	situated in the Wrangell Mountains
Cleveland	USA–Canada	10,479	highest peak of the Lewis range in the northern Rockies
Clingman's Dome	USA	6,643	highest point in Tennessee, situated in the Great Smoky Mountains National Park
Cloud Peak	USA	13,165	highest peak of the Bighorn Mountains in the northern Rocky Mountains, southern Montana
Communism Peak	Tajikistan	24,590	highest point of the Pamirs, and highest point of Tajikistan
Cook	New Zealand	12,349	situated in the Southern Alps, the highest peak of New Zealand
Cooke	Australia	1,910	highest peak in the Darling range of Western Australia
Coombe Hill	England	825	highest peak of the Chilterns
Corn Ddu	Wales	2,863	twin peak, with Pen-y-Fan, of the Brecon Beacons
Cotopaxi	Ecuador	19,347	active volcano situated in the Andes, last eruption in 1975
Crêt de la Neige	France	5,636	situated in the French segment of the Jura Mountains
Cristóbal Colón	Colombia	18,947	situated in the Santa Marta Mountains and is the highest peak in Colombia
Cross Fell	England	2,930	highest peak in the Pennines

Name	Area	Height (ft)	Details
Curcubắta Marc	Romania	6,063	highest peak of the Bihor Massif in the Apuneni Mountains
Dandenong	Australia	2,077	highest peak in the Dandenong range of southern Victoria
Davis	USA	3,213	highest point in Pennsylvania, part of the Allegheny Mountains
Dhaulagiri	Nepal	26,795	Himalayan mountain; name means 'White Mountain' in Sanskrit
Djebel Chélia	Algeria	7,638	situated in the Aurès range of Northern Algeria
Doda Betta	India	8,652	highest peak in Tamil Nãdu state, south-eastern India, and 2nd highest peak in the Western Ghãts
Dom Mountain	Indonesia	4,396	situated on the island of New Guinea, there is also a Dom Peak in the Apennines
Dome Fuji Peak	Antarctica	12,487	situated on Queen Maud Land
Dome Mountain	Canada	896	situated south of Lake Melville in Newfoundland
Dufourspitze	Switzerland	15,203	highest peak in Switzerland, in the Monte Rosa Massif
Dunkery Beacon	England	1,750	highest peak of Exmoor, on the border of Somerset and Devon
Eagle	USA	2,300	highest peak in Minnesota
Ebal	Palestine	3,084	situated in the West Bank just north of Mt Gerizim
Edith	USA	9,504	highest peak of the Big Belt Mountains, a segment of the northern Rocky Mountains
Egmont	New Zealand	8,260	extinct volcano on the Taranaki peninsula of North Island
Eiger	Switzerland	13,026	first climbed in 1858 by Charles Barrington and Christian Almer. The 6,000' North Face was first climbed in July 1938 by Heinrich Harrer, Fritz Kasparek, Anderl Heckmair and Ludwig Vorg; the difficulty of this climb earned the Eiger Nordwand many nicknames, including 'The White Spider', 'The White Cobra' and 'Murder Wall'
El Capitan	USA	3,604	highest peak in Yosemite National Park, central California. El Capitan is a granite buttress, part of Sierra Nevada range
El Misti	Ecuador	19,233	volcano situated in the Ecuadorean Andes; last eruption in 1878
Elbert	USA	14,433	situated in the Sawatch range of the Rockies in central Colorado, the highest point in Colorado and the Rockies
Elbright Road	USA	442	situated in New Castle County, the highest point in Delaware
Elbrus	Russia	18,510	highest peak in the Caucasus and highest in Russia, just north of the Georgia border
Elgon	Kenya/Uganda	14,140	extinct volcano on the Kenya/Uganda border, first climbed by Sir Frederick Jackson and Ernest Gedge in 1890, highest peak is Wagagai
Encuolo	Ethiopia	14,144	situated in the Eastern Highlands north of the Shebele river
Erebus	Antarctica	12,448	volcano situated on Ross Island, discovered by Sir James Ross in 1841 and named after his ship
Etna	Italy	10,855	situated on the island of Sicily, this volcano, the highest in Europe, had a major eruption in 1669 when 20,000 people were killed and the city of Catania was devastated
Evans	USA	14,264	highest peak of the Front range in the central Rocky Mountains
Everest	Nepal/Tibet	29,035	highest point on Earth, named after George Everest, Surveyor General of India (1830–43), and called Peak XV until 1865; Dalai Lama 1st gave permission to climb in 1920 and Sir John Hunt led the 1953 successful expedition; Dougal Haston and Doug Scott in 1976 became the first British climbers; Reinhold Messner was the first to make a successful climb without oxygen; Junko Tabei of Japan became the first woman to climb Everest on 16 May 1975; Alison Hargreaves became first woman to climb Everest without oxygen but died soon after on K2; Everest is also called Goddess Mother of the World (Chomolungma in the Tibetan language); previously believed to be 29,028'; remeasured on 5 May 1999 with GPS equipment
Fairweather	North America	15,299	situated in the St. Elias Mountains, on the British Columbia/Alaska border, and first climbed in 1931
Fan Si Pan	Vietnam	10,308	highest peak in Vietnam
Fanthams Peak	New Zealand	6,438	extinct volcano on the Taranaki peninsula of North Island
Fichtelberg	Germany	3,983	highest peak on the German side of the Ore Mountains
Finsteraarhorn	Switzerland	14,022	highest peak of the Bernese Alps
Foraker	USA	17,400	situated in the Alaska range, and first climbed in 1934
Francs Peak	USA	13,140	highest peak of the Absaroka range of the northern Rocky Mountains in northwestern Wyoming and southern Montana
Fremont Peak	USA	13,730	situated in the Wind River range of Wyoming
Galtymore	Ireland	3,018	highest peak of the Galty Mountains of Western Ireland
Gannett Peak	USA	13,763	highest peak in the Wind River range and also the highest peak in Wyoming
Gerizim (Jabal At-Tur)	Palestine	2,890	Since 1967 has been part of the West Bank of Judaea and Samaria, under Israeli administration, it is twinned with Mt Ebal, which is just north of Gerizim

GEOGRAPHY

Name	Area	Height (ft)	Details
Gerlach	Slovakia	8,711	situated in the Tatra segment of the Carpathian Mountains and is the highest peak of the Carpathians
Glittertinden	Norway	8,110	situated in the Jotunheimen (Giant's Home) Mountain and although twelve feet higher than Galdhopiggen the peak is a 65 ft thick permanent, glacial ice cap
Golyam (Great) Perelik	Balkans	7,188	highest peak in the Rhodope Mountains
Goodsir	Canada	11,683	situated in the Yoho National Park of eastern British Columbia
Grandfather	USA	5,964	situated in North Carolina, part of the Blue Ridge Mountains
Granite Peak	USA	12,799	highest peak in Montana, part of the Beartooth range
Greylock	USA	3,491	situated in the Berkshire Hills, the highest point in Massachusetts
Guadalupe Peak	USA	8,749	highest point in Texas
Guge	Ethiopia	13,790	situated west of Lake Abaya
Guru Sikhar	India	5,650	See Mt Abu
Hagen	New Guinea	12,392	situated in the Central Highlands of New Guinea Island, Papua New Guinea
Harney Peak	USA	7,242	highest peak in South Dakota situated in the Black Hills
Hartz Mountain	Australia	4,111	highest peak of the Hartz Mountain range in Southern Tasmania
Harvard	USA	14,420	situated in the Sawatch Mountains, a segment of the Rockies running through Colorado
Hermon	Syria/Lebanon	9,232	aka Jabal ash-Shaikh, and situated west of Damascus, Hermon means 'Forbidden Place'
High Peak	Philippines	6,683	highest peak of the Zambales Mountains
High Point	USA	1,803	highest peak in New Jersey
High Willhays	England	2,039	highest peak in the Dartmoor National Park of Devon
Hochgolling	Austria	9,393	highest peak of the Niedere Tauern range of the Eastern Alps
Hood	USA	11,235	situated in the Cascade range, highest peak in Oregon
Huascarán	Peru	22,205	extinct volcano in west Peru, in the Peruvian Andes, highest peak in Peru
Hubbard	North America	15,015	situated in the St Elias Mountains, on the Yukon/Alaska border, and first climbed in 1951
Humphrey's Peak	USA	12,633	one of the three San Francisco Peaks, the highest peak in Arizona
Hunter	USA	14,573	situated in the Alaska range
Ida	Crete	8,058	highest peak on the island at 2,456m, it is just three metres higher than Mt Pachnes, the second highest peak
Ingleborough	England	2,376	one of the so called Three Peaks of the Yorkshire Dales National Park
Ironstone	Australia	4,736	highest peak of the Great Western Mountains in Tasmania
Isto	USA	9,058	highest peak of the Brooks range in the northern Rocky Mountains near the Canadian border
Iztaccíhuatl	Mexico	17,159	dormant volcano which last erupted in 1868, situated on the México-Puebla state line in central Mexico, 10 miles north of its twin, Popocatépetl
Jerimoth Hill	USA	812	highest peak in Rhode Island, less than a mile from the Connecticut border
Juliana Top	Suriname	4,199	highest peak of the Wilhelmina Gebergte range of central Suriname
Jungfrau	Switzerland	13,642	situated in the Bernese Alps 11 miles south-east of Interlaken; first climbed by two Swiss brothers, Rudolf and Hieronymus Meyer, in 1811
K2	Pakistan	28,250	situated in the Karakorum range in the Himalayas, on the western side of the Indian/Pakistani line of control in Jammu and Kashmir, first climbed by Compagnoni and Lacedelli in 1954 K2 is also known as Mt Godwin Austen, Dapsang, and Chogori
Kanchenjunga	Nepal/India	28,208	on the border of Nepal and Sikkim, the 3rd highest mountain in the world was first climbed in 1955, although Charles Evans stopped short of the summit in deference to Sikkimese religious beliefs; Kanchenjunga means 'Five Treasuries of the Great Snow' (Sikkim)
Karisimbi	Dem Rep Congo/ Rwanda	14,787	highest peak of the Virunga range
Katahdin	USA	5,268	highest peak in Maine
Kellerwand	Austria	9,121	highest peak of the Carnic Alps
Kennedy Peak	Myanmar	2,704	situated on the Tropic of Cancer near the Indian border
Kennesaw	USA	551	situated in Atlanta, Georgia
Kenya (Batian Peak)	Kenya	17,057	extinct volcano, first climbed in 1899 by Halford and Mackinder of Great Britain
Kerintji	Indonesia	12,484	highest peak in the West Sumatran/Java range
Kilimanjaro	Tanzania	19,340	Volcanic mountain near the Kenyan border, the Kibo peak being the highest point in Tanzania and probably the only snow-covered point on the equator; the other main peak is Mawenzi

Name	Area	Height (ft)	Details
Kimpō	Japan	8,514	situated in the Chichibu Mountains, the northern extension of the Kwanto range
Kinabalu	Malaysia	13,455	highest peak in the Malay Archipelago, situated on the island of Borneo, it was formerly known as St Peter's Mount
Kinder Scout	England	2,088	highest point in the Peak District
King	Canada	16,972	situated in the St Elias Mountains, Yukon Territory, and first climbed in 1952
Kings Peak	USA	13,528	highest point in Utah, situated in the Uintas range
Kirkpatrick	Antarctica	14,856	highest point of the Queen Alexandra range
Klinovec	Czech Republic	4,080	highest peak in the Ore Mountains
Klyuchevskaya Sopka	Russia	15,584	highest active volcano in Asia, situated in Kamchatka Peninsula
Kompasberg	South Africa	8,215	highest peak of the Sneeuberg (Snow Mountain) range in central Cape Province
Kosciusko	Australia	7,316	situated in the Snowy Mountains of New South Wales, the highest peak in Australia
Krakatoa	Indonesia	2,667	famous for the eruption of 1883 when 163 villages were destroyed and 36,417 people were killed. Despite the title of the 1968 film, Krakatoa is actually west of Java
Kriván	East Europe	8,182	one of the highest peaks of the High Tatras on the Poland/Slovakia border
Kusotuy	Russia	5,512	highest point of the Yablonovy range
Kyparissovouno	Cyprus	3,360	highest point of the Kyrenia Mountains
La Dôle	Switzerland	5,545	situated in the Swiss segment of the Jura Mountains
Lascar	Chile	18,508	Volcano situated in the Chilean Andes, last eruption in 1969
Lassen	USA	10,457	Volcano situated in the Cascade range in California
Latrobe	Australia	2,475	highest point of Wilson's Promontory in southern Victoria
Le Reculet	France	5,633	situated in the French segment of the Jura Mountains
Les Écrins	France	13,461	highest peak of the Dauphiné Alps
Lhotse (E)	Nepal/Tibet	27,923	situated just south of Everest, to which it is joined by a 25,000′ ridge; The 'E' of its original name stands for Everest
Llullaillaco	S America	22,058	Dormant volcano situated in the Andes on the Argentina/Chile border, last eruption in 1877
Logan	Yukon	19,550	2nd highest peak in North America, first climbed in 1925 by MacCarthy and Lambert; mountains with the same name in Quebec, Arizona and Washington
Lomnicky	East Europe	8,635	one of the highest peaks of the High Tatras on the Poland/Slovakia border
Lozère	France	5,584	highest peak of the Cévennes range of southern France
Lucania	Canada	17,146	situated in the St Elias Mountains, Yukon Territory, and first climbed in 1937
Lugnaquilla	Ireland	3,039	highest peak of the Wicklow Mountains
Lyavirdyr	Tajikistan	20,837	highest point of the Sarykol range
Magazine	USA	2,753	highest peak in Arkansas
Mansfield	USA	4,393	highest point in Vermont
Marcy	USA	5,344	highest peak of the Adirondacks, and the highest peak of New York state
Mariveles	Philippines	4,659	Most southerly peak of the Zambales Mountains, lying opposite Manila Bay
Markham	Antarctica	14,272	highest point of the Queen Elizabeth range
Marmolada	Italy	10,964	highest peak in the Dolomites
Mary's Peak	USA	4,097	South-west of Corvallis, the highest point of the Oregon Coastal range
Massive	USA	14,421	situated in the Sawatch Mountains, a segment of the Rockies running through Colorado
Matterhorn	Switzerland/Italy	14,691	First climbed 14 Jul 1865 by British explorer Edward Whymper, although the Italian ridge was scaled 3 days later by Giovanni Carrel; Matterhorn was named after the Swiss city of Zermatt; Italian name is Monte Cervino
Mauna Kea	USA	13,796	Dormant volcano situated on Hawaii Island, the highest point in Hawaii state, in fact, its 32,000′ height from the seafloor makes it the world's highest peak from base to tip
Mauna Loa	USA	13,678	situated on Hawaii Island, the actual height of the volcano from its base on the seafloor is second only to Mauna Kea; last erupted in 1988
McIntyre	USA	5,114	situated in the Adirondack range of New York state; highest peak is Algonquin
McKinley	USA	20,320	situated in the Alaska range, and first climbed in 1913, the highest peak of North America
Mercedario	Argentina	22,211	situated in the Andes, first climbed in 1934
Meru	Tanzania	14,980	located near the Kenyan border, south-west of Kilimanjaro

GEOGRAPHY

Name	Area	Height (ft)	Details
Mikeno	Dem Rep Congo/ Rwanda	14,557	situated in the Virunga Mountains
Miller	Antarctica	13,646	situated in the Queen Elizabeth range
Mitchell	USA	6,684	highest point in North Carolina, situated in the Black Mountains, part of the Blue Ridge Mountains; highest peak east of the Mississippi
Moldoveanu	Romania	8,346	situated in the Transylvanian Alps, the highest peak in Romania
Mönch	Switzerland	13,448	flanked by the Eiger and Jungfrau in the Bernese Alps
Mount Darwin	Zimbabwe	4,951	situated in northern Zimbabwe, locals call it Pfura, meaning 'rhinoceros'
Mulhacén	Spain	11,421	situated in the Sierra Nevadas of southern Spain, the highest mountain of the Iberian Peninsula
Nanda Devi	India	25,643	situated in the Uttar Pradesh segment of the Himalayas
Nanga (Naked) Parbat	Kashmir	26,660	often regarded as the first major peak of the western Himalayas; the local name is Diamir (King of the Mountains)
Neblina	Brazil	9,889	situated in the Serra Tapirapeó, Amazonas state, highest peak in Brazil
Nebo	Jordan	2,631	highest point of the Pisgah Ridge, from which Moses viewed the Promised Land
North Baldy	USA	9,131	Twin peak, with Mt Baden-Powell, and situated in the San Gabriel Mountains of southern California
Ojos del Salado	S America	22,588	Although the mountain straddles the Chile/Argentina border, the highest peak is totally in Chile and is the highest point, first climbed in 1937. Ojos del Salado is also the highest active volcano in the world. It was previously designated as dormant but it started to 'steam' in 1981 and has recently produced vents
Olga	Australia	3,507	situated in Uluru National Park, Mt Olga is the most westerly of Australia's 3 giant tors, the others being Ayers Rock at 2,845' and Mt Conner
Orizaba (Citlaltépetl)	Mexico	18,406	dormant volcano situated in Altiplano de Mexico, last erupted in 1687, the highest point in Mexico
Pelée	Martinique	4,582	In 1902 the town of St Pierre was destroyed by this volcano's eruption, which killed all 26,000 inhabitants, except for a prisoner who survived in the thick-walled prison
Pen-y-Fan	Wales	2,906	highest point of the Brecon Beacons
Pen-y-Gader	Wales	2,927	highest point of the Cader Idris range
Pen-y-Ghent	England	2,278	one of the so called Three Peaks of the Yorkshire Dales National Park
Pinátubo	Philippines	5,723	situated in Luzon, this volcano last erupted in 1991, when 847 people were killed – the most lethal eruption of the 20th century
Pissis	Argentina	22,241	situated in the Andes, first climbed in 1937
Popocatépetl	Mexico	17,930	volcano which last erupted in 1997, the first eruption since 1802, although it does emit large clouds of smoke periodically; known locally as Nahuatl (smoking mountain)
Poroshiri	Japan	6,732	highest peak of the Hidaka–Sammyaku range on Hokkaido
Profitis	Greece	1,857	volcanic mountain on the island of Thera in the Cyclades, the highest point on the island
Punta Pora	Paraguay	2,296	second-highest peak in Paraguay
Puy de Sancy	France	6,184	highest peak of the Massif Central
Rainier	USA	14,410	dormant volcano, highest peak of the Cascade range and also the highest peak in Washington state, first climbed in 1870
Ramlo	Ethiopia	6,988	situated inland of the Red Sea coast, north of Djibouti
Revelstoke	Canada	6,375	situated in the Selkirk Mountains of south-eastern British Columbia
Rock Creek Butte	USA	9,105	highest peak of the Blue Mountains, situated on the Elkhorn Ridge on the Oregon/Washington border
Rogers	USA	5,729	highest point in Virginia, part of the Blue Ridge Mountains
Rosa	Switzerland/Italy	15,203	situated SE of Zermatt, often identified with Dufourspitze, although Monte Rosa has many other named peaks
Round	Australia	5,300	highest peak of the New England range, NSW
Ruapehu	New Zealand	9,177	active volcano and highest point on North Island
Rushmore	South Dakota	6,040	situated in the Black Hills, and famous for its carved faces (60' high) of Washington, Lincoln, Jefferson and Roosevelt, executed by Gutzon Borglum between 1927 and 1941
St Helens	USA	8,360	volcano situated in Washington state (Cascades); it erupted in 1980 after lying dormant from 1857
St Mary	Australia	3,825	highest peak in the Flinders ranges
Sajama	Bolivia	21,391	situated in the Andes, first climbed in 1939, the highest peak of Bolivia

Name	Area	Height (ft)	Details
Sakesar	Pakistan	4,992	highest peak of the Salt range in the northern Punjab
San Antonio	USA	10,080	Nicknamed 'Old Baldy' and the highest peak of the San Gabriel Mountains of southern California
San Bernardino	USA	10,630	situated in the San Bernardino Mountains of southern California
San Gorgonio	USA	11,502	situated in the San Bernardino Mountains, highest point in southern California
San Jacinto Peak	USA	10,804	highest point of the San Jacinto Mountains of southern California
San Pedro	Chile	20,339	volcano situated in the Chilean Andes, last eruption in 1960
Sanford	USA	16,237	situated in the Wrangell Mountains of south-eastern Alaska, first climbed in 1938
Santorini	Greece	1,960	see Thera
Sassafras	USA	3,560	highest point in South Carolina, part of the Blue Ridge Mountains
Scafell	England	3,162	south-west of Scafell Pike, the 2nd-highest peak in England
Scafell Pike	England	3,210	situated in the Lake District of Cumbria, highest point in England
Scott Peak	USA	11,394	highest peak of the Bitterroot range in the northern Rocky Mountains, Idaho
Shasta	USA	14,162	extinct volcano situated in the Cascade range of northern California
Shirane	Japan	10,472	highest mountain of the Japanese Alps, on Honshu island; the peak of the mountain is named Ontake
Shishaldin	USA	9,387	volcanic mountain in the Unimak Islands, the highest point in the Aleutian range of Alaska
Sierra Blanca	USA	12,003	highest peak of the Sacramento Mountains in the southern Rockies
Sinai	Egypt	7,497	situated on the Sinai Peninsula, under Israeli administration from the Six-Day War of 1967 until 1979, when it was returned to Egypt; God is purported to have given Moses the Ten Commandments here
Sir James McBrien	Canada	9,061	highest peak of the Mackenzie Mountains in the Yukon Territory
Sir Sanford	Canada	11,590	highest peak of the Selkirk Mountains
Sir Wilfrid Laurier	Canada	11,299	highest peak of the Cariboo range of British Columbia
Slide	USA	4,204	highest point of the Catskill Mountains
Slieve Donard	N Ireland	2,796	highest peak of the Mourne Mountains
Snaefell	Isle of Man	2,034	highest peak of the Isle of Man
Snowdon	Wales	3,560	situated in Snowdonia National Park, Clwyd and Gwynedd, highest peak in Wales
Solomon's Throne	Pakistan	18,481	situated in the Sulaimân range of central Pakistan
Spruce Knob	USA	4,862	highest point in West Virginia, part of the Allegheny Mountains
Stanley	Dem Rep Congo/ Uganda	16,795	highest mountain in the Ruwenzori range (highest peak named after Queen Margherita of Italy), first climbed in 1906 by Luigi Abruzzi
Steele	Canada	16,644	situated in the St Elias Mountains, Yukon Territory, and first climbed in 1935
Sugar Loaf	Brazil	1,325	overlooking the entrance of Guanabara Bay, south-eastern Brazil
Sunflower	USA	4,039	highest point in Kansas, situated south-east near the Colorado border
Table (Tafelberg)	South Africa	3,563	Flat-topped mountain overlooking Cape Town and Table Bay; the highest peak is Maclear's Beacon, subsidiary peaks include Lion's Head (2,195′) and Devil's Peak (3,281′)
Tahan	Malaysia	7,175	situated in Taman Negara National Park, West Malaysia
Tahat	Algeria	9,852	situated in the Hoggar Massif of the southern Saharan Atlas mountains
Talo	Ethiopia	14,478	situated in central Ethiopia in the Gojam Massif
Tambora	Indonesia	9,350	situated on Sumbawa and famous for its eruption of 1815 when over 90,000 people perished
Tapuaenuku	New Zealand	9,465	highest peak of the Kaikoura range on South Island
Taum Sauk	USA	1,772	highest peak of the Ozark Mountains, and highest point in Missouri
Teide	Spain	12,190	volcanic mountain situated on the island of Tenerife in the Canaries, last erupted in 1909
Tendre	Switzerland	5,550	situated in the Swiss segment of the Jura Mountains
Thabana Ntlenyana	Lesotho	11,425	highest peak in the Drakensberg Mountains
Thera	Greece	1,960	southernmost island of the Cyclades group, aka Santorini, and famous for its volcanic eruption c1550 BC which possibly gave rise to the legend of the lost city of Atlantis
Timpanogos	USA	12,008	highest peak of the Wasatch range in the south central Rocky Mountains

Name	Area	Height (ft)	Details
Tirich Mir	Pakistan	25,230	highest peak in the Hindu Kush range, lying 155 miles north of Peshawar
Titano	San Marino	2,424	highest peak and dominant feature of San Marino
Toluca	Mexico	4,577	volcano situated in Mexico state, central Mexico near Toluca, the crater partly filled by a lake
Triglav	Slovenia	9,396	highest peak of the Julian Alps of Slovenia, first climbed in 1778
Tsiafajavona	Madagascar	8,671	situated in the Ankaratra Mountain region, 2nd-highest peak of Madagascar
Tupungato	S. America	22,310	situated in the Andes, on the Argentina/Chile border, first climbed in 1897
Tyree	Antarctica	16,289	situated in the Sentinel range of the Ellsworth Mountains, first climbed in 1967
Vancouver	North America	15,700	situated in the St Elias Mountains, on the Yukon/Alaska border, and first climbed in 1949
Veleta	Spain	11,128	situated in the Sierra Nevadas of southern Spain, the 2nd highest mountain of mainland Spain
Vesuvius	Italy	4,198	volcano situated in the Bay of Naples, first major eruption in AD 79 and the last in 1944
Victoria	Myanmar	10,150	highest peak of the Arakan Yoma range separating Myanmar from the Indian subcontinent
Vikhren	Bulgaria	9,564	situated in the Rhodope Mountains; second-highest peak in Bulgaria
Vinson Massif	Antarctica	16,864	situated in the Sentinel range of the Ellsworth Mountains, first climbed in 1966
Waddington	Canada	13,104	highest peak of the Coast Mountains of British Columbia
Walsh	Canada	14,780	situated in the St Elias Mountains, Yukon Territory, and first climbed in 1941
Warren	USA	13,720	situated in the Wind River range of Wyoming
Washington	USA	6,288	highest peak in the Presidential range of the White Mountains, and the highest peak in New Hampshire
Waun Fach	Wales	2,660	highest peak of the Black Mountains of east Gwent
Wheeler Peak	USA	13,161	situated in the Sangre de Cristo Mountains, the highest point in New Mexico
Whernside	England	2,416	one of the so-called Three Peaks of the Yorkshire Dales National Park
White Butte	USA	3,506	highest peak in North Dakota
Whiteface	USA	4,865	situated in the Adirondacks of New York
Whitney	USA	14,494	highest peak of Sierra Nevada range in California and the highest peak of the 48 coterminous United States of America
Wilson	USA	5,710	situated in the San Gabriel Mountains of southern California
Wood	Canada	15,886	situated in the St Elias Mountains, Yukon Territory, and first climbed in 1941
Woodroffe	Australia	4,724	highest peak of South Australia situated in the Musgrave ranges
Worcester Beacon	England	1,395	highest peak of the Malverns
Wrangell	USA	14,163	situated in the Wrangell Mountains of south-eastern Alaska
Wu-t'ai	China	10,033	situated in north-east Shansi Province, the name meaning 'five terraces'
Yes Tor	England	2,028	situated in the Dartmoor National Park of Devon, and twinned with High Willhays
Zengö	Hungary	2,237	highest peak of the Mecsek Mountains of southern Hungary
Ziel	Australia	4,954	highest peak of the MacDonnell ranges of Australia
Zomba	Malawi	6,846	highest point of the Zomba Massif in southern Malawi
Zugspitze	Germany	9,721	part of the Wettersteingebirge in the Bavarian Alps, lying on the Austrian border, the highest point in Germany

Oceans

	Area (Sq Miles)	% of Earth's Water	Deepest Point
Pacific	64,186,300	46.0	Challenger Deep
Atlantic	33,420,000	23.9	Milwaukee Deep
Indian	28,350,500	20.3	Planet Deep
Arctic	5,105,700	3.6	Eurasia Basin

British Place Names:
meanings of suffixes and prefixes

Name	Meaning	Name	Meaning	Name	Meaning
aber	river mouth	dal	field	kyle	strait
ac	oak or acorn	dar	water	lade	river mouth
agh	field	dean	wooded vale	law	rising ground
aig	nook or creek	dearg	red	lea	meadow
aird	height	del	dale	leck	field of corpses
ald	old	den	wooded vale	lee	meadow
alt	brook	dene	wooded vale	leigh	woodland glade or meadow
alt	steep place	der	water		
an	terminal diminutive	dhu	black	ley	woodland glade or meadow
ard	height	don	hill or water		
ath	ford	dor	water	linn	waterfall
auch	field	dour	water	lis	enclosure
auchter	summit	drom	ridge	litch	field of corpses
avon	river	drum	ridge	llan	church
ax	water	dum	fortress	llech	smooth cliff
ay	island	dun	hill (England)	llwyd	grey or hoary
bal	village or town	dun	fortress (Scotland + Ireland)	llwyn	wood
balloch	pass			llyn	lake
bally	village or town	dur	water	loch	lake
ban	white or fair	dwfr	water	lough	lake
bar	point or projecting height	dyke	ditch	low	rising ground or mound
		ea	island	lynn	waterfall
beath	birch tree	eccles	church	madah	wolf
beck	brook	egles	church	madan	fair
bedd	grave	ennis	island	maen	stone
beg	little	esk	water	magh	plain
ben	mountain	ex	water	mawr	great
bere	barley	ey	island	mere	lake or marsh
blair	plain	fell	mountain	mickle	great or much
borough	fortified place	field	clearing	minster	monastic establishment
bourne	stream	fin	white or fair		
brae	promontory	fleet	river	moor	lake or marsh
bre	promontory	force	waterfall	mor	great
brogh	fortified place	ford	shallow river crossing	moss	bog
bruach	slope or brae	gair	short	mull	headland
bryn	ridge	garth	enclosure	nant	brook or valley
burg	fortified place	gate	passage	ness	promontory
burn	brook	ghyll	ravine	ock	water
bury	fortified place	gill	ravine	oke	water
by	village	glen	narrow valley	or	river or sea shore
caer	camp or fortified place	ham	home or enclosure	pen	hill or headland
cairn	pile of stones	hampton	home farm or village	pike	mountain summit
cambus	crooked	hanger	wood on hillside	pont	bridge
carn	pile of stones	haugh	meadow between hills	port	harbour
carrick	cliff	hause	pass or col	pwil	pool
caster	walled camp	hay	hedge	rath	round earthwork
cefn	ridge	head	headland or hill	rhos	moor
cester	walled camp	hithe	haven	rhyd	ford
cheap	market	holme	river island	rigg	ridge
chester	walled camp	holt	small wood	ross	promontory
chipping	market place	hoo	heel of land	royd	ridded of trees
clach	stone	hurst	thick wood on a hill	scar	cliff
clere	hill	inch	island	seat	cultivated place or dwelling
clon	meadow	ing	meadow		
coe	narrow	ing	son of	set	settlement
coln	colony	ing	people of	sex	Saxon
combe	grassy hollow	innis	island	shan	mountain
cote	mud cottage	inver	river mouth	shaw	shady place
craig	rock or cliff	keld	spring	shot	protruding land
crick	cliff	ken	head	shott	protruding land
croe	sheepfold	kil	church	slievh	mountain
croft	enclosure	kirk	church	staple	store or market
cwm	grassy valley	knock	knoll	stead	place or holding
dal	dale	knoll	hill top	stock	palisaded place

GEOGRAPHY

Name	Meaning	Name	Meaning	Name	Meaning
stoke	palisaded place	ton	farm or town	walt	wood
stow	holy place or enclosure	tor	rocky hill	weald	wood
strat	roman road	tre	dwelling or small town	wich	marshy meadow
strath	broad valley	tree	post, cross or crucifix	wick	village or farm
tam	wide	try	dwelling	win	plain
thorpe	farm or village	twistle	boundary	wold	wood
thwaite	clearing	ty	house	worth	protected enclosure
tober	well	ux	water	ystrad	vale
toft	enclosure	wald	wood		

British Place Names: meanings

Name	Meaning	Name	Meaning
Accrington	Acorn Farm	Oundle	Non-sharing Ones
Crawley	Crows Wood	Pontypridd	Bridge by the Earthen House
Croydon	Saffron Valley		
Cumbernauld	Meeting of the Streams	Powys	Provincial
Cumbria	Fellow Countrymen	Prestatyn	Priest's Village
Derby	Deer Village	Preston	Priest's Village
Derwent	Oak River	Prestwick	Priest's Outlying Farm
Devizes	Boundaries	Purbeck	Bittern's Beak
Diss	Ditch	Purley	Pear-Tree Wood
Ely	Eel	Ramsey	Land of Wild Garlic
Epping	Look-out Place	Ramsgate	Raven's Gap
Falkirk	Speckled Church	Redhill	Red Slope
Gateshead	Goat's Head	Reigate	Doe Gate
Gatwick	Goat Farm	Renfrew	Current Point
Harlow	Army Mound	Rhondda	Noisy One
Harrogate	Heap of Stones Road	Ribble	Tearing One
Harwich	Military Settlement	Rievaulx	Rye Valley
Hendon	High Hill	Salford	Willow-Tree Ford
Hythe	Landing Place	Selby	Village by the Willows
Kesteven	Wood Meeting Place	Sherborne	Bright Stream
Lampeter	St Peter's Church	Skye	Wing
Leatherhead	Grey Ford	Snaefell	Snow Mountains
Lerwick	Mud Bay	Soho	Hunting Cry (named after)
Lichfield	Open Land by the Grey Forest	Solihull	Muddy Hill
		Staines	Stone
Llanfair- Pwllgwyngyllgogerych wyrndrobwillantysiliogog- ogoch	St Mary's Church in the hollow of the White Hazel	Stevenage	Place at the firm Oak
		Stranraer	Fat Peninsula
		Streatham	Home by a Roman Road
		Surrey	Southern District
Lundy	Puffin (Norse meaning)	Sussex	South Saxons
Malpas	Bad Step	Sutton	Southern Farm
March	Boundary	Swindon	Pig Hill
Margate	Sea Gate	Tay	Silent One
Matlock	Assembly Oak	Tees	Seething One
Melrose	Bare Moor	Tenby	Little Fort
Menai	Carrying	Tintagel	Throat Fort
Merton	Farm by a Pool	Tobermory	St Mary's Well
Morecambe	Curved Sea	Tranmere	Cranes
Morpeth	Murder Path	Tresco	Elder-Tree Farm
Moulton	Mule's Settlement	Tring	Tree-covered Hillside
Neasden	Nose-shaped Hill	Trossachs	Transverse Hills
Neath	Shining One	Unst	Abode of Eagles
Nottingham	Home of Snot's People		

World Place Names: meanings

Name	Meaning	Name	Meaning
Aachen	Water Springs	Bruges	Bridge
Acapulco	Conquered City	Brussels	Marsh Room
Accra	Ant	Bulawayo	Place of the Massacre
Aceldama	Field of Blood	Bulgaria	Mixed Race
Acropolis	Citadel	Burkina Faso	Land of the Worthy Men
Addis Ababa	New Flower	Cairo	The Fort
Africa	People of the Dusty Land	Calvary	Skull
Agadir	Wall	Cambrai	Crayfish
Agulhas, Cape	Needle	Canada	Camp
Ajaccio	Resting Place	Canberra	Meeting Place
Alamo	Cottonwood	Carlow	Four Lakes
Alaska	Great Land	Carmel	Garden
Amritsar	Immortal Lake	Carthage	New Town
Anatolia	Sunrise East	Casablanca	White House
Angostura	Strait Narrows	Cayman Islands	Alligator
Anguilla	Eel	Ceylon	Lion
Annapurna	Abundant Food	Chattanooga	Rock Rising to a Point
Antananarivo	City of a Thousand	Chicago	Garlic Place
Antofagasta	Hidden Copper	Chittagong	White Village
Antrim	One House	Clonmel	Meadow of Honey
Antwerp	Wharfside	Comoros	Moon
Appenzell	Abbot's Cell	Conakry	Over the Water
Aquitaine	Water Land	Coney Island	Rabbit Island
Arabia	Tent Dweller	Copenhagen	Merchant's Port
Aral Sea	Island Sea	Cork	Marsh
Aran Islands	Kidney Islands	Costa Dorada	Gold Coast
Ararat	Mountain of Sorrow	Costa Rica	Rich Coast
Ardennes	Land of Forests	Cotonou	Dead Person Lagoon
Argentina	Land of Silver	Cotopaxi	Shining Mountain
Arizona	Dry Region	Cyprus	Copper
Arnhem	Sand Homestead	Dahomey	On the Stomach of Dan
Asturias	Rock Water	Dalmatia	Young Animal
Atacama	Black Duck	Danube	River of Sheep
Australia	Southern Land	Dar es Salaam	House of Peace
Austria	Eastern Borderland	Darjeeling	Diamond Island (literal)
Azores	Goshawks		aka Place of the
Babylon	Gate of the Gods		Thunderbolt
Baden	Baths	Davos	Behind
Baghdad	Gift of God	Deauville	Damp Plain
Bahrain	Two Seas	Dijon	Divine
Baku	Windward	Djibouti	Plate
Bangkok	Region of Olive Trees	Dnieper	Far River
(see Krung Thep)		Dodecanese	Twelve Islands
Bangui	Rapids	Dominica	Lord's Day
Banjui	Rope Matting	Donegal	Fort of Foreigners
Barbados	Bearded	Drakensberg	Dragon Mountain
Basse-Terre	Low Land	Druk Yul (see Bhutan)	Land of the Dragon
Baton Rouge	Red Stick	Dublin	Black Pool
Beijing	Northern Capital	Dubrovnik	Oak Forest
Beirut	The Wells	Dumbarton	Fort of the Britons
Belfast	Mouth of the Sandbank	Dunkirk	Dune Church
Belgrade	White City	Dunsinane	Hill of the Teat
Belorussia	White Russia	Dushanbe	Monday
Bern	Bear	Egypt	Temple of Soul Ptah
Bethany	House of Poverty	Eindhoven	End Property
Bethlehem	House of Bread	Ephesus	Overseer
Bethphage	House of Figs	Eritrea	Red
Betws-y-Coed	Chapel in the Woods	Ethiopia	Burnt Appearance
Bhutan (see Druk Yul)	End of Tibet	Faeroes	Islands of Sheep
Bihar	Monastery	Fair Isle	Islands of Sheep
Bikini	Surface Coconut	Formosa	Beautiful
Bizerta	Stable Flowing Through	Franche-Comté	Free County
Bloemfontein	Fountain of Flowers	Fray Bentos	Brother Benedict
Boise	Wooded	Galapagos	Giant Tortoise
Bosporus	Oxford	Gallipoli	Beautiful Town
Brindisi	Deer	Galway	Stony
Brno	Clay	Gangtok	Hill Summit

G
E
O
G
R
A
P
H
Y

Name	Meaning	Name	Meaning
Geelong	Marshy Place	Lesbos	Wooded
Gelderland	Yellow Mountain	Levant	Rising
Georgia	Fertile Earth/Tilled Land	Lhasa	City of the Gods
Ghent	Confluence	Liepaja	Lime Tree
Gibraltar	Mountain of Tariq	Limburg	Lime-Tree Fortress
Grasse	Fat	Limerick	Bare Area of Ground
Graubunden	Grey League	Limoges	Elm-Tree Village
Graz	Small Fort	Limpopo	Crocodile River
Greece	Venerable	Linkoping	Flax Market
Gretna	Gravel Hill	Linz	Lime Tree
Groningen	Green	Lisburn	Fort of the Gamblers
Grozny	Awesome	Lodz	Boat
Guadalajara	River of Stones	Lofoten	Fox Foot
Guadalupe	River Wolf	Lombardy	Long Beards/Axes
Guatemala	Land of the Eagle	Longjumeau	New Market
Haarlem	Height Silt	Los Angeles	City of Angels
Haiphong	Sea Room	Luanda	Tax
Haiti	Mountain Land/Nest	Luxembourg	Little Fort
Hanoi	Inside the River	Machu Picchu	Old Man Peak
Hanover	High Bank	Malaga	Queen
Harbin	Place Where Fish is Dried	Malmo	Mineral Island
Harfleur	High Estuary	Managua	Rain Spirit
Harlech	Beautiful Rock	Manama	Place of Rest/Dreams
Harz	Forest	Mandalay	Circle
Hawaii	Place of the Gods	Marathan	Fennel
Hebron	To Unite	Marianske Lazne	Mary's Springs
Hekla	Cloak	Marmara	Marble
Hokkaido	North Sea Province	Marrakesh	Fortified
Holm	Island	Massachusetts	People of the Big Hill
Honshu	Main District	Mato Grosso	Dense Forest
Huang Hai	Yellow Sea	Matsuyama	Pine Mountain
Huang Ho	Yellow River	Mayo	Plain of the Yew Tree
Hunan	South of the Lake	Meath	Middle
Hyderabad	Lion Town	Mecca	Ruined/Sanctuary
Ibadan	Worship	Mechelen	Meeting Place
Ibiza	Island of Perfumes	Medina	The City
Inchon	Virtue River	Melanesia	Black Islands
Iona	Yew Tree	Memphis	His Beauty
Irian Jaya	Cloud-Covered Victory	Mesopotamia	Between the Rivers
Jaffa	Beautiful	Monaghan	Little Thickets
Japan	Sun Origin	Monte Carlo	Charles's Mountain
Jericho	Moon Month	Montenegro	Black Mountain
Johore	To Tie	Montreal	Royal Mountain
Kanchenjunga	Five Treasures of the Snow	Morocco	Far West
Kara Kum	Black Sands	Munich	Monk
Katmandu	Wooden Temples	Munster	Monastery
Kattegat	Boat Way	Muscat	Hidden
Kawasaki	River Cape	Myanmar	The Strong
Kazan	Cauldron	Nairobi	Marsh
Khartoum	End of Elephant's Trunk	Nanking	Southern Capital
Kildare	Church of the Oak	Narvik	Narrow Bay
Kilimanjaro	Mountain of the God of Cold	Natal	Christmas
Killarney	Church of the Sloes	N'Djamena	Resting Place
Kobe	House of God	Negev	South
Koblenz	Confluence	Nepal	Fly Down
Kosovo	Blackbird	Netherlands	Lower Land
Kronstadt	Crown City	Neuchâtel	New Castle
Krung Thep (see Bangkok)	City of Angels	Neustria	New Western Kingdom
		Nevada	Snowy
		New York (named after)	Future James II
Kuala Lumpur	Mouth of the Muddy River	Newry	Yew Tree
Kyushu	Nine Provinces	Nicosia	Victory
Kyzyl Kum	Red Sand	Nijmegen	New Market
Labrador	Labourer	Nîmes	Sanctuary
Lagos	Lakes	Norrkoping	Northern Trading Place
Las Vegas	Meadows	Nova Scotia	New Scotland
Latakia	People Ruler	Nullarbor	No Trees
Lebanon	White	Oahu	Place of Assembly
Leipzig	Lime Tree	Omaha	Those Who Live Upstream on the River
Leitrim	Grey Ridge		

Name	Meaning	Name	Meaning
Omsk	Calm	Saskatoon	Fruit of Tree of Many Branches
Orinoco	Place of Paddling		
Oruro	Black and White	Schaffhausen	Sheep House
Osnabrück	Current Bridge	Shaba	Copper
Pacific	Calm	Shikoku	Four Provinces
Padua	Pine	Shiraz	Good Grape
Pagalu	Father Cockerel	Sichuan	Four Rivers
Pakistan	Land of the Pure	Sierra Leone	Lion Mountains
Palermo	Safe Anchorage	Sierra Madre	Mother Range
Palestine	Land of the Philistines	Sierra Nevada	Snowy Mountains
Pamplona	Pompey's City	Sikkim	Summit
Panmunjom	Floor Gate Shop	Singapore	Lion House
Papeete	Water Basket	Smolensk	Tar
Pemba	Green Island	Society Islands (after)	Royal Society
Peshawar	Frontier Town	Solferino	Sulphur
Petra	Rock	Soweto (acronym)	South Western Townships
Philadelphia	Brotherly Love	Sporades	Disseminated
Philippines (named after)	Philip II of Spain	Sri Lanka	Island of the Blessed
Phnom Penh	Mountain of Plenty	Srinagar	City of Happiness
Picardy	Pike	Stromboli	Round
Piedmont	Foot of the Mountain	Stuttgart	Mares Garden
Plovdiv	Philip's Town	Sudan	Land of the Blacks
Po	Pines	Sulawesi	Spear Iron
Pomerania	By the Sea	Surabaya	Hero Danger
Pompeii	Five	Tabor	Navel
Pont-L'Évêque	Bishop's Bridge	Taipei	Northern Taiwan
Popocatepetl	Smoking Mountain	Taiwan	Terrace Bay
Port Louis (named after)	Louis XV of France	Tegucigalpa	Silver Mountain
Portugal	Warm Harbour	Tehran	Level
Potomac	Where Goods are Brought in	Tel Aviv	Hill Spring
Potsdam (Germany)	Under the Oaks	Temirtau	Mountain of Iron
Prague	Threshold	Teplice	Warm
Praia	Beach	Texas	Friends
Prince Edward Isle (named after)	Father of Queen Victoria	Thailand	Free People
		Tigris	Arrow
Puerto Rico	Rich Harbour	Timor	East
Punta Arenas	Sandy Point	Tiruchchirappalli	Town of the Sacred Rock
Pusan	Pot Mountain	Tokyo	Eastern Capital
Pyongyang	Flat Land	Topeka	A Good Place to Dig Potatoes
Quebec	Place Where Waters Narrow		
		Transylvania	Beyond the Forest
Quemoy	Golden Gate	Trieste	Trade Market
Rajasthan	Land of Kings	Trinidad	Trinity
Reykjavik	Bay of Smoke	Tripoli	Three Towns
Rio de Janeiro	River of January	Tsushima	Pair of Horses
Rio Muni	Silent River	Turku	Market Place
Riyadh	Gardens	Tuscany (named after)	Etruscans
Robben Island	Seal Island	Tuvalu	Eight Standing Together
Roncesvalles	Bramble Valley	Tyre	Stone
Roquefort	Strong Rock	Ukraine	Border Country
Roscoff	Hill of the Blacksmith	Ulan Bator	Town of the Red Hero
Roubaix	Horse Stream	Ulm	Marsh
Rub-al-Khali	Empty Quarter	Utah	Mountain Men
Ryukyu	Ball of Precious Stones	Uttar Pradesh	North State
'sHertogenbosch	Duke's Wood	Xinjiang	New Frontier
Sahara	Desert	Yucatan	Massacre
Sakhalin	Black River	Zagreb	Beyond the Bank
Samos	Dune	Zamora	Emerald
Santo Domingo	Holy Sunday	Zanzibar	Black Coast
Sapporo	Pavillion of Banknotes	Zermatt	At the Pasture
Saratov	Yellow Mountain	Zhengzhou	Solemn Region
Sarayevo	Palace	Zimbabwe	House of Stones
Saskatchewan	Rapid Flowing River		

GEOGRAPHY

Places: alternative names

Aachen	Aix-La-Chapelle	Lake Constance	Bodensee
Almaty	Alma-Ata	Lake Geneva	Lac Léman
Banaba	Ocean Island	Lake Gennesaret	Sea of Galilee
Bangkok	Krung Thep	Lake Tiberias	Sea of Galilee
Bavaria	Bayern	Le Havre	Newhaven
Belarus	Belorussia	Lhasa	Forbidden City
Belfast	Athens of Ireland	Liberec	Reichenburg
Bermuda	Somers Islands	Lindisfarne	Holy Island
Bhutan	Druk Yul	Livorno	Leghorn
Bioko	Fernando Po	London	The Smoke
Bogotá	Santa Fé de Bogotá	Lushun	Port Arthur
Boston	Athens of the New World	Macao	Aomin
Bulgaria	Narodna Republic	Munich	München
Burma	Myanmar	New Orleans	The Big Easy
Cairo	Al-Qāhirah	New York	The Big Apple
China	Cathay	New Zealand	Pig Island
Christiansted	Bassin	Niue	Savage Island
Cordoba	Athens of the West	Osaka	Venice of Japan
Croagh Patrick, Mt	Reek	Peking	Beijing – Celestial City
Edinburgh	Athens of the North	Persian Gulf	Arabian Gulf
Egypt	Misr	Regensburg	Ratisbon
Florence	Firenze	Rio Grande	Rio Bravo
Gambier Islands	Mangareva Islands	Rome	Eternal City
Godthaab	Nuuk	Sousse	Susa
Golgotha	Calvary	Sweden	Sverige
Gravelly Hill Interchange	Spaghetti Junction	Switzerland	Confederation
Grenada	Isle of Spice		of Helvetia
Istanbul	Stamboul	Sydney	The Big Smoke
Japan	Nihon – Nippon	Thessaloníki	Salonika
K2	Godwin Austen	Turin	Torino
Korea	Choson	Victoria (Mt)	Tomaniivi (Fiji)

Places: former names

Albany (NY)	Fort Orange	Duarte (Mt)	Trujillo (Dominican Republic)
Almaty	Zailiyskoye (1854–55), Verny (1855–1921)	Dunaujváros	Sztalinvaros (Hungary)
		Dushanbe	Stalinabad
Alvernia (Mt)	Como Hill (Bahamas)	East Timor	Portuguese Timor
Annapolis	Providence, Town of Proctor's, Town at the Severn, Anne Arundel Town	Edirne	Adrianople
		Equatorial Guinea	Spanish Guinea
		Ethiopia	Abyssinia
Astana	Akmola	Frunze	Pishpek
Bangladesh	East Bengal (until 1947), East Pakistan (1947–70)	Ghana	Gold Coast
		Grenada	Conception
Belize	British Honduras (until 1973)	Guinea	French Guinea
Benin	Dahomey (until 1975)	Guinea-Bissau	Portuguese Guinea
Bermuda	Somers Islands	Guyana	British Guiana
Bioko	Macias Nguema Biyogo (1973–79)	Harare	Salisbury
Black Sea	The Euxine	Hawaii	Sandwich Islands
Bodrum	Halicarnassus	Ho Chi Minh City	Saigon
Bolivia	Upper Peru	Indonesia	Dutch East Indies
Botswana	Bechuanaland (until 1966)	Iran	Persia
Bujumbura	Usumbura	Iraq	Mesopotamia
Burkina Faso	Upper Volta (until 1984)	Istanbul	Constantinople, Byzantium
Burundi	Urundi	Izmir	Smyrna
Cambodia	Kampuchea, Khmer Empire	Iznik	Niacaea
Canada	New France	Jordan	Transjordan
Cape Horn	Elizabetha	Kathmandu	Manju-Patan
Central African Republic	Ubanghi Shari	Katowice	Stalinogrod
		Kinshasa	Léopoldville (until 1966)
Congo, Dem	Zaïre, Belgian Congo, Congo	Kiribati	Gilbert Islands
Dardanelles	Hellespont	Klagenfurt	Chlagenvurt
Djakarta	Sunda Kelapa	Klondyke	River of Fish
Djibouti	French Somaliland	Kota Kinabalu	Jesselton
Donetsk	Stalino	Kyrgyzstan	Khirgizia

Ladoga	Neva
Ladysmith	Windsor
Lahore	Lava
Lahti	Bay (Finland)
Le Mans	Cenomannis
Le Puy	Podium
Leningrad	St Petersburg (1703–1914 and 1991 to present), Petrograd (1914–24)
Lesotho	Basutoland
Malawi	Nyasaland
Mali	French Sudan
Maputo	Lourenço Marques
Marianske Lazne	Marienbad
Mariupol	Zhdanov
Marseille	Ville-sans-Nom
Mauritius	Île de France
Micronesia	Caroline Islands
Moldova	Moldavia, Bessarabia
Mongolian People's Republic	Outer Mongolia
Montreal	Ville Marie
Myanmar	Burma
Namibia	South West Africa
N'Djamena	Fort-Lamy
New Britain	Neu-Pommern
New York	New Amsterdam (1625–64)
Novokuznetsk	Stalinsk
Novomoskovsk	Stalinogorsk
Nuuk	Godthaab
Olympia	Smithfield
Oman	Muscat and Oman
Oslo	Kristiania
Ottawa	Bytown
Palm Beach	Palm City
Palm Springs	Agua Caliente
Palmyra	Tadmor
Pittsburgh	Fort Duquesne
Prince Edward Island	Île Saint-Jean
Princeton	Stony Brook
Puerto Rico	San Juan (Puerto Rico was then capital)

Réunion	Île Bonaparte, Île Bourbon, Île Mascareigne
Richmond (Eng)	Sheen
Seychelles	Seven Sisters
Shaba	Katanga
Shenyang	Mukden
Sofia	Serdica
Sousse	Hadrumetum
Sparta	Lacedaemonia
Sri Lanka	Ceylon, Serendip
Stepanakert	Khankendy
Suriname	Dutch Guiana
Tahiti	King George III Island, Nouvelle-Cythère
Taiwan	Formosa
Tanzania	Tanganyika
Tasmania	Van Diemen's Land
Thailand	Siam
Tiruchchirappalli	Trichinopoly
Toronto	York
Troy	Ilium
Tuvalu	Ellice Islands
Ubangi-Shari	French Equatorial Africa
Ulyanovsk	Simbirsk
Uskudar	Scutari
United Arab Emirates	Trucial States
Vanuatu	New Hebrides
Volgograd	Tsaritsyn (1589–1925) Stalingrad (1925–61)
Western Sahara	Spanish Sahara
Yangon	Rangoon
Yemen	Aden
Zambia	Northern Rhodesia
Zanzibar	Shirazi
Zimbabwe	Southern Rhodesia (1911–64) Rhodesia (1964–79) Zimbabwe Rhodesia (1979–80)

GEOGRAPHY

World's Longest Rivers

		Source	Length (miles)	Course and Outflow
1	Nile	Kagera River, Burundi	4,145	Tanzania/Uganda/Sudan/Egypt to eastern Mediterranean.
2	Amazon	Apurimac River, Peru	4,007	Colombia to Brazil to South Atlantic (Canal do Sul).
3	Mississippi-Missouri	Jefferson (Red Rock) River, Montana	3,710	N and S Dakota/Nebraska/Iowa/Missouri/ Kansas/Illinois/Kentucky/Tennessee/ Arkansas/Mississippi/Louisiana to Gulf of Mexico. Although the Missouri is a tributary of the Mississippi, it is also an extension via Lake Itasca (see individual entries), so the system is made up of the total length of the Missouri and 1,395 miles of the Mississippi.
4	Yenisey	Selenga River, Mongolia	3,442	Flows due north through central Russia to the Kara Sea.
5	Yangtze (Chang-Jiang)	Kunlun Mts, China	3,436	Flows in an easterly course across China to the East China Sea near Shanghai.
6	Yellow River (Huang Ho)	Qinghai, China	3,395	Flows north of the Yangtze in an easterly course to the Yellow Sea.
7	Ob'-Irtysh	Altai Mts, Russia	3,361	Northern course touching Kazakhstan and through Russia to Kara Sea.
8	Paraná	Paranáiba and Grande confluence, Brazil	3,032	Flows south via Paraguay border and Argentina into confluence with River Uruguay to the Rio de la Plata (River Plate) estuary in the South

		Source	Length (miles)	Course and Outflow
9	Zaïre (Congo)	Chambeshi River, Zambia	2,920	Atlantic near Buenos Aires. The system is aka Rio de la Plata-Paraná. Called Lualaba in Dem Rep of Congo. Runs along Congo border into Atlantic at Angola.
10	Amur-Argun	China	2,782	See individual entries of the 2 rivers.
11	Lena	Kirenga River, Siberia	2,734	Russia and northward to Laptev Sea in the Arctic Ocean.
12	Mackenzie-Peace	Finlay/Parsnip confluence, BC	2,635	Flows eastwards to Alberta and then north via NWT to Beaufort Sea. The system is linked by the Slave River between Lake Athabasca and the Great Slave Lake.
13	Mekong	Lants'ang, Tibet	2,600	China/Burma/Laos/Thailand/Cambodia/Vietnam to South China Sea.
14	Niger	Loma Mts, Guinea	2,590	Flows through Mali, Niger and along Benin border into Nigeria before discharging into the Gulf of Guinea in the Atlantic.
15	Murray-Darling	New England Plateau, NSW/Queensland	2,330	See individual entries of the 2 rivers.
16	Zambesi	Kalene Hill, Zambia	2,200	Flows south across Angola and western Zambia, then north-eastward forming the border between Zambia and Zimbabwe, and finally south-eastward across Mozambique to its delta on the Indian Ocean.
17	Volga	Valdai Hills, nr Moscow	2,193	Flows generally south-eastward to discharge into the Caspian Sea in Russia. The Volga is considered the longest river in Europe as the longer Russian rivers flow east of the Urals which are considered the boundary into Asia.
18	Madeira	Mamoré and Beni Rivers, Bolivia	2,082	Joins the Amazon 90 miles east of Manaus, it is the 2nd longest tributary in the world.
19	Jurua	Puerto Portillo, Peru	2,040	Flows east and north into Brazil before joining the Amazon south of Fonte Boa.
20	Purus	Loreto Department, Peru	1,995	Flows north and east into Brazil to join the Amazon upstream from Manaus (Solimões River).

NB: A usual definition of a river might be 'a freshwater channelled body of water that flows from its source into another river, a lake, the sea, or an inland desert', in which case the Missouri and Mississippi Rivers would make the above listing as separate entries. However, the table above includes the system as a whole and both the rivers are dealt with individually below. The alphabetic listing is for ease of reference, as in many of the sections, but is in no way an attempt to be fully comprehensive; it is merely a useful gazetteer of some interesting rivers.

Other Notable Rivers

	Source	Length (miles)	Course and Outflow
Achelous (Akhelóös)	Pindus Mountains	140	Divides Aetolia from Acarnania and discharges into the Ionian Sea.
Amu Darya (Oxus)	Eastern Pamirs	1,578	Follows the Afghanistan/Tajikistan border and then the Turkmenistan/Uzbekistan border before discharging into the Aral Sea. The source of the Amu Darya is often thought to be the confluence of the Vakhsh and Pyandzh rivers but in fact its longest headstream is the Daryã-ye Vãkhjir in the Eastern Pamirs.
Amur	Russia/China	1,755	Tatar Strait of the Pacific Ocean.
Argun	Khingan range, China	1,007	Joins Amur at the confluence of the Shilka.
Arkansas	Sawatch range of Rocky Mountains	1,459	Flows east-southeastward to the Mississippi at Arkansas City via Kansas and Oklahoma.
Arno	Monte Falterona, Tuscan Apennines	150	Flows westwards via Florence and Pisa to the Ligurian Sea area of the Mediterranean.
Athabasca	Columbia Icefield, Canadian Rockies	765	Forms the southernmost part of the Mackenzie River system in northern Alberta and discharges into Lake Athabasca.
Avon	Devizes, Wiltshire	48	Aka Hampshire Avon or East Avon, flows generally south via Salisbury to the English Channel at Christchurch Harbour.

	Source	Length (miles)	Course and Outflow
Avon (Lower)	Cotswolds	75	Aka Bristol Avon, flows through Gloucester, Wiltshire, and Avon before entering the Bristol Channel via the Severn estuary, at Avonmouth, the ocean port of Bristol.
Avon (Upper)	Naseby, Leicester/Northants border	96	Aka Warwickshire Avon, flows generally south-westward through Northants, Leicestershire, Warwickshire, and Hereford and Worcester before joining the Severn at Tewkesbury, Gloucs.
Axe	Beaminster, Dorset	24	Flows westward to form the boundary between Dorset and Somerset before reaching Axminster in Devon and entering the English Channel south of Axmouth.
Bann	Co Down, NI	76	Longest river of Northern Ireland; flows into the Atlantic Ocean.
Black	Yunnan Province, China	498	Flows south-east into northern Vietnam parallel to the Red River, which it joins near Hanoi.
Black	Ozark Mountains, Missouri	280	Flows south-eastward to Poplar Bluff, Missouri, and then flows south-west before entering the White River near Newport, Arkansas.
Black Volta (Mouhoun)	Bobo Dioulasso, Burkina Faso	720	Flows along the border of Burkina Faso and Côte D'Ivoire with Ghana before discharging into Lake Volta in northern Ghana.
Boyne	Bog of Allen, Co Kildare	70	Flows north-east to enter the Irish Sea just south of Drogheda.
Brahmaputra	Tibetan Himalayas	1,800	Confluence with the Ganges as the Jamuna and into the Bay of Bengal in Bangladesh.
Bug	Western Ukraine	516	Flows into Poland via Brest in Belarus and discharges into the Vistula just south of Warsaw.
Camel	Davidstow, Cornwall	30	Generally flows northward into the Celtic Sea at Padstow.
Cher	North-west Massif Central, France	217	Flows north across the Combrailles Plateau, eventually reaching the Loire at Cinq-Mars-la-Pile.
Cimarron	Capulin Mt Monument, New Mexico	698	Flows eastwards past the Black Mesa peak in Oklahoma and into Kansas via Colorado before re-entering Oklahoma and discharging into the Arkansas River near Tulsa.
Clyde	Lowther Hills, Strathclyde	98	Flows north-westerly into the Firth of Clyde.
Colorado	Rockies, Colorado	1,450	Flows south-west to the Gulf of California.
Colorado	Grande and Barrancas confluence	530	Flows south-eastward across Patagonia and into the Atlantic Ocean south of Bahia Blanca.
Columbia	Rockies, British Columbia	1,243	Flows south through central Washington to the Oregon border and then due west before discharging into the Pacific Ocean.
Danube	Black Forest, Germany	1,775	Flows through Germany, Austria, Czech Republic, Hungary, Croatia, Yugoslavia, Bulgaria, Romania, Moldova, and into the Black Sea in the Ukraine.
Darling	New England Plateau, NSW Queensland	1,702	Follows the NSW/Queensland border into NSW to join the Murray at Wentworth, on the Victoria border. Longest river of Australia.
Dee	Cairngorms	87	Famous for its salmon, the Dee flows easterly to the North Sea at Aberdeen. The 17-mile stretch of the Dee between Braemar and Ballater has become known as 'Royal Deeside' because Balmoral Castle is a popular holiday retreat of the Royal Family.
Dee	Snowdonia National Park	70	Flows via Lake Bala and then north-east to Corwen and eastward past Llangollen before travelling northward to Chester and out to the Irish Sea at Flint.
Dee	Dumfries and Galloway	50	Flows south and enters the Solway Firth at Kircudbright.
Delaware	Schoharie County, New York	405	Flows along the border between New York and Pennsylvania, New Jersey and Pennsylvania, and Delaware and New Jersey before discharging into the Atlantic Ocean at Delaware Bay.
Demerara	Central Guyana	215	Flows northward to the Atlantic Ocean at Georgetown.
Derwent	Tasmania	107	Flows south-east to the Tasman Sea.
Derwent	Peak District	60	Flows south-east through Derby to the River Trent.

GEOGRAPHY

	Source	Length (miles)	Course and Outflow
Derwent	Fylingdales Moor	57	Flows south joining the Ouse just west of the Humber estuary.
Derwent	Borrowdale Fells, Cumbria	34	Flows north and west to the Irish Sea.
Dnestr	Carpathian Mountains	877	Flows south from Ukraine into Moldova before emptying into the Black Sea.
Dnieper (Dnepr)	Valdai Hills, Smolensk	1,367	Flows through Russia, Belarus and the Ukraine into the Black Sea.
Don	Novomoskovsk, Russia	1,224	Flows south and discharges into the Gulf of Taganrog in the Sea of Azov.
Don	Grampians	78	Flows south-eastward into the North Sea at the Bridge of Don.
Douro	Sierra de Urbión, Spain	556	Flows across Spain and northern Portugal to the Atlantic Ocean at Foz do Douro.
Dunajec	Tatra Mountains, Czech/Polish border	156	Flows north-east across Poland into the Vistula.
Ebro	Fontibre, Cantabrian Mts	565	Longest river in Spain. Flows in a south-easterly direction via Zaragosa and into the Balearic Sea area of the Mediterranean.
Eden	Lake District Fells	90	Flows north-westward to the Irish Sea at the Solway Firth inlet.
Elbe	Czech/Polish border	724	Flows westward through Czech Republic (where it is known as the Labe) until it starts a north-westerly run east of Prague through Germany to discharge into the North Sea.
Euphrates	South-west Turkey	1,700	Flows in south-easterly direction through northern Syria and Iraq to the Persian Gulf.
Exe	The Chains, Somerset	60	Flows south across Devon and into the English Channel at Exmouth.
Forth	Ben Lomond	65	Flows eastward into the Firth of Forth, near Kincardine.
Frome	Evershot, Dorset	40	Flows eastward into Poole Harbour at Wareham.
Gambia	Guinea Republic	700	Flows westwards via the Gambia into the Atlantic Ocean.
Ganges	Indian Himalayas	1,553	Confluence with the Brahmaputra as the Jamuna and into the Bay of Bengal in Bangladesh.
Garonne	Spanish Pyrenees	357	Flows north-east to Toulouse then north-west to the Bay of Biscay via the Gironde estuary.
Great Ouse	Brackley, Northants	150	Flows through Buckinghamshire, Bedfordshire and Cambridgeshire before discharging into the North Sea at the Wash.
Hudson	Lake Tear of Clouds, New York State	315	Flows south-eastward to Corinth in Saratoga County and then north-eastwards to Hudson Falls before travelling south to New York Bay.
Hunter	Mt Royal Range, New South Wales	287	Flows south-west through Glenbawn Reservoir before entering the Tasman Sea at Newcastle.
Iguaçu	Serra do Mar, Brazil	808	Flows westward before joining the Paraná at border of Argentina, Brazil and Paraguay.
Indus	Tibet	1,790	Runs through Pakistan from north to south and discharges into the Arabian Sea.
Irrawaddy	Northern Myanmar	1,337	Flows south through Mandalay and eventually west of Yangon into the Andaman Sea.
Isar	Karwendelgebirge, Innsbruck, Austria	183	Flows into Germany at Scharnitz Pass then after travelling through Munich enters the Danube.
James	Jackson and Cowpasture confluence, Virginia	340	Flows in an easterly direction, crossing the Blue Ridge Mountains near Lynchburg and continuing past Richmond into the southern end of Chesapeake Bay at the Hampton Roads.
Jordan	Mount Hermon, Syria	223	Lowest river in the world, flows south across Israel and into Jordan before draining into the Dead Sea. The distance between the Sea of Galilee and the Dead Sea is approximately 100 miles and yet the Jordan's length is double that distance due to its meandering course. The Jordan became the cease-fire line during the Israeli–Jordanian hostilities.
Jumna (Yamuna)	Jamnotri, Himalayas	855	Flows from Uttar Pradesh along the border with Haryăna and then via Delhi to the Agra Canal before joining the Ganges at its most sacred point.
Liffey	Wicklow Mountains	50	Flows through Co Wicklow, Kildare and Dublin before entering the Irish Sea at Dublin Bay.

	Source	Length (miles)	Course and Outflow
Limpopo	Witwatersrand, South Africa	1,100	Rises as the Crocodile River and flows in an arc first north-east and then east, forming the border between Transvaal and Botswana and then Transvaal and Zimbabwe before veering south-east into Mozambique and into the Indian Ocean north of Maputo. It becomes the Limpopo at the Crocodile's confluence with the Marico on the Transvaal/Botswana border.
Loire	Southern Massif Central	634	Longest river in France. Flows north and west towards the Brittany peninsula, where it discharges into the Bay of Biscay in the Atlantic Ocean.
Mackenzie	Great Slave Lake, NWT, Canada	1,060	Beaufort Sea in Arctic Ocean.
Magdalena	Colombian Andes	930	Flows northward to the Caribbean Sea.
Manzanares	El Pardo Reservoir, Madrid	42	Minor river that discharges into a canal system south of Madrid, it is notable only for being the river on which Madrid stands (at over 2,100′ the highest capital of Europe).
Marañón	Peruvian Andes	879	Flows northwest from northeast Peru before receiving the Huallaga River and combining with the Ucayali River, to form the Amazon.
Marne	Langres, Plateau de Langres, France	326	Flows north-northwest past Chaumont and Saint-Dizier, then turns west-northwest to Epernay before veering south of Paris and discharging into the Seine at Charenton.
Medina	St Catherine's Downs	13	Flows from the south of the Isle of Wight to its northern outflow into the Solent.
Medway	East Grinstead, West Sussex	70	Follows the Sussex/Kent boundary to Ashurst before turning north-east to the Thames at the Sheerness delta. Traditionally those born in Kent west of the Medway are called Kentish Men, and those born east of the Medway, Men of Kent.
Merrimack	White Mts, New Hampshire	110	Flows southward into Massachusetts before veering north-east to empty into the Atlantic.
Mersey	Confluence of Goyt, Etherow, Tame	70	Flows eastward to the Irwell and the Manchester Ship Canal.
Meuse	Pouilly, Plateau de Langres, France	590	Flowing north through Belgium and the Netherlands to the North Sea.
Mississippi	Lake Itasca, Minnesota	2,348	Gulf of Mexico.
Missouri (Big Muddy)	Beaverhead Co, Montana	2,315	Joins Mississippi 10 miles north of St Louis; it is the longest tributary in the world.
Motagua	Chichicastenango	250	Longest river in Guatemala, flowing east-north-east into the Gulf of Honduras.
Murray	Snowy Mts, NSW	1,609	Flows along the boundary of NSW and Victoria, bends south at Morgan, South Australia, and discharges into the Indian Ocean at Encounter Bay in the Great Australian Bight.
Negro	Eastern Colombia	1,400	Major tributary of the Amazon that follows the Colombian/Venezuelan border and into Brazil to join the Amazon at the Solimões confluence.
Negro	Bagé, Brazil	500	Flows south-westward into Uruguay before joining the Uruguay River at Soriano.
Negro	Chilean Andes	400	Flows south-eastward across northern Patagonia and discharges into the Atlantic Ocean south-east of Viedma and Carmen de Patagones.
Neisse (Nysa)	Sudeten Mountains	157	Forms part of the German/Polish frontier before joining the Oder River. There is another Neisse which also rises in the Sudeten Mountains but lies totally in Poland.
Nene	Northants/Leics	102	Flows north-easterly via Peterborough to the North Sea in the Wash.
Oder	Oder Mountains, Czechoslovakia	531	Flows north-east then north when it picks up the Neisse and flows into the Baltic Sea.
Ohio	Allegheny and Monongahela, Pittsburgh	981	Flows north-west out of Pennsylvania then south-westward, forming boundaries between Ohio/Kentucky, Indiana/Kentucky, and Illinois/Kentucky before joining the Mississippi at Cairo, Illinois.
Omo	Ethiopian Highlands	290	Flows south across Ethiopia before emptying into Lake Rudolf on the Ethiopia/Sudan border.

GEOGRAPHY

	Source	Length (miles)	Course and Outflow
Orange	Sinqu River, Lesotho	1,300	Flows west along the Orange Free State/Cape Province border through Upington and along the southern border of Namibia before discharging into the Atlantic Ocean at Alexander Bay.
Orinoco	Venezuela–Brazil border	1,700	Flows in a northern arc forming the boundary between Venezuela and Colombia before veering north-eastward across Venezuela and into the Atlantic Ocean near Trinidad.
Ouse	Swale and Ure Confluence	57	Flows south-east to the Humber estuary.
Parramatta	Sydney	15	Meaning 'plenty of eels'. Flows through Sydney and into Port Jackson on the Tasman Sea.
Patuca	Guayape and Guayambre confluence	200	Flows from north-eastern Honduras and crosses the Mosquito Coast before discharging into the Caribbean at Patuca Point.
Peace	Finlay River, BC, Canada	1,195	Slave River in Wood Buffalo National Park.
Pechora	Northern Urals	1,124	Flows south and then west and north across Russia before emptying into the Barents Sea.
Pecos	Mora County, New Mexico	735	Flows into Texas and empties into the Rio Grande at the Amistad National Recreation Area.
Piddle	Alton Pancras, Dorset	21	Aka the Trent, and flowing south-eastward to Poole Harbour.
Po	Monte Viso Mts, Cottian Alps	405	Longest river in Italy. Flows eastwards in its upper course then northward through Turin and finally eastward to its delta on the Gulf of Venice in the Adriatic area of the Mediterranean.
Potomac	Appalachian Mts, West Virginia	383	Forms boundary between Maryland and Virginia via Washington DC and into Chesapeake Bay.
Red River	New Mexican Plains	1,270	Flows south-eastward through Texas, Oklahoma and Louisiana and into the Gulf of Mexico via the Mississippi River near Baton Rouge.
Red River (Hong)	Yunnan Province, SW China	750	Principal river of northern Vietnam, flowing south-east across the Tonkin region through Hanoi before discharging into the Gulf of Tonkin.
Red Volta	NW of Ouagadougou, Burkina Faso	200	Flows south-south-east to join the White Volta near the Gambaga scarp, northern Ghana.
Rhine	Swiss Alps	865	Forms the boundary between Switzerland, Liechtenstein and Germany and then runs north, bordering France and Germany and finally north-westward towards the North Sea via the Netherlands.
Rhône	Swiss Alps	505	Flows into Lake Geneva and then through France, merging with the Saône at Lyons, before entering the Mediterranean west of Marseille in the Golfe du Lion.
Ribble	Gayle and Cam confluence, Yorkshire	75	Flows south into Lancashire after rounding Whernside, at 2,419′ the highest peak in the Yorkshire Dales National Park; on entering Preston it flows due west towards the Irish Sea near Lytham St Annes.
Rio Grande	Rockies, Colorado	1,885	Forms the boundary between Texas and Mexico before discharging into the Gulf of Mexico. The Rio Grande is known in Mexico as the Rio Bravo.
Salween	Eastern Tibet	1,500	Flows east and south through China and forms the border between Myanmar and Thailand before emptying into the Gulf of Martaban
São Francisco	Serra da Canastra, Minais Gerais, Brazil	1,811	The longest river totally in Brazil flows in a north-easterly direction to the Atlantic.
Sava	Triglav Mts, Slovenia	584	Flows south-east through Slovenia and Croatia and follows border of Bosnia and Herzegovina into northern Yugoslavia to discharge into the Danube at Belgrade.
Scheldt	Northern France	270	Flows north and north-east through western Belgium to Antwerp, then north-west to the North Sea in the Netherlands.
Seine	Langres Plateau, nr Dijon	485	Flows north-westerly through Paris before emptying into the English Channel near Le Havre.
Severn	Finger Lakes, Ontario	610	Flows north-east through Severn Lake to Hudson Bay.

	Source	Length (miles)	Course and Outflow
Severn (Hafren)	Plynlimon, Northern Powys	220	Flows south via Shropshire, Worcestershire, Gloucestershire, and into Bristol Channel in the Atlantic Ocean. It is the longest river in Britain.
Shannon	Tiltinbane Mts, Co Cavan	240	Flows through Leitrim and boundaries of Roscommon, Longford, Westmeath, Offaly, Galway, Tipperary, Clare, Limerick, and discharges into the Atlantic Ocean at Loop Head, Co Clare.
Shenandoah	Virginia	370	Flows north to meet the Potomac at Harper's Ferry.
Spey	Corrieyairack Forest	107	Flows north-east across the Highlands into the North Sea, east of the Moray Firth.
Spree	Lusatian Mts, Germany	250	Rising near the Czech/Polish border, the Spree flows north through Berlin and into the Havel River, a tributary of the Elbe, at Spandau.
St Lawrence	St Louis River, Minnesota	1,945	Gulf of St Lawrence in Quebec. (The St Lawrence proper is 760 miles in length, as the remainder runs from its source via the Great Lakes, except Lake Michigan.)
Stour	East Cambridgeshire	47	Flows eastward through East Anglia, forming most of the Suffolk/Essex boundary, and discharges into the North Sea at Harwich.
Stour (Dorset)	Stourhead, Wiltshire	51	Flows south-eastward through Blandford Forum and into the English Channel at Christchurch Harbour.
Stour (Great)	South of Ashford	40	Aka Kentish Stour, flows through the Weald, past Ashford to Canterbury and Sandwich and into the English Channel.
Suir	Devil's Bit Mountains	114	Flows south across Co Tipperary through Thurles before discharging into Waterford Harbour.
Susquehanna	Otsego Lake, New York State	444	Flows south through western Pennsylvania and into Chesapeake Bay in Maryland.
Sutlej (Zaradros)	Lan-ka Ts'o, SW Tibet	900	Longest of the Punjab's 'Five Rivers', flowing into India and Pakistan, where it joins the Chenāb River, west of Bahāwalpur.
Swan	Corrigin, Western Australia	224	Rises as the Avon and flows through Perth to the Indian Ocean at Fremantle.
Syr Darya	Naryn and Karadarya confluence	1,374	The Syr Darya is 1,876 miles long including the 500 miles of the Naryn. On leaving the Fergana Valley the river flows north-west via Kyrgyzstan and into the Aral Sea at Kazakhstan.
Taff	Brecon Beacons	38	Flows southwards through Merthyr Tydfil, Pontypridd and finally Cardiff.
Tagus	Sierra de Albarracin, Spain	626	Flows westward into Portugal before discharging into the Atlantic Ocean near Lisbon.
Tamar	Woolley, Morwenstow	61	Flows south along the border between Devon and Cornwall and into the English Channel at Plymouth Sound.
Tay	Ben Lui, southern Grampians	117	Longest river in Scotland flows out to the Firth of Tay in the North Sea.
Tees	Cross Fell, Pennines	70	Flows eastwards defining the boundary of Cumbria and Durham then into Cleveland, passing through Stockton and Middlesbrough and into the North Sea.
Teifi	Strata Florida, Cambrian Mts	56	Famous for the many castle ruins along its banks, the Teifi flows generally south-westward through Lampeter and Cenarth Falls, where salmon can be seen climbing the artificial ladder up the falls, before discharging into the bay at Cardigan.
Test	Overton, nr Basingstoke, Hants	45	Famous trout river that flows southward via Winchester into Southampton Water, the last 16 miles between Romsey and Southampton Water are famous for their salmon.
Thames	Cotswolds, Gloucs	215	Flows easterly into the North Sea at Tilbury. Tributaries include the Churn, Coln, Windrush, Evenlode, Cherwell, Ock, Thame, Kennett, Loddon, Colne, Wey and Mole.
Tiber (Tevere)	Monte Fumaiolo, Apennines	252	Flows in a southerly direction through the city of Rome and into the Tyrrhenian Sea area of the Mediterranean near Ostia Antica.

GEOGRAPHY

	Source	Length (miles)	Course and Outflow
Tigris	South-west Turkey	1,180	Flows south into Iraq, through Baghdad and joins Euphrates before discharging into the Persian Gulf between Iraq and Iran.
Towy (Tywi)	Rhandirmwyn, Cambrian Mts	65	The longest river wholly in Wales, although since the damming of its main headwater in 1972 to form Llyn Brianne Reservoir it is slightly shorter than before.
Trent	Pennines, Staffordshire	170	Historically the boundary between north and south England, running south-east through the Potteries and Stoke-on-Trent, then north-east via Burton-on-Trent and Nottingham before entering the North Sea by the Humber estuary.
Tweed	Peebles	96	Flows easterly into the North Sea.
Tyne	River Rede, nr Hexham	62	Flows eastward along the Northumberland/Co Durham border before discharging into the North Sea at the Tyne estuary in Newcastle.
Urubamba	Peruvian Andes	450	Flows northward to meet the Apurimac to become the Ucayali.
Uruguay	Southern Brazil	990	Flows west through Brazil and then south-westward forming the Argentina/Brazil border before veering southward to form the Argentina/Uruguay border and discharging into the Rio de la Plata estuary at its confluence with the Paraná.
Usk	Black Mountain, Brecon Beacons	57	Flows generally south via Abergavenny and into the Bristol Channel at Newport.
Vistula (Wisła)	Beskidy Mts, Poland	664	Longest river of Poland, flows northwards via Kracow and Warsaw before entering the Baltic Sea on the Gulf of Gdansk; it is the longest river that empties into the Baltic Sea.
Vltava (Moldau)	South-west Bohemia	270	Longest river of the Czech Republic, flows north through Prague before discharging into the Elbe (Labe) at Melnik, just north of Prague.
Volta	Black and White Voltas	1,000	The extension of the Black and White Voltas through Lake Volta, discharging into the Gulf of Guinea in Ghana, near the Togo border.
Wear	Waskerley Beck, Co Durham	65	Flows south-east towards Bishop Auckland then north-east to Durham before discharging into the North Sea at Sunderland.
White Volta (Nakambe)	Ouagadougou, Burkina Faso	400	Flows generally southward into Lake Volta in northern Ghana.
Witham	Leicestershire	80	Flows through Lincoln and then south-east into the North Sea at the Wash.
Wye	Plynlimon, Northern Powys	130	Rises within 2 miles of the Severn and flows south-west into England at Hay before travelling through Hereford and back into Wales just south of Monmouth and finally through Tintern and Chepstow to discharge into the Bristol Channel at the Severn estuary.
Yare	Norfolk Broads	55	Flows through the middle of Broadland into Yarmouth and the North Sea; its tributary the Wensum flows through Norwich City.
Yarqon	Rosh ha-'Ayin	16	Flows westward north of Tel Aviv via the Plain of Sharon to the Mediterranean.
Yarra	Mt Matlock, Victoria	153	Flows west to Melbourne and discharges into Hobson's Bay, at the head of Port Phillip Bay.
Yellowstone	Yount Peak, Wyoming	671	Flows northeasterly via the Yellowstone National Park into Montana before joining the Missouri River on the border of Montana and North Dakota.
Yukon	Tagish Lake, Yukon-BC	1,875	Flows north-west into Alaska and discharges into the Bering Sea at Norton Sound.
Zaradros (Sutlej)	Lan-ka Ts'o, SW Tibet	900	Longest of the Punjab's 'Five Rivers', flowing into India and Pakistan where it joins the Chenāb River, west of Bahāwalpur.
Zeravshan	Eastern Turkestan Range	545	Flows west through Tajikistan and south-eastern Uzbekistan to Chardzhou.

Seas of the World

	Details	Sq Miles	Ocean
Adriatic	arm of the Mediterranean between Italy, Slovenia, Croatia and Yugoslavia	50,590	inland
Aegean	arm of the Mediterranean between Greece and Turkey; Crete is its southern boundary	83,000	inland
Andaman	bounded by Myanmar, Thailand, Malay Peninsula, Sumatra and the Andaman and Nicobar Islands	218,100	Indian
Arabian	bounded to the east by India, to the north by Pakistan and Iran and to the west by the Arabian Peninsula and the Horn of Africa	1,490,000	Indian
Arafura	situated between the north coast of Australia, the Gulf of Carpentaria and the south coast of New Guinea, it lies east of the Timor Sea, from which it is separated by the Torres Strait	250,000	Pacific
Azov	inland sea north of the Black Sea between Ukraine and Russia	15,000	inland
Baltic	bordered by Norway, Sweden, Denmark, Germany, Poland, Lithuania, Latvia, Estonia, Russia and Finland	147,500	Atlantic
Banda	bounded by the Moluccas and Lesser Sunda Islands	180,000	Pacific
Barents	formerly known as the Murmean Sea, bounded by the Russian and Norwegian mainlands to the south, Franz Josef Land to the north, the Norwegian and Greenland seas to the west, Spitsbergen to the north-west and the Novaya Zemlya archipelago to the east	542,000	Arctic
Beaufort	situated north of Alaska and Canada	184,000	Arctic
Bering	separates the Asian and North American continents and contains St Lawrence Island, St Matthew Island, Nunivak Island and the Pribilof Islands and the northern border of the Aleutians	875,750	Pacific
Bismarck	lies north of the Solomon Sea off the north-east coast of Papua New Guinea	15,000	Pacific
Black	inland sea lying between Turkey, Bulgaria, Romania, Moldova, Ukraine, Russia and Georgia	196,100	inland
Caribbean	deepest sea in the world, average depth about 8,000′ and maximum depth 30,249′	971,400	Atlantic
Celebes (Sulawesi)	bounded to the north by the Sulu Sea, to the east by the Sangi Islands, to the south by Celebes and to the west by Borneo	110,000	Pacific
Chukchi	situated north of the Bering Sea separating Alaska and Russia	225,000	Arctic
Coral	lies off the east coast of Australia north of the Tasman Sea	1,886,000	Pacific
East China	bounded by South Korea, Japan, Taiwan and China	256,600	Pacific
East Siberian	lying between the Laptev Sea and the Chukchi Sea	361,000	Arctic
English Channel	separates the southern coast of England from the northern coast of France; the French call the Channel 'La Manche' (the sleeve) and its minimum width of 21 miles lies between Dover and Calais	34,700	Atlantic
Flores	situated between the Lesser Sunda Islands to the south and Sulawesi (Celebes) Island to the north	93,000	Pacific
Greenland	borders Greenland to the west, Iceland and the Norwegian Sea to the south and the Arctic Ocean to the north	465,000	Arctic
Ionian	arm of the Mediterranean between Greece to the east, Sicily to the south-west and the Italian mainland to the west	49,500	inland
Irish	bounded by Scotland on the north, England on the east, Wales on the south and Ireland on the west	34,200	Atlantic
Japan	northern extension of the East China Sea, bounded by Japan and Sakhalin Island to the east and by Korea and Russia to the west	391,100	Pacific
Java	bounded by Borneo to the north and Java to the south	167,000	Pacific
Kara	situated off the northern coast of Russia between the Barents Sea and the Laptev Sea	340,000	Arctic
Laccadive	bordering the south-west coast of mainland India, Lakshadweep Islands and the Maldives	209,000	Indian
Laptev	until 1935 known as the Siberian Sea, lying between the Kara Sea and East Siberian Sea	276,000	Arctic
Ligurian	arm of the Mediterranean between the north-west coast of Italy and Corsica to the south	9,800	inland
Mediterranean	largest inland sea in the world, linked to the Atlantic in the west by the Strait of Gibraltar; it encompasses many named sea areas	966,500	inland
Molucca	merges with the Ceram Sea to the south-east and the Banda Sea to the south	77,000	Pacific
North	extends southward from the Norwegian Sea between Norway and the UK, connecting the Skagerrak with the English Channel	164,900	Atlantic
Norwegian	bordered by the Greenland and Barents seas, Norwegian mainland, Shetland and Faeroe islands, Icelandic mainland, Jan Mayen Island, North Sea and Atlantic Ocean	712,000	Atlantic
Okhotsk	bounded by the east Russian mainland, Japan and the Kuril Islands	537,500	Pacific

GEOGRAPHY

Details		Sq Miles	Ocean
Philippine	lying east of the Philippines and Japan, its southern boundary includes the Caroline Islands, its western boundary includes Guam, and the northern boundary by the Volcano Islands to the north-east and Honshu to the north-west	400,000	Pacific
Red	inland sea extending from Suez in Egypt to the Strait of Bāb el-Mandeb in the south, it washes the shores of Egypt, Sudan, Eritrea, Ethiopia, Djibouti, Saudi Arabia and Yemen	174,900	inland
Savu	situated in the Lesser Sunda Islands between Timor and Sumba Islands	41,000	Pacific
Sea of Marmara (Propontis)	inland sea separating parts of Asian Turkey from European Turkey	4,429	inland
Solomon	lies north of the Coral Sea off the east coast of New Guinea	280,000	Pacific
South China	bounded by the Malay Peninsula, Taiwan, Philippines, Borneo, China and Vietnam	1,148,500	Pacific
Sulu	situated in the Philippine Islands north of the Celebes Sea	100,000	Pacific
Tasman	situated between the south-east coast of Australia and New Zealand	900,000	Pacific
Timor	lies south-west of the Arafura Sea off the north-west coast of Australia	235,000	Indian
Tyrrhenian	bounded by Sicily and the Italian mainland to the east and Corsica and Sardinia to the west	51,000	inland
White	lying south of the Barents Sea off the north-west coast of Russia	35,000	Arctic
Yellow	lying between the People's Republic of China to the north and west, and Korea to the east	113,500	Pacific
Zuiderzee (Southern Sea)	inlet of the North Sea washing the shores of the Netherlands	2,000	Atlantic

NB: The areas given for the above seas, as well as the following gulfs, straits and bays, are as produced by the latest world statistics, which are open to interpretation because it is not always clear at what point the waters merge. Most lists of seas only include those recognised by the International Hydrographic Bureau, and this is a controversial area as, although the reasoning is that seas not recognised are either parts of larger seas or oceans, in fact many of the seas that are recognised – e.g. the Caribbean – are also part of larger sea areas. Surely the Panama Canal links the Atlantic to the Pacific and not merely the Caribbean to the Pacific! The criterion used by the Bureau appears to be that a sea must be surrounded by large areas of land to enable it to be separately identifiable from the oceans but, apart from the inland seas noted above, all other seas are purely geographical markings. In order not to be too controversial I have given the best judgements possible of the areas usually considered as seas by cartographers in the list above, but have remained true to tradition when listing the seas by size elsewhere in this section. This will mean that although the South China Sea will be listed as the world's largest sea in the relevant section, this is inconsistent with the above table which shows the Coral Sea as the largest. If the question is asked, 'What is the largest sea in the world?' then the safe answer would be the South China Sea, which is part of the much larger Malay Sea, no longer recognised by the Bureau, but one has to be aware that large sea areas such as the Coral Sea and Arafura Sea are, rather ambiguously, classed as parts of oceans.

Seas: world's largest

		Area (Sq Miles)
1	South China	1,148,500
2	Caribbean	971,400
3	Mediterranean	966,500
4	Bering	875,750
5	Gulf of Mexico	582,100
6	Okhotsk	537,500
7	Sea of Japan	391,100
8	Hudson Bay	281,900
9	East China	256,600
10	Andaman	218,100
11	Black	196,100
12	Red	174,900

NB: The Malay Sea, which embraced the South China Sea and the Strait of Malacca, is no longer recognised by the International Hydrographic Bureau. Similarly, many other large seas (e.g. the Coral and the Arafura) would normally be included in the list but are also not recognised by the Bureau.

Straits of the World

Bass	Named by English navigator Matthew Flinders after the surgeon-explorer George Bass, the strait is 180 miles in length with an area of 28,950 sq mi; it separates the Tasman Sea area of the Pacific from the Indian Ocean. Technically it is the Tasman Sea that separates Victoria from Tasmania, but the whole of the northern coast of Tasmania borders the waters of the Bass Strait.
Belle Isle Strait	Links the Atlantic to the Gulf of St Lawrence between Newfoundland and Labrador; it is 90 miles long.
Bosporus (Bosphorus)	Links the Black Sea and the Sea of Marmara, and separates part of Asian Turkey from European Turkey. The strait is 19 miles in length.
Cabot	A 60-mile-long channel linking the Gulf of St Lawrence to the Atlantic between Newfoundland and Nova Scotia.
Cook	Links the Tasman Sea to the South Pacific between North Island and South Island, New Zealand. The Cook Strait is 14 miles wide at its narrowest point.
Dardanelles (Hellespont)	Formerly called the Hellespont, they are 38 miles long and link the Aegean Sea with the Sea of Marmara.
Davis	Links Baffin Bay and the Labrador Sea between Greenland and Baffin Island, part of the Northwest Passage linking the Atlantic to the Pacific, it is approximately 400 miles long and wide.
Denmark	Links the Greenland Sea to the North Atlantic between Greenland and Iceland. The British battleship *Hood* was sunk by the German battleship *Bismarck* in the strait on 24 May 1941.
Dover	Links the English Channel (Fr. La Manche) to the North Sea. Its width is approximately 20 miles. The French refer to this stretch of water as the Pas-de-Calais.
Florida	Links the Gulf of Mexico and the Atlantic between Florida and Cuba; it is 110 miles in length. The Spanish explorer Ponce de León was the first European to navigate the strait, in 1513.
Foveaux	Links the Tasman Sea to the South Pacific between South Island and Stewart Island, New Zealand.
Gibraltar	Links the Mediterranean Sea to the Atlantic Ocean. The western extreme is 27 miles wide between the capes of Trafalgar and Spartel and the eastern extreme is 14 miles wide between the Rock of Gibraltar (Pillars of Hercules) and Mount Hacho. The length of the strait is 36 miles and it is also known as Fretum Herculeum.
Hormuz	Links the Persian Gulf to the Gulf of Oman between Iran and the Arabian Peninsula.
Hudson	Links Hudson Bay and the Labrador Sea between Baffin Island and Quebec and is approximately 500 miles in length.
Johore	The northern arm of the Singapore Strait between Singapore Island and Johor State, Malaysia, it is 30 miles in length.
Kattegat	Links the Baltic to the North Sea (Skagerrak inlet) and separates Denmark and Sweden; it is 137 miles in length.
Magellan	Links the Atlantic and Pacific Oceans, between the mainland southern tip of South America and Tierra del Fuego. It is 350 miles in length.
Makassar	Links the Celebes Sea to the Java Sea between Borneo and Celebes; it stretches for approximately 500 miles.
Malacca	Links the Andaman Sea to the South China Sea between Sumatra and the Malay Peninsula; it is 500 miles in length and has an area of 25,000 sq miles.
Messina	Links the Tyrrhenian Sea and the Ionian Sea between Sicily and mainland Italy; it is 20 miles in length and ranges from 2 to 10 miles in width.
North Channel	Links the Irish Sea and the North Atlantic Ocean and washes the shores of Northern Ireland and Scotland. The minimum width of 13 miles lies between the Mull of Kintyre and Torr Head; it is 52 miles long.
Otranto	Links the Adriatic Sea and the Ionian Sea between Albania and Italy. Capo d'Otranto is the most easterly point in Italy and from that point the width of the strait is 40 miles.
St George's Channel	Links the Irish Sea to the Celtic Sea in the North Atlantic, its minimum width of 47 miles lies between Carnsore Point, near Rosslare, Ireland and St David's Head in Dyfed, Wales. It is 100 miles in length.
Singapore	Links the Strait of Malacca and the South China Sea between Singapore Island and the Riau Islands of Indonesia; it is 65 miles in length and 10 miles in width.
Taiwan (Formosa)	Links the South China Sea and the East China Sea between Fukien Province of China and Taiwan; its former name of Formosa means 'beautiful' in Portuguese.
Torres	Links the Coral Sea and the Arafura Sea between New Guinea to the north and Cape York Peninsula, Queensland, Australia, to the south. It is about 80 miles wide between these points. The many islands in the Torres Strait may be remnants of a land bridge that once linked Asia and Australia.
Yucatán Channel	Although not actually called a strait, it links the Gulf of Mexico and the Caribbean Sea between Cuba and Mexico, and is 135 miles in length.

GEOGRAPHY

Towns and Cities on Rivers

Town/City	River	Town/City	River	Town/City	River
Abbotsford	Tweed	Colchester	Colne	Jarrow	Tyne
Aberdeen	Dee and Don	Coldstream	Tweed	Kathmandu	Vishnumati
Adelaide	Torrens	Coleraine	Bann	Kelso	Tweed and Teviot
Albuquerque	Rio Grande	Cologne	Rhine	Khartoum	White Nile and Blue Nile
Alexandria	Nile	Concord, NH	Merrimack	Kidderminster	Stour
Alloa	Forth	Cork	Lee	Kiev	Dnieper
Amsterdam	Amstel	Cowes	Medina	Kilkenny	Nore
Anstruther	Forth	Delft	Schie	Kilmarnock	Irvine
Antwerp	Scheldt	Derby	Derwent	King's Lynn	Great Ouse
Astrakhan	Caspian Sea	Derry	Foyle	Lahore	Ravi
Augusta	Savannah	Detroit	Lake St Clair	Lancaster	Lune
Aviemore	Spey	Dewsbury	Calder	Langholm	Esk
Avignon	Rhône	Doncaster	Don	Le Havre	Seine
Babylon	Euphrates	Dorchester	Frome	Leamington Spa	Warwickshire Avon
Baghdad	Tigris	Dorking	Mole	Leeds	Aire
Baku	Caspian Sea	Dresden	Elbe	Leicester	Soar
Balmoral	Dee	Dublin	Liffey	Leipzig	Pleisse, Parthe, Elster
Bamako, Mali	Niger	Dumbarton	Clyde	Lima	Rimac
Bangkok	Chao Phraya	Dumfries	Nith	Limerick	Shannon
Bangui	Ubangi	Dundee	Tay	Limoges	Vienne
Basel	Rhine	Dunoon	Clyde	Lincoln	Witham
Basra	Shatt al Arab	Durham	Wear	Linz	Danube
Bath	Bristol Avon	Düsseldorf	Rhine	Lisbon	Tagus
Baton Rouge	Mississippi	Edinburgh	Forth, Firth of	Lisburn	Lagan
Bedford	Great Ouse	Ennis	Fergus	Littlehampton	Arun
Belfast	Lagan	Enniskillen	Erne	Liverpool	Mersey
Belgrade	Danube, Sava	Evesham	Warwickshire Avon	London	Thames
Benares	Ganges			Loughborough	Soar
Berlin	Spree	Exeter	Exe	Louisville	Ohio
Berne	Aare	Falmouth	Fa	Luton	Lea
Berwick	Tweed	Florence	Arno	Lyons	Rhône and Saône
Birkenhead	Mersey	Frankfurt am Main	Main		
Blandford Forum	Dorset Stour	Frankfurt an der Oder	Oder	Madrid	Manzanares
Bonn	Rhine and Seig	Fremantle	Swan	Maidstone	Medway
Bootle	Mersey	Geneva	Rhône	Maldon	Blackwater
Bordeaux	Garonne	Geneva	Lake Geneva	Mallow	Blackwater
Bowness	Forth	Gillingham	Medway	Manchester	Irwell
Bratislava	Danube	Glasgow	Clyde	Manchester, NH	Merrimack
Brecon	Usk	Gloucester	Severn	Mandalay	Irrawaddy
Bremen	Weser	Godalming	Wey	Maputo	Delagoa Bay
Brest, Belarus	Bug	Grantchester	Granta	Marlow	Thames
Brighouse	Calder	Grantham	Witham	Melbourne	Yarra
Bristol	Bristol Avon	Gravesend	Thames	Middlesbrough	Tees
Brussels	Senne	Greenock	Clyde	Midhurst	Rother
Bucharest	Danube tributary: Dimbovita	Grenoble	Isère	Milan	Olono
		Grimsby	Humber	Mold	Alyn
Buckhaven	Forth	Guangzhou	Zhujiang	Montreal	St Lawrence and Ottawa
Buckingham	Ouse	Guildford	Wey	Morpeth	Wansbeck
Budapest	Danube	Hamburg	Elbe	Moscow	Moskva
Buenos Aires	Rio de la Plata	Hanoi	Song-Koi (Red)	Munich	Isar
Buffalo	Lake Erie	Harrogate	Nidd	Nantes	Loire
Cairo	Nile (Rosetta and Damietta)	Harwich	Stour	Nantwich	Weaver
Calcutta	Hoogly	Haverfordwest	Cleddau	Nashville	Cumberland
Cambridge	Cam (aka Granta)	Hawick	Teviot and Slitrig	New Delhi	Jumna
Canterbury	Stour	Heidelberg	Neckar	New Orleans	Mississippi Gulf of Mexico
Cardiff	Taff	Helensburgh	Clyde		
Carlisle	Eden	Hereford	Wye	New York	Hudson
Carmarthen	Towy	Hertford	Lea	Newbury	Kennet
Chester	Dee	Ho Chi-Minh City	Saigon	Newcastle	Tyne
Chicago	Lake Michigan	Hull	Humber	Newport (Gwent)	Usk
Chichester	Lavant	Huntingdon	Ouse	Newport (I of W)	Medina
Chongqing	Yangzi	Hyderabad	Indus	Niamey, Niger	Niger
Cincinnati	Ohio	Ilkley	Wharfe	Northampton	Nene
Cockermouth	Derwent and Cocker	Indianapolis	White		
		Inverness	Ness		
		Ipswich	Orwell		

Norwich	Wensum	Rome	Tiber	Swansea	Tawe
Nottingham	Trent	Rotterdam	Rhine, Maas,	Taunton	Tone
Nuneaton	Anker		Scheldt	Tewkesbury	Severn,
Omdurman	Nile	Rugby	Warwickshire		Warwickshire
Oporto	Douro		Avon		Avon
Orléans	Loire	Rye	Rother	Thebes (Egypt)	Nile
Oxford	Thames	Salisbury	Hampshire Avon	Tidmarsh	Pang
	(Isis and		and Wily	Tintern Abbey	Wye
	Cherwell)	São Paulo	Tiete	Tipperary	Ara
Pangbourne	Thames	Seoul	Han	Tiverton	Exe
Paris	Seine	Shanghai	Hwangpu	Tonbridge	Medway
Patna	Ganges	Sheffield	Don, and Sheaf	Totnes	Dart
Peebles	Tweed	Shoreham-	Adur	Turin	Po
Perth, Australia	Swan	by-Sea		Vienna	Danube
Perth, Scotland	Tay	Shrewsbury	Severn	Wakefield	Calder
Peterborough	Nene	Sligo	Garavogue	Wareham	Frome
Philadelphia	Delaware	Southampton	Test, and Itchen	Warsaw	Vistula
Phnom Penh	Mekong	Southend-	Thames	Warwick	Warwickshire
Pisa	Arno	on-Sea			Avon
Pittsburgh	Ohio	Spalding	Welland	Washington DC	Potomac
Plock	Vistula	St Albans	Ver	Waterford	Suir
Prague	Vltava	St Ives (Cambs)	Ouse	Whalley	Calder
Preston	Ribble	St Louis	Mississippi	Whitby	Esk
Quebec	St Lawrence,	St Petersburg	Neva	Wimborne	Stour and Allen
	St Charles	Stafford	Sow	Winchester	Itchen
Reading	Thames and	Stoke	Trent	Windsor	Thames
	Kennet	Strabane	Mourne	Worcester	Severn
Richmond	Swale	Strasbourg	Ill	Wuhan	Han and Yangzi
(Yorks)		Stratford	Warwickshire	Yonkers	Hudson
Richmond (Va)	James		Avon	York	Ouse
Ripon	Ure	Stuttgart	Neckar	Zagreb	Sava
Rochester	Medway	Sunderland	Wear	Zurich	Limmat

Trenches: deepest

Trench	Deepest Point
Marianas Trench (Pacific)	Challenger Deep 35,840′
Puerto Rico Trench (Atlantic)	Milwaukee Deep 28,232′
Java Trench (Indian)	Planet Deep 23,376′
Eurasia Basin (Arctic)	Eurasia Basin 17,880′

Waterways

Aden Links the Red Sea to the Arabian Sea and borders Yemen to the north and Somalia to the south. The gulf is 920 miles in length and has an area of 205,000 sq miles.

Alaska Inlet of the North Pacific on the south coast of Alaska, and bordered by Kodiak Island to the west and Cape Spencer to the east, it has an area of 592,000 sq miles.

Alphonse XIII Canal Opened in 1926 and runs for 53 miles, linking Seville to the Atlantic via the Gulf of Cadiz.

Angel Falls Situated in the Guiana Highlands in Bolivar state, south-eastern Venezuela, on the Rio Churún, a tributary of the Caroni. At 3,212′ the falls are the highest in the world.

Aqaba North-eastern arm of the Red Sea between Saudi Arabia and the Sinai Peninsula. The gulf is 100 miles in length.

Baffin Bay Inlet of the North Atlantic with an area of 266,000 sq miles, situated between Greenland and Baffin Island.

Bengal, Bay of Inlet of the Indian Ocean bordering India, Myanmar, Sri Lanka, and the Andaman and Nicobar Islands; it occupies an area of 839,000 sq miles.

Biscay, Bay of Inlet of the North Atlantic bordering northern Spain and south-west France; it has an area of 86,000 sq miles.

Biscayne Bay Inlet of the Atlantic in south-eastern Florida; it is 40 miles in length and between 2 and 10 miles in width.

Bothnia Northern arm of the Baltic between Sweden on the west and Finland on the east.

Boyoma Falls Formerly called the Stanley Falls; situated on the Lualaba River in the Democratic Republic of Congo, it has a drop of 200′ and is the world's greatest waterfall by volume of water.

Bridgewater Canal Opened in 1761 and named after Francis Egerton, 3rd Duke of Bridgewater. The canal was built by James Brindley and originally ran for 10 miles, carrying barges over the Irwell at Barton; it was extended to Liverpool in 1776, joining the Mersey at Runcorn.

Bristol Channel Inlet of the Atlantic between South Wales and the English counties of Somerset, Devon and Cornwall.

GEOGRAPHY

Caledonian Canal   Built by Thomas Telford in 1803–21 and opened in 1822, it has 29 locks and links the east and west coasts of Scotland via the lakes of the Great Glen.

California   Aka Sea of Cortés and situated in northwestern Mexico, it is 750 miles in length and has an area of 62,000 sq miles.

Carpentaria   Inlet of the Arafura Sea indenting the north-eastern coast of Australia. The gulf has an area of 120,000 sq miles.

Cauldron Snout   Situated on the River Tees, Cumbria/Durham border, the highest waterfall in England (200′).

Churchill Falls   Discovered in 1839 by John McLean and known as the Grand Falls until 1965, when they were renamed in honour of Winston Churchill. Situated on the Churchill River, in west Labrador, Newfoundland, the falls have a drop of 245′.

Corinth   Inlet of the Ionian Sea separating the Peloponnese from mainland Greece.

Delagoa Bay   Situated on the south-east coast of Mozambique, it is 19 miles in length and 16 miles wide.

Eas a' Chuàl Aluinn   Situated in Sutherland in the Scottish Highlands in Glas Bheinn, the highest waterfall in the British Isles (658′).

False Bay   Inlet of the Atlantic, south of Cape Town, South Africa.

Finland   Eastern arm of the Baltic between Finland to the north, Estonia to the south, and Russia to the east.

Florida Bay   Triangular-shaped body of water at the southern tip of mainland Florida stretching from Cape Sable in the west, Key Largo in the east and Long Key in the south.

Fundy, Bay of   Inlet of the Atlantic between New Brunswick and Nova Scotia; it stretches for 94 miles.

Genoa   Inlet of the Ligurian Sea stretching eastwards for 90 miles around the north-west coast of Italy from Imperia to La Spezia.

Grand Canal   Waterway that splits the city of Venice from St Mark's Cathedral to Sta Chiara church; it is 2.1 miles in length.

Grand Canal (China)   Often considered a river system rather than a canal system, but much of its 1,107 miles is artificial waterway made by damming rivers and lakes. Nowadays it is treated in the same fashion as the St Lawrence Seaway and not included in lists of canals. It runs from Beijing to Hangzhou, was opened in AD 610 and has been regularly reconstructed ever since.

Grand Union Canal   Before 1929 was known as the Grand Junction Canal but was enlarged by amalgamating several canals and is now a main line between London and Birmingham and has several forks, the largest connecting to Leicester. The main sideshoots of the system are the Regent's Canal (Little Venice), the Paddington Arm to Brentford, the Aylesbury Arm, the Northampton Arm, and the Erewash Canal, which extends to the Leicester branch.

Great Australian Bight   Inlet of the Indian Ocean extending eastwards from West Cape, Western Australia, to South-West Cape, Tasmania.

Guinea   Inlet of the Atlantic washing the coasts of Liberia (Grain Coast), Côte D'Ivoire (Ivory), Ghana (Gold), Togo (Slave), Benin (Slave), Nigeria (Slave), Equatorial Guinea, Gabon, and Cameroon (Bight of Bonny).

Hauraki (North Wind)   Inlet of the South Pacific indenting eastern North Island, New Zealand, covering an area of 884 sq miles.

Houston Canal   Shipping channel running through Houston, Texas, into Galveston Bay and ultimately the Gulf of Mexico after a journey of 56.7 miles. The Houston Canal has no locks.

Hudson Bay   Inland sea bordering Manitoba, Ontario, Quebec, and Northwest Territories; it has an area of 281,900 sq miles and contains Belcher Islands, Mansel Island, Coats Island and Southampton Island. The southern section has an inlet between Ontario and Quebec (James Bay).

Islands, Bay of   Situated in the north of North Island, New Zealand, it has a shoreline of 500 miles.

James Bay   Southern extension of the larger Hudson Bay; it is 275 miles in length and 135 miles in width and contains many islands the largest being, Akimiski.

Khone Falls   Situated on the Mekong River, Laos, on the border with Cambodia, it has a drop of 45′ and is the world's second greatest waterfall by volume.

Kiel Canal (North Sea)   Stretches for 60.9 miles and links the North Sea (at the mouth of the Elbe) to Kiel Harbour on the Baltic.

Love Canal   Not a canal at all nowadays but an area of Niagara Falls, New York, which, in 1978, was the scene of the worst environmental disaster involving chemical wastes in US history. The area, which had become a dumping ground for nuclear waste, has become a byword for similar areas.

Manchester Ship Canal   Opened in 1894 and runs for 39.7 miles linking Manchester to the Irish Sea.

Mexico, Gulf of   Large body of water occupying an area of 582,000 square miles situated on the southeast coast of North America and connected to the Atlantic Ocean by the Straits of Florida and to the Caribbean Sea by the Yucatan Channel.

Mozambique Channel   Channel of the Indian Ocean between Madagascar and Mozambique which stretches for about 1,000 miles.

Niagara Falls   Situated on the Niagara River, the falls are divided into two cataracts divided by Goat Island. The larger cataract is called the Horseshoe Falls with its drop of 162′ and crest line of 2,600′; the smaller is called the American Falls with its drop of 167′ but much smaller crest line of 1,000′ across. Niagara Falls is the world's third greatest waterfall by volume of water.

Oman   Northwestern arm of the Arabian Sea between Oman and Iran, it is 350 miles in length and is linked to the Persian Gulf via the Strait of Hormuz.

Panama Canal   Connecting the Atlantic and Pacific oceans and stretching for 50.71 miles, the canal was begun by Ferdinand de Lesseps in 1879, but numerous difficulties caused its cancellation until the Hay-Bunau-Varilla Treaty of 1903 between Panama and the USA granted the United States the building rights. The engineer, John F Stevens, drafted the final plan in 1906 but was succeeded as chief engineer by George Washington Goethals in 1907. The canal opened on 15 August 1914, and under the Carter-Torrijos Treaty of 1977 was officially handed back to Panama on 31 December 1999 by US President Bill Clinton. The 6 locks are the Gatún Locks (a set of three), Pedro Miguel Lock and Miraflores Locks (a set of two) . The Caribbean entrance is at Limón Bay and its southern entrance is in the Bay of Panama. Vessels cannot navigate the waters under their own power.

Persian Gulf   Shallow body of water between the Arabian Peninsula and Iran. The surface area of this inlet of the Indian Ocean is approximately 88,800 square miles.

Pistyll-y-Llyn Situated on the Powys/Dyfed border, at 240' the highest waterfall in Wales.

Port Phillip Bay Inlet of Bass Strait on the south central coast of Victoria, Australia. Its entrance is known as 'the Rip'.

Powerscourt Falls Situated in the River Dargle, Co Wicklow, the highest waterfall in Ireland (350').

Prince William Sound Inlet of the Gulf of Alaska with Hinchinbrook and Montague islands at its entrance.

Princess Charlotte Bay Inlet of the Coral Sea off the coast of Queensland; named after the daughter of George IV, it is bounded by Cape Melville to the east and Claremont Point to the west.

Ribbon Falls Situated in the Yosemite National Park, California.

Riga Inlet of the Baltic bounded by the northern coast of Latvia and the western coast of Estonia, it has an area of 7,000 sq miles.

Saint Lawrence Truly, a sea area of 91,800 sq miles with borders on Quebec, Newfoundland, Nova Scotia and New Brunswick; and containing Prince Edward Island.

Saint Lawrence Seaway Stretching from the Atlantic Ocean to the western end of the Great Lakes, the seaway was begun in August 1954, completed in April 1959 and measures 2,342 miles in length. It is a series of nearly 60 canals, of which the Welland is the longest.

Saint Vincent Inlet of the Indian Ocean on the south-east coast of South Australia, it is 90 miles in length.

Saronic (Aegina) Inlet of the Aegean Sea lying east of the Gulf of Corinth from which it is separated by the Corinth Canal.

Skagerrak Arm of the North Sea between Norway and the Jutland peninsula of Denmark on the south.

Spencer Inlet of the Great Australian Bight between the Eyre and Yorke peninsulas of South Australia, it contains many small islands including Gambier, Thistle, Sir Joseph Banks, and Neptune.

Suez North-western arm of the Red Sea between Africa and the Sinai Peninsula, it is 195 miles in length and its most northerly point at Suez marks the beginning of the Suez Canal.

Suez Canal The first fact to determine about the Suez Canal is its length, a subject that is one of the most frequently asked quiz questions. It is officially 100.6 miles long, but many reputable sources will have it listed anywhere between 100 and 105 miles; this difference is mainly due to alterations to accommodate larger vessels. The canal was built by Ferdinand de Lesseps (1805–94) and opened in 1869; its extremities are Port Said at the northern end and Suez to the south; it links two broad areas of sea, the Mediterranean and the Red Sea (via the Gulf of Suez), and is therefore technically, like many canals, a strait. It has no locks.

Sutherland Falls Situated in the Arthur River near Milford Sound, Otago, South Island, New Zealand; at 1,904' the fifth-highest waterfall in the world.

Tadjoura Situated at the western end of the Gulf of Aden around the port of Djibouti. The gulf is 50 miles in length.

Taranto Arm of the Ionian Sea in southern Italy between Cape Santa Maria di Leuca and Cape Colonne, forming the hollow in front of the 'boot' of Italy.

Thailand (Siam) Bordering Thailand, Cambodia, and South Vietnam, the gulf is 350 miles wide and 450 miles in length.

Thérmai Inlet of the Aegean Sea in north eastern Greece between Macedonia, Thessaly, and the Chalcidice Peninsula.

Tonkin Inlet of the South China Sea bounded by China, Hainan Island, and North Vietnam. The gulf is 300 miles in length and 150 miles in width.

Tugela Falls Situated in the Tugela River, Natal, South Africa; at 3,110' the second highest cataract in the world.

Utigård Falls Situated in the Jostedal Glacier, Nesdale, Norway, the highest of the many great waterfalls of Norway and with a total drop of 2,625' the third highest in the world.

Victoria Falls Truly breathtaking waterfall on the Zambesi River on the border between Zambia and Zimbabwe, its drop is 355' and it is known locally as 'The Smoke That Thunders'.

Volga–Don Shipping Canal Runs from Kalach on the Tsimlyansk Reservoir on the Don 62.2 miles to Krasnoarmeysk on the Volga; it was completed in 1952 and joins the Black Sea to the Caspian Sea.

Welland Canal Completed in 1932 and now part of the St Lawrence Seaway, it is 27.6 miles in length and is situated in southern Ontario between Lake Erie to the south and Lake Ontario to the north; it was built as an alternative route through the River Niagara because of the impassable falls.

White Sea–Baltic Canal Longest ship canal in the world (141 miles), between Povenets and Belomorsk in Russia; it has 19 locks and was opened in 1933 as the Stalin Canal.

Yosemite Falls Situated in Yosemite National Park, central California, USA. The Upper Yosemite Fall drops 1,430' and the Lower Falls 320' with the cascades between making a total drop of 2,425'.

GEOGRAPHY

Definitions of Waterways

bay a wide semicircular indentation of a shoreline, especially between two headlands or peninsulas.

canal an artificial waterway constructed for navigational aid, irrigation, or hydro-electric power.

lake a body of water, either freshwater or salt, completely surrounded by land.

ocean very large stretch of sea, especially one of the 4 main oceans of the world, i.e. Pacific, Atlantic, Indian, Arctic. The Antarctic Ocean is made up of the southern extremities of the Atlantic, Pacific and Indian Oceans.

river see definition in relevant section.

sea a mass of salt water that may be part of one of the Earth's oceans or part of a larger sea area.

strait a narrow channel of the sea, bordered by land and linking two larger sea areas. It is often confusing to think of a strait as connecting waters, as opposed to land, because it is usually the land boundaries of the strait that are better known. To give a typical example, most people realise that the Bass Strait lies between mainland Australia and Tasmania, but few will know that the strait links the Tasman Sea area of the Pacific and the Indian Ocean.

Sea Areas

Weather forecasts are broadcast on a regular basis for the Shipping Forecast Areas around the British coast and neighbouring countries. It should be noted that the areas listed below are the boundaries set by Britain and are not universally accepted by other countries who have their own boundary limits and names.

The areas will be described firstly by clockwise coastal areas around Great Britain, starting with the northernmost point of Scotland, and then the coastal regions of Ireland, starting with the northernmost point, before describing other areas and their locations relative to one another.

German Bight was previously called Heligoland until 1956 and FitzRoy (named after the Met office founder and HMS *Beagle* captain, Admiral Robert Fitzroy) was called Finisterre until 2002.

Around Great Britain

Fair Isle: southeast of Faeroes, west of Viking, northeast of Hebrides, northwest of Forties
Cromarty: west of Forties
Forth: west of Forties
Tyne: west of Dogger
Humber: west of German Bight and touching the coast of the Netherlands
Thames: bordering the Netherlands and touching the coast of Belgium
Dover: bordering France and Belgium
Wight: bordering France
Portland: bordering France
Plymouth: east of Sole and bordering France
Lundy: east of Fastnet and touching the coast of Ireland
Irish Sea: surround Anglesey and the Isle of Man
Hebrides: east of Bailey, northeast of Rockall and containing the Outer Hebrides
Malin: east of Rockall and containing the Inner Hebrides

Around Ireland

Malin: east of Rockall and containing the Inner Hebrides
Irish Sea: surround Angelsey and the Isle of Man
Lundy: east of Fastnet and touching the coast of Ireland
Fastnet: north of Sole and bordering the southern coast of Ireland
Shannon: north of Sole
Rockall: south of Bailey and touching the western coast of Ireland

South-East Iceland: most northerly sea area; north of Bailey and northwest of Faeroes and bordering Iceland
Faeroes: southeast of SE Iceland, northwest of Fair Isle, northeast of Bailey, north of Hebrides
Viking: east of Fair Isle, west of North Utsire, north of Forties, northwest of South Utsire
North Utsire: east of Viking, north of South Utsire, and bordering the coast of Norway
South Utsire: southeast of Viking, south of North Utsire, north of Fisher and bordering the coast of Norway
Fisher: south of South Utsire, north of German Bight, east of Forties, and bordering the Skaggerak
Forties: bordered by Fair Isle, Viking, South Utsire, Fisher, Dogger, Forth, and Cromarty
German Bight: south of Fisher, east of Dogger, east of Humber, and bordering Denmark and Germany
Dogger: south of Forties, west of German Bight, north of Humber, east of Tyne
Biscay: south of Plymouth, east of FitzRoy, and bordering France and Spain
FitzRoy: west of Biscay, south of Sole, north of Trafalgar and bordering Spain
Trafalgar: south of FitzRoy and bordering Spain and Portugal
Sole: west of Plymouth and south of Shannon and Fastnet
Bailey: south of SE Iceland, southwest of Faeroes, west of Hebrides, north of Rockall

Beaufort Scale

0	Calm
1	Light air
2	Light breeze
3	Gentle breeze
4	Moderate breeze
5	Fresh breeze
6	Strong breeze
7	Moderate gale
8	Fresh gale
9	Strong gale
10	Whole gale
11	Storm
12	Hurricane

(Devised in 1805 by Francis Beaufort. Force 13 to 17 were added in 1955 by the US Weather Bureau but are seldom used.)

Flags of the World

Afghanistan	horizontal bands of green, white and black, with the national arms in the centre in gold.
Albania	black double-headed eagle on a red background.
Algeria	red star and crescent on a green and white background split vertically.
Andorra	vertical stripes of blue, yellow (gold) and red, with the national arms in the central yellow band.
Angola	yellow (gold) star, machete and half cog wheel on a red and black background split horizontally.
Antigua & Barbuda	red with an inverted triangle divided horizontally black over blue over white, with a rising yellow (gold) sun on the black band.
Argentina	horizontal bands of blue, white and blue, with a yellow (gold) sun on white band.
Armenia	horizontal tricolour of red, blue and orange.
Aruba	blue with two narrow yellow (gold) horizontal bands near the bottom and a red four-pointed star, bordered white, in the top left hoist.
Australia	The British Blue Ensign in the canton, with five white stars of the Southern Cross in the fly, and the white Commonwealth star of seven points beneath the Union Flag.
Austria	horizontal bands of red, white and red, sometimes depicting the national emblem in the centre.
Azerbaijan	horizontal bands of blue, red and green, with a white crescent and eight-pointed star on the red band.
Bahamas	horizontal bands of blue, yellow (gold) and blue, with a black equilateral triangle on the hoist.
Bahrain	red, with vertical serrated white bar on the hoist.
Bangladesh	red circle on a green background.
Barbados	vertical stripes of blue, yellow (gold) and blue, with a trident head on central gold stripe.
Belarus	red, with a green horizontal band in the lower third, and a red and white ornamental vertical stripe on the hoist.
Belgium	vertical tricolour of black, yellow (gold) and red.
Belize	white disc containing the coat of arms surrounded by a green garland, the disc being on a blue background with a red edge top and bottom.
Benin	two horizontal bands of yellow (gold) over red with a larger vertical green stripe on the hoist.
Bermuda	red with a British Blue Ensign in the canton and shield of arms in the fly.
Bhutan	silver-grey dragon on a background of yellow (gold) over orange triangles split from top right to bottom left.
Bolivia	horizontal tricolour of red, yellow (gold) and green, occasionally showing the national emblem in centre.
Bosnia-Hercegovina	blue with a yellow (gold) triangle in the fly with a series of white stars running diagonally across the hypotenuse top left to bottom right. Prior to 1998 the flag was white with a blue shield in the centre with white diagonal and six yellow (gold) fleurs-de-lys.
Botswana	blue, with a horizontal black stripe in centre with a white edge top and bottom.
Brazil	green with yellow (gold) lozenge containing a blue sphere with a white girdle often displaying the motto *Ordem e Progresso*.
Brunei	yellow (gold), with two diagonal stripes white over black running from just below top left corner to just above bottom right hand corner, with the coat of arms in the centre.
Bulgaria	horizontal tricolour of white, green and red.
Burkina Faso	two horizontal bands of red over green with yellow (gold) star in the centre.
Burma/Myanmar	red with a dark blue canton containing a cogwheel and two rice ears surrounded by 14 white stars.
Burundi	white saltire with red background top and bottom and green background on fly and hoist, a central white disc containing a triangle of three red six-pointed stars edged in green.
Cambodia	horizontal bands of blue, red and blue, with the red of double width and containing a depiction of the temple of Angkor in white.
Cameroon	vertical tricolour of green, red and yellow (gold), with a five-pointed yellow (gold) star on the central red band.
Canada	red maple leaf in a white square, with vertical red stripes on fly and hoist.
Cape Verde	blue, with three horizontal narrow bands of white, red and white in the third quarter, and a circle of ten yellow (gold) stars running through the bands near the hoist.
Central African Republic	four horizontal bands of blue, white, green and yellow (gold), with a vertical red stripe in centre and a five-pointed yellow (gold) star in top left of blue band.
Chad	vertical tricolour of blue, yellow (gold) and red.
Chile	two horizontal bands of white over red, with a five-pointed white star in a blue square covering the first third of the white band.
China	red with large five-pointed yellow (gold) star in the upper left quarter, four smaller stars of the same colour forming an arc around the larger one.
Colombia	horizontal tricolour of yellow (gold), blue and red, the yellow (gold) band being twice the width of the other two.
Comoros	central vertical white crescent with four white stars between its horns and facing the fly, on a green background, the name of Allah in the upper fly and Muhammad in the lower hoist both in Arabic script.

Congo, Dem Rep of	blue, with a large yellow (gold) five-pointed star in the centre, with six smaller stars of the same colour running vertically down the hoist.
Congo, Republic of	green equilateral triangle over red equilateral triangle with a yellow (gold) diagonal stripe separating them running from the top right fly to the bottom left hoist.
Costa Rica	five horizontal bands of blue, white, red, white and blue, the red central band being twice the width of the others and containing the national emblem in the centre.
Croatia	horizontal bands of red, white and blue, with the national emblem in the centre.
Cuba	five horizontal bands of blue, white, blue, white and blue, with red equilateral triangle on hoist with white five-pointed star in centre.
Cyprus	white, with a yellow (gold) outline of Cyprus in the centre above a wreath of olive.
Czech Republic	two horizontal bands of white over red, with a blue equilateral triangle on the hoist.
Denmark	white cross on a red background, the vertical stripe being slightly nearer the hoist than the fly.
Djibouti	two horizontal bands of blue over green, with a white equilateral triangle on the hoist with a red five-pointed star in the centre.
Dominica	cross of yellow (gold), black and white stripes on a green background, and in the centre a red disc charged with a Sisserou parrot encircled by ten green stars.
Dominican Republic	blue and red quarters, with a white cross overlapping and the national emblem in the centre.
East Timor	red with a yellow triangle with its base the full length of the hoist and its apex at the centre of the flag. Within this triangle is another black triangle sharing a base but apex midway to the base and apex of the larger triangle, within the black triangle is a white five-pointed star.
Ecuador	horizontal bands of yellow (gold), blue and red, the yellow (gold) band being twice the width of the other two and the national emblem in the centre.
Egypt	horizontal bands of red, white and black, with an eagle in the centre.
El Salvador	horizontal bands of blue, white and blue, with coat of arms on white band.
England	red cross of St George on a white background.
Equatorial Guinea	horizontal bands of green, white and red, with a blue equilateral triangle on the hoist and coat of arms in the centre.
Eritrea	red triangle with a yellow (gold) olive wreath on the hoist, green triangle over blue triangle on the fly.
Estonia	horizontal tricolour of blue, black and white.
Ethiopia	horizontal bands of green, yellow (gold), and red, with blue disc in the centre containing a yellow (gold) pentagram.
Faroe Islands	red cross, bordered blue on a white background the vertical stripe being nearer the hoist than the fly.
Fiji	Union flag in top left quarter on a blue background and the shield of Fiji in the fly.
Finland	blue cross on a white background, the vertical stripe being slightly nearer the hoist than the fly.
France	vertical tricolour of blue, white and red.
Gabon	horizontal tricolour of green, yellow (gold), and blue.
Gambia	five horizontal bands of red, white, blue, white and green, the white bands being much narrower than the others.
Georgia	cherry red, with a black over white rectangle in the upper hoist.
Germany	horizontal tricolour of black, red and yellow (gold).
Ghana	horizontal bands of red, yellow (gold) and green, with black five-pointed star in the centre.
Greece	nine blue and white horizontal stripes with a white cross on a blue background in the canton.
Greenland	two horizontal bands of white over red, with a large circle near the hoist and the colours reversed within, being red over white.
Grenada	two green equilateral triangles with apex towards the centre and separated by a yellow (gold) five-pointed star in a red disc, the area between the triangles is yellow (gold), the flag has a red border with three yellow (gold) stars on the top and three yellow (gold) stars on the bottom, the green triangle in the hoist has a nutmeg in its centre.
Guatemala	vertical stripes of blue, white and blue, with a coat of arms in the central white band.
Guinea	horizontal tricolour of red, yellow (gold) and green.
Guinea-Bissau	horizontal bands of yellow (gold) over green, with vertical red band in the hoist, charged with a black star.
Guyana	green with a yellow, white-bordered triangle from the hoist to the fly, with an equilateral red triangle on the hoist with a black border.
Haiti	two horizontal bands of blue over red, with the national emblem in the centre.
Honduras	horizontal bands of blue, white and blue, with five blue five-pointed stars arranged as a saltire in the white band.
Hong Kong	red ground with a white bauhinia flower of five petals in the centre, each petal containing a red star.
Hungary	horizontal tricolour of red, white and green.
Iceland	blue with a white-bordered red cross, the vertical stripe being nearer the hoist than the fly.
India	horizontal bands of saffron (orange-yellow), white and green, with a blue Asoka wheel in the central white band.
Indonesia	two horizontal bands of red over white.
Iran	horizontal tricolour of green, white and red, with the words Allahu Akbar (God is great) repeated 22 times in white on the lower green and upper red bands, and the national emblem in red in the central white band.

Iraq	horizontal bands of red, white and black, with three green five-pointed stars in the central white band and the words Allahu Akbar written between the stars.
Ireland	vertical tricolour of green, white and orange.
Israel	two horizontal blue bands near the top and bottom with a blue shield of David in the centre, all on a white background.
Italy	vertical tricolour of green, white and red.
Ivory Coast	vertical tricolour of orange, white and green.
Jamaica	yellow (gold) diagonal cross forming background triangles of green top and bottom and black on the hoist and fly.
Japan	white with a large red disc representing the sun in the centre.
Jordan	horizontal bands of black, white and green, with a red equilateral triangle on the hoist containing a seven-pointed white star.
Kazakhstan	blue with a yellow (gold) sun in the centre and a soaring eagle wrapped around the lower hemisphere, a gold (yellow) stripe adorns the hoist.
Kenya	five horizontal bands of black, white, red, white and green, the white bands being much narrower than the others, a red and black oval shield adorns the centre with two white crossed spears behind the shield.
Kiribati	red representing the sky and six white and blue wavy lines representing the sea, a yellow (gold) rising sun in the centre with a flying frigate bird above in the same colour.
Korea, North (Chosun)	five horizontal bands of blue, white, red, white and blue, the white bands being much narrower than the others and the central red band being twice the width of the blue bands, a large red five-pointed star within a white circle adorns the central band on the hoist.
Korea, South	white with a red over blue yin-yang symbol in the centre, and four black trigrams emanating from the symbol diagonally.
Kuwait	horizontal bands of green, white and red, with a black trapezoid in the hoist.
Kyrgyzstan	red with a yellow (gold) sun in the centre containing a representation of a yurt.
Laos	horizontal bands of red, blue and red, the central blue band being twice the width of the other two and containing a white circle.
Latvia	horizontal bands of red, white and red, the central white band being half the width of the other two.
Lebanon	horizontal bands of red, white and red, the central white band being twice the width of the other two and containing a green and brown cedar tree.
Lesotho	split diagonally from bottom to top, the top half being white and the bottom half mainly green with a blue band at the top, the upper white triangle contains an assegai and knobkerrie behind a Basotho shield in brown, in the hoist.
Liberia	eleven alternate red and white horizontal bands (six red and five white), with a blue canton containing a white five-pointed star.
Libya	emerald green.
Liechtenstein	two horizontal bands of blue over red with a yellow (gold) crown in the blue band near the hoist.
Lithuania	horizontal tricolour of yellow (gold), green and red.
Luxembourg	horizontal tricolour of red, white and blue.
Macedonia	red with a yellow (gold) disc in the centre representing the sun and eight yellow (gold) flares emanating from the sun in the shape of a cross and saltire.
Madagascar	two horizontal bands of red over green with a broad white stripe in the hoist.
Malawi	horizontal tricolour of black, red and green with a red rising sun on the black band.
Malaysia	fourteen alternating horizontal bands of red and white with a yellow (gold) fourteen-pointed star inside a crescent of the same colour in a large blue canton.
Maldives	green with a large red border and a white crescent in the centre with horns facing the fly.
Mali	vertical tricolour of green, yellow (gold) and red.
Malta	two vertical stripes of white and red with a representation of the George Cross in the canton of the white stripe.
Marshall Islands	blue with a diagonal ray divided orange over white running from the lower hoist to the upper fly, a white sun in the canton.
Mauritania	green with a yellow (gold) crescent in the centre with horns facing the top, a five-pointed yellow (gold) star situated within the horns of the crescent.
Mauritius	four horizontal bands of red, blue, yellow (gold), and green.
Mexico	vertical stripes of green, white and red with the Mexican emblem of an eagle on a cactus devouring a snake in the centre.
Moldova	vertical stripes of blue, yellow (gold) and red with the national arms in the centre.
Monaco	horizontal bands or red over white.
Mongolia	vertical stripes of red, blue and red with the Soyombo symbol in yellow (gold) on the red band in the hoist.
Morocco	red with a green pentagram, representing the Seal of Solomon, in the centre.
Mozambique	horizontal bands of green, black and yellow (gold) with the central black band having a white border, a red equilateral triangle in the hoist charged with the national emblem.
Namibia	split diagonally from bottom to top by a red stripe with a white border, the upper blue triangle containing a yellow (gold) 12-pointed sun in the canton, and the lower triangle being plain green.
Nauru	blue ground with a yellow (gold) horizontal narrow band in the centre representing the Equator, and a white 12-pointed star representing the 12 original Nauruan tribes in the lower hoist.

GEOGRAPHY

Nepal	double pennant of red with a blue border, the lower pennant containing a white rayed sun and the upper pennant containing a white recumbent crescent and quarter moon.
Netherlands	horizontal tricolour of red, white and blue.
New Zealand	blue ground with Union Flag in canton and four five-pointed red stars with white borders on the fly.
Nicaragua	horizontal bands of blue, white and blue, with the national coat of arms in the centre.
Niger	horizontal bands of orange, white and green, with an orange disc in the central white band.
Nigeria	vertical stripes of green, white and green.
Norway	blue cross bordered with white on a red background, the vertical stripe being slightly nearer the hoist than the fly.
Oman	red with a white panel in the upper fly and a green one in the lower fly, the national emblem in white in the upper hoist.
Pakistan	green with a large white crescent with horns facing the upper fly in the centre and a small five-pointed white star in between the horns, a large white vertical stripe running along the hoist.
Palau	light blue with a large yellow (gold) disc just off centre near the hoist.
Panama	quartered, the white canton containing a five-pointed blue star, a red upper fly, blue lower staff and a white lower fly containing a five-pointed red star.
Papua New Guinea	diagonally split from upper hoist to lower fly red over black, a soaring Bird of Paradise in yellow (gold) in the red fly and five white stars of the Southern Cross on the black hoist.
Paraguay	horizontal bands of red, white and blue with the national seal in the central white band, and the Treasury seal on the reverse central white band. The Paraguayan flag is the only national flag to have different obverse and reverse designs.
Peru	a shield of arms on a central band surrounded by a laurel wreath. The shield includes a *vicuña*, the *keno* tree and the cornucopia apportioning gold and silver coins, representing the three kingdoms: animal, vegetable and mineral.
Philippines	two horizontal bands of blue over red, with a white equilateral triangle running the length of the hoist; the triangle containing a yellow (gold) sun in the centre and three small five-pointed stars of the same colour, one in each angle.
Poland	equal horizontal bands of white over red.
Portugal	vertical stripes of green and red, the green stripe being a little smaller than the red fly; the national emblem just off centre overlapping the two colours.
Qatar	maroon, with vertical serrated white bar on the hoist.
Romania	vertical tricolour of blue, yellow (gold) and red.
Russia	horizontal tricolour of white, blue and red.
Rwanda	vertical stripes of red, yellow (gold) and green with bold letter R in the yellow (gold) stripe.
St Christopher & Nevis (aka St Kitts)	green over red triangles divided by a diagonal black bar running from the staff to the upper fly, the black bar is bordered yellow (gold) and contains two white stars, one in the staff and one in the upper fly.
St Lucia	blue with three triangles in the centre, yellow (gold) over black over white, all with a common base, the white appearing to border the black but the yellow (gold) being right-angled at its apex.
St Vincent & Grenadines	vertical stripes of blue, yellow (gold) and green with the central yellow (gold) band being twice the width of the other two, and three green diamonds in the shape of a V in the centre.
Samoa	red with a blue canton of five white stars of the Southern Cross.
San Marino	equal horizontal bands of white over blue.
São Tomé & Principe	horizontal bands of green, yellow (gold) and green, with the yellow (gold) band wider than the other two and containing two large black five-pointed stars nearer the fly than the hoist; a red equilateral triangle runs along the hoist.
Saudi Arabia	green with a white scimitar in the centre with the Arabic writing 'There is no God but God and Muhammad is the Prophet of God' also in white, above the scimitar.
Scotland	white diagonal cross of St Andrew on a blue background.
Senegal	vertical tricolour of green, yellow (gold) and red with green five-pointed star in central yellow (gold) band.
Seychelles	five rays extending from the lower hoist, from left to right, blue, yellow (gold), red, white, and green.
Sierra Leone	horizontal tricolour of green, white and blue.
Singapore	equal horizontal bands of red over white with white crescent in the canton with horns facing the fly and five small white five-pointed stars in a pentagon shape between the horns.
Slovakia	horizontal tricolour of white, blue and red with the national coat of arms off centre near the hoist.
Slovenia	horizontal tricolour of white, blue and red with the national coat of arms over the white and blue bands in the upper hoist.
Solomon Islands	split diagonally from bottom to top by a yellow stripe, the upper blue triangle containing five white stars and the lower triangle being plain green.
Somalia	blue with a white five-pointed star in the centre.
South Africa	divided red over blue by a horizontal green Y bordered white, inside the V of the Y a black triangle bordered yellow (gold).
Spain	horizontal bands of red, yellow (gold) and red with the national emblem being optionally depicted on the yellow (gold) band near the hoist.
Sri Lanka	on a dark red field with yellow (gold) border a yellow (gold) lion passant holding a sword in its right paw, and a representation of a bo leaf in each corner; to its left two vertical stripes of green and saffron also with a yellow (gold) border.

Sudan	horizontal bands of red, white and black, with a green equilateral triangle on the hoist.
Suriname	five horizontal bands of green, white, red, white and green, the red band being twice the width of the green bands and the white bands being a mere border to the red; a yellow (gold) five-pointed star in the centre.
Swaziland	five horizontal bands of blue, yellow (gold), crimson, yellow (gold) and blue, the crimson band being twice the width of the blue bands and the yellow (gold) bands being a mere border to the crimson; an emblem of a shield and two spears is depicted all over the central band.
Sweden	yellow (gold) cross on a blue background, the vertical stripe being slightly nearer the hoist than the fly.
Switzerland	red square flag with a large central white cross.
Syria	horizontal bands of red, white and black, with two green five-pointed stars either side of the centre of the white band running horizontally.
Taiwan	red with a blue canton containing a 12-rayed white sun.
Tajikistan	horizontal bands of red, white and green, the white band being twice the width of the other two; a crown adorned with a crescent of seven yellow (gold) stars is depicted in the centre.
Tanzania	green over blue triangles divided by a diagonal black bar running from the staff to the upper fly, the bar having a yellow (gold) border.
Thailand	five horizontal bands of red, white, blue, white and red, the blue band being twice the width of the others.
Togo	five horizontal bands of green, yellow (gold), green, yellow (gold) and green, a large white five-pointed star within a red canton in the upper hoist.
Tonga	red with a white canton containing a red cross.
Trinidad & Tobago	red with a black diagonal bar, bordered white, running from right of the upper hoist to left of the bottom fly.
Tunisia	red with a central white disc containing a red five-pointed star within a red crescent, horns facing the fly.
Turkey	red with a central white skewed five-pointed star within a white crescent, horns facing the fly.
Turkmenistan	green with an ornamental carpet pattern running vertically near the hoist; a crescent and five stars in white are depicted to the right of the upper hoist, the horns facing the hoist and stars forming a diagonal cross within the horns.
Tuvalu	light blue with Union Flag in canton and nine yellow (gold) five-pointed stars in the fly.
Uganda	six horizontal bands of black, yellow (gold), red, black, yellow (gold), red; with a white disc in central two bands containing a depiction of a crested crane.
Ukraine	equal horizontal bands of blue over yellow (gold).
United Arab Emirates	horizontal bands of green, white and black, with a wide red stripe running down the hoist.
United Kingdom	Union Flag consisting of the English and Scottish flags and the red saltire of St Patrick on a white ground representing Northern Ireland.
USA	thirteen alternating horizontal bands of red and white with a blue canton containing fifty white stars in a six, five, six, five, six, five, six, five, six pattern, each star representing one of the fifty constituent states.
Uruguay	nine alternating horizontal bands of white and blue with a 16-rayed yellow (gold) sun in a white canton, the sun often depicted with eyes and full mouth.
Uzbekistan	horizontal bands of blue, white and green, the central white band being fimbriated with red, and the blue band containing a white crescent in the hoist, facing the fly and three rows of white stars, three, four, five, making 12 in all.
Vanuatu	divided red over green by a horizontal yellow (gold) Y bordered black, inside the V of the Y a black triangle containing a boar's tusk overlaid by two crossed fern leaves.
Vatican City	square flag divided vertically, yellow (gold) in the hoist and white in the fly; crossed keys and triple crown device in the centre of the white stripe.
Venezuela	vertical stripes of yellow (gold), blue and red, with an arc of seven white stars in the central blue band and the national emblem in the canton.
Vietnam	red with a large yellow (gold) five-pointed star in the centre.
Wales	equal horizontal bands of white over green with large red dragon all over the field.
Yemen	horizontal tricolour of red, white and black.
Yugoslavia	horizontal tricolour of blue, white and red.
Zambia	green with three vertical stripes of red, black and orange in the fly topped by a depiction of an eagle.
Zimbabwe	seven horizontal bands of green, yellow (gold), red, black, red, yellow (gold) and green; a white equilateral triangle running down the hoist, bordered black, and containing the national emblem.
Definition of terms	Canton: small rectangular charge in the top left-hand corner. Charge: a shield or emblem within a field or canton. Field: the whole of the ground of a flag. Fly: the outer edge of a flag away from the hoist. Hoist: the inner edge of a flag next to the staff. Staff: the flagpole.

GEOGRAPHY

Roman Place Names of Britain

Roman Name	British Name
Abone	Sea Mills, Avon
Aballava	Burgh by Sands, Cumbria
Ad Ansam	Higham, Suffolk
Ad Pontem	East Stoke, Nottinghamshire
Aesica	Great Chesters, Northumberland
Ageloco	Littleborough, Lancashire
Alabum	Llandovery, Dyfed
Alauna	Maryport, Cumbria
	Ardoch, Tayside
	Watercrook, Cumbria
Albion	England
Anderitum	Pevensey, East Sussex
Aquae Arnemetiae	Buxton, Derbyshire
Aquae Sulis	Bath, Avon
Arbeia	South Shields, Tyne & Wear
Ardotalia	Melandra Castle, Derbyshire
Ariconium	Weston-under-Penyard, Hereford &Worcestershire
Banna	Birdoswald, Cumbria
Bannaventa	Whilton Lodge, Northamptonshire
Bannovalum	Horncastle, Lincolnshire
Bibra	Beckfoot, Cumbria
Blatobulgium	Birrens, Dumfries and Galloway
Bovio	Holt, Cheshire
Bovivum	Tilston, Cheshire
Branodunum	Brancaster, Norfolk
Bravoniacum	Kirkby Thore, Cumbria
Bravonium	Leintwardine, Hereford & Worcestershire
Bremenium	High Rochester, Northumberland
Bremetenacum Veteranorum	Ribchester, Lancashire
Bremia	Llanio, Dyfed
Brocavum	Brougham, Cumbria
Brocolitia	Carrawburgh, Northumberland
Burrium	Usk, Gwent
Caesaria	Sark
	Jersey
Caesaromagus	Chelmsford, Essex
Calacum	Burrow in Lonsdale, Lancashire
Calcaria	Tadcaster, North Yorkshire
Caledonia	Scotland
Calleva atrebatum	Silchester, Hampshire
Camboglanna	Castlefields, Cumbria
Camboritum	Lackford, Suffolk
Cambria	Wales
Camulodunum	Colchester, Essex
	Slack, West Yorkshire
Canonium	Kelvedon, Essex
Canovium	Caerhun, Gwynedd
Castra Exploratorum	Netherby, Cumbria
Cataractonium	Catterick, North Yorkshire
Causennis	Saltersford, Lincolnshire
Cecucmum	Y Gaer, Powys
Cilurnum	Chesters, Northumberland
Clausentum	Bitterne, Hampshire
Combretovium	Baylham House, Suffolk
Concangis	Chester-le-Street, Durham
Concavata	Drumburgh, Cumbria
Condate	Northwich, Cheshire
Condercum	Benwell, Tyne & Wear
Coria	Corbridge, Northumberland
Corinium Dobunnorum	Cirencester, Gloucestershire
Crococalana	Brough, Nottinghamshire
Cunetio	Mildenhall, Wiltshire

Roman Name	British Name
Danum	Doncaster, South Yorkshire
Delgovicia	Millington, East Yorkshire
Derventio	Malton, North Yorkshire
	Littlechester, Derbyshire
	Papcastle, Cumbria
Deva	Chester, Cheshire
Dubris	Dover, Kent
Dunum	Hod Hill, Dorset
Durnovaria	Dorchester, Dorset
Durobrivae	Rochester, Kent
	Water Newton, Cambridgeshire
Durocobrivis	Dunstable, Bedfordshire
Durocornovium	Wanborough, Wilts
Duroliponte	Cambridge, Cambs
Durovernum Cantiacorum	Canterbury, Kent
Durovigutum	Godmanchester, Cambridgeshire
Eboracum	York, North Yorkshire
Epiacum	Whitley Castle, Northumberland
Esmeduna	Liverpool
Fanumcocium	Bewcastle, Cumbria
Gabrosentum	Moresby, Cumbria
Galava	Ambleside, Cumbria
Gariannum	Burgh Castle, Norfolk
Gernemuta magna	Great Yarmouth
Glanibanta	Ambleside, Cumbria
Glevum	Gloucester, Gloucestershire
Gobanneum	Abergavenny, Gwent
Granta	Cambridge
Habitancum	Risingham, Northumberland
Hibernia	Ireland
Isca	Caerleon, Gwent
Isca Dumnoniorum	Exeter, Devon
Isurium Brigantum	Aldborough, North Yorkshire
Itunocelum	Ravenglass, Cumbria
Lactodurum	Towcester, Northamptonshire
Lagentium	Castleford, West Yorkshire
Launa	Learchild, Northumberland
Lavatris	Bowes, Durham
(Portus) Lemanis	Lympne, Kent
Letocetum	Wall, Staffordshire
Leucarum	Loughor, West Glamorgan
Leucomagus	East Anton, Hampshire
Levobrinta	Forden Gear, Powys
Lindinis	Ilchester, Somerset
Lindum	Lincoln, Lincolnshire
Londinium	London, Greater London
Longovicium	Lanchester, Durham
Luentinum	Pumsaint, Dyfed
Luguvalium	Carlisle, Cumbria
Lunecastrum	Lancaster
Magiovinium	Dropshort, Buckinghamshire
Magis	Burrow Walls, Cumbria
Maglona	Old Carlisle, Cumbria
Magna	Carvoran, Northumberland
Magnis	Kenchester, Herefordshire
Maia	Bowness-on-Solway, Cumbria
Mamucium/ Mancunium	Manchester, Greater Manchester
Manavia	Isle of Man
Manduessedum	Mancetter, Warwickshire
Margidunum	Castle Hill, Nottinghamshire
Mediobogdum	Hardknott, Cumbria
Mediolanum	Whitchurch, Shropshire
Mona	Isle of Anglesey
Morbium	Piercebridge, Co. Durham
Moridunum	Carmarthen, Dyfed
	Seaton, Devon

Navio	Brough, Derbyshire	Sorviodunum	Old Sarum, Wiltshire
Nemeto Statio	North Tawton, Devon	Sullon Iacis	Brockley Hill, Greater London
Nidum	Neath, West Glamorgan	Trimontium	Newstead, Borders
Noviomagus	Chichester, West Sussex	Tripontium	Cave's Inn, Warwickshire
Regnorum		Uxacona	Redhill, Shropshire
Noviomagus	Crayford, Greater London	Uxelodunum	Stanwix, Cumbria
Olenacum	Elslack, North Yorkshire	Vagniacis	Springhead, Kent
Onnum	Halton, Northumberland	Varis	St Asaph, Clwyd
Orcades Insulae	Orkney Islands	Vectis	Isle of Wight
Othona	Bradwell-on-Sea, Essex	Veluniate	Carriden, Falkirkshire
Pennocrucium	Water Eaton, Staffordshire	Venonis	High Cross, Leicestershire
Petuarea	Brough on Humber,	Venta Belgarum	Winchester, Hampshire
	Humberside	Venta Icenorum	Caistor St Edmund, Norfolk
Pons Aelius	Newcastle, Tyne & Wear	Venta Silurum	Caerwent, Gwent
Pontes	Staines, Surrey	Verbeia	Ilkley, West Yorkshire
Portus Ardaoni	Portchester, Hants (also	Vercovicium	Housesteads, Northumberland
	Portus Ardurni)	Verlucio	Sandy Lane, Wiltshire
Portus Dubris	Dover, Kent	Vernemetum	Willoughby, Nottinghamshire
Ranatis/Tanatus	Thanet	Verteris	Brough, Cumbria
Ratae Corieltavorum	Leicester, Leicestershire	Verulamium	St Albans, Hertfordshire
Regodunum	Castleshaw, Greater	Vigornia	Worcester
	Manchester	Vindobala	Rudchester, Northumberland
Regulbium	Reculver, Kent	Vindocladia	Badbury, Dorset
Riduna	Alderney, Channel Islands	Vindolanda	Chesterholm, Northumberland
Rutupiae	Richborough, Kent	Vindomora	Ebchester, Durham
Salinae	Droitwich, Worcestershire	Vinovia	Binchester, Durham
	Middlewich, Cheshire	Viroconium	Wroxeter, Shropshire
Sarnia	Guernsey	Cornoviorum	
Segedunum	Wallsend, Tyne & Wear	Virosidum	Brough-by-Bainbridge,
Segelocum	Littleborough, Nottinghamshire		North Yorkshire
Segontium	Caernarfon, Gwynedd	Voreda	Old Penrith, Cumbria

NB The above are sites of Roman cities during their occupation in the first four centuries AD. A few of the situations are doubtful and alternatives are given in areas of uncertainty.

GEOGRAPHY

Roman Place Names of the World

Roman Name	British Name	Roman Name	British Name
Abbatis Cella (Abbot's Cell)	Appenzell	Italia	Italy
Aegyptus	Egypt	Langobardus	Lombardy
Africa	Libya / Tunisia	Lausodunum	Lausanne
Aquincum	Budapest	Limonum	Poitiers
Arabia Felix	Arabia	Lugdunum	Lyon
Arabona	Gyor	Lusitania	Portugal
Arenacum	Arnhem	Lutetia	Paris
Ariminum	Rimini	Massilia	Marseilles
Augusta Taurinorum	Turin	Matisco	Macon
Aurelianum	Orléans	Mauretania	Morocco
Caesarea Augusta	Zaragoza	Mediolanum	Milan
Caesaria	Jersey	Noviomagus	Longjumeau
Caesaria Maritima	Palestine	Noviomagus	Nijmegen
Candia	Crete	Olisipo	Lisbon
Cibinium	Sibiu	Patavium	Padua
Crassus	Grasse	Pinciacum	Poissy
Curicum	Krk	Portus Cale	Oporto
Dacia	Romania	Portus Veneris	Port-Vendres
Fiscamnum	Fécamp	Praenestum	Palestrina
Fretum Herculaneum	Gibraltar (Strait of)	Puteoli	Pozzuoli
Gades	Cadiz	Sexantaprista	Ruse
Gallia	France	Sparnacum	Epernay
Germania	Germany	Trajectum Castrum	Utrecht
Graecia	Greece	Turicum	Zurich
Helvetia	Switzerland	Vapincum	Gap
Hibernia	Ireland	Vasconia	Gascony
Hispania	Spain	Vindobona	Vienna

World Table: Geographical Gazetteer

Country	GMT	Currency	Split into 100	UN Member	Common-wealth	Europe	Official Languages	Highest Point	Area Sq Km	Area Sq Miles	Population
Afghanistan	+4	afghani	puls	1946			Pashto, Dari Persian	Noshaq (24,581')	647,497	249,999	22,132,000
Albania	+1	Lek	qindarka	1955			Albanian	Korabi (9,028')	28,748	11,100	3,731,000
Algeria	+1	dinar	centimes	1962			Arabic, Berber, French	Tahat (9,852')	2,381,741	919,591	29,272,344
Andorra	+1	euro	cents	1993			Catalan, French, Spanish	Pla del'Estany (9,678')	468	181	65,971
Angola	+1	kwanza	lweis	1976			Portuguese	Serra Moco (8,563')	1,246,700	481,351	11,569,000
Antigua and Barbuda	-4	East Caribbean dollar	cents	1981	1981		English	Boggy Peak (1,319')	442	171	70,000
Argentina	-3	peso	austral	1945			Spanish	Aconcagua (22,834')	2,766,889	1,068,297	35,672,000
Armenia	+4	dram	louma	1992			Armenian	Aragats (13,418')	29271	11,302	3,800,000
Australia	+8-+11	dollar	cents	1945	1931		English	Kosciusko (7,316')	7,686,848	2,967,895	19,603,500
Austria	+1	euro	cents	1955		1995	German	Grossglockner (12,462')	83,849	32,374	8,110,244
Azerbaijan	+4	manat	gopik	1992			Azeri	Bazar-dyuzi (15,156')	86,600	33,436	8,100,000
Bahamas	-5	dollar	cents	1973	1973		English	Alvernia (on Cat Island) (206')	13,935	5,380	289,000
Bahrain	+3	dinar	fils (1,000)	1971			Arabic	Jabal ad-Dukhan (440')	622	240	620,000
Bangladesh	+6	taka	poisha	1974	1972		Bengali	Keokradong (4,034')	143,998	55,598	123,100,000
Barbados	-4	dollar	cents	1966	1966		English	Hillaby (1,115')	430	166	262,000
Belarus	+2	rouble	kopeks	1945			Belarussian	Dzerzhinsky (1,135')	207,600	80,154	10,000,000
Belgium	+1	euro	cents	1945		1958	Dutch, French, German	Botrange (2,277')	30,513	11,781	10,188,000
Belize	-6	dollar	cents	1981	1981		English	Victoria Peak (3,681')	22,965	8,867	230,000
Benin	+1	franc	centimes	1960			French, Fon, Adja, Yoruba	Atacora Massif (2,103')	122,622	47,344	5,828,000
Bermuda	-4	dollar	cents				English	Gibb's Hill (245')	53	20	60,000
Bhutan	+6	ngultrum	chetrum	1971			Dzongkha, Bumthangka	Khula Kangri (24,784')	47,000	18,147	1,862,000
Bolivia	-4	boliviano	centavos	1945			Spanish, Quechua, Amyara	Nevado Sajama (21,391')	1,098,581	424,163	8,140,000
Bosnia-Hercegovina	+1	marka	fening	1992			Bosnian	Bobotov Kuk (8,274')	51,129	19,741	3,784,000
Botswana	+2	pula	thebes	1966	1966		Setswana, English	Otse (4,886')	581,730	224,606	1,533,000
Brazil	-2--5	real	centavos	1945			Portuguese	Pico da Bandeira (9,482')	8,511,965	3,286,473	159,884,000
Brunei	+8	dollar	sen	1984	1984		Malay, English	Bukit Belalong (3,098')	5,765	2,226	307,000
Bulgaria	+2	lev	stotinki	1955			Bulgarian	Musala (9,596')	110,912	42,823	8,306,000
Burkina Faso	0	franc	centimes	1960			French, Mossi	Tema (2,457')	274,200	105,869	11,087,000
Burundi	+2	franc	centimes	1962			Rundi, French, Swahili	Muramvya (8,809')	27,834	10,747	6,194,000
Cambodia	+7	riel	sen	1955			Khmer, English	Ka-Kup (5,722')	181,035	69,898	11,437,656
Cameroon	+1	franc	centimes	1960	1995		French, English	Cameroon (13,350')	475,442	183,568	13,937,000
Canada	-4--8	dollar	cents	1945	1931		English, French	Logan (19,550')	9,976,185	3,851,809	30,491,294
Cape Verde	-1	escudo	centavos	1975			Portuguese, Crioulo	Pico do Cano (9,285')	4,033	1,557	406,000
Central African Rep	+1	franc	centimes	1960			French, Sangho	Gaou (4,659')	622,984	240,534	3,245,000

Country	GMT	Currency	Split into 100	UN Member	Common-wealth	Europe	Official Languages	Highest Point	Area Sq Km	Area Sq Miles	Population
Chad	+1	franc	centimes	1960			French, Arabic	Emi Koussi (11,204')	1,284,000	495,753	6,702,000
Chile	-3--5	peso	centavos	1945			Spanish	Ojos del Salado (22,588')	756,945	292,257	14,622,000
China	+8	yuan	fen	1945			Mandarin Chinese	Everest (29,035')	9,596,961	3,705,390	1,248,540,000
Colombia	-5	peso	centavos	1945			Spanish	Pico Cristobal Colon (18,947')	1,141,748	440,829	41,539,000
Comoros	+3	franc	centimes	1975			French, Arabic, Comoran	Kartala (7,746')	2,171	838	651,000
Congo, Dem Rep of	+1--+2	franc	centimes	1960			French, Lingala, Kiswahili	Stanley (Ngaliema) (16,795')	2,345,409	905,563	48,040,000
Congo, Rep of	+1	franc	centimes	1960			French	Foungouti (3,412')	342,000	132,046	2,745,000
Costa Rica	-6	colon	centimos	1945			Spanish	Chirripo (12,533')	50,700	19,575	3,943,204
Croatia	+1	kuna	lipas	1993			Croatian	Velika Peak (7,200')	56,538	21,829	4,498,000
Cuba	-5	peso	centavos	1945			Spanish	Pico Turquino (6,467')	110,861	42,803	11,059,000
Cyprus	+2	pound	cents	1960	1961		Greek, Turkish	Olympus (6,401')	9,251	3,572	766,000
Czech Republic	+1	koruna	haléru	1993		1973	Czech, Slovak	Snezka (5,256')	78,644	30,364	10,304,000
Denmark	+1	krone	ore	1945			Danish	Yding Skovhoj (568')	43,069	16,629	5,284,000
Djibouti	+3	franc	centimes	1977			French, Arabic, Afar, Somali	Mousa (6,769')	22,000	8,494	634,000
Dominica	-4	East Caribbean $	cents	1978	1978		English	Imray's View (4,747')	748	289	71,200
Dominican Republic	-4	peso	centavos	1945			Spanish	Pico Duarte (10,417')	48,734	18,816	8,097,000
East Timor	+9	US dollar	cents				Portuguese	Tata Mailau (9,679')	14,874	5,743	839,719
Ecuador	-5	US dollar	cents	1945			Spanish	Chimborazo (20,561')	283,561	109,483	13,839,978
Egypt	+2	pound	piastres	1945			Arabic	Jebel Katherina (8,651')	1,001,449	386,660	69,536,644
El Salvador	-6	colon	centavos	1945			Spanish	Santa Ana (7,812')	21,041	8,124	6,237,662
Equatorial Guinea	+1	franc (was epkwele)	centimos	1968			Spanish	Moka (9,350')	28,051	10,831	486,060
Eritrea	+3	nafka	cents	1993			English, Arabic	Ramlo (7,235')	93,679	36,169	4,298,269
Estonia	+2	kroon	sent	1991			Estonian	Munamagi (1,042')	45,125	17,423	1,423,316
Ethiopia	+3	birr	cents	1945			Amharic, Galla, Somali	Ras Dashen (15,158')	1,128,221	435,607	65,891,874
Fiji	+13	dollar	cents	1970 left 1987	1970		English, Fijian	Victoria (Tomanivi) 4,341'	18,274	7,056	844,330
Finland	+2	euro	cents	1955		1995	Finnish, Swedish	Haltiatunturi (4,344')	338,000	130,502	5,175,783
France	+1	euro	cents	1945		1958	French	Blanc (15,771')	547,026	211,207	59,551,227
Gabon	+1	franc	centimes	1960			French, Fang, Eshira, Mbete	Iboundji (5,185')	267,667	103,346	1,221,175
Gambia	0	dalasi	butut	1965	1965		English	No land above 66'	11,295	4,361	1,411,205
Georgia	+4	lari	tetri	1992			Georgian, Russian, Armenian	Shkhara (16,627')	69,700	26,911	4,989,285
Germany	+1	euro	cents	1973		1958	German	Zugspitze (9,721')	357,050	137,857	83,029,536
Ghana	0	cedi	pesewas	1957	1957		English, Asante, Ewe, Fante	Afadjato (2,860')	238,537	92,099	19,894,014
Greece	+2	euro	cents	1945		1981	Greek	Olympus (9,550')	131,944	50,944	10,623,855
Greenland	-3	krone	ore				Greenlandic, Danish	Gunnbjorns Field (12,139)	2,175,600	840,000	56,000

GEOGRAPHY

Country	GMT	Currency	Split into 100	UN Member	Common-wealth	Europe	Official Languages	Highest Point	Area Sq Km	Area Sq Miles	Population
Grenada	-4	East Caribbean $	cents	1974	1974		English	St Catherine (2,756')	344	133	89,227
Guatemala	-6	quetzal	centavos	1945			Spanish	Tajumulco (13,881')	108,889	42,042	12,974,361
Guinea	0	franc	centimes	1958			French	Nimba (5,748')	245,857	94,925	7,613,870
Guinea-Bissau	0	franc	centimes	1974			Portuguese, Creole, Fulani	Fouta Djallon (600')	36,125	13,948	1,315,822
Guyana	-4	dollar	cents	1966	1966		English, Hindu, Urdu	Roraima (9,094')	214,969	83,000	697,181
Haiti	-5	gourde	centimes	1945			French, Creole	Pic La Selle (8,793')	27,750	10,714	6,964,549
Honduras	-6	lempira	centavos	1945			Spanish	Cerro Las Minas (9,400')	112,088	43,277	6,406,052
Hong Kong	+8	dollar	cents				Chinese, English	no named mountains	1,071	414	6,724,900
Hungary	+1	forint	filler	1955			Magyar	Kekes (3,330')	93,030	35,919	10,106,017
Iceland	0	krona	aurar	1946			Icelandic	Hvannadalshnukur (6,952')	103,000	39,768	277,906
India	+5.5	rupee	paisa	1945	1947		Hindi, English	Nanda Devi (25,645')	3,287,590	1,269,340	1,027,015,247
Indonesia	+7–+9	rupiah	sen	1950			Bahasa Indonesia	Puncak Jaya (16,020')	1,904,569	735,355	228,437,870
Iran	+3.5	rial	dinars	1945			Farsi	Qolleh-ye Damavand (18,386')	1,648,000	636,293	66,128,965
Iraq	+3	dinar	fils-1000	1945			Arabic	Kurdistan Range (12,000')	434,924	167,924	23,331,985
Ireland	0	euro	cents	1955	left 1949	1973	Irish, English	Carrantuohill (3,414')	70,283	27,136	3,626,087
Israel	+2	Shekel	Agorot	1949			Hebrew, Arabic	Atzmon (Har Meron) 3,963'	20,770	8,019	6,100,000
Italy	+1	euro	cents	1955		1958	Italian	Blanc (15,616')	301,225	116,303	57,523,000
Ivory Coast	0	franc	centimes	1960			French	Toukui (6,900')	322,463	124,503	14,300,000
Jamaica	-5	dollar	cents	1962	1962		English	Blue Mountain Peak (7,402')	10,991	4,244	2,665,636
Japan	+9	yen	sen	1956			Japanese	Fuji (12,388')	369,792	142,777	126,771,612
Jordan	+2	dinar	fils–1,000	1955			Arabic	Jabal Ramm (5755')	97,740	37,737	5,153,378
Kazakhstan	+4–+6	tenge	tyin	1992			Kazakh, Russian	Khan-Tengri Peak (5,000')	2,717,300	1,049,151	15,049,100
Kenya	+3	shilling	cents	1963	1963		Swahili, English, Kikuyu	Kenya (17,057')	582,646	224,960	30,765,916
Kiribati	+12–+13	Australian $	cents	1979	1979		English, Kiribati (Gilbertese)	Banaba Peak (265')	728	281	96,335
Korea, North (Chosun)	+9	won	chon	1991			Korean	Pektu San (9,003')	120,538	46,540	21,968,228
Korea, South	+9	won	jeon	1991			Korean	Halla-san (6,398')	98,477	38,022	47,904,370
Kuwait	+3	dinar	fils–1000	1963			Arabic	Ash-Shaqaya (951')	17,818	6,880	2,041,961
Kyrgyzstan	+5	som	tyiyn	1992			Kirghiz, Russian	Victory Peak (24,406') (Pik Pobedy)	198,500	76,641	4,753,003
Laos	+7	kip	at	1955			Lao, French	Phou Bia (9252')	231,800	89,498	5,635,967
Latvia	+2	lat	santims	1991			Latvian	Vidzeme (Livonia) 1020'	63,935	24,685	2,385,231
Lebanon	+2	pound	piastres	1945			Arabic	Qurnat as-Sawda (10131')	10,400	4,015	3,627,774
Lesotho	+2	loti	lisente	1966	1966		Sesotho, English	Thabana Ntlenyana (11425')	30,355	11,720	2,177,062
Liberia	0	dollar	cents	1945			English	Peak of Mt Nimba (4500')	111,369	43,000	3,225,837
Libya	+1	dinar	dirhams-1000	1955			Arabic	Pico Bette (7500')	1,759,540	679,359	5,240,599
Liechtenstein	+1	Swiss franc	rappen/ centimes	1993			German	Grauspitze (8526')	158	61	32,528
Lithuania	+2	litas	centas	1991			Lithuanian	Juozapine (964')	65,200	25,174	3,483,972

Country	GMT	Currency	Split into 100	UN Member	Common-wealth	Europe	Official Languages	Highest Point	Area Sq Km	Area Sq Miles	Population
Luxembourg	+1	euro	cents	1945		1958	French, German, Letzeburgesch	Bourgplatz (1833')	2,586	998	442,972
Macedonia	+1	denar	denis	1993			Macedonian, Albanian	Kajmakcalan (8271')	25,713	9,928	2,046,209
Madagascar	+3	franc	centimes	1960			Malagasy, French	Maromokotro (9436')	587,041	226,657	15,982,563
Malawi	+2	kwacha	tambala	1964	1964		English, Chichewa	Mlanje Sapitwa (9843')	118,484	45,747	10,548,250
Malaysia	+8	ringgit	sen	1957	1957		Malay, Chinese, English	Kinabalu (13455')	329,749	127,316	22,229,040
Maldives	+5	rufiyaa	laaris	1965	1982		Divehi	no land above 8'	298	115	310,764
Mali	0	franc	centimes	1960			French, Bambara, Fulani	Hombori Tondo (3789')	1,240,000	478,764	11,008,518
Malta	+1	lira	cents	1964	1964		Maltese, English, Italian	Sceberras (816')	246	95	382,525
Marshall Islands	+12	US dollar	cents	1991			Marshallese, English	no land above 20'	181	70	70,822
Mauritania	0	ouguiya	khoums-5	1961			Arabic, French, Hassaniya	Kediet Ijill (3,002')	1,030,700	397,954	2,747,312
Mauritius	+4	rupee	cents	1968	1968		English	Black River Mountain (2,711')	2,045	790	1,199,881
Mexico	-6/-8	peso	centavos	1945			Spanish	Orizaba (18,406')	1,972,547	761,601	97,483,412
Moldova	+2	leu	bani	1992			Moldovan, Russian	Balaneshty (1,409)	33,700	13,012	4,335,000
Monaco	+1	euro	cents	1993			French	On Chemin de Revoires (533')	1.9	0.73	31,842
Mongolia	+8	tugrik	möngö	1961			Khalkha Mongolian	Monh Hayrhan Uul (14,311')	1,565,000	604,247	2,654,999
Morocco	0	dirham	centimes	1956			Arabic, French, Berber	Jebel Toubkal (13,655')	446,550	172,413	30,645,305
Mozambique	+2	metical	centavos	1975	1995		Portuguese	Monte Binga (7,992')	801,590	309,494	19,371,057
Myanmar (Burma)	+6	kyat	pyas	1948			Burmese, English	Hkakado Razi (19,296')	676,552	261,217	41,994,678
Namibia	+2	namibian $	cents	1990	1990		Afrikaans, English	Brandberg (8,461')	824,292	318,259	1,797,677
Nauru	+12	Australian $	cents	1968	1968		English	Nauru Peak (225')	21	8	12,088
Nepal	+5.75	rupee	paisa	1955			Nepali	Everest (29,035')	140,747	54,342	25,284,463
Netherlands	+1	euro	cents	1945		1958	Dutch	Vaalserberg (1,053')	40,844	15,770	15,981,472
New Zealand	+13	dollar	cents	1945	1931		English, Maori	Cook (12,349')	268,867	103,810	3,864,129
Nicaragua	-6	cordoba	centavos	1945			Spanish	Pico Mogoton (6,913')	130,000	50,193	4,918,393
Niger	+1	franc	centimes	1960			French, Hausa, Tuareg	Greboun (6,562')	1,267,000	489,189	10,335,156
Nigeria	+1	naira	kobo	1960	1960		English, Hausa, Ibo, Yoruba	Dimlang (6,700')	923,768	356,667	126,635,626
Norway	+1	krone	ore	1945			Norwegian	Galdhopiggen (8,098')	386,958	149,405	4,504,000
Oman	+4	rial omani	baizas-1000	1971			Arabic	Jabal ash Sham (10,400')	212,457	82,030	2,400,000
Pakistan	+5	rupee	paisa	1947	1947		Urdu	K2 (Godwin Austen) 28,250'	883,254	341,025	144,616,639
Panama	-5	balboa	centesimos	1945			Spanish	Chiriqui (11,467')	77,082	29,761	2,815,644
Papua New Guinea	+10	kina	toea	1975	1975		English, Pidgin, Moru	Wilhelm (15,400')	461,691	178,259	5,049,055
Paraguay	-3	guarani	céntimos	1945			Spanish, Guarani	Cerro Tatug (2,297')	406,752	157,047	5,734,139
Peru	-5	new sol	cents	1945			Spanish, Quechua	Huascaran (22,205')	1,285,216	496,222	27,483,864
Philippines	+8	peso	centavos	1945			Pilipino, English	Apo (9,690')	3000,00	115,830	82,841,518
Poland	+1	zloty	groszy	1945			Polish	Rysy (8,199)	312,677	120,725	38,633,912
Portugal	0	euro	cents	1955		1986	Portuguese	Estrela (6,539')	88,880	34,317	9,920,760
Qatar	+3	riyal	dirhams	1971			Arabic	no named mountains	11,000	4,247	769,152

GEOGRAPHY

Country	GMT	Currency	Split into 100	Common-wealth	Europe	UN Member	Official Languages	Highest Point	Area Sq Km's	Area Sq Miles	Population
Romania	+2	leu	bani			1955	Romanian	Moldoveanu (8,346')	237,500	91,699	22,430,457
Russia	+2–+12	rouble	kopeks			1991	Russian	Elbrus (18,510')	17,075,400	6,592,819	144,200,000
Rwanda	+2	franc	centimes			1962	French, Kinyarwanda	Karisimbi (14,787')	26,338	10,169	7,312,756
St Kitts and Nevis	-4	East Caribbean $	cents	1983		1983	English	Liamuiga Nevis (3,792')	269	104	38,756
St Lucia	-4	East Caribbean $	cents	1979		1979	English	Gimie (3,145')	616	238	158,178
St Vincent	-4	East Caribbean $	cents	1979		1980	English	Soufrière (4,048')	388	150	109,022
Samoa	-11	tala	sene	1970		1976	Samoan, English	Mauga Silisli (6,094')	1,714	662	168,000
San Marino	+1	euro	cents			1992	Italian	Titano (2,424')	61	24	26,336
São Tomé	0	dobra	centavos			1975	Portuguese	Pico Gago Coutinho (6,640')	964	372	165,034
Saudi Arabia	+3	riyal	halalah			1945	Arabic	Jebel Razikh (12,002')	2,149,640	829,977	22,757,092
Senegal	0	franc	centimes			1960	French, Wolof, Fulani	Gounou (4,970')	196,192	75,750	10,284,929
Seychelles	+4	rupee	cents	1976		1976	Creole, English, French	Seychellois (2,992')	456	176	79,725
Sierra Leone	0	leone	cents	1961		1961	English, Krio, Mende	Bintimani (6,390')	71,740	27,699	5,426,618
Singapore	+8	dollar	cents	1965		1965	Malay, Chinese, Tamil, English	Bukit Timah (581')	639	247	4,017,733
Slovakia	+1	koruna	hallers			1993	Slovak, Hungarian, Czech	Gerlachovsky (8,711')	49,035	18,932	5,414,937
Slovenia	+1	tolar	stotin			1993	Slovene, Hungarian	Triglav (9,396')	20,251	7,819	1,987,000
Solomon Islands	+11	dollar	cents	1978		1978	English, Pidgin	Makarakombou (8,028')	28,446	10,983	480,442
Somalia	+3	shilling	cents			1960	Somali, Arabic, English	Surud Ad (7,894')	637,657	246,200	7,488,773
South Africa	+2	rand	cents	1931		1945	Afrikaans, English, Xhosa, Zulu	Injasuti (11,182')	1,221,031	471,441	43,686,000
Spain	+1	euro	cents		1986	1955	Spanish	Teide (12,190') Canaries	504,782	194,897	40,037,995
Sri Lanka	+6	rupee	cents	1948		1955	Sinhalese, Tamil	Pidurutalagala (8,292')	65,610	25,332	19,408,635
Sudan	+3	dinar	pounds=10			1956	Arabic	Kinyeti (10,456')	2,505,813	967,495	30,080,373
Suriname	-3	guilder/florin	cents			1975	Dutch, Hindustani, Sranang Tongo	Julianatop (4,218')	163265	63,037	433,998
Swaziland	+2	lilangeni	cents	1968		1968	English, Swazi	Emlembe (6,113')	17,363	6,704	1,104,343
Sweden	+1	krona	ore		1995	1946	Swedish, Finnish	Kebnekaise (6,965')	449,964	173,731	8,875,053
Switzerland	+1	Swiss francs	centimes/rappen				German, French, Italian, Romansch	Dufourspitze (15,203')	41,293	15,943	7,283,274
Syria	+2	pound	piastres			1945	Arabic, Kurdish, Armenian	Jabal ash–Shaikh (Hermon) (9,232')	185,180	71,498	16,728,808
Taiwan	+8	dollar	cents				Mandarin Chinese	Yu Shan (Morrison) (13,113')	35,742	13,800	22,350,000
Tajikistan	+5	somoni	dirams			1992	Tajik, Uzbek, Russian	Communism Peak (24,590')	143,100	55,251	6,578,681
Tanzania	+3	shilling	cents	1961		1964	English, Kiswahili	Kilimanjaro (19,340')	945,087	364,898	36,232,074
Thailand	+7	baht	satang			1946	Thai	Doi Inthanon (8,452')	514,000	198,456	61,797,751
Togo	0	franc	centimes			1960	French, Ewe, Kabiye	Baumann (3,235') aka Agou	56,785	21,925	5,153,088
Tonga	+14	pa'anga	seniti	1970		1970	Tongan, English	Kao (3,380')	699	270	104,227

Country	GMT	Currency	Split into 100	UN Member	Common-wealth	Europe	Official Languages	Highest Point	Area Sq Km's	Area Sq Miles	Population
Trinidad and Tobago	-4	dollar	cents	1962	1962		English, Hindi, French, Spanish	Cerro Aripo (3,085')	4,828	1864	1,169,682
Tunisia	+1	dinar	millemes–1,000	1956			Arabic, French	Djebel Chambi (5,066')	164,150	63,378	9,660,000
Turkey	+2	lira	kurus	1945			Turkish	Buyuk Agridagi (Ararat) (17,011')	814,578	314,509	66,493,970
Turkmenistan	+5	manat	tenge	1992			Turkmenian, Russian, Uzbek	Koitendag Peak (11,293)	488,100	188,456	5,500,000
Tuvalu	+12	dollar	cents	1978	1978		Tuvaluan, English	no land above 15'	16	6	10,991
Uganda	+3	shilling	cents	1962	1962		English, Swahili, Luganda	Stanley (16,795')	236,036	91,134	23,985,712
Ukraine	+2	hryvna	kopiykas	1945			Ukrainian, Russian	Kamul (1,549')	603,700	233,089	48,900,000
United Arab Emirates	+4	dirham	fils	1971			Arabic	Western Al-Hajar (3,900')	83,600	32,278	2,407,460
United Kingdom	0	pound	pence	1945	1931	1973	English	Ben Nevis (4,406')	240,883	93,005	59,647,790
USA	-5/--10	dollar	cents	1945			English	McKinley (20,320')	9,158,960	3,536,278	281,421,906
Uruguay	-3	peso	centesimos	1945			Spanish	Cerro de Las Animas (1,643')	176,215	68,037	3,360,105
Uzbekistan	+5	sum	tiyin	1992			Uzbek, Russian, Tajik	Beshtor (14,104')	447,400	172,741	25,000,000
Vanuatu	11	vatu	centimes	1981	1980		Bislama, French, English	Tabwebesana (6,195')	12,190	4,707	192,910
Vatican City	+1	euro	cents				Italian, Latin, Polish	none	0.44	0.17	890
Venezuela	-4	bolivar	centimos	1945			Spanish	La Pico Columna (Bolivar) (16,427')	912,050	352,143	25,160,000
Vietnam	+7	dong (=10 Hao)	xu	1977			Vietnamese	Fan si Pan (10,308')	329,556	127,242	79,939,014
Yemen	+3	riyal	fils	1947			Arabic	Jabalan Nabi Shu'ayb (12,336')	527,969	203,849	18,078,035
Yugoslavia	+1	dinar	paras	1945			Serbo Croat, Macedonian, Slovenic	Daravica (8,714')	102,350	39,517	10,766,290
Zambia	+2	kwacha	ngwee	1964	1964		English, Bemba, Nyanja	Muchinga (7,350')	752,614	290,585	9,770,199
Zimbabwe	+2	dollar	cents	1980	1980		English, Sindebele, Chishona	Inyangani (8,503')	390,580	150,803	11,365,366

NB: Of the 54 Commonwealth members, 16 have Queen Elizabeth II as head of state, 33 are republics and five have their own monarchies. Pakistan left the Commonwealth in 1972 but rejoined in 1989, but was suspended on 18 October 1999. Zimbabwe was suspended on 20 March 2002.

GEOGRAPHY

Country	International Car Registration	Drives	International Civil Aircraft Markings	Type of Government	Religion	National Day	IDD Codes from UK	IDD Codes to UK
Afghanistan	AFG	right	YA	democratic republic	Islam	19 Aug	0093	operator
Albania	AL	right	ZA	socialist republic	Islam	11 Jan	00355	0044
Algeria	DZ	right	7T	democratic republic	Islam	1 Nov	00213	0044
Andorra	AND	right	C3	unicameral co-principality	RC	8 Sept	00376	0044
Angola		right	D2	people's republic	none	11 Nov	00244	0044
Antigua and Barbuda			V2	constitutional monarchy	none	1 Nov	001268	01144
Argentina	RA	right	LQ, and LV	federal republic	RC	25 May	0054	0044
Armenia		right		federal state	none	21 Sept	00374	81044
Australia	AUS	left	V8	federal parliamentary state	none	26 Jan	0061	001144
Austria	A	right	OE	federal republic	none	26 Oct	0043	0044
Azerbaijan		right		federal republic	Shia Muslim	28 May	00994	81044
Bahamas	BS	left	C6	constitutional monarchy	none	10 July	001242	01144
Bahrain	BRN	right	A9	monarchy	Islam	16 Dec	00973	044
Bangladesh	BD	left	S2	people's republic	Islam	26 Mar	00880	0044
Barbados	BDS	left	8P	constitutional monarchy	none	30 Nov	001246	01144
Belarus	BER	right		federal republic	RC	27 July	00375	81044
Belgium	B	right	00	constitutional monarchy	RC	21 July	0032	0044
Belize	BH	right	V3	constitutional monarchy	none	21 Sept	00501	01144
Benin	DY	right	TY	people's republic	none	30 Nov	00229	0044
Bermuda			VR-B	British colony	none		001441	01144
Bhutan		right	A5	constitutional monarchy	Buddhism	17 Dec	00975	0044
Bolivia		right	CP	republic	RC	6 Aug	00591	0044
Bosnia-Hercegovina		left		federal republic	Islam	1 Mar	00396	9944
Botswana	RB	right	A2	republic	none	30 Sept	00267	0044
Brazil	BR	right	PP, and PT	federal republic	RC	7 Sept	0055	0044
Brunei	BRU	left	V8	monarchy (sultanate)	Islam	23 Feb	00673	0144
Bulgaria	BG	right	LZ	socialist republic	none	3 Mar	00359	0044
Burkina Faso	XT	right	9U	military regime	none	11 Dec	00226	0044
Burundi	RU	right	XU	military regime	none	1 July	00257	9044
Cambodia	K			people's republic	Buddhism	9 Nov	00855	0044
Cameroon	TJ			republic	none	20 May	00237	0044
Canada	CDN	right	CF, and CG	federal parliamentary state	none	1 July	001	01144
Cape Verde	D4			republic	RC	5 July	00238	044
Central African Rep	RCA	right	TL	republic	none	1 Dec	00236	0044
Chad	TT			republic	none	13 Apr	00235	0044
Chile	RCH	right	CC	military regime	RC	18 Sept	0056	0044
China	B			republic	none	1 Oct	0086	0044
Colombia	CO	right	HK	republic	RC	20 July	0057	9044
Comoros	D6			federal republic	Islam	6 July	00269	1044
Congo, Dem Rep of	ZRE	right	9Q	republic	RC	24 Nov	00243	0044
Congo, Rep of	RCB	right	TN	people's republic	RC	15 Aug	00242	0044

Country	International Car Registrations	Drives	International Civil A/C Markings	Type of government	Religion	National Day	IDD Codes from UK	IDD Codes to UK
Costa Rica	CR	right	TI	republic	RC	15 Sept	00506	0044
Croatia	HR	right		republic	RC	30 May	00385	9944
Cuba	C	right	CU	socialist republic	none	1 Jan	0053	11944
Cyprus	CY	left	5B	republic (unicameral parliament)	Greek Orthodox	1 Oct	00357	0044
Czech republic	CS	right	OK	federal republic	RC	28 Oct	00420	0044
Denmark	DK	right	OY	constitutional monarchy	Evangelical Lutheran	5 June	0045	0044
Djibouti			J2	republic	none	27 June	00253	0044
Dominica	WD	left	J7	republic	none	3 Nov	001809	01144
Dominican republic	DOM	left	HI	republic	none	27 Feb	001809	01144
East Timor	RI	right	PK	republic	RC	20 May	0062	00144
Ecuador	EC	right	HC	republic	none	10 Aug	00593	0144
Egypt	ET	right	SU	republic	Islam	23 July	0020	0044
El Salvador	ES	right	YS	republic	none	15 Sept	00503	0044
Equatorial Guinea			3C	republic	none	12 Oct	00240	1944
Eritrea		right		republic	none	24 May	00291	operator
Estonia	EW	right	CCCP	unicameral republic	Lutheran	24 Feb	00372	80044
Ethiopia	E	right	ET	people's republic	none	28 May	00251	0044
Falkland Islands			VP-F		none		00500	0144
Fiji	FJI	left	DQ	republic	none	10 Oct	00679	0544
Finland	SF	right	OH	republic	none	6 Dec	00358	99044
France	F	right	F	republic	none	14 July	0033	0044
Gabon		right	TR	republic	none	17 Aug	00241	0044
Gambia	WAG	right	C5	republic	none	18 Feb	00220	0044
Georgia			GRU	republic	none	26 May	00995	81O44
Germany	D	right	D	republic	none	3 Oct	0049	0044
Ghana	GH	right	9G	republic	none	6 Mar	00233	0044
Gibraltar	GBZ	right	VR-G	republic	none		00350	0044
Greece	GR	right	SX	republic	Eastern Orthodox	25 Mar	0030	0044
Greenland				constitutional monarchy (Denmark)	Evangelical Lutheran		00299	00944
Grenada	WG	left	J3	constitutional monarchy	none	7 Feb	001809	01144
Guatemala	GCA	right	TG	republic	none	15 Sept	00502	0044
Guinea			3X	republic	none	2 Oct	00224	0044
Guinea-Bissau			J5	republic	none	24 Sept	00245	operator
Guyana	GUY	left	8R	republic	none	26 May	00592	00144
Haiti	RH	right	HH	republic	none	1 Jan	00509	operator
Honduras		left	HR	republic	none	15 Sept	00504	0044
Hong Kong	HK	left	VR-H	territory of China	none		00852	00144
Hungary	H	right	HA	people's republic	none	15 Mar, 20 Aug; 23 Oct	0036	0044
Iceland	IS	right	TF	republic	Evangelical Lutheran	17 June	00354	0044
India	IND	left	VT	republic	none	26 Jan	0091	0044
Indonesia	RI	left	PK	republic	Monotheism	17 Aug	0062	00144

GEOGRAPHY

Country	International Car Registrations	Drives	International Civil A/C Markings	Type of government	Religion	National Day	IDD Codes from UK	IDD Codes to UK
Iran	IR	right	EP	republic	Islam	11 Feb	0098	0044
Iraq	IRQ	right	YI	republic	Islam	17 July	00964	0044
Ireland	IRL	left	EI, and EJ	republic	none	17 Mar	00353	0044
Israel	IL	right	4X	republic	none		00972	0044
Italy	I	right	I	republic	none	2 June	0039	0044
Ivory Coast	CI	right	TU	republic	none	7 Dec	00225	0044
Jamaica	JA	left	6Y	constitutional monarchy	none	Aug 1st Mon	001879	01144
Japan	J	left	JA	constitutional monarchy	none	23 Dec	0081	00144
Jordan	HKJ	right	JY	Hashemite kingdom	Islam	25 May	00962	0044
Kazakhstan			CCCP	republic	Islam	16 Dec	007	81044
Kenya	EAK	left	5Y	republic	none	12 Dec	00254	00044
Kiribati			T3	republic	none	12 July	00686	0044
Korea, North	P			democratic people's republic	none	8 Sept	00850	01044
Korea, South	ROK	right	HL	republic	none	15 Aug	0082	00144
Kuwait	KWT	right	9K	constitutional monarchy	Islam	25 Feb	00965	0044
Kyrgyzstan			CCCP	republic	Islam	31 Aug	00996	81044
Laos	LAO	right	RDPL	democratic people's republic	Islam	2 Dec	00856	operator
Latvia	LR	right	CCCP	republic	Lutheran	18 Nov	00371	81044
Lebanon	RL	right	OD	republic	none	22 Nov	00961	0044
Lesotho	LS	left	7P	constitutional monarchy	none	4 Oct	00266	0044
Liberia	LB	right	EL	republic	none	26 July	00231	0044
Libya	LAR	right	5A	socialist republic	Islam	1 Sept	00218	0044
Liechtenstein	FL	right	HB	principality	RC	15 Aug	0041	0044
Lithuania			CCCP	republic	RC	16 Feb	00370	81044
Luxembourg	L	right	LX	grand duchy	none	23 June	00352	0044
Macedonia				republic	none	18 Sept	00389	9944
Madagascar	RM	right	5R	democratic republic	none	26 June	00261	0044
Malawi	MW	left	7Q	republic	none	6 July	00265	10144
Malaysia	MAL	left	9M	constitutional monarchy	Islam	31 Aug	0060	0044
Maldives			8Q	republic	Islam	26 July	00960	0044
Mali	RMM	right	TZ	republic	none	22 Sept	00223	0044
Malta	M	left	9H	republic	RC	31 Mar	00356	0044
Marshall Islands			MI	republic	none	21 Oct	00692	01244
Mauritania	RIM	right	5T	Islamic republic	Islam	28 Nov	00222	0044
Mauritius	MS	left	3B	constitutional monarchy	none	12 Mar	00230	0044
Mexico	MEX	right	XA, XB, XC	federal republic	none	16 Sept	0052	9844
Micronesia				federal states	none		00691	01144
Moldova	MOL		MOL	republic	none	27 Aug	00373	81044
Monaco	MC	right	3A	principality	none	19 Nov	0037793	0044
Mongolia				people's republic	none	11 July	00976	operator
Morocco	MA	right	CN	kingdom	Islam	3 Mar	00212	0044

Country	International Car Registrations	Drives	International Civil A/C Markings	Type of government	Religion	National Day	IDD Codes from UK	IDD Codes to UK
Mozambique			C9	people's republic	none	25 June	00258	0044
Myanmar (Burma)	BUR	right	XY, XZ	military regime	none	4 Jan	0095	044
Namibia	SWA	left		federal state	none	21 Mar	00264	0944
Nauru			C2	republic	none	31 Jan	00674	0044
Nepal		right	9N	kingdom	Hinduism	18 Feb	00977	0044
Netherlands	NL	right	PH	kingdom	none	30 April	0031	0044
New Zealand	NZ	left	ZK	constitutional monarchy	none	6 Feb	0064	0044
Nicaragua	NIC	right	YN	republic	none	15 Sept	00505	0044
Niger	RN	right	5U	republic	none	18 Dec	00227	0044
Nigeria	WAN	right	5N	federal republic	none	1 Oct	00234	00944
Norway	N	right	LN	constitutional monarchy	Evangelical Lutheran	17 May	0047	09544
Oman			A40	Sultanate	Islam	18 Nov	00968	0044
Pakistan	PAK	left	AP	republic	Islam	23 Mar & 14 Aug	0092	0044
Panama	PA	right	HP	republic	none	3 Nov	00507	0044
Papua New Guinea	PNG	left	P2	constitutional monarchy	none	16 Sept	00675	0544
Paraguay	PY	right	ZP	republic	RC	15 May	00595	00244
Peru	PE	right	OB	republic	RC	28 July	0051	0044
Philippines	RP	right	RP	republic	RC	12 June	0063	0044
Poland	PL	right	SP	republic	none	3 May	0048	0044
Portugal	P	right	CS	republic	RC	10 June	00351	0044
Qatar			A7	constitutional monarchy	Islam	3 Sept	00974	044
Romania	RO	right	YR	republic	none	1 Dec	0040	0044
Russia	RUS		CCCP	federal republic	none	12 June	007	81044
Rwanda	RWA	right	9XR	republic	none	1 July	00250	0044
Samoa	WS	right	5W	constitutional monarchy	none	1 June	00685	144
San Marino	RSM	right	T7	serene republic	RC	3 Sept	00378	0044
São Tomé			S9	republic	RC	12 July	00239	0044
Saudi Arabia			HZ	kingdom	Islam	23 Sept	00966	0044
Senegal	SN	right	6V	republic	none	4 Apr	00221	0044
Seychelles	SY	left	S7	republic	RC	5 June	00248	044
Sierra Leone	WAL	right	9L	republic	none	27 Apr	00232	044
Singapore	SGP	left	9V	republic	none	9 Aug	0065	00544
Slovak republic			SQ	republic	RC	1 Jan	0042	0044
Slovenia			SLO	republic	RC	25 June	00386	0044
Solomon Islands			H4	constitutional monarchy	none	7 July	00677	0044
Somalia			6O	democratic republic	Islam	tba	00252	operator
South Africa	ZA	left	ZS	republic	none	27 April	0027	0944
Spain	E	right	EC	kingdom	none	12 Oct	0034	0744
Sri Lanka	CL	left	4R	democratic socialist republic	none	4 Feb	0094	0044

GEOGRAPHY

Country	International Car Registrations	Drives	International Civil A/C Markings	Type of government	Religion	National Day	IDD Codes from UK	IDD Codes to UK
St Kitts and Nevis			VP-LKA/ LLZ	constitutional monarchy	none	19 Sept	001869	operator
St Lucia	WL	left	J6	constitutional monarchy	none	22 Feb	001758	044
St Vincent	WV	left	J8	constitutional monarchy	none	27 Oct	001809	0044
Sudan			ST	republic	none	1 Jan	00249	0044
Surinam	SME	left	PZ	republic	none	25 Nov	00597	00144
Swaziland	SD	left	3D	kingdom	none	6 Sept	00268	0044
Sweden	S	right	SE	constitutional monarchy	Lutheran	6 June	0046	00744
Switzerland	CH	right	HB	federal republic	none	1 Aug	0041	0044
Syria	SYR	right	YK	republic	none	17 Apr	00963	0044
Taiwan	RC	right	B	republic	none	10 Oct	00886	00244
Tajikistan			CCCP	republic	Islam	9 Sept	007	81044
Tanzania	EAT/EAZ	left	5H	republic	none	26 Apr	00255	0044
Thailand	T	left	HS	constitutional monarchy	Buddhism	5 Dec	0066	00144
Togo	TG	right	5V	republic	none	13 Jan	00228	0044
Tonga			A3	constitutional monarchy	none	4 June	00676	0044
Trinidad and Tobago	TT	left	9Y	republic	none	31 Aug	001868	01144
Tunisia	TN	right	TS	republic	Islam	20 Mar	00216	0044
Turkey	TR	right	TC	republic	none	29 Oct	0090	0044
Turkmenistan			CCCP	republic	Islam	27 Oct	00993	81044
Tuvalu			T2	constitutional monarchy	Protestant	1 Oct	00688	0044
Uganda	EAU	left	5X	republic	none	9 Oct	00256	0044
UK	GB	left	G	constitutional monarchy	None			
Ukraine	UKR		CCCP	republic	RC	24 Aug	00380	81044
UAE			A6	federal monarchy	Islam	2 Dec	00971	0044
Uruguay	ROU	right	CX	republic	RC	25 Aug	00598	0044
USA	USA	right	N	federal republic	none	4 July	001	01144
Uzbekistan			CCCP	republic	Islam	1 Sept	007	81044
Vanuatu			YJ	republic	none	30 July	00678	0044
Vatican City				state	RC	22 Oct	003966982	0044
Venezuela	YV	right	YV	republic	none	5 July	0058	0044
Vietnam	VN	right	VN	socialist republic	none	2 Sept	0084	0044
Yemen	ADN	right	4W	people's democratic republic	Islam	22 May	00967	9944
Yugoslavia	YU		YU	socialist federal republic	none	29 Nov	00381	0044
Zambia	Z	left	9J	republic	none	24 Oct	00260	0044
Zimbabwe	ZW	left	Z	republic	none	18 Apr	00263	11044

NB: Any gaps in the World Geographical Gazetteer or table above indicate information that has not been verifiable.

National Anthems

Country	National Anthem	Country	National Anthem
Afghanistan	Soroud-e-Melli	**Germany**	Unity and Right and Freedom
	First line: As long as the earth and heavens exist	**Ghana**	God bless our Homeland, Ghana
		Greece	Hymn to Freedom
Albania	The Flag that in Battle United Us	**Guatemala**	Happy Guatemala
Algeria	Qassaman	**Guinea**	People of Africa
	First line: We swear by the lightning that destroys	**Guyana**	Dear land of Guyana
		Haiti	La Dessalinienne
Andorra	Great Charlemagne, My Father	**Honduras**	Your Flag is a Heavenly Light
Angola	Angola Avante	**Hungary**	God Bless the Hungarians
Antigua and Barbuda	Fair Antigua and Barbuda	**Iceland**	O God of Our Country
		India	Jana-gana-mana
Argentina	Hear, Oh Mortals, the Sacred Cry of Liberty	**Indonesia**	Indonesia, Our Native Land
		Iran	Sorood-e Jomhoori-e Eslami
Australia	Advance Australia Fair	**Iraq**	Salute of the Republic
Austria	Land of Mountains, Land on the River (from Mozart's 'Little Masonic Cantata')	**Ireland**	The Soldier's Song
		Israel	The Hope (Hatikvah)
		Italy	Inno di Mameli
Bahamas	March on, Bahamaland	**Ivory Coast**	L'Abidjanaise
Bangladesh	Amar Sonar Bangla	**Jamaica**	First line: Jamaica, Land We Love
	First line: My golden Bengal, I love you	**Japan**	Kimi ga yo Wa (May Your Peaceful Reign Last Long)
Barbados	In Plenty and in Time of Need		First line: The reign of our emperor
Belarus	Soviet anthem with words omitted	**Jordan**	Long Live the King
Belgium	La Brabançonne	**Kenya**	Ee Mungu nguvu yetu (Oh God of all creation)
Belize	O Land of the Free		
Benin	The New Dawn	**Kiribati**	Stand up, Kiribati
Bolivia	Oh Bolivia, Our Long-Felt Desires	**Korea, North**	Shine Bright O Dawn on This Land So Fair
	First line: Bolivians, propitious fate has crowned our hopes		
		Korea, South	Aegukka
Botswana	Fatshe Leno La Rona	**Laos**	Xatlao tangtae dayma Lao
	First line: Blessed be this noble land		First line: thook thuana nentxoo soo tehay (for the whole of time the Lao people glorified their Fatherland)
Brazil	From Peaceful Ypiranga's Banks		
Brunei	O God, Long Live Our Majesty the Sultan		
		Latvia	God Bless Latvia
Bulgaria	Stara Planina's Peaks Proudly Rise	**Lebanon**	We All Belong to the Homeland
Burkina Faso	Against the Humiliating Bars, a Thousand Years Ago	**Lesotho**	Lesotho fatsela bontat'a rona (Lesotho, land of our fathers)
Burundi	Dear Burundi, O Pleasant Land	**Liberia**	All Hail, Liberia, Hail
Cambodia	Nokoreach	**Liechtenstein**	High on the Rhine
Cameroon	O Cameroon Thou Cradle of Our Forefathers	**Lithuania**	Lietuva tevyne musu (Lithuania, Our land)
Canada	O Canada, Our Home and Native Land	**Luxembourg**	Our Homeland
		Macedonia	Today over Macedonia
Chile	Dulce Patria, Recibe Los Votos	**Madagascar**	Ry tanindrazanay Malala o (O beloved Fatherland)
China	March of the Volunteers		
Colombia	Oh Gloria Inmarcesible	**Malawi**	O God Bless our Land of Malawi
Croatia	Our Beautiful Homeland	**Malaysia**	Negara-Ku (My Country)
Cuba	To Battle, Men of Bayamo	**Maldives**	Qawmee Salaam
Cyprus	Ode to Freedom	**Mali**	A ton appel, Mali (at your call Mali)
Czech Republic	Where is my Motherland	**Malta**	L-Innu Malti
		Mauritius	Glory to Thee, Motherland
Denmark	King Christian Stood by the Lofty Mast	**Mexico**	Mexicans, the War Cry
		Monaco	Hymne Monégasque
Dominica	Isle of Beauty	**Morocco**	Hymn of the Sharif
Dominican Rep	Brave men of Quisqueya, Let Us Raise Our Song	**Mozambique**	Long Live Frelimo
		Myanmar (Burma)	We Shall Love Burma Evermore
East Timor	Patria Patria (Fatherland, fatherland)		
Egypt	Biladi	**Nepal**	May Glory Crown Our Illustrious Sovereign
El Salvador	Let Us Proudly Hail the Fatherland		
Estonia	My Fatherland	**Netherlands**	Wilhelmus van Nassaue
Ethiopia	Ityopya, Ityopya Kidemi	**New Zealand**	God Defend New Zealand/God Save the Queen
Fiji	God bless Fiji		
Finland	Oi aamme Suomi (Our Land, Finland)	**Nicaragua**	Hail, Nicaragua
		Nigeria	Arise, O Compatriots
France	La Marseillaise	**Norway**	Yes, We Love This Country
Gabon	Uni dans la Concorde	**Oman**	God Save Our Sultan Said
Gambia, The	For The Gambia, Our Homeland	**Pakistan**	Quami Tarana

GEOGRAPHY

Country	National Anthem
Panama	Victory Is Ours at Last
Papua New Guinea	Arise, All You Sons of This Land
Paraguay	Paraguayans, Republic or Death
Peru	We Are Free, Let Us Remain So Forever
Philippines	Bayang Magiliw First line: Beloved land, pearl of the Orient
Poland	Poland Has Not Yet Been Destroyed
Portugal	A Portuguesa
Romania	Desteaptate, Romane, din somnul cel de moarte (wake up Romanians, from your deadly slumber)
Russia	Slavsya (Be Great)
Samoa	The Banner of Freedom
Saudi Arabia	Long Live Our Beloved King
Seychelles	Koste Seselwa (Seychelles Unite)
Sierra Leone	High We Exalt Thee, Realm of the Free
Singapore	Majulah Singapura
Slovak Republic	Storm over the Tatras
Slovenia	A Toast
Solomon Islands	God Bless our Solomon Islands
South Africa	The Call of South Africa, and God Bless South Africa
Spain	Marcha Real Española
Sri Lanka	Sri Lanka Matha, Apa Sri Lanka (Mother Sri Lanka, thy Sri Lanka)
St Kitts and Nevis	O Land of Beauty
St Lucia	Sons and Daughters of Saint Lucia
St Vincent	St Vincent, Land So Beautiful
Sudan	We Are the Army of God
Swaziland	Ingoma Yesive

Country	National Anthem
Sweden	Thou Ancient, Thou Freeborn
Switzerland	Step into the Rosy Dawn
Syria	Defenders of the Homeland, Greetings
Tanzania	God Bless Africa
Thailand	Pleng Chart
Togo	Terre de nos aieux (Land of our forefathers)
Tonga	Oh Almighty God Above
Trinidad and Tobago	Forged from the Love of Liberty
Tunisia	Humata Al Hima First line: Immortal and precious the blood we have shed
Turkey	The Independence March First line: Korkma Sünmez bu safaklarda yüzen al sancak (Be not afraid! Our flag will never fade)
Tuvalu	Tuvalu for the Almighty
Uganda	Oh, Uganda First line: Pearl of Africa
UK	God Save the Queen
Uruguay	Easterners, the Fatherland or Death
USA	The Star-Spangled Banner
Vanuatu	First line: Yumi, yumi, yumi i glat blong tale se, yumi, yumi, yumi i man blong Vanuatu (We, we, we are glad to tell, we, we we are the people of Vanuatu)
Venezuela	Glory to the Brave People
Vietnam	Soldiers of Vietnam, We Are Advancing
Yugoslavia	Oh Slavs, Our Ancestors' Words Still Live
Zambia	Stand and Sing of Zambia, Proud and Free
Zimbabwe	Blessed be the Country of Zimbabwe

HISTORY

Chronicles of World History

AD 1 The accepted year of Jesus' birth as calculated by Dionysius Exiguus in AD 525. (The more probable date is now considered to be 4 or possibly 6 BC.)
The King of the Trinovantes tribe, in Southern England, Addedomarus, dies and is succeeded by Dubnovellaunus.

2 Lucius Caesar (the 1st grandson of Augustus) dies.

3 The future Roman Emperor Galba is born.

4 Gaius Caesar (2nd grandson of Augustus) dies leaving Tiberius, the Emperor's newly adopted grandson, as heir.

5 Romans defeat the Lombard tribes on the lower Elbe.

6 Chinese initiate 'Civil Service' examinations for prospective politicians.

7 Ovid works on his masterpiece, *Metamorphoses*.

8 Ovid is exiled to Tomis (now Constanta, in present-day Romania) by the Emperor Augustus for reasons unknown.

9 Germans under Arminius wipe out 3 Roman legions in the Teutoburg Forest. Titus Livius (Livy), from Padua, completes his 142-volume *History of Rome*.

10 Cunobelinus (Cymbeline) rules over most of southern England from his HQ at Camulodunum (Colchester).

12 Gaius Caesar (later nicknamed Caligula, meaning 'little boots') is born.

13 Tiberius is appointed his successor by Augustus.

14 Death of Augustus. His adopted son Agrippa Postumus is immediately executed, and Tiberius becomes emperor.

15 The law of 'Maiestas', making it a crime to harm the interests of Rome, and therefore of the Emperor, is brought back by Tiberius to ensure that his sovereign power is not undermined.

16 An attempt to overthrow Tiberius is thwarted when a slave of Agrippa Postumus, named Clemens, is killed.

17 The poet Ovid dies in exile. Livy dies in Patavium (Padua).

18 In China, the usurper Emperor Wang Mang's forces fail to subdue the rebel band known as the Red Eyebrows at Shandong.

19 Tiberius' nephew Germanicus is poisoned in Syria, possibly by Gnaeus Calpurnius Piso, the governor of Syria.

20 Piso commits suicide during his trial.

21 A revolt by the Gallic tribes, the Treveri and the Aedui, is put down by Gaius Silius.

22 Wang Mang is defeated and killed, during a revolt by followers of the Han regime.

23 Drusus, the son of Tiberius, is poisoned by Lucius Aelius Sejanus, commander of the Praetorian Guard.

24 Tacfarinas, king of the Numidians, is killed by the Romans after a 7-year revolt.

25 Tiberius retires to Capri on the advice of the increasingly dominating Sejanus. Buddha is represented in human form for the first time at Gandhara.

26 Pontius Pilate becomes the 5th Roman procurator of Judaea and Samaria.

27 Tiberius leaves Rome and settles on Capri.

29 Agrippina, widow of Germanicus, is arrested on the orders of Tiberius.

30 Jesus of Nazareth is crucified at Golgotha. Dionysius Exiguus, the inventor of the Christian calendar, wrongly dated the birth of Jesus according to the Roman system, i.e. 754 years after the founding of Rome.

31 Sejanus is executed by Tiberius when the extent of his plotting emerges.

32 In Rome, interest rates rocket as a result of a currency shortage. The Emperor Otho is born.

35 Tiberius makes Caligula and Tiberius Gemellus heirs to his private estate.

36 The future Emperor Nerva is born.

37 Tiberius dies at Misenum and is succeeded by Gaius Caesar (Caligula). The Emperor Nero is born.

38 Drusilla, beloved sister and consort of Caligula, dies, and is deified.

39 Caligula puts down a conspiracy by the governor of higher Germany, Gaetulicus.

40 King Ptolemy of Mauretania is assassinated by order of Caligula.

41 Caligula declares himself a god and is assassinated shortly afterwards. Claudius succeeds him.

42 Cunobelinus, ruler of most of Southern England, dies.

43 The Romans, on the orders of Claudius, invade Britain.

44 James becomes the first Christian apostle to be martyred.

45 The philosopher Philo dies.

46 The kingdom of Thrace becomes a province of Rome.

47 Messalina, wife of the Emperor Claudius, is acquiring a reputation as a sexual profligate.

48 Emperor Guang Wudi re-establishes Chinese domination of the people of inner Mongolia. Claudius has Messalina executed for infidelity.

49 Claudius expels Jewish Christians from Rome.

50 Claudius adopts his stepson Nero.

51 Caractacus, son of Cunobelinus, is captured by the Romans at Ludlow.

52 The future Emperor Domitian is born.

53 Nero marries his stepsister Octavia.

54 Claudius dies after eating poisoned mushrooms administered by the Empress Agrippina. Nero succeeds him.

55 Britannicus, son of Claudius, dies, possibly poisoned by Nero.

57	Paul is arrested at Caesarea and held for trial.
58	Paul writes an epistle to the Romans.
59	Nero has his mother, Agrippina, killed.
60	Mark, a disciple of Jesus, chronicles the life of his master, from baptism by his cousin, John, to his eventual death.
61	During a rebellion led by Queen Boudicca of the Iceni, the Trinovantes and Iceni tribes sack Roman Colchester, St Albans and London. Boudicca commits suicide after defeat by Suetonius Paulinus.
62	Paul is put under 'house arrest' in Rome.
63	The Armenian throne is returned to Tiridates after the peace of Rhandeia.
64	Paul of Tarsus is executed, as is Peter the apostle. Fire destroys over half of the city of Rome.
65	Nero's pregnant wife dies after being kicked by him.
66	The courtier Gaius Petronius is accused of treason and has to commit suicide.
67	The Jews rise up against the Romans.
68	Nero commits suicide to end the Julio-Claudian line of Roman Emperors. He is succeeded by Servius Sulpicius Galba.
69	The year of 4 Roman emperors, Galba, Vitellius, Otho and Vespasian.
70	Vespasian's son, Titus, sacks Jerusalem, destroying most of the 3rd Temple; only the 'Wailing Wall' is left standing.
71	The 'Arch of Titus', in celebration of the sacking of Jerusalem, is erected in Rome.
73	Chinese forces under General Ban Chao gain control over the 'Oasis' states. After a two-year siege, the fortress of Masada in Judea falls to the Romans.
74	Vespasian institutes 'Latin Rights' which give inhabitants of towns identical civil rights to 'Citizens' except for holding public office.
75	Vespasian completes his Temple of Peace in Rome.
76	Johanan Ben Zakkai re-establishes the Sanhedrin, the Jewish religious court.
77	Gnaeus Julius Agricola arrives in Britain to complete the conquest.
78	Vima Kadphises, the Kushan king, who rules India from Benares, sends a delegation to Rome to arrange a surprise attack on the Parthians.
79	Vesuvius erupts, destroying Pompeii and the neighbouring towns of Herculaneum and Stabiae. Pliny the Elder is one of the victims. Vespasian dies, and his son Titus succeeds him.
80	The apostle Luke begins to write his gospel. The Colosseum is opened in Rome.
81	Titus dies of the plague and is succeeded by his brother, Titus Flavius Domitianus (Domitian). Domitian consecrates the triumphal arch to celebrate Titus's victory over the Jews.
82	Spanish poet Marcus Valerius Martialis (Martial) begins his *Epigrams*.
83	Agricola defeats the Caledonians at Mount Graupius.
84	Agricola is called back to Rome.
85	Domitian appoints himself censor for life, thereby giving himself complete control of the composition of the Senate.
86	The future Emperor Antoninus is born.
87	The Romans suffer a serious setback in the Dacian War.
88	The revolt of Saturninus, governor of Upper Germany, leads to Domitian declaring that only one legion is to be quartered in each Roman camp, to prevent any local commander from gaining excessive influence over troops.
89	Domitian is forced to sign a peace treaty with the Dacian king, Decebalus.
90	Domitian begins the persecution and execution of opponents.
91	Chinese general Ban Chao defeats the Indian Kushans.
92	The Iazyges, a nomadic tribe, invade Dacia. Domitian leads his soldiers in person and succeeds in repelling them.
94	General Ban Chao completes his conquest of the Tarim basin.
95	Malaria appears in rural areas around Rome.
96	Emperor Domitian is stabbed to death by plotters led by his wife, Domitia. Senator Marcus Cocceius Nerva succeeds him.
97	Emperor Nerva recalls General Marcus Ulpius Trajanus (Trajan) from Upper Germany and adopts him.
98	Emperor Nerva dies, and is succeeded by Trajan.
99	Julius Frontinus, a former governor of Britain, surveys and describes the aqueducts of Rome in his capacity as superintendent of Rome's water supply.
100	The Sun and Moon pyramids are begun at Teotihuacán in Mexico.
101	Trajan invades Dacia (in present-day Romania), fearing the increasing dominance of Decebalus.
102	Sarmizegethusa, capital of Dacia, is taken by Trajan; Decebalus agrees to become a Roman ally.
104	Martial dies at Bibilis, in Spain.
105	Tsai Lun, a Chinese eunuch, invents a kind of paper made from tree bark, hemp and rags.
106	Dacia becomes a Roman province after King Decebalus and his chiefs commit suicide.
110	Pliny the Younger is appointed governor of Bithynia. Juvenal publishes his first book of *Satires* in Rome, highlighting corruption, vice and the unjust treatment of the poor.
114	Trajan's Column and Basilica are built. Armenia is annexed to the Roman Empire.
115	Mesopotamia is occupied by the Romans.
116	Assyria is annexed to the Roman Empire.
117	Trajan dies and is succeeded by Publius Aelius Hadrianus (Hadrian). Cornelius Tacitus, the celebrated historian, dies.
120	Construction of the Pantheon in Rome is begun.
122	Construction of Hadrian's Wall is begun.
123	Emperor Hadrian meets the king of Parthia, thus averting war.

125	Plague and famine in North Africa.
128	The Greek physician Galen is born.
132	The Jewish population of Jerusalem revolts over the construction of a shrine to Jupiter on the site of the Temple.
135	The Romans retake and demolish Jerusalem; Jewish leader Simon Bar-Kokhba killed near Caesarea; diaspora begins.
138	Hadrian dies and is succeeded by his recently adopted son Antonius Pius.
139	The Romans advance northwards under governor Quintus Lollius Urbicus from Hadrian's Wall to the Clyde–Forth line.
142	Construction of the Antonine Wall is begun.
154	Brigantian revolt in Pennines put down by governor Julius Verus, but troops withdrawn from Caledonia as a result.
155	Partial destruction by indigenous Picts of the Antonine Wall.
161	Antonius dies and is succeeded by his adopted son Marcus Annius Verus (Marcus Aurelius).
163	Antonine Wall abandoned.
167	Barbarians attack Rome, but are repelled by Marcus Aurelius. The Marcomanni and Quadi cross the Danube into Roman territory.
168	The Marcomanni, who have occupied North-western Italy, are conquered by Marcus Aurelius.
169	The Marcomanni revolt, but the revolt is crushed.
174	The Germanic Quadi tribe defeated by Marcus Aurelius.
175	Avidius Cassius encourages the legions in Asia to revolt, but is assassinated and his head sent to Marcus Aurelius.
177	Persecution of Christians recommences in Rome; they adopt the fish symbol as an emblem of their faith.
180	Marcus Aurelius dies and is succeeded by his son Commodus.
185	Mass mutiny of the Roman army in Britain eventually quelled by newly appointed governor Publius Helvius Pertinax.
192	Commodus murdered by his mistress and chamberlain, who found their names on an execution list.
193	Pertinax is chosen as emperor by the senate, but his strict rule leads to his assassination. Didius Julianus becomes emperor after an auction but has already been deposed and killed by the time that Septimius Severus, the Pannonian legate, invades Rome and is declared emperor.
197	Clodius Albinus, the British legate, revolts, but is defeated and killed by Severus at Lyons.
200	Japanese empress, Jingu, sends a fleet to invade Korea, which surrenders on sight of it.
205	Plotinus, founder of Neoplatonism, is born.
209	Roman legions under Severus and Caracalla march against the Caledonii, advancing as far as Aberdeen; forts built on Firths of Forth and Tay.
211	Septimius Severus dies at York; he is succeeded by his sons Caracalla and Geta.
212	Caracalla murders Geta and slaughters thousands of his brother's supporters. He extends Roman citizenship to all free inhabitants of the Empire by the Edict of Caracalla.
215	Manes, who develops the dualist philosophy known as Manichaeism, is born in southern Mesopotamia.
216	Britannia is divided into two provinces – Upper Britain (south and west) and Lower Britain (north).
217	Caracalla is murdered by his officers, and is succeeded by Macrinus.
218	Macrinus is defeated in battle near Antioch and executed. He is succeeded by Varius Avitus Bassianus, who takes the name Heliogabalus.
220	Fall of the Han Dynasty in China, which splits into a number of smaller states.
222	Heliogabalus is murdered by the Praetorian Guard. His cousin and adopted son Bassianus succeeds him, taking the name Severus Alexander.
225	Southern India breaks up into several kingdoms with the end of the Andgra dynasty.
226	The rebel prince Ardashir takes control of Persia, founding the Sassanid dynasty.
234	Severus Alexander decrees that bread, rather than grain, be given to Rome's poor.
235	The Alemanni invade Gaul, but are bought off by Severus Alexander. As a result, he is murdered by his army, who proclaim Maximinus as Emperor.
238	The African provinces set up Gordianus I, a descendant of Trajan, as Emperor. Gordianus commits suicide when his son is killed by supporters of Maximinus, but when Maximinus is assassinated by the Praetorian Guard, Gordianus' grandson, Gordianus III, becomes emperor.
244	Gordianus III defeats the Persians at Resaena, but soon after is murdered during a mutiny by Marcus Philippus, who replaces him and makes peace with the Persians.
248	Games are held to celebrate Rome's millennium.
249	Decius usurps the throne from Philippus, who is killed. The Goths cross the River Danube and lay waste several Roman provinces.
250	Decius initiates further persecution of Christians.
251	Decius dies in battle against the Goths; his successor Gallus bribes the Goths to return from whence they came.
253	Aemilian revolts against Gallus, who dies by the hand of his own troops. Aemilian dies and Valerianus becomes Emperor.
254	Origen, one of the leading Christian scholars, dies.
255	Plague sweeps across Europe.
257	The Goths move into the Black Sea area.
258	The Alemanni and Suevi invade Northern Italy, but are repulsed at Milan.
260	Valerianus seized by the Persians and dies in captivity; his son Gallienus succeeds him.
267	Prince Odenathus of Palmyra assassinated with Gallienus' complicity.
268	Gallienus murdered by his own troops at Milan. Claudius II becomes emperor.
269	The Goths invade the Balkans, sacking Athens, Sparta and Corinth, but are defeated in battle by Claudius II.

HISTORY

270	Claudius II dies. His brother Quintillus succeeds him, but commits suicide when his troops desert him. Aurelian becomes emperor.
271	Aurelian ejects the Alemanni from Italy, and rebuilds the walls of Rome.
272	Aurelian conquers the kingdom of Palmyra.
274	A rebellion at Châlons is put down by Aurelian, who returns to Rome in triumph.
275	The Romans pull back to the Danube and Rhine, which are established as the Empire's frontier. Aurelian is assassinated by his officers, and Tacitus succeeds him as emperor.
276	Tacitus killed by his own troops after defeating the Goths in Asia Minor. His brother Florianus succeeds, only to be killed also. Marcus Aurelius Probus becomes Emperor. Mani is crucified on the grounds of heresy.
282	The Franks and Alemanni invade Gaul, but are repulsed by Probus, who is killed by his troops in Egypt. Marcus Aurelius Carus replaces him.
283	Marcus Aurelius Carus dies, to be succeeded by his son Numerianus.
284	Numerianus is assassinated, to be replaced by Diocletian.
285	Diocletian partitions the Empire – he rules in the East, to counter the barbarian threat there, while Maximian is appointed to run the Western portion.
286	Carausius, commander of the Channel fleet, revolts and seizes Britain, where construction begins on a series of forts to guard the south-eastern coast (the Saxon Shore forts).
290	Construction begins on the amphitheatre in Verona.
291	Persian King Vahram II kills the Manichaean Sisih.
293	Carausius murdered by Allectus, his finance minister, who seizes power in Britain.
296	Allectus defeated and killed by Constantius Chlorus in battle near Silchester.
300	Diocletian builds a palace at Ragusa (later Dubrovnik).
301	Christianity proclaimed the state religion in Armenia.
303	The notary Genesius is martyred. Diocletian begins a general persecution of Christians.
304	The Kingdom of Cheng Han is founded in Sichuan.
305	Diocletian and his co-ruler Maximian abdicate and are succeeded by Galerius and Constantius Chlorus respectively.
306	Constantius Chlorus dies near York. His son Constantine is proclaimed Emperor, but Galerius raises Severus instead.
307	Severus dies; Galerius raises Licinius to co-Emperor.
308	Maxentius, son of Maximian, becomes despot in Rome.
311	Galerius attempts to expel Maxentius, but is defeated and dies soon after.
312	Constantine defeats Maxentius, his rival Western emperor, at the Milvian Bridge.
313	Christianity tolerated in the Roman Empire by the Edict of Milan.
316	The Xiongnu, later identified with the Huns, invade China.
323	Constantine and Licinius at war; Constantine victorious.
324	Licinius executed; Constantine becomes sole ruler. Christianity declared the official religion of the Roman Empire.
325	Council of Nicaea declares Christ and God are of the same substance – 'consubstantial'.
330	Constantinople (formerly Byzantium; known today as Istanbul) is dedicated as the new capital of the Roman Empire.
335	Church of the Holy Sepulchre consecrated in Jerusalem.
337	Constantine I dies, not long after taking Christian baptism; he is succeeded by his three sons, Constantine II, Constantius II and Constans.
338	Jewish calendar reformed by establishing variable year lengths.
340	Constantine II killed at Aquileia fighting Constans; Empire splits into East under Constantius II and West under Constans.
350	Constans murdered by General Magnentius in a coup.
352	Magnentius is defeated by Constantius II at Mursa in Mesopotamia.
353	Magnentius commits suicide. Constantius II reunites Empire.
356	All pagan temples in the Roman Empire ordered closed by Constantius II.
360	Lo-tsun founds the Caves of the Thousand Buddhas in Gansu, China. The Huns invade Europe for the first time.
361	Constantius II dies, and is succeeded by his pagan cousin Julian.
363	Julian dies in battle against the Persians; Jovian, captain of the Imperial Bodyguard, succeeds to the throne.
364	Jovian cedes Armenia to Shah Shapur II of Persia, and dies on his return. Valentinian I becomes emperor, and appoints his brother Valens to rule in the Eastern half.
367	Picts, Scots, Angles and Saxons invade Britain in a joint attack.
369	Theodosius, a Roman general, re-establishes order in Britain.
372	Buddhism reaches Korea from China.
375	Valentinian I dies. His 4-year-old son Valentinian II nominally succeeds him in the West but his older half-brother Gratian has effective control.
376	The Huns invade Russia and defeat the Visigoths. From now on, tribes pushed westward by the Huns press harder into the Roman Empire.
378	Visigoths defeat and kill the Emperor Valens at the battle of Adrianople.
379	Gratian's general, Theodosius becomes Emperor in the East.
382	Visigoths settled as Foederati (military allies) in the Balkans by Theodosius.
383	Magnus Maximus mutinies against Gratian, who is assassinated. Magnus rules in Britain, Gaul and Spain.
386	Hymn singing introduced by St Ambrose, Bishop of Milan.
388	Magnus Maximus invades Italy, to be defeated by Theodosius and murdered. Valentinian II established in power in the West.

391	The library at Alexandria is destroyed in a fire started by a Christian mob seeking to eradicate non-Christian works.
392	The Frankish general Arbogast organises the assassination of Valentinian II and replaces him with a puppet emperor, Eugenius.
394	Eugenius defeated and killed by Theodosius, who reunites the Empire. Arbogast commits suicide.
395	Theodosius dies, and the Roman Empire splits in two for good. His son Arcadius rules in the East, Honorius in the West.
396	Alaric the Visigoth invades Greece.
397	Stilicho, regent to Honorius, ejects the Visigoths from Greece and crushes a rebellion in North Africa.
401	The Visigoths invade Northern Italy.
402	Visigoths halted by Stilicho at the battle of Pollentia.
405	The Colosseum closed by Honorius.
406	Stilicho halts barbarian invasion of Italy. Vandals under Gunderic invade Gaul.
407	Roman troops depart Britain under the pretender Constantine III; Britain left to fend for itself.
408	Stilicho is murdered on Honorius' orders. Arcadius dies. His son Theodosius II becomes emperor in Constantinople.
409	The Vandals cross the Pyrenees and enter Spain.
410	Visigoths under Alaric sack Rome. Alaric dies shortly afterwards; his brother Ataulf takes command.
411	Constantine III defeated and executed by troops loyal to Honorius. Pelagius calls on St Augustine at Hippo but Augustine refuses to see him.
412	The Visigoths enter Gaul from Italy and establish a kingdom there.
415	Neoplatonist philosopher Hypatia is killed in Alexandria by a Christian mob who scraped her to death with oyster shells.
416	Vandal kingdom of Spain falls to the Visigoths.
418	Franks enter Gaul and settle.
420	Nanjing becomes the capital of northern China once more. Eastern Qin state in China is overthrown by its general Liu Yu, who founds the Liu Song state. St Jerome dies.
422	Theodosius II makes peace with Shah Varahran of Persia, and agrees an annual tribute with the Huns.
423	Death of Honorius, emperor of the West.
425	Constantinople University founded.
426	Yash Kukhmol arrives from Teotihuacán in Copán, founding a Mayan dynasty.
427	Korean capital moved to Pyongyang by King Changsu.
429	Vandals invade Africa, led by King Gaiseric. The British, led by Bishop Germanus, defeat barbarian invaders (the 'Alleluia Victory').
430	Cunedda, chief of the Gododdin, moves at the Welsh King Vortigern's behest from Scotland to Gwynedd, whose royal house he thereby founds.
431	Council of Ephesus deposes Patriarch Nestorius of Constantinople for his belief that Jesus had two natures, one human and one divine.
432	Saint Patrick sent as a missionary to Ireland.
433	Attila becomes co-ruler of the Huns.
439	Carthage taken by Gaiseric's Vandals, who make it their capital.
440	The town of Ys in Armorica (later Brittany) is submerged in a great flood. The Vandals invade Sicily.
441	Britain invaded by Angles, Saxons and Jutes.
443	The Alemanni settle in Alsace.
444	The wheelbarrow developed in China.
446	Britain told to fend for itself when it appeals to Rome for help against barbarian invaders.
450	Theodosius II dies, to be succeeded by Marcian, who refuses to continue paying tribute to the Huns to prevent them from attacking.
451	Huns defeated at battle of Châlons by Romans and Visigoths under Flavius Aetius.
452	Venice founded by refugees from the Huns.
453	Death of Attila on his wedding night.
455	The Vandals sack Rome.
457	Marcian dies, to be succeeded by Leo I.
460	Roman fleet destroyed by the Vandals off Cartagena.
461	Severus III becomes Western emperor.
466	Theodoric II of the Visigoths killed by his brother Euric, who succeeds him.
467	Anthemius elected Western emperor at Leo I's behest; they mount a joint expedition against the Vandals in North Africa.
468	The Vandals successfully repulse the Roman invasion.
471	Goths and Eastern Romans clash due to a feud caused by the failure of the expedition against the Vandals.
472	Ricimer the Visigoth captures Anthemius, and appoints Olybrius in his stead. Both Ricimer and Olybrius subsequently die; Gundobad the Burgundian takes control.
473	Gundobad names Glycerinus Western emperor, but he is deposed by Julius Nepos, a protégé of Leo I.
474	Leo I dies, to be succeeded by his son-in-law Zeno.
475	Orestes deposes Julius Nepos and makes his son Romulus Augustulus Western emperor.
476	Romulus Augustulus deposed by Odoacer at Ravenna; Western Roman Empire ends.
477	Sussex founded by Aelle, who lands with his sons at Selsey.
478	Shinto shrines appear in Japan.
481	At the age of 15, Clovis I succeeds his father Childeric I as king of the Franks.
484	Armenia revolts successfully against the Persians led by Vahan Mamikonian. Freedom of religious worship was restored to them by the Treaty of Nvarsag.

486	Clovis defeats governor Syriagus at Soissons and takes control of Northern Gaul.
488	The Ostrogoths, led by Theodoric and prompted by Zeno, invade Italy, now ruled by Odoacer.
491	Zeno dies, to be succeeded by Anastasius, who marries his widow. The South Saxons under Aelle capture Pevensey Castle.
493	Odoacer surrenders to Theodoric at Ravenna after a siege, and is murdered by him. Theodoric founds the Ostrogoth kingdom of Italy.
495	Cerdic, founder of Wessex, lands near Southampton.
496	Clovis defeats the Alemanni near Strasbourg, and converts to Christianity, being baptised by Bishop Remigius of Rheims.
500	The Marcomanni invade Bavaria from Bohemia, which is settled by the Czechs. Incense is added to Christian services to cover the smell of unwashed worshippers.
502	King Gundobad of Burgundy issues a legal code that establishes equality before the law for Burgundians and Romans.
507	Clovis defeats the Visigoths, killing King Alaric II at Vouillé, near Poitiers, and goes on to conquer Southern Gaul.
508	The Ostrogoths under Theodoric conquer Provence and Septimania.
511	Death of Clovis. His kingdom of Francia is divided into four to provide kingdoms for his four sons.
516	The British comprehensively defeat the Saxons at Mons Badonicus.
517	Emperor Wudi introduces Buddhism to central China.
518	Emperor Anastasius I dies, to be succeeded by Justin I, chief of the imperial guard, who entrusts much imperial policy to his nephew Justinian.
519	Eastern and Western Churches reconciled.
520	Priscian codifies Latin grammar with his long treatise, the *Institutiones Grammaticae*.
522	The philosopher and statesman Boethius arrested on a charge of conspiring against Theodoric.
523	King Thrasamund of the Vandals dies and is succeeded by Hilderic.
524	Boethius writes *The Consolation of Philosophy* and is executed shortly after.
525	Yemen invaded by Abyssinians under Caleb. Dionysius Exiguus wrongly sets the date of Christ's birth as 25 December in the 753rd year of Rome.
526	Theodoric the Ostrogoth dies, and is succeeded by his 10-year-old grandson Athalaric.
527	Death of Justin I; his nephew Justinian succeeds him.
528	Hun King Grod converted to Christianity and was killed. The Korean state of Silla officially recognised Buddhism.
529	Benedict of Nursia founds the monastery of Monte Cassino. Justinian closes the non-Christian Academy at Athens.
530	The great Byzantine general Belisarius defeats the Persians at Dara. King Hilderic of the Vandals dies, to be succeeded by Gelimer.
531	Chosroes I becomes Shah of Persia. The Franks conquer Thuringia.
532	Burgundy invaded by the Franks.
533	Belisarius conquers the Vandal kingdom of North Africa, reclaiming it for Byzantium.
534	Toledo made capital of the Visigoth kingdom of Spain. Malta captured by the Byzantine army.
535	Belisarius invades and captures Sicily, and moves into Southern Italy.
536	Belisarius takes Rome from the Ostrogoths.
537	Arthur and Medrault fall at the battle of Camlann.
539	Witigis, leader of the Ostrogoths, is captured by Belisarius at Ravenna. Belisarius recalled to Constantinople.
540	Totila, an Ostrogoth leader, expels the Byzantines from Italy. The Roman statesman and author Cassiodorus founds the monastery at Vivarium in Calabria and retires there.
541	Totila succeeds to the Ostrogothic throne on the death of his uncle Hildebad. The bubonic 'Plague of Justinian' pandemic starts in Constantinople.
542	The Welsh monk Gildas writes *De Excidio et Conquestu Britanniae*, a history of the Roman conquest and Anglo-Saxon invasion of Britain.
543	Justinian condemns the writings of Origen.
546	Totila captures Rome. Audoin establishes a new Lombard kingdom in Austria.
547	The Plague of Justinian reaches Britain. The Angle king Ida accedes to the throne of Bernicia, in north-east England.
549	The last games are held in Rome.
550	The Toltecs overrun Teotihuacán. St David converts the Welsh.
551	The Byzantines defeat an Ostrogothic fleet in a naval battle.
552	Totila killed at Taginae fighting the Byzantines under Narses. Justinian sends missionaries to China to smuggle silkworms out. Buddhism arrives in Japan from Korea.
553	Rome and Naples annexed by Narses for Byzantium.
554	Narses appointed Exarch of Italy.
558	Reunification of Francia by Chlothar I after the death of his brother Childebert I.
559	The Bulgars attack Constantinople, but are repelled by Belisarius.
560	Aethelbert I becomes king of Kent. Ceawlin becomes king of Wessex.
561	Death of Chlothar I – Francia again split in four by his sons.
563	Foundation of monastery on Iona by Columcille (Saint Columba).
565	St Columba subdues a monster on Loch Ness. Belisarius dies. Justinian I dies, and is succeeded by his nephew Justin II.
567	With the death of Charibert, Francia reorganised into Austrasia in the east, Neustria in the west and Burgundy in the south.
568	Alboin founds a Lombard kingdom in Northern and Central Italy.

570	Muhammad born in Mecca. The Persians take the Yemen from the Abyssinians.
571	Foundation of the kingdom of East Anglia.
572	War breaks out between Persia and Byzantium.
573	Sigebert of Austrasia attacks Chilperic of Neustria over the murder of Galswintha, sister of Sigebert's wife Brunhilda.
574	Aidan ordained king of the Argyll Scots by St Columba.
575	King Sigebert assassinated on the orders of Chilperic's wife and former mistress Fredegunde; Brunhilda seeks revenge.
577	Celtic kings Coinmail, Condidan and Farinmail killed at the battle of Dyrham by West Saxons under Cuthwine and Ceawlin.
578	Death of Justin II, to be succeeded by Tiberius II.
579	Death of Shah Chosroes of Persia.
581	China's Sui dynasty founded by Emperor Wendi (Yang Jian).
582	Death of Tiberius II, to be succeeded by his son-in-law Maurice.
583	Wendi moves into the new city of Chang'an, soon to become the world's largest city.
584	Death of Chilperic of Neustria, who is succeeded by his son Chlothar II.
585	King Leovigild of the Visigoths puts down a revolt by his son Hermenegild, whom he kills, and proceeds to conquer the rest of the Iberian peninsula.
586	King Leovigild dies, leaving the Visigothic throne to his son Recared. Disputes in Japan between Shinto and Buddhist adherents.
587	The Visigoths convert from Arianism to Catholicism. The first Buddhist monastery is built in Japan.
588	Shah Hormizd of Persia deposed and murdered after defeats by Byzantines; replaced by his son Chosroes II.
589	Wendi defeats the Chen at Jian-Kang and reunites China. Chosroes II deposed in Persia, fleeing to Constantinople.
590	Gregory I the Great becomes Pope and undertakes reforms in Rome, as well as helping to expel the plague from the city.
591	Maurice helps restore Chosroes II to the Persian throne in return for territorial concessions.
592	Ceawlin of Wessex deposed by Ceol. The Bretwaldaship (overlordship) of the English peoples south of the Humber passes to Aethelbert of Kent.
593	The newly crowned Aethelfrith unites Bernicia and Deira to create the kingdom of Northumbria.
594	The 'Plague of Justinian' pandemic comes to an end. Gregory of Tours dies.
596	St Augustine dispatched by Pope Gregory to convert Britain.
597	Saint Augustine arrives in Kent, converts King Aethelbert and founds the archdiocese of Canterbury.
600	Tibet begins to develop into a unitary state.
602	Emperor Maurice killed and replaced by Phocas.
603	Battle of Catraeth (Catterick): Aethelfrith of Northumbria defeats a coalition of British from Lothian, North Wales and North West England.
604	The Japanese code of Prince Shotoku Taishi demands the veneration of Buddha, his priests and his laws.
606	Harsha of Thanesar founds an empire in Northern India, the last indigenous ruler to do so for several centuries.
607	Horyuji temple and hospital, the oldest surviving wooden building in the world, constructed in Japan.
609	Consecration of the Pantheon in Rome.
610	Emperor Phocas deposed and killed by Heraclius. Muhammad has a vision of the angel Gabriel on Mount Hira.
611	Death of Ceolwulf of Wessex, succeeded by Cynegils.
612	Harsha of Thanesar takes the title of Emperor of the Five Indies. St Gall founds the hermitage, later a monastery of St Gallen in Switzerland.
613	Francia reunited under Chlothar II after his conquest of Austrasia.
614	Chlothar II issues the *Edictum Chlotacharii*, which defines the rights of kings, nobles and Church within Francia.
615	Jerusalem sacked by the Persians, who take the 'True Cross' as booty.
616	Aethelbert of Kent dies; Raedwald of East Anglia becomes Bretwalda; he kills Aethelfrith of Northumbria at the River Idle, replacing him by the exiled Edwin.
618	Sui dynasty replaced by the Tang.
619	Publication of the *Suan-Ching*, textbooks for use in public examinations in China.
620	Chosroes II takes Rhodes, thus restoring the Persian Empire to the extent it reached under Darius I.
622	In July Muhammad flees from Mecca to Medina (the hegira, from which the Islamic calendar year 1 is dated).
623	Samo, a Frankish merchant, frees Slav tribes in Carinthia from Avar overlordship and becomes their ruler.
625	Death of Raedwald; Edwin of Northumbria becomes Bretwalda.
626	Chinese Emperor Gaozu abdicates in favour of his son Taizong.
627	The Byzantines decisively defeat the Persians at Nineveh.
628	Chosroes II murdered by his son Kavadh II, who succeeds him.
629	Chlothar II dies, to be succeeded by his son Dagobert I. Emperor Heraclius recovers Jerusalem from the Persians.
630	Mecca falls to Muhammad who writes letters on the principles of Islam to various rulers.
632	Death of Muhammad; Abu Bakr chosen as Caliph.
633	Edwin of Northumbria killed by Mercian/Welsh forces at Hatfield. They proceed to ravage the kingdom, which splits back in two.
634	Abu Bakr dies; Umar becomes Caliph. Oswald re-establishes the kingdom of Northumbria and becomes Bretwalda.

635	Islamic forces take Damascus, which becomes the capital of the Caliphate. Harsha invades the land of the Chalukyas, but is repulsed.
638	Jerusalem falls to Islamic forces under Umar.
639	Dagobert I of Francia dies; the kingdom is split again.
641	Great Library at Alexandria destroyed in a fire.
642	Oswald of Northumbria dies in battle at Maserfelth (near Oswestry) fighting King Penda of Mercia; he is succeeded in Bernicia by Oswy. Persia is conquered and made subject to the Caliphate.
644	Byzantine forces capture Alexandria, which revolted against Islamic rule, but the Arabs retake it. Caliph Umar dies, to be succeeded by Uthman.
646	The Taikwa reform in Japan establishes centralised government under Imperial control.
647	Harsha of Thanesar dies, and his Northern Indian empire fragments as a result.
649	Cyprus falls to Islamic forces.
650	The Bulgarian Empire, then in Southern Russia, conquered by the Khazars.
652	Arabs come to an agreement with the Nubians, establishing Aswan as the southern limit of the Caliphate in Egypt.
653	The Visigothic king Recesswinth of Spain draws up a legal code for his domains, the *Liber Iudicorium*.
654	Penda of Mercia, Aethelhere of East Anglia and various other royals are killed in the battle of the River Winwaed by Oswy of Bernicia, who re-establishes Northumbria.
655	A Byzantine fleet led by Constans II defeated at Lycia by an Arab fleet.
656	Caliph Uthman is murdered in Medina. Muhammad's son-in-law Ali replaces him. Grimoald attempts to usurp the throne of Austrasia after the death of Clovis II.
657	Mercia released from Northumbrian rulership; Wulfhere son of Penda becomes king.
661	Ali deposed and murdered; the Umayyad dynasty, founded by Muawiya, assumes the Caliphate at Damascus.
664	The English Church adopts the Roman liturgy in preference to the Irish at the Synod of Whitby.
668	Emperor Constans II dies mysteriously in his bath at Syracuse.
669	Theodore of Tarsus ordained Archbishop of Canterbury, and proceeds to reform the English Church.
670	Death of Oswy of Northumbria, the last Bretwalda; his son Ecgfrith succeeds him.
671	The weapon Greek fire – an inflammable liquid that could be propelled through bronze tubes – invented by Kallinikos of Byzantium.
672	The see of Canterbury given authority over the church in England by the Synod of Hertford.
674	The Arabs penetrate as far as the Indus.
678	After several years' siege, the Arabs fail to take Constantinople and establish a 30-year peace with the Byzantine Empire.
680	Caliph Yaezid puts down a revolt by Hussain, son of Ali, who is killed.
682	Islamic forces overrun Tripoli, Carthage and Tangiers, expelling the Byzantines from North Africa.
685	Ecgfrith of Northumbria falls in battle against the Picts at Nechtanesmere; he is succeeded by Aldfrith.
687	Pepin II of Hérstal defeats his foes at Tertry and gains effective control of all of Francia. He and his successors rule as 'mayors of the palace', holding real power under figurehead Merovingian kings.
688	Caedwalla of Wessex resigns the kingship and goes on pilgrimage to Rome, succeeded by Ine.
689	Justinian II defeats Slavic forces in Thrace, and deports many of them to Anatolia.
690	Wihtred becomes King of Kent.
692	Brihtwold becomes the first native Archbishop of Canterbury; the Irish church accepts the authority of Rome at the Synod of Tara.
694	King Ine codifies the laws of Wessex.
695	Emperor Justinian II deposed by his officers, who cut off his nose and exile him; he is replaced by Leontius.
696	Paoluccio Anafesto is appointed the first doge of Venice.
697	Carthage destroyed by the Arabs.
698	Emperor Leontius deposed and replaced by Tiberius III.
700	The Agilofings, dukes of Bavaria, make Ratisbon their capital.
701	The Japanese emperor passes a law making him the sole proprietor of land in the country.
705	Justinian II restored as emperor.
709	Deaths of bishops Aldhelm of Sherborne, who converted Wessex, and St Wilfrid of Hexham.
710	Nara established as the capital of Japan.
711	Fall of the Visigothic kingdom in Spain to the invading Arab and Moorish forces after the defeat and death of King Roderick; only Asturias remains a Christian kingdom. Justinian II murdered by Philip Bardanes, who takes the throne as Philippicus.
712	The Arabs take Samarkand, where they discover the art of making paper, and Sind.
713	Emperor Philippicus deposed and replaced by Anastasius II.
714	Death of Pepin II in Francia. His son, Charles Martel, begins to unify the Frankish kingdom.
715	Winfrith, the future St Boniface, begins his missionary work among the Germans.
716	Emperor Anastasius II deposed; he is replaced by Theodosius III. Aethelbald becomes king of Mercia, succeeding Ceolred.
717	Theodosius III deposed by Leo III. The Arabs besiege Constantinople. Omar II becomes caliph and grants a tax exemption to true believers.
718	Constantinople fights off the Arab siege; Greek fire is spectacularly used to decimate the Arab fleet.
720	The Arabs conquer Sardinia and cross the Pyrenees, taking Narbonne.
722	St Boniface made the first bishop among the Germans.
725	The heathen Oak of Thor felled by St Boniface.
726	Ine of Wessex dies on pilgrimage in Rome; succeeded by Aethelheard.
730	Emperor Leo III excommunicated by Pope Gregory II over his iconoclastic policies, which forbid making images of Christ, the Virgin Mary or the saints.
731	Bede completes his *Ecclesiastical History of the English People*.

732	Charles Martel defeats the Arabs at the battle of Tours (or Poitiers), their furthest incursion into Europe.
735	Burgundy conquered by Charles Martel. The Venerable Bede dies.
737	Death of King Theuderic IV of Francia.
739	Bishoprics at Passau, Ratisbon and Salzburg founded by St Boniface. Charles Martel and his Lombard allies expel the Moors and Arabs from Provence.
741	Death of Charles Martel, who divides his mayoralty between his sons Carloman in Neustria and Pepin in Austrasia.
743	Childeric III becomes king of Francia after a six-year interregnum.
744	Swabia added to territory of Francia.
746	Constantine V retakes Cyprus from the Arabs. Carloman retires to a monastery, leaving Pepin as mayor of all of Francia.
748	The first printed newspaper published in what is now Beijing.
749	The Neighing Stallion sculpted out of fire-clay in China. As-saffah establishes Abbasid rule in Baghdad.
750	Umayyad Caliph Marwan II deposed and killed by the Abbasids, descended from the Prophet's uncle.
751	Childeric III, last Merovingian monarch, replaced as king by Pepin III the Short, who founds the Carolingian dynasty.
754	Pepin III assists Pope Stephen III against the Lombards.
756	Abd-al-Rahman establishes the Umayyad Emirate of Cordoba.
757	Offa succeeds Aethelbald as king of Mercia after the latter's murder.
758	King Edbriht of Northumbria abdicates to become a monk, succeeded by his son Osulf.
759	Narbonne retaken from the Moors by Frankish troops.
760	Turkish empire founded by a Tartar tribe in Armenia.
762	Caliph Mansur founds Baghdad as capital of the Abbasid Caliphate.
765	China invaded by a Tibetan army.
768	Pepin III dies; Francia is split between his sons Charles (later Charlemagne) and Carloman.
770	Death of the poet Tu Fu.
771	Carloman dies; kingdom reunited under Charlemagne.
772	Charlemagne invades and subdues Saxony.
773	Charlemagne invades and subdues Lombardy.
774	Charlemagne confims the Donation of Pepin, a grant of lands made by his father to Pope Stephen II in 757, which creates the Papal States.
775	Tibet and China confirm a boundary agreement.
776	Kent gains temporary independence from Mercia as a result of winning the battle of Otford.
778	Roland, Lord of the Breton Marches, killed by Basques at Roncesvalles as Charlemagne's army withdraws from a venture in Spain.
779	Offa defeats Cynewulf of Wessex near Benson and becomes de facto ruler of England.
780	On the death of her husband, Leo IV, the Empress Irene becomes Regent of the Byzantine Empire and restores Image Worship.
781	Nestorian Christians in China develop monasteries.
782	Charlemagne executes 4,500 Saxon hostages at Verdun and annexes Saxony.
783	Widukind leads a Saxon revolt against Frankish rule.
784	Work commences on Offa's Dyke.
785	Widukind submits to Charlemagne and is baptised.
786	Harun al-Rashid becomes Caliph, succeeding his brother al-Hadi.
787	First Viking raid on England, near Wareham.
788	Charlemagne annexes Bavaria, deposing Duke Tassilo.
789	Frankish ports closed to English merchants due to a dispute between Charlemagne and Offa.
790	Irish monks sail to Iceland in skin-frame vessels.
792	Offa has King Aethelbert of East Anglia beheaded, and annexes his kingdom.
793	Lindisfarne and Jarrow sacked by the Vikings.
794	The Japanese capital moves from Nara to Heian (later known as Kyoto).
795	First Viking attacks on Ireland.
796	Death of Offa brings his son Ecgfrith to the throne. He dies soon after, and Cenwulf succeeds him.
797	Empress Irene of Byzantium deposes and blinds her son Constantine VI.
798	Revolt in Kent against Mercian rule subdued by King Cenwulf, who blinds the Kentish royal leader Eadbert and cuts off his hands.
799	Charlemagne captures and destroys Fiume.
800	Charlemagne crowned Holy Roman Emperor on Christmas Day.
802	Empress Irene deposed by her finance minister Nicephorus; Egbert succeds Brihtric as king of Wessex.
803	The Bulgarians free themselves from Tartar overlordship.
804	Charlemagne finally defeats the Saxons.
805	The Japanese Buddhist priest Saicho brings tea to Japan.
807	Monastery founded by Cellach of Iona at Kells.
808	Foundation of Fez, in Morocco, as a tent colony.
809	Death of Harun al-Rashid, succeeded by his son al-Amin.
810	Musa al-Khwarazmi writes a book on equations, introducing the Hindu numerals now known as Arabic.
812	Byzantine Empire recognises Charlemagne as emperor in the West.
813	Al-Mamun murders and succeeds his brother Caliph al-Amin.
814	Death of Charlemagne. His son Louis the Pious succeeds him.
815	Cornwall conquered by Egbert of Wessex.
817	Louis the Pious partitions the Holy Roman Empire amongst his sons and makes Lothair, his eldest son, co-emperor.

821	Tibetan independence from China ratified by treaty at Chang'an.
825	Egbert of Wessex defeats Beornred of Mercia at Ellandun, near Swindon, and briefly controls all England.
826	Islamic pirates capture Crete and use it as a base for raids in the Aegean. Nominoë becomes Count of Brittany.
827	Sicily invaded by Arab forces.
829	Louis the Pious invests his son Charles the Bald with the dukedom of Swabia, upsetting the status quo.
830	The Great Moravian Empire founded by Prince Moimir.
831	Anskar is created bishop of Hamburg, with responsibility for converting Scandinavia.
832	Emperor Theophilus issues an edict banning the worship of images.
833	Louis the Pious defeated by his elder sons at Colmar and imprisoned.
834	Louis the Pious restored to his throne by loyalists; his eldest son Lothair retires to his Italian sub-kingdom.
838	The Arabs sack Marseilles and also cross to Southern Italy.
839	Egbert of Wessex dies, and is succeeded by his son Aethelwulf.
840	Death of Louis the Pious. The Holy Roman Empire splits into three, but the new emperor, Lothair, seeks to conquer his brothers' portions.
841	Lothair defeated by his brothers Louis the German and Charles the Bald at Fontenoy, thus frustrating his imperial plans. The Vikings found the city of Dublin in Ireland.
842	Emperor Theophilus dies, and is succeeded by his son Michael III. Under the regency of his mother, Theodora, image worship is restored.
843	Treaty of Verdun establishes the territories of the three remaining sons of Louis the Pious, thus dividing for good the lands of the Holy Roman Empire. Kenneth MacAlpin, king of Dalriada since 840, unites the Picts and Scots into a single kingdom (Alba), the forerunner of Scotland.
845	Buddhism suppressed in China by Emperor Wu Tsung.
846	Rome is attacked and badly damaged by Arab forces.
847	Al-Mutawakkil succeeds his brother al-Wathiq as caliph.
849	Birth of Alfred the Great of Wessex, at Wantage.
850	Rurik the Norseman becomes the ruler of Kiev.
851	The Vikings sack London and Canterbury, but are halted in their depredations by Aethelwulf of Wessex and his son Aethelbald at Aclea.
852	Muhammad I succeeds to the Emirate of Cordoba on the death of his father Abdul-Rahman II.
853	Kudawara Kudanari, the first major Japanese painter, dies.
855	Holy Roman Emperor Lothair I dies; his portion of the empire is divided amongst his three sons; Louis II succeeds his father as Emperor.
856	Aethelbald replaces Aethelwulf as king in Wessex, Kent, Surrey and Sussex. Vikings burn Paris.
857	Ergotism epidemics, caused by poisoned grain, begin to appear in Europe.
858	Death of Aethelwulf of Wessex. Aethelbald becomes sole king of Wessex but grants his brother Aethelbert an under-kingship.
859	Norse marauders enter the Mediterranean and cause havoc.
860	Aethelbald of Wessex dies, to be succeeded by his brother Aethelbert.
861	Cologne, Paris, Aix-la-Chapelle, Toulouse and Worms sacked by Viking raiders.
862	Novgorod, capital of Kiev Rus, founded by Rurik.
863	The Cyrillic alphabet is developed by Cyril and his brother Methodius in Moravia.
864	King Boris I of Bulgaria converts to Christianity.
865	Ivar the Boneless and his brother Halfdan arrive in England in an attempt to conquer the country. Aethelbert of Wessex dies; his brother Aethelred I succeeds him.
867	Basil I, the Macedonian, murders Michael III and becomes Byzantine emperor.
868	Ahmad ibn Tulun establishes the Tulunid dynasty in Egypt.
869	Malta captured by Islamic forces.
870	Martyrdom of King (later St) Edmund of East Anglia at the hands of the Vikings.
871	Vikings defeated by Wessex at Ashdown but victorious at Reading, Basing, Merton and Wilton. Alfred succeeds Aethelred I as king of Wessex.
874	The Vikings begin to colonise Iceland. Burgred, last independent English king of Mercia, forced to abdicate by the Vikings, who replace him with their puppet Ceolwulf II.
875	Holy Roman Emperor Louis II dies; his uncle Charles the Bald establishes himself as his successor.
876	Louis the German dies; his portion of the Holy Roman Empire is divided amongst his three sons.
877	Charles the Bald dies; he is succeeded as French king by his son Louis II the Stammerer. The imperial throne is left unfilled.
878	Alfred, after a period in hiding at Athelney, decisively defeats the Vikings at Edington, Wiltshire, and preserves Wessex as an English kingdom.
879	The treaty of Wedmore establishes the Danelaw in parts of England: Danish laws and customs will prevail there. Louis II dies; his sons Louis III and Carloman jointly succeed him.
880	Southern Italy reconquered from the Arabs by the Byzantine Emperor Basil.
881	Charles III, king of Swabia, crowned Holy Roman Emperor.
882	Louis III of France dies; his brother Carloman reigns alone. Kiev replaces Novgorod as capital of Kiev Rus under Oleg.
883	The Zenj rebellion of African slaves in Chaldea, which has lasted fourteen years, finally suppressed by al-Muwaffiq, brother of Caliph al-Mu'tamid.
884	Carloman of France dies while hunting. Emperor Charles III the Fat takes control, temporarily reuniting most of the Holy Roman Empire.
885	Ashot IV, Prince of Armenia, assumes the title King Ashot I.
886	Paris besieged by Vikings, who are paid off by Charles the Fat. London retaken by Alfred, who gives it and English Mercia to his son-in-law Aethelred.

887 Charles III deposed as emperor at Tribur; the Carolingian Empire falls apart.
888 Odo Count of Paris elected king of France; Berengar I of Friuli, grandson of Louis the Pious, becomes king of Italy. Rudolf I becomes king of a reformed Burgundy.
889 Donald II succeeds his cousin Eochaid as king of Scotland. Guido of Spoleto replaces Berengar I as king of Italy.
890 Alfred the Great establishes an English navy and militia. Harald I Finehair defeats his opponents at Hafursfjord and claims the sovereignty of Norway.
891 Guido of Spoleto crowned first non-Carolingian Holy Roman Emperor. Arnulf of Germany drives the Vikings from his country.
892 Caliph al-Mu'tamid dies; he is succeeded by his nephew al-Mu'tadid. The Vikings launch another invasion attempt on England.
893 The Vikings are decisively defeated by Alfred's son, Edward the Elder, at Farnham. Asser writes his life of Alfred.
894 Guido of Spoleto dies; his son Lambert succeeds him in Italy and as Emperor. Svatopluk I of Moravia, who has created the greater Moravian kingdom dies; his sons Moimir I and Svatopluk II jointly succeed him.
895 The Magyars, expelled from southern Russia, move under Arpad into Hungary.
896 By request of Pope Formosus, Arnulf of Germany replaces Lambert of Spoleto as Holy Roman Emperor, re-establishing Carolingian rule. Alfred defeats the Vikings at sea and ends their threat.
897 Pope Formosus' body is exhumed, dressed in papal vestments and tried for perjury; found guilty, it has three fingers cut off and is thrown into the Tiber.
898 Odo of France dies. The Carolingian pretender Charles III the Simple replaces him. Lambert of Spoleto dies and Berengar I reclaims the Italian crown.
899 Alfred the Great dies, and his son Edward succeeds him. Emperor Arnulf dies, and is succeeded in Germany by his son Louis III the Child.
900 Gunbjorn discovers Greenland. The Arab physician al-Razi identifies measles, smallpox, plague, consumption and rabies.
901 Louis III of Provence, grandson of Emperor Louis II, crowned Holy Roman Emperor. Edward the Elder takes the title 'King of the Angles and Saxons'.
902 With the fall of Taormina to the Arabs, Sicily is lost to Byzantium.
903 Pope Leo V is deposed after one month as Pontiff by Christopher, who lasts a year.
904 Leo of Tripoli commands an Arab fleet that sacks Thessalonica. The election of Pope Sergius III leads to a period of pornocracy in the Vatican.
905 Emperor Louis III surprised and blinded by insurgents, leading to his deposition from the imperial throne. Sancho I of Navarre succeeds his brother Fortun Garces and makes the county a kingdom. Shaiban succeeds his nephew Harun as king of Egypt, but is deposed shortly after; the Tulunid dynasty falls as a result.
906 Annam gains independence from China.
907 Fall of the Tang dynasty following conquest by Khitan Mongols. The Later Liang Dynasty under Taizu replaces it. The Magyars invade and destroy the Moravian empire of Moimir I, who perishes in the invasion.
909 The Fatimid dynasty is founded in Tunisia when al-Mahdi claims the caliphate.
910 The Byzantine Emperor Leo VI is forced to pay tribute to the Magyars. The kingdom of Asturias is renamed the kingdom of León its new capital. The Abbey of Cluny is founded.
911 Normandy established as a Norse province by the treaty of Saint-Clair-sur-Epte; Hrolf (Rollo) becomes duke. Louis III of Germany dies, the Carolingians die out and Conrad I of Franconia is elected king in his place.
912 Abdul-Rahman III succeeds his grandfather Abdullah as emir of Cordoba. The Byzantine Emperor Leo VI dies; his brother Alexander II succeeds him.
913 Emperor Alexander II dies; his nephew Constantine VII, still a child, succeeds him. Byzantium refuses to pay its tribute to Symeon of Bulgaria, who calls himself Emperor of the Romans but fails to take Constantinople.
914 With the death of Pope Lando, no Pope until John Paul I in 1978 will take a name that has not been used by a Pope before, starting with Lando's successor, John X.
915 Berengar I of Italy is crowned Holy Roman Emperor, the last Carolingian to hold the title.
916 Essex taken from the Vikings by Edward the Elder.
917 Symeon of Bulgaria overruns Thrace and now controls the Balkans.
918 Deaths of Conrad I of Germany and Lady Aethelflaed of the Mercians. The latter acknowledge Edward the Elder as their king; he now controls all England south of the Humber.
919 Henry the Fowler, duke of Saxony, elected king of Germany. Ragnald the Viking seizes York, and makes himself king.
920 Edward the Elder acknowledged as overlord by the kings of Scotland, York and Strathclyde.
921 Sitric Caoch of Dublin succeeds Ragnald as king of York.
922 Charles III of France deposed by his barons, who elect Robert Capet, duke of Francia, king in his place; Charles raises an army to contest this.
923 Robert of France killed at the battle of Soissons, but Charles III is defeated and imprisoned; Duke Rudolf of Burgundy, Robert's son-in-law, is elected by the barons as king. Fall of the Later Liang dynasty in China, Li Cunxu of the Later Tang replacing Modi as emperor, taking the name Zhuengzong.
924 Edward the Elder of Wessex and England dies; his son Athelstan is hailed king in Mercia but Wessex disputes the succession. Symeon of Bulgaria unsuccessfully attacks Constantinople. Emperor Berengar, king of Italy, dies; the Imperial crown falls into abeyance.
925 Athelstan crowned king of England, having finally been accepted by Wessex. Henry the Fowler conquers Lorraine.
926 Symeon of Bulgaria defeated by Croat allies of the Byzantine Empire. Hugh of Arles becomes king of Italy after Rudolf II of Burgundy resigns the throne.

927	Symeon of Bulgaria dies. His son Peter succeeds him and signs a peace treaty with the Byzantines. Sitric of York dies. He is succeeded by his brother Guthfrith who is forced to flee when Athelstan conquers York and Southern Northumbria. The kings of Scotland and Strathclyde acknowledge Athelstan as their overlord.
928	Cornwall subdued by Athelstan, who sets the River Tamar as its boundary.
929	Duke Wenceslas of Bohemia murdered by non-Christians led by his brother Boleslav I, who succeeds him. Charles III of France dies, leaving Rudolf II as sole king. Emir Abdul-Rahman III of Corboba proclaims himself caliph.
930	The Black Stone stolen from the Kaaba in Mecca by the Carmathians, a Muslim sect.
931	Rameiro II succeeds his brother Alfonso IV as king of León.
932	William Longsword succeeds his father Rollo as duke of Normandy.
933	Henry the Fowler defeats Magyar raiders at the battle of Merseburg.
934	Scotland invaded by Athelstan, whose fleet ravages the coast as far as Caithness.
936	Louis IV (d'Outremer) returns from exile in England to be king of France after the death of Duke Rudolf of Burgundy. Henry the Fowler dies, and is succeeded by his son Otto I. The Tang dynasty falls in China; Shi Jing-tang of the Later Jin replaces Feidi as emperor, taking the name Gaozu.
937	Athelstan defeats a coalition of his foes at Brunanburh (whereabouts unknown), cementing his power in Britain. King Rudolf of Burgundy dies, his son Conrad succeeding him.
938	Yenching (later Peking and Beijing) founded as a Khitan capital.
939	Athelstan dies, and is succeeded by his half-brother Edmund (the Elder). Olaf Guthricson retakes York for the Vikings. Otto I defeats Eberhard of Franconia and his ducal allies at Andernach, confirming his monarchical authority in Germany.
940	Olaf of York invades the Midlands. By the treaty of Leicester much of the old Danelaw is ceded to him.
941	Igor of Kiev attacks Constantinople by way of the River Dnieper and the Black Sea, but his fleet is destroyed by Greek fire. Olaf of York dies; his cousin Olaf Sitricsson succeeds him.
942	Richard the Old succeeds his father William Longsword as duke of Normandy after the latter's murder by Arnold I of Flanders. The Five Boroughs of Derby, Leicester, Lincoln, Nottingham and Stamford are recovered by Edmund the Elder. Erik Bloodaxe succeeds his father Harald I Finehair as king of Norway on the latter's abdication at the age of 80.
943	Constantine I of Scotland abdicates and retires to a monastery, his son Malcolm I succeeds him. Byzantine troops recover the Mandylion.
944	Edmund the Elder recovers York, expelling Ragnald Guthricson, who had usurped the throne from his cousin Olaf the previous year.
945	Igor of Kiev dies; he is succeeded by his wife Olga. Mozambique attacked by Indonesians. Imad ibn-Buwayhid conquers Baghdad, keeping Caliph al-Mustaqfi as a figurehead. Louis IV taken prisoner by Hugh the Great, duke of France.
946	Caliph al-Mustaqfi deposed and blinded by the Buwayhids; his cousin al-Muti replaces him. Edmund the Elder and Otto I act in support of Louis IV, who is freed. Edmund the Elder assassinated at Pucklechurch; his brother Eadred succeeds him.
947	Eric Bloodaxe deposed as king of Norway by his brother Haakon I due to his violence. He flees to England where Wulfstan of York makes him king of that city. Hugh of Arles dies; his son Lothair of Arles succeeds him as king of Italy. The Later Jin dynasty falls in China, Emperor Chudi being replaced by Gaozu of the Later Han.
948	Eadred ravages Northumbria in response to their crowning of Eric Bloodaxe, who is forced to flee.
949	Olaf Sitricsson is invited to return as king of York.
950	Hywel Dda, prince of Deheubarth and Gwynedd and creator of a Welsh law code, dies; Gwynedd and Deheubarth separate. Mixcoatl, Toltec emperor, is assassinated and deified as a result; Lothair of Arles dies; Italy ruled jointly by Berengar II of Ivrea and his son Adalbert.
951	The Later Han dynasty falls in China; Emperor Yindi is replaced by Guo Wei of the Later Zhou, who takes the name Taizu.
952	Eric Bloodaxe returns to York and resumes the kingship.
954	Louis IV of France dies; his son Lothair succeeds him. Eric Bloodaxe forced to flee from York and is killed soon after; Eadred now rules all England.
955	Otto I decisively defeats the Magyars at the battle of Lechfeld. Eadred of England dies; his nephew Eadwig succeeds him.
956	St Dunstan, abbot of Glastonbury, exiled from England after a quarrel with King Eadwig.
957	Mercia and Northumbria rebel against Eadwig and choose his younger brother Edgar as their king.
959	Eadwig of Wessex dies; his brother Edgar the Peaceable succeeds him and reunites the kingdom of England. Emperor Constantine VII dies, his son Romanus II succeeds him.
960	Northern Song dynasty established by Zhao Kuangyin, who takes the name Taizu, replacing Gongdi of the Later Zhou. The kingdom of Poland created by King Mieszko I, who founds the Piast dynasty.
961	A Byzantine fleet commanded by Nicephorus Phocas recaptures Crete from the Arabs. Caliph Abdul-Rahman III of Cordoba dies; his son al-Hakam II succeeds him.
962	Otto I of Germany is crowned Holy Roman Emperor, re-establishing that title.
963	The Byzantine Emperor Romanus II is poisoned by his wife Theophano, who marries Nicephorus Phocas, elevating him to the imperial crown.
965	Cyprus recaptured from the Arabs by Byzantine forces. Al-Mutannabi, the Arab poet, is murdered by bandits.
966	Sancho I of León dies; he is succeeded by his son Ramiro III. King Dub of Scotland dies; he is succeeded by his third cousin Culen.
967	Duke Boleslav I of Bohemia dies; he is succeeded by his son Boleslav II.
968	Dinh Tien-Hoang De becomes king of North Vietnam, founding the Dinh dynasty.

969	Byzantine Emperor Nicephorus II Phocas murdered by his wife's lover, John Tzimisces, who rules in his stead. Cairo founded by the Fatimids, who have conquered Egypt.
970	Garcia II of Navarre dies, and is succeeded by his son Sancho II.
971	Culen of Scotland dies; he is succeeded by his third cousin Kenneth II. St Swithin reinterred inside Winchester Cathedral; 40 days of rain follow.
972	Boris II of Bulgaria forced to abdicate by the invading Byzantines, ending the Krum dynasty's reign in that country.
973	Holy Roman Emperor Otto I dies; he is succeeded by his son Otto II. Edgar of England crowned king at Bath.
975	Edgar dies, and is succeeded by his son Edward. Modern arithmetical notation introduced into Europe by the Arabs.
976	Byzantine Emperor John I Tzimisces dies; succeeded by Basil II, son of Romanus II. Leopold I of the house of Babenberg made Margrave of Austria. Caliph al-Hakam II of Cordoba dies; his son Hisham II succeeds him. Samuel makes himself Tsar of Bulgaria. Duke Henry the Quarrelsome of Bavaria deposed by Otto II.
978	Edward (the Martyr) assassinated at Corfe and succeeded by his half-brother Aethelred II (Unraed). Mohammad ibn abi-Amir al-Mansur, regent of Cordoba, takes effective control of the Caliphate there.
979	Dinh Tien-Hoang De of Dai Vet (Vietnam) dies; succeeded by his son Dinh De-Toan.
980	Le Dai-Hanh Hoang-De usurps the Dai Vet throne from Dinh De-Toan, establishing the Earlier Le Dynasty. Vladimir of Novgorod seizes Kiev from his brother Yaropolk I.
981	León made tributary to the Caliphate of Cordoba. Italy invaded by Arabs; Otto II marches against them but the Byzantines offer them support.
982	Otto II defeated by a combination of Byzantine and Arab forces at Basientello. Eric the Red settles in Greenland.
983	Emperor Otto II dies, his three-year-old son Otto III succeeds him.
984	Henry the Quarrelsome seizes Otto III in an attempt to make himself regent, but is thwarted by Otto II's widow Theophano of Byzantium.
985	Henry the Quarrelsome returned to the dukedom of Bavaria. Harald I Bluetooth of Denmark dies, and is succeeded by his son Sweyn I Forkbeard. Otto-William, a Carolingian prince, establishes the county of Burgundy.
986	Lothair of France dies, he is succeeded by his son Louis V. Sultan Sabuk-Tigan of Ghazni invades India. Bjarni Herjolfsson sights the coast of Labrador.
987	Louis V dies; the Carolingians are replaced as kings of France by the Capetians, when Hugh I is crowned King.
988	Vladimir of Kiev converts to Christianity, marries Anne, sister of Emperor Basil II, and sets about converting his subjects.
989	Emperor Basil II, with the aid of Russian troops, defeats Anatolian insurgents led by Bardas Phocas.
990	William IV of Aquitaine dies; succeeded by his son William V. Ghanaian forces take Awdaghost and establish the king of Ghana as the most powerful ruler in non-Islamic Africa.
991	Norsemen raid England led by Olaf Tryggvesson, defeating English forces under Ealdorman Byrhtnoth at Maldon; they are paid to leave by Danegeld.
992	Mieszko I of Poland dies, and is succeeded by his son Boleslav I the Brave, who invades Pomerania to gain access to the Baltic.
993	Khitan Mongols annex Korea .
994	Sweyn of Denmark, assisted by Olaf Tryggvesson, raids England, unsuccessfully besieges London and is paid off by Aethelred II. Olaf Tryggvesson converts to Christianity.
995	Syria retaken by the Byzantine Empire. Olaf Tryggvesson succeeds to the throne of Norway, and forcibly attempts to convert his subjects to Christianity.
996	Otto III crowned Holy Roman Emperor by his cousin Pope Gregory V. Hugh I of France dies, and is succeeded by his son Robert II. Richard I the Old, Duke of Normandy dies; succeeded by his son Richard II the Good. Emperor Basil II defeats the Bulgarians and recovers Greece.
997	Duke Geza of Hungary dies; succeeded by his son Stephen I. Sultan Sabuk-Tagin of Ghazni, in modern Afghanistan, dies; succeeded by his son Ismail.
998	Sultan Ismail of Ghazni dies; succeeded by his brother Mahmud.
999	Boleslav I of Poland conquers Silesia. Gerbert of Aurillac becomes Pope, taking the name Sylvester II; he is the first French Pope. Brian Boru conquers Dublin from the Norse settlers.
1000	Ceylon conquered by King Rajaraja of the Cholas. Stephen I of Hungary becomes king with Papal approval. Olaf Tryggvesson commits suicide after his defeat by the kings of Denmark and Sweden at the naval battle of Svolder; Erik Jarl of Lade replaces him as king of Norway.
1002	Emperor Otto III dies of malaria; succeeded by his cousin Henry II. Al-Mansur, chief minister of Cordoba dies, the Caliphate begins to decline. Aethelred II marries Emma, sister of Richard II of Normandy, and orders the massacre of Danish settlers in southern England.
1003	King Sweyn of Denmark raids England in revenge for the massacre of his countrymen, exacting tribute from Aethelred.
1004	China pays tribute to the Khitan Mongols as the result of a peace treaty. Emperor Henry II defeats Ardoin of Lombardy and is crowned king of that country.
1005	Kenneth III of Scotland is killed in battle against his cousin Malcolm II, who succeeds him.
1006	Islamic settlers arrive in north-western India. Mount Metrop erupts in Java, killing King Dharmawangs.
1007	Danegeld of £36,000 paid by Aethelred II to protect England from raids for two years.
1008	Sultan Mahmud of Ghazni defeats Hindu forces at Peshawar and expands his realms.
1009	Caliph al-Hakim of Egypt sacks the Church of the Holy Sepulchre in Jerusalem. Caliph Hisham II of Cordoba deposed by his cousin Muhammad II, who is deposed in his turn by his cousin Suleiman.
1010	The 'Peace of God' established in France by Robert II. Danish forces under Thorkell the Tall defeat the East

Anglians at Ringmere. Muhammad II regains the caliphate of Cordoba from Suleiman, but is ousted again, this time by a returning Hisham II.

1011	Canterbury taken by the Danes, who capture Archbishop Alphege.
1012	Danegeld of £48,000 paid to the Danes, who nevertheless kill Alphege before they leave. Thorkell the Tall defects to the English. Persecution of heretics in Germany commences.
1013	Sweyn Forkbeard conquers England, helped by Thorkell, who redefects. Aethelred II flees to Normandy. Hisham II of Cordoba dies, and is succeeded by Suleiman.
1014	Sweyn dies, and Aethelred returns from exile. Brian Boru wins the battle of Clontarf but is killed. Emperor Basil II seizes Western Bulgaria and blinds the resisting native army.
1015	Olaf II succeeds Eric as king of Norway and establishes its independence from Denmark. Cnut invades England and Wessex submits to him.
1016	Aethelred II dies, succession disputed between his son Edmund Ironside and Cnut. Cnut wins the battle of Ashingdon; Edmund allowed to reign in Wessex but dies shortly afterwards.
1017	Cnut divides England into four earldoms, Wessex, East Anglia, Mercia and Northumbria, for administrative purposes.
1018	The treaty of Bautzen ends the war between Germany and Poland. Macedonia regained by the Byzantines after the submission of the Bulgarians.
1019	Yaroslav I the Wise succeeds his brother Sviatopolk I as prince of Kiev. Cnut becomes king of Denmark on the death of his brother Harald II.
1020	Corsica annexed by Pisa. Faroes, Shetlands and Orkneys recognise Olaf II of Norway as king. Godwin becomes earl of Wessex.
1021	Emperor Basil II invades Armenia. An epidemic of St Vitus' Dance sweeps Europe.
1022	Emperor Henry II defeats a Byzantine army in Southern Italy. The Synod of Pavia decrees celibacy for higher clergy.
1023	Abdul-Rahman V becomes caliph of Cordoba, replacing the Hammudid al-Qasim of Malaga.
1024	Emperor Henry II dies. He is succeeded by his second cousin twice removed, Conrad II of Franconia. Boleslav I of Poland is crowned king of that country.
1025	Emperor Basil II dies, and is succeeded by his brother Constantine VIII. Boleslav I of Poland dies and is succeeded by his son Mieszko II and reverts to the title of prince.
1026	Cnut thwarts a combined Norwegian and Swedish attack at the sea battle of the Holy River. Guido d'Arezzo introduces solmisation in music.
1027	Robert I the Devil becomes duke of Normandy on the death of his brother Richard III.
1028	Cnut conquers Norway and sends his son Sweyn to rule it. Emperor Constantine VIII dies, succeeded by his daughter Zoë. Romanus III becomes co-emperor upon marrying her. Sancho III of Navarre conquers Castile.
1030	Olaf II of Norway attempts to win back his throne, but is defeated and killed by Cnut's forces at Stiklestad. Sultan Mahmud of Ghazni dies, and is succeeded by his son Muhammad.
1031	Muhammad of Ghazni deposed and blinded by his brother Masud I. Caliph Hisham III deposed, ending the Umayyad Caliphate of Cordoba, which fragments. Robert II the Pious of France dies; succeeded by his son Henry I.
1032	Rudolf III of Burgundy dies without an heir, and Conrad II unites the kingdom with the Empire.
1033	Mieszko II of Poland defeated by combined German and Russian forces and his realm forced to become a fief of the Empire. Castile granted independence from Navarre.
1034	Empress Zoe murders Romanus III and marries Michael IV, who becomes co-Emperor. Mieszko of Poland dies; his son Kasimir I succeeds him but the country plunges into civil war. Malcolm II of Scotland dies, and is succeeded by his grandson Duncan I.
1035	Duke Robert the Magnificent of Normandy dies on pilgrimage to Jerusalem. His illegitimate son William (the future 'Conqueror') succeeds, sparking a succession dispute. Sancho III of Navarre dies, and is succeeded in Navarre by his son Garcia IV and in Castile by his son Ferdinand I. Cnut dies. Harthacnut succeeds him in Denmark and England, but his brother Harold seizes England for himself. Magnus I the Good, son of Olaf II, regains Norwegian independence, defeating Sweyn.
1036	Alfred, son of Aethelred II, returns to England but is murdered by Godwin of Wessex. Harold I (Harefoot) proclaimed Regent of England.
1037	Harold I proclaimed king of England. Ferdinand I of Castile conquers León, deposing Vermudo III. The Islamic philosopher and physician Avicenna dies.
1038	King Stephen of Hungary dies, and is succeeded by his nephew by marriage Peter Orseolo.
1039	Emperor Conrad II dies, succeeded by his son Henry III. Gruffydd ap Llywelyn, prince of Gwynedd, defeats an English invading force on the River Severn.
1040	Macbeth defeats and kills King Duncan of Scotland and assumes the crown. Harold I dies; Harthacnut successfully claims the English crown by right of succession.
1041	Samuel Aba usurps the Hungarian throne from Peter Orseolo. Co-Emperor Michael IV dies; his nephew Michael V fills the breach.
1042	Harthacnut dies; his half-brother Edward the Confessor is elected king whilst Magnus of Norway takes Denmark. Michael V imprisons the Empress Zoë, but a rebellion blinds him, locks him in a monastery and frees Zoë, who marries Constantine IX and makes him co-Emperor.
1043	Samuel Aba of Hungary invades Bavaria, where he is countered by Emperor Henry III. Coventry Abbey founded by Leofric of Mercia.
1044	Emperor Henry III defeats Samuel Aba's Hungarians and restores Peter Orseolo to his throne. Anawrata founds the Pagan dynasty in Burma.
1045	The deposed Pope Benedict IX retakes the throne from Sylvester III by force, and then sells it to Gregory VI.
1046	Peter Orseolo of Hungary deposed by his second cousin Andras I. Emperor Henry III forces Gregory VI to

1046   abdicate on grounds of simony, ratifies the depositions of his two predecessors and installs Clement II at the Synod of Rome.

1047   Norman rebels defeated at Val-ès-Dunes by Duke William, who thus lies secure in his rule. King Magnus dies. Sweyn II, a nephew of Cnut, succeeds him in Denmark, whilst Harald III Hardrada, Magnus' uncle, succeeds him in Norway.

1048   Last Viking raid on south-east England, the raiders flee to Flanders, which is attacked by Edward the Confessor and Emperor Henry III.

1049   Leo IX elected Pope after the death of Damasus II.

1050   Empress Zoë dies, her older sister Theodora succeeding her. Robert of Jumièges becomes Archbishop of Canterbury.

1051   Earl Godwin of Wessex rebels unsuccessfully against Edward the Confessor, he and his family flee to Flanders.

1052   Earl Godwin and his family return to power in England. Stigand uncanonically becomes Archbishop of Canterbury as Archbishop Robert is forced to flee. Pisa takes Sardinia from the Arabs.

1053   Robert Guiscard defeats Papal forces at Civitate, capturing Leo IX, before taking Benevento from the Byzantines and founding a Norman state in Southern Italy. Godwin of Wessex dies, his son Harold succeeding him as earl.

1054   Final schism between Roman Catholic and Orthodox churches. Henry I of France invades Normandy and is defeated at Mortemer. Macbeth defeated by Malcolm Canmore and Earl Siward of Northumbria at Dunsinane.

1055   Seljuk Turks led by Togril-Beg enter Baghdad to liberate the Abbasid Caliphate from Shiite control; Togril-Beg makes himself the Caliph's temporal master. Co-Emperor Constantine IX dies, Theodora reigns alone. Earl Siward of Northumbria dies, and is succeeded six-year-old by Tostig Godwinson.

1056   Emperor Henry III dies, succeeded by his son Henry IV. Empress Theodora dies, ending the reign of the Macedonian dynasty in Byzantium. Michael VI succeeds her.

1057   Macbeth killed by Malcolm III Canmore at Lumphanan, but is succeeded by his stepson Lulach. Isaac Comnenus overthrows Emperor Michael VI.

1058   Lulach killed by Malcolm III Canmore, who becomes king of Scotland. Prince Kasimir I of Poland dies; succeeded by his son Boleslav II.

1059   By the treaty of Melfi Robert Guiscard becomes Duke of Apulia and Sicily and swears fealty to the Papacy. Emperor Isaac Comnenus abdicates in favour of Constantine X.

1060   Andras I of Hungary deposed by his brother Bela I. Henry I of France dies; succeeded by his son Philip I.

1061   Northumbria raided by Malcolm III of Scotland. Duke Spitihnev II of Bohemia dies, succeeded by his brother Vratislav II.

1062   By the Coup d'Etat of Kaiserswerth, Emperor Henry IV seized by Archbishop Anno of Cologne, who takes power in Germany alongside Archbishop Adalbert of Bremen.

1063   Gwynedd conquered by Earls Harold and Tostig; Prince Gruffydd killed by his own men. Bela I of Hungary dies, succeeded by his nephew Salomon, son of deposed king Andras. Alp Arslan succeeds his uncle Togril-Beg as sultan of the Seljuk Turks.

1064   Belgrade seized by the Hungarians from Byzantium. Armenia conquered by Alp Arslan.

1065   Ferdinand I of Castile and León dies; succeeded by his sons Sancho II in Castile and Alfonso VI in León. Westminster Abbey is consecrated.

1066   Death of Edward the Confessor causes succession dispute in England. Harold II Godwinson chosen king, defeats and kills Harald Hardrada at Stamford Bridge but is defeated and killed at Hastings by William of Normandy, who becomes king.

1067   Emperor Constantine X dies; his widow marries Romanus IV Diogenes, who becomes Emperor. Boleslav II of Poland captures Kiev. El Cid founds the world's first leper hospital in Castile.

1068   Earls Edwin and Morcar rebel against William I, but are defeated in York.

1069   Northumbrians and Mercians rebel, with Danish help, against William I, but the risings are put down and William devastates Northumbria ('the harrying of the North').

1070   The Order of the Knights of St John founded in Jerusalem by Amalfian merchants. Sweyn II of Denmark attacks England, but is bought off by William I, who puts down the revolt of Hereward the Wake.

1071   Robert Guiscard captures Bari, thus expelling the Byzantines from Italy. Byzantine forces heavily defeated at Manzikert under Alp Arslan, by Seljuk Turks who capture Emperor Romanus. When released he is blinded by the Byzantines, who select Michael VII as Emperor, and dies soon after. The Seljuqs now control Asia Minor.

1072   Sancho II of Castile murdered at the siege of Zamora whilst fighting Navarrese forces. He is succeeded by his brother Alfonso VI of León. Palermo taken by Robert and Roger Guiscard. Alp Arslan murdered by a captive while campaigning in Transoxiana; his son Malik Shah becomes sultan.

1073   Hildebrand of Soana elected Pope, taking the title Gregory VII.

1074   Salomon of Hungary deposed by his cousin Geza I. Robert Guiscard excommunicated by Gregory VII, who also excommunicates all married priests.

1075   Malik Shah subdues Syria and Palestine. Gregory VII bans simony and declares the Pope to be absolute sovereign of the Church.

1076   German bishops at the Synod of Worms declare Gregory VII deposed and Henry IV demands Gregory's abdication. Gregory excommunicates the bishops and Henry, whom he declares deposed. Thus the 'Investiture Contest' begins between Emperor and Pope, over the right of the Emperor to appoint bishops, who hold secular as well as spiritual power.

1077   When Henry IV does penance at Canossa to Gregory VII, the Germans declare him deposed and elect Rudolf of Swabia as anti-king. Geza I of Hungary dies, and is succeeded by his brother Ladislas I.

1078   Emperor Michael VII abdicates; Nicephorus III elected in his place.

1079   King Boleslav II of Poland excommunicated by Bishop (later Saint) Stanislas of Cracow, who is assassinated on Boleslav's orders. Gregory VII excommunicates Boleslav, who is deposed by a revolt by his nobles and succeeded by his brother Vladislav I Herman, who reverts to the title Prince.

1080 Anti-king Rudolf of Swabia defeated and killed by Henry IV's forces. Gregory VII again excommunicates and deposes Henry IV, who then seeks to depose Gregory, replacing him with the Archbishop of Ravenna as Clement III.

1081 Emperor Nicephorus III abdicates in favour of Alexius I Comnenus. Emperor Henry IV invades Italy seeking to establish Clement III as Pope.

1082 Bishop Odo, Earl of Kent, revolts against his half-brother William I, but is stripped of his earldom and imprisoned.

1083 The Kiyowara family revolt in northern Japan; Yoshiiye Minamoto sent to quell the rebellion.

1084 The Synod of Rome deposes Gregory VII and recognises Clement III, but Henry IV and Clement III are forced to withdraw when Robert Guiscard advances in support of Gregory from Southern Italy.

1085 Toledo taken from the Arabs by Alfonso VI of Castile. Pope Gregory VII dies at Salerno. Robert Guiscard dies, and is succeeded as duke of Apulia by his son Roger Borsa. William I commissions the Domesday Book.

1086 Islamic rule in Southern Spain rejuvenated by the Almoravids of Morocco, who defeat Alfonso VI of Castile at Zallaka. The Domesday Book is compiled. Cnut IV of Denmark dies, ending an invasion threat to England. His brother Olaf IV succeeds him.

1087 William I dies of an injury sustained at the siege of Mantes, and is succeeded by his sons Robert in Normandy and William II Rufus in England.

1088 Urban II elected Pope, but only partially recognised. Bishop Odo and various Norman barons in England rebel against William II, but the revolt is crushed.

1089 Archbishop Lanfranc of Canterbury dies, but no successor is chosen, so William II can enjoy the revenues of the see.

1090 Count Roger Guiscard of Sicily captures Malta from the Arabs.

1091 William II of England and Robert of Normandy make their peace by the treaty of Caen. Malcolm III of Scotland invades Northumbria, but is repulsed by William and Robert and acknowledges William as his overlord.

1092 The Seljuk vizier Nizam al-Malik assassinated by the Ismailite sect, the Hashishin (Assassins). King Vratislav of Bohemia dies. He is succeeded for a short while by his brother Conrad and then his son Bretislav II, who reverts to the title Duke. William II takes Cumberland from the Scots and refounds Carlisle as his north-western outpost.

1093 William II falls gravely ill and appoints St Anselm to the see of Canterbury, recovering soon after. Malcolm III invades Northumbria again but is killed near Alnwick; his wife Margaret dies 4 days later. He is succeeded by his brother Donald III Bane.

1094 Rodrigo Diaz de Vivar, El Cid, takes Valencia from the Moors. Donald Bane is deposed from the Scottish throne by his nephew Duncan II, who dies after six months. Donald Bane returns to the throne.

1095 Ladislas I of Hungary conquers Croatia and Dalmatia but dies soon after, and is succeeded by his nephew Koloman. Olaf IV of Denmark dies, and is succeeded by his brother Erik I. First Crusade launched by Pope Urban II at the council of Clermont, aiming to take Jerusalem and the Holy Land from the Seljuk Turks.

1096 Peter the Herrmit preaches the crusade in France and Germany, assembling a rag-tag force which goes East. Germans such as Ermich of Leiningen take advantage of crusade hysteria to persecute Jews in the Holy Roman Empire. Robert of Normandy leases his duchy to William II in order to go on crusade.

1097 Peter the Hermit's crusaders massacred near Nicaea in Asia Minor by Seljuk Turks, but the main crusading force wins major victories both there and at Dorylaeum. Donald Bane of Scotland deposed with William II's help, and replaced by his nephew Edgar.

1098 Robert de Molesme founds the monastery of Cîteaux, and thereby the Cistercian order. Magnus III of Norway seizes the Orkneys, Hebrides and Isle of Man. Crusaders take Antioch after a lengthy siege.

1099 Jerusalem captured by the crusaders; Godfrey of Bouillon becomes Advocate of the Holy Sepulchre. El Cid dies at Cuenca after defeat by the Almoravids.

1100 Godfrey of Bouillon dies, and his brother Baldwin succeeds him and founds the Kingdom of Jerusalem. William II of England dies whilst hunting, and is succeeded by his brother Henry I.

1101 Robert of Normandy invades England to take the throne from brother Henry, but is bought off by the treaty of Alton. Roger d'Hauteville, count of Sicily, dies; succeeded by his son Simon.

1102 Vladislav I of Poland abdicates, and is succeeded after a power struggle by his son Boleslav III. Alfonso VI of Castile raises the year-long siege of Valencia.

1103 Magnus III of Norway invades Ireland, but is killed in battle; his son Eysten I succeeds him. Bohemund of Otranto ransomed from captivity by the Danishmend Emir.

1104 Acre taken by crusaders under Baldwin I of Jerusalem. Mount Hekla in Iceland erupts violently.

1105 Emperor Henry IV is captured by his son Henry and is forced to abdicate in favour of him; when he breaks the terms of his abdication he is imprisoned.

1106 Henry IV escapes from prison but dies whilst raising an army against his son, who succeeds him. Henry of England defeats Robert of Normandy at Tinchebrai, dispossessing Robert of his duchy and imprisoning him.

1107 King Edgar of Scotland dies, and is succeeded by his brother Alexander I.

1108 Philip I of France dies, and is succeeded by his son Louis VI. Bohemund of Otranto defeated by the Emperor Alexius at Durazzo.

1109 Boleslav III of Poland defeats Emperor Henry V at Hundsfeld. Crusaders led by Raymond of St Gilles take Tripoli and Beirut; Raymond founds the County of Tripoli.

1110 The earliest known miracle play performed at Dunstable.

1111 Henry V crowned emperor under duress by Pope Paschal II. Bohemund of Otranto dies, and is succeeded as prince of Antioch by his nephew Tancred. Count Roger of Apulia dies; his son William II succeeds him.

1112 Emperor Henry V excommunicated. Tancred of Antioch dies, and is succeeded by his nephew Roger of Salerno. Henry of Burgundy, count of Portugal, dies, and is succeeded by his son Alfonso I.

1113 Pisa conquers the Balearic Islands. Sviatopolk of Kiev dies, and is succeeded by his cousin Vladimir II Monomach. The Knights Hospitaller resolve to defend the Holy Land.

1114 Pipe rolls introduced by Bishop Roger of Salisbury as a means of recording Exchequer accounts.

1115 St Bernard founds a monastery at Clairvaux and becomes its first abbot. The Juchens create the Chinese state of Jin under their chieftain Aguda.

1116 Coloman of Hungary dies; succeeded by his son Stephen II.

1117 St Magnus, earl of Orkney, murdered on the island of Egilsay on the orders of his cousin Earl Haakon.

1118 The Knights Templar founded in Jerusalem by Hugh de Payens. Emperor Alexius I dies, and is succeeded by his son John II. Baldwin I of Jerusalem dies, and is succeeded by his great-nephew Baldwin II. Alfonso I of Aragon takes Zaragoza from the Almoravids and makes it his capital.

1119 Count Baldwin VII of Flanders dies; succeeded by his cousin Charles the Good. Crusading armies are heavily defeated at the Field of Blood in Syria. Roger of Antioch is killed.

1120 Prince William, heir and only legitimate son of Henry I, drowns in the wreck of the *White Ship*.

1121 Peter Abelard's teachings on the Trinity condemned at the Synod of Soissons.

1122 Emperor John II wipes out the Pecheneg Turks in the Balkans. The Investiture Question is finally settled with the Concordat of Worms; Emperor Henry V renounces the right of investiture.

1123 Emperor John II defeats the Serbs in the Balkans. Marriage of priests banned by the First Lateran Council. The Augustinian canon Rahere founds St Bartholomew's Hospital in London.

1124 Emperor John II defeats the Hungarians. Alexander I of Scotland dies; succeeded by his brother David I.

1125 Emperor Henry V dies, leaving no successor; Lothair of Saxony is elected to succeed him. Morocco conquered by the Almohads.

1126 Emperor Lothair III makes his son-in-law, Henry X the Proud, duke of Bavaria, succeeding Henry's father, Henry IX. Chinese Emperor Huizong dies after being captured by the Jin; his son Qinzong succeeds him.

1127 The Jin overrun Northern China and Emperor Qinzong perishes; his brother Gaozong flees south and establishes the Southern Song dynasty. Count William III of Apulia dies, Roger of Sicily claims overlordship, but the inhabitants appeal to the Pope for protection. Roger is excommunicated.

1128 Count Charles the Good of Flanders is murdered; Louis VI attempts to impose Robert of Normandy on the county but the inhabitants install Thierry of Alsace, a cousin of Charles. The Templars gain papal recognition; St Bernard draws up their rule. Alfonso I of Portugal defeats Alfonso VII of Castile at São Mamede and shakes off Castilian overlordship. Pope Honorius accepts Roger of Sicily's claim to Apulia and invests him as count.

1129 First Cistercian abbey founded in England, at Waverley. Henry of Blois becomes Bishop of Winchester. Count Fulk V of Anjou resigns the county to his son Geoffrey and goes to Jerusalem to marry Melisande, heiress to King Baldwin II.

1130 Pope Honorius II dies. Innocent II is elected to succeed him but the election is disputed and an antipope, Anacletus II, is also elected. Innocent II flees to France, where he is championed by St Bernard, while Anacletus is backed by Roger II of Sicily, whom he crowns king of that country.

1131 Baldwin II of Jerusalem dies, and is succeeded by his son-in-law Fulk V. Rievaulx Abbey founded.

1132 Fountains Abbey founded.

1133 Lothair III crowned Emperor by Innocent II in the Lateran while the antipope Anacletus II is established in St Peter's. St Bartholomew's Fair founded in London.

1134 Emperor Lothair makes Albert the Bear margrave of Brandenburg and head of the North March.

1135 Henry I of England dies of a surfeit of lampreys; although he made his barons swear that his daughter Matilda would succeed him, his nephew Stephen of Blois engineers his own coronation as king.

1136 Emperor Lothair takes Apulia from Roger II of Sicily. Peter Abelard writes his *Historia calamitatum mearum*.

1137 Louis VI of France dies, and is succeeded by his son Louis VII. Gruffydd ap Cynan, prince of Gwynedd, dies, and is succeeded by his son Owain Gwynedd. Emperor Lothair III dies.

1138 Conrad III of Hohenstaufen elected emperor to succeed Lothair III. When Boleslav III of Poland dies, his country is divided amongst his four sons. David I of Scotland invades England in support of Matilda but is defeated at the battle of the Standard.

1139 The Second Lateran Council ends the schism in the Church. Innocent II is now universally recognised as Pope. Alfonso I crowned king of Portugal. Matilda lands at Arundel, staking her claim to the English throne; anarchy breaks out in the country.

1140 Prince Sobeslav I of Bohemia dies, and is succeeded by his son Vladislav II. Peter Abelard is condemned for heresy at the council of Sens, on a motion railroaded through by St Bernard.

1141 Stephen of England taken prisoner after defeat at Lincoln. Matilda proclaimed queen, but her high-handed behaviour alienates many, in particular London. Stephen is released in exchange for Robert, earl of Gloucester, and Matilda is forced back on the defensive.

1142 The duchy of Bavaria is conferred by Conrad III on Margrave Henry II of Austria. Peter Abelard dies, worn out by the Church's ill-treatment.

1143 Emperor John II of Byzantium dies, and is succeeded by his son Manuel I. Fulk V of Jerusalem dies; his son Baldwin III succeeds him.

1144 Geoffrey of Anjou subdues Normandy and is proclaimed duke. Imad-ud-Din Zangi, sultan of Mosul, captures Edessa, in eastern Turkey, causing alarm in Outremer and in Western Europe.

1145 Arnold of Brescia establishes a republic in Rome; the newly-crowned Pope Eugenius III is forced to flee. St Bernard takes the lead in proclaiming the Second Crusade, to avenge the fall of Edessa.

1146 Zangi of Mosul is murdered, and succeeded by his formidable son Nur-ud-Din, who consolidates the conquest of Edessa.

1147 The Second Crusade collapses in chaos as the crusaders attack Damascus, an ally of Jerusalem, thus alienating it. Lisbon however is taken from the Moors by King Alfonso of Portugal. Matilda leaves England; her son Henry is left to carry on the fight, though only fourteen.

1148 Sugar brought back from the Middle East by returning crusaders.

1149 Raymond of Poitiers, prince of Antioch, killed by Nur-ud-Din.

1150 The University of Paris is founded. *The Black Book of Carmarthen*, an anthology of ancient Welsh poetry, is compiled.

1151 Geoffrey of Anjou dies, and is succeeded in Anjou, Normandy and associated domains by his son Henry. Fire and plague insurance policies are developed in Iceland.

1152 Emperor Conrad III dies and is succeeded by his nephew Frederick I Barbarossa. Louis VII divorces Eleanor of Aquitaine, who promptly marries Henry of Anjou.

1153 David I of Scotland dies; succeeded by his grandson Malcolm IV. Ascalon falls to Baldwin III of Jerusalem. St Bernard of Clairvaux dies. The Treaty of Wallingford brings the English anarchy to an end by recognising Henry of Anjou as Stephen's heir.

1154 Roger II of Sicily dies; succeeded by his son William I. Damascus surrenders to Nur-ud-Din, who now controls most of Syria. Stephen of England dies and is succeeded by Henry, who now rules half of France as well as England. On the death of Anastasius IV, Nicholas Breakspear is elected Pope, taking the name Adrian IV.

1155 Ireland bestowed on Henry II by Pope Adrian IV. Adrian IV restores papal authority in Rome. Arnold of Brescia is hanged as a heretic by Emperor Frederick. St Berthold founds the Carmelite order of monks.

1156 Austria made a duchy with special status by Emperor Frederick. William I of Sicily recovers Bari from the Greeks and makes his peace with Rome.

1157 Erik IX of Sweden conquers and forcibly converts Finland. Alfonso VII of Castile dies; he is succeeded by his sons Sancho III in Castile and Ferdinand II in León.

1158 Prince Vladislav of Bohemia elevated to king by Emperor Frederick. Sancho III of Castile dies, and is succeeded by his infant son Alfonso VIII.

1159 Pope Adrian IV dies, and is succeeded by Alexander III. John of Salisbury writes the *Policraticus*, a treatise on government.

1160 Emperor Frederick, incensed by witnessing the inhabitants of Crema dismembering their prisoners during his siege, hurls his own prisoners over the walls before entering and destroying the city.

1161 Edward the Confessor is canonised.

1162 Emperor Frederick destroys Milan. Thomas Becket is chosen as Archbishop of Canterbury. Danegeld – by now just a general tax – is collected in England for the final time.

1163 The Welsh rebel against Henry II, but the revolt is suppressed and Prince Rhys ap Gruffydd is imprisoned. Henry II and Thomas Becket quarrel over the Church's status vis-à-vis the monarch.

1164 Legal rights of Church and State codified by Henry II at the council of Clarendon; Becket rejects the code and is forced to flee after he is condemned at the council of Northampton. Héloïse dies and is buried next to Abelard.

1165 Emperor Manuel allies with Venice against Emperor Frederick. Malcolm IV of Scotland dies, and is succeeded by his brother William the Lion. Charlemagne is canonised.

1166 *The Song of Cnut* written down by a monk of Ely. The erection of jails in all English counties ordered by the Assize of Clarendon. William I of Sicily dies, and is succeeded by his son William II.

1167 Oxford University is created when English students are barred from attending Paris.

1168 Milan is rebuilt. Prince Andrei I Bogoliubsky of Vladimir-Suzdal sacks Kiev and assumes the title Grand Prince.

1169 Saladin becomes vizier to the Fatimid caliph al-'Adid of Cairo, effectively controlling Egypt. Norman-Welsh barons land at Wexford supporting King Dermot of Leinster's efforts to regain his throne.

1170 Henry II has his son Henry crowned joint-king (the 'Young King'). Richard Strongbow, earl of Pembroke, takes Waterford and marries Dermot of Leinster's daughter. Thomas Becket returns to Canterbury, but is murdered four weeks later.

1171 Dermot of Leinster dies, and is succeeded by his son-in-law Richard Strongbow, who is forced to accept Henry II as his overlord when Henry crosses to Ireland. Saladin abolishes the Fatimid caliphate and rules Egypt himself.

1172 Henry II receives homage from the Irish at Cashel, but his wife Eleanor raises Aquitaine against him, forcing him to seek a reconciliation with Pope Alexander at Avranches.

1173 Henry II's wife and sons revolt against him, supported by William the Lion of Scotland and Louis VII of France. Eleanor of Aquitaine is captured and imprisoned. Thomas Becket is canonised.

1174 Henry II does public penance for Becket's murder and subdues the revolt against him. Nur-ud-Din dies and a fight for power in the Arab world ensues. Saladin takes Damascus. Amalric I of Jerusalem dies, and is succeeded by his leper son Baldwin IV.

1175 By the treaty of Windsor Rory O'Connor recognised as High King of Ireland under Henry II's overlordship.

1176 The Lombard League defeats Emperor Frederick at Legnano. The first eisteddfod is held at Cardigan Castle. Construction starts at London Bridge.

1177 Baldwin IV of Jerusalem defeats Saladin at Ramleh. Angkor Wat, capital of the Khmer empire, falls to Champa invaders.

1178 Construction starts on the bridge at Avignon.

1179 The Waldensians, Roman Catholic reformers are forbidden to preach by the Pope without the permission of bishops. The Third Lateran Council rules that popes will henceforth be elected by a two-thirds majority of the College of Cardinals.

1180 Louis VII of France dies, and is succeeded by his son Philip Augustus. Emperor Manuel I dies, and is succeeded by his son Alexius II. Henry II reforms the English coinage.

1181 Pope Alexander III dies; Lucius III succeeds him.

1182	Valdemar I of Denmark dies, and is succeeded by his son Cnut VI. Revolts in Byzantium force Emperor Alexius II to make his father's cousin Andronicus co-Emperor.
1183	Emperor Alexius II murdered, and replaced by his co-emperor, Andronicus I. Emperor Frederick, the Pope and the Lombard League make the Peace of Constance. Saladin takes Aleppo. Henry the 'Young King', rebellious son of Henry II of England, dies.
1184	Cyprus gains freedom from Byzantium. Giorgi III of Georgia dies, and is succeeded by his daughter Thamar. Glastonbury Abbey burns down.
1185	Emperor Andronicus I killed by rioters and succeeded by Isaac II Angelus. Bulgarians under Peter and Ivan Asen revolt against Byzantium. Saladin takes Mosul. Prince John sent to govern Ireland, antagonises the local lords and is recalled.
1186	Emperor Frederick marries his son Henry to Constance, heiress of Sicily, and has him crowned Caesar. Baldwin V of Jerusalem dies. The crown passes to Guy of Lusignan.
1187	Saladin defeats a crusader army at Hattin and takes Jerusalem. The Punjab conquered by the Ghaznavid Mohammad of Ghur. Bulgaria becomes independent under Ivan Asen.
1188	The Third Crusade is proclaimed; to this end the first general tax, the Saladin Tithe, is levied in France. Henry II quarrels with his son Richard and Philip II of France over his French lands and the succession.
1189	Henry II dies, and is succeeded by his son Richard, whose coronation is accompanied by a massacre of Jews. William II of Sicily dies; his bastard cousin Tancred takes the throne.
1190	Emperor Frederick I Barbarossa drowns in Cilicia whilst on crusade, he is succeeded by his son Henry VI. The Jews in York are massacred, but the city is fined.
1191	Richard I conquers Cyprus from the Byzantines and sells it to the Templars, before capturing Acre. Philip II returns to France after falling ill. Richard defeats Saladin at Arsuf. The Order of Germanic Hospitallers is founded at Acre. Zen Buddhism is introduced to Japan.
1192	Richard I, realizing he cannot win in Palestine, makes a truce with Saladin, ending the Third Crusade. On his return home, he is captured and imprisoned by Leopold, duke of Austria. Sultan Muhammad of Ghur captures Delhi, which becomes the Muslim capital in India. Yoritomo Minamoto becomes the first shogun (warlord) of Japan, effectively ruling under a figurehead emperor.
1193	Richard I is handed over to Emperor Henry VI, who demands ransom for his release. Prince John takes the opportunity to foment rebellion whilst Hubert Walter, archbishop of Canterbury, raises the sum. Saladin dies, and is succeeded in Cairo by his son Imad-ud-Din, whilst his relatives rule elsewhere in Arabia.
1194	The Yellow River changes course. Spitsbergen discovered by Norsemen. Richard I is freed after the ransom is paid, returns to England briefly to put down John's rebellion and leaves the country permanently for France. Emperor Henry VI conquers Sicily, deposing William III, son of Tancred. Prince Dafydd of Gwynedd dies, and is succeeded by his nephew Llywelyn ap Iorwerth the Great.
1195	Emperor Isaac II deposed, blinded and imprisoned by his brother Alexius III.
1196	Alfonso II of Aragon dies, and is succeeded by his son Pedro II. Bela III of Hungary dies; his son Imre succeeds him.
1197	Emperor Henry VI dies, sparking a succession dispute. Peter Asen of Bulgaria is murdered, and succeeded by his brother Kalojan. Prince Rhys of Deheubarth dies, and is succeeded by his son Gruffydd.
1198	Pope Celestine III dies. He is succeeded by Innocent III, who excommunicates Philip II of France for repudiating his wife Ingeborg of Denmark. Two rival emperors are established: Philip of Swabia, brother of Henry VI, and Otto, Duke of Saxony.
1199	Richard I dies after an injury at the siege of Chalus. He is succeeded by his brother John, although Philip II goes to war in France in support of John's nephew Arthur of Brittany. The Declaration of Speyer gives the German princes the right to elect their king.
1200	John of England and Philip II of France make peace at Le Goulet, with John confirmed in the Angevin lands in France under Philip's overlordship. Llywelyn the Great seizes Anglesey.
1201	The St Gotthard Pass is opened in Switzerland.
1202	The Fourth Crusade is proclaimed by Innocent III, with leadership given to Count Boniface III of Montferrat. The crusaders get into debt with Venice, whose doge, Enrico Dandolo, persuades them to take Zara for Venice. For this the crusaders are excommunicated by Innocent III.
1203	John murders his nephew, Arthur of Brittany, causing his French possessions to revolt. Crusaders and Venetians agree to help Isaac II regain the Byzantine throne from Alexius III, and are successful.
1204	Emperor Isaac II and his son Alexius IV deposed by Alexius V Ducas. The crusaders conquer Constantinople, and Alexius V flees to Morea, where he is captured and executed. Baldwin of Flanders is elected emperor, but the Byzantine empire disintegrates as relatives of the former ruling families set up independent states. Eleanor of Aquitaine dies. Normandy is captured by Philip Augustus.
1205	The Duchy of Athens is founded by Othon de la Roche. William of Champlitte founds the Principate of Achaea. Emperor Baldwin is defeated and executed by Kalojan of Bulgaria at Adrianople; he is succeeded by his brother Henry. Ladislas III of Hungary deposed by his uncle Andras II.
1206	The Mongol leader Temujin is proclaimed Genghis Khan at Karakorum. Qutb-ud-Din Aibak kills Sultan Muhammad and founds the Sultanate of Delhi. Theodore I Lascaris elected Legitimist Emperor at Nicaea.
1207	Marco I Sanudo founds the duchy of Naxos. Boniface of Montferrat, king of Thessalonica dies, and is succeeded by his son Demetrius.
1208	Philip of Swabia, pretender to the Holy Roman Empire, murdered by Otto of Wittelsbach, who is elected to succeed him and betrothed to his daughter. England placed under interdict by Innocent III. The Albigensian Crusade is proclaimed by Innocent III against Cathar heretics in Languedoc.
1209	The Albigensian fortress of Carcassonne is brutally taken by crusaders under Simon de Montfort. Otto of Wittelsbach crowned Emperor Otto IV in Rome. King John is excommunicated by Innocent III. Cambridge University founded by students leaving Oxford due to town and gown clashes.
1210	The order of the Friars Minor, founded by Francis of Assisi, approved by Innocent III. *Tristan und Isolde* written by Gottfried von Strassburg.

1211   Genghis Khan invades China. Sancho I of Portugal dies, and is succeeded by his son Alfonso II. Emperor Otto deposed by the German princes.

1212   Frederick II elected king by the German princes. Alfonso VIII of Castile decisively defeats the Moors at Las Navas de Tolosa. Stephen of Cloyes leads the Children's Crusade to its doom: many of the children who sail from Marseilles for the Holy Land end up in slavery.

1213   King John submits to the Papacy. Simon de Montfort invades Aragon, defeating the Aragonese at Muret and killing Pedro II, whose infant son James I is put into the care of the Templars.

1214   King John, Otto IV and other lords form alliance against Philip Augustus, who defeats the allied troops at Bouvines, Flanders. William the Lion of Scotland dies, and is succeeded by his son Alexander II.

1215   A revolt by barons in England leads to the signing under duress by King John of Magna Carta; rebel barons later capture Rochester Castle but John retakes it. Frederick II crowned emperor at Aachen. St Dominic founds the Dominican Order.

1216   Baronial revolts against King John gather force and the Dauphin Louis is invited to become king of England. John loses his baggage in the Wash and dies at Newark; he is succeeded by his son Henry III, with William Marshal, earl of Pembroke, proclaimed Regent. Pope Innocent III dies, and is succeeded by Honorius III.

1217   William Marshal defeats baronial rebels at Lincoln; the French fleet is later defeated off Sandwich and Prince Louis sues for peace. Henry III established as unchallenged king of England. The Fifth Crusade is launched under the leadership of John de Brienne.

1218   Persia overrun by Genghis Khan's Mongols. Deposed Emperor Otto IV dies, leaving Frederick II unchallenged. The Dannebrog is adopted as the flag of Denmark.

1219   Sultan Ka'us I of Rum dies, and is succeeded by his brother Kubadh I. Robert succeeds his mother Yolande as emperor in Constantinople. William Marshal dies.

1220   The Dresden Boys' choir founded. Building commences on Salisbury and Amiens cathedrals.

1221   Samarkand sacked by Genghis Khan. The Fifth Crusade ends in failure.

1222   University of Oxford establishes St George's Day, 23 April, as national holiday of England.

1223   Philip Augustus of France dies, and is succeeded by his son Louis VIII. Russians defeated by the Mongols at Kalka River. Alfonso II of Portugal dies, and is succeeded by his son Sancho II.

1224   The Jodo Shin (True Pure Land) sect founded in Japan by Shinran Shonin. Poitou and Gascony, possessions of Henry III of England, invaded by Louis VIII of France.

1225   Magna Carta is reissued in definitive form.

1226   Louis VIII of France dies, and is succeeded by his son Louis IX. St Francis of Assisi dies. The Teutonic Knights are commissioned to conquer and convert Prussia.

1227   Genghis Khan dies; his empire is divided among his three sons. Pope Honorius III dies, and is succeeded by Gregory IX. Frederick II embarks upon crusade, but is forced back by illness and excommunicated by Gregory IX for temporizing.

1228   Frederick II embarks upon crusade whilst Pope Gregory IX invades his realm. Francis of Assisi canonised.

1229   Frederick II reaches an agreement with Sultan Malik-al-Kamil, gaining Jerusalem, Bethlehem, Nazareth and an access corridor from Acre with a 15-year truce, and has himself crowned king of Jerusalem in Jerusalem. Returning from Palestine, Frederick defeats his enemies in Italy. The Balearic Islands conquered by Aragon.

1230   Frederick II and Pope Gregory IX reach an agreement at San Germano and Frederick's excommunication is lifted. Alfonso IX of León; dies his son Ferdinand III of Castile unites the two kingdoms.

1231   The Japanese shogun Fujiwara Yoritsune forbids the selling of children into slavery. Frederick II founds a medical school at Salerno.

1232   Muhammad I al-Ghalib comes to power in Granada, founding the Nasrid dynasty. Anthony of Padua canonised a year after his death.

1233   Pope Gregory IX founds the Papal Inquisition for the suppression of heresy and entrusts it to the Dominicans. The earl of Pembroke, aided by Llywelyn of Wales, leads a baronial revolt against Henry III.

1234   The earl of Pembroke is murdered in Ireland defending his Leinster estates against royalist attacks. Henry III and Llywelyn of Wales make peace.

1235   The Jin state in China falls to the Great Khan Ogedei's Mongols. Andras II of Hungary dies, and is succeeded by his son Bela IV.

1236   Alexander Nevsky succeeds to the Grand Duchy of Novgorod.

1237   The Mongols, led by Subutai and Ogedei, invade Russia, capture Moscow and devastate Poland.

1238   Moorish Valencia surrenders to James I of Aragon.

1239   Emperor Frederick II excommunicated again by Gregory IX.

1240   Prince Llywelyn of Gwynedd dies, and is succeeded by his son Dafydd. Richard of Cornwall and his brother-in-law Simon de Montfort lead a crusade to the Holy Land. The Mongol leader Batu, a grandson of Genghis Khan, takes and destroys Kiev.

1241   The Mongols advance into Eastern Europe, routing the Germans at Liegnitz in Silesia, but the death of Khan Ogedei saves Europe from invasion. Pope Gregory IX dies, and is succeeded by Celestine IV, who dies after seventeen days as Pontiff.

1242   Batu establishes the Golden Horde Mongols at Sarai on the Volga. Alexander Nevsky defeats the Teutonic Knights on the frozen Lake Peipus.

1243   Innocent IV elected Pope after an eighteen-month delay due to quarrels with Emperor Frederick II.

1244   Pasha Khwarazmi of Egypt recaptures Jerusalem for the Arabs. The Cathar stronghold of Montségur falls to Catholic besiegers and a mass execution of the defenders takes place outside.

1245   The Council of Lyon declares Frederick II deposed, causing civil war in Germany. Sancho II of Portugal deposed by Pope Innocent IV, who offers the throne to Sancho's brother Alfonso III.

1246   Landgrave Henry Raspe of Thuringia is elected German king. He defeats Frederick II's son Conrad at Nidda but is driven out of Thuringia by Conrad and Duke Otto II of Bavaria. Duke Frederick II of Austria dies; Emperor Frederick II seizes his duchy.

1247	Buda founded by Bela IV of Hungary to replace Pest, destroyed by the Mongols. With the demise of Henry of Thuringia, William II of Holland is elected anti-king in Germany.
1248	Louis IX of France sets off on the Seventh Crusade. Rhodes taken from the Byzantines by the Genoese. Moorish Seville falls after a two-year siege to Ferdinand III of Castile.
1249	The crusaders land in Egypt and take Damietta. Alexander II of Scotland dies, and is succeeded by his son Alexander III.
1250	Louis IX of France captured by Caliph Turan Shah of Egypt at the battle of Fariskur but released after paying ransom. The Mamluks depose and kill Turan Shah; Musa, a cousin of Turan Shah, becomes Caliph but rules in name only. Emperor Frederick II dies, and is succeeded by his son Conrad IV.
1251	Ottokar, margrave of Moravia, elected duke of Austria.
1252	Ferdinand III of Castile dies; his son Alfonso X succeeds him. Duke Andrei II of Vladimir deposed by the Great Khan Mongka in favour of his younger brother Alexander Nevsky.
1253	Wenceslas I of Bohemia dies, and is succeeded by his son Ottokar II, duke of Austria. The Buddhist monk Nichiren founds his own sect in Japan.
1254	Pope Innocent IV offers the Sicilian throne to Edmund, son of Henry III, who accepts on his behalf. Louis IX of France returns from crusade. Emperor Conrad IV dies. The succession of his infant son Conradin is blocked by opponents of the Hohenstaufens.
1255	Prince Llywelyn of Gwynedd ousts his brother Owen from joint rulership of the Principality.
1256	Venice and Genoa go to war. The order of Augustinian Hermits is founded. Hulagu, a grandson of Genghis Khan, conquers Persia.
1257	Richard, earl of Cornwall, is elected Holy Roman Emperor, but his election is disputed by Alfonso X of Castile.
1258	Hulagu Khan conquers Baghdad, killing Caliph al-Musta'sim and bringing the Abbasid Caliphate to an end. The Provisions of Oxford establish a form of parliamentary government in England. Manfred, regent of Sicily, crowns himself king, deposing his nephew Conradin, and is excommunicated by Pope Alexander IV.
1259	By the treaty of Paris Henry III gives up his claim to Normandy, Anjou and Poitou, and does homage for Gascony and Aquitaine to Louis IX.
1260	The Mamluk Baibars I becomes sultan in Egypt and defeats the Mongols at Ain Jalut in Palestine, saving Egypt from invasion and turning the tide of Mongol attacks. Kublai Khan comes to power in China.
1261	The Greeks reconquer Constantinople, driving the Latin Emperor Baldwin II from the city. The Nicaean Emperor Michael VIII Palaeologus succeeds him.
1262	Haakon IV of Norway unites Greenland and Iceland with his kingdom. Cadiz taken from the Moors.
1263	Alexander III of Scotland defeats Haakon IV of Norway at Largs and takes the Hebrides. Haakon dies on his way home and is succeeded by his son Magnus VI.
1264	Civil war erupts in England between Henry III and a baronial alliance led by Simon de Montfort; de Montfort defeats and captures Henry at Lewes, becoming de facto ruler of England.
1265	Charles of Anjou granted crusading privileges to conquer Sicily by Pope Clement IV. Simon de Montfort summons parliament, but is defeated and killed at Evesham by Prince Edward, who has escaped from imprisonment.
1266	Charles of Anjou defeats and kills Manfred of Sicily at Benevento and becomes king of Sicily. The Hebrides and the Isle of Man granted to Scotland by Norway under the terms of the Treaty of Perth.
1267	Llewelyn of Gwynedd, recognised as Prince of Wales by the treaty of Montgomery, pays homage to Henry III.
1268	Sultan Baibars captures Jaffa and Antioch. Conradin attempts to reclaim Sicily from Charles of Anjou, but is captured and executed. Pope Clement IV dies; the Papacy is left vacant.
1269	Louis IX of France orders Jews in his country to wear a purple wheel on their clothing.
1270	Louis IX of France dies in Tunisia whilst leading the Eighth Crusade; he is succeeded by his son Philip III. The poet Tannhäuser dies.
1271	Pope Gregory X elected to the three-years-vacant papal throne. Marco Polo accompanies his father and uncle to the Far East.
1272	Richard of Cornwall, king of the Romans, dies. Henry III of England dies, and is succeeded by his son Edward I, who is on crusade.
1273	Rudolf, count of Habsburg, elected German king and Holy Roman Emperor.
1274	Thomas Aquinas dies, leaving unfinished his *Summa Theologiae*. Kublai Khan sends an invasion fleet to Japan, but it is destroyed by a typhoon.
1275	Moses de León completes the Jewish mystical text the *Zohar*. Prince Llywelyn of Wales refuses homage to Edward I.
1276	Pope Gregory dies, followed by his successors Innocent V and Hadrian V; John XXI becomes 4th Pope of the year. Ottokar of Bohemia outlawed by Rudolf of Habsburg, but submits to him and is allowed to keep Bohemia and Moravia.
1277	Roger Bacon imprisoned for heresy. Sultan Baibars I of Egypt dies, and is succeeded by his son Baraka Khan. Llywelyn of Gwynedd forced to submit to Edward I by the treaty of Conway.
1278	Ottokar of Bohemia defeated and killed by Rudolf of Habsburg at Dürnkrut. He is succeeded by his son Wenceslas II. The glass mirror is invented.
1279	Alfonso III of Portugal dies near Macao, and is succeeded by his son Diniz. Kublai Khan defeats the Southern Song dynasty in a sea battle and reunites China under the rule of his Yuan dynasty.
1280	Magnus VI of Norway dies; his son Erik II succeeds him.
1281	When Kublai Khan sends a second invasion fleet to Japan it is again decimated by a typhoon, which the Japanese call *kamikaze*, divine wind.
1282	When his younger brother David starts a rebellion against Edward I, Llywelyn of Gwynedd is forced to take part, but is killed near Builth. His brother succeeds him. In the Sicilian Vespers, Sicilian nobles revolt

against Charles of Anjou, who flees whilst his countrymen are massacred. Pedro III of Aragon is offered the Sicilian crown and arrives to accept it.

1283   Prussia subdued by the Teutonic Knights. Edward I conquers Wales. Prince David of Gwynedd is surrendered by his men and executed by Edward.

1284   Kublai Khan invades Vietnam, but his army is destroyed by local guerrillas. Edward I settles Welsh affairs by the Statute of Rhuddlan and arranges for his son Edward to be born in Caernarfon castle.

1285   Charles of Anjou, king of Naples, dies whilst preparing to invade Sicily, succeeded by his son Charles II. Philip III of France dies, and is succeeded by his son Philip IV the Fair. Pedro III of Aragon and Sicily dies, to be succeeded in Aragon by his son Alfonso III and in Sicily by his son James.

1286   Alexander III of Scotland dies on a night ride; his heir is his granddaughter Margaret, the Maid of Norway.

1287   Kublai Khan invades Burma.

1288   Charles II of Naples is released from custody in Aragon on the condition that he accepts Aragonese rule in Sicily.

1289   Tripoli falls to Egyptian forces. Block printing is introduced to Europe at Ravenna.

1290   Edward I expels the Jews from England. Richard of Haldingham draws the *Mappa Mundi*. Margaret of Norway dies whilst on board ship to Scotland; the throne is vacant.

1291   Acre falls to Egyptian forces, ending crusader interest in Outremer. The Knights Hospitallers settle in Cyprus. Rudolf of Habsburg dies. The cantons of Uri, Schwyz and Unterwalden form the Everlasting League, the beginnings of Switzerland.

1292   Adolf, count of Nassau, elected German king. Edward I grants the Scottish throne to John de Balliol.

1293   Kublai Khan sends an expedition to take Java, but it fails.

1294   Philip IV of France confiscates Gascony; Edward I declares war but preparations are disrupted by revolt in Wales. Kublai Khan dies, and is succeeded by his grandson Temür.

1295   A Welsh revolt collapses after defeat at Maes Moydog. Scotland, resentful of a summons to help Edward I, forms the Auld Alliance with France. The Model Parliament convenes at Westminster.

1296   The Genoese defeat the Venetian fleet at Curzola; Marco Polo is amongst those captured. Edward I invades Scotland, forces John de Balliol to abdicate and takes the Stone of Scone, where Scottish kings are crowned, to Westminster.

1297   William Wallace leads a Scottish revolt against Edward I, defeating the English at Stirling Bridge and invading Northumberland and Cumberland. Giant moas become extinct on New Zealand's North Island.

1298   Adolf of Nassau is dethroned by his electors and killed at the battle of Göllheim; Albrecht of Austria, son of Rudolf of Habsburg, replaces him as German king. Edward I invades Scotland, defeating the Scots at Falkirk; Wallace flees abroad.

1299   Osman I, first of the Ottomans, becomes sultan of Turkey.

1300   Arnaud de Villeneuve distils brandy at Montpellier. Edward I invades Scotland again, but makes a truce after a Papal appeal to withdraw. Henry of Great Poland is deposed; Wenceslas II of Bohemia is elected to succeed him.

1301   Andras III of Hungary dies, ending the rule of the Arpad dynasty. Wenceslas II of Bohemia becomes king in his stead, but civil war breaks out. Edward I makes his son Edward Prince of Wales.

1302   The Black faction drive the Whites from Florence; Dante is exiled as a result. The Estates-General of France meet for the first time. Flemish burghers defeat the French at the battle of the Spurs.

1303   Philip IV of France sends Guillaume de Nogaret to capture Pope Boniface VIII and bring him to face trial in France. De Nogaret is thwarted by the Roman citizens, but Boniface dies a virtual prisoner and a broken man in the Vatican shortly after.

1304   The Scottish barons submit to Edward I at St Andrews whilst Stirling Castle only submits after a siege.

1305   Bertrand de Got, Archbishop of Bordeaux, elected Pope as Clement V. Wenceslas II of Bohemia, Poland and Hungary dies. He is succeeded in Bohemia and Poland by his son Wenceslas III, but in Hungary by Otto III of Bavaria. William Wallace is captured, tried and executed by the English.

1306   Wenceslas III of Bohemia and Poland is murdered. Albrecht of Austria invests his son Rudolf with Bohemia whilst Ladislas IV of Kujavia succeeds in Poland. Jews expelled from France. Rhodes purchased by the Knights Hospitallers. Robert Bruce murders John Comyn and is subsequently crowned king of Scots at Scone. The English invade Scotland and force Bruce to flee.

1307   Edward I of England dies, and is succeeded by his son Edward II, who creates Piers Gaveston earl of Cornwall. Philip IV seizes the property of the Knights Templar in France so as to replenish his treasury, but some of the Templar treasure is hidden away.

1308   The Templars are suppressed in England. Parliament forces Edward II to banish Piers Gaveston, who is created Lieutenant in Ireland. Albrecht of Austria is murdered on orders of his nephew John; Henry IV of Luxembourg is elected his successor.

1309   Clement V moves the Papacy to Avignon, thus beginning The 'Babylonian Captivity'.

1310   Parliament forces Edward II to appoint 21 Lords Ordainers to reform the government. A Council of Ten is appointed to rule Venice.

1311   The English Parliament orders baronial consent to appointments by Edward II. Robert Bruce raids Northumberland.

1312   The Knights Templar are abolished in France. Lyons is incorporated into France by the treaty of Vienne. Piers Gaveston is captured by barons and executed.

1313   Perth, Roxburgh, Edinburgh and the Isle of Man taken by the Scots, who besiege Stirling Castle. Emperor Henry VII dies.

1314   Jacques de Molay, Grand Master of the Knights Templar, is burned as a heretic; he curses Philip IV and Pope Clement V at the stake, both of whom die before the year is out. Edward II invades Scotland, but is routed at Bannockburn. Louis X succeeds his father Philip. Louis of Bavaria is elected German king, but a faction elects his rival Frederick of Austria as anti-king; civil war breaks out in Germany.

1315	Edward Bruce, Robert's brother, is offered the High Kingship of Ireland; he sails to Ireland and defeats the Earl of Ulster near Connor.
1316	Edward Bruce, is crowned high king of Ireland. Louis X of France dies. He is briefly succeeded by his son Jean I, who dies soon after his father, and then by his brother Philip V. John XXII elected Pope after a two year hiatus.
1317	The Salic Law is adopted by the French royal family: from now on females and descendants of the female line may not inherit the crown or other titles.
1318	Edward Bruce is killed in the battle of Faughart.
1319	Scots raid into England, defeating an army at the battle of Myton-in-Swaledale; a truce is subsequently made between the English and Scots.
1320	Vladislav IV is crowned king of Poland. The Declaration of Arbroath asserts Scots independence and loyalty to Robert Bruce. Tughluq Shah I founds the Tughluq dynasty as rulers of the sultanate of Delhi, overthrowing Khusraw Shah of the Khalji dynasty.
1321	Parliament forces Edward II to banish his close supporters Hugh Despenser and his son, but he recalls them and raises an army. Dante Alighieri dies.
1322	Philip V of France dies, and is succeeded by his brother Charles IV. Edward II defeats his cousin Thomas, earl of Lancaster, at Boroughbridge; Lancaster is executed and Edward's opponents punished. Frederick of Austria defeated and taken prisoner by Louis of Bavaria at the battle of Mühldorf.
1323	Thomas Aquinas is canonised.
1324	Marco Polo dies. Charles IV of France invades Gascony.
1325	Tughluq Shah I of Delhi is murdered by his son Muhammad Shah I, who replaces him as Sultan. Louis of Bavaria accepts Frederick of Austria as co-regent of Germany, but the move is unsuccessful.
1326	Osman I of Turkey dies; his son Orkhan succeeds him. Queen Isabella of England and her lover Roger Mortimer invade England; Edward II is captured and the Despensers executed.
1327	Edward II is forced to abdicate in favour of his son Edward III, and is murdered 8 months later in Berkeley Castle. Munich is devastated by fire.
1328	Charles IV of France dies, and is succeeded by his cousin Philip VI, first of the Valois dynasty. Robert Bruce is recognised as king of the Scots by the treaty of Northampton; Pope John XXII also recognises him.
1329	Robert Bruce dies of leprosy; he is succeeded by his son David II.
1330	Frederick of Austria dies; by the treaty of Hagenau Louis of Bavaria is recognised as emperor by the Habsburg faction. Edward III takes control of government in England, capturing and executing Roger Mortimer.
1331	Stephen Urosh III of Serbia is overthrown and murdered by his son Stephen Urosh IV Dushan, who replaces him as king.
1332	Lucerne joins the Swiss League. Edward Balliol invades Scotland, defeating loyalist forces at Dupplin Moor, and is crowned king, but is then defeated by loyalists and flees to England.
1333	Vladislav IV of Poland dies, and is succeeded by his son Casimir III the Great. Edward III and Edward Balliol besiege Berwick and defeat a relieving force at Halidon Hill. The Isle of Man is seized by England.The Black Death pandemic – a combination of bubonic and pneumonic plague passed on by fleas from infected rats – emerges in China.
1334	Casimir III of Poland encourages Jewish immigration. David II of Scotland flees to France and loyalist revolts break out. Berwick ceded to England by Edward Balliol. Pope John XXII dies, and is succeeded by Benedict XII.
1335	Emperor Andronicus III conquers Thessaly.
1336	Alfonso IV of Aragon dies, and is succeeded by his son Pedro IV. The Vijayanagar Empire is founded in southern India by Harihara I of the Yadava dynasty.
1337	Edward III claims the throne of France, thus precipitating the Hundred Years War.
1338	The French initiate hostilities against England, burning Portsmouth and Southampton. Edward III and Emperor Louis IV enter into an alliance. The university of Pisa is founded. Ashikaga Takaufi founds the Ashikaga shogunate.
1339	Venice conquers Treviso, thus gaining its first mainland possession.
1340	Waldemar IV, youngest son of the deposed Christopher II, ascends the Danish throne, ending eight years of anarchy. The English win a decisive naval victory over the French at Sluys.
1341	David II returns to Scotland, forcing the withdrawal of Edward Balliol. Emperor Andronicus III dies, and is succeeded by his 9-year-old son John V. When John's guardian, John Cantacuzene, attempts to set himself up as emperor, civil war erupts.
1342	Edward III conquers most of Brittany. Charles Robert, king of Hungary dies, and is succeeded by his son Louis I the Great.
1343	The Peruzzi banking house of Florence collapses as Edward III defaults on his loan repayments. The Black Death spreads amongst the Tartars in the Crimea.
1344	The Bardi banking house in Florence collapses. The Yellow River floods 16,000 square km of China and changes its course. Alfonso XI of Castile conquers Algeciras from the Moors.
1345	Stephen Urosh IV Dushan proclaims himself emperor of the Serbs and prepares to attack Byzantium.
1346	The French annihilated at Crécy by English bowmen. John of Luxembourg perishes in the battle, and is succeeded by his son Charles I, who is subsequently crowned German king. Scottish forces under David II invade England but are routed at Neville's Cross with David II taken prisoner.
1347	John Cantacuzene is victorious in the Byzantine civil war and reigns, nominally as co-emperor with John V, as John VI. Cola di Rienzi overthrows the Roman plutocracy, but attracts the enmity of Pope Clement VI and is forced to abdicate. Calais surrenders to Edward III after an 11-month siege. Emperor Louis IV dies during a bear hunt, and is succeeded by his rival Charles I of Luxembourg. The Black Death reaches the Black Sea, Sicily and Marseilles.

HISTORY

1348	The Black Death sweeps across Europe and has entered England by summer. Despite Pope Clement VI absolving them of blame, Jews are blamed in areas of France, Germany and Switzerland for the plague pandemic and are persecuted. Many leave for Poland and Russia which are more tolerant. Edward III founds the Order of the Garter.
1349	The Black Death reaches Scotland, Ireland and Poland. A flagellant movement appears as a response to the plague pandemic, but it is denounced and suppressed by Clement VI.
1350	Philip VI of France dies, and is succeeded by his son Jean II. Alfonso XI of Castile dies of the plague whilst besieging Gibraltar, and is succeeded by his son Pedro I the Cruel. Cola di Rienzi appears in Prague, where he is imprisoned by Charles of Luxembourg.
1351	Zurich joins the Swiss League. Florence and Milan go to war over Tuscany. The Statute of Labourers fixes wage rates and restricts movement of labourers in England, as a result of Black Death depopulation and the economic strain of war.
1352	Glarus and Zug join the Swiss League. The Black Death penetrates Russia. Cola di Rienzi is sentenced to death at Avignon, but is saved when Clement VI dies and his successor Innocent VI pardons him.
1353	Bern joins the Swiss League. Giovanni Boccaccio completes *The Decameron*.
1354	The Ottoman Turks take Gallipoli. Innocent VI grants Cola di Rienzi the title Senator and sends him to Rome, but he is killed in a riot within two months. The Genoese defeat a Venetian fleet at Sapienza.
1355	Stephen Urosh IV Dushan of Serbia dies, and is succeeded by his son Stephen Urosh V. The St Scholastica's Day riots in Oxford last three days, with many students killed in 'town and gown' clashes.
1356	Jean II of France captured by the English at the battle of Poitiers, where the Black Prince Edward Prince of Wales, gains a crushing victory.
1357	Parisian merchants, led by Etienne Marcel and Robert le Coq, revolt against the dauphin's administration. David II of Scotland ransomed by the treaty of Berwick.
1358	French peasants revolt in the Jacquerie uprising in the Beauvais but it is suppressed with English assistance. Etienne Marcel is assassinated in Paris by a supporter of the dauphin.
1359	Revolutionaries in red hats storm Bruges in an unsuccessful attempt to overthrow the patrician government. Ivan II of Muscovy dies, and is succeeded by his son Dimitri Donskoy.
1360	England and France sign the treaty of Brétigny, which gives England territorial gains and stipulates the payment of a ransom for Jean II. When the ransom cannot be raised Jean II voluntarily goes back into captivity. Sultan Orkhan of Turkey dies, and is succeeded by Murad I.
1361	Murad I takes Adrianople and makes it the Ottoman capital. The Black Death reappears in England and France.
1362	The Black Prince is appointed ruler of Aquitaine.
1363	Tughlug Timur, shah in Turkestan, dies; he is succeeded by his son Ilyas Khoja, establishing Zungarian Chaghatai rule.
1364	Jean II of France dies in captivity in England, and is succeeded by his son Charles V.
1365	By the Statute of Praemunire the English parliament repudiates Papal overlordship of the country and forbids appeals to the Papal court.
1366	Amadeus of Savoy takes Gallipoli as part of his crusade against the Turks. Pedro the Cruel of Castile is deposed in favour of his half-brother Henry of Trastamara.
1367	Pedro I of Portugal dies and is succeeded by his son Ferdinand. The Black Prince invades Castile in support of Pedro the Cruel, defeating Castilian and French forces at Najera and restoring Pedro's crown.
1368	Chinese Yuan Emperor Shundi is deposed by the Ming Zhu Yuanzhang, who takes the throne with the name Hongwu.
1369	Pedro the Cruel of Castile offends the Black Prince, who abandons him. Besieged by Henry of Trastamara at Montiel, Pedro is defeated and killed by Henry who replaces him as king. France declares war on England.
1370	The Mongol ruler Timur the Lame (Tamburlaine) takes the throne of Samarkand. The Black Prince sacks Limoges. Casimir III of Poland dies in a hunting accident; the last Piast king, he is succeeded by his nephew Louis of Anjou, the king of Hungary.
1371	David II of Scotland dies; he is succeeded by his nephew Robert II, the first of the Stuarts. Sultan Murad I wins the battle of Chernomen – Macedonia, Bulgaria and the Byzantines are forced to admit his suzerainty.
1372	The English defeated by Castilian forces at sea off La Rochelle, which falls, along with Poitou, to the French.
1373	Brandenburg annexed by Emperor Charles IV from Otto V of Bavaria, and is given to his son Wenceslas to rule.
1374	A mysterious dancing craze affects Aix-La-Chapelle, when the inhabitants inexplicably dance themselves to exhaustion.
1375	England and France sign the truce of Bruges – English possessions in France much reduced as a result. The Mamluks take Sis from the Armenian King León V, ending Armenian independence.
1376	Edward, the Black Prince, dies. The Good Parliament is convened; Sir Peter de la Mare is chosen Speaker for the House of Commons.
1377	Pope Gregory XI returns the Papacy to Rome. Edward III dies, and is succeeded by his grandson Richard II; John of Gaunt becomes Regent. The French raid Sussex and Kent, burning Rye and Hastings.
1378	Pope Gregory XI dies. Urban VI is elected his successor but tries to reform the College of Cardinals, leading the French Cardinals to create Robert of Geneva Pope Clement VII at Anagni. He moves his Curia to Avignon and the Great Schism begins. Emperor Charles IV dies, and is succeeded by his son Wenceslas.
1379	Henry II of Castile dies, and is succeeded by his son Juan I.
1380	St Catherine of Siena dies. Charles V of France dies, and is succeeded by his son Charles VI the Mad. Dmitri III Donskoi, prince of Moscow, defeats the Mongols at Kulikovo.
1381	Wat Tyler and John Ball lead the Peasants' Revolt in England. Archbishop Sudbury is murdered outside the Tower by a mob but Tyler is stabbed to death by William Walworth, mayor of London, on meeting Richard II at Smithfield. Ball is executed and the rising is suppressed. Venice defeats Genoa in the war of Chioggia.

1382	The religious reformer John Wycliffe is condemned by Archbishop William Courtenay and barred from teaching at Oxford. Louis of Anjou, king of Hungary and Poland, dies, and is succeeded by his daughters Mary in Hungary and Jadwiga in Poland.
1383	The Bishop of Norwich leads the 'Norwich Crusade' to Flanders in support of Pope Urban VI, but is repulsed and impeached at home by Chancellor Michael de la Pole. Ferdinand of Portugal dies, and is succeeded by his daughter Beatrix.
1384	Juan I of Castile marries Beatrix of Portugal, but the Portuguese resist his claim to their throne. John Wycliffe dies.
1385	Scottish forces, aided by the French, raid Northumbria. Portuguese forces defeat Juan of Castile at the battle of Aljubarrota; João of Aviz, an illegitimate son of Pedro I, takes the kingship.
1386	England and Portugal sign the treaty of Windsor, sealed by the marriage of João I with John of Gaunt's daughter Philippa. Jadwiga of Poland marries Jagiello of Lithuania, who takes the name Vladislav V. Leopold III of Styria and Tyrol defeated and killed by the Swiss at the battle of Sempach; his 4 sons jointly succeed him.
1387	Olaf V of Denmark and Norway dies, and is succeeded by his mother Margaret I. Sigismund of Luxembourg, margrave of Brandenburg, marries Mary of Hungary, becoming king. Geoffrey Chaucer begins *The Canterbury Tales*.
1388	At the battle of Otterburn (Chevy Chase) the Scots under the earl of Douglas defeat and capture Henry 'Hotspur' Percy, though Douglas himself is killed.
1389	Margaret I of Denmark and Norway is offered the Swedish throne, invades and defeats King Albert II of Mecklenburg at Falköping, and thereby unites the Scandinavian thrones. Sultan Murad I defeats a Serb-led coalition at Kosovo and conquers Serbia. Murad is subsequently assassinated by the Serb noble Lazar, who is captured and put to death by Murad's son and successor Bayazid I.
1390	Byzantine Emperor John V is deposed by his grandson John VII, but his son Manuel restores him to the throne. Robert II of Scotland dies, and is succeeded by his son Robert III. Juan I of Castile dies, and is succeeded by his son Henry III.
1391	Emperor John V dies, and is succeeded by his son Manuel II. Jews persecuted in Andalusia and Barcelona, as scapegoats for plague. Gedun Truppa is the first Dalai Lama in Tibet.
1392	Charles VI of France suffers his first fit of madness. Yi Songgye founds the Yi Dynasty in Korea, supplanting the Koryo Dynasty and making Kyongsong (later known as Seoul) the capital.
1393	Bulgaria subdued by Sultan Bayazid I. Timur the Lame takes Baghdad. Emperor Wenceslas IV tortures and murders St John of Nepomuk in Prague.
1394	Emperor Wenceslas taken prisoner by his cousin Jobst of Moravia. Anti-Pope Clement VII dies, and is replaced by Benedict XXIII. Richard II goes to Ireland and sets the limit of the territory later known as 'The Pale'.
1395	Richard II receives the submission of 80 Irish chiefs and returns to England. Albert of Mecklenburg renounces the Swedish throne, confirming Margaret of Denmark as queen.
1396	England and France agree a 28-year truce. Sigismund of Hungary leads a Crusade to Nicopolis, where his army is routed by the Ottoman Turks. Gian Galeazzo Visconti buys the title Duke of Milan from Emperor Wenceslas.
1397	Scandinavian nobles assembled in the Union of Kalmar officially recognise the union of Denmark, Norway and Sweden under Queen Margaret. Sultan Bayazid besieges Constantinople but withdraws when Timur the Lame appears in his lands.
1398	Richard II orders a duel to settle the dispute between John of Gaunt's son Henry Bolingbroke and the duke of Norfolk; he then intercedes and banishes the pair. Timur the Lame conquers and sacks Delhi.
1399	John of Gaunt dies. Richard II confiscates the Lancastrian inheritance of Gaunt. Bolingbroke returns from exile, engineers the deposition of Richard II, and is crowned Henry IV in his stead.
1400	Richard II murdered in Pontefract Castle. Emperor Wenceslas is deposed for drunkenness and incompetence; Rupert III of the Palatinate elected to replace him. Owain Glyndwr attacks Lord Grey of Ruthin, proclaims himself prince of Wales and engineers a revolt in the Principality.
1401	Baghdad and Damascus fall to Timur the Lame.
1402	Sultan Bayazid defeated and captured by Timur the Lame at the battle of Ankara; Bayazid is forced to become Timur's footstool while his favourite wife Despina is made a naked waitress. Duke Gian Galeazzo Visconti of Milan dies whilst besieging Florence, and is succeeded by his son Giovanni Maria. The earl of Northumberland and his son Hotspur capture the earl of Douglas at the battle of Homildon Hill.
1403	Sultan Bayazid dies in captivity at Timur's camp; his sons Suleiman and Muhammad dispute the succession. The Doge of Venice imposes quarantine as an attempt to ward off the Black Death. The earl of Northumberland rebels against Henry IV but is defeated at Shrewsbury, where his son Hotspur perishes.
1404	Owain Glyndwr holds a Welsh parliament at Dolgellau.
1405	Timur the Lame dies, and is succeeded by his sons Miran Shah and Shah Rukh and by Miran Shah's son Khalil Sultan in his domains. Owain Glyndwr is defeated at Grosmont by John Talbot and at Usk by Henry, Prince of Wales. Richard Scrope, Archbishop of York, leads a revolt against Henry IV, but the rebellion collapses and Scrope is executed.
1406	Robert III of Scotland sends his son James to France for safety, fearing his brother Albany, but James is captured by the English at sea and imprisoned. Robert III dies and Albany becomes regent as James is kept captive.
1407	Louis, duke of Orléans, is assassinated on the orders of John the Fearless, duke of Burgundy, causing a feud between Burgundian and Armagnac followers in France.
1408	The last threat to Henry IV in England is extinguished by the Sheriff of Yorkshire's victory at Bramham Moor; the earl of Northumberland dies in the battle.
1409	Henry, prince of Wales, captures Harlech castle, kills Edmund Mortimer and subdues the Welsh revolt. In

an attempt to end the Great Schism a conclave of cardinals announces that both Gregory XII and Benedict XIII are deposed, and elects Alexander V in their stead. Both Gregory and Benedict refuse to accept this election, and there are now three contending popes. Dalmatia recovered by Venice.

1410   Anti-Pope Alexander V dies and John XXIII replaces him as the third pope. Emperor Rupert dies. Sigismund of Hungary, brother of the deposed Wenceslas, is elected to succeed him. The Teutonic Knights are decisively defeated by a Polish-Lithuanian force at Tannenberg.

1411   Portugal and Castile make peace. Poland and the Teutonic Knights make the Peace of Thorn.

1412   Duke Giovanni Visconti of Milan is assassinated, and succeeded by his brother Filippo Maria of Pavia. Margaret of Denmark, Sweden and Norway dies, and is succeeded by her great-nephew Erik of Pomerania.

1413   Henry IV of England dies; his son Henry V succeeds him. Civil war amongst the Ottomans ends when Muhammad I defeats and kills his brother Musa outside Constantinople.

1414   The Lollards, radical religious reformers, under Sir John Oldcastle, revolt against Henry V, but are suppressed. The Council of Constance is convened by John XXIII at the instigation of Sigismund of Hungary, in an attempt to end the Great Schism.

1415   The Council of Constance deposes John XXIII and accepts the abdication of Gregory XII, but Benedict XIII refuses to abdicate. Jan Hus is burnt for heresy, causing outrage in Bohemia. Henry V goes to war with France after the failure of negotiations to marry Catherine of Valois, and gains a crushing victory at Agincourt.

1416   Jerome of Prague, a follower of Hus, is burned for heresy. The Venetians defeat the Ottomans in the Dardanelles.

1417   Caen falls to Henry V. Oddo, Colonna is elected Pope, taking the name Martin V, and the Great Schism comes to an end, although Benedict XIII and a small number of clerics hold out.

1418   Madeira discovered by Portuguese explorers under the aegis of Henry the Navigator. John the Fearless of Burgundy takes control of the French government, but the Dauphin Charles sets up a rival administration at Bourges.

1419   Rouen, and subsequently Normandy fall to Henry V. Hussites rebel in Bohemia, defenestrating Catholic councillors in Prague. John the Fearless of Burgundy is assassinated by Armagnacs supporting Dauphin Charles, driving his successor Philip the Good to an alliance with England.

1420   The Anglo-Burgundian alliance makes the treaty of Troyes with Charles VI of France; Henry is made Charles' heir and marries his daughter Catherine. Chinese Emperor Yongle moves his capital to Dadu and renames it Beijing ('northern capital').

1421   Sultan Muhammad I dies, and is succeeded by his son Murad II. Florence buys the city of Livorno. The Zuider Zee is formed by an irruption of the North Sea; 100,000 perish in the process.

1422   Henry V dies, and is succeeded by his nine month-old son Henry VI. Charles VI of France dies and his son Charles VII declares himself king, but Henry VI is proclaimed king by Protector Bedford in the Anglo-Burgundian areas in accordance with the treaty of Troyes.

1423   Thessalonica is purchased from the Byzantines by Venice in an attempt to prevent the Ottomans taking it. James I of Scotland is freed from captivity by the treaty of London on payment of a ransom.

1424   Chinese Emperor Yongle dies and is succeeded by his son Hongxi. James I returns to Scotland and takes up government from his uncle Albany. The English defeat Charles VII at Verneuil.

1425   James I of Scotland executes his uncle Albany and his family. Emperor Manuel II dies, and is succeeded by his son John VIII. Le Mans falls to the English. Henry the Navigator takes the Canary Islands from Castile.

1426   Venice and Milan go to war.

1427   Yeshak of Ethiopia attempts to form an anti-Islamic alliance with Aragon and France.

1428   By the terms of the Treaty of Delft, Duke Phillip of Burgundy is made governor of Hainault, Holland and Zeeland and heir to Jacqueline of Bavaria, Countess of these lands.

1429   French lose to the English at Rouvray (battle of the Herrings) but under the leadership of Jeanne d'Arc relieve Orleans and are victorious at Patay, where Talbot is captured. Charles VII is crowned at Rheims.

1430   Thessalonica falls to the Ottomans of Murad II. Jeanne d'Arc is captured by the Burgundians at Compiègne and sold to the English, who imprison her at Rouen.

1431   A Lollard conspiracy led by 'Jack Sharp' is crushed by the duke of Gloucester. Jeanne d'Arc is burned as a witch at Rouen.

1432   The Azores are discovered by the Portuguese sailor Gonzalo Cabral. Sultan Murad II takes Albania.

1433   Lucca defeats Florence. Timbuktu falls to the Tuaregs. João I of Portugal dies, and is succeeded by his son Duarte. Duke Phillip of Burgundy forces Jacqueline of Bavaria to abdicate in Hainault, Holland and Zeeland after she had incited a failed revolt against him.

1434   The Khmer move their capital from Angkor to Phnom Penh. Cosimo de Medici is recalled from exile to rule Florence. Vladislav V of Poland dies, and is succeeded by his son Vladislav VI. Jan Van Eyck paints Giovanni Arnolfini and his wife.

1435   The Riksdag of Sweden meets for the first time and makes Engelbrecht Engelbrechtson regent for the ineffectual King Erik. Alfonso V of Aragon attempts to capture Naples, thus reuniting Naples and Sicily under one crown but is captured and later released. France and Burgundy are reconciled by the peace of Arras.

1436   The Compact of Iglau ends the Hussite wars in Bohemia and Emperor Sigismund is acknowledged king. Paris falls to the French. The Scots fail to capture Roxburgh Castle.

1437   James I of Scotland is murdered at Perth by Sir Robert Graham, who is executed for the deed. James II succeeds his father. Emperor Sigismund dies, and is succeeded by his son-in-law Albrecht II of Habsburg.

1438   Pahacutec founds the Inca dynasty in Peru. Erik of Denmark, Norway and Sweden flees from rebellions to Gotland, where he takes up piracy.

1439   Serbia falls to Sultan Murad II. The Council of Florence ratifies the union of Roman and Byzantine churches under Rome's primacy. German King Albrecht II dies, leaving his wife pregnant.

1440 Frederick III of Styria is elected German king. Ladislas Posthumus is born and succeeds his late father Albrecht in Austria and Bohemia; in Hungary Vladislav VI of Poland is invited to be king. Eton College is founded by Henry VI.

1441 The Churches of Rome and Ethiopia sign an act of union. The Portuguese sell Africans as slaves in Lisbon: from this the slave trade will develop.

1442 Eleanor Cobham, duchess of Gloucester, is divorced and imprisoned on charge of attempting to kill Henry VI by sorcery.

1443 The Ottomans defeated by the Hungarian hero Janos Hunyadi at Nish; George Castriota, governor of Albania, takes advantage of this defeat by declaring his province independent.

1444 Christians and Ottomans declare a truce at Adrianople and George Brankovich is restored to his principality of Serbia; Hungarians break the truce but are defeated at Varna; Vladislav VI of Poland perishes there and Ladislas Posthumus succeeds to the Hungarian throne.

1445 Cape Verde discovered by Diniz Diaz of Portugal. Copenhagen becomes the capital of Denmark.

1446 Corinth falls to the Ottomans. Janos Hunyadi is elected regent of Hungary for Ladislas.

1447 Casimir of Lithuania, a brother of the late Vladislav VI, is elected king of Poland. Milan becomes a republic on the death of Filippo Maria Visconti. Shah Rukh, Lord of Turkestan dies, and is succeeded by his son Ulugh Beg.

1448 With the death of Christopher of Bavaria, king of Sweden, Denmark and Norway, the Union of Kalmar dissolves. Christian of Oldenburg reigns in Denmark and Norway whilst Karl Knutsen is elected king of Sweden. Sultan Murad defeats the Hungarians under Janos Hunyadi at the second battle of Kosovo. Emperor John VIII dies, and is succeeded by his brother Constantine XI.

1449 Ulugh Beg, Lord of Turkestan, is executed by his son Abd al-Latif, who also puts his brother Abd al-Aziz to death. The Timurid provinces in Turkestan fragment as a result, and Babur ibn Baisonqur, a nephew of Ulugh Beg, takes power in Khurasan.

1450 Abd al-Latif dies; his cousin Abdullah Mirza succeeds him as Lord of Turkestan. Francesco Sforza overthrows the republic in Milan and makes himself duke. Normandy reconquered by France. Jack Cade leads a revolt in Kent and Sussex; it fails and Cade is killed, but Henry VI is forced to flee for safety to Kenilworth for a while.

1451 Gascony reconquered by the French. Sultan Murad II dies, and is succeeded by his son Muhammad II.

1452 Borso of Este is created duke of Modena by Emperor Frederick III. James II of Scotland murders the earl of Douglas at Stirling. John Talbot leads an expedition to Gascony and reconquers much of it.

1453 Constantinople falls to the Ottoman Sultan Muhammad II; Emperor Constantine XI perishes in the fighting and the Byzantine Empire is no more. The French win a decisive victory over the English at Castillon, where Talbot dies. Gascony is reconquered and the English hold only Calais in France. The Hundred Years War is thus brought to an end. Henry VI has a bout of insanity.

1454 The duke of York is appointed protector during Henry VI's incapacity. The Peace of Lodi is reached between Venice and Milan and their allies. Venice signs a treaty with Sultan Muhammad II.

1455 Henry VI recovers his sanity and dismisses the duke of York from the post of Protector. The Wars of the Roses begin when York and the earl of Warwick raise an army and defeat and capture Henry VI at St Albans. York is made Constable of England but pro-Lancastrian riots break out. Johannes Gutenberg produces the first printed Bible, using the movable metal type that he started to perfect in the 1450s.

1456 The Ottomans capture Athens but are repulsed from Belgrade by Janos Hunyadi, who dies soon after from plague. Vlad III the Impaler retakes the Wallachian throne from Vladislav II.

1457 Karl VIII of Sweden is driven out and replaced by Christian I of Denmark. Laszlo Hunyadi, son of Janos, is arrested and beheaded in Buda, sparking outrage in Hungary; Ladislas Posthumus is forced to flee to Prague, where he dies suddenly. Emperor Frederick III succeeds in Austria; George Podiebrad, leader of the Hussites, is elected king in Bohemia.

1458 Matthias Corvinus, second son of Janos Hunyadi, is elected king of Hungary. Alfonso V of Aragon dies, and is succeeded in Aragon and Sicily by his brother Juan II and in Naples by his bastard son Ferdinand.

1459 Civil war is renewed in England. The Yorkists are victorious at Blore Heath but defeated at Ludford Bridge. The Irish come out in support of the Yorkists.

1460 Henry VI defeated and captured by the Yorkists at Northampton; the duke of York is named heir to Henry but dies at the battle of Wakefield, where the Lancastrians are victorious. James II of Scotland dies when a cannon misfires at Roxburgh, and is succeeded by his son James III. Henry the Navigator dies.

1461 Yorkists victorious at Mortimer's Cross, where Owen Tudor is captured and executed, but defeated at St Albans. Henry VI is rescued by the Lancastrians. Edward of York deposes Henry VI and crushes the Lancastrians at Towton; Henry VI and his family flee to Scotland. Charles VII of France dies, and is succeeded by his son Louis XI. Trebizond falls to the Ottomans.

1462 Vlad III the Impaler of Wallachia is deposed and replaced by his pro-Turkish brother Radu III. Prince Vasili of Moscow dies, and is succeeded by his son Ivan III the Great.

1463 Bosnia conquered by the Ottomans, who go to war with the Venetians. England, France and Burgundy sign the Truce of Hesdin, the latter two recognizing Edward IV of York as king of England.

1464 Yorkists victorious at Hedgeley Moor and Hexham, and gain control of Northern England. Louis XI of France founds the *Poste Royale*. Cosimo de Medici dies, and is succeeded by his son Piero I.

1465 Henry VI captured in Ribblesdale and imprisoned in the Tower. Louis XI of France defeated by a coalition of royal dukes at Montlhéry and is forced to sign the treaty of Conflans.

1466 The Medicis form an alliance with the Vatican to finance alum mining in the Papal States. George Podiebrad, king of Bohemia, excommunicated by Pope Paul II.

1467 Philip the Good of Burgundy dies, and is succeeded by his son Charles the Bold.

1468 Zara Ya'kob Constantine of Ethiopia dies, and is succeeded by his son Ba'eda Maryam I. James III of Scotland contracts to marry Margaret, daughter of Christian of Denmark; the Orkneys and Shetlands are pledged as security for her dowry.

1469   Rebellion develops in England against Edward IV and the power of his wife's family. Edward is imprisoned after his army deserts him at Olney, and is released with a promise to appease the rebels. Piero de Medici dies; his sons Lorenzo the Magnificent and Giuliano succeed him. Ferdinand, heir to the throne of Aragon, marries Isabella, heiress of Castile.

1470   Portuguese seafarers reach the Gold Coast. Edward IV defeats a rebel army at Empingham, but Warwick and the Lancastrians reach an accord and invade, forcing Edward to flee to Burgundy. Henry VI is restored to the throne.

1471   Edward IV returns to England, defeats and kills Warwick at Barnet and then decisively defeats the Lancastrians at Tewkesbury, where Edward Prince of Wales perishes. Henry VI is murdered in the Tower. Louis XI of France and Charles the Bold of Burgundy go to war.

1472   Lopo Gonçalves is the first European to cross the Equator. Ivan III of Moscow marries Zoe, niece of Emperor Constantine XI, thus attempting to transfer imperial lustre to himself.

1473   Charles the Bold of Burgundy occupies Lorraine and Alsace. Cyprus falls under Venetian rule.

1474   The Union of Constance is formed against Charles the Bold of Burgundy, who makes an anti-French alliance, via the treaty of London, with Edward IV. Henry IV of Castile dies, and is succeeded by his half-sister Isabella and her husband Ferdinand, son of Juan II of Aragon.

1475   Edward IV invades France but is let down by his absent ally Charles the Bold and goes on to sign a 7-year truce with Louis XI via the treaty of Picquigny.

1476   Charles the Bold makes war on the Swiss, but is defeated at Granson, and later at Morat. Duke Galeazzo Sforza of Milan is assassinated by republicans, but is succeeded by his son Gian Galeazzo. William Caxton establishes the first English printing press.

1477   Edward IV bans early forms of skittles and cricket due to their interference with archery practice. Charles the Bold of Burgundy dies fighting the Swiss at the battle of Nancy; his state implodes and is effectively shared between Louis XI and Charles' son-in-law Maximilian, son of Emperor Frederick III.

1478   The duke of Clarence is drowned in a butt of Malmsey while imprisoned in the Tower of London. Novgorod subdued by Ivan the Great of Muscovy. Isabella of Castile unleashes the Inquisition on Jewish converts. Pope Sixtus VI and the Pazzi family plot to assassinate the Medicis; Giuliano is killed but Lorenzo escapes and decimates the Pazzis in revenge.

1479   Juan II of Aragon dies. His son Ferdinand succeeds him and the thrones of Castile and Aragon are thus united. The treaty of Constantinople ends the war between Venice and the Ottoman Empire.

1480   Ivan III frees Muscovy from Tartar domination. Duke René of Anjou dies; his domains, including Provence, are annexed by Louis XI. Otranto is taken by the Ottomans.

1481   Sultan Muhammad II dies, and is succeeded by his son Bayazid II. Alfonso V of Portugal dies, and is succeeded by his son João II.

1482   Venice goes to war with Ferrara. Louis XI and the Habsburgs make the Peace of Arras, partitioning the Burgundian domains.

1483   Edward IV dies, and is succeeded by his son Edward V, who disappears along with his brother Richard in the Tower. Their uncle Richard assumes the kingship. Louis XI of France dies, and is succeeded by his son Charles VIII. The Dominican Tomás de Torquemada takes control of the Spanish Inquisition.

1484   Diogo Cão discovers the mouth of the River Congo. Pope Innocent VIII issues the bull *Summis Desiderantes* against witchcraft.

1485   Emperor Frederick III expelled from Vienna by Matthias Corvinus of Hungary. Henry Tudor invades England against Richard III, defeats and kills him at Bosworth Field, and takes the throne. Caxton publishes Malory's *Morte d'Arthur*.

1486   Matthias Corvinus devises a law code for Hungary. Henry VII marries Elizabeth of York and unites the houses of Lancaster and York. Krämer and Spränger publish the *Malleus Maleficarum* attacking witches and witchcraft.

1487   Lambert Simnel leads revolt against Henry VII, claiming to be Edward IV's nephew, but is defeated at Stoke and sent to work in the royal kitchens. Bartholomew Diaz sails around the Cape of Good Hope, which he names the Cape of Storms.

1488   James III of Scotland is murdered; his son James IV succeeds him. Duke Francis of Brittany dies, and is succeeded by his daughter Anne. Johann Widmann develops the use of the symbols (+), (&), and (-). Bartholomew Diaz returns to Lisbon, where João II gives the Cape of Good Hope its name.

1489   Typhus is brought to Aragon by soldiers returning from Cyprus. Catherine Cornaro of Cyprus is forced to sell her kingdom to Venice. Henry VII signs the anti-French treaty of Redon with Brittany.

1490   Matthias Corvinus of Hungary dies without an heir, and is succeeded by Ladislas of Bohemia.

1491   Perkin Warbeck claims to be Richard, duke of York, and rallies support for his cause in France and Ireland. Charles VIII of France annexes Brittany by forcing Anne of Brittany to marry him.

1492   Granada, the last Moorish city, conquered by Ferdinand and Isabella; Spain effectively one country. Lorenzo the Magnificent of Florence dies, and is succeeded by his son Piero II. Casimir IV of Poland and Lithuania dies, and is succeeded by his sons John Albert in Poland and Alexander in Lithuania. Rodrigo Borgia elected Pope as Alexander VI. Henry VII invades France and is bought off by Charles VIII under the treaty of Étaples, with compensation for Brittany's annexation and the expulsion of Warbeck. Jews in Spain are ordered to convert or quit the country. Christopher Columbus discovers Cuba and Hispaniola.

1493   Columbus returns home from the Indies, and is sent back as governor of the new lands by Isabella of Castile, discovering Dominica. Pope Alexander VI publishes the bull *Inter Cetera Divina* dividing the New World between Spain and Portugal. Emperor Frederick III dies, and is succeeded by his son Maximilian I.

1494   Emperor Maximilian I recognises Warbeck as king of England. Spain and Portugal divide the New World by the treaty of Tordesillas. Charles VIII of France invades Italy, deposes Piero de Medici in Florence and takes Rome. Duke Gian Galeazzo of Milan dies, probably poisoned by his uncle Lodovico, who succeeds him.

1495   Charles VIII of France expels Alfonso II of Naples and is crowned king of the state, but is forced to retreat by Alfonso's son Ferdinand II, who assumes the kingship. Syphilis strikes the state and the French soldiers are badly affected by it. The Diet of Worms is established to modernise the Holy Roman Empire. João II of Portugal dies, and is succeeded by his cousin Manuel the Fortunate. Warbeck received by James IV of Scotland. A dry-dock is built in Portsmouth, establishing the dockyard there.

1496 Henry VII commissions John Cabot to search for new lands. The Canary Islands conquered by Spain. Ferdinand II of Naples dies, and is succeeded by his uncle Frederick IV. James IV invades Northumberland in support of Warbeck. Manuel I of Portugal expels the Jews from his country.

1497 John and Sebastian Cabot reach Labrador and Newfoundland. The Cornish rebel against taxation but are defeated at Blackheath; Warbeck lands in Cornwall but is captured. John of Denmark defeats the Swedish at Brunkeberg and revives the Union of Kalmar. Savonarola stages a bonfire of vanities in Florence. Vasco da Gama rounds the Cape of Good Hope and gives Natal its name as he discovers it on Christmas Day.

1498 Charles VIII of France dies, and is succeeded by his second cousin once removed Louis XII, duke of Orléans. Savonarola burned at the stake for heresy. Vasco da Gama reaches Malindi in East Africa and then Calicut in India. Columbus embarks on a third voyage, discovering Trinidad and the Orinoco River.

1499 Louis XII of France divorces his wife Jeanne and marries Anne of Brittany to keep the duchy in French hands. Emperor Maximilian and the Swiss go to war; by the Peace of Basel, Swiss independence is granted. Venice and the Ottomans go to war; the Venetian fleet is defeated at Sapienza. Montenegro falls to the Ottomans. Louis XII takes Milan, forcing Ludovico Sforza to flee to the Tyrol. Perkin Warbeck is executed.

1500 Ludovico Sforza recaptures Milan, but the French return and capture Sforza on retaking the city. Pedro Cabral discovers Brazil when blown off course en route for India.

1501 Lithuania invaded by Ivan III of Moscow. Basel and Schaffhausen admitted to the Swiss Confederation. Frederick IV of Naples dies; Pope Alexander VI declares Louis XII Frederick's successor. Ismail I, sheikh of Ardabil, defeats Shah Alwand of Persia at Shurur and establishes Safavid rule in the country. Emperor Maximilian I recognises the French conquests in Italy by the Peace of Trent.

1502 St Helena discovered by João de Nova. Arthur, prince of Wales, dies at Ludlow.

1503 Louis XII of France abandons his claim to the Neapolitan throne after his alliance with Ferdinand of Aragon collapses. Gonzalo de Cordoba defeats a French army and enters Naples. James IV of Scotland marries Margaret Tudor, daughter of Henry VII. Pope Alexander VI dies, and is succeeded briefly by Pius III, and then by Julius II.

1504 Albert of Bavaria defeats Rupert, son of the Elector Palatine in the Bavarian War, during which at Landshut the Frankonian knight Götz von Berlichingen loses his right hand and has it replaced by one of iron. Michelangelo's statue of David is put on display in Florence.

1505 Ivan III of Muscovy dies, and is succeeded by his son Vasili III.

1506 Niccolò Machiavelli forms a Florentine militia, the first national army established in Italy. Christopher Columbus dies. 4,000 Jews perish in a riot in Lisbon. Philip the Handsome, son of the Emperor Maximilian and husband of the de jure Castilian Queen Juana (Joanna) dies, sending his wife mad.

1507 Cesare Borgia dies whilst besieging Viana, in Spain.

1508 Juan Ponce de León colonises Puerto Rico. Pope Julius II confirms that the German King will automatically become Holy Roman Emperor. Michelangelo starts painting the ceiling of the Sistine Chapel.

1509 Francisco de Almeida destroys a Muslim fleet at the battle of Diu, guaranteeing Portuguese control of the spice trade. Pope Julius II excommunicates the Venetian Republic, which is defeated by the French at Agnadello. Henry VII dies, and is succeeded by his son Henry VIII.

1510 Afonso de Albuquerque seizes Goa for Portugal. Sir Richard Empson and Edmund Dudley beheaded by Henry VIII for their unpopular fiscal policies under his father.

1511 Portuguese forces under Albuquerque seize Malacca, the centre of the spice trade. Julius II forms the Holy League with Venice to drive the French from Italy and enlists the support of Ferdinand of Aragon and Henry VIII.

1512 Forces of the Holy League are defeated by the French at Ravenna, but the French are then driven from Milan; Massimiliano Sforza, son of the deposed Duke Ludovico, becomes duke. Sultan Bayazid dies mysteriously after being deposed by his Janissaries; his son Selim I the Grim succeeds him.

1513 Juan Ponce de León discovers Florida. John of Denmark dies, and is succeeded by his son Christian II, who is rejected by the Swedes. Pope Julius II dies, and is succeeded by Leo X. Henry VIII invades France, where he and Emperor Maximilian are successful in the battle of Guinegatte (the Spurs). James IV of Scotland takes advantage of the English in France to invade, but his army is routed at Flodden and James is killed, to be succeeded by his infant son James V.

1514 The Henry Grace a Dieu, the largest warship in the world, is launched in England. Thomas Wolsey becomes Archbishop of York. The Ottoman Sultan Selim invades Persia and routs the Persian army at Chaldiran.

1515 Louis XII of France dies, and is succeeded by his son-in-law François I, who defeats the Swiss and Venetians at Marignano and takes Milan.

1516 Ferdinand II of Aragon dies, and is succeeded on the Spanish throne by his grandson Charles I. Pope Leo X and François I of France sign the Concordat of Bologna, giving France freedom in ecclesiastical appointments. Sultan Selim I defeats the Mamluks at Marjdabik and takes Syria. Thomas More publishes Utopia.

1517 Egypt falls to the Ottoman Turks, to whom the Sharif of Mecca submits, leaving Arabia under Ottoman control. Martin Luther nails 95 theses to the door of Wittenberg Cathedral attacking the sale of indulgences.

1518 Huldrych Zwingli forces the expulsion from Zurich of Barnardin Samson, a Franciscan seller of indulgences. Wolsey negotiates the Peace of London between England, France, the Holy Roman Empire, Spain and the Papacy; they agree to crusade against the Turks.

1519 Emperor Maximilian dies, and is succeeded by his grandson Charles V (I of Spain). Vasco de Balboa is beheaded in Panama as he loses the power struggle amongst the Spanish in Central America. Hernán

Cortés enters Tenochtitlán, the Aztec capital, and is received by Emperor Montezuma, whom he takes prisoner.

1520   Christian II of Denmark invades Sweden and is successful at Tiveden and Uppsala before taking Stockholm; despite proclaiming an amnesty he executes numerous leading Swedes. Henry VIII and François I meet at the Field of the Cloth of Gold near Calais. Cortés driven from Tenochtitlán by Cuauhtemoc. Sultan Selim I dies, and is succeeded by his son Suleiman I the Magnificent. Ferdinand Magellan sails through the Strait of Magellan and names the Pacific.

1521   Martin Luther is interrogated by the Diet of Worms; refusing to recant he is put in the castle of Wartburg for his own protection by Frederick of Saxony and begins a German translation of the Bible. Ferdinand Magellan dies in a skirmish in the Philippines. Cortés overthrows the Aztec empire; Montezuma II dies in the fighting. Sultan Suleiman I takes Belgrade. Henry VIII is awarded the title 'Defender of the Faith' by Leo X for an anti-Lutheran work.

1522   Luther returns to Wittenberg and initiates church services in German. Sultan Suleiman takes Rhodes from the Knights of St John. Juan Sebastiano del Cano returns home after finishing Magellan's circumnavigation of the world.

1523   Christian II of Denmark deposed by his nobles for cruelty and replaced by his uncle Frederick I. Gustavus Vasa takes advantage of the situation to be crowned king of Sweden. Sir Thomas More elected Speaker of the House of Commons. Zwingli publishes his 67 Articles in Zurich.

1524   Giovanni da Verrazano discovers New York Bay, naming Manhattan Angoulême. Denmark confirms Swedish independence by the treaty of Malmö. Shah Ismail I of Persia dies, and is succeeded by his son Tahmasp I.

1525   Emperor Charles V defeats François I of France at Pavia, imprisons him and establishes control over Italy. Albert von Brandenburg, Grand Master of the Teutonic Knights, makes himself duke of Prussia. A peasants' revolt in Germany is suppressed, and its leader Thomas Müntzer executed. Cardinal Wolsey gives Hampton Court to Henry VIII.

1526   François I of France signs the treaty of Madrid, ceding various lands to Charles V, but renounces it because the terms were extorted from him, and allies himself with Sultan Suleiman, who defeats and kills Louis II of Hungary at the battle of Mohacs. Ferdinand, brother of Emperor Charles V is chosen to succeed Louis II in Hungary and Bohemia, but the Hungarians elect John Zapolya as king. Zahir-ud-Din Babur defeats Sultan Ibrahim Lodi of Delhi at Panipat, takes Agra and founds the Mughal Empire.

1527   The Mughal Emperor Babur defeats Rajput forces at Kanvaha. England and France ally via the treaty of Westminster. Imperial troops sack Rome; Pope Clement VII is imprisoned in the Castel Sant' Angelo. Holbein paints Thomas More and his family.

1528   The physician and alchemist Paracelsus is forced from Basel due to his unorthodox medical opinions and treatments.

1529   François I of France and Emperor Charles V make peace via the treaty of Cambrai. Suleiman the Magnificent takes Buda and besieges Vienna but fails to take it. Cardinal Wolsey falls from power due to his inability to secure a divorce for Henry VIII from Catherine of Aragon. Sir Thomas More replaces him as Lord Chancellor, the first layman to hold the post.

1530   The Knights of St John are settled in Malta by Emperor Charles V. Melanchthon prepares the *Confession of Augsburg* as a statement of faith for the German Protestant princes, who form the Schmalkaldic League against Emperor Charles V. Cardinal Wolsey is arrested for treason, but dies whilst on his way to trial. The Mughal Emperor Babur dies, and is succeeded by his son Humayun.

1531   Lisbon is destroyed by an earthquake. The Catholic Swiss Cantons attack and defeat Zurich in the battle of Kappel; Zwingli dies in the fighting.

1532   The English clergy recognise Henry VIII as Supreme Head of the Church. Sultan Suleiman invades Hungary. The Inca chief Atahualpa seized by Pizarro, who reintroduces horses to South America. François Rabelais publishes *Pantagruel*.

1533   Henry VIII divorces Catherine of Aragon and marries Anne Boleyn with the sanction of Thomas Cranmer, newly appointed archbishop of Canterbury; this leads to Henry's excommunication. Pizarro executes Atahualpa by strangling and causes the downfall of the Incas. Holbein paints *The Ambassadors*. Vasili III of Moscow dies, and is succeeded by his son Ivan IV the Terrible.

1534   John of Leiden sets up the radical Protestant Anabaptist kingdom of Zion at Münster. Jacques Cartier sails for the New World by command of François I and reaches the Gulf of St Lawrence. Ignatius Loyola founds the Society of Jesus (Jesuits). The Act of Supremacy marks the final break between England and Rome, comfirming Henry VIII as Supreme Head of the Church of England.

1535   Jacques Cartier sails up the St Lawrence to Montreal. Thomas Cromwell is appointed Vicar-General to investigate religious houses in England. Francis of Waldeck retakes Münster from the Anabaptists. John Fisher, Bishop of Rochester, and Sir Thomas More executed for refusing to take an oath supporting Henry VIII's acts. Emperor Charles V conquers Tunis, defeating the pirate leader Khair ad-Din. Duke Francesco Sforza of Milan dies; the duchy reverts to Emperor Charles V.

1536   John of Leiden is executed in Münster. The Anabaptist Jacob Hutter is burned at the stake. Dissolution of the monasteries commences in England, leading to a rising under Robert Aske (the Pilgrimage of Grace). Henry VIII executes Anne Boleyn on the grounds of adultery and marries Jane Seymour. Wales is formally united with England. William Tyndale is executed for heresy.

1537   Pope Paul III prohibits enslavement of New World natives and excommunicates Catholic slave traders. Robert Aske is received by Henry VIII and Cromwell, but is later executed for treason. Jane Seymour dies after bearing the future Edward VI.

1538   Pope Paul III allies with Charles V and the Venetians in a Holy League against the Ottoman Empire, but the combined Venetian, Genoese and papal fleet is defeated at Prevesa by the Ottomans.

1539   Charles V and François I make peace with the treaty of Toledo. The Six Articles are passed in England, enforcing Catholic orthodoxy. Dissolution of the monasteries ends; the abbots of Reading, Colchester and Glastonbury are executed in the process.

1540 Henry VIII marries Anne of Cleves but quickly repudiates her. The marriage is annulled and he marries Catherine Howard. Thomas Cromwell falls from grace over the Cleves marriage and is executed. The Jesuits are recognised by Pope Paul III. The Norse colony of Greenland comes to an end, with the last colonist discovered dead outside his hut with a dagger in his hand.

1541 John Calvin sets up a theocratic government in Geneva. Henry VIII is accepted by the Irish Parliament as king of Ireland and head of the Irish Church.

1542 Henry VIII executes Catherine Howard for adultery. Pope Paul III establishes the Universal Inquisition to repress the Reformation. James V of Scotland raids Cumberland, but is defeated badly at Solway Moss. He dies soon after and is succeeded by his six-day-old daughter, Mary.

1543 Pope Paul III establishes an index of prohibited books. The Spanish Inquisition commences burning Protestants at the stake. Henry VIII marries Catherine Parr. Copernicus publishes his *De revolutionibus orbium coelestrium*, stating his belief that the planets orbit a stationary Sun.

1544 Henry VIII captures Boulogne, but subsequently retires from France when his ally Charles V and François I make peace with the treaty of Crépy-en-Valois.

1545 The *Mary Rose* capsizes off Portsmouth. Charles V and Suleiman the Magnificent make a truce with the treaty of Adrianople. The Council of Trent meets, in an attempt by the Catholic church to establish a Counter-Reformation.

1546 England and France make peace with the treaty of Ardres, by which England holds Boulogne for eight years before returning it to France. The Paris printer Etienne Dolet is executed for heresy and blasphemy as a result of publishing humanist works by the likes of Erasmus.

1547 Ivan IV the Terrible of Moscow crowned Tsar of Russia. Henry VIII dies, and is succeeded by his nine-year-old-son Edward VI. François I laughs on receiving news of Henry's death, develops a fever and dies, to be succeeded by his son Henri II. John Knox is captured at St Andrews and sent to work on a French galley. Protector Somerset, ruling on behalf of his nephew Edward, invades Scotland and defeats the Scots at Pinkie.

1548 Francis Xavier founds a Jesuit mission in Japan. Sigismund I of Poland dies, and is succeeded by his son Sigismund II Augustus.

1549 Ivan IV summons the first Russian national assembly. The Protestant Book of Common Prayer is imposed in England, leading to risings in Devon and Cornwall. Robert Kett leads a revolt in Norfolk against land enclosures, but is defeated at Dussindale.

1550 England makes peace with France and Scotland by the treaty of Boulogne; Boulogne is returned to France and John Knox released from galley labour. Cricket is first referred to.

1551 Henri II of France disavows the Council of Trent and renews the war against Charles V. The Ottomans attack Malta, but are repulsed and take Tripoli instead.

1552 The duke of Somerset is executed. Tsar Ivan IV takes Kazan and attacks Astrakhan. The second Book of Common Prayer is introduced.

1553 Richard Chancellor opens a trade route to Moscow via the White Sea and Archangel. Edward VI dies, and is succeeded by his Catholic half-sister Mary, despite the duke of Northumberland's efforts to install Lady Jane Grey, his daughter-in-law, as a Protestant queen. Northumberland is later executed.

1554 Sir Thomas Wyatt leads revolt from Kent over Mary I's proposed marriage to Philip of Spain, but is defeated and executed. Lady Jane Grey is also executed, whilst Mary's half-sister Elizabeth is imprisoned in the Tower.

1555 Pope Julius III dies, his successor Marcellus II dies after a month, and Paul IV succeeds. Paul walls in Rome's Jewish quarter, creating a ghetto. John Knox returns to Scotland. Tobacco is brought to Europe from America. Mary I persecutes Protestants; Latimer and Ridley are burned at the stake in Oxford. Charles V hands sovereignty of the Netherlands to his son Philip.

1556 Thomas Cranmer is dismissed as Archbishop of Canterbury and burned at the stake. Emperor Charles V abdicates; his brother Ferdinand succeeds him as Emperor whilst his son Philip II succeeds in Spain. Indian Mughal emperor Humayun dies after falling from his library roof, and is succeeded by his son Jalal-ud-Din Akbar I.

1557 Tsar Ivan IV invades Poland. Macao founded by the Portuguese, whose King João III dies, and is succeeded by his grandson Sebastian. The Spanish drive the French from Italy after victory at the battle of St Quentin.

1558 Calais, England's last continental possession, falls to the French. Mary I dies, and is succeeded by her half-sister Elizabeth. William Cecil becomes Secretary of State. John Knox writes his *First Blast of the Trumpet Against the Monstrous Regiment of Women*.

1559 Christian III of Denmark dies, and is succeeded by his son Frederick II; Christian's imprisoned predecessor Christian II also dies. The Act of Supremacy restores the Church of England. The war between England, Spain and France is ended by the treaty of Cateau-Cambrésis. Henri II of France dies after a jousting accident, and is succeeded by his son François II.

1560 The treaty of Berwick is made between England and the Protestant Scottish lords against the French, whose troops are forced to return home; the Scots Parliament approves Knox's Calvinistic Confession of Faith. Louis de Bourbon organises the Huguenot Conspiracy of Amboise against the Catholic Guises, but is thwarted by the Dowager Queen Catherine de Medici. François II of France dies, and is succeeded by his brother Charles IX.

1561 Philip II declares Madrid the capital of Spain. Persecution of French Huguenots suspended by the Edict of Orléans. Flemish Calvinist refugees settle in England. St Paul's Cathedral damaged by fire after a lightning strike.

1562 The duc de Guise orders the massacre of Huguenots at Vassy, thus precipitating the Wars of Religion in France. The English establish the 39 Articles of Religion.

1563 The duc de Guise is murdered by a Huguenot; Catherine de Medici is left in charge of the Catholic faction and grants limited toleration to the Huguenots by the Peace of Amboise, ending the First War of Religion. John Foxe's *Book of Martyrs* is published. The Council of Trent comes to an end.

1564   England and France make peace by the treaty of Troyes: in return for 220,000 crowns Elizabeth renounces claim to Calais. Emperor Ferdinand I dies, and is succeeded by his son Maximilian II.

1565   The Ottomans besiege Malta, but 700 Knights of St John under Jean de La Valette hold them off for 4 months before Spanish troops relieve them and force the Ottomans to withdraw. Mary Queen of Scots marries her cousin Henry, Lord Darnley.

1566   Mary Queen of Scots' secretary, David Rizzio, is murdered at Holyrood. Calvinists riot in the Netherlands and petition the Regent, Margaret of Palma, to abolish the Inquisition. Suleiman the Magnificent dies, and is succeeded by his son Selim II.

1567   Lord Darnley is murdered at Kirk o'Field; the earl of Bothwell, who is believed to have ordered the assassination, marries Mary Queen of Scots. The earl of Morton discovers the possibly fabricated Casket Letters incriminating Bothwell and Mary; the Scots Lords rebel against Mary, imprison her in Lochleven Castle and force her abdication in favour of her son James VI, with Moray as Regent. Philip II sends the duke of Alba to eliminate Protestant resistance in the Netherlands, where he begins a reign of terror. Regent Margaret resigns.

1568   The Second War of Religion in France is ended by the treaty of Longjumeau. Mary Queen of Scots escapes Lochleven, raises an army, but is defeated by Moray at Langside and flees to England. Alba beheads Counts Egmont and Hoorn in Brussels for opposing the Inquisition and confiscates the estates of those who failed to attend the Council of Blood. Erik XIV of Sweden is deposed due to mental illness and replaced by his brother John III. The first modern Eisteddfod is held at Caerwys.

1569   Elizabeth orders Mary of Scots' detention in Tutbury Castle and imprisons the duke of Norfolk, who seeks to marry Mary. Catholics under the duc d'Anjou defeat Huguenot forces at Jarnac. Mercator publishes his map of the world and establishes his projection. The Union of Lublin unites Poland and Lithuania. Catholic earls of Northumberland and Westmorland revolt, seize Durham, but are forced to flee by Baron Hunsdon. Cosimo de Medici is made the Grand duke of Tuscany by Pope Pius V.

1570   Regent Moray is assassinated; the earl of Lennox takes over the regency. Elizabeth I is excommunicated. The third War of Religion is ended by the Peace of St Germain-en-Laye. Tsar Ivan IV establishes a reign of terror in Great Novgorod and violently purges his government in Moscow. Denmark recognises Swedish independence by the Peace of Stettin.

1571   Pope Pius V establishes the anti-Turkish Maritime League with Spain, Venice, Malta and Genoa; its fleet gains a decisive victory over the Turks at Lepanto. Roberto di Ridolfi plots to free Mary Queen of Scots and depose Elizabeth I, but the plots are exposed and fail. Sir Thomas Gresham's bourse is chartered as the Royal Exchange. Regent Lennox is murdered at Stirling; the earl of Mar replaces him.

1572   The duke of Norfolk is executed for treason in assisting the Ridolfi plot. Sigismund II of Poland dies without an heir; the Polish estates declare the crown elective. Catherine de Medici organises the Massacre of St Bartholomew's Day against the Huguenots; Admiral Gaspard de Coligny is disembowelled and defenestrated while still living. 3,000 Protestants die; Pope Gregory XIII congratulates Catherine. The fourth War of Religion commences. Regent Mar dies, replaced by the earl of Morton.

1573   The Peace of Constantinople ends the war between Venice and the Turks. Poland elects Henri, duc d'Anjou as king. The Edict of Boulogne ends the fourth War of Religion. Francis Walsingham is appointed Elizabeth's Secretary of State.

1574   The fifth War of Religion breaks out. Charles IX of France dies, and is succeeded by his brother Henri III, who abandons the Polish throne. Juan Fernandez discovers the Juan Fernandez Islands. Sultan Selim II dies after a fall in his bath, succeeded by his son Murad III.

1575   Dutch rebels fail to reach agreement with the Spanish Governor-General Requesens at Breda. The duc de Guise defeats the Huguenots at Dormans. Stephen Bathory of Transylvania is elected king of Poland.

1576   The Peace of Chastenoy ends the fifth War of Religion, but grants so many concessions to the Huguenots that the French Catholics ally with Philip II; Henri III outlaws Protestantism to appease them. Spanish troops rampage in the Netherlands, sacking Antwerp; the Pacification of Ghent allies the Lowland provinces in a pact for independence as a result. Emperor Maximilian II dies, and is succeeded by his son Rudolf II. Shah Tahmasp is murdered, and succeeded by his son Ismail II. The Theatre, England's first playhouse, is opened by Richard Burbage in Shoreditch.

1577   The sixth War of Religion breaks out; Catholic forces are victorious but to curb the power of the Holy League Henri III grants the Huguenots terms via the Peace of Bergerac. Don John of Austria arrives to take up the Governorship of the Netherlands, but his Perpetual Edict is rejected by William the Silent, who enters Brussels in triumph.

1578   Alessandro Farnese, duke of Parma, sent with an army to the Netherlands, where he defeats the Dutch at Gemblours and succeeds as governor on the death of Don John. Shah Isma'il II dies, and is succeeded by his brother Muhammad Kundabanda. King Sebastian of Portugal invades Morocco, but perishes along with most of his army at Al Kasr al Kebir, although the king of Fez is also killed. A cult develops around the dead king and four pretenders appear, who are all executed. Sebastian's great-uncle Henry succeeds him.

1579   The Union of Arras unites the Walloons of the Netherlands whilst the Dutch provinces unite under the Union of Utrecht and sign a military alliance with England. Francis Drake lands in California and claims English sovereignty over the area he calls 'New Albion'.

1580   The seventh War of Religion breaks out in France, but is ended by the treaty of Fleix. The Spanish invade Portugal led by the duke of Alva, defeat the Portuguese at Alcantara and conquer the country. Francis Drake completes a circumnavigation of the world.

1581   Stephen Bathory of Poland invades Russia. William the Silent appoints François, duc d'Alençon, king of the Netherlands. Tsar Ivan the Terrible kills his heir with his own hands. The Jesuit Edmund Campion is arrested, tortured, tried and executed.

1582   Tsar Ivan the Terrible makes peace with Poland and Sweden with the Peace of Jam-Zapolski and abandons Livonia and Estonia to Poland. James VI of Scotland kidnapped by pro-English nobles at Ruthven. Pope Gregory XIII introduces the Gregorian calendar, devised by Aloysius Lilius.

1583 James VI of Scotland escapes from his captors after 10 months. Humphrey Gilbert founds a colonial settlement in Newfoundland at St John's, but drowns on the return journey. Plots against Elizabeth I by John Somerville and Francis Throckmorton are foiled.

1584 Walter Raleigh founds a colony on Roanoke Island, Virginia. Tsar Ivan the Terrible dies, and is succeeded by his son Feodor I. François, duc d'Alencon dies, leaving Henri III with no direct heir; Henri of Navarre becomes nearest male heir. William the Silent is assassinated at Delft by Balthazar Gérard, but his son Maurice of Nassau continues the struggle against Spain.

1585 The Eighth War of Religion (the War of the Three Henris) breaks out in France as the Holy League under Henri, duc de Guise, attempt to stop Henri of Navarre from succeeding to the throne. The Netherlands are taken under English protection by the treaty of Nonsuch and a force under the earl of Leicester is sent to assist them.

1586 Kashmir annexed by the Emperor Akbar. Francis Drake raids Spanish New World colonies and rescues the survivors from the failed Roanoke settlement. Anglo-Dutch forces defeat the Spanish at Zutphen but Sir Philip Sidney dies as a result of a wound sustained there. Sir Anthony Babington plots against Elizabeth I, but Walsingham uncovers the plot and Babington is executed. Mary Queen of Scots is tried for her involvement and sentenced to death. Stephen Bathory of Poland dies.

1587 Mary Queen of Scots executed at Fotheringhay Castle. Sir Francis Drake raids Cadiz, 'singeing the king of Spain's beard' and disrupting preparations for the Armada. Sir Christopher Hatton is appointed Lord Chancellor. Poland elects Sigismund, son of John of Sweden, as king. Henri of Navarre defeats the Catholic League at Coutras.

1588 Frederick II of Denmark dies, and is succeeded by his son Christian IV. Henri, duc de Guise, enters Paris and forces Henri III to flee. The Spanish Armada sails for England under the duke of Medina Sidonia, but is defeated by the English and the weather. Although the tonnage of the 2 fleets was similar the Spanish lost nearly half of their 130 ships and the English none. Henri III arranges for Guise's assassination.

1589 The Russian Orthodox Church makes itself independent of Constantinople. Henri III of France is assassinated at St Cloud by Jacques Clément, a Dominican monk; he nominates Henri of Navarre as his successor, who founds the Bourbon line and defeats the Catholic League at Arques. The Rev. William Lee invents the first knitting machine, whilst Sir John Harington invents the Ajax, a flushing toilet.

1590 Shah Akbar conquers Orissa. Shah Abbas of Persia and Sultan Murad make peace, with Georgia, Azerbaijan and other provinces passing to the Turks. The Catholic League proclaim the cardinal Charles de Bourbon king of France; he dies soon after whilst Henri IV defeats them at Ivry. Edmund Spenser writes the first three books of The Faerie Queene. Shakespeare writes the Henry VI trilogy.

1591 The Tsarevich Dmitri is murdered, probably on order of the Regent Boris Godunov. Sir Richard Grenville dies after his ship, Revenge, battles a Spanish squadron single-handed for 15 hours.

1592 Galileo Galilei is forced to move from Pisa to Padua after publishing his results on falling weights. The Japanese warlord Hideyoshi invades Korea and takes Seoul and Pyongyang. John III of Sweden dies, and is succeeded by his son Sigismund, king of Poland.

1593 The Chinese enter Korea and force Hideyoshi to retreat to the south coast. Christopher Marlowe is stabbed to death in Deptford by Ingram Frizer during a tavern brawl. Henri IV converts to Catholicism to win over his subjects (saying 'Paris is well worth a mass'). Salisbury Cathedral's organist strikes the Dean in a fit of rage and is dismissed from his post.

1594 Henri IV enters Paris and grants Huguenots freedom of worship by the Edict of St Germain-en-Laye. John Lancaster returns to Britain after sailing to the East Indies and establishes a spice trade. The philosopher Giordano Bruno is seized by the Vatican for espousing the Copernican theory of the Solar System.

1595 Sultan Murad III dies, and is succeeded by his son Muhammad III. Henri IV drives the Spanish from Burgundy after victory at Fontaine-Française. Spanish forces attack Cornwall, burning Penzance and Mousehole. Francis Drake and John Hawkins leave Plymouth to raid Panama; Hawkins dies en route near Puerto Rico.

1596 Francis Drake dies of dysentery off Panama. The tomato is introduced to England. The Catholic League submit to Henri IV, ending the Wars of Religion. Willem Barents discovers Spitsbergen. The English sack Cadiz whilst Spain captures Calais. The Ottomans defeat the Hungarians at Erlau and Keresztes.

1597 Philip II sends a second Armada to England, but it is scattered by storms and fails. Transylvania ceded to Emperor Rudolf II by Sigmund Bathory.

1598 Tsar Feodor I dies; his brother-in-law Boris Godunov seizes the throne and forces the national assembly to accept him. Henri IV of France grants rights to Huguenots by the Edict of Nantes. France and Spain make peace by the treaty of Vervins. Philip II of Spain dies, and is succeeded by his son Philip III.

1599 The Globe Theatre is built in London. The earl of Essex is made Lord Lieutenant of Ireland, but after signing an unauthorised truce with the earl of Tyrone returns to England and is arrested by Elizabeth I. The Swedish Diet deposes Sigismund III and makes Karl of Sodermanlund, uncle of Sigismund, regent for Sigismund's younger brother John.

1600 The East India Company is founded. Giordano Bruno is burned at the stake for heresy in Rome due to his support for the Copernican system. Ieyasu Tokugawa defeats his rivals at Sekigahara and takes control of Japan, moving the capital from Kyoto to Edo (Tokyo); the shipwrecked English mariner Will Adams becomes an adviser to him. Will Kemp morris-dances from London to Norwich.

1601 The earl of Essex leads a revolt against Elizabeth I, which fails and Essex is executed for treason. Moghul Emperor Akbar the Great annexes Berar, Ahmadnagar and Khandesh. A Spanish army lands in Ireland to support Tyrone's revolt.

1602 The Spaniards in Ireland surrender to Mountjoy at Kinsale. The Dutch East India Company is founded. Emperor Rudolf II suppresses the Moravian Brethren.

1603 Elizabeth I dies, her cousin twice removed; James VI of Scotland, succeeds her. Tyrone submits to Mountjoy in Ireland, where James proclaims an amnesty. Walter Raleigh attempts to put Arabella Stuart on the throne rather than James, and is imprisoned for treason. Ieyasu founds the Tokugawa Shogunate in Japan. Sultan Muhammad III dies, and is succeeded by his son Ahmed I.

1604   The Hampton Court Conference convenes to discuss religious matters, and commissions an English translation of the Bible. Regent Karl becomes king of Sweden after his nephew John renounces the throne. England and Spain make peace. Ostend falls to the Spanish after a three-year siege.

1605   Tsar Boris Godunov dies; his son Feodor II succeeds him but is assassinated. A pretender, Dmitri, who claims to be a son of Ivan the Terrible, enters Moscow and is crowned Tsar. Akbar the Great dies, and is succeeded by his son Jahangir. Shogun Ieyasu retires in favour of his son Hidetada. Robert Catesby leads a plot to assassinate James I, but the plot fails and Guy Fawkes is caught red-handed under the House of Lords. Miguel de Cervantes publishes part one of *Don Quixote.*

1606   Tsar Dmitri is assassinated by the boyar (noble) Vasili Shuisky, who is elected Tsar. The Virginia Company is set up and 120 colonists leave London, led by Captain Christopher Newport. Shakespeare's *Macbeth* and *King Lear* are first performed.

1607   The English Parliament rejects the union of England and Scotland. Jamestown, Virginia is founded by Christopher Newport, who returns to England leaving Captain James Smith in charge; captured by the Algonquin, Smith's life is saved by the chief's daughter Pocahontas.

1608   Tsar Vasili Shuisky is defeated by a second 'False Dmitri', who advances on Moscow. Frederick IV of the Palatinate organises a Protestant Union in Germany. Emperor Rudolf II is forced to cede Hungary, Austria and Moravia to his brother Matthias. The Jesuit state of Paraguay is established.

1609   Philip III of Spain signs a 12-year truce with the Dutch, effectively recognising their independence. Duke Maximilian of Bavaria organises a Catholic League to oppose the Protestant Union in Germany. John-William of Jülich-Cleves dies without an heir; Brandenburg and Neuburg quarrel over the territory. James I begins settling Protestants in Ulster.

1610   Galileo observes four moons orbiting Jupiter. Henri IV of France is assassinated by François Ravaillac; he is succeeded by his son Louis XIII. The Jamestown colonists abandon their settlement, but on meeting a ship of new settlers return and try again. Tsar Vasili Shuisky is deposed by Sigismund III of Poland and abducted to Warsaw; Vladislav, Sigismund's son, is offered the throne. Frederick IV of the Palatinate dies, and is succeeded by his son Frederick V.

1611   Henry Hudson is marooned by mutineers whilst searching for the North-west Passage and is never heard of again. Denmark declares war on Sweden. Emperor Rudolf II is forced to resign the Bohemian crown in favour of his brother Matthias. Karl IX of Sweden dies, and is succeeded by his son Gustavus II Adolphus.

1612   Emperor Rudolf II dies, and is succeeded as Holy Roman Emperor by his brother Matthias. Prince Dmitri Pojarsky forces the Polish in Moscow to surrender, thwarting Vladislav of Poland's claim for the throne. Henry, prince of Wales, dies of typhoid.

1613   Sweden and Denmark make the Peace of Knärod; Sweden gives up Finland. Mikhail Romanov, son of the Patriarch of Moscow, is elected Tsar by the boyars. The Globe Theatre burns down during a performance of Shakespeare's *Henry VIII.*

1614   Pocahontas marries John Rolfe, a settler. The 'Addled Parliament' meets, but is dissolved after clashes with James I over finance. The French parliament, the Estates-General convene, but is dismissed by the duc de Richelieu. The Virginian colonists resist French colonial attempts in Maine and Nova Scotia. Jülich-Cleves is divided between Brandenburg and Neuburg by the treaty of Xanten. John Napier publishes a book of logarithms.

1615   The Moluccas seized from the Portuguese by the Dutch, whilst the English defeat a Portuguese fleet off Bombay. Osaka falls to the Tokugawa shogunate. Lady Arabella Stuart starves herself to death in the Tower of London.

1616   Baffin Bay discovered by William Baffin. Francis Beaumont and Miguel de Cervantes die. William Shakespeare dies on his 52nd birthday. Manchurian Tartars invade China. Walter Raleigh is released from the Tower to search for El Dorado. James I sells peerages to raise funds. Maximilian of Tyrol and Archduke Albert renounce their claims to the Imperial throne in favour of Ferdinand of Styria. Galileo is arrested for heresy.

1617   Russia and Sweden make the Peace of Stolbovo; Novgorod is returned to Russia but Karelia is ceded to Sweden. Pocahontas is received by James I at court, but dies of smallpox soon after. Sultan Ahmad I dies, and is succeeded by his brother Mustafa I.

1618   Richelieu is exiled to Avignon after conspiring with the Queen Mother. Bohemian rebels throw the regents, Jaroslav von Martinitz and William Slawata, out of the Hradcany Palace in the Defenestration of Prague, an act which precipitates the Thirty Years War, as rebels led by Heinrich von Thurn advance on Austria and an Imperial army is raised to face them. Duke Albert Frederick of Prussia dies, his duchy passes to John Sigismund of Brandenburg. Francis Bacon is made Lord Chancellor. Walter Raleigh returns from his fruitless expedition to South America, and is executed by James I for treason to appease the Spaniards. Sultan Mustafa I is declared unfit to rule and is replaced by his nephew Osman II.

1619   Emperor Matthias dies. His cousin Ferdinand II of Styria succeeds him, but is deposed by the Bohemian Diet in favour of Frederick V of the Palatinate. A Bohemian army under Count von Thurn besieges Vienna, but is forced to withdraw. Louis XIII recalls Richelieu to subdue a revolt by Marie de Medici; the treaty of Angoulême ends the conflict. William Harvey establishes the circulation of the blood.

1620   Gustavus Adolphus of Sweden occupies Livonia after declaring war on Poland. The Pilgrim Fathers depart from Plymouth to America; the *Speedwell* is forced to turn back but the *Mayflower* arrives at Cape Cod; the settlement is called New Plymouth. Count Von Tilly leads a Catholic Union army to victory in the battle of the White Mountain against Frederick of Bohemia, who is deposed; the Bohemian revolt is suppressed by Emperor Frederick. Oliver Cromwell is denounced for playing cricket.

1621   Frederick V of the Palatinate is placed under Imperial Ban and his electorate invaded. The Huguenots rebel against Louis XIII. Philip III of Spain dies, and is succeeded by his son Philip IV, who resumes the war with the Netherlands. Count Olivares becomes chief minister of Spain. The Dutch West India Company is founded. Francis Bacon is impeached by Parliament for corruption, but is pardoned by James I.

1622 Richelieu is created a cardinal by Louis XIII, who makes peace with the Huguenots by reaffirming the Edict of Nantes. Count von Tilly is defeated at Wiesloch, but defeats Baden at Wimpfen and Brunswick at Höchst. Sultan Osman II is murdered by his Janissaries after planning to reform them and Mustafa I is restored to the throne.

1623 Abbas I of Persia takes Baghdad and Mosul from the Ottomans. Sultan Mustafa I is removed again from the throne and replaced by his nephew Murad IV. Count von Tilly defeats Brunswick at Stadtlohn and advances on Westphalia. Shogun Hidetada abdicates in favour of his son Iemitsu. Velázquez is appointed Court Painter to Philip IV of Spain. The First Folio of Shakespeare's plays is published.

1624 Cardinal Richelieu is made the chief minister of Louis XIII of France.

1625 James I dies, and is succeeded by his son Charles I. Sir William Courteen establishes a settlement on Barbados. Henri duc de Rohan leads a Huguenot rebellion against Louis XIII. Emperor Ferdinand II makes Wallenstein general of the Imperial forces and duke of Friedland. Breda falls to the Spanish after an eleven-month siege. Count von Tilly invades Saxony.

1626 Peter Minuit buys Manhattan from the Wappinger Confederacy for 60 guilders, founding New Amsterdam. The French colonise Madagascar. Louis XIII and the Huguenots make the Peace of La Rochelle. Wallenstein defeats a Protestant army at the Bridge of Dessau. The Duchy of Urbino is bequeathed to the Pope.

1627 Pirates attack Reykjavik. The Huguenots rise again; Richelieu besieges La Rochelle, which the duke of Buckingham tries but fails to relieve. Imperial forces conquer Silesia, Brunswick, Mecklenburg, Schleswig, Holstein and Jutland, forcing Christian IV of Denmark to retire from the war. Shah Jahangir dies, and is succeeded by his grandson Dawar Bakhsh.

1628 Wallenstein obtains the Duchy of Mecklenburg, assumes the title Admiral of the Baltic, but fails to take Stralsund. Shah Dawar Bahsh is removed from the throne by his uncle Shah Jahan I. Gustavus Adolphus enters the Thirty Years War. The duke of Buckingham is assassinated by John Felton at Portsmouth. La Rochelle capitulates to Louis XIII. Ignatius Loyola is canonised.

1629 Shah Abbas of Persia dies, and is succeeded by his grandson Safi I. Charles I dissolves Parliament and assumes direct rule. Emperor Ferdinand II issues the Edict of Restitution, restoring Church estates and permitting freedom of worship only to adherents of the Confession of Augsburg, which the Catholic League ruthlessly enforces. Christian IV of Denmark regains his lands by the Peace of Lübeck, on condition he refrains from intervening in Imperial affairs. Sweden and Poland make the Peace of Altmark. Bethlen Gabor of Transylvania dies, and is succeeded by his wife Catherine of Brandenburg.

1630 Gustavus Adolphus invades Germany whilst Emperor Ferdinand II dismisses Wallenstein and replaces him with Tilly. Boston founded by John Winthrop. Sultan Murad IV defeats the Persians and captures Hamadan. Anglo-French hostilities are ended by the treaty of Madrid. George Rakoczy I is elected prince of Transylvania on the death of Stephen Bethlen.

1631 Richelieu and the German Protestant princes ally with Gustavus Adolphus against Emperor Ferdinand II. Urbino is annexed by the Papacy. Tilly brutally sacks Magdeburg, burns Halle and invades Saxony, but is defeated by Gustavus Adolphus at the battle of Breitenfeld. Gustavus Adolphus takes Frankfurt-am-Oder, Würzburg and Mainz. Wallenstein is reappointed by Emperor Ferdinand II.

1632 Gustavus Adolphus defeats Tilly, who is mortally wounded, at the Lech and takes Munich. At the battle of Lützen, he defeats Walenstein but is killed in action. His daughter Christina succeeds him on the Swedish throne. Shah Jehan orders the destruction of Hindu temples. Charles I issues a charter for the colony of Maryland under the governorship of Lord Baltimore. The first coffee shop opens in London. Sigismund III of Poland dies, and is succeeded by his son Vladislav VII.

1633 Wallenstein defeats Bernard of Saxe-Weimar and a Swedish army at Steinau and occupies Bohemia. Galileo is forced by the Inquisition to abjure the theories of Copernicus.

1634 The Oberammergau Passion Play is enacted for the first time. Russia and Poland make peace via the treaty of Polianovska; Vladislav VII renounces his claim to Russia. Emperor Ferdinand II relieves Wallenstein of command, replacing him with Matthias Gallas. Wallenstein is assassinated soon after, whilst Imperial troops defeat the Swedes at Nördlingen and conquer Württemberg and Franconia.

1635 Cardinal Richelieu founds the Académie Française. Emperor Ferdinand II settles differences with Elector John George of Saxony via the Peace of Prague, after France and Sweden formally ally against him, formally bringing France into the Thirty Years War. Sweden and Poland agree a 20-year truce via the treaty of Stuhmsdorf. France and Saxe-Weimar ally by the treaty of St Germain-en-Laye. The first General Post Office in England opens in Bishopsgate, London.

1636 Persia and the Ottoman Empire make peace. Olivares invades Picardy. Swedish troops defeat the Saxons at the battle of Wittstock. Harvard College is founded in Cambridge, Massachusetts.

1637 Emperor Ferdinand II dies, and is succeeded by his son Ferdinand III. Bogislav XIV of Pomerania dies without an heir; his lands are divided between Sweden and Prussia. The Dutch under Frederick Henry of Orange recapture Breda.

1638 The Scottish Covenant is drawn up and signed, forcing Charles I to withdraw Laud's liturgy in Scotland. Bernhard of Saxe-Weimar takes Freiburg and Breisach. Sultan Murad IV retakes Baghdad from the Persians. Torture is abolished in England.

1639 The First Bishops' War erupts in Scotland between the Covenanters and Charles I. Peace comes by the Pacification of Berwick, and Charles I grants the Scots a General Assembly and Parliament, which he dissolves at the end of the year. Dutch admiral Maarten Tromp destroys a Spanish fleet in the decisive battle of the Downs.

1640 Catalonia revolts against Spanish taxes and control. Sultan Murad IV dies, and is succeeded by his brother Ibrahim. Charles I is forced to reconvene Parliament but the 'Short Parliament' refuses to authorise any taxes and is dissolved. The Scots revolt in the Second Bishops' War, defeating the English at Newburn. Thomas Wentworth is created earl of Strafford. The Great Council of Peers summoned by Charles I concludes the treaty of Ripon, paying off the Scots, and insists on the election of Parliament. The 'Long

Parliament', is duly elected. João of Braganza is elected king of Portugal, which breaks free from Spain, but Spain refuses to recognise this. Elector George William of Brandenburg dies, and is succeeded by his son Frederick William, the 'Great Elector'. Strafford and Laud are impeached.

1641 Tsar Michael I forbids the sale and use of tobacco, yet makes the substance a State monopoly. Strafford is executed. Parliament abolishes the Star Chamber. Parliament sends the Grand Remonstrance to Charles I, who is infuriated. The comte de Soissons plots against Louis XIII, but Jean d'Orléans, the king's brother, exposes him. The Irish Catholics revolt.

1642 Charles I enters the House of Commons to arrest Hampden, Pym, Holles, Haselrig and Strode for treason, but the quintet have been warned and take refuge in the City of London. Charles I flees London, rejects Parliament's 19 Propositions and raises his standard in Nottingham, triggering the Civil War. Rupert of the Rhine defeats the Parliamentarians at Powick Bridge and Edgehill. Blaise Pascal invents an adding machine. Cardinal Richelieu dies; Cardinal Mazarin replaces him as first minister of France. Abel Tasman discovers Van Diemen's Land (Tasmania) and New Zealand.

1643 Evangelista Torricelli develops the barometer. Parliamentarians under Fairfax take Leeds. Cromwell is victorious at Grantham, but Hampden is defeated and killed at Chalgrove Field. Louis XIII of France dies, and is succeeded by his son Louis XIV. French troops defeat a combined Spanish, Italian, Dutch and Flemish army at the battle of Rocroi. Royalists are victorious at Roundway Down and take Bristol, but are defeated at Gloucester, Newbury and Winceby. John Pym dies of cancer. Olivares falls from power in Spain.

1644 Ming Emperor Chongzhen commits suicide as Peking falls to the bandit Li Zicheng, thus ending his dynasty's rule. Li proclaims himself emperor, but is driven out by the Manchus, who found the Qing dynasty with Shunzhi as Emperor. John Milton writes his pamphlet the *Areopagitica*, on press freedom. The Scottish Covenanters join the Civil War on the Parliamentarian side. After a Royalist victory at Cropredy Bridge, Cromwell heavily defeats Prince Rupert at Marston Moor and takes York. Scottish royalists under Montrose defeat the Covenanters at Tippermuir, Charles captures Fowey, whilst the second battle of Newbury is indecisive.

1645 Archbishop Laud is executed. Montrose defeats the Covenanters at Inverlochy. The Ottomans and Venice war over Crete. Armistice talks between Charles I and Parliament fail at Uxbridge. John Lilburne publicizes Leveller ideas. Swedish troops defeat the Imperial army at Jankau and take Moravia. The Dutch occupy St Helena. Parliament creates the New Model Army under Fairfax and Cromwell which decisively defeats the royalists at Naseby. Tsar Michael I dies, and is succeeded by his son Alexei. The French defeat the Bavarians at Nördlingen. Prince Rupert surrenders Bristol, incurring his uncle's wrath. Covenanters rout Montrose at Philiphaugh.

1646 The Swedes take Prague, and in concert with the French invade Bavaria. Royalist armies in Exeter and Oxford capitulate to Parliamentarians; Charles surrenders to the Covenanters at Southwell. Held in Newcastle, Charles fails to reach agreement with Parliament and tries, but fails, to escape.

1647 George Fox founds the 'Friends of the Truth', later to become the Quakers. Matthew Hopkins, the 'Witchfinder General', is found guilty of witchcraft himself and hanged. Bear baiting and folk dancing are banned in England. The Scots hand over Charles I to Parliament in return for £400,000. Stadtholder Frederick Henry of Holland dies, and is succeeded by his son William II. Naples revolts against Spanish rule. Bavaria and Cologne state their neutrality in the Thirty Years War by the treaty of Ulm, but Emperor Ferdinand III gains their support. Mainz and Hesse withdraw from the fray.

1648 Parliament loses patience with Charles I after he makes a secret treaty with the Scots, who rebel along with the Welsh. Spain reasserts its rule over Naples. Ukrainians under Bogdan Chmielnicki lead a pogrom of Jews in a bid to establish independence from Poland. Sultan Ibrahim is deposed and killed by his Janissaries for lifting the siege of Heraklion, and is succeeded by his son Muhammad IV. The Second Civil War is short-lived, Cromwell defeating the Scots at Preston, and Colonel Thomas Pride purges Parliament to ensure Charles I is put on trial. The Fronde riots break out in Paris asserting the rights of the Paris Parlement (Parliament). The Peace of Westphalia ends the Thirty Years War, but is condemned by Pope Innocent X.

1649 Charles I is tried by Parliament and executed; Parliament abolishes the monarchy and the House of Lords, proclaiming a 'Commonwealth'. The War of the Fronde is ended by the treaty of Rueil; however a second Fronde uprising breaks out. The Levellers and Diggers are suppressed. Royalists rebel in Ireland; Cromwell sacks Drogheda and Wexford.

1650 Mazarin allies himself with the leaders of the first Fronde, and imprisons the leaders of the second. René Descartes dies whilst in the service of Queen Christina. Montrose leads a Scottish uprising against Parliament but is defeated at Carbisdale, betrayed by Neil McLeod and hanged. Archbishop James Ussher calculates that the Earth was created in 4004 BC. Charles II arrives in Scotland. Cromwell invades Scotland and is victorious at Dunbar. Stadtholder William II dies of smallpox, leaving a posthumously born heir, William III. The Holy Roman Empire and Sweden reach an accord with the treaty of Nuremberg.

1651 Charles II is crowned at Scone and invades England but is defeated by Cromwell at Worcester, evades capture and flees to France. Thomas Hobbes publishes *Leviathan*, and John Playford *The English Dancing Master*. Paris Parlement votes for the release of the Great Condér, leader of the Fronde, forcing Mazarin from the country, but he returns with an army to suppress the rebellion. Shogun Iemitsu dies, and is succeeded by his son Ietsuna, who quickly suppresses two rebellions.

1652 Jan Van Riebeck founds Cape Town. The Great Condé defeats a royalist army at Bléneau and is welcomed in Paris, where a rebel government is formed; however, the government quarrels with the Parisian middle class, which lets Louis XIV into the city. Parliament publishes the reconciliatory Act of Pardon and Oblivion. Admiral Robert Blake defeats Maarten Tromp off Dover, and England and Holland go to war, but Blake is defeated off Dungeness.

1653 The pirate Zheng Chenkong ravages the Chinese coast in his war with the Manchus. Mazarin returns to Paris and suppresses the Fronde. Lorenzo Tonti devises the Tontine system of life insurance. The English fleet defeats the Dutch off Portland, North Foreland and Texel. Cromwell dissolves the Long Parliament, and after the unsuccessful Barebones Parliament is made Lord Protector. Izaak Walton publishes *The Compleat Angler.*

1654   The treaty of Westminster ends the Anglo-Dutch War. Queen Christina of Sweden abdicates, and is succeeded by her cousin Karl X. Bogdan Chmielnicki swears allegiance to Russia, which goes to war with Poland, taking Smolensk.

1655   Colonel Penruddock leads a rising against Cromwell in Wiltshire, which is suppressed. The English under Vice-Admiral Penn take Jamaica from the Spanish. Karl X of Sweden invades Poland, precipitating the first Northern War. Elector Frederick William of Brandenburg invades Prussia. Cromwell divides England into 11 districts, each governed by a major-general. Cromwell readmits Jews into England.

1656   Sweden and Prussia ally by the treaty of Königsberg, whilst Denmark, Russia and the Holy Roman Empire declare war on Sweden. Spain declares war on Britain. Sweden defeats Poland at the battle of Warsaw. Baruch Spinoza is excommunicated for heresy. João IV of Portugal dies, and is succeeded by his son Alfonso VI.

1657   Christiaan Huygens develops the pendulum clock. Cromwell rejects an offer of the crown and establishes a nominated House of Lords. Emperor Ferdinand dies, and is succeeded by his son Leopold I. Admiral Blake destroys a Spanish treasure fleet at Santa Cruz. Brandenburg allies with Poland against Sweden by the treaty of Bromberg.

1658   The stage coach service is established in England. Jan Swammerdam observes red blood cells for the first time. The treaty of Roskilde ends the first Northern War, but Charles X of Sweden starts a second by unsuccessfully attacking Copenhagen. An Anglo-French force defeats the Spanish at the battle of the Dunes and England acquires Dunkirk. Shah Jahan I is imprisoned by his son Aurangzeb Alamgir I, who replaces him as Mughal emperor. Oliver Cromwell dies; his son Richard becomes Lord Protector.

1659   Elector Frederick William of Brandenburg drives the Swedes from Prussia. Richard Cromwell resigns as Lord Protector; conflict between army and Parliament leads to a state of near-anarchy. France and Spain make the Peace of the Pyrenees.

1660   General Monck, commanding general in Scotland, leads his troops to London to call for a new Parliament, which meets and votes for the restoration of the monarchy under Charles II. Karl X of Sweden dies, and is succeeded by his son Karl XI. Charles II makes the Declaration of Breda promising religious toleration and returns to England. The Peace of Oliva ends the hostilities between Sweden, Poland, Brandenburg and the Holy Roman Empire. Denmark reaches peace with and cedes Skania to Sweden by the treaty of Copenhagen. The Royal Society for the Promotion of Natural Knowledge is founded. George Racoczy II of Transylvania dies in battle against the Turks.

1661   Michael Apafi I is elected to replace the deceased George Racoczy III as Prince of Transylvania. Chinese living within 10 miles of the coast are ordered to move inland in an attempt to deter pirate Zheng Chenkong. Cardinal Mazarin dies, letting Louis XIV begin personal rule. The Cavalier Parliament meets in England. The Peace of Kardis between Sweden and Russia finally ends the second Northern War. Tangier and Bombay are ceded to England by Portugal in a treaty of alliance.

1662   France and Holland ally against England. The revised Prayer Book is imposed on Anglicans. The Royal Society is granted a Royal Charter by Charles II. Dunkirk is sold to France by Charles II for £400,000.

1663   The Theatre Royal, Drury Lane, opens with a performance of John Fletcher's *The Humorous Lieutenant.* Colbert founds the Académie des Inscriptions et Belles Lettres in Paris. The Ottomans declare war on the Holy Roman Empire and invade Hungary. Colbert makes New France into a colony with Quebec as the capital.

1664   France and Saxony make an alliance. The Conventicle Act bans unauthorised religious meetings of more than 5 people in England, in an attempt to suppress nonconformism. Austrian troops defeat the Turks at St Gotthard on the Raab River and make the Truce of Vasvar. New Amsterdam under Peter Stuyvesant surrenders to the English, who rename it New York.

1665   The Great Plague hits London. The second Anglo-Dutch War opens; the Dutch are defeated off Lowestoft. Anglo-Portuguese forces defeat the Spanish at Villaviciosa and Montes Claros, securing Portuguese independence. Philip IV of Spain dies, and is succeeded by his son Charles II.

1666   Louis XIV founds a French Academy of Sciences. Holland allies with Brandenburg, Brunswick and Denmark to secure its safety, whilst France declares war on England. The English and Dutch fleets meet in the inconclusive Four Days Battle before an English victory at Orford Ness. London is ravaged by a Great Fire starting in Pudding Lane.

1667   Russia and Poland make peace with the treaty of Andrusovo, ending their 13-year war; Kiev, Smolensk and the Eastern Ukraine are ceded to Russia. John Milton's *Paradise Lost* is published. French troops invade Flanders and Hainault, starting the War of Devolution. The Dutch sail up the Medway to Chatham, sinking several ships and taking the English flagship back to Holland. England, Holland and France make peace by the treaty of Breda. The Medway débâcle leads to the fall of Clarendon, and the Cabal administration under Clifford, Arlington, Buckingham, Ashley and Lauderdale is formed. (Cabal is a mnemonic for its members but the word does not derive from them.) The Regent Pedro banishes Alfonso VI of Portugal to the Azores.

1668   England, Holland and Sweden ally by the treaty of the Hague. John Dryden is appointed the first Poet Laureate. Spain recognises Portuguese independence by the treaty of Lisbon. The War of Devolution is ended by the Peace of Aix-La-Chapelle, whilst Louis XIV and Emperor Leopold I reach an agreement over future partition of Spanish realms. John Kasimir of Poland abdicates.

1669   The Lithuanian Michael Wisniowecki is elected king of Poland. The Mughal Aurangzeb bans Hinduism in India and destroys Hindu temples, leading to widespread revolts. Crete falls to the Ottomans. The Hanseatic League holds its last meeting. Antonio Stradivari makes his first violin. Samuel Pepys ceases writing his diary.

1670   Frederick III of Denmark dies, and is succeeded by his son Christian V. The Ukrainian Cossacks rebel against Polish rule, but are suppressed by Jan Sobieski. Gabriel Mouton, a French clergyman, proposes

H
I
S
T
O
R
Y

the establishment of decimal measurements. France and Bavaria make a defensive alliance, whilst Charles II makes the secret treaty of Dover with Louis XIV, pledging anti-Dutch collaboration and conversion to Roman Catholicism at an appropriate moment.

1671   The buccaneer Henry Morgan captures Panama City, is tried for piracy but pardoned and knighted by Charles II and later becomes Deputy Governor of Jamaica. The Ottomans declare war on Poland. The Don Cossacks under Stenka Razin revolt, but their rising is quelled and Razin executed. Milton publishes *Paradise Regained* and Aphra Behn *The Forced Marriage*.

1672   The Russian serfs rebel. Charles II issues the Declaration of Indulgence. Louis XIV declares war on the Dutch and sends his troops in; an English fleet defeats the Dutch at Southwold Bay. The Dutch Grand Pensionary Jan de Witt and his brother Cornelius are murdered by a mob, after William III of Orange has been appointed to the revived office of Stadtholder and put in charge of the Dutch army.

1673   Parliament forces Charles II to revoke the Declaration of Indulgence and instead passes the Test Act. Brandenburg pledges to refuse assistance to enemies of France by the treaty of Vossen, whilst Leopold I declares war on France. Michael Wisniowecki of Poland dies; the next day Jan Sobieski defeats the Ottomans at Khorzim.

1674   France devastates the Palatinate whilst Spain deters the anti-French coalition. Jan Sobieski is elected king of Poland. England and Holland make peace by the the treaty of Westminster. The bandit Sivaji Bhonsala founds a Marāthā state as independent from the Mughal Empire.

1675   France recovers Alsace after victory at Turkheim. Sweden goes to war with Denmark and Brandenburg, but is defeated by the latter at Fehrbellin. The Royal Greenwich Observatory is founded, with John Flamsteed as first Astronomer Royal.

1676   Tsar Alexis dies, and is succeeded by his son Feodor III. Jan Sobieski of Poland makes peace with the Ottomans under the treaty of Zuravno, ceding the Polish Ukraine. The Swedes defeat the Danes at Lunden.

1677   The Dutch are defeated by the French at Cassel, but with the Danes defeat a Swedish fleet at Öland. Jean Racine's tragedy *Phèdre* is first performed. Edmund Halley returns from St Helena, having catalogued the Southern Night Sky.

1678   France captures Ghent and Ypres. Russia joins the war against Sweden. France, Spain and Holland make the peace of Nijmegen; Holland regains its lost territories. False allegations made by Titus Oates and others of a 'Popish Plot' to kill Charles II lead to severe anti-Catholic measures. Hungarians under Emeric Tokolyi rebel against Imperial rule. Brandenburg takes Stralsund from the Swedes. The factional terms Whig and Tory enter use in Parliament.

1679   The Cavalier Parliament is dissolved. Archbishop Sharp of St Andrews murdered by Covenanters, whose rising is defeated by Monmouth at Bothwell Brig. Louis XIV forces the Peace of St Germain-en-Laye on Sweden and Brandenburg; the latter relinquishes its conquests. Sweden and Denmark make peace by the treaty of Lund. Henry Purcell is appointed organist of Westminster Abbey.

1680   Sivaji Bhonsala dies, and is succeeded by his son Sambhaji I, but Emperor Aurangzeb attempts to reconquer the Marathas. Shogun Ietsuna dies, and is succeeded by his brother Tsunayoshi.

1681   Charles II grants Pennsylvania as a nonconformist colony to William Penn. Emperor Kangxi suppresses the Rebellion of the Three Feudatories. France annexes Strasbourg. Bank cheques are issued for the first tiime in England.

1682   Louis XIV moves his court to Versailles. The Chelsea Hospital is founded. La Salle reaches the mouth of the Mississippi, names the surrounding area 'Louisiana' claiming it for France. Tsar Feodor III of Russia dies. His sister Sophia becomes regent for her younger brothers, Ivan V, who is mentally defective, and her half-brother Peter I, and seeks to kill Peter's supporters as a threat to her position.

1683   By the League of The Hague, Spain and the Holy Roman Empire join Holland and Sweden in an anti-French coalition. The Rye House Plot against Charles II and James, duke of York is unmasked; Lord William Russell and Algernon Sidney are executed for their roles in the plot and the earl of Essex commits suicide. Alfonso VI of Portugal dies, and is succeeded by his brother Pedro II. Ottomans besiege Vienna, but are forced to withdraw by Jan Sobieski of Poland and Charles, duke of Lorraine. China captures Formosa (Taiwan).

1684   The Japanese poet Saikaku composes 23,500 verses in 24 hours. The Holy Roman Empire, Poland and Venice form the Holy League of Linz against the Turks. Jews are expelled from Bordeaux.

1685   Charles II dies, and is succeeded by his brother James II, but his illegitimate son the duke of Monmouth leads an uprising which ends in defeat at Sedgemoor. Monmouth is beheaded and Judge Jeffreys conducts the 'Bloody Assizes' against Monmouth's followers. Louis XIV revokes the Edict of Nantes, forcing Huguenots to flee abroad and damaging the French economy.

1686   The Institut de Saint Louis is founded by Madame de Maintenon to educate the daughters of poor gentlefolk; the curriculum includes cookery; graduates are given a blue ribbon – the *cordon bleu*. The League of Augsburg is formed against Louis XIV by the Holy Roman Empire, Spain, Sweden, Saxony, Bavaria and the Palatinate. Buda is liberated from the Ottomans, whilst Russia declares war on them.

1687   Shogun Sunayoshi forbids the killing of animals in Japan. James II proclaims freedom of worship and receives the Papal Nuncio. Ottomans defeated by Charles of Lorraine at Mohács who expell them from Hungary, they lose the Greek Peloponnese and Athens to the Venetians. Sultan Muhammad IV is deposed by his Janissaries and replaced by his brother Suleiman III. Newton's *Principia* is published.

1688   Elector Frederick William of Brandenburg dies, and is succeeded by his son Frederick III. An heir to James II is born. To forestall a Catholic succession William of Orange is invited to replace James, which he does in the 'Glorious Revolution'. James II flees to exile in France. The Ottomans surrender Belgrade to the Austrians. France invades the Palatinate. A marine insurance society is founded in Edward Lloyd's Coffee House in London.

1689   Natal becomes a Dutch colony. Louis XIV declares war on Britain whilst James II arrives in Ireland and besieges Londonderry. A Jacobite rising in Scotland defeats a Covenanter army at Killiecrankie before being defeated at Dunkeld. Regent Sophia is deposed in Russia after conspiring to abduct Peter I, who is established as tsar. The Declaration of Rights is proclaimed in England.

1690   Marlborough captures Cork and Kinsale from Jacobite supporters. Spain and Savoy join the League of Augsburg, which is defeated at Fleurus. The French defeat an Anglo-Dutch fleet off Beachy Head and burn Teignmouth. William III defeats James II at the battle of the Boyne, forcing James back to France. Calcutta is founded by the East India Company. The Ottomans retake Transylvania, Serbia, Belgrade and Bulgaria.

1691   The first directory of addresses is published in Paris. Sultan Suleiman III dies, and is succeeded by his brother Ahmad II, whose reign starts poorly with defeat at Slankamen and expulsion from Hungary. The Irish Jacobites are defeated at Aughrim and pacified by the treaty of Limerick.

1692   The Campbells massacre the MacDonalds at Glencoe. Marlborough is briefly imprisoned for suspected treasonable contact with James II. The Salem witch trials commence. The English defeat a French invasion fleet at La Hogue, but an Anglo-Dutch army is defeated at Steenkirk. Ernst Augustus of Brunswick is made Elector of Hanover.

1693   William III borrows £1 million, instigating the National Debt. French fleet defeats an Anglo-Dutch one at Cape St Vincent and Lagos; French armies are also successful at Neerwinden and Marsaglia.

1694   William Paterson leads the founding of the Bank of England, with Sir John Houblon as its first Governor. Shah Suleiman I of Persia dies, and is succeeded by his son Husain I. Mary II of England dies.

1695   Princess Anne returns to court to act as hostess for her brother-in-law William III. Sultan Ahmad II dies, and is succeeded by his nephew Mustafa II. William Paterson helps found the Bank of Scotland. Peter the Great besieges Azov, but is forced to withdraw by the Turks with heavy losses. William III takes Namur.

1696   Jan Sobieski of Poland dies. Peter the Great takes Azov and conquers Kamchatka. The Window Tax is introduced in England, whilst John Locke and Isaac Newton reform the coinage.

1697   Peter the Great travels incognito from Russia to study European ways of life. Karl XI of Sweden dies, and is succeeded by his son Karl XII. Elector Frederick-Augustus I of Saxony is elected king of Poland, taking the title Augustus II. France, Britain, Spain and the Holy Roman Empire make peace by the treaty of Ryswick. Eugene of Savoy heavily defeats the Turks at Zenta.

1698   Elector Ernst Augustus of Hanover dies, and is succeeded by his son George. Leopold of Anhalt-Dessau introduces goose-stepping to the Prussian army. Whitehall Palace is largely destroyed by fire. The Streltzy, elite musketeer regiments, revolt in Moscow, but the rising is quelled.

1699   Turkey signs the Peace of Karlowitz with Austria, to which it cedes Hungary, Croatia and Transylvania. Turkey also cedes its portion of the Ukraine to Poland, and Morea and Dalmatia to Venice. Christian V of Denmark dies, and is succeeded by his son Frederick IV. Denmark, Russia, Poland and Saxony sign the treaty of Preobrazhenskoe to carve up the Swedish Empire. William Dampier explores the western Australian coast. Henry Winstanley builds the first Eddystone Lighthouse.

1700   The German Protestant states adopt the Gregorian calendar. The Great Northern War opens with concerted attacks on Sweden; Saxony invades Livonia and Denmark invades Schleswig, but Sweden invades Zeeland, forces the Danes from the war by the treaty of Travendal, and defeats Russia at Narva. The duke of Gloucester dies, leaving no direct Stuart heir after Princess Anne (James Stuart being unacceptable). Charles II of Spain dies, the Habsburg line ends with him and the throne goes to Philip V, grandson of Louis XIV.

1701   Elector Frederick of Brandenburg makes himself king of Prussia; Emperor Leopold acquiesces in return for military aid. The War of the Spanish Succession opens; England, Holland and Savoy join the Holy Roman Empire in the Grand Alliance. Karl XII of Sweden invades Poland. Eugene of Savoy defeats the French at Carpi and Chiara. Antoine Cadillac founds Detroit. The Act of Settlement provides for the succession in England to pass to Electress Sophia of Hanover after Princess Anne. Jethro Tull develops the seed drill.

1702   William III dies, and is succeeded in England by his sister-in-law Anne, whilst in Holland the Stadtholdership is put into abeyance. The *Daily Courant* becomes London's first daily newspaper. Karl XII of Sweden takes Warsaw and Cracow. Marlborough captures Venlo, Roermond and Liège, and is raised from an earl to a Duke. Protestant peasants, the Camisards, revolt in the Cévennes.

1703   The Swedish defeat the Russians at Pulutsk. Marlborough takes Cologne and Bonn. Peter the Great founds St Petersburg. The Grand Alliance proclaims Archduke Charles of Austria king of Spain. Portugal joins the Grand Alliance and signs the Methuen treaty with England. The Eddystone Lighthouse is destroyed as a great storm hits Southern England.

1704   Sweden secures the deposition of Augustus II of Poland in favour of Stanislas Leszczynski. Gibraltar is captured by the English, who defeat a relieving force at Velez Malaga. Marlborough and Eugene of Savoy heavily defeat the French at Blenheim. Beau Nash becomes Master of Ceremonies at Bath.

1705   Edmund Halley predicts the return in 1758 of the comet that will bear his name. Emperor Leopold dies, and is succeeded by his son Joseph I. Peter the Great's westernization provokes revolts in Astrakhan. Barcelona falls to the Grand Alliance.

1706   Karl XII of Sweden defeats a Russo-Saxon army at Fraustadt. Marlborough defeats the French at Ramillies; Brussels, Antwerp, Ghent and Ostend quickly capitulate to him. Archduke Charles is installed in Madrid, but is driven out after 3 months by Philip V of Spain. Eugene of Savoy defeats the French at Turin and drives them from Lombardy. Augustus II of Poland abdicates, recognizing his usurper Stanislas I.

1707   Emperor Aurangzeb dies, and is succeeded by his son A'zam Shah, whose death soon after puts his brother Bahadur Shah I on the throne. A French army under the duke of Berwick defeats an Anglo-Portuguese force at Almanza. England and Scotland formally unite with the Act of Union. Prussia and Sweden sign a Perpetual Alliance. Admiral Sir Cloudesley Shovell's squadron runs aground in the Scillies, only one man survives. Fortnum & Mason's opens in Piccadilly.

1708   Marlborough and Eugene of Savoy defeat the French at Oudenarde; Marlborough subsequently captures Lille. Minorca captured by the British. The East India Company and the New East India Company merge. The Sikh guru Govind Singh is assassinated by order of the Mughal Bahadur Shah. Karl XII of Sweden invades the Ukraine.

1709   The *Tatler* is launched by Richard Steele and Joseph Addison. Tsar Peter defeats Karl XII of Sweden at Poltava, forcing Karl to take refuge in Anatolia and breaking Sweden's power. Augustus II takes advantage of this by driving Stanislas I from Poland and regaining the throne. Marlborough and Eugene of Savoy take Tournai and Mons and defeat the French at Malplaquet. Abraham Darby develops coke-fuelled iron smelting at Coalbrookdale.

1710   Stanhope is victorious at Almenara and Saragossa but is defeated and captured at Brihuega. Handel is appointed Kapellmeister to Elector George of Hanover. Christopher Wren completes St Paul's Cathedral.

1711   Addison and Steele launch the *Spectator*. Queen Anne establishes Ascot racecourse. Emperor Joseph I dies, and is succeeded by his brother Charles VI, who guarantees a Hungarian constitution by the Peace of Szathmar. Russia and Turkey sign the treaty of Pruth; Tsar Peter is forced to return Azov to the Turks. Rio de Janeiro is captured by the French. The South Sea Company is established. Marlborough is dismissed from command and replaced by Ormonde.

1712   Civil war breaks out in Switzerland; the Protestant cantons are victorious at Villmergen and peace is re-established by the treaty of Aarau. The Mughal Emperor Bahadur Shah I dies; his sons quarrel over the succession.

1713   Farrukhsiyar, grandson of Bahadur Shah, establishes himself as Mughal emperor. Karl XII of Sweden is taken prisoner by the Ottomans at Bender in Moravia. Frederick I of Prussia dies and is succeeded by his son Frederick William I. The treaties of Utrecht end the War of the Spanish Succession, with Philip V allowed to keep the throne, establishing the Bourbon dynasty in the country; the thrones of France and Spain are never to be united. Emperor Charles VI does not sign. Charles VI issues the Pragmatic Sanction, allowing female succession in Habsburg domains. Shogun Ienobu dies, and is succeeded by his infant son Ietsugu.

1714   The Board of Longitude promises a £20,000 reward for anybody who can discover a method of divining longitude. Russia gains control of Finland after victory at the battle of Storkyro. Charles VI makes peace with France at Rastatt and Baden. Queen Anne dies, and is succeeded by her second cousin George I, as his mother Sophia had died shortly before. Karl XII of Sweden is released by the Turks.

1715   Louis XIV dies, and is succeeded by his great-grandson Louis XV. Mir Vais, chief of Kandahar, dies; his son Mir Maahmoud succeeds him, but is assassinated by his uncle Mir Abdullah who takes power. The earl of Mar leads a Jacobite rising in Scotland; the Old Pretender James lands at Peterhead to support the rising, but his supporters are defeated at Sheriffmuir and Preston.

1716   The Old Pretender returns to France as the '15 rebellion fizzles out. Shogun Ietsugu dies aged seven and is succeeded by Yoshimune, a distant relation. Eugene of Savoy defeats the Ottomans at Peterwardein; Emperor Charles VI joins the war and Temesvar, the last Ottoman possession in Hungary, falls. The Tsarevich Alexei flees Russia and places himself under the protection of Charles VI.

1717   The Grand Lodge of the Freemasons is established at the Goose and Gridiron Tavern, Covent Garden. School attendance is made compulsory in Prussia. Lhasa is occupied by Mongols. Eugene of Savoy defeats the Ottomans at Belgrade.

1718   Edward Teach, Blackbeard, is killed in a fight in North Carolina. The first English banknotes are issued. Philip V of Spain sends troops into Sicily; the Quadruple Alliance of the Empire, France, England and Holland is formed to counter him. Tsarevich Alexei is killed by order of Peter the Great and his friends executed. Karl XII is killed at Fredriksten during an expedition into Norway, and is succeeded by his sister Ulrika.

1719   Liechtenstein becomes an independent principality under Count Hans von Liechtenstein, who has bought the territory. Herat rebels against Shah Hussein, and defeats an army sent to subdue the area. Sweden and Hanover make the Peace of Stockholm. The Mughal emperor Farrukhsiyar dies, creating a succession dispute which is eventually resolved when his cousin Muhammad ascends the throne.

1720   The Great Northern War is brought to an end as Sweden makes peace with her neighbours. Ulrika of Sweden abdicates in favour of her husband Frederick of Hesse. A plague outbreak in Marseille is the final time the Black Death pandemic strikes. The South Sea Company collapses (South Sea Bubble), as does John Law's Mississippi Company, bringing ruin to many. China makes Tibet a protectorate.

1721   A revolt in Formosa is suppressed by China. A regular postal service is established between London and New England. John Aislabie, Chancellor of the Exchequer, is dismissed and imprisoned for fraud. Robert Walpole is appointed First Lord of the Treasury by George I, becoming the first prime minister. Sweden and Russia sign the treaty of Nystadt; Russia gains Estonia. Peter the Great is proclaimed Emperor of All the Russias.

1722   Mir Mahmoud of Kandahar conquers Afghanistan, defeats the Persians at Gulnabad, and takes Isfahan. Shah Hussein abdicates in favour of his son Tahmasp, but Mahmoud proclaims himself Shah. Russia and the Ottoman Empire exploit the situation and invade; the Russians withdraw after an outbreak of ergotism. Hungary rejects Emperor Charles' Pragmatic Sanction. Jacob Roggeveen discovers Rapa Nui, naming it Easter Island.

1723   Louis XV of France attains his majority, ending the Regency period. Britain and Prussia sign the treaty of Charlottenburg, arranging marriages between the two royal houses.

1724   Philip V of Spain abdicates in favour of his son Luis, who dies some months after, and Philip returns to the throne. Russia and the Ottoman Empire make a treaty for the dismemberment of Persia, where Mir Mahmoud goes insane.

1725   Tsar Peter the Great dies, and is succeeded by his widow Catherine I. The Pragmatic Sanction is guaranteed by the treaty of Vienna. Tabriz falls to the Ottomans. Mir Mahmoud kills 39 Persian princes; the surviving nobles elect his cousin Ashraf to replace the insane Shah, who is murdered on order of Ashraf. The treaty of Hanover allies Britain, Prussia and France against Austria and Spain.

1726   Voltaire is exiled in England. General George Wade commences a programme of road-building in Scotland. Montevideo is founded. Cardinal Fleury becomes chief minister to Louis XV.

1727   Spain besieges Gibraltar, but does not formally declare war on Britain. Shah Ashraf defeats an Ottoman army and the two powers make peace. Catherine I of Russia dies, and is succeeded by Peter II, a grandson of Peter I. George I dies of apoplexy, and is succeeded by his son George II.

1728 The Kiakhta treaty sets the border and terms of trade between China and Russia. Spain abandons its siege of Gibraltar when the Convention of the Prado settles a truce with Britain. Roman Catholics are disenfranchised in Ireland. Vitus Bering discovers the Bering Strait. The Empire and Prussia make the treaty of Berlin. A Freemasons' Lodge is founded in Madrid, but is quickly suppressed by the Inquisition.

1729 Emperor Yongzheng bans opium smoking in China. Corsica temporarily becomes independent of Genoa. France, Britain and Spain end hostilities with the treaty of Seville. Charles Wesley founds the Holy Club at Oxford with his brother John and George Whitehead.

1730 Peter II of Russia dies of smallpox; his cousin Anne takes power in a coup. Shah Ashraf is murdered after defeat near Shiraz; Tahmasp II returns to power. Viscount Townshend improves crop husbandry with the use of turnips after leaving Walpole's government. Crown Prince Frederick of Prussia is imprisoned at Küstrin after attempting to flee to England. Sultan Ahmad III is deposed, and replaced by his nephew Mahmud I. Frederick IV of Denmark dies, and is succeeded by his son Christian VI.

1731 John Hadley invents the reflecting quadrant. Shah Tahmasp is defeated by the Ottomans at Arijan and sues for peace, ceding large tracts of land to the Ottomans. Tahmasp is imprisoned by his brother-in-law Nadir Kuli and his infant son Abbas III set up as Shah. The Holy Roman Empire makes the treaty of Vienna with Britain, Holland and Spain, securing support for the Pragmatic Sanction.

1732 Genoa regains control of Corsica.

1733 James Oglethorpe establishes a colony at Savannah, founding the state of Georgia. John Kay invents a flying shuttle loom. Augustus II of Poland dies; France persuades Polish nobles to restore Stanislas I but Austria and Russia demand that Augustus' son, Frederick Augustus of Saxony, succeed his father. In the War of the Polish Succession, they invade Poland.

1734 Persia and the Ottoman Empire go to war. France and Spain defeat Austrian armies in Naples and Parma. Danzig falls to the invading Russian army, but Stanislas I escapes to Prussia.

1735 William Pitt is elected MP for Old Sarum. The treaty of Vienna ends the War of the Polish Succession, and Augustus III is established on the Polish throne. Russia allies with the Persian Nadir Kuli against the Ottoman Empire; Nadir defeats the Ottomans at Baghavand and takes Tiflis. John Harrison develops his chronometer. Linnaeus publishes *Systema naturae*, the origin of modern classification of plants and animals.

1736 Shah Abbas III dies, and Nadir Kuli succeeds him. Claudius Aymond performs the first successful appendectomy. Freemasonry is condemned by Pope Clement XII. Statutes against witchcraft are repealed in England. Emperor Yongzheng dies, and is succeeded by his son Qianlong.

1737 Benjamin Franklin creates the Philadelphia police force, the first of its kind. The Licensing Act orders all plays to submit to the Lord Chamberlain's censorship. Gian Gastone di Medici dies, last of his line. The Grand Duchy of Tuscany passes to Francis of Lorraine, whilst Lorraine passes to Stanislas I of Poland as a reward for renouncing his claim to the Polish throne.

1738 Orsova falls to the Ottomans, who drive the Imperial troops back to Belgrade. Jean H.L. Orry imposes the corvée, compulsory labour, to construct roads in France. John and Charles Wesley form the Methodist Society.

1739 Dick Turpin is hanged at York. Shah Nadir of Persia sacks Delhi, drastically diminishing Mughal power in India. Nadir seizes the Koh-i-Noor diamond. Emperor Charles VI makes peace with the Ottomans by the treaty of Belgrade, ceding the city to the Ottomans. England and Spain go to war (the War of Jenkins' Ear) over alleged Spanish transgressions. Porto Bello in Panama is seized by Admiral Vernon.

1740 Frederick William I of Prussia dies, and is succeeded by his son Frederick II the Great, who invades Silesia. Emperor Charles VI dies; he is succeeded in his kingdoms by his daughter Maria Theresa, but Saxony, Bavaria and Spain dispute her right to succeed and the War of the Austrian Succession begins. Tsarina Anna dies, and is succeeded by her infant great-nephew Ivan VI.

1741 Frederlck the Great defeats the Austrians at Mollwitz and captures Brieg, Neisse, Glatz and Olmütz before the British mediate. Prague is occupied by a French, Bavarian and Saxon army. Elizabeth, daughter of Peter the Great, deposes Tsar Ivan VI and rules herself.

1742 Anders Celsius develops the centigrade thermometer system. Elector Charles Albert of Bavaria is elected to the vacant title of Holy Roman Emperor. Robert Walpole resigns as Prime Minister, replaced by the earl of Wilmington. Prussia defeats the Austrians at Chotusitz, before signing treaty of Berlin with Austria, gaining upper and lower Silesia. Britain and Prussia sign the treaty of Westminster, safeguarding Hanover.

1743 George II leads a multinational Pragmatic Army to victory over the French at Dettingen. Pogroms of Jews occur in Russia. Persia and the Ottoman Empire go to war. Austria and Saxony ally, whilst Bavaria is conquered by Austria.

1744 Frederick the Great invades Saxony and Bohemia, taking Prague before being driven back to Saxony. Maria Theresa launches a series of pogroms in Moravia and Bohemia against the Jews.

1745 Emperor Charles VII dies. Francis of Lorraine, grand duke of Tuscany and husband of Maria Theresa, is elected the new Emperor. The French defeat an army led by the duke of Cumberland at Fontenoy and advance into the Austrian Netherlands. The Prussians defeat the Austrians and Saxons at Hohenfriedberg and the Austrians at Soor. Charles Edward Stuart lands on Eriskay, proclaiming his father king. He gains support from various Scottish clans, takes Edinburgh and is victorious at Prestonpans, but loses his nerve on reaching Derby and withdraws.

1746 The retreating Jacobites are victorious at Falkirk but are routed by Cumberland at Culloden. The Young Pretender escapes, and helped by Flora MacDonald reaches Skye, from where he returns to France. Cumberland severely represses the Scots, and the wearing of tartan is outlawed. Canaletto moves to England. Philip V of Spain dies, and is succeeded by his son Ferdinand VI. France defeats Austria at Raucoux and takes the Austrian Netherlands.

1747 The Republic of the United Provinces is overthrown by the French and William IV of Orange-Nassau resumes the post of Stadtholder. Prussia and Sweden form a defensive alliance. The French defeat an Anglo-Dutch army at Laufeld. Shah Nadir is murdered in Afghanistan; his nephew Adil succeeds him whilst

Ahmed Shah Durrani takes advantage of the situation to establish an independent Afghanistan. Lord Lovat is beheaded for Jacobitism on Tower Hill, the last man to be executed there.

1748   The treaty of Aix-la-Chapelle ends the War of the Austrian Succession with a stalemate peace. This gives general recognition to the Pragmatic Sanction and the Prussian conquest of Silesia.

1749   Thomas Chippendale opens a workshop. Admiral Anson reforms the Royal Navy. Henry Fielding publishes *Tom Jones.*

1750   Henry Fielding and his brother John found the Bow Street Runners. Thomas Gray's 'Elegy Written in a Country Churchyard' is written in Stoke Poges. The Jockey Club is founded in the Star and Garter Coffee House, Pall Mall. JS Bach dies. João V of Portugal dies, and is succeeded by his son Jose I, who appoints the marquis of Pombal as his chief minister. Pombal strips the Inquisition of its power.

1751   China invades Tibet. Robert Clive seizes Arcot from the French. Stadtholder William IV dies, and is succeeded by his infant son William V. Britain adopts January 1 as the beginning of the New Year, instead of 25 March.

1752   Britain adopts the Gregorian calendar system; 11 days disappear from September. Benjamin Franklin invents the lightning conductor. Ahmed Shah of Afghanistan takes Lahore. Spain and the Holy Roman Empire sign the treaty of Aranjuez.

1753   Sir Hans Sloane dies; his legacy of books and collections are used to found the British Museum and British Library. The Marriage Act forbids unlicensed weddings in Britain. The Jewish Naturalisation Act seeks to remove disabilities for Jews in Britain, but the hostility it engenders leads to its repeal.

1754   The Royal and Ancient Golf Club is founded at St Andrews, and codifies the rules of the sport. William Cookworthy pioneers English porcelain production. The first iron-rolling mill is built, in Fareham, Hampshire. In North America the Albany Convention is convened by several colonies and the Iroquois to form a joint defence against the French, who defeat two expeditions led by George Washington. The Convention agrees to Franklin's proposal for the union of the 13 colonies. Sultan Mahmud I dies while dismounting from his horse, and is succeeded by his brother Osman III.

1755   Casanova is imprisoned in Venice for spying. Pasquale de Paoli is elected general in Corsica, and leads a revolt against Genoa. In North America, General Braddock is killed in the battle of the Wilderness, as the French rout a British expedition, but the French are subsequently defeated at Lake George. Lisbon is devastated by an earthquake and tidal wave; 30,000 die.

1756   A porcelain factory is founded at Sèvres. John Smeaton builds a new Eddystone Lighthouse. England and Prussia ally by the treaty of Westminster. Minorca surrenders to Franco-Spanish forces after Admiral Byng breaks off a naval action. Britain declares war on France, but Montcalm drives the British from the Great Lakes. Siraj-ud-Daula, a French ally, seizes Calcutta, imprisoning 146 Britons in a small guardroom (Black Hole of Calcutta); according to English propaganda, only 23 emerge alive the next morning. Seven Years War erupts as Prussia invades Saxony, which has allied with France, Austria, Russia and Sweden against it.

1757   John Campbell invents the sextant. Ahmed Shah of Afghanistan takes Delhi and the Punjab. Robert Clive recovers Calcutta and defeats Siraj-ud-Daula at Plassey. For his role in losing Minorca, Admiral Byng is shot 'pour encourager les autres' at Portsmouth. Frederick the Great defeats the Austrians at Prague, but is defeated at Kolin before further victories at Rossback and Leuthen. Cumberland is routed by the French at Hastenbeck and is forced by the Convention of Klosterzeven to surrender Hanover to them. Sultan Osman III dies, and is succeeded by his cousin Mustafa III.

1758   Britain promises assistance to Prussia by the treaty of London. Samuel Johnson founds *The Idler*. Clive becomes governor of Bengal. An English army fighting for Frederick II of Prussia defeats the French at Krefeld, and Frederick crushes the Russians at Zorndorf but is defeated by the Austrians at Hochkirch. Fort Duquesne is captured from the French by George Washington and John Forbes and renamed Pittsburgh.

1759   Handel dies. Guadeloupe is captured by the British. Samuel Johnson publishes *Rasselas*. The French defeat Brunswick at Brunswick, but are defeated by an Anglo-Prussian army at Minden. Ferdinand VI of Spain dies, and is succeeded by his half-brother Charles III. Frederick the Great is defeated by an Austro-Russian army at Kunersdorf. General Wolfe defeats Montcalm on the Plains of Abraham outside Quebec; both generals die in battle. Quebec falls to the British. Admiral Hawke destroys a French squadron off Quiberon.

1760   Earl Ferrers is hanged at Tyburn, the last peer to be executed in Britain. Austria defeats Prussia at Landshut, but is defeated at Liegnitz. Amherst captures Montreal. Russian troops capture and burn Berlin. George II dies, and is succeeded by his grandson George III. Prussia defeats the Austrians at Torgau. John Harrison develops his H-4 chronometer.

1761   Ahmed Shah of Afghanistan defeats the Marathas at Panipat. Pondicherry, the French base in southern India, falls to Sir Eyre Coote. France and Spain invade Portugal; Portugal asks for British help. Spain and the Bourbon Italian states ally with France against Britain.

1762   Tsarina Elizabeth dies, and is succeeded by her nephew Peter III who withdraws from the Seven Years War and returns Pomerania to Prussia. St Vincent, Martinique Grenada and St Lucia seized by the British under Rodney. Jean-Jacques Rousseau writes the *Social Contract*. Sweden and Prussia ally by the treaty of Hamburg. Peter is assassinated on behalf of his wife, who succeeds him as Catherine II.

1763   The treaty of Paris ends the Seven Years War. Spain cedes Florida to Britain. The *Almanach de Gotha* is first published. Augustus III of Poland and Saxony dies; he is succeeded in Saxony only by his son Frederick-Christian, who also dies, and is succeeded by his son Frederick-Augustus III.

1764   James Hargreaves invents the spinning jenny. Stanislas Poniatowski is elected to the vacant Polish throne. Hyder Ali takes Mysore. Sir Hector Monro defeats the Nawab of Oudh at Buxar, and takes control of Bengal. Ex-Tsar Ivan VI is murdered in prison.

1765   Frederick the Great founds the Bank of Prussia. The Stamp Act imposes taxation on the American colonists, much to their disgust. Emperor Francis I dies, and is succeeded by his son Joseph II. The auto-da-fé is abolished in Lisbon.

1766   On the death of ex-king Stanislas, duke of Lorraine, the duchy reverts to France. The Stamp Act is repealed, but the Declaratory Act affirms the right of Parliament to tax the American colonists. Frederick V of Denmark dies, and is succeeded by his son Christian VII.

1767   Siam is invaded by the Burmese. Nevil Maskelyne, the Astronomer Royal, issues the first Nautical Almanac. Clive leaves India.

1768   The Royal Academy of Arts is founded, with Joshua Reynolds as the first president. The first edition of the *Encyclopaedia Britannica* is published. The Gurkha king Prithvi Naryan Shah makes Nepal a unitary kingdom. Corsica is bought by the French from Genoa. Austria renounces all claims to Silesia.

1769   Austria occupies the Lvov and Zips regions of Poland. Frederick the Great and Emperor Joseph II meet at Neisse to discuss the partition of Poland. Richard Arkwright develops the spinning frame. James Watt patents a steam engine. Josiah Wedgwood opens his pottery works at Etruria. Wellington, Napoleon, Ney and Soult are born.

1770   Joseph Cugnot constructs a steam-powered road vehicle in France. Lord North replaces Grafton as prime minister. The 'Boston Massacre', a brawl between civilians and troops, leaves 3 dead. All taxes, bar that on tea, on the American colonists are repealed. An Anglo-Spanish dispute over the Falklands is resolved by French mediation. Captain James Cook lands at Botany Bay, Australia. A Russian fleet defeats the Ottomans at the battle of Chesme.

1771   The Crimea is conquered by Russian Cossacks. Duke Charles-Emmanuel III of Savoy abolishes serfdom. Adolphus Frederick of Sweden dies, and is succeeded by his son Gustav III. The Marathas drive the Afghans from Delhi.

1772   The Danish nobility rebel against Count Johann von Struensee, who has held absolute power for a year, torturing and beheading him. George III secures the passage of the Royal Marriages Act to control whom the royal family may marry. Russia, Prussia and Austria perform the first partition of Poland. Gustav III of Sweden re-establishes absolute monarchy. Carl Wilhelm Scheele discovers oxygen (Priestley discovers it independently in 1774); Daniel Rutherford, Joseph Priestley, Henry Cavendish and Carl Wilhelm Scheele independently discover nitrogen.

1773   Emperor Joseph II expels the Jesuits, prompting Pope Clement XIV to dissolve the order. Tea is thrown into the sea in the protest known as the Boston Tea Party as a protest against the tea duty. The first Stock Exchange opens in London. Captain Cook enters the Antarctic Circle. Denmark cedes Oldenburg to Russia. Thomas Pritchard constructs the Ironbridge at Coalbrookdale.

1774   The Coercive Acts against Massachusetts include closing the port of Boston. Lord North is robbed by a highwayman at Chiswick. Louis XV of France dies, and is succeeded by his grandson Louis XVI. Sultan Mustafa III dies, and is succeeded by his brother Abdul-Hamid I. Russia acquires the northern Black Sea coast by the treaty of Kuchuk-Kainardji with Turkey. Joseph Priestley discovers oxygen. Austria occupies Bukovina. The Continental Congress, comprising all the America colonies bar Georgia, convenes, deciding to ban imports from and exports to Britain.

1775   Paul Revere rides to Lexington to warn of British troop movements. The American War of Independence opens. The colonists win victories at Concord, Fort Ticonderoga and Crown Point. The Second Continental Congress convenes and John Hancock is elected its president. The British defeat the rebels at Bunker Hill.

1776   Adam Smith publishes *The Wealth of Nations*. The St Leger is first run (founded by Colonel Barry St Leger). Grigori Potemkin organises a Russian Black Sea Fleet. Russia and Denmark sign the treaty of Copenhagen. The American colonists issue the Declaration of Independence. After defeat at Long Island and on Lake Champlain they score a major victory at Trenton.

1777   Spain and Portugal settle their differences over their South American colonies. The Americans are victorious at Princeton, Ridgefield and Bennington, but lose at the Brandywine and Germantown before victory at Bemis Heights provokes Burgoyne to surrender at Saratoga. Elector Maximilian III of Bavaria dies; with no direct heir, the Electorship passes to Count Karl Theodor of the Palatine.

1778   Joseph Bramah patents an improved water closet. Captain Cook discovers and names the Sandwich Islands. France signs treaties of alliance with the United States. Frederick the Great opens the War of the Bavarian Succession by invading Bohemia. The British take Savannah.

1779   Samuel Crompton develops the spinning mule. Captain Cook is killed by natives in Hawaii. The Oaks is first run (named after the house at Epsom leased by the 12th earl of Derby). Warren Hastings sends British troops against the Marathas. The Peace of Teschen settles the War of the Bavarian Succession. British troops are defeated at Baton Rouge by an augmented American army. Spain declares war on Britain.

1780   Admiral Rodney defeats the Spanish off Cape St Vincent. Lord George Gordon whips up anti-Catholic hysteria in London into the Gordon riots. The Americans are defeated at Camden, but are victorious at Kings Mountain. Emperor Joseph II abolishes serfdom in Bohemia and Hungary. Maria Theresa dies, and is succeeded in Habsburg territories by her son Emperor Joseph. The Derby is first run. Peruvian Indians rebel against Spanish rule, led by the Inca descendant Tupac Amaru, who is executed next year as the revolt is suppressed.

1781   William Herschel discovers Uranus. Warren Hastings plunders the treasure of the Nabob of Oudh. Emperor Joseph II grants religious tolerance in the Holy Roman Empire and abolishes serfdom in Austria. General Cornwallis surrenders to the Americans at Yorktown, ending British military operations in America.

1782   Spain captures Minorca from Britain, and completes the conquest of Florida. Lord North resigns as prime minister, and is succeeded by Rockingham; on his death Shelburne replaces him, and Pitt the Younger becomes chancellor of the exchequer. Admiral Rodney defeats the French at the battle of the Saints. Rama I founds the Chakri dynasty as kings of Siam, ruling from Bangkok. The *Royal George* sinks off Portsmouth, with the loss of 800 men.

1783   Shelburne resigns as prime minister, succeeded by Portland, whose government falls; Pitt the Younger becomes prime minister at the age of 24. Henry Cort develops a method of puddling iron. The treaty of Versailles recognises American Independence and cedes Florida to Spain. The Montgolfier brothers make the first balloon flight at Annonay. Potemkin annexes the Crimea for Russia.

HISTORY

1784   Turkey is forced to accept the Russian annexation of the Crimea by the treaty of Constantinople. John Wesley draws up his 'Deed of Declaration', providing for the continuance of the Methodist movement. A revolt in Transylvania persuades Emperor Joseph II to suspend the Hungarian constitution. The East India Company is put under government control.

1785   Jean Blanchard and John Jefferies cross the English Channel by balloon. *The Daily Universal Register*, later renamed *The Times*, is founded. The prince of Wales secretly weds Maria Fitzherbert. Warren Hastings resigns as governor-general of India. The Diamond Necklace affair discredits Marie Antoinette and leads to the arrest of Cardinal de Rohan. Austria and Holland settle their differences by the treaty of Fontainebleau.

1786   Jacques Balmat and Michel-Gabriel Paccard make the first ascent of Mont Blanc. Penang is ceded by the Rajah of Kedah to Britain. Frederick the Great of Prussia dies, and is succeeded by his nephew Frederick William II.

1787   The Marylebone Cricket Club is founded, and Thomas Lord opens his first cricket ground. Warren Hastings is impeached by Edmund Burke. George Washington chairs a Constitutional Convention in America which draws up the constitution. Russia and Turkey go to war. Delaware, Pennsylvania and New Jersey are the first states to join the union of the United States.

1788   William Symington develops a workable steamboat. The First Fleet lands convicts at Botany Bay and Sydney is founded to house them. The trial for corruption of Warren Hastings begins. Gustavus III of Sweden invades Russian Finland. Louis XVI is persuaded to summon the Estates-General in France. George III suffers a bout of mental illness.

1789   Sultan Abdul Hamid I is poisoned and succeeded by his nephew Selim III. George Washington is elected the first president of the United States. A mutiny takes place, led by Fletcher Christian, on HMS *Bounty*; Christian and the mutineers settle on Pitcairn Island; Captain Bligh, set adrift, navigates across 3,600 miles of ocean to Timor. George III recovers from his illness The Estates-General meet at Versailles; the Third Estate declares itself a National Assembly and swears not to dissolve until a constitution is granted. The Paris mob storm the Bastille, starting a revolution. Feudalism is abolished in France. The National Assembly issues the Declaration of the Rights of Man. Louis XVI and his family are forced to go to Paris as the mob attacks Versailles. Belgrade and Bucharest are taken by Austria.

1790   Emperor Joseph II dies, and is succeeded by his brother Leopold II. Louis XVI accepts a revolutionary constitution. Philadelphia becomes the American capital. Alexander Hamilton founds Washington DC.

1791   Marie Harel develops Camembert cheese. The *Observer* begins publication. Boswell's *Life of Johnson* and Tom Paine's *Rights of Man* are published. John Wesley dies. The Canada Constitutional Act splits Canada into Upper and Lower Canada, with legislatures in Ontario and Quebec. Louis XVI flees Paris, but is captured at Varennes and forced to return. Mozart's *The Magic Flute* is 1st performed. The Bill of Rights, consisting of the first ten amendments to the American constitution, is codified.

1792   Denmark abjures slavery. The Democratic Republican and Federalist parties are founded in America. Russia and Turkey make the Peace of Jassy. Cornwallis defeats Tipu Sultan of Mysore at Seringapatam and takes half of Mysore. Emperor Leopold II dies, and is succeeded by his son Francis II. Gustavus III of Sweden is assassinated in Stockholm Opera House, and is succeeded by his son Gustavus IV. Prussia and Austria ally against France, which declares war on them and Sardinia. Prussia takes Verdun but the French are victorious at Valmy and conquer the Austrian Netherlands. The Paris mob storms the Tuileries; the Swiss Guard fire on them. Louis XVI is imprisoned in the Temple and the National Convention abolishes the monarchy. The Jacobins seize power and the guillotine is put into use.

1793   Louis XVI is executed, as are his cousin Philippe Égalité, duke of Orléans, and Queen Marie Antoinette. France declares war on Britain, Holland and Spain, which join the First Coalition against France. The Vendée rises against republican excesses, but a rebel army is routed at Savenay. America declares its neutrality, unable to decide which side to back. The Committee of Public Safety take power; Robespierre heads a government which embarks on the Reign of Terror. Prussia and Russia perform the Second Partition of Poland, seizing half of Poland's territory. Marat is murdered by Charlotte Corday. Toulon is occupied by the British, but recaptured by a force including Napoleon.

1794   King Kamehameha of Polynesia cedes Hawaii to George III, but the cession is not ratified. Shah Lutf Ali of Persia is defeated and killed by Agha Muhammad, who founds the Qajar dynasty. Kosciusko leads a rising of Polish patriots, which is suppressed by the Russians. The Reign of Terror reaches a height as Danton and Desmoulins are executed. Habeas Corpus is suspended in Britain. Admiral Howe defeats the French fleet on the 'Glorious First of June', but the French have revenge at Charleroi and Fleurus. Robespierre holds the Festival of the Supreme Being; Thermidorean moderates stage a coup – Robespierre and St Just are executed and the Jacobin Club closed.

1795   The French capture the Dutch fleet in the River Texel; Stadtholder William V is forced to flee to England and the French form the Batavian republic in the Netherlands. Prussia makes peace with France by the treaty of Basel. The Speenhamland magistrates devise a new form of poor relief. Warren Hastings is acquitted. The Chouan uprising occurs in Brittany. Cape Town and Trincomalee are taken by the British. The Directory, led by Barras, comes to power in France. Austria, Prussia, and Russia perform the Third Partition of Poland; Stanislas II is forced to abdicate as his country ceases to exist.

1796   Colombo is taken by the British, establishing British control over Ceylon. Emperor Qianlong abdicates, and is succeeded by his son Jiaqing. Napoleon leads an army into Italy; it defeats the Austrians at Millesimo, Lodi and Arcol and establishes the Lombard Republic. François Babeuf leads a conspiracy to overthrow the Directory, but it fails. Edward Jenner discovers a vaccine against smallpox. Elba is captured by Britain. Robert Burns dies aged 37. Spain and Britain go to war. Tsarina Catherine the Great dies, and is succeeded by her son Paul I.

1797   Napoleon defeats the Austrians at Rivoli, seizes Mantua, and founds the Ligurian republic in Genoa and the Cisalpine Republic. Trinidad and St Lucia are taken by the British from the French. Admiral Jervis defeats the Spanish at Cape St Vincent. French troops are landed at Fishguard, but are quickly captured. The first £1 banknotes are issued. John Adams succeeds George Washington as American President. The

Royal Navy suffers mutinies at the Nore and Spithead, but defeats a Franco-Dutch fleet at Camperdown. Barras thwarts a royalist reaction by the coup d'état of Fructidor. By the Peace of Campo Formio, the Austrian Netherlands are annexed by France whilst Venice and its territories are passed to Austria; Venice thus loses its independence. Frederick William II of Prussia dies, and is succeeded by his son Frederick William III.

1798   Thomas Malthus produces his *Essay on the Principles of Population*. Coleridge and Wordsworth publish *Lyrical Ballads*. Napoleon captures Rome, proclaiming the Roman Republic and forcing Pope Pius VI into custody at Valence. The Helvetic Republic, encouraged by the French, is proclaimed in Bern. Napoleon then captures Malta en route to Egypt, where he defeats the Mamluks at the battle of the Pyramids, but Nelson destroys his fleet at the battle of the Nile. Irish rebels are defeated at Vinegar Hill, whilst French troops landing in support are forced to surrender at Ballinamuck. The Irish nationalist Wolfe Tone is captured, condemned, but commits suicide. Ferdinand IV of Naples enters Rome, but is driven out by the French and Naples overrun. Income Tax is introduced in Britain.

1799   Napoleon invades Syria, but is repulsed by Sir Sidney Smith at Acre. The Rosetta Stone is discovered. Britain and Hyderabad share Mysore after Tipu Sultan is killed at Seringapatam. The Second Coalition against France is organised by Pitt. Russian troops defeat the French at Zurich, but are eventually driven out; after victory at Cassano they overthrow the Cisalpine Republic. Napoleon defeats an Anglo-Turkish army at Aboukir. On 18 Brumaire Napoleon overthrows the Directory and becomes First Consul.

1800   The American capital is transferred from Philadelphia to Washington DC. The French defeat the Turks at Heliopolis. Austrian troops starve Genoa into submission, but are defeated at Marengo, giving Napoleon control of Italy. Malta is captured by the British.

1801   Great Britain and Ireland unite. France adopts a metric system of weights and measures. The Bank of France is founded. Austria and France make the peace of Lunéville, which destroys the viability of the Holy Roman Empire. Thomas Jefferson becomes American president. Pitt the Younger resigns as prime minister over Catholic Emancipation, and is replaced by Addington. Tsar Paul I is assassinated, succeeded by his son Alexander I. Nelson defeats the Danish fleet at Copenhagen (after the famous incident of him turning a blind eye to Parker's orders). The French troops in Egypt surrender to the English.

1802   William Cobbett founds the *Political Register*. The *Charlotte Dundas*, the world's first steamship, is built by William Symington. Madame Tussaud mounts her first waxworks exhibition in London. Napoleon becomes president of the Italian Republic, which has superseded the Cisalpine Republic. Britain and France make peace by the treaty of Amiens. Napoleon creates the Légion d'Honneur, is made First Consul for life and annexes Piedmont, Parma and Piacenza.

1803   The Swiss cantons regain their independence by the Act of Mediation. Henry Shrapnel develops an explosive shell. The United States purchase the Louisiana territory – over 800,000 sq. miles of land west of the Mississippi – from France. Thomas Telford commences building the Caledonian Canal. France and Britain resume hostilities; France occupies Hanover. Arthur Wellesley (the future duke of Wellington) leads British troops to victory against Sindhia of Gwalior in the Second Maratha War.

1804   Richard Trevithick develops a steam locomotive. The duc d'Enghien is executed for plotting a Bourbon restoration. The Code Napoleon comes into force. Addington is forced to resign by Pitt the Younger, who replaces him. Napoleon is proclaimed Emperor of the French, crowning himself in the presence of Pope Pius VII. A revolt forces the French to withdraw from Haiti. Former US treasury secretary Alexander Hamilton is killed in a duel with Vice-President Aaron Burr.

1805   Francis Beaufort devises the Beaufort Scale. Mungo Park explores the Upper Niger. Muhammad Ali is proclaimed Pasha of Egypt. Napoleon crowns himself king of Italy in Milan wih the old Lombard crown. Austria, Russia, Sweden and Britain form the Third Coalition against France. The British fleet is victorious at Trafalgar over a Franco-Spanish fleet, but Nelson is mortally wounded. On the same day Napoleon defeats an Austro-Russian army at Ulm, and is subsequently victorious at Austerlitz. France and Austria make peace by the treaty of Pressburg; Austria is forced to yield the Tyrol and her Italian possessions whilst Bavaria and Württemberg become kingdoms and Baden a grand duchy.

1806   Britain occupies the Cape of Good Hope. Pitt the Younger dies; Grenville forms a coalition, the 'Ministry of All the Talents', to replace him. Britain establishes a blockade of the European coastline; Napoleon retaliates by the Berlin Decree establishing the Continental System to bar European ports to British ships. Napoleon makes his brothers Joseph and Louis kings of Naples and Holland respectively. France organises the Confederation of the Rhine; the Holy Roman Empire thus ceases to exist and Francis II is merely Emperor of Austria. Prussia joins the Third Coalition. Napoleon defeats the Prussians at Jena and Auerstadt and enters Berlin. Saxony becomes a kingdom by the Peace of Posen.

1807   Charles and Mary Lamb's *Tales from Shakespeare* is published; Charles is guardian to his sister, who stabbed their mother during a bout of insanity. Slavery is prohibited in Britain. Sultan Selim III is deposed by his Janissaries and succeeded by his cousin Mustapha IV. HMS *Leopard* takes deserters from USS *Chesapeake*, enraging the Americans. Napoleon meets Tsar Alexander at Tilsit and makes the peace by the treaty of Tilsit. Napoleon makes his brother Jerome king of Westphalia. Copenhagen is bombarded by the British. Baron von Stein becomes Prussian prime minister and emancipates the serfs there. France invades Portugal, which has refused to join the Continental System; the Portuguese royal family flees to Brazil.

1808   French troops under Murat invade Spain. Charles IV of Spain abdicates in favour of his son Ferdinand VII, but Napoleon orders Murat to force Joseph Bonaparte upon them. Spanish resistance puts Joseph to flight, but Napoleon takes Madrid and restores him. Grand Vizier Bairakdar attempts to restore Sultan Selim III, who is strangled by the janissaries. Bairakdar deposes and murders Sultan Mustafa IV, replacing him with his brother Mahmud II. Murat replaces Joseph as king of Naples.

1809   Sir John Moore is mortally wounded as British troops evacuate Corunna. Gustavus IV of Sweden is captured in a coup; the Duke of Sudermania forms a government and Gustavus is forced to abdicate. Gustavus IV's uncle Karl XIII eventually succeeds him. Britain and the Sikhs make a pact of friendship by the treaty of Amritsar. Napoleon annexes the Papal States, taking Pope Pius VII prisoner, and to further his dynastic ambitions, divorces Josephine. Wellington defeats Soult at Oporto and Jourdan at Talavera. Napoleon is defeated by the Austrians at Aspern, but is victorious at Wagram and makes peace with Austria by the treaty of Schönbrunn. Canning, British foreign secretary, and Castlereagh, war minister, fight a duel on Putney Heath and resign from office. Metternich becomes Austrian minister of foreign affairs. Austria joins the Continental System.

1810   Napoleon marries Marie Louise of Austria. Andreas Hofer leads an Austrian rebellion, but is executed at Mantua. Napoleon annexes Holland when his brother Louis abdicates, and later annexes Hanover and various German ports. Jean Bernadotte is invited to become heir to the Swedish throne as Karl XIII has no children. The Krupp steel works open in Essen.

1811   George III descends into madness and the prince of Wales is declared Regent. Belgrade is seized by the Russians. Pasha Muhammad Ali massacres the Mamluks at Cairo. Luddism erupts in the Midlands. Wellington defeats the French at Fuentes de Onoro and Albuera. Francisco de Miranda declares Venezuelan independence; Paraguay follows suit. William Harrison defeats the Shawnee at Tippecanoe.

1812   In Spain, Wellington takes Ciudad Rodrigo and Badajoz, defeats Marmont at Salamanca and enters Madrid. Prime minister Spencer Perceval is assassinated by John Bellingham, and is succeeded by the earl of Liverpool. America declares war on Britain. Napoleon leads his Grand Army into Russia. Britain, Russia and Sweden ally via the treaty of Örebro. De Miranda is made dictator of Venezuela after an earthquake, but is captured by the Spanish. After victory at Smolensk and an inconclusive outcome at Borodino Napoleon takes an evacuated Moscow, which is then burned down by Russian saboteurs. He orders a retreat, and has to suffer terrible losses in crossing the River Berezina. General Claude Malet attempts to depose Napoleon in his absence, but is executed as the conspiracy fails.

1813   The locomotive 'Puffing Billy' is developed by William Hedley. Prussia declares war on France, but is defeated, along with Russia, by Napoleon at Lützen, Bautzen and Wurschen. Wellington defeats Jourdan at Vittoria and crosses into France. Simon Bolívar becomes dictator of Venezuela. Austria declares war on France. Prusso-Russian troops defeat Napoleon at Grossbeeren and Wahlstatt, but are defeated at Dresden before further victory at Dennewitz. An Austro-Prusso-Russian army defeats Napoleon at Leipzig, and drives him back across Germany. Mexico declares independence from Spain. The French are expelled from Holland.

1814   Denmark cedes Heligoland to Britain by the treaty of Kiel. Murat deserts Napoleon and joins the Allies, who inflict defeats on Napoleon at La Rothière, Laon, Arcis and Fère-Champenoise before entering Paris. Wellington defeats the French at Toulouse. Napoleon abdicates, is banished to Elba, and is granted its sovereignty. Louis XVIII returns from exile. Ferdinand VII returns to the Spanish throne. The Austrian Netherlands and Holland unite to form the kingdom of the Netherlands. The White House is burned down by British troops. The Cape of Good Hope becomes a British colony. The Congress of Vienna opens. The treaty of Ghent ends hostilities between Britain and America.

1815   Napoleon returns from Elba, forcing Louis XVIII to flee to Ghent. His forces under Ney are victorious at Quatre Bras, but Wellington defeats him at Waterloo. After surrendering to the British, he is exiled to St Helena. Louis XVIII returns, Ney is executed and Murat deposed from Naples; he is executed when trying to regain his throne. Spanish troops reconquer Venezuela, forcing Bolívar to flee. To protect domestic growers against cheaper imports, the Corn Laws are passed in Britain. The treaty of Vienna draws up a new political map of Europe: Norway is passed to Denmark, the Rhineland to Prussia, Poland to Russia and various monarchs restored to their thrones.

1816   Argentina declares itself independent, as does Brazil under the Portuguese prince João, who succeeds to the Portuguese throne on the death of his mother Maria I, but remains in Brazil. The first Diet of the German Confederation opens in Frankfurt. Cobbett's *Political Register* increases its radical influence after a price cut to 2d.

1817   José de San Martín and Bernardo O'Higgins defeat the Spanish at Chacabuco and establish an independent Chile. The last major Luddite attack takes place in Loughborough. The 'Blanketeers' march from Manchester to protest against the suspension of the Habeas Corpus Act, but are halted at Stockport; there are similar riots elsewhere. Bolivar reestablishes an independent Venezuela. The Ottomans grant partial autonomy to the Serbs.

1818   The Rajput states and Indore come under British control by the treaty of Mundosir. Karl XIII of Sweden dies, and is succeeded by Bernadotte, who takes the name Karl XIV. The American-Canadian border is defined along the 49th parallel. James Blundell performs the first successful blood transfusion. At the Congress of Aix-la-Chapelle, the victorious allies agree to withdraw their troops from France, which has paid the war indemnity imposed in 1815.

1819   Stamford Raffles founds the city of Singapore. The United States take over Florida from Spain. The reactionary Karlsbad Decrees are promulgated in Germany. The Peterloo Massacre kills 11 people in Manchester, when yeomen attack a reformist crowd. The reactionary Six Acts are passed in England. Simon Bolivar becomes president of the newly independent Colombia.

1820   Liberia is founded for the repatriation of American Negroes. There are revolts in Spain, where Ferdinand VII is forced to restore the constitution of 1812, and in Portugal, demanding a constitution. George III dies, and is succeeded by his son George IV. The duc de Berry, heir to the French throne, is assassinated; a son, the comte de Chambord, is born posthumously. At the Congress of Troppau, Prussia, Austria and Russia discuss concerted action against revolutionary movements with Britain and France. The Cato Street Conspiracy to murder British cabinet ministers is discovered and its leaders executed. Keats publishes *Lamia, Isabella, The Eve of St Agnes and other Poems*.

1821   A Carbonarist uprising in Naples is put down by the Austrians, sanctioned by the Congress of Laibach. Bolívar defeats the Spanish at Carabobo, ensuring Venezuelan independence. Peru declares independence under José de San Martín. El Salvador, Honduras, Costa Rica, Guatemala and Panama follow suit. Greeks start an insurgence against the Ottomans in an attempt to gain independence. Victor

Emmanuel of Piedmont is forced to abdicate in favour of his more liberal brother Charles Felix. The Austrians intervene, defeating the Piedmontese at Novara and reasserting control over the country.

1822   Viceroy Wellesley is attacked by Orangemen in Dublin in the 'Bottle Riots'. The Ottomans capture Chios and massacre its inhabitants. Agostín de Itúrbide is declared emperor of Mexico. A Greek flotilla burns an Ottoman fleet, bringing further reprisals. British foreign secretary Castlereagh commits suicide. Regent Pedro, son of João VI of Portugal, declares Brazil independent.

1823   Michael Faraday succeeds in liquefying chlorine. Emperor Agostín de Itúrbide is forced to abdicate as Mexico declares itself a republic. The Lancet is first published. A revolt in Spain is quelled with French assistance. President Monroe issues the Monroe Doctrine, closing the Americas to European colonialism.

1824   The RNLI is founded. The First Burmese War between Britain and Burma commences; Rangoon is taken by the British. Lord Byron dies at Missolonghi whilst assisting the Greeks. Beethoven's 9th Symphony is first performed. Louis XVIII of France dies, and is succeeded by his brother Charles X.

1825   Ferdinand I of the Two Sicilies dies, and is succeeded by his son Francis I. John Quincy Adams is elected American president by the House of Representatives after none of the four candidates gains a majority in the election. Bolivia under Jose de Sucre declares independence from Peru, and Uruguay, with Argentine support, from Brazil. The Stockton–Darlington railway opens, the first passenger-carrying line. The Erie Canal links the Hudson River to the Great Lakes and the American Midwest. Tsar Alexander I dies, and is succeeded by his brother Nicholas I, who is confronted by the Decembrist revolt of officers, which he puts down.

1826   The First Burmese War is ended by the treaty of Yandabo. João VI of Portugal dies, and is succeeded by his son Pedro IV, who abdicates in favour of his daughter Maria II and remains in Brazil. Persia and Russia go to war; the Russians are victorious at Ganja. Stamford Raffles founds the Royal Zoological Society in London.

1827   Peru secedes from Colombia. Count Kapodistrias is elected president of Greece as Britain, France and Russia sign the treaty of London pledging support for the Greeks; an allied fleet crushes an Ottoman and Egyptian fleet at Navarino. Russia defeats Persia and takes Yerevan.

1828   Wellington becomes prime minister. Russia makes peace with Persia by the treaty of Turkmanchai, and subsequently declares war on the Ottomans. Maria II of Portugal is deposed by her uncle, the Regent Dom Miguel, and flees to England as civil war breaks out. The treaty of Rio de Janeiro confirms Uruguayan independence. Thomas Arnold becomes headmaster of Rugby School.

1829   The Catholic Emancipation Act is passed in Britain. Wellington fights a duel with the earl of Winchelsea. The Metropolitan Police is founded by Robert Peel. The first Boat Race takes place at Henley. The London Protocol establishes Greek independence; the treaty of Adrianople ends Russo-Turkish hostilities. Stephenson's Rocket wins the Rainhill Trials. Slavery is abolished in Mexico.

1830   Joseph Smith founds the Church of Jesus Christ of Latter-Day Saints. The Swing riots, caused by the introduction of threshing machines and rural unemployment, start in Kent and spread west and north. George IV dies, and is succeeded by his brother William IV. Algeria is conquered by France, but an uprising in Paris forces Charles X to abdicate in favour of his grandson, however Louis-Philippe, duc d'Orléans, usurps the throne. Belgium secedes from the Kingdom of the Netherlands. Wellington is ousted as prime minister after a general election, and replaced by earl Grey.

1831   Independence agitations in Italy are quelled by Austrian troops. Pedro I of Brazil abdicates, and is succeeded by his son Pedro II. A Polish revolt is put down after Russian troops are victorious at Ostroleka. Leopold of Saxe-Coburg is elected king of the Belgians. Charles Felix of Piedmont dies, and is succeeded by his distant relation Charles Albert. The Greek President Kapodistrias is assassinated. Faraday invents the dynamo. The defeat of Grey's Reform Bill in the Lords causes anti-clerical agitation. Mazzini founds Young Italy.

1832   The First Reform Act is passed, doubling the franchise. Otto of Bavaria is elected king of Greece.

1833   Britain annexes the Falkland Islands. The Convention of Kutahya passes control of Syria to Muhammad Ali of Egypt. Slavery is abolished in the British Empire. Ferdinand VII of Spain dies, and is succeeded by his infant daughter Isabella II. Santa Anna becomes President of Mexico whilst civil war looms in the country.

1834   The Zollverein customs union comes into operation in Germany. The Spanish Inquisition is abolished. To protect their constitutions, Portugal and Spain form a Quadruple Alliance with France and Britain. Don Carlos attempts to usurp the Spanish throne from his niece Isabella II, plunging the country into civil war, whilst in Portugal Dom Miguel is forced to flee as troops led by his brother Pedro restore Maria II to her throne. For forming a trade union, the Tolpuddle Martyrs are arrested and transported to Australia. Fire destroys the Houses of Parliament.

1835   Francis II of Austria dies, and is succeeded by his son Ferdinand I. Juan de Rosas becomes dictator of Argentina. The Boers begin the 'Great Trek'. Texas attempts to secede from Mexico.

1836   Santa Anna takes the Alamo at San Antonio; Davy Crockett and Jim Bowie are killed. Sam Houston defeats and captures Santa Anna at San Jacinto; Texas gains independence with Houston as president. Louis Napoleon Bonaparte attempts a revolt at Strasbourg, and is banished to America.

1837   William IV dies, and is succeeded in England by his niece Victoria and in Hanover by his brother Ernst Augustus, duke of Cumberland, who promptly cancels the constitution of 1833 there. Brunel launches the Great Western. Births, marriages and deaths are officially registered in England and Wales. Isaac Pitman develops shorthand. French Canadians revolt against British rule.

1838   Chopin begins his liaison with George Sand. Richard Cobden establishes the Anti-Corn Law League. The 'People's Charter' is published. Grace Darling assists in the rescue from the wreck of the Forfarshire. The First Afghan War begins; the British capture Kabul and imprison the Emir Dost Muhammad. The Boers defeat the Zulus at Blood River.

1839   The Rebecca Riots against the Poor Law Amendment Act take place in Wales (rioters disguise themselves as women). Goodyear discovers how to vulcanise rubber. Argentina and Uruguay go to war. The Ottomans invade Syria but are defeated by Ibrahim Pasha at Nezib. The treaty of London guarantees Belgian independence and neutrality. Sultan Mahmud II is poisoned, and succeeded by his son Abdul Mejid. Chinese attempts to stop the importation of opium lead to the Opium War with Britain. Frederick VI of Denmark dies, and is succeeded by his nephew, Christian VIII. Bradshaw's provides first railway timetables.

1840   The Maoris cede sovereignty of New Zealand to England by the treaty of Waitangi. Rowland Hill introduces the Penny Post. Frederick William III of Prussia dies, and is succeeded by his son Frederick William IV. Britain, Austria, Prussia and Russia ally against Muhammad Ali of Egypt by the treaty of London; after Beirut and Acre are captured, Muhammad agrees to return Syria to Ottoman rule. Lower and Upper Canada are united under a single legislature. Rafael Carrera becomes dictator of Guatemala. Louis Napoleon Bonaparte is imprisoned at Ham after another attempt to foment revolt fails. William I of Holland abdicates, and is succeeded by his son William II.

1841   Hong Kong is taken by the British. William Harrison dies after catching cold giving his inaugural address as US president, and is succeeded by John Tyler. Thomas Cook arranges his first excursion, to a temperance meeting. The Straits Convention closes the Bosporus to warships. Carlos Lopez becomes President of Paraguay. The first issue of *Punch* is published.

1842   Crawford W Long performs the first operation under anaesthesia. British troops in Afghanistan are massacred. The second Chartist petition is rejected. Civil war erupts in Uruguay. The Webster-Ashburton treaty defines the US–Canadian border. The treaty of Nanking ends the Opium War; Hong Kong is ceded to Britain. Alexander Karageorgevich deposes Michael Obrenovich as prince of Serbia. Marx meets Engels. Britain withdraws from Afghanistan.

1843   The Thames Tunnel opens, first underwater tunnel in the world. Brunel launches the *Great Britain*. Sind is conquered by General Charles Napier. Hawaii becomes independent, with recognition from France and Britain.

1844   George Williams founds the YMCA. Karl XIV of Sweden dies, and is succeeded by his son Oscar I. The Factory Act fixes maximum workdays of 6½ hours for children, 12 hours for women. Samuel Morse transmits his first telegraph message. The Dominican Republic gains independence from Haiti. The Co-operative movement is founded in Rochdale.

1845   The Irish famine begins as the potato crop fails. Henry Newman converts to Catholicism. Sir John Franklin sets out with the *Erebus* and *Terror* to find the North-West Passage. British incursions in the Punjab and Kashmir cause the Anglo-Sikh War. The Sonderbund is formed when 7 Catholic cantons secede from the Confederation in Switzerland.

1846   The Anglo-Sikh War is ended by the treaty of Lahore. Cracow is annexed by Austria. Louis Napoleon Bonaparte escapes from prison and moves to London. The treaty of Washington settles the Oregon–Canada border along the 49th Parallel. America goes to war with Mexico after failing to purchase New Mexico; after victories at Palo Alto and Resaca de la Palma New Mexico is annexed by the United States. Peel repeals the Corn Laws, fatally splitting his party and forcing him to resign as prime minister; Lord John Russell replaces him. Charles Dickens founds the *Daily News*.

1847   Mexican troops under Santa Anna are defeated by the Americans at Buena Vista and Cerro Gordo. Liberia is proclaimed an independent republic. The Catholic cantons refuse to dissolve the Sonderbund, precipitating war in Switzerland.

1848   Christian VIII of Denmark dies, and is succeeded by his son Frederick III. Gold is discovered in California. The treaty of Guadalupe Hidalgo ends the conflict between America and Mexico, which is forced to yield its lands north of the Rio Grande. Marx and Engels publish the *Communist Manifesto*. Paris erupts in revolt, forcing Louis Philippe to abdicate. The Second French Republic is formed; a workers' revolt is put down (the June Days) and Louis Napoleon Bonaparte is elected President. The revolution in France inspires a wave of revolts across Europe: Metternich falls in Austria; Milan, Parma, Venice, Hungary and the Czechs revolt against Austrian dominion; liberals rise across Germany, creating a National Assembly; Rome rises against Papal war, forcing Pope Pius IX to flee to Gaeta. Piedmont declares war on Austria, but after victories at Goito and Pastrengo is defeated by Radetzky at Custozza. Windischgrätz suppresses the Czech rising; nevertheless, Emperor Ferdinand I is forced to abdicate in favour of his nephew Franz Josef. The Second Anglo-Sikh war breaks out. The third Chartist petition is presented amid a meeting which collapses in farce, and is rejected. Switzerland becomes a federal union. The Pre-Raphaelite Brotherhood is founded.

1849   The Sikhs are defeated by the British at Chillianwalla and forced to surrender at Rawalpindi; the Punjab is annexed by Britain. A Roman republic under Mazzini is formed, but French, Austrian, Spanish, Neapolitan and Tuscan troops capture Rome and restore Pope Pius IX. Radetzky defeats the Piedmontese at Novara. Charles Albert of Piedmont abdicates in favour of his son Victor Emmanuel II and the Peace of Milan ends hostilities. The German National Assembly elects Frederick William IV 'Emperor of the Germans', but he refuses the title and the Assembly collapses in chaos. Hungary proclaims independence under Kossuth, but Russian troops invade and are victorious at Temesvar; Kossuth flees and Hungary returns to Austrian rule. Venice submits to the Austrians.

1850   Palmerston blockades Piraeus over the Don Pacifico Affair, forcing the Greeks to comply with his wishes, but is censured in parliament. Prussia and Denmark reach an accord on Schleswig-Holstein by the treaty of Berlin. Hong Xiuquan leads the Taiping rebellion in China. Count Camillo Cavour becomes chief minister of Piedmont.

1851   Danilo II succeeds Peter II in Montenegro and makes the state a principality. The Great Exhibition is held in Hyde Park. The Americas Cup yacht race is first held around the Isle of Wight. The Australian Gold Rush begins. Louis Napoleon Bonaparte stages a coup d'état in France.

1852   Juan Manuel de Rosas, Argentine dictator, is forced to flee after defeat by insurgents with Uruguayan and Brazilian help at Caseros. The Second Burmese War breaks out between Britain and Burma. Louis Napoleon Bonaparte proclaims the Second Empire, crowning himself Napoleon III.

1853   Pegu is taken by Britain as the Second Burmese War ends. Shogun Ieyoshi dies, and is succeeded by his son Iesada, who opens two Japanese ports to foreign trade. Russia invades the Ottoman Danubian principalities and destroys the Turkish fleet at Sinope. Maria II of Portugal dies, and is succeeded by her son Pedro V.

1854   The Convention of Bloemfontein leaves the Orange Free State free for the Boers and withdraws the British south of the Orange River. America makes the treaty of Kanagawa with Japan over trade and the Elgin treaty with Britain over Canadian trade. Britain and France declare war on Russia in support of Turkey and are victorious at the Alma, Balaklava (where the Charge of the Light Brigade takes place), and Inkerman, before besieging Sebastopol.

1855   Piedmont joins the anti-Russian alliance in the Crimean War by the treaty of Turin. Aberdeen resigns as prime minister over the conduct of the war, and is replaced by Palmerston. Tsar Nicholas I dies, and is succeeded by his son Alexander II. Britain and Afghanistan sign the anti-Persian treaty of Peshawar. The *Daily Telegraph* is first published. Sebastopol falls to the allied armies.

1856   The Victoria Cross is instituted. Britain annexes Oudh and establishes Natal as a Crown Colony. The Crimean War is ended by the treaty of Paris; the integrity of the Ottoman Empire is recognised and the Black Sea demilitarised. The Chinese board the *Arrow* off Canton over suspected piracy; British ships bombard Canton in response. Marthinius Pretorius establishes the Transvaal republic. Henry Bessemer introduces his steel-making converter.

1857   Britain forces Afghani independence on the Persians by the treaty of Paris. The Sepoys in Meerut revolt, sparking a general Indian Mutiny; the inhabitants of Cawnpore are massacred and Lucknow besieged for six months. Garibaldi forms the Italian National Association. British and French forces occupy Canton.

1858   Felice Orsini attempts to assassinate Napoleon III, causing Anglo-French tension and turning Napoleon's mind towards Italy; he has secret meetings at Plombières with Cavour. Anglo-Chinese hostilities are ended by the treaty of Tianjin. The Indian Mutiny is suppressed; the East India Company is wound up and its powers transferred to the British crown. Frederick William IV is declared insane; his brother William is made Regent. Alexander Karageorgevich is deposed by the Serbian Diet and replaced by Milos Obrenovich. France launches *La Gloire*, a naval vessel partially clad in iron.

1859   Piedmont traps Austria into war, and backed by Napoleon III is victorious at Magenta and Solferino. Ferdinand of the Two Sicilies dies, and is succeeded by his son Francis II. Napoleon III and Franz Josef of Austria make the Peace of Villafranca; Lombardy is passed to Piedmont. John Brown raids Harpers Ferry. Darwin publishes the *Origin of Species*. Queensland is established as a separate colony with Brisbane as its capital.

1860   Piedmont cedes Nice and Savoy to France by the treaty of Turin. Plebiscites in the Italian duchies favour union with Piedmont. Garibaldi and his 1,000 redshirts sail from Genoa to Sicily, take the island and then progress to Naples, where he proclaims Victor Emmanuel II of Piedmont king of Italy. Piedmontese troops invade the Papal States en route to the Two Sicilies, which Garibaldi hands to Victor Emmanuel II; Garibaldi retires to Caprera. South Carolina secedes from the Union in protest at the election of Abraham Lincoln as president. The Second Maori War breaks out in New Zealand. Richard Cobden negotiates an Anglo-French trade treaty. Anglo-French forces bombard Sinho, occupy the Tagu forts, defeat the Chinese army at Ba Lizhao and burn the Summer Palace in Peking in retaliation for Chinese treaty breaches and cruelty to captives; the treaty of Peking forces further concessions on the Chinese.

1861   Frederick William IV of Prussia dies and is succeeded by his brother Wilhelm I. Tsar Alexander II emancipates the Russian serfs. The kingdom of Italy is proclaimed, with its capital at Florence, as Rome refuses to join. The Confederate States of America are proclaimed at the Congress of Montgomery and go to war with the Union by bombarding Fort Sumter: the Civil War begins. The Confederates are victorious at Bull Run. Prince Albert dies. With the commissioning into the Royal Navy of the iron-hulled HMS *Warrior*, all other naval vessels are rendered effectively obsolete.

1862   In America the Union launches the ironclad USS *Monitor*, which fights the Confederate ironclad *Merrimack* to a draw in Hampton Roads. The battle of Shiloh is a bloody draw, whilst the Confederates are subsequently victorious at the second battle of Bull Run and Fredericksburg. Napoleon III sends French troops to establish a Catholic empire in Mexico, forcing the withdrawal of British and Spanish troops; the French are heavily defeated at Puebla. Bismarck is appointed prime minister of Prussia. A military revolt forces Otto I of Greece to abdicate and return to Bavaria.

1863   The first underground railway, from Farringdon Street to Paddington, is opened. The Greeks elect Prince Alfred of Britain as their new king, but he is forced to reject the position; William of Denmark is elected instead, taking the title George I. The Confederates are victorious at Chancellorsville, but are routed at Gettysburg, which proves a turning point. The Union has further victories at Vicksburg and Chattanooga but is defeated at Chickamauga. Lincoln gives the Gettysburg Address at the dedication of the cemetery there. Mexico City falls to the French, who invite Archduke Maximilian of Austria to become emperor of the country. Japan closes its ports and expels foreign traders, prompting Britain to bombard Kagoshima. Frederick VII of Denmark dies, and is succeeded by his nephew Christian IX, who incorporates Schleswig into the country after German pressure on the area. The English Football Association is founded.

1864   Austrian and Prussian troops invade Schleswig-Holstein, defeating the Danes at Düppel. A conference in London fails to settle the dispute, and Prussia and Austria force Denmark to cede the area by the treaty of Vienna. Archduke Maximilian accepts the Mexican crown. Brazil invades Uruguay after a dispute with Paraguay. The Taiping Rebellion is suppressed, with help from General Gordon's troops; Hong Xiuquan commits suicide. Ulysses S Grant takes command of the Union army. In the Wilderness campaign in Virginia, the Union loses 60,000 of an army of over 100,000, the Confederacy 20,000 of its 60,000 men. Sherman takes Atlanta and Savannah as his Union army marches through Georgia. General George Thomas wipes out a Confederate army under JB Hood at Nashville.

1865   The Confederate states surrender to the Unionists at Appomattox; five days later Abraham Lincoln is assassinated by John Wilkes Booth. William Booth founds the Christian Revival Association (later the Salvation Army). Edward Whymper climbs the Matterhorn. Edward Lister's use of carbolic acid founds modern antiseptic surgery. Lord Palmerston dies in office, and is succeeded as prime minister by Lord

John Russell. Leopold I of Belgium dies, and is succeeded by his son Leopold II. The Thirteenth Amendment abolishes slavery in the US.

1866   Prince Alexander of Romania is dethroned and replaced by Carol I of Hohenzollern. Bismarck, with Italian assistance, engineers war against Austria and allied German states, defeating the Austrians at Sadowa, although the Italians are defeated at Custozza and the naval battle of Lissa. The Peace of Prague gives Prussia Hanover, Hesse, Nassau, Frankfurt and Holstein. Shogun Iemochi dies, and is succeeded by his kinsman Yoshinobu. The treaty of Vienna cedes Venetia to Italy.

1867   The Ausgleich creates the Dual Monarchy of Austria-Hungary. Alaska is sold by Russia to America. The Dominion of Canada is created. Emperor Maximilian of Mexico surrenders to insurgents after the French abandon him and is executed. Prussia forms the North German Confederation. The Second Reform Act doubles the British electorate. Garibaldi marches on Rome, but is defeated by a Franco-Papal army at Mentana and taken prisoner. The Queensberry Rules on boxing are drawn up.

1868   The Shogunate is abolished in Japan; by the Meiji Restoration power passes to Emperor Matsuhito. Disraeli becomes prime minister, but is defeated in a general election by Gladstone, who replaces him. Prince Michael of Serbia is assassinated, succeeded by his kinsman Milan II Isabella II of Spain is deposed after a revolution in Spain. The first Trades Union Congress meets in Manchester. The last public hangings in England take place.

1869   The first Nihilist Congress meets in Basel. The *Cutty Sark* is launched. Napoleon III reintroduces a parliamentary system into France. The Suez Canal is opened.

1870   Papal infallibility is proclaimed. Isabella II of Spain abdicates in favour of her son Alfonso XII but the throne is offered to Leopold of Hohenzollern, who is forced to decline it after French protests. These protests are edited by Bismarck into the 'Ems telegram' and used to foment war between France and Prussia. After a French victory at Saarbrücken, Prussia is victorious at Weissenberg, Wörth, Mars-la-Tour, Gravelotte and Sedan. Napoleon III surrenders and abdicates as Paris revolts and proclaims the Third Republic. Paris is besieged by the Prussians. Italian troops enter Rome and absorb it into the kingdom; it is made the capital. Amadeus of Savoy accepts the Spanish throne.

1871   Wilhelm I of Prussia is proclaimed emperor of a federal Germany at Versailles. Paris surrenders to the Prussians. The leftist Commune takes power there, and is repressed with the loss of 20,000 lives. The Convention of London abolishes the demilitarization of the Black Sea. Britain and America settle differences by the treaty of Washington. France and Germany make the Peace of Frankfurt; Alsace-Lorraine is ceded to Germany and an indemnity paid by France. Stanley meets Livingstone at Ujiji (now in Tanzania). Bank holidays are introduced.

1872   Wanderers win the first FA Cup final. Don Carlos invades Spain, but is routed at Oroquista and forced to withdraw. The secret ballot is introduced in Britain. Germany, Austria-Hungary and Russia form the Three Emperors League. The *Marie Celeste* is found deserted.

1873   A Spanish republic is proclaimed and Amadeus I forced to abdicate. Sultan Bargash Sayyid closes the slave markets in Zanzibar. The cities of Buda and Pest are united to form the Hungarian capital. WC Wingfield invents Sphairistike (lawn tennis).

1874   Disraeli defeats Gladstone in the General Election. Japan invades Formosa, and withdraws on payment of compensation by China. Fiji is annexed by Britain. Alfonso XII of Spain proclaims his reign at Sandhurst.

1875   Bismarck foments tension between Germany and France ('Is War in Sight?' article in the *Berlin Post*). Bosnia-Herzegovina revolts against Turkish rule. Matthew Webb swims the English Channel. Disraeli arranges the purchase of shares in the Suez Canal. Sir Joseph Bazalgette completes the London sewerage system. The MCC codifies the rules of lawn tennis.

1876   Korea becomes independent from China. Alexander Graham Bell patents the telephone. Bulgaria rises against Turkey, but is savagely repressed, drawing Gladstone out of retirement. Queen Victoria is proclaimed Empress of India and is officially inaugurated in January 1877. Sultan Abdul Aziz is deposed in favour of his nephew Murad V and commits suicide; Murad is himself deposed in favour of his brother Abdul Hamid II. General Custer is defeated and killed by the Sioux at the battle of Little Big Horn. Serbia and Montenegro declare war on Turkey, but the Serbs are routed at Alexinatz. Wild Bill Hickok is shot dead.

1877   Rutherford B Hayes is elected American president after an electoral commission decides in his favour. Russia declares war on Turkey and takes Kars and Plevna. Britain warns Russia off taking Constantinople. Serbia also declares war on Turkey. Australia beats England in the first cricket Test match. The first Lawn Tennis Championships are held at Wimbledon.

1878   Victor Emmanuel II of Italy dies, and is succeeded by his son Umberto I. Russia takes Adrianople; the Turks capitulate and sign the treaty of San Stefano, in which Bulgarian, Romanian and Serbian independence is fully established. The provisions are unacceptable to other European powers; differences are resolved at the Congress of Berlin, where the San Stefano provisons are reduced in scale.

1879   The Irish Land League is founded. Britain goes to war with the Zulus, who massacre the British at Isandhlwana but are held at Rorke's Drift and defeated at Ulundi. Their king Cetewayo is captured and deported and the Zulu wars end; the Prince Imperial, heir of Napoleon III, is a casualty. Britain occupies the Khyber Pass by the treaty of Gandamak with Afghanistan and invades when the legation in Kabul is massacred, taking the city and deposing Emir Yakub. Khedive Ismail of Egypt is deposed in favour of his son Tewfik. The Tay Bridge collapses in a storm; 78 lives are lost as a train crossing the bridge falls into the river.

1880   Andrew Carnegie presents Dunfermline with a free library. Gladstone defeats Disraeli in the General Election. Tahiti is annexed by France. Morocco gains independence. Captain Boycott is ostracised by his tenants in County Mayo. Paul Kruger declares the Transvaal an independent republic.

1881   Boers repulse the British at Laing's Neck and defeat them at Majuba Hill; peace is made by the treaty of Pretoria, which recognises an independent Transvaal as the South African Republic. James Garfield is inaugurated as American president but is shot and fatally wounded soon after. Tsar Alexander II is assassinated; he is succeeded by his son Alexander III, who responds by introducing repressive measures. Tunisia is made a French protectorate.

1882   Prince Milan II of Serbia declares himself king. The Hague Convention establishes a three-mile limit for territorial waters. The Fenians assassinate two British ministers in Phoenix Park, Dublin. Nationalist riots in Egypt led by Arabi Pasha lead to the British fleet bombarding Alexandria; Sir Garnet Wolseley defeats Arabi at Tel-el-Kebir and occupies Cairo.

1883   Paul Kruger becomes president of the South African Republic. Krakatoa erupts in spectacular fashion. Khedive Tewfik appoints a British agent to assist his government; Sir Evelyn Baring takes up the post. The Orient Express makes its first run. The Mahdi stirs up a revolt in Sudan and defeats an Anglo-Egyptian army at El Obeid.

1884   The Fabian Society is established. General Gordon reaches Khartoum intent on evacuating the city but decides to stay. China declares war on France after the latter bombards Formosa as a reprisal for China's refusal to acknowledge a French protectorate over Indo-China. The Third Reform Act is passed in Britain.

1885   Wolseley defeats the Mahdi's followers at Abu Klea but reaches Khartoum two days after its fall and Gordon's death. Wolseley is forced to withdraw and the news helps contribute to the fall of Gladstone's government. The Congo becomes the personal possession of Leopold II of Belgium. Germany annexes Tanganyika and Zanzibar. The Mahdi dies, but his successor Abdullah el Tasshi gains control over Sudan. Alfonso XII of Spain dies; his pregnant widow Maria Christina becomes regent.

1886   General Boulanger becomes French war minister. Gladstone's conversion to Irish Home Rule splits the Liberals; Joseph Chamberlain leads the Liberal Unionists into partnership with the Conservatives. Alfonso XIII of Spain is born king. France banishes the Bonaparte and Orléans families. Prince Alexander of Bulgaria abdicates after a coup. Randolph Churchill resigns as chancellor in a fit of pique and destroys his political career in the process. The discovery of gold in Transvaal transforms the politics of southern Africa.

1887   The First Colonial Conference opens in London. Germany and Russia make the secret Reinsurance Treaty. Zululand is annexed by Britain. Ferdinand of Saxe-Coburg is elected prince of Bulgaria. Italy and Abyssinia go to war; the Italians are routed at Dogali. Macao is ceded to Portugal.

1888   Kaiser Wilhelm I dies; his son Frederick III succeeds him, but dies soon after and is succeeded by his son Wilhelm II. Brazil frees its slaves. The Jack the Ripper murders take place in London. The first beauty contest is held in Spa, Belgium. The Suez Canal Convention, guaranteeing freedom of access to the canal, is signed in Constantinople.

1889   Urged by his supporters to stage a coup d'état, Boulanger refuses and flees abroad. Crown Prince Rudolf of Austria shoots his mistress and commits suicide at Mayerling. Milan II of Serbia abdicates in favour of his son Alexander II. Gustave Eiffel completes the Eiffel Tower for the Paris Exhibition. The first Pan-American Conference meets in Washington. The Brazilian army deposes King Pedro II and installs General Manuel de Fonseca as president.

1890   The Forth Railway Bridge opens. Kaiser Wilhelm forces Bismarck's resignation as Chancellor. Social insurance is introduced in Switzerland. Heligoland is exchanged for the German colonies of Zanzibar and Pemba by Britain. The first Japanese elections are held. William III of Holland dies, and is succeeded by his daughter Wilhelmina. Luxembourg separates from the Netherlands under Duke Adolf of Nassau. Sitting Bull is captured and killed; American troops massacre 200 Sioux at Wounded Knee.

1891   WL Judson invents the zip. President Fonseca of Brazil is ousted in favour of Vice-President Floriano Peixoto.

1892   Khedive Tewfik of Egypt dies, and is succeeded by his son Abbas II. Lizzie Borden murders her parents. Gladstone forms his fourth administration at the age of 82 after victory in the general election.

1893   The Independent Labour Party is founded in Bradford. Natal is granted self-government. The Matabele rise against the British South Africa Company, but Jameson crushes the revolt and takes Bulawayo, forcing King Lobengula into exile. Gladstone's Irish Home Rule Bill is defeated in the House of Lords. Transvaal annexes Swaziland.

1894   The Manchester Ship Canal is opened. Gladstone resigns from office, and is replaced as prime minister by Lord Rosebery. Uganda becomes a British protectorate. The Ottomans massacre thousands of Armenians in suppressing a revolt. President Carnot of France is assassinated by an Italian anarchist at Lyon. Korea and Japan declare war on China. Albert Dreyfus is arrested on a treason charge; convicted, he is imprisoned on Devil's Island.

1895   The treaty of Shimonoseki ends the Sino-Japanese War after the Japanese crush the Chinese at Wei hai wei; Formosa and Port Arthur are ceded to Japan but returned in exchange for an indemnity. Italy invades Abyssinia, but is defeated at Amba Alagi. The British South Africa Company's land south of the Zambezi is renamed Rhodesia. Premier Stamboulov of Bulgaria is assassinated. The Kiel Canal is opened. Wilhelm Röntgen discovers X-rays. The first public film show takes place. Jameson raids Transvaal, but fails to foment a rebellion against its Boer rulers.

1896   Jameson is captured by the Boers at Doorn Kop. Kaiser Wilhelm sends the Kruger Telegram, inflaming Anglo-German relations. Becquerel discovers radioactivity in uranium. Italy is defeated by the Abyssinians at Adowa and withdraws by the treaty of Addis Ababa. The first modern Olympic Games are held in Athens. Shah Nasir-ud-Din of Persia is assassinated; he is succeeded by his son Muzaffir-ud-Din. Marconi patents wireless telegraphy. Kitchener leads an Anglo-Egyptian force into the Sudan. Over 50,000 Armenians are massacred by the Turks.

1897   Crete proclaims union with Greece, prompting a war between Greece and Turkey; the Turks are victorious and the island stays under Turkish hands by the treaty of Constantinople. Hawaii is annexed by the United States. The first Zionist Congress meets in Basel.

1898   Zola publishes 'J'accuse' over the Dreyfus affair, proved to have been fabricated by anti-Semitic army officers. The USS *Maine* explodes in Havana harbour, Spanish involvement is suspected, and war breaks out between America and Spain; the Spanish fleet in Manila Bay is destroyed and the Americans are successful at San Juan and Santiago Bay; peace is made by the treaty of Paris, by which Spain cedes

Cuba, Puerto Rico, Guam and the Philippines in return for $20m. Empress Elizabeth of Austria is murdered by an Italian anarchist. Kitchener defeats the Sudanese at Omdurman, retakes Khartoum and advances to Fashoda, where he discovers a French force which is ordered to withdraw after the British government protests to the French.

1899   The First Hague Peace Conference meets. Dreyfus is pardoned by presidential decree after being found guilty again in a second trial prompted by public opinion. Transvaal declares war on Britain; the Orange Free State allies with Transvaal. The Boers besiege Kimberley, Mafeking and Ladysmith and are victorious at Stormberg, Magersfontein and Colenso.

1900   The Boers are victorious at Spion Kop, but Kimberley, Ladysmith and Mafeking are relieved and Bloemfontein, Johannesburg and Pretoria are taken by the British, who annex the Orange Free State and Transvaal. Kruger flees to Germany but is refused an audience by Kaiser Wilhelm II. The Labour Representation Committee is established, with Ramsay MacDonald as secretary. The Boxer Rebellion against foreign influence in China breaks out; the German ambassador is murdered and the foreign legations in Beijing besieged, but are subsequently relieved. The first Zeppelin airship takes to the air. Umberto I of Italy is assassinated by an anarchist; his son Victor Emmanuel III succeeds him.

1901   The Commonwealth of Australia is created. The Boers begin guerrilla warfare against the British. The first British submarine, Holland I, is launched. Queen Victoria dies, and is succeeded by her son Edward VII. US President William McKinley is assassinated by an anarchist; Vice-President Theodore Roosevelt succeeds him. The Boxer Rebellion is ended by the Peace of Beijing. The first Nobel Prizes are awarded. Marconi, who is in Newfoundland receives a wireless message from Cornwall.

1902   Britain allies with Japan. St Pierre, Martinique, is destroyed by the eruption of Mount Pelée. The treaty of Vereeniging ends the Boer War with British sovereignty imposed. Trotsky escapes from prison in Siberia and flees to London, where he meets Lenin. The Order of Merit is established.

1903   King Alexander I and Queen Draga of Serbia are assassinated by supporters of the rival Karageorgevich dynasty, whose heir Peter I ascends the throne in their place. The first Tour de France takes place. The Russian Social Democratic Party splits into Mensheviks and Bolsheviks at its London conference. The Wright Brothers perform the first successful powered flight.

1904   The wireless distress signal CQD is adopted. The Japanese attack the Russians in Port Arthur, setting off war between the two countries; the Japanese are subsequently victorious at Liaoyang. Britain and France ally by the 'Entente Cordiale'. The Rolls-Royce motor company is founded. Vycheslav Plehve, Russian minister of the interior, is assassinated. The British enter Tibet by imposing the treaty of Lhasa; they aim to safeguard it from Russian penetration. The Russian fleet attacks Hull trawlers off the Dogger Bank, mistaking them for Japanese warships; the French mediate between Britain and Russia and the matter is resolved.

1905   Port Arthur surrenders to the Japanese; the resulting protests in St Petersburg are brutally crushed (Bloody Sunday); revolts flare up in Russia as a result, exacerbated by defeats at Mukden and the Tsushima Strait, where the navy is annihilated; the battleship Potemkin mutinies; the Russo-Japanese war is ended by the treaty of Portsmouth, a Soviet is established in St Petersburg and Tsar Nicholas II issues a liberal policy (the October Manifesto). Crete revolts against Turkish rule. Kaiser Wilhelm II visits Tangier, where he emphasizes German interests, to the alarm of other countries. Norway separates from Sweden; Prince Charles of Denmark is elected king, taking the name Haakon VII. The Conservative Party splits over tariff reform; Balfour resigns as PM as a result and Campbell-Bannerman replaces him. Albert Einstein publishes his special theory of relativity.

1906   The Liberals gain a landslide victory in the General Election. HMS Dreadnought is launched in Britain, making all other warships outdated and precipitating a naval arms race. The Algeciras Conference settles the Moroccan question and defuses European tension. San Francisco is hit by a severe earthquake. The Duma meets in Russia, but it is too liberal for the Tsar's liking and is dissolved. As the Tsar's control is re-established over the country, he backtracks on his liberal reforms. Dreyfus is rehabilitated in France and awarded the Légion d'Honneur. South Sinai is ceded to Egypt by the Turks under British pressure. Transvaal and the Orange River colonies are granted self-government.

1907   Sinn Fein ('We ourselves') is established. France and Japan reach agreement on an 'open door' policy in China. The Second Hague Peace Conference meets. Emperor Ko-jong of Korea is forced to abdicate by the Japanese, who establish a protectorate over the country with his son Sun-jong as a figurehead emperor. Britain and Russia reach an entente, forming the Triple Entente with France as a counterweight to the Triple Alliance of Germany, Italy and Austria-Hungary. New Zealand becomes a dominion.

1908   Carlos I of Portugal and his heir are assassinated; his younger son Manuel II succeeds him. The Young Turks revolt at Resina before gaining a majority in the new Ottoman parliament and introducing reforms. The first Ford Model T is sold. Bulgaria declares independence; Prince Ferdinand assumes the title of Tsar. Austria annexes Bosnia-Herzegovina, to international consternation. Crete declares union with Greece again.

1909   Turkey and Serbia are forced to accept the Austrian annexation of Bosnia-Herzegovina. Sultan Abdul Hamid II is deposed by the Young Turks in favour of his brother Muhammad V. Shah Muhammad Ali of Persia is deposed in favour of his son Ahmad by Ali Kuli Khan. Louis Blériot crosses the English Channel by aeroplane. The House of Lords rejects Lloyd-George's 'People's Budget', causing a constitutional crisis; Asquith calls a general election .

1910   Liberals and Tories tie in a General Election; Asquith's government depends on Labour and Irish Nationalist votes. Premier Boutros Ghali of Egypt is assassinated by a nationalist fanatic, whilst Islamic agitation increases. Edward VII dies, and is succeeded by his son George V, who inherits a constitutional crisis. South Africa becomes a dominion. Japan annexes Korea. Montenegro declares itself a kingdom under Nicholas I. Manuel II of Portugal is deposed by a revolution which declares Portugal a republic headed by Teofilo Braga. A second election produces another hung parliament.

1911   Electric escalators are installed for the first time at Earl's Court Station. Germany sends the gunboat Panther to Agadir, creating another international crisis. The Parliament Bill is passed by the Lords, under duress, settling the constitutional crisis. Italy declares war on Turkey as it attempts to invade Tripolitania (Libya). Sun Yat-sen leads a revolution overthrowing the Manchu monarchy in China and establishing a republic, with himself as its first president. The Mexican Civil War is ended by the establishment in power of the revolutionary, Francisco Madero. Roald Amundsen becomes the first man to reach the South Pole.

1912   The *Titanic* sinks on its maiden voyage, with the loss of over 1,500 lives. It becomes the first ship to use the newly adopted SOS distress signal. Emperor Meiji (Mutsuhito) of Japan dies, and is succeeded by his son Yoshihito. The treaty of Lausanne makes peace between Italy and Turkey, and accepts Italy's conquest of Tripolitania. The first Balkan War takes place when Serbia, Montenegro and Bulgaria declare war on Turkey, whose remaining European possessions are overrun.

1913   Greece joins the anti-Turkish alliance in the Balkans. George I of Greece is assassinated; his son Constantine I succeeds him. The great powers force the treaty of London on the combatants, which leaves none of them satisfied. Suffragette Emily Davison throws herself under the king's horse at the Derby. A Second Balkan War, precipitated by Bulgaria, erupts, with Serbia, Greece, Russia and Turkey against the country; this war is resolved by the treaty of Bucharest but tensions still simmer.

1914   Archduke Franz Ferdinand of Austria is assassinated by a Serb extremist in Sarajevo. Austria seeks to punish Serbia, but merely succeeds in dragging most of Europe into World War I. The British Expeditionary Force lands to support the French. Russia invades Germany, but is repulsed at Tannenberg and defeated at the Masurian Lakes. Germany invades Belgium and France, but is held at the Marne. The First battle of Ypres is a bloody draw and the trench system of warfare emerges on the Western Front. The British fleet is defeated by the Germans at Coronel but victorious at the Falkland Islands. Ireland is pushed to the brink of civil war over Home Rule, but the onset of war diverts attention away from the crisis. The Panama Canal opens.

1915   Germany uses poison gas for the first time at the Second battle of Ypres. The British attempt to surprise Turkey at Gallipoli, but are repulsed. German U-boat sinks the *Lusitania*, causing international outrage. Italy is enticed on to the Entente side in the war by the secret treaty of London and attacks Austria, but fails to advance. Edith Cavell is shot after accusations that she helped Allied soldiers escape from Brussels.

1916   The Mexican revolutionary Pancho Villa raids New Mexico. Germany and France fight a bloody draw over Verdun, which remains in French hands. Irish republicans stage the Easter Rising in Dublin, but the coup fails and the leaders are executed. American troops act as peacekeepers in the Dominican Republic. The British and German fleets fight the battle of Jutland, which proves indecisive but the German fleet withdraws to Kiel and remains there. Allied troops mount a major offensive on the Somme, which gains them some ground after 5 months of bloody battle. Emperor Franz Joseph of Austria dies, and is succeeded by his great-nephew Charles I. The Russian monk Rasputin is assassinated by a group of nobles concerned about his influence at court. Einstein publishes his general theory of relativity.

1917   The Orders of the Companions of Honour and of the British Empire are established. America, Cuba and China enter the war on the Allied side. The Allies are victorious at Arras and Passchendaele, although with much loss of life at the latter. Constantine I of Greece abdicates in favour of his son Alexander I. Mata Hari is executed as a spy. The Balfour Declaration over a Jewish homeland in Palestine is issued. Tanks are used for the first time with any effect at Cambrai. Troops mutiny in Russia; the worsening situation prompts Tsar Nicholas II to abdicate in favour of his brother Grand Duke Michael, who refuses the throne and the Tsardom collapses. A provisional government is set up, but fails to manage the war any better. Revolts against it in July are suppressed, as is Brusilov's coup attempt. However, the Bolsheviks succeed in a coup in November, forcing prime minister Kerensky to flee. Lenin is established in power.

1918   In Britain, a Representation of the People Act gives the vote to all men over 21 and all women over 30. Russia withdraws from the war by making the treaty of Brest-Litovsk with Germany; Finland, Poland and the Baltic States are given independence. A coalition of Bolshevik opponents declare war on them, starting civil war in Russia. The Bolsheviks murder the Tsar and his family. A German offensive is successful on the Western Front, but the Allies regroup and push them back, being victorious at the marne and Amiens. Ferdinand I of Bulgaria abdicates in favour of his son Boris III. The Austro-Hungarian Empire collapses; Emperor Charles I abdicates and the Empire becomes several republics. Allied forces remove the Turks from the Middle East. The Czechs declare independence under Tomas Masaryk. The German navy mutinies. Kaiser Wilhelm II abdicates; Germany becomes a republic. An armistice is signed ending action in World War I. The kingdom of Yugoslavia, under Peter I of Serbia, is proclaimed. A Spanish Influenza pandemic begins.

1919   The Eighteenth Amendment is passed, establishing Prohibition in America. The Allies convene in Paris to settle the world map after World War I; the treaties of Versailles with Germany, Saint-Germain with Austria and Neuilly with Bulgaria are imposed. The Bolsheviks establish the Third International. The League of Nations is founded. Alcock and Brown become the first men to fly the Atlantic. The German fleet is scuttled in Scapa Flow. In India, British troops kill 379 demonstrators in the Amritsar Massacre. Austria exiles the Habsburgs.

1920   Irish republicans begin guerrilla war against continued British rule. President Venustiano Carranza of Mexico is assassinated; he is succeeded by Adolfo de la Huerta. The treaties of Trianon with Hungary and Sèvres with Turkey are imposed. The International Court of Justice is established at The Hague. The Little Entente of Czechoslovakia and Yugoslavia (joined next year by Romania) is formed. King Alexander I of Greece dies; his father Constantine I resumes the throne.

1921   The first All-India parliament is opened in Delhi. Reza Khan Pahlevi organises a coup d'etat in Persia. Ex-Emperor Charles fails to regain the Hungarian throne. The Bolsheviks are victors in the Russian Civil War, but the economy is ruined, forcing Lenin to adopt the New Economic Policy. The Allied Reparations Commission levies compensation of £6,650m on Germany. Britain and Irish republicans reach an accord; Northern Ireland is granted its own parliament with Sir James Craig as prime minister. Spanish troops in Morocco are annihilated by Berber rebels, at Anual. Faisal I is elected king of Iraq after a plebiscite. Eduardo Iradier, prime minister of Spain is assassinated by an anarchist. Takashi Hara, prime minister of Japan, is assassinated.

1922   The treaties of Washington establish a Pacific status quo. The Irish Free State is established, but the IRA declares civil war against the government in Dublin and assassinates Prime Minister Michael Collins. The kingdom of Egypt is established under Fuad I. Mustafa Kemal evicts the Greeks from Smyrna. The Arabs in Palestine reject the British mandate. Constantine I of Greece abdicates again, in favour of his son George II. The Conservatives withdraw from the coalition government, bringing down Lloyd George. Bonar Law becomes prime minister. Mussolini leads the Fascists in a March on Rome and succeeds in forming a government. Mustafa Kemal proclaims Turkey a republic; Sultan Muhammad VI is deposed; his cousin Abdul-Majid II maintains the title Caliph. Howard Carter opens Tutankhamun's tomb. The BBC begins its radio broadcasts. The Union of Soviet Socialist Republics (USSR) is formed.

1923   The French occupy the Ruhr after the Germans default on reparations. Prime minister Stamboliski of Bulgaria is removed from office by a coup and shot while trying to escape. The treaty of Lausanne resolves the war between Greece and Turkey. President Warren Harding of America dies in office, and is succeeded by his laconic Vice-President Calvin Coolidge. Germany is hit by hyper-inflation. Primo de Rivera establishes a dictatorship in Spain with the approval of Alfonso XIII. Mustafa Kemal moves the Turkish capital to Ankara. Hitler mounts the 'Beer Hall Putsch'; it fails and he is imprisoned. The Greek army deposes George II.

1924   Venizelos becomes prime minister of Greece. Lenin dies; a triumvirate of Stalin, Kamenev and Zinoviev replaces him in power. After a general election produces a hung parliament, Ramsay MacDonald forms the first Labour government in Britain; he is defeated in a subsequent election, in which the Conservatives are helped by the forged Zinoviev Letter. Kemal abolishes the Caliphate and exiles the Ottomans from Turkey.

1925   Norway renames its capital Oslo and annexes Spitsbergen. Sun Yat-sen dies; Chiang Kai-shek is appointed his replacement by the Guomindang (Chinese Nationalist Party). Hindenburg is elected president of Germany. Hitler sets up the SS (Schutzstaffel) as his personal bodyguard. Reza Khan Pahlavi deposes Shah Ahmad of Persia and ascends the throne himself. The Locarno treaties are signed, guaranteeing the common borders of Belgium, France and Germany, and demilitarizing the Rhineland.

1926   Abdul-Aziz II Ibn Saud of Najd becomes king of the Hijaz. The General Strike is called in Britain, but fails to achieve much. Pilsudski stages a coup d'état in Poland. Lebanon is proclaimed a republic. Stalin forces the banishment of Trotsky and Zinoviev from Moscow as he assumes control of Russia. Emperor Yoshihito of Japan dies, and is succeeded by his son Hirohito. John Logie Baird develops television.

1927   Charles Lindbergh makes the first solo flight across the Atlantic. Trotsky is expelled from the Communist Party. Ferdinand I of Romania dies, and is succeeded by his infant nephew Michael.

1928   In Britain, all women receive the vote. The anti-war Kellogg-Briand Pact is signed. Albania becomes a kingdom under Ahmed Bey Zogu, who takes the title Zog I. The first Five Year Plan is outlined by Stalin. Chiang Kai-shek is formally elected president of China.

1929   Alexander I of Yugoslavia suppresses the constitution and proclaims a dictatorship. Italy and the Vatican make the Lateran Treaties, establishing an independent Vatican City. The St Valentine's Day Massacre of gangsters occurs in Chicago. Labour wins a general election for the first time and Ramsay MacDonald returns to office as prime minister. The Wall Street Crash leads to a collapse of share prices and the onset of severe economic depression in America.

1930   France starts work on the Maginot Line of defences. Primo de Rivera resigns office through ill health and dies soon after. Brüning forms a right-wing coalition government in Germany. Haile Selassie becomes king of Abyssinia. Carol II of Romania replaces his young son Michael as King. President Leguia of Peru is forced from office by a military coup. José Uriburu leads a military coup in Argentina. The R101 airship crashes and burns. Getulio Vargas leads a revolution in Brazil and is named President. The Youth Hostels Association is founded.

1931   Oswald Mosley leaves the Labour Party and forms the short-lived New Party. Alfonso XIII of Spain abdicates and leaves the country. The Credit-Anstalt bank of Austria collapses, creating a financial crisis in central Europe. The Invergordon mutiny over pay cuts occurs. Japan occupies Manchuria. MacDonald forms a National Government to deal with the deteriorating economic situation, but the Labour Party mostly splits from him. The Statute of Westminster defines dominion statutes and creates the Commonwealth.

1932   Gandhi is arrested after the Indian National Congress is declared illegal. President Doumer of France is assassinated by a Russian émigré. The Nazis win the German general election, but refuse to serve under President Hindenburg's nominee as Chancellor, Von Papen, who is later forced to resign. Iraq ceases to be a British mandate. Mosley founds the British Union of Fascists. Franklin D Roosevelt defeats President Hoover in a landslide victory in the American presidential elections.

1933   Hitler is appointed German Chancellor. Prohibition is abolished in America. The Reichstag, Germany's parliament, building burns down; Communists are blamed. Chancellor Dollfuss of Austria rules by decree, provoking riots from Austrian Nazis. The first German concentration camps are opened. Hitler takes dictatorial powers; systematic persecution of Jews begins; the Gestapo is founded. Nadir Shah of Afghanistan is assassinated, succeeded by his son Muhammad Zahir Shah.

1934   Hitler purges the Nazi party in the 'Night of the Long Knives'. Austrian Nazis assassinate Dollfuss in a failed putsch; Schuschnigg becomes chancellor. Hitler becomes German president on the death of Hindenburg. The USSR joins the League of Nations. King Alexander of Yugoslavia is assassinated together with the French foreign minister, Louis Barthou, at Marseille by a Croat revolutionary based in Hungary; he is succeeded by his son Peter II. Mao Zedong leads the Chinese Communists on the Long March. Sergei Kirov is assassinated in Leningrad, giving Stalin a pretext to purge the Russian Communists of his opponents.

1935   The Saar is returned to Germany after a plebiscite; Hitler repudiates the Versailles treaty and passes the Nuremberg decrees against Jews. Persia is renamed Iran by order of the Shah. Alcoholics Anonymous is established. Japan withdraws from the League of Nations. Italy invades Abyssinia; the League of Nations imposes sanctions against Italy but the Anglo-French Hoare–Laval plan proposes partial acquiescence in the conquest. George II of Greece returns to his throne. The US creates the Commonwealth of the Philippines, a step towards Filipino independence.

1936 George V dies, his son Edward VIII succeeds him but abdicates in favour of his brother George VI after falling in love with Wallis Simpson. The Japanese army attempts a coup, but fails. Germany reoccupies the Rhineland. King Fuad of Egypt dies, and is succeeded by his son Farouk. Italy completes its conquest of Abyssinia. Spanish generals, led by Franco, revolt against the Republican government; this leads to civil war. Television broadcasts start in Britain.

1937 Guernica is destroyed by aircraft of the German Condor Legion assisting Franco's rebels. The Peel Commission on Palestine proposes partition into Arab and Jewish states with a British mandate for Jerusalem and Bethlehem. Amelia Earhart disappears on a Pacific flight. Japan invades China, surprising the Chinese at the Marco Polo Bridge and capturing Beijing, Nanjing, Tianjin and Shanghai; the Chinese government moves to Chongqing. The legitimate Spanish government moves to Barcelona. Italy withdraws from the League of Nations.

1938 Austria is forced to unite with Germany (the Anschluss). Continuing his Great Purge of all potential opposition, Stalin tries and executes former colleagues including Buthasin, Rykor and Yagoda. The Sudeten Germans demand secession from Czechoslovakia; Britain and France appease Hitler at Munich and allow this, to much public disgust. Britain drops the Peel proposals on Palestine, prompting terrorist attacks in the area. Hungary annexes southern Slovakia. The anti-Jewish Kristallnacht takes place in Germany. Kemal Ataturk dies, and is succeeded as Turkish president by Ismet Inonu.

1939 Germany occupies the rump Czech lands and places Slovakia under protection. Franco's insurgents capture Madrid and are victorious in the Spanish Civil War. Italy invades Albania. Hungary and Spain quit the League of Nations. Germany and Russia conclude a non-aggression pact and carve up Poland between themselves. Poland is invaded by the two countries; Britain and France, who have pledged to guarantee Poland, declare war on Germany as a result. A German u-Boat sinks HMS *Royal Oak* in Scapa Flow. Russia invades Finland and the Baltic States and is expelled from the League of Nations. The *Graf Spee* is scuttled after losing the battle of the River Plate.

1940 Finland and Russia make peace. Germany invades Norway, Denmark, Benelux and France. Churchill replaces Chamberlain as prime minister. Allied troops are evacuated at Dunkirk. Italy declares war on Britain and France. The puppet Vichy France is established. The British destroy the French fleet at Mers-el-Kebir to prevent it falling into Vichy hands. The Home Guard is founded. A German aerial assault on Britain is repulsed (the Battle of Britain). Trotsky is assassinated in Mexico, possibly on Stalin's orders. Germany, Italy and Japan form the 'Axis'.

1941 British troops help the Abyssinians expel the Italians; Haile Selassie is restored to his throne. The pro-Nazi Regent Paul of Yugoslavia is deposed; Germany invades the country. Reich Marshal Hermann Göring instructs Reinhard Heydrich, deputy chief of the SS, 'to carry out the final solution of the Jewish question'. Iran is invaded by Britain and Russia; Reza Shah abdicates in favour of his pro-Allied son Muhammad Reza. Mass deportations begin to death camps such as Auschwitz, Chelmno and Treblinka. Japan bombs Pearl Harbor and invades the Philippines; America thereby enters the war. Hong Kong falls to the Japanese.

1942 The Japanese take the Philippines, Dutch East Indies, Singapore and Burma, but lose the naval battles of the Coral Sea and Midway to the Americans. Two Czech resistance men sent from Britain assassinate Reinhard Heydrich; the Nazis burn Lidice as revenge. Rommel, after taking Tobruk, is defeated at El Alamein and forced to retreat across North Africa. The battle of Stalingrad begins.

1943 Churchill, Roosevelt and De Gaulle meet at Casablanca. The Germans surrender at Stalingrad and are driven back West. Guadal canal falls to the US. Allied aircraft destroy a Japanese convoy at the Bismarck Sea. The Warsaw Ghetto is attacked by the Germans, falls after a siege, and survivors are deported to concentration camps. The Allies drive the Germans from North Africa and cross into Sicily and Italy. The Soviets score a major victory at Kursk in the largest-ever tank battle. Mussolini is forced to resign and Badoglio replaces him. Italy signs an armistice with the Allies, but the Germans keep up the fight in the country. Churchill, Stalin and Roosevelt meet at Tehran.

1944 The Allies land at Anzio and take Rome. Leningrad is relieved by the Russians. The Solomon and Marshall Islands fall to the Americans, who defeat the Japanese at the Philippine Sea. The D-Day landings provide the springboard for the reconquest of France. Iceland gains independence from Denmark. Warsaw rises against the Germans. Guam falls to the Americans. The Russians enter Romania, Czechoslovakia, Bulgaria and Hungary. Stauffenberg leads a failed attempt on Hitler's life; Rommel is implicated and forced to commit suicide. The Germans fight back at the battle of the Bulge. North Burma is retaken by the British.

1945 The Allies enter Germany. The Americans take the Philippines and Okinawa. The League of Arab States is founded. FD Roosevelt dies, and is succeeded as American president by Truman. Mussolini is killed by partisans. Hitler commits suicide. Burma is recaptured by the British. Germany surrenders to the Allies. Churchill, Truman and Stalin meet at Potsdam to consider the future. Attlee replaces Churchill after a Labour landslide at the general election. America drops atomic bombs on Hiroshima and Nagasaki and Japan surrenders. Ho Chi Minh declares Vietnam an independent republic. The United Nations is founded. The Nuremberg trials commence. Peter II of Yugoslavia is deposed by the Communists.

1946 The United Nations convenes in London, as the League of Nations is formally wound up. Jewish terrorism recommences in Palestine. Juan Perón becomes president of Argentina. Mao Zedong proclaims war against the Guomindang regime in China. Victor Emmanuel III of Italy abdicates in favour of his son Umberto II, who is exiled when a referendum votes to abolish the monarchy. Transjordan becomes an independent state under King Abdullah. Bulgaria votes to abolish its monarchy and becomes a communist state. The Fourth Republic is established in France.

1947 The Dead Sea Scrolls are discovered. Mount Hekla erupts in Iceland. The Palestine question is passed to the United Nations for resolution after British partition proposals are rejected there. United Nations partition proposals are rejected by the Arabs. George II of Greece dies, and is succeeded by his brother Paul I. India, Pakistan and Burma become independent states. Michael of Romania is forced to abdicate by the communists.

HISTORY

1948   Gandhi is assassinated by a Hindu fundamentalist. The communists mount a coup in Czechoslovakia. The British leave Palestine once their mandate expires; Ben Gurion proclaims the state of Israel, which is immediately attacked by its Arab neighbours but fights them off. The Russians blockade West Berlin; the Allies respond by an airlift. Apartheid laws are passed in South Africa. Wilhelmina of Holland abdicates in favour of her daughter Juliana. Nehru sends Indian troops to force Hyderabad to join India, and the Nizam gives way under force.

1949   NATO is created. The Republic of Ireland is proclaimed. The Council of Europe is created. West and East Germany are created. Transjordan is renamed Jordan. The Chinese communists drive the Guomindang from China; it takes refuge on Formosa. Mao Zedong becomes the head of state of China. Indonesia is granted independence; Sukarno is elected president.

1950   North Korea invades South Korea, but the United Nations sends troops to defend it; when North Korea is forced to withdraw, China sends troops to assist it. Leopold III of Belgium returns from exile, but decides to abdicate after protests against him. China invades Tibet.

1951   MacArthur is replaced as UN commander in Korea, as the war develops into stalemate. The spies Burgess and Maclean flee to Moscow. King Abdullah of Jordan is assassinated, and is succeeded by his son Talal. Japan is granted independence after military occupation. A general election makes Churchill prime minister again.

1952   George VI dies, and is succeeded by his daughter Elizabeth II. Kenyatta heads the Mau Mau resistance to drive the British from Kenya. General Naguib leads a coup in Egypt; King Farouk is forced to abdicate in favour of his infant son Fa'ad II. King Talal of Jordan is deposed after being declared unfit to rule and is succeeded by his son Hussein. Britain produces an atomic bomb. America develops the H-bomb.

1953   Stalin dies; Malenkov succeeds to his posts; Khrushchev is appointed First Secretary. Hillary and Tensing achieve the first successful ascent of Mount Everest. A republic is proclaimed in Egypt and Naguib is granted dictatorial powers. The combatants in the Korean War sign an armistice at Panmunjon, ending the active war. The Federation of Rhodesia and Nyasaland is established.

1954   The Vietnamese communists defeat the French at Dien Bien Phu and occupy Hanoi. Alfredo Stroessner is elected president of Paraguay on the death of President Lopez. Vietnam is split into two at a conference in Geneva. SEATO is established. Rebellion breaks out in French Algeria. Colonel Nasser seizes power in Egypt from General Naguib. Laos gains independence from France.

1955   Malenkov resigns in Russia, and is replaced by Bulganin. Churchill resigns as prime minister, and is replaced by Eden. The Warsaw Pact is established as a communist counterweight to NATO. Austrian independence is restored by the Vienna Treaty. Juan Perón is ousted by a military coup in Argentina.

1956   The first Eurovision Song Contest is won by Switzerland. Sudan and Tunisia become independent republics. Morocco becomes an independent kingdom. Archbishop Makarios and Cypriot Enosis (union with Greece) agitators are deported to the Seychelles. Nasser nationalizes the Suez Canal. Imre Nagy is returned to power in Hungary after demonstrations, but proves too independent for Russia. Israel invades the Sinai, encouraged by Britain and France, who send troops to the Suez Canal to 'protect' it. Under international pressure, they withdraw when UN forces arrive. Russian troops are sent to Hungary; Nagy is seized and executed.

1957   Eden resigns as prime minister after the Suez fiasco, and is succeeded by Harold Macmillan. Ghana is granted independence. The European Economic Community is established by the treaty of Rome. Russia launches Sputnik I, the first space satellite. Mao Zedong decrees the disastrous Great Leap Forward in Chinese agriculture and rural industry.

1958   Egypt and Sudan unite as the United Arab Republic under Nasser. Khrushchev ousts Bulganin as Chairman of the Council of Ministers in Russia and has effective control of the government. The Fourth Republic in France collapses through the ramifications of the Algerian crisis; De Gaulle forms a government, establishes the Fifth Republic and is elected president. General Kassem stages a coup in Iraq, assassinating King Faisal, his son and the premier and taking power.

1959   Fidel Castro ousts President Batista from Cuba and creates a communist state there. The Dalai Lama is forced to flee Tibet as China represses the indigenous population. Mao Zedong resigns as China's head of state in favour of Liu Shaoqi, but remains in power as chairman of the communists. Singapore gains independence under prime minister Lee Kuan Yew. Cyprus is granted independence; Archbishop Makarios is elected president.

1960   The South African police fire on a protest in Sharpeville, killing 69. Gary Powers is shot down over Russia, causing US/Russian tension. Belgium grants independence to the Congo. Mrs Bandaranaike becomes prime minister in Ceylon, the first woman anywhere to hold such a post.

1961   Yuri Gagarin is launched into space in *Vostok 1*. Cuban rebels, assisted by America, land at the Bay of Pigs, but are repulsed by the Cuban army. South Africa leaves the Commonwealth. The Berlin Wall is constructed. UN Secretary-General Dag Hammarskjöld is killed in a plane crash in the Congo; U Thant is elected as his successor.

1962   Algeria is granted independence by France. Former SS administrator Adolf Eichmann is hanged by Israel for war crimes. Russia attempts to send arms to Cuba and establish a missile base there; President Kennedy blockades the island and forces Khrushchev to withdraw; for a few days the spectre of nuclear war looms large.

1963   Kim Philby flees to Moscow after his espionage activities are uncovered. The Profumo crisis develops in Britain, weakening Macmillan's government. Doctor Beeching's report initiates harsh cuts in the British railway system. The nuclear submarine USS *Thresher* sinks. A nuclear test ban treaty is signed by the US, USSR and Britain. Martin Luther King makes his 'I have a dream' speech. Macmillan resigns through ill health, and is replaced by Alec Douglas-Home. A military coup succeeds in South Vietnam. President Kennedy is assassinated; his assumed killer Lee Harvey Oswald is shot dead days later by Jack Ruby.

1964   Fighting breaks out in Cyprus between the Greek and Turkish communities; Greece refuses direct talks while the UN sends peacekeeping troops. King Paul of Greece dies, and is succeeded by his son Constantine II. Ian Smith becomes prime minister of Southern Rhodesia. Nelson Mandela, found guilty in the Rivonia treason trial, is sentenced to life imprisonment. Nyasaland gains independence as Malawi.

America escalates operations against North Vietnam. Malta gains independence. Khrushchev is ousted from power in the USSR; Brezhnev and Kosygin take over. Northern Rhodesia becomes independent as Zambia.

1965 Nicolae Ceausescu becomes premier of Romania. In reprisals after a failed communist coup, the Indonesian army kills half a million people. Rhodesia declares independence from Britain; sanctions are imposed on it as an illegal state. General Mobutu takes power in the Belgian Congo in a coup.

1966 Mrs Gandhi becomes prime minister of India. France withdraws from NATO. England win the football World Cup, defeating West Germany 4–2. South African prime minister Hendrik Verwoerd is assassinated, replaced by Vorster. Harold Wilson and Ian Smith discuss the Rhodesia affair on HMS *Tiger*, but the talks come to nothing.

1967 A military coup in Greece removes Constantine II from the throne; he is forced to flee as a counter-coup fails. Arab nations invade Israel, but Israel forces them back and captures Sinai, the West Bank and the Golan Heights in the Six Days War. Colour television begins in Britain. Jerusalem is proclaimed a united city under Israeli rule. General de Gaulle encourages the secession of Quebec whilst on a visit there, causing a diplomatic storm. Che Guevara is captured and shot in Bolivia. South Yemen gains independence.

1968 The communists begin the Tet Offensive in Vietnam. America commits the My Lai Massacre. Martin Luther King and Robert Kennedy are assassinated. Alexander Dubcek comes to power in Czechoslovakia, but his liberalization policies are unpopular in Russia, which sends in troops to re-establish a government more to its liking. Dubcek is arrested. Student riots in Paris destabilise the government, but de Gaulle uses his personal authority to reestablish effective government.

1969 Yasser Arafat is elected chairman of the PLO. General de Gaulle resigns as President of France, and is replaced by Georges Pompidou. America begins to withdraw troops from Vietnam. America lands men on the moon. Civil unrest in Northern Ireland spills over into fighting and terrorism; troops are sent to maintain order. Colonel Gaddafi deposes King Idris of Libya and assumes power.

1970 The Nigerian civil war ends with the capitulation of Biafra. Brazil win the football World Cup with the best team ever according to the popular press. The Portuguese dictator Salazar dies, and is succeeded as premier by Marcello Caetano. King Hussein of Jordan and Pope Paul VI survive assassination attempts. Salvador Allende is elected President of Chile. President Nasser of Egypt dies, and is succeeded by Anwar Sadat. The Japanese novelist Yukio Mishima commits suicide after failing to launch a military coup to purge the disgrace of defeat in 1945.

1971 Idi Amin seizes power in Uganda. The Vietnam war spreads into Laos and Cambodia. Decimal coinage is introduced in Britain. President François Duvalier of Haiti dies, and is succeeded by his son Jean-Claude (Baby Doc). Internment is introduced in Northern Ireland. The Congo is renamed Zaïre by President Mobutu. East Pakistan gains independence as Bangladesh.

1972 The Bloody Sunday shootings take place in Londonderry. President Nixon's visit to China initiates US-Chinese détente. Direct rule is imposed in Northern Ireland. Ceylon becomes the republic of Sri Lanka. The Democratic headquarters in the Watergate building, Washington are burgled; President Nixon is implicated, but is re-elected for a 2nd term. Palestinian terrorists seize and kill Israeli athletes at the Munich Olympics. Idi Amin expels Asians from Uganda.

1973 Britain, Ireland and Denmark join the EEC. A ceasefire is proclaimed in the Vietnam War, but fighting still continues in the area. The Cod War between Britain and Iceland develops. General Pinochet ousts President Allende of Chile in a violent coup, in which Allende perishes. Egypt and Syria attack Israel in the Yom Kippur War, but Israel repulses them. Vice-President Spiro Agnew of America resigns over income tax evasion; Gerald Ford replaces him. Arab oil producers embargo shipments to the West, which supports Israel in the war, causing an energy crisis. A coal strike in Britain forces the government to declare a three-day working week.

1974 After a coup In Portugal, Portuguese Guinea gains independence as Guinea-Bissau. Chancellor Willy Brandt of West Germany resigns when one of his aides is unmasked as an East German spy. Cypriot rebels overthrow Archbishop Makarios; Turkish forces invade Cyprus and occupy much of the north. The military junta in Greece resigns and a civilian government under Karamanlis is restored. President Nixon is forced to resign as a result of the Watergate affair; Gerald Ford replaces him and grants a pardon.

1975 North Vietnam overruns South Vietnam; America withdraws and Vietnam is reunited under a communist leadership. Portugal grants independence to Angola and Mozambique. Eritrean secessionists begin a guerrilla war in Ethiopia. King Faisal of Saudi Arabia is assassinated by his nephew Prince Faisal, who is beheaded for murder; the King's brother Khalid succeeds him. Chiang Kai-Shek dies, and is succeeded as President of Taiwan by Yan Jiangan. The Khmer Rouge declare Year Zero in Cambodia and embark on a programme of mass executions. General Franco dies; the country reverts to a monarchy under Juan Carlos I, grandson of Alfonso XIII.

1976 Chou En-lai and Mao Zedong die in China; the 'Gang of Four' attempt to take over but are arrested. Spain withdraws from Spanish Sahara, which is promptly seized by Morocco; Mauritania also takes a portion. Concorde enters regular passenger service. Harold Wilson resigns as prime minister and is succeeded by James Callaghan. Palestinian terrorists hijack an Air France plance, but Israeli commandos storm it at Entebbe.

1977 President Bante of Ethiopia and 10 aides are killed in a gun battle in a council meeting in Addis Ababa; Colonel Mengistu fills the void. Two Boeing 747s collide on the runway at Tenerife; 577 die. Deng Xiaoping assumes power in China. President Sadat of Egypt visits Israel. Jean Bedel Bokassa crowns himself Emperor of the Central African Empire (Republic) in an extravagant ceremony.

1978 Secessionist rebels, backed by Angola, Cuba and Russia, invade Katanga in Zaïre, but are repulsed with American help. Red Brigade terrorists abduct and kill former Italian premier Aldo Moro. Communists seize control in South Yemen, and assassinate the President of North Yemen. Pope Paul VI dies, as does his successor John Paul I after 33 days; Karol Wojtyla is elected the first non-Italian Pope for 455 years and takes the name John Paul II. The first transatlantic balloon crossing is made. In Nicaragua the Sandinista guerrillas begin a campaign of violence against President Somoza. Israel and Egypt sign the Camp David accords. The Shah of Iran imposes martial law to curb dissent.

1979   The Khmer Rouge are overthrown in Cambodia. The Shah of Iran flees to Egypt and an Islamic fundamentalist regime under Ayatollah Khomeini is established; when the seriously ill Shah is allowed into America, extremists seize the American embassy in Tehran. Former prime minister Bhutto of Pakistan is hanged by the regime of General Zia. Margaret Thatcher comes to power in Britain. Saddam Hussein comes to power in Iraq, replacing Hassan al-Bakr. The Sandinistas overthrow Somoza and establish a junta in Nicaragua. Lord Mountbatten is assassinated by the IRA. Emperor Bokassa is deposed and the Central African Republic restored. Soviet troops enter Afghanistan, supposedly at the request of the government there, igniting civil war.

1980   Zimbabwe gains independence; Robert Mugabe comes to power. Queen Juliana of Holland abdicates in favour of her daughter Beatrix. President Tito of Yugoslavia dies, leaving a power vacuum. The SAS retake the Iranian Embassy, which had been taken by opponents of the Islamic regime. Mount St Helens erupts. The Moscow Olympic Games are boycotted by America and other countries in protest over Afghanistan. Solidarity is formed by shipyard workers in Gdansk. Iran and Iraq go to war.

1981   Ronald Reagan becomes US president. Iran releases the American Embassy hostages. The Space Shuttle makes its maiden space flight. Pope John Paul II is wounded in an assassination attempt in Rome by an extremist Turk. Several attacks on Iranian government officials leave many of the government dead, but it survives. President Sadat of Egypt is assassinated by extremists; Hosni Mubarak replaces him. Jerry Rawlings takes power in Ghana after a coup.

1982   Argentina invades the Falklands, but Britain sends a task force and retakes them; the military junta in Argentina falls as a result of this defeat. Israel withdraws from Sinai, but becomes enmeshed in Lebanon by trying to subdue the PLO's activities there. The Lebanese President Bashir Gemayel is assassinated; his brother Amin succeeds him. Leonid Brezhnev dies; Yuri Andropov replaces him as Soviet leader.

1983   Benigno Aquino is killed on returning to the Philippines in a government conspiracy to muzzle opposition. The Soviets shoot down a Boeing 747 that had strayed into Soviet airspace off Sakhalin. A coup in Grenada leaves prime minister Maurice Bishop and most of his cabinet dead; America sends troops in to restore order, to some anger in Britain.

1984   Yuri Andropov dies; Konstantin Chernenko replaces him as Soviet leader. Sikh extremists occupy the Golden Temple at Amritsar; over 200 die when Mrs Gandhi sends troops in to clear them. York Minster catches fire shortly after the modernist David Jenkins is enthroned as bishop of Durham. Britain agrees to hand Hong Kong back to China in 1997 on the expiration of the lease on the New Territories. Sikhs in revenge organise the assassination of Mrs Gandhi; her son Rajiv succeeds her as prime minister.

1985   Uruguay returns to civilian rule under President Sanguinetti. Chernenko dies; Mikhail Gorbachev succeeds him as Soviet leader and undertakes policies of openness (Glasnost) and reform (Perestroika). Brazil returns to civilian rule under President José Sarney. Enver Hoxha dies, and is succeeded by Ramiz Alia as President of Albania. A military coup removes Milton Obote from power in Uganda. The army, under General Babangida, takes power in Nigeria. The cruise liner *Achille Lauro* is hijacked by Palestinian guerrillas.

1986   All 7 crew die when the space shuttle *Challenger* explodes shortly after take-off. President Jean-Claude Duvalier of Haiti resigns and flees to Paris after revolts against his regime. The government of President Marcos of the Philippines falls; Cory Aquino is elected his successor. Prime minister Olof Palme of Sweden is mysteriously assassinated. America bombs Libya in reprisal for Libyan-sponsored terrorist actions. The nuclear power station in Chernobyl, Ukraine, suffers meltdown and explodes. The London Stock Exchange is computerised in the 'big bang'.

1987   Terry Waite is taken hostage in Lebanon whilst seeking to free others. *The Herald of Free Enterprise* capsizes outside Zeebrugge. A great storm crosses southern England, causing much damage. Boris Yeltsin is dismissed in Moscow for complaining at the slow pace of reform. An escalator catches fire at King's Cross; 31 die in the ensuing conflagration. America and Russia sign a nuclear weapons reduction treaty.

1988   The USSR begins withdrawal from Afghanistan. Iran and Iraq end their 8-year war. Iraq gasses dissident Kurds. General Zia of Pakistan is killed in a plane crash. Benazir Bhutto is subsequently elected prime minister of Pakistan. A terrorist bomb brings down a Pan-Am 747 over Lockerbie. USS *Vincennes* mistakenly shoots down an Iranian Airbus.

1989   Emperor Hirohito of Japan dies, and is succeeded by his son, Akihito. Alfredo Stroessner, dictator of Paraguay, is overthrown. General Noriega is defeated in the Panama general elections but ignores the result, causing the Americans to send in troops to remove him. Ayatollah Khomeini dies and Hojatolislam Rafsanjani becomes president of Iran. Communist governments collapse in Poland, Hungary, Czechoslovakia and Romania. The Berlin Wall comes down. President Ceausescu is executed in Romania.

1990   Nelson Mandela is released from prison. Lithuania secedes from the USSR, which sends troops in an attempt to bring it to heel. East and West Germany are reunited. Iraq invades and annexes Kuwait. Sanctions are imposed by the UN, which sends troops to expel Iraq. The premiership of Mrs Thatcher collapses; John Major is elected to replace her.

1991   Somali rebels overthrow President Barre. The UN force expels Iraq from Kuwait, but leaves Saddam Hussein in power in Iraq. Rajiv Gandhi is assassinated by Tamil extremists while campaigning in the Indian general election. Croatia and Slovenia declare independence from Yugoslavia; Serbs and Croats begin a series of ethnic wars. Hard-line Communists attempt to overthrow President Gorbachev, but fail, and communism in Russia collapses. The Baltic states are granted independence. Gorbachev resigns as Russian president and Boris Yeltsin is elected his successor. The USSR dissolves into its constituent parts.

1992   Algerian general elections are declared void when Islamic fundamentalists win; the latter begin a terrorist campaign. The sovereignty of Bosnia-Herzegovina is recognised by the EC and US, but Bosnian Serbs declare independence under Radovan Karadzic, and a vicious civil war develops; 'ethnic cleansing' kills thousands of Albanians and displaces hundreds of thousands. Hindu militants destroy the mosque at Ayodhya.

1993   Czechoslovakia splits into the Czech Republic and Slovakia. Israel and the PLO sign a peace accord. Cultists led by David Koresh kill American government officials at Waco and commit suicide after being besieged. President Premadasa of Sri Lanka is killed by a Tamil terrorist. The Russian communists rebel against President Yeltsin, but the revolt is quelled.

1994   Nelson Mandela is elected President of South Africa. The US invades Haiti. Jordan and Israel sign a peace treaty. Russia invades Chechnya.

1995   The World Trade Organization is founded. The Russians take the Chechen capital, Grozny; resistance continues elsewhere, but peace is agreed. Prime minister Yitzhak Rabin of Israel is assassinated by a Jewish fanatic; Shimon Peres succeeds him.

1996   Yasser Arafat is elected first president of Palestine. Benjamin Netanyahu defeats Shimon Peres in the Israeli general election; his hardline policies set back the peace process.

1997   Deng Xiaoping dies; Jiang Zemin takes power in China. Hong Kong is passed to China. Diana, Princess of Wales, is killed in a car crash. Labour wins a landslide victory in the general election; Tony Blair becomes prime minister. President Mobutu is overthrown in Zaïre, which the new government renames the Democratic Republic of Congo. The treaty of Amsterdam, providing for further European integration, is signed. Mother Teresa of Calcutta dies in her adopted city, aged 87. Jenny Shipley is sworn in as New Zealand's first woman prime minister.

1998   Frank Sinatra dies following a long illness. Frenchman Benoit Lecomte becomes the first man to swim the Atlantic; his 3,716-mile swim from Cape Cod to Quiberon, takes 72 days. Gerhard Schröder, the Social Democrat leader, replaces Christian Democrat leader Helmut Kohl as German Chancellor.

1999   Bill Clinton was impeached but cleared of high crimes and misdemeanours. The Australian people voted to 're-elect' the Queen as their Head of State. Cardinal Basil Hume, Archbishop of Westminster died.

2000   General Augusto Pinochet, who was to stand trial in Britain for human rights violations, was allowed home to Santiago, Chile, following medical opinion that he was not fit enough to face the ordeal. Pope John-Paul II made an historic visit to the Holy Land and began it by standing on Mount Nebo in Jordan, the peak from where Moses is said to have seen the Promised Land. The Right Reverend Lord (Donald) Coggan, Archbishop of Canterbury, 1974–80, died.

NB. The chronology above is a brief cross-section of British and world events of the last two thousand years. Some of the data will inevitably be duplicated in other sections but it is useful to be reminded of the order of events relative to other happenings of the day.

In a book that endeavours to seek the truth it seems incongruous to chronicle prehistorical events which by definition must be open to some doubt, even with all the latest DNA and radiocarbon dating techniques. The approach adopted is to give a brief overview of the order of events that are likely to be of interest to the reader and to chronicle other events, although still open to interpretation, of a more definite nature.

Every schoolchild learns to classify prehistory into Stone Age, Bronze Age and Iron Age but it is very difficult to be pedantic and say when one age started and another ended. In fact, of course the Stone and Bronze ages never really ended anyway. The Paleolithic Period or Old Stone Age is deemed to have commenced over two million years ago with evidence of the use of rudimentary chipped stone tools, probably by a distant relative of modern man. Fossil remains of this precursor of *Homo sapiens* were found at Olduvai Gorge, Tanzania, in 1964 and variously assigned the names *Homo habilis*, *Australopithecus africanus*, or *Australopithecus robustus*, although the latter two names are often applied to an even older relative of modern man thought to have existed millions of years earlier. Fossil remains of Peking Man and Java Man suggested another forerunner of modern man, *Homo erectus*, dated from over a million years ago until 300,000 years ago. From about 300,000 BC other species of early man evolved and were given the general name of *Homo sapiens*. In 1856 the remains of a species of *Homo sapiens* was discovered in the Neander Valley in Germany and dated between 200,000 BC and 30,000 BC. The species of *Homo sapiens* that archaeologists and prehistorians call 'Modern Man' appears to date from circa 38,000 BC. The period from the identification of 'Modern Man' to the end of the Old Stone Age was characterised by the production of Paleolithic cave drawings, the oldest of which, the Chauvet paintings of southeast France, were discovered in 1994 and dated circa 29,000 BC, making them circa 15,000 years older than the Lascaux paintings, Dordogne. This period also saw the beginning of organised tool-making industries beginning with the Aurignacian Culture and developing via the Gravettian (Périgordian), Solutrean, and Magdalenian Cultures to the Azilian industry which specialised in microlith tools for catching fish, birds and small mammals as the big game of the last ice age disappeared.

The next classification of prehistory is the Neolithic Period or New Stone Age, characterised by stone tools shaped by polishing or grinding. This period of our history corresponds to the geological Holocene Epoch circa 8,000 BC, the most recent interval of the Earth's geological history. This period also corresponds to the end of the last ice age. In circa 10,400 BC a major climatic warming occurred, the Bolling interstadial, which lasted for approximately 400 years and this was followed by the Allerod interstadial between circa 9,800 BC and circa 9,000 BC. This intermittent global warming became constant in circa 8,000 BC and can be classified as the end of the last ice age, which began around the same time as the emergence of 'Modern Man', and the beginning of the New Stone Age. The first free-standing stone buildings were built during the Neolithic Period, the oldest of which is Cgantija, a temple on the edge of the Xaghra plateau in the middle of the Maltese island of Gozo, circa 3,600 BC. The most recent archaeological find attributed to the Neolithic Period was the ice-man 'Otzi', discovered in the Otzal Alps on the Austrian–Italian border at an altitude of 3,210 metres, in 1991. Modern technology has established 'Otzi's size, looks, apparel and enabled a reconstruction in the Museum of Archaeology in Bolzano, Italy, the country that claimed him. The consensus opinion is that 'Otzi' lived circa 3,300 BC. It is very difficult to approximate the beginning of the Bronze Age as there was a long period of quasi-copper-based tools being produced. This period is referred to as the Chalcolithic (Copper-Stone) Age and even this period was precursed by the use of pure copper in Anatolia by 6,500 BC. The speculative classification of a Bronze Age perhaps can be dated to circa 3,000 BC, when it is established that the Greeks first added tin to copper, although this practice only became widespread a thousand years later. The last technological and cultural period in our classification is the Iron Age, which once again is very difficult to give a definite date of identification as there was a long period of overlapping with the Bronze Age. There is evidence of sparse use of iron in the Middle East as early as 3,000 BC, but it did not replace bronze as a superior metal until circa 1,200 BC.

5508	The year of creation as adopted in Constantinople in 7th century and used by the Eastern Orthodox Church for 1,000 years.
5490	The year of creation as calculated by early Christians in Syria.
4004	James Ussher's 17th-century postulate as being the date of the creation of the universe.
3150	Egypt is united under Menes, the first king of the First Dynasty, and the first prehistoric human whose name we know. Sumerians invent a primitive writing system.
3100	Stonehenge is laid out.
3000	Egyptians pioneer the use of hieroglyphs.
2650	Pyramid of Zoser at Saqqara is built by Imhotep.
2566	The Great Pyramid of Khufu (aka Cheops), at Giza, is built and stands 480 feet high.
2500	A mysterious cult of 'Beaker folk' spreads throughout Europe, warriors being buried with their ornate cups.
2100	In Mesopotamia the first code of law is devised by Ur-Nammu and his son, Shulgi.
1700	Abraham, a prince of Ur, moves to Canaan and founds a religion.
1650	Jewish religion is developed by Abraham's grandson, Jacob.
1349	The young Pharaoh, Tutankhamun, is buried at Thebes.
1237	Ramesses II of Egypt dies and is succeeded by his son Merneptah.
1198	Ramesses III rallies the Egyptians against Mediterranean invaders known as 'Sea Peoples'.
1193	King Priam's city of Troy falls to the Greeks under Agamemnon.
1025	Samuel anoints Saul as king of Hebron.
1012	Saul and his son, Jonathan, are killed at the battle of Mount Gilboa, and succeeded by David.
1005	Jerusalem falls to King David who is anointed King of Judea by Samuel.
1000	The Rig Veda (Hindu hymns) are written.
990	Absalom, 3rd son of King David, kills Amnon in revenge for the rape of his sister, Tamar, and is banished by David.
978	Absalom leads a rebellion but is killed by David's nephew, Joab.
961	David dies and is succeeded by his son, Solomon, who executes Joab for killing Absalom.
922	Solomon is succeeded by his son, Rehoboam, but 10 northern tribes establish Israel, with Jeroboam as king.
850	In Babylon an epic poem 'When on High' is dedicated to the great god, Marduk.
800	The Vedas are written.
776	The first Olympic Games are held in Olympia, Greece.
753	Rome is founded by Romulus and Remus.
750	*Iliad* and *Odyssey* become popular in Greece. Etruscans settle in Tuscany from the Middle East.
722	Israel's capital since 879 BC, the Hill of Samaria, falls to Assyrian forces.
721	The 27,000 Israelites are taken off by the Assyrians and become known as 'The Lost Tribes of Israel'.
658	Byzantium is founded by Greek colonists from Megara.
630	*The Shi Jing (Book of Songs)*, an early book of Chinese poems is written.
629	King Ashurbanipal of Assyria dies, leaving a library of over 25,000 books.
621	The Athenian lawgiver Draco issues a code of laws that makes almost every offence punishable by death.
597	Jerusalem falls to Nebuchadnezzar II, who exiles Jews in what becomes known as 'The Babylonian Captivity'.
586	The transportation of Judaeans to Babylon, known as the Babylon Exile or Captivity.
582	The first Pythian games are held.
563	Siddhartha Gautama (Buddha) is born.
550	The Temple of Artemis is built at Ephesus in Turkey.
551	Kung Fu-tse (Confucius) is born.
538	Cyrus allows the Jews to return to Jerusalem, thus ending the Babylonian Exile.
528	Buddhism is founded in India.
509	Tarquinius Superbus, King of Rome, is overthrown and Rome becomes a republic.
490	Battle of Marathon gives Athens victory over the Persians.
483	Siddhartha Gavtama (Budda) dies.
480	Battle of Thermopylae gives the Persians, under Xerxes, victory over the Spartans and Thespians, under Leonidas. Battle of Salamis gives the Greeks (400 ships) victory over the Persians (1,000 ships).
456	Aeschylus dies after writing 90 plays, of which only 7 are to survive.
356	The Temple of Artenus, built by Croesus, king of Lydia, is burned by a madman, Herostratus.
354	Mausoleum at Halicarnassus is built.
336	Alexander the Great succeeds his father on the Macedonian throne.
323	Alexander the Great dies, aged 32, in Babylon.
276	First Syrian War begins.
265	Archimedes invents his 'Archimedean Screw' for raising irrigation water.
264	The First Punic War between Rome and Carthage begins.
237	Hamilcar Barca leads a Carthaginian army in an invasion of Spain.
228	Hamilcar Barca is killed and his command in Spain passes to his son-in-law Hasdrubal.
221	Hasdrubal is assassinated and his command passes to Hannibal, the 26-year-old son of Hamilcar Barca.
220	The Flaminian Way between Rome and Rimini is completed.

218 The second Punic War begins.
217 Battle of Lake Trasimene in Umbria gives Hannibal victory over Gaius Flaminius and 16,000 Romans.
216 Battle of Cannae gives Hannibal a resounding victory over the Romans.
190 Battle of Magenta, near Smyrna, gives Rome a victory over Antiochus III of Syria.
183 Hannibal poisons himself.
160 Judas Maccabaeus is killed, his brother, Jonathan is destined to make Judaea a largely independent state.
149 Romans invade North Africa and besiege Carthage.
135 Rome's first Slave War begins.
102 Julius Caesar is born. (It is possible he was born up to 2 years later.)
83 Mark Antony is born.
73 Third Slave War breaks out under the leadership of Spartacus, a Thracian slave. Herod the Great is born.
63 Cicero, a Roman Consul, unmasks a conspiracy led by Catiline, the former governor of Africa.
60 The first Roman Triumvirate is formed by Julius Caesar, Pompey, and Crassus.
55 Julius Caesar's first invasion of Britain.
54 Julius Caesar's second invasion of Britain; Cassivellaunus agrees to pay tribute.
52 Gang warfare in Rome between supporters of Clodius and Milo results in the death of Clodius in a brawl.
49 Julius Caesar leads his legions across the Rubicon into Italy to begin the civil war.
47 Julius Caesar leads his legions across Asia Minor where he defeats Pharnaces III, King of Pontus, near Zela. announcing his victory in the dispatch 'Veni, Vidi, Vici' (I came, I saw, I conquered).
45 Julian calendar introduced by Sosigenes.
44 Julius Caesar is assassinated on the Ides of March.
43 The second Roman Triumvirate is formed by Octavian, Mark Antony, and Marcus Lepidus.
Cicero is beheaded on the orders of Mark Antony.
42 Brutus and Cassius are defeated at Philippi in Macedonia; Cassius orders his shield-bearer to cut his throat, while Brutus runs on to the sword of his friend, Strato.
41 Mark Antony meets Cleopatra at Tarsus and as Julius Caesar had before him, he forms an alliance.
37 Herod the Great becomes King of Judea.
31 Battle of Actium gives victory to Octavian but Cleopatra escapes to Egypt.
30 Mark Antony commits suicide and Cleopatra follows soon after; her son, Caesarion is murdered. Egypt becomes a Roman province.
27 Augustus becomes the first Roman Emperor after changing his name from Octavian.

Modern History

Agent Orange Notorious herbicide used by the US military machine in Vietnam in the 1960s and 1970s; its active ingredient 245-T was also used in weedkillers and caused devastation.

A6 Murder Michael Gregsten and Valerie Storie were shot in their car in a lay-by off the A6 between Luton and Bedford in August 1961. Storie, who survived the shooting, picked out James Hanratty at an identity parade, which led to his hanging in April 1962. Journalist Paul Foot has campaigned on behalf of Hanratty pointing out that Peter Alphon confessed to the murder.

Balfour Declaration A milestone on the way to establishing the state of Israel. Arthur Balfour, the former Conservative PM, served as foreign secretary in 1916–19, and in November 1917 wrote to Lord Rothschild, leader of the British Jewish community, to the effect that Britain favoured a national home for the Jewish people provided that it did not prejudice the civil and religious rights of existing non-Jewish communities in Palestine.

Barlow Clowes Fraudulent investment company, details of which came to light in 1988. Elizabeth Barlow disappeared but Peter Clowes was sentenced to 10 years imprisonment in 1992. The government at first refused to pay compensation, but the Ombudsman found maladministration by the Department of Trade and Industry so £150 m was provided.

Beveridge Report Report laying down the framework for the development of the Welfare State. Published in 1942 and accepted by the coalition government in 1944, it became operational in 1948.

Big Bang Transformation of the London Stock Exchange in October 1986 which reflected the advent of global stock and bond trading networks and of round-the-clock trading. It also abolished the different categories of stockbrokers and jobbers.

Birmingham Six Patrick Hill, Richard McIlkenny, John Walker, William Power, Gerard Hunter and Hugh Callaghan wrongly imprisoned for IRA activities following the bombing of 2 public houses in Birmingham in November 1974. Their convictions were quashed in the Appeal Court in March 1991.

Bloody Sunday A day of serious conflict in the Bogside area of Londonderry on 30 January 1972 when the security forces opened fire on a civil rights march, killing 13 civilians.

Blue Streak British rocket which in the 1950s was expected to provide a nuclear delivery capability independent of US technological expertise; abandoned in 1960 in favour of the US Skybolt missile.

Bridgewater Four Michael and Vincent Hickey, James Robinson and Patrick Molloy were convicted of killing newspaper delivery boy Carl Bridgewater at Yew Tree Farm in Staffordshire, largely because of a confession made by Molloy, who died in prison in 1981. The remaining 3 were released on 20 February 1997 after evidence of police corruption.

Chiltern Hundreds British MPs cannot resign directly, but they may not hold an office of profit under the crown. The solution is to apply for the stewardship of various crown sinecures, of which the Chiltern Hundreds is the best-known.

Citizens' Charter Government charter instigated by John Major in 1991 with the intention of improving standards of public services in the UK.

Cod War A series of disputes between UK and Iceland in the 1960s over fishing rights.

Cuban Missile Crisis   US hostility towards the Cuban revolution, together with Castro's open espousal of communism, had brought Cuba into a close relationship with USSR. Following the US-sponsored Bay of Pigs invasion, Castro requested Soviet atomic weaponry to improve their defences. When US reconnaissance spotted missile sites being built, President Kennedy declared a blockade, on 22 October 1961. For several days a confrontation of superpowers appeared likely, but the Russians backed off, and the blockade ended on 20 November.

Dikko Affair   UK customs found the exiled Nigerian politician Umari Dikko drugged in a crate at Stansted airport in July 1984. Three Israelis and a Nigerian diplomat concealed in another crate were charged with kidnapping and administering drugs.

Doomsday Clock   Picture of a clock, the hands of which indicate the time estimated to remain before nuclear war (midnight), which has been printed in every issue of the *Bulletin of Atomic Scientists* since its founding in 1945. It stood at 11.58 during the cold war but was put back to 11.50 in 1989.

Echo 1   First US communications satellite; a large aluminium-coated balloon that reflected radio signals. Launched on 12 August 1960 by NASA as part of the US effort to close the satellite telecommunications lead achieved by the USSR with the Sputnik.

Elgin Marbles   Sculptures from the Parthenon obtained cheaply from the occupying Turks by the British Ambassador Lord Elgin in 1801 and later sold to the British Museum. The continuing Greek campaign for their return was spearheaded by Melina Mercouri as Minister for Culture and the injustice is often highlighted by the well-known television producer and quiz show host, William G Stewart.

Fourth Estate   Term used in modern times to describe the power of the press. The Middle Ages divided society into 3 estates: nobility, church and commons.

Fourth Man   Anthony Blunt was given this epithet when revealed as a spy in 1979 following the defections to the USSR of the spies Burgess and Maclean in 1951 and Kim Philby in 1963.

Gaza Strip   A 146-sq-mile area of land bordered by the Mediterranean, Israel and Egypt, captured by Israel from Egypt during the Six-Day War of 1967 and inhabited by 700,000 people, mostly stateless Palestinians living in refugee camps.

General Strike   Staged by the TUC from 3 to 13 May 1926 in an unsuccessful attempt to support coalminers. The strike provoked retaliatory legislation against trade unions.

Geneva Summit 1985   First of a series of bilateral superpower summit meetings held in the later 1980s involving Mikhail Gorbachev and Ronald Reagan (followed by George Bush).

Golan Heights   Range of strategic hills in south-west Syria overlooking northern Israel, captured by Israel from Syria in the Six-Day War of 1967.

Gold Standard   Economic system in which a country's paper currency is supported by gold, anyone having the right to demand from the national bank the same amount of gold as the face value of a banknote. Britain was on the gold standard from 1821 to 1914, partly returned to it in 1925 as a result of Churchill's wishes, but finally abandoned it in 1931 under the chancellorship of Philip Snowden.

Great Leap Forward   Campaign undertaken by Mao Zedong between 1957 and 1960 to organise China's vast population into large-scale rural communes and local manufacturing units, to meet the country's economic problems.

Guildford Four   Patrick Armstrong, Gerard Conlon, Carole Richardson and Paul Hill were sentenced to life imprisonment in 1975 for the murder of 7 people in 1974 after the bombing of 2 public houses in Guildford and 1 in Woolwich. They were released on appeal in 1989 after police evidence was found to be misleading.

Herald of Free Enterprise   British car ferry owned by Townsend Thoresen which overturned and sank off the Belgian port of Zeebrugge on 6 March 1987 with the loss of 193 lives after the bow doors were left open.

Heysel Stadium Disaster   Death of 39 Belgian and Italian spectators on 29 May 1985 at the final of the European Cup football competition between Liverpool and Juventus in Belgium's Heysel Stadium when visiting British fans caused a wall and safety barriers to collapse.

Hiroshima   Southern Japanese city destroyed on 6 August 1945 by the first atomic bomb, nicknamed Little Boy and dropped from the US B-29 bomber *Enola Gay*.

Hiss Case   Legal case which typified US anti-communist paranoia. On 29 January 1950 Alger Hiss, accused by Whittaker Chambers of being a communist during the 1930s while working for the US State Department, was given a 5-year prison term.

Ho Chi Minh Trail   Network of concealed tracks through eastern Laos developed during the early stages of the Vietnam War as a supply route for North Vietnamese and Viet Cong forces in South Vietnam.

Holt Drowning   Disappearance and presumed death of Australian PM and Liberal Party leader Harold Holt while swimming at Portsea near Melbourne on 17 December 1967.

Human Shield   After Iraq's occupation of Kuwait in August 1990 Saddam Hussein used Western nationals captured there as a defence against possible action by the opposing coalition forces during operation Desert Shield.

100 Flowers Bloom   Political slogan adopted by Mao Zedong (Mao Tse-tung) in 1956 and launched as a movement in February 1957 to allow more free speech in Communist China. The high level of strikes that followed caused Mao to retract his original statement and suggested that the campaign was a means of identifying reactionary elements.

Hungarian Uprising   Popular uprising against Soviet domination in 1956 when after 4 days of demonstrations in Budapest, on 24 October the former communist PM, Imre Nagy, formed a revolutionary multi-party government and proclaimed Hungary's withdrawal from the Warsaw Pact. The Soviet Union crushed the uprising and Janos Kadar took over as head of a pro-Soviet regime and supervised the normalisation policy. Nagy was executed by the new government in 1958.

In Place of Strife   Document published by the Labour government of the UK on 17 January 1969 setting out its policy for controlling industrial relations through legal sanctions.

Intifada   (Arabic: 'shaking off') Palestinian mass popular uprising in the Gaza Strip and West Bank which started in December 1987 with demonstrations, strikes and violent confrontation between Palestinian youths and Israeli occupying forces. Israel responded with an iron-fist approach which included beatings and deportations.

Iranian Embassy Siege Storming of the Iranian embassy in London by the SAS after it was seized on 30 April 1980 by Iranian dissidents seeking to draw attention to the plight of the Arab minority in Iran and demanding the release of 91 of their comrades imprisoned in Khuzestan.

Iron Curtain Frontier dividing the Eastern Europe of the communist bloc from the capitalist West. Winston Churchill popularised the phrase, using it in a 1946 speech at Westminster College, Fulton, Missouri when he said: 'From Stettin in the Baltic to Trieste in the Adriatic, an iron curtain has descended across the continent'. Joseph Goebbels has been credited with inventing the term.

ITT Scandal Scandal involving the activities of International Telephone and Telegraph in the USA and overseas. The scandal broke in 1972 when a plan to nationalise the Chilean Telephone Company (Chitelco) was sabotaged; ITT's collusion with the CIA culminated in the 1973 coup which overthrew the Allende government.

JAL Air Disaster World's worst air crash involving a single aircraft: a Boeing 747 on a Japan Airlines flight from Tokyo to Osaka crashed in mountainous terrain near Tokyo on 12 August 1985 and killed 520 of the 524 passengers and crew.

Jamahiriya Term coined by Colonel Gaddafi, who in 1977 changed the name of Libya to 'Socialist People's Libyan Arab Jamahiriya'. The word means 'State of the masses'.

Jonestown Massacre Mass death of 913 children, men and women at Jonestown, in the Guyana jungle, on 29 November 1978. The Rev. Jim Jones, founder of the People's Temple in Indianapolis in 1957, had set up a commune in Guyana in 1977. After murdering investigators, he led and apparently enforced a mass suicide using cyanide.

Khaki Election General election of October 1900, called by Salisbury's Conservative-Unionist government, and named after the new khaki uniform worn by the British army in the Boer war.

Korean War War in 1950–3 between communist North Korea (supported by the USSR and China) and South Korea (supported by the USA and UN).

Lame-Duck President Term used to describe an outgoing US president between the elections in November and the beginning of the new president's term on 20 January the following year.

Lancaster House Agreement UK Foreign and Commonwealth Secretary Lord Carrington brokered this agreement which ended UDI and heralded the independence of Zimbabwe. It was signed on 21 December 1979 by former Rhodesian leader Ian Smith, PM Bishop Abel Muzorewa, Robert Mugabe and Joshua Nkomo, as well as by Carrington and Sir Ian Gilmour representing the British delegation. Lord Soames became governor during the transitional period.

LDC Least Developed Country, a category used by the UN to describe many of its poorer member states. According to UN estimates, over 500 million people lived in LDCs in 1990.

Limehouse Declaration Political statement issued on 25 January 1981 by four senior members of the British Labour Party, Roy Jenkins, David Owen, William Rodgers and Shirley Williams, who became popularly known as the 'gang of four', effectively launching the Social Democratic Party (SDP).

Lockerbie Scottish town on which a Pan Am airliner PA103 en route from London to New York crashed after a mid-air explosion on 21 December 1988, killing all 259 passengers and crew as well as 11 townspeople. Two Libyans went on trial in Holland in 2000, accused of organising the bombing. Abdelbaset Ali Mohamed Al Megrahi was found guilty and sentenced to life but Al Amin Khalifa Fhimah was freed due to lack of evidence.

Lockheed Scandal Political scandal which emerged in Japan in 1976, involving the acceptance of bribes by Kakuei Tanaka, PM 1972–4, from the Lockheed Aircraft Corporation.

Long March The 6,000-mile journey undertaken in 1934–5 by forces of the Chinese Communist Party from Jiangxi province to Yan'an in north Shaanxi to avoid encirclement by the forces of the nationalist Guomindang.

Los Angeles Riots Major disturbances which occurred in LA between 29 April and 4 May 1992 involving widespread destruction and ethnic violence that brought 58 deaths. The riots were sparked off when an all-white jury acquitted 4 white police officers who had been filmed beating black motorist Rodney King in March 1991.

Maastricht Netherlands town where the 12 EU member states met in December 1991 for the summit that concluded the treaty on European Union. They returned on 7 Feb 1992 for the formal signing of what became the Maastricht Treaty, which was an accord on European political union and on EMU (European Monetary Union).

MAD Mutually Assured Destruction, which would result from a full-scale nuclear war between the superpowers according to the theorists of deterrence by the 'balance of terror'.

Markov Affair Controversy associated with the death in London on 15 September 1978 of Georgi Markov, a Bulgarian journalist employed by the BBC World Service, who was injected with the poison ricin from a specially adapted umbrella by an agent of the Bulgarian security service.

Marshall Plan Plan to assist the economic recovery of post-war Europe, proposed by US Secretary of State George Marshall in June 1947. The scheme offered US funding to European countries (eventually over $12 billion) if they co-operated with each other in drafting recovery programmes.

Mason-Dixon Line Boundary between the US states of Maryland and Pennsylvania which marks the border between former slave states of the south and northern states where slavery was illegal.

McCarthyism Anti-communist hysteria endemic in the USA in the early 1950s, built upon a foundation established by the House Committee on Un-American Activities. Senator Joseph McCarthy of Wisconsin made a speech in Wheeling, West Virginia, in February 1952 which began the series of anti-communist witch hunts.

Messina Conference June 1955 meeting between the foreign ministers of Belgium, France, Italy, Luxembourg, Netherlands and West Germany which led to the Rome Treaty of March 1957.

Mildenhall Treasure Hoard of Roman silver of the 4th century AD, discovered during ploughing in Suffolk in 1942. The main item of value is the 'Great Dish'.

HISTORY

Montgomery Bus Boycott   Year-long boycott of the public transport system in Montgomery, Alabama, which provided a key early victory for the US civil rights movement. It began on 5 December 1955, after a black woman, Rosa Parks, was arrested for refusing to give up her seat on a bus to a white passenger.

Montreal Protocol   Agreement signed in September 1987 by 24 countries which undertook to halve their CFC production by 1999. The protocol aims to reduce damage to the ozone layer.

Moro Affair   Circumstances surrounding the kidnapping on 16 March 1978 of Aldo Moro, president of the Italian Christian Democratic Party, by the left-wing Brigate Rosse, and his assassination on 9 May after the government refused to meet the kidnappers' demands.

Nagasaki   Target city on 9 August 1945 of the second atomic bomb which caused the Japanese surrender in World War II.

Normalisation   Sinister name for the programme aimed at stabilising communist rule in Czechoslovakia after the suppression of the 1968 Prague Spring. Under Gustav Husak, Normalisation featured a purge of tens of thousands of politically unreliable professionals and communist party members as well as an end to freedom of speech.

Pairing   Convention whereby pairs of MPs, one each from the government and opposition sides, agree that if one is unable to be present to vote, the other will abstain.

Peacock Throne   Metaphor for the pre-1979 Iranian monarchy and a reference to the throne used by the two Pahlavi shahs at their coronations. The original Peacock Throne was stolen by the Iranian conqueror Nadir Shah during a raid on the Mughal bastion, the Red Fort, in Delhi in 1793.

Perestroika   Restructuring, slogan adopted by Soviet leader Mikhail Gorbachev in late 1986 to denote his policies of pragmatic reform.

Pieds Noirs **(Black Feet)**   Term used to describe white French settlers resident in France's North African colonies, especially Algeria, and who returned to France after decolonisation in the 1960s.

Ponting Affair   Trial and acquittal of Clive Ponting in the UK in 1985 under the 1911 Official Secrets Act. Ponting, a high-flying civil servant in the MOD, was accused of leaking classified information to Labour MP Tam Dalyell, relating to the sinking of the Argentinian cruiser *Belgrano* during the 1982 Falklands War.

Potsdam   Conference held from 17 July to 2 August 1945 between the USSR, UK and USA, the Big Three allied powers of World War II, to decide the treatment of defeated Germany.

Poulson Affair   The events leading to the resignation on 18 July 1972 of Reginald Maudling as home secretary in the UK Conservative Cabinet. John Poulson was an architect who built up a major international practice in the 1960s and increased his standing through contacts with influential politicians. By the early 1970s he faced bankruptcy and was subsequently charged with corruption relating to bribes given to national and local politicians aimed at winning contracts. Poulson was sentenced to 7 years whilst Maudling, who had been chaiman of the Poulson company, resigned.

Profumo Affair   Scandal leading to the resignation in 1963 of John Profumo as secretary of state for war in the UK Conservative Cabinet. Profumo had formed a liaison with Christine Keeler, who

simultaneously was having a relationship with a Soviet military attaché in London, Eugene Ivanov.

Rivers of Blood   Controversial speech made by UK Conservative MP Enoch Powell on 20 April 1968 in which he warned of what he saw as the social and economic consequences of continued immigration into the UK of black people from the Commonwealth. Powell compared himself to a Roman in Virgil's Aeneid who had a vision of the River Tiber foaming with blood.

Roe v Wade   The landmark 1973 Supreme Court decision which made abortion legal in the USA.

Rosenbergs   US couple, Julius and Ethel, who were executed in Sing Sing prison in 1953 for having allegedly supplied the Soviet Union with atomic bomb secrets.

San Francisco Conference   International conference held April–June 1945 after which participants signed the UN charter. The conference was attended by 47 fully independent states as well as Byelorussia and Ukraine, which were Soviet constituents, and India and the Philippines, which had not at that stage achieved full independence.

Scarman Report   Serious racial disturbances in South-East London in April 1981 led to Lord Scarman carrying out a thorough public inquiry, whose findings were published in November.

Schuman Plan   Proposal advanced by French foreign minister Robert Schuman on 9 May 1950 which formed the European Coal and Steel Community.

Seles stabbing   Tennis player Monica Seles was stabbed by a crazed fan of her rival, Steffi Graf, during a match in Hamburg on 30 April 1993.

Sellafield   Site on the west coast of England, in Cumbria, run by British Nuclear Fuels. The first nuclear power station opened here, at Calder Hall, in 1956. At that time the area was known as Windscale, but on 10 October 1957 an atomic pile overheated, causing a near-catastrophe and some long-term fatalities. To protect the image of the industry the name of the site was changed.

Sharpeville Massacre   In this South African township 50 miles from Johannesburg on 21 March 1960 the police killed 69 peaceful demonstrators protesting against the Pass Laws. The UN subsequently called for the abandonment of apartheid.

Six-Day War   Threatened by a build-up of hostile Arab forces, between 5 and 10 July 1967 Israel attacked Egypt, Jordan and Syria and occupied the Sinai peninsula, the Gaza Strip, East Jerusalem, the West Bank and the Golan Heights, before declaring a ceasefire.

Social Contract   Informal agreement between the UK Labour government and the TUC in the mid-1970s aiming to balance wage restraint against a loosening of legal restrictions on trade unions.

Spin Doctor   In politics, a public relations expert working behind the scenes to have the media interpret events from the viewpoint favoured by a particular individual, faction of party.

Stockholm Syndrome   Psychological condition in which hostages grow to empathise with their captors' political or personal convictions. The term derives from a bank robbery in Stockholm in 1973 when several people taken as hostages lent their support to the robbers.

Suez Crisis   Middle East crisis precipitated by the nationalisation of the mainly British and French-owned Suez Canal by Egyptian President Gamal Abdel Nasser on 26 July 1956. Nasser acted after the USA had reneged on a commitment to help finance the construction of the Aswan High Dam. Israel invaded on 29 October; acting in collusion, French and British forces intervened a week later, under guise of keeping the peace. By March 1957, all 3 had withdrawn under strong UN pressure.

Sutton Hoo Ship Burial Anglo-Saxon treasure unearthed in 1939 at Sutton Hoo in Suffolk and believed to have been the tomb of an Anglo-Saxon king buried about 625, possibly Raedwald. Mrs Pretty, who owned the land and hence the treasure, kindly donated the find to the British Museum.

TD Gaelic for Teachta Dála, a member of the Irish Dáil or lower house of parliament.

Territorial Waters The offshore area in which a coastal state claims sovereign jurisdiction, save for the customary rights of freedom of navigation for merchant shipping. At present 12 miles is the accepted boundary of territorial waters, with a few exceptions, mostly in Africa and Central and South America.

Third Man Kim Philby, a UK journalist and former intelligence officer who defected to the Soviet Union in January 1963, was given this epithet after the earlier defections of Guy Burgess and Donald Maclean in 1951.

***Tiger*Talks** Negotiations held aboard HMS *Tiger* off Gibraltar on 2–4 December 1966 between Harold Wilson and Ian Smith, which failed to end Rhodesian UDI.

Trident Multiple-warhead submarine-launched nuclear missile with a range of 4,500 miles, introduced in 1979 by the US Navy in refitted Poseidon submarines, and in larger *Ohio*-class submarines first delivered in 1981. A more powerful Trident 2 missile was introduced in 1990.

Union Carbide Disaster In December 1984 a leak of toxic gas from Union Carbide pesticide plant near Bhopal, India, killed 2,500 and injured 200,000.

Vatican II The 2nd Vatican Council (the first was in 1869-70), which met in 4 sessions between 11 October 1962 and 8 December 1965. Launched by Pope John XXIII, it was concluded by his successor Pope Paul VI. Vatican II was the 21st Ecumenical Council in the history of the Roman Catholic Church and brought a reformist, liberalising outlook to existing dogma.

Vietnam War The 1954–75 war between North and South Vietnam, the latter assisted from 1961 by the USA. The war resulted in victory for the North and the union of the two Vietnams in 1976.

Vincennes On 3 July 1988 the US warship *Vincennes*, serving in the Persian Gulf, mistook an Iran Air A3000 Airbus for an attacking bomber and shot it down, costing 290 civilian lives.

Waco Siege A 51-day siege of the HQ of the Branch Davidian religious cult near Waco, Texas, began on 28 February 1993 and ended on 19 April when the FBI stormed the compound and fire broke out, killing its leader David Koresh and 70 of its members.

Warnock Report UK report published in July 1984 on bio-ethics as well as the social and legal implications of recent and potential developments in the field of human-assisted reproduction. Chaired by Dame Mary Warnock, the committee recommended that certain forms of infertility treatment should be viewed as ethically acceptable.

Warren Commission Chaired by the head of the US Supreme Court, Chief Justice Earl Warren, the Commission investigated circumstances surrounding the assassination of President JF Kennedy in Dallas on 22 November 1963. The Commission's report concluded on 22 September 1964 that Lee Harvey Oswald had been solely responsible for the killing.

West Bank Territory of Palestine west of the River Jordan, claimed from 1949 to 1988 as part of Jordan, but occupied by Israel since the Six-Day War of 1967. The territory, excluding East Jerusalem, is widely referred to within Israel by its biblical names, Judea and Samaria, and is considered part of Eretz Israel. In September 1993 Israeli forces withdrew from the West Bank but the territory is still disputed by many Israelis.

Winter of Discontent Time of industrial unrest in the UK over the severe winter of 1978–9.

Wolfenden Report Report of the UK Committee on Homosexual Offences and Prostitution, chaired by Sir John Wolfenden, which recommended in particular the decriminalisation of homosexual acts between consenting adult males and an increase in penalties for soliciting by prostitutes. The landmark report published on 4 September 1957 led to the Street Offences Act of 1959 and to the Sexual Offences Act of 1967.

Year Zero Slogan adopted by the Khmer Rouge to denote the start of their 4-year period of rule in Cambodia in April 1975.

Yom Kippur War On 6 October 1973 Syria and Egypt mounted a surprise attack on Israel as it observed Yom Kippur (the Jewish Day of Atonement), aiming to regain territory lost during the Six-Day War of 1967. Although Israel was caught off guard initially, by 24 October the Israelis were advancing on Cairo and Damascus and a ceasefire was declared, restoring the status quo.

Zeebrugge Disaster see *Herald of Free Enterprise*.

HISTORY

LANGUAGE

Foreign Words and Phrases

ab initio (L.)   from the beginning

à bon marché (Fr.)   a good bargain, cheap (lit. at a good market)

a cappella (It.)   without instrumental accompaniment (lit. in chapel style)

à cheval (Fr.)   on horseback (also denotes two roulette numbers)

achtung (Ger.)   look out, beware, take heed (lit. attention)

ad astra (L.)   to the stars

ad hoc (L.)   for this special purpose (lit. to this)

ad libitum (L.)   at pleasure

ad rem (L.)   to the purpose, to the point (lit. to the matter)

à la carte (Fr.)   each dish priced separately (lit. according to the menu)

à la mode (Fr.)   according to custom or fashion

Agnus Dei (L.)   lamb of God

al dente (It.)   firm when bitten (lit. to the teeth)

al fresco (It.)   in the open air (lit. in the fresh)

alloi kamon, alloi onanto (Gr.)   some toil, others reap the advantage

Alma Mater (L.)   applied to former school, university, or college, (lit. fostering or bounteous mother)

alter ego (L.)   other self

amor vincit omnia (L.)   love conquers all

Angst (Ger.)   anxiety

annus mirabilis (L.)   a remarkable year (lit. year of wonder)

Anschauung (Ger.)   point of view (lit. looking around)

Anschluss (Ger.)   joining together

ante bellum (L.)   before the war

a priori (L.)   from cause to effect (lit. from the previous)

à propos (Fr.)   to the purpose

auberge (Fr.)   inn, tavern

au courant (Fr.)   fully acquainted with (lit. in the current)

Aufklärung (Ger.)   clarification, enlightenment

auf Wiedersehen (Ger.)   till we meet again

au pair (Fr.)   home-help from a foreign country (lit. on an equal basis)

au revoir (Fr.)   till we meet again

auto-da-fé (Port.)   act of faith

avant-garde (Fr.)   progressive or radical artists and thinkers (lit. vanguard)

bain-marie (Fr.)   a double saucepan (lit. bath of Maria)

baksheesh (Pers.)   gratuity or tip (lit. a present)

banzai (Jap.)   a Japanese battle-cry (lit. 10,000 years)

barrio (Sp.)   district, suburb (lit. open country)

bas bleu (Fr.)   literary woman, blue-stocking worker (lit. under blue)

batik (Malay)   cloth dyeing method using wax, the cloth itself, (lit. painted)

bête noire (Fr.)   a bugbear, pet aversion (lit. black beast)

bibelot (Fr.)   trinket, curio, knick-knack (lit. small book)

bidet (Fr.)   bestridable bath (lit. small horse)

Bildungsroman (Ger.)   novel concerning early development of its central figure, (lit. education novel)

billet-doux (Fr.)   love letter (lit. sweet note)

Blitzkrieg (Ger.)   intense military attack (lit. lightning war)

Boche (Fr.)   French slang for a German soldier (lit. rascal)

bois brûlé (Fr.)   French-Canadian Indian (lit. burnt wood)

bona fide (L.)   with good faith

bona-roba (It.)   prostitute, wench (lit. good dress)

bona vacantia (L.)   goods without any apparent owner and to which the Crown has the rights (lit. ownerless goods)

bonheur du jour (Fr.)   small writing-table (lit. happiness of the day)

bonhomie (Fr.)   good-nature (lit. good man)

bon mot (Fr.)   witty remark (lit. good word)

bonsai (Jap.)   miniature tree in a pot (lit. bowl growing)

bourgeois (Fr.)   middle-class person (lit. town dweller)

cacoethes (Gr)   bad habit, mania (lit. evil habit)

carabiniere (It.)   member of Italian police force

carpe diem (L.)   seize the day

carte blanche (Fr.)   freedom of action, card hand with no court cards (lit. blank card)

caveat emptor (L.)   let the buyer beware

cave canem (L.)   beware of the dog

cela va sans dire (Fr.)   needless to say, that goes without saying

c'est la vie (Fr.)   that's life

ceteris paribus (L.)   other things being equal

cinquecento (Fr.)   classical style of art of the 16th century (lit. five hundred)

cire perdue (Fr.)   bronze casting using wax technique (lit. lost wax)

cogito, ergo sum (L.)   I think, therefore I am

compos mentis (L.)   sound of mind

corpus delicti (L.)   body or substance of a crime

corregidor (Sp.)   chief magistrate of a Spanish town (lit. to correct)

corrida (Sp.)   a bullfight (lit. corral)

corrigenda (L.)   things to be corrected

coup de foudre (Fr.)   love at first sight, sudden event (lit. flash of lightning)

coup de grâce (Fr.)   action that puts an end to something, (lit. stroke of mercy)

coup d'état (Fr.)   sudden and violent change of government, (lit. stroke of state)

cri de coeur (Fr.)   heartfelt appeal or protest (lit. cry from the heart)

cru (Fr.)   French vineyard (lit. growth)

cucullus non facit monachum (L.)   the cowl does not make the monk

cui bono (L.)   to whose benefit

cul-de-sac (Fr.)   road with one end blocked off, dead end (lit. bottom of the bag)

cum grano salis (L.)   with a grain of salt

curriculum vitae (L.)   course of life

dacha (Rus.)   Russian country villa (lit. gift)

de facto (L.)   in fact

déjà vu (Fr.)   already seen

de jure (L.)   by right (lit. from the law)

de profundis (L.)   out of the depths

de rigueur (Fr.)   required by etiquette (lit. of strictness)

Dei gratia (L.)   by God's grace

Deo volente (L.)   God willing

dernier cri (Fr.)   latest fashion, last word (lit. last cry)

de trop (Fr.) superfluous, not wanted (lit. too much)
die dulci fruere (L.) have a nice day
Doppelgänger (Ger.) wraith, look-a-like (lit. double goer)
dos-à-dos (Fr.) a seat on which the users sit back to back, (lit. back to back)
dramatis personae (L.) cast of a play
duce (It.) leader
duende (Sp.) Imp, goblin, ghost
Dummkopf (Ger.) dumb-head
e pluribus unum (L.) one out of many
Ecce Homo (L.) artistic representation of Christ crowned with thorns. From the words of Pontius Pilate to his accusers, (lit. behold the man)
echt (Ger.) real, genuine, authentic
effendi (Turk.) mister (lit. master)
emeritus (L.) honourably retired (lit. meritorious)
ersatz (Ger.) replacement, substitute, imitation
esprit de corps (Fr.) pride in belonging to a group (lit. spirit of a body)
eureka (Gr.) I have found it
ex cathedra (L.) with authority
ex officio (L.) by virtue of his office (lit. out of duty)
fabricati diem (L.) make my day
fac ut gaudeam (L.) make my day
fait accompli (Fr.) thing already done (lit. accomplished fact)
fartlek (Swed.) interval athletics training (lit. speed play)
fatwa (Arab.) a legal decision
faux pas (Fr.) social blunder, indiscretion (lit. false step)
Fidei Defensor (L.) defender of the faith
flagrante delicto (L.) in the act of a crime
floreat (L.) let it flourish
force de frappe (Fr.) French nuclear deterrent (lit. striking force)
Führer (Ger.) leader
Gastarbeiter (Ger) person with temporary permission to work, in a foreign country (lit. guest-worker)
Gauleiter (Ger.) district leader
gestalt (Ger.) organised whole in which each part affects every other part (lit. shape)
Gesundheit (Ger.) your health (lit. healthy sound)
glasnost (Rus.) openness
Götterdämmerung (Ger.) In German mythology the final destruction of the world (lit. twilight of the gods)
goût (Fr.) taste, artistic discernment
gravitas (L.) solemn demeanour
gringo (Sp.) term used by Latin-Americans for foreigners, (lit. foreigner)
gulag (Rus.) labour camp
habeas corpus (L.) a writ to produce a prisoner before a court, (lit. you should have the body)
haiku (Jap.) amusement verse
hajj (Arab.) pilgrimage
Hakenkreuz (Ger.) swastika (lit. hooked cross)
halal (Arab.) cooked according to Muslim law (lit. lawful)
haute couture (Fr.) high fashion (lit. high dressmaking)
haute cuisine (Fr.) high-class cooking
haute école (Fr.) classic style of riding (lit. high school)
hic et nunc (L.) here and now
hic et ubique (L.) here and everywhere
hic jacet (L.) here lies
hic sepultus (L.) here buried
hoi polloi (Gr.) common people or rabble (lit. the many)
hominis est errare (L.) to err is human
homme d'affaires (Fr.) businessman
homme d'esprit (Fr.) man of wit or genius

honi soit qui mal y pense (Fr.) shamed be he who thinks evil
honores mutant mores (L.) honours change manners
hors de combat (Fr.) disabled or injured (lit. out of the fight)
hors d'oeuvre (Fr.) savoury appetiser (lit. out of the course)
hwyl (W.) fervour
Ibidem (L.) in the same place
Ich dien (Ger.) I serve
id est (L.) that is
ignorantia juris neminem excusat (L.) ignorance of the law excuses no one
illegitimi non carborundum (L.) don't let the bastards grind you down
in camera (L.) in secret (Lit. in the chamber)
incunabulum (L.) book printed before 1501 (lit. from cradle), original Latin meaning was 'swaddling clothes'
in extremis (L.) at the point of death (lit. in the last)
in flagrante delicto (L.) in the act of a crime or red-handed, (lit. with the crime still ablaze), sometimes written 'flagrante delicto'
infra dig(nitatem) (L.) beneath one's dignity
in loco parentis (L.) in place of a parent
in petto (It.) when a cardinal is selected by the pope but not yet anounced (lit. in the breast)
inshallah (Arab.) equivalent to the term 'touch wood' (lit. if Allah wills)
inter alia (L.) among other things
intra vires (L.) within the powers of
in utero (L.) before birth (lit. in the womb)
in vino veritas (L.) drunken people often speak the truth, (lit. in wine, truth)
in vitro (L.) in a test tube (lit. in glass)
ipso facto (L.) by the fact itself
jacquerie (Fr.) a peasants' revolt as in France in 1358 (lit. peasant)
j'adoube (Fr.) I adjust (chess term)
je ne sais quoi (Fr.) indefinable quality (lit. I know not what)
jeune premier (fem. -ière) (Fr.) juvenile lead in musical play or theatrical production (lit. first youth)
jeunesse dorée (Fr.) rich and fashionable young people (lit. gilded youth)
jihad (Arab.) a Muslim holy war (lit. conflict)
joie de vivre (Fr.) joy of living
Jugendstil (Ger.) art nouveau (lit. youth style)
Junker (Ger.) class of Prussian land-owning aristocracy (lit. young lord)
juste milieu (Fr.) happy medium or golden mean (lit. the right mean or the right course)
kamikaze (Jap.) Japanese suicide pilots in WWII (lit. divine wind)
Kapellmeister (Ger.) person in charge of an orchestra (lit. chapel master)
karaoke (Jap.) Japanese entertainment of singing to backing tapes, (lit. empty orchestra)
Katzenjammer (Ger.) colloquial term for a hangover (lit. cat's wailing)
kia ora (Maori) good luck (lit. be well)
kibbutz (Heb.) Jewish community in Israel (lit. gathering)
kibitzer (Yid.) person who gives unwanted advice especially at a card game, (lit. lapwing or plover)
kitsch (Ger.) worthless art
kolkhoz (Rus.) Russian collective farm
kulak (Rus.) land-owning peasant (lit. fist)
Kulturkampf (Ger.) culture struggle
la dolce vita (It.) the sweet life
laissez-faire (Fr.) unrestricted commerce (lit. allow to do)
Langlauf (Ger.) cross-country skiing (lit. long run)

LANGUAGE

lapsus calami (L.) slip of the pen
lapsus linguae (L.) slip of the tongue
lares et penates (L.) household goods
l'chaim (Heb.) a Jewish toast (lit. to life)
Lebensraum (Ger.) territory needed by a state for its natural development, (lit. living space)
Lederhosen (Ger.) leather trousers
lèse-majesté (Fr.) high treason (lit. injured majesty)
lex scripta (L.) written law
lex talionis (L.) law of retaliation (lit. such law)
litterae humaniores (L.) name given to study of classics at Oxford University (lit. more humane letters)
locum tenens (L.) a deputy (lit. place held)
locus classicus (L.) authoritive and oft-quoted passage from a standard text (lit. classical place)
lycée (Fr.) in France, a state secondary school (lit. pupil)
magnum opus (L.) a great work of art or literature
maharishi (Hin.) Hindu teacher of religious doctrine (lit. great sage)
mahatma (Sans.) Brahman sage (lit. great soul)
maillot (Fr.) tights worn for balet or gymnastics (lit. swaddling clothes)
mal de mer (Fr.) seasickness
mañana (Sp.) tomorrow
manqué (Fr.) unfulfilled potential (lit. having missed)
maven (Yid.) a connoisseur (lit. understanding)
mazel tov (Heb.) congratulations or good luck (lit. good star)
mea culpa (L.) by my own fault
memento mori (L.) reminder of death
mene, mene, tekel, upharsin (Aram.) words that appeared on the wall during Belshazzar's Feast (lit. numbered, numbered, weighed, divided)
mens rea (L.) criminal intent (lit. guilty mind)
modus operandi (L.) method of working
mot juste (Fr.) appropriate word
multum in parvo (L.) much in little
mutatis mutandis (L.) with required changes
né(e) (Fr.) born
ne plus ultra (L.) extreme perfection (lit. not more beyond)
nil desperandum (L.) never despair (lit. nothing to be despaired)
nisi (L.) coming into effect unless otherwise stated (lit. unless)
noblesse oblige (Fr.) obligation of nobility or privileged to be honourable (lit. nobility obliges)
nom de guerre (Fr.) an assumed name (lit. name of war)
nom de plume (Fr.) pen-name
non sequitur (L.) statement that has no relevance to what went before (lit. it does not follow)
nota bene (L.) note well
nuit blanche (Fr.) sleepless night (lit. white night)
Nunc Dimittis (L.) the Canticle of Simeon (Luke 2:29–32), (lit. now depart)
obiter dictum (L.) said in passing
objet d'art (Fr.) small object of artistic worth (lit. object of art)
objet trouvé (Fr.) ordinary object seen from an artistic viewpoint, (lit. found object)
oeuvre (Fr.) total output of an artist or writer
om mani padme hum (Sans.) Tibetan Buddhists meditational chant. Aka Shadakshari mantra (lit. hail, jewel in the lotus)
omnia vincit amor (L.) love conquers all
panem et circenses (L.) bread and circuses (written by Juvenal of the loves of the typical Roman citizen)
parador (Sp.) Inn or tavern
par avion (Fr.) by airmail (lit. by air)

parvenu (Fr.) an upstart or social climber (lit. to attain)
paterfamilias (L.) male head of a household (lit. father of the family)
patois (Fr.) dialect
pax vobiscum (L.) peace be with you
per ardua ad astra (L.) through adversity to the stars
perestroika (Rus.) reconstruction
per se (L.) In itself
persona non grata (L.) unacceptable person
petit bourgeois (Fr.) lower middle-class
petit four (Fr.) small rich, sweet cakes, usually with icing (lit. little oven)
petit mal (Fr.) mild form of epilepsy with short bouts of unconsciousness (lit. little illness)
pied à terre (Fr.) temporary lodging (lit. foot to the ground)
pince-nez (Fr.) spectacles without ear-pieces (lit. pinch nose)
pinxit (L.) an inscription found after an artist's name on a painting (lit. painted)
pis aller (Fr.) a compromise or last resort (lit. the worst going)
plongeur (Fr.) washer-up (lit. plunger)
poco a poco (It.) little by little
poilu (Fr.) French equivalent of 'Tommy', an infantryman (lit. hairy)
posada (Sp.) an inn in a Spanish-speaking country (lit. place for stopping)
pose plastique (Fr.) theatrical presentation of the motionless nude female form (lit. flexible pose)
post meridiem (L.) after midday
pousse-café (Fr.) small glass of spirits especially brandy or a liqueur (lit. push-coffee)
prêt-à-porter (Fr.) ready to wear or off the peg
prima donna (It.) leading female operatic star (lit. first lady)
prima facie (L.) at first sight (lit. first face)
primus inter pares (L.) first among equals
pro tempore (L.) for the time being
quattrocento (It.) the 15th century especially in relation to Italian arts (lit. four hundred) short for milquattrocento '1400'
que será será (Sp.) whatever will be will be
quidnunc (L.) person eager to learn news or scandal, a gossipmonger, (lit. what now)
quid pro quo (L.) one thing for another
qui tacet consentit (L.) silence implies consent
quod erat demonstrandum (L.) which was to be demonstrated
quod vide (L.) usually seen as qv after a word treated more fully elsewhere (lit. which see)
raison d'être (Fr.) reason for being
rapporteur (Fr.) person appointed by a committee to prepare reports of meetings, (lit. reporter)
Realpolitik (Ger.) ruthlessly realistic and opportunist approach to statesmanship
repéchage (Fr.) heat of a contest in which eliminated contestants compete again (lit. fishing out again)
requiescat in pace (L.) rest in peace
res ipsa loquitur (L.) the thing speaks for itself
rien ne va plus (Fr.) roulette term meaning no more bets are to be placed (lit. nothing further goes)
Risorgimento (It.) the 19th century movement for the political unification of Italy (lit. to rise again)
roman à clef (Fr.) novel in which real people are depicted under disguised names (lit. novel with a key)
sang-froid (Fr.) composure in the face of danger (lit. cold blood)
sanpaku (Jap.) visibility of the white of the eye below the iris and on both sides (lit. three white)

sansculotte (Fr.) low-class Republican during the French Revolution (lit. without knee breeches)

sans souci (Fr.) without cares

sasquatch America's equivalent of the abominable snowman, aka big foot

satyagraha (Sans.) a policy of non-violent resistance to British rule in India, (lit. truth pertinacity)

savoir-faire (Fr.) knowing how to act

sayonara (Jap.) goodbye

Schadenfreude (Ger.) delighting in another's misfortune (lit. harm joy)

schlock (Yid.) cheap or shoddy (lit. damaged merchandise)

schmaltz (Yid.) sentimentality (lit. melted fat)

schmuck (Yid.) contemptible person (lit. penis)

schweinhund (Ger.) term of abuse (lit. pig dog)

seicento (It.) the 17th century especially in relation to Italian arts (lit. six hundred) short for milseicento '1600'

semper eadem (L.) always the same (motto of Elizabeth I and Anne Boleyn)

semper fidelis (L.) always faithful

semper ubi sub ubi (L.) always wear underwear (Latin scholar's joke)

seppuku (Jap.) the correct term in Japan for hara-kiri, which is a colloquialism (lit. cut open the stomach)

shiatsu (Jap.) acupuncture using fingers instead of needles (lit. finger pressure)

shmatte (Yid.) shabbiness especially of clothes (lit. rag)

sic (L.) bracketed insert in a text to indicate questionable word is correct (lit. thus or so)

sic transit gloria mundi (L.) thus passes the glory of the world

Sieg Heil (Ger.) Nazi salute accompanied by the raising of the right arm (lit. hail to victory)

sine die (L.) without a fixed date (lit. without a day)

sine prole (L.) without offspring

sine qua non (L.) an essential condition or requirement (lit. without which not)

son et lumière (Fr.) entertainment staged at night to set off a building artistically (lit. sound and light)

sotto voce (It.) musical term 'In an undertone' (lit. under voice)

soupçon (Fr.) trace, hint, small amount (lit. suspicion)

sputnik (Rus.) unmanned artificial Earth satellite (lit. travelling companion)

stet (L.) literary mark in proofing meaning correction should be ignored (lit. let it stand)

Sturm und Drang (Ger.) late 18th century German literary style (lit. storm and stress)

subbotnik (Rus.) voluntary Saturday work to assist economy (lit. Saturday)

sub judice (L.) under consideration of a judge

sub poena (L.) writ compelling a court attendance (lit. under a penalty)

sub rosa (L.) in secret (lit. under the rose)

summa cum laude (L.) with the highest praise

table d'hôte (Fr.) fixed-price meal with set courses (lit. host's table)

tabula rasa (L.) clean slate (lit. scraped table)

tai chi (Chin.) Chinese system of callisthenics (lit. great fist)

tempus fugit (L.) time flies

terra firma (L.) firm ground

tête-bêche (Fr.) double-headed stamp (lit. head to double-head)

tot homines, quot sententiae (L.) so many men, so many minds

tour de force (Fr.) masterly accomplishment (lit. show of strength)

trecento (It.) the 14th century especially in relation to Italian arts (lit. three hundred) short for miltrecento '1300'

tricoteuse (Fr.) woman who knitted at executions during French Revolution (lit. knitter)

trompe l'oeil (Fr.) appearance of reality in art (lit. deceives the eye)

ultra vires (L.) beyond the powers of

urbi et orbi (L.) to the city and the world

veni, vidi, vici (L.) I came, I saw, I conquered

verbum sat sapienti (L.) a word is enough for a wise man

victor ludorum (L.) overall winner of a competition (lit. winner of the games)

videlicet (L.) namely

vis-à-vis (Fr.) in relation to (lit. face to face)

viva voce (L.) orally (lit. with the living voice)

vox populi (L.) voice of the people

Wanderjahr (Ger.) wonder year

Wehrmacht (Ger.) German forces 1921–45 (lit. defence force)

Wunderkind (Ger.) a highly talented child (lit. wonder child)

yordim (Heb.) emigrants from the state of Israel

Zaibatsu (Jap.) family business conglomerate (lit. wealthy clique)

Zeitgeist (Ger.) spirit of the times

L
A
N
G
U
A
G
E

Cockney Rhyming Slang

Cockney–Standard

Cockney	Standard	Cockney	Standard
Abergavenny	penny		tools
Adam and Eve	believe		football pools
airs and graces	faces	April showers	flowers
	braces	Aristotle	bottle
	Epsom Races	army and navy	gravy
alderman's nail	tail	artful dodger	lodger
alligator	later	Auntie Ella	umbrella
almond rocks	socks	Auntie Nellie	belly
Alphonse	ponce	babbling brook	cook
Andy Cain	rain		crook
Anna Maria	fire	bacon and eggs	legs
'apenny dip	ship	ball of chalk	walk
apple fritter	bitter (beer)	balloon car	saloon bar
apples and pears	stairs	band in the box	pox
April fools	stools	band of hope	soap

Barnaby Rudge	judge	dog and bone	phone
Barnet Fair	hair	do me goods	Woods (Woodbines)
bat and wicket	ticket	Duchess of Fife	wife
Bath bun	son	Duke of York	chalk
	sun		cork
battle-cruiser	boozer		fork
bazaar	bar (pub)	dustbin lids	kids
bear's paw	saw	early hours	flowers
Beecham's Pill	bill	earwig	twig (understand)
	still (photo)	eighteen pence	sense
bees and honey	money	elephant's trunk	drunk
beggar my neighbour	on the labour (dole)	field of wheat	street
bird lime	time	fife and drum	bum
biscuits and cheese	knees	fine and dandy	brandy
bladder of lard	card	fisherman's daughter	water
boat race	face	flowery dell	cell
Bob Squash	wash	four by two	Jew
Bo-Peep	sleep	frog and toad	road
boracic lint	skint	front wheel skid	yid
bottle and glass	arse	garden gate	magistrate
bow and arrow	sparrow	gay and frisky	whisky
bread and butter	gutter	German bands	hands
bread and cheese	sneeze	ginger beer	queer
Bristol Cities	titties		engineer
Brussels sprouts	scouts	Glasgow Rangers	strangers
bubble and squeak	beak (magistrate)	God forbids	kids
	Greek	goose's neck	cheque
bucket and pail	jail	Gordon and Gotch	watch
bull and cow	row	grasshopper	copper
burnt cinder	window	greengages	wages
Burton-on-Trent	rent	Hampstead Heath	teeth
bushel and peck	neck	Hampton Wick	prick
Bushey Park	lark	Harry Randall	candle
butcher's hook	look	Harvey Nichols	pickles
Cain and Abel	table	hearts of oak	broke
canal boat	tote	hit and miss	kiss
Cape of Good Hope	soap		piss
Captain Cook	book	holy friar	liar
carving knife	wife	iron hoof	pouf
cash and carried	married	iron tank	bank
cat and mouse	house	Isle of Wight	right
Chalk Farm	arm	I suppose	nose
cheerful giver	liver	Jack and Jill	hill
Cherry Hogg	dog		bill
Chevy Chase	face		till
china plate	mate	jackdaw	jaw
chop sticks	six	Jack Jones	alone
clickety click	sixty-six	Jack Tar	bar
cobbler's awls	balls	Jack the Ripper	kipper
cock linnet	minute	jam jar	car
cockroach	coach	Jerry O'Gorman	Mormon
cock sparrow	barrow	Jimmy Riddle	piddle
cocoa	say so	Jim Skinner	dinner
Conan Doyle	boil	Joanna	piano
country cousin	dozen	Johnnie Horner	corner
crust of bread	head	Kate and Sydney	steak and kidney
cuddle and kiss	miss	Kate Karney	army
currant bun	son	Khyber Pass	arse
	sun	kidney punch	lunch
custard and jelly	telly	la-di-dah	car
cuts and scratches	matches	Lilian Gish	fish
daffydown dilly	silly	Lilley and Skinner	dinner
Daily Mail	tale		beginner
daisy roots	boots	linen draper	paper
dickory dock	clock	lion's lair	chair
dicky bird	word	loaf of bread	head
Dicky Dirt	shirt	loop the loop	soup
dig in the grave	shave	Lord Lovell	shovel
ding dong	song	Lord Mayor	swear
ding dong bell	hell	lousy brown	Rose and Crown
dinky doo	twenty-two	Lucy Locket	pocket
Doctor Crippen	dripping	macaroni	pony

Marie Corelli	telly	read and write	fight
Mickey Mouse	house	Richard the Third	bird
mince pies	eyes	Rory O'More	door
Molly Malone	phone	Rosy Lee	tea
monkeys' tails	nails	round the houses	trousers
Mother Hubbard	cupboard	rub-a-dub-dub	pub
mother's ruin	gin	Salford Docks	rocks
Mrs Chant	aunt	salmon and trout	stout
Mutt and Jeff	deaf	sausage and mash	cash
nanny goat	boat		crash
	tote		
	coat	Scapa Flow	go
near and far	bar	Scotch pegs	legs
	car	Sexton Blake	cake
needle and pin	gin		fake
Nervo and Knox	pox	skin and blister	sister
	goggle box	sky rocket	pocket
Newington Butts	guts	sorry and sad	bad
Noah's ark	park	stammer and stutter	butter
	nark	stand at ease	cheese
north and south	mouth	tea leaf	thief
oily rag	fag	tea pot lid	yid
old pot and pan	old man		quid
Oliver Twist	fist		kid
on the floor	poor	tiddly wink	drink
orchestra stalls	balls	tit for tat	hat
Owen Nares	chairs	Tod Sloan	(on one's) own
Oxford scholar	dollar	Tom and Dick	sick
peas in the pot	hot	Tommy Tucker	supper
pen and ink	stink	Tom Thumb	rum
piccolo and flute	suit	trouble and strife	wife
pig's ear	beer	two and eight	state
pimple and blotch	scotch	Uncle Bert	shirt
pitch and toss	boss	Uncle Fred	bread
plates of meat	feet	Uncle Ned	bed
pleasure and pain	rain	weasel and stoat	coat
potatoes in the mould	cold	weeping willow	pillow
rabbit and pork	talk	whistle and flute	suit
		you and me	tea

Cockney Rhyming Slang

Standard–Cockney

alone	Jack Jones	boil	Conan Doyle
arm	Chalk Farm	book	Captain Cook
army	Kate Karney	boots	daisy roots
arse	bottle and glass	boozer	battle-cruiser
	Khyber Pass	boss	pitch and toss
aunt	Mrs Chant	bottle	Aristotle
bad	sorry and sad	braces	airs and graces
balls	cobbler's awls	brandy	fine and dandy
	orchestra stalls	bread	Uncle Fred
bank	iron tank	broke	hearts of oak
bar	Jack Tar	bum	fife and drum
	near and far	butter	stammer and stutter
bar (pub)	bazaar	cake	Sexton Blake
barrow	cock sparrow	candle	Harry Randall
beak (magistrate)	bubble and squeak	car	jam jar
bed	Uncle Ned		La-Di-Dah
beer	pig's ear		near and far
beginner	Lilley and Skinner	card	bladder of lard
believe	Adam and Eve	cash	sausage and mash
belly	Auntie Nellie	cell	flowery dell
bill	Jack and Jill	chair	lion's lair
	Beecham's pill	chairs	Owen Nares
bird	Richard the Third	chalk	Duke of York
bitter (beer)	apple fritter	cheese	stand at ease
boat	nanny goat	cheque	goose's neck

LANGUAGE

Word	Rhyming slang	Word	Rhyming slang
clock	dickory dock	liar	holy friar
coach	cockroach	liver	cheerful giver
coat	nanny goat	lodger	artful dodger
	weasel and stoat	look	butcher's hook
cold	potatoes in the mould	lunch	kidney punch
cook	babbling brook	magistrate	garden gate
copper	grasshopper	married	cash and carried
cork	Duke of York	matches	cuts and scratches
corner	Johnnie Horner	mate	china plate
crash	sausage and mash	minute	cock linnet
crook	babbling brook	miss	cuddle and kiss
cupboard	Mother Hubbard	money	bees and honey
deaf	Mutt and Jeff	Mormon	Jerry O'Gorman
dinner	Jim Skinner	mouth	north and south
	Lilley and Skinner	nails	monkeys' tails
dog	Cherry Hogg	nark	Noah's ark
dollar	Oxford Scholar	neck	bushel and peck
door	Rory O'More	nose	I suppose
dozen	country cousin	old man	old pot and pan
drink	tiddly wink	on the labour (dole)	beggar my neighbour
dripping	Doctor Crippen	(on one's) own	Tod Sloan
drunk	elephant's trunk	paper	linen draper
engineer	ginger beer	park	Noah's ark
Epsom Races	airs and graces	penny	Abergavenny
eyes	mince pies	phone	Molly Malone
face	boat race	piano	dog and bone
	Chevy Chase		Joanna
faces	airs and graces	pickles	Harvey Nichols
facts	brass tacks	piddle	Jimmy Riddle
fag	oily rag	pillow	weeping willow
fake	Sexton Blake	piss	hit and miss
feet	plates of meat	pocket	sky rocket
fight	read and write		Lucy Locket
fire	Anna Maria	ponce	Alphonse
fish	Lilian Gish	pony	macaroni
fist	Oliver Twist	poor	on the floor
flowers	April showers	pouf	iron hoof
	early hours	pox	band in the box
football pools	April fools		Nervo and Knox
fork	Duke of York	prick	Hampton Wick
gin	needle and pin	pub	rub-a-dub-dub
	mother's ruin	queer	ginger beer
go	Scapa Flow	quid	tea pot lid
goggle box	Nervo and Knox	rain	Andy Cain
gravy	army and navy		pleasure and pain
Greek	bubble and squeak	rent	Burton-on-Trent
guts	Newington Butts	right	Isle of Wight
gutter	bread and butter	road	frog and toad
hair	Barnet Fair	rocks	Salford Docks
hands	German bands	Rose and Crown	lousy brown
hat	tit for tat	row	bull and cow
head	crust of bread	rum	Tom Thumb
	loaf of bread	saloon bar	balloon car
hell	ding dong bell	saw	bear's paw
hill	Jack and Jill	say So	cocoa
hot	peas in the pot	scotch	pimple and blotch
house	cat and mouse	scouts	brussels sprouts
	Mickey Mouse	sense	eighteen pence
jail	bucket and pail	shave	dig in the grave
jaw	jackdaw	ship	'apenny dip
Jew	four by two	shirt	Dicky Dirt
judge	Barnaby Rudge		Uncle Bert
kid	tea pot lid	shovel	Lord Lovell
kids	dustbin lids	sick	Tom and Dick
	God forbids	silly	daffydown dilly
kipper	Jack the Ripper	sister	skin and blister
kiss	hit and miss	six	chop sticks
knees	biscuits and cheese	sixty-six	clickety click
lark	Bushey Park	skint	boracic lint
later	alligator	sleep	Bo-Peep
legs	bacon and eggs	sneeze	bread and cheese
	Scotch pegs	soap	Cape of Good Hope

	band of hope	telly	Marie Corelli
socks	almond rocks		custard and jelly
son	Bath bun	thief	tea leaf
	currant bun	ticket	bat and wicket
song	ding dong	till	Jack and Jill
soup	loop the loop	time	bird lime
sparrow	bow and arrow	titties	Bristol Cities
stairs	apples and pears	tools	April fools
state	two and eight	tote	nanny goat
steak and kidney	Kate and Sydney		canal boat
still (photo)	Beecham's pill	trousers	round the houses
stink	pen and ink	twenty-two	dinky doo
stools	April fools	twig (understand)	earwig
stout	salmon and trout	umbrella	Auntie Ella
strangers	Glasgow Rangers	wages	greengages
street	field of wheat	walk	ball of chalk
suit	whistle and flute	wash	Bob Squash
	piccolo and flute	watch	Gordon and Gotch
sun	Bath bun	water	fisherman's daughter
	currant bun	whisky	gay and frisky
supper	Tommy Tucker	wife	Duchess of Fife
swear	Lord Mayor		trouble and strife
table	Cain and Abel		carving knife
tail	alderman's nail	window	burnt cinder
tale	Daily Mail	Woods (Woodbines)	do me goods
talk	rabbit and pork	word	Dicky Bird
tea	you and me	yid	front wheel skid
	Rosy Lee		tea pot lid
teeth	Hampstead Heath		

Greek Alphabet

A	α	alpha	N	ν	nu		
B	β	beta	Ξ	ξ	xi		
Γ	γ	gamma	O	o	omicron		
Δ	δ	delta	Π	π	pi		
E	ε	epsilon	P	ρ	rho		
Z	ζ	zeta	Σ	σ	sigma		
H	η	eta	T	τ	tau		
Θ	θ	theta	Y	υ	upsilon		
I	ι	iota	Φ	φ	phi		
K	κ	kappa	X	χ	chi		
Λ	λ	lambda	Ψ	ψ	psi		
M	μ	mu	Ω	ω	omega		

LANGUAGE

Hebrew Alphabet

Tet (T) Chet (Ch) Zayin (Z) Vav (V/O/U) He (H) Dalet (D) Gimel (G) Bet (B/V) Alef (Silent)

Samech (S) Nun (N) Mem (M) Lamed (L) Kaf (K/Kh) Yod (Y)

Tav (T/S) Shin (Sh/S) Resh (R) Qof (Q) Tzade (Tz) Pe (P/F) Ayin (Silent)

NB There are 22 letters in the alef-bet and Hebrew script is written from right to left, alef being the first letter and tav the last. Kaf, mem, nun, pe and tzade have different characters when used at the end of a word.

Americanisms

English word	American equivalent	English word	American equivalent
A (film rating)	M (Mature film rating)	cravat	Ascot
AA (film rating)	R (Restricted film rating)	cream cracker	soda cracker
accumulator bet	parlay	crisps	chips
Akela	Den Mother	cupboard	closet
Alf Garnett	Archie Bunker	current account	checking account
Alsatian	German Shepherd	curriculum vitae	résumé
aluminium	aluminum	curtains	drapes
anorak	parka	curtains (net)	sheers/underdrapes
approved school	reform school	death duties	estate tax
Armistice Day	Veteran's Day	dinner jacket	tuxedo
articulated lorry	trailer truck	directory inquiries	information
aubergine	eggplant	district	precinct
autumn	fall	docker	longshoreman
avocado	alligator pear	double cream	whipping cream
baby's liquid feed	formula	drainpipe	downspout
baby's dummy	pacifier	draughts	checkers
bag	sack	drawing pin	thumb tack
baking tray	cookie sheet	dress circle	mezzanine/loge
bank account	checking account	dressing gown	bathrobe
bank holiday	legal holiday	dual carriageway	divided highway
bank note	bill	dustbin	garbage pail
bed (folding)	murphy bed	earth wire	ground wire
beggar	pan handler	eiderdown	comforter
big wheel	ferris wheel	elastic band	rubber band
biscuit	cookie	estate agent	realtor
Black Maria	patrol wagon	estate car	station wagon
blue-eyed boy (pet)	fair-haired boy (pet)	Europe	yarrup
bottom drawer	hope chest	evening classes	night school
bowler hat	derby	fan light	transom
box room	lumber room	fill in (a form)	fill out (a form)
braces	suspenders	fire hydrant	fire plug
broad bean	Lima bean	firework	firecracker
budgerigar	parakeet	flannel	wash cloth
bullseye	zinger	flat (leased or owned)	apartment
bum	fanny	flat (owned)	condominium
bum-bag	fanny pack	flatterer	apple polisher
by-law	ordinance	flautist	flutist
camp bed	cot	flex	wire
candy floss	cotton candy	flick knife	switchblade
car bonnet	hood	floor	deck
car boot	trunk	flyover	overpass
car park	parking lot	foot and mouth	hoof and mouth
caravan site	trailer park	foyer	lobby
caretaker	janitor	frying pan	skillet
cashier	teller	full stop	period
casserole	pot roast	funny bone	crazy bone
catapult	slingshot	garage	bodyshop
cattle grid	Texas gate	garden	yard
chat	confab	gardening	yard work
cheat	gyp	gear lever	gearshift
chemist's shop	drug store	girl guide	girl scout
cheque	check	glow worm	lightning bug
chest of drawers	bureau	goods van (train)	box car
chick-pea	garbanzo bean	goods wagon (train)	freight car
chimney	smokestack	gossip	scuttle butt
chips	french fries	got	gotten
chiropodist	podiatrist	greaseproof paper	wax paper
cigar box	humidor	green fingers	green thumb
city centre	down town	grill	broil
class/form	grade	gundog	birddog
commis waiter	bus boy	guttering	eavestrough
complimentary ticket	Annie Oakley	haberdashery	notions
condom	rubber	handbag	pocketbook
convict	yardbird		purse
coriander	cilantro	hat (woollen)	toque
cos lettuce	romaine lettuce	Heath Robinson	Rube Goldberg
courgette	zucchini	hire purchase	instalment plan

English word	American equivalent	English word	American equivalent
hob	burner	plaster (medical dressing)	Band-Aid
homeless woman	bag lady	plus fours	knickers
hot dog	weenie	police patrol car	prowl car
housewife	homemaker	policeman (uniformed)	patrolman
housing estate	sub-division	porter	bellhop
hymen	cherry	post code	zip code
ice lolly	popsicle	pouffe	hassock
icing sugar	confectionery sugar	primary school	grade school
	powdered sugar	public convenience	comfort station
ignorant person	redneck	public school	private school
illegal immigrant	wet-back	pushchair	stroller
income support	relief	queue	line
influenza	grippe	quilt	comforter
jam	jelly	railway porter	redcap
jelly	jello	receptionist	desk clerk
jemmy	jimmy	reef knot	square knot
jug	pitcher	refrigerator	icebox
jumble sale	rummage sale	reserve price	upset price
knacker's yard	glue factory	residential area	uptown
ladder (in stockings)	run (in tights)	revision (for exams)	review
ladybird	ladybug	riding whip	quirt
lame	gimpy	ring doughnut	cruller
lantern	jacklight	road	pavement
lay-by	pull-off	rosé wines	blush wines
level crossing	grade crossing	rota	roster
lift	elevator	roundabout	traffic circle
limited (company)	incorporated (inc)	rubbish	garbage
lodger	roomer	sack	fire
long jump	broad jump	sailor (US navy)	bluey jacket
lorry	truck	saloon car	sedan
lovebite	hickey	salt beef	corned beef
lucky dip	grab bag	sandpit	sand box
maize	corn	sausages	links
megaphone	bullhorn	scarf	neckerchief
men's outfitter	haberdasher	season ticket	commuter ticket
merry-go-round	carousel	second-hand	pre-owned
minced meat	hamburger meat	self-catering	cook-in
	ground meat	semi-detached	duplex
money paid illicitly	kickback	short-hand typist	stenographer
motorway	throughway	short trousers	knee pants
	freeway	sideboards	sideburns
	expressway	skipping rope	jumping rope
	superhighway	skirting board	base board
mudguard (car)	fender		mopboard
music-hall	vaudeville	smoked salmon	lox
muslin	cheesecloth	smoking jacket	lounge jacket
Naafi	PX (Post Exchange)	sofa	davenport
nappy	diaper	solicitor	attorney
non-alcoholic drink	root beer	sorbet	sherbet
notepad	scratchpad	spanner	wrench
noughts & crosses	tic tac toe	spare room	glory hole
offal	variety meat	stalls	orchestra seats
okra	gumbo	state school	public school
open air stands	bleachers	states on Gulf of Mexico	Gulf States
oven	range	stiletto heels	spike heels
oven gloves	pot holders	stock	inventory
packed lunch	sack lunch	streaming (in schools)	tracking
pageboy (hotel)	bellhop	string	cord
paraffin	kerosene	striptease artist	peeler
patience (card game)	solitaire,	suitcase	valise
paunch (spare tyre)	bay window	surgical spirit	rubbing alcohol
pavement	sidewalk	swede	rutabaga
pedestrian crossing	crosswalk	sweet potato	yam
pelmet	valance	sweets	candy
Perspex (trade name)	Plexiglas	Swiss roll	jelly roll
persuade	buffalo	tallboy	highboy
petrol	gas	tap	faucet
petrol station	filling station	telephone box	phone booth
pharmacist	druggist	television	boot tube
phone-in	call-in	tennis shoes	sneakers
pimple	zit	ticket (free)	Annie Oakley

LANGUAGE

English word	American equivalent	English word	American equivalent
tie-pin	stick-pin	US marine	leatherneck
tobacconist's shop	cigar store	use hindsight after the	second-guess
toilet (Domestic)	restroom	event	
toilet (outdoor)	out-house	verruca	plantar wart
torch	flashlight	vest	undershirt
tornado	twister	VIP address book	blue book
training camp (military)	boot camp	waistcoat	vest
tram	streetcar	waiter (apprentice)	bus boy
trilby	fedora	walk with style	sashay
trousers	pants	wallet	billfold
truncheon	nightstick	washing up bowl	dishpan
turn-ups (trousers)	cuffs	wedding ring	wedding band
U (Universal film rating)	G (General film rating)	wet paint	fresh paint
underground (tube)	subway	wheelbarrow	pushcart
underpants	shorts	wholemeal biscuit	graham cracker
undertaker	mortician	windscreen	windshield
up to you	down to you	zed (z)	zee

Forenames: Meanings

Aaron high mountain/bright
Abdullah servant of God
Abel breath
Abelard resolute
Abigail father rejoices
Abner father of light
Abraham father on high/father of a multitude
Absalom father of peace
Ada noble/happy/prosperous
Adam red earth
Adolph noble wolf
Adrian dark one of the Adriatic
Aesop burnt faced
Agatha good
Agnes lamb/chaste
Ahab uncle
Ajax eagle
Akram excellent
Alan harmony/handsome
Alaric ruler of all
Alastair form of Alexander
Albert nobly bright
Alexander defender of men
Alfred elf/wise counsellor
Algernon bearded
Ali protected by God/the greatest
Alison of noble kind
Alma apple/norishing/loving
Amadeus lover of God
Amanda fit to be loved
Ambrose immortal
Amelia hard-working
Amos burden
Amy beloved
Andrea female form of Andrew
Andrew manly
Angela messenger/angel
Anita grace, mercy
Anne English form of Hannah
Anthea flowery
Anthony inestimable
April name of a month
Arnold eagle power

Arthur bear/stone/valorous
Audrey noble strength
Aziz famous
Barbara strange/foreign land
Barry fair-headed/spear
Baruch blessed
Basil royal/kingly
Beatrice bringer of joy
Belinda beautiful and pretty
Benjamin son of my right hand
Berenice one who brings victory
Bernard brave bear
Bertram glorious raven
Beth pet form of Elizabeth
Betty pet form of Elizabeth
Bill pet form of William
Bipin forest
Bjorn bear
Bob pet form of Robert
Boris fighter
Brandon broom-covered hill
Brenda burning/a flame
Brian hill/strength
Bronwyn white breasted
Bud brother
Byron from the cottage
Carl man/husbandman
Cameron crooked nose/awesome
Carmen garden/song
Carol female form of Charles
Casper treasure
Catherine pure
Cecilia blind
Charles man/husbandman
Cher beloved
Christine anointed
Christopher carrier of Christ
Claire bright/shining
Colette victorious
Colin form of Nicholas
Cordelia jewel of the sea
Craig rock
Cressida golden

Cyril lord
Damian to tame
Daniel God is my judge
Danielle female form of Daniel
Darius wealthy
Darren beloved
David beloved/friend
Dean valley/leader
Deborah bee/eloquent
Declan man of prayer
Dennis of Dionysus (Greek God of wine)
Derek gifted ruler (form of Theodonic)
Dermot free man
Derry red-haired
Diane divine
Donald world ruler
Donna lady
Donovan dark warrior
Doris gift of the sea
Dorothy gift of God
Douglas from the dark water
Dudley of the people's meadows
Eamon rich protector
Ebenezer stone of help
Edward prosperous guardian
Eileen Irish form of Helen
Eldridge wise ruler
Elijah Jehovah is my God
Elizabeth my God is bountiful
Elvis all wise
Emily industrious
Emma all-embracing
Emmanuel God with us
Enoch dedicated
Eric ruler of all
Erasmus lovable
Esther star
Ethan firm/strong
Eugenie well born
Evelyn pleasant
Ezekiel God will strengthen
Ezra helper
Felipe lover of horses
Felix fortunate
Ferdinand adventuresome
Fidel faithful
Finlay fair hero
Floyd grey-haired
Frank Frenchman/freeman
Franklin freeholder
Frederick peaceful ruler
Gabriel God is my strength
Gail pet form of Abigail
Gareth gentle/firm spear
Garth protector
Gary spear/form of Gareth
Gavin hawk
Gemma gem
Geoffrey peaceful ruler/God's peace
George husbandman/farmer
Gerard bold spear
Graham warlike person
Gregory on the watch
Griselda grey battle maid

Gudrun God secret
Gulliver glutton
Guy lovely
Habib beloved
Hamish (variant of Jacob)
Hanif believer
Hannah grace/favour
Hans (variant of John)
Harold leader of armies
Harry pet form of Henry
Hayley hay-meadow
Hector steadfast
Helen bright/shining one
Henry household ruler
Hermione well-born lady
Hilary joyful
Hilda battle maid
Hiram most noble
Homer pledge
Horace keeper of the hours
Hortense gardener
Howard guardian
Hubert bright minded
Hugh heart/mind
Humphrey warrior peace
Ian Scottish form of John
Ichabod departed glory
Ida work
Imran strong
Ira watchful
Irene peace
Iris rainbow
Irvin handsome/fair
Isaac he will laugh
Isaiah God is salvation
Ishmael God will hear
Ivan his favour
Jacqueline female form of James
James one who takes by the heel
Jane female form of John
Jared descending
Jason to heal
Javier owner of a new horse
Jed hard
Jemima dove
Jennifer fair
Jeremy Jehovah exalts/appointed by God
Jess wealthy
Jessica God beholds
Jethro superabundance
Jezebel domination
Joab God is the father
Joachim God will judge
Joan helper
John Jehovah has been gracious
Jonathan Jehovah's gift
Joseph Jehovah adds
Joyce joyful
Julie descended from Jove/youthful
Julian descended from Jove/youthful
Karen from Katarina/pure
Katarina (form of Catherine)
Keir dark skinned
Keith of the forest

Kelly   warlike one
Kenneth   handsome; fair one or fire sprung
Kevin   handsome at birth
Lakisha   woman
Latoya   Antonia
Laura   bay/laurel
Leah   gazelle
Lee   of the meadow
Leila   night
Leonard   strong lion
Leslie   of the grey, fortress
Letitia   joy
Lilith   of the night
Linda   pretty
Lindsay   pool on the island
Lloyd   grey
Loretta   pure
Lucille   light
Lyn   cascade
Madhur   sweet
Madison   warrior's son
Magnus   great
Malcolm   dove
Mandy   much loved
Marcus   war-like
Margaret   pearl
Mario   war-like
Mark   Mars (god of war)
Martin   Mars (god of war)
Marvin   sea friend
Mary   'bitterness' or wished-for child
Matilda   battle maiden
Matthew   gift of the Lord
Maureen   little Mary
Maurice   dark-skinned
Melissa   bee/honey
Merill   famous
Michael   like the Lord
Miranda   fit to be wondered at
Moses   saved
Nadia   hope
Nancy   pet form of Anne
Natalie   birthday of the Lord
Neil   champion
Nicholas   victory of the people
Noah   rest/comfort
Omar   first son
Pamela   all honey
Patricia   noble
Paul   small
Peter   stone/rock
Philip   lover of horses
Quentin   fifth born child

Rachel   ewe
Randolph   edge wolf/house wolf
Raphael   God has healed
Raymond   counsel for the defence/wise protection
Rebecca   noose/one who brings peace
Rhoda   rose
Richard   strong ruler
Robert   bright fame
Roger   famous spear
Rolf   swift wolf
Ronald   counsel/power
Ronan   little seal
Rowan   red
Roxane   dawn
Ruth   vision of beauty
Samuel   heard/name of God
Sarah   princess
Saskia   protector of the universe
Sean   (form of John)
Sebastian   revered
Sharon   the plain
Shirley   bright clearing
Simon   listening attentively
Stacey   resurrection
Stephen   crown
Stuart   steward
Susan   lily
Sylvia   forest
Teresa   woman of Theresia/reaper
Theodoric   gifted ruler
Thomas   twin
Tiffany   manifestation of God
Timothy   honouring God
Tracy   pet form of Teresa
Trevor   big village/prudent
Tristan   the noisy one
Ursula   she bear
Vera   faith/truth
Victoria   victory
Vincent   conquer
Virgil   flourishing
Virginia   maiden
Vladimir   possess peace
Walter   ruling people
Wayne   wagon maker
William   helmet of resolution
Xavier   bright
Yuri   farmer
Yusuf   one chosen by God
Zachariah   God's remembrance
Zadok   just
Zia   enlightened
Zoe   life

LITERATURE

Autobiographies in Title Order

Title	Author	Title	Author
Absolutely Mahvelous	Billy Crystal	Cider With Rosie (1959)	Laurie Lee
Absolutely Now	Lynn Franks	Citizen Jane	Jane Fonda
Accidental MP, An	Martin Bell	Cleared for Take Off (1996)	Dirk Bogarde
Actor and His Time, An	John Gielgud	Clear Water Stream, A (1958)	Henry Williamson
Acts of Defiance	Jack Ashley	Closing Ranks (1997)	Dirk Bogarde
Acts of Faith	Adam Faith	Coal Miner's Daughter, The	Loretta Lynn
Against Goliath	David Steel	Coming Attraction (1988)	Terence Stamp
Against the Grain	Boris Yeltsin	Confessions	Jean-Jacques
Alderman's Tale, The	Don Mosey		Rousseau
All Above Board	Wilfrid Brambell	Confessions of an Actor	John Barrymore
All Creatures Great and Small	James Herriott	Confessions of an Actor	Laurence Olivier
Alliss in Wonderland	Peter Alliss	Confessions of an English	Thomas De Quincey
All My Yesterdays	Edward G Robinson	Opium-Eater	
All Those Tomorrows	Mai Zetterling	Courting Triumph	Virginia Wade
Almost a Gentleman (1991)	John Osborne	Crying with Laughter	Bob Monkhouse
Along My Line	Gilbert Harding	Cuban Rebel Girls (1959)	Errol Flynn
Also Known as Shirley (1987)	Shelley Winters	Dancing in the Light (1985)	Shirley MacLaine
Always Playing	Nigel Kennedy	Dancing in the Moonlight	Ronnie Barker
An Actor's Life for Me	Lilian Gish	Dear Me	Peter Ustinov
An American Comedy	Harold Lloyd	Diet for Life	Lynn Redgrave
Animal Days	Desmond Morris	Don't Fall off the Mountain (1970)	Shirley MacLaine
Another Part of the Wood (1974)	Kenneth Clark	Don't Laugh at Me	Norman Wisdom
Anything for a Quiet Life	Jack Hawkins	Door Marked Summer, The	Michael Bentine
Apple Sauce	Michael Wilding	Double Feature (1989)	Terence Stamp
Arias and Raspberries	Sir Harry Secombe	Drums under the Window (1945)	Sean O' Casey
As I Remember Them (1962)	Eddie Cantor	Duke, The	David Nicholson
As I Walked Out One	Laurie Lee (1929)	Ecstasy and Me	Hedy Lamarr
Midsummer's Morning		Ed Wynn's Son	Keenan Wynn
As It Happened (1954)	Clement, Attlee	80 Not Out	Patrick Moore
As It Happens (1975)	Jimmy Savile	Eternal Male, The	Omar Sharif
As It Seemed to Me	John Cole	Evening All	Ted Willis
Astronomer by Chance	Bernard Lovell	Every Other Inch a Lady	Beatrice Lilley
Backward Glance, A	Edith Wharton	Every Shot I Take	Davis Love III
Banjaxed	Terry Wogan	Eye of the Tiger	Frank Bruno
Bardot, Deneuve, and Fonda	Roger Vadim	Facing the Music	Jane Torvill &
Battling for Peace	Shimon Peres		Christopher Dean
Beam Ends (1934)	Errol Flynn	Falling towards England	Clive James
Beating Time	Antony Hopkins	Farce about Face	Brian Rix
	(conductor)	Final Dress (1983)	John Houseman
Before I Forget	James Mason	Fire over England (1994)	Ken Russell
Before the Dawn	Gerry Adams	First Interval	Donald Wolfit
Beginning	Kenneth Branagh	Five Lives (1964)	Lord Longford
Being Myself	Martina Navratilova	For Dogs and Angels	Chili Boucher
Beneath the Underdog	Charlie Mingus	Free House, A	Walter Sickert
Best of Times, Worst of Times	Shelley Winters	From a Bundle of Rags	Jim Bowen
Better Class of Person, A	John Osborne	Front and Center (1980)	John Houseman
(1981)		Full Monty, The	Jim Davidson
Blessings in Disguise (1985)	Alec Guinness	Fun in a Chinese Laundry	Josef von Sternberg
Bonus of Laughter, The	Leslie Crowther	Future Indefinite (1954)	Noel Coward
Born Lucky	John Francome	Gay Illiterate, The (1944)	Louella Parsons
Born to Believe (1953)	Lord Longford	Gift of Joy, A (1965)	Helen Hayes
Bound for Glory	Woody Guthrie	Girl Power	Spice Girls
Boy	Roald Dahl	Glorious Uncertainty	Jenny Pitman
Bring on the Empty Horses	David Niven	Good Vibrations	Jacqueline Gold (Ann
British Picture, A (1985)	Ken Russell		Summers)
Buried Day, The	Cecil Day Lewis	Good Vibrations	Evelyn Glennie
By Myself	Lauren Bacall	Goodbye to All That	Robert Graves
Can You Have It All	Nicola Horlick	Goodness Had Nothing to	Mae West (1959)
Caught in the Act (1986)	Richard Todd	Do with It	
Change Lobsters and Dance	Lili Palmer	Good, the Bad and the Bubbly,	George Best
Changing	Liv Ullmann	The	
Child of My Love	Sue Ryder	Grace Abounding	John Bunyan
Choices	Liv Ullmann	Grain of Wheat (1974)	Lord Longford
Chronicles of Wasted Time	Malcolm Muggeridge	Grand Inquisitor	Robin Day

Title	Author	Title	Author
Greatest Game of All, The (1969)	Jack Nicklaus	Life of an American Workman, The	Walter Percy Chrysler
Great Meadow (1992)	Dirk Bogarde	Life on Film (1971)	Mary Astor
Great Morning (1947)	Osbert Sitwell	Life, Sex and ESP (1975)	Mae West
Halfway Through the Door	Alan Arkin	Life Wish (1987)	Jill Ireland
Happy Go Lucky (1959)	Kenneth More	Limelight and After	Claire Bloom
Happy Hooker, The	Xavier Hollander	Little Clown, The	Reg Varney
Haunted Life, A	Anthony Perkins	Little Girl Lost	Drew Barrymore
Have Tux Will Travel (1958)	Bob Hope	Little Wilson and Big God (1987)	Anthony Burgess
Here Lies	Eric Ambler		
His Eye Is on the Sparrow	Ethel Waters	Lonely Life, The (1962)	Bette Davis
Hitting across the Line	Viv Richards	Long Banana Skin, The	Michael Bentine
Hollywood in a Suitcase (1980)	Sammy Davis Jnr	Long Walk to Freedom	Nelson Mandela
		Lorenzo Goes to Hollywood	Edward Arnold
Hons and Rebels	Jessica Mitford	Love Is a Many-Splendoured Thing	Han Suyin
Hundred Different Lives, A	Raymond Massey		
I Can't Stay Long (1975)	Laurie Lee	Love Is an Uphill Thing (1975)	Jimmy Savile
I.E. (1965)	Mickey Rooney	Man Who Listens to Horses, The	Monty Roberts
I Knock at the Door (1939)	Sean O' Casey		
I Like What I Know	Vincent Price	Martha, Jane and Me	Mavis Nicholson
I'm Still Here	Yvonne De Carlo	Mask or Face (1958)	Michael Redgrave
I'm Still Here (1989)	Eartha Kitt	Master of None	Gilbert Harding
In and Out of Character	Basil Rathbone	Me	Katherine Hepburn
In Camera (1989)	Richard Todd	Mein Kampf	Adolf Hitler
In Darkness and Light	Anthony Hopkins	Memoirs of an Unfit Mother	Anne Robinson
Inishfallen Fare Thee Well (1949)	Sean O' Casey	Memoirs of a Professional Cad	George Sanders
		Memories	Ethel Barrymore
In My Father's Court	Isaac Bashevis Singer	Middle of My Century, The (1989)	Shelley Winters
In My Mind's Eye (1983)	Michael Redgrave	Mingled Chime, A	Thomas Beecham
In Search of History: A Personal Adventure	Theodore H White	Minnie the Moocher and Me	Cab Calloway
		Mirror in My House (1956)	Sean O' Casey
Inside the Third Reich	Albert Speer	Moab Is My Washpot	Stephen Fry
Intermission	Anne Baxter	Moment of War, A	Laurie Lee
I Owe Russia $2000 (1963)	Bob Hope	Moon's a Balloon, The	David Niven
I Paid Hitler	Baron Von Thyssen	More or Less (1978)	Kenneth More
I Reach for the Stars	Barbara Cartland	Mother Goddam (1975)	Bette Davis
I Search for Rainbows (1967)	Barbara Cartland	Movies, Mr Griffith and Me, The	Lilian Gish
I Seek the Miraculous (1978)	Barbara Cartland	Mr Nice	Howard Marks
		Musician at Large	Steve Race
I Was Born Greek	Melina Mercouri	My American Journey	Colin Powell
Is It Me	Terry Wogan	My Days and Dreams	Edward Carpenter
Isthmus Years, The (1943)	Barbara Cartland	My Double Life	Sarah Bernhardt
It Doesn't Take a Hero	Norman Schwarzkopf	My Early Life (1981)	Ronald Reagan
It's All in the Playing (1987)	Shirley MacLaine	My Life	Richard Wagner
It's Been Fun (1949)	Anna Neagle	My Life Line	Lady Isobel Barnett
It's Me, O Lord! (1957)	AE Coppard	My Lucky Stars: A Hollywood Memory (1989)	Shirley Maclaine
Jack of All Trades	Jack Warner		
Jacob's Ladder	David Jacob	My Many Lives	Lotte Lehmann
Jump Jockeys Don't Cry	Sharron Murgatroyd	My Name Escapes Me (1996)	Alec Guinness
Just Resting	Leo McKern	My Story (1959)	Mary Astor
Just Williams	Kenneth Williams	My Ten Years in the Studios (1940)	George Arliss
Kentish Lad, A	Frank Muir		
King's Story, A (1951)	Duke of Windsor	My Turn	Nancy Reagan
Kink	Dave Davies	My Wicked Wicked Ways (1955)	Errol Flynn
Knock Wood	Candice Bergen		
Last Christmas Show, The (1976)	Bob Hope	Naked Civil Servant, The	Quentin Crisp
		Nice One Cyril	Cyril Fletcher
Laugh Is on Me, The	Phil Silvers	Noa-Noa	Paul Gaugin
Laughter in the Next Room (1948)	Osbert Sitwell	No Bed of Roses	Joan De Havilland
		No Bells on Sunday	Rachel Roberts
Leaving a Doll's House	Claire Bloom	Noble Essences (1950)	Osbert Sitwell
Left Hand: Right Hand (1944)	Osbert Sitwell	No Minor Chords	André Previn
Let's Get through Wednesday	Reginald Bosanquet	Nostalgia Isn't What It Used to Be	Simone Signoret
Let the Chips Fall	Rudy Vallee		
Life for Life's Sake	Richard Aldington	Nothing's Impossible	Brian Blessed
Life in Movies, A	Michael Powell	Not the Whole Truth	Patrick Lichfield
Life in Movies, A	Fred Zinneman	Now and Then	Roy Castle
Life Is a Banquet	Rosalind Russell	Oak and the Calf, The	Alexander Solzhenitsyn
Life Is Too Short (1991)	Mickey Rooney		
Life Lines (1989)	Jill Ireland	Odd Man Out	Ronnie Biggs

Title	Author	Title	Author
Odd Woman Out	Muriel Box	Straight Man, The	Nicholas Parsons
On and Off the Fairway (1979)	Jack Nicklaus	Straight Shooting	Robert Stack
One Day at a Time	Bernie Winters	Suite in Four Movements	Eric Coates
One Hump or Two	Frank Worthington	Summoned by Bells	John Betjeman
One Man Tango	Anthony Quinn	Sunday Night at Seven	Jack Benny
One Small Footprint (1980)	Molly Weir	Sunset and Evening Star (1955)	Sean O'Casey
On and Off the Lee	Dorothy Hamill	Surprised by Joy	CS Lewis
On My Way to the Club	Ludovic Kennedy	Take It Like a Man	Boy George
On Reflection (1969)	Helen Hayes	Take My Life (1957)	Eddie Cantor
On the Other Hand	Fay Wray	Taken on Trust	Terry Waite
On the Stage (1926)	George Arliss	Tall, Dark and Gruesome	Christopher Lee
Open Book, An	John Huston	Tell It to Louella (1962)	Louella Parsons
Opening Up	Mike Atherton	Testament of Youth	Vera Brittain
Ordeal	Linda Lovelace	Testing Times	Graham Gooch
Orderly Man, An (1983)	Dirk Bogarde	There's Always Tomorrow (1974)	Anna Neagle
Original Sin, The	Anthony Quinn	There's Lovely	Johnny Morris
Other Half, The (1977)	Kenneth Clark	Things I Had to Learn, The	Loretta Young
Other Side of the Street, The	Jean Alexander	Those Twentieth Century	Michael Tippett
Outline	Paul Nash	Blues	
Out of Africa	Isak Dinesen / Karen Blixen	Thursday's Child	Eartha Kitt
		Time and Chance	James Callaghan
Out on a Limb	Heather Mills	Time to Declare	David Owen
Out on a Limb (1983)	Shirley MacLaine	To Hell and Back	Niki Lauda
Peacework (1991)	Spike Milligan	To Hell and Back	Audie Murphy
People	Edgar Wallace	To Keep the Ball Rolling	Anthony Powell
Pictures in the Hallway (1942)	Sean O' Casey	Travelling Player	Michael York
Please Don't Hate Me	Dmitri Tiomkin	Tree Is a Tree, A	King Vidor
Poet in the Family, A	Dannie Abse	Twenty Questions	Norman Hackforth
Point of View, A	Barry Took	Twice Over Lightly (1981)	Helen Hayes
Polly Wants a Zebra	Michael Aspel	Two-Way Story	Cliff Michelmore & Jean Metcalfe
Postillion Struck by Lightning, A (1977)	Dirk Bogarde	Unreliable Memoirs	Clive James
Precious Little Sleep	Wayne Sleep	Up from Slavery	Booker T Washington
Present Indicative (1937)	Noël Coward	Up in the Clouds, Gentlemen Please	John Mills
Prick up Your Ears	Joe Orton		
Prima Donna's Progress, A	Joan Sutherland	Up the Ladder to Obscurity	David Lodge
Quite Contrary	Mary Whitehouse	Up the Years from Bloomsbury (1927)	George Arliss
Ragman's Son, The	Kirk Douglas		
Rebel with a Cause	Hans Eysenck	Vanished World, The (1969)	HE Bates
Reluctant Jester, The	Michael Bentine	Vie d'Henri Brulard, La	Stendhal
Road to Hollywood (1977)	Bob Hope	Voyage (1978)	Sterling Hayden
Roamin' in the Gloaming	Sir Harry Lauder	Walking in the Shade	Doris Lessing
Roar of the Crowd	Gentleman Jim Corbett	Walking Tall	Simon Weston
		Wanderer (1963)	Sterling Hayden
Runthrough (1972)	John Houseman	Way I See It, The (1959)	Eddie Cantor
Scarlet Tree, The (1946)	Osbert Sitwell	Wet Flanders Plain, The (1929)	Henry Williamson
Screening History	Gore Vidal	What Falls Away	Mia Farrow
Second Act	Joan Collins	What's It All About	Michael Caine
Self Consciousness	John Updike	When I Was Young	Raymond Massey
Self Portrait	Gene Tierney	Where Have All the Bullets Gone (1985)	Spike Milligan
Shelley (1980)	Shelley Winters		
Shoes Were for Sunday (1970)	Molly Weir	Where's Harry	Harry Carpenter
Shooting the Actor	Simon Callow	Where's the Rest of Me	Ronald Reagan
Short Walk from Harrods, A (1994)	Dirk Bogarde	Why Me (1989)	Sammy Davis Jnr
		Will This Do	Auberon Waugh
Silver and Gold	Norman Hartnell	With Nails	Richard E Grant
Snakes and Ladders (1978)	Dirk Bogarde	Words	Jean-Paul Sartre
Some Other Rainbow	John McCarthy and Jill Morrell	World Elsewhere, A	Michael Hordern
		World of Yesterday, The	Stefan Zweig
Spend Spend Spend	Vivian Nicholson	World Within World	Stephen Spender
Stamp Album (1987)	Terence Stamp	Years of Opportunity, The (1947)	Barbara Cartland
Stand By Your Man	Tammy Wynette	Yes I Can (1966)	Sammy Davis Jnr
Stare Back and Smile	Joanna Lumley	Yo Yo Man, The	Bill Maynard
Steps in Time	Fred Astaire	You Can Get There from Here (1975)	Shirley MacLaine
Still Dancing	Lew Grade		
Still on My Way to Hollywood	Ernie Wise	Yours Indubitably	Robertson Hare
Story of a Bad Man	Thomas Aldrich	You've Had Your Time (1990)	Anthony Burgess
Story of a Soul, The	Thérèse of Lisieux	Zero to Hero	Frank Bruno

L
I
T
E
R
A
T
U
R
E

NB: Dates are only provided when authors listed have more than one volume of autobiography or in instances where an author's identity may need clarification.

First lines of books and poems

Adams, Richard *Shardik* Even in the dry heat of summer's end, the great forest was never silent.

Agee, James *A Death in the Family* We are talking now of summer evenings in Knoxville, Tennessee in the time that I lived there so successfully disguised to myself as a child.

Alcott, Louisa May *Good Wives* In order that we may start afresh and go to Meg's wedding with free minds, it will be well to begin with a little gossip about the Marches.

Alcott, Louisa May *Little Men* Please, sir, is this Plumfield? asked a ragged boy of the man who opened the great gate at which the omnibus left him.

Alcott, Louisa May *Little Women* Christmas won't be Christmas without any presents, grumbled Jo, lying on the rug.

Angelou, Maya *I Know Why the Caged Bird Sings* When I was three and Bailey was four, we had arrived in the musty little town.

Arnold, Matthew 'Dover Beach' The sea is calm tonight. The tide is full, the moon lies fair.

Ashford, Daisy *The Young Visiters* Mr Salteena was an elderly man of 42 and was fond of asking peaple (sic) to stay with him.

Asimov, Isaac *Foundation* His name was Gaal Dornick and he was just a country boy who had never seen Trantor before.

Asimov, Isaac *I, Robot* I looked at my notes and I didn't like them. I'd spent three days at U.S. Robots and might as well have spent them at home with the Encyclopedia Tellurica.

Atwater, Richard & Florence *Mr. Popper's Penguins* It was an afternoon in late September. In the pleasant city of Stillwater, Mr. Popper, the house painter, was going home from work.

Atwood, Margaret *Cat's Eye* Time is not a line but a dimension, like the dimensions of space.

Auden, WH *Night Mail* This is the Night Mail crossing the border, bringing the cheque and the postal order.

Austen, Jane *Emma* Emma Woodhouse, handsome, clever, and rich, with a comfortable home and happy disposition, seemed to unite some of the best blessings of existence.

Austen, Jane *Mansfield Park* About thirty years ago, Miss Maria Ward of Huntingdon with only seven thousand pounds had the good luck to captivate Sir Thomas Bertram.

Austen, Jane *Northanger Abbey* No one who had ever seen Catherine Morland in her infancy would have supposed her born to be an heroine.

Austen, Jane *Persuasion* Sir Walter Elliot, of Kellynch Hall, in Somersetshire, was a man who, for his own amusement, never took up any book but the Baronetage . . .

Austen, Jane *Pride and Prejudice* It is a truth universally acknowledged, that a single man in possession of a good fortune, must be in want of a wife.

Austen, Jane *Sense and Sensibility* The family of Dashwood has long been settled in Sussex.

Baldwin, James *Go Tell It on the Mountain* Everyone had always said that John would be a preacher when he grew up, just like his father.

Banks, Lynne Reid *The Indian in the Cupboard* It was not that Omri didn't appreciate Patrick's birthday present to him.

Barrie, JM *Peter Pan* All children, except one, grow up.

Barth, John *Giles Goat-Boy* George is my name; my deeds have been heard of in Tower Hall, and my childhood has been chronicled in the *Journal of Experimental Psychology*.

Barth, John *The Sot-Weed Factor* In the last years of the seventeenth century there was to be found among the fops & fools of the London coffee-houses one rangy, gangling flitch called Ebenezer Cooke, more ambitious than talented, and yet more talented than prudent.

Baum, Frank *The Wonderful Wizard of Oz* Dorothy lived in the midst of the great Kansas prairies, with Uncle Henry, who was a farmer, and Aunt Em, who was the farmer's wife.

Bellow, Saul *Herzog* If I am out of my mind, it's all right with me thought Moses Herzog.

Bellow, Saul *Humboldt's Gift* The book of ballads published by Von Humboldt Fleisher in the Thirties was an immediate hit.

Bemelmans, Ludwig *Madeline* In an old house in Paris that was covered with vines lived 12 little girls in two straight lines.

Benchley, Peter *Jaws* The great fish moved silently through the night water, propelled by short sweeps of its crescent tail.

Berryman, John *Homage to Mistress Bradstreet* The Governor your husband lived so long.

Bester, Alfred *The Stars My Destination* This was a Golden Age, a time of high adventure, rich living, and hard dying . . . but nobody thought so.

Betjeman, John 'A Subaltern's Love-Song' Miss J. Hunter Dunn, Miss J. Hunter Dunn, Furnish'd and burnish'd by Aldershot sun.

Blake, William 'Tyger!' Tyger! Tyger! burning bright In the forests of the night, What immortal hand or eye Could frame thy fearful symmetry?

Blatty, William Peter *The Exorcist* Like the brief doomed flare of exploding suns that registers dimly on blind men's eyes, the beginning of the horror passed almost unnoticed.

Böll, Heinrich *The Clown* It was dark by the time I reached Bonn, and I forced myself not to succumb to the series of mechanical actions which had taken hold of me in five years of travelling back and forth.

Boyle, T Coraghessan *The Road to Wellville* Dr. John Harvey Kellogg, inventor of the cornflake and peanut butter, not to mention caramel-cereal coffee, Bromose, Nuttolene and some seventy-five other gastronomically correct foods, paused to level his gaze on the heavyset women in front of him.

Bradbury, Ray *Fahrenheit 451* It was a pleasure to burn.

Bradley, Marion Zimmer *Mists of Avalon* Even in high summer, Tintagel was a haunted place; Igraine, Lady of Duke Gorlois, looked out over the sea from the headland.

Braine, John *Life at the Top* She woke me up by lifting my eyelids; then she slipped under the bed clothes beside me and lay there smiling.

Brautigan, Richard *A Confederate General from Big Sur* When I first heard about Big Sur I didn't know that it was a member of the Confederate States of America.

Brontë, Anne *Agnes Grey* All true histories contain instruction, though in some, the treasure may be hard to find, and when found, so trivial in quantity that the dry shrivelled kernel scarcely compensates for the trouble of cracking the nut.

Brontë, Anne *The Tenant of Wildfell Hall* You must go back with me to the autumn of 1827.

Brontë, Charlotte *Jane Eyre* There was no possibility of taking a walk that day.

Brontë, Charlotte *The Professor* The other day, in looking over my papers, I found in my desk the following copy of a letter.

Brontë, Charlotte *Villette* My Godmother lived in a handsome house in the clean and ancient town of Bretton.

Brontë, Emily *Wuthering Heights* 1801 – I have just returned from a visit to my landlord.

Brooke, Rupert 'The Soldier' If I should die, think only this of me: That there's some corner of a foreign field That is forever England.

Brown, Margaret Wise *Goodnight Moon* In the great green room, there was a telephone and a red balloon.

Brown, Rita Mae *Rubyfruit Jungle* No one remembers her beginnings.

Brown, Rita Mae *Venus Envy* Dying's not so bad. At least I won't have to answer the telephone.

Browning, Elizabeth Barrett 'How Do I Love Thee' How do I love thee? Let me count the ways. .

Browning, Robert 'Childe Roland to the Dark Tower Came' My first thought was, he lied in every word.

Browning, Robert 'Home-Thoughts: from Abroad' Oh, to be in England now that April's there . . .

Buchan, John *The Thirty-Nine Steps* I returned from the city about three o'clock on that May afternoon, pretty well disgusted with life.

Buck, Pearl *The Good Earth* It was Wang Lung's marriage day.

Bulwer-Lytton, Edward *Paul Clifford* It was a dark and stormy night and the rain fell in torrents – except at occasional intervals, when it was checked by a violent gust of wind which swept up the streets (for it is in London that our scene lies), rattling along the housetops, and fiercely agitating the scanty flame of the lamps that struggled against the darkness.

Bunyan, John *The Pilgrim's Progress* As I walked through the wilderness of this world, I lighted on a certain place where was a Den, and I laid me down in that place to sleep: and, as I slept, I dreamed a dream.

Burgess, Anthony *A Clockwork Orange* What's it going to be then, eh?

Burgess, Anthony *Earthly Powers* It was the afternoon of my eighty-first birthday and I was in bed with my catamite when Ali announced that the Archbishop had come to see me.

Burnett, Frances Hodgson *A Little Princess* Once on a dark winter's day, when the yellow fog hung so thick and heavy in the streets of London that the lamps were lighted and the shop windows blazed with gas as they do at night, an odd-looking little girl sat in a cab with her father and was driven rather slowly through the big thoroughfares.

Burnett, Frances Hodgson *The Secret Garden* When Mary Lennox was sent to Misselthwaite Manor to live with her uncle everybody said she was the most disagreeable-looking child ever seen.

Burns, Robert 'A Red Red Rose' O my luve's like a red, red rose, That's newly sprung in June.

Burns, Robert 'To a Field Mouse' Wee, sleekit, cow'rin', tim'rous beastie, O what a panic's in thy breastie.

Butler, Samuel *The Way of All Flesh* When I was a small boy at the beginning of the century I remember an old man who wore knee-breeches and worsted stockings, and used to hobble about the street of our village with the help of a stick.

Byron, Lord 'She Walks in Beauty' She walks in beauty, like the night Of cloudless climes and starry skies.

Caldwell, Taylor *Great Lion of God* He is very ugly, said his mother.

Camus, Albert *The Stranger* Mother died today. Or perhaps it was yesterday, I don't know.

Capote, Truman *Breakfast at Tiffany's* I am always drawn back to the places where I have lived, the houses & their neighborhoods.

Capote, Truman *In Cold Blood* The village of Holcomb stands on the high wheat plains of western Kansas, a lonesome area that other Kansans call 'out there'.

Carey, Peter *Jack Maggs* It was a Saturday night when the man with the red waistcoat arrived in London.

Carroll, Lewis *Alice's Adventures in Wonderland* Alice was beginning to get very tired of sitting by her sister on the bank, and of having nothing to do: once or twice she had peeped into the book her sister was reading, but it had no pictures or conversations in it, 'and what is the use of a book, thought Alice 'without pictures or conversation?'

Carroll, Lewis *Through the Looking Glass and What Alice Found There;* One thing was certain, that the white kitten had had nothing to do with it – it was the black kitten's fault entirely.

Castaneda, Carlos *The Teachings of Don Juan* My notes on my first session with don Juan are dated June 23,1961.

Cather, Willa *My Ántonia* I first heard of Ántonia on what seemed to me an interminable journey across the great midland plains of North America.

Cervantes, Miguel de *Don Quixote* At a village of La Mancha, whose name I do not wish to remember, there lived a little while ago one of those gentlemen who are wont to keep a lance in the rack, an old buckler, a lean horse and a swift greyhound.

Chandler, Raymond *The Big Sleep* It was about eleven o'clock in the morning, mid-October, with the sun not shining and a look of hard wet rain in the clearness of the foothills.

Chang, Jung *Wild Swans* At the age of fifteen my grandmother became the concubine of a warlord general.

Chaucer, Geoffrey *The Canterbury Tales* Whan that Aprill with his shoures soote The droghte of March hath perced to the roote.

Chesterton, GK *The Man Who Was Thursday* The suburb of Saffron Park lay on the sunset side of London, as red and ragged as a cloud of sunset.

Chesterton, GK *The Donkey* When fishes flew and forests walked and figs grew upon thorn.

Chopin, Kate *The Awakening* A green and yellow parrot, which hung in a cage outside the door, kept repeating over and over: 'Allez vous-en! Allez vous-en ! Sapristi ! That's all right !'

LITERATURE

Christie, Agatha   *The Mirror Crack'd*   Miss Jane Marple was sitting by her window.

Clarke, Arthur C   *Childhood's End*   The Volcano that had reared Taratua up from the Pacific depths had been sleeping now for half a million years. Yet in a little while, thought Reinhold, the island would be bathed in fires fiercer than any that had attended its birth.

Clarke, Arthur C   *The City and the Stars*   Like a glowing jewel, the city lay upon the breast of the desert. Once it had known change and alteration, but now time passed it by. Night and day fled across the desert's face, but in Diaspar it was always afternoon, and darkness never came.

Clarke, Arthur C   *2001: A Space Odyssey*   The drought had lasted now for ten million years, and the reign of the terrible lizards had long since ended.

Cleland, John   *Fanny Hill*   Madam, I sit down to give you an undeniable proof of my considering your desires as indispensable orders.

Collins, Wilkie   *The Moonstone*   In the first part of Robinson Crusoe, at page one hundred and twenty-nine, you will find it thus written: 'Now I saw, though too late, the Folly of beginning a Work before we count the Cost, and before we judge rightly of our own strength to go through with it.'

Collins, Wilkie   *The Woman in White*   This is the story of what a Woman's patience can endure, and what a Man's resolution can achieve.

Condon, Richard   *Prizzi's Honor*   Corrado Prizzi's granddaughter was being married before the baroque altar of Santa Grazia de Traghetto, the lucky church of the Prizzi family.

Conrad, Joseph   *Heart of Darkness*   Nellie, a cruising yawl, swung to her anchor without a flutter of sails, and was at rest.

Conrad, Joseph   *Lord Jim*   He was an inch, perhaps two, under six feet, powerfully built, and he advanced straight at you with a slight stoop of the shoulders, head forward, and a fixed from-under stare which made you think of a charging bull.

Conrad, Joseph   *Nostromo*   In the time of Spanish rule, and for many years afterwards, the town of Sulaco – the luxuriant beauty of the orange gardens bears witness to its antiquity – had never been commercially anything more important than a coasting port with a fairly large local trade in ox-hides and indigo.

Conrad, Joseph   *An Outcast of the Islands*   When he stepped off the straight and narrow path of his peculiar honesty, it was with an inward assertion of unflinching resolve.

Conrad, Joseph   *The Secret Agent*   Mr Verloc, going out in the morning, left his shop nominally in charge of his brother-in-law.

Coolidge, Susan   *What Katy Did Next*   The September sun was glinting cheerfully into a pretty bedroom furnished with blue.

Cooper, James Fenimore   *The Last of the Mohicans*   It was a feature peculiar to the colonial wars of North America, that the toils and dangers of the wilderness were to be encountered before the adverse hosts could meet.

Crane, Stephen   *The Red Badge of Courage*   The cold passed reluctantly from the earth, and the retiring fogs revealed an army stretched out on the hills, resting.

Dahl, Roald   *Charlie and the Chocolate Factory*   These two very old people are the father and mother of Mr. Bucket.

Dante, Alighieri   *Divine Comedy*   Midway along the path of life.

Davies, Robertson   *The Cunning Man*   Should I have taken the false teeth?

Davies, WH   'Leisure'   What is this life if, full of care, We have no time to stand and stare?

Defoe, Daniel   *Robinson Crusoe*   I was born in the year 1632, in the city of York, of a good family, though not of that country, my father being a foreigner of Bremen, who settled first at Hull. He got a good estate by merchandise, and leaving off his trade lived afterward at York, from whence he had married my mother, whose relations were named Robinson, a good family in that country, and from whom I was called Robinson Kreutznear.

Deighton, Len   *Catch a Falling Spy*   Smell that air, said Major Mann.

Deighton, Len   *The Ipcress File*   They came through on the hot line at about half past two in the afternoon.

De La Mare, Walter   'The Listeners'   'Is there anybody there?' said the Traveller, Knocking on the moonlit door.

Dick, Philip K   *Do Androids Dream of Electric Sheep?*   A merry little surge of electricity piped by automatic alarm from the mood organ beside his bed awakened Rick Deckard.

Dickens, Charles   *Barnaby Rudge*   In the year 1775, there stood upon the borders of Epping Forest, at a distance of about twelve miles from London – measuring the Standard in Cornhill, or rather from the spot on or near to which the Standard used to be in days of yore – a house of public entertainment called the Maypole; which fact was demonstrated to all such travellers as could neither read nor write (and at that time a vast number both of travellers and stay-at-homes were in this condition) by the emblem reared on the roadside over and against the house, which, if not of those goodly proportions that Maypoles were wont to present in olden times, was a fair young ash, thirty feet in height, and straight as any arrow that ever English yeoman drew.

Dickens, Charles   *Bleak House*   London. Michaelmas term lately over, and the Lord Chancellor sitting in Lincoln's Inn Hall.

Dickens, Charles   *A Christmas Carol*   Marley was dead, to begin with. There is no doubt whatever about that.

Dickens, Charles   *David Copperfield*   Whether I shall turn out to be the hero of my own life, or whether that station will be held by anybody else, these pages must show.

Dickens, Charles   *Dombey and Son*   Dombey sat in the corner of the darkened room in the great armchair by the bedside, and Son lay tucked up in a warm little basket bedstead, carefully disposed on a low settee immediately in front of the fire and close to it, as if his constitution were analogous to that of a muffin, and it was essential to toast him brown while he was very new.

Dickens, Charles   *Great Expectations*   My father's family name being Pirrip, and my christian name Philip, my infant tongue could make of both names nothing longer or more explicit than Pip.

Dickens, Charles   *Hard Times*   Now, what I want is Facts.

Dickens, Charles   *Little Dorrit*   Thirty years ago, Marseilles lay burning in the sun, one day.

Dickens, Charles   *Martin Chuzzlewit*   As no lady or

gentleman, with any claims to polite breeding, can possibly sympathise with the Chuzzlewit Family without being first assured of the extreme antiquity of the race, it is a great satisfaction to know that it undoubtedly descended in a direct line from Adam and Eve; and was, in the very earliest times, closely connected with the agricultural interest.

Dickens, Charles *The Mystery of Edwin Drood* An ancient English Cathedral Tower?

Dickens, Charles *Nicholas Nickleby* There once lived, in a sequestered part of the county of Devonshire, one Mr Godfrey Nickleby: a worthy gentleman, who, taking it into his head rather late in life that he must get married, and not being young enough or rich enough to aspire to the hand of a lady of fortune, had wedded an old flame out of mere attachment, who in her turn had taken him for the same reason.

Dickens, Charles *The Old Curiosity Shop* Night is generally my time for walking.

Dickens, Charles *Oliver Twist* Among other public buildings in a certain town, which for many reasons it will be prudent to refrain from mentioning, and to which I will assign no fictitious name, there is one anciently common to most towns, great or small – to wit, a workhouse; and in this workhouse was born, on a day and date which I need not trouble myself to repeat, inasmuch as it can be of no possible consequence to the reader, in this stage of the business at all events, the item of mortality whose name is prefixed to the head of this chapter.

Dickens, Charles *Our Mutual Friend* In these times of ours, though concerning the exact year there is no need to be precise, a boat of dirty and disreputable appearance, with two figures in it, floated on the Thames, between Southwark Bridge which is of iron, and London Bridge which is of stone, as an autumn evening was closing in.

Dickens, Charles *Pickwick Papers* The first ray of light which illumines the gloom, and converts into a dazzling brilliancy that obscurity in which the earlier history of the public career of the immortal Pickwick would appear to be involved, is derived from the perusal of the following entry in the transactions of the Pickwick Club, which the editor of these papers feels the highest pleasure in laying before his readers as a proof of the careful attention, indefatigable assiduity, and nice discrimination, with which his search among the multifarious documents confided to him has been conducted.

Dickens, Charles *A Tale of Two Cities* It was the best of times, it was the worst of times, it was the age of wisdom, it was the age of foolishness, it was the epoch of belief, it was the epoch of incredulity, it was the season of Light, it was the season of Darkness, it was the spring of hope, it was the winter of despair, we had everything before us, we had nothing before us, we were all going direct to Heaven, we were all going direct the other way – in short, the period was so.

Dickinson, Emily untitled poem I heard a Fly buzz – when I died . . .

Doctorow, EL *Ragtime* In 1902 Father built a house at the crest of the Broadview Avenue hill in New Rochelle, New York.

Dos Passos, John *1919* Oh the infantree the infantree With the dirt behind their ears
ARMIES CLASH AT VERDUN IN GLOBE'S GREATEST BATTLE 150,000 MEN AND WOMEN PARADE

but another question and a very important one is raised.

Dostoevsky, Fyodor *The Brothers Karamazov* Alexey Fyodorovitch Karamazov was the third son of Fyodor Pavlovitch Karamazov, a landowner well known in our district in his own day, and still remembered among us owing to his gloomy and tragic death, which happened thirteen years ago, and which I shall describe in its proper place.

Dostoevsky, Fyodor *Crime and Punishment* On an exceptionally hot evening early in July a young man came out of the garret in which he lodged in S. Place and walked slowly, as though in hesitation, towards K. bridge.

Doyle, Sir Arthur Conan *The Hound of the Baskervilles* Mr. Sherlock Holmes, who was usually very late in the mornings, save upon those not infrequent occasions when he was up all night, was seated at the breakfast table.

Dryden, John *Absalom and Achitophel* In pious times, ere priestcraft did begin. . .

Du Maurier, Daphne *The King's General* September 1653. The last of summer. The first chill winds of autumn.

Du Maurier, Daphne *Rebecca* Last night I dreamt I went to Manderley again.

Dumas, Alexandre *The Count of Monte Cristo* On the 24th of February, 1815, the lookout of Notre Dame de la Garde signalled the three-master, the *Pharaon*, from Smyrna, Trieste, and Naples. As usual, a pilot put off immediately, and rounding the Chateau d'If, got on board the vessel between Cape Morgion and the Isle of Rion.

Dumas, Alexandre *The Three Musketeers* On the first Monday of the month of April, 1625, the town of Meung, in which the author of The Romance of the Rose was born, appeared to be in a perfect state of revolution as if the Huguenots had just made a second Rochelle of it.

Eliot, George *Middlemarch* Miss Brooke had that kind of beauty which seems to be thrown into relief by poor dress.

Eliot, George *The Mill on the Floss* A wide plain, where the broadening Floss hurries on between its green banks to the sea, and the loving tide, rushing to meet it, checks its passage with an impetuous embrace.

Eliot, George *Silas Marner* In the days when the spinning-wheels hummed busily in the farmhouses – and even great ladies, clothed in silk and thread-lace, had their toy spinning-wheels of polished oak – there might be seen in districts far away among the lanes, or deep in the bosom of the hills, certain pallid undersized men, who, by the side of the brawny country-folk, looked like the remnants of a disinherited race.

Eliot, TS *East Coker* In my beginning is my end.

Eliot, TS 'The Love Song of J. Alfred Prufrock' Let us go then, you and I . . .

Ellison, Ralph *Invisible Man* I am an invisible man.

Farmer, Philip Jose *To Your Scattered Bodies Go* His wife had held him in her arms as if she could keep death away from him. He had cried out, 'My God, I am a dead man!'

Faulkner, William *Go Down, Moses* Isaac McCaslin, 'Uncle Ike', past seventy and nearer eighty than he ever corroborated any more, a widower now and uncle to half a country and father to one.

Faulkner, William *Sanctuary* From behind the screen of bushes which surrounded the spring, Popeye watched the man drinking.

LITERATURE

Faulkner, William *The Sound and the Fury* Through the fence, between the curling flower spaces, I could see them hitting.

Fielding, Henry *Tom Jones* An author ought to consider himself not as a gentleman who gives a private or eleemosynary treat.

Fitzgerald, F Scott *The Great Gatsby* In my younger and more vulnerable years my father gave me some advice that I've been turning over in my mind ever since.

Flaubert, Gustave *Madame Bovary* We were in the study-hall when the headmaster entered, followed by a new boy not yet in school uniform and by the handyman carrying a large desk.

Fleming, Ian *Chitty-Chitty-Bang-Bang* Most motorcars are conglomerations (this is a long word for bundles) of steel and wire and rubber and plastic, and electricity and oil and gasoline and water, and the toffee papers you pushed down the crack in the back seat last Sunday.

Fleming, Ian *Goldfinger* James Bond, with two double bourbons inside him, sat back in the final departure lounge of Miami Airport and thought about life and death.

Ford, Ford Madox *The Good Soldier* This is the saddest story I have ever heard.

Forster, EM *A Passage to India* Except for the Marabar Caves – and they are twenty miles off – the city of Chandrapore presents nothing extraordinary.

Forsyth, Frederick *The Odessa File* Everybody seems to remember what they were doing on November 22nd 1963, when Kennedy was shot.

Fowles, John *The French Lieutenant's Woman* An easterly is the most disagreeable wind in Lyme Bay – Lyme Bay being that largest byte from the underside of England's outstretched southwestern leg – and a person of curiosity could at once have deduced several strong probabilities about the pair who began to walk down the quay at Lyme Regis, the small but ancient eponym of the inbite, one incisively sharp and blustery morning in the late March of 1867.

Gallico, Paul *The Poseidon Adventure* At seven o'clock, the morning of the 26th of December, the S.S. Poseidon, 81,000 tons, homeward bound for Lisbon after a month-long Christmas cruise to African and South American ports, suddenly found herself in the midst of an unaccountable swell, 400 miles southwest of the Azores, and began to roll like a pig.

Galsworthy, John *The Man of Property* Those privileged to be present at a family festival of the Forsythes have seen that charming and instructive sight – an upper middle class family in full plumage.

Gardner, John *Grendel* The old ram stands looking down over rockslides, stupidly triumphant.

Gibson, William *Neuromancer* The sky above the port was the color of television, tuned to a dead channel.

Gide, André *The Fruits of the Earth* Do not hope, Nathaniel, to find God here or there – but everywhere.

Gipson, Fred *Old Yeller* We called him Old Yeller.

Golding, William *Lord of the Flies* The boy with fair hair lowered himself down the last few feet of rock and began to pick his way towards the lagoon.

Golding, William *The Princess Bride* This is my favorite book in all the world, though I have never read it.

Goldman, William *Marathon Man* Everytime he drove through Yorkville, Rosenbaum got angry, just on general principles.

Goldsmith, Oliver 'Elegy on the Death of a Mad Dog' Good people all, of every sort, Give ear unto my song.

Grahame, Kenneth *The Wind in the Willows* The Mole had been working very hard all the morning, spring-cleaning his little home.

Grass, Günter *The Tin Drum* Granted: I am an inmate of a mental hospital; my keeper is watching me, he never lets me out of his sight; there's a peephole in the door, and my keeper's eye is the shade of brown that can never see through a blue-eyed type like me.

Graves, Robert *I, Claudius* I, Tiberius Claudius Drusus Nero Germanicus This-that-and-the-other (for I shall not trouble you yet with all my titles) who was once, and not so long ago either, known to my friends and relatives and associates as 'Claudius the Idiot', or 'That Claudius', or 'Claudius the Stammerer', or 'Clau-Clau-Claudius' or at best as 'Poor Uncle Claudius', am now about to write this strange history of my life; starting from my earliest childhood and continuing year by year until I reach the fateful point of change where, some eight years ago, at the age of fifty-one, I suddenly found myself caught in what I may call the 'golden predicament' from which I have never since become disentangled.

Gray, Thomas 'Elegy Written in a Country Churchyard' The curfew tolls the knell of parting day . . .

Gray, Thomas 'The Progress of Poesy' Awake, Aeolian lyre, awake

Greene, Graham *The Power and the Glory* Mr Tench went out to look for his ether cylinder, into the blazing Mexican sun.

Greene, Graham *The Quiet American* After dinner I sat and waited for Pyle in my room over the rue Catinat: he had said, 'I'll be with you at latest by ten,' and when midnight had struck I couldn't stay quiet any longer and went down into the street.

Guterson, David *Snow Falling on Cedars* The accused man, Kabuo Miyamoto, sat proudly upright with a rigid grace.

Høeg, Peter *Miss Smilla's Feeling for Snow* It's freezing – an extraordinary 0º fahrenheit – and it's snowing, and in the language that is no longer mine the snow is qanik –

Haggard, H Rider *King Solomon's Mines* It is a curious thing that at my age, fifty-five last birthday, I should find myself taking up a pen to try and write a history.

Haggard, H Rider *She* There are some events of which each circumstance and surrounding detail seem to be graven on the memory in such a fashion that we cannot forget them.

Hailey, Arthur *Airport* At half-past six on a Friday evening in January, Lincoln International Airport, Illinois, was functioning, though with difficulty.

Haley, Alex *Roots* Early in the spring of 1750, in the village of Juffure, four days upriver from the coast of Gambia, West Africa, a manchild was born to Omoro and Binta Kinte.

Hammett, Dashiell *The Maltese Falcon* Samuel Spade's jaw was long and bony, his chin a jutting 'V' under the more flexible 'V' of his mouth.

Hammett, Dashiell *The Thin Man* I was leaning against a bar in a speak-easy on Fifty-second Street, waiting for Nora to finish her Christmas shopping, when a girl got up from the table where she had been sitting.

Hardy, Thomas *Far from the Madding Crowd* When

Farmer Oak smiled, the corners of his mouth spread till they were within an unimportant distance of his ears, his eyes were reduced to chinks, and diverging wrinkles appeared round them, extending upon his countenance like the rays in a rudimentary sketch of the rising sun.

Hardy, Thomas *Jude the Obscure* The schoolmaster was leaving the village, and everybody seemed sorry.

Hardy, Thomas *The Mayor of Casterbridge* One evening of late summer, before the nineteenth century had reached one-third of its span, a young man and woman, the latter carrying a child, were approaching the large village of Weydon-Priors, in Upper Wessex, on foot.

Hardy, Thomas *Tess of the D'Urbervilles* On an evening in the latter part of May a middle-aged man was walking homeward from Shaston to the village of Marlott, in the adjoining Vale of Blakemore or Blackmoor.

Harris, Robert *Fatherland* Thick cloud had pressed down on Berlin all night and now it was lingering into what passed for morning.

Hartley, LP *The Go-Between* The past is a foreign country, they do things differently there.

Hawthorne, Nathaniel *The House of the Seven Gables* Halfway down a bystreet of one of our New England towns stands a rusty wooden house, with seven acutely peaked gables, facing towards various points of the compass, and a huge, clustered chimney in the midst.

Hawthorne, Nathaniel *The Scarlet Letter* A throng of bearded men, in sad-colored garments and gray, steeple-crowned hats, intermixed with women, some wearing hoods, and others bareheaded, was assembled in front of a wooden edifice, the door of which was heavily timbered with oak, and studded with iron spikes.

Heinlein, Robert *The Moon Is a Harsh Mistress* I see in *Lunaya Pravda* that Luna City Council has passed on first reading a bill to examine, license, inspect – and tax – public food vendors operating inside municipal pressure.

Heinlein, Robert *Stranger in a Strange Land* Once upon a time there was a Martian named Valentine Michael Smith.

Heller, Joseph *Catch-22* It was love at first sight.

Heller, Joseph *Something Happened* I get the willies when I see closed doors.

Hemans, Felicia 'Casabianca' The boy stood on the burning deck, Whence all but he had fled.

Hemingway, Ernest *The Old Man and the Sea* He was an old man who fished alone in a skiff in the Gulf stream and he had gone 84 days now without taking a fish.

Herrick, Robert 'To the Virgins, to Make Much of Time' Gather ye rosebuds while ye may, Old Time is still a-flying.

Hesse, Hermann *Siddhartha* In the shade of the house, in the sunshine on the river bank by the boats, in the shade of the sallow wood and the fig tree, Siddharta, the handsome Brahmin's son, grew up with his friend Govinda.

Higgins, Colin *Harold and Maude* Harold Chasen stepped up on the chair and placed the noose about his neck.

Hoban, Russell *Riddley Walker* On my naming day when I come 12 I gone front spear and kilt a wyld boar he parbly ben the las wyld pig on the Bundel.

Homer *The Odyssey* By now the other warriors, those that had escaped head-long ruin by sea or in a battle, were safely home.

Hopkins, Gerard Manley 'The Wreck of the Deutschland' Thou mastering me . . .

Hughes, Thomas *Tom Brown's Schooldays* The Browns have been illustrious by the pen of Thackeray and the pencil of Doyle.

Hugo, Victor *The Hunchback of Notre-Dame* It was three hundred forty-eight years, six months, and nineteen days ago today that the citizens of Paris were awakened by the pealing of all the bells in the triple precincts of the City, the University, and the Town.

Hugo, Victor *Les Misérables* In 1815, M. Charles-François-Bienvenu Myriel was Bishop of D—.

Hurston, Zora Neale *Their Eyes Were Watching God* Ships at a distance have every man's wish on board.

Huxley, Aldous *Brave New World* A squat gray building of only thirty-four stories. Over the main entrance the words CENTRAL LONDON HATCHERY AND CONDITIONING CENTRE, and in a shield the World State's motto, Community, Identity, Stability.

Huxley, Aldous *Crome Yellow* Along this particular stretch of line, no express had ever passed.

Irving, John *The Hotel New Hampshire* The summer my father bought the bear, none of us was born – we weren't even conceived: not Frank, the oldest; not Fanny, the loudest; not me, the next; and not the youngest of us, Lilly and Egg.

Irving, John *A Prayer for Owen Meany* I am doomed to remember a boy with a wrecked voice – not because of his voice, or because he was the smallest person I ever knew, or even because he was the instrument of my mother's death, but because he is the reason I believe in God; I am a Christian because of Owen Meany.

Irving, John *The World According to Garp* Garp's mother, Jenny Fields, was arrested in Boston in 1942 for wounding a man in a movie theater.

Jacques, Brian *Redwall* Mathias cut a comical figure as he hobbled his way along the cloisters, with his large sandals flip-flopping and his tail peeping from beneath the baggy folds of an oversized novice's habit.

James, Henry *The Turn of the Screw* The story had held us, round the fire, sufficiently breathless, but except the obvious remark that it was gruesome, as, on Christmas Eve in an old house, a strange tale should essentially be, I remember no comment uttered till somebody happened to say that it was the only case he had met in which such a visitation had fallen on a child.

Jong, Erica *Fear of Flying* There were 117 psychoanalysts on the Pan Am flight to Vienna and I'd been treated by at least six of them.

Jonson, Ben 'To Celia' Drink to me only with thine eyes: and I will pledge with mine.

Joyce, James *Dubliners* There was no hope for him this time: it was the third stroke.

Joyce, James *Portrait of the Artist as a Young Man* Once upon a time and a very good time it was there was a moocow coming down along the road and this moocow that was coming down along the road met a nicens little boy named baby tuckoo.

Joyce, James *Ulysses* Stately plump Buck Mulligan came from the stairhead, bearing a bowl of lather on which a mirror and a razor lay crossed.

L I T E R A T U R E

Juster, Norton *The Phantom Tollbooth* There was a boy named Milo who didn't know what to do with himself . . .

Kafka, Franz 'Metamorphosis' As Gregor Samsa awoke one morning from uneasy dreams, he found himself transformed into a giant insect.

Kafka, Franz *The Trial* Someone must have been telling lies about Joseph K, for without having done anything wrong he was arrested one fine morning.

Keats, John 'La Belle Dame Sans Merci' Oh, What can ail thee, knight at arms Alone and palely loitering.

Keats, John *Hyperion* Deep in the shady sadness of a vale . . .

Keats, John 'On First Looking into Chapman's Homer' Much have I travell'd in the realms of gold, And many goodly states and kingdoms seen.

Keats, John 'To Autumn' Season of mists and mellow fruitfulness, close bosom-friend of the maturing sun.

Kennedy, William *Quinn's Book* I, Daniel Quinn, neither the first nor the last of a line of such Quinn's, set eyes on Maud the wondrous on a late December day in 1849 on the banks of the river of the aristocrats and paupers, just as the great courtesan Magdalena Colón, also known as La Última, a woman whose presence turned men into spittling, masturbating pigs, boarded a skiff to carry her across the river's icy water from Albany to Greenbush, her first stop en route to the city of Troy, a community of iron, where later that evening she was scheduled to enact, yet again, her role as the lascivious Lais, that fabled prostitute who spurned Demosthenes' gold and yielded free to Diogenes, the virtuous, impecunious tub-dweller.

King, Stephen *Carrie* Nobody was really surprised when it happened, not really, not on the subconscious level where savage things grow.

King, Stephen *Cujo* Not so long ago, a monster came to the small town of Castle Rock, Maine.

Kingsolver, Barbara *The Bean Trees* I have been afraid of putting air in a tire ever since I saw a tractor tire blow up and throw Newt Hardbines's father over the top of the Standard Oil sign.

Kingsolver, Barbara *Pigs in Heaven* Women on their own run in Alice's family.

Kipling, Rudyard 'Gunga Din' You may talk o'gin and beer, when you're quartered safe out 'ere.

Kipling, Rudyard 'If' If you can keep your head when all about you are losing theirs and blaming it on you.

Kipling, Rudyard *The Jungle Book* It was seven o'clock of a very warm evening in the Seeonee hills when Father Wolf woke up from his day's rest, scratched himself, yawned, and spread out his paws one after the other to get rid of the sleepy feeling in their tips.

Kipling, Rudyard *Kim* He sat in defiance of municipal orders, astride the gun of Zam-Zammeh on her brick platform opposite the old Ajaibgher – the Wonder House, as the natives called the Lahore Museum.

Kipling, Rudyard *Stalky and Co* In summer all right-minded boys built huts in the furze-hill behind the College – little lairs whittled out of the heart of the prickly bushes, full of stumps, odd root-ends, and spikes, but, since they were strictly forbidden, palaces of delight.

Knowles, John *A Separate Peace* I went back to the Devon School not long ago, and found it looking oddly newer than when I was a student there fifteen years before.

Kosinski, Jerzy *The Painted Bird* In the first weeks of World War II, in the fall of 1939, a six year old boy from a large city in Eastern Europe was sent by his parents, like thousands of other children, to the shelter of a distant village.

Kundera, Milan *The Unbearable Lightness of Being* The idea of eternal return is a mysterious one, and Nietzsche has often perplexed other philosophers with it: to think that everything recurs as we once experienced it, and that the recurrence itself recurs ad infinitum! What does this mad myth signify?

L'Engle, Madeline *A Wrinkle In Time* It was a dark and stormy night.

Lawrence, DH *Lady Chatterley's Lover* Ours is essentially a tragic age, so we refuse to take it tragically.

Lawrence, DH *Sons and Lovers* 'The Bottoms' succeeded to 'Hell Row'.

Lawrence, DH *Women In Love* Ursula and Gudrun Brangwen sat one morning in the window-bay of their father's house in Beldover, working and talking.

Le Carré, John *The Honourable Schoolboy* Afterwards, in the dusty little corners where London's secret servants drink together, there was argument about where the Dolphin case history should really begin.

Le Carré, John *The Russia House* In a broad Moscow street not two hundred yards from the Leningrad station, on the upper floor of an ornate and hideous hotel built by Stalin in the style known to Muscovites as Empire During the Plague, the British Council's first ever audio fair for the teaching of the English language and the spread of British culture was grinding to its excruciating end.

Le Carré, John *The Spy Who Came in from the Cold* The American handed Leamas another cup of coffee and said, 'Why don't you go back and sleep? We can ring you if he shows up.'

Le Carré, John *Tinker, Tailor, Soldier, Spy* The truth is, if old Major Dover hadn't dropped dead at Taunton races Jim would never have come to Thursgood's at all.

Lee, Harper *To Kill a Mockingbird* When he was nearly thirteen, my brother Jem got his arm badly broken at the elbow.

Le Guin, Ursula *The Dispossessed* There was a wall.

Le Guin, Ursula *The Left Hand of Darkness* I'll make my report as if I told a story, for I was taught as a child on my homeworld that Truth is a matter of the imagination.

Leroux, Gaston *The Phantom of the Opera* It was the evening on which MM. Debienne and Poligny, the managers of the Opera, were giving a last gala performance to mark their retirement.

Levin, Ira *Rosemary's Baby* Rosemary and Guy Woodhouse had signed a lease on a five-room apartment in a geometric white house on First Avenue when they received word, from a woman named Mrs. Cortez, that a four-room apartment in Bramford had become available.

Lewis, CS *The Lion, the Witch and the Wardrobe* Once there were four children whose names were Peter, Susan, Edmond, and Lucy.

Lewis, Sinclair *Babbitt* The tower of Zenith aspired above the morning mist; austere towers of steel and cement and limestone, sturdy as cliffs and delicate as silver rods.

Lewis, Sinclair *Elmer Gantry* Elmer Gantry was drunk. He was eloquently drunk, lovingly and pugnaciously drunk.

Lewis, Sinclair *Main Street* This is America – a town of a few thousand, in a region of wheat and corn and dairies and little groves. The town is, in our tale, called 'Gopher Prairie, Minnesota.' But its Main Street is the continuation of Main Streets everywhere.

London, Jack *The Call of the Wild* Buck did not read the newspapers or he would have known that trouble was brewing.

Longfellow, Henry Wadsworth *The Song of Hiawatha* Should you ask me, whence these stories?

Longfellow, Henry Wadsworth 'The Village Blacksmith' Under a spreading chestnut tree The village smithy stands.

Lovecraft, HP *The Call Of Cthulhu* The most merciful thing in the world, I think, is the inability of the human mind to correlate all its contents.

Macaulay, Rose *The Towers of Trebizond* 'Take my camel dear', said my aunt Dot, as she climbed down from this animal on her return from High Mass.

McCloskey, Robert *Make Way for Ducklings* Mr. and Mrs. Mallard were looking for a place to live.

McCullers, Carson *The Heart Is a Lonely Hunter* In the town there were two mutes, and they were always together.

McCullough, Colleen *The First Man in Rome* Having no personal commitment to either of the new consuls, Gaius Julius Caesar and his son simply tacked themselves onto the procession which started nearest to their own house, the procession of the senior consul, Marcus Minucius Rufus.

McCullough, Colleen *The Thorn Birds* On December 8th, 1915, Meggie Cleary had her fourth birthday.

McCullough, Colleen *Caesar's Women* Brutus, I don't like the look of your skin. Come here to the light, please.

MacDonald, Betty *Mrs. Piggle Wiggle* I expect I might as well begin by telling you about Mrs. Piggle-Wiggle.

McEwan, Ian *Enduring Love* The beginning is simple to mark.

McKenna, Richard *The Sand Pebbles* Hello, ship, Jake Holman said under his breath.

McMillan, Terry *Waiting to Exhale* Right now I'm supposed to be all geeked up because I'm getting ready for a New Year's Eve party that some guy named Lionel invited me to.

McMurtry, Larry *Terms of Endearment* The success of a marriage invariably depends on the woman, Mrs. Greenway said.

Malamud, Bernard *The Fixer* From the small crossed window of his room above the stable in the brickyard, Yakov Bok saw people in their long overcoats running somewhere early that morning, everybody in the same direction.

Mann, Thomas *Buddenbrooks* And – and – what comes next? Oh, yes, yes, what the dickens does come next? C'est la question, ma très chère demoiselle! Frau Consul Buddenbrooks shot a glance at her husband and came to the rescue of her daughter.

Márquez, Gabriel García *One Hundred Years of Solitude* Many years later, as he faced the firing squad, Colonel Aureliano Buendía was to remember that distant afternoon when his father took him to discover ice.

Marvell, Andrew 'To His Coy Mistress' Had we but world enough, and time, This coyness, Lady, were no crime.

Masefield, John 'Sea-Fever' I must go down to the seas again, to the lonely sea and the sky, And all I ask is a tall ship and a star to steer her by . . .

Maugham, W Somerset *Of Human Bondage* The day broke grey and dull.

Melville, Herman *Billy Budd* In the time before steamships, or then more frequently than now, a stroller along the docks of any considerable sea-port would occasionally have his attention arrested by a group of bronzed mariners, man-of-war's men or merchant-sailors in holiday attire ashore on liberty.

Melville, Herman *Moby-Dick* Call me Ishmael.

Metalious, Grace *Peyton Place* Indian summer is like a woman. Ripe, hotly passionate, but fickle, she comes and goes as she pleases so that one is never sure whether she will come at all, nor for how long she will stay.

Michener, James A *The Source* On Tuesday the freighter steamed through the Straits of Gibraltar and for five days plowed eastward through the Mediterranean, past islands and peninsulas rich in history, so that on Saturday night the steward advised Dr. Cullinane, 'If you wish an early sight of the Holy Land you must be up at dawn.'

Miller, Henry *Tropic of Cancer* I am living at the Villa Borghese. There is not a crumb of dirt anywhere nor a chair misplaced. We are alone here and we are dead.

Miller Jr, Walter *A Canticle for Leibowitz* Brother Francis Gerard of Utah might never have discovered the blessed documents, had it not been for the pilgrim with girded loins who had appeared during that young novice's Lenten fast in the desert.

Milton, John *Lycidas* Yet once more, O ye laurels, and once more, Ye myrtles brown, with ivy never sere.

Milton, John 'On His Blindness' When I consider how my light is spent, Ere half my days, in this dark world and wide.

Milton, John *Paradise Lost* Of man's first disobedience, and the fruit Of that forbidden tree, whose mortal taste Brought death into the world, and all our woe, With loss of Eden.

Mitchell, Margaret *Gone with the Wind* Scarlett O'Hara was not beautiful, but men seldom realized it when caught by her charm as the Tarleton twins were.

Montgomery, Lucy Maud *Anne of Green Gables* Mrs. Rachel Lynde lived just where the Avonlea main road dipped down into a little hollow.

Morrison, Toni *Beloved* 124 was spiteful.

Morrison, Toni *Sula* In that place, where they tore the night shade and blackberry patches from their roots to make room for the Medallion City Golf Course, there was once a neighborhood.

Nabokov, Vladimir *Lolita* Lolita, light of my life, fire of my loins.

Naylor, Gloria *The Women of Brewster Place* Brewster Place was the bastard child of several clandestine meetings between the alderman of the sixth district and the managing director of the Unico Realty Company.

Niven, Larry *Ringworld* In the night time heat of Beirut in one of a row of general address transfer booths, Louis Wu flicked into reality.

Norton, Mary *The Borrowers* It was Mrs May who first told me about them.

LITERATURE

Oates, Joyce Carol *Because It Is Bitter, and Because It Is My Heart* Little Red Garlock, sixteen years old, skull smashed soft as a rotted pumpkin and body dumped into the Cassadaga River near the foot of Pitt Street, must not have sunk as deep as he'd been intended to sink, or floated as far.

Oates, Joyce Carol *Bellefleur* It was many years ago in that dark, chaotic, unfathomable pool of time before Germaine's birth (nearly twelve months before her birth), on a night in late September stirred by innumerable frenzied winds, like spirits contending with one another.

Oates, Joyce Carol *Expensive People* I was a child murderer.

O'Connor, Flannery *The Violent Bear It Away* Francis Marion Tarwater's uncle had been dead for only half a day when the boy got too drunk to finish digging his grave.

Orwell, George *1984* It was a bright cold day in April, and the clocks were striking thirteen.

Owen, Wilfred 'Anthem for Doomed Youth' What passing-bells for these who die as cattle?

Pasternak, Boris *Doctor Zhivago* On they went, singing 'Rest Eternal,' and whenever they stopped, their feet, the horses, and the gusts of wind seemed to carry on their singing.

Paterson, Katherine *Bridge to Terabitha* Ba-room, ba-room, ba-room, baripity, baripity, baripity, baripity – Good.

Piercy, Marge *Small Change* Beth was looking in the mirror of her mother's vanity.

Piper, Watty *The Little Engine That Could* Chug, chug, chug. Puff, puff, puff. Ding-dong, ding-dong.

Plath, Sylvia *The Bell Jar* It was a queer, sultry summer, the summer they electrocuted the Rosenbergs, and I didn't know what I was doing in New York.

Pohl, Frederick *Gateway* My name is Robinette Broadhead, in spite of which I am male.

Pope, Alexander *The Dunciad* The Mighty Mother, and her Son, who brings The Smithfield muses to the ear of kings, I sing.

Porter, Katherine Anne *Ship of Fools* August, 1931 – The port town of Veracruz is a little purgatory between land and sea.

Portis, Charles *True Grit* People do not give it credence that a fourteen-year-old girl could leave home and go off in the wintertime to avenge her father's blood.

Potok, Chaim *The Chosen* For the first fifteen years of our lives, Danny and I lived within five blocks of each other and neither of us knew of the other's existence.

Puzo, Mario *The Godfather* Amerigo Bonasera sat in New York Criminal Court Number 3 and waited for justice; vengeance on the men who had so cruelly hurt his daughter.

Pynchon, Thomas *Gravity's Rainbow* A screaming comes across the sky.

Rand, Ayn *Atlas Shrugged* Who is John Galt?.

Remarque, Erich Maria *All Quiet on the Western Front* We are five miles behind the front.

Renault, Mary *The King Must Die* The Citadel of Troizen, where the Palace stands, was built by giants before anyone remembers.

Rey, HA *Curious George* This is George. He lived in Africa.

Robbins, Tom *Even Cowgirls Get the Blues* Amoebae leave no fossils.

Robbins, Tom *Jitterbug Perfume* The beet is the most intense of vegetables.

Robbins, Tom *Still Life with Woodpecker* In the last quarter of the twentieth century, at a time when Western civilization was declining too rapidly for comfort and yet too slowly to be exciting, much of the world sat on the edge of an increasingly expensive theater seat, waiting – with various combinations of dread, hope, and ennui – for something momentous to occur.

Robinson, Marilynne *Housekeeping* My name is Ruth. I grew up with my sister, Lucille, under the care of my grandmother,.

Rölvaag, OE *Giants in the Earth* Bright, clear sky over a plain so wide that the rim of the heavens cut down on it around the entire horizon.

Roth, Philip *Portnoy's Complaint* She was so deeply imbedded in my consciousness that for the first year of school I seemed to have believed that each of my teachers was my mother in disguise.

Rushdie, Salman *The Satanic Verses* To be born again, sang Gibreel Farishta tumbling from the heavens, 'first you have to die'.

Salinger, JD *The Catcher in the Rye* If you really want to hear about it, the first thing you'll probably want to know is where I was born, and what my lousy childhood was like.

Schaefer, Jack *Shane* He rode into our valley in the summer of '89.

Scott, Sir Walter *Old Mortality* 'Most Readers,' says the Manuscript of Mr Pattieson, 'must have witnessed with delight the joyous burst which attends the dismissing of a village-school on a fine summer evening.'

Segal, Erich *Love Story* What can you say about a 25 year old girl who died?

Selden, George *The Cricket in Times Square* A mouse was looking at Mario. The mouse's name was Tucker.

Service, Robert *The Shooting of Dan McGrew* A bunch of the boys were whooping it up in the Malarnute saloon.

Sewell, Anna *Black Beauty* The first place that I can well remember was a large pleasant meadow with a pond of clear water in it.

Sharpe, Tom *The Midden* It was Timothy Bright's ambition to make a fortune.

Shaw, Irwin *Rich Man, Poor Man* Mr. Donnelly, the track coach, ended the day's practice early because Henry Fuller's father came down to the high-school field to tell Henry that they had just got a telegram from Washington announcing that Henry's brother had been killed in action in Germany.

Shelley, Mary *Frankenstein* You will rejoice to hear that no disaster has accompanied the commencement of an enterprise which you have regarded with such evil forebodings.

Shelley, Percy Bysshe 'Ozymandias of Egypt' I met a traveller from an antique land . . .

Sholokhov, Mikhail *And Quiet Flows the Don* The Melekhov farm was right at the end of the Tatarsk village.

Shute, Nevil *On the Beach* Lt Commander Peter Holmes of the Royal Australian Navy woke soon after dawn.

Simak, Clifford *City* Gramp Stevens sat in a lawn chair, watching the mower at work, feeling the warm, soft sunshine seep into his bones.

Simak, Clifford *Way Station* The noise was ended

now. The smoke drifted like thin gray wisps of fog above the tortured earth and the shattered fences.

Sims, George R   *In the Workhouse – Christmas Day*   It is Christmas Day in the Workhouse.

Singer, Isaac Bashevis   *Shosha*   I was brought up on three dead languages – Hebrew, Aramaic, and Yiddish (some consider the last not a language at all) – and in a culture that developed in Babylon: the Talmud.

Smith, Betty   *A Tree Grows in Brooklyn*   Serene was a word you could put to Brooklyn, New York.

Smith, Dodie   *101 Dalmatians*   Not long ago, there lived in London a young married couple of Dalmatian dogs named Pongo and Misses Pongo.

Solzhenitsyn, Alexander   *The Gulag Archipelago*   How do people get to this clandestine Archipelago?

Sontag, Susan   *Death Kit*   Diddy the Good was taking a business trip.

Spencer, Scott   *Endless Love*   When I was seventeen and in full obedience to my heart's most urgent commands, I stepped far from the pathway of normal life and in a moment's time ruined everything I loved – I loved so deeply, and when the love was interrupted, when the incorporeal body of love shank back in terror and my own body was locked away, it was hard for others to believe that a life so new could suffer so irrevocably.

Spenser, Edmund   *The Faerie Queene*   A Gentle Knight was pricking on the plaine.

Steinbeck, John   *Cannery Row*   Cannery Row in Monterey in California is a poem, a stink, a grating noise, a quality of light, a tone, a habit, a nostalgia, a dream.

Steinbeck, John   *The Grapes of Wrath*   To the red country and part of the gray country of Oklahoma, the last rains came gently, and they did not cut the scarred earth.

Steinbeck, John   *Of Mice and Men*   A few miles south of Soledad, the Salinas River drops in close to the hill-side bank and runs deep and green.

Steinbeck, John   *The Pearl*   Kino awakened in the near dark.

Stevenson, Robert Louis   *The Strange Case of Dr Jekyll and Mr Hyde*   Mr. Utterson the lawyer was a man of a rugged countenance, that was never lighted by a smile; cold, scanty and embarrassed.

Stevenson, Robert Louis   *Kidnapped*   I will begin the story of my adventures with a certain morning early in the month of June, the year of grace 1751, when I took the key for the last time out of the door of my father's house.

Stevenson, Robert Louis   *Treasure Island*   Squire Trelawney, Dr. Livesey, and the rest of these gentlemen having asked me to write down the whole particulars about Treasure Island.

Stevenson, RL & L Osbourne   *The Wrong Box*   How very little does the amateur, dwelling at home at ease, comprehend the labours and perils of the author.

Stewart, Mary   *The Crystal Cave*   I am an old man now, but then I was already past my prime when Arthur was crowned King.

Stoker, Bram   *Dracula*   3 May. Bistritz. – Left Munich at 8:35 P.M., on 1st May, arriving at Vienna early next morning; should have arrived at 6:46, but the train was an hour late. Buda-Pesth seems a wonderful place, from the glimpse which I got from the train and the little I could walk through the streets.

Stone, Irving   *Lust for Life*   Monsieur Van Gogh, it's time to wake up.

Stout, Rex   *The Hand in Glove*   It was not surprising that Sylvia Raffray, on that Saturday in September, had occasion for discourse with various men, none of them utterly ordinary, and with one remarkable young woman; it was not surprising that all this happened without any special effort on Sylvia's part, for she was rich, personable to an extreme, an orphan, and six months short of twenty-one years.

Stowe, Harriet Beecher   *Uncle Tom's Cabin*   Late in the afternoon of a chilly day in February, two gentlemen were sitting alone over their wine, in a well-furnished dining parlour, in the town of P——, in Kentucky.

Sturgeon, Theodore   *More Than Human*   The idiot lived in a black and gray world, punctuated by the white lightning of hunger and the flickering of fear.

Styron, William   *The Confessions of Nat Turner*   To the public – The late insurrection in Southampton has greatly excited the public mind and led to a thousand idle, exaggerated and mischievous reports.

Swift, Jonathan   *Gulliver's Travels*   My father had a small estate in Nottinghamshire; I was the third of five sons.

Tan, Amy   *The Hundred Secret Senses*   My sister Kwan believes she has yin eyes.

Tan, Amy   *The Joy Luck Club*   My father asked me to be the fourth corner at the Joy Luck Club.

Thackeray, William M   *Vanity Fair*   While the present century was in its teens, and on one sunshiny morning in June, there drove up to the great iron gate of Miss Pinkerton's academy for young ladies, on Chiswick Mall, a large family coach, with two fat horses in blazing harness, driven by a fat coachman in a three cornered hat and wig, at the rate of four miles an hour.

Theroux, Paul   *The Mosquito Coast*   We drove past Tiny Polski's mansion house to the main road, and then the five miles into Northampton, Father talking the whole way about savages and the awfulness of America – how it got turned into a dope-taking, door-locking, ulcerated danger zone of rabid scavengers and criminal millionaires and moral sneaks.

Thomas, Dylan   *Under Milk Wood*   To begin at the beginning, It is spring, moonless night in the small town, starless and bible-black . . .

Thompson, Flora   *Lark Rise to Candleford*   The hamlet stood on a gentle rise in the flat, wheat-growing north-east corner of Oxfordshire.

Thoreau, Henry David   *Walden*   When I wrote the following pages, or rather the bulk of them, I lived alone, in the woods, a mile from any neighbor, in a house which I had built myself, on the shore of Walden Pond, in Concord, Massachusetts, and earned my living by the labor of my hands only.

Thurber, James   *The Thirteen Clocks*   Once upon a time, in a gloomy castle on a lonely hill, where there were thirteen clocks that wouldn't go, there lived a cold, aggressive Duke, and his niece, the Princess Saralinda.

Tolkien, JRR   *The Hobbit*   In a hole in the ground there lived a hobbit.

Tolstoy, Leo   *Anna Karenina*   All happy families are alike, but an unhappy family is unhappy after its own fashion.

Tolstoy, Leo   *War and Peace*   Well, Prince, so Genoa and Lucca are now just family estates of the Buonapartes.

Travers, PL   *Mary Poppins*   If you want to find Cherry Tree Lane all you have to do is ask a policeman at the crossroads.

Twain, Mark　*The Adventures of Huckleberry Finn*
You don't know about me, without you have read a
book by the name of *The Adventures of Tom Sawyer*,
but that ain't no matter.

Twain, Mark　*The Adventures of Tom Sawyer*　TOM!

Tyler, Anne　*Breathing Lessons*　Maggie and Ira
Moran had to go to a funeral in Deer Lick,
Pennsylvania.

Undset, Sigrid　*Kristin Lavransdatter*　When the
lands and goods of Ivar Gjesling the younger, of
Sundbu, were divided after his death in 1306, his
lands in Sil of Gudbrandsdal fell to his daughter
Ragnfrid and her husband Lavrans Björngulfsön.

Updike, John　*Rabbit at Rest*　Standing amid the
tan, excited post-Christmas crowd at the Southwest
Florida Regional Airport, Rabbit Angstrom has a
funny sudden feeling that what he has come to meet,
what's floating in unseen about to land, is not his son
Nelson and daughter-in-law Pru and their two
children but something more ominous and intimately
his: his own death, shaped vaguely like an airplane.

Updike, John　*Rabbit Is Rich*　Running out of gas,
Rabbit Angstrom thinks as he stands behind the
summer-dusty windows of the Springer Motors display.

Updike, John　*Rabbit Redux*　Men emerge pale from
the little printing plant at four sharp, ghosts for an
instant, blinking, until the outdoor light overcomes
the look of constant indoor light clinging to them.

Updike, John　*Rabbit, Run*　Boys are playing
basketball around a telephone pole with a backboard
bolted to it.

Uris, Leon　*Exodus*　The airplane plip-plopped down
the runway to a halt before the big sign: WELCOME
TO CYPRUS.

Verne, Jules　*Around the World in 80 Days*　Mr
Phileas Fogg lived, in 1872, at No. 7, Savile Row,
Burlington Gardens, the house in which Sheridan
died in 1814.

Vidal, Gore　*Creation*　I am blind. But I am not deaf.
Becuase of the incompleteness of my misfortune, I
was obliged yesterday to listen for nearly six hours to
a self-styled historian whose account of what the
Athenians call 'the Persian Wars' was nonsense of a
sort that were I less old and more privileged, I would
have risen in my seat at the Odeon and scandalized
all Athens by answering him.

Vidal, Gore　*Lincoln*　Elihu B. Washburne opened his
gold watch.

Vidal, Gore　*Myra Breckinridge*　I am Myra
Breckinridge whom no man will ever possess.

Virgil　*Aeneid*　I sing of arms and the man.

Voltaire　*Candide*　In the country of Westphalia, in
the castle of the most noble Baron of Thunder-ten-
tronckh, lived a youth whom Nature had endowed
with a most sweet disposition.

Vonnegut, Kurt　*Breakfast of Champions*　This is a
tale of a meeting of two lonesome, skinny, fairly old
white men on a planet which was dying fast.

Vonnegut, Kurt　*Cat's Cradle*　Call me Jonah.

Vonnegut, Kurt　*Slapstick*　To whom it may concern:
It is springtime.

Vonnegut, Kurt　*Slaughterhouse-Five*　All this
happened, more or less.

Walker, Alice　*The Color Purple*　You better not
never tell nobody but God.

Walker, Alice　*Possessing the Secret of Joy*　I did
not realize for a long time that I was dead.

Waller, Robert　*The Bridges of Madison County*　On
the morning of August 8, 1965, Robert Kincaid

locked the door to his small two-room apartment on
the third floor of a rambling house in Bellingham,
Washington.

Warren, Robert Penn　*A Place To Come To*　I was
the only boy, or girl either, in the public school in the
town of Dugton, Claxford County, Alabama, whose
father had ever got killed in the middle of the night
standing up in the front of his wagon to piss on the
hindquarters of one of a span of mules and, being
drunk, pitching forward on his head, still hanging
onto his dong, and hitting the pike in such a position
and condition that both the left front and left rear
wheels of the wagon rolled, with perfect precision,
over his unconscious neck, his having passed out
being, no doubt, the reason he took the fatal plunge
in the first place.

Waugh, Evelyn　*Brideshead Revisited*　When I
reached C Company lines, which were at the top of
the hill, I paused and looked back at the camp, just
coming into full view before me through the grey mist
of early morning.

Waugh, Evelyn　*Scoop*　While still a young man,
John Courteney Boot had, as his publisher
proclaimed, 'achieved an assured and enviable
position in contemporary letters'.

Wells, HG　*The Island of Doctor Moreau*　I do not
propose to add anything to what has already been
written concerning the loss of the 'Lady Vain'.

Wells, HG　*The Time Machine*　The Time Traveller
(for so it will be convenient to speak of him) was
expounding a recondite matter to us.

Wells, HG　*The War of the Worlds*　No one would
have believed in the last years of the nineteenth
century that this world was being watched keenly
and closely by intelligences greater than man's and
yet as mortal as his own; that as men busied
themselves about their various concerns they were
scrutinised and studied, perhaps almost as narrowly
as a man with a microscope might scrutinise the
transient creatures that swarm and multiply in a drop
of water.

Welty, Eudora　*The Optimist's Daughter*　A nurse
held the door open for them. Judge McKelva going
first, then his daughter Laurel, then his wife Fay, they
walked into the windowless room where the doctor
would make his examination.

Wharton, Edith　*Ethan Frome*　I had the story, bit
by bit, from various people, and, as generally
happens in such cases, each time it was a different
story.

White, EB　*Charlotte's Web*　Where's Papa going
with that ax? said Fern to her mother as they were
setting the table for breakfast.

White, EB　*Stuart Little*　When Mrs. Frederick C.
Little's second son arrived, everybody noticed that
he was not much bigger than a mouse.

Wibberley, Leonard　*The Mouse That Roared*　The
Duchy of Grand Fenwick lies in a precipitous fold of
the northern Alps and embraces in its tumbling
landscape portions of three valleys, a river, one
complete mountain with an elevation of two
thousand feet and a castle.

Wilde, Oscar　*The Ballad of Reading Gaol*　He did
not wear his scarlet coat.

Wilde, Oscar　*The Picture of Dorian Gray*　The
studio was filled with the rich odour of roses, and
when the light summer wind stirred amidst the trees
of the garden there came through the open door the
heavy scent of the lilac, or the more delicate perfume
of the pink-flowering thorn.

Wilder, Thornton *The Bridge of San Luis Rey* On Friday noon, July the twentieth, 1714, the finest bridge in all Peru broke and precipitated five travelers into the gulf below.

Wolfe, Thomas *You Can't Go Home Again* It was the hour of twilight on a soft spring day toward the end of April in the year of Our Lord 1929, and George Webber leaned his elbows on the sill of his back window and looked out at what he could see of New York.

Wolfe, Thomas *Look Homeward, Angel* A destiny that leads the English to the Dutch is strange enough; but one that leads from Epsom into Pennsylvania, and thence into the hills that shut in Altamont over the proud coral cry of the cock, and the soft stone smile of the angel, is touched by that dark miracle of chance which makes new magic in a dusty world.

Woolf, Virginia *Orlando* He – for there could be no doubt of his sex, though the fashion of the time did something to disguise it – was in the act of slicing at the head of a Moor which swung from the rafters.

Wordsworth, William *The Prelude* Oh there is blessing in this gentle breeze.

Wouk, Herman *The Winds of War* Commander Victor Henry rode a taxi-cab home from the Navy building on Constitution Avenue, in a gusty gray March rainstorm that matched his mood.

Wright, Richard *Native Son* Brrrrrriiiiiiiiiiiiiiiiiiinng! An alarm clock clanged in the dark and silent room. A bed spring creaked. A woman's voice sang out impatiently. 'Bigger, shut that thing off!'

Wyndham, John *The Day of the Triffids* When a day that you happen to know is Wednesday starts off by sounding like Sunday, there is something seriously wrong somewhere.

Wyss, Johann *The Swiss Family Robinson* For many days we had been tempest-tossed.

Yeats, WB 'When You are Old' When you are old and grey and full of sleep, And nodding by the fire, take down this book . . .

Zelazny, Roger *Lord of Light* His followers called him Mahasamatman and said he was a god. He preferred to drop the Maha- and the -atman, however, and called himself Sam.

NB: This is another section where it is only possible to list a good cross-section of works rather than a fully comprehensive catalogue. It is hoped that many of the better-known openings are included, as well as some more obscure but interesting ones. In the cases of works written in a foreign language and translated into English, the wording will vary according to the translator.

Closing Words of Books and Poems

Arnold, Mathew 'Dover Beach' Swept with confused alarms of struggle and flight, where ignorant armies clash by night.

Arnold, Mathew 'The Scholar Gipsy' Shy traffickers, the dark Iberians come, And on the beach undid his corded bales.

Asimov, Isaac *I Robot* She died last month at the age of Eighty Two.

Austen, Jane *Emma* But, in spite of these deficiencies, the wishes, the hopes, the confidence, the predictions of the small band of true friends who witnessed the ceremony, were fully answered in the perfect happiness of the union.

Austen, Jane *Lady Susan* I confess that I can pity only Miss Manwaring, who coming to town and putting herself to an expense in clothes, which impoverished her for two years, on purpose to secure him, was defrauded of her due by a woman ten years older than herself.

Austen, Jane *Mansfield Park* Fanny had never been able to approach but with some painful sensation of restraint or alarm, soon grew as dear to her heart, and as thoroughly perfect in her eyes, as everything else within the view and patronage of Mansfield Park had long been.

Austen, Jane *Northanger Abbey* I leave it to be settled by whomsoever it may concern, whether the tendency of this work be altogether to recommend parental tyranny or reward filial disobedience.

Austen, Jane *Persuasion* She gloried in being a sailor's wife, but she must pay the tax of quick alarm for belonging to that profession which is, if possible, more distinguished in its domestic virtues than in its national importance.

Austen, Jane *Pride and Prejudice* And they were both ever sensible of the warmest gratitude towards the persons who, by bringing her into Derbyshire, had been the means of uniting them.

Austen, Jane *Sanditon* It was impossible not to feel him hardly used; to be obliged to stand back in his own house and see the best place by the first constantly occupied by Sir Harry Denham.

Austen, Jane *Sense and Sensibility* Between Barton and Delaford, there was that constant communication which strong family affection would naturally dictate; and among the merits and the happiness of Elinor and Marianne, let it not be ranked as the least considerable, that though sisters and living almost within sight of each other, they could live without disagreement between themselves, or producing coolness between their husbands.

Austen, Jane *The Watsons* Emma was of course un-influenced, except to greater esteem for Elizabeth, by such representations – and the visitors departed without her.

Bellow, Saul *Henderson the Rain King* I guess I felt it was my turn now to move, and so went running – leaping, leaping, pounding, and tingling over the pure white lining of the gray Arctic silence.

Bennett, Arnold *Clayhanger* He braced himself to the exquisite burden to life.

Bennett, Arnold *The Old Wives' Tale* She glanced at the soup plate, and, on the chance that it might after all contain something worth inspection, she awkwardly balanced on her old legs and went to it again.

Brontë, Anne *Agnes Grey* And now I think I have said sufficient.

Brontë, Anne *The Tenant of Wildfell Hall* Till then, farewell, Gilbert Markham Staningley, June 10th 1847.

Brontë, Charlotte *Jane Eyre* Amen; even so come, Lord Jesus.

Brontë, Charlotte *The Professor* Papa, Come!

Brontë, Charlotte *Villette* Madame Walravens fulfilled her ninetieth year before she died. Farewell.

Brontë, Emily *Wuthering Heights* I lingered around

them under that benign sky; watched the moths fluttering among the heath and harebells, listening to the soft wind breathing through the grass, and wondered how anyone could ever imagine unquiet slumbers for the sleepers in that quiet earth.

Buchan, John *The Thirty-Nine Steps* But I had done my best service, I think, before I put on khaki.

Carey, Peter *Jack Maggs* Affectionately Inscribed to Percival Clarence Buckle, A man of letters, A patron of the arts.

Carroll, Lewis *Alice's Adventures in Wonderland* And how she would feel with all their simple sorrows, and find a pleasure in all their simple joys, remembering her own child-life, and the happy summer days.

Carroll, Lewis *Through the Looking Glass* But the provoking kitten only began on the other paw, and pretended it hadn't heard the question. Which do *you* think it was?

Cervantes, Miguel de *Don Quixote* Farewell.

Clarke, Arthur C *2001* But he would think of something.

Cleland, John *Fanny Hill* I shall see you soon, and in the meantime think candidly of me, and believe me ever, madam, Yours, etc, etc, etc.

Collins, Wilkie *The Moonstone* Who can tell?

Conrad, Joseph *Lord Jim* While he waves his hand sadly at his butterflies.

Conrad, Joseph *An Outcast of the Islands* And Almayer, who stood waiting, with a smile of tipsy attention on his lips, heard no other answer.

Cookson, Catherine *The Maltese Angel* Oh, let me cry. Let me cry, my love.

Cookson, Catherine *The Year of the Virgins* Listen to me, Flo Coulson, your mother loves me. Do you hear that? Your mother loves me. Everything comes to him who waits. Your mother loves me.

Cooper, James Fenimore *The Pioneers* Who are opening the way for the march of the Nation across the Continent.

Defoe, Daniel *Robinson Crusoe* And here, resolving to harass myself no more, I am preparing for a longer journey than all these, having lived 72 years, a life of infinite variety, and learn'd sufficiently to know the value of retirement, and the blessing of ending our days in peace.

Dickens, Charles *David Copperfield* Oh Agnes, Oh my soul, so may thy face be by me when I close my life indeed; so may I, when realities are melting from me like the shadows which I now dismiss, still find thee near me, pointing upward!

Dickens, Charles *Great Expectations* And had given her a heart to understand what my heart used to be.

Dickens, Charles *Oliver Twist* These, and a thousand looks and smiles, and turns of thought and speech – I would fain recall them every one.

Dickens, Charles *Oliver Twist (supplementary)* I believe it none the less because that nook is in a church, and she was weak and erring.

Dickens, Charles *A Tale of Two Cities* It is a far, far better thing that I do, than I have ever done: it is a far, far better rest that I go to, than I have ever known.

Dostoevsky, Fyodor *Crime and Punishment* That might be the subject of a new story, but our present story is ended.

Doyle, Arthur Conan *The Hound of the Baskervilles* We can stop at Mancini's for a little dinner on the way.

Dumas, Alexander *The Three Musketeers* The opinion of those who thought themselves the best informed was that he was boarded and lodged in

some royal castle at the expense of his generous eminence.

Fielding, Henry *Tom Jones* Who doth not most gratefully bless the day when Mr Jones was married to Sophia.

Greene, Graham *Brighton Rock* She walked rapidly in the thin June sunlight towards the worst horror of all.

Harris, Robert *Fatherland* Then he tugged the gun from his waistband, checked to make sure it was loaded and moved towards the silent trees.

Hartley, LP *Eustace and Hilda* But the cold crept onwards and he did not wake.

Heller, Joseph *Catch-22* The knife came down missing him by inches, and he took off.

Hughes, Thomas *Tom Brown's School Days* We can come to the knowledge of him in whom alone, the love and the tenderness, and the purity, and the strength, the courage, and the wisdom of all these, dwell for ever and ever in perfect fullness.

Huxley, Aldous *Crome Yellow* He climbed into the hearse.

Le Carré, John *The Honourable Schoolboy* And nor does Guillam, for George's sake.

Le Carré, John *The Russia House* It's going to be alright Harry, he assured me as he showed me off the premises. Tell them that. Spying is waiting.

Lewis, CS *The Lion, The Witch and The Wardrobe* But if the Professor was right it was only the beginning of the adventures of Narnia.

Lewis, Sinclair *Arrowsmith* We'll plug along on it for two or three years, and maybe we'll get something permanent – and probably we'll fail!

Longfellow, Henry Wadsworth 'The Villlage Blacksmith' Thus on its sounding anvil shaped Each burning deed and thought.

Longfellow, Henry Wadsworth 'The Wreck of the Hesperus' Christ saves us all from a death like this, on the reef of Norman's woe.

Lowry, Malcolm *Under the Volcano* Somebody threw a dead dog after him down the ravine.

Marvell, Andrew 'To His Coy Mistress' Thus though we cannot make our Sun, stand still, yet we will make him run.

McEwan, Ian *Enduring Love* So now, Rachael said. Tell Leo as well. Say it again slowly, that thing about the river.

Melville, Herman *Billy Budd* I am sleepy, and the oozy weeds about me twist.

Milton, John *On His Blindness* They also serve who only stand and wait.

Mitchell, Margaret *Gone With the Wind* After all, Tomorrow is another day.

O'Brien, Flann *At Swim-Two-Birds* He went home one evening and drank three cups of tea with three lumps of sugar in each, cut his jugular with a razor three times and scrawled with a dying hand on a picture of his wife, goodbye, goodbye, goodbye.

Service, Robert 'The Shooting of Dan McGrew' The woman that kissed him and pinched his poke, was the lady that's known as Lou.

Sewell, Anna *Black Beauty* I am still in the orchard at Birtwick standing with my old friends under the apple trees.

Shaw, Irwin *The Young Lions* Because he knew he had to deliver Noah Ackerman, personally, to Captain Green.

Solzhenitsyn, Alexander *One Day in the Life of Ivan Denisovich* The three extra days were because of the leap years.

Steel, Danielle *Kaleidoscope* He held her tightly in his arms and she knew he was telling the truth. 'Everything's going to be all right now.'

Steel, Danielle *Star* Home at last. Together.

Swift, Jonathan *Gulliver's Travels* And therefore, I here entreat those who have any tincture of this absurd vice, that they will not presume to appear in my sight.

Thompson, Flora *Lark Rise to Candleford* They were spun of love and kinship and cherished memories.

Tolstoy, Leo *War and Peace* In the present case, it is an essential to surmount a consciousness of an unreal freedom and to recognise a dependence not perceived by our senses.

Tremain, Rose *Restoration* Before I have grown too frail to climb the stairs – I shall bring you back.

Waugh, Evelyn *Brideshead Revisited* 'You're looking unusually cheerful today,' said the second-in-command.

Wilde, Oscar *The Ballad of Reading Gaol* The coward does it with a kiss, The brave man with a sword.

Wood, Mrs Henry *East Lynne* Oh Barbara, never forget – never forget that the only way to ensure peace in the end, is to strive always to be doing right, unselfishly, under God.

Wyndham, John *The Day of the Triffids* Until we have wiped the last one of them from the face of the land they have usurped.

NB: This section is much shorter than the opening lines, merely because closing lines tend to be less memorable than opening lines, and consequently, rarely crop up in any form of quiz.

Index of Books (in title order)

(* denotes author's first book)

Book	Author	Book	Author
Aaron's Rod	DH Lawrence	Animal Farm	George Orwell
The Abbot	Walter Scott	Anna Karenina	Leo Tolstoy
Absalom, Absalom!	William Faulkner	Anna of the Five Towns	Arnold Bennett
The Absentee	Maria Edgeworth	Anne of Green Gables*	LM Montgomery
The Acid House	Irvine Welsh	Antic Hay	Aldous Huxley
The Actual	Saul Bellow	Any Old Iron	Anthony Burgess
Adam Bede*	George Eliot	Appassionata	Jilly Cooper
Adolphe	Benjamin Constant	Armageddon	Leon Uris
The Adventures of Huckleberry Finn	Mark Twain	Around the World in 80 Days	Jules Verne
The Adventures of Peregrine Pickle	Tobias Smollett	As I Lay Dying	William Faulkner
		At Mrs Lippincote's*	Elizabeth Taylor
The Adventures of Sherlock Holmes	Arthur Conan Doyle	Atlas Shrugged	Ayn Rand
The Aeneid	Virgil	August 1914	Alexander Solzhenitsyn
Affliction	Fay Weldon	The Awakening	Kate Chopin
The African Queen	CS Forester	An Awfully Big Adventure	Beryl Bainbridge
Afternoon Men*	Anthony Powell	The Bad Place	Dean R Koontz
The Age of Innocence	Edith Wharton	The Ballad of Peckham Rye	Muriel Spark
The Age of Reason	Thomas Paine	The Ballad of the Sad Café	Carson McCullers
Agnes Grey*	Anne Brontë	Bambi	Felix Salten
The Agony and the Ecstasy	Irving Stone	Barchester Towers	Anthony Trollope
Airframe	Michael Crichton	Barnaby Rudge	Charles Dickens
Airport	Arthur Hailey	Baron Münchhausen	RE Raspe
The Alexandria Quartet	Lawrence Durrell	The Battle of the Books	Jonathan Swift
Alias Grace	Margaret Atwood	The Beach	Alex Garland
Alice's Adventures in Wonderland	Lewis Carroll	Beasts and Superbeasts	Hector Hugh Munro (Saki)
Allan Quatermain	Henry Rider Haggard	Beau Geste	PC Wren
All Quiet on the Western Front	Erich Maria Remarque	The Beautiful and Damned	F Scott Fitzgerald
All the Conspirators*	Christopher Isherwood	The Beauty Myth	Naomi Wolf
		Behind the Scenes at the Museum	Kate Atkinson
Almayer's Folly*	Joseph Conrad	Belinda	Maria Edgeworth
Alphabats	Paul Sellers	The Bell Jar	Sylvia Plath
Altered States	Anita Brookner	Beloved	Toni Morrison
The Ambassadors	Henry James	Bend in the River	VS Naipaul
Amelia	Henry Fielding	Bend Sinister	Vladimir Nabokov
An American Dream	Norman Mailer	Ben Hur	Lew Wallace
American Pastoral	Philip Roth	Beware of Pity	Stefan Zweig
American Psycho	Brett Easton Ellis	The BFG	Roald Dahl
An American Tragedy	Theodore Dreiser	Biggles	Capt. WE Johns
An Evil Cradling	Brian Keenan	The Big Sleep	Raymond Chandler
And Quiet Flows the Don	Mikhail Sholokhov	Big Sur	Jack Kerouac
Angel Pavement	JB Priestley	Billy Budd	Herman Melville
Angela's Ashes	Frank McCourt	Billy Bunter	Frank Richards
		Billy Liar	Keith Waterhouse

LITERATURE

Book	Author
Birds of Prey	Wilbur Smith
Birdsong	Sebastian Faulks
Black Ajax	George MacDonald Fraser
Black Beauty	Anna Sewell
The Black Prince	Iris Murdoch
The Black Stallion	Walter Farley
The Blinder	Barry Hines
Bliss, and other stories	Katherine Mansfield
The Bloody Ground	Bernard Cornwell
Blott on the Landscape	Tom Sharpe
The Blue Angel	Heinrich Mann
Bluebeard	Charles Perrault
Bondage of Love	Catherine Cookson
The Bonfire of the Vanities	Tom Wolfe
Bonjour Tristesse	Françoise Sagan
The Book of Nonsense	Edward Lear
The Borrowers	Mary Norton
The Bostonians	Henry James
The Bottle Factory Outing	Beryl Bainbridge
The Box of Delights	John Masefield
Boyhood	Leo Tolstoy
The Boys from Brazil	Ira Levin
Branded Man	Catherine Cookson
Brave New World	Aldous Huxley
Bravo Two Zero	Andy McNab
Breakfast at Tiffany's	Truman Capote
Breaking Hearts	Simon Gray
The Bride of Lammermoor	Walter Scott
Brideshead Revisited	Evelyn Waugh
The Bridesmaid	Ruth Rendell
The Bridge of San Luis Rey	Thornton Wilder
The Bridge on the River Kwai	Pierre Boulle
The Bridges of Madison County	Robert James Waller
Bridget Jones's Diary: A Novel	Helen Fielding
A Brief History of Time	Stephen Hawking
Brigadier Gerard, The Exploits of	Arthur Conan Doyle
Brighton Rock	Graham Greene
The British Museum Is Falling Down	David Lodge
Broca's Brain	Carl Sagan
The Brothers Karamazov	Fyodor Dostoyevsky
The Buccaneers	Edith Wharton
Buddenbrooks*	Thomas Mann
The Buddha of Suburbia	Hanif Kureishi
Bulldog Drummond	Herman Cyril McNeile (Sapper)
Busman's Honeymoon	Dorothy L Sayers
The Cabala*	Thornton Wilder
Cakes and Ale	William Somerset Maugham
Call for the Dead*	John Le Carré
Call of the Wild	Jack London
The Call of Wings	Agatha Christie
Camilla	Fanny Burney
The Camomile Lawn	Mary Wesley
Campbell's Kingdom	Ralph Hammond Innes
Cancer Ward	Alexander Solzhenitsyn
Candide	Voltaire
The Canterbury Tales	Geoffrey Chaucer
The Captain and the Kings	Taylor Caldwell
Captain Corelli's Mandolin	Louis de Bernières
Captain Slaughterboard Drops Anchor*	Mervyn Peake
The Carpetbaggers	Harold Robbins
The Carpet People*	Terry Pratchett
The Case of the Velvet Claws	Earl Stanley Gardner

Book	Author
The Castle	Franz Kafka
The Castle of Otranto	Horace Walpole
Castle Rackrent*	Maria Edgeworth
The Casuarina Tree	William Somerset Maugham
Cat and Mouse	Günther Grass
Catch-22	Joseph Heller
The Catcher in the Rye*	JD Salinger
Catherine Herself*	James Hilton
Catriona	Robert Louis Stevenson
The Cauldron	Colin Forbes
Cause Celeb	Helen Fielding
The Caves of Steel	Isaac Asimov
Cecilia	Fanny Burney
A Celebration of Mass	Pope John Paul II
The Celestine Prophecy	James Redfield
Central Line – (short story)	Maeve Binchy
Centuries	Nostradamus
A Certain Justice	PD James
Charity	Len Deighton
Charlie and the Chocolate Factory	Roald Dahl
Charlotte's Friends	Sarah Kennedy
Chatterton	Peter Ackroyd
Chérie	Colette
Childhood	Leo Tolstoy
Childhood	Maxim Gorky
Children of the New Forest	Capt. Frederick Marryat
The Children of Violence	Doris Lessing
Child Whispers*	Enid Blyton
Chitty Chitty Bang Bang	Ian Fleming
Chocolat	Joanne Harris
Chomolungma Sings the Blues	Ed Douglas
Christmas Carol, A	Charles Dickens
Chronicles of Thomas Covenant	Stephen Donaldson
Cider With Rosie	Laurie Lee
The Citadel	AJ Cronin
The City and the Stars	Arthur C Clarke
Clarissa	Samuel Richardson
Claudia	Arnold Zweig
Claudine (series)	Colette
Clayhanger	Arnold Bennett
A Clockwork Orange	Anthony Burgess
The Cloister and the Hearth	Charles Reade
Close Relations	Deborah Moggach
Coastliners	Joanne Harris
Cocaine Nights	JG Ballard
Cold Mountain	Charles Frazier
The Collector	John Fowles
Colonel Sun	Robert Markham
The Color Purple	Alice Walker
La Comédie Humaine	Honoré de Balzac
The Comforters	Muriel Spark
The Commitments*	Roddy Doyle
Common Sense	Thomas Paine
Confessions of an English Opium Eater	Thomas De Quincey
Coningsby	Benjamin Disraeli
A Cool Million	Nathanael West
Coral Island	RM Ballantyne
The Corridors of Power	CP Snow
The Count of Monte Cristo	Alexandre Dumas (Père)
The Country Diary of an Edwardian Lady	Edith Holden
The Country Girls	Edna O'Brien
Cover Her Face*	PD James

LITERATURE

Book	Author
First Among Equals	Jeffrey Archer
The First Circle	Alexander Solzhenitsyn
First Men in the Moon	HG Wells
The Fisher King	Anthony Powell
The Flute-Player	DM Thomas
The Fog	James Herbert
Forsyte Saga	John Galsworthy
For Want of a Nail*	Melvyn Bragg
For Whom the Bell Tolls	Ernest Hemingway
Foucault's Pendulum	Umberto Eco
The Foundation Trilogy	Isaac Asimov
The Fourth Estate	Jeffrey Archer
The Fourth Protocol	Frederick Forsyth
The Foxglove Saga*	Auberon Waugh
Framley Parsonage	Anthony Trollope
Frankenstein*	Mary Shelley
Frankenstein Unbound	Brian Aldiss
The French Lieutenant's Woman	John Fowles
Frenchman's Creek	Daphne Du Maurier
From Doon with Death*	Ruth Rendell
From Here to Eternity	James Jones
Full Circle: A Pacific Journey	Michael Palin
Funeral in Berlin	Len Deighton
Fungus the Bogeyman	Raymond Briggs
Furnace	Muriel Gray
The Game	AS Byatt
Game, Set and Match	Len Deighton
Gamesmanship	Stephen Potter
The Garden of Eden	Ernest Hemingway
The Garden Party & Other Stories	Katherine Mansfield
Gargantua	François Rabelais
The Garrick Year	Margaret Drabble
Gaudy Night	Dorothy L Sayers
Gentlemen Marry Brunettes	Anita Loos
Gentlemen Prefer Blondes	Anita Loos
George's Marvellous Medicine	Roald Dahl
Georgy Girl	Margaret Forster
Germinal	Émile Zola
Get Shorty	Elmore Leonard
Ghost	Danielle Steele
The Ghost in the Machine	Arthur Koestler
The Ghost Road	Pat Barker
Gigi	Colette
Gil Blas	Alain Le Sage
The Ginger Man*	JP Donleavy
Giovanni's Room	James Baldwin
The Gladiators	Arthur Koestler
The Glass Bead Game	Herman Hesse
The Glass Key	Dashiell Hammett
The Go-Between	LP Hartley
The Godfather	Mario Puzo
The God of Small Things	Arundhati Roy
God's Little Acre	Erskine Caldwell
The Golden Apples of the Sun	Ray Bradbury
The Golden Bowl	Henry James
Gone With the Wind	Margaret Mitchell
Goodbye Mr Chips	James Hilton
Goodbye to Berlin	Christopher Isherwood
The Good Companions	JB Priestley
The Good Earth	Pearl Buck
The Good Soldier Svejk	Jaroslav Hasek
Good Wives	Louisa May Alcott
The Gormenghast Trilogy	Mervyn Peake
Go Tell It on the Mountain	James Baldwin
Grapefruit	Yoko Ono
The Grapes of Wrath	John Steinbeck

Book	Author
The Grass is Singing*	Doris Lessing
Gravity's Rainbow	Thomas Pynchon
Great Apes	Will Self
Great Expectations	Charles Dickens
The Great Fire of London*	Peter Ackroyd
The Great Gatsby	F Scott Fitzgerald
The Green Hat	Michael Arlen
Greenmantle	John Buchan
Greybeard	Brian Aldiss
Gridlock	Ben Elton
Grimus*	Salman Rushdie
The Group	Mary McCarthy
Gulag Archipelago	Alexander Solzhenitsyn
Gulliver's Travels	Jonathan Swift
The Gun Seller	Hugh Laurie
The Gunpowder Plot: Terror and Faith in 1605	Antonia Fraser
The Guns of Navarone	Alistair Maclean
Guys and Dolls	Damon Runyon
The Haj	Leon Uris
The Handmaid's Tale	Margaret Atwood
Haphazard House	Mary Wesley
The Happy Return	CS Forester
Harper of Heaven	Robert Service
Harpoon at a Venture	Gavin Maxwell
Harry Potter and the Chamber of Secrets	JK Rowling
Harry Potter and the Goblet of Fire	JK Rowling
Harry Potter and the Philosopher's Stone	JK Rowling
Harry Potter and the Prisoner of Azkaban	JK Rowling
Harvest	Celia Brayfield
Hatter's Castle*	AJ Cronin
Hawksmoor	Peter Ackroyd
Headlong Hall	Thomas Love Peacock
Hearing Secret Harmonies (A Dance to the Music of Time)	Anthony Powell
The Heart Is a Lonely Hunter*	Carson McCullers
Heart of Darkness	Joseph Conrad
Heart of Midlothian	Walter Scott
The Heart of the Matter	Graham Greene
Heavy Weather	PG Wodehouse
Heidi	Johanna Spyri
Helliconia Trilogy	Brian Aldiss
Hemingway's Chair	Michael Palin
The History of Henry Esmond	WM Thackeray
The Heretic's Apprentice	Ellis Peters
Hereward the Wake	Charles Kingsley
Herzog	Saul Bellow
High Fidelity	Nick Hornby
High Rise	JG Ballard
A High Wind in Jamaica	Richard Hughes
The High Window	Raymond Chandler
The Hireling	LP Hartley
A History of Tom Jones A Foundling	Henry Fielding
The History Man	Malcolm Bradbury
The History of Mr Polly	HG Wells
The Hitchhiker's Guide to the Galaxy*	Douglas Adams
HMS Ulysses*	Alistair MacLean
The Hobbit	JRR Tolkien
Hogfather	Terry Pratchett
Hollywood Wives	Jackie Collins
The Honorary Consul	Graham Greene
Hope	Len Deighton
Hornblower (series)	CS Forester

LITERATURE

Book	Author	Book	Author
The Lord of the Rings (Trilogy)	JRR Tolkien	Moby-Dick	Herman Melville
Lorna Doone	RD Blackmore	Moll Flanders	Daniel Defoe
Lost Continent: Travels in Small Town America	Bill Bryson	A Month in the Country	Ivan Turgenev
		The Moon and Sixpence	William Somerset Maugham
Lost Horizon	James Hilton		
The Lost World of the Kalahari	Laurens Van Der Post	The Moonstone	Wilkie Collins
		The Moor's Last Sigh	Salman Rushdie
The Lost World	Michael Crichton	Mort	Terry Pratchett
The Lost World	Arthur Conan Doyle	Le Morte D'Arthur	Thomas Malory
Love in a Cold Climate	Nancy Mitford	Mother	Maxim Gorky
Love in Another Town	Barbara Taylor Bradford	Mother, Can You Hear Me?	Margaret Forster
		Mother Goose	Charles Perrault
Love in the Time of Cholera	Gabriel García Márquez	Mother Goose Treasury	Raymond Briggs
		Mourning Doves	Helen Forrester
Love on the Dole	Walter Greenwood	Mr Men	Roger Hargreaves
Love Story	Eric Segal	Mr Midshipman Easy	Capt. Frederick Marryat
The L-Shaped Room	Lynne Reid Banks		
The Luck of Barry Lyndon	WM Thackeray	Mr Nice	Howard Marks
Lucky Jim*	Kingsley Amis	Mr Norris Changes Trains	Christopher Isherwood
Lust for Life	Irving Stone		
The Macdermots of Ballycloran*	Anthony Trollope	Mrs Dalloway	Virginia Woolf
		Mr Sponge's Sporting Tour	Robert Smith Surtees
Madame Bovary	Gustave Flaubert		
Mad Cows	Kathy Lette	Murder Must Advertise	Dorothy L Sayers
Made in America	Bill Bryson	The Murder of Roger Ackroyd	Agatha Christie
The Magic Mountain	Thomas Mann	'The Murders in the Rue Morgue'	Edgar Allan Poe
The Magus	John Fowles		
The Maid of Buttermere	Melvyn Bragg	My Cousin Rachel	Daphne Du Maurier
Maigret	Georges Simenon	My Family and Other Animals	Gerald Durrell
Making History	Stephen Fry	My Son, My Son	Howard Spring
The Maltese Falcon	Dashiell Hammett	The Mysterious Affair at Styles	Agatha Christie
The Man from the North*	Arnold Bennett	The Mystery of Edwin Drood	Charles Dickens
A Man Lay Dead*	Ngaio Marsh	The Mystic Masseur*	VS Naipaul
The Man Who Listens to Horses	Monty Roberts	My Universities	Maxim Gorky
		The Naked and the Dead*	Norman Mailer
Man Who Was Thursday	GK Chesterton		
The Man Who Watched the Trains Go By	Georges Simenon	The Naked Lunch	William Burroughs
		The Name of the Rose	Umberto Eco
Manhattan Transfer	John Dos Passos	Nana	Émile Zola
Mansfield Park	Jane Austen	The Napoleon of Notting Hill	GK Chesterton
The Martian	George Du Maurier	National Velvet	Enid Bagnold
Martin Chuzzlewit*	Charles Dickens	Nausea	Jean-Paul Sartre
Mary Barton*	Elizabeth Gaskell	Neither Here Nor There	Bill Bryson
The Mary Deare	Ralph Hammond Innes	Never Love a Stranger	Harold Robbins
		The New Machiavelli	HG Wells
Mary Poppins	PL Travers	Next of Kin	Joanna Trollope
The Mask of Dimitrios	Eric Ambler	Nexus	Henry Miller
Maskerade	Terry Pratchett	Nicholas Nickleby	Charles Dickens
Master and Commander	Patrick O'Brian	The Nigger of the Narcissus	Joseph Conrad
The Master and Margarita	Mikhail Bulgakov	Night and Day	Virginia Woolf
Matilda	Roald Dahl	The Night Manager	John Le Carré
The Mayor of Casterbridge	Thomas Hardy	Nightmare Abbey	Thomas Love Peacock
Meet the Tiger	Leslie Charteris		
Melincourt	Thomas Love Peacock	Night Train	Martin Amis
		The Nine Billion Names of God	Arthur C Clarke
Memoirs of a Fox-Hunting Man	Siegfried Sassoon	The Nine Tailors	Dorothy L Sayers
The Memory Game	Nicci French	Nineteen Eighty-Four	George Orwell
Men Are from Mars, Women Are from Venus	John Gray	Noble House	James Clavell
		Noddy	Enid Blyton
Men at Arms	Terry Pratchett	Non-Stop	Brian Aldiss
Message from Malaga	Helen MacInnes	North and South	Mrs Elizabeth Gaskell
The Metamorphosis	Franz Kafka		
Metroland	Julian Barnes	Northanger Abbey	Jane Austen
The Midden	Tom Sharpe	Nostromo	Joseph Conrad
Midnight Cowboy	James Herlihy	Not a Penny More, Not a Penny Less*	Jeffrey Archer
Midnight's Children	Salman Rushdie		
The Midwich Cuckoos	John Wyndham	Notes From a Small Island	Bill Bryson
Miguel Street	VS Naipaul	Now We Are Six	AA Milne
Mildred Pierce	James M Cain	The Oak and the Calf	Alexander Solzhenitsyn
The Mill on the Floss	George Eliot		
Miss Lonelyhearts	Nathanael West	Oblomov	Ivan Goncharov

LITERATURE

Book	Author
Right Ho, Jeeves	PG Wodehouse
The Rights of Man	Thomas Paine
Ring of Bright Water	Gavin Maxwell
Riotous Assembly*	Tom Sharpe
Rip Van Winkle	Washington Irving
Rites of Passage	William Golding
Road Rage	Ruth Rendell
The Roads to Freedom (Trilogy)	Jean-Paul Sartre
The Road to Wigan Pier	George Orwell
Robinson Crusoe	Daniel Defoe
Rob Roy	Walter Scott
Rockets Galore	Compton Mackenzie
The Adventures of Roderick Random	Tobias Smollett
Rogue Justice	Geoffrey Household
Rogue Male	Geoffrey Household
Romola	George Eliot
Rookwood	William Harrison Ainsworth
Room at the Top	John Braine
A Room with a View	EM Forster
Rosemary's Baby	Ira Levin
Runaway Jury	John Grisham
Rupert of Hentzau	Anthony Hope
Rural Rides	William Cobbett
The Sailor Who Fell from Grace with the Sea	Yukio Mishima
The Saint	Leslie Charteris
Salammbô	Gustave Flaubert
Salar the Salmon	Henry Williamson
Salmagundi	Washington Irving
Sard Harker	John Masefield
The Satanic Verses	Salman Rushdie
Saturday Night and Sunday Morning*	Alan Sillitoe
Say Cheese and Die Again!	RL Stine
The Scarlatti Inheritance	Robert Ludlum
The Scarlet Letter	Nathaniel Hawthorne
The Scarlet Pimpernel	Baroness Orczy
The Screwtape Letters	CS Lewis
The Sea, The Sea	Iris Murdoch
Sea-Wolf	Jack London
The Second Sex	Simone de Beauvoir
Secret Diary of Adrian Mole Aged 13 3/4*	Sue Townsend
The Secret Garden	Frances Hodgson Burnett
The Secret Life of Walter Mitty	James Thurber
The Secret Seven	Enid Blyton
The Seed and the Sower	Laurens Van Der Post
Seize the Day	Saul Bellow
The Selfish Gene	Richard Dawkins
Sense and Sensibility*	Jane Austen
The Sentinel	Arthur C Clarke
Seventh Avenue	Norman Bogner
79 Park Avenue	Harold Robbins
Shadow Baby	Margaret Forster
Shadow of a Sun*	AS Byatt
Sharpe's Devil	Bernard Cornwell
She	Henry Rider Haggard
The Shipping News	E Annie Proulx
Shogun	James Clavell
Shout at the Devil	Wilbur Smith
The Sign of Four	Arthur Conan Doyle
Silas Marner	George Eliot
The Silence of the Lambs	Thomas Harris
The Silmarillion	JRR Tolkien
The Simisola	Ruth Rendell
Sins	Judith Gould

Book	Author
Sir Charles Grandison	Samuel Richardson
Slaughterhouse-Five	Kurt Vonnegut
Sleepers	Lorenzo Carcaterra
The Sleeping Beauty	Charles Perrault
Small Is Beautiful	Ernst Schumacher
A Small Town in Germany	John Le Carré
The Snow Goose	Paul Gallico
The Snowman	Raymond Briggs
Snow White and the Seven Dwarfs	Grimm Brothers
Soldiers' Pay*	William Faulkner
Some Other Rainbow	John McCarthy and Jill Morrell
Song of the Light: Rameses	Christian Jacq
Sons and Lovers	DH Lawrence
Sophie's World	Jostein Gaarder
The Sorrows of Young Werther	Johann Goethe
The Sound and the Fury	William Faulkner
A Spell of Winter	Helen Dunmore
The Spirit Level	Seamus Heaney
Spycatcher	Peter Wright
The Spy Who Came in from the Cold	John Le Carré
Stamboul Train	Graham Greene
The Stand	Stephen King
Stanley and the Women	Kingsley Amis
Stark*	Ben Elton
A Start in Life*	Anita Brookner
The State We're In	Will Hutton
Stay With Me Till Morning	John Braine
The Stepford Wives	Ira Levin
Steppenwolf	Herman Hesse
Still Life	AS Byatt
A Stone For Danny Fisher	Harold Robbins
The Story of Esther Costello	Nicholas Monsarrat
The Strange Case of Dr Jekyll and Mr Hyde	Robert Louis Stevenson
The Strange House*	Raymond Briggs
Strangers and Brothers	CP Snow
Studs Lonigan Trilogy	James Farrell
Stuff	Joseph Connolly
The Subjection of Women	John Stuart Mill
A Suitable Boy	Vikram Seth
A Summer Birdcage*	Margaret Drabble
The Sun Also Rises	Ernest Hemingway
Superwoman	Shirley Conran
Swallows and Amazons	Arthur Ransome
Swan	Naomi Campbell
Sweet William	Beryl Bainbridge
The Swiss Family Robinson	Johann Wyss
The Sword in the Stone	TH White
Sword of Honour Trilogy	Evelyn Waugh
Sybil	Benjamin Disraeli
The System of Logic	John Stuart Mill
The Tailor of Panama	John Le Carré
Take a Girl Like You	Kingsley Amis
A Tale of a Tub	Jonathan Swift
The Tale of Genji	Lady Murasaki
The Tale of Jemima Puddle-Duck	Beatrix Potter
The Tale of Mr Jeremy Fisher	Beatrix Potter
The Tale of Squirrel Nutkin,	Beatrix Potter
A Tale of Two Cities	Charles Dickens
Tales from Shakespeare	Charles and Mary Lamb
Tales of My Landlord	Walter Scott
Tales of the City	Armistead Maupin
Tales of the South Pacific*	James Michener
The Talisman	Walter Scott
Talking to the Dead	Helen Dunmore
Tancred	Benjamin Disraeli

LITERATURE

Book	Author	Book	Author
Winnie-the-Pooh	AA Milne	Worst Fears	Fay Weldon
Winnie-the-Pooh: Now We Are Six	AA Milne	A Wreath of Roses	Elizabeth Taylor
		Wreckers Must Breathe	Ralph Hammond Innes
Winsome Winnie	Stephen Leacock		
The Witches of Eastwick	John Updike	Wuthering Heights	Emily Brontë
The Witching Hour	Anne Rice	The X Files	Les Martin
With These Hands	Pam Ayres	A Year in Cricklewood	Alan Coren
Witness for the Prosecution	Agatha Christie	A Year in Provence	Peter Mayall
The Woman in White	Wilkie Collins	Year of the Tiger	Jack Higgins
The Woman Who Walked into Doors	Roddy Doyle	The Young Fur Traders	RM Ballantyne
		The Young Man*	Stephen Potter
Women in Love	DH Lawrence	Youth	Leo Tolstoy
The Wonderful Adventures of Nils	Selma Lagerlöf	Zen and the Art of Motorcycle Maintenance	Robert Pirsig
Worrals of the WAAF	Capt. WE Johns		

NB: The list above is a good cross-section of popular works, but by no means comprehensive. Many popular books are included and some interesting less-known works. For ease of reference, the list is re-sorted below by author.

Index of Books By Author

(* denotes author's first book)

Author	Book	Author	Book
Paul Ableman	I Hear Voices	Margaret Atwood	Alias Grace
Peter Ackroyd	Chatterton		The Handmaid's Tale
	The Great Fire of London*	Jane Austen	Emma
	Hawksmoor		Mansfield Park
	The Last Testament of Oscar Wilde		Northanger Abbey
			Persuasion
Douglas Adams	Hitchhiker's Guide to the Galaxy*		Pride and Prejudice
		Pam Ayres	Sense and Sensibility*
Richard Adams	Watership Down	Richard Bach	With These Hands
William Harrison Ainsworth	Rookwood		Jonathan Livingston Seagull
		Enid Bagnold	National Velvet
Louisa May Alcott	Little Men	Beryl Bainbridge	An Awfully Big Adventure
	Good Wives		The Bottle Factory Outing
	Little Women		
Brian Aldiss	Dracula Unbound		The Dressmaker
	Enemies of the System		English Journey
	Frankenstein Unbound		Every Man for Himself
	Greybeard		Filthy Lucre
	Helliconia Trilogy		Sweet William
	Non-Stop		A Weekend with Claud*
	Remembrance Day	James Baldwin	Go Tell It on the Mountain
Eric Ambler	The Dark Frontier*		Giovanni's Room
	The Mask of Dimitrios		Just Above My Head
Kingsley Amis	Jake's Thing	RM Ballantyne	Coral Island
	Lucky Jim*		The Young Fur Traders
	The Old Devils	JG Ballard	Cocaine Nights
	One Fat Englishman		High Rise
	Stanley and the Women		Empire of the Sun
	Take a Girl Like You		The Drowned World*
	That Uncertain Feeling	Honoré de Balzac	La Comédie Humaine
Martin Amis	Night Train	Iain Banks	The Wasp Factory
Jeffrey Archer	The Eleventh Commandment	Lynne Reid Banks	The L-Shaped Room
	First Among Equals	Pat Barker	The Ghost Road
	The Fourth Estate	Julian Barnes	Metroland
	Not a Penny More, Not a Penny Less*	JM Barrie	The Little Minister
			A Window in Thrums
Michael Arlen	The Green Hat	HE Bates	The Two Sisters *
	Piracy		Fair Stood the Wind for France
Isaac Asimov	The Foundation Trilogy		The Jacaranda Tree
	The Caves of Steel		The Darling Buds of May
	I, Robot	Charles Baudelaire	La Fanfarlo
Kate Atkinson	Behind the Scenes at the Museum	Aphra Behn	Oroonoko
		William Beckford	Vathek

LITERATURE

Author	Book
	The Lady in the Lake
Jung Chang	Wild Swans
Henri Charrière	Papillon
Leslie Charteris	Meet the Tiger
	The Saint
Geoffrey Chaucer	The Canterbury Tales
GK Chesterton	The Napoleon of Notting Hill
	The Innocence of Father Brown
	The Man Who Was Thursday
Kate Chopin	The Awakening
Agatha Christie	The Call of Wings
	Curtain
	Hound of Death
	The Murder of Roger Ackroyd
	The Mysterious Affair at Styles
	Witness for the Prosecution
Tom Clancy	Executive Orders
Arthur C Clarke	The City and the Stars
	The Nine Billion Names of God
	Prelude to Space*
	The Sentinel
	3001: The Final Odyssey
	2001: A Space Odyssey
	2061: Odyssey Three
	2010: Odyssey Two
Mary Higgins Clark	Pretend You Don't See Her
James Clavell	King Rat
	Noble House
	Shogun
John Cleland	Fanny Hill
William Cobbett	Rural Rides
Colette	Chérie
	Claudine (series)
	Gigi
Jackie Collins	Hollywood Wives
Joan Collins	Prime Time
Wilkie Collins	The Moonstone
	The Woman in White
William Congreve	Incognita, or Love and Duty Reconciled*
Joseph Connolly	Stuff
Joseph Conrad	Almayer's Folly*
	Heart of Darkness
	Lord Jim
	The Nigger of the Narcissus
	Nostromo
	An Outcast of the Islands
	Under Western Eyes
Shirley Conran	Lace
	Superwoman
Benjamin Constant	Adolphe
Catherine Cookson	Bondage of Love
	Branded Man
	Kate Hannigan*
	The Upstart
Susan Coolidge	What Katy Did
James Fenimore Cooper	The Last of the Mohicans
	Leatherstocking stories
	Precaution*
Jilly Cooper	Appassionata
	Emily*

Author	Book
Alan Coren	The Dog It Was That Died*
	A Year in Cricklewood
Bernard Cornwell	The Bloody Ground
	Excalibur
	Sharpe's Devil
Patricia Cornwell	The Hornet's Nest
	Unnatural Exposure
Stephen Crane	The Red Badge of Courage
Michael Crichton	Airframe
	Jurassic Park
	The Lost World
Richmal Crompton	Just William
AJ Cronin	The Citadel
	Hatter's Castle*
	The Keys of the Kingdom
Edwina Currie	Parliamentary Affair
Roald Dahl	The BFG
	Charlie and the Chocolate Factory
	George's Marvellous Medicine
	James and the Giant Peach
	Matilda
Richard Dana Jr	To Cuba and Back
	Two Years Before the Mast
Charles Darwin	The Descent of Man
	The Origin of Species
Robertson Davies	What's Bred in the Bone
Richard Dawkins	The Selfish Gene
Simone De Beauvoir	The Second Sex
Daniel Defoe	A Journal of the Plague Year
	Moll Flanders
	Robinson Crusoe
Len Deighton	Charity
	Faith
	Funeral in Berlin
	Game, Set and Match
	Hope
	The Ipcress File*
	Only When I Larf
Shelagh Delaney	A Taste of Honey
RF Delderfield	A Horseman Riding By
	To Serve Them All My Days
Thomas De Quincey	Confessions of an English Opium Eater
Colin Dexter	Death Is Now My Neighbour
Charles Dickens	Barnaby Rudge
	Bleak House
	A Christmas Carol
	David Copperfield
	Dombey and Son
	Great Expectations
	Little Dorritt
	Martin Chuzzlewit
	The Mystery of Edwin Drood (unfinished)
	Nicholas Nickleby
	The Old Curiosity Shop
	Oliver Twist
	Our Mutual Friend
	Pickwick Papers
	A Tale of Two Cities
James Dickey	Deliverance
Benjamin Disraeli	Coningsby

LITERATURE

Author	Book	Author	Book
Johann Goethe	The Sorrows of Young Werther	Roger Hargreaves	Mr Men
	Wilhem Meister's Apprenticeship	Joanne Harris	Chocolat
			Coastliners
	Wilhem Meister's Travels	Joel Chandler Harris	Uncle Remus stories
Nikolai Gogol	Dead Souls	Thomas Harris	The Silence of the Lambs
	The Diary of a Madman	LP Hartley	The Go-Between
	The Overcoat		The Hireling
William Golding	Lord of the Flies*	Jaroslav Hasek	The Good Soldier Svejk
	Pincher Martin	Stephen Hawking	A Brief History of Time
	Rites of Passage	Nathaniel Hawthorne	Fanshawe*
Oliver Goldsmith	The Vicar of Wakefield		The Scarlet Letter
Ivan Goncharov	Oblomov	Seamus Heaney	The Spirit Level
Maxim Gorky	Childhood	Joseph Heller	Catch-22
	Mother		Picture This
	My Universities	Ernest Hemingway	Death in the Afternoon
Judith Gould	Sins		A Farewell to Arms
Winston Graham	Poldark		For Whom the Bell Tolls
Kenneth Grahame	The Wind in the Willows		The Garden of Eden
Günther Grass	Cat and Mouse		The Old Man and the Sea
	Dog Years		The Sun Also Rises
	The Tin Drum*		The Torrents of Spring*
	A Wide Field	Frank Herbert	Dune
Robert Graves	I, Claudius	James Herbert	The Rats
John Gray	Men are From Mars, Women are From Venus		The Fog
		James Herlihy	Midnight Cowboy
Muriel Gray	Furnace	Herman Hesse	The Glass Bead Game
Simon Gray	Breaking Hearts		Peter Camenzind*
Graham Greene	Brighton Rock		Steppenwolf
	The Heart of the Matter	Jack Higgins	The Eagle Has Landed
	The Honorary Consul		The President's Daughter
	Our Man in Havana		The Year of the Tiger
	The Power and the Glory	Richard Hillary	The Last Enemy
	Stamboul Train	James Hilton	Catherine Herself*
	The Third Man		Goodbye Mr Chips
Walter Greenwood	Love on the Dole		Lost Horizon
Zane Grey	Riders of the Purple Sage	Barry Hines	The Blinder
Brothers Grimm	Snow White and the Seven Dwarfs		A Kestrel for a Knave
		Edith Holden	The Country Diary of an Edwardian Lady
John Grisham	The Partner		
	Runaway Jury	AM Homes	The End of Alice
Richard D Gross	Psychology, the Science of Mind and Behaviour	Anthony Hope	The Prisoner of Zenda
			Rupert of Hentzau
George and Weedon Grossmith	The Diary of a Nobody	Nick Hornby	Fever Pitch*
			High Fidelity
Henry Rider Haggard	Allan Quatermain	EW Hornung	Raffles
	King Solomon's Mines	Geoffrey Household	Rogue Justice
	She		Rogue Male
Arthur Hailey	Airport	Richard Hughes	A High Wind in Jamaica
	Hotel	Thomas Hughes	Tom Brown's Schooldays
	Wheels	Victor Hugo	The Hunchback of Notre Dame
Radcliffe Hall	The Well of Loneliness		Les Misérables
Willis Hall	The Long and the Short and the Tall	Will Hutton	The State We're In
		Aldous Huxley	Antic Hay
Dashiell Hammett	The Glass Key		Brave New World
	The Maltese Falcon		Crome Yellow
	The Thin Man		The Devils of Loudun
Ralph Hammond Innes	Campbell's Kingdom		The Doors of Perception
	The Mary Deare		Eyeless in Gaza
	Wreckers Must Breathe		Point Counter Point
Thomas Hardy	Desperate Remedies*	John Irving	A Prayer For Owen Meany
	Far from the Madding Crowd		
		Washington Irving	The Legend of Sleepy Hollow
	Jude the Obscure		
	The Mayor of Casterbridge		Rip Van Winkle
			Salmagundi
	The Return of the Native	Christopher Isherwood	All the Conspirators*
	Tess of the D'Urbervilles		Goodbye to Berlin
	The Trumpet Major		Mr Norris Changes Trains
	Under the Greenwood Tree		Prater Violet
		Kazuo Ishiguro	The Remains of the Day

LITERATURE

Author	Book
	Peter Simple
Ngaio Marsh	A Man Lay Dead*
	Overture to Death
Les Martin	The X Files
John Masefield	The Box of Delights
	Sard Harker
William Somerset Maugham	Cakes and Ale
	The Casuarina Tree
	Liza of Lambeth*
	The Moon and Sixpence
	Of Human Bondage
	The Razor's Edge
Armistead Maupin	Tales of the City
Gavin Maxwell	Ring of Bright Water
	Harpoon at a Venture
Peter Mayall	A Year in Provence
Mary McCarthy	The Group
Frank McCourt	Angela's Ashes
Carson McCullers	The Heart Is a Lonely Hunter*
	The Ballad of the Sad Café
Andy McNab	Bravo Two Zero
	Immediate Action
	Remote Control*
Herman Cyril McNeile (Sapper)	Bulldog Drummond
Herman Melville	Billy Budd
	Moby-Dick
	Typee*
Grace Metalious	Peyton Place
James Michener	Tales of theSouth Pacific*
John Stuart Mill	The Subjection of Women
	The System of Logic
Henry Miller	Tropic of Cancer
	Tropic of Capricorn
	Nexus
AA Milne	Now We Are Six
	Winnie-the-Pooh
Yukio Mishima	The Sailor Who Fell from Grace with the Sea
Margaret Mitchell	Gone With the Wind
Nancy Mitford	Love in a Cold Climate
Deborah Moggach	Close Relations
Nicholas Monsarrat	The Cruel Sea
	The Story of Esther Costello
LM Montgomery	Anne of Green Gables*
Michael Moorcock	A Cure for Cancer
	The English Assassin
	The Final Programme
George Moore	Esther Waters
Thomas More	Utopia
Jan Morris	Fifty Years of Europe
Toni Morrison	Beloved
John Mortimer	Felix in the Underworld
	Paradise Postponed
Andrew Morton	Diana: Her New Life
Hector Hugh Munro (Saki)	The Unbearable Bassington
	Beasts and Superbeasts
Murasaki Shikibu	The Tale of Genji
Iris Murdoch	The Black Prince
	The Sea, The Sea
	The Time of the Angels
	Under the Net*
Vladimir Nabokov	Bend Sinister
	Lolita
VS Naipaul	A Bend in the River
	A House for Mr Biswas

Author	Book
	In a Free State
	Miguel Street
	The Mystic Masseur*
Edith Nesbit	The Railway Children
	The Lark
	The Treasure Seekers
Mavis Nicholson	What Did You Do in the War, Mummy?
Mary Norton	The Borrowers
Nostradamus	Centuries
Patrick O'Brian	Master and Commander
Edna O'Brien	The Country Girls
Ben Okri	Dangerous Love
Michael Ondaatje	The English Patient
Yoko Ono	Grapefruit
Baroness Orczy	The Scarlet Pimpernel
George Orwell	Animal Farm
	Down and Out in Paris and London
	The Lion and the Unicorn
	Nineteen Eighty-Four
	The Road to Wigan Pier
Thomas Paine	The Age of Reason
	Common Sense
	Public Good
	The Rights of Man
Michael Palin	Full Circle: A Pacific Journey
	Hemingway's Chair
Sara Paretsky	Toxic Shock
John Dos Passos	Manhattan Transfer
Anna Pasternak	Princess in Love
Boris Pasternak	Doctor Zhivago*
Alan Paton	Cry, the Beloved Country
	Too Late the Phalarope
Thomas Love Peacock	Headlong Hall
	Melincourt
	Nightmare Abbey
Mervyn Peake	The Gormenghast Trilogy
	Captain Slaughterboard Drops Anchor*
	Titus Groan
Charles Perrault	The Sleeping Beauty
	Bluebeard
	Little Red Riding Hood
	Mother Goose
	Puss in Boots
Ellis Peters	The Heretic's Apprentice
Robert Pirsig	Zen and the Art of Motor cycle Maintenance
Sylvia Plath	The Bell Jar
Edgar Allan Poe	'The Fall of the House of Usher'
	'The Murders in the Rue Morgue'
	'The Pit and the Pendulum'
Pope John Paul II	A Celebration of Mass
Beatrix Potter	The Tale of Jemima Puddle-Duck
	The Tale of Mr Jeremy Fisher
	The Tale of Squirrel Nutkin
Stephen Potter	Gamesmanship
	One-Upmanship
	The Young Man*
Anthony Powell	Afternoon Men*
	A Dance to the Music of Time (12 volumes)
	The Fisher King

Author	Book	Author	Book
CP Snow	The Corridors of Power	Hunter S Thompson	Fear and Loathing in Las Vegas
	Strangers and Brothers		
Dava Sobel	Longitude	Henry Thoreau	Walden, or Life in the Woods
Alexander Solzhenitsyn	August 1914		
	Cancer Ward	James Thurber	The Secret Life of Walter Mitty
	The First Circle		
	The Gulag Archipelago	JRR Tolkien	The Hobbit
	The Oak and the Calf		The Lord of the Rings (trilogy)
	One Day in the Life of Ivan Denisovich*		
			The Silmarillion
Muriel Spark	The Ballad of Peckham Rye	Leo Tolstoy	Anna Karenina
			Boyhood
	The Comforters		Childhood
	The Prime of Miss Jean Brodie		War and Peace
Mickey Spillane	I, The Jury		Youth
Howard Spring	Fame Is the Spur	Sue Townsend	The Secret Diary of Adrian Mole Aged 13 ¾*
	My Son, My Son	Berick Traven	The Treasure of the Sierra Madre
Johanna Spyri	Heidi		
Danielle Steele	Ghost	PL Travers	Mary Poppins
John Steinbeck	East of Eden	Robert Tressell	The Ragged Trousered Philanthropists
	The Grapes of Wrath		
	Of Mice and Men	Anthony Trollope	Barchester Towers
	Tortilla Flat		Framley Parsonage
Stendhal	La Chartreuse de Parme		The Macdermots of Ballycloran*
	Le Rouge et le Noir		
Julia Stephenson	Pandora's Diamond		The Pallisers
Laurence Sterne	The Life and Opinions of Tristram Shandy		The Warden
		Joanna Trollope	Next of Kin
Robert Louis Stevenson	Catriona	Ivan Turgenev	Fathers and Sons
	Kidnapped		A Month in the Country
	The Strange Case of Dr Jekyll and Mr Hyde	Mark Twain	The Adventures of Huckleberry Finn
	Weir of Hermiston		The Adventures of Tom Sawyer
RL Stine	Say Cheese and Die Again!	John Updike	In the Beauty of the Lilies
Bram Stoker	Dracula		Rabbit
Irving Stone	The Agony and the Ecstasy		The Witches of Eastwick
		Leon Uris	Armageddon
	Lust for Life		Exodus
Rex Stout	A Question of Proof		The Haj
Harriet Beecher Stowe	Uncle Tom's Cabin	Laurens Van Der Post	The Lost World of the Kalahari
Lytton Strachey	Eminent Victorians		
Robert Smith Surtees	Jorrocks's Jaunts and Jollities		The Seed and the Sower
	Mr Sponge's Sporting Tour	Jules Verne	Around the World in 80 Days
Patrick Susskind	Perfume		Journey to the Centre of the Earth
Graham Swift	Last Orders		
Jonathan Swift	The Battle of the Books		Twenty Thousand Leagues Under the Sea
	Gulliver's Travels		
	Journal to Stella	Virgil	The Aeneid
	A Tale of a Tub	Voltaire	Candide
Elizabeth Taylor	At Mrs Lippincote's*	Kurt Vonnegut	Player Piano*
	A Wreath of Roses		Slaughterhouse 5
WM Thackeray	Denis Duval (Thackeray's last)	Alice Walker	The Color Purple
		Lew Wallace	Ben Hur
	The History of Henry Esmond	Robert James Waller	The Bridges of Madison County
	The Luck of Barry Lyndon	Horace Walpole	The Castle of Otranto
	Pendennis	Keith Waterhouse	Billy Liar
	Vanity Fair: A Novel Without a Hero	Alec Waugh	The Loom of Youth*
			Island in the Sun
	The Virginians	Auberon Waugh	The Foxglove Saga*
DM Thomas	The Flute-Player	Evelyn Waugh	Brideshead Revisited
	The White Hotel		Decline and Fall*
Dylan Thomas	Portrait of the Artist as a Young Dog		Sword of Honour (trilogy)
		Fay Weldon	Affliction
Leslie Thomas	Dangerous Davies		Down Among the Women
	Tropic of Ruislip		The Fat Woman's Joke*
	The Virgin Soldiers*		The Life and Loves of a She-Devil
Flora Thompson	Lark Rise to Candleford		

Author	Book	Author	Book
	Worst Fears	Henry Williamson	Salar the Salmon
HG Wells	The First Men in the Moon		Tarka the Otter
	The History of Mr Polly	Paul Wilson	Little Book of Calm
	The Invisible Man	PG Wodehouse	Heavy Weather
	The New Machiavelli		Right Ho, Jeeves
	The Time Machine*	Tom Wolfe	The Bonfire of the
	The War of the Worlds		Vanities
Irvine Welsh	The Acid House	Naomi Wolf	The Beauty Myth
	Ecstasy		Promiscuities
	Trainspotting	Virginia Woolf	Jacob's Room
Mary Wesley	The Camomile Lawn		Mrs Dalloway
	Haphazard House		Night and Day
	Jumping the Queue		To the Lighthouse
Nathanael West	A Cool Million		The Voyage Out*
	The Day of the Locust	Herman Wouk	The Winds of War
	The Dream Life of Balso	PC Wren	Beau Geste
	Snell	Peter Wright	Spycatcher
	Miss Lonelyhearts	Elizabeth Wurtzel	Prozac Nation
Edith Wharton	The Age of Innocence	John Wyndham	The Day of the Triffids*
	The Buccaneers		The Kraken Wakes
	Ethan Frome		The Midwich Cuckoos
Dennis Wheatley	The Devil Rides Out	Johann Wyss	The Swiss Family
TH White	The Once and Future King		Robinson
	The Sword in the Stone	Émile Zola	Germinal
Oscar Wilde	The Picture of Dorian Gray		J'Accuse
Thornton Wilder	The Bridge of San Luis		Nana
	Rey		Thérèse Raquin
	The Cabala*	Arnold Zweig	Claudia
John Williams	Victory	Stefan Zweig	Beware of Pity
(pictures by Tom Stoddart)			Kaleidoscope

Books: General Information

The Admirable Crichton Master: Lord Loam. Ship: The Bluebell.

Alexandria Quartet Justine, Balthazar, Mountolive, Clea (who had her right hand cut off to save her from drowning after it was pinned underwater by a harpoon gun).

Alice in Wonderland In the croquet game, the mallets were flamingoes and the balls were hedgehogs.

The Anglo-Saxon Chronicle Early record in English of events in England from the arrival of Christianity to 1154, surviving in seven manuscripts and begun about 890, possibly by Alfred the Great. Entries include the arrival of Hengist and Horsa, the story of Cynewulf and Cyneheard, and Alfred's last series of Danish wars. One famous passage is a poem about the battle of Brunanburh (937). The chronicle was expanded and continued, particularly in the late 16th and early 17th century.

Animal Farm The manor farm was owned by Mr Jones, Napoleon the pig became the leader, Boxer was the horse.

Anna Karenina Anna's death: She threw herself under a train.

Anne of Green Gables Prince Edward Island was the setting for Anne Shirley's adventures.

Antic Hay Title comes from a line in Edward II by Christopher Marlowe.

Around the World in 80 Days Central character is Phileas Fogg and his valet is Passepartout. They start and finish at the Reform Club in London. The Indian Widow is Aouda.

Baedeker Books Named after Karl Baedeker of Essen (1801–59), who started the issue of the famous guidebooks in Koblenz. The tradition was continued by his son Fritz, who transferred the business to Leipzig. The term 'Baedeker raids' was applied to the deliberate bombing in the Second World War of provincial cities of great historic and cultural significance, such as Bath, Exeter and Norwich.

Bildungsroman (lit. education novel) Novels portraying a person's formative years, a favourite genre with German authors. Agathon (1766) is considered the first example, but Goethe's Wilhelm Meister's Apprenticeship (1796) is outstanding.

Bleak House Court case was Jarndyce v Jarndyce, the rag and bone man was Krook (who died of spontaneous combustion).

Book of the Century Lord of the Rings was voted Book of the Century in a survey of 25,000 people carried out in 1997 by Channel 4 and Waterstone's.

Bookshop First WH Smith: Euston Station.

The Borrowers The Names: Pod, Homily, Arrietty.

Bradshaw's Railway Guide First published in 1839 in the form of Railway Time Tables by George Bradshaw (1801–53), a Quaker printer and engraver. These developed into Bradshaw's Monthly Railway Guide in 1841 and continued to be published until May 1961.

Brave New World Title from The Tempest by William Shakespeare.

The Brothers Karamazov Alyosha, Dmitry, Ivan, Smolykov.

Cakes and Ale Title from a line in Twelfth Night by William Shakespeare.

The Call of the Wild Dog's name Buck.

Candide Dr Pangloss's famous quote: 'All is for the best in the best of possible worlds.'

Canterbury Tales   The pilgrims met at the Tabard Inn, Southwark. The host on the pilgrimage was Harry Bailly. The summoner's tale tells of a corrupt mendicant friar who is tricked into accepting a donation of a fart.

Catch-22   Set in Pianosa in the Mediterranean. Captain Yossarian had the predicament. Kid Sampson died: cut in half by a low-flying aircraft. Catch-22 is the predicament faced by US bomber crews: You don't have to fly any more missions if you're crazy, but if you ask to be grounded you prove you're not crazy.

The Catcher in the Rye   Central character Holden Caulfield.

Children's Laureate   Quentin Blake became the first in 1999 and Ann Fine replaced him in May 2001.

Clayhanger Trilogy   Clayhanger, Hilda, Lessways, These Twain. A fourth novel, The Roll Call, is loosely connected to the trilogy.

Cold Comfort Farm   Cows' names: Aimless, Feckless, Graceless, Pointless.

The Corridors of Power   War Minister was Roger Quaife.

The Count of Monte Cristo   The Count was Edmond Dantès, imprisoned in the Château d'If. He inherited a fortune left by Abbé Faria.

Crime and Punishment   Crime: murder of a female pawnbroker. Criminal: Raskolnikov. Investigating Inspector: Petrovitch.

David Copperfield   Headmaster of Salem House School: Mr Creakle. Aunt: Betsy Trotwood. Wives: Dora Spenlow and Agnes Wickfield.

Death in Venice   Gustav von Aschenbach dies of cholera.

Dickens   Only novel with female narrator: Bleak House.

Doctor Zhivago   Title character: Dr Yuri Zhivago. Wife: Tania Gromeko. Lover: Lara Antipova.

Dombey and Son   Captain Cuttle's famous quote: 'When found, make a note of.'

Don Quixote   Horse: Rosinante. Squire: Sancho Panza. Lady: Dulcinea.

East of Eden   Based on the story of Cain and Abel.

Emma   Emma Woodhouse marries Mr Knightley.

Every Man For Himself   Story of the Titanic disaster told by Morgan, a well connected young man.

Fair Stood the Wind for France   Title from 'Ballad of Agincourt' by Michael Drayton.

Far from the Madding Crowd   Bathsheba Everdene marries Sergeant Troy and Gabriel Oak. Title from 'Elegy Written in a Country Church-yard' by Thomas Gray.

Feet of Clay   Main character Commander Sir Samuel Vimes, head of Ankh-Morpork City Guard.

Finnegans Wake   Central character is Humphrey Chimpden Earwicker, a publican; the action takes place during one night.

Forsyte Saga Trilogy   A Man of Property, In Chancery, To Let.

For Whom the Bell Tolls   Title from a sermon by John Donne.

Foundation Trilogy   Foundation, Foundation and Empire, Second Foundation.

Gargantua and Pantagruel   Published under name 'Alcofri bas Nasier' (anagram of François Rabelais).

George Smiley   First appeared in Call for the Dead.

Glass of Blessings (Barbara Pym)   Title from 'The Pulley' by George Herbert.

Gone with the Wind   Scarlett O'Hara marries Charles Hamilton, Frank Kennedy, Rhett Butler.

Gothic Novel: 1st   The Castle of Otranto by Horace Walpole (1764).

Grapes of Wrath   The Joad family – Tom, Al, Noah, Ruthie, Winfield and Rosasharn leave Oklahoma for California.

Gravity's Rainbow   Central character Tyrone Slothrop.

The Great Gatsby   Jay Gatsby loves Daisy Buchanan, cousin of narrator Nick Carraway.

Gulliver's Travels   Horses: Houyhnms. Humans: Yahoos. Lands visited: Lilliput, Brobdingnag, Laputa, Blefuscu. Subtitle: 'Travels into Several Remote Nations of the World'.

Hardy's last novel   Jude the Obscure.

Harleian Manuscripts   Collection of manuscripts made by Robert Harley, first earl of Oxford (1661–1724). It consisted of over 50,000 books, 350,000 pamphlets, and 7,000 manuscripts of biblical texts and other historical data. The manuscripts were bought by Parliament in 1753 and placed in the British Museum. They are now housed in the British Library.

Harry Potter Books   Illustrated by Mary Grandpré. First in the series titled Harry Potter and the Sorcerer's Stone in the USA.

Heavy Metal   Phrase coined by William Burroughs in The Naked Lunch.

Helliconia Trilogy   Helliconia Spring, Helliconia Summer, Helliconia Winter.

The History Man   Title character Howard Kirk.

Howard's End   House owners Mr and Mrs Wilcox.

Incunabula   Books printed before 1501 (means 'swaddling clothes').

Interior Monologue   Extended representation in prose or verse of a character's unspoken thoughts, memories and impressions, rendered as if directly overheard by the reader without the intervention of a summarising narrator.

Ivanhoe   Love interest: Lady Rowena.

James Bond books not by Fleming   Colonel Sun and The James Bond Dossier by Kingsley Amis, writing as Robert Markham.

Jane Eyre   Mr Rochester lives at Thornfield Hall. Jane's school is Lowood. Jane's bullying cousin is John Reed. Her home until aged 10 is Gateshead Hall. Dedicated to William Makepeace Thackery.

The Jewel in the Crown   First novel in the Raj Quartet. Plot revolves around the alleged rape in the Bibighar Gardens of Daphne Manners.

Jude the Obscure   Jude Fawley aspires to go to Christminster (Oxford), but fails to get into Sarcophagus College.

Kidnapped   Central character is David Balfour. His friend is the Jacobite Alan Breck. The ship that is meant to take David to the Carolina is the Covenant.

Kipps   Central character Arthur Kipps. Occupation: draper's assistant.

The Last Tycoon   Allegedly based on the Hollywood film producer Irving Thalberg.

Leather-Stocking stories   Hero: Natty Bumppo, also called 'Hawkeye', 'Pathfinder' and 'Deerslayer'. The Last of the Mohicans was Uncas and his father was Chingachgook.

Little Lord Fauntleroy   Title character: Cedric Errol.

Little Women   They are the March sisters: Amy, Beth, Jo and Meg.

Lolita   Title character: Dolores Haze.

The Longest Journey (EM Forster)   Title from Epipsychidion by Percy Bysshe Shelley.

Look Homeward, Angel (Thomas Wolfe) from *Lycidas* by John Milton.

The Lord of the Rings Setting: Middle Earth. Hobbit: Bilbo Baggins. Bilbo's nephew: Frodo. Maker of the One Ring: Sauron. Sauron's land: Mordor. Wizard: Gandalf. Gandalf's horse: Shadowfax. Books in the trilogy: *The Fellowship of the Ring*, *The Two Towers*, *The Return of the King*.

Madame Bovary Title character née Emma Rouault.

Mansfield Park Heroine Fanny Price.

The Mayor of Casterbridge Mayor: First Michael Henchard then Donald Farfrae. Setting: Wessex. 'Casterbridge' is Dorchester. Henchard sells his wife and daughter for five guineas.

The Memory Game Nicci Gerrard and Sean French are co-writers.

The Mill on the Floss Central characters: Tom and Maggie Tulliver. Setting: Dorlcote Mill.

Mirror Crack'd From Side to Side (Agatha Christie) Title from 'The Lady of Shalott' by Alfred Lord Tennyson.

Moby Dick Captain: Ahab. Narrator: Ishmael. Ship: Pequod.

The Moon and Sixpence Inspired by the life of Paul Gauguin.

The Moonstone Title is the name of a diamond.

Morse Christian name Endeavour (revealed in *Death Is Now My Neighbour*).

Mort Main character, Mort, is Death's hopelessly inept teenage apprentice.

Mr Weston's Good Wine (TF Powys) Title from *Emma*, by Jane Austen.

My Son, My Son Original title *Oh Absalom*.

Nicholas Nickleby Nicholas marries Madeline Bray. School: Dotheboys Hall. Schoolmaster: Wackford Squeers. Friend: Smike.

The Nine Tailors Are church bells that cause Geoffrey Deacon's death.

Nineteen Eighty-Four Hero: Winston Smith. His lover: Julia (junior member of the anti-Sex League). Britain depicted as Airstrip One (part of Oceania).

Northanger Abbey Heroine Catherine Morland.

Our Mutual Friend Title character: John Harmon. Marries: Bella Wilfe. Villain: Silas Wegg the peg-leg.

Pale Fire (Nabokov) Title from *Timon of Athens* by William Shakespeare.

A Passage to India Setting: Chandrapore. Central characters: Dr Aziz and Cyril Fielding. Aziz accused of rape by Adela Quested.

Peter Rabbit's father Killed and made into a pie by Mrs McGregor.

The Pickwick Papers Cricket match: All-Muggleton v Dingley Dell.

The Pilgrim's Progress Hero: Christian. Castle: Doubting. Giant: Despair. Goal: Celestial City.

The Portrait of a Lady Title character Isabel Archer.

Power and the Glory Set in Mexico.

The Prime of Miss Jean Brodie Art teacher: Teddy Lloyd.

The Prince and the Pauper Title characters – Prince: Edward, Prince of Wales, later Edward VI; Pauper: Tom Canty.

Prison: authors in

Brendan Behan for IRA activities.

William Blake in Chichester for fighting with a soldier.

John Bunyan in Bedford gaol for preaching without a licence.

Daniel Defoe after writing *The Shortest Way with Dissenters* (a satire on High Church attitudes to religious nonconformism).

John Donne in the Fleet for marrying Anne Moore (a minor) in 1576. Hence his comment: 'John Donne – Anne Donne – Undone.'

Fyodor Dostoyevsky was condemned to death for belonging to a revolutionary organisation but was reprieved and served 4 years hard labour in Siberia.

Ben Jonson was imprisoned for killing Gabriel Spenser, but after pleading benefit of clergy was merely branded on the left thumb.

Ezra Pound was charged with treason for delivering radio broadcasts on behalf of the Axis powers during the Second World War, but was found unfit to plead and instead imprisoned in an asylum.

Alexander Solzhenitsyn spent 8 years in a prison camp for criticising Stalin's conduct of the war against Nazi Germany.

Oscar Wilde was imprisoned for 2 years in Reading Gaol for homosexual offences. He wrote *De Profundis* while incarcerated, not *The Ballad of Reading Gaol*.

The Prisoner of Zenda Title character: King Rudolf. Kingdom: Ruritania. Imprisoned by: Duke Michael.

Quentin Durward Marries Isabelle de Croye.

Rabbit Tetralogy *Rabbit, Run*; *Rabbit Redux*; *Rabbit Is Rich*; *Rabbit at Rest*.

The Railway Children Names: Peter, Phyllis, Roberta.

The Raj Quartet *The Jewel in the Crown*, *The Day of the Scorpion*, *A Division of the Spoils*, *The Towers of Silence*.

The Red and The Black (Stendhal's *Le Rouge et le Noir*). Colours symbolise respectively the Army and the Church.

The Red Badge of Courage Set in the American Civil War.

Rip Van Winkle Set in the Catskill Mountains. Rip sleeps for 20 years.

Room 101 In Orwell's *Nineteen Eighty-Four*, this room contained rats used to help interrogate Winston Smith, as they were his great fear.

The Scarlet Letter Central character: Hester Prynne. The Scarlet Letter: A for Adultery.

The Scarlet Pimpernel Title character: Sir Percy Blakeney.

Scriblerus Club Literary group including Swift, Pope, Gay, Arbuthnot and Thomas Parnell, which met from January to July 1714 to 'ridicule all the false tastes in learning'. Martinos Scriblerus was a pseudonym occasionally used by Pope.

The Seed and the Sower Filmed as *Merry Christmas Mr Lawrence*.

Sense and Sensibility Characters who represent these quallities: Sense – Elinor Dashwood. Sensibility – Marianne Dashwood.

Sherlock Holmes Landlady: Mrs Hudson.

Shogun Central character: John Blackthorne.

Slaughterhouse-Five Hero: Billy Pilgrim.

Sons and Lovers Son: Paul Morel.

The Sound and the Fury Title from: *Macbeth* by William Shakespeare. Family: Benjy, Caddy, Jason and Quentin Compson.

Spanish Civil War Served as stretcher bearer: WH Auden (for the Republicans).

The Spy Who Came in from the Cold Title character: Leamas.

LITERATURE

Stammered   Somerset Maugham.

Steppenwolf   Central character: Harry Haller.

Stream of Consciousness   Term coined in William James's (1842–1910) *Principles of Psychology* (1890) and used to describe the continuity of impressions and thoughts in the human mind. The literary sense of the term was introduced in 1918 by May Sinclair (1863–1946) in a review of early volumes of Dorothy Richardson's (1873–1957) novel sequence *Pilgrimage* (1915–38) and is a method for representing the aforementioned psychological principle in unpunctuated or fragmentary forms of interior monologue.

The Sun Also Rises   Source of the term: 'The Lost Generation'.

Swiss Family Robinson   Johann David Wyss wrote the story and his son Johann Rudolf completed and edited it. The Robinsons' names: Fritz, Ernest, Franz and Jack.

Sword of Honour Trilogy   *Men at Arms, Officers and Gentlemen, Unconditional Surrender.*

The Tailor of Panama   Tailor: Harry Pendel.

The Tale of Two Cities   Cities: Paris and London. Sentenced to guillotine: Charles Darnay. Sacrificed himself in Darnay's place: Sydney Carton.

Tender Is the Night   Title from 'Ode to a Nightingale' by John Keats.

Tess of the D'Urbervilles   Tess marries Angel Clare.

The Thirty-Nine Steps   Hannay's servant: Paddock.

Three Men in a Boat   Title characters: George, Harris, Montmorency (Dog).

Thrums   Name given in JM Barrie to disguise Kirriemuir, his home town.

The Tin Drum   Hero: Oskar Matzerath (a dwarf).

Tobacco Road   Sharecropper: Jeeter Lester. Jeeter's wife: Ada.

Tom Jones   Tom's wife: Sophia Western. Her servant: Mrs Honour.

The Trial   Central character: Joseph K.

The Turn of the Screw   Children: Miles and Flora. Ghosts: Miss Jessel and Peter Quint.

2001: A Space Odyssey   Book based on the film of the same name.

Ulysses   Central characters: Leopold and Molly Bloom and Stephen Daedalus. Set during 18 hours in Dublin on 16 June 1904.

Uncle Tom's Cabin   Slave owner: Simon Legree.

Unnatural Exposure   Plot: Bodies are being dumped in rubbish and bin men demand stress counselling.

Vanity Fair   Central character: Becky Sharp marries: Rawdon Crawley. Becky's friend: Amelia Sedley. she marries: (1) George Osborne; (2) Captain Dobbin. School: Miss Pinkerton's. Illustrated by: W.M. Thackeray.

Victory (John Williams)   Set during Tony Blair's campaign for the 1997 election (pictures by Tom Stoddart).

Villette   Villette is a city based on Brussels.

The Water-Babies   Set in Vendale.

Watership Down   Rabbits   Bigwig, Fiver, General Woundwort, Hazel.

The Well of Loneliness   Originally banned for lesbian content.

Westward Ho!   Hero: Amyas Leigh. His love: Rose of Torridge.

What Katy Did   Heroine's full name: Katy Carr.

Whisky Galore   Setting: Great and Little Todday.

Whitbread Awards: Man and Wife   Michael Frayn and Claire Tomalin became the first married couple to win Whitbread Awards, in 2003.

White Fang   offspring of a wolf-dog and a dog.

WH Smith   *The End of Alice,* banned for its content of child abuse

The Wind in the Willows   Characters: Badger, Mole, Toad, Water Rat.

Winnie-the-Pooh   Title character: Edward (Pooh). Boy: Christopher Robin. Donkey: Eeyore. Elephant: Heffalump. Kidnapped baby: Roo (kangaroo). Illustrator: EH Shepard.

Woman publishers   Virago (run by women for women).

Women in Love   Gudrun Brangwen and Gerald Crich were based on Katherine Mansfield and John Middleton Murry.

Wuthering Heights   Narrated by Mr Lockwood and Nelly Deane.

Wyss, Johann Rudolf   Wrote the Swiss National Anthem 'Rufst du mein Vaterland'.

Zuleika Dobson (Max Beerbohm)   Servant: Mélisande.

Plays and Playwrights

(* denotes playwright's first play)

Playwright	Play
Aeschylus (c. 525–456 BC)	Oresteia Trilogy
	The Persians
	Prometheus Bound
	Seven Against Thebes
	Suppliants
Edward Albee (1928–)	The American Dream
	A Delicate Balance
	Three Tall Women
	Tiny Alice
	Who's Afraid of Virginia Woolf?
	The Zoo Story
Maxwell Anderson (1888–1959)	Anne of the Thousand Days
Jean Anouilh (1910–87)	Antigone
	Becket
	Eurydice
	The Lark (L'Alouette)
	L'Hermine*
	L'Invitation au Château
	Thieves' Carnival
	Waltz of the Toreadors
John Arden (1930–)	All Fall Down*
	Ironhand
	Live Like Pigs
	Serjeant Musgrave's Dance
	Vandaleur's Folly
	The Workhouse Donkey
Aristophanes (c448–388 BC)	The Acharnians
	The Birds
	Clouds
	Ecclesiazusae
	The Frogs
	The Knights
	Lysistrata
	The Peace
	Plutus
	Thesmophoriazusae
	The Wasps
W H Auden (1907–73)	The Ascent of F6
	The Dance of Death
Alan Ayckbourn (1939–)	Absent Friends
	Absurd Person Singular
	Bedroom Farce
	Callisto 5
	A Chorus of Disapproval
	Communicating Doors
	How the Other Half Loves
	Jeeves
	Joking Apart
	Just Between Ourselves
	Living Together
	Man of the Moment
	Mr Whatnot*
	The Norman Conquests
	Relatively Speaking
	Round and Round the Garden
	Season's Greetings
	Sisterly Feelings
	A Small Family Business
	Table Manners
	Ten Times Table
	Time and Time Again
	Time of My Life

Playwright	Play
	Way Upstream
	Woman in Mind
J M Barrie (1860–1937)	The Admirable Crichton
	The Boy David (last)
	Dear Brutus
	Mary Knows
	Peter Pan
	Quality Street
	Walker, London*
	What Every Woman Knows
H E Bates (1905–74)	The Last Bread
Pierre Beaumarchais (1732–99)	The Barber of Seville
	Eugénie*
	The Marriage of Figaro
Samuel Beckett (1906–89)	Breath
	Endgame
	Happy Days
	Ill Seen Ill Said
	Not I
	Waiting for Godot
Brendan Behan (1923–64)	The Hostage
	The Quare Fellow*
Aphra Behn (1640–89)	The Feigned Courtizans
	The Forced Marriage
	The Rover
Alan Bennett (1934–)	An Englishman Abroad
	Forty Years On*
	Getting On
	Habeas Corpus
	Kafka's Dick
	The Madness of George III
	The Old Country
	On the Margin (1st TV play)
	A Question of Attribution
	Talking Heads
Alan Bleasdale (1946–)	Are You Lonesome Tonight?
	Boys from the Blackstuff
	Having a Ball
	It's a Madhouse
	The Monocled Mutineer
	No More Sitting on the Old School Bench*
	On the Ledge
Simon Block	Chimps
Edward Bond (1934–)	Early Morning
	Narrow Road to the Deep North
	The Pope's Wedding*
Dion Boucicault (c. 1820–90)	The Colleen Bawn
	The Corsican Brothers
	London Assurance (written under name of Lee Morton)
	The Octoroon
	The Shaughraun
Bertolt Brecht (1898–1956)	Baal
	The Caucasian Chalk Circle
	Drums in the Night*
	Fear and Misery in the Third Reich
	The Good Woman of Setzuan
	Mother Courage
	The Preventable Rise of Arturo Ui

LITERATURE

Playwright	Play	Playwright	Play
	The Threepenny Opera	(1888–1965)	The Confidential Clerk
Abe Burrows	Cactus Flower		The Elder Statesman
(1910–85)			The Family Reunion
Jim Cartwright	Bed		Murder in the Cathedral
(1958–)	The Rise and Fall of Little		The Rock
	Voice		Sweeney Agonistes*
	Road	Ben Elton	Gasping
Anton Chekhov	The Bear	(1959–)	Silly Cow
(1860–1904)	The Cherry Orchard	George Etherege	The Comical Revenge, or
	Ivanov*	(c. 1635–92)	Love in a Tub
	The Island of Sakhalin		The Man of Mode, or
	The Seagull		Sir Fopling Flutter
	The Three Sisters		She Would If She Could
	Uncle Vanya	Euripides	Alcestis*
	The Wood Demon	(c. 484–406 BC)	Andromache
Caryl Churchill	Cloud Nine		The Bacchae
(1938–)	Fen		Electra
	Icecream		Hecuba
	Light Shining*		Helen
	Light Shining in		Hippolytus
	Buckinghamshire		Ion
	Serious Money		Iphigenia in Aulis
	Softcops		Iphigenia in Tauris
	Top Girls		Medea
Jean Cocteau	L'Aigle à deux têtes		The Phoenician Women
(1889–1963)	Les Mariés de la Tour Eiffel		The Trojan Women
	Orpheus	George Farquhar	The Beaux' Stratagem
William Congreve	The Double Dealer	(c. 1677–1707)	The Constant Couple
(1670–1729)	Love for Love		Love and a Bottle*
	The Mourning Bride		The Recruiting Officer
	The Old Bachelor*	Georges Feydeau	An Absolute Turkey
	The Way of the World	(1862–1921)	A Flea in her Ear
Pierre Corneille	Andromède		Hotel Paradiso
(1606–84)	Le Cid		Ladies' Tailor*
	Cinna		Pig in a Poke
	Clitandre	Eduardo de Filippo	Filumena
	La Galerie du Palais	(1900–84)	La Grande Magia
	Horace		Saturday, Sunday, Monday
	The Liar (Le Menteur)	Alistair Foot and	No Sex Please, We're British
	Mélite*	Anthony Marriot	
	La Mort de Pompée	John Ford	The Broken Heart
	Nicomède	(c. 1586–1640)	The Lady's Trial
	Polyeucte		The Lover's Melancholy
	Pulchérie		Perkin Warbeck
	Rodogune		'Tis Pity She's a Whore
	Théodore	Dario Fo	The Accidental Death of an
	La Veuve	(1926–)	Anarchist
Noël Coward	Bitter Sweet	Michael Frayn	Alphabetical Order
(1899–1973)	Blithe Spirit	(1933–)	Benefactors
	Cavalcade		Clouds
	Design for Living		Donkeys' Years
	Easy Virtue		Here
	Fallen Angels		Look, Look
	This Happy Breed		Make and Break
	Hay Fever		Noises Off
	I'll Leave it to You*		The Sandboy
	Nude with Violin		The Two of Us*
	Peace in Our Time	Brian Friel	Dancing at Lughnasa
	Post Mortem	(1929–)	The Enemy Within
	Present Laughter		Faith Healer
	Private Lives		The Freedom of the City
	Relative Values		Molly Sweeney
	The Vortex		Philadelphia, Here I Come!
John Dryden	All for Love		Translations
(1631–1700)	The Indian Emperor		Wonderful Tennessee
	Marriage à-la-Mode	Christopher Fry	The Boy With a Cart
	The Rival Ladies	(1907–)	Curtmantle
	The State of Innocence		The Lady's Not for Burning
Alexander Dumas (Fils)	Camille		A Phoenix Too Frequent
(1824–95)			Thursday's Child
T S Eliot	The Cocktail Party		The Tower

Playwright	Play
	Venus Observed
John Galsworthy	The Silver Box
(1867–1933)	The Skin Game
Jean Genet	The Balcony
(1910–86)	The Maids
	The Screens
John Godber	April in Paris
(1956–)	Bouncers
	Happy Families
	Happy Jack
	Lucky Sods
	The Office Party
	On the Piste
	Salt of the Earth
	September in the Rain
	Shakers
	Teechers
	Up 'N' Under
Johann W von Goethe	Götz von Berlichingen
(1749–1832)	Die Mitschuldigen
	Egmont
	Erwin und Elmire
	Faust (Parts I & II)
	Iphigenie auf Tauris
	Torquato Tasso
Nikolai Gogol	The Inspector General
(1809–52)	
William Golding	The Brass Butterfly
(1911–93)	
Oliver Goldsmith	She Stoops to Conquer
(1728–74)	
Maxim Gorky	The Lower Depths
(1868–1936)	
Harley Granville Barker	The Madras House
(1877–1946)	The Marrying of Ann Leete
	The Voysey Inheritance
	Waste
Simon Gray	Butley
(1936–)	Cell Mates
	The Common Pursuit
	Dog Days
	Dutch Uncle
	Hidden Laughter
	The Idiot
	Life Support
	Molly
	Otherwise Engaged
	Plaintiffs and Defendants
	Quartermaine's Terms
	The Rear
	Simply Disconnected
	Sleeping Dog
	Spoiled
	Stagestruck
	Two Sundays
	Wise Child*
John Guare	The House of Blue Leaves
(1938–)	Six Degrees of Separation
Patrick Hamilton	Gaslight (aka: Angel Street)
(1904–62)	Rope (US title: Rope's End)
Christopher Hampton	After Mercer
(1946–)	Les Liaisons Dangereuses
	The Philanthropist
	Savages
	Total Eclipse
	Treats
	When Did You Last See My Mother?*
David Hare	The Absence of War
(1947–)	Knuckle
	Licking Hitler (TV play)

Playwright	Play
	Man Above Men (TV play)
	Murmuring Judges
	Racing Demon
	The Secret Rapture
	Slag*
Richard Harris	The Business of Murder
(1934–)	Dead Guilty
	The Maintenance Man
	Outside Edge
	Stepping Out
Harold Harwood	The Grain of Mustard Seed
(1874–1959)	
Ronald Harwood	After the Lions
(1934–)	Another Time
	Country Matters*
	The Dresser
	The Handyman
	Poison Pen
	Reflected Glory
	Taking Sides
Victor Hugo	Angelo
(1802–85)	Cromwell
	Hernani
	Lucrèce Borgia
	Marie Tudor
	Marion Delorme
	Le Roi s'amuse
	Ruy Blas
Henrik Ibsen	An Enemy of the People
(1828–1906)	Catiline*
	A Doll's House
	Ghosts
	Hedda Gabler
	John Gabriel Borkman
	Love's Comedy
	The Master Builder
	Peer Gynt
	The Wild Duck
Eugène Ionesco	The Bald Prima Donna
(1912–94)	Rhinoceros
	The Lesson
Alfred Jarry	Ubu Roi
(1873–1907)	
Terry Johnson	Dead Funny
(1955–)	Hysteria
	Imagine Drowning
	Insignificance
	Unsuitable for Adults
Ben Jonson	The Alchemist
(1572–1637)	Bartholomew Fair
	Catiline
	Cynthia's Revels
	Every Man in His Humour
	Every Man Out of His Humour
	The Poetaster
	The Sad Shepherd (unfinished)
	Sejanus
	The Silent Woman
	Volpone
Tom Kempinski	Duet for One
(1938–)	Separation
Joseph Kesselring	Arsenic and Old Lace
(1902–67)	
Thomas Kyd	The Spanish Tragedy
(1558–94)	
Mike Leigh	Abigail's Party
(1943–)	Babies Grow Old
	Big Basil
	The Box Play*
	Greek Tragedy

LITERATURE

Playwright	Play	Playwright	Play
	Individual Fruit Pies		Chez Nous
	My Parents Have Gone to Carlisle		Daddy Kiss It Better
			A Day in the Death of Joe Egg*
	Nuts in May		
Alain-René Lesage (1668–1747)	Turcaret		Forget-Me-Not Lane
			The Freeway
Ira Levin (1929–)	Deathtrap		The Heart of the Country
	Veronica's Room		The National Health
Frederick Lonsdale (1881–1954)	Aren't We All?		Passion Play
	Canaries Sometimes Sing		A Piece of My Mind
	The Last of Mrs Cheyney		Poppy
	On Approval		Privates on Parade
Federico García Lorca (1898–1936)	Blood Wedding		Walk on the Grass (first TV play)
	The House of Bernarda Alba		
	Yerma		When the Wind Blows
Compton Mackenzie (1883–1972)	The Gentleman in Grey	Edna O'Brien (1932–)	Flesh and Blood
			Madame Bovary
Maurice Maeterlinck (1862–1949)	The Blue Bird		Virginia
	La Princesse Maleine	Sean O'Casey (1880–1964)	The Bishop's Bonfire
	Mary Magdalene		Cockadoodle Dandy
	Pelléas et Mélisande		Juno and the Paycock
David Mamet (1947–)	American Buffalo		The Plough and the Stars
	The Cryptogram		The Shadow of a Gunman
	Duck Variations		The Silver Tassie
	Glengarry Glen Ross	Clifford Odets (1906–63)	Awake and Sing!
	A Life in the Theater		Golden Boy
	Oleanna		Till the Day I Die
	Sexual Perversity in Chicago		Waiting for Lefty
	The Shawl	Eugene O'Neill (1888–1953)	Ah, Wilderness
	Speed-the-Plow		Anna Christie
Christopher Marlowe (1564–93)	Doctor Faustus		Beyond the Horizon
	Edward II		Desire under the Elms
	The Jew of Malta		The Emperor Jones
	The Massacre at Paris		The Great God Brown
	Tamburlaine the Great		The Hairy Ape
Conor McPherson	The Weir		The Iceman Cometh
Thomas Middleton (c. 1570–1627)	Blurt		Lazarus Laughed
	The Changeling (with William Rowley)		Long Day's Journey into Night
	A Game at Chess		Marco Millions
	Master Constable		Mourning Becomes Electra
	The Spanish Gypsy (with William Rowley)		Strange Interlude
			A Touch of the Poet
	Women Beware Women		The Web*
Arthur Miller (1915–)	After the Fall	Joe Orton (1933–67)	Entertaining Mr Sloane*
	All My Sons*		The Erpingham Camp
	Broken Glass		Loot
	The Crucible		The Ruffian on the Stair
	Danger: Memory!		What the Butler Saw
	Death of a Salesman	John Osborne (1929–94)	The Entertainer
	The Last Yankee		Epitaph for George Dillon
	The Man Who Had All the Luck		The Hotel in Amsterdam
			Inadmissible Evidence
	The Price		Jill and Jack (TV play)
	The Ride Down Mount Morgan		Look Back in Anger
			Luther
	A View from the Bridge		A Patriot for Me
Molière (1622–1673)	The Blue-Stockings		West of Suez (TV play)
	Le Bourgeois Gentilhomme	Arthur Wing Pinero (1855–1934)	The Cabinet Minister
	The Impostor		Dandy Dick
	Le Malade Imaginaire		The Gay Lord Quex
	Le Misanthrope		His House in Order
	The Miser		The Magistrate
	The School for Wives		Mid-Channel
	Tartuffe		The Profligate
Nicholas Monsarrat (1910–79)	The Visitors		The Schoolmistress
			The Second Mrs Tanqueray
John Mortimer (1923–)	The Dock Brief		The Squire
	A Voyage Round My Father		Trelawny of the 'Wells'
Peter Nichols (1927–)	Ben Spray		£200 a Year*
	Born in the Gardens	Harold Pinter	Betrayal

Playwright	Play	Playwright	Play
(1930–)	The Birthday Party	(1759–1805)	Don Carlos
	The Caretaker		The Maid of Orleans
	The Homecoming		Maria Stuart
	Hothouse		The Robbers*
	Moonlight		Wallenstein Trilogy
	No Man's Land		William Tell
	One for the Road	Anthony Shaffer	The Case of the Oily
	Other Places	(1926–)	Levantine
	The Room*		Murderer
Luigi Pirandello	Come Tu Mi Vuoi		Sleuth
(1867–1936)	Enrico IV	Peter Shaffer	Amadeus
	Six Characters in Search of	(1926–)	Black Comedy
	an Author		Equus
Sylvia Plath	Three Women		Five-Finger Exercise*
(1932–63)			The Gift of the Gorgon
JB Priestley	Dangerous Corner*		Lettice and Lovage
(1894–1984)	I Have Been Here Before		The Private Ear
	An Inspector Calls		The Public Eye
	Laburnum Grove		The Royal Hunt of the Sun
	The Linden Tree		Yonadab
	Time and the Conways	George Bernard Shaw	Androcles and the Lion
	When We Are Married	(1856–1950)	Arms and the Man
Alexander Pushkin	Boris Godunov		Back to Methuselah
(1799–1837)			Caesar and Cleopatra
Jean Racine	Alexandre le Grand		Candida
(1639–99)	Andromaque		Captain Brassbound's
	Athalie		Conversion
	Bajazet		The Devil's Disciple
	Bérénice		The Doctor's Dilemma
	Britannicus		Getting Married
	Esther		Heartbreak House
	Iphigénie		John Bull's Other Island
	La Thébaïde, ou Les Frères		Major Barbara
	ennemis		Man and Superman
	Mithridate		The Millionairess
	Phèdre		Mrs Warren's Profession
Terence Rattigan	Adventure Story		Pygmalion
(1911–77)	The Browning Version		Saint Joan
	Cause Célèbre		Widowers' Houses
	The Deep Blue Sea		You Never Can Tell
	Flare Path	Sam Shepard	Buried Child
	French Without Tears	(1943–)	Cowboys*
	Harlequinade		The Curse of the Starving
	Ross		Class
	Separate Tables		Dog and Rocking Chair
	The Winslow Boy		Fool for Love
Edmond Rostand	Chantecler		A Lie of the Mind
(1868–1918)	Cyrano de Bergerac		The Rock Garden
William Rowley	A New Wonder: A Woman		Simpatico
(c. 1585–1642)	Never Vext		The Tooth of Crime
Willy Russell	Blind Scouse Trilogy*		True West
(1947–)	Blood Brothers	Richard Brinsley	The Critic
	Boy with Transistor Radio	Sheridan	Jupiter
	Breezeblock Park	(1751–1816)	The Rivals
	Educating Rita		St Patrick's Day
	I Read the News Today (radio)		The School for Scandal
	John, Paul, George	R C Sherriff	Home at Seven
	Ringo . . . and Bert	(1896–1975)	Journey's End*
	King of the Castle (TV play)	Alan Sillitoe (1928–)	All Citizens Are Soldiers
	One for the Road	and Ruth Fainlight	
	Our Day Out	(1931–)	
	Shirley Valentine	Neil Simon	Barefoot in the Park
	Stags and Hens	(1927–)	Biloxi Blues
Jean-Paul Sartre	In Camera		California Suite
(1905–80)	The Condemned of Altona		Come Blow Your Horn*
James Saunders	Bodies		The Gingerbread Lady
(1925–)	Making It Better		The Good Doctor
	Next Time I'll Sing to You		Last of the Red Hot Lovers
	Retreat		Little Me
	A Scent of Flowers		Lost in Yonkers
Friedrich von Schiller	Demetrius (unfinished)		The Odd Couple

LITERATURE

Playwright	Play	Playwright	Play
	Plaza Suite		The Tinker's Wedding
	The Prisoner of Second		The Well of the Saints
	Avenue	Peter Terson	Zigger Zagger
	Promises, Promises	Brandon Thomas	Charley's Aunt
	The Sunshine Boys	(1856–1914)	
	Sweet Charity	Dylan Thomas	Under Milk Wood
	They're Playing Our Song	(1914–53)	
Sophocles	Ajax	John Vanbrugh	The Confederacy
(c. 496–405 BC)	Antigone	(1664–1726)	The Provok'd Husband
	Electra		The Provok'd Wife
	Ichneutae		(both above completed by
	Oedipus at Colonus		Colley Cibber)
	Oedipus Rex		The Relapse, or Virtue in
	Philoctetes		Danger
	Trachiniae	John Webster	The Devil's Law Case
Tom Stoppard	After Magritte	(1580–1625)	The Duchess of Malfi
(1937–)	Albert's Bridge (radio)		The White Devil
	Dirty Linen	Frank Wedekind	Earth Spirit
	The Dissolution of Dominic	(1864–1918)	Pandora's Box
	Boot (radio)		Spring Awakening
	Enter a Free Man	Arnold Wesker	Annie Wobbler
	Jumpers	(1932–)	Chicken Soup With Barley
	M Is for Moon Among Other		Chips With Everything
	Things (radio)		I'm Talking About Jerusalem
	Night and Day		The Kitchen
	Professional Foul (TV play)		Roots
	The Real Inspector Hound	Hugh Whitemore	The Best of Friends
	Rosencrantz and	(1936–)	Breaking the Code
	Guildenstern Are Dead		It's Ralph
	Separate Peace (first TV play)		Pack of Lies
	Travesties		Stevie*
	A Walk on the Water*	Oscar Wilde	The Duchess of Padua
Tom Stoppard and	Every Good Boy Deserves	(1854–1900)	An Ideal Husband
André Previn (1929–)	Favour		The Importance of Being
David Storey	The Changing Room		Ernest
(1933–)	The Contractor		Lady Windermere's Fan
	Cromwell		Salome
	Early Days		A Woman of No Importance
	The Farm	Thornton Wilder	The Angel that Troubled the
	Home	(1897–1975)	Waters
	In Celebration		The Long Christmas Dinner
	Life Class		The Matchmaker
	The March on Russia		Our Town
	Mother's Day		The Skin of Our Teeth
	The Restoration of Arnold		The Trumpet Shall Sound
	Middleton*	Tennessee Williams	Battle of Angels*
	Sisters	(1911–83)	Camino Real
August Strindberg	The Creditors		Cat on a Hot Tin Roof
(1849–1912)	The Dance of Death		The Glass Menagerie
	A Dream Play		The Night of the Iguana
	The Father		The Rose Tattoo
	Master Olof		A Streetcar Named Desire
	Miss Julie		Suddenly Last Summer
	To Damascus		Sweet Bird of Youth
J M Synge	In the Shadow of the Glen	William Wycherley	The Country Wife
(1871–1909)	The Playboy of the Western	(1640–1716)	The Gentleman Dancing
	World		Master
	Riders to the Sea		The Plain Dealer

Plays and Playwrights (in Play Order)

(for playwrights' dates see previous section)

Play	Playwright	Play	Playwright
Abigail's Party	Mike Leigh	Absurd Person Singular	Alan Ayckbourn
The Absence of War	David Hare	The Accidental Death	Dario Fo
Absent Friends	Alan Ayckbourn	of an Anarchist	
An Absolute Turkey	Georges Feydeau	The Acharnians	Aristophanes

Play	Playwright	Play	Playwright
The Admirable Crichton	J M Barrie	The Birds	Aristophanes
Adventure Story	Terence Rattigan	The Birthday Party	Harold Pinter
After Magritte	Tom Stoppard	The Bishop's Bonfire	Sean O'Casey
After Mercer	Christopher Hampton	Bitter Sweet	Noël Coward
After the Fall	Arthur Miller	Black Comedy	Peter Shaffer
After the Lions	Ronald Harwood	Blind Scouse Trilogy*	Willy Russell
Ah, Wilderness	Eugene O'Neill	Blithe Spirit	Noël Coward
Ajax	Sophocles	Blood Brothers	Willy Russell
Albert's Bridge (radio)	Tom Stoppard	Blood Wedding	Federico García Lorca
Alcestis*	Euripides	The Blue Bird	Maurice Maeterlinck
The Alchemist	Ben Jonson	The Blue-Stockings	Molière
Alexandre le Grand	Jean Racine	Blurt	Thomas Middleton
All Citizens Are Soldiers	Alan Sillitoe and Ruth Fainlight	Bodies	James Saunders
		Boris Godunov	Alexander Pushkin
All Fall Down*	John Arden	Born in the Gardens	Peter Nichols
All for Love	John Dryden	Bouncers	John Godber
All My Sons*	Arthur Miller	Le Bourgeois Gentilhomme	Molière
Alphabetical Order	Michael Frayn		
Amadeus	Peter Shaffer	The Box Play*	Mike Leigh
American Buffalo	David Mamet	The Boy David (last)	J M Barrie
The American Dream	Edward Albee	The Boy with a Cart	Christopher Fry
An Enemy of the People	Henrik Ibsen	Boy with Transistor Radio	Willy Russell
An Englishman Abroad	Alan Bennett	Boys from the Blackstuff	Alan Bleasdale
Androcles and the Lion	George Bernard Shaw	The Brass Butterfly	William Golding
Andromache	Euripides	Breaking the Code	Hugh Whitemore
Andromaque	Jean Racine	Breath	Samuel Beckett
Andromède	Pierre Corneille	Breezeblock Park	Willy Russell
The Angel that Troubled the Waters	Thornton Wilder	Britannicus	Jean Racine
		Broken Glass	Arthur Miller
Angelo	Victor Hugo	The Broken Heart	John Ford
Anna Christie	Eugene O'Neill	The Browning Version	Terence Rattigan
Anne of the Thousand Days	Maxwell Anderson	Buried Child	Sam Shepard
		The Business of Murder	Richard Harris
Annie Wobbler	Arnold Wesker	Butley	Simon Gray
Another Time	Ronald Harwood	The Cabinet Minister	Arthur Wing Pinero
Antigone	Jean Anouilh	Cactus Flower	Abe Burrows
Antigone	Sophocles	Caesar and Cleopatra	George Bernard Shaw
April in Paris	John Godber	California Suite	Neil Simon
Are You Lonesome Tonight?	Alan Bleasdale	Callisto 5	Alan Ayckbourn
		Camille	Alexander Dumas (Fils)
Aren't We All?	Frederick Lonsdale	Camino Real	Tennessee Williams
Arms and the Man	George Bernard Shaw	Canaries Sometimes Sing	Frederick Lonsdale
Arsenic and Old Lace	Joseph Kesselring		
The Ascent of F6	W H Auden and Christopher Isherwood	Candida	George Bernard Shaw
		Captain Brassbound's Conversion	George Bernard Shaw
Athalie	Jean Racine		
Awake and Sing	Clifford Odets	The Caretaker	Harold Pinter
Baal	Bertolt Brecht	The Case of the Oily Levantine	Anthony Shaffer
Babies Grow Old	Mike Leigh		
The Bacchae	Euripides	Cat on a Hot Tin Roof	Tennessee Williams
Back to Methuselah	George Bernard Shaw	Catiline*	Henrik Ibsen
Bajazet	Jean Racine	Catiline	Ben Jonson
The Balcony	Jean Genet	The Caucasian Chalk Circle	Bertolt Brecht
The Bald Prima Donna	Eugène Ionesco		
The Barber of Seville	Pierre Beaumarchais	Cause Célèbre	Terence Rattigan
Barefoot in the Park	Neil Simon	Cavalcade	Noël Coward
Bartholomew Fair	Ben Jonson	Cell Mates	Simon Gray
Battle of Angels*	Tennessee Williams	The Changeling	Thomas Middleton and William Rowley
The Bear	Anton Chekhov		
The Beaux' Stratagem	George Farquhar	The Changing Room	David Storey
Becket	Jean Anouilh	Chantecler	Edmond Rostand
Bed	Jim Cartwright	Charley's Aunt	Brandon Thomas
Bedroom Farce	Alan Ayckbourn	The Cherry Orchard	Anton Chekhov
Ben Spray	Peter Nichols	Chez Nous	Peter Nichols
Benefactors	Michael Frayn	Chicken Soup With Barley	Arnold Wesker
Bérénice	Jean Racine		
The Best of Friends	Hugh Whitemore	Chimps	Simon Block
Betrayal	Harold Pinter	Chips With Everything	Arnold Wesker
Beyond the Horizon	Eugene O'Neill	A Chorus of Disapproval	Alan Ayckbourn
Big Basil	Mike Leigh	Le Cid	Pierre Corneille
Biloxi Blues	Neil Simon	Cinna	Pierre Corneille

LITERATURE

Play	Playwright	Play	Playwright
Claude Gueux	Victor Hugo	Drums in the Night*	Bertolt Brecht
Clitandre	Pierre Corneille	The Duchess of Malfi	John Webster
Cloud Nine	Caryl Churchill	The Duchess of Padua	Oscar Wilde
Clouds	Michael Frayn	Duck Variations	David Mamet
Clouds	Aristophanes	Duet for One	Tom Kempinski
Cockadoodle Dandy	Sean O'Casey	Dutch Uncle	Simon Gray
The Cocktail Party	T S Eliot	Early Days	David Storey
The Colleen Bawn	Dion Boucicault	Early Morning	Edward Bond
Come Blow Your Horn*	Neil Simon	Earth Spirit	Frank Wedekind
		Easy Virtue	Noël Coward
Come Tu Mi Vuoi	Luigi Pirandello	Ecclesiazusae	Aristophanes
The Comical Revenge, or Love in a Tub	Sir George Etherege	Educating Rita	Willy Russell
		Edward II	Christopher Marlowe
The Common Pursuit	Simon Gray	Egmont	Johann Wolfgang von Goethe
Communicating Doors	Alan Ayckbourn		
The Condemned of Altona	Jean-Paul Sartre	The Elder Statesman	T S Eliot
		Electra	Euripides
The Confederacy	John Vanbrugh	Electra	Sophocles
The Confidential Clerk	T S Eliot	The Emperor Jones	Eugene O'Neill
The Constant Couple	George Farquhar	Endgame	Samuel Beckett
The Contractor	David Storey	The Enemy Within	Brian Friel
The Corsican Brothers	Dion Boucicault	Enrico IV	Luigi Pirandello
Country Matters*	Ronald Harwood	Enter a Free Man	Tom Stoppard
The Country Wife	William Wycherley	The Entertainer	John Osborne
Cowboys*	Sam Shepard	Entertaining Mr Sloane*	Joe Orton
The Creditors	August Strindberg	Epitaph for George Dillon	John Osborne
The Critic	Richard Brinsley Sheridan	Equus	Peter Shaffer
Cromwell	David Storey	The Erpingham Camp	Joe Orton
Cromwell	Victor Hugo	Erwin und Elmire	Johann Wolfgang von Goethe
The Crucible	Arthur Miller		
The Cryptogram	David Mamet	Esther	Jean Racine
The Curse of the Starving Class	Sam Shepard	Eugénie*	Pierre Beaumarchais
		Eurydice	Jean Anouilh
Curtmantle	Christopher Fry	Every Good Boy Deserves Favour	Tom Stoppard and André Previn
Cynthia's Revels	Ben Jonson		
Cyrano de Bergerac	Edmond Rostand	Every Man in his Humour	Ben Jonson
Daddy Kiss It Better	Peter Nichols	Every Man Out of his Humour	Ben Jonson
The Dance of Death	W H Auden		
The Dance of Death	August Strindberg	Faith Healer	Brian Friel
Dancing at Lughnasa	Brian Friel	Fallen Angels	Noël Coward
Dandy Dick	Arthur Wing Pinero	The Family Reunion	T S Eliot
Dangerous Corner*	J B Priestley	The Farm	David Storey
Danger: Memory!	Arthur Miller	The Father	August Strindberg
A Day in the Death of Joe Egg*	Peter Nichols	Faust (Parts I & II)	Johann Wolfgang von Goethe
Dead Funny	Terry Johnson	Fear and Misery in the Third Reich	Bertolt Brecht
Dead Guilty	Richard Harris		
Dear Brutus	J M Barrie	The Feigned Courtizans	Aphra Behn
Death of a Salesman	Arthur Miller	Fen	Caryl Churchill
Deathtrap	Ira Levin	Filumena	Eduardo de Filippo
The Deep Blue Sea	Terence Rattigan	Five-Finger Exercise*	Peter Shaffer
A Delicate Balance	Edward Albee	Flare Path	Terence Rattigan
Demetrius (unfinished)	Friedrich von Schiller	A Flea in her Ear	Georges Feydeau
Design for Living	Noël Coward	Flesh and Blood	Edna O'Brien
Desire under the Elms	Eugene O'Neill	Fool for Love	Sam Shepard
The Devil's Disciple	George Bernard Shaw	The Forced Marriage	Aphra Behn
The Devil's Law Case	John Webster	Forget-Me-Not Lane	Peter Nichols
Dirty Linen	Tom Stoppard	Forty Years On*	Alan Bennett
The Dissolution of Dominic Boot (radio)	Tom Stoppard	The Freedom of the City	Brian Friel
		The Freeway	Peter Nichols
The Dock Brief	John Mortimer	French Without Tears	Terence Rattigan
The Doctor's Dilemma	George Bernard Shaw	The Frogs,	Aristophanes
Dog and Rocking Chair	Sam Shepard	La Galerie du Palais	Pierre Corneille
Dog Days	Simon Gray	A Game at Chess	Thomas Middleton
A Doll's House	Henrik Ibsen	Gaslight (aka: Angel Street)	Patrick Hamilton
Don Carlos	Friedrich von Schiller		
Donkeys' Years	Michael Frayn	Gasping	Ben Elton
The Double Dealer	William Congreve	The Gay Lord Quex	Arthur Wing Pinero
Doctor Faustus	Christopher Marlowe	The Gentleman Dancing Master	William Wycherley
A Dream Play	August Strindberg		
The Dresser	Ronald Harwood	The Gentleman in Grey	Compton Mackenzie

Play	Playwright	Play	Playwright
Getting Married	George Bernard Shaw	In the Shadow of the Glen	J M Synge
Getting On	Alan Bennett		
Ghosts	Henrik Ibsen	Inadmissible Evidence	John Osborne
The Gift of the Gorgon	Peter Shaffer	The Indian Emperor	John Dryden
The Gingerbread Lady	Neil Simon	Individual Fruit Pies	Mike Leigh
The Glass Menagerie	Tennessee Williams	Insignificance	Terry Johnson
Glengarry Glen Ross	David Mamet	An Inspector Calls	J B Priestley
Golden Boy	Clifford Odets	The Inspector General	Nikolai Gogol
The Good Doctor	Neil Simon	L'Invitation au Château	Jean Anouilh
The Good Woman of Setzuan	Bertolt Brecht	Ion	Euripides
		Iphigenia in Aulis	Euripides
Götz von Berlichingen	Johann W von Goethe	Iphigenia in Tauris	Euripides
The Grain of Mustard Seed	Harold Harwood	Iphigénie	Jean Racine
		Iphigenie auf Tauris	Johann Wolfgang von Goethe
La Grande Magia	Eduardo de Filippo		
The Great God Brown	Eugene O'Neill	Ironhand	John Arden
Greek Tragedy	Mike Leigh	The Island of Sakhalim	Anton Chekov
Habeas Corpus	Alan Bennett	It's a Madhouse	Alan Bleasdale
The Hairy Ape	Eugene O'Neill	It's Ralph	Hugh Whitemore
The Handyman	Ronald Harwood	Ivanov*	Anton Chekhov
This Happy Breed	Noël Coward	Jeeves	Alan Ayckbourn
Happy Days	Samuel Beckett	The Jew of Malta	Christopher Marlowe
Happy Families	John Godber	Jill and Jack (TV play)	John Osborne
Happy Jack	John Godber	John Bull's Other Island	George Bernard Shaw
Harlequinade	Terence Rattigan	John Gabriel Borkman	Henrik Ibsen
Having a Ball	Alan Bleasdale	John, Paul, George, Ringo . . . and Bert	Willy Russell
Hay Fever	Noël Coward		
The Heart of the Country	Peter Nichols	Joking Apart	Alan Ayckbourn
Heartbreak House	George Bernard Shaw	Journey's End*	R C Sherriff
Hecuba	Euripides	Jumpers	Tom Stoppard
Hedda Gabler	Henrik Ibsen	Juno and the Paycock	Sean O'Casey
Helen	Euripides	Jupiter	Richard Brinsley Sheridan
Here	Michael Frayn	Just Between Ourselves	Alan Ayckbourn
Hernani	Victor Hugo	Kafka's Dick	Alan Bennett
Hidden Laughter	Simon Gray	King of the Castle (TV play)	Willy Russell
Hippolytus	Euripides		
His House in Order	Arthur Wing Pinero	The Kitchen	Arnold Wesker
Home	David Storey	The Knights	Aristophanes
Home at Seven	R C Sherriff	Knuckle	David Hare
The Homecoming	Harold Pinter	La Princess Maleine	Count Maurice Maeterlinck
Horace	Pierre Corneille	Laburnum Grove	J B Priestley
The Hostage	Brendan Behan	Ladies' Tailor*	Georges Feydeau
The Hotel in Amsterdam	John Osborne	Lady Windermere's Fan	Oscar Wilde
Hotel Paradiso	Georges Feydeau	The Lady's Not for Burning	Christopher Fry
Hothouse	Harold Pinter	The Lady's Trial	John Ford
The House of Bernarda Alba	Federico García Lorca	L'Aigle à deux têtes	Jean Cocteau
		The Lark (L'Alouette)	Jean Anouilh
The House of Blue Leaves	John Guare	The Last Bread	H E Bates
		Last of Mrs Cheyney	Frederick Lonsdale
How the Other Half Loves	Alan Ayckbourn	The Last of the Red Hot Lovers	Neil Simon
Hysteria	Terry Johnson	The Last Yankee	Arthur Miller
I Have Been Here Before	J B Priestley	Lazarus Laughed	Eugene O'Neill
I Read the News Today (radio)	Willy Russell	Les Mariés de la Tour Eiffel	Jean Cocteau
Icecream	Caryl Churchill	Les Liaisons Dangereuses	Christopher Hampton
The Iceman Cometh	Eugene O'Neill		
Ichneutae	Sophocles	The Lesson	Eugène Ionesco
An Ideal Husband	Oscar Wilde	Lettice and Lovage	Peter Shaffer
The Idiot	Simon Gray	L'Hermine*	Jean Anouilh
I'll Leave it to You*	Noël Coward	The Liar(Le Menteur)	Pierre Corneille
Ill Seen Ill Said	Samuel Beckett	Licking Hitler (TV play)	David Hare
I'm Talking About Jerusalem	Arnold Wesker	A Lie of the Mind	Sam Shepard
		Life Class	David Storey
Imagine Drowning	Terry Johnson	A Life in the Theater	David Mamet
The Importance of Being Ernest	Oscar Wilde	Life Support	Simon Gray
		Light Shining*	Caryl Churchill
The Impostor	Molière	Light Shining in Buckinghamshire	Caryl Churchill
In Camera	Jean-Paul Sartre		
In Celebration	David Storey	The Linden Tree	J B Priestley

LITERATURE

Play	Playwright	Play	Playwright
Little Me	Neil Simon	The Monocled Mutineer	Alan Bleasdale
Live Like Pigs	John Arden	Moonlight	Harold Pinter
Living Together	Alan Ayckbourn	La Mort de Pompée	Pierre Corneille
London Assurance	Dion Boucicault	Mother Courage	Bertolt Brecht
The Long Christmas Dinner	Thornton Wilder	Mother's Day	David Storey
		Mourning Becomes Electra	Eugene O'Neill
Long Day's Journey into Night	Eugene O'Neill	The Mourning Bride	William Congreve
Look Back in Anger	John Osborne	Mr Whatnot*	Alan Ayckbourn
Look, Look	Michael Frayn	Mrs Warren's Profession	George Bernard Shaw
Loot	Joe Orton	Murder in the Cathedral	T S Eliot
Lost in Yonkers	Neil Simon	Murderer	Anthony Shaffer
Love and a Bottle*	George Farquhar	Murmuring Judges	David Hare
Love for Love	William Congreve	My Parents Have Gone to Carlisle	Mike Leigh
The Lover's Melancholy	John Ford		
Love's Comedy	Henrik Ibsen	Narrow Road to the Deep North	Edward Bond
The Lower Depths	Maxim Gorky		
Lucky Sods	John Godber	The National Health	Peter Nichols
Lucrèce Borgia	Victor Hugo	A New Wonder: A Woman Never Vext	William Rowley
Luther	John Osborne		
Lysistrata	Aristophanes	Next Time I'll Sing to You	James Saunders
M Is for Moon Among Other Things (radio)	Tom Stoppard	Nicomède	Pierre Corneille
		Night and Day	Tom Stoppard
Madame Bovary	Edna O'Brien	The Night of the Iguana	Tennessee Williams
The Madness of George III	Alan Bennett	No Man's Land	Harold Pinter
		No More Sitting on the Old School Bench*	Alan Bleasdale
The Madras House	Harley Granville Barker		
The Magistrate	Arthur Wing Pinero	No Sex Please, We're British	Alistair Foot and Anthony Marriot
The Maid of Orleans	Friedrich von Schiller		
The Maids	Jean Genet	Noises Off	Michael Frayn
The Maintenance Man	Richard Harris	Norman Conquests	Alan Ayckbourn
Major Barbara	George Bernard Shaw	Not I	Samuel Beckett
Make and Break	Michael Frayn	Nude with Violin	Nöel Coward
Making It Better	James Saunders	Nuts in May	Mike Leigh
Le Malade Imaginaire	Molière	The Octoroon	Dion Boucicault
Man Above Men (TV play)	David Hare	The Odd Couple	Neil Simon
		Oedipus at Colonus	Sophocles
Man and Superman	George Bernard Shaw	Oedipus Rex	Sophocles
The Man of Mode, or Sir Fopling Flutter	George Etherege	The Office Party	John Godber
		The Old Bachelor*	William Congreve
Man of the Moment	Alan Ayckbourn	The Old Country	Alan Bennett
The Man Who Had All the Luck,	Arthur Miller	Oleanna	David Mamet
		On Approval	Frederick Lonsdale
The March on Russia	David Storey	On the Ledge	Alan Bleasdale
Marco Millions	Eugene O'Neill	On the Margin (first TV play)	Alan Bennett
Marie Tudor	Victor Hugo		
Marion Delorme	Victor Hugo	On the Piste	John Godber
The Marriage of Figaro	Pierre Beaumarchais	One for the Road	Harold Pinter
Marriage à-la-Mode	John Dryden	One for the Road	Willy Russell
The Marrying of Ann Leete	Harley Granville Barker	Oresteia Trilogy	Aeschylus
		Orpheus	Jean Cocteau
Mary Knows	J M Barrie	Other Places	Harold Pinter
Mary Magdalene	Maurice Maeterlinck	Otherwise Engaged	Simon Gray
Maria Stuart	Friedrich von Schiller	Our Day Out	Willy Russell
The Massacre at Paris	Christopher Marlowe	Our Town	Thornton Wilder
The Master Builder	Henrik Ibsen	Outside Edge	Richard Harris
Master Constable	Thomas Middleton	Pack of Lies	Hugh Whitemore
Master Olof	August Strindberg	Pandora's Box	Frank Wedekind
The Matchmaker	Thornton Wilder	Passion Play	Peter Nichols
Medea	Euripides	A Patriot for Me	John Osborne
Mélite	Pierre Corneille	Peace in Our Time	Noël Coward
Mid-Channel	Arthur Wing Pinero	A Piece of My Mind	Peter Nichols
The Millionairess	George Bernard Shaw	The Peace	Aristophanes
Le Misanthrope	Molière	Peer Gynt	Henrik Ibsen
The Miser	Molière	Pelléas et Mélisande	Count Maurice Maeterlinck
Miss Julie	August Strindberg	Perkin Warbeck	John Ford
Mithridate	Jean Racine	The Persians	Aeschylus
Die Mitschuldigen	Johann Wolfgang von Goethe	Peter Pan	J M Barrie
		Phèdre	Jean Racine
Molly	Simon Gray	Philadelphia Here I Come	Brian Friel
Molly Sweeney	Brian Friel	The Philanthropist	Christopher Hampton

Play	Playwright
Philoctetes	Sophocles
The Phoenician Women	Euripides
A Phoenix Too Frequent	Christopher Fry
A Piece of My Mind	Peter Nichols
Pig in a Poke	Georges Feydeau
The Plain Dealer	William Wycherley
Plaintiffs and Defendants	Simon Gray
The Playboy of the Western World	J M Synge
Plaza Suite	Neil Simon
The Plough and the Stars	Sean O'Casey
Plutus	Aristophanes
The Poetaster	Ben Jonson
Poison Pen	Ronald Harwood
Polyeucte	Pierre Corneille
The Pope's Wedding*	Edward Bond
Poppy	Peter Nichols
Post Mortem	Noël Coward
Present Laughter	Noël Coward
The Preventable Rise of Arturo Ui	Bertolt Brecht
The Price	Arthur Miller
The Prisoner of Second Avenue	Neil Simon
The Private Ear	Peter Shaffer
Private Lives	Noël Coward
Privates on Parade	Peter Nichols
Professional Foul (TV play)	Tom Stoppard
The Profligate	Arthur Wing Pinero
Prometheus Bound	Aeschylus
Promises, Promises	Neil Simon
The Provok'd Husband	John Vanbrugh (completed by Colley Cibber)
The Provok'd Wife	John Vanbrugh (completed by Colley Cibber)
The Public Eye	Peter Shaffer
Pulchérie	Pierre Corneille
Pygmalion	George Bernard Shaw
Quality Street	J M Barrie
The Quare Fellow*	Brendan Behan
Quartermaine's Terms	Simon Gray
A Question of Attribution	Alan Bennett
Racing Demon	David Hare
The Real Inspector Hound	Tom Stoppard
The Rear	Simon Gray
The Recruiting Officer	George Farquhar
Reflected Glory	Ronald Harwood
The Relapse	John Vanbrugh
Relative Values	Noël Coward
Relatively Speaking	Alan Ayckbourn
The Restoration of Arnold Middleton*	David Storey
Retreat	James Saunders
Rhinoceros	Eugène Ionesco
The Ride Down Mount Morgan	Arthur Miller
Riders to the Sea	J M Synge
The Rise and Fall of Little Voice	Jim Cartwright
The Rival Ladies	John Dryden
The Rivals	Richard Brinsley Sheridan
Road	Jim Cartwright
The Robbers*	Friedrich von Schiller
The Rock Garden	Sam Shepard
The Rock	T S Eliot
Rodogune	Pierre Corneille
Le Roi s'amuse	Victor Hugo
The Room*	Harold Pinter
Roots	Arnold Wesker
Rope (US title: Rope's End)	Patrick Hamilton
The Rose Tattoo	Tennessee Williams
Rosencrantz and Guildenstern Are Dead	Tom Stoppard
Ross	Terence Rattigan
Round and Round the Garden	Alan Ayckbourn
The Rover	Aphra Behn
The Royal Hunt of the Sun	Peter Shaffer
The Ruffian on the Stair*	Joe Orton
Ruy Blas	Victor Hugo
The Sad Shepherd (unfinished)	Ben Jonson
Saint Joan	George Bernard Shaw
Saint Patrick's Day	Richard Brinsley Sheridan
Salome	Oscar Wilde
Salt of the Earth	John Godber
The Sandboy	Michael Frayn
Saturday, Sunday, Monday	Eduardo de Filippo
Savages	Christopher Hampton
A Scent of Flowers	James Saunders
The School for Scandal	Richard Brinsley Sheridan
The School for Wives	Molière
The Schoolmistress	Arthur Wing Pinero
The Screens	Jean Genet
The Seagull	Anton Chekhov
Season's Greetings	Alan Ayckbourn
The Second Mrs Tanqueray	Arthur Wing Pinero
The Secret Rapture	David Hare
Sejanus	Ben Jonson
Separate Peace (first TV Play)	Tom Stoppard
Separate Tables	Terence Rattigan
Separation	Tom Kempinski
September in the Rain	John Godber
Sergeant Musgrave's Dance	John Arden
Serious Money	Caryl Churchill
Seven Against Thebes	Aeschylus
Sexual Perversity in Chicago	David Mamet
The Shadow of a Gunman	Sean O'Casey
Shakers	John Godber
The Shaughraun	Dion Boucicault
The Shawl	David Mamet
She Stoops to Conquer	Oliver Goldsmith
She Would If She Could	George Etherege
Shirley Valentine	Willy Russell
The Silent Woman	Ben Jonson
Silly Cow	Ben Elton
The Silver Box	John Galsworthy
The Silver Tassie	Sean O'Casey
Simpatico	Sam Shepard
Simply Disconnected	Simon Gray
Single Spies	Alan Bennett
Sisterly Feelings	Alan Ayckbourn
Sisters	David Storey
Six Characters in Search of an Author	Luigi Pirandello
Six Degrees of Separation	John Guare
The Skin Game	John Galsworthy
The Skin of Our Teeth	Thornton Wilder
Slag*	David Hare
Sleeping Dog	Simon Gray

LITERATURE

Play	Playwright	Play	Playwright
Sleuth	Anthony Shaffer	The Trumpet Shall	Thornton Wilder Sound
A Small Family Business	Alan Ayckbourn	Turcaret	Alain-René Lesage
Softcops	Caryl Churchill	£200 a Year*	Arthur Wing Pinero
The Spanish Gypsy	Thomas Middleton and William Rowley	The Two of Us*	Michael Frayn
		Two Sundays	Simon Gray
The Spanish Tragedy	Thomas Kyd	Ubu Roi	Alfred Jarry
Speed-the-Plow	David Mamet	Uncle Vanya	Anton Chekhov
Spoiled	Simon Gray	Under Milk Wood	Dylan Thomas
Spring Awakening	Frank Wedekind	Unsuitable for Adults	Terry Johnson
The Squire	Arthur Wing Pinero	Up 'N' Under	John Godber
Stagestruck	Simon Gray	Vandaleur's Folly	John Arden
Stags and Hens	Willy Russell	Venus Observed	Christopher Fry
State of Innocence	John Dryden	Veronica's Room	Ira Levin
Stepping Out	Richard Harris	La Veuve	Pierre Corneille
Stevie*	Hugh Whitemore	A View from the Bridge	Arthur Miller
Strange Interlude	Eugene O'Neill	Virginia	Edna O'Brien
A Streetcar Named Desire	Tennessee Williams	The Visitors	Nicholas Monsarrat
		Volpone (The Fox)	Ben Jonson
Suddenly Last Summer	Tennessee Williams	The Vortex	Noël Coward
The Sunshine Boys	Neil Simon	A Voyage Round My Father	John Mortimer
Suppliants	Aeschylus		
Sweeney Agonistes*	T S Eliot	The Voysey Inheritance	Harley Granville Barker
Sweet Bird of Youth	Tennessee Williams		
Sweet Charity	Neil Simon	Waiting for Godot	Samuel Beckett
Table Manners	Alan Ayckbourn	Waiting for Lefty	Clifford Odets
Taking Sides	Ronald Harwood	Walk on the Grass (first TV Play)	Peter Nichols
Talking Heads	Alan Bennett		
Tamburlaine the Great	Christopher Marlowe	A Walk on the Water*	Tom Stoppard
Tartuffe	Molière	Walker, London*	J M Barrie
Teechers	John Godber	Wallenstein Trilogy	Friedrich von Schiller
La Thébaïde, ou Les Frères ennemis	Jean Racine	Waltz of the Toreadors	Jean Anouilh
		The Wasps	Aristophanes
Ten Times Table	Alan Ayckbourn	Waste	Harley Granville–Barker
Théodore	Pierre Corneille	The Way of the World	William Congreve
Thesmophoriazusae	Aristophanes	Way Upstream	Alan Ayckbourn
They're Playing Our Song	Neil Simon	The Web*	Eugene O'Neill
		The Weir	Conor McPherson
Thieves' Carnival	Jean Anouilh	The Well of the Saints	J M Synge
The Three Sisters	Anton Chekhov	West of Suez (TV play)	John Osborne
Three Tall Women	Edward Albee	What Every Woman Knows	J M Barrie
Three Women	Sylvia Plath		
The Threepenny Opera	Bertolt Brecht	What the Butler Saw	Joe Orton
Thursday's Child	Christopher Fry	When Did You Last See My Mother?*	Christopher Hampton
Till the Day I Die	Clifford Odets		
Time and the Conways	J B Priestley	When the Wind Blows	Peter Nichols
Time and Time Again	Alan Ayckbourn	When We Are Married	J B Priestley
Time of My Life	Alan Ayckbourn	The White Devil	John Webster
The Tinker's Wedding	J M Synge	Who's Afraid of Virginia Woolf ?	Edward Albee
Tiny Alice	Edward Albee		
'Tis Pity She's a Whore	John Ford	Widowers' Houses	George Bernard Shaw
To Damascus	August Strindberg	The Wild Duck	Henrik Ibsen
The Tooth of Crime	Sam Shepard	William Tell	Friedrich von Schiller
Top Girls	Caryl Churchill	The Winslow Boy	Terence Rattigan
Torquato Tasso	Johann Wolfgang von Goethe	Wise Child*	Simon Gray
		Woman in Mind	Alan Ayckbourn
Total Eclipse	Christopher Hampton	A Woman of No	Oscar Wilde Importance
A Touch of the Poet	Eugene O'Neill	Women Beware Women	Thomas Middleton
The Tower	Christopher Fry	Wonderful Tennessee	Brian Friel
Trachiniae	Sophocles	The Wood Demon	Anton Chekhov
Translations	Brian Friel	The Workhouse Donkey	John Arden
Travesties	Tom Stoppard	Yerma	Federico García Lorca
Treats	Christopher Hampton	Yonadab	Peter Shaffer
Trelawny of the 'Wells'	Arthur Wing Pinero	You Never Can Tell	George Bernard Shaw
The Trojan Women	Euripides	Zigger Zagger	Peter Terson
True West	Sam Shepard	The Zoo Story	Edward Albee

Theatre: General Information

After the Fall Central character: Quentin. Former wife: Maggie (modelled on Marilyn Monroe).

Arms and the Man Setting: Bulgaria. Family: Petkoffs.

Banned by Lord Chamberlain *Early Morning* by Edward Bond (1968) was the last play to be banned by the Lord Chamberlain, whose office was abolished on 26 Sept. 1968.

The Birthday Party Party for: Stanley. Boarding house owners: Meg and Petey.

The Blue Bird Children: Mytyl and Tyltyl.

Broadway theatre named after Neil Simon is the only living American playwright to be so honoured.

Camille Central character Marguerite Gautier.

Candida Candida's husband: Reverend Morell. Poet: Marchbanks.

The Caretaker Title character Davies.

Cat on a Hot Tin Roof Title character: Maggie Pollitt. Husband: Brick. Location: St Louis.

Cell Mates Took over from Stephen Fry: Simon Ward.

Charley's Aunt Title character: Donna Lucia d'Alvadores. Charley's surname: Wykeham.

Chips with Everything Setting: RAF.

Comedy Meaning: Revel-song.

Comedy of Intrigue Founder: Sir George Etherege.

Death of a Salesman Salesman: Willie Loman.

Doll's House Doll's name: Nora. Nora's husband: Torvald Helmer.

Entertainer Title character Archie Rice.

Equus Psychiatrist: Dysart. Stableboy: Alan Strang.

The Gingerbread Lady Filmed as: *Only When I Laugh*.

The Glass Menagerie Family: Wingfields.

Hedda Gabler Husband: Professor George Tessman.

The Iceman Cometh Salesman: Hickey. Setting: Harry Hope's saloon (NY).

The Importance of Being Ernest Title character: Jack Worthing (real name Ernest Moncrieff). Governess: Miss Prism. Jack found in handbag at station. Left in baby's place: novel. Algernon Moncrieff's fictional friend: Bunbury.

In Camera Setting: Hell. Characters: Garcin, Estelle, Inez.

The Inspector General Impostor: Khlestakov.

Japanese theatre Two main types: Nō (lit: talent) was developed in the 14th century from a court dance and the acrobatics of the sarugaku troupes. Kabuki (lit: singing and dancing art) was developed in the 17th century and was originally only performed by women. The costumes worn come from the Edo period (1603–1868).

The Jew of Malta Title character: Barabas.

Journey's End Setting: First World War.

Jumpers Professor: George Moore. George's Wife: Dotty.

Juno and the Paycock Paycock: Jack Boyle.

Killed by Tortoise Aeschylus was allegedly killed when an eagle dropped a tortoise on his head.

Killed fellow actor in duel Ben Jonson.

Le Bourgeois Gentilhomme Title character: Monsieur Jourdain.

Lady Windermere's Fan Mother: Mrs Erlynne.

The Lady's Not for Burning Setting: Cool Clary.

Famous Lines Brazil, where the nuts come from (*Charley's Aunt*).

He is the very pineapple of politeness (Mrs Malaprop in *The Rivals*).

Heav'n has no rage, like love to hatred burn'd, Nor Hell a fury, like a woman scorned (*The Mourning Bride*).

Music hath charms to soothe a savage breast (*The Mourning Bride*).

Our civil community is founded on the pestiferous soil of falsehood (Dr Stockman in *An Enemy of the People*).

Very flat, Norfolk (*Private Lives*).

The Long Day's Journey into Night Family: Tyrones.

Look Back in Anger Central character: Jimmy Porter. Jimmy's wife: Alison.

Lyceum Managed by Sir Henry Irving 1878–99.

The Maids Title characters: Claire and Solange.

Le Misanthrope Title character: Alceste.

The Miser Lead character: Harpagon.

Mourning Becomes Electra Based on the Oresteia Trilogy by Aeschylus.

Norman Conquests *Table Manners*, *Round and Round the Garden*, *Living Together*.

Oresteia Trilogy (Aeschylus) *Agamemnon*, *Choephoroe* (*The Libation-Bearers*), *Eumenides*.

Peter Pan Children: John, Michael and Wendy Darling. Hook educated at Eton. Dog: Nana.

Phèdre Based on *Hippolytus* by Euripides.

The Playboy of the Western World Title character: Christie Mahon.

Prison Written in: *Our Lady of the Flowers* by Jean Genet.

Private Lives Written for Gertrude Lawrence.

Pushkin's 'Little Tragedies' *Mozart and Salieri*, *The Covetous Knight*, *The Stone Guest*, *The Feast during the Plague*.

Pygmalion Professor: Henry Higgins. Flowergirl: Eliza Doolittle. Higgins home: Wimpole St. Scandal over: use of the word 'bloody'.

The Quare Fellow Set in a Dublin prison.

The Rivals Rivals: Captain Absolute (Ensign Beverley) and Sir Lucius O'Trigger (Bob Acres). Setting: Bath. Lady: Lydia Languish. Her Aunt: Mrs Malaprop.

Roots Central character: Beatie Bryant. Setting: Norfolk.

Seagull Central characters: Irina, Nina, Trigorin the novelist.

Second Mrs Tanqueray Title character: Paula Ray.

She Stoops to Conquer Central character: Marlow. Marlow's love: Miss Hardcastle.

State of Innocence Based on *Paradise Lost* by John Milton.

A Streetcar Named Desire Central character: Blanche Du Bois. Blanche's sister: Stella. Stella's husband: Stanley Kowalsky. Setting: New Orleans.

Sturm und Drang (Storm and Stress) German literary movement that preceded Romanticism, taking its name from the play by Max Klinger *Der Wirrwarr, oder Sturm und Drang*.

Subtitle *Man and Superman* 'A Comedy and a Philosophy'.

Theatre of Cruelty Name given by Antonin Artaud to his use of lighting effects, screams and oversized puppets to induce audience reaction, as in *Les Cenci*.

Theatre of Fact Aka Documentary Theatre: a German movement founded in the early 1960s by

L
I
T
E
R
A
T
U
R
E

Rolf Hochuth, Peter Weiss and Heinar Kipphardt, highlighting the political propaganda of post-Second World War Germany.

Theatre of the Absurd   Name given to the pessimistic vision of humanity struggling vainly to find a purpose as depicted in works by Beckett (*Waiting for Godot*), Ionesco (*The Bald Soprano*), and such diverse dramatists as Jean Genet, Arthur Adamov and Harold Pinter.

The Three Sisters   Title characters: Irina, Masha, Olga.

Tragedy   Meaning: goat-song.

Travesties   Setting: Zurich.

Volpone   Servant: Mosca.

Waiting for Godot   Tramps: Vladimir (Didi), Estragon (Gogo).

Waiting for Lefty   Title character: Lefty Costello.

Wallenstein Trilogy   *Wallensteins Lager, Die Piccolomini, Wallensteins Tod.*

The Way of the World   Central characters: Mirabell, Millamant, Lady Wishford.

Wesker Trilogy   *Chicken Soup with Barley, Roots, I'm Talking About Jerusalem.*

What the Butler Saw   Setting: Psychiatrist's clinic.

The Winslow Boy   Based on Archer–Shee case.

Theatres of the British Isles

(excluding London, see separate section; English unless stated otherwise)

Aberdeen, Music Hall (Sco)
Aldeburgh, Snape Maltings
Alnwick, Playhouse
Andover, Cricklade Theatre
Andover, Winton Studio Theatre
Armagh, The Marketplace Theatre (Ire)
Averham, Robin Hood Theatre
Aylesbury, Limelight Theatre
Barnstaple, Queens Theatre
Basildon, Towngate Theatre
Basingstoke, The Anvil
Basingstoke, Haymarket
Bath, Rondo Studio Theatre
Bath, Theatre Royal
Belfast, The Grand Opera House (Ire)
Belfast, Group Theatre (Ire)
Belfast, Lyric Theatre (Ire)
Belfast, Waterfront (Ire)
Bexhill, De La Warr Pavilion
Birmingham, Alexandra
Birmingham, Crescent
Birmingham, Hippodrome
Birmingham, Repertory Theatre
Birmingham, Symphony Hall
Blackburn, King George's Hall
Blackburn, Opera House
Blackpool, Grand Theatre
Blackpool, Opera House
Bolton, Albert Hall
Bournemouth, Pavilion Theatre
Bradford, St George's Hall
Brighton, Brighton Centre
Brighton, Dome
Brighton, Komedia Theatre
Brighton, Theatre Royal
Bristol, Colston Hall
Bristol, Old Vic Theatre
Bristol, Theatre Royal
    (oldest in Britain: built 1766)
Bromley, Churchill Theatre
Bury St Edmunds, Theatre Royal
Buxton, Opera House
Cambridge, ADC Theatre
Cambridge, Corn Exchange
Canterbury, Gulbenkian Theatre
Cardiff, St David's Hall (Wal)
Carlisle, Sands Centre
Carshalton, Charles Cryer Studio

Theatre
Chatham, Theatre Royal
Cheltenham, Everyman Theatre
Cheltenham, Playhouse Theatre
Chester, Gateway Theatre
Chesterfield, Pomegranate Theatre
Chichester, Festival Theatre
Cockermouth, Kirkgate Centre
Coleraine, Riverside Theatre (Ire)
Cork, Cork Opera House (Ire)
Cork, Everyman Palace Theatre (Ire)
Cork, Granary Theatre (Ire)
Cork, Half Moon Theatre (Ire)
Cork, Savoy Theatre (Ire)
Coventry, Belgrade Theatre
Coventry, Warwick Arts Centre
Crawley, The Hawth
Crewe, Lyceum
Croydon, Fairfield Hall & Ashcroft Theatre
Darlington, Civic Theatre – Arts Centre
Derby, Assembly Rooms
Derby, Playhouse Theatre
Dublin, Abbey Theatre (Ire)
Dublin, Andrews Theatre (Ire)
Dublin, Dublin Gate Theatre (Ire)
Dublin, Gaiety Theatre (Ire)
Dublin, Olympia Theatre (Ire)
Dublin, Peacock Theatre (Ire)
Dublin, Tivoli Theatre (Ire)
Dumfries, Theatre Royal (Sco)
Edinburgh, Festival Theatre (Sco)
Edinburgh, Gilded Balloon (Sco)
Edinburgh, King's Theatre (Sco)
Edinburgh, Playhouse (Sco)
Edinburgh, Royal Lyceum Theatre (Sco)
Edinburgh, Traverse (Sco)
Eltham, Bob Hope Theatre
Exeter, Northcott Theatre
Felixstowe, Spa Pavilion Theatre
Galway, Blackbox Theatre (Ire)
Galway, Druid Theatre (Ire)
Glasgow, Citizens Theatre (Sco)
Glasgow, Pavilion Theatre (Sco)
Glasgow, Royal Concert Hall (Sco)
Glasgow, Theatre Royal (Sco)
Glasgow, Tramway (Sco)
Glasgow, Tron Theatre (Sco)

Glyndebourne, Opera House
Grimsby, Auditorium
Great Yarmouth, Britannia Theatre
Great Yarmouth, New Wellington Theatre
Great Yarmouth, St George's Theatre
Guildford, Civic Theatre
Guildford, Yvonne Arnaud Theatre
Halifax, Victoria Theatre
Hanley, The Royal
High Wycombe, Wycombe Swan Theatre
Hitchin, The Queen Mother Theatre
Hornchurch, Queen's Theatre
Harrogate, Harrogate Theatre
Huddersfield, Lawrence Batley Theatre
Hull, Hull Truck Theatre
Ifield, Barn Theatre
Ilford, Kenneth More Theatre
Ilfracombe, The Landmark Theatre
Inverness, Eden Court Theatre (Sco)
Isle of Man, Gaiety Theatre
Ipswich, Regent Theatre
Keswick, Theatre By The Lake
Lancaster, Grand Theatre
Lancaster, Nuffield Theatre
Leeds, City Varieties
Leeds, Grand Theatre
Leeds, West Yorkshire Playhouse
Leicester, De Montfort Hall
Leicester, Haymarket Theatre
Leicester, Phoenix Arts
Liverpool, Empire
Liverpool, Everyman Theatre
Liverpool, Neptune Theatre
Liverpool, Playhouse
Liverpool, Royal Court Theatre
Liverpool, Royal Philharmonic Hall
Liverpool, St George's Hall
Llandudno, North Wales Theatre (Wal)
Manchester, Apollo
Manchester, Bridgewater Hall
Manchester, Contact Theatre
Manchester, Library Theatre
Manchester, Lowry Centre
Manchester, Palace Theatre-Opera House

Manchester, Royal Exchange Theatre
Mansfield, Palace Theatre
Milton Keynes, Milton Keynes Theatre
Mold, Theatre Clwyd (Wal)
Mull, Little Theatre (Sco)
Newark, Palace Theatre
Newbury, Corn Exchange
Newbury, Watermill Theatre
Newcastle, Opera House
Newcastle, Playhouse
Newcastle, Theatre Royal
Northampton, Derngate Theatre
Northampton, Royal Theatre
Norwich, The Maddermarket
Norwich, Playhouse
Norwich, Theatre Royal
Nottingham, Lace Market Theatre
Nottingham, Playhouse
Nottingham, Royal Centre
Oldham, Sixth Form College Theatre
Oxford, Apollo Theatre
Oxford, Playhouse Theatre
Perth, Perth Theatre (Sco)
Pitlochry, Festival Theatre (Sco)
Plymouth, Theatre Royal

Poole, The Lighthouse
Porthcurno (Cornwall), Minack (open-air)
Portsmouth, Guildhall
Preston, Guildhall & Charter Theatre
Reading, The Hexagon
Redhill, Harlequin
Rhyl, Pavilion Theatre (Wal)
St Helens, Theatre Royal
Salford, The Lowry
Salisbury, Playhouse
Scarborough, Stephen Joseph Theatre
Sheffield, City Hall
Sheffield, Crucible
Sligo, Hawk's Well Theatre (Ire)
South Shields, Custom House
Southampton, The Gantry
Southampton, The Mayflower
Southampton, The Nuffield Theatre
Stevenage, Gordon Craig Theatre
Stoke-on-Trent, New Victoria Theatre
Stoke-on-Trent, The Royal
Stoke-on-Trent, Victoria Hall
Stratford-upon-Avon, The Other Place

Stratford-upon-Avon, Royal Shakespeare Theatre
Stratford-upon-Avon, Swan Theatre
Sunderland, Empire Theatre
Swansea, Grand Theatre (Wal)
Swindon, Wyvern Theatre
Tamworth, Arts Centre
Taunton, Brewhouse Theatre
Tewkesbury, Roses Theatre
Truro, Hall For Cornwall
Wakefield, Theatre Royal & Opera House
Warrington, Parr Hall
Watford, Palace Theatre
Wavendon, The Stables
Wellingborough, The Castle
Weymouth, Pavilion
Winchester, Theatre Royal
Woking, Ambassadors / New Victoria
Wolverhampton, Grand Theatre
Worcester, Swan Theatre
Worthing, Northbrook Theatre
Wythenshaw, Forum Theatre
York, Barbican
York, Theatre Royal

Poetry: By Poet

Peter Ackroyd (1949–)
Anna Akhmatova (1889–66)
Matthew Arnold (1822–88)

Margaret Atwood (1939–)
W H Auden (1907–73)

Richard Harris Barham (1788–1845)
Charles Baudelaire (1821–67)
Hilaire Belloc (1870–1953)

John Betjeman

Country Life
London Lickpenny
Anno Domini
White Flock
Dover Beach
Empedocles on Etna
The Forsaken Merman
The Scholar Gypsy
Sohrab and Rustum
The Strayed Reveller
Thyrsis
Tristram and Iseult
The Circle Game

About the House
The Age of Anxiety
Another Time
City Without Walls
The Double Man
Homage to Clio
In Memory of W.B. Yeats
Look, Stranger!
Miss Gee
New Year Letter
Night Mail
On This Island
The Orators
Paid on Both Sides
The Shield of Achilles
Spain
Stop All the Clocks
The Ingoldsby Legends
The Jackdaw of Rheims
Les Fleurs du mal

The Bad Child's Book of Beasts
Cautionary Tales
Matilda
Continual Dew

(1906–84)

Laurence Binyon (1869–1943)
William Blake (1757–1827)

Aleksandr Blok (1880–1921)

Edmund Blunden (1896–1974)

Wilfrid Scawen Blunt (1840–1922)
Gordon Bottomley (1874–1948)
Robert Bridges (1844–1930)

Emily Brontë

Death in Leamington
A Few Late Chrysanthemums
Highland Low
The Metropolitan Railway
Mount Zion
New Bats in Old Belfries
A Nip in the Air
Old Lights for New Chancels
A Subaltern's Love Song
For the Fallen
Tristram's End
Jerusalem
Milton
The Sick Rose
Songs of Experience
Songs of Innocence
The Tyger
Nocturnal Hours
The Rose and the Cross
The Scythians
Songs About the Lady Fair
The Twelve
Almswomen
Bonadventure
Pastorals
Undertones of War
The Waggoner
The Old Squire

Poems of Thirty Years
To Ironfounders and Others
Eros and Psyche
The Growth of Love
London Snow
October
Prometheus the Firegiver
The Spirit of Man
The Testament of Beauty
Gondal

(1818–48)
Last Lines
Plead for Me
Remembrance
To Imagination

Rupert Brooke
(1887–1915)
1914
The Old Vicarage,
Grantchester
The Soldier

Elizabeth Barrett
Browning
(1806–61)
Aurora Leigh
The Battle of Marathon
Casa Guidi Windows
The Cry of the Children
How Do I Love Thee?
Poems before Congress
The Seraphim
Sonnets from the
Portuguese

Robert Browning
(1812–89)
Andrea del Sarto
Bells and Pomegranates
Childe Roland to the Dark
Tower Came
Fra Lippo Lippi
Home Thoughts From
Abroad
Home-Thoughts, from the
Sea
How They Brought the Good
News from Ghent to Aix
Men and Women
My Last Duchess
Paracelsus
Pauline
The Pied Piper of Hamelin
Pippa Passes
Rabbi Ben Ezra
The Ring and the Book
Soliloquy of the Spanish
Cloister
Sordello

John Bunyan
(1628–88)
The Pilgrim

Robert Burns
(1759–96)
Address to a Mouse
Auld Lang Syne
Comin' Through the Rye
The Cotter's Saturday Night
Death and Doctor Hornbook
Despondency
Desolate and Pale Moonlight
Epistle to Davie
Ae Fond Kiss
For a' that and a' that
Halloween
The Holy Fair
Holy Willie's Prayer
The Jolly Beggars
Kilmarnock Poems
The Lament
A Red, Red Rose
Scots Musical Museum
Tam O'Shanter
To a Field Mouse
The Twa Herds

Samuel Butler
(1612–80)

Hudibras

Lord Byron
(1788–1824)
Beppo
Childe Harold's Pilgrimage
The Destruction of
Sennacherib
Don Juan
Hours of Idleness
Lara
The Prisoner of Chillon

She Walks in Beauty
The Siege of Corinth
The Vision of Judgment
We'll Go No More A-Roving

Luis de Camoes
(1524–1580)
The Lusiads
Rimas

Roy Campbell
(1901–1957)
The Flaming Terrapin
Flowering Rifle
Soldier's Reply to the Poet
The Wayzgoose

Thomas Campbell
(1777–1844)
Gertrude of Wyoming

Lewis Carroll
(1832–98)
The Hunting of the Snark
Jabberwocky
Phantasmagoria and other
Poems
The Walrus and the
Carpenter

Sydney Carter
(1915–)
Lord of the Dance

Charles Causley
(1917–)
Farewell, Aggie Weston
Figure of 8
RIJP
Survivor's Leave
Underneath the Water
Union Street
The Young Man of Cury

Thomas Chatterton
(1752–70)
The Rowley Poems

Geoffrey Chaucer
(c. 1343–1400)
The Canterbury Tales
Troilus and Criseyde

G K Chesterton
(1874–1936)
The Donkey
Greybeards at Play
The Wild Knight

John Clare
(1793–1864)
First Love
The Rural Muse
The Shepherd's Calendar
Village Minstrel

Samuel Taylor
Coleridge (1772–1834)
The Ancient Mariner
Christabel
Dejection: An ode
Kubla Khan
Ode to France
The Rime of the Ancient
Mariner

William Cory
(1823–92)
Heraclitus
Ionica

William Cowper
(1731–1800)
John Gilpin
The Task

George Crabbe
(1754–1832)
The Borough
The Village

Hart Crane
(1899–1932)
The Bridge
White Buildings

Dante Alighieri
(1265–1321)
Banquet
Canzoniere
The Divine Comedy

W H Davies
(1871–1940)
Leisure
Money
School's Out
A Soul's Destroyer

Emily Dickinson
(1830–86)
A Bird Came Down the Walk
A Narrow Fellow in the Grass
Parting

Austin Dobson
(1840–1921)
At the Sign of the Lyre
A Fancy From Fontenelle
Proverbs in Porcelain
Vignettes in Rhyme

John Donne
(c. 1572–1631)
Anniversaries
The Canonization
The Exstasie
The Good-Morrow
Metempsychosis

A Nocturnall upon St Lucies
  Day
Song
The Sun Rising
A Valediction: Forbidding
  Mourning

Ernest Dowson
(1867–1900)
Decorations
Non Sum Qualis Eram
Vitae Sumina Brevis

John Dryden
(1631–1700)
Absalom and Achitophel
Alexander's Feast
Annus Mirabilis: The Year of
  Wonders, 1666
Astræ Redux
Fables, Ancient and Modern
The Hind and the Panther
The Medal
Religio Laici
A Song for St Cecilia's Day
Sylvia the Fair

T S Eliot
(1888–1965)
Ash Wednesday
Four Quartets
Gerontion
The Hollow Men
The Journey of the Magi
The Love Song of J. Alfred
  Prufrock
The Waste Land

Ralph Waldo Emerson
(1803–82)
Brahma
Give All to Love
May–Day
The Problem

William Empson
(1906–84)
The Gathering Storm

Quintus Ennius
(239–169 BC)
Annales

Gavin Ewart
(1916–95)
Poets

Edward Fitzgerald
(1809–83)
The Rubaiyat of Omar
  Khayyam (translation from
  Persian)

James Elroy Flecker
(1884–1915)
The Bridge of Fire
The Golden Journey to
  Samarkand
The Old Ships

Robert Lee Frost
(1874–1963)
After Apple-Picking
Birches
A Boy's Will
The Death of the Hired Man
Dust of Snow
Fire and Ice
A Further Range
The Gift Outright
A Lone Striker
Mountain Interval
Mowing
Neither Out Far Nor In
  Deep
New Hampshire
North of Boston
The Oven Bird
Pan With Us
The Silken Tent
Steeple Bush
Stopping by Woods on a
  Snowy Evening
The Tuft of Flowers
West-Running Brook
A Witness Tree

Jean Genet
(1910–86)
Chant Secret

Allen Ginsberg
Empty Mirror

(1926–97)
Howl*
Kaddish
Planet News
Reality Sandwiches

Johann Wolfgang
von Goethe
(1749–1832)
Erlkönig
Kennst du das Land
Roman Elegies

Oliver Goldsmith
(1728–74)
The Deserted Village
Elegy on the Death of a Mad
  Dog
The Traveller

Robert Graves
(1895–1985)
Fairies and Fusiliers
Over the Brazier
A Slice of Wedding Cake

Thomas Gray
(1716–71)
The Bard
The Descent of Odin
Elegy Written in a Country
  Churchyard
The Fatal Sisters
Ode on a Distant Prospect of
  Eton College
The Progress of Poesy

Graham Greene
(1904–91)
Bubbling April

Julian Grenfell
(1888–1915)
Into Battle

William Hamilton
(1665–1751)
Last Dying Words of Bonny
  Heck

William Hamilton
(1704–54)
The Braes of Yarrow

Thomas Hardy
(1840–1928)
The Darkling Thrush
The Dynasts
Wessex Poems
Winter Words

Seamus Heaney
(1929–)
Beowulf (translation)
Field Work
Death of a Naturalist
Door into the Dark
Haw Lantern
Seeing Things
The Spirit Level (collection)
Sweeney's Flight

Felicia Hemans
(1793–1835)
Casabianca
The Landing of the Pilgrim
  Fathers

William Henley
(1849–1903)
England, My England
For England's Sake
Hawthorn and Lavender
In Hospital
Invictus
A Song of Speed
Song of the Sword

Robert Herrick
(1591–1674)
Cherry-Ripe
Delight in Disorder
To the Virgins, To Make
  Much of Time
Upon Julia's Clothes

Friedrich Hölderlin
(1770–1843)
Friedensfeier (Celebration of
  Peace)

Homer
(8th century BC)
The Iliad
The Odyssey

Thomas Hood
(1799–1845)
Autumn, Ode to
The Dream of Eugene
  Aram
Faithless Sally Brown
Lycus the Centaur
National Tales
Ruth
The Song of the Shirt
Tim Turpin
Whims and Oddities

Gerard Manley Hopkins
Felix Randal

(1844–89)
- Pied Beauty
- The Windhover
- The Wreck of the Deutschland

A E Housman (1859–1936)
- Epitaph on an Army of Mercenaries
- Fancy's Knell
- Last Poems
- More Poems
- A Shropshire Lad

Ted Hughes (1930–98)
- Cave Birds
- Crow
- The Hawk in the Rain
- Lupercal
- Moortown
- The Remains of Elmet
- Wodwo
- Birthday Letters collection

Victor Hugo (1802–85)
- Les Châtiments
- Les Contemplations

James Leigh Hunt (1784–1859)
- Abou Ben Adhem
- Jenny Kissed Me
- Juvenilia
- The Nile

Henrik Ibsen (1828–1906)
- Brand

Elizabeth Jennings (1926–)
- The Animals' Arrival
- Lucidities
- One Flesh
- Relationships
- Song for a Birth or a Death
- A Way of Looking

Samuel Johnson (1709–84)
- London
- The Vanity of Human Wishes

Ben Jonson (1572–1637)
- Drink to Me Only With Thine Eyes
- To Celia

John Keats (1795–1821)
- Endymion
- The Eve of St Agnes
- Grecian Urn, Ode on a
- Hymn to Pan
- Hyperion
- Isabella or the Pot of Basil
- La Belle Dame Sans Merci
- Lamia
- Ode on Melancholy
- Ode to a Nightingale
- On First Looking into Chapman's Homer
- Ode to Psyche
- To Autumn

Rudyard Kipling (1865–1936)
- The Ballad of East and West
- Barrack-Room Ballads
- The Betrothed
- Cities and Thrones and Powers
- The Female of the Species
- The Gods of the Copybook Headings
- Gunga Din
- If
- Mandalay
- The Way Through the Woods
- The White Man's Burden

Walter Savage Landor (1775–1864)
- Gebir
- Rose Aylmer

William Langland (c. 1322–1400)
- Piers Plowman

Philip Larkin (1922–85)
- High Windows
- Church Going
- The North Ship
- This Be the Verse
- The Whitsun Weddings

Emma Lazarus (1849–87)
- Admetus
- By the Waters of Babylon
- The New Colossus

Edward Lear (1812–88)
- The Owl and the Pussycat

Laurie Lee (1914–97)
- April Rise
- The Bloom of Candles
- My Many–Coated Man
- The Sun My Monument

Cecil Day Lewis (1904–72)
- Beechen Vigil
- Overtures to Death

C S Lewis (1898–1963)
- Dymer

Henry Wadsworth Longfellow (1807–82)
- The Belfry of Bruges
- The Courtship of Miles Standish
- Evangeline
- Excelsior
- Kalevala
- The Golden Legend
- The Song of Hiawatha
- Paul Revere's Ride
- The Skeleton in Armour
- The Village Blacksmith
- Voices of the Night
- Wayside Inn, Tales of a
- The Wreck of the Hesperus

Federico García Lorca (1898–1936)
- Canciones
- Romancero Gitano

Richard Lovelace (1618–57)
- To Althea
- To Lucasta, On Going to the Wars

Hugh MacDiarmid (1892–1978)
- A Drunk Man Looks at the Thistle
- Sangschaw

Louis MacNeice (1907–63)
- Autumn Sequel
- Bagpipe Music
- Blind Fireworks
- The Burning Perch
- Solstices

Stéphane Mallarmé (1842–98)
- L'Après-midi d'un Faune

Osip Mandelstam (1891–1938)
- Kamen Stone
- Tristia

Walter de la Mare (1873–1956)
- The Listeners
- O Lovely England
- Peacock Pie
- Silver
- Songs of Childhood
- The Veil

Leo Marks
- Code Poem for the French Resistance

Christopher Marlowe (1564–93)
- Come Live With Me and Be My Love
- Hero and Leander (unfinished)
- The Passionate Shepherd to His Love

Andrew Marvell (1621–78)
- The Definition of Love
- The Garden
- An Horatian Ode
- To His Coy Mistress

John Masefield (1878–1967)
- Cargoes
- Dauber
- The Everlasting Mercy
- Gallipoli
- Nan
- Reynard the Fox
- Sea Fever
- Shakespeare

	The Widow in the Bye-Street
Vladimir Mayakovsky (1894–1930)	*The Backbone Flute*
	A Cloud in Trousers
	150,000,000
John McCrae (1872–1918)	*In Flanders Fields*
William McGonagall (1830–1902)	*Poetic Gems*
	The Tay Bridge Disaster
Alice Meynell (1847–1922)	*Renouncement*
	The Shepherdess
John Milton (1608–74)	*At a Solemn Music*
	Comus
	De Doctrina Christiana
	Il Penseroso
	L'Allegro
	Let Us with a Gladsome Mind
	Lycidas
	Nativity Ode
	On His Blindness
	On the Late Massacre in Piedmont
	Paradise Lost
	Paradise Regained
	Samson Agonistes
E G Moll (1900–93)	*Returned Soldier*
Clement Moore (1779–1863)	*A Visit from St Nicholas*
Thomas Moore (1779–1852)	*Irish Melodies*
	Lalla Rookh
	The Last Rose of Summer
	The Light of Other Days
Pete Morgan (1939–)	*My Enemies Have Sweet Voices*
Edwin Muir (1887–1959)	*Chorus of the Newly Dead*
	The Confirmation
	Journeys and Places
	The Labyrinth
Ogden Nash (1902–71)	*Bed Riddance*
	I'm a Stranger Here Myself
	Versus
Henry Newbolt (1862–1938)	*The Death of Admiral Blake*
	Drake's Drum
	The Island Race
	Songs of the Sea
Cardinal J H Newman (1801–90)	*The Dream of Gerontius*
Alfred Noyes (1880–1958)	*Drake*
	The Flower of Old Japan
	The Forest of Wild Thyme
	Forty Singing Seamen
	The Highwayman
	The Torchbearers
Arthur O'Shaughnessy (1844–81)	*An Epic of Women*
	Lays of France
	Music and Moonlight
	Ode (We Are The Music-Makers)
	Songs of a Worker
Wilfred Owen (1893–1918)	*Anthem For Doomed Youth*
	Disabled
	Dulce et Decorum Est
Francis Palgrave (1824–97)	*Idylls and Songs*
Boris Pasternak (1890–1960)	*Above the Barriers*
	Lieutenant Shmidt
Coventry Patmore (1823–96)	*Amelia*
	The Toys
	The Unknown Eros
	The Victories of Love

George Peele (1556–96)	*A Farewell to Arms*
Sylvia Plath (1932–63)	*Ariel*
	The Colossus
	Crossing the Water
	A Winter Ship
	Winter Trees
Edgar Allan Poe (1809–49)	*Annabel Lee*
	The Bells
	Eureka
	Israfel
	Lenore
	The Raven
	Tamerlane
	To My Mother
Alexander Pope (1688–1744)	*The Dunciad*
	Eloisa to Abelard
	An Epistle to Doctor Arbuthnot
	An Essay on Man
	Of the Use of Riches
	The Rape of the Lock
	Windsor Forest
Ezra Pound (1885–1972)	*A Lume Spento*
	The Cantos
	Exultations
	Homage to Sextus Propertius
	Hugh Selwyn Mauberley
	If This Be Treason
	Pisan Cantos
	Quia Pauper Amavi
	Umbra
John Pudney (1909–77)	*For Johnny*
Alexander Pushkin (1799–1837)	*The Bronze Horseman*
	Egyptian Nights
	Eugene Onegin
	Poltava
	The Prisoner of the Caucasus
	The Robber Brothers
	Ruslan and Lyudmilla
	Tzigani
Francis Quarles (1592–1644)	*Argalus and Parthenia*
	Divine Fancies
Manuel Quintana (1772–1857)	*Al combate de Trafalgar*
Rainer Maria Rilke (1875–1926)	*Die Sonnette an Orpheus*
Arthur Rimbaud (1854–91)	*Le Bateau ivre (The Drunken Boat)*
	Les Illuminations
Pierre de Ronsard (1524–85)	*Amours*
	Le Bocage
Isaac Rosenberg (1890–1918)	*On Receiving News of the War*
	Trench Poems
Christina Rossetti (1830–94)	*A Birthday*
	Goblin Market
	A Pageant
	The Prince's Progress
	Remember
	Uphill
Dante Gabriel Rossetti (1828–82)	*The Blessed Damozel*
	The House of Life
	The King's Tragedy
	The White Ship
Siegfried Sassoon (1886–1967)	*Aftermath*
	Attack
	Counter-Attack
	Everyone Sang
	The Old Huntsman

LITERATURE

Alan Seeger (1888–1916) — *Rendezvous*

Robert Service (1874–1958) — *Rhymes of a Rolling Stone* / *The Shooting of Dan McGrew*

William Shakespeare (1564–1616) — *Let Me Not to the Marriage of True Minds* (Sonnet 116) / *Shall I Compare Thee to a Summer's Day* (Sonnet 18)

P B Shelley and Elizabeth Shelley — *Original Poetry by Victor and Cazire*

Percy Bysshe Shelley (1792–1822) — *Adonais* / *Alastor* / *Epipsychidion* / *Hellas* / *Julian and Maddalo* / *Love's Philosophy* / *To Naples* / *Ode to the West Wind* / *Ozymandias of Egypt* / *Prometheus Unbound* / *Queen Mab* / *To a Skylark* / *To Liberty* / *The Witch of Atlas*

Sir Philip Sidney (1554–86) — *Arcadia* / *Astrophel and Stella*

Alan Sillitoe (1928–) — *Marmalade Jim at the Farm* / *The Rats and Other Poems* / *Snow on the North Side of Lucifer* / *Storm* / *Sun Before Departure* / *Tides and Stone Walls*

Stevie Smith (1902–71) — *Not Waving But Drowning*

Charles Hamilton Sorley (1895–1915) — *All the Hills and Vales Along* / *Marlborough*

Robert Southey (1774–1843) — *The Battle of Blenheim* / *Bishop Bruno* / *Bishop Hatto* / *The Inchcape Rock* / *The Old Man's Comforts* / *The Fanfarlo*

Muriel Spark (1918–)

Edmund Spenser (c. 1552–99) — *The Faerie Queene* / *Mother Hubberds Tale* / *The Shepheardes Calender*

James Stephens (1882–1950) — *The Crock of Gold* / *In the Poppy Field* / *Insurrections*

Robert Louis Stevenson (1850–94) — *A Child's Garden of Verses* / *A London Sabbath Morn* / *Underwoods* / *The Vagabond* / *The Woodman*

John Still (1543–1608) — *Jolly Good Ale and Old*

Rabindranath Tagore (1861–1941) — *The Crescent Moon* / *Gitanjali* / *The Golden Boat* / *Manasi*

Ann Taylor (1782–1866) and Jane Taylor (1783–1824) — *Twinkle Twinkle Little Star*

Alfred, Lord Tennyson (1809–92) — *The Charge of the Light Brigade* / *Crossing the Bar* / *Idylls of the King* / *In Memoriam* / *The Lady of Shalott* / *Locksley Hall* / *The Lotos-Eaters* / *Maud* / *Oenone* / *The Princess* / *The Revenge* / *Rizpah* / *Timbuctoo* / *To Virgil* / *Ulysses*

William Makepeace Thackeray (1811–63) — *The Sorrows of Werther*

Dylan Thomas (1914–53) — *After the Funeral* / *Altarwise by Owl-Light* / *And Death Shall Have No Dominion* / *Deaths and Entrances* / *Do Not Go Gentle into That Good Night* / *Especially When the October Wind* / *In Country Sleep* / *In the White Giant's Thigh* / *I See the Boys of Summer* / *Light Breaks Where No Sun Shines* / *Over Sir John's Hill* / *Poem in October* / *We Lying by Seasand*

Edward Thomas (1878–1917) — *Adlestrop*

Henry David Thoreau (1817–62) — *Independence* / *Smoke*

Rose Thorpe (1850–1939) — *Curfew Must Not Ring Tonight*

John Updike (1932–) — *The Carpentered Hen and Other Tame Creatures*

Paul Valéry (1871–1945) — *La Jeune Parque*

Edward de Vere 17th Earl of Oxford (1550–1604) — *What Cunning Can Express*

Emile Verhaeren (1855–1916) — *Les Débâcles* / *Les Flamandes* / *La Multiple Splendeur*

Paul Verlaine (1844–96) — *La Bonne Chanson* / *Fêtes Galantes* / *Sagesse*

François Villon (1431–1463) — *Ballade des pendus* / *Le Grand Testament* / *Le Petit Testament*

Virgil (70–19 BC) — *The Aeneid* / *The Bucolics* / *The Georgics (or Art of Husbandry)* / *Vers de Société*

Vincent Voiture (1597–1648)

Voltaire (1694–1778) — *La Henriade*

Walt Whitman (1819–92) — *Drum-Taps* / *Leaves of Grass* / *O Captain! My Captain!* / *Song of Myself* / *When Lilacs Last in the Dooryard Bloom'd*

John Greenleaf Whittier (1807–92) — *At Sundown* / *Barbara Frietchie* / *The Battle Autumn of 1862* / *In War Time* / *Laus deo* / *Snow-bound*

Oscar Wilde — *The Ballad of Reading Gaol*

(1854–1900)

Tennessee Williams
(1911–83)
William Wordsworth
(1770–1850)

Ravenna
To Milton
The Summer Belvedere
In the Winter of Cities
The Affliction of Margaret
The Borderers
To the Cuckoo
Daffodils
Ode to Duty
The Excursion
Guilt and Sorrow
Intimations of Immortality
I Wandered Lonely as a
  Cloud
The Lucy Poems
My Heart Leaps Up
Nutting
The Prelude
Resolution and
  Independence
She Was a Phantom of
  Delight
The Solitary Reaper

W B Yeats
(1865–1939)

Sergey Yesenin
(1895–1925)

Yevgeny Yevtushenko
(1933–)

Tintern Abbey
Upon Westminster Bridge
Vaudracour and Julia
Brown Penny
Byzantium
Ego Dominus Tuus
He Wishes For the Cloths of
  Heaven
An Irish Airman Foresees
  His Death
The Lake Isle of Innisfree
Sailing to Byzantium
When You Are Old
Confessions of a Hooligan
Moscow of the Taverns
Desolate and Pale
  Moonlight
The Black Man
Babi Yar
Heavy Soils
Ivan the Terrible
A Wave of the Hand
Zima Junction

Poetry: By Poem

(for poets' dates see previous section)

Abou Ben Adhem	James Leigh Hunt	Ariel	Sylvia Plath
About the House	W H Auden	Ash Wednesday	T S Eliot
Above the Barriers	Boris Pasternak	Astræa Redux	John Dryden
Absalom and Achitophel	John Dryden	Astrophel and Stella	Sir Philip Sidney
Address to a Mouse	Robert Burns	At a Solemn Music	John Milton
Adlestrop	Edward Thomas	At Sundown	John Greenleaf Whittier
Admetus	Emma Lazarus	Attack	Siegfried Sassoon
Adonais	Percy Bysshe Shelley	At the Sign of the Lyre	Austin Dobson
The Aeneid	Virgil	Auld Lang Syne	Robert Burns
The Affliction of Margaret	William Wordsworth	Aurora Leigh	Elizabeth Barrett
L'Allegro	John Milton		Browning
After Apple-Picking	Robert Lee Frost	Autumn Sequel	Louis MacNeice
Aftermath	Siegfried Sassoon	Babi Yar	Yevgeny Yevtushenko
After the Funeral	Dylan Thomas	The Backbone Flute	Vladimir Mayakovsky
The Age of Anxiety	W H Auden	The Bad Child's Book of	Hilaire Belloc
Alastor	Percy Bysshe Shelley	Beasts	
Al Combate de Trafalgar	Manuel Quintana	Bagpipe Music	Louis MacNeice
Alexander's Feast	John Dryden	Ballade des pendus	François Villon
All the Hills and Vales	Charles Hamilton	Ballad of East and West	Rudyard Kipling
Along	Sorley	The Ballad of Reading	Oscar Wilde
Almswomen	Edmund Blunden	Gaol	
Altarwise by Owl-Light	Dylan Thomas	Banquet	Dante Alighieri
To Althea	Richard Lovelace	Barbara Frietchie	John Greenleaf Whittier
Amelia	Coventry Patmore	The Bard	Thomas Gray
Amours	Pierre de Ronsard	Barrack-Room Ballads	Rudyard Kipling
And Death Shall Have	Dylan Thomas	Le Bateau Ivre	Arthur Rimbaud
No Dominion		The Battle Autumn	John Greenleaf Whittier
Andrea del Sarto	Robert Browning	of 1862	
The Animals' Arrival	Elizabeth Jennings	The Battle of Blenheim	Robert Southey
Annabel Lee	Edgar Allan Poe	The Battle of Marathon	Elizabeth Barrett
Annales	Quintus Ennius	Browning	
Anniversaries	John Donne	Bed Riddance	Ogden Nash
Anno Domini	Anna Akhmatova	Beechen Vigil	Cecil Day Lewis
Annus Mirabilis:	John Dryden	The Belfry of Bruges	Henry Wadsworth
The Year of Wonders,			Longfellow
1666		Bells and Pomegranates	Robert Browning
Another Time	W H Auden	The Bells	Edgar Allan Poe
Anthem For Doomed	Wilfred Owen	Beppo	Lord George Byron
Youth		The Betrothed	Rudyard Kipling
April Rise	Laurie Lee	Birches	Robert Lee Frost
Arcadia	Sir Philip Sidney	A Bird Came Down the	Emily Dickinson
Argalus and Parthenia	Francis Quarles	Walk	

LITERATURE

A Birthday	Christina Rossetti	The Crescent Moon	Rabrindranath Tagore
Bishop Bruno	Robert Southey	The Crock of Gold	James Stephens
Bishop Hatto	Robert Southey	Crossing the Bar	Alfred, Lord Tennyson
The Black Man	Sergey Yesenin	Crossing the Water	Sylvia Plath
The Blessèd Damozel	Dante Gabriel Rossetti	Crow	Ted Hughes
Blind Fireworks	Louis MacNeice	The Cry of the Children	Elizabeth Barrett
On His Blindness	John Milton	Browning	
The Bloom of Candles	Laurie Lee	Curfew Must Not Ring	Rose Thorpe
Le Bocage	Pierre de Ronsard	Tonight	
Bonadventure	Edmund Blunden	Daffodils	William Wordsworth
La Bonne Chanson	Paul Verlaine	The Darkling Thrush	Thomas Hardy
The Borderers	William Wordsworth	Dauber	John Masefield
The Borough	George Crabbe	Death and Doctor	Robert Burns
A Boy's Will	Robert Lee Frost	Hornbook	
The Braes of Yarrow	William Hamilton	Death in Leamington	John Betjeman
Brahma	Ralph Waldo Emerson		
Brand	Henrik Ibsen	The Death of Admiral	Henry Newbolt
The Bridge of Fire	James Elroy Flecker	Blake	
The Bridge	Hart Crane	Death of a Naturalist	Seamus Heaney
The Bronze Horseman	Alexander Pushkin	The Death of the	Robert Lee Frost
Brown Penny	W B Yeats	Hired Man	
Bubbling April	Graham Greene	Deaths and Entrances	Dylan Thomas
The Bucolics	Virgil	Decorations	Ernest Dowson
The Burning Perch	Louis MacNeice	The Definition of Love	Andrew Marvell
By the Waters of Babylon	Emma Lazarus	De Doctrina Christiana	John Milton
Byzantium	W B Yeats	Dejection: An Ode	Samuel Taylor Coleridge
Canciones	Federico Garcia Lorca	Delight in Disorder	Robert Herrick
The Canonization	John Donne	The Descent of Odin	Thomas Gray
The Canterbury Tales	Geoffrey Chaucer	The Deserted Village	Oliver Goldsmith
The Cantos	Ezra Pound	Desolate and Pale	Robert Burns
Canzoniere	Dante Alighieri	Moonlight	
Cargoes	John Masefield	Despondency	Robert Burns
Carpentered Hen and	John Updike	Destruction of	Lord Byron
Other Tame Creatures		Sennacherib	
Casa Guidi Windows	Elizabeth Barrett Browning	Disabled	Wilfred Owen
Casabianca	Felicia Hemans	The Divine Comedy	Dante Alighieri
Cautionary Tales	Hilaire Belloc	Divine Fancies	Francis Quarles
Cave Birds	Ted Hughes	Don Juan	Lord George Byron
Chant Secret	Jean Genet	The Donkey	G K Chesterton
The Charge of the Light	Alfred, Lord Tennyson	Do Not Go Gentle into	Dylan Thomas
Brigade		That Good Night	
Cherry-Ripe	Robert Herrick	Door into the Dark	Seamus Heaney
Childe Harold's	Lord Byron	The Double Man	W H Auden
Pilgrimage		Dover Beach	Matthew Arnold
Childe Roland to the	Robert Browning	Drake	Alfred Noyes
Dark Tower Came		Drake's Drum	Henry Newbolt
A Child's Garden of	Robert Louis Stevenson	The Dream of Gerontius	Cardinal J H Newman
Verses		Drink to Me Only with	Ben Jonson
Chorus of the Newly Dead	Edwin Muir	Thine Eyes	
Christabel	Samuel Taylor Coleridge	Drum-Taps	Walt Whitman
The Circle Game	Margaret Atwood	The Drunken Boat	Arthur Rimbaud
Cities and Thrones and	Rudyard Kipling	A Drunk Man Looks at	Hugh MacDiarmid
Powers		the Thistle	
City Without Walls	W H Auden	Dulce et Decorum Est	Wilfred Owen
A Cloud in Trousers	Vladimir Mayakovsky	The Dunciad	Alexander Pope
Code Poem for the	Leo Marks	Dust of Snow	Robert Lee Frost
French Resistance		Duty, Ode to	William Wordsworth
The Colossus	Sylvia Plath	Dymer	C S Lewis
Come Live With Me	Christopher Marlowe	The Dynasts	Thomas Hardy
and Be My Love		Ego Dominus Tuus	W B Yeats
Comin' Through the Rye	Robert Burns	Egyptian Nights	Alexander Pushkin
Comus	John Milton	Elegy on the Death of a	Oliver Goldsmith
Confessions of a	Sergey Yesenin	Mad Dog	
Hooligan		Elegy Written in a	Thomas Gray
The Confirmation	Edwin Muir	Country Churchyard	
Continual Dew	John Betjeman	Eloisa to Abelard	Alexander Pope
The Cotter's Saturday	Robert Burns	Empedocles on Etna	Matthew Arnold
Night		Empty Mirror	Allen Ginsberg
Counter-Attack	Siegfried Sassoon	Endymion	John Keats
Country Life	Peter Ackroyd	England, My England	William Henley
The Courtship of Miles	Henry Wadsworth	An Epic of Women	Arthur O'Shaughnessy
Standish	Longfellow	Epipsychidion	Percy Bysshe Shelley

Epistle to Davie	Robert Burns
An Epistle to Doctor	Alexander Pope*Arbuthnot*
Epitaph on an Army of Mercenaries	A E Housman
Erlkönig	Johann Wolfgang von Goethe
Eros and Psyche	Robert Bridges
Especially When the October Wind	Dylan Thomas
An Essay on Man	Alexander Pope
Eugene Aram	Thomas Hood
Eugene Onegin	Alexander Pushkin
Eureka	Edgar Allan Poe
Evangeline	Henry Wadsworth Longfellow
The Eve of St Agnes	John Keats
The Everlasting Mercy	John Masefield
Everyone Sang	Siegfried Sassoon
Excelsior	Henry Wadsworth Longfellow
The Excursion	William Wordsworth
The Exstasie	John Donne
Exultations	Ezra Pound
Fables, Ancient and Modern	John Dryden
The Faerie Queene	Edmund Spenser
Fairies and Fusiliers	Robert Graves
Faithless Sally Brown	Thomas Hood
A Fancy From Fontenelle	Austin Dobson
Fancy's Knell	A E Housman
Fanfarlo	Muriel Spark
Farewell, Aggie Weston	Charles Causley
A Farewell to Arms	George Peele
The Fatal Sisters	Thomas Gray
Felix Randal	Gerard Manley Hopkins
The Female of the Species	Rudyard Kipling
Fêtes Galantes	Paul Verlaine
A Few Late Chrysanthemums	John Betjeman
Field Work	Seamus Heaney
Figure of 8	Charles Causley
Fire and Ice	Robert Lee Frost
First Love	John Clare
The Flaming Terrapin	Roy Campbell
Flowering Rifle	Roy Campbell
The Flower of Old Japan	Alfred Noyes
Ae Fond Kiss	Robert Burns
For a' that and a' that	Robert Burns
For England's Sake	William Henley
For Johnny	John Pudney
For the Fallen	Laurence Binyon
The Forest of Wild Thyme	Alfred Noyes
The Forsaken Merman	Matthew Arnold
Forty Singing Seamen	Alfred Noyes
Four Quartets	T S Eliot
Fra Lippo Lippi	Robert Browning
Friedensfeier (celebration of peace)	Friedrich Hölderlin
A Further Range	Robert Lee Frost
Gallipoli	John Masefield
The Garden	Andrew Marvell
The Gathering Storm	William Empson
Gebir	Walter Savage Landor
The Georgics (or Art of Husbandry)	Virgil
Gerontion	T S Eliot
Gertrude of Wyoming	Thomas Campbell
The Gift Outright	Robert Lee Frost
Gitanjali	Rabindranath Tagore
Give All to Love	Ralph Waldo Emerson
Goblin Market	Christina Rossetti
The Gods of the Copybook	Rudyard Kipling
The Golden Boat	Rabindranath Tagore
The Golden Journey to Samarkand	James Elroy Flecker
The Golden Legend	Henry Wadsworth Longfellow
Gondal	Emily Brontë
The Good Morrow	John Donne
Le Grand Testament	François Villon
Greybeards at Play	G K Chesterton
The Growth of Love	Robert Bridges
Guilt and Sorrow	William Wordsworth
Gunga Din	Rudyard Kipling
Halloween	Robert Burns
Haw Lantern	Seamus Heaney
The Hawk in the Rain	Ted Hughes
Hawthorn and Lavender	William Henley
He Wishes For the Cloths of Heaven	W B Yeats
Heavy Soils	Yevgeny Yevtushenko
Hellas	Percy Bysshe Shelley
La Henriade	Voltaire
Heraclitus	William Cory
Hero and Leander (unfinished)	Christopher Marlowe
The Song of Hiawatha	Henry Wadsworth Longfellow
High and Low	John Betjeman
The Highwayman	Alfred Noyes
High Windows	Philip Larkin
The Hind and the Panther	John Dryden
The Hollow Men	T S Eliot
The Holy Fair	Robert Burns
Holy Willie's Prayer	Robert Burns
Homage to Clio	W H Auden
Homage to Sextus Propertius	Ezra Pound
Home-Thoughts, from Abroad	Robert Browning
Home-Thoughts, from the Sea	Robert Browning
An Horatian Ode	Andrew Marvell
Hours of Idleness	Lord Byron
The House of Life	Dante Gabriel Rossetti
How Do I Love Thee?	Elizabeth Barrett Browning
Howl*	Allen Ginsberg
How They Brought the Good News from Ghent to Aix	Robert Browning
Hudibras	Samuel Butler
Hugh Selwyn Mauberley	Ezra Pound
The Hunting of the Snark	Lewis Carroll
Hymn to Pan	John Keats
Hyperion	John Keats
I See the Boys of Summer	Dylan Thomas
I Wandered Lonely as a Cloud	William Wordsworth
Idylls and Songs	Francis Palgrave
Idylls of the King	Alfred, Lord Tennyson
If	Rudyard Kipling
If This Be Treason	Ezra Pound
The Iliad	Homer
Il Penseroso	John Milton
I'm a Stranger Here Myself	Ogden Nash
To Imagination	Emily Brontë
The Inchcape Rock	Robert Southey
In Country Sleep	Dylan Thomas
Independence	Henry David Thoreau
The Ingoldsby Legends	Richard Harris Barham
In Flanders Field	John McCrae

L
I
T
E
R
A
T
U
R
E

In Hospital	William Henley
In Memoriam	Alfred, Lord Tennyson
In Memory of W.B. Yeats	W H Auden
Insurrections	James Stephens
In the Poppy Fields	James Stephens
In the White Giant's Thigh	Dylan Thomas
Intimations of Immortality	William Wordsworth
Into Battle	Julian Grenfell
Invictus	William Henley
In War Time	John Greenleaf Whittier
Ionica	William Cory
An Irish Airman Foresees His Death	W B Yeats
Irish Melodies	Thomas Moore
Isabella or the Pot of Basil	John Keats
The Island Race	Henry Newbolt
Israfel	Edgar Allan Poe
Ivan the Terrible	Yevgeny Yevtushenko
Jabberwocky	Lewis Carroll
The Jackdaw of Rheims	Richard Harris Barham
Le Jardin des Tuileries	Oscar Wilde
Jenny Kissed Me	James Leigh Hunt
Jerusalem	William Blake
La Jeune Parque	Paul Valéry
John Gilpin	William Cowper
The Jolly Beggars	Robert Burns
Jolly Good Ale and Old	John Still
The Journey of the Magi	T S Eliot
Journeys and Places	Edwin Muir
Julian and Maddalo	Percy Bysshe Shelley
Juvenilia	James Leigh Hunt
Kaddish	Allen Ginsberg
Kamen	Osip Mandelstam
Kalevala	Henry Wadsworth Longfellow
Kennst du das Land	Johann Wolfgang von Goethe
Kilmarnock Poems	Robert Burns
The King's Tragedy	Dante Gabriel Rossetti
Kubla Khan	Samuel Taylor Coleridge
L'Après-midi d'un Faune	Stéphane Mallarmé
La Belle Dame Sans Merci	John Keats
La Nymphe de la Seine	Jean Racine
The Labyrinth	Edwin Muir
The Lady of Shalott	Alfred, Lord Tennyson
The Lake Isle of Innisfree	W B Yeats
Lalla Rookh	Thomas Moore
The Lament	Robert Burns
Lamia	John Keats
The Landing of the Pilgrim Fathers	Felicia Hemans
Lara	Lord Byron
Last Dying Words of Bonny Heck	William Hamilton
Last Lines	Emily Brontë
Last Poems	A E Housman
The Last Rose of Summer	Thomas Moore
Laus Deo	John Greenleaf Whittier
Lays of France	Arthur O'Shaughnessy
Leaves of Grass	Walt Whitman
Leisure	W H Davies
Lenore	Edgar Allan Poe
Les Châtiments	Victor Hugo
Les Contemplations	Victor Hugo
Les Débâcles	Emile Verhaeren
Les Flamandes	Emile Verhaeren
Les Fleurs du mal	Charles Baudelaire
Les Illuminations	Arthur Rimbaud
Let Me Not to the Marriage of True Minds (Sonnet 116)	William Shakespeare
Let Us with a Gladsome Mind	John Milton
To Liberty	Percy Bysshe Shelley
Lieutenant Shmidt	Boris Pasternak
Light Breaks Where No Sun Shines	Dylan Thomas
The Light of Other Days	Thomas Moore
The Listeners	Walter de la Mare
Locksley Hall	Alfred, Lord Tennyson
London	Samuel Johnson
London Lickpenny	Peter Ackroyd
A London Sabbath Morn	Robert Louis Stevenson
London Snow	Robert Bridges
A Lone Striker	Robert Lee Frost
Look, Stranger!	W H Auden
Lord of the Dance	Sydney Carter
The Lotos-Eaters	Alfred, Lord Tennyson
The Love Song of J. Alfred Prufrock	T S Eliot
Love's Philosophy	Percy Bysshe Shelley
Lucasta	Richard Lovelace
Lucidities	Elizabeth Jennings
The Lucy Poems	William Wordsworth
A Lume Spento	Ezra Pound
Lupercal	Ted Hughes
The Lusiads	Luis de Camoes
Lycidas	John Milton
Lycus the Centaur	Thomas Hood
Manasi	Rabindranath Tagore
Mandalay	Rudyard Kipling
Marlborough	Charles Hamilton Sorley
Marmalade Jim at the Farm	Alan Sillitoe
Matilda	Hilaire Belloc
Maud	Alfred, Lord Tennyson
May-Day	Ralph Waldo Emerson
Medal, The	John Dryden
Men and Women	Robert Browning
Metempsychosis	John Donne
The Metropolitan Railway	John Betjeman
Milton	William Blake
Miss Gee	W H Auden
Money	W H Davies
Moortown	Ted Hughes
More Poems	A E Housman
Moscow of the Taverns	Sergey Yesenin
Mother Hubberds Tale	Edmund Spenser
Mountain Interval	Robert Lee Frost
Mount Zion	John Betjeman
Mowing	Robert Lee Frost
La Multiple Splendeur	Emile Verhaeren
Music and Moonlight	Arthur O'Shaughnessy
The Music-Makers	Arthur O'Shaughnessy
My Enemies Have Sweet Voices	Pete Morgan
My Heart Leaps Up	William Wordsworth
My Last Duchess	Robert Browning
My Many-Coated Man	Laurie Lee
Nan	John Masefield
A Narrow Fellow in the Grass	Emily Dickinson
National Tales	Thomas Hood
Nativity Ode	John Milton
Neither Out Far Nor in Deep	Robert Lee Frost
New Bats in Old Belfries	John Betjeman
The New Colossus	Emma Lazarus
New Hampshire	Robert Lee Frost
New Year Letter	W H Auden
Night Mail	W H Auden
The Nile	James Leigh Hunt

LITERATURE

The Vanity of Human	Samuel Johnson *Wishes*	*What Cunning Can*	Edward de Vere, 17th Earl
The Veil	Walter de la Mare	*Express*	of Oxford
Vers de Société	Vincent Voiture	*When Lilacs Last in the*	Walt Whitman
Versus	Ogden Nash	*Dooryard Bloom'd*	
The Victories of Love	Coventry Patmore	*When You Are Old*	W B Yeats
Vignettes in Rhyme	Austin Dobson	*Whims and Oddities*	Thomas Hood
The Village	George Crabbe	*The White Flock*	Anna Akhmatova
The Village Blacksmith	Henry Wadsworth	*The White Man's Burden*	Rudyard Kipling
	Longfellow	*White Buildings*	Hart Crane
Village Minstrel	John Clare	*The White Ship*	Dante Gabriel Rossetti
The Vision of Judgment	Lord Byron	*The Whitsun Weddings*	Philip Larkin
A Visit from St Nicholas	Clement Moore	*The Widow in the*	John Masefield
Vitae Sumina Brevis	Ernest Dowson	*Bye-Street*	
Voices of the Night	Henry Wadsworth	*The Wild Knight*	G K Chesterton
	Longfellow	*The Windhover*	Gerard Manley Hopkins
The Waggoner	Edmund Blunden	*Windsor Forest*	Alexander Pope
The Walrus and the	Lewis Carroll	*A Winter Ship*	Sylvia Plath
Carpenter		*Winter Trees*	Sylvia Plath
The Waste Land	T S Eliot	*Winter Words*	Thomas Hardy
A Wave of the Hand	Yevgeny Yevtushenko	*The Witch of Atlas*	Percy Bysshe Shelley
A Way of Looking	Elizabeth Jennings	*A Witness Tree*	Robert Lee Frost
The Way Through	Rudyard Kipling	*Wodwo*	Ted Hughes
the Woods		*The Woodman*	Robert Louis Stevenson
The Wayzgoose	Roy Campbell	*The Wreck of the*	Gerard Manley Hopkins
We'll Go No More	Lord Byron	*Deutschland*	
A-Roving		*The Wreck of the*	Henry Wadsworth
We Lying by Seasand	Dylan Thomas	*Hesperus*	Longfellow
Wessex Poems	Thomas Hardy	*The Young Man of Cury*	Charles Causley
West-Running Brook	Robert Lee Frost	*Zima Junction*	Yevgeny Yevtushenko

Poetry: General Information

L
I
T
E
R
A
T
U
R
E

alexandrine Iambic or trochaic hexameter (line of 12 syllables or 6 feet) with, usually, a caesura (break) at the 6th syllable.

allegory Narrative or description in prose or verse with an underlying meaning or moral message as in *The Faerie Queene* or *The Pilgrim's Progress*.

apocope Omission of the final letter, syllable or sound of a word, e.g. the poetic use of th' instead of the.

assonance Use of the same or similar vowel sounds close together for the sake of euphony, memorability or emotional effect, e.g. 'And deep asleep he seemed'.

asylum, committed to John Clare from 1837 until his death.

W H Auden Friend and collaborator: Christopher Isherwood.

The Ballad of Reading Gaol Famous extract: 'And all men kill the thing they love, by all let this be heard, Some do it with a bitter look, Some with a flattering word. The coward does it with a kiss, The brave man with a sword!'

ballade Poem of three eight-line stanzas, rhyming ababbcbc, and one four-line *envoi* (final stanza) rhyming bcbc, with a refrain at the end of each of its four sections. François Villon was a great exponent of the ballade in French, Hilaire Belloc in English.

Bastille Imprisoned for a year in 1717: Voltaire (François Marie Arouet).

bathos Anticlimax or sudden descent, intended or not, from the sublime to the commonplace, e.g. the last 2 lines of Tennyson's *Enoch Arden*: 'And when they buried him the little port, Had seldom seen a costlier funeral.'

Beat Poets Lawrence Ferlinghetti, Allen Ginsberg, Jack Kerouac, Gregory Corso.

Belloc Many of his works illustrated by G K Chesterton.

The Betrothed Extract: A woman is only a woman, but a good cigar is a Smoke.

Elizabeth Barrett Browning Pet name: She was affectionately known as 'My Little Portuguese' by her husband Robert Browning.

Brunanburh Poem in Old English, included in four manuscripts of the *Anglo-Saxon Chronicle* under the year 937 and dealing with the battle of that name.

catachresis Misuse or incorrect application of a word, e.g. 'chronic' to mean 'severe', or 'refute' to mean 'deny'.

Christian Poet First English: Caedmon.

Clerihew Comic biographical poem in the form of a quatrain with lines of various length, rhyming aabb, named after its inventor Edmund Clerihew Bentley (1875–1956). Example: The Art of Biography is different from Geography. Geography is about maps, Biography is about chaps.

dithyramb Song or poem in honour of Dionysus.

The Donkey Describes itself as 'the devil's walking parody On all four-footed things'.

Dover Beach First lines 'The sea is calm tonight The tide is full.'

duels Ben Jonson killed fellow actor Gabriel Spencer. To defend his wife's honour, Alexander challenged and was killed by Baron d'Anthès.

Dymer C S Lewis published this work under the name of Clive Hamilton.

Elegy Written in a Country Churchyard Opening: 'The curfew tolls the knell of parting day, The lowing herd wind slowly o'er the lea . . .' Extract: 'Far from the madding crowd's ignoble strife . . .'

elision Suppression of a vowel or syllable in verse for the sake of metrical correctness, e.g. 'ta'en' (one syllable) replacing 'taken' (two).

enjambement Running-on of one line of verse into

another without a grammatical break, e.g.: 'Nay, but this dotage of our general's / O'erflows the measure . . . ' (*Antony and Cleopatra*).

epigram Pointed, witty saying or verse that may be aphoristic, sarcastic, complimentary or amusing.

euphuism Highly elaborate prose style as found in John Lyly's *Euphues* (1580).

The Exeter Book Important manuscript containing Old English poetry, copied about 940 and given by Bishop Leofric (d. 1072) to Exeter Cathedral. The best-known poems include *The Wanderer, The Seafarer, Widsith, The Ruin, Wulf and Eadwacer, The Wife's Lament, The Husband's Message* and *Resignation*.

Four Quartets (T S Eliot) *Burnt Norton, East Coker, The Dry Salvages, Little Gidding.*

The Four Boileau, La Fontaine, Molière, Racine.

Georgian Poets Writing during the reign of *George V*: Lascelles Abercrombie, Hilaire Belloc, Rupert Brooke, W H Davies, Ernest Dowson, John Drinkwater, James Elroy Flecker, Robert Graves, Ralph Hodgson, John Masefield, Walter de la Mare, Harold Monro, Siegfried Sassoon, Sir John Squire, Edward Thomas.

Gertrude of Wyoming Poem by Thomas Campbell in Spenserian stanzas, published 1809. Describes the destruction of the settlement of Wyoming in Pennsylvania by a force of Indians.

The Golden Treasury of best songs and Lyrical poems in the English language Editor: Francis Palgrave edited the classic book of poetic works (1861) with the help of his friend Tennyson, but controversially omitted all of William Blake's poems.

Griffin Poetry Prize Inaugurated in 2001 in Canada. $40,000 awarded to best Canadian collection and $40,000 to best international collection.

haiku Japanese verse form of seventeen syllables in three lines of five, seven and five syllables, encapsulating an idea, image or mood.

Home-Thoughts, From Abroad Opening: 'Oh, to be in England Now that April's there . . .'

Imagism Poetic movement and theory (1909–17) which emphasised direct treatment of subject-matter, concreteness, extreme economy of language and the rhythm of phrases rather than the rhythm of regular metres. Poets include Richard Aldington, HD, F S Flint, James Joyce, Amy Lowell and Ezra Pound.

Keats's epitaph By himself: 'Here lies one whose name was writ in water.'

Kubla Khan Sacred river: Alph.

Lake Poets Wordsworth, Coleridge and Southey.

Leisure Opening: 'What is this life if, full of care, We have no time to stand and stare?'

limerick Five-line nonsense verse popularised by Edward Lear and following a rhyming scheme of aabba. Example: There was a young lady of Wilts Who walked up to Scotland on stilts When they said it was shocking To show so much stocking She answered 'Then what about kilts?'

The Listeners First line: '"Is there anybody there?" said the traveller . . .'

Maud Classic lines: 'Come into the garden, Maud, For the black bat, night, has flown . . .'

Metaphysical Poets A group of English poets of the 17th century, who include John Donne, George Herbert, Henry Vaughan, Richard Crashaw and Andrew Marvell (term first used by Samuel Johnson, possibly influenced by a phrase of Dryden's).

metre Measure of lines of verse which in English is basically accentual, determined by stress, each group of syllables, usually two or three, forms a metrical unit called a foot.

Milton called Athens 'Mother of arts and eloquence'.

The New Colossus Lines from this sonnet, inscribed on the Statue of Liberty: 'Give me your tired, your poor, Your huddled masses, yearning to breathe free, The wretched refuse of your teeming shore. Send these, the homeless, tempest-tost to me, I lift my lamp beside the golden door'.

Night Mail Opening: 'This is the Night Mail crossing the Border, Bringing the cheque and the postal order.'

Ode on a Distant Prospect of Eton College Extract: 'Ye distant spires, ye antique towers . . .'

Ode to Autumn Opening: 'Season of mists and mellow fruitfulness, Close bosom-friend of the maturing sun'.

Old English poem, 1st *Beowulf* (probably composed orally in the 8th century; written down in 10th century).

The Old Vicarage, Grantchester Details: Contains German and Greek lines (Jeffrey Archer purchased the property).

On his Blindness First line: 'When I consider how my light is spent'.

Ozymandias First line: 'I met a traveller from an antique land . . .'

pathetic fallacy The ascription of human emotions to non-human objects and phenomena, e.g. 'the cruel sea'.

The Pilgrim's Progress Extract: 'The name of the Slough was Despond'.

Pléiade, La Group of seven French poets and writers of the 16th century, led by Pierre de Ronsard. The name was taken from that given by the Alexandrian critics to seven tragic poets of the reign of Ptolemy III Philadelphus (285–246 BC). The other six members of La Pléiade were Joachim du Bellay, Jean-Antoine de Baif, Jean Dorat, Rémy Belleau, Etienne Jodelle and Pontis de Tyard.

Poet Laureate Deposed: John Dryden, who became a Catholic in 1685 and was deposed in 1689 after the Glorious Revolution. Longest in office: Alfred, Lord Tennyson (1850–92).

Pott's disease Suffered by Alexander Pope, who was only 4' 6" tall.

prisoner poets François Villon – for his various criminal activities. James Leigh Hunt: 2 years (1813–15) for libelling the Prince Regent. Jean Genet: for theft, male prostitution, and other crimes. Richard Lovelace: in 1642, for being a Royalist.

The Rape of the Lock Two Catholic families quarrel after a male member of one steals a lock of hair from a female member of the other.

Sally Brown (Thomas Hood) Extract: 'They went and told the sexton, and The sexton toll'd the bell'.

Sea Fever Opening: 'I must go down to the seas again, to the lonely sea and the sky, And all I ask is a tall ship and a star to steer her by . . .'

Shall I compare thee to a summer's day Next lines: 'Thou art more lovely and more temperate. Rough winds do shake the darling buds of May, And summer's lease hath all too short a date . . .'

The Soldier First line: 'If I should die think only this of me'.

Song (John Donne) First line: 'Go and catch a falling star . . .'

Songs of Childhood Published by Walter de la Mare using the pseudonym Walter Ramal.

sonnets Three basic types: Spenserian, Shakespearian and Petrarchan.

Spasmodic School Term coined by William Aytoun (1813–65) in his *Firmilian, or The Student of Badajoz* (1854) as an attack on the intensely melodramatic poems of such as P J Bailey, J W Marston, S T Dobell and Alexander Smith.

Spenserian stanza Eight iambic pentameters followed by one iambic hexameter, rhyming ababbcbcc.

spondee Metrical foot consisting of two long or stressed syllables.

The Star-Spangled Banner By Francis Scott Key (1779–1843). First line: 'Oh say can you see by the dawn's early light . . .'

Stella (from *Astrophel and Stella*) Thought to be Penelope Devereux.

A Subaltern's Love-song Beloved: Miss Joan Hunter Dunn. Towns mentioned: Aldershot and Camberley. Car mentioned: Hillman.

Tennyson quotes 'In the Spring a young man's fancy lightly turns to thoughts of love.'
'Man is the hunter; woman is his game . . .'
''Tis better to have loved and lost Than never to have loved at all.'

tercet Three-line stanza, particularly as used in terza rima.

terza rima Verse-form of three-line stanzas rhyming aba, bcb, cdc, and so on, usually iambic pentameters, e.g. *Ode to the West Wind*.

To a Field Mouse Opening: 'Wee, sleekit, cow'rin', tim'rous beastie, O what a panic's in thy breastie ! Extract: 'The best laid schemes o' mice an' men. Gang aft a-gley.'

To a Skylark Opening: 'Hail to thee, blithe Spirit'!

To the Virgins, To Make Much of Time First line: 'Gather ye rosebuds while ye may . . .'

Transcendentalists A mid 19th-century New England movement of writers, poets and philosophers who believed in the unity of all creation, the innate goodness of man and the supremacy of insight over logic and experience. Notable adherents were Ralph Waldo Emerson and Henry David Thoreau.

Upon Westminster Bridge Opening: 'Earth has not anything to show more fair . . .'

The Village Blacksmith Opening: Under the spreading chestnut tree The village smithy stands . . .'

A Visit from St Nicholas Opening: ''Twas the night before Christmas . . .'

Whitbread Literary Award Winners

Category		Title	Author
1971	Novel	*The Destiny Waltz*	Gerda Charles
	Biography	*Henrik Ibsen*	Michael Meyer
	Poetry	*Mercia Hymns*	Geoffrey Hill
1972	Novel	*The Bird of Night*	Susan Hill
	Biography	*Trollope*	James Pope-Hennessy
	Children's book	*The Diddakoi*	Rumer Godden
1973	Novel	*The Chip-Chip Gatherers*	Shiva Naipaul
	Biography	*CB: A Life of Sir Henry Campbell-Bannerman*	John Wilson
	Children's book	*The Butterfly Ball & the Grasshopper's Feast*	Alan Aldridge and William Plomer
1974	Novel	*The Sacred and Profane Love Machine*	Iris Murdoch
	Biography	*Poor Dean Brendan*	Andrew Boyle
	Children's book (joint)	*How Tom Beat Captain Najork and His Hired Sportsmen*	Russell Hoban and Quentin Blake
		The Emperor's Winding Sheet	Jill Paton Walsh
1975	Novel	*Docherty*	William McIlvanney
	Autobiography	*In Our Infancy*	Helen Corke
	First book	*The Improbable Puritan: A Life of Bulstrode Whitelocke*	Ruth Spalding
1976	Novel	*The Children of Dynmouth*	William Trevor
	Biography	*Elizabeth Gaskell*	Winifred Gerin
	Children's book	*A Stitch in Time*	Penelope Lively
1977	Novel	*Injury Time*	Beryl Bainbridge
	Biography	*Mary Curzon*	Nigel Nicolson
	Children's book	*No End to Yesterday*	Shelagh Macdonald
1978	Novel	*Picture Palace*	Paul Theroux
	Biography	*Lloyd George: The People's Champion*	John Grigg
	Children's book	*The Battle of Bubble and Squeak*	Philippa Pearce
1979	Novel	*The Old Jest*	Jennifer Johnston
	Autobiography	*About Time*	Penelope Mortimer
	Children's novel	*Tulku*	Peter Dickinson
1980	Novel & Book of the Year	*How Far Can You Go?*	David Lodge
	Biography	*On the Edge of Paradise: A.C. Benson the Diarist*	David Newsome
	Children's novel	*John Diamond*	Leon Garfield
1981	Novel	*Silver's City*	Maurice Leitch
	Biography	*Monty: The Making of a General*	Nigel Hamilton
	Children's novel	*The Hollow Land*	Jane Gardam
	First novel	*A Good Man in Africa*	William Boyd

LITERATURE

Year	Category	Title	Author
1982	Novel	*Young Shoulders*	John Wain
	Biography	*Bismarck*	Edward Crankshaw
	Children's novel	*The Song of Pentecost*	W J Corbett
	First novel	*On the Black Hill*	Bruce Chatwin
1983	Novel	*Fools of Fortune*	William Trevor
	Biography	*Vita*	Victoria Glendinning
	(joint)	*King George V*	Kenneth Rose
	Children's novel	*The Witches*	Roald Dahl
	First novel	*Flying to Nowhere*	John Fuller
1984	Novel	*Kruger's Alp*	Christopher Hope
	Biography	*T.S. Eliot*	Peter Ackroyd
	Children's novel	*The Queen of the Pharisees' Children*	Barbara Willard
	First novel	*A Parish of Rich Women*	James Buchan
	Short story	*Tomorrow is Our Permanent Address*	Diane Rowe
1985	Novel	*Hawksmoor*	Peter Ackroyd
	Biography	*Hugh Dalton*	Ben Pimlott
	Children's novel	*The Nature of the Beast*	Janni Howker
	First novel	*Oranges Are Not the Only Fruit*	Jeanette Winterson
	Poetry & Book of the year	*Elegies*	Douglas Dunn
1986	Novel & Book of the Year	*An Artist of the Floating World*	Kazuo Ishiguro
	Biography	*Gilbert White*	Richard Mabey
	Children's novel	*The Coal House*	Andrew Taylor
	First novel	*Continent*	Jim Crace
	Poetry	*Stet*	Peter Reading
1987	Novel	*The Child in Time*	Ian McEwan
	Biography & Book of the Year	*Under the Eye of the Clock*	Christopher Nolan
	First novel	*The Other Garden*	Francis Wyndham
	Poetry	*The Haw Lantern*	Seamus Heaney
1988	Novel	*The Satanic Verses*	Salman Rushdie
	Biography	*Tolstoy*	A N Wilson
	Children's novel	*Awaiting Developments*	Judy Allen
	First novel & Book of the Year	*The Comforts of Madness*	Paul Sayer
	Poetry	*The Automatic Oracle*	Peter Porter
1989	Novel	*The Chymical Wedding*	Lindsay Clarke
	Biography and Book of the Year	*Coleridge: Early Visions*	Richard Holmes
	Children's novel	*Why Weeps the Brogan?*	Hugh Scott
	First novel	*Gerontius*	James Hamilton
	Poetry	*Shibboleth*	Michael Donaghy
1990	Novel & Book of the Year	*Hopeful Monsters*	Nicholas Mosley
	Biography	*A.A. Milne: His Life*	Ann Thwaite
	Children's novel	*A.K.*	Peter Dickinson
	First novel	*The Buddha of Suburbia*	Hanif Kureishi
	Poetry	*Daddy, Daddy*	Paul Durcan
1991	Novel	*The Queen of the Tambourine*	Jane Gardam
	Biography & Book of the Year	*A Life of Picasso*	John Richardson
	Children's novel	*Harvey Angell*	Diana Hendry
	First novel	*Alma Cogan*	Gordon Burn
	Poetry	*Gorse Fires*	Michael Longley
1992	Novel	*Poor Things*	Alasdair Gray
	Biography	*Trollope*	Victoria Glendinning
	Children's novel	*The Great Elephant Chase*	Gillian Cross
	First novel & Book of the Year	*Swing Hammer Swing!*	Jeff Torrington
	Poetry	*The Gaze of the Gorgon*	Tony Harrison
1993	Novel & Book of the Year	*Theory of War*	Joan Brady
	Biography	*Philip Larkin*	Andrew Motion
	Children's novel	*Flour Babies*	Anne Fine
	First novel	*Saving Agnes*	Rachel Cusk
	Poetry	*Mean Time*	Carol Ann Duffy
1994	Novel & Book of the Year	*Felicia's Journey*	William Trevor
	Biography	*The Married Man*	Brenda Maddox
	Children's novel	*Gold Dust*	Geraldine McCaughrean
	First novel	*The Longest Memory*	Fred D'Aguiar
	Poetry	*Out of Danger*	James Fenton
1995	Novel	*The Moor's Last Sigh*	Salman Rushdie
	Biography	*Gladstone*	Roy Jenkins
	Children's novel	*The Wreck of the Zanzibar*	Michael Morpurgo
	First novel & Book of the Year	*Behind the Scenes at the Museum*	Kate Atkinson
	Poetry	*Gunpowder*	Bernard O'Donoghue
1996	Novel	*Every Man for Himself*	Beryl Bainbridge
	Biography	*Thomas Cranmer: A Life*	Diarmaid MacCulloch
	First novel	*The Debt to Pleasure*	John Lancaster
	Poetry & Book of the Year	*The Spirit Level*	Seamus Heaney

	Children's Book of the Year	*The Tulip Touch*	Anne Fine
1997	Novel	*Quarantine*	Jim Crace
	Biography	*Victor Hugo*	Graham Robb
	First novel	*The Ventriloquist's Tale*	Pauline Melville
	Poetry & Book of the Year	*Tales from Ovid*	Ted Hughes
	Children's Book of the Year	*Aquila*	Andrew Norriss
1998	Novel	*Leading the Cheers*	Justin Cartwright
	Biography	*Georgiana, Duchess of Devonshire*	Amanda Foreman
	First novel	*The Last King of Scotland*	Giles Foden
	Children's Book of the Year	*Skellig*	David Almond
	Poetry & Book of the Year	*Birthday Letters*	Ted Hughes
1999	Novel	*Music and Silence*	Rose Tremain
	Biography	*Berlioz: Servitude and Greatness*	David Cairns
	First novel	*White City Bloc*	Tim Lott
	Children's Book of the Year	*Harry Potter and the Prisoner of Azkaban*	J K Rowling
	Poetry & Book of the Year	*Beowulf*	Seamus Heaney
2000	Novel & Book of the Year	*English Passengers*	Mathew Kneale
	Biography	*Bad Blood: A memoir*	Lorna Sage
	First novel	*White Teeth*	Zadie Smith
	Children's Book of the Year	*Coram Bay*	Jamila Gavin
	Poetry	*The Asylum Dance*	John Burnside
2001	Novel	*Twelve Bar Blues*	Patrick Neate
	Biography	*Selkirk's Island*	Diana Souhami
	First novel	*Something Like A House*	Sid Smith
	Children's Book & Book of the Year	*The Amber Spyglass*	Philip Pullman
	Poetry	*Bunny*	Selima Hill
2002	Novel	*Spies*	Michael Frayn
	Biography & Book of the Year	*Samuel Pepys: The Unequalled Self*	Claire Tomalin
	First Novel	*The Song of Names*	Norman Lebrecht
	Children's Book of the Year	*Saffy's Angel*	Hilary McKay
	Poetry	*The Ice Age*	Paul Farley

Pulitzer Prize for Fiction

Year	Book	Author	Year	Book	Author
1918	*His Family*	Ernest Poole	1946	No Award	
1919	*The Magnificent Ambersons*	Booth Tarkington	1947	*All the King's Men*	Robert Penn Warren
1920	No Award		1948	*Tales of the South Pacific*	James A Michener
1921	*The Age of Innocence*	Edith Wharton			
1922	*Alice Adams*	Booth Tarkington	1949	*Guard of Honor*	James Gould Cozzens
1923	*One of Ours*	Willa Cather	1950	*The Way West*	A B Guthrie Jr
1924	*The Able McLaughlins*	Margaret Wilson	1951	*The Town*	Conrad Richter
1925	*So Big*	Edna Ferber	1952	*The Caine Mutiny*	Herman Wouk
1926	*Arrowsmith*	Sinclair Lewis	1953	*The Old Man and the Sea*	Ernest Hemingway
1927	*Early Autumn*	Louis Bromfield			
1928	*The Bridge at San Luis Rey*	Thornton Wilder	1954	No Award	
1929	*Scarlet Sister Mary*	Julia Peterkin	1955	*A Fable*	William Faulkner
1930	*Laughing Boy*	Oliver LaFarge	1956	*Andersonville*	Mackinlay Kantor
1931	*Years of Grace*	Margaret Ayer Barnes	1957	No Award	
1932	*The Good Earth*	Pearl S Buck	1958	*A Death in the Family*	James Agee
1933	*The Store*	T S Stribling	1959	*The Travels of Jamie McPheeters*	Robert Lewis Taylor
1934	*Lamb in his Bosom*	Caroline Miller			
1935	*Now in November*	Josephine Winslow Johnson	1960	*Advise and Consent*	Allen Drury
			1961	*To Kill a Mockingbird*	Harper Lee
1936	*Honey in the Horn*	Harold L Davis	1962	*The Edge of Sadness*	Edwin O'Connor
1937	*Gone with the Wind*	Margaret Mitchell	1963	*The Reivers*	William Faulkner
1938	*The Late George Apley*	John Phillips Marquand	1964	No Award	
			1965	*The Keepers of the House*	Shirley Ann Grau
1939	*The Yearling*	Marjorie Kinnan Rawlings	1966	*Collected Stories of Katherine Anne Porter*	Katherine Anne Porter
1940	*The Grapes of Wrath*	John Steinbeck	1967	*The Fixer*	Bernard Malamud
1941	No Award				
1942	*In This Our Life*	Ellen Glasgow	1968	*The Confessions of Nat Turner*	William Styron
1943	*Dragon's Teeth*	Upton Sinclair			
1944	*Journey in the Dark*	Martin Flavin	1969	*House Made of Dawn*	N Scott Momaday
1945	*A Bell for Adano*	John Hersey			

LITERATURE

1970	Collected Stories	Jean Stafford	1988	Beloved	Toni Morrison
1971	No Award		1989	Breathing Lessons	Anne Tyler
1972	Angle of Repose	Wallace Stegner	1990	The Mambo King Plays	Oscar Hijuelos
1973	The Optimist's Daughter	Eudora Welty		Songs of Love	
1974	No Award		1991	Rabbit at Rest	John Updike
1975	The Killer Angels	Michael Shaara	1992	A Thousand Acres	Jane Smiley
1976	Humboldt's Gift	Saul Bellow	1993	A Good Scent from a	Robert Olen
1977	No Award			Strange Mountain	Butler
1978	Elbow Room	James Alan	1994	The Shipping News	E Annie Proulx
		McPherson	1995	The Stone Diaries	Carol Shields
1979	The Stories of John	John Cheever	1996	Independence Day	Richard Ford
	Cheever		1997	Martin Dressler: Tale of	Steven
1980	The Executioner's Song	Norman Mailer		an American Dreamer	Millhauser
1981	A Confederacy of Dunces	John Kennedy	1998	American Pastoral	Philip Roth
		Toole	1999	The Hours	Michael
1982	Rabbit is Rich	John Updike			Cunningham
1983	The Color Purple	Alice Walker	2000	Interpreteur of Maladies	Jhumpa Lahiri
1984	Ironweed	William Kennedy	2001	The Amazing Adventures	Michael Chabon
1985	Foreign Affairs	Alison Lurie		of Kavalier & Clay	
1986	Lonesome Dove	Larry McMurty	2002	Empire Falls	Richard Russo
1987	A Summons to Memphis	Peter Taylor			

Booker Prize for Fiction

Year	Book	Author	Year	Book	Author
1969	Something to Answer For	P H Newby	1984	Hotel Du Lac	Anita Brookner
1970	The Elected Member	Bernice Rubens	1985	The Bone People	Keri Hulme
1971	In a Free State	V S Naipaul	1986	The Old Devils	Kingsley Amis
1972	G	John Berger	1987	Moon Tiger	Penelope Lively
1973	The Siege of Krishnapur	J G Farrell	1988	Oscar and Lucinda	Peter Carey
1974	The Conservationist	Nadine Gordimer	1989	The Remains of the Day	Kazuo Ishiguro
	Holiday	Stanley	1990	Possession	A S Byatt
		Middleton	1991	The Famished Road	Ben Okri
		(joint)	1992	Sacred Hunger	Barry Unsworth
1975	Heat and Dust	Ruth Prawer		The English Patient	Michael Ondaatje
		Jhabvala			(joint)
1976	Saville	David Storey	1993	Paddy Clarke Ha Ha Ha	Roddy Doyle
1977	Staying On	Paul Scott	1994	How Late it Was, How Late	James Kelman
1978	The Sea, The Sea	Iris Murdoch	1995	The Ghost Road	Pat Barker
1979	Offshore	Penelope	1996	Last Orders	Graham Swift
		Fitzgerald	1997	The God of Small Things	Arundhati Roy
1980	Rites of Passage	William Golding	1998	Amsterdam	Ian McEwan
1981	Midnight's Children	Salman Rushdie	1999	Disgrace	J M Coetzee
1982	Schindler's Ark	Thomas Keneally	2000	The Blind Assassin	Margaret Atwood
1983	The Life and Times of	J M Coetzee	2001	True History of the Kelly Gang	Peter Carey
	Michael K		2002	Life of Pi	Yann Martel

NB: The Man Booker Prize is awarded for a novel by a citizen of the UK, Eire, South Africa, or any Commonwealth country, with the proviso that it was first published in Britain.

Orange Prize for Fiction

The Orange Award was launched in January 1996 and is restricted to female novelists. As well as the annual prize of £30,000 the winner receives a bronze figurine created by Griznel Niven known as the 'Betsie'.

Winners	Year	Title
Helen Dunmore	1996	A Spell of Winter
Anne Michaels	1997	Fugitive Pieces
Carol Shields	1998	Larry's Party
Suzanne Berne	1999	A Crime in the Neighbourhood
Linda Grant	2000	When I Lived in Modern Times
Kate Grenville	2001	The Idea of Perfection
Ann Patchett	2002	Bel Canto

Fictional Literary Characters

(except Dickens and Shakespeare)

Captain Absolute	*The Rivals*
Captain Ahab	*Moby-Dick*
Roderick Alleyn	created by Ngaio Marsh
Charlie Allnutt	*The African Queen*
Squire Allworthy	*Tom Jones*
Andy Capp	drawn by Reg Smythe
Andy Pandy	created by Maria Bird
Harry Angstrom	the Rabbit Tetralogy
Lara Antipova	*Doctor Zhivago*
Aouda	*Around the World in 80 Days*
John Appleby	created by Michael Innes
Isobel Archer	*The Portrait of a Lady*
Jack Aubrey	*Master and Commander* (& others)
Steve Austin	*Cyborg* (by Martin Caidin)
Ayesha	*She*
Dr Aziz	*A Passage to India*
Babar	created by Jean de Brunhoff
Badger	*The Wind in the Willows*
Bilbo Baggins	*The Hobbit, Lord of the Rings*
David Balfour	*Kidnapped*
The Baron (John Mannering)	created by Anthony Morton (John Creasey)
Oliver Barrett IV	*Love Story*
Bastable Family	*The Treasure-Seekers* (by E Nesbit)
Batman	created by Bob Kane
Dr Jim Bayliss	*All My Sons*
Bazarov	*Fathers and Sons*
Belinda	*The Rape of the Lock*
Elizabeth Bennet	*Pride and Prejudice*
Inspector Bertozzo	*Accidental Death of an Anarchist*
Rev. Edmund Bertram	*Mansfield Park*
Sir Thomas Bertram	*Mansfield Park*
Margot Beste-Chetwynde	*Decline and Fall*
Big Daddy	*Cat on a Hot Tin Roof*
Bigwig (rabbit)	*Watership Down*
Ernie Bilko	created by Nat Hiken
Mr Bingley	*Pride and Prejudice*
John Blackthorne	*Shogun*
Modesty Blaise	created by Peter O'Donnell
Sir Percy Blakeney	*The Scarlet Pimpernel*
Colonel Blimp	created by David Low
Leopold Bloom	*Ulysses*
Prince Andrey Bolkonsky	*War and Peace*
James Bond	created by Ian Flemming
Bosinney	*The Forsyte Saga*
Boxer the Horse	*Animal Farm*
Jack Boyle	*Juno and the Paycock*
Lady Bracknell	*The Importance of Being Ernest*
Ben Braddock	*The Graduate*
Colonel Brandon	*Sense and Sensibility*
Alan Breck	*Kidnapped*
Brer Rabbit	the Uncle Remus stories
Dorothea Brooke	*Middlemarch*
Father Brown	created by G K Chesterton
Pinkie Brown	*Brighton Rock*
Beatrice Bryant	*Roots*
Daisy Buchanan	*The Great Gatsby*
Charlie Bucket	*Charlie and the Chocolate Factory*
Buck (the Dog)	*The Call of the Wild*

Natty Bumppo	the Leatherstocking stories
Albert Campion	created by Margery Allingham
Tom Canty	*The Prince and the Pauper*
Sir Danvers Carew	*Dr Jekyll and Mr Hyde*
William Carey	*Of Human Bondage*
Katy Carr	*What Katy Did*
Captain Cat	*Under Milk Wood*
Anne Catherick	*The Woman in White*
Catherine	*The Bell*
Holden Caulfield	*The Catcher in the Rye*
Jenny Cavillieri	*Love Story*
Professor Challenger	*The Lost World*
Canon Chasuble	*The Importance of Being Ernest*
Chauntecleer (the hen)	*Nun's Priest's Tale*
Jack Chesney	*Charley's Aunt*
Harvey Cheyne	*Captains Courageous*
Chichikov	*Dead Souls*
Chingachgook	the Leatherstocking stories
Mr Charles Chipping	*Goodbye, Mr Chips*
Christian	*The Pilgrim's Progress*
Frank Churchill	*Emma*
Petty Officer Claggart	*Billy Budd*
Angel Clare	*Tess of the D'Urbervilles*
Eric Claudin	*The Phantom of the Opera*
Darius Clayhanger (printer)	*Clayhanger*
Clegg	*The Collector*
Robert James Colley	*Rites of Passage*
Compson family	*The Sound and the Fury* and *Absalom, Absalom!*
Hugh Conway	*Lost Horizon*
Mr Crawford	*Mansfield Park*
Guy Crouchback	*Men at Arms*
Lenina Crowne	*Brave New World*
Isabelle de Croye	*Quentin Durward*
Sergeant Cuff	*The Moonstone*
Curdie (miner)	*The Princess and the Goblin*
Stephen Daedalus	*Ulysses*
Adam Dalgleish	created by P D James
Edmond Dantès	*Count of Monte Christo*
Mrs Danvers	*Rebecca*
Dapper	*The Alchemist*
Mr Fitzwilliam Darcy	*Pride and Prejudice*
Dashwood family	*Sense and Sensibility*
Anne Deever	*All My Sons*
Danny Deever	*Barrack-Room Ballads*
Maxim De Winter	*Rebecca*
James Dixon	*Lucky Jim*
Captain Dobbin	*Vanity Fair*
Eliza Doolittle	*Pygmalion*
Paul Drake	created by Erle Stanley Gardner
Abel Drugger	*The Alchemist*
Blanche Du Bois	*A Streetcar Named Desire*
Lady Dulcinea	*Don Quixote*
Auguste Dupin	created by Edgar Allan Poe
Albus Dumbledore	Harry Potter books
Dudley Dursley	Harry Potter books
Catherine Earnshaw	*Wuthering Heights*
Humphrey Chimpden Earwicker	*Finnegans Wake*
Eeyore	*Winnie-the-Pooh*
Montague Egg	created by Dorothy L Sayers
Anne Elliot	*Persuasion*

Sir Walter Elliot	*Persuasion*
Mrs Erlynne	*Lady Windermere's Fan*
Cedric Errol	*Little Lord Fauntleroy*
Esmeralda	*The Hunchback of Notre Dame*
Estragon	*Waiting for Godot*
Etienne	*Germinal*
Bathsheba Everdene	*Far from the Madding Crowd*
Face	*The Alchemist*
Jane Fairfax	*Emma*
Jude Fawley	*Jude the Obscure*
Gervase Fenn	created by Edmund Crispin
Cyril Fielding	*A Passage to India*
Fiver	*Watership Down*
Pegeen Flaherty	*The Playboy of the Western World*
Flashman	*Tom Brown's Schooldays*
Henry Fleming	*The Red Badge of Courage*
Phileas Fogg	*Around the World in 80 Days*
Fossil family	*Ballet Shoes* (Noel Streatfeild)
Frodo	*The Lord of the Rings*
Archdeacon Frollo	*The Hunchback of Notre Dame*
Gandalf	*The Lord of the Rings*
James Gatz (Jay Gatsby)	*The Great Gatsby*
Marguerite Gautier	*Camille*
Gerard	*The Cloister and the Hearth*
Inspector Ghote	created by H R F Keating
Roderick Glossop (psychiatrist)	the Jeeves stories
Anthony Gloster (shipowner)	*The Mary Gloster* (Kipling)
Holly Golightly	*Breakfast at Tiffany's*
Gollum	*The Lord of the Rings*
Hermione Granger	Harry Potter books
Cordelia Gray	created by P D James
Grendel	*Beowulf*
Jack Grey	*Pale Fire*
Joan Griffin	*The Invisible Man*
Clyde Griffiths	*An American Tragedy*
Captain Grimes	*Decline and Fall*
Tania Gromeko	*Doctor Zhivago*
Gunga Din	created by Rudyard Kipling
Tod Hackett	*The Day of the Locust*
Harry Haller	*Steppenwolf*
Basil Hallward	*The Picture of Dorian Gray*
Charles Hamilton	*Gone With the Wind*
Richard Hannay	*The Thirty-Nine Steps*
Miss Hardcastle	*She Stoops to Conquer*
Hawkeye	the Leatherstocking stories
Bill Haydon (spy)	*Tinker, Tailor, Soldier, Spy*
Dolores Haze	*Lolita*
Hazel (rabbit)	*Watership Down*
Nora Helmer	*A Doll's House*
Michael Henchard	*The Mayor of Casterbridge*
Frederic Henry	*A Farewell to Arms*
Hickey	*The Iceman Cometh*
Henry Higgins	*Pygmalion*
Charles Highway	*The Rachel Papers*
Bridget Hitler	*Young Adolf* by Beryl Bainbridge
Captain Hook	*Peter Pan*
Houyhnhnms (horses)	*Gulliver's Travels*
Humbert Humbert	*Lolita*
Humpty Dumpty	*Through the Looking Glass*
Injun Joe	*Tom Sawyer*
Mrs Jennings	*Sense and Sensibility*
Mrs Jessel	*The Turn of the Screw*
Tom Joad	*The Grapes of Wrath*
Jocasta	*Oedipus the King*
Victoria Jones	*Bhowani Junction* (John Masters)
Robert Jordan	*For Whom the Bell Tolls*
Monsieur Jourdain	*Le Bourgeois Gentilhomme*
Joseph K	*The Trial*
Alyosha Karamazov	*The Brothers Karamazov*
Dmitri Karamazov	*The Brothers Karamazov*
Ivan Karamazov	*The Brothers Karamazov*
Chris Keller	*All My Sons*
Frank Kennedy	*Gone With the Wind*
Khlestakov	*The Inspector General*
Kipps (draper's assistant)	*Kipps*
Howard Kirk	*The History Man*
Joseph Knecht	*The Glass Bead Game* (aka *Magister Ludi*)
Mr Knightley	*Emma*
Kostoglotov	*Cancer Ward*
Stanley Kowalsky	*A Streetcar Named Desire*
Lydia Languish	*The Rivals*
Leamas	*The Spy Who Came in from the Cold*
Simon Legree	*Uncle Tom's Cabin*
Amyas Leigh	*Westward Ho!*
Jeeter Lester	*Tobacco Road*
Adrian Leverkühn (composer)	*Doctor Faustus*
Levin	*Anna Karenina*
Ligia	*Quo Vadis?*
Teddy Lloyd	*The Prime of Miss Jean Brodie*
Lord Loam	*The Admirable Crichton*
Willy Loman	*Death of a Salesman*
Lovewit	*The Alchemist*
Frank Lubey	*All My Sons*
Lucky	*Waiting for Godot*
Tertius Lydgate (surgeon)	*Middlemarch*
Lt Macaulay	*Bhowani Junction* (John Masters)
Christie Mahon	*The Playboy of the Western World*
Major Major	*Catch-22*
Mrs Malaprop	*The Rivals*
Draco Malfoy	Harry Potter books
Captain Charles Mallison	*Lost Horizon*
Daphne Manners	*The Jewel in the Crown*
Stephen Maturin	created by Patrick O'Brian
Oskar Matzerath	*The Tin Drum*
Oliver Mellors	*Lady Chatterley's Lover*
Merrylegs (pony)	*Black Beauty*
Messala	*Ben Hur*
Duke Michael	*The Prisoner of Zenda*
Mildew	*Fungus the Bogeyman*
Millamant	*The Way of the World*
George Milton	*Of Mice and Men*
Minnehaha	*Hiawatha*
Mirabell	*The Way of the World*
Mold	*Fungus the Bogeyman*
Mole	*The Wind in the Willows*
Algernon Moncrieff	*The Importance of Being Ernest*
Montmorency (the dog)	*Three Men in a Boat*
Dr Monygham	*Nostromo*
Paul Morel	*Sons and Lovers*
Dean Moriarty	*On the Road*
Catherine Morland	*Northanger Abbey*
Mother's Younger Brother	*Ragtime* (E L Doctorow)
Mowgli	*The Jungle Book*

Matthew Mugg (catsmeat man)	*Doctor Dolittle*
Prince Myshkin	*The Idiot*
Mytyl	*The Blue Bird*
Nana	*Peter Pan*
Napoleon the Pig	*Animal Farm*
Nawab of Satipur	*Heat and Dust* (Ruth Prawer Jhabvala)
Nayland-Smith	*Fu Manchu*
Captain Nemo	*Twenty Thousand Leagues Under the Sea*
Norah Nesbit	*Of Human Bondage*
Gabriel Oak	*Far from the Madding Crowd*
Kitty Oblonsky	*Anna Karenina*
Julia O'Brien	*Nineteen Eighty-Four*
Mrs Ogmore-Pritchard	*Under Milk Wood*
O-Lan	*The Good Earth*
Oompa Loompas	*Charlie and the Chocolate Factory*
George Osborne	*Vanity Fair*
Mr Palmer	*Sense and Sensibility*
Doctor Pangloss	*Candide*
Panurge	*Gargantua and Pantagruel*
Sancho Panza	*Don Quixote*
Passepartout	*Around the World in 80 Days*
Paul Pennyfeather	*Decline and Fall*
Pertelote (the cock)	*The Nun's Priest's Tale*
Ronald Osprey Petrefact	*Ancestral Vices* (Tom Sharpe)
Petrovitch	*Crime and Punishment*
Alexander Petrovsky	*Russian Hide-and-Seek* (Kingsley Amis)
Phaedrus	*Zen and the Art of Motorcycle Maintenance*
Aunt Peturia	*Harry Potter books*
Piggy	*Lord of the Flies*
Billy Pilgrim	*Slaughterhouse-Five*
Captain Pissani	*Accidental Death of an Anarchist*
Maggie Pollitt	*Cat on a Hot Tin Roof*
Polynesia (parrot)	*Doctor Dolittle*
Ernest Pontifex	*The Way of All Flesh*
Jimmy Porter	*Look Back in Anger*
Claude (Mustard) Pott	created by P G Wodehouse
Harry Potter	*Harry Potter books*
Pozzo	*Waiting for Godot*
Ford Prefect	*The Hitchhiker's Guide to the Galaxy*
Private Prewitt	*From Here to Eternity*
Fanny Price	*Mansfield Park*
Dr Primrose	*The Vicar of Wakefield*
Miss Prism	*The Importance of Being Ernest*
Dr Proudie	*Barchester Towers*
Mrs Proudie	*Barchester Towers*
Hester Prynne	*The Scarlet Letter*
Pushmi-Pullyu (two-headed llama)	*Doctor Dolittle*
Roger Quaife	*The Corridors of Power*
Quasimodo	*The Hunchback of Notre Dame*
Queen of Hearts	*Alice's Adventures in Wonderland*
Adela Quested	*A Passage to India*
Quint	*The Turn of the Screw*
Ralph	*Lord of the Flies*
Elwin Ransome	*Perelandra* by C S Lewis
Raskolnikov	*Crime and Punishment*
Paul Ray	*The Second Mrs Tanqueray*
Red Queen	*Through the Looking Glass*
Ignatius J Reilly	*Confederacy of Dunces* (John K Toole)

Archie Rice	*The Entertainer*
Rico Bandello	*Little Caesar* (W R Burnett)
John Ridd	*Lorna Doone*
Sir Colenso Ridgeon	*The Doctor's Dilemma*
Rikki Tikki Tavi	*The Jungle Book*
Christopher Robin	*Winnie-the-Pooh*
Fanny Robin	*Far from the Madding Crowd*
Mr Rochester	*Jane Eyre*
Mildred Rodgers	*Of Human Bondage*
Rose of Torridge	*Westward Ho!*
Emma Rouault	*Madame Bovary*
Lady Rowena	*Ivanhoe*
Roxane	*Cyrano de Bergerac*
Nicholas Rubashov	*Darkness at Noon*
King Rudolf	*The Prisoner of Zenda*
Mrs Rushworth	*Mansfield Park*
Captain Charles Ryder	*Brideshead Revisited*
Iris Aroon St Charles	*Good Behaviour* (Molly Keane)
Sauron	*The Lord of the Rings*
Rose Sayer	*The African Queen*
Scamper	*The Secret Seven*
Basil Seal	*Black Mischief*
Amelia Sedley	*Vanity Fair*
John Francis Shade	*Pale Fire*
Shadowfax (horse)	*The Lord of the Rings*
Shalimar	*The Arabian Nights*
Becky Sharp	*Vanity Fair*
Anne Shirley	*Anne of Green Gables*
Napoleon Bonaparte Simpson	*The Spectacles* (Edgar Allan Poe)
Saleem Sinai	*Midnight's Children*
Dr Slop	*Tristram Shandy*
Obadiah Slope	*Barchester Towers*
Tyrone Slothrop	*Gravity's Rainbow*
Lennie Small	*Of Mice and Men*
Pavel Smedyakov	*The Brothers Karamazov*
George Smiley	created by John le Carré
Smith	*Loneliness of the Long Distance Runner*
Winston Smith	*Nineteen Eighty-Four*
Lady Sneerwell	*The School for Scandal*
Julian Sorel	*The Red and the Black*
Bertie Stanhope	*Barchester Towers*
Steerpike	*Titus Groan*
Alan Strang	*Equus*
Subtle	*The Alchemist*
Joseph Surface	*The School for Scandal*
Svengali	*Trilby*
Tadzio	*Death in Venice*
John Tanner	*Man and Superman*
Tatiana	*Eugene Onegin*
Lady Teazle	*The School for Scandal*
Professor George Tessman	*Hedda Gabler*
Becky Thatcher	*Tom Sawyer*
Henry Tilney	*Northanger Abbey*
Timmy	*The Famous Five*
Tinker Bell	*Peter Pan*
Tiresias	*Oedipus the King*
Toad	*The Wind in the Willows*
Uncle Toby	*Tristram Shandy*
Kenneth Marchal Toomey	*Earthly Powers*
Topsy	*Uncle Tom's Cabin*
Rev. John Treherne	*The Admirable Crichton*
Trigorin	*The Seagull*
Trilby (artist's model)	*Trilby*
Disko Troop	*Captains Courageous*
Sergeant Troy	*Far from the Madding Crowd*
Maggie Tulliver	*The Mill on the Floss*
Tom Tulliver	*The Mill on the Floss*

L
I
T
E
R
A
T
U
R
E

Tweedledum and Tweedledee	Through the Looking Glass	Mr Weston	Emma
Tyltyl	The Blue Bird	Reg Wexford	created by Ruth Rendell
Uncas	the Leatherstocking stories	Ann Whitefield	Man and Superman
Andrew Undershaft (arms maker)	Major Barbara	White Queen	Through the Looking Glass
		Mr Wickham	Pride and Prejudice
Jean Valjean	Les Misérables	Ashley Wilkes	Gone With the Wind
Piet van der Valk	created by Nicolas Freeling	Aaron Winthrop	Silas Marner
Harriet Vane	created by Dorothy L Sayers	Willy Nilly	Under Milk Wood
Uncle Vernon	Harry Potter books	Willy Wonka	Charlie and the Chocolate Factory
Vladimir	Waiting for Godot		
Gustav Von Aschenbach	Death in Venice	Nero Wolfe	created by Rex Stout
Voldemort	Harry Potter books	Emma Woodhouse	Emma
Count Vronsky	Anna Karenina	Ernest Wooley	The Admirable Crichton
Alice Walker	The Color Purple	Wormold	Our Man in Havana
The Walrus and the Carpenter	Through the Looking Glass	Jack Worthing	The Importance of Being Ernest
Wang Lung	The Good Earth	General Woundwort (rabbit)	Watership Down
Maria Ward	Mansfield Park	Charles Wykeham	Charley's Aunt
Water Rat	The Wind in the Willows	Yahoos (humans)	Gulliver's Travels
Ronald Weasley	Harry Potter books	Mary Yellan	Jamaica Inn
Captain Wentworth	Persuasion	Captain Yossarian	Catch-22
Sophia Western	Tom Jones	Falther Zossima	The Brothers Karamazov

Chaucer's Canterbury Pilgrims

1	The Knight's Tale		13	The Physician's Tale
2	The Miller's Tale		14	The Pardoner's Tale
3	The Reeve's Tale		15	The Shipman's Tale
4	The Cook's Tale		16	The Prioress's Tale
5	The Man of Law's Tale		17	Chaucer's Tale of Sir Thopas
6	The Wife of Bath's Tale		18	Chaucer's Tale of Melibeus
7	The Friar's Tale		19	The Monk's Tale
8	The Summoner's Tale		20	The Nun's Priest's Tale
9	The Clerk's Tale		21	The Second Nun's Tale
10	The Merchant's Tale		22	The Canon's Yeoman's Tale
11	The Squire's Tale		23	The Manciple's Tale
12	The Franklin's Tale		24	The Parson's Tale

NB: The Canterbury Tales was an unfinished collection of tales told in the course of a pilgrimage to Thomas Becket's shrine at Canterbury. In addition to the 22 story-tellers listed above, the party included a dyer, weaver, arrowmaker, haberdasher, carpenter, ploughman and guidesman, making a total of 29. Chaucer himself may be included as a pilgrim to give a definitive total of 30.

Charles Dickens's Characters (the Novels)

Barnaby Rudge: fifth published novel (1841), originally as serial in weekly magazine Master Humphrey's Clock

Benjamin   Member of the Prentice Knights with Simon Tappertit.

Chester, Edward   Son of John, eventually overcomes the opposition of his father and marries Emma Haredale. The couple relocate to the West Indies.

Chester, Sir John   Father of Edward, tries to prevent Edward's marriage to Emma Haredale. Becomes a member of Parliament. Killed in a duel by Emma's uncle Geoffrey.

Cobb, Tom   Friend of John Willet at the Maypole Inn.

Daisy, Solomon   Clerk and bell-ringer at the parish church in Chigwell. Friend of John Willet at the Maypole Inn. Daisy tells the story of Reuben Haredale's murder.

Dennis, Ned   Executioner at Tyburn, becomes involved in the Gordon Riots and is executed.

Fielding, Sir John   Blind half-brother of novelist Henry Fielding. Magistrate at Bow Street. Dickens has him at the scene of the Gordon Riots when, in fact, Fielding was on his deathbed at the time of the riots.

Gashford   Lord George Gordon's hypocritical secretary. He urges the rioters to exact revenge on Geoffrey Haredale, who had exposed his treacherous ways. He abandons Lord Gordon when the riots are suppressed by soldiers and becomes a government spy.

Gordon, Lord George   1751–93 Historical figure and leader of the Gordon (anti-Catholic) Riots of 1780.

Grip   Barnaby Rudge's pet raven, who carried his head on one side and seemed to embody the spirit of all-knowingness with his sound unwitting advice.

Grueby, John   Loyal servant of Lord George Gordon who tries to isolate Gordon from the rioters when the protest turns to violence.

Haredale, Emma   Daughter of the murdered Reuben and niece of Geoffrey. She eventually marries Edward Chester.

Haredale, Geoffrey   Brother of the murdered Reuben and uncle of Emma. Suspected of being responsible for the murder of his brother, he spends his life in pursuit of the real killer. A Catholic, his house is burned in the Gordon Riots. He fights a duel with Sir John Chester.

Haredale, Reuben Brother of Geoffrey, father of Emma. Murdered before the story begins.

Hugh Ostler at the Maypole. Joins the rioters in London and is later hanged. Revealed to be the son of Sir John Chester.

Langdale Kindly vintner and distiller in Holborn based on an historical figure. The Catholic Langdale shelters Geoffrey Haredale from the rioters. His home and warehouse are burned in the riots, his stores of spirits are consumed by the mob.

Miggs, Miss Maid in the Varden household. Comically allies with Martha Varden against her husband. Miggs aids the rioters when they attempt to capture Gabriel. She is discharged after the riots and becomes a jailer in a women's prison.

Parkes, Phil Friend of John Willet at the Maypole Inn.

Philips Constable who the Lord Mayor of London suggests might help to protect Langdale during the Gordon Riots.

Rudge, Barnaby Main character, a simple but good-hearted boy who unwittingly gets involved in the Gordon Riots when he falls into bad company. He is later arrested and sentenced to death but gains reprieve through the help of Gabriel Varden.

Rudge, Barnaby Sr Father of Barnaby and husband of Mary. He was the Steward at the Warren and murdered his employer, Reuben Haredale. He went into hiding after the murder and resurfaces years later trying to extort money from his wife. He is finally captured by Geoffrey Haredale.

Rudge, Mary Barnaby's mother, goes to great lengths to keep Barnaby away from his father who has murdered Reuben Haredale.

Stagg Blind member of the Prentice Knights with Simon Tappertit. He joins Barnaby Rudge Sr trying to extort money from Mary Rudge. Killed when he tries to run from officers arresting Hugh, Barnaby, and Rudge Sr.

Tappertit, Simon Locksmith Gabriel Varden's apprentice, who is in love with Gabriel's daughter, Dolly. He becomes a leader of the rioters during the Gordon Riots and during the fighting loses his slender legs, long his pride and joy.

Varden, Dolly Daughter of Gabriel and Martha, friend of Emma Haredale, loved by Joe Willet, whom she eventually marries.

Varden, Gabriel Honest locksmith and owner of the Golden Key where Simon Tappertit is apprenticed. Father of Dolly and long-suffering husband of Martha. He is a friend of Barnaby's mother and, after the Gordon Riots, helps clear Barnaby's name.

Varden, Martha Overbearing wife of Gabriel, mother of Dolly. A woman of 'uncertain temper' and a fanatical Protestant, her fanaticism is tempered after the riots when she witnesses the heroics of her husband.

Willet, Joe Son of John who resents his father's treatment of him. He joins the army and loses an arm in the American Revolution. Later he marries Dolly Varden. The couple become proprietors of the rebuilt Maypole Inn.

Willet, John Proprietor of the Maypole Inn and father of Joe. Father and son quarrel when John treats the adult Joe as a child and Joe leaves, joining the army. John witnesses the destruction of the Maypole by the rioters. He is later reconciled with his son.

Bleak House: ninth novel published in 20 monthly parts between March 1852 and September 1853

Badger, Bayham Doctor, cousin of Kenge, to whom Richard Carstone is apprenticed. Badger's wife Laura talks incessantly about her two former husbands, Captain Swosser and Professor Dingo.

Bagnet Family Musical, military family headed by Matthew, an old army friend of George Rouncewell. Bagnet's wife, the old girl, knows Matthew so well that he always calls upon her to supply his opinion. The Bagnet children, Quebec, Malta and Woolwich, are named after the bases where the family have been stationed. Matthew is guarantor to George's loan from Smallweed. When Smallweed calls in the debt George is forced to deliver a document Smallweed needs to help Tulkinghorn learn Lady Dedlock's secret.

Barbary, Miss Godmother who raises Esther Summerson. Later found to be Esther's aunt, the sister of Lady Dedlock.

Bogsby, James George 'Highly respectable' landlord of the Sol's Arms.

Boodle, Lord Politician who attends Sir Leicester Dedlock's social gatherings. Like Buffy he speculates on governmental machinations, including Coodle, Doodle and so on through the alphabet up to Quoodle.

Boythorn, Lawrence Friend of John Jarndyce whom Dickens based on writer Walter Savage Landor (1775-1864)

Bucket, Inspector Detective in charge of finding Tulkinghorn's murderer. After Lady Dedlock's disappearance Sir Leicester hires Bucket to find her. He later uncovers the will that is instrumental in clearing up the Jarndyce and Jarndyce Chancery case.

Buffy, the Right Hon. William MP who attends Sir Leicester Dedlock's social gatherings. Like Lord Boodle he speculates on governmental machinations, including Cuffy, Duffy and so on through the alphabet up to Puffy.

Carstone, Richard Ward of John Jarndyce and a party to the case of Jarndyce and Jarndyce. He marries Ada Clare and later dies when his health declines as the estate he hopes to acquire is consumed in court costs.

Chadband, Reverend Typical Dickensian hypocritical reverend, admonishing Jo in the spirit while he starves. Marries the former Mrs Rachael.

Clare, Ada Ward of John Jarndyce, friend of Esther Summerson, cousin of Richard Carstone, whom she marries but is soon widowed.

Darby Police constable on duty in Tom-all-Alone's, who accompanies Inspector Bucket and Mr Snagsby

Dedlock, Lady Honoria Wife of Sir Leicester Dedlock and, unknown to her husband, mother of Esther Summerson. A tainted woman who lives a life of lies. When Tulkinghorn, the family lawyer, learns the secret she runs away and is found dead by Esther at the gates of the cemetery in which Esther's father, Captain Hawdon, lies buried.

Dedlock, Sir Leicester Husband of Lady Dedlock, a baronet who is 20 years older than his wayward wife. Owner of Chesney Wold, and guardian of the status quo.

Dedlock, Volumnia Poor relation of Sir Leicester Dedlock. 'Rouged and necklaced' hanger-on at Chesney Wold.

Dingo, Professor Mrs Bayham Badger's second husband, who was said to have been 'of European reputation'.

Doyce, Daniel Smith and engineer who has

perfected the ultimate invention, involving a very curious secret process, but is constantly thwarted by the government in his attempt to get it developed. The invention goes unexplained.

Flite, Miss   A slightly mad old woman who is a regular attendant at the court of Chancery, expecting to receive a favourable judgement in a case that no one is sure has ever existed.

Gridley   Known as the 'Man from Shropshire' and another casualty of Chancery.

Grub, Mr   President of the Umbugology and Ditchwaterisics session at the second meeting of the Mudfog Association.

Grubble, Mr   Landlord of the Dedlock Arms, who never wore a coat except at church. His wife was a beautiful woman who broke her ankle but it never healed.

Guppy, William   Clerk for Kenge and Carboy. Proposes marriage to Esther Summerson, which she refuses. Guppy is involved in the investigation of Lady Dedlock's secret.

Hawdon, Captain   *See* Nemo.

Hortense, Mademoiselle   Lady Dedlock's French maid. She is dismissed in favour of Rosa and aids Tulkinghorn in discovering Lady Dedlock's secret. When Tulkinghorn spurns her she murders him. Hortense is based on Mrs Manning, a murderer whose execution Dickens witnessed in 1849.

Jarndyce, John   Owner of Bleak House and party in the Chancery suit of Jarndyce and Jarndyce. He adopts Esther Summerson, who becomes close friends with John's cousins, Ada Clare and Richard Carstone. John hates the lawsuit which has gone on for so long with no end in sight. Richard, however, becomes totally consumed by the case, hoping it will make him his fortune. This obsession causes Carstone and Jarndyce to suffer a falling out. Jarndyce falls in love with Esther and asked her to marry him, but although she originally consents, she subsequently falls in love with Allan Woodcourt.

Jellyby, Caroline (Caddy)   Neglected daughter of Mrs Jellyby and acts as her personal secretary ('I'm pen and ink to ma'). Caddy leaves home and marries Prince Turveydrop.

Jellyby, Mrs   Mrs Jellyby is involved in many causes and charities but neglects her large family. Dickens modelled Mrs Jellyby on Caroline Chisholm.

Jellyby, Peepy   Little brother of Caddy and son of Mrs Jellyby whose clothes were either too big or too small.

Jenny   Brickmaker's wife, befriended by Esther Summerson after Jenny's child dies. Later exchanges coats with Lady Dedlock, throwing Bucket off in his pursuit of Lady Dedlock as she flees following the revealing of her secret.

Jo   The crossing sweeper. When Jo shows Lady Dedlock the haunts of Captain Hawdon, lawyer Tulkinghorn has Jo kept moving from place to place. He befriends Esther Summerson at Bleak House and communicates smallpox to Charlie, and then Esther. Jo later dies at George's Shooting Gallery.

Jobling, Tony (Weevle)   Friend of Guppy who takes Nemo's room at Krook's after Nemo's death. Jobling and Guppy discover the spectacular death of Krook and are temporary celebrities, drinking for free at the Sol's Arms.

Kenge   Solicitor for John Jarndyce in the firm Kenge and Carboy. Known as 'Conversation Kenge'.

Krook   Drunken and illiterate proprietor of a rag and bottle shop. Known as the 'Lord Chancellor', Krook collects court documents. A will instrumental in the Jarndyce and Jarndyce court case is found among

his holdings by Mr Smallweed, who inherits Krook's possessions following his demise by spontaneous combustion. Krook is Mrs Smallweed's brother.

Lord Chancellor   A high legal figure in the Court of Chancery (of course).

Mooney   Beadle who is summoned to Krook's home on Hawdon's (Nemo's) death and gives evidence at the inquest.

Neckett, Mr   Sheriff's officer who arrests debtors and delivers them to Coavin's sponging house (temporary debtor's prison). Thus Skimpole gives Neckett the nickname 'Coavinses'. Neckett dies leaving three orphans: Charlotte (Charley), Emma and Tom.

Neckett, Charlotte (Charley)   Daughter of sheriff's officer Neckett. When her father dies Charley cares for her two younger siblings, Emma and Tom. Charley becomes Esther Summerson's maid, nursing Esther through smallpox. She later marries a miller.

Nemo   Alias of Captain Hawdon (Nemo is Latin for 'nobody'). Nemo is doing some law copying for Snagsby and is a boarder in Krook's rag and bottle shop when he dies of an opium overdose. He is later found to be the former lover of Lady Dedlock and the father of Esther Summerson.

Pardiggle, Mrs   Associate of Mrs Jellyby in her charitable works.

Quale, Mr   Part of Mrs Jellyby's circle of friends, although interested in Caddy Jellyby. Eventually weds Miss Wisk.

Rachael, Mrs   Esther Summerson's nurse. Later marries Reverend Chadband.

Rosa   Personal maid to Lady Dedlock after Hortense is dismissed. Marries Mrs Rouncewell's grandson.

Rouncewell, George   Son of the Dedlock's housekeeper Mrs Rouncewell. George ran away to join the army and cut himself off from his mother. After leaving the army he buys a shooting gallery in London with money borrowed from Smallweed. Smallweed pressures George to give over examples of Captain Hawdon's handwriting in order to help Tulkinghorn learn Lady Dedlock's secret. Charged with the murder of Tulkinghorn by Bucket, later George is exonerated of the crime and is reunited with his mother.

Rouncewell, Mrs   Longtime housekeeper of Chesney Wold, home of Sir Leicester Dedlock. Mother of George and another son, who is an important ironmaster in northern England.

Skimpole, Harold   Friend of John Jarndyce who claims he is a mere child who understands nothing of money, and through this smooth act manages to have everyone else pay his way through life. Dickens modelled Skimpole on Leigh Hunt.

Smallweed, Mr Joshua   Grandfather Smallweed is a usurer to whom Rouncewell owes money. Smallweed uses this leverage to obtain from George a sample of Nemo's handwriting in an attempt to help Tulkinghorn learn Lady Dedlock's secret. Also in the Smallweed family are grandmother – Krook's sister, at whom grandfather throws cushions when she mentions money – and the twin grandchildren, Bartholomew and Judy.

Snagsby   Law stationer near Chancery Lane who hires Nemo to do some copy work. Snagsby's wife is a zealous supporter of Rev. Chadband.

Squod, Phil   George Rouncewell's ugly little assistant at the shooting gallery. Formerly a travelling tinker.

Summerson, Esther   Principal character in the story and one of the narrators. She is brought up an orphan by her aunt, Miss Barbary. On her aunt's death she is adopted by John Jarndyce and becomes companions to his wards, Ada Clare and Richard Carstone. It is revealed that Esther is the illegitimate daughter of Captain Hawdon and Lady Dedlock. John Jarndyce falls in love with her and asks her to marry him. She consents out of respect for Jarndyce, but during the engagement she falls in love with Allan Woodcourt.

Tangle, Mr Barrister who is the leading living authority on the case of Jarndyce v Jarndyce having read nothing else since his schooldays.

Tulkinghorn, Mr Family lawyer to the Dedlocks. When he finds out Lady Dedlock's secret past, and tries to gain from it, he is murdered by Lady Dedlock's former maid, Hortense.

Turveydrop, Mr Owner of a dance academy on Newman Street and a 'model of deportment'.

Turveydrop, Prince Son of Mr Turveydrop, owner of a dance academy. Prince, named for the Prince Regent, gives dancing lessons and supports his father.

Vholes Richard Carstone's solicitor in Symond's Inn, recommended by Skimpole, who lures Richard deeper into the Chancery case that will ultimately lead to Richard's despair and death.

Wisk, Miss Feminist who eventually accepts Mr Quale as her husband.

Woodcourt, Allan A young surgeon who falls in love with Esther Summerson before going away as ship's doctor to India. On his return to England he learns that Esther is engaged to John Jarndyce. When Jarndyce learns that Esther is in love with Woodcourt he releases her to marry him.

A Christmas Carol: **Christmas book published December 1843 by Chapman and Hall; illustrated by John Leech; too short to be classified as a novel and perhaps more correctly categorised as a novella**

Belle Scrooge's former fiancée, whom he had forgotten until reminded by the Ghost of Christmas Past.

Cratchit, Bob Long-suffering clerk of Ebenezer Scrooge and father of Tiny Tim. Bob endures his employer's mistreatment until Scrooge, reformed by the visit of the three spirits, raises his salary and vows to help his struggling family.

Cratchit, Caroline Wife of Bob and mother of four children, Peter, Belinda, Martha and the youngest, Tiny Tim.

Cratchit, Tiny Tim Crippled son of Bob Cratchit. The forecast of Tim's death by the Ghosts of Christmas Present and Future is instrumental in Scrooge's reformation, after which Tim is afforded proper medical attention and is cured.

Dilber, Mrs A laundress whom Ebenezer Scrooge meets in his vision of Christmas Future, selling his belongings after his death.

Fan Scrooge's sister, mother of his nephew Fred. She has died before the story begins, but lives again in the 'shadows' shown to Scrooge by the Ghost of Christmas Past.

Fezziwig, Mr Scrooge was apprenticed to 'Old Fezziwig' after he left school. Scrooge visits his old employer with the Ghost of Christmas Past and is reminded of what a kind, generous man he was.

Fezziwig, Mrs Wife of the merchant 'Old Fezziwig'.

Fred Ebenezer Scrooge's nephew who is ignored in his invitation to Scrooge to attend Christmas dinner, but the Ghost of Christmas Present shows Fred saying some good-natured things about his uncle.

Ghost of Christmas Future Shows Scrooge the demise of Tiny Tim and of himself, leading to Scrooge's reformation.

Ghost of Christmas Past Shows Scrooge his lonely and difficult childhood and gradual decline into the miser he will become.

Ghost of Christmas Present Shows Scrooge the joy that Christmas brings, both at the poor household of the Cratchits and at the home of his nephew Fred.

Joe A fence (seller of stolen goods).

Marley, Jacob Scrooge's former partner, who died seven Christmas Eves ago. Jacob, in life, was a penny-pinching miser like Scrooge and is suffering for it in the afterlife. His ghost comes to haunt Scrooge, hoping to change Scrooge's life and therefore help him to avoid Marley's fate.

Scrooge, Ebenezer Probably Dickens' best-known character, the miserly Scrooge, with his familiar cry of 'Bah, Humbug!', is visited by the ghost of his former partner, Jacob Marley, who sends three more spirits in hopes of reforming Scrooge's heartless and penny-pinching ways. It is a tough assignment for them and he fights the inevitable, but he is eventually transformed into a benevolent humanitarian.

Topper, Mr A bachelor who is a guest at Fred's Christmas dinner.

Wilkins, Dick Scrooge's fellow apprentice at Mr Fezziwig's.

David Copperfield: **eighth novel published in 20 monthly parts between May 1849 and November 1850**

Babley, Richard *See* Mr Dick.

Bailey, Captain Army officer who makes David Copperfield jealous by dancing with the eldest Miss Larkins.

Barkis A carrier between Blunderstone and Yarmouth. He marries Clara Peggotty. Famous quote: 'Barkis is willing', denoting his desire to marry Peggotty.

Charley The 'dreadful old man' who owns a marine shop at Chatham. David Copperfield sells his jacket to Charley for eighteen pence.

Chestle, Mr Elderly Kentish hop-grower, who marries the eldest Miss Larkins.

Chillip, Doctor Attends Mrs Copperfield at David's birth.

Copperfield, Clara Mother of David Copperfield. A widow when David is born, she later is lured into marriage by Edward Murdstone, who destroys her spirit. She dies along with her newborn son while David is away at school.

Copperfield, David Main character and narrator of the story, modelled after Dickens's life. Begins life with his widowed mother and their maid, Peggotty. When his mother marries Mr Murdstone his life becomes miserable. He is sent to Creakle's school, where he meets Steerforth and Traddles. After the death of his mother he goes to work at Murdstone and Grinby and is lodged with the Micawbers. David runs away to live with his aunt Betsey Trotwood in Dover. He marries Dora Spenlow and then Agnes Wickfield.

Creakle, Mr Severe headmaster of Salem House Academy, where David first goes to school. He was based on William Jones, headmaster of Wellington Academy, which Dickens attended from 1825 to 1827.

Creakle, Mrs Mr Creakle's wife (unnamed). They have a daughter (unnamed also) who attracts David and Steerforth.

Crewler, Reverend Horace A curate in Devonshire. Father of Sophy Crewler.

Crewler, Sophy Daughter of the Reverend Horace Crewler and fiancée of Tommy Traddles.

Crupp, Mrs   David Copperfield's brandy-loving landlady at the Adelphi.

Dartle, Rosa   Companion to Mrs Steerforth, possessively attached to Steerforth, who has marked her face when a child by throwing a hammer in a fit of temper. Rosa hates Little Em'ly for running away with Steerforth.

Demple, George   A doctor's son and fellow pupil of David Copperfield at Salem House.

Dick, Mr   Kite-making, memoir-writing companion to Betsey Trotwood, who gives good advice but is not all there. Mr Dick's real name was Richard Babley but he was always referred to as plain Mr Dick. His insight is uncanny and he becomes a friend of David's.

Em'ly, Little   Mr Peggotty's niece and David's childhood friend. She is later engaged to Ham but is lured away by the charms of Steerforth. Mr Peggotty is heartbroken and searches for her, finally finding her when Steerforth tires of her and she leaves him. She later emigrates to Australia with her uncle.

Endell, Martha   A girl whose ruin foreshadows Little Em'ly's and helps to prevent her falling into the same trap. She eventually emigrates to Australia with Little Em'ly, Mr Peggotty and Mrs Gummidge.

Fibbitson, Mrs   Elderly inmate of the almshouses where Mrs Mell lives.

Gummidge, Mrs   Widow of Mr Peggotty's former partner in a boat concern, who had died very poor. She lives with Mr Peggotty and later emigrates to Australia with him.

Heep, Uriah   A hypocritical clerk of Mr Wickfield's who is continually citing his humbleness. He deviously plots to ruin Wickfield but is later undone by Mr Wilkins Micawber. On their first meeting, David describes him as 'a red-haired person – a youth of fifteen, as I take it now, but looking much older – whose hair was cropped as close as the closest stubble; who had hardly any eyebrows, and no eyelashes'.

Jip   Dora Spenlow's pet spaniel, whose name was short for Gypsy. He dies at David Copperfield's feet at the very moment of Dora's death.

Joram   Assistant to Mr Omer in his capacity as the Yarmouth undertaker, who, after marrying Omer's daughter, Minnie, becomes a partner in the business.

Jorkins, Mr   Partner of Francis Spenlow in the firm of proctors where David Copperfield is articled. Jorkins is largely unseen, although Spenlow finds it expedient to refer to his opinion to justify his own conduct.

Kidgerbury, Mrs   Domestic help of David and Dora, described as 'the oldest inhabitant of Kentish Town who went out charring'.

Larkins Family   Mr Larkins and his two daughters, the youngest Miss Larkins and the eldest Miss Larkins. The eldest Miss Larkins would be about 30 years old when David, as a young 17-year-old, had a crush on her.

Littimer   Manservant to Steerforth, involved in the concealment of the elopement of Steerforth and Emily. He is later guilty of embezzlement and is captured with the help of Miss Mowcher. David says of him: 'I believe there never existed in his station a more respectable-looking man. He was taciturn, soft-footed, very quiet in his manner, deferential, observant, always at hand when wanted, and never near when not wanted; but his great claim to consideration was his respectability'.

Maldon, Jack   Annie Strong's cousin, who goes to India; he may have been dishonourable in his intentions to Annie without her reciprocating.

Mealy Potatoes   Boy who works at Murdstone and Grinby's warehouse, whose name derived from the complexion of his skin.

Mell, Charles   Assistant schoolmaster at Salem House Academy. David Copperfield befriends Mell and finds that his mother lives in an almshouse, which he innocently relates to Steerforth. Steerforth uses this information to discredit Mell and have him dismissed. Mell later emigrates to Australia and becomes headmaster at Colonial Salem House Grammar School in Port Middlebay.

Micawber, Emma   Long-suffering wife of Mr Micawber, whom she swears she will never leave despite his financial difficulties. David describes her as 'a thin and faded lady, not at all young, with a baby at her breast. This baby was one of twins; and I may remark here that I hardly ever, in all my experience of the family, saw both the twins detached from Mrs Micawber at the same time. One of them was always taking refreshment'.

Micawber, Wilkins   David lodges at his home. Always in debt and waiting for 'something to turn up', he ends up in debtor's prison. On his release he has various occupations but is eventually employed at Mr Wickfield's office, where he exposes the deeds of Uriah Heep. In gratitude for this his debts are paid and he emigrates to Australia, where he prospers. Famous quote: 'Annual income £20, annual expenditure £19 19/6, result, happiness. Annual income £20, annual expenditure £20 0/6d, result, misery'.

Mills, Julia   Friend and confidante of Dora Spenlow and David's go-between during his courtship with Dora. She later goes to live in India.

Mowcher, Miss   Steerforth's friend; a dwarf who sells cosmetics; his relations with her give the reader insight into the pity that dominates Steerforth's character (which includes self-pity).

Murdstone, Edward   Second husband of Clara Copperfield whom David dislikes. He is a stern disciplinarian with a violent nature, who sends David off to Salem House School and later consigns him to the warehouse of Murdstone and Grinby.

Murdstone, Jane   The equally stern sister of Edward Murdstone who moves in with David and his mother after her marriage to Murdstone.

Omer, Minnie   Daughter of Mr Omer, who marries his foreman, Joram.

Omer, Mr   Draper, tailor, haberdasher and furnisher, who resided in Yarmouth and arranged the funeral of Clara Murdstone and her baby son.

Peggotty, Clara   David's devoted nurse and sister to Daniel Peggotty. After the death of David's mother she is discharged and marries Barkis. When Barkis dies she goes to live with David and Betsey Trotwood.

Peggotty, Daniel   Crotchety fisherman brother of Clara. He lives in an overturned boat on the beach at Yarmouth with Little Em'ly, Ham and Mrs Gummidge. When Em'ly abandons them to elope with Steerforth, Daniel vows to find her. Steerforth later leaves Em'ly and she is reunited with Daniel. At the end of the novel Daniel, Em'ly and Mrs Gummidge resettle in Australia.

Peggotty, Ham   Orphaned nephew of Daniel Peggotty and fiancé of Little Em'ly. A fisherman and boatbuilder. He drowns trying to rescue Steerforth. 'He was a huge, strong fellow of six feet high, broad in proportion, and round-shouldered; but with a simpering boy's face and curly light hair that gave him quite a sheepish look.'

Shepherd, Miss Boarder at Misses Nettingall's educational establishment and a brief early romantic fixation of young David Copperfield.

Spenlow, Dora Daughter of David's employer, Francis Spenlow. She and David are married and David tries to teach her to keep house, but she has no head for it. She becomes ill with an unspecified illness and dies young.

Spenlow, Francis Proctor at Doctor's Commons where David is apprenticed. David says of him: 'He was a little light-haired gentleman, with undeniable boots, and the stiffest of white cravats and shirt-collars. He was buttoned up mighty trim and tight, and must have taken a great deal of pains with his whiskers, which were accurately curled.'

Steerforth, James Friend of David, whom he often calls 'Daisy', at the Salem House school where his engaging charm makes him everyone's favourite. David later runs into him again in London and he accompanies David on a trip to Yarmouth, where he charms Little Em'ly into eloping with him. They go abroad and Steerforth soon tires of Em'ly and deserts her. He is later drowned in a shipwreck where Ham Peggotty, from whom Steerforth stole Em'ly away, dies trying to save him.

Strong, Annie Young wife of Dr Strong who has a strong affiliation to Jack Maldon.

Strong, Dr David's teacher who is writing a dictionary; his wife is much younger and David's observance of their relationship shapes his early doubts about marriage.

Tiffey, Mr Chief clerk at Spenlow and Jorkins, who tells David Copperfield of Mr Spenlow's accidental death.

Tipp Carman at Murdstone and Grinby's, who addressed David Copperfield as 'David' whereas the other workers referred to him as 'the little gent' or 'the young Suffolker'.

Topsawyer According to a story told to David Copperfield at the inn in Yarmouth, Topsawyer ordered a glass of ale like that ordered by David, drank it and fell dead.

Traddles, Tommy Downtrodden pupil with David Copperfield and Steerforth at Salem House. David's best friend and best man at David's wedding to Dora Spenlow. He later becomes a lawyer and marries Sophy Crewler.

Trotwood, Betsey David Copperfield's great aunt. David runs away from London, when he is installed at Murdstone and Grinby's warehouse, and goes to Dover to live with Betsey. She helps David get a start in life and, when she loses her fortune, goes to London to live with David.

Wickfield, Agnes Childhood friend of David Copperfield and daughter of Betsey Trotwood's lawyer. Becomes David's wife after the death of Dora.

Wickfield, Mr Father of Agnes and lawyer to Betsey Trotwood. His overindulgence of wine causes him to be vulnerable to the schemes of Uriah Heep, who becomes his partner and attempts to ruin him.

Yawler Friend of Tommy Traddles at Salem House 'with his nose on one side'.

***Dombey and Son*: seventh novel, published in monthly parts by Bradbury and Evans, from October 1846 to April 1848**

Bagstock, Joe Dombey's friend who sets him up with Edith Granger.

Blimber, Cornelia Prim and proper daughter of Dr and Mrs Blimber.

Blimber, Dr Pompous and pedantic headmaster of the school in Brighton where Paul Dombey was a pupil.

Blimber, Mrs Proud and devoted wife of Dr Blimber who feigned learnedness.

Bokum, Mrs Widow, and 'dearest friend' of Mrs MacStinger. She kept a close eye on Captain Bunsby on his way to his wedding to Mrs MacStinger in case he attempted escape.

Briggs One of Paul Dombey's fellow pupils at Doctor Blimber's school.

Brogley, Mr The 'sworn broker and appraiser' who took possession of The Wooden Midshipman after Solomon Gills fell into debt.

Brown, Conversation Acquaintance of Cousin Feenix, who was a 'four-bottle man at the Treasury Board'.

Brown, Good Mrs An ugly old rag and bone vendor and mother of Alice Marwood (Brown). She kidnaps Florence Dombey and steals her clothes.

Bunsby, Captain Jack Commander of the *Cautious Clara* and friend of Captain Cuttle, who marries Mrs MacStinger.

Burgess and Co. Mr Toots's tailors, who were 'fash'nable but very dear'.

Carker, Harriet Takes pity on Alice Marwood, who at first shuns her when she finds out that she is James Carker's sister but eventually becomes her friend. Harriet marries Mr Morfin.

Carker, James Manager at Dombey and Son who is employed to convey messages to Edith but not content with seducing her also contrives to bring the firm to ruin. Blessed with a set of extremely white teeth, he is the brother of John and Harriet Carker. He is eventually killed under a train whilst in flight from Dombey.

Carker, John Referred to as Carker the Junior, due to his lowly position, although in actual fact is older than James by nearly three years. John stole money from the firm but was kept on by Dombey, although his brother never lets him forget the indiscretion. John is devoted to his sister Harriet.

Chick, Louisa Sister of Paul Dombey Snr and friend to Mrs Tox. Her famous quote is 'make an effort'.

Chick, Mr Husband of Louisa Chick and therefore Mr Dombey's brother-in-law.

Cuttle, Captain Seafaring friend of Sol Gills, whose shop he cares for when Sol goes in search of his lost nephew, Walter Gay. His famous quote is 'When found, make a note of'.

Daws, Mary Young kitchen-maid in Paul Dombey's household.

Diogenes Dog owned by the Blimber family originally but given to Florence Dombey by Toots, with the Blimbers' blessing.

Dombey, Florence Neglected daughter of Paul Dombey and sister of little Paul, whom she nurses in his illness. She marries Walter Gay and eventually cares for her bankrupt and invalid father.

Dombey, Paul Jnr The long-hoped-for heir to the house of Dombey and Son. His mother dies at his birth, leaving him a frail and sickly child. His father sends him to Brighton in the care of Mrs Pipchin, hoping the sea air will bolster his failing health. He lives only six years.

Dombey, Paul Snr Powerful head of the House of Dombey shipping firm. He wants a son and when a daughter (Florence) is born he despises her. His second child, a son (Paul), is weak and sickly and dies a child. Paul's first wife dies with the birth of Paul Jnr and he remarries.

Feenix, Cousin Referred to as 'Cousin' although in actuality a Lord. He is nephew to Cleopatra Skewton.

LITERATURE

Flowers Cleopatra Skewton's personal maid.

Game Chicken, The Pugilist employed by Mr Toots in the 'cultivation of those gentle arts which refine and humanise existence'.

Gay, Walter Sol Gill's nephew, he is employed in the house of Dombey and Son. When Walter befriends Florence Dombey her father is displeased and sends him to the firm's branch in Barbados. The ship in which he sails is lost and Sol goes to search for him.

Gills, Solomon Uncle of Walter Gay and owner of a ship's chandler shop called 'The Wooden Midshipman'. When Walter's ship is lost at sea Solomon goes in search of him, leaving the care of the shop to his friend, Captain Cuttle.

Glubb, Old Old, crab-faced man who influences Paul Dombey with his stories of fish and sea monsters.

Granger, Colonel First husband of Edith Granger.

Granger, Edith Paul Dombey's second wife is the widow of Colonel Granger and the daughter of Mrs Skewton. She marries Dombey but does not love him. She later elopes with John Carker, a manager at Dombey's firm, to punish her husband.

Howler, the Rev. Melchisedech Officiates at the wedding of Captain Bunsby and Mrs MacStinger.

MacStinger, Mrs Captain Cuttle's irascible landlady, who is a widow with three children: Charles (known as Chowley), Juliana and Alexander.

Marwood, Alice Good Mrs Brown's daughter, who was John Carker's mistress and Edith's cousin.

Morfin, Mr The assistant manager of Dombey and Son who marries Harriet Carker.

Nipper, Susan Florence's companion who speaks her mind and later marries Mr Toots.

Pankey, Miss Young lady who is the only other boarder at Mrs Pipchin's when Paul Dombey lives there.

Perch, Mr Timid messenger in the firm of Dombey and Son.

Pipchin, Mrs Keeper of 'an infantine Boarding House of a very select description' in Brighton.

Rob the Grinder Robin Toodle, who has a miscreant youth then works at first for Captain Cuttle and then James Carker.

Skewton, Cleopatra Mother of Edith Granger. She dies after having a stroke.

Toodle, Mr Husband of Polly Toodle and father of Rob the Grinder. He is a stoker on the railway and later an engine driver.

Toodle, Polly Little Paul Dombey's nurse, known in the Dombey household as Richards, dismissed when she takes Paul to visit her family in a poorer section of London. She re-enters the story when Captain Cuttle asks her to look after Sol Gill's Shop 'The Wooden Midshipman'.

Toots, Mr A student at Dr Blimber's school who loves Florence but marries Susan.

Tox, Lucretia Close friend of Mrs Chick, Paul Dombey Snr's sister. She has hopes to marry Paul Snr after his first wife dies. Paul marries Mrs Granger instead, breaking Miss Tox's heart, but she stays loyal to him through later hardships.

Withers Mrs Skewton's page, who pushes her around in her wheelchair.

***Great Expectations*: thirteenth novel published in 36 weekly parts in 1860 / 1861**

Avenger, The Pip's name for Pepper, a servant boy hired by him. Pip has such a hard time finding things to keep him busy 'that I sometimes sent him to Hyde Park Corner to see what o'clock it was.'

Barley, Clara Herbert Pocket's secret sweetheart. She is secret because Herbert knows his mother would say she is below his 'station'. She's actually a sweet, fairy-like girl who takes care of her dying drunk of a father.

Barley, Old Bill Clara's father, an unseen 'sad old rascal' who used to be a ship's purser.

Biddy A kind, intelligent girl Pip's age who works for Mr Wopsle's great aunt at the school. Later, she comes to work for Joe, taking care of Mrs Joe Gargery. She loves Pip but he ignores her as his expectations are realised. When Pip eventually realises he loves her too it is too late as she has married Joe.

Black Bill A prisoner Wemmick recognises in Newgate Prison 'behind the cistern' when he takes Pip on a visit to the prison.

Brandley, Mrs Friend of Miss Havisham, whom Estella boarded with at Richmond.

Camilla Ageing relative of Miss Havisham who doesn't have an inch of love for the woman but is greedy for her money. She buzzes around Miss Havisham like a sycophantic fly. Matthew Pocket's sister.

Compeyson Con man who deceives Miss Havisham to get her money and then leaves her at the altar. He is an accomplice of Magwitch in the original prison break. He later exposes Magwitch and accidentally drowns when Magwitch is recaptured.

Drummle, Bentley Pip's fellow student at Matthew Pocket's. He marries Estella for her money and abuses her. He is killed when kicked by a horse that he has mistreated.

Estella Pip meets Estella at Satis House and falls in love with her, but she is cruel to him. Pip goes to London and becomes a gentleman and continues to adore Estella, but she warns him that she is incapable of love. She later marries Bentley Drummle, who mistreats her and she leaves him. Drummle dies and Estella and Pip meet two years later and vow to remain together.

Gargery, Joe Blacksmith, friend and adoptive father to Pip. Joe is also the husband of Pip's sister, Georgiana Mary, who mistreats him as badly as she does Pip. After his wife's death Joe comes to London and nurses Pip through an illness. Later he marries Pip's friend Biddy.

Gargery, Mrs Joe Wife of Joe Gargery and sister of Pip; a bitter, angry woman who brings up Pip 'by hand' – that is, she whips him whenever she can, often employing 'the tickler'. She is ultimately beaten to death by Orlick.

Georgiana Ageing relative of Miss Havisham.

Handel Herbert Pocket's affectionate name for Pip.

Havisham, Miss A very rich and grim old woman who lives in seclusion at Satis House. She is the adopted mother of Estella, whom she teaches to break men's hearts to avenge her own misfortune at being left at the altar by Compeyson years before. She continues to wear her wedding dress and even keeps the mouldy wedding cake. Pip goes to Miss Havisham's to play and meets and falls in love with Estella. Pip believes Miss Havisham is his secret benefactor as he goes to London and becomes a gentleman. She dies in a house fire.

Hubble, Mr and Mrs Simple, silly folks from Pip's village. Mr Hubble is a wheelwright.

Jaggers Lawyer who serves Miss Havisham and Magwitch, as he specialises in getting convicts light sentences. It is through Jaggers that Pip receives the benefits of the great expectations that he assumes are from Miss Havisham but in reality are from the convict Magwitch.

Magwitch, Abel   A convict whom Pip helps in the marshes after his escape from the prison ship. He is recaptured and transported to Australia, where he gains a fortune which he secretly uses to increase Pip's 'expectations'. He secretly returns to England as Provis and confronts Pip with the secret source of his good fortune. Magwitch is recaptured and dies before he can be executed. Magwitch is also the father of Estella.

Molly   Jaggers' housekeeper, Magwitch's wife and Estella's mother.

Orlick, Dolge   Joe Gargery's journeyman blacksmith, he quarrels with Mrs Joe and later attacks her, leaving her with injuries of which she later dies. He falls in with a bad lot and tries to murder Pip.

Pip (Philip Pirrip)   The narrator as well as the protagonist of the story. Pip is an orphan being raised by his sister, Mrs Joe Gargery, and her husband, Joe Gargery, a blacksmith.

Pocket, Herbert   Pip goes to London and meets Herbert, who he discovers is the 'pale young gentleman' with whom he fought at Miss Havisham's as a child. Pip and Herbert become best friends and share chambers at Barnard's Inn and at the Temple. Herbert helps teach Pip 'city manners'. Pip helps Herbert become a partner in the firm of Clarriker and Co., which enables Pocket to marry Clara Barley.

Pocket, Matthew   Father of Herbert and cousin of Miss Havisham. He is the only one of Miss Havisham's relatives who speaks honestly of her and has been banished from her presence. Matthew is Pip's tutor in London. He has no control over his large family and has a habit of pulling himself up by his hair in frustration. Pip tells Miss Havisham of Matthew's good character and she leaves him 4,000 pounds in her will. Matthew's wife, Belinda, is obsessed with social position, having been the daughter of a knight.

Pocket, Sarah   Ageing relative of Miss Havisham.

Pumblechook, Uncle   Joe's uncle, a well-to-do corn-chandler in the village. He considers himself upper-class and is actually a bombastic fool: 'A large hard-breathing middle-aged slow man, with a mouth like a fish, dull staring eyes, and sandy hair standing upright on his head, so that he looked as if he had just been all but choked'.

Raymond, Cousin   Ageing relative of Miss Havisham.

Skiffins, Miss   Very partial to the Aged Wemmick and eventually marries John Wemmick at a church in Camberwell Green.

Startop   Student and boarder of Matthew Pocket. He is a good friend of Pip's.

Trabb   Tailor who makes Pip a new suit of clothes before he goes to London, also in charge of the mourners at Pip's sister's funeral.

Trabb's Boy   Assistant to Trabb, the tailor, who terrorises Pip. He later leads Herbert to the limekiln to rescue Pip from Orlick.

Wemmick, John   Jagger's confidential clerk, friend of Pip (in private) who lives in a delightfully strange house with 'an aged parent'. 'A dry man, rather short in stature, with a square wooden face, whose expression seemed to have been imperfectly chipped out with a dull-edged chisel.'

Wemmick, 'The Aged'   Wemmick's elderly, and quite deaf, relative (commonly held to be Wemmick's father, but not described as such by Dickens). The Aged lives with Wemmick in his castle and is quite happy when you nod at him.

Whimple, Mrs   Landlady of the house where Old Barley and his daughter Clara had lodgings.

Wopsle's Great-Aunt   A 'ridiculous old lady' who runs the so-called school in town out of a cottage.

Wopsle, Mr   Parish clerk, friend of the Gargerys. He aspires to enter the Church and preach in the pulpit but instead becomes an actor with the stage name of Waldengarver. Pip sees him perform *Hamlet* in London.

Hard Times: tenth novel, written for *Household Words* from April to August 1854

Bitzer   A student in Gradgrind's school of hard facts. Later a light porter in Bounderby's bank.

Blackpool, Stephen   A worker in Bounderby's mill. His wife is a drunk and he befriends Rachael, but falls out with his employer and leaves to look for work elsewhere. He is accused of robbing the bank, and before his name is cleared he falls down a well and dies. Later he is cleared with the discovery that the robbery was committed by young Tom Gradgrind.

Bounderby, Josiah   Coketown Banker, mill owner and 'self-made man', abandoned as a child. His story is exposed as a sham when Mrs Pegler, his loving mother whom he has discarded, is found. Bounderby marries his friend Gradgrind's daughter Louisa and later discards her.

Childers, EWB   Young man who is an equestrian in Sleary's Circus. He marries Sleary's daughter Josephine and has a son, who at three years old is, according to Sleary, 'The Little Wonder of Thcolaththic Equitation'.

Gordon, Emma   Tightrope-walker, who comforts Sissy Jupe when her father vanishes.

Gradgrind, Louisa   Oldest daughter of Thomas and like him a victim of utilitarianism. She marries Bounderby, whom she doesn't love. She later leaves her husband and returns to her father.

Gradgrind, Adam Smith and Malthus   The two youngest sons of Thomas Gradgrind, named by their father after famous political economists.

Gradgrind, Mrs   Wife of Thomas and mother of their five children.

Gradgrind, Thomas   A mill owner retired from business and father of Louisa and Tom. He runs a school and emphasises the importance of facts and figures over fancy to his students and his children. By the end of the story he learns that facts and figures must be tempered by love and forbearance.

Gradgrind, Tom   Son of Thomas, nicknamed 'The Whelp' by Harthouse. He is employed at Bounderby's bank, from which he later steals; the blame is set on Stephen Blackpool. He finally leaves the country with the aid of Sleary and his circus troupe.

Harthouse, James   A Parliamentary candidate visiting Coketown, he befriends Tom Gradgrind in an attempt to seduce his sister Louisa, who is in an unhappy marriage to Bounderby. As a result of the attempted seduction Louisa runs home to her father, refuses to return to her husband, and is later disowned by him.

Jupe, Cecilia (Sissy)   Daughter of Signor Jupe, a clown in Sleary's Circus, who is deserted by her father and taken in by Gradgrind. She befriends Louisa.

Kidderminster   Small boy with an old face, who played the part of Childers's infant son in 'his daring vaulting act as the Wild Huntsman of the North American Prairies'.

M'Choakumchild   Schoolmaster in Gradgrind's school where fancy and imagination are discouraged in favour of hard facts.

Merrylegs   Signor Jupe's highly trained performing

LITERATURE

dog which makes its way to Sleary's Circus at Chester following Jupe's disappearance and dies at Sleary's feet.

Pegler, Mrs Revealed at the end of the story to be Bounderby's loving mother, exposing as a sham his claim to be a 'self-made man', who raised himself in the streets.

Rachael Friend of Stephen Blackpool, who loves her but cannot gain release from his drunken wife. She defends Stephen when he is accused of theft from the bank.

Slackbridge Rabble-rousing trade union delegate who persuades the Coketown millworkers to shun Stephen Blackpool.

Sladdery, Mr Fashionable London librarian who boasts of having a high connection.

Sleary Proprietor of Sleary's Circus. Speaks with a lisp ('People mutht be amuthed'). He helps Tom Gradgrind escape abroad after the bank robbery.

Sparsit, Mrs Housekeeper of Bounderby with aristocratic connections. She is a busybody, causing dissension between Bounderby and his wife Louisa Gradgrind.

Little Dorrit: eleventh novel, published in 1857

Bangham, Mrs Charwoman and messenger at the Marshalsea Prison who attended Mrs Dorrit at the birth of Amy.

Barnacle, Tite A senior official in the Circumlocution Office, where everything goes round in circles, and nothing ever gets done.

Barroneau, Madame The widow whom Rigaud married and was accused of murdering, although his version of events is that she leapt over a cliff-top after a violent quarrel.

Casby, Christopher Formerly town-agent to Tite Barnacle. His benevolent appearance leads to him being referred to as the 'last of the Patriarchs'. Father of Flora Finchina.

Charlotte The 'false young friend' of Miss Wade when they were schoolgirls.

Chivery, John and Young John The two sons of the turnkey at the Marshalsea. John Chivery was dubbed the 'sentimental son' whilst Young John loves Amy Dorrit and assists in finding her father's fortune.

Chivery, Mr and Mrs John John Chivery was a turnkey at the Marshalsea Prison who never opened his mouth 'without occasion'. His wife ran a tobacconist shop.

Clennam, Arthur Returns to England from abroad, where he has spent years with his father in the family business. On his father's death he falls out with his mother and gives up his share of the business. He befriends Amy Dorrit at the Marshalsea and becomes business partner to Daniel Doyce. After losing everything in a banking scam by Merdle he is himself imprisoned in the Marshalsea. His health fails and Amy cares for him in the prison. The novel ends with Arthur and Amy's marriage.

Clennam, Mrs Invalid mother of Arthur, with whom she has a falling-out over the family business. She avoids a blackmail scheme by Rigaud/Blandois when her tumbledown house tumbles down on him.

Dawes, Mary Nurse in the poor nobleman's household where Miss Wade was employed as a governess.

Dorrit, Amy Title character, daughter of William Dorrit, born in the Marshalsea debtors' prison. She works for Mrs Clennam and befriends Arthur. Her father inherits a fortune and they leave the prison and travel abroad. After her father's death she discovers that the fortune has been lost in a banking

scam. She nurses Arthur in the Marshalsea when his fortune is lost in the same banking scam, and eventually marries him.

Dorrit, Edward (Tip) Ne'er-do-well brother of Amy Dorrit and son of Edward Dorrit.

Dorrit, Fanny Sister of Amy. A dancer with social aspirations, Fanny marries Mr Sparkler, stepson of Mr Merdle. Fanny and Sparkler lose everything in the Merdle banking scam.

Dorrit, Frederick Brother of William, uncle of Fanny, Edward and Amy. He plays clarionet in a small-time theatre. He is due an inheritance but the knowledge is kept from him by the intrigues of Mrs Clennam.

Dorrit, William Father of Amy, Fanny and Edward, and long-time inmate of the Marshalsea debtors' prison. He inherits an estate and leaves the prison, travelling in style with his daughters. After his death Amy learns that his fortune has been lost in the Merdle banking scam.

Doyce, Daniel Inventor of an unspecified mechanical wonder which he is unable to get a patent for in the Circumlocution Office. He enters a partnership with Arthur Clennam, who loses the firm's money in the Merdle scandal. Doyce later sells the invention abroad and returns to liberate Arthur from the Marshalsea.

Finching, Flora Former sweetheart of Arthur Clennam who reappears 20 years later, 'grown to be very broad, and short of breath'. Dickens modelled the character of Flora after his own early sweetheart, Maria Beadnell, who reappears later in Dickens's life but not quite the way he remembered her.

Flintwinch, Mrs Jeremiah, née Affery Wife of Mrs Clennam's clerk who sees the evil doings of the house in dreams.

Flintwinch, Ephraim Brother of Jeremiah whose looks are almost identical.

Flintwinch, Jeremiah Mrs Clennam's clerk to whom her son Arthur relinquishes his share of the family business.

Gowan, Henry Arthur Clennam first meets him when Gowan is idly tossing stones into the Thames. The always affable Henry marries Pet Meagles.

Haggage, Doctor Prisoner who attends at the birth of Amy Dorrit.

Jenkinson Messenger in the Circumlocution Office.

Lion Henry Gowan's Newfoundland dog, who dies by poison probably administered by Blandois.

Maggy Simple-minded granddaughter of Mrs Bangham.

Meagles, Mr and Mrs Kind-hearted retired banker Mr Meagles, his wife and daughter Minnie 'Pet', befriend Arthur Clennam, Amy Dorrit and Daniel Doyce. The Meagleses adopt Tattycoram from the Foundling Hospital.

Merdle, Mr and Mrs Mr Merdle is an unscrupulous banker. Investing in his enterprises ruins the Dorrits, Arthur Clennam and others. Merdle commits suicide when his fraud is uncovered. Mrs Merdle is the mother of Mr Sparkler by a previous marriage.

Mr F's Aunt Companion to Flora Finching (aunt to her late husband) and one of the funniest characters in Dickens. Dickens describes her as 'an amazing little old woman, with a face like a staring wooden doll too cheap for expression, and a stiff yellow wig perched unevenly on the top of her head, as if the child who owned the doll had driven a tack through it anywhere, so that it only got fastened on'. She has a great propensity for uttering totally nonsensical barbs.

Pancks Clerk and rent collector for Mr Casby. He assists in finding William Dorrit's fortune. A comical character who does everything 'with a puff and a snort'.

Plornish, Mr   A simple, good-natured plasterer.

Rigaud/Blandois   Villain of the novel. Rigaud attempts to blackmail Mrs Clennam and has her house fall and crush him for his efforts.

Slingo   Dealer in horses who vowed to give Tip Dorrit 'a berth' on his release from the Marshalsea.

Sparkler, Mr Edmund   Son of Mrs Merdle by her first marriage. Edmund is one of the Lords of the Circumlocution Office and marries Fanny Dorrit.

Tattycoram/Harriet Beadle   Adopted by the Meagleses from the Foundling Hospital, Harriet is given the name Tattycoram and is maid to the Meagleses daughter, Pet. She exhibits fits of temper and is counselled by Mr Meagles to 'count five and twenty'.

Wade, Miss   Dark figure who lures Tattycoram away from the kind-hearted Meagles.

Wobbler, Mr   Member of the Secretarial Department of the Circumlocution Office.

Martin Chuzzlewit: sixth novel published in 1843–4 as The Life and Adventures of Martin Chuzzlewit

Bailey, Christopher   Impish 'small boy with a large red head, and no nose to speak of' who worked as boot-boy and porter at Mrs Todgers's Commercial Boarding House.

Brick, Jefferson   War correspondent on the *New York Rowdy Journal*.

Buffum, Oscar   One of the deputation who arranges the 'le-vee' in honour of Elijah Pogram at the National Hotel in an American town.

Bullamy   Porter at the offices of Montague Tigg's fraudulent Anglo-Bengalee Disinterested Loan and Assurance Company. Following Tigg's murder Bullamy and Crimple make off with the firm's money.

Chiggle   An 'immortal' American sculptor who made a statue of Elijah Pogram.

Choke, General Cyrus   American swindler, who introduces Martin Chuzzlewit to Scadder.

Chollop, Major Hannibal   American 'worshipper of freedom', who meets Martin Chuzzlewit and Mark Tapley in Eden.

Chuzzlewit, Jonas   Son of Anthony Chuzzlewit, he kills his father to gain his inheritance, marries Mercy Pecksniff and, through his cruelty, breaks her spirit. He murders Tigg and, on the way to prison, kills himself.

Chuzzlewit, Martin   Grandson of Martin Sr. He has a falling-out with his grandfather over his love for Mary Graham. Becomes a pupil of Pecksniff who, because of pressure from the grandfather, throws young Martin out.

Chuzzlewit, Old Martin   Grandfather of Martin, cousin of Pecksniff, brother of Anthony, uncle of Jonas. Martin is suspicious of his hypocritical relatives, chiefly Pecksniff, whose hypocrisy Martin exposes and is reconciled with his grandson, young Martin.

Crimple, David   Officer at the offices of Montague Tigg's Anglo-Bengalee Disinterested Loan and Assurance Company. He and Bullamy steal the firm's money after Tigg's murder.

Diver, Colonel   Editor of the *New York Rowdy Journal*.

Dunkle, Doctor Ginery   A 'gentleman of great poetical elements' who acts as the spokesman of the committee that welcomes Elijah Pogram.

Fips, Mr   Lawyer in Austin Friars, who was secretly commissioned by Old Martin to employ Tom Pinch to arrange and catalogue books at £100 per year.

Gamp, Sarah   A midwife, nurse and 'layer-out' of the dead. She is a fixture in the story and appears to be much more concerned with her own creature comforts than those of her patients.

Gill, Mrs   Client of Mrs Gamp, who could calculate exactly when the birth of her babies was due.

Graham, Mary   Mary cares for old Martin Chuzzlewit with the knowledge that she will not profit from Martin's wealth after his death. Chuzzlewit's grandson Martin falls in love with Mary, which displeases his grandfather, who disinherits young Martin but eventually gives them his blessing to marry.

Harris, Mrs   Sarah Gamp's alluded-to but unseen friend. Betsey Prig expresses disbelief as to her existence.

Hominy, Mrs   Pretentious so-called philosopher and authoress whom Martin Chuzzlewit meets in America.

Izzard, Mr   Member of the committee that welcomes Elijah Pogram.

Jinkins, Mr   Boarder at Mrs Todgers's who, although talking of splendid things, was a fish-salesman's book-keeper.

Jobling, Doctor John   Doctor who attended Anthony Chuzzlewit and Lewsome and who became the medical officer of the Anglo-Bengalee Disinterested Loan and Life Assurance Company.

Kedgick, Captain   Landlord of the National Hotel in an American town.

Kettle, La Fayette   Secretary of the Watertoast Association, whom Martin Chuzzlewit encounters on his travels to Eden.

Lewsome   Young surgeon attended by Doctor Jobling and nursed by Sarah Gamp during a serious illness.

Lupin, Mrs   Landlady of the Blue Dragon who eventually marries Mark Tapley.

Mould, Mr   Undertaker whose countenance often belied the seriousness of his job.

Nadgett   Inquiry agent employed at a salary of £1 per week by Tigg's fraudulent company. Discovers Jonas Chuzzlewit's intention to poison Anthony Chuzzlewit and later Jonas's guilt in the murder of Tigg, by fishing his blood-stained clothes from the river.

Pecksniff, Seth   Sanctimonious surveyor and architect, and one of the biggest hypocrites in fiction. A cousin of old Martin Chuzzlewit and the father of Mercy and Charity.

Pinch, Tom   Devoted admirer and assistant to Pecksniff. A kindly, sweet-tempered fellow, completely blind to Pecksniff's hypocrisy despite a multitude of evidence of it. He finally becomes aware of Pecksniff's true character and is dismissed.

Pogram, Hon. Elijah   American Congressman who meets Martin Chuzzlewit on a steamboat on the way back from Eden.

Prig, Mrs Betsey   Nurse who is a friend and colleague of Sarah Gamp and who comically doubts the existence of Mrs Harris.

Scadder, Zephania   Agent of the Eden Land Corporation who is introduced to Martin Chuzzlewit by Cyrus Choke.

Tacker   Chief mourner for Mr Mould the undertaker.

Tamaroo   Slow-witted old woman who replaced Young Bailey at Todgers's.

Tapley, Mark   Ostler at the Blue Dragon Inn and servant to young Martin Chuzzlewit. He accompanies Martin to America and later marries Mrs Lupin, the Blue Dragon's landlady. The inn is renamed The Jolly Tapley.

Tigg, Montague   Disreputable adventurer, who changes his name to Tigg Montague. Tigg discovers the murderous intentions of Jonas Chuzzlewit via his agent, Nadgett, and is killed by Jonas.

Todgers, Mrs   Proprietor of a Commercial Boarding House in London in which she welcomes Charity and Mercy Pecksniff despite her rule of only receiving gentlemen boarders.

Wolf, Mr   One of Montague Tigg's guests at a dinner attended by Jonas Chuzzlewit.

The Mystery of Edwin Drood: fifteenth novel unfinished at Dickens's death in 1870

Bazzard   Clerk to Hiram Grewgious who writes an unproduced tragedy, 'The Thorn of Anxiety'. Grewgious admits that Bazzard has a strange power over him.

Billickin, Mrs   London landlady of Rosa Bud and her chaperone, Miss Twinkleton. She insists on using the title 'Billickin' in business matters, fearing being taken advantage of because she is a woman. Mrs Billickin and Miss Twinkleton take a comical dislike for one another.

Brobity, Miss   The owner of a school in Cloisterham. Miss Brobity married Mr Sapsea.

Bud, Rosa   Betrothed to Edwin Drood in childhood, they later agree that they cannot marry. Edwin disappears and John Jasper declares his love for Rosa. In terror she flees to London to her guardian, Grewgious. 'The pet pupil of the Nuns' House is Miss Rosa Bud, of course called Rosebud; wonderfully pretty, wonderfully childish, wonderfully whimsical'.

Chinaman, Jack   Keeper of a London opium den in competition with Princess Puffer's den.

Crisparkle, Septimus   Minor canon of Cloisterham Cathedral. 'Mr Crisparkle, Minor Canon, early riser, musical, classical, cheerful, kind, good-natured, social, contented, and boy-like'. He takes Neville Landless as a pupil and helps Neville flee to London when suspicion is cast on him for the disappearance of Edwin Drood.

Datchery, Dick   Mysterious visitor to Cloisterham whose 'white head was unusually large, and his shock of white hair was unusually thick and ample'. Datchery keeps an eye on John Jasper after the disappearance of Edwin Drood. The true identity of Datchery is one of the most contested points of the uncompleted mystery. It is widely believed that Datchery is one of the characters in the book in disguise; most likely candidates include Neville, Bazzard, Tartar, Grewgious, Helena, or even Edwin Drood himself.

Deputy (Winks)   Boy hired by Durdles to throw stones at him when he is wandering drunk at night. 'Sometimes the stones hit him, and sometimes they miss him, but Durdles seems indifferent to either fortune. The hideous small boy, on the contrary, whenever he hits Durdles, blows a whistle of triumph through a jagged gap, convenient for the purpose in the front of his mouth, where half his teeth are wanting; and whenever he misses him, yelps out "Mulled agin!"'

Drood, Edwin   He is an orphan and had been betrothed by his father to Rosa Bud since early childhood. Later Edwin and Rosa rebel against the arrangement. Rosa is also wooed by Edwin's uncle John Jasper. Edwin turns up missing and his watch is found in the river. Jasper hints suspicion of Neville Landless in the disappearance when the novel stops short with the death of Dickens in 1870.

Durdles   Drunken stonemason who engraves tombstones for Cloisterham Cathedral. John Jasper is interested in Durdles's ability to tap on the tombs and discover their contents. Durdles hires Deputy to throw stones at him when he catches him wandering about drunk at night. No man is better known in Cloisterham.

Giggles, Miss   Pupil at Miss Twinkleton's school who is described as 'so deficient in sentiment' that she professes to pull faces at any young man paying homage.

Grewgious, Hiram   Guardian of Rosa Bud. He is upset at John Jasper's advances to Rosa and finds her lodging in London at an apartment owned by Mrs Billickin. He later investigates the disappearance of Edwin Drood and is suspicious of Jasper. 'An angular man with no conversational powers' is how he describes himself.

Honeythunder, Luke   Loud, overbearing philanthropist and guardian of Neville and Helena Landless.

Jasper, John   Uncle of Edwin Drood who has an opium habit. He cares for his nephew but harbours secret feelings for Edwin's fiancée Rosa Bud. Edwin disappears and the story ends prematurely with Dickens's death, but many believe that it was Jasper who killed Edwin Drood. 'Mr Jasper is a dark man of some six-and-twenty, with thick, lustrous, well-arranged black hair and whiskers. He looks older than he is, as dark men often do. His voice is deep and good, his face and figure are good, his manner is a little sombre.' He is said to be capable of mesmerism.

Landless, Helena   Twin sister of Neville who, as the story ends prematurely, is falling in love with Canon Crisparkle.

Landless, Neville   Twin brother of Helena. He and his sister are brought to Cloisterham by their guardian, Mr Honeythunder. Neville is attracted to Rosa Bud and, being set up by Jasper, quarrels with Edwin Drood. After Drood's disappearance Jasper casts blame on Neville, who has no alibi and flees to London with his sister.

Puffer, Princess   Old hag who runs the London opium den that John Jasper frequents.

Sapsea, Thomas   Pompous auctioneer turned mayor of Cloisterham. 'The purest Jackass in Cloisterham.'

Tartar   Retired navy man and friend of Crisparkle. He befriends Neville in London and works with Grewgious and Crisparkle in protecting Neville from John Jasper.

Tisher, Mrs   Miss Twinkleton's assistant at the school for girls at Nun's House.

Tope, Mr   Chief verger and showman of Cloisterham Cathedral. His wife acts as John Jasper's housekeeper.

Twinkleton, Miss   Principal of a school for girls at Nun's House in Cloisterham (Cloisterham was based on Rochester) where Rosa Bud and Helena Landless attend. She is assisted by Mrs Tisher. Miss Twinkleton later becomes Rosa's chaperone in London.

Nicholas Nickleby: third published novel (1839) as *The Life and Adventures of Nicholas Nickleby*

Alphonse   Mrs Wititterly's page whose appearance belied his name.

Bolder   Pupil at Dotheboys Hall whose father was 'two pound ten short' in the payment of his fees.

Bonney, Mr   The promoter of The United Metropolitan Hot Muffin and Crumpet Baking and Punctual Delivery Company.

Bravassa, Miss   Beautiful actress in Mr Crummles's company.

Bray, Madeline   Cares for her selfish invalid father

who tries to sell her in marriage to his creditor Arthur Gride, assisted by Ralph Nickleby. Her father dies and the scheme is exposed. She marries Nicholas at the end of the story.

Bray, Walter Father of Madeline whose sudden death on the morning of his daughter's sham of a wedding day prevents the marriage.

Brooker, Mr Ralph Nickleby's former clerk, who took charge of his employer's son and named him Smike. On returning to England following an eight-year sentence of transportation he reveals Smike's real identity.

Browdie, John Bluff Yorkshire corn factor and stalwart friend of Nicholas Nickleby and Smike. He marries Matilda Price.

Browndock, Miss Mr Nickleby's cousin's sister-in-law.

Bulph, Mr Pilot in whose house the Crummleses live when they visit Portsmouth.

Cheeryble Brothers Charles and Edwin (Ned). Benevolent businessmen who employ and befriend Nicholas Nickleby and his family.

Cheeryble, Frank Nephew of the Cheeryble twins, who marries Kate Nickleby.

Chowser, Colonel Disreputable acquaintance of Ralph Nickleby. He was a Colonel 'of the Militia . . . and the race-courses'.

Crummles, Mr Vincent Manager of a touring acting company who hires Nicholas Nickleby and Smike and becomes their friend.

Dibabs, Jane Former acquaintance of Mrs Nickleby, who cites her as an example of a woman who 'married a man who was a great deal older than herself'.

Dick Blind blackbird owned by Tim Linkinwater and kept in the Cheeryble Brothers' counting-house.

Folair, Mr Pantomimist in Mr Crummles's touring company.

Gallanbile, Mr MP who seeks a cook through the General Agency Office which Nicholas also uses.

Gride, Arthur Old miserly character who tries to buy a marriage to Madeline Bray with the help of her father.

Grudden, Mrs General helper at the Crummles's touring company who could turn her hand to anything.

Hawk, Sir Mulberry Friend of Ralph Nickleby who has lecherous designs on Kate and assaults her. Hawk is a man of fashion and a gambler. He shoots and kills Lord Frederick Verisopht in a duel.

Kenwigs Family Mr Kenwigs was a turner in ivory and he and his family lodged in the same house as Newman Noggs.

Knag, Miss Madame Mantalini's forewoman who ultimately becomes the proprietor of the business.

Knag, Mortimer Brother of Miss Knag, who works as an ornamental stationer and small circulating library keeper in a street off the Tottenham Court Road.

La Creevy, Miss Miniature painter in the Strand. The Nicklebys lease lodging from her briefly and she becomes their faithful friend. In the end she marries the Cheeryble Brothers' old clerk, Tim Linkinwater.

Ledbrook, Miss Actress in Mr Crummles's touring company and a friend of Miss Snevellici.

Lillyvick, Mr Collector of water rates, and Mrs Kenwig's uncle, who marries Henrietta Petowker.

Linkinwater, Tim Faithful clerk to the Cheeryble Brothers and friend of the Nicklebys. He marries Miss La Creevy.

Mantalini, Madame Milliner and dressmaker who employs Kate Nickleby. Her business is ruined by her husband's extravagances and is transferred to Miss Knag.

Mantalini, Mr Husband of Madame Mantalini who ultimately separates from her and becomes bankrupt and imprisoned where he is taken by a laundress to turn a mangle in a cellar. 'My life is one demd horrid grind.'

Nickleby, Kate Sister of Nicholas. She is placed by her uncle, Ralph Nickleby, with Madame Mantalini. She is the object of the undesirable attentions of some of the evil-minded clients of her uncle, who is using her to his advantage.

Nickleby, Mrs Mother of Nicholas and Kate. Absent-minded and self-absorbed, she continues to 'put on airs' even in the reduced situation of her family after the financial ruin and death of her husband. The character is heavily drawn from Dickens's mother.

Nickleby, Nicholas Brother to Kate, nephew of Ralph, and the principal character of the story. Hoping to provide support for his mother and sister after the death of his father, he turns to his uncle Ralph for assistance.

Nickleby, Ralph Uncle to Nicholas and Kate (and later we find, father of Smike). A rich and miserly moneylender who feigns to help his late brother's family but, in reality, tries to humiliate Nicholas and use Kate to his own advantage.

Noggs, Newman Once a well-to-do gentleman but he squanders his money and is reduced to serving Ralph Nickleby as clerk. He befriends Nicholas and eventually helps him escape the designs of Ralph.

Petowker, Miss Henrietta Actress at the Theatre Royal, Drury Lane, who meets Mr Lillyvick at the Kenwigs' home and marries him.

Price, Matilda Miller's daughter, who marries John Browdie.

Pupker, Sir Matthew The chairman of The United Metropolitan Hot Muffin and Crumpet Baking and Punctual Delivery Company.

Sliderskew, Peg Arthur Gride's housekeeper who steals a box of documents from her master, including a will relating to Madeline Bray's inheritance. Peg is apprehended for the theft and sentenced to transportation.

Smike Abandoned at Dotheboys Hall in the care of the evil Squeers, Smike is mistreated for years before being rescued by Nicholas. He later dies from the treatment he received as a child. After his death it is discovered that he was Ralph Nickleby's son.

Snevellici, Miss Actress in Mr Crummles's touring company and a friend of Miss Ledbrook.

Squeers, Wackford Proprietor of Dotheboys Hall, he took in boys who were not wanted by their families and mistreated them. Nicholas Nickleby becomes his assistant master but sees the way he treats his charges, gives him a sound thrashing, and leaves.

Timberry, Snittle Actor who presides at Vincent Crummles's farewell dinner before the family leaves for America.

Tix, Tom Broker who takes possession of the Mantalinis' business.

Verisopht, Lord Frederick Young nobleman in Ralph Nickleby's circle who is killed in a duel with Sir Mulberry Hawk.

Witterly, Henry and Julia Married couple living in Cadogan Place, Sloane Street. Kate Nickleby was employed briefly as Mrs Witterly's companion.

Wrymug, Mrs A 'genteel female' who is a client at the General Agency Office.

The Old Curiosity Shop: **fourth published novel in 1841**

Barbara 'Little servant-girl', 'very tidy, modest and demure, but very pretty too'.

Brass, Sally Sister and partner of Quilp's unscrupulous attorney, Sampson Brass. She is the mother of the Marchioness, the below-stairs maid.

Brass, Sampson 'An attorney of no good repute', Brass served as Daniel Quilp's lawyer. He helps Quilp get the Curiosity Shop from Nell's grandfather and when he tries to help Quilp frame Kit Nubbles he is undone with the help of his clerk Dick Swiveller.

Cheggs, Mr and Miss Friends of Sophy Wackles, the sweetheart of Dick Swiveller. Mr Cheggs is a market gardener, who eventually marries Sophy, much to the chagrin of Dick.

Codlin and Short Proprietors of a travelling Punch and Judy show that Nell and her grandfather meet on their travels through the English countryside.

Edwards, Miss Student-teacher at Miss Monflathers' Boarding and Day Establishment who lodged for nothing but also received no pay.

Foxey Revered father of Sally and Sampson Brass. His maxim was 'always suspect everybody'.

Grinder, Mr A travelling entertainer who followed behind a couple in Highland dress on stilts, with a drum on his back.

Jarley, Mrs Proprietor of a travelling waxworks who employs Nell and her grandfather. When the grandfather schemes to steal from Mrs Jarley, in order to support a gambling habit, Nell persuades him that they should take to the road again.

Jiniwin, Mrs Mrs Quilp's mother, who has many unsuccessful verbal run-ins with Daniel Quilp.

Monflathers, Miss Head of the Boarding and Day Establishment in the town where Mrs Jarley sets up her waxwork exhibition.

Nell's Grandfather Owner of the Old Curiosity Shop. He has a secret gambling habit, hoping to make a fortune for his granddaughter. He borrows money to gamble from Quilp. When he cannot pay he takes Nell and escapes London to the country. When Nell dies he is heart-broken.

Nubbles, Kit Kit is shop boy at the Curiosity Shop owned by Nell's grandfather.

Quilp, Daniel An evil dwarf who lends money to Nell's grandfather who gambles it away and flees London with Nell in an attempt to avoid Quilp. Quilp attempts to find the pair as they travel through the country. Later Quilp is pursued by the police and, lost in the fog, he drowns in the Thames.

Single Gentleman, The Mysterious lodger of the Brasses who is trying to find Nell and her grandfather. He is revealed to be the brother of the grandfather and finds the pair shortly before his brother's death.

Slum, Mr Tallish gentleman who composes verses to advertise products for a fee.

Sweet William Travelling conjuror met by Little Nell and her grandfather at the Jolly Sandboys.

Swiveller, Dick Friend of Fred Trent who has designs to marry Nell Trent but is encouraged to wait until Nell has inherited her grandfather's money. When Nell and her grandfather leave London Swiveller is befriended by Quilp, who helps him gain employment.

The Marchioness Dick Swiveller's nickname for the little servant kept locked below stairs by the Brasses. Swiveller later marries her.

Trent, Fred Nell's brother, a gambler, would like to get his hands on his grandfather's money through his friend Dick Swiveller.

Trent, Nelly Known as Little Nell, she is the principal character in the story. She lives with her grandfather, when he falls into the clutches of Daniel Quilp she helps him escape London. The hardships endured during their wanderings are too much for the delicate Nell.

Wackles, Sophy First love of Dick Swiveller. Swiveller reluctantly leaves her and enters into a scheme, hatched by Nell's brother Fred Trent, to marry Nell and inherit the grandfather's money. Sophy marries Cheggs, a market gardener.

Whisker Self-willed pony who, from being the most obstinate and opinionated pony on the face of the earth, was, in Kit Nubbles's hands, the meekest and most tractable of animals.

Oliver Twist: second published novel, originally in *Bentley's Miscellany* between February 1837 and April 1839 in 24 monthly instalments

Artful Dodger, The *See* Jack Dawkins.

Bates, Charley Member of Fagin's band of thieves. He mends his ways after Fagin is captured.

Bedwin, Mrs A 'motherly old lady' who is Mr Brownlow's housekeeper.

Betsy (Bet) Prostitute and friend of Nancy. Goes mad after identifying Nancy's body.

Blathers Bow Street Runner (London policeman) who, along with Duff, investigates the attempted robbery of the Maylie home.

Brittles Despite being over 30 years old, described as a 'lad of all work' residing at Mrs Maylie's.

Brownlow, Mr Adopts Oliver after he is charged with pickpocketing. He later establishes Oliver's true identity.

Bull's-eye Bill Sikes's white shaggy dog who falls to his death at the same time as Sikes accidentally hangs himself on Jacob's Island, Bermondsey.

Bumble, Mr Beadle at the workhouse where Oliver is born. He mistreats the residents in his care and becomes the symbol of Dickens's distaste for the workhouse system. Bumble names the foundling Twist due to his coming next alphabetically after the last 'Swabble'. In fact he says the next one will be 'Unwin' and then 'Vilkins'. He marries Mrs Corney and later is disgraced and becomes a resident in the same workhouse. Famous quote when told by Mr Brownlow that the law supposes that your wife acts under your directions: 'If the law supposes that, then the law is a ass . . . a idiot.'

Charlotte Maidservant to Mr and Mrs Sowerberry. She is very partial to Noah Claypole, whom she feeds with oysters.

Chickweed, Conkey According to Blathers, he was a publican who carried out a fake burglary on himself, althought the crime was detected by Jem Spyers.

Chitling, Tom Member of Fagin's gang and Betsy's sweetheart.

Claypole, Noah Assistant at Sowerberry's with whom Oliver fights. Noah later joins Fagin's band and spies on Nancy. After Fagin's capture he testifies against him and becomes an informer for the police.

Corney, Mrs Matron of the workhouse where Oliver is born. She marries Bumble, making him miserable. The Bumbles are disgraced and end up as paupers in the workhouse they once ruled over.

Dawkins, Jack The most successful and interesting of Fagin's thieves. He shows Oliver the ropes of the pickpocket game and is later captured and sentenced to transportation. Dawkins is better known as The Artful Dodger.

Duff Bow Street Runner (London policeman) who, along with Blathers, investigates the attempted robbery of the Maylie home.

Fagin A crafty old Jew who runs a thieves' school near Field Lane in Saffron Hill. Oliver falls in with

Fagin's band when he runs away from the workhouse. When Fagin attempts to help Monks destroy Oliver's reputation he is arrested and executed at Newgate.

Fleming, Agnes Mother of Oliver, whom she gives birth to out of wedlock with Edwin Leeford and subsequently dies at the workhouse. Agnes is also the sister of Rose Maylie.

Gamfield, Mr Cruel chimney sweep who does not let the safety of his sweeps concern him. 'Even if they've stuck in a chimbley, roasting their feet makes 'em struggle to hextricate themselves.'

Grimwig, Mr Cantankerous friend of Mr Brownlow. Quote: 'I'll eat my head!'

Kags Robber who was in the house on Jacob's Island when Bill Sikes sought refuge there.

Leeford, Edward Villainous son of Edwin and half-brother of Oliver Twist who plots with Fagin to corrupt Oliver, in which case Leeford will inherit all of their father's property. After the plan is foiled Leeford is forced to emigrate to America, where he dies in prison. Leeford is referred to as Monks.

Leeford, Edwin Father of Oliver, whom he has fathered out of wedlock with Agnes Fleming. Also father of Edward (Monks) from a previous marriage. Edwin has died before the story begins.

Losberne, Dr Impetuous doctor who treats Oliver and Rose in illness. A friend of the Maylie family.

Mann, Mrs Matron of a workhouse farm where Oliver is raised until he is nine years old.

Maylie, Harry Son of Mrs Maylie, he marries Rose.

Maylie, Mrs Mother of Harry and the adopted mother of Rose.

Maylie, Rose A poor girl adopted by Mrs Maylie. She and Mr Brownlow endeavour to help Oliver through Nancy. When Nancy's conversation with Rose on London Bridge is overheard by Claypole, Nancy is murdered by Sikes. She later marries Harry.

Monks *See* Edward Leeford.

Nancy Prostitute and member of Fagin's band of thieves. Befriends Oliver and is eventually murdered by Sikes trying to help Oliver escape Fagin's clutches.

Sally, Old Old hag present at Oliver's birth. She steals the locket and ring from Oliver's mother as she lies dying.

Sikes, Bill A vicious thief working on the fringes of Fagin's band of pickpockets. He uses Oliver in an attempt to burgle the Brownlow home. When Nancy tries to help Oliver she is found out by Fagin who relates the information to Sikes. He murders Nancy, and later hangs himself by accident while trying to escape a hue-and-cry.

Slout Master of the workhouse where Oliver was born, replaced by Mr Bumble following his death.

Sowerberry, Mr Undertaker to whom Oliver is apprenticed. Oliver is mistreated and runs away to London.

Spyers, Jem Bow Street Runner who detected the deception of Conkey Chickweed's fake burglary.

Twist, Oliver Principal character in the story. He is born in a workhouse, where he is mistreated by Bumble, the beadle (quote: 'Please sir, may I have some more?'). He is apprenticed to Sowerberry, the undertaker, and runs away to London where he falls in with Fagin.

Our Mutual Friend: fourteenth novel, published in 1865

Blight Mortimer Lightwood's office boy, often referred to as 'young Blight'.

Blogg, Mr Beadle who permits Betty Higden to adopt Sloppy

Boffin, Mrs Henrietta Noddy Boffin's wife, who, unlike her husband, enjoyed the good life.

Boffin, Nicodemus John Harmon's servant. When John's son is supposed drowned, Boffin and his wife inherit the Harmon fortune, for a time.

Boots and Brewer Guests at the Veneerings' social gatherings.

Dolls, Mr Father of Jenny Wren, whose real name is Cleaver but is called Mr Dolls by Eugene Wrayburn.

Gliddery, Bob Pot-boy at the Six Jolly Fellowship Porters.

Goody, Mrs The Reverend Mr Milvey suggests that the Boffins adopt her grandchild but his wife disagrees, as she is an 'inconvenient woman, who drank eleven cups of tea the previous Christmas, and grumbled all the time'.

Handford, Julius Alias taken by John Harmon in order to investigate his own supposed drowning.

Harmon, John Son of a wealthy dust contractor and heir to his fortune if he agrees to marry Bella Wilfer. He is away from England when his father dies, and on the way home he is supposed drowned in a case of mistaken identity.

Headstone, Bradley A schoolteacher and master of the boys department of a school on the borders of Kent and Surrey. He becomes obsessed with Lizzie Hexam. Lizzie wants nothing to do with him and he becomes jealous.

Hexam, Charley Brother of Lizzie and son of Gaffer, who becomes Bradley Headstone's pupil.

Hexam, Gaffer Waterman, father of Lizzie, who plies the Thames looking for dead bodies. He finds a body thought to be John Harmon, the central character in the story.

Hexam, Lizzie Daughter of waterman Gaffer Hexam and sister of Charley. She is opposed to her father's business of combing the Thames looking for drowned bodies but is true to him. When her father drowns she goes to live with Jenny Wren. Eventually she marries Eugene Wrayburn.

Higden, Betty Almost 80 years old but still very active. She keeps 'a Minding School' for children.

Kibble, Jacob Fellow-passenger with John Harmon on the voyage from the Cape to London.

Lightwood, Mortimer A lawyer, too lazy to take on much work, and friend of Eugene Wrayburn. His only clients are the Boffins, which puts him in the middle of much of the story.

Milvey, Mrs Margaretta Wife of the Reverend Milvey and mother of their six children.

Milvey, the Reverend Frank The Boffins' clergyman, whom they consult when they decide to adopt an orphan.

Potterson, Miss Abbey Proprietor of the Six Jolly Fellowship Porters, on the Thames.

Riah 'An old Jewish man, in an ancient coat, long of skirt and wide of pocket' who fronts a money-lending business. He befriends Lizzie Hexam and Jenny Wren.

Riderhood, Rogue Waterman and former partner of Gaffer Hexam who tries to pin blame on Gaffer for the Harmon murder to gain a reward. Riderhood later becomes a lock-keeper and tries to blackmail Bradley Headstone after Bradley tries to murder Eugene Wrayburn.

Rokesmith, John Alias used by John Harmon when he is employed as secretary to the Boffins.

Sloppy Orphan boy adopted by Betty Higden and given the job of turning the mangle at her Minding School.

Tootle, Tom Gentleman who tells Miss Abbey Potterson that a man has been run down in a wherry,

LITERATURE

by a foreign steamer, on the Thames. The man turns out to be Rogue Riderhood.

Veneering, Hamilton & Anastasia High society couple at whose frequent dinner parties the story of John Harmon is discovered. Hamilton buys his way into Parliament and is later bankrupt and the couple flee to France.

Venus, Mr Taxidermist and dealer in bones and skeletons who owned a 'little dark greasy' shop in Clerkenwell.

Wegg, Silas Rascally street vendor hired by Mr Boffin to read to him. Wegg is illiterate and makes the stories up as he goes along. After installing himself in the Boffin household he goes about trying to get a piece of the Boffin fortune.

Wilfer, Bella Girl specified in old Harmon's will as the one that his son John should marry in order to gain his inheritance. When John disappears and is presumed drowned she is left 'a widow without ever being married'. She leaves her home and goes to live with the Boffins.

Williams, William Regular customer of Miss Abbey Potterson at the Six Jolly Fellowship Porters.

Wrayburn, Eugene Lawyer and friend of Mortimer Lightwood. 'If there is a word in the dictionary under any letter from A to Z that i abominate, it is energy.' He becomes interested in the Harmon case and meets Lizzie Hexam and falls in love with her. She loves him also but tries to distance herself from him because they come from different classes of society.

Wren, Jenny aka Fanny Cleaver Crippled dolls' dressmaker with whom Lizzie Hexam lives after the death of her father. She helps Lizzie escape London when pursued by Headstone and Wrayburn.

Pickwick Papers: **first published novel and serialised between April 1836 and November 1837 as *The Posthumous Papers of the Pickwick Club***

Allen, Arabella Sister of Benjamin, who attempted to marry her to his friend Bob Sawyer. Arabella eventually marries Nathaniel Winkle.

Allen, Benjamin Medical student and close friend of Bob Sawyer.

Bagman, The Appears twice in the novel, first at the Peacock, Eatanswill, and then at the Bush Inn, Bristol, reciting a story on each occasion: 'The Bagman's Story' and 'The Bagman's Uncle'.

Bantam, Angelo Cyrus Master of Ceremonies at Bath.

Bardell, Mrs Martha Mr Pickwick's landlady in Goswell Street.

Betsy Mrs Raddle's dirty and slipshod maid.

Bladud, Prince Legendary founder of Bath, the subject of 'The True Legend of Prince Bladud' that Mr Pickwick reads in his bedroom.

Boffer A Stock Exchange broker, on whose probable methods and timing of committing suicide Wilkins Flasher and Frank Simmery placed bets.

Boldwig, Captain 'Little fierce man in a stiff black neckerchief and blue surtout', who discovered Mr Pickwick asleep in a wheelbarrow on his land.

Bolo, Miss Mr Pickwick's whist partner whilst at Bath, who 'went straight home in a flood of tears, and a sedan chair' due to his bad play.

Brooks Pieman who could 'make pies out o' anything' including cats. He lodged at Sam Weller's.

Brown The Muggleton shoemaker, whose name on Rachael Wardle's shoes, which had been left with Sam Weller for cleaning, showed Mr Wardle that she was staying at the White Hart.

Budger, Mrs Elderly widow with whom Mr Jingle dances at the Rochester ball, in Mr Winkle's dress-suit, to the jealous fury of Doctor Slammer, who consequently challenges the unfortunate Winkle to a duel.

Bulder, Colonel Head of the Rochester garrison who attends the charity ball also attended by the Pickwickians. Bulder also commands the military review at Chatham when Mr Pickwick gets in the way.

Bullman Plaintiff in the case discussed by Dodson and Fogg's clerks in the hearing of Mr Pickwick and Sam Weller.

Burton, Thomas Member of the Brick Lane Branch of the United Grand Junction Ebenezer Temperance Association. 'Purveyor of cat's meat to the Lord Mayor and Sheriffs, and several members of the Common Council.'

Buzfuz, Sergeant Bullying counsel for Mrs Bardell, who is a wicked caricature of a type of histrionic advocate frequently encountered in those days.

Charley Dishevelled, red-headed pot-boy at the Magpie and Stump where Mr Pickwick and Sam Weller go in search of Mr Lowten.

Cripps, Tom Errand-boy to Benjamin Allen and Bob Sawyer.

Crookey Servant at Namby's sponging-house.

Dodson and Fogg Mrs Bardell's attorneys who commit her to prison for non-payment of their costs.

Dowler, Mr and Mrs Army officer and his wife who travelled with Mr Pickwick to Bath.

Dumkins, Mr A formidable cricketer who played for the All-Muggleton club.

Fizkin, Horatio Buff candidate in the Eatanswill election, who was defeated by the Honourable Samuel Slumkey.

Flasher, Wilkins A Stock Exchange broker who, with Frank Simmery, placed bets on Boffer's probable methods and timing of committing suicide.

Groffin, Thomas Chemist, who attempts, unsuccessfully, to be excused jury duty in the case of Bardell v Pickwick.

Grub, Gabriel Subject of 'The Story of the Goblins who stole a Sexton' as told by Mr Wardle.

Grundy, Mr Gentleman who refuses to oblige the company with a song at the Magpie and Stump where Mr Pickwick and Sam Weller have arranged to meet Mr Lowten.

Harris Greengrocer in whose shop the Bath footmen hold their party.

Humm, Mr Anthony President of the Brick Lane Branch of the United Grand Junction Ebenezer Temperance Association.

Hunt Head gardener to Captain Boldwig, who is receiving orders from his master when the appearance of Mr Pickwick asleep in a wheelbarrow on his land is brought to the attention of Boldwig.

Isaac A 'shabby man in black leggings' who accompanies Mr Jackson when he arrests Mrs Bardell.

Jackson, Mr Dodson and Fogg's clerk who arrests Mrs Bardell and serves the Pickwickians with subpoenas to attend the trial.

Jingle, Alfred A wandering rascal who befriends Mr Pickwick and accompanies the group to the Wardle home at Dingley Dell. He entices Miss Rachael to elope with him and is run down and bought off by Rachael's brother. Pickwick eventually exposes Jingle, who uses the alias of Charles Fitz-Marshall when tricking Pickwick into thinking he is planning another elopement.

Jinkins, Mr Suitor of the widow in 'The Bagman's Story'.

Jinks, Mr Dishevelled-looking clerk who worked for Mr Nupkins as the magistrate's adviser.

Lowten, Mr Mr Perker's clerk who first meets Mr Pickwick after singing a comic song at the Magpie and Stump.

Muzzle Mr Nupkins's footman who challenges Job Trotter to a fight over the affections of the cook.

Namby, Mr Sheriff's deputy of Bell Alley, Coleman Street, who arrests Mr Pickwick at the suit of Mrs Bardell.

Nupkins, Mr George Magistrate in attendance on the Pickwickian expedition to Ipswich.

Perker, Mr Mr Wardle's lawyer at Gray's Inn, who looks after Mr Pickwick's interests in the case of Bardell v Pickwick.

Pickwick, Samuel Founder and Chairman of the Pickwick Club. Pickwick, along with his friends Tupman, Snodgrass and Winkle and his servant Sam Weller, travel around England in search of adventure. Pickwick is one of Dickens's most loved characters.

Porkenham Family Close friends of the Nupkins family. George Nupkins is horrified at the possibility that they might know the true identity of Captain Fitz-Marshall.

Roker, Tom Turnkey at the Fleet, who shows Mr Pickwick his accommodation for the next three months.

Samba, Quanko Bowler in the West Indies cricket match described by Alfred Jingle at Dingley Dell. He apparently bowled Jingle out but never recovered from his exertions and died.

Sawyer, Bob Medical student and close friend of Benjamin Allen. 'Sawyer, late Nockemorf', who eventually gains a medical appointment in India.

Simmery, Frank A Stock Exchange broker, who, with Wilkins Flasher, placed bets on Boffer's probable methods and timing of committing suicide.

Skimpin, Mr Sergeant Buzfuz's assistant during the trial of Bardell v Pickwick.

Slammer, Dr Surgeon who is infuriated when Alfred Jingle, wearing Nathaniel Winkle's coat, dances with Mrs Budger, and consequently challenges Winkle to a duel, but discovers the mistaken identity before any damage is done.

Slasher, Dr Surgeon at St Bartholomew's Hospital, who was said to be the best operator alive. 'Took a boy's leg out of the socket last week, boy ate five apples and a gingerbread cake exactly two minutes after it was all over, boy said that he wouldn't lie there to be made game of and he'd tell his mother if they didn't begin.'

Slumkey, the Hon. Samuel Blue candidate in the Eatanswill election, who defeated Horatio Fizkin.

Slurk, Mr Editor of the *Eatanswill Independent* who has a furious quarrel with a rival editor.

Snodgrass, Augustus A member of the Pickwick Club and party to the adventures of Pickwick's travels. He falls in love with Emily Wardle and marries her at the end of the story.

Snubbin, Sergeant Mr Pickwick's counsel for defence in the trial of Bardell v Pickwick, who proves out of his depth against the redoubtable Sergeant Buzfuz.

Struggles, Mr Extremely passionate but unsuccessful bowler for the Dingley Dell cricket team.

Trotter, Job Servant to Alfred Jingles who has a couple of run-ins with Sam Weller, who takes a dislike to him, not least because he has a habit of calling him Mr Walker.

Trundle, Mr Partner of Isabel Wardle in a game of cards and ultimately becomes her partner in marriage.

Tupman, Tracy A member of the Pickwick Club, and travelling companion to Mr Pickwick in the story's adventures.

Upwitch, Richard Greengrocer who was a jury member in the trial of Bardell v Pickwick.

Wardle, Emily Daughter of Mr Wardle and niece of Rachael, who marries Augustus Snodgrass.

Wardle, Isabella Daughter of Mr Wardle and niece of Rachael, who marries Mr Trundle.

Wardle, Mr Yeoman farmer and owner of Manor Farm at Dingley Dell. Pickwick and his friends visit Manor Farm frequently. Wardle's daughter marries Pickwickian Augustus Snodgrass. Jingle tries to elope with Miss Rachael, Wardle's sister, but is caught and bought off.

Wardle, Rachael Sister of Mr Wardle who was persuaded to elope by Mr Jingle but is accosted by Mr Pickwick at the White Hart Inn and Jingle is bought off for £120.

Weller, Sam Mr Pickwick's servant is one of the most popular characters in Dickens's works. He counsels his master with Cockney wisdom and is thoroughly devoted to Pickwick. Sam has an unfortunate habit of transposing Ws and Vs to comical effect.

Weller, Tony Samuel's father, Tony Weller, is equally entertaining, also having the same unfortunate habit of transposing Ws and Vs to comical effect.

Whiffers, Mr Footman who resigns at the 'swarry' at Bath because the requirement for him to eat cold meat was a manly outrage.

Wicks, Mr One of Dodson and Fogg's clerks.

Wildspark, Tom Tony Weller's example of the importance of an alibi 'Ve got Tom Vildspark off that 'ere manslaughter, with a alleybi, ven all the bigvigs to a man said as nothing couldn't save him.'

Wilkins Gardener to Captain Boldwig, who brings to the attention of his master the appearance of Mr Pickwick asleep in a wheelbarrow on his land.

Winkle, Nathaniel Member of the Pickwick Club and travelling companion to Pickwick and his friends. He marries Arabella Allen, which upsets his father. Later Winkle's father comes to London and sees his daughter-in-law for himself, and is reconciled to the marriage.

Wugsby, Mrs Colonel One of the ladies that Mr Pickwick plays cards with at Bath.

A Tale of Two Cities: **twelfth novel, serialised in** *All the Year Round* **in weekly parts from April to November 1859**

Carton, Sydney Lawyer who is able to get a charge of treason reversed for Charles Darnay due to a strong physical resemblance. He later takes Darnay's place at the guillotine. Quote: 'It is a far, far better thing I do than I have ever done.'

Cruncher, Jerry Messenger for Tellson's Bank who moonlights as a grave robber.

Darnay, Charles Nephew of Marquis St Evrémonde. He is tried for treason in London and is acquitted due to his resemblance to Sydney Carton. He marries Lucie Manette, daughter of Dr Manette. He returns to Paris to help a friend imprisoned there and is arrested once more.

Defarge, Ernest Husband of Madame Defarge and keeper of a wine shop in Paris. He is a leader among the revolutionaries.

Defarge, Madame Thérèse Wife of wine-shop keeper Ernest Defarge, and a leader among the revolutionaries. She records enemies of the Republic in her knitting. She accidentally shoots herself dead in a struggle with Miss Pross in Paris.

Foulon, Joseph-François Unscrupulous financier of the ancien régime who is seized by a mob and decapitated.

Gabelle, Théophile Postmaster in the village of St Evrémonde who is arrested when the French Revolution begins. Dickens named the character after the salt tax imposed in the pre-revolutionary days.

Jacques Name by which several of the French revolutionaries are known. Defarge is 'Jacques Four'.

Lorry, Jarvis A clerk in Tellson's bank who is instrumental in bringing Dr Manette, who is imprisoned in Paris, back to England. He returns to Paris to look after the bank's interest after the Revolution starts and while there helps Lucie and Charles Darnay in their predicament.

Manette, Dr Alexandre A prisoner in the Bastille in Paris for eighteen years. He is released and accompanies his daughter, Lucie, and Jarvis Lorry to England. He returns to Paris after the outbreak of the Revolution and, as a former prisoner, is able to secure Darnay's release.

Manette, Lucie Daughter of Dr Manette. She is taken to Paris by Jarvis Lorry when her father is released from prison. She marries Charles Darnay but is adored from afar by Sydney Carton, who feels unfit for her. Darnay and Lucie have a daughter, also named Lucie. When Darnay is imprisoned in Paris by the revolutionaries Carton takes his place at the guillotine, thereby fulfilling his promise to help Lucie.

Pross, Miss Lucie Manette's loyal maid. In the end of the novel she struggles with Madame Defarge and Defarge is killed in the scuffle.

Pross, Solomon/John Barsad Miss Pross's brother, who sneaks Carton into the prison to trade places with Darnay.

Stryver, Mr Solicitor friend of Sydney Carton who helps to defend Charley Darnay from the charges of treason.

'Vengeance, The' Fiery woman friend of Madame Defarge who regularly attended the executions at the guillotine.

Mr Men and Little Misses

Mr Men

1	Mr Bounce is round and yellow and very cuddly. He is forever turning somersaults while landing on his head.
2	Mr Brave proves that looks can be deceiving, bespectacled and yellow-looking but utterly fearless.
3	Mr Bump is always having accidents of all sorts, and so is always wrapped in bandages from his latest injury.
4	Mr Busy always has something to do, and like Mr Rush this blue character simply cannot relax.
5	Mr Chatterbox never ever stops talking, not even for a moment. It is impossible to get a word in edgeways.
6	Mr Cheeky is extremely rude. When he meets people in the street he insults them unashamedly. (Not one of the original 43 characters but introduced in 2001 as a result of a nationwide competition to celebrate the 30th anniversary of their birth. Gemma Almond, 8, from Shropshire won the competition.)
7	Mr Cheerful is always looking on the bright side of life and is there to cheer you up when you are down.
8	Mr Christmas was not one of the original 43 Mr Men books but was created for a Christmas special.
9	Mr Clever is wide-eyed and bespectacled, and of course knows absolutely everything.
10	Mr Clumsy means well but really is very clumsy indeed, so don't let him near Mr Bump's children.
11	Mr Daydream is in a world of his own most of the time, his imagination running rife.
12	Mr Dizzy lives in a land where pigs and elephants are clever, and he just can't get his head around it all.
13	Mr Forgetful is big and blue and egg-shaped and very very absent-minded.
14	Mr Funny lives in a teapot-shaped house, and drives a shoe-shaped car. He is a practical joker par excellence.
15	Mr Fussy likes things to be neat and tidy, and even irons his shoelaces. He is green and fastidious.
16	Mr Greedy is the greediest person alive. When he comes to visit, make sure there's no food lying around!
17	Mr Grumble is never content. On a lovely day he hates the hot sun, and when it snows he's too cold!
18	Mr Grumpy is always in a bad mood, no matter what. He can't stand it when other people have fun.
19	Mr Happy lives in Happyland where everyone and everything is always happy. Big and yellow with a grin to match.
20	Mr Impossible really can do the impossible! Mauve in colour, there is nothing up his sleeve!
21	Mr Jelly is scared of everything and anything. The quivering red blob is also known as Mr Nervous.
22	Mr Lazy likes nothing more than to do absolutely nothing. He'll laze about in the sun all day if he can.
23	Mr Mean is not very nice really. He's tall and slim but with short arms and long pockets.
24	Mr Messy needs to get his act together. His garden is overgrown and his washing up is never done.
25	Mr Mischief is a bigger practical joker than Mr Fun. He is always sniggering over his latest prank.
26	Mr Muddle just can't get things right, so if you meet him in the morning, he'll say 'Good Afternoon!'
27	Mr Noisy is always shouting. He's utterly incapable of talking quietly.
28	Mr Nonsense looks like a clown and acts like one, his big red nose protruding from a nonsensical grin.
29	Mr Nosey is incapable of minding his own business. His long green nose is taller than himself.
30	Mr Perfect is as his name implies. He has a perfect house with a perfect garden and his lawn is always perfect.
31	Mr Quiet can't stand noisy people or places. Unfortunately he lives in Loudland and it's very trying for him.
32	Mr Rush is always in a hurry and this mauve, triangular-faced flash is heading for a fall unless he slows down.
33	Mr Silly is just plain daft! Even his large red hat is pulled down over his eyes so he cannot see properly.
34	Mr Skinny is long, yellow and as skinny as a rake – literally! Perhaps he should help Mr Messy with his garden!
35	Mr Slow is in no hurry. His moustachioed face gives him a distinguished look . . . but don't rush him!
36	Mr Small really is very tiny, his little red features barely discernible unless you are looking down!

37   Mr Sneeze lives in Coldland, and always has a cold and a very red nose and a blue face from all his sneezing.
38   Mr Snow is the personification of all the snowmen you have ever made in wintertime.
39   Mr Strong can lift entire buildings. He eats a lot of eggs, too, to keep his strength up. He is Big and Square.
40   Mr Tall is as tall as a cliff. He has very long legs, so he can walk a long way very very quickly.
41   Mr Tickle likes to tickle people but his long arms can make breakfast while lying in bed! He was the first Mr Man.
42   Mr Topsy-Turvy reads books upside-down and has a clock that goes anti-clockwise. He greets people he meets by saying 'Morning Good' and he also wears his hat upside-down.
43   Mr Uppity is an outrageous snob, although his black topper makes him look rather distinguished and dapper.
44   Mr Worry is always deep in thought, with a deep frown upon his round blue face.
45   Mr Wrong just can't get things right. He can't even choose a pair of gloves of the same colour!

Little Misses

1   Little Miss Bossy can't stop ordering people around and shouting at them. When she says jump you jump.
2   Little Miss Brainy is the female counterpart of Mr Clever.
3   Little Miss Busy is always busy cleaning the house, shopping, gardening, cooking. She never stops!
4   Little Miss Chatterbox is the female counterpart of Mr Chatterbox and is equally talkative.
5   Little Miss Contrary is always deep in thought but will never agree about anything!
6   Little Miss Curious cannot help but have an inquiring mind.
7   Little Miss Dotty lives in nonsenseland, where Mr Silly and Mr Nonsense live, and she is equally dotty.
8   Little Miss Fickle changes her mind constantly and who knows what or where the mood takes her.
9   Little Miss Fun is a party animal! She's always ready to go out and have fun somewhere.
10   Little Miss Giggles can't stop giggling. She giggles so much that when she's around, everyone else starts too!
11   Little Miss Greedy is as greedy as Mr Greedy. In the earliest books she was also called Little Miss Plump.
12   Little Miss Helpful tries her hardest to be as helpful as she possibly can be. She really does try . . . so hard!
13   Little Miss Late is never on time and punctuality is certainly not her byword.
14   Little Miss Lucky doesn't seem quite as lucky as her name implies, but things always come out all right in the end.
15   Little Miss Magic can do magic! I suppose Mr Impossible would be her male equivalent
16   Little Miss Naughty is very naughty and her naughty ways do not make her very many friends!
17   Little Miss Neat can't stand any sort of mess. She is bespectacled, round and green.
18   Little Miss Quick doesn't hang around at all, and whatever she does she does it very quickly indeed.
19   Little Miss Scatterbrain is very absent-minded and her male equivalent would be Mr Forgetful.
20   Little Miss Shy is very unassuming and would rather be left alone so I won't embarrass her any longer.
21   Little Miss Somersault has very long legs and is very gymnastic. She is forever turning somersaults.
22   Little Miss Splendid looks a little aloof but is quite splendid really although a little prim and proper.
23   Little Miss Star is round and blue with lovely green shoes. She is a real star through and through.
24   Little Miss Stubborn will not listen. No matter how silly her ideas are she is determined to follow them through.
25   Little Miss Sunshine is a vision in yellow and her beaming smile is sure to cheer the hardest heart.
26   Little MissTidy is not green like Little Miss Neat but yellow, and she doesn't wear glasses either.
27   Little Miss Tiny is very small indeed. In fact she is smaller than Mr Small!
28   Little Miss Trouble cannot help but find trouble. She is the female equivalent of Mr Mischief.
29   Little Miss Twins do everything in pairs, and say things twice twice. They live in Twoland. The Little Miss Twins were inspired by Roger Hargreaves's twin daughters.
30   Little Miss Wise is the person to consult if you want some sound advice, as she is very wise indeed.

Note

Mr Men and Little Misses are to get six new friends 15 years after the death of their creator Roger Hargreaves. His son has penned the tales of Mr Cool, Mr Rude, Mr Good, Little Miss Bad, Little Miss Scary and Little Miss Whoops. Adam Hargreaves took over the running of the Mr Men empire after his father died of a stroke in 1988 at the age of 53. Adam had been the original inspiration for the books when he asked his father what a tickle looked like. The result was Mr Tickle, the first in a series which went on to sell over 100 million copies worldwide. The first four new books were due to be published in April and the two others in September. The books were written by Adam, but he will still credit his father as author to keep his father's memory alive.

LITERATURE

Poets Laureate

John Dryden (1668-88)
Thomas Shadwell (1688–92)
Nahum Tate (1692–1715)
Nicholas Rowe (1715–18)
Laurence Eusden (1718–30)
Colley Cibber (1730–57)
William Whitehead (1757–85)
Thomas Wharton (1785–90)
Henry James Pye (1790–1813)
Robert Southey (1813–43)

William Wordsworth (1843–50)
Alfred, Lord Tennyson (1850–92)
Alfred Austin (1896–1913)
Robert Bridges (1913–30)
John Masefield (1930–67)
Cecil Day-Lewis (1968–72)
Sir John Betjeman (1972–84)
Ted Hughes (1984–1998)
Andrew Motion (1999–)

NB: Ben Jonson was the first to be granted a pension as poet, to James I (1616), and in 1630 Charles I added an annual butt of canary wine, which was discontinued by Henry Pye who preferred money. Sir William Davenant succeeded Jonson but the position was only made official in 1668. William Whitehead appointed after Thomas Gray declined the honour. Similarly Alfred, Lord Tennyson became laureate after Samuel Rogers declined.

Servants (and Masters)

Lugg	Campion	Françoise	Marcel Family
Bunter	Lord Peter Wimsey		(*Remembrance of Things*
Miss Lemon	Poirot		*Past*)
Mrs Hudson	Sherlock Holmes	Anatole	Aunt Dahlia (Jeeves stories)
Reginald Jeeves	Bertie Wooster	Mary Ann	White Rabbit
Launcelot Gobbo	Shylock	Eurycleia	Ulysses
Passepartout	Phileas Fogg	Feers	Madame Ranevsky (*Cherry*
Sancho Panza	Don Quixote		*Orchard*)
Mélisande	Zuleika Dobson	Mrs Honour	Sophia Western (*Tom Jones*)
Paddock	Richard Hannay	Corporal Trim	Uncle Toby (*Tristram Shandy*)

Other Literary Prizewinners in 2002

Agatha (mystery award)	Best Novel: *Murphy's Law* by Rhys Bowen
Arthur C Clarke (science fiction)	Best Novel published in Britain: *Bold As Love* by Gwyneth Jones
Betty Trask Prize	For first novels in English, published in the UK, by Commonwealth citizens under the age of 35. The £8,000 first prize in 2002 went to Hari Kunzru for *The Impressionist*
British Book Awards (Nibbies)	Author of the year: Philip Pullman
Crime Writers Association	Gold Dagger (Fiction) *The Athenian Murders* by Jose Carlos Samoza
Hugo (science fiction)	Best US Novel: *American Gods* by Neil Gaiman
Kate Greenaway (children's illustration)	*Pirate Diary* illustrated by Chris Riddell (2001 book)
Nestlé Smarties Prize	Awarded by the Youth Libraries Group to the most outstanding children's book published in the UK across three age groups.
	Age 0–5 *Jazzy in the Jungle* by Lucy Cousins
	Age 6–8 *That Pesky Rat* by Lauren Child
	Age 9–11 *Mortal Engines* by Philip Reeve
Samuel Johnson Prize	Established in December 1998. The £30,000 prize is awarded to non-fiction works published in the UK between 1 January and 30 April of the year of the prize. 2002 winner was Margaret Macmillan's *Peacemakers Paris 1919: Six Months That Changed the World*

LONDON

Theatres

Name	Address	Post	Details
Adelphi	Strand	WC2	Opened by John Scott in 1806 and originally called the Sans Pareil. First performance on 17 November 1806, *The Rout,* recitations by Miss Jane M Scott. Recently showing *Chicago* (Olivier Award: Best Musical 1998).
Albery	St Martin's Lane	WC2	Designed in 1903 by W G R Sprague and called the New Theatre till 1923. Recently showing *The Master Builder* (by Henrik Ibsen).
Aldwych	Aldwych	WC2	Designed 1905 by W G R Sprague. Home of Ben Travers farces 1925–33. Recently showing *Fame: The Musical* (by David de Silva).
Almeida	Almeida St	N1	Fringe theatre built for other purposes in 1837.
Apollo	Shaftesbury Ave	W1	Designed in 1901 by Lewen Sharp.
Apollo Victoria	Victoria	SW1	Opened in 1930 as a cinema; theatre since 1979. Recently showing *Starlight Express* from 27 March 1984–12 January 2002 and since 19 June 2002 *Bombay Dreams* (by Meera Syal).
Arts	Strand	WC2	Opened in 1927 as an avant-garde theatre challenging the censorial constraints of the Lord Chamberlain's Office. Recently showing *Madness of George Dubya* (by Justin Butcher).
Barbican (and Pit)	Silk St	EC2	Opened in 1982, since when the London Symphony Orchestra has been in residence at Barbican Hall. Also home of the Royal Shakespeare Company.
Bloomsbury	Off Tottenham Ct Rd	WC1	Fringe theatre that shows a wide spectrum of work.
Bridewell	Bride Lane	EC4	Fringe theatre.
Bush	Shepherd's Bush	W12	Fringe theatre founded in 1972.
Cambridge	Earlham St	WC2	Designed in 1930. Recently showing *Grease* (transferred from the Dominion) and since 28 October 2002 *Our House* (by Tim Firth).
Coliseum	St Martin's Lane	WC2	Largest theatre in the West End, seating nearly 2,500. Interior designed in 1904 by Frank Matcham. Home of the English National Opera since 1968.
Comedy	Panton St	SW1	Designed in 1881 by Thomas Verity. Recently showing *Sexual Perversity in Chicago* (by David Mamet).
Criterion	Piccadilly	W1	Current home of the Reduced Shakespeare Company. Designed in 1874 by Thomas Verity.
Dominion	Tottenham Ct Rd	WC1	Built 1929 by William and T R Millburn. Recently showing *We Will Rock You* (by Ben Elton).
Donmar Warehouse	Earlham St	WC2	Recently showing *After Miss Julie* (by Patrick Marber).
Drury Lane Theatre Royal	Catherine St	WC2	Designed in 1812 by Benjamin Wyatt. Designed in 1929 by Ewen Barr. Recently showing *My Fair Lady* (by Lerner and Loewe) and from 7 October *Anything Goes.*
Duchess	Catherine St	WC2	Recently showing *Through The Leaves* (by Franz Xaver Kroetz).
Duke of York's	St Martin's Lane	WC2	Designed by Walter Emden in 1892 and called the Trafalgar Square till 1895. Recently showing *Stones In His Pockets* (by Marie Jones).
Fortune	Russell St	WC2	Designed in 1924 by Ernest Schaufelberg. Recently showing *The Woman in Black.*
Gaiety	Strand	WC2	Opened in 1868 and had England's first electric lighting system in 1878.
Garrick	Charing Cross Road	WC2	Designed by Walter Emden and C J Phipps in 1889. Recently showing *Just Like That* (by John Fisher).
Gate (Prince Albert Pub)	Pembridge Rd	W11	Reputation for high-quality productions of neglected European classics.
Gielgud	Shaftesbury Ave	W1	Designed 1906 by W G R Sprague. Originally the Hick's Theatre: then the Globe (1909–95). Recently showing *Tell Me On A Sunday* (by Andrew Lloyd Webber).
Greenwich	Crooms Hill	SE10	Open since 1969 in reconstructed Victorian music hall.
Hampstead Theatre Club	Swiss Cottage	NW3	Fringe theatre.
Her Majesty's	Haymarket	SW1	Original building designed by Sir John Vanbrugh in 1705; present theatre designed 1896 by C J Phipps. Recently showing *Phantom of the Opera.*
King's Head	Upper St	N1	Founded as a pub theatre in 1970.
Lyceum	Wellington St	WC2	Designed by James Payne in 1771. Recently showing *Lion King* (songs by Elton John and Tim Rice).

Name	Address	Post	Details
Lyric	King St Hammersmith	W6	Designed in 1979. Usually performances of planned short-season runs.
Lyric	Shaftesbury Ave	W1	Designed in 1888 by C J Phipps. Recently showing *Hitchcock Blonde* (by Terry Johnson).
Mayfair	Mayfair Hotel	W1	Part of the hotel complex.
Mermaid	Puddle Dock	EC4	Founded in 1959 by Sir Bernard Miles.
New Ambassadors	West St	WC2	Designed in 1913 by W G R Sprague. Ivor Novello made debut here in *Deburau*.
New End	New End	NW3	Fringe theatre.
New London	Drury Lane	WC2	Designed in 1973 by Paul Turkovic. Recently showing *Joseph And The Amazing Technicolor Dreamcoat*.
Old Vic	Waterloo Rd	SE1	Designed 1818 by Rudolf Cabanel. Currently owned by the Old Vic Theatre Trust 2000 Ltd.
Palace	Cambridge Circus	WC2	Built by T E Collcutt and G H Holloway, opened in 1891 as The Royal English Opera House showing Sir Arthur Sullivan's *Ivanhoe*. Recently showing *Les Misérables*.
Palladium	Argyll St	WC1	Opened in 1910 as a music hall. Recently showing *Chitty Chitty Bang Bang*.
Peacock	Portugal St	WC2	Sadler's Wells theatre.
Phoenix	Charing Cross Road	WC2	Designed by Giles Gilbert Scott and Bertie Crewe and opened in 1930. Recently showing *Blood Brothers* (by Willy Russell).
Piccadilly	Denman St	W1	Designed in 1928 by Bertie Crewe and Edward Stone. Recently showing *Ragtime*.
Players	Off Villiers St	SW1	Several locations since 1936. Now situated underneath Charing Cross arches.
Playhouse	Northumberland Ave	WC2	Designed by Sefton Parry in 1882. Recently showing *Three Sisters* (by Anton Chekhov).
Prince Edward	Old Compton St	W1	Opened in 1930. Recently showing *Mamma Mia!*
Prince of Wales	Coventry St	W1	Designed 1937 by Robert Cromie. Recently showing *Cliff – The Musical* (by Mike Reid and Trevor Payne).
Queen's	Shaftesbury Ave	W1	Interior designed 1907 by W G R Sprague, new exterior redesigned by Bryan Westwood and Hugh Casson after bomb damage in 1940, reopened 1959.
Regent's Park (open air)	Regent's Park	NW1	Founded in 1932. Stages annual productions of *A Midsummer Night's Dream*.
Royal Court Downstairs	Sloane Square	SW3	Recently showing *Topdog/Underdog* (by Suzan-Lori Parks).
Royal Court Upstairs	Sloane Square	SW3	Recently showing *Food Chain* (by Mick Mahoney).
Royal National Theatre	South Bank	SE1	Designed by Denys Lasdun, opened 1976. Three auditoriums, the Olivier (large and open-spaced), the Lyttelton (proscenium arched) and the Cottesloe (small but flexible).
Royal Opera	Bow St	WC2	Designed by Edward Shepherd in 1732. Redesigned by E M Barry in 1858 and called The Covent Garden Opera Company. Renamed the Royal Opera House in 1968.
Sadler's Wells	Rosebery Ave	EC1	Opened in 1683 by Thomas Sadler but sadly recently demolished.
Savoy	Strand	WC2	Designed in 1881 by C J Phipps and financed by Richard D'Oyly Carte for the production of Gilbert and Sullivan Operas. First public building to be lit by electricity, although the Gaiety theatre had experimented in 1878.
Shaftesbury	Shaftesbury Ave	WC1	Designed in 1911 by Bertie Crewe. Recently showing *Calamity Jane*.
Shakespeare's Globe	Southwark	SE1	Sam Wanamaker's dream of a theatre for all was opened in 1997 with Mark Rylance playing Henry V.
St Martin's	West St	WC2	Designed in 1916 by W G R Sprague. Recently showing *The Mousetrap*.
Strand	Aldwych	WC2	Designed 1905 by W G R Sprague. Recently showing *The Rat Pack*.
Theatre Royal, Haymarket	Haymarket	SW1	Built in 1821 by John Nash.
Theatre Royal, Stratford	Gerry Raffles Square	E15	Built in 1884 by James George Buckle.
Tricycle	Kilburn High Rd	NW6	Fringe theatre.
Unicorn	Great Newport St	WC2	Presently a travelling company following the closure of its theatre in Great Newport Street.
Vaudeville	Strand	WC2	Designed by C J Phipps 1870. Recently showing *Stomp* (by Luke Cresswell and Steve McNicholas).
Venue	Leicester Square	WC2	Opened in November 2001, the brainchild of Adam Kenwright. Was specifically designed to show the musical *Taboo*, based on the life of pop singer Boy George.
Victoria Palace	Victoria St	SW1	Designed in 1911 by Frank Hatcham. Recently showing *Grease* (by Jim Jacobs and Warren Casey).

Name	Address	Post	Details
Westminster	Palace St	SW1	Possibly the nearest theatre to Buckingham Palace.
Whitehall	Whitehall	SW1	Built in 1930. Formerly to the design of E A Stone. Known for its farces.
Wyndham's	Charing Cross Road	WC2	Designed by W G R Sprague and opened in 1899. Recently showing *Absolutely!! (Perhaps)* adapted from Luigi Pirandello's *Right You Are If You Think So.*
Young Vic	The Cut	SE1	Built in 1970. Recently showing *Hobson's Choice* (by Harold Brighouse).

NB: Notable London fringe theatres (and pubs) not listed above include Half Moon, Old Red Lion, Orange Tree, Bird's Nest, Landor, Hen & Chickens, Pentameters, Albany, Etcetera, Oval House, Pleasance, Richmond (The Green) and Riverside Studios.

Statues

Site	Person(s) Depicted
Albert Hall (SW7)	*Prince Albert* by Joseph Durham (1863).
Bank of England (EC2)	Stone statues of *Sir John Soane* by Sir William Reid Dick (1937) and *King William III* by Sir Henry Cheere (1735).
Banqueting House, Whitehall (SW1)	Lead bust of *Charles I* by unknown sculptor.
Belgrave Square (SW1)	Bronze of *Simon Bolivar* by Hugo Daini (1974).
Birdcage Walk (SW1)	Bronze of *Field Marshal Earl Alexander of Tunis* by James Butler (1985).
Bloomsbury Square, (WC1)	*Charles James Fox* by Richard Westmacott (1816).
Cannon St (EC4)	Bronze mask of *Winston Churchill* by Frank Dobson (1959) over the entrance to Bracken House.
Carey St / Serle St (WC2)	Stone figure of *Sir Thomas More* by Robert Smith (1866).
Carlton Gardens (SW1)	Bronze of *General Charles de Gaulle* and *George VI* by William McMillan.
Cavendish Square (W1)	Bronze of *William George Bentinck* by Thomas Campbell (1851).
Charing Cross Rd (WC2)	Bronze of *Sir Henry Irving* by Thomas Brock (1910) by the St Martin's Place side of the National Portrait Gallery.
Chelsea Embankment (SW3)	Bronze of *Thomas Carlyle* by Sir Joseph Boehm (1882); seated bronze of *Sir Thomas More* by L Cubitt Bevis (1969).
Chelsea Hospital (SW3)	*Bronze of King Charles II in Roman Costume*, by Grinling Gibbons (1676).
Chiswick House (W4)	Stone figure of *Inigo Jones* by John Rysbrack (1729).
City Rd (EC1)	*John Wesley* by John Adams-Acton (1891).
Cockspur St (SW1)	Bronze equestrian of *George III* by Matthew Cotes Wyatt.
Commercial Rd (E1)	Bronze of *Clement Attlee* by Frank Forster (1988) outside Limehouse Library.
Cornhill (No 32) EC3	Mahogany carving of *The Brontë sisters in Conversation with William Makepeace Thackeray* by Walter Gilbert (1939).
Crystal Palace Park (SE19)	Marble bust of *Sir Joseph Paxton* by W F Woodington (1869).
Downing St (SW1)	*Mountbatten* outside Foreign Office.
Euston Station (NW1)	Bronze of *Robert Stephenson* by Baron Marochetti (1871).
Festival Hall (SE1)	Bronze of *Frederic Chopin*, beside the Festival Hall, by B Kubica (1975).
Fleet St (EC4)	Stone of *Elizabeth I* by William Kerwin (1586) over the vestry porch of St Dunstan in the West. This is the oldest statue of a monarch in London and, in fact, the oldest outdoor statue of any kind.
Fleet St (Nos 143–4) EC4	Stone of *Mary, Queen of Scots*, placed by an admirer, Sir John Tollemache Sinclair (1880).
Greenwich Park (SE10)	Samuel Nixon's Foggit Tor granite of *William IV*, erected in King William IV St in 1844 and moved to present site in 1938.
Grosvenor Gardens (SW1)	Bronze equestrian of *Marechal Foch* by G. Mallisard (1930).
Grosvenor Square (W1)	Bronze of *F.D. Roosevelt* by Sir William Reid Dick; bronze of *General Dwight D. Eisenhower* by Robert Dean (1989).
Guildhall (EC2)	Limewood carvings of mythical giants, *Gog and Magog*, by David Evans, replacing those burned in 1940.
Hamilton Gardens (W1)	Bronze of *George Gordon Byron* by Richard Belt (1880).
Hanover Square (W1)	Bronze of *William Pitt the Younger* by Francis Chantrey (1831).
Highgate Cemetery (N6)	Bronze of *Karl Marx* by Laurence Bradshaw (1956).
Holborn Circus (EC1)	Equestrian bronze of *Prince Albert* by Charles Bacon (1874).
Horse Guards Parade (SW1)	Bronze of *Field Marshal Earl Kitchener* by John Tweed (1926); bronze equestrian of *Field Marshal Viscount Wolseley* by Sir William Goscombe John (1920).
Houses of Parliament (SW1)	Equestrian bronze of *Richard I* in Old Palace Yard by Carlo Marochetti (1861); bronze of *Oliver Cromwell* outside Westminster Hall by Sir Hamo Thornycroft (1899). Statue of *George VI* stands opposite the *Richard I* outside the grounds and was sculpted by William Reid Dick (1947).
Hyde Park Corner (SW1)	Bronze of *The Duke of Wellington* on his horse, Copenhagen, by J E Boehm (1888).
Kensington Gardens (SW7)	Bronze of *Sir Winston and Lady Churchill* by Oscar Nemon (1981) situated near

L
O
N
D
O
N

Site	Person(s) Depicted
	Hyde Park Gate; seated statue of *Queen Victoria* by her daughter, Princess Louise (1893); Albert Memorial designed by George Gilbert Scott, with seated statue of Albert begun by Baron Marochetti and completed in 1876 by John Foley.
Kensington Palace (W8)	Bronze of *William III* by Heinrich Baucke (1907) presented by Kaiser Wilhelm II to his uncle, Edward VII.
King Charles Street (SW1)	Bronze figure of *Robert Clive* by John Tweed (1912).
King Edward Street (EC1)	Granite figure of *Sir Rowland Hill*, founder of the Penny Post, by R Onslow Ford (1881).
Leicester Square: Centre (WC2)	Marble of *William Shakespeare* by Giovanni Fontana (1874); bronze of *Charlie Chaplin* by John Doubleday (unveiled by Ralph Richardson in 1981).
Leicester Square: Gates (WC2)	Memorial gates, to *John Hunter* by Thomas Woolner, *Isaac Newton* by William Calder Marshall, *Joshua Reynolds* by Henry Weekes (all 1874) and *William Hogarth* by Joseph Durham (1875), all of whom have commemorative busts.
The Mall (near Admiralty Arch, SW1)	Bronze of *Captain James Cook* by Sir Thomas Brock (1914).
	Seated marble statue of Queen Victoria by Sir Thomas Brock (1911).
Marylebone Rd (NW1)	Bronze of *John Fitzgerald Kennedy* by Jacques Lipchitz (1965).
Millbank (SW1)	Bronze of *Sir John Everett Millais* by Sir Thomas Brock (1904).
Old Bailey (EC4)	Gilt of *Justice* by F W Pomeroy (1907).
Park Crescent (W1)	Bronze of *Edward Augustus, Duke of Kent* (Queen Victoria's father) by S S Gahagen (1827).
Park Lane (W1)	*Achilles* (20′ bronze cast in 1822 by Sir Richard Westmacott) 'Erected by the women of England to Arthur, Duke of Wellington and his brave companions in arms'.
Parliament Square (SW1)	Bronzes of *George Canning*, in a toga, by Richard Westmacott (1832); *Sir Robert Peel* by Matthew Noble (1876); *Field Marshal Jan Christian Smuts* by Jacob Epstein (1958); *Abraham Lincoln* (copy of the statue by Augustus Saint-Gaudens in Chicago); *Winston Churchill* by Ivor Roberts Jones (1973); *Benjamin Disraeli* by Mario Raggi (1883); *Lord Palmerston* by Thomas Woolner (1876).
Piccadilly Circus (W1)	*Shaftesbury Memorial Fountain*, better known as *Eros* although Alfred Gilbert's 1893 aluminium statue in fact depicts *The Angel of Christian Charity*, in honour of Lord Shaftesbury himself.
Pimlico Gardens (SW1)	Stone of *William Huskisson* in a Roman toga, by John Gibson (1836).
Prudential Assurance (Holborn EC1)	Cupronised plaster bust of *Charles Dickens* by Percy Fitzgerald (1907).
Red Lion Square (WC1)	Bronze bust of *Bertrand Russell* by Marcelle Quinton (1980).
Royal Exchange (EC2)	Equestrian bronze of *Wellington* begun by Francis Chantrey & completed by Henry Weekes (1844); and stone figure of *Richard Whittington* by J E Carew (1845).
Royal Geographical Society, Kensington Gore (SW7)	Bronzes of *David Livingstone* by T B Huxley-Jones (1953) and *Sir Ernest Shackleton* by C Sarjeant Jagger (1932).
St Bartholomew's Hospital (EC1)	Stone figure of *Henry VIII*, the founder, by Francis Bird (1702) stands over the gateway.
St Giles Cripplegate	Memorial statue of *John Milton* by Montford (1904).
St James's Square (SW1)	*William III*, equestrian bronze by John Bacon the Elder (1808).
St Martin's Place (WC2)	Marble statue of *Edith Cavell* by Sir George Frampton (1920). Famous inscription reads: 'Patriotism is not enough. I must have no hatred or bitterness for anyone.'
St Thomas's Hospital (SE1)	Statue of *Sir Robert Clayton*, the hospital's benefactor. The only outdoor stone statue by Grinling Gibbons.
Savoy Place (WC2)	Bronze of *Michael Faraday* by J H Foley (1889) situated outside the Institution of Electrical Engineers.
Soho Square (W1)	Stone statue of *King Charles II* by Caius Gabriel Cibber once owned by W S Gilbert.
Somerset House,	Baroque fountain in bronze, including a figure of *King George III* by John Bacon the
Strand (WC2)	Elder (1788).
South Africa House (Trafalgar Square)	Large stone figure of *Bartholomew Diaz* by Coert Steynberg (1934).
South Square, Gray's Inn (WC1)	*Francis Bacon* by F W Pomeroy (1912).
Strand (WC2)	Bronzes of *Air Chief Marshal Lord Dowding* and *Sir Arthur 'Bomber' Harris* by Faith Winter (1988) opposite St Clement Danes, the RAF church, and *Dr Samuel Johnson* by Percy Fitzgerald (1910).
Tavistock Square (WC1)	Bronze of *Mahatma Gandhi* by Fredda Brilliant (unveiled by Harold Wilson in 1968).
Tooting Broadway (SW17)	Bronze of *King Edward VII* by L F Roselieb (1911).
Trafalgar Square (WC2)	Bronzes outside National Gallery of *George Washington* by Jean-Antoine Houdon and *James II* in Roman dress by Grinling Gibbons; *Sir Henry Havelock* by William Behnes (1861); bronze equestrians of *George IV* by Sir Francis Chantrey (1834) and *Charles I* by Hubert Le Sueur (1633); *Nelson's column* (170′ 2″), with statue of Nelson by E H Bailey (1843) and Landseer's lions cast in 1868 from guns recovered from the wreck of the *Royal George*. On the north wall of the Square are

Site	Person(s) Depicted
	bronze busts of Admirals *Lord Beatty* by William McMillan (1984), *Lord Cunningham*, by Franta Belsky (1967) and *Lord Jellicoe* by Sir Charles Wheeler (1948).
University College London (WC1)	Bronze tablet and medallion of *Richard Trevithick* by L S Merrifield (1933).
Victoria Embankment (WC2)	*Isambard Kingdom Brunel* by Carlo Marochetti (1877); *Cleopatra's Needle* (68 ½').
Victoria Embankment	Bronzes of *John Stuart Mill* by Thomas Woolner (1878); *Robert Burns* by Sir John
Gardens (WC2)	Steel (1884); *Sir Arthur Sullivan* by W Goscombe John (1903), with a mourning female on the plinth; *Robert Raikes* by Sir Thomas Brock (1880).
Victoria Tower Gardens, Westminster (SW1)	*Burghers of Calais* by Rodin, copy (installed 1915) of original in Calais, created 1895. Emmeline and Christabel Pankhurst by A G Walker (1930).
Waterloo Place (SW1)	*Duke of York Column* memorial to Frederick, 2nd son of George III, statue by Sir Richard Westmacott 1834; bronze equestrian of *King Edward VII* by Sir Bertram Mackennal (1922); bronze of *Captain Robert Falcon Scott* by Lady Scott (1915); *Florence Nightingale* by Walker.
Westminster Bridge (SE1)	Thomas Thornycroft's *Boadicea* at the north-eastern end.
Whitehall (SW1)	Bronzes of *Sir Walter Raleigh* by William McMillan (1959); *Field Marshal Montgomery of Alamein* by Oscar Nemon (unveiled by Queen Mother in 1980); *Field Marshal the Viscount Alanbrooke* and *Field Marshal the Viscount Slim*, both by Ivor Roberts Jones.
Woodford Green (E18)	Bronze of *Winston Churchill* by David McFall (unveiled by Field Marshal Montgomery in October 1959).
Woolwich, Royal Arsenal (SE18)	Stone figure of *Wellington* by Thomas Milnes (1848).

Bridges

From East to West	Type	Opened	
Queen Elizabeth II	Road	1991	Clockwise route of M25; the Dartford Tunnel is the anti-clockwise route.
Tower	Road	1894	Built by John Wolfe-Barry to a design by Sir Horace Jones, the furthest bridge downstream in London.
London	Road	1831	Rebuilt by John Rennie but moved to Lake Havasu City, Arizona, in 1967; new bridge opened by Queen Elizabeth II, 16 March 1973.
Alexandra	Rail	1866	Cannon St in the north to Clink St in the south.
Southwark	Road	1819	Built by John Rennie; rebuilt 1921.
Millennium	Foot	2000	Built by an amalgamation of Norman Foster, Anthony Caro and Ove Enge. Links St Paul's Cathedral and the Tate Modern.
Blackfriars	Rail	1864	Upper Thames St in the north to Southwark St in the south.
Blackfriars	Road	1769	Rebuilt 1869 and widened 1910.
Waterloo	Road	1817	Built by John Rennie but rebuilt by LCC between 1937 and 1944 to plans of Sir Giles Gilbert Scott, opened by Herbert Morrison 1945.
Hungerford	Rail & Foot	1863	Suspension bridge built by Brunel 1845 but rebuilt 1863 as Rail & Foot bridge designed by Sir John Hawkshaw.
Westminster	Road	1750	Leads from Westminster Abbey and Houses of Parliament to the former County Hall and St Thomas' Hospital. The bridge was rebuilt in 1862.
Lambeth	Road	1862	Leads from Millbank in the north to Lambeth Palace. Rebuilt in 1932.
Vauxhall	Road	1816	Leads from Millbank in the north to Kennington Lane. Rebuilt in 1906.
Grosvenor	Rail	1860	Rebuilt 1967.
Chelsea	Road	1934	Built 1858 but rebuilt as suspension bridge 1934 and widened 1937.
Albert	Road	1873	Restructured by Sir Joseph Bazalgette in 1884 and strengthened 1973.
Battersea	Road	1772	Built of wood by Henry Holland and rebuilt by Bazalgette 1890.
Battersea	Rail	1863	
Wandsworth	Road	1873	Rebuilt 1940.
Putney	Rail	1889	
Putney	Road	1729	Rebuilt by Bazalgette 1886.
Hammersmith	Road	1827	Rebuilt by Bazalgette 1887 and the first London suspension bridge.
Barnes	Rail & Foot	1849	Restructured 1893.
Chiswick	Road	1933	Built by Sir Herbert Baker and Alfred Dryland.
Kew	Rail	1869	
Kew	Road	1759	Rebuilt and renamed The King Edward VII Bridge 1903.
Richmond Lock	Foot	1894	
Twickenham	Road	1933	
Richmond	Rail	1848	Restructured 1908.
Richmond	Road	1777	Widened 1937.

Teddington Lock	Foot	1889	
Kingston	Road	1828	Widened 1914.
Hampton Court	Road	1753	Replaced by iron bridge 1865 and rebuilt 1933.

Postal Areas

E1	Whitechapel	SW1	Belgravia		EC4	Fleet St
E2	Bethnal Green	SW2	Brixton			
E3	Bow	SW3	Chelsea		SE1	Southwark
E4	Chingford	SW4	Clapham		SE2	Abbey Wood
E5	Clapton	SW5	Earls Court		SE3	Blackheath
E6	East Ham	SW6	Fulham		SE4	Brockley
E7	Forest Gate	SW7	South Kensington		SE5	Camberwell
E8	Hackney	SW8	South Lambeth		SE6	Catford
E9	Homerton	SW9	Stockwell		SE7	Charlton
E10	Leyton	SW10	West Brompton		SE8	Deptford
E11	Leytonstone	SW11	Battersea		SE9	Eltham
E12	Manor Park	SW12	Balham		SE10	Greenwich
E13	Plaistow	SW13	Barnes		SE12	Lee
E14	Poplar	SW14	Mortlake		SE13	Lewisham
E15	Stratford	SW15	Putney		SE14	New Cross
E16	Victoria Docks	SW16	Streatham		SE15	Peckham
E17	Walthamstow	SW17	Tooting		SE16	Rotherhithe
E18	South Woodford	SW18	Wandsworth		SE17	Walworth
		SW19	Wimbledon		SE18	Woolwich
N1	Islington	SW20	West Wimbledon		SE19	Norwood
N2	East Finchley				SE20	Anerley
N3	Finchley (Church End)	W1	Mayfair		SE21	Dulwich
N4	Finsbury Park	W2	Paddington		SE22	East Dulwich
N5	Highbury	W3	Acton		SE23	Forest Hill
N6	Highgate	W4	Chiswick		SE24	Herne Hill
N7	Holloway	W5	Ealing		SE25	South Norwood
N8	Hornsey	W6	Hammersmith		SE26	Sydenham
N9	Lower Edmonton	W7	Hanwell		SE27	West Norwood
N10	Muswell Hill	W8	Kensington		SE28	Thamesmead
N11	New Southgate	W9	Maida Vale			
N12	North Finchley	W10	North Kensington		NW1	Camden Town
N13	Palmers Green	W11	Notting Hill		NW2	Cricklewood
N14	Southgate	W12	Shepherds Bush		NW3	Hampstead
N15	South Tottenham	W13	West Ealing		NW4	Hendon
N16	Stoke Newington	W14	West Kensington		NW5	Kentish Town
N17	Tottenham				NW6	Kilburn
N18	Upper Edmonton	WC1	Bloomsbury		NW7	Mill Hill
N19	Upper Holloway	WC2	St James		NW8	Marylebone
N20	Whetstone				NW9	Kingsbury
N21	Winchmore Hill	EC1	Finsbury		NW10	Willesden
N22	Wood Green	EC2	City		NW11	Golders Green
		EC3	Spitalfields			

General Information

Admiralty Arch (SW1) Built in 1910 to the design of Sir Aston Webb (who also designed the façade of Buckingham Palace) and consisting of 3 identical arches. Situated where the Mall leads into Trafalgar Square.

Alexandra Palace (N22) Sited in Muswell Hill and built in 1875 by Meeson and Johnson.

Alsop, William Designer of North Greenwich Jubilee Line Station.

Art galleries Tate Gallery, Millbank; Tate Modern, Bankside; National Gallery, Trafalgar Square; National Portrait Gallery, St Martin's Place; Wallace Collection, W1; Courtauld Institute, Strand; Sir John Soane's Museum, Lincoln's Inn Fields; William Morris Gallery, Forest Rd, E17; Queen's Gallery in Buckingham Palace; Dulwich Picture Gallery built by Sir John Soane 1811–13, England's oldest public art gallery.

Banqueting House Designed by Inigo Jones in 1622 and the only part of Whitehall Palace still standing.

Belfast, HMS (SE1) Built in 1939 and situated at Symon's Wharf in Vine Lane, this 11,000-ton cruiser, the largest ever built was opened to the public in 1971.

Big Ben Housed in St Stephen's Tower within the Houses of Parliament (Palace of Westminster) Big Ben, weighing in at 13.5 tons, is the name of the large bell housed in the clock tower and named after, either Benjamin Caunt, a popular boxer of the day (1858), or more likely Sir Benjamin Hall, the Chief Commissioner of Works.

Billingsgate Market (EC3) Fish market in Lower

Thames St, in use for over 7 centuries, which closed on 16 Jan 1982.

Billingsgate Market (E14) Opened on the Isle of Dogs 3 days after the original market closed.

Birdcage Walk (SW1) Here stood the aviary of James I.

Birkbeck College (WC1) Founded in 1823 as the London mechanics' Institution. Took its present name in 1907 and became part of the University of London in 1920. Situated in Malet Street.

Bishop of London, first St Mellitus, c. AD 604.

Blackfriars Bridge Roberto Calvi, an Italian banker, found hanging beneath it on 19 June 1982.

Blue Plaques William Ewart had the idea of using these to commemorate famous people, and Lord Byron was the first to have a plaque conferred on the house where he was born in Holles St, Westminster.

British Library Formed in 1973 from the amalgamation of the British Museum Library, National Central Library and National Lending Library. Now situated at St Pancras.

British Museum (WC1) Founded in 1753, initially to house the collection of Hans Sloane (1660–1753), it was opened to the public in 1759 at Montague House. The present museum was built on the same site in 1823–47 to a design of Robert Smirke. The ethnographical department of the museum is called The Museum of Mankind. Among the best known of the museum's treasures are the Elgin Marbles, Portland Vase, Mildenhall Treasure, Rosetta Stone, Sutton Hoo, Lewis Chessman, and the Lindow Man. Recent millennium renovations include the museum's inner courtyard, hidden from the public for 150 years being turned into the '*Great Court*' covered with a spectacular glass and steel roof designed by Norman Foster.

British Telecom Tower Designed by Eric Bedford and stands 580′ high with a 40′ mast giving an overall height of 620′. Originally called the Post Office Tower and nowadays simply the Telecom Tower.

Burghers of Calais **replica** Sited in Victoria Tower Gardens.

Canary Wharf Tower Designed by Cesar Pelli and at 850 feet exceeds the British Telecom Tower as Britain's tallest structure. Officially called No. 1 Canada Square.

Centre of London Charing Cross is now used as the point for measuring distances to other places.

Charing Cross Station (WC2) Situated just off the Strand and designed by Sir John Hawkshaw in 1864.

Clink Street (SE1) Site of the Bishop of Winchester's London estate and synonymous with the name of his Ecclesiastical prison.

Clubs Boodle's; Brooks's; Carlton; White's (all situated in St James's St, SW1); Beefsteak; Garrick; Pratt's (all the waiters are called George); Reform (Pall Mall), Athenaeum, Portland, Savile, Travellers, Groucho.

Coal Tax Christopher Wren's 50 new churches were paid for by a tax on coal entering London.

Cockneys Must be born within the sound of the church bells of St Mary le Bow.

Congestion charge From 17 February 2003 motorists driving into central London pay £5 for the privilege!

Courtauld Institute of Art Owned by the University of London and situated at Somerset House on the Strand.

Covent Garden Market (WC2) London's main wholesale fruit, flower and vegetable market. Congestion in Central London caused its closure in 1974 after 340 years trading. The New Covent Garden Market was opened immediately at the former railway yard at Nine Elms, Battersea.

Denmark St Aka Tin Pan Alley; home of the music publishing industry.

Docklands Light Railway Opened in 1987 and now extended from the Isle of Dogs to Bank.

Drainage system Designed by Joseph Bazalgette between 1859 and 1875 and still serving as the basis of London's sewage system.

Eel Pie Island, Twickenham Joined to the mainland by an old rickety concrete bridge, about 3′ wide. Made famous in the 1960s when the Rolling Stones played a concert there.

Football clubs: oldest Fulham (formed in 1879); Leyton Orient (1881); Spurs (1882); QPR (1885); Millwall (1885); Arsenal (1886); Brentford (1889); Wimbledon (1889); West Ham (1900); Chelsea (1905); Crystal Palace (1905); Charlton (1905).

Fulham Palace Official residence of the Bishop of London until 1973.

Greater London Consists of 31 boroughs and the cities of Westminster and London.

Greater London Council Created in 1965, but abolished in 1986. Originally called the London County Council, formed 1889.

Greenwich Palace (SE10) Built by Humphrey Deele of Gloucester in 1426 and now the site of the Royal Naval Hospital.

Gun salutes A salute of 62 guns is fired at the Tower of London on the birthdays of HRH Prince Philip, HM Queen Elizabeth, the Queen Mother and HM the Queen, who also has a 62-gun salute on accession and coronation day. A 42-gun salute is fired at the Tower of London and Hyde Park on other state occasions, e.g. opening and dissolution of Parliament, the birth of a royal infant, or a royal procession through London.

Hampton Court Maze Constructed for William and Mary (1690).

Highgate Hill Dick Whittington supposedly 'turned' here and became Lord Mayor.

Hyde Park Corner (SW1) Historic entrance to London from the west via the tollgate through Kensington and Knightsbridge.

Imperial War Museum Opened in 1920, and since 1935 occupying the remaining part of the old Bethlehem Royal Hospital, opened in 1815.

Livery Companies Craft guilds set up to promote the various trades of London. The Weavers are the oldest established guild whilst the Mercers are thought of as the senior guild. At present there are 102 city guilds, The Water Conservators being the latest set up in 2000.

Lloyd's of London Insurance underwriting corporation functional since the late 17th century, housed since 1986 in a headquarters designed by Richard Rogers.

London Eye Situated on the South Bank between the Hungerford and Westminster bridges. The British Airways London Eye is administered by the Tussauds Group. The diameter of the wheel is 135 metres (450 feet) and the architects were David Marks and Julia Barfield. The eye is also known as The Millennium Wheel.

London Gazette Henry Muddiman started it in 1665. It is published on Tuesdays and Fridays, as the

L
O
N
D
O
N

official organ of Britain's government. It was known as the *Oxford Gazette* for the first 23 bulletins.

London Stone Now set in the wall of the Bank of China, Cannon St, and possibly once used by the Romans as a measuring point.

Marble Arch Designed by John Nash to commemorate Nelson's victories, erected on side of Buckingham Palace in 1827, moved to Hyde Park in 1851.

Marylebone Road Site of Madame Tussaud's and the Planetarium.

May Day Parade Traditional parade through Hyde Park.

Mayor Ken Livingstone.

Monument (EC2) Contains 311 steps and commemorates the nearby spot in Pudding Lane where the Great Fire started in 1666. Designed by Christopher Wren, the total height is 202 feet.

Museum: Childhood Situated in Bethnal Green. Administered by the Victoria and Albert Museum, opened in 1872.

Museum of London (EC2) Opened in 1976 and illustrating the history of London from prehistoric times to the present day.

Museum: Wellington Apsley House, Hyde Park Corner. Administered by the Victoria and Albert Museum.

National History Museum (SW7) Situated near the V & A Museum in Cromwell Rd and opened in 1881 to a design of Alfred Waterhouse. Merged with the Ecological Museum in 1985.

National Maritime Museum (SE10) Founded in 1932.

New Scotland Yard (SW1) Metropolitan Police HQ situated near Victoria Street since 1967. The previous Scotland Yard building on the North Bank near Westminster Bridge was completed by Norman Shaw in 1890, after the original building at the top of Whitehall was damaged by a Fenian bomb in 1884.

Oldest club White's, founded 1693.

Palace of Westminster (SW1) The first palace was built for Edward the Confessor, not completed till 1858, but after the fire of 1834 its replacement was designed to become the home of both Houses of Parliament. Charles Barry's design was preferred to 96 other entrants, and he brought in Augustus Pugin to provide the Gothic interiors. The House of Commons was rebuilt by Giles Gilbert Scott after the bombing of 1941. St Stephen's Tower tops the Commons building, whilst the Victoria Tower stands at the southern end, at the other extreme from Big Ben.

Parks (central London) Green, Hyde, Regent's, St James's, Kensington Gardens.

Pelicans Live in St James's Park.

Peter Pan Statue in Kensington Gardens sculpted by George Frampton in 1912.

Petticoat Lane (E1) East London's long-established Sunday market (8am to 2pm) on Middlesex Street. Originally called Hog Lane Market in the 15th century. Given the name Petticoat Lane around 1600 because of its clothes stalls.

Piccadilly Circus Junction of Haymarket, Regent St, Piccadilly, Shaftesbury Avenue, Coventry Street.

Planetarium Opened in 1958 in Marylebone Rd, next to Madame Tussaud's.

Pool of London A reach of Thames consisting of two parts: the Lower running from Limekiln Creek to Cherry Garden Pier, and the Upper, from Cherry Garden Pier to London Bridge. Tower Bridge divides the two.

Queen's House, Greenwich Started by Inigo Jones during the reign of James I, as a gift to his wife Anne of Denmark; eventually completed in 1640. Now the centrepiece of the National Maritime Museum.

Ratcliff Highway Murders Seven victims were murdered in 2 incidents on this street in present-day Stepney in Dec. 1811. John Williams, a lodger at the Pear Tree public house, was arrested but hanged himself before his trial. The incident was a spur to the eventual forming of the Metropolitan Police in 1829.

Richard II Oldest painting of an English monarch from life (late 14th century), in Westminster Abbey.

Roman Gates of London Wall Aldgate; Aldersgate; Bishopsgate; Cripplegate; Ludgate; Newgate.

Royal Academy Founded by Joshua Reynolds in 1768, and originally site at Somerset House. Established in 1868 at Burlington House. Piccadilly Sackler Galleries added in 1990 by Norman Foster.

Royal Courts of Justice Designed by George Street in 1868 and situated on the north side of the Strand, the courts hear civil cases and criminal appeals. Opened by Queen Victoria in 1882 the Supreme Court is made up of the High Court, Court of Appeal and Crown Court. The High Court has 3 divisions: Queen's Bench, Family and Chancery. There are over 150 judges in the Royal Courts of Justice, a corridor known as the Chicken Run, and a recent wing named after St Thomas More. A tributary of the River Fleet is reputed to run under the building.

Royal Exchange (EC3) Founded by Thomas Gresham in 1566 as the 'Bourse' and proclaimed the Royal Exchange by Elizabeth I in 1570. First building destroyed in the Great Fire in 1666; second burned down in 1838; third completed 1842.

Royal National Theatre Building on the South Bank opened in 1976 and designed by Denys Lasdun. Lyttelton was 1st of the 3 auditoria to open, followed by the Olivier and Cottesloe.

Science Museum (SW7) Originally housed in the Victoria and Albert Museum but moved into its own building, across Exhibition Road, in 1913. The museum is the world's pre-eminent museum of science, medicine and technology. The Wellcome Wing, designed by Richard MacCormac, was opened in 2000 in partnership with the Wellcome Trust, Science Museum, and the Heritage Lottery Fund.

St James's Palace (SW1) Built by Henry VIII.

St Paul's Cathedral The new St Paul's Cathedral was built by Sir Christopher Wren between 1675 and 1710. The frescoes depicting the life of St Paul, above the Whispering Gallery on the underside of the dome are by James Thornhill. In the lower part of the south-west tower stands William Kempster's Geometrical Staircase and the clock room in the upper part houses Great Tom, the largest of three bells. The original St Paul's was built in 604 in the reign of St Ethelbert of Kent, the first Christian king in England, only to be destroyed by fire soon after. Two more rebuildings took place, culminating in the destruction by the Great Fire of 1666, when the only monument to survive was that of John Donne, the poet, who had been Dean of St Paul's for the last 10 years of his life. From pavement to the top of the cross on the tower of the dome, St Paul's is 365 feet high.

Silent Change   Annual ceremony to admit the new Lord Mayor.

Smithfield Market (EC1)   London's largest meat market which, although in decline, employs its own police force.

Somerset House   Designed by Sir William Chambers in the late 18th century and situated on the Strand.

Stock Exchange (EC2)   The new Stock Exchange opened in June 1973, replacing a building opened in 1888.

Strawberry Hill   Horace Walpole's Twickenham residence, built in 1748 and much extended, which is now the Roman Catholic St Mary's College of Higher Education.

Thames   No native name is known before Julius Caesar called the river 'Tamesis'. After Kent it is the oldest place name in England. Since 1996 it has been controlled by the Environment Agency.

Thames Embankments   Victoria Embankment on the north side of the river, running from Westminster to Blackfriars, the Albert Embankment on the south side from Westminster Bridge to Vauxhall, and the Chelsea Embankment, from Chelsea Bridge to Battersea Bridge were constructed by Sir J W Bazalgette.

Thames tunnels   The first tunnel under the Thames, completed in 1843, and linking Wapping and Rotherhithe, was called the 'Thames Tunnel' and is still in existence as a railway tunnel. The oldest road tunnel is the old Blackwall, opened in 1897; other road tunnels include the new Blackwall (1967), Rotherhithe (1908), and Dartford (1963 and 1980). The only foot tunnel still in existence runs from Greenwich to the Isle of Dogs.

Thames reaches   Starting from the mouth and proceeding upriver, the reaches are: Sea Reach (Yantlet Creek to West Blyth Buoy); Lower Hope (to Coalhouse Point); Gravesend (to Tilburyness); Northfleet Hope (to Broadness); St Clement's or Fiddlers' (to Stoneness); Long (to Dartford Creek); Erith Rands (to Coalharbour Point); Erith (to Jenningtree Point); Halfway (to Crossness); Barking (to Tripcock Point); Gallions (to Woolwich Hoba Wharf); Woolwich (to Lyle Park); Bugsby's (to Blackwell Point); Blackwall (to Dudgeon's Dock); Greenwich (to Deptford Creek); Limehouse (to Limekiln Creek); Lower Pool (to Cherry Garden Pier); Upper Pool (to London Bridge); London Bridge to Westminster Bridge and Westminster Bridge to Vauxhall Bridge (both nameless); Nine Elms (to Chelsea Bridge); Chelsea (to Battersea Bridge); Battersea (to Wandsworth Bridge); Wandsworth (to Putney Bridge); Barn Elms (to Hammersmith Bridge); Chiswick (to Chiswick Ferry); Corney (to Barnes Railway Bridge); and Mortlake (to Kew Bridge).

Theatre: largest   Coliseum.

Tourism Awards 2002
   Top Attraction – London Eye
   Top Hotel – Claridge's
   Top Restaurant – Rules (Strand)
   Top Retailer – Selfridges

Tower of London: first foundation   White Tower built by Gundul, bishop of Rochester, between 1078 and 1098.

Tower of London: Crown Jewels first housed   During reign of Henry III.

Tower of London: last beheading   Simon Fraser, Lord Lovat, in 1747. Last execution: Joseph Jacobs (15 Aug 1941).

Tower of London: last Monarch to occupy   James I.

Tower of London: Towers   Beauchamp; Bell; Bloody; Bowyer; Brick; Broad Arrow; Byward; Constable; Cradle; Devereux; Develin; Flint; Lanthorn; Martin; Middle; Salt; St Thomas's; Wakefield; Wardrobe (no longer standing); Well, White (the oldest).

Underground   First stretch of underground electric railway between City and Stockwell opened in 1890. John Fowler and Sir Benjamin Baker engineered the work.

Other British Underground systems in Glasgow, Liverpool, and Newcastle.

Metropolitan Railway, using steam locomotives, opened in 1863 and ran from Paddington to Farringdon St. Harry Beck (1902–74) redesigned the map in 1931 and his use of straight lines and a colour-coding system for the different lines is still in use.

Underground Map   Albert Stanley, Lord Ashfield, issued first map in 1908. The present colour-coded map was implemented in 1933 from a design by Harry Beck.

Unknown Warrior's Tomb   Westminster Abbey.

Victoria and Albert Museum (SW7)   The national museum of fine and applied art and design. Founded in 1852, and moved to its present site in 1857, being known then as the South Kensington Museum. The building was designed by Aston Webb and given its current name in 1899.

Wallace Collection   Art collection in Hertford House, Manchester Square, W1. Most famous work: *The Laughing Cavalier.*

Wardour St   Once used as a term to denote the British film industry.

Westminster Abbey: founder   St Edward the Confessor.

Westminster Abbey: Nave   At the end of the Nave, just in front of the Great West Door, is a memorial to Winston Churchill and nearby is the grave of the Unknown Warrior, commemorating those who were killed in WW1. The graves and memorials in the Nave include those of David Livingstone, David Lloyd George, Clement Attlee, Ramsay MacDonald, Isaac Newton, Lord and Lady Baden-Powell and F D Roosevelt.

Westminster Abbey: Poets' Corner   Graves and memorials of most of the major English poets and some writers and musicians. The foremost tomb is that of Geoffrey Chaucer, the first to be buried there, and the foremost memorial is that of William Shakespeare. Among the 20th-century poets commemorated are W H Auden, Dylan Thomas and T S Eliot. Gerard Manley Hopkins (1844–89), although buried in Glasnevin Cemetery, Dublin, has a commemorative plaque. Samuel Johnson, Charles Dickens and G F Handel are also buried there, and Oscar Wilde has been commemorated on floor and window.

Westminster Abbey: Royal Tombs   Elizabeth I; Mary I; Edward the Confessor; Henry VII; James I; Edward VI; George II; Henry III; Edward I; Edward III; Richard II; Henry V; Anne; Charles II; William III; Mary II and Mary Stewart; Queen of Scotland and France.

Westminster Abbey: Tomb of Elizabeth & Mary   Latin inscription on their tomb reads: 'Consorts both in throne and grave, here sleep we two sisters, Elizabeth and Mary, in the hope of one resurrection.'

Westminster Cathedral (SW1)   Roman Catholic Cathedral in Francis St, SW1, built of brick and

LONDON

Portland stone, to the design of John Francis Bentley and completed in 1903.

Westminster Hall Built by William Rufus between 1097 and 1099, home of the Royal Courts of Justice till they moved to the Strand in 1882, and incorporated in the Houses of Parliament.

White Lodge Built in 1727–8 in Richmond Park and formerly a royal residence, it is now the Royal Ballet School.

Whitehall Palace Tudor Palace much used by Henry VIII (died there in 1547) but William III found the river air exacerbated his asthma so transferred the royal residence to Kensington Palace. Only the Banqueting House, a later addition, survived the fire that destroyed the palace in 1698.

Zoo Founded by Sir Stamford Raffles; opened in 1828 after his death. Aviary designed by Lord Snowdon and opened in 1965.

MEDICINE

Medical Discoveries

Discovery	Date	Discoverer	Nationality
adrenal gland: function of	1856	Alfred Vulpian	French
adrenalin	1901	Jokichi Takamine	Japanese
AIDS	1981	Lost Angeles scientists	American
antisepsis	1865	Joseph Lister	British
blood circulation	1628	William Harvey	British
blood groups	1901	Karl Landsteiner	Austrian
chloroform	1847	James Simpson	British
chromosomes	1888	Thomas Morgan	American
corpuscles, red	1684	Antoni van Leeuwenhoek	Dutch
cortisone	1934	Edward Kendall	American
diabetes, cause of	1901	Eugene Opic	American
diphtheria bacillus	1884	Edwin Klebs and Friedrich Löffler	German
DNA, structure of	1953	Francis Crick and James Watson	British/American
Down's Syndrome, cause of	1959	Dr Jerome, Lejeune	French
electro-encephalogram	1929	Hans Berger	German
endorphins	1975	Hughes, Guillemin	American
enzymes	1833	Anselme Payen, Jean-François Persoz	French
ether as anaesthetic	1846	William Morton	American
heparin	1915	Jay McLean	American
heredity	1865	Gregor Mendel	Austrian
HIV virus, isolated	1983	Luc Montagnier (among others)	French
insulin, isolated	1921	F G Banting, C H Best, J J R McLeod	Canadian
interferon	1957	A Isaacs, J Lindemann	UK/Swiss
leprosy bacillus	1869	Gerhard Hansen	Norwegian
microbes	1762	M A Plenciz	Austrian
morphine	1805	Friedrich Sertürner	German
nitrous oxide	1776	Joseph Priestley	British
nucleic acid	1869	J F Miescher	Swiss
penicillin	1928	Alexander Fleming	British
protozoa	1675	Antoni van Leeuwenhoek	Dutch
rabies vaccination	1885	Louis Pasteur	French
Rhesus factor	1939	Karl Landsteiner, A S Wiener	Austrian
scurvy, treatment of	1740	James Lind	British
sleeping sickness transmission	1895	David Bruce	British
smallpox vaccination	1796	Edward Jenner	British
streptomycin	1943	Selman Waksman	American
tomography	1915	André Bocage	French
tuberculosis bacillus	1882	Robert Koch	German
typhus bacillus	1880	Karl Eberth	German
vitamin A	1913	E McCollum, M Davis, T Osborne, L Mendel	American
vitamin B (niacin)	1913	Casimir Funk	Polish
vitamin B1 (thiamin)	1897	Christiaan Eijkman	Dutch
vitamin B2 (riboflavin)	1933	R Kuhn, A von Szent-Gyorgi, J Wagner-Jauregg	Austrian/ Hungarian/ Austrian
vitamin B3	1937	Madden, Strong, Wooley, Elvehjem	British/American
vitamin B5	1933	R J Williams	American
vitamin B6	1936	Birch, A von Szent-Gyorgi	US/Hungarian
vitamin B9	1938	Day	British
vitamin B12	1937	G R Minot, W P Murphy	British
vitamin C (isolated)	1928	A von Szent-Gyorgi	Hungarian
vitamin D (isolated)	1924	Steenbock, Hess, Weinstock	German
vitamin E	1923	H M Evans, Bishop	American
vitamin K1	1934	Carl Peter Henrik Dam	Danish
vitamins, necessity of	1906	Sir Frederick Hopkins	British
X-rays	1892	Heinrich Hertz	German
X-rays, properties of	1895	Wilhelm Röntgen	German
yellow fever, mosquito transmission	1881	Ronald Ross	British

Bones in the Human Body

skull		
occipital		1
parietal – 1 pair		2
sphenoid		1
ethmoid		1
inferior nasal conchae – 1 pair		2
frontal – 1 pair fused		1
nasal – 1 pair		2
lacrimal – 1 pair		2
temporal – 1 pair		2
maxilla – 1 pair		2
zygomatic – 1 pair		2
vomer		1
palatine – 1 pair		2
mandible – 1 pair fused		1
		22

arms		
upper arm:	humerus – 1 pair	2
lower arm:	radius –1 pair	2
	ulna – 1 pair	2
carpus:	scaphoid – 1 pair	2
	lunate – 1 pair	2
	triquetral – 1 pair	2
	pisiform – 1 pair	2
	trapezium – 1 pair	2
	trapezoid – 1 pair	2
	capitate – 1 pair	2
	hamate – 1 pair	2
metacarpals – 5 pairs		10
phalanges:	1st digit – 2 pairs	4
	2nd digit – 3 pairs	6
	3rd digit – 3 pairs	6
	4th digit – 3 pairs	6
	5th digit – 3 pairs	6
		60

hip bones (pelvic girdle)	
ilium fused with ischium and pubis – 1 pair	2

ears	
malleus	2
incus	2
stapes	2
	6

vertebrae	
cervical	7
thoracic	12
lumbar	5
sacral – 5 fused to form sacrum	1
coccyx – fused joint	1
	26

ribs	
true ribs – 7 pairs	14
false ribs – 5 pairs (2 floaters)	10
	24

sternum	
manubrium	1
sternebrae	1
xiphisternum	1
	3

throat	
hyoid	1

pectoral girdle	
clavicle – 1 pair	2
scapula – 1 pair	2
	4

legs		
upper leg:	femur – 1 pair	2
lower leg:	tibia – 1 pair	2
	fibula – 1 pair	2
tarsus:	talus – 1 pair	2
	calcaneus – 1 pair	2
	navicular – 1 pair	2
	medial cuneiform – 1 pair	2
	intermediate cuneiform – 1 pair	2
	lateral cuneiform – 1 pair	2
	cuboid – 1 pair	2
metatarsals – 5 pairs		10
phalanges	1st digit – 2 pairs	4
	2nd digit – 3 pairs	6
	3rd digit – 3 pairs	6
	4th digit – 3 pairs	6
	5th digit – 3 pairs	6
		58

Total	
skull	22
arms	60
hips	2
ears	6
vertebrae	26
ribs	24
sternum	3
throat	1
pectoral girdle	4
legs	58
	206

General Information

abdomen   contains most of the digestive system. It is the biggest cavity in the body, extending from underneath the diaphragm to the groin area and bounded at the back of the body by the spine, and round its upper sides by the ribs. The abdomen contains the alimentary canal, liver, spleen, kidneys and pancreas.

acid in stomach   hydrochloric.

acupuncture   Traditional acupuncture is based on the principle that our health is dependent on the bal-anced functioning of the body's motivating energy, known as Qi (ch'i). This Qi flows throughout the body, but is concentrated in channels beneath the skin, known as meridians. The aim of treatment is to restore the balance between the equal and opposite qualities of Qi, namely the Yin and Yang.

The Human body is composed of 12 meridians that mirror themselves on the left and right side of the body. Each of these meridians contains / is a part of muscles, tendons, ligaments and a surrounding facia that stretches all along the meridian, a bit like a string of sausages. From childhood there were times when we felt that powerful emotions would overwhelm us. We learnt to suppress these overwhelming emotions by contracting muscles within us. These contractions become habitual and are thought to have an effect on the body structure affecting bone alignment in the joints, spine and cranium. When the body structure is distorted (extremely common) nerves can get pinched or stretched, internal body organs become distorted, hormonal glands under- or overproduce, joints can wear out quicker, and various muscles and tendons may become shortened or overstretched. Stress is the most common cause of this distortion, but there are other common factors that will also affect our health and well-being. These include diet, drugs and lack of appropriate exercise.

Acupuncture treats the body as a whole – the physical, mental (emotional) & psychic (spirit) levels, not only the disease or ailment. It is an ancient art of healing developed over thousands of years and works by stimulating the Qi and eliminating all toxins from the body. This is achieved by stimulation of specific energy points. Acupuncture can be done without needle – laser, electro-acupuncture, finger pressure (shiatsu) or ultrasound. It is not a substitute for conventional medicine but acts to compliment it. It was popularised in the Western world in 1972 following Richard Nixon's visit to China and his championing of its benefits.

There are hundreds of acupuncture points throughout the body, but here is a list of the main 12 meridians:
(1) the Lung Channel of Hand, (2) the Large Intestine Channel of Hand, (3) the Stomach Channel of Foot, (4) the Spleen Channel of Foot, (5) the Heart Channel of Hand, (6) the Small Intestine Channel of Hand, (7) the Urinary Bladder Channel of Foot, (8) the Kidney Channel of Foot, (9) the Pericardium Channel of Hand, (10) the Triple Burner Channel of Hand, (11) the Gall Bladder Channel of Foot, (12) the Liver Channel of Foot.
Notes: The lungs (Yin) and large intestine (Yang) are paired organs. Their opening is the nose, and they govern skin and hair. The main function of the large intestine is the metabolism of water and the passing of water. The spleen (Yin) and the stomach (Yang) are paired organs. Their opening is the mouth and they control the flesh and the limbs. The spleen is the main organ of digestion. Its function is to transport nutrients and regulate the blood (keep it within the channels). It is responsible for the transformation of food into nourishment. The stomach receives food while the spleen transports nutrients. The stomach moves things downward while the spleen moves things upward.

The heart (Yin) and the small intestine (Yang) are paired organs. Their point of entry is the tongue. They control the blood vessels and are reflected in the face. The heart governs the blood vessels and is responsible for moving blood through them. It also stores the spirit, and is the organ usually associated with mental processes. The major function of the small intestine is to separate waste material from the nutritious elements in food. The nutritious elements are then distributed throughout the body and the waste is sent on to the large intestine. The kidneys (Yin) and the urinary bladder (Yang) are paired organs. Their opening is the urethra. They control the bones, marrow, and brain, and their health is

reflected in the hair of the head. The kidneys store Original Essence (Yuan Jing) and are therefore responsible for growth, development, and reproductive functions. They play the primary role in water metabolism and control the body's liquids, and also hold the body's most basic Yin and Yang. The main function of the urinary bladder is to transform fluids into urine and excrete it from the body. The pericardium (Yin) and the triple burner (Yang) are paired organs. Though the pericardium has no separate physiological functions, it is generally mentioned with regard to the delirium induced by high fevers. The triple burner is regarded as 'having a name but no form' but is considered to be an organ that coordinates all the functions of water metabolism.

The liver (Yin) and the gall bladder (Yang) are considered paired organs. Their point of entry is the eyes. They control the sinews (muscles and joints), and their health is reflected in the finger and toe nails. The main task of the liver is spreading and regulating Qi throughout the entire body. Its unique character is flowing and free, so depression or frustration can disturb its functioning. In addition, the liver is responsible for storing blood when the body is at rest. This characteristic, together with its control over the lower abdomen, makes it the most critical organ in terms of women's menstrual cycle and sexuality. The main function of the gall bladder is storing and excreting the bile produced by the liver.

adrenal glands   glands that produce adrenalin, which prepares the body for stress by increasing heart rate and blood pressure. They also produce cortisone, which has a variety of metabolic effects.

allergy   term used by Clemens von Pirquet (1874–1929) in 1906 following his observations of the skin reaction to his test for tuberculosis.

allopathy   treatment of disease by conventional means – i.e. with drugs having opposite effects to the symptoms (opposite of homoeopathy).

Alzheimer's disease   serious disorder of the brain manifesting itself in premature senility. Named after the German neurologist Alois Alzheimer (1864–1915), who first identified it.

analeptic drug   restores and invigorates.

anaphylaxis   an extreme, often life-threatening reaction to an antigen, e.g. to a bee sting, due to hypersensitivity following an earlier dose.

anaplasty   medical name for plastic surgery.

anatomy   The science of the bodily structure of animals and plants.

angioplasty   surgical technique for restoring normal blood flow through an artery by means of laser therapy or insertion of a balloon into the narrowed section.

artery   tubular thick-walled muscular vessel that conveys oxygenated blood from the heart, the largest being the aorta.

Asperger's syndrome   mild variant of autism diagnosed in 1994. Sufferers may have extraordinary compensating talents, e.g. musical prodigy Joseph Erber (born 1984).

axilla   anatomical name for the armpit.

biology   the study of living organisms.

blepharitis   inflammation of the eyelids.

blood: circulation time   23 seconds on average.

blood content in body   varies slightly, but average man has 12 pts (5.6 litres) and woman 7 pts (3.3 litres), making the average 9 pints in general. An approximate calculation for adults is 60 millilitres per kilogram of body weight.

MEDICINE

blood groups A, B, AB, O. Blood groups may also be divided into Rhesus negative and positive. The most common group is O, which is universally given, and AB can receive from any group.

blood pressure: readings systolic is highest blood pressure reading; diastolic is lowest. Abnormally high or low conditions are called hypertension and hypotension respectively.

body builds the classification system is called somatotype and consists of: ectomorph (tall), endomorph (fat), mesomorph (muscular).

bones consist mainly of collagen, calcium phosphate and inorganic salts, mainly hydroxyapatite. The smallest is the stapes and the largest the femur. The only non-connected bone is the hyoid in the throat.

bradycardia abnormally slow heart action.

brain the brain contains 10,000 million nerve cells, each of which has a potential 25,000 inter-connections with other cells. Average weight of the brain is 3lb (1.4 kg). The left side is the rational side.

calcaneus heel bone.

cells the smallest cell in the human body is the male sperm, the largest is the female ovum.

central nervous system brain and spinal cord (vertebrates).

Chinese restaurant syndrome the so-called illness caused by monosodium glutamate. There is no evidence that the symptoms of dizziness and headaches affect more than a tiny proportion of people.

cholangiography X-ray examination of the bile ducts used to locate obstructions.

cholecystography X-ray examination of the gall bladder used to detect the presence of gall stones.

chromosomes there are 23 pairs in the human body, the female having two X sex chromosomes while the male has one XY pair. They carry the gene sequence and, therefore, full genetic blueprint.

collagen protein of great tensile strength present in bones, cartilage, tendons, ligaments and the skin.

colostrum mother's first breast-product after a birth before milk flow begins. Contains antibodies that bring important immunities.

comedo medical name for a blackhead.

conjunctivitis aka pink eye.

cornea convex transparent membrane that forms the forward covering of the eyeball; it is the only part of the body devoid of blood supply.

couéism form of auto-suggestion propagated by Emile Coué (1857–1926). A key phrase was: 'Every day, and in every way, I am becoming better and better.'

coxa (aka innominate bone) hip bone or joint (contrast ilium).

Crohn's disease chronic inflammatory disease of the intestines, especially the colon and ileum, causing ulcers and fistulae. Named after B B Crohn, US pathologist (1874–1983).

crural of the leg.

cubital of the forearm.

dentine calcified tissue of tooth.

diaphragm dome-shaped muscular partition that separates the abdominal and thoracic cavities.

disease: most widespread tooth and gum disease.

Down's syndrome: cause extra chromosome (three number 21s instead of the usual two, hence the medical name, Trisomy 21).

Economo's disease trypanosomiasis (sleeping sickness).

English disease aka bronchitis.

enuresis Involuntary urination.

epiglottis thin cartilaginous flap that covers the entrance to the larynx during swallowing, preventing food from entering the trachea.

epilepsy: categories petit mal, grand mal, psychomotor.

epistaxis a nose bleed.

erysipelas aka St Anthony's Fire.

erythrocyte red blood cell that contains the pigment haemoglobin and transports oxygen and carbon dioxide to and from the tissues.

eye chart, standard Snellen chart.

folic acid another name for vitamin B.

gall bladder muscular membranous sac; its function is to store and concentrate bile, a fluid that is received from the liver and is important in digestion. In humans, it is situated on the underside of the liver and is pear-shaped and expendable, with a capacity of about 1.7 fluid ounces (50 ml).

gland: largest the liver.

glandular fever infectious viral disease characterised by swelling of the lymph glands and prolonged lassitude. Aka infectious mononucleosis.

Government Chief Medical Officer Professor Liam Donaldson.

Graves disease exophthalmic goitre with characteristic swelling of the neck and protrusion of the eyes, resulting from an overactive thyroid gland.

haemoglobin red oxygen-carrying protein containing iron and present in the red blood cells of vertebrates.

haemophilia male-only disease that prevents the blood from clotting. Women may be carriers. Aka Royal Disease.

hallux big toe.

hardest substance in body tooth enamel.

Harefield Britain's leading hospital for heart and heart-and-lung operations, situated 20 miles west of London.

hemicrania migraine.

hernia the projection of an organ through the lining of the cavity in which it is normally situated. The two most common forms of hernia are femoral (upper thigh) and inguinal (groin).

heroin: made from morphine, an opium derivative.

herpes zoster shingles, an acute painful inflammation of the nerve ganglia, with a skin eruption, often forming a girdle around the waist, and caused by the same virus as chickenpox.

homoeopathy treatment of disease by minute doses of drugs that in a healthy person would produce symptoms of the disease. Opposite of allopathy.

hormones: female sex oestrogen and progesterone.

hospice movement: founder Dame Cicely Saunders.

housemaid's knee inflammation and swelling of the bursa in front of the kneecap, often caused by continual kneeling on hard surfaces. Aka prepatellar bursitis.

humerus bone extending from the shoulder to the elbow.

humours obsolete name for the four chief fluids of the body, i.e. blood, phlegm, yellow bile and black bile, that were once thought to determine a person's physical and mental qualities. Aka cardinal humours.

Hurler's syndrome defect in metabolism resulting in mental retardation, a protruding abdomen and bone deformities, including an abnormally large head. Aka gargoylism.

hypermetropia the condition of having long sight.

illium bone forming the upper part of each half of the human pelvis (contrast coxa).

inferiority complex named by Alfred Adler.

innominate bone (aka coxa) bone formed from the fusion of the ilium, ischium and pubis, aka the hip bone.

insulin: gland that produces pancreas (in cells called the islets of Langerhans).

interferon proteins made by cells in response to virus infection.

iridology diagnosis by examination of the iris of the eye (used mainly in alternative medicine).

iris the coloured muscular diaphragm that surrounds and controls the size of the pupil.

jaw bones maxilla (upper jaw), mandible (lower jaw).

joints: lubricating fluid synovial fluid.

keloid/cheloid overgrown scar tissue.

kidney organ that maintains water balance and expels metabolic wastes. The kidneys consist of two series of specialised tubules that empty into two collecting ducts, the Wolffian ducts. The two kidneys are positioned on the back wall of the abdomen.

kissing disease glandular fever.

kyphosis excessive outward curvature of the thoracic spine causing hunching of the back.

larynx cartilaginous and muscular hollow organ forming part of the air passage to the lungs. Aka Adam's apple, voice-box.

Lassa fever acute and often fatal febrile viral haemorrhagic disease of tropical Africa, named from the village in Nigeria where first reported.

Legionnaires' disease form of bacterial pneumonia first identified after an outbreak at an American Legion meeting in Philadelphia in 1976 and spread by water droplets through air-conditioning systems and similar devices.

leucocyte colourless amoeboid cell of blood and lymph, containing a nucleus and important in fighting disease. Aka white blood cell/white corpuscle.

leucoderma (aka vitiligo) skin condition characterized by loss of melanin pigmentation.

leucoma a white opacity in the cornea of the eye.

leucotomy surgical cutting of white nerve fibres within the brain, especially prefrontal lobotomy.

leukaemia malignant disease in which the bone marrow and other blood-forming organs produce too many leucocytes.

ligament short band of tough flexible fibrous connective tissue linking bones together.

ligature tie or bandage used in surgery for a bleeding artery.

lingua the tongue.

lipids organic compounds that are esters of fatty acids and are found in blood, cell membranes and elsewhere.

lithotomy surgical removal of a calculus (stony secretion) from the bladder or urinary tract.

lithotripsy removal of a calculus from the bladder or urinary tract by means of ultrasound techniques that shatter the stone so that fragments passs naturally from the body.

liver largest organ in the human body, composed of a spongy mass of wedge-shaped lobes that has numerous metabolic and secretory functions. It is tucked beneath the diaphragm, protected from damage by the lower ribs of the right side. Its average weight is 3 to 4 lb (1.36 to 1.81 kg).

liver: functions production of bile to emulsify fat in the bowel. Reception of all the products of food absorption and the subsequent release as energy sources. Carbohydrates are stored as glycogen, and the liver uses insulin from the pancreas to control the body's glucose level. Purification of blood. Production of proteins needed for blood clotting.

liver transplants: hospital Addenbrooke's Hospital near Cambridge was the pioneer.

lordosis inward curvature of the spine.

lungs the 700 million air sacs are called alveoli, and the right lung is heavier than the left.

lunula crescent-shaped white area at the base of the fingernail.

Lyme disease form of arthritis caused by spirochaete bacteria transmitted by ticks. Named after a town in Connecticut, USA, where an outbreak occurred in 1975.

Mantoux test intradermal tuberculin test named after French physician Charles Mantoux 1877–1947.

mastoid process conical prominence on the temporal bone behind the ear, to which muscles are attached.

Ménière's syndrome inner ear disorder characterised by ringing in ear, dizziness and impaired hearing.

miner's disease pneumoconiosis (caused by inhalation of coal dust).

mnemonic for nerves in the superorbital tissue: Lazy French Tarts Lie Naked In Anticipation (Lacrimal, Frontal, Trochlear, Lateral, Nasociliary, Internal, Abduceris).

mons pubis rounded mass of fatty tissue lying over the joint of the pubic bones.

mons veneris rounded mass of fatty tissue on a woman's abdomen above the vulva (Latin: Mount of Venus).

Moorfields (London EC1) Britain's leading hospital specialising in eye injuries.

MRSA general term for a group of bacteria that are penicillin-resistant. It particularly attacks the weak and infirm and is prevalent in hospital environments among patients with open wounds.

Munchausen's syndrome medical name for feigned symptoms brought on with a view to gaining admission into hospital.

Munchausen's syndrome by proxy mental condition in which a person seeks attention by inducing illness in another person, especially a child. Named after R E Raspe's literary hero.

muscae volitantes moving black specks seen before the eyes, caused by opaque fragments floating in the vitreous humour ('floaters') or a defect in the lens.

muscle: not attached at both ends tongue.

muscles: smile or frown debate although smiling is more beneficial to one's wellbeing, in fact, frowning uses more muscles.

myeloid tissue term for bone marrow, found in the or spinal cord and elsewhere.

myopia short-sightedness.

naevus birthmark in the form of a raised red patch on the skin.

nosology branch of medical science dealing with the classification of diseases.

obstetrics of or relating to childbirth and associated processes.

oedema condition characterised by an excess of watery fluid collecting in the cavities or tissues of the body. Aka dropsy.

oesophagus part of the alimentary canal between the pharynx and the stomach. Aka gullet.

MEDICINE

olfactory   of or relating to the sense of smell.

organs: largest   the skin is the largest and heaviest organ of the human body, but the largest and heaviest organ within the human body is the liver.

Paget's cancer   cancer of the nipple and surrounding tissue. Named after Sir James Paget (1814–99) the English surgeon and pathologist who described this disease.

Paget's disease   chronic disease of the bones characterised by inflammation and deformation. Aka *osteitis deformans*.

pancreas   gland secreting the hormone insulin, which regulates glucose levels in the body. Deficiency of insulin causes diabetes mellitus (sugar diabetes). The pancreas lies across the upper part of the abdomen, in front of the spine and on top of the aorta and the vena cava (the body's main artery and vein). The basic structures in the pancreas are the acini, collections of secreting cells round the blind end of a small duct. Among the acini are small groups of cells called the 'islets of Langerhans'. These constitute the whole 'other life' of the pancreas as an endocrine organ secreting the insulin required by the body to control its sugar level. The pancreas also has an exocrine gland which produces essential alkali in the form of sodium bicarbonate to neutralise the acidic content of the stomach.

pathology   study of causes and nature of diseases.

phlebitis   inflammation of a vein.

phlegm: medical name   sputum.

plasma   clear yellowish fluid portion of blood or lymph in which the corpuscles and cells are suspended.

prescription charge   from 1 April 2003 £6.30p.

purkinje effect   As light intensity decreases red objects are perceived to fade faster than blue objects of similar brightness.

radius   outer and slightly shorter of the two bones of the forearm.

retina   light-sensitive portion of the eyeball.

retrovir   brand name of zidovudine (AZT), used in treating HIV and AIDS.

rubella   German measles.

rubeola   medical name for measles.

Schick test   identifies susceptibility to diphtheria.

sclera   the white part of the eye.

sex change operation: first   George (Christine) Jorgensen (1952).

Siamese twins: called after most famous conjoined twins to survive into adulthood: Chang and Eng (1811–74), born in Siam.

singultus   hiccup.

skin   accounts for 16% of the body's weight and has an average surface area of 2,800 sq in (18,000 sq cm); as such, it is the largest and heaviest organ of the human body.

spleen   main function is to act as a filter for the blood and to make antibodies. It lies just below the diaphragm at the top of the left-hand side of the abdomen. It is normally about 5 inches (13 cm) long and weighs about ½ lb (240 g) and lies along the line of the 10th rib.

Stockholm syndrome   psychological term for process of bonding between hostage and captors.

Stoke Mandeville   Britain's leading hospital for the treatment of spinal injuries.

stomach capacity   about 2–2½ pints (0.94–1.18 litres).

stomatology   study of mouth diseases.

strabismus   medical name for a squint.

syncope   technical name for a faint.

talipes   club foot.

talus   the ankle bone.

teeth   By the age of 2–3 a child will usually have a complete set of 20 deciduous (milk) teeth. A full set of 32 permanent teeth develops after the age of six. The front four teeth in each jaw are called incisors, the next two are the canines (eyeteeth), the next four are premolars (the hindmost being the third molar or wisdom teeth), the outer teeth are called molars.

teeth: mnemonic   4 canines ('dogs' 4 letters)
8 incisors (8 letters in word)
8 premolars (8 letters in word)
12 molars (remaining teeth)
C is before I and M in alphabet and premolar implies that they come before molars.

tendon   cord or strand of strong fibrous tissue attaching a muscle to a bone.

testes   two glands that produce sperms and the male hormone testosterone.

test tube baby: first   Louise Brown in 1978 (doctors were Steptoe and Edwards).

thalassotherapy   ancient medical treatment of lying in sea water.

thorax   anatomical name for the chest.

thyroid gland   situated in the neck in front of the windpipe. Controls the metabolism.

tincture   medicinal extract in a solution of alcohol.

tongue   medical name lingua. Studding the tongue are many small projections called papillae. Inside these are some 9,000 taste buds which respond to only four basic tastes i.e. sweet, sour, salt and bitter.

Tourette's syndrome   neurological disorder characterised by tics, involuntary vocalisation, and in some cases the compulsive utterance of obscenities. The syndrome is named after French neurologist Gilles de la Tourette.

trachea   the windpipe.

trachoma   contagious disease of the eye with inflamed granulation on the inner surface of the lids, caused by chlamydiae.

trench foot   medical condition prevalent throughout the First World War caused by standing around in cold, wet and unsanitary conditions and in severe cases resulting in amputation of the feet.

trismus   variety of tetanus with tonic spasms of the jaw muscles causing the mouth to remain tightly closed. Aka lockjaw.

ulna   inner and longer of the two bones of the forearm.

urticaria   hives or nettle rash.

varicella   chickenpox.

variola   smallpox.

vascular   relating to blood vessels.

venereal disease: most common   gonorrhea.

vitiligo (aka leucoderma)   skin disease characterised by loss of melanin pigmentation.

vitamin   term coined by Casimir Funk (1884–1967) in 1911 for the unidentified substances present in food that could prevent the diseases scurvy, beriberi and pellagra.

Wasserman test: used for   testing for syphilis.

white death   tuberculosis.

yellow fever   tropical virus disease with fever and jaundice, transmitted by the mosquito and often fatal.

Phobias

abluto	bathing	cremno	precipices		satellites
acaro	itching	cryo	ice, frost	kineso	motion
acero	sourness	cymo	sea swell	kineto	motion
achulo	darkness	cyno	dogs	klepto	stealing
acro	heights	cyprido	venereal disease	koni	dust
aero	air	demo	crowds	kopo	fatigue
agora	open spaces	demono	demons	kristallo	ice
aichuro	points	dendro	trees	kypho	stooping
ailuro	cats	dermato	skin	lachano	vegetables
akoustico	sound	dermatosio	skin disease	lalo	stuttering
alektoro	chickens	didaskaleino	school	leuko	white
algo	pain	dike	justice	limno	lakes
amaka	carriages	dipso	drinking	linono	string
amatho	dust	dora	fur	logo	words
amaxo	vehicles	dromo	crossing streets	lysso	insanity
ambulo	walking	dysmorpho	deformity	maieusio	pregnancy
amycho	being scratched	eisoptro	mirror	mania	insanity
andro	men	electro	electricity	mastigo	flogging
anemo	wind	eleuthero	freedom	mechano	machinery
angino	narrowness	emeto	vomiting	melano	black
anglo	England and the	enete	pins	melo	music
	English	entomo	insects	merintho	being bound
anthro	flowers	eoso	dawn	metallo	metals
anthropo	man	eremo	solitude	meteoro	meteors
antlo	flood	ergasio	surgery	metro	poetry
apeiro	infinity	erythro	blushing	myso	contamination
api	bees	frigo	being cold	mono	being alone
arachno	spiders	gallo	France and the	musico	music
astheno	weakness		French	muso	mice
astra	lightning	gato	cats	myso	dirt
ataxio	disorder	gameto	marriage	myxo	slime
ate	ruin	gelio	laughter	necro	corpses
atelo	imperfection	genio	chins	negro	black people
aulo	flute	geno	sex	nelo	glass
aurora	Northern Lights	genu	knees	neo	newness
automyso	being dirty	gephyro	crossing bridges	nepho	clouds
bacilli	microbes	geuma	taste	nosema	illness
ballisto	missiles	gnosio	knowledge	noso	disease
baro	gravity	grapho	writing	nycto	darkness
baso	walking	gymno	nudity	ochlo	crowds
batho	depth	gyno	women	ocho	vehicles
batracho	reptiles	hade	Hell	odonto	teeth
belone	needles	haemato	blood	oiko	home
blenno	slime	halo	speaking	olfacto	smell
bronto	thunder	hamartio	sin	ombro	rain
caino	novelty	haphe	being touched	ommeta	eyes
carcino	cancer	hapto	touch	oneiro	dreams
cardio	heart condition	harpaxo	robbers	ophidio	snakes
carno	meat	hedono	pleasure	ornitho	birds
cathiso	sitting	helmintho	worms	osmo	odours
catoptro	mirrors	hiero	sacred things	osphresio	body odours
chaeto	hair	hippo	horses	ostracono	shellfish
cheima	cold	hodo	travel	ourano	Heaven
chero	cheerfulness	homichlo	fog	paedo	children or dolls
chiono	snow	homo	homosexuals	panto	everything
chrometo	money	horme	shock	paralipo	neglect of duty
chromo	colour	hyalinopygo	glass bottoms	paraskavedekatria	
chrono	duration	hydro	water		Friday the 13th
chronometro	clocks	hygro	dampness	partheno	girls
cibo	food	hypegia	responsibility	patho	disease
crystallo	crystals	hypno	sleep	patroio	heredity
claustro	closed spaces	hypso	high places	peccato	sinning
clino	going to bed	ideo	ideas	pediculo	lice
cnido	stings	io	rust	pelado	bald people
coito	sexual	kakorraphia	failure	penia	poverty
	intercourse	katagelo	ridicule	phago	swallowing
cometo	comets	keno	void	phasmo	ghosts
copro	faeces	keraunothneto	fall of man-made	phengo	daylight

MEDICINE

phobo	fears	**scoliono**	school	**terato**	monsters
phono	speaking aloud or noise	**scopo**	being stared at	**terdeka**	the number 13
		seia	flash	**thaaso**	sitting
photo	light	**sela**	flashes	**thalasso**	sea
phronemo	thinking	**sidero**	stars	**thanato**	death
phthisio	tuberculosis	**siderodromo**	travelling by train	**theo**	God
phyllo	leaves			**thermo**	heat
pnigero	smothering	**sino**	China	**thixo**	touching
pogono	beards	**sito**	food	**toco**	childbirth
poine	punishment	**sopho**	learning	**toxi**	poison
poly	many things	**sperma**	germs	**traumato**	injury
potamo	rivers	**spermato**	semen	**tremo**	trembling
poto	alcohol	**sphekso**	wasps	**trichopatho**	hair
pterono	feathers	**staso**	standing	**triskaideka**	the number 13
pyro	fire	**stygio**	hell	**trypano**	injections
rhabdo	being beaten	**syphilo**	syphilis	**xantho**	yellow
russo	Russia	**tacho**	speed	**xeno**	foreigners
rypo	soiling	**tapho**	graves and being buried alive	**zelo**	jealousy
satano	Satan			**zoo**	animals
scio	shadows				

Operations: Military and Social

Accolade Unfulfilled 1943 plan for capture of Rhodes and other Aegean islands.

Acrobat Original name for Operation Torch and the name used in the 1943 film *Tunisian Victory*, it was the planned British operation to advance from Cyrenaica to Tripoli, 1941.

Adlertag (Eagle Day) Start of main German air offensive on 13 August 1940, which led to the Adlerangriff (German plan for Battle of Britain).

A Go Japanese plan for a counterattack against possible US recapture of the Marianas during 1944.

Alaric First German codename for their possible military takeover in Italy.

Allied Force Began on 24 March 1999 when United States military forces, acting with Nato allies, commenced air strikes against Serbian military targets in the former Yugoslavia. The multinational force was tasked by Nato to bring an end to crimes committed by the Federal Republic of Yugoslavia against ethnic Albanians in the southern province of Kosovo. On 20 June 1999 Operation Allied Force was officially terminated. This was in response to the departure of all FRY military and police forces from Kosovo in compliance with the Military Technical Agreement, which was signed by the Commander of KFOR and representatives of the FRY Government on 9 June 1940.

Alpen Veilchen (Alpine Violet) Proposed plan for Italians to break out from Albania into Greece. Cancelled on 19 January 1940.

Anakim First Allied plan for amphibious reconquest of Burma, abandoned in 1943.

Anton German occupation of Vichy France on 11 November 1942, first codenamed Attila.

Anvil Original codename for Allied landing on the French coast between Toulon and Cannes, later changed to Dragoon.

Aphrodite American scheme to load surplus bombers with explosives and fly them to the south coast of Britain, where the two-man crew would bail out and another plane would guide the plane to crash into a V-1 site. Joe Kennedy, elder brother of JFK, was blown up on a test run over Norfolk.

Apostle I Allied return to Norway on 10 May 1945.

Arcadia Codename for the conference between Churchill and F.D. Roosevelt in Washington, 22 December 1941–14 January 1942.

Aufbau Ost Prior to Barbarossa, this was the German buildup in the east.

Autumn Mist (Herbstnebel) Codename for the Ardennes Offensive (Battle of the Bulge) in 1944.

Avalanche US and British forces landing in the Gulf of Salerno causing the Germans to withdraw to the Gustav Line across the peninsula north of Naples, 9–19 September 1943.

Avonmouth Failed Allied expedition to Narvik May–June 1940.

Axis (Achse) Originally called 'Alaric', the disarming of the Italian army after their surrender to the Germans on 8 September 1943.

Babylon 7 June 1981, destruction of Osirak nuclear reactor in Iraq by Israeli F16s.

Badr 6 October 1973, Arab assault in Yom Kippur War.

Bagration Successful Soviet offensive in the central part of the German-occupied Russian Front, 23 June–29 August 1944.

Barbarossa German invasion of the USSR on 22 June 1941, supported by Romanian troops.

Battleaxe 15 June 1941, the first British offensive into 'Hellfire' (Halfaya) Pass, which failed to recapture Tobruk.

Baytown British landing at Reggio, 3 September 1943, and advance into the south-west Italian mainland, reaching Auletta on 19 September and Potenza on 20 September.

Bernhard Failed German plan to flood Britain with forged money during the Second World War, by means of an air drop, and thereby ruin the British economy.

Bigot Security classification for Normandy landing planning documents.

Birdcage Airborne leaflet drop on POW camps in the Far East announcing Japanese surrender.

Blackbuck 1 1 May 1982, bombing of Port Stanley runway by a Vulcan bomber.

Blackcock XII British Corps attack at Roermond, southeast Holland, 16–26 January 1945.

Black (Schwarz) The German occupation of Italy in 1943.

Blue Book Following an unexplained UFO sighting in Roswell, New Mexico, in 1947 the US Air Force set up a study group code-named Project Sign. Of the 147 reported sightings all but 12 were explained. A further rush of sightings prompted the set up of Project Grudge on 11 February 1949. The USAF attempted to explain every UFO sighting but of the 273 official sightings, 231 were classed as unidentified. In March 1952 Project Grudge went public as Project Blue Book and for the next 17 years remained the USAF's official UFO Study Program. Investigations ceased in 1969 as the US government advised the USAF that the project was no longer justifiable.

Bluecoat Normandy Operation of 30 July 1944, which concerned the initial British diversionary breakout from their American boundary, followed by the US 3rd Army, under Patton, breaking through the German defences at Avranches, the gateway from Normandy into Brittany.

Bodenplatte Luftwaffe offensive operation against Allied airfields in north-western Europe during December 1944.

Bodyguard Overall codename for multiple Allied deception tactics in 1944, but usually associated with the diversionary operation to deceive the Germans into thinking that the invasion was to be Kent-based and aimed at the Pas de Calais. Originally codenamed Jael.

Bolero The build up of US troops in the UK in 1942.

Bolo During Vietnam War, an ambush operation by American F-4 fighters, flying like bombers, which knocked out 7 North Vietnamese Migs in one go.

Brassard Allied amphibious landings launched from Corsica on Elba, 17 June 1944.

Brevity 15 May 1941, the first British offensive into Hellfire Pass.

Buckshot Planned British attack in Libya, May 1942.

Bumblebee Anti-burglary device instigated by the Metropolitan Police on 1 June 1993 and sponsored by Yellow Pages. Bumblebee has several aspects to its 'sting'. The aim is to target known burglars in an effort to 'fight back' against criminals. In 1995 the Bumblebee Imaging System was implemented whereby stolen property recovered by the police can be matched against photographs supplied by the victim. Bumblebee has also run a campaign to make people aware that covert police patrols are carried out at car boot sales. Another key factor in Bumblebee operations is the personalisation of belongings. The increase in computer and mobile phone companies having tracing methods has meant their products are no longer worth stealing.

Cartwheel Phase One US troops recapture important islands in the Solomon Island Group from 1 July to 25 November 1943.

Cartwheel Phase Two US and Australian forces invasion of north-east New Guinea from 4 September 1943 to 23 March 1944.

Catapult 3 July 1940, British naval attack on French fleet at Mers-el-Kebir, destroying or damaging most of its ships to prevent them from falling into German or Italian hands.

Catherine British plan for forcing a passage into the Baltic to aid Poland, before the country's invasion by Germany and the Soviet Union in September 1939.

Cedar Falls The US clearance of Vietcong from Iron Triangle, Vietnam, in 1967.

Centaur Crackdown on Britain's 'black economy' by Customs and Excise from 1985 onwards. Lester Piggott was a famous catch.

Cerberus Channel dash of the German ships *Scharnhorst*, *Prinz Eugen* and *Gneisenau* from Brest to Germany in February 1942.

Chariot 27–28 March 1942, British Commando raid on St Nazaire to destroy the Normandie Dock.

Charnwood Normandy operation of 7 July 1944: attack north of Caen following a massive RAF bombardment.

Chastise British bombers led by Wing-Commander Guy Gibson attacked three dams in the Ruhr region of Germany in May 1943, using the spinning or 'bouncing' bombs designed by Barnes Wallis. Two dams were breached. Aka the Dambusters' Raid.

Cheshire British equivalent of Operation 'Provide Promise', i.e. the RAF flights into Sarajevo.

Chicken Little Abortive attempt to predict time and place of Skylab's return to Earth in 1979.

Chromite 15 September 1950, General MacArthur's successful amphibious landing at Inchon during the Korean War.

Clean Hands Launched by Milan magistrates in February 1992 to halt corruption in the city, especially collusion between the Mafia and the Christian Democratic Party.

Cobra Allied Normandy USAAF breakout of July 25 1944, following massive bombardment by USAAF.

Cockade Part of Allied deception plan to convince Germans that invasion of Europe would be anywhere but Normandy in summer of 1944. Brittany, northern Norway and the Pas de Calais were false objectives.

Colossus First British airborne operation (unsuccessful), Tragino viaduct, Campagne, Italy, on 10 February 1941.

Compass 9 December 1940, British 8th Army attack at Sidi Barrani, Egypt, which began the destruction of the Italian 10th Army.

Corkscrew Allied operations against the Mediterranean island of Pantelleria in June 1943.

Coronet Proposed US invasion of Japanese island of Honshu in March 1946 overtaken by Japanese surrender the year before.

Corporate British recapture of the Falklands in May/June 1982.

Countryman Investigation into alleged corruption in the Metropolitan Police.

Cromwell Not an operation but a British codeword for 'Invasion Imminent' used from 1940.

Crossbow Operation using fighters, anti-aircraft batteries and barrage balloons against German V-1 flying bombs in 1944, and later to bomb the V-2 rocket launch sites.

Crusader The 8th Army's first offensive (as 8th Army) in Libya, 18 November to 12 December 1941.

Culverin Allied plan for recapture of northern Sumatra in 1943 – never carried out.

Deliberate Force Nato's air campaign against Bosnian Serbs from 30 August to 14 September 1995.

Deny Flight UN denial of Bosnian airspace to warring parties, began on 12 April 1993. On 28 February 1994 four Bosnian Serb warplanes violating the no-fly zone were shot down by Nato aircraft. This was the first military engagement ever undertaken by the UN/NATO Alliance.

Desert Sabre Official name for the ground war in the Persian Gulf January–February 1991, although US media often used the term 'Desert Sword'.

Desert Shield US-led multinational force, whose establishment was formally announced on 9 November 1990 and whose aim was to secure the withdrawal of Iraqi troops from Kuwait.

Desert Storm Air offensive launched by US-led allied forces on the night of 17 January 1991 against targets in Iraq and Iraqi-occupied Kuwait. The campaign lasted until 27 February 1991.

Detachment US capture of the Japanese island of Iwo Jima from 19 February to 1 March 1945.

Diadem Allied offensive that began on 11 May 1944, and broke the German Gustav Line, capturing Rome on 4 June 1944.

Dickens The 3rd Battle of Cassino, Italy, 15 March 1944. The original codename was Bradman, a cricket reference.

Diver British anti-V-1 measures.

Downfall Projected Allied invasion of mainland Japan, planned for 1 November 1945 and never carried out.

Dragoon Launched on 15 August 1944; Allied invasion of southern France, subsequent to Operation Anvil. When the US 7th Army and the French 1st Army landed on the French Riviera the Americans drove through the Alps to take Grenoble, while the French took Marseilles and advanced up the Rhône valley to rejoin the Americans near Lyons and move northeastward into Alsace in September 1944.

Dracula Liberation of Rangoon completed on 3 May 1945.

Dynamo Evacuation of Anglo-French forces from Dunkirk, 26 May to 4 June 1940.

Eclipse Proposed dropping of Allied airborne army on Berlin in April 1945.

Edelweiss German Army Group A's operations against Baku area of the Caucasus during the summer of 1942.

Eisenhammer Planned Luftwaffe attack on Soviet power stations during February 1945.

El Dorado Canyon 14 April 1986, 24 USAF F-111 bombers attacked Tripoli in reprisal raid.

Epsom Normandy operation in the last 5 days of June 1944, a british move to outflank Caen from the West.

Eureka Codename for the Tehran conference of November 1943 between Churchill, Roosevelt and Stalin.

Exporter British and Free French invasion of Vichy-ruled Lebanon and Syria from 8 June to 12 July 1941.

Felix Proposed German plan to capture Gibraltar and the Canary and Cape Verde Islands with Spanish aid in November 1940. Spain's neutrality ruled it out.

Firebrand Allied occupation of Corsica, largely by Free French forces, from September to October 1943.

Flash Codename for attempt on Hitler's life in March 1943 when a bomb placed in his plane by Fabian von Schlabrendorff failed to explode.

Flintlock US invasion of Marshall Islands and Kwajalein Atoll from 31 January to 7 February 1944.

Forager US invasion of the Marianas between J11 and 26 June 1944.

Fortitude, North and South Deception campaigns to suggest that invasion of Northern Europe would be directed at either Norway or the Pas de Calais in 1944.

Freeborn 8th Army provision for withdrawal to Egyptian frontier in 1941.

Frequent Wind US evacuation of Saigon, Vietnam, in April 1975.

Fritz Initial plan for German invasion of the Soviet Union in December 1940, precursor of Barbarossa.

Fuller Attempt to prevent the German warships *Scharnhorst* and *Gneisenau* escaping from Brest in December 1943.

Full Flow Greatest UK exercise since 1945 involving transfer of 57,000 troops from UK to Germany for Lionheart/Cold Fire exercises; began 3 September 1984.

Galvanic US occupation of Tarawa, Makin and Apamama, in the Gilbert Islands, on 20–21 November 1943.

Gemsbock Anti-partisan drive in Greece, July 1944.

Gomorrah RAF fire-storm raid on Hamburg, 25 July 1943, when anti-radar chaff, codenamed 'Window', was used for the first time.

Goodwood Normandy offensive of 18 July 1944: an attack by the British Second Army south-east of Caen following massive bombardment by RAF.

Granby British contribution to the Gulf War from Operation Desert Storm to the ceasefire on 11 April 1991.

Granite US offensive operations in the Central Pacific, beginning March 1944.

Grapeshot Allied attack on German-occupied northern Italy in 1944.

Grenade Operation that linked Lieutenant General William Simpson's 9th US Army to the Canadian offensive against the lower Rhine (Operation Veritable) in February 1945.

Gymnast Proposed British landings in Tunisia and Algeria in 1941, superseded by Torch.

Hammer Proposed Allied attack on Trondheim, central Norway, April 1940, abandoned as impracticable.

Hercules Proposed German airborne invasion of

Malta in the spring of 1942 involving airborne and sea landings. The operation was cancelled.

Horrido German anti-partisan drive in Yugoslavia during the spring of 1944.

Husky US and British troops landing in Sicily on 10 July 1943; total occupation achieved by 17 August 1943.

Icarus Proposed German invasion of Iceland in 1940; not carried out.

Iceberg US capture of Okinawa from 1 April to 22 June 1945.

I Go Japanese codename for naval counter-offensive in the Pacific during April 1943.

I – Go Sakusen Japanese air offensive in south-west Pacific, 7 to 16 April 1945 (aka Operation A).

Iltis German anti-partisan drive in Greece during March 1944.

Infatuate Allied operation to capture Walcheren Island in the Scheldt estuary on 1–18 November 1944.

Irma Media term for the airlift of some 40 people seriously injured in the war in Bosnia-Herzegovina to hospitals in the UK, Sweden and Italy in August 1993. Named after Irma Hadzimuratovic, a wounded 5-year-old whose plight was given huge media coverage after Prime Minister John Major arranged for her flight out of Sarajevo.

Ironclad British occupation of Diego Suarez, Madagascar, 8 May 1942.

Isabella (Ilona) Abortive German plans to occupy Atlantic coasts of Spain and Portugal in 1941.

Jael See Bodyguard.

Jericho RAF Mosquito raid on Amiens jail to release Resistance prisoners, 18 February 1944.

Joint Guardian In the aftermath of Operation Allied Force the Joint Guardian operation continues to pursue the ultimate goal of a peaceful multi-ethnic and democratic Kosovo. The original five-point plan of Allied Force was to stop the Serb offensive, force a Serb withdrawal, establish democratic self-government in Kosovo, allow a Nato-led peacekeeping force and to allow the safe return of Kosovar Albanian refugees.

Jubilee Disastrous Anglo-Canadian amphibious raid on Dieppe on 19 August 1942.

Junction City Only US para assault of Vietnam War, 22 February–14 May 1967.

Jupiter Projected Allied invasion of northern Norway in 1942; not carried out.

Just Cause Code name for the US military invasion of Panama between 20 December 1989 and 13 February 1990. It saw the first operational use of the stealth bomber.

Ka Go Japanese reinforcement of Guadalcanal in August 1942 resulting in the battle of the Eastern Solomons.

Kathleen A German-planned invasion of Ireland in the summer of 1940, with the support of the IRA. Preparing work on this plan was made by the IRA themselves, but aborted.

Konstantin German operation to seize control of Italian-controlled Balkans during September 1943.

Koralle German anti-partisan drive in Greece during July 1944.

Kreuzoller German anti-partisan drive in Greece during August 1944.

Kugelblitz German anti-partisan drive in Yugoslavia during latter half of 1943.

Kutuzov Soviet counter-offensive in the Kursk salient of July 1943.

MILITARY

Leopard German assault on the island of Leros, Greece, in 1943.

Lightfoot General Montgomery's plan for the breakthrough phase of the 2nd Battle of El Alamein, 23 October 1942. It failed to break the German defences.

Lila German operation to seize the French fleet at Toulon. They found the fleet scuttled on 27 November 1942.

Limerick British attack in Libya, June 1942.

Linebacker II The 1972 Christmas bombing offensive against North Vietnam by US B-52 bombers.

Little Saturn Soviet offensive against the German relief forces trying to break through to the encircled 6th Army at Stalingrad, launched on 16 December 1942.

Lumberjack Advances by US First Army to the Rhine at Cologne and by US Third Army further south in February 1945.

Lustre British transfer of forces from Western Desert to Greece in March 1941.

Luttich German attempt to cut off the Americans breaking out of Normandy by attacking at Mortain 17 August 1944.

Magic Name given to the overall US Intelligence programme before and during the Second World War devoted to breaking Japanese codes.

Magic Carpet Airlift of some 50,000 Jews from Yemen to Israel in the late 1940s and early 1950s.

Magnet Codename for the arrival of US forces in Northern Ireland in February 1942.

Mailfist Planned Allied recapture of Singapore, in 1945.

Manhattan District Cover name for the USA's atomic bomb project begun in June 1942.

Mannah Dropping of food supplies to occupied Holland by RAF in April and May 1945. Also codename for British intervention in the Greek civil war in October 1944.

Marita German assault on Yugoslavia and Greece in May 1941.

Maritime Monitor Royal Navy blockade of Serbia.

Market Garden The disastrous Allied airborne attack near Arnhem on 17 September 1944 which failed to link up with the British Second Army. Market was the airborne operation in which Allied paratroops were to seize key river crossings in advance of Second Army's tanks. Garden was the ground phase.

Menace Failed Anglo-Free French attempt to capture Vichy Dakar in West Africa with help from De Gaulle in September 1940.

Mercury German airborne assault on Crete in May 1941.

Midsummer Night's Dream Probing attack by Rommel in Libya, 14 September 1941.

Millennium RAF Bomber Command's 30/31 May 1942, 1,000-bomber raid on Cologne.

Mincemeat Aka The Man Who Never Was. Precursor of Operation Husky, whereby the aim was to deceive the German general staff into believing the proposed Allied attack on Sicily was, in fact, to be on Sardinia and Corsica in the west and the Greek mainland in the east. The deception was the plan of two relatively junior officers, Squadron Leader Sir Archibald Cholmondley and intelligence officer Lt Cmdr Ewen Montagu. It was Cholmondley who first suggested planting a series of subtle clues on a dead body and ensuring the Germans would be privy to this information, and it was Montagu who gave the plan

its feasibility. The dead body, whose true identity was never revealed, was given the name of Captain (acting major) William Martin of the Royal Marines, and his mode of death was a plane crash at sea off the Spanish coast, where the Abwehr (German Intelligence) was known to be very active. The plan was a total success and 'Husky' gave the Allies control of the Mediterranean.

Mongoose Operation launched by President John F Kennedy and his brother Robert Kennedy, the Attorney-General, in December 1961, with the aim of overthrowing Fidel Castro of Cuba.

Moonlight Sonata German air-raid on Coventry on 14 and 15 November 1940.

Moses Secret airlift of Ethiopian Jews, or Falashas, to Israel from refugee camps in Sudan 1984–5.

Musketeer Anglo-French assault on Suez on 5 November 1956, first ever use of helicopters in amphibious landing.

Myth Soviet investigation into the death of Hitler in 1946, with aim of ensuring that he was in fact dead.

Neptun German anti-partisan drive, Greece 1944.

Neptune Naval side of Operation Overlord, involving 7,000 Allied ships.

No Ball Air attacks on German rocket-launching sites in 1944–5.

Nordlicht (Northern Lights) German operation against Leningrad during the summer of 1942.

Nordwind German counter-attack in Alsace (west of Strasbourg) in January 1945.

Oak Rescue of former prime minister Benito Mussolini from captivity in the Abruzzi mountains on 12 September 1943 by a small German force under Otto Skorzeny.

Olive Allied attack on the Gothic Line, Italy, in August 1944.

Olympic Proposed Allied plan to invade Kyushu in October 1945, precursor of projected Operation Downfall, the assault on Japan itself.

Ore The ongoing investigation into paedophilia via the Internet. The police have been able to track down downloaders of child pornography, via their credit card details, and specifically target those that have regular contact with children. So far the operation has unmasked over a thousand offenders in the UK, many of whom live a middle-class suburban lifestyle ranging from businessmen to pop musicians.

Overcast US plan launched in July 1945 to spirit German weapon scientists away from Europe to work in US laboratories.

Overlord Code name for the Allied invasion of Normandy in 1944. Originally planned for May, the day finally chosen was 5 June but the operation was delayed 24 hours by bad weather.

Panther German anti-partisan drive in Yugoslavia during spring of 1944.

Paperclip American project authorised by Harry S Truman in September 1946 whereby a selection of German scientists was brought to America to work on behalf of the US Government during the 'Cold War' following the end of the Second World War.

Paraquat British recapture of South Georgia from Argentina on 25 April 1982.

Peace for Galilee Codename for Israel's full-scale invasion of Lebanon in June 1982, launched with aim of eradicating the PLO from Lebanon.

Pedestal British convoy to supply Malta in August 1942, involving 2 battleships (*Nelson* and *Rodney*), 3 aircraft carriers (*Victorious* and *Eagle* were sunk and

Indomitable damaged), 2 ferry carriers (*Argus* and *Furious* carrying Spitfires), to Malta, 14 merchantmen (9 sunk, 5 arrived, including tanker, *Ohio* which was literally dragged into Malta sandwiched between 2 destroyers.

Pegasus 15 April 1968, relief by US and South Vietnamese forces of Khe Sanh combat base, Vietnam, besieged since mid-January.

Plan Blue (Fall Blau) Originally, the name given to a 1938 study from the Luftwaffe about aerial warfare in England, but more commonly the German offensive in southern Russia in the spring of 1942. Aka 'Case Blue'.

Plan Green (Fall Grün) In 1937 the plan to attack and occupy Czechoslovakia, which was executed without resistance in May 1938, after the Munich conference. In 1940 it was the name given to the plan for a frontal attack on the Maginot Line, later called Fall Braun.

Plan Red (Fall Rot) In 1935 Fall Rot was a study to defend against a surprise attack by France while defending the borders against Czechoslovakia and Poland. The 1937 version of Fall Rot included offensive operations against Czechoslovakia with the aim of preventing a prolonged two-front war. In 1940 it was the second part of the western campaign; after the destruction of the British Expeditionary Force and the northern army of France, it was, with Fall Braun, the attack on the rest of the French army, which was still entrenched in the Maginot Line.

Plan White (Fall Weiss) German invasion of Poland in September 1939. Aka 'Case White'.

Plan Yellow (Fall Gelb) German assault in the Low Countries and France launched on 10 May 1940. Aka 'Case Yellow'.

Platinum Part of 'Barbarossa' comprising operations towards Murmansk in the north.

Plunder Montgomery's crossing of the Rhine at the head of the 21st Army Group on 23 March 1945.

Pointblank Bombing campaign against German military, industrial and economic targets from May 1943.

Polar Bear German assault on the island of Kos, Greece, in 1943.

Provide Assistance Codename for the US relief operation launched on 23 July 1994 to deliver humanitarian relief to Rwandan refugees in Zaïre, prompted by an outbreak of cholera, aka Operation Support Hope.

Provide Comfort Code name for an emergency relief programme announced by Western allied forces on 16 April 1991, for the besieged Kurdish population of northern Iraq.

Provide Promise USAF flights into Sarajevo during conflict. Began on 2 July 1992 with 21 nations forming a coalition to resupply a war-ravaged Sarajevo. The longest humanitarian airlift in history ended on 9 January 1996.

Puma Proposed British operation to seize Canary Islands in 1941.

Punishment German air attacks on Yugoslav capital of Belgrade from 6 to 8 April 1941.

Quadrant Codename of the Quebec conference of August 1943, attended by Churchill and Roosevelt.

Rankin Allied plans for return to European continent. Rankin A involved possible return in advance of scheduled Normandy invasion, B was response in case of German withdrawal from France or Norway, C in case of German unconditional surrender.

Ratweek RAF and Yugoslav partisans launch attacks on roads and railways intending to prevent German withdrawal from Yugoslavia, September 1944.

Reckless US operation against Hollandia, New Guinea, in April 1944.

Regenbogen (Rainbow) Scuttling of German U-boats at the end of the Second World War. 231 scuttled during May 1945.

Restore Hope Codename given to the December 1992 deployment of a US-led 35,000-strong multinational force in Somalia to ensure the safe delivery of international aid to Somalis who were starving as a result of the year-long civil war.

Rhine Exercise The one and only cruise of the German battleship *Bismarck* from 19 to 27 May 1941, when she sank in the Bay of Biscay.

Rhubarb RAF Fighter Command sweeps over the English Channel and occupied French coastline from late 1940 onwards.

Richard German plan for intervention in Spain in the event of a Republican victory in the Civil War.

Ring Soviet operation to destroy encircled German 6th Army at Stalingrad in January 1943.

Rösselsprung (Knight's Move) German attack on Tito's HQ, Hvar, Yugoslavia, 25 May 1944.

Rolling Thunder Programme of sustained US bombing of North Vietnam mounted by administration of President Lyndon Johnson, March 1965–November 1968.

Rosario Argentine invasion of the Falkland Islands on 3 April 1982.

Roundup Allied plan to land in France between the Somme and the Seine (Dieppe and Le Havre) in spring 1943 by 30 US and 18 British divisions; replaced by Overlord.

Rumpelkammer (Junk Room) German V1 campaign against UK 1944–5.

Rumyantsev Soviet counter-offensive following Operation Citadel, August 1943, mounted at southern end of the Kursk salient.

Salmon Trap Abortive German plan to cut Murmansk railway in 1942.

Sandstone Codename for the US Army's nuclear testing series of 1948.

Schneesturm (Snowstorm) German anti-partisan drive in Yugoslavia late 1943.

Scorcher British occupation of Crete after withdrawal from Greece, May–June 1941.

Sea-Lion Proposed German invasion of England in 1940.

Sextant Cairo conference held just before and after the British–Soviet–US Tehran conference. At Cairo were US, British and Chinese heads of state, November and December 1943.

Sharp Guard Nato-WEU restriction on shipping to the Federal Republic of Yugoslavia in 1994.

Sheepskin Invasion of Anguilla in March 1969 by 300 British troops and 50 police to restore British rule from St Kitts-Nevis.

Shingle Amphibious landing at Anzio, 22 January 1944, sealed off by Germans until Operation Diadem broke through the Gustav Line.

Sho Go (Victory) Japanese defence plan in the summer of 1944, embracing several plans which could be put into effect once the axis of Allied advance became clear. Plan 1 provided for the defence of the Philippines, Plan 2 for the defence of Formosa and the Ryukyus, Plan 3 for the defence of

Japan itself, Plan 4 for the defence of the Kuriles and Hokkaido. After Plan 1 was triggered, the Battle of Leyte Gulf ensued.

Shrapnel Abortive British plan of 1940 to seize the Cape Verde Islands in the event of Spain entering the war on Germany's side and threatening Gibraltar.

Sickle Cover name for the build-up of the US Eighth Air Force in Britain from 1942.

Slapstick British landing at Taranto on the heel of Italy and advance along the coast towards the German Gustav Line 9 September–30 November 1943.

Sledgehammer Proposed British–American contingency plan to invade Normandy and Brittany in Autumn 1942 if the Soviet Union appeared about to collapse.

Source British midget submarine attack on German battleship *Tirpitz*, 22 September 1943.

Spring Canadian breakout in Normandy July 1944, coordinated with Operations Goodwood and Cobra.

Starfish British deception plan early in the Second World War to simulate the effects of marker incendiaries dropped by bombers, and lure German bombers away from real targets.

Starkey Allied invasion practice in English Channel, September 1943, part of the Cockade deception plan.

Starvation US naval operation, launched in March 1945, to mine Japan's home waters.commenced March.

Steinadler German anti-partisan drive in Greece during July 1944.

Steinbock (Ibex) Luftwaffe bombing attacks on Britain in the spring of 1944.

Stosser German parachute operations during the Ardennes Offensive in 1944.

Strangle Air attacks destroying German communications in Italy before Operation Diadem in March 1944.

Student The German occupation of Rome in 1943. Part of Operation Black.

Sunrise Secret negotiations with the German command in Italy for surrender of German forces in May 1945.

Supercharge I British break-out in the 2nd Battle of El Alamein 2–4 November 1942.

Super-Gymnast Plan for an Allied landing in north-west Africa in 1942, which evolved into Operation Torch.

Symbol Anglo–American Casablanca Conference 14–23 January 1943.

Taxable RAF drop window off the Pas de Calais, as diversion for D-Day, 5–6 June 1944.

Terminal Allied conference at Potsdam 16 July to 2 August 1945.

Thunderbolt 3 July 1976, Israeli commando raid to release hostages of hijacked Palestinian terrorists to Entebbe. Thunderbolt was also codename in the Second World War for Luftwaffe cover for 'Cerberus'.

Thunderclap Plan favoured by 'Bomber' Harris for an all-out bombing assault on Germany, as a war winning *coup de grâce*, applied in particular to the bombing of Dresden in February 1945.

Tidal Wave USAAF bombing of the oil refineries at Ploesti, Romania, 1 August 1943.

Tiger British fast convoy loaded with war material which passed the length of the Mediterranean during May 1941, bringing tanks and fighter planes to the 8th Army in Egypt.

Torch Final codename for Allied landings in north-west Africa, 8 November 1942.

Totalize Normandy Operation of 7 Aug 1944, concerning Canadian attack towards Falaise, Normandy, aiming to link with US forces closing in from the south to trap German troops concentrated southward in the 'Falaise pocket'.

Tractable Canadian follow-up attack towards Falaise of 14 August 1944, an extension of Totalize.

Trident Anglo–American summit conference, Washington 12–25 May 1943. Operation Trident is also the name of a Metropolitan Police initiative begun in March 1998 to end a spate of shootings among the black communities in London.

Turquoise Codename for the French military operation in Rwanda launched on 23 June 1994 following the death in a plane crash of President Juvenal Habyarimana and the violence that followed.

Typhoon (Taifun) German push to capture Moscow, September–December 1941.

U Go Japanese drive on India, from Burma in March 1944.

UNOSOM II The aftermath of Operation Restore Hope in Somalia in 1994.

Uphold Democracy 19 September 1994, USA ousting of Haitian Junta in favour of exiled President Jean-Bertrand Aristide.

Uranus Soviet attack which trapped the Germans 6th Army in Stalingrad, November 1942.

Urgent Fury Codename for the military invasion of the Caribbean island of Grenada in October 1983 by 7,000 US Marines in order to rescue medical students embroiled in political chaos following the murder of PM Maurice Bishop by hardline Stalinists.

Valkyrie Codeword for anti-Nazi uprising planned to follow the failed assassination attempt on Adolf Hitler by Claus von Stauffenberg on 20 July 1944.

Varsity Airborne assault that accompanied Montgomery's crossing of the Rhine on 24 March 1945.

Velvet Unrealised offer made late in 1942, to base 20 Anglo–American air force squadrons in Soviet Caucasus.

Vengeance Assassination of Admiral Yamamoto, Japanese naval commander in chief, by American P-38 fighters on 18 April 1943.

Veritable Opening of the Allied Rhineland campaign on 8 February 1945 with Canadians driving south from Nijmegen in the Netherlands to capture land between the Rhine and Maas and so clear German troops from the west bank of the Upper Rhine.

Vittles US name for Berlin Airlift, 26 June 1948 to 30 September 1949.

Vulcan Final Allied offensive in Tunisia, 6 May 1943.

Warden RAF flights over northern Iraq, post Gulf War.

Watch on the Rhine The German counter-offensive in the Ardennes commencing 16 December 1944, aka the Battle of the Bulge.

Watchtower 7 August 1942, US capture of airstrip on Guadalcanal and the naval and seaplane base Tulagi in Solomon Isles, leading to a 6-month campaign to expel the Japanese from Guadalcanal.

Weiss 1 and 2 German anti-partisan drive in Bosnia, February 1943.

Weser Exercise The German invasion of Norway in April 1940.

Wilfred Proposed British plan to mine neutral Norwegian waters in April 1940, which was pre-empted by German invasion of Norway, though not before one minefield was laid.

Winter Storm   General Von Manstein's unsuccessful operation to relieve Germany's encircled 6th Army at Stalingrad, December 1942.

Wolf   German anti-partisan drive in Yugoslavia in the spring of 1944.

Zeppelin   Abortive German plot to assassinate Stalin in July 1944.

Zipper   Projected British assault on Japanese-occupied Malaya in 1945, which was pre-empted by their surrender.

Zitadelle   German attack that led to the Battle of Kursk (central Russia) in July 1943, the largest tank battle in history.

Zorba   Codename for the ongoing investigation into Freemasonry within the Police Force.

General Information

aerobatics team: RAF   Red Arrows.

army: European country without one   Liechtenstein.

army: largest   China.

bugle calls   Reveille (first), Last Post (Penultimate), Lights Out (Last).

concentration camp: first   British in the Boer War.

decorations: highest UK civilian   George Cross.

decorations: highest UK military   Victoria Cross.

Foreign Legion   Founded by King Louis-Philippe (1831) as an aid to controlling French colonial possessions. The Legion's unofficial motto is *Legio Patria Nostra* (The Legion is Our Fatherland). Its monthly magazine is called *Képi Blanc* (White Kepi). Its HQ was formerly in Sidi Ben Abbas (Algeria) but is now in Aubagne, near Marseilles.

guards regiments   Grenadiers, Coldstream, Scots, Irish and Welsh.

home guard: original name   Local Defence Volunteers.

Household Cavalry regiments   Life Guards, Blues and Royals.

Marines: attached to   Admiralty (although classified as soldiers). The Royal Marines were founded in 1664.

Monty's double   Clifford James.

National Service   Commencing in 1947 and initially for men of 18+ and for a two-year term (lowered to 18 months); abolished in 1960. Last recruits passed out in 1962.

Officer Training School: Army   Sandhurst.

Officer Training School: Navy   Dartmouth.

Officer Training School: RAF   Cranwell.

Parachute Regiment: nickname   Red Devils.

private army: only force allowed in UK   Duke of Atholl Highlanders.

RAF: formed   Initially the Royal Flying Corps formed 13 May (1912) but amalgamated with the Royal Naval Air Service on 1 Apil 1918 to form the RAF.

salutes   Queen's Birthday 62 guns, opening of Parliament 42 guns.

SAS (Special Air Service): Founder   David Stirling.

Special Forces equivalents   Delta Force (US), SAS and SBS (Britain), Spetznaz (Russia).

US Air Force Academy (Colorado Springs)   Founded in 1954 and is the Officer Training School for the US Air Force.

US Marines: founded   1775.

US Military Academy (West Point)   Founded in 1802 and is the Officer Training School for the US Army.

US Naval Academy (Annapolis)   Founded in 1845 and is the Officer Training School for the US Navy and Marine Corps.

Victoria Cross: most won in a single action   Eleven at Rorke's Drift (22 January 1879) during the Zulu Wars.

MILITARY

Comparative Ranks in the Armed Forces

OFFICERS

Royal Navy	Army	RAF
Admiral of the Fleet	Field Marshal	Marshal of the Royal Air Force
Admiral	General	Air Chief Marshal
Vice-Admiral	Lieutenant-General	Air Marshal
Rear-Admiral	Major-General	Air Vice-Marshal
Commodore	Brigadier	Air Commodore
Captain	Colonel	Group Captain
Commander	Lieutenant-Colonel	Wing Commander
Lt-Commander	Major	Squadron Leader
Lieutenant	Captain	Flight Lieutenant
Sub-Lieutenant	Lieutenant	Flying Officer
Acting Sub-Lieutenant	Second Lieutenant	Pilot Officer

NONCOMMISSIONED OFFICERS

Fleet Chief Petty Officer	Warrant Officer Class 1	Warrant Officer
	Warrant Officer Class 2	
Chief Petty Officer	Staff Sergeant	Flight Sergeant/Chief Technician
Petty Officer	Sergeant	Sergeant
Leading Rate	Corporal	Corporal
	Lance-Corporal	

Battles

Battle	War	Date	Details
Aachen	Second World War	21 Oct. 1944	Eight-day battle culminating in Allies capturing first major German city in the war.
Abensberg	Napoleonic Wars	20 Apr. 1809	French and Bavarians under Napoleon defeat Austrians under Archduke Charles.
Aberdeen	English Civil War	13 Sept. 1644	Royalists under marquis of Montrose defeated the Covenanters under Lord Burleigh.
Aboukir Bay/Nile	French Revolutionary Wars	1 Aug. 1798	Nelson destroyed 11 French ships in harbour, nullifying Napoleon's Egyptian land successes.
Abraham, Plains of	Seven Years' War	13 Sept. 1759	British secured Quebec; British and French leaders' James Wolfe and Marquis de Montcalm, were killed.
Actium	Second Triumvirate War	2 Sept. 31 BC	Octavia defeated Antony and Cleopatra on a promontory in Acarnania, Greece.
Adrianople	Roman/Visigoth War	9 Aug. AD 378	The Visigoth Fritigern defeated Romans led by Emperor Valens.
Adowa/Adwa	Italian Invasion of Ethiopia	1 Mar. 1896	King Menelik II's decisive defeat of General Baratieri forced Treaty of Addis Ababa on Italy, October 1896.
Adwalton Moor	English Civil War	30 June 1643	Royalists under the earl of Newcastle defeated Lord Fairfax's parliamentarians.
Aegospotami	Peloponnesian War	405 BC	The final battle of the Peloponnesian War in which the fleets of the two Greek rival powers fought a sea battle in the Hellespont and the Spartan leader Lysander using better tactics eventually defeated the Athenians under Conon.
Agincourt	Hundred Years' War	25 Oct. 1415	Henry V's archers laid foundations for defeat of French, under Constable Charles d'Albret.
Alamo	Texan/Mexican War	6 Mar. 1836	Col. Travis, Jim Bowie and Davy Crockett were among 183 Texans killed by Santa Anna's Mexican troops.
Åland	Great Northern War	July 1714	Russian fleet under Apraksin and Peter the Great defeated the Swedes under Ehrenskjold.
Alarcos	Spanish/Muslim Wars	18 July 1195	Moors under Yakub el Mansur defeated Spaniards under Alfonso VIII of Castile.
Aleppo	Tatar Invasion of Syria	11 Nov. 1400	Tatars under Tamerlane defeated Turks under the Syrian Emirs.
Alesia	Gallic Wars	c. 52 BC	Romans under Julius Caesar defeated Gauls under Vercingetorix.
Alexandria	British invasion of Egypt	21 Mar. 1801	British under Sir Ralph Abercromby (killed) defeated French under General Menou.
Algeciras Bay	French Revolutionary Wars	8 July 1801	Two sea battles between British under Saumarez and French under Linois; the first was indecisive but the second won a victory for Saumarez.
Alicante	War of Spanish Succession	29 June 1706	Admiral Sir George Byng commanded a fleet of 5 ships that attacked the city walls causing severe damage.
Aliwal	First Anglo-Sikh War	28 Jan. 1846	General Sir Harry Smith led a joint British/Indian force to victory against Sikhs.
Alkmaar	Eighty Years' War	8 Oct. 1573	Siege was laid, 21 August 1573, by 1,000 Spaniards but Dutch defended successfully.
Alma	Crimean War	20 Sept. 1854	Indecisive battle between Russian and a joint British/French/Turkish army.
Alnwick	Anglo-Scottish Wars	13 Nov. 1093	Malcolm Canmore, king of Scotland, and his son Edward were both slain.
Alsen	Schleswig-Holstein War	29 June 1864	In this last engagement of the war, the Prussians defeated the Danes.
Amphipolis	Peloponnesian War	422 BC	Indecisive attempt by the Athenians under Cleon to recapture Amphipolis from the Spartans.
Ankara	Ottoman Wars	20th July 1402	Mongols under Tamerlane defeated Ottomans under the sultan Bayezid I.
Antietam	US Civil War	17 Sept. 1862	A decisive battle that halted the Confederates in their advance on Maryland.
Antioch	First Crusade	3 June 1098	Siege started on 21 October 1097; Saracens held out against crusaders for 7 months.
Antwerp	Eighty Years' War	4 Nov. 1576	Known as the Spanish Fury; Sancho d'Avila's Spaniards slaughtered 8,000 Walloons.

Battle	War	Date	Details
Anzio	Second World War	22 Jan. 1944	A surprise landing near Rome by nearly 50,000 British/American troops.
Appomattox	US Civil War	9 Apr. 1865	Confederate army was surrounded in the Court House and Lee surrendered to Grant.
Arausio	Teutonic Wars	105 BC	Germanic tribes defeated Romans under Quintus Servilius Caepio and Gnaeus Mallius Maximus.
Arbela	Alexander's Asiatic Wars	1 Oct. 331 BC	Macedonians defeated Persians under Darius, making Alexander master of Asia.
Arcot	Carnatic War	Aug. 1751	Robert Clive captured fortress and held it for 7 weeks, delaying French advance in India.
Ardennes	Second World War	16 Jan. 1945	Aka Battle of the Bulge (coined by Churchill), the last German offensive on the Western Front.
Armada	Anglo-Spanish War	July 1588	Spanish Armada of 130 ships defeated by English fleet of 197, under Lord Howard.
Arnhem	Second World War	17 Sept. 1944	While airborne US troops secured bridges over Maas and Waal, British Arnhem landing severely defeated.
Arques	French Religious Wars	21 Sept. 1589	Henry of Navarre, later King Henry IV, led Huguenots to victory against Catholic League.
Arsuf	Third Crusade	7 Sept. 1191	King Richard I gained notable tactical victory against the Saracens.
Ascalon/Ashqelon	First Crusade	19 Aug. 1099	Crusaders under Godefroi de Bouillon gained a victory against Saracens under Kilidj Arslan.
Ashdown	Danish invasion of Britain	8 Jan. 871	King Ethelred of Wessex aided by Alfred the Great defeated the Danes.
Ashingdon	Danish invasion of Britain	18 Oct. 1016	Canute of Denmark defeated Edmund Ironside, which led to him becoming King.
Aspern	Napoleonic Wars	22 May 1809	French retreated to the island of Lobau in the Danube; they had few supplies and Napoleon rejected his generals' advice to retreat. Napoleon's first defeat, by an Austrian army.
Aughrim	War of English Succession	12 July 1691	William III's army led by Godert de Ginkel scattered a Jacobite army in Galway.
Auldearn	English Civil War	9 May 1645	Royalists under the marquis of Montrose defeated Covenanters east of Nairn.
Austerlitz	Napoleonic Wars	2 Dec. 1805	Aka Battle of the Three Emperors (Russian, French, Austrian). Napoleon defeated Kutuzov.
Bāhādurpur	Mughal Civil War	24 Feb 1658	Conflict between the four sons of Shāh Jehan, Mughal emperor of India, over the succession. The shah's second son, Shujā, set himself up as the governor of Bengal but was defeated in battle by the son of Dārā Shikoh, the eldest son of Shah Jehan. The third son, Aurangzeb, later executed his nephew, Sulaymān Shīkoh.
Balaclava	Crimean War	25 Oct. 1854	Allied victory over the Russians, but disastrous charge of British Light Brigade prompted General Bosquet to say 'This is not war.'
Ball's Bluff	US Civil War	21 Oct. 1861	Confederates under General Evans defeated Union army under General Stone.
Baltimore	War of 1812	11 Sept. 1814	British under General Ross (killed) defeated Americans under General Winder.
Bannockburn	Scottish Independence	24 June 1314	Robert the Bruce defeated English invaders under King Edward II.
Barāri Ghāt	Afghan-Marāthā War	9 Jan. 1760	Afghan army under Ahmad Shāh Durrāni defeated the Marāthās under Dattāji Sindhia (died).
Barnet	Wars of the Roses	14 Apr. 1471	Yorkists under King Edward IV defeated Lancastrians under earl of Warwick (killed).
Beachy Head	War of English Succession	29–30 June 1690	English and Dutch under Lord Torrington defeated by French under Tourville.
Belleau Wood	First World War	6 June 1918	First major US – German clash of the war, a hard-won victory by General Bundy over Ludendorff.
Bellevue	Franco-Prussian War	18 Oct. 1870	Marshal Bazaine was driven back from Metz by Germans.
Berwick	Scottish Independence	28 Mar. 1296	Edward I's troops killed thousands after John de Balliol's refusal to supply men for Gascon War.
Beymaroo	First British-Afghan War	23 Nov. 1841	General Elphinstone allowed only 1 gun for Brigadier Shelton to dislodge Afghans.

Battle	War	Date	Details
Bismarck	Second World War	27 May 1941	After sinking the cruiser *Hood*, Lutjens' battleship was sunk near Brest by British torpedo planes and warships.
Blenheim	War of Spanish Succession	13 Aug. 1704	Duke of Marlborough and Eugene of Savoy defeated French under Marshal Tallard in Bavarian town.
Blood River	Afrikaner-Zulu War	16 Dec. 1838	Zulus under King Dingaan (Dingane) were routed by the Transvaal Boers.
Blore Heath	Wars of the Roses	23 Sept. 1459	Yorkists under the earl of Salisbury dispersed Lancastrians under Lord Audley.
Borodino	Napoleonic Wars	7 Sept. 1812	Napoleon paved the way for his triumphant march on Moscow by defeating Kutuzov.
Bosworth Field	Wars of the Roses	21 Aug. 1485	Henry, Duke of Richmond, later Henry VII, defeated and killed Richard III to end wars.
Boudicca	Roman invasion of Britain	AD 61	Suetonius routed Queen Boudicca of the Iceni, who took poison on the battlefield.
Boyne	War of English Succession	1 July 1690	Decisive battle of the war; William III defeated James II.
Brandywine	US War of Independence	11 Sept. 1777	British under General Howe forced George Washington's troops to retreat.
Breitenfeld	Thirty Years' War	17 Sept. 1631	First major Protestant victory of the war, in which the Roman Catholic Habsburg emperor Ferdinand II and the Catholic League under Johan Isaclaes Graf von Tilly were defeated by the Swedish-Saxon army under King Gustavus II Adolphus of Sweden.
Brill	Eighty Years' War	1 Apr. 1572	De La Marck's *Wetergeuzen* (sea beggars) took Dutch port from Spain to gain first Dutch victory of war.
Britain	Second World War	June 1940 –Apr. 1941	German air raids intended to prepare for invasion of Britain but repulsed by RAF
Bronkhurst Spruit	First Boer War	20 Dec. 1880	Opening engagement of the war, a British column of 259 was ambushed and defeated.
Bull Run (Manassas) (First)	US Civil War	21 July 1861	Beauregard defeated McDowell's Union army, Confederate General Jackson gained nickname 'Stonewall'.
Bull Run (Manassas) (Second)	US Civil War	29–30 Aug. 1862	Confederates Lee and Jackson routed troops under General Pope.
Bunker Hill	US War of Independence	17 June 1775	British troops under Howe gained Breed's Hill and Bunker Hill but suffered heavy losses.
Burlington Heights	War of 1812	5 May 1813	British under Col. Proctor attacked by Clay but eventually gained the day.
Bussaco	Peninsular War	27 Sept. 1810	Wellington defeated pursuing French army under Marshals Masséna and Ney.
Buxar/Baksar	British/Bengal War	23 Oct.1764	Major Munro's victory over a confederation of Indian pirates gave the East India Company control of Bengal and Bihar.
Cadiz	Anglo-Spanish War	29 Apr. 1587	Drake destroyed over 100 ships in his famous singeing of the Spanish king's beard.
Caer Caradoc	Roman invasion of Britain	AD 50	Romans under Ostorius Scapula defeated Caratacus, king of the British tribe of Trinovantes.
Calais	Anglo-French Wars	6 Jan. 1558	Last English stronghold in France lost, causing Mary I to say 'When I am dead and opened, you shall find Calais will be writ on my heart'.
Cambodia	Vietnamese invasion	7 Jan. 1979	Vietnamese army captured Phnom Penh and formed People's Republic of Kampuchea.
Cambrai	First World War	20 Nov.– 7 Dec. 1917	Brig.-Gen. Elles led world's first massed tank attack: dramatic breakthrough but soon reversed.
Camden	US War of Independence	16 Aug. 1780	British under Cornwallis defeated Americans under General Gates.
Camperdown	French Revolutionary Wars	11 Oct.1797	British fleet under Duncan intercepted and routed a Dutch convoy on its way to support a French invasion of Ireland.
Campo Santo	War of Austrian Succession	8 Feb. 1743	Indecisive battle between Spaniards under Mortemar and Imperialists under Count Traum.
Camulodunum	Second Roman invasion of Britain	C. AD 43	Romans under Emperor Claudius accepted surrender of local tribes after defeat on the Medway.

Battle	War	Date	Details
Cannae	Second Punic War	3 Aug. 216 BC	Hannibal gained a devastating victory over Romans under Varro due to superior cavalry.
Cape Matapan	Second World War	28 Mar. 1941	Small British fleet sank six or seven Italian ships off Cape Matapan, Greece (aka Cape Tainaron).
Cape St Vincent	French Revolutionary Wars	14 Feb. 1797	Spaniards were totally defeated by fleet of Sir John Jervis, who was made earl of St Vincent.
Carabobo	Latin American Wars	24 June 1921	South American rebels under Antonio Simon Bolivar defeated Spanish royalists under General La Torre.
Carbisdale	English Civil War	27 Apr. 1650	Marquis of Montrose captured by parliamentary force and executed the following month.
Carchemish	Syrian War	605 BC	Babylonian troops led by Crown Prince Nebuchadrezzar II captured Carchemish from the Egyptians.
Carlisle	Jacobite Rebellion of '45	9 Nov. 1745	Young Pretender, Charles Edward Stuart, Bonny Prince Charlie, defeated duke of Cumberland.
Carrhae	Roman/Mesopotamia War	53 BC	Romans under Marcus Licinius Crassus (killed) invaded Mesopotamia but were defeated by the Parthians.
Carrical	Seven Years' War	2 Aug. 1758	British under Admiral Pocock defeated French under Comte d'Ache but with few gains.
Cartagena	War of Austrian Succession	9 Mar. 1741	Port blockaded by British under Admiral Vernon but extensive losses forced his withdrawal.
Cassino	Second World War	Jan./May 1944	Fierce and protracted battle during which Allies blew up the Benedictine monastery, 15 February, believing it to be German-occupied.
Castillon	Hundred Years' War	17 July 1453	John Talbot, earl of Shrewsbury, was killed, and the English lost Gascony, in the last battle of the war.
Cedar Creek	US Civil War	19 Oct. 1864	Union General Sheridan defeated Confederates under General Early.
Cedar Mountain	US Civil War	9 Aug. 1862	Union Corps under Banks attacked Confederates under Jackson but forced to withdraw.
Cerignola	Franco-Spanish Wars	28 Apr. 1503	Spanish under Cordoba defeated French troops under Louis XII.
Chaeronea	Philippan Campaigns	338 BC	Macedonian army under Philip II defeated the joint Theban/Athenian army.
Chaldiran	Ottoman Wars	23 Aug.1514	Ottomans under Sultan Selim I defeated Safavid army under Shah Esma'il northeast of Lake Van.
Châlons	Attila Conquests	451 AD	Aka Battle of the Catalaunian Plains. Joint force of Romans and Visigoths defeated the Huns under Attila.
Chevy Chase	Scottish Independence	15 Aug. 1388	Aka Otterburn. Henry Percy's (Hotspurs) superior forces were soundly beaten by Scots.
Chickahominy	US Civil War	3 June 1864	General Lee's Confederates soundly repulsed Union attacks under Grant.
Chippenham	Danish Invasion of Britain	Jan. 878	Danes under Guthrum attacked King Alfred on 12th Night; he was forced to hide at Athelney.
Chongju	Russo-Japanese War	Apr. 1904	First land battle of war; Cossacks were driven back with few losses.
Chorillos	Peruvian-Chilean War	13 Jan. 1861	Chileans comprehensively defeated Peruvians.
Christianople	Danish-Swedish Wars	Autumn 1611	First military exploit of the 16-year-old King Gustavus Adolphus of Sweden was a total success.
Chrysler's Farm	War of 1812	11 Nov. 1813	British under Colonel Morrison defeated Americans under General Boyd.
Cold Harbour	US Civil War	3 June 1864	Grant's frontal attack on entrenched Confederate forces repulsed but counter-assault was disastrously defeated by Lee.
Colenso	Second Boer War	15 Dec. 1899	Sir Redvers Buller's first move to relieve Ladysmith repelled by Gen. Botha.
Copenhagen	French Revolutionary Wars	2 Apr. 1801	Nelson turned his blind eye to Admiral Hyde Parker's signal to retire and gained the day.
Coral Sea	Second World War	8 May 1942	Naval conflict fought mainly by aircraft from carriers. US carrier *Lexington* lost, but Japanese withdrew.
Coronel	First World War	1 Nov. 1914	Von Spee's *Scharnhorst* and *Gneisenau* sank the British ships *Monmouth* and *Good Hope*.

MILITARY

Battle	War	Date	Details
Corunna	Peninsular War	16 Jan. 1809	French under Marshal Soult defeated by British under Sir John Moore (killed).
Crécy	Hundred Years' War	26 Aug. 1346	Edward III's archers and cannon defeated French cavalry under Philip VI.
Cropredy Bridge	English Civil War	29 June 1644	Royalists under Charles I defeated Sir William Waller's parliamentarians near Banbury.
Cross Keys	US Civil War	8 June 1862	Confederates under Ewell fought successful rearguard action against Fremonts' Federals.
Cuba	Castro Revolt	26 July 1953	Fidel and Raul Castro led unsuccessful raid on armoury at Santiago and were imprisoned.
Culloden	Jacobite Rebellion of '45	16 Apr. 1746	Aka Drumossie Moor. Duke of Cumberland earned epithet 'Butcher' for treatment of Jacobite Rebels after his crushing victory.
Custoza (First)	Italian War of Independence	24 July 1848	Crushing defeat for the forces of Charles Albert, king of Sardinia-Piedmont by the Austrian veteran Field Marshal Joseph Radetzky.
Custoza (Second)	Italian War of Independence	24 June 1866	An 80,000-man Austrian army under Archduke Albert defeated a 120,000-man Italian army under Victor Emmanuel II.
Cyprus	Turkish Invasion	20 July 1974	Turkey invaded northern Cyprus and established a beachhead around Kyrenia.
D-Day	Second World War	6 June 1944	The launching of Operation Overlord, the Allied Invasion of Normandy, was a major turning point of the war.
Dettingen	War of Austrian Succession	27 June 1743	Anglo-Austrian-German victory over French; the last occasion that a British sovereign (George II) led his troops into battle.
Diamond Hill	Second Boer War	11 June 1900	Lord Roberts attacked General Botha near Pretoria and drove him from his position.
Dien Bien Phu	French-Vietnamese War	13 Mar.– 7 May 1954	General Giap's siege and capture of key stronghold ended French power in Indochina and caused partition of Vietnam.
Dieppe	Second World War	19 Aug. 1942	Daytime Allied raid testing German Atlantic defences; 2nd Canadian Division suffered terrible losses.
Dingaan's Day	Afrikaner-Zulu War	16 Dec. 1838	Zulus under Dingaan were routed by the Transvaal Boers.
Dominica	US War of Independence	12 Apr. 1782	Aka Battle of Les Saintes. Admiral Rodney defeated French fleet, preserved British hold on Jamaica.
Dorylaeum	First Crusade	1 July 1097	Victory for Crusaders under Bohemond and Raymond of Toulouse over Seljuk Turks.
Douro	Peninsular War	12 May 1809	Wellington crossed the Douro and drove Marshal Soult's French troops out of Oporto.
Dover	Anglo-Dutch Wars	29 Nov. 1652	Dutch fleet under van Tromp victorious over Admiral Blake's English fleet at Dover and at Dungeness shortly after.
Dresden	Napoleonic Wars	26 Aug. 1813	Napoleon victorious over Russians, Prussians and Austrians.
Ebro River	Spanish Civil War	July–Nov. 1938	General Franco's Nationalists won a counter-offensive against Republicans under Modesto.
Edgecote	Wars of the Roses	26 July 1469	Lancastrian victory over Yorkists under the earl of Pembroke.
Edgehill	English Civil War	24 Oct. 1642	Indecisive first battle of Civil War between Charles I and parliamentarians under earl of Essex.
El Alamein	Second World War	Oct.–Nov. 1942	Montgomery's 8th Army drove Germans out of Egypt.
Elands River	Second Boer War	4 Aug. 1900	Australians under Col. Hore held out under fire until relieved by Kitchener.
Empingham	Wars of the Roses	12 Mar. 1470	Aka Losecoat Field. King Edward IV routed Sir Robert Welles's rebels.
Entholm	Northern Wars	11 June 1676	Swedes were defeated by Danish fleet under Admiral van Tromp.
Erbach	French Revolutionary Wars	15 May 1800	French under Sainte-Suzanne held out against Austrians under General Baron Kray.
Evesham	Second Barons' War	4 Aug. 1265	Prince Edward defeated the Barons, killed Simon de Montfort and restored Henry III.
Eylau	Napoleonic Wars	7–8 Feb. 1807	Indecisive battle between French troops under Napoleon and a joint Russian and Prussian army under Leonty Leontyevich Bennigsen.

Battle	War	Date	Details
Falkirk (First)	Scottish Independence	22 July 1298	English under Edward I defeated Scots under Sir William Wallace, who became a fugitive.
Falkirk (Second)	Jacobite Rebellion of '45	17 Jan. 1746	Jacobite army under Charles Edward Stuart (Young Pretender) defeated royalist forces under Henry Hawley.
Falkland Islands	First World War	8 Dec. 1914	Sturdee's squadron sank most of German Pacific squadron under von Spee (died).
Falkland Islands	British-Argentine War	2 Apr. 1982	Argentinian armed forces under General Galtieri invaded Falklands. On 3 April South Georgia was taken and on 5 April Rear Adm. Sandy Woodward led task force to free islands. On May 2 the *General Belgrano* was sunk by the sub *Conqueror*, and on 4 May the destroyer *Sheffield* was hit, and sank on 10 May. On 21 May 5,000 troops under Major-Gen. Jeremy Moore went ashore at Port San Carlos, and Argentinian surrender terms were eventually signed on 14 June, 10 weeks and 3 days after invasion.
Ferrybridge	Wars of the Roses	28 Mar. 1461	Lancastrians under Lord Clifford defeated Yorkists under Lord Fitzwalter (killed).
Fisher's Hill	US Civil War	22 Sept. 1864	Union force under Sheridan defeated Confederates under General Early.
Five Forks	US Civil War	1 Apr.1865	Sheridan and Warren defeated Pickett's Confederates causing Lee's withdrawal from Richmond and surrender at Appomattox on 9 April.
Flodden	Anglo-Scottish Wars	9 Sept. 1513	English under the earl of Surrey (Thomas Howard) defeated Scots under James IV (killed).
Fontenoy	War of Austrian Succession	11 May 1745	French under Marshal de Saxe repulsed duke of Cumberland's abortive drive to relieve Tournai.
Formigny	Hundred Years' War	15 Apr. 1450	French under the comte de Clermont defeated English under Kyrielle, restoring Normandy to France.
Fort Frontenac	Seven Years' War	27 Aug. 1758	Colonel Bradstreet defeated French under Noyan, who lost control of Lake Ontario.
Gebora	Peninsular War	19 Feb. 1811	Spaniards under Mendizabal were routed by French under Marshal Soult.
Gettysburg	US Civil War	1–3 July 1863	Greatest battle of the war between Meade's army of the Potomac and Lee's army of Virginia. Only a narrow Union victory, but it stopped Lee's invasion of the North.
Gibraltar	War of Spanish Succession	24 July 1704	British and Dutch fleet under Sir George Rooke defeated Spanish under marquis de Salinas and took Gibraltar.
Gitschin	Seven Weeks' War	29 June 1866	Prussians under Prince Frederick Charles defeated Austrians and Saxons under Clam-Gallas.
Glorious 1st of June	French Revolutionary Wars	1 June1794	Aka Ushant. British under Lord Howe defeated French and sank the *Vengeur*.
Golden Spurs	Flemish War	11 July 1302	Aka Courtrai. Untrained Flemish guild workers defeated French cavalry in Flanders and took their spurs as a trophy of their victory.
Graf Spee	Second World War	17 Dec. 1939	The pride of the German fleet, the pocket battleship *Graf Spee* was scuttled by Captain Hans Langsdorf after being harried by three British cruisers *Achilles*, *Ajax* and *Exeter* and forced into Montevideo harbour. The Uruguayan government ordered the ship to sea but, rather than face a certain defeat, Hitler himself ordered the scuttling and Langsdorf shot himself.
Granada	Moorish Wars	Jan. 1492	Moors under Boabdil were defeated and the city came under Catholic rule of Ferdinand II of Aragon and Isabella I of Castille.
Grant's Hill	Seven Years' War	14 Sept. 1758	Major Grant with 800 Highlanders defeated by French under de Ligneris at Fort Duquesne.
Gravelines	Franco-Spanish Wars	13 July 1558	Spanish under comte d'Egmont, backed by an English fleet, defeated French under Marshal de Thermes.

MILITARY

Battle	War	Date	Details
Guadalajara	Spanish Civil War	8 Mar. 1937	Republicans defeated Nationalists under Franco and Italian Fascists under General Roatta.
Guadalcanal	Second World War	Aug. 1942– Jan. 1943	Americans eventually gained victory over Japanese after 5 months' fighting on land and sea.
Guadeloupe	French Revolutionary Wars	3 July 1794	Sir John Jervis captured island but it was recaptured by the French on 10 December.
Guilford Courthouse	US War of Independence	15 Mar. 1781	British under Lord Cornwallis defeated Americans under General Greene.
Halidon Hill	Scottish Independence	19 July 1333	English troops under Edward III defeated Scottish forces attempting to relieve Berwick-upon-Tweed.
Han Ko/Hangö	Great Northern War	4–6 Aug. 1714	Peter the Great commanded a fleet against Swedes, the first major Russian victory at sea.
Harfleur	Hundred Years' War	Aug.–Sept. 1415	English under Henry V defeated the French troops after a 6-week siege of the port.
Harpers Ferry	US Civil War	15 Sept. 1862	Confederates under General Thomas Stonewall Jackson forced Union garrison to surrender.
Hastings	Norman Conquest	14 Oct. 1066	Aka Battle of Senlac Hill. Harold II of England (killed) defeated by William, duke of Normandy.
Hedgeley Moor	Wars of the Roses	25 Apr. 1464	Yorkist Lord Montagu routed Lancastrians under Margaret of Anjou and Ralph Percy (killed).
Heligoland	Napoleonic Wars	31 Aug. 1807	British squadron under Admiral Thomas Russell captured island from Danes.
Heligoland Bight	First World War	28 Aug. 1914	Admiral Beatty's battle cruiser Lion sank the German cruisers Mainz and Koln.
Heliopolis	French Revolutionary Wars	20 Mar. 1800	Turks in Egypt under Ibrahim Bey routed by French under General Kléber.
Herrings	Hundred Years War	12 Feb. 1429	Sir John Fastolfe defeated the comte de Clermont at Rouvray.
Hexham	Wars of the Roses	15 May 1464	Yorkists under Lord Montagu defeated and executed duke of Somerset.
Homildon Hill	Scottish Independence	14 Sept. 1402	English troops under Sir Henry Percy (Hotspur) defeated the Scots under the 4th earl of Douglas.
Hydaspes	Alexander's Asiatic Wars	326 BC	Fourth and last pitched battle fought by Alexander the Great during his Asiatic Campaign. Despite overwhelming numerical superiority of the Persian army led by Porus, and the 200 elephants that Porus had at his disposal, Alexander's tactical genius won the day.
Hyderabad	Conquest of Sind	24 Mar. 1843	British under Sir Charles Napier defeated Baluchis under Shir Mohammed.
Ilipa	Second Punic War	206 BC	Romans under Publius Cornelius Scipio (Africanus) defeated Carthaginians under Hasdrubal. Gisco and Mago in the Spanish town near Seville.
Imola	French Revolutionary Wars	3 Feb. 1797	French and Italian troops under Marshal Victor defeated Papal troops under General Colli.
Imphal	Second World War	29 Mar. 1944	Japanese troops besieged the city of Imphal in Assam, north-east India.
Inchon	Korean War	15 Sept. 1950	Amphibious landing by General Almond's X Corps drove the North Korean troops inland and seized Kimpo airfield.
Ingogo River	First Boer War	8 Feb. 1881	Boers defeated a small British column of 5 companies, 4 guns and a mounted force.
Inhlobane Mountain	Zulu War	28 Mar. 1879	British force of 1,300 under Cols Buller and Russell defeated by Zulus.
Inkerman	Crimean War	5 Nov. 1854	Russians under Prince Menshikov defeated by Franco-British troops under Raglan.
Ipsus	Macedonian-Egyptian War	301 BC	The combined forces of Lysimachus king of Thrace and Seleucus I Nicator of Babylon defeated the Macedonian army under Antigonus (killed) and his son Demetrius.
Isandhlwana	Zulu War	22 Jan. 1879	Six companies of 24th Regiment under Col. Durnford overwhelmed by Zulus under Matyana.
Issus	Alexander's Asiatic War	333 BC	Alexander the Great defeated Persians under King Darius.

Battle	War	Date	Details
Ivry	French Religious Wars	14 Mar. 1590	Henry IV's Huguenots defeated Catholic League under duc de Mayenne.
Iwo Jima	Second World War	19 Feb. 1945	General Schmidt's US V Amphibious Corps assaulted and secured the small island (8 sq miles) by 26 March.
Jajau	Mughal Civil War	12 June 1707	Family conflict to decide the successor to the Mughal emperor Aurangzeb; eventually his eldest surviving son Bahādur Shāh succeeded after a bloody battle with his brother Azam Shāh.
Jarnac	French Religious Wars	13 Mar. 1569	Catholics under the duke of Anjou defeated Huguenots under the prince de Condé.
Jena	Napoleonic Wars	14 Oct. 1806	Napoleon defeated the prince of Hohenlohe's Prussian army.
Jutland	First World War	31 May 1916	(Aka Skagerrak) Only major clash betwen British and German fleets in the war. British lost two ships, but German High Seas fleet did not seek battle thereafter.
Kadesh	Egyptian/Hittite War	1299 BC	Seeking to recapture the Syrian city of Kadesh, Ramses II engaged the Hittite leader Muwatallis without success and was forced to retreat; the Hittites moving southward into Damascus.
Kambula	Zulu War	29 Mar. 1879	British under Colonel Wood defeated Zulus under Cetewayo.
Karbalā	Muslim Wars	10 Oct. 680	Husayn ibn Ali, grandson of the Prophet Muhammad was defeated and killed by an army sent by the Umayyad Caliph Yazid I.
Karnāl	Mughal Civil Wars	24 Feb. 1739	Persian forces under Nāder Shāh defeated the Mughals under Emperor Muhammad Shāh.
Kemendine	First Burma War	10 June 1824	British under Sir Archibald Campbell defeated Burmese troops.
Khartoum	British-Sudan Campaign	26 Jan. 1885	General Gordon killed defending the city against the Mahdi after Beresford's troops were delayed.
Killiecrankie	Jacobite Rising	27 July 1689	Highland Jacobites under 'Bonny' Dundee defeated William III's troops under General Mackay, but Dundee's death undid the victory.
Kilsyth	English Civil War	15 Aug. 1645	Royalists under marquis of Montrose defeated Covenanters under General Baillie.
Kimberley	Second Boer War	15 Oct. 1899	Gen. French relieved town on 15 Feb. 1900 from Boer siege led by General Cronje.
Kioge	Northern War	July 1677	Danish fleet under Admiral Juel defeated Swedes under Admiral Horn.
Kissingen	Seven Weeks War	10 July 1866	Prussians under General Falkstein defeated Bavarians under General Zoller.
Kiu-lien-Cheng	Russo-Japanese War	1 May 1904	Japanese under Marshal Kuroki defeated Russians under General Sassulitch.
Königgrätz	Seven Weeks War	3 July 1866	Aka Battle of Sadowa. Decisive battle of the conflict in which Helmuth von Moltke's Prussian army defeated the Austrian army led by General Benedek, which led to Austria's exclusion from a Prussian-dominated Germany. The war was formally concluded on 23 August 1866 by the Treaty of Prague. Bismarck's alliance with Italy meant Venetia was ceded to the Italians.
Kosovo	Byzantine Wars	June 1389	Battle fought at Kosovo Polje (Field of the Blackbirds) between Serbs under Prince Lazar and Turks under Sultan Murad I, who gained a hard-fought victory.
Kursk Salient	Second World War	5–13 July 1943	Largest tank battle of the war, in which Russians smashed massive German offensive.
Ladysmith	Second Boer War	2 Nov. 1899	Sir George White defended against Boers until Redvers Buller relieved town 27 Feb. 1900.
Laings Nek	First Boer War	28 Jan. 1881	British under Gen Colley repulsed by Boers.
Lake Erie	War of 1812	10 Sept. 1813	Master Commandant Oliver Hazard Perry's fleet of 9 ships engaged 6 British warships under Captain Robert Heriot Barclay and although having to transfer from his flagship

MILITARY

Battle	War	Date	Details
			Lawrence to its sister ship *Niagara*, Perry sailed directly into the British line and firing broadsides as he went eventually forced the British to surrender.
Lake Trasimeno	Second Punic War	217 BC	The Carthaginian General Hannibal defeated the Roman army under Gaius Flaminius (killed) on the north shore of the Italian lake.
Landau	War of Spanish Succession	29 July 1702	French under de Melac lost the fortress to Prince Louis of Baden.
Langport	English Civil War	10 July 1645	Parliamentarians under Thomas Fairfax defeated Royalists under Lord Goring.
Langside	Anti-Marian Uprising	13 May 1568	Mary Queen of Scots's army was defeated by earl of Moray; Mary escaped to England.
Lansdowne	English Civil War	5 July 1643	Royalists under Sir Ralph Hopton defeated parliamentarians under Sir William Waller.
La Rochelle	Hundred Years' War	1372	A Castilian fleet under Bocanegra, acting in support of the French, defeated the English under Pembroke.
Lauffeld	War of Austrian Succession	2 July 1747	French under Marshal Saxe defeated allied Austrian and British army under Cumberland.
Leck	Thirty Years' War	5 Apr. 1632	Gustavus Adolphus's Swedish/German army defeated Imperialists under Tilly (mortally wounded).
Leghorn	Anglo-Dutch Wars	31 Mar. 1653	Admiral Van Gelen (killed) destroyed 6 English ships commanded by Commodore Appleton.
Leipzig	Napoleonic Wars	16–19 Oct. 1813	Napoleon defeated, and forced into decisive retreat, by Coalition of Blücher, Schwarzenberg and Bernadotte.
Le Mans	Franco-Prussian War	10–11 Jan. 1871	French under Chanzy were completely routed by Germans under Prince Frederick Charles.
Leningrad	Second World War	15 Jan. 1944	(Now St Petersburg) Russians relieved the 30-month blockade of the city after 5 days' fighting.
Lepanto	Cyprus War	7 Oct. 1571	Last major battle using oared ships brought decisive victory for the Holy League fleet under Don John of Austria over Ottoman Turks.
Leuctra	Boeotian-Athenian War	371 BC	Boeotian army under Epaminondas defeated a Spartan army under King Cleombrotus.
Lewes	English Barons' War	14 May 1264	Simon de Montfort defeated Henry III and Prince Edward and signed the Mise of Lewes.
Lexington	US War of Independence	19 Apr. 1775	First battle of the war resulted in minor victory for British troops under Lt-Col. Francis Smith.
Leyte Gulf	Second World War	24–26 Oct. 1944	Biggest ever naval battle. United States defeated Japanese comprehensively, losing 6 ships to Japan's 28.
Liaoyang	Russo-Japanese War	25 Aug.–3 Sept. 1904	Japanese army under Marshal Oyama forced Russians under General Kuropatkin to retreat.
Lille	War of Spanish Succession	12 Aug. 1708	French under Marshal de Boufflers surrendered to Prince Eugene on 25 Oct. 1708.
Lindley	Second Boer War	27 May 1900	Colonel Spragge surrendered to superior Boer force.
Little Bighorn	Sioux Rising	25 June 1876	Col. Custer (killed) and his 7th US Cavalry wiped out by Sioux and Cheyenne warriors under Sitting Bull.
Loudoun Hill	Scottish Independence	10 May 1307	Robert the Bruce defeated earl of Pembroke's cavalry by his spearmen's steadfastness.
Lucknow	Indian Mutiny	June–Nov. 1857	Siege relieved by General Sir Colin Campbell.
Lundy's Lane	War of 1812	25 July 1814	Americans under General Brown unsuccessfully attacked British under Sir George Drummond.
Lützen	Thirty Years' War	16 Nov. 1632	Indecisive battle in which Gustavus II Adolphus of Sweden lost his life while engaging the Habsburg forces of Albrecht von Wallenstein.
Madrid	Spanish Civil War	7 Nov. 1936	Nationalists under General Mola attacked the Republican forces of General Miaja causing the government to flee to Valencia.
Mafeking	Second Boer War	Oct. 1899	Colonel Baden-Powell resisted Boers under General Cronje in siege not raised till 17 May 1900.
Magdeburg	Thirty Years' War	Mar. 1631	Imperialists under Field Marshal Tilly besieged the city and von Falkenberg was killed.

Battle	War	Date	Details
Magenta	Italian Independence Wars	4 June 1859	French under General MacMahon defeated Austrians under Marshal Gyulai.
Majuba Hill	First Boer War	27 Feb. 1881	Boers under General Joubert defeated British under Sir George Colley (killed).
Maldon	Danish Invasion of Britain	AD 991	Danish army under Tryggvason defeated Anglo-Saxons under Brithnoth.
Malplaquet	War of Spanish Succession	11 Sept. 1709	German and British forces under Marlborough defeated French under Villars in costly victory.
Malvern Hill	US Civil War	1 July 1862	Union repelled fierce Confederate attacks during 7 days' battle.
Mantineia	Peloponnesian War	418 BC	Spartan forces under King Agis defeated the Athenians.
Manzikert	Anatolian Wars	AD 1071	Byzantines under the emperor Romanus IV Diogenes were defeated by the Seljuq Turks led by Sultan Alp-Arslan.
Marathon	Persian-Greek Wars	Sept. 490 BC	Athenians under Miltiades, 10,000 in number, defeated 50,000 Persians.
Marengo	French Revolutionary Wars	14 June 1800	Napoleon with aid of General Desaix (killed) defeated Austrians under General Mélas.
Margate	Hundred Years' War	24 Mar. 1387	Earls of Arundel and Nottingham repelled invasion threat from Franco-Castilian force.
Marne	First World War	6–9 Sept. 1914 and July 1918	Two bloody battles. In both cases the Germans were forced to retreat.
Marston Moor	English Civil War	2 July 1644	Prince Rupert's royalists defeated by Cromwell's Ironsides under Fairfax and Manchester.
Medellín	Peninsular War	28 Mar. 1809	French under Marshal Victor comprehensively defeated Spanish under Cuesta.
Medway	Second invasion of Britain	c. AD 43	Romans under Emperor Claudius defeated Britons under Caratacus and his brother Togodumnus (died)
Megiddo	Palestinian War	c.1468 BC	The Palestinian town of Megiddo was captured by the Egyptian king Thutmosis III.
Metauro River	Second Punic War	207 BC	Romans under Marcus Livius Salinator and Claudius Nero defeated Carthaginians under Hasdrubal (died), the brother of Hannibal.
Midway	Second World War	3–6 June 1942	In battle fought mainly by aircraft, Japanese attack on US base repelled, US carrier *Yorktown* lost, but 4 Japanese carriers sunk.
Missolonghi (First)	Greek War of Independence	Jan. 1823	The Ottomans were forced to withdraw after failing to take the key fortress of Missolonghi (Mesolóngion).
Missolonghi (Second)	Greek War of Independence	23 Apr. 1826	Joint Turkish/Egyptian forces under Ibrahim Pasha defeated a smalll Greek garrison under Mavrocordatos.
Mohács	Ottoman Wars	29 Aug. 1526	Turks under Suleyman I defeated Hungarians under Louis II.
Molinos del Rey	Peninsular War	21 Dec. 1808	French under General St Cyr defeated Spanish under Reding.
Monongahela	French-Indian War	9 July 1755	British army under General Edward Braddock was routed by the joint French and Indian forces under Captain Daniel de Beaujeu and, after his death, by Captain Jean Dumas. The survivors of the battle near Fort Duquesne (Pittsburgh) included George Washington.
Mons Lactarius	Ostrogoth War	AD 553	Byzantine General Narses defeated the Goths under Teias (died), near Naples, Italy.
Morat	Swiss-Burgundy War	22 June 1476	Victory for the Swiss Confederation over the Burgundians under Charles the Bold.
Morgarten	Swiss War of Independence	15 Nov. 1315	Swiss Confederation's first military success against the Austrians under Leopold I.
Mortimer's Cross	Wars of the Roses	2 Feb. 1461	Edward, duke of York, defeated Lancastrians under earls of Pembroke and Wiltshire.
Mukden	Russo-Japanese War	19 Feb.–10 Mar. 1905	Russian stronghold in Manchuria that finally fell to the Japanese.
Munda	Roman Civil War	45 BC	Decisive battle of the Roman Civil War when Julius Caesar conclusively defeated the Pompeians.
Mylae	First Punic War	260 BC	Romans destroyed 50 Carthaginian ships.
Nahāvand	Arabian Wars	AD 642	Arab forces under Nu'mān defeated Sāsānian troops under Firuzan.

MILITARY

Battle	War	Date	Details
Nancy	Swiss-Burgundy War	1477	Victory for the Swiss Confederation over the Burgundians under Charles the Bold (died).
Nanjing	Chinese Civil War	22 Apr. 1949	Communists captured Chiang Kai-shek's Nationalist capital, enabling communists under Mao Zedong to take control of China.
Naseby	English Civil War	14 June 1645	Parliamentarians under Fairfax routed Prince Rupert's royalists.
Nashville	US Civil War	15–16 Dec. 1864	Union army under General Thomas defeated Confederates under General Hood.
Navarino	Greek War of Independence	20 Oct. 1827	Last action between wooden ships. Britain, France and Russia defeated Turks and Egyptians.
Nemea	Corinthian War	394 BC	After the victory of Sparta in the Peloponnesian War against Athens it maintained its military superiority against a coalition of troops from Thebes, Corinth, Athens and Argos, largely due to their skill in hoplite warfare (use of heavy infantry).
Neva River	Swedish Holy War	15 July 1240	Novgorod army under Prince Alexander Yaroslavich defeated the Swedes under earl Birger on the banks of the Neva. Yaroslavich was given the name Nevsky in honour of his victory.
Neville's Cross	Anglo-Scottish Wars	17 Oct. 1346	Scots under David II routed by Henry de Percy and Ralph de Neville.
Newbury (First)	English Civil War	20 Sept. 1643	Charles I failed to prevent the parliamentarians under the earl of Essex from marching to London.
Newbury (Second)	English Civil War	27 Oct. 1644	Charles I's inconclusive encounter with parliamentary force under the earl of Manchester spurred formation of the New Model Army.
New Orleans	War of 1812	Jan. 1815	Andrew Jackson defeated English force under General Sir Edward Pakenham (killed).
New Orleans	US Civil War	Apr. 16th 1862	Union fleet under Commodore Farragut bombarded Forts Jackson and forced surrender of city.
Niagara	Seven Years' War	June 1759	British under General Prideaux (killed) besieged the Canadian fort and William Johnson successfully repulsed Ligneris.
Nicopolis	Ottoman Wars	25 Sept. 1396	Turks under Sultan Bayezid I defeated a Christian Allied army under Sigismund, king of Hungary.
Nile/Aboukir Bay	French Revolutionary Wars	1–2 Aug. 1798	French fleet destroyed and Admiral Brueys killed by Nelson, checking Napoleon's plans in Middle East.
Nong Sa Rai	Thai War of Independence	1593	The final battle between the Thai troops under Prince Naresuen and Burmese troops under King Nanda Bayin. The Burmese Crown Prince was slain by Naresuen and Thai independence was safe for 150 years.
Nördlingen	Thirty Years' War	5–6 Sept. 1634	Decisive victory for the Holy Roman Empire and Spain under Matthias Gallas over the Swedish army led by Gustav Karlsson Horn and Bernhard of Saxe-Weimar, which led to the dissolution of the Heilbronn alliance and forced Cardinal Richelieu to bring France into the war.
Northampton	Wars of the Roses	10 July 1460	Earl of March, later Edward IV, routed the Lancastrians, captured Henry VI and executed supporters, including Buckingham and Shrewsbury.
Novara	Italian War of Independence	23 Mar. 1849	Austrian troops under Marshal Joseph Radetzky routed Piedmontese army.
Okinawa	Second World War	1 Apr.–21 June 1945	US amphibious landing met fierce and protracted resistance inland, losing over 7,000 men to Japan's 100,000 killed. US and Japanese commanders Bruckner and Ushiima.
Omdurman	British-Sudan Campaigns	2 Sept. 1898	General Kitchener destroyed the Mahdi's army. Last full-scale cavalry charge by 21st Lancers, including Winston Churchill.

Battle	War	Date	Details
Opequan	US Civil War	19 Sept. 1864	Confederates under General Early defeated by General Sheridan and Lt-Col. George Custer.
Oporto	Peninsular War	28 Mar. 1809	French under Marshal Soult defeated Portuguese under Lima and Pareiras.
Orléans	Hundred Years' War	12 Oct. 1428–8 May 1429	Decisive siege in which English were forced to withdraw after Joan of Arc captured key siege forts.
Oswego	Seven Years' War	11 Aug. 1756	French under marquis of Montcalm took English fort held by Col. Mercer (killed).
Otterburn	Scottish Independence	15 Aug. 1388	Aka Chevy Chase. Scots under earls Douglas (killed) and Murray defeated Henry Percy (Hotspur).
Oudenarde	War of Spanish Succession	11 July 1708	British and Imperialists under Marlborough and Prince Eugene defeated French under Ventome and Burgundy.
Palo Alto	Mexican War	8 May 1846	First clash of the Mexican War in which the Americans under General Zachary Taylor defeated the Mexican army under General Mariano Arista.
Panipat (First)	Indian Wars	21 Apr. 1526	Mughal chief Bābur defeated Sultan Ibrāhim Lodo of Delhi (died).
Panipat (Second)	Indian Wars	5 Nov. 1556	Bayram Khān, the guardian of Mughal emperor Akbar, defeated the Hindu General Hemu.
Panipat (Third)	Indian Wars	14 Jan. 1761	Afghan chief Ahmad Shāh Durrāni defeated the Marāthā army under the Bhāo Sahib.
Parma	War of Polish Succession	29 June 1734	French under Marshal de Coigny defeated Imperialists under Count Claudius de Mercy (killed).
Passchendaele	First World War	30 Oct. 1917	Aka 3rd Battle of Ypres. Canadian 3rd and 4th Division and British pushed back Germans but suffered heavy casualties.
Patay	Hundred Years War	18 June 1429	French under Joan of Arc and duc d'Alençon defeated English under Talbot and Fastolfe.
Pea Ridge	US Civil War	6–8 Mar. 1862	Aka Elk Horn Tavern. First key Union victory west of Mississippi. Confederate General Ben McCulloch killed.
Pearl Harbor	Second World War	7 Dec. 1941	Japanese carrier-based planes attacked US Pacific fleet without declaring war, sank 19 ships. USA forced into the war.
Pharsalus	Roman Civil War	48 BC	Julius Caesar defeated the much larger force of Pompey. Caesar, who had only minor losses, exclaimed 'Hoc voluerunt' ('They would have it so').
Philippi	Brutus' Rebellion	42 BC	Republicans under Brutus and Cassius (both committed suicide) defeated by Octavian and Mark Antony, exposing Rome to autocratic rule.
Pichincha	Latin-American Wars	24 May 1822	South American rebels under Antonio José de Sucre overcame Spanish royalists.
Pinkie Cleugh	Anglo-Scottish Wars	10 Sept. 1547	Scots under the earls of Arran and Huntly defeated by English under Protector Somerset.
Plains of Abraham	Seven Years' War	13 Sept. 1759	French under Montcalm defeated by Wolfe and lost Quebec. Both generals killed.
Plassey	Seven Years' War	23 June 1757	British under Robert Clive defeated nawab of Bengal and assured East India Company's rule there.
Poitiers	Hundred Years' War	19 Sept. 1356	English archers under Edward the Black Prince defeated French under King John II.
Plataea	Persian-Greek Wars	479 BC	Greeks under Pausanias won a decisive victory over the Persians under Mardonius.
Port Arthur	Sino-Japanese War	21 Nov. 1894	(Now called Lushun.) Japanese defeated Chinese with very few casualties.
Port Arthur	Russo-Japanese War	8 Feb. 1904	Japanese fleet attacked Russian squadron without declaring war. Japan eventually won the port after almost a year's fighting (treaty of Portsmouth).
Preston	English Civil War	17–19 Aug. 1648	Cromwell's Roundheads defeated royalists under duke of Hamilton and Sir Marmaduke Langdale, ending the Second Civil War.
Preston	Jacobite Rebellion 1715	13 Nov. 1715	General Will Thomas's royalists defeated Jacobites under Thomas Forster.

MILITARY

Battle	War	Date	Details
Prestonpans	Jacobite Rebellion 1745	21 Sept. 1745	Aka Gladsmuir. Jacobites under Young Pretender Charles Edward Stuart defeated royalists in a 10-minute battle.
Princeton	US War of Independence	3 Jan. 1777	Americans under George Washington defeated British under Cornwallis.
Pydna	Third Macedonian War	22 June 168 BC	Romans under Lucius Aemilius Paullus defeated the Macedonians under king Perseus.
Pyramids	French Revolutionary Wars	21 July 1798	Napoleon defeated Mamelukes under Murad Bey and went on to occupy Cairo.
Quatre Bras	Napoleon's Hundred Days	16 June 1815	Marshal Ney engaged Wellington, causing his withdrawal to Waterloo.
Quebec	Seven Years' War	27 June 1759	First of two battles of Seven Years' War, which decided the future of Canada.
Queenston Heights	War of 1812	13 Oct. 1812	British in Canada under General Brock (killed) defeated Americans under General Van Rensselaer.
Quiberon Bay	Seven Years' War	20 Nov. 1759	British fleet under Admiral Hawke defeated French under Marshal de Conflans.
Radcot Bridge	Richard II's Barons' War	20 Dec. 1387	Earl of Derby, later Henry IV, defeated Richard II's supporter Robert de Vere, earl of Oxford.
Ramillies	War of Spanish Succession	23 May 1706	British and Imperialists under Marlborough defeated French under Villeroi.
Rieti	Italian War of Independence	7 Mar. 1821	Austrians defeated Pepe's Neapolitans, entered Naples and reinstated Ferdinand IV on throne.
Rio Salado		30 Oct. 1340	Castilian forces under Alfonso XI and Portuguese forces under Alfonso IV defeated Muslim Marinids of North Africa.
River Plate	Second World War	13 Dec. 1939	The battle in Uruguayan waters between British and German warships ended on 17 December with the scuttling of the German pocket battleship *Graf Spee*
Roanoke Island	US Civil War	7 Feb. 1862	Union General Burnside defeated Confederates under General Wise.
Rocroi	Thirty Years War	19 May 1643	French army under the Duc d'Enghien (later known as the Great Condé) routed a Spanish army under Don Francisco de Melo, ending the Spanish ascendancy in Europe.
Rorke's Drift	Zulu-British War	22 Jan. 1879	Lts Chard and Bromhead led a company from 24th Regiment to repulse numerically far superior Zulu attack. 11 VCs awarded.
Ruhr Pocket	Second World Warl	1 Apr. 1945	US 9th Army surrounded remnants of Field Marshal Model's Army Group B, causing mass surrender and Model's suicide.
Sadowa	Seven Weeks' War	3 July 1866	See Königgrätz.
St Albans (First)	Wars of the Roses	22 May 1455	First battle in these wars. Duke of York defeated Lancastrians. Henry VI captured. Northumberland and Somerset killed.
St Albans (Second)	Wars of the Roses	17 Feb. 1461	Lancastrians under Margaret of Anjou defeated Yorkists and released Henry VI.
Saintes	US War of Independence	12 Apr. 1782	British under Admiral Sir George Rodney gained a decisive naval victory in the West Indies over a French fleet under the Comte de Grasse.
Salamanca	Peninsular War	22 July 1812	Wellington's Allied army defeated Marshal Auguste Marmont's force, the main French army in Spain.
Salamis (First)	Persian-Greek Wars	480 BC	Greeks under Themistocles won a naval victory over the Persians under Xerxes.
Salamis (Second)	Macedonian-Egyptian War	306 BC	Demetrius I Poliorcetes of Macedonia won a naval encounter with the Egyptians under Ptolemy I.
Salerno	Second World War	Sept. 1943	In Allied amphibious landing, 5th Army reinforced by US 82nd Airborne and British 7th Armoured took port and had entered Naples by 1 October.
Samaria	Palestinian War	722 BC	The capital of the Hebrew kingdom of Israel was destroyed by the Assyrians under Sargon II.
Samugarh	Mughal Civil War	29 May 1658	Decisive battle of the struggle for the Mughal throne between Aurangzeb and Murād Bakhsh, the third and fourth sons of Shah Jehan, on

Battle	War	Date	Details
			the one side, and the eldest son, Dārā Shikoh, on the other. Aurangzeb ultimately triumphed and began his long rule as emperor.
San Jacinto	Texan Rising	21 Apr. 1836	General Houston defeated Mexicans under Santa Anna, which led to admission of Texas to US states 1845.
Santa Cruz (First)	Anglo-Spanish Wars	1657	British fleet under Robert Blake destroyed the harboured Spanish fleet.
Santa Cruz (Second)	Anglo-Spanish Wars	1797	Horatio Nelson lost his right arm during his unsuccessful assault on the Tenerife port.
Saratoga (First)	US War of Independence	19 Sept. 1777	Aka Battle of Freeman's Farm. British army under General Burgoyne unsuccessfully attempted to gain access to Albany.
Saratoga (Second)	US War of Independence	7 Oct. 1777	Aka Battle of Bemis Heights or Second Battle of Freeman's Farm. General Burgoyne's continued engagement of American troops was thwarted by General Benedict Arnold.
Saratoga (Third)	US War of Independence	17 Oct. 1777	Decisive battle of the war whereby the British army under General Burgoyne was defeated by the Americans under Gates; the outcome encouraged the French into the war.
Sauchie Burn	Barons' Rebellion	18 June 1488	James III of Scotland (killed) defeated by rebel barons under the earl of Angus.
Sedan	Franco-Prussian War	1 Sept.1870	General von Moltke's German Army defeated French, Emperor Napoleon III surrendered, French Second Empire fell.
Sedgemoor	Monmouth's Rebellion	6 July 1685	Royal troops under the earl of Feversham defeated James, duke of Monmouth.
Selby	English Civil War	11 Apr. 1644	Sir Thomas Fairfax defeated royalists under Col. John Bellasis.
Seringapatam	Fourth Mysore War	1799	British army under Richard Wellesley defeated the Indians under Tipu Sultan (died).
Sevastopol	Crimean War	Sept. 1854–Sept. 1855	Successful Allied siege of Russian naval base.
Seven Days battle	US Civil War	26 June–2 July 1862	Confederates under General Lee staved off Union campaign to capture Richmond after a week-long series of battles.
Sevenoaks	Cade's Rebellion	18 June 1450	Rebels under Jack Cade defeated royal troops under Sir Humphrey Stafford (died).
Shanghai	Sino-Japanese War	8 Aug. 1937	Chinese defended this port for three months but eventually succumbed to Japanese.
Shannon and Chesapeake	War of 1812	1 June 1813	British frigate *Shannon* under Capt. Broke captured US frigate *Chesapeake* under Capt. Lawrence (killed).
Sheerness	Anglo-Dutch Wars	7 June 1667	Dutch fleet under Admiral de Ruyter sailed up the Medway to Upnor Castle and sank 7 ships.
Sheriffmuir	Jacobite Rebellion 1715	13 Nov. 1715	Indecisive battle between 10,000 Jacobite rebels under the earl of Mar and 3,300 loyalist Scots under the duke of Argyll.
Shiloh	US Civil War	6–7 Apr. 1862	Major engagement with even casualties, but Confederates under General Johnston (killed) eventually left the field to Grant's Federal troops.
Shirogawa	Satsuma Rebellion	24 Sept. 1876	Imperial army under Prince Taruhito defeated rebels under Takamori Saigo (killed).
Shrewsbury	Percy's Rebellion	21 July 1403	Royalists under Henry IV defeated Henry Percy (Hotspur), who was killed in battle.
Six Day War	Israeli–Arab War	5–10 June 1967	Victory over United Arab Republic, Syria and Jordan brought Israel control of Golan Heights, West Bank, Gaza Strip, Sinai Peninsula and the Old City of Jerusalem.
Sluys	Hundred Years' War	24 June 1340	English archers under Edward III defeated French in the Zwyn estuary in the main naval engagement of the war.
Solferino	Italian War of Independence	24 June 1859	Indecisive but bloody battle that led to the peace of Villafranca and the Austrian loss of Lombardy to Italy.
Solway Moss	Anglo-Scottish Wars	25 Nov. 1542	Scots under Oliver Sinclair were routed by English under Thomas Dacre and John Musgrave.
Somme	First World War	1 July–19 Nov.	Franco-British offensive cost over 1 million

MILITARY

Battle	War	Date	Details
			casualties, made small territory gains. First tank attack of war on 15 Sept. In 1918 Germans made the Somme target for their last offensive.
Stamford Bridge	Norse Invasion of Britain	25 Sept. 1066	English under Harold II defeated Norsemen under Harold Hardrada and Tostig (both killed).
Stirling Bridge	Scottish Independence	11 Sept. 1297	Scots under Sir William Wallace defeated the invading English under the earl of Surrey.
Stoke	Lambert Simnel's Rebellion	16 June 1487	Royal troops under Henry VII defeated rebels under John de la Pole, earl of Lincoln.
Talavera	Peninsular War	28 July 1809	Arthur Wellesley was made Viscount Wellington after defeating the French under King Joseph Bonaparte and Marchand Jourdan.
Tālikota	Muslim Wars	Jan. 1565	Muslim sultans of Bijāpur, Bidar, Ahmadnagar, and Golconda defeated the forces of the Hindu raja of Vijayanagar.
Tearless Battle	Spartan Wars	368 BC	Arcadians attempted to cut off Spartan army under Archidamus but no Spartans were killed.
Tel-el-Kebir	Egyptian Revolt	13 Sept. 1882	Sir Garnet Wolseley defeated Egyptian nationalists under Arabi Pasha.
Teutoburg Forest	German-Roman War	AD 9	The Germanic Cherusci tribe, led by the young German prince Arminius, ambushed and slaughtered the Roman army under General Quinctilius Varus (committed suicide).
Tewkesbury	Wars of the Roses	4 May 1471	Yorkists under Edward IV defeated Lancastrians under Queen Margaret and Somerset. Prince Edward, son of Henry VI (killed).
Thapsus	Roman Civil War	6 Feb. 46 BC	Romans under Julius Caesar slaughtered the troops of Quintus Metellus Scipio, the father-in-law of Pompey the Great, and within weeks had conquered the rest of Roman Africa.
Thermopylae	Third Persian Invasion	19 Aug. 480 BC	Spartans and Thespians under Leonidas defeated by Persians under Xerxes.
Thorn	Great Northern War	22 Sept. 1702	Swedes under Charles XII defeated Poles and elected Stanislas Leszczynski king of Poland.
Tinchebrai	Norman Civil War	28 Sept. 1106	English under Henry I defeated his brother duke Robert of Normandy, annexing Normandy.
Toulon	French Revolutionary Wars	Aug.–Dec. 1793	Notable for being the engagement that earned Napoleon Bonaparte his reputation as a military tactician when he forced the withdrawal of the Anglo-Spanish fleet.
Tours/Poitiers	Muslim Invasion of France	10 Oct. 732	Franks under Charles Martel defeated Saracens under Abderrahman Ibn Abdillah (killed), halting Moorish conquest of Europe.
Towton	Wars of the Roses	29 Mar. 1461	Edward IV defeated Lancastrians under Henry VI and was crowned on 28 June.
Trafalgar	Napoleonic Wars	21 Oct. 1805	British fleet under Nelson (died) and Collingwood defeated Spanish and French under Villeneuve, losing no ships and capturing half of the enemy's.
Trenton	US War of Independence	26 Dec. 1776	Notable as the first success of George Washington in open warfare.
Tsushima Strait	Russo-Japanese War	27–28 May 1905	Admiral Togo routed Russian fleet under Rozlidestrenski, making first use of naval radio.
Ulm	Napoleonic Wars	20 Oct. 1805	Napoleon defeated Austrians under General Baron Mack von Leiberich (court-martialled).
Ulundi	Zulu-British War	4 July 1879	Final battle of the Anglo-Zulu War, in which Cetshwayo (Cetewayo) was defeated and taken prisoner.
Ushant			See Glorious 1st of June.
Valmy	French Revolutionary Wars	20 Sept. 1792	French under Dumouriez and Kellerman defeated Prussians under Duke of Brunswick.
Verdun	First World War	21 Feb.– 20 Dec. 1916	German General von Falkenhayn's war of attrition against French, with combined casualties of over 650,000 and no conclusive outcome.
Vienna	Ottoman Wars	July–Sept. 1683	The Siege of Vienna by the Turks against the Habsburg Holy Roman Emperor Leopold I. On 12 September a combined force led by John III Sobieski defeated the Turks.
Vinegar Hill	Irish Rebellion	21 June 1798	Irish loyalists under General Lake defeated Catholic rebels under Father Murphy.

Battle	War	Date	Details
Virginia Capes	US War of Independence	5 Sept. 1781	French naval victory over a British fleet under Admiral Thomas Graves near Chesapeake Bay.
Vitoria	Peninsular War	21 June 1813	British under Wellington defeated French and expelled Joseph Bonaparte from Spain.
Vyborg	Russo-Finnish War	24 Apr. 1918	General Mannerheim's Finnish White Army defeated Bolsheviks.
Wakefield	Wars of the Roses	30 Dec. 1460	Lancastrians under Somerset defeated Yorkists under Richard of York (killed).
Wandiwāsh	Seven Years' War	22 Jan. 1760	British under Sir Eyre Coote defeated the French under the Comte de Lally in what was the decisive battle in the Anglo-French conflict in southern India.
Warburg	Seven Years' War	31 July 1760	French under Chevalier du Muy forced to retire by joint Prussian/British force.
Waterloo	Napoleon's Hundred Days	18 June 1815	Wellington aided by Prussians under Blücher defeated Napoleon who abdicated on 22 June.
Worcester	English Civil War	3 Sept. 1651	Last pitched battle of civil war in which Cromwell defeated royalists under Charles II.
Yarmuk River	Palestinian Wars	20 Aug. 636	Arabian army under Khālid ibn al-Walid defeated a Byzantine army under Theodorus.
Yom Kippur	Israeli-Arab War	6–24 Oct. 1973	Syrian and Egyptian surprise offensive along Golan Heights and Suez Canal defeated after heavy fighting.
Yorktown	US War of Independence	19 Oct. 1781	General Cornwallis forced to surrender to US and French troops, ending war.
Ypres (First)	First World War	14 Oct.1914	General von Falkenhayn's push to reach ports of Calais and Dunkirk halted by the British Expeditionary Force under Sir John French.
Ypres (Second)	First World War	22 Apr.– late May 1915	General Falkenhayn used lethal chlorine gas for the first time, causing many Allied deaths and advancing about 3 miles.
Ypres (Third)	First World War		See Passchendaele.
Zama	Second Punic War	202 BC	Carthaginians under Hannibal were defeated by Romans under Scipio Africanus in final battle of this war.
Zenta	Ottoman Wars	11 Sept. 1697	Ottoman army under Sultan Mustafa II was engaged by an Austrian army under Prince Eugene of Savoy while crossing the Tisza river and comprehensively defeated.
Zutphen	Dutch War of Independence	22 Sept. 1586	Spanish victory over English force under Leicester notable for death of Sir Philip Sidney.

MILITARY

MUSIC: CLASSICAL

Opera: Précis of Plots

Aida (Verdi, 1871)   Aida, a captive Ethiopian princess, is servant to the Egyptian princess Amneris. Both are in love with General Radamès, who loves Aida. Radamès goes to war against the Ethiopians, defeats them and is given Amneris's hand in marriage, but Radames is suspected of having betrayed his country in trying to help Aida and sentenced to death. Aida conceals herself in the tomb where both of them are buried alive, while above them, Amneris prays.

The Barber of Seville (Rossini, 1816)   Count Almaviva, aided by his barber Figaro, is pursuing Rosina. Her guardian, Bartolo, who wants to marry her himself, tries to stop them but is unsuccessful, and Rosina marries the count.

The Bartered Bride (Smetana, 1866)   Marenka loves Jenik, whose parents want to marry her to the halfwit son of Micha. Jenik is offered money to give her up, and accepts on condition she marries Micha's eldest son. This turns out to be Jenik himself; Marenka can marry him after all.

La Bohème (Puccini, 1896)   Mimi, who is consumptive, falls in love with a Bohemian poet, Rodolfo, and for a while they live together, but constant quarrels drive them apart. Then Rodolfo's friends discover that Mimi is dying and bring her to him, but it is too late and she dies in his arms.

Carmen (Bizet, 1875)   The soldier Don José deserts the army to follow the gypsy girl Carmen, who leaves him for the toreador Escamillo. Mad with jealousy, Don José follows her to the bullring and kills her.

Cavalleria Rusticana (Mascagni, 1890)   Brokenhearted because her lover, Turiddu, has abandoned her for another woman, Santuzza tells the other woman's husband what is going on. He kills Turiddu in a duel.

The Coronation of Poppaea (Monteverdi, 1643)   Emperor Nero resolves to marry his mistress Poppaea. One by one, he murders everyone who stands in their way until Poppaea is crowned empress.

Così fan tutte (Mozart, 1790)   The sisters Fiordiligi and Dorabella swear to be faithful to their lovers Ferrando and Guglielmo, so to try their fidelity the latter pretend to go off to the wars. But they return in disguise and each proceeds to make advances to the other's girl, who both respond. The men then reveal their disguise, but forgive their wayward sweethearts, and both couples are reunited.

Don Giovanni (Mozart, 1787)   Foiled in his attempts to seduce Donna Anna, the libertine Don Giovanni (aka Don Juan) kills her father, the Commendatore. Anna and her fiancé Don Ottavio vow to avenge him. They are joined by Donna Elvira, another former victim of the Don. In a gesture of defiance, Don Giovanni has confronted a statue of the Commendatore and invited him to dinner. The Commendatore duly accepts, arrives at the Don's house and drags him down to hell.

Eugene Onegin (Tchaikovsky, 1879)   Tatyana, young and open-hearted, falls in love with the worldly Eugene Onegin and confesses her feelings, but he rejects her. Years later they meet again and this time he falls in love with her, but by now she is married and, though still attracted to him, sends him away for ever.

Falstaff (Verdi, 1893)   Shakespeare's fat knight, Sir John Falstaff, is simultaneously wooing two wives of Windsor, Mistress Ford and Mistress Page, who discover what he is up to and contrive to pay him back, but Falstaff eventually takes it in good part and the opera finishes with a happy ending for a young couple involved in the plotting – Nannetta Ford and her lover, Fenton.

Faust (Gounod, 1859)   Faust has been given back his youth by the devil, Mephistopheles, so he can pursue the beautiful Marguerite. They fall in love and she has a child, but Faust then deserts her. She kills the child and is condemned to death. Faust returns to save her, but he is too late, and she dies and is borne to heaven.

Fidelio (Beethoven, 1805)   When Florestan is unjustly imprisoned, his wife Leonora disguises herself as a young man called Fidelio and gets a job inside the prison, from where she succeeds in getting him freed.

The Flying Dutchman (Wagner, 1843)   A Dutch sea captain has been condemned by the Devil to sail the seas for ever, unless he can find a woman who will love him until death. Once in every seven years he is allowed to land in search of her. He meets Senta, who declares her love for him, but leaves her owing to a misunderstanding, whereupon she throws herself into the sea and drowns, thus freeing him.

Gloriana (Britten, 1953)   The libretto was based on Lytton Strachey's *Elizabeth and Essex* and concerns the decline of Essex in the affections of Queen Elizabeth. The opening act tells of a fight between Essex and Lord Montjoy at the court of Elizabeth. They are rebuked, but the rebellious nature of Essex is recognised by the Queen. Essex is appointed Deputy of Ireland and given the charge of subduing Tyrone, but fails miserably. On his return to England the disgraced Essex rebels and is arrested as a traitor. At his trial at Whitehall, Essex is given a death sentence, which is eventually signed by Elizabeth after an injudicious word from Lady Rich. The final act depicts the Queen reflecting on her life to the audience.

Lohengrin (Wagner, 1850)   The heroine, Elsa, falsely accused, will lose her life if she cannot find a champion. When one appears (Lohengrin, a knight searching for the Holy Grail), he agrees to defend her so long as she never asks his name. Eventually they marry, but an enemy dupes her into asking her husband's name. Now she has broken her vow and he leaves her for ever.

Lucia di Lammermoor (Donizetti, 1835)   Lucy Ashton is in love with Edgar, but is tricked by her brother into marrying someone else. On her wedding night she goes mad and kills her husband. When he learns of her subsequent death, Edgar kills himself.

Madame Butterfly (Puccini, 1904)   The American naval Lieutenant Pinkerton has married the innocent Japanese girl Cio-Cio-San. He regards the arrangements as only temporary and leaves her when the time comes, but she loves him and longs for his return. When he does, with an American wife, Butterfly promises to give him their child and then kills herself.

The Magic Flute (Mozart, 1791)   This is a contest between Good (the high priest Sarastro) and Evil (the Queen of the Night). Prince Tamino falls in love with the Queen of the Night's daughter, Pamina, and has to undergo many tests and temptations, helped by a gift of a magic flute, before he conquers Evil and wins the hand of his beloved.

Manon (Massenet, 1884)   Manon Lescaut and the Chevalier Des Grieux fall in love and run away together, but she prefers luxury to poverty and leaves him for a rich man. She is eventually deported for being a prostitute. Des Grieux follows her, but she is overwhelmed by her suffering and dies in his arms.

The Marriage of Figaro (Mozart, 1786)   Figaro, barber to the womanising Count Almaviva, is about to be married to Susanna, the countess's maid, but discovers the count has designs on her. Figaro, Susanna, the countess and her page Cherubino hatch a plot to unmask the count, and all ends happily with the wedding of Figaro and Susanna.

The Mastersingers of Nuremberg (Wagner, 1868)   The Mastersingers of Nuremberg are to hold a song contest, the prize being the hand of Eva. The knight Walther arrives, falls in love with Eva and decides to compete, coached by Hans Sachs the cobbler. Although his rival Beckmesser does his best to discredit him, he wins both the contest and Eva.

Norma (Bellini,1831)   The Druid priestess Norma has had two children by the Roman general Pollione, who has now fallen in love with a younger priestess, Adalgisa. Norma incites a Gallo-Roman war, Pollione is captured and sentenced to death, and they both go to be sacrificed together.

Otello (Verdi, 1887)   Otello, the Moor of Venice, is tricked by the evil Iago into believing his wife, Desdemona, has been unfaithful to him. In a fit of jealousy he kills her, learns the truth, then kills himself.

I Pagliacci (Leoncavallo, 1893)   A troupe of strolling players enact a real-life drama. The clown, Canio, does not know that his wife, Nedda, is having an affair with Silvio, a villager, although he is suspicious. At that night's performance, in which Canio plays a jealous husband, reality gets the better of him, the play becomes a real quarrel, and he stabs both Nedda and Silvio to death.

The Pearl Fishers (Bizet, 1863)   Pearl fishers Zurga and Nadir have long loved the priestess, Leila, but have vowed not to let this destroy their friendship. Then Leila arrives to conduct a religious ceremony, and she and Nadir confess their love. They are discovered and sentenced to death. Zurga helps them escape but loses his own life as a result.

Peter Grimes (Britten, 1945)   The lone fisherman, Peter Grimes, is an outsider in the East Coast fishing community where he lives. Already under suspicion after the mysterious death of his young apprentice, when a second boy dies unaccountably, Grimes is forced to take to sea and drowns himself.

Rigoletto (Verdi, 1851)   The hunchback jester Rigoletto has helped his master, the Duke of Mantua, to seduce the daughter of the courtier Monterone, who curses him. The duke believes that Rigoletto has a mistress (actually his daughter), Gilda, and seduces her. In revenge, Rigoletto plots to have the duke murdered, but the plot misfires and Gilda is killed instead. The curse has been fulfilled.

The Ring Cycle (Wagner, 1876)   *The Rhinegold*: The magic Rhinegold is at the bottom of the River Rhine, guarded by the Rhinemaidens. Alberich, the wicked dwarf, steals it and makes a ring from it to become all-powerful. Meanwhile, the god Wotan is looking for money to pay for his castle of Valhalla and plots to steal the gold. He tricks Alberich into parting with it, but it is cursed and results in a death. *The Valkyrie*: Wotan has fathered nine warrior-maidens, the Valkyries; his favourite is Brünnhilde. He also has a son and a daughter, Siegmund and Sieglinde, who were separated at birth. In a storm, Siegmund takes shelter in a hut where Sieglinde lives with her husband Hunding. The two fall in love and run away but are pursued by Hunding, who kills Siegmund. Brünnhilde carries Siegmund off to Valhalla in defiance of her father, who condemns her to sleep in a ring of fire until a hero comes to rescue her. *Siegfried*: Sieglinde has died giving birth to a son, Siegfried, who has been brought up by the dwarf Mime in the hope that he will one day get the Ring back. With the help of Wotan and Brünnhilde, Siegfried is led to the magic rock where he awakes Brünnhilde and they fall in love. *Twilight of the Gods*: Siegfried has taken the Ring from the dragon that was guarding it and now gives it to Brünnhilde while he goes in search of further adventure. He reaches the Hall of the Gibichungs, who hope to marry him to their sister Gutrune. Although Brünnhilde comes with the Ring to rescue him, he is killed. Brünnhilde builds a funeral pyre for him and climbs on to it herself. The Rhinemaidens arrive in a flood and snatch back the Ring, while Valhalla is consumed in flames. It is the end of the gods.

Der Rosenkavalier (Strauss, 1911)   The young Count Octavian is having an affair with an older woman, the Marschallin, although she knows it cannot last. Octavian is sent to bear a silver rose as a symbol of the forthcoming marriage of the beautiful young Sophie von Faninal to a much older man, Baron Ochs. The two young people fall in love, their elders realise that it is better to let them go, and Octavian and Sophie face a future together.

Ruslan and Lyudmila (Glinka, 1842)   Svyetozar is hosting a wedding celebration for his daughter Lyudmila, who is betrothed to the knight Ruslan. The bard Bayan sings but foretells ill fortune for the newly-weds. A thunderclap followed by total darkness interrupts the festivities. Light returns but Lyudmila has disappeared. Lyudmila's former suitors search in vain. Ruslan encounters the wise magician Finn, who tells him of Lyudmila's abduction by the evil dwarf Chernomor. Ruslan acquires a magic sword and challenges Chernomor to a duel. The dwarf casts a sleeping spell on Lyudmila before encountering Ruslan, who defeats him by cutting off his beard, the source of power. Ruslan awakens Lyudmila with a magic ring.

The Tales of Hoffmann (Offenbach, 1881)   The poet Hoffmann relates the stories of the three loves of his life, all destroyed by the same evil genius. First, there is Olympia, who, he does not realize until too late, is only a mechanical doll. Then the courtesan Giulietta, who leaves him for another, and finally Antonia, a pure young girl who knows she will die if she tries to sing but is tricked into doing so. The story of loss is about to be repeated with the opera singer Stella, and Hoffmann is left alone to drown his sorrows in beer.

M
U
S
I
C

C
L
A
S
S
I
C
A
L

Tosca (Puccini, 1900)   The opera singer Floria Tosca is loved by the political agitator Cavaradossi and desired by the evil police chief Scarpia. Cavaradossi is arrested, but Scarpia promises Tosca he will free him if she agrees to give herself to him. She kills Scarpia, but he has tricked her and Cavaradossi is shot, whereupon Tosca throws herself to her death from the prison battlements.

La Traviata (The Fallen Woman) (Verdi, 1853)   Violetta, a courtesan, has fallen in love with a young aristocrat, Alfredo, but Alfredo's father begs her to break off the relationship as it will bring disgrace to his family, and she goes back to her old life. Alfredo confronts and denounces her, but she is dying of consumption, and when, too late, he returns to her side, she dies in his arms.

Tristan und Isolde (Wagner, 1865)   Isolde is to be married to King Mark of Cornwall and his nephew Tristan is sent to fetch her, but the two fall in love. After the wedding they meet, but they are discovered and Tristan is wounded. Isolde comes to him as he dies, then herself falls lifeless over his body.

Il Trovatore (The Troubadour) (Verdi, 1853)   Leonora is being serenaded by a mysterious troubador, regarded as a rival by Count di Luna, who is in love with her. The troubador turns out to be Manrico, apparently the son of the gypsy Azucena. But Azucena explains that years ago, in revenge for the agony of seeing her mother burned to death, she threw the Count's abducted baby brother into the flames – but by mistake threw her own baby instead. Manrico and Leonora run away but are pursued by the Count, who imprisons Manrico. Leonora agrees to marry the Count as the price of Manrico's freedom, but then kills herself. The Count executes Manrico, then is told by Azucena that he has killed his own brother.

Turandot (Busoni, 1917)   The cruel Chinese princess Turandot will marry only if a suitor prince can solve her three riddles. If he cannot, he will die. An unknown prince answers the riddles correctly but tells her that if she can discover his name by morning, he will agree to die. Turandot tortures the slave girl Liu, who knows the name but will not reveal it, and Liu eventually dies. The prince tells Turandot his name. It is 'Love,' and she accepts him as her husband.

NB: The above is only a small selection of operas but offers a flavour of the moods and emotions that can be explored in others.

Composers
(Chronological order)

Name	Principal works	Details
Hildegard of Bingen 1098–1179	Church music departing from traditional plainsong style	Saint and abbess
Pérotin c. 1160–c. 1205	Christmas and St Stephen's Day graduals (1198, 1199)	aka Perotinus Magnus; maître de chapelle at Notre Dame; exponent of *ars antiqua*
Adam de la Halle c. 1250–?1306	*Le jeu de Robin et de Marion* anticipated the genre of opéra comique	Aka Adam the Hunchback; born Arras, France and died in Naples; court musician of the Comte d'Artois
Machaut, Guillaume de c. 1300–c.1377	*Messe de Notre Dame* (for four violins); *Voir Dit* (Tale of Truth), collection of ballads; 23 motets	Born and died in Reims; leading French composer of free-flowing *ars nova* style of 14th century; canon of Reims Cathedral
Landini, Francesco c. 1325–1397	Various madrigals; over 140 ballads	Born and died in Florence; blinded in youth from smallpox; noted for 'Landini Cadence' in which sixth degree octave is inserted between leading note and octave
Dunstable, John c. 1390–1453	Masses and motets	Aka Dunstaple; internationally renowned in his day
Du Fay, Guillaume c. 1400–1474	8 masses; 87 motets; 59 French chansons	Composed earliest requiem mass; possibly originated Fauxbourdon style; canon of Cambrai
Ockeghem, Johannes c. 1430–1495	14 masses; 10 motets; 20 chansons	Born Flanders and died Tours; composer to 3 successive French kings: Charles VII, Louis XI, Charles VIII
Josquin des Prés c. 1445–1521	18 masses; 100 motets	Born Picardy and died Hainault; Luther called him 'Master of the Notes'
Isaac, Heinrich c. 1450–1517	36 masses; 'Innsbruck I Must Leave You' (song) reworked by J.S. Bach and Brahms	Born Brabant and died Florence; taught in household of Medici family
Taverner, John c. 1490–1545	8 masses (inc. *Westron Wynde*); other church music	Occasionally alleged to have given up music to persecute Catholics under Thomas Cromwell; subject of opera by Peter Maxwell Davies
Cabezón, Antonio de c. 1510–1566	'El Caballero variation'	Born Burgos and died Madrid; blind from birth
Tallis, Thomas c. 1510–1585	'Spem in alium nunquam habui' (In no other is my Hope) (motet)	Elizabeth I granted monopoly of sheet music to Tallis and William Byrd

MUSIC CLASSICAL

Name	Principal works	Details
Gabrieli, Andrea c. 1510–1586	7 masses and numerous motets	Born and died in Venice
Palestrina, Giovanni 1525–1594	Over 100 masses and 250 motets, including Stabat Mater	Took his name from his birthplace; lost his family in Italian plague
Lassus, Orlande 1532–1594	Wrote some 2,000 madrigals, motets, chansons, canzonas, masses, lieder, etc.	Born at Mons, died at Munich; preceded Palestrina as chapelmaster of Papal Church of St John Lateran, Rome
Byrd, William 1543–1623	Prolific composer and pioneer of madrigals but also composed motets, masses and music for organ and virginals, his most famous work being the collection of 42 virginal pieces My Lady Nevells Book	Pupil of Thomas Tallis and favoured by Queen Elizabeth despite being a Catholic; granted monopoly of all sheet music in England along with Tallis
Victoria Tomás Luis de 1548–1611	Composed in a similar style to that of Palestrina but distinguished by his use of Spanish melody. His total output consisted of church music including the motets Vexilla Regis and Magnum Mysterium, the acclaimed Officium Hebdonadae Sanctae, and the Requiem Mass composed at the death of Empress Maria	Spanish composer, born in Avila; studied for priesthood in Rome and in 1576 became chaplain to the widowed Empress Maria, sister of Philip II, returning with her to Madrid in 1583 to the convent of the Descalzas Reales, where he remained as choirmaster until his death
Morley, Thomas 1557–1602	Father of the English madrigal who edited the collection The Triumphs of Oriana; his last work was The First Book of Ayres	Pupil of Byrd who became organist at St Paul's Cathedral and Gentleman of the Chapel Royal in 1592
Sweelinck, Jan Piterszoon 1562–1621	Wrote over 250 vocal works and 70 for keyboard. His fantasias were the first example of fully worked-out fugues. He founded the North German school which later included Diderik Buxtehude and J S Bach	Dutch composer, organist and harpsichordist. Succeeded his father as organist of the Oude Kerk (old church), Amsterdam in 1580, a position he held until his death
Bull, John c. 1562–1628	Although Bull's reputation was as a performer rather than a composer, he, along with William Byrd and Orlando Gibbons, published the first book of keyboard music in England, the aptly named Parthenia (Maidenhood), 1611. His other works include the virginal pieces Walsingham and God Save the King, although the attribution of our present National Anthem to Bull is perhaps not from this piece but a later untitled work	English musician. Appointed organist in the Queen's Chapel in 1586 and became the first music lecturer at Gresham College in 1597, and organist to James I in 1607. His Catholicism led him to flee England in 1613 to become organist of the Chapel Royal, Brussels and in 1615 became organist at Antwerp Cathedral, where he remained until his death
Dowland, John 1562–1626	Published 87 songs as well as Lachrimae (1604), 21 dance pieces containing 7 pavanes, all beginning with the theme of Dowland's song 'Flow my tears'	Lutenist and singer/songwriter for the king of Denmark (1598–1606) and Lord Howard de Walden (1606–12) as well as Anne of Denmark and Charles I
Monteverdi, Claudio 1567–1643	First opera La Favola d'Orfeo (1607) is earliest opera in the regular repertoire; last opera: L'Incoronazione di Poppea (1642); many operas lost; other works listed in tables	Son of a barber/surgeon who wed the singer Claudia Cattaneo; he was a pupil of Ingegneri and was patronised by the duke of Mantua; took holy orders for a short time
Gibbons, Orlando 1583–1625	Composer of madrigals, e.g. 'The Silver Swan', and anthems, e.g. 'This is the Record of John'; also contributed to the first book of keyboard music printed in England, Parthenia	Organist of Chapel Royal from 1604 and Westminster Abbey from 1623
Frescobaldi, Girolamo	In 1612 he published 12 fantasias, and in 1624 a collection of 10 ricercari,	Italian virtuoso organist, born in Ferrara. Became organist

1583–1643	five canzoni and 11 capriccios. Frescobaldi was a strong influence of the German Baroque school through the work of his pupils Froberger and Tunder	at St Peter's, Rome, where 30,000 people are said to have attended his first performance
Schütz, Heinrich 1585–1672	Christmas Oratorio; settings of the Passion	German composer and organist who studied law and was one of Bach's influences
Froberger, Johann Jakob 1616–67	Froberger was the first important German composer for the harpsichord and a leading light of early Baroque music	German composer, born in Stuttgart. He became a court organist in Vienna, 1637, and later that year travelled to Rome to study under Frescobaldi
Lully, Jean-Baptiste 1632–1687	Composed 20 operas and ballets, including Alceste (1684), Psyché (1678), Roland (1685), Armide et Rénaud (1686), Achille et Polixène (posthumous collaboration with Colasse) and Le Bourgeois Gentilhomme (collaboration with Molière)	Italian-born but took French nationality in 1661; from 1664 collaborated with Molière in series of comedy-ballets which were forerunners of French opera; danced role of the Mufti in Le Bourgeois Gentilhomme; died accidentally by stabbing himself in the foot with long pole used to conduct (wound turned gangrenous)
Buxtehude, Diderik c. 1637–1707	20 cantatas, of which the cycle of seven Membra Jesu Nostri, are the most famous. He also wrote toccatas, preludes, fugues and chaconnes. Most of his harpsichord music has been lost	Danish organist and composer. In 1688 he became organist of Mary's Church, Lübeck, where his fame spread throughout Northern Germany. Handel visited him in 1703 and in 1705 J S Bach was known to have walked the 200 miles from Arnstadt to hear him play
Blow, John 1649–1708	Wrote over 100 anthems and 13 services but best known work was masque Venus and Adonis (1682)	One of the first choirboys of Chapel Royal after Restoration and organist at Westminster Abbey (1668–79), preceding Henry Purcell
Corelli, Arcangelo 1653–1713	First composition: Sonata for Violin and Lute. 60 sonatas (48 trio and 12 solo) 12 Concerti Grossi (published posthumously) the most famous being his Christmas Concerto	Italian violinist, conductor and composer. From 1687 he was under the patronage of Cardinal Pamphili. Corelli was a skilled conductor and is often thought of as a pioneer of modern orchestral direction
Purcell, Henry 1659–1695	Only opera Dido and Aeneas (1683); fantasias for strings (1680); 'My Heart is Inditing' for Coronation of James II (1685); semi-operas include The Fairy Queen, King Arthur, The Tempest and the unfinished The Indian Queen	Succeeded Matthew Locke as composer to the king's violins and John Blow as organist of Westminster Abbey (1679); in 1682 became one of the three organists of the Chapel Royal
Scarlatti, Alessandro 1660–1725	First of 115 operas Gli Equivoci; his greatest considered to be Mitridate Eupatore (1707); only comic opera Il Trionfo dell'Onore (1718); last opera La Griselda (1721)	Founder of Neapolitan School of composers; father of Domenico Scarlatti
Couperin, François 1668–1733	Composed 230 harpsichord pieces, also chamber music	Wrote textbook The Art of Touching the Keyboard, known as 'Couperin the Great' on account of quantity of musicians in the family
Vivaldi, Antonio 1678–1741	First opera Ottone in Villa (1713); first Venetian opera Orlando Finto Pazzo; best known opera Orlando Furioso (1727); most famous work The Four	Nicknamed the Red Priest after taking holy orders in 1703; taught violin at Ospedale della Pietà, an orphanage, from

Name	Principal works	Details
Telemann, Georg Philipp 1681–1767	*Seasons* (1725); most famous oratorio *Juditha Triumphans* (1716) Often considered the most prolific of all composers with 600 overtures and 44 passions to his name as well as 40 operas (best known being *Pimpinone*, 1725)	1703; died and buried in a pauper's grave in Vienna; Peter Ryom catalogued works, Leipzig, 1974 with prefix RV (Ryom Verzeichnis) German composer and organist who had no formal training but studied Lully and André Campra; appointed Kantor at the Thomaskirche, Leipzig, in preference to J S Bach
Bach, Johann Sebastian 1685–1750	Orchestral and keyboard works include: *Brandenburg Concertos (Nos 1–6)* (1717); *The Well-Tempered Klavier* (48 preludes and fugues); *Goldberg Variations* (30 variations on original theme); English suites and French suites, as well as the unfinished *Die Kunst der Fuge* (The Art of Fugue); famous oratorios include *St John Passion, St Matthew Passion* and *Christmas Oratorio*	Born Eisenach and died in Leipzig; orphaned at age of 10 and lived with elder brother at Ohrdruf; married his cousin Maria Barbara Bach in 1707 and after her death in 1720 married Anna Magdalena Wilcken (December 1721); almost totally blind during last year of life; Wagner described his work as 'The most stupendous miracle in all music'; catalogues have BWV nos (Bach Werke Verzeichnis)
Scarlatti, Domenico 1685–1757	About 550 harpsichord sonatas; also operas and oratorios	Long-time friend of Handel; powerful influence on modern keyboard technique
Handel, George Frederick 1685–1759	First opera *Almira* (1705) and last *Deidamia* (1740); other notable operas include *Agrippina* (1709), *Rinaldo* (1711), *Teseo* (1712), *Radamisto* (1720), *Tamerlano* (1724), *Orlando* (1733), *Ariodante* (1735), *Alcina* (1735), *Berenice* (1737), *Serse* (1738); orchestral works include *Water Music* (1717) and *Music for Royal Fireworks* (1749) played in Green Park to mark the Peace of Aix-la-Chapelle; oratorios include *Esther* (1732), *Athalia* (1733), *Alexander's Feast* (1736), *Israel in Egypt* (1739), *Messiah* (1741), *Judas Maccabaeus* (1746); church music includes *Dettingen Te Deum* (1743), *Chandos Anthems* (1718), *Zadok the Priest* (1737); other famous work is 5th Harpsichord Suite, nicknamed *The Harmonious Blacksmith* (1720)	Born in Halle and died in London; son of a barber/surgeon; studied law until his father died; became English citizen in 1726; received pension of £200 p.a. for life from Queen Anne (1712), which was increased to £600 by King George I for whom he wrote his famous *Water Music* suite in 1717; blind for last 7 years of his life and aided by his agent and friend, John Christopher Smith
Arne, Thomas Augustine 1710–1778	First opera was *Rosamond* (1733); composed settings for Shakespeare songs including 'Under the Greenwood Tree', 'Where the Bee Sucks' and 'Blow Blow thou Winter Wind'; most famous work is 'Rule Britannia', originally written for *The Masque of Alfred*	Born and died in London; son of an upholsterer and educated at Eton; his sister was famous actress Mrs Cibber; son Michael wrote 'The Lass with a delicate air'; married a singer, Cecilia Young (1736)
Boyce, William 1711–1779	Most famously associated with the song 'Heart of Oak', composed in 1759 for pantomime *Harlequin's Invasion* to words by David Garrick; 8 symphonies and 12 overtures	Master of the King's Musick from 1755
Gluck, Christoph Willibald 1714–1787	First opera *Artaserse* (1741); best known opera is *Orfeo et Eurydice* (1762); other operas include *La Clemenza di Tito* (1752), *Alceste* (1767) and *Armide* (1777); his best-known ballet is *Don Juan* (1761); opera comiques include *The Pilgrimage to Mecca*	Born Erasbach, Germany and died in Vienna; German composer under patronage of Prince Lobkowitz in his formative years; in 1754 Empress Maria Theresa appointed him opera Kapellmeister to court theatre in Vienna

Haydn, Franz Joseph
1732–1809

Austrian-born son of a farmer-wheelwright; precocious talent as a child; from 1761 was patronised by Prince Paul Esterházy, working as Vice-Kapellmeister at Eisenstadt, Hungary; mutual admiration for Mozart influenced his work from 1781; Beethoven was his pupil for a short period; regarded as the father of the symphony only because of his prolific output; his works are often given Hob nos., after Anthony van Hoboken (1887–1983), who catalogued them

Composed 104 numbered symphonies; Symphony in D Major No 96 is called the 'Miracle' because it was thought that after its first performance the audience flocking to applaud him escaped injury when a chandelier fell on their empty seats. In fact, this incident occurred on 2 February 1795 while his 102nd Symphony was playing; composed 20 operas, the first *La Canterina* 1766 and the last *Orfeo ed Euridice* (1791); other works include numerous masses, cantatas, sonatas, oratorios, concertos and chamber music

Cimarosa, Domenico
1749–1801

Court composer to Catherine II of Russia; in 1791 succeeded Salieri as Kapellmeister to Leopold II in Vienna; sentenced to death in 1799 for supporting French Republican army but reprieved on condition he left Naples

First of 65 operas was *Le Stravaganze del Conti* (1772); best known opera *The Secret Marriage* (1792); other operas include *Artaserse* (1784), *Penelope* (1795) and *L'Apprensivo Raggirato* (1798); also wrote 30 keyboard sonatas

Mozart, Wolfgang Amadeus
1756–1791

Born in Salzburg and died in Vienna; Johannes Chrysostomus Wolfgangus Theophilus was baptismal name; son of Leopold, Vice-Kapellmeister to Prince Archbishop of Salzburg; sister was Maria Anna (Nannerl; 1751–1829); in Rome in 1769 he heard Allegri's *Miserere* and wrote it out from memory; married Constance Weber in August 1782; his *Requiem Mass* for Count von Walsegg was completed after his death by Franz Süssmayr; work was catalogued by Ludwig von Köchel, an Austrian botanist and mineralogist

First opera was *Apollo et Hyacinthus* (1767); other operas include *Bastien und Bastienne* (1768), *Idomeneo* (1780), *The Marriage of Figaro* (1786), *Don Giovanni* (1787), *Così fan tutte* (1789), *Die Zauberflöte* (The Magic Flute) (1791); last opera *La Clemenza di Tito* (1791); of the 41 symphonies the last 3 were composed in a matter of a few weeks; also wrote numerous orchestral pieces and concertos for both piano and violin as well as horn concertos, string quartets, 40 songs and many sonatas; *Eine kleine Nachtmusik* (1787) is a popular orchestral piece, being theme tune for *Brain of Britain* quiz

Beethoven, Ludwig van
1770–1827

Born in Bonn and buried in Central Friedhof, Vienna; father was court singer to the elector of Cologne; dedicated his 3rd Symphony to Napoleon but retracted it on hearing he had made himself emperor; learned he was going deaf in 1798; mystery cloaks identity of his 'Immortal Beloved', although Antonie Brentano is a candidate as he dedicated his *Diabelli Variations* to her; freedom of Vienna bestowed on him in 1815

Only opera *Fidelio* (1805) was originally called *Leonora*; nine complete symphonies, but Dr Barry Cooper, a music lecturer at Aberdeen University, has pieced together, from sketches, a 10th Symphony by making projections of existing themes; composed 32 piano sonatas, including No. 14 in C sharp minor (*Moonlight*) and No. 15 in D major (*Pastoral*); best-known piano concerto was No. 5 (*Emperor*); numerous songs, sonatas and masses; one violin concerto

Paganini, Niccolò
1782–1840

Born in Genoa, died of cancer of the larynx in Nice; regarded as greatest genius of the violin; successful gambler who owned a casino and lent money to struggling musicians, e.g. Berlioz; Mephistophelean looks fostered stories of satanic powers

Six violin concertos remain but various others lost; composed many variations on existing works, such as *God Save the King*, an aria from *La Cenerentola* and *Witches' Dance*, based on an air by Sussmayr; popular work is *Variations on a Theme of Rossini* and *24 Caprices*; also wrote 12 sonatas for violin and guitar

Weber, Carl Maria
1786–1826

Born Eutin in Oldenburg, Germany, the son of a musician and actor-manager; died of tuberculosis while staying with Sir George Smart in his Great Portland St home and re-buried in Dresden in 1844

First of 9 operas *Das Waldmädchen* (1800); other operas include *Silvana* (1810), *Abu Hassan* (1811), *Der Freischütz* (1821), *Euryanthe* (1823) and his final opera *Oberon* (1826); also composed symphonies, songs and masses

Meyerbeer, Giacomo

German operatic composer, born in Berlin and originally named

First opera *Jephtas Gelübde* (1812). Other notable operas include *Robert*

MUSIC CLASSICAL

Name	Principal works	Details
1791–1864	le Diable (1831), Les Huguenots (1836), Le Prophète (1940), L'Etoile du Nord (1854) and L'Africaine (1864). Also wrote oratorio, marches, songs, and church music	Jakob Liebmann Beer. He was a child prodigy pianist, playing a Mozart concerto at the age of 11. Meyerbeer's pageant-like operas were attacked by the anti-Semitism of Wagner
Rossini, Gioachino Antonio 1792–1868	First of 35 operas was Demetrio e Polibio (1806); best-known operas include Tancredi (1813), Otello (1816), Elizabeth of England (1815), La Gazza Ladra, Cinderella (1817) and his last opera William Tell (1829); also composed cantatas, sonatas and orchestral works although retired completely from opera as a result of neurasthenia; late works include Petite Messe Solennelle and a variety of pieces he called 'Sins of my Old Age'; notable prodigy: 6 string sonatas date from his early teens	Born in Pesaro in Italy, died in Paris; buried in Père Lachaise cemetery, but reinterred in Florence in 1887; son of a trumpeter and a singer; married soprano Isabella Colbran (1821) and then after divorcing her, Olympe Pélissier; court composer to Charles X of France in 1825; famous for his 'Samedi Soirs' performances; a gourmand:Tournedos Rossini is named after him; nicknamed Monsieur Crescendo
Schubert, Franz Peter 1797–1828	Wrote 9 numbered symphonies although 7th and 8th were unfinished, as were some unnumbered ones; first opera Des Teufels Lustschloss (1814); prolific output included over 600 songs of which 144 were written in 1815 (8 in one day); some popular songs include 'Death and the Maiden (1817), the Winterreise (Winter Journey) song cycle (1827) and settings of Shakespearean songs, e.g. 'Who is Sylvia?' and 'Hark, Hark the Lark', also notable Goethe settings; of his oratorios, Lazarus (1820), his setting of psalm 23, is best known, although 'Wanderer Fantasy' is popular; unusually did not compose any concertos	Born and died in Vienna, buried near to Beethoven at Währing, and later exhumed and reburied in the Central Cemetery of Vienna; father was schoolmaster and his first teacher; the celebrated baritone Michael Vogl sang many of his lieder; Schubert was a torchbearer at Beethoven's funeral in 1827; his works were catalogued by Otto Deutsch
Donizetti, Gaetano 1797–1848	First opera Il Pigmalione (1816); other operas include Enrico di Borgogna (1818), Zoraide di Grenate (1822), Ann Boleyn (1830), Lucretia Borgia (1833), Lucia di Lammermoor (1835), Mary Stuart (1835), Roberto Devereux (1837), Don Pasquale (1843) and (last) Dom Sébastien (1843); also wrote church music, string quartets and symphonies	Born and died in Bergamo; joined the Austrian army and composed in his spare time until 1822 when he left and became full-time composer; became insane in later life due to syphilis
Bellini, Vincenzo 1801–1835	First opera Adelson e Salvini (1825); others include The Sleepwalker (1831), Norma (1831) and, last opera, I Puritani (1835)	Born in Catania, Sicily, died in Puteaux, near Paris, reinterred in Catania 1876; studied under Niccolò Zingarelli at San Sebastiano in Naples
Berlioz, Hector 1803–1869	Operas: Benvenuto Cellini (1837), Les Troyens (1858) and Béatrice et Bénédict (1862); famous orchestral works include Waverley (1828), King Lear (1831), Le Corsaire (1831), Rob Roy (1832), Harold in Italy (1834), Symphonie Funèbre et Triomphale (1840); best known work is Symphony Fantastique (1830); famous dramatic cantata is The Damnation of Faust	Born Grenoble and died in Paris; son of a provincial doctor but dropped out of medical school for a music career; married Irish actress Harriet Smithson (1833); Paganini paid him 20,000 francs for Harold in Italy; formed liaison with singer Marie Recio (1841)
Strauss the Elder, Johann 1804–1849	Composed 251 works of which 152 were waltzes; Radetzky March (1848), named after an Austrian field-marshal, easily his best known work	Born and died (scarlet fever) in Vienna
Glinka, Mikhail 1804–1857	Two operas Life for the Tsar (1836) – aka Ivan Susanin – and Ruslan and Lyudmila (1842); orchestral works include Kamarinskaya (1848) and Night in Madrid (1848)	Born in Smolensk and died in Berlin; first Russian composer to be recognised outside Russia; worked in Communications Ministry 1824–8

Composer	Biography	Works
Mendelssohn, Felix 1809–1847	Born Hamburg and died in Leipzig, probably due to overwork and blow of sister's death; grandson of philosopher Moses Mendelssohn; wrote *Hebrides Overture* (aka *Fingal's Cave*) after visit to Britain in 1829; eldest sister was Fanny, a piano virtuoso; at 12 became friend of the 72-year-old Goethe	Twelve early string symphonies, also 5 mature symphonies and concertos (e.g. for violin); dramatic works include *Midsummer Night's Dream* and the unfinished opera *Lorelei*; best known oratorios *Elijah* (1846) and *St Paul* (1836); hymns include 'Hear My Prayer' (1844), which contains the section 'O for the Wings of a Dove'
Chopin, Frédéric 1810–1849	Born in Zelazowa Wola, Poland, of French father and Polish mother, died in Paris; all works involve a piano; though a piano virtuoso, gave only about 30 public performances; lover of novelist George Sand (1837–47)	Piano works include the 'Funeral March' Sonata (1837), *Krakowiak Rondo* (1828) and *Là ci darem variations*; famous for his nocturnes, preludes, mazurks, études, written for solo piano; Waltz in D flat, known as the Minute Waltz
Schumann, Robert 1810–1856	Born in Zwickau and died in Endenich; studied law at Leipzig and Heidelberg; married Clara Wieck in 1840; attempted suicide in 1854 by throwing himself in the Rhine and was committed to an asylum	Only opera *Genoveva* (1849); incidental music to Byron's verse-drama *Manfred* 1849; 4 symphonies, songs and song-cycles, and numerous piano pieces, including *Abegg Variations* (dedicated to Meta Abegg and written using notes of her surname in 1830)
Liszt, Franz 1811–1886	Born in Raiding in Hungary, died in Bayreuth; child prodigy who gave first piano recital aged 9; lived with Countess Marie d'Agoult from 1833 and had 3 children, one of whom, Cosima, first married Hans Bülow and then Wagner; Kapellmeister at Weiner court 1848–59, and championed Wagner and Berlioz; in 1865 he took minor orders and became Abbé Liszt	One opera *Don Sanche* (1825) in collaboration with Ferdinando Paer; 2 symphonies *Faust* (1857) and *Dante* (1856); piano works include 19 composed 'Hungarian Rhapsodies', 1846–85, *Années de pèlerinage* (1848–77) and concertos; symphonic poems include *Les Préludes* (1848), *Orpheus* (1854), *Prometheus* (1850) and *Hamlet* (1858); also composed numerous études, songs and oratorios
Wagner, Richard 1813–1883	Born Leipzig and died in Venice, buried at Wahnfried; attended school in Dresden and Thomasschule in Leipzig; married actress Minna Planer in 1836 but had affair with Mathilde Wesendonck; King Ludwig of Bavaria became his patron; Minna died in 1866 and he started affair with Cosima, wife of Hans Bülow, who bore him 2 daughters (Isolde and Eva); Cosima's marriage was annulled in 1869 and she gave birth to Wagner's son, Siegfried; Wagner and Cosima were married in 1870	Composed only 1 symphony, in C (1832); first opera *Die Feen* (The Fairies 1834) although he did compose earlier work *Die Hochzeit* but destroyed it; other operas include *Rienzi*, *The Flying Dutchman*, *Lohengrin*, *Tannhäuser*, *Der Ring des Nibelungen*, *The Mastersingers of Nuremberg* and *Parsifal* (his last); the opera *Tristan und Isolde* reflected his emotional turmoil over Mathilde Wesendonck; orchestral works include overture based on 'Rule, Britannia', *Faust* overture, *Siegfried Idyll* and concert overture *Polonia*; also composed 7 Songs From Goethe's Faust, as well as many books on music; pioneer of the Le tmotiv
Verdi, Giuseppe 1813–1901	Born Parma, died in Milan leaving bulk of his money to a home he had founded for elderly musicians; innkeeper's son first taught by local organist Antonio Barezzi, a wholesaler whose daughter he married; between 1838 and 1840 his wife and 2 children died; married soprano, Giuseppina Strepponi in 1859; in 1860, after Italian independence from Austria, elected deputy in first National Parliament	First opera *Oberto, Conte di San Bonifacio* (1838) although an earlier one, *Rocester*, is lost; other operas include *Nabucco* (1841), *Ernani* (1843), *Attila* (1846), *Macbeth* (1847), *Luisa Miller* (1849), *Stiffelio* (1850), *Rigoletto* (1851), *Il Trovatore* (1852), *Otello* (1886) and *Falstaff* (1892); Verdi's *Requiem* composed in memory of poet Manzoni and played at funeral of Diana, Princess of Wales (1997)
Gounod, Charles 1818–1893	Born in Paris, died in St Cloud; won Grand Prix de Rome in 1839; studied for priesthood but chose a life in music	First opera *Sapho* (1851); best known *Faust* (1859); 3 symphonies and various oratorios and cantatas; also *Funeral March of a Marionette* (1872)
Offenbach, Jacques	Born in Deutz, near Cologne, and died in Paris; son of a cantor	First opera *Die Rheinnixen* (1864); only grand opera *The Tales of Hoffmann*

Name	Principal works	Details
1819–1880	(1881); only ballet *Le Papillon* (1860); operettas include *Orpheus in the Underworld* (1858), *La Belle Hélène* (1864) and *Daphnis et Chloé* (1860)	in Cologne synagogue; surname Offenbach came from the name of family's home town
Bruckner, Anton 1824–1896	Ten symphonies, last unfinished; masses in D Minor (1864), E Minor (1869) and F Minor (1872) as well as cantatas and chamber music; many works edited by composer and others, and exist in various versions	Born in Ansfelden, died in Vienna; known internationally as a virtuoso organist; first (unnumbered) symphony written in his late thirties
Smetana, Bedřich 1824–1884	First opera *The Brandenburgers in Bohemia* (1863); other operas include *The Bartered Bride* (1866), *The Secret* (1878), *The Kiss* (1876) and *Two Widows* (1874); cycle of 6 symphonic poems, *Má Vlast* (My Country 1874–9)	Born in Litomyšl, died in Prague; regarded as founder of Czech music; active in founding national opera house; venereal disease caused deafness and later insanity
Strauss the Younger, Johann 1825–1899	Composed nearly 400 waltzes of which the best known include *Blue Danube*, *Tales from the Vienna Woods* (1868), *Roses From the South* (1880) and *Emperor Waltz* (1888); most famous operetta *Die Fledermaus* (The Bat 1874); also composed various polkas and an unfinished ballet, *Cinderella* (completed by Joseph Bayer)	Born and died in Vienna; worked as a bank clerk in early career; known as the Waltz King; in 1848 revolution supported opposite side to his father
Borodin, Alexander 1833–1887	Only opera *Prince Igor* left unfinished and completed by Rimsky-Korsakov and Alexander Glazunov; 3 symphonies, the 3rd completed by Glazunov; 2 string quartets; tone poem *In The Steppes of Central Asia*; music used in Forrest and Wright's musical *Kismet*	Born and died in St Petersburg; illegitimate son of Russian prince; doctor and professor of chemistry; feminist who founded a school of medicine for women
Brahms, Johannes 1833–1897	Four symphonies and 4 concertos; orchestral works include *Tragic Overture* (1880), *Academic Festival Overture* (1880) and *Variations on a Theme by Haydn* (1873); key choral works, *German Requiem* (1866) and *Schickalslied* (1871); no operas, but nearly 200 songs as well as chamber music, organ works and piano works, including *Variations on a Theme by Paganini* (1866)	Born in Hamburg, died in Vienna; son of professional double-bass player; hailed as genius by Schumann in essay 'New Paths' 1853 and succeeded him as teacher to Princess Friederike of Lippe-Detmold
Saint–Saëns, Camille 1835–1921	First opera *La Princesse Jaune* (1872); most famous opera *Samson and Delilah* (1868); 3 symphonies (2 other symphonies were withdrawn); symphonic poems include *Danse Macabre* (1874); popular orchestral piece *Carnival of the Animals* (1886), its performance forbidden in the composer's lifetime (movement 13, 'The Swan', most popular piece); also composed *Variations on a Theme of Beethoven* (1874) and *Polonaise* for 2 pianos; various oratorios and masses include Psalm 150 (1907); 5 piano concertos, No. 2 best known	Born in Paris and died in Algiers; symphony No. 3 dedicated to Liszt's memory; wrote coronation march for Edward VII, 1902; *Carnival of the Animals* in 14 movements i.e. 'Royal March of the Lion', 'Hens & Cocks', 'Wild Asses', 'Tortoises', 'The Elephant', 'Kangaroos', 'Aquarium', 'Persons with Long Ears', 'Cuckoo in the Depths of Woods', 'Aviary', 'Pianists', 'Fossils', 'The Swan', 'Finale'; the tortoises are represented by the can-can in slow motion, the 'Dance of the Sylphs' on double-basses for the elephant and the fossils is a parody of *Danse Macabre*
Bizet, Georges 1838–1875	First opera *Le Docteur Miracle* (1856); last and most famous opera *Carmen* (1874); one symphony; orchestral suite *L'Arlésienne*	Born in Paris, died in Bougival; entered Paris Conservatory at age 9; Won Grand Prix de Rome in 1857
Mussorgsky, Modest 1839–1881	First opera *Salammbô* (unfinished); *Boris Godunov* (1869) only completed opera, piano works *Pictures at an Exhibition*; orchestral *A Night on the*	Born in Karevo, Pskov, died in St Petersburg; one of the Russian 5 or Mighty Handful (the others: Balakirev, Cui, Borodin,

Bare Mountain

Rimsky-Korsakov)

Tchaikovsky, Pyotr
1840–1893

Born in Votkinsk, died in St Petersburg of cholera, although he may have taken poison to avoid a homosexual scandal; read Law in St Petersburg and became civil servant; married Antonina Miliukova 1877 but left her a month later and attempted suicide in his guilt; Countess Nadezhda von Meck was his patron although they never met (it is said that he crossed the street once to avoid a meeting); it is said that he used to hold his head while conducting, lest it fall off!

First opera *Voyevoda* (1868); others include *Eugene Onegin* (1879) and *The Queen of Spades* (1890); last opera *Yolanta* (1891); 3 ballets *Swan Lake* (1876), *Sleeping Beauty* (1889) and *Nutcracker* (1892); other works include 6 symphonies, 2 piano concertos, a violin concerto, a number of tone poems including *Romeo and Juliet* and *Italian Caprice*, as well as an unnumbered *Manfred Symphony* (1885); *Rococo Variations* for cello and orchestra

Dvořák, Antonín
1841–1904

Born in Nelahozeves, Bohemia, died in Prague; son of a village butcher; joined National Theatre of Prague as viola player in 1866

Opera *Alfred* (1870); best-known *Rusalka* (1900); last opera *Armida* (1903); 9 symphonies, including No. 9 in E Minor, *From the New World*, and other cello concertos

Sullivan, Arthur
1842–1900

Born in Lambeth and died, appropriately, on St Cecilia's Day, at Westminster; son of Irish bandmaster at Sandhurst; first to win Mendelssohn Scholarship of the Royal Academy of Music, 1856; knighted in 1883; *Thespis* in 1871 was 1st collaboration with Gilbert; Savoy Theatre, opened during run of *Patience*, specialized in Gilbert and Sullivan; the two fell out during a run of *The Gondoliers* supposedly over a choice of carpet for the theatre; they were reconciled for *Utopia Ltd* and *The Grand Duke* (1896)

Only grand opera *Ivanhoe* (1890); composed tune for hymn 'Onward Christian Soldiers'; 14 operettas in collaboration with W.S. Gilbert; songs include 'The Lost Chord'; first operetta *Cox and Box* (1866, librettist Burnand); last operetta *The Emerald Isle* left unfinished (completed by Edward German to Basil Hood's libretto); oratorios include *The Prodigal Son* (1869); cantatas include *Kenilworth* (1864); composed a symphony in E (the 'Irish'); incidental music to various Shakespeare plays

Grieg, Edvard
1843–1907

Born and died in Bergen; married his cousin, soprano Nina Hagerup, in 1867 when he also founded the Norwegian Academy of Music; Ibsen commissioned incidental music to *Peer Gynt*

Orchestral works include *Peer Gynt Suite* (1875), *Lyric Suite* (1904) and *Holberg Suite* (1884); wrote *Norwegian Dances* (4 hands) and numerous songs for piano; 1 symphony, 1 piano concerto

Rimsky-Korsakov, Nikolay
1844–1908

Born in Tikhvin, died in Lyubensk; navy cadet as child, hoping to become a sailor; slow movement of 1st Symphony written off Gravesend; wrote 1st opera whilst serving as a naval lieutenant; edited *100 Russian Folk-Songs* 1877

First opera *The Maid of Pskov* (aka: *Ivan the Terrible*) 1872; last opera (of 14) *The Golden Cockerel* (1907); 3 symphonies – first major Russian symphonies; famous orchestral works include *Spanish Caprice* (1887) and *Sheherazade* (1888)

Janáček, Leoš
1854–1928

Born in Moravia, died in Moravská, Ostrava; Czech composer who had his success late in life; inspired by an affair with Kamila Stösslova

First opera *Šárka* (1888); others *Jenůfa* (1904) and *From the House of the Dead* (1930: his last); Glagolitic Mass; rhapsody *Taras Bulba*; 2 string quartets; song-cycle *Diary of One Who Disappeared*

Elgar, Edward
1857–1934

Born in Broadheath, Worcestershire, died in Worcester; son of an organist and music shop proprietor in Worcester; married General's daughter Caroline Roberts who died in 1920; knighted in 1904 as first English composer of International repute since Purcell

Composed 2 symphonies and an unfinished 3rd; cantata, *The Dream of Gerontius* (1900); orchestral works *Pomp and Circumstance* marches (1901–30), *Enigma Variations* (1899); Violin Concerto in B Minor (1910); Cello Concerto in E Minor (1919); unfinished opera *The Spanish Lady*

Name	Principal works	Details
Puccini, Giacomo 1858–1924	First opera *Le Villi* (The Willis) 1883; best-known opera *Manon Lescaut* (1893), *La Bohème* (1896), *Tosca* (1900), *Madame Butterfly* (1904), *Turandot* (unfinished, but completed by Franco Alfano)	Born in Lucca, Italy, died in Brussels; came from a long line of church musicians
Mahler, Gustav 1860–1911	Ten symphonies (one unfinished, completed by Deryck Cooke, 1st 8 of which Mahler conducted first performances); song symphony *Song of the Earth* (1909); song-cycle *Kindertotenlieder* (1904); cantata *Das Klagende Lied* (1880); only opera was completion of Weber's *The Three Pintos*	Born in Kalist, Bohemia, died in Vienna; brilliant conductor who headed Hamburg Opera from 1891; then Vienna State Opera, New York Metropolitan Opera, New York Philharmonic; converted from Judaism to Roman Catholicism 1897; married musician Alma Schindler in 1902
Debussy, Achille-Claude 1862–1918	Most famous opera *Pelléas et Mélisande*; orchestral works *Prélude à l'après-midi d'un Faune* (1894); *La Mer* (1905); *Nocturnes* (1899)	Born in St Germain-en-Laye, died (cancer) in Paris; won Prix de Rome in 1884 with cantata *L'Enfant prodigue*; influenced by Javanese gamelan music at Paris Exposition; as well as by impressionist painters; married Lily Texier 1899 but left her 5 years later for a singer, Emma Bardac and married her in 1908; part of *La Mer* written in Eastborne
Delius, Frederick 1862–1934	First opera *Irmelin* (1892); last opera *Fennimore and Gerda* (1910); others *The Magic Fountain* (1895), *Koanga* (1897), *A Village Romeo and Juliet* (1901), and *Margot-la-Rouge* (1902); orchestral pieces *Brigg Fair* (1907), *On Hearing the First Cuckoo in Spring* (1912); choral works *Sea Drift* (1909), *A Mass of Life* (1909); various Norwegian songs, as well as concertos, piano pieces and melodramas	Born in Bradford, Yorkshire, died in Grez-sur-Loing; reinterred in May 1935 at Limpsfield, Surrey; until 1904 composed under name of Fritz Delius; influenced by lasting friendship with Grieg; married Jelka Rosen 1903 and lived near Fontainebleau; became blind (probably due to syphilis) and continued composing helped by a young Yorkshire musician, Eric Fenby
Szymanowski, Karol 1882–1937	Operas *Hagith* (1913), *King Roger* (1924); 4 symphonies, 2 violin concertos, 2 ballets; voices and orchestra *Love Songs of Hafiz* (1911), *Stabat Mater* (1926); violin and piano, *Myths* (1915); also songs	Born in Tymoslowska, Ukraine, died in Lausanne; leading figure at turn of century in composer's association 'Young Poland in Music'; later influenced both by Stravinsky and by folk music of Tatra Mountains
Strauss, Richard 1864–1949	First of 15 operas *Guntram* (1893); others *Salome* (1905), *Electra* (1909), *Der Rosenkavalier* (1911), *Die Frau ohne Schatten* (1919); last opera *Capriccio* (1941); ballets include *Josephslegende* (1914); tone poems include *Till Eulenspiegel*, *Don Quixote* and *Also sprach Zarathustra*	Born in Munich, died in Garmisch-Partenkirchen; son of a horn player in Munich Court Orchestra; married soprano Pauline de Ahna, 1894; became Austrian citizen in 1947
Dukas, Paul 1865–1935	One opera *Ariane et Barbe-Bleu* (1906); 1 ballet *La Péri* (1912); most famous work, symphonic poem *The Sorcerer's Apprentice* (1897); 1 symphony, 1 piano sonata	Born and died in Paris; never prolific, he burned at least 15 years of unpublished work before he died; helped Saint-Saëns complete Guiraud's opera *Frédégonde*
Sibelius, Jean 1865–1957	Tone poem *Finlandia* became voice of his country; others *En Saga* (1901), *The Swan of Tuonela* (1893); 7 symphonies, 1 violin concerto	Born in Hämeenlinna (Tavastehus), died in Järvenpää; received State pension for life in 1897 to free him to compose; 5th Symphony written on his 50th birthday; did not compose for the last 27 years of his life

Composer	Works	Biography
Nielsen, Karl 1865–1931	Six symphonies for violin, flute and clarinet; concertos, string quartets, piano music, songs; operas: *Saul and David* (1902), *Maskarade* (1906)	Born in Nøatre-Lyndelse, Denmark, died in Copenhagen; wife a sculptor; developed 'progressive tonality' in which a work may change its key as it develops; in 5th symphony, sidedrummer is instructed to improvise so as to halt progress of orchestra
Satie, Erik 1866–1925	Three ballets *Parade* (1917), *Mercure*, and *Relâche* (1924). *Parade* was scored for typewriters, airplane propellers, sirens, ticker-tape, steamship whistle and lottery wheel. A marionette opera *Geneviève de Brabant* (1899). Piano pieces, include *Trois morceaux en forme de poire* (Three pear-shaped pieces) a work for four hands (1903) and *Gymnopédies* (1888) a trio of piano pieces Nos 1 and 3 orchestrated by Debussy and No. 2 by Roland-Manuel.	French composer and pianist, born in Honfleur, of a French father and Scottish mother. In 1893, he had a stormy affair with the artist Suzanne Valadon but lived as a recluse for some years. Satie parodied the orthodoxy and stiffness of established music using whimsical titles and musical directions. He was a major influence on many French composers including Debussy, Ravel and 'Les Six'
Vaughan Williams, Ralph 1872–1958	First opera *Hugh the Drover* (1914); last *The Pilgrim's Progress* (1951); orchestral works *In the Fen Country* (1904), *Fantasia on a Theme by Thomas Tallis* (1910); 9 symphonies, also concertos, ballets, songs and chamber music	Born in Down Ampney, Gloucestershire, died in London; lived in Dorking in Surrey 1929–53
Rachmaninoff, Sergei 1873–1943	Three symphonies; 4 piano concertos, notably the 2nd in C minor; *Rhapsody on a Theme of Paganini* (1934) for piano and orchestra; many piano pieces; first opera *Aleko* (1892), last *Monna Vanna* (1907)	Born in Semyonovo, Starorussky, died in Beverly Hills; virtuoso pianist; became US citizen in 1943; lifelong friend of the celebrated bass Chaliapin; underwent hypnosis when experiencing creative block – 2nd piano concerto dedicated to hypnotist
Holst, Gustav 1874–1934	Best known for orchestral suite *The Planets* (1918); also for orchestra: *Egdon Heath* (1927), *Book Green Suite* (1930) last opera *The Wandering Scholar*	Born in Cheltenham, died in London; worked as trombonist for Carl Rosa Opera (1898–1900); learned Sanskrit to translate hymns from *Rig Veda*
Schoenberg, Arnold 1874–1951	First opera (the monodrama): *Erwartung* (1909), last *Moses und Aron* (19051) other significant works include: *Gurrelieder, Pierrot Lunaire, A Survivor from Warsaw* and *Verklarte Nacht*	Revolutionised music to reach atonality and serialism; had a phobia about the number 13, and '*Moses und Aron*' is spelled thus so as to only have 12 letters; teacher of Webern and Berg; became a US citizen in 1941
Ives, Charles 1874–1954	Four symphonies and the so-called first orchestral set (New England Symphony); 'Universe' Symphony was never completed in his lifetime but Johnny Reinhard completed it and performed it in 1996; also wrote the song 'Shall We Gather at the River'	Born in Danbury, Connecticut, died in New York; wrote symphony while at Yale; formed his own insurance company (1907); 3rd symphony won Pulitzer Prize (1947)
Ravel, Maurice 1875–1937	Operas: *L'Heure Espagnole* (1907), *L'Enfant et les Sortilèges* (1925); ballets: *Daphnis et Chloé* (1911), *Boléro* (1928); 2 piano concertos (written simultaneously); also for piano: *Pavane pour une infante défunte* (1899), *Le Tombeau de Couperin* (1917); chamber music	Born in Ciboure, died in Paris; orchestrated Mussorgsky's *Pictures at an Exhibition*; repeated failure to win Prix de Rome led to resignation of director of Paris Conservatoire, which awards it
Respighi, Ottorino 1879–1936	Roman trilogy of symphonic poems: *Pines of Rome, Fountains of Rome, Roman Festivals*; also *Three Botticelli Pictures*; concertos and operas	Born in Bolgna, died in Rome; studied under Rimsky-Korsakov in St Petersburg and Max Binch in Berlin
Bridge, Frank	One opera: *The Christmas Rose* (1929). Orchestral suite *The Sea* (1911)	Born in Brighton, died in Eastbourne; English composer, conductor,

Name	Principal works	Details
1879–1941	String Quartets: *Sir Roger de Coverley* (1922), *Scherzo Phantastick* (1901), and *Sally in our Alley* (1916)	violist and violinist. In 1927 taught the 14-year-old Benjamin Britten. Conducted the New Symphony Orchestra from its inception at Covent Garden. Best known for his string quartets
Ireland, John 1879–1962	Orchestral prelude *The Forgotten Rite* (1913). Symphonic rhapsody *Mai-Dun* (1921); the title refers to the prehistoric Dorset fortification, Maiden Castle. Comic overture *Satyricon* 1946). Tone poem *Sea Fever* (1913)	English composer and pianist, born in Bowden, Cheshire, and died in Washington, West Sussex. Established his reputation with his Violin Sonata in A (1917) but is best remembered for his settings of poems by Hardy, Housman and Masefield
Bartók, Béla 1881–1945	*Music for Strings, Percussion and Celesta* (1936); *Concerto for Orchestra* (1943); only opera *Duke Bluebeard's Castle* (1911); ballets: *The Wooden Prince* (1911) and *The Miraculous Mandarin* (1919); 3 piano concertos; 2 violin concertos; 6 string quartets	Born in Nagyszentmiklós, Hungary (now Romania), died (leukaemia) in New York; dedicated collector of Hungarian and other East European folk music; anti-Nazi who emigrated to USA in 1940
Kodály, Zoltán 1882–1967	Three operas *Háry János* (1926), *Spinning Room* (1932), and *Czinka Panna* (1948). Choral and orchestral work *Psalmus Hungaricus* (1923) was based on text of Psalm 55 and commissioned for the 50th anniversary of the union of Buda and Pest. Two sets of Hungarian dances for orchestra *Marosszék Dances* (1930) and *Dances of Galánta* (1933)	Hungarian composer born in Kecskemét and died in Budapest. Wrote collections of folksongs with Béla Bartók between 1906 and 1921, although these were not published until 1951 as *Corpus Musicae Popularis Hungariae*. He carried out reforms in musical education and developed an evolutionary system of training and sight-singing
Stravinsky, Igor 1882–1971	Ballets include *The Firebird* (1910), *Petrushka* (1911), *The Rite of Spring* (1913), *Agon* (1953); first opera *The Nightingale* (1909), last *The Rake's Progress* (1951); important works in all the major forms include *Symphony of Psalms* (1930), *Ebony Concerto* (1946), *Septet* (1953), *Threni* (1958)	Born Oranienbaum, died New York; most influential classical composer of 20th century; became French citizen 1934, American 1945; first performance of *The Rite of Spring* in Paris caused famous riot by unattuned listeners
Webern, Anton 1883–1945	String quartet (1938); *Variations* for orchestra (1940); 3 cantatas; 1 symphony	Studied under Schoenberg and became rigorous exponent of serial music; born in Vienna, died in Mittersill after being shot accidentally by American sentry
Bax, Arnold 1883–1953	One ballet *Between Dusk and Dawn* (1917); seven symphonies. orchestral tone poem *Tintagel* (1919) first performed 1920; other orchestral works include *November Woods* (1917) and *Mourning Song* (1946)	Born in Streatham and died in Cork; English composer and pianist; master of the Kings/Queens; Music 1942–53. Knighted in 1937. His autobiography *Farewell My Youth* (1943) is an acclaimed work
Varèse, Edgard 1883–1965	Orchestral works include *Amériques* (1921), *Octandre* (1923) *Intégrales* (1925), *Arcana* (1927) and *Ionisation* (1931). Known for his experimental use of instrument combinations and unconventional percussion. His *Désert* (1954) employs tape-recorded sound; concentrated on electronic music later	French composer and conductor, born in Paris and died in New York. Became an American citizen in 1926. He organised the international Composers' Guild in 1921 and co-founded the Pan-American Association of Composers in 1927
Berg, Alban 1885–1935	Two operas, *Wozzeck* (1922) and *Lulu* (1935); *Lyric Suite* for string quartet (1926); violin concerto (1935)	Born and died in Vienna (insect bite); quit civil servant career to compose; *Lulu* completed by Friedrich Cerha, many years after Berg's death, due to reluctance of his widow
Prokofiev, Sergey 1891–1953	Seven symphonies, also concerti and string quartets; symphonic tale *Peter and the Wolf* (1936); ballets include *The Buffoon* (1920), *Age of Steel* (1926),	Born Sontsovka, died in Moscow; lived in Paris 1920–33; wrote film scores, e.g. *Lieutenant Kijé* and *Alexander Nevsky*, died

Composer	Works	Notes
	Romeo and Juliet (1936); operas include *The Gambler* (1917), *Love for Three Oranges* (1919), *War and Peace* (1943)	on the same day as Stalin
Bliss, Arthur 1891–1975	First opera *The Olympians* (1949); last opera *Tobias and the Angel* (1960); first ballet *Checkmate* (1937); last ballet *The Lady of Shalott* (1958); first symphony: *Colour Symphony*	Born and died in London; wrote music for Korda's film based on H G Wells's *Things to Come*; knighted in 1950; became master of the Queen's Musick in 1953
Hindemith, Paul 1895–1963	Operas include *Murder, the Hope of Women* (1919), *Mathis der Maler* (1935), *The Long Christmas Dinner* (1960); ballets: *Der Dämon* (1922), *Nobilissima Visione* (1938), *Hérodiade* (1944); several symphonies; a wealth of string quartets and sonatas	Born in Hanau, died in Frankfurt; married Gertrud Rottenberg in 1924; satirical opera *News of the Day* (1929) featured soprano singing in her bath; founded a music school in Ankara; associated with Gebrauchsmusik ('utility music', written for some social purpose)
Gershwin, George 1898–1937	First 'hit' song was 'Swanee' (1919); 1 opera: *Porgy and Bess*; *Rhapsody in Blue* for piano, jazz band and orchestra (1924); tone poem for *An American in Paris* (1928)	Born in Brooklyn, NY, died in Beverly Hills, California; turned pro musician aged 14; many collaborations with his elder brother, lyricist Ira Gershwin
Poulenc, Francis 1899–1963	First opera: *Les Mamelles de Tirésias* (1944), last *La Voix Humaine* (1958); ballet *Les Biches* (1923); solo piano works, concertos, sonatas and many songs; church music including *Gloria* and *Stabat Mater*	Born and died in Paris; had independent income (related to family in Rhône-Poulenc pharmaceuticals); longtime companion of baritone Pierre Bernac
Copland, Aaron 1900–1990	First ballet *Grohg* (1925); others *Billy the Kid* (1938), *Rodeo* (1942), *Appalachian Spring* (1944); 5 symphonies; orchestral work *El Salon Mexico* (1936); only opera *The Tender Land* (1954)	Born in Brooklyn, NY, died in New York; symphony finale based on *Fanfare for the Common Man*
Walton, William 1902–1983	Two symphonies; 4 concertos; oratorio *Belshazzar's Feast* (1931); 2 operas *Troilus and Cressida* (1954) and *The Bear* (1967); first ballet *The First Shoot* (1935)	Born in Oldham, died in Forio d'Ischia; son of choirmaster and singing teacher; wrote *Façade* to accompany Edith Sitwell; film scores include *First of the Few* and *Henry V*
Tippett, Michael 1905–1998	First opera *The Midsummer Marriage* (1955), also *The Knot Garden* (1969), *The Ice Break* (1976), last *New Year* (1989); 4 symphonies, 5 string quartets, concertos etc.; oratorio *A Child of Our Time* includes negro spirituals	Born and died in London; wrote own libretti; committed pacifist – acted as page-turner for Britten and Pears while imprisoned in Wormwood Scrubs as conscientious objector
Shostakovich, Dmitry 1906–1975	Fifteen symphonies, 15 string quartets, 6 concertos; piano preludes; first opera *The Nose* (1928); first ballet *The Age of Gold* (1930)	Born in St Petersburg, died in Moscow; twice severely criticised for formalism by Stalinist regime; fire fighter in Nazi siege of Leningrad 1941; wrote much film music
Messiaen, Olivier 1908–1992	One symphony *Turangalîla* (premiered by Bernstein, 1948); *L'Ascension* for orchestra (1935); much organ music; 1 opera *St Francis of Assisi*	Born in Avignon, died in Paris; many works inspired by birdsong; *Quartet for the End of Time* (1941) written and premiered in POW camp
Carter, Elliott 1908–	Ballets *Pocahontas* (1939), *The Minotaur* (1947); concertos and symphonic works; many sonatas; *Night Fantasies* for piano (1980); 3 string quartets	Born in New York; encouraged by Ives; studied under Nadia Boulanger in Paris 1932–5
Barber, Samuel 1910–1981	Three operas and three symphonies; two ballets *Medea* (1946), revised as *Cave of the Heart* in 1947, and *Souvenirs* (1952); tone poem *Knoxville: Summer of 1915* (1947)	American composer and pianist; born in West Chester, Pennsylvania, and died in New York. Reputation made with his tone poem based on Arnold's 'Dover Beach' (1931)

Name	Principal works	Details
Britten, Benjamin 1913–1976	First opera *Paul Bunyan* (1941); others include *Peter Grimes* (1945), *Billy Budd* (1951), *The Turn of the Screw* (1954) and last *Death in Venice* (1973); *Variations on a Theme of Frank Bridge* for string orchestra (1937); *War Requiem* for choir and orchestra (1961); only ballet *The Prince of the Pagodas* (1956)	Born at Lowestoft on St Cecilia's Day (22 Nov.) and died at Aldeburgh; lifelong friendship with Peter Pears; founded Aldeburgh Festival in 1948; became Lord Britten of Aldeburgh in 1976; first composer to be created life peer
Lutoslawski, Witold 1913–1994	Four symphonies; *Concerto for Orchestra* (1954); concertos for violin, cello, etc.; *Venetian Games* for orchestra (1961)	Warsaw café pianist in Second World War; regularly wrote controlled aleatory music, leaving certain things to chance; refused to write opera as could not see why people should sing rather than talk
Bernstein, Leonard 1918–1990	Three symphonies, 1 violin concerto (called *Serenade*); operas, *Trouble in Tahiti*, later became part of *A Quiet Place*; musicals: *On the Town, West Side Story, Candide*	Born in Lawrence, Massachusetts, died in New York; celebrated conductor and teacher; wrote film music for *On the Waterfront* (1954)
Simpson, Robert 1921–1997	11 symphonies; two piano sonatas *Variations and Finale on a Theme of Haydn* (1948) and *Variations and Finale on a Theme of Beethoven* (1990)	English composer, musicologist and author; on BBC music staff 1951–80. Wrote books on several composers, including Carl Nielsen, Anton Bruckner and Jean Sibelius
Arnold, Malcolm 1921–	Nine symphonies; ballets: *Homage to the Queen* (1953), *Rinaldo and Armida* (1955) and *Electra* (1963); concert overture *Beckus the Dandipratt* (1948)	Born in Northampton; English composer, trumpeter, and conductor. Like Richard Rodney Bennett composed several film scores including *The Bridge on the River Kwai*; knighted in 1922
Boulez, Pierre 1921–	*Le Marteau sans Maître* for voice and chamber orchestra (1957); *Pli Selon Pli* for voice and orchestra (1962); *Éclats/Multiples* (1976)	Born in Montbrison; leader of French 12-tone music school; once suggested burning down opera houses, but now conducts in them regularly; continually revises a small number of works
Ligeti, György 1923–	Opera *Le Grand Macabre* (1978), *Kammerkonzert* (1970); 2 string quartets, piano études; various orchestral works	Born in Discőszentmáron; left Hungary in 1956; music used in film *2001*, though he only found out when he went to see it; one work is for 100 metronomes
Berio, Luciano 1925–	Orchestral music; many pieces for voice and various instruments include *Circles* (1960); operas include *La Veria Storia* (1982); most famous work *Sinfonia* (1969)	Exponent of serial and electronic music; one movement of *Sinfonia* mixes a movement of Mahler's *Resurrection* with much other music and spoken text
Henze, Hans Werner 1926–	Nine symphonies; prolific in most musical forms; first opera *Das Wundertheater* (1949), others include *Boulevard Solitude* (1951), *The Bassarids* (1965), *The English Cat* (1983); latest opera *Venus and Adonis* (1997)	Born in Gütersloh; equally at home with atonal, aleatory and conventional techniques; much influenced by Italy, living there for some years; many works have left-wing inspiration
Stockhausen, Karlheinz 1928–	Many works for varying ensembles, e.g. *Gruppen* for 3 orchestras and *Stimmung* for singers and tape; piano pieces, also electronic music; ongoing operatic project: *Licht* (cycle of 7 operas each linked to a day of the week)	Born in Mödrath, near Cologne; studied under Frank Martin, Messiaen and Milhaud; experimental works include a string quartet for players in helicopters

Rautavaara, Einojuhani
1928–

Operas include *Vincent* (based on Van Gogh); latest opera *Aleksis Kivi* (1997); 7 symphonies, concertos, etc.

Born in Helsinki; a number of works invoke angels; *Cantus Arcticus* is a concerto for birds (recorded) and orchestra

Sondheim, Stephen
1930–

First musical *Saturday Night* (1957, but premiered in 1998); also *Company* (1970), *A Little Night Music* (1973), *Sweeney Todd* (1979); latest musical *Passion* (1995)

Born in New York; writes lyrics and music; wrote lyrics for *West Side Story* and *Gypsy*; writes film scores, plays and film scripts; works often presented by opera companies

Górecki, Henryk
1933–

Three symphonies – the 3rd (*Symphony of Sorrowful Songs*) catapulted him to fame; also 2 string quartets, *Lerchenmusik*, *Kleines Requiem für ein Polka*, etc.

Born in Czernice, Poland; earlier work in a much more modern style; now exploring medieval influences

Maxwell Davies, Peter
1934–

Eight symphonies as of 2001; 10 Strathclyde Concertos for Scottish Chamber Orchestra, among other concertos; first opera *Taverner* (1970), latest *The Doctor of Myddfai* (1996); recent works include the tone poem *Mavis in Las Vegas* and *Mr Emmet Takes a Walk*

Born in Salford, very prolific; lives in Orkney, many works inspired by Orcadian writer George Mackay Brown; surname is really Davies; universally known as Max; his 8th symphony, 'Antarctic Symphony' was composed after visiting the Antarctic peninsula between 20 December 1997 and 8 January 1998

Birtwistle, Harrison
1934–

First opera *Punch and Judy* (1967), latest *The Second Mrs Kong* (1994); one ballet: *Pulsefield* (1977); *Pulse Shadow* (1996) for soprano, ensemble and strings; *The Last Supper* (1999) for 14 soloists, chorus, orchestra and tape

Born in Accrington; *Panic* (concertante work for saxophone and drum kit) commissioned for last night of centenary Prom season 1995; co-founded Pierrot Players with Maxwell Davies; knighted in 1998

Schnittke, Alfred
1934–1998

Eight symphonies, several concerti, including concerti grossi; first opera *Life with an Idiot* (1992), *The Eleventh Commandment* (1962), latest *Gesualdo* (1994); ballets include *Peer Gynt* (1986); also *Faust* cantata

Born in Engels, USSR, died in Hamburg; Russian-born of German origin; name linked to 'polystylism', where many styles of music appear in one piece; symphony No. 5 is also Concerto Grosso No. 4

Pärt, Arvo
1935–

Three symphonies, plus concerti; choral works include *St John's Passion* (1982), *Miserere* (1989) and *Berlin Mass* (1991)

Born in Paide, Estonia; emigrated to West Berlin in 1982; his early works were influenced by Shostakovich but developed his own austere style

Bennett, Richard Rodney
1936–

Four operas; *The Ledge* (1961), *The Mines of Sulphur* (1965), *Penny for a Song* (1966); *Victory* (1939); ballets: *Jazz Calendar* (1964) and *Isadora* (1981); setting of poems by Kathleen Raine for soprano, chorus and orchestra *Spells* (1974)

Born in Broadstairs, Kent; English composer and pianist educated at the Royal Academy of Music and in Paris under Pierre Boulez; ventured into the jazz field with his 1964 ballet *Jazz Calendar*, and followed this with *Jazz Pastoral* (1969); knighted in 1998.

Tavener, John
1944–

Operas include *Thérèse* (1979), *Mary of Egypt* (1992); many works for various instrumental groupings; *The Whale* (1967) was in first ever concert by London Sinfonietta; cello and strings piece *The Protecting Veil* (1987); choral work: *We Shall See Him as He Is* (1990)

Born in London; recent work pervaded by religious sentiment of Greek Orthodox Church; claims descent from John Taverner

Martland, Steven
1958–

Most famous orchestral work to date *Babi Yar* (1983); ensemble piece *Remembering Lennon* (1981)

English composer born in Liverpool; professed aim 'to return music to the streets'

Adès, Thomas
1971–

Chamber Symphony (1990) first performed in 1993; *Five Eliot Landscapes* (1990); *The Origin of the Harp* (1994); *The Premises Are Alarmed* (1996) for the opening of the Bridgewater Hall in which the Hallé was conducted by Kent Nagano; *Powder Her Face* (1995) Chamber Opera; *Asyla* (1997)

English composer and pianist; second in piano section of the BBC Young Musician of the Year in 1989; graduated from Cambridge in 1992 with a double-starred first and established himself as a leading light both as a virtuoso and composer; Made his Proms debut in 1998 and the following year conducted the BBC Symphony Orchestra in the London premiere of *Asyla*

Operatic Characters (by character)

Character	Opera	Composer	Role
Abdallo	Nabucco	Verdi	Nabucco's officer
Abdullah	Oberon	Weber	Pirate
Abigaille	Nabucco	Verdi	Nabucco's adopted daughter
Abimelech	Samson et Dalila	Saint-Saëns	Satrap of Gaza
Abraham	Háry János	Kodály	Innkeeper
Adalgisa	Norma	Bellini	Temple virgin
Adele	Die Fledermaus	Johann Strauss II	Eisenstein's maid
Adelma	Turandot	Busoni	Turandot's slave
Admetus	Alceste	Gluck	Alceste's husband
Adriano	Rienzi	Wagner	Colonna's son
Aegisth	Elektra	Richard Strauss	Klytemnestra's lover
Aeneas	Dido and Aeneas	Purcell	Trojan general
Agathe	Der Freischütz	Weber	Cuno's daughter
Ahmed	Marouf	Rabaud	Pastry cook
Aida	Aida	Verdi	Ethiopian princess
Alberich	Der Ring des Nibelungen	Wagner	Nibelung dwarf
Albert Herring	Albert Herring	Britten	Greengrocer's assistant
Albrecht von Brandenburg	Mathis der Maler	Hindemith	Archbishop of Mainz
Alceste	Alceste	Gluck	Wife of Admetus
Alcindoro	La Bohème	Puccini	Musetta's escort
Alfio	Cavalleria Rusticana	Mascagni	Teamster
Don Alfonso	Così fan tutte	Mozart	Don
Alfonso d'Este	Lucrezia Borgia	Donizetti	Lucrezia's third husband
Alfonso XI	La Favorita	Donizetti	King of Castile
Alfredo Germont	La Traviata	Verdi	Violetta's lover (a singer)
Ali	Marouf	Rabaud	Marouf's friend
Alice/Alisa	Lucia di Lammermoor	Donizetti	Lucy's companion
Alice Ford	Falstaff	Verdi	Citizen of Windsor
Alidoro	La Cenerentola	Rossini	Philosopher and magician
Almaviva	The Barber of Seville	Rossini	Count
Almaviva	The Marriage of Figaro	Mozart	Count
Emperor Altoum	Turandot	Puccini	Turandot's father
Don Alvaro	La Forza del Destino	Verdi	Leonora's lover
Alwa	Lulu	Berg	Writer
Amaryllus	The Poisoned Kiss	Vaughan Williams	Empress's son
Ambrogio	The Barber of Seville	Rossini	Bartolo's servant
Amelia	A Masked Ball	Verdi	Riccardo's lover, wife of Renato
Amfortas	Parsifal	Wagner	King of the Grail
Amina	The Sleepwalker	Bellini	The sleepwalking girl
Amneris	Aida	Verdi	Egyptian princess
Amonasro	Aida	Verdi	Aida's father (King of Ethiopia)
Amor	Orfeo ed Euridice	Gluck	God of love
Andromaque	The Trojans (Les Troyens)	Berlioz	Hector's widow
Angèle	The Tsar Has His Photograph Taken	Weill	Photographer
Angelica	The Poisoned Kiss	Vaughan Williams	Tormentilla's maid
Angelina	La Cenerentola	Rossini	Don Magnifico's step-daughter, Cinderella
Donna Anna	Don Giovanni	Mozart	Don Ottavio's fiancée
Annina	Der Rosenkavalier	Richard Strauss	Valzacchi's partner
Annina	La Traviata	Verdi	Violetta's confidante
Annius	La Clemenza di Tito	Mozart	Patrician
Antonio	The Marriage of Figaro	Mozart	Gardener
Apollyon	The Pilgrim's Progress	Vaughan Williams	Fallen angel
Arbace	Idomeneo	Mozart	Idomeneo's confidante
Mr Archdale	Porgy and Bess	Gershwin	White man
Arthur Bucklaw/Arturo	Lucia di Lammermoor	Donizetti	Lord
Arthur Jones	Billy Budd	Britten	Seaman
Ashby	The Girl of the Golden West	Puccini	Wells-Fargo agent
Avosmediano	Palestrina	Pfitzner	Bishop of Cadiz
Azucena	Il Trovatore	Verdi	Gypsy woman
Baba the Turk	The Rake's Progress	Stravinsky	Bearded lady
Babekan	Oberon	Weber	Saracen prince
Balthasar Zorn	The Mastersingers of Nuremberg	Wagner	Mastersinger and pewterer
Balthazar	La Favorita	Donizetti	Superior of the monastery
Barak	Turandot	Busoni	Servant

Character	Opera	Composer	Role
Barak	Die Frau ohne Schatten	Richard Strauss	Dyer
Barbarina	The Marriage of Figaro	Mozart	Antonio's daughter
Barnaba	La Gioconda	Ponchielli	Spy
Baron Ochs	Der Rosenkavalier	Richard Strauss	Sophie's would-be suitor
Baroncelli	Rienzi	Wagner	Roman citizen
Bartolo	The Barber of Seville	Rossini	Rosina's guardian
Basilio	The Barber of Seville	Rossini	Singing teacher
Don Basilio	The Marriage of Figaro	Mozart	Organist
Bayan	Ruslan and Lyudmila	Glinka	Bard
Sixtus Beckmesser	The Mastersingers of Nuremberg	Wagner	Mastersinger and town clerk
Beelzebub	Doktor Faust	Busoni	Spirit voice
Belinda	Dido and Aeneas	Purcell	Lady in waiting
Lady Bellows	Albert Herring	Britten	Elderly autocrat
Ben Budge	The Beggar's Opera	Pepusch	Highwayman
Benôit	La Bohème	Puccini	Landlord
Beppe	I Pagliacci	Leoncavallo	Harlequin
Berta	The Barber of Seville	Rossini	Housekeeper
Bess	Porgy and Bess	Gershwin	Porgy's mistress, formerly Crown's
Betty Doxy	The Beggar's Opera	Pepusch	Lady of the town
Bianca	The Rape of Lucretia	Britten	Nurse
Bianca	La Rondine	Puccini	Magda's friend
Lady Billows	Albert Herring	Britten	Elderly autocrat
Billy Budd	Billy Budd	Britten	Seaman and stammerer
Billy Jackrabbit	The Girl of the Golden West	Puccini	Red indian
Biterolf	Tannhäuser	Wagner	Knight
Dr Blind	Die Fledermaus	Johann Strauss II	Eisenstein's attorney
Bob Boles	Peter Grimes	Britten	Fisherman
Boniface	Le Jongleur de Notre Dame	Massenet	Cook
The Bonze	Madame Butterfly	Puccini	Priest
Brangäne	Tristan und Isolde	Wagner	Isolde's maid
Brünnhilde	Der Ring des Nibelungen	Wagner	Valkyrie
Brutus Jones	Emperor Jones	Gruenberg	Escaped convict, tribal ruler
Bussy	Zazà	Leoncavallo	Journalist
Calaf	Turandot	Busoni	Suitor to Turandot
Calaf	Turandot	Puccini	Suitor to Turandot
Canio	I Pagliacci	Leoncavallo	Pagliaccio (clown)
Wolfgang Capito	Mathis der Maler	Hindemith	Councillor
Cardillac	Cardillac	Hindemith	Goldsmith
Don Carlos	Don Carlos	Verdi	Heir to Spanish throne
Don Carlos	Ernani	Verdi	King of Castile
Carmen	Carmen	Bizet	Gypsy
Carolina	The Secret Marriage	Cimarosa	Geronimo's daughter
Cascart	Zazà	Leoncavallo	Music-hall performer
Cassio	Otello	Verdi	Lieutenant
Catarina	Madame Sans-Gêne	Giordano	Laundress
Cavaradossi	Tosca	Puccini	Painter
Sir Robert Cecil	Gloriana	Britten	Secretary to the Council
Celio	The Love for Three Oranges	Prokofiev	Magician
Cesare Angelotti	Tosca	Puccini	Escaped political prisoner
Charlemagne	Oberon	Weber	Emperor of the Franks
Charles Gérard	Andrea Chénier	Giordano	Revolutionary leader
Chernomor	Ruslan and Lyudmila	Glinka	An evil dwarf
Cherubino	The Marriage of Figaro	Mozart	Page
Chevalier des Grieux	Manon	Massenet	Manon's love
Chochenille	The Tales of Hoffmann	Offenbach	Spalanzani's servant
Chorèbe	The Trojans (Les Troyens)	Berlioz	Cassandra's lover
Christine	Intermezzo	Richard Strauss	Storch's wife
Chrysothemis	Elektra	Richard Strauss	Elektra's sister
Cio-Cio-San	Madame Butterfly	Puccini	Pinkerton's wife
Cirillo	Fedora	Giordano	Coachman
Claggart	Billy Budd	Britten	Master-at-arms
Claison	Capriccio	Richard Strauss	Actress
Clara	Porgy and Bess	Gershwin	Jake's wife
Princess Clarissa	The Love for Three Oranges	Prokofiev	King's niece
Clorinda	La Cenerentola	Rossini	Don Magnifico's daughter
Clotilde	Norma	Bellini	Norma's friend
Mrs Coaxer	The Beggar's Opera	Pepusch	Lady of the town
Comtesse de Coigny	Andrea Chénier	Giordano	Madeleine's mother
Cola Rienzi	Rienzi	Wagner	Papal legate
Collatinus	The Rape of Lucretia	Britten	Soldier
Colline	La Bohème	Puccini	Philosopher

Character	Opera	Composer	Role
Commendatore	*Don Giovanni*	Mozart	Donna Anna's father
Comte de Grieux	*Manon*	Massenet	Chevalier's father
Conrad Nachtigall	*The Mastersingers of Nuremberg*	Wagner	Mastersinger and bucklemaker
Coppelius	*The Tales of Hoffmann*	Offenbach	Scientist
Count de Luna	*Il Trovatore*	Verdi	Count of aragon
Crébillon	*La Rondine*	Puccini	Perichaud's friend
Creon	*Oedipus Rex*	Stravinsky	Jocasta's brother
Crown	*Porgy and Bess*	Gershwin	Stevedore
Don Curzio	*The Marriage of Figaro*	Mozart	Lawyer
Daland	*The Flying Dutchman*	Wagner	Sea captain
El Dancairo	*Carmen*	Bizet	Smuggler
Dandini	*La Cenerentola*	Rossini	Valet
Daniello	*Johnny Spielt Auf*	Krenek	Artist
Dansker	*Billy Budd*	Britten	Seaman
Dapertutto	*The Tales of Hoffmann*	Offenbach	Sorcerer
The Dark Fiddler	*A Village Romeo and Juliet*	Delius	Real owner of land
David	*The Mastersingers of Nuremberg*	Wagner	Hans Sachs' apprentice
David	*L'Amico Fritz*	Mascagni	Rabbi
de Bretigny	*Manon*	Massenet	A nobleman
Désiré	*Fedora*	Giordano	Valet
Despina	*Così fan tutte*	Mozart	Maid
Dickson	*La Dame Blanche*	Boieldieu	Tenant of the White Lady
Dido	*Dido and Aeneas*	Purcell	Queen of Carthage
Dimitri	*Fedora*	Giordano	Groom
Dipsacus	*The Poisoned Kiss*	Vaughan Williams	Magician
Dolly Trull	*The Beggar's Opera*	Pepusch	Lady of the town
Donald	*Billy Budd*	Britten	Seaman
Donner	*Der Ring des Nibelungen*	Wagner	Norse god
Dorabella	*Così fan tutte*	Mozart	Fiordiligi's sister
Douphol	*La Traviata*	Verdi	Baron
Duclou	*Zazà*	Leoncavallo	Stage manager
Mme Dufresne	*Zazà*	Leoncavallo	Milio's wife
Dumas	*Andrea Chénier*	Giordano	President of the tribunal
Earl of Essex	*Gloriana*	Britten	The Queen's favorite
Principessa Eboli	*Don Carlos*	Verdi	Lady-in-waiting
Edgar/Edgardo	*Lucia di Lammermoor*	Donizetti	Edgar of Ravenswood
Edmondo	*Manon Lescaut*	Puccini	Student
Elettra	*Idomeneo*	Mozart	Greek princess
Elektra	*Elektra*	Richard Strauss	Agamemnon's daughter
Elisabeth	*Tannhäuser*	Wagner	Hermann's niece
Elizabeth of England	*Gloriana*	Britten	Queen of England
Elisetta	*The Secret Marriage*	Cimarosa	Geronimo's older daughter
Ellen Orford	*Peter Grimes*	Britten	Schoolteacher
Elvino	*The Sleepwalker*	Bellini	Farmer, Amina's love
Elvira	*Ernani*	Verdi	Ernani's beloved
Donna Elvira	*Don Giovanni*	Mozart	Lady from Burgos
Enzo	*La Gioconda*	Ponchielli	Sea captain
Erda	*Der Ring des Nibelungen*	Wagner	Earth goddess
Ernesto	*Don Pasquale*	Donizetti	Don Pasquale's nephew
Eroshka	*Prince Igor*	Borodin	Gudok player
Escamillo	*Carmen*	Bizet	Bullfighter
Esmerelda	*The Bartered Bride*	Smetana	Dancer
Estrella	*Háry János*	Kodály	Lady-in-waiting
Euridice	*Orfeo ed Euridice*	Gluck	Orfeo's wife
Eva	*The Mastersingers of Nuremberg*	Wagner	Pogner's daughter
Fafner	*Der Ring des Nibelungen*	Wagner	Giant, builder of Valhalla
Dr Falke	*Die Fledermaus*	Johann Strauss II	Eisenstein's Friend
Faninal	*Der Rosenkavalier*	Richard Strauss	Sophie's father
Farfarello	*The Love for Three Oranges*	Prokofiev	A devil
Farlaf	*Ruslan and Lyudmila*	Glinka	Warrior, suitor to Lyudmila
Fasolt	*Der Ring des Nibelungen*	Wagner	Giant, builder of Valhalla
Fata Morgana	*The Love for Three Oranges*	Prokofiev	Witch
Fatima	*Oberon*	Weber	Reiza's companion
Fatimah	*Marouf*	Rabaud	Marouf's wife
Fenena	*Nabucco*	Verdi	Nabucco's daughter
Fenton	*Falstaff*	Verdi	In Love with Nanetta
Feodor	*Boris Godunov*	Mussorgsky	Son of Boris Godunov
Ferrando	*Così fan tutte*	Mozart	Dorabella's fiancé
Ferrando	*Il Trovatore*	Verdi	Captain of the Guard
Fidalma	*The Secret Marriage*	Cimarosa	Geronimo's sister
Figaro	*The Barber of Seville*	Rossini	Barber

Character	Opera	Composer	Role
Figaro	The Marriage of Figaro	Mozart	Servant to Almaviva
Filch	The Beggar's Opera	Pepusch	Pickpocket
Filipievna	Eugene Onegin	Tchaikovsky	Nurse
Finn	Ruslan and Lyudmila	Glinka	Wizard
Fiordiligi	Così fan tutte	Mozart	Dorabella's sister
Fiorello	The Barber of Seville	Rossini	Servant
Flamand	Capriccio	Richard Strauss	Musician
Flavio	Norma	Bellini	Centurion
Florestan	Fidelio	Beethoven	Spanish nobleman
Flosshilde	Der Ring des Nibelungen	Wagner	Rhinemaiden
Frank Ford	Falstaff	Verdi	Alice's husband
Frank	Die Fledermaus	Johann Strauss II	Prison governor
Frantz	The Tales of Hoffmann	Offenbach	Crespel's servant
Frasquita	Carmen	Bizet	Gypsy
Frasquita	Der Corregidor	Wolf	Tio Lucas' wife
Frazier	Porgy and Bess	Gershwin	Catfish Row 'lawyer'
Freia	Der Ring des Nibelungen	Wagner	Goddess of youth and beauty
Fricka	Der Ring des Nibelungen	Wagner	Wotan's wife
Fritz Kothner	The Mastersingers of Nuremberg	Wagner	Mastersinger and baker
Froh	Der Ring des Nibelungen	Wagner	Norse god
Frosch	Die Fledermaus	Johann Strauss II	Jailer
Gallanthus	The Poisoned Kiss	Vaughan Williams	Amaryllus's sister
Mr Gedge	Albert Herring	Britten	Vicar
Geneviève	Pelléas et Mélisande	Debussy	Mother of Pelléas
Gennaro	Lucrezia Borgia	Donizetti	Venetian nobleman, Lucrezia's son
Gennaro	The Jewels of the Madonna	Wolf-Ferrari	Blacksmith
Georges Brown	La Dame Blanche	Boieldieu	English officer
Gérald	Lakmé	Delibes	English officer
Gerhilde	Der Ring des Nibelungen	Wagner	Valkyrie
Geronimo	The Secret Marriage	Cimarosa	Citizen of Bologna
Gertrude	Hänsel and Gretel	Humperdinck	Mother of Hansel and Gretel
Gilda	Rigoletto	Verdi	Rigoletto's daughter
La Gioconda	La Gioconda	Ponchielli	Street singer, Enzo's love
Giorgetta	Il Tabarro	Puccini	Michele's wife
Godfrey	Lohengrin	Wagner	Elsa's brother
Golaud	Pelléas et Mélisande	Debussy	Arkel's grandson
Gorislava	Ruslan and Lyudmila	Glinka	Ratmir's lover
Goro	Madame Butterfly	Puccini	Marriage broker
Grech	Fedora	Giordano	Policeman
Prince Gremin	Eugene Onegin	Tchaikovsky	General
Grigorij	Boris Godunov	Mussorgsky	False Dimitri
Grimgerde	Der Ring des Nibelungen	Wagner	Valkyrie
Gubetta	Lucrezia Borgia	Donizetti	Servant to Lucrezia
Guglielmo	Così fan tutte	Mozart	Fiordiligi's fiancé
Gunther	Der Ring des Nibelungen	Wagner	Hagen's half-brother
Gutrune	Der Ring des Nibelungen	Wagner	Gunther's sister
Gzak	Prince Igor	Borodin	Polovtsian Khan
Hadji	Lakmé	Delibes	Nilakantha's servant
Hagen	Der Ring des Nibelungen	Wagner	Alberich's Descendant
Hans Foltz	The Mastersingers of Nuremberg	Wagner	Mastersinger and coppersmith
Hans Sachs	The Mastersingers of Nuremberg	Wagner	Mastersinger and cobbler
Hans Schwarz	The Mastersingers of Nuremberg	Wagner	Mastersinger and stocking weaver
Happy	The Girl of the Golden West	Puccini	Miner
Haroun al Rashid	Oberon	Weber	Caliph of Baghdad
Harry Paddington	The Beggar's Opera	Pepusch	Highwayman
Helmwige	Der Ring des Nibelungen	Wagner	Valkyrie
Henry Ashton	Ennio Lucia di Lammermoor	Donizetti	Lord of Lammermoor
Hermann	Tannhäuser	Wagner	Landgrave of Thuringia
Hermann	The Tales of Hoffmann	Offenbach	Student
Hermann Ortel	The Mastersingers of Nuremberg	Wagner	Mastersinger and soap boiler
Herod	Salome	Richard Strauss	Ruler of Galileo
Herodias	Salome	Richard Strauss	Herod's wife
Hob	The Poisoned Kiss	Vaughan Williams	Servant of Dipsacus
Hoffmann	The Tales of Hoffmann	Offenbach	Poet
Hunding	Der Ring des Nibelungen	Wagner	Siegmund's enemy
Hylas	The Trojans (Les Troyens)	Berlioz	Trojan sailor
Idamente	Idomeneo	Mozart	Idomeneo's son
Idomeneo	Idomeneo	Mozart	King of Crete
Ighino	Palestrina	Pfitzner	Palestrina's son
Prince Igor	Prince Igor	Borodin	Prince of Seversk
Ilia	Idomeneo	Mozart	Trojan princess

Character	Opera	Composer	Role
Ilka	*Háry János*	Kodály	Háry's fiancée
Incredible	*Andrea Chénier*	Giordano	Spy
Iopas	*The Trojans (Les Troyens)*	Berlioz	Poet
Irene	*Rienzi*	Wagner	Rienzi's sister
Isolde	*Tristan und Isolde*	Wagner	Irish princess
Jacquino	*Fidelio*	Beethoven	Rocco's assistant
Jago	*Ernani*	Verdi	Silva's squire
Jake	*Porgy and Bess*	Gershwin	Fisherman
Aunt Jane	*Hugh the Drover*	Vaughan Williams	Sister of the constable
Jaroslavna	*Prince Igor*	Borodin	Prince Igor's wife
Jean	*Le Jongleur de Notre Dame*	Massenet	A poor juggler
Jemmy Twitcher	*The Beggar's Opera*	Pepusch	Highwayman
Jenik	*The Bartered Bride*	Smetana	Micha's son
Jenny	*La Dame Blanche*	Boieldieu	Dickson's wife
Jenny Diver	*The Beggar's Opera*	Pepusch	Lady of the night
Jim	*Porgy and Bess*	Gershwin	Cotton picker
Jocasta	*Oedipus Rex*	Stravinsky	Wife of Oedipus
Joe	*The Girl of the Golden West*	Puccini	Miner
John	*Peter Grimes*	Britten	Peter's apprentice
John the Butcher	*Hugh the Drover*	Vaughan Williams	Mary's fiancé
John the Baptist	*Salome*	Richard Strauss	Jewish prophet
Johnny	*Johnny Spielt Auf*	Krenek	Artist
Don José	*Carmen*	Bizet	Corporal in the Guard
Juan Lopez	*Der Corregidor*	Wolf	Mayor
Judith	*Duke Bluebeard's Castle*	Bartók	Bluebeard's last wife
Junius	*The Rape of Lucretia*	Britten	Roman general
Justizrat	*Intermezzo*	Richard Strauss	Storch's friend
Kammersänger	*Intermezzo*	Richard Strauss	Storch's friend
Kate	*Madame Butterfly*	Puccini	Pinkerton's wife
Kathinka	*The Bartered Bride*	Smetana	Marenka's mother
Kecal	*The Bartered Bride*	Smetana	Marriage broker
King of Clubs	*The Love for Three Oranges*	Prokofiev	Ruler of the kingdom
Klingsor	*Parsifal*	Wagner	Magician
Kontchak	*Prince Igor*	Borodin	Polovtsian Khan
Kontchakovna	*Prince Igor*	Borodin	Kontchak's daughter
Kruschev	*Boris Godunov*	Mussorgsky	Boyard
Kundry	*Parsifal*	Wagner	Bewitched woman
Kunz Vogelgesang	*The Mastersingers of Nuremberg*	Wagner	Mastersinger and furrier
Kurvenal	*Tristan und Isolde*	Wagner	Tristan's retainer
Lakmé	*Lakmé*	Delibes	Nilakantha's daughter
Larina	*Eugene Onegin*	Tchaikovsky	Tatyana's mother
Larkens	*The Girl of the Golden West*	Puccini	Miner
Lartigen	*Zazà*	Leoncavallo	Monologist
Lawrence	*The Wreckers*	Smyth	Lighthouse keeper
Leandro	*The Love for Three Oranges*	Prokofiev	King of Spades and PM
Lenski	*Eugene Onegin*	Tchaikovsky	Olga's fiancé
Leonara di Gusman	*La Favorita*	Donizetti	King's mistress
Leonora	*Il Trovatore*	Verdi	Beloved of Manrico
Leonora	*Fidelio*	Beethoven	Florestan's wife
Leporello	*Don Giovanni*	Mozart	Servant
Lescaut	*Manon*	Massenet	A gambler
Lillas Pastia	*Carmen*	Bizet	Innkeeper
Lily	*Porgy and Bess*	Gershwin	Strawberry woman
Lindorf	*The Tales of Hoffmann*	Offenbach	Councillor of Nuremberg
Linette	*The Love for Three Oranges*	Prokofiev	Princess hidden in an orange
Lisette	*La Rondine*	Puccini	Magda's maid
Liù	*Turandot*	Puccini	Slave girl
Lob	*The Poisoned Kiss*	Vaughan Williams	Assistant of Dipsacus
Lockit	*The Beggar's Opera*	Pepusch	Jailer
Lodovico	*Otello*	Verdi	Venetian ambassador
Loge	*Der Ring des Nibelungen*	Wagner	Norse god
Lohengrin	*Lohengrin*	Wagner	Parsifal's son
Lola	*Cavalleria Rusticana*	Mascagni	Alfio's wife
Lorek	*Fedora*	Giordano	Surgeon
Loris Ipanov	*Fedora*	Giordano	Count
Lucia	*The Rape of Lucretia*	Britten	Lucretia's attendant
Lucretia	*Palestrina*	Pfitzner	Palestrina's wife
Lucretia	*The Rape of Lucretia*	Britten	Wife of Collatinus
Lucrezia Borgia	*Lucrezia Borgia*	Donizetti	Duchess of Ferrara
Lucy/Lucia	*Lucia di Lammermoor*	Donizetti	Ashton's sister
Lucy Lockit	*The Beggar's Opera*	Pepusch	Jailer's daughter

MUSIC CLASSICAL

Character	Opera	Composer	Role
Luigi	Il Tabarro	Puccini	Stevedore, Giorgetta's father
Lulu	Lulu	Berg	Prostitute
Luther	The Tales of Hoffmann	Offenbach	Innkeeper
Lyudmila	Ruslan and Lyudmila	Glinka	A noblewoman
Macheath	The Beggar's Opera	Pepusch	Highwayman
MacIrton	La Dame Blanche	Boieldieu	Justice of the Peace
Mad Margaret	Ruddigore	Sullivan	Mad woman
Maddalena	Rigoletto	Verdi	Sparafucile's sister
Madeleine de Coigny	Andrea Chénier	Giordano	In love with Andrea Chénier
Madelon	Andrea Chénier	Giordano	Old woman
Maffio Orsini	Lucrezia Borgia	Donizetti	Lucrezia's enemy
Magda	La Rondine	Puccini	Rambaldo's mistress
Magdalena	The Mastersingers of Nuremberg	Wagner	Nurse
Don Magnifico	La Cenerentola	Rossini	Baron of Montflagon
Mahomet	Der Rosenkavalier	Richard Strauss	Negro page
Dr Malatesta	Don Pasquale	Donizetti	Don Pasquale's friend
Maliella	The Jewels of the Madonna	Wolf-Ferrari	Gennaro's adopted sister
Mallika	Lakmé	Delibes	Lakmé's slave
Mama Lucia	Cavalleria Rusticana	Mascagni	Turiddu's mother
Manon	Manon	Massenet	Lescaut's cousin
Manrico	Il Trovatore	Verdi	Troubador
Duke of Mantua	Rigoletto	Verdi	Nobleman
Manuela	Der Corregidor	Wolf	Maid
Manz	A Village Romeo and Juliet	Delius	Farmer
Marcellina	Fidelio	Beethoven	Rocco's daughter
Marcellina	The Marriage of Figaro	Mozart	Housekeeper
Marcello	La Bohème	Puccini	Painter
Marco	Zazà	Leoncavallo	Dufresne's butler
Marenka	The Bartered Bride	Smetana	In love with Jenik
Marguerite	La Dame Blanche	Boieldieu	Servant
Marguérite	Faust	Gounod	Beloved of Faust
Maria	Porgy and Bess	Gershwin	Cookshop keeper
Marianne	Der Rosenkavalier	Richard Strauss	Sophie's duenna
Marie	Wozzeck	Berg	Prostitute
Marie-Louise	Háry János	Kodály	Napoleon's second wife
Marina Mnishek	Boris Godunov	Mussorgsky	Daughter of Voyevode of Sandomir
Mario Cavaradossi	Tosca	Puccini	Painter
King Marke	Tristan und Isolde	Wagner	King of Cornwall
Marlardot	Zazà	Leoncavallo	Music-Hall owner
Marouf	Marouf	Rabaud	Shoemaker
Marschallin	Der Rosenkavalier	Richard Strauss	Princess
Martha Schwerlein	Faust	Gounod	Marguérite's neighbour
Marti	A Village Romeo and Juliet	Delius	Farmer
Cavaliere Marullo	Rigoletto	Verdi	Courtier
Mary	Hugh the Drover	Vaughan Williams	Constable's daughter
Marzci	Háry János	Kodály	Marie's coachman
Masetto	Don Giovanni	Mozart	Peasant
Mat of the Mint	The Beggar's Opera	Pepusch	Highwayman
Mathieu	Andrea Chénier	Giordano	Waiter
Mathis	Mathis der Maler	Hindemith	Painter (Grünewald)
Matteo Borsa	Rigoletto	Verdi	Courtier
Matteo del Sarto	Arlecchino	Busoni	Tailor
Max	Johnny Spielt Auf	Krenek	Composer
Mélisande	Pelléas et Mélisande	Debussy	Golaud's wife
Melot	Tristan und Isolde	Wagner	Courtier
Melusine	Háry János	Kodály	Countess
Mercedes	Carmen	Bizet	Gypsy
Micaela	Carmen	Bizet	Village girl
Micha	The Bartered Bride	Smetana	Jenik's father
Michele	Il Tabarro	Puccini	Barge owner
Michelin	Zazà	Leoncavallo	Journalist
Milio Dufresne	Zazà	Leoncavallo	Zaza's lover
Mime	Der Ring des Nibelungen	Wagner	A Nibelung
Mimi	La Bohème	Puccini	Seamstress
Minnie	The Girl of the Golden West	Puccini	Barmaid
Dr Miracle	The Tales of Hoffmann	Offenbach	Doctor
Missail	Boris Godunov	Mussorgsky	Vagrant
Mistrust	The Pilgrim's Progress	Vaughan Williams	Neighbour
Molly Brazen	The Beggar's Opera	Pepusch	Lady of the town
Monostatos	The Magic Flute	Mozart	Servant

Character	Opera	Composer	Role
Montano	Otello	Verdi	Otello's predecessor
Morales	Carmen	Bizet	Officer of the Guard
Augustin Moser	The Mastersingers of Nuremberg	Wagner	Mastersinger and tailor
Muff	The Bartered Bride	Smetana	Comedian
Musetta	La Bohème	Puccini	In love with Marcello
Nabucco	Nabucco	Verdi	Nebuchadnezzar, King of Babylon
Naina	Ruslan and Lyudmila	Glinka	Witch
Namouna	Oberon	Weber	Fatima's grandmother
Nancy	Albert Herring	Britten	Baker's assistant
Nanetta	Falstaff	Verdi	Ford's daughter
Narbal	The Trojans (Les Troyens)	Berlioz	Dido's minister
Narraboth	Salome	Richard Strauss	Captain of the Guard
Natalia	Zazà	Leoncavallo	Zazà's maid
Nathanael	The Tales of Hoffmann	Offenbach	Student
Ned Keene	Peter Grimes	Britten	Apothecary
Nedda	I Pagliacci	Leoncavallo	Canio's wife
Nick	The Girl of the Golden West	Puccini	Bartender
Nicklaus	The Tales of Hoffmann	Offenbach	Hoffmann's friend
Nicola	Fedora	Giordano	Footman
Nicoletta	The Love for Three Oranges	Prokofiev	Princess hidden in an orange
Nilakantha	Lakmé	Delibes	Brahmin priest
Nimming Ned	The Beggar's Opera	Pepusch	Highwayman
Ninetta	The Love for Three Oranges	Prokofiev	Princess hidden in an orange
Norina	Don Pasquale	Donizetti	Widow
Norma	Norma	Bellini	Druid priestess
Norman	Lucia di Lammermoor	Donizetti	Follower of Ashton
Obstinate	The Pilgrim's Progress	Vaughan Williams	Neighbour
Octavian	Der Rosenkavalier	Richard Strauss	Bearer of the Rose
Oedipus	Oedipus Rex	Stravinsky	King of Thebes
Olga	Eugene Onegin	Tchaikovsky	Tatiana's sister
Olivier	Capriccio	Richard Strauss	Poet
Olympia	The Tales of Hoffmann	Offenbach	Mechanical doll
One-Arm	Die Frau ohne Schatten	Richard Strauss	Barak's brother
One-Eye	Die Frau ohne Schatten	Richard Strauss	Barak's brother
Orest	Elektra	Richard Strauss	Elektra's brother
Orfeo	Orfeo ed Euridice	Gluck	Singer-poet
Orlovsky	Die Fledermaus	Johann Strauss II	Rich Russian
Oroveso	Norma	Bellini	Norma's father
Ortlinde	Der Ring des Nibelungen	Wagner	Valkyrie
Ortrud	Lohengrin	Wagner	Wife of Frederick
Oscar	A Masked Ball	Verdi	Riccardo's page
Ovlour	Prince Igor	Borodin	Polovtsian traitor
Palestrina	Palestrina	Pfitzner	Composer
Pamina	The Magic Flute	Mozart	Daughter of Queen of the Night
Pang	Turandot	Puccini	Lord of Provisions
Pantalone	Turandot	Busoni	Minister
Pantaloon	The Love for Three Oranges	Prokofiev	King's friend
Panthée	The Trojans (Les Troyens)	Berlioz	Priest
Paolino	The Secret Marriage	Cimarosa	Carolina's secret husband
Paolo Orsini	Rienzi	Wagner	Patrician
Papagena	The Magic Flute	Mozart	Destined to be Papageno's wife
Papageno	The Magic Flute	Mozart	Bird catcher
Parpignol	La Bohème	Puccini	Toy vendor
Parsifal	Parsifal	Wagner	Knight of the Holy Grail
Peachum	The Beggar's Opera	Pepusch	Fence
Pelléas	Pelléas et Mélisande	Debussy	Arkel's grandson
Périchaud	La Rondine	Puccini	Rambaldo's friend
Peter	Porgy and Bess	Gershwin	Honey-man
Peter	Hänsel and Gretel	Humperdinck	Father of Hansel and Gretel
Peter Grimes	Peter Grimes	Britten	Fisherman
Pilgrim	The Pilgrim's Progress	Vaughan Williams	Pilgrim
Pimen	Boris Godunov	Mussorgsky	Hermit
Ping	Turandot	Puccini	Chinese Grand Chancellor
Lt Pinkerton	Madame Butterfly	Puccini	Lt in US Navy
Pittichinaccio	The Tales of Hoffmann	Offenbach	Giulietta's admirer
Don Pizarro	Fidelio	Beethoven	Prison governor
Pliable	The Pilgrim's Progress	Vaughan Williams	Neighbour
Veit Pogner	The Mastersingers of Nuremberg	Wagner	Mastersinger and goldsmith (Eva's father)
Pollione	Norma	Bellini	Proconsul of Rome

MUSIC CLASSICAL

Character	Opera	Composer	Role
Polly Peachum	*The Beggar's Opera*	Pepusch	Peachum's daughter, Macheath's wife
Polyxène	*The Trojans (Les Troyens)*	Berlioz	Priam's daughter
Pong	*Turandot*	Puccini	Lord of the Imperial Kitchen
Porgy	*Porgy and Bess*	Gershwin	A crippled beggar
Priam	*The Trojans (Les Troyens)*	Berlioz	King of Troy
Prince	*Lulu*	Berg	Traveller in Africa
Prince	*The Love for Three Oranges*	Prokofiev	Hypochondriac
Prunier	*La Rondine*	Puccini	Poet
Publius	*La Clemenza di Tito*	Mozart	Captain of Praetorian Guard
Queen Mother of Samarkand	*Turandot*	Busoni	Negress
Rafaele	*The Jewels of the Madonna*	Wolf-Ferrari	Leader of the Camorra
Raimondo	*Rienzi*	Wagner	Papal legate
Rambaldo	*La Rondine*	Puccini	Banker
Ramfis	*Aida*	Verdi	High priest
Don Ramiro	*La Cenerentola*	Rossini	Prince of Salerno
Jack Rance	*The Girl of the Golden West*	Puccini	Sheriff
Rangoni	*Boris Godunov*	Mussorgsky	Jesuit
Ratmir	*Ruslan and Lyudmila*	Glinka	Suitor to Lyudmila
Raymond/ Raimondo	*Lucia di Lammermoor*	Donizetti	Chaplain, Lucy's tutor
Mr Redburn	*Billy Budd*	Britten	First lieutenant
Red Whiskers	*Billy Budd*	Britten	Impressed seaman
Reinmar von Zweter	*Tannhäuser*	Wagner	Knight
Reiza	*Oberon*	Weber	Haroun el Rashid's daughter
El Remondado	*Carmen*	Bizet	Smuggler
Renato	*A Masked Ball*	Verdi	Riccardo's secretary
Repela	*Der Corregidor*	Wolf	Valet to magistrate
Rhadames	*Aida*	Verdi	Captain of the Guard
Riccardo	*A Masked Ball*	Verdi	Governor of Louisiana
Riedinger	*Mathis der Maler*	Hindemith	Rich Lutheran
Rigoletto	*Rigoletto*	Verdi	Gilda's father, a jester
Rocco	*Fidelio*	Beethoven	Chief jailer
Rodolfo	*La Bohème*	Puccini	Poet
Rosalinda	*Die Fledermaus*	Johann Strauss II	Eisenstein's wife
Rose	*Lakmé*	Delibes	An English lady
Rosina	*The Barber of Seville*	Rossini	Dr Bartolo's ward
Rossweisse	*Der Ring des Nibelungen*	Wagner	Valkyrie
Roucher	*Andrea Chénier*	Giordano	Andrea's friend
Ruggero	*La Rondine*	Puccini	Son of Rambaldo's childhood friend
Ruslan	*Ruslan and Lyudmila*	Glinka	Suitor to Lyudmila
Rustighello	*Lucrezia Borgia*	Donizetti	Alfonso's henchman
Sali	*A Village Romeo and Juliet*	Delius	Mary's daughter
Salome	*Salome*	Richard Strauss	Daughter of Herodias
Santuzza	*Cavalleria Rusticana*	Mascagni	In love with Turiddu
Sarastro	*The Magic Flute*	Mozart	High priest
Baron Scarpia	*Tosca*	Puccini	Chief of police
Dr Schön	*Lulu*	Berg	Editor
Senta	*The Flying Dutchman*	Wagner	Daland's daughter
Sharpless	*Madame Butterfly*	Puccini	US consul in Nagasaki
Sid	*Albert Herring*	Britten	Butcher's assistant
Siegfried	*Der Ring des Nibelungen*	Wagner	Son of Siegmund and Sieglunde
Sieglunde	*Der Ring des Nibelungen*	Wagner	Siegmund's twin sister
Siegmund	*Der Ring des Nibelungen*	Wagner	Mortal son of Wotan
Silvano	*A Masked Ball*	Verdi	A young sailor
Silvio	*I Pagliacci*	Leoncavallo	In love with Nedda
Sophie	*Der Rosenkavalier*	Richard Strauss	Daughter of von Faninal
Spalanzani	*The Tales of Hoffmann*	Offenbach	Inventor
Sportin' Life	*Porgy and Bess*	Gershwin	Dope dealer
Stella	*The Tales of Hoffmann*	Offenbach	Opera singer
Robert Storch	*Intermezzo*	Richard Strauss	Musical conductor
Suky Tawdry	*The Beggar's Opera*	Pepusch	Lady of the town
Susan B Anthony	*The Mother of Us All*	Thomson	American suffragette
Susanna	*The Marriage of Figaro*	Mozart	Maid
Suzuki	*Madame Butterfly*	Puccini	Servant
Suzy	*La Rondine*	Puccini	Magda's friend
Svyetor	*Ruslan and Lyudmila*	Glinka	Lyudmila's father
Talpa	*Il Tabarro*	Puccini	Stevedore
Tannhäuser	*Tannhäuser*	Wagner	Knight
Tatiana	*Eugene Onegin*	Tchaikovsky	In love with Eugene
Telramund	*Lohengrin*	Wagner	Count of Brabant

Character	Opera	Composer	Role
Thisbe	La Cenerentola	Rossini	Don Magnifico's daughter
Timorous	The Pilgrim's Progress	Vaughan Williams	Neighbour
Tinca	Il Tabarro	Puccini	Stevedore
Tio Lucas	Der Corregidor	Wolf	Miller
Tiresias	Oedipus Rex	Stravinsky	Blind soothsayer
Titurel	Parsifal	Wagner	Father of Amfortas
Titus	La Clemenza di Tito	Mozart	Emperor of Rome
Tom Rakewell	The Rake's Progress	Stravinsky	The Rake
Tonio	I Pagliacci	Leoncavallo	Clown
Tonuelo	Der Corregidor	Wolf	Court messenger
Tormentilla	The Poisoned Kiss	Vaughan Williams	Daughter of Dipsacus
Tosca	Tosca	Puccini	Singer
Toto	Zazà	Leoncavallo	Dufresne's child
Mrs Trapes	The Beggar's Opera	Pepusch	Tally woman
Trim	The Girl of the Golden West	Puccini	Miner
Tristan	Tristan und Isolde	Wagner	Cornish knight
Trouble	Madame Butterfly	Puccini	Cio-Cio-San's child
Truchsess von Waldburg	Mathis der Maler	Hindemith	Leader of the army
Trulove	The Rake's Progress	Stravinsky	Anne's father
Princess Turandot	Turandot	Puccini	Daughter of Altoum
Turiddu	Cavalleria Rusticana	Mascagni	Soldier
Ulrica	A Masked Ball	Verdi	Fortune teller
Ulrich Eisslinger	The Mastersingers of Nuremberg	Wagner	Mastersingers and grocer
Mr Upfold	Albert Herring	Britten	Mayor
Ursula	Mathis der Maler	Hindemith	Riedinger's daughter
Valzacchi	Der Rosenkavalier	Richard Strauss	Scandalmonger
Varlaam	Boris Godunov	Mussorgsky	Vagrant
Vasek	The Bartered Bride	Smetana	Micha's second son
Venus	Tannhäuser	Wagner	Supernatural seductress
Captain Vere	Billy Budd	Britten	Ship's captain
Violetta Valery	La Traviata	Verdi	Courtesan
Vitellia	La Clemenza di Tito	Mozart	Daughter of deposed emperor
Vitellozzo	Lucrezia Borgia	Donizetti	Nobleman
Miss Vixen	The Beggar's Opera	Pepusch	Lady of the town
Vizier	Marouf	Rabaud	Sultan's adviser
Vladimir Igorevitch	Prince Igor	Borodin	Igor's son
Vladimir Yaroslavovitch	Prince Igor	Borodin	Yaroslavna's brother
Vreli	A Village Romeo and Juliet	Delius	Marti's daughter
Jake Wallace	The Girl of the Golden West	Puccini	Minstrel
Sir Walter Raleigh	Gloriana	Britten	Courtier
Walter von Stolzing	The Mastersingers of Nuremberg	Wagner	Franconian knight
Walther von der Vogelweide	Tannhäuser	Wagner	Knight
Waltraute	Der Ring des Nibelungen	Wagner	Valkyrle
Watchful	The Pilgrim's Progress	Vaughan Williams	Porter
Wellgunde	Der Ring des Nibelungen	Wagner	Rhine maiden
Woglinde	Der Ring des Nibelungen	Wagner	Rhine maiden
Wolfram	Tannhäuser	Wagner	Knight
Wotan	Der Ring des Nibelungen	Wagner	Norse god
Wowkle	The Girl of the Golden West	Puccini	Billy's squaw
Wozzeck	Wozzeck	Berg	Soldier
Xenia	Boris Godunov	Mussorgsky	Boris Godunov's daughter
Yamadori	Madame Butterfly	Puccini	Rich Japanese
Yniold	Pelléas et Mélisande	Debussy	Golaud's son
Yvette	La Rondine	Puccini	Magda's friend
Yvonne	Jonny Spielt Auf	Krenek	Chambermaid
Zaccaria	Nabucco	Verdi	High Priest of Jerusalem
Zazà	Zazà	Leoncavallo	Music-hall singer
Zerlina	Don Giovanni	Mozart	Engaged to Matteo
Zuniga	Carmen	Bizet	Captain of the Guard

MUSIC CLASSICAL

Operatic Characters (by opera)

Opera	Composer	Character	Role
Aida	Verdi	Aida	Ethiopian princess
		Amneris	Egyptian princess
		Amonasro	Aida's father (King of Ethiopia)
		Ramfis	High priest
		Rhadames	Captain of the Guard
Albert Herring	Britten	Albert Herring	Greengrocer's assistant
		Lady Bellows	Elderly autocrat
		Mr Gedge	Vicar
		Mr Upfold	Mayor
		Nancy	Baker's assistant
		Sid	Butcher's assistant
Alceste	Gluck	Admetus	Alceste's husband
		Alceste	Wife of Admetus
L'Amico Fritz	Mascagni	David	Rabbi
Andrea Chénier	Giordano	Charles Gérard	Revolutionary leader
		Comtesse de Coigny	Madeleine's mother
		Dumas	President of the tribunal
		Incredible	Spy
		Madeleine de Coigny	In love with Andrea Chénier
		Madelon	Old woman
		Mathieu	Waiter
		Roucher	Andrea's friend
Arlecchino	Busoni	Matteo del Sarto	Tailor
The Barber of Seville	Rossini	Almaviva	Count
		Ambrogio	Bartolo's servant
		Bartolo	Rosina's guardian
		Basilio	Singing teacher
		Berta	Housekeeper
		Figaro	Barber
		Fiorello	Servant
		Rosina	Dr Bartolo's ward
The Bartered Bride	Smetana	Esmerelda	Dancer
		Jenik	Micha's son
		Kathinka	Marenka's mother
		Kecal	Marriage broker
		Marenka	In love with Jenik
		Micha	Jenik's father
		Muff	Comedian
		Vasek	Micha's second son
The Beggar's Opera	Pepusch	Ben Budge	Highwayman
		Betty Doxy	Lady of the town
		Dolly Trull	Lady of the town
		Filch	Pickpocket
		Harry Paddington	Highwayman
		Jemmy Twitcher	Highwayman
		Jenny Diver	Lady of the night
		Lockit	Jailer
		Lucy Lockit	Jailer's daughter
		Macheath	Highwayman
		Mat of the Mint	Highwayman
		Miss Vixen	Lady of the town
		Molly Brazen	Lady of the town
		Mrs Coaxer	Lady of the town
		Mrs Trapes	Tally woman
		Nimming Ned	Highwayman
		Peachum	Fence
		Polly Peachum	Peachum's daughter, Macheath's wife
		Suky Tawdry	Lady of the town
Billy Budd	Britten	Arthur Jones	Seaman
		Billy Budd	Seaman and stammerer
		Captain Vere	Ship's captain
		Claggart	Master-at-arms
		Dansker	Seaman
		Donald	Seaman
		Mr Redburn	First lieutenant
		Red Whiskers	Impressed seaman

Opera	Composer	Character	Role
La Bohème	Puccini	Alcindoro	Musetta's escort
		Benoît	Landlord
		Colline	Philosopher
		Marcello	Painter
		Mimi	Seamstress
		Musetta	In love with Marcello
		Parpignol	Toy Vendor
		Rodolfo	Poet
Boris Godunov	Mussorgsky	Feodor	Son of Boris Godunov
		Grigorij	False Dimitri
		Kruschev	Boyar
		Marina Mnishek	Daughter of Voyevode Sandomir
		Missail	Vagrant
		Pimen	Hermit
		Rangoni	Jesuit
		Varlaam	Vagrant
		Xenia	Boris Godunov's daughter
Capriccio	Richard Strauss	Claison	Actress
		Flamand	Musician
		Olivier	Poet
Cardillac	Hindemith	Cardillac	Goldsmith
Carmen	Bizet	Carmen	Gypsy
		Don José	Corporal in the Guard
		El Dancairo	Smuggler
		El Remondado	Smuggler
		Escamillo	Bullfighter
		Frasquita	Gypsy
		Lillas Pastia	Innkeeper
		Mercedes	Gypsy
		Micaela	Village girl
		Morales	Officer of the Guard
		Zuniga	Captain of the Guard
Cavalleria Rusticana	Mascagni	Alfio	Teamster
		Lola	Alfio's wife
		Mama Lucia	Turiddu's mother
		Santuzza	In love with Turiddu
		Turiddu	Soldier
La Cenerentola	Rossini	Alidoro	Philosopher and magician
		Angelina	Don Magnifico's stepdaughter, Cinderella
		Clorinda	Don Magnifico's daughter
		Dandini	Valet
		Don Magnifico	Baron of Montflagon
		Don Ramiro	Prince of Salerno
		Thisbe	Don Magnifico's daughter
La Clemenza di Tito	Mozart	Annius	Patrician
		Publius	Captain of Praetorian Guard
		Titus	Emperor of Rome
		Vitellia	Daughter of deposed emperor
Der Corregidor	Wolf	Frasquita	Tio Lucas' wife
		Juan Lopez	Mayor
		Manuela	Maid
		Repela	Valet to magistrate
		Tio Lucas	Miller
		Tonuelo	Court messenger
Così fan tutte	Mozart	Despina	Maid
		Don Alfonso	Don
		Dorabella	Fiordiligi's sister
		Ferrando	Dorabella's fiancé
		Fiordiligi	Dorabella's sister
		Guglielmo	Fiordiligi's fiancé
La Dame Blanche	Boieldieu	Dickson	Tenant of the White Lady
		Georges Brown	English officer
		Jenny	Dickson's wife
		MacIrton	Justice of the Peace
		Marguerite	Servant
Dido and Aeneas	Purcell	Aeneas	Trojan general
		Belinda	Lady-in-waiting
		Dido	Queen of Carthage
Don Carlos	Verdi	Don Carlos	Heir to Spanish throne
		Principessa Eboli	Lady in waiting

M
U
S
I
C

C
L
A
S
S
I
C
A
L

Opera	Composer	Character	Role
Don Giovanni	Mozart	Commendatore	Donna Anna's father
		Donna Anna	Don Ottavio's fiancée
		Donna Elvira	Lady from Burgos
		Leporello	Servant
		Masetto	Peasant
		Zerlina	Engaged to Matteo
Don Pasquale	Donizetti	Dr Malatesta	Don Pasquale's friend
		Ernesto	Don Pasquale's nephew
		Norina	Widow
Duke Bluebeard's Castle	Bartók	Judith	Bluebeard's last wife
Elektra	Richard Strauss	Aegisth	Klytemnestra's lover
		Chrysothemis	Elektra's sister
		Elektra	Agamemnon's daughter
		Orest	Elektra's brother
Emperor Jones	Gruenberg	Brutus Jones	Escaped convict, tribal leader
Ernani	Verdi	Don Carlos	King of Castile
		Elvira	Ernani's beloved
		Jago	Silva's squire
Eugene Onegin	Tchaikovsky	Filipievna	Nurse
		Prince Gremin	General
		Larina	Tatyana's mother
		Lenski	Olga's fiancé
		Olga	Tatiana's sister
		Tatiana	In love with Eugene
Falstaff	Verdi	Alice Ford	Citizen of Windsor
		Fenton	In love with Nanetta
		Frank Ford	Alice's husband
		Nanetta	Ford's daughter
Faust	Gounod	Marguérite	Beloved of Faust
		Martha Schwerlein	Marguérite's neighbour
La Favorita	Donizetti	Alfonso XI	King of Castile
		Balthazar	Superior of the monastery
		Leonara di Gusman	King's mistress
Fedora	Giordano	Cirillo	Coachman
		Désiré	Valet
		Dimitri	Groom
		Grech	Policeman
		Lorek	Surgeon
		Loris Ipanov	Count
		Nicola	Footman
Fidelio	Beethoven	Don Pizarro	Prison governor
		Florestan	Spanish nobleman
		Jacquino	Rocco's assistant
		Leonora	Florestan's wife
		Marcellina	Rocco's daughter
		Rocco	Chief jailer
Die Fledermaus	Johann Strauss II	Adele	Eisenstein's maid
		Dr Blind	Eisenstein's attorney
		Dr Falke	Eisenstein's friend
		Frank	Prison governor
		Frosch	Jailer
		Orlovsky	Rich Russian
		Rosalinda	Eisenstein's wife
The Flying Dutchman	Wagner	Daland	Sea captain
		Senta	Daland's daughter
Die Frau ohne Schatten	Richard Strauss	Barak	Dyer
		One-Arm	Barak's brother
		One-Eye	Barak's brother
La Forza del Destino	Verdi	Don Alvaro	Leonora's lover
Der Freischütz		Agathe	Cuno's daughter
La Gioconda	Ponchielli	Barnaba	Spy
		Enzo	Sea captain
		La Gioconda	Street singer, Enzo's love
The Girl of the Golden West		Ashby	Wells-Fargo agent
		Billy Jackrabbit	Red Indian
		Happy	Miner
		Jack Rance	Sheriff
		Jake Wallace	Minstrel
		Joe	Mine
		Larkens	Miner
		Minnie	Barmaid

Opera	Composer	Character	Role
		Nick	Bartender
		Trim	Miner
		Wowkle	Billy's squaw
Gloriana	Britten	Earl of Essex	The Queen's favourite
		Elizabeth of England	Queen of England
		Sir Robert Cecil	Secretary to the Council
		Sir Walter Raleigh	Courtier
Hänsel and Gretel	Humperdinck	Gertrude	Mother of Hansel and Gretel
		Peter	Father of Hansel and Gretel
Háry János	Kodály	Abraham	Innkeeper
		Estrella	Lady-in-waiting
		Ilka	Háry's fiancée
		Marie-Louise	Napoleon's second wife
		Marzci	Marie's coachman
		Melusine	Countess
Hugh the Drover	Vaughan Williams	Aunt Jane	Sister of the constable
		John the Butcher	Mary's fiancé
		Mary	Constable's daughter
Idomeneo	Mozart	Arbace	Idomeneo's confidante
		Elettra	Greek princess
		Idamente	Idomeneo's son
		Idomeneo	King of Crete
		Ilia	Trojan princess
Intermezzo	Richard Strauss	Christine	Storch's wife
		Justizrat	Storch's friend
		Kammersänger	Storch's friend
		Robert Storch	Musical conductor
The Jewels of the Madonna	Wolf-Ferrari	Gennaro	Blacksmith
		Maliella	Gennaro's adopted sister
		Rafaele	Leader of the Camorra
Le Jongleur de Notre Dame	Massenet	Boniface	Cook
Jonny Spielt Auf	Krenek	Daniello	Artist
(Jonny Plays on)		Jonny	Artist
		Max	Composer
		Yvonne	Chambermaid
Lakmé	Delibes	Gérald	English officer
		Hadji	Nilakantha's servant
		Lakmé	Nilakantha's daughter
		Mallika	Lakmé's slave
		Nilakantha	Brahmin priest
		Rose	An English lady
Lohengrin		Godfrey	Elsa's brother
		Lohengrin	Parsifal's son
		Ortrud	Wife of Frederick
		Telramund	Count of Brabant
The Love for Three Oranges	Prokofiev	Celio	Magician
		Farfarello	A devil
		Fata Morgana	Witch
		King of Clubs	Ruler of the kingdom
		Leandro	King of Spades and prime minister
		Linette	Princess hidden in an orange
		Nicoletta	Princess hidden in an orange
		Ninetta	Princess hidden in an orange
		Pantaloon	King's friend
		Prince	Hypochondriac
		Princess Clarissa	King's niece
Lucia di Lammermoor	Donizetti	Alice/Alisa	Lucia's companion
		Arthur Bucklaw/Arturo	Lord
		Henry Ashton/Enrico	Lorn of Lammermoor
		Edgar/Edgardo	Edgar of Ravenswood
		Norman/Normando	Follower of Ashton
		Raymond/Raimondo	Chaplain, Lucy's tutor
Lucrezia Borgia	Donizetti	Alfonso d'Este	Duke of Ferrara, Lucrezia's third husband
		Gennaro	Venetian nobleman, Lucrezia's son
		Gubetta	Servant to Lucrezia
		Lucrezia Borgia	Duchess of Ferrara
		Maffio Orsini	Lucrezia's enemy
		Rustighello	Alfonso's henchman
		Vitellozzo	Nobleman, Gennaro's friend

MUSIC
CLASSICAL

Opera	Composer	Character	Role
Lulu	Berg	Alwa	Writer
		Dr Schön	Editor
		Lulu	Prostitute
		Prince	Traveller in Africa
Madame Butterfly	Puccini	The Bonze	Priest
		Cio-Cio-San	A geisha, Pinkerton's wife
		Goro	Marriage broker
		Kate	Pinkerton's American wife
		Lt Pinkerton	Lieutenant in US Navy
		Sharpless	US consul in Nagasaki
		Suzuki	Servant
		Trouble	Cio-Cio-San's child
		Yamadori	Rich Japanese
Madame Sans-Gêne	Giordano	Catarina	Laundress
The Magic Flute	Mozart	Monostatos	Servant
		Pamina	Daughter of Queen of the Night
		Papagena	Destined to be Papageno's wife
		Papageno	Bird catcher
		Sarastro	High priest
Manon	Massenet	Chevalier des Grieux	Manon's love
		Comte des Grieux	Chevalier's father
		de Bretigny	A nobleman
		Lescaut	A gambler
		Manon	Lescaut's cousin
Marouf	Rabaud	Ahmed	Pastry cook
		Ali	Marouf's friend
		Fatimah	Marouf's wife
		Marouf	Shoemaker
		Vizier	Sultan's adviser
The Marriage of Figaro	Mozart	Almaviva	Count
		Antonio	Gardener
		Barbarina	Antonio's daughter
		Cherubino	Page
		Don Basilio	Organist
		Don Curzio	Lawyer
		Figaro	Servant to Almaviva
		Marcellina	Housekeeper
		Susanna	Maid
A Masked Ball	Verdi	Amelia	Riccardo's love, wife of Renato
		Oscar	Riccardo's page
		Renato	Riccardo's secretary
		Riccardo	Governor of Louisiana
		Silvano	A young sailor
		Ulrica	Fortune teller
The Mastersingers of Nuremberg	Wagner	Augustin Moser	Mastersinger and tailor
		Balthasar Zorn	Mastersinger and pewterer
		Sixtus Beckmesser	Mastersinger and town clerk
		Conrad Nachtigall	Mastersinger and bucklemaker
		David	Hans Sachs's apprentice
		Eva	Pogner's daughter
		Fritz Kothner	Mastersinger and baker
		Hans Foltz	Mastersinger and coppersmith
		Hans Sachs	Mastersinger and cobbler
		Hans Schwarz	Mastersinger and stocking weaver
		Hermann Ortel	Mastersinger and soap boiler
		Kunz Vogelgesang	Mastersinger and furrier
		Magdalena	Nurse
		Ulrich Eisslinger	Mastersinger and grocer
		Veit Pogner	Mastersinger and goldsmith (Eva's father)
		Walter von Stolzing	Franconian knight
Mathis der Maler	Hindemith	Albrecht von Brandenburg	Archbishop of Mainz
		Mathis	Painter (Grünewald)
		Riedinger	Rich Lutheran
		Truchsess von Waldburg	Leader of the army
		Ursula	Riedinger's daughter
		Wolfgang Capito	Councillor
The Mother of Us All	Thomson	Susan B Anthony	American suffragette
Nabucco	Verdi	Abdallo	Nabucco's officer
		Abigaille	Nabucco's adopted daughter

Opera	Composer	Character	Role
		Fenena	Nabucco's daughter
		Nabucco	Nebuchadnezzar, King of Babylon
		Zaccaria	High Priest of Jerusalem
Norma	Bellini	Adalgisa	Temple virgin
		Clotilde	Norma's friend
		Flavio	Centurion
		Norma	Druid priestess
		Oroveso	Norma's father
		Pollione	Proconsul of Rome
Oberon	Weber	Abdullah	Pirate
		Babekan	Saracen prince
		Charlemagne	Emperor of the Franks
		Fatima	Reiza's companion
		Haroun al Rashid	Calif of Baghdad
		Namouna	Fatima's grandmother
		Reiza	Haroun el Rashid's daughter
Oedipus Rex	Stravinsky	Creon	Jocasta's brother
		Jocasta	Wife of Oedipus
		Oedipus	King of Thebes
		Tiresias	Blind soothsayer
Orfeo et Euridice	Gluck	Amor	God of love
		Euridice	Orfeo's wife
		Orfeo	Singer poet
Otello	Verdi	Cassio	Lieutenant
		Lodovico	Venetian ambassador
		Montano	Otello's predecessor
I Pagliacci	Leoncavallo	Beppe	Harlequin
		Canio	Pagliaccio (clown)
		Nedda	Canio's wife
		Silvio	In love with Nedda
		Tonio	Clown
Palestrina	Pfitzner	Avosmediano	Bishop of Cadiz
		Ighino	Palestrina's son
		Lucretia	Palestrina's wife
		Palestrina	Composer
Parsifal	Wagner	Amfortas	King of the Grail
		King Titurel	Father of Amfortas
		Klingsor	Magician
		Kundry	Bewitched woman
		Parsifal	Knight of the Holy Grail
Pelléas et Mélisande	Debussy	Geneviève	Mother of Pelléas
		Golaud	Arkel's grandson
		Mélisande	Golaud's wife
		Pelléas	Arkel's grandson
		Ynlold	Golaud's son
Peter Grimes	Britten	Bob Boles	Fisherman
		Ellen Orford	Schoolteacher
		John	Peter's apprentice
		Ned Keene	Apothecary
		Peter Grimes	Fisherman
The Pilgrim's Progress	Vaughan Williams	Apollyon	Fallen angel
		Mistrust	Neighbour
		Obstinate	Neighbour
		Pilgrim	Pilgrim
		Pliable	Neighbour
		Timorous	Neighbour
		Watchful	Porter
The Poisoned Kiss	Vaughan Williams	Amaryllus	Empress's son
		Angelica	Tormentilla's maid
		Dipsacus	Magician
		Gallanthus	Amaryllus's sister
		Hob	Servant of Dipsacus
		Lob	Assistant of Dipsacus
		Tormentilla	Daughter of Dipsacus
Porgy and Bess	Gershwin	Bess	Porgy's mistress, formerly Crown's
		Clara	Jake's wife
		Crown	Stevedore
		Frazier	Catfish Row 'lawyer'
		Jake	Fisherman
		Jim	Cotton picker
		Lily	Strawberry woman

MUSIC CLASSICAL

Opera	Composer	Character	Role
		Maria	Cookshop keeper
		Mr Archdale	White man
		Peter	Honey-man
		Porgy	A crippled beggar
		Sportin' Life	Dope dealer
Prince Igor	Borodin	Eroshka	Gudok player
		Gzak	Polovtsian Khan
		Jaroslavna	Prince Igor's wife
		Kontchak	Polovtsian Khan
		Kontchakovna	Kontchak's daughter
		Ovlour	Polovtsian traitor
		Prince Igor	Prince of Seversk
		Vladimir Igorevitch	Igor's son
		Vladimir Yaroslavovitch	Yaroslavna's brother
The Rake's Progress	Stravinsky	Baba the Turk	Bearded lady
		Tom Rakewell	The Rake
		Trulove	Anne's father
The Rape of Lucretia	Britten	Bianca	Nurse
		Collatinus	Soldier
		Junius	Roman general
		Lucia	Lucretia's attendant
		Lucretia	Wife of Collatinus
Rienzi	Wagner	Adriano	Colonna's son
		Baroncelli	Roman citizen
		Cola Rienzi	Papal legate
		Irene	Rienzi's sister
		Paolo Orsini	Patrician
		Raimondo	Papal legate
Rigoletto	Verdi	Cavaliere Marullo	Courtier
		Duke of Mantua	Nobleman
		Gilda	Rigoletto's daughter
		Maddalena	Sparafucile's sister
		Matteo Borsa	Courtier
		Rigoletto	Gilda's father, a jester
Der Ring des Nibelungen	Wagner	Alberich	Nibelung dwarf
		Brünnhilde	Valkyrie
		Donner	Norse god
		Erda	Earth goddess
		Fafner	Giant, builder of Valhalla
		Fasolt	Giant, builder of Valhalla
		Flosshilde	Rhinemaiden
		Freia	Goddess of youth and beauty
		Fricka	Wotan's wife
		Froh	Norse god
		Gerhilde	Valkyrie
		Grimgerde	Valkyrie
		Gunther	Hagen's half-brother
		Gutrune	Gunther's sister
		Helmwige	Valkyrie
		Hunding	Siegmund's enemy
		Loge	Norse god
		Mime	A Nibelung
		Ortlinde	Valkyrie
		Rossweisse	Valkyrie
		Siegfried	Son of Siegmund and Sieglunde
		Sieglunde	Siegmund's twin sister
		Siegmund	Mortal son of Wotan
		Waltraute	Valkyrie
		Wellgunde	Rhine maiden
		Woglinde	Rhine maiden
		Wotan	Norse god
La Rondine	Puccini	Bianca	Magda's friend
		Crébillon	Perichaud's friend
		Lisette	Magda's maid
		Magda	Salon owner, Rambaldo's mistress
		Périchaud	Rambaldo's friend
		Prunier	Poet
		Rambaldo	Banker
		Ruggero	Son of Rambaldo's childhood friend
		Suzy	Magda's friend
		Yvette	Magda's friend

Opera	Composer	Character	Role
Der Rosenkavalier	Richard Strauss	Annina	Valzacchi's partner
		Baron Ochs	Sophie's would-be suitor
		Faninal	Sophie's father
		Mahomet	Negro page
		Marianne	Sophie's duenna
		Marschallin	Princess
		Octavian	Bearer of the Rose
		Sophie	Daughter of Faninal
		Valzacchi	Scandalmonger
Ruddigore	Sullivan	Mad Margaret	Mad woman
Ruslan and Lyudmila	Glinka	Bayan	Bard
		Chernomor	An evil dwarf
		Farlaf	Warrior
		Finn	Wizard
		Gorislava	Ratmir's lover
		Lyudmila	a noblewoman
		Naina	Witch
		Ratmir	Knight, suitor to Lyudmila
		Ruslan	Suitor to Lyudmila
		Svyetozer	Lyudmila's father
Salome	Richard Strauss	Herod	Ruler of Galilee
		Herodias	Herod's wife
		John the Baptist	Jewish prophet
		Narraboth	Captain of the Guard
		Salome	Daughter of Herodias
Samson et Dalila	Saint-Saëns	Abimielech	Satrap of Gaza
The Secret Marriage	Cimarosa	Carolina	Geronimo's daughter
		Elisetta	Geronimo's older daughter
		Fidalma	Geronimo's sister
		Geronimo	Citizen of Bologna
		Paolino	Carolina's secret husband
The Sleepwalker	Bellini	Amina	The sleepwalking girl
(La Sonnambula)		Elvino	Farmer
Il Tabarro	Puccini	Giorgetta	Michele's wife
		Luigi	Stevedore, Giorgetta's lover
		Michele	Barge owner
		Talpa	Stevedore
		Tinca	Stevedore
The Tales of Hoffmann	Offenbach	Chochenille	Spalanzani's servant
		Coppelius	Scientist
		Dapertutto	Sorcerer
		Dr Miracle	Doctor
		Frantz	Crespel's servant
		Hermann	Student
		Hoffmann	Poet
		Lindorf	Councillor of Nuremberg
		Luther	Innkeeper
		Nathanael	Student
		Nicklaus	Hoffmann's friend
		Olympia	Mechanical doll
		Pittichinaccio	Giulietta's admirer
		Spalanzani	Inventor
		Stella	Opera singer
Tannhäuser	Wagner	Biterolf	Knight
		Elisabeth	Hermann's niece
		Hermann	Landgrave of Thuringia
		Reinmar von Zweter	Knight
		Tannhäuser	Knight
		Venus	Supernatural seductress
		Walther von der Vogelweide	Knight
		Wolfram	Knight
Tosca	Puccini	Baron Scarpia	Chief of Police
		Cavaradossi	Painter
		Cesare Angelotti	Escaped political prisoner
		Mario Cavaradossi	Painter
		Tosca	Singer
La Traviata	Verdi	Alfredo Germont	Violetta's lover (a singer)
		Annina	Violetta's confidante
		Douphol	Baron
		Violetta Valery	Courtesan

MUSIC CLASSICAL

Opera	Composer	Character	Role
Tristan und Isolde	Wagner	Brangäne	Isolde's maid
		Isolde	Irish princess
		King Marke	King of Cornwall
		Kurvenal	Tristan's retainer
		Melot	Courtier
		Tristan	Cornish knight
The Trojans (Les Troyens)	Berlioz	Andromaque	Hector's widow
		Chorèbe	Cassandra's lover
		Hylas	Trojan sailor
		Iopas	Poet
		Narbal	Dido's minister
		Panthée	Priest
		Polyxène	Priam's daughter
		Priam	King of Troy
Il Trovatore	Verdi	Azucena	Gypsy woman
		Count de Luna	Count of Aragon
		Ferrando	Captain of the Guard
		Manrico	Troubadour
		Leonora	Beloved of Manrico
The Tsar Has His Photograph Taken	Weill	Angèle	Photographer
Turandot	Busoni	Adelma	Turandot's slave
		Barak	Servant
		Calaf	Suitor to Turandot
		Pantalone	Minister
		Queen Mother of Samarkand	Negress
Turandot	Puccini	Calaf	Suitor to Turandot
		Emperor Altoum	Turandot's father
		Liù	Slave girl
		Pang	Lord of Provisions
		Ping	Chinese Grand Chancellor
		Pong	Lord of the Imperial Kitchen
		Princess Turandot	Daughter of Altoum
A Village Romeo and Juliet	Delius	The Dark Fiddler	Real owner of land
		Manz	Farmer
		Marti	Farmer
		Sali	Manz's daughter
		Vreli	Marti's daughter
Wozzeck	Berg	Marie	Prostitute
		Wozzeck	Soldier
The Wreckers	Smyth	Lawrence	Lighthouse keeper
Zazà	Leoncavallo	Bussy	Journalist
		Cascart	Music-hall performer
		Duclou	Stage manager
		Mme Dufresne	Milio's wife
		Lartigen	Monologist
		Marco	Dufresne's butler
		Marlardot	Music-hall owner
		Michelin	Journalist
		Milio Dufresne	Zaza's lover
		Natalia	Zazà's maid
		Toto	Dufresne's child
		Zazà	Music-hall singer

Operas and Operettas

Operas and operettas	Composer	First performance	Librettist	General information
Adriana Lecouvreur	Francesco Cilea	1902	Milan	Colautti	
L'Africaine	Giacomo Meyerbeer	1865	London, Paris, New York	Scribe	
Ägyptische Helena	Richard Strauss	1928	Dresden	Hofmannsthal	
Aida	Giuseppe Verdi	1871	Cairo	Ghislanzoni	
Akhnaten	Philip Glass	1984	Stuttgart	Glass (Richard Riddell, Robert Israel and Shalom Goldman helped with the libretto)	
Albert Herring	Benjamin Britten	1947	Glyndebourne	Crozier	
Alceste	Christoph Gluck	1767	Vienna	Calzabigi	
Aleko	Sergei Rachmaninov	1893	Moscow	Nemirovich-Danchenko	
Alfred	Thomas Arne	1740	London	Thomson and Mallet	Contains song 'Rule, Britannia'
Almira	George Frederick Handel	1705	Hamburg	Feustking	Handel's first opera
Alzira	Giuseppe Verdi	1845	Naples	Cammarano	
Amahl and the Night Visitors	Gian Carlo Menotti	1951	New York	Menotti	First opera written for TV
Amelia Goes to the Ball	Gian Carlo Menotti	1937	Berlin	Menotti	
L'Amico Fritz	Pietro Mascagni	1891	Rome	Daspuro	
Amleto (Hamlet)	Franco Faccio	1865	Genoa	Boito	
Andrea Chénier	Umberto Giordano	1896	Milan	Illica	
Aniara	Karl-Birger Blomdahl	1959	Stockholm	Lindegren	
Anne Boleyn	Gaetano Donizetti	1830	Milan	Romani	
Antar	Gabriel Dupont	1921	Paris	Dupont	
Antony and Cleopatra	Samuel Barber	1966	New York (Met)	Zeffirelli and Barber	
Arabella	Richard Strauss	1933	Dresden	Hofmannsthal	
Ariadne auf Naxos	Richard Strauss	1916	Vienna	Hofmannsthal	
Ariane et Barbe-bleu	Paul Dukas	1907	Paris	Maeterlinck	
Arlecchino (Harlequin)	Ferruccio Busoni	1917	Zurich	Busoni	
Armide	Christoph Gluck	1777	Paris	Quinault	
Artaxerxes	Thomas Arne	1762	London	Metastasio	
At the Boar's Head	Gustav Holst	1925	Manchester	Holst	
The Barber of Seville	Giovanni Paisiello	1782	St Petersburg	Petrosellini	
The Barber of Seville	Gioachino Rossini	1816	Rome	Sterbini	Based on Beaumarchais comedy
The Bartered Bride	Bedrich Smetana	1866	Prague	Sabina	
The Bassarids	Hans Werner Henze	1966	Salzburg	Auden and Kallman	
The Bear	William Walton	1967	Aldeburgh	Dehn	
Beatrice Cenci	Berthold Goldschmidt	1988	London	Esslin	Prizewinner in Festival of Britain Competition 1951
Béatrice et Bénédict	Hector Berlioz	1862	Baden-Baden	Berlioz	
The Beautiful Galathea	Franz von Suppe	1865	Vienna	Henrion	
The Beggar's Opera	Christoph Pepusch	1728	London	Gay	
Belfagor	Ottorino Respighi	1923	Milan	Morselli and Gaustalla	
Belisario	Gaetano Donizetti	1836	Venice	Cammarano	
La Belle Hélène	Jacques Offenbach	1864	Paris	Meilhac and Halévy	

Operas and operettas	Composer	First performance		Librettist	General information
The Bells of Corneville	Robert Planquette	Paris and New York	1877	Clairville and Gabet	
Benvenuto Cellini	Hector Berlioz	Paris	1838	Wailly and Barbier	
Berenice	George Frederick Handel	London	1737	Salvi	
Billy Budd	Benjamin Britten	London	1951	Forster and Crozier	Ship: HMS Indomitable
The Black Mask	Krzysztof Penderecki	Salzburg	1986	Kupfer and Penderecki	
Blond Eckbert	Judith Weir	London	1994	Weir	
Boccaccio	Franz von Suppé	Vienna	1879	Zell and Génée	
La Bohème	Ruggiero Leoncavallo	Venice	1897	Leoncavallo	
La Bohème	Giacomo Puccini	Turin	1896	Giacosa and Illica	Title translates as La Bohème, though not the same story
The Bohemian Girl	Michael Balfe	London	1843	Bunn	
Boris Godunov	Modeste Mussorgsky	St Petersburg	1874	Mussorgsky	
Boulevard Solitude	Hans Werner Henze	Hanover	1952	Henze and Weil	
Die Brautwahl	Ferruccio Busoni	Hamburg	1912	Busoni, after Hoffmann	
The Burning Fiery Furnace	Benjamin Britten	Orford	1966	Plomer	
The Caliph of Baghdad	François Boieldieu	Paris	1800	Saint-Just	
La Calisto	Pietro Francesco Cavalli	Venice	1651	Faustini	
La Campana Sommersa	Ottorino Respighi	Hamburg	1927	Guastalla	Title translates as The Submerged Bell
Candide	Leonard Bernstein	Boston	1956	Hellmann	
El Capitán	John Philip Sousa	New York and Boston	1896	Klein	
Capriccio	Richard Strauss	Munich	1942	Krauss and Strauss	
I Capuleti e i Montecchi	Vincenzo Bellini	Venice	1830	Romani	The Capulets and the Montagues, i.e. Romeo and Juliet
Cardillac	Paul Hindemith	Dresden	1926	Lion	
Caritas	Robert Saxton	Wakefield	1991	Wesker	
Carmen	Georges Bizet	Paris	1875	Meilhac and Halévy	Carmen dies by stabbing (at the hands of Don José)
Castor and Pollux	Jean-Philippe Rameau	Paris	1737	Bernard	
The Catiline Conspiracy	Iain Hamilton	Stirling	1974	Hamilton	
Cavalleria Rusticana	Pietro Mascagni	Rome	1890	Menasci and Targioni-Tozzetti	
Cendrillon (Cinderella)	Nicolò Isouard	Paris	1810	Étienne	
Cendrillon (Cinderella)	Jules Massenet	Paris	1899	Henry Cain	
La Cenerentola (Cinderella)	Gioachino Rossini	Rome	1817	Ferretti	
Chérubin	Jules Massenet	Monte Carlo	1905	Henry Cain and Francis de Croisset	The story of Cherubino after the marriage of Figaro
Cheryomushki	Dmitry Shostakovich	Moscow	1959	Mass and Chervinsky	Shostakovich's only operetta
The Chocolate Soldier	Oscar Straus	Vienna	1908	Jacobson and Bernauer	Based on G B Shaw's play Arms and the Man
Christmas Eve	Nikolay Rimsky-Korsakov	St Petersburg	1895	Rimsky-Korsakov	Based on Gogol story
Le Cid	Jules Massenet	Paris	1885	D'Ennery, Gallet and Blau	
La Clemenza di Tito	Wolfgang Amadeus Mozart	Prague	1791	Metastasio	Mozart's last opera
Comedy on the Bridge	Bohuslav Martinu	Prague (Radio)	1937	Martinu	
Conchita	Riccardo Zandonai	Milan	1911	Vaucaire and Zangarini	
Confessions of a Justified Sinner	Thomas Wilson	York	1976	John Currie	Based on the novel by James Hogg
The Consul	Gian Carlo Menotti	Philadelphia	1950	Menotti	The Consul represents bureaucratic red tape

Operas and operettas	Composer	First performance	Librettist	General information
Le Coq d'Or	Nikolay Rimsky-Korsakov	1909	Moscow	Belsky	Rimsky-Korsakov's 14th and last opera
The Coronation of Poppaea	Claudio Monteverdi	1643	Venice	Busenello	Monteverdi's last opera
Der Corregidor (The Magistrate)	Hugo Wolf	1896	Mannheim	Mayreder	Based on The Three-Cornered Hat by Alarcón
Il Corsaro	Giuseppe Verdi	1848	Trieste	Piave	Based on Byron's poem The Corsair
Così fan tutte	Wolfgang Amadeus Mozart	1790	Vienna	da Ponte	Role of Fiordiligi long regarded as unsingable
The Count of Luxemburg	Franz Lehár	1909	Vienna	Willner and Bodanzky	
Cox and Box	Arthur Sullivan	1867	London	Burnand	
The Cunning Little Vixen	Leoš Janáček	1924	Brno	Janáček	
Curlew River	Benjamin Britten	1964	Orford	Plomer	A church parable
Dafne	Jacopo Peri	1598	Florence	Rinuccini	Generally regarded to be the earliest opera
Dalibor	Bedrich Smetana	1868	Prague	Spindler	Translation of German text by Joseph Wenzig
La Dame Blanche (White Lady)	François Boieldieu	1825	Paris	Scribe	Based on Scott's The Monastery and Guy Mannering
Danton's Death	Gottfried Von Einem	1947	Salzburg	Blacher and Von Einem	Based on drama by Büchner
Daphne	Richard Strauss	1938	Dresden	Gregor	
Dardanus	Jean-Philipe Rameau	1739	Paris	De La Bruyère	
The Daughter of the Regiment	Gaetano Donizetti	1840	Paris	Saint-Georges and Bayard	
David	Darius Milhaud	1954	Jerusalem	Lunel	
Day of Peace (Friedenstag)	Richard Strauss	1938	Munich	Gregor	
Death in Venice	Benjamin Britten	1973	Aldeburgh	Myfanwy Piper	
Debora e Jaële	Ildebrando Pizzetti	1922	Milan	Pizzetti	
Deidamia	George Frederick Handel	1741	London	Rolli	Handel's last opera
The Deserted Island	Franz Joseph Haydn	1779	Esterháza	Metastasio	Also the title of an opera by G Scarlatti
Les Deux Journées (The Two Days)	Luigi Cherubini	1800	Paris	Bouilly	Known in Britain as The Water Carrier
Les Dialogues des Carmélites	Francis Poulenc	1957	Milan, Paris, San Francisco	Lavery	
Dido and Aeneas	Henry Purcell	1689	Chelsea	Nahum Tate	
A Dinner Engagement	Lennox Berkeley	1954	Aldeburgh	Paul Dehn	
Doctor Miracle	Georges Bizet	1857	Paris	Battu and Halévy	Joint winner of the Offenbach Prize with Lecocq
Doctor Miracle	Charles Lecocq	1857	Paris	Battu and Halévy	Joint winner of the Offenbach Prize with Bizet
The Doctor of Myddfai	Peter Maxwell Davies	1996	Cardiff	Pountney	
Doktor Faust	Ferruccio Busoni	1925	Dresden	Busoni	Completed after Busoni's death by Jarnach
Dollar Princess	Leo Fall	1907	Vienna	Willner and Grünbaum	
Don Carlos	Giuseppe Verdi	1867	Paris	Méry and Du Locle	Also known as Don Carlo
Don Giovanni	Wolfgang Amadeus Mozart	1787	Prague	Da Ponte	Based on Bertati's Don Juan (1775)
Don Pasquale	Gaetano Donizetti	1843	Paris and London	Ruffini	
Don Quixote	Jules Massenet	1910	Monte Carlo	Henry Cain	
The Duenna	Roberto Gerhard	1949	BBC Radio	Gerhard and Hassall	Based on Sheridan work
The Duenna	Sergey Prokofiev	1946	Leningrad	Prokofiev and Mendelson	Based on Sheridan work
Duke Bluebeard's Castle	Béla Bartók	1918	Budapest	Béla Balázs	
Duke of Alba	Gaetano Donizetti	1882	Rome	Scribe	Completed by Salvi
The Dwarf (Der Zwerg)	Alexander Zemlinsky	1922	Cologne	G C Klaren	Based on Oscar Wilde's The Birthday of the Infanta
Edgar	Giacomo Puccini	1889	Milan	Fontana	
Einstein on the Beach	Philip Glass	1976	Avignon	Knowles, Childs, Johnson	Composed in collaboration with Robert Wilson
Electrification of the Soviet Union	Nigel Osborne	1987	Glyndebourne	Craig Raine	Based on Pasternak's 'Last Summer' and

MUSIC CLASSICAL

Operas and operettas	Composer	First performance	Librettist	General information
Elegy for Young Lovers	Hans Werne Henze	Schwetzingen 1961	Auden and Kallman	'Spectorsky'
Elektra	Richard Strauss	Dresden 1909	Hofmannsthal	
L'Elisir d'Amore	Gaetano Donizetti	Milan 1832	Romani	
Elizabeth, Queen of England	Gioachino Rossini	Naples 1815	Giovanni Schmidt	Based on Sophia Lee's novel The Recess
The Emerald Isle	Arthur Sullivan	London (Savoy) 1901	Basil Hood	Posthumous comic opera completed by Edward German
The Emperor Jones	Louis Gruenberg	New York 1933	de Jaffa	
L'Enfant et les Sortilèges	Maurice Ravel	Monte Carlo 1925	Colette	
The English Cat	Hans Werner Henze	Schwetzingen 1983	Edward Bond	
Ernani	Giuseppe Verdi	Venice 1844	Piave	Based on Victor Hugo's play Hernani
Esclarmonde	Jules Massenet	Paris 1889	Blau and de Gramont	
L'Étoile (The Star)	Emmanuel Chabrier	Paris 1877	Leterrier and Vanloo	
L'Étoile du Nord (The North Star)	Giacomo Meyerbeer	Paris 1854	Scribe	
Eugene Onegin	Pyotr Tchaikovsky	Moscow 1879	Shilovsky and Tchaikovsky	
Euryanthe	Carl Maria Weber	Vienna 1823	Helmina von Chézy	
The Excursions of Mr Brouček	Leoš Janáček	Prague 1920	Janáček	
The Fair Maid of Perth	Georges Bizet	Paris 1867	St George and Adenis	Based on Sir Walter Scott's play of the same name
The Faithful Shepherd	George Frederick Handel	London 1712	Rossi	Based on Guarini's play
The Fall of the House of Usher	Claude Debussy	New Haven 1977	Debussy	Based on Edgar Allan Poe work but left unfinished and reconstructed by W Harwood
Falstaff	Giuseppe Verdi	Milan 1893	Boito	Verdi's last opera
Fanny Robin	Edward Harper	Edinburgh 1975	Harper	Based on Wessex poems and Far From the Madding Crowd
Faust	Ludwig Spohr	Prague 1816	J K Bernard	Not based on Goethe's Faust
Faust	Charles Gounod	Paris 1859	Barbier and Carré	Based on Carré's Faust et Marguerite and Goethe's Faust
La Favola d'Orfeo	Claudio Monteverdi	Mantua 1607	Striggio	
La Favorite	Gaetano Donizetti	Paris 1840	Royer, Vaëz and Scribe	
Fedora	Umberto Giordano	Milan 1898	Colautti	Based on Sardou's play of the same name
Die Feen (The Fairies)	Richard Wagner	Munich 1888	Wagner	Wagner's first opera
Fennimore and Gerda	Frederick Delius	Frankfurt 1919	Delius	Delius's 6th and last opera
Der Ferne Klang	Franz Schreker	Frankfurt 1912	Schreker	
La Fiamma	Ottorino Respighi	Rome 1934	Guastalla	
Fidelio, or the Triumph of Married Love	Ludwig van Beethoven	Vienna 1805	Josef Sonnleithner	Beethoven's only opera
Fidelity Rewarded	Franz Joseph Haydn	Esterháza 1781	G Lorenzi	
The Fiery Angel	Sergey Prokofiev	Paris 1954	Prokofiev	Prokofiev's Symphony No. 3 uses themes from this opera
La Finta Giardiniera (The Feigned Garden Girl)	Wolfgang Amadeus Mozart	Munich 1775	Uncertain	Mozart's first significant opera
Die Fledermaus (The Bat)	Johann Strauss II	Vienna and New York 1874	Hafner and Genée	Opera in 3 acts although often played in one
The Flying Dutchman	Richard Wagner	Dresden 1843	Wagner	
Die Frau ohne Schatten	Richard Strauss	Vienna 1919	Hofmannsthal	English title: The Woman without a Shadow
From One Day to the Next	Arnold Schoenberg	Frankfurt 1930	Max Blonda	Max Blonda was Gertrud Schoenberg

Operas and operettas	Composer	First performance		Librettist	General information
From the House of the Dead	Leoš Janáček	1930	Brno	Janáček	Based on Dostoyevsky's novel
The Gambler	Sergey Prokofiev	1929	Brussels	Prokofiev	Based on Dostoyevsky's short story
The Gamblers	Dmitry Shostakovich	1978	Leningrad	Shostakovich	Unfinished opera completed by Krzysztof Meyer
Gawain	Harrison Birtwistle	1991	London	David Harsent	
Genoveva	Robert Schumann	1850	Leipzig	Reinick and Schumann	Also the name of an opera by Detlev Müller-Siemens
Gesualdo	Alfred Schnittke	1994	Vienna	Bletschacher	Based on life of the composer Gesualdo
Der Gewaltige Hahnrei	Berthold Goldschmidt	1992	Berlin	Goldschmidt	Composed in 1930
Gianni Schicchi	Giacomo Puccini	1918	New York	Forzano	The third part of Puccini's Il Trittico
La Gioconda	Amilcare Ponchielli	1876	Milan	'Tobia Gorrio' (Arrigo Boito)	Contains the ballet Dance of the Hours (Act 3)
Un Giorno di Regno	Giuseppe Verdi	1840	Milan	Romani	
The Girl of the Golden West (La Fanciulla del West)	Giacomo Puccini	1910	New York (Met)	Civinini and Zangarini	Based on Belasco's play The Girl of the Golden West
Giuditta	Franz Lehár	1934	Vienna	Knepler and Löhner	Lehár's only opera
Gloriana	Benjamin Britten	1953	London	W Plomer	Commissioned for coronation of Elizabeth II
Golem	John Casken	1989	London	Casken and Audi	
Golem	Larry Sitsky	1993	Sydney	Larry Sitsky	
The Gondoliers	Arthur Sullivan	1889	London	W S Gilbert	Aka: 'The King of Barataria'
Götterdämmerung (The Twilight of the Gods)	Richard Wagner	1876	Bayreuth	Wagner	Final opera in his tetralogy Der Ring des Nibelungen
The Government Inspector	Werner Egk	1957	Schwetzingen	Egk	Based on Gogol's story
The Grand Duke	Arthur Sullivan	1896	London and Berlin	W S Gilbert	Aka: 'The Statutory Duel'
Grande Duchesse de Gérolstein	Jacques Offenbach	1867	Paris	Meilhac and Halévy	
The Grand Macabre	György Ligeti	1978	Paris, New York & London	Meschke	
Greek	Mark-Anthony Turnage	1988	Munich	Turnage and Jonathan Moore	Based on Berkoff's play Greek
The Greek Passion	Bohuslav Martinů	1961	Zurich	Martinů and Kazantzakis	Based on Kazantzakis novel Christ Recrucified
Griséldis	Jules Massenet	1901	Paris	Silvestre and Morand	Based on a story in Boccaccio's Decameron
The Growing Castle	Malcolm Williamson	1968	Dynevor	Williamson	Based on Strindberg's dream play
Guntram	Richard Strauss	1894	Weimar	Strauss	Strauss's first opera
Gwendoline	Emmanuel Chabrier	1886	Brussels	Mendès	
The Gypsy Baron (Zigeunerbaron)	Johann Strauss II	1885	Vienna	Schnitzer	
Halka	Stanislaw Moniuszko	1848	Vilnius (Wilno)	Wolski	
Hamlet (3 acts)	Humphrey Searle	1968	Hamburg	Searle	
Hamlet (5 acts)	Ambroise Thomas	1868	Paris	Barbier and Carré	Other operas on the subject by Scarlatti, Gasparini, Mercadante, Grandi, Szokolay
Hans Heiling	Heinrich Marschner	1833	Berlin	Devrient	
Hänsel and Gretel	Engelbert Humperdinck	1893	Weimar	Adelheid Wette	Based on the story by the Brothers Grimm
The Happy Prince	Malcolm Williamson	1965	Farnham	Williamson	
Harmony of the World	Paul Hindemith	1957	Munich	Hindemith	Based on life of Johann Kepler
Henry VIII	Camille Saint-Saëns	1883	Paris	Détroyat and Silvestre	
Hérodiade	Jules Massenet	1881	Brussels	Millet and Grémont	
L'Heure Espagnole	Maurice Ravel	1911	Paris	Franc-Nohain	
Higglety Pigglety Pop!	Oliver Knussen	1985	Glyndebourne	Knussen and Sendak	
Hin und Zurück (There and Back)	Paul Hindemith	1927	Baden Baden	Schiffer	

MUSIC CLASSICAL

Operas and operettas	Composer	First performance	Librettist	General information
Hippolyte et Aricie	Jean-Philippe Rameau	1733	Paris	Abbé Pellegrin	
Historia von D. Johann Fausten	Alfred Schnittke	1995	Hamburg	Morgener and Schnittke	
HMS Pinafore	Arthur Sullivan	1878	London	W S Gilbert	Aka: 'The Lass That Loved a Sailor'
The Horseman	Aulis Sallinen	1975	Savonlinna	Haavikko	
Hugh the Drover	Ralph Vaughan Williams	1924	London	Harold Child	Aka: 'Love in the Stocks'
Les Huguenots	Giacomo Meyerbeer	1836	Paris	Scribe and Deschamps	
The Ice Break	Michael Tippett	1977	Covent Garden	Tippett	
Idomeneo, King of Crete	Wolfgang Amadeus Mozart	1781	Munich	G B Varesco	
Imeneo	George Frederick Handel	1740	London	Anonymous	
The Immortal Hour	Rutland Boughton	1914	Glastonbury	Boughton	
Importance of Being Earnest	Mario Castelnuovo-Tedesco	1975	New York	Castelnuovo-Tedesco	
L'Incoronazione di Poppea	Claudio Monteverdi	1642	Venice	Busenello	
The Indian Queen	Henry Purcell	1695	London	Dryden and R Howard	Concerns Mexican–Peruvian rivalry
Inès de Castro	James MacMillan	1996	Edinburgh	Clifford	
L'infedeltà delusa (Deceit Outwitted)	Franz Joseph Haydn	1773	Eszterháza	Coltellini	
Intermezzo	Richard Strauss	1924	Dresden	Strauss	Two main characters portrayed are Strauss and his wife
Intolleranza	Luigi Nono	1961	Venice	Nono	
The Invisible City of Kitezh	Nikolay Rimsky-Korsakov	1907	St Petersburg	Belsky	
Iolanthe	Arthur Sullivan	1882	London and New York	W S Gilbert	Aka: 'The Peer and the Peri'
Iphigénie en Aulide	Christoph Gluck	1774	Paris	Du Roullet	
Iphigénie en Tauride	Christoph Gluck	1778	Paris	Guillard and Du Roullet	
Iris	Pietro Mascagni	1898	Rome	Illica	
Irish Legend	Werner Egk	1955	Salzburg	Egk	Based on W B Yeats's 'Countess Cathleen'
Irmelin	Frederick Delius	1953	Oxford	Delius	
The Italian Girl in Algiers	Gioachino Rossini	1813	Venice	Anelli	Libretto taken from Mosca's opera of the same name
Ivan IV	Georges Bizet	1951	Bordeaux	F H Leroy and H Trianon	Originally written for Gounod
Ivanhoe	Arthur Sullivan	1891	London	J Sturgis	Based on Sir Walter Scott's novel
The Jacobin	Antonín Dvořák	1889	Prague	M Cervinková-Riegrová	
Jenůfa	Leoš Janáček	1904	Brno	Janáček	Retains title of 'Her Foster-Daughter' in Czech Republic
Jérusalem	Giuseppe Verdi	1847	Paris	Royer and Vaëz	
The Jewels of the Madonna	Ermanno Wolf-Ferrari	1911	Berlin	Golisciani and Zangarini	
The Jewess (La Juive)	Jacques Halévy	1835	Paris	Scribe	
Joan of Arc	Giuseppe Verdi	1845	Milan	Solera	
Le Jongleur de Notre Dame	Jules Massenet	1902	Monte Carlo	Léna	
Jonny Spielt Auf	Ernst Krenek	1927	Leipzig	Krenek	
The Journey to Rheims	Gioachino Rossini	1825	Paris	Balocchi	Full title: The Journey to Rheims or Inn of the Golden Lily
Judith	Arthur Honegger	1926	Monte Carlo	R Morax	
Judith	Eugene Goossens	1929	London and Philadelphia	Arnold Bennett	
Juha	Aarre Merikanto	1958	Finland	Ackté and Aho	
Julien	Gustave Charpentier	1913	Paris	Charpentier	Sequel to Louise
Julietta	Bohuslav Martinů	1938	Prague	Martinů	

Operas and operettas	Composer	First performance		Librettist	General information
Julius Caesar in Egypt	George Frederick Handel	London	1724	N F Haym	Numerous other operas on the theme of Julius Caesar
The Jumping Frog of Calaveras County	Lukas Foss	Indiana	1950	J Karsavina	Based on Mark Twain story
Der Junge Lord (The Young Lord)	Hans Werner Henze	Berlin	1965	I Bachmann	
Der Kaiser von Atlantis	Viktor Ullmann	Terezin	1943	Kien	Premiere in Terezin prison camp banned
Kashchey the Immortal	Nikolay Rimsky-Korsakov	Moscow	1902	Rimsky-Korsakov	
Kate and the Devil	Antonín Dvořák	Prague	1899	A Wenig	
Katerina Izmaylova	Dmitry Shostakovich	Moscow	1934	A Preys and Shostakovich	Revision of Lady Macbeth of the Mtsensk District
Die Kathrin	Erich Korngold	Stockholm	1939	Korngold	
Katya Kabanova	Leoš Janáček	Brno	1921	Janáček	Based on Ostrovsky's play The Storm
Khovanshchina (The Khovansky Affair)	Modest Mussorgsky	St Petersburg	1886	V Stasov and Mussorgsky	Completed by Rimsky-Korsakov
King Arthur, or the British Worthy	Henry Purcell	London	1691	Dryden	Semi-opera, but in reality a play with extensive music
The King Goes Forth to France	Aulis Sallinen	Savonlinna	1984	P Haavikko	
The King of Lahore	Jules Massenet	Paris	1877	L Gallet	
The King of Ys	Édouard-Victor-Antoine Lalo	Paris	1888	Blau	
King Priam	Michael Tippett	Coventry	1962	Tippett	Based on Homer's Iliad
King Roger	Karol Szymanowski	Warsaw	1926	J Iwaszkiewicz	
The King's Children	Engelbert Humperdinck	Munich and London	1897	Ernst Rosmer	Rosmer the pseudonym of Else Bernstein-Porges
The Kiss	Bedrich Smetana	Prague	1876	E Krásnohorská	Based on story by Joanna Muzakova
Die Kluge (The Clever Girl)	Carl Orff	Frankfurt	1943	Orff	Aka The Wise Woman
The Knot Garden	Michael Tippett	Covent Garden	1970	Tippett	
Koanga	Frederick Delius	Elberfeld	1904	C F Keary	Based on G W Gable's novel The Grandissimes
König Hirsch (King Stag)	Hans Werner Henze	Berlin	1956	H von Cramer	
Lady Macbeth of Mtsensk District	Dmitry Shostakovich	Leningrad	1963	A Preys and Shostakovich	See Katerina Izmaylova
Lakmé	Léo Delibes	Paris and Chicago	1883	Gondinet and Gille	
The Lambton Worm	R Sherlaw Johnson	Oxford	1978	Anne Ridler	
The Land of Smiles	Franz Lehár	Vienna	1923	L Herzer and F Löhner	
The Last Temptations	Joonas Kokkonen	Helsinki	1975	L Kokkonen	Based on life of Finnish evangelist Paavo Ruotsalainen
Lear	Aribert Reimann	Munich	1978	Claus Henneberg	
The Legend of Tsar Sultan	Nikolay Rimsky-Korsakov	Moscow	1900	Belsky	Based on Pushkin poem; contains 'The Flight of the Bumble Bee'
Leonora, or Married Love	Pierre Gaveaux	Paris	1798	J N Bouilly	
Let's Make An Opera	Benjamin Britten	Aldeburgh	1949	Eric Crozier	
Das Liebesverbot	Richard Wagner	Magdeburg	1836	Wagner	Based on Shakespeare's Measure for Measure
Life for the Tsar	Mikhail Glinka	St Petersburg	1836	Baron Yegor Rosen	
Life with an Idiot	Alfred Schnittke	Amsterdam	1992	Erofeyev	
The Light Cavalry	Franz von Suppé	Vienna	1866	C Costa	
The Lighthouse	Peter Maxwell Davies	Edinburgh	1980	Davies	
Linda di Chamounix	Gaetano Donizetti	Vienna	1842	Rossi	
The Lodger	Phyllis Tate	London	1960	David Franklin	
Lodoiska	Luigi Cherubini	Paris	1791	Fillette-Loraux	
Lohengrin	Richard Wagner	Weimar	1850	Wagner	Liszt was the conductor at the first performance

Operas and operettas	Composer	First performance	Librettist	General information
I Lombardi	Giuseppe Verdi	1843 Milan	Solera	
The Long Christmas Dinner	Paul Hindemith	1961 Mannheim	Thornton Wilder	
Louise	Gustave Charpentier	1900 Paris	Charpentier	
The Love for Three Oranges	Sergey Prokofiev	1921 Chicago	Prokofiev	
The Love of Danae	Richard Strauss	1952 Salzburg	J Gregor	
The Love of the Three Kings	Italo Montemezzi	1913 La Scala	Benelli	
Lowland (Tiefland)	Eugen D'Albert	1903 Prague	R Lothar	
Lucia di Lammermoor	Gaetano Donizetti	1835 Naples	Cammarano	Based on Scott's novel Bride of Lammermoor (1819)
Lucio Silla	Wolfgang Amadeus Mozart	1772 Milan	G da Gamerra	
Lucrezia Borgia	Gaetano Donizetti	1833 Milan	Romani	
Luisa Miller	Giuseppe Verdi	1849 Naples	Cammarano	
Lulu	Alban Berg	1937 Zurich	Berg	
Macbeth	Giuseppe Verdi	1847 Florence	Plave	
Macbeth	Ernest Bloch	1910 Paris	Edmond Fleg	
Macbeth	Lawrance Collingwood	1934 London	Collingwood	
Madame Angot's Daughter	Charles Lecocq	1872 Brussels	Clairville, Siraudin and Koning	
Madame Butterfly	Giacomo Puccini	1904 Milan	Giacosa and Illica	Based on Belasco's play
Madame Sans-Gêne	Umberto Giordano	1915 New York and Turin	Simoni	
Maddalena	Sergey Prokofiev	1978 Manchester	Prokofiev	Completed by Edward Downes
The Magic Flute	Wolfgang Amadeus Mozart	1791 Vienna	Schikaneder	
The Magic Fountain	Frederick Delius	1977 London	Delius; Jutta Bell and Delius	
The Magic Island (Die Zauberinsel)	Heinrich Sutermeister	1942 Dresden	Sutermeister	Based on Shakespeare's The Tempest
The Maid of Orleans	Pyotr Tchaikovsky	1881 St Petersburg	Tchaikovsky	
The Maid of Pskov	Nikolay Rimsky-Korsakov	1873 St Petersburg	Rimsky-Korsakov	
The Makropulos Affair	Leoš Janáček	1926 Brno	Janáček	Based on Karel Čapek's play
Les Mamelles de Tirésias	Francis Poulenc	1947 Paris	Poulenc	Based on Apollinaire play
Manon	Jules Massenet	1884 Paris	Meilhac and Gille	Based on Prévost's novel Manon Lescaut
Manon Lescaut	Giacomo Puccini	1893 Turin	Giacosa, Illica, Ricordi, Praga and Oliva	
Margot la Rouge	Frederick Delius	1981 BBC Radio	Rosenval	Composed 1902
Maria di Rohan	Gaetano Donizetti	1843 Vienna	Cammarano	
Maria Golovin	Gian Carlo Menotti	1958 Brussels and New York	Menotti	
Maria Stuarda	Gaetano Donizetti	1835 Milan	G Bardari	Based on Schiller's play
Maritana	Vincent Wallace	1845 London	E Fitzball	
Marouf	Henri Rabaud	1914 Paris	Népoty	
The Marriage	Bohuslav Martinů	1954 Hamburg	Martinů	First airing was on American television (NBC) in 1953
The Marriage	Modest Mussorgsky	1917 Petrograd	Mussorgsky	
The Marriage of Figaro	Wolfgang Amadeus Mozart	1786 Vienna	Da Ponte	Based on Beaumarchais play
Martha, or Richmond Fair	Friedrich von Flotow	1847 Vienna	W Friedrich	
The Martyrdom of St Magnus	Peter Maxwell Davies	1977 Kirkwall	Davies	First performance, St Magnus Cathedral, Kirkwall, Orkney
Mary of Egypt	John Tavener	1992 Aldeburgh	Mother Thekla	
Mary, Queen of Scots	Thea Musgrave	1977 Edinburgh	Musgrave	Also the name of a ballet by John McCabe

Operas and operettas	Composer	First performance		Librettist	General information
The Mask of Orpheus	Harrison Birtwistle	1986	London	Peter Zinovieff	
Maskarade	Carl Nielsen	1906	Copenhagen	V Andersen	
A Masked Ball	Giuseppe Verdi	1859	Rome	Antonio Somma	
I Masnadieri (The Robbers)	Giuseppe Verdi	1847	London	Maffei	Based on incident in Cervantes' Don Quixote
Master Peter's Puppet Show	Manuel de Falla	1923	Seville	Falla	
The Mastersingers of Nuremberg	Richard Wagner	1868	Munich	Wagner	
Mathis der Maler (Matthias the Painter)	Paul Hindemith	1938	Zurich	Hindemith	Based on life of Matthias Grünewald
Mavra	Igor Stravinsky	1922	Paris	Kochno	
May Night	Nikolay Rimsky-Korsakov	1880	St Petersburg	Rimsky-Korsakov	Based on Gogol story
Mazeppa	Pyotr Tchaikovsky	1884	Moscow	Tchaikovsky and Burenin	
Medea (Médée)	Luigi Cherubini	1797	Paris	F B Hoffman	
The Medium	Gian Carlo Menotti	1946	Columbia University	Menotti	
Mephistopheles	Arrigo Boito	1868	Milan	Boito	Based on Goethe's Faust
Merrie England	Edward German	1902	London (Savoy)	Basil Hood	
The Merry Widow	Franz Lehár	1905	Vienna	V Léon and L Stein	Widow's name is Hanna Glawari
The Merry Wives of Windsor	Otto Nicolai	1849	Berlin	S H Mosenthal	
The Midsummer Marriage	Michael Tippett	1955	London	Tippett	
A Midsummer Night's Dream	Benjamin Britten	1960	Aldeburgh	Pears and Britten	Based on Goethe's novel Wilhelm Meisters Lehrjahre
Mignon	Ambroise Thomas	1866	Paris	Barbier and Carré	Aka: The Town of Titipu
The Mikado	Arthur Sullivan	1885	London	W S Gilbert	
The Mines of Sulphur	Richard Rodney Bennett	1965	London	Beverley Cross	
Mireille	Charles Gounod	1864	London and Paris	Carré	
The Miserly Knight	Sergei Rachmaninov	1906	Moscow	Rachmaninov	Based on Strindberg's play
Miss Donnithorne's Maggot	Peter Maxwell Davies	1974	Adelaide	Randolph Stow	Other version by Rorem and Bibalo
Miss Julie	Ned Rorem	1965	New York	Kenward Elmslie	
Miss Julie	William Alwyn	1976	Broadcast	Alwyn	
Mitridate, Rè di Ponto	Wolfgang Amadeus Mozart	1770	Milan	V A Cigna-Santi	
Mlada	Nikolay Rimsky-Korsakov	1892	St Petersburg	Rimsky-Korsakov	
Monday From Light	Karlheinz Stockhausen	1988	Milan	Stockhausen	
Monsieur Beaucaire	André Messager	1919	Birmingham	Lonsdale and Ross	Based on Booth Tarkington's story
The Moon (Der Mond)	Carl Orff	1939	Munich	Orff	
Moses in Egypt	Gioachino Rossini	1818	Naples	A L Tottola	
Moses und Aron	Arnold Schoenberg	1954	Hamburg	Schoenberg	
The Mother (Matka)	Alois Hába	1931	Munich	Hába	
The Mother of Us All	Virgil Thomson	1947	New York	Stein	Gertrude Stein and Virgil Thomson are characters
Mozart and Salieri	Nikolay Rimsky-Korsakov	1898	Moscow	Rimsky-Korsakov	
La Muette de Portici	Daniel Auber	1828	Paris	Scribe and Delavigne	Aka: Masaniello
Nabucco (Nebuchadnezzar)	Giuseppe Verdi	1842	Milan	T Solera	
La Navarraise	Jules Massenet	1894	Covent Garden	Jules Claretie and Henri Cain	
Nelson	Lennox Berkeley	1953	London	Alan Pryce-Jones	
Nero (Nerone)	Arrigo Boito	1924	Milan	Boito	
Nero (Nerone)	Pietro Mascagni	1935	Milan	Targioni-Tozzetti	
Neues vom Tage (News of the Day)	Paul Hindemith	1929	Berlin	Marcellus Schiffer	

Operas and operettas	Composer	First performance		Librettist	General information
New Year	Michael Tippett	1989	Houston	Tippett	
A Night at the Chinese Opera	Judith Weir	1987	Cheltenham	Weir	
The Night Bell	Gaetano Donizetti	1836	Naples	Donizetti	
A Night in Paris	Frederick Delius	1982	London	Rosenval	
A Night in Venice	Johann Strauss II	1883	Berlin	F Zell (Camillo Walzel) and Génée	
The Nightingale (Le Rossignol)	Igor Stravinsky	1914	Paris and London	Stravinsky and S Mitusov	
Nixon in China	John Adams	1987	Houston	Alice Goodman	
Norma	Vincenzo Bellini	1831	Milan	Romani	
The Nose	Dmitry Shostakovich	1930	Leningrad	Zamyatin, Yunin, Preys	Based Gogol story. Shostakovich wrote part of libretto
Notre Dame	Franz Schmidt	1914	Vienna	Leopold Wilk and Schmidt	
Noye's Fludde	Benjamin Britten	1958	Aldeburgh	Britten	Based on Chester miracle play
Oberon, or the Elf-King's Oath	Carl Maria Weber	1826	Covent Garden	J R Planché	
L'Oca del Cairo	Wolfgang Amadeus Mozart	1860	Frankfurt	Varesco	Unfinished opera buffa
Oedipus	George Enescu	1936	Paris	E Fleg	
Oedipus Rex	Igor Stravinsky	1927	Paris	J Cocteau	From Sophocles
The Olympians	Arthur Bliss	1949	London	J B Priestley	
The Opera Ball	Richard Heuberger	1898	Vienna	Léon and Waldeberg	Contains the aria 'Geh'n wir in's Chambre séparée'
The Oracle	Franco Leoni	1905	Covent Garden	C Zanoni	Based on story The Cat and the Cherub by C B Fernald
Orfeo ed Euridice	Christoph Gluck	1762	Vienna	Calzabigi	
Orlando	George Frederick Handel	1733	London	Anon	Based on Ariosto's 16th-century poem, Orlando Furioso
Orlando Furioso	Antonio Vivaldi	1727	Venice	Braccioli	
Orlando Paladino	Franz Joseph Haydn	1782	Eszterháza	N Porta	
Orpheus in the Underworld	Jacques Offenbach	1858	Paris	Crémieux and Halévy	
Osud (Fate)	Leoš Janáček	1958	Brno	Janáček	Janáček and Fedora Bartosová
Otello	Giuseppe Verdi	1887	Milan	Boito	
Ottone	George Frederick Handel	1723	London	N Haym	
Our Man in Havana	Malcolm Williamson	1963	London	Sidney Gilliat	Based on Graham Greene's novel
Padmâvatî	Albert Roussel	1923	Paris	L Laloy	Opera-ballet
I Pagliacci	Ruggiero Leoncavallo	1892	Milan	Leoncavallo	Famous aria 'Vesti la giubba' ('On with the motley') refers to clown's attire
Palestrina	Hans Pfitzner	1917	Munich	Pfitzner	
Paradise Lost	Krzysztof Penderecki	1978	Chicago	Christopher Fry	Based on Milton's poem
Paris and Helen	Christoph Gluck	1770	Vienna	Calzabigi	
Parisian Life (La Vie Parisienne)	Jacques Offenbach	1866	Paris	Meilhac and Halévy	
Parsifal	Richard Wagner	1882	Bayreuth	Wagner	Wagner's last opera
Partenope	George Frederick Handel	1730	London	Stampiglia	
Patience	Arthur Sullivan	1881	London	W S Gilbert	Aka: Bunthorne's Bride
Paul Bunyan	Benjamin Britten	1941	New York	W H Auden	
The Pearl Fishers	Georges Bizet	1863	Paris	Cormon and Carré	Action set in Ceylon (Sri Lanka)
Penelope	Rolf Liebermann	1954	Salzburg	H Strobel	Based on the story of Ulysses' wife in Homer's

Operas and operettas	Composer	First performance		Librettist	General information
Pénélope	Gabriel Fauré	1913	Monte Carlo and Paris	René Fauchois	Odyssey
A Penny For a Song	Richard Rodney Bennett	1967	London	Colin Graham	
The Perfect Fool	Gustav Holst	1923	Covent Garden	Holst	
Peter Grimes	Benjamin Britten	1945	London	Montagu Slater	Based on George Crabbe's poem 'The Borough'
Peter Schmoll and his Neighbours	Carl Maria Weber	1803	Augsburg	Joseph Türk	
The Pilgrim's Progress	Ralph Vaughan Williams	1951	Covent Garden	Vaughan Williams	Christian's name in Bunyan's novel is changed to Pilgrim
The Pirate	Vincenzo Bellini	1827	Milan	Romani	
The Pirates of Penzance	Arthur Sullivan	1879	Paignton, Devon, and New York	W S Gilbert	Aka: *The Slave of Duty*
The Poacher or the Voice of Nature	Albert Lortzing	1842	Leipzig	Lortzing	Aka: *The Empress and the Necromancer*
The Poisoned Kiss	Ralph Vaughan Williams	1936	London and Cambridge	Evelyn Sharp	
Polly	Christoph Pepusch	1777	London	John Gay	
Porgy and Bess	George Gershwin	1935	Boston and New York	DuBose Heyward and Ira Gershwin	
Powder her Face	Thomas Adès	1995	Cheltenham	Philip Hensher	Shown on British television on Christmas Day 1999
Il Prigioniero (The Prisoner)	Luigi Dallapiccola	1949	Italy	Dallapiccola	
Prima Donna	Arthur Benjamin	1949	London	Cedric Cliffe	
Prima la Musica e Poe le Parole	Antonio Salieri	1786	Vienna	Casti	First performed in double bill with Mozart's *Der Schauspieldirektor*
Prince Igor	Alexander Borodin	1890	St Petersburg	Borodin	Completed by Rimsky-Korsakov and Glazunov
The Prince of Homburg	Hans Werner Henze	1960	Hamburg	Bachmann	
Princess Ida	Arthur Sullivan	1884	London and Boston	W S Gilbert	Aka: *Castle Adamant*
The Prodigal Son	Benjamin Britten	1968	Orford	Plomer	A church parable
Le Prophète	Giacomo Meyerbeer	1849	Paris and London	Scribe	
Punch and Judy	Harrison Birtwistle	1968	Aldeburgh	Stephen Pruslin	
Purgatory	Gordon Crosse	1966	Cheltenham	W B Yeats	
I Puritani (di Scozia)	Vincenzo Bellini	1835	London and Paris	C Pepoli	Bellini's last opera
I Quattro Rusteghi (The Four Rustics)	Ermanno Wolf-Ferrari	1906	Munich	Sugano and Pizzolato	
The Queen of Sheba	Károly Goldmark	1875	Vienna	S H Mosenthal	
The Queen of Spades (Pique Dame)	Pyotr Tchaikovsky	1890	St Petersburg	M Tchaikovsky and Pyotr Tchaikovsky	
Quiet Flows the Don	Ivan Dzerzhinsky	1935	Leningrad	Dzerzhinsky	
A Quiet Place	Leonard Bernstein	1983	Houston	S Wadsworth	Revised in 3 acts incorporating Bernstein's *Trouble in Tahiti*
Radamisto	George Frederick Handel	1720	London	N Haym	
The Rajah's Diamond	Alun Hoddinott	1979	BBC TV	Myfanwy Piper	
The Rake's Progress	Igor Stravinsky	1951	Venice	Chester Kallman and W H Auden	
The Rape of Lucretia	Benjamin Britten	1946	Glyndebourne	Ronald Duncan	
The Red Line	Aulis Sallinen	1978	Helsinki	Sallinen	
Regina	Marc Blitzstein	1949	New Haven	Blitzstein	Based on Lillian Hellman's play *The Little Foxes*
Il Rè Pastore (The Shepherd King)	Wolfgang Amadeus Mozart	1775	Salzburg	Metastasio	

MUSIC CLASSICAL

Operas and operettas	Composer	First performance	Librettist	General information
Resurrection	Peter Maxwell Davies	1987	Maxwell Davies	
Das Rheingold (The Rhine Gold)	Richard Wagner	1869	Wagner	Became the prologue to the The Ring cycle
Richard the Lionhearted	André Grétry	1784	M J Sedaine	
Riders to the Sea	Ralph Vaughan Williams	1937	J M Synge	Faithful setting of Synge's play
Rienzi	Richard Wagner	1842	Wagner	Based on Bulwer-Lytton's novel
Rigoletto	Giuseppe Verdi	1851	Piave	Based on Hugo's play Le Roi s'Amuse
Rinaldo	George Frederick Handel	1711	Rossi	Handel's first opera in England
Der Ring des Nibelungen	Richard Wagner	1876	Wagner	
Der Ring des Polykrates	Erich Korngold	1916	J Korngold	
The Rise and Fall of the City of Mahagonny	Kurt Weill	1930	Brecht	Composed 1914
The Rising of the Moon	Nicholas Maw	1970	Beverley Cross	
Il Ritorno d'Ulisse in Patria	Claudio Monteverdi	1640	G Badoaro	English title: Ulysses' Return to His Native Land
Robert Devereux, Earl of Essex	Gaetano Donizetti	1837	Cammarano	
Robert the Devil	Giacomo Meyerbeer	1831	Scribe and Delavigne	
Rodelinda	George Frederick Handel	1725	Salvi and Haym	
Le Roi l'a dit	Léo Delibes	1873	Gondinet	
Le Roi malgré lui	Emmanuel Chabrier	1887	De Najac and Buroni	
Romeo and Juliet	Charles Gounod	1867	Barbier and Carré	
Romeo and Juliet	Heinrich Sutermeister	1940	Sutermeister	
La Rondine (The Swallow)	Giacomo Puccini	1917	Giuseppe Adami	
Der Rosenkavalier	Richard Strauss	1911	Hofmannsthal	Adapted from a German libretto by Alfred Lillner and Heinze Reichart
The Royal Hunt of the Sun	Iain Hamilton	1977	Hamilton	Based on Peter Shaffer's play
Ruddigore	Arthur Sullivan	1887	W S Gilbert	Aka: The Witch's Curse
Rusalka	Alexander Dargomyzhsky	1856	Dargomyzhsky	
Rusalka	Antonin Dvořák	1901	J Kvapil	
Ruslan and Lyudmila	Mikhail Glinka	1842	Shirkov and Bakhturin	Based on Pushkin's poem
Ruth	Lennox Berkeley	1956	Crozier	
Sadko	Nikolay Rimsky-Korsakov	1898	Rimsky-Korsakov, Stasov and Belsky	
St François d'Assise	Olivier Messiaen	1983	Messiaen	Messiaen's only opera
The Saint of Bleecker Street	Gian Carlo Menotti	1954	Menotti	
Salome	Antoine Mariotte	1908	Oscar Wilde	Based on Oscar Wilde's play
Salome	Richard Strauss	1905	Hedwig Lachmann	Based on Wilde's play
Samson et Dalila	Camille Saint-Saëns	1877	Lemaire	
Sapho	Jules Massenet	1897	Cain and Bernède	
Šárka	Zdeněk Fibich	1897	Schulzová	
Šárka	Leoš Janáček	1925	Zeyer	
Saturday from Light	Karlheinz Stockhausen	1984	Stockhausen	
Saul and David	Carl Nielsen	1902	Christiansen	
Der Schauspieldirektor (The Impresario)	Wolfgang Amadeus Mozart	1786	G Stephanie	
Schwanda the Bagpiper	Jaromir Weinberger	1927	Kares and Brod	
Die Schweigsame Frau	Richard Strauss	1935	Stefan Zweig	Translates as 'The Silent Woman'

Operas and operettas	Composer	First performance		Librettist	General information
The Secret	Bedřich Smetana	Prague	1878	Krásnohorská	
The Secret Marriage	Domenico Cimarosa	Vienna	1792	G Bertati	
Semele	John Eccles	Oxford	1964	Congreve	Based on Ovid's Metamorphoses
Semele	George Frederick Handel	London	1744	Congreve	Includes aria 'Where'er you walk'
Semiramide	Gioachino Rossini	Venice	1823	G Rossi	Many other operas based on Voltaire's Sémiramis
Semyon Kotko	Sergey Prokofiev	Moscow	1940	Prokofiev	
The Short Life (La Vida Breve)	Manuel De Falla	Nice	1913	Fernández Shaw	
The Sicilian Vespers	Giuseppe Verdi	Paris	1855	Scribe and Duveyrier	
The Siege of Corinth	Gioachino Rossini	Paris	1826	Balocchi and Soumet	
Siegfried	Richard Wagner	Bayreuth	1876	Wagner	Third part of Der Ring das Nibelungen
Sigurd	Ernest Reyer	Brussels and London	1884	Du Locle and Blau	
The Silken Ladder	Gioachino Rossini	Venice	1812	G M Foppa	
Simon Boccanegra	Giuseppe Verdi	Venice	1857	Piave and Montanelli	
Sir John in Love	Ralph Vaughan Williams	London	1929	Vaughan Williams	'Greensleeves' is sung by Mistress Ford in Act 3
The Sleepwalker	Vincenzo Bellini	Milan and London	1831	Romani	Italian title: La Sonnambula
The Small Venetian Square	Ermanno Wolf-Ferrari	Milan	1936	Ghisalberti	
The Snow Maiden (Snegurochka)	Nikolay Rimsky-Korsakov	St Petersburg	1882	Rimsky-Korsakov	
Die Soldaten (The Soldiers)	Bernd Alois Zimmermann	Cologne	1965	Zimmermann and Bernd Alois	
Son and Stranger	Felix Mendelssohn	Leipzig	1851	Klingemann	German title: Die Heimkehr aus der Fremde
The Sorcerer	Arthur Sullivan	London	1877	W S Gilbert	
Sorochintsy Fair	Modest Mussorgsky	Moscow	1913	Mussorgsky	Unfinished opera based on Gogol story
The Spanish Lady	Edward Elgar	Never performed		Elgar	Incomplete. Based on Jonson's The Devil is an Ass
Stiffelio	Giuseppe Verdi	Trieste	1850	Piave	
The Stone Guest	Alexander Dargomyzhsky	St Petersburg	1872	Pushkin	Same story as Don Giovanni
The Story of a Real Man	Sergey Prokofiev	Leningrad	1948	Mira Mendelson and Prokofiev	
La Straniera	Vincenzo Bellini	Milan	1829	Romani	
Suor Angelica (Sister Angelica)	Giacomo Puccini	New York	1918	Forzano	The second part of Puccini's Il Trittico
Susanna's Secret	Ermanno Wolf-Ferrari	Munich	1909	Zangarini and Golisciani	Secret is that Susanna smokes
Il Tabarro (The Cloak)	Giacomo Puccini	New York	1918	Adami	The first part of Puccini's Il Trittico
A Tale of Two Cities	Arthur Benjamin	London	1957	Cedric Cliffe	
The Tales of Hoffmann	Jacques Offenbach	Paris	1881	Barbier and Carré	Three acts: Olympia, Antonia and Giulietta ('Barcarolle' in Act 3)
Tamerlane (Tamerlano)	George Frederick Handel	London	1724	N F Haym	
The Taming of the Shrew	Hermann Goetz	Mannheim	1874	J V Widmann	
Tancredi	Gioachino Rossini	Venice	1813	Rossi	
Tannhäuser	Richard Wagner	Dresden	1845	Wagner	Full title: Tannhäuser and the Singing Contest on the Wartburg
Taras Bulba	Arturo Berutti	Buenos Aires	1895	Berutti	
Taverner	Peter Maxwell Davies	Covent Garden	1972	Maxwell Davies	
The Telephone	Gian Carlo Menotti	New York	1947	Menotti	
The Tempest (Der Sturm)	Frank Martin	Vienna	1956	Martin	
The Tender Land	Aaron Copland	New York	1954	H Everett	

Operas and operettas

Operas and operettas	Composer	First performance		Librettist	General information
Thaïs	Jules Massenet	1894	Paris	L Gallet	Based on Anatole France novel (1890)
Theseus (Teseo)	George Frederick Handel	1713	London	N F Haym	
Thespis	Arthur Sullivan	1871	London	W S Gilbert	Aka: The Gods Grown Old
The Thieving Magpie	Gioachino Rossini	1817	Milan	Gherardini	Italian title: La Gazza Ladra
The Threepenny Opera	Kurt Weill	1928	Berlin	Brecht	Based on The Beggar's Opera by John Gay and Christoph Pepusch
Tom Jones	Edward German	1907	London and Manchester	Thompson and Courtneidge	
Tom Jones	Stephen Oliver	1976	Snape	Oliver	
Tom Jones	François Philidor	1765	Paris	Poinsinet and Davesne	
Tosca	Giacomo Puccini	1900	London and Rome	Giacosa and Illica	Based on Sardou's play
Die Tote Stadt (The Dead City)	Erich Korngold	1920	Hamburg and Cologne	Paul Schott	Paul Schott is the pseudonym for Erich Korngold and his father Julius Korngold
The Travelling Companion	Charles Villiers Stanford	1925	Liverpool	Henry Newbolt	
La Traviata (The Fallen Woman)	Giuseppe Verdi	1853	Venice	Piave	Based on Dumas fils' novel Lady of the Camellias
The Trial (Der Prozess)	Gottfried von Einem	1953	Salzburg	Blacher and H von Cramer	From Franz Kafka's novel
Trial by Jury	Arthur Sullivan	1875	London	W S Gilbert	Only grand opera produced by the collaboration
Tristan und Isolde	Richard Wagner	1865	Munich	Wagner	
Troilus and Cressida	William Walton	1954	Covent Garden	Christopher Hassall	Based on Chaucer's story, as opposed to Shakespeare's
The Trojans (Les Troyens)	Hector Berlioz	1863	Paris	Berlioz	
Trouble in Tahiti	Leonard Bernstein	1952	New York	Bernstein	
Il Trovatore (The Troubadour)	Giuseppe Verdi	1853	Rome	Cammarano and Bardare	Fourth act completed by Bardare, after death of Cammarano
The Tsarevich (Der Zarewitsch)	Franz Lehár	1927	Berlin	Reichart and Jenbach	
The Tsar Has His Photograph Taken	Kurt Weill	1928	Leipzig	Kaiser	
The Tsar's Bride	Nikolay Rimsky-Korsakov	1899	Moscow	L A Mey	Adaptation of L A Mey's play, extra scene by Tumenev
Turandot	Ferruccio Busoni	1917	Zurich	Busoni	Based on Gozzi's play
Turandot (unfinished)	Giacomo Puccini	1926	Milan	Adami and Simoni	Final scene completed by Franco Alfano
Il Turco in Italia	Gioachino Rossini	1814	Milan	Romani	
The Turn of the Screw	Benjamin Britten	1954	Venice and London	Myfanwy Piper	Based on Henry James's story
The Twin Brothers	Franz Schubert	1820	Vienna	G von Hofmann	
The Two Widows	Bedrich Smetana	1874	Prague	Emanuel Züngel	
Ulisse	Luigi Dallapiccola	1968	Berlin	Dallapiccola	Based on Homer
Ulysses	Reinhard Keiser	1722	Copenhagen	F M Lersner	
Ulysses	John C Smith	1733	London	S Humphreys	Based on Homer
Utopia Limited	Arthur Sullivan	1893	London	W S Gilbert	Aka: The Flowers of Progress
Vakula the Smith	Pyotr Tchaikovsky	1876	St Petersburg	Y Polonsky	Based on Gogol's story Christmas Eve
The Valkyrie (Die Walküre)	Richard Wagner	1870	Munich	Wagner	The Valkyrie is Brünnhilde
The Vampire	Heinrich Marschner	1828	Leipzig	W A Wohlbrück	Based on John Polidori's story 'The Vampyre'
Vanessa	Samuel Barber	1958	New York	Menotti	Based on Dinesen's Seven Gothic Tales
Venus and Adonis	John Blow	1683	London	Anon	
La Vera Constanza (True Constancy)	Franz Joseph Haydn	1779	Eszterháza	F Puttini	
Véronique	André Messager	1898	Paris	Vanloo and Duval	

Operas and operettas	Composer	First performance		Librettist	General information
Das Verratene Meer (The Sea Betrayed)	Hans Werner Henze	1990	Berlin	Treichel	
La Vestale	Gaspare Spontini	1807	Paris	De Jouy	
Victory	Richard Rodney Bennett	1970	Covent Garden	Beverley Cross	Based on Joseph Conrad's novel
A Village Romeo and Juliet	Frederick Delius	1907	Berlin	Delius	
Le Villi (The Willis)	Giacomo Puccini	1884	Milan	F Fontana	
Violanta	Erich Korngold	1916	Munich	Müller	
The Violins of Saint-Jacques	Malcolm Williamson	1966	London	William Chappell	
The Visit of the Old Lady	Gottfried von Einem	1971	Vienna	Dürrenmatt	
The Voice of Ariadne	Thea Musgrave	1974	Snape Maltings	A Elguera	
La Voix Humaine (The Human Voice)	Francis Poulenc	1959	Paris	Cocteau	
La Wally	Alfredo Catalani	1892	Milan	Illica	
The Wandering Scholar	Gustav Holst	1934	Liverpool	Clifford Bax	
War and Peace	Sergey Prokofiev	1944	Moscow	Mira Mendelson and Prokofiev	
Wat Tyler	Alan Bush	1974	Sadler's Wells	Nancy Bush	
We Come to the River	Hans Werner Henze	1976	London	Edward Bond	
The Wedding of the Camacho	Felix Mendelssohn	1827	Berlin	F Voight	Based on an episode in Don Quixote
Werther	Jules Massenet	1892	Vienna	Blau, Milliet, Hartmann	Based on Goethe's novel The Sorrows of Young Werther
Where the Wild Things Are	Oliver Knussen	1980	Brussels	Maurice Sendak and Knussen	
William Tell	Gioachino Rossini	1829	Paris	De Jouy and Bis	
The World on the Moon	Franz Joseph Haydn	1777	Eszterháza	Goldoni	
Wozzeck	Alban Berg	1925	Berlin	Berg	
The Wreckers	Ethel Smyth	1906	Leipzig	'H B' (Harry Brewster) Laforestier	
Das Wunder der Heliane	Erich Korngold	1927	Hamburg	Müller	
Wuthering Heights	Bernard Herrmann	1982	Portland, Oregon	Lucille Fletcher	
Xerxes (Serse)	George Frederick Handel	1738	London	Stampiglia	
Yan Tan Tethera	Harrison Birtwistle	1986	London	T Harrison	
The Yeomen of the Guard	Arthur Sullivan	1888	London and NY	W S Gilbert	Aka: The Merryman and his Maid
Yolanta (Iolanta)	Pyotr Tchaikovsky	1892	St Petersburg	M Tchaikovsky	
Zampa, or the Marble Bride	Ferdinand Hérold	1831	Paris	Mélesville	
Zar und Zimmermann	Albert Lortzing	1837	Leipzig	Lortzing	André Grétry and B A Weber composed operas on same subject / English translation: Tsar and Carpenter
Zazà	Ruggiero Leoncavallo	1900	Milan	Leoncavallo	

MUSIC CLASSICAL

Operatic Suicides and Deaths

Character	Opera	Composer	Method
Aida	Aida	Verdi	Conceals herself in vault in which her lover is immured so as to share his death.
Andrey	Khovanshchina	Mussorgsky	Climbs a funeral pyre and perishes in the flames.
Brünnhilde	Götterdämmerung	Wagner	Rides her horse Grane on to Siegfried's funeral pyre.
Carmen	Carmen	Bizet	Stabbed by Don José.
Cio-Cio-San	Madame Butterfly	Puccini	Commits hara-kiri.
Cleopatra	Antony and Cleopatra	Barber	Presses an asp to her bosom.
Dido	Dido and Aeneas	Purcell	Stabs herself and mounts a funeral pyre.
Edgardo	Lucia di Lammermoor	Donizetti	Stabs himself with a dagger at Lucia's tomb.
Ernani	Ernani	Verdi	Stabs himself in fulfilment of a pledge to die when his enemy, Silva, sounds his horn.
Fenella	La Muette de Portici	Auber	Throws herself into the sea when she learns that her brother Masaniello has been killed.
Gioconda	La Gioconda	Ponchielli	Stabs herself to frustrate the lust of the spy Barnaba.
Gwendoline	Gwendoline	Chabrier	Stabs herself to join her Danish lover, Harald, in death.
Herman	Queen of Spades (Pique Dame)	Tchaikovsky	Stabs himself when he sees the ghost of an old countess whose death he has caused.
Iris	Iris	Mascagni	Throws herself into a sewer after unjustly being accused of becoming a geisha.
Katerina Ismailova	Lady Macbeth of Mtsensk District	Shostakovich	Drowns herself in a river en route to a Siberian prison camp.
La Wally	La Wally	Catalani	Throws herself from a precipice during an avalanche in the Alps.
Lakmé	Lakmé	Delibes	Poisons herself with the juice of an exotic flower when she loses her lover, Gerald.
Leonora	Il Trovatore	Verdi	Takes poison from a ring and swallows it rather than submit to the Count di Luna.
Liù	Turandot	Puccini	Stabs herself rather than reveal under torture the name of the Unknown Prince, Calaf.
Magda Sorel	The Consul	Menotti	Seals her kitchen and turns on the gas.
Manfredo	The Love of Three Kings	Montemezzi	Deliberately kisses the poisoned lips of his murdered wife Fiora in her tomb.
Marfa	Khovanshchina	Mussorgsky	Climbs a funeral pyre and perishes in the flames.
Margared	Le Roi d'Ys	Lalo	Leaps from precipice in remorse for aiding enemies to open dikes that protect city from sea.
Mizgir	The Snow Maiden (Snegurochka)	Rimsky-Korsakov	Flings himself into a lake when his beloved Snow Maiden is melted by a ray of sunlight.
Otello	Otello	Verdi	Stabs himself with a dagger following his murder of Desdemona.
Pollione	Norma	Bellini	Joins the Druid priestess on her funeral pyre.
Salome	Hérodiade	Massenet	Stabs herself upon learning that John the Baptist has been executed.
Selika	L'Africaine	Meyerbeer	Inhales the perfume of the manchinel tree, deadly to all who breathe it.
Seneca	L'Incoronazione di Poppea	Monteverdi	Opens his veins in the bath at the command of Emperor Nero.
Sister Angelica	Suor Angelica	Puccini	Swallows a poisonous potion she has concocted from the herbs in her convent's garden.
Tosca	Tosca	Puccini	Leaps to her death from parapet of the castle of Sant' Angelo in Rome after her lover is shot.
Violetta	La Traviata	Verdi	Dies of consumption.
Werther	Werther	Massenet	Shoots himself with a pistol.
Wozzeck	Wozzeck	Berg	Stabs his wife then walks into a pond and drowns.

Opera: General Information

aria (air) Solo vocal piece in A-B-A form.

bleeding chunks Operatic extracts played out of context. Term coined by Sir Donald Tovey.

burletta A comic operetta.

Camerata Society of 16th-century Florentine poets and musicians who developed opera.

canon Counterpoint in which one melodic strand gives the rule to another.

cantata Musical setting of a text, often religious, consisting of arias and choruses interspersed with recitatives.

canticle Bible hymn, other than a psalm, used in church liturgy.

cantor 1) Leading singer in a synagogue. 2) Director of music in Lutheran Church.

caoine (pronounced 'keen') Irish funeral song accompanied by wailing.

castrato Male soprano or contralto whose voice was preserved by castration before puberty.

'Catalogue Aria' Nickname for Leporello's aria in Act 1 Scene 2 of Mozart's *Don Giovanni* in which he recounts to Donna Elvira a list of his master Don Giovanni's conquests.

coloratura Word applied both to a florid virtuoso aria and to the voice required for such a passage.

Don Giovanni: conquests Italian 640, German 231, French 100, Turkish 91, Spanish 1003 = 2,065 (according to Leporello, although in the opera he has none).

English National Opera Assumed name in 1974, six years after moving into Coliseum in St Martin's Lane from previous London HQ at Sadler's Wells, Rosebery Avenue.

Gilbert and Sullivan: row over Librettist and composer fell out over choice of carpet for the Savoy.

Gluck and Piccinni war Divided Paris into French and Italian opera fans in the 1770s.

grand opera Opera on a large scale, usually entirely sung.

intermezzo Instrumental interlude used in course of an opera or play. Term also used for short opera performed between the acts of a larger one.

La Scala, Milan Built in 1778 and named after Regina della Scala, wife of a Duke of Milan. The opera house (lit. the staircase) opened on 3 August 1778 with operas of Salieri.

The Legend of Tsar Saltan Orchestral interlude 'The Flight of the Bumble Bee' appears in Act 3.

leitmotif (leading theme) Recurring theme written for a specific character or event in opera or television and film music.

libretto The words of any vocal piece such as an oratorio, but particularly the text of an opera.

'Love-Death' Wagner's name given to love duet in Act 2 of *Tristan und Isolde*, although more generally regarded as Isolde's aria at end of Act 3.

Mastersingers: thirteen Sixtus Beckmesser – Town Clerk, Fritz Kothner – Baker, Balthasar Zorn – Pewterer, Ulrich Eisslinger – Grocer, Hans Sachs – Cobbler, Veit Pogner – Goldsmith, Kunz Vogelgesang – Furrier, Conrad Nachtigal – Buckle-maker, Augustin Mosler – Tailor, Hermann Ortel – Soap boiler, Hans Schwarz – Stocking weaver, Hans Foltz – Coppersmith, Walther von Stolzing – Unemployed.

Moody-Manners Opera Co Touring opera company formed in 1898 by Charles Manners and his wife Fanny Moody but disbanded in 1916.

opera buffa (Fr. *opera bouffe*) Comic opera; the opposite of *opera seria*.

opéra-comique 1) Second opera house of Paris; originally opened 1715; has a history of name changes and re-location; it is currently known as Salle Favart. 2) Term describing opera with spoken dialogue.

operetta Light opera, sometimes of a comic nature, e.g. Gilbert and Sullivan operettas.

overture Introductory music for an opera, oratorio or ballet.

Paris Opéra (Académie de Musique) Latest building opened in 1875 and commonly known as Garnier or Salle Garnier, after its architect. After the opening of the Opéra Bastille in 1990, the Garnier Opéra is now used mainly for ballet. The term Paris Opéra is now used to mean the Garnier and the Bastille.

pasticcio/pastiche Opera in which each act is by a different composer. Although these terms are often used synonymously, pastiche describes a work written in the style of another period or manner.

patter song Rapid, sometimes tongue-twisting song often found in comic opera and now in pop music.

polo Andalusian folk song accompanied with dance and performed in 3/8 with syncopations and vocal coloraturas on words, e.g. 'Ole' and 'Ay', as performed in several operas.

prima donna (first lady) Most important female singer in an opera.

prologue Introductory piece that presents the background for an opera.

Puccini: unfinished opera *Turandot* (completed by Franco Alfano).

Rhinemaidens: three Flosshilde, Wellgunde, Woglinde.

Singspiel German light opera with spoken dialogue.

soubrette Soprano comedienne.

surtitle A printed translation of part of the text of an opera, usually projected on a screen above the stage. This innovation was first used on 21 January 1983 by the Canadian Opera company for *Electra*.

travesti Term used to describe operatic roles whereby character parts are sung by the opposite gender, e.g. Cherubino in *The Marriage of Figaro* or Prince Orlofsky in *Die Fledermaus*. Such parts are often called breeches or trouser-roles.

Turandot: three riddles What is born each night and dies each dawn ... hope. What flickers red and is warm like a flame, yet is not fire ... blood. What is like ice but burns ... Turandot.

TV opera: first *Amahl and the Night Vistors* (Magi) by Menotti (1951).

Valkyries Brünnhilde, Gerhilde, Grimgerde, Helmwige, Ortlinde, Rossweise, Schwertleite, Siegrune, Waltraute.

Venice Opera House Teatro La Fenice, opened in 1792 and destroyed by fire 1836, rebuilt 1837 but seriously damaged again in 1996.

voice registers Chest, head and middle voice; so called because the notes seem to come from these areas.

MUSIC CLASSICAL

Hymns, Anthems, Songs and Ballads

Abide With Me   Henry Francis Lyte.

America the Beautiful   Katherine Lee Bates (words); Samuel Augustus Ward (music).

America (My Country 'tis of Thee)   Samuel Francis Smith (tune of 'God Save the Queen').

Annie Laurie   William Douglas. First line: Maxwelton's braes are bonnie, where early fa's the dew.

Auld Lang Syne   Robert Burns.

Battle Hymn of the Republic   Julia Ward Howe. First line: Mine eyes have seen the glory of the coming of the Lord (tune of 'John Brown's body')

Beer Barrel Polka (Roll out the barrel)   Tune by Jaromir Vejvoda.

Caller Herrin'   Tune by Nathaniel Gow blends fishwives' cry with bells of St Andrew's Church; words by Lady Nairne.

Calm Sea and Prosperous Voyage   J W Goethe.

The Campbells are Coming   Anon.

Columbia, the Gem of the Ocean   Thomas à Becket (1808–90).

Eternal Father, Strong To Save   William Whiting (words); J B Dykes (music); aka 'The Navy's Hymn'. First line, 'O thou who bidd'st the ocean deep'.

Evening Hymn   Purcell (music); Fuller (words). First line, 'Now that the sun hath veiled his light'.

The Flowers that Bloom in the Springtime   W S Gilbert (words); Arthur Sullivan (music).

For the Fallen   3rd movement of Elgar's choral work Spirit of England with words by Laurence Binyon.

Funiculì Funiculà   Luigi Denza's song composed for the opening of the Naples funicular railway in 1880.

General William Booth Enters into Heaven   Ives (music); Vachel Lindsay (words).

Girl I Left Behind Me, The   Played in the British Army on occasions of departure and sometimes known as 'Brighton Camp'.

God Bless the Prince of Wales   Henry Brinley Richards (music); Ceiriog Hughes (words).

God Preserve the Emperor Francis (Emperor's Hymn)   Lorenz Haschka (words); Haydn (music); known as 'Austria' in hymn-books and became Austrian anthem. The German anthem 'Deutschland über Alles' adopted the tune.

Greensleeves   Old English tune popularly attributed to Henry VIII but no evidence of this is available, although it may have been written during his reign. Mentioned by Shakespeare in The Merry Wives of Windsor and tune used by Holst in St Paul's Suite and by Busoni in Turandot.

Habañera   Cuban song and dance of African origins, which became popular in Spain. Famous example is the habañera in Bizet's Carmen.

Happy Birthday to You   Composed in USA by Mildred Hill and published by Clayton F Summy as 'Good Morning to All'.

Hark, the Herald Angels Sing   Words by Charles Wesley.

Hear My Prayer   Hymn by Mendelssohn containing section 'O for the wings of a dove'.

Heart of Oak   Written by actor David Garrick in 1759 to music by William Boyce. It was a topical song from the pantomime Harlequin's Invasion and commemorated the British victories at Minden, Quiberon Bay and Quebec.

Home, Sweet Home   Henry Bishop composed the music (1821) and the words were by J H Payne.

Internationale   Socialist song composed by P Degeyter to words by Eugène Pottier; it was the official anthem of Communist Russia until 1 January 1944 and often confused with 'The Red Flag'.

Jerusalem   Music by Hubert Parry (1916); words by William Blake.

Jubilate   Psalm 100 (Anglican service), alternative to Benedictus; set to music by various composers.

Keel Row   Quoted by Debussy in the 3rd movement of his Images. This song, of unknown origin, first appeared in a collection of favourite Scots tunes and is principally identified with the North-east of England.

keen (caoine)   Irish funeral song with wailing. Represented in Vaughan Williams's opera Riders to the Sea.

Land of Hope and Glory   Finale of Elgar's Coronation Ode with words by A C Benson. The tune adapts the melody of the trio section of Pomp and Circumstance March No. 1 in D.

Land of My Fathers (Hen Wlad fy Nhadau)   National anthem of Wales (words by Evan James; music by his son James); originally called 'Glan Rhondda'.

Lass of Richmond Hill   James Hook (music); L McNally (words). The song refers to Richmond in Yorkshire.

Last Rose of Summer, The   Adaption of R A Millihin's 'The Groves of Barley' by Thomas Moore (1779-1852), famously heard in Friedrich von Flotow's opera Martha.

Let Us Garlands Bring   Song-cycle by Gerald Finzi to words by Shakespeare, first performed in 1942 for the 70th birthday of Vaughan Williams. The five songs are 1) 'Come Away Death', 2) 'Who Is Sylvia?' 3) 'Fear No More the Heat O' the Sun', 4) 'O Mistress Mine', 5) 'It Was a Lover and His Lass'.

Lilliburlero   Song of unknown origin, which is the tune of Northern Ireland's 'Orange' party, set to different words as 'Protestant Boys'.

Lincoln, the Great Commoner   Song by Charles Ives; words by Edwin Markham.

Londonderry Air   Irish folk tune first published in the Petrie collection of 1855, the most famous words being those of 'Danny Boy' by F E Weatherly.

The Lost Chord   Song by Arthur Sullivan composed in 1877 in sorrow at his brother's death.

Magnificat   Canticle of the Virgin Mary, 'My Soul Doth Magnify the Lord', as it appears in St Luke's Gospel. Latin name is the first word of the Vulgate translation, i.e. Magnificat anima mea Dominum.

La Marseillaise   French national anthem, words and music by Claude Rouget de Lisle; written in 1792 under the title 'War Song for the Rhine Army'. Famously quoted in Tchaikovsky's 1812 Overture.

Nearer, My God, to Thee   Hymn existing in British and American versions, both set to verses by Sarah Flower Adams. The English version was composed by John Dykes, and the American version is sung to the tune 'Bethany,' by Lowell Mason.

O Canada!   Canadian national anthem; originally a hymn in honour of St John the Baptist; music composed by Calixa Lavallée in 1880.

O Come All Ye Faithful   John Francis Wade wrote both the words and music in the early 1740s.

O God, Our Help in Ages Past   Based on Psalm 90 by Isaac Watts to a tune by William Croft, this hymn is particularly associated with Remembrance Day services.

Old Folks at Home By Stephen Foster. First line: 'Way down upon the Swanee River, far, far away'.

Onward, Christian Soldiers Reverend Sabine Baring-Gould published the words in 1868 and Arthur Sullivan the music in 1871.

Pammelia (All Honey) First collection of rounds, catches and canons published in England, by T Ravenscroft in 1609.

Rock of Ages, Cleft For Me Hymn; words by Reverend Augustus Montague Toplady; music by Richard Redhead.

Rule, Britannia! Music by Thomas Arne to words of James Thomson and first played in *The Masque of Alfred* at Maidenhead on 1 August 1740. It has become a nationalistic English anthem and is also often considered to be the hidden theme of Elgar's *Enigma Variations*.

St Anne English hymn tune of uncertain origin but possibly composed by William Croft. It is usually sung to the words 'O God, Our Help in Ages Past'.

Seven Gypsy Songs Dvořák (music), Heyduk (words). 1) 'My Song Resounds', 2) 'My Triangle is Singing', 3) 'Silent the Woods', 4) 'Songs My Mother Taught Me', 5) 'Sound the Fiddle', 6) 'Clean Cotton Clothes', 7) 'To the Heights of Tatra'.

Sheep May Safely Graze Air by J S Bach subsequently arranged by several composers, notably William Walton in *The Wise Virgins*.

Simple Gifts Shaker hymn composed by Joseph Brackett (1848) and quoted by Copland in *Appalachian Spring*.

Song of Destiny (Schicksalslied) Brahms (music); Hölderlin (words).

Song of the Fates (Gesang der Farzen) Brahms (music); Goethe (words).

The Star-Spangled Banner National anthem of USA. Words by Francis Scott Key (1814), written during the war of 1812, and music adapted from John Stafford Smith's *Anacreon in Heaven*.

Sumer is Icumen In (Summer is coming in) Dating from *c.* 1240 and often quoted as the oldest extant canon. Aka 'The Reading Rota' as the author is thought to have been John of Fornsete, a monk of Reading Abbey.

Tea for Two Song by Vincent Youmans, written for *No, No, Nanette* (1925). An orchestral version by Shostakovich (1928) was given the name 'Tahiti Trot'.

'Tis the Last Rose of Summer Old Irish air originally called 'Castle Hyde'.

While Shepherds Watched Their Flocks Words by Nahum Tate.

Ballets

Name	Music by	Choreographer	First performance	
The Age of Gold	Dmitry Shostakovich	Kaplan and Vaynonen	1930	Leningrad
Agon	Igor Stravinsky	Balanchine	1957	Los Angeles
El Amor brujo (Love the Magician)	Manuel de Falla	Falla (as pantomime) La Argentinita (as ballet in 1931)	1915	Madrid
Apollo Musagetes (Apollo, Leader of the Muses)	Igor Stravinsky	Bolm Balanchine	1928 1928	Washington Paris
Appalachian Spring	Aaron Copland	Martha Graham	1944	Washington
L'Après-midi d'un faune	Claude Debussy	Nijinsky Robbins	1912 1946	Paris New York
Bacchus and Ariadne	Albert Roussel	Lifar	1931	Paris
La Bayadère	Léon Minkus	Petipa	1877	St Petersburg
Les Biches	Francis Poulenc	Nijinskaya	1924	Monte Carlo
Billy the Kid	Aaron Copland	Loring	1938	Chicago
Boléro	Maurice Ravel	Nijinskaya	1928	Paris
The Bolt	Dmitry Shostakovich	Lopokov	1931	Leningrad
La Boutique Fantastique	Ottorino Respighi (arr. of Rossini's music)	Massine	1919	London
The Box of Toys	Claude Debussy	André Hellé	1919	Paris
Caroline Mathilde	Peter Maxwell Davies	Flindt	1991	Amsterdam
Checkmate	Arthur Bliss	de Valois	1937	Paris
Cinderella	Sergey Prokofiev	Ashton	1948	Moscow
Coppélia	Léo Delibes	Saint-Léon	1870	Paris
La Création du Monde	Darius Milhaud	Börlin	1923	Paris
The Creatures of Prometheus	Ludwig van Beethoven	Viganò Ashton	1801 1970	Vienna Bonn
Daphnis et Chloé	Maurice Ravel	Fokine Ashton	1912 1957	Paris London
Les Deux Pigeons	André Messager	Mérante	1886	Paris
Don Quixote	Léon Minkus	Petipa	1869	St Petersburg
Edward II	John McCabe	Bintley	1996	Stuttgart
Façade	William Walton	Ashton	1931	London
The Fairy's Kiss	Igor Stravinsky	Nijinskaya MacMillan	1928 1980	Paris London
Fall River Legend	Morton Gould	de Mille	1948	New York
Fancy Free	Leonard Bernstein	Robbins	1944	New York
Le Festin de l'araignée (Spider's Banquet)	Albert Roussel	Staats	1913	Paris

Name	Music by	Choreographer	First Performance	
La Fille mal gardée (The Unchaperoned Girl)	John Lanchbery (arr. of Ferdinand Hérold's music)	Ashton	1960	London
Firebird	Igor Stravinsky	Fokine	1910	Paris
The Four Temperaments	Paul Hindemith	Balanchine	1946	New York
Gaîté Parisienne	Manuel Rosenthal (arr. of Offenbach's music)	Massine	1938	Monte Carlo
Gayane	Aram Khachaturian	Anisimova	1942	Leningrad
Giselle, or the Wilis	Adolphe Adam	Coralli and Perrot	1841	Paris
		Petipa	1884	St Petersburg
The Good-Humoured Ladies	Domenico Scarlatti (arr. by Tommasini)	Massine	1917	Rome
The Haunted Ballroom	Geoffrey Toye	de Valois	1934	London
Homage to the Queen	Malcolm Arnold	Ashton	1953	London (Coronation Night)
Horoscope	Constant Lambert	Ashton	1938	London
Jeux (Games)	Claude Debussy	Nijinsky	1913	Paris
Josephslegende (Legend of Joseph)	Richard Strauss	Fokine	1914	London and Paris
Madame Chrysanthème	Alan Rawsthorne	Ashton	1955	London
Les Mariés de la Tour Eiffel	Les Six (excluding Durey)	Börlin	1921	Paris
Miracle in the Gorbals	Arthur Bliss	Helpmann	1944	London
Miss Julie	Andrzej Panufnik	MacMillan	1970	Stuttgart
Nobilissima Visione	Paul Hindemith	Massine	1938	Monte Carlo
Nutcracker	Pyotr Tchaikovsky	Ivanov	1892	St Petersburg
Ondine (Undine)	Hans Werner Henze	Ashton	1958	London
Orpheus	Igor Stravinsky	Balanchine	1948	New York
Parade	Erik Satie	Massine	1917	Paris
Le Pas d'Acier	Sergey Prokofiev	Massine	1927	Paris
Paul Bunyan	William Bergsma	Ballet for puppets	1939	San Francisco
Peer Gynt	Alfred Schnittke	Neumeier	1986	Hamburg
The Peri	Paul Dukas	Clustine	1912	Paris
Perséphone	Igor Stravinsky	Jooss	1934	Paris
		Ashton	1962	London
Les Petits Riens	Wolfgang Amadeus Mozart	Jean Noverre	1778	Paris
Petrushka	Igor Stravinsky	Fokine	1911	Paris
Pineapple Poll	Arthur Sullivan (arr. by Mackerras)	Cranko	1951	Sadler's Wells
The Prince of the Pagodas	Benjamin Britten	Cranko	1957	Covent Garden
		MacMillan	1995	London
The Prodigal Son	Sergey Prokofiev	Balanchine	1929	Paris
Pulcinella	Igor Stravinsky	Massine	1920	Paris
The Rake's Progress	Gavin Gordon	de Valois	1935	London
Raymonda	Alexander Glazunov	Petipa	1898	Paris
The Rite of Spring	Igor Stravinsky	Nijinsky	1913	London and Paris
		MacMillan	1962	London
Rodeo	Aaron Copland	de Mille	1942	New York
Romeo and Juliet	Sergey Prokofiev	Psota	1938	Brno
		MacMillan	1965	London
Salome	Peter Maxwell Davies	Flindt	1978	Copenhagen
The Sanguine Fan	Edward Elgar	Hynd (1976 revival)	1917	London
Scaramouche	Jean Sibelius	Walbom	1922	Copenhagen
Scheherazade	Nikolay Rimsky-Korsakov	Fokine	1910	Paris
Schlagobers (Whipped Cream)	Richard Strauss	Kröller	1924	Vienna and Breslau
The Seven Deadly Sins	Kurt Weill	Balanchine	1933	Paris
The Sleeping Beauty	Pyotr Tchaikovsky	Petipa	1890	St Petersburg
The Song of the Earth	Gustav Mahler	MacMillan	1965	London
Spartacus	Aram Khachaturian	Jacobson	1956	Leningrad
Le Spectre de la Rose	Carl Maria Weber	Fokine	1911	Monte Carlo
The Stone Flower	Sergey Prokofiev	Lavrovsky	1954	Moscow
Swan Lake	Pyotr Tchaikovsky	Reisinger	1877	Moscow
		Petipa and Ivanov	1895	St Petersburg
Les Sylphides	Frederic Chopin	Mérante	1876	Paris
Sylvia, ou La Nymph de Diane	Léo Delibes	Fokine	1907	St Petersburg
		Ashton	1952	London
The Tales of Hoffmann	Jacques Offenbach (arr. Lanchbery)	Darrell	1973	London
The Three-Cornered Hat	Manuel de Falla	Massine	1919	London
Tiresias	Constant Lambert	Ashton	1951	London
The Triumph of Neptune	Lord Berners	Balanchine	1926	London
La Ventana	Holm Lumbye	Bournonville	1854	Copenhagen

A Wedding Bouquet	Lord Berners	Ashton	1936	London
The Wedding (Les Noces)	Igor Stravinsky	Nijinskaya	1923	Paris
The Wise Virgins	William Walton	Ashton	1940	Sadler's Wells
The Wooden Prince	Bela Bartók	Balázs	1917	Budapest

NB: Where ballets have been re-choreographed, both original and better-known modern versions are listed.

Ballet: General Information

ballet: first   *Balet Comique de la Royne* (Paris 1581), produced by violinist Balthasar de Beaujoyeux.

Ballets Russes   Founded in Paris in 1909 by Serge Diaghilev (Mikhail Fokine was his choreographer).

ballet terms   Jeté – leap from one foot to another; arabesque – one leg raised behind and arms extended; entrechat – leap while striking heels together; pirouette – rapid whirling round on the point of one foot.

Bolshoi Theatre (Great Theatre)   Oldest theatre in Moscow, originally called the Petrovsky, built by Maddox (1780), home of the Bolshoi Ballet.

classic ballet: first   *Le Bourgeois Gentilhomme* (1670).

comédie-ballet   French musico-dramatic entertainment devised by Molière and Lully in the late 17th century.

corps de ballet   The ballet troupe excluding the principal dancers.

Dance Theatre of Harlem   Founded by Arthur Mitchell (1968); first black classical ballet company; presented season at Covent Garden 1981.

defections from USSR   Mikhail Baryshnikov while dancing with the Kirov in Toronto (1974); Natalia Makarova while dancing with the Kirov in London (1972); Rudolf Nureyev while dancing with the Kirov in Paris (1961).

La Fille mal gardée (*The Unchaperoned Girl*)   Adaptation of a work based on French songs and airs originally produced in Bordeaux 1789.

Marie Taglioni (1804–1884)   First ballerina to dance on points and to wear a tutu.

professional ballet dancer: first female   La Fontaine in Lully's *Le Triomphe de l'Amour* at the Paris Opera House 1681.

Pulcinella   Scenes and costumes by Picasso.

ritual dances: four dances (*The Midsummer Marriage*)   'The Earth in Autumn', 'Waters in Winter', 'Air in Spring', 'Fire in Summer'.

Ritual Fire Dance   From Falla's *El Amor brujo* (*Love the Magician*).

Royal Ballet   Name bestowed by Royal Charter in 1956 on the former Sadler's Wells Ballet, Covent Garden. Touring company originally known as Sadler's Wells Royal Ballet is now based in Birmingham and since 1991 is known as Birmingham Royal Ballet.

Le Spectre de la Rose   Weber's *Invitation to the Dance* used as musical score.

Dance Types

allemande   German dance, moderately paced in 4/4 rhythm, and performed in a cheerful fashion.

anglaise   English country dance in quick duple metre.

apache   French dance, often violent, imitating a Parisian gangster and his girlfriend.

badinage   Playful dance or dance movement of a suite.

beguine   Sensuous Latin ballroom dance originating in the Caribbean and danced to a bolero rhythm.

bergamasque (bergomask)   Peasant dance of Bergamo, Italy, resembling a tarantella.

black bottom   Popular dance of the late 1920s, originally in North America, involving lively rotation of the hips.

bolero   Spanish dance in triple rhythm, said to have been invented in Cadiz around 1780.

bossa-nova   Brazilian variation of the samba.

bourrée   French dance, in quadruple time, performed in a lively style very like the gavotte.

branle   French country dance of the 15th century characterised by a swaying motion and performed in a linked circle.

break bance   Energetic solo dance frequently involving spinning on the floor on the back or head; originating in the USA in the 1980s.

cachucha   Andalusian dance in triple metre similar to a bolero, for solo dancer.

cakewalk   Popularised in the 1890s when black slaves parodied the white method of dance, a cake being awarded to best dancers.

calinda   Negro dance, which was basis for an orchestral dance-interlude by Delius in his second opera *Koanga*.

calypso   West Indian folk dance but better known in its sung form.

canaries   Old 17th-century dance similar to a gigue and so called because it imitated Canary Island rituals.

can-can   Boisterous Parisian dance of quadrille pattern originating in Algeria in the 1830s.

carmagnole   Round dance, popular in the French Revolutionary period.

cha-cha-cha   Cuban dance developed from the mambo in early 1950s.

chaconne   Slow and dignified dance, probably originating in Spain.

Charleston   Fast foxtrot named after Charleston, South Carolina, and popularised in New York in 1922.

conga   Latin American dance of three steps and kick to the side, performed in chain with hands on the next person's hips.

cotillon   Lively French formation dance of the 18th century similar to a quadrille.

MUSIC CLASSICAL

courante From the French meaning 'running', a courante is moderate to lively in pace, with shifting rhythms.

csárdás Hungarian dance in two sections: 1) Slow and melancholy, 2) quick and lively.

cushion dance Dance where one partner dropped a cushion before the other, who then knelt on it and bestowed a kiss on the bearer.

danse champêtre French rustic dance performed in the open air.

divertissement Dance or ballet with or without lyric, included in an opera or play to add variety.

ezcudantza Basque festival dance for two performers with accompaniment of pipe and tabor.

fandango Old Spanish courtship dance in triple time.

farandole French line dance in 6/8 time usually to the accompaniment of galoubet and tambourin.

flamenco Spanish dance with lively toe and heel steps, usually accompanied by guitar and castanets.

foxtrot Ballroom dance in quadruple time combining short and long steps in various sequences, originated in North America in the early 20th century.

funk Style of popular dance music of US black origin, popularised by singers such as James Brown. The staccato body movements follow the heavy syncopation of the music.

galliard Spirited dance popular in Tudor times, performed in a gay, rollicking manner, in triple time.

galop (galopade) Mid-19th-century dance with lively rhythm, executed with hopping movements.

gavotte French dance in 4/4 time, starting on the third beat of the bar.

gigue Formal dance for two in the 16th and 17th centuries; derived from the jig and usually with violin accompaniment.

gitana Spanish gypsy dance.

gopak Lively Russian folk dance in duple time.

guajira Spanish dance with alternating rhythm between 6/8 and 3/4.

guaracha Spanish and Mexican folk dance in two sections, one in triple time and the other in duple. Dancer usually plays guitar.

habañera Cuban dance named after the city of Havana. Performed in 2/4 time.

halling Norwegian dance possibly originating in the Hallingdal. It is a frantic dance accompanied by Hardanger fiddle and other violins.

hanacca Moravian dance in simple triple time; a sort of quick polonaise.

haute danse Old term for a dance where feet are lifted, as opposed to *basse danse* in which they stay close to the floor.

hay Traditional country dance for two or more partners, with interweaving steps.

hob-and-nob Scottish country dance (1745) tune developed into 'The Campbells are Coming'.

hopak (gopak) Ukrainian folk dance, once for men only but later danced by couples. Steps are improvised but in 2/4 time.

hornpipe Lively English sailors' dance in 4/4 time.

jabo/jaleo Spanish dance for solo performer in a slow triple rhythm.

jarabe Spanish tap dance.

jig Lively British folk dance, usually in 6/8 time.

jitterbug Energetic dance, popular in the 1940s, performed chiefly to swing music.

jive Lively and jerky dance performed to jazz and,

later, to rock and roll, popular in the 1940s and 1950s. Nowadays a generic term for any lively dance.

joropo Latin dance in rapid 3/4 time.

jota Spanish dance in rapid triple time with castanets and accompanied by guitar and voice.

krakoviak Polish dance from Krakow district, in lively 2/4 time.

kujawiak Polish dance for two, slower variant of the mazurka.

lambada Fast erotic Brazilian dance in which couples frequently touch hips. (lit: A beating)

lancer Quadrille for 8 or 16 pairs, popular in 19th-century England.

Ländler Traditional couple dance of Bavaria and Alpine Austria which greatly influenced the evolution of the waltz.

lezginka Dance of the Lezghins, a Muslim tribe on the Iran border.

loure French dance, similar to a gigue but slower and graver, usually with bagpipe accompaniment.

malagueña Spanish dance from Málaga and Murcia, similar to fandango and exported to Mexico by Spanish settlers.

mambo Latin American ballroom dance.

matelotte Dutch sailors' dance similar to hornpipe but danced in clogs, with arms interlinked behind the dancers' backs.

maxixe Brazilian dance, precursor of the tango.

mazurka Polish national dance in triple time.

merengue Latin American ballroom dance.

minuet Stately court dance of 17th century in triple time. The style was adopted by classical composers in suites and overtures, and as third movement of symphonies and quartets.

morris English folk dance for men with accompaniment of fiddle, tabor, pipe, concertina and accordion, long associated with Whitsuntide. The dancers wear bells on their knees and often represent characters, e.g. the Fool or the Queen of the May.

musette Dance with a drone bass accompaniment.

nachtanz (after-dance) Term applied to the second of the two dance tunes which were commonly paired from the 15th to 16th centuries, i.e. pavane and salliard, sarabande and gigue, and passamezzo and salfarello.

new Jack swing Type of funk dance, often with rap.

paso doble Spanish dance with double steps in rapid 2/4 time.

passacaglia Almost indistinguishable from the chaconne in its slow triple-time steps.

passamezzo Italian dance of the 16th and 17th centuries, similar to pavane but faster and less serious.

passepied Lively minuet of Breton origin in triple time and popular in the 17th century.

pavane Slow, stately dance of Spanish origin, often danced in conjunction with the galliard.

polka Bohemian dance, popular in 19th century and comprising three steps and a hop in fast duple time.

polonaise Polish dance in 3/4 time performed as a march in a ceremonial style.

polska Scandinavian dance in simple triple time that derives from the Mazurka and dates from the union of the Polish and Swedish crowns (1587).

quadrille Square dance in five movements, for four or more couples.

quick-step Fast version of the foxtrot. Also a lively march in 2/4, also known as a quick march.

rant Old English 17th-century dance of the jig variety, originating in the north of England and Scotland.

redowa Bohemian dance resembling the Polish mazurka.

rigaudon (rigadoon) Light and graceful dance performed in 4/4 time and in a lively spirit, originating in Provence.

rondeña Fandango of southern Spain, named after Ronda in Andalusia.

rueda Spanish round dance in quintuple time, popular in Castile.

rumba Cuban dance in 8/8 time, originating in the 1920s and extending into the jazz age and into ballroom dancing.

running set English folk dance still popular in the Appalachian mountains of America.

salsa Latin American dance style combining Latin rhythms with rock.

saltarello Traditional Italian dance usually in compound duple time and as the name suggests incorporates a series of jumps and leaps.

samba Lively, modern ballroom dance from Brazil, developed from the maxixe. The samba was popularized in Britain in the 1940s and 1950s by Edmundo Ros.

saraband(e) Originating in 17th century Spain and performed in slow, dignified triple metre.

sardana National dance of Catalonia performed to the accompaniment of the fluvial.

schottische (Scottish) A 19th-century German dance resembling a slow polka. Introduced to England in 1848 and known as the 'German polka'.

seguidilla Andalusian national dance in fast triple metre.

Sir Roger de Coverley English country dance of uncertain origin.

springer Norwegian folk dance in 3/4 time.

Strathspey Scottish dance, slower than a reel, in 4/4 time using the Scotch snap rhythm.

tango Syncopated, faster version of habañera, originating in Argentina c. 1900; characterised by long gliding steps and sudden pauses.

tarantella Neapolitan peasant dance in 6/8 time.

tirana Spanish song/dance in 6/8 time, usually to guitar accompaniment; popular in Andalusia.

torch Dance (Fackeltanz) More often a torchlight procession to music, usually performed at weddings.

trepak Quick Russian dance in 2/4 time, most often associated with Cossacks.

veleta (valeta) Ballroom dance in triple-time. (Lit. weather-vane).

verbunkos Hungarian soldiers' dance used in the late 18th century to attract recruits for the army.

volta Lively Italian dance resembling a galliard and popular in the 16th and 17th centuries. Also known as lavolta. Britten's *Gloriana* includes a volta.

waltz Developed from the ländler around 1800 and performed in triple time whilst couples spin around the dance floor.

zamba Argentinian scarf dance (originated in Peru) in 6/8 time.

zapateado Spanish dance in triple time, characterised by rhythmic heel stamping.

zortziko Basque folk dance in 5/4 time, similar to the rueda.

zydeco Style of popular dance music that mixes cajun and Afro-Caribbean with rhythm and blues.

Organ Stops

Two types are flue pipes and reed pipes. Pipes may vary from 32 feet in length to less than an inch, giving the organ a range of nine octaves, larger than any other instrument. Below are listed some common stops.

Aeolina	Eighteenth	Jubal	Octavin	Seventeenth
Amoroso	Eleventh	Jula	Olseau	Seventy-first
Bassoon	Eoline	Jungfernstime	Open Diapason	Third
Bible-Regal	Fernflöte (Distant	Keen Strings	Ottavina	Thiry-first
Bird Whistle	Flute)	Keraulophon	Parade Drum	Thunder
Block-flute	Fifteenth	Kerophone	Parforce	Tibia
Canary	Flageolet	Kleine Mixture	Pfeife	Twelfth
Carillon	Flûte à Pavillon	Koppel	Phoneuma	Tympani
Celesta	Forty-third	Labial Oboe	Piano	Ucceli
Clarabella	Furniture	Largo	Piccolo	Unda Maris (Wave
Clarinet Flute	Gamba	Larigot	Plein Jeu	of the Sea)
Clarion	Gedackt	Ludwigtone	Point-Flute	Untersatz
Cor de Nuit	Gemshorn	Magnaton	Portunal	Vidula
Corno di Bassetto	Grave Mixture	Major Bass	Quadragesima	Viola di Samba
Corno Dolce	Grobregal	Major Flute	Quincena	Vox Angelica
Cornopean	Hahn	Marimba	Quint	Vox Humana
Cor-Oboe	Harmonic Bass	Melodia	Racket	Wald Quint
Cremona	Harmonic Flute	Melophone	Rain	Woodland Flute
Crumhorn	Harmonic Piccolo	Mixture Stop	Reed Flute	Xylophone
Cuckoo	Harp	Montre	Resultant	Zauberflöte
Cymbel	Hautboy	Musette	Sackbut	Ziflot
Diaphone	Hohlflöte	Night Horn	Sadt	Zimbelstern
Docena	Horn Diapason	Nightingale	Salamine	Zünk
Doppelflöte	Hummel	Nineteenth	Salicional	
Dulciana Mixture	Infra Bass	Ninth	Scarf	
Duophone	Italian Principal	None	Septime	
Echo Gamba	Iula	Oboe	Serpent	

MUSIC CLASSICAL

Ballet Dancers and Choreographers

Alvin Ailey Jr (1931–89)
Alicia Alonso (1921–)
Frederick Ashton (1904–88)
George Balanchine (1904–83)
Mikhail Baryshnikov (1948–)
Maurice Béjart (1927–)
Svetlana Beriosova (1932–98)
David Bintley (1957–)
Carlo de Blaisis (1795–1878)
August Bournonville (1805–79)
Darcy Bussell (1969–)
Maria Anna de Camargo (1710–70)
Enrico Cecchetti (1850–1928)
Harold Christensen (1904–89)
Lew Christensen (1909–84)
John Cranko (1927–73)
Birgit Cullberg (1908–99)
Merce Cunningham (1919–)
Patrick Delcroix (1963–)
Agnes De Mille (1905–93)
Charles-Louis Didelot (1797–1837)
Anton Dolin (1904–83)
Anthony Dowell (1943–)
Nacho Duato (1957–)
Isadora Duncan (1878–1927)

Mats Elk (1945–)
Garth Fagan (1940–)
Suzanne Farrell (1945–)
Mikhail Fokine (1880–1942)
Margot Fonteyn (1919–91)
William Forsythe (1949–)
Loie Fuller (1862–1928)
Martha Graham (1894–1991)
Beryl Grey (1927–)
Carlotta Grisi (1819–99)
Sylvie Guillem (1965–)
Hanya Holm (1893–1992)
Doris Humphrey (1895–1958)
Kurt Jooss (1920–)
Tamara Karsavina (1885–1978)
Gelsey Kirkland (1952–)
Jirì Kylàn (1947–)
Rudolf von Laban (1879–1958)
Serge Lifar (1905–86)
Paul Lightfoot (1966–)
Kenneth MacMillan (1929–)
Natalia Makarova (1940–)
Hans van Manen (1932–)
Alicia Markova (1910–)
Léonide Massine (1896–1979)

Mikhail Mordkin (1880–1944)
Bronislava Nijinska (1891–1972)
Vaclav Nijinsky (1890–1950)
Alwin Nikolais (1910–93)
Rudolf Nureyev (1939–93)
Gideon Obarzanek (1966–)
Anna Pavlova (1885–1931)
Marius Petipa (1818–1910)
Roland Petit (1924–)
Maya Plisetskya (1925–)
Jerome Robbins (1918–98)
Marie Sallé (1707–56)
Antoinette Sibley (1939–)
Maria Taglioni (1808–84)
Glen Tetley (1926–)
Twyla Tharp (1941–)
Antony Tudor (1908–87)
Galina Ulanova (1910–98)
Ninette de Valois (1898–2001)
Auguste Vestris (1760–1842)
Gaetano Vestris (1729–1808)
Charles Weidman (1901–75)
Mary Wigman (1886–1973)

Orchestral Positions
(can vary with conductor's preference)

Section	Position
First violins	Left of conductor and to the right of second violins
Second violins	Left of first violins and in front but slightly left of conductor
Cellos	Right of conductor and to the left of the violas
Violas	Right of cellos and in front but slightly right of the conductor
Double basses	Behind the violas and cellos
Trumpets	Behind the double basses and double bassoons
Horns	Behind the clarinets and bassoons
Harp	Behind the bass clarinet and in front of percussion
Piccolo	Left of second violin and in front of bass clarinet
Flutes	Left of piccolo and in front of clarinets
Cor anglais	Right of double basses and back of violas
Oboes	Right of cor anglais and left of the flutes
Bassoons	Behind the oboes and in front of the horns
Double bassoon	Behind the cor anglais and in front of the trumpets
Clarinets	Behind the flutes and in front of the horns
Bass clarinet	Behind the piccolo and to the left of second violins
Percussion	Behind the harp and to the right of timpani
Timpani	Behind the horns and between percussion and trombones
Trombones	Behind horns and trumpets
Tuba	Behind trumpets and to the left of trombones

NB: All positions are viewed relative to the section and not the front.

Master of the King's/Queen's Music

1625	Nicholas Lanier	1834	Christian Kramer
1666	Louis Grabu	1848	George Frederick Anderson
1674	Nicholas Staggins	1870	William George Cusins
1700	John Eccles	1893	Walter Parratt
1735	Maurice Greene	1924	Edward Elgar
1755	William Boyce	1934	Walford Davies
1779	John Stanley	1942	Arnold Bax
1786	William Parsons	1953	Arthur Bliss
1817	William Shield	1975	Malcolm Williamson (died 2 March 2003)

Classical Works

Music	Composer	Music	Composer
Abegg Variations	Robert Schumann	Éclats (Fragments)	Pierre Boulez
Academic Festival	Johannes Brahms	Egdon Heath	Gustav Holst
Overture		Eight Songs for a Mad	Peter Maxwell Davies
An Alpine Symphony	Richard Strauss	King	
Also sprach Zarathustra	Richard Strauss	Eine Kleine Nachtmusik	Wolfgang Amadeus
(Thus Spake Zoroaster)		(A Little Night Music)	Mozart
Alto Rhapsody	Johannes Brahams	Elegy For JFK	Igor Stravinsky
The Apostles (oratorio)	Edward Elgar	Elijah Oratorio	Felix Mendelssohn
Appassionata Sonata	Ludwig van Beethoven	Emperor March	Richard Wagner
Archduke Trio	Ludwig van Beethoven	(Kaisermarsch)	
Ariana a Naxos	Franz Joseph Haydn	Emperor Waltz	Johann Strauss II
(cantata)		The Enclosed Garden	Gabriel Fauré
The Art of Fugue	Johann Sebastian Bach	L'Enfant prodigue	Claude Debussy
Asrael (symphony)	Josef Suk	(cantata)	
Aurora's Wedding	Pyotr Tchaikovsky	An English Suite	Parry, Hubert
Bergomask Suite	Claude Debussy	España	Emmanuel Chabrier
Brandenburg Concertos	Johann Sebastian Bach	Esther	George Frederick Handel
El Capitán (march)	John Philip Sousa	Façade	William Walton
Capriccio Espagnol	Nikolay Rimsky-Korsakov	The Fair Melusina	Felix Mendelssohn
Carmina Burana	Carl Orff	Fanfare for the Common	Aaron Copland
(part 1 of Trionfi trilogy)		Man	
Carnaval	Robert Schumann	Fantasia on a Theme by	Ralph Vaughan Williams
Carnival	Antonín Dvořák	Thomas Tallis	
The Carnival of Animals	Camille Saint-Saëns	Fantasia on a Theme	Michael Tippett
Catulli Carmina (cantata)	Carl Orff	of Handel	
Caucasian Sketches	Mikhail Ippolitov-Ivanov	Fantasia on Christmas	Ralph Vaughan Williams
Celtic Requiem	John Tavener	Carols	
Chagall Windows	John McCabe	Fantasia on	Ralph Vaughan Williams
Chamber Symphony	Arnold Schoenberg	Greensleeves	
(name of two works)		Faust Overture	Richard Wagner
Chandos Anthems	George Frederick Handel	Fêtes galantes	Claude Debussy
A Child of Our Time	Sir Michael Tippett	Finlandia	Jean Sibelius
The Childhood of Christ	Hector Berlioz	Fireworks	Igor Stravinsky
Children's Corner	Claude Debussy	Fireworks Music	George Frederick Handel
A Children's Overture	Roger Quilter	Five Tudor Portraits	Ralph Vaughan Williams
Christmas Oratorio	Johann Sebastian Bach	The Flight of the Bumble	Nikolay Rimsky-Korsakov
Clair de Lune	Claude Debussy	Bee	
The Cloud Messenger	Gustav Holst	Four Last Songs	Richard Strauss
Cockaigne (In	Edward Elgar	Four Sea Interludes	Benjamin Britten
London Town)		The Four Seasons	Antonio Vivaldi
Colonel Bogey	Kenneth Alford	Four Serious Songs	Johannes Brahms
Colour Symphony	Arthur Bliss	French Suites	Johann Sebastian Bach
Concertino Pastorale	John Ireland	Froissart	Edward Elgar
Construction in Metal	John Cage	From Stone to Thorn	Peter Maxwell Davies
(name of three works)		From the Diary of	Dominick Argento
Coronation Mass	Wolfgang Amadeus	Virginia Woolf	
	Mozart	Funeral March of a	Charles Gounod
Coronation Ode	Edward Elgar	Marionette	
The Creation	Franz Joseph Haydn	The Garden of Fand	Arnold Bax
Crown Imperial	William Walton	Gaspard de la Nuit	Maurice Ravel
The Crown of India	Edward Elgar	A German Requiem	Johannes Brahms
The Crucifixion	John Stainer	The Girl With the Flaxen	Claude Debussy
The Curlew (song cycle)	Peter Warlock	Hair	
The Damnation of Faust	Hector Berlioz	Gold and Silver (waltz)	Franz Lehár
Dance of Death	Franz Liszt	The Golden Spinning	Antonín Dvořák
(Totentanz)		Wheel	
Danse Macabre	Camille Saint-Saëns	Golliwogg's Cakewalk	Claude Debussy
Dante Symphony	Franz Liszt	Good Friday Music	Richard Wagner
Davidde Penitente	Wolfgang Amadeus	Gymnopédies	Erik Satie
	Mozart	Gypsy Songs	Johannes Brahms
Death and the Maiden	Franz Schubert	(Zigeunerlieder)	
Death and Transfiguration	Richard Strauss	Habañera	Maurice Ravel
The Death of Cleopatra	Hector Berlioz	Hail to the Chief	James Sanderson
Deborah	George Frederick Handel	Hamlet (fantasy	Pyotr Tchaikovsky
Diabelli Variations	Ludwig van Beethoven	overture)	
The Dream of Gerontius	Edward Elgar	Hamlet (symphonic	Franz Liszt
Ebony Concerto	Igor Stravinsky	poem)	

MUSIC

CLASSICAL

Music	Composer	Music	Composer
Harold in Italy	Hector Berlioz	Lady Radnor's Suite	Hubert Parry
L'Heure Espagnole (The Spanish Hour)	Maurice Ravel	Land of the Mountain and the Flood	Hamish MacCunn
Hiawatha	Samuel Coleridge-Taylor	The Lark Ascending	Ralph Vaughan Williams
Hodie (On This Day)	Ralph Vaughan Williams	The Last Sleep of the Virgin	Jules Massenet
Holberg Suite	Edvard Grieg		
The Holy Boy	John Ireland	Late Swallows	Frederick Delius
Holy Sonnets of John Donne	Benjamin Britten	Lazarus (oratorio)	Franz Schubert
		The Legend of St Elizabeth	Franz Liszt
L'Horizon chimérique	Gabriel Fauré	Lélio, or the Return to Life	Hector Berlioz
Hungarian Dances	Johannes Brahms	Lie Strewn the White Flocks (pastoral)	Arthur Bliss
Hungarian Rhapsodies	Franz Liszt		
The Hymn of Jesus	Gustav Holst	Lieutenant Kijé	Sergey Prokofiev
Hymn of Paradise	Herbert Howells	The Light of Life	Edward Elgar
Hymn to St Magnus	Peter Maxwell Davies	A Lincoln Portrait	Aaron Copland
Hymns from the Rig Veda	Gustav Holst	Little Suite	Claude Debussy
Iberia	Isaac Albéniz	Little Symphony	Charles Gounod
Imaginary Landscape	John Cage	A London Overture	John Ireland
In a Summer Garden	Frederick Delius	A London Symphony	Ralph Vaughan Williams
Indian Diary	Ferruccio Busoni	The Love Feast of the Apostles	Richard Wagner
Indian Fantasy	Ferruccio Busoni		
In Honour of the City	George Dyson	Love-Dreams (Liebesträume)	Franz Liszt
In Honour of the City of London	William Walton		
		Love-Song Waltzes	Johannes Brahms
In the Faery Hills	Arnold Bax	The Magic Island	William Alwyn
In the South	Edward Elgar	Makrokosmos	George Crumb
In the Steppes of Central Asia	Alexander Borodin	Mantra	Karlheinz Stockhausen
		The Mask of Time	Michael Tippett
Invitation to the Dance	Carl Maria Weber	Mass of Christ the King	Malcolm Williamson
In Windsor Forest	Ralph Vaughan Williams	A Mass of Life	Frederick Delius
Irish Symphony	Hamilton Harty	Má Vlast (My Country)	Bedřich Smetana
Islamey	Mily Balakirev	Mazeppa	Franz Liszt
The Island of Joy	Claude Debussy	Memento Vitae (Memory of Life)	Thea Musgrave
The Isle of the Dead	Sergei Rachmaninov		
Israel in Egypt	George Frederick Handel	Mephisto Waltzes	Franz Liszt
Israel Symphony	Ernest Bloch	La Mer (The Sea)	Claude Debussy
Italian Caprice	Pyotr Tchaikovsky	Messiah (oratorio)	George Frederick Handel
Italian Serenade	Hugo Wolf	Metamorphosen	Richard Strauss
Jacob's Ladder	Arnold Schoenberg	A Midsummer Night's Dream (1826)	Felix Mendelssohn
Jamaican Rumba	Arthur Benjamin		
Jeux d'Eau (Fountains)	Maurice Ravel	A Midsummer Night's Dream	Carl Orff (1939)
Jeux d'Enfants (Children's Games)	Georges Bizet		
		Mikrokosmos	Béla Bartók
Joan of Arc at the Stake (oratorio)	Arthur Honegger	The Miraculous Mandarin	Béla Bartók
		Mládí (Youth)	Leoš Janáček
Joan of Arc at the Stake (concert aria)	Franz Liszt	Moby Dick (cantata)	Bernard Herrmann
		Moby Dick (concertato)	Peter Mennin
Johannesburg Festival Overture	William Walton	Moby Dick (symphonic poem)	Douglas Moore
Joshua	George Frederick Handel	Morning Heroes	Arthur Bliss
Judas Maccabaeus	George Frederick Handel	Mother Goose Suite	Maurice Ravel
Judith (oratorio)	Thomas Arne (1761)	Name Day (Namensfeier)	Ludwig van Beethoven
Judith (oratorio)	Hubert Parry (1888)	Natural Histories	Maurice Ravel
Judith Triumphant	Antonio Vivaldi	New England Holidays	Charles Ives
Kakadu Variations	Ludwig van Beethoven	Night and Dreams	Franz Schubert
Kamarinskaya (Wedding Song)	Mikhail Glinka	Night on the Bare Mountain	Modest Mussorgsky
Karelia Suite	Jean Sibelius	Noble and Sentimental Waltzes	Maurice Ravel
Kinderscenen (Scenes From Childhood)	Robert Schumann		
		The Noonday Witch	Antonín Dvořák
King David	Arthur Honegger	Norfolk Rhapsody	Ralph Vaughan Williams
The Kingdom (oratorio)	Edward Elgar	North Country Sketches	Frederick Delius
King of Prussia Quartets	Wolfgang Amadeus Mozart	Nursery Suite	Edward Elgar
		The Oceanides	Jean Sibelius
King Stephen	Ludwig van Beethoven	Ode For St Cecilia's Day	Henry Purcell (1683–92)
Kontakte (Contacts)	Karlheinz Stockhausen	Ode For St Cecilia's Day	George Frederick Handel (1739)
Lachrimae	John Dowland		
Lachrymae	Benjamin Britten	Ode For St Cecilia's Day	Hubert Parry (1889)
Lady in the Dark	Kurt Weill	Ode to Death	Gustav Holst
The Lady of Shalott	Maurice Jacobson	Ode to Napoleon Bonaparte	Arnold Schoenberg
The Lady of Shalott	Phyllis Tate		

Music	Composer	Music	Composer
Odyssey	Nicholas Maw	Russian Easter Festival Overture	Nikolay Rimsky-Korsakov
Oiseaux Exotiques	Olivier Messiaen	Rustic Wedding	Károly Goldmark
Omar Khayyám	Granville Bantock	Rustle of Spring	Christian Sinding
On Hearing the First Cuckoo in Spring	Frederick Delius	St Anthony Variations	Johannes Brahms
Orb and Sceptre March	William Walton	St John Passion	Johann Sebastian Bach
Organ Solo Mass	Wolfgang Amadeus Mozart	St Ludmila	Antonín Dvořák
		St Matthew Passion	Johann Sebastian Bach
Orpheus	Franz Liszt	St Nicolas	Benjamin Britten
Othello	Antonín Dvořák	St Paul	Felix Mendelssohn
An Oxford Elegy	Ralph Vaughan Williams	St Paul's Suite	Gustav Holst
Pacific 231	Arthur Honegger	St Thomas Wake	Peter Maxwell Davies
Pan and Syrinx	Carl Nielsen	Samson (oratorio)	George Frederick Handel
Papillons (Butterflies)	Robert Schumann		
Paradise Lost (cantata)	Christopher Steel	Sarnia	John Ireland
Pavane	Gabriel Fauré	Satyricon	John Ireland
Pavane For a Dead Infanta	Maurice Ravel	Scapino	William Walton
Peacock Variations	Zoltán Kodály	Scaramouche	Darius Milhaud
Peasant Cantata	Johann Sebastian Bach	Scenes from the Bavarian Highlands	Edward Elgar
Peer Gynt	Edvard Grieg	Scenes From the Saga of King Olaf	Edward Elgar
Pelléas et Mélisande	Gabriel Fauré		
Pelléas et Mélisande	Arnold Schoenberg	Scottish Fantasy	Max Bruch
Pelléas et Mélisande	Jean Sibelius	Scythian Suite	Sergey Prokofiev
Peter and the Wolf	Sergey Prokofiev	The Sea	Frank Bridge
Phaëton	Camille Saint-Saëns	Sea Drift	Frederick Delius
Phoebus and Pan	Johann Sebastian Bach	Sea Fever	John Ireland
Pierrot Lunaire	Arnold Schoenberg	Sea Pictures	Edward Elgar
Pines of Rome	Ottorino Respighi	The Seasons	Franz Joseph Haydn
The Planets	Gustav Holst	Serenade for Tenor, Horn and Strings	Benjamin Britten
The Pleasure Dome of Kubla Khan	Charles Griffes		
Poet & Peasant Overture	Franz von Suppé	Severn Suite	Edward Elgar
Pohjola's Daughter	Jean Sibelius	Sheherazade	Nikolay Rimsky-Korsakov (1889)
Polovtsian Dances	Alexander Borodin		
Portsmouth Point	William Walton	Shéhérazade	Maurice Ravel (1904)
Prélude à l'Après-midi d'un faune	Claude Debussy	Shepherd Fennel's Dance	Balfour Gardiner
		Shylock	Gabriel Fauré
Préludes	Claude Debussy	Siegfried Idyll	Richard Wagner
Les Préludes	Ferencz Liszt	Simple Symphony	Benjamin Britten
Procession	Karlheinz Stockhausen	Slavonic Dances	Antonín Dvořák
The Prodigal Son	Benjamin Britten	Slavonic Rhapsodies	Antonín Dvořák
The Prodigal Son	Claude Debussy	The Soldier's Tale	Igor Stravinsky
The Prodigal Son (oratorio)	Arthur Sullivan	A Song for the Lord Mayor's Table	William Walton
Prometheus	Franz Liszt	The Song of Sorrow	Gustav Mahler
Queen Mary's Funeral Music	Henry Purcell	The Song of the Earth	Gustav Mahler
		Song of the Flea	Modest Mussorgsky
Quiet City	Aaron Copland	Song of the High Hills	Frederick Delius
Radetzky March	Johann Strauss the Elder	Song of the Young Boys	Karlheinz Stockhausen
Raft of the Medusa, The	Hans Werner Henze	Songs Without Words	Felix Mendelssohn
Rakastava (The Lover)	Jean Sibelius	Songs and Dances of Death	Modest Mussorgsky
Ramifications	György Ligeti		
Rapsodie Espagnole	Franz Liszt	Songs My Mother Taught Me	Antonín Dvořák
Rapsodie Espagnole (including Habañera)	Maurice Ravel		
		Songs of Travel	Ralph Vaughan Williams
Renard (The Fox)	Igor Stravinsky	The Sorcerer's Apprentice (based on Goethe poem)	Paul Dukas
Rhapsody in Blue	George Gershwin		
Rhapsody on a Theme of Paganini	Sergei Rachmaninov		
		The Spectre's Bride	Antonín Dvořák
Roman Festivals	Ottorino Respighi	The Spirit of England	Edward Elgar
Romeo and Juliet (fantasy overture)	Pyotr Tchaikovsky	Spitfire Prelude and Fugue	William Walton
		A Spring Symphony	Benjamin Britten
Romeo and Juliet (symphony)	Hector Berlioz	Spring (Printemps)	Claude Debussy
		The Starlight Express	Edward Elgar
Roses From the South	Johann Strauss II	La Stravaganza (The Extraordinary)	Antonio Vivaldi
Le Rouet d'Omphale	Camille Saint-Saëns		
Rugby	Arthur Honegger	Street Corner	Alan Rawsthorne
Ruins of Athens	Ludwig van Beethoven	Such a Day, Such a Night	Francis Poulenc
Rule, Britannia! (from the masque Alfred)	Thomas Arne	Suite bergamasque	Claude Debussy
		Summer Night on the River	Frederick Delius
Running Set	Ralph Vaughan Williams		

MUSIC

CLASSICAL

Music	Composer	Music	Composer
Summer's Last Will and Testament	Constant Lambert	Ultimos Ritos (Last Rites)	John Tavener
The Swan of Tuonela	Jean Sibelius	Ulysses (cantata)	Mátyás Seiber
Swan Song	Franz Schubert	The Unanswered Question	Charles Ives
The Swan-Turner	Paul Hindemith	Universal Prayer	Andrzej Panufnik
Symphonia Domestica	Richard Strauss	Vallée d'Obermann (Obermann Valley)	Franz Liszt
Symphonic Dances	Sergei Rachmaninov		
Symphonic Metamorphosis of Themes by Weber	Paul Hindemith	La Valse (The Waltz)	Maurice Ravel
		Valse Triste (Sad Waltz)	Jean Sibelius
Symphonie Espagnole	Édouard-Victor-Antoine Lalo	Variations on a Rococo Theme	Pyotr Tchaikovsky
Symphonie Fantastique	Hector Berlioz		
Symphonie Funèbre et Triomphale	Hector Berlioz	Variations on a Theme by Haydn	Johannes Brahms
Symphonies of Wind Instruments	Igor Stravinsky	Variations on a Theme of Frank Bridge	Benjamin Britten
Symphony in Three Movements	Igor Stravinsky	Variations on a Theme of Hindemith	William Walton
Symphony of Psalms	Igor Stravinsky	Venetian Games	Witold Lutoslawski
Syrinx	Claude Debussy	A Vision of Aeroplanes	Ralph Vaughan Williams
Tahiti Trot	Dmitry Shostakovich	The Vision of Judgement	Peter Racine Fricker
Tales from the Vienna Woods	Johann Strauss II	The Vision of St Augustine	Michael Tippett
		Visions Fugitives (Fleeting Visions)	Sergey Prokofiev
Tam O'Shanter	Malcolm Arnold		
Taras Bulba	Leoš Janáček	The Wand of Youth	Edward Elgar
The Tempest	Pyotr Tchaikovsky (1873)	War Requiem	Benjamin Britten
The Tempest	Jean Sibelius (1925)	The Wasps	Ralph Vaughan Williams
Theodora	George Frederick Handel	Water Music	George Frederick Handel
Three Pear-Shaped Pieces	Erik Satie	The Water Sprite	Antonín Dvořák
		Wedding Day at Troldhaugen	Edvard Grieg
Three Places in New England	Charles Ives		
		Welles Raises Kane	Bernard Herrmann
Three Screaming Popes	Mark-Anthony Turnage	The Whale	John Tavener
Till Eulenspiegel	Richard Strauss	The White Peacock	Charles Griffes
Tintagel	Arnold Bax	Wine	Alban Berg
To the Children	Sergei Rachmaninov	Winterreise (Winter Journey)	Franz Schubert
The Tomb of Couperin	Maurice Ravel		
Tragic Overture	Johannes Brahms	The Wood Dove	Antonín Dvořák
Transcendental Studies	Franz Liszt	The Young Person's Guide to the Orchestra	Benjamin Britten
Turandot	Carl Maria Weber		
Tzigane (Gypsy)	Maurice Ravel	Zyklus (Cycle)	Karlheinz Stockhausen

Musical Instructions

a cappella   In the chapel style (unaccompanied).

accarezzevole   Caressingly.

accelerando   Becoming faster.

ad libitum   At will, improvised.

adagietto   Not quite as slow as adagio.

adagio   At ease. Slow tempo between largo (slower) and andante (faster).

adagissimo   Very slow.

addolorato   Sorrowfully.

à demi-jeu   With half the power.

à demi-voix   With half the voice, whispered.

affábile   Gently, pleasingly.

afflito   Sorrowfully, mournfully, sadly.

affrettando   Hurrying.

allegramente   Brightly, gaily.

allegretto   Moderately quick.

allegro   Quick.

ancora   Repeat, again.

andante   Moving along, flowing (slowish but not slow).

andantino   Diminutive of andante although nowadays usually means a little faster.

arcato   Bowed.

arpeggio   Playing of the notes of a chord individually in quick succession.

ballabile   In a dance style.

bariolage   Rapid alternation of open and stopped strings in violin playing.

barré   Playing a chord on the guitar with finger across all strings raising their pitch equally.

bisbigliando   Both hands playing adjacent strings of harp repeatedly pianissimo.

bouche fermée   Closed-mouth singing, i.e. humming.

brio   Vigour, spirit.

calando   Diminishing gradually – softer and slower.

calcando   Quickening gradually (literally, trampling).

col legno   With the wood; using the stick part of the bow to strike the string.

common time   4/4 metre.

comodo   Leisurely, moderate speed.

con brio   With vigour.

con fuoco   With fire; using both force and speed.

con lancio   With verve.

con sordini   On stringed instruments – with mutes; on keyboard instruments – with dampers.

coperti Covered; relates to drums being muted by being covered with a cloth.

crescendo Becoming louder.

da capo From the beginning (literally, from the head).

dal segno From the sign, meaning return to the sign and repeat.

diminuendo Becoming quieter.

diminution Opposite of augmentation, i.e shortening of the time-values of notes of melodic parts.

dolce Sweet, with an implication of 'soft'.

forte Loudly.

fortissimo Very loudly.

gedämpft (damped) Therefore muted for strings and horns; muffled for drums; soft-pedalled for piano.

giocoso Merry, playful.

grazioso Graceful.

jeté (flung) Bowing technique whereby the upper part of the bow is bounced on the string.

larghetto Slow tempo, a little faster than largo.

largo Broad, slow tempo.

legato Smoothly, with no breaks between successive notes.

lento Slow.

maestoso Majestically or stately.

martelé (hammered) Playing the violin with short strokes and never lifting the bow from the strings.

mezza voce Subdued tone between piano and forte (literally, middle voice).

moderato Moderate pace.

morendo Dying away, fading.

muta Direction to change keys, frequently found in timpani and horn parts.

piacere (pleasure) At the performer's discretion.

pianissimo (pp) Very soft.

pianississimo (ppp) Very, very soft.

piano (p) Soft.

pianoforte Soft-loud.

pizzicato (pinched) On string instruments, plucking the string.

poco a poco Little by little, gradually.

portamento Carrying, i.e. the carrying of the sound from one note to another (very legato).

portato Halfway between staccato and legato.

prestissimo Very, very fast; the fastest tempo.

presto Fast.

rake On guitar, dragging the pick across muted strings in an arpeggiated fashion.

rallentando Becoming gradually slower.

ritardando Delaying, becoming gradually slower.

rubato (robbed) Freely slowing down and speeding up the tempo without changing the basic pulse.

saltato (saltando) Bowing technique where the bow is bounced lightly on the string. Means 'jumping'.

scherzando (scherzhaft) Playful, light-hearted.

scherzo Piece in a lively tempo; 'joke'.

sostenuto Sustained.

sotto voce Under the voice, in a quiet soft voice.

spiccato (detached) Bouncing the bow on the strings.

stringendo Tightening, increasing the tension by hurrying the tempo.

strophic Describes a song that has identical music in each verse.

subito Suddenly, at once.

sul ponticello On the bridge: playing a stringed instrument with the bow as near as possible to the bridge.

sul tasto Instruction to take the bow over the fingerboard. Means 'on the fingerboard'.

sur la touche Bow over the fingerboard. Means 'on the touch', synonymous with *sul tasto*.

susurrando Whispering, murmuring.

tacet Stop playing and be silent.

tutti (all) Instruction for the whole orchestra to play.

una corda One string, i.e. the use of the soft pedal which causes the hammers of a piano to.strike only one string per note instead of three.

vibrato Rapid alteration of pitch or intensity of a note to impart 'expression'.

vivace Vivacious, i.e. fast and lively.

Names and Nicknames of Symphonies

The Age of Anxiety	Bernstein's Symphony No. 2
Alleluiasymphonie	Haydn's Symphony No. 30 in C
America	Bloch's 'Epic Rhapsody' Symphony (1926)
Andante Cantabile	Tchaikovsky's Symphony No. 5 in E minor (2nd movement)
Antar	Rimsky-Korsakov's Symphony No. 2 Op. 9 (Oriental Suite)
Antarctica	Vaughan Williams's Symphony No. 7
Apocalyptic	Bruckner's Symphony No. 7
Asrael	Suk's Symphony No. 2 in C minor Op. 27
Babi Yar	Shostakovich's Symphony No. 13 in B flat minor Op. 113
The Bear (L'Ours)	Haydn's Symphony No. 82 in C
The Bells of Zlonice	Dvořák's Symphony No. 1 in C minor Op. 3
The Bell	Khachaturian's Symphony No. 2 in A minor
The Camp Meeting	Ives's Symphony No. 3
Capricieuse	Berwald's Symphony No. 2
Celestial Railroad	Ives's Symphony No. 4, 2nd movement, fantasy piece for piano
Cello Symphony	Britten's Opus 68 Symphony dedicated to Rostropovich
La Chasse (The Hunt)	Haydn's Symphony No. 73 in D
Choral	Beethoven's Symphony No. 9 in D minor Op. 125
Christmas	Haydn's Symphony No. 26 in D minor
Classical	Prokofiev's Symphony No. 1 in D Op. 25
Clock	Haydn's Symphony No. 101 in D
Decoration Day	Ives's 2nd Movement of his 'New England Holidays'
Deliciae Basiliensis	Honegger's Symphony No. 4
The Distraught Man	Haydn's Symphony No. 60 in C major

MUSIC CLASSICAL

The Divine Poem	Scriabin's Symphony No. 3 in C minor Op. 43
Le Double	Dutilleux's Symphony No. 3
Dreams of Gandalf	Sallinen's Symphony No. 7
Drumroll	Haydn's Symphony No. 103 in E flat
Eroica	Beethoven's Symphony No. 3 in E flat major
Espansiva (Expansive)	Nielsen's Symphony No. 3
Fantaisies	Martinu's Symphony No. 6
Farewell (Abschied)	Haydn's Symphony No. 45 in F sharp minor
Fate	Beethoven's Symphony No. 5 in C minor Op. 67
Fate	Tchaikovsky's Symphony No. 4 in F minor Op. 36
Festive	Smetana's Symphony in E
Fire	Haydn's Symphony No. 59 in A
First of May	Shostakovich's Symphony No. 3 in E flat Op. 20
Four Seasons	Malipiero's Symphony No. 1
The Four Temperaments	Nielsen's Symphony No. 2 in C minor Op. 16
Fourth of July	Ives's 3rd Movement of his 'New England Holidays'
From a New Zealand Diary	Sallinen's Symphony No. 6
From the New World	Dvořák's Symphony No. 9 (formerly No. 5) in E minor
Funeral March	Beethoven's Symphony No. 3 in E flat Op. 55 (2nd movement)
Gothic	Havergal Brian's Symphony No. 1 in D minor
Great C Major	Schubert's Symphony No. 9 in C major
Great G Minor	Mozart's Symphony No. 40 in G minor, K550
Haffner	Mozart's Symphony No. 35 in D, K385
Heavenly Length	Schubert's Symphony No. 9 in C major
The Hen	Haydn's Symphony No. 83 in G minor
Holidays	Ives's Symphony (1904–13)
Horn Signal	Haydn's Symphony No. 31 in D
The Hunt (La Chasse)	Haydn's Symphony No. 73 in D
Hydriotaphia	Alwyn's Symphony No. 5
Hymn of Praise	Mendelssohn's Symphony No. 2 in B flat Op. 52
Ilya Murometz	Glière's Symphony No. 3
Imperial	Haydn's Symphony No. 53 in D
The Inextinguishable	Nielsen's Symphony No. 4, Op. 29
Irish	Stanford's Symphony No. 3 in F minor Op. 28
Irish	Sullivan's Symphony in E minor
Israel	Bloch's Symphony (1916)
Italian	Mendelssohn's Symphony No. 4 in A major Op. 90
Jeremiah	Bernstein's Symphony No. 1
Jupiter	Mozart's Symphony No. 41 in C major, K551
Kaddish	Bernstein's Symphony No. 3
Lamentations	Haydn's Symphony No. 26 in D minor
Largo	Dvořák's Symphony No. 5 (No. 9) in E minor (2nd movement)
Loudon	Haydn's Symphony No. 69 in C
Leningrad	Shostakovich's Symphony No. 7 in C major Op. 60
Linz	Mozart's Symphony No. 36 in C, K425
Little C Major	Schubert's Symphony No. 6 in C major
Little G Minor	Mozart's Symphony No. 25 in G minor, K183
Little Russian	Tchaikovsky's Symphony No. 2 in C minor Op. 17
Liturgique	Honegger's Symphony No. 3
Lobgesang (Hymn of Praise)	Mendelssohn's Symphony No. 2 in B flat Op. 52
London	Vaughan Williams's Symphony No. 2
London	Haydn's Symphony No. 104 in D
London Symphonies	Haydn's Symphonies Nos 93–104
Maria Theresia	Haydn's Symphony No. 48 in C
Mathis der Maler	Hindemith's Symphony (1934)
Le Matin (Morning)	Haydn's Symphony No. 6 in D
Mercury	Haydn's Symphony No. 43 in E flat
Michelangelo	Kancheli's Symphony No. 4
Le Midi (Noon)	Haydn's Symphony No. 7 in C
Military	Haydn's Symphony No. 100 in G
Miracle	Haydn's Symphony No. 96 in D
Mysterious Mountain	Hovahness' Symphony No. 2 Op. 132
New England Holidays	Ives's Symphony (1904–13)
New World	Dvořák's Symphony No. 9 (formerly No. 5) in E minor
1917 Symphony	Shostakovich's Symphony No. 12 in D minor
Nordic	Hanson's Symphony No. 1 in E minor Op. 21
Die Nullte	Bruckner's Symphony No. 0 in D minor
October	Shostakovichs' Symphony No. 2 in B major Op. 14
Ode to Joy	Beethoven's Symphony No. 9 in D Op. 125 (4th movement)
Organ	Saint-Saëns' Symphony No. 3 in C minor
L'Ours (The Bear)	Haydn's Symphony No. 82 in C
Oxford	Haydn's Symphony No. 92 in G

Palindrome	Haydn's Symphony No. 47 in G
Paris	Mozart's Symphony No. 31 in D, K297
Paris Symphonies	Haydn's Symphonies Nos 82–87
La Passione	Haydn's Symphony No. 49 in F minor
Pastoral	Beethoven's Symphony No. 6 in F major
Pastoral	Vaughan Williams's Symphony No. 3
Pathétique	Tchaikovsky's Symphony No. 6 in B minor Op. 74
The Philosopher	Haydn's Symphony No. 22 in E flat
Pittsburgh	Hindemith's Symphony (1958)
Polish	Tchaikovsky's Symphony No. 3 in D Op. 29
La Poule (The Hen)	Haydn's Symphony No. 83 in G minor
Prague	Mozart's Symphony No. 38 in D, K504
Reformation	Mendelssohn's Symphony No. 5 in D minor
La Reine (The Queen)	Haydn's Symphony No. 85 in B flat
Requiem	Hanson's Symphony No. 4 Op. 34
Resurrection	Mahler's Symphony No. 2 in C minor
Resurrection	Rubbra's Symphony No. 9
Rhenish	Schumann's Symphony No. 3 in E flat major Op. 97
Romantic	Bruckner's Symphony No. 4 in E Flat major
Romantic	Hanson's Symphony No. 2 Op. 30
La Roxelane	Haydn's Symphony No. 63 in C major
Rustic Wedding	Goldmark's Symphony Op. 26
St Florian	Schnittke's Symphony No. 2
Salomon	Haydn's Symphony No. 104 in D
Salomon Symphonies	Haydn's Symphonies Nos 93–104
Schoolmaster	Haydn's Symphony No. 55 in E flat
Scotch (Scottish)	Mendelssohn's Symphony No. 3 in A minor Op. 56
Sea	Hanson's Symphony No. 7
Sea	Vaughan Williams's Symphony No. 1 in C
The Seasons	Spohr's Symphony No. 9 in B minor
Serena	Hindemith's Symphony (1946)
Sérieuse	Berwald's Symphony No. 1
Das Siegeslied	Brian's Symphony No. 4
Simple	Britten's Symphony Op. 4
Simple	Nielsen's Symphony No. 6
Sinfonia Antarctica	See *Antarctica*
Sinfonia Boreale	Holmboe's Symphony No. 8
Sinfonia da Requiem	Britten's Symphony Op. 20
Sinfonia di Sfere	Panufnik's Symphony No. 5
Sinfonia Elegiaca	Malipiero's Symphony No. 2
Sinfonia Elegiaca	Panufnik's Symphony No. 2
Sinfonia Mistica	Panufnik's Symphony No. 6
Sinfonia Rustica	Holmboe's Symphony No. 3
Sinfonia Rustica	Panufnik's Symphony No. 1
Sinfonia Sacra	Holmboe's Symphony No. 4
Sinfonia Sacra	Panufnik's Symphony No. 3
Sinfonia Sacra	Rubbra's Symphony No. 9
Sinfonia Votiva	Panufnik's Symphony No. 8
Singulière	Berwald's Symphony No. 3 in C minor
Le Soir (Evening)	Haydn's Symphony No. 8 in G
Song in the Night	Szymanowski's Symphony No. 3
Spring	Schumann's Symphony No. 1 in B flat Op. 38
Stimmen Verstummen	Gubaildulina's Symphony (1986)
Study	Bruckner's Symphony in F minor
Summer Music	Mathias's Symphony No. 2
Surprise	Haydn's Symphony No. 94 in G major
Symphony of a Thousand	Mahler's Symphony No. 8 in E flat major
Tempest	Haydn's Symphony No. 8 in G, Fourth movement
Tempora Mutantur	Haydn's Symphony No. 64 in A
Thanksgiving Day	Ives's 4th movement of his 'New England Holidays'
Titan	Mahler's Symphony No. 1 in D major
To the Memory of Lenin	Shostakovich's Symphony No. 12 in D minor Op. 112
Tragic	Schubert's Symphony No. 4 in C minor
Trauer (Mourning)	Haydn's Symphony No. 44 in E minor
Di Tre Re	Honegger's Symphony No. 5
Triumph	Smetana's Symphony in E
Ukrainian	Tchaikovsky's Symphony No. 2 in C minor
Unfinished	Schubert's Symphony No. 8 in B minor
Vigil	MacMillan's Symphony (1997)
Wagner	Bruckner's Symphony No. 3 in D minor
Washington Mosaics	Sallinen's Symphony No. 5
Washington's Birthday	Ives's 1st movement of his 'New England Holidays'

MUSIC CLASSICAL

Waves	Kernis' Symphony No. 1
Winter Daydreams	Tchaikovsky's Symphony No. 1 in G minor Op. 13
The Year 1905	Shostakovich's Symphony No. 11 in G minor Op. 103
The Year 1917	Shostakovich's Symphony No. 12 in D minor Op. 112

Names and Nicknames of Symphonies (by composer)

Alwyn's Symphony No. 5	*Hydriotaphia*
Beethoven's Symphony No. 3 in E flat major	*Eroica*
Beethoven's Symphony No. 3 in E flat Op. 55 (2nd movement)	*Funeral March*
Beethoven's Symphony No. 5 in C minor Op. 67	*Fate*
Beethoven's Symphony No. 6 in F major	*Pastoral*
Beethoven's Symphony No. 9 in D minor Op. 125	*Choral*
Beethoven's Symphony No. 9 in D Op. 125 (4th movement)	*Ode to Joy*
Bernstein's Symphony No. 1	*Jeremiah*
Bernstein's Symphony No. 2	*The Age of Anxiety*
Bernstein's Symphony No. 3	*Kaddish*
Berwald's Symphony No. 1	*Sérieuse*
Berwald's Symphony No. 2	*Capricieuse*
Berwald's Symphony No. 3 in C major	*Singulière*
Bloch's 'Epic Rhapsody' Symphony (1926)	*America*
Bloch's Symphony (1916)	*Israel*
Brian's Symphony No. 1 in D minor	*Gothic*
Brian's Symphony No. 4	*Das Siegeslied*
Britten's Op. 68 dedicated to Rostropovich	*Cello Symphony*
Britten's Symphony Op. 20	*Sinfonia da Requiem*
Britten's Symphony Op. 4	*Simple*
Bruckner's Symphony in F minor	*Study*
Bruckner's Symphony No. 0 in D minor	*Die Nullte*
Bruckner's Symphony No. 3 in D minor	*Wagner*
Bruckner's Symphony No. 4 in E flat major	*Romantic*
Bruckner's Symphony No. 7	*Apocalyptic*
Dutilleux's Symphony No. 3	*Le Double*
Dvořák's Symphony No. 1 in C minor Op. 3	*The Bells of Zlonice*
Dvořák's Symphony No. 5 (No. 9) in E minor (2nd movement)	*Largo*
Dvořák's Symphony No. 9 (formerly No. 5) in E minor	*From the New World*
Glière's No. 3	*Ilya Murometz*
Goldmark's Symphony Op. 26	*Rustic Wedding*
Gubaildulina's Symphony (1986)	*Stimmen Verstummen*
Hanson's Symphony No. 1 in E minor Op. 21	*Nordic*
Hanson's Symphony No. 2 Op. 30	*Romantic*
Hanson's Symphony No. 4 Op. 34	*Requiem*
Hanson's Symphony No. 7	*Sea*
Haydn's Symphony No. 6 in D	*Le Matin (Morning)*
Haydn's Symphony No. 7 in C	*Le Midi (Noon)*
Haydn's Symphony No. 8 in G	*Le Soir (Evening)*
Haydn's Symphony No. 8 in G (4th movement)	*Tempest*
Haydn's Symphony No. 22 in E flat	*The Philosopher*
Haydn's Symphony No. 26 in D minor	*Christmas*
Haydn's Symphony No. 26 in D minor	*Lamentation*
Haydn's Symphony No. 30 in C	*Alleluiasymphonie*
Haydn's Symphony No. 31 in D	*Horn Signal*
Haydn's Symphony No. 43 in E flat	*Mercury*
Haydn's Symphony No. 44 in E minor	*Trauer (Mourning)*
Haydn's Symphony No. 45 in F sharp minor	*Farewell (Abschied)*
Haydn's Symphony No. 47 in G	*Palindrome*
Haydn's Symphony No. 48 in C	*Maria Theresia*
Haydn's Symphony No. 49 in F minor	*La Passione*
Haydn's Symphony No. 53 in D	*Imperial*
Haydn's Symphony No. 55 in E flat	*Schoolmaster*
Haydn's Symphony No. 59 in A	*Fire*
Haydn's Symphony No. 60 in C major	*The Distraught Man*
Haydn's Symphony No. 63 in C major	*La Roxolane*
Haydn's Symphony No. 64 in A	*Tempora Mutantur*
Haydn's Symphony No. 69 in C	*Laudon*
Haydn's Symphony No. 73 in D	*The Hunt (La Chasse)*
Haydn's Symphonies Nos 82–87	*Paris Symphonies*
Haydn's Symphony No. 82 in C	*The Bear (L'Ours)*
Haydn's Symphony No. 83 in G minor	*The Hen (La Poule)*
Haydn's Symphony No. 85 in B flat	*La Reine (The Queen)*

Haydn's Symphony No. 92 in G	*Oxford*
Haydn's Symphonies Nos 93–104	*London Symphonies*
Haydn's Symphonies Nos 93–104	*Salomon Symphonies*
Haydn's Symphony No. 94 in G major	*Surprise*
Haydn's Symphony No. 96 in D	*Miracle*
Haydn's Symphony No. 100 in G	*Military*
Haydn's Symphony No. 101 in D	*Clock*
Haydn's Symphony No. 103 in E flat	*Drumroll*
Haydn's Symphony No. 104 in D	*London*
Haydn's Symphony No. 104 in D	*Salomon*
Hindemith's Symphony (1934)	*Mathis der Maler*
Hindemith's Symphony (1946)	*Serena*
Hindemith's Symphony (1958)	*Pittsburgh*
Holmboe's Symphony No. 3	*Sinfonia Rustica*
Holmboe's Symphony No. 4	*Sinfonia Sacra*
Holmboe's Symphony No. 8	*Sinfonia Boreale*
Honegger's Symphony No. 3	*Liturgique*
Honegger's Symphony No. 4	*Deliciae Basiliensis*
Honegger's Symphony No. 5	*Di Tre Re*
Hovahness' Symphony No. 2 Op. 132	*Mysterious Mountain*
Ives's 1st movement of his 'New England Holidays'	*Washington's Birthday*
Ives's 2nd movement of his 'New England Holidays'	*Decoration Day*
Ives's 3rd movement of his 'New England Holidays'	*Fourth of July*
Ives's 4th movement of his 'New England Holidays'	*Thanksgiving Day*
Ives's Symphony No. 3	*The Camp Meeting*
Ives's Symphony No. 4, 2nd movement; fantasy piece for piano	*Celestial Railroad*
Ives's Symphony (1904–13)	*Holidays*
Ives's Symphony (1904–13)	*New England Holidays*
Kanchell's Symphony No. 4	*Michelangelo*
Kernis's Symphony No. 1	*Waves*
Khachaturian's Symphony No. 2 in A minor	*The Bell*
MacMillan's Symphony (1997)	*Vigil*
Mahler's Symphony No. 1 in D major	*Titan*
Mahler's Symphony No. 2 in C minor	*Resurrection*
Mahler's Symphony No. 8 in E flat major	*Symphony of a Thousand*
Malipiero's Symphony No. 1	*Four Seasons*
Malipiero's Symphony No. 2	*Sinfonia Elegiaca*
Martinu's Symphony No. 6	*Fantaisies*
Mathias's Symphony No. 2	*Summer Music*
Mendelssohn's Symphony No. 2 in B flat Op. 52	*Lobgesang (Hymn of Praise)*
Mendelssohn's Symphony No. 3 in A minor Op. 56	*Scotch (Scottish)*
Mendelssohn's Symphony No. 4 in A major Op. 90	*Italian*
Mendelssohn's Symphony No. 5 in D minor	*Reformation*
Mozart's Symphony No. 25 in G minor, K183	*Little G Minor*
Mozart's Symphony No. 31 in D, K297	*Paris*
Mozart's Symphony No. 35 in D, K385	*Haffner*
Mozart's Symphony No. 36 in C, K425	*Linz*
Mozart's Symphony No. 38 in D, K504	*Prague*
Mozart's Symphony No. 40 in G minor, K550	*Great G Minor*
Mozart's Symphony No. 41 in C major, K551	*Jupiter*
Nielsen's Symphony No. 2 in C minor Op. 16	*The Four Temperaments*
Nielsen's Symphony No. 3	*Espansiva (Expansive)*
Nielsen's Symphony No. 4, Op. 29	*The Inextinguishable*
Nielsen's Symphony No. 6	*Simple*
Panufnik's Symphony No. 1	*Sinfonia Rustica*
Panufnik's Symphony No. 2	*Sinfonia Elegiaca*
Panufnik's Symphony No. 3	*Sinfonia Sacra*
Panufnik's Symphony No. 5	*Sinfonia di Sfere*
Panufnik's Symphony No. 6	*Sinfonia Mistica*
Panufnik's Symphony No. 8	*Sinfonia Votiva*
Prokofiev's Symphony No. 1 in D Op. 25	*Classical*
Rimsky-Korsakov's Symphony No. 2 Op. 9 (Oriental Suite)	*Antar*
Rubbra's Symphony No. 9	*Resurrection*
Rubbra's Symphony No. 9	*Sinfonia Sacra*
Saint-Saëns's Symphony No. 3 in C minor	*Organ*
Sallinen's Symphony No. 5	*Washington Mosaics*
Sallinen's Symphony No. 6	*From a New Zealand Diary*
Sallinen's Symphony No. 7	*Dreams of Gandalf*
Schnittke's Symphony No. 2	*St Florian*
Schubert's Symphony No. 4 in C minor	*Tragic*
Schubert's Symphony No. 6 in C major	*Little C Major*
Schubert's Symphony No. 8 in B minor	*Unfinished*

MUSIC CLASSICAL

Schubert's Symphony No. 9 in C major	*Great C Major*
Schubert's Symphony No. 9 in C major, D944	*Heavenly Length*
Schubert's Symphony No. 1 in B flat Op. 38	*Spring*
Schubert's Symphony No. 3 in E flat major Op. 97	*Rhenish*
Scriabin's Symphony No. 3 in C minor Op. 43	*The Divine Poem*
Shostakovich's Symphony No. 2 in B major Op. 14	*October*
Shostakovich's Symphony No. 3 in E flat Op. 20	*First of May*
Shostakovich's Symphony No. 7 in C major Op. 60	*Leningrad*
Shostakovich's Symphony No. 11 in G minor Op. 103	*The Year 1905*
Shostakovich's Symphony No. 12 in D minor Op. 112	*The Year 1917*
Shostakovich's Symphony No. 12 in D minor Op. 12	*To the Memory of Lenin*
Shostakovich's Symphony No. 13 in B flat minor Op. 113	*Babi Yar*
Smetana's Symphony in E	*Festive/Triumph*
Spohr's Symphony No. 9 in B minor	*Seasons*
Stanford's Symphony No. 3 in F minor Op. 28	*Irish*
Suk's Symphony No. 2 in C minor Op. 27	*Asrael*
Sullivan's Symphony in E minor	*Irish*
Szymanowski's Symphony No. 3	*Song in the Night*
Tchaikovsky's Symphony No. 1 in G minor Op. 13	*Winter Daydreams*
Tchaikovsky's Symphony No. 2 in C minor Op. 17	*Little Russian/Ukrainian*
Tchaikovsky's Symphony No. 3 in D Op. 29	*Polish*
Tchaikovsky's Symphony No. 4 in F minor Op. 36	*Fate*
Tchaikovsky's Symphony No. 6 in B minor Op. 74	*Pathétique*
Vaughan Williams's Symphony No. 1 in C	*Sea*
Vaughan Williams's Symphony No. 2	*London*
Vaughan Williams's Symphony No. 3	*Pastoral*
Vaughan Williams's Symphony No. 7	*Antarctica*

Nicknames of Classical Works

Actus Tragicus	Bach's church cantata No. 106 ('God's time is the best')
Adieux Sonata	Beethoven's Piano Sonata No. 26 in E flat major, which he called 'The Farewell'
African	Saint-Saën's Piano Concerto No. 5
Air on the G String	Wilhelmj's arrangement of Bach Suite for Orchestra No. 3 in D (2nd movement)
American Quartet	Dvořák's String Quartet in F Op. 96
Andante Cantabile	Tchaikovsky's String Quartet No. 1 in D Op. 11 (2nd movement)
Appassionata Sonata	Beethoven's Piano Sonata No. 23 in F minor Op. 57
Archduke Trio	Beethoven's Piano Trio in B flat Op. 97, dedicated to Archduke Rudolf of Austria
Arpeggione	Schubert's Sonata in A minor for cello and piano
Basle Concerto	Stravinsky's Concerto in D for strings
Battle Symphony	Beethoven's orchestral work 'Wellington's Victory' Op. 91
The Bell	Haydn's String Quartet in D minor Op. 76 No. 2
The Bird	Haydn's String Quartet in C Op. 33 No. 3
The Black Mass	Scriabin's Piano Sonata No. 9 in F Op. 68
Black-key Étude	Chopin's Étude in G flat major for piano Op. 10 No. 5
Brandenburg Concertos	Bach's 6 concertos for various instruments, BWV 1046–1051
Bridal Chorus	Wagner's chorus from Act 3 of *Lohengrin*
Butterfly	Chopin's Étude in G flat for piano Op. 25 No. 9
Cat Waltz	Chopin's Waltz in F for piano Op. 34 No. 3
Cat's Fugue	Scarlatti's Fugue in G minor for harpsichord
La Chasse	Haydn's String Quartet in B flat Op. 1 No. 1
Chopsticks	Anonymous quick waltz tune for piano, first published in London 1877
Coffee Cantata	Bach's Cantata No. 211
Colas Breugnon	Kabalevsky's opera *The Craftsman of Clamecy*
Concord Sonata	Ives's Piano Sonata No. 2
Contemplation of Nothing Serious	Ives's orchestral piece *Central Park in the Dark in the Good Old Summertime*
Coronation Concerto	Mozart's Piano Concerto No. 26 in D, K537
The Cuckoo and the Nightingale	Handel's second set of six concertos for organ and orchestra
Dance Before the Golden Calf	Schoenberg's climax of Act 2 of his opera *Moses und Aron*
Dance of the Blessed Spirits	Gluck's slow dance in Act 2 of *Orfeo ed Euridice*, noted for its flute solo
Dance of the Comedians	Smetana's dance episode in Act 3 of *The Bartered Bride*, featuring clowns
Dance of the Hours	Episode, frequently played separately, in Act 3 of Ponchielli's *La Gioconda* and representing the conflict between darkness and light
Dance of the Seven Veils	Dance episode during Strauss's opera *Salome*
Dance of the Sylphs	Berlioz's orchestral episode during *La Damnation de Faust*, which forms part of Faust's dream on the banks of the Elbe

Dance of the Tumblers	Rimsky-Korsakov's episode during *The Snow Maiden* in which acrobats dance for the Tsar Berendey
Dead March in Saul	Handel's Funeral March from the oratorio *Saul*
Death and the Maiden	Schubert's String Quartet No. 14 in D minor
Dettingen Te Deum	Handel's *Te Deum* in D
Devil's Trill	Tartini's Violin Sonata in G minor
Diabelli Variations	Beethoven's 33 variations on a waltz by Diabelli in C for piano Op. 120
The Difficult Decision	Beethoven's String Quartet in F Op. 135 (4th movement)
Dissonance Quartet	Mozart's String Quartet No. 19 in C major, K465
Dog Waltz	Chopin's Waltz in D flat for piano Op. 64 No. 1
Dominicus Mass	Mozart's Mass in C, K66
Donkey Quartet	Haydn's String Quartet in D minor Op. 76 No. 2
Dorian Toccata and Fugue	Bach Toccata and Fugue in D minor for organ, BWV 538
A Dream	Haydn's String Quartet in F Op. 50 No. 5 (2nd movement)
Dumbarton Oaks	Stravinsky's Concerto in E flat for chamber ensemble
Dumky Trio	Dvořák's Piano Trio in E minor Op. 90
Ebony	Stravinsky's Concerto for clarinet and jazz band
Edward	Brahms's Ballade in D minor for piano Op. 10 No. 1
Eine Kleine Nachtmusik	Mozart's Divertimento in G for strings, K525
Eine Kleine Trauermusik	Schubert's Nonet in E flat minor for wind instuments
Elegy	Massenet's orchestral selection in E minor from his opera *Les Érinnyes*
Elvira Madigan	Mozart's Piano Concerto No. 21 in C
Emperor Concerto	Beethoven's Piano Concerto No. 5 in E flat major Op. 73
Emperor Quartet	Haydn's String Quartet in C major Op. 76 No. 3
English Suites	Bach's 6 Suites for harpsichord, BWV 806-811
Erdödy Quartets	Haydn's 6 String Quartets
Eroica Variations	Beethoven's 15 Variations and fugue on an Original Theme in E flat major Op. 76 Nos 75–80 for piano
Eyeglass Duo	Beethoven's Duo in E flat for viola and cello
Fall of Warsaw	Chopin's Étude in C minor for piano Op. 10 No. 12
Il Favorito	Vivaldi's Violin Concerto in E minor Op. 11 No. 2
Fiddle Fugue	Bach's Fugue in D minor for organ, BWV 539
Fifths	Haydn's String Quartet in D minor Op. 76 No. 2
Fingal's Cave	Mendelssohn's Overture for orchestra Op. 26, originally named *The Lonely Island*
The Forty-eight	Bach's *Well-Tempered Clavier*
The Four Seasons	Vivaldi's 4 Violin Concertos Op. 8 Nos 1–4
The Four Temperaments	Hindemith's Theme and Variations for string and piano: melancholic, sanguine, phlegmatic, choleric
French Suites	Bach's 6 Suites for harpsichord, BWV 812–817
The Frog	Haydn's String Quartet in D Op. 50 No. 6
From My Life	Smetana's String Quartets No. 1 in E minor (especially) and No. 2 in D minor
Funeral Anthem	Handel's anthem in G minor, *The Ways of Zion Do Mourn*
Funeral March	Chopin's Piano Sonata No. 2 in B flat minor Op. 35 (3rd movement)
Funeral March	Beethoven's Piano Sonata No. 12 in A flat Op. 26 (3rd movement)
Für Elise	Beethoven's Bagatelle in A minor for piano
Il Gardellino	Vivaldi's Flute Concerto in D Op. 10 No. 3
Gassenhauer Trio	Beethoven's Trio in B flat for clarinet, cello and piano Op. 11
German Suites	Bach's set of 6 keyboard partitas
Ghost Trio	Beethoven's Piano Trio in D major Op. 70 No. 1
The Girl With Enamel Eyes	Delibes 3-act ballet *Coppelia*
Goldberg Variations	Bach's Aria with Diverse Variations for harpsichord, BWV 988
Golden Sonata	Purcell's Sonata in F for two violins, viola da gamba and organ
Grand Duo	Schubert's Sonata in C major for piano (4 hands)
Grande Valse Brillante	Chopin's Waltz in E flat for piano Op. 18
Grazer Fantasie	Schubert's Fantasy in C for piano
Great Fugue	Beethoven's Fugue in B flat major for String Quartet Op. 133
Great Organ Mass	Haydn's Mass in E flat, Hob. XXII:4
Grief	Chopin's Étude in E for piano Op. 10 No. 3
Gypsy Rondo	Haydn's Piano Trio in G, Hob. XV:25 (3rd movement)
Haffner Serenade	Mozart's Suite in D major for orchestra, K250
Hallelujah Chorus	Handel's Chorus in D from his oratorio *Messiah*, No. 44
Hallelujah Concerto	Handel's Organ Concerto in B flat Op. 106
Hammerklavier	Beethoven's Piano Sonata No. 29 in B flat major Op. 106
Handel Variations	Brahms's Variations and Fugue on a Theme by Handel in B flat for Piano
Handel's Largo	Handel's aria 'Ombre mai fù', from his opera *Serse* (*Xerxes*)
Harmonious Blacksmith	Handel's Harpsichord Suite No. 5 in E (4th movement) Air with 5 variations
Harmonious Inspiration	Vivaldi's 12 concertos for various instruments Op. 3
Harmony Mass	Haydn's Mass No. 12 in B flat, H XXII:14
Harp Étude	Chopin's Étude in A flat for piano Op. 25 No. 1
Harp Quartet	Beethoven's String Quartet in E flat major Op. 74
Haydn Quartets	Mozart's 6 String Quartets Op. 10, K387–465

M
U
S
I
C

C
L
A
S
S
I
C
A
L

Haydn Variations	Brahms's Variations on a Theme by Joseph Haydn in B flat
The Hebrides	Mendelssohn's Overture for orchestra Op. 26
Heiliger Dankgesang	Beethoven's String Quartet in A minor Op. 132 (3rd movement)
Heiligmesse	Haydn's Mass in B flat, Hob. XXII:10
Hexenmenuet	Haydn's String Quartet in D minor Op. 76 No. 2 (3rd movement)
Hoffmeister Quartet	Mozart's String Quartet in D, K499
Hornpipe (aka Lark)	Haydn's String Quartet in D Op. 64 No. 5
Hornpipe Concerto	Handel's Concerto Grosso in B minor Op. 6, No. 12
Horn Trio	Brahms's Trio in E flat for violin, horn and piano Op. 40
Horseman (aka The Rider)	Haydn's String Quartet in G minor Op. 74 No. 3
Housatonic at Stockbridge	Ives's 'Three Places in New England' (3rd movement)
Humoresque	Dvořák's piano piece in G flat Op. 101 No. 7
Hunt Cantata	Bach Cantata 208 'Was mir behagt, ist nur die munter Jagd!'
The Hunt	Mozart's String Quartet No. 17 in B flat, K458
The Hunt	Haydn's String Quartet in B flat Op. 1 No. 1
Imperial Mass	Haydn's Mass No. 9 in D minor, Hob. XXII:11
Italian Concerto	Bach's Concerto for solo harpsichord, BWV 971
Jesu, Joy of Man's Desiring	Bach's chorale prelude from Cantata 147, 'Herz und Mund und Tat und Leben'
Jeunehomme Concerto	Mozart's Piano Concerto in E flat Op. 33 No. 2
Jig Fugue	Bach's Fugue in G for organ, BWV 577
The Joke	Haydn's String Quartet in E flat Op. 33 No. 2
Jungfernquartette	Haydn's 6 String Quartets Op. 33
Kaiser (aka Emperor)	Haydn's String Quartet in C Op. 76 No. 3
Kamennoi-Ostrov	Rubinstein's piece for piano in F sharp No. 22
Kettledrum Mass (Paukenmesse)	Haydn's Mass No. 7 in C major, Hob. XXII:9
Kreutzer Sonata	Beethoven's Violin Sonata No. 9 in A major Op. 47
Kreutzer Sonata Quartet	Janáček's String Quartet No. 1
Lark (aka Hornpipe)	Haydn's String Quartet in D Op. 64 No. 5
Late Quartets	Beethoven's String Quartets Op. 127, 130–133 and 135
Liebestraum	Liszt's Nocturne in A flat for piano; No. 3 of 3 of that title
Little Fugue in G Minor	Bach's Fugue for organ, BWV 578
Little Organ Mass	Haydn's Mass in B flat No. 5, Hob. XXII:7
Lobkowitz Quartets	Haydn's 2 String Quartets Op. 77 Nos 81–82
La Malinconia	Beethoven's String Quartet in B flat Op. 18 No. 6 (4th movement)
Manzoni Requiem	Verdi's Requiem, in memory of poet Alessandro Manzoni
Marche Militaire	Schubert's March in D for piano duet Op. 51 No. 1
Mariazell Mass	Haydn's Mass in C, Hob. XXII:8
Mass in Time of War	Haydn's Mass No. 7 in C, Hob. XXII:9
Mazeppa Études	Liszt's Transcendental Études for piano No. 4
Meditation	Massenet's selection in D for violin and orchestra from the opera Thaïs
Melody in F	Rubinstein's Piano Piece No. 1 of 2 melodies Op. 3
Military Polonaise	Chopin's Polonaise in A for piano Op. 40 No. 1
Minuet in G	Beethoven's 6 Minuets, WoO 10 No. 2
Minuet in G	Paderewski's Minuet for piano Op. 14 No. 1
Minuet in G	Bach's 'Notebook for Anna Magdalena Bach', 1st selection
Minute Waltz	Chopin's Waltz in D flat for piano Op. 64 No. 1
Missa Solemnis	Beethoven's Mass in D Op. 123
Moonlight Sonata	Beethoven's Piano Sonata No. 14 in C sharp minor Op. 27 No. 2
The Mount of Olives	Beethoven's Oratorio Christ on the Mount of Olives Op. 85
Mozartiana	Tchaikovsky's Suite No. 4 for orchestra
A Musical Joke	Mozart's Divertimento in F for chamber ensemble, K522
Muss es sein? Es muss sein! Es muss sein!	Beethoven's String Quartet in F major Op. 135 (4th movement)
Nelson Mass	Haydn's Mass No. 9 in D minor, Hob. XXII:11
New England	Ives's first orchestral set
Nicolai Mass	Haydn's Mass in G, Hob. XXII:6
Organ Solo Mass	Mozart's Mass in C, K259
Paganini Études	Liszt's 6 Études for piano on themes of Paganini
Paganini Variations	Brahms's Variations on a Theme of Paganini in A minor for piano
Pastoral Sonata	Beethoven's Piano Sonata No. 15 in D major Op. 28
Pastoral Symphony	Handel's interlude from his oratorio Messiah, No. 13
Pathétique	Beethoven's Piano Sonata No. 8 in C minor Op. 13
Paukenmesse (Kettledrum Mass)	Haydn's Mass in C major, Hob. XXII:9
Peasant Cantata	Bach's Cantata 212 'Mer hahn en neue Oberkeet'
Pomp and Circumstance	Elgar's March in D major, from a set of 5 with that title, Op. 39 No. 1
Posthorn Serenade	Mozart's Serenade in D for orchestra, K320
Prelude in C	Bach's Well-Tempered Clavier Volume I, 1st selection
Prelude in C sharp minor	Rachmaninoff's Prelude for piano, Op. 3 No. 2
Prussian Quartets	Mozart's 3 String Quartets, K575, 589, 590
Prussian Quartets	Haydn's 6 String Quartets Op. 50 Nos 1–6
Quartetto Serioso	Beethoven's String Quartet in F minor Op. 95
Quartettsatz	Schubert's String Quartet No. 12 in C minor

Quintenquartett	Haydn's String Quartet in D minor Op. 76 No. 2
Rage over a Lost Penny	Beethoven's Rondo a Capriccio in G for piano Op. 129
Raindrop Prelude	Chopin's Prelude in D flat for piano Op. 28 No. 15
Rain Sonata	Brahms's Violin Sonata No. 1 in G Op. 78
Ratswahl Cantata	Bach's Cantata 71, 'Gott ist mein König'
Razor Quartet	Haydn's String Quartet in F minor Op. 55 No. 2
Razumovsky Quartets	Beethoven's 3 String Quartets Op. 59
Recitative	Haydn's String Quartet in G Op. 17 No. 5
Reliquie Sonata	Schubert's Piano Sonata No. 13 in C
Rêve Angélique	Rubinstein's piano piece in F sharp No. 22 from Kamennoi-Ostrov
Revolutionary Étude	Chopin's Étude in C minor for piano Op. 10 No. 12
The Rider (aka Horseman)	Haydn's String Quartet in G minor Op. 74 No. 3
Rondo a Capriccio	Beethoven's Piano Sonata in G Op. 129
Rondo alla Turca	Mozart's Piano Sonata in A, K331 (3rd movement)
Russian Quartets	Haydn's 6 String Quartets Op. 33 Nos 1–6
Russian Quartets	Beethoven's 3 String Quartets Op. 59
St Anne Fugue	Bach's Fugue in E flat for organ, BWV 552
St Anthony Chorale	Haydn's Divertimento in B flat for wind, instruments II:46 (2nd movement)
St Cecilia Mass	Haydn's Mass in C, XXII:5
St Joseph Mass	Haydn's Mass in E flat, Hob. XXII:4
Gli Scherzi	Haydn's 6 String Quartets Op. 33 Nos 37–42
Scherzoso	Beethoven's String Quartet in B flat Op. 130
Schübler Chorales	Bach's 6 Chorale Preludes for organ, BWV 645–50
Serenade	Haydn's String Quartet in F Op. 3 No. 5
Sheep May Safely Graze	Bach's Cantata 208, 'Was mir behagt ist nur die muntre Jagd'
Shepherd Boy Étude	Chopin's Étude in A flat for piano Op. 25 No. 1
Six-Four-Time Mass	Haydn's Mass in G, Hob. XXII:6
Solemn Vespers	Mozart's Vesperae Solennes de Confessore in C, K339
Sonata Facile	Mozart's Piano Sonata in C, K545
Sonata quasi una Fantasia	Beethoven's Piano Sonata No. 13 in E flat and No. 14 in C sharp minor
Spatzenmesse	Mozart's Mass in G, K220
Spaur Mass	Mozart's Mass in C, K258
Spring Sonata	Beethoven's Violin and Piano Sonata No. 5 in F Op. 24
Spring Song	Mendelssohn's 'Lied ohne Worte' (Song Without Words)
La Stravaganza	Vivaldi's 12 Violin Concertos Op. 4
Street Song Trio	Beethoven's Trio in B flat for clarinet, cello and piano Op. 11
Sun Quartets	Haydn's 6 String Quartets Op. 20 Nos 1–6
Sunrise Quartet	Haydn's String Quartet in B flat Op. 76 No. 4
Swedish Rhapsody	Alfvén's Midsommarvaka for orchestra Op. 19
Tempest	Beethoven's Piano Sonata No. 17 in D
Theresia Mass	Haydn's Mass No. 10 in B flat, Hob. XXII:12
Three Places in New England	Ives's first orchestral set
Timpani Mass	Haydn's Mass in C, Hob. XXII:9
To the Memory of an Angel	Berg's Violin Concerto
The Torrent	Chopin's Étude in C sharp Minor for piano Op. 10 No. 4
Tost Quartets	Haydn's 12 String Quartets Op. 54, 55, and 64
Trauer-Ode	Bach's Cantata 198, 'Lass, Fürstin, lass noch einen Strahl'
Ein Traum	Haydn's String Quartet in F Op. 50 No. 5 (2nd movement)
Triangle Concerto	Liszt's Piano Concerto No. 1 in E flat
Triple Concerto	Beethoven's Concerto in C for piano, violin and cello Op. 56
Tristesse	Chopin's Étude in E for piano Op. 10 No. 3
Trout Quintet	Schubert's Quintet in A for piano, violin, viola, cello and double bass
Trumpet Tune	Purcell's harpsichord piece in C
Trumpet Voluntary	Jeremiah Clarke's instrumental piece in D
Turkish March	Beethoven's incidental music to The Ruins of Athens for orchestra
Turkish Rondo	Mozart's Piano Sonata in A, K331 (3rd movement)
Twinkle Twinkle Variations	Mozart's Variation on 'Ah, vous dirai-je, maman' in C for piano
Two-Cello Quintet	Schubert's String Quintet in C Op. 163
Utrecht Jubilate	Handel's Jubilate in D
Utrecht Te Deum	Handel's Te Deum in D
Villanelle	Chopin's Étude in G flat for piano Op. 25 No. 9
Voces Intimae (Friendly Voices)	Sibelius' String Quartet in D minor Op. 56
Waisenhausmesse	Mozart's Mass in C minor, K139
Waldstein	Beethoven's Piano Sonata No. 21 in C major Op. 53
Wedding March	Mendelssohn's incidental music to A Midsummer Night's Dream for orchestra Op. 61 (9th movement)
Wedge Fugue	Bach's Fugue in E minor for organ
The White Mass	Scriabin's Piano Sonata No. 7 in F sharp Op. 64
Wind-Band Mass	Haydn's Mass No. 12 in B flat, Hob. XXII:14
Winter Wind Étude	Chopin's Etude in A minor for piano Op. 25 No. 11
Witches' Minuet	Haydn's String Quartet in D minor Op. 76 No. 2 (3rd movement)
WTC	Bach's Well-Tempered Clavier

MUSIC CLASSICAL

General Information

acciaccatura   A short grace note played simultaneously with the principal note and released immediately.

Aldeburgh Festival   Founded by Benjamin Britten in 1948, held in Aldeburgh, Suffolk, with concert hall, the Maltings, at nearby Snape.

Amati family   Violin makers in Cremona, 16th–18th century. Nicola Amati taught Stradivari and Guarneri.

arpeggio   Chord spread, i.e. notes played one after the other as on the harp.

Ars Antiqua (Old Art)   Refers to music of 12th and 13th centuries derived from the school of Paris.

Ars Nova (New Art)   Style of music developed in 14th-century France and Italy. Term coined by Philippe de Vitry.

attempted suicide: Debussy's wife   Rosalie 'Lily' Texier shot herself during a bout of depression.

attempted suicide: Tchaikovsky   Walked into the freezing River Neva at dead of night following his disastrous marriage in 1877.

Aurora's Wedding   Divertissement of last act of *Sleeping Beauty*, sometimes performed separately.

bagatelle   Short, plain composition especially for pianoforte e.g. Für Elise.

Baroque   Musical era roughly from 1600 to around 1750.

Battle Symphony   Beethoven's orchestral work *Wellington's Victory* Op. 91 (includes 'Rule, Britannia!' and 'God Save the King').

berceuse   Lullaby.

Boehm system   Theobald Boehm (1794–1881) devised an acoustically superior system of placing and sizing the holes in the flute, and of using the keys to cover them, now universally used.

Boosey and Hawkes Ltd   London music publishers (amalgamated 1930).

Boston Symphony Orchestra   Founded in October 1881 by Henry Lee Higginson.

Brahms: personal motto   *Frei aber Froh* (free but happy). He used the initial letters as the thematic structure of his 3rd Symphony.

Brandenburg Concertos   Bach's 6 Concerti Grossi dedicated to Christian Ludwig, Margrave of Brandenburg.

brindisi   Drinking song usually accompanying a toast.

Canterbury degrees (Lambeth degrees)   Music degrees conferred traditionally by the Archbishop of Canterbury.

capriccio   Musical composition that has original and unexpected effects. Janáček and Stravinsky both wrote works called 'Capriccio'.

Carnegie Hall   Largest concert-hall in New York, designed by W B Tuthill and opened in 1891.

castrato   Male soprano castrated before puberty to preserve the voice.

cataloguers of works   Schubert – Deutsch; Haydn – Hoboken; Scarlatti – Kirkpatrick (Longo numbers are also still used); Mozart – Köchel; Vivaldi – Ryom (Pincherle & Fanna also catalogued works); J S Bach – Schmieder (used initials BWV: Bach-Werke-Verzeichnis); Liszt – both R and S numbers; Nielsen – FS (Fog and Schousboe); Frank Bridge – H numbers; Holmboe – Rapoport (M for Meta numbers, after Holmboe's wife); Bartók – Sz numbers; Beethoven – Kinsky (used WoO numbers for works without an opus) and Hess (used Hn numbers for other works); Purcell – Zimmerman; Handel – Baselt (HMV numbers); Dvorak – Burghauser; Donizetti – Inzaghi; Chopin – Brown.

catch   Type of round whose words may sound comical when sung. A catch club was formed in London in 1761.

chamber music   Term coined by Charles Burney in 1805 to describe music not intended for the church, theatre or public concert room, but now applied to ensemble music written for small groups, such as string quartets.

Cheltenham Festival   Music festival started in 1945 as Festival of British Contemporary Music but since 1969 drawing music from international sources.

J. & W. Chester Ltd   Music publishers founded in Brighton (1874) and specialising in Russian and other foreign composers.

Chetham's School of Music   Founded in 1656, by a bequest from Humphrey Chetham (1580–1653), situated in Long Millgate, Manchester; Chetham's is Britain's only full-scale music school for children, with over 280 boys and girls aged 8–18.

Chicago Symphony Orchestra   Founded in 1891 by Theodore Thomas; it is the third oldest orchestra in USA.

children: most born to one composer   Twenty to J S Bach.

Children's Corner   Six piano pieces dedicated by Debussy to his daughter: 1) Dr Gradus ad Parnassum, 2) Jimbo's Lullaby, 3) Serenade for the Doll, 4) Snow is Dancing, 5) The Little Shepherd, 6) Golliwogg's Cakewalk.

clam   Playing a wrong note in a performance.

Classic FM: top 100, most popular work   Max Bruch's 1st Violin Concerto (1996 and 1997).

Classical Period   Ranges from the late 18th to the early 19th century.

Colour Symphony (Arthur Bliss): movements   The four movements: *Purple, Red, Blue* and *Green*.

Composers' Guild of Great Britain   Founded in 1944 to protect the rights of composers; affiliated to the Society of Authors. First president was Vaughan Williams.

concerto   Work, usually in three movements, which contrasts and integrates a solo instrument with the orchestra.

conductor with 36 names   Louis Julien (1812–60) was sponsored at his baptism by 36 members of the local philharmonic society.

coronach (corranach)   Funeral dirge of Ireland and Highland Scotland.

Crossover Chart   Established in 1996 and includes popular light classical pieces.

deaf composers   Beethoven, Fauré, Smetana.

deaf percussionist   Evelyn Glennie.

Diabelli Variations   Beethoven's Thirty-Three Variations on a Waltz by Diabelli.

Dido's Lament   Aria from Act 3 of Purcell's *Dido and Aeneas*, played annually at Remembrance Day service at the Cenotaph and beginning with the words 'When I am laid in earth'.

The Divine Poem   Scriabin's Symphony No. 3 in C minor Op. 43 (three movements entitled *Struggles, Delights* and *Divine Play*).

Dvořák: son-in-law   Josef Suk.

Early Music Consort   Founded by David Munrow in 1967 to perform Renaissance and medieval music on original instruments.

Edinburgh Festival   Founded in 1947 with Rudolf Bing as director. Three-week festival of music held in August–September now teems with other arts and entertainments.

Eighteen-Twelve (1812)   Concert overture Op. 49 by Tchaikovsky commemorating the defeat of Napoleon's Grande Armée on its retreat from Moscow. It incorporates 'La Marseillaise'.

English Chamber Orchestra   Founded in 1948 as the Goldsbrough Orchestra (after its founder); present name adopted in 1960.

English Folk Dance and Song Society   Amalgamation in 1932 of Folk Song Society (founded 1898) and English Folk Dance Society (founded 1911); HQ in Cecil Sharp House, London, NW1 7AY.

Enigma Variations: musical portraits   1) Lady Elgar (C.A.E.); 2) Hew Steuart-Powell (H.D.S.-P.); 3) RB Townshend (R.B.T.); 4) W. Meath Baker (W.M.B.); 5) Richard P. Arnold (R.P.A.); 6) Isabel Fitton (Ysobel); 7) A. Troyte Griffith (Troyte); 8) Winifred Norbury (W.N.); 9) AJ Jaeger (Nimrod); 10) Dora Penny (Dorabella); 11) GR Sinclair (G.R.S.); 12) Basil Nevinson (B.G.N.); 13) Lady Mary Lygon; 14) Elgar (E.D.U.).

Estampes (Engravings)   Three piano pieces by Debussy: *Pagodas, Evening in Granada*, and *Gardens in the Rain*.

étude (study)   Composition intended to test and extend the performer's technique.

eurhythmics   Method invented by Émile Jaques-Dalcroze (1865–1950) for expressing rhythmical aspect of music through gymnastic exercises.

Faust Symphony (Liszt)   Movements portray three characters: *Faust, Gretchen* and *Mephistopheles*.

Fireworks Music   Handel wrote the music to celebrate the Peace of Aix-La-Chapelle (1749); first played in Green Park, London.

First Post   British Army bugle call, a summons back to the barracks, sounded at 9.30 p.m.

The Five (aka The Mighty Handful)   Russian composers Balakirev, Borodin, Cui, Mussorgsky and Rimsky-Korsakov.

Frankfurt Group   English composers who were pupils of Iwan Knorr in the 1890s; they were Norman O'Neill, Roger Quilter, Cyril Scott and Balfour Gardiner.

funeral marches   Famous ones include the 3rd movement of Chopin's 2nd piano sonata; Handel's Dead March in *Saul*; 2nd movement of Beethoven's *Eroica*; Siegfried's Funeral March from Wagner's *Götterdämmerung*.

Gagliano family   18th-century family of violin-makers from Naples. Key members: Alessandro, his sons, Niccolò and Gennaro, and grandsons Ferdinando and Giuseppe.

gamelan   A kind of orchestra widespread in south-east Asia, especially Indonesia, whose range of percussion includes gongs, drums, marimbas and chimes.

Gebrauchsmusik (utility music)   Term associated in the 1920s with works by Hindemith, Weill and Krenek, influenced by Brecht and designed for social and educational purposes.

Gesamtkunstwerk   Wagner's term for a dramatic work in which drama, music, poetry, song and painting would be united into a single artistic whole.

glee   Vocal music for three or four parts, unaccompanied and homophonic, popular in late 18th- and early 19th-century England.

Goldberg Variations   J S Bach's 30 variations on a theme for two-manual harpsichord.

Grove, Sir George   English music writer (1820–1900) who, after training as a civil engineer, turned to musical studies and compiled *Grove's Dictionary of Music and Musicians*, then published in 4 volumes, now expanded into 20.

Guarneri Quartet   American string quartet formed in 1964 in Vermont. Members are Arnold Steinhardt and John Dally (violins), Michael Tree (viola) and Peter Wiley (cello), who replaced founding member David Soyer in 2000.

Hail to the Chief   March traditionally played at formal American events to announce the arrival of the President, first used at the inauguration of Martin Van Buren in 1837. The words came from Sir Walter Scott's *Lady of the Lake* but are no longer used. Derived from an old Gaelic tune, the melody was adapted by the English composer, James Sanderson (1769–1841) for a scene in Scott's play.

hairpins   Nickname for the signs < (crescendo) and > (diminuendo).

Hallé Orchestra   Founded in 1857 by Charles Hallé and based in Manchester. Sir John Barbirolli was the principal conductor from 1943 to his death in 1970. Kent Nagano has been the conductor since 1992.

Haydn's Symphony No. 45   Haydn directed his musicians to gradually leave the stage during the last movement, hence the nickname 'Farewell'.

Henry Wood: pseudonym   Paul Klenovsky was the cryptic name (Klen means maple tree) under which Wood transcribed for orchestra Bach's Toccata and Fugue in D minor.

Hexameron   Six variations for piano on a march from Bellini's *I Puritani*, each written by a different composer/pianist, i.e. Liszt, Pixis, Herz, Thalberg, Czerny and Chopin, each of whom played his variation at the first performance of the work in a charity concert in Paris in 1837 (first of the super groups one might say!). Liszt later added orchestral accompaniments and played whole series at recitals.

humoresque   Humorous or capricious instrumental piece. Famous examples are by Dvořák and Schumann.

Images   Title used by Debussy for two works: 1) *Images* for Orchestra, including *Gigues, Ibéria* and *Rondes de Printemps*; 2) two sets for solo piano: *Reflets dans l'eau, Hommage à Rameau, Movement, Cloches à travers les feuilles, Et la lune descend sur le temple qui fut* and *Poissons d'or*.

Jena Symphony   A work found by Fritz Stein in 1909 in Jena, Germany, and linked until 1957 with Beethoven; it turned out that Friedrich Witt was the composer.

La Jeune France (Young France)   Group of four French composers (Yves Baudrier, André Jolivet, Daniel Lesur and Olivier Messiaen) who resolved in Paris in 1936 to carry out 'a return to the human' in composition.

jubilate   Hymn of praise, usually based on Psalm 100 (in Roman Catholic Psalter, Psalm 99).

Juilliard Quartet   Founded by William Schuman in New York in 1946; the line-up as at April 2001 is Joel Smirnoff and Ronald Copes (violins), Samuel Rhodes (viola) and Joel Krosnick (cello).

MUSIC CLASSICAL

K numbers Named after the cataloguers of two composers: Mozart – Ludwig von Köchel; Scarlatti – Ralph Kirkpatrick.

karaoke (empty orchestra) Singing along with recorded accompaniment.

Kneller Hall Headquarters, founded in 1857 at Twickenham, Middlesex, of Royal Military School of Music.

La Scala (The Staircase) Milan opera house built in 1778 on the site of a church founded in the 18th century by Regina della Scala, wife of a Duke of Milan.

Last Post British Army bugle call sounded at 10 p.m. that ends the day. It is customary to play the Last Post at military funerals.

Leeds Piano Competition Established in 1963 by Fanny Waterman and Marion Thorpe and held triennially. The first winner was Michael Roll, and many placed pianists have won international reputations, notably Peter Donohoe, who was placed sixth in 1981.

Leitmotiv Term first used by A W Ambrose (c.1865) in an article about Wagner's operas and Liszt's symphonic poems; it was later used by F W Jähns, to denote a short and recurrent musical figure standing for an idea or character.

Les Six Term coined by Henri Collet in 1920 to describe the avant-garde French composers Georges Auric (1899–1983), Louis Durey (1888–1979), Arthur Honegger (1892–1955), Darius Milhaud (1892–1974), Francis Poulenc (1899–1963) and Germaine Tailleferre (1892–1983).

Leventritt Competition International competition alternately for pianists and violinists, established in 1939 by Leventritt Foundation, New York. Winner's prize consists of engagements with prominent orchestras and offer of recording contract.

Lincoln Center for the Performing Arts New York arts centre consisting of Metropolitan Opera House, Avery Fisher Hall, Juilliard School and various theatres and societies.

London Philharmonic Orchestra Founded by Sir Thomas Beecham in 1932.

London Symphony Orchestra Founded by players who seceded from Henry Wood's Queen's Hall orchestra in 1904 and run by its own members ever since.

Má Vlast Cycle of 6 symphonic poems by Smetana: 1) *The High Citadel* (*Vysehrad*); 2) *River Moldau* (*Vltava*); 3) *Sàrka*; 4) *From Bohemia's Meadows and Forests* (*Z Ceskych Luhu a Haju*); 5) *Tabor*, 6) *Blánik* (*The Valhalla of the Hussite heroes*).

madrigal Song form for two or more voices developed in 13th- and 14th-century Italy, most often secular and unaccompanied; revived and enhanced during the Renaissance into an expressive, polyphonic form introduced into Elizabethan England.

Manchester School Name given to group of composers (Maxwell Davies, Harrison Birtwistle, Alexander Goehr and John Ogdon) taught in Manchester by Richard Hall in the late 1950s.

masque Courtly entertainment that evolved in 17th-century England, incorporating music, acting and spectacular costumes and scenery.

Mighty Handful (aka The Five) Alternative name for 'The Five' (coined by Vladimir Stasov).

minimalism Style of music that developed in the 1960s, involving repetition of short musical motifs in simple harmonic idiom. Prominent members include Philip Glass, Steve Reich and Terry Riley.

minuet Movement (usually the 3rd) in sonatas and symphonies of the classical period, derived from the dance of the same name.

Miserere Psalm 51 (50 in Roman Catholic Psalter) set to music by various composers.

most prolific composer Georg Philipp Telemann is often assigned this title; among his output are over 600 overtures, 44 Passions, 40 operas and numerous other works.

motet Choral composition, generally on a sacred text.

motif Short melodic pattern or musical idea that runs throughout a piece.

Mourning Music (*Trauermusik*) Paul Hindemith work composed within hours of the death of George V in 1936.

Mozart: wrote down on first hearing Gregorio Allegri's *Miserere* was supposedly sacrosanct to the Vatican; Mozart went to a service there and went home and wrote it down from memory, thereby risking excommunication. It is however very likely that Mozart had heard the piece on at least one occasion prior to his visit to Rome.

Mozart's Piano Concerto No. 21 in C Given nickname of 'Elvira Madigan' in 1967 because it was the theme tune of the film of that name.

Mozart's Piano Concerto No. 26 in D Given nickname of 'Coronation' because it was played at King Leopold II of Prussia's coronation.

Mozart's String Quartets 14–19 Dedicated to Haydn with the words 'I send my six sons to you'.

Mozart: work falsely attributed to *Adélaïde* violin concerto. In 1977 Marius Casadesus admitted he composed it.

musical epochs Medieval 600–1425; Renaissance 1425–1600; Baroque 1600–1750; Classical 1750–1825; Romantic 1820–80; Post-Romantic 1880–1910; Modern since 1910; some historians also identify a Nationalist epoch 1860–1910 and an Impressionist epoch 1890–1920.

musique concrète Music composed by manipulating recorded sounds, especially natural sounds rather than electronic.

National Gallery Recitals During the Second World War Dame Myra Hess founded and directed a series of lunchtime recitals, which became very popular and helped to sustain morale.

New Symphony Orchestra London orchestra founded by Sir Thomas Beecham in 1905 and became Royal Albert Hall Orchestra in 1920 and later disbanded.

New York Philharmonic Orchestra Oldest US symphony orchestra, founded in 1842 as Philharmonic Society of New York; merged with New York Symphony Orchestra in 1928 to become Philharmonic Symphony Orchestra of New York; now known as the NYPO.

nocturne Night-piece, serenade.

notes of the scale: English to Italian A=la, B=si, C=do, D=re, E=mi, F=fa, G=sol.

octet A group of 8 musicians, or a piece of music written for such a group. A string octet is usually a double string quartet.

opus (work) Opus numbers are used to designate the order in which a given composer's works were written or published.

oratorio Musical setting for voices and orchestra of a text based on the Scriptures or an epic theme. Could be described as an opera without staging, scenery or costumes.

Parthenia Title of the first book of keyboard music printed in England (1611), collecting pieces by William Byrd, John Bull and Orlando Gibbons.

pastorale Either a musical play based on a rustic subject, or a composition with rustic overtones.

Performing Right Society Association of composers, authors, and music publishers founded in Britain in 1914 to collect royalties for non-dramatic public performance and broadcasting of members' works.

Philharmonia Orchestra English symphony orchestra founded in 1945 by Walter Legge.

piano quartet Piano, violin, viola and cello.

piano quintet Usually string quartet plus piano.

piano trio Piano, violin, and cello.

Pictures at an Exhibition Mussorgsky's versions in music of 10 pictures displayed at a memorial exhibition for Russian artist Victor Hartmann: 1) *The Gnome*; 2) *The Old Castle*; 3) *Tuileries*; 4) *Bydlo* (a farm cart); 5) *Unhatched Chickens*; 6) *Samuel Goldenberg and Shmuyle*; 7) *Market-Place at Limoges*; 8) *Catacombs*; 9) *Baba-Yaga (The Hut on Fowl's Legs)*; 10) *The Great Gate of Kiev*.

Pierrot Players Instrument ensemble founded in 1967 by Maxwell Davies and Harrison Birtwistle, regrouped to form the Fires of London in 1970 before disbanding in 1987.

Pomp and Circumstance Elgar's title (taken from Act 3 of *Othello*) for his set of five marches for symphony orchestra, the first of which was the basis for 'Land of Hope and Glory' (words by A C Benson).

Pre-classical Term applied to composers such as C P E Bach who are considered to be later than baroque and leading to the 'Classical' style of Haydn and Mozart.

Promenade Concerts Although promenade concerts (at which listeners could saunter around) were put on in London as early as 1838, it was not until 1895 that they became a regular annual feature when Robert Newman began a series at Queen's Hall with Henry Wood as conductor. Wood's name became synonymous with the Proms, and after his death in 1944, Malcolm Sargent became principal conductor (1948–67). Royal Albert Hall became venue in 1941 on the destruction of Queen's Hall.

Proms: centenary 1995; Harrison Birtwistle composed *Panic*.

Proms: last four directors Sir William Glock, Robert Ponsonby, Sir John Drummond and, the present incumbent, Nicholas Kenyon.

Queen's Hall Once London's chief concert hall, situated in Langham Place, opened in 1893 and destroyed by fire in 1941, following a Nazi bombing raid.

rāga Indian musical form that represents a mood, concept or occasion by one of many patterns of notes presented as an ascending and descending scale used as a basis for improvisation.

Ring Cycle Full title *Der Ring des Nibelungen* (*The Ring of the Nibelung*). Often referred to as the tetralogy although Wagner himself called the first opera, *Das Rheingold*, the prologue. After it comes *Die Walküre* (*The Valkyrie*), followed by *Siegfried* and finally, *Götterdämmerung* (*Twilight of the Gods*).

Royal Academy of Music Founded in London in 1822 and situated in Tenterden Street but moved to Marylebone Road in 1912. The RAM has about 700 students and 150 staff.

Royal College of Music Founded in 1882 but moved to its present site at Prince Consort Road, South Kensington in 1894.

Royal Philharmonic Orchestra Founded in 1946 by Sir Thomas Beecham, who was principal conductor until his death in 1961.

St Louis Symphony Orchestra Founded in March 1881, the second oldest symphony orchestra in the USA.

Scottish Chamber Orchestra Founded in 1974 with headquarters in Queen's Hall, Edinburgh.

secular music Any music that is not sacred music.

septet Make-up varies, but typical format would be violin, viola, French horn, clarinet, bassoon, cello and double bass.

sextet Group of 6 musicians; a string sextet usually two each of violins, violas and cellos.

sonata Instrumental composition usually in three or four movements for unaccompanied piano or, more rarely, for another stringed instrument with piano accompaniment.

stanza One of a number of sections of a song, two or more lines long, characterised by a common metre, rhyme and number of lines.

string quartet Violins (1st and 2nd), viola and cello.

string quintet String quartet with added viola or cello.

string trio Violin, viola and cello.

Sturm und Drang (Storm and Stress) Term applied to a period (*c.*1760–80) of great emotional intensity in German literature and music. Musically, it is particularly associated with F J Haydn's works around the time of his Symphonies 40–59.

Suite bergamasque Piano suite by Debussy, its 4 movements: *Prélude, Menuet, Clair de Lune*, and *Passepied*.

symphonic structure In the Classical model, 4 movements: 1) a fast sonata; 2) a slow movement; 3) a minuet scherzo; 4) a fast movement, mostly a rondo.

Tchaikovsky Piano Competition Quadrennial competition first held in Moscow in 1954. Famous winners include Van Cliburn, John Ogdon, Vladimir Ashkenazy.

Three Bs Bach, Beethoven, Brahms (term coined by Hans von Bülow).

Three Choirs Festival Annual meeting that rotates among the 3 cathedral choirs of Gloucester, Hereford and Worcester, held almost continuous since the early 18th century.

tonic sol-fa System of sight-singing and notation devised by Sarah Ann Glover in England in the 1840s, though much the same system had been introduced in the USA by D Sower in 1832.

toy symphony Term for a symphony in which toy instruments are used as well as strings and piano; the most popular example is a work by Leopold Mozart, with toy instruments now thought to have been added by Michael Haydn.

train wreck Colloquial term for what happens when the parts in an ensemble collide because the musicians are not playing together.

The Triumphs of Oriana Collection of 5- and 6-part English madrigals by 24 composers assembled by Thomas Morley in 1601 in honour of Elizabeth I.

trumpet voluntary Piece that imitates a trumpet but is, in fact, played using a similar sounding organ stop. The best known version is a transcription by

MUSIC CLASSICAL

Henry Wood of a piece originally ascribed to Purcell but now credited to Jeremiah Clarke. He called it 'The Prince of Denmark's March', but Wood's title has superseded Clarke's.

Tuning of Strings Cello: C, G, D, A (octave lower than the viola). Violin: G, D, A, E. Double-bass: E, A, D, G. Banjo: 4 strings C, G, D, A; 5 strings G, D, G, B, D. Viola: C, G, D, A (5th lower than violin).

Tweedledum and Tweedledee Name coined by John Byrom (1692–1763) to satirise the public feuding between composers G F Handel and G Bononcini.

violinists: known for revealing garments Vanessa Mae, Anne-Sophie Mutter, Linda Lampenius.

Wagner's patron Ludwig II, King of Bavaria (1845–86).

The Walk to the Paradise Garden Intermezzo before concluding scene of Delius's opera *A Village Romeo and Juliet*. The Paradise Garden is actually a public house.

Wedding March Played at the end of Act 4 of Mendelssohn's *Midsummer Night's Dream* and traditionally used on exit from the church. The Bridal Chorus from *Lohengrin* commonly announces the entry.

Wigmore Hall London concert hall in Wigmore Street, opened in 1901 as Bechstein Hall.

WoO Werk ohne Op. zahl (work without opus number): system of catalogue numbers used to identify composer's works that lack opus numbers.

woodwind quintet Usually flute, clarinet, oboe, French horn and bassoon.

Musical Instruments

accordion Invented by Friedrich Buschmann of Berlin in 1822.

Aeolian harp Box and strings that sound when hit by a current of air.

aeolina Mouth organ.

angelica Instrument of the lute family with 16 or 17 strings.

arpeggione Six-stringed cello invented by G Staufer of Vienna in 1823. Aka *guitare d'amour*.

aulos Double-reed wind instrument of ancient Greece.

autoharp Zither on which chord keys are pressed by one hand and strings strummed by the other.

Bach trumpet Valveless trumpet in either C or D.

backfall Part of an organ that connects the rods to the keyboard.

bagpipes Ancient instrument popular throughout the world but particularly identified with Scotland. The Scottish Highland bagpipe has two tenor drones and a bass drone, tuned an octave apart. The chanter is the pipes that plays the tune. Versions of the bagpipe around the world include the Bulgarian *gaida*, the *cornemuse* of France and Belgium, the *gaita* of northwestern Spain and the Irish Uilleann pipes.

balalaika Russian three-stringed instrument of the lute family with a triangular belly and moveable frets on the arm. The balalaika was developed in the 18th century from the *domra*.

bamboula West Indian tambourine.

bandoneon Argentinian variant of the accordion.

baritone horn Brass instrument in B flat, related to the euphonium with a smaller bore and 3 valves.

baryton Stringed instrument similar to viola da gamba but with sympathetic strings. Played by Prince Esterházy (Haydn's patron); it has made a revival in recent years.

Basque drum Tambourine.

bassanello Shawm-like woodwind instrument, no longer played.

bassoon Bass member of the double-reed oboe family, pitched in C.

bell lyra Type of portable glockenspiel.

bissex Twelve-string guitar invented in 1770 by Vanhecke.

bodhran Irish frame drum played with a double-ended stick.

bombard Alto-pitched shawm.

bombardon Form of bass tuba with 3 piston valves.

boobams Percussion instrument using a varying number of bamboo tubes.

bottleneck Tube that fits over a finger on the fretting hand used for slide-guitar playing.

bouzouki Greek fretted string instrument with a long neck and 4 sets of strings.

cabaca/cabasa Latin American percussion instrument, around or pear-shaped gourd covered with beads and fitted with a handle.

calliope Literally meaning 'beautiful-voiced' after the Muse of epic poetry; US name for a steam-driven organ.

campanelle Glockenspiel.

canale Psaltery.

canntaireachd Ancient Highland bagpipe notation, using syllables to represent a group of notes.

carillon Alternative name for glockenspiel, so called by Handel in 1739 when he first used the instrument in *Saul*.

castanets Twin cup-shaped clappers; name derives from the Spanish *castaña*, chestnut wood.

celesta Small keyboard instrument patented by Auguste Mustel in 1886 and famously used in Tchaikovsky's 'Dance of the Sugar Plum Fairy'.

cello: full name Violoncello.

cembalo Short for clavicembalo, the Italian word for harpsichord.

cetera Zither.

chalumeau Forerunner of the clarinet with 6 to 8 finger-holes.

chanterelle The E string on a violin, or the highest string on any instrument in the violin or lute family.

charivari Cacophonous, extemporised music produced with any household utensil or object that will make a noise.

chitarrone Lute similar to a theorbo but longer.

choke cymbal: aka High-hat cymbal.

chromatic harp Harp built by Pleyel in 1897; equipped with a string for every semitone, it needed no pedals.

cimbalom Form of dulcimer native to Hungary, made up of a box on which strings are hit with mallets.

cittern A 15th-century forerunner of the lute with metal strings tuned in pairs and plucked.

clapper Striker in the middle of a bell.

clarinet Single-reed woodwind instrument developed

by J C Denner of Nuremberg in the late 17th century.

clàrsach Ancient small Celtic harp having brass strings instead of gut or nylon ones.

clavecin Harpsichord.

claves Cuban percussion instruments consisting of round wooden sticks that are stuck together.

clavichord/clarichord Small keyboard instrument invented in 14th century. Aka manichord or chekker.

colascione European version of oriental long-necked lute popular in the Tudor period.

colophony Bow rosin (named after Colophon in Asia Minor, the source of the best rosin).

concertina Invented by Charles Wheatstone in 1829 as the 'Symphonium'. Similar to accordion but no keyboard.

console Part of organ by which the musician operates the instrument.

cor anglais French for English horn, but in fact an alto oboe; invented by Ferlandis of Bergamo.

cor de chasse Hunting horn developed in France in 17th century.

cornopean Late 19th-century brass instrument similar to a trumpet.

crembalum Type of Jew's harp.

crook Tube inserted into a brass instrument to lengthen its tube and change its pitch.

crotales Ancient Greek percussion instrument in form of a rattle or clapper.

crumhorn Early and widely used Renaissance double-reed instrument. Name means 'curved horn'.

crwth Welsh medieval instrument with 6 strings, a bowed lyre.

cuckoo Two-note wind instrument imitating the bird.

damper Felt piece that damps the vibration of the string on a piano until the key is depressed.

didjeridu (didgeridoo) Native Australian wind instrument, which allows player to breathe through nose while playing.

digitorium Small keyboard machine usually having 5 keys, which are sprung more severely than usual so as to strengthen fingers. Invented by Myer Marks in the mid-19th century.

domra Type of early balalaika with a round body and two or three metal strings tuned a fourth apart.

double bass: aka Bull-fiddle, doghouse.

Dudelsack German form of bagpipe.

dulcimer Ancient instrument with wire strings stretching over a shallow box which are struck with rods.

dulcitone Instrument similar to celesta but with steel tuning forks instead of steel plates.

duplex-coupler piano Invented by Emanuel Moór in 1921; has 2 keyboards, upper tuned an octave higher.

electronde Electronic instrument invented by Martin Taubman in 1933, like the theremin but can create staccato effect.

embouchure Mouthpiece of a brass instrument.

emicon Electric instrument invented in USA in 1931 and producing notes from air in graded chromatic scale.

English flute: aka Recorder.

English horn Alto oboe, pitched a 5th lower and having a conical shape and bulbous bell.

euphonium Tenor tuba in B flat. Also name of instrument made of glass plates and rods by Ernst Chladni in 1790.

fagotto Bassoon.

fipple Mouthpiece for all wind instruments.

flageolet Small type of recorder.

flexatone Patented in 1922 and consisting of a flexible metal sheet suspended in a wire frame with handle. Shaking produces a tremolo sound.

flugelhorn Brass instrument in the cornet family but with a wider bore and larger bell.

flûte à bec (beak flute) Type of recorder.

French harp Harmonica.

French horn Coiled brass wind intrument extending to 11ft when uncoiled with a bell of 14in diameter. Early form supposedly introduced to the orchestra by Lully; modern form uses valves introduced in the 1820s.

frog On bowed instruments, the end of the bow that is held in the hand. Aka nut.

Geigenwerk Type of hurdy-gurdy invented in Nuremberg in 1575 by Hans Haiden.

gekkin Japanese instrument with circular body like banjo but with 9 frets and 4 strings tuned in pairs.

gemshorn Type of flute made of horn, not used since 16th century. Aka chamois horn.

gittern Medieval ancestor of guitar.

glockenspiel (lit. bell play) Musical instrument consisting of hanging metal bars, which are struck with a hammer.

gong Ancient percussion instrument first found in China, a metal disc generally with upturned edges, usually with indefinite pitch but sometimes tuned.

grelots Little bells, e.g. sleigh bells, used as percussion.

gusla One-stringed bowed instrument long popular in Slavonic cultures.

gusli Ancient Russian instrument of the zither family.

harmonica Mouth organ with metal reeds, first produced by Friedrich Buschman of Berlin in 1821 as the 'Mundäoline'. The two main types of harmonicas are the chromatic and the diatonic. The chromatic harmonica is preferred by blues players such as Bob Dylan and Neil Young. The diatonic harmonica has a wider range and more suited to the virtuoso such as Larry Adler.

harmonium Small portable reed organ perfected by Alexandre Debain of Paris in the early 1840s.

harp Forty-seven-stringed instrument whose modern orchestral version with a pedal mechanism was developed by Sébastien Érard.

harpsichord Wing-shaped keyboard instrument in which the strings are mechanically plucked rather that struck with a hammer.

hautbois French name for oboe, (lit. 'high wood').

Hawaiian guitar Ukulele (also nickname of steel guitar) introduced by the Portuguese.

heckelphone Double-reed, baritone oboe with a conical bore and bulbous bell.

helicon Tuba with a circular construction that can be wrapped around the body for marching bands.

hellertion Electric instrument developed in Frankfurt in 1936 by Bruno Helberger and Peter Lertes, similar to Theremin but with a range of 6 octaves.

hitschiriki Japanese instrument like a bamboo flute with 7 finger-holes and 2 thumb-holes.

hityokin Japanese vertical flute made of bamboo.

hornpipe Wind instrument with a single reed and a cow's horn fitted on the end.

hummel Swedish zither.

hurdy-gurdy Medieval instrument resembling a viol but whose sound is produced by friction of hand-cranked wooden wheel on strings that could be stopped by keys.

huruk Hourglass-shaped Indian drum.

hydraulis Ancient instrument, aka water organ, supposedly invented in Greece by Ktesibios in the 3rd century BC.

idiophone Term used for instrument whose own material makes a characteristic sound such as castanets, gongs, bells, etc.

Irish harp Small harp played while held in the lap.

Japanese fiddle One-stringed instrument played by street performers.

Jew's harp Folk instrument consisting of a metal frame that contains a flexible strip of metal. The frame is held between the player's teeth while the metal strip is twanged.

kazoo Short tube open at both ends, with a vibrating membrane in between, played by humming into it; a kind of mirliton.

kin Japanese string instrument, a small koto.

kithara Ancient but sophisticated Greek lyre, which is finger plucked.

klavier Keyboard instrument (with strings).

knollhorn Soft-sounding herald horn from the mid-western region of the US.

Korean temple block Oriental addition to the 20th-century dance-band drummer's equipment, constituting a skull-shaped hollow block of wood, in several sizes, and struck with a drumstick.

koto Japanese instrument resembling a zither, with 7 to 13 silk strings plucked by the fingers.

lira A 16th-century string instrument with drones, played with a bow.

loure French bagpipe.

lute Ancient musical instrument with a pear-shaped belly and a long, fretted fingerboard and played like a modern guitar.

lutherie The art of making string instruments – not only lutes, but also guitars and the violin family.

luthier One who practises lutherie.

lyra (lyre) Ancient Greek instrument with a 4-sided frame, encompassing strings attached from a soundbox to a crossbar. Played like a harp.

machete Portuguese 4-string folk guitar.

mandocello Bass mandolin.

mandola/mandora Small, early precursor of the lute and mandolin with 9 frets and up to 6 strings.

mandolin Instrument in the lute family, fretted and with 8 wire strings tuned in four pairs, G, D, A, E.

maracas Latin American percussion instrument consisting of two seed-filled gourds, which are shaken by handles.

mardakion Accordion-like instrument from the mid-west US.

marimba African percussion instrument introduced to Latin America, a deeper pitched version of the xylophone with metal resonators.

m'bira African 'thumb piano' made up of a number of metal or cane tongues held in position with a bar attached to a box or board. The free ends are twanged with the thumbs.

mellophone Variation of the French horn constructed for marching.

melodeon Related to the concertina, with 10 treble keys on the right, bellows and 4 bass keys on the left.

metallophone Percussion instrument consisting of tuned metal bars arranged in single or double rows.

mirliton Instrument containing a membrane to modify a sound made when the player hums or sings into or against it.

monochord Musical instrument with one string, used for determining the ratios of musical intervals.

Moog synthesizer Earliest commercial, voltage-controlled synthesizer, invented by Robert Moog in 1965.

mouth organ The term covers many instruments with metal reeds but nowadays is synonymous with the harmonica.

musetta Bellows-operated French bagpipe popular in the court of Louis XIV.

mute Device usually conical in shape, that muffles a brass instrument's sound.

nightingale Toy instrument used in by Scarlatti in an oratorio by Scarlatti and by Leopold Mozart in his *Toy Symphony*.

nose flute Originating in Polynesia, a bamboo flute blown through the nostrils.

nut On bowed instruments, device fitted on to the end of the bow that is held in the hand, and used to adjust the bow's tension.

oboe Double-reed woodwind instrument with a conical bore in C and a natural scale of D.

oboe d'amore Slightly bigger than the normal oboe, with a pear-shaped bell, and pitched a minor third lower.

ocarina (little goose) Small, round, wind instrument with finger holes, and made out of clay or porcelain; so named by Giuseppe Donati in mid-1800s; aka sweet potato.

oliphant Small medieval horn made from an elephant's tusk.

ondes Martenot Electronic keyboard instrument developed by Maurice Martenot in the 1920s; shaped like a spinet.

ophicleide Large, brass, keyed bass bugle played in the upright position, developed from the serpent (name is Greek for 'serpent with keys') but displaced by the bass tuba.

panharmonicon Mechanical orchestra invented by Johann Maelzel in 1805; inspiration of Beethoven's *Battle Symphony*.

panpipes (aka syrinx) Ancient wind instrument consisting of several pipes of graduated lengths bound together.

pegbox Box at the end of the neck on string instruments into which the pegs that adjust the strings are inserted.

phagotum Type of bellows-blown bagpipe invented by Canon Afranio of Ferrara in the early 1500s.

pianoforte Full name of the piano, with 88 keys, first made in Florence around 1700 by Bartolomeo Cristofori; name is Italian for soft-loud.

pianola Player piano manufactured in the early 1900s by the Aeolian Corporation; the first of the kind was the Welte-Mignon.

piccolo Small flute that sounds an octave higher than written (piccolo in C) or, less often, a minor ninth higher than written (piccolo in D flat).

point Tip of the bow of a string instrument.

poliphant Thirty-seven-stringed instrument of early 17th century; a cross between harp, lute and theorbo.

posthorn Cylindrical, valveless straight horn used by coachmen and mailcarriers to announce arrival.

psaltery Ancient string instrument, similar to the dulcimer.

purfling Decorative strip inlaid around the edges of a string instrument.

pyiba Pear-shaped, four-stringed, ancient Chinese lute.

racket Double-reed instrument consisting of short, thick cylinder of wood drilled along its length with a bore-holes connected into a single air channel.

raspa Cuban percussion instrument made out of gourd with notches that are scraped with a stick.

ratamacue Drum rudiment consisting of an alternating-hand sticking pattern.

ratchet/rattle Percussion instrument with a cogwheel that strikes one or more metal or wooden projections when twirled.

rebab An ancient North African and Middle Eastern short-necked fiddle with two strings.

rebec Small, pear-shaped, medieval bowed instrument, a development of the Arab rebab, with a short neck and three to five strings.

recorder End-blown wooden flute without keys, with a tapering bore.

reed(s) Clarinet is a single-reed instrument; oboe and bassoon are double-reed.

regal Portable reed organ of the 16th century.

Rhodes piano Electric piano developed by Harold Rhodes.

rhythmicon Keyboard percussion instrument using photoelectric cell and devised by Lev Theremin and Henry Cowell in 1931.

rosin Block of hardened tree resin that is rubbed across the bow hairs to enhance the friction.

rote (rotta) Lyre-type instrument from the Middle Ages.

sackbut Renaissance name for the slide trombone, which then had a smaller bell and narrower bore.

saddle On guitar, a thin strip of ivory, bone or plastic set into the bridge.

saltbox Charivari instrument used by flipping the lid and beating the side with a rolling pin or spoon.

samisen Flat-backed, long-necked lute from Japan with a skin-covered belly and three silk strings.

sarangi Northern Indian fiddle with short, thick neck and 3 to 4 bowed strings plus sympathetic strings.

sarod Indian instrument usually having 6 main strings and 12 to 15 sympathetic strings.

sarrusophone Double-reed woodwind instrument related to the oboe but made of brass, invented by French bandleader Sarrus in 1856.

saxophone Single-reed family of instruments, usually metal but sometimes plastic, invented by Adolphe Sax around 1840 and patented in 1846.

scordatura Changing the tuning of one or more strings from their standard pitch.

scroll Ornamental curled portion at the end of the pegbox on instruments of the violin family.

Scruggs picking Banjo finger-picking style developed by Earl Scruggs, using the thumb and two fingers.

serpent S-curved wooden horn with a conical bore, finger holes and a cup-shaped mouthpiece.

seven-string guitar Has an extra, high A string.

shakuhachi End-blown bamboo flute from Japan.

shawm Family of high-pitched, double-reed woodwind instruments of the Middle Ages; precursors of the oboe.

sheng Chinese mouth organ made up of wind chamber fitted with pipes with reeds that vibrate.

shofar Ancient Hebrew ceremonial wind instrument made of a ram's horn.

simandl bow For string basses; a bow configured to be held with the palm up.

sistrum Ancient percussion instrument made up of metal disc rattles threaded on rods.

sitar Long-necked Indian lute with moveable arched frets, a gourd resonator close to the pegboard, and 3 to 7 strings, below which are sympathetic strings, often as many as 12. Made popular in the West by Ravi Shankar.

skirl On bagpipe, the sounds made by the upper pipes.

sousaphone Tuba that encircles the body and made specifically for John Philip Sousa's band.

spinet Small Renaissance keyboard instrument with a plucking action like a harpsichord.

steel drums Made out of various-sized oil drums, with deeply incised patterns with different pitches.

stick, Chapman Electric 10-stringed (5 bass and 5 guitar) instrument that utilises tapping technique on strings.

swell Mechanical device on some keyboard instruments for adjusting the volume of sound.

switch Percussion instrument, made up of wires bound at one end, that is struck against the hand.

sympathetic string String that vibrates in an instrument without being plucked in response to the vibrations of strings that are plucked, or to a percussion impact.

tablas Asymmetrical pair of conical, tuned, wooden Indian drums, beaten with the hands.

tabor Earliest form of the snare drum, which evolved into a military instrument.

talon The nut end of the bow used to play string instruments.

tambour Type of drum.

tambourine Percussion instrument of Arab origin consisting of a small, shallow, circular drum with metal discs inserted into its frame. The discs are known as jingles.

tambur(a) Long-necked, round-bodied lute. Indian tamburas have 4 strings, drones and a moveable ivory bridge to adjust pitch; Balkan tamburas are fretted.

tam-tam Large, flat, thin metal saucer suspended on a frame and struck with a soft beater.

theorbo Sixteenth-century arch-lute with numerous stopped and unstopped strings attached to separate pegbox.

Theremin Electronic instrument developed by Lev Theremin (1920); the hands do not touch the instrument but produce oscillations when they move around the antenna.

ti tzu Chinese flute with 6 finger-holes and a 7th hole covered with thin membrane whose vibration dictates the tone.

timbrel Ancient Middle Eastern tambourine, and its medieval European descendant.

tin whistle High-pitched, end-blown Irish flute with 6 holes, made out of metal.

tonette Wood or plastic end-blown flute with finger-holes.

tremolo arm Device that changes the pitch of the strings by moving the bridge with a type of spring action.

trombone Brass instrument, larger than a trumpet, and with a sliding tube to extend notes.

trumpet Brass wind instrument consisting of a long tubular central piece with a cup-shaped mouth-piece and wide, bell-shaped base. A trumpet has three valves.

MUSIC CLASSICAL

tuba Bass instrument patented by W Wieprecht and Moritz in Berlin (1835).

tubular bells Percussion instrument in the form of suspended tubes, tuned to the diatonic scale, and struck with a hammer.

tuning-fork Two-pronged metal instrument invented in 1711 by the trumpeter John Shore. The pure tone that it emits when set vibrating helps to give the pitch to singers or instruments.

uilleann pipes Irish bagpipes worked by bellows held under one arm.

ukelele (ukulele) Four-stringed instrument developed in Hawaii in the 1870s from a kind of Portugese guitar

upright piano Piano in which strings are vertical. John Isaac Hawkins of Philadelphia first built iron-framed uprights in 1800.

vibraphone (vibes) Xylophone with metal bars and a wide vibrato effect produced by electrically operated fans.

vihuela Six-string Spanish instrument of the 1600s that looks like a guitar but is tuned as a lute.

vina Indian stringed instrument, those from northern India having a long stick-like unfretted fingerboard resting on two resonating gourds, those from southern India having a much broader fingerboard and a wooden body in place of one of the gourds.

viola da braccio Tenor viol played under the arm.

viola da gamba Bass viol played between the knees.

viola d'amore Unfretted tenor instrument with 7 strings and 7 to 14 sympathetic strings.

violin Treble stringed instrument with 4 strings tuned to G, D, A, E.

violoncello Tenor stringed instrument of the violin family, played between the knees, using bass clef, with 4 strings tuned to C, G, D, A.

virginal Small, soft-sounding harpsichord of the 16th and 17th centuries, with one string to a note.

Wagner tuba Invented by Richard Wagner specifically for his *Ring Cycle*; look is more of a horn than a tuba.

whammy bar Another name for tremolo arm.

woodwind Recorders, flutes, clarinets, saxophones, oboes, piccolos, cor anglais and bassoons (lowest pitch).

xylophone (lit. wood sound) Percussion instrument consisting of graduated, tuned wooden bars played by being struck with a hammer.

xylorimba Combination of xylophone and marimba.

zither Family of plucked string instruments including the dulcimer, hummel, koto, autoharp and psaltery, where the (up to 45) strings run the entire length of a flat body.

Famous Musicians

Bassoonists
Archie Camden
John Hebden
D Kern Holoman
Jacques Hotteterre
Edwin James
John Lampe
William Waterhouse

Cellists
Hugo Becker
Luigi Boccherini
Anner Bylsma
Pablo Casals
Gaspar Cassadó
Mischel Cherniavsky
Myung-Wha Chung
Robert Cohen
Christopher Coin
Karl Davidoff
Jean Louis Dufort
Jean Pierre Dufort
Jacqueline Du Pré
Maurice Eisenberg
Emanuel Feuermann
Amaryllis Fleming
Pierre Fournier
Auguste Franchomme
Carl Fuchs
Karine Georgian
Georg Goltermann
Bernard Greenhouse
Natalia Gutman
Lynn Harrell
Beatrice Harrison
Nicola Haym
John Hebden
Thomas Igloi

Steven Isserlis
Giuseppe Maria
  Jacchini
Ivor James
Antonio Janigro
Hans Kindler
Ralph Kirshbaum
Anton Kraft
Nicolaus Kraft
Robert Lindley
Julian Lloyd Webber
Martin Lovett
Antonio Lysy
Yo-Yo Ma
Enrico Mainardi
Mischa Maisky
António Meneses
Howard Mitchell
May Mukle
André Navarra
Charles Neate
Zara Nelsova
Arto Noras
Vladimir Orloff
Siegfried Palm
Stephen Paxton
Boris
  Pergamenschikov
Gregor Piatigorsky
Alfredo Piatti
Anthony Pini
William Pleeth
David Popper
Julius Rietz
Bernhard Romberg
Leonard Rose
Mstislav Rostropovich
Milos Sádlo

Felix Salmond
Samuil Samosud
Heinrich Schiff
Johann Schlick
Georg Schnéevoigt
Mátyás Seiber
Adrien François Servais
Raphael Sommer
William Henry Squire
János Starker
Guilhermina Suggia
Paul Tortelier
Arturo Toscanini
Christopher Van
  Kampen
Alfred Wallenstein
Raphael Wallfisch
Moray Welsh
August Wenzinger
Hanus Wihan

Clarinettists
John Adams
Heinrich Bärmann
Jack Brymer
Louis Cahuzac
Benny Goodman
Woody Herman
Janet Hilton
Emma Johnson
Reginald Kell
Thea King
Hyacinth Klosé
Henry Lewis
Richard Mühlfeld
Gervase de Peyer
Artie Shaw
Anton Stadler

Richard Stolzman
Morton Subotnick
Frederick Thurston
Bernard Walton

Double Bass
Giovanni Bottesini
Ida Carroll
Eugene Cruft
Domenico Dragonetti
Barry Guy
Gary Karr
Franz Kotzwara
Serge Koussevitzky

Flautists
Richard Adeney
Bruno Bartoletti
Michel Blavet
Theobald Boehm
Giulio Briccialdi
Franz Doppler
Karl Doppler
Louis François Fleury
James Galway
Severino Gazzelloni
Geoffrey Gilbert
Dave Heath
Hans-Joachim
  Koellreutter
Hans-Martin Linde
Johann Bernhard
  Logier
Edward McGuire
Susan Milan
Gareth Morris
Marcel Moyse
Aurèle Nicolet

Johann Quantz
Jean-Pierre Rampal
Elaine Shaffer
Fritz Spiegl
Adolf Terschak
David Van Vactor

French Horn
Hermann Baumann
Aubrey Brain
Dennis Brain
Alan Civil
Anthony Halstead
David Pyatt
Barry Tuckwell

Guitarists
Julian Bream
Leo Brouwer
Cornelius Cardew
Ferdinando Carulli
Mauro Giuliani
Miguel Llobet
Carlos Montoya
Gaspar Sanz
Andrés Segovia
Philip Selby
Fernando Sor
Francisco Tárrega
Jason Vieaux
John Williams
Narciso Yepes

Harpists
Osian Ellis
Félix Godefroid
Marie Goossens
Sidonie Goossens
Alphonse Hasselmans
Ursula Holliger
Alfred Holý
Maria Korchinska
Johann Krumpholtz
François Naderman
Elias Parish-Alvars
John Parry
Nansi Richards
Marisa Robles
Carlos Salzédo
Marcel Tournier
Nicanor Zabaleta

Horns
David Amram
Johannes Amon
Adolph Borsdorf
Alan Civil
Louis-François Dauprat
John Denison
Heinrich Domnich
Anton Joseph Hampel
Maurice Handford
Ifor James
Ignaz Leutgeb
Giovanni Punto
Timothy Reynish
Franz Joseph Strauss
Barry Tuckwell

Mouth Organists
Larry Adler
Tommy Reilly

Oboists
Evelyn Barbirolli (née
   Rothwell)
Neil Black
Janet Craxton
John Cruft
Johann Fischer
Leon Goossens
Heinz Holliger
John Lancie
Ludwig August Lebrun
Charles Mackerras
Jean-Claude Malgoire
Friedrich Ramm
Ray Still
Edo de Waart

Organists
Herbert Andrews
Jennifer Bate
Jonathan Battishill
William Best
E Power Biggs
John Birch
John Blitheman
John Blow
Léon Boëllmann
Georg Böhm
Kevin Bowyer
John Dykes Bower
Ernest Bullock
Charles Burney
John Camidge
Matthew Camidge
Thomas Camidge
Melville Cook
George Cunningham
Carlo Curley
John Danby
Thurston Dart
Christopher Dearnley
William Done
Maurice Dupré
Hermann Finck
Grattan Flood
Virgil Fox
Alfred Gaul
Nicolas Gigault
Eugène Gigout
Johann Goldberg
John Goss
Alan Gray
Nicolas de Grigny
Douglas Guest
George Guest
Christopher Herrick
Edward Hopkins
Karl Friedrich Horn
Francis Jackson
Geraint Jones
Johann Kerll
Jacob Kirckman
Leonhard Kleber
Carlmann Kolb
Johann Krebs
Jean Langlais
Philip Ledger
Edwin Lemare
Henry Ley
Gaston Litaize
Charles Lloyd
Vincent Lübeck

David Lumsden
André Marchal
Louis Marchand
Giovanni Martini
Olivier Messiaen
Georg Monn
James Nares
Edward Naylor
Martin Neary
Sydney Nicholson
Thomas Noble
Vincent Novello
Herbert Oakeley
Boris Ord
Johann Pachelbel
Jane Parker-Smith
Peter Pears
Simon Preston
Daniel Purcell
Henry Purcell
James Pyne
Helmuth Rilling
Edward Rimbault
Alec Robertson
Douglas Robinson
Lionel Rogg
Cyril Rootham
Barry Rose
Bernard Rose
Francisco de Salinas
Sir Malcolm Sargent
Heinrich Scheidemann
Samuel Scheidt
Albert Schweitzer
John Scott
George Sinclair
Johann Staden
Paul Steinitz
Leopold Stokowski
Karl Straube
Herbert Sumsion
Richard Terry
George Thalben-Ball
David Titterington
Thomas Trotter
David Tudor
Franz Tunder
Denis Vaughan
Louis Vierne
Helmut Walcha
William Walond
Henry Watson
Gillian Weir
Charles Wesley
Allan Wicks
Charles-Marie Widor
David Willcocks
Charles Lee Williams
Malcolm Williamson
Arthur Wills
Philipp Wolfrum
Leslie Woodgate
Henry Wood
Pietro Alessandro Yon
Pietro Ziani

Percussionists
James Blades
Evelyn Glennie
Stomu Yamashita

Pianists

Jacques Abram
Joaquin Achucarro
Thomas Ades
Daniel Adni
Roy Agnew
Martha Argerich
Vladimir Ashkenazy
Stefan Askenase
Victor Babin
Gina Bachauer
Paul Badura-Skoda
Daniel Barenboim
Hans Barth
Ethel Bartlett
Harold Bauer
Malcolm Bilson
Christian Blackshaw
Marc Blitzstein
Michel Block
Susan Bradshaw
Alfred Brendel
Yefim Bronfman
Bruno Canino
Teresa Carreño
Jean Casadesus
Robert Marcel
   Casadesus
Shura Cherkassky
Aldo Ciccolini
Van Cliburn
Harriet Cohen
Elizabeth Coolidge
Imogen Cooper
Joseph Cooper
Alfred Cortot
Johann Cramer
Paul Crossley
Clifford Curzon
Karl Czerny
György Cziffra
Michel Dalberto
Edward Dannreuther
Bella Davidovich
Peter Donohoe
Ania Dorfmann
Barry Douglas
Karl Engel
John Field
Margaret Fingerhut
Rudolf Firkusny
Annie Fischer
Edwin Fischer
Leon Fleisher
Myers Foggin
Andor Foldes
Hubert Foss
Ian Fountain
Fou Ts'ong
Philip Fowke
Homero Francesch
Samson François
Peter Frankl
Justus Frantz
Géza Frid
Ignaz Friedman
Benjamin Frith
Liza Fuchsova
Ossip Gabrilowitsch
Irwin Gage
Andrei Gavrilov
Walter Gieseking
Emil Gilels

Arabella Goddard
Leopold Godowsky
Anthony Goldstone
Richard Goode
Glenn Gould
Gary Graffman
Percy Grainger
Arthur de Greef
Gordon Green
Horacio Gutiérrez
Monique Haas
Ingrid Haebler
Charles Hallé
Mark Hambourg
Paul Hamburger
Iain Hamilton
Clara Haskil
Claude Helffer
Clifton Helliwell
Myra Hess
Rolf Hind
Alfred Hipkins
Ludwig Hoffman
Vladimir Horowitz
Colin Horsley
Louis Horst
Mieczyslaw Horszowski
Stephen Hough
Andrew Imbrie
John Ireland
Edward Isaacs
Leonard Isaacs
Michael Isador
Martin Isepp
Eugene Istomin
Paul Jacobs
Byron Janis
Grant Johannesen
Graham Johnson
Eileen Joyce
Terence Judd
Jeffrey Kahane
Joseph Kalichstein
Friedrich Kalkbrenner
William Kapell
Jean-Rodolphe Kars
Julius Katchen
Peter Katin
Mindru Katz
Wilhelm Kempff
John Kirkpatrick
Evgeny Kissin
Bernhard Klee
Walter Klien
Karl Klindworth
Zoltán Kocsis
Alfons Kontarsky
Aloys Kontarsky
Lili Kraus
Katia Labèque
Marielle Labèque
Frederic Lamond
Alicia de Larrocha
Philip Ledger
Yvonne Lefébure
Theodor Leschetizky
Oscar Levant
Raymond Lewenthal
Hans Leygraf
Josef Lhévinne
Rosina Lhévinne
John Lill

Eugene List
Kathleen Long
Marguérite Long
Alessandro Longo
Yvonne Loriod
Radu Lupu
Moura Lympany
Alexei Lyubimov
Joanna McGregor
Witold Malcuzynski
Leopold Mannes
Tobias Matthay
Denis Matthews
Florence May
Fanny Mendelssohn
Hephzibah Menuhin
Frank Merrick
Noel Mewton-Wood
Nina Milkina
Benno Moiseiwitsch
Federico Mompou
David Money
Stephen Montague
Gerald Moore
Angus Morrison
Ignaz Moscheles
Charles Neate
Marc Neikrug
Ivor Newton
Joaquin Nin
David Owen Norris
Lev Oborin
Noriko Ogawa
John Ogdon
Garrick Ohlsson
Mercedes Olivera
Georges Onslow
Ursula Oppens
Rafael Orozco
Leslie Orrey
Cristina Ortiz
George Osborne
Cécile Ousset
Vladimir Ovchinikov
Vladimir de Pachmann
Ignacy Jan Paderewski
Kun Woo Paik
Maria von Paradis
    (blind)
Jon Kimura Parker
Eric Parkin
Geoffrey Parsons
Leonard Pennario
Murray Perahia
Vlado Perlemuter
Egon Petri
Nikolai Petrov
Isidor Philipp
Maria-João Pires
Johann Peter Pixis
Artur Pizarro
Barbara von Ployer
Ivo Pogorelich
Maurizio Pollini
Jean-Bernard Pommier
Viktoria Postnikova
Leff Pouishnoff
Ferdinand Praeger
André Previn
Stephen Pruslin
Gwenneth Pryor
Anne Queffélec

Ruth Railton
Thomas Rajna
Dezsö Ránki
Clarence Raybould
Julius Reubke
Robert Riefling
Ferdinand Ries
Bernard Roberts
Rae Robertson
Pascal Rogé
Michael Roll
Martin Roscoe
Charles Rosen
Moriz Rosenthal
Mstislav Rostropovich
Anton Rubinstein
Arthur Rubinstein
Nikolay Rubinstein
Mikhail Rudy
Christian Rummel
Walter Rummel
Harold Rutland
Vasily Safonov
Harold Samuel
György Sándor
Jesús Maria Sanromá
Vasily Sapellnikov
Sir Malcolm Sargent
Irene Scharrer
Xaver Scharwenka
Ernest Schelling
Heinrich Schenker
Andras Schiff
Allan Schiller
Artur Schnabel
Karl Ulrich Schnabel
Irina Schnittke
Clara Schumann
Phyllis Sellick
Yitkin Seow
Peter Serkin
Rudolf Serkin
Shulamith Shafir
William Shakespeare
Howard Shelley
Maxim Shostakovich
Béla Siki
Constantin Silvestri
Abbey Simon
Leonard Slatkin
Jan Smeterlin
Cyril Smith
Ronald Smith
Yonty Solomon
Georg Solti
Peter Stadlen
Bernhard Stavenhagen
Wilhelm Stenhammar
Ronald Stevenson
Soulima Stravinsky
Walter Susskind
Roberto Szidon
Carl Tausig
André Tchaikowsky
Boris Tchaikovsky
Alec Templeton
Sigismond Thalberg
Jean-Yves Thibaudet
Michael Tilson Thomas
Martino Tirimo
Donald Tovey
Valerie Tryon

Norman Tucker
David Tudor
Rosalyn Tureck
Mitsuko Uchida
Sergio Varella-Cid
Tamás Vásáry
Bálint Vazsonyi
Isabelle Vengerova
Adela Verne
Mathilde Verne
Roger Vignoles
Ricardo Viñes
Lucille Wallace
Peter Wallfisch
Fanny Waterman
Sydney Watson
André Watts
Daniel Wayenberg
Joseph Weingarten
Erik Werba
Jósef Wieniawski
Earl Wild
David Wilde
Malcolm Williamson
Paul Wittgenstein
Roger Woodward
Enloc Wu
Friedrich Wührer
Marie Wurm
Jürg Wyttenbach
Théophile Ysaye
Carlo Zecchi
Géza Zichy
Alexander Ziloti
Krystian Zimerman
Jan Zimmer
Agnes Zimmermann

Trumpeters
Maurice André
Malcolm Arnold
Ernest Hall
Håkan Hardenberger
Philip Jones
Humphrey Lyttelton
Johann Petzold
Gerard Schwarz
Crispian Steel-Perkins
Edward Tarr
John Wilbraham

Tuba
Eleazar de Carvalho

Violists
Yuri Bashmet
Paul Doktor
Watson Forbes
Rivka Golani
Karel Hába
Nobuko Imai
Allan Pettersson
Jean Pougnet
William Primrose
Frederick Riddle
Hermann Ritter
Peter Schidlof
Bernard Shore
Lionel Tertis
Walter Trampler
Efrem Zimbalist

Violinists
Joseph Achron
Delphin Alard
Pierre Amoyal
Jelly Arányi
Alexandre-Joseph Artôt
Thomas Baltzar
John Banister
Angel Barrios
Richard Barth
Yuri Bashmet
Rudolf Baumgartner
Hugh Bean
Paul Beard
Boris Belkin
Joshua Bell
Norbert Brainin
George Bridgetower
Adolph Brodsky
Ole Bull
Alfredo Campoli
John Carrodus
Marius Casadesus
Arthur Catterall
Levon Chilingiran
Kyung-Wha Chung
Raymond Cohen
Béla Dekany
Gioconda De Vito
Augustine Dumay
John Ella
Mischa Elman
Devy Erlih
Adila Fachiri
Carlo Farina
Alfonso Ferrabosco
Christian Ferras
Michael Festing
Carl Flesch
Giovanni Fontana
Zino Francescatti
Miriam Fried
Joseph Fuchs
Mayumi Fujikawa
Ivan Galamian
Saschko Gawriloff
André Gertler
Rivka Golani
Szymon Goldberg
Stephane Grappelli
Hyam Greenbaum
Sidney Griller
Frederick Grinke
Ida Haendel
Marie Hall
Jascha Heifetz

Joseph Hellmesberger
Willy Hess
Ulf Hoelscher
Karl Hoffmann
Ralph Holmes
Henry Holst
Yuzuko Horigome
Jenő Hubay
Bronislaw Huberman
Monica Huggett
Shizuka Ishikawa
Feliks Janiewicz
Joseph Joachim
Leila Josefowicz
Joseph Kaminski
Mark Kaplan
Louis Kaufman
Hans Keller
Nigel Kennedy
Willem Kes
Isabelle van Keulen
Young-Uck Kim
Pawel Kochánski
Leonid Kogan
Franz Kotzwara
Fritz Kreisler
Gidon Kremer
Rodolphe Kreutzer
Wenzel Krumpholtz
Oleg Krysa
Jan Kubelik
Sigiswald Kuijken
Georg Kulenkampff
Franz Lamotte
Linda Lampenius
Jaime Laredo
Cho-Liang Lin
Tasmin Little
Alan Loveday
Mark Lubotsky
Anne Macnaghten
Vanessa Mae
André Mangeot
Mantovani
Alessandro Marcello
Silvia Marcovici
Johanna Martzy
Joseph Massart
Nicola Matteis
Eduard Melkus
Isolde Menges
Yehudi Menuhin
Goto Midori
Stoika Milanova
Nathan Milstein
Shlomo Mintz

Lydia Mordkovitch
Viktoria Mullova
Charles Munch
Anne-Sophie Mutter
Pietro Nardini
Yfrah Neaman
Wilma Neruda
Ginette Neveu
Sigmund Nissel
David Oistrakh
Igor Oistrakh
Raphael Oleg
Frantisek Ondncek
Igor Ozim
Niccolò Paganini
Manoug Parikian
György Pauk
Edith Peinemann
Itzhak Perlman
George Frederic Pinto
Adolf Pollitzer
Jean Pougnet
Maud Powell
William Primrose
Gaetano Pugnani
Giovanni Punto
Michael Rabin
John Ravenscroft
Ede Reményi
Vadim Repin
Ruggiero Ricci
Franz Anton Ries
Hubert Ries
Alexander Ritter
Andreas Jakob
  Romberg
Arnold Rosé
Carl Rosiers
Max Rostal
Christian Rummel
George Saint-George
Prosper Sainton
Johann Peter Salomon
Albert Sammons
Eugene Sarbu
Emile Sauret
Rosario Scalero
Anton Schindler
Alexander Schneider
Wolfgang Schneiderhan
Jaap Schröder
Franz Schubert
Ignaz Schuppanzigh
Otakar Sevcik
Emily Shinner
Oscar Shumsky

Joseph Silverstein
Dmitry Sitkovetzky
Camillo Sivori
Nikolay Sokoloff
Paolo Spagnoletti
Albert Spalding
Theodore Spiering
Johann Wenzel Stamitz
Simon Standage
Isaac Stern
Julius Stern
Frederick Stock
George Stratton
Josef Suk
Zoltán Székely
Henryk Szeryng
Josef Szigeti
Gabor Takács-Nagy
Václav Talich
Giuseppe Tartini
Vilmos Tátrai
Charles Taylor
Arve Tellefsen
Emil Telmányi
Henri Temianka
Klaus Tennstedt
Carlo Tessarini
Jacques Thibaud
César Thomson
Luigi Tomasini
Giuseppe Torelli
Yan Pascal Tortelier
Roman Totenberg
Berthold Tours
Chrétien Urhan
Tibór Varga
Sándor Végh
Maxim Vengerov
Henri Verbrugghen
Henri Vieuxtemps
H. Waldo Warner
Joseph Miroslav Weber
Henryk Wieniawski
Wanda Wilkomirska
Marie Wilson
Michael Zacharewitsch
Christian Zacharias
Zvi Zeitlin
Jakob Zeugheer
Efrem Zimbalist
Frank Peter Zimmermann
Louis Zimmermann
Yossi Zivoni
Olive Zorian
Pinchas Zukerman
Paul Zukofsky

MUSIC CLASSICAL

Famous Singers

Sopranos
Aïno Ackté
Roberta Alexander
Jeannine Altmeyer
Elly Ameling
Marie Angel
Sheila Armstrong
Martina Arroyo
Florence Austral
Lilian Bailey
Isobel Baillie

Josephine Barstow
Kathleen Battle
Hildegard Behrens
Elizabeth Billington
Judith Blegen
Hannelore Bode
Barbara Bonney
Lucrezia Bori
Inge Borkh
Gré Brouwenstijn
Norma Burrowes

Montserrat Caballé
Teresa Cahill
Maria Callas
Emma Calvé
Maria Caniglia
Maria Caradori-Allan
Margherita Carosio
Katharina Cavalieri
Maria Cebotari
Maria Chiara
Gina Cigna

Mimi Coertse
Isabella Colbran
Elizabeth Connell
Mary Costa
Régine Crespin
Joan Cross
Lella Cuberli
Maud Cunitz
Toti Dal Monte
Suzanne Danco
Barbara Daniels

Gloria Davy
Anne Dawson
Lynne Dawson
Lisa Della Casa
Joséphine De Reszke
Emmy Destinn
Libuse Domaninska
Helen Donath
Dorothy Dorow
Dorothy Dow
Elizabeth Duparc
Denise Duval
Noël Eadie
Jean Eaglen
Emma Eames
Florence Easton
Christiane Eda-Pierre
Mary Ellis
Anne Evans
Carole Farley
Geraldine Farrar
Eileen Farrell
Helen Field
Sylvia Fischer
Kirsten Flagstad
Mirella Freni
Elizabeth Fretwell
Marya Freund
Marta Fuchs
Johanna Gadski
Amelita Galli-Curci
Mary Garden
Lesley Garrett
Catherine Gayer
Mechthild Gessendorf
Sona Ghazarian
Christel Goltz
Jill Gomez
Linda Esther Gray
Silvia Greenberg
Giulia Grisi
Reri Grist
Edita Gruberova
Nora Gruhn
Elisabeth Grümmer
Hilde Gueden
Nancy Gustafson
Marie Gutheil-Schoder
Alison Hagley
Joan Hammond
Heather Harper
Eiddwen Harrhy
Kathryn Harries
Elizabeth Harwood
Minnie Hauk
Cynthia Haymon
Lorna Haywood
Frieda Hempel
Elvira de Hidalgo
Judith Howarth
Karen Huffstodt
Rita Hunter
Maria Ivogün
Gundula Janowitz
Maria Jeritza
Sumi Jo
Eva Johannson
Gwyneth Jones
Ava June
Sena Jurinac
Raina Kabaivanska
Kiri Te Kanawa

Julie Kaufmann
Adelaide Kemble
Barbra Kemp
Yvonne Kenny
Adele Kern
Emma Kirkby
Dorothy Kirsten
Katharina Klafsky
Anny Konetzni
Hilde Konetzni
Annelies Kupper
Selma Kurz
Dora Labbette
Aloysia Lange
Nanny Larsén-Todsen
Magda Laszló
Marjorie Lawrence
Evelyn Lear
Lilli Lehmann
Liza Lehmann
Lotte Lehmann
Frida Leider
Adèle Leigh
Hellen Lemmens
Tiana Lemnitz
Mary Lewis
Miriam Licette
Caterina Ligendza
Jenny Lind
Berit Lindholm
Wilma Lipp
Pilar Lorengar
Victoria de Los Angeles
Felicity Lott
Germaine Lubin
Pauline Lucca
Sylvia McNair
Catherine Malfitano
Mathilde Mallinger
Blanche Marchesi
Lois Marshall
Margaret Marshall
Eva Marton
Valerie Masterson
Amalie Materna
Edith Mathis
Karita Mattila
Johanna Meier
Nellie Melba
Janine Micheau
Julia Migenes
Zinka Milanov
Anna von Mildenburg
Audrey Mildmay
Aprile Millo
Nelly Miricioiu
Martha Mödl
Anna Moffo
Fanny Moody
Grace Moore
Elsie Morison
Edda Moser
Maria Müller
Carol Neblett
Judith Nelson
Mignon Nevada
Agnes Nicholls
Birgit Nilsson
Christine Nilsson
Alda Noni
Elizabeth Norberg
Lillian Nordica

Jessye Norman
Clara Novello
Jarmila Novotná
Magda Olivero
Elaine Padmore
Felicity Palmer
Euphrosyne Parepa
Anne Pashley
Giuditta Pasta
Adelina Patti
Rose Pauly
Fanny Persiani
Roberta Peters
Helga Pilarczyk
Rosalind Plowright
Deborah Polaski
Lily Pons
Rosa Ponselle
Lucia Popp
Leontyne Price
Margaret Price
Yvonne Printemps
Ana Pusar
Ashley Putnam
Louisa Pyne
Rosa Raisa
Hildegard Ranczak
Judith Raskin
Aulikki Rautawaara
Delia Reinhardt
Maria Reining
Elisabeth Rethberg
Esther Réthy
Katia Ricciarelli
Margaret Ritchie
Faye Robinson
Joan Rodgers
Amanda Roocroft
Annaliese Rothenberger
Hermine Rudersdorff
Leonie Rysanek
Hilde Sadek
Sibyl Sanderson
Sylvia Sass
Bidú Sayão
Marianne Schech
Erna Schlüter
Elisabeth Schumann
Vera Schwarz
Elisabeth Schwarzkopf
Graziella Sciutti
Renata Scotto
Nadine Secunde
Irmgard Seefried
Meta Seinemeyer
Marcella Sembrich
Luciana Serra
Ellen Shade
Honor Sheppard
Margaret Sheridan
Amy Shuard
Margarethe Siems
Anja Silja
Dorothy Silk
Beverly Sills
Jeannette Sinclair
Victoria Sladen
Oda Slobodskaya
Elisabeth Söderström
Henriette Sontag
Elena Souliotis
Maria Stader

Eleanor Steber
Hanny Steffek
Sophie Stehle
Anna Steiger
Teresa Stich-Randall
Lilian Stiles Allen
Teresa Stolz
Anna Storace
Rosina Storchio
Teresa Stratas
Rita Streich
Cheryl Studer
Rosa Sucher
Elsie Suddaby
Susan Sunderland
Joan Sutherland
Helena Tattermuschová
Renata Tebaldi
Giusto Tenducci (male)
Milka Ternina
Margarete
   Teschemacher
Eva Tetrazzini
Luisa Tetrazzini
Maggie Teyte
Thérèse Tietjens
Pauline Tinsley
Anna Tomowa-Sintow
Helen Traubel
Carrie Tubb
Eva Turner
Dawn Upshaw
Viorica Ursuleac
Leontina Vaduva
Benita Valente
Anita Välkki
Ninon Vallin
Carol Vaness
Julia Varady
Astrid Varnay
Elizabeth Vaughan
Galina Vishnevskaya
Jennifer Vyvyan
Johanna Wagner
Yoko Watanabe
Claire Watson
Janice Watson
Lilian Watson
Aloysia Weber
Gillian Webster
Lucie Weidt
Ljuba Welitsch
Ruth Welting
Catherine Wilson
Marie Wittich
Sophie Wyss
Rachel Yakar
Mara Zampieri
Ruth Ziesak
Teresa Zylis-Gara

Mezzo-Soprano
Janet Baker
Agnes Baltsa
Cecilia Bartoli
Teresa Berganza
Faustina Bordoni
Olga Borodina
Marianne Brandt
Marie Brema
Grace Bumbry
Sally Burgess

Majorano Caffarelli
Sarah Jane Cahier
Susanna Cibber
Katherine Ciesinski
Cynthi Clarey
Girolamo Crescentini
Claire Croiza
Janice De Gaetani
Astra Desmond
Oralia Dominguez
Nancy Evans
Maria Ewing
Brigitte Fassbaender
Linda Finnie
Muriel Forster
Elena Gerhardt
Rita Gorr
Bernadette Greevy
Giuditta Grisi
Barbara Hendricks
Jane Henschel
Alfreda Hodgson
Grace Hoffman
Elisabeth Höngen
Marilyn Horne
Anne Howells
Eirian James
Della Jones
Fiona Kimm
Louise Kirkby-Lunn
Gillian Knight
Nadezda Kniplová
Kathleen Kuhlmann
Lotte Lenya
Marjana Lipovsek
Martha Lipton
Jean Madeira
Maria Malibran
Mathilde Marchesi
Waltraud Meier
Susanne Mentzer
Kerstin Meyer
Yvonne Minton
Diana Montague
Ann Murray
Hyacinth Nicholls
Elena Obraztsova
Maria Olczewska
Anne Sofie von Otter
Rosa Papier
Anna Pollak
Florence Quivar
Eva Randová
Nell Rankin
Regina Resnik
Anna Reynolds
Jean Rigby
Vera Rozsa
Trudeliese Schmidt
Hanna Schwarz
Constance Shacklock
Mitsuko Shirai
Giulietta Simionato
Monica Sinclair
Doris Soffel
Frederica von Stade
Risë Stevens
Ebe Stignani
Conchita Supervia
Gladys Swarthout
Klara Takács
Blanche Thebom

Kerstin Thorborg
Jennie Tourel
Zélia Trebelli
Tatiana Troyanos
Lucia Valentini-Terrani
Josephine Veasey
Shirley Verrett
Pauline Viardot-Garcia
Sieglinde Wagner
Edyth Walker
Penelope Walker
Sarah Walker
Carolyn Watkinson
Lucie Weidt
Eugenia Zareska
Delores Ziegler

Counter-tenors
James Bowman
Michael Chance
Alfred Deller
Jochen Kowalski
Andreas Scholl

Contraltos
Muriel Brunskill
Clara Butt
Giovanni Carestini
Kathleen Ferrier
Birgit Finnilä
Maureen Forrester
Louise Homer
Mary Jarred
Sigrid Onegin
Norma Procter
Gladys Ripley
Charlotte Sainton-Dolby
Ernestine
   Schumann-Heink
Antoinette Sterling
Caroline Unger
Lucia Elizabeth Vestris
Mary Wakefield
Helen Watts

Baritones
Pasquale Amato
Thomas Allen
Ettore Bastianini
Pierre Bernac
John Brownlee
Sesto Bruscantini
Renato Bruson
Delme Bryn-Jones
Renato Capecchi
Piero Cappuccilli
Clive Carey
Ulrik Cold
Brian Cooke
Peter Dawson
Giuseppe De Luca
Willi
   Domgraf-Fassbänder
Geraint Evans
Keith Falkner
David Ffrangcon-Davies
Dietrich Fischer-Dieskau
Lucien Fugère
Peter Glossop
Tito Gobbi
John Goss
Franz Grundheber

Hakan Hagegard
Derek Hammond-Stroud
Thomas Hampson
Percy Heming
Thomas Hemsley
Roy Henderson
George Henschel
Jason Howard
Neil Howlett
Gerhard Hüsch
Dmitri Hvorostovsky
Jorma Hynninen
Richard Jackson
Herbert Janssen
Phillip Joll
Dimitri Kharitonov
Peter Knapp
Otakar Kraus
Tom Krause
Jean-Louis Lassalle
Sergei Leiferkus
François Le Roux
George London
Benjamin Luxon
Donald McIntyre
James Maddalena
Victor Maurel
Donald Maxwell
Michael Maybrick
Yury Mazurok
Robert Merrill
Johannes Messchaert
Dennis Noble
John Noble
Alan Opie
Rolando Panerai
Charles Panzéra
Kostas Paskalis
Antonio Pini-Corsi
Juan Pons
Hermann Prey
Gino Quilico
Louis Quilico
Frederick Ranalow
John Rawnsley
Theodor Reichmann
Maurice Renaud
Marko Rothmüller
Titta Ruffo
Kennerley Rumford
Karel Salomon
Mario Sammarco
Charles Santley
Heinrich Schlusnus
Andreas Schmidt
Paul Schöffler
Antonio Scotti
William Shimell
John Shirley-Quirk
Paolo Silveri
Knut Skram
Russell Smythe
Gérard Souzay
Oley Speaks
Mariano Stabile
Thomas Stewart
Richard Stilwell
Julius Stockhausen
Jonathan Summers
Giuseppe Taddei
Carlo Tagliabue
Antonio Tamburini

Lawrence Tibbett
Alan Titus
Hermann Uhde
Theodor Uppman
Giuseppe Valdengo
Anton Van Rooy
Ramón Vinay
Michael Vogl
Eberhard Wächter
Ian Wallace
Jess Walters
William Warfield
Leonard Warren
Bernd Weikl
Willard White
Clarence Whitehill
David Wilson-Johnson
Ingvar Wixell
Ekkerhard Wlaschiha
Gregory Yurisich
Giorgio Zancanaro

Tenors
Valentin Adamberger
John Aler
John Alexander
Luigi Alva
Max Alvary
Francisco Araiza
John Beard
Karl Beck
Kim Begley
Jussi Björling
Beno Blachut
Rockwell Blake
Dino Borgioli
Stuart Burrows
José Carreras
Enrico Caruso
Richard Cassilly
Graham Clark
John Coates
Vinson Cole
Peter Cornelius
Jean Cox
Charles Craig
Richard Crooks
Hugues Cuénod
Arthur Davies
Ben Davies
Ryland Davies
Tudor Davies
Mario Del Monaco
François Delsarte
Fernando De Lucia
Gregory Dempsey
Jean De Reszke
Anton Dermota
Plácido Domingo
Nigel Douglas
Ronald Dowd
Warren Ellsworth
Poul Elming
Gervase Elwes
Karl Erb
Bruce Ford
Paul Frey
Manuel del Garcia
Nicolai Gedda
Giuseppe Giacomelli
Beniamino Gigli
Reiner Goldberg

Karl Graun
Donald Grobe
Jerry Hadley
Ben Heppner
Martyn Hill
Joseph Hislop
Werner Hollweg
Hans Hopf
Walter Hyde
Hermann Jadlowker
Neil Jenkins
Siegfried Jerusalem
Edward Johnson
Parry Jones
Manfred Jung
Michael Kelly
Jan Kiepura
Waldemar Kmentt
Heinrich Knote
Alfredo Kraus
Werner Krenn
David Kuebler
Charles Kullman
Gary Lakes
Philip Langridge
Mario Lanza
Giacomo Lauri-Volpi
Jeffrey Lawton
Richard Leech
Keith Lewis
Richard Lewis
Luis Lima
Edward Lloyd
Max Lorenz
Veriano Lucheti
John McCormack
James McCracken
Giovanni Mario
Giovanni Martinelli
Yury Marusin
Helmut Melchert
Lauritz Melchior
Chris Merritt
Thomas Moser
Frank Mullings
Heddle Nash
Angelo Neumann
Albert Niemann
Adolphe Nourrit
Karl Oestvig

Alexander Oliver
Joseph O'Mara
Juan Oncina
Dennis O'Neill
Ian Partridge
Julius Patzak
Luciano Pavarotti
Peter Pears
Jan Peerce
Aureliano Pertile
Alfred Piccaver
Vilém Pribyl
Josef Protschka
Anton Raaff
Torsten Ralf
Thomas Randle
Sims Reeves
Alberto Remedios
David Rendall
Kenneth Riegel
Anthony Rolfe Johnson
Vladimir Rosing
Helge Roswaenge
Robert Rounseville
Giovanni-Battista
  Rubini
Thomas Salignac
Giovanni-Battista
  Sbriglia
Benedikt Schack
Aksel Schiotz
Tito Schipa
Erik Schmedes
Ludwig Schnorr
Rudolf Schock
Peter Schreier
Peter Seiffert
William Shakespeare
George Shirley
Léopold Simoneau
Leo Slezak
Fritz Soot
Gerhard Stolze
Kurt Streit
Ludwig Suthaus
Set Svanholm
Ferruccio Tagliavini
Francesco Tamagno
Enrico Tamberlik
Richard Tauber

John Templeton
Jess Thomas
Joseph Tichatschek
Richard Tucker
Fritz Uhl
Ragnar Ulfung
Georg Unger
Gerhard Unger
Jon Vickers
Ramón Vinay
Heinrich Vogl
Joseph Ward
Spas Wenkoff
Walter Widdop
Steuart Wilson
Gösta Winbergh
Wolfgang Windgassen
Hermann Winkelmann
Hermann Winkler
Ludwig Wüllner
Fritz Wunderlich
Alexander Young
Heinz Zednik
Giovanni Zenatello
Ivo Zidek

Castrato
Domenico Annibali
Majorano Caffarelli
Girolano Crescentini
Carlo Farinelli
Gaetano Guadagni
Domenico Mustafa
Senesino

Bass
Donald Adams
Paul Bender
Kurt Böhme
Kim Borg
Fyodor Chaliapin
Boris Christoff
Henry Cooke
Stafford Dean
Otto Edelmann
Signor Foli
David Franklin
Gottlob Frick
Manuel Garcia
Nicolai Ghiaurov

Nicola Ghiuselev
Josef Greindl
Paul Hillier
Robert Holl
Gwynne Howell
Marcel Journet
Manfred Jungwirth
Alexander Kipnis
Paul Knüpfer
Luigi Lablache
Charles Manners
Josef von Manowarda
Kurt Moll
Paolo Montarsolo
Yevgeny Nesterenko
Robert Newman
Siegmund Nimsgern
Ezio Pinza
Pol Plançon
Paul Plishka
Robert Radford
Ruggero Raimondi
Karl Ridderbusch
Michael Rippon
Paul Robeson
Forbes Robinson
Nicola Rossi-Lemeni
Joseph Rouleau
Kurt Rydl
Matti Salminen
Manfred Schenk
Andrew Shore
Cesare Siepi
Hans Sotin
Roger Soyer
Horace Stevens
Fyodor Stravinsky
Mihály Székely
Italo Tajo
Martti Talvela
Bryn Terfel
David Thomas
John Tomlinson
Richard Van Allan
José Van Dam
Norman Walker
Gustavus Waltz
David Ward
Ludwig Weber
Nicola Zaccaria

Conductors

Claudio Abbado
Komei Abe
Hermann Abendroth
Maurice Abravanel
Byron Adams
John Adams
Kurt Adler
Peter Adler
Yuri Ahronovitch
Gerd Albrecht
John Alldis
Antonio Almeida
Petr Altricher
Carl Alwin
Gilbert Amy
Karel Ancerl
Géza Anda

Karsten Andersen
Martin André
Volkmar Andreae
Paul Angerer
Enrique Arbós
Richard Armstrong
Vladimir Ashkenazy
David Atherton
Moshe Atzmon
Daniel Barenboim
Thomas Beecham
Jiri Belohlavek
Richard Bernas
Leonard Bernstein
Henry Bishop
Stanley Black
Richard Blackford

Nadia Boulanger
Pierre Boulez
Adrian Boult
Martyn Brabbins
Joly Braga-Santos
Nicholas Braithewaite
Warwick Braithewaite
Max Bruch
Hans Bülow
Fritz Busch
Ferruccio Busoni
Basil Cameron
Philip Cannon
Guido Cantelli
André Caplet
Franco Capuana
John Carewe

Mosco Carner
Jean-Claude
  Casadesus
Fritz Cassirer
Aldo Ceccato
Zdenek Chalabala
Harry Christophers
Myung-Whun Chung
Nicholas Cleobury
Stephen Cleobury
André Cluytens
Albert Coates
James Conlon
Emil Cooper
Michael Costa
Robert Craft
John Crosby

Edric Cundell
William Cusins
Henryk Czyz
Frank Damrosch
Leopold Damrosch
Walter Damrosch
Paul Daniel
Oskar Danon
Stephen Darlington
Dennis Russell Davies
Andrew Davis
Colin Davis
Jacques Delacôte
Norman Del Mar
Gaetano Delogu
John DeMain
Neville Dilkes
Christoph von Dohnányi
Antal Dorati
Clive Douglas
Edward Downes
Sian Edwards
Karl Elmendorff
Alberto Erede
Mark Ermler
Franco Faccio
Bryan Fairfax
Charles Farncombe
Robert Farnon
Vladimir Fedoseyev
Frederick Fennell
Arthur Fiedler
Max Fiedler
Adam Fischer
Ivan Fischer
Anatole Fistoulari
Grzegorz Fitelberg
Claus Peter Flor
Lawrence Foster
Myer Fredman
Ferenc Fricsay
Oskar Fried
Lionel Friend
Janos Fürst
Wilhelm Furtwängler
Piero Gamba
John Eliot Gardiner
Valery Gergiev
Alexander Gibson
Michael Gielen
Carlo Maria Giulini
Jane Glover
Daniel Godfrey
Walter Goehr
Georg Göhler
Vladimir Golschmann
Reginald Goodall
Roy Goodman
Ron Goodwin
Eugene Goossens
  (Belg.)
Eugene Goossens (Fr.)
Eugene Goossens (GB)
Hans Graf
Michael Graubart
Noah Greenberg
Bohumil Gregor
Charles Groves
Hermann Grunebaum
Marco Guidarini
Karl Haas
Robert Haas

François Habeneck
Alan Hacker
Hartmut Haenchen
Bernard Haitink
Charles Hallé
Louis Halsey
Simon Halsey
Maurice Handford
Vernon Handley
Nikolaus Harnoncourt
Trevor Harvey
László Heltay
Philippe Herreweghe
Bernard Herrmann
Alfred Hertz
Leslie Heward
Richard Hickox
Alfred Hill
Jun'ichi Hirokami
Irwin Hoffman
Christopher Hogwood
Heinrich Hollreiser
Imogen Holst
Bo Holten
Anthony Hopkins
John Hopkins
Jascha Horenstein
Milan Horvat
Anthony Hose
Elgar Howarth
Owain Arwel Hughes
Donald Hunt
George Hurst
Eliahu Inbal
Michiyoshi Inoue
Ernest Irving
Robert Irving
José Iturbi
Hiroyuki Iwaki
René Jacobs
Reginald Jacques
Jussi Jalas
Marek Janowski
Arvid Jansons
Mariss Jansons
Neeme Järvi
Paavo Järvi
Graeme Jenkins
Newell Jenkins
Eugen Jochum
Jullien Joly
Simon Joly
Enrique Jordá
Armin Jordan
James Judd
Louis Julien
Jürgen Jürgens
Robert Kajanus
Okko Kamu
Herbert von Karajan
Jacek Kasprzyk
Bernard Keeffe
Christopher Keene
Joseph Keilberth
Rudolf Kempe
Paul van Kempen
István Kertész
Willem Kes
Hans Kindler
Robert King
Bernhard Klee
Carlos Kleiber

Erich Kleiber
Otto Klemperer
Paul Kletzki
Berislav Klobucar
Hans Knappertsbusch
Kazuhiro Koizumi
Kyril Kondrashin
Franz Konwitschny
Kazimierz Kord
Zdenek Kosler
André Kostelanetz
Serge Koussevitzky
Jiri Kout
Karel Kovarovic
Clemens Krauss
Yakov Kreizberg
Jan Krenz
Henry Krips
Josef Krips
Jaroslav Krombholc
Karl Krueger
Rafael Kubelik
Gustav Kuhn
Efrem Kurtz
Franz Lachner
Charles Lamoureux
Michael Lankester
Joseph Lanner
Lars-Erik Larsson
Eduard Lassen
Ashley Lawrence
Alexander Lazarev
Philip Ledger
Michel Legrand
György Lehel
Erich Leinsdorf
Lawrence Leonard
Raymond Leppard
Hermann Levi
James Levine
Anthony Lewis
Henry Lewis
András Ligeti
Andrew Litton
Grant Llewellyn
David Lloyd-Jones
James Lockhart
Alain Lombard
Jesus Lopez-Cobos
James Loughran
Ferdinand Löwe
John Lubbock
Leighton Lucas
Leopold Ludwig
Alexandre Luigini
Peter Maag
Lorin Maazel
Zdenek Macal
Denis McCaldin
Nicholas McGegan
Charles Mackerras
Ernest MacMillan
Fritz Mahler
Gustav Mahler
Jerzy Maksymiuk
Jean-Claude Malgoire
Nikolay Malko
Luigi Mancinelli
August Manns
Mantovani
Gino Marinuzi
Neville Marriner

Odaline de la Martinez
Jean Martinon
Giuseppe Martucci
Diego Masson
Kurt Masur
Eduardo Mata
Lovro von Matacic
Muir Mathieson
John Mauceri
Peter Maxwell Davies
Zubin Mehta
Willem Mengelberg
Herbert Menges
Howard Mitchell
Bernardino Molinari
Francesco
  Molinari-Pradelli
Pierre Monteux
Kenneth Montgomery
Rudolf Moralt
Wyn Morris
Felix Mottl
Evgeny Mravinsky
Karl Muck
Michael Mudie
Leopoldo Mugnone
Charles Munch
Karl Münchinger
Riccardo Muti
Kent Nagano
Garcia Navarro
Boyd Neel
John Nelson
Woldemar Nelsson
Frantisek Neumann
Václav Neumann
Roy Newsome
Harry Newstone
Arthur Nikisch
Roger Norrington
David Oistrakh
Sakari Oramo
Eugene Ormandy
Tadaaki Otaka
Willem van Otterloo
Seiji Ozawa
Ettore Panizza
Paul Paray
Alain Paris
Andrew Parrott
Jules-Étienne
  Pasdeloup
Giuseppe Patanè
Bernhard Paumgartner
Emil Paur
Wilfrid Pelletier
Murray Perahia
Libor Pesek
Zoltán Peskó
Trevor Pinnock
Percy Pitt
Michel Plasson
Giorgio Polacco
Egon Pollak
John Poole
Frederik Prausnitz
Georges Prêtre
André Previn
Fernando Previtali
Brian Priestman
Klaus Pringsheim
John Pritchard

MUSIC CLASSICAL

Felix Prohaska
Eve Queler
Peter Raabe
Ruth Railton
Karl Rankl
Simon Rattle
Clarence Raybould
Ernest Read
Hans Redlich
Leopold Reichwein
Fritz Reiner
Edouard van Remoortel
Timothy Reynish
Hans Richter
Karl Anton
  Rickenbacher
Kathleen Riddick
Hugo Rignold
Helmuth Rilling
Carlo Rizzi
James Robertson
Christopher Robinson
Stanford Robinson
Arthur Rodzinski
Landon Ronald
Karl Rosa
Hans Rosbaud
Albert Rosen
Joseph Rosenstock
Antoni Ros Marbá
Mario Rossi
Mstislav Rostropovich
Walter Rothwell
Tony Rowe
Witold Rowicki
Gennady
  Rozhdestvensky
Julius Rudel
Max Rudolf
Christian Rummel
Donald Runnicles
John Rutter
Paul Sacher
Vasily Safonov
Karel Salomon
Esa-Pekka Salonen
Samuil Samosud
Kurt Sanderling
Nello Santi
Gabriele Santini
Nino Sanzogno
Jukka-Pekka Saraste
Sir Malcolm Sargent
Wolfgang Sawallisch
Franz Schalk

Xaver Scharwenka
Hermann Scherchen
Heinrich Schiff
Anton Schindler
Thomas Schippers
Erich Schmid
Ole Schmidt
Hans Schmidt-Isserstedt
Georg Schnéevoigt
Alexander Schneider
Max Schönherr
Michael Schonwandt
Hans-Hubert Schönzeler
Peter Schreier
Ernst von Schuch
Ignaz Schuppanzigh
Carl Schuricht
Gerard Schwarz
Rudolf Schwarz
Claudio Scimone
Christopher Seaman
Uri Segal
Leif Segerstam
Karel Sejna
Jerzy Semkow
Tullio Serafin
Robert Shaw
Howard Shelley
Maxim Shostakovich
Oscar Shumsky
Joseph Silverstein
Constantin Silvestri
Geoffrey Simon
Yury Simonov
Vassily Sinaisky
George Sinclair
Dmitri Sitkovetsky
Stanislaw
  Skrowaczewski
Leonard Slatkin
Nicolas Slonimsky
Alexander Smallens
George Smart
Václav Smetácek
Nicholas Smith
Ethel Smyth
Nikolay Sokoloff
Georg Solti
Marc Soustrot
Theodore Spiering
Peter Stadlen
Simon Standage
Bernhard Stavenhagen
Erwin Stein
Fritz Stein

Horst Stein
Emil Steinbach
Fritz Steinbach
Pinchas Steinberg
William Steinberg
Markus Stenz
Fritz Stiedry
Frederick Stock
Leopold Stokowski
Josef Stransky
George Stratton
Karl Straube
Eduard Strauss I
Eduard Strauss II
Richard Strauss
Igor Stravinsky
Simon Streatfeild
Wolfgang Stresemann
Frank van der Stucken
Otmar Suitner
Walter Susskind
Yevgeny Svetlanov
Hans Swarowsky
Ward Swingle
Tadeusz Sygietynski
Georg Szell
Eugen Szenkar
Michel Tabachnik
Václav Talich
Egisto Tango
Jeffrey Tate
Vilem Tausky
Pyotr Tchaikovsky
Yuri Temirkanov
Klaus Tennstedt
Richard Terry
Christian Thielemann
Michael Tilson Thomas
Theodore Thomas
Bryden Thomson
Heinz Tietjen
Martino Tirimo
Paul Tortelier
Yan Pascal Tortelier
Arturo Toscanini
Geoffrey Toye
Barry Tuckwell
Rosalyn Tureck
Martin Turnovsky
Erik Tuxen
Heinz Unger
Eduard Van Beinum
André Vandernoot
Osmo Vanska
Silvio Varviso

Tamás Vásáry
Denis Vaughan
Sándor Végh
Henri Verbrugghen
Gilbert Vinter
Jaroslav Vogel
Hans Vonk
Edo de Waart
Roger Wagner
Siegfried Wagner
Alfred Wallenstein
Bruno Walter
Günter Wand
Volker Wangenheim
Guy Warrack
Akeo Watanabe
Sydney Watson
Joseph Miroslav Weber
Martin Wegelius
Bruno Weil
Felix Weingartner
George Weldon
Walter Weller
Franz Welser-Möst
August Wenzinger
Ian Whyte
Günther Wich
Allan Wicks
Mark Wigglesworth
David Wilde
Stephen Wilkinson
Jósef Wilkomirski
David Willcocks
Malcolm Williamson
Antoni Wit
Albert Wolff
Hugh Wolff
Henry Wood
David Wooldridge
Barry Wordsworth
Franz Wüllner
Jürg Wyttenbach
Arvid Yansons
Simone Young
Eugène Ysaye
Takuo Yuasa
Lothar Zagrosek
Carlo Zecchi
Hans Zender
Jakob Zeugheer
Alexander Ziloti
David Zinman
Pinchas Zukerman
Paul Zukofsky
Herman Zump

Show and Film Songs: by Song

Song	Show/Film	Song	Show/Film
Ac-cent-tchu-ate the Positive	Here Come the Waves	All Through the Night	Anything Goes
Adelaide	Guys and Dolls	All Time High	Octopussy
Afraid to Dream	You Can't Have Everything	All You Need Is Love	Yellow Submarine
		Almost Like Being in Love	Brigadoon
After the Ball	The Jolson Story	Always	Christmas Holiday
	A Trip to Chinatown (show)		Blue Skies
	Lillian Russell	Always True to You in My Fashion	Kiss Me Kate
After You Get What You Want You Don't Want it	There's No Business Like Showbusiness	Among My Souvenirs	The Best Years of Our Lives
Again	Road House		Paris
Ain't Got a Dime to My Name	Road to Morocco	And This Is My Beloved	Kismet
Ain't Got No – I Got Life	Hair	Animal Crackers in My Soup	Curly Top
Ain't It a Shame About Mame	Rhythm on the River	The Anniversary Song	The Jolson Story
Ain't Misbehavin'	Atlantic City	Another Brick in the Wall	The Wall
	Gentlemen Marry Brunettes	Another Suitcase in Another Hall	Evita (show)
	You Were Meant For Me	Anything You Can Do	Annie Get Your Gun
	Hot Chocolates (show)	Any Time's Kissing Time	Chu Chin Chow
	The Strip	Anywhere I Wander	Hans Christian Andersen
	Follow the Band		
	Stormy Weather	April in Paris	April in Paris
Ain't She Sweet?	You Were Meant For Me		Paris Holiday
	You're My Everything		Both Ends of the Candle
Alabamy Bound	With a Song in My Heart	April Played the Fiddle	If I Had My Way
	Broadway	April Showers	The Jolson Story
	The Great American Broadcast		Jolson Sings Again
	Show Business		The Eddie Duchin Story
Alexander's Ragtime Band	Alexander's Ragtime Band		April Showers
	There's No Business Like Show Business	Aquarius	Hair
		Arriverderci Darling	The Seven Hills of Rome
Alice Blue Gown	Irene	As I Love You	The Big Beat
All Alone	Alexander's Ragtime Band	As Long As He Needs Me	Oliver
		As Time Goes By	Everybody's Welcome (show)
All God's Chillun Got Rhythm	A Day at the Races		Casablanca
All I Ask of You	Phantom of the Opera (show)	At Last	Sun Valley Serenade
			The Glenn Miller Story
All I Do Is Dream of You	Sadie McKee		Orchestra Wives
	Broadway Melody of 1936	At Long Last Love	At Long Last Love
	The Boy Friend		You Never Know (show)
	Singin' in the Rain	Auf Wiederseh'n	The Blue Paradise
All My Loving	A Hard Day's Night		Deep in My Heart
All of Me	Meet Danny Wilson	Avalon	The Benny Goodman Story
	Lady Sings the Blues		The Jolson Story
All of You	Silk Stockings		Both Ends of the Candle
All or Nothing At All	Weekend Pass		
All Over the Place	Sailors Three		
All the Things You Are	Broadway Rhythm	Baby Doll	The Belle of New York
	Because You're Mine	Baby Face	Glorifying the American Girl
	Till The Clouds Roll By		Jolson Sings Again
All the Time in the World	On Her Majesty's Secret Service		Thoroughly Modern Millie
All the Way (1957)	The Joker Is Wild		

Song	Show/Film	Song	Show/Film
Baby I Don't Care	Jailhouse Rock	Blue Skies	Glorifying the
Baby It's Cold Outside (1949)	Neptune's Daughter		American Girl
Bachelor Boy	Summer Holiday		The Jazz Singer
Bali Ha'i	South Pacific		Blue Skies
Basin Street Blues	The Glenn Miller Story		Alexander's Ragtime
	The Strip		Band
Baubles, Bangles and Beads	Kismet		White Christmas
Be a Clown	The Pirate	Boogie Woogie Bugle Boy	Swingtime Johnny
	Singin' in the Rain		Buck Privates
	(show)	Boots and Saddle	Call of the Canyon
Beale Street Blues	St Louis Blues	Born Free (1966)	Born Free
	It's Trad, Dad	The Boys in the Backroom	Destry Rides Again
Beat Out Dat Rhythm	Carmen Jones	Brazil	The Eddie Duchin
on a Drum			Story
Beautiful Dreamer	Swanee River		The Girl He Left
Be-Bop-A-Lula	The Girl Can't Help It		Behind
Be Careful, It's My Heart	Holiday Inn		Saludos Amigos
Because the Night	That Summer	The Breeze and I	Cuban Pete
Begin the Beguine	Broadway Melody of	Bright Eyes	Watership Down
	1940	Broken Hearted	The Best Things in Life
	Night and Day		Are Free
	Jubilee (show)	Brother, Can You Spare	Americana
Beginner's Luck	Shall We Dance	a Dime?	
Bei Mir Bist Du Schöhn	Love, Honour and	Buckle Down, Winsocki	Best Foot Forward
	Behave	Burlington Bertie from Bow	Mother Wore Tights
Be My Love	Looking For Love		Star
	The Toast of New	Bushel and a Peck	Guys and Dolls (show)
	Orleans	Bustopher Jones	Cats (show)
The Best Things In Life	The Best Things In Life	But Beautiful	Road to Rio
Are Free	Are Free	But Not for Me	Girl Crazy
	Good News	Buttons and Bows	The Paleface
Bewitched, Bothered	Pal Joey		Son of Paleface
and Bewildered		Button Up Your Overcoat	Follow Through
Bibbidi-Bobbidi-Boo	Cinderella		The Best Things in Life
Bidin' My Time	Girl Crazy		Are Free
	Rhapsody in Blue	Bye Bye Blackbird	Pete Kelly's Blues
	The Glenn Miller Story		The Eddie Cantor
Big Spender	Sweet Charity		Story
Bill	Showboat		Rainbow Round My
	The Man I Love		Shoulder
	Both Ends of the	By Strauss	An American in Paris
	Candle		The Show Is On (show)
The Birth of the Blues	Painting the Clouds	By the Light of the Silvery	The Jolson Story
	with Sunshine	Moon	Two Weeks with Love
	The Best Things in Life		The Birth of the Blues
	Are Free		Sunbonnet Sue
	The Birth of the Blues	By the Sleepy Lagoon	Sleepy Lagoon
The Black Bottom	George White's		
	Scandals (show)	Ça C'est l'Amour	Les Girls
	A Star Is Born	California, Here I Come	Lucky Boy
The Black Hills of Dakota	Calamity Jane		Jolson Sings Again
Bless Yore Beautiful Hide	Seven Brides for		With a Song in My
	Seven Brothers		Heart
Blow, Gabriel, Blow	Anything Goes		You're My Everything
Blueberry Hill	The Singing Hill		The Jolson Story
Blue Moon	This Could Be the Night		Rose of Washington
	Words and Music		Square
	Kiss Them for Me	Call Me	American Gigolo
	Grease	Call Me Irresponsible (1963)	Papa's Delicate
	Torch Song		Condition
	With a Song in My	Candy Kisses	Down Dakota Way
	Heart	Can I Forget You	High, Wide and
Blues in the Night	The Birth of the Blues		Handsome

Song	Show/Film	Song	Show/Film
The Canoe Song	Sanders of the River		Oh Kay (show)
Can't Buy Me Love	A Hard Day's Night		Both Ends of the
Can't Help Falling in Love	Blue Hawaii		Candle
Can't Help Lovin' Dat Man	Both Ends of the		Tea for Two
	Candle	Do I Love You Because	Cinderella (show)
	Show Boat	You're Beautiful	
	Till The Clouds Roll By	Do I Love You, Do I	Night and Day
Carolina in the Morning	The Dolly Sisters		DuBarry Was a Lady
	Jolson Sings Again	Doin' What Comes Naturally	Annie Get Your Gun
	April Showers	Do I Worry	Pardon My Sarong
	I'll See You in My	Dominique	The Singing Nun
	Dreams	The Donkey Serenade	The Firefly
C'est Magnifique	Can-Can	Don't Cry for Me, Argentina	Evita
C'est Si Bon	Latin Quarter (show)	Don't Ever Leave Me	Sweet Adeline
	New Faces		Both Ends of the
Charmaine	Sunset Boulevard		Candle
The Charm of You	Anchors Aweigh	Don't Fence Me In	Don't Fence Me In
Chattanooga Choo Choo	The Glenn Miller Story		Hollywood Canteen
	Springtime in the	Don't It Make My Brown Eyes	Convoy
	Rockies	Blue	
	Sun Valley Serenade	Don't Laugh at Me	Trouble in Store
Chattanooga Shoeshine Boy	Indian Territory	Don't Rain on My Parade	Funny Girl
Cheek to Cheek	Top Hat	Do-Re-Mi	The Sound of Music
Cheerful Little Earful	Sweet and Low (show)	Down among the Sheltering	That Midnight Kiss
Chica Chica Boom Chic	That Night in Rio	Palms	Some Like It Hot
Chim Chim Cheree (1964)	Mary Poppins	Do You Know Where You're	Mahogany
Clap Hands, Here Comes	Funny Lady	Going To?	
Charley		The Drinking Song	The Student Prince
Clap Yo' Hands	Oh Kay (show)	Duelling Banjos	Deliverance
	Rhapsody in Blue		
	Funny Face	Edelweiss	The Sound of Music
Climb Ev'ry Mountain	The Sound of Music	Eleanor Rigby	Yellow Submarine
Close as Pages in a Book	Up in Central Park	Embraceable You	An American in Paris
A Cock-Eyed Optimist	South Pacific		Girl Crazy
Colonel Bogey March	The Bridge on the		Nancy Goes to Rio
	River Kwai		Rhapsody in Blue
Come and Get It	The Magic Christian		Sincerely Yours
Come Back to Sorrento	Paramount on Parade		With a Song in My
Consider Yourself	Oliver		Heart
The Continental (1934)	The Gay Divorcee	Emotions	The Stud
Cool Water	Hands across the	Empty Chairs at Empty Tables	Les Misérables (show)
	Water	The Entertainer	The Sting
A Couple of Swells	Easter Parade	Evergreen	A Star is Born
		Everybody's Doing It	The Fabulous Dorseys
Dance to the Music	Woodstock		Alexander's Ragtime
Dancing in the Street	Cooley High		Band
Dancing on the Ceiling	Evergreen		Easter Parade
Dat's Love	Carmen Jones	Everybody's Talkin'	Midnight Cowboy
Day by Day	Godspell	Everything's Coming Up Roses	Gypsy
Days of Wine and Roses	Days of Wine and	Ev'ry Time We Say Goodbye	Seven Lively Arts
(1962)	Roses		(show)
The Deadwood Stage	Calamity Jane	Experiment	Nymph Errant (show)
Dear Little Cafe	Bitter-Sweet	Eye of the Tiger	Rocky III
Deep in the Heart of Texas	With a Song in My		
	Heart	Falling in Love Again	The Blue Angel
	Hi Neighbour	Falling in Love with Love	The Boys from
Delta Lady	Mad Dogs and		Syracuse
	Englishmen	Fame	Fame
Diamonds Are a Girl's	Gentlemen Prefer	Fascinating Rhythm	Girl Crazy
Best Friend	Blondes		Lady, Be Good!
Ding Dong the Witch Is Dead	The Wizard of Oz		Rhapsody in Blue
D.I.V.O.R.C.E.	Five Easy Pieces		Singin' in the Rain
Do Do Do	Star		(show)

M
U
S
I
C

P
O
P

Song	Show/Film	Song	Show/Film
Feather Your Nest	Tip Top (show)	Here Comes the Sun	John, Paul, George,
Feed the Birds	Mary Poppins		Ringo and Bert
A Fellow Needs a Girl	Allegro (show)	Here in My Arms	Tea for Two
Fever	Hey Boy! Hey Girl!	Hernando's Hideaway	The Pajama Game
Five Foot Two, Eyes of Blue	Has Anybody Seen My Gal?	Hi-Diddle-Dee-Dee (An Actor's Life For Me)	Pinocchio
Flash Bang Wallop	Half a Sixpence (show)	High Hopes (1959)	Hole in the Head
Flashdance – What a Feeling (1983)	Flashdance	High Noon (1952)	High Noon
A Foggy Day	A Damsel in Distress	Hold the Line	Yesterday's Heroes
Foggy Mountain Breakdown	Bonnie and Clyde	Honeysuckle Rose	Thousands Cheer
The Folks Who Live on the Hill	High, Wide and Handsome		Tin Pan Alley
		Hong Kong Blues	To Have and Have Not
For All We Know (1970)	Lovers and Other Strangers	Hopelessly Devoted to You	Grease
		Hound Dog	Grease
For Every Man There's a Woman	Casbah	How Are Things in Glocca Morra	Finian's Rainbow
For You, for Me, for Everyone	The Shocking Miss Pilgrim	How Could You Believe Me?	Wedding Bells
		How High the Moon?	Two for the Show
French Military Marching Song	The Desert Song	How Long Has This Been Going On	Funny Face
Friendship	DuBarry Was a Lady		Rosalie (show)
From the Top of Your Head	Two for Tonight	How to Handle a Woman	Camelot
Genie with the Light Brown Lamp	Aladdin and His Wonderful Lamp	I Cain't Say No	Oklahoma!
The Gentleman is a Dope	Allegro (show)	I Concentrate on You	Broadway Melody of 1940
Get Me to the Church on Time	My Fair Lady	I Could Have Danced All Night	My Fair Lady
		I Could Write a Book	Pal Joey
Get Out and Get Under	Hullo Tango (show)	Ida, Sweet as Apple Cider	Babes in Arms
	The Pleasure Seekers (show)		The Eddie Cantor Story
Get Out of Town	Leave It to Me (show)		Incendiary Blonde
Getting to Know You	The King and I	I Didn't Know What Time It Was	Pal Joey
Gigi (1958)	Gigi		Too Many Girls
The Gipsy in Me	Anything Goes (show)	I'd Do Anything	Oliver
Give Me the Moonlight	Hullo America	I Don't Know How to Love Him	Jesus Christ Superstar
	The Dolly Sisters	I Feel Pretty	West Side Story
The Glory of Love	Karate Kid II	If Ever I Would Leave You	Camelot
God on High	Les Misérables	If I Didn't Care	The Great American Broadcast
Gonna Build a Mountain	Stop the World – I Want To Get Off	If I Had a Talking Picture of You	The Best Things In Life Are Free
Good Morning Starshine	Hair		Sunny Side Up
Goodnight, Sweetheart	The Big Broadcast of 1936	If I Loved You	Carousel
	You Were Meant for Me	If I Ruled The World	Pickwick (show)
		If I Were A Bell	Guys and Dolls
		If I Were A Rich Man	Fiddler on the Roof
Happy Days Are Here Again	Chasing Rainbows	I Get a Kick Out of You	Anything Goes
	Rain or Shine		Night and Day
Happy Holiday	Holiday Inn		Sunny Side of the Street
Happy Talk	South Pacific		
Harry Lime Theme	The Third Man	I Got Plenty of Nuttin'	Porgy and Bess
Have You Met Miss Jones	Gentlemen Marry Brunettes	I Got Rhythm	Girl Crazy
			Rhapsody in Blue
			An American in Paris
Have Yourself a Merry Little Christmas	Meet Me in St Louis	I Got the Sun in the Morning	Annie Get Your Gun
		I Hate Men	Kiss Me, Kate
The Heat Is on	Beverly Hills Cop	I Just Called to Say I Love You (1984)	Woman in Red
Hello, Hello, Who's Your Lady Friend?	The Story of Vernon and Irene Castle	I Know Him So Well	Chess (show)
Hello, Young Lovers	The King and I	I Like to Recognize the Tune	Too Many Girls (show)
Help	Help!		Meet the People
	John, Paul, George, Ringo and Bert		

Song	Show/Film
I'll Be with You in Apple Blossom Time	Buck Privates
I'll Build a Stairway to Paradise	Rhapsody in Blue
	Stop Flirting (show)
	An American in Paris
	George White's Scandals of 1922 (show)
I'll Never Fall in Love Again	Promises, Promises (show)
I'll See You Again	Bitter-Sweet
I'll See You in My Dreams	Follow the Boys
	I'll See You In My Dreams
	Pardon My Rhythm
I Love a Piano	Easter Parade
I Love Paris	Can-Can
I Love You (Archer and Thompson)	Little Jesse James (show)
	The Sun Also Rises
I Love You (Porter)	Mexican Hayride
I Love You, Samantha	High Society
I'm Always Chasing Rainbows	The Dolly Sisters
	Oh, Look (show)
	The Ziegfeld Girl
I'm Forever Blowing Bubbles	On Moonlight Bay
I'm Free	Tommy
I'm Getting Sentimental over You	DuBarry Was a Lady
I'm Gonna Wash that Man Right out of My Hair	South Pacific
I'm in Love With a Wonderful Guy	South Pacific
I'm Looking over a Four-Leaf Clover	The Jazz Singer
	Jolson Sings Again
I'm Riding for a Fall	Thank Your Lucky Stars
I'm Sitting on Top of the World	I'll Cry Tomorrow
	The Jolson Story
	Love Me Or Leave Me
	The Singing Fool
The Impossible Dream	Man of La Mancha
Indian Love Call	One Night of Love
	Rose Marie
Inka Dinka Doo	The Great Schnozzle
	This Time for Keeps
	Two Girls and a Sailor
In the Cool, Cool, Cool of the Evening (1951)	Here Comes the Groom
In the Mood	The Glenn Miller Story
	Sun Valley Serenade
In the Still of the Night	Night and Day
	Rosalie
I Remember You	The Fleet's In
Irresistible You	Broadway Rhythm
Isn't It Kinda Fun	State Fair
Isn't It Romantic?	Love Me Tonight
Isn't This a Lovely Day	Top Hat
It Ain't Necessarily So	Porgy and Bess
I Talk to the Trees	Paint Your Wagon
It Could Happen to You	And the Angels Sing
It Had to Be You	Her Kind of Man

Song	Show/Film
	I'll See You In My Dreams
It Might As Well Be Spring (1945)	State Fair
It's a Hap-Hap-Happy Day	Gulliver's Travels
It's a Lovely Day Today	Call Me Madam
It's All Right with Me	Can-Can
It's d'Lovely	Anything Goes
	The Fleet's Lit Up (show)
	Red Hot and Blue (show)
It's Easy to Remember	Mississippi
It's Only a Paper Moon	Too Young to Know
	Take a Chance
I've Been a Bad Bad Boy	Privilege
I've Got a Crush on You	Three for the Show
	Meet Danny Wilson
	Strike Up the Band (show)
	Both Ends of the Candle
I've Got a Gal in Kalamazoo	Kiss Them for Me
	Orchestra Wives
I've Got Five Dollars	Gentlemen Marry Brunettes
I've Got My Eyes on You	Broadway Melody of 1940
I've Got You on My Mind	The Gay Divorcee
I've Got You under My Skin	Born to Dance
	Night and Day
	This Could Be the Night
I've Grown Accustomed to Her Face	My Fair Lady
I Wanna Be Loved by You	Gentleman Marry Brunettes
	Good Boy (show)
	Some Like It Hot
	Three Little Words
I Want to Be Happy	No, No, Nanette
	Tea for Two
I Whistle a Happy Tune	The King and I
I Wish I Didn't Love You So	The Perils of Pauline
I Wish I Were in Love Again	Babes in Arms (show)
	Words and Music
I Wonder Who's Kissing Her Now	I Wonder Who's Kissing Her Now
	Moonlight in Havana
	Prince for Tonight (show)
	The Time, the Place and the Girl
I Won't Dance	Lovely to Look At
	Roberta
	Till the Clouds Roll By
I Yi Yi Yi Yi I Like You Very Much	That Night in Rio
The James Bond Theme	Doctor No

MUSIC POP

Song	Show/Film	Song	Show/Film
Jean	The Prime of Miss Jean Brodie		George White's Scandals of 1945
Jeepers Creepers	Going Places		The Jolson Story
Jenny	Lady in the Dark		The Man I Love
	Star		Rhapsody in Blue
Jezebel	The Seven Hills of Rome		Show Girl (show)
			Starlift
Johnny One Note	Words and Music	Long Ago and Far Away	Cover Girl
	Babes in Arms (show)		Till the Clouds Roll By
		Looking for a Boy	Tip-Toes (show)
June in January	Here Is My Heart	Look of Love	Casino Royale
June Is Busting Out All Over	Carousel	Louise	Innocents of Paris
Just in Time	Bells Are Ringing		The Stooge
Just One of Those Things	Can-Can	Love Changes Everything	Aspects of Love (show)
	The Eddie Duchin Story	Love in Bloom	She Loves Me Not
	Jubilee (show)	Love Is a Many-Splendored Thing	Grease
	Lullaby of Broadway		Love Is a Many-Splendored Thing
	Night and Day		
	Panama Hattie	Love Is Sweeping the Country	Of Thee I Sing (show)
	Young at Heart		
		Love Steals Your Heart	The Wicked Lady
Keep the Home Fires Burning	Variety Jubilee	Love Thy Neighbour	We're Not Dressing
Keep Young and Beautiful	Roman Scandals	Love Walked In	Rhapsody in Blue
Kiss in Your Eyes	The Emperor Waltz		The Goldwyn Follies
Knockin' on Heaven's Door	Pat Garrett and Billy the Kid	Luck Be a Lady Tonight	Guys and Dolls
		Lucky in Love	Good News
			The Best Things in Life Are Free
The Lady Is a Tramp	Babes in Arms (show)		
	Pal Joey	Lucy in the Sky with Diamonds	John, Paul, George, Ringo and Bert
	Words and Music	Lullaby of Broadway	Gold Diggers of 1935
The Lambeth Walk	Me and My Girl		
Lara's Theme (aka Somewhere My Love)	Dr Zhivago		Lullaby of Broadway
		Lulu's Back in Town	Broadway Gondolier
The Last Time I Saw Paris	Paris Holiday	Lydia the Tattooed Lady	At the Circus
	Till the Clouds Roll By		
	Lady, Be Good!	Mack the Knife	The Threepenny Opera (show)
Lavender Blue	So Dear to My Heart		Satchmo the Great
Leaning on a Lamp Post	Me and My Girl	Mad About the Boy	Words and Music (show)
	Feather Your Nest		
Let Me Be Loved	The James Dean Story		Set to Music (show)
Let's Be Buddies	Black Vanities (show)	Make Believe	Till the Clouds Roll By
	Panama Hattie		
Let's Call the Whole Thing Off	Shall We Dance?		Show Boat
Let's Do It (Let's Fall in Love)	Night and Day	The Man I Love	Both Ends of the Candle
	Can-Can		The Eddy Duchin Story
	Wake Up and Dream (show)		
	Paris (show)		Lady Sings the Blues
Let's Face the Music and Dance	Follow the Fleet		The Man I Love
Let's Hear It for the Boy	Footloose		Rhapsody in Blue
Life Is Just a Bowl of Cherries	George White's Scandals		Sincerely Yours
	The Best Things In Life Are Free		Will o' the Whispers (show)
			Young at Heart
Little April Shower	Bambi		
Little Girl Blue	Jumbo	The March of the Siamese Children	The King and I
A Little Of What You Fancy	Variety Jubilee		
Living Doll	Serious Charge	Maria	West Side Story
Liza	An American in Paris	Marta	The Big Broadcast
		Maybe	Oh Kay (show)

Song	Show/Film	Song	Show/Film
Me and My Shadow	Hold That Ghost	Oh, What a Circus	Evita
Memories Are Made of This	The Seven Hills of Rome	Oh, You Beautiful Doll	Wharf Angel
			Oh, You Beautiful Doll
Memory	Cats (show)		The Story of Vernon and Irene Castle
Memo to Turner	Performance		
Mimi	Love Me Tonight		For Me and My Gal
	Pepe	Ol' Man River	Show Boat
Minnie the Moocher	The Big Broadcast		Till the Clouds Roll By
Miss Otis Regrets	Hi Diddle Diddle (show)	Once upon a Dream	Play it Cool
	Night and Day	One Night in Bangkok	Chess (show)
Mister Snow	Carousel	Only a Rose	The Vagabond King
Mona Lisa (1950)	After Midnight	Only You	Rock around the Clock
Moonlight Becomes You	Road to Morocco	On the Atchison, Topeka and Santa Fe	The Harvey Girls
Moon River (1961)	Breakfast at Tiffany's		
The More I See You	The Diamond Horseshoe	On the Beach	Wonderful Life
		On the Good Ship Lollipop	Bright Eyes
The Most Beautiful Girl in the World	Jumbo	On the Street Where You Live	My Fair Lady
		On the Sunny Side of the Street	Swing Parade of 1946
Most Gentlemen Don't Like Love	Black Velvet (show)		Is Everybody Happy
	Leave it to Me (show)		Both Ends of the Candle
Mountain Greenery	Words and Music		The Benny Goodman Story
Mr Mistoffolees	Cats (show)		
Mrs Robinson	The Graduate		The Eddie Duchin Story
Music, Maestro, Please	These Foolish Things (show)		On the Sunny Side of the Street
Music of the Night	Phantom of the Opera (show)	Our Love Is Here to Stay	An American in Paris
			The Goldwyn Follies
My Baby Just Cares for Me	Whoopee		Lady Sings the Blues
My Favourite Things	Sound of Music	Out of My Dreams	Oklahoma!
My Funny Valentine	Pal Joey	Over My Shoulder	Evergreen
	Babes in Arms (show)	Over the Rainbow (1939)	The Wizard of Oz
	Gentlemen Marry Brunettes		
My Heart Belongs to Daddy	Let's Make Love	Pack up Your Troubles in Your Old Kit Bag	Her Soldier Boy (show)
	Love Thy Neighbour		Wait Till the Sun Shines Nellie
	Night and Day	People Will Say We're in Love	Oklahoma!
My Heart Stood Still	Words and Music	The Physician	Nymph Errant (show)
	A Connecticut Yankee		Star
My One and Only	Funny Face	Pinball Wizard	Tommy
My Resistance Is Low	Las Vegas Story	Please Do It Again	The French Doll (show)
My Romance	Jumbo		
My Sin	The Best Things in Life Are Free		Thoroughly Modern Millie
			Rhapsody in Blue
The Nearness of You	Romance in the Dark		Mayfair and Montmartre (show)
Never on Sunday (1960)	Never on Sunday		
New York, New York	On the Town		Back to the Future
Nice Work If You Can Get it	An American in Paris	The Power of Love	Road to Utopia
	A Damsel in Distress	Put It There, Pal	Blue Skies
Night and Day	Lady on a Train	Puttin' on the Ritz	Idiot's Delight
	The Gay Divorcee		Puttin' on the Ritz
	Night and Day		
	Reveille with Beverley	Que Sera, Sera (1956)	The Man Who Knew Too Much
The Night They Invented Champagne	Gigi		
Nobody Does It Better	The Spy Who Loved Me	Raindrops Keep Falling on My Head	Butch Cassidy and the Sundance Kid
Oh, Lady Be Good	Lady, Be Good!	Red Sails in the Sunset	Province Town Follies (show)
	Rhapsody in Blue		
Oh, What a Beautiful Morning	Oklahoma!		

MUSIC POP

Song	Show/Film
Return to Sender	Girls! Girls! Girls!
Rhapsody in Blue	The King of Jazz
	Rhapsody in Blue
Rhythm of Life	Sweet Charity
Rhythm of the Rain	The Man from the
	Folies Bergère
The Riff Song	The Desert Song
Right Back Where We Started	The World is Full of
From	Married Men
River Kwai March	The Bridge on the
	River Kwai
Road Runner	Cooley High
Rock around the Clock	Rock around the
	Clock
	The Blackboard Jungle
Roll Along, Prairie Moon	Here Comes the Band
Say You, Say Me (1985)	White Nights
Second-Hand Rose	Funny Girl
	My Man
	The Ziegfeld Follies of
	1921 (show)
The Second Time Around	High Time
Secret Love (1953)	Calamity Jane
Send in the Clowns	A Little Night Music
	(show)
September Song	Knickerbocker Holiday
	Pepe
	September Affair
Seventy-Six Trombones	Music Man
The Shadow of Your Smile	The Sandpiper
(1965)	
Shaft (1971)	Shaft
Shall We Dance?	The King and I
The Sheik of Araby	Make it Snappy (show)
	Tin Pan Alley
She Loves You	A Hard Day's Night
She's So Beautiful	Time
Ship Without a Sail	Heads Up
Shoes with Wings On	The Barkleys of
	Broadway
Short'nin' Bread	Jericho
Sing For Your Supper	The Boys from
	Syracuse
Singin' in the Rain	Hollywood Revue of
	1929
	Little Nellie Kelly
	Singin' in the Rain
Sit Down You're Rocking	Guys and Dolls
the Boat	
Slap That Bass	Shall We Dance?
Slaughter on Tenth Avenue	On Your Toes
	Words and Music
Smoke Gets in Your Eyes	Roberta
	Till the Clouds Roll
	By
	Lovely to Look At
So Am I	Lady Be Good!
	(show)
So in Love	Kiss Me Kate
Somebody Loves Me	George White's
	Scandals of 1924
	(show)

Song	Show/Film
	Broadway Rhythm
	Pete Kelly's Blues
	Somebody Loves Me
	Lullaby of Broadway
Some Day	Rhapsody in Blue
	The Vagabond King
Some Day My Prince Will	Snow White and the
Come	Seven Dwarfs
Some Enchanted Evening	South Pacific
Someone to Watch over Me	Rhapsody in Blue
	Young at Heart
	Three for the Show
	Both Ends of the
	Candle
	Beau James
Something's Coming	Star
Somewhere	West Side Story
Sonny Boy	West Side Story
	The Singing Fool
	Jolson Sings Again
	The Best Things in Life
	Are Free
Soon	Strike Up the Band
	(show)
A Spoonful of Sugar	Mary Poppins
Spring Is Here	I Married an Angel
Stardust	The Eddie Duchin
	Story
Stay as Sweet as You Are	College Rhythm
Staying Alive	Saturday Night Fever
Straighten Up and Fly Right	Here Comes Elmer
	On Stage Everybody
Strange Music	Song of Norway
Stranger in Paradise	Kismet
Strangers in the Night	A Man Could Get
	Killed
Suicide Is Painless	M.A.S.H.
Summer Nights	Grease
Summertime	Porgy and Bess
Sunny Disposish	Americana (show)
Sunrise Sunset	Fiddler on the Roof
Supercalifragilisticexpiali-	Mary Poppins
docious	
The Surrey with the Fringe on	Oklahoma!
Top	
Swanee	Jolson Sings Again
	Sinbad (show)
	Rhapsody in Blue
	Jigsaw (show)
	The Glorious Days
	(show)
	The Jolson Story
	Sincerely Yours
	A Star Is Born
Sweeping the Clouds Away	Paramount on Parade
Sweet and Lowdown	Tip-Toes (show)
Sweet Georgia Brown	Some Like It Hot
Sweet Leilani (1937)	Waikiki Wedding
Swingin' on a Star (1944)	Going My Way
S'Wonderful	Funny Face
	Rhapsody in Blue
	An American in Paris
	Starlift

Song	Show/Film	Song	Show/Film
Take My Breath Away (1986)	Top Gun	The Ugly Duckling	Hans Christian Andersen
Talk to the Animals (1967)	Doctor Dolittle		
Tara's Theme	Gone with the Wind	Up Where We Belong (1982)	An Officer and a Gentleman
Tea for Two	With a Song in My Heart		
	Sincerely Yours	Varsity Drag	Good News
	Jazz on a Summer's Day		
	Tea for Two	Wanderin' Star	Paint Your Wagon
	No, No, Nanette	Wanting You	The New Moon
Thank Heaven for Little Girls	Gigi	Watch the Birdie	Hellzapoppin
Thanks for the Memory (1938)	The Big Broadcast of 1938	The Way We Were (1973)	The Way We Were
		The Way You Look Tonight (1936)	Swing Time
That Certain Feeling	Tip-Toes (show)		
	That Certain Feeling	We Kiss in the Shadow	The King and I
That Old Black Magic	Star Spangled Rhythm	Welcome to My Dream	Road to Utopia
	Radio Stars on Parade	Well, Did You Evah?	High Society
	Here Come the Waves		DuBarry Was a Lady (show)
	Meet Danny Wilson	We'll Gather Lilacs	Lilacs in the Spring
That's Amore	The Caddy		Perchance to Dream (show)
That's Entertainment	The Band Wagon		
That's for Me	State Fair	We're in the Money	Painting the Clouds with Sunshine
There Is Nothing Like a Dame	South Pacific		
There's A Small Hotel	On Your Toes (show)		Gold Diggers of 1933
	Words and Music		
	Pal Joey	What is This Thing Called Love?	Starlift
			Wake Up and Dream
There's No Business Like Show Business	There's No Business Like Show Business		Night and Day
	Annie Get Your Gun		The Eddie Duchin Story
They All Laughed	Shall We Dance?	Whatever Lola Wants	What Lola Wants
They Call the Wind Maria	Paint Your Wagon		Damn Yankees (show)
They Can't Take That Away From Me	The Barkleys of Broadway	What Kind of Fool Am I?	Stop the World – I Want to Get Off
	Shall We Dance?	What'll I Do?	Alexander's Ragtime Band
This Can't Be Love	Words and Music		
	The Boys from Syracuse	When I Fall in Love	Istanbul
	Jumbo		One Minute to Zero
This Is My Song	Countess from Hong Kong	When I Grow Too Old to Dream	The Night is Young
			Deep in My Heart
This Nearly Was Mine	South Pacific	When I Take My Sugar to Tea	Monkey Business
Thou Swell	A Connecticut Yankee	When the Going Gets Tough	Jewel of the Nile
	Words and Music	When the Red Red Robin	I'll Cry Tomorrow
Three Coins in the Fountain (1954)	Three Coins in the Fountain		Has Anybody Seen My Gal?
			The Jolson Story
Till There Was You	Music Man	When Will I See You Again?	Black Joy
Time of My Life (1987)	Dirty Dancing	When You're Smiling	Meet Danny Wilson
Together	The Best Things in Life Are Free	When You Wish upon A Star	Pinocchio
		Where or When	Words and Music
	Since You Went Away		Babes In Arms
To-Kay	Bitter-Sweet	Where's That Rainbow?	Words and Music
To Keep My Love Alive	A Connecticut Yankee (show)	Where the Blue of the Night	The Big Broadcast
		Whistle While You Work	Snow White and the Seven Dwarfs
Tonight	West Side Story		
Too Darn Hot	Kiss Me Kate	White Christmas	White Christmas
Trail of the Lonesome Pine	Way Out West		Blue Skies
The Trolley Song	Meet Me in St Louis		Holiday Inn
True Love	High Society	Who's Sorry Now?	Three Little Words
Tubular Bells	The Exorcist		A Night in Casablanca
Tutti Frutti	Don't Knock the Rock	Who Wants to Be a Millionaire?	High Society
Two Little Blue Birds	Sunny	Why Can't You Behave?	Kiss Me, Kate
		Why Do I Love You?	Show Boat

MUSIC POP

Song	Show/Film	Song	Show/Film
Why Was I Born?	Sweet Adeline (show)	You'll Never Know (1943)	Hello, 'Frisco, Hello
Wind beneath My Wings	Beaches	You'll Never Walk Alone	Carousel
Windmills of Your Mind (1968)	The Thomas Crown Affair	You Light up My Life (1977)	You Light Up My Life
Wish Me Luck As You Wave Me Goodbye	Shipyard Sally	You Made Me Love You	Broadway Melody of 1938
With a Little Bit of Luck	My Fair Lady		Wharf Angel
With a Little Help from My Friends	Woodstock		The Jolson Story
	Stardust		Syncopation
	All This and World War II		Jolson Sings Again
	Sgt Pepper's Lonely Hearts Club Band		Love Me Or Leave Me
	Yellow Submarine	You Make Me Feel So Young	I'll Get By
With a Song in My Heart	Words and Music		Three Little Girls in Blue
	With a Song in My Heart	You Must Have Been a Beautiful Baby	Hard to Get
	This Is The Life		My Dream Is Yours
	Spring Is Here		The Eddie Cantor Story
	Painting the Clouds with Sunshine	Younger Than Springtime	South Pacific
	Young Man of Music	You're the Cream in My Coffee	The Cockeyed World
With Every Breath I Take	Here Is My Heart		The Best Things in Life Are Free
Won't You Come Home Bill Bailey?	The Five Pennies	You're the One That I Want	Grease
		You're the Top	Night and Day
Woodchoppers' Ball	What's Cooking?		Anything Goes
Wooden Heart	G.I. Blues	You Started Something	Moon over Miami
Wouldn't It Be Loverly	My Fair Lady	You Stepped out of a Dream	The Ziegfeld Girl
Wunderbar	Kiss Me, Kate	You Took Advantage of Me	Present Arms
			On Your Toes (show)
			A Star Is Born
Yes Sir, That's My Baby	The Eddie Cantor Story	You've Lost That Lovin' Feelin'	Stardust
	Broadway (show)		
You Are Beautiful	Flower Drum Song	Zip-a-dee-doo-dah (1947)	Song of the South
You'd Be So Nice to Come Home to	Something to Shout About	Zorba's Dance	Zorba the Greek

Show and Film Songs: by Show or Film

Show/Film	Song	Show/Film	Song
A Connecticut Yankee	My Heart Stood Still Thou Swell	All This and World War II	With a Little Help from My Friends
A Connecticut Yankee (show)	To Keep My Love Alive	Allegro (show)	A Fellow Needs a Girl
A Damsel in Distress	A Foggy Day Nice Work If You Can Get It		The Gentleman Is a Dope
A Day at the Races	All God's Chillun Got Rhythm	A Man Could Get Killed	Strangers in the Night
		American Gigolo	Call Me
After Midnight	Mona Lisa (1950)	Americana	Brother, Can You Spare a Dime
A Hard Day's Night	All My Loving		
	Can't Buy Me Love	Americana (show)	Sunny Disposish
	She Loves You	An American in Paris	By Strauss
Aladdin and His Wonderful Lamp	Genie With the Light Brown Lamp		Embraceable You
			I Got Rhythm
Alexander's Ragtime Band	Alexander's Ragtime (1970) Band		I'll Build a Stairway to Paradise
	All Alone		Liza
	Blue Skies		Nice Work If You Can Get It
	Everybody's Doing It		Our Love Is Here to Stay
	What'll I Do		S'Wonderful
A Little Night Music (show)	Send in the Clowns	A Night in Casablanca	Who's Sorry Now?

Show/Film	Song	Show/Film	Song
An Officer and a Gentleman	Up Where We Belong (1982)	Black Joy	When Will I See You Again?
Anchor's Aweigh	The Charm of You	Black Vanities (show)	Let's Be Buddies
And the Angels Sing	It Could Happen to You	Black Velvet (show)	Most Gentlemen Don't Like Love
Annie Get Your Gun	Anything You Can Do		
	Doin' What Comes Naturally	Blue Hawaii	Can't Help Falling in Love
	I Got the Sun in the Morning	Blue Skies	Always
	There's No Business Like Show Business		Blue Skies
			Puttin' on the Ritz
Anything Goes	All Through the Night		White Christmas
	Blow, Gabriel, Blow	Bonnie and Clyde	Foggy Mountain Breakdown
	I Get a Kick out of You		
	It's d'Lovely	Born Free	Born Free (1966)
	You're the Top	Born to Dance	I've Got You under My Skin
Anything Goes (show)	The Gipsy in Me		
April in Paris	April in Paris	Both Ends of the Candle	April in Paris
April Showers	April Showers		Avalon
	Carolina in the Morning		Bill
Aspects of Love (show)	Love Changes Everything		Can't Help Loving Dat Man
A Star Is Born	Evergreen (1976)		Do Do Do
	The Black Bottom		Don't Ever Leave Me
	Swanee		I've Got a Crush on You
	You Took Advantage of Me		The Man I Love
			On the Sunny Side of the Street
Atlantic City	Ain't Misbehavin'		Someone to Watch Over Me
At Long Last Love	At Long Last Love		
A Trip to Chinatown (show)	After the Ball	Breakfast at Tiffany's	Moon River (1961)
At the Circus	Lydia the Tattooed Lady	Bridge on the River Kwai	Colonel Bogey March
		Brigadoon	Almost Like Being in Love
Babes in Arms	Ida, Sweet as Apple Cider	Bright Eyes	On the Good Ship Lollipop
	Where or When	Broadway	Alabamy Bound
Babes in Arms (show)	I Wish I Were in Love Again	Broadway (show)	Yes, Sir, That's My Baby
	Johnny One Note	Broadway Gondolier	Lulu's Back in Town
	The Lady Is a Tramp	Broadway Melody of 1936	All I Do Is Dream of You
	My Funny Valentine	Broadway Melody of 1938	You Made Me Love You
Back to the Future	The Power of Love	Broadway Melody of 1940	Begin the Beguine
Bambi	Little April Shower		I Concentrate on You
The Band Wagon	That's Entertainment		I've Got My Eyes on You
The Barkleys of Broadway	They Can't Take That Away from Me	Broadway Rhythm	All the Things You Are
			Irresistible You
	Shoes With Wings On		Somebody Loves Me
Beaches	Wind beneath My Wings	Buck Privates	Boogie Woogie Bugle Boy
Beau James	Someone to Watch over Me		I'll Be with You in Apple Blossom Time
Because You're Mine	All the Things You Are	Butch Cassidy and the Sundance Kid	Raindrops Keep Falling On My Head
The Belle of New York	Baby Doll		
Bells Are Ringing	Just in Time		
Best Foot Forward	Buckle Down, Winsocki	Calamity Jane	The Black Hills of Dakota
The Best Things in Life Are Free	The Best Things in Life are Free		The Deadwood Stage
Beverly Hills Cop	The Heat Is On		Secret Love (1953)
Birth of the Blues	Blues in the Night	Call Me Madam	It's a Lovely Day Today
	By the Light of the Silvery Moon	Call of the Canyon	Boots and Saddle
Bitter-Sweet	Dear Little Cafe	Camelot	How to Handle a Woman
	I'll See You Again		If Ever I Would Leave You
	To-Kay		
The Blackboard Jungle	Rock around the Clock		

Show/Film	Song	Show/Film	Song
Can-Can	C'est Magnifique	DuBarry Was a Lady	Do I Love You, Do I
	I Love Paris		Friendship
	It's All Right with Me		I'm Getting Sentimental
	Just One of Those		over You
	Things	DuBarry Was a Lady (show)	Well, Did You Evah?
	Let's Do It (Let's Fall in		
	Love)	Easter Parade	A Couple of Swells
Careless Lady	All of Me		Everybody's Doing It
Carmen Jones	Beat Out Dat Rhythm		I Love a Piano
	on a Drum	Evergreen	Dancing on the Ceiling
	Dat's Love		Over My Shoulder
Carousel	If I Loved You	Everybody's Welcome (show)	As Time Goes By
	June Is Busting Out All	Evita	Don't Cry For Me,
	Over		Argentina
	Mister Snow		Oh, What a Circus
	You'll Never Walk Alone	Evita (show)	Another Suitcase in
Casablanca	As Time Goes By		Another Hall
Casbah	For Every Man There's		
	Woman	Fame	Fame (1980)
Casino Royale	The Look of Love	Feather Your Nest	Leaning on a Lamp Post
Cats	Bustopher Jones	Fiddler on the Roof	Sunrise, Sunset
	Mr Mistofolees		If I Were a Rich Man
	Memory	Finian's Rainbow	How Are Things in
Chasing Rainbows	Happy Days Are Here		Glocca Morra?
	Again	Five Easy Pieces	D.I.V.O.R.C.E.
Chess (show)	I Know Him So Well	Flashdance	Flashdance – What a
	One Night in Bangkok		Feeling (1983)
Christmas Holiday	Always	Flower Drum Song	You Are Beautiful
Chu Chin Chow	Any Time's Kissing	Follow the Band	Ain't Misbehavin'
	Time	Follow The Boys	I'll See You in My
Cinderella	Bibbidi-Bobbidi-Boo		Dreams
Cinderella (show)	Do I Love You Because	Follow the Fleet	Let's Face the Music
	You're Beautiful?		and Dance
College Rhythm	Stay as Sweet as You	Follow Through	Button Up Your
	Are		Overcoat
Convoy	Don't It Make My Brown	Footloose	Let's Hear It for the Boy
	Eyes Blue	For Me and My Gal	Oh, You Beautiful Doll
Cooley High	Dancing in the Street	Funny Face	Clap Yo' Hands
	Road Runner		How Long Has This
Countess from Hong Kong	This Is My Song		Been Going On?
Cover Girl	Long Ago and Far Away		My One and Only
Cuban Pete	The Breeze and I		S'Wonderful
Curly Top	Animal Crackers in My	Funny Girl	Don't Rain on My
	Soup		Parade
			Second-Hand Rose
Damn Yankees (show)	Whatever Lola Wants	Funny Lady	Clap Hands, Here
Days of Wine and Roses	Days of Wine and		Comes Charley
	Roses (1962)		
Deep in My Heart	Auf Wiederseh'n	Gentlemen Marry Brunettes	Have You Met Miss
	When I Grow Too Old to		Jones
	Dream		I Wanna Be Loved by
Deliverance	Duelling Banjos		You
Destry Rides Again	The Boys in the		I've Got Five Dollars
	Backroom		My Funny Valentine
Dirty Dancing	Time of My Life (1987)		Ain't Misbehavin'
Doctor Dolittle	Talk to the Animals	Gentlemen Prefer Blondes	Diamonds Are a Girl's
	(1967)		Best Friend
Doctor No	The James Bond Theme	George White's Scandals	Life Is Just a Bowl of
Don't Fence Me In	Don't Fence Me In		Cherries
Don't Knock the Rock	Tutti Frutti	George White's Scandals of	I'll Build a Stairway To
Down Dakota Way	Candy Kisses	1922 (show)	Paradise
Dr Zhivago	Lara's Theme (aka	George White's Scandals of	Somebody Loves Me
	Somewhere My Love)	1924 (show)	

Show/Film	Song
George White's Scandals of 1945	Liza
George White's Scandals (show)	The Black Bottom
G.I. Blues	Wooden Heart
Gigi	Gigi (1958)
	The Night They Invented Champagne
	Thank Heaven for Little Girls
Girl Crazy	Bidin' My Time
	But Not for Me
	Embraceable You
	Fascinating Rhythm
	I Got Rhythm
Girls! Girls! Girls!	Return to Sender
Glorifying the American Girl	Baby Face
	Blue Skies
Godspell	Day by Day
Going My Way	Swingin' on a Star (1944)
Going Places	Jeepers Creepers
Gold Diggers of 1933	We're in the Money
Gold Diggers of 1935	Lullaby of Broadway
Gone with the Wind	Tara's Theme
Good Boy (show)	I Wanna Be Loved by You
Good News	The Best Things in Life Are Free
	Lucky in Love
	Varsity Drag
Grease	Blue Moon
	Hopelessly Devoted to You
	Hound Dog
	Love Is a Many-Splendored Thing
	Summer Nights
	You're the One That I Want
Gulliver's Travels	It's A Hap-Hap-Happy Day
Guys and Dolls	Adelaide
	If I Were a Bell
	Luck Be a Lady Tonight
	Sit Down You're Rocking the Boat
Guys and Dolls (show)	Bushel and a Peck
Gypsy	Everything's Coming Up Roses
Hair	Ain't Got No – Got Life
	Aquarius
	Good Morning Starshine
Half a Sixpence (show)	Flash Bang Wallop
Hands across the Water	Cool Water
Hans Christian Andersen	Anywhere I Wander
	The Ugly Duckling
Hard to Get	You Must Have Been a Beautiful Baby
Has Anybody Seen My Gal?	Five Foot Two, Eyes of Blue

Show/Film	Song
	When the Red Red Robin
Heads Up	Ship Without a Sail
Hello, 'Frisco, Hello	You'll Never Know (1943)
Hellzapoppin	Watch the Birdie
Help!	Help
Here Comes Elmer	Straighten Up and Fly Right
Here Comes the Band	Roll Along, Prairie Moon
Here Comes the Groom	In the Cool, Cool, Cool of the Evening
Here Come the Waves	That Old Black Magic
	Ac-cent-tchu-ate the Positive
Here Is My Heart	June in January
	With Every Breath I Take
Her Kind of Man	It Had to Be You
Her Soldier Boy (show)	Pack Up Your Troubles in Your Old Kit Bag
Hey Boy! Hey Girl!	Fever
Hi Diddle Diddle (show)	Miss Otis Regrets
High Noon	High Noon (1952)
High Society	I Love You, Samantha
	True Love
	Well, Did You Evah?
	Who Wants to Be a Millionaire?
High Time	The Second Time Around
High, Wide and Handsome	Can I Forget You
	The Folks Who Live on the Hill
Hi Neighbour	Deep in the Heart of Texas
Hold That Ghost	Me and My Shadow
Hole in the Head	High Hopes (1959)
Holiday Inn	Be Careful, It's My Heart
	Happy Holiday
	White Christmas 1942)
Hollywood Canteen	Don't Fence Me In
Hollywood Revue of 1929	Singin' in the Rain
Hot Chocolates (show)	Ain't Misbehavin'
Hullo America	Give Me the Moonlight
Hullo Tango (show)	Get Out and Get Under
Idiot's Delight	Puttin' on the Ritz
If I Had My Way	April Played the Fiddle
I'll Cry Tomorrow	I'm Sitting on Top of the World
	When the Red Red Robin
I'll Get By	You Make Me Feel So Young
I'll See You in My Dreams	Carolina in the Morning
	I'll See You in My Dreams
	It Had to Be You
I Married an Angel	Spring Is Here

MUSIC POP

Show/Film	Song	Show/Film	Song
Incendiary Blonde	Ida, Sweet as Apple Cider	Knickerbocker Holiday	September Song
	It Had to Be You	Lady, Be Good!	Fascinating Rhythm
Indian Territory	Chattanoogie Shoeshine Boy		The Last Time I Saw Paris (1941)
Innocents of Paris	Louise		Oh, Lady Be Good
Irene	Alice Blue Gown	Lady, Be Good (show)	So Am I
Is Everybody Happy	On the Sunny Side of the Street	Lady in the Dark	Jenny
		Lady on a Train	Night and Day
Istanbul	When I Fall in Love	Lady Sings the Blues	All of Me
It's Trad, Dad	Beale Street Blues		The Man I Love
I Wonder Who's Kissing Her Now	I Wonder Who's Kissing Her Now		Our Love Is Here to Stay
		Las Vegas Story	My Resistance Is Low
Jailhouse Rock	Baby I Don't Care	Latin Quarter (show)	C'est Si Bon
Jazz on a Summer's Day	Tea for Two	Leave It to Me (show)	Get Out of Town
The Jazz Singer	I'm Looking Over a Four-Leaf Clover		Most Gentlemen Don't Like Love
Jericho	Short'nin' Bread	Les Misérables	Empty Chairs at Empty Tables
Jesus Christ Superstar	I Don't Know How to Love Him		God on High
Jewel of the Nile	When the Going Gets Tough	Les Girls	Ça C'est l'Amour
Jigsaw (show)	Swanee	Let's Make Love	My Heart Belongs to Daddy
John, Paul, George, Ringo and Bert	Help	Lilacs in the Spring	We'll Gather Lilacs
	Here Comes the Sun	Lillian Russell	After the Ball
	Lucy in the Sky with Diamonds	Little Jesse James (show)	I Love You (Archer and Thompson)
Jolson Sings Again	April Showers	Little Nellie Kelly	Singin' in the Rain
	Baby Face	Looking for Love	Be My Love
	California, Here I Come	Love, Honour and Behave	Bei Mir Bist Du Schön
	Carolina in the Morning	Love Is a Many-Splendored Thing	Love is a Many-Splendored Thing
	I'm Looking Over a Four-Leaf Clover	Lovely to Look At	I Won't Dance
	Sonny Boy		Smoke Gets in Your Eyes
	Swanee		
	You Made Me Love You	Love Me Or Leave Me	I'm Sitting on Top of the World
Jubilee (show)	Begin the Beguine		You Made Me Love You
	Just One of Those Things	Love Me Tonight	Isn't It Romantic?
Jumbo	Little Girl Blue		Mimi
	The Most Beautiful Girl in the World	Lovers and Other Strangers	For All We Know (1970)
	My Romance	Love Thy Neighbour	My Heart Belongs to Daddy
	This Can't Be Love	Lucky Boy	California, Here I Come
Karate Kid II	The Glory of Love	Lullaby of Broadway	Just One of Those Things
Kismet	And This Is My Beloved		Somebody Loves Me
	Baubles, Bangles and Beads		Lullaby of Broadway (1935)
	Stranger in Paradise		
Kiss Me, Kate	Always True to You in My Fashion	Mad Dogs and Englishmen	Delta Lady
	I Hate Men	Mahogany	Do You Know Where You're Going To?
	So in Love		
	Too Darn Hot	Make It Snappy (show)	The Sheik of Araby
	Why Can't You Behave?	Man of La Mancha	The Impossible Dream
	Wunderbar		
Kiss Them for Me	Blue Moon	Mary Poppins	Chim Chim Cheree (1964)
	I've Got a Gal in Kalamazoo		

Show/Film	Song	Show/Film	Song
	Feed the Birds		Night and Day
	A Spoonful of Sugar		What Is This Thing
	Supercalifragilisticexpia		Called Love
	alidocious		You're the Top
M.A.S.H.	Suicide Is Painless	No, No, Nanette	I Want To Be Happy
Mayfair and Montmartre	Please Do it Again		Tea for Two
(show)		Nymph Errant (show)	Experiment
Me and My Girl	The Lambeth Walk		The Physician
	Leaning on a Lamp Post		
Meet Danny Wilson	All of Me	Octopussy	All Time High
	I've Got a Crush on You	Of Thee I Sing (show)	Love Is Sweeping the
	That Old Black Magic		Country
	When You're Smiling	Oh Kay (show)	Clap Yo' Hands
Meet Me in St Louis	Have Yourself a Merry		Do Do Do
	Little Christmas		Maybe
	The Trolley Song	Oh, Look (show)	I'm Always Chasing
Meet the People	I Like to Recognise		Rainbows
	the Tune	Oh, You Beautiful Doll	Oh You Beautiful Doll
Mexican Hayride	I Love You (Porter)	Oklahoma!	I Cain't Say No
Midnight Cowboy	Everybody's Talkin'		Oh What a Beautiful
Mississippi	It's Easy to Remember		Morning
Monkey Business	When I Take My Sugar		Out of My Dreams
	to Tea		People Will Say We're in
Moonlight in Havana	I Wonder Who's Kissing		Love
	Her Now		The Surrey With the
Moon over Miami	You Started Something		Fringe On Top
Mother Wore Tights	Burlington Bertie from	Oliver	As Long As He Needs
	Bow		Me
Music Man	Seventy-Six Trombones		Consider Yourself
	Till There Was You		I'd Do Anything
My Dream Is Yours	You Must Have Been	When I Fall in Love	
	Beautiful Baby	One Minute to Zero	When I Fall in Love
My Fair Lady	Get Me to the Church	One Night of Love	Indian Love Call
	On Time	On Her Majesty's Secret	All the Time in the
	I Could Have Danced All	Service	World
	Night	On Moonlight Bay	I'm Forever Blowing
	I've Grown Accustomed		Bubbles
	to Her Face	On Stage Everybody	Straighten Up and Fly
	On the Street Where You		Right
	Live	On the Sunny Side of the	On the Sunny Side of
	With a Little Bit of Luck	Street	the Street
	Wouldn't It Be Loverly	On the Town	New York, New York
My Man	Second-Hand Rose	On Your Toes	Slaughter on Tenth
			Avenue
		On Your Toes (show)	There's a Small Hotel
Nancy Goes to Rio	Embraceable You		You Took Advantage of
Neptune's Daughter	Baby It's Cold Outside		Me
	(1949)	Orchestra Wives	At Last
Never on Sunday	Never on Sunday		I've Got a Gal in
	(1960)		Kalamazoo
New Faces	C'est Si Bon		
Night and Day	Begin the Beguine	Painting the Clouds with	The Birth of the Blues
	Do I Love You, Do I	Sunshine	We're in the Money
	I Get a Kick out of You		With a Song in My
	In the Still of the Night		Heart
	I've Got You under My	Paint Your Wagon	I Talk to the Trees
	Skin		They Call the Wind
	Just One of Those		Maria
	Things		Wanderin' Star
	Let's Do It (Let's Fall in	Pal Joey	Bewitched, Bothered
	Love)		and Bewildered
	Miss Otis Regrets		I Could Write a Book
	My Heart Belongs to		I Didn't Know What Time
	Daddy		It Was

M
U
S
I
C

P
O
P

Show/Film	Song	Show/Film	Song
	The Lady is a Tramp		Love Walked In
	My Funny Valentine		The Man I Love
	There's a Small Hotel		Oh, Lady Be Good
Panama Hattie	Just One of Those Things		Please Do It Again
			Rhapsody in Blue
	Let's Be Buddies		Somebody Loves Me
Papa's Delicate Condition	Call Me Irresponsible (1963)		Someone to Watch over Me
Paramount on Parade	Come Back to Sorrento		Swanee
	Sweeping the Clouds Away		S'Wonderful
		Rhythm on the River	Ain't It a Shame about Mame
Pardon My Rhythm	I'll See You in My Dreams	Road House	Again
Pardon My Sarong	Do I Worry	Road to Morocco	Ain't Got a Dime to My Name
Paris	Among My Souvenirs		
Paris (show)	Let's Do it (Let's Fall in Love)		Moonlight Becomes You
		Road to Rio	But Beautiful
Paris Holiday	April in Paris	Road to Utopia	Put It There, Pal
	The Last Time I Saw Paris		Welcome to My Dream
		Roberta	I Won't Dance
Pat Garrett and Billy the Kid	Knockin' on Heaven's Door		Smoke Gets in Your Eyes
Pepe	Mimi	Rock around the Clock	Only You
	September Song		Rock around the Clock
Perchance to Dream (show)	We'll Gather Lilacs	Rocky III	Eye of the Tiger
Performance	Memo to Turner	Romance in the Dark	The Nearness of You
Pete Kelly's Blues	Bye Bye Blackbird	Roman Scandals	Keep Young and Beautiful
	Somebody Loves Me		
Phantom of the Opera (show)	All I Ask of You	Rosalie	In the Still of the Night
	Music of the Night	Rosalie (show)	How Long Has This Been Going On
Pickwick (show)	If I Ruled the World		
Pinocchio	Hi-Diddle-Dee-Dee (An Actor's Life For Me)	Rose Marie	Indian Love Call
		Rose of Washington Square	California, Here I Come
	When You Wish upon a Star (1940)	Sadie McKee	All I Do Is Dream of You
Play It Cool	Once upon a Dream		
Porgy and Bess	I Got Plenty of Nuttin'		All Over the Place
	It Ain't Necessarily So	Sailors Three	Beale Street Blues
	Summertime	St Louis Blues	
Present Arms	You Took Advantage of Me	Saludos Amigos	Brazil
		Sanders of the River	The Canoe Song
		Satchmo the Great	Mack the Knife
Prince for Tonight (show)	I Wonder Who's Kissing Her Now	Saturday Night Fever	Staying Alive
		September Affair	September Song
Privilege	I've Been a Bad Bad Boy	Sergeant Pepper's Lonely Hearts Club Band	With a Little Help from My Friends
Promises, Promises (show)	I'll Never Fall in Love Again		
		Serious Charge	Living Doll
Province Town Follies (show)	Red Sails in the Sunset	Set to Music (show)	Mad about the Boy
Puttin' on the Ritz	Puttin' on the Ritz	Seven Brides for Seven Brothers	Bless Yore Beautiful Hide
Radio Stars on Parade	That Old Black Magic	The Seven Hills of Rome	Arriverderci Darling
Rain or Shine	Happy Days Are Here Again		Jezebel
			Memories are Made of This
Rainbow Round My Shoulder	Bye Bye Blackbird		
Red Hot and Blue (show)	It's d'Lovely	Seven Lively Arts (show)	Ev'ry Time We Say Goodbye
Reveille with Beverley	Night and Day		
Rhapsody in Blue	Bidin' My Time	Shaft	Shaft (1971)
	Clap Yo' Hands	Shall We Dance?	Beginner's Luck
	Embraceable You		Let's Call the Whole Thing Off
	Fascinating Rhythm		
	I Got Rhythm		Slap That Bass
	I'll Build a Stairway to Paradise		They All Laughed
	Liza		They Can't Take That Away from Me

Show/Film	Song	Show/Film	Song
She Loves Me Not	Love in Bloom	Star	Burlington Bertie from Bow
Shipyard Sally	Wish Me Luck As You Wave Me Goodbye		Do Do Do
Show Boat	Bill		Jenny
	Can't Help Loving Dat Man		The Physician
	Make Believe		Someone to Watch over Me
	Ol' Man River	Stardust	With a Little Help from My Friends
	Why Do I Love You?		You've Lost That Lovin' Feelin'
Show Business	Alabamy Bound		
	It Had to Be You	Starlift	Liza
Show Girl (show)	Liza		S'Wonderful
Silk Stockings	All of You		What Is This Thing Called Love?
Sinbad (show)	Swanee		
Sincerely Yours	Embraceable You	Star Spangled Rhythm	That Old Black Magic
	The Man I Love	State Fair	Isn't It Kinda Fun
	Swanee		It Might As Well Be Spring (1945)
	Tea for Two		
Since You Went Away	Together		That's For Me
Singin' in the Rain	All I Do Is Dream of You	Stop Flirting (show)	I'll Build a Stairway to Paradise
	Singin' in the Rain		
Singin' in the Rain (show)	Be a Clown	Stop the World – I Want To Get Off	What Kind of Fool Am I?
	Fascinating Rhythm		
Sleepy Lagoon	By the Sleepy Lagoon		Gonna Build a Mountain
Snow White and the Seven Dwarfs	Some Day My Prince Will Come	Stormy Weather	Ain't Misbehavin'
	Whistle While You Work	Strike Up the Band (show)	I've Got a Crush on You
So Dear to My Heart	Lavender Blue		
Somebody Loves Me	Somebody Loves Me		Soon
Some Like It Hot	Down among the Sheltering Palms	Summer Holiday	Bachelor Boy
	Sweet Georgia Brown	Sunbonnet Sue	By the Light of the Silvery Moon
	I Wanna Be Loved by You		
Something to Shout About	You'd Be So Nice to Come Home to	Sunny	Two Little Blue Birds
Song of Norway	Strange Music	Sunny Side of the Street	I Get a Kick Out of You
Song of the South	Zip-a-dee-doo-dah (1947)	Sunny Side Up	If I Had a Talking Picture of You
Son of Paleface	Buttons and Bows	Sunset Boulevard	Charmaine
The Sound of Music	Climb Ev'ry Mountain	Sun Valley Serenade	At Last
	Do-Re-Mi		Chattanooga Choo Choo
	Edelweiss		In the Mood
	My Favourite Things	Swanee River	Beautiful Dreamer
South Pacific	Bali Ha'i	Sweet Adeline	Don't Ever Leave Me
	A Cock-Eyed Optimist	Sweet Adeline (show)	Why Was I Born?
	Happy Talk	Sweet and Low (show)	Cheerful Little Earful
	I'm Gonna Wash That Man Right Out of My Hair	Sweet Charity	Big Spender
			Rhythm of Life
	I'm in Love with a Wonderful Guy	Swing Parade of 1946	On the Sunny Side of the Street
	Some Enchanted Evening	Swing Time	The Way You Look Tonight (1936)
	There Is Nothing Like A Dame	Swingtime Johnny	Boogie Woogie Bugle Boy
	This Nearly Was Mine		
	Younger Than Springtime	Syncopation	You Made Me Love You
Spring Is Here	With a Song in My Heart	Take a Chance	It's Only a Paper Moon
Springtime in the Rockies	Chattanooga Choo Choo	Tea for Two	Do Do Do
			Here in My Arms

M
U
S
I
C

P
O
P

Show/Film	Song	Show/Film	Song
	I Want to Be Happy		You Must Have Been a
	Tea for Two		Beautiful Baby
Thank Your Lucky Stars	I'm Riding for a Fall	The Eddie Duchin Story	April Showers
That Certain Feeling	That Certain Feeling		Brazil
That Midnight Kiss	Down among the		Just One of Those
	Sheltering Palms		Things
That Night in Rio	Chica Chica Boom		On the Sunny Side of
	Chic		the Street
	I Yi Yi Yi Yi I Like You		Stardust
	Very Much		What Is This Thing
That Summer	Because the Night		Called Love?
The Benny Goodman Story	Avalon		The Man I Love
	On the Sunny Side of	The Emperor Waltz	Kiss in Your Eyes
	the Street	The Exorcist	Tubular Bells
The Best Things in Life	The Birth of the Blues	The Fabulous Dorseys	Everybody's Doing It
Are Free	Broken Hearted	The Firefly	The Donkey Serenade
	Button Up Your	The Five Pennies	Won't You Come Home
	Overcoat		Bill Bailey
	If I Had a Talking Picture	The Fleet's In	I Remember You
	of You	The Fleet's Lit Up (show)	It's d'Lovely
	Life is Just a Bowl of	The French Doll (show)	Please Do It Again
	Cherries	The Gay Divorcee	The Continental
	Lucky in Love		I've Got You on My
	My Sin		Mind
	Sonny Boy		Night and Day
	Together	The Girl Can't Help It	Be-Bop-A-Lula
	You're the Cream in My	The Girl He Left Behind	Brazil
	Coffee	The Glenn Miller Story	At Last
The Best Years of Our Lives	Among My Souvenirs		Basin Street Blues
The Big Beat	As I Love You		Bidin' My Time
The Big Broadcast	Marta		Chattanooga Choo
	Minnie the Moocher		Choo
	Where the Blue of the		In the Mood
	Night	The Glorious Days (show)	Swanee
The Big Broadcast of 1936	Goodnight, Sweetheart	The Goldwyn Follies	Love Walked In
The Big Broadcast of 1938	Thanks for the Memory		Our Love Is Here to
	(1938)		Stay
The Blue Angel	Falling in Love Again	The Graduate	Mrs Robinson
The Blue Paradise	Auf Wiederseh'n	The Great American	Alabamy Bound
The Boy Friend	All I Do Is Dream of	Broadcast	
	You		If I Didn't Care
The Boys from Syracuse	Falling in Love with	The Great Schnozzle	Inka Dinka Doo
	Love	The Harvey Girls	On the Atchison, Topeka
	Sing for Your Supper		and Santa Fe
	This Can't Be Love	The James Dean Story	Let Me Be Loved
The Bridge on the River Kwai	River Kwai March	The Jazz Singer	Blue Skies
The Caddy	That's Amore	The Joker Is Wild	All the Way (1957)
The Cockeyed World	You're the Cream in My	The Jolson Story	After the Ball
	Coffee		The Anniversary Song
The Desert Song	French Military		April Showers
	Marching		Avalon
	Song		By the Light of the
	The Riff Song		Silvery Moon
The Diamond Horseshoe	The More I See You		California, Here I
The Dolly Sisters	Carolina in the Morning		Come
	Give Me the Moonlight		I'm Sitting on Top of the
	I'm Always Chasing		World
	Rainbows		Liza
The Eddie Cantor Story	Bye Bye Blackbird		Swanee
	Ida, Sweet as Apple		When the Red Red
	Cider		Robin
	Yes Sir, That's My		You Made Me Love
	Baby		You

Show/Film	Song	Show/Film	Song
The King and I	Getting to Know You	*The Wall*	Another Brick in the Wall
	The March of the Siamese Children	*The Way We Were*	The Way We Were (1973)
	Hello, Young Lovers	*The Wicked Lady*	Love Steals Your Heart
	I Whistle a Happy Tune	*The Wizard of Oz*	Over the Rainbow (1939)
	Shall We Dance?	*The World Is Full of Married Men*	Right Back Where We Started From
	We Kiss in the Shadow		
The King of Jazz	Rhapsody in Blue	*The Ziegfeld Follies of 1921* (show)	Second-Hand Rose
The Magic Christian	Come and Get It		
The Man from the Folies Bergere	Rhythm of the Rain	*The Ziegfeld Girl*	I'm Always Chasing Rainbows
The Man I Love	Bill		You Stepped Out of a Dream
	Liza		
	The Man I Love	*There's No Business Like Show Business*	Alexander's Ragtime Band
The Man Who Knew Too Much	Que Sera, Sera (1956)		There's No Business Like Show Business
The New Moon	Wanting You		After You Get What You Want You Don't Want It
The Night Is Young	When I Grow Too Old to Dream	*These Foolish Things* (show)	Music, Maestro, Please
The Pajama Game	Hernando's Hideaway	*This Could Be the Night*	I've Got You under My Skin
The Paleface	Buttons and Bows		
The Perils of Pauline	I Wish I Didn't Love You So		Blue Moon
The Pirate	Be a Clown	*This Is the Life*	With a Song in My Heart
The Pleasure Seekers (show)	Get Out and Get Under		
The Prime of Miss Jean Brodie	Jean	*This Time for Keeps*	Inka Dinka Doo
		Thoroughly Modern Millie	Baby Face
The Sandpiper	The Shadow of Your Smile (1965)		Please Do It Again
		Thousands Cheer	Honeysuckle Rose
The Seven Hills of Rome	Arriverderci Darling	*Three Coins in the Fountain*	Three Coins in the Fountain (1954)
	Memories Are Made of This		
The Shocking Miss Pilgrim	For You, for Me, for Everyone	*Three for the Show*	I've Got a Crush on You
			Someone to Watch over Me
The Show Is On (show)	By Strauss		
The Singing Fool	I'm Sitting on Top of the World	*Three Little Girls in Blue*	You Make Me Feel So Young
	Sonny Boy	*Three Little Words*	I Wanna Be Loved by You
The Singing Hill	Blueberry Hill		
The Singing Nun	Dominique		Who's Sorry Now?
The Spy Who Loved Me	Nobody Does It Better	*Till the Clouds Roll By*	Long Ago and Far Away
The Sting	The Entertainer		All the Things You Are
The Stooge	Louise		Can't Help Loving Dat Man
The Story of Vernon and Irene Castle	Hello, Hello, Who's Your Lady Friend?		I Won't Dance
	Oh, You Beautiful Doll		The Last Time I Saw Paris
The Strip	Ain't Misbehavin'		Make Believe
	Basin Street Blues		Ol' Man River
The Stud	Emotions		Smoke Gets in Your Eyes
The Student Prince	The Drinking Song		
The Sun Also Rises	I Love You (Archer and Thompson)	*Time*	She's So Beautiful
		Tin Pan Alley	Honeysuckle Rose
The Third Man	Harry Lime Theme		The Sheik of Araby
The Thomas Crown Affair	Windmills of Your Mind (1968)	*Tip-Toes* (show)	Looking for a Boy
			Sweet and Lowdown
The Threepenny Opera (show)	Mack the Knife		That Certain Feeling
The Time, the Place and the Girl	I Wonder Who's Kissing Her Now	*Tip Top* (show)	Feather Your Nest
The Toast of New Orleans	Be My Love	*To Have and Have Not*	Hong Kong Blues
The Vagabond King	Only a Rose	*Tommy*	I'm Free
	Some Day		Pinball Wizard

M
U
S
I
C

P
O
P

Show/Film	Song
Too Many Girls	I Didn't Know What Time It Was
Too Many Girls (show)	I Like to Recognize the Tune
Too Young to Know	It's Only a Paper Moon
Top Gun	Take My Breath Away (1986)
Top Hat	Cheek to Cheek
	Isn't This a Lovely Day
Torch Song	Blue Moon
Trouble in Store	Don't Laugh at Me
Two for the Show	How High the Moon?
Two for Tonight	From the Top of Your Head
Two Girls and a Sailor	Inka Dinka Doo
Two Weeks with Love	By the Light of the Silvery Moon
Up in Central Park	Close As Pages in a Book
Variety Jubilee	Keep the Home Fires Burning
	A Little of What You Fancy
Waikiki Wedding	Sweet Leilani (1937)
Wait Till the Sun Shines, Nellie	Pack Up Your Troubles in Your Old Kit Bag
Wake Up and Dream	What Is This Thing Called Love?
Wake Up and Dream (show)	Let's Do It (Let's Fall in Love)
Watership Down	Bright Eyes
Way Out West	Trail of the Lonesome Pine
Wedding Bells	How Could You Believe Me?
Weekend Pass	All or Nothing at All
We're Not Dressing	Love Thy Neighbour
West Side Story	I Feel Pretty
	Maria
	Something's Coming
	Somewhere
	Tonight
Wharf Angel	Oh, You Beautiful Doll
	You Made Me Love You
What Lola Wants	Whatever Lola Wants
What's Cooking?	Woodchoppers' Ball
White Christmas	Blue Skies
	White Christmas
White Nights	Say You, Say Me (1985)
Whoopee	My Baby Just Cares for Me
Will o' the Whispers (show)	The Man I Love,
With a Song in My Heart	California, Here I Come
	Deep in the Heart of Texas

Show/Film	Song
	Embraceable You
	Tea for Two
	Alabamy Bound
	Blue Moon
	With a Song in My Heart
The Wizard of Oz	Ding Dong the Witch Is Dead
	Over th Rianbow (1939)
Woman in Red	I Just Called to Say I Love You
Wonderful Life	On the Beach
Woodstock	Dance to the Music
	With a Little Help from My Friends
Words and Music	Slaughter on Tenth Avenue
	Blue Moon
	I Wish I Were in Love Again
	Johnny One Note
	The Lady Is a Tramp
	Mountain Greenery
	My Heart Stood Still
	There's a Small Hotel
	This Can't Be Love
	Thou Swell
	Where or When
	Where's That Rainbow?
	With a Song in My Heart
Words and Music (show)	Mad about the Boy
Yellow Submarine	All You Need Is Love
	Eleanor Rigby
	With a Little Help from My Friends
Yesterday's Heroes	Hold the Line
You Can't Have Everything	Afraid to Dream
You Light Up My Life	You Light Up My Life (1977)
You Never Know (show)	At Long Last Love
Young at Heart	Just One of Those Things
	The Man I Love
	Someone to Watch over Me
Young Man of Music	With a Song in My Heart
You're My Everything	Ain't She Sweet?
	California, Here I Come
You Were Meant for Me	Ain't Misbehavin'
	Ain't She Sweet?
	Goodnight, Sweetheart
Zorba the Greek	Zorba's Dance

Theme Songs or Signature Tunes

Song/Tune	Artiste	Song/Tune	Artiste
Back to Those Happy Days	Herman Darewski	Louise	Maurice Chevalier
Be My Love	Mario Lanza	Love in Bloom	Jack Benny
Because of You	Tony Bennett	Love Is Like a Violin	Ken Dodd
Begin the Beguine	Leslie (Hutch) Hutchinson	Lullaby of Broadway	George Shearing
		Makin' Whoopee	Eddie Cantor
Bei Mir Bist Du Schön	Andrews Sisters	Mañana Is Soon	Peggy Lee
Bewitched Bothered and Bewildered	Bill Snyder	Enough For Me	
		Marigold	Billy Mayerl
Bill	Helen Morgan	Marta	Arthur Tracy (The Street Singer)
Blue Flame (opening theme)	Woody Herman		
Bugle Call Rag	Harry Roy	Minnie the Moocher	Cab Calloway
Ciribiribin	Harry James	Moonlight Serenade	Glenn Miller
Clap Hands Here Comes Charlie	Charlie Kunz	Mother Machree	John MacCormack
		Music, Maestro, Please	Harry Leader
Cocktails for Two	Carl Brisson	My Blue Heaven	Gene Austin
Coquette	Guy Lombardo	My Heart Belongs to Daddy	Mary Martin
Cry	Johnnie Ray	My Mammy	Al Jolson
Cuban Love Song	Edmundo Ros	My Time Is Your Time	Rudy Vallee
Dancing Time	Oscar Rabin	Near You	Francis Craig
Darling, Je Vous Aime Beaucoup	Hildegarde	Nightmare	Artie Shaw
		Oh Monah	Lew Stone
Dear Old Southland	Layton and Johnstone	O Mein Papa	Eddie Calvert
Deep Forest	Earl Hines	One O'Clock Jump	Count Basie
Dinah	Dinah Shore	On the Air	Carroll Gibbons
Don't Laugh at Me	Norman Wisdom	Over the Rainbow	Judy Garland
Dream	The Pied Pipers	Paper Doll	Mills Brothers
Dream Along with Me	Perry Como	Rags, Bottles or Bones	Syd Walker
Everybody Loves Somebody	Dean Martin	Red Sails in the Sunset	Suzette Tarri
Give Me the Moonlight	Frankie Vaughan	Rhapsody in Blue	Paul Whiteman
Give My Regards to Broadway	George M Cohen	Rose of Washington Square	Fanny Brice
Goodbye (closing theme)	Benny Goodman	Sally	Gracie Fields
Goodnight	Cavan O'Connor	Say It With Music	Jack Payne
Goodnight, Sweetheart (closing theme)	Ray Noble	Sentimental Journey	Les Brown
		She's My Lovely	Billy Ternent
Here's to the Next Time	Henry Hall	Shine On Harvest Moon	Nora Bayes
How High the Moon	Les Paul and Mary Ford	Skyliner	Charlie Barnet
Hurry on Down	Nellie Lutcher	Sleepy Serenade	Cyril Stapleton
Ida, Sweet as Apple Cider	Eddie Cantor	Smoke Rings	Glen Gray
I Do Like to Be Beside the Seaside	Reginald Dixon	Some of These Days	Sophie Tucker
		Somebody Stole My Gal	Billy Cotton
I Don't Care	Eva Tanguay	So Rare (closing theme)	Jimmy Dorsey
If I Didn't Care	Ink Spots	So Tired	Russ Morgan
I Got Rhythm	Ethel Merman	Speak to Me of Love	Lucienne Boyer
I'll See You Again	Noël Coward	Stage Coach	Eric Winstone
I'll See You in My Dreams	Tony Martin	Stormy Weather	Lena Horne
I Love a Lassie	Harry Lauder	Straighten Up and Fly Right	Nat King Cole
I'm Getting Sentimental Over You	Tommy Dorsey	Sugar Blues	Clyde McCoy
		Summertime	Bob Crosby
Inka Dinka Doo	Jimmy Durante	Sunrise Serenade	Frankie Carle
In the Mood	Joe Loss	Sweet and Lovely	Russ Columbo
I Used to Sigh for the Silvery Moon	G H Elliott (Chocolate-coloured Coon)	Take Me to Your Heart Again	Edith Piaf
		Take the 'A' Train	Duke Ellington
J'Attendrai	Jean Sablon	Tenderly	Rosemary Clooney
Just an Old-Fashioned Girl	Eartha Kitt	Thanks for the Memory	Bob Hope
Just Like a Melody from Out of the Sky	Jay Wilbur	That Old Black Magic	Stanley Black
			Billy Daniels
La Mer	Charles Trenet	That's What I Like about the South	Phil Harris
Leaning on a Lamp Post	George Formby		
Let's Dance (opening theme)	Benny Goodman	The Dicky Bird Hop	Ronald Gourlay
Life Is Nothing without Music	Fred Hartley	The Donkey Serenade	Monte Rey

MUSIC POP

Song/Tune	Artiste	Song/Tune	Artiste
The Jolly Brothers	Albert Whelan	Down South	
The Sweetest Music This Side of Heaven	Maurice Winnick	When My Baby Smiles At Me	Ted Lewis
The Very Thought of You (opening theme)	Ray Noble	When the Moon Comes Over the Mountain	Kate Smith
The Wheel of Fortune	Kay Starr	When You're Smiling	George Elrick
Tumbling Tumbleweeds	Sons of the Pioneers	Where the Blue of the Night	Bing Crosby
We'll Be Together Again	Frankie Laine	Whispering	Roy Fox
What's New	Billy Butterfield	Woodchoppers' Ball	Woody Herman
When Day Is Done	Ambrose	You're Dancing on My Heart	Victor Sylvester
When It's Sleepy Time	Louis Armstrong	Yours	Vera Lynn

NB: The theme tunes or signature tunes above are the ones the people themselves considered to be so, and not always the one most readily identifiable with the artist. For example, few would consider 'Yours' to be more identifiable with Vera Lynn than 'The White Cliffs of Dover'. Similarly, 'Take Me To Your Heart Again' is certainly not the most famous Edith Piaf song.

It is probably a good idea at this stage to lay to rest once and for all the most common source of frustration for quiz players on the topic of signature tunes, i.e. is Glenn Miller's signature tune 'In the Mood' or 'Moonlight Serenade'? The problem arises because 'In the Mood' was one of Glenn Miller's most popular tunes and was featured in both *Sun Valley Serenade* and *The Glenn Miller Story*; however, Glenn Miller himself composed 'Moonlight Serenade' and always considered this to be his signature tune. Joe Loss did, in fact, record 'In the Mood' and subsequently adopted it as his signature.

TV and Radio Theme Tunes

Programme	Tune (and/or composer)	Programme	Tune (and/or composer)
Absolutely Fabulous	'This Wheel's on Fire' by Julie Driscoll	Desert Island Discs	'By the Sleepy Lagoon' by Eric Coates
The Archers	'Barwick Green' (from *My Native Heath*) suite written in 1922 by Arthur Wood	Doctor Kildare	'Three Stars Will Shine Tonight' (vocal version by Richard Chamberlain)
		Dr Who	Theme by Ron Grainer
Auf Wiedersehen Pet	'That's Living Alright' (sung by Joe Fagin)	The Dukes of Hazzard	Theme tune by Waylon Jennings
The Avengers	Theme by Laurie Johnson	Eastenders	Theme tune by Simon May
Big Brother	Theme tune by Element Four (aka Paul Oakenfold and Andy Gray)	Eastenders: vocal version	'Anyone Can Fall in Love' sung by Anita Dobson
		Equaliser	Theme tune by Stewart Copeland
Billy Cotton Band Show	'Somebody Stole My Gal'		
Blake's 7	Music by Dudley Simpson	Friends	'I'll Be There For You' by The Rembrandts
Blue Peter	'Barnacle Bill the Sailor' by Robison and Luther (famous adaptation by Mike Oldfield)	Grand Prix	BBC – 'The Chain' by Fleetwood Mac
		Great Antiques Hunt	Theme tune by the Brodsky Quartet
Bonanza	Music by David Rose		
Bootsie and Snudge	'Pop Goes the Weasel'	Harry's Game	Theme by Clannad
Brain of Britain	Mozart's *Eine kleine Nachtmusik*	Have Gun, Will Travel	'The Ballad of the Paladin'
		Hawaii Five O	Music by Morton Stevens
Captain Pugwash	'Hornblower' (played on the accordion by Tommy Edwards)	Horse of the Year Show	Mozart's 'A Musical Joke'
		Howards Way	Theme tune by Simon May
Crossroads	Theme by Tony Hatch and later adapted by Paul McCartney	Howards Way: vocal version	'Always There' by Marti Webb
		I'm Sorry I'll Read That Again	'The Angus Prune Tune'
Dad's Army	'Who Do You Think You're Kidding, Mr Hitler?' sung by Bud Flanagan		
		Inspector Morse	Theme tune by Barrington Pheloung
Danger Man	Music by Edwin Astley		

Programme	Tune (and/or composer)	Programme	Tune (and/or composer)
Ironside	Theme by Quincy Jones	Rawhide	Theme sung by Frankie Laine
Jason King	Theme by Laurie Johnson		
Juke Box Jury	'Hit and Miss' by John Barry	Ready Steady Go!	'Wipe Out' (The Surfaris); '5-4-3-2-1' (Manfred Mann)
Just a Minute	Minute Waltz by Chopin	The Saint	Music by Edwin Astley
The Killing Game	'Tom Hark' by the Piranhas	The Seven Faces of Woman	'She' (sung by Charles Aznavour)
Kojak	Theme by Billy Goldenberg	The Sky at Night	At the Castle Gate by Sibelius (from Pelléas et Mélisande)
Life and Times of David Lloyd George	'Chi Mai' by Ennio Morricone	The Snowman	'Walking in the Air' (sung by Aled Jones)
Light of Experience	Theme by Doina De Jale	South Bank Show	Variations on a Theme of Paganini by Julian Lloyd Webber
The Lone Ranger	William Tell Overture by Rossini		
M.A.S.H.	'Suicide Is Painless' by Mash	Star Trek	Music by Alexander Courage
Mastermind	'Approaching Menace' by Neil Richardson	Stingray	'Aquamarina' (sung by Garry Miller)
Match of the Day	Drum Majorette	Supergran	Theme composed and sung by Billy Connolly
Miami Vice	'Miami Vice Theme' and 'Crockett's Theme' (both by Jan Hammer)	Test Match Special	'Soul Limbo' by Booker T & The MGs
Minder	'I Could Be So Good For You' by Pat Waterman and Gerard Kenny	That Was the Week That Was	Sung by Millicent Martin
Mission Impossible	Theme by Lalo Schifrin	The Third Man	'Harry Lime Theme' by Anton Karas
Mistral's Daughter	'Only Love' (sung by Nana Mouskouri)	Tinker, Tailor, Soldier, Spy	Nunc Dimittis, arranged by Geoffrey Burgon
Monty Python's Flying Circus	'Liberty Bell' by John Paul Souza	Top of the Pops	'Yellow Pearl' by Phil Lynott (co-written by Lynott and Ray Davies); 'Whole Lotta Love' by CCS (instrumental version of Led Zeppelin song); 'The Wizard' by Paul Hardcastle
Moonlighting	'Moonlighting Theme' by Al Jarreau		
Neighbours	Theme by Tony Hatch		
Noddy	Paul K Joyce		
No Honestly	'No Honestly' by Lynsey de Paul	Top Secret	'Sucu Sucu'
		Two-Way Family Favourites	'With a Song in My Heart' by Richard Rodgers
Onedin Line	Spartacus by Khatchaturian		
One Foot in the Grave	Composed and sung by Eric Idle	Van Der Valk	'Eye Level' by Simon Park
		What the Papers Say	From the Cornish Dances by Malcolm Arnold
Owen MD	'Sleepy Shores' by Johnny Pearson		
Perry Mason	Theme by Fred Steiner	X Files	Music by Mark Snow
The Persuaders	Music by John Barry		
The Prisoner	Music by Ron Grainer	Yes Honestly	'Yes Honestly' by Georgie Fame
Prisoner Cell Block H	'On the Inside' (sung by Lynne Hamilton)		
Protectors	'Avenues and Alleyways' by Tony Christie	Z Cars	'Theme from Z Cars' aka 'Johnny Todd' by the Johnny Keating Orchestra
Randall and Hopkirk (Deceased)	Music by Edwin Astley		

MUSIC POP

Eurovision Song Contest Winners

Year	Song	Country (and Singer)	UK Entry	UK Posn
1956	Refrain	Switzerland (Lys Assia)	No entry	
1957	Net Als Toen	Holland (Corry Brokken)	All (Patricia Breden)	6th
1958	Dors, Mon Amour	France (André Claveau)	No entry	
1959	Een Beetje	Holland (Teddy Scholten)	Sing Little Birdie (Pearl Carr and Teddy Johnson)	2nd
1960	Tom Pillibi	France (Jacqueline Boyer)	Looking High, High, High (Bryan Johnson)	2nd
1961	Nous, les Amoureux	Luxembourg (Jean-Claude Pascal)	Are You Sure (Allisons)	2nd
1962	Un Premier Amour	France (Isabelle Aubret)	Ring-a-ding Girl (Ronnie Carroll)	4th
1963	Dansevise	Denmark (Grethe Jorgen Ingmann)	Say Wonderful Things (Ronnie Carroll)	4th
1964	Non Ho L'Eta (This Is My Prayer)	Italy (Gigliola Cinquetti)	I Say the Little Things (Matt Monro)	2nd
1965	Poupée de Cire, Poupée de Son	Luxembourg (France Gall)	I Belong (Kathy Kirby)	2nd
1966	Merci Chérie	Austria (Udo Jurgens)	A Man without Love (Kenneth McKellar)	7th
1967	Puppet on a String	UK (Sandie Shaw)	Puppet on a String	1st
1968	La La La	Spain (Massiel)	Congratulations (Cliff Richard)	2nd
1969	Viva Cantando	Spain (Salome)	Boom Bang-A-Bang	1st
	Boom Bang-A-Bang	UK (Lulu)		
	De Troubadour	Holland (Lennie Kuhr)		
	Un Jour Un Enfant	France (Frida Boccara)		
1970	All Kinds of Everything	Ireland (Dana)	Knock Knock (Mary Hopkin)	2nd
1971	Un Banc, Un Arbre, Une Rue	Monaco (Séverine)	Jack in the Box (Clodagh Rodgers)	4th
1972	Après Toi (Come What May)	Luxembourg (Vicky Leandros)	Beg, Steal or Borrow (New Seekers)	2nd
1973	Tu Te Reconnaîtras (Wonderful Dream)	Luxembourg (Anne-Marie David)	Power to all our Friends (Cliff Richard)	3rd
1974	Waterloo	Sweden (Abba)	Long Live Love (Olivia Newton-John)	4th
1975	Ding A Dong	Holland (Teach In)	Let Me Be the One (Shadows)	2nd
1976	Save Your Kisses for Me	UK (Brotherhood of Man)	Save Your Kisses For Me	1st
1977	L'Oiseau et L'Enfant	France (Marie Myriam)	Rock Bottom (Lynsey de Paul)	2nd
1978	A-ba-ni-bi	Israel (Izhar Cohen and the Alpha-Beta)	The Bad Old Days (Coco)	11th
1979	Hallelujah	Israel (Milk and Honey featuring Gali Atari)	Mary Ann (Black Lace)	7th
1980	What's Another Year?	Ireland (Johnny Logan)	Love Enough for Two (Prima Donna)	3rd
1981	Making Your Mind Up	UK (Buck's Fizz)	Making Your Mind Up	1st
1982	Ein Bisschen Frieden (A Little Peace)	Germany (Nicole)	One Step Further (Bardo)	7th
1983	Si la Vie Est Cadeau	Luxembourg (Corinne Hermes)	I'm Never Giving Up (Sweet Dreams)	6th
1984	Diggi loo-Diggi Ley	Sweden (Herreys)	Love Games (Belle and the Devotions)	7th
1985	La Det Swinge (Let it Swing)	Norway (Bobbysocks)	Love Is (Vikki)	4th
1986	J'aime la Vie	Belgium (Sandra Kim)	Runner in the Night (Ryder)	7th
1987	Hold Me Now	Ireland (Johnny Logan)	Only the Light (Rikki)	13th
1988	Ne Partez Pas Sans Moi	Switzerland (Celine Dion)	Go (Scott Fitzgerald)	2nd
1989	Rock Me	Yugoslavia (Riva)	Why Do I Always Get It Wrong (Live Report)	2nd
1990	Insieme:1992	Italy (Toto Cutugno)	Give a Little Love Back to the World (Emma)	6th
1991	Fångad Av En Stormvind	Sweden (Carola)	A Message to Your Heart (Samantha Janus)	10th

Year	Song	Country (and Singer)	UK Entry	UK Posn
1992	Why Me?	Ireland (Linda Martin)	One Step Out of Time (Michael Ball)	2nd
1993	In Your Eyes	Ireland (Niamh Kavanagh)	Better the Devil You Know (Sonia)	2nd
1994	Rock 'n' Roll Kids	Ireland (Paul Harrington and Charlie McGettigan)	We Will Be Free (Lonely Symphony) (Frances Ruffelle)	10th
1995	Nocturne	Norway (Secret Garden)	Love City Groove (Love City Groove)	10th
1996	The Voice	Ireland (Eimear Quinn)	Just a Little Bit (Gina G)	8th
1997	Love Shine a Light	UK (Katrina and the Waves)	Love Shine a Light	1st
1998	Diva	Israel (Dana International)	Where Are You? (Imaani)	2nd
1999	Take Me to Your Heaven	Sweden (Charlotte Nilsson)	Say It Again (Precious)	12th
2000	Fly on the Wings of Love	Denmark (Olsen Brothers)	Don't Play That Song Again (Nikki French)	16th
2001	Everybody	Estonia (Tanel Pader and Dave Benton)	No Dream Impossible (Lindsay Dracass)	15th
2002	I Wanna	Latvia (Marija Naumova)	Come Back (Jessica Garlick)	3rd equal
2003	Every Way That I Can	Turkey (Sertab Erener)	Cry Baby (Jemini)	Last

Classical-based Pop Tunes

Baubles, Bangles and Beads Adapted from the String Quartet in D major by Alexander Borodin

Beat Out Dat Rhythm on a Drum Based on 'The Gypsy Song' from the opera *Carmen* by Georges Bizet

Can Can (Bad Manners) Adapted from *Orpheus in the Underworld* by Jacques Offenbach

Can't Help Falling in Love Based on *Plaisir d'Amour* by Giovanni Martini

Capstick Comes Home Based on Dvořák's Symphony No. 9 in E minor (2nd movement, Largo)

Danny Boy Lyrics by Frederick Weatherly (1848–1929) and based on 'The Londonderry Air'

Dat's Love Based on 'Habañera' from the opera *Carmen* by Georges Bizet

Fanfare for the Common Man (ELP) Based on Aaron Copland's orchestral piece of the same name

Hello Muddah, Hello Fadduh Adapted from 'Dance of the Hours', Act 3 of *La Gioconda* by Amilcare Ponchielli

Hot Diggity Adapted from *España* (Spanish Rhapsody) by Emmanuel Chabrier

I Believe in Father Christmas Adapted from the *Lieutenant Kijé Suite*, Op. 60 by Sergei Prokofiev

I'd Climb the Highest Mountain Based on *Humoresque* Opus 101 No. 7 by Antonín Dvořák

If I Had Words Adapted from the 3rd movement of Symphony No. 3 Op. 78 by Charles Camille Saint-Saëns

If You Are But a Dream Adapted from *Romance* in E flat by Anton Rubinstein

I'm Always Chasing Rainbows Adapted from *Fantaisie Impromptu* in C sharp minor Op. 66 by Frederic Chopin

In An Eighteenth-century Drawing Room Adapted from Piano Sonata No. 3 in C by Wolfgang Amadeus Mozart

Joybringer Adapted from the 4th movement of *The Planets Suite* Op. 32 by Gustav Holst ('Jupiter – Bringer of Jollity')

Kiss in Your Eyes Adapted from *Une Chambre séparée* by Richard Heuberger

Lamp Is Low Adapted from *Pavane pour une infante défunte* by Maurice Ravel

Land of Hope and Glory Based on *Pomp and Circumstance March* No. 1 by Edward Elgar

Like I Do Adapted from 'Dance of the Hours', Act 3 of *La Gioconda* by Amilcare Ponchielli

Moon Love Based on the 2nd movement of Tchaikovsky's Symphony No. 5

More Than Love Adapted from the 2nd movement of the Sonata for Piano No. 8 in C minor, Op. 13 by Ludwig van Beethoven

My Reverie Based on Debussy's *Rêverie*

Narcissus Adapted from the *Water Scenes Suite*, Op. 13 No. 4 by Ethelbert Nevin

Nut Rocker Adapted from the March from *Casse-noisette Suite*, Op. 71 by Tchaikovsky

On the Isle of May Based on Tchaikovsky's Andante Cantabile

Our Love Based on Tchaikovsky's *Romeo and Juliet Overture*

Question and Answer Adapted from *Petite Suite de Concert*, Op. 77 by Samuel Coleridge-Taylor

River Kwai March Based on 'Colonel Bogey March' by Kenneth Alford

Rodrigo's Concerto An arrangement of the 2nd movement of the *Concerto for Guitar and Orchestra in D major* by Joaquin Rodrigo

Sabre Dance Adapted from *Gayaneh Ballet* by Aram Khatchaturian

So Deep Is the Night Adapted from Etude in E minor, Op. 10 No. 3 by Frédéric Chopin

Song of India Adapted from *Chanson indoue* by Nikolai Rimsky-Korsakov

The Story of a Starry Night Based on the 1st movement of Symphony No. 6 by Tchaikovsky

Strange Music Adapted from *Wedding-Day in Troldhaugen* by Edvard Grieg

Stranger in Paradise Adapted from a theme of the *Polovtsian Dances* by Alexander Borodin

Suddenly (Tony Bennett) Adapted from *Une Chambre Séparée* by Richard Heuberger

Surrender (Elvis Presley) Adapted from 'Torna A Surriento' by Ernesto De Curtis

The Things I Love Based on Melodie in E flat major, Op. 42 No 3 by Tchaikovsky

MUSIC POP

Till the End of Time Based on Chopin's Polonaise No. 6 in A flat for piano
Toccata and Fugue (Vanessa Mae) Variation of a Toccata and Fugue by Johann Sebastian Bach
Under the Lilac Bough From the musical *Lilac Time*, based on various pieces of music of Franz Schubert

Wagon Wheels Adapted from the 2nd movement of Dvorak's Symphony No. 9 in E minor
Wild Horses Based on 'Wilder Reiter' by Robert Schumann
Wooden Heart Adapted from the German folk song 'Muss I denn'

Composers of Pop Songs and Tunes

Song	Composer
Alexander's Ragtime Band	Irving Berlin
Alfie	Burt Bacharach and Hal David
All along the Watchtower	Bob Dylan
All of You	Cole Porter
All the Young Dudes	David Bowie
Alternate Title	Mickey Dolenz
Always Something There To Remind Me	Burt Bacharach and Hal David
And I Love You So	Don McLean
Anything You Can Do	Irving Berlin
Automatically Sunshine	William 'Smokey' Robinson
Baby I Don't Care	Leiber and Stoller
Bad To Me	Lennon and McCartney
Batdance	Prince
Beautiful Dreamer	Stephen Foster
Begin the Beguine	Cole Porter
Boat That I Row, The	Neil Diamond
Born Free	Don Black and John Barry
Bright Eyes	Mike Batt
Bring it on Home to Me	Sam Cooke
Brown Eyed Handsome Man	Chuck Berry
Carnival Is Over	Tom Springfield
Chain Reaction	Bee Gees
Chantilly Lace	J P Richardson (The Big Bopper)
Cheek to Cheek	Irving Berlin
Close to You	Burt Bacharach and Hal David
Come and Get It	Paul McCartney
A Couple of Swells	Irving Berlin
Cupid	Sam Cooke
Dancing in the Street	Marvyn Gaye and William Stevenson
Dancing on a Saturday Night	Barry Blue and Lynsey De Paul
The Day I Met Marie	Hank Marvin
Dick-A-Dum Dum (Kings Road)	Jim Dale
Do They Know It's Christmas?	Bob Geldof and Midge Ure
Do You Know Where You're Going To?	Gerry Goffin and Michael Masser
Do You Love Me	Berry Gordy Jr
Do You Want To Know a Secret	Lennon and McCartney
Doctorin' the Tardis	Gary Glitter, Ron Grainer, Chapman and Chinn

Song	Composer
Doin' What Comes Naturally	Irving Berlin
Don't Cry Out Loud	Carole Bayer Sager and Peter Allen
Don't Give Up On Us	Tony Macaulay
Don't Sleep in the Subway	Tony Hatch and Jackie Trent
Easter Parade	Irving Berlin
Eloise	Paul Ryan
Fascinating Rhythm	George and Ira Gershwin
First Cut Is the Deepest	Cat Stevens
Floy Joy	William 'Smokey Robinson'
For the Good Times	Kris Kristofferson
Genie with the Light Brown Lamp	Marvin, Welch, Bennett, Rostill (Shadows)
Georgy Girl	Jim Dale and Tom Springfield
Giving It All Away	Leo Sayer and David Courtney
Goldfinger	Tony Newley, John Barry and Leslie Bricusse
Goodbye	Lennon and McCartney
Goodbye (Mary Hopkin)	Lennon and McCartney
Got to Get You into My Life	Lennon and McCartney
Grease	Barry Gibb
A Groovy Kind of Love	Carole Bayer Sager and Tony Wine
Halfway to Paradise	Gerry Goffin and Carole King
Happy Holiday	Irving Berlin
A Hard Rain's Gonna Fall	Bob Dylan
Have I Told You Lately	Van Morrison
Help Me Make It through The Night	Kris Kristofferson
Hey, Good Looking	Hank Williams
Hopelessly Devoted to You	John Farrar
The Hustle	Van McCoy
I Don't Wanna Fight	Lulu
I Don't Want to Talk About it	Cat Stevens and Danny Whitten
If Not for You	Bob Dylan
I Get a Kick Out of You	Cole Porter
I Got Plenty of Nuttin'	George and Ira Gershwin
I Got Rhythm	George and Ira Gershwin
I Got the Sun in the Morning	Irving Berlin

Song	Composer	Song	Composer
I Just Don't Know What to do with Myself	Burt Bacharach and Hal David	Mama Told Me Not to Come	Randy Newman
I'll Keep You Satisfied	Lennon and McCartney	The Man Who Sold the World	David Bowie
I'll Never Fall in Love Again	Burt Bacharach and Hal David	The March of the Siamese Children	Richard Rodgers
I'll Never Fall in Love Again (Tom Jones)	Lonnie Donegan and Jimmie Currie	Mighty Quinn	Bob Dylan
I Love You, Samantha	Cole Porter	Miss Otis Regrets	Cole Porter
I'm a Believer	Neil Diamond	Mr Tambourine Man	Bob Dylan
I'm a Tiger	Marty Wilde and Ronnie Scott	Money (That's What I Want)	Berry Gordy Jr and Janie Bradford
I'm into Something Good	Gerry Goffin and Carole King	Mrs Brown You've Got a Lovely Daughter	Trevor Peacock
I Say a Little Prayer	Burt Bacharach and Hal David	My Guy	William 'Smokey' Robinson
I Shot the Sheriff	Bob Marley	My Heart Belongs to Daddy	Cole Porter
Isn't This a Lovely Day	Irving Berlin	My Resistance Is Low	Hoagy Carmichael and Harold Adamson
It Doesn't Matter Anymore	Paul Anka		
It Don't Mean a Thing	Duke Ellington and Irving Mills	Needles and Pins	Sonny Bono and Jack Nitzche
It Might as Well Rain until September	Gerry Goffin and Carole King	A Nice Cup Of Tea	A P Herbert
It's All in the Game	Charles Dawes and Carl Sigman	Night and Day	Cole Porter
		Nothing Compares 2 U	Prince
I've Got You under My Skin	Cole Porter		
I Wanna Be Your Man	Lennon and McCartney	Oh, Carol	Neil Sedaka and Howard Greenfield
I Will Drink the Wine	Paul Ryan	Oh No, Not My Baby	Gerry Goffin and Carole King
Jackie Wilson Said	Van Morrison		
Jambalaya	Hank Williams	Photograph	Ringo Starr and George Harrison
The James Bond Theme	Monty Norman		
Just Like a Woman	Bob Dylan	Pink Cadillac	Bruce Springsteen
		The Purple People Eater	Sheb Wooley
Killing Me Softly with His Song	Charles Fox and Norman Gimbel	Puttin' on the Ritz	Irving Berlin
Knockin' on Heaven's Door	Bob Dylan	Rhapsody in Blue	George Gershwin
		River Kwai March	Malcolm Arnold
Lady	Lionel Richie	Roamin' in the Gloamin'	Harry Lauder
The Lady is a Tramp	Rodgers and Hart	Rocket Man	Elton John and Bernie Taupin
Leaning on a Lamp Post	Noel Gay	Roll Over Beethoven	Chuck Berry
Leavin' on a Jet Plane	John Denver	Running Bear	J P Richardson (The Big Bopper)
Legend of the Glass Mountain	Nino Rota		
Let's Call the Whole Thing Off	George and Ira Gershwin	Saving All My Love for You	Gerry Goffin and Michael Masser
Let's Do It (Let's Fall in Love)	Cole Porter	September Song	Maxwell Anderson and Kurt Weill
Let's Face the Music and Dance	Irving Berlin	Simon Smith and His Amazing Dancing Bear	Randy Newman
Little Bit Me, Little Bit You	Neil Diamond		
Living Doll	Lionel Bart	Something's Gotten Hold of My Heart	Roger Cook and Roger Greenaway
The Locomotion	Gerry Goffin and Carole King	Something Tells Me	Roger Cook and Roger Greenaway
Love and Marriage	Sammy Cahn and Jimmy Van Heusen	Sophisticated Lady	Duke Ellington, Irving Mills and Mitchell Parish
MacArthur Park	Jim Webb		
Mack the Knife	Weill, Brecht, Blitzstein	Step Inside Love	Lennon and McCartney
Mad about the Boy	Noël Coward	The Stripper	David Rose
Mad Dogs and Englishmen	Noël Coward	S'Wonderful	George and Ira Gershwin
Magic Moments	Burt Bacharach and Hal David		

MUSIC POP

Take Five	Paul Desmond and Lola Brubeck	What'll I Do	Irving Berlin
Take Good Care of My Baby	Gerry Goffin and Carole King	What's New, Pussycat?	Burt Bacharach and Hal David
Tara's Theme	Max Steiner	When I'm Dead and Gone	Gallagher and Lyle
Tears of a Clown	Smokey Robinson, Stevie Wonder, Henry Cosby	When I Need You	Carole Bayer Sager and Albert Hammond
This Guy's in Love With You	Burt Bacharach and Hal David	Wherever I Lay My Hat	Marvin Gaye and Norman Whitfield
This is My Song	Charlie Chaplin	A Whiter Shade of Pale	Keith Richard and Gary Brooker
This Wheel's on Fire	Bob Dylan and Rick Danko	Who Wants to Be a Millionaire	Cole Porter
Throw Down A Line	Hank B Marvin	Wild Thing	Chip Taylor
To Keep My Love Alive	Rodgers and Hart	Wild World	Cat Stevens
To Know Him is To Love Him	Phil Spector	Will You Love Me Tomorrow	Gerry Goffin and Carole King
To Love Somebody	Barry and Robin Gibb	A Winter's Tale	Mike Batt
Too Darn Hot	Cole Porter	Wired for Sound	B A Robertson and Alan Tarney
Trains and Boats and Planes	Burt Bacharach and Hal David	Without You	Peter Ham and Tony Evans (Badfinger)
True Love	Cole Porter		
Twent-Four Hours from Tulsa	Burt Bacharach and Hal David	Wichita Lineman	Jim Webb
Twisting the Night Away	Sam Cooke	Woman in Love	Barry and Robin Gibb
		Woodstock	Joni Mitchell
		A World Without Love	Lennon and McCartney
Up on the Roof	Gerry Goffin and Carole King	Wunderbar	Cole Porter
Up Where We Belong	Buffy St Marie, Jack Nitzche, William Jennings	You Make Me Feel So Young	Mack Gordon and Joseph Myrow
		Your Cheating Heart	Hank Williams
		You're the One That I Want	John Farrar
We Are the World	Michael Jackson and Lionel Richie	You're the Top	Cole Porter
Well, Did You Evah?	Cole Porter	You've Got Your Troubles	Roger Cook and Roger Greenaway

Derivations of Names

Group	Derivation	Where from
Abba (1972)	The initials of of its members' Christian names	Sweden/Norway
Adam and the Ants (1977)	Adopted his surname as collective name for his group of four	London
A-Ha (1982)	Keyboardist Mags Furuholmen chose name as it was a universally accepted expression	Norway
Alice Cooper (1965)	Spelt out by a ouija board	USA
America (1967)	Met at London school; all 3 members were sons of US Air Force officers stationed in UK	USA
Archies (1967)	Named after a popular CBS cartoon series based on John Goldwater comic book characters	USA
Art of Noise (1983)	The name of an Italian futurist manifesto	UK
Aswad (1983)	Arabic for 'Black'	UK
Bachman-Turner Overdrive (1973)	Added name of a trucking magazine, *Overdrive*, to those of its founding members	Canada
Bad Company (1973)	From a Jeff Bridges film	UK
Bangles (1981)	Forced to change name from the Bangs because of existing band	Los Angeles
Bauhaus (1980)	Named after the German art movement	UK
Bay City Rollers (1970)	Chosen by sticking pin in map of USA and pricking Bay City	UK
Bee Gees (1959)	From the initials of their founder Barry Gibb. There is no substance to the myth that a racetrack promoter (Bill Goode) and a DJ (Bill Gates) inspired the name	Australia
B-52's	Southern US nickname for a bouffant hairstyle adopted by its female members	Georgia
Blondie (1975)	Lead singer's hair colour	New York
Boomtown Rats (1978)	Originally Nightlife Thugs; changed name to phrase in Woody Guthrie biography *Bound For Glory*	Dublin
Bread (1968)	Chosen after they were stuck behind a Wonder Bread truck in a traffic jam	Los Angeles
Buffalo Springfield (1966)	A make of steamroller	California
Canned Heat (1966)	From 1928 song by Mississipi bluesman Tommy Johnson, 'Canned Heat Blues'	Los Angeles
Captain And Tennille (1971)	Mike Love of the Beach Boys called Daryl Dragon 'Captain Keyboards' and the name stuck; other member Toni Tennille	San Francisco
CCS (1970)	Collective Consciousness Society, a collaboration between Alexis Korner, Mickie Most and John Cameron	UK
Clannad (1981)	Gaelic for 'Family'	Ireland
Commodores (1968)	Random choice from dictionary (nearly called the Commodes, so they say)	USA
Cream (1966)	Thought themselves the best so named themselves accordingly	UK
Creedence Clearwater Revival (1968)	Creedence was a friend of the band and Clearwater came from a beer commercial	USA
Crystals (1961)	After Crystal Bates, daughter of their first songwriter, Leroy Bates	USA
Cult (1982)	Originally called Southern Death Cult, taken from a newspaper headline	UK
Cure (1976)	Originally called the Easy Cure, a stock phrase of the day	Crawley
Damned (1976)	From the Dracula-style fancy dress worn by lead singer Dave Vanian	UK
Deacon Blue (1987)	From a Steely Dan record	UK
Dead Kennedys (1978)	Name was designed to shock, as it refers to the Kennedy brothers John and Robert	San Francisco
Deep Purple (1968)	Chosen as a contrast to Vanilla Fudge, on whom they based their early music	UK
Def Leppard (1977)	Corruption of Deaf Leopard, proposed by band's lead singer Joe Elliott	Sheffield

MUSIC POP

Group	Derivation	Where from
Depeche Mode (1980)	From a French fashion magazine, meaning 'Fast Fashion'	UK
Devo (1972)	From video Truth about De-evolution, award winner at Ann Arbor Film Festival	Akron, Ohio
Dexy's Midnight Runners (1978)	Slang term for the pep pill Dexedrine	Birmingham
Dire Straits (1977)	From the financial plight of the group when formed	UK
Doobie Brothers (1970)	After 'doobie' the Californian nickname for a marijuana cigarette	San Jose, California
Doors (1965)	From Aldous Huxley book The Doors of Perception (Huxley took title from Blake work)	Los Angeles
Dr Feelgood (1971)	From 1962 US hit 'Doctor Feel-Good' by bluesman Piano Red	UK
Dr Hook (1968)	Prompted by the eye patch (as in Captain Hook) worn by lead singer Ray Sawyer	New Jersey
Duran Duran (1978)	First gig was at Barbarella's in Birmingham so used a name from the Jane Fonda film	Birmingham
Earth, Wind and Fire (1969)	Singer and drummer Maurice White named band after 3 of the ancient elements	USA
The Easybeats	From a BBC Light programme pop show hosted by Brian Matthews	USA
Echo and the Bunnymen (1977)	Echo was the nickname for their drum machine, which was replaced by Pete de Freitas	Liverpool
Eurythmics (1977)	Named in 1980 after 'Rhythm Gymnastics' style devised by Emile Jaques-Dalcroze	UK
Everything But the Girl (1982)	Took their misleading name from a local second-hand furniture store	Hull
Faces (1969)	Steve Marriot left the Small Faces to form Humble Pie and the 'Small' was dropped	London
Fairport Convention (1967)	After the house, 'Fairport', in which its guitarist Simon Nicol lived in Muswell Hill	London
Faith No More (1980)	After a greyhound on which they had a bet	Los Angeles
Fifth Dimension (1966)	Originally called Versatiles changed name to reflect being beyond the 4th dimension	Los Angeles
Fine Young Cannibals (1984)	From the Robert Wagner/Natalie Wood film All the Fine Young Cannibals	UK
Fixx (1980)	Originally called the Portraits but changed it to Fix then to Fixx because of drug slur	UK
Fleetwood Mac (1967)	From 2 members, drummer Mick Fleetwood and bassist John McVie	UK
Flock of Seagulls (1979)	From cult novel by Richard Bach, Jonathan Livingstone Seagull (1970)	Liverpool
Frankie Goes to Hollywood (1980)	Headline in Variety magazine about Sinatra moving from Las Vegas to Hollywood	Liverpool
Genesis (1965)	Originally Garden Wall; Jonathan King renamed them in 1967 as they were being 'born'	London
Grateful Dead (1963)	Said to come from an Egyptian prayer book	San Francisco
Guess Who (1965)	Forerunner of Bachman-Turner Overdrive; name based on British band The Who	Canada
Guns N' Roses (1985)	Combination of former guitarist Tracii Guns and the lead singer's assumed name	Los Angeles
Harpers Bizarre (1963)	Variation on the magazine Harper's Bazaar (Harper's and Queen)	San Francisco
Headgirl (1981)	Motorhead and Girlschool united for one-hit wonder 'The St Valentine's Day Massacre'	UK
Heaven 17 (1980)	Named after a group in Anthony Burgess's novel A Clockwork Orange	Sheffield
Herman's Hermits (1961)	The Herman was derived from Sherman, the flying squirrel in Rocky and Bullwinkle Show	Manchester
Hollies (1962)	Tribute to Buddy Holly	Manchester
Hot Chocolate (1969)	Named by an agent from the Apple record company as a pun on their colour and style	London
Human League (1977)	From a science-fiction computer game	Sheffield
Humble Pie (1969)	Superstars Frampton and Marriott named band to contrast with their pop idol status	London
Icehouse (1980)	Originally Flowers; changed name to that of their 1st album so as not to clash with existing group	Sydney
INXS (1977)	Originally called Farriss Brothers after 3 members but changed to a pun on In Excess	Australia
Iron Maiden (1976)	From a medieval instrument of torture	London

MUSIC POP

Group	Derivation	Where from
Jefferson Airplane (1965)	Hippie jargon for a paper match split at one end to hold a reefer; subsequently changed name to Jefferson Starship (1974) then Starship (1985)	San Francisco
Jesus and Mary Chain (1983)	After Alan McGee's club in London, where they performed early hits	Scotland
Jethro Tull (1967)	From the famous agriculturist, author of *Horse Hoeing Husbandry*	Blackpool
Joy Division (1977)	Nazi slang term for a military brothel	UK
Judas Priest (1973)	From Bob Dylan song, 'Ballad of Frankie Lee and Judas Priest'	Birmingham
Kajagoogoo (1983)	Supposedly from original surname of film director Elia Kazan 'Kazanjoglou'	UK
KC and the Sunshine Band (1973)	Named after founder Harry Wayne Casey	Florida
Kinks (1963)	Named by pop impresario Larry Page, based on 'Kinky', a vogue word of swinging London	London
Kraftwerk (1970)	German for power plant referring to their electronic synthesisers	Düsseldorf
Level 42 (1980)	From the answer to the meaning of life in Douglas Adams's *The Hitch Hiker's Guide to the Galaxy*	UK
Lovin' Spoonful (1965)	From a line in a song by bluesman John Hurt	USA/Canada
Lynyrd Skynyrd (1966)	Named after the gym teacher who had expelled them from school	Jacksonville, Florida
Madness (1976)	From a Prince Buster song	UK
Mamas and the Papas (1965)	Named from 2 married couples in group, John and Michelle Phillips and Cass Elliot and John Hendricks	New York
Manhattan Transfer (1969)	From novel by Jon Dos Passos	New York
Men at Work (1979)	From road sign 'Danger Men at Work'	Melbourne
Metallica (1981)	Adopted a name to suit their particular type of rock music	Los Angeles
Mindbenders (1965)	The name of a Dirk Bogarde film	UK
Mothers of Invention (1965)	Originally called the Muthers but changed to echo proverb 'necessity is the . . .'	Los Angeles
Motley Crue (1981)	Play on phrase motley crew, which was an apt name for their bizarre appearance	USA
Motorhead (1975)	Song written by Ian 'Lemmy' Kilminster for Hawkwind, group he was sacked from	UK
Mott the Hoople (1968)	From an obscure novel by Willard Manus published in 1967	Hereford
Move (1966)	From the 5 members various moves from their prior bands	Birmingham
New Kids on the Block (1984)	Named by manager Maurice Starr as a white equivalent to his other band, New Edition	Massachusetts
New Order (1980)	After suicide of Ian Curtis, Joy Division became New Order, which was also a Nazi term	UK
Pet Shop Boys (1981)	Named by its members for friends who worked in an Ealing pet shop	London
Pink Floyd (1965)	Named as tribute to bluesmen Pink Anderson and Floyd Council	London
Planxty (1972)	From an Irish folk dance	Ireland
Platters (1953)	Black American group tock their name from the slang term for gramophone records	Los Angeles
Poco (1968)	Originally called Pogo after a comic strip but forced to amend it when creator objected	Los Angeles
Pogues (1983)	Original name was Pogue Mahone ('Kiss my arse'); changed after BBC banned them	UK/Ireland
Pretenders (1978)	Named by Chrissie Hynde after a Platters hit, 'The Great Pretender'	UK/USA
Pretty Things (1963)	After the Bo Diddley hit 'Pretty Thing'	Sidcup, Kent
Procul Harum (1967)	Originally called the Paramounts, said to have been renamed after someone's cat	Southend, Essex
Psychedelic Furs (1977)	From Velvet Underground hit 'Venus in Furs'	London
R.E.M. (1980)	Although an abbreviation for rapid eye movement, the name was arbitrarily arrived at	Athens, Georgia
REO Speedwagon (1967)	From an early make of fire engine, Ransom E. Olds Speedwagon	Champaign, Illinois

Group	Derivation	Where from
Righteous Brothers (1962)	Originally called Paramours; took their name from the slang for excellent performers	Anaheim, California
Rolling Stones (1962)	From the Muddy Waters song 'Rolling Stone'	London
Ronettes (1959)	From the nickname of Veronica Bennett (Ronnie), one of the founder members	New York
Roxy Music (1971)	Based on the Roxy cinema chain	London
Run DMC (1982)	Nicknames of their 2 lead singers, Joseph 'Run' Simmons and Darryl 'D' McDaniels	New York
Scritti Politti (1977)	Based on the Italian phrase for 'political writings'	Leeds
Searchers (1961)	Named after the John Wayne film	Liverpool
Selecter (1979)	From the 'B' side of their debut single 'Gangsters', written by Noel Davies	Coventry
Sex Pistols (1975)	Malcolm McLaren named them after his boutique 'Sex' and Shakespeare character	London
Shadows (1959)	Originally called the Drifters; Jet Harris changed name in a Ruislip pub in 1959	London
Shakatak (1980)	From a local boutique	London
Shakespears Sister (1989)	From a Smiths' song (spelt wrongly)	UK
Shalamar (1977)	Named after the Shalimar Gardens near Lahore in Pakistan	Los Angeles
Shirelles (1957)	Name based on their lead singer Shirley Owens	Passaic, New Jersey
Showaddywaddy (1973)	From 'Bop bop showaddywaddy' backing of 'Little Darlin'' by the Diamonds	Leicester
Simple Minds (1977)	Self-deprecatory name adopted during the Punk era	Glasgow
Simply Red (1985)	Named after the red hair of its lead singer Mick Hucknall	Manchester
Slade (1969)	Originally Ambrose Slade among other names, shortened to Slade in 1969	Wolverhampton
Smiths (1982)	Suggests the anonymity its members are said to have sought	Manchester
Soft Cell (1979)	Pun on 'soft sell', a term used for selling by inducement	Leeds
Soft Machine (1966)	After the William Burroughs novel of 1961	Canterbury
Spandau Ballet (1979)	Name derived from 2 contrasting words as an oxymoron to give effect	London
Split Enz (1972)	Originally called Split Ends after hair that has split, but changed spelling in 1975	Auckland, NZ
Squeeze (1974)	From a Velvet Underground Album	London
Steeleye Span (1969)	Name adopted from the traditional Lincolnshire ballad 'Horkston Grange'	UK
Steely Dan (1972)	Name of steam-powered dildo in novel The Naked Lunch by William Burroughs	Los Angeles
Steppenwolf (1968)	From the Herman Hesse novel	USA/Canada
Stone Roses (1980)	Originally played as Patrol and English Rose; chose similar name to Rolling Stones	Manchester
Stranglers (1974)	Originally the Guildford Strangler; shortened name when gaining following	Guildford
Strawbs (1967)	Originally the Strawberry Hill Boys, from the area of London they were from	London
Supertramp (1969)	From the W H Davies book Autobiography of a Super-tramp	London
Supremes (1959)	Originally called the Primettes as they supported the Primes (Temptations)	Detroit
Sweet (1966)	Originally called Wainwright's Gentlemen then Sweetshop	UK
Swinging Blue Jeans (1958)	Originally called Bluegenes; changed name on gaining sponsorship from jeans company	Liverpool
Take That (1994)	From the caption beside a Madonna poster	UK
Talking Heads (1975)	From the television jargon for a kind of static presentation	New York
Teardrop Explodes (1978)	From a caption in a Marvel science fiction comic	Liverpool
Tears for Fears (1981)	From Arthur Janov's book on primal therapy Prisoners of Pain	UK

Group	Derivation	Where from
Ten cc (10cc) (1972)	Named by Jonathan King, because the average male semen ejaculation was 9 cc	Manchester
Ten Thousand Maniacs (1981)	Name resulted from mishearing of film title *12,000 Maniacs*	Jamestown, New York
Ten Years After (1965)	Originally called Jaybirds changed name in 1966 on 10th anniversary of rock 'n' roll	Nottingham
The The (1980)	Parody of the many rock groups whose name begins with 'The'	London
Thin Lizzy (1969)	From 'Tin Lizzy', colloquial name for an old car	Dublin
Thompson Twins (1977)	From the characters in the Tintin cartoons by Hergé	Sheffield
Three Dog Night (1968)	Australian expression for a cold night when 3 dogs are needed to keep warm	USA
Toto (1978)	Corruption of real name of lead singer, Toteaux, to give the name of dog in *The Wizard of Oz*	Los Angeles
TPau (1986)	Carol Decker named group from the high priestess of Vulcan, a character in *Star Trek*	London
U2 (1977)	Said to be suggestive of the words 'You too'	Dublin
UB40 (1978)	From designation of Unemployment Benefit form	Birmingham
Ultravox (1976)	Name means 'beyond the voice', but may also refer to founder John Foxx	London
Velvet Underground (1965)	From the title of a pornographic publication	London
Wet Wet Wet (1986)	From a lyric on a Scritti Politti record	UK
X (1977)	From group's lead singer Exene Cervenka, nicknamed X	Los Angeles
XTC (1977)	Suggests 'ecstasy', but last 2 letters are initials of their drummer Terry Chambers	Swindon
Yardbirds (1963)	From the jazzman Charlie Parker, nicknamed Yardbird	Kingston-upon-Thames
Yazoo (1982)	From an early blues record label	UK

MUSIC POP

Singles

(number in brackets = top chart position)

NB: The listings below include all Top 10 singles released between the inception of the UK charts in November 1952 and 31 December 2002.
Other records that did not make the Top 10, but are notable for some other reason, are also included. Solo artistes are listed by surname.
The alphabetical listing of song titles includes the year of release of the single after the artiste's name. Other information is given where appropriate.

Title	Group/Artiste
Abacab (9)	Genesis (1981)
Abba-Esque EP (1)	Erasure (1992)
ABC (8)	Jackson 5 (1970)
Abracadabra (2)	Steve Miller Band (1982)
Abraham Martin And John (9)	Marvin Gaye (1970)
Absolute Beginners (2)	David Bowie (1986)
Absolute Beginners (4)	Jam (1981)
Absolutely Everybody (7)	Vanessa Amorosi (2000)
Absolutely Fabulous (6)	Pet Shop Boys (1994)
Accidents (46) second and only other hit	Thunderclap Newman (1970)
Achilles Heel (re-issue) (8)	Toploader (2000)
Achy Breaky Heart (3) first hit	Billy Ray Cyrus (1992)
Activ 8 (Come With Me) (3)	Altern 8 (1991)
Addam's Groove (4)	MC Hammer (1991)
Addicted To Bass (2)	Puretone (2002)
Addicted To Love (5)	Robert Palmer (1986)
Addictive (3)	Truth Hurts featuring Rakim (2002)
Adelante (2)	Sash (2000)
Adoration Waltz (9)	David Whitfield (1957)
Affirmation (8)	Savage Garden (2000)
Africa (3)	Toto (1983)
African Waltz (9)	Johnny Dankworth (1961)
Afrika Shox (7)	Leftfield / Bambaataa (1999)
After The Love Has Gone (4)	Earth Wind & Fire (1979)
After The Love Has Gone (5)	Steps (1999)
After You're Gone/Sacred Trust (2) first hit	One True Voice (2002)
Agadoo (2)	Black Lace (1984)
Again (6)	Janet Jackson (1993)
Against All Odds (1)	Mariah Carey & Westlife (2000)
Against All Odds (Take A Look At Me Now) (2)	Phil Collins (1984)
Ain't Gonna Bump No More (With No Big Fat Woman) (2)	Joe Tex (1977)
Ain't Got No – I Got Life / Do What You Gotta Do (2)	Nina Simone (1968)
Ain't It Fun (9)	Guns 'N' Roses (1993)
Ain't It Funny (3)	Jennifer Lopez (2001)
Ain't It Funny (remix) (4)	Jennifer Lopez (2002)

Title	Group/Artiste
Ain't Misbehavin' (3)	Tommy Bruce & The Bruisers (1960)
Ain't No Doubt (1)	Jimmy Nail (1992)
Ain't No Love (Ain't No Use) (3)	Sub Sub and Melanie Williams (1993)
Ain't No Mountain High Enough (6)	Diana Ross (1970)
Ain't No Pleasing You (2)	Chas & Dave (1982)
Ain't No Stoppin' Us (8)	DJ Luck & MC Neat featuring JJ (2000)
Ain't No Stoppin' Us Now (5)	McFadden & Whitehead (1979)
Ain't No Sunshine (8)	Michael Jackson (1972)
Ain't Nobody (1)	LL Cool J (1997)
Ain't Nobody (8)	Course (1997)
Ain't Nobody (8)	Rufus & Chaka Khan (1984)
Ain't Nobody Better (10)	Inner City (1989)
Ain't Nobody (remix) (6)	Rufus & Chaka Khan (1989)
Ain't Nothing Goin' On But The Rent (5)	Gwen Guthrie (1986)
Ain't Talkin' 'Bout Dub (7)	Apollo Four Forty (1997)
Ain't That A Shame (7) first hit	Pat Boone (1955)
Ain't That Funny (8)	Jimmy Justice (1962)
Ain't That Just The Way (6)	Lutricia McNeal (1997)
Air That I Breathe, The (2)	Hollies (1974)
Air That I Breathe, The (6)	Simply Red (1998)
Airport (4)	Motors (1978)
Airwave (10)	Rank 1 (2000)
Aisha (9)	Death In Vegas (2000)
Albatross (1)	Fleetwood Mac (1968)
Albatross (re-issue) (2)	Fleetwood Mac (1973)
Alcoholic (10)	Starsailor (2001)
Alfie (9)	Cilla Black (1966)
Alice I Want You Just For Me (9)	Full Force (1985)
Alive (5)	S Club (2002)
Alive And Kicking (7)	Simple Minds (1985)
All About Us (3)	Peter Andre (1997)
All Alone Am I (7)	Brenda Lee (1963)
All Along The Watchtower (5)	Jimi Hendrix Experience (1968)
All Around My Hat (5)	Steeleye Span (1975)
All Around The World (1)	Oasis (1998)
All Around The World (1)	Lisa Stansfield (1989)
All Because Of You (6)	Geordie (1973)
All By Myself (6)	Celine Dion (1996)
All Cried Out (8)	Alison Moyet (1984)

Title	Group/Artiste
All Day And All Of The Night (2)	Kinks (1964)
All Day And All Of The Night (7)	Stranglers (1988)
All For Love (2)	Bryan Adams, Rod Stewart & Sting (1994)
All For You (3)	Janet Jackson (2001)
All 4 Love (5)	Color Me Badd (1991)
All Hooked Up (7)	All Saints (2001)
All I Ask Of You (3)	Cliff Richard and Sarah Brightman (1986)
All I Ever Need Is You (8)	Sonny & Cher (1972)
All I Have To Do Is Dream (3)	Bobbie Gentry & Glen Campbell (1969)
All I Have To Do Is Dream / Claudette (1)	Everly Brothers (1958)
All I Have To Give (2)	Backstreet Boys (1998)
All I Really Want To Do (4)	Byrds (1965)
All I Really Want To Do (9) first solo hit	Cher (1965)
All I See Is You (9)	Dusty Springfield (1966)
All I Wanna Do (4)	Sheryl Crow (1994)
All I Wanna Do (4)	Dannii Minogue (1997)
All I Wanna Do Is Make Love To You (8)	Heart (1990)
All I Want (2)	Mis-Teeq (2001)
All I Want For Christmas Is You (2)	Mariah Carey (1994)
All I Want Is You (4)	911 (1998)
All I Want Is You (4)	U2 (1989)
All Kinds Of Everything (1) first hit	Dana (1970)
All Mine (8)	Portishead (1997)
All My Life (5)	Foo Fighters (2002)
All My Life (8)	K-Ci & JoJo (1998)
All My Love (6)	Cliff Richard (1967)
All Night Holiday (20)	Russ Abbot (1985)
All Night Long (5)	Rainbow (1980)
All Night Long (All Night) (2)	Lionel Richie (1983)
(All Of A Sudden) My Heart Sings (10)	Paul Anka (1959)
All Of Me Loves All Of You (4)	Bay City Rollers (1974)
All Of My Heart (5)	ABC (1982)
All Of My Life (9)	Diana Ross (1974)
All Or Nothing (4)	O-Town (2001)
All Or Nothing (1)	Small Faces (1966)
All Out Of Love / Beauty And The Beast (10)	H & Claire (2002)
All Right Now (2)	Free (1970)
All Right Now (remix) (8)	Free (1991)
All Rise (4) first hit	Blue (2001)
All She Wants Is (9)	Duran Duran (1989)
All Shook Up (re-entry) (1)	Elvis Presley with The Jordanaires (1957)
All Star Hit Parade (2)	Various Artists (1956)
All Stood Still (8)	Ultravox (1981)
All That I Need (1)	Boyzone (1998)
All That She Wants (1) first hit	Ace Of Base (1993)
All The Love In The World (10)	Dionne Warwick (1982)
All The Small Things (2)	Blink 182 (2000)
All The Things She Said (9)	Simple Minds (1986)

Title	Group/Artiste
All The Time And Everywhere (9)	Dickie Valentine (1953)
All The Way From Memphis (10)	Mott The Hoople (1973)
All The Way (re-entry) (3)	Frank Sinatra (1957)
All The Young Dudes (3)	Mott The Hoople (1972)
All Time High (75)	Rita Coolidge (1983)
All Together Now (4)	Farm (1990)
All You Good Good People EP (8)	Embrace (1997)
All You Need Is Love (1)	Beatles (1967)
Ally's Tartan Army (6)	Andy Cameron (1978)
Almaz (4)	Randy Crawford (1986)
Almost There (2)	Andy Williams (1965)
Almost Unreal (7)	Roxette (1993)
Alone (5)	Bee Gees (1997)
Alone (8)	Petula Clark (1957)
Alone (3)	Heart (1987)
Alone (7)	Lasgo (2002)
Alone Again (Naturally) (3)	Gilbert O'Sullivan (1972)
Alone Without You (8)	King (1985)
Alphabet Street (9)	Prince (1988)
Alright (6)	Jamiroquai (1997)
Alright / Time (2)	Supergrass (1995)
Alright Alright Alright (3)	Mungo Jerry (1973)
Also Sprach Zarathustra (2001) (7)	Deodato (1973)
Alternate Title (2)	Monkees (1967)
Always (3)	Atlantic Starr (1987)
Always (2)	Bon Jovi (1994)
Always (4)	Erasure (1994)
Always And Forever / Mind Blowing Decisions (remix) (9)	Heatwave (1978)
Always Be My Baby (3)	Mariah Carey (1996)
Always Breaking My Heart (8)	Belinda Carlisle (1996)
Always Come Back To Your Love (3)	Samantha Mumba (2001)
Always Look On The Bright Side Of Life (3)	Monty Python (1991)
Always On My Mind (1)	Pet Shop Boys (1987)
Always On My Mind (9)	Elvis Presley (1972)
Always On Time (6)	Ja Rule featuring Ashanti (2002)
Always There (6)	Incognito featuring Jocelyn Brown (1991)
Always Yours (1)	Gary Glitter (1974)
Am I That Easy To Forget (3)	Engelbert Humperdinck (1968)
AM To PM (3)	Christina Milian (2002)
Amateur Hour (7)	Sparks (1974)
Amazing Grace (5)	Judy Collins (1970)
Amazing Grace (1)	Pipes & Drums & Military Band Of The Royal Scots Dragoon Guards (1972)
America: What Time Is Love (4)	KLF (1992)
American Dream (55) first and only hit	Crosby, Stills, Nash and Young (1989)
American Dream (3)	Jakatta (2001)
American Pie (1)	Madonna (2000)

Title	Group/Artiste	Title	Group/Artiste
American Pie (2) first hit	Don McLean (1972)	Another Step (Closer To You) (6)	Kim Wilde & Junior (1987)
Americanos (4)	Holly Johnson (1989)	Another Suitcase In Another Hall (7)	Madonna (1997)
Amigo (9)	Black Slate (1980)	Answer Me (9) first hit	Barbara Dickson (1976)
Amnesia (10)	Chumbawamba (1998)		
Amoureuse (13) first hit	Kiki Dee (1973)	Answer Me (1)	Frankie Laine (1953)
An American Trilogy (8)	Elvis Presley (1972)	Answer Me (1)	David Whitfield (1953)
An Everlasting Love (10)	Andy Gibb (1978)		
An Innocent Man (8)	Billy Joel (1984)	Ant Rap (3)	Adam & The Ants (1981)
Anarchy In The UK (38) first hit	Sex Pistols (1976) re-issued 1992 (No. 33)	Ante Up (7)	MOP featuring Busta Rhymes (2001)
And I Love You So (3)	Perry Como (1973)		
And The Beat Goes On (2)	Whispers (1980)	Antmusic (EP) (2)	Adam & The Ants (1980)
And The Heavens Cried (6)	Anthony Newley (1961)	Any Dream Will Do (1)	Jason Donovan (1991)
Anfield Rap (Red Machine In Full Effect) (3)	Liverpool FC (1988)	Any Old Iron (21) first hit	Peter Sellers (1957) re-issue reached No. 17
Angel (5)	Madonna (1985)		
Angel (1)	Shaggy featuring Rayvon (2001)	Any Way That You Want Me (8)	Troggs (1966)
Angel (4)	Simply Red (1996)	Anyone Can Fall In Love (4)	Anita Dobson (1986)
Angel / What Made Milwaukee Famous (Has Made A Loser Out Of Me) (4)	Rod Stewart (1972)	Anyone Of Us (Stupid Mistake) (1)	Gareth Gates (2002)
Angel Eyes (4)	Roxy Music (1979)	Anyone Who Had A Heart (1)	Cilla Black (1964)
Angel Eyes / Voulez Vous (3)	Abba (1979)	Anything (5)	Culture Beat (1994)
Angel Eyes (Home And Away) (5)	Wet Wet Wet (1987)	Anything (2)	3T (1996)
Angel Face (4)	Glitter Band (1974)	Anything For You (10)	Gloria Estefan and The Miami Sound Machine (1988)
Angel Fingers (1)	Wizzard (1973)		
Angel Of Harlem (9)	U2 (1988)	Anything Is Possible / Evergreen (1)	Will Young (2002)
Angel Of Mine (4)	Eternal (1997)	Anytime You Need A Friend (8)	Mariah Carey (1994)
Angel Street (8)	M People (1998)		
Angela Jones (7)	Michael Cox (1960)	Anyway Anyhow Anywhere (10)	Who (1965)
Angelo (1)	Brotherhood Of Man (1977)	Anywhere For You (4)	Backstreet Boys (1997)
Angels (4)	Robbie Williams (1997)	Anywhere Is (7)	Enya (1995)
Angie (5)	Rolling Stones (1973)	Apache (1)	Shadows (1960)
Angie Baby (5)	Helen Reddy (1975)	Apeman (5)	Kinks (1970)
Animal (6)	Def Leppard (1987)	Applejack (4)	Jet Harris & Tony Meehan (1963)
Animal Nitrate (7)	Suede (1993)		
Annie I'm Not Your Daddy (2)	Kid Creole & The Coconuts (1982)	April Love (7)	Pat Boone (1957)
		April Skies (8)	Jesus & Mary Chain (1987)
Annie's Song (1)	John Denver (1974)		
Annie's Song (3)	James Galway (1978)	Are Friends Electric (1)	Tubeway Army (1979)
Anniversary Waltz – Part 1, The (2)	Status Quo (1990)	Are You Gonna Go My Way (4)	Lenny Kravitz (1993)
		Are You Lonesome Tonight (1)	Elvis Presley with The Jordanaires (1961)
Another Brick In The Wall Part II (1)	Pink Floyd (1979)		
Another Chance (1)	Roger Sanchez (2001)	Are You Ready To Rock (8)	Wizzard (1974)
		Are You Sure (2)	Allisons (1961)
Another Day (2)	Paul McCartney (1971)		
Another Day (7)	Whigfield (1994)	Aria (5)	Mr Acker Bilk, his Clarinet & Strings (1976)
Another Day In Paradise (5)	Brandy & Ray J (2001)		
		Arms Around The World (4)	Louise (1997)
Another Day In Paradise (2)	Phil Collins (1989)	Arms Of Mary (5)	Sutherland Brothers & Quiver (1976)
Another Lover (9)	Dane (2001)		
Another Night (2)	MC Sar & The Real McCoy (1994)	Army Of Me (10)	Björk (1995)
		Around The World (5)	Bing Crosby (1957)
		Around The World (5)	Daft Punk (1997)
Another One Bites The Dust (5)	Queen featuring Wyclef Jean, Pras Michel and Free (1998)	Around The World (7)	East 17 (1994)
		Around The World (8)	Gracie Fields (1957)
		Around The World (4)	Ronnie Hilton (1957)
Another One Bites The Dust (7)	Queen (1980)	Art For Art's Sake (5)	10CC (1975)
Another Rock And Roll Christmas (7)	Gary Glitter (1984)	Arthur's Theme (Best That You Can Do) (7)	Christopher Cross (1982)

Title	Group/Artiste	Title	Group/Artiste
As (4)	George Michael & Mary J Blige (1999)	Baby It's You (7)	Beatles (1995)
		Baby Jane (1)	Rod Stewart (1983)
		Baby Jump (re-entry) (1)	Mungo Jerry (1971)
As I Love You (re-entry) (1)	Shirley Bassey (1959)	Baby Let Me Take You Home (21) first hit	Animals (1964)
As Long As He Needs Me (2)	Shirley Bassey (1960)	Baby Love (1)	Supremes (1964)
As Long As You Love Me (3)	Backstreet Boys (1997)	Baby Make It Soon (9)	Marmalade (1969)
		Baby Now That I've Found You (1)	Foundations (1967)
As Tears Go By (9)	Marianne Faithfull (1964)	Baby One More Time (1)	Britney Spears (1999)
As Time Goes By (5)	Dooley Wilson (1977)	Baby Please Don't Go (10)	Them (1965)
As Usual (5)	Brenda Lee (1964)	Babylon (5)	David Gray (2000)
As You Like It (5)	Adam Faith (1962)	Babylon's Burning (7) first hit	Ruts (1979)
Ashes To Ashes (1)	David Bowie (1980)	Baby's Got A Temper (5)	Prodigy (2002)
At My Most Beautiful (10)	REM (1999)	Back For Good (1)	Take That (1995)
At Night (6)	Shakedown (2002)	Back Here (re-issue) (5)	BBMak (2001)
At The Club / Saturday Night At The Movies (re-entry) (3)	Drifters (1972)	Back Home (1)	England World Cup Squad (1970)
At The Hop (3)	Danny & The Juniors (1958)	Back In My Life (4)	Alice Deejay (1999)
		Back Off Boogaloo (2)	Ringo Starr (1972)
Atlantis (2)	Shadows (1963)	Back Street Luv (4) first and only hit	Curved Air (1971)
Atmosphere (7)	Russ Abbot (1984)	Back To Life (However Do You Want Me)(1)	Soul II Soul featuring Caron Wheeler (1989)
Atomic (1)	Blondie (1980)		
Attention To Me (9)	Nolans (1981)	Back To The Sixties (4)	Tight Fit (1981)
Auf Weidersehen (10)	Vera Lynn (1952)	Back Together Again (3)	Roberta Flack & Donny Hathaway (1980)
Australia (7)	Manic Street Preachers (1996)		
Autobahn (11) first hit	Kraftwerk (1975)	Backstage (4)	Gene Pitney (1966)
Automatic (2)	Pointer Sisters (1984)	Bad (3)	Michael Jackson (1987)
Automatic High (2)	S Club Juniors (2002)	Bad Actress (10)	Terrorvision (1996)
		Bad Bad Boy (10)	Nazareth (1973)
Automatic Lover (4)	Dee D Jackson (1978)	Bad Boy (7)	Marty Wilde (1959)
		Bad Boys (2)	Wham! (1983)
Automatically Sunshine (10)	Supremes (1972)	Bad Girl (10)	Madonna (1993)
Autumn Almanac (3)	Kinks (1967)	Bad Intentions (4)	Dr Dre featuring Knoc-Turn'al (2002)
Avenging Angels (6)	Space (1998)		
Axel F (2)	Harold Faltermeyer (1985)	Bad Moon Rising (1)	Creedence Clearwater Revival (1969)
Axel F / Keep Pushin' (7)	Clock (1995)		
Ay Ay Ay Ay Moosey (10)	Modern Romance (1981)	Bad To Me (1)	Billy J Kramer And The Dakotas (1963)
B With Me (5)	Mis-Teeq (2002)	Bad Touch, The (4)	Bloodhound Gang (2000)
Babe (6)	Styx (1980)		
Babe (1)	Take That (1993)	Bag It Up (1)	Geri Halliwell (2000)
Babooshka (5)	Kate Bush (1980)	Baggy Trousers (3)	Madness (1980)
Baby Baby (5)	Corona (1995)	Bailamos (4)	Enrique Iglesias (1999)
Baby Baby (4)	Frankie Lymon & Teenagers (1957)		
		Baker Street (3) first hit	Gerry Rafferty (1978)
Baby Baby (2)	Amy Grant (1991)	Baker Street (2)	Undercover (1992)
Baby Can I Hold You / Shooting Star (2)	Boyzone / Stephen Gately (1997)	Ball Of Confusion (7)	Temptations (1970)
Baby Come Back (1)	Pato Banton (1994)	Ball Park Incident (6) first hit	Wizzard (1972)
Baby Come Back (1)	Equals (1968)	Ballad Of Bonnie And Clyde (1)	Georgie Fame (1967)
Baby Come On Over (5)	Samantha Mumba (2001)	Ballad Of Davy Crockett (2)	Bill Hayes (1956)
Baby Don't Change Your Mind (4)	Gladys Knight & The Pips (1977)	Ballad Of Davy Crockett, The (3)	Tennessee Ernie Ford (1956)
Baby Face (2)	Little Richard (1959)	Ballad Of John And Yoko (1)	Beatles (1969)
Baby I Don't Care (3)	Transvision Vamp (1989)	Ballad Of Paladin (10)	Duane Eddy (1962)
		Ballad Of Tom Jones, The (4)	Space with Cerys of Catatonia (1998)
Baby I Know (10)	Rubettes (1977)		
Baby I Love You (8)	Dave Edmunds (1973)	Ballroom Blitz, The (2)	Sweet (1973)
		Bamboogie (2)	Bamboo (1998)
Baby I Love You (8)	Ramones (1980)	Banana Boat Song (8) first hit	Shirley Bassey (1957)
Baby I Love Your Way (2)	Big Mountain (1994)		
Baby I Love Your Way – Freebird (6)	Will To Power (1989)	Banana Boat Song (Day-O) (2) first hit	Harry Belafonte (1957)

Title	Group/Artiste	Title	Group/Artiste
Banana Republic (3)	Boomtown Rats (1980)	Beautiful (10)	Matt Darey with Marcella Woods (2002)
Banana Rock (9)	Wombles (1974)		
Banana Splits (7)	Dickies (1979)	Beautiful Day (1)	U2 (2000)
Band Of Gold (6) first and only hit	Don Cherry (1956)	Beautiful Ones (8)	Suede (1996)
		Beautiful Stranger (2)	Madonna (1999)
Band Of Gold (1)	Freda Payne (1970)	Beauty And The Beast (9) first hit	Celine Dion & Peabo Bryson (1992)
Band On The Run (3)	Paul McCartney & Wings (1974)	Because I Got High (1)	Afroman (2001)
Bang Bang (2) first hit	B A Robertson (1979)	Because I Love You (The Postman Song) (6)	Stevie B (1991)
Bang Bang (My Baby Shot Me Down) (3)	Cher (1966)	Because Of You (3)	Scanty Sandwich (2000)
Bangers And Mash (22)	Peter Sellers and Sophia Loren (1961)	Because The Night (5)	Patti Smith Group (1978)
		Because They're Young (2)	Duane Eddy (1960)
Bangin' Man (3)	Slade (1974)	Because We Want To (1) first hit	Billie (1998)
Bangla-Desh (10)	George Harrison (1971)	Because You Loved Me (5)	Celine Dion (1996)
		Because You're Mine (3)	Mario Lanza (1952)
Banks Of The Ohio (6)	Olivia Newton-John (1971)	Because You're Mine (6)	Nat 'King' Cole (1952)
Banner Man (3)	Blue Mink (1971)	Because You're Mine (re-entry) (10)	Nat 'King' Cole (1953)
Barbados (1)	Typically Tropical (1975)	Bed Sitter (4)	Soft Cell (1981)
Barbara Ann (3)	Beach Boys (1966)	Beds Are Burning (48) first hit	Midnight Oil (1988)
Barber's Adagio For Strings (4)	William Orbit (1999)	Beds Are Burning (re-issue) (6)	Midnight Oil (1989)
Barbie Girl (1) first hit	Aqua (1997)	Bedtime Story (4)	Madonna (1995)
Barcelona (2)	Freddy Mercury & Montserrat Caballé (1987)	Beetlebum (1)	Blur (1997)
		Before (7)	Pet Shop Boys (1996)
Barcelona (re-issue) (2)	Freddy Mercury & Montserrat Caballé (1992)	Beg Steal Or Borrow (2)	New Seekers (1972)
		Begin The Beguine (1)	Julio Iglesias (1981)
		Behind A Painted Smile (5)	Isley Brothers (1969)
Barrel Of A Gun (4)	Depeche Mode (1997)	Behind The Groove (6)	Teena Marie (1980)
		Being Boiled (6)	Human League (1982)
Bartender And The Thief, The (3)	Stereophonics (1998)	Being Brave (10)	Menswear (1996)
Basket Case (7)	Green Day (1995)	Being With You (1)	Smokey Robinson (1981)
Bat Out Of Hell (re-issue) (8)	Meat Loaf (1993)		
Batdance (2)	Prince (1989)	Belfast (8)	Boney M (1977)
Battle (10)	Wookie featuring Lain (2000)		
		Belfast Child (1)	Simple Minds (1989)
Battle Of New Orleans (2)	Lonnie Donegan & His Skiffle Group (1959)	Believe (1)	Cher (1998)
		Believe In Me (8)	Utah Saints (1993)
		Belissima (4)	DJ Quicksilver (1997)
Be Alone No More (6) first hit	Another Level (1998)	Bell Bottom Blues (4) first hit	Alma Cogan (1954)
Be Careful (7)	Sparkle featuring R Kelly (1998)	Ben (7)	Michael Jackson (1972)
Be Cool (7)	Paffendorf (2002)		
Be Mine (4)	Lance Fortune (1960)	Ben (5)	Marti Webb (1985)
Be My Baby (6)	Vanessa Paradis (1992)	Bend It (2)	Dave Dee, Dozy, Beaky, Mick & Tich (1966)
Be My Baby (4)	Ronettes (1963)		
Be My Girl (2)	Jim Dale (1957)	Bend Me Shape Me (3)	Amen Corner (1968)
Be Quick Or Be Dead (2)	Iron Maiden (1992)	Bernadette (8)	Four Tops (1967)
Be The First To Believe (6) first hit	A1 (1999)	Best Disco In Town, The (10)	Ritchie Family (1976)
		Best In Me (8)	Let Loose (1995)
Be There (8)	UNKLE featuring Ian Brown (1999)	Best Of Me, The (2)	Cliff Richard (1989)
		Best Of My Love (4)	Emotions (1977)
Beat Dis (2) first and biggest hit	Bomb The Bass (1988)	Best Thing That Ever Happened To Me (7)	Gladys Knight & The Pips (1975)
Beat Goes On (11) first hit	All Seeing I, The (1998)	Best Things In Life Are Free (remix), The (7)	Luther Vandross & Janet Jackson (1995)
Beat It (3)	Michael Jackson (1983)	Best Things In Life Are Free, The (2)	Luther Vandross & Janet Jackson with BBD and Ralph Tresvant (1992)
Beat Mama (9)	Cast (1999)		
Beat Surrender (1)	Jam (1982)		
Beat The Clock (10)	Sparks (1979)	Best Years Of Our Lives (4)	Modern Romance (1982)
Beatles Movie Medley (10)	Beatles (1982)		
Beatnik Fly (8)	Johnny & The Hurricanes (1960)	Best, The (5)	Tina Turner (1989)

Title	Group/Artiste	Title	Group/Artiste
Betcha By Golly Wow (13) first hit	Stylistics (1972)	Blackberry Way (1)	Move (1968)
Bette Davis Eyes (10) first and biggest hit	Kim Carnes (1981)	Blame It On The Boogie (4) first hit	Big Fun (1989)
Better Best Forgotten (2)	Steps (1999)	Blame It On The Boogie (8)	Jacksons (1978)
Better Day (9)	Ocean Colour Scene (1997)	(Blame It) On The Pony Express (7)	Johnny Johnson & The Bandwagon (1970)
Better Love Next Time (8)	Dr Hook (1980)	Blame It On The Weatherman (1)	B*Witched (1999)
Better Off Alone (2)	DJ Jurgen presents Alice DeeJay (1999)	Blanket On The Ground (6)	Billie Jo Spears (1975)
Better The Devil You Know (2)	Kylie Minogue (1990)	Blaze Of Glory (13) first solo hit	Jon Bon Jovi (1990)
Better Watch Out (10)	Ant & Dec (1996)	Bless You (5)	Tony Orlando (1961)
Beyond The Stars (8)	David Whitfield (1955)	Blind Vision (10)	Blancmange (1983)
Big Apple (8)	Kajagoogoo (1983)	Blinded By The Light (6)	Manfred Mann's Earth Band (1976)
Big Bad John (2)	Jimmy Dean (1961)		
Big Big World (5)	Emilia (1998)	Blinded By The Sun (7)	Seahorses (1997)
Big Boys Don't Cry / Rockin' Robin (10)	Lolly (1999)	Block Rockin' Beats (1)	Chemical Brothers (1997)
Big Brother UK TV Theme (4)	Element Four (2000)	Blockbuster (1)	Sweet (1973)
Big Fun (4)	Gap Band (1986)	Blood On The Dancefloor (1)	Michael Jackson (1997)
Big Fun (8) first hit	Inner City (1988)		
Big Hunk O' Love, A (4)	Elvis Presley with The Jordanaires (1959)	Bloodnok's Rock 'N' Roll Call / Ying Tong Song (3)	Goons (1956)
Big In Japan (8) first and only hit	Alphaville (1984)	Blossom Fell, A (10)	Ronnie Hilton (1955)
Big Love (9)	Fleetwood Mac (1987)	Blossom Fell, A (3)	Nat 'King' Cole (1955)
		Blossom Fell, A (9)	Dickie Valentine (1955)
Big Man (2)	Four Preps (1958)	Blow The House Down (10)	Living In A Box (1989)
Big Mistake (2)	Natalie Imbruglia (1998)	Blow Ya Mind (6)	Lock 'N' Load (2000)
Big Seven (8)	Judge Dread (1972)	Blowing Wild (2)	Frankie Laine (1954)
Big Ship (8)	Cliff Richard (1969)		
Billie Jean (1)	Michael Jackson (1983)	Blue Angels (6)	Pras (1998)
		Blue Bayou / Mean Woman Blues (3)	Roy Orbison (1963)
Bills Bills Bills (6)	Destiny's Child (1999)	Blue (Da Ba Dee) (1)	Eiffel 65 (1999)
Billy Don't Be A Hero (1)	Paper Lace (1974)	Blue Eyes (8)	Elton John (1982)
Bimbo (7)	Ruby Wright (1954)	Blue Eyes (3)	Don Partridge (1968)
Bionic Santa (10)	Chris Hill (1976)	Blue Guitar (8)	Justin Hayward & John Lodge (1975)
Bird Dog (2)	Everly Brothers (1958)	Blue Is The Colour (5)	Chelsea FC (1972)
Bird Of Paradise (6)	Snowy White (1983)	Blue Jean (6)	David Bowie (1984)
Birdhouse In Your Soul (6)	They Might Be Giants (1990)	Blue Monday (re-entry) (9)	New Order (1983)
		Blue Monday (remix) (3)	New Order (1988)
Birdie Song (The Birdie Dance) (2)	Tweets (1981)	Blue Moon (1)	Marcels (1961)
Bitch (6)	Meredith Brooks (1997)	Blue Moon (9)	Elvis Presley (1956)
		Blue Moon / Only You (9)	John Alford (1996)
Bits And Pieces (2)	Dave Clark Five (1964)	Blue Room (8)	Orb (1992)
Bitter Sweet Symphony (2)	Verve (1997)	Blue Savannah (3)	Erasure (1990)
Bitterest Pill (I Ever Had To Swallow) (2)	Jam (1982)	Blue Star (The Medic Theme) (2)	Cyril Stapleton Orchestra (1955)
Black And White (6)	Greyhound (1971)	Blue Suede Shoes (10)	Carl Perkins (1956)
Black Betty (7)	Ram Jam (1977)	Blue Suede Shoes (9)	Elvis Presley (1956)
Black Coffee (1)	All Saints (2000)	Blue Tango (8)	Ray Martin Orchestra (1952)
Black-Eyed Boy (5)	Texas (1997)		
Black Hills Of Dakota (7)	Doris Day (1954)	Blue Tango (re-entry) (10)	Ray Martin Orchestra (1952)
Black Is Black (2)	La Belle Epoque (1977)	Blue Velvet (2)	Bobby Vinton (1990)
Black Is Black (2)	Los Bravos (1966)	Blueberry Hill (re-entry) (6)	Fats Domino (1956)
Black Night (2) first hit	Deep Purple (1970)	Blurred (6)	Pianoman (1996)
Black Or White (1)	Michael Jackson (1991)	Blurry (8)	Puddle Of Mudd (2002)
Black Skin Blue-Eyed Boys (9)	Equals (1970)	Bo Diddley (4)	Buddy Holly (1963)
Black Suits Comin' (Nod Ya Head) (3)	Will Smith featuring Tra-Knox (2002)	Boat That I Row, The (6)	Lulu (1967)
		Bobby's Girl (3)	Susan Maughan (1962)
Black Superman (Muhammad Ali) (7)	Johnny Wakelin & Kinshasa Band (1975)	Body And Soul (9)	Mai Tai (1985)
		Body Groove (3)	Architechs featuring Nana (2000)
Black Velvet (2)	Alannah Myles (1990)	Body II Body (5)	Samantha Mumba (2000)

M
U
S
I
C

P
O
P

Title	Group/Artiste	Title	Group/Artiste
Body Talk (4)	Imagination (1981)	Boys Are Back In Town, The (8)	Thin Lizzy (1976)
Bodyshakin' (3)	911 (1997)	Boys Cry (8)	Eden Kane (1964)
Bohemian Like You (re-issue) (5)	Dandy Warhols (2001)	Boys Keep Swinging (7)	David Bowie (1979)
		Boys (Summertime Love) (3)	Sabrina (1988)
Bohemian Rhapsody (1)	Queen (1975)	Brand New Key (4)	Melanie (1972)
Bohemian Rhapsody (re-issue) / These Are The Days Of Our Lives (1)	Queen (1991)	Brass In Pocket (1)	Pretenders (1979)
		Break Away (6)	Beach Boys (1969)
Bomb Diggy (6)	Another Level (1999)	Break My Stride (4)	Matthew Wilder (1984)
Bomb! (These Sounds Fall Into My Mind)(5)	Bucketheads (1995)	Break The Rules (8)	Status Quo (1974)
		Breakaway (4)	Tracey Ullman (1983)
Boney M Megamix (7)	Boney M (1992)		
Boogie Nights (2)	Heatwave (1977)	Breakdance Party (9)	Break Machine (1984)
Boogie Oogie Oogie (3)	A Taste Of Honey (1978)	Breakfast At Tiffany's (1)	Deep Blue Something (1996)
Boogie Wonderland (4)	Earth Wind & Fire with The Emotions (1979)	Breakfast In America (9)	Supertramp (1979)
		Breakfast In Bed (6)	UB40 featuring Chrissie Hynde (1988)
Book Of Days (10)	Enya (1992)		
Book Of Love (8)	Mudlarks (1958)	Breakin' ... There's No Stopping Us Now (5)	Ollie & Jerry (1984)
Book (re-entry), The (10)	David Whitfield (1954)	Breakin' Down The Walls Of Heartache (4)	Johnny Johnson & The Bandwagon (1968)
Book, The (5)	David Whitfield (1954)		
Boom Bang-A-Bang (2)	Lulu (1969)	Breaking Up Is Hard To Do (3)	Partridge Family (1972)
Boom Boom Boom (1)	Outhere Brothers (1995)	Breaking Up Is Hard To Do (7)	Neil Sedaka (1962)
Boom Boom Boom Boom (1)	Vengaboys (1999)	Breakout (4)	Swing Out Sister (1986)
Boom! Shake The Room (1)	Jazzy Jeff & The Fresh Prince (1993)	Breakthru (7)	Queen (1989)
Boombastic (1)	Shaggy (1995)	Breath Of Life (8)	Erasure (1992)
Bootie Call (1)	All Saints (1998)	Breathe (1)	Prodigy (1996)
Bootylicious (2)	Destiny's Child (2001)	Breathe Again (2)	Toni Braxton (1994)
		Breathless (1)	Corrs (2000)
Bop Bop Baby (5)	Westlife (2002)	Breathless (8)	Jerry Lee Lewis (1958)
Borderline (2)	Madonna (1986)		
Born Free (6)	Vic Reeves & The Roman Numerals (1994)	Breeze And I, The (5)	Caterina Valente (1955)
Born Slippy (2)	Underworld (1996)	Bridge Of Sighs, The (9) first hit	David Whitfield (1953)
Born To Be Alive (10)	Patrick Hernandez (1979)	Bridge Over Troubled Water (1)	Simon & Garfunkel (1970)
Born To Be With You (8)	Chordettes (1956)	Bridget The Midget (Queen of the Blues) (2)	Ray Stevens (1971)
Born To Be With You (5)	Dave Edmunds (1973)		
Born To Make You Happy (1)	Britney Spears (2000)	Bright Eyes (1)	Art Garfunkel (1979)
		Brimful Of Asha (remix) (1)	Cornershop (1998)
Born Too Late (5)	Poni-Tails (1958)	Bring A Little Water Sylvie/ Dead Or Alive (7)	Lonnie Donegan & His Skiffle Group (1956)
Born With A Smile On My Face (2) first hit	Stephanie De Sykes with Rain (1974)		
Boss Drum (4)	Shamen (1992)	Bring It All Back (1) first hit	S Club 7 (1999)
Both Sides Now (14) first hit	Judy Collins (1970)	Bring It On Home To Me (7)	Animals (1965)
Both Sides Of The Story (7)	Phil Collins (1993)	Bring Me Edelweiss (5)	Edelweiss (1989)
Bouncer, The (7)	Kicks Like A Mule (1992)	Bring The Noise (14) biggest hit	Anthrax featuring Chuck D (1991)
Bound 4 Da Reload (Casualty) (1)	Oxide & Neutrina (2000)	Bring Your Daughter ... To The Slaughter (1)	Iron Maiden (1991)
Bow Wow (That's My Name) (6)	Lil Bow Wow (2001)	Bringing On Back The Good Times (9)	Love Affair (1969)
Boxer Beat (3)	Jo Boxers (1983)		
Boxer, The (6)	Simon & Garfunkel (1969)	Britannia Rag (re-entry) (5)	Winifred Atwell (1953)
Boy From New York City (2)	Darts (1978)	British Hustle / Peace On Earth (8)	Hi Tension (1978)
Boy From Nowhere, A (2)	Tom Jones (1987)	Brits 1990, The (2)	Various Artists (1990)
Boy Is Mine, The (2)	Brandy & Monica (1998)		
Boy Named Sue, A (4)	Johnny Cash (1969)	Broken Down Angel (9)	Nazareth (1973)
Boy You Knock Me Out (3)	Tatyana Ali featuring Will Smith (1999)	Broken Hearted Melody (7)	Sarah Vaughan (1959)
Boys (7)	Britney Spears featuring P Williams (2002)	Broken Wings (6)	Art & Dotty Todd (1953)
		Broken Wings (4)	Mr Mister (1985)
		Broken Wings (re-entry) (1)	Stargazers (1953)

Title	Group/Artiste	Title	Group/Artiste
Brontosaurus (7)	Move (1970)	Call, The (8)	Backstreet Boys
Brother Louie (7)	Hot Chocolate		(2001)
	(1973)	Calling (7)	Geri Halliwell (2001)
Brother Louie (4)	Modern Talking	Calling All The Heroes (6)	It Bites (1986)
	(1986)	Calling Occupants Of	
Brown Sugar/Bitch/Let It	Rolling Stones	Interplanetary Craft (9)	Carpenters (1977)
Rock (2)	(1971)	Calling Your Name (4)	Marilyn (1983)
Brown-eyed Handsome Man (3)	Buddy Holly (1963)	Camels (9)	Santos (2001)
Buck Rogers (5)	Feeder (2001)	Camouflage (4)	Stan Ridgway (1986)
Buddy/The Magic Number (7)	De La Soul (1989)	Can Can (3)	Bad Manners (1981)
biggest hit		Can Can You Party (8)	Jive Bunny & The
Buffalo Gals (9)	Malcolm McLaren		Mastermixers
	and The World		(1990)
	Famous	Can I Play With Madness (3)	Iron Maiden (1988)
	Supreme Team	Can I Take You Home Little	
	(1982)	Girl (10)	Drifters (1975)
Buffalo Soldier (4)	Bob Marley & The	Can I Touch You ... There (6)	Michael Bolton
	Wailers (1983)		(1995)
Buffalo Stance (3) first hit	Neneh Cherry (1988)	Can The Can (1)	Suzi Quatro (1973)
Bug A Boo (9)	Destiny's Child	Can We Fix It? (1)	Bob The Builder
	(1999)		(2000)
Buggin' Me (6)	True Steppers with	Can You Feel It (6)	Jacksons (1981)
	Dane Bowers	Can You Feel The Force (5)	Real Thing (1979)
	(2000)	Can You Forgive Her (7)	Pet Shop Boys
Build Me Up Buttercup (2)	Foundations (1968)		(1993)
Bullet In The Gun (2000 remix)	Planet Perfecto	Candida (9) first hit	Dawn (1971)
(7)	(2000)	Candle In The Wind 97 /	Elton John (1997)
Bulls On Parade (8)	Rage Against The	Something About	
	Machine (1996)	The Way You Look Tonight (1)	
Bump N' Grind (8)	R Kelly (1995)	Candle In The Wind (re-issue) (5)	Elton John (1988)
Bump, The (3)	Kenny (1974)	Candy (6)	Mandy Moore (2000)
Bunsen Burner (9)	John Otway (2002)	Candy Girl (1)	New Edition (1983)
Buona Sera (7)	Acker Bilk & His	Candy Man (6)	Brian Poole & The
	Paramount Jazz		Tremeloes (1964)
	Band (1960)	Canned Heat (4)	Jamiroquai (1999)
Burning Bridges	Status Quo (1988)	Can't Be With You Tonight (2)	Judy Boucher (1987)
(On And Off And On Again) (5)		Can't Buy Me Love (1)	Beatles (1964)
Burning Down The House (7)	Tom Jones & The	Can't Fight The Moonlight (1)	LeAnn Rimes (2000)
	Cardigans (1999)	Can't Get By Without You (2)	Real Thing (1976)
Burning Heart (5)	Survivor (1986)	Can't Get By Without You	Real Thing (1986)
Burning Love (7)	Elvis Presley (1972)	(The Second Decade Remix) (6)	
Bus Stop (5)	Hollies (1966)	Can't Get Enough (8)	Soulsearcher (1999)
But I Do (3)	Clarence 'Frogman'	Can't Get Enough Of Your Love	Barry White (1974)
	Henry (1961)	Babe (8)	
Butterfingers (re-entry) (8)	Tommy Steele (1957)	Can't Get Used To Losing You (3)	Beat (1983)
Butterfly (3)	Crazy Town (2001)	Can't Get Used To Losing You (2)	Andy Williams (1963)
Butterfly (1) first hit	Andy Williams (1957)	Can't Get You Out Of My	Kylie Minogue (2001)
By The Way (2)	Red Hot Chili	Head (1)	
	Peppers (2002)	Can't Give You Anything	Stylistics (1975)
Bye Bye Baby (1)	Bay City Rollers	(But My Love) (1)	
	(1975)	Can't Help Falling In Love (4)	Stylistics (1976)
Bye Bye Baby (7)	TQ (1999)	Can't Help Falling In Love (3)	Andy Williams
Bye Bye Bye (3)	N Sync (2000)		(1970)
Bye Bye Love (6) first hit	Everly Brothers	Can't I (9)	Nat 'King' Cole
	(1957)		(1953)
C U When You Get There (3)	Coolio featuring 40	Can't I (re-entry) (6)	Nat 'King' Cole
	Thevz (1997)		(1953)
Ca Plane Pour Moi (8)	Plastic Bertrand	Can't I (re-entry) (10)	Nat 'King' Cole
	(1978)		(1953)
Calendar Girl (8)	Neil Sedaka (1961)	Can't Keep This Feeling In (10)	Cliff Richard (1998)
California Dreamin' (re-entry) (9)	Mamas & The Papas	Can't Shake The Feeling (8)	Big Fun (1989)
	(1997)	Can't Stand Losing You	Police (1979)
California Love (6)	2Pac featuring Dr	(re-release) (2)	
	Dre (1996)	Can't Stay Away From You (7)	Gloria Estefan &
California Man (7)	Move (1972)		Miami Sound
Call Me (1)	Blondie (1980)		Machine (1989)
Call Me (2)	Spagna (1987)	Can't Take My Eyes Off You (4)	Boystown Gang
(Call Me) Number One (2)	Tremeloes (1969)		(1982)
Call Up The Groups (3) first hit	Barron Knights with	Can't Take My Eyes Off You (5)	Andy Williams
	Duke D'Mond		(1968)
	(1964)	Can't Wait Another Minute (7)	Five Star (1986)

Title	Group/Artiste	Title	Group/Artiste
Can't You See That She's Mine (10)	Dave Clark Five (1964)	Change (4)	Tears For Fears (1983)
Captain Beaky / Wilfred The Weasel (5)	Keith Michell (1980)	Change Would Do You Good, A (8)	Sheryl Crow (1997)
Captain Of Her Heart, The (8)	Double (1986)	Changes (3)	2Pac (1999)
Car 67 (7)	Driver 67 (1978)	Changing Partners (10)	Bing Crosby (1954)
Car Wash (9) first hit	Rose Royce (1976)	Changing Partners (4)	Kay Starr (1954)
Cara Mia (1)	David Whitfield with Mantovani (1954)	Changing Partners (re-entry) (9)	Bing Crosby (1954)
Caramel (9)	City High featuring Eve (2002)	Changingman, The (7)	Paul Weller (1995)
		Chanson D'Amour (1)	Manhattan Transfer (1977)
Caravan Of Love (1)	Housemartins (1986)		
Careless Hands (6)	Des O'Connor (1967)	Chant No. 1 (I Don't Need This Pressure On) (3)	Spandau Ballet (1981)
Careless Whisper (1) first solo hit	George Michael (1984)	Charlie Brown (6)	Coasters (1959)
Caribbean Disco Show, The (8)	Lobo (1981)	Charly (3) first hit	Prodigy (1991)
Caribbean Queen (No More Love On The Run) (6)	Billy Ocean (1984)	Charmaine (6) first hit	Bachelors (1963)
		Charmless Man (5)	Blur (1996)
		Chase The Sun (5)	Planet Funk (2001)
Carnation (6) B side of Going Underground	Liam Gallagher and Steve Craddock (1999)	Check Out The Groove (10)	Bobby Thurston (1980)
Carnaval De Paris (5)	Dario G (1998)	Check This Out (6)	LA Mix (1988)
Carnival (72) first hit	Cardigans (1995)	Cheeky Song (Touch My Bum) (2)	Cheeky Girls (2002)
Carnival Is Over, The (1)	Seekers (1965)	Chequered Love (4)	Kim Wilde (1981)
Carolina Moon / Stupid Cupid (1)	Connie Francis (1958)	Cherish (4)	Kool & The Gang (1985)
Caroline (5)	Status Quo (1973)	Cherish (3)	Madonna (1989)
Carrie (4)	Cliff Richard (1980)	Cherish/Could It Be Forever (2) first hit	David Cassidy (1972)
Carrie-Anne (3)	Hollies (1967)	Cherry Pink And Apple Blossom White (1)	Eddie Calvert (1955)
Carry Me Home (9)	Gloworm (1994)		
Cars (1)	Gary Numan (1979)	Cherry Pink And Apple Blossom White (1)	Perez 'Prez' Prado (King of the Mambo) (1955)
Cartoon Heroes (7)	Aqua (2000)		
Casanova (9)	Levert (1987)		
Case Of The Ex (3)	Mya (2001)	Chi Mai (The Theme From The Life And Times Of Lloyd George) (2)	Ennio Morricone (1981)
Cassius (7)	Cassius 1999 (1999)		
Cast Your Fate To The Wind (5)	Sounds Orchestral (1964)	Chicka Boom (5)	Guy Mitchell (1953)
		Chicka Boom (re-entry) (4)	Guy Mitchell (1954)
Castles In The Sky (3)	Ian Van Dahl (2001)	Chicken Song, The (1)	Spitting Image (1986)
Cat Amongst The Pigeons / Silent Night (2)	Bros (1988)		
Cat Crept In, The (2)	Mud (1974)	Child (3)	Mark Owen (1996)
Catch A Falling Star (9)	Perry Como (1958)	Children (2)	Robert Miles (1996)
Catch The Wind (4) first hit	Donovan (1965)	Children Of The Revolution (2)	T Rex (1972)
Catch Us If You Can (5)	Dave Clark Five (1965)	Child's Prayer, A (7)	Hot Chocolate (1975)
Cathy's Clown (1)	Everly Brothers (1960)	China Girl (2)	David Bowie (1983)
		China In Your Hand (1)	T'Pau (1987)
Cats In The Cradle (7)	Ugly Kid Joe (1993)	China Tea (5)	Russ Conway (1959)
Caught In The Middle (2)	A1 (2002)		
Caught Out There (4)	Kelis (2000)	Chiquitita (2)	Abba (1979)
Causing A Commotion (4)	Madonna (1987)	Chirpy Chirpy Cheep Cheep (1)	Middle Of The Road (1971)
Cecilia (4)	Suggs and Louchie Lou & Michie One (1996)		
		Chocolate Box (9)	Bros (1989)
		Chocolate Salty Balls (1)	Chef (1998)
Celebration (7)	Kool & The Gang (1980)	Choose Life (6)	PF Project featuring Ewan McGregor (1997)
Centerfold (3)	J Geils Band (1982)		
Certain Smile, A (4)	Johnny Mathis (1958)	Chorus (3)	Erasure (1991)
		Chosen Few, The (7)	Dooleys (1979)
C'est La Vie (1) first hit	B*Witched (1998)	Christmas Alphabet (1)	Dickie Valentine (1955)
C'est La Vie (3)	Robbie Nevil (1986)		
Chain Gang (9)	Sam Cooke (1960)	Christmas Island (8)	Dickie Valentine (1956)
Chain Gang (9)	Jimmy Young (1956)		
Chain Reaction (1)	Diana Ross (1986)	Church Of The Poison Mind (2)	Culture Club (1983)
Chain Reaction / One For Sorrow (remix) (2)	Steps (2001)	Cigarettes And Alcohol (7)	Oasis (1994)
		Cinderella Rockefella (1)	Esther & Abi Ofarim (1968)
Chains (6) first and biggest hit	Tina Arena (1994)		
Chance (9)	Big Country (1983)	Cindy Incidentally (2)	Faces (1973)
Change (10)	Lisa Stansfield (1991)	Cindy Oh Cindy (5)	Eddie Fisher (1956)
		Circle In The Sand (4)	Belinda Carlisle (1988)

Title	Group/Artiste	Title	Group/Artiste
Circle, The (6)	Ocean Colour Scene (1996)	Come Outside (1)	Mike Sarne with Wendy Richard (1962)
Circles (4)	New Seekers (1972)	Come Play With Me (10)	Wedding Present (1992)
Circus, The (6)	Erasure (1987)	Come Prima (2)	Marino Marini & His Quartet (1958)
Clair (1)	Gilbert O'Sullivan (1972)	Come Softly To Me (6)	Fleetwoods (1959)
Clairvoyant, The (6)	Iron Maiden (1988)	Come Softly To Me (9)	Frankie Vaughan & The Kaye Sisters (1959)
Clapping Song, The (6)	Shirley Ellis (1965)		
Classic (8)	Adrian Gurvitz (1982)	Come Tomorrow (4)	Manfred Mann (1965)
Classical Gas (9)	Mason Williams (1968)	Come What May (2)	Vicky Leandros (1972)
Cleanin' Out My Closet (4)	Eminem (2002)		
Clementine (8)	Bobby Darin (1960)	Come With Me (2)	Puff Daddy featuring Jimmy Page (1998)
Clementine (3)	Mark Owen (1997)		
Cleopatra's Theme (3) first hit	Cleopatra (1998)	Come With Us / The Test (14)	Chemical Brothers (2002)
Clint Eastwood (4)	Gorillaz (2001)		
Close The Door (6)	Stargazers (1955)	Comes A-Long A-Love (1)	Kay Starr (1952)
Close (To The Edit) (8) first hit	Art Of Noise (1984)	Coming Around (5)	Travis (2000)
Close To You (9)	Marti Pellow (2001)	Coming Around Again (10)	Carly Simon (1987)
Close To You (7)	Maxi Priest (1990)	Comin' Home (16) first solo hit	Eric Clapton (1969)
Closer Than Close (4)	Rosie Gaines (1997)	Coming Home Now (4)	Boyzone (1996)
Closer to Me (4)	Five (2001)	Coming Up (2)	Paul McCartney (1980)
Cloud Lucky Seven (2)	Guy Mitchell (1953)		
Cloud Number 9 (6)	Bryan Adams (1999)	Common People (2)	Pulp (1995)
Clouds Across The Moon (6)	Rah Band (1985)	Communication (Somebody Answer The) (5)	Mario Piu (1999)
Club Tropicana (4)	Wham! (1983)	Complex (6)	Gary Numan (1979)
C'Mon Everybody (6)	Eddie Cochran (1959)	Complicated (3)	Avril Lavigne (2002)
		Compliments On Your Kiss (2)	Red Dragon with Brian & Tony Gold (1994)
C'Mon Everybody (3)	Sex Pistols (1979)		
Co-Co (2)	Sweet (1971)		
Coco Jamboo (8)	Mr President (1997)	Computer Love / The Model (re-entry) (1)	Kraftwerk (1981)
Cognoscenti Vs Intelligentsia (4)	Cuban Boys (1999)		
Cold As Ice (4)	MOP (2001)	Concrete And Clay (1)	Unit Four Plus Two (1965)
Colette (9)	Billy Fury (1960)		
Colourblind (1)	Darius (2002)	Condemnation (9)	Depeche Mode (1993)
Colours (4)	Donovan (1965)		
Combine Harvester (Brand New Key) (1)	Wurzels (1976)	Confessin' (1)	Frank Ifield (1963)
		Confide In Me (2)	Kylie Minogue (1994)
Come And Get It (4) first and biggest hit	Badfinger (1970)	Confusion / Last Train To London (8)	Electric Light Orchestra (1979)
Come And Stay With Me (4)	Marianne Faithfull (1965)	Congratulations (1)	Cliff Richard (1968)
		Constantly (4)	Cliff Richard (1964)
Come As You Are (9)	Nirvana (1992)	Contact (6)	Edwin Starr (1979)
Come Baby Come (3)	K7 (1993)	Controversy (5)	Prince (1993)
Come Back And Shake Me (3)	Clodagh Rodgers (1969)	Conversations (7)	Cilla Black (1969)
		Convoy (2)	C W McCall (1976)
Come Back And Stay (4)	Paul Young (1983)	Convoy G.B. (4)	Laurie Lingo & The Dipsticks (1976)
Come Back Brighter (8)	Reef (1997)		
Come Back Darling (10)	UB40 (1998)	Cool For Cats (2)	Squeeze (1979)
Come Back My Love (2)	Darts (1978)	Cool Water (2)	Frankie Laine (1955)
Come Back To What You Know (6)		Cornflake Girl (4)	Tori Amos (1994)
Come In Out Of The Rain (8)	Wendy Moten (1994)	Coronation Rag (re-entry) (5)	Winifred Atwell (1953)
Come Into My Life (7)	Joyce Sims (1988)		
Come Into My World (8)	Kylie Minogue (2002)	Cosmic Girl (6)	Jamiroquai (1996)
		Cotton Eye Joe (1)	Rednex (1994)
Come Live With Me (5)	Heaven 17 (1983)	Cottonfields (5)	Beach Boys (1970)
Come On (21) first hit	Rolling Stones (1963)	Could Have Told You So (6)	Halo James (1989)
		Could I Have This Kiss Forever (7)	Whitney Houston & Enrique Iglesias (2000)
Come On Eileen (1)	Dexy's Midnight Runners (1982)		
Come On Over Baby (All I Want Is You) (8)	Christina Aguilera (2000)	Could It Be Forever / Cherish (2) first hit	David Cassidy (1972)
Come On Let's Go (10)	Tommy Steele (1958)	Could It Be I'm Falling In Love (5)	David Grant & Jaki Graham (1985)
Come On Over To My Place (re-issue) (9)	Drifters (1972)	Could It Be Magic (3)	Take That (1992)
Come On You Reds (1)	Manchester United Football Club (1994)	Could You Be Loved (5)	Bob Marley & The Wailers (1980)

MUSIC POP

Title	Group/Artiste	Title	Group/Artiste
Couldn't Get It Right (10)	Climax Blues Band (1976)	Crying In The Chapel (1)	Elvis Presley with The Jordanaires (1965)
Could've Been (4)	Tiffany (1988)	Crying In The Chapel (re-entry) (7)	Lee Lawrence (1953)
Counting Teardrops (4)	Emile Ford & The Checkmates (1960)	Crying Over You (11) only other hit	Ken Boothe (1974)
Country House (1)	Blur (1995)	Crystal (8)	New Order (2001)
Country Roads (7)	Hermes House Band (2001)	Cubik / Olympic (10)	808 State (1990)
Cover Girl (4)	New Kids On The Block (1990)	Cuddly Toy (re-issue) (4)	Roachford (1989)
		Cuff Of My Shirt (9)	Guy Mitchell (1954)
Coward Of The County (1)	Kenny Rogers (1980)	Cult Of Snap (8)	Snap (1990)
		Cum On Feel The Noize (1)	Slade (1973)
Cowpuncher's Cantata (11) first hit	Max Bygraves (1952)	Cumberland Gap (1)	Lonnie Donegan & His Skiffle Group (1957)
Cowpuncher's Cantata (re-entry) (6)	Max Bygraves (1953)	Cumberland Gap (10)	Vipers Skiffle Group (1957)
Cowpuncher's Cantata (re-entry) (8)	Max Bygraves (1953)	Cupid (7)	Sam Cooke (1961)
Cowpuncher's Cantata (re-entry) (10)	Max Bygraves (1953)	Cupid (6)	Johnny Nash (1969)
Coz I Luv You (1)	Slade (1971)	Cupid – I've Loved You For A Long Time (4)	Detroit Spinners (1980)
Crackers International EP (2)	Erasure (1988)	Cut Some Rug / Castle Rock (7)	Bluetones (1996)
Cracklin' Rosie (3) first hit	Neil Diamond (1970)	Cutter, The (8)	Echo And The Bunnymen (1983)
Cradle Of Love (2)	Johnny Preston (1960)	D.I.S.C.O. (2)	Ottowan (1980)
Crash (5)	Primitives (1988)	D.I.V.O.R.C.E. (1) first hit	Billy Connolly (1975)
Crazy (2)	Seal (1990)	Da Da Da (2)	Trio (1982)
Crazy Crazy Nights (4)	Kiss (1987)	Da Doo Ron Ron (5)	Crystals (1963)
Crazy For You (2)	Let Loose (1994)	Da Funk / Musique (7)	Daft Punk (1997)
Crazy For You (2)	Madonna (1985)	Da Ya Think I'm Sexy? (7)	N-Trance featuring Rod Stewart (1997)
Crazy For You (remix) (2)	Madonna (1991)		
Crazy Horses (2)	Osmonds (1972)	Da Ya Think I'm Sexy? (1)	Rod Stewart (1978)
Crazy Little Party Girl (7)	Aaron Carter (1998)	Daddy Cool (6) first hit	Boney M (1976)
Crazy Little Thing Called Love (2)	Queen (1979)	Daddy Cool / The Girl Can't Help It (6) first hit	Darts (1977)
Crazy Love (10)	M J Cole (2000)		
Crazy Rap (10)	Afroman (2002)	Daddy's Home (2)	Cliff Richard (1981)
Crazy (remix) (6)	Mark Morrison (1996)	Dance Away (2)	Roxy Music (1979)
		Dance Dance Dance (Yowsah Yowsah Yowsah) (6) first hit	Chic (1977)
Creep (7)	Radiohead (1993)		
Creep (re-entry), The (10)	Ken Mackintosh Orchestra (1954)	Dance For Me (6)	Sisqo (2001)
		Dance Into The Light (9)	Phil Collins (1996)
Creep (re-issue) (6)	TLC (1996)	Dance Little Lady Dance (6)	Tina Charles (1976)
Creeque Alley (9)	Mamas & The Papas (1967)	Dance On (1)	Shadows (1962)
		Dance The Night Away (4)	Mavericks (1998)
Criticize (4)	Alexander O'Neal (1987)	Dance To The Music (7)	Sly & The Family Stone (1968)
Crockett's Theme (2)	Jan Hammer (1987)		
Crocodile Rock (5)	Elton John (1972)	Dance With Guitar Man (4)	Duane Eddy & The Rebelettes (1962)
Crocodile Shoes (4)	Jimmy Nail (1994)		
Cross My Broken Heart (6)	Sinitta (1988)	Dance With Me (10)	Debelah Morgan (2001)
Crossroads (1)	Blazin' Squad (2002)		
Crown, The (6)	Gary Byrd & The GB Experience (1983)	Dance With The Devil (3)	Cozy Powell (1973)
		Dance Yourself Dizzy (2)	Liquid Gold (1980)
Cruel Summer (8)	Ace Of Base (1998)	Dancin' Party (4)	Showaddywaddy (1977)
Cruel Summer (8)	Bananarama (1983)		
Cruise Into Christmas (10)	Jane McDonald (1998)	Dancing In The City (3)	Marshall Hain (1978)
Crunch, The (6)	Rah Band (1977)		
Crush (4)	Jennifer Paige (1998)	Dancing In The Dark (re-entry) (4)	Bruce Springsteen (1985)
Crush On You (9)	Aaron Carter (1997)	Dancing In The Moonlight (remix) (7)	Toploader (2000)
Crush On You (5)	Jets (1987)		
Cry For Help (7)	Rick Astley (1991)	Dancing In The Street (1)	David Bowie & Mick Jagger (1985)
Cry Just A Little Bit (3)	Shakin' Stevens (1983)		
Cry Wolf (5)	A-Ha (1986)	Dancing In The Street (re-issue) (4)	Martha Reeves & The Vandellas (1969)
Cryin' In The Rain (6)	Everly Brothers (1962)		
		(Dancing) On A Saturday Night (2) first and biggest hit	Barry Blue (1973)
Crying (1)	Don McLean (1980)		
Crying Game, The (5)	Dave Berry (1964)	Dancing On The Ceiling (7)	Lionel Richie (1986)

Title	Group/Artiste	Title	Group/Artiste
Dancing On The Floor (Hooked On Love) (10)	Third World (1981)	Delaware (3)	Perry Como (1960)
Dancing Queen (1)	Abba (1976)	Delilah (2)	Tom Jones (1968)
Dancing Tight (4)	Galaxy featuring Phil Fearon (1983)	Delilah (7)	Sensational Alex Harvey Band (1975)
Dancing With Tears In My Eyes (3)	Ultravox (1984)	Delta Lady (10)	Joe Cocker (1969)
Dancing With The Captain (8)	Paul Nicholas (1976)	Dem Girlz (I Don't Know Why) (10)	Oxide & Neutrino featuring Kowdean (2002)
Danger Games (8)	Pinkees (1982)		
Daniel (4)	Elton John (1973)	Denis (2) first hit	Blondie (1978)
Darlin' (6)	Frankie Miller (1978)	Desiderata (7)	Les Crane (1972)
Dat (6)	Pluto Shervington (1976)	Design For Life, A (2)	Manic Street Preachers (1996)
Daughter Of Darkness (5)	Tom Jones (1970)	Desire (1)	U2 (1988)
Davy's On The Road Again (6)	Manfred Mann's Earth Band (1978)	Detroit City (8)	Tom Jones (1967)
Day After Day (10)	Badfinger (1972)	Devil Gate Drive (1)	Suzi Quatro (1974)
Day And Night (1)	Billie Piper (2000)	Devil In Disguise (1)	Elvis Presley with The Jordanaires (1963)
Day I Met Marie, The (10)	Cliff Richard (1967)		
Day The Rains Came, The (1)	Jane Morgan (1958)	Devil Woman (9)	Cliff Richard (1976)
Day Trip To Bangor (Didn't We Have A Lovely Time) (3)	Fiddler's Dram (1979)	Devil Woman (5)	Marty Robbins (1962)
		Devil You Know, The (10)	Jesus Jones (1993)
		Devil's Answer, The (4)	Atomic Rooster (1971)
Day Tripper / We Can Work It Out (1)	Beatles (1965)	Diamonds (1)	Jet Harris & Tony Meehan (1963)
Day We Caught The Train, The (4)	Ocean Colour Scene (1996)	Diana (1) first hit	Paul Anka (1957)
Day We Find Love, The (4)	911 (1997)	Diane (1)	Bachelors (1964)
Day Without Love, A (6)	Love Affair (1968)	Diary Of Horace Wimp, The (8)	Electric Light Orchestra (1979)
Daydream (2)	Lovin' Spoonful (1966)		
Daydream Believer (5)	Monkees (1967)	Did You Ever (2)	Nancy Sinatra & Lee Hazlewood (1971)
Daydreamer / The Puppy Song (1)	David Cassidy (1973)	Die Another Day (3)	Madonna (2002)
Daydreamin' (6)	Tatyana Ali (1998)	Different Beat, A (1)	Boyzone (1996)
Days Of Pearly Spencer, The (4)	Marc Almond (1992)	Different Corner, A (1)	George Michael (1986)
Daysleeper (6)	REM (1998)	Dilemma (1)	Nelly featuring Kelly Rowland (2002)
D-Days (10)	Hazel O'Connor (1981)	Dime And A Dollar (8)	Guy Mitchell (1954)
De Do Do Do De Da Da Da (5)	Police (1980)	Dime And A Dollar (re-entry) (8)	Guy Mitchell (1954)
Dead End Street (5)	Kinks (1966)	Dirty (1)	Christina Aguilera featuring Redman (2002)
Dead From The Waist Down (7)	Catatonia (1999)		
Dead Giveaway (8)	Shalamar (1983)	Dirty Cash (2)	Adventures Of Stevie V (1990)
Dead Ringer For Love (5)	Meat Loaf (1981)	Dirty Diana (4)	Michael Jackson (1988)
Dean And I, The (10)	10CC (1973)		
Dear Jessie (5)	Madonna (1989)	Disappointed (6)	Electronic (1992)
Dear John (10)	Status Quo (1982)	Disco Connection (10)	Isaac Hayes (1976)
Dear Lonely Hearts (4)	Nat 'King' Cole (1962)	Disco Duck (Part One) (6)	Rick Dees & His Cast Of Idiots (1976)
Dear Prudence (3)	Siouxsie & The Banshees (1983)		
Death Of A Clown (3)	Dave Davies (1967)	Disco Stomp (6)	Hamilton Bohannon (1975)
Debora / One Inch Rock (re-issue) (7)	Tyrannosaurus Rex (1972)	Disco 2000 (7)	Pulp (1995)
December 1963 (Oh What A Night) (1)	Four Seasons (1976)	Disco's Revenge (9)	Gusto (1996)
		Discotheque (1)	U2 (1997)
Deck Of Cards (re-entry) (5)	Wink Martindale (1963)	Distant Drums (1)	Jim Reeves (1966)
Dedicated Follower Of Fashion (4)	Kinks (1966)	Divine Emotions (8)	Narada (1988)
Dedicated To The One I Love (2)	Mamas & The Papas (1967)	Dizzy (1)	Tommy Roe (1969)
Dedicated To The One I Love (6)	Bitty McLean (1994)	Dizzy (1)	Vic Reeves & The Wonder Stuff (1991)
Deep (5)	East 17 (1993)		
Deep Deep Trouble (7)	Simpsons featuring Bart & Homer (1991)	DJ (3)	H & Claire (2002)
		Do Anything You Wanna Do (9)	Eddie & The Hotrods (1977)
Deeper And Deeper (6)	Madonna (1992)	Do I Do (10)	Stevie Wonder (1982)
Deeper Love, A (5)	Aretha Franklin (1994)		
Deeper Shade Of Blue (4)	Steps (2000)	Do It Again (1)	Beach Boys (1968)
Deeper Underground (1)	Jamiroquai (1998)	Do It Do It Again (9)	Raffaella Carra (1978)
Deeply Dippy (1)	Right Said Fred (1992)		

MUSIC POP

Title	Group/Artiste	Title	Group/Artiste
Do Nothing / Maggie's Farm (4)	Specials (1980)	Don Quixote (10)	Nik Kershaw (1985)
Do That To Me One More Time (7)	Captain & Tennille (1980)	Donald Where's Your Troosers (re-issue) (4)	Andy Stewart (1989)
Do The Bartman (1)	Simpsons (1991)	Donna (2) first hit	10CC (1972)
Do The Conga (10)	Black Lace (1984)	Donna (3)	Marty Wilde (1959)
(Do) The Hucklebuck (5)	Coast To Coast (1981)	Don't (2)	Elvis Presley with The Jordanaires (1958)
(Do The) Spanish Hustle (10)	Fatback Band (1976)		
Do They Know It's Christmas (1)	Band Aid (1984)	Don't Answer Me (6)	Cilla Black (1966)
Do They Know It's Christmas (1)	Band Aid II (1989)	Don't Be A Stranger (3)	Dina Carroll (1993)
Do They Know It's Christmas (re-entry) (3)	Band Aid (1985)	Don't Be Cruel (42) first hit	Bobby Brown (1988)
Do U Still (7)	East 17 (1996)	Don't Be Stupid (You Know I Love You) (5)	Shania Twain (2000)
Do Wah Diddy (9)	DJ Otzi (2001)	Don't Blame Me (8)	Frank Ifield (1964)
Do Wah Diddy Diddy (1)	Manfred Mann (1964)	Don't Break My Heart (3)	UB40 (1985)
		Don't Bring Me Down (6)	Animals (1966)
Do What You Do (6)	Jermaine Jackson (1985)	Don't Bring Me Down (3)	Electric Light Orchestra (1979)
Do Ya Do Ya (Wanna Please Me) (10)	Samantha Fox (1986)	Don't Bring Me Down (10)	Pretty Things (1964)
Do You Feel My Love (8)	Eddy Grant (1980)	Don't Call Me Baby (re-issue) (1)	Madison Avenue (2000)
Do You Know (6)	Michelle Gayle (1997)	Don't Cry (8)	Guns 'N' Roses (1991)
Do You Know The Way To San Jose (8)	Dionne Warwick (1968)	Don't Cry Daddy (8)	Elvis Presley (1970)
Do You Love Me (1)	Brian Poole & The Tremeloes (1963)	Don't Cry For Me Argentina (1)	Julie Covington (1976)
Do You Love Me (30) first hit	Dave Clark Five (1963)	Don't Cry For Me Argentina (3)	Madonna (1996)
		Don't Cry For Me Argentina (5)	Shadows (1978)
Do You Mind (1)	Anthony Newley (1960)	Don't Do It Baby (9)	Mac & Katie Kissoon (1975)
Do You Really Like It (1)	DJ Pied Piper & Master of Ceremonies (2001)	Don't Ever Change (5)	Crickets (1962)
		Don't Forbid Me (2)	Pat Boone (1957)
Do You Really Want To Hurt Me (1) first hit	Culture Club (1982)	Don't Forget To Remember (2)	Bee Gees featuring Colin Peterson (1969)
Do You See The Light (Looking For) (10)	Snap featuring Niki Harris (1993)	Don't Get Me Wrong (10)	Pretenders (1986)
Do You Wanna Dance (7)	Barry Blue (1973)	Don't Give Me Your Life (2)	Alex Party (1995)
Do You Wanna Touch Me? (Oh Yeah) (2)	Gary Glitter (1973)	Don't Give Up (1)	Chicane featuring Bryan Adams (2000)
Do You Want Me (5)	Salt-N-Pepa (1991)	Don't Give Up (9)	Peter Gabriel & Kate Bush (1986)
Do You Want To Know A Secret (2)	Billy J Kramer And The Dakotas (1963)	Don't Give Up On Us (1)	David Soul (1976)
		Don't Go (3)	Yazoo (1982)
Doctor Doctor (3)	Thompson Twins (1984)	Don't Go Breaking My Heart (1)	Elton John & Kiki Dee (1976)
Doctor Jones (1)	Aqua (1998)	Don't Go Breaking My Heart (7)	Elton John & RuPaul (1994)
Doctor My Eyes (9)	Jackson 5 (1973)		
Doctorin' The House (6)	Coldcut with Yazz & Plastic Population (1988)	Don't It Make My Brown Eyes Blue (5)	Crystal Gayle (1977)
		Don't Knock The Rock (7)	Bill Haley & His Comets (1957)
Doctorin' The Tardis (1)	Timelords (1988)	Don't Know Much (2)	Linda Ronstadt with Aaron Neville (1989)
Doctor's Orders (7)	Sunny (1974)		
Does Your Chewing Gum Lose Its Flavour (On The Bedpost Overnight) (3)	Lonnie Donegan & His Skiffle Group (1959)	Don't Laugh At Me (3)	Norman Wisdom (1954)
Does Your Mother Know (4)	Abba (1979)	Don't Leave Me (6)	Blackstreet (1997)
Doesn't Really Matter (5)	Janet Jackson (2000)	Don't Leave Me This Way (5)	Harold Melvin & The Bluenotes (1977)
Dog Eat Dog (4)	Adam & The Ants (1980)	Don't Leave Me This Way (1)	Communards (1986)
Doin' The Do (7)	Betty Boo (1990)	Don't Let Go (Love) (5)	En Vogue (1997)
Doing Alright With The Boys (6)	Gary Glitter (1975)	Don't Let It Die (2)	Hurricane Smith (1971)
Dolce Vita (5)	Ryan Paris (1983)		
Dolly My Love (10)	Moments (1975)	Don't Let Me Be Misunderstood (3)	Animals (1965)
Dolphins Were Monkeys (5)	Ian Brown (2000)	Don't Let Me Down / You And I (2)	Will Young (2002)
Dominique (7)	Singing Nun (Soeur Sourire) (1963)	Don't Let Me Get Me (6)	Pink (2002)
Domino Dancing (7)	Pet Shop Boys (1988)	Don't Let The Stars Get In Your Eyes (1) first hit	Perry Como (1953)

Title	Group/Artiste	Title	Group/Artiste
Don't Let The Sun Catch You Crying (6)	Gerry & The Pacemakers (1964)	Doo Wap (That Thing) (3)	Lauryn Hill (1998)
Don't Let The Sun Go Down On Me (1)	George Michael with Elton John (1991)	Doodah! (7)	Cartoons (1999)
Don't Look Any Further (9)	M People (1993)	Dooms Night (8)	Azzido Da Bass (2000)
Don't Look Back In Anger (1)	Oasis (1996)	Doop (1)	Doop (1994)
Don't Make Me Wait (10)	911 (1996)	Double Barrel (1) first hit	Dave & Ansil Collins (1971)
Don't Make My Baby Blue (10)	Shadows (1965)	Double Dutch (3)	Malcolm McLaren (1983)
Don't Marry Her (8)	Beautiful South (1996)	Dove (I'll Be Loving You) (9)	Moony (2002)
Don't Miss The Partyline (7)	Bizz Nizz (1990)	Down Boy (2)	Holly Valance (2002)
Don't Need The Sun To Shine (To Make Me Smile) (9)	Gabrielle (2001)	Down Deep Inside (Theme From The Deep) (5)	Donna Summer (1977)
Don't Pay The Ferryman (48) first hit	Chris De Burgh (1982)	Down Down (1)	Status Quo (1974)
Don't Play Your Rock 'N' Roll To Me (8)	Smokie (1975)	Down 4 U (4)	Irv Gotti Presents (2002)
Don't Speak (1)	No Doubt (1997)	Down On The Beach Tonight (7)	Drifters (1974)
Don't Stand So Close To Me (1)	Police (1980)	Down On The Street (9)	Shakatak (1984)
Don't Stay Away Too Long (3)	Peters & Lee (1974)	Down To Earth (3)	Curiosity Killed The Cat (1986)
Don't Stop (3)	ATB (1999)	Down Under (1)	Men At Work (1983)
Don't Stop Me Now (9)	Queen (1979)	Down Yonder (8)	Johnny & The Hurricanes (1960)
Don't Stop Movin' (5)	Livin' Joy (1996)	Downhearted (3)	Eddie Fisher (1953)
Don't Stop Movin' (1)	S Club 7 (2001)	Downtown (2)	Petula Clark (1964)
Don't Stop The Music (7)	Yarbrough & Peoples (1980)	Downtown (remix) (10)	Petula Clark (1988)
Don't Stop Till You Get Enough (3)	Michael Jackson (1979)	Downtown Train (10)	Rod Stewart (1990)
Don't Stop (Wiggle Wiggle) (1)	Outhere Brothers (1995)	Dr Beat (6)	Miami Sound Machine (1984)
Don't take Away The Music (4)	Tavares (1976)	Dr Kiss Kiss (8)	5000 Volts (1976)
Don't Talk Just Kiss (3)	Right Said Fred with Jocelyn Brown (1991)	Dr Love (4)	Tina Charles (1976)
		Dragnet (7)	Ray Anthony (1953)
Don't Talk To Him (2)	Cliff Richard & The Shadows (1963)	Dragnet (re-entry) (9)	Ted Heath Orchestra (1953)
Don't Talk To Me About Love (7)	Altered Images (1983)	Drama! (4)	Erasure (1989)
		Dreadlock Holiday (1)	10CC (1978)
Don't Tell Me (8)	Blancmange (1984)	Dream Baby (2)	Roy Orbison (1962)
Don't Tell Me (4)	Madonna (2000)	Dream Lover (1)	Bobby Darin (1959)
Don't That Beat All (8)	Adam Faith (1962)	Dream On (6)	Depeche Mode (2001)
Don't Think I'm Not (9)	Kandi (2000)	Dream To Me (9)	Dario G (2001)
Don't Throw Your Love Away (1)	Searchers (1964)	Dreamboat (1)	Alma Cogan (1955)
Don't Treat Me Like A Child (3) first hit	Helen Shapiro (1961)	Dreamer (remix) (1)	Livin' Joy (1995)
Don't Turn Around (5)	Ace Of Base (1994)	Dreamin' (5)	Johnny Burnette (1960)
Don't Turn Around (1)	Aswad (1988)	Dreamin' (8)	Cliff Richard (1980)
Don't Walk Away (7)	Jade (1993)	Dreaming (2)	Blondie (1979)
Don't Wanna Let You Go (9)	Five (2000)	Dreaming (9)	Glen Goldsmith (1988)
Don't Wanna Lose You (6)	Gloria Estefan (1989)	Dreaming (10)	Ruff Driverz presents Arrola (1998)
Don't Want To Forgive Me Now (7)	Wet Wet Wet (1995)	Dreaming Of Me (57) first hit	Depeche Mode (1981)
Don't Waste My Time (8)	Paul Hardcastle featuring Carol Kenyon (1986)	Dreamlover (9)	Mariah Carey (1993)
		Dreams (6)	Corrs (1998)
Don't Worry (2) first solo hit	Kim Appleby (1990)	Dreams (1)	Gabrielle (1993)
Don't Worry Be Happy (2)	Bobby McFerrin (1988)	Dream's A Dream, A (6)	Soul II Soul (1990)
		Dreams Can Tell A Lie (10)	Nat 'King' Cole (1956)
Don't You (Forget About Me) (7)	Simple Minds (1985)	Dress You Up (5)	Madonna (1985)
Don't You Love Me (3)	Eternal (1997)	Drifting Away (9)	Lange featuring Skye (2002)
Don't You Rock Me Daddy-O (4)	Lonnie Donegan & His Skiffle Group (1957)	Drinking In L.A. (re-issue) (3)	Bran Van 3000 (1999)
Don't You Rock Me Daddy-O (10)	Vipers Skiffle Group (1957)	Drive (5)	Cars (1984)
Don't You Think It's Time (6)	Mike Berry & The Outlaws (1963)	Drive (re-entry) (4)	Cars (1985)
		Drive-In Saturday (3)	David Bowie (1973)
Don't You Want Me (6)	Felix (1992)	Driven By You (6)	Brian May (1991)
Don't You Want Me (1)	Human League (1981)	Driving In My Car (4)	Madness (1982)
		Drop Dead Gorgeous (7)	Republica (1997)
Don't You Want Me (remix) (10)	Felix (1995)	Drop The Boy (2)	Bros (1988)

Title	Group/Artiste	Title	Group/Artiste
Drops Of Jupiter (Tell Me) (10)	Train (2001)	Emotion (3)	Destiny's Child (2001)
Drowned World (Substitute For Love) (10)	Madonna (1998)	Emotional Rescue (9)	Rolling Stones (1980)
Drowning (4)	Backstreet Boys (2002)	Encore Une Fois (2)	Sash (1997)
		End Is The Beginning Is The End, The (10)	Smashing Pumpkins (1997)
Drowning In Berlin (9)	Mobiles (1982)	End Of The Line (5)	Honeyz (1998)
Drugs Don't Work, The (1)	Verve (1997)	End Of The Road (1)	Boyz II Men (1992)
Dry County (9)	Bon Jovi (1994)	Endless Love (3)	Luther Vandross & Mariah Carey (1994)
Dub Be Good To Me (1)	Beats International with Lindy Layton (1990)		
Dude (Looks Like A Lady) (20) first hit; first release 1987, No 45	Aerosmith (1990)	Endless Love (7)	Diana Ross & Lionel Richie (1981)
		Endless Sleep (4) first hit	Marty Wilde (1958)
Duke Of Earl (6)	Darts (1979)	Endlessly (28) first and biggest hit	Brook Benton (1959)
Dyna-Mite (4)	Mud (1973)		
Dy-Na-Mi-Tee (5)	Ms Dynamite (2002)	England's Irie (6)	Black Grape, Joe Strummer & Keith Allen (1996)
D'You Know What I Mean? (1)	Oasis (1997)		
Each Time (2)	E-17 (1998)	English Country Garden (5)	Jimmie Rodgers (1962)
Each Time You Break My Heart (5)	Nick Kamen (1986)		
Early In The Morning (8)	Vanity Fare (1969)	Enjoy The Silence (6)	Depeche Mode (1990)
Earth Angel (4)	Crew Cuts (1955)		
Earth Dies Screaming, The/ Dream A Lie (10)	UB40 (1980)	Enjoy Yourself (5)	A+ (1999)
		Enola Gay (8)	Orchestral Manoeuvres In The Dark (1980)
Earth Song (1)	Michael Jackson (1995)		
Easy (9)	Commodores (1977)	Enter Sandman (5)	Metallica (1991)
Easy Lover (1)	Philip Bailey duet with Phil Collins (1985)	Erase / Rewind (7)	Cardigans (1999)
		Erasure-ish (25) first hit	Björn Again (1992)
Ebb Tide (9)	Frank Chacksfield (1954)	Ernie (The Fastest Milkman In The West) (1)	Benny Hill (1971)
Ebeneezer Goode (1)	Shamen (1992)	Erotica (3)	Madonna (1992)
Ebony And Ivory (1)	Paul McCartney with Stevie Wonder (1982)	Escape (3)	Enrique Iglesias (2002)
		Escaping (3)	Dina Carroll (1996)
E-Bow The Letter (4)	REM (1996)	Especially For You (3)	Denise & Johnny (1998)
Echo Beach (10)	Martha & The Muffins (1980)		
		Especially For You (1)	Kylie Minogue & Jason Donovan (1988)
Ecuador (2)	Sash featuring Rodriguez (1997)	Et Les Oiseaux Chantaient (And The Birds Were Singing) (4)	Sweet People (1980)
Edelweiss (2)	Vince Hill (1967)		
Edge Of Heaven, The / Where Did Your Heart Go (1)	Wham! (1986)	Eternal Flame (1)	Atomic Kitten (2001)
		Eternal Flame (1)	Bangles (1989)
Egyptian Reggae (5)	Jonathan Richman & Modern Lovers (1977)	Eternally (8)	Jimmy Young (1953)
		Eternity / The Road To Mandalay (1)	Robbie Williams (2001)
Eighteen Strings (9)	Tinman (1994)	Eton Rifles, The (3)	Jam (1979)
Eighteen With A Bullet (7)	Pete Wingfield (1975)	European Female (9)	Stranglers (1983)
		Evapor 8 (6)	Altern 8 (1992)
Eighth Day (5)	Hazel O'Connor (1980)	Eve Of Destruction (3)	Barry McGuire (1965)
Einstein A Go-Go (5)	Landscape (1981)	Eve Of War (remix), The (3)	Jeff Wayne's War Of The Worlds (1989)
Elected (4)	Alice Cooper (1972)		
Election Day (7) first hit	Arcadia (1985)	Even After All (10)	Finley Quaye (1997)
Electric Avenue (2)	Eddy Grant (1983)	Even Better Than The Real Thing (remix) (8)	U2 (1992)
Electric Avenue (remix) (5)	Eddy Grant (2001)		
Electrical Storm (5)	U2 (2002)	Even The Bad Times Are Good (4)	Tremeloes (1967)
Electricity (5)	Suede (1999)	Ever Fallen In Love (9)	Fine Young Cannibals (1987)
Elenore (5)	Turtles (1968)		
Elephant Stone (8)	Stone Roses (1990)	Ever Fallen In Love (With Someone You Shouldn't've) (12) biggest hit	Buzzcocks (1978)
Elevation (3)	U2 (2001)		
Eloise (3)	Damned (1986)		
Eloise (2)	Barry Ryan (1968)	Evergreen/Anything Is Possible (1)	Will Young (2002)
Elusive Butterfly (5)	Val Doonican (1966)		
Elusive Butterfly (5)	Bob Lind (1966)	Everlasting Love (5)	Cast From Casualty (1998)
Embarrassment (4)	Madness (1980)		
Emma (3)	Hot Chocolate (1974)	Everlasting Love (1)	Love Affair (1968)

Title	Group/Artiste	Title	Group/Artiste
Evermore (3)	Ruby Murray (1955)	Everything Is Alright (Uptight) (10)	C J Lewis (1994)
Every Beat Of My Heart (2)	Rod Stewart (1986)	Everything Is Beautiful (6) first hit	Ray Stevens (1970)
Every Breath You Take (1)	Police (1983)	Everything Must Change (9)	Paul Young (1984)
Every Day Hurts (3)	Sad Cafe (1979)	Everything Must Go (5)	Manic Street Preachers (1996)
Every Day (I Love You More) (2)	Jason Donovan (1989)	Everything's Alright (9)	Mojos (1964)
Every Day Of My Life (5)	Malcolm Vaughan (1955)	Everything's Gonna Be Alright (5)	Sweetbox (1998)
Every Little Step (6)	Bobby Brown (1989)	Everytime / Ready Or Not (3)	A1 (1999)
Every Little Thing She Does Is Magic (1)	Police (1981)	Everytime You Need Me (3)	Fragma featuring Maria Rubia (2001)
Every Loser Wins (1)	Nick Berry (1986)	Everywhere (4)	Fleetwood Mac (1988)
Every Morning (10)	Sugar Ray (1999)		
Every Time You Go Away (4)	Paul Young (1985)	Evil Hearted You / Still I'm Sad (3)	Yardbirds (1965)
Everybody (6)	Clock (1995)	Evil That Men Do, The (5)	Iron Maiden (1988)
Everybody (4)	Hear'Say (2001)	Evil Woman (10)	Electric Light Orchestra (1976)
Everybody (7)	Progress presents The Boy Wunda (1999)	Ev'rywhere (3)	David Whitfield (1955)
Everybody (9)	Tommy Roe (1963)	Excerpt From A Teenage Opera (2)	Keith West (1967)
Everybody (Backstreet's Back) (3)	Backstreet Boys (1997)	Ex-Factor (4)	Lauryn Hill (1999)
Everybody Dance (9)	Chic (1978)	Exodus (Theme From 'Exodus') (6)	Ferrante & Teicher (1961)
Everybody Get Together (8)	Dave Clark Five (1970)	Experiments With Mice (7)	Johnny Dankworth (1956)
Everybody Get Up (2)	Five (1998)	Express Yourself (5)	Madonna (1989)
Everybody Gonfi-Gon (7)	Two Cowboys (1994)	Extended Play EP (7)	Bryan Ferry (1976)
Everybody Hurts (7)	REM (1993)	Exterminate (2)	Snap featuring Niki Harris (1993)
Everybody In The Place (EP) (2)	Prodigy (1992)	Eye Level (re-entry) (1)	Simon Park Orchestra (1973)
Everybody Knows (2)	Dave Clark Five (1967)	Eye Of The Tiger (1)	Survivor (1982)
Everybody Wants To Rule The World (2)	Tears For Fears (1985)	F.L.M. (7)	Mel & Kim (1987)
Everybody Wants To Run The World (5)	Tears For Fears (1986)	Fable (7)	Robert Miles (1996)
Everybody's Free (To Feel Good) (6)	Rozalla (1991)	Fabulous (8)	Charlie Gracie (1957)
Everybody's Free (To Wear Sunscreen) (1)	Baz Luhrmann (1999)	Faces (8)	2 Unlimited (1993)
Everybody's Got To Learn Sometime (5)	Korgis (1980)	Fade To Grey (8)	Visage (1980)
(Everybody's Got To Learn Sometime) I Need Your Loving (3)	Baby D (1995)	Fairground (1)	Simply Red (1995)
Everybody's Laughing (10)	Phil Fearon & Galaxy (1984)	Fairytale Of New York (2)	Pogues featuring Kirsty MacColl (1987)
Everybody's Somebody's Fool (5)	Connie Francis (1960)	Faith (2)	George Michael (1987)
Everyday (5)	Bon Jovi (2002)	Faith Can Move Mountains (7)	Johnnie Ray & The Four Lads (1952)
Everyday (3)	Slade (1974)	Faith Can Move Mountains (re-entry) (9)	Johnnie Ray & The Four Lads (1953)
Everyday I Love You (3)	Boyzone (1999)	Faith Can Move Mountains (re-entry) (10)	Nat 'King' Cole (1953)
Everyday Is Like Sunday (9)	Morrissey (1988)	Faith Can Move Mountains (re-entry) (9)	Johnnie Ray & The Four Lads (1953)
Everyone Says Hi (20)	David Bowie (2002)	Faith Can Move Mountains (11) first hit	Jimmy Young (1953)
Everyone's Gone To The Moon (4)	Jonathan King (1965)	Fall In Love With You (2)	Cliff Richard & The Shadows (1960)
Everything (6)	Mary J Blige (1997)	Fallin' (3)	Alicia Keys (2001)
Everything About You (3) first hit	Ugly Kid Joe (1992)	Falling (7)	Julie Cruise (1990)
Everything Changes (1)	Take That (1994)	Falling (9)	Roy Orbison (1963)
Everything Counts (6)	Depeche Mode (1983)	Falling Apart At The Seams (9)	Marmalade (1976)
Everything I Am (6)	Plastic Penny (1968)	Falling In Love Again (8)	Eagle-Eye Cherry (1998)
(Everything I Do) I Do It For You (1)	Bryan Adams (1991)	Falling Into You (10)	Celine Dion (1996)
(Everything I Do) I Do It For You (7)	Fatima Mansions (1992)	Fame (1)	Irene Cara (1982)
Everything I Have Is Yours (re-entry) (8)	Eddie Fisher (1953)	Family Affair (8)	Mary J Blige (2001)
Everything I Own (1) first hit	Ken Boothe (1974)	Fancy Pants (4)	Kenny (1975)
Everything I Own (1) first solo hit	Boy George (1987)	Fanfare For The Common Man (2) only hit	Emerson Lake & Palmer (1977)
		Fantastic Day (9)	Haircut 100 (1982)
		Fantasy (2)	Appleton (2002)

Title	Group/Artiste	Title	Group/Artiste
Fantasy (5)	Black Box (1990)	Find The Time (7)	Five Star (1986)
Fantasy (4)	Mariah Carey (1995)	Fine Time (9)	Yazz (1989)
Fantasy Island (5)	Tight Fit (1982)	Finger Of Suspicion (1)	Dickie Valentine with
Far Far Away (2)	Slade (1974)		The Stargazers
Farewell – Bring It On Home	Rod Stewart (1974)		(1954)
To Me / You Send Me (7)		Fings Ain't Wot They Used To	Max Bygraves (1960)
Farewell Is A Lonely Sound (8)	Jimmy Ruffin (1970)	Be (5)	
Farewell My Summer Love (7)	Michael Jackson	Fire (1)	Crazy World Of
	(1984)		Arthur Brown
Fascinating Rhythm (9)	Bass-O-Matic (1990)		(1968)
Fashion (5)	David Bowie (1980)	Fire (35) first hit	U2 (1981)
Fast Car (5)	Tracy Chapman	Fire Brigade (3)	Move (1968)
	(1988)	Firestarter (1)	Prodigy (1996)
Fast Love (1)	George Michael	Firewire (9)	Cosmic Gate (2001)
	(1996)	First Cut Is The Deepest (18)	P P Arnold (1967)
Fat Lip (8)	Sum 41 (2001)	first hit	
Fat Neck (10)	Black Grape (1996)	First Night, The (6)	Monica (1998)
Father (10)	LL Cool J (1998)	First Of May (6)	Bee Gees (1969)
Father And Son (2)	Boyzone (1995)	First Time, The (1)	Robin Beck (1988)
Fattie Bum Bum (8)	Carl Malcolm (1975)	first and only hit	
Favourite Shirts (Boy Meets	Haircut 100 (1981)	First Time, The (5)	Adam Faith with The
Girl) (4)			Roulettes (1963)
FBI (6)	Shadows (1961)	5-4-3-2-1 (5) first hit	Manfred Mann (1964)
Fear Of The Dark (live) (8)	Iron Maiden (1993)	Five Live EP (1)	George Michael,
Feel (4)	Robbie Williams		Queen, Lisa
	(2002)		Stansfield (1993)
Feel Good (7)	Phats & Small	5-7-0-5 (8)	City Boy (1978)
	(1999)	Fix (7)	Blackstreet (1997)
Feel It (1)	Tamperer featuring	Flash (5)	BBE (1997)
	Maya (1998)	Flash (10)	Queen (1980)
Feel It Boy (9)	Beenie Man featuring	Flashdance ... What A Feeling (2)	Irene Cara (1983)
	Janet (2002)	Flat Beat (1)	Mr Oizo (1999)
(Feel Like) Heaven (6)	Fiction Factory	Flava (1)	Peter Andre (1996)
	(1984)	Flawless (7)	Ones (2001)
Feel So Good (10)	Mase (1997)	Flirtation Waltz (re-entry) (10)	Winifred Atwell
Feel So Real (5)	Steve Arrington		(1953)
	(1985)	Float On (1)	Floaters (1977)
Feel The Beat (5)	Darude (2000)	Floral Dance, The (2) first and	Brighouse & Rastrick
Feel The Need In Me (4) first hit	Detroit Emeralds	only hit	Brass Band (1977)
	(1973)	Floral Dance (21) first and only	Terry Wogan (1978)
Feelings (4)	Morris Albert (1975)	hit	
Feels Like Heaven (5)	Urban Cookie	Flowers (2)	Sweet Female
	Collective (1993)		Attitude (2000)
Feels Like I'm In Love (1)	Kelly Marie (1980)	Flowers In The Rain (2)	Move (1967)
Feels So Good (5)	Melanie B (2001)	Floy Joy (9)	Supremes (1972)
Feet Up (2) first hit	Guy Mitchell (1952)	Fly Away (1)	Lenny Kravitz (1999)
Fernando (1)	Abba (1976)	Fly By II (6)	Blue (2002)
Ferry 'Cross The Mersey (8)	Gerry & The	Fly, The (1)	U2 (1991)
	Pacemakers (1964)	Flying (4)	Cast (1996)
Ferry 'Cross The Mersey (1)	Christians, Holly	Flying Without Wings (1)	Westlife (1999)
	Johnson, Paul	Fog On The Tyne (Revisited) (2)	Gazza & Lindisfarne
	McCartney,		(1990)
	Gerry Marsden &	Folk Singer, The (4)	Tommy Roe (1963)
	Stock Aitken	Follow Da Leader (5)	Nigel & Marvin
	Waterman (1989)		(2002)
Fever (5)	Peggy Lee with Jack	Follow Me (3)	Uncle Kracker (2001)
	Marshall's Music	Follow The Rules (9)	Livin' Joy (1996)
	(1958)	Follow You Follow Me (7)	Genesis (1978)
Fever (6)	Madonna (1993)	Food For Thought/King (4)	UB40 (1980)
Fields Of Fire (400 Miles) (10)	Big Country (1983)	first hit	
first hit		Fool Again (1)	Westlife (2000)
Figaro (1)	Brotherhood Of Man	Fool (If You Think It's Over) (30)	Chris Rea
	(1978)	first hit	
Fill Me In (1)	Craig David (2000)	Fool Such As I, A/I Need Your	Elvis Presley with
Filmstar (9)	Suede (1997)	Love Tonight (1)	The Jordanaires
Final Countdown, The (1)	Europe (1986)		(1959)
Finally Found (4)	Honeyz (1998)	Fool To Cry (6)	Rolling Stones
Finally (re-issue) (2)	Ce Ce Peniston		(1976)
	(1992)	Foolish (4)	Ashanti (2002)
Find My Love (7)	Fairground Attraction	Foolish Beat (9)	Debbie Gibson
	(1988)		(1988)

Title	Group/Artiste	Title	Group/Artiste
Foot Tapper (1)	Shadows (1963)	French Kiss (2)	Lil' Louis (1989)
Footloose (6)	Kenny Loggins (1984)	French Kissin' In The USA (8)	Deborah Harry (1986)
Footsee (9)	Wigan's Chosen Few (1975)	Fresh! (6)	Gina G (1997)
Footsteps (4)	Steve Lawrence (1960)	Friday I'm In Love (6)	Cure (1992)
		Friday On My Mind (6)	Easybeats (1966)
For All We Know (6)	Shirley Bassey (1971)	Friend Or Foe (9)	Adam Ant (1982)
For America (10)	Red Box (1986)	Friendly Persuasion (3)	Pat Boone (1956)
For Once In My Life (3)	Stevie Wonder (1968)	Friends (8)	Arrival (1970)
For The Good Times (7)	Perry Como (1973)	Friends And Neighbours (re-entry) (3)	Billy Cotton & His Band (1954)
For Whom The Bell Tolls (4)	Bee Gees (1993)	Friends Forever (5)	Thunderbugs (1999)
(For You) I'll Do Anything You		Frightened City (3)	Shadows (1961)
Want Me To (5)	Barry White (1975)	From A Distance (6)	Bette Midler (1991)
For Your Babies (9)	Simply Red (1992)	From A Jack To A King (2)	Ned Miller (1963)
For Your Eyes Only (8)	Sheena Easton (1981)	From A Window (10)	Billy J Kramer And The Dakotas (1964)
For Your Love (3)	Yardbirds (1965)	From Me To You (1)	Beatles (1963)
Forest, A (31)	Cure (1980)	From New York To L.A. (6)	Patsy Gallant (1977)
Forever (6)	Damage (1996)	From The Heart (6)	Another Level (1999)
Forever (6)	N-Trance (2002)	From The Underworld (6)	Herd (1967)
Forever (8)	Roy Wood (1973)	From This Moment On (9)	Shania Twain (1998)
Forever And Ever (1)	Slik (1976)	Frozen (1)	Madonna (1998)
Forever Autumn (5)	Jeff Wayne's War Of The Worlds featuring Justin Hayward (1978)	Frozen Orange Juice (10)	Peter Sarstedt (1969)
		Full Metal Jacket (I Wanna Be Your Drill Instructor) (2)	Abigail Mead & Nigel Goulding (1987)
Forever Love (1) first solo hit	Gary Barlow (1996)	Funeral Pyre (4)	Jam (1981)
Forget Me Not (3)	Eden Kane (1962)	Funkin' For Jamaica (N.Y.) (10)	Tom Browne (1980)
Forget Me Not (7)	Vera Lynn (1952)	Funky Gibbon / Sick Man Blues (4)	Goodies (1975)
Forget Me Not (re-entry) (5)	Vera Lynn (1952)		
Forget Me Nots (8)	Patrice Rushen (1982)	Funky Moped / Magic Roundabout (5) first and only hit	Jasper Carrott (1975)
Forgot About Dre (7)	Dr Dre featuring Eminem (2000)	Funky Town (8)	Pseudo Echo (1987)
		Funky Weekend (10)	Stylistics (1976)
Forgotten Town (22) first hit	Christians (1987)	Funkytown (2)	Lipps Inc (1980)
48 Crash (3)	Suzi Quatro (1973)	Funny Familiar Forgotten Feeling (7)	Tom Jones (1967)
Found A Cure (6)	Ultra Naté (1998)		
Found That Soul (9)	Manic Street Preachers (2001)	Funny Funny (13) first hit	Sweet (1971)
		Funny How Love Can Be (8)	Ivy League (1965)
Four Bacharach And David Songs EP (2)	Deacon Blue (1990)	G.H.E.T.T.O.U.T. (10)	Changing Faces (1997)
Four From Toyah EP (4)	Toyah (1981)	G.L.A.D. (10)	Kim Appleby (1991)
Four Letter Word (6)	Kim Wilde (1988)	Gambler (4)	Madonna (1985)
4 My People (5)	Missy Elliott (2002)	Gamblin' Man / Putting On The Style (1)	Lonnie Donegan & His Skiffle Group (1957)
4 Seasons Of Loneliness (10)	Boyz II Men (1997)		
Fox On The Run (5)	Manfred Mann (1968)	Game Of Love (2)	Wayne Fontana & The Mindbenders (1965)
Fox On The Run (2)	Sweet (1975)		
Frankie (1)	Sister Sledge (1985)		
Freak Like Me (1)	Sugababes (2002)	Games People Play (6)	Joe South (1969)
Freak Me (1)	Another Level (1998)	Games Without Frontiers (4)	Peter Gabriel (1980)
Free (7)	DJ Quicksilver (1997)	Gangsta Lovin' (6)	Eve featuring Alicia Keys (2002)
Free (4)	Ultra Naté (1997)	Gangsta's Paradise (1)	Coolio featuring LV (1995)
Free (1) first hit	Deniece Williams (1977)	Gangster Trippin' (3)	Fatboy Slim (1998)
Free As A Bird (2)	Beatles (1995)	Gangsters (6)	Special AKA (1979)
Free Me (7)	Cast (1997)	Garden Of Eden (1)	Frankie Vaughan (1957)
Freed From Desire (3)	Gala (1997)		
Freedom (1)	Wham! (1984)	Gaye (8)	Clifford T Ward (1973)
Freedom (2) first hit	Robbie Williams (1996)	Gee Baby (4)	Peter Shelley (1974)
Freedom Come Freedom Go (6)	Fortunes (1971)	Gee Whiz It's You (4)	Cliff Richard & The Shadows (1961)
Freeek! (7)	George Michael (2002)	Genie In A Bottle (1)	Christina Aguilera (1999)
Freestyler (2)	Bomfunk MCs (2000)		
Freight Train (5)	Charles McDevitt Skiffle Group and Nancy Whiskey (1957)	Geno (1)	Dexy's Midnight Runners (1980)
		Gentle On My Mind (2)	Dean Martin (1969)

MUSIC
POP

Title	Group/Artiste	Title	Group/Artiste
Georgy Girl (3)	Seekers (1967)	Girl All The Bad Guys Want (8)	Bowling For Soup (2002)
Get A Life (3)	Soul II Soul (1989)	Girl Can't Help It, The/Daddy Cool (6) first hit	Darts (1977)
Get Away (1)	Georgie Fame & The Blue Flames (1966)	Girl Can't Help It, The (9)	Little Richard (1957)
Get Back (1)	Beatles with Billy Preston (1969)	Girl Crazy (7)	Hot Chocolate (1982)
Get Dancing (8) first hit	Disco Tex & Sex-O-Lettes (1974)	Girl Don't Come (3)	Sandie Shaw (1964)
Get Down (1)	Gilbert O'Sullivan (1973)	Girl I'm Gonna Miss You (2)	Milli Vanilli (1989)
Get Down On It (3)	Kool & The Gang (1981)	Girl Is Mine, The (8)	Michael Jackson & Paul McCartney (1982)
Get Get Down (5)	Paul Johnson (1999)	Girl Like You, A (4)	Edwyn Collins (1995)
Get Here (4)	Oleta Adams (1991)		
Get It (10)	Darts (1979)	Girl Like You, A (3)	Cliff Richard & The Shadows (1961)
Get It On (1)	T Rex (1971)		
Get Lost (10)	Eden Kane (1961)	Girl Of My Best Friend, The (9)	Elvis Presley with The Jordanaires (1976)
Get Off Of My Cloud (1)	Rolling Stones (1965)		
Get Outta My Dreams Get Into My Car (3)	Billy Ocean (1988)	Girl On TV (6)	Lyte Funkie Ones (2000)
Get Over You / Move This Mountain (3)	Sophie Ellis-Bextor (2002)	Girl You Know It's True (3)	Milli Vanilli (1988)
Get Ready (10)	Temptations (1969)	Girlfriend (1)	Billie (1998)
Get Ready For This (2)	2 Unlimited (1991)	Girlfriend (2)	N Sync (2002)
Get The Girl! Kill The Baddies! (9)	Pop Will Eat Itself (1993)	Girlfriend (8)	Pebbles (1988)
Get The Message (8)	Electronic (1991)	Girlie Girlie (7)	Sophia George (1985)
Get The Party Started (2)	Pink (2002)	Girls (3)	Moments & Whatnauts (1975)
Get Up And Boogie (7)	Silver Convention (1976)	Girls And Boys (5)	Blur (1994)
Get Up (Before The Night Is Over) (2)	Technotronic featuring Ya Kid K (1990)	Girls Girls Girls (7)	Sailor (1976)
		Girls Just Want To Have Fun (2)	Cyndi Lauper (1984)
Get UR Freak On (4)	Missy Elliott (2001)	Girls Like Us (7)	B15 Project with Chrissy D & Lady G (2000)
Get-A-Way (4)	Maxx (1994)		
Gett Off (4)	Prince & The New Power Generation (1991)	Girls On Film (5)	Duran Duran (1981)
		Girls Talk (4)	Dave Edmunds (1979)
Gettin' Jiggy Wit It (3)	Will Smith (1998)	Give A Little Love (1)	Bay City Rollers (1975)
Ghetto Child (7)	Detroit Spinners (1973)	Give A Little Love (7)	Daniel O'Donnell (1998)
Ghetto Heaven (10)	Family Stand (1990)	Give In To Me (2)	Michael Jackson (1993)
Ghetto Romance (7)	Damage (2000)		
Ghetto Superstar (2)	Pras Michel, Ol' Dirty Bastard and Mya (1998)	Give It Away (9)	Red Hot Chili Peppers (1994)
		Give It To You (5)	Jordan Knight (1999)
Ghost Town (1)	Specials (1981)	Give It Up (1)	KC & The Sunshine Band (1983)
Ghostbusters (2)	Ray Parker Jr (1984)		
Ghosts (5)	Japan (1982)	Give It Up (re-entry) (5)	Goodmen (1993)
Giddy-Up-A-Ding-Dong (4)	Freddie Bell & The Bellboys (1956)	Give Me A Little More Time (5)	Gabrielle (1996)
		Give Me Back My Heart (4)	Dollar (1982)
Gift Of Christmas, The (9) first and only hit	Childliners (1995)	Give Me Just A Little More Time (3) first hit	Chairmen Of The Board (1970)
Gigi (8)	Billy Eckstine (1959)	Give Me Just A Little More Time (2)	Kylie Minogue (1992)
Gilly Gilly Ossenfeffer Katzenellen Bogen By The Sea (7)	Max Bygraves (1954)	Give Me Love (Give Me Peace On Earth) (8)	George Harrison (1973)
Gimme All Your Lovin' (10)	ZZ Top (1984)	Give Me The Night (7)	George Benson (1980)
Gimme Dat Ding (6)	Pipkins (1970)		
Gimme Gimme Gimme (a man after midnight) (3)	Abba (1979)	Give Me Your Word (1)	Tennessee Ernie Ford (1955)
Gimme Hope Jo'Anna (7)	Eddy Grant (1988)	Give Peace A Chance (2)	John Lennon & The Plastic Ono Band (1969)
Gimme Little Sign (8)	Brenton Wood (1967)		
Gimme Some Loving (2)	Spencer Davis Group (1966)	Giving It All Away (5) first solo hit	Roger Daltrey (1973)
		Glad All Over (1)	Dave Clark Five (1963)
Gimme Some More (5)	Busta Rhymes (1999)	Glad It's All Over / Damned On 45 (6)	Captain Sensible (1984)
Gin House Blues (12) first hit	Amen Corner (1967)		
Ginny Come Lately (5)	Brian Hyland (1962)	Glass Of Champagne, A (2)	Sailor (1975)

Title	Group/Artiste	Title	Group/Artiste
Globetrotter (5)	Tornados (1963)	Good Heart, A (1)	Feargal Sharkey (1985)
Gloria (6)	Laura Branigan (1982)	Good Life (4)	Inner City (1988)
Glorious (4)	Andreas Johnson (2000)	Good Life (Buena Vida) (remix) (10)	Inner City (1999)
Glory Of Love (3)	Peter Cetera (1986)	Good Luck Charm (1)	Elvis Presley with The Jordanaires (1962)
Glow Worm (10)	Mills Brothers (1953)		
Go (10)	Moby (1991)		
Go Away Little Girl (6)	Mark Wynter (1962)	Good Morning Freedom (10)	Blue Mink (1970)
Go (Before You Break My Heart) (8)	Gigliola Cinquetti (1974)	Good Morning Judge (5)	10CC (1977)
		Good Morning Starshine (6)	Oliver (1969)
Go For The Eyes (2)	KP (1974)	Good Old Arsenal (16) first hit	Arsenal FC First Team Squad (1971)
Go Let It Out (1)	Oasis (2000)		
Go Now (1) first hit	Moody Blues (1964)	Good Old Rock 'N' Roll (7)	Dave Clark Five (1969)
Go On Move (7)	Reel 2 Real with The Mad Stuntman (1994)	Good The Bad And The Ugly, The (1)	Hugo Montenegro (1968)
Go West (2)	Pet Shop Boys (1993)	Good Thing (8)	Eternal (1996)
		Good Thing (7)	Fine Young Cannibals (1989)
Go Wild In The Country (7)	Bow Wow Wow (1982)	Good Thing Going (We've Got A Good Thing Going) (4)	Sugar Minott (1981)
God Gave Rock And Roll To You (4)	Kiss (1992)		
God Is A DJ (6)	Faithless (1998)	Good Times (5)	Chic (1979)
God Only Knows (2)	Beach Boys (1966)	Good Timin' (1)	Jimmy Jones (1960)
God Save The Queen (2)	Sex Pistols (1977)	Good Tradition (10) first hit	Tanita Tikaram (1988)
Goin' Down (4)	Melanie C (1999)		
Goin' Home (4)	Osmonds (1973)	Good Vibrations (1)	Beach Boys (1966)
Going Back (10)	Dusty Springfield (1966)	Good Year For The Roses, A (6)	Elvis Costello (1981)
		Goodbye (2)	Mary Hopkin (1969)
Going Back To My Roots (4)	Odyssey (1981)	Goodbye (1)	Spice Girls (1998)
Going Back To My Roots / Rich In Paradise (9)	FPI Project present Rich In Paradise and Paolo Dini (1989)	Goodbye Jimmy Goodbye (10)	Ruby Murray (1959)
		Goodbye My Love (2)	Glitter Band (1975)
		Goodbye My Love (4)	Searchers (1965)
		Goodbye Sam Hello Samantha (6)	Cliff Richard (1970)
Going For Gold (8)	Shed Seven (1996)		
Going In With My Eyes Open (2)	David Soul (1977)	Goodbye Stranger (9)	Pepsi & Shirlie (1987)
Going Nowhere (9)	Gabrielle (1993)		
Going Out (5)	Supergrass (1996)	Goodbye Yellow Brick Road (6)	Elton John (1973)
Going Underground / Carnation (6)	Buffalo Tom / Liam Gallagher & Steve Cradock (1999)	Goodness Gracious Me (4)	Peter Sellers and Sophia Loren (1960)
		Goodnight Girl (1)	Wet Wet Wet (1992)
Going Underground / Dreams Of Children (1)	Jam (1980)	Goodnight Midnight (4)	Clodagh Rodgers (1969)
Gold (10)	Artist Formerly Known As Prince (1995)	Goodnight Tonight (5)	Wings (1979)
		Goody Two Shoes (1)	Adam Ant (1982)
		Google Eye (10)	Nashville Teens (1964)
Gold (2)	Spandau Ballet (1983)	Got My Mind Set On You (2)	George Harrison (1987)
Golden Brown (2)	Stranglers (1982)	Got The Feelin' (3)	Five (1998)
Golden Lights (21) second and only other hit	Twinkle (1965)	Got 'Til It's Gone (6)	Janet Jackson (1997)
		Got To Be Certain (2)	Kylie Minogue (1988)
Golden Years (8)	David Bowie (1975)	Got To Be There (5)	Michael Jackson (1972)
Golden Years EP, The (8)	Motorhead (1980)		
Goldeneye (10)	Tina Turner (1995)	Got To Get It (4)	Culture Beat (1993)
Goldfinger (5)	Ash (1996)	Got To Get You Into My Life (6)	Cliff Bennett & The Rebel Rousers (1966)
Gone Till November (3)	Wyclef Jean (1998)		
Gonna Get Along Without You Now (8)	Viola Wills (1979)	Got To Give It Up (7)	Marvin Gaye (1977)
		Got To Have Your Love (2)	Liberty X (2002)
Gonna Make You A Star (1)	David Essex (1974)	Got To Have Your Love (4)	Mantronix featuring Wondress (1990)
Gonna Make You An Offer You Can't Refuse (8)	Jimmy Helms (1973)		
Gonna Make You Sweat (Everybody Dance Now) (3)	C & C Music Factory (1990)	Gotham City (9)	R Kelly (1997)
		Gotta Be You (10)	3T (1997)
Goo Goo Barabajagal (Love Is Hot) (12)	Jeff Beck (1969) biggest hit	Gotta Get Thru This (1)	Daniel Bedingfield (2001)
Good Enough (4)	Dodgy (1996)	Gotta Have Something In The Bank Frank (8)	Frankie Vaughan & The Kaye Sisters (1957)
Good Golly Miss Molly (8)	Little Richard (1958)		

Title	Group/Artiste	Title	Group/Artiste
Gotta Have Something In The Bank Frank (8)	Kaye Sisters (1957)	Guitar Tango (4)	Shadows (1962)
Gotta Pull Myself Together (9)	Nolans (1980)	Gym And Tonic (1)	Spacedust (1998)
Gotta Tell You (2)	Samantha Mumba (2000)	Gypsies Tramps And Thieves (4)	Cher (1971)
		Gypsy Woman (La Da Dee) (2)	Crystal Waters (1991)
Govinda (7)	Kula Shaker (1996)	H.A.P.P.Y. Radio (9)	Edwin Starr (1979)
Granada (10)	Frankie Laine (1954)	Ha Ha Said The Clown (4)	Manfred Mann (1967)
Granada (re-entry) (9)	Frankie Laine (1954)		
Grand Coolie Dam (6)	Lonnie Donegan & His Skiffle Group (1958)	Half A Heart (8)	H & Claire (2002)
		Half As Much (3) first hit	Rosemary Clooney (1952)
Grand Piano (9)	Mixmaster (1989)	Halfway Down The Stairs (7)	Muppets (1977)
Grandad (1)	Clive Dunn (1970)	Halfway To Paradise (3)	Billy Fury (1961)
Grandma's Party (9)	Paul Nicholas (1976)	Hallelujah (5)	Milk & Honey featuring Gali Atari (1979)
Gravel Pit (6)	Wu-Tang Clan (2000)		
Grease (3)	Frankie Valli (1978)	Hallelujah Freedom (10)	Junior Campbell (1972)
Grease Megamix (3)	John Travolta & Olivia Newton-John (1990)	Hallowed Be Thy Name (live) (9)	Iron Maiden (1993)
		Halo (10)	Texas (1997)
Great Balls Of Fire (1)	Jerry Lee Lewis (1957)	Hammer To the Heart (6)	Tamperer featuring Maya (2000)
Great Beyond, The (3)	REM (2000)	Hand On Your Heart (1)	Kylie Minogue (1989)
Great Pretender, The / Only You (5) first hit	Platters (1956)	Handbags And Gladrags (4)	Stereophonics (2001)
Great Pretender, The (4)	Freddie Mercury (1987)	Hands Clean (12)	Alanis Morissette (2002)
Great Pretender, The (9)	Jimmy Parkinson (1956)	Hands Off – She's Mine (9)	Beat (1980)
Greatest Love Of All (8)	Whitney Houston (1986)	Hands To Heaven (4)	Breathe (1988)
		Hands Up (Give Me Your Heart) (3)	Ottowan (1981)
Green Door (8)	Jim Lowe (1956)		
Green Door (1)	Shakin' Stevens (1981)	Handy Man (3)	Jimmy Jones (1960)
Green Door (2)	Frankie Vaughan (1956)	Hang On In There Baby (3)	Johnny Bristol (1974)
		Hang On In There Baby (3)	Curiosity (1992)
Green Green Grass Of Home (1)	Tom Jones (1966)	Hang On Sloopy (5)	McCoys (1965)
Green Leaves Of Summer, The (7)	Kenny Ball & His Jazzmen (1962)	Hang On To Your Love (8)	Jason Donovan (1990)
Green Manalishi (With The Two Pronged Crown), The (10)	Fleetwood Mac (1970)	Hangin' Tough (1)	New Kids On The Block (1990)
		Hanging On The Telephone (5)	Blondie (1978)
Green Onions (7)	Booker T & The MG's (1979)	Hanky Panky (2)	Madonna (1990)
		Happenin' All Over Again (4)	Lonnie Gordon (1990)
Green Tambourine (7)	Lemon Pipers (1968)	Happening, The (6)	Supremes (1967)
Grey Day (4)	Madness (1981)	Happy (8)	MN8 (1995)
Groove Is In The Heart / What Is Love (2)	Deee-Lite (1990)	Happy Birthday (2)	Altered Images (1981)
Groove, The (7)	Rodney Franklin (1980)	Happy Birthday (2)	Stevie Wonder (1981)
		Happy Birthday Sweet Sixteen (3)	Neil Sedaka (1961)
Groovejet (If This Ain't Love) (1)	Spiller (2000)	Happy Days And Lonely Nights (6)	Ruby Murray (1955)
Groover, The (4)	T Rex (1973)	Happy Hour (3)	Housemartins (1986)
Groovin' (8)	Young Rascals (1967)	Happy Jack (3)	Who (1966)
		Happy Talk (1) first hit	Captain Sensible (1982)
Groovin' With Mr Bloe (2)	Mr Bloe (1970)		
Groovin' (You're The Best Thing) / Big Boss Groove (5)	Style Council (1984)	Happy To Be On An Island In The Sun (5)	Demis Roussos (1975)
Groovy Kind Of Love, A (1)	Phil Collins (1988)	Happy Together (10)	Jason Donovan (1991)
Groovy Kind Of Love, A (2)	Mindbenders (1966)	Happy Wanderer (Der Fröhliche Wanderer) (2)	Obernkirchen Children's Choir (1954)
Groovy Train (6)	Farm (1990)		
Guaglione (2)	Perez 'Prez' Prado & His Orchestra (1995)	Happy Wanderer (Der Fröhliche Wanderer) (re-entry) (8)	Obernkirchen Children's Choir (1954)
Guantanamera (7)	Sandpipers (1966)		
Gudbuy T'Jane (2)	Slade (1972)	Happy Whistler, The (8)	Don Robertson (1956)
Guess I Was A Fool (5)	Another Level (1998)		
Guiding Star (9)	Cast (1997)	Happy Xmas (War Is Over) (4)	John Lennon, Yoko Ono & The Plastic Ono Band with The Harlem Community Choir (1972)
Guilty (10)	Pearls (1974)		
Guilty Conscience (5)	Eminem featuring Dr Dre (1999)		
Guitar Boogie Shuffle (10)	Bert Weedon (1959)		

Title	Group/Artiste	Title	Group/Artiste
Happy Xmas (War Is Over) (re-entry) (2)	John Lennon, Yoko Ono & The Plastic Ono Band with The Harlem Community Choir (1980)	Heart And Soul (4) first hit	T'Pau (1987)
		Heart Full Of Soul (2)	Yardbirds (1965)
		Heart Of A Man, The (5)	Frankie Vaughan (1959)
Hard Day's Night, A (1)	Beatles (1964)	Heart Of A Teenage Girl, The (10)	Craig Douglas (1960)
Hard Day's Night, A (14)	Peter Sellers (1965)	Heart Of Asia (3)	Watergate (2000)
Hard Habit To Break (8)	Chicago (1984)	Heart Of Glass (1)	Blondie (1979)
Hard Headed Woman (2)	Elvis Presley with The Jordanaires (1958)	Heart Of Gold (10)	Neil Young (1972)
		Heart Of My Heart (7)	Max Bygraves (1954)
Hard Knock Life (Ghetto Anthem) (2)	Jay-Z (1998)	Heart On My Sleeve (6)	Gallagher & Lyle (1976)
Hard Rain's Gonna Fall, A (10) first solo hit	Bryan Ferry (1973)	Heartache (2)	Pepsi & Shirlie (1987)
Hard To Say I'm Sorry (7)	Az Yet featuring Peter Cetera (1997)	Heartache Avenue (7)	Maisonettes (1982)
		Heartaches By The Number (re-entry) (5)	Guy Mitchell (1959)
Hard To Say I'm Sorry (4)	Chicago (1982)	Heartbeat (2)	Nick Berry (1992)
Harder I Try, The (2)	Brother Beyond (1988)	Heartbeat (3) first hit	Ruby Murray (1954)
		Heartbeat (7)	Showaddywaddy (1975)
Hardest Part Is The Night (68) first hit	Bon Jovi (1985)	Heartbeat / Tragedy (1)	Steps (1998)
Harlem Shuffle (7) first and only hit	Bob & Earl (1969)	Heartbreak Hotel (2) first hit	Elvis Presley (1956)
		Heartbreak Hotel / Hound Dog (re-issue) (10)	Elvis Presley (1971)
Harvest For The World (8)	Christians (1988)		
Harvest For The World (10)	Isley Brothers (1976)	Heartbreaker (5)	Mariah Carey featuring Jay-Z (1999)
Haters (8)	So Solid Crew presents Mr Shabz (2002)		
		Heartbreaker (2)	Dionne Warwick (1982)
Hats Off To Larry (6)	Del Shannon (1961)		
Have A Drink On Me (8)	Lonnie Donegan & His Group (1961)	Heart-Shaped Box (5)	Nirvana (1993)
		Heatseeker (12) biggest hit	AC/DC (1988)
Have A Nice Day (5)	Stereophonics (2001)	Heaven (1)	DJ Sammy & Yanou featuring Do (2002)
Have I The Right (6)	Dead End Kids (1977)	Heaven For Everyone (2)	Queen (1995)
		Heaven Is A Halfpipe (4)	OPM (2001)
Have I The Right (1)	Honeycombs (1964)	Heaven Is A Place On Earth (1) first hit	Belinda Carlisle (1987)
Have I Told You Lately (5)	Rod Stewart (1993)		
Have You Ever (1)	S Club 7 (2001)	Heaven Knows I'm Miserable Now (10)	Smiths (1984)
Have You Ever Been In Love (10)	Leo Sayer (1982)		
Have You Ever Really Loved A Woman (4)	Bryan Adams (1995)	Heaven Must Be Missing An Angel (4) first hit	Tavares (1976)
Have You Seen Her (3)	Chi-Lites (1972)	Heaven Must Have Sent You (3)	Elgins (1971)
Have You Seen Her (8)	MC Hammer (1990)	Heaven's What I Feel (4)	Gloria Estefan (1998)
Have You Seen Her / Oh Girl (re-issue) (5)	Chi-Lites (1975)	Hell Raiser (2)	Sweet (1973)
Have You Seen Your Mother Baby Standing In The Shadow (5)	Rolling Stones (1966)	Hello (1)	Lionel Richie (1984)
		Hello Goodbye (1)	Beatles (1967)
		Hello Hello I'm Back Again (2)	Gary Glitter (1973)
Hawkeye (7)	Frankie Laine (1955)	Hello Hurray (6)	Alice Cooper (1973)
Hazard (3)	Richard Marx (1992)	Hello Little Girl (9)	Fourmost (1963)
He Ain't Heavy He's My Brother (3)	Hollies (1969)	Hello Mary Lou / Travellin' Man (2)	Ricky Nelson (1961)
		Hello Suzie (4)	Amen Corner (1969)
He Ain't Heavy He's My Brother (re-issue) (1)	Hollies (1988)	Hello This Is Joanie (The Telephone Answering Machine Song) (6)	Paul Evans (1978)
He Ain't No Competition (6)	Brother Beyond (1988)	Hello, Dolly! (4)	Louis Armstrong and the All Stars (1964)
He Wasn't Man Enough (5)	Toni Braxton (2000)	Help / La Na Nee Nee Noo Noo(3)	Bananarama (1989)
Head Over Feet (7)	Alanis Morissette (1996)	Help Me Make It Through The Night (6)	John Holt (1974)
Heal The World (2)	Michael Jackson (1992)	Help The Aged (8)	Pulp (1997)
Hear The Drummer (Get Wicked) (3)	Chad Jackson (1990)	Help Yourself (5)	Tom Jones (1968)
Heard It All Before (9)	Sunshine Anderson (2001)	Help! (1)	Beatles (1965)
		Here And Now / You'll Be Sorry (4)	Steps (2001)
Heart (1)	Pet Shop Boys (1988)	Here Comes My Baby (4)	Tremeloes (1967)
		Here Comes Summer (1)	Jerry Keller (1959)
Heart And Soul (75)	Cilla Black with Dusty Springfield (1993)	Here Comes That Feeling (5)	Brenda Lee (1962)
		Here Comes The Hotstepper (4)	Ini Kamoze (1995)

Title	Group/Artiste	Title	Group/Artiste
Here Comes The Night (2)	Them (1965)	Hideaway (10)	Dave Dee, Dozy, Beaky, Mick & Tich (1966)
Here Comes The Rain Again (8)	Eurythmics (1984)		
Here Comes The Sun (10)	Steve Harley (1976)		
Here I Am (5)	Bryan Adams (2002)	Hideaway (9)	De'Lacy (1995)
		Hi-Fidelity (5)	Kids From Fame (1982)
Here I Go Again (4)	Hollies (1964)		
Here I Go Again (remix) (9)	Whitesnake (1987)	High (8)	Cure (1992)
Here I Stand (10)	Bitty McLean (1994)	High (4)	Lighthouse Family (1998)
Here In My Heart (1)	Al Martino (1952)		
Here It Comes Again (4)	Fortunes (1965)	High Class Baby (7)	Cliff Richard with The Drifters (1958)
Here We Go Round The Mulberry Bush (8)	Traffic (1967)		
		High Energy (5)	Evelyn Thomas (1984)
Here With Me (4)	Dido (2001)		
Here's Where The Story Ends (7)	Tin Tin Out featuring Shelley Nelson (1998)	High Hopes (re-entry) (6)	Frank Sinatra (1959)
		High In The Sky (6)	Amen Corner (1968)
Hernando's Hideaway (1)	Johnston Brothers (1955)	High Life (8)	Modern Romance (1983)
Hero (7)	Mariah Carey (1993)	High Noon (Do Not Forsake Me) (7) first hit	Frankie Laine (1952)
Hero (1)	Enrique Iglesias (2002)		
		High Time (4)	Paul Jones (1966)
Hero (4)	Chad Kroeger featuring Josey Scott (2002)	High Voltage / Points Of Authority (9)	Linkin Park (2002)
		Higher Ground (8)	UB40 (1993)
Heroes And Villains (8)	Beach Boys (1967)	Higher State Of Consciousness (8)	Josh Wink (1995)
Hersham Boys (6)	Sham 69 (1979)		
He's Gonna Step On You Again (4)	John Kongos (1971)	Higher State Of Consciousness (remix) (7)	Josh Wink (1996)
He's In Town (3)	Rockin' Berries (1964)		
		Hillbilly Rock Hillbilly Roll (7)	Woolpackers (1996)
He's Misstra Know It All (10)	Stevie Wonder (1974)	Hindu Times, The (1)	Oasis (2002)
		Hippy Chick (re-entry) (8)	Soho (1991)
He's So Fine (16) first hit	Chiffons (1963)	Hippy Hippy Shake (2)	Swinging Blue Jeans (1963)
He's The Greatest Dancer (6)	Sister Sledge (1979)		
Hey Baby (2)	No Doubt (2002)	History (8)	Mai Tai (1985)
Hey Baby (Unofficial World Cup Remix) (10)	DJ Otzi (2002)	History / Ghosts (5)	Michael Jackson (1997)
Hey Baby (Uuh, Aah) (1)	DJ Otzi (2001)	Hit And Miss (10)	John Barry Seven (1960)
Hey Boy Hey Girl (3)	Chemical Brothers (1999)		
Hey Child (3)	East 17 (1997)	Hit 'Em High (The Monstars' Anthem) (8)	B Real / Busta Rhymes / Coolio / LL Cool J / Method Man (1997)
Hey DJ I Can't Dance To That Music You're Playing (7)	Beatmasters featuring Betty Boo (1989)		
		Hit Me With Your Rhythm Stick (1)	Ian Dury & The Blockheads (1978)
Hey Dude (2)	Kula Shaker (1996)		
Hey Girl (10)	Small Faces (1966)	Hit That Perfect Beat (3)	Bronski Beat (1985)
Hey Girl Don't Bother Me (1)	Tams (1971)	Hit The Road Jack (6)	Ray Charles (1961)
Hey Joe (6)	Jimi Hendrix Experience (1967)	Hold Back The Night (5)	Trammps (1975)
		Hold Me (3)	P J Proby (1964)
Hey Joe (1)	Frankie Laine (1953)	Hold Me Close (1)	David Essex (1975)
Hey Jude (1)	Beatles (1968)	Hold Me In Your Arms (10)	Rick Astley (1989)
Hey Little Girl (2)	Del Shannon (1962)	Hold Me Now (2)	Johnny Logan (1987)
Hey Matthew (9)	Karel Fialka (1987)		
Hey Music Lover (6)	S Express (1989)	Hold Me Now (4)	Thompson Twins (1983)
Hey Now (Girls Just Want To Have Fun) (4)	Cyndi Lauper (1994)		
		Hold Me Thrill Me Kiss Me (3)	Muriel Smith (1953)
Hey Paula (8)	Paul & Paula (1963)	Hold Me Thrill Me Kiss Me Kill Me (2)	U2 (1995)
Hey Rock And Roll (2) first hit	Showaddywaddy (1974)		
		Hold Me Tight (5) first hit	Johnny Nash (1968)
Hey Sexy Lady (10)	Shaggy (2002)	Hold My Hand (1)	Don Cornell (1954)
Hey There (4)	Rosemary Clooney (1955)	Hold On (5) first hit	En Vogue (1990)
		Hold On (6)	Wilson Phillips (1990)
Hey There (5)	Johnnie Ray (1955)		
(Hey There) Lonely Girl (4)	Eddie Holman (1974)	Hold On Tight (4)	Electric Light Orchestra (1981)
(Hey You) The Rocksteady Crew (6)	Rocksteady Crew (1983)	Hold On To My Love (7)	Jimmy Ruffin (1980)
Hey! Baby (2)	Bruce Channel (1962)		
		Hold Tight (4)	Dave Dee, Dozy, Beaky, Mick & Tich (1966)
Hi Hi Hi / C Moon (5)	Wings (1972)		
Hi Ho Silver (5)	Jim Diamond (1986)		
Hi-Ho Silver Lining (14) first hit	Jeff Beck (1967)		
Hide U (6)	Kosheen (2001)		

Title	Group/Artiste	Title	Group/Artiste
Hold Your Head Up (5) first and biggest hit	Argent (1972)	House Of Love (10) first hit	East 17 (1992)
Holding Back The Years (2)	Simply Red (1986)	House Of The Rising Sun (1)	Animals (1964)
Holding On For You (5)	Liberty X (2002)	House Of The Rising Sun (4)	Frijid Pink (1970)
Holding Out For A Hero (2)	Bonnie Tyler (1985)	House That Jack Built, The (4)	Alan Price Set (1967)
Hole In My Shoe (2)	Neil (1984)		
Hole In My Shoe (2)	Traffic (1967)	House That Jack Built, The (9)	Tracie (1983)
Hole In The Ground (9) first hit	Bernard Cribbins (1962)	Housecall (remix) (8)	Shabba Ranks featuring Maxi Priest (1993)
Holiday (6)	Madonna (1984)	How About That! (4)	Adam Faith (1960)
Holiday Rap (6)	MC Miker G & Deejay Sven (1986)	How Am I Supposed To Live Without You (3) first hit	Michael Bolton (1990)
Holiday (re-entry) (2)	Madonna (1985)	How Bizarre (5)	OMC (1996)
Holiday (re-issue) (5)	Madonna (1991)	How 'Bout Us (5) first and only hit	Champaign (1981)
Holidays In The Sun (8)	Sex Pistols (1977)		
Holler / Let Love Lead The Way (1)	Spice Girls (2000)	How Can I Be Sure (1)	David Cassidy (1972)
Holy Cow (6)	Lee Dorsey (1966)	How Can I Love You More (remix) (8)	M People (1996)
Holy Smoke (3)	Iron Maiden (1990)	How Can We Be Lovers (10)	Michael Bolton (1990)
Homburg (6)	Procol Harum (1967)		
Home Lovin' Man (7)	Andy Williams (1970)	How Come, How Long (10)	Babyface featuring Stevie Wonder (1997)
Homely Girl (5)	Chi-Lites (1974)		
Homely Girl (6)	UB40 (1989)	How Deep Is Your Love (3)	Bee Gees (1977)
Homeward Bound (9)	Simon & Garfunkel (1966)	How Deep Is Your Love (9)	Dru Hill (1998)
Homing Waltz (9)	Vera Lynn (1952)	How Deep Is Your Love (1)	Take That (1996)
Honey (3)	Mariah Carey (1997)	How Do I Live (7)	LeAnn Rimes (1998)
Honey (2)	Bobby Goldsboro (1968)	How Do You Do It (1)	Gerry & The Pacemakers (1963)
Honey Come Back (4)	Glen Campbell (1970)	How Do You Want Me To Love You? (10)	911 (1998)
Honey Honey (10)	Sweet Dreams (1974)	(How Does It Feel To Be) On Top Of The World (9)	England United (1998)
Honey (re-issue) (2)	Bobby Goldsboro (1975)	How High (6)	Charlatans (1997)
Honey To The Bee (3)	Billie (1999)	How Many Tears (10)	Bobby Vee (1961)
Hong Kong Garden (7)	Siouxsie & The Banshees (1978)	(How Much Is) That Doggie In The Window (9)	Patti Page (1953)
Honky Tonk Women (1)	Rolling Stones (1969)	(How Much Is) That Doggie In The Window (1)	Lita Roza (1953)
Hooked On Classics (2)	Royal Philharmonic Orchestra (1981)	How Much Love (10)	Leo Sayer (1977)
Hooray Hooray It's A Holi-Holiday (3)	Boney M (1979)	How Soon (10)	Henry Mancini Orchestra (1964)
Hoots Mon (1)	Lord Rockingham's XI (1958)	How Will I Know (5)	Whitney Houston (1986)
Hopelessly Devoted To You (2)	Olivia Newton-John (1978)	How Wonderful You Are (2)	Gordon Haskell (2001)
Horny (5)	Mark Morrison (1996)	How You Remind Me (4)	Nickelback (2002)
		Howzat (4)	Sherbet (1976)
Horny (2)	Mousse T vs Hot 'N' Juicy (1998)	Human (8)	Human League (1986)
Horse With No Name (re-entry) (3)	America (1972)	Human Nature (10)	Gary Clail On U-Sound System (1994)
Hot Diggity (Dog Ziggity Boom) (4)	Perry Como (1956)	Human Nature (8)	Madonna (1995)
Hot In Herre (4)	Nelly (2002)	Humpin' Around (remix) (8)	Bobby Brown (1995)
Hot Love (1)	T Rex (1971)	Hundred Mile High City (4)	Ocean Colour Scene (1997)
(Hot S**t) Country Grammar (7)	Nelly (2000)		
Hot Stuff (9)	Arsenal FC (1998)	Hundred Pounds Of Clay, A (9)	Craig Douglas (1961)
Hot Toddy (6)	Ted Heath Orchestra (1953)	Hungry Like The Wolf (5)	Duran Duran (1982)
		Hunting High And Low (5)	A-Ha (1986)
Hotel California (8)	Eagles (1977)	Hurdy Gurdy Man (4)	Donovan (1968)
Hotlegs / I Was Only Joking (5)	Rod Stewart (1978)	Hurry Up Harry (10)	Sham 69 (1978)
Hound Dog (2)	Elvis Presley (1956)	Hurt (4)	Manhattans (1976)
House Arrest (3)	Krush (1987)	Hurt So Good (4)	Susan Cadogan (1975)
House Nation (re-entry) (8)	Housemaster Boyz and The Rude Boy Of The House (1987)	Hush (2)	Kula Shaker (1997)
		Hustle, The (3)	Van McCoy & Soul City Symphony (1975)
House Of Fun (1)	Madness (1982)		

M
U
S
I
C

P
O
P

Title	Group/Artiste	Title	Group/Artiste
Hymn To Her (8)	Pretenders (1986)	I Could Be Happy (7)	Altered Images (1981)
Hyperballad (8)	Björk (1996)	I Could Be So Good For You (3)	Dennis Waterman with The Dennis Waterman Band (1980)
Hypnotize (10)	Notorious BIG (1997)		
I Ain't Gonna Stand For It (10)	Stevie Wonder (1980)		
I Am A Cider Drinker (Paloma Blanca) (3)	Wurzels (1976)	I Could Easily Fall (In Love With You) (9)	Cliff Richard & The Shadows (1964)
I Am Blessed (7)	Eternal (1995)	I Couldn't Live Without Your Love (6)	Petula Clark (1966)
I Am The Law (32) first hit	Anthrax (1987)		
I Am The Beat (6)	Look (1980)	I Did What I Did For Maria (2)	Tony Christie (1971)
I Am ... I Said (4)	Neil Diamond (1971)	I Didn't Know I Loved You (Til I Saw You Rock 'N' Roll) (4)	Gary Glitter (1972)
I Beg Your Pardon (5)	Kon Kan (1989)		
I Believe (2)	Bachelors (1964)	I Didn't Mean To Turn You On (9)	Robert Palmer (1986)
I Believe (11) first hit	Marcella Detroit (1994)	I Die: You Die (6)	Gary Numan (1980)
I Believe (6)	EMF (1991)	I Don't Believe In If Anymore (8)	Roger Whittaker (1970)
I Believe (1)	Frankie Laine (1953)		
I Believe / Up On The Roof (1)	Robson & Jerome (1995)	I Don't Care (7)	Shakespears Sister (1992)
I Believe I Can Fly (1)	R Kelly (1997)	I Don't Know Anybody Else (4)	Black Box (1990)
I Believe In Christmas (9)	Tweenies (2001)	I Don't Know Why (7)	Eden Kane (1962)
I Believe In Father Christmas (2)	Greg Lake (1975)	I Don't Like Mondays (1)	Boomtown Rats (1979)
I Believe (In Love) (8)	Hot Chocolate (1971)	I Don't Wanna Dance (1)	Eddy Grant (1982)
		I Don't Wanna Fight (7)	Tina Turner (1993)
I Believe (re-issue) (7)	Happy Clappers (1995)	I Don't Wanna Get Hurt (7)	Donna Summer (1989)
I Belong To You (6)	Gina G (1996)		
I Breathe Again (5)	Adam Rickett (1999)	I Don't Wanna Lose You (8)	Tina Turner (1989)
I Can Do It (7)	Rubettes (1975)	I Don't Want A Lover (8)	Texas (1989)
I Can Hear Music (10)	Beach Boys (1969)	I Don't Want Our Loving To Die (5)	Herd (1968)
I Can Hear The Grass Grow (5)	Move (1967)	I Don't Want To (9)	Toni Braxton (1997)
I Can Help (6)	Billy Swan (1974)	I Don't Want To Miss A Thing (4)	Aerosmith (1998)
I Can Make You Feel Good (8)	Kavana (1997)	I Don't Want To Put A Hold On You (3)	Berni Flint (1977)
I Can Make You Feel Good (7)	Shalamar (1982)		
I Can Only Disappoint U (8)	Mansun (2000)	I Don't Want To Talk About It (3)	Everything But The Girl (1988)
I Can Prove It (8)	Phil Fearon (1986)		
I Can See Clearly Now (5)	Johnny Nash (1972)	I Don't Want To Talk About It / First Cut Is The Deepest (1)	Rod Stewart (1977)
I Can See For Miles (10)	Who (1967)		
I Can't Control Myself (2)	Troggs (1966)	I Drove All Night (7)	Cyndi Lauper (1989)
I Can't Dance (7)	Genesis (1992)	I Drove All Night (7)	Roy Orbison (1992)
I Can't Explain (8) first hit	Who (1965)	I Eat Cannibals Part 1 (8)	Toto Coelo (1982)
(I Can't Get No) Satisfaction (1)	Rolling Stones (1965)	I Feel Fine (1)	Beatles (1964)
		I Feel For You (1)	Chaka Khan (1984)
I Can't Go For That (No Can Do) (8)	Daryl Hall & John Oates (1982)	I Feel For You (9)	Bob Sinclair (2000)
		I Feel Like Buddy Holly (7)	Alvin Stardust (1984)
(I Can't Help) Falling In Love With You (1)	UB40 (1993)	I Feel Love (1)	Donna Summer (1977)
I Can't Help Myself (7)	Lucid (1998)	I Feel Love (re-issue) (8)	Donna Summer (1995)
I Can't Help Myself (re-issue) (10)	Four Tops (1970)	I Feel Love (medley) (3)	Bronski Beat with Marc Almond (1985)
I Can't Leave You Alone (9)	George McCrae (1974)		
		I Feel The Earth Move (7)	Martika (1989)
I Can't Let Go (2)	Hollies (1966)	I Feel You (1)	Peter Andre (1996)
I Can't Let Maggie Go (8)	Honeybus (1968)	I Feel You (8)	Depeche Mode (1993)
I Can't Stand It (7)	Captain Hollywood Project (1990)		
		I Finally Found Someone (10)	Barbra Streisand & Bryan Adams (1997)
I Can't Stand The Rain (5)	Eruption (1978)		
I Can't Stand Up For Falling Down (4)	Elvis Costello (1980)	I Found Lovin' (7)	Fatback Band (1987)
		I Found Lovin' (9)	Steve Walsh (1987)
I Can't Stop Lovin' You (Though I Try) (6)	Leo Sayer (1978)	I Found Someone (5)	Cher (1987)
		I Get A Kick Out Of You (7)	Gary Shearston (1974)
I Can't Stop Loving You (1)	Ray Charles (1962)		
I Can't Take The Power (7)	Off-Shore (1990)	I Get A Little Sentimental Over You (5)	New Seekers (1974)
I Can't Tell A Waltz From A Tango (5)	Alma Cogan (1954)		
		I Get Around (3)	Beach Boys (1964)
I Can't Tell The Bottom From The Top (7)	Hollies (1970)	I Get Lonely (5)	Janet Jackson (1998)
I Can't Wait (2)	Nu Shooz (1986)		
I Close My Eyes And Count To Ten (4)	Dusty Springfield (1968)	I Get So Lonely (5)	Nat 'King' Cole & The Four Knights (1954)

Title	Group/Artiste	Title	Group/Artiste
I Understand (5)	Freddie & The Dreamers (1964)	I Was Made To Love Her (5)	Stevie Wonder (1967)
I Wanna Be A Hippy (6)	Technohead (1996)	I (Who Have Nothing) (6)	Shirley Bassey (1963)
I Wanna Be The Only One (1)	Eternal featuring BeBe Winans (1997)	I Will (4)	Ruby Winters (1977)
I Wanna Be U (6)	Chocolate Puma (2001)	I Will Always Love You (1)	Whitney Houston (1992)
I Wanna Be Your Lover (41) first hit	Prince (1980)	I Will Always Love You (6)	Rik Waller (2002)
		I Will Come To You (5)	Hanson (1997)
I Wanna Be Your Man (12)	Rolling Stones (1963)	I Will Return (5)	Springwater (1971)
I Wanna Dance Wit Choo (6)	Disco Tex & Sex-O-Lettes (1975)	I Will Survive (16)	Arrival (1970)
		I Will Survive (1)	Gloria Gaynor (1979)
I Wanna Dance With Somebody (Who Loves Me) (1)	Whitney Houston (1987)	I Will Survive (remix) (5)	Gloria Gaynor (1993)
I Wanna Do It With You (8)	Barry Manilow (1982)	I Wish (5)	Stevie Wonder (1976)
(I Wanna Give You) Devotion (2)	Nomad (1991)	(I Wish I Knew How It Would Feel To Be) Free / One (6)	Lighthouse Family (2001)
I Wanna Go Home (The Wreck Of The John 'B') (5)	Lonnie Donegan & Wally Stott Orchestra (1960)	I Wish It Could Be Christmas Everyday (4)	Wizzard (1973)
I Wanna Hold Your Hand (9)	Dollar (1979)	I Wish It Would Rain Down (7)	Phil Collins (1990)
(I Wanna) Love My Life Away (26) first hit	Gene Pitney (1961)	I Wonder (4)	Dickie Valentine (1955)
		I Wonder Why (2)	Showaddywaddy (1978)
I Wanna Love You Forever (7)	Jessica Simpson (2000)	I Wonder Why (5)	Curtis Stigers (1992)
I Wanna Sex You Up (1) first hit	Color Me Badd (1991)	I Won't Forget You (3)	Jim Reeves (1964)
		I Won't Last A Day Without You / Goodbye To Love (9)	Carpenters (1972)
I Wanna Stay With You (6)	Gallagher & Lyle (1976)	I Won't Let The Sun Go Down On Me (re-issue) (2)	Nik Kershaw (1984)
I Want Candy (9)	Bow Wow Wow (1982)	I Won't Let You Down (3)	PhD (1982)
I Want It All (3)	Queen (1989)	I Won't Run Away (7)	Alvin Stardust (1984)
I Want It That Way (1)	Backstreet Boys (1999)	I Wouldn't Trade You For The World (4)	Bachelors (1964)
I Want Love (9)	Elton John (2001)	I.O.U. (2)	Freeez (1983)
(I Want To Be) Elected (9)	Mr Bean and The Smear Campaign with Bruce Dickinson (1992)	Ice Ice Baby (1)	Vanilla Ice (1990)
		Ice In The Sun (8)	Status Quo (1968)
		I'd Do Anything For Love (But I Won't Do That) (1)	Meat Loaf (1993)
I Want To Be Free (8)	Toyah (1981)	I'd Lie For You (And That's The Truth) (2)	Meat Loaf (1995)
I Want To Break Free (3)	Queen (1984)	I'd Like To Teach The World To Sing (1)	New Seekers (1971)
I Want To Hold Your Hand (1)	Beatles (1963)		
I Want To Know What Love Is (1)	Foreigner (1984)	I'd Love You To Want Me (5)	Lobo (1974)
I Want To Stay Here (3)	Steve & Eydie (1963)	I'd Never Find Another You (5)	Billy Fury (1961)
I Want To Wake Up With You (1)	Boris Gardiner (1986)	I'd Rather Jack (8)	Reynolds Girls (1989)
I Want You Back (1) first hit	Melanie B featuring Missy 'Misdemeanor' Elliott (1998)	Idle Gossip (3)	Perry Como (1954)
		If (1)	Telly Savalas (1975)
		If Anyone Finds This I Love You (4)	Ruby Murray with Anne Warren (1955)
I Want You Back (5)	Bananarama (1988)	If I Can't Have You (4)	Yvonne Elliman (1978)
I Want You Back (4)	Cleopatra (1998)		
I Want You Back (2)	Jackson 5 (1970)	If I Could Turn Back The Hands Of Time (3)	R Kelly (1999)
I Want You Back (5)	N Sync (1999)	If I Could Turn Back Time (6)	Cher (1989)
I Want You Back (remix) (8)	Michael Jackson & The Jackson 5 (1988)	If I Didn't Care (9)	David Cassidy (1974)
I Want You For Myself (2)	Another Level / Ghostface Killah (1999)	If I Give My Heart To You (4)	Doris Day (1954)
		If I Give My Heart To You (re-entry) (3)	Joan Regan (1954)
I Want Your Love (10)	Atomic Kitten (2000)	If I Had A Hammer (4)	Trini Lopez (1963)
I Want Your Love (4)	Chic (1979)	If I Had Words (3)	Scott Fitzgerald and Yvonne Keely with The St Thomas More School Choir (1978)
I Want Your Love (5)	Transvision Vamp (1988)		
I Want Your Sex (3)	George Michael (1987)		
I Was Kaiser Bill's Batman (5)	Whistling Jack Smith (1967)	If I Let You Go (1)	Westlife (1999)
		If I Never See You Again (3)	Wet Wet Wet (1997)
I Was Made For Dancin' (4)	Leif Garrett (1979)	If I Only Had Time (3)	John Rowles (1968)

Title	Group/Artiste	Title	Group/Artiste
If I Said You Have A Beautiful Body Would You Hold It Against Me (3)	Bellamy Brothers (1979)	I'll Be Loving You (Forever) (5)	New Kids On The Block (1990)
If I Told You That (9)	Whitney Houston & George Michael (2000)	I'll Be Missing You (1)	Puff Daddy & Faith Evans with 112 (1997)
If I Was (1)	Midge Ure (1985)	I'll Be Satisfied (10)	Shakin' Stevens (1982)
If I Were A Carpenter (9)	Bobby Darin (1966)	I'll Be There (2)	Mariah Carey (1992)
If I Were A Carpenter (7)	Four Tops (1968)	I'll Be There (4)	Jackson 5 (1970)
If I Were A Rich Man (9)	Topol (1967)	I'll Be There For You – You're All I Need To Get By (10)	Method Man featuring Mary J Blige (1995)
If It Happens Again (9)	UB40 (1984)		
If It Makes You Happy (9)	Sheryl Crow (1996)		
If Not For You (7) first hit	Olivia Newton-John (1971)	I'll Be There For You (re-entry) (5)	Rembrandts (1997)
If Not You (5)	Dr Hook (1976)	I'll Be There For You (Theme From Friends) (3)	Rembrandts (1995)
If Only I Could (3)	Sydney Youngblood (1989)	I'll Be Your Baby Tonight (6)	Robert Palmer & UB40 (1990)
(If Paradise Is) Half As Nice (1)	Amen Corner (1969)	I'll Come When You Call (6)	Ruby Murray (1955)
If She Should Come To You (4)	Anthony Newley (1960)	I'll Find My Way Home (6)	Jon & Vangelis (1981)
If The Kids Are United (9)	Sham 69 (1978)	I'll Fly For You (9)	Spandau Ballet (1984)
If The Whole World Stopped Loving (3)	Val Doonican (1967)	I'll Get By (10)	Shirley Bassey (1961)
If Tomorrow Never Comes (1)	Ronan Keating (2002)	I'll Keep You Satisfied (4)	Billy J Kramer And The Dakotas (1963)
If Ya Gettin' Down (2)	Five (1999)		
If You Believe (re-entry) (7)	Johnnie Ray (1955)	I'll Make Love To You (5)	Boyz II Men (1994)
If You Buy This Record Your Life Will Be Better (3)	Tamperer featuring Maya (1998)	I'll Never Break Your Heart (re-issue) (8)	Backstreet Boys (1996)
If You Can't Give Me Love (4)	Suzi Quatro (1978)	I'll Never Fall In Love Again (1)	Bobbie Gentry (1969)
If You Can't Stand The Heat (10)	Bucks Fizz (1982)		
If You Come Back (1)	Blue (2001)	I'll Never Fall In Love Again (2)	Tom Jones (1967)
If You Don't Know Me By Now (9)	Harold Melvin & The Bluenotes (1973)	I'll Never Find Another You (1) first hit	Seekers (1965)
If You Don't Know Me By Now (2)	Simply Red (1989)	I'll Never Get Over You (4)	Johnny Kidd & The Pirates (1963)
If You Ever (2)	East 17 featuring Gabrielle (1996)	I'll Pick A Rose For My Rose (10)	Marv Johnson (1969)
If You Go Away (8)	Terry Jacks (1974)		
If You Go Away (9)	New Kids On The Block (1991)	I'll Remember (Theme From 'With Honours') (7)	Madonna (1994)
If You Gotta Go Go Now (2)	Manfred Mann (1965)	I'll Say Forever My Love (7)	Jimmy Ruffin (1970)
If You Gotta Make A Fool Of Somebody (3)	Freddie & The Dreamers (1963)	I'll Stand By You (10)	Pretenders (1994)
If You Had My Love (4)	Jennifer Lopez (1999)	I'll Stop At Nothing (4)	Sandie Shaw (1965)
If You Leave Me Now (1)	Chicago (1976)	I'll Take You Home Again Kathleen (7)	Slim Whitman (1957)
If You Let Me Stay (7) first hit	Terence Trent D'Arby (1987)	I'm A Believer (3)	EMF & Reeves & Mortimer (1995)
If You Love Me (8)	Brownstone (1995)	I'm A Believer (1)	Monkees (1967)
If You Only Let Me In (6)	MN8 (1995)	I'm A Boy (2)	Who (1966)
If You Think You Know How To Love Me (3)	Smokie (1975)	I'm A Clown / Some Kind Of Summer (3)	David Cassidy (1973)
If You Tolerate This Your Children Will Be Next (1)	Manic Street Preachers (1998)	I'm A Man (8) first hit	Chicago (1970)
If You Wanna Party (9)	Molella with The Outhere Brothers (1995)	I'm A Man (9)	Spencer Davis Group (1967)
		I'm A Man Not A Boy (7)	North & South (1997)
If You Were With Me Now (4)	Kylie Minogue & Keith Washington (1991)	I'm A Slave For You (4)	Britney Spears (2001)
		I'm A Tiger (9)	Lulu (1968)
If You're Looking For A Way Out (6)	Odyssey (1980)	I'm a Wonderful Thing Baby (4)	Kid Creole & The Coconuts (1982)
If You're Not The One (1)	Daniel Bedingfield (2002)	I'm Alive (1)	Hollies (1965)
Iko Iko (10)	Natasha (1982)	I'm Alive (6)	Stretch 'N' Vern present Maddogg (1996)
Il Silenzio (8)	Nini Rosso (1965)		
I'll Be (9)	Foxy Brown featuring Jay-Z (1997)	(I'm Always Hearing) Wedding Bells (5)	Eddie Fisher (1955)
I'll Be Back (5) first and only hit	Arnee & The Terminators (1991)	(I'm Always Touched By Your) Presence Dear (10)	Blondie (1978)
I'll Be Home (1)	Pat Boone (1956)	I'm Coming Home (2)	Tom Jones (1967)

MUSIC POP

Title	Group/Artiste	Title	Group/Artiste
I'm Crying (8)	Animals (1964)	I'm Walking Behind You (1)	Eddie Fisher with Hugo Winterhalter's Orchestra and Sally Sweetland (1953)
I'm Doing Fine Now (4)	Pasadenas (1992)		
I'm Easy / Be Aggressive (3)	Faith No More (1993)		
I'm Every Woman (4)	Whitney Houston (1993)		
I'm Every Woman (remix) (8)	Chaka Khan (1989)	I'm Your Angel (3)	Celine Dion & R Kelly (1998)
I'm Free (5)	Soup Dragons (1990)	I'm Your Baby Tonight (5)	Whitney Houston (1990)
I'm Gonna Be Alright (3)	Jennifer Lopez (2002)	I'm Your Man (1)	Wham! (1985)
I'm Gonna Be Strong (2)	Gene Pitney (1964)	Imagine (6)	John Lennon (1975)
I'm Gonna Get Me A Gun (6)	Cat Stevens (1967)	Imagine (re-entry) (1)	John Lennon (1980)
I'm Gonna Get You (3)	Bizarre Inc featuring Angie Brown (1992)	Imagine (re-issue) (3)	John Lennon (1999)
I'm Gonna Getcha Good (4)	Shania Twain (2002)	Imitation Of Life (6)	REM (2001)
I'm Gonna Make You Love Me (3)	Diana Ross & The Supremes and The Temptations (1969)	Immortality (5)	Celine Dion with The Bee Gees (1998)
		In A Broken Dream (3)	Python Lee Jackson (1972)
I'm Gonna Make You Mine (2)	Lou Christie (1969)	In A Golden Coach (3)	Billy Cotton & His Band (1953)
I'm Gonna Run Away From You (4)	Tami Lynn (1971)	In A Golden Coach (7)	Dickie Valentine (1953)
I'm Gonna Tear Your Playhouse Down (9)	Paul Young (1984)	In All The Right Places (8)	Lisa Stansfield (1993)
I'm In The Mood For Dancing (3)	Nolans (1979)	In Betweenies, The / Father Christmas Do Not Touch Me (7)	Goodies (1974)
I'm Into Something Good (1)	Herman's Hermits (1964)		
I'm Leaving It (All) Up To You (2)	Donny & Marie Osmond (1974)	In Demand (6)	Texas (2000)
		In Dreams (6)	Roy Orbison (1963)
I'm Like A Bird (5)	Nelly Furtado (2001)	In Dulce Jubilo / On Horseback (4)	Mike Oldfield (1975)
I'm Looking Out The Window / Do You Want To Dance (2)	Cliff Richard with Norrie Paramor / Cliff Richard & The Shadows (1962)	In My Defence (8)	Freddie Mercury (1992)
		In My Eyes (9)	Milk Inc (2002)
I'm Mandy Fly Me (6)	10CC (1976)	In My Own Time (4)	Family (1971)
I'm Not A Girl Not Yet A Woman (2)	Britney Spears (2002)	In My Place (2)	Coldplay (2002)
		In Our Lifetime (4)	Texas (1999)
I'm Not In Love (1)	10CC (1975)	In Summer (5)	Billy Fury (1963)
I'm Not Scared (7)	Eighth Wonder (1988)	In The Air Tonight (2) first solo hit	Phil Collins (1981)
I'm On Fire (4)	5000 Volts (1975)	In The Air Tonight (remix) (4)	Phil Collins (1988)
I'm On Fire / Born In The USA (5)	Bruce Springsteen (1985)	In The Army Now (2)	Status Quo (1986)
		In The Bad Bad Old Days (8)	Foundations (1969)
I'm Only Sleeping / Off On Holiday (7)	Suggs (1995)	In The Closet (8)	Michael Jackson (1992)
I'm Outta Love (6)	Anastacia (2000)	In The Country (6)	Cliff Richard & The Shadows (1966)
I'm Over You (2)	Martine McCutcheon (2000)	In The End (8)	Linkin Park (2001)
I'm Real (4)	Jennifer Lopez (2001)	In The Ghetto (2)	Elvis Presley (1969)
		In The Middle Of Nowhere (8)	Dusty Springfield (1965)
I'm Right Here (5)	Samantha Mumba (2002)	In The Name Of The Father (8)	Black Grape (1995)
I'm Still Standing (4)	Elton John (1983)	In The Navy (2)	Village People (1979)
I'm Still Waiting (1)	Diana Ross (1971)		
I'm Stone In Love With You (10)	Johnny Mathis (1975)	In The Summertime (1) first hit	Mungo Jerry (1970)
I'm Stone In Love With You (9)	Stylistics (1972)	In The Summertime (5)	Shaggy featuring Rayvon (1995)
I'm Telling You Now (2)	Freddie & The Dreamers (1963)	In The Year 2525 (Exordium And Terminus) (1)	Zager & Evans (1969) only hit
I'm The Leader Of The Gang (I Am) (1)	Gary Glitter (1973)	In These Arms (9)	Bon Jovi (1993)
		In Thoughts Of You (9)	Billy Fury (1965)
I'm The Lonely One (8)	Cliff Richard & The Shadows (1964)	In Too Deep (6)	Belinda Carlisle (1996)
I'm The One (2)	Gerry & The Pacemakers (1964)	In Yer Face (9)	808 State (1991)
I'm The Urban Spaceman (5)	Bonzo Dog Doo-Dah Band (1968)	In Your Arms (Rescue Me) (8)	Nu Generation (2000)
I'm Too Sexy (2) first hit	Right Said Fred (1991)	In Your Eyes (7)	George Benson (1983)
		In Your Eyes (3)	Kylie Minogue (2002)
I'm Walking Backwards For Christmas / Bluebottle Blues (4)	Goons (1956)	In Your Room (8)	Depeche Mode (1994)
		In Zaire (4)	Johnny Wakelin (1976)

Title	Group/Artiste	Title	Group/Artiste
Incommunicado (6)	Marillion (1987)	It Hurts So Much (8)	Jim Reeves (1965)
Incredible (remix) (8)	M-Beat featuring General Levy (1994)	It Is Time To Get Funky (9)	D Mob (1989)
		It Keep Rainin' (Tears From Eyes) (2)	Bitty McLean (1993)
Independent Women Part 1 (1)	Destiny's Child (2000)	It Miek (7)	Desmond Dekker & Aces (1969)
Indian Love Call (7)	Slim Whitman (1955)	It Might As Well Rain Until September (3)	Carole King (1962)
Indian Reservation (3)	Don Fardon (1970)		
Indiana Wants Me (2)	R Dean Taylor (1971)	It Must Be Him (2) first and biggest hit	Vikki Carr (1967)
Infinite Dreams (6)	Iron Maiden (1989)		
Infinity (5)	Guru Josh (1990)	It Must Be Love (4)	Madness (1981)
Informer (2)	Snow (1993)	It Must Be Love (re-issue) (6)	Madness (1992)
Inner Smile (6)	Texas (2001)	It Must Have Been Love (3)	Roxette (1990)
Innuendo (1)	Queen (1991)	It Must Have Been Love (re-issue) (10)	Roxette (1993)
Insanity (3)	Oceanic (1991)		
Insatiable (8)	Darren Hayes (2002)	It Only Takes A Minute (9)	One Hundred Ton And A Feather (1976)
Inside (1)	Stiltskin (1994)		
Inside Out (3)	Odyssey (1982)		
Insomnia (3)	Faithless (1996)	It Only Takes A Minute (7)	Take That (1992)
Instant Karma (5)	John Lennon & The Plastic Ono Band (1970)	It Only Took A Minute (6)	Joe Brown & The Bruvvers (1962)
		It Should Have Been Me (5)	Yvonne Fair (1976)
Instant Replay (8)	Dan Hartman (1978)	It Started With A Kiss (5)	Hot Chocolate (1982)
Instant Replay (10)	Yell! (1990)		
Instinction (10)	Spandau Ballet (1982)	It Takes More (7)	Ms Dynamite (2002)
		It Takes Two (5)	Rod Stewart & Tina Turner (1990)
Interesting Drug (9)	Morrissey (1989)		
Intergalactic (5)	Beastie Boys (1998)	It Wasn't Me (1)	Shaggy featuring Rikrok (2001)
International Bright Young Thing (7)	Jesus Jones (1991)		
Into The Groove (1)	Madonna (1985)	Itchycoo Park (3)	Small Faces (1967)
Into The Valley (10)	Skids (1979)	Itchycoo Park (re-issue) (9)	Small Faces (1975)
Intuition (7)	Linx (1981)	It'll Be Me (2)	Cliff Richard & The Shadows (1962)
Invisible Sun (2)	Police (1981)		
Invisible Touch (live) (7)	Genesis (1992)	It's A Fine Day (5)	Opus III (1992)
Ire Feelings (Skanga) (9)	Rupie Edwards (1974)	It's A Hard Life (6)	Queen (1984)
		It's A Heartache (4)	Bonnie Tyler (1977)
Irish Rover, The (8)	Pogues & The Dubliners (1987)	It's A Love Thing (9)	Whispers (1981)
		It's A Miracle (4)	Culture Club (1984)
Iron Lion Zion (5)	Bob Marley & The Wailers (1992)	It's A Sin (1)	Pet Shop Boys (1987)
		It's All Coming Back To Me Now (3)	Celine Dion (1996)
Is There Anybody Out There (5)	Bassheads (1991)	It's All Gravy (9)	Romeo featuring Christina Milian (2002)
Is There Something I Should Know (1)	Duran Duran (1983)		
Is This Love (9)	Bob Marley & The Wailers (1978)	It's All In The Game (1)	Tommy Edwards (1958)
Is This Love (9)	Whitesnake (1987)	It's All In The Game (5)	Four Tops (1970)
Is This Love? (3)	Alison Moyet (1986)	It's All In The Game (2)	Cliff Richard & The Shadows (1963)
Island In The Sun (3)	Harry Belafonte (1957)		
Island Of Dreams (5)	Springfields (1962)	It's All Over (9)	Cliff Richard (1967)
Islands In The Stream (7)	Kenny Rogers & Dolly Parton (1983)	It's All Over Now (1)	Rolling Stones (1964)
Isle Of Innisfree (3) first hit	Bing Crosby (1952)	It's Almost Tomorrow (1) first and only hit	Dreamweavers (1956)
Isn't It A Wonder (2)	Boyzone (1997)	It's Alright (3)	East 17 (1993)
Isn't She Lovely (4)	David Parton (1977)	It's Alright (5)	Pet Shop Boys (1989)
Israelites (1)	Desmond Dekker & Aces (1969)		
		It's Been So Long (4)	George McCrae (1975)
Israelites (re-issue) (10)	Desmond Dekker (1975)	It's Different For The Girls (5)	Joe Jackson (1980)
It Ain't What You Do It's The Way That You Do It (4)	Fun Boy Three & Bananarama (1982)	It's For You (7)	Cilla Black (1964)
		It's Four In The Morning (3)	Faron Young (1972)
		It's Getting Better (8)	Mama Cass (1969)
It Began In Afrika (8)	Chemical Brothers (2001)	It's Goin' Down (7)	X-Ecutioners (2002)
		It's Gonna Be A Cold Cold Christmas (4)	Dana (1975)
It Didn't Matter (9)	Style Council (1987)		
It Doesn't Have To Be This Way (5)	Blow Monkeys (1987)	It's Gonna Be Me (9)	N Sync (2000)
		It's Good News Week (5)	Hedgehoppers Anonymous (1965)
It Doesn't Matter (3)	Wyclef Jean (2000)		
It Doesn't Matter Anymore (1)	Buddy Holly (1959)	It's Grim Up North (10)	Justified Ancients Of Mu Mu (1991)
It Don't Come Easy (4)	Ringo Starr (1971)		
It Feels So Good (remix) (1)	Sonique (2000)	It's Impossible (4)	Perry Como (1971)

Title	Group/Artiste	Title	Group/Artiste
Joanna / Tonight (2)	Kool & The Gang (1984)	Just My Imagination (Running Away With Me) (8)	Temptations (1971)
Joe Le Taxi (3)	Vanessa Paradis (1988)	Just One Look (2)	Hollies (1964)
John And Julie (6)	Eddie Calvert (1955)	Just One More Night (8)	Yellow Dog (1978)
Johnny Come Home (8)	Fine Young Cannibals (1985)	Just One Smile (8)	Gene Pitney (1966)
		Just Say No (5)	Grange Hill Cast (1986)
Johnny Reggae (3)	Piglets (1971)		
Johnny Remember Me (1)	John Leyton (1961)	Just The Two Of Us (2)	Will Smith (1998)
Johnny Will (4)	Pat Boone (1961)	Just The Way You Are (8)	Milky (2002)
Join In And Sing Again (9)	Johnston Brothers (1955)	Just Walkin' In The Rain (1)	Johnnie Ray (1956)
		Just What I Always Wanted (8)	Mari Wilson (1982)
Join Together (9)	Who (1972)	Just When I Needed You Most (8)	Randy Vanwarmer (1979)
Joker, The (1)	Steve Miller Band (1990)	Just Who Is The Five O'Clock Hero (8)	Jam (1982)
Jolene (7)	Dolly Parton (1976)		
Journey, The (3)	911 (1997)	Justified And Ancient (2)	KLF with Tammy Wynette (1991)
Joy (4)	Soul II Soul (1992)		
Joy And Pain (10)	Donna Allen (1989)	Justify My Love (2)	Madonna (1990)
Joybringer (9)	Manfred Mann's Earth Band (1973)	Karma Chameleon (1)	Culture Club (1983)
		Karma Police (8)	Radiohead (1997)
Joyride (4)	Roxette (1991)	Kate Bush On Stage EP (10)	Kate Bush (1979)
Judy In Disguise (With Glasses) (3)	John Fred & The Playboy Band (1968)	Kayleigh (2)	Marillion (1985)
		(Keep Feeling) Fascination (2)	Human League (1983)
Judy Teen (5)	Cockney Rebel (1974)	Keep On Dancin' (8)	Gary's Gang (1979)
		Keep On Dancing (9) first hit	Bay City Rollers (1971)
Juke Box Jive (3)	Rubettes (1974)		
Julia Says (3)	Wet Wet Wet (1995)	Keep On Jumpin' (7)	Lisa Marie Experience (1996)
Julie Ann (10)	Kenny (1975)	Keep On Jumpin' (8)	Todd Terry with Martha Wash and Jocelyn Brown (1996)
Julie Do Ya Love Me (8)	White Plains (1970)		
Juliet / Tell Me Girl (What Are You Gonna Do) (1)	Four Pennies (1964)		
		Keep On Loving You (7)	REO Speedwagon (1981)
Jump (2)	Kris Kross (1992)		
Jump (7)	Van Halen (1984)	Keep On Movin' (1)	Five (1999)
Jump Around (re-issue) / Top O' The Morning (8)	House Of Pain (1993)	Keep On Moving (5)	Soul II Soul featuring Caron Wheeler (1989)
Jump (For My Love) (6)	Pointer Sisters (1984)	Keep On Running (1)	Spencer Davis Group (1965)
Jump They Say (9)	David Bowie (1993)		
Jump To The Beat (3)	Stacy Lattisaw (1980)	Keep On Walkin' (10)	Ce Ce Peniston (1992)
Jump To The Beat (8)	Dannii Minogue (1991)	Keep Searchin' (We'll Follow The Sun) (3)	Del Shannon (1965)
		Keep The Faith (5)	Bon Jovi (1992)
Jumpin' Jumpin' (5)	Destiny's Child (2000)	Kernkraft 400 (2)	Zombie Nation (2000)
Jumping Jack Flash (1)	Rolling Stones (1968)		
		Ketchup Song (Asereje), The (1)	Las Ketchup (2002)
Jungle Rock (3)	Hank Mizell (1976)	Kevin Carter (9)	Manic Street Preachers (1996)
Just A Girl (re-issue) (3)	No Doubt (1997)		
Just A Little (1)	Liberty X (2002)	Kewpie Doll (9)	Perry Como (1958)
Just A Step From Heaven (8)	Eternal (1994)	Kewpie Doll (10)	Frankie Vaughan (1958)
Just An Illusion (2)	Imagination (1982)		
Just Another Day (5)	Jon Secada (1992)	Key The Secret, The (2)	Urban Cookie Collective (1993)
Just Around The Hill (8)	Sash (2000)		
Just Can't Get Enough (8)	Depeche Mode (1981)	Key To My Life (3)	Boyzone (1995)
		Kids (2)	Robbie Williams & Kylie Minogue (2000)
Just Don't Want To Be Lonely (9)	Freddie McGregor (1987)		
Just For You (10)	Glitter Band (1974)	Kids In America (2) first hit	Kim Wilde (1981)
Just For You (8)	M People (1997)	Kid's Last Fight, The (3)	Frankie Laine (1954)
Just Got Lucky (7)	Jo Boxers (1983)	Killer (1)	Adamski (1990)
Just Like A Pill (1)	Pink (2002)	Killer (4)	ATB (2000)
Just Like A Woman (10)	Manfred Mann (1966)	Killer (EP) (8)	Seal (1991)
		Killer On The Loose (10)	Thin Lizzy (1980)
Just Like Eddie (5)	Heinz (1963)	Killer Queen (2)	Queen (1974)
(Just Like) Starting Over (1)	John Lennon (1980)	Killing Me Softly (1)	Fugees (1996)
Just Looking (4)	Stereophonics (1999)	Killing Me Softly With His Song (6)	Roberta Flack (1973)
		Killing Moon (9)	Echo And The Bunnymen (1984)
Just Loving You (6)	Anita Harris (1967)		

M
U
S
I
C

P
O
P

Title	Group/Artiste	Title	Group/Artiste
Killing Of Georgie (Parts 1 And 2), The (2)	Rod Stewart (1976)	Koochy (4)	Armand Van Helden (2000)
Kind Of Magic, A (3)	Queen (1986)	Kowalski (8)	Primal Scream (1997)
King / Food For Thought (4) first hit	UB40 (1980)	Kung Fu Fighting (8)	Bus Stop featuring Carl Douglas (1998)
King Creole (2)	Elvis Presley with The Jordanaires (1958)	Kung Fu Fighting (1)	Carl Douglas (1974)
King Of My Castle (1)	Wamdue Project (1999)	Kung-Fu (9)	187 Lockdown (1998)
King Of Rock 'N' Roll, The (7)	Prefab Sprout (1988)	La Bamba (1)	Los Lobos (1987)
King Of The Cops (6)	Billy Howard (1975)	La Dee Dah (4)	Jackie Dennis (1958)
King Of The Road (1)	Roger Miller (1965)	La Isla Bonita (1)	Madonna (1987)
King Of The Road (EP) (9)	Proclaimers (1990)	La La La Hey Hey (7)	Outhere Brothers (1995)
Kings Of The Wild Frontier (2)	Adam & The Ants (1981)	La Mer (Beyond The Sea) (8)	Bobby Darin (1960)
Kingston Town (4)	UB40 (1990)	La Primavera (3)	Sash (1998)
Kinky Afro (5)	Happy Mondays (1990)	Labelled With Love (4)	Squeeze (1981)
		Labour Of Love (6)	Hue & Cry (1987)
Kinky Boots (5)	Patrick MacNee & Honor Blackman (1990)	Ladies Knight (9)	Kool & The Gang (1979)
		Lady D'Arbanville (8)	Cat Stevens (1970)
Kiss (5)	Art Of Noise featuring Tom Jones (1988)	Lady Eleanor (3)	Lindisfarne (1972)
		Lady (Hear Me Tonight) (1)	Modjo (2000)
Kiss (9)	Dean Martin (1953)	Lady In Red, The (1)	Chris De Burgh (1986)
Kiss (6)	Prince & The Revolution (1986)	Lady Lynda (6)	Beach Boys (1979)
		Lady Madonna (1)	Beatles (1968)
Kiss And Say Goodbye (4)	Manhattans (1976)	Lady Marmalade (1)	Christina Aguilera, Lil' Kim, Mya & Pink (2001)
Kiss From A Rose (re-issue) / I'm Alive (4)	Seal (1995)		
Kiss Kiss (1)	Holly Valance (2002)	Lady Rose (5)	Mungo Jerry (1971)
Kiss Me (4)	Sixpence None The Richer (1999)	Lady Willpower (5)	Union Gap featuring Gary Puckett (1968)
Kiss Me (4)	Stephen 'Tin Tin' Duffy (1985)	Ladyboy Is Mine, The (10)	Stuntmasters (2001)
Kiss Me Honey Honey Kiss Me (3)	Shirley Bassey (1958)	Lambada (4)	Kaoma (1989)
		Lamplight (7)	David Essex (1973)
Kiss (re-entry) (5)	Dean Martin (1953)	Land Of Make Believe, The (9)	Allstars (2002)
Kiss The Girl (9)	Peter Andre (1998)	Land Of Make Believe, The (1)	Bucks Fizz (1981)
Kiss The Rain (4)	Billie Myers (1998)	Larger Than Life (5)	Backstreet Boys (1999)
Kiss (When The Sun Don't Shine) (3)	Vengaboys (1999)	Last Christmas / Everything She Wants (2)	Wham! (1984)
Kiss You All Over (6)	Exile (1978)	Last Christmas (re-issue) (6)	Wham! (1985)
Kisses Sweeter Than Wine (7)	Jimmie Rodgers (1957)	Last Farewell, The (2)	Roger Whittaker (1975)
Kisses Sweeter Than Wine (8)	Frankie Vaughan (1957)	Last Goodbye / Be With You (2)	Atomic Kitten (2002)
Kissin' Cousins (10)	Elvis Presley with The Jordanaires (1964)	Last Kiss, The (6)	David Cassidy (1985)
Kissin In The Back Row Of The Movies (2)	Drifters (1974)	Last Night In Soho (8)	Dave Dee, Dozy, Beaky, Mick & Tich (1968)
Kites (9)	Simon Dupree & The Big Sound (1967)	Last Night On Earth (10)	U2 (1997)
		Last Night Was Made For Love (4)	Billy Fury (1962)
Klubbhopping (10)	Klubbheads (1996)	Last Of The Famous International Playboys (6)	Morrissey (1989)
Knee Deep In The Blues (3)	Guy Mitchell (1957)		
Knock Knock Who's There (2)	Mary Hopkin (1970)	Last One Standing (8)	Girl Thing (2000)
Knock On Wood (10)	David Bowie (1974)	Last Resort (3)	Papa Roach (2001)
Knock On Wood (6)	Amii Stewart (1979)	Last Thing On My Mind (6)	Steps (1998)
Knock On Wood / Light My Fire (remix) (7)	Amii Stewart (1985)	Last Time, The (1)	Rolling Stones (1965)
Knock Three Times (1)	Dawn (1971)	Last Train To San Fernando (2)	Johnny Duncan & Blue Grass Boys (1957)
Knocked It Off (8)	B A Robertson (1979)		
Knockin' On Heaven's Door (2)	Guns 'N' Roses (1992)	Last Train To Trancentral (2)	KLF (1991)
Knockin' On Heaven's Door / Throw These Guns Away (1)	Dunblane (1996)	Last Waltz, The (1)	Engelbert Humperdinck (1967)
Knowing Me Knowing You (1)	Abba (1977)	Lately (6)	Samantha Mumba (2001)
Kon-Tiki (1)	Shadows (1961)		

Title	Group/Artiste	Title	Group/Artiste
Lately (3)	Stevie Wonder (1981)	Let Me Entertain You (3)	Robbie Williams (1998)
Laugh At Me (9)	Sonny (1965)	Let Me Go Lover (9) (first hit)	Teresa Brewer with The Lancers (1955)
Laughing Gnome, The (6)	David Bowie (1973)		
Launch, The (2)	DJ Jean (1999)	Let Me Go Lover (10)	Kathy Kirby (1964)
Lavender (5)	Marillion (1985)	Let Me Go Lover (3)	Dean Martin (1955)
Lay All Your Love On Me (7)	Abba (1981)	Let Me Go Lover (5)	Ruby Murray (1955)
Lay All Your Love On Me (3)	Racey (1978)		
Lay Down Your Arms (1)	Anne Shelton (1956)	Let Me In (2)	Osmonds (1973)
Lay Lady Lay (5)	Bob Dylan (1969)	Let Me Live (9)	Queen (1996)
Layla (7)	Derek & The Dominoes (1972)	Let Me Show You (5)	Camisra (1998)
		Let Me Try Again (5)	Tammy Jones (1975)
Layla (re-issue) (4)	Derek & The Dominoes (1982)	Let The Beat Control Your Body (6)	2 Unlimited (1994)
Lazy (9)	Suede (1997)	Let The Heartaches Begin (1) first hit	Long John Baldry (1967)
Lazy (2)	X-Press 2 featuring David Byrne (2002)	Let The Music Play (9)	Barry White (1975)
		Let There Be Drums (3)	Sandy Nelson (1961)
Lazy Days (8)	Robbie Williams (1997)	Let There Be Love (6)	Simple Minds (1991)
Lazy River (2)	Bobby Darin (1961)		
Lazy Sunday (2)	Small Faces (1968)	Let Your Love Flow (7) first hit	Bellamy Brothers (1976)
Le Freak (7)	Chic (1978)		
Leader Of The Pack (re-issue) (3)	Shangri-Las (1972)	Let Your Yeah Be Yeah (5)	Pioneers (1971)
Leader Of The Pack (re-issue) (7)	Shangri-Las (1976)	Let's All Chant (8)	Michael Zager Band (1978)
Lean On Me (3)	Club Nouveau (1987)		
		Let's Dance (1)	David Bowie (1983)
Lean On Me (7)	Mud (1976)	Let's Dance (1)	Five (2001)
Lean On Me (Ah-Li-Ayo) (3)	Red Box (1985)	Let's Dance (2)	Chris Montez (1962)
Learnin' The Blues (2)	Frank Sinatra with Nelson Riddle (1955)	Let's Dance (re-entry) (9)	Chris Montez (1972)
		Let's Get Ready To Rhumble (9)	PJ & Duncan (1994)
		Let's Get Rocked (2)	Def Leppard (1992)
Leave A Light On (4)	Belinda Carlisle (1989)	Let's Get Serious (8)	Jermaine Jackson (1980)
Leave A Little Love (8)	Lulu (1965)	Let's Get Together Again (8)	Glitter Band (1974)
Leave Home (17) first hit	Chemical Brothers (1995)	Let's Get Together No. 1 (6)	Big Ben Banjo Band (1954)
Leave Me Alone (2)	Michael Jackson (1989)	Let's Go All The Way (3)	Sly Fox (1986)
Leave Them All Behind (9)	Ride (1992)	Let's Go Crazy / Take Me With You (7)	Prince & The Revolution (1985)
Leavin' On A Jet Plane (2)	Peter Paul & Mary (1970)	Let's Go Round Again (10)	Louise (1997)
		Let's Go To San Francisco (4)	Flowerpot Men (1967)
Leeds United (10)	Leeds United FC (1972)	Let's Groove (3)	Earth Wind & Fire (1981)
Left To My Own Devices (4)	Pet Shop Boys (1988)	Let's Hang On! (4)	Four Seasons featuring The Sound Of Frankie Valli (1965)
Legacy EP (7)	Mansun (1998)		
Legend Of Xanadu (1)	Dave Dee, Dozy, Beaky, Mick & Tich (1968)		
		Let's Have A Ball (4)	Winifred Atwell (1957)
Lenny (10)	Supergrass (1995)	Let's Have A Ding Dong (3)	Winifred Atwell (1955)
Les Bicyclettes De Belsize (5)	Engelbert Humperdinck (1968)	Let's Have A Party (2)	Winifred Atwell (1953)
Lessons In Love (3)	Level 42 (1986)	Let's Have A Quiet Night In (8)	David Soul (1977)
Let 'Em In (2)	Wings (1976)	Let's Have Another Party (1)	Winifred Atwell (1954)
Let Forever Be (9)	Chemical Brothers (1999)	Let's Hear It For The Boy (2)	Deniece Williams (1984)
Let It Be (2)	Beatles (1970)		
Let It Be (1)	Ferry Aid (1987)	Let's Make A Night To Remember (10)	Bryan Adams (1996)
Let It Rain (10)	East 17 (1995)		
Let It Rock / Memphis Tennessee (6)	Chuck Berry (1963)	Let's Party (1)	Jive Bunny & The Mastermixers (1989)
Let Love Be Your Energy (10)	Robbie Williams (2001)		
		Let's Put It All Together (9)	Stylistics (1974)
Let Me Be Your Fantasy (1)	Baby D (1994)	Let's Spend The Night Together/ Ruby Tuesday (7)	Rolling Stones (1967)
(Let Me Be Your) Teddy Bear (3)	Elvis Presley with The Jordanaires (1957)	Let's Stay Together (7)	Al Green (1972)
		Let's Stay Together (6)	Tina Turner (1983)
Let Me Blow Ya Mind (4)	Eve featuring Gwen Stefani (2001)	Let's Stick Together (Let's Work Together) (4)	Bryan Ferry (1976)
Let Me Clear My Throat (8)	DJ Kool (1997)		

MUSIC POP

Title	Group/Artiste	Title	Group/Artiste
Let's Talk About Sex (2)	Salt-N-Pepa featuring Psychotropic (1991)	Liquidator (9)	Harry J Allstars (1969)
		Listen To What The Man Said (6)	Wings (1975)
Let's Think About Living (6)	Bob Luman (1960)	Listen To Your Heart (10)	Sonia (1989)
Let's Try Again / Didn't I Blow Your Mind (8)	New Kids On The Block (1990)	Listen To Your Heart / Dangerous (6)	Roxette (1990)
Let's Twist Again / The Twist (re-issue) (5)	Chubby Checker (1975)	Little Arrows (2)	Leapy Lee (1968)
Let's Twist Again (remix) (2)	Chubby Checker (1961)	Little Bird / Love Song For A Vampire (3)	Annie Lennox (1993)
		Little Bit Me A Little Bit You, A (3)	Monkees (1967)
Let's Wait Awhile (3)	Janet Jackson (1987)	Little Bit More, A (2)	Dr Hook (1976)
		Little Bit More, A (1)	911 (1999)
Let's Walk Thata-Way (4)	Doris Day & Johnnie Ray (1953)	Little Bit Of Lovin' (8)	Kele Le Roc (1998)
		Little Bit Of Luck, A (9)	DJ Luck & MC Neat (1999)
Let's Work Together (2)	Canned Heat (1970)	Little Bit Of Soap, A (5)	Showaddywaddy (1978)
Letter From America (3)	Proclaimers (1987)		
Letter To You, A (10)	Shakin' Stevens (1984)	Little Bitty Tear, A (9)	Burl Ives (1962)
		Little By Little / She Is Love (2)	Oasis (2002)
Letter, The (5)	Box Tops (1967)	Little Children (1)	Billy J Kramer And The Dakotas (1964)
Licence To Kill (6)	Gladys Knight (1989)		
Lie To Me (10)	Bon Jovi (1995)	Little Darlin' (3)	Diamonds (1957)
Life (8)	Des'ree (1998)	Little Devil (9)	Neil Sedaka (1961)
Life (6)	Haddaway (1993)	Little Donkey (3)	Nina & Frederick (1960)
Life Ain't Easy (4)	Cleopatra (1998)		
Life Is A Flower (5)	Ace Of Base (1998)	Little Drummer Boy (6)	Beverley Sisters (1959)
Life Is A Minestrone (7)	10CC (1975)		
Life is A Rollercoaster (1)	Ronan Keating (2000)	Little Fluffy Clouds (10)	Orb (1993)
Life Is Too Short Girl (9)	Sheer Elegance (1976)	Little L (5)	Jamiroquai (2001)
		Little Less Conversation, A (1)	Elvis vs JXL (2002)
Life Less Ordinary, A (10)	Ash (1997)	Little Lies (5)	Fleetwood Mac (1987)
Life On Mars (3)	David Bowie (1973)		
Lifeline (7)	Spandau Ballet (1982)	Little Love And Understanding, A (10)	Gilbert Becaud (1975)
Lift Me Up (1)	Geri Halliwell (1999)	Little Loving, A (6)	Fourmost (1964)
Lifted (4)	Lighthouse Family (1996)	Little Man (4)	Sonny & Cher (1966)
Light My Fire (7)	Clubhouse featuring Carl (1994)	Little Miss Lonely (8)	Helen Shapiro (1962)
Light My Fire (6)	Jose Feliciano (1968)	Little More Love, A (4)	Olivia Newton-John (1978)
Light My Fire (1)	Will Young (2002)	Little Peace, A (1)	Nicole (1982)
Light My Fire / 137 Disco Heaven (medley) (5)	Amii Stewart (1979)	Little Red Monkey (10)	Frank Chacksfield (1953)
Light My Fire (re-issue) (7)	Doors (1991)	Little Red Rooster (1)	Rolling Stones (1964)
(Light Of Experience) Doina De Jale (4)	Georghe Zamfir (1976)	Little Respect, A (4)	Erasure (1988)
Light Of My Life (8) first hit	Louise (1995)	Little Respect, A (3)	Wheatus (2001)
Like A Baby (10)	Len Barry (1966)	Little Shoemaker, The (7) first hit	Petula Clark (1954)
Like A Prayer (3)	Madhouse (2002)	Little Things (5)	Dave Berry (1965)
Like A Prayer (1)	Madonna (1989)	Little Things Mean A Lot (1)	Kitty Kallen (1954)
Like A Rolling Stone (4)	Bob Dylan (1965)	Little Time, A (1)	Beautiful South (1990)
Like A Rose (6)	A1 (2000)		
Like A Virgin (3)	Madonna (1984)	Little Town Flirt (4)	Del Shannon (1963)
Like Clockwork (6)	Boomtown Rats (1978)	Little White Bull (6)	Tommy Steele (1959)
Like I Do (3)	Maureen Evans (1962)	Little Willy (4)	Sweet (1972)
		Live And Let Die (5)	Guns 'N' Roses (1991)
Like I Love You (2)	Justin Timberlake (2002)	Live And Let Die (9)	Paul McCartney & Wings (1973)
Like I've Never Been Gone (3)	Billy Fury (1963)		
Like Sister And Brother (7)	Drifters (1973)	Live Forever (10)	Oasis (1994)
Like To Get To Know You Well (4)	Howard Jones (1984)	Live In Trouble (7)	Barron Knights (1977)
Lily The Pink (1)	Scaffold (1968)	Live Is Life (6)	Opus (1985)
Lily Was Here (6)	Dave A Stewart with Candy Dulfer (1990)	Live It Up (3)	Mental As Anything (1987)
Lion Sleeps Tonight, The (1)	Tight Fit (1982)	Live Like Horses (9)	Elton John & Luciano Pavarotti (1996)
Lipstick On Your Collar (3)	Connie Francis (1959)		
Liquid Dreams (3)	O-Town (2001)	Live The Dream (7)	Cast (1997)

Title	Group/Artiste	Title	Group/Artiste
Live To Tell (2)	Madonna (1986)	Look At That Girl (1)	Guy Mitchell (1953)
Live Together (10)	Lisa Stansfield (1990)	Look Away (7)	Big Country (1986)
		Look For A Star (7)	Garry Mills (1960)
Liverpool Lou (7)	Scaffold (1974)	Look Homeward Angel (7)	Johnnie Ray (1957)
Livin' It Up (re-issue) (5)	Ja Rule featuring Case (2002)	Look Mama (10)	Howard Jones (1985)
Livin' La Vida Loca (1)	Ricky Martin (1999)	Look Of Love, The (4)	ABC (1982)
Livin' On A Prayer (4)	Bon Jovi (1986)	Look Of Love, The (9)	Madonna (1987)
Livin' Thing (4)	Electric Light Orchestra (1976)	Look Through Any Window (4)	Hollies (1965)
		Look Wot You Dun (4)	Slade (1972)
Living Daylights, The (5)	A-Ha (1987)	Look, The (7) first hit	Roxette (1989)
Living Doll (1)	Cliff Richard & The Drifters (1959)	Lookin' Through The Windows (9)	Jackson 5 (1972)
Living Doll (1)	Cliff Richard & The Young Ones with Hank Marvin (1986)	Looking After No. 1 (11) first hit	Boomtown Rats (1977)
		Looking For Love (8)	Karen Ramirez (1998)
Living In A Box (5)	Living In A Box (1987)	Looking Through The Eyes Of Love (9)	Partridge Family starring David Cassidy (1973)
Living In America (5)	James Brown (1986)		
Living In The Past (3)	Jethro Tull (1969)	Looking Through The Eyes Of Love (3)	Gene Pitney (1965)
Living Next Door To Alice (5)	Smokie (1976)		
Living Next Door To Alice (Who The F**K Is Alice) (3)	Smokie featuring Roy 'Chubby' Brown (1995)	Loop Di Love (4)	Shag (1972)
		Loop-De-Loop (5)	Frankie Vaughan (1963)
Living On My Own (1)	Freddie Mercury (1993)	Lorelei (10)	Lonnie Donegan (1960)
Living On The Ceiling (7)	Blancmange (1982)	Lose Yourself (1)	Eminem (2002)
Living On Video (9)	Trans X (1985)	Losing My Mind (6)	Liza Minnelli (1989)
Living Years, The (2)	Mike & The Mechanics (1989)	Losing You (10)	Brenda Lee (1963)
		Losing You (9)	Dusty Springfield (1964)
LK (Carolina Carol Bela) (17)	DJ Marky & XRS with Stamina MC (2002)	Lost In France (9) first hit	Bonnie Tyler (1976)
		Lost In Music (remix) (4)	Sister Sledge (1984)
L-L-Lucy (10)	Mud (1975)	Lost In Space (4)	Apollo Four Forty (1998)
Loadsamoney (4)	Harry Enfield (1988)		
Loco (5)	Fun Lovin' Criminals (2001)	Lost In Space (6)	Lighthouse Family (1998)
Loco In Acapulco (7)	Four Tops (1988)	Lost John / Stewball (2)	Lonnie Donegan Skiffle Group (1956)
Locomotion (5)	Orchestral Manoeuvres In The Dark (1984)		
		Loungin' (7)	LL Cool J (1996)
Loco-Motion, The (2)	Little Eva (1962)	Love Action (I Believe In Love) (3)	Human League (1981)
Loco-Motion, The (2)	Kylie Minogue (1988)		
Logical Song, The (2)	Scooter (2002)	Love Ain't Here Anymore (3)	Take That (1994)
Logical Song, The (7)	Supertramp (1979)	Love And Affection (10) first and biggest hit	Joan Armatrading (1976)
Lola (2)	Kinks (1970)		
Lollipop (6)	Chordettes (1958)	Love And Kisses (8)	Dannii Minogue (1991)
Lollipop (2)	Mudlarks (1958)		
London Nights (2)	London Boys (1989)	Love And Marriage (3)	Frank Sinatra (1956)
Lone Ranger, The (5)	Quantum Jump (1979)	Love And Pride (2)	King (1985)
		Love And Understanding (10)	Cher (1991)
Lonely (6)	Peter Andre (1997)	Love At First Sight (2)	Kylie Minogue (2002)
Lonely Boy (3)	Paul Anka (1959)	Love Can Build A Bridge (1)	Cher, Chrissie Hynde, Neneh Cherry and Eric Clapton (1995)
Lonely Bull, The (3)	Herb Alpert & The Tijuana Brass (1963)		
Lonely Pup (In A Christmas Shop) (4)	Adam Faith with The Children (1960)	Love Can't Turn Around (10)	Farley 'Jackmaster' Funk and Jessie Saunders (1986)
Lonely This Christmas (1)	Mud (1974)		
Long And Winding Road, The / Suspicious Minds (1)	Will Young & Gareth Gates (2002)	Love Cats, The (7)	Cure (1983)
		Love Changes Everything (2) first hit	Michael Ball (1989)
Long-Haired Lover From Liverpool (1)	Little Jimmy Osmond (1972)		
		Love Changes Everything (2)	Climie Fisher (1988)
Long Hot Summer / Paris Match (3)	Style Council (1983)	Love City Groove (7) first and only hit	Love City Groove (1995)
Long Live Love (1)	Sandie Shaw (1965)		
Long Tall Glasses (4)	Leo Sayer (1974)	Love Come Down (7)	Evelyn 'Champagne' King (1982)
Long Tall Sally (3)	Little Richard (1957)		
Long Train Runnin (7)	Doobie Brothers (1993)	Love Don't Cost A Thing (1)	Jennifer Lopez (2001)
Look At Me (2) first solo hit	Geri Halliwell (1999)	Love Don't Live Here Anymore (3)	Jimmy Nail (1985)
		Love Don't Live Here Anymore (2)	Rose Royce (1978)

Title	Group/Artiste	Title	Group/Artiste
Love Grows (Where My Rosemary Goes) (1)	Edison Lighthouse (1970)	Love Spreads (2)	Stone Roses (1994)
Love Guaranteed (7)	Damage (1997)	Love Theme From A Star Is Born (Evergreen) (3)	Barbra Streisand (1977)
Love Hangover (10)	Diana Ross (1976)	Love Theme From The Thornbirds (10)	Juan Martin (1984)
Love Hurts (4)	Jim Capaldi (1975)		
Love I Lost, The (3)	West End featuring Sybil (1993)	Love To Hate You (4)	Erasure (1991)
Love In An Elevator (13)	Aerosmith (1989)	Love To Love You Baby (4) first hit	Donna Summer (1976)
Love In The First Degree (3)	Bananarama (1987)	Love Town (6)	Booker Newbury III (1983)
Love Is A Many-Splendoured Thing (2)	Four Aces featuring Al Alberts (1955)	Love Train (4)	Holly Johnson (1989)
Love Is A Stranger (6)	Eurythmics (1983)	Love Train (9)	O'Jays (1973)
Love Is All Around (5)	Troggs (1967)	Love Will Save The Day (10)	Whitney Houston (1988)
Love Is All Around (1)	Wet Wet Wet (1994)		
Love Is Contagious (7)	Taja Seville (1988)	Love Won't Wait (1)	Gary Barlow (1997)
Love Is In The Air (5)	John Paul Young (1978)	Love Worth Waiting For, A (2)	Shakin' Stevens (1984)
Love Is Life (6)	Hot Chocolate (1970)	Love X Love (10)	George Benson (1980)
Love Is Like A Violin (8) first hit	Ken Dodd (1960)		
Love Is Like Oxygen (9)	Sweet (1978)	Love You Save, The (7)	Jackson 5 (1970)
Love Is The Drug (2)	Roxy Music (1975)	Love ... Thy Will Be Done (9)	Martika (1991)
Love Is The Law (3)	Seahorses (1997)	Lovefool (2)	Cardigans (1997)
(Love Is) The Tender Trap (2)	Frank Sinatra (1956)	Lovely Day (7)	Bill Withers (1978)
Love Kills (10)	Freddie Mercury (1984)	Lovely Day (remix) (4)	Bill Withers (1988)
Love Letters (4)	Ketty Lester (1962)	Lover's Concerto, A (5)	Toys (1965)
Love Letters (4)	Alison Moyet (1987)	Lovers Of The World Unite (7)	David & Jonathan (1966)
Love Letters (6)	Elvis Presley (1966)	Love's Been Good To Me (8)	Frank Sinatra (1969)
Love Letters In The Sand (2)	Pat Boone (1957)	Love's Got A Hold On My Heart (2)	Steps (1999)
Love Like A Man (10)	Ten Years After (1970)	Love's Gotta Hold On Me (4)	Dollar (1979)
Love Like You And Me (10)	Gary Glitter (1975)	Love's Just A Broken Heart (5)	Cilla Black (1966)
Love Machine (3)	Miracles (1976)	Love's Theme (10)	Love Unlimited Orchestra (1974)
Love Makes The World Go Round (6)	Perry Como (1958)	Love's Unkind (3)	Donna Summer (1977)
Love Me (6)	Yvonne Elliman (1976)	Lovesick Blues (1)	Frank Ifield (1962)
Love Me Do (17) first hit	Beatles (1962)	Lovestruck (10)	Madness (1999)
Love Me Do (re-entry) (4)	Beatles (1982)	Lovin' Each Day (2)	Ronan Keating (2001)
Love Me For A Reason (2) first hit	Boyzone (1994)	Lovin' Is Easy (6)	Hear'Say (2002)
Love Me For A Reason (1)	Osmonds (1974)	Lovin' Things (6) first hit	Marmalade (1968)
Love Me Forever (5)	Marion Ryan (1958)	Loving You (2)	Minnie Riperton (1975)
Love Me Like I Love You (4)	Bay City Rollers (1976)	LSI (6)	Shamen (1992)
Love Me Love My Dog (3)	Peter Shelley (1975)	Lucille (10)	Little Richard (1957)
Love Me Or Leave Me (8)	Sammy Davis Jr (1955)	Lucille (1)	Kenny Rogers (1977)
Love Me Tonight (9)	Tom Jones (1969)	Lucille / So Sad (to watch good love go bad) (4)	Everley Brothers (1960)
Love Missile F1-11 (3)	Sigue Sigue Sputnik (1986)	Lucky (5)	Britney Spears (2000)
Love Of A Lifetime (9)	Honeyz (1999)		
Love Of My Life (9)	Dooleys (1977)	Lucky Lips (4)	Cliff Richard & The Shadows (1963)
Love Of The Common People (9)	Nicky Thomas (1970)	Lucky Man (7)	Verve (1997)
Love Of The Common People (2)	Paul Young (1983)	Lucky Number (3)	Lene Lovich (1979)
Love Of The Loved (35) first hit	Cilla Black (1963)	Lucky Stars (3)	Dean Friedman (1978)
Love On A Mountain Top (10)	Robert Knight (1973)		
Love On The Line (6)	Blazin' Squad (2002)	Lucy In The Sky With Diamonds (10)	Elton John (1974)
Love On Your Side (9)	Thompson Twins (1983)	Lullaby (5)	Cure (1989)
Love Plus One (3)	Haircut 100 (1982)	Lullaby (9)	Shawn Mullins (1999)
Love Really Hurts Without You (2)	Billy Ocean (1976)		
Love Resurrection (10)	Alison Moyet (1984)	Luv Me Luv Me (5)	Shaggy (2001)
Love Rollercoaster (7)	Red Hot Chili Peppers (1997)	Luv U Better (7)	LL Cool J (2002)
Love Shack (2)	B-52's (1990)	Luvstruck (9)	Southside Spinners (2000)
Love Shine A Light (3)	Katrina & The Waves (1997)	Lyin' Eyes (23)	Eagles (1975)
Love Song / Alive And Kicking (re-issues) (6)	Simple Minds (1992)	Ma Baker (2)	Boney M (1977)
		Ma (He's Making Eyes At Me) (2)	Johnny Otis Show (1957)

Title	Group/Artiste	Title	Group/Artiste
Ma (He's Making Eyes At Me) (10)	Lena Zavaroni (1974)	Mambo No 5 (1)	Bob The Builder (2001)
Macarena (2)	Los Del Rio (1996)	Mambo No 5 (A Little Bit Of ...) (1)	Lou Bega (1999)
Macarthur Park (4)	Richard Harris (1968)	Mamma Mia (1)	Abba (1975)
		Man From Laramie, The (1)	Jimmy Young (1955)
Macarthur Park (5)	Donna Summer (1978)	Man Of Mystery / The Stranger (5)	Shadows (1960)
		Man Of The World (2)	Fleetwood Mac (1969)
Machine Gun (20) first hit	Communards (1974)		
Mack The Knife (1)	Bobby Darin (1959)	Man On Fire / Wanderin' Eyes (6)	Frankie Vaughan (1957)
Mad About You (9)	Bruce Ruffin (1972)		
Mad Passionate Love (6)	Bernard Bresslaw (1958)	Man On The Edge (10)	Iron Maiden (1995)
		Man (Uh-Huh) (7)	Rosemary Clooney (1954)
Mad World (3) first hit	Tears For Fears (1982)		
		Man Who Sold The World, The (3)	Lulu (1974)
Maggie May (1)	Rod Stewart (1971)	Man With The Child In His Eyes (6)	Kate Bush (1978)
Magic Fly (2)	Space (1977)	Man Without Love, A (2)	Engelbert Humperdinck (1968)
Magic Moments (1)	Perry Como (1958)		
Magic Number, The / Buddy (7) biggest hit	De La Soul (1989)		
		Man! I Feel Like A Woman (3)	Shania Twain (1999)
Magic Roundabout/Funky Moped (5)	Jasper Carrott (1975)	Manchild (5)	Neneh Cherry (1989)
		Mandy (9)	Eddie Calvert (1958)
Magical Mystery Tour EP (2)	Beatles (1967)	Maneater (6)	Daryl Hall & John Oates (1982)
Mah Na Mah Na (8)	Piero Umiliani (1977)		
Maid Of Orleans (The Waltz Joan Of Arc) (4)	Orchestral Manoeuvres In The Dark (1982)	Manic Monday (2) first hit	Bangles (1986)
		Marblehead Johnson (7)	Bluetones (1996)
		March Of The Siamese Children (4)	Kenny Ball & His Jazzmen (1962)
Main Title Theme From Man With The Golden Arm (9)	Billy May Orchestra (1956)	Marcheta (8) first hit	Karl Denver (1961)
Make It A Party (7)	Winifred Atwell (1956)	Marguerita Time (3)	Status Quo (1983)
		Maria (1)	Blondie (1999)
Make It Easy On Yourself (1)	Walker Brothers (1965)	Maria (8)	P J Proby (1965)
		Maria Elena (5)	Los Indios Tabajaras (1963)
Make It Good (11)	A1 (2002)		
Make It Soon (9)	Tony Brent (1953)	Maria Maria (6)	Santana featuring The Product G&B (2000)
Make It Soon (re-entry) (9)	Tony Brent (1953)		
Make It With You (5)	Bread (1970)		
Make It With You (7)	Let Loose (1996)	Marie (9)	Bachelors (1965)
Make Love To Me (8)	Jo Stafford (1954)	(Marie's The Name) His Latest Flame / Little Sister (1)	Elvis Presley (1961)
Make Me An Island (3)	Joe Dolan (1969)		
Make Me Smile (Come Up And See Me) (1)	Steve Harley & Cockney Rebel (1975)	Marjorine (48) first hit	Joe Cocker (1968)
		Marrakesh Express (17) first and only hit	Crosby, Stills and Nash (1969)
Make The World Go Away (8) first hit	Eddy Arnold (1966)	Martha's Harbour (10)	All About Eve (1988)
		Mary Had A Little Boy (8)	Snap (1990)
Makin' Love (9)	Floyd Robinson (1959)	Mary Had A Little Lamb (9)	Wings (1972)
		Mary's Boy Child (1)	Harry Belafonte (1957)
Making Up Again (7)	Goldie (1978)		
Making Your Mind Up (1) first hit	Bucks Fizz (1981)	Mary's Boy Child – Oh My Lord (1)	Boney M (1978)
Male Stripper (4)	Man 2 Man meet Man Parrish (1987)	Mary's Boy Child (re-entry) (10)	Harry Belafonte (1958)
		Mary's Prayer (3)	Danny Wilson (1988)
Malt And Barley Blues (5)	McGuinness Flint (1971)	Mas Que Nada (10)	Echobeatz (1998)
		Massachusetts (1)	Bee Gees (1967)
Mama (5)	Dave Berry (1966)	Masses Against The Classes, The (1)	Manic Street Preachers (2000)
Mama (4)	Genesis (1983)		
Mama – Who Da Man? (3)	Richard Blackwood (2000)	Master And Servant (9)	Depeche Mode (1984)
Mama / Robot Man (2)	Connie Francis (1960)	Masterblaster (Jammin') (2)	Stevie Wonder (1980)
Mama / Who Do You Think You Are (1)	Spice Girls (1997)	Masterblaster 2000 (5)	DJ Luck & MC Neat featuring JJ (2000)
Mama Told Me Not To Come (4)	Tom Jones & The Stereophonics (2000)	Matchstalk Men And Matchstalk Cats And Dogs (1) first and only hit	Brian & Michael (1978)
Mama Told Me Not To Come (3)	Three Dog Night (1970)	Material Girl (3)	Madonna (1985)
		Matthew And Son (2)	Cat Stevens (1967)
Mama Used To Say (7)	Junior (1982)	May I Have The Next Dream With You (8)	Malcolm Roberts (1968)
Mama Weer All Crazee Now (1)	Slade (1972)		
Mambo Italiano (1)	Rosemary Clooney & The Mellomen (1954)	May You Always (9)	Joan Regan (1959)
		Maybe (12)	Enrique Iglesias (2002)

Title	Group/Artiste	Title	Group/Artiste
Maybe Baby (4)	Crickets (1958)	Midnight Train To Georgia (10)	Gladys Knight & The Pips (1976)
Me And My Life (4)	Tremeloes (1970)		
Me And You And A Dog Named Boo (4)	Lobo (1971)	Mighty Joe (43) second and only other hit	Shocking Blue (1970)
Me And You Versus The World (9)	Space (1996)	Mighty Quinn (1)	Manfred Mann (1968)
Me Julie (2)	Shaggy & Ali G (2002)	Milk (10)	Garbage featuring Tricky (1996)
Me No Pop (32)	Kid Creole and the Coconuts (1981)	Milk And Alcohol (9)	Dr Feelgood (1979)
Me The Peaceful Heart (9)	Lulu (1968)	Millennium (1)	Robbie Williams (1998)
Mean Streak (10)	Cliff Richard & The Drifters (1959)	Millennium Prayer, The (1)	Cliff Richard (1999)
Meet Me On The Corner (2)	Max Bygraves (1955)	Million Love Songs, A (7)	Take That (1992)
Meet Me On The Corner (5)	Lindisfarne (1972)	Mind Of It's Own, A (6)	Victoria Beckham (2002)
(Meet) The Flintstones (3)	BC-52s (1994)		
Megablast / Don't Make Me Wait (6)	Bomb The Bass featuring Merlin & Antonia / Lorraine & Lose (1988)	Minute You're Gone, The (1)	Cliff Richard (1965)
		Mirror In The Bathroom (4)	Beat (1980)
		Mirror Man (2)	Human League (1982)
Megamix (6)	Technotronic (1990)	Mirror Mirror (4)	Dollar (1981)
Mellow Yellow (8)	Donovan (1967)	Mirror Mirror (9)	Pinkerton's Assorted Colours (1966)
Melody Of Love (10)	Ink Spots (1955)		
Melting Pot (3) first hit	Blue Mink (1969)	Misfit (7)	Curiosity Killed The Cat (1987)
Memories Are Made Of This (5)	Dave King featuring The Keynotes (1956)	Miss Sarajevo (6)	Passengers (1995)
		Miss You / Far Away Eyes (3)	Rolling Stones (1978)
Memories Are Made Of This (1)	Dean Martin (1956)	Miss You Like Crazy (2)	Natalie Cole (1989)
Memory (6)	Elaine Paige (1981)	Mis-Shapes / Sorted For E's And Wizz (2)	Pulp (1995)
Memphis Tennessee (19) first hit	Dave Berry (1963)		
Men In Black (1) first hit	Will Smith (1997)	Missing (remix) (3)	Everything But The Girl (1994)
Mercy Mercy Me – I Want You (9)	Robert Palmer (1991)		
Merry Christmas Everyone (1)	Shakin' Stevens (1985)	Missing You (3)	Chris De Burgh (1988)
Merry Gentle Pops (9)	Barron Knights with Duke D'Mond (1965)	Missing You (9)	John Waite (1984)
		Mississippi (1)	Pussycat (1976)
Merry Xmas Everybody (1)	Slade (1973)	Mistletoe And Wine (1)	Cliff Richard (1988)
Mess Of Blues, A (2)	Elvis Presley with The Jordanaires (1960)	Misty (2)	Ray Stevens (1975)
		Misty Blue (5)	Dorothy Moore (1976)
Message In A Bottle (1)	Police (1979)		
Message To You Rudy, A / Nite Club (10)	Specials featuring Rico (1979)	Mmm Mmm Mmm Mmm (2) first hit	Crash Test Dummies (1994)
Message Understood (6)	Sandie Shaw (1965)	Mmmbop (1)	Hanson (1997)
Message, The (8)	Grandmaster Flash & The Furious Five (1982)	Mo Money Mo Problems (6)	Notorious BIG featuring 112 (1997)
Metal Guru (1)	T Rex (1972)	Moan And Groan (7)	Mark Morrison (1997)
Mexicali Rose (8)	Karl Denver (1961)		
Mexico (15)	Long John Baldry (1968)	Mobile (4)	Ray Burns with Eric Jupp and Orchestra (1955)
MFEO (8)	Kavana (1997)		
Mi Chico Latino (1)	Geri Halliwell (1999)	Mockingbird Hill (10)	Migil Five (1964)
Miami (3)	Will Smith (1998)	Modern Girl (8)	Sheena Easton (1980)
Miami Hit Mix / Xmas Through Your Eyes (8)	Gloria Estefan (1992)	Modern Love (2)	David Bowie (1983)
		Moi ... Lolita (9)	Alizee (2002)
Miami Vice Theme (5)	Jan Hammer (1985)	Moments In Soul (7)	JT & The Big Family (1990)
Michael (1)	Highwaymen (1961)		
Michael Row The Boat / Lumbered (6)	Lonnie Donegan & His Group (1961)	Mona (2)	Craig McLachlan & Check 1-2 (1990)
Michelle (1)	Overlanders (1966)	Mona Lisa (5)	Conway Twitty (1959)
Mickey (2)	Toni Basil (1982)		
Mickey (4)	Lolly (1999)	Monday Monday (3)	Mamas & The Papas (1966)
Midas Touch (8)	Midnight Star (1986)		
Midlife Crisis (10)	Faith No More (1992)	Money (5)	Flying Lizards (1979)
		Money (5)	Jamelia featuring Beenie Man (2000)
Midnight In Chelsea (4)	Jon Bon Jovi (1997)	Money For Nothing (4)	Dire Straits (1985)
Midnight In Moscow (2)	Kenny Ball & His Jazzmen (1961)	Money Honey (3)	Bay City Rollers (1975)
Midnight Rider (10)	Paul Davidson (1975)	Money Money Money (3)	Abba (1976)

Title	Group/Artiste	Title	Group/Artiste
Money's Too Tight (To Mention) (13)	Simply Red (1985) first hit	Moulin Rouge (re-entry) (10)	Mantovani & His Orchestra (1953)
Monkey Spanner (7) only other hit	Dave & Ansel Collins (1971)	Mountain Greenery (re-entry) (4)	Mel Tormé (1956)
Monsieur Dupont (6)	Sandie Shaw (1969)	Move Any Mountain (remix) (4)	Shamen (1991)
Monster Mash (3)	Bobby 'Boris' Pickett & the Crypt-Kickers (1973)	Move Away (7)	Culture Club (1986)
		Move Closer (1)	Phyllis Nelson (1985)
		Move It (2) first hit	Cliff Richard and The Drifters (1958)
Montego Bay (3) first hit	Bobby Bloom (1970)		
Mony Mony (7)	Billy Idol (1987)	Move Mania (8)	Sash featuring Shannon (1998)
Mony Mony (1)	Tommy James & The Shondells (1968)	Move Move Move (The Red Tribe) (6)	1996 Manchester Utd FA Cup Squad (1996)
Moody Blue (6)	Elvis Presley (1977)		
Moon River (1)	Danny Williams (1961)	Move On Baby (7)	Cappella (1994)
		Move Over Darling (8)	Doris Day (1964)
Moonglow / Theme From Picnic (7)	Morris Stoloff (1956)	Move Over Darling (8)	Tracey Ullman (1983)
Moonlight Shadow (4)	Mike Oldfield featuring Maggie Reilly (1983)	Move Your Body (3)	Eiffel 65 (2000)
		Move Your Body (Elevation) (7)	Xpansions (1991)
Moonlighting (2)	Leo Sayer (1975)	Movies (5)	Alien Ant Farm (2002)
Moonlighting Theme (8)	Al Jarreau (1987)		
Moonshine Sally (10)	Mud (1975)	Movin' Too Fast (2)	Artful Dodger & Romina Johnson (2000)
More (10)	Perry Como (1956)		
More (4)	Jimmy Young (1956)		
More And More Party Pops (5)	Russ Conway (1959)	Moving (9)	Supergrass (1999)
More I See You, The (3)	Chris Montez (1966)	Moving On Up (2)	M People (1993)
More More More (5)	Andrea True Connection (1976)	Mozart Symphony No. 40 in G Minor (5)	Waldo De Los Rios (1971)
More Party Pops (10)	Russ Conway (1958)	Mr Blobby (1)	Mr Blobby (1993)
More Than A Woman (1)	Aaliyah (2002)	Mr Blue Sky (6)	Electric Light Orchestra (1978)
More Than A Woman (2)	911 (1998)		
More Than A Woman (7)	Tavares (1978)	Mr Hankey The Christmas Poo (4)	Mr Hankey (1999)
More Than Ever (Coma Prima) (5)	Malcolm Vaughan with The Mike Sammes Singers (1958)	Mr Loverman (re-issue) (3)	Shabba Ranks (1993)
		Mr Sandman (11) first hit	Chordettes (1954)
		Mr Sandman (9)	Four Aces featuring Al Alberts (1955)
More Than I Can Say (2)	Leo Sayer (1980)		
More Than I Can Say / Staying In (4)	Bobby Vee (1961)	Mr Sandman (5)	Dickie Valentine (1954)
More Than I Needed To Know (5)	Scooch (2000)	Mr Sleaze (3)	Stock Aitken Waterman (1987)
More Than In Love (2)	Kate Robbins & Beyond (1981)		
		Mr Soft (8)	Cockney Rebel (1974)
More Than This (5)	Emmie (1999)		
More Than This (6)	Roxy Music (1982)	Mr Tambourine Man (1) first hit	Byrds (1965)
More Than Words (2)	Extreme (1991)	Mr Vain (1)	Culture Beat (1993)
More To This World (8)	Bad Boys Inc (1994)	Mr Wendal / Revolution (4)	Arrested Development (1993)
More You Ignore Me The Closer I Get, The (8)	Morrissey (1994)		
		Mr Wonderful (5)	Peggy Lee (1957)
Morning Has Broken (9)	Cat Stevens (1972)	Mr Writer (5)	Stereophonics (2001)
Morning Side Of The Mountain (5)	Donny & Marie Osmond (1974)		
		Mrs Robinson (4)	Simon & Garfunkel (1968)
Morningtown Ride (2)	Seekers (1966)		
Most Beautiful Girl In The World, The (1)	Artist Formerly Known As Prince (1994)	Mrs Robinson (EP) (9)	Simon & Garfunkel (1969)
		Ms Grace (1)	Tymes (1974)
Most Beautiful Girl, The (2)	Charlie Rich (1974)	Ms Jackson (2)	Outkast (2001)
Most Girls (5)	Pink (2000)	(Mucho Mambo) Sway (2)	Shaft (1999)
Mother And Child Reunion (5) first solo hit	Paul Simon (1972)	Mulder And Scully (3)	Catatonia (1998)
		Mull Of Kintyre / Girls' School (1)	Wings (1977)
Mother Nature And Father Time (7)	Nat 'King' Cole (1953)	Multiplication (5)	Bobby Darin (1961)
		Murder On The Dancefloor (2)	Sophie Ellis-Bextor (2001)
Mother Of Mine (2)	Neil Reid (1972)		
Motorhead Live (6)	Motorhead (1981)	Musclebound / Glow (10)	Spandau Ballet (1981)
Motown Song, The (10)	Rod Stewart with The Temptations (1991)		
		Music (1)	Madonna (2000)
		Music (3)	John Miles (1976)
Mouldy Old Dough (1)	Lieutenant Pigeon (1972)	Music And Lights (5)	Imagination (1982)
		Music Gets The Best Of Me (14)	Sophie Ellis Bextor (2002)
Moulin Rouge (1)	Mantovani & His Orchestra (1953)	Music Is My Radar (10)	Blur (2000)

MUSIC POP

Title	Group/Artiste	Title	Group/Artiste
Music Of The Night, The (7)	Michael Crawford (1987)	My Name Is (2) first hit	Eminem (1999)
Music Of Torvill And Dean EP, The (9)	Richard Hartley & Mike Reed Orchestra (1984)	My Name Is Jack (8)	Manfred Mann (1968)
Music Sounds Better With You (2)	Stardust (1998)	My Name Is Prince (7)	Prince & The New Power Generation (1992)
Music To Watch Girls By (9)	Andy Williams (1999)	My Oh My (6)	Aqua (1998)
Music's No Good Without You, The (8)	Cher (2001)	My Oh My (2)	Slade (1983)
Must Be The Music (8)	Joey Negro featuring Taka Boom (2000)	My Old Man's A Dustman (Ballad Of A Refuse Disposal Officer) (1)	Lonnie Donegan & His Group (1960)
Must To Avoid, A (6)	Herman's Hermits (1965)	My Old Piano (5)	Diana Ross (1980)
		My One Temptation (7)	Mica Paris (1988)
My All (4)	Mariah Carey (1998)	My Perfect Cousin (9)	Undertones (1980)
My Baby Just Cares For Me (5)	Nina Simone (1987)	My Prayer (9)	Gerry Monroe (1970)
My Baby Loves Lovin' (9)	White Plains (1970)	My Prayer (4)	Platters (1956)
My Best Friend's Girl (3) first and biggest hit	Cars (1978)	My Prerogative (6)	Bobby Brown (1988)
		My Pretty One (6)	Cliff Richard (1987)
My Boy (5)	Elvis Presley (1974)	My Resistance Is Low (3)	Robin Sarstedt (1976)
My Boy Lollipop (2)	Millie (1964)		
My Brother Jake (4)	Free (1971)	My Sentimental Friend (2)	Herman's Hermits (1969)
My Camera Never Lies (1)	Bucks Fizz (1982)		
My Cherie Amour (4)	Stevie Wonder (1969)	My September Love (re-entry) (3)	David Whitfield (1956)
My Coo-Ca-Choo (2) first hit	Alvin Stardust (1973)	My Sharona (6)	Knack (1979)
My Culture (9)	1 Giant Leap featuring Maxi Jazz and Robbie Williams (2002)	My Ship Is Coming In (3)	Walker Brothers (1965)
		My Simple Heart (9)	Three Degrees (1979)
My Destiny (7)	Lionel Richie (1992)	My Son My Son (1)	Vera Lynn with The Frank Weir Orchestra (1954)
My Ding-A-Ling (1)	Chuck Berry (1972)		
My Dixie Darling (10)	Lonnie Donegan & His Skiffle Group (1957)	My Special Angel (3)	Malcolm Vaughan (1957)
		My Star (5)	Ian Brown (1998)
My Ever Changing Moods (5)	Style Council (1984)	My Sweet Lord (1)	George Harrison (1971)
My Eyes Adored You (5)	Frankie Valli (1975)		
My Favourite Mistake (9)	Sheryl Crow (1998)	My Sweet Lord (re-issue) (1)	George Harrison (2002)
My Favourite Waste Of Time (3)	Owen Paul (1986)		
My Friend (3)	Frankie Laine (1954)	My Toot Toot (6)	Denise La Salle (1985)
My Friend Stan (2)	Slade (1973)		
My Friend The Sea (7)	Petula Clark (1961)	My True Love (9)	Jack Scott (1958)
My Generation (2)	Who (1965)	My Vision (6)	Jakatta featuring Seal (2002)
My Girl (3)	Madness (1980)		
My Girl Lollipop (My Boy Lollipop) (9)	Bad Manners (1982)	My Way (10)	Dorothy Squires (1970)
My Girl (re-issue) (2)	Temptations (1992)	My Way (6)	Limp Bizkit (2001)
My Guy (5)	Mary Wells (1964)	My Way (9)	Elvis Presley (1977)
My Happiness (4)	Connie Francis, David Rose Orchestra (1959)	My Way (9)	Frank Sinatra (1969)
		My Way Of Thinking / I Think It's Going To Rain (6)	UB40 (1980)
My Heart Has A Mind Of It's Own (3)	Connie Francis (1960)	My Weakness Is None Of Your Business (9)	Embrace (1998)
My Heart Will Go On (1)	Celine Dion (1998)		
My Kind Of Girl (5)	Matt Monro (1961)	Mysterious Girl (2)	Peter Andre featuring Bubbler Ranx (1996)
My Little Lady (6)	Tremeloes (1968)		
My Little One (6)	Marmalade (1971)	Mysterious Times (2)	Sash featuring Tina Cousins (1998)
My Love (4)	Petula Clark (1966)		
My Love (8)	Kele Le Roc (1999)	Na Na Hey Hey Kiss Him Goodbye (5)	Bananarama (1983)
My Love (9)	Paul McCartney & Wings (1973)	Na Na Hey Hey Kiss Him Goodbye (5)	Steam (1970)
My Love (1)	Westlife (2000)	Na Na Is The Saddest Word (5)	Stylistics (1975)
My Love (5)	Julio Iglesias featuring Stevie Wonder (1988)	Na Na Na (10)	Cozy Powell (1974)
		Nairobi (3)	Tommy Steele (1958)
My Love And Devotion (10)	Doris Day (1952)		
My Love For You (9)	Johnny Mathis (1960)	Naked (5)	Louise (1996)
		Naked In The Rain (4)	Blue Pearl (1990)
My Love Is Your Love (2)	Whitney Houston (1999)	Name Of The Game, The (1)	Abba (1977)
My Lovin' (4)	En Vogue (1992)	Nancy Boy (4)	Placebo (1997)
My Mind's Eye (4)	Small Faces (1966)	Nathan Jones (5)	Supremes (1971)

Title	Group/Artiste	Title	Group/Artiste
National Express (8)	Divine Comedy (1999)	Next Episode, The (3)	Dr Dre featuring Snoop Dogg (2001)
Native New Yorker (5) first hit	Odyssey (1977)	Next Time, The / Bachelor Boy (1)	Cliff Richard and The Shadows (1962)
Natural (6)	Peter Andre (1997)	Nice Guy Eddie (10)	Sleeper (1996)
Natural (3)	S Club 7 (2000)	Night Birds (9)	Shakatak (1982)
Natural Born Bugie (4)	Humble Pie (1969)	Night Chicago Died, The (3)	Paper Lace (1974)
Natural Sinner (6)	Fair Weather (1970)	Night Fever (1)	Bee Gees (1978)
Naughty Lady Of Shady Lane (6)	Ames Brothers (1955)	Night Games (6)	Graham Bonnet (1981)
Naughty Lady Of Shady Lane (5)	Dean Martin (1955)	Night Has A Thousand Eyes, The (3)	Bobby Vee (1963)
Neanderthal Man (2)	Hotlegs (1970)		
Need You Tonight (2)	INXS (1988)	Night Of Fear (2) first hit	Move (1967)
Needin' U (8)	David Morales presents The Face (1998)	Night Owl (5)	Gerry Rafferty (1979)
		Night They Drove Old Dixie Down, The (6)	Joan Baez (1971)
Needles And Pins (1)	Searchers (1964)	Night To Remember, A (5)	Shalamar (1982)
Needles And Pins (10)	Smokie (1977)	Night, The (7)	Frankie Valli & The Four Seasons (1975)
Nellie The Elephant (4)	Toy Dolls (1984)		
Nelson Mandela (9)	Special AKA (1984)	Nights In White Satin (re-entry) (9)	Moody Blues (1972)
Nessaja (4)	Scooter (2002)	Nights On Broadway (6)	Candi Staton (1977)
Nessun Dorma (2)	Luciano Pavarotti (1990)	Nightshift (3)	Commodores (1985)
		Nikita (3)	Elton John (1985)
Never / These Dreams (re-issue) (8)	Heart (1988)	911 (9)	Wyclef Jean featuring Mary J Blige (2000)
Never Be The Same Again (1)	Melanie C with Lisa Left Eye Lopes (2000)		
		9pm (Till I Come) (1)	ATB (1999)
Never Can Say Goodbye (4)	Communards (1987)	Nine Times Out Of Ten (3)	Cliff Richard & The Shadows (1960)
Never Can Say Goodbye (2) first hit	Gloria Gaynor (1974)	9 To 5 (3)	Sheena Easton (1980)
Never Do A Tango With An Eskimo (6)	Alma Cogan (1955)	Nineteen (1)	Paul Hardcastle (1985)
Never Ending Song Of Love (2)	New Seekers (1971)	19 / 2000 (6)	Gorillaz (2001)
Never Ending Story (4)	Limahl (1984)	1999 / Little Red Corvette (re-issue) (2)	Prince (1985)
Never Ever (1)	All Saints (1997)		
Never Forget (1)	Take That (1995)	1999 (re-entry) (10)	Prince (1999)
Never Gonna Give You Up (1) first hit	Rick Astley (1987)	Nineteenth Nervous Breakdown (2)	Rolling Stones (1966)
Never Gonna Give You Up (6)	Musical Youth (1983)	99 Red Balloons (1)	Nena (1984)
Never Gonna Let You Go (7)	Tina Moore (1997)	99 Ways (5)	Tab Hunter (1957)
Never Had A Dream Come True (1)	S Club 7 (2000)	No Arms Can Ever Hold You (7)	Bachelors (1964)
Never Had A Dream Come True (6)	Stevie Wonder (1970)	No Charge (1)	J J Barrie (1976)
		No Diggity (9)	Blackstreet (1996)
Never Knew Love Like This Before (4)	Stephanie Mills (1980)	No Doubt About It (2)	Hot Chocolate (1980)
Never Let Her Slip Away (5)	Andrew Gold (1978)	No Fronts (9)	Dog Eat Dog (1996)
Never Let Her Slip Away (5)	Undercover (1992)	No Good 4 Me (6)	Oxide & Neutrino featuring Megaman (2000)
Never Let You Down (7)	Honeyz (1999)		
Never Never (4)	Assembly (1983)	No Good (Start The Dance) (4)	Prodigy (1994)
Never Never Never (8)	Shirley Bassey (1973)	No Honestly (7)	Lynsey De Paul (1974)
Never Say Goodbye (9)	Karl Denver (1962)	No Limit (1)	2 Unlimited (1993)
Never Too Late (4)	Kylie Minogue (1989)	No Matter How I Try (5)	Gilbert O'Sullivan (1971)
Never Trust A Stranger (7)	Kim Wilde (1988)	No Matter What (5)	Badfinger (1971)
New Beginning / Bright Eyes (3)	Stephen Gately (2000)	No Matter What (1)	Boyzone (1998)
New Beginning (Mamba Seyra) (8)	Bucks Fizz (1986)	No Milk Today (7)	Herman's Hermits (1966)
New Day Has Come, A (7)	Celine Dion (2002)	No More (6)	A1 (2001)
New Direction (2)	S Club Juniors (2002)	No More (Baby I'Ma Do Right) (6)	3LW (2001)
		No More Drama (9)	Mary J Blige (2002)
New England, A (7)	Kirsty MacColl (1985)	No More Heroes (8)	Stranglers (1977)
New Moon On Monday (9)	Duran Duran (1984)	No More (I Can't Stand It) (8)	Maxx (1994)
New Song (3) first hit	Howard Jones (1983)	No More I Love Yous (2)	Annie Lennox (1995)
New Years Day (10)	U2 (1983)	No More Lonely Nights (2)	Paul McCartney (1984)
New York Groove (9)	Hello (1975)		
New York Mining Disaster 1941 (12) first hit	Bee Gees (1967)	No More Mr Nice Guy (10)	Alice Cooper (1973)

MUSIC
POP

Title	Group/Artiste	Title	Group/Artiste
No More Tears (Enough Is Enough) (3)	Donna Summer & Barbra Streisand (1979)	Now That We Found Love (2)	Heavy D & The Boyz (1991)
No More The Fool (5)	Elkie Brooks (1986)	Now That We've Found Love (10)	Third World (1978)
No No No (5) first hit	Destiny's Child (1998)	Now Those Days Are Gone (8)	Bucks Fizz (1982)
		N-R-G (12) first hit	Adamski (1990)
No One But You (3)	Billy Eckstine (1954)	Nu Flow (3)	Big Brovaz (2002)
No One Is Innocent / My Way (7)	Sex Pistols (1978)	Nuff Vibes EP (5)	Apache Indian (1993)
No One Quite Like Grandma (1)	St Winifred's School Choir (1980)	Number 1 (6)	Tweenies (2000)
No Other Love (1)	Ronnie Hilton (1956)	Numero Uno (9)	Starlight (1989)
No Particular Place To Go (3)	Chuck Berry (1964)	Nut Rocker (1)	B Bumble and the Stingers (1962)
No Regrets (9) first solo hit	Midge Ure (1982)		
No Regrets (7)	Walker Brothers (1976)	Nutbush City Limits (4)	Ike & Tina Turner (1973)
No Regrets / Antmusic (4)	Robbie Williams (1998)	O L'Amour (7)	Dollar (1987)
No Scrubs (3)	TLC (1999)	O Superman (2)	Laurie Anderson (1981)
No Son Of Mine (6)	Genesis (1991)	O.T.B (On The Beach) / Reachers Of Civilisation (4)	York (2000)
No Surprises (4)	Radiohead (1998)		
No Woman No Cry (2)	Fugees (1996)	Ob-La-Di Ob-La-Da (1)	Marmalade (1968)
No Woman No Cry (re-entry) (8)	Bob Marley & The Wailers (1981)	Oblivious (47) first hit	Aztec Camera (1983)
		Obsession (5) first and only hit	Animotion (1985)
Nobody Does It Better (7)	Carly Simon (1977)	Off The Wall (7)	Michael Jackson (1979)
Nobody I Know (10)	Peter & Gordon (1964)	Oh Babe What Would You Say? (4)	Hurricane Smith (1972)
Nobody Knows (4)	Tony Rich Project (1996)	Oh Baby I... (4)	Eternal (1994)
		Oh Boy (3)	Crickets (1957)
Nobody Needs Your Love (2)	Gene Pitney (1966)	Oh Boy (1)	Mud (1975)
Nobody Told Me (6)	John Lennon (1984)	Oh Boy (The Mood I'm In) (8)	Brotherhood Of Man (1977)
Nobody Wants To Be Lonely (4)	Ricky Martin & Christina Aguilera (2001)	Oh Carol (3)	Neil Sedaka (1959)
		Oh Carol (5)	Smokie (1978)
Nobody's Child (6)	Karen Young (1969)	Oh Carolina (1) first hit	Shaggy (1993)
Nobody's Darlin' But Mine (4)	Frank Ifield (1963)	Oh Diane (9)	Fleetwood Mac (1982)
Nobody's Diary (3)	Yazoo (1983)		
Nobody's Fool (9)	Haircut 100 (1982)	Oh Happy Day (2)	Edwin Hawkins Singers (1969)
North Country Boy (4)	Charlatans (1997)		
Northern Lights (10)	Renaissance (1978)	Oh Happy day (4)	Johnston Brothers (1953)
Northern Star (4)	Melanie C (1999)		
Not A Dry Eye In The House (7)	Meat Loaf (1996)	Oh Julie (1)	Shakin' Stevens (1982)
Not Fade Away (3)	Rolling Stones (1964)		
Not Over Yet (6)	Grace (1995)	Oh Lori (8)	Alessi (1977)
Not Over Yet (9)	Diana Ross (1999)	Oh Mein Papa (1) first hit	Eddie Calvert (1953)
Not Such An Innocent Girl (6)	Victoria Beckham (2001)	Oh My Papa (9)	Eddie Fisher (1954)
(Nothin' Serious) Just Buggin' (7)	Whistle (1986)	Oh My Papa (re-entry) (10)	Eddie Fisher (1954)
Nothing (9)	A (2002)	Oh No Not My Baby (6)	Rod Stewart (1973)
Nothing Can Divide Us (5)	Jason Donovan (1988)	Oh Pretty Woman (1)	Roy Orbison (1964)
		Oh Well (2)	Fleetwood Mac (1969)
Nothing Compares 2 U (1)	Sinead O'Connor (1990)	Oh What A Circus (3)	David Essex (1978)
Nothing Else Matters (6)	Metallica (1992)	Oh Yeah (6)	Ash (1996)
Nothing Lasts Forever (8)	Echo And The Bunnymen (1997)	Oh Yeah (On The Radio) (5)	Roxy Music (1980)
		Oh Yes! You're Beautiful (2)	Gary Glitter (1974)
Nothing Really Matters (7)	Madonna (1999)	Ohh! What A Life (10)	Gibson Brothers (1979)
Nothing Rhymed (8) first hit	Gilbert O'Sullivan (1970)	Oi (8)	Platinum 45 featuring More Fire Crew (2002)
Nothing's Gonna Change My Love For You (1)	Glenn Madeiros (1988)		
Nothing's Gonna Stop Me Now (8)	Samantha Fox (1987)	OK? (10)	Julie Covington, Rula Lenska, Charlotte Cornwell and Sue Jones-Davies (1977)
Nothing's Gonna Stop Us Now (1)	Starship (1987)		
Notorious (7)	Duran Duran (1986)		
November Rain (4)	Guns 'N' Roses (1992)	Okay! (4)	Dave Dee, Dozy, Beaky, Mick & Tich (1967)
Novocaine For The Soul (10)	Eels (1997)		
Now (3)	Al Martino (1953)	Ol' Rag Blues (9)	Status Quo (1983)
Now Is The Time (5)	Jimmy James & The Vagabonds (1976)	Old Before I Die (2)	Robbie Williams (1997)

Title	Group/Artiste	Title	Group/Artiste
Older / I Can Make You Love Me (3)	George Michael (1997)	One More Time (2)	Daft Punk (2000)
Oldest Swinger In Town (6)	Fred Wedlock (1981)	One More Try (8)	George Michael (1988)
Ole Ola (Mulher Brasilieira) (4)	Rod Stewart and Scottish World Cup Football Squad '78 (1978)	One Nation Under A Groove (9)	Funkadelic (1978)
		One Night / I Got Stung (1)	Elvis Presley (1959)
		One Night In Heaven (6)	M People (1993)
		One Night Stand (5)	Mis-Teeq (2001)
Oliver's Army (2)	Elvis Costello & The Attractions (1979)	One Of These Nights (23) first hit	Eagles (1975)
On A Carousel (4)	Hollies (1967)	One Of Us (3)	Abba (1981)
On A Night Like This (2)	Kylie Minogue (2000)	One Of Us (6)	Joan Osborne (1996)
On A Ragga Tip (2)	SL2 (1992)		
On A Saturday Night (45) only other hit	Terry Dactyl and the Dinosaurs (1973)	One Shining Moment (10)	Diana Ross (1992)
		One Step Beyond (7)	Madness (1979)
On a Slow Boat To China (3)	Emile Ford & The Checkmates (1960)	One Step Closer (2)	S Club Juniors (2002)
On Her Majesty's Secret Service (7)	Propellerheads / David Arnold (1997)	One Step Further (2)	Bardo (1982)
		One Step Too Far (6)	Faithless featuring Dido (2002)
On My Own (2)	Patti LaBelle & Michael McDonald (1986)	One Sweet Day (6)	Mariah Carey & Boyz II Men (1995)
		One To Another (3)	Charlatans (1996)
On My Radio (8)	Selecter (1979)	1-2-3 (3) first hit	Len Barry (1965)
On Our Own (Theme from Ghostbusters II) (4)	Bobby Brown (1989)	1-2-3 (9)	Gloria Estefan & Miami Sound Machine (1988)
On The Beach (7)	Cliff Richard & The Shadows (1964)	1-2-3-4 Get With The Wicked (10)	Richard Blackwood (2000)
On The Inside (3)	Lynne Hamilton (1989)	1-2-3 O'Leary (4)	Des O'Connor (1968)
On The Radio (7)	Martine McCutcheon (2001)	One Vision (7)	Queen (1985)
On The Rebound (1)	Floyd Cramer (1961)	One Way Love (9)	Cliff Bennett & The Rebel Rousers (1964)
On The Road Again (8) first hit	Canned Heat (1968)		
On The Ropes (EP) (10)	Wonder Stuff (1993)	One Way Ticket (9)	Eruption (1979)
On The Street Where You Live (1)	Vic Damone (1958)	One Week (5)	Barenaked Ladies (1999)
On Your Own (5)	Blur (1997)	One Wild Night (10)	Bon Jovi (2001)
Once Around The Block (46)	Badly Drawn Boy (1999)	One, The (8)	Backstreet Boys (2000)
Once Upon A Dream (7)	Billy Fury (1962)	One, The (10)	Elton John (1992)
Once Upon A Long Ago (10)	Paul McCartney (1987)	Onion Song (9)	Marvin Gaye & Tammi Terrell (1969)
One (7)	U2 (1992)		
One And One (3)	Robert Miles featuring Maria Nayler (1996)	Only Fools (Never Fall In Love) (10)	Sonia (1991)
One And One Is One (3)	Medicine Head (1973)	Only Living Boy In New Cross, The (7)	Carter The Unstoppable Sex Machine (1992)
One And Only, The (1)	Chesney Hawkes (1991)	Only Love (2)	Nana Mouskouri (1986)
One By One (7)	Cher (1996)	Only One I Know, The (9) first hit	Charlatans (1990)
One Day At A Time (1)	Lena Martell (1979)	Only One Road (8)	Celine Dion (1995)
One Day I'll Fly Away (2)	Randy Crawford (1980)	Only One Woman (5)	Marbles (1968)
One Day In Your Life (1)	Michael Jackson (1981)	Only Rhyme That Bites, The (10)	MC Tunes vs 808 State (1990)
One For Sorrow (2)	Steps (1998)	Only Sixteen (1)	Craig Douglas (1959)
One In Ten (7)	UB40 (1981)	Only The Lonely (re-entry) (1)	Roy Orbison (1960)
One Kiss From Heaven (9)	Louise (1996)	Only Thing That Looks Good On Me Is You, The(6)	Bryan Adams (1996)
One Love (3)	Blue (2002)		
One Love (8)	Prodigy (1993)	Only Way Is Up, The (1)	Yazz & The Plastic Population (1988)
One Love (4)	Stone Roses (1990)		
One Love / People Get Ready (5)	Bob Marley & The Wailers (1984)	Only Way Out, The (10)	Cliff Richard (1982)
		Only When You Leave (3)	Spandau Ballet (1984)
One Man Band (6)	Leo Sayer (1974)	Only Yesterday (2)	Carpenters (1975)
One Minute Man (10)	Missy Elliott featuring Ludacris (2001)	Only You (1)	Flying Pickets (1983)
		Only You (3)	Hilltoppers (1956)
		Only You / The Great Pretender (5)	Platters (1956)
One Moment In Time (1)	Whitney Houston (1988)		
		Only You (4)	Praise (1991)
One More Night (4)	Phil Collins (1985)	Only You (2)	Yazoo (1982)

MUSIC POP

Title	Group/Artiste	Title	Group/Artiste
Only You Can (3)	Fox (1975)	Pandora's Box (7)	Orchestral Manoeuvres In The Dark (1991)
Ooh Aah ... Just A Little Bit (1)	Gina G (1996)		
Ooh La La (2)	Wiseguys (1999)		
Ooh La La La (Let's Go Dancin') (6)	Kool & The Gang (1982)	Papa Don't Preach (1)	Madonna (1986)
		Papa Don't Preach (3)	Kelly Osbourne (2002)
Ooh Stick You! (8)	Daphne & Celeste (2000)	Papa's Got A Brand New Pigbag (3)	Pigbag (1982)
Ooh To Be Ah (7)	Kajagoogoo (1983)		
Ooh-Wakka-Doo-Wakka-Day (8)	Gilbert O'Sullivan (1972)	Paper Plane (8)	Status Quo (1973)
		Paper Roses (7)	Kaye Sisters (1960)
Ooops (42) first hit	Björk (1991)		
Oops (Oh My) (5)	Tweet (2002)	Paper Roses (2)	Marie Osmond (1973)
Oops Up (5)	Snap (1990)		
Oops Up Side Your Head (6)	Gap Band (1980)	Paper Sun (5)	Traffic (1967)
Oops! ... I Did It Again (1)	Britney Spears (2000)	Paperback Writer (1)	Beatles (1966)
		Paradise City (6)	Guns 'N' Roses (1989)
Open Arms (4)	Mariah Carey (1996)		
Open Road (7)	Gary Barlow (1997)	Paralysed (8)	Elvis Presley (1957)
Open You Mind (7)	Usura (1993)	Paranoid (4) first and biggest hit	Black Sabbath (1970)
Open Your Heart (6)	Human League (1981)		
		Paranoid Android (3)	Radiohead (1997)
Open Your Heart (9)	M People (1995)	Parisienne Walkways (8)	Gary Moore (1979)
Open Your Heart (4)	Madonna (1986)	Parklife (10)	Blur (1994)
Operation Blade (Bass In The Place) (5)	Public Domain (2000)	Part Of The Union (2)	Strawbs (1973)
		Part-Time Lover (3)	Stevie Wonder (1985)
Opposites Attract (2)	Paula Abdul with The Wild Pair (1990)	Party (2)	Elvis Presley with The Jordanaires (1957)
Ordinary World (5)	Aurora featuring Naimee Coleman (2000)	Party Fears Two (9) first and biggest hit	Associates (1982)
Ordinary World (6)	Duran Duran (1993)	Party People ... Friday Night (5)	911 (1997)
Original Prankster (6)	Offspring (2000)	Party Pops (24) first hit	Russ Conway (1957)
Orinoco Flow (1)	Enya (1988)	Party's Over, The (9)	Lonnie Donegan (1962)
Orville's Song (4)	Keith Harris & Orville (1982)	Pasadena (4)	Temperance Seven (1961)
Ossie's Dream (Spurs Are On Their Way To Wembley) (5)	Tottenham Hotspur FA Cup Final Squad (1981)	Pass And Move (It's The Liverpool Groove) (4)	Liverpool FC & The Boot Room Boyz (1996)
Our Favourite Melodies (9)	Craig Douglas (1962)	Pass The Dutchie (1)	Musical Youth (1982)
Our House (5)	Madness (1982)	Passengers (5)	Elton John (1984)
Our Lips Are Sealed (7)	Fun Boy Three (1983)	Passion (remix) (6)	Gat Decor (1996)
Out In The Fields (5)	Gary Moore & Phil Lynott (1985)	Patches (2)	Clarence Carter (1970)
Out Of Reach (4)	Gabrielle (2001)	Patience (10)	Guns 'N' Roses (1989)
Out Of Space / Ruff In The Jungle Bizness (5)	Prodigy (1992)	Patricia (8)	Perez Prado & His Orchestra (1958)
Out Of Time (1)	Chris Farlowe (1966)	Peace (8)	Sabrina Johnston (1991)
Out Of Your Mind (2)	True Steppers, with Dane Bowers and Victoria Beckham (2000)	Peace In Our Time (8)	Cliff Richard (1993)
		Peace On Earth / Little Drummer Boy (3)	David Bowie & Bing Crosby (1982)
Outside (2)	George Michael (1998)	Peaches (8)	Presidents of the United States of America (1996)
Outside Of Heaven (1)	Eddie Fisher (1953)		
Over Under Sideways Down (10)	Yardbirds (1966)	Peaches / Go Buddy Go (8)	Stranglers (1977)
Over You (5)	Roxy Music (1980)	Peacock Suit (5)	Paul Weller (1996)
Overload (6)	Sugababes (2000)	Pearl In The Shell (7)	Howard Jones (1984)
Overprotected (4)	Britney Spears (2002)	Pearl's A Singer (8) first hit	Elkie Brooks (1977)
Oxygene Part IV (4)	Jean-Michel Jarre (1977)	Peek-A-Boo (7)	New Vaudeville Band (1967)
Pacific (10)	808 State (1989)	Peggy Sue (6)	Buddy Holly (1957)
Paint It Black (1)	Rolling Stones (1966)	Penny Lane / Strawberry Fields Forever (2)	Beatles (1967)
Painter Man (10)	Boney M (1979)	People Are People (4)	Depeche Mode (1984)
Pale Shelter (5)	Tears For Fears (1983)		
Paloma Blanca (10)	George Baker Selection (1975)	People Everyday (2)	Arrested Development (1992)

MUSIC POP

Title	Group/Artiste	Title	Group/Artiste
Power Of Love, The (1)	Frankie Goes To Hollywood (1984)	Puppy Love / Sleigh Ride (6)	S Club Juniors (2002)
Power Of Love, The (1)	Jennifer Rush (1985)	Pure And Simple (1)	Hear'Say (2001)
Power Rangers (3)	Mighty Morphin Power Rangers (1994)	Pure Morning (4)	Placebo (1998)
		Pure Shores (1)	All Saints (2000)
Power To All Our Friends (4)	Cliff Richard (1973)	Purple Haze (3)	Jimi Hendrix Experience (1967)
Power To The People (7)	John Lennon & The Plastic Ono Band (1971)	Purple Pills / Purple Hills (2)	D12 (2001)
		Purple Rain (8)	Prince & The Revolution (1984)
Power, The (1) first hit	Snap (1990)	Purple People Eater, The (12)	Sheb Wooley (1958)
Praise You (1)	Fatboy Slim (1999)	Push It (9)	Garbage (1998)
Pray (8)	MC Hammer (1990)	Push It / Tramp (2)	Salt-N-Pepa (1988)
Pray (1)	Take That (1993)	Push The Feeling On (remix) (3)	Nightcrawlers featuring John Reid (1995)
Praying For Time (6)	George Michael (1990)		
Pretend (2)	Nat 'King' Cole (1953)	Pushbike Song, The (2)	Mixtures (1971)
Pretend (4)	Alvin Stardust (1981)	Puss 'N' Boots (5)	Adam Ant (1983)
Pretty Blue Eyes (4)	Craig Douglas (1960)	Put The Needle On It (7)	Dannii Minogue (2002)
Pretty Flamingo (1)	Manfred Mann (1966)	Put Your Arms Around Me (10)	Texas (1997)
		Put Your Hands Together (7)	D Mob (1990)
Pretty Fly (For A White Guy) (1)	Offspring (1999)	Put Your Head On My Shoulder (7)	Paul Anka (1959)
Pretty Good Year (7)	Tori Amos (1994)		
Pretty Little Angel Eyes (5)	Showaddywaddy (1978)	Put Your Love In Me (10)	Hot Chocolate (1977)
Pretty Little Black-Eyed Susie (2)	Guy Mitchell (1953)	Putting On The Style / Gambling Man (1)	Lonnie Donegan (1957)
Pretty Paper (6)	Roy Orbison (1964)		
Pretty Vacant (6)	Sex Pistols (1977)	Pyjamarama (10)	Roxy Music (1973)
Price Of Love, The (2)	Everly Brothers (1965)	Pyramid Song (5)	Radiohead (2001)
Pride (In The Name Of Love) (3)	U2 (1984)	Quarter To Three (7)	Gary US Bonds (1961)
Prince Charming (1)	Adam & The Ants (1981)		
		Que Sera Mi Vida (5)	Gibson Brothers (1979)
Princess In Rags (9)	Gene Pitney (1965)	Queen Of Clubs (7)	KC & The Sunshine Band (1974)
Private Emotion (9)	Ricky Martin featuring Meja (2000)		
		Queen Of My Heart (1)	Westlife (2001)
		Queen Of New Orleans (10)	Jon Bon Jovi (1997)
Private Investigations (2)	Dire Straits (1982)	Question (2)	Moody Blues (1970)
Private Number (8)	Judy Clay & William Bell (1968)	Quiereme Mucho (Yours) (3)	Julio Iglesias (1982)
		Quit Playing Games (With My Heart) (2)	Backstreet Boys (1997)
Private Number (3)	911 (1999)		
Prize Of Gold (6)	Joan Regan (1955)	Rabbit (8)	Chas & Dave (1980)
Problems (6)	Everly Brothers (1959)	Race With The Devil (8)	Gun (1968)
		Race, The (7)	Yello (1988)
Professional Widow (remix) (1)	Tori Amos (1997)	Rachel (10)	Al Martino (1953)
Promise Me (3)	Beverley Craven (1991)	Rachmaninoff's Variation On A Theme (9)	Winifred Atwell (1954)
Promised Land (9)	Elvis Presley (1975)	Radancer (6)	Marmalade (1972)
Promises (6)	Ken Dodd (1966)	Radar Love (7)	Golden Earring (1973)
Promises (38) first hit	Take That (1991)		
Protect Your Mind (For The Love Of A Princess) (4)	DJ Sakin & Friends (1999)	Radio Gaga (2)	Queen (1984)
		Rag Doll (2)	Four Seasons featuring Frankie Valli (1964)
Proud Mary (8) first hit	Creedence Clearwater Revival (1969)		
		Ragamuffin Man (8)	Manfred Mann (1969)
Proud One, The (5)	Osmonds (1975)	Rage Hard (4)	Frankie Goes To Hollywood (1986)
Prove Your Love (8)	Taylor Dayne (1988)		
		Rags To Riches (9)	Elvis Presley (1971)
Pub With No Beer, A (3)	Slim Dusty (1959)	Rags To Riches (re-entry) (3)	David Whitfield (1954)
Public Image (9)	Public Image Ltd (1978)		
		Rain (7)	Madonna (1993)
Pump Up The Jam (2)	Technotronic featuring Felly (1989)	Rain (7)	Status Quo (1976)
		Rain And Tears (29)	Aphrodite's Child (1968)
Pump Up The Volume / Anitina (The First Time) (1)	Marrs (1987)	Rain Or Shine (2)	Five Star (1986)
Puppet On A String (1)	Sandie Shaw (1967)	Rain Rain Rain (8)	Frankie Laine, The Four Lads and The Buddy Cole Quartet (1954)
Puppy Love (1) first solo hit	Donny Osmond (1972)		

Title	Group/Artiste	Title	Group/Artiste
Rain, The (4)	Oran 'Juice' Jones (1986)	Red River Rock (3)	Johnny & The Hurricanes (1959)
Rain (Supa Dupa Fly), The (first hit)	Missy 'Misdemeanor' Elliott (1997)	Reet Petite (The Sweetest Girl In Town) (6)	Jackie Wilson (1957)
Rainbow (3)	Marmalade (1970)	Reet Petite (The Sweetest Girl In Town) (re-issue) (1)	Jackie Wilson (1986)
Rainbow Valley (5)	Love Affair (1968)	Reflections (5)	Diana Ross & The Supremes (1967)
Raincloud (6)	Lighthouse Family (1997)		
Raindrops Keep Falling On My Head (10)	Sacha Distel (1970)	Reflections Of My Life (3)	Marmalade (1969)
Rainy Day Women Nos 12 And 35 (7)	Bob Dylan (1966)	Reflex, The (1)	Duran Duran (1984)
		Reggae Tune (10)	Andy Faithweather-Low (1974)
Ramblin' Rose (5)	Nat 'King' Cole (1962)	Regret (4)	New Order (1993)
Ramona (4)	Bachelors (1964)	Regulate (5)	Warren G & Nate Dogg (1994)
Randy (9)	Blue Mink (1973)		
Rapper's Delight (3)	Sugarhill Gang (1979)	Relax (1) first hit	Frankie Goes To Hollywood (1983)
Rapture (5)	Blondie (1981)	Relax (re-issue) (5)	Frankie Goes To Hollywood (1993)
Rapture (2)	IIO (2001)	Release Me (1)	Engelbert Humperdinck (1967)
Rasputin (2)	Boney M (1978)		
Rat Race / Rude Boys Outa Jail (5)	Specials (1980)	Relight My Fire (1)	Take That featuring Lulu (1993)
Rat Trap (1)	Boomtown Rats (1978)	Remember Me (8)	Blue Boy (1997)
		Remember Me (7)	Diana Ross (1971)
Rave On (5)	Buddy Holly (1958)	Remember Me This Way (3)	Gary Glitter (1974)
Raving I'm Raving (2)	Shut Up & Dance (1992)	Remember (Sha-La-La) (6)	Bay City Rollers (1974)
Rawhide (6)	Frankie Laine (1959)		
Ray Of Light (2)	Madonna (1998)	Remember The Time / Come Together (3)	Michael Jackson (1992)
Reach (2)	S Club 7 (2000)	Remember You're A Womble (3)	Wombles (1974)
Reach For The Stars / Climb Ev'ry Mountain (1)	Shirley Bassey (1961)	Remember You're Mine / There's A Goldmine In The Sky (5)	Pat Boone (1957)
Reach Out I'll Be There (1)	Four Tops (1966)		
Reach Up (Papa's Got A Brand New Pig Bag) (6)	Perfecto Allstarz (1995)	Renaissance (5)	M People (1994)
Ready Or Not (5)	Course (1997)	Rendezvous (8)	Craig David (2001)
Ready Or Not (1)	Fugees (1996)	Rendez-Vu (4)	Basement Jaxx (1999)
Ready Willing And Able (7)	Doris Day (1955)		
Real Gone Kid (8)	Deacon Blue (1988)	Renegade Master '98 (remix) (3)	Wildchild (1998)
Real Good Time (7)	Alda (1998)		
Real Love (4)	Beatles (1996)	Rent (8)	Pet Shop Boys (1987)
Real Love (8)	Time Frequency (1993)	Renta Santa (10)	Chris Hill (1975)
		Requiem (4)	London Boys (1989)
Real Slim Shady, The (1)	Eminem (2000)	Re-Rewind The Crowd Say Bo Selecta (2)	Artful Dodger featuring Craig David (1999)
Real Thing, The (1)	Tony Di Bart (1994)		
Real Thing, The (9)	Lisa Stansfield (1997)	Rescue Me (3)	Madonna (1991)
Real Thing, The (6)	2 Unlimited (1994)	Rescue Me (8)	Ultra (1999)
Real Wild Child (Wild One) (10)	Iggy Pop (1986)	Respect (10)	Aretha Franklin (1967)
Really Free (27) first hit	John Otway and Wild Willy Barrett (1977)	Respect Yourself (7)	Bruce Willis (1987)
		Respectable (1)	Mel & Kim (1987)
Really Saying Something (5)	Bananarama with Fun Boy Three (1982)	Resurrection (3)	PPK (2001)
		Resurrection Shuffle, The (3)	Ashton Gardner & Dyke (1971)
Reason (8)	Ian Van Dahl (2002)		
Reasons To Be Cheerful (Part 3) (3)	Ian Dury & The Blockheads (1979)	Return Of Django / Dollar In The Teeth (5)	Upsetters (1969)
		Return Of The Los Palmas Seven, The (7)	Madness (1981)
Reason To Believe (19) first hit	Rod Stewart (1971)	Return Of The Mack (1)	Mark Morrison (1996)
Rebel Rebel (5)	David Bowie (1974)		
Rebel Yell (6)	Billy Idol (1985)	Return To Innocence (3)	Enigma (1994)
Red Alert (5)	Basement Jaxx (1999)	Return To Me (2)	Dean Martin (1958)
		Return To Sender (1)	Elvis Presley with The Jordanaires (1962)
Red Balloon (7)	Dave Clark Five (1968)		
Red Dress (7)	Alvin Stardust (1974)	Reunited (4)	Peaches & Herb (1979)
Red Letter Day, A (9)	Pet Shop Boys (1997)		
Red Light Spells Danger (2)	Billy Ocean (1977)	Reverence (10)	Faithless (1997)
Red Red Wine (1)	UB40 (1983)		

Title	Group/Artiste	Title	Group/Artiste
Reverence (10)	Jesus & Mary Chain (1992)	Rocafella (13)	Cam'ron featuring Juelz Santana (2002)
Reverend Black Grape (9)	Black Grape (1995)		
Reward (6)	Teardrop Explodes (1981)	Rock A Hula Baby / Can't Help Falling in Love(1)	Elvis Presley with The Jordanaires (1962)
Rhinestone Cowboy (4)	Glen Campbell (1975)	Rock And Roll (Parts 1 And 2) (2)	Gary Glitter (1972)
Rhythm Is A Dancer (1)	Snap (1992)	Rock And Roll Waltz (1)	Kay Starr (1956)
Rhythm Is A Mystery (3)	K-Klass (1991)	Rock Around The Clock (re-entry) (1)	Bill Haley & His Comets (1955)
Rhythm Of My Heart (3)	Rod Stewart (1991)		
Rhythm Of The Night (4)	DeBarge (1985)	Rock Around The Clock (re-entry) (5)	Bill Haley & His Comets (1956)
Rhythm Of The Night, The (2)	Corona (1994)		
Rhythm Of The Rain (5)	Cascades (1963)	Rock DJ (1)	Robbie Williams (2000)
Rhythm Of The Rain (9)	Jason Donovan (1990)	Rock Island Line (8) first hit	Lonnie Donegan Skiffle Group (1956)
Richard III (2)	Supergrass (1997)		
Ricochet (8)	Joan Regan & The Squadronaires (1953)	Rock Me Amadeus (1)	Falco (1986)
		Rock Me Gently (2)	Andy Kim (1974)
		Rock My Heart (9)	Haddaway (1994)
Ricochet (re-entry) (9)	Joan Regan & The Squadronaires (1954)	Rock 'N' Roll (8)	Status Quo (1981)
		Rock 'N' Roll Damnation (24) first hit	AC/DC (1978)
Riddle, The (3)	Nik Kershaw (1984)		
Ride A White Swan (2)	T Rex (1970)	Rock 'N' Roll Winter (6)	Wizzard (1974)
Ride Like The Wind (3)	East Side Beat (1991)	Rock On (3) first hit	David Essex (1973)
		Rock The Boat (4)	Forrest (1983)
Ride On Time (1) first hit	Black Box (1989)	Rock The Boat (6)	Hues Corporation (1974)
Ride Wit Me (3)	Nelly featuring City Spud (2001)		
		Rock This Town (9)	Stray Cats (1981)
Riders In The Sky (8)	Ramrods (1961)	Rock With You (7)	Michael Jackson (1980)
Right Back Where We Started From (8)	Maxine Nightingale (1975)		
		Rock Your Baby (8)	KWS (1992)
Right Back Where We Started From (4)	Sinitta (1989)	Rock Your Baby (1) first hit	George McCrae (1974)
Right By Your Side (10)	Eurythmics (1983)	Rock-A-Beatin' Boogie (4)	Bill Haley & His Comets (1955)
Right Here (3)	SWV (1993)		
Right Here Right Now (2)	Fatboy Slim (1999)	Rock-A-Billy (1)	Guy Mitchell (1957)
Right Here Waiting (2)	Richard Marx (1989)	Rockafeller Shank, The (6)	Fatboy Slim (1998)
Right In The Night (Fall In Love With Music) (re-issue) (10)	Jam & Spoon featuring Plavka (1995)	Rockaria! (9)	Electric Light Orchestra (1977)
		Rocket (6)	Mud (1974)
Right Now (10) first hit	Atomic Kitten (1999)	Rocket Man (2)	Elton John (1972)
Right Said Fred (10)	Bernard Cribbins (1962)	Rockin' All Over The World (3)	Status Quo (1977)
		Rockin' Around The Christmas Tree (6)	Brenda Lee (1962)
Ring My Bell (1) first and only hit	Anita Ward (1979)		
Ring Ring (Ha Ha Hey) (10)	De La Soul (1991)	Rockin' Around The Christmas Tree (3)	Mel & Kim (1987)
Rio (9)	Duran Duran (1982)		
Rip It Up (4)	Bill Haley & His Comets (1956)	Rockin' Good Way, A (5)	Shakin' Stevens & Bonnie Tyler (1984)
Rip It Up (8)	Orange Juice (1983)	Rockin' Over The Beat (9)	Technotronic featuring Ya Kid K (1990)
Rise (1)	Gabrielle (2000)		
Rise And Fall Of Flingel Bunt, The (5)	Shadows (1964)	Rockin' Robin (3)	Michael Jackson (1972)
Rise To The Occasion (10)	Climie Fisher (1987)	Rockin' Roll Baby (6)	Stylistics (1974)
River Deep Mountain High (3)	Ike & Tina Turner (1966)	Rockin' Through The Rye (3)	Bill Haley & His Comets (1956)
River Of Dreams, The (3)	Billy Joel (1993)	Rocking Goose (3)	Johnny & The Hurricanes (1960)
River, The (3)	Ken Dodd (1965)		
Riverdance (9)	Bill Whelan and Anuna and RTE Concert Orchestra (1994)	Rockit (8)	Herbie Hancock (1983)
		Rocks / Funky Jam (7)	Primal Scream (1994)
Rivers Of Babylon / Brown Girl In The Ring (1)	Boney M (1978)	Rodrigo's Guitar Concerto De Aranjuez (3)	Manuel & The Music Of The Mountains (1976)
Road Rage (5)	Catatonia (1998)		
Road To Hell (Part 2), The (10)	Chris Rea (1989)	Rok Da House (5)	Beatmasters with The Cookie Crew (1988)
Road To Nowhere (6)	Talking Heads (1985)		
Robert De Niro's Waiting (3)	Bananarama (1984)		
Robin Hood (10)	Gary Miller (1956)	Roll Away The Stones (8)	Mott The Hoople (1973)
Robin (The Hooded Man) (42)	Clannad (1984)		

Title	Group/Artiste	Title	Group/Artiste
Roll On / This Is How We Do It (7)	Mis-Teeq (2002)	Running Scared (9)	Roy Orbison (1961)
Roll Over Beethoven (6)	Electric Light Orchestra (1973)	Running Up That Hill (3)	Kate Bush (1985)
		Running With The Night (9)	Lionel Richie (1983)
Roll Over Lay Down (9)	Status Quo (1975)	Rush Rush (6)	Paula Abdul (1991)
Roll With It (2)	Oasis (1995)	Rushes (5)	Darius (2002)
Rollercoaster (1)	B*Witched (1998)	S Club Party (2)	S Club 7 (1999)
Rollin' (1)	Limp Bizkit (2001)	S**t On You (10)	D12 (2001)
Rollin' Home (9)	Status Quo (1986)	S.O.S. (6)	Abba (1975)
Rolling Stone (5)	David Essex (1975)	Sabre Dance (5)	Love Sculpture (1968)
Romeo (6)	Basement Jaxx (2001)	Sacred Trust / After You're Gone (2) first hit	One True Voice (2002)
Romeo (3)	Petula Clark (1961)	Sacrifice (re-issue) / Healing Hands (1)	Elton John (1990)
Romeo (3)	Romeo Dunn (2002)		
Romeo (4)	Mr Big (1977)	Sad Songs (Say So Much) (7)	Elton John (1984)
Romeo And Juliet (8)	Dire Straits (1981)	Sad Sweet Dreamer (1)	Sweet Sensation (1974)
Roobarb And Custard (7)	Shaft (1991)		
Room In Your Heart (5)	Living In A Box (1989)	Saddle Up (9) first and only hit	David Christie (1982)
		Sadness Part 1 (1)	Enigma (1990)
Rose Garden (3)	Lynn Anderson (1971)	Safety Dance, The (6)	Men Without Hats (1983)
Rose Marie (1) first hit	Slim Whitman (1955)	Sail On (8)	Commodores (1979)
Roses Are Red (3)	Ronnie Carroll (1962)	Sailing (1)	Rod Stewart (1975)
Roses Are Red (8)	Mac Band with McCampbell Brothers (1988)	Sailing On The Seven Seas (3)	Orchestral Manoeuvres In The Dark (1991)
Rosie (4)	Don Partridge (1968)	Sailing (re-entry) (3)	Rod Stewart (1976)
Rotterdam (5)	Beautiful South (1996)	Sailor (1)	Petula Clark (1961)
		Sailor (10)	Anne Shelton (1961)
Roulette (1)	Russ Conway (1959)	Saint, The (3)	Orbital (1997)
Round And Round (9)	Jaki Graham (1985)	Saints Rock 'N' Roll, The (5)	Bill Haley & His Comets (1956)
Round Round (1)	Sugababes (2002)		
Roussos Phenomenon EP, The (1)	Demis Roussos (1976)	Sale Of The Century (10)	Sleeper (1996)
		Sally (4)	Gerry Monroe (1970)
Rubber Ball (4) first hit	Bobby Vee (1961)	Salsoul Nugget (If U Wanna) (6)	M & S presents The Girl Next Door (2001)
Rubber Ball (9)	Marty Wilde (1961)		
Rubber Bullets (1)	10CC (1973)	Saltwater (6)	Julian Lennon (1991)
Ruby Don't Talk Your Love To Town (2)	Kenny Rogers & The First Edition (1969)	Saltwater (6)	Chicane with Maire Brennan of Clannad (1999)
Ruby Tuesday (9)	Melanie (1970)	Salva Mea (remix) (9)	Faithless (1996)
Ruby Tuesday / Let's Spend The Night Together (3)	Rolling Stones (1967)	Sam (6)	Olivia Newton-John (1977)
		Samba De Janeiro (8)	Bellini (1997)
Rumble In The Jungle (3)	Fugees featuring A Tribe Called Quest, Busta Rhymes and Forte (1997)	Same Old Brand New You (1)	A1 (2000)
		San Bernadino (7)	Christie (1970)
		San Franciscan Nights (7)	Eric Burdon & The Animals (1967)
Run Away (6)	MC Sar & The Real McCoy (1995)	San Francisco (Be Sure To Wear Some Flowers In Your Hair) (1)	Scott McKenzie (1967)
Run Baby Run (10)	Newbeats (1971)		
Run For Home (10)	Lindisfarne (1978)	Sanctify Yourself (10)	Simple Minds (1986)
Run Run Away (7)	Slade (1984)	Sandstorm (8)	Cast (1996)
Run Run Run (6)	Jo Jo Gunne (1972)	Sandstorm (3)	Darude (2000)
Run To Him (6)	Bobby Vee (1961)	Sandy (2)	John Travolta (1978)
Run To Me (9)	Bee Gees (1972)	Santa Bring My Baby Back (To Me) (7)	Elvis Presley (1957)
Run To The Hills (7)	Iron Maiden (1982)		
Run To The Hills (re-issue) (9)	Iron Maiden (2002)	Santa Claus Is Comin' To Town / My Hometown (9)	Bruce Springsteen (1985)
Run To The Sun (6)	Erasure (1994)		
Run To You (11) first hit	Bryan Adams (1985)	Santo Natale (2)	David Whitfield (1954)
Run To You (3)	Rage (1992)		
Runaway (2)	Corrs (1999)	Satan (3)	Orbital (1997)
Runaway (6)	Janet Jackson (1995)	Satisfy You (8)	Puff Daddy featuring R Kelly (2000)
Runaway (1) first hit	Del Shannon (1961)		
Runaway Boys (9)	Stray Cats (1980)	Saturday Love (6)	Cherelle with Alexander O'Neal (1985)
Runaway Train (re-entry) (7)	Soul Asylum (1993)		
Runner, The (10)	Three Degrees (1979)	Saturday Night (6)	Suede (1997)
Running Bear (1)	Johnny Preston (1960)	Saturday Night (1)	Whigfield (1994)
Running In The Family (6)	Level 42 (1987)	Saturday Night's Alright For Fighting (7)	Elton John (1973)

MUSIC POP

Title	Group/Artiste	Title	Group/Artiste
Savage, The (10)	Shadows (1961)	Sealed With A Kiss (3)	Brian Hyland (1962)
Save A Prayer (2)	Duran Duran (1982)	Sealed With A Kiss (re-issue) (7)	Brian Hyland (1975)
Save Me (4)	Dave Dee, Dozy, Beaky, Mick & Tich (1966)	Search For The Hero (9)	M People (1995)
		Searchin' (30) first hit	Coasters (1957)
Save Our Love (8)	Eternal (1994)	Searchin' (I Gotta Find A Man) (6)	Hazell Dean (1984)
Save The Best For Last (3)	Vanessa Williams (1992)	Searchin' My Soul (10)	Vonda Shepard (1998)
Save The Last Dance For Me (2)	Drifters (1960)	Searching (4)	China Black (1994)
Save Tonight (6) first and biggest hit	Eagle-Eye Cherry (1998)	Seaside Shuffle (2)	Terry Dactyl & The Dinosaurs (1972)
Save Your Kisses For Me (1)	Brotherhood Of Man (1976)	Seasons In The Sun (1)	Terry Jacks (1974)
		Secret (5)	Madonna (1994)
Save Your Love (1)	Renee & Renato (1982)	Secret Love (5)	Bee Gees (1991)
		Secret Love (1)	Doris Day (1954)
Saved By The Bell (2)	Robin Gibb (1969)	Secret Love (4)	Kathy Kirby (1963)
Saving All My Love For You (1) first hit	Whitney Houston (1985)	Secret Lovers (10)	Atlantic Starr (1986)
		Secrets (9)	Eternal (1996)
Saviour's Day (1)	Cliff Richard (1990)	Secrets That You Keep, The (3)	Mud (1975)
Say A Little Prayer (10)	Bomb The Bass featuring Maureen (1988)	See Emily Play (6)	Pink Floyd (1967)
		See My Baby Jive (1)	Wizzard (1973)
Say Hello Wave Goodbye (3)	Soft Cell (1982)	See My Friend (10)	Kinks (1965)
Say I Won't Be There (5)	Springfields (1963)	See The Day (3)	Dee C Lee (1985)
Say I'm Your No.1 (7)	Princess (1985)	See Ya (6)	Atomic Kitten (2000)
Say It Again (6)	Precious (1999)	See You (6)	Depeche Mode (1982)
Say It Again (7)	Jermaine Stewart (1988)	See You Later Alligator (7)	Bill Haley & His Comets (1956)
Say It Isn't So (10)	Bon Jovi (2000)	Self Control (5)	Laura Branigan (1984)
Say My Name (3)	Destiny's Child (2000)	Semi-Detached Suburban Mr James (2)	Manfred Mann (1966)
Say Say Say (2)	Paul McCartney & Michael Jackson (1983)	Send In The Clowns (6)	Judy Collins (1975)
		Senses Working Overtime (10)	XTC (1982)
		Sentinel (10)	Mike Oldfield (1992)
Say What You Want (3)	Texas (1997)	Senza Una Donna (Without A Woman) (4)	Zucchero & Paul Young (1991)
Say What You Want / Insane (re-recording) (4)	Texas featuring The Wu-Tang Clan (1998)	Separate Lives (4)	Phil Collins & Marilyn Martin (1985)
Say Wonderful Things (6)	Ronnie Carroll (1963)	September (3)	Earth Wind & Fire (1978)
Say You Love Me (7)	Simply Red (1998)	Serenade (re-entry) (8)	Slim Whitman (1956)
Say You Say Me (8)	Lionel Richie (1985)	Serious (8)	Donna Allen (1987)
Say You'll Be Mine (1)	Spice Girls (1996)	Sesame's Treet (2)	Smart Es (1992)
Say You'll Be Mine / Better The Devil You Know (4)	Steps (1999)	Set Adrift On Memory Bliss (3)	PM Dawn (1991)
		Set Me Free (7)	Jaki Graham (1986)
Say You're Mine Again (10)	June Hutton with Axel Stordahl (1953)	Set Me Free (9)	Kinks (1965)
		Set You Free (remix) (2)	N-Trance (1995)
Say You're Mine Again (re-entry) (6)	June Hutton with Axel Stordahl (1953)	Set You Free (2nd remix) (4)	N-Trance (2001)
		Setting Sun (1)	Chemical Brothers (1996)
Scarlett O'Hara (2)	Jet Harris & Tony Meehan (1963)	7 Days (1)	Craig David (2000)
		Seven Days And One Week (3)	BBE (1996)
Scatman (3)	Scatman John (1995)	Seven Drunken Nights (7)	Dubliners (1967)
		Seven Little Girls Sitting In The Back Seat (3)	Avons (1959)
Scatman's World (10)	Scatman John (1995)		
School Day (Ring! Ring! Goes The Bell) (24) first hit	Chuck Berry (1957)	Seven Lonely Days (re-entry) (6)	Gisele McKenzie (1953)
School's Out (1) first hit	Alice Cooper (1972)	Seven Seas Of Rye (10) first hit	Queen (1974)
Scientist, The (10)	Coldplay (2002)	7 Seconds (3)	Youssou N'Dour featuring Neneh Cherry (1994)
Scotch On The Rocks (8)	Band Of The Black Watch (1975)		
Scream (3)	Michael Jackson & Janet Jackson (1995)	Seven Tears (1)	Goombay Dance Band (1982)
		7 Ways To Love (8)	Cola Boy (1991)
Scream If You Wanna Go Faster (8)	Geri Halliwell (2001)	Sex On The Beach (2)	T-Spoon (1998)
		Sexbomb (3)	Tom Jones & Mousse T (2000)
Se A Vide (That's The Way Life Is) (8)	Pet Shop Boys (1996)	Sexcrime (Nineteen Eighty-Four) (4)	Eurythmics (1984)
Sea Of Love (3)	Marty Wilde (1959)	(Sexual) Healing (4)	Marvin Gaye (1982)
Sealed With A Kiss (1)	Jason Donovan (1989)	Sexy Eyes (4)	Dr Hook (1980)

Title	Group/Artiste	Title	Group/Artiste
Sexy MF / Strollin' (4)	Prince & The New Power Generation (1992)	She's The One / It's Only Us (1)	Robbie Williams (1999)
Sha La La (3)	Manfred Mann (1964)	Shindig (6)	Shadows (1963)
Sha La La La Lee (3)	Small Faces (1966)	Shine (5)	Aswad (1994)
Shackles (Praise You) (5)	Mary Mary (2000)	Shine A Little Love (6)	Electric Light Orchestra (1979)
Shaddup You Face (1)	Joe Dolce Music Theatre (1981)	Shine On (8)	Degrees Of Motion featuring Biti (1994)
Shake Rattle And Roll (4) first hit	Bill Haley & His Comets (1954)	Shining Light (8)	Ash (2001)
		Shiny Happy People (6)	REM (1991)
Shake Ur Body (7)	Shy FX & T Power featuring Di (2002)	Ship Of Fools (6)	Erasure (1988)
Shake You Down (6)	Gregory Abbott (1986)	Shirley (6)	Shakin' Stevens (1982)
Shake Your Body (Down To The Ground) (4)	Jacksons (1979)	Shocked (6)	Kylie Minogue (1991)
		Shoop Shoop Song (It's In His Kiss), The (1)	Cher (1991)
Shake Your Head (4)	Was (Not Was) (1992)	Shoot Me With Your Love (7)	D:Ream (1995)
		Shooting Star (3)	Flip & Fill (2002)
Shake Your Love (7)	Debbie Gibson (1988)	Shortsharpshock EP (9)	Therapy? (1993)
Shakin' All Over (1)	Johnny Kidd & The Pirates (1960)	Shotgun Wedding (6) first and only hit	Roy C (1966)
Shakin' Stevens EP, The (2)	Shakin' Stevens (1982)	Shotgun Wedding (re-issue) (8)	Roy C (1972)
		Should I Stay Or Should I Go (re-issue) (1)	Clash (1991)
Shalala Lala (5)	Vengaboys (2000)		
Shame Shame Shame (6)	Shirley & Company (1975)	Shoulda Woulda Coulda (10)	Beverley Knight (2002)
Shang-A-Lang (2)	Bay City Rollers (1974)	Shout (10)	Ant & Dec (1997)
		Shout (7)	Louchie Lou & Michie One (1993)
Shape Of My Heart (4)	Backstreet Boys (2000)	Shout (8)	Lulu (1986)
Shapes Of Things (3)	Yardbirds (1966)	Shout (7) first hit	Lulu & The Luvvers (1964)
Sharing You (10)	Bobby Vee (1962)		
Shattered Dreams (5)	Johnny Hates Jazz (1987)	Shout (4)	Tears For Fears (1984)
Shazam! (4)	Duane Eddy (1960)	Shout To The Top (7)	Style Council (1984)
She (1)	Charles Aznavour (1974)	Show Me Heaven (1)	Maria McKee (1990)
		Show Me Love (8)	Robyn (1998)
She Bangs (3)	Ricky Martin (2000)	Show Me Love (6)	Robin S (1993)
She Don't Let Nobody (4)	Chaka Demus & Pliers (1993)	Show Me Love (remix) (9)	Robin S (1997)
She Drives Me Crazy (5)	Fine Young Cannibals (1989)	Show Me The Meaning Of Being Lonely (3)	Backstreet Boys (2000)
She Loves You (1)	Beatles (1963)	Show Me The Way (10)	Peter Frampton (1976)
She Makes My Day (6)	Robert Palmer (1988)		
She Makes My Nose Bleed (9)	Mansun (1997)	Show Me You're A Woman (8)	Mud (1975)
She Means Nothing To Me (9)	Phil Everly / Cliff Richard (1983)	Show Must Go On, The (2) first hit	Leo Sayer (1973)
She Wants To Dance With Me (6)	Rick Astley (1988)	Show You The Way To Go (1)	Jacksons (1977)
She Wants You (3)	Billie (1998)	Show, The (7)	Doug E Fresh & The Get Fresh Crew (1985)
She Wears My Ring (3)	Solomon King (1968)		
She Wears Red Feathers (1)	Guy Mitchell (1953)	Showing Out (Get Fresh At The Weekend) (3)	Mel & Kim (1986)
She'd Rather Be With Me (4)	Turtles (1967)		
Sheffield Grinder/Capstick Comes Home, The (3)	Tony Capstick (1981)	Shuffle, The (4)	Van McCoy (1977)
		Shut Up (7)	Madness (1981)
Sheila (3) first hit	Tommy Roe (1962)	Shut Up And Forget About It (9)	Dane (2001)
Sheila Take A Bow (10)	Smiths (1987)	Shut Your Mouth (20)	Garbage (2002)
Sherry (10) first and only hit	Adrian Baker (1975)	Shy Boy (4)	Bananarama (1982)
Sherry (8)	Four Seasons (1962)	Shy Guy (2)	Diana King (1995)
She's A River (9)	Simple Minds (1995)	Side By Side (7)	Kay Starr (1953)
She's A Star (9)	James (1997)	Side Saddle (1)	Russ Conway (1959)
She's Got Claws (6)	Gary Numan (1981)	Sideshow (3)	Barry Biggs (1976)
She's Got That Vibe (3)	R Kelly (1994)	Sight For Sore Eyes (6)	M People (1994)
She's Leaving Home (1)	Billy Bragg with Cara Tivey (1988)	Sign O' The Times (10)	Prince (1987)
		Sign Of The Times (3)	Belle Stars (1983)
She's Not You (1)	Elvis Presley with The Jordanaires (1962)	Sign Your Name (2)	Terence Trent D'Arby (1988)
		Sign, The (2)	Ace Of Base (1994)
She's On It (10)	Beastie Boys (1987)	Signature Tune Of 'The Army Game', The (5)	Michael Medwin, Bernard Bresslaw, Alfie Bass and Leslie Fyson (1958)
She's Out Of My Life (3)	Michael Jackson (1980)		

M
U
S
I
C

P
O
P

Title	Group/Artiste	Title	Group/Artiste
Silence Is Golden (1)	Tremeloes (1967)	Slave To Love (10)	Bryan Ferry (1985)
Silence (remixes) (3)	Delirium featuring Sarah McLachlan (2000)	Sledgehammer (4)	Peter Gabriel (1986)
		Sleeping Satellite (1)	Tasmin Archer (1992)
Silent Night (8)	Bing Crosby (1952)		
Silhouettes (3)	Herman's Hermits (1965)	Sleepy Shores (8)	Johnny Pearson Orchestra (1971)
Silhouettes (10)	Cliff Richard (1990)	Slight Return (2)	Bluetones (1996)
Silly Games (2)	Janet Kay (1979)	Slightest Touch, The (4)	Five Star (1987)
Silly Love Songs (2)	Wings (1976)	Sloop John B (2)	Beach Boys (1966)
Silly Thing (6)	Sex Pistols (1979)	Slow Down (10)	John Miles (1977)
Silver Dream Machine (4)	David Essex (1980)	Slowhand (10)	Pointer Sisters (1981)
Silver Lady (1)	David Soul (1977)		
Silver Machine (3)	Hawkwind (1972)	Smack My Bitch Up (8)	Prodigy (1997)
Silver Star (3)	Four Seasons (1976)	Smalltown Boy (3) first hit	Bronski Beat (1984)
Simon Says (2)	1910 Fruitgum Co (1968)	Smarty Pants (9)	First Choice (1973)
		Smells Like Teen Spirit (7)	Nirvana (1991)
Simon Smith and his Amazing Dancing Bear (4)	Alan Price Set (1967)	Smile (2)	Nat 'King' Cole (1954)
Simon Templar / Two Pints Of Lager And A Packet Of Crisps Please (7)	Splodgeness-abounds (1980)	Smoke (5)	Natalie Imbruglia (1998)
		Smoke Gets In Your Eyes (1)	Platters (1959)
Simple Game (3)	Four Tops (1971)	Smooth (3)	Santana featuring Rob Thomas (2000)
Since I Don't Have You (10)	Guns 'N' Roses (1994)		
Since Yesterday (5)	Strawberry Switchblade (1984)	Smooth Criminal (3)	Alien Ant Farm (2001)
Since You've Been Gone (6)	Rainbow (1979)	Smooth Criminal (8)	Michael Jackson (1988)
Sing (3)	Travis (2001)		
Sing Baby Sing (3)	Stylistics (1975)	Smurf Song, The (2)	Father Abraham & Smurfs (1978)
Sing It Back (4)	Moloko (1999)		
Sing Me (8)	Brothers (1977)	Snap Megamix (10)	Snap (1991)
Sing Our Own Song (5)	UB40 (1986)	Snooker Loopy (6)	Matchroom Mob with Chas & Dave (1986)
Singing The Blues (1)	Guy Mitchell (1956)		
Singing The Blues (1)	Tommy Steele (1956)	Snoopy Vs The Red Baron (4)	Hotshots (1973)
Sir Duke (2)	Stevie Wonder (1977)	Snoopy Vs The Red Baron (8)	Royal Guardsmen (1967)
Sister (10)	Bros (1989)	Snot Rap (9)	Kenny Everett (1983)
Sister Jane (9)	New World (1972)	Snow Coach (7)	Russ Conway (1959)
Sisters Are Doin' It For Themselves (9)	Eurythmics & Aretha Franklin (1985)	So Cold The Night (8)	Communards (1986)
Sit Down (2)	James (1991)	So Emotional (5)	Whitney Houston (1987)
Sit Down (remix) (7)	James (1998)		
(Sittin' On) The Dock Of The Bay (3)	Otis Redding (1968)	So Good (3)	Boyzone (1995)
		So Good To Be Back Home Again (8)	Tourists (1980)
Sitting Down Here (5)	Lene Marlin (2000)	So Hard (4)	Pet Shop Boys (1990)
Six Teens, The (9)	Sweet (1974)		
6 Underground (remix) (9)	Sneaker Pimps (1997)	So Lonely (8)	Jakatta (2002)
		So Lonely (6)	Police (1980)
16 Bars (7)	Stylistics (1976)	So Long Baby (10)	Del Shannon (1961)
Sixteen Reasons (9)	Connie Stevens (1960)	So Macho / Cruising (2)	Sinitta (1986)
		So Pure (3)	Baby D (1996)
Sixteen Tons (10)	Frankie Laine (1956)	So Why So Sad (8)	Manic Street Preachers (2001)
Sixteen Tons (1)	Tennessee Ernie Ford (1956)	So You Win Again (1)	Hot Chocolate (1977)
68 Guns (17) first and biggest hit	Alarm (1983)		
Size Of A Cow, The (5)	Wonder Stuff (1991)	So Young (6)	Corrs (1998)
Sk8er Boi (9)	Avril Lavigne (2002)	Softly As I Leave You (10)	Matt Monro (1962)
Skin Deep (7)	Duke Ellington (1954)	Softly Softly (1)	Ruby Murray (1955)
		Softly Whispering I Love You (4)	Congregation (1971)
Skin Deep (9)	Ted Heath Orchestra (1954)	Soldier Blue (7)	Buffy St Marie (1971)
Skweeze Me Pleeze Me (1)	Slade (1973)		
Sky (2)	Sonique (2000)	Soley Soley (5)	Middle Of The Road (1971)
Sky High (9)	Jigsaw (1975)		
Skye Boat Song, The (10)	Roger Whittaker & Des O'Connor (1986)	Solid (3)	Ashford & Simpson (1985)
		Solid Gold Easy Action (2)	T Rex (1972)
Slam Dunk (Da Funk) (10)	Five (1997)	Solitaire (4)	Andy Williams (1973)
Slam Jam (4)	WWF Superstars (1992)	Solomon Bites The Worm (10)	Bluetones (1998)
		Some Girls (2)	Racey (1979)
		Some Girls (9)	Ultimate Kaos (1994)

Title	Group/Artiste	Title	Group/Artiste
Some Kinda Fun (10)	Chris Montez (1963)	Somewhere (9)	Pet Shop Boys (1997)
Some Might Say (1)	Oasis (1995)	Somewhere (6)	P J Proby (1964)
Some Of Your Lovin' (8)	Dusty Springfield (1965)	Somewhere Along The Way (3) first hit	Nat 'King' Cole (1952)
Some People (3)	Cliff Richard (1987)	Somewhere In My Heart (3)	Aztec Camera (1988)
Somebody Help Me (1)	Spencer Davis Group (1966)	Somewhere Out There (8)	Linda Ronstadt & James Ingram (1987)
Somebody Stole My Gal (6)	Johnnie Ray (1953)		
Somebody Stole My Gal (re-entry) (6)	Johnnie Ray (1953)	Somewhere Somehow (7)	Wet Wet Wet (1995)
Somebody To Love (2)	Queen (1976)	Son Of A Gun (remix) (6)	JX (1995)
Somebody's Watching Me (6)	Rockwell (1984)	Son Of A Preacher Man (9)	Dusty Springfield (1968)
Someday (4)	Eternal (1996)		
Someday (9)	Ricky Nelson (1958)	Son Of Hickory Holler's Tramp (2)	O C Smith (1968)
Someday I'll Be Saturday Night (7)	Bon Jovi (1995)	Son Of My Father (1) first hit	Chicory Tip (1972)
Someday (I'll Come Back) (10)	Lisa Stansfield (1992)	Song For Guy (4)	Elton John (1978)
		Song For The Lovers, A (3)	Richard Ashcroft (2000)
Someone (6)	Johnny Mathis (1959)	Song For Whoever (2) first hit	Beautiful South (1989)
Someone Else's Baby (2)	Adam Faith (1960)		
Someone Else's Roses (5)	Joan Regan (1954)	Song Of The Dreamer (10)	Johnnie Ray (1955)
Someone Like You (10)	Russell Watson & Faye Tozer (2002)	Song 2 (2)	Blur (1997)
		Sorrow (3)	David Bowie (1973)
Someone Loves You Honey (9)	Lutricia McNeal (1998)	Sorrow (4)	Merseys (1966)
		Sorry I'm A Lady (8)	Baccara (1978)
Someone Someone (2)	Brian Poole & The Tremeloes (1964)	Sorry Seems To Be The Hardest Word (1)	Blue featuring Elton John (2002)
Someone's Looking At You (4)	Boomtown Rats (1980)	Sorry Suzanne (3)	Hollies (1969)
		Sound (9)	James (1991)
Somethin' Stupid (1)	Robbie Williams & Nicole Kidman (2001)	Sound And Vision (3)	David Bowie (1977)
		Sound Of Drums (3)	Kula Shaker (1998)
Somethin' Stupid (1)	Nancy Sinatra & Frank Sinatra (1967)	Sound Of Silence, The (3)	Bachelors (1966)
		Sound Of The Underground (1) first hit	Girls Aloud (2002)
Something (4)	Shirley Bassey (1970)	Southern Freeez (8)	Freeez (1981)
Something (4)	Lasgo (2002)	Souvenir (3)	Orchestral Manoeuvres In The Dark (1981)
Something / Come Together (4)	Beatles (1969)		
Something About You (6)	Level 42 (1985)		
Something Better Change / Straighten Out (9)	Stranglers (1977)	Sowing The Seeds Of Love (5)	Tears For Fears (1989)
Something 'Bout You Baby I Like (9)	Status Quo (1981)	Space Jungle, The (7)	Adamski (1990)
		Space Oddity (5)	David Bowie (1969)
Something Changed (10)	Pulp (1996)	Space Oddity (re-issue) (1)	David Bowie (1975)
Something Deep Inside (4)	Billie Piper (2000)	Spaceman (1) first hit	Babylon Zoo (1996)
Something Else / Friggin' In The Riggin' (3)	Sex Pistols (1979)	Spanish Eyes (re-issue) (5)	Al Martino (1973)
		Spanish Flea (3)	Herb Alpert & The Tijuana Brass (1965)
Something For The Pain (8)	Bon Jovi (1995)		
Something Goin' On (5)	Todd Terry (1997)	Spanish Harlem (14)	Aretha Franklin (1971)
Something Good (4)	Utah Saints (1992)		
Something In The Air (1)	Thunderclap Newman (1969)	Speak Like A Child (4)	Style Council (1983)
		Speak To Me Pretty (3)	Brenda Lee (1962)
(Something Inside) So Strong (4)	Labi Siffre (1987)	Special AKA Live EP, The (1)	Special AKA (1980)
Something Old Something New (9)	Fantastics (1971)	Special Brew (3)	Bad Manners (1980)
		Special Years, The (7)	Val Doonican (1965)
		Speedy Gonzales (2)	Pat Boone (1962)
Something Tells Me (Something Is Gonna Happen Tonight) (3)	Cilla Black (1971)	Spice Up Your Life (1)	Spice Girls (1997)
		Spin The Black Circle (10)	Pearl Jam (1994)
Something's Burning (8)	Kenny Rogers & The First Edition (1970)	Spinning Around (1)	Kylie Minogue (2000)
		Spinning The Wheel (2)	George Michael (1996)
Something's Gotten Hold Of My Heart (1)	Marc Almond featuring Gene Pitney (1989)	Spirit In The Sky (1)	Dr & The Medics (1986)
Something's Gotten Hold Of My Heart (5)	Gene Pitney (1967)	Spirit In The Sky (1)	Norman Greenbaum (1970)
Something's Happening (6)	Herman's Hermits (1968)	Splish Splash (18) first hit	Bobby Darin (1958)
		Splish Splash (7)	Charlie Drake (1958)
Sometimes (2)	Erasure (1986)	Squeeze Box (10)	Who (1976)
Sometimes (3)	Britney Spears (1999)	S-S-Single Bed (4)	Fox (1976)
		St Elmo's Fire (Man In Motion) (6)	John Parr (1985)

Title	Group/Artiste	Title	Group/Artiste
St Therese Of The Roses (re-entry) (3)	Malcolm Vaughan (1956)	Steal My Sunshine (8)	Len (1999)
St Valentine's Day Massacre EP (5)	Motorhead & Girlschool (1981)	Steam (7)	East 17 (1994)
Staccato's Theme (4)	Elmer Bernstein (1959)	Steam (10)	Peter Gabriel (1993)
		Step Back In Time (4)	Kylie Minogue (1990)
Stagger Lee (7)	Lloyd Price (1959)	Step By Step (2)	New Kids On The Block (1990)
Stairway Of Love (3)	Michael Holliday (1958)	Step Inside Love (8)	Cilla Black (1968)
Stairway To Heaven (8)	Far Corporation (1985)	Step Off (Part 1) (8)	Grandmaster Melle Mel & Furious Five (1984)
Stairway To Heaven (7)	Rolf Harris (1993)	Step On (5)	Happy Mondays (1990)
Stairway To Heaven (8)	Neil Sedaka (1960)	Steppin' Out (6)	Joe Jackson (1983)
Stan (1)	Eminem (2000)	Stereotype / International Jet Set (6)	Specials (1980)
Stand And Deliver (1)	Adam & The Ants (1981)	Stereotypes (7)	Blur (1996)
Stand By Me (2)	Oasis (1997)	Stick It Out (4)	Right Said Fred & Friends (1993)
Stand By Me (re-issue) (1)	Ben E King (1987)	Still (4)	Commodores (1979)
Stand By Your Man (1) first hit	Tammy Wynette (1975)	Still D.R.E. (6)	Dr Dre featuring Snoop Doggy Dogg (2000)
Stand Tough (7)	Point Break (2000)		
Stand Up For Your Love Rights (2)	Yazz (1988)	Still On Your Side (8)	BBMak (2001)
Standing In The Road (4)	Blackfoot Sue (1972)	Still Water (Love) (10)	Four Tops (1970)
Standing In The Shadows Of Love (6)	Four Tops (1967)	Stillness In Time (9)	Jamiroquai (1995)
Standing On The Corner (4)	King Brothers (1960)	Stomp (6)	Brothers Johnson (1980)
Star Guitar (8)	Chemical Brothers (2002)	Stomp (1)	Steps (2000)
		Stoned Love (3)	Supremes (1971)
Star People '97 (2)	George Michael (1997)	Stonk, The (1)	Hale & Pace & The Stonkers (1991)
Star 69 (10)	Fatboy Slim (2001)	Stool Pigeon (7)	Kid Creole & The Coconuts (1982)
Star Trekkin' (1)	Firm (1987)		
Star Wars Theme / Cantina Band (7)	Meco (1977)	Stop (4)	Sam Brown (1989)
Stardust (7)	David Essex (1974)	Stop (2)	Spice Girls (1998)
Staring At The Sun (3)	U2 (1997)	Stop Crying Your Heart Out (2)	Oasis (2002)
Starlight (2)	Supermen Lovers with Mani Hoffman (2001)	Stop In The Name Of Love (7)	Supremes (1965)
		Stop Stop Stop (2)	Hollies (1966)
Starmaker (3)	Kids From Fame (1982)	Stop The Cavalry (3)	Jona Lewie (1980)
Starman (10)	David Bowie (1972)	Stop The Rock (10)	Apollo Four Forty (1999)
Starry Eyed (1)	Michael Holliday (1960)	Storm In A Teacup (7)	Fortunes (1972)
Starry-Eyed Surprise (6)	Oakenfold (2002)	Story Of My Life, The (1)	Michael Holliday (1958)
Stars (8)	Simply Red (1991)	Story Of The Blues, The (3)	Wah (1982)
Stars On 45 (2)	Starsound (1981)	Story Of Tina, The (10)	Al Martino (1954)
Stars On 45 Vol.2 (2)	Starsound (1981)	Straight From The Heart (9)	Doolally (1999)
Start (1)	Jam (1980)	Straight Up (3)	Paula Abdul (1989)
Start Me Up (7)	Rolling Stones (1981)	Stranded (3)	Lutricia McNeal (1998)
Starting Together (2)	Su Pollard (1986)		
Stay (4)	Eternal (1993)	Strange And Beautiful (7)	Aqualung (2002)
Stay (8)	Hollies (1963)	Strange Currencies (9)	REM (1995)
Stay (2)	Sash featuring La Trec (1997)	Strange Kind Of Woman (8)	Deep Purple (1971)
		Strange Lady In Town (6)	Frankie Laine (1955)
Stay (1)	Shakespears Sister (1992)	Strange Little Girl (7)	Stranglers (1982)
Stay Another Day (1)	East 17 (1994)	Stranger In Moscow (4)	Michael Jackson (1996)
Stay (Faraway So Close) (4)	U2 (1993)	Stranger In Paradise (1) first hit	Tony Bennett (1955)
Stay (I Missed You) (6)	Lisa Loeb & Nine Stories (1994)	Stranger In Paradise (6)	Four Aces featuring Al Alberts (1955)
Stay On These Roads (5)	A-Ha (1988)	Stranger In Paradise (6)	Tony Martin (1955)
Stay Out Of My Life (9)	Five Star (1987)	Stranger On The Shore (2)	Acker Bilk with Leon Young Strings (1961)
Stay Together (3)	Suede (1994)		
Stay With Me (6)	Faces (1971)	Strangers In The Night (1)	Frank Sinatra (1966)
Stay With Me (Baby) (10)	Rebecca Wheatley (2000)	Strawberry Fair (3)	Anthony Newley (1960)
Stayin' Alive (4)	Bee Gees (1978)	Strawberry Fields Forever (3)	Candy Flip (1990)
Stayin' Alive (2)	N-Trance featuring Ricardo Da Force (1995)	Streak, The (1)	Ray Stevens (1974)
		Street Dance (3)	Break Machine (1984)

Title	Group/Artiste	Title	Group/Artiste
Street Life (5)	Crusaders (1979)	Sultans Of Swing (8) first hit	Dire Straits (1979)
Street Life (9)	Roxy Music (1973)	Summer Holiday (1)	Cliff Richard and The Shadows (1963)
Street Spirit (Fade Out) (5)	Radiohead (1996)		
Street Tuff (3)	Rebel MC & Double (1989)	Summer In The City (8)	Lovin' Spoonful (1966)
Streets Of London (2)	Ralph McTell (1974)	Summer Night City (5)	Abba (1978)
Streets Of Philadelphia (2)	Bruce Springsteen (1994)	Summer Nights (10)	Marianne Faithfull (1965)
Strong (4)	Robbie Williams (1999)	Summer Nights (1)	John Travolta & Olivia Newton-John (1978)
Strong Enough (5)	Cher (1999)		
Stronger (7)	Britney Spears (2000)	Summer Of Love (8)	Lonyo (2000)
Stronger / Angels With Dirty Faces (7)	Sugababes (2002)	Summer Of My Life (7)	Simon May (1976)
		Summer Set (5) first hit	Acker Bilk and his Paramount Jazz Band (1960)
Strummin' (52) first hit	Chas and Dave (1978)		
Strut Your Funky Stuff (10)	Frantique (1979)	Summer Son (5)	Texas (1999)
Stuck In A Moment You Can't Get Out Of (2)	U2 (2001)	Summer (The First Time) (9)	Bobby Goldsboro (1973)
Stuck In The Middle (4)	Louise (2001)	Summerlove Sensation (3)	Bay City Rollers (1974)
Stuck In The Middle With You (8)	Stealer's Wheel (1973)	Summertime (7)	Another Level featuring TQ (1999)
Stuck On You (3)	Elvis Presley with The Jordanaires (1960)	Summertime (8)	Jazzy Jeff & The Fresh Prince (1991)
Stuck On You (9)	Trevor Walters (1984)	Summertime Blues (18) first hit	Eddie Cochran (1958)
Stupid Cupid / Carolina Moon (1)	Connie Francis (1958)	Summertime City (4)	Mike Batt (1975)
Stupid Girl (4)	Garbage (1996)	Summertime Of Our Lives (5)	A1 (1999)
Stutter (5)	Joe (2001)	Sun Ain't Gonna Shine Anymore, The (1)	Walker Brothers (1966)
Stutter Rap (No Sleep 'Til Bedtime) (4)	Morris Minor & The Majors (1987)	Sun Always Shines On TV, The (1)	A-Ha (1985)
Substitute (2)	Clout (1978)	Sun And The Rain, The (5)	Madness (1983)
Substitute (8)	Liquid Gold (1980)	Sun Arise (3)	Rolf Harris (1962)
Substitute (5)	Who (1966)	Sun Goes Down (Living It Up), The (10)	Level 42 (1983)
Substitute (re-issue) (7)	Who (1976)		
Subterranean Homesick Blues (9)	Bob Dylan (1965)	Sun Hits The Sky (10)	Supergrass (1997)
Suburbia (8)	Pet Shop Boys (1986)	Sun Is Shining (3)	Bob Marley vs Funkstar De Luxe (1999)
Such A Night (1)	Johnnie Ray (1954)		
Sucu Sucu (9)	Laurie Johnson (1961)	Sunchyme (2)	Dario G (1997)
		Sunday Girl (1)	Blondie (1979)
Suddenly (3)	Angry Anderson (1988)	Sunday Morning Call (4)	Oasis (2000)
		Sunny (3)	Boney M (1977)
Suddenly (4)	Billy Ocean (1985)	Sunny Afternoon (1)	Kinks (1966)
Suddenly There's A Valley (7)	Petula Clark (1955)	Sunset (Bird Of Prey) (9)	Fatboy Slim (2000)
Suddenly You Love Me (6)	Tremeloes (1968)	Sunshine (9)	Gabrielle (1999)
Suedehead (5) first hit	Morrissey (1988)	Sunshine After The Rain (10)	Elkie Brooks (1977)
Sugar And Spice (2)	Searchers (1963)	Sunshine After The Rain, The (4)	Berri (1995)
Sugar Baby Love (1) first hit	Rubettes (1974)	Sunshine Girl (8)	Herman's Hermits (1968)
Sugar Candy Kisses (3)	Mac & Katie Kissoon (1975)	Sunshine Of Your Smile, The (9)	Mike Berry (1980)
Sugar Me (5) first hit	Lynsey De Paul (1972)	Sunshine On A Rainy Day (re-mix) (4)	Zoe (1991)
Sugar Moon (6)	Pat Boone (1958)	Sunshine Superman (2)	Donovan (1966)
Sugar Sugar (1) first and only hit	Archies (1969)	Super Trouper (1)	Abba (1980)
		Superfly Guy (5)	S Express (1988)
Sugar Town (8)	Nancy Sinatra (1967)	Superman (Gioca Jouer) (9)	Black Lace (1983)
Sugarbush (8)	Doris Day & Frankie Laine (1952)	Supermarioland (8)	Ambassadors Of Funk with MC Mario (1992)
Sugarbush (re-entry) (8)	Doris Day & Frankie Laine (1952)	Supernature (8)	Cerrone (1978)
		Supreme (4)	Robbie Williams (2000)
Sukiyaki (10)	Kenny Ball & His Jazzmen (1963)	Sure (1)	Take That (1994)
		Surfin' USA (34) first hit	Beach Boys (1963)
Sukiyaki (6)	Kyu Sakamoto (1963)	Surrender (10)	Diana Ross (1971)
Sultana (5)	Titanic (1971)	Surrender (7)	Swing Out Sister (1987)

MUSIC POP

Title	Group/Artiste	Title	Group/Artiste
Surrender (Torna Surriento) (1)	Elvis Presley with The Jordanaires (1961)	Sylvias Mother (2) first hit	Dr Hook (1972)
		Sympathy For The Devil (9)	Guns 'N' Roses (1995)
Surrender Your Love (7)	Nightcrawlers featuring John Reid (1995)	Synth And Strings (8)	Yomanda (1999)
		System Addict (3)	Five Star (1986)
Surround Yourself With Sorrow (3)	Cilla Black (1969)	Taboo (10)	Glamma Kid featuring Shola Ama (1999)
Survivor (1)	Destiny's Child (2001)	Tahiti (8)	David Essex (1983)
Susan's House (9)	Eels (1997)	Tainted Love (5)	Marilyn Manson (2002)
Suspicion (9)	Elvis Presley (1976)		
Suspicious Minds (8)	Fine Young Cannibals (1986)	Tainted Love (1)	Soft Cell (1981)
		Tainted Love (5)	Soft Cell / Marc
Suspicious Minds (2)	Elvis Presley (1969)		Almond (1991)
Suspicious Minds / The Long and Winding Road (1)	Will Young and Gareth Gates (2002)	Take A Chance On Me (1)	Abba (1978)
		(Take A Little) Piece Of My Heart (9)	Erma Franklin (1992)
Sven Sven Sven (7)	Bell & Spurling (2001)	Take A Look Around (Theme From MI 2) (3) first hit	Limp Bizkit (2000)
Swallowed (7)	Bush (1997)	Take Five (6)	Dave Brubeck Quartet (1961)
Swamp Thing (3)	Grid (1994)		
Sway (6)	Dean Martin (1954)	Take Good Care Of My Baby (3)	Bobby Vee (1961)
Swear It Again (1) first hit	Westlife (1999)	Take Good Care Of Yourself (9)	Three Degrees (1975)
Sweat (A La La La La Long) (re-entry) (3)	Inner Circle (1993)	Take It To The Limit (12)	Eagles (1976)
Swedish Rhapsody (2)	Mantovani & His Orchestra (1953)	Take Me Bak 'Ome (1)	Slade (1972)
		Take Me Home (2) first hit	Sophie Ellis-Bextor (2001)
Swedish Rhapsody (10)	Ray Martin Orchestra (1953)	Take Me I'm Yours (19) first hit	Squeeze (1978)
Swedish Rhapsody (re-entry) (4)	Ray Martin Orchestra (1953)	Take Me There (7)	Blackstreet & Mya featuring Mase and Blinky Blink (1998)
Sweet Caroline (8)	Neil Diamond (1971)		
Sweet Child O' Mine (remix) (6)	Guns 'N' Roses (1989)	Take Me To The Mardi Gras (7)	Paul Simon (1973)
Sweet Dream (7)	Jethro Tull (1969)	Take Me To Your Heart (8)	Rick Astley (1988)
Sweet Dreams (Are Made Of This) (2)	Eurythmics (1983)	Take My Breath Away (1) first hit	Berlin (1986)
		Take My Breath Away (5)	Emma Bunton (2001)
Sweet Harmony (8)	Beloved (1993)	Take My Breath Away (re-entry) (3)	Berlin (1990)
Sweet Inspiration (10)	Johnny Johnson & The Bandwagon (1970)	Take My Heart (9)	Al Martino (1952)
		Take On Me (1)	A1 (2000)
Sweet Like Chocolate (1)	Shanks & Bigfoot (1999)	Take On Me (2) first hit	A-Ha (1985)
Sweet Little Mystery (5)	Wet Wet Wet (1987)	Take That Look Off Your Face (3)	Marti Webb (1980)
Sweet Love 2K (3)	Fierce (2000)		
Sweet Lullaby (10)	Deep Forest (1994)	Take These Chains From My Heart (5)	Ray Charles (1963)
Sweet Nothin's (4)	Brenda Lee (1960)		
Sweet Old-Fashioned Girl (3)	Teresa Brewer (1956)	Take Your Time (10)	Mantronix featuring Wondress (1990)
Sweet Soul Music (7)	Arthur Conley (1967)	Taken For Granted (10)	Sia (2000)
Sweet Surrender (6)	Wet Wet Wet (1989)	Takes Two To Tango (6) first hit	Louis Armstrong (1952)
Sweet Talkin' Guy (re-issue) (4)	Chiffons (1972)		
Sweet Talkin' Woman (6)	Electric Light Orchestra (1978)	Talk Of The Town (8)	Pretenders (1980)
		Talking In Your Sleep / Love Me (6)	Martine McCutcheon (1999)
Sweetest Smile (8)	Black (1987)		
Sweetest Thing (3)	U2 (1998)	Tammy (2)	Debbie Reynolds (1957)
Sweetness (4)	Michelle Gayle (1994)	Tap Turns On The Water (5)	CCS (1971)
Sweets For My Sweet (3)	C J Lewis (1994)	Tarzan Boy (3) first and only hit	Baltimora (1985)
Sweets For My Sweet (1) first hit	Searchers (1963)	Taste Of Aggro, A (3)	Barron Knights (1978)
Swing The Mood (1)	Jive Bunny & The Mastermixers (1989)	Tattva (4)	Kula Shaker (1996)
		Tea For Two Cha Cha (3)	Tommy Dorsey Orchestra and Warren Covington (1958)
Swing Your Daddy (4)	Jim Gilstrap (1975)		
Swingin' Shepherd Blues (3)	Ted Heath Orchestra (1958)		
Swinging On A Star (7)	Big Dee Irwin (1963)	Teacher / The Witches Promise (4)	Jethro Tull (1970)
Swiss Maid (2)	Del Shannon (1962)	Tear Fell, A (2)	Teresa Brewer (1956)
Swords Of A Thousand Men (6)	Ten Pole Tudor (1981)		
Sylvia (4)	Focus (1973)	Teardrop (10)	Massive Attack (1998)

Title	Group/Artiste	Title	Group/Artiste
Teardrops (5)	Shakin' Stevens (1984)	Tetris (6) first and only hit	Doctor Spin (1992)
Teardrops (3)	Womack & Womack (1988)	Tha Crossroads (8)	Bone Thugs-N-Harmony (1996)
Tearin' Up My Heart (9)	N Sync (1999)	Thank Abba For The Music (4)	Steps, Tina Cousins, Cleopatra, B*Witched and Billie (1999)
Tears (1)	Ken Dodd (1965)		
Tears I Cried, The (8)	Glitter Band (1975)		
Tears In Heaven (5)	Eric Clapton (1992)	Thank God I Found You (10)	Mariah Carey (2000)
Tears Of A Clown / Ranking Full Stop (6)	Beat (1979)	Thank U (5)	Alanis Morissette (1998)
Tears Of A Clown, The (1)	Smokey Robinson & The Miracles (1970)	Thank U Very Much (4) first hit	Scaffold (1967)
		Thank You (3)	Dido (2001)
Tears On My Pillow (1)	Kylie Minogue (1990)	Thanks For The Memory (Wham Bam Thank You Mam) (7)	Slade (1975)
Tears On My Pillow (1)	Johnny Nash (1975)	That Don't Impress Me Much (3)	Shania Twain (1999)
Tease Me (3) first hit	Chaka Demus & Pliers (1993)	That Girl Belongs To Yesterday (7)	Gene Pitney (1964)
		That Look In Your Eye (5)	Ali Campbell (1995)
Teddy Bear (4)	Red Sovine (1981)	That Ole Devil Called Love (2)	Alison Moyet (1985)
Teen Beat (9)	Sandy Nelson (1959)	That Same Old Feeling (5)	Pickettywitch (1970)
Teenage Dirtbag (2)	Wheatus (2001)	That Sounds Good To Me (4)	Jive Bunny & The Mastermixers (1990)
Teenage Kicks (31) first hit	Undertones (1978)		
Teenage Rampage (2)	Sweet (1974)		
Teenager On Love, A (2)	Marty Wilde (1959)	That'll Be The Day (1) first hit	Crickets (1957)
Telegram Sam (1)	T Rex (1972)	That's Amore (2)	Dean Martin and Dick Stabile Orchestra (1954)
Telephone Line (8)	Electric Light Orchestra (1977)		
Telephone Man (6)	Meri Wilson (1977)	That's Livin' Alright (3)	Joe Fagin (1984)
Teletubbies Say Eh-Oh! (1)	Teletubbies (1997)	That's My Home (7)	Mr Acker Bilk & his Paramount Jazz Band (1961)
Tell Her About It (4)	Billy Joel (1983)		
Tell Him (10)	Billie Davis (1963)		
Tell Him (3)	Barbra Streisand & Celine Dion (1997)	That's The Way (I Like It) (4)	KC & The Sunshine Band (1975)
Tell Him (6)	Hello (1974)	That's The Way It Is (10)	Mel & Kim (1988)
Tell It To My Heart (3) first hit	Taylor Dayne (1988)	That's The Way Love Goes (2)	Janet Jackson (1993)
Tell It To My Heart (9)	Kelly Llorenna (2002)	That's The Way Love Is (8)	Ten City (1989)
Tell Laura I Love Her (1)	Ricky Valance (1960)	That's What Friends Are For (8)	Deniece Williams (1977)
Tell Me (4)	Melanie B (2000)		
Tell Me A Story (5)	Jimmy Boyd (1953)	That's What I Like (1)	Jive Bunny & The Mastermixers (1989)
Tell Me A Story (5)	Jimmy Boyd & Frankie Laine (1953)	That's What Love Will Do (3)	Joe Brown & The Bruvvers (1963)
Tell Me What He Said (2)	Helen Shapiro (1962)	That's You (10)	Nat 'King' Cole (1960)
Tell Me When (7) first and biggest hit	Applejacks (1964)	Them Girls Them Girls (5)	Zig & Zag (1994)
Tell Me When (6)	Human League (1995)	Theme For a Dream (3)	Cliff Richard & The Shadows (1961)
Tell Me Why (The Riddle) (7)	Paul Van Dyk featuring Saint Etienne (2000)	Theme From A Summer Place (2)	Percy Faith & his Orchestra (1960)
Telstar (1)	Tornados (1962)	Theme From A Threepenny Opera (Mack The Knife) (8)	Louis Armstrong and his All-Stars (1956)
Temma Harbour (6)	Mary Hopkin (1970)		
Temple Of Love (3)	Sisters Of Mercy (1992)	Theme From Dixie (7)	Duane Eddy (1961)
Temptation (1)	Everly Brothers (1961)	Theme From Harry's Game (5) first hit	Clannad (1982)
Temptation (2)	Heaven 17 (1983)	Theme From M.A.S.H. (Suicide Is Painless) (7)	Manic Street Preachers (1992)
Temptation (remix) (4)	Heaven 17 (1992)	Theme From M.A.S.H. (Suicide Is Painless) (1)	MASH (1980)
10538 Overture (9)	Electric Light Orchestra (1972)	Theme From Mahogany (Do You Know Where You're Going To) (5)	Diana Ross (1976)
Tender (2)	Blur (1999)		
Tenderly (10)	Nat 'King' Cole (1954)		
Tennessee Wig Walk (4)	Bonnie Lou (1954)	Theme From Mission Impossible (7)	Adam Clayton and Larry Mullen (1996)
Tequila (5)	Champs (1958)	Theme From New York New York (re-issue) (4)	Frank Sinatra (1986)
Tequila (2)	Terrorvision (1999)		
Terry (4) first hit	Twinkle (1964)	Theme From S-Express (1)	S-Express (1988)
Terrys Theme From Limelight (3)	Ron Goodwin Orchestra (1953)	Theme From Shaft (4)	Isaac Hayes (1971)
Terry's Theme From Limelight (2)	Frank Chacksfield (1953)	Theme From The Deerhunter (Cavatina) (9)	Shadows (1979)

Title	Group/Artiste
Theme From The Legion's Last Patrol (4)	Ken Thorne Orchestra (1963)
Theme From The Threepenny Opera (9)	Dick Hyman Trio (1956)
Theme From Z Cars (8)	Johnny Keating Orchestra (1962)
Then He Kissed Me (2)	Crystals (1963)
Then I Kissed Her (4)	Beach Boys (1967)
There Are More Questions Than Answers (9)	Johnny Nash (1972)
There But For Fortune (8)	Joan Baez (1965)
There By The Grace Of God (6)	Manic Street Preachers (2002)
There Goes My Everything (2)	Engelbert Humperdinck (1967)
There Goes My Everything (6)	Elvis Presley (1971)
There Goes My First Love (3)	Drifters (1975)
There Goes The Fear (3)	Doves (2002)
There Is A Mountain (8)	Donovan (1967)
There It Is (5)	Shalamar (1982)
There Must Be A Reason (9)	Frankie Laine (1954)
There Must Be A Way (7)	Frankie Vaughan (1967)
There Must Be An Angel (Playing With My Heart) (1)	Eurythmics (1985)
There There My Dear (7)	Dexy's Midnight Runners (1980)
There You Go (6)	Pink (2000)
There You'll Be (3)	Faith Hill (2001)
There's A Ghost In My House (3)	R Dean Taylor (1974)
There's A Heartache Following Me (6)	Jim Reeves (1964)
There's A Kind Of Hush (7)	Herman's Hermits (1967)
There's A Whole Lot Of Loving (2)	Guys & Dolls (1975)
(There's) Always Something There To Remind Me (1) first hit	Sandie Shaw (1964)
There's No Other Way (8)	Blur (1991)
There's Nothing I Won't Do (4)	JX (1996)
These Are The Times (4)	Dru Hill (1999)
These Boots Are Made For Walking (1)	Nancy Sinatra (1966)
These Days (7)	Bon Jovi (1996)
They Don't Care About Us (4)	Michael Jackson (1996)
They Don't Know (3)	So Solid Crew (2001)
They Don't Know (2)	Tracey Ullman (1983)
(They Long To Be) Close To You (6) first hit	Carpenters (1970)
They're Coming To Take Me Away Ha-Haaa! (4)	Napoleon XIV (1966)
Thieves In The Temple (7)	Prince (1990)
Thing Called Love, A (4)	Johnny Cash (1972)
Things (2)	Bobby Darin (1962)
Things Can Only Get Better (6)	Howard Jones (1985)
Things Can Only Get Better (remix) (1)	D:Ream (1994)
Things I've Seen (6)	Spooks (2001)
Things That Make You Go Hmmm ... (4)	C & C Music Factory (1991)
Things We Do For Love, The (6)	10CC (1976)
Think Of You (7)	Whigfield (1995)
Think Twice (1)	Celine Dion (1994)
Thinking About Your Love (4)	Kenny Thomas (1991)
Thinking It Over (5)	Liberty (2001)

Title	Group/Artiste
This Ain't A Love Song (6)	Bon Jovi (1995)
This Charming Man (re-issue) (8)	Smiths (1992)
This Corrosion (7)	Sisters Of Mercy (1987)
This Guy's In Love With You (3)	Herb Alpert (1968)
This Is A Call (5)	Foo Fighters (1995)
This Is It (10)	Dannii Minogue (1993)
This Is It (9)	Melba Moore (1976)
This Is My Song (1)	Petula Clark (1967)
This Is My Song (2)	Harry Secombe (1967)
This Is Not A Love Song (5)	Public Image Ltd (1983)
This Is Tomorrow (9)	Bryan Ferry (1977)
This Little Bird (6)	Marianne Faithfull (1965)
This Old Heart Of Mine (4)	Rod Stewart (1975)
This Old Heart Of Mine (Is Weak For You) (3)	Isley Brothers (1968)
This Ole House (4)	Billie Anthony with Eric Jupp Orchestra (1954)
This Ole House (1)	Rosemary Clooney (1954)
This Ole House (1)	Shakin' Stevens (1981)
This One's For The Children (9)	New Kids On The Block (1990)
This Time I Know It's For Real (3)	Donna Summer (1989)
This Time (We'll Get It Right) / England We'll Fly The Flag (2)	England World Cup Squad (1982)
This Town Ain't Big Enough For Both Of Us (2)	Sparks (1974)
This Used To Be My Playground (3)	Madonna (1992)
This Wheel's On Fire (5)	Julie Driscoll, Brian Auger & The Trinity (1968)
Thong Song (3)	Sisqo (2000)
Thorn In My Side (5)	Eurythmics (1986)
Those Were The Days (1)	Mary Hopkin (1968)
Thought I'd Died And Gone To Heaven (8)	Bryan Adams (1992)
Thousand Miles, A (6)	Vanessa Carlton (2002)
Three Bells, The (6)	Browns (1959)
Three Coins In The Fountain (5)	Four Aces featuring Al Alberts (1954)
Three Coins In The Fountain (1)	Frank Sinatra (1954)
3 Is Family (9)	Dana Dawson (1995)
3 Lions (1)	Baddiel & Skinner and Lightning Seeds (1996)
3 Lions '98 (1)	Baddiel & Skinner and Lightning Seeds (1998)
Three Little Pigs (5)	Green Jelly (1993)
Three Steps To Heaven (1)	Eddie Cochran (1960)
Three Steps To Heaven (2)	Showaddywaddy (1975)
Three Times A Lady (1)	Commodores (1978)
3 x 3 EP (10)	Genesis (1982)
3AM Eternal (1)	KLF featuring Children of The Revolution (1991)
Thriller (10)	Michael Jackson (1983)

Title	Group/Artiste	Title	Group/Artiste
Through The Barricades (6)	Spandau Ballet (1986)	Tokoloshe Man (4)	John Kongos (1971)
Through The Rain (8)	Mariah Carey (2002)	Tokyo Melody (9)	Helmut Zacharias (1964)
Throw Down The Line (7)	Cliff Richard & Hank Marvin (1969)	Tom Dooley (5)	Kingston Trio (1958)
Thunder (4)	East 17 (1995)	Tom Dooley (3)	Lonnie Donegan & His Skiffle Group (1958)
Thunder In The Mountains (4)	Toyah (1981)		
Thunderbirds Are Go (5)	FAB featuring MC Parker (1990)	Tom Hark (2)	Elias & His Zigzag Jive Flutes (1958)
Ticket To Ride (1)	Beatles (1965)	Tom Hark (6)	Piranhas (1980)
Tide Is High (Get The Feeling), The (1)	Atomic Kitten (2002)	Tom Tom Turnaround (6)	New World (1971)
		Tom Traubert's Blues (Waltzing Matilda) (6)	Rod Stewart (1992)
Tide Is High, The (1)	Blondie (1980)		
Tie a Yellow Ribbon Round the Old Oak Tree (1)	Dawn featuring Tony Orlando (1973)	Tomboy (10)	Perry Como (1959)
Tie Me Kangaroo Down Sport (9) first hit	Rolf Harris (1960)	Tomorrow (8)	Johnny Brandon, The Phantoms, and Norman Warren (1955)
Tiger Feet (1)	Mud (1974)		
(Til) I Kissed You (2)	Everly Brothers (1959)	Tomorrow (9)	Sandie Shaw (1966)
		Tomorrow's (Just Another Day) / Madness (Is All In My Mind) (8)	Madness (1983)
Till (2)	Tom Jones (1971)		
Till The End Of The Day (8)	Kinks (1965)		
Time (9)	Craig Douglas (1961)	Tom's Diner (2)	DNA featuring Suzanne Vega (1990)
Time After Time (3)	Cyndi Lauper (1984)		
Time (Clock Of The Heart) (3)	Culture Club (1982)	Tonight (3)	New Kids On The Block (1990)
Time Drags By (10)	Cliff Richard & The Shadows (1966)		
		Tonight I Celebrate My Love (2)	Peabo Bryson & Roberta Flack (1983)
Time Has Come, The (4)	Adam Faith (1961)		
Time Is Now, The (2)	Moloko (2000)		
Time Is Tight (4)	Booker T & The MG's (1969)	Tonight I'm Yours (Don't Hurt Me) (8)	Rod Stewart (1981)
		Tonight Tonight (7)	Smashing Pumpkins (1996)
Time To Burn (3)	Storm (2000)		
Time To Say Goodbye (Con Te Partiro) (2)	Sarah Brightman & Andrea Bocelli (1997)	Tonight's The Night (Gonna Be Alright) (5)	Rod Stewart (1976)
		Too Bad (9)	Nickelback (2002)
Time Warp (remix), The (7)	Damian (1989)	Too Blind To See It (5)	Kym Sims (1991)
Times They Are A-Changin' (9) first hit	Bob Dylan (1965)	Too Busy Thinking 'Bout My Baby (5)	Marvin Gaye (1969)
Tin Soldier (9)	Small Faces (1967)		
Tired Of Being Alone (4)	Al Green (1971)	Too Close (1)	Blue (2001)
Tired Of Waiting For You (1)	Kinks (1965)	Too Funky (4)	George Michael (1992)
To Be Or Not To Be (9)	B A Robertson (1980)		
To Be With You (3)	Mr Big (1992)	Too Good To Be Forgotten (5)	Amazulu (1986)
To Be With You Again (10)	Level 42 (1987)	Too Good To Be Forgotten (10)	Chi-Lites (1974)
To Cut A Long Story Short (5) first hit	Spandau Ballet (1980)	Too Hot (9)	Coolio (1996)
		Too Late For Goodbyes (6)	Julian Lennon (1984)
To Earth With Love (10)	Gay Dad (1999)	Too Many Broken Hearts (1)	Jason Donovan (1989)
To Know Him Is To Love Him (2)	Teddy Bears (1958)		
To Know You Is To Love You (5)	Peter & Gordon (1965)	Too Much (2)	Bros (1989)
		Too Much (6)	Elvis Presley with The Jordanaires (1957)
To Live And Die In L.A. (10)	Makaveli (1997)		
To Love Somebody (5)	Nina Simone (1969)	Too Much (1)	Spice Girls (1997)
To Love Somebody (8)	Jimmy Somerville (1990)	Too Much Heaven (3)	Bee Gees (1978)
		Too Much Love Will Kill You (5)	Brian May (1992)
To The Moon And Back (3)	Savage Garden (1998)	Too Much Too Little Too Late (3)	Johnny Mathis & Deniece Williams (1978)
To You I Belong (1)	B*Witched (1998)		
Tobacco Road (6)	Nashville Teens (1964)	Too Nice To Talk To (7)	Beat (1980)
		Too Shy (1)	Kajagoogoo (1983)
Toca's Miracle (1)	Fragma (2000)	Too Soon To Know (3)	Roy Orbison (1966)
Toccata (5)	Sky (1980)	Too Young (5)	Donny Osmond (1972)
Together (6)	Connie Francis (1961)		
		Too Young To Die (10)	Jamiroquai (1993)
Together (8)	P J Proby (1964)	Too Young To Go Steady (8)	Nat 'King' Cole (1956)
Together Again (4)	Janet Jackson (1997)		
		Top Of The World (2)	Brandy featuring Mase (1998)
Together Forever (2)	Rick Astley (1988)		
Together In Electric Dreams (3)	Giorgio Moroder & Phil Oakey (1984)	Top Of The World (5)	Carpenters (1973)
Together We Are Beautiful (1)	Fern Kinney (1980)	Torch (2)	Soft Cell (1982)

M
U
S
I
C

P
O
P

Title	Group/Artiste	Title	Group/Artiste
Torn (2)	Natalie Imbruglia (1997)	Tu M'Aimes Encore (To Love Me Again) (7)	Celine Dion (1995)
Torn Between Two Lovers (4)	Mary MacGregor (1977)	Tubthumping (2)	Chumbawamba (1997)
Tossing And Turning (3)	Ivy League (1965)	Tumbling Dice (5)	Rolling Stones (1972)
Total Eclipse Of The Heart (5)	Nicki French (1995)	Tunnel Of Love (10)	Fun Boy Three (1983)
Total Eclipse Of The Heart (1)	Bonnie Tyler (1983)	Turn (8)	Travis (1999)
Touch Me (1)	Rui Da Silva featuring Cassandra (2001)	Turn Around (3)	Phats & Small (1999)
Touch Me (3)	49ers (1989)	Turn Back Time (1)	Aqua (1998)
Touch Me (All Night Long) (5)	Cathy Dennis (1991)	Turn It On Again (8)	Genesis (1980)
Touch Me (I Want Your Body) (3) first hit	Samantha Fox (1986)	Turn It Up / Fire It Up (2)	Busta Rhymes (1998)
Touch Me In The Morning (9)	Diana Ross (1973)	Turn Off The Light (4)	Nelly Furtado (2001)
Touch Too Much, A (8)	Arrows (1974)	Turn On Tune In Cop Out (re-issue) (3)	Freak Power (1995)
Tower Of Strength (1)	Frankie Vaughan (1961)	Turn The Music Up (8)	Players Association (1979)
Town Called Malice / Precious (1)	Jam (1982)	Turning Japanese (3)	Vapors (1980)
Toxygene (4)	Orb (1997)	Turtle Power (1)	Partners In Kryme (1990)
Toy Balloons (7)	Russ Conway (1961)	Tusk (6)	Fleetwood Mac (1979)
Toy Boy (4)	Sinitta (1987)		
Toy Soldiers (5)	Martika (1989)	Tweedle Dee (4)	Little Jimmy Osmond (1973)
Tracks Of My Tears, The (9)	Smokey Robinson & The Miracles (1969)	Tweedle Dee Tweedle Dum (2)	Middle Of The Road (1971)
Tracy (4)	Cufflinks (1969)	Twelfth Of Never, The (1)	Donny Osmond (1973)
Tragedy (1)	Bee Gees (1979)		
Trail Of The Lonesome Pine, The (2)	Laurel & Hardy with The Avalon Boys (1975)	Twelfth Of Never, The (8)	Cliff Richard (1964)
		20th Century Boy (3)	T Rex (1973)
Train Of Thought (8)	A-Ha (1986)	Twenty Four Hours From Tulsa (5)	Gene Pitney (1963)
Trains and Boats and Planes (4)	Burt Bacharach (1965)	Twenty Four Seven (6)	Artful Dodger featuring Melanie Blatt (2001)
Trapped (3)	Colonel Abrams (1985)		
Trash (3)	Suede (1996)	Twenty Tiny Fingers (4)	Stargazers (1955)
Travellers Tune (5)	Ocean Colour Scene (1997)	25 Or 6 To 4 (7)	Chicago (1970)
		21 Seconds (1)	So Solid Crew (2001)
Travellin' Band (8)	Creedence Clearwater Revival (1970)	Twilight Time (3)	Platters (1958)
		Twilight Zone (2)	2 Unlimited (1992)
Travellin' Light (1)	Cliff Richard & The Shadows (1959)	Twist And Shout (1)	Chaka Demus & Pliers (1993)
Tribal Dance (4)	2 Unlimited (1993)	Twist And Shout (10)	Deacon Blue (1991)
Tribute (Right On) (5)	Pasadenas (1988)	Twist And Shout (4) first hit	Brian Poole & The Tremeloes (1963)
Trip To Trumpton, A (6)	Urban Hype (1992)		
Trippin' (8)	Mark Morrison (1996)	Twist And Shout (4)	Salt-N-Pepa (1988)
		Twist In My Sobriety (22)	Tanita Tikaram (1988)
Trouble (10)	Coldplay (2000)	Twist (Yo Twist), The (2)	Fat Boys & Chubby Checker (1988)
True (1)	Spandau Ballet (1983)		
True Blue (1)	Madonna (1986)	Twistin' The Night Away (6)	Sam Cooke (1962)
True Faith (4)	New Order (1987)	2 Become 1 (1)	Spice Girls (1996)
True Faith (remix) (9)	New Order (1994)	Two Can Play That Game (re-entry) (3)	Bobby Brown (1995)
True Love (4)	Bing Crosby & Grace Kelly (1956)	2 Faced (3)	Louise (2000)
True Love (2)	Elton John – duet with Kiki Dee (1993)	2-4-6-8 Motorway (5) first hit	Tom Robinson Band (1977)
		Two Hearts (6)	Phil Collins (1988)
True Love Never Dies (re-issue) (7)	Flip & Fill featuring Kelly Llorenna (2002)	Two In A Million / You're My Number One (2)	S Club 7 (1999)
		Two Kinds Of Teardrops (5)	Del Shannon (1963)
True Love Ways (8)	Cliff Richard (1983)	Two Little Boys (1)	Rolf Harris (1969)
True Love Ways (2)	Peter & Gordon (1965)	Two Princes (3)	Spin Doctors (1993)
		2 Times (2)	Ann Lee (1999)
Truly (6)	Lionel Richie (1982)	Two Tribes (1)	Frankie Goes To Hollywood (1984)
Truly Madly Deeply (4)	Savage Garden (1998)	U And Me (10)	Cappella (1994)
		U Can't Touch This (3)	MC Hammer (1990)
Try Again (5)	Aaliyah (2000)	U Got It Bad (5)	Usher (2001)
Try Me Out (6)	Corona (1995)	U Got 2 Let The Music (2)	Cappella (1993)

Title	Group/Artiste	Title	Group/Artiste
U Know What's Up (2)	Donell Jones (2000)	Up Where We Belong (7)	Joe Cocker & Jennifer Warnes (1983)
U R The Best Thing (remix) (4)	D:Ream (1994)		
U Remind Me (3)	Usher (2001)		
U Sure Do (re-entry) (4)	Strike (1995)	Upside Down (10)	A Teens (2001)
Ugly (7)	Bubba Sparxxx (2001)	Upside Down (2)	Diana Ross (1980)
		Uptown Girl (1)	Billy Joel (1983)
Ugly Duckling, The (10)	Mike Reid (1975)	Uptown Girl (1)	Westlife (2001)
Uh La La La (10)	Alexia (1998)	Use It Up And Wear It Out (1)	Odyssey (1980)
Um Um Um Um Um Um (5)	Wayne Fontana & The Mindbenders (1964)	Vacation (10)	Connie Francis (1962)
		Valentine (9)	T'Pau (1988)
Un Banc Un Arbre Une Rue (9)	Severine (1971)	Vaya Con Dios (7)	Les Paul & Mary Ford (1953)
(Un Dos Tres) Maria (6)	Ricky Martin (1997)		
Una Paloma Blanca (5)	Jonathan King (1975)	Venus (8)	Bananarama (1986)
Unbelievable (3)	EMF (1990)	Venus (4)	Don Pablo's Animals (1990)
Un-Break My Heart (2)	Toni Braxton (1996)		
Unbreakable (1)	Westlife (2002)	Venus (8) first hit	Shocking Blue (1970)
Unchained Melody (10) first and only hit	Les Baxter his Chorus and Orchestra (1955)	Venus In Blue Jeans (4)	Mark Wynter (1962)
		Victim Of Love (7)	Erasure (1987)
Unchained Melody (1)	Gareth Gates (2002)	Victims (3)	Culture Club (1983)
		Video Killed The Radio Star (1) first hit	Buggles (1979)
Unchained Melody (2)	Al Hibbler (1955)		
Unchained Melody (1)	Jimmy Young (1955)	Vienna (2)	Ultravox (1981)
Unchained Melody/(There'll Be Bluebirds Over) The White Cliffs Of Dover (1)	Robson & Jerome (1995)	Vienna Calling (10)	Falco (1986)
		View To A Kill, A (2)	Duran Duran (1985)
		Vincent (1)	Don McLean (1972)
Unchained Melody (re-issue) (1)	Righteous Brothers (1990)	Vindaloo (2)	Fat Les (1998)
		Virginia Plain (4) first hit	Roxy Music (1972)
Uncle John From Jamaica (6)	Vengaboys (2000)	Virtual Insanity (3)	Jamiroquai (1996)
Under Pressure (1)	Queen & David Bowie (1981)	Vision Of Love (9) first hit	Mariah Carey (1990)
		Visions (7)	Cliff Richard (1966)
Under The Boardwalk (2)	Bruce Willis (1987)	Viva Bobby Joe (6)	Equals (1969)
Under The Bridge / Lady Marmalade (1)	All Saints (1998)	Viva Forever (1)	Spice Girls (1998)
		Viva La Radio (6)	Lolly (1999)
Under The Bridges Of Paris (7)	Eartha Kitt (1955)	Viva Las Vegas (10)	ZZ Top (1992)
Under The Bridges Of Paris (6)	Dean Martin (1955)	Vogue (1)	Madonna (1990)
Under The Moon Of Love (1)	Showaddywaddy (1976)	Voice In The Wilderness (2)	Cliff Richard & The Shadows (1960)
Under Your Thumb (3)	Godley & Creme (1981)	Volare (2)	Dean Martin (1958)
		Volare (10)	Domenico Modugno (1958)
Underneath Your Clothes (3)	Shakira (2002)		
Underwater Love (4)	Smoke City (1997)	Voodoo Chile (1)	Jimi Hendrix Experience (1970)
Undivided Love (5)	Louise (1996)		
Unforgettable Fire, The (6)	U2 (1985)	Voyage Voyage (5)	Desireless (1988)
Union Of The Snake (3)	Duran Duran (1983)	Wait (7)	Robert Howard & Kym Mazelle (1989)
United States Of Whatever (10)	Liam Lynch (2002)		
United We Stand (10) first hit	Brotherhood Of Man (1970)		
		Waiting For A Girl Like You (8)	Foreigner (1981)
Universal, The (5)	Blur (1995)	Waiting For A Star To Fall (9)	Boy Meets Girl (1988)
Unleash The Dragon (6)	Sisqo (2000)		
Unpretty (6)	TLC (1999)	Waiting For An Alibi (9)	Thin Lizzy (1979)
Until It Sleeps (5)	Metallica (1996)	Waiting For The Train (7)	Flash & The Pan (1983)
Until It's Time For You To Go (5)	Elvis Presley (1972)		
Until The End Of Time (4)	2Pac (2001)	Waiting For Tonight (5)	Jennifer Lopez (1999)
Until The Time Is Through (2)	Five (1998)		
Up And Down (4)	Vengaboys (1998)	Wake Me Up Before You Go Go (1)	Wham! (1984)
Up Around The Bend (3)	Creedence Clearwater Revival (1970)		
		Wake Up Boo! (9)	Boo Radleys (1995)
Up Middle Finger (7)	Oxide & Neutrino (2001)	Wake Up Little Susie (2)	Everly Brothers (1957)
		Walk Away (4)	Matt Monro (1964)
Up On The Roof (10)	Kenny Lynch (1962)	Walk Away From Love (10)	David Ruffin (1976)
Up The Junction (2)	Squeeze (1979)	Walk Away Renee (3)	Four Tops (1967)
Up The Ladder To The Roof (6)	Supremes (1970)	Walk Don't Run (8)	Ventures (1960)
Up To The Wildstyle (10)	Porn Kings vs DJ Supreme (1999)	Walk Hand In Hand (2)	Tony Martin (1956)
		Walk In The Black Forest, A (3)	Horst Jankowski (1965)
Up Town Top Ranking (1) first and only hit	Althia & Donna (1977)		
Up Up And Away (6)	Johnny Mann Singers (1967)	Walk Like A Panther '98 (10)	The All Seeing I, with Tony Christie (1999)

M
U
S
I
C

P
O
P

Title	Group/Artiste	Title	Group/Artiste
Walk Like An Egyptian (3)	Bangles (1986)	Water Water / Handful Of Songs (5)	Tommy Steele (1957)
Walk Of Life (2)	Dire Straits (1986)	Waterfalls (9)	Paul McCartney (1980)
Walk On (5)	U2 (2001)		
Walk On By (7)	Gabrielle (1997)	Waterfalls (4)	TLC (1995)
Walk On By (6)	Sybil (1990)	Waterloo (1) first hit	Abba (1974)
Walk On By (5)	Leroy Van Dyke (1962)	Waterloo Sunset (2)	Kinks (1967)
		Way Down (1)	Elvis Presley (1977)
Walk On By (9)	Dionne Warwick (1964)	Way Down Yonder In New Orleans (3)	Freddy Cannon (1960)
Walk On The Wild Side (10)	Lou Reed (1973)	Way I Am, The (8)	Eminem (2000)
Walk On Water (10)	Milk Inc (2002)	Way It Used To Be, The (3)	Engelbert Humperdinck (1969)
Walk Right Back / Ebony Eyes (1)	Everly Brothers (1961)	Way Of Life (6)	Family Dogg (1969)
Walk Right In (10)	Rooftop Singers (1963)	Way To Your Love, The (1)	Hear'Say (2001)
Walk Right Now (7)	Jacksons (1981)	Way We Were, The / Try To Remember (4)	Gladys Knight & The Pips (1975)
Walk Tall (3) first hit	Val Doonican (1964)	Way You Make Me Feel, The (3)	Michael Jackson (1987)
Walk The Dinosaur (10)	Was (Not Was) (1987)		
Walk This Way (8)	Run DMC (1986)	Way You Make Me Feel, The (6)	Ronan Keating (2000)
Walk With Me (10)	Seekers (1966)		
Walkaway (9)	Cast (1996)	Wayward Wind (9)	Gogi Grant (1956)
Walkin' (7)	CCS (1971)	Wayward Wind (1)	Frank Ifield (1963)
Walkin' Back To Happiness (1)	Helen Shapiro (1961)	Wayward Wind (8)	Tex Ritter (1956)
Walkin' Miracle, A (6)	Limmie & The Family Cookin (1974)	We All Follow Man United (10)	Manchester United Football Club (1985)
Walkin' To Missouri (9) first hit	Tony Brent (1952)	We All Stand Together (3)	Paul McCartney & The Frog Chorus (1984)
Walkin' To Missouri (re-entry) (7)	Tony Brent (1953)		
Walking Away (3)	Craig David (2000)		
Walking In The Air (5)	Aled Jones (1985)	We Are Detective (7)	Thompson Twins (1983)
Walking In The Rain (7)	Modern Romance (1983)		
		We Are Family (8)	Sister Sledge (1979)
Walking In The Rain (10)	Partridge Family starring David Cassidy (1973)	We Are Family (remix) (5)	Sister Sledge (1993)
		We Are Glass (5)	Gary Numan (1980)
Walking On Broken Glass (8)	Annie Lennox (1992)	We Are The Champions (2)	Queen (1977)
Walking On Sunshine (10)	Bad Manners (1981)	We Are The World (1)	USA For Africa (1985)
Walking On Sunshine (8)	Katrina & The Waves (1985)	We Call It Acieed (3)	D Mob (1988)
Walking On Sunshine (4)	Rocker's Revenge (1982)	We Can Work It Out / Day Tripper (1)	The Beatles (1965)
Walking On The Moon (1)	Police (1979)	We Close Our Eyes (5) first hit	Go West (1985)
Walking Wounded (6)	Everything But The Girl (1996)	We Come 1 (3)	Faithless (2001)
		We Didn't Start The Fire (7)	Billy Joel (1989)
Wall Street Shuffle, The (10)	10CC (1974)	We Do It (5)	R & J Stone (1976)
Walls Come Tumbling Down (6)	Style Council (1985)	We Don't Have To ... (2)	Jermaine Stewart (1986)
Waltz Away Dreaming (10)	Toby Bourke with George Michael (1997)	We Don't Need Another Hero (Thunderdome) (3)	Tina Turner (1985)
Wanderer, The (10)	Dion (1962)	We Don't Talk Anymore (1)	Cliff Richard (1979)
Wanderer, The (7)	Status Quo (1984)	We Got A Love Thang (6)	Ce Ce Peniston (1992)
Wanderin' Eyes (6)	Charlie Gracie (1957)	We Gotta Get Out Of This Place (2)	Animals (1965)
Wand'rin' Star (1)	Lee Marvin (1970)	We Have A Dream (5)	Scotland World Cup Squad (1982)
Wanna Be Startin' Something (8)	Michael Jackson (1983)	We Have All The Time In The World (3)	Louis Armstrong (1994)
Wannabe (1) first hit	Spice Girls (1996)	We Like To Party! (Vengabus) (3)	Vengaboys (1999)
Wanted (4)	Perry Como (1954)	We Love You / Dandelion (8)	Rolling Stones (1967)
Wanted (3)	Dooleys (1979)		
Wanted (re-entry) (4)	Al Martino (1954)	We Shall Overcome (26) first hit	Joan Baez (1965)
War (3)	Edwin Starr (1970)	We Should Be Together (10)	Cliff Richard (1991)
War Baby (6)	Tom Robinson (1983)	We Take Mystery (To Bed) (9)	Gary Numan (1982)
War Of Nerves (7)	All Saints (1998)	(We Want) The Same Thing (6)	Belinda Carlisle (1990)
War Song, The (2)	Culture Club (1984)		
Warpaint (5)	Brook Brothers (1961)	We Will Make Love (2)	Russ Hamilton (1957)
Watching Me Watching You (10)	David Grant (1983)		
Watching The Detectives (15) first hit	Elvis Costello (1977)	We Will Rock You (1)	Five & Queen (2000)

Title	Group/Artiste	Title	Group/Artiste
Weak In The Presence Of Beauty (6)	Alison Moyet (1987)	What Can I Say (10)	Boz Scaggs (1977)
Wear My Ring Around Your Neck (3)	Elvis Presley with The Jordanaires (1958)	What Can You Do For Me (10)	Utah Saints (1991)
		What Do I Do (5)	Phil Fearon & Galaxy (1984)
Weather With You (7)	Crowded House (1992)	What Do I Get (37) first hit	Buzzcocks (1978)
Wedding Bells (7)	Godley & Creme (1981)	What Do I Have To Do (6)	Kylie Minogue (1991)
		What Do You Want (1)	Adam Faith (1959)
Wedding, The (3)	Julie Rogers (1964)	What Do You Want To Make Those Eyes At Me For (1)	Emile Ford & The Checkmates (1959)
Wee Rule (6)	Wee Papa Girl Rappers (1988)		
Welcome Home (1)	Peters & Lee (1973)	What Do You Want To Make Those Eyes At Me For (5)	Shakin' Stevens (1987)
Welcome To My World (6)	Jim Reeves (1963)		
Welcome To the Cheap Seats (EP) (8)	Wonder Stuff (1992)	What Have I Done To Deserve This (2)	Pet Shop Boys & Dusty Springfield (1987)
(Welcome) To The Dance (5)	Des Mitchell (2000)		
Welcome To The Pleasure Dome (2)	Frankie Goes To Hollywood (1985)	What Have You Done For Me Lately (3)	Janet Jackson (1986)
Welcome To Tomorrow (6)	Snap featuring Summer (1994)	What I Am (2)	Tin Tin Out featuring Emma Bunton (1999)
We'll Bring The House Down (10)	Slade (1981)		
We'll Find Our Day (17) only other hit	Stephanie De Sykes (1975)	What I Go To School For (3)	Busted (2002)
		What If (6)	Kate Winslet (2001)
Well I Ask You (1)	Eden Kane (1961)	What Is Love (2)	Haddaway (1993)
We're All Alone (6) first hit	Rita Coolidge (1977)	What Is Love (2)	Howard Jones (1983)
We're Going To Ibiza! (1)	Vengaboys (1999)		
We're Gonna Do It Again (6)	Manchester Utd Football Squad & Stryker (1995)	What It Feels Like For A Girl (7)	Madonna (2001)
		What I've Got In Mind (4)	Billie Jo Spears (1976)
We're On The Ball (3)	Ant & Dec (2002)	What Kinda Boy You Looking For Girl (10)	Hot Chocolate (1983)
We're Through (7)	Hollies (1964)		
West End Girls (1) first hit	Pet Shop Boys (1985)	What Makes A Man (2)	Westlife (2000)
		What My Heart Wants To Say (5)	Gareth Gates (2002)
Westside (4)	TQ (1999)	What Now My Love (5)	Shirley Bassey (1962)
Wet Dream (10) first and only hit	Max Romeo (1969)	What The World Is Waiting For / Fool's Gold (8)	Stone Roses (1989)
We've Got It Goin' On (3)	Backstreet Boys (1996)		
		What Time Is Love (5)	KLF with Children of The Revolution (1990)
We've Got Tonight (4)	Ronan Keating featuring Lulu (2002)		
		What Took You So Long (1)	Emma Bunton (2001)
Wham Rap (8)	Wham! (1983)	What Would I Be (2)	Val Doonican (1966)
What (3)	Soft Cell (1982)	What Would You Do (3)	City High (2001)
What A Difference A Day Made (6)	Esther Phillips (1975)	What You Got (4)	Abs (2002)
What A Girl Wants (3)	Christina Aguilera (2000)	What You're Proposing (2)	Status Quo (1980)
		What'd I Say (10)	Jerry Lee Lewis (1961)
What A Waste (9) first hit	Ian Dury & The Blockheads (1978)	Whatever (3)	Oasis (1994)
		Whatever I Do (Wherever I Go) (4)	Hazell Dean (1984)
What A Wonderful World / Cabaret (1)	Louis Armstrong Orchestra & Chorus / Louis Armstrong and his All-Stars (1968)	Whatever Will Be Will Be (1)	Doris Day (1956)
		Whatever You Want (4)	Status Quo (1979)
		What's Another Year (1)	Johnny Logan (1980)
What About Us (4)	Brandy (2002)	What's Going On (6)	Artists Against Aids Worldwide (2001)
What Am I Gonna Do (3)	Rod Stewart (1983)		
		What's It Gonna Be?! (6)	Busta Rhymes featuring Janet (1999)
What Am I Gonna Do With You (5)	Barry White (1975)		
		What's Love Got To Do With It (2)	Warren G featuring Adina Howard (1996)
What Are You Doing Sunday (3)	Dawn featuring Tony Orlando (1971)		
What Becomes Of The Broken Hearted (10)	Jimmy Ruffin (1966)	What's Love Got To Do With It (3)	Tina Turner (1984)
What Becomes Of The Broken Hearted/Saturday Night At The Movies / You'll Never Walk Alone (1)	Robson & Jerome (1996)	What's Luv (4)	Fat Joe featuring Ashanti (2002)
		What's So Different (10)	Ginuwine (1999)
		What's The Colour Of Money (7)	Hollywood Beyond (1986)
What Becomes Of The Broken Hearted (re-issue) (4)	Jimmy Ruffin (1974)	What's The Frequency Kenneth (9)	REM (1994)
What Can I Do (3)	Corrs (1998)	What's Up (6)	DJ Miko (1994)

MUSIC POP

Title	Group/Artiste
What's Up (2)	4 Non Blondes (1993)
What's Your Flava (8)	Craig David (2002)
Whatta Man (7)	Salt-N-Pepa with En Vogue (1994)
Wheels (8)	String-A-Longs (1961)
When (1)	Kalin Twins (1958)
When (3)	Showaddywaddy (1977)
When A Child Is Born (1)	Johnny Mathis (1976)
When A Man Loves A Woman (8)	Michael Bolton (1991)
When A Man Loves A Woman (4)	Percy Sledge (1966)
When A Man Loves A Woman (re-issue) (2)	Percy Sledge (1987)
When A Woman (6)	Gabrielle (2000)
When Doves Cry (10)	Ginuwine (1997)
When Doves Cry (4)	Prince (1984)
When Forever Has Gone (2)	Demis Roussos (1976)
When I Fall In Love (2)	Nat 'King' Cole (1957)
When I Fall In Love (4)	Donny Osmond (1973)
When I Fall In Love / My Arms Keep Missing You (2)	Rick Astley (1987)
When I Fall In Love (re-issue) (4)	Nat 'King' Cole (1987)
When I Grow Up (9)	Garbage (1999)
When I Lost You (6)	Sarah Whatmore (2002)
When I Need You (5)	Will Mellor (1998)
When I Need You (1)	Leo Sayer (1977)
When I Said Goodbye / Summer Of Love (5)	Steps (2000)
When I Think Of You (10)	Janet Jackson (1986)
When I'm Dead And Gone (2)	McGuinness Flint (1970)
When I'm Good And Ready (5)	Sybil (1993)
When Johnny Comes Marching Home / Made You (5)	Adam Faith with John Barry Orchestra (1960)
When Julie Comes Around (10)	Cufflinks (1970)
When Love And Hate Collide (2)	Def Leppard (1995)
When Love Comes To Town (6)	U2 with B B King (1989)
When Mexico Gave Up The Rumba (6)	Mitchell Torok (1956)
When My Little Girl Is Smiling (9)	Craig Douglas (1962)
When My Little Girl Is Smiling (9)	Jimmy Justice (1962)
When She Was My Girl (3)	Four Tops (1981)
When The Girl In Your Arms Is The Girl In Your Heart (3)	Cliff Richard with the Norrie Paramor Orchestra (1961)
When The Going Gets Tough (1)	Boyzone (1999)
When The Going Gets Tough The Tough Get Going (1)	Billy Ocean (1986)
When The Heartache Is Over (10)	Tina Turner (1999)
When The Lights Go Out (4)	Five (1998)
When We Dance (9)	Sting (1994)
When We Were Young (10)	Bucks Fizz (1983)
When Will I Be Famous (2)	Bros (1988)
When Will I Be Loved (4)	Everly Brothers (1960)
When Will I See You Again (1)	Three Degrees (1974)
When Will You Say I Love You (3)	Billy Fury (1963)
When You Ask About Love (4)	Matchbox (1980)
When You Believe (4)	Mariah Carey &

Title	Group/Artiste
	Whitney Houston (1998)
When You Come Back To Me (2)	Jason Donovan (1989)
When You Look At Me (3)	Christina Milian (2002)
When You Lose The One You Love (7)	David Whitfield with Mantovani (1955)
When You Say Nothing At All (1)	Ronan Keating (1999)
(When You Say You Love Somebody) In The Heart (7)	Kool & The Gang (1984)
When You Tell Me That You Love Me (2)	Diana Ross (1991)
When You Walk In The Room (3)	Searchers (1964)
When You're Gone (3)	Bryan Adams featuring Melanie C (1998)
When You're In Love With A Beautiful Woman (1)	Dr Hook (1979)
(When You're) Young And In Love (7)	Flying Pickets (1984)
Whenever Wherever (2)	Shakira (2002)
Whenever You Need Somebody (3)	Rick Astley (1987)
Where Are You Baby (3)	Betty Boo (1990)
Where Are You Now (My Love) (1)	Jackie Trent (1965)
Where Did Our Love Go (8)	Donnie Elbert (1972)
Where Did Our Love Go (3) first hit	Supremes (1964)
(Where Do I Begin) Love Story (4)	Andy Williams (1971)
Where Do You Go (2)	No Mercy (1997)
Where Do You Go To My Lovely (1)	Peter Sarstedt (1969)
Where Love Lives (remix) (9)	Alison Limerick (1996)
Where The Boys Are / Baby Roo (5)	Connie Francis (1961)
Where The Streets Have No Name (4)	U2 (1987)
Where The Streets Have No Name (Can't Take My Eyes Off You) / How Can You Expect To Be Taken Seriously (4)	Pet Shop Boys (1991)
Where The Wind Blows (2)	Frankie Laine (1953)
Where Will The Baby's Dimple Be (6)	Rosemary Clooney and Mellomen, with the Buddy Cole Quartet (1955)
Where's The Love (4)	Hanson (1997)
Where's Your Head At? (9)	Basement Jaxx (2001)
Wherever I Lay My Hat (That's My Home) (1) first hit	Paul Young (1983)
Wherever You Will Go (3)	Calling (2002)
Which Way You Goin' Billy (7)	Poppy Family (1970)
Whiskey In The Jar (6) first hit	Thin Lizzy (1973)
Whispering Grass (1)	Windsor Davies & Don Estelle (1975)
Whistle Song (Blow My Whistle B***h) (5)	DJ Aligator Project (2002)
White Christmas (5)	Bing Crosby (1977)
White Christmas (6)	Mantovani & His Orchestra (1952)
White Horses (10)	Jacky (1968)
White Lines (Don't Do It) (7)	Grandmaster & Melle Mel (1984)
White Sport Coat, A (6)	King Brothers (1957)

Title	Group/Artiste	Title	Group/Artiste
White Wedding (6)	Billy Idol (1985)	Wild Boys (2)	Duran Duran (1984)
Whiter Shade Of Pale, A (1)	Procol Harum (1967)	Wild In The Country / I Feel	Elvis Presley with
Who Am I (10)	Beenie Man (1998)	So Bad (4)	The Jordanaires
Who Am I / This Is It! (5)	Adam Faith (1961)		(1961)
Who Are We (6)	Ronnie Hilton (1956)	Wild One (7)	Bobby Rydell (1960)
Who Do You Love Now	Riva featuring Dannii	Wild One, The (7)	Suzi Quatro (1974)
(Stringer) (3)	Minogue (2001)	Wild Side Of Life (9)	Status Quo (1976)
Who Feels Love? (4)	Oasis (2000)	Wild Thing (2) first hit	Troggs (1966)
Who Found Who (10)	Jellybean featuring	Wild West Hero (6)	Electric Light
	Elisa Fiorillo (1987)		Orchestra (1978)
Who Is It (10)	Michael Jackson	Wild Wild West (2)	Will Smith featuring
	(1992)		Dru Hill (1999)
Who Killed Bambi (6)	Ten Pole Tudor	Wild Wind (2)	John Leyton (1961)
	(1979)	Wild World (8)	Jimmy Cliff (1970)
Who Let The Dogs Out (2)	Baha Men (2000)	Wild World (5)	Maxi Priest (1988)
Who Loves You (6)	Four Seasons (1975)	Will I Ever (7)	Alice Deejay (2000)
Who Needs Love Like That (10)	Erasure (1992)	Will I? (5)	Ian Van Dahl (2001)
Who The Hell Are You (10)	Madison Avenue	Will 2K (2)	Will Smith (1999)
	(2000)	Will You (8)	Hazel O'Connor
Whodunit (5)	Tavares (1977)		(1981)
Whole Again (1)	Atomic Kitten (2001)	Will You Be There (9)	Michael Jackson
Whole Lotta Love (3)	Goldbug (1996)		(1993)
Whole Lotta Shakin' Goin' On (8)	Jerry Lee Lewis	Will You Love Me Tomorrow (4)	Shirelles (1961)
	(1957)	Wimoweh (4)	Karl Denver (1962)
Whole Lotta Woman (1)	Marvin Rainwater	Winchester Cathedral (4)	New Vaudeville Band
	(1958)		(1966)
Whole Of The Moon (re-issue),	Waterboys (1991)	Wind Beneath My Wings (3)	Steven Houghton
The (3)			(1997)
Whoomph! (There It Is) (4)	Clock (1995)	Wind Beneath My Wings (5)	Bette Midler (1989)
Whoops Now / What'll I Do (9)	Janet Jackson	Wind Cries Mary, The (6)	Jimi Hendrix
	(1995)		Experience (1967)
Who's In The House (8)	Beatmasters	Wind Me Up (Let Me Go) (2)	Cliff Richard & The
	featuring Merlin		Shadows (1965)
	(1989)	Wind Of Change (2)	Scorpions (1991)
Who's Leaving Who (4)	Hazell Dean (1988)	Windmills Of Your Mind (8)	Noel Harrison (1969)
Who's Sorry Now (1)	Connie Francis	Wings Of A Dove (2)	Madness (1983)
	(1958)	Winner Takes It All, The (1)	Abba (1980)
Who's That Girl (3)	Eurythmics (1983)	Winter In July (7)	Bomb The Bass
Who's That Girl (6)	Eve (2001)		(1991)
Who's That Girl (1)	Madonna (1987)	Winter World Of Love (7)	Engelbert
Why (10)	Glamma Kid (1999)		Humperdinck
Why (5)	Annie Lennox (1992)		(1969)
Why (8)	Mis-Teeq (2001)	Winter's Tale, A (2)	David Essex (1982)
Why (1)	Anthony Newley	Winter's Tale, A (6)	Queen (1995)
	(1960)	Wipe Out (5)	Surfaris (1963)
Why (3)	Donny Osmond	Wipeout (2)	Fat Boys & The
	(1972)		Beach Boys (1987)
Why (10)	Carly Simon (1982)	Wired For Sound (4)	Cliff Richard (1981)
Why (2)	3T featuring Michael	Wish You Were Here (8)	Eddie Fisher (1953)
	Jackson (1996)	Wishful Thinking (9)	China Crisis (1984)
Why? (6)	Bronski Beat (1984)	Wishing (10)	Buddy Holly (1963)
Why Can't I Wake Up With	Take That (1993)	Wishing I Was Lucky (6)	Wet Wet Wet (1987)
You (2)		Wishing (If I Had A Photograph	A Flock Of Seagulls
Why Can't This Be Love (8)	Van Halen (1986)	Of You) (10)	(1982)
Why Do Fools Fall In Love (1)	Frankie Lymon &	Wishing On A Star (10)	Fresh 4 featuring
	Teenagers (1956)		Lizz E (1989)
Why Do Fools Fall In Love (4)	Diana Ross (1981)	Wishing On A Star (3)	Rose Royce (1978)
Why Does It Always Rain On		Wishing Well (7)	Free (1973)
Me? (10)	Travis (1999)	Wishing Well (4)	Terence Trent D'Arby
Why Don't You Get A Job? (2)	Offspring (1999)		(1987)
Why Oh Why Oh Why (6)	Gilbert O'Sullivan	Wishing You Were Somehow	Sarah Brightman
	(1973)	Here Again (7)	(1987)
Wichita Lineman (7) first hit	Glen Campbell	Witch Doctor (2)	Cartoons (1999)
	(1969)	Witch Doctor (5)	Don Lang & His
Wicked Game (10)	Chris Isaak (1990)		Frantic Five (1958)
Wicker Man, The (9)	Iron Maiden (2000)	Witch Queen Of New Orleans,	Redbone (1971)
Wide Boy (9)	Nik Kershaw (1985)	The (2)	
Wide-Eyed And Legless (6)	Andy Faithweather-	Witch, The (8)	Rattles (1970)
	Low (1975)	With A Girl Like You (1)	Troggs (1966)
Wiggle It (3)	2 In A Room (1991)	With A Little Help From	Young Idea (1967)
Wig-Wam Bam (4)	Sweet (1972)	Friends (10)	

MUSIC POP

Title	Group/Artiste	Title	Group/Artiste
With A Little Help From My Friends (1)	Joe Cocker (1968)	Work It (6)	Missy Elliott (2002)
With A Little Help From My Friends (1)	Wet Wet Wet (1988)	Work It Out (7)	Beyonce (2002)
		Work Rest And Play EP (6)	Madness (1980)
With A Little Luck (5)	Wings (1978)	Work That Body (7)	Diana Ross (1982)
With All My Heart (4)	Petula Clark (1957)	Workaholic (4)	2 Unlimited (1992)
With My Own Eyes (10)	Sash (2000)	Working In A Coalmine (8)	Lee Dorsey (1966)
With Or Without You (4)	U2 (1987)	Working My Way Back To You / Forgive Me Girl (1)	Detroit Spinners (1980)
With You I'm Born Again (2)	Billy Preston & Syreeta (1979)	World (9)	Bee Gees (1967)
Without Love (10)	Tom Jones (1969)	World In Motion (1)	Englandneworder (1990)
Without Me (1)	Eminem (2002)	World Of Our Own (1)	Westlife (2002)
Without You (1)	Mariah Carey (1994)	World Of Our Own, A (3)	Seekers (1965)
Without You (1)	Nilsson (1972)	World Without Love, A (1) first hit	Peter & Gordon (1964)
Woman (9)	Neneh Cherry (1996)		
Woman (1)	John Lennon (1981)	World's Greatest, The (4)	R Kelly (2002)
Woman In Love (1)	Barbra Streisand (1980)	Would I Lie To You (1)	Charles & Eddie (1992)
Woman In Love (3)	Three Degrees (1979)	Would You? (3)	Touch & Go (1998)
Woman In Love, A (1)	Frankie Laine (1956)	Wouldn't Change A Thing (2)	Kylie Minogue (1989)
Woman Trouble (6)	Artful Dodger & Robbie Craig with Craig David (2000)	Wouldn't It Be Good (4)	Nik Kershaw (1984)
		Wrapped Around Your Finger (7)	Police (1983)
Woman (Uh-Huh) (7)	Jose Ferrer (1954)	Written In The Stars (10)	Elton John & LeAnn Rimes (1999)
Wombling Merry Christmas (2)	Wombles (1974)		
Wombling Song, The (4) first hit	Wombles (1974)	Wrong (8)	Everything But The Girl (1996)
Wonder Of You, The (1)	Elvis Presley (1970)	Wrong Impression (10)	Natalie Imbruglia (2002)
Wonderful Christmastime (6)	Paul McCartney (1979)	Wuthering Heights (1) first hit	Kate Bush (1978)
Wonderful Copenhagen (5)	Danny Kaye (1953)	Xanadu (1)	Olivia Newton-John and ELO (1980)
Wonderful Land (1)	Shadows (1962)	X-Files (8)	DJ Dado (1996)
Wonderful Life (8)	Black (1987)	X-Files, The (2)	Mark Snow (1996)
Wonderful Time Up There, A (2)	Pat Boone (1958)	Y Viva Espana (4)	Sylvia (1974)
Wonderful Tonight (3)	Damage (1997)	Y.M.C.A. (1)	Village People (1978)
Wonderful World (7)	Herman's Hermits (1965)		
		Years May Come Years May Go (7)	Herman's Hermits (1970)
Wonderful World Beautiful People (6) first hit	Jimmy Cliff (1969)	Yeh Yeh (1)	Georgie Fame & The Blue Flames (1964)
Wonderful World Of The Young (8)	Danny Williams (1962)	Yellow (4)	Coldplay (2000)
Wonderful World (re-issue) (2)	Sam Cooke (1986)	Yellow River (1) first hit	Christie (1970)
Wonderland (8)	Big Country (1984)	Yellow Rose Of Texas (2)	Mitch Miller (1955)
Wondrous Stories (7) first hit	Yes (1977)	Yellow Submarine / Eleanor Rigby (1)	Beatles (1966)
Wonderwall (2)	Mike Flowers Pops (1995)	Yes (8)	McAlmont & Butler (1995)
Wonderwall (2)	Oasis (1995)		
Won't Get Fooled Again (9)	Who (1971)	Yes I Will (9)	Hollies (1965)
Won't Take It Lying Down (7)	Honeyz (2000)	Yes My Darling Daughter (10)	Eydie Gorme (1962)
Won't Talk About It (9)	Beats International (1990)	Yes Sir I Can Boogie (1)	Baccara (1977)
		Yes Tonight Josephine (1)	Johnnie Ray (1957)
Wood Beez (Pray Like Aretha Franklin) (10)	Scritti Politti (1984)	Yesterday (8)	Beatles (1966)
Wooden Heart (1)	Elvis Presley (1961)	Yesterday (8)	Matt Monro (1965)
Woodstock (1)	Matthews Southern Comfort (1970)	Yesterday (4)	Wet Wet Wet (1997)
		Yesterday Has Gone (4)	Cupid's Inspiration (1968)
Woo-Hah!! Got You All In Check (8)	Busta Rhymes (1996)	Yesterday Man (3)	Chris Andrews (1965)
Word Girl, The (6)	Scritti Politti featuring Ranking Ann (1985)	Yesterday Once More (2)	Carpenters (1973)
		Yesterdays / November Rain (8)	Guns 'N' Roses (1992)
Word Up (3)	Cameo (1986)	Yester-Me Yester-You Yesterday (2)	Stevie Wonder (1969)
Word Up (8)	Gun (1994)	Ying Tong Song (re-issue) (9)	Goons (1973)
Words (8)	Bee Gees (1968)	You (2)	S Club 7 (2002)
Words (1)	Boyzone (1996)	You (10)	Ten Sharp (1992)
Words (2)	F R David (1983)	You Ain't Seen Nothing Yet (2)	Bachman-Turner Overdrive (1974)
Words Are Not Enough/I Know Him So Well (5)	Steps (2001)	You Always Hurt The One You Love (6)	Clarence 'Frogman' Henry (1961)
Wordy Rappinghood (7)	Tom Tom Club (1981)		

Title	Group/Artiste	Title	Group/Artiste
You Are Alive (4)	Fragma (2001)	You Held The World In Your Arms (9)	Idlewild (2002)
You Are Everything (5)	Diana Ross & Marvin Gaye (1974)	You Just Might See Me Cry (2)	Our Kid (1976)
You Are My Destiny (6)	Paul Anka (1958)	You Keep It All In (8)	Beautiful South (1989)
You Are My World (30)	Communards (1985)	You Keep Me Hangin' On (8)	Supremes (1966)
You Are Not Alone (1)	Michael Jackson (1995)	You Keep Me Hangin' On (2)	Kim Wilde (1986)
You Are The Sunshine Of My Life (7)	Stevie Wonder (1973)	You Little Thief (5)	Feargal Sharkey (1986)
You Belong To Me (1)	Jo Stafford (1952)	You Make It Move (26) first hit	Dave Dee, Dozy, Beaky, Mick & Tich (1965)
You Better You Bet (9)	Who (1981)		
You Came (3)	Kim Wilde (1988)	You Make Me Feel Brand New (2)	Stylistics (1974)
You Can Call Me Al (4)	Paul Simon (1986)		
You Can Do Magic (3)	Limmie & The Family Cookin (1973)	You Make Me Feel Like Dancing (2)	Leo Sayer (1976)
You Can Get It If You Really Want (2)	Desmond Dekker (1970)	You Make Me Feel (Mighty Real) (5)	Jimmy Somerville (1990)
You Can Never Stop Me Loving You (10)	Kenny Lynch (1963)	You Make Me Feel (Mighty Real) (8)	Sylvester (1978)
You Can't Hurry Love (1)	Phil Collins (1982)	You Make Me Sick (9)	Pink (2001)
You Can't Hurry Love (3)	Supremes (1966)	You Make Me Wanna (1)	Usher (1998)
You Could Be Mine (3)	Guns 'N' Roses (1991)	You Might Need Somebody (4)	Shola Ama (1997)
You Do Something To Me (9)	Paul Weller (1995)	You Must Have Been A Beautiful Baby (10)	Bobby Darin (1961)
You Don't Bring Me Flowers (5)	Barbra & Neil (1978)	You Must Love Me (10)	Madonna (1996)
You Don't Care About Us (5)	Placebo (1998)	You Need Hands / Tulips From Amsterdam (3)	Max Bygraves with The Clark Brothers (1958)
You Don't Have To Be A Baby To Cry (6)	Caravelles (1963)		
You Don't Have To Be A Star (To Be In My Show) (7)	Marilyn McCoo & Billy Davis Jr (1977)	You Needed Me (1)	Boyzone (1999)
You Don't Have To Go (3)	Chi-Lites (1976)	You Only Tell Me You Love Me When You're Drunk (8)	Pet Shop Boys (2000)
You Don't Have To Say You Love Me (5)	Guys & Dolls (1976)	You Really Got Me (1)	Kinks (1964)
You Don't Have To Say You Love Me (9)	Elvis Presley (1971)	You Rock My World (2)	Michael Jackson (2001)
You Don't Have To Say You Love Me (1)	Dusty Springfield (1966)	You See The Trouble With Me (1)	Black Legend (2000)
You Don't Know (1)	Helen Shapiro (1961)	You See The Trouble With Me (2)	Barry White (1976)
You Don't Know Me (9)	Ray Charles (1962)	You Send Me (29) first hit	Sam Cooke (1958)
You Don't Know Me (1)	Armand Van Helden (1999)	You Sexy Thing (2)	Hot Chocolate (1975)
You Don't Love Me (No No No) (3)	Dawn Penn (1994)	You Sexy Thing (re-issue) (6)	Hot Chocolate (1997)
(You Drive Me) Crazy (5)	Britney Spears (1999)	You Sexy Thing (remix) (10)	Hot Chocolate (1987)
You Drive Me Crazy (2)	Shakin' Stevens (1981)	You Should Be Dancing (5)	Bee Gees (1976)
You Gave Me Love (10)	Crown Heights Affair (1980)	You Should Be ... (3)	Blockster (1999)
		You Showed Me (8)	Lightning Seeds (1997)
You Get What You Give (5)	New Radicals (1999)	You Spin Me Round (Like A Record) (1)	Dead Or Alive (1985)
You Got It (3)	Roy Orbison (1989)		
You Got It (The Right Stuff) (1)	New Kids On The Block (1989)	You Stole The Sun From My Heart (5)	Manic Street Preachers (1999)
You Got Soul (6)	Johnny Nash (1969)	You Take Me Up (2)	Thompson Twins (1984)
You Got The Love (4)	Source featuring Candi Staton (1991)	You To Me Are Everything (1) first hit	Real Thing (1976)
You Got The Love (3) (re-entry)	Source featuring Candi Staton (1997)	You To Me Are Everything (The Decade Remix 76–86) (5)	Real Thing (1986)
U Got 2 Know (6)	Cappella (1993)	You Wear It Well (1)	Rod Stewart (1972)
You Got What It Takes (7)	Marv Johnson (1960)	You Were Made For Me (3)	Freddie & The Dreamers (1963)
You Got What It Takes (2)	Showaddywaddy (1977)	You Were On My Mind (2)	Crispian St Peters (1966)
You Gotta Be (re-issue) (10)	Des'ree (1999)	You Were Right (9)	Badly Drawn Boy (2002)
(You Gotta) Fight For Your Right (To Party) (11) first hit	Beastie Boys (1987)	You Win Again (1)	Bee Gees (1987)
		You Won't Find Another Fool Like Me (1)	New Seekers (1973)
You Have Been Loved / The Strangest Thing '97 (2)	George Michael (1997)	You You You (6)	Alvin Stardust (1974)
		You'll Answer To Me (5)	Cleo Laine (1961)
		You'll Never Find Another Love Like Mine (10)	Lou Rawls (1976)
		You'll Never Know (6)	Shirley Bassey (1961)

MUSIC POP

Title	Group/Artiste
You'll Never Stop Me From Loving You (1) first hit	Sonia (1989)
You'll Never Walk Alone (1)	Crowd (1985)
You'll Never Walk Alone (1)	Gerry & The Pacemakers (1963)
You'll See (5)	Madonna (1995)
Young And Foolish (10)	Edmund Hockridge (1956)
Young At Heart (8)	Bluebells (1984)
Young At Heart (re-issue) (1)	Bluebells (1993)
Young At Heart (12) first hit	Frank Sinatra (1954)
Young Gifted And Black (5)	Bob & Marcia (1970)
Young Girl (1)	Union Gap featuring Gary Puckett (1968)
Young Girl (re-issue) (6)	Gary Puckett & The Union Gap (1974)
Young Guns (Go For It) (3) first hit	Wham! (1982)
Young Hearts Run Free (2) first hit	Candi Staton (1976)
Young Love (1)	Tab Hunter (1957)
Young Love (1)	Donny Osmond (1973)
Young Lovers (9)	Paul & Paula (1963)
Young New Mexican Puppeteer, The (6)	Tom Jones (1972)
Young Ones, The (1)	Cliff Richard & The Shadows (1962)
Young Parisians (9)	Adam & The Ants (1980)
Your Christmas Wish (8)	Smurfs (1996)
Your Love Is King (6)	Sade (1984)
Your Loving Arms (remix) (6)	Billie Ray Martin (1995)
Your Song (7)	Elton John (1971)
Your Song (4)	Elton John & Alessandro Safina (2002)
Your Woman (1)	White Town (1997)
You're A Lady (3)	Peter Skellern (1972)
You're A Superstar (7)	Love Inc (2002)
You're All That Matters To Me (6)	Curtis Stigers (1992)
You're Driving Me Crazy (1)	Temperance Seven (1961)
You're Gorgeous (3)	Babybird (1996)
(You're) Having My Baby (6)	Paul Anka featuring Odia Coates (1974)
You're History (7)	Shakespears Sister (1989)
You're In My Heart (3)	Rod Stewart (1977)
You're Makin' Me High (7)	Toni Braxton (1996)
You're More Than A Number In My Little Red Book (5)	Drifters (1976)
You're Moving Out Today (6)	Carole Bayer Sager

Title	Group/Artiste
only hit	(1977)
You're My Best Friend (7)	Queen (1976)
You're My World (1)	Cilla Black (1964)
You're No Good (3)	Swinging Blue Jeans (1964)
You're Not Alone (1)	Olive (1997)
You're Sixteen (3)	Johnny Burnette (1961)
You're Sixteen (4)	Ringo Starr (1974)
You're So Vain (3)	Carly Simon (1972)
You're Still The One (10) first hit	Shania Twain (1998)
You're The First The Last My Everything (1)	Barry White (1974)
You're The One I Love (3)	Shola Ama (1997)
You're The One That I Want (1)	John Travolta & Olivia Newton-John (1978)
You're The One That I Want (re-issue) (4)	John Travolta & Olivia Newton-John (1998)
You're The Voice (6)	John Farnham (1987)
You've Got A Friend (9)	Brand New Heavies (1997)
You've Got A Friend (4)	James Taylor (1971)
You've Got It Bad (7)	Ocean Colour Scene (1996)
You've Got Me Dangling On A String (5)	Chairmen of the Board (1970)
You've Got Your Troubles (2)	Fortunes (1965)
You've Lost That Lovin' Feelin' (2)	Cilla Black (1965)
You've Lost That Lovin' Feelin' (1) first hit	Righteous Brothers (1965)
You've Lost That Lovin' Feelin' (re-issue) (3)	Righteous Brothers (1990)
You've Lost That Lovin' Feelin' (re-issue) (10)	Righteous Brothers (1969)
Yummy Yummy Yummy (5)	Ohio Express (1968)
Zabadak! (3)	Dave Dee, Dozy, Beaky, Mick & Tich (1967)
Zambesi (2) first and only hit	Lou Busch and his Orchestra (1956)
Zambesi (17) second and only other hit	Pirhanas featuring Boring Bob Grover
Zephyr Song, The (11)	Red Hot Chili Peppers (2002)
Ziggy Stardust (15) biggest hit	Bauhaus (1982)
Zing A Little Zong (10)	Bing Crosby & Jane Wyman (1952)
Zombie (14)	Cranberries (1994)
Zoom (2)	Fat Larry's Band (1982)
Zorba's Dance (6)	Marcello Minerbi (1965)

Singles: by Group/Artiste

Group/Artiste	Title
A	Nothing (9)
A Flock Of Seagulls	Wishing (If I Had A Photograph Of You) (10)
A1	Be The First To Believe (6)
	Caught In The Middle (2)
	Everytime / Ready Or Not (3)
	Like A Rose (6)
	Make It Good (11)

Group/Artiste	Title
	No More (6)
	Same Old Brand New You (1)
	Summertime Of Our Lives (5)
	Take On Me (1)
A Teens	Upside Down (10)
A Tribe Called Quest	Rumble In The Jungle (3)
A+	Enjoy Yourself (5)
Aaliyah	More Than A Woman (1)

Group/Artiste	Title	Group/Artiste	Title
	Try Again (5)		Space Jungle, The (7)
Abba	Angel Eyes / Voulez Vous (3)	Adventures Of	Dirty Cash (2)
	Chiquitita (2)	Stevie V	
	Dancing Queen (1)	Aerosmith	Dude (Looks Like A Lady) (20)
	Does Your Mother Know (4)		I Don't Want To Miss A Thing (4)
	Fernando (1)		Love In An Elevator (13)
	Gimme Gimme Gimme (A Man	Afroman	Because I Got High (1)
	After Midnight) (3)		Crazy Rap (10)
	I Have A Dream (2)	Aguilera, Christina	Come On Ever Baby (All I
	Knowing Me Knowing You (1)		Want Is You) (8)
	Lay All Your Love On Me (7)		Dirrty (1)
	Mamma Mia (1)		Genie In A Bottle (1)
	Money Money Money (3)		Lady Marmalade (1)
	Name Of The Game, The (1)		Nobody Wants To Be Lonely
	One Of Us (3)		(4)
	S.O.S. (6)		What A Girl Wants (3)
	Summer Night City (5)	A-Ha	Cry Wolf (5)
	Super Trouper (1)		Hunting High And Low (5)
	Take A Chance On Me (1)		I've Been Losing You (8)
	Waterloo (1)		Living Daylights, The (5)
	Winner Takes It All, The (1)		Stay On These Roads (5)
Abbot, Russ	All Night Holiday (20)		Sun Always Shines On TV, The
	Atmosphere (7)		(1)
Abbott, Gregory	Shake You Down (6)		Take On Me (2)
ABC	All Of My Heart (5)		Train Of Thought (8)
	Look Of Love, The (4)	Alan Price Set	House That Jack Built, The (4)
	Poison Arrow (6)		I Put A Spell On You (9)
Abdul, Paula	Opposites Attract (2)		Simon Smith And His Amazing
	Rush Rush (6)		Dancing Bear (4)
	Straight Up (3)	Alarm	68 Guns (17)
Abrams, Colonel	Trapped (3)	Albert, Morris	Feelings (4)
Abs	What You Got (4)	Alberts, Al	Love Is A Many Splendoured
AC/DC	Heatseeker (12)		Thing (2)
	Rock 'N' Roll Damnation (24)		Mr Sandman (9)
Ace Of Base	All That She Wants (1)		Stranger In Paradise (6)
	Cruel Summer (8)		Three Coins In The Fountain (5)
	Don't Turn Around (5)	Alda	Real Good Time (7)
	Life Is A Flower (5)	Alessi	Oh Lori (8)
	Sign, The (2)	Alex Party	Don't Give Me Your Life (2)
Aces	Israelites (1)	Alexia	Uh La La La (10)
	It Miek (7)	Alford, John	Blue Moon / Only You (9)
Adam & The Ants	Ant Rap (3)	Ali, Tatyana	Boy You Knock Me Out (3)
	Antmusic (EP) (2)		Daydreamin' (6)
	Dog Eat Dog (4)	Alien Ant Farm	Movies (5)
	Kings Of The Wild Frontier (2)		Smooth Criminal (3)
	Prince Charming (1)	Alizee	Moi ... Lolita (9)
	Stand And Deliver (1)	All About Eve	Martha's Harbour (10)
	Young Parisians (9)	All Saints	All Hooked Up (7)
Adams, Bryan	All For Love (2)		Black Coffee (1)
	Cloud Number 9 (6)		Bootie Call (1)
	Don't Give Up (1)		I Know Where It's At (4)
	(Everything I Do) I Do It For		Never Ever (1)
	You (1)		Pure Shores (1)
	Have You Ever Really Loved A		Under The Bridge / Lady
	Woman (4)		Marmalade (1)
	Here I Am (5)		War Of Nerves (7)
	I Finally Found Someone (10)	All Seeing I, The	Beat Goes On (11)
	It's Only Love (29)		Walk Like A Panther '98 (10)
	Let's Make A Night To	Allen, Donna	Joy And Pain (10)
	Remember (10)		Serious (8)
	Only Thing That Looks Good	Allen, Keith	England's Irie (6)
	On Me Is You, The (6)	All-4-One	I Swear (1)
	Please Forgive Me (2)	Allisons	Are You Sure (2)
	Run To You (11)	Allstars	Land Of Make Believe, The (9)
	Thought I'd Died And Gone To	Almond, Marc	Days Of Pearly Spencer, The
	Heaven (8)		(4)
	When You're Gone (3)		I Feel Love (medley) (3)
Adams, Oleta	Get Here (4)		Something's Gotten Hold Of My
Adamski	Killer (1)		Heart (1)
	N-R-G (12)		Tainted Love (5)

Group/Artiste	Title	Group/Artiste	Title
Alpert, Herb	Lonely Bull, The (3)		Guess I Was A Fool (5)
	Spanish Flea (3)		I Want You For Myself (2)
	This Guy's In Love With You (3)		Summertime (7)
Alphaville	Big In Japan (8)	Ant & Dec	Better Watch Out (10)
Altered Images	Don't Talk To Me About Love (7)		Let's Get Ready To Rhumble (9)
	Happy Birthday (2)		Shout (10)
	I Could Be Happy (7)		We're On The Ball (3)
Altern 8	Activ 8 (Come With Me) (3)	Ant, Adam	Friend Or Foe (9)
	Evapor 8 (6)		Goody Two Shoes (1)
Althia & Donna	Up Town Top Ranking (1)		Puss 'N' Boots (5)
Ama, Shola	Taboo (10)	Anthony, Billie	This Ole House (4)
	You Might Need Somebody (4)	Anthrax	Bring The Noise (14)
	You're The One I Love (3)		I Am The Law (32)
Amazulu	Too Good To Be Forgotten (5)	Anuna	Riverdance (9)
Ambassadors Of Funk	Supermarioland (8)	Apache Indian	Nuff Vibes EP (5)
Amen Corner	Bend Me Shape Me (3)	Aphrodite's Child	Rain And Tears (29)
	Gin House Blues (12)	Apollo Four Forty	Ain't Talkin' 'Bout Dub (7)
	Hello Suzie (4)		Lost In Space (4)
	High In The Sky (6)		Stop The Rock (10)
	(If Paradise Is) Half As Nice (1)	Appleby, Kim	Don't Worry (2)
America	Horse With No Name (re-entry) (3)		G.L.A.D. (10)
Ames Brothers	Naughty Lady Of Shady Lane (6)	Applejacks	Tell Me When (7)
		Appleton	Fantasy (2)
Amorosi, Vanessa	Absolutely Everybody (7)	Aqua	Barbie Girl (1)
Amos, Tori	Cornflake Girl (4)		Cartoon Heroes (7)
	Pretty Good Year (7)		Doctor Jones (1)
	Professional Widow (remix) (1)		My Oh My (6)
Anastacia	I'm Outta Love (6)		Turn Back Time (1)
Anderson, Angry	Suddenly (3)	Aquagen	Phatt Bass (9)
Anderson, Laurie	O Superman (2)	Aqualung	Strange And Beautiful (7)
Anderson, Lynn	Rose Garden (3)	Arcadia	Election Day (7)
Anderson, Sunshine	Heard It All Before (9)	Archer, Tasmin	Sleeping Satellite (1)
Andre, Peter	All About Us (3)	Archies	Sugar Sugar (1)
	Flava (1)	Architechs	Body Groove (3)
	I Feel You (1)	Arena, Tina	Chains (6)
	Kiss The Girl (9)	Argent	Hold Your Head Up (5)
	Lonely (6)	Armatrading, Joan	Love And Affection (10)
	Mysterious Girl (2)	Armstrong, Louis	Hello, Dolly! (4)
	Natural (6)		Takes Two To Tango (6)
Andrea True Connection	More More More (5)		Theme From A Threepenny Opera (Mack The Knife) (8)
Andrews, Chris	Yesterday Man (3)		We Have All The Time In The World (3)
Aneka	Japanese Boy (1)		What A Wonderful World / Cabaret (1)
Animals	Baby Let Me Take You Home (21)	Arnee & The Terminators	I'll Be Back (5)
	Bring It On Home To Me (7)	Arnold, David	On Her Majesty's Secret Service (7)
	Don't Bring Me Down (6)		
	Don't Let Me Be Misunderstood (3)	Arnold, Eddy	Make The World Go Away (8)
	House Of The Rising Sun (1)	Arnold, P P	First Cut Is The Deepest (18)
	I'm Crying (8)	Arrested Development	Mr Wendal / Revolution (4)
	It's My Life (7)		People Everyday (2)
	San Franciscan Nights (7)	Arrington, Steve	Feel So Real (5)
	We Gotta Get Out Of This Place (2)	Arrival	Friends (8)
Animotion	Obsession (5)		I Will Survive (16)
Anka, Paul	(All Of A Sudden) My Heart Sings (10)	Arrows	Touch Too Much, A (8)
	Diana (1)	Arsenal FC	Hot Stuff (8)
	I Love You Baby (3)	Arsenal FC First Team Squad	Good Old Arsenal (16)
	Lonely Boy (3)		
	Put Your Head On My Shoulder (7)	Art & Dotty Todd	Broken Wings (6)
	You Are My Destiny (6)	Art Of Noise	Close (To The Edit) (8)
	(You're) Having My Baby (6)		Kiss (5)
Another Level	Be Alone No More (6)		Peter Gunn (8)
	Bomb Diggy (6)	Artful Dodger	Movin' Too Fast (2)
	Freak Me (1)		Please Don't Turn Me On (4)
	From The Heart (6)		Re-Rewind The Crowd Say Bo Selecta (2)
			Twenty Four Seven (6)
			Woman Trouble (6)

Group/Artiste	Title
Artists Against Aids Worldwide	What's Going On (6)
Ash	Goldfinger (5)
	Life Less Ordinary, A (10)
	Oh Yeah (6)
	Shining Light (8)
Ashanti	Always On Time (6)
	Foolish (4)
	What's Luv (4)
Ashcroft, Richard	Song For The Lovers, A (3)
Ashford & Simpson	Solid (3)
Ashton Gardner & Dyke	Resurrection Shuffle, The (3)
Assembly	Never Never (4)
Associates	Party Fears Two (9)
Astley, Rick	Cry For Help (7)
	Hold Me In Your Arms (10)
	Never Gonna Give You Up (1)
	She Wants To Dance With Me (6)
	Take Me To Your Heart (8)
	Together Forever (2)
	When I Fall In Love / My Arms Keep Missing You (2)
	Whenever You Need Somebody (3)
Aswad	Don't Turn Around (1)
	Shine (5)
ATB	Don't Stop (3)
	Killer (4)
	9pm (Till I Come) (1)
Atlantic Starr	Always (3)
	Secret Lovers (10)
Atomic Kitten	Eternal Flame (1)
	I Want Your Love (10)
	It's OK (3)
	Last Goodbye / Be With You (2)
	Right Now (10)
	See Ya (6)
	Tide Is High (Get The Feeling), The (1)
	Whole Again (1)
Atomic Rooster	Devil's Answer, The (4)
Attractions	Oliver's Army (2)
Atwell, Winifred	Britannia Rag (re-entry) (5)
	Coronation Rag (re-entry) (5)
	Flirtation Waltz (re-entry) (10)
	Let's Have A Ball (4)
	Let's Have A Ding Dong (3)
	Let's Have A Party (2)
	Let's Have Another Party (1)
	Make It A Party (7)
	Piano Party (10)
	Poor People Of Paris (1)
	Rachmaninoff's Variation On A Theme (9)
Auger, Brian	This Wheel's On Fire (5)
Aurora	Ordinary World (5)
Avalon Boys	Trail Of The Lonesome Pine, The (2)
Average White Band	Pick Up The Pieces (6)
Avons	Seven Little Girls Sitting In The Back Seat (3)
Axel Stordahl	Say You're Mine Again (10)
	Say You're Mine Again (re-entry) (6)
Az Yet	Hard To Say I'm Sorry (7)
Aznavour, Charles	She (1)
Aztec Camera	Oblivious (47)
	Somewhere In My Heart (3)

Group/Artiste	Title
Azzido Da Bass	Dooms Night (8)
B Bumble and the Stingers	Nut Rocker (1)
B15 Project	Girls Like Us (7)
B Real	Hit 'Em High (The Monstars' Anthem) (8)
B*Witched	Blame It On The Weatherman (1)
	C'est La Vie (1)
	Jesse Hold On (4)
	Rollercoaster (1)
	Thank Abba For The Music (4)
	To You I Belong (1)
B, Melanie	Feels So Good (5)
	I Want You Back (1)
	Tell Me (4)
B, Stevie	Because I Love You (The Postman Song) (6)
Baby D	(Everybody's Got To Learn Sometime) I Need Your Loving (3)
	Let Me Be Your Fantasy (1)
	So Pure (3)
Babybird	You're Gorgeous (3)
Babyface	How Come, How Long (10)
Babylon Zoo	Spaceman (1)
Baccara	Sorry I'm A Lady (8)
	Yes Sir I Can Boogie (1)
Bacharach, Burt	Trains and Boats and Planes (4)
Bachelors	Charmaine (6)
	Diane (1)
	I Believe (2)
	I Wouldn't Trade You For The World (4)
	Marie (9)
	No Arms Can Ever Hold You (7)
	Ramona (4)
	Sound Of Silence, The (3)
Bachman-Turner Overdrive	You Ain't Seen Nothing Yet (2)
Backstreet Boys	All I Have To Give (2)
	Anywhere For You (4)
	As Long As You Love Me (3)
	Call, The (8)
	Drowning (4)
	Everybody (Backstreet's Back) (3)
	I Want It That Way (1)
	I'll Never Break Your Heart (re-issue) (8)
	Larger Than Life (5)
	One, The (8)
	Quit Playing Games (With My Heart) (2)
	Shape Of My Heart (4)
	Show Me The Meaning Of Being Lonely (3)
	We've Got It Goin' On (3)
Bad Boys Inc	More To This World (8)
Bad Manners	Can Can (3)
	My Girl Lollipop (My Boy Lollipop) (9)
	Special Brew (3)
	Walking On Sunshine (10)
Baddiel & Skinner	3 Lions (1)
	3 Lions '98 (1)
Badfinger	Come And Get It (4)
	Day After Day (10)
	No Matter What (5)

MUSIC POP

Group/Artiste	Title
Badly Drawn Boy	Once Around The Block (46)
	You Were Right (9)
Baez, Joan	Night They Drove Old Dixie Down, The (6)
	There But For Fortune (8)
	We Shall Overcome (26)
Baha Men	Who Let The Dogs Out (2)
Bailey, Philip	Easy Lover (1)
Baker Selection, George	Paloma Blanca (10)
Baker, Adrian	Sherry (10)
Ball, Kenny & His Jazzmen	Green Leaves Of Summer, The (7)
	March Of The Siamese Children (4)
	Midnight In Moscow (2)
	Sukiyaki (10)
Ball, Michael	Love Changes Everything (2)
Baltimora	Tarzan Boy (3)
Bambaataa	Afrika Shox (7)
Bamboo	Bamboogie (2)
Bananarama	Cruel Summer (8)
	Help (3)
	I Want You Back (5)
	It Ain't What You Do It's The Way That You Do It (4)
	Love In The First Degree (3)
	Na Na Hey Hey Kiss Him Goodbye (5)
	Really Saying Something (5)
	Robert De Niro's Waiting (3)
	Shy Boy (4)
	Venus (8)
Band Aid	Do They Know It's Christmas (1)
	Do They Know It's Christmas (re-entry) (3)
Band Aid II	Do They Know It's Christmas (1)
Band Of The Black Watch	Scotch On The Rocks (8)
Bangles	Eternal Flame (1)
	Manic Monday (2)
	Walk Like An Egyptian (3)
Banton, Pato	Baby Come Back (1)
Barber's Jazz Band, Chris	Petite Fleur (9)
Bardo	One Step Further (2)
Bardot	Poison (45)
Barenaked Ladies	One Week (5)
Barlow, Gary	Forever Love (1)
	Love Won't Wait (1)
	Open Road (7)
Barron Knights	Call Up The Groups (3)
	Live In Trouble (7)
	Merry Gentle Pops (9)
	Pop Go The Workers (5)
	Taste Of Aggro, A (3)
Barry, John	As You Like It (5)
	How About That! (4)
	When Johnny Comes Marching Home / Made You (5)
Barry, Len	Like A Baby (10)
	1-2-3 (3)
Basement Jaxx	Red Alert (5)
	Rendez-Vu (4)
	Romeo (6)
	Where's Your Head At? (9)
Basil, Toni	Mickey (2)
Bass, Alfie	Signature Tune Of 'The Army Game', The (5)

Group/Artiste	Title
Bassey, Shirley	As I Love You (re-entry) (1)
	As Long As He Needs Me (2)
	Banana Boat Song (8)
	For All We Know (6)
	I (Who Have Nothing) (6)
	I'll Get By (10)
	Kiss Me Honey Honey Kiss Me (3)
	Never Never Never (8)
	Reach For The Stars / Climb Ev'ry Mountain (1)
	Something (4)
	What Now My Love (5)
	You'll Never Know (6)
Bassheads	Is There Anybody Out There (5)
Bass-O-Matic	Fascinating Rhythm (9)
Batt, Mike	Summertime City (4)
Bauhaus	Ziggy Stardust (15)
Baxter, Les	Unchained Melody (10)
Bay City Rollers	All Of Me Loves All Of You (4)
	Bye Bye Baby (1)
	Give A Little Love (1)
	I Only Wanna Be With You (4)
	Keep On Dancing (9)
	Love Me Like I Love You (4)
	Money Honey (3)
	Remember (Sha-La-La) (6)
	Shang-A-Lang (2)
	Summerlove Sensation (3)
BBD	Best Things In Life Are Free, The (2)
BBE	Flash (5)
	Seven Days And One Week (3)
BBMak	Back Here (re-issue) (5)
	Still On Your Side (8)
BC-52s	(Meet) The Flintstones (3)
Beach Boys	Barbara Ann (3)
	Break Away (6)
	Cottonfields (5)
	Do It Again (1)
	God Only Knows (2)
	Good Vibrations (1)
	Heroes And Villains (8)
	I Can Hear Music (10)
	I Get Around (7)
	Lady Lynda (6)
	Sloop John B (2)
	Surfin' USA (34)
	Then I Kissed Her (4)
	Wipeout (2)
Beastie Boys	Intergalactic (5)
	She's On It (10)
	(You Gotta) Fight For Your Right (To Party) (11)
Beat	Can't Get Used To Losing You (3)
	Hands Off – She's Mine (9)
	Mirror In The Bathroom (4)
	Tears Of A Clown / Ranking Full Stop (6)
	Too Nice To Talk To (7)
Beatles	All You Need Is Love (1)
	Baby It's You (7)
	Ballad Of John And Yoko (1)
	Beatles Movie Medley (10)
	Can't Buy Me Love (1)
	Day Tripper / We Can Work It Out (1)
	Free As A Bird (2)
	From Me To You (1)
	Get Back (1)

Group/Artiste	Title
	Hard Day's Night, A (1)
	Hello Goodbye (1)
	Help! (1)
	Hey Jude (1)
	I Feel Fine (1)
	I Want To Hold Your Hand (1)
	Lady Madonna (1)
	Let It Be (2)
	Love Me Do (17)
	Love Me Do (re-entry) (4)
	Magical Mystery Tour EP (2)
	Paperback Writer (1)
	Penny Lane / Strawberry Fields Forever (2)
	Please Please Me (2)
	Real Love (4)
	She Loves You (1)
	Something / Come Together (4)
	Ticket To Ride (1)
	Yellow Submarine / Eleanor Rigby (1)
	Yesterday (8)
Beatmasters	Hey DJ I Can't Dance To That Music You're Playing (7)
	Rok Da House (5)
	Who's In The House (8)
Beats International	Dub Be Good To Me (1)
	Won't Talk About It (9)
Beautiful South	Don't Marry Her (8)
	Little Time, A (1)
	Perfect 10 (2)
	Rotterdam (5)
	Song For Whoever (2)
	You Keep It All In (8)
Becaud, Gilbert	Little Love And Understanding, A (10)
Beck, Jeff	Goo Goo Barabajagal (Love Is Hot) (12)
	Hi-Ho Silver Lining (14)
Beck, Robin	The First Time (1)
Beckham, Victoria	Mind Of It's Own, A (6)
	Not Such An Innocent Girl (6)
	Out Of Your Mind (2)
Bedingfield, Daniel	Gotta Get Thru This (1)
	If You're Not The One (1)
	James Dean (I Wanna Know) (4)
Bee Gees	Alone (5)
	Don't Forget To Remember (2)
	First Of May (6)
	For Whom The Bell Tolls (4)
	How Deep Is Your Love (3)
	Immortality (5)
	I've Gotta Get A Message To You (1)
	Jive Talkin' (5)
	Massachusetts (1)
	New York Mining Disaster 1941 (12)
	Night Fever (1)
	Run To Me (9)
	Secret Love (5)
	Stayin' Alive (4)
	Too Much Heaven (3)
	Tragedy (1)
	Words (8)
	World (9)
	You Should Be Dancing (5)
	You Win Again (1)
Beenie Man	Feel It Boy (9)
	Money (5)

Group/Artiste	Title
	Who Am I (10)
Bega, Lou	Mambo No 5 (A Little Bit Of ...) (1)
Belafonte, Harry	Banana Boat Song (2)
	Island In The Sun (3)
	Mary's Boy Child (1)
	Mary's Boy Child (re-entry) (10)
Bell & Spurling	Sven Sven Sven (7)
Bell, William	Private Number (8)
Bellamy Brothers	If I Said You Have A Beautiful Body Would You Hold It Against Me (3)
	Let Your Love Flow (7)
Belle Stars	Sign Of The Times (3)
Bellini	Samba De Janeiro (8)
Beloved	Sweet Harmony (8)
Bennett, Tony	Stranger In Paradise (1)
Benson, George	Give Me The Night (7)
	In Your Eyes (7)
	Love X Love (10)
Benton, Brook	Endlessly (28)
Berlin	Take My Breath Away (1)
	Take My Breath Away (re-entry) (3)
Bernard Ebbinghouse Orchestra	It's All Over (9)
Bernstein, Elmer	Staccato's Theme (4)
Berri	Sunshine After The Rain, The (4)
Berry, Chuck	Let It Rock / Memphis Tennessee (6)
	My Ding-A-Ling (1)
	No Particular Place To Go (3)
	School Day (Ring! Ring! Goes The Bell) (24)
Berry, Dave	Crying Game, The (5)
	Little Things (5)
	Mama (5)
	Memphis Tennessee (19)
Berry, Mike	Sunshine Of Your Smile, The (9)
Berry, Nick	Every Loser Wins (1)
	Heartbeat (2)
Beverley Sisters	I Saw Mommy Kissing Santa Claus (re-entry) (6)
	Little Drummer Boy (6)
Beyonce	Work It Out (7)
B-52's	Love Shack (2)
Big Ben Banjo Band	Let's Get Together No. 1 (6)
Big Brovaz	Nu Flow (3)
Big Country	Chance (9)
	Fields Of Fire (400 Miles) (10)
	Look Away (7)
	Wonderland (8)
Big Dee Irwin	Swinging On A Star (7)
Big Fun	Blame It On The Boogie (4)
	Can't Shake The Feeling (8)
Big Mountain	Baby I Love Your Way (2)
Bigfoot	Sweet Like Chocolate (1)
Biggs, Barry	Sideshow (3)
Bilk, Mr Acker	Aria (5)
	Buona Sera (7)
	Stranger On The Shore (2)
	Summer Set (5)
	That's My Home (7)
Bill Haley & His Comets	Don't Knock The Rock (7)
	Rip It Up (4)
	Rock Around The Clock (re-entry) (1)
	Rock Around The Clock (re-entry) (5)

M
U
S
I
C

P
O
P

Group/Artiste	Title	Group/Artiste	Title
	Rock-A-Beatin' Boogie (4)		Family Affair (8)
	Rockin' Through The Rye (3)		I'll Be There For You – You're
	Saints Rock 'N' Roll, The (5)		All I Need To Get By (10)
	See You Later Alligator (7)		911 (9)
	Shake Rattle And Roll (4)		No More Drama (9)
Billie	Because We Want To (1)	Blink 182	All The Small Things (2)
	Girlfriend (1)	Blinky Blink	Take Me There (7)
	Honey To The Bee (3)	Blockster	You Should Be ... (3)
	She Wants You (3)	Blondie	Atomic (1)
	Thank Abba For The Music (4)		Call Me (1)
Birkin, Jane	Je T'Aime ... Moi Non Plus (2)		Denis (2)
	Je T'Aime ... Moi Non Plus (re-		Dreaming (2)
	issue) (1)		Hanging On The Telephone (5)
Biti	Shine On (8)		Heart Of Glass (1)
Bizarre Inc	I'm Gonna Get You (3)		(I'm Always Touched By Your)
	Playing With Knives (4)		Presence Dear (10)
Bizz Nizz	Don't Miss The Partyline (7)		Maria (1)
Björk	Army Of Me (10)		Picture This (12)
	Hyperballad (8)		Rapture (5)
	It's Oh So Quiet (4)		Sunday Girl (1)
	Ooops (42)		Tide Is High, The (1)
Björn Again	Erasure-ish (25)	Bloodhound Gang	Bad Touch, The (4)
Black	Sweetest Smile (8)	Bloom, Bobby	Montego Bay (3)
	Wonderful Life (8)	Blow Monkeys	It Doesn't Have To Be This
Black Box	Fantasy (5)		Way (5)
	I Don't Know Anybody Else (4)	Blue	All Rise (4)
	Ride On Time (1)		Fly By II (6)
Black Grape	England's Irie (6)		If You Come Back (1)
	Fat Neck (10)		One Love (3)
	In The Name Of The Father (8)		Sorry Seems To Be The
	Reverend Black Grape (9)		Hardest Word (1)
Black Lace	Agadoo (2)		Too Close (1)
	Do The Conga (10)	Blue Boy	Remember Me (8)
	Superman (Gioca Jouer) (9)	Blue Flames	Get Away (1)
Black Legend	You See The Trouble With Me		Yeh Yeh (1)
	(1)	Blue Grass Boys	Last Train To San Fernando (2)
Black Sabbath	Paranoid (4)	Blue Mink	Banner Man (3)
Black Slate	Amigo (9)		Good Morning Freedom (10)
Black, Cilla	Alfie (9)		Melting Pot (3)
	Anyone Who Had A Heart (1)		Randy (9)
	Conversations (7)	Blue Pearl	Naked In The Rain (4)
	Don't Answer Me (6)	Blue, Barry	(Dancing) On A Saturday Night
	Heart and Soul (75)		(2)
	It's For You (7)		Do You Wanna Dance (7)
	Love Of The Loved (35)	Bluebells	Young At Heart (8)
	Love's Just A Broken Heart (5)		Young At Heart (re-issue) (1)
	Something Tells Me	Bluenotes	Don't Leave Me This Way (5)
	(Something Is Gonna Happen		If You Don't Know Me By Now
	Tonight) (3)		(9)
	Step Inside Love (8)	Bluetones	Cut Some Rug / Castle Rock
	Surround Yourself With Sorrow		(7)
	(3)		Marblehead Johnson (7)
	You're My World (1)		Slight Return (2)
	You've Lost That Lovin' Feelin'		Solomon Bites The Worm (10)
	(2)	Blur	Beetlebum (1)
Blackfoot Sue	Standing In The Road (4)		Charmless Man (5)
Blackstreet	Don't Leave Me (6)		Country House (1)
	Fix (7)		Girls And Boys (5)
	No Diggity (9)		Music Is My Radar (10)
	Take Me There (7)		On Your Own (5)
Blackwood, Richard	Mama – Who Da Man? (3)		Parklife (10)
	1-2-3-4 Get With The Wicked		Song 2 (2)
	(10)		Stereotypes (7)
Blancmange	Blind Vision (10)		Tender (2)
	Don't Tell Me (8)		There's No Other Way (8)
	Living On The Ceiling (7)		Universal, The (5)
Blatt, Melanie	Twenty-Four Seven (6)	Bob & Earl	Harlem Shuffle (7)
Blazin' Squad	Crossroads (1)	Bob and Marcia	Pied Piper (11)
	Love On The Line (6)		Young Gifted And Black (5)
Blige, Mary J	As (4)	Bob The Builder	Can We Fix It? (1)
	Everything (6)		Mambo No 5 (1)

Group/Artiste	Title	Group/Artiste	Title
Boris Pickett & Crypt-Kickers	Monster Mash (3)		Looking After No. 1 (11)
Bocelli, Andrea	Time To Say Goodbye (Con Te Partiro) (2)		Rat Trap (1)
			Someone's Looking At You (4)
Bohannon, Hamilton	Disco Stomp (6)	Boone, Pat	Ain't That A Shame (7)
Bolton, Michael	Can I Touch You ... There (6)		April Love (7)
	How Am I Supposed To Live Without You (3)		Don't Forbid Me (2)
			Friendly Persuasion (3)
	How Can We Be Lovers (10)		I'll Be Home (1)
	When A Man Loves A Woman (8)		It's Too Soon To Know (7)
			Johnny Will (4)
Bomb The Bass	Beat Dis (2)		Love Letters In The Sand (2)
	Megablast / Don't Make Me Wait (6)		Remember You're Mine / There's A Goldmine In The Sky (5)
	Say A Little Prayer (10)		
	Winter In July (7)		Speedy Gonzales (2)
Bombalurina	Itsy Bitsy Teeny Weeny Yellow Polka Dot Bikini (1)		Sugar Moon (6)
			Wonderful Time Up There, A (2)
Bomfunk MCs	Freestyler (2)	Boot Room Boyz	Pass And Move (It's The Liverpool Groove) (4)
Bon Jovi	Always (2)		
	Dry County (9)	Boothe, Ken	Crying Over You (11)
	Everyday (5)		Everything I Own (1)
	Hardest Part Is The Night (68)	Bootzilla Orchestra	Double Dutch (3)
	In These Arms (9)	Boswell, Eve	Pickin' A Chicken (9)
	It's My Life (3)	Boucher, Judy	Can't Be With You Tonight (2)
	Keep The Faith (5)	Boulevard, DB	Point Of View (3)
	Lie To Me (10)	Bourke, Toby	Waltz Away Dreaming (10)
	Livin' On A Prayer (4)	Bow Wow Wow	Go Wild In The Country (7)
	One Wild Night (10)		I Want Candy (9)
	Please Come Home For Christmas (7)	Bowers, Dane	Buggin' Me (6)
			Out Of Your Mind (2)
	Say It Isn't So (10)	Bowie, David	Absolute Beginners (2)
	Someday I'll Be Saturday Night (7)		Ashes To Ashes (1)
			Blue Jean (6)
	Something For The Pain (8)		Boys Keep Swinging (7)
	These Days (7)		China Girl (2)
	This Ain't A Love Song (6)		Dancing In The Street (1)
Bon Jovi, Jon	Blaze of Glory (13)		Drive-In Saturday (3)
	Midnight In Chelsea (4)		Everyone Says Hi (20)
	Queen Of New Orleans (10)		Fashion (5)
Bone Thugs-N-Harmony	Tha Crossroads (8)		Golden Years (8)
			Jean Genie, The (2)
Boney M	Belfast (8)		Jump They Say (9)
	Boney M Megamix (7)		Knock On Wood (10)
	Daddy Cool (6)		Laughing Gnome, The (6)
	Hooray Hooray It's A Holi-Holiday (3)		Let's Dance (1)
			Life On Mars (3)
	Ma Baker (2)		Modern Love (2)
	Mary's Boy Child – Oh My Lord (1)		Peace On Earth / Little Drummer Boy (3)
	Painter Man (10)		Rebel Rebel (5)
	Rasputin (2)		Sorrow (3)
	Rivers Of Babylon / Brown Girl In The Ring (1)		Sound And Vision (3)
			Space Oddity (5)
	Sunny (3)		Space Oddity (re-issue) (1)
Bonnet, Graham	Night Games (6)		Starman (10)
Bono	I've Got You Under My Skin (4)		Under Pressure (1)
Bonzo Dog Doo-Dah Band	I'm The Urban Spaceman (5)	Bowling For Soup	Girl All The Bad Guys Want (8)
		Box Tops	Letter, The (5)
Boo Radleys	Wake Up Boo! (9)	Boy Meets Girl	Waiting For A Star To Fall (9)
Boo, Betty	Doin' The Do (7)	Boyd, Jimmy	I Saw Mommy Kissing Santa Claus (3)
	Hey DJ I Can't Dance To That Music You're Playing (7)		
			Tell Me A Story (5)
	Where Are You Baby (3)	Boystown Gang	Can't Take My Eyes Off You (4)
Boogie Box High	Jive Talkin' (7)	Boyz II Men	End Of The Road (1)
Booker Newbury III	Love Town (6)		4 Seasons Of Loneliness (10)
Booker T & The MG's	Green Onions (7)		I'll Make Love To You (5)
	Time Is Tight (4)		One Sweet Day (6)
Boomtown Rats	Banana Republic (3)	Boyzone	All That I Need (1)
	I Don't Like Mondays (1)		Baby Can I Hold You / Shooting Star (2)
	Like Clockwork (6)		Coming Home Now (4)

MUSIC

POP

Group/Artiste	Title
	Different Beat, A (1)
	Everyday I Love You (3)
	Father And Son (2)
	I Love The Way You Love Me (2)
	Isn't It A Wonder (2)
	Key To My Life (3)
	Love Me For A Reason (2)
	No Matter What (1)
	Picture Of You (2)
	So Good (3)
	When The Going Gets Tough (1)
	Words (1)
	You Needed Me (1)
Bragg, Billy	She's Leaving Home (1)
Bran Van 3000	Drinking In L.A. (re-issue) (3)
Brand New Heavies	You've Got A Friend (9)
Brandon, Johnny	Tomorrow (8)
Brandy	Another Day In Paradise (5)
	Boy Is Mine, The (2)
	Top Of The World (2)
	What About Us (4)
Branigan, Laura	Gloria (6)
	Self Control (5)
Braxton, Toni	Breathe Again (2)
	He Wasn't Man Enough (5)
	I Don't Want To (9)
	Un-Break My Heart (2)
	You're Makin' Me High (7)
Bread	Make It With You (5)
Break Machine	Breakdance Party (9)
	Street Dance (3)
Breathe	Hands To Heaven (4)
Brent, Tony	Make It Soon (9)
	Make It Soon (re-entry) (9)
	Walkin' To Missouri (9)
	Walkin' To Missouri (re-entry) (7)
Bresslaw, Bernard	Mad Passionate Love (6)
	Signature Tune Of 'The Army Game', The (5)
Brewer, Teresa	Let Me Go Lover (9)
	Sweet Old-Fashioned Girl (3)
	Tear Fell, A (2)
Brian & Michael	Matchstalk Men And Matchstalk Cats And Dogs (1)
Brighouse & Rastrick Brass Band	Floral Dance, The (2)
Brightman, Sarah	All I Ask Of You (3)
	I Lost My Heart To A Starship Trooper (6)
	Phantom Of The Opera, The (7)
	Pie Jesu (3)
	Time To Say Goodbye (Con Te Partiro) (2)
	Wishing You Were Somehow Here Again (7)
Bristol, Johnny	Hang On In There Baby (3)
Bronski Beat	Hit That Perfect Beat (3)
	I Feel Love (medley) (3)
	Smalltown Boy (3)
	Why? (6)
Brook Brothers	Warpaint (5)
Brooks, Elkie	No More The Fool (5)
	Pearl's A Singer (8)
	Sunshine After The Rain (10)
Brooks, Meredith	Bitch (6)
Bros	Cat Amongst The Pigeons / Silent Night (2)
	Chocolate Box (9)

Group/Artiste	Title
	Drop The Boy (2)
	I Owe You Nothing (1)
	I Quit (4)
	Sister (10)
	Too Much (2)
	When Will I Be Famous (2)
Brother Beyond	Harder I Try, The (2)
	He Ain't No Competition (6)
Brotherhood Of Man	Angelo (1)
	Figaro (1)
	Oh Boy (The Mood I'm In) (8)
	Save Your Kisses For Me (1)
	United We Stand (10)
Brothers	Sing Me (8)
Brothers Johnson	Stomp (6)
Brown, Angie	I'm Gonna Get You (3)
Brown, Bobby	Don't Be Cruel (42)
	Every Little Step (6)
	Humpin' Around (remix) (8)
	My Prerogative (6)
	On Our Own (Theme from Ghostbusters II) (4)
	Two Can Play That Game (re-entry) (3)
Brown, Foxy	I'll Be (9)
Brown, Ian	Be There (8)
	Dolphins Were Monkeys (5)
	My Star (5)
Brown, James	Living In America (5)
Brown, Jocelyn	Always There (6)
	Don't Talk Just Kiss (3)
	Keep On Jumpin' (8)
Brown, Sam	Stop (4)
Browne, Tom	Funkin' For Jamaica (N.Y.) (10)
Browns	Three Bells, The (6)
Brownstone	If You Love Me (8)
Brubeck Quartet, Dave	Take Five (6)
Bruce, Tommy	Ain't Misbehavin' (3)
Bruisers	Ain't Misbehavin' (3)
Bryson, Peabo	Beauty And The Beast (9)
	Tonight I Celebrate My Love (2)
Bubbler Ranx	Mysterious Girl (2)
Bucketheads	Bomb! (These Sounds Fall Into My Mind), The (5)
Bucks Fizz	If You Can't Stand The Heat (10)
	Land Of Make Believe, The (1)
	Making Your Mind Up (1)
	My Camera Never Lies (1)
	New Beginning (Mamba Seyra) (8)
	Now Those Days Are Gone (8)
	When We Were Young (10)
Buddy Cole & his Orchestra	Hey There (4)
	This Ole House (1)
Buddy Cole Quartet	Rain Rain Rain (8)
	Where Will The Baby's Dimple Be (6)
Buffalo Tom	Going Underground / Carnation (6)
Buggles	Video Killed The Radio Star (1)
Bunton, Emma	Take My Breath Away (5)
	What I Am (2)
	What Took You So Long (1)
Burdon, Eric	San Franciscan Nights (7)
Burl Ives	Little Bitty Tear, A (9)
Burnette, Johnny	Dreamin' (5)
	You're Sixteen (3)
Burns, Ray	Mobile (4)

Group/Artiste	Title
Bus Stop	Kung Fu Fighting (8)
Bush	Swallowed (7)
Bush, Kate	Babooshka (5)
	Don't Give Up (9)
	Kate Bush On Stage EP (10)
	Man With The Child In His Eyes (6)
	Running Up That Hill (3)
	Wuthering Heights (1)
Busted	What I Go To School For (3)
Buzzcocks	Ever Fallen In Love (With Someone You Shouldn't've) (12)
	What Do I Get (37)
BVSMP	I Need You (3)
Bygraves, Max	Cowpuncher's Cantata (re-entry) (6)
	Cowpuncher's Cantata (re-entry) (8)
	Cowpuncher's Cantata (re-entry) (10)
	Fings Ain't Wot They Used To Be (5)
	Gilly Gilly Ossenfeffer Katzenellen Bogen By The Sea (7)
	Heart Of My Heart (7)
	Jingle Bell Rock (7)
	Meet Me On The Corner (2)
	You Need Hands / Tulips From Amsterdam (3)
Byrd, Gary	Crown, The (6)
Byrds	All I Really Want To Do (4)
	Mr Tambourine Man (1)
Byrne, David	Lazy (2)
C & C Music Factory	Gonna Make You Sweat (Everybody Dance Now) (3)
	Things That Make You Go Hmmm ... (4)
C J Lewis	Everything Is Alright (Uptight) (10)
	Sweets For My Sweet (3)
C W McCall	Convoy (2)
C, Melanie	Goin' Down (4)
	I Turn To You (1)
	Never Be The Same Again (1)
	Northern Star (4)
	When You're Gone (3)
C, Roy	Shotgun Wedding (6)
	Shotgun Wedding (re-issue) (8)
Cadogan, Susan	Hurt So Good (4)
Calling	Wherever You Will Go (3)
Calvert, Eddie	Cherry Pink And Apple Blossom White (1)
	John And Julie (6)
	Mandy (9)
	Oh Mein Papa (1)
Cameo	Word Up (3)
Cameron, Andy	Ally's Tartan Army (6)
Camisra	Let Me Show You (5)
Campbell, Ali	That Look In Your Eye (5)
Campbell, Glen	All I Have To Do Is Dream (3)
	Honey Come Back (4)
	It's Only Make Believe (4)
	Rhinestone Cowboy (4)
	Wichita Lineman (7)
Campbell, Junior	Hallelujah Freedom (10)
Cam'ron	Rocafella (13)
Candy Flip	Strawberry Fields Forever (3)
Canned Heat	Let's Work Together (2)
	On The Road Again (8)

Group/Artiste	Title
Cannon, Freddy	Way Down Yonder In New Orleans (3)
Capaldi, Jim	Love Hurts (4)
Cappella	Move On Baby (7)
	U And Me (10)
	U Got 2 Let The Music (2)
	U Got 2 Know (6)
Capstick, Tony	Sheffield Grinder / Capstick Comes Home, The (3)
Captain	Do That To Me One More Time (7)
Captain Hollywood Project	I Can't Stand It (7)
Captain Sensible	Glad It's All Over / Damned On 45 (6)
	Happy Talk (1)
Cara Tivey	She's Leaving Home (1)
Cara, Irene	Fame (1)
	Flashdance ... What A Feeling (2)
Caravelles	You Don't Have To Be A Baby To Cry (6)
Cardigans	Burning Down The House (7)
	Carnival (72)
	Erase / Rewind (7)
	Lovefool (2)
Carey, Mariah	Against All Odds (1)
	All I Want For Christmas Is You (2)
	Always Be My Baby (3)
	Anytime You Need A Friend (8)
	Dreamlover (9)
	Endless Love (3)
	Fantasy (4)
	Heartbreaker (5)
	Hero (7)
	Honey (3)
	I'll Be There (2)
	My All (4)
	One Sweet Day (6)
	Open Arms (4)
	Thank God I Found You (10)
	Through The Rain (8)
	Vision Of Love (9)
	When You Believe (4)
	Without You (1)
Carl	Light My Fire (7)
Carlisle, Belinda	Always Breaking My Heart (8)
	Circle In The Sand (4)
	Heaven Is A Place On Earth (1)
	I Get Weak (10)
	In Too Deep (6)
	Leave A Light On (4)
	(We Want) The Same Thing (6)
Carlton, Vanessa	Thousand Miles, A (6)
Carnes, Kim	Bette Davis Eyes (10)
Carpenters	Calling Occupants Of Interplanetary Craft (9)
	I Won't Last A Day Without You / Goodbye To Love (9)
	Only Yesterday (2)
	Please Mr Postman (2)
	(They Long To Be) Close To You (6)
	Top Of The World (5)
	Yesterday Once More (2)
Carr, Vikki	It Must Be Him (2)
Carra, Raffaella	Do It Do It Again (9)
Carroll, Dina	Don't Be A Stranger (3)
	Escaping (3)
	It's Too Late (8)

M
U
S
I
C

P
O
P

Group/Artiste	Title
	Perfect Year, The (5)
Carroll, Ronnie	Roses Are Red (3)
	Say Wonderful Things (6)
Carrott, Jasper	Funky Moped / Magic Roundabout (5)
Cars	Drive (5)
	Drive (re-entry) (4)
	My Best Friend's Girl (3)
Carter The Unstoppable Sex Machine	Only Living Boy In New Cross, The (7)
Carter, Aaron	Crazy Little Party Girl (7)
	Crush On You (9)
Carter, Clarence	Patches (2)
Cartoons	Doodah! (7)
	Witch Doctor (2)
Cascades	Rhythm Of The Rain (5)
Case	Livin' It Up (re-issue) (5)
Cash, Johnny	Boy Named Sue, A (4)
	Thing Called Love, A (4)
Cass, Mama	It's Getting Better (8)
Cassandra	Touch Me (1)
Cassidy, David	Breaking Up Is Hard To Do (3)
	Could It Be Forever / Cherish (2)
	Daydreamer / The Puppy Song (1)
	How Can I Be Sure (1)
	If I Didn't Care (9)
	I'm A Clown / Some Kind Of Summer (3)
	Last Kiss, The (6)
Cassius 1999	Cassius (7)
Cast	Beat Mama (9)
	Flying (4)
	Free Me (7)
	Guiding Star (9)
	Live The Dream (7)
	Sandstorm (8)
	Walkaway (9)
Cast From Casualty	Everlasting Love (5)
Casuals	Jesamine (2)
Catatonia	Dead From The Waist Down (7)
	Mulder And Scully (3)
	Road Rage (5)
Caterina Valente	Breeze And I, The (5)
CCS	Tap Turns On The Water (5)
	Walkin' (7)
Ce Ce Peniston	Finally (re-issue) (2)
	Keep On Walkin' (10)
	We Got A Love Thang (6)
Cerrone	Supernature (8)
Cerys of Catatonia	Ballad Of Tom Jones, The (4)
Cetera, Peter	Glory Of Love (3)
	Hard To Say I'm Sorry (7)
Chacksfield, Frank	Ebb Tide (9)
	Little Red Monkey (10)
	Terry's Theme From Limelight (2)
Chairmen Of The Board	Give Me Just A Little More Time (3)
	You've Got Me Dangling On A String (5)
Chaka Demus & Pliers	She Don't Let Nobody (4)
	Tease Me (3)
	Twist And Shout (1)
Champaign	How 'Bout Us (5)
Champs	Tequila (5)
Changing Faces	G.H.E.T.T.O.U.T. (10)
Channel, Bruce	Hey! Baby (2)

Group/Artiste	Title
Chapman, Tracy	Fast Car (5)
Charlatans	How High (6)
	North Country Boy (4)
	One To Another (3)
	Only One I Know, The (9)
Charlene	I've Never Been To Me (1)
Charles & Eddie	Would I Lie To You (1)
Charles McDevitt Skiffle Group	Freight Train (5)
Charles, Ray	Hit The Road Jack (6)
	I Can't Stop Loving You (1)
	Take These Chains From My Heart (5)
	You Don't Know Me (9)
Charles, Tina	Dance Little Lady Dance (6)
	Dr Love (4)
	I Love To Love (1)
Chas and Dave	Ain't No Pleasing You (2)
	Rabbit (8)
	Snooker Loopy (6)
	Strummin' (52)
Check 1-2	Mona (2)
Checker, Chubby	Let's Twist Again / The Twist (re-issue) (5)
	Let's Twist Again (remix) (2)
	Twist (Yo Twist), The (2)
Checkmates	Counting Teardrops (4)
	On a Slow Boat To China (3)
	What Do You Want To Make Those Eyes At Me For (1)
Cheeky Girls	Cheeky Song (Touch My Bum) (2)
Chef	Chocolate Salty Balls (1)
Chelsea FC	Blue Is The Colour (5)
Chemical Brothers	Block Rockin' Beats (1)
	Come With Us / The Test (14)
	Hey Boy Hey Girl (3)
	It Began In Afrika (8)
	Leave Home (17)
	Let Forever Be (9)
	Setting Sun (1)
	Star Guitar (8)
Cher	All I Ever Need Is You (8)
	All I Really Want To Do (9)
	Bang Bang (My Baby Shot Me Down) (3)
	Believe (1)
	Gypsies Tramps And Thieves (4)
	I Found Someone (5)
	I Got You Babe (1)
	If I Could Turn Back Time (6)
	Little Man (4)
	Love And Understanding (10)
	Love Can Build A Bridge (1)
	Music's No Good Without You, The (8)
	One By One (7)
	Shoop Shoop Song (It's In His Kiss), The (1)
	Strong Enough (5)
Cherelle	Saturday Love (6)
Cherry, Don	Band Of Gold (6)
Cherry, Eagle-Eye	Falling In Love Again (8)
	Save Tonight (6)
Cherry, Neneh	Buffalo Stance (3)
	Love Can Build A Bridge (1)
	Manchild (5)
	7 Seconds (3)
	Woman (9)
Chic	Dance Dance Dance (Yowsah

M
U
S
I
C

P
O
P

Group/Artiste	Title
	Both Sides Of The Story (7)
	Dance Into The Light (9)
	Easy Lover (1)
	Groovy Kind Of Love, A (1)
	I Wish It Would Rain Down (7)
	In The Air Tonight (2)
	In The Air Tonight (remix) (4)
	One More Night (4)
	Separate Lives (4)
	Two Hearts (6)
	You Can't Hurry Love (1)
Color Me Badd	All 4 Love (5)
	I Wanna Sex You Up (1)
Commodores	Easy (9)
	Nightshift (3)
	Sail On (8)
	Still (4)
	Three Times A Lady (1)
Communards	Don't Leave Me This Way (1)
	Machine Gun (20)
	Never Can Say Goodbye (4)
	So Cold The Night (8)
	You Are My World (30)
Como, Perry	And I Love You So (3)
	Catch A Falling Star (9)
	Delaware (3)
	Don't Let The Stars Get In Your Eyes (1)
	For The Good Times (7)
	Hot Diggity (Dog Ziggity Boom) (4)
	Idle Gossip (3)
	It's Impossible (4)
	Kewpie Doll (9)
	Love Makes The World Go Round (6)
	Magic Moments (1)
	More (10)
	Tomboy (10)
	Wanted (4)
Company	Shame Shame Shame (6)
Congregation	Softly Whispering I Love You (4)
Conley, Arthur	Sweet Soul Music (7)
Connolly, Billy	D.I.V.O.R.C.E. (1)
Conway, Russ	China Tea (5)
	More And More Party Pops (5)
	More Party Pops (10)
	Party Pops (24)
	Roulette (1)
	Side Saddle (1)
	Snow Coach (7)
	Toy Balloons (7)
Cooke, Sam	Chain Gang (9)
	Cupid (7)
	Twistin' The Night Away (6)
	Wonderful World (re-issue) (2)
	You Send Me (29)
Cookie Crew	Rok Da House (5)
Cool J, LL	Ain't Nobody (1)
	Father (10)
	Hit 'Em High (The Monstars' Anthem) (8)
	I Need Love (8)
	Loungin' (7)
	Luv U Better (7)
	Phenomenon (9)
Coolidge, Rita	All Time High (75)
	We're All Alone (6)
Coolio	C U When You Get There (3)
	Gangsta's Paradise (1)

Group/Artiste	Title
	Hit 'Em High (The Monstars' Anthem) (8)
	Too Hot (9)
Cooper, Alice	Elected (4)
	Hello Hurray (6)
	No More Mr Nice Guy (10)
	Poison (2)
	School's Out (1)
Cornell, Don	Hold My Hand (1)
Cornershop	Brimful Of Asha (remix) (1)
Cornwell, Charlotte	OK? (10)
Corona	Baby Baby (5)
	Rhythm Of The Night, The (2)
	Try Me Out (6)
Corrs	Breathless (1)
	Dreams (6)
	Runaway (2)
	So Young (6)
	What Can I Do (3)
Cosmic Gate	Firewire (9)
Costello, Elvis	Good Year For The Roses, A (6)
	I Can't Stand Up For Falling Down (4)
	Oliver's Army (2)
Cotton, Billy & His Band	Friends And Neighbours (re-entry) (3)
	In A Golden Coach (3)
Course	Ain't Nobody (8)
	Ready Or Not (5)
Cousins, Tina	Mysterious Times (2)
	Thank Abba For The Music (4)
Covington, Julie	Don't Cry For Me Argentina (1)
	OK? (10)
Cox, Michael	Angela Jones (7)
Cradock, Steve	Going Underground / Carnation (6)
Craig, Robbie	Woman Trouble (6)
Cramer, Floyd	On The Rebound (1)
Cranberries	Zombie (14)
Crane, Les	Desiderata (7)
Crash Test Dummies	Mmm Mmm Mmm Mmm (2)
Craven, Beverley	Promise Me (3)
Crawford, Michael	Music Of The Night, The (7)
Crawford, Randy	Almaz (4)
	One Day I'll Fly Away (2)
Crazy Town	Butterfly (3)
Crazy World Of Arthur Brown	Fire (1)
Creedence Clearwater Revival	Bad Moon Rising (1)
	Proud Mary (8)
	Travellin' Band (8)
	Up Around The Bend (3)
Crew Cuts	Earth Angel (4)
Cribbins, Bernard	Hole In The Ground (9)
	Right Said Fred (10)
Crickets	Don't Ever Change (5)
	Maybe Baby (4)
	Oh Boy (3)
	That'll Be The Day (1)
Crosby, Stills and Nash	Marrakesh Express (17)
Crosby, Stills, Nash and Young	American Dream (55)
Crosby, Bing	Around The World (5)
	Changing Partners (10)
	Changing Partners (re-entry) (9)
	Isle Of Innisfree (3)
	Peace On Earth / Little Drummer Boy (3)
	Silent Night (8)

Group/Artiste	Title	Group/Artiste	Title
	True Love (4)		Wonderful Tonight (3)
	White Christmas (5)	Damian	Time Warp (remix), The (7)
	Zing A Little Zong (10)	Damned	Eloise (3)
Cross, Christopher	Arthur's Theme (Best That You Can Do) (7)	Damone, Vic	On The Street Where You Live (1)
Crow, Sheryl	All I Wanna Do (4)	Dana	All Kinds Of Everything (1)
	Change Would Do You Good, A (8)		It's Gonna Be A Cold Cold Christmas (4)
	If It Makes You Happy (9)		Please Tell Him That I Said Hello (8)
	My Favourite Mistake (9)	Dane	Another Lover (9)
Crowd	You'll Never Walk Alone (1)		Shut Up And Forget About It (9)
Crowded House	Weather With You (7)	Dankworth, Johnny	African Waltz (9)
Crown Heights Affair	You Gave Me Love (10)		Experiments With Mice (7)
Cruise, Julie	Falling (7)	Danny & The Juniors	At The Hop (3)
Crusaders	Street Life (5)	Daphne & Celeste	Ooh Stick You! (8)
Crystals	Da Doo Ron Ron (5)	Darey, Matt	Beautiful (10)
	Then He Kissed Me (2)	Darin, Bobby	Clementine (8)
Cuban Boys	Cognoscenti Vs Intelligentsia (4)		Dream Lover (1)
			If I Were A Carpenter (9)
Cufflinks	Tracy (4)		La Mer (Beyond The Sea) (8)
	When Julie Comes Around (10)		Lazy River (2)
Cult Of Ant	Better Watch Out (10)		Mack The Knife (1)
Culture Beat	Anything (5)		Multiplication (5)
	Got To Get It (4)		Splish Splash (18)
	Mr Vain (1)		Things (2)
Culture Club	Church Of The Poison Mind (2)		You Must Have Been A Beautiful Baby (10)
	Do You Really Want To Hurt Me (1)		
	I Just Wanna Be Loved (4)	Darius	Colourblind (1)
	It's A Miracle (4)		Rushes (5)
	Karma Chameleon (1)	Darts	Boy From New York City (2)
	Move Away (7)		Come Back My Love (2)
	Time (Clock Of The Heart) (3)		Daddy Cool / The Girl Can't Help It (6)
	Victims (3)		Duke Of Earl (6)
	War Song, The (2)		Get It (10)
Cupid's Inspiration	Yesterday Has Gone (4)		It's Raining (2)
Cure	A Forest (31)	Darude	Feel The Beat (5)
	Friday I'm In Love (6)		Sandstorm (3)
	High (8)	Daryl Hall &	I Can't Go For That
	Love Cats, The (7)	John Oates	(No Can Do) (8)
	Lullaby (5)		Maneater (6)
Curiosity	Hang On In There Baby (3)	Dave & Ansil Collins	Double Barrel (1)
Curiosity Killed	Down To Earth (3)		Monkey Spanner (7)
The Cat	Misfit (7)	Dave Clark Five	Bits And Pieces (2)
Curved Air	Back Street Luv (4)		Can't You See That She's Mine (10)
Cutting Crew	(I Just) Died In Your Arms Tonight (4)		Catch Us If You Can (5)
Cyril Stapleton	Blue Star (The Medic Theme)		Do You Love Me (30)
Orchestra	(2)		Everybody Get Together (8)
Cyrus, Billy Ray	Achy Breaky Heart (3)		Everybody Knows (2)
D Mob	It Is Time To Get Funky (9)		Glad All Over (1)
	Put Your Hands Together (7)		Good Old Rock 'N' Roll (7)
	We Call It Acieed (3)		Red Balloon (7)
D12	Purple Pills / Purple Hills (2)	Dave Dee, Dozy,	Bend It (2)
	S**t On You (10)	Beaky, Mick and	Hideaway (10)
D:Ream	Shoot Me With Your Love (7)	Tich	Hold Tight (4)
	Things Can Only Get Better (remix) (1)		Last Night In Soho (8)
			Legend Of Xanadu (1)
	U R The Best Thing (remix) (4)		Okay! (4)
Da Force, Ricardo	Stayin' Alive (2)		Save Me (4)
Da Silva, Rui	Touch Me (1)		You Make It Move (26)
Dactyl, Terry and the	On A Saturday Night (45)		Zabadak! (3)
Dinosaurs	Seaside Shuffle (2)	David & Jonathan	Lovers Of The World Unite (7)
Daft Punk	Around The World (5)	David Morales	Needin' U (8)
	Da Funk / Musique (7)	David Rose & His	My Happiness (4)
	One More Time (2)	Orchestra	
Dale, Jim	Be My Girl (2)	David Whitfield &	Adoration Waltz (9)
Daltrey, Roger	Giving It All Away (5)	Roland Shaw	
Damage	Forever (6)	David, Craig	Fill Me In (1)
	Ghetto Romance (7)		Rendezvous (8)
	Love Guaranteed (7)		

Group/Artiste	Title	Group/Artiste	Title
	Re-Rewind The Crowd Say Bo Selecta (2)	Deep Blue Something	Breakfast At Tiffany's (1)
		Deep Forest	Sweet Lullaby (10)
	7 Days (1)	Deep Purple	Black Night (2)
	Walking Away (3)		Strange Kind Of Woman (8)
	What's Your Flava (8)	Def Leppard	Animal (6)
	Woman Trouble (6)		Let's Get Rocked (2)
David, F R	Words (2)		When Love And Hate Collide (2)
Davidson, Paul	Midnight Rider (10)		
Davies, Dave	Death Of A Clown (3)	Degrees Of Motion	Shine On (8)
Davies, Windsor	Whispering Grass (1)	Dekker, Desmond	Israelites (1)
Davis Jr, Billy	You Don't Have To Be A Star (To Be In My Show) (7)		Israelites (re-issue) (10)
			It Miek (7)
Davis Jr, Sammy	Love Me Or Leave Me (8)		You Can Get It If You Really Want (2)
Davis, Billie	Tell Him (10)		
Dawn	Candida (9)	De'Lacy	Hideaway (9)
	Knock Three Times (1)	Delirium	Silence (remixes) (3)
	Tie A Yellow Ribbon Round The Old Oak Tree (1)	Denise & Johnny	Especially For You (3)
		Dennis, Cathy	Touch Me (All Night Long) (5)
	What Are You Doing Sunday (3)	Dennis, Jackie	La Dee Dah (4)
		Denver, John	Annie's Song (1)
Dawson, Dana	3 Is Family (9)	Denver, Karl	Marcheta (8)
Day, Doris	Black Hills Of Dakota (7)		Mexicali Rose (8)
	If I Give My Heart To You (4)		Never Say Goodbye (9)
	Let's Walk Thata-Way (4)		Wimoweh (4)
	Move Over Darling (8)	Deodato	Also Sprach Zarathustra (2001) (7)
	My Love And Devotion (10)		
	Ready Willing And Able (7)	Depeche Mode	Barrel Of A Gun (4)
	Secret Love (1)		Condemnation (9)
	Sugarbush (8)		Dream On (6)
	Sugarbush (re-entry) (8)		Dreaming Of Me (57)
	Whatever Will Be Will Be (1)		Enjoy The Silence (6)
Dayne, Taylor	Prove Your Love (8)		Everything Counts (6)
	Tell It To My Heart (3)		I Feel You (8)
De Burgh, Chris	Don't Pay The Ferryman (48)		In Your Room (8)
	Lady In Red, The (1)		It's No Good (5)
	Missing You (3)		Just Can't Get Enough (8)
De La Soul	Magic Number, The / Buddy (7)		Master And Servant (9)
	Ring Ring (Ha Ha Hey) (10)		People Are People (4)
De Paul, Lynsey	No Honestly (7)		See You (6)
	Sugar Me (5)	Derek & The Dominoes	Layla (7)
De Sykes, Stephanie	Born With A Smile On My Face (2)		Layla (re-issue) (4)
		Desireless	Voyage Voyage (5)
	We'll Find Our Day (17)	Des'ree	Life (8)
Deacon Blue	Four Bacharach And David Songs EP (2)		You Gotta Be (re-issue) (10)
		Destiny's Child	Bills Bills Bills (6)
	Real Gone Kid (8)		Bootylicious (2)
	Twist And Shout (10)		Bug A Boo (9)
Dead End Kids	Have I The Right (6)		Emotion (3)
Dead Or Alive	You Spin Me Round (Like A Record) (1)		Independent Women Part 1 (1)
			Jumpin' Jumpin' (5)
Dean, Hazell	Searchin' (I Gotta Find A Man) (6)		No No No (5)
			Say My Name (3)
	Whatever I Do (Wherever I Go) (4)		Survivor (1)
		Marcella Detroit	I Believe (11)
	Who's Leaving Who (4)	Detroit Emeralds	Feel The Need In Me (4)
Dean, Jimmy	Big Bad John (2)	Detroit Spinners	Cupid – I've Loved You For A Long Time (4)
Death In Vegas	Aisha (9)		
DeBarge	Rhythm Of The Night (4)		Ghetto Child (7)
Dec	Better Watch Out (10)		Working My Way Back To You / Forgive Me Girl (1)
Decker, Diana	Poppa Piccolino (2)		
	Poppa Piccolino (re-entry) (5)	Deuce	I Need You (10)
Dee C Lee	See The Day (3)	Dexy's Midnight Runners	Come On Eileen (1)
Dee D Jackson	Automatic Lover (4)		Geno (1)
Dee, Kiki	Amoureuse (13)		Jackie Wilson Said (I'm In Heaven When You Smile) (5)
	Don't Go Breaking My Heart (1)		
	True Love (2)		There There My Dear (7)
Deee-Lite	Groove Is In The Heart / What Is Love (2)	Di	Shake Ur Body (7)
		Di Bart, Tony	Real Thing, The (1)
Deejay, Alice	Back In My Life (4)	Diamond, Jim	Hi Ho Silver (5)
	Will I Ever (7)		I Should Have Known Better (1)
Deejay, Sven	Holiday Rap (6)		

Group/Artiste	Title	Group/Artiste	Title
Diamond, Neil	Cracklin' Rosie (3)	DNA	Tom's Diner (2)
	I Am ... I Said (4)	Do	Heaven (1)
	Sweet Caroline (8)	Dobson, Anita	Anyone Can Fall In Love (4)
	You Don't Bring Me Flowers (5)	Doctor Spin	Tetris (6)
Diamonds	Little Darlin' (3)	Dodd, Ken	Love Is Like A Violin (8)
Dick Stabile & his Orchestra	That's Amore (2)		Promises (6)
			River, The (3)
Dickies	Banana Splits (7)		Tears (1)
Dickinson, Bruce	(I Want To Be) Elected (9)	Dodgy	Good Enough (4)
Dickson, Barbara	Answer Me (9)	Dog Eat Dog	No Fronts (9)
	I Know Him So Well (1)	Dogg, Nate	Regulate (5)
Dido	Here With Me (4)	Doh, Ken	I Need A Lover Tonight (7)
	One Step Too Far (6)	Dolan, Joe	Make Me An Island (3)
	Thank You (3)	Dolce Music Theatre, Joe	Shaddup You Face (1)
Dini, Paolo	Going Back To My Roots / Rich In Paradise (9)		
		Dollar	Give Me Back My Heart (4)
Dinosaurs	Seaside Shuffle (2)		I Wanna Hold Your Hand (9)
Dion	Wanderer, The (10)		Love's Gotta Hold On Me (4)
Dion, Celine	All By Myself (6)		Mirror Mirror (4)
	Beauty And The Beast (9)		O L'Amour (7)
	Because You Loved Me (5)	Domino, Fats	Blueberry Hill (re-entry) (6)
	Falling Into You (10)	Don Lang & His Frantic Five	Witch Doctor (5)
	I'm Your Angel (3)		
	Immortality (5)	Don Pablo's Animals	Venus (4)
	It's All Coming Back To Me Now (3)	Donegan, Lonnie	I Wanna Go Home (The Wreck Of The John 'B') (5)
	My Heart Will Go On (1)		Lorelei (10)
	New Day Has Come, A (7)		Party's Over, The (9)
	Only One Road (8)	Donovan	Catch The Wind (4)
	Power Of Love, The (4)		Colours (4)
	Tell Him (3)		Hurdy Gurdy Man (4)
	Think Twice (1)		Jennifer Juniper (5)
	Tu M'Aimes Encore (To Love Me Again) (7)		Mellow Yellow (8)
			Sunshine Superman (2)
Dire Straits	Money For Nothing (4)		There Is A Mountain (8)
	Private Investigations (2)	Donovan, Jason	Any Dream Will Do (1)
	Romeo And Juliet (8)		Especially For You (1)
	Sultans Of Swing (8)		Every Day (I Love You More) (2)
	Walk Of Life (2)		
Dirty Rotten Scoundrels	People Hold On (4)		Hang On To Your Love (8)
			Happy Together (10)
Disco Tex	Get Dancing (8)		Nothing Can Divide Us (5)
	I Wanna Dance Wit Choo (6)		Rhythm Of The Rain (9)
Distel, Sacha	Raindrops Keep Falling On My Head (10)		Sealed With A Kiss (1)
			Too Many Broken Hearts (1)
Divine Comedy	National Express (8)		When You Come Back To Me (2)
Divinyls	I Touch Myself (10)		
DJ Aligator Project	Whistle Song (Blow My Whistle B***h), The (5)	Doobie Brothers	Long Train Runnin' (7)
		Doolally	Straight From The Heart (9)
DJ Dado	X-Files (8)	Dooleys	Chosen Few, The (7)
DJ Jean	Launch, The (2)		Love Of My Life (9)
DJ Jurgen presents Alice DeeJay	Better Off Alone (2)		Wanted (3)
		Doonican, Val	Elusive Butterfly (5)
DJ Kool	Let Me Clear My Throat (8)		If The Whole World Stopped Loving (3)
DJ Luck & MC Neat	Ain't No Stoppin Us (8)		
	Little Bit Of Luck, A (9)		Special Years, The (7)
	Masterblaster 2000 (5)		Walk Tall (3)
DJ Marky & XRS	LK (Carolina Carol Bela) (17)		What Would I Be (2)
DJ Miko	What's Up (6)	Doop	Doop (1)
DJ Otzi	Do Wah Diddy (9)	Doors	Light My Fire (re-issue) (7)
	Hey Baby (Unofficial World Cup Remix) (10)	Dorothy Squires	My Way (10)
		Dorsey, Lee	Holy Cow (6)
	Hey Baby (Uuh, Aah) (1)		Working In A Coalmine (8)
DJ Pied Piper & The MC	Do You Really Like It (1)	Double	Captain Of Her Heart, The (8)
		Doug E Fresh & Get Fresh Crew	Show, The (7)
DJ Quicksilver	Belissima (4)		
	Free (7)	Douglas, Carl	Kung Fu Fighting (1)
DJ Sakin & Friends	Protect Your Mind For The Love Of A Princess) (4)		Kung Fu Fighting (8)
		Douglas, Craig	Heart Of A Teenage Girl, The (10)
DJ Sammy	Heaven (1)		
DJ Supreme	Up To The Wildstyle (10)		Hundred Pounds Of Clay, A (9)

Group/Artiste	Title	Group/Artiste	Title
	Only Sixteen (1)	Dunblane	Knockin' On Heaven's Door /
	Our Favourite Melodies (9)		Throw These Guns Away (1)
	Pretty Blue Eyes (4)	Duncan, Johnny	Last Train To San Fernando (2)
	Time (9)	Dundas, David	Jeans On (3)
	When My Little Girl Is Smiling	Dunn, Clive	Grandad (1)
	(9)	Dunn, Romeo	Romeo (3)
Doves	There Goes The Fear (3)	Duran Duran	All She Wants Is (9)
Dr & The Medics	Spirit In The Sky (1)		Girls On Film (5)
Dr Alban	It's My Life (2)		Hungry Like The Wolf (5)
Dr Dre	Bad Intentions (4)		Is There Something I Should
	California Love (6)		Know (1)
	Forgot About Dre (7)		New Moon On Monday (9)
	Guilty Conscience (5)		Notorious (7)
	Next Episode, The (3)		Ordinary World (6)
	Still D.R.E. (6)		Planet Earth (12)
Dr Feelgood	Milk And Alcohol (9)		Reflex, The (1)
Dr Hook	Better Love Next Time (8)		Rio (9)
	If Not You (5)		Save A Prayer (2)
	Little Bit More, A (2)		Union Of The Snake (3)
	Sexy Eyes (4)		View To A Kill, A (2)
	Sylvias Mother (2)		Wild Boys (2)
	When You're In Love With A	Dusty, Slim	Pub With No Beer, A (3)
	Beautiful Woman (1)	Dylan, Bob	Lay Lady Lay (5)
Drake, Charlie	Splish Splash (7)		Like A Rolling Stone (4)
Dreamers	I Understand (5)		Positively Fourth Street (8)
	If You Gotta Make A Fool Of		Rainy Day Women Nos 12 And
	Somebody (3)		35 (7)
	I'm Telling You Now (2)		Subterranean Homesick Blues
	You Were Made For Me (3)		(9)
Dreamweavers	It's Almost Tomorrow (1)		Times They Are A-Changin' (9)
Drifters	At The Club / Saturday Night At	Dynamite, Ms	Dy-Na-Mi-Tee (5)
	The Movies (3)		It Takes More (7)
	Can I Take You Home Little Girl	E-17	Each Time (2)
	(10)	Eagles	Hotel California (8)
	Come On Over To My Place		Lyin' Eyes (23)
	(re-issue) (9)		One Of These Nights (23)
	Down On The Beach Tonight		Take It To The Limit (12)
	(7)	Earth Wind & Fire	After The Love Has Gone (4)
	High Class Baby (7)		Let's Groove (3)
	Kissin In The Back Row Of The		September (3)
	Movies (2)	Earth Wind & Fire	Boogie Wonderland (4)
	Like Sister And Brother (7)	with Emotions	
	Living Doll (1)	East Of Eden	Jig A Jig (7)
	Mean Streak (10)	East 17	Around The World (7)
	Move It (2)		Deep (5)
	Save The Last Dance For Me		Do U Still (7)
	(2)		Hey Child (3)
	There Goes My First Love (3)		House Of Love (10)
	You're More Than A Number In		If You Ever (2)
	My Little Red Book (5)		It's Alright (3)
Driscoll, Julie	This Wheel's On Fire (5)		Let It Rain (10)
Driver 67	Car 67 (7)		Stay Another Day (1)
Dru Hill	How Deep Is Your Love (9)		Steam (7)
	These Are The Times (4)		Thunder (4)
	Wild Wild West (2)	East Side Beat	Ride Like The Wind (3)
Duane Eddy	Ballad Of Paladin (10)	Easton, Sheena	For Your Eyes Only (8)
	Because They're Young (2)		Modern Girl (8)
	Dance With Guitar Man (4)		9 To 5 (3)
	Pepe (2)	Easybeats	Friday On My Mind (6)
	Peter Gunn (8)	Echo And The	Cutter, The (8)
	Peter Gunn Theme (6)	Bunnymen	Killing Moon (9)
	Play Me Like You Play Your		Nothing Lasts Forever (8)
	Guitar (9)	Echobeatz	Mas Que Nada (10)
	Shazam! (4)	Eckstine, Billy	Gigi (8)
	Theme From Dixie (7)		No One But You (3)
Dubliners	Irish Rover, The (8)		Circus, The (6)
	Seven Drunken Nights (7)		Crackers International EP (2)
Duke D'Mond	Call Up The Groups (3)		Drama! (4)
	Merry Gentle Pops (9)		Little Respect, A (4)
	Pop Go The Workers (5)		Love To Hate You (4)
Dulfer, Candy	Lily Was Here (6)		Run To The Sun (6)

Group/Artiste	Title	Group/Artiste	Title
	Ship Of Fools (6)		Claudette (1)
	Sometimes (2)		Bird Dog (2)
	Victim Of Love (7)		Bye Bye Love (6)
	Who Needs Love Like That (10)		Cathy's Clown (1)
Ellis Bextor, Sophie	Music Gets The Best Of Me (14)		Cryin' In The Rain (6)
Eric Jupp & His Orchestra	This Ole House (4)		Lucille / So Sad (To Watch Good Love Go Bad) (4)
Eric Rodgers & His Orchestra	You Need Hands / Tulips From Amsterdam (3)		Price Of Love, The (2)
Eruption	I Can't Stand The Rain (5)		Problems (6)
	One Way Ticket (9)		Temptation (1)
Essex, David	Gonna Make You A Star (1)		(Til) I Kissed You (2)
	Hold Me Close (1)		Wake Up Little Susie (2)
	Lamplight (7)		Walk Right Back / Ebony Eyes (1)
	Oh What A Circus (3)		When Will I Be Loved (4)
	Rock On (3)	Everly, Phil	She Means Nothing To Me (9)
	Rolling Stone (5)	Everything But The Girl	I Don't Want To Talk About It (3)
	Silver Dream Machine (4)		Missing (remix) (3)
	Stardust (7)		Walking Wounded (6)
	Tahiti (8)		Wrong (8)
	Winter's Tale, A (2)	Exile	Kiss You All Over (6)
Estefan, Gloria	Anything For You (10)	Extreme	More Than Words (2)
	Can't Stay Away From You (7)	FAB	Thunderbirds Are Go (5)
	Don't Wanna Lose You (6)	Faces	Cindy Incidentally (2)
	Heaven's What I Feel (4)		Pool Hall Richard / I Wish It Would Rain (8)
	Miami Hit Mix / Christmas Through Your Eyes (8)		Stay With Me (6)
	1-2-3 (9)	Fagin, Joe	That's Livin' Alright (3)
Estelle, Don	Whispering Grass (1)	Fair Weather	Natural Sinner (6)
Esther & Abi Ofarim	Cinderella Rockefella (1)	Eddie & The Hotrods	Do Anything You Wanna Do (9)
Eternal	Angel Of Mine (4)	Edelweiss	Bring Me Edelweiss (5)
	Don't You Love Me (3)	Edison Lighthouse	Love Grows (Where My Rosemary Goes) (1)
	Good Thing (8)		
	I Am Blessed (7)	Edmund Hockridge	Young And Foolish (10)
	I Wanna Be The Only One (1)	Edmunds, Dave	Baby I Love You (8)
	Just A Step From Heaven (8)		Born To Be With You (5)
	Oh Baby I ... (4)		Girls Talk (4)
	Power Of A Woman (5)		I Hear You Knocking (1)
	Save Our Love (8)	Edwards, Rupie	Ire Feelings (Skanga) (9)
	Secrets (9)	Edwards, Tommy	It's All In The Game (1)
	Someday (4)	Eels	Novocaine For The Soul (10)
	Stay (4)		Susan's House (9)
Europe	Final Countdown, The (1)	Eiffel 65	Blue (Da Ba Dee) (1)
Eurythmics	Here Comes The Rain Again (8)		Move Your Body (3)
	Love Is A Stranger (6)	808 State	Cubik / Olympic (10)
	Right By Your Side (10)		In Yer Face (9)
	Sexcrime (Nineteen Eighty-Four) (4)		Only Rhyme That Bites, The (10)
	Sisters Are Doin' It For Themselves (9)		Pacific (10)
	Sweet Dreams (Are Made Of This) (2)	Eighth Wonder	I'm Not Scared (7)
	There Must Be An Angel (Playing With My Heart) (1)	Eirc Jupp & His Orchestra	Mobile (4)
	Thorn In My Side (5)	Elbert, Donnie	Where Did Our Love Go (8)
	Who's That Girl (3)	Electric Light Orchestra	Confusion / Last Train To London (8)
Evans, Faith	I'll Be Missing You (1)		Diary Of Horace Wimp, The (8)
Evans, Maureen	Like I Do (3)		Don't Bring Me Down (3)
Evans, Paul	Hello This Is Joanie (The Telephone Answering Machine Song) (6)		Evil Woman (10)
			Hold On Tight (4)
Eve	Caramel (9)		Livin' Thing (4)
	Gangsta Lovin' (6)		Mr Blue Sky (6)
	Let Me Blow Ya Mind (4)		Rockaria! (9)
	Who's That Girl (6)		Roll Over Beethoven (6)
Evelyn 'Champagne' King	Love Come Down (7)		Shine A Little Love (6)
			Sweet Talkin' Woman (6)
Everett, Kenny	Snot Rap (9)		Telephone Line (8)
Everly Brothers	All I Have To Do Is Dream /		10538 Overture (9)
			Wild West Hero (6)
			Xanadu (1)
		Electronic	Disappointed (6)
			Get The Message (8)

M
U
S
I
C

P
O
P

Group/Artiste	Title	Group/Artiste	Title
Element Four	Big Brother UK TV Theme (4)		Shop) (4)
Elgins	Heaven Must Have Sent You (3)		Poor Me (1)
			Someone Else's Baby (2)
Elias & His Zigzag Jive Flutes	Tom Hark (2)		Time Has Come, The (4)
			What Do You Want (1)
Elliman, Yvonne	If I Can't Have You (4)		When Johnny Comes Marching
	Love Me (6)		Home / Made You (5)
Ellington, Duke	Skin Deep (7)		Who Am I / This Is It! (5)
Ellis, Shirley	Clapping Song, The (6)	Faithfull, Marianne	As Tears Go By (9)
Ellis-Bextor, Sophie	Get Over You / Move This		Come And Stay With Me (4)
	Mountain (3)		Summer Nights (10)
	Murder On The Dancefloor (2)		This Little Bird (6)
	Take Me Home (2)	Faithless	God Is A DJ (6)
Embrace	All You Good Good People EP (8)		Insomnia (3)
			One Step Too Far (6)
	Come Back To What You Know (6)		Reverence (10)
			Salva Mea (remix) (9)
	My Weakness Is None Of Your Business (9)		We Come 1 (3)
Emerson Lake & Palmer	Fanfare For The Common Man (2)	Faithweather-Low, Andy	Reggae Tune (10)
			Wide-Eyed And Legless (6)
EMF	I Believe (6)	Falco	Rock Me Amadeus (1)
	I'm A Believer (3)		Vienna Calling (10)
	Unbelievable (3)	Faltermeyer, Harold	Axel F (2)
Emilia	Big Big World (5)	Fame, Georgie	Ballad Of Bonnie And Clyde (1)
Eminem	Cleanin' Out My Closet (4)		Get Away (1)
	Forgot About Dre (7)		Yeh Yeh (1)
	Guilty Conscience (5)	Family	In My Own Time (4)
	Lose Yourself (1)	Family Dogg	Way Of Life (6)
	My Name Is (2)	Family Stand	Ghetto Heaven (10)
	Real Slim Shady, The (1)	Fantastics	Something Old Something New (9)
	Stan (1)	Far Corporation	Stairway To Heaven (8)
	Way I Am, The (8)	Fardon, Don	Indian Reservation (3)
	Without Me (1)	Farley 'Jackmaster' Funk	Love Can't Turn Around (10)
Emmie	More Than This (5)		
Emotions	Best Of My Love (4)	Farlowe, Chris	Out Of Time (1)
	Boogie Wonderland (4)	Farm	All Together Now (4)
En Vogue	Don't Let Go (Love) (5)		Groovy Train (6)
	Hold On (5)	Farnham, John	You're The Voice (6)
	My Lovin' (4)	Fat Boys	Twist (Yo Twist), The (2)
	Whatta Man (7)		Wipeout (2)
Enfield, Harry	Loadsamoney (4)	Fat Joe	What's Luv (4)
England United	(How Does It Feel To Be) On Top Of The World (9)	Fat Larry's Band	Zoom (2)
		Fat Les	Vindaloo (2)
England World Cup Squad	Back Home (1)	Fat Les 2000	Jerusalem (10)
	This Time (We'll Get It Right) / England We'll Fly The Flag (2)	Fatback Band	(Do The) Spanish Hustle (10)
			I Found Lovin' (7)
Englandneworder	World In Motion (1)	Fatboy Slim	Gangster Trippin' (3)
Enigma	Return To Innocence (3)		Praise You (1)
	Sadness Part 1 (1)		Right Here Right Now (2)
Enya	Anywhere Is (7)		Rockafeller Shank, The (6)
	Book Of Days (10)		Star 69 (10)
	Orinoco Flow (1)		Sunset (Bird Of Prey) (9)
Equals	Baby Come Back (1)	Father Abraham	Smurf Song, The (2)
	Black Skin Blue-Eyed Boys (9)	Fatima Mansions	(Everything I Do) I Do It For You (7)
	Viva Bobby Joe (6)		
Erasure	Abba-Esque EP (1)	Fearon, Phil	Dancing Tight (4)
	Always (4)		Everybody's Laughing (10)
	Blue Savannah (3)		I Can Prove It (8)
	Breath Of Life (8)		What Do I Do (5)
	Chorus (3)	Feeder	Buck Rogers (5)
Fair, Yvonne	It Should Have Been Me (5)	Feliciano, Jose	Light My Fire (6)
Fairground Attraction	Find My Love (7)	Felix	Don't You Want Me (6)
	Perfect (1)		Don't You Want Me (remix) (10)
Faith No More	I'm Easy / Be Aggressive (3)	Felly	Pump Up The Jam (2)
	Midlife Crisis (10)	Ferrante & Teicher	Exodus (Theme From 'Exodus') (6)
Faith, Adam	As You Like It (5)		
	Don't That Beat All (8)	Ferrer, Jose	Woman (Uh-Huh) (7)
	First Time, The (5)	Ferry Aid	Let It Be (1)
	How About That! (4)	Ferry, Bryan	Extended Play EP (7)
	Lonely Pup (In A Christmas		Hard Rain's Gonna Fall, A (10)

Group/Artiste	Title	Group/Artiste	Title
	Let's Stick Together (Let's Work Together) (4)	Flint, Berni	I Don't Want To Put A Hold On You (3)
	Slave To Love (10)	Flip & Fill	Shooting Star (3)
	This Is Tomorrow (9)		True Love Never Dies (re-issue) (7)
Fialka, Karel	Hey Matthew (9)		
Fiction Factory	(Feel Like) Heaven (6)	Floaters	Float On (1)
Fiddler's Dram	Day Trip To Bangor (Didn't We Have A Lovely Time) (3)	Flowerpot Men	Let's Go To San Francisco (4)
		Flowers Pops, Mike	Wonderwall (2)
Fields, Gracie	Around The World (8)	Flying Lizards	Money (5)
Fierce	Sweet Love 2K (3)	Flying Pickets	Only You (1)
Fine Young Cannibals	Ever Fallen In Love (9)		(When You're) Young And in Love (7)
	Good Thing (7)		
	Johnny Come Home (8)	Focus	Sylvia (4)
	She Drives Me Crazy (5)	Fontana, Wayne	Game Of Love (2)
	Suspicious Minds (8)		Um Um Um Um Um Um (5)
Fiorillo, Elisa	Who Found Who (10)	Foo Fighters	All My Life (5)
Firm	Star Trekkin' (1)		This Is A Call (5)
First Choice	Smarty Pants (9)	Ford, Emile	Counting Teardrops (4)
First Edition	Ruby Don't Talk Your Love To Town (2)		On a Slow Boat To China (3)
			What Do You Want To Make Those Eyes At Me For (1)
	Something's Burning (8)		
Fisher, Climie	Love Changes Everything (2)	Ford, Mary	Vaya Con Dios (7)
	Rise To The Occasion (10)	Foreigner	I Want To Know What Love Is (1)
Fisher, Eddie	Cindy Oh Cindy (5)		
	Downhearted (3)		Waiting For A Girl Like You (8)
	Everything I Have Is Yours (re-entry) (8)	Forrest	Rock The Boat (4)
		Forte	Rumble In The Jungle (3)
	(I'm Always Hearing) Wedding Bells (5)	Fortune, Lance	Be Mine (4)
		Fortunes	Freedom Come Freedom Go (6)
	I'm Walking Behind You (1)		
	Oh My Papa (9)		Here It Comes Again (4)
	Oh My Papa (re-entry) (10)		Storm In A Teacup (7)
	Outside Of Heaven (1)		You've Got Your Troubles (2)
	Wish You Were Here (8)	40 Thevz	C U When You Get There (3)
Fitzgerald, Scott	If I Had Words (3)	49ers	Touch Me (3)
Five	Closer to Me (4)	Foundations	Baby Now That I've Found You (1)
	Don't Wanna Let You Go (9)		
	Everybody Get Up (2)		Build Me Up Buttercup (2)
	Got The Feelin' (3)		In The Bad Bad Old Days (8)
	If Ya Gettin' Down (2)	Four Aces	Love Is A Many-Splendoured Thing (2)
	Keep On Movin' (1)		
	Let's Dance (1)		Mr Sandman (9)
	Slam Dunk (Da Funk) (10)		Stranger In Paradise (6)
	Until The Time Is Through (2)		Three Coins In The Fountain (5)
	We Will Rock You (1)		
	When The Lights Go Out (4)	Four Knights	I Get So Lonely (5)
Five Star	Can't Wait Another Minute (7)		I Get So Lonely (re-entry) (10)
	Find The Time (7)	Four Lads	Faith Can Move Mountains (7)
	Rain Or Shine (2)		Faith Can Move Mountains (re-entry) (9)
	Slightest Touch, The (4)		
	Stay Out Of My Life (9)		Rain Rain Rain (8)
	System Addict (3)	4 Non Blondes	What's Up (2)
5000 Volts	Dr Kiss Kiss (8)	Four Pennies	Juliet / Tell Me Girl (What Are You Gonna Do) (1)
	I'm On Fire (4)		
Flack, Roberta	Back Together Again (3)	Four Preps	Big Man (2)
	Killing Me Softly With His Song (6)	Four Seasons	December 1963 (Oh What A Night) (1)
	Tonight I Celebrate My Love (2)		Let's Hang On! (4)
Flash & The Pan	Waiting For The Train (7)		Night, The (7)
Fleetwood Mac	Albatross (1)		Rag Doll (2)
	Albatross (re-issue) (2)		Sherry (8)
	Big Love (9)		Silver Star (3)
	Everywhere (4)		Who Loves You (6)
	Green Manalishi, The (With The Two-Pronged Crown) (10)	Four Tops	Bernadette (8)
			I Can't Help Myself (re-issue) (10)
	Little Lies (5)		
	Man Of The World (2)		If I Were A Carpenter (7)
	Oh Diane (9)		It's All In The Game (5)
	Oh Well (2)		Loco In Acapulco (7)
	Tusk (6)		Reach Out I'll Be There (1)
Fleetwoods	Come Softly To Me (6)		Simple Game (3)

MUSIC

POP

Group/Artiste	Title	Group/Artiste	Title
	Standing In The Shadows Of Love (6)		All Right Now (remix) (8)
	Still Water (Love) (10)		Another One Bites The Dust (5)
	Walk Away Renee (3)		My Brother Jake (4)
	When She Was My Girl (3)		Wishing Well (7)
Fourmost	Hello Little Girl (9)	Freeez	I.O.U. (2)
	Little Loving, A (6)		Southern Freeez (8)
Fox	Only You Can (3)	French, Nicki	Total Eclipse Of The Heart (5)
	S-S-Single Bed (4)	Fresh 4	Wishing On A Star (10)
Fox, Samantha	Do Ya Do Ya (Wanna Please Me) (10)	Fresh Prince	Boom! Shake The Room (1)
			Summertime (8)
	Nothing's Gonna Stop Me Now (8)	Friedman, Dean	Lucky Stars (3)
		Frijid Pink	House Of The Rising Sun (4)
	Touch Me (I Want Your Body) (3)	Frog Chorus	We All Stand Together (3)
FPI Project	Going Back To My Roots / Rich In Paradise (9)	Fugees	Killing Me Softly (1)
			No Woman No Cry (2)
Fragma	Everytime You Need Me (3)		Ready Or Not (1)
	Toca's Miracle (1)		Rumble In The Jungle (3)
	You Are Alive (4)	Full Force	Alice I Want You Just For Me (9)
Frampton, Peter	Show Me The Way (10)	Fun Boy Three	It Ain't What You Do It's The Way That You Do It (4)
Francis, Connie	Carolina Moon / Stupid Cupid (1)		
			Our Lips Are Sealed (7)
	Everybody's Somebody's Fool (5)		Really Saying Something (5)
			Tunnel Of Love (10)
	Lipstick On Your Collar (3)	Fun Lovin' Criminals	Loco (5)
	Mama / Robot Man (2)	Funk Masters	It's Over (8)
	My Happiness (4)	Funkadelic	One Nation Under A Groove (9)
	My Heart Has A Mind Of It's Own (3)	Funkstar De Luxe	Sun Is Shining (3)
		Furious Five	Message, The (8)
	Together (6)		Step Off (Part 1) (8)
	Vacation (10)	Furtado, Nelly	I'm Like A Bird (5)
	Where The Boys Are / Baby Roo (5)		Turn Off The Light (4)
		Fury, Billy	Colette (9)
	Who's Sorry Now (1)		Halfway To Paradise (3)
Frank Weir Orchestra	My Son My Son (1)		I'd Never Find Another You (5)
Frankie Goes To Hollywood	Power Of Love (re-issue), The (6)		In Summer (5)
			In Thoughts Of You (9)
	Power Of Love (re-issue), The (10)		It's Only Make Believe (10)
			Jealousy (2)
	Power Of Love, The (1)		Last Night Was Made For Love (4)
	Rage Hard (4)		
	Relax (1)		Like I've Never Been Gone (3)
	Relax (re-issue) (5)		Once Upon A Dream (7)
	Two Tribes (1)		When Will You Say I Love You (3)
	Welcome To The Pleasure Dome (2)	Fyson, Leslie	Signature Tune Of 'The Army Game', The (5)
Frankie Lymon & Teenagers	Baby Baby (4)	G, Ali	Me Julie (2)
	Why Do Fools Fall In Love (1)	G, Dario	Carnaval De Paris (5)
Franklin, Aretha	Deeper Love, A (5)		Dream To Me (9)
	I Knew You Were Waiting (For Me) (1)		Sunchyme (2)
		G, Gina	Fresh! (6)
	I Say A Little Prayer (4)		I Belong To You (6)
	Respect (10)		Ooh Aah ... Just A Little Bit (1)
	Sisters Are Doin' It For Themselves (9)	G, Warren	I Shot The Sheriff (2)
			Regulate (5)
	Spanish Harlem (14)		What's Love Got To Do With It (2)
Franklin, Erma	(Take A Little) Piece Of My Heart (9)		
		Gabriel, Peter	Don't Give Up (9)
Franklin, Rodney	Groove, The (7)		Games Without Frontiers (4)
Frantique	Strut Your Funky Stuff (10)		Sledgehammer (4)
Freak Power	Turn On Tune In Cop Out (re-issue) (3)		Steam (10)
		Gabrielle	Don't Need The Sun To Shine (To Make Me Smile) (9)
Freddie	I Understand (5)		
	If You Gotta Make A Fool Of Somebody (3)		Dreams (1)
			Give Me A Little More Time (5)
	I'm Telling You Now (2)		Going Nowhere (9)
	You Were Made For Me (3)		If You Ever (2)
Freddie Bell & The Bellboys	Giddy-Up-A-Ding-Dong (4)		Out Of Reach (4)
			Rise (1)
Free	All Right Now (2)		Sunshine (9)
			Walk On By (7)

Group/Artiste	Title	Group/Artiste	Title
	When A Woman (6)		Invisible Touch (live) (7)
Gaines, Rosie	Closer Than Close (4)		Mama (4)
Gainsbourg, Serge	Je T'Aime ... Moi Non Plus (2)		No Son Of Mine (6)
	Je T'Aime ... Moi Non Plus (re-issue) (1)		3 x 3 EP (10)
			Turn It On Again (8)
Gala	Freed From Desire (3)	Gentry, Bobbie	All I Have To Do Is Dream (3)
Galaxy	Dancing Tight (4)		I'll Never Fall In Love Again (1)
	Everybody's Laughing (10)	Geordie	All Because Of You (6)
	What Do I Do (5)	George, Boy	Everything I Own (1)
Gali Atari	Hallelujah (5)	George, Sophia	Girlie Girlie (7)
Gallagher & Lyle	Heart On My Sleeve (6)	Gerry & The	Don't Let The Sun Catch You
	I Wanna Stay With You (6)	Pacemakers	Crying (6)
Gallagher, Liam &	Carnation (6)		Ferry Cross The Mersey (8)
Steve Cradock			How Do You Do It (1)
Gallant, Patsy	From New York To L.A. (6)		I Like It (1)
Galway, James	Annie's Song (3)		I'm The One (2)
Gap Band	Big Fun (4)		You'll Never Walk Alone (1)
	Oops Up Side Your Head (6)	Ghostface Killah	I Want You For Myself (2)
Garbage	I Think I'm Paranoid (9)	Gibb, Andy	An Everlasting Love (10)
	Milk (10)	Gibb, Robin	Saved By The Bell (2)
	Push It (9)	Gibson Brothers	Ohh! What A Life (10)
	Shut Your Mouth (20)		Que Sera Mi Vida (5)
	Stupid Girl (4)	Gibson, Debbie	Foolish Beat (9)
	When I Grow Up (9)		Shake Your Love (7)
Gardiner, Boris	I Want To Wake Up With You (1)	Gilstrap, Jim	Swing Your Daddy (4)
		Ginuwine	What's So Different (10)
Garfunkel, Art	Bright Eyes (1)		When Doves Cry (10)
	I Only Have Eyes For You (1)	Giorgio Moroder	Together In Electric Dreams (3)
Garrett, Leif	I Was Made For Dancin' (4)	Girl Thing	Last One Standing (8)
Gary Clail On	Human Nature (10)	Girls Aloud	Sound Of The Underground (1)
U-Sound System		Girlschool	St Valentine's Day Massacre
Gary US Bonds	Quarter To Three (7)		EP (5)
Gary's Gang	Keep On Dancin' (8)	Glamma Kid	Taboo (10)
Gaskin, Barbara	It's My Party (1)		Why (10)
Gat Decor	Passion (remix) (6)	Glen Somers & His	Pickin' A Chicken (9)
Gately, Stephen	Baby Can I Hold You /	Orchestra	
	Shooting Star (2)	Glitter Band	Angel Face (4)
	New Beginning / Bright Eyes (3)		Goodbye My Love (2)
Gates, Gareth	Anyone Of Us (Stupid Mistake) (1)		Just For You (10)
			Let's Get Together Again (8)
	Long And Winding Road, The / Suspicious Minds (1)		People Like You People Like Me (5)
	Unchained Melody (1)		Tears I Cried, The (8)
	What My Heart Wants To Say (5)	Glitter, Gary	Always Yours (1)
Gay Dad	To Earth With Love (10)		Another Rock And Roll Christmas (7)
Gaye, Marvin	Abraham Martin And John (9)		Do You Wanna Touch Me? (Oh Yeah) (2)
	Got To Give It Up (7)		Doing Alright With The Boys (6)
	I Heard It Through The Grapevine (1)		Hello Hello I'm Back Again (2)
	I Heard It Through The Grapevine (re-issue) (8)		I Didn't Know I Loved You (Til I Saw You Rock 'N' Roll) (4)
	Onion Song (9)		I Love You Love Me Love (1)
	(Sexual) Healing (4)		I'm The Leader Of The Gang (I Am) (1)
	Too Busy Thinking 'Bout My Baby (5)		Love Like You And Me (10)
	You Are Everything (5)		Oh Yes! You're Beautiful (2)
Gayle, Crystal	Don't It Make My Brown Eyes Blue (5)		Remember Me This Way (3)
Gayle, Michelle	Do You Know (6)		Rock And Roll (Parts 1 And 2) (2)
	Sweetness (4)	Gloworm	Carry Me Home (9)
Gaynor, Gloria	I Will Survive (1)	Go West	We Close Our Eyes (5)
	I Will Survive (remix) (5)	Godley & Creme	Under Your Thumb (3)
	Never Can Say Goodbye (2)		Wedding Bells (7)
Gazza	Fog On The Tyne (Revisited) (2)	Gold, Andrew	Never Let Her Slip Away (5)
		Gold, Brian	Compliments On Your Kiss (2)
GB Experience	Crown, The (6)	Gold, Tony	Compliments On Your Kiss (2)
General Levy	Incredible (remix) (8)	Goldbug	Whole Lotta Love (3)
Genesis	Abacab (9)	Golden Earring	Radar Love (7)
	Follow You Follow Me (7)	Goldie	Making Up Again (7)
	I Can't Dance (7)		

Group/Artiste	Title
Goldsboro, Bobby	Honey (2)
	Honey (re-issue) (2)
	Summer (The First Time) (9)
Goldsmith, Glen	Dreaming (9)
Goldtrix presents Andrea Brown	It's Love (Trippin') (6)
Goodies	Funky Gibbon / Sick Man Blues (4)
	In Betweenies, The / Father Christmas Do Not Touch Me (7)
Goodmen	Give It Up (re-entry) (5)
Goodwin, Ron Orchestra	Terry's Theme From Limelight (3)
Goombay Dance Band	Seven Tears (1)
Goons	Bloodnok's Rock 'N' Roll Call / Ying Tong Song (3)
	I'm Walking Backwards For Christmas / Bluebottle Blues (4)
	Ying Tong Song (re-issue) (9)
Gordon, Lonnie	Happenin' All Over Again (4)
Gore, Lesley	It's My Party (9)
Gorillaz	Clint Eastwood (4)
	19 / 2000 (6)
Gorme, Eydie	Yes My Darling Daughter (10)
Goulding, Nigel	Full Metal Jacket (I Wanna Be Your Drill Instructor) (2)
Grace	Not Over Yet (6)
Gracie, Charlie	Fabulous (8)
	Wanderin' Eyes (6)
Graham, Jaki	Could It Be I'm Falling In Love (5)
	Round And Round (9)
	Set Me Free (7)
Grandmaster	White Lines (Don't Do It) (7)
Grandmaster Flash	Message, The (8)
Grandmaster Melle Mel	Step Off (Part 1) (8)
Grange Hill Cast	Just Say No (5)
Grant, Amy	Baby Baby (2)
Grant, David	Could It Be I'm Falling In Love (5)
	Watching Me Watching You (10)
Grant, Eddy	Do You Feel My Love (8)
	Electric Avenue (2)
	Electric Avenue (remix) (5)
	Gimme Hope Jo'Anna (7)
	I Don't Wanna Dance (1)
Grant, Gogi	Wayward Wind (9)
Gray, David	Babylon (5)
Gray, Macy	I Try (7)
Green Day	Basket Case (7)
Green Jelly	Three Little Pigs (5)
Green, Al	Let's Stay Together (7)
	Tired Of Being Alone (4)
Greenbaum, Norman	Spirit In The Sky (1)
Greyhound	Black And White (6)
Grid	Swamp Thing (3)
Gun	Race With The Devil (8)
	Word Up (8)
Guns 'N' Roses	Ain't It Fun (9)
	Don't Cry (8)
	Knockin' On Heaven's Door (2)
	Live And Let Die (5)
	November Rain (4)
	Paradise City (6)
	Patience (10)

Group/Artiste	Title
	Since I Don't Have You (10)
	Sweet Child O' Mine (remix) (6)
	Sympathy For The Devil (9)
	Yesterdays / November Rain (8)
	You Could Be Mine (3)
Guru Josh	Infinity (5)
Gurvitz, Adrian	Classic (8)
Gusto	Disco's Revenge (9)
Guthrie, Gwen	Ain't Nothing Goin' On But The Rent (5)
Guys & Dolls	There's A Whole Lot Of Loving (2)
	You Don't Have To Say You Love Me (5)
H & Claire	All Out Of Love / Beauty And The Beast (10)
	DJ (3)
	Half A Heart (8)
Haddaway	I Miss You (9)
	Life (6)
	Rock My Heart (9)
	What Is Love (2)
Haircut 100	Fantastic Day (9)
	Favourite Shirts (Boy Meets Girl) (4)
	Love Plus One (3)
	Nobody's Fool (9)
Hale & Pace & The Stonkers	Stonk, The (1)
Halliwell, Geri	Bag It Up (1)
	Calling (7)
	It's Raining Men (1)
	Lift Me Up (1)
	Look At Me (2)
	Mi Chico Latino (1)
	Scream If You Wanna Go Faster (8)
Halo James	Could Have Told You So (6)
Hamilton, Lynne	On The Inside (3)
Hamilton, Russ	We Will Make Love (2)
Hammer, Jan	Crockett's Theme (2)
	Miami Vice Theme (5)
Hancock, Herbie	Rockit (8)
Hanson	I Will Come To You (5)
	Mmmbop (1)
	Where's The Love (4)
Happy Clappers	I Believe (re-issue) (7)
Happy Mondays	Kinky Afro (5)
	Step On (5)
Hardcastle, Paul	Don't Waste My Time (8)
	Nineteen (1)
Harlem Community Choir	Happy Xmas (War Is Over) (4)
	Happy Xmas (War Is Over) (re-entry) (2)
Harley, Steve	Here Comes The Sun (10)
	Make Me Smile (Come Up And See Me) (1)
	Phantom Of The Opera, The (7)
Harris, Anita	Just Loving You (6)
Harris, Jet	Applejack (4)
	Diamonds (1)
	Scarlett O'Hara (2)
Harris, Niki	Do You See The Light (Looking For) (10)
	Exterminate (2)
Harris, Richard	Macarthur Park (4)
Harris, Rolf	Stairway To Heaven (7)
	Sun Arise (3)
	Tie Me Kangaroo Down Sport

MUSIC POP

Group/Artiste	Title	Group/Artiste	Title
	Knock Knock Who's There (2)		Oh My Papa (re-entry) (10)
	Temma Harbour (6)		Outside Of Heaven (1)
	Those Were The Days (1)	Human League	Being Boiled (6)
Hot Butter	Popcorn (5)		Don't You Want Me (1)
Hot Chocolate	Brother Louie (7)		Human (8)
	Child's Prayer, A (7)		(Keep Feeling) Fascination (2)
	Emma (3)		Love Action (I Believe In Love)
	Girl Crazy (7)		(3)
	I Believe (In Love) (8)		Mirror Man (2)
	It Started With A Kiss (5)		Open Your Heart (6)
	Love Is Life (6)		Tell Me When (6)
	No Doubt About It (2)	Humble Pie	Natural Born Bugie (4)
	Put Your Love In Me (10)	Humperdinck,	Am I That Easy To Forget (3)
	So You Win Again (1)	Engelbert	Last Waltz, The (1)
	What Kinda Boy You Looking		Les Bicyclettes De Belsize (5)
	For Girl (10)		Man Without Love, A (2)
	You Sexy Thing (2)		Release Me (1)
	You Sexy Thing (re-issue) (6)		There Goes My Everything (2)
	You Sexy Thing (remix) (10)		Way It Used To Be, The (3)
Hot Gossip	I Lost My Heart To A Starship		Winter World Of Love (7)
	Trooper (6)	Hunter, Tab	99 Ways (5)
Hot 'N' Juicy	Horny (2)		Young Love (1)
Hotlegs	Neanderthal Man (2)	Hutton, June	Say You're Mine Again (10)
Hotshots	Snoopy Vs The Red Baron (4)		Say You're Mine Again (re-
Houghton, Steven	Wind Beneath My Wings (3)		entry) (6)
House Of Pain	Jump Around (re-issue) / Top	Hyland, Brian	Ginny Come Lately (5)
	O' The Morning (8)		Itsy Bitsy Teeny Weeny Yellow
Housemartins	Caravan Of Love (1)		Polka Dot Bikini (8)
	Happy Hour (3)		Sealed With A Kiss (3)
Housemaster Boyz	House Nation (re-entry) (8)		Sealed With A Kiss (re-issue)
Houston, Whitney	Could I Have This Kiss Forever		(7)
	(7)	Hyman Trio, Dick	Theme From The Threepenny
	Greatest Love Of All (8)		Opera (9)
	How Will I Know (5)	Hynde, Chrissie	Breakfast In Bed (6)
	I Have Nothing (3)		I Got You Babe (1)
	I Wanna Dance With		Love Can Build A Bridge (1)
	Somebody (Who Loves Me)	Ian Dury & The	Hit Me With Your Rhythm Stick
	(1)	Blockheads	(1)
	I Will Always Love You (1)		Reasons To Be Cheerful (Part
	If I Told You That (9)		3) (3)
	I'm Every Woman (4)		What A Waste (9)
	I'm Your Baby Tonight (5)	Idlewild	You Held The World In Your
	It's Not Right But It's OK (3)		Arms (9)
	Love Will Save The Day (10)	Idol, Billy	Mony Mony (7)
	My Love Is Your Love (2)		Rebel Yell (6)
	One Moment In Time (1)		White Wedding (6)
	Saving All My Love For You (1)	Ifield, Frank	Confessin' (1)
	So Emotional (5)		Don't Blame Me (8)
	When You Believe (4)		I Remember You (1)
Howard, Adina	What's Love Got To Do With It		Lovesick Blues (1)
	(2)		Nobody's Darlin' But Mine (4)
Howard, Billy	King Of The Cops (6)		Wayward Wind (1)
Hudson-Ford	Pick Up The Pieces (8)	Iglesias, Enrique	Bailamos (4)
Hue & Cry	Labour Of Love (3)		Could I Have This Kiss Forever
Hues Corporation	Rock The Boat (6)		(7)
Huey Lewis & The	Power Of Love /		Escape (3)
News	Do You Believe In Love (re-		Hero (1)
	issue), The (9)		Maybe (12)
Hugo Montenegro	Good The Bad And The Ugly,	Iglesias, Julio	Begin The Beguine (1)
	The (1)		My Love (5)
Hugo Winterhalter	Naughty Lady Of Shady Lane		Quiereme Mucho (Yours) (3)
	(6)	IIO	Rapture (2)
Hugo Winterhalter's	Downhearted (3)	Ike	Nutbush City Limits (4)
Orchestra	I'm Walking Behind You (1)		River Deep Mountain High (3)
	Wish You Were Here (8)	Imagination	Body Talk (4)
	Cindy Oh Cindy (5)		Just An Illusion (2)
	Everything I Have Is Yours		Music And Lights (5)
	(re-entry) (8)	Imbruglia, Natalie	Big Mistake (2)
	(I'm Always Hearing) Wedding		Smoke (5)
	Bells (5)		Torn (2)
	Oh My Papa (9)		Wrong Impression (10)

M
U
S
I
C

P
O
P

	Start (1)	Joel, Billy	An Innocent Man (8)
	Town Called Malice / Precious (1)		River Of Dreams, The (3)
Jam & Spoon	Right In The Night (Fall In Love With Music) (re-issue) (10)		Tell Her About It (4)
			Uptown Girl (1)
Jamelia	Money (5)		We Didn't Start The Fire (7)
James	She's A Star (9)	John Barry Seven	Hit And Miss (10)
	Sit Down (2)	John Fred & Playboy Band	Judy In Disguise (With Glasses) (3)
	Sit Down (remix) (7)		
	Sound (9)	John, Elton	Blue Eyes (8)
James, Etta	I Just Want To Make Love To You (5)		Candle In The Wind 97 / Something About The Way You Look Tonight (1)
James, Tommy	Mony Mony (1)		Candle In The Wind (re-issue) (5)
Jamiroquai	Alright (6)		
	Canned Heat (4)		Crocodile Rock (5)
	Cosmic Girl (6)		Daniel (4)
	Deeper Underground (1)		Don't Go Breaking My Heart (1)
	Little L (5)		Don't Go Breaking My Heart (7) with RuPaul & Kiki Dee
	Love Foolosophy (14)		
	Stillness In Time (9)		Don't Let The Sun Go Down On Me (1)
	Too Young To Die (10)		
	Virtual Insanity (3)		Goodbye Yellow Brick Road (6)
Janet	Feel It Boy (9)		I Guess That's Why They Call It The Blues (5)
	What's It Gonna Be?! (6)		
Jankowski, Horst	Walk In The Black Forest, A (3)		I Want Love (9)
Japan	Ghosts (5)		I'm Still Standing (4)
	I Second That Emotion (9)		Live Like Horses (9)
Jarre, Jean-Michel	Oxygene Part IV (4)		Lucy In The Sky With Diamonds (10)
Jarreau, Al	Moonlighting Theme (8)		
Jay-Z	Hard Knock Life (Ghetto Anthem) (2)		Nikita (3)
			One, The (10)
	Heartbreaker (5)		Passengers (5)
	I'll Be (9)		Pinball Wizard (7)
Jazzy Jeff	Boom! Shake The Room (1)		Rocket Man (2)
	Summertime (8)		Sacrifice (re-issue) / Healing Hands (re-issue) (1)
Jean, Wyclef	Another One Bites The Dust (5)		
	Gone Till November (3)		Sad Songs (Say So Much) (7)
	It Doesn't Matter (3)		Saturday Night's Alright For Fighting (7)
	911 (9)		
	Perfect Gentleman (4)		Song For Guy (4)
Jeff Wayne's War Of The Worlds	Eve Of War (remix), The (3)		Sorry Seems To Be The Hardest Word (1)
	Forever Autumn (5)		
Jellybean	Who Found Who (10)		True Love (2)
Jesus & Mary Chain	April Skies (8)		Written In The Stars (10)
	Reverence (10)		Your Song (4) with Alessandro Safina
Jethro Tull	Living In The Past (3)		
	Sweet Dream (7)		Your Song (7)
	Teacher / The Witches Promise (4)	Johnny & The Hurricanes	Beatnik Fly (8)
			Down Yonder (8)
Jets	Crush On You (5)		Red River Rock (3)
Jigsaw	Sky High (9)		Rocking Goose (3)
Jilted John	Jilted John (4)	Johnny Hates Jazz	Shattered Dreams (5)
Jimmy Boyd & Frankie Laine	Tell Me A Story (5)	Johnny Johnson & The Bandwagon	(Blame It) On The Pony Express (7)
Jimmy James & The Vagabonds	Now Is The Time (5)		Breakin' Down The Walls Of Heartache (4)
			Sweet Inspiration (10)
Jive Bunny & The Mastermixers	Can Can You Party (8)		Theme From Z Cars (8)
	Let's Party (1)	Johnny Keating Orchestra	
	Swing The Mood (1)		
	That Sounds Good To Me (4)	Johnny Kidd & The Pirates	I'll Never Get Over You (4)
	That's What I Like (1)		Shakin' All Over (1)
JJ	Ain't No Stoppin Us (8)	Johnny Pearson Orchestra	Sleepy Shores (8)
	Masterblaster 2000 (5)		
Jo Boxers	Boxer Beat (3)	Johnson, Andreas	Glorious (4)
	Just Got Lucky (7)	Johnson, Holly	Americanos (4)
Jo Jo Gunne	Run Run Run (6)		Ferry 'Cross The Mersey (1)
Joan Jett & The Blackhearts	I Love Rock 'N' Roll (4)		Love Train (4)
		Johnson, Laurie	Sucu Sucu (9)
Joe	Stutter (7)	Johnson, Marv	I'll Pick A Rose For My Rose (10)
Joe Brown & The Bruvvers	It Only Took A Minute (6)		
	Picture Of You, A (2)		You Got What It Takes (7)
	That's What Love Will Do (3)	Johnson, Paul	Get Get Down (5)

Group/Artiste	Title
Johnson, Romina	Movin' Too Fast (2)
Johnston Brothers	Hernando's Hideaway (1)
	Join In And Sing Again (9)
	Oh Happy Day (4)
Johnston, Sabrina	Peace (8)
Jon & Vangelis	I Hear You Now (8)
	I'll Find My Way Home (6)
Jonathan Richman	Egyptian Reggae (5)
Jones, Aled	Walking In The Air (5)
Jones, Donell	U Know What's Up (2)
Jones, Howard	Like To Get To Know You Well (4)
	Look Mama (10)
	New Song (3)
	Pearl In The Shell (7)
	Things Can Only Get Better (6)
	What Is Love (2)
Jones, Jesus	Devil You Know, The (10)
	International Bright Young Thing (7)
Jones, Jimmy	Good Timin' (1)
	Handy Man (3)
Jones, Paul	High Time (4)
	I've Been A Bad Bad Boy (5)
Jones, Tammy	Let Me Try Again (5)
Jones, Tom	Boy From Nowhere, A (2)
	Burning Down The House (7)
	Daughter Of Darkness (5)
	Delilah (2)
	Detroit City (8)
	Funny Familiar Forgotten Feeling (7)
	Green Green Grass Of Home (1)
	Help Yourself (5)
	I'll Never Fall In Love Again (2)
	I'm Coming Home (2)
	It's Not Unusual (1)
	Kiss (5)
	Love Me Tonight (9)
	Mama Told Me Not To Come (4)
	Sexbomb (3)
	Till (2)
	Without Love (10)
	Young New Mexican Puppeteer, The (6)
Jones-Davies, Sue	OK? (10)
JT & The Big Family	Moments In Soul (7)
Judge Dread	Big Seven (8)
	Je T'Aime (Moi Non Plus) (9)
Junior	Another Step (Closer To You) (6)
	Mama Used To Say (7)
Justice, Jimmy	Ain't That Funny (8)
	When My Little Girl Is Smiling (9)
Justified Ancients Of Mu Mu	It's Grim Up North (10)
JX	Son Of A Gun (remix) (6)
	There's Nothing I Won't Do (4)
JXL	Little Less Conversation, A (1)
K7	Come Baby Come (3)
Kaci	I Think I Love You (10)
Kajagoogoo	Big Apple (8)
	Ooh To Be Ah (7)
	Too Shy (1)
Kalin Twins	When (1)
Kallen, Kitty	Little Things Mean A Lot (1)
Kamen, Nick	Each Time You Break My Heart (5)
Kamoze, Ini	Here Comes The Hotstepper

Group/Artiste	Title
	(4)
Kandi	Don't Think I'm Not (9)
Kane, Eden	Boys Cry (8)
	Forget Me Not (3)
	Get Lost (10)
	I Don't Know Why (7)
	Well I Ask You (1)
Kaoma	Lambada (4)
Kate Robbins & Beyond	More Than In Love (2)
Katrina & The Waves	Love Shine A Light (3)
	Walking On Sunshine (8)
Kavana	I Can Make You Feel Good (8)
	MFEO (8)
Kay, Janet	Silly Games (2)
Kaye Sisters	Come Softly To Me (9)
	Gotta Have Something In The Bank Frank (8)
	Gotta Have Something In The Bank Frank (8) with Frankie Vaughan
	Paper Roses (7)
Kaye, Danny	Wonderful Copenhagen (5)
KC & The Sunshine Band	Give It Up (1)
	Please Don't Go (3)
	Queen Of Clubs (7)
	That's The Way (I Like It) (4)
K-Ci & JoJo	All My Life (8)
Keating, Johnny	Don't That Beat All (8)
Keating, Ronan	I Love It When We Do (5)
	If Tomorrow Never Comes (1)
	Life is A Rollercoaster (1)
	Lovin' Each Day (2)
	Way You Make Me Feel, The (6)
	We've Got Tonight (4)
	When You Say Nothing At All (1)
Keely, Yvonne	If I Had Words (3)
Keith Harris & Orville	Orville's Song (4)
Kelis	Caught Out There (4)
Keller, Jerry	Here Comes Summer (1)
Kelly, Grace	True Love (4)
Kelly, R	Be Careful (7)
	Bump 'N' Grind (8)
	Gotham City (9)
	I Believe I Can Fly (1)
	If I Could Turn Back The Hands Of Time (3)
	I'm Your Angel (3)
	Satisfy You (8)
	She's Got That Vibe (3)
	World's Greatest, The (4)
Ken Mackintosh Orchestra	Creep (re-entry), The (10)
Ken Thorne Orchestra	Theme From The Film The Legion's Last Patrol (4)
Kenny	Bump, The (3)
	Fancy Pants (4)
	Julie Ann (10)
Kenyon, Carol	Don't Waste My Time (8)
Kershaw, Nik	Don Quixote (10)
	I Won't Let The Sun Go Down On Me (2)
	Riddle, The (3)
	Wide Boy (9)
	Wouldn't It Be Good (4)
Keynotes	Memories Are Made Of This (5)
Keys, Alicia	Fallin' (3)
	Gangsta Lovin' (6)
Khan, Chaka	Ain't Nobody (8)

M
U
S
I
C

P
O
P

	Ain't Nobody (remix) (6)	Kongos, John	He's Gonna Step On You Again (4)
	I Feel For You (1)		Tokoloshe Man (4)
	I'm Every Woman (remix) (8)	Kool & The Gang	Celebration (7)
Kicks Like A Mule	Bouncer, The (7)		Cherish (4)
Kid Creole & The Coconuts	Annie I'm Not Your Daddy (2)		Get Down On It (3)
	I'm a Wonderful Thing Baby (4)		Joanna / Tonight (2)
	Me No Pop (32)		Ladies Knight (9)
	Stool Pigeon (7)		Ooh La La La (Let's Go Dancin') (6)
Kidman, Nicole	Somethin' Stupid (1)		(When You Say You Love Somebody) In The Heart (7)
Kids From Fame	Hi-Fidelity (5)	Korgis	Everybody's Got To Learn Sometime (5)
	Starmaker (3)	Kosheen	Hide U (6)
Kim, Andy	Rock Me Gently (2)	Kowdean	Dem Girlz (I Don't Know Why) (10)
King	Alone Without You (8)	KP	Go For The Eyes (2)
	Love And Pride (2)	Kraftwerk	Autobahn (11)
King Brothers	Standing On The Corner (4)		Computer Love / The Model (re-entry) (1)
	White Sport Coat, A (6)	Kramer, Billy J and The Dakotas	Bad To Me (1)
King, B B	When Love Comes To Town (6)		Do You Want To Know A Secret (2)
King, Ben E	Stand By Me (re-issue) (1)		From A Window (10)
King, Carole	It Might As Well Rain Until September (3)		I'll Keep You Satisfied (4)
	It's Too Late (6)		Little Children (1)
King, Dave	Memories Are Made Of This (5)	Kravitz, Lenny	Are You Gonna Go My Way (4)
King, Diana	Shy Guy (2)		Fly Away (1)
King, Jonathan	Everyone's Gone To The Moon (4)	Kris Kross	Jump (2)
		Kroeger, Chad	Hero (4)
	Una Paloma Blanca (5)	Krush	House Arrest (3)
King, Solomon	She Wears My Ring (3)	Kula Shaker	Govinda (7)
Kingston Trio	Tom Dooley (5)		Hey Dude (2)
Kinks	All Day And All Of The Night (2)		Hush (2)
	Apeman (5)		Sound Of Drums (3)
	Autumn Almanac (3)		Tattva (4)
	Dead End Street (5)	KWS	Please Don't Go / Game Boy (1)
	Dedicated Follower Of Fashion (4)		Rock Your Baby (8)
	Lola (2)	Kyu Sakamoto	Sukiyaki (6)
	See My Friend (10)	La Belle Epoque	Black Is Black (2)
	Set Me Free (9)	LA Mix	Check This Out (6)
	Sunny Afternoon (1)	La Na Nee Nee Noo Noo	Help (3)
	Till The End Of The Day (8)		
	Tired Of Waiting For You (1)	La Salle, Denise	My Toot Toot (6)
	Waterloo Sunset (2)	La Trec	Stay (2)
	You Really Got Me (1)	LaBelle, Patti	On My Own (2)
Kinney, Fern	Together We Are Beautiful (1)	Lain	Battle (10)
Kinshasa Band	Black Superman (Muhammad Ali) (7)	Laine, Cleo	You'll Answer To Me (5)
Kirby, Kathy	Let Me Go Lover (10)	Laine, Frankie	Answer Me (1)
	Secret Love (4)		Blowing Wild (2)
Kiss	Crazy Crazy Nights (4)		Cool Water (2)
	God Gave Rock And Roll To You (4)		Granada (10)
			Granada (re-entry) (9)
Kitt, Eartha	Under The Bridges Of Paris (7)		Hawkeye (7)
K-Klass	Rhythm Is A Mystery (3)		Hey Joe (1)
KLF	America: What Time Is Love (4)		High Noon (Do Not Forsake Me) (7)
	Justified And Ancient (2)		I Believe (1)
	Last Train To Trancentral (2)		Kid's Last Fight, The (3)
	3AM Eternal (1)		My Friend (3)
	What Time Is Love (5)		Rain Rain Rain (8)
Klubbheads	Klubbhopping (10)		Rawhide (6)
Knack	My Sharona (6)		Sixteen Tons (10)
Knight, Beverley	Shoulda Woulda Coulda (10)		Strange Lady In Town (6)
Knight, Gladys	Baby Don't Change Your Mind (4)		Sugarbush (8)
	Best Thing That Ever Happened To Me (7)		Sugarbush (re-entry) (8)
	Licence To Kill (6)		There Must Be A Reason (9)
	Midnight Train To Georgia (10)		Where The Wind Blows (2)
	Way We Were, The / Try To Remember (4)		Woman In Love, A (1)
Knight, Jordan	Give It To You (5)		
Knight, Robert	Love On A Mountain Top (10)		
Knoc-Turn'al	Bad Intentions (4)		
Kon Kan	I Beg Your Pardon (5)	Lake, Greg	I Believe In Father Christmas

Group/Artiste	Title	Group/Artiste	Title
	(2)	Leon Young String Chorale	Stranger On The Shore (2)
Lambrettas	Poison Ivy (7)	Lester, Ketty	Love Letters (4)
Lancers	Let Me Go Lover (9)	Let Loose	Best In Me (8)
Landscape	Einstein A Go-Go (5)		Crazy For You (2)
Lange	Drifting Away (9)		Make It With You (7)
Lanza, Mario	Because You're Mine (3)	Level 42	It's Over (10)
Las Ketchup	Ketchup Song (Asereje), The (1)		Lessons In Love (3)
			Running In The Family (6)
Lasgo	Alone (7)		Something About You (6)
	Something (4)		Sun Goes Down (Living It Up),
Lattisaw, Stacy	Jump To The Beat (3)		The (10)
Lauper, Cyndi	Girls Just Want To Have Fun (2)		To Be With You Again (10)
	Hey Now (Girls Just Want To	Levert	Casanova (9)
	Have Fun) (4)	Lewie, Jona	Stop The Cavalry (3)
	I Drove All Night (7)	Lewis, Donna	I Love You Always Forever (5)
	Time After Time (3)	Lewis, Linda	It's In His Kiss (6)
Laurel & Hardy	Trail Of The Lonesome Pine, The (2)	Leyton, John	Johnny Remember Me (1)
			Wild Wind (2)
Laurie Lingo & The Dipsticks	Convoy G.B. (4)	Liam Gallagher	Going Underground / Carnation (6)
Lavigne, Avril	Complicated (3)	Liberty X	Got To Have Your Love (2)
	Sk8er Boi (9)		Holding On For You (5)
Lawrence, Lee	Crying In The Chapel (re-entry) (7)		Just A Little (1)
			Thinking It Over (5)
Lawrence, Steve	Footsteps (4)	Lieutenant Pigeon	Mouldy Old Dough (1)
Layton, Lindy	Dub Be Good To Me (1)	Lifford	Please Don't Turn Me On (4)
Le Roc, Kele	Little Bit Of Lovin' (8)	Lighthouse Family	High (4)
	My Love (8)		(I Wish I Knew How It Would
Leandros, Vicky	Come What May (2)		Feel To Be) Free / One (6)
Lee Lewis, Jerry	Breathless (8)		Lifted (4)
	Great Balls Of Fire (1)		Lost In Space (6)
	What'd I Say (10)		Raincloud (6)
	Whole Lotta Shakin' Goin' On (8)	Lightning Seeds	3 Lions (1)
			3 Lions '98 (1)
Lee, Ann	2 Times (2)		You Showed Me (8)
Lee, Brenda	All Alone Am I (7)	Lil Bow Wow	Bow Wow (That's My Name) (6)
	As Usual (5)		
	Here Comes That Feeling (5)	Lil' Kim	Lady Marmalade (1)
	Losing You (10)	Lil' Louis	French Kiss (2)
	Rockin' Around The Christmas Tree (6)	Limahl	Never Ending Story (4)
		Limerick, Alison	Where Love Lives (remix) (9)
	Speak To Me Pretty (3)	Limmie & The Family Cookin	Walkin' Miracle, A (6)
	Sweet Nothin's (4)		
Lee, Leapy	Little Arrows (2)		You Can Do Magic (3)
Lee, Peggy	Fever (5)	Limp Bizkit	My Way (6)
	Mr Wonderful (5)		Rollin' (1)
Leeds United FC	Leeds United (10)		Take A Look Around (Theme
Leftfield	Afrika Shox (7)		From MI 2) (3)
Lemon Pipers	Green Tambourine (7)	Lind, Bob	Elusive Butterfly (5)
Len	Steal My Sunshine (8)	Lindisfarne	Fog On The Tyne (Revisited) (2)
Lennon, John	Give Peace A Chance (2)		Lady Eleanor (3)
	Happy Xmas (War Is Over) (4)		Meet Me On The Corner (5)
	Happy Xmas (War Is Over) (re-entry) (2)		Run For Home (10)
		Linkin Park	High Voltage / Points Of
	Imagine (6)		Authority (9)
	Imagine (re-entry) (1)		In The End (8)
	Imagine (re-issue) (3)	Linx	Intuition (7)
	Instant Karma (5)	Lipps Inc	Funkytown (2)
	(Just Like) Starting Over (1)	Liquid Gold	Dance Yourself Dizzy (2)
	Nobody Told Me (6)		Substitute (8)
	Power To The People (7)	Lisa Left Eye Lopes	Never Be The Same Again (1)
	Woman (1)	Lisa Loeb	Stay (I Missed You) (6)
Lennon, Julian	Saltwater (6)	Lisa Marie Experience	Keep On Jumpin' (7)
	Too Late For Goodbyes (6)	Little Eva	Loco-Motion, The (2)
Lennox, Annie	Little Bird / Love Song For A Vampire (3)	Little Richard	Baby Face (2)
			Girl Can't Help It, The (9)
	No More I Love Yous (2)		Good Golly Miss Molly (8)
	Walking On Broken Glass (8)		Long Tall Sally (3)
	Why (5)		Lucille (10)
Lenska, Rula	OK? (10)	Liverpool FC	Anfield Rap (Red Machine In

M
U
S
I
C

P
O
P

Group/Artiste	Title
	Full Effect) (3)
	Pass And Move (It's The Liverpool Groove) (4)
Livin' Joy	Don't Stop Movin' (5)
	Dreamer (remix) (1)
	Follow The Rules (9)
Living In A Box	Blow The House Down (10)
	Living In A Box (5)
	Room In Your Heart (5)
Lizz E	Wishing On A Star (10)
Llorenna, Kelly	Tell It To My Heart (9)
	True Love Never Dies (re-issue) (7)
Lobo	Caribbean Disco Show, The (8)
	I'd Love You To Want Me (5)
	Me And You And A Dog Named Boo (4)
Lock 'N' Load	Blow Ya Mind (6)
Locklin, Hank	Please Help Me I'm Falling (9)
Lodge, John	Blue Guitar (8)
Logan, Johnny	Hold Me Now (2)
	What's Another Year (1)
Loggins, Kenny	Footloose (6)
Lolly	Big Boys Don't Cry / Rockin' Robin (10)
	Mickey (4)
	Viva La Radio (6)
London Boys	London Nights (2)
	Requiem (4)
London Philharmonic Orchestra	True Love Ways (8)
Londonbeat	I've Been Thinking About You (2)
Long John Baldry	Let The Heartaches Begin (1)
	Mexico (15)
Lonnie Donegan	Battle Of New Orleans (2)
	Bring A Little Water Sylvie / Dead Or Alive (7)
	Cumberland Gap (1)
	Does Your Chewing Gum Lose Its Flavour (On The Bedpost Overnight) (3)
	Don't You Rock Me Daddy-O (4)
	Gamblin' Man / Putting On The Style (1)
	Grand Coolie Dam (6)
	Have A Drink On Me (8)
	Lost John / Stewball (2)
	Michael Row The Boat / Lumbered (6)
	My Dixie Darling (10)
	My Old Man's A Dustman (Ballad Of A Refuse Disposal Officer) (1)
	Rock Island Line (8)
	Tom Dooley (3)
Lonyo	Summer Of Love (8)
Look	I Am The Beat (6)
Loon	I Need A Girl (Part One) (4)
Lopez, Jennifer	Ain't It Funny (3)
	Ain't It Funny (remix) (4)
	If You Had My Love (4)
	I'm Gonna Be Alright (3)
	I'm Real (4)
	Jenny From The Block (3)
	Love Don't Cost A Thing (1)
	Play (3)
	Waiting For Tonight (5)
Lopez, Trini	If I Had A Hammer (4)
Lord Rockingham's XI	Hoots Mon (1)

Group/Artiste	Title
Loren, Sophia	Goodness Gracious Me (4)
Lorraine & Lose	Megablast / Don't Make Me Wait (6)
Los Bravos	Black Is Black (2)
Los Del Rio	Macarena (2)
Los Indios Tabajaras	Maria Elena (5)
Los Lobos	La Bamba (1)
Lou Busch	Zambesi (2)
Lou, Bonnie	Tennessee Wig Walk (4)
Louchie Lou	Cecilia (4)
	Shout (7)
Louise	Arms Around The World (4)
	Let's Go Round Again (10)
	Light Of My Life (8)
	Naked (5)
	One Kiss From Heaven (9)
	Stuck In The Middle (4)
	2 Faced (3)
	Undivided Love (5)
Love Affair	Bringing On Back The Good Times (9)
	Day Without Love, A (6)
	Everlasting Love (1)
	Rainbow Valley (5)
Love City Groove	Love City Groove (7)
Love Inc	You're A Superstar (7)
Love Sculpture	Sabre Dance (5)
Love Unlimited Orchestra	Love's Theme (10)
Lovich, Lene	Lucky Number (3)
Lovin' Spoonful	Daydream (2)
	Summer In The City (8)
Lowe, Jim	Green Door (8)
Lowe, Nick	I Love The Sound Of Breaking Glass (7)
Lucid	I Can't Help Myself (7)
Ludacris	One Minute Man (10)
	Rollout (My Business) (20)
Luhrmann, Baz	Everybody's Free (To Wear Sunscreen) (1)
Lulu	Boat That I Row, The (6)
	Boom Bang-A-Bang (2)
	I'm A Tiger (9)
	Leave A Little Love (8)
	Man Who Sold The World, The (3)
	Me, The Peaceful Heart (9)
	Relight My Fire (1)
	Shout (7)
	Shout (8) remake
	We've Got Tonight (4)
Luman, Bob	Let's Think About Living (6)
Luniz	I Got 5 On It (3)
Luvvers	Shout (7)
LV	Gangsta's Paradise (1)
Lynch, Kenny	Up On The Roof (10)
	You Can Never Stop Me Loving You (10)
Lynch, Liam	United States Of Whatever (10)
Lynn, Tami	I'm Gonna Run Away From You (4)
Lynn, Vera	Auf Wiedersehen (10)
	Forget Me Not (7)
	Forget Me Not (re-entry) (5)
	Homing Waltz (9)
	My Son My Son (1)
Lynott, Phil	Out In The Fields (5)
Lyte Funkie Ones	Girl On TV (6)
M	Pop Muzik (2)
M & S presents Girl Next Door	Salsoul Nugget (If U Wanna) (6)

Group/Artiste	Title	Group/Artiste	Title
M J Cole	Crazy Love (10)		Hanky Panky (2)
M People	Angel Street (8)		Holiday (6)
	Don't Look Any Further (9)		Holiday (re-entry) (2)
	How Can I Love You More (remix) (8)		Holiday (re-issue) (5)
			Human Nature (8)
	Just For You (8)		I'll Remember (Theme From 'With Honours') (7)
	Moving On Up (2)		
	One Night In Heaven (6)		Into The Groove (1)
	Open Your Heart (9)		Justify My Love (2)
	Renaissance (5)		La Isla Bonita (1)
	Search For The Hero (9)		Like A Prayer (1)
	Sight For Sore Eyes (6)		Like A Virgin (3)
Mac & Katie Kissoon	Don't Do It Baby (9)		Live To Tell (2)
	Sugar Candy Kisses (3)		Look Of Love, The (9)
Mac Band	Roses Are Red (8)		Material Girl (3)
MacColl, Kirsty	Fairytale Of New York (2)		Music (1)
	New England, A (7)		Nothing Really Matters (7)
MacGregor, Mary	Torn Between Two Lovers (4)		Open Your Heart (4)
Macneal	I See A Star (8)		Papa Don't Preach (1)
MacNee, Patrick	Kinky Boots (5)		Power Of Good-Bye / Little Star, The (6)
Mad Stuntman	Go On Move (7)		
	I Like To Move It (5)		Rain (7)
Madhouse	Like A Prayer (3)		Ray Of Light (2)
Madison Avenue	Don't Call Me Baby (re-issue) (1)		Rescue Me (3)
			Secret (5)
	Who The Hell Are You (10)		This Used To Be My Playground (3)
Madness	Baggy Trousers (3)		
	Driving In My Car (4)		True Blue (3)
	Embarrassment (4)		Vogue (1)
	Grey Day (4)		What It Feels Like For A Girl (7)
	House Of Fun (1)		Who's That Girl (1)
	It Must Be Love (4)		You Must Love Me (10)
	It Must Be Love (re-issue) (6)		You'll See (5)
	Lovestruck (10)	Mai Tai	Body And Soul (9)
	My Girl (3)		History (8)
	One Step Beyond (7)	Maire Brennan of Clannad	Saltwater (6)
	Our House (5)		
	Return Of The Los Palmas Seven, The (7)	Maisonettes	Heartache Avenue (7)
		Majors	Stutter Rap (No Sleep 'Til Bedtime) (4)
	Shut Up (7)		
	Sun And The Rain, The (5)	Makaveli	To Live And Die In L.A. (10)
	Tomorrow's (Just Another Day) / Madness (Is All In My Mind) (8)	Malcolm Vaughan/ Mike Sammes	More Than Ever (Coma Prima) (5)
		Malcolm, Carl	Fattie Bum Bum (8)
	Wings Of A Dove (2)	Mamas & The Papas	California Dreamin' (re-entry) (9)
	Work Rest And Play EP (6)		
Madonna	American Pie (1)		Creeque Alley (9)
	Angel (5)		Dedicated To The One I Love (2)
	Another Suitcase In Another Hall (7)		
			Monday Monday (3)
	Bad Girl (10)	Man 2 Man meet Man Parrish	Male Stripper (4)
	Beautiful Stranger (2)		
	Bedtime Story (4)	Manchester Utd Football Club	Come On You Reds (1)
	Borderline (2)		Move Move Move (The Red Tribe) (6)
	Causing A Commotion (4)		
	Cherish (3)		We All Follow Man United (10)
	Crazy For You (2)		We're Gonna Do It Again (6)
	Crazy For You (remix) (2)	Manfred Mann	Come Tomorrow (4)
	Dear Jessie (5)		Do Wah Diddy Diddy (1)
	Deeper And Deeper (6)		5-4-3-2-1 (5)
	Die Another Day (3)		Fox On The Run (5)
	Don't Cry For Me Argentina (3)		Ha Ha Said The Clown (4)
	Don't Tell Me (4)		If You Gotta Go Go Now (2)
	Dress You Up (5)		Just Like A Woman (10)
	Drowned World (Substitute For Love) (10)		Mighty Quinn (1)
			My Name Is Jack (8)
	Erotica (3)		Pretty Flamingo (1)
	Express Yourself (5)		Ragamuffin Man (8)
	Fever (6)		Semi-Detached Suburban Mr James (2)
	Frozen (1)		
	Gambler (4)		Sha La La (3)

Group/Artiste	Title	Group/Artiste	Title
Manfred Mann's Earth Band	Blinded By The Light (6)	Marrs	Pump Up The Volume / Anitina (The First Time) (1)
	Davy's On The Road Again (6)	Marsden, Gerry	Ferry 'Cross The Mersey (1)
	Joybringer (9)	Marsha	Piece Of My Heart (7)
Manhattan Transfer	Chanson D'Amour (1)	Marshall Hain	Dancing In The City (3)
Manhattans	Hurt (4)	Martell, Lena	One Day At A Time (1)
	Kiss And Say Goodbye (4)	Martha & The Muffins	Echo Beach (10)
Manic Street Preachers	Australia (7)	Martika	I Feel The Earth Move (7)
	Design For Life, A (2)		Love ... Thy Will Be Done (9)
	Everything Must Go (5)		Toy Soldiers (5)
	Found That Soul (9)	Martin, Billie Ray	Your Loving Arms (remix) (6)
	If You Tolerate This Your Children Will Be Next (1)	Martin, Dean	Gentle On My Mind (2)
	Kevin Carter (9)		Kiss (9)
	Masses Against The Classes, The (1)		Kiss (re-entry) (5)
			Let Me Go Lover (3)
	So Why So Sad (8)		Memories Are Made Of This (1)
	Theme From M.A.S.H. (Suicide Is Painless) (7)		Naughty Lady Of Shady Lane (5)
	There By The Grace Of God (6)		Return To Me (2)
	You Stole The Sun From My Heart (5)		Sway (6)
			That's Amore (2)
Manilow, Barry	I Wanna Do It With You (8)		Under The Bridges Of Paris (6)
Mann Singers, Johnny	Up Up And Away (6)		Volare (2)
		Martin, Juan	Love Theme From The Thornbirds (10)
Manson, Marilyn	Tainted Love (5)	Martin, Marilyn	Separate Lives (4)
Mansun	I Can Only Disappoint U (8)	Martin, Ricky	Livin' La Vida Loca (1)
	Legacy EP (7)		Nobody Wants To Be Lonely (4)
	She Makes My Nose Bleed (9)		Private Emotion (9)
Mantovani & His Orchestra	Cara Mia (1)		She Bangs (3)
	Moulin Rouge (1)		(Un Dos Tres) Maria (6)
	Moulin Rouge (re-entry) (10)	Martin, Tony	Stranger In Paradise (6)
	Swedish Rhapsody (2)		Walk Hand In Hand (2)
	When You Lose The One You Love (7)	Martindale, Wink	Deck Of Cards (re-entry) (5)
	White Christmas (6)	Martino, Al	Here In My Heart (1)
Mantronix	Got To Have Your Love (4)		Now (3)
	Take Your Time (10)		Rachel (10)
Manuel and The Music Of The Mountains	Rodrigo's Guitar Concerto De Aranjuez (3)		Spanish Eyes (re-issue) (5)
			Story Of Tina, The (10)
Marbles	Only One Woman (5)		Take My Heart (9)
Marcels	Blue Moon (1)		Wanted (re-entry) (4)
Marie, Kelly	Feels Like I'm In Love (1)	Marvin, Hank	Living Doll (1)
Marie, Teena	Behind The Groove (6)		Throw Down The Line (7)
Marillion	Incommunicado (6)	Marvin, Lee	Wand'rin' Star (1)
	Kayleigh (2)	Marx, Richard	Hazard (3)
	Lavender (5)		Right Here Waiting (2)
Marilyn	Calling Your Name (4)	Mary, Mary	Shackles (Praise You) (5)
Marino Marini & His Quartet	Come Prima (2)	Mase	Feel So Good (10)
			Take Me There (7)
Marley, Bob	Sun Is Shining (3)		Top Of The World (2)
Marley, Bob, & The Wailers	Buffalo Soldier (4)	MASH	Theme From M.A.S.H. (Suicide Is Painless) (1)
	Could You Be Loved (5)	Mason Williams	Classical Gas (9)
	Iron Lion Zion (5)	Massive Attack	Teardrop (10)
	Is This Love (9)	Master Of Ceremonies	Do You Really Like It (1)
	Jamming / Punky Reggae Party (9)	Matchbox	When You Ask About Love (4)
		Matchroom Mob	Snooker Loopy (6)
	No Woman No Cry (re-entry) (8)	Mathis, Johnny	Certain Smile, A (4)
	One Love / People Get Ready (5)		I'm Stone In Love With You (10)
Marlin, Lene	Sitting Down Here (5)		My Love For You (9)
Marmalade	Baby Make It Soon (9)		Someone (6)
	Falling Apart At The Seams (9)		Too Much Too Little Too Late (3)
	Lovin' Things (6)		When A Child Is Born (1)
	My Little One (6)	Matthews Southern Comfort	Woodstock (1)
	Ob-La-Di Ob-La-Da (1)		
	Radancer (6)	Maughan, Susan	Bobby's Girl (3)
	Rainbow (3)	Maureen	Say A Little Prayer (10)
	Reflections Of My Life (3)	Mavericks	Dance The Night Away (4)

Group/Artiste	Title
Maxi Jazz	My Culture (9)
Maxx	Get-A-Way (4)
	No More (I Can't Stand It) (8)
May Orchestra, Billy	Main Title Theme From Man With The Golden Arm (9)
May, Brian	Driven By You (6)
	Too Much Love Will Kill You (5)
May, Simon	Summer Of My Life (7)
Maya	Feel It (1)
	Hammer To the Heart (6)
	If You Buy This Record Your Life Will Be Better (3)
Mazelle, Kym	Wait (7)
M-Beat	Incredible (remix) (8)
MC Hammer	Addam's Groove (4)
	Have You Seen Her (8)
	Pray (8)
	U Can't Touch This (3)
MC Mario	Supermarioland (8)
MC Miker G	Holiday Rap (6)
MC Neat	Little Bit Of Luck, A (9)
MC Parker	Thunderbirds Are Go (5)
MC Sar	Another Night (2)
	Run Away (6)
MC Tunes	Only Rhyme That Bites, The (10)
McAlmont & Butler	Yes (8)
McCampbell Brothers	Roses Are Red (8)
McCartney, Paul	Another Day (2)
	Band On The Run (3)
	Coming Up (2)
	Ebony And Ivory (1)
	Ferry 'Cross The Mersey (1)
	Girl Is Mine, The (8)
	Jet (7)
	Live And Let Die (9)
	My Love (9)
	No More Lonely Nights (2)
	Once Upon A Long Ago (10)
	Pipes Of Peace (1)
	Say Say Say (2)
	Waterfalls (9)
	We All Stand Together (3)
	Wonderful Christmastime (6)
McCoo, Marilyn	You Don't Have To Be A Star (To Be In My Show) (7)
McCoy, Van	Hustle, The (3)
	Shuffle, The (4)
McCoys	Hang On Sloopy (5)
McCrae, George	I Can't Leave You Alone (9)
	It's Been So Long (4)
	Rock Your Baby (1)
McCutcheon, Martine	I'm Over You (2)
	I've Got You (6)
	On The Radio (7)
	Perfect Moment (1)
	Talking In Your Sleep / Love Me (6)
McDonald, Jane	Cruise Into Christmas (10)
McDonald, Michael	On My Own (2)
McFadden & Whitehead	Ain't No Stoppin' Us Now (5)
McFerrin, Bobby	Don't Worry Be Happy (2)
McGregor, Ewan	Choose Life (6)
McGregor, Freddie	Just Don't Want To Be Lonely (9)
McGuinness Flint	Malt And Barley Blues (5)
	When I'm Dead And Gone (2)
McGuire, Barry	Eve Of Destruction (3)
McKee, Maria	Show Me Heaven (1)
McKenzie, Gisele	Seven Lonely Days (re-entry)

Group/Artiste	Title
	(6)
McKenzie, Scott	San Francisco (1)
McLachlan, Craig	Mona (2)
McLachlan, Sarah	Silence (remixes) (3)
McLaren, Malcolm	Buffalo Gals (9)
	Double Dutch (3)
McLean, Bitty	Dedicated To The One I Love (6)
	Here I Stand (10)
	It Keep Rainin' (Tears From Eyes) (2)
McLean, Don	American Pie (2)
	Crying (1)
	Vincent (1)
McNeal, Lutricia	Ain't That Just The Way (6)
	Someone Loves You Honey (9)
	Stranded (3)
McTell, Ralph	Streets Of London (2)
Mead, Abigail	Full Metal Jacket (I Wanna Be Your Drill Instructor) (2)
Meat Loaf	Bat Out Of Hell (re-issue) (8)
	Dead Ringer For Love (5)
	I'd Do Anything For Love (But I Won't Do That) (1)
	I'd Lie For You (And That's The Truth) (2)
	Not A Dry Eye In The House (7)
Meco	Star Wars Theme / Cantina Band (7)
Medeiros, Glenn	Nothing's Gonna Change My Love For You (1)
Medicine Head	One And One Is One (3)
Medley, Bill	(I've Had) The Time Of My Life (6)
	(I've Had) The Time Of My Life (re-entry) (8)
Meehan, Tony	Applejack (4)
	Diamonds (1)
	Scarlett O'Hara (2)
Megaman	No Good 4 Me (6)
Meja	Private Emotion (9)
Mel & Kim	F.L.M. (7)
	Respectable (1)
	Rockin' Around The Christmas Tree (3)
	Showing Out (Get Fresh At The Weekend) (3)
	That's The Way It Is (10)
Melanie	Brand New Key (4)
	Ruby Tuesday (9)
Melle Mel	White Lines (Don't Do It) (7)
Mellomen	Mambo Italiano (1)
	Where Will The Baby's Dimple Be (6)
Mellor, Will	When I Need You (5)
Melvin, Harold	Don't Leave Me This Way (5)
	If You Don't Know Me By Now (9)
Men At Work	Down Under (1)
Men Without Hats	Safety Dance, The (6)
Menswear	Being Brave (10)
Mental As Anything	Live It Up (3)
Mercury, Freddie	Great Pretender, The (4)
	In My Defence (8)
	Living On My Own (1)
	Love Kills (10)
Mercury, Freddy	Barcelona (2)
	Barcelona (re-issue) (2)
Meri Wilson	Telephone Man (6)

M
U
S
I
C

P
O
P

Group/Artiste	Title	Group/Artiste	Title
Merlin	Who's In The House (8)	Miles-Kingston, Paul	Pie Jesu (3)
Merlin & Antonia	Megablast / Don't Make Me	Milian, Christina	AM to PM (3)
	Wait (6)		It's All Gravy (9)
Merseybeats	I Think Of You (5)		When You Look At Me (3)
Merseys	Sorrow (4)	Milk & Honey	Hallelujah (5)
Metallica	Enter Sandman (5)	Milk Inc	In My Eyes (9)
	Nothing Else Matters (6)		Walk On Water (10)
	Until It Sleeps (5)	Milky	Just The Way You Are (8)
Method Man	Hit 'Em High (The Monstars'	Millard Thomas	Banana Boat Song (2)
	Anthem) (8)	Miller Band, Steve	Abracadabra (2)
	I'll Be There For You – You're		Joker, The (1)
	All I Need To Get By (10)	Miller, Frankie	Darlin' (6)
Miami Sound	Anything For You (10)	Miller, Gary	Robin Hood (10)
Machine	Can't Stay Away From You (7)	Miller, Ned	From A Jack To A King (2)
	Dr Beat (6)	Miller, Roger	King Of The Road (1)
	1-2-3 (9)	Milli Vanilli	Girl I'm Gonna Miss You (2)
Michael Medwin	Signature Tune Of 'The Army		Girl You Know It's True (3)
	Game', The (5)	Millie	My Boy Lollipop (2)
Michael Reed	Music Of Torvill And Dean EP,	Mills Brothers	Glow Worm (10)
Orchestra	The (9)	Mills, Garry	Look For A Star (7)
Michael, George	As (4)	Mills, Stephanie	Never Knew Love Like This
	Careless Whisper (1)		Before (4)
	Different Corner, A (1)	Mindbenders	Game Of Love (2)
	Don't Let The Sun Go Down		Groovy Kind Of Love, A (2)
	On Me (1)		Um Um Um Um Um Um (5)
	Faith (2)	Minerbi, Marcello	Zorba's Dance (6)
	Fast Love (1)	Minnelli, Liza	Losing My Mind (6)
	Five Live EP (1)	Minogue, Dannii	All I Wanna Do (4)
	Freeek! (7)		Jump To The Beat (8)
	I Knew You Were Waiting (For		Love And Kisses (8)
	Me) (1)		Put The Needle On It (7)
	I Want Your Sex (3)		This Is It (10)
	If I Told You That (9)		Who Do You Love Now
	Jesus To A Child (1)		(Stringer) (3)
	Older / I Can Make You Love	Minogue, Kylie	Better The Devil You Know (2)
	Me (3)		Can't Get You Out Of My Head
	One More Try (8)		(1)
	Outside (2)		Come Into My World (8)
	Praying For Time (6)		Confide In Me (2)
	Spinning The Wheel (2)		Especially For You (1)
	Star People '97 (2)		Give Me Just A Little More
	Too Funky (4)		Time (2)
	Waltz Away Dreaming (10)		Got To Be Certain (2)
	You Have Been Loved / The		Hand On Your Heart (1)
	Strangest Thing '97 (2)		I Should Be So Lucky (1)
Michel, Pras	Another One Bites The Dust (5)		If You Were With Me Now (4)
	Ghetto Superstar That Is What		In Your Eyes (3)
	You Are (2)		Je Ne Sais Pas Pourquoi (2)
Michell, Keith	Captain Beaky / Wilfred The		Kids (2)
	Weasel (5)		Loco-Motion, The (2)
Michie One	Cecilia (4)		Love At First Sight (2)
	Shout (7)		Never Too Late (4)
Middle Of The Road	Chirpy Chirpy Cheep Cheep (1)		On A Night Like This (2)
	Soley Soley (5)		Please Stay (10)
	Tweedle Dee Tweedle Dum (2)		Shocked (6)
Midler, Bette	From A Distance (6)		Spinning Around (1)
	Wind Beneath My Wings (5)		Step Back In Time (4)
Midnight Oil	Beds Are Burning (re-issue) (6)		Tears On My Pillow (1)
Midnight Star	Midas Touch (8)		What Do I Have To Do (6)
Mighty Morphin	Anything For You (10)		Wouldn't Change A Thing (2)
Power Rangers		Minott, Sugar	Good Thing Going
Migil Five	Mockingbird Hill (10)		(We've Got A Good Thing
Mike & The	Living Years, The (2)		Going) (4)
Mechanics		Miracles	Love Machine (3)
Mike Berry &	Don't You Think It's Time (6)		Tears Of A Clown, The (1)
The Outlaws			Tracks Of My Tears, The (9)
Miles, John	Music (3)	Mirage	Jack Mix II / III (4)
	Slow Down (10)		Jack Mix IV (8)
Miles, Robert	Children (2)	Mirror, Danny	I Remember Elvis Presley (The
	Fable (7)		King Is Dead) (4)
	One And One (3)	Missy Elliott	4 My People (5)

Group/Artiste	Title	Group/Artiste	Title
	Get UR Freak On (4)		Let's Dance (re-entry) (9)
	One Minute Man (10)		More I See You, The (3)
	Rain (Supa Dupa Fly), The (16)		Some Kinda Fun (10)
	Work It (6)	Montserrat Caballé	Barcelona (2)
Missy 'Misdemeanor' Elliott	Don't You Think It's Time (6)		Barcelona (re-issue) (2)
Mis-Teeq	All I Want (2)	Monty Python	Always Look On The Bright Side Of Life (3)
	B With Me (5)	Moody Blues	Go Now (1)
	One Night Stand (5)		Nights In White Satin (re-entry) (9)
	Roll On / This Is How We Do It (7)		Question (2)
	Why (8)	Moony	Dove (I'll Be Loving You) (9)
Mitch Miller	Yellow Rose Of Texas (2)	Moore, Dorothy	Misty Blue (5)
Mitchell, Des	(Welcome) To The Dance (5)	Moore, Gary	Out In The Fields (5)
Mitchell, Guy	Chicka Boom (5)		Parisienne Walkways (8)
	Chicka Boom (re-entry) (4)	Moore, Mandy	Candy (6)
	Cloud Lucky Seven (2)	Moore, Melba	This Is It (9)
	Cuff Of My Shirt (9)	Moore, Tina	Never Gonna Let You Go (7)
	Dime And A Dollar (8)	MOP	Ante Up (7)
	Dime And A Dollar (re-entry) (8)		Cold As Ice (4)
	Feet Up (2)	More Fire Crew	Oi (8)
	Heartaches By The Number (re-entry) (5)	Morgan, Debelah	Dance With Me (10)
	Knee Deep In The Blues (3)	Morgan, Jane	Day The Rains Came, The (1)
	Look At That Girl (1)	Morissette, Alanis	Hands Clean (12)
	Pretty Little Black-Eyed Susie (2)		Head Over Feet (7)
	Rock-A-Billy (1)		Thank U (5)
	She Wears Red Feathers (1)	Morricone, Ennio	Chi Mai (Theme From TV Series The Life And Times Of Lloyd George) (2)
	Singing The Blues (1)		
Mixmaster	Grand Piano (9)	Morris Minor	Stutter Rap (No Sleep 'Til Bedtime) (4)
Mixtures	Pushbike Song, The (2)	Morrison, Mark	Crazy (remix) (6)
Mizell, Hank	Jungle Rock (3)		Horny (5)
MN8	Happy (8)		Moan And Groan (7)
	If You Only Let Me In (6)		Return Of The Mack (1)
	I've Got A Little Something For You (2)		Trippin' (8)
Mobiles	Drowning In Berlin (9)	Morrissey	Everyday Is Like Sunday (9)
Moby	Go (10)		Interesting Drug (9)
	James Bond Theme (Moby's Re-Version) (8)		Last Of The Famous International Playboys (6)
	Porcelain (5)		More You Ignore Me The Closer I Get, The (8)
Modern Romance	Ay Ay Ay Ay Moosey (10)		Suedehead (5)
	Best Years Of Our Lives (4)	Mortimer, Bob	I'm A Believer (3)
	High Life (8)	Moten, Wendy	Come In Out Of The Rain (8)
	Walking In The Rain (7)	Motorhead	Golden Years EP, The (8)
Modern Talking	Brother Louie (4)		Motorhead Live (6)
Modjo	Lady (Hear Me Tonight) (1)		St Valentine's Day Massacre EP (5)
Modugno, Domenico	Volare (10)		
Mojos	Everything's Alright (9)	Motors	Airport (4)
Molella	If You Wanna Party (9)	Mott The Hoople	All The Way From Memphis (10)
Moloko	Sing It Back (4)		All The Young Dudes (3)
	Time Is Now, The (2)		Roll Away The Stones (8)
Moments	Dolly My Love (10)	Mouskouri, Nana	Only Love (2)
	Girls (3)	Mousse T	Horny (2)
	Jack In The Box (7)		Sexbomb (3)
Monica	Boy Is Mine, The (2)	Mouth	I See A Star (8)
	First Night, The (6)	Move	Blackberry Way (1)
Monkees	Alternate Title (2)		Brontosaurus (7)
	Daydream Believer (5)		California Man (7)
	I'm A Believer (1)		Fire Brigade (3)
	Little Bit Me A Little Bit You, A (3)		Flowers In The Rain (2)
Monro, Matt	My Kind Of Girl (5)		I Can Hear The Grass Grow (5)
	Portrait Of My Love (3)		Night Of Fear (2)
	Softly As I Leave You (10)	Moyet, Alison	All Cried Out (8)
	Walk Away (4)		Is This Love? (3)
	Yesterday (8)		Love Letters (4)
Monroe, Gerry	My Prayer (9)		Love Resurrection (10)
	Sally (4)		That Ole Devil Called Love (2)
Montez, Chris	Let's Dance (2)		Weak In The Presence Of

MUSIC POP

Group/Artiste	Title	Group/Artiste	Title
	Beauty (6)	Narada	Divine Emotions (8)
Mr Bean	(I Want To Be) Elected (9)	Narada Michael	I Shoulda Loved Ya (8)
Mr Big	Romeo (4)	Walden	
	To Be With You (3)	Nash, Johnny	Cupid (6)
Mr Blobby	Mr Blobby (1)		Hold Me Tight (5)
Mr Bloe	Groovin' With Mr Bloe (2)		I Can See Clearly Now (5)
Mr Hankey	Mr Hankey The Christmas Poo		Tears On My Pillow (1)
	(4)		There Are More Questions
Mr Mister	Broken Wings (4)		Than Answers (9)
Mr Oizo	Flat Beat (1)		You Got Soul (6)
Mr President	Coco Jamboo (8)	Nashville Teens	Google Eye (10)
Mud	Cat Crept In, The (2)		Tobacco Road (6)
	Dyna-Mite (4)	Nat 'King' Cole	Because You're Mine (6)
	Lean On Me (7)		Because You're Mine (re-entry)
	L-L-Lucy (10)		(10)
	Lonely This Christmas (1)		Blossom Fell, A (3)
	Moonshine Sally (10)		Can't I (9)
	Oh Boy (1)		Can't I (re-entry) (6)
	Rocket (6)		Can't I (re-entry) (10)
	Secrets That You Keep, The (3)		Dear Lonely Hearts (4)
	Show Me You're A Woman (8)		Dreams Can Tell A Lie (10)
	Tiger Feet (1)		Faith Can Move Mountains (re-
Mudlarks	Book Of Love (8)		entry) (10)
	Lollipop (2)		I Get So Lonely (5)
Mullen, Larry	Theme From Mission		I Get So Lonely (re-entry) (10)
	Impossible (7)		Mother Nature And Father Time
Mullins, Shawn	Lullaby (9)		(7)
Mumba, Samantha	Always Come Back To Your		Pretend (2)
	Love (3)		Ramblin' Rose (5)
	Baby Come On Over (5)		Smile (2)
	Body II Body (5)		Somewhere Along The Way (3)
	Gotta Tell You (2)		Tenderly (10)
	I'm Right Here (5)		That's You (10)
	Lately (6)		Too Young To Go Steady (8)
Mungo Jerry	Alright Alright Alright (3)		When I Fall In Love (2)
	Baby Jump (re-entry) (1)		When I Fall In Love (re-issue)
	In The Summertime (1)		(4)
	Lady Rose (5)	Natasha	Iko Iko (10)
Muppets	Halfway Down The Stairs (7)	Nayler, Maria	One And One (3)
Murray, Ruby	Evermore (3)	Nazareth	Bad Bad Boy (10)
	Goodbye Jimmy Goodbye (10)		Broken Down Angel (9)
	Happy Days And Lonely Nights	N'Dour, Youssou	7 Seconds (3)
	(6)	Negro, Joey	Must Be The Music (8)
	Heartbeat (3)	Neil	Hole In My Shoe (2)
	If Anyone Finds This I Love You	Nelly	Dilemma (1)
	(4)		Hot In Herre (4)
	I'll Come When You Call (6)		(Hot S**t) Country Grammar (7)
	Let Me Go Lover (5)		Ride Wit Me (3)
	Softly Softly (1)	Nelson Riddle & His	Learnin' The Blues (2)
Musical Youth	Never Gonna Give You Up (6)	Orchestra	
	Pass The Dutchie (1)	Nelson, Phyllis	Move Closer (1)
Mya	Case Of The Ex (3)	Nelson, Ricky	Hello Mary Lou / Travellin' Man
	Ghetto Superstar That Is What		(2)
	You Are (2)		It's Late (3)
	Lady Marmalade (1)		Poor Little Fool (4)
	Take Me There (7)		Someday (9)
Myers, Billie	Kiss The Rain (4)	Nelson, Sandy	Let There Be Drums (3)
Myles, Alannah	Black Velvet (2)		Teen Beat (9)
N Sync	Bye Bye Bye (3)	Nena	99 Red Balloons (1)
	Girlfriend (2)	Nevil, Robbie	C'est La Vie (3)
	I Want You Back (5)	Neville, Aaron	Don't Know Much (2)
	It's Gonna Be Me (9)	Nevins, Jason	It's Like That (1)
	Pop (9)	New Edition	Candy Girl (1)
	Tearin' Up My Heart (9)	New Kids On The	Cover Girl (4)
Nail, Jimmy	Ain't No Doubt (1)	Block	Hangin' Tough (1)
	Crocodile Shoes (4)		If You Go Away (9)
	Love Don't Live Here Anymore		I'll Be Loving You (Forever) (5)
	(3)		Let's Try Again / Didn't I Blow
Nana	Body Groove (3)		Your Mind (8)
Napoleon XIV	They're Coming To Take Me		Step By Step (2)
	Away Ha-Haaa! (4)		This One's For The Children (9)

Group/Artiste	Title	Group/Artiste	Title
	Tonight (3)	Nirvana	Come As You Are (9)
	You Got It (The Right Stuff) (1)		Heart-Shaped Box (5)
New Order	Blue Monday (re-entry) (9)		Smells Like Teen Spirit (7)
	Blue Monday (remix) (3)	N-Joi	Anthem (8)
	Crystal (8)	No Doubt	Don't Speak (1)
	Regret (4)		Hey Baby (2)
	True Faith (4)		Just A Girl (re-issue) (3)
	True Faith (remix) (9)	No Mercy	Please Don't Go (4)
New Power	Gett Off (4)		Where Do You Go (2)
Generation	My Name Is Prince (7)	Nolans	Attention To Me (9)
	Sexy MF / Strollin' (4)		Gotta Pull Myself Together (9)
New Radicals	You Get What You Give (5)		I'm In The Mood For Dancing
New Seekers	Beg Steal Or Borrow (2)		(3)
	Circles (4)	Nomad	(I Wanna Give You) Devotion
	I Get A Little Sentimental Over		(2)
	You (5)	North & South	I'm A Man Not A Boy (7)
	I'd Like To Teach The World To	Notorious BIG	Hypnotize (10)
	Sing (1)		Mo Money Mo Problems (6)
	Never Ending Song Of Love (2)	N-Trance	Da Ya Think I'm Sexy? (7)
	You Won't Find Another Fool		Forever (6)
	Like Me (1)		Set You Free (remix) (2)
New Vaudeville Band	Peek-A-Boo (7)		Set You Free (2nd remix) (4)
	Winchester Cathedral (4)		Stayin' Alive (2)
New World	Sister Jane (9)	Nu Generation	In Your Arms (Rescue Me) (8)
	Tom Tom Turnaround (6)	Nu Shooz	I Can't Wait (2)
Newbeats	Run Baby Run (10)	Numan, Gary	Cars (1)
Newley, Anthony	And The Heavens Cried (6)		Complex (6)
	Do You Mind (1)		I Die: You Die (6)
	If She Should Come To You (4)		She's Got Claws (6)
	I've Waited So Long (3)		We Are Glass (5)
	Personality (6)		We Take Mystery (To Bed) (9)
	Strawberry Fair (3)	Oakenfold	Starry-Eyed Surprise (6)
	Why (1)	Oakey, Phil	Together In Electric Dreams (3)
Newton-John, Olivia	Banks Of The Ohio (6)	Oasis	All Around The World (1)
	Grease Megamix (3)		Cigarettes And Alcohol (7)
	Hopelessly Devoted To You (2)		Don't Look Back In Anger (1)
	If Not For You (7)		D'You Know What I Mean? (1)
	Little More Love, A (4)		Go Let It Out (1)
	Physical (7)		Hindu Times, The (1)
	Sam (6)		Little By Little / She Is Love (2)
	Summer Nights (1)		Live Forever (10)
	Xanadu (1)		Roll With It (2)
	You're The One That I Want (1)		Some Might Say (1)
	You're The One That I Want		Stand By Me (2)
	(re-issue) (4)		Stop Crying Your Heart Out (2)
Nicholas, Paul	Dancing With The Captain (8)		Sunday Morning Call (4)
	Grandma's Party (9)		Whatever (3)
Nickelback	How You Remind Me (4)		Who Feels Love? (4)
	Too Bad (9)		Wonderwall (2)
Nicole	Little Peace, A (1)	Obernkirchen	Happy Wanderer (Der
Nigel & Marvin	Follow Da Leader (5)	Children's Choir	Fröhliche Wanderer) (2)
Nightcrawlers	Push The Feeling On (remix)		Happy Wanderer (Der
	(3)		Fröhliche Wanderer) (re-
	Surrender Your Love (7)		entry) (8)
Nightingale, Maxine	Right Back Where We Started	Ocean Colour Scene	Better Day (9)
	From (8)		Circle, The (6)
Nilsson	Without You (1)		Day We Caught The Train, The
Nina & Frederick	Little Donkey (3)		(4)
911	All I Want Is You (4)		Hundred Mile High City (4)
	Bodyshakin' (3)		Traveller's Tune (5)
	Day We Find Love, The (4)		You've Got It Bad (7)
	Don't Make Me Wait (10)	Ocean, Billy	Caribbean Queen (No More
	How Do You Want Me To Love		Love On The Run) (6)
	You? (10)		Get Outta My Dreams Get Into
	Journey, The (3)		My Car (3)
	Little Bit More, A (1)		Love Really Hurts Without Me
	More Than A Woman (2)		(2)
	Party People … Friday Night (5)		Red Light Spells Danger (2)
	Private Number (3)		Suddenly (4)
Nine Stories	Stay (I Missed You) (6)		When The Going Gets Tough
1910 Fruitgum Co	Simon Says (2)		The Tough Get Going (1)

Group/Artiste	Title	Group/Artiste	Title
Oceanic	Insanity (3)	Orbital	Saint, The (3)
O'Connor, Des	Careless Hands (6)		Satan (3)
	I Pretend (1)	OMD	Enola Gay (8)
	1-2-3 O'Leary (4)		Joan Of Arc (5)
	Skye Boat Song, The (10)		Locomotion (5)
O'Connor, Hazel	D-Days (10)		Maid Of Orleans (The Waltz
	Eighth Day (5)		Joan Of Arc) (4)
	Will You (8)		Pandora's Box (7)
O'Connor, Sinead	Nothing Compares 2 U (1)		Sailing On The Seven Seas (3)
O'Donnell, Daniel	Give A Little Love (7)		Souvenir (3)
Odyssey	Going Back To My Roots (4)	Original	I Luv U Baby (remix) (2)
	If You're Looking For A Way	Orlando, Tony	Bless You (5)
	Out (6)		Tie A Yellow Ribbon Round The
	Inside Out (3)		Old Oak Tree (1)
	Native New Yorker (5)		What Are You Doing Sunday
	Use It Up And Wear It Out (1)		(3)
Off-Shore	I Can't Take The Power (7)	Osborne, Joan	One Of Us (6)
Offspring	Original Prankster (6)	Osbourne, Kelly	Papa Don't Preach (3)
	Pretty Fly (For A White Guy) (1)	Osmond, Donny	I'm Leaving It (All) Up To You
	Why Don't You Get A Job? (2)		(2)
Ohio Express	Yummy Yummy Yummy (5)		Morning Side Of The Mountain
O'Jays	Love Train (9)		(5)
Ol' Dirty Bastard	Ghetto Superstar That Is What		Puppy Love (1)
	You Are (2)		Too Young (5)
Oldfield, Mike	In Dulce Jubilo / On Horseback		Twelfth Of Never, The (1)
	(4)		When I Fall In Love (4)
	Moonlight Shadow (4)		Why (3)
	Portsmouth (3)		Young Love (1)
	Sentinel (10)	Osmond, Little Jimmy	Long-Haired Lover From
Olive	You're Not Alone (1)		Liverpool (1)
Oliver	Good Morning Starshine (6)		Tweedle Dee (4)
Ollie & Jerry	Breakin' ... There's No Stopping	Osmond, Marie	I'm Leaving It (All) Up To You
	Us Now (5)		(2)
OMC	How Bizarre (5)		Morning Side Of The Mountain
187 Lockdown	Kung-Fu (9)		(5)
1 Giant Leap	My Culture (9)		Paper Roses (2)
One Hundred Ton	It Only Takes A Minute (9)	Osmonds	Crazy Horses (2)
and a Feather			Goin' Home (4)
112	I'll Be Missing You (1)		Let Me In (2)
	Mo Money Mo Problems (6)		Love Me For A Reason (1)
One True Voice	Sacred Trust / After You're		Proud One, The (5)
	Gone (2)	O'Sullivan, Gilbert	Alone Again (Naturally) (3)
O'Neal, Alexander	Criticize (4)		Clair (1)
	Saturday Love (6)		Get Down (1)
Ones	Flawless (7)		No Matter How I Try (5)
Ono, Yoko	Happy Xmas (War Is Over) (4)		Nothing Rhymed (8)
	Happy Xmas (War Is Over) (re-		Ooh-Wakka-Doo-Wakka-Day
	entry) (2)		(8)
	Instant Karma (5)		Why Oh Why Oh Why (6)
OPM	Heaven Is A Halfpipe (4)	Otis Show, Johnny	Ma (He's Making Eyes At Me)
Opus	Live Is Life (6)		(2)
Opus III	It's A Fine Day (5)	O-Town	All Or Nothing (4)
Oran 'Juice' Jones	Rain, The (4)		Liquid Dreams (3)
Orange Juice	Rip It Up (8)	Ottowan	D.I.S.C.O. (2)
Orb	Blue Room (8)		Hands Up (Give Me Your
	Little Fluffy Clouds (10)		Heart) (3)
	Toxygene (4)	Otway, John	Bunsen Burner (9)
Orbison, Roy	Blue Bayou / Mean Woman	Otway, John & Wild	Really Free (27)
	Blues (3)	Willy Barrett	
	Dream Baby (2)	Our Kid	You Just Might See Me Cry (2)
	Falling (9)	Outhere Brothers	Boom Boom Boom (1)
	I Drove All Night (7)		Don't Stop (Wiggle Wiggle) (1)
	In Dreams (6)		If You Wanna Party (9)
	It's Over (1)		La La La Hey Hey (7)
	Oh Pretty Woman (1)	Outkast	Ms Jackson (2)
	Only The Lonely (re-entry) (1)	Overlanders	Michelle (1)
	Pretty Paper (6)	Owen, Mark	Child (3)
	Running Scared (9)		Clementine (3)
	Too Soon To Know (3)	Oxide & Neutrina	Bound 4 Da Reload (Casualty)
	You Got It (3)		(1)
Orbit, William	Barber's Adagio For Strings (4)	Oxide & Neutrino	Up Middle Finger (7)

Group/Artiste	Title
Oxide & Neutrino with Kowdean	Dem Girlz (I Don't Know Why) (10)
Oxide & Neutrino with Megaman	No Good 4 Me (6)
Paffendorf	Be Cool (7)
Page, Jimmy	Come With Me (2)
Page, Patti	(How Much Is) That Doggie In The Window (9)
Paige, Elaine	I Know Him So Well (1)
	Memory (6)
Paige, Jennifer	Crush (4)
Palmer, Robert	Addicted To Love (5)
	I Didn't Mean To Turn You On (9)
	I'll Be Your Baby Tonight (6)
	Mercy Mercy Me – I Want You (9)
	She Makes My Day (6)
Papa Roach	Last Resort (3)
Paper Lace	Billy Don't Be A Hero (1)
	Night Chicago Died, The (3)
Paradis, Vanessa	Be My Baby (6)
	Joe Le Taxi (3)
Paramount Jazz Band	Buona Sera (7)
	Summer Set (5)
	That's My Home (7)
Paris, Mica	My One Temptation (7)
Paris, Ryan	Dolce Vita (5)
Parker Jr, Ray	Ghostbusters (2)
Parkinson, Jimmy	Great Pretender, The (9)
Parr, John	St Elmo's Fire (Man In Motion) (6)
Partners In Kryme	Turtle Power (1)
Parton, David	Isn't She Lovely (4)
Parton, Dolly	Islands In The Stream (7)
	Jolene (7)
Partridge Family	Breaking Up Is Hard To Do (3)
	Looking Through The Eyes Of Love (9)
	Walking In The Rain (10)
Partridge, Don	Blue Eyes (3)
	Rosie (4)
Pasadenas	I'm Doing Fine Now (4)
	Tribute (Right On) (5)
Passengers	Miss Sarajevo (6)
Pat & Mick	I Haven't Stopped Dancing Yet (9)
Paul & Paula	Hey Paula (8)
	Young Lovers (9)
Paul, Les	Vaya Con Dios (7)
Paul, Owen	My Favourite Waste Of Time (3)
Pavarotti, Luciano	Live Like Horses (9)
	Nessun Dorma (2)
Payne, Freda	Band Of Gold (1)
Peaches & Herb	Reunited (4)
Pearl Jam	Spin The Black Circle (10)
Pearls	Guilty (10)
Pebbles	Girlfriend (8)
Peers, Donald	Please Don't Go (3)
Pellow, Marti	Close To You (9)
Penn, Dawn	You Don't Love Me (No No No) (3)
Peppers	Pepper Box (6)
Pepsi & Shirlie	Goodbye Stranger (9)
	Heartache (2)
Percy Faith & His Orchestra	Half As Much (3)
	Theme From A Summer Place (2)
Perez Prado & His Orchestra	Patricia (8)

Group/Artiste	Title
Perez 'Prez' Prado Orchestra	Cherry Pink And Apple Blossom White (1)
	Guaglione (2)
Perfecto Allstarz	Reach Up (Papa's Got A Brand New Pig Bag) (6)
Perkins, Carl	Blue Suede Shoes (10)
Pet Shop Boys	Absolutely Fabulous (6)
	Always On My Mind (1)
	Before (7)
	Can You Forgive Her (7)
	Domino Dancing (7)
	Go West (2)
	Heart (1)
	It's A Sin (1)
	It's Alright (5)
	Left To My Own Devices (4)
	Red Letter Day, A (9)
	Rent (8)
	Se A Vide (That's The Way Life Is) (8)
	So Hard (4)
	Somewhere (9)
	Suburbia (8)
	West End Girls (1)
	What Have I Done To Deserve This (2)
	Where The Streets Have No Name (Can't Take My Eyes Off You) / How Can You Expect To Be Taken Seriously (4) You Only Tell Me You Love Me When You're Drunk (8)
Peter & Gordon	Nobody I Know (10)
	To Know You Is To Love You (5)
	True Love Ways (2)
	World Without Love, A (1)
Peter Paul & Mary	Leavin' On A Jet Plane (2)
Peters & Lee	Don't Stay Away Too Long (3)
	Welcome Home (1)
Peterson, Colin	Don't Forget To Remember (2)
PF Project	Choose Life (6)
Phantoms	Tomorrow (8)
Phats & Small	Feel Good (7)
	Turn Around (3)
PhD	I Won't Let You Down (3)
Phillips, Esther	What A Difference A Day Made (6)
Pianoman	Blurred (6)
Pickettywitch	That Same Old Feeling (5)
Pigbag	Papa's Got A Brand New Pigbag (3)
Piglets	Johnny Reggae (3)
Pilot	January (1)
Pink	Don't Let Me Get Me (6)
	Get The Party Started (2)
	Just Like A Pill (1)
	Lady Marmalade (1)
	Most Girls (5)
	There You Go (6)
	You Make Me Sick (9)
Pink Floyd	Another Brick In The Wall Part II (1)
	See Emily Play (6)
Pinkees	Danger Games (8)
Pinkerton's Assorted Colours	Mirror Mirror (9)
Pioneers	Let Your Yeah Be Yeah (5)
Piper, Billie	Day And Night (1)
	Something Deep Inside (4)
Royal Scots Dragoon	Amazing Grace (1)

MUSIC POP

Group/Artiste	Title	Group/Artiste	Title
Guards			Every Little Thing She Does Is
Pipkins	Gimme Dat Ding (6)		Magic (1)
Pips	Baby Don't Change Your Mind		Invisible Sun (2)
	(4)		Message In A Bottle (1)
	Best Thing That Ever		So Lonely (6)
	Happened To Me (7)		Walking On The Moon (1)
	Midnight Train To Georgia (10)		Wrapped Around Your Finger
	Way We Were, The / Try To		(7)
	Remember (4)	Pollard, Su	Starting Together (2)
Piranhas	Tom Hark (6)	Poni-Tails	Born Too Late (5)
	Zambesi (17)	Poole, Brian	Candy Man (6)
Pitney, Gene	Backstage (4)		Do You Love Me (1)
	I Must Be Seeing Things (6)		Someone Someone (2)
	(I Wanna) Love My Life Away		Twist And Shout (4)
	(26)	Pop Will Eat Itself	Get The Girl! Kill The Baddies!
	I'm Gonna Be Strong (2)		(9)
	Just One Smile (8)	Pop, Iggy	Real Wild Child (Wild One) (10)
	Looking Through The Eyes Of	Poppy Family	Which Way You Goin' Billy (7)
	Love (3)	Porn Kings	Up To The Wildstyle (10)
	Nobody Needs Your Love (2)	Portishead	All Mine (8)
	Princess In Rags (9)	Powell, Cozy	Dance With The Devil (3)
	Something's Gotten Hold Of My		Na Na Na (10)
	Heart (1) with Marc Almond	PPK	Resurrection (3)
	Something's Gotten Hold Of My	Praise	Only You (4)
	Heart (5)	Pras	Blue Angels (6)
	That Girl Belongs To Yesterday	Precious	Say It Again (6)
	(7)	Prefab Sprout	King Of Rock 'N' Roll, The (7)
	Twenty-Four Hours From Tulsa	Presidents Of The	Peaches (8)
	(5)	United States	
Piu, Mario	Communication (Somebody	Presley, Elvis	All Shook Up (re-entry) (1)
	Answer The) (5)		Always On My Mind (9)
PJ & Duncan	Let's Get Ready To Rhumble		An American Trilogy (8)
	(9)		Are You Lonesome Tonight (1)
Placebo	Nancy Boy (4)		Big Hunk O' Love, A (4)
	Pure Morning (4)		Blue Moon (9)
	You Don't Care About Us (5)		Blue Suede Shoes (9)
Planet Funk	Chase The Sun (5)		Burning Love (7)
Planet Perfecto	Bullet In The Gun (2000 remix)		Crying In The Chapel (1)
	(7)		Devil In Disguise (1)
Plastic Bertrand	Ca Plane Pour Moi (8)		Don't (2)
Plastic Ono Band	Give Peace A Chance (2)		Don't Cry Daddy (8)
	Happy Xmas (War Is Over) (4)		Fool Such As I / I Need Your
	Happy Xmas (War Is Over) (re-		Love Tonight, A (1)
	entry) (2)		Girl Of My Best Friend, The (9)
	Instant Karma (5)		Good Luck Charm (1)
	Power To The People (7)		Hard-Headed Woman (2)
Plastic Penny	Everything I Am (6)		Heartbreak Hotel (2)
Plastic Population	Doctorin' The House (6)		Heartbreak Hotel / Hound Dog
	Only Way Is Up, The (1)		(re-issue) (10)
Platinum 45	Oi (8)		Hound Dog (2)
Platters	Great Pretender / Only You,		I Just Can't Help Believing (6)
	The (5)		In The Ghetto (2)
	My Prayer (4)		It's Now Or Never (1)
	Smoke Gets In Your Eyes (1)		It's Only Love / Beyond The
	Twilight Time (3)		Reef (3)
Plavka	Right In The Night (Fall In Love		I've Lost You (9)
	With Music) (re-issue) (10)		Jailhouse Rock (1)
Players Association	Turn The Music Up (8)		King Creole (2)
PM Dawn	Set Adrift On Memory Bliss (3)		Kissin' Cousins (10)
Pogues	Fairytale Of New York (2)		(Let Me Be Your) Teddy Bear
	Irish Rover, The (8)		(3)
Point Break	Stand Tough (7)		Little Less Conversation, A (1)
Pointer Sisters	Automatic (2)		Love Letters (6)
	Jump (For My Love) (6)		(Marie's The Name) His Latest
	Slowhand (10)		Flame / Little Sister (1)
Police	Can't Stand Losing You (re-		Mess Of Blues, A (2)
	release) (2)		Moody Blue (6)
	De Do Do Do De Da Da Da (5)		My Boy (5)
	Don't Stand So Close To Me		My Way (9)
	(1)		One Night / I Got Stung (1)
	Every Breath You Take (1)		Paralysed (8)

Group/Artiste	Title	Group/Artiste	Title
	Party (2)	Proclaimers	King Of The Road (EP) (9)
	Promised Land (9)		Letter From America (3)
	Rags To Riches (9)	Procol Harum	Homburg (6)
	Return To Sender (1)		Whiter Shade Of Pale, A (1)
	Rock A Hula Baby / Can't Help Falling In Love (1)	Prodigy	Baby's Got A Temper (5)
			Breathe (1)
	Santa Bring My Baby Back (To Me) (7)		Charly (3)
			Everybody In The Place (EP) (2)
	She's Not You (1)		Firestarter (1)
	Stuck On You (3)		No Good (Start The Dance) (4)
	Surrender (Torna Surriento) (1)		One Love (8)
	Suspicion (9)		Out Of Space / Ruff In The Jungle Bizness (5)
	Suspicious Minds (2)		
	There Goes My Everything (6)		Smack My Bitch Up (8)
	Too Much (6)	Product G&B	Maria Maria (6)
	Until It's Time For You To Go (5)	Progress presents Boy Wunda	Everybody (7)
	Way Down (1)	Propellerheads	On Her Majesty's Secret Service (7)
	Wear My Ring Around Your Neck (3)		
		Pseudo Echo	Funky Town (8)
	Wild In The Country / I Feel So Bad (4)	Psychotropic	Let's Talk About Sex (2)
		Public Domain	Operation Blade (Bass In The Place) (5)
	Wonder Of You, The (1)		
	Wooden Heart (1)	Public Image Ltd	Public Image (9)
	You Don't Have To Say You Love Me (9)		This Is Not A Love Song (5)
		Puckett, Gary	Lady Willpower (5)
Preston, Billy	Get Back (1)		Young Girl (1)
	With You I'm Born Again (2)		Young Girl (re-issue) (6)
Preston, Johnny	Cradle Of Love (2)	Puddle Of Mudd	Blurry (8)
	Running Bear (1)	Puff Daddy	Come With Me (2)
Pretenders	Brass In Pocket (1)		I Need A Girl (Part One) (4)
	Don't Get Me Wrong (10)		I'll Be Missing You (1)
	Hymn To Her (8)		Satisfy You (8)
	I Go To Sleep (7)	Pulp	Common People (2)
	I'll Stand By You (10)		Disco 2000 (7)
	Talk Of The Town (8)		Help The Aged (8)
Pretty Things	Don't Bring Me Down (10)		Mis-Shapes / Sorted For E's And Wizz (2)
Price, Alan	Jarrow Song (6)		
Price, Lloyd	Personality (9)		Something Changed (10)
	Stagger Lee (7)	Puretone	Addicted To Bass (2)
Priest, Maxi	Close To You (7)	Pussycat	Mississippi (1)
	Housecall (remix) (8)	Python Lee Jackson	In A Broken Dream (3)
	Wild World (5)	Quantum Jump	Lone Ranger, The (5)
Primal Scream	Kowalski (8)	Quartz introducing Dina Carroll	It's Too Late (8)
	Rocks / Funky Jam (7)		
Primitives	Crash (5)	Quatro, Suzi	Can The Can (1)
Prince	Alphabet Street (9)		Devil Gate Drive (1)
	Batdance (2)		48 Crash (3)
	Controversy (5)		If You Can't Give Me Love (4)
	Gett Off (4)		Wild One, The (7)
	Gold (10)	Quaye, Finley	Even After All (10)
	I Wanna Be Your Lover (41)	Queen	Another One Bites The Dust (5)
	Kiss (6)		Another One Bites The Dust (7)
	Let's Go Crazy / Take Me With You (7)		Bohemian Rhapsody (1)
			Bohemian Rhapsody (re-issue) / These Are The Days Of Our Lives (1)
	Most Beautiful Girl In The World, The (1)		
	My Name Is Prince (7)		
	1999 / Little Red Corvette (re-issue) (2)		Breakthru (7)
			Crazy Little Thing Called Love (2)
	1999 (re-entry) (10)		
	Purple Rain (8)		Don't Stop Me Now (9)
	Sexy MF / Strollin' (4)		Five Live EP (1)
	Sign O' The Times (10)		Flash (10)
	Thieves In The Temple (7)		Heaven For Everyone (2)
	When Doves Cry (4)		I Want It All (3)
Princess	Say I'm Your No.1 (7)		I Want To Break Free (3)
Proby, P J	Hold Me (3)		Innuendo (1)
	Maria (8)		It's A Hard Life (6)
	Somewhere (6)		Killer Queen (2)
	Together (8)		Kind Of Magic, A (3)

M
U
S
I
C

P
O
P

Group/Artiste	Title	Group/Artiste	Title
	Let Me Live (9)		Can't Get By Without You (2)
	One Vision (7)		Can't Get By Without You
	Radio Gaga (2)		(The Second Decade Remix)
	Seven Seas Of Rye (10)		(6)
	Somebody To Love (2)		You To Me Are Everything (1)
	Under Pressure (1)		You To Me Are Everything
	We Are The Champions (2)		(The Decade Remix 76-86)
	We Will Rock You (1)		(5)
	Winter's Tale, A (6)	Rebel MC & Double	Street Tuff (3)
	You're My Best Friend (7)	Rebelettes	Dance With Guitar Man (4)
Quiver	Arms Of Mary (5)		Play Me Like You Play Your
R & J Stone	We Do It (5)		Guitar (9)
Racey	Lay All Your Love On Me (3)	Red Box	For America (10)
	Some Girls (2)		Lean On Me (Ah-Li-Ayo) (3)
Radiohead	Creep (7)	Red Dragon	Compliments On Your Kiss (2)
	Karma Police (8)	Red Hot Chili Peppers	By The Way (2)
	No Surprises (4)		Give It Away (9)
	Paranoid Android (3)		Love Rollercoaster (7)
	Pyramid Song (5)		Zephyr Song, The (11)
	Street Spirit (Fade Out) (5)	Redbone	Witch Queen Of New Orleans,
Rafferty, Gerry	Baker Street (3)		The (2)
	Night Owl (5)	Redding, Otis	(Sittin' On) The Dock Of The
Rage	Run To You (3)		Bay (3)
Rage Against The	Bulls On Parade (8)	Reddy, Helen	Angie Baby (5)
Machine		Redman	Dirrty (1)
Rah Band	Clouds Across The Moon (6)	Rednex	Cotton Eye Joe (1)
	Crunch, The (6)	Reed, Lou	Walk On The Wild Side (10)
Rainbow	All Night Long (5)	Reef	Come Back Brighter (8)
	I Surrender (3)		Place Your Hands (6)
	Since You've Been Gone (6)	Reel 2 Real	Go On Move (7)
Rainwater, Marvin	Whole Lotta Woman (1)		I Like To Move It (5)
Rakim	Addictive (3)		Jazz It Up (7)
Ram Jam	Black Betty (7)	Reeves, Jim	Distant Drums (1)
Ramirez, Karen	Looking For Love (8)		I Love You Because (5)
Ramones	Baby I Love You (8)		I Won't Forget You (3)
Ramrods	Riders In The Sky (8)		It Hurts So Much (8)
Rank 1	Airwave (10)		There's A Heartache Following
Ranking Ann	Word Girl, The (6)		Me (6)
Ranks, Shabba	Housecall (remix) (8)		Welcome To My World (6)
	Mr Loverman (re-issue) (3)	Reeves, Martha	Dancing In The Street (re-
Rattles	Witch, The (8)		issue) (4)
Rawls, Lou	You'll Never Find Another Love	Reeves, Vic	Born Free (6)
	Like Mine (10)		Dizzy (1)
Ray Anthony	Dragnet (7)		I'm A Believer (3)
Ray Martin Orchestra	Blue Tango (8)	Regan, Joan	If I Give My Heart To You (re-
	Blue Tango (re-entry) (10)		entry) (3)
	Swedish Rhapsody (10)		May You Always (9)
	Swedish Rhapsody (re-entry)		Prize Of Gold (6)
	(4)		Ricochet (8)
Ray, Johnnie	Faith Can Move Mountains (7)		Ricochet (re-entry) (9)
	Faith Can Move Mountains (re-		Someone Else's Roses (5)
	entry) (9)	Reid, John	Push The Feeling On (remix)
	Hey There (5)		(3)
	If You Believe (re-entry) (7)		Surrender Your Love (7)
	Just Walkin' In The Rain (1)	Reid, Mike	Ugly Duckling, The (10)
	Let's Walk Thata-Way (4)	Reid, Neil	Mother Of Mine (2)
	Look Homeward Angel (7)	Reilly, Maggie	Moonlight Shadow (4)
	Somebody Stole My Gal (6)	REM	At My Most Beautiful (10)
	Somebody Stole My Gal (re-		Daysleeper (6)
	entry) (6)		E-Bow The Letter (4)
	Song Of The Dreamer (10)		Everybody Hurts (7)
	Such A Night (1)		Great Beyond, The (3)
	Yes Tonight Josephine (1)		Imitation Of Life (6)
Rayvon	Angel (1)		Shiny Happy People (6)
	In The Summertime (5)		Strange Currencies (9)
Rea, Chris	Fool (If You Think It's Over)		What's The Frequency Kenneth
	(30)		(9)
	Road To Hell (Part 2), The (10)	Rembrandts	I'll Be There For You (re-entry)
Real McCoy	Another Night (2)		(5)
	Run Away (6)		I'll Be There For You (Theme
Real Thing	Can You Feel The Force (5)		From Friends) (3)

Group/Artiste	Title	Group/Artiste	Title
Renaissance	Northern Lights (10)		Please Don't Tease (1)
Renee & Renato	Save Your Love (1)		Power To All Our Friends (4)
REO Speedwagon	Keep On Loving You (7)		Saviour's Day (1)
Republica	Drop Dead Gorgeous (7)		She Means Nothing To Me (9)
Revolution	Kiss (6)		Silhouettes (10)
	Let's Go Crazy / Take Me With You (7)		Some People (3)
			Summer Holiday (1)
	Purple Rain (8)		Theme For a Dream (3)
Reynolds Girls	I'd Rather Jack (8)		Throw Down The Line (7)
Reynolds, Debbie	Tammy (2)		Time Drags By (10)
Rhymes, Busta	Ante Up (7)		Travellin' Light (1)
	Gimme Some More (5)		True Love Ways (8)
	Hit 'Em High (The Monstars' Anthem) (8)		Twelfth Of Never, The (8)
			Visions (7)
	Rumble In The Jungle (3)		Voice In The Wilderness (2)
	Turn It Up / Fire It Up (2)		We Don't Talk Anymore (1)
	What's It Gonna Be?! (6)		We Should Be Together (10)
	Woo-Hah!! Got You All In Check (8)		When The Girl In Your Arms Is The Girl In Your Heart (3)
Rich In Paradise	Going Back To My Roots / Rich In Paradise (9)		Wind Me Up (Let Me Go) (2)
			Wired For Sound (4)
Rich Project, Tony	Nobody Knows (4)		Young Ones, The (1)
Rich, Charlie	Most Beautiful Girl, The (2)	Richard, Wendy	Come Outside (1)
Richard, Cliff	All I Ask Of You (3)	Richie, Lionel	All Night Long (All Night) (2)
	All My Love (6)		Dancing On The Ceiling (7)
	Best Of Me, The (2)		Endless Love (7)
	Big Ship (8)		Hello (1)
	Can't Keep This Feeling In (10)		My Destiny (7)
	Carrie (4)		Running With The Night (9)
	Congratulations (1)		Say You Say Me (8)
	Constantly (4)		Truly (6)
	Daddy's Home (2)	Rick Dees & His Cast Of Idiots	Disco Duck (Part One) (6)
	Day I Met Marie, The (10)		
	Devil Woman (9)	Rickett, Adam	I Breathe Again (5)
	Don't Talk To Him (2)	Rico	Message To You Rudy, A / Nite Club (10)
	Dreamin' (8)		
	Fall In Love With You (2)	Ride	Leave Them All Behind (9)
	Gee Whiz It's You (4)	Ridgway, Stan	Camouflage (4)
	Girl Like You, A (3)	Right Said Fred	Deeply Dippy (1)
	Goodbye Sam Hello Samantha (6)		Don't Talk Just Kiss (3)
			I'm Too Sexy (2)
	High Class Baby (7)	Right Said Fred & Friends	Stick It Out (4)
	I Could Easily Fall (In Love With You) (9)		
		Righteous Brothers	Unchained Melody (re-issue) (1)
	I Just Don't Have The Heart (3)		
	I Love You (1)		You've Lost That Lovin' Feelin' (1)
	I Still Believe In You (7)		
	I'm Looking Out The Window / Do You Want To Dance (2)		You've Lost That Lovin' Feelin' (re-issue) (3)
	I'm The Lonely One (8)		You've Lost That Lovin' Feelin' (re-issue) (10)
	In The Country (6)		
	It'll Be Me (2)	Rikrok	It Wasn't Me (1)
	It's All In The Game (2)	Rimes, LeAnn	Can't Fight The Moonlight (1)
	It's All Over (9)		How Do I Live (7)
	Living Doll (1)		Written In The Stars (10)
	Living Doll (1) with The Young Ones	Riperton, Minnie	Loving You (2)
		Ritchie Family	Best Disco In Town, The (10)
	Lucky Lips (4)	Ritter, Tex	Wayward Wind (8)
	Mean Streak (10)	Riva	Who Do You Love Now (Stringer) (3)
	Millennium Prayer, The (1)		
	Minute You're Gone, The (1)	Roachford	Cuddly Toy (re-issue) (4)
	Mistletoe And Wine (1)	Robbins, Marty	Devil Woman (5)
	Move It (2)	Robert Howard	Wait (7)
	My Pretty One (6)	Roberts, Malcolm	May I Have The Next Dream With You (8)
	Next Time / Bachelor Boy, The (1)		
		Robertson, B A	Bang Bang (2)
	Nine Times Out Of Ten (3)		Knocked It Off (8)
	On The Beach (7)		To Be Or Not To Be (9)
	Only Way Out, The (10)	Robertson, Don	Happy Whistler, The (8)
	Peace In Our Time (8)	Robinson, Floyd	Makin' Love (9)
	Please Don't Fall In Love (7)	Robinson, Smokey	Being With You (1)

MUSIC POP

Group/Artiste	Title	Group/Artiste	Title
	Tears Of A Clown, The (1)		(6)
	Tracks Of My Tears, The (9)		All Of My Life (9)
Robinson, Tom	War Baby (6)		Chain Reaction (1)
Robson & Jerome	I Believe / Up On The Roof (1)		Endless Love (7)
	Unchained Melody / (There'll Be Bluebirds Over) The White Cliffs Of Dover (1)		I'm Gonna Make You Love Me (3)
	What Becomes Of The Broken Hearted / Saturday Night At The Movies / You'll Never Walk Alone (1)		I'm Still Waiting (1)
			Love Hangover (10)
			My Old Piano (5)
			Not Over Yet (9)
			One Shining Moment (10)
Robyn	Show Me Love (8)		Reflections (5)
Rocker's Revenge	Walking On Sunshine (4)		Remember Me (7)
Rockin' Berries	He's In Town (3)		Surrender (10)
	Poor Man's Son (5)		Theme From Mahogany (Do You Know Where You're Going To) (5)
Rocksteady Crew	(Hey You) The Rocksteady Crew (6)		
Rockwell	Somebody's Watching Me (6)		Touch Me In The Morning (9)
Rodgers, Clodagh	Come Back And Shake Me (3)		Upside Down (2)
	Goodnight Midnight (4)		When You Tell Me That You Love Me (2)
	Jack In The Box (4)		
Rodgers, Jimmie	English Country Garden (5)		Why Do Fools Fall In Love (4)
	Kisses Sweeter Than Wine (7)		Work That Body (7)
Rodriguez	Ecuador (2)		You Are Everything (5)
Roe, Tommy	Dizzy (1)	Rosso, Nini	Il Silenzio (8)
	Everybody (9)	Roulettes	First Time, The (5)
	Folk Singer, The (4)	Roussos, Demis	Happy To Be On An Island In The Sun (5)
	Sheila (3)		
Rogers, Julie	Wedding, The (3)		Roussos Phenomenon EP, The (1)
Rogers, Kenny	Coward Of The County (1)		
	Islands In The Stream (7)		When Forever Has Gone (2)
	Lucille (1)	Rowland, Kelly	Dilemma (1)
	Ruby Don't Talk Your Love To Town (2)	Rowles, John	If I Only Had Time (3)
		Roxette	Almost Unreal (7)
	Something's Burning (8)		It Must Have Been Love (3)
Rolling Stones	Angie (5)		It Must Have Been Love (re-issue) (10)
	Brown Sugar / Bitch / Let It Rock (2)		
	Come On (21)		Joyride (4)
	Emotional Rescue (9)		Listen To Your Heart / Dangerous (6)
	Fool To Cry (6)		
	Get Off My Cloud (1)		Look, The (7)
	Have You Seen Your Mother Baby Standing In the Shadow (5)	Roxy Music	Angel Eyes (4)
			Dance Away (2)
			Jealous Guy (1)
	Honky Tonk Women (1)		Love Is The Drug (2)
	(I Can't Get No) Satisfaction (1)		More Than This (6)
	I Wanna Be Your Man (12)		Oh Yeah (On The Radio) (5)
	It's All Over Now (1)		Over You (5)
	It's Only Rock And Roll (10)		Pyjamarama (10)
	Jumping Jack Flash (1)		Street Life (9)
	Last Time, The (1)		Virginia Plain (4)
	Let's Spend The Night Together / Ruby Tuesday (3)	Roy 'Chubby' Brown	Living Next Door To Alice (Who The F**K Is Alice) (3)
		Royal Guardsmen	Snoopy Vs The Red Baron (8)
	Little Red Rooster (1)	Royal Philharmonic	All I Ask Of You (3)
	Miss You / Far Away Eyes (3)	Orchestra	Hooked On Classics (2)
	Nineteenth Nervous Breakdown (2)	Royce, Rose	Car Wash (9)
			Love Don't Live Here Anymore (2)
	Not Fade Away (3)		
	Paint It Black (1)		Wishing On A Star (3)
	Start Me Up (7)	Roza, Lita	(How Much Is) That Doggie In The Window (1)
	Tumbling Dice (5)		
	We Love You / Dandelion (8)	Rozalla	Everybody's Free (To Feel Good) (6)
Roman Numerals	Born Free (6)		
Romeo	It's All Gravy (9)	RTE Concert	Riverdance (9)
Romeo, Max	Wet Dream (10)	Orchestra	
Ronettes	Be My Baby (4)	Rubettes	Baby I Know (10)
Ronstadt, Linda	Don't Know Much (2)		I Can Do It (7)
	Somewhere Out There (8)		Juke Box Jive (3)
Rooftop Singers	Walk Right In (10)		Sugar Baby Love (1)
Ross, Diana	Ain't No Mountain High Enough	Rubia, Maria	Everytime You Need Me (3)

Group/Artiste	Title
Ruff Driverz presents Arrola	Dreaming (10)
Ruffin, Bruce	Mad About You (9)
Ruffin, David	Walk Away From Love (10)
Ruffin, Jimmy	Farewell Is A Lonely Sound (8)
	Hold On To My Love (7)
	I'll Say Forever My Love (7)
	It's Wonderful (To Be Loved By You) (6)
	What Becomes Of The Broken Hearted (10)
	What Becomes Of The Broken Hearted (re-issue) (4)
Rufus	Ain't Nobody (8)
	Ain't Nobody (remix) (6)
Run DMC	It's Like That (1)
	Walk This Way (8)
RuPaul	Don't Go Breaking My Heart (7)
Rush, Jennifer	Power Of Love, The (1)
Rushen, Patrice	Forget Me Nots (8)
Ruts	Babylon's Burning (7)
Ryan, Barry	Eloise (2)
Ryan, Marion	Love Me Forever (5)
Rydell, Bobby	Wild One (7)
S Club	Alive (5)
S Club Juniors	Automatic High (2)
	New Direction (2)
	One Step Closer (2)
	Puppy Love / Sleigh Ride (6)
S Club 7	Bring It All Back (1)
	Don't Stop Movin' (1)
	Have You Ever (1)
	Natural (3)
	Never Had A Dream Come True (1)
	Reach (2)
	S Club Party (2)
	Two In A Million / You're My Number One (2)
	You (2)
S Express	Hey Music Lover (6)
	Superfly Guy (5)
	Theme From S'Express (1)
S, Robin	Show Me Love (6)
	Show Me Love (remix) (9)
Sabrina	Boys (Summertime Love) (3)
Sad Cafe	Every Day Hurts (3)
Sade	Your Love Is King (6)
Safina, Alessandro	Your Song (4)
Safri Duo	Played A Live (The Bongo Song) (6)
Sager, Carole Bayer	You're Moving Out Today (6)
Sailor	Girls Girls Girls (7)
	Glass Of Champagne, A (2)
Saint Etienne	Tell Me Why (The Riddle) (7)
Sally Sweetland (soprano)	I'm Walking Behind You (1)
Salt-N-Pepa	Do You Want Me (5)
	Let's Talk About Sex (2)
	Push It / Tramp (2)
	Twist And Shout (4)
	Whatta Man (7)
Sanchez, Roger	Another Chance (1)
Sandpipers	Guantanamera (7)
Santana	Maria Maria (6)
	Smooth (3)
Santana, Juelz	Rocafella (13)
Santos	Camels (9)
Sarne, Mike	Come Outside (1)
Sarstedt, Peter	Frozen Orange Juice (10)
	Where Do You Go To My

Group/Artiste	Title
	Lovely (1)
Sarstedt, Robin	My Resistance Is Low (3)
Sash	Adelante (2)
	Ecuador (2)
	Encore Une Fois (2)
	Just Around The Hill (8)
	La Primavera (3)
	Move Mania (8)
	Mysterious Times (2)
	Stay (2)
	With My Own Eyes (10)
Saunders, Jessie	Love Can't Turn Around (10)
Savage Garden	Affirmation (8)
	I Knew I Loved You (10)
	To The Moon And Back (3)
	Truly Madly Deeply (4)
Savalas, Telly	If (1)
Sayer, Leo	Have You Ever Been In Love (10)
	How Much Love (10)
	I Can't Stop Lovin' You (Though I Try) (6)
	Long Tall Glasses (4)
	Moonlighting (2)
	More Than I Can Say (2)
	One Man Band (6)
	Show Must Go On, The (2)
	When I Need You (1)
	You Make Me Feel Like Dancing (2)
Scaffold	Lily The Pink (1)
	Liverpool Lou (7)
	Thank U Very Much (4)
Scaggs, Boz	What Can I Say (10)
Scanty Sandwich	Because Of You (3)
Scatman John	Scatman (3)
	Scatman's World (10)
Scooch	More Than I Needed To Know (5)
Scooter	Logical Song, The (2)
	Nessaja (4)
Scorpions	Wind Of Change (2)
Scott, Jack	My True Love (9)
Scott, Josey	Hero (4)
Scott, Linda	I've Told Every Little Star (7)
Scottish World Cup Football Squad	Ole Ola (Mulher Brasilieira) (4)
	We Have A Dream (5)
Scritti Politti	Wood Beez (Pray Like Aretha Franklin) (10)
	Word Girl, The (6)
Seahorses	Blinded By The Sun (7)
	Love Is The Law (3)
Seal	Crazy (2)
	Killer (EP) (8)
	Kiss From A Rose (re-issue) / I'm Alive (4)
	My Vision (6)
Searchers	Don't Throw Your Love Away (1)
	Goodbye My Love (4)
	Needles And Pins (1)
	Sugar And Spice (2)
	Sweets For My Sweet (1)
	When You Walk In The Room (3)
Secada, Jon	Just Another Day (5)
Secombe, Harry	This Is My Song (2)
Sedaka, Neil	Breaking Up Is Hard To Do (7)
	Calendar Girl (8)
	Happy Birthday Sweet Sixteen (3)

MUSIC

POP

Group/Artiste	Title	Group/Artiste	Title
	I Go Ape (9)		Voice In The Wilderness (2)
	Little Devil (9)		Wind Me Up (Let Me Go) (2)
	Oh Carol (3)		Wonderful Land (1)
	Stairway To Heaven (8)		Young Ones, The (1)
Seekers	Carnival Is Over, The (1)	Shaft	(Mucho Mambo) Sway (2)
	Georgy Girl (3)		Roobarb And Custard (7)
	I'll Never Find Another You (1)	Shag	Loop Di Love (4)
	Morningtown Ride (2)	Shaggy	Angel (1)
	Walk With Me (10)		Boombastic (1)
	World Of Our Own, A (3)		Hey Sexy Lady (10)
Selecter	On My Radio (8)		In The Summertime (5)
Sellers, Peter	Any Old Iron (17)		It Wasn't Me (1)
	Bangers And Mash (22)		Luv Me Luv Me (5)
	Goodness Gracious Me (4)		Me Julie (2)
	Hard Day's Night, A (14)		Oh Carolina (1)
Sensational Alex	Delilah (7)		Piece Of My Heart (7)
Harvey Band		Shakatak	Down On The Street (9)
Severine	Un Banc Un Arbre Une Rue (9)		Night Birds (9)
Sex Pistols	Anarchy In The UK (33)	Shakedown	At Night (6)
	C'Mon Everybody (3)	Shakespears Sister	I Don't Care (7)
	God Save The Queen (2)		Stay (1)
	Holidays In The Sun (8)		You're History (7)
	No One Is Innocent / My Way	Shakira	Underneath Your Clothes (3)
	(7)		Whenever Wherever (2)
	Pretty Vacant (6)	Shalamar	Dead Giveaway (8)
	Silly Thing (6)		I Can Make You Feel Good (7)
	Something Else / Friggin' In		Night To Remember, A (5)
	The Riggin' (3)		There It Is (5)
Sex-O-Lettes	Get Dancing (8)	Sham 69	Hersham Boys (6)
	I Wanna Dance Wit Choo (6)		Hurry Up Harry (10)
Shadows	Apache (1)		If The Kids Are United (9)
	Atlantis (2)	Shamen	Boss Drum (4)
	Dance On (1)		Ebeneezer Goode (1)
	Don't Cry For Me Argentina (5)		LSI (6)
	Don't Make My Baby Blue (10)		Move Any Mountain (remix) (4)
	Don't Talk To Him (2)		Phorever People (5)
	Fall In Love With You (2)	Shangri-Las	Leader Of The Pack (re-issue)
	FBI (6)		(3)
	Foot Tapper (1)		Leader Of The Pack (re-issue)
	Frightened City (3)		(7)
	Gee Whiz It's You (4)	Shanice	I Love You Smile (2)
	Girl Like You, A (3)	Shanks	Sweet Like Chocolate (1)
	Guitar Tango (4)	Shannon	Move Mania (8)
	I Could Easily Fall (In Love	Shannon, Del	Hats Off To Larry (6)
	With You) (9)		Hey Little Girl (2)
	I Love You (1)		Keep Searchin' (We'll Follow
	I'm Looking Out The Window /		The Sun) (3)
	Do You Want To Dance (2)		Little Town Flirt (4)
	I'm The Lonely One (8)		Runaway (1)
	In The Country (6)		So Long Baby (10)
	It'll Be Me (2)		Swiss Maid (2)
	It's All In The Game (2)		Two Kinds Of Teardrops (5)
	Kon-Tiki (1)	Shapiro, Helen	Don't Treat Me Like A Child (3)
	Lucky Lips (4)		Little Miss Lonely (8)
	Man Of Mystery / The Stranger		Tell Me What He Said (2)
	(5)		Walkin' Back To Happiness (1)
	Next Time / Bachelor Boy, The		You Don't Know (1)
	(1)	Sharkey, Feargal	Good Heart, A (1)
	Nine Times Out Of Ten (3)		You Little Thief (5)
	On The Beach (7)	Shaw, Sandie	Girl Don't Come (3)
	Please Don't Tease (1)		I'll Stop At Nothing (4)
	Rise And Fall Of Flingel Bunt,		Long Live Love (1)
	The (5)		Message Understood (6)
	Savage, The (10)		Monsieur Dupont (6)
	Shindig (6)		Puppet On A String (1)
	Summer Holiday (1)		(There's) Always Something
	Theme For a Dream (3)		There To Remind Me (1)
	Theme From The Deerhunter		Tomorrow (9)
	(Cavatina) (9)	Shearston, Gary	I Get A Kick Out Of You (7)
	Time Drags By (10)	Shed Seven	Going For Gold (8)
	Travellin' Light (1)	Sheer Elegance	Life Is Too Short Girl (9)

Group/Artiste	Title
Shelley Nelson	Here's Where The Story Ends (7)
Shelley, Peter	Gee Baby (4)
	Love Me Love My Dog (3)
Shelton, Anne	Lay Down Your Arms (1)
	Sailor (10)
Shepard, Vonda	Searchin' My Soul (10)
Sherbet	Howzat (4)
Shervington, Pluto	Dat (6)
Shirelles	Will You Love Me Tomorrow (4)
Shirley	Shame Shame Shame (6)
Shocking Blue	Mighty Joe (43)
	Venus (8)
Shondells	Mony Mony (1)
Showaddywaddy	Dancin' Party (4)
	Heartbeat (7)
	Hey Rock And Roll (2)
	I Wonder Why (2)
	Little Bit Of Soap, A (5)
	Pretty Little Angel Eyes (5)
	Three Steps To Heaven (2)
	Under The Moon Of Love (1)
	When (3)
	You Got What It Takes (2)
Shut Up & Dance	Raving I'm Raving (2)
Shy FX & T Power	Shake Ur Body (7)
Sia	Taken For Granted (10)
Siffre, Labi	(Something Inside) So Strong (4)
Sigue Sigue Sputnik	Love Missile F1-11 (3)
Silver Convention	Get Up And Boogie (7)
Simon & Garfunkel	Boxer, The (6)
	Bridge Over Troubled Water (1)
	Homeward Bound (9)
	Mrs Robinson (4)
	Mrs Robinson (EP) (9)
Simon Dupree & The Big Sound	Kites (9)
Simon Park Orchestra	Eye Level (re-entry) (1)
Simon, Carly	Coming Around Again (10)
	Nobody Does It Better (7)
	Why (10)
	You're So Vain (3)
Simon, Paul	Mother And Child Reunion (5)
	Take Me To The Mardi Gras (7)
	You Can Call Me Al (4)
Simone, Nina	Ain't Got No – I Got Life / Do What You Gotta Do (2)
	My Baby Just Cares For Me (5)
	To Love Somebody (5)
Simple Minds	Alive And Kicking (7)
	All The Things She Said (9)
	Belfast Child (1)
	Don't You (Forget About Me) (7)
	Let There Be Love (6)
	Love Song / Alive And Kicking (re-issues) (6)
	Sanctify Yourself (10)
	She's A River (9)
Simply Red	Air That I Breathe, The (6)
	Angel (4)
	Fairground (1)
	For Your Babies (9)
	Holding Back The Years (2)
	If You Don't Know Me By Now (2)
	Money's Too Tight (To Mention) (13)
	Say You Love Me (7)
	Stars (8)

Group/Artiste	Title
Simpson, Jessica	I Wanna Love You Forever (7)
Simpsons	Do The Bartman (1)
Simpsons featuring Bart & Homer	Deep Deep Trouble (7)
Sims, Joyce	Come Into My Life (7)
Sims, Kym	Too Blind To See It (5)
Sinatra, Frank	All The Way (re-entry) (3)
	High Hopes (re-entry) (6)
	I've Got You Under My Skin (4)
	Learnin' The Blues (2)
	Love And Marriage (3)
	(Love Is) The Tender Trap (2)
	Love's Been Good To Me (8)
	My Way (5)
	Somethin' Stupid (1)
	Strangers In The Night (1)
	Theme From New York New York (re-issue) (4)
	Three Coins In The Fountain (1)
	Young At Heart (12)
Sinatra, Nancy	Did You Ever (2)
	Somethin' Stupid (1)
	Sugar Town (8)
	These Boots Are Made For Walking (1)
Sinclair, Bob	I Feel For You (9)
Singing Nun (Soeur Sourire)	Dominique (7)
Sinitta	Cross My Broken Heart (6)
	Right Back Where We Started From (4)
	So Macho / Cruising (2)
	Toy Boy (4)
Siouxsie & The Banshees	Dear Prudence (3)
	Hong Kong Garden (7)
Sisqo	Dance For Me (6)
	Thong Song (3)
	Unleash The Dragon (6)
Sister Sledge	Frankie (1)
	He's The Greatest Dancer (6)
	Lost In Music (remix) (4)
	We Are Family (8)
	We Are Family (remix) (5)
Sisters Of Mercy	Temple Of Love (3)
	This Corrosion (7)
Sixpence None The Richer	Kiss Me (4)
Skellern, Peter	You're A Lady (3)
Skids	Into The Valley (10)
Sky	Toccata (5)
Skye	Drifting Away (9)
SL2	On A Ragga Tip (2)
Slade	Bangin' Man (3)
	Coz I Luv You (1)
	Cum On Feel The Noize (1)
	Everyday (3)
	Far Far Away (2)
	Gudbuy T'Jane (2)
	Look Wot You Dun (4)
	Mama Weer All Crazee Now (1)
	Merry Xmas Everybody (1)
	My Friend Stan (2)
	My Oh My (2)
	Run Run Away (7)
	Skweeze Me Pleeze Me (1)
	Take Me Bak 'Ome (1)
	Thanks For The Memory (Wham Bam Thank You Mam) (7)

M
U
S
I
C

P
O
P

Group/Artiste	Title
	We'll Bring The House Down (10)
Sledge, Percy	When A Man Loves A Woman (4)
	When A Man Loves A Woman (re-issue) (2)
Sleeper	Nice Guy Eddie (10)
	Sale Of The Century (10)
Slik	Forever And Ever (1)
Sly & The Family Stone	Dance To The Music (7)
Sly Fox	Let's Go All The Way (3)
Small Faces	All Or Nothing (1)
	Hey Girl (10)
	Itchycoo Park (3)
	Itchycoo Park (re-issue) (9)
	Lazy Sunday (2)
	My Mind's Eye (4)
	Sha La La La Lee (3)
	Tin Soldier (9)
Smart Es	Sesame's Treet (2)
Smashing Pumpkins	End Is The Beginning Is The End, The (10)
	Tonight Tonight (7)
Smear Campaign	(I Want To Be) Elected (9)
Smith Group, Patti	Because The Night (5)
Smith, Hurricane	Don't Let It Die (2)
	Oh Babe What Would You Say? (4)
Smith, Muriel	Hold Me Thrill Me Kiss Me (3)
Smith, O C	Son Of Hickory Holler's Tramp (2)
Smith, Will	Black Suits Comin' (Nod Ya Head) (3)
	Boy You Knock Me Out (3)
	Gettin' Jiggy Wit It (3)
	Just The Two Of Us (2)
	Men In Black (1)
	Miami (3)
	Wild Wild West (2)
	Will 2K (2)
Smiths	Heaven Knows I'm Miserable Now (10)
	Sheila Take A Bow (10)
	This Charming Man (re-issue) (8)
Smoke City	Underwater Love (4)
Smokie	Don't Play Your Rock 'N' Roll To Me (8)
	If You Think You Know How To Love Me (3)
	It's Your Life (5)
	Living Next Door To Alice (5)
	Living Next Door To Alice (Who The F**K Is Alice) (3)
	Needles And Pins (10)
	Oh Carol (5)
Smurfs	I've Got A Little Puppy (4)
	Smurf Song, The (2)
	Your Christmas Wish (8)
Snap	Cult Of Snap (8)
	Do You See The Light (Looking For) (10)
	Exterminate (2)
	Mary Had A Little Boy (8)
	Oops Up (5)
	Power, The (1)
	Rhythm Is A Dancer (1)
	Snap Megamix (10)
	Welcome To Tomorrow (6)
Sneaker Pimps	6 Underground (remix) (9)

Group/Artiste	Title
Snoop Dogg	Next Episode, The (3)
Snoop Doggy Dogg	Still D.R.E. (6)
Snow	Informer (2)
Snow, Mark	X-Files, The (2)
So Solid Crew	They Don't Know (3)
	21 Seconds (1)
So Solid Crew presents Mr Shabz	Haters (8)
Soft Cell	Bed Sitter (4)
	Say Hello Wave Goodbye (3)
	Tainted Love (1)
	Tainted Love (5) with Marc Almond
	Torch (2)
	What (3)
Soho	Hippy Chick (re-entry) (8)
Somerville, Jimmy	To Love Somebody (8)
	You Make Me Feel (Mighty Real) (5)
Sonia	Listen To Your Heart (10)
	Only Fools (Never Fall In Love) (10)
	You'll Never Stop Me From Loving You (1)
Sonique	I Put A Spell On You (re-issue) (8)
	It Feels So Good (remix) (1)
	Sky (2)
Sonny	All I Ever Need Is You (8)
	I Got You Babe (1)
	Laugh At Me (9)
	Little Man (4)
Soul Asylum	Runaway Train (re-entry) (7)
Soul City Symphony	Hustle, The (3)
Soul II Soul	Back To Life (However Do You Want Me) (1)
	Dream's A Dream, A (6)
	Get A Life (3)
	Joy (4)
	Keep On Moving (5)
Soul, David	Don't Give Up On Us (1)
	Going In With My Eyes Open (2)
	Let's Have A Quiet Night In (8)
	Silver Lady (1)
Soulsearcher	Can't Get Enough (8)
Sounds Orchestral	Cast Your Fate To The Wind (5)
Soup Dragons	I'm Free (5)
Source	You Got The Love (3)
	You Got The Love (4)
South, Joe	Games People Play (6)
Southside Spinners	Luvstruck (9)
Sovine, Red	Teddy Bear (4)
Space	Avenging Angels (6)
	Ballad Of Tom Jones, The (4)
	Magic Fly (2)
	Me And You Versus The World (9)
Spacedust	Gym And Tonic (1)
Spagna	Call Me (2)
Spandau Ballet	Chant No. 1 (I Don't Need This Pressure On) (3)
	Gold (2)
	I'll Fly For You (9)
	Instinction (10)
	Lifeline (7)
	Musclebound / Glow (10)
	Only When You Leave (3)
	Through The Barricades (6)
	To Cut A Long Story Short (5)
	True (1)

Group/Artiste	Title	Group/Artiste	Title
Sparkle	Be Careful (7)	Springfields	Island Of Dreams (5)
Sparks	Amateur Hour (7)		Say I Won't Be There (5)
	Beat The Clock (10)	Springsteen, Bruce	Dancing In The Dark (re-entry) (4)
	This Town Ain't Big Enough For Both Of Us (2)		I'm On Fire / Born In The USA (5)
Sparxxx, Bubba	Ugly (7)		Santa Claus Is Comin' To Town / My Hometown (9)
Spears, Billie Jo	Blanket On The Ground (6)		Streets Of Philadelphia (2)
	What I've Got In Mind (4)	Springwater	I Will Return (5)
Spears, Britney	Baby One More Time (1)	Squadronaires	Ricochet (8)
	Born To Make You Happy (1)		Ricochet (re-entry) (9)
	Boys (7)	Squeeze	Cool For Cats (2)
	I'm A Slave For You (4)		Labelled With Love (4)
	I'm Not A Girl Not Yet A Woman (2)		Take Me I'm Yours (19)
	Lucky (5)		Up The Junction (2)
	Oops ... I Did It Again (1)	St Marie, Buffy	Soldier Blue (7)
	Overprotected (4)	St Peters, Crispian	Pied Piper (5)
	Sometimes (3)		You Were On My Mind (2)
	Stronger (7)	St Thomas More	If I Had Words (3)
	(You Drive Me) Crazy (5)	School Choir	
Special AKA	Gangsters (6)	St Winifred's School	No One Quite Like Grandma
	Nelson Mandela (9)	Choir	(1)
	Special AKA Live EP, The (1)	Stafford, Jo	Make Love To Me (8)
Specials	Do Nothing / Maggie's Farm (4)		You Belong To Me (1)
	Ghost Town (1)		Stomp (1)
	Message To You Rudy / Nite Club, A (10)		Thank Abba For The Music (4)
	Rat Race / Rude Boys Outa Jail (5)		When I Said Goodbye / Summer Of Love (5)
	Stereotype / International Jet Set (6)		Words Are Not Enough / I Know Him So Well (5)
Spencer Davis Group	Gimme Some Loving (2)	Stamina MC	LK (Carolina Carol Bela) (17)
	I'm A Man (9)	Stanley Black & His	Book (re-entry), The (10)
	Keep On Running (1)	Orchestra	Book, The (5)
	Somebody Help Me (1)		Rags To Riches (re-entry) (3)
Spice Girls	Goodbye (1)	Stansfield, Lisa	All Around The World (1)
	Holler / Let Love Lead The Way (1)		Change (10)
	Mama / Who Do You Think You Are (1)		Five Live EP (1)
			In All The Right Places (8)
	Say You'll Be Mine (1)		Live Together (10)
	Spice Up Your Life (1)		People Hold On (4)
	Stop (2)		Real Thing, The (9)
	Too Much (1)		Someday (I'll Come Back) (10)
	2 Become 1 (1)	Stardust	Music Sounds Better With You (2)
	Viva Forever (1)		
	Wannabe (1)	Stardust, Alvin	I Feel Like Buddy Holly (7)
Spiller	Groovejet (If This Ain't Love) (1)		I Won't Run Away (7)
			Jealous Mind (1)
Spin Doctors	Two Princes (3)		My Coo-Ca-Choo (2)
Spitting Image	Chicken Song, The (1)		Pretend (4)
Splodgenessabounds	Simon Templar / Two Pints Of Lager And A Packet Of Crisps Please (7)		Red Dress (7)
			You You You (6)
		Stargazers	Broken Wings (re-entry) (1)
Spooks	Things I've Seen (6)		Close The Door (6)
Springfield, Dusty	All I See Is You (9)		Finger Of Suspicion (1)
	Going Back (10)		I See The Moon (1)
	Heart and Soul (75)		Twenty Tiny Fingers (4)
	I Close My Eyes And Count To Ten (4)	Starlight	Numero Uno (9)
		Starr, Edwin	Contact (6)
	I Just Don't Know What To Do With Myself (3)		H.A.P.P.Y. Radio (9)
			War (3)
	I Only Want To Be With You (4)	Starr, Freddie	It's You (9)
	In The Middle Of Nowhere (8)	Starr, Kay	Changing Partners (4)
	Losing You (9)		Comes A-Long A-Love (1)
	Some Of Your Lovin' (8)		Rock And Roll Waltz (1)
	Son Of A Preacher Man (9)		Side By Side (7)
	What Have I Done To Deserve This (2)	Starr, Ringo	Back Off Boogaloo (2)
			It Don't Come Easy (4)
	You Don't Have To Say You Love Me (1)		Photograph (8)
			You're Sixteen (4)
		Starsailor	Alcoholic (10)

M
U
S
I
C

P
O
P

Group/Artiste	Title	Group/Artiste	Title
Starship	Nothing's Gonna Stop Us Now (1)		Pick A Part That's New (4)
		Steve & Eydie	I Want To Stay Here (3)
Starsound	Stars On 45 (2)	Steve 'Silk' Hurley	Jack Your Body (1)
	Stars On 45 Vol.2 (2)	Stevens, Cat	I'm Gonna Get Me A Gun (6)
Staton, Candi	Nights On Broadway (6)		Lady D'Arbanville (8)
	You Got The Love (4)		Matthew And Son (2)
	You Got The Love (re-entry) (3)		Morning Has Broken (9)
	Young Hearts Run Free (2)	Stevens, Connie	Sixteen Reasons (9)
Status Quo	Anniversary Waltz – Part 1, The (2)	Stevens, Ray	Bridget The Midget (The Queen Of The Blues) (2)
	Break The Rules (8)		Everything Is Beautiful (6)
	Burning Bridges (On And Off And On Again) (5)		Misty (2)
			Streak, The (1)
	Caroline (5)	Stevens, Shakin'	Cry Just A Little Bit (3)
	Dear John (10)		Green Door (1)
	Down Down (1)		I'll Be Satisfied (10)
	Ice In The Sun (8)		It's Raining (10)
	In The Army Now (2)		Letter To You, A (10)
	Marguerita Time (3)		Love Worth Waiting For, A (2)
	Ol' Rag Blues (9)		Merry Christmas Everyone (1)
	Paper Plane (8)		Oh Julie (1)
	Pictures Of Matchstick Men (7)		Rockin' Good Way, A (5)
	Rain (7)		Shakin' Stevens EP, The (2)
	Rock 'N' Roll (8)		Shirley (6)
	Rockin' All Over The World (3)		Teardrops (5)
	Roll Over Lay Down (9)		This Ole House (1)
	Rollin' Home (9)		What Do You Want To Make Those Eyes At Me For (5)
	Something 'Bout You Baby I Like (9)		You Drive Me Crazy (2)
	Wanderer, The (7)	Stewart, Amii	Knock On Wood (6)
	What You're Proposing (2)		Knock On Wood / Light My Fire (remix) (7)
	Whatever You Want (4)		Light My Fire / 137 Disco Heaven (medley) (5)
	Wild Side Of Life (9)	Stewart, Andy	Donald Where's Your Troosers (re-issue) (4)
Stealer's Wheel	Stuck In The Middle With You (8)		
Steam	Na Na Hey Hey Kiss Him Goodbye (9)	Stewart, Dave	It's My Party (1)
Steele, Tommy	Butterfingers (re-entry) (8)	Stewart, Dave A	Lily Was Here (6)
	Come On Let's Go (10)	Stewart, Jermaine	Say It Again (7)
	Little White Bull (6)		We Don't Have To ... (2)
	Nairobi (3)	Stewart, Rod	All For Love (2)
	Singing The Blues (1)		Angel / What Made Milwaukee Famous (Has Made A Loser Out Of Me) (4)
	Water Water / Handful Of Songs (5)		Baby Jane (1)
Steeleye Span	All Around My Hat (5)		Da Ya Think I'm Sexy? (1)
Stefani, Gwen	Let Me Blow Ya Mind (4)		Da Ya Think I'm Sexy? (7) with N-Trance
Stephen 'Tin Tin' Duffy	Kiss Me (4)		Downtown Train (10)
Steps	After The Love Has Gone (5)		Every Beat Of My Heart (2)
	Better Best Forgotten (2)		Farewell – Bring It On Home To Me / You Send Me (7)
	Chain Reaction / One For Sorrow (remix) (2)		Have I Told You Lately (5)
	Deeper Shade Of Blue (4)		Hotlegs / I Was Only Joking (5)
	Heartbeat / Tragedy (1)		I Don't Want To Talk About It / First Cut Is The Deepest (1)
	Here And Now / You'll Be Sorry (4)		It Takes Two (5)
	It's The Way You Make Me Feel / Too Busy Thinking 'Bout My Baby (2)		Killing Of Georgie (Parts 1 And 2), The (2)
	Last Thing On My Mind (6)		Maggie May (1)
	Love's Got A Hold On My Heart (2)		Motown Song, The (10)
	One For Sorrow (2)		Oh No Not My Baby (6)
	Say You'll Be Mine / Better The Devil You Know (4)		Ole Ola (Mulher Brasilieira) (4)
			Reason to Believe (19)
Stereophonics	Bartender And The Thief, The (3)		Rhythm Of My Heart (3)
			Sailing (1)
	Handbags And Gladrags (4)		Sailing (re-entry) (3)
	Have A Nice Day (5)		This Old Heart Of Mine (4)
	Just Looking (4)		Tom Traubert's Blues (Waltzing Matilda) (6)
	Mama Told Me Not Come (4)		Tonight I'm Yours (Don't Hurt
	Mr Writer (5)		

Group/Artiste	Title	Group/Artiste	Title
	Me) (8)		(2)
	Tonight's The Night (Gonna Be Alright) (5)	Styx	Babe (6)
		Sub Sub	Ain't No Love (Ain't No Use) (3)
	What Am I Gonna Do (3)	Suede	Animal Nitrate (7)
	You Wear It Well (1)		Beautiful Ones (8)
	You're In My Heart (3)		Electricity (5)
Stigers, Curtis	I Wonder Why (5)		Filmstar (9)
	You're All That Matters To Me (6)		Lazy (9)
			Saturday Night (6)
Stiltskin	Inside (1)		Stay Together (3)
Sting	All For Love (2)		Trash (3)
	When We Dance (9)	Sugababes	Freak Like Me (1)
Stock Aitken Waterman	Ferry 'Cross The Mersey (1)		Overload (6)
	Mr Sleaze (3)		Round Round (1)
Stoloff, Morris	Moonglow / Theme From Picnic (7)		Stronger / Angels With Dirty Faces (7)
Stone Roses	Elephant Stone (8)	Sugar Ray	Every Morning (10)
	Love Spreads (2)	Sugarhill Gang	Rapper's Delight (3)
	One Love (4)	Suggs	Cecilia (4)
	What The World Is Waiting For / Fool's Gold (8)		I'm Only Sleeping / Off On Holiday (7)
Storm	Time To Burn (3)	Sum 41	Fat Lip (8)
Stranglers	All Day And All Of The Night (7)	Summer	Welcome To Tomorrow (6)
	European Female (9)	Summer, Donna	Down Deep Inside (Theme From The Deep) (5)
	Golden Brown (2)		I Don't Wanna Get Hurt (7)
	No More Heroes (8)		I Feel Love (1)
	Peaches / Go Buddy Go (8)		I Feel Love (re-issue) (8)
	Something Better Change / Straighten Out (9)		I Love You (10)
	Strange Little Girl (7)		Love To Love You Baby (4)
Strawberry Switchblade	Since Yesterday (5)		Love's Unkind (3)
			Macarthur Park (5)
Strawbs	Part Of The Union (2)		No More Tears (Enough Is Enough) (3)
Stray Cats	Rock This Town (9)		This Time I Know It's For Real (3)
	Runaway Boys (9)		
Streisand, Barbra	I Finally Found Someone (10)	Sunny	Doctor's Orders (7)
	Love Theme From A Star Is Born (Evergreen) (3)	Supergrass	Alright / Time (2)
			Going Out (5)
	No More Tears (Enough Is Enough) (3)		Lenny (10)
	Tell Him (3)		Moving (9)
	Woman In Love (1)		Richard III (2)
	You Don't Bring Me Flowers (5)		Sun Hits The Sky (10)
Stretch 'N' Vern present Maddogg	I'm Alive (6)	Supermen Lovers	Starlight (2)
		Supertramp	Breakfast In America (9)
Strike	U Sure Do (re-entry) (4)		Logical Song, The (7)
String-A-Longs	Wheels (8)	Supremes	Automatically Sunshine (10)
Strummer, Joe	England's Irie (6)		Baby Love (1)
Stryker	We're Gonna Do It Again (6)		Floy Joy (9)
Stuntmasters	Ladyboy Is Mine, The (10)		Happening, The (6)
Style Council	Groovin' (You're The Best Thing) / Big Boss Groove (5)		I'm Gonna Make You Love Me (3)
	It Didn't Matter (9)		Nathan Jones (5)
	Long Hot Summer / Paris Match (3)		Reflections (5)
			Stoned Love (3)
	My Ever Changing Moods (5)		Stop In The Name Of Love (7)
	Shout To The Top (7)		Up The Ladder To The Roof (6)
	Speak Like A Child (4)		Where Did Our Love Go (3)
	Walls Come Tumbling Down (6)		You Can't Hurry Love (3)
Stylistics	Betcha By Golly Wow (13)		You Keep Me Hangin' On (8)
	Can't Give You Anything (But My Love) (1)	Surfaris	Wipe Out (5)
		Survivor	Burning Heart (5)
	Can't Help Falling In Love (4)		Eye Of The Tiger (1)
	Funky Weekend (10)	Sutherland Brothers	Arms Of Mary (5)
	I'm Stone In Love With You (9)	Swan, Billy	I Can Help (6)
	Let's Put It All Together (9)	Sweet	Ballroom Blitz, The (2)
	Na Na Is The Saddest Word (5)		Blockbuster (1)
	Rockin' Roll Baby (6)		Co-Co (2)
	Sing Baby Sing (3)		Fox On The Run (2)
	16 Bars (7)		Funny Funny (13)
	You Make Me Feel Brand New		Hell Raiser (2)

MUSIC

POP

Group/Artiste	Title
	Little Willy (4)
	Love Is Like Oxygen (9)
	Six Teens, The (9)
	Teenage Rampage (2)
	Wig-Wam Bam (4)
Sweet Dreams	Honey Honey (10)
Sweet Female Attitude	Flowers (2)
Sweet People	Et Les Oiseaux Chantaient (And The Birds Were Singing) (4)
Sweet Sensation	Sad Sweet Dreamer (1)
Sweetbox	Everything's Gonna Be Alright (5)
Swing Out Sister	Breakout (4)
	Surrender (7)
Swinging Blue Jeans	Hippy Hippy Shake (2)
	You're No Good (3)
SWV	Right Here (3)
Sybil	Love I Lost, The (3)
	Walk On By (6)
	When I'm Good And Ready (5)
Sylvester	You Make Me Feel (Mighty Real) (8)
Sylvia	Y Viva Espana (4)
Syreeta	With You I'm Born Again (2)
T Rex	Children Of The Revolution (2)
	Get It On (1)
	Groover, The (4)
	Hot Love (1)
	Jeepster (2)
	Metal Guru (1)
	Ride A White Swan (2)
	Solid Gold Easy Action (2)
	Telegram Sam (1)
	20th Century Boy (3)
Taffy	I Love My Radio (My Deejay's Radio) (6)
Taja Seville	Love Is Contagious (7)
Taka Boom	Must Be The Music (8)
Take That	Babe (1)
	Back For Good (1)
	Could It Be Magic (3)
	Everything Changes (1)
	How Deep Is Your Love (1)
	It Only Takes A Minute (7)
	Love Ain't Here Anymore (3)
	Million Love Songs, A (7)
	Never Forget (1)
	Pray (1)
	Promises (38)
	Relight My Fire (1)
	Sure (1)
	Why Can't I Wake Up With You (2)
Talking Heads	Road To Nowhere (6)
Tamperer	Feel It (1)
	Hammer To The Heart (6)
	If You Buy This Record Your Life Will Be Better (3)
Tams	Hey Girl Don't Bother Me (1)
Taste Of Honey, A	Boogie Oogie Oogie (3)
Tavares	Don't Take Away The Music (4)
	Heaven Must Be Missing An Angel (4)
	More Than A Woman (7)
	Whodunit (4)
Taylor, James	You've Got A Friend (4)
Taylor, R Dean	Indiana Wants Me (2)
	There's A Ghost In My House (3)

Group/Artiste	Title
Teardrop Explodes	Reward (6)
Tears For Fears	Change (4)
	Everybody Wants To Rule The World (2)
	Everybody Wants To Run The World (5)
	Mad World (3)
	Pale Shelter (5)
	Shout (4)
	Sowing The Seeds Of Love (5)
Technohead	I Wanna Be A Hippy (6)
Technotronic	Get Up (Before The Night Is Over) (2)
	Megamix (6)
	Pump Up The Jam (2)
	Rockin' Over The Beat (9)
Ted Heath Orchestra	Dragnet (re-entry) (9)
	Hot Toddy (6)
	Skin Deep (9)
	Swingin' Shepherd Blues (3)
Teddy Bears	To Know Him Is To Love Him (2)
Teletubbies	Teletubbies Say Eh-Oh! (1)
Temperance Seven	Pasadena (4)
	You're Driving Me Crazy (1)
Temptations	Ball Of Confusion (7)
	Get Ready (10)
	I'm Gonna Make You Love Me (3)
	Just My Imagination (Running Away With Me) (8)
	Motown Song, The (10)
	My Girl (re-issue) (2)
10CC	Art For Art's Sake (5)
	Dean And I, The (10)
	Donna (2)
	Dreadlock Holiday (1)
	Good Morning Judge (5)
	I'm Mandy Fly Me (6)
	I'm Not In Love (1)
	Life Is A Minestrone (7)
	Rubber Bullets (1)
	Things We Do For Love, The (6)
	Wall Street Shuffle, The (10)
Ten City	That's The Way Love Is (8)
Ten Pole Tudor	Swords Of A Thousand Men (6)
	Who Killed Bambi (6)
Ten Sharp	You (10)
Ten Years After	Love Like A Man (10)
Tennessee Ernie Ford	Ballad Of Davy Crockett, The (3)
	Give Me Your Word (1)
	Sixteen Tons (1)
Tennille	Do That To Me One More Time (7)
Terrell, Tammi	Onion Song (9)
Terrorvision	Bad Actress (10)
	Perseverance (5)
	Tequila (2)
Terry, Todd	Keep On Jumpin' (8)
	Something Goin' On (5)
Tex, Joe	Ain't Gonna Bump No More (With No Big Fat Woman) (2)
Texas	Black-Eyed Boy (5)
	Halo (10)
	I Don't Want A Lover (8)
	In Demand (6)
	In Our Lifetime (4)
	Inner Smile (6)
	Put Your Arms Around Me (10)

Group/Artiste	Title
	Say What You Want (3)
	Say What You Want / Insane (re-recording) (4)
	Summer Son (5)
Them	Baby Please Don't Go (10)
	Here Comes The Night (2)
Therapy?	Shortsharpshock EP (9)
They Might Be Giants	Birdhouse In Your Soul (6)
Thin Lizzy	Boys Are Back In Town, The (8)
	Killer On The Loose (10)
	Waiting For An Alibi (9)
	Whiskey In The Jar (6)
Third World	Dancing On The Floor (Hooked On Love) (10)
	Now That We've Found Love (10)
Thomas, Evelyn	High Energy (5)
Thomas, Kenny	Thinking About Your Love (4)
Thomas, Nicky	Love Of The Common People (9)
Thomas, Rob	Smooth (3)
Thompson Twins	Doctor Doctor (3)
	Hold Me Now (4)
	Love On Your Side (9)
	We Are Detective (7)
	You Take Me Up (2)
Three Degrees	My Simple Heart (9)
	Runner, The (10)
	Take Good Care Of Yourself (9)
	When Will I See You Again (1)
	Woman In Love (3)
Three Dog Night	Mama Told Me Not To Come (3)
3LW	No More (Baby I'Ma Do Right) (6)
3T	Anything (2)
	Gotta Be You (10)
	Why (2)
Thunderbugs	Friends Forever (5)
Thunderclap Newman	Accidents (46)
	Something In The Air (1)
Thurston, Bobby	Check Out The Groove (10)
Tiffany	Could've Been (4)
	I Saw Him Standing There (8)
	I Think We're Alone Now (1)
Tight Fit	Back To The Sixties (4)
	Fantasy Island (5)
	Lion Sleeps Tonight, The (1)
Tijuana Brass	Lonely Bull, The (3)
	Spanish Flea (3)
Tikaram, Tanita	Good Tradition (10)
	Twist In My Sobriety (22)
Tillotson, Johnny	Poetry In Motion (1)
Timberlake, Justin	Like I Love You (2)
Time Frequency	Real Love (8)
Timelords	Doctorin' The Tardis (1)
Tin Tin Out	Here's Where The Story Ends (7)
	What I Am (2)
Tinman	Eighteen Strings (9)
Titanic	Sultana (5)
TLC	Creep (re-issue) (6)
	No Scrubs (3)
	Unpretty (6)
	Waterfalls (4)
Tom Robinson Band	2-4-6-8 Motorway (5)
Tom Tom Club	Wordy Rappinghood (7)
Tommy Dorsey Orchestra	Tea For Two Cha Cha (3)
Tony Osborne & His Orchestra	Around The World (8)

Group/Artiste	Title
Tony Scott's Orchestra	Banana Boat Song (2)
Toploader	Achilles Heel (re-issue) (8)
	Dancing In The Moonlight (remix) (7)
Topol	If I Were A Rich Man (9)
Tormé, Mel	Mountain Greenery (re-entry) (4)
Tornados	Globetrotter (5)
	Telstar (1)
Torok, Mitchell	When Mexico Gave Up The Rumba (6)
Toto	Africa (3)
Tottenham Hotspur FC	Ossie's Dream (Spurs Are On Their Way To Wembley) (5)
Touch & Go	Would You? (3)
Tourists	I Only Want To Be With You (4)
	So Good To Be Back Home Again (8)
Toy Dolls	Nellie The Elephant (4)
Toyah	Four From Toyah EP (4)
	I Want To Be Free (8)
	Thunder In The Mountains (4)
Toys	Lover's Concerto, A (5)
Tozer, Faye	Someone Like You (10)
T'Pau	China In Your Hand (1)
	Heart And Soul (4)
	Valentine (9)
TQ	Bye Bye Baby (7)
	Summertime (7)
	Westside (4)
Tracie	House That Jack Built, The (9)
Traffic	Here We Go Round The Mulberry Bush (8)
	Hole In My Shoe (2)
	Paper Sun (5)
Train	Drops Of Jupiter (Tell Me) (10)
Tra-Knox	Black Suits Comin' (Nod Ya Head) (3)
Trammps	Hold Back The Night (5)
Trans X	Living On Video (9)
Transvision Vamp	Baby I Don't Care (3)
	I Want Your Love (5)
Travis	Coming Around (5)
	Sing (3)
	Turn (8)
	Why Does It Always Rain On Me? (10)
Travolta, John	Grease Megamix (3)
	Sandy (2)
	Summer Nights (1)
	You're The One That I Want (1)
	You're The One That I Want (re-issue) (4)
Tremeloes	(Call Me) Number One (2)
	Candy Man (6)
	Do You Love Me (1)
	Even The Bad Times Are Good (4)
	Here Comes My Baby (4)
	Me And My Life (4)
	My Little Lady (6)
	Silence Is Golden (1)
	Someone Someone (2)
	Suddenly You Love Me (6)
	Twist And Shout (4)
Trent D'Arby, Terence	If You Let Me Stay (7)
	Sign Your Name (2)
	Wishing Well (4)
Trent, Jackie	Where Are You Now (My Love)

M
U
S
I
C

P
O
P

Group/Artiste	Title	Group/Artiste	Title
	(1)	Tyrannosaurus Rex	Debora / One Inch Rock (re-issue) (7)
Tresvant, Ralph	Best Things In Life Are Free, The (2)	UB40	Breakfast In Bed (6)
Tricky	Milk (10)		Come Back Darling (10)
Trinity	This Wheel's On Fire (5)		Don't Break My Heart (3)
Trio	Da Da Da (2)		Earth Dies Screaming / Dream
Troggs	Any Way That You Want Me (8)		A Lie, The (10)
	I Can't Control Myself (2)		Higher Ground (8)
	Love Is All Around (5)		Homely Girl (6)
	Wild Thing (4)		(I Can't Help) Falling In Love
	With A Girl Like You (1)		With You (1)
True Steppers	Buggin' Me (6)		I Got You Babe (1)
	Out Of Your Mind (2)		If It Happens Again (9)
Truth Hurts	Addictive (3)		I'll Be Your Baby Tonight (6)
T-Spoon	Sex On The Beach (2)		King / Food For Thought (4)
Tubeway Army	Are Friends Electric (1)		Kingston Town (4)
Turner, Tina	Best, The (5)		My Way Of Thinking / I Think
	Goldeneye (10)		It's Going To Rain (6)
	I Don't Wanna Fight (7)		One In Ten (7)
	I Don't Wanna Lose You (8)		Please Don't Make Me Cry (10)
	It Takes Two (5)		Red Red Wine (1)
	It's Only Love (29)		Sing Our Own Song (5)
	Let's Stay Together (6)	Ugly Kid Joe	Cats In The Cradle (7)
	Nutbush City Limits (4)		Everything About You (3)
	River Deep Mountain High (3)	Ullman, Tracey	Breakaway (4)
	We Don't Need Another Hero (Thunderdome) (3)		Move Over Darling (8)
			They Don't Know (2)
	What's Love Got To Do With It (3)	Ultimate Kaos	Some Girls (9)
		Ultra	Rescue Me (8)
	When The Heartache Is Over (10)	Ultra Naté	Found A Cure (6)
			Free (4)
Turtles	Elenore (7)		All Stood Still (8)
	She'd Rather Be With Me (4)	Ultravox	Dancing With Tears In My Eyes
Twain, Shania	Don't Be Stupid (You Know I Love You) (5)		(3)
			Vienna (2)
	From This Moment On (9)	Umiliani, Piero	Mah Na Mah Na (8)
	I'm Gonna Getcha Good (4)	Uncle Kracker	Follow Me (3)
	Man! I Feel Like A Woman (3)	Undercover	Baker Street (2)
	That Don't Impress Me Much (3)		Never Let Her Slip Away (5)
		Undertones	My Perfect Cousin (9)
	You're Still The One (10)		Teenage Kicks (31)
Tweenies	I Believe In Christmas (9)	Underworld	Born Slippy (2)
	Number 1 (6)	Union Gap	Lady Willpower (5)
Tweet	Oops (Oh My) (5)		Young Girl (1)
Tweets	Birdie Song (The Birdie Dance) (2)		Young Girl (re-issue) (6)
		Unit Four Plus Two	Concrete And Clay (1)
Twinkle	Golden Lights (21)	UNKLE	Be There (8)
	Terry (4)	Upsetters	Return Of Django / Dollar In
Twitty, Conway	It's Only Make Believe (1)		The Teeth (5)
	Mona Lisa (5)	Urban Cookie	Feels Like Heaven (5)
Two Cowboys	Everybody Gonfi-Gon (7)	Collective	Key The Secret, The (2)
2 In A Room	Wiggle It (3)	Urban Hype	Trip To Trumpton, A (6)
2Pac	California Love (6)	Ure, Midge	If I Was (1)
	Changes (3)		No Regrets (9)
	Until The End Of Time (4)	USA For Africa	We Are The World (1)
2 Unlimited	Faces (8)	Usher	I Need A Girl (Part One) (4)
	Get Ready For This (2)		Pop Ya Colla (2)
	Let The Beat Control Your Body (6)		U Got It Bad (5)
			U Remind Me (3)
	No Limit (1)		You Make Me Wanna (1)
	Real Thing, The (6)	Usura	Open You Mind (7)
	Tribal Dance (4)	Utah Saints	Believe In Me (8)
	Twilight Zone (2)		Something Good (4)
	Workaholic (4)		What Can You Do For Me (10)
Tyler, Bonnie	Holding Out For A Hero (2)	U2	All I Want Is You (4)
	It's A Heartache (4)		Angel Of Harlem (9)
	Lost In France (9)		Beautiful Day (1)
	Rockin' Good Way, A (5)		Desire (1)
	Total Eclipse Of The Heart (1)		Discotheque (1)
Tymes	Ms Grace (1)		Electrical Storm (5)
Typically Tropical	Barbados (1)		Elevation (3)

Group/Artiste	Title	Group/Artiste	Title
	Even Better Than The Real Thing (remix) (8)		Green Door (2)
	Fire (35)		Heart Of A Man, The (5)
	Fly, The (1)		Kewpie Doll (10)
	Hold Me Thrill Me Kiss Me Kill Me (2)		Kisses Sweeter Than Wine (8)
	I Still Haven't Found What I'm Looking For (6)		Loop-De-Loop (5)
			Man On Fire / Wanderin' Eyes (6)
	Last Night On Earth (10)		There Must Be A Way (7)
	New Years Day (10)		Tower Of Strength (1)
	One (7)	Vaughan, Malcolm	Every Day Of My Life (5)
	Please (7)		My Special Angel (3)
	Pride (In The Name Of Love) (3)		St Therese Of The Roses (re-entry) (3)
	Staring At The Sun (3)	Vaughan, Sarah	Broken Hearted Melody (7)
	Stay (Faraway So Close) (4)	Vee, Bobby	How Many Tears (10)
	Stuck In A Moment You Can't Get Out Of (2)		More Than I Can Say / Staying In (4)
	Sweetest Thing (3)		Night Has A Thousand Eyes, The (3)
	Unforgettable Fire, The (6)		Rubber Ball (4)
	Walk On (5)		Run To Him (6)
	When Love Comes To Town (6)		Sharing You (10)
	Where The Streets Have No Name (4)		Take Good Care Of My Baby (3)
	With Or Without You (4)	Vega, Suzanne	Tom's Diner (2)
Valance, Holly	Down Boy (2)	Vengaboys	Boom Boom Boom Boom (1)
	Kiss Kiss (1)		Kiss (When The Sun Don't Shine) (3)
Valance, Ricky	Tell Laura I Love Her (1)		Shalala Lala (5)
Valentine, Dickie	All The Time And Everywhere (9)		Uncle John From Jamaica (6)
	Blossom Fell, A (9)		Up And Down (4)
	Christmas Alphabet (1)		We Like To Party! (Vengabus) (3)
	Christmas Island (8)		We're Going To Ibiza! (1)
	Finger Of Suspicion (1)	Ventures	Perfidia (4)
	I Wonder (4)		Walk Don't Run (8)
	In A Golden Coach (7)	Verve	Bitter Sweet Symphony (2)
	Mr Sandman (5)		Drugs Don't Work, The (1)
Valli, Frankie	Grease (3)		Lucky Man (7)
	Let's Hang On! (4)	Village People	In The Navy (2)
	My Eyes Adored You (5)		Y.M.C.A. (1)
	Night, The (7)	Vinton, Bobby	Blue Velvet (2)
	Rag Doll (2)	Vipers Skiffle Group	Cumberland Gap (10)
Van Dahl, Ian	Castles In The Sky (3)		Don't You Rock Me Daddy-O (10)
	Reason (8)		
	Will I? (5)	Visage	Fade To Grey (8)
Van Dyk, Paul	Tell Me Why (The Riddle) (7)	Wah	Story Of The Blues, The (3)
Van Dyke, Leroy	Walk On By (5)	Waite, John	Missing You (9)
Van Halen	Jump (7)	Wakelin, Johnny	Black Superman (Muhammad Ali) (7)
	Why Can't This Be Love (8)		In Zaire (4)
Van Helden, Armand	Koochy (4)	Waldo De Los Rios	Mozart Symphony No. 40 in G Minor (7)
	You Don't Know Me (1)	Walker Brothers	Make It Easy On Yourself (1)
Vandellas	Dancing In The Street (re-issue) (4)		My Ship Is Coming In (3)
Vandross, Luther	Best Things In Life Are Free (remix), The (7)		No Regrets (7)
			Sun Ain't Gonna Shine Anymore, The (1)
	Best Things In Life Are Free, The (2)	Walker, Scott	Jackie (22)
	Endless Love (3)		Joanna (7)
Vanilla Ice	Ice Ice Baby (1)	Waller, Rik	I Will Always Love You (6)
	Play That Funky Music (10)	Wally Stott Orchestra	I Wanna Go Home (The Wreck Of The John 'B') (5)
Vanity Fare	Early In The Morning (8)		
Vanwarmer, Randy	Just When I Needed You Most (8)	Walsh, Steve	I Found Lovin' (9)
Vapors	Turning Japanese (3)	Walters, Trevor	Stuck On You (9)
Various Artists	All Star Hit Parade (2)	Wamdue Project	King Of My Castle (1)
	Brits 1990, The (2)	Ward, Anita	Ring My Bell (1)
	Perfect Day (1)	Ward, Clifford T	Gaye (8)
Vaughan, Frankie	Come Softly To Me (9)	Warhols, Dandy	Bohemian Like You (re-issue) (5)
	Garden Of Eden (1)		
	Gotta Have Something In The Bank Frank (8)	Warnes, Jennifer	(I've Had) The Time Of My Life

M
U
S
I
C

P
O
P

Group/Artiste	Title
	(6)
	(I've Had) The Time Of My Life (re-entry) (8)
	Up Where We Belong (7)
Warp Brothers	Phatt Bass (9)
Warren, Anne	If Anyone Finds This I Love You (4)
Warwick, Dionne	All The Love In The World (10)
	Do You Know The Way To San Jose (8)
	Heartbreaker (2)
	Walk On By (9)
Was (Not Was)	Shake Your Head (4)
	Walk The Dinosaur (10)
Wash, Martha	Keep On Jumpin' (8)
Washington, Keith	If You Were With Me Now (4)
Waterboys	Whole Of The Moon (re-issue), The (3)
Watergate	Heart Of Asia (3)
Waterman, Dennis	I Could Be So Good For You (3)
Waters, Crystal	Gypsy Woman (La Da Dee) (2)
Watson, Russell	Someone Like You (10)
Weather Girls	It's Raining Men (3)
Webb, Marti	Ben (5)
	Take That Look Off Your Face (3)
Wedding Present	Come Play With Me (10)
Wedlock, Fred	Oldest Swinger In Town (6)
Wee Papa Girl Rappers	Wee Rule (6)
Weedon, Bert	Guitar Boogie Shuffle (10)
Weller, Paul	Changingman, The (7)
	It's Written In The Stars (7)
	Peacock Suit (5)
	You Do Something To Me (9)
Wells, Mary	My Guy (5)
West End	Love I Lost, The (3)
West, Keith	Excerpt From A Teenage Opera (2)
Westlife	Against All Odds (1)
	Bop Bop Baby (5)
	Flying Without Wings (1)
	Fool Again (1)
	I Have A Dream / Seasons In The Sun (1)
	If I Let You Go (1)
	My Love (1)
	Queen Of My Heart (1)
	Swear It Again (1)
	Unbreakable (1)
	Uptown Girl (1)
	What Makes A Man (2)
	World Of Our Own (1)
Wet Wet Wet	Angel Eyes (Home And Away) (5)
	Don't Want To Forgive Me Now (7)
	Goodnight Girl (1)
	If I Never See You Again (3)
	Julia Says (3)
	Love Is All Around (1)
	Somewhere Somehow (7)
	Sweet Little Mystery (5)
	Sweet Surrender (6)
	Wishing I Was Lucky (6)
	With A Little Help From My Friends (1)
	Yesterday (4)
Wham!	Bad Boys (2)
	Club Tropicana (4)

Group/Artiste	Title
	Edge Of Heaven / Where Did Your Heart Go, The (1)
	Freedom (1)
	I'm Your Man (1)
	Last Christmas / Everything She Wants (2)
	Last Christmas (re-issue) (6)
	Wake Me Up Before You Go Go (1)
	Wham Rap (8)
	Young Guns (Go For It) (3)
Whatmore, Sarah	When I Lost You (6)
Whatnauts	Girls (3)
Wheatley, Rebecca	Stay With Me (Baby) (10)
Wheatus	Little Respect, A (3)
	Teenage Dirtbag (2)
Wheeler, Caron	Back To Life (However Do You Want Me) (1)
	Keep On Moving (5)
Whelan, Bill	Riverdance (9)
Whigfield	Another Day (7)
	Saturday Night (1)
	Think Of You (7)
Whiskey, Nancy	Freight Train (5)
Whispers	And The Beat Goes On (2)
	It's A Love Thing (9)
Whistle	(Nothin' Serious) Just Buggin' (7)
Whistling Jack Smith	I Was Kaiser Bill's Batman (5)
White Plains	Julie Do Ya Love Me (8)
	My Baby Loves Lovin' (9)
White Town	Your Woman (1)
White, Barry	Can't Get Enough Of Your Love Babe (8)
	(For You) I'll Do Anything You Want Me To (5)
	Let The Music Play (9)
	What Am I Gonna Do With You (5)
	You See The Trouble With Me (2)
	You're The First The Last My Everything (1)
White, Snowy	Bird Of Paradise (6)
Whitesnake	Here I Go Again (remix) (9)
	Is This Love (9)
Whitfield, David	Answer Me (1)
	Beyond The Stars (8)
	Book (re-entry), The (10)
	Book, The (5)
	Bridge Of Sighs (9)
	Cara Mia (1)
	Ev'rywhere (3)
	My September Love (re-entry) (3)
	Rags To Riches (re-entry) (3)
	Santo Natale (2)
	When You Lose The One You Love (7)
Whitman, Slim	I'll Take You Home Again Kathleen (7)
	Indian Love Call (7)
	Rose Marie (1)
	Serenade (re-entry) (8)
Whittaker, Roger	I Don't Believe In If Anymore (8)
	Last Farewell, The (2)
	Skye Boat Song, The (10)
Who	Anyway Anyhow Anywhere (10)
	Happy Jack (3)
	I Can See For Miles (10)

Group/Artiste	Title
	I Can't Explain (8)
	I'm A Boy (2)
	Join Together (9)
	My Generation (2)
	Pictures Of Lily (4)
	Pinball Wizard (4)
	Squeeze Box (10)
	Substitute (5)
	Substitute (re-issue) (7)
	Won't Get Fooled Again (9)
	You Better You Bet (9)
Wigan's Chosen Few	Footsee (9)
Wild Cherry	Play That Funky Music (7)
Wild Pair	Opposites Attract (2)
Wildchild	Renegade Master '98 (remix) (3)
Wilde, Kim	Another Step (Closer To You) (6)
	Chequered Love (4)
	Four Letter Word (6)
	Kids In America (2)
	Never Trust A Stranger (7)
	You Came (3)
	You Keep Me Hangin' On (2)
Wilde, Marty	Bad Boy (7)
	Donna (3)
	Endless Sleep (4)
	Rubber Ball (9)
	Sea Of Love (3)
	Teenager On Love, A (2)
Wilder, Matthew	Break My Stride (4)
Will To Power	Baby I Love Your Way – Freebird (6)
Williams, Alyson	I Need Your Lovin' (8)
Williams, Andy	Almost There (2)
	Butterfly (1)
	Can't Get Used To Losing You (2)
	Can't Help Falling In Love (3)
	Can't Take My Eyes Off You (5)
	Home Lovin' Man (7)
	Music To Watch Girls By (9)
	Solitaire (4)
	(Where Do I Begin) Love Story (4)
Williams, Danny	Moon River (1)
	Wonderful World Of The Young (8)
Williams, Deniece	Free (1)
	Let's Hear It For The Boy (2)
	That's What Friends Are For (8)
	Too Much Too Little Too Late (3)
Williams, Melanie	Ain't No Love (Ain't No Use) (3)
Williams, P	Boys (7)
Williams, Robbie	Angels (4)
	Eternity / The Road To Mandalay (1)
	Feel (4)
	Freedom (2)
	Kids (2)
	Lazy Days (8)
	Let Love Be Your Energy (10)
	Let Me Entertain You (3)
	Millennium (1)
	My Culture (9)
	No Regrets / Antmusic (4)
	Old Before I Die (2)
	Rock DJ (1)
	She's The One / It's Only Us (1)
	Somethin' Stupid (1)
	Strong (4)
	Supreme (4)

Group/Artiste	Title
Williams, Vanessa	Save The Best For Last (3)
Willis, Bruce	Respect Yourself (7)
	Under The Boardwalk (2)
Wills, Viola	Gonna Get Along Without You Now (8)
Wilson Phillips	Hold On (6)
Wilson, Danny	Mary's Prayer (3)
Wilson, Dooley	As Time Goes By (5)
Wilson, Jackie	I Get The Sweetest Feeling (9)
	I Get The Sweetest Feeling / (Your Love Keeps Lifting Me) Higher and Higher (re-issue) (3)
	Reet Petite (The Sweetest Girl In Town) (6)
	Reet Petite (The Sweetest Girl In Town) (re-issue) (1)
Wilson, Mari	Just What I Always Wanted (8)
Winans, BeBe	I Wanna Be The Only One (1)
Wingfield, Pete	Eighteen With A Bullet (7)
Wings	Band On The Run (3)
	Goodnight Tonight (5)
	Hi Hi Hi / C Moon (5)
	Jet (7)
	Let 'Em In (2)
	Listen To What The Man Said (6)
	Live And Let Die (9)
	Mary Had A Little Lamb (9)
	Mull Of Kintyre / Girls' School (1)
	My Love (9)
	Silly Love Songs (2)
	With A Little Luck (5)
Wink, Josh	Higher State Of Consciousness (8)
	Higher State Of Consciousness (remix) (7)
Winslet, Kate	What If (6)
Winters, Ruby	I Will (4)
Wisdom, Norman	Don't Laugh At Me (3)
Wiseguys	Ooh La La (2)
Withers, Bill	Lovely Day (7)
	Lovely Day (remix) (4)
Wizzard	Angel Fingers (1)
	Are You Ready To Rock (8)
	Ball Park Incident (6)
	I Wish It Could Be Christmas Everyday (4)
	Rock 'N' Roll Winter (6)
	See My Baby Jive (1)
Wogan, Terry	Floral Dance (21)
Womack & Womack	Teardrops (3)
Wombles	Banana Rock (9)
	Remember You're A Womble (3)
	Wombling Merry Christmas (2)
	Wombling Song, The (4)
Wonder Stuff	Dizzy (1)
	On The Ropes (EP) (10)
	Size Of A Cow, The (5)
	Welcome To the Cheap Seats (EP) (8)
Wonder, Stevie	Do I Do (10)
	Ebony And Ivory (1)
	For Once In My Life (3)
	Happy Birthday (2)
	He's Misstra Know It All (10)
	How Come, How Long (10)
	I Ain't Gonna Stand For It (10)
	I Just Called To Say I Love You (1)
	I Was Made To Love Her (5)

M
U
S
I
C

P
O
P

Group/Artiste	Title	Group/Artiste	Title
	I Wish (5)		Stand Up For Your Love Rights (2)
	Lately (3)	Yell!	Instant Replay (10)
	Masterblaster (Jammin') (2)	Yello	Race, The (7)
	My Cherie Amour (4)	Yellow Dog	Just One More Night (8)
	My Love (5)	Yes	Wonderous Stories (7)
	Never Had A Dream Come True (6)	Yomanda	Synth And Strings (8)
	Part-Time Lover (3)	York	O.T.B (On The Beach) / Reachers Of Civilisation (4)
	Sir Duke (2)		
	Yester-Me Yester-You Yesterday (2)	Young Idea	With A Little Help From Friends (10)
	You Are The Sunshine Of My Life (7)	Young Ones	Living Doll (1)
Wondress	Got To Have Your Love (4)	Young Rascals	Groovin' (8)
	Take Your Time (10)	Young, Faron	It's Four In The Morning (3)
Wood, Brenton	Gimme Little Sign (8)	Young, Jimmy	Chain Gang (9)
Wood, Roy	Forever (8)		Eternally (8)
Woods, Marcella	Beautiful (10)		Faith Can Move Mountains (11)
Wookie	Battle (10)		Man From Laramie, The (1)
Wooley, Sheb	Purple People Eater, The (12)		More (4)
Woolpackers	Hillbilly Rock Hillbilly Roll (7)		Unchained Melody (1)
World's Famous Supreme Team	Buffalo Gals (9)	Young, John Paul	Love Is In The Air (5)
		Young, Karen	Nobody's Child (6)
Wright, Ruby	Bimbo (7)	Young, Neil	Heart Of Gold (10)
Wurzels	Combine Harvester (Brand New Key) (1)	Young, Paul	Come Back And Stay (4)
			Every Time You Go Away (4)
	I Am A Cider Drinker (Paloma Blanca) (3)		Everything Must Change (9)
			I'm Gonna Tear Your Playhouse Down (9)
Wu-Tang Clan	Gravel Pit (6)		Love Of The Common People (2)
	Say What You Want / Insane (re-recording) (4)		Senza Una Donna (Without A Woman) (4)
WWF Superstars	Slam Jam (4)		Wherever I Lay My Hat (That's My Home) (1)
Wyman, Jane	Zing A Little Zong (10)		
Wynette, Tammy	Justified And Ancient (2)	Young, Will	Anything Is Possible / Evergreen (1)
	Stand By Your Man (1)		
Wynter, Mark	Go Away Little Girl (6)		Don't Let Me Down / You And I (2)
	Venus In Blue Jeans (4)		
X-Ecutioners	It's Goin' Down (7)		Light My Fire (1)
Xpansions	Move Your Body (Elevation) (7)		Long And Winding Road, The / Suspicious Minds (1)
X-Press 2	Lazy (2)		
XTC	Senses Working Overtime (10)	Youngblood, Sydney	If Only I Could (3)
Ya Kid K	Get Up (Before The Night Is Over) (2)	Zacharias, Helmut	Tokyo Melody (9)
		Zager & Evans	In The Year 2525 (Exordium And Terminus) (1)
	Rockin' Over The Beat (9)		
Yanou	Heaven (1)	Zager Band, Michael	Let's All Chant (8)
Yarbrough & Peoples	Don't Stop The Music (7)	Zamfir, Georghe	(Light Of Experience) Doina De Jale (4)
Yardbirds	Evil Hearted You / Still I'm Sad (3)		
	For Your Love (3)	Zavaroni, Lena	Ma (He's Making Eyes At Me) (10)
	Heart Full Of Soul (2)		
	Over Under Sideways Down (10)	Zig & Zag	Them Girls Them Girls (5)
		Zoe	Sunshine On A Rainy Day (re-mix) (4)
	Shapes Of Things (3)		
Yazoo	Don't Go (3)	Zombie Nation	Kernkraft 400 (2)
	Nobody's Diary (3)	Zucchero	Senza Una Donna (Without A Woman) (4)
	Only You (2)		
Yazz	Doctorin' The House (6)	ZZ Top	Gimme All Your Lovin' (10)
	Fine Time (9)		Viva Las Vegas (10)
	Only Way Is Up, The (1)		

Christmas No. 1s

1952	Here in My Heart – Al Martino
1953	Answer Me – Frankie Laine
1954	Let's Have Another Party – Winifred Atwell
1955	The Christmas Alphabet – Dickie Valentine.
1956	Just Walkin' in the Rain – Johnnie Ray
1957	Mary's Boy Child – Harry Belafonte
1958	It's Only Make Believe – Conway Twitty
1959	What Do You Want to Make Those Eyes at Me For – Emile Ford and the Checkmates
1960	I Love You – Cliff Richard and the Shadows
1961	Moon River – Danny Williams
1962	Return to Sender – Elvis Presley
1963	I Want to Hold Your Hand – Beatles
1964	I Feel Fine – Beatles
1965	Day Tripper/We Can Work It Out – Beatles
1966	Green Green Grass of Home – Tom Jones
1967	Hello Goodbye – Beatles
1968	Lily the Pink – Scaffold
1969	Two Little Boys – Rolf Harris
1970	I Hear You Knockin' – Dave Edmunds
1971	Ernie (The Fastest Milkman in the West) – Benny Hill
1972	Long Haired Lover from Liverpool – Little Jimmy Osmond
1973	Merry Xmas Everybody – Slade
1974	Lonely This Christmas – Mud
1975	Bohemian Rhapsody – Queen
1976	When a Child Is Born – Johnny Mathis
1977	Mull of Kintyre/Girls' School – Wings
1978	Mary's Boy Child – Boney M
1979	Another Brick in the Wall – Pink Floyd
1980	There's No One Quite Like Grandma – St Winifred's School Choir
1981	Don't You Want Me – Human League
1982	Save Your Love – Renee and Renato
1983	Only You – Flying Pickets
1984	Do They Know It's Christmas – Band Aid
1985	Merry Christmas Everyone – Shakin' Stevens
1986	Reet Petite – Jackie Wilson
1987	Always on My Mind – Pet Shop Boys
1988	Mistletoe and Wine – Cliff Richard
1989	Do They Know It's Christmas? – Band Aid II
1990	Saviour's Day – Cliff Richard
1991	Bohemian Rhapsody / These are the Days of Our Lives – Queen
1992	I Will Always Love You – Whitney Houston
1993	Mr. Blobby – Mr. Blobby
1994	Stay Another Day – East 17
1995	Earth Song – Michael Jackson
1996	2 Become 1 – Spice Girls
1997	Too Much – Spice Girls
1998	Goodbye – Spice Girls
1999	I Have a Dream/Seasons in the Sun – Westlife
2000	Can We Fix It – Bob The Builder
2001	Somethin' Stupid – Robbie Williams and Nicole Kidman
2002	Sound Of The Underground – Girls Aloud

LPs

Title	Group/artiste	Title	Group/artiste
Abacab	Genesis	Attack of the Grey Lantern	Mansun
Abbey Road	Beatles	Auberge	Chris Rea
According to My Heart	Jim Reeves	Autobahn	Kraftwerk
Achtung Baby	U2	Automatic for the People	R.E.M.
Actually	Pet Shop Boys	Avalon	Roxy Music
Adrenalize	Def Leppard	Babylon and On	Squeeze
Affection	Lisa Stansfield	Back in Black	AC/DC
Afterburner	ZZ Top	Back to Front (1)	Gilbert O'Sullivan (1972)
Aftermath	Rolling Stones		
The Age of Consent	Bronski Beat	Back to Front (1)	Lionel Richie (1992)
Agent Provocateur	Foreigner	Bad	Michael Jackson
Aja	Steely Dan	Bagsy Me	Wannadies
Aladdin Sane	David Bowie	Band of Gypsies	Jimi Hendrix
Album of the Year	Faith No More	Band on the Run	Wings
Alf	Alison Moyet	Batman	Prince
All Change	Cast	Bat Out Of Hell	Meat Loaf
All Things Must Pass	George Harrison	Before the Rain	Eternal
Ancient Heart	Tanita Tikaram	Beggars Banquet	Rolling Stones
Andromeda Heights	Prefab Sprout	Be Here Now (1)	Oasis
Another Time, Another Place	Bryan Ferry	Behind the Mask	Fleetwood Mac
Anthem	Toyah	Big Bang	We've Got a Fuzzbox and We're Gonna Use it
The Anvil	Visage		
Appetite for Destruction	Guns 'N' Roses		
Are You Experienced?	Jimi Hendrix Experience	Big River	Jimmy Nail
		Billion Dollar Babies	Alice Cooper
Are You Gonna Go My Way	Lenny Kravitz	Black Tie White Noise	David Bowie
Argus	Wishbone Ash	Blast	Holly Johnson
Armed Forces	Elvis Costello	Blonde on Blonde	Bob Dylan
Arrival	Abba	Blondes Have More Fun	Rod Stewart
Astral Weeks	Van Morrison	Blood on the Dance Floor (1)	Michael Jackson
Atlantic Crossing	Rod Stewart	Blood Sugar Sex Magik	Red Hot Chili Peppers
Atom Heart Mother	Pink Floyd		

Title	Group/artiste	Title	Group/artiste
Bloody Tourists	10cc		Orchestra
Blue for You	Status Quo	Disraeli Gears	Cream
Blue Is the Colour	Beautiful South	Diva	Annie Lennox
Blue Sky on Mars	Matthew Sweet	The Division Bell	Pink Floyd
Bookends	Simon and Garfunkel	Dizzy Heights	Lightning Seeds
Both Sides	Phil Collins	Do It Yourself	The Seahorses
Boys and Girls	Bryan Ferry	Don't Be Cruel	Bobby Brown
Breakfast In America	Supertramp	Don't Shoot Me, I'm Only the	Elton John
Breathless	Kenny G	Piano Player	
Bridge of Spies	T'Pau	Dookie	Green Day
Bridge Over Troubled Water	Simon and Garfunkel	Double Fantasy	John Lennon
British Steel	Judas Priest	Down Drury Lane to Memory	One Hundred and
Brothers in Arms	Dire Straits	Lane	One Strings
Buddah and the Chocolate Box	Cat Stevens	Drag	kd lang
Bursting at the Seams	Strawbs	Dreamland	Robert Miles
Business as Usual	Men at Work	Dreams Are Nothin' More	David Cassidy
Cafe Bleu	Style Council	Than Wishes	
Can't Slow Down	Lionel Richie	Dr Feelgood	Motley Crue
Captain Fantastic and the	Elton John	Duke	Genesis
Brown Dirt Cowboy		Eat to the Beat	Blondie
Captain Paralytic and the		Electric Ladyland	Jimi Hendrix
Brown Ale Cowboy	Mike Harding		Experience
Caribou	Elton John	Electric Warrior	T Rex
Carry On up the Charts	Beautiful South	Elegantly Wasted	INXS
Catch Bull at Four	Cat Stevens	Eliminator	ZZ Top
China Town	Thin Lizzy	Emergency on Planet Earth	Jamiroquai
Chorus	Erasure	Emotional Rescue	Rolling Stones
Circle of One	Oleta Adams	Endless Flight	Leo Sayer
The Circus	Erasure	English Settlement	X-Ray Specs
Cloud Nine	George Harrison	Enjoy Yourself	Kylie Minogue
Colour	Christians	Every Good Boy Deserves	Moody Blues
The Colour and the Shape	Foo Fighters	Favour	
Colour By Numbers	Culture Club	Every Picture Tells a Story	Rod Stewart
The Colour of My Love	Celine Dion	Everybody Else Is Doing it,	Cranberries
Come On Over	Shania Twain	So Why Can't We	
Coming Up	Suede	Everything Changes	Take That
Communiqué	Dire Straits	Everything Must Go	Manic Street
Connected	Stereo MCs		Preachers
Conscience	Womack and	Exile on Main Street	Rolling Stones
	Womack	Extra Virgin	Olive
Conversation Peace	Stevie Wonder	Façades	Sad Cafe
Cosmo's Factory	Creedence	Face Value	Phil Collins
	Clearwater	Falling Into You	Celine Dion
	Revival	Fantastic!	Wham!
Cracked Rear View	Hootie and the	Faster Than the Speed of Night	Bonnie Tyler
	Blowfish	The Fat of the Land (1)	The Prodigy
Crazy You	G.U.N.	Fear of the Dark	Iron Maiden
Cricklewood Green	Ten Years After	Fever In Fever Out	Luscious Jackson
Crime of the Century	Supertramp	The Final Cut	Pink Floyd
Crocodiles	Echo and the	Fireball	Deep Purple
	Bunnymen	Flaming Pie (1)	Paul McCartney
Cross of Changes	Enigma	Flesh and Blood	Roxy Music
Crossroads	Tracy Chapman	Flowers in the Dirt	Paul McCartney
Culture Club	Colour by Numbers	Flying Colours	Chris De Burgh
Cuts Both Ways	Gloria Estefan	Fog on the Tyne	Lindisfarne
Dancin' in the Key of Life	Steve Arrington	Foreign Affair	Tina Turner
Dangerous	Michael Jackson	Forever	Damage
Dare	Human League	Forever Changes	Love
Dark Side of the Moon	Pink Floyd	461 Ocean Boulevard	Eric Clapton
A Day at the Races	Queen	Four Symbols	Led Zeppelin
Daydream	Mariah Carey	Foxtrot	Genesis
Days of Future Passed	Moody Blues	Fresh	Gina G
Destination Anywhere	Jon Bon Jovi	Fresh Cream	Cream
Destiny	Gloria Estefan	From the Cradle	Eric Clapton
Devil Without a Cause	Kid Rock	The Game	Queen
Diamond Dogs	David Bowie	Germ Free Adolescents	X-Ray Specs
Diamond Life	Sade	Ghost in the Machine	Police
A Different Beat	Boyzone	The Gift	Jam
Different Class	Pulp	Give Me the Reason	Luther Vandross
Dig Your Own Hole	Chemical Brothers	Glittering Prize	Simple Minds
Discovery	Electric Light	Goat's Head Soup	Rolling Stones

Title	Group/artiste	Title	Group/artiste
Going for the One	Yes	John Wesley Harding	Bob Dylan
Going to a Go-Go	Smokey Robinson and the Miracles	Jollification	Lightning Seeds
		The Joshua Tree	U2
Gold Blade	Hometurf	Journey Through the Secret Life of Plants	Stevie Wonder
Goodbye	Cream		
Goodbye Cruel World	Elvis Costello	Journey to the Centre of the Earth	Rick Wakeman
Goodbye Yellow Brick Road	Elton John		
Goodnight Vienna	Ringo Starr	Ju Ju	Siouxsie and the Banshees
Graceland	Paul Simon		
Graffiti Bridge	Prince	Junction Seven	Steve Winwood
The Great Escape	Blur	K	Kula Shaker
Great Expectations	Tasmin Archer	Kaleidoscope	Siouxsie and the Banshees
The Great Rock 'N' Roll Swindle	Sex Pistols		
Guilty	Barbra Streisand	Kavana	Kavana
Happy Nation	Ace of Base	Keep the Faith	Bon Jovi
Harvest	Neil Young	Kimono My House	Sparks
Headquarters	Monkees	Kings of the Wild Frontier	Adam Ant
The Healing Game	Van Morrison	Koo Koo	Debbie Harry
Hearsay	Alexander O'Neal	L	Steve Hillage
Heaven and Hell	Vangelis	Labour of Love	UB40
Heavy Soul (1)	Paul Weller	La Passione	Chris Rea
Hedgehog Sandwich	Not the 9 O'Clock News Cast	Ladies and Gentlemen	George Michael
		The Last Waltz	The Band
Hello	Status Quo	L.A. Woman	Doors
Help!	Beatles	Legend	Bob Marley and the Wailers
Hergest Ridge	Mike Oldfield		
High on the Happy Side	Wet Wet Wet	Let It Bleed	Rolling Stones
Highway 61 Revisited	Bob Dylan	Let's Talk About Love	Celine Dion
History – Past Present and Future Book	Michael Jackson	The Lexicon of Love	ABC
		Lie	Charles Manson
Hit	Wannadies	Life	Simply Red
Horses	Patti Smith	Life After Death	Notorious B.I.G.
Hotel California	Eagles	Life Thru a Lens	Robbie Williams
Hot Rats	Frank Zappa	Lil' Darlin'	Thomas Ribeiro
Hounds of Love	Kate Bush	The Lion and the Cobra	Sinead O'Connor
Houses of the Holy	Led Zeppelin	Little Creatures	Talking Heads
Human Racing	Nik Kershaw	Live at the BBC	Beatles
Human's Lib	Howard Jones	Live in the City of Light	Simple Minds
Human Touch	Bruce Springsteen	Liverpool	Frankie Goes to Hollywood
Hunky Dory	David Bowie		
Hunting High and Low	A-Ha	Living in Oz	Rick Springfield
The Hurting	Tears for Fears	Living in the Material World	George Harrison
Hypnotised	Undertones	Living in the Past	Jethro Tull
Hysteria (1)	Def Leppard	The Lone Ranger	Suggs
Hysteria (3)	Human League	Love at the Greek	Neil Diamond
I Am	Earth Wind and Fire	Love de Luxe	Sade
I Do Not Want What I Haven't Got	Sinead O'Connor	Love Hurts	Cher
		Love over Gold	Dire Straits
If the Beatles Had Read Hunter . . . The Singles	Wonder Stuff	Lovesexy	Prince
		Machine Head	Deep Purple
The Immaculate Collection	Madonna	Mad Dogs and Englishmen	Joe Cocker
In Blue	Corrs	Made in Heaven	Queen
In It for the Money	Supergrass	Make It Big	Wham!
Innervisions	Stevie Wonder	Makin' Movies	Dire Straits
An Innocent Man	Billy Joel	Manifesto	Roxy Music
The Innocents	Erasure	The Man Who	Travis
Innuendo	Queen	Meat is Murder	Smiths
In Search of the Lost Chord	Moody Blues	Meaty, Beaty, Big and Bouncy	Who
In Square Circle	Stevie Wonder	Medusa	Annie Lennox
In Through the Out Door	Led Zeppelin	Middle of Nowhere (1)	Hanson
Into the Gap	Thompson Twins	Millennium	Backstreet Boys
Invisible Touch	Genesis	The Miracle	Queen
I Say I Say I Say	Erasure	Mirror Ball	Neil Young
I Should Coco	Supergrass	Misplaced Childhood	Marillion
It Doesn't Matter Anymore	Supernaturals	Missing ... Presumed Having a Good Time	Notting Hillbillies
It's Better to Travel	Swing Out Sister		
It's Great When You're ... Straight Yeah!	Black Grape	Mondo Bongo	Boomtown Rats
		Monster	R.E.M.
I've Been Expecting You	Robbie Williams	The More Things Change	Machine Head
Jagged Little Pill	Alanis Morissette	Morning Glory	Oasis
Jam	Little Angels	Mother Nature Calls	Cast

MUSIC

POP

Title	Group/artiste	Title	Group/artiste
Mr Fantasy	Traffic	Physical Graffiti	Led Zeppelin
Mr Wonderful	Fleetwood Mac	Picture This	Wet Wet Wet
Mud Slide Jim and the	James Taylor	Pieces of You	Jewel
Blue Horizon		Pills 'N' Thrills and Bellyaches	Happy Mondays
Music Box	Mariah Carey	Pin-Ups	David Bowie
Music for the Jilted Generation	Prodigy	Piper at the Gates of Dawn	Pink Floyd
Music from Big Pink	The Band	Pisces, Aquarius, Capricorn	Monkees
My Aim Is True	Elvis Costello	and Jones Ltd	
Naked	Talking Heads	Play (1)	Moby
Nashville Skyline	Bob Dylan	The Pleasure Principle	Gary Numan
Natural	Peter Andre	Pocketful of Kryptonite	Spin Doctors
Never a Dull Moment	Rod Stewart	Pop	U2
Never for Ever	Kate Bush	Popped in Souled Out	Wet Wet Wet
Nevermind	Nirvana	Porcupine	Echo and the
Never Mind the Bollocks Here's	Sex Pistols		Bunnymen
the Sex Pistols		Pornography	Cure
New Boots and Panties!!	Ian Dury & the	Postcard	Mary Hopkin
	Blockheads	Pot Luck	Elvis Presley
A New Flame	Simply Red	Presence	Led Zeppelin
New Jersey	Bon Jovi	Private Collection	Cliff Richard
A New World Record	Electric Light	Private Dancer	Tina Turner
	Orchestra	Promises and Lies	UB40
A Night at the Opera	Queen	Prophets, Seers and Sages	T, Rex
Night Birds	Shakatak	Protection	Massive Attack
Night Flight to Venus	Boney M	Pulse	Pink Floyd
A Night on the Town	Rod Stewart	Pump	Aerosmith
Night Owl	Gerry Rafferty	Pump Up the Jam	Technotronic
Nine Lives	Aerosmith	Push	Bros
1982	Status Quo	A Question of Balance	Moody Blues
Nobody Else	Take That	Quick Step and Side Kick	Thompson Twins
A Nod's as Good as a Wink	Faces	Rage	T'Pau
To a Blind Horse		Rage in Eden	Ultravox
No Fences	Garth Brooks	Ram	Paul and Linda
No Jacket Required	Phil Collins		McCartney
No More Heroes	Stranglers	Rattle and Hum	U2
No Need to Argue	Cranberries	The Raw and the Cooked	Fine Young Cannibals
No Parlez	Paul Young	Real Things	2 Unlimited
No Sleep till Hammersmith	Motorhead	Red River Valley	Slim Whitman
No Strings Attached	'N Sync	Regatta de Blanc	Police
Nothing Like the Sun	Sting	Reload	Tom Jones
The Number of the Beast	Iron Maiden	Reminiscing	Buddy Holly and the
Ocean Drive	Lighthouse Family		Crickets
Oceans of Fantasy	Boney M	Replicas	Tubeway Army
Odds and Sods	Who	Republic	New Order
Off the Wall	Michael Jackson	Return of the Space Cowboy	Jamiroquai
Ogden's Nut Gone Flake	Small Faces	Return to Fantasy	Uriah Heep
OK Computer (1)	Radiohead	Revenge	Eurythmics
Old New Borrowed and Blue	Slade	Revolver	Beatles
Older	George Michael	Rhythm of the Saints	Paul Simon
Once Upon a Star	Bay City Rollers	The Riddle	Nik Kershaw
Once Upon a Time	Simple Minds	Rising from the East	Bally Sagoo
One Hot Minute	Red Hot Chili Peppers	Roping the Wind	Garth Brooks
On Every Street	Dire Straits	Rubber Soul	Beatles
On the Level	Status Quo	Rumours	Fleetwood Mac
On the Threshold of a Dream	Moody Blues	Rum, Sodomy and the Lash	Pogues
Only Human	Dina Carroll	Runaway Horses	Belinda Carlisle
Only Yesterday	Carpenters	Said and Done	Boyzone
Ooh-La-La	Faces	Saturday Night	Zhane
Open Road (1)	Gary Barlow	Savage	Eurythmics
Our Favourite Shop	Style Council	Scary Monsters and Super	David Bowie
Out of Time	R.E.M.	Creeps	
Outlandos d'Amour	Police	Script for a Jester's Tear	Marillion
Oxygene	Jean-Michel Jarre	The Secret of Association	Paul Young
Parallel Lines	Blondie	The Seeds of Love	Tears for Fears
Paranoid	Black Sabbath	Sensational	Michelle Gayle
Parklife	Blur	Sentimental Journey	Ringo Starr
Pastpresent	Clannad	Sergeant Pepper's Lonely	Beatles
Pearl	Janis Joplin	Hearts Club Band	
Pearls	Elkie Brooks	Seven and the Ragged Tiger	Duran Duran
Pet Sounds	Beach Boys	Seventh Son of a Seventh Son	Iron Maiden
Phuq	Wildhearts	Share My World	Mary J. Blige

Title	Group/artiste	Title	Group/artiste
Shaved Fish	John Lennon	Tarkus	Emerson, Lake and Palmer
Shelter	Brand New Heavies		
Shepherd Moons	Enya	Tears and Laughter	Johnny Mathis
She's So Unusual	Cyndi Lauper	Tease Me	Chaka Demus and Pliers
She's the Boss	Mick Jagger		
Silk and Steel	Five Star	Teaser and the Firecat	Cat Stevens
Singles	Alison Moyet	Technique	New Order
The Six Wives of Henry VIII	Rick Wakeman	Telekon	Gary Numan
Sleeping with the Past	Elton John	Tell Me on a Sunday	Marti Webb
The Slider	T Rex	Tellin' Stories	The Charlatans
Slippery When Wet	Bon Jovi	10	Wet Wet Wet
Slowhand	Eric Clapton	Ten	Pearl Jam
Smiler	Rod Stewart	Ten Good Reasons	Jason Donovan
The Smoker You Drink The Player You Get	Joe Walsh	Tennis	Chris Rea
		The Man and His Music	Sam Cooke
So	Peter Gabriel	Thriller	Michael Jackson
So Far So Good	Bryan Adams	Through the Barricades	Spandau Ballet
Solitude Standing	Suzanne Vega	Thunder and Lightning	Thin Lizzy
So Long So Wrong	Alison Krauss and Union Station	Time for Healing	Sounds of Blackness
		Timeless	Sarah Brightman
Some Friendly	Charlatans	To the Extreme	Vanilla Ice
Song Bird	Eva Cassidy	To the Faithful Departed	Cranberries
The Song Remains the Same	Led Zeppelin	Touch	Eurythmics
Songs in the Key of Life	Stevie Wonder	Tragic Kingdom	No Doubt
Songs of Faith and Devotion	Depeche Mode	Transformer	Lou Reed
The Soul Cages	Sting	Travelling without Moving	Jamiroquai
Soul Provider	Michael Bolton	Trout Mask Replica	Captain Beefheart and his Magic Band
Sound of Lies	The Jayhawks		
Sparkle in the Rain	Simple Minds	True Stories	Talking Heads
Spartacus	Farm	Tubular Bells	Mike Oldfield
Speak and Spell	Depeche Mode	Tuesday Night Music Club	Sheryl Crow
Spellbound	Paula Abdul	Tug of War	Paul McCartney
Spirits Having Flown	Bee Gees	Tunnel of Love	Bruce Springsteen
Sports Car	Judie Tzuke	Turn Back the Clock	Johnny Hates Jazz
Standing Stone	Paul McCartney	Turn It Upside Down	Spin Doctors
Stand Up	Jethro Tull	Tusk	Fleetwood Mac
Stanley Road	Paul Weller	12 Gold Bars	Status Quo
Staring at the Sun	U2	21 Today	Cliff Richard
Stars	Simply Red	U.F. Orb	Orb
Station to Station	David Bowie	Ultra	Depeche Mode
Stay on These Roads	A-Ha	Under the Pink	Tori Amos
Steel Wheels	Rolling Stones	The Unforgettable Fire	U2
Steeltown	Big Country	Universal Soldier	Donovan
Step by Step	New Kids on the Block	Up	Right Said Fred
		Upstairs at Eric's	Yazoo
Sticky Fingers	Rolling Stones	Urban Hymns (1)	Verve
Still Crazy after All These Years	Paul Simon	Use Your Illusion	Guns 'N' Roses
Still Waters	Bee Gees	Vauxhall and I	Morrissey
Stranded	Roxy Music	Very	Pet Shop Boys
The Stranger	Billy Joel	Viva Hate	Morrissey
Street Fighting Years	Simple Minds	Voice of Love	Diana Ross
String of Hits	Shadows	Voices from the Holy Land	Aled Jones
Stripped	Rolling Stones	Voodo Lounge	Rolling Stones
Stupidity	Dr Feelgood	Voulez-Vous	Abba
Supernatural	Santana	Wake Up!	Boo Radleys
Surrealistic Pillow	Jefferson Airplane	Waking Up the Neighbours	Bryan Adams
Sweet Baby James	James Taylor	Walking Wounded	Everything But the Girl
Symbol	Prince	Walthamstow	East 17
Synchronicity	Police	Wanted	Yazz
Take Two	Robson and Jerome	War	U2
Tales from Topographic Oceans	Yes	Water Sign	Chris Rea
		Watermark	Enya
Talk On Corners	Corrs	We All Had Doctors' Papers	Max Boyce
Talking Back to the Night	Steve Winwood	We Can Make It	Peters and Lee
Talking Book	Stevie Wonder	We Can't Dance	Genesis
Talking with the Taxman about Poetry	Billy Bragg	We Have All the Time in the World	Louis Armstrong
Tango in the Night	Fleetwood Mac	We Too Are One	Eurythmics
Tanx	T Rex	Welcome to the Pleasuredome	Frankie Goes to Hollywood
Tapestry	Carole King		
A Tapestry of Dreams	Charles Aznavour	Welcome to Wherever You Are	INXS

MUSIC POP

Title	Group/artiste	Title	Group/artiste
Whatever You Want	Status Quo	*Wish You Were Here*	Pink Floyd
When the World Knows Your Name	Deacon Blue	*Women and Captain First*	Captain Sensible
Where We Belong	Boyzone	*Words of Love*	Buddy Holly and the Crickets
Whipped Cream and Other Delights	Herb Alpert and the Tijuana Brass	*Wu-Tang Forever*	Wu-Tang Clan
White Feathers	Kajagoogoo	*You and Me Both*	Yazoo
White on Blonde	Texas	*Young Americans*	David Bowie
The Whole Story	Kate Bush	*Your Secret Love*	Luther Vandross
Wicked Game	Chris Isaak	*You Showed Me*	Lightning Seeds
Wild!	Erasure	*Youthquake*	Dead or Alive
Wild Wood	Paul Weller	*Zenyatta Mondatta*	Police
Wish	Cure	*Zooropa*	U2

Nationalities of Pop Groups and Soloists

Abba   Sweden and Norway
AC/DC   UK and Australia
Adamski   UK
Air Supply   UK and Australia
Alphaville   Germany
Aneka   UK
Angry Anderson   Australia
Anthrax   USA
Aphrodite's Child   Greece
Aqua   Denmark
Baccara   Spain
Basia   Poland
Belle Stars   UK
Black Box   Italy
Boney M   Jamaica, Antilles, Montserrat
Boris Gardiner   Jamaica
Cappella   Italy
Cardigans   Sweden
Catatonia   Wales
Champs Boys   France
Chicory Tip   UK
Crowded House   Australia and New Zealand
Curved Air   UK
Cutting Crew   UK and Canada
Danny Mirror   Holland
Darts   UK
Deee-Lite   USA, Russia and Japan
Del Amitri   UK
Eddy Grant   Guyana
Edmund Hockridge   Canada
Emile Ford   UK
Enigma   Germany and Romania
Enya   Ireland
Europe   Sweden
Father Abraham   Holland
Fleetwood Mac   UK and USA
Foreigner   UK and USA
Fox   UK and USA
FPI Project   Italy
Funkadelic   USA
Gallagher and Lyle   UK
Gibson Brothers   Martinique
Go-Gos   USA
Golden Earring   Holland
Greyhound   Jamaica
Guess Who   Canada
Hawkwind   UK (German dancer)
Helmut Zacharias   Germany

Hothouse Flowers   Ireland
Human Resource   Holland
Icehouse   New Zealand
Incognito   UK and France
Inner Circle   Jamaica
Jam and Spoon   Germany
Jam Machine   Italy
Jam Tronik   Germany
Jan Hammer   Czechoslovakia
John Farnham   Australia
John Parr   UK
John Paul Young   Australia
JT and the Big Family   Italy
Kaoma   France
Kraftwerk   Germany
Lobo (70s band)   USA
Lobo (80s band)   Holland
Mai Tai   Holland
Manfred Mann   South Africa
M/A/R/R/S   UK
Martha and the Muffins   Canada
Martika   USA
Men at Work   Australia
Men Without Hats   Canada
Mental As Anything   Australia
Metallica   USA and Denmark
Mezzoforte   Iceland
Midnight Oil   Australia
Milk and Honey   Israel
Millie   Jamaica
Milli Vanilli   France and Germany
Mixmaster   Italy
Modern Talking   Germany
Mouth and MacNeal   Holland
New Seekers   UK
Norman Greenbaum   USA
Opus   Austria
Ottawan   France
Pasadenas   UK
Patsy Gallant   Canada
Peppers   France
Percy Faith   Canada
Perez Prado   Cuba
Plastic Bertrand   Belgium
Poppy Family   Canada
Praga Khan   Belgium
Prefab Sprout   UK
Pseudo Echo   Australia

Python Lee Jackson Australia
Rob 'N' Raz (featuring Leila K) Sweden
Roxette Sweden
Rozalla Zimbabwe
Rush Canada
Shocking Blue Holland
Silver Convention Germany and USA
Snap Germany and USA
Soeur Sourire (Singing Nun) Belgium
Spagna Italy
Split Enz New Zealand and UK
Starlight Italy
Starsound Holland
Stereophonics Wales
Sweet People France

Sylvia Sweden
Teach-In Holland
Technotronic Belgium
Ten Sharp Holland
Third World Jamaica
Thomas Dolby UK
Thompson Twins New Zealand and UK
2 Unlimited Holland
Vanessa Paradis France
Van Halen Holland and USA
Whigfield Denmark
Wigan's Chosen Few USA
Yello Switzerland
Zucchero Italy

Composition of Pop Groups

A1
Ben Adams
Christian Ingebrigtsen
Paul Marazzi
Mark Read

ABBA
Benny Andersson
Agnetha Fältskog
Anni-Frid Lyngstad
Björn Ulvaeus
Swedish group except for the Norwegian brunette
Anni-Frid Lyngstad

ABC
Martin Fry – Vocals
Mark Lickley – Bass
Dave Robinson – Drums
Steve Singleton – Saxophone
Mark White – Guitar

AC/DC
Dave Evans – Vocals (left 1977)
Mark Evans – Bass
Brian Johnson – Vocals (replaced Bon Scott)
Phil Rudd – Drums (Left in 1982)
Bon Scott – Vocals (previously drums, died 1980)
Chris Slade
Cliff Williams (replaced Dave Evans)
Simon Wright (replaced Phil Rudd)
Angus Young – Lead Guitar
Malcolm Young – Guitar

Ace of Base
Jonas 'Joker' Berggren
Jenny Berggren
Linn Berggren
Ulf 'Buddha' Ekberg

Adam and the Ants
Matthew Ashman – Guitar and Piano
Dave Barbe 'Barbarossa' – Drums
Johnny Bivouac – Guitar
Stuart Goddard (Adam) – Lead Vocals and Guitar
Jordan – Vocals
Andy Warren – Bass

Aerosmith
Jimmy Crespo – Guitar (joined after Whitfield left)
Rick Dufay – Guitar (joined after Whitfield left)
Tom Hamilton – Bass
Joey Kramer – Drums
Joe Perry – Guitar
Ray Tabano – Guitar (replaced by Brad Whitfield)
Steve Tyler – Lead Vocals
Brad Whitfield – Guitar (left in 1980)

A-Ha
Magne Furuholmen – Keyboards, Guitar, Backing Vocals
Morten Harket – Lead Vocals
Paul Waaktaar-Savoy – Guitar and Backing Vocals

Airforce
Ginger Baker – Drums and Percussion
Graham Bond – Saxophone
Rick Grech – Bass and Violin
Jeanette Jacobs – Vocals
Remi Kabaka – Percussion
Denny Laine – Guitar
Steve Winwood – Guitar, Keyboards and Vocals
Chris Wood – Saxophone and Flute

Alarm, The
Eddie MacDonald – Guitar and Vocals
Mike Peters – Bass and Vocals
Dave Sharp – Guitar and Vocals
Mark Taylor – Keyboards
Nigel Twist – Drums

All Saints
Natalie Appleton
Nicole Appleton
Melanie Blatt
Shaznay Lewis

Altered Images
Michael 'Tich' Anderson – Drums
Caesar – Guitar
Claire Grogan – Vocals
Tony McDaid – Guitar
Johnny McElhone – Bass

Amazulu
Sharon Bailey – Percussion
Lesley Beach – Saxophone
Debbie Evans – Drums
Clare Henny – Bass
Rose Minor – Vocals
Margo Sagov – Guitar

MUSIC
POP

Amen Corner
Dennis Bryon – Drums
Andy Fairweather Lowe – Guitar and Lead Vocals
Alan Jones – Saxophone
Neil Jones – Guitar
Mike Smith – Saxophone
Clive Taylor – Bass
Blue Weaver – Guitar

Animals
Vic Briggs – Bass
George Bruno – Keyboards and Vocals
Eric Burdon – Vocals
Charles 'Chas' Chandler – Bass
Luke Francis – Guitar and Vocals
Barry Jenkins – Drums and Percussion
Danny McCullough – Bass, Guitar and Vocals
Zoot Money – Organ
Alan Price – Piano and Vocals
Dave Rowberry – Organ
Andy Somers – Guitar
John Steele – Drums
Hilton Valentine – Guitar
John Weider – Guitar, Violin and Bass

Another Level
Mark Baron
Dane Bowers
Bobak Kianoush
Wayne Williams

Aphrodite's Child
Silver Koulouris – Guitar and Percussion
Vangelis Papathanassiou – Keyboards, Flute and
  Vocals
Demis Roussos – Vocals
Lucas Sideras – Drums and Vocals

Aqua
René Dif – Bald-headed Vocalist Claus Noreen
Lene Nystrom – Lead Vocalist
Soren Rasted
Danish group except for Nystrom, who is Norwegian

Argent
Rod Argent – Keyboards and Vocals
Russ Ballard – Guitar, Piano and Vocals
Jim Grimaldi – Guitar
Robert Henrit – Drums and Percussion
Jim Rodford – Bass and Vocals
John Verity – Guitar and Vocals

Art of Noise
Anne Dudley – Keyboards
JJ Jeczalik – Keyboards

Ash
Mark Hamilton – Bass
Charlotte Hatherly – Guitar
Rick 'Rock' McMurray – Drums
Tim Wheeler – Vocals, Guitar

Asia
Geoff Downes – Keyboards
Steve Howe – Guitar
Greg Lake – Vocals and Bass
Mandy Meyer – Guitar
Carl Palmer – Drums
John Payne – Vocals and Bass
Al Pitrelli – Guitar
John Wetton – Vocals and Bass

Aswad
Donnal Benjamin – Guitar and Vocals
Brinsley Forde – Guitar and Vocals
Tony Gadd – Bass
Angus 'Drummie Zeb' Gaye – Drums
Donald 'Dee' Griffiths – Guitar
Courtney Hemmings – Keyboards
Bunny McKenzie – Harmonica and Vocals
Candy McKenzie – Vocals
George 'Ras' Oban – Bass
Tony Robinson – Bass and Keyboards

Atomic Kitten
Jenny Frost
Natasha Hamilton
Liz McLarnon
Kerry McFadden (née Katona) – replaced by Jenny
Frost

Atomic Rooster
Steve Bolton – Guitar
John Cann – Guitar and Vocals
Vincent Crane – Keyboards and Vocals
Chris Farlowe – Vocals
Pete Frenchy – Vocals
Paul Hammond – Drums and Percussion
Johnny Mandala – Guitar
Carl Palmer – Drums and Percussion
Ric Parnell – Drums and Percussion

Average White Band
Roger Ball – Keyboards and Saxophone
Malcolm Duncan – Saxophone
Alan Gorrie – Vocals
Robbie Mcintosh – Drums and Percussion
Onnie Mcintyre – Guitar and Vocals
Hamish Stuart – Bass, Guitar and Vocals

Aztec Camera
Roddy Frame – Guitar and Vocals
Dave Mulholland – Drums
Campbell Owens – Bass

B-52s, The
Fred Schneider – Keyboards and Vocals
Kate Pierson – Organ and Vocals
Keith Strickland – Drums
Cindy Wilson – Guitar and Vocals
Ricky Wilson – Guitar

Bachelors
Con Cluskey
Declan Cluskey
John Stokes

Backstreet Boys
Nick Carter
Howie Dorough
Brian Littrell
AJ McLean
Kevin Richardson

Bad Manners
Buster Bloodvessel – Vocals
Louis Cook – Guitar and Vocals
Dave Farren – Bass
Paul Hyman – Trumpet
Chris Kane – Tenor Sax
Andrew Marson – Alto Sax
Alan Sayag – Harmonica and Vocals
Martin Stewart – Keyboards
Brian Tuitt – Drums

Badfinger
Tom Evans – Bass, Guitar and Vocals
Mike Gibbons – Drums
Pete Ham – Vocals
Joey Molland – Guitar and Vocals

Bananarama
Sarah Dallin
Siobhan Fahey (left 1987 and formed
    Shakespears Sister)
Jacquie O'Sullivan (1988-1991)
Keren Woodward

Band, The
Rick Danko – Bass and Vocals
Levon Helm – Drums, Keyboards and Vocals
Garth Hudson – Accordion, Keyboards and
    Saxophone
Robbie Robertson – Guitar, Keyboards and
    Vocals

Band of Gypsies, The
Billy Cox – Bass
Jimi Hendrix – Guitar and Vocals
Buddy Miles – Drums

Bangles, The
Lyne Elklnad – Guitar, Vocals
    (replaced by Susanna Hoffs)
Susanna Hoffs – Vocals, Rhythm Guitar
Amanda Mills – Vocals, Bass
    (replaced by Annette Zilinkas)
Debbi Peterson – Vocals, Drums
Vicki Peterson – Vocals, Lead Guitar
Michael 'Mickis' Steele – Bass and Vocals
Annette Zilinkas – Bass, Harmonica

Bardot
Belinda Chapple
Sophie Monk
Sally Polyhronas
Katie Underwood (left in May 2001)
Tiffany Wood
Winners of the Australian 'Popstars', disbanded in
    May 2002

Barron Knights, The
Barron Anthony – Vocals
Butch Baker – Guitar and Vocals
Dave Ballinger – Drums
Duke D'Mond – Vocals
Peanuts Langford – Guitar and Vocals

Bay City Rollers
Eric Faulkner – Guitar, Mandolin and Vocals
Alan Longmuir – Accordion, Bass, Piano and
    Vocals
Derek Longmuir – Drums and Percussion
Les McKeown – Guitar and Lead Vocals
Ian Mitchell – Guitar and Vocals
Stuart Wood – Bass, Guitar, Piano and Vocals

Beach Boys
Glen Campbell – Guitar and Vocals
Blondie Chapman
Ricky Fataar
Al Jardine – Rhythm Guitar and Vocals
Bruce Johnstone
Mike Love – Lead Vocals
David Marks
John Stamos
Brian Wilson – Vocals, Keyboard and Bass

Carl Wilson – Vocals and Guitar
Dennis Wilson – Drums

Beastie Boys
Michael Diamond
Adam Horowitz
Adam Yauch

Beatles, The
Pete Best – Drums
George Harrison – Lead Guitar and Vocals
John Lennon – Vocals, Guitar and Piano
Paul McCartney – Vocals, Bass, Guitar and Piano
Ringo Starr – Drums
Stu Sutcliffe – Guitar and Vocals
Brian Epstein – Manager (died in 1967)

Beautiful South
Jacqui Abbot – Vocals
Briana Corrigan – Vocals (replaced by Jacqui Abbot
    in 1994)
Paul Heaton – Vocals
David Hemmingway – Drums
David Rotheray – Guitar
David Stead – Drums
Sean Welch – Bass

Bee Gees
Barry Gibb
Maurice Gibb (died 12 Jan 2003)
Robin Gibb

Bellamy Brothers, The
David Bellamy – Vocals
Howard Bellamy – Vocals
Richard Bennett – Guitar
King Errison – Percussion
Alan Estes – Drums
Emory Gordy – Bass

B*witched
Lindsay Armaou
Edele Lynch
Keavy Lynch
Sinead O'Carroll

Big Brother and the Holding Company
Peter Albin – Bass and Vocals
Sam Andrew – Guitar and Vocals
David Getz – Drums and Vocals
James Gurley – Guitar and Vocals
Janis Joplin – Lead Vocals

Big Country
Stuart Adamson – Lead Vocals and Guitar (died
    2001)
Pat Ahern – Drums
Mark Brzezicki – Drums
Tony Butler – Bass and Vocals
Bruce Watson – Guitar and Vocals

Björn Again
Benny Anderwear
Agnetha Falstart
Frida Longstokin
Bjorn Volvo-us
Australian tribute-band backed by Ola Drumkitt and
    Rutger Sonofagunn

Black Box
Daniele Davoli – Lead Vocals
Mirko Limoni

MUSIC POP

Valeno Semplici

Black Sabbath
Vinnie Apice – Drums
Terry 'Geezer' Butler – Bass
Ian Gillan – Vocals
Glen Hughes – Vocals
Tony Iommi – Guitar
Ronnie James – Vocals (replaced by Ian Gillan)
Geoff Nicols – Keyboards
Ozzy Osbourne – Vocals and Harmonica
　　(replaced by James)
Cozy Powell – Drums
Eric Singer – Drums
Dave Spitz – Bass
Rick Wakeman – Keyboard
Bill Ward – Drums

Blind Faith
Ginger Baker – Drums
Eric Clapton – Lead Guitar
Rick Grech – Bass and Violin
Steve Winwood – Vocals

Blodwyn Pig
Mick Abrahams – Guitar and Vocals
Ron Berg – Drums and Percussion
Jack Lancaster – Cornet, Saxophone and Violin
Andy Pile – Bass

Blondie
Clement Burke – Drums
Paul Carbonara – Guitar
James Destri – Keyboard
Leigh Foxx – Bass
Debbie Harry – Lead Vocals
Nigel Harrison – Bass
Frank Infante – Guitar
Chris Stein – Guitar

Blood, Sweat and Tears
Dave Bergeron – Trombone and Tuba
David Clayton-Thomas – Vocals
Bobby Colomby – Drums
Jim Fielder – Bass
Jerry Hyman – Trombone
Steve Katz – Guitar, Harmonica and Vocals
Tom Klatka – Trumpet
Al Kooper – Guitar, Keyboards and Vocals
Jerry La Croix – Saxophone and Vocals
Fred Lipsius – Saxophone and Piano
Ron McLure – Bass
Dick Nalligan – Keyboards
Alan Rubin – Trumpet
Lou Soloff – Trumpet
William Tillman – Saxophone
George Wadenius – Guitar
Larry Willis – Keyboards
Chuck Winfield – Trumpet

Blue
Anthony Costa
Duncan James
Lee Ryan
Simon Webbe

Blur
Damon Albarn – Lead Vocals and Keyboards
Graham Coxon – Guitar
Alex James – Bass
Dave Rowntree – Drums

Bon Jovi
Jon Bon Jovi – Lead Vocals and Guitar
Richie Sambora – Lead Guitar
Dave Bryan – Keyboardist
Tico Torres – Drums
Alec John Such – Bass
　　(replaced by Hugh McDonald)
Hugh McDonald – Bass

Boney M
Marcia Barrett
Bobby Farrell
Liz Mitchell
Maisie Williams

Bonzo Dog Doo-Dah Band
Vernon Dudley Bowhay-Nowell – Percussion
Glen Colson – Drums
Neil Innes – Guitar, Piano and Vocals
Rodney Slater – Saxophone
Larry 'Legs' Smith – Drums
Roger Ruskin Spear – Percussion, Saxophone,
　　Trumpet
Sam Spoons – Acoustic Bass and Percussion
Vivian Stanshall – Lead Vocals and Various
　　Instruments

Boomtown Rats
Pete Briquette – Bass and Vocals
Gerry Cott – Guitar
Simon Crowe – Drums and Vocals
Johnny Fingers – Keyboards
Bob Geldof – Lead Vocals
Gary Roberts – Guitar and Vocals

Bow Wow Wow
Matthew Ashman – Guitar and Vocals
Dave Barbe 'Barbarossa' – Drums
Leigh Gorman – Bass and Vocals
Annabella Lu-Win – Lead Vocals

Boyz II Men
Mike McCaryl
Nathan Morris
Wanya Morris
Shawn Stockman

Boyzone
Keith Duffy
Stephen Gately
Mikey Graham
Ronan Keating
Shane Lynch

Bread
Mike Botts – Drums and Percussion
David Gates – Lead Vocals, Guitar, Keyboards,
　　Violin, Bass
James Griffin – Guitar, Keyboards and Vocals
Larry Knechtel – Harmonica (replaced Rob Royer)
Rob Royer – Vocals, Guitar and Keyboards

Bronski Beat
Steve Bronski – Keyboards
John Foster – Vocals (replaced Jimmy Somerville in
　　1986)
Jimmy Somerville – Lead Vocals
Larry Steinbeck – Keyboards

Bros
Matt Goss
Luke Goss

Craig Logan

Brotherhood of Man
Tony Burrows
(founder member left before Eurovision success)
Sue Glover
(founder member left before Eurovision success)
Johnny Goodison
(founder member left before Eurovision success)
Roger Greenaway
(founder member left before Eurovision success)
Martin Lee (Eurovision winner)
Sunny Leslie
(founder member left before Eurovision success)
Lee Sheriden (Eurovision winner)
Nicky Stevens (Eurovision winner)
Sandra Stevens (Eurovision winner)
Russell Stone
(founder member left before Eurovision success)
Tony Burrows was also lead singer with The Ivy
League, White Plains, Flowerpot Men, Pipkins and
Edison Lighthouse

Bucks Fizz
Jay Aston
Cheryl Baker
Bobby G (real name Robert Gubby)
Mike Nolan
Shelley Preston (replaced Jay Aston in 1985)
David Van Day (ex Dollar) replaced Mike Nolan in
1995 but then formed another version of the band
with Nolan, whilst Bobby G continued as the only
founder member of his version. When Nolan left after
a dispute with Van Day, Bobby G sued for improper
use of name and although it was originally found in
favour of Van Day in 2001 the verdict was set aside
out of court in 2002 and Bobby G was given the
proprietary use of the group's name whilst the other
version is now called David Van Day's Bucks Fizz.

Buffalo Springfield
Richie Furay – Guitar and Vocals
Doug Hastings – Vocals
Dewey Martin – Drums
Jim Messina – Bass and Vocals
Bruce Palmer – Bass
Stephen Stills – Guitar and Piano
Neil Young – Guitar and Vocals

Buggles
Geoff Downes – Keyboards
Trevor Horn – Vocals and Various Instruments

Busted
Charlie Simpson
Matt Jay
James Bourne

Buzzcocks
Garth Davies – Bass
Howard Deveto – Vocals
Steve Diggle – Bass and Guitar
Steve Garvey – Bass
John Maher – Drums
Pete Shelley – Guitar and Vocals

Byrds, The
Skip Battin
Gene Clark
(co-founder but left in 1966 and died in 1991)
Michael Clarke – Drums
(founding member, died in 1993)

David Crosby – Guitar and Vocals
John Guerin
Chris Hillman – Bass and Mandolin
(founding member)
Kevin Kelley
Roger McGuinn – Lead Vocals and Guitar
(founding member)
Gene Parsons – Drums (replaced David Crosby)
Gram Parsons – Guitar
Clarence White – Guitar
John York
Two of the five founding members have now died,
but the other three get together with various
combinations of the above-named musicians to
perform as The Byrds, although the last gig by the
original five was in 1991.

Calling, The
Alex Band – Lead Vocals
Aaron Kamin – Guitar
Billy Mohler – Bass
Nate Wood – Drums
Sean Woolstenhulme – Guitar

Captain and Tennille
Daryl Dragon – Keyboards
Toni Tennille – Lead Vocals

Carpenters, The
Karen Carpenter – Vocals and Drums
Richard Carpenter – Vocals and Piano

Catatonia
Paul Jones – Bass
Dafydd Ieuan – Drums
(left 1995 to join Super Furry Animals)
Cerys Matthews – Lead Vocals
Clancy Pegg – Keyboard (left in 1995)
Owen Powell – Guitar
(joined after Ieuan and Pegg left)
Aled Richards – Drums (replaced Dafydd Ieuan)
Mark Roberts – Guitar

Chairmen of the Board
General Norman Johnson – Lead Vocals
Ken Knox – Saxophone
Danny Woods – Vocals

Charlatans
John Baker – Guitar
Martin Blunt – Bass
(nervous breakdown after Baker left)
Jon Brookes – Drums
Tim Burgess – Lead Vocals
Mark Collins – Guitar (replaced John Baker)
Rob Collins – Organ
(died in a car crash 23 July 1996)
Tony Rogers – Keyboards

Chemical Brothers
Tom Rowlands
Ed Simons

Chic
Bernard Edwards – Bass (died 1996)
Nile Rodgers – Guitar

Chicago
DaWane Bailey
(joined temporarily between 1991 and 1993)
Peter Cetera – Vocals & Bass
(founding member left 1985)

Bill Champlin – Keyboards (joined in 1982)
Donnie Dacus – Guitar
(replaced Kath after shooting accident)
Marty Grebb – Saxophone and Guitars
(briefly played in 1981)
Keith Howland – Guitars (joined in 1995)
Tris Imboden – Drums
(replaced Danny Seraphine in 1991)
Terry Kath – Guitar and Vocals
(founding member died 1978)
Robert Lamm – Keyboard and Vocals
(founding member)
Lee Loughnane – Trumpet and Percussion
(founding member)
Laudir De Oliveira – Congas, Bongos and
Percussion (1974–82)
James Pankow – Trombone (founding member)
Walter Parazaider (Walt Perry) – Saxophone
(founding member)
Chris Pinnick – Guitar
(replaced Dacus in 1980, left in 1981)
Jason Scheff – (replaced Peter Cetera in 1985)
Danny Seraphine – Drums and Percussion
(founding member)
Steven Stills – Guitar (replaced by Chris Pinnick)
Originally named Chicago Transit Authority when
having their first hit 'I'm a Man' but forced to change
it after being threatened with legal action by Mayor
Richard Daley.

Clash, The
Terry Chimes – Drums
(replaced by Topper Headon in 1977)
Topper Headon – Drums
Mick Jones – Guitar and Vocals
Paul Simonon – Bass
Joe Strummer – Lead Vocals and Guitar (died
December 2002)

Cliff Richard and The Shadows
Cliff Richard – Vocals
See separate entry for The Shadows

Coldcut
Matt Black
Jonathan Moore

Coldplay
Guy Berryman – Bass
Jon Buckland – Guitar
Will Champion – Drums
Chris Martin – Lead Vocals, Keyboard

Commodores, The
William King – Trumpet
Ronald LaPread – Bass
Thomas McClary – Guitar
JD Nicholas –
(formerly of Heatwave, replaced Lionel Richie)
Walter 'Clyde' Orange – Drums
Lionel Richie – Lead Vocals, Piano and Saxophone
Milan Williams – Keyboards

Communards
Richard Coles – Keyboard
Jimmy Somerville – Vocals

Corrs, The
Andrea Corr – Lead Vocals
Caroline Corr – Drums and Vocals
Jim Corr – Guitar and Keyboard
Sharon Corr – Violin and Vocals

Cranberries
Mike Hogan – Bass
Noel Hogan – Guitarist (main song writer)
Feargal Lawler – Drums
Dolores O'Riordan – Lead Vocals

Cream
Peter 'Ginger' Baker – Drums
Jack Bruce – Bass and Vocals
Eric Clapton – Guitar and Vocals

Crickets
Jerry Allison – Drums
Sonny Curtis – Guitar and Vocals
(joined in circa 1961)
Buddy Holly – Guitar and Lead Vocals
Joe B Mauldin – Bass
Niki Sullivan – Rhythm Guitar
(founding member left in 1958)

Crowded House
Neil Finn (New Zealander founding member)
Tim Finn
(songwriting brother of Neil joined band 1989–91)
Mark Hart – Guitarist (American joined in 1993)
Paul Hester – Drums (Australian founding member)
Craig Hooper – Guitar (founding member 1985–6)
Nick Seymour – Bass (Australian founding member)
Formed in 1985 as the Mullanes (founder Neil Finn's
middle name) but became Crowded House in 1986.
Disbanded 1996.

Culture Club
Mikey Craig – Bass
Boy George – Lead Vocals
Rob Hay – Guitar
Jon Moss – Drums

Cure, The
Andy Anderson – Drums
Perry Bamonte – Guitar
Jason Cooper – Drums
Michael Dempsey – Bass
Simon Gallup – Bass
Roger O'Donnell – Keyboards
Robert Smith – Guitar and Vocals
Porl Thompson – Guitar
Phil Thornalley – Bass
Lol Tolhurst – Keyboards
Boris Williams – Drums

Cutting Crew
Martin 'Frosty' Beedle – Drummer
Nick Van Eede – Lead Vocals
Colin Farley – Bass
Kevin MacMichael – Guitar

Damned, The
Brian James – Guitar
Rat Scabies – Drums
Captain Sensible – Bass
Dave Vanian – Vocals

Dave Clark Five
Dave Clark – Drums
Lenny Davidson Guitar
Rick Huxley – Guitar
Denis Payton – Saxophone
Mike Smith – Keyboards and Lead Vocals

Dave Dee, Dozy, Beaky, Mick and Tich
Ian Amey (Tich) – Guitar

Trevor Davies (Dozy) – Bass
John Dymond (Beaky) – Guitar
David Harman (Dave Dee) – Vocals
Michael Wilson (Mick) – Drums

Dawn

Telma Hopkins
Tony Orlando
Pam Vincent
Joyce Vincent-Wilson

Deacon Blue

Guy Barker – Trumpet
Pete Beachill – Trombone
Dave Bishop – Baritone Saxophone
Stuart Elliot – Bodhran
Mark Feltham – Harmonica
Simon Gardener – Trumpet
Graham Kelling – Guitar (founding member)
Lorraine Mcintosh – Vocals (founding member)
James Prime – Piano
Ricky Ross – Vocals (founding member)
Neil Sidwell – Trombone
Jamie Talbot – Baritone Saxophone
Phil Todd – Tenor Saxophone
Ewen Vernal – Bass
Douglas Vipond – Drums (founding member)
Chris White – Tenor Saxophone
Gavin Wright – Fiddle
Husband and wife team of Ricky Ross and Lorraine
Mcintosh played with various artists on LPs and the
above are mostly session musicians.

Deep Purple

Don Airey – Keyboards (joined in 2002)
Ritchie Blackmore – Guitar
    (founder left 1975 returned 1989–92)
Tommy Bolin – Guitar and Vocals
    (replaced Blackmore 1975)
David Coverdale – Guitar and Vocals
    (replaced Gillan 1973–6)
Rod Evans – Vocals (founding member)
Ian Gillan – Vocals
    (replaced Evans 1969 left, returned 1994)
Roger Glover – Bass
    (replaced Nick Semper in June 1969)
Glenn Hughes – Bass
    (replaced Roger Glover in 1973)
John Lord – Keyboards (founding member)
Steve Morse – Guitar (joined in 1994)
Ian Paice – Drums (founding member)
Joe Satriani – Guitar (1993–4)
Nick Semper – Bass (founding member)
Joe Lyn Turner – Vocals (1989-92)
Founded in 1968 as Roundabout but changed name
in April to Deep Purple

Def Leppard

Richard Allen – Drums (lost left arm in car accident)
Vivian Campbell – Guitar (replaced Steve Clark)
Steve Clark – Guitar joined in 1977, died 1991)
Phil Cohen – Guitar (replaced Pete Willis)
Joe Elliott – Vocals (joined in 1977)
Rick Savage – Bass
Pete Willis – Guitar (fired from the band for alcoholism)

Depeche Mode

Vince Clarke – Synthesiser
    (replaced by Wilder in 1982)
Andy Fletcher – Keyboard and Backing Vocals
David Gahan – Lead Vocals
Martin Gore – Guitar, Keyboard and Backing Vocals

Alan Wilder – Keyboard, Piano and Drums
    (left in 1995)

Destiny's Child

Beyonce Knowles
Kelly Rowland
Michelle Williams

Dexy's Midnight Runners

Kevin 'Billy' Adams – Guitar and Banjo
Kevin 'Al' Archer – Keyboards and Vocals
    (founding member)
Mickey Billingham – Keyboards
Geoff Blythe – Tenor Saxophone
Steve Brennan – Violin
Andy 'Stoker' Growcott – Drums
    (replaced Bobby Junlor)
Bobby Junior – Drums
Giorgio Kilkenny – Bass (replaced Steve Wynn)
Andy Leek – Keyboards
Roger MacDuff – Violin
Brian Maurice – Alto Saxophone
Helen O'Hara – Violin
Jim Paterson – Trombone
Kevin Rowlands – Lead Vocals (founding member)
Peter Saunders – Alto Saxophone
Seb Shelton – Drums
Paul Speare – Tenor Saxophone
Steve 'Babyface' Spooner – Alto Sax
    (replaced Saunders)
Mick Talbot – Keyboards
Pete Williams – Bass
Steve Wynn – Bass

Dire Straits

John Illsley – Bass
Dave Knopfler – Guitar
Mark Knopfler – Lead Vocals and Guitar
Pick Withers – Drums

Dollar

Thereze Bazar
David Van Day

Doobie Brothers

Mike Hossack – Drums
Tom Johnston – Guitar
Keith Knudsen – Drums and Vocals
Michael McDonald – Vocals
John McFee – Guitar and Violin
Patrick Simmons – Guitar and Vocals

Drifters

Willie Ferbie
Ben E King
Rudy Lewis (died in 1964)
Clyde McPhatter (founder died in 1972)
Johnny Moore (died 1998)
Bill Pinkney (only living founding member in 1953)
Charlie Thomas
Andrew Thrasher
Gearhardt Thrasher
Since 1958 Pinkney has used the name The
Original Drifters to differentiate themselves from a
British group that became The Shadows

Duran Duran

Simon Le Bon – Lead Vocals
Nick Rhodes – Keyboards
Andy Taylor – Guitar
John Taylor – Bass
Roger Taylor – Drums

Eagles
Dan Felder – Guitar and Lead Vocals
Glenn Frey – Guitar, Piano, Keyboard and Vocals
Don Henley – Drums
Timothy B Schmit – Bass
Joe Walsh – Guitar, Organ and Vocals

Earth, Wind and Fire
Philip Bailey – Drums and Vocals (founding member)
Ronald Bautista – Guitar and Vocals
Michael Beal – Guitar and Harmonica
Leslie Drayton – Trumpet
Larry Dunn – Keyboards
Sonny Emory – Drums
Wade Flemons – Backing Vocals
John Graham – Guitar
Yackov Ben Israel – Conga and Percussion
Ralph Johnson – Drums
Ronnie Laws – Saxophone and Flute
Al McKay – Rhythm Guitar (founding member)
Sheldon Reynolds – Backing Vocals
Sherry Scot – Backing Vocals
Alexander Thomas – Trombone
Chet Washington – Tenor Saxophone
Fred White – Drums and Percussion
Maurice White – Drums and Vocals
   (founder 1970)
Verdine White – Bass
Don Whitehead – Keyboards and Backing Vocals
Andrew Woolfolk – Saxophone
Band's name derived from the astrological signs of
the three founding members

East 17
Terry Caldwell – Vocals
Brian Harvey – Lead Singer
John Hendy – Vocals
Tony Mortimer – Keyboards

Electric Light Orchestra
Michael De Albuquerque – Bass and Cello
Phil Bates – Guitar and Backing Vocals
Bev Bevan – Drums, Percussion and Backing
   Vocals
Louis Clark – Keyboards and Backing Vocals
Mike Edwards – Cello
Melvyn Gale – Cello
Wilf Gibson – Violin
Kelly Groucutt – Bass and Backing Vocals
Pete Haycock – Bass and Backing Vocals
Parthenon Huxley – Guitar and Backing Vocals
Mik Kaminski – Violin
Neil Lockwood – Backing Vocals
Jeff Lynne – Guitar, Keyboards and Vocals
Hugh McDowell – Cello
Richard Tandy – Piano, Harmonica and Backing
   Vocals
Eric Troyer – Keyboards and Backing Vocals
Colin Walker – Cello
Roy Wood – Guitar, Banjo, Sitar and Vocals

EMF
James Atkin – Lead Vocals
Derry Brownson – Keyboards
Mark Decloedt – Drums
Ian Dench – Guitar and Keyboards
Zac Foley – Bass

En Vogue
Terry Ellis
Cindy Herron-Braggs
Maxine Jones
Dawn Robinson (left in 1995)

Erasure
Andy Bell
Vince Clarke

Eternal
Easther Bennett
Vernette Bennett
Kelle Bryan
Louise Redknapp (née Nurding)

Eurythmics
Annie Lennox
Dave Stewart

Faces, The
Kenney Jones – Drums
Ronnie Lane – Bass
Ian McLagan – Keyboards
Rod Stewart – Lead Vocals
Ronnie Wood – Guitar and Backing Vocals
Following Marriott's defection to form Humble Pie in
1969, Ron Wood and Rod Stewart were brought in
and the Small Faces became The Faces

Fairground Attraction
Roy Dodds – Drums
Simon Edwards – Bass
Mark Nevin – Guitar
Eddi Reader – Lead Vocals

Feeder
Taka Hirose – Bass
Jon Lee – Drums
Grant Nicholas – Vocals, Guitar

Fine Young Cannibals
Andy Cox – Guitar
Roland Gift – Lead Vocals
David Steele – Bass

Five
Richard Abidin Breen 'Abs'
Jason Brown 'J'
Sean Conlon
Ritchie Neville
Scott Robinson

Five Star
Delroy Pearson
Deniece Pearson
Doris Pearson
Lorraine Pearson
Stedman Pearson

Fleetwood Mac
Lindsey Buckingham – Vocals and Guitar
   (joined in 1974)
Mick Fleetwood – Drums
Peter Green – Guitar
Christine McVie née Perfect – Keyboards and Vocals
John McVie – Bass
Stevie Nicks – Vocals

Foo Fighters
William Goldsmith – Drums
Dave Grohl – Vocals and Guitar
Nate Mendel – Bass
Pat Smear – Guitar

Foreigner
Thom Gimbel – Saxophone, Guitar
Lou Gramm – Lead Vocals
Jeff Jacobs – Piano, Vocals
Mick Jones – Guitar, Piano, Vocals
Mark Schulman – Drums
Bruce Turgon – Bass

Four Tops
Renaldo Benson
Abdul Fakir
Lawrence Payton
Levi Stubbs

Frankie Goes to Hollywood
Peter Gill – Drums
Holly Johnson – Lead Vocals
Nasher Nash – Guitar
Mark O'Toole – Bass
Paul Rutherford – Vocals

Frankie Lymon and the Teenagers
Sherman Garnet – Vocals
Frankie Lymon – Vocals
James Merchant – Vocals
Joe Negroni – Vocals
Herman Santiago – Vocals

Free
Andy Fraser – Bass
Simon Kirke – Drums
Paul Kossoff – Guitar
Paul Rodgers – Vocals

Fugees
Lauryn 'L' Hill
Wyclef 'Clef' Jean
Prakazrel 'Pras' Michel

Fun Boy Three
Lynval Golding – Guitar and Vocals
Terry Hall – Vocals
Neville Staples – Vocals

Fun Lovin' Criminals
Steve 'O' Borovini – Drums
(left 1999 replaced by Jayson)
Maxwell 'Mackie' Jayson – Drums
Brian 'Fast, Fisty, etc' Leiser – Guitar
Huey 'DiFontaine' Morgan – Lead Vocals and Guitar

Genesis
Tony Banks – Keyboard
Phil Collins – Drums (joined in 1970, left in 1996)
Peter Gabriel – Lead Vocals (left in 1975)
Steve Hackett – Guitar (joined in 1970, left in 1977)
Anthony Philips – Guitar (left in 1970)
Mike Rutherford – Bass
John Silver – Drums (replaced by Collins)
Chris Stewart – Drums (replaced by John Silver)
Ray Wilson – Drums (replaced Phil Collins)

Gerry and the Pacemakers
Les Chadwick – Bass
Arthur Mack – Piano (replaced by Les Maguire)
Les Maguire – Piano
Freddie Marsden – Drums
Gerry Marsden – Lead Vocals and Guitar

Girls Aloud
Nadine Coyle
Sarah Harding
Nicola Roberts
Cheryl Tweedy
Kimberley Walsh
Girl Group formed through ITV's *Popstars: The Rivals*

Gladys Knight and the Pips
William Guest – Vocals
Gladys Knight – Lead Vocals
Merald Knight – Vocals
Edward Patten – Vocals

Go West
Peter Cox – Vocals
Richard Drummie – Guitar, Keyboards and Vocals

Green Day
Billie Joe Armstrong – Vocals and Guitar
Tre Cool – Drums
Mike Dirnt – Bass
John Kiffmeyer – Drums (replaced by Tre Cool)

Guns 'N' Roses
Steven Adler – Drums (replaced by Matt Sorum)
Duff 'Rose' McKagan – Bass
Dizzy Read – Keyboard (added in 1990)
Axl Rose – Lead Vocals
Slash – Guitar
Matt Sorum – Drums
Izzy Stradlin – Guitar

Happy Mondays
Bez – Percussion
Paul Davis – Keyboards
Mark 'Cow' Day – Guitar
Paul Ryder – Bass
Shaun Ryder – Vocals
Gary Whelan – Drums

Hawkwind
Dave Brock – Guitar and Vocals
Robert Calvert – Vocals
Ian 'Lemmy' Kilmister – Lead Vocals and Bass
Stacia – Dancer
Nik Turner – Saxophone and Flute
Memorable for Lemmy's vocals on 'Silver Machine'
and the nude gyrations of six-foot dancer Stacia

Hear'Say
Danny Foster
Mylenne Klass
Kim Marsh (left in 2001 and was replaced by
Shentall)
Suzanne Shaw
Johnny Shentall
Noel Sullivan

Heaven 17
Glenn Gregory – Vocals
Ian Craig Marsh – Keyboards
(previously in Human League)
Martin Ware – Keyboards
(previously in Human League)
Carol Kenyon was the uncredited vocalist on
'Temptation'

Hollies, The
Bernard Calvert – Bass
(replaced Eric Haydock in 1966)
Alan Clarke – Lead Vocals (founding member)
Bobby Elliott – Drums (replaced Rathbone in 1963)
Eric Haydock – Bass (founding member 1962–6)
Tony Hicks – Guitar (founding member)

Graham Nash – Guitar and Vocals
(founder 1962–8, and 1983)
Don Rathbone – Drums
(founding member 1962–3)
Mikael Rikfors – Lead Vocals
(replaced Alan Clarke 1971–3)
Terry Sylvester – Guitar and Vocals
(replaced Nash in 1968)
Founded in 1962

Hot Chocolate
Franklyn De Allie – Guitar
Errol Brown – Lead Vocals
Tony Connor – Drums
Larry Ferguson – Pianist
Harvey Hinsley – Guitar
Ian King – Drums (replaced by Tony Connor)
Patrick Olive – Percussionist
Tony Wilson – Bass (left in 1976)

Housemartins, The
Stan Cullimore – Bass
Norman Cook – Guitar
Paul Heaton – Vocals and Guitar
(later formed Beautiful South)
David Hemmingway – Drums
(later formed Beautiful South)
Ted Key – Guitar
(replaced by Norman 'Fat Boy Slim' Cook)
Hugh Whitaker – Drums
(replaced by David Hemmingway)

Hue and Cry
Greg Kane
Pat Kane

Huey Lewis and the News
Mario Cipollina – Bass
Johnny Colla – Guitar and Saxophone
Bill Gibson – Drums
Chris Hayes – Guitar
Sean Hopper – Keyboards
Huey Lewis – Lead Vocals

Human League, The
Ian Burden (joined in 1981)
Jo Callis – Synthesizer (joined in 1981)
Joanne Catherall
Ian Craig Marsh (left in 1980 to form Heaven 17)
Philip Oakley
Susan Anne Sulley
Martyn Ware (left in 1980 to form Heaven 17)
Adrian Wright – Synthesizer

Humble Pie
Dave 'Clem' Clempson – Guitar and Vocals
(replaced Frampton)
Dave 'Bucket' Colwell (member of Humble Pie 2000)
Peter Frampton – Guitar and Vocals (left in 1971)
Steve Marriott – Guitar and Lead Vocals
Zoot Money – Keyboards
(member of Humble Pie 2000)
Greg Ridley – Bass and Vocals
Jerry Shirley – Drums
Bob Tench – Guitar (member of Humble Pie 2000)

Ink Spots
Jerry Daniels (founding member)
Charles Fuqua (founding member)
Orville 'Hoppy' Jones (founding member)
Bill Kenny (replaced Jerry Daniels in 1936)
Jim 'Mr inkspots' Nabbie

(replaced Kenny 1945, died 1992)
Ivory 'Deek' Watson (founding member)
Founded in 1932

Inspiral Carpets
Clint Boon – Organ
Craig Gill – Drums
Stephen Holt – Vocals
Graham Lambert – Guitar
David Swift – Bass

INXS
Michael Hutchence – Lead Vocals (died in 1997)
Garry Beers – Bass, Vocals
Andrew Farriss – Keyboard
Jon Farriss – Drums
Tim Farriss – Guitar
Kirk Pengilly – Guitar, Saxophone and Vocals

Isley Brothers
Ernie Isley – Drums, Guitar and Percussion
Marvin Isley – Bass and Percussion
O'Kelly Isley – Vocals
Ronald Isley – Vocals
Rudolph Isley – Vocals
Chris Jasper – Drums and Keyboards

Jackson Five
Jackie Jackson (born Sigmund Jackson)
Jermaine Jackson – Bass and Lead Vocals
Marion Jackson
Michael Jackson – Lead Vocals
Randy Jackson – (replaced Jermaine 1976)
Tito Jackson (born Toriano Jackson) – Guitar

Jam, The
Rick Buckler – Drums (replaced David Waller in 1978)
Bruce Foxton – Bass
David Waller – Drums
Paul Weller – Vocals, Guitar

James
Tim Booth – Vocals
Saul Davies – Violin (added 1990)
Andy Diagram – Trumpet (added 1990)
Paul Gilbertson – Guitar
Jim Glennie – Bass
Larry Gott – Guitar (replaced Paul Gilbertson 1985)
Mark Hunter – Keyboard (added 1990)
Michael Kulas – Guitar (added 1999)
Adrian Oxaal – Guitar (added 1997)
David Baynton-Power – Drums (replaced Gavan Whelan 1990)
Gavan Whelan – Drums

Jamiroquai
Wallis Buchanan – Vibraphone
Nick Fyffe – (replaced Stuart Zender)
J (Jason) K (Kay) – Lead Vocals
Derrick McKenzie – Drums
Toby Smith – Keyboard
Stuart Zender – Bass (left October 1998)

Jethro Tull
Mick Abrahams – Guitar and Vocals
Ian Anderson – Flute, Guitar, Mandolin, Saxophone and Vocals
Barriemore Barlow – Drums
(replaced Clive Bunker in 1971)
Clive Bunker – Drums
Glen Cornick – Bass

Martin Barre – Flute and Guitar
John Evan – Keyboards
John Glascock – Bass and Vocals
(replaced Hammond, 1976)
Jeffrey Hammond – Bass
(replaced Glen Cornick in 1971)
David Palmer – Keyboard

King Crimson
Robert Fripp – Guitar and Melotron
Michael Giles – Drums and Vocals
Greg Lake – Bass and Vocals
Ian McDonald – Flute, Keyboards and Saxophone

Kinks, The
Mick Avory – Drums
John Beecham – Trombone and Tuba
Laurie Brown – Vocals
Mike Cotton – Trumpet
John Dalton – Bass (left in 1976)
Dave Davies – Guitar, Vocals
Raymond Douglas Davies – Vocals, Guitar, Piano
John Gosling – Keyboards
Alan Holmes – Saxophone and Clarinet
Davy Jones – Saxophone and Clarinet
Peter Quaife – Bass
(left in 1969 and replaced by Dalton)

Kiss
Peter Criss – Drums and Vocals
Ace Frehley – Guitar and Vocals
Gene Simmons – Bass and Vocals
Paul Stanley – Guitar

Kool & The Gang
Clifford Adams – Trombone
Robert 'Kool' Bell – Bass
Robert 'The Captain' Bell – Keyboards and Saxophone
Gary Brown – Vocals
'Funky' George Brown – Drums
Skip Martin – Vocals
Odeen Mays – Vocals
Robert 'Spike' Mickens – Trumpet
Michael Ray – Trumpet
Pharoah Sanders
Charles 'Calydes' Smith – Guitar
James 'JT' Taylor – Vocals (joined in 1979, left after Toon)
Dennis 'DT' Thomas – Saxophone
Leon Thomas
Earl Toon Jnr – Vocals
(left and Taylor became front man)

Kraftwerk
Klaus Dinger
Wolfgang Flur – Electronic Drums
Thomas Homann (left the band)
Ralf Hutter – Organ
Eberhardt Khranemann – Bass (left the band)
Klaus Roeder – Guitar, Violin, Keyboards
Michael Rother – Guitar
Florian Schneider – Woodwind

Kula Shaker
Alonza Bevan – Bass
Jay Darlington – Keyboard
Crispian Mills – Lead Vocals
Paul Winterhart – Drums

Led Zeppelin
Jason Bonham – Drums

(replaced his father in 1980)
John 'Bonzo' Bonham – Drums (died in 1980)
John Paul Jones – Bass
Jimmy Page – Lead Guitar
Robert Plant – Lead Vocals
Jimmy Page decided to reform the Yardbirds under the name of the New Yardbirds. Keith Moon commented that it would go down like a lead balloon, in fact, a Le(a)d Zeppelin.

Level 42
Boon Gould – Guitar
Phil Gould – Drums
Mark King – Bass and Vocals
Mark Lindup – Keyboards and Vocals

Liberty X
Michelle Heaton
Tony Lundon
Kevin Simm
Jessica Taylor
Kelli Young

Lighthouse Family, The
Tunde Baiyewu – Lead Vocals
Paul Tucker – Keyboards

Lightning Seeds
Ian Broudie – Lead Vocals and Guitar
Martyn Campbell – Bass
Paul Hemmings – Guitar
Ali Kane – Keyboards
(replaced by Angie Pollock in 1996)
Angie Pollock – Keyboards
Mat Priest – Drums
Chris Sharrock – Drums
(replaced by Mat Priest in 1996)

Limp Bizkit
Wes Borland – Guitar
Fred Durst – Lead Vocals
DJ Lethal (joined in 1996)
John Otto – Drums
Sam Rivers – Bass

Love Affair
Maurice Bacon – Drums
Rex Brayley – Guitar
Steve Ellis – Vocals
Morgan Fisher – Organ
Lynton Guest – Organ
Mick Jackson – Bass
A less well-known US band had the same name

Lynyrd Skynyrd
Bob Burns – Drums
Allen Collins – Guitar
Steve Gaines – Guitar
Ed King – Guitar
Billy Powell – Keyboards
Gary Rossington – Guitar
Leon Williams – Bass
Ronnie Van Zant – Vocals

M People
Paul Heard
Mike Pickering
Heather Small

Madness
Mike 'Barso' Barson – Keyboards
Mark 'Bedders' Bedford – Bass

MUSIC POP

Chris 'Chrissy Boy' Foreman – Guitar
Graham 'Suggs' McPherson – Lead Vocals
Carl 'Chas' Smash – Trumpet and Backing Vocals
Lee 'Kix' Thompson – Saxophone and Vocals
Daniel 'Woody' Woodgate – Drums and Percussion

Mamas and the Papas
Denny Doherty – Vocals
Mama Cass Elliot – Vocals
John Phillips – Guitar and Vocals
Michelle Phillips – Vocals

Manfred Mann
Michael D'Abo – Lead Vocals
  (replaced Paul Jones in 1966)
Mike Hugg – Drums and Percussion
Paul Jones – Lead Vocals
Tom McGuinness – Bass
Manfred Mann – Keyboards
Mike Vickers – Guitar

Manhattan Transfer
Tim Hauser
Laurel Masse
Alan Paul
Janis Siegel

Manic Street Preachers
James Dean Bradfield – Lead Vocals, Lead and
  Rhythm Guitar
Richey Edwards – Rhythm Guitar
  (went missing in 1995)
Sean Moore – Drums
Nicky Wire – Bass

Marillion
Fish – Vocals (left in 1988)
Steve Hogarth – Vocals (replaced Fish in 1989)
Mark Kelly – Keyboards
Ian Mosley – Drums
Mick Pointer – Drums
Steve Rothery – Guitar
Pete Trewavas – Bass

Marmalade
William 'Junior' Campbell – Guitar and Vocals
  (founding member)
Raymond Duffy – Drums (founding member)
Patrick Fairley – Guitar (founding member)
Dean Ford – Lead Vocals (founding member)
Graham Knight – Bass and Vocals
  (founding member)
Alan Whitehead – Drums
  (replaced Duffy in late 1966)
Founded in 1966 having previously been named
Dean Ford and the Gaylords

Martha Reeves and the Vandellas
Rosalind Ashford
Betty Kelly
Lols Reeves
Martha Reeves

Middle of the Road
Phil Anderson – Guitar and Vocals
Ken Andrew – Drums and Vocals
  (founding member)
Eric Campbell-Lewis – Guitar (founding member)
Ian Campbell-Lewis – Guitar (founding member)
Sally Carr – Lead Vocals (founding member)
Shug Devun – Keyboards
Derek Hall – Guitar and Vocals

Neil Henderson – Bass and Vocals
Kenny McKay – Guitar and Vocals
Pat Monaghan – Guitar and Vocals

Mindbenders
Wayne Fontana – Lead Vocals
Graham Gouldman – Guitar
Paul Hancox – Drums
James O'Neill – Guitar
Eric Stewart – Guitar, Piano and Vocals

Mis-Teeq
Alesha Dixon
Su-Elise Nash
Sabrina Washington

Monkees, The
Mickey Dolenz – Drums and Vocals
Davy Jones – Tambourine and Vocals
Mike Nesmith – Guitar and Vocals
Peter Tork – Bass and Vocals

Moody Blues
Graeme Edge – Drums and Vocals
  (founder member)
Justin Hayward – Guitar and Vocals
  (replaced Laine)
Denny Laine – Guitar and Vocals
  (founder member left, 1966)
John Lodge – Bass, Cello, Guitar and Vocals
Mike Pinder – Keyboards and Vocals
  (founder member)
Ray Thomas – Reeds and Vocals
  (founder member)
Clint Warwick – Guitar (founder member left in 1966)

Motorhead
Phil Campbell – Guitar
Mikkey Dee – Drums
Ian 'Lemmy' Kilmister – Lead Vocals and Bass

Mott the Hoople
Dale Griffin – Drums and Vocals
Ian Hunter – Piano, Guitar and Lead Vocals
Mick Ralphs – Guitar and Vocals
Overend Watts – Bass and Vocals

Move, The
Bev Bevan – Drums
Trevor Burton – Guitar and Vocals
Chris Kefford – Bass
Jeff Lynn – Guitar and Vocals
Rick Pride – Bass and Vocals
Carl Wayne – Guitar and Vocals
Roy Wood – Guitar, Banjo, Sitar and Vocals

Mud
Rob Davies
Les Gray
Dave Mount
Ray Stiles

Mugwumps
Denny Doherty – Vocals
Cass Elliot – Vocals
James Hendricks – Vocals
Zal Yanovsky – Guitar and Vocals

Mungo Jerry
Mike Cole – Bass
Ray Dorset – Vocals, Guitar
Colin Earl – Piano, Vocals

Paul King – Banjo, Guitar, Vocals

'N Sync
Lance Bass
JC Chasez
Joey Fatone
Chris Kirkpatrick
Justin Timberlake

Nazareth
Pete Agnew – Bass (founding member)
Manny Charlton – Guitar (founding member)
Zal Cleminson – Guitar (1979–81)
Ronnie Leahy – Keyboards
John Locke – Keyboards (replaced Zal Cleminson)
Dan McCafferty – Vocals (founding member)
Jimmy Murrison – Guitar
Bill Rankin – Guitar and Keyboards
(replaced Locke in 1981)
Darrell Sweet – Drummer (founding member)

New Christy Minstrels, The
Karen Black (better known nowadays as an actress)
Bob Buchanan
Gene Clark (left to join The Byrds)
Barry McGuire – Lead Vocals
Larry Ramos
Kenny Rogers – Vocals (1966–7)
Mike Settle
(left 1967 to start First Edition with Rogers)
Randy Sparks (founder of the group)

New Kids on the Block
Jonathan Knight
Jordan Knight
Joe McIntyre
Donnie Wahlberg
Danny Wood

New Seekers
Chris Barrington – Bass
(founding member left in 1970)
Peter Doyle (joined in 1970)
Eve Graham (founding member)
Sally Graham (founding member left in 1970)
Laurie Heath – Guitar (founding member left in
1970)
Marty Kristian (founding member)
Paul Layton (joined in 1970)
Peter Oliver (replaced Peter Doyle in 1973)
Lyn Paul (joined in 1970)
Keith Potger (founder but only played on one LP)

Nice, The
Brian 'Blinky' Davison – Drums
Keith Emerson – Keyboards
Lee Jackson – Bass
David O'List – Guitar and Vocals

Nickelback
Chad Kroeger – Vocals and Guitar
Mike Kroeger – Guitar
Ryan Peake – Guitar and Vocals
Ryan Vikedal – Bass

911
Lee Brennan
Jimmy Constable
Simon 'Spike' Dawbarn

Nirvana
Kurt Cobain – Lead Vocals and Guitar (died in 1994)

David Grohl – Drums and Vocals
Chris Novoselic – Bass and Vocals

Oasis
Gem Archer – Guitar
(replaced Paul Arthurs in 1999)
Paul 'Bonehead' Arthurs – Rhythm Guitar
Andy Bell – Bass (replaced Paul McGuigan)
Liam Gallagher – Vocals
Noel Gallagher – Vocals and Guitar
Tony McCarroll – Drums
Paul 'Guigsy' McGuigan – Bass
Alan White – Drums
(replaced Tony McCarroll in 1994)

Ocean Colour Scene
Steve Craddock – Lead Guitar, Keyboards and
Vocals
Simon Fowler – Lead Vocals, Guitar and Harmonica
Oscar Harrison – Drums and Vocals
Damon Minchela – Bass

O'Jays
Bill Isles
Eddie Levert
Bobby Massey
William Powell
Walter Williams
Formed in 1958 as the Mascots and became the
O'Jays in honour of Cleveland DJ Eddie O'Jay

One True Voice
Anton Gordon
Matt Johnson
Daniel Pearce
Keith Semple
Jamie Shaw
Vocal harmony group formed via ITV's *Popstars:
The Rivals*

Orchestral Manoeuvres in the Dark (OMD)
Malcolm Holmes – Keyboards
Dave Hughes – Drums and Percussion
Paul Humphreys – Keyboards
Andy McCluskey – Bass and Vocals

Osmonds, The
Donny Osmond
Alan Osmond
Little Jimmy Osmond
Wayne Osmond
Jay Osmond
Merrill Osmond

Pet Shop Boys
Chris Lowe
Neil Tennant – Lead Vocals

Peter, Paul and Mary
Paul Stookey – Guitar and Vocals
Mary Travers – Vocals
Peter Yarrow – Guitar and Vocals

Pink Floyd
Syd Barrett – Guitar and Vocals
Dave Gilmour – Guitar and Vocals
Nick Mason – Drums and Percussion
Roger Waters – Bass, Piano and Percussion
Rick Wright – Keyboards

Plastic Ono Band
Eric Clapton – Guitar

MUSIC

POP

John Lennon – Vocals, Guitar and Piano
Yoko Ono – Vocals
Ringo Starr – Drums
Klaus Voorman – Bass
Alan White – Drums

Platters
Alex Hodge
David Lynch (died in 1981)
Herb Reed
Paul Robi (died in 1989)
Zola Taylor
Sonny Turner
Tony Williams (died in 1992)
Managed by Sam 'Buck' Ram

Pogues, The
James Feamley – Piano Accordion and Guitar
Jim Finer – Banjo and Mandolin
Darryl Hunt – Bass
Shane MacGowan – Lead Vocals
 (replaced by Joe Strummer)
Cait O'Riordan – Bass (replaced by Darryl Hunt)
Andrew Ranken – Drums
Peter 'Spidey' Stacy – Tin Whistle
Joe Strummer – Lead Vocals
Terry Woods

Police
Stewart Copeland – Drums
Sting (Gordon Sumner) – Lead Vocals and Bass
Andy Summers – Guitar
Miles Copeland – Manager

Pretenders, The
Martin Chambers – Drums
Pete Farndon – Bass (left 1982, died 1983)
Malcolm Foster – Bass (added 1983)
James Honeyman-Scott – Guitar
 (died in 1982)
Chrissie Hynde – Lead Vocals
Robbie McIntosh – Guitar (added 1983)

Proclaimers
Charlie Reid
Craig Reid

Procol Harum
Gary Brooker – Piano and Lead Vocals
Alan Cartwright – Bass
Chris Copping – Bass and Organ
Matthew Fisher – Guitar and Organ
Mick Grabham – Guitar
Bobby Harrison – Drums and Percussion
David Knights – Bass
Ray Royer – Guitar
Peter Solley – Organ
Robin Trower – Guitar and Vocals
BJ Wilson – Drums and Percussion

Prodigy
Graham 'Gizz' Butt – Guitar
Keith Flint – Lead Vocals
Liam Howlett – Keyboards
Alison 'Alli' MacInnes – Guitar
Sharky – Dancer and Backing Vocals
Leeroy Thornhill – Dancer
MC Maxim Reality (born Keith Palmer)

Public Image Ltd
Keith Levine – Guitar
John Lydon (Johnny Rotten) – Lead Vocals

Jim Walker – Drums
Jah Wobble – Bass

Pulp
Jarvis Cocker – Lead Vocals and Guitar
Peter Dalton – Keyboard
Wayne Furniss – Drums
Jamie Pinchbeck – Bass

Quarrymen, The
George Harrison – Lead Guitar and Vocals
John Lennon – Rhythm Guitar and Vocals
Paul McCartney – Bass and Vocals
Pete Best – Drums
Formed 1958 and became The Silver Beatles in
1959 when Tony Sheridan joined them. Whatever
became of them?

Queen
John Deacon – Bass
Brian May – Guitar and Vocals
Freddie Mercury (born Freddie Bulsara) – Vocals
 and Keyboard
Roger Taylor – Drums

Q-Tips, The
Stewart Blandmer – Saxophone and Vocals
Steve Farr – Saxophone and Vocals
Tony Hughes – Trumpet
Mick Pearl – Bass
Garth Watt Roy – Guitar and Vocals
Barry Watts – Drums
Paul Young – Guitar and Lead Vocals

Radiohead
Johnny Greenwood – Lead Guitar
Colin Greenwood – Bass
Ed O'Brien – Rhythm Guitar
Phil Selway – Drums
Thom Yorke – Lead Vocals and Rhythm Guitar

Rainbow
Don Airey – Keyboards (replaced David Stone)
Jimmy Bain – Bass (replaced Craig Gruber)
Ritchie Blackmore – Guitar
Graham Bonnet – Vocals
 (replaced Ronnie James Dio)
Tony Carey – Keyboards
 (replaced Mickey Lee Soule)
Mark Clarke – Bass (replaced Jimmy Bain)
Bob Daisley – Bass (replaced Mark Clarke)
Ronnie James Dio – Vocals
Gary Driscoll – Drums
Roger Glover – Bass (replaced Bob Daisley)
Craig Gruber – Bass
Cozy Powell – Drums (replaced Gary Driscoll)
Mickey Lee Soule – Keyboards
David Stone – Keyboards (replaced Tony Carey)

The Red Hot Chili Peppers
Flea (Michael Balzary) – Trumpet, Bass (founding
 member)
John Frusciante – (replaced Duane 'Blackbird'
 McKnight, left and rejoined)
Jack Irons – Drums (left to form What Is This)
Anthony Kiedis – Vocals (founding member)
Duane 'Blackbird' McKnight – Guitar (replaced Hillel
 Slovak)
Arik Marshall – Guitar (replaced John Frusciante)
Cliff Martinez – Bass
Dave Navarro – (replaced Jesse Tobias)
DH Peligro – Drums (formerly with Dead Kennedys)

Jack Sherman – Guitar
Hillel Slovak – Guitar (died 25 June 1988)
Chad Smith – Drums (replaced DH Peligro)
Jesse Tobias – Guitar (replaced Arik Marshall)
The Red Hot Chili Peppers were once known as
Tony Flow and the Miraculously Majestic Masters of
Mayhem

REM
Bill Berry – Drums (left in 1996)
Peter Buck – Lead Guitar, Mandolin and Banjo
Mike Mills – Bass, Keyboard
Michael Stipe – Lead Vocals and Guitar

Righteous Brothers
Bobby Hatfield
Bill Medley
Jimmy Walker (replaced Bill Medley in 1968)

Right Said Fred
Fred Fairbrass
Richard Fairbrass
Rob Manzoli

Rolling Stones, The
Mick Jagger – Lead Vocals
Brian Jones – Guitar (died in 1969)
Darryl Jones – Bass (joined in 1994)
Keith 'The Human Riff' Richards – Guitar
Ian Stewart – Piano (died 12 December 1985)
Mick Taylor – Guitar (1969–74)
Charlie Watts – Drums
Ron Wood – Bass (joined in 1975)
Bill Wyman – Bass (left in 1992)
Andrew Loog Oldham – Manager

Ronettes
Estelle Bennett
Veronica 'Ronnie' Bennett
Nedra Talley

Roxette
Marie Fredriksson – Vocals
Per Gessle – Guitar and Vocals

Roxy Music
Roger Bunn – Guitar
Brian Eno – Synthesizer
Bryan Ferry – Lead Vocals and Keyboards
John Gustafson – Bass (replaced Sal Maida)
Eddie Jobson – Keyboards
Rik Kenton – Bass (replaced Graham Simpson)
Andy MacKay – Saxophone
Sal Maida – Bass (replaced John Porter)
Phil Manzanera – Guitar
David O'List – Guitar
John Porter – Bass (replaced Rik Kenton)
Graham Simpson – Bass
David Skinner – Keyboards
Paul Thompson – Drums
Gary Tibbs – Bass (replaced John Wetton)
John Wetton – Bass

Rutles, The
Dirk McQuickly (Eric Idle)
Ron Nasty (Neil Innes)
Stig O'Hara (Ricky Fataar)
Barry Wom (John Halsey)
Leggy Mountbatten (Terence Bayler) – Manager
Spoof group invented by Eric Idle and Gary Weiss
and modelled on The Beatles. Had a minor hit in
actuality with 'I Must Be In Love'

S Club
Tina Barrett
Paul Cattermole (left 2002)
Jon Lee
Bradley McIntosh
Jo O'Meara
Hannah Spearritt
Rachel Stevens
Formerly known as S Club 7 until Paul Cattermole
left

S Club Juniors
Aaron
Calvin
Daisy
Frankie
Hannah
Jay
Rochelle
Stacey

Salt-N-Pepa
Sandra 'Pepa' Denton
DJ Pamela Green
Cheryl 'Salt' James
DJ Dee Dee 'Spinderella' Roper (replaced Pamela
Green)

Savage Garden
Darren Hayes – Lead Vocals
Daniel Jones – Guitar

Scaffold
John Gorman
Mike McGear
Roger McGough

Searchers, The
Chris Curtis
Tony Jackson
John McNally
Mike Pinder

Seekers
Judith Durham – Vocal
Athol Guy – Bass
Keith Potger – Guitar
Bruce Woodley – Guitar

Sex Pistols
Paul Cook – Drums
Steve Jones – Guitar
Glen Matlock – Bass
    (replaced by Sid Vicious in 1977)
Wally Nightingale – Lead Vocals
Jonny Rotten – Vocals
Sid Vicious – Bass (died in 1979)
Malcolm McLaren – Manager
Reformed in 1996 for the 'Filthy Lucre' tour

Shadows, The
Brian Bennett – Drums (founding member)
Warren Bennett – Guitar and Keyboards (son of
    Brian)
John Farrar – Bass Guitar
    (replaced Alan Tarney in 1977)
Mo Foster – Bass (classed as an honorary Shadow)
Mark Griffiths – Bass (replaced Alan Jones in
    1987)
Cliff Hall – Piano (from 1978 an honorary Shadow)
Jet Harris – Bass
    (replaced by Brian Locking in 1962)

MUSIC POP

Alan Hawkshaw – Piano and Keyboards (joined
   1968)
Alan Jones – Bass
   (from 1977 an honorary Shadow)
Brian 'Licorice' Locking – Bass
   (left for religious reasons 1964)
Ben Marvin – Guitar (son of Hank)
Hank Marvin – Lead Guitar
Tony Meehan – Drums
   (replaced by Brian Bennett in 1961)
John Rostill – Bass Guitar
   (joined 1964, died in 1973)
Alan Tarney – Bass Guitar and Piano (1973–7)
Bruce Welch – Rhythm Guitar

Shakespears Sister
Marcella Detroit
Siobhan Fahey

Shalamar
Jeffrey Daniel
Howard Hewett
Jody Watley

Shamen, The
Colin Angus
Derek McKenzie (replaced by William Sinnott)
Keith McKenzie
William Sinnott (drowned in 1991)
Peter Stephenson
Richard 'Mr C' West

Simply Red
Tony Bowers – Bass
Mick 'Red' Hucknall – Lead Vocals
Chris Joyce – Drums
Tim Kellett – Brass, Keyboards
Fritz McIntyre – Keyboards
Sylvan Richardson – Guitar

Slade
Dave Hill – Lead Guitar and Backing Vocals
Noddy Holder – Lead Vocals and Guitar
Jim Lea – Bass and Violin
Don Powell – Drums

Small Faces
Kenney Jones – Drums
Ronnie Lane – Bass
Ian McLagan – Keyboards
Steve Marriott – Vocals and Guitar
Following Marriott's defection to form Humble Pie in
1969, Ron Wood and Rod Stewart were brought in
and the Small Faces became The Faces

Smashing Pumpkins
Jimmy Chamberlin – Drums
Billy Corgan – Lead Vocals and Guitar
James Iha – Lead Guitar
Melissa Auf Der Maur – Bass
D'Arcy Wretzky – Bass (replaced by Melissa Auf
   Der Maur)

Smiths
Mike Joyce – Drums
Johnny Marr – Guitar
Stephen Morrissey – Vocals
Andy Rourke – Bass

Smokey Robinson and the Miracles
Bill Griffin – Vocals
Pete Moore – Vocals

Smokey Robinson – Lead Vocals
Bobby Rogers – Vocals
Ronny White – Vocals

So Solid Crew
Harvey
Lisa
Romeo
Band is reputed to have at least 30 transient mem-
bers

Soft Cell
Marc Almond – Lead Vocals
Dave Ball – Synthesizer

Spandau Ballet
Tony Hadley – Lead Vocals
John Keeble – Drums
Gary Kemp – Guitar
Martin Kemp – Bass
Steve Norman – Guitar, Saxophone and Percussion
Steve Dagger – Manager

Spencer Davis Group
Spencer Davis – Guitar and Vocals
   (founding member)
Ray Fenwick – Guitar (replaced Phil Sawyer)
Eddie Hardin – Keyboards (replaced Phil Sawyer)
Phil Sawyer – Guitar and Keyboards
   (joined 1967 after Steve Winwood left)
Muff Winwood – Bass
   (founding member left in 1967)
Steve Winwood – Vocals, Guitar and Piano
   (founding member)
Peter York – Drums (founding member)
Steve Winwood left in 1967 to form Traffic

Spice Girls
Victoria Beckham (née Adams) 'Posh Spice'
Melanie 'B' Brown 'Scary Spice'
Emma Bunton 'Baby Spice'
Melanie 'C' Chisholm 'Sporty Spice'
Geri Halliwell 'Ginger Spice' (left the group in 1999)

Spinal Tap
Joe 'Mama' Bessemer – Drums
   (replaced Mick Shrimpton)
Peter James Bond
   (replaced Childs, spontaneously combusted)
Eric 'Stumpy Joe' Childs – Drums
   (died in 1974 after choking)
Ian Faith – Manager (replaced Hampton)
Glyn Hampton – Manager (left in 1975)
Ross MacLochness – Keyboards
   (replaced Denny Upham)
John 'Stumpy' Pepys – Drums
   (died in gardening accident 1969)
Jeanine Pettibone – Manager (replaced Ian Faith)
Ronnie Pudding – Bass
David St Hubbins (Michael McKean)
Viv Savage – Keyboards (replaced MacLochness)
Mick Shrimpton – Drums
   (replaced Bond but suffered same fate)
Ric Shrimpton – Drums
   (played in the 1992 revival group)
Derek Smalls (Harry Shearer) – Bass
Nigel Tufnel (Christopher Guest)
Denny Upham – Keyboards
CJ Vanston – Keyboards
   (played in the 1992 revival group)
Fictitious group played by McKean, Guest and
Shearer in the 1984 satirical film *This Is Spinal Tap*,

although spawning minor hits such as 'Bitch School' and 'The Majesty of Rock'.

Squeeze
Paul Carrack – Keyboards and Vocals
Chris Difford – Guitar and Vocals
Paul Gunn – Drums (replaced by Gilson Lavis)
Jools Holland – Keyboards and Vocals
Gilson Lavis – Drums
Glenn Tilbrook – Guitar and Vocals
Miles Copeland – Manager (in the early days)

Status Quo
John Coghlan – Drums
Alan Lancaster – Bass
Roy Lynes – Keyboards
Rick Parfitt – Guitar and Vocals
Francis Rossi – Guitar and Vocals
The above are the five founding members, although various other musicians have played with the Quo over the years

Steps
Lee Latchford-Evans
Claire Richards
Lisa Scott-Lee
Faye Tozer
Ian 'H' Watkins

Stereophonics
Stuart Cable – Drummer
Kelly Jones – Lead Vocals and Guitar
Richard Jones – Bass

Stone Roses
Ian Brown – Vocals
Andy Couzens – Guitar
Pete Garner – Bass
  (replaced by Gary 'Mani' Mounfield)
Gary 'Mani' Mounfield – Bass
John Squire – Guitar
Simon Wolstencroft – Drums
  (replaced by Alan 'Reni' Wren)
Alan 'Reni' Wren – Drums

Stranglers, The
Jet Black – Drums
Jean-Jacques Burnel – Bass and Vocals
Hugh Cornwell – Guitar and Vocals
Dave Greenfield – Keyboards

Strokes, The
Julian Casablancas – Lead Vocals
Nikolai Fraiture – Bass
Albert Hammond Jr – Guitar
Fabrizio Moretti – Drums
Nick Valensi – Guitar

Suede
Brett Anderson – Lead Vocalist
Bernard Butler – Guitar
  (replaced by Richard Oakes)
Neil Codling – Keyboard, Vocals
Justine Frischmann – Guitar (left)
Simon Gilbert – Drums
Richard Oakes – Guitar
Mat Osman – Bass

Sugarbabes, The
Keisha Buchanan
Mutya Buena
Sioban Donaghy (left in 2001)

Heidi Range (replaced Sioban Donaghy)

Super Furry Animals
Huw 'Bunf' Bunford – Guitar and Vocals
Cian Ciaran – Keyboards
Dafydd Ieuan – Drums
Guto Pryce – Bass
Gruff Rhys – Lead Vocals and Guitar

Supergrass
Gaz Coombes – Lead Vocals and Guitar
Danny Goffey – Drums
Micky Quinn – Bass

Supertramp
Rick Davies – Keyboards, Harmonica and Vocals
Mark Hart – Keyboards and Vocals
John Helliwell – Keyboards and Saxophones
Cliff Hugo – Bass
Bob Sjebenberg – Drums
Jesse Sjebenberg – Keyboards, Guitar, Percussion
  and Vocals
Dougie Thompson – Bass
Lee Thornburg – Trumpet and Trombone
Carl Verheyen – Guitar and Vocals

Supremes
Florence Ballard
Cindy Birdsong
Diana Ross
Jean Terrell (joined after Ross left)
Mary Wilson (replaced by Birdsong on becoming
  Supremes)
Jean Terrell (joined after Ross left)
Originally called Primettes

Sweet
Brian Connolly – Vocals
  (founding member, died in 1997)
Steve Priest – Bass (founding member)
Andy Scott – Guitar
Mick Stewart – Guitar
Frank Torpey – Guitar (founding member)
Mick Tucker – Drums (founding member)
Phil Wainman – Drums

Take That
Gary Barlow – Lead Vocals, Piano and Composer
Howard Donald
Jason Orange
Mark Owen
Robbie Williams (left in 1995)
Disbanded in February 1996

Talking Heads
David Byrne – Guitar and Lead Vocals
Chris Frantz – Drums
Jerry Harrison – Guitar, Keyboards and Vocals
Martina Weymouth – Bass

Tears For Fears
Oleta Adams – Vocals
Roland Orzabal – Guitar, Keyboards and Vocals
  (founder)
Curt Smith – Bass and Vocals (founding member)
Ian Stanley – Keyboards
Basically a duo that became a one-man band when
Curt Smith left in 1991

Temptations
Dennis Edwards
Mel Franklin

Eddie Kendricks
David Ruffin
Otis Williams
Paul Williams

10 CC
Lol Creme – Guitar and Keyboards
Kevin Godley – Drums, Percussion and Vocals
Graham Gouldman – Bass, Guitar and Vocals
Eric Stewart – Guitar, Piano and Vocals

Ten Years After
Chick Churchill – Keyboards
Alvin Lee – Guitar and Vocals
Ric Lee – Drums and Percussions
Leo Lyons – Bass

Texas
Eddie Campbell – Keyboards
Richard Hynde – Drums
Stuart Kerr – Drums
Johnny McElhone – Bass
Ally McErlaine – Guitar
Tony McGovern – Guitar
Sharleen Spiteri – Lead Vocals and Guitar
Mykey Wilson – Drums

Them
Jim Armstrong – Sitar, Guitar and Drums
Peter Bardens – Organ
Ray Elliot – Organ, Flute, Saxophone
Billy Harrison – Guitar
David Harvey – Drums
Alan Henderson – Bass
John McAuley – Drums, Harmonica and Vocals
Ray Ken McPowell – Vocals
Van Morrison – Harmonica, Tenor Saxophone and
    Vocals

Thin Lizzy
Eric Bell – Guitar (founding member 1970–74)
Brian Downey – Drums (founding member 1970–83)
John DuCann – Guitar (January to April 1974)
Dave Flett – Guitar (1979–80)
Andy Gee – Guitar (January to April 1974)
Scott Gorham – Guitar (1974–83)
Phil Lynott – Bass and Vocals
    (founding member, died 1986)
Gary Moore – Guitar
    (January to April 1974 and 1977–9)
Mark Nauseef – Drums (1978–9)
Brian 'Robbo' Robertson – Guitar and Vocals
    (1974–8)
Midge Ure – Guitar (1979–80)
Darren Wharton – Keyboards (1980-83)
Snowy White – Guitar (1980–82)
Eric Wrixon – Keyboards (founding member, 1970)

Thompson Twins
Tom Bailey – Synthesizer and Vocals
Chris Bell – Drums
Alannah Currie – Percussion, Saxophone and
    Vocals
Joe Leeway – Percussion
John Roog – Guitar
Matthew Seligman – Bass
Pete Todd – Guitar

Three Degrees
Sheila Ferguson
Valerie Holiday
Fayette Pinkney

Three Dog Night
Michael Allsup – Guitar
Jimmy Greenspoon – Keyboards
Danny Hutton – Vocals
Chuck Negren – Vocals
Joe Schermie – Bass
Floyd Sneed – Drums and Percussion
Cory Wells – Vocals

Thunderclap Newman
Speedy Keen – Drums, Guitar and Vocals
Jimmy McCulloch – Guitar
Andy Newman – Keyboards

TLC
Lisa 'Left-eye' Lopes (died in 2002)
Rozonda 'Chilli' Thomas
Tionne 'T-Boz' Watkins

Toploader
Julian Deane – Lead Guitar and Vocals
Rob Green – Drums
Dan Hipgrave – Rhythm and Acoustic Guitar
Matt Knight – Bass
Joseph Washbourn – Lead Vocals, Piano and Organ

T'Pau
Tim Burgess – Drums
Michael Chetwood – Keyboards
Carol Decker – Vocals
Paul Jackson – Bass
Ron Rogers – Guitar
Taj Wyzgowski – Guitar

Traffic
Reebop Kwaku Baah – Percussion
Barry Beckett – Keyboards
Jim Capaldi – Drums, Percussion and Vocals
Jim Gordon – Drums
Rick Grech – Bass and Violin
Roger Hawkins – Drums
David Hood – Bass
Dave Mason – Bass, Guitar, Sitar and Vocals
Steve Winwood – Lead Vocals, Guitar and
    Keyboard
Chris Wood – Flute, Organ, Percussion, Saxophone,
    Vocals)

Travelling Wilburys
Bob Dylan
George Harrison
Jeff Lynne
Roy Orbison
Tom Petty

Travis
Andy Dunlop – Lead Guitar
Fran Healey – Lead Vocals and Guitar
Douglas Payne – Bass
Neil Primrose – Drums

Tremeloes, The
Alan Blakely – Guitar
Dave Munden – Drums
Len 'Chip' Hawkes – Bass and Vocals
Rick West – Guitar
Formed 1959 and began life as backing group to
Brian Poole. Signed by Decca in preference to The
Beatles, who auditioned on the same day. When
Poole went solo in 1966 they became equally
successful in their own right.

T-Rex

Miller Anderson – Guitar
Marc Bolan – Guitar and Vocals (died 1977)
Steve Currie – Bass
Dino Dines – Keyboards
Mickey Finn – Drums and Percussion
Herbie Flowers – Bass
Jack Green – Guitar
Gloria Jones – Vocals and Clarinet
Bill Legend – Drums
Dave Lutton – Drums
Tony Newman – Drums
Tyrone Scott – Keyboards
Steve 'Peregrine' Took – Percussion
    (replaced by Finn in 1969)
Tony Visconti
Formed in 1968 as Tyrannosaurus Rex but short-ened to T-Rex by the time of their first number one, 'Hot Love', in 1971

Troggs

Ronnie Bond – Drums and Percussion
Chris Britton – Guitar
Reg Presley – Lead Vocals
Peter Staples – Bass

2 Unlimited

Anita Doth (stage name of Anita Dells)
Ray Slijngaard

U2

Adam Clayton
Dave 'The Edge' Evans
Paul 'Bono' Hewson
Larry Mullen Jr

UB4O

Astro – Trumpet, Vocals
James Brown – Drums
Ali Campbell – Lead Vocals
Robin Campbell – Guitar and Vocals
Earl Falconer – Bass and Vocals
Norman Hassan – Percussion and Vocals
Martin Meredith – Saxophone and Keyboards
Laurence Parry – Trumpet and Trombone
Brian Travers – Saxophone and Horn
Michael Virtue – Keyboards

Velvet Underground

Willie 'Loco' Alexander – (replaced Lou Reed)
John Cale – Vocals and various stringed
    instruments
Sterling Morrison – Guitar
Nico – Occasional Lead Singer (died 1988)
Lou Reed – Lead Vocals, Keyboards, Guitar
Maureen Tucker – Vocals, Guitar and Drums
Doug Yule – Vocals and Bass (replaced John Cale)

Vengaboys

DJ Dansky
DJ Delmundo
Denice
Kim
Robin
Roy
Yorick (replaced Robin in 1999)
Formed by Spanish DJs Dansky and Delmundo but the four singer / dancers from Hungary, Trinidad, Brazil and Holland became the live performers. Vengaboys became the first Netherlands-based act to score six successive Top 5 singles.

Verve

Richard Ashcroft – Lead Vocals and Guitar
Simon Jones – Bass
Nick McCable – Lead Guitar
Peter Salisbury – Drums
Simon Tang – Guitars, Keyboard

Village People

Eric Anzalone – Biker (replaced Glenn Hughes)
Alexander Briley – G.I.
David Hodo – Construction Worker
Glenn Hughes – Biker
Jeff Olson – Cowboy
Felipe Rose – Indian
Ray Simpson – Cop (replaced Victor Willis)
Victor Willis – Cop

Vixen

Janet 'Patricia' Gardner – Vocals
Laurie Hedlund – Drums
Tamara Ivanov – Rhythm Guitar
Pia Koko – Bass
Jan 'Lynn' Kuehnemund – Lead Guitar and Founder
Sharon 'Share' Pederson – Bass
    (replaced Pia Koko)
Maxine Petrucci – Bass (replaced Share Pederson)
Roxy Petrucci – Drums (replaced Laurie Hedlund)
Rana Ross – Bass (replaced Maxine Petrucci)
Gina Stile – Rhythm Guitar
    (replaced Tamara Ivanov)

Wailers

Aston Barrett – Bass, Guitar and Percussion
Carlton Barrett – Drums and Percussion
Tyrone Downie – Bass, Keyboards and Percussion
Bob Marley – Guitar, Percussion and Lead Vocals
    (died in 1981)
Alvin Patterson – Percussion
Earl Smith – Guitar and Percussion
I-Threes – Marcia Griffiths, Rita Marley, Judy Mowati
I-Threes were a vocal trio that backed Marley

Walker Brothers

Scott Engel (assumed the name Scott Walker)
Gary Leeds – Drums
John Maus – Guitar and Vocals
In fact none of the group were brothers or named Walker

Was (Not Was)

Don Fagenson
David Weiss

Weather Girls

Izora Redman
Martha Wash

Weezer

Brian Bell – Guitar and Vocals
Rivers Cuomo – Lead Vocals and Rhythm Guitar
Matt Sharp – Bass and Vocals
Patrick Wilson – Drums

Westlife

Nicky Byrne
Klan Egan – Piano
Mark Feehily
Shane Filan – Lead Vocals
Bryan McFadden
Only act to reach number one with their first seven releases, all entered at the top, and only band to have four number ones in a single year.

MUSIC

POP

Wet Wet Wet
Graeme Clark – Bass and Vocals
Tom Cunningham – Drums
Neil Mitchell – Keyboard and Vocals
Marti Pellow (born Mark McLoughlin) – Lead Vocals

Wham!
George Michael
Andrew Ridgeley

Whitesnake
Tommy Aldridge – Drums
Richard Bailey – Keyboards
Vivian Campbell – Guitar
Denny Carmassi – Drums
David Coverdale – Guitar and Vocals
Warren DeMartini – Guitar
David Dowle – Drums
Aynsley Dumber – Drums
Mel Galley – Guitar
Colin Hodgkinson – Bass
Brian Johnston – Keyboards
Jon Lord – Keyboards
Bernie Marsden – Guitar
Micky Moody – Guitar
Neil Murray – Bass
Ian Paice – Drums
Cozy Powell – Drums
Guy 'Starka' Pratt
Rudy Sarzo – Bass
Rick Serrate – Keyboards
Pete Solley – Keyboards
John Sykes – Guitar
Brett Tuggle – Keyboards
Steve Vai – Guitar
Adrian Vandenberg – Guitar

White Stripes, The
Jack White – Lead Vocals, Guitar and Piano
Meg White – Drums and Vocals

Who, The
Roger Daltrey – Lead Vocals
John Entwistle – Bass, Vocals, Piano and Brass
(died in 2002)
Kenny Jones – Drums (replaced Keith Moon)
Keith Moon – Drums and Percussion
(died in 1978)
Pete Townshend – Guitar, Organ, Synthesizer
and Vocals

Wings
Geoff Britton – Drums
Joe English – Vocals, Drums
(1975–6 replaced Sewell)
Denny Laine – Vocals, Keyboards, Guitar
Linda McCartney – Vocals, Keyboard (died in 1998)
Paul McCartney – Vocals, Piano, Bass
Jimmy McCulloch – Guitar and Vocals
Denny Sewell – Drums, Percussion and Vocals
(1971–5)

Wizzard
Mike Burney – Saxophone
Charlie Grima – Drums and Percussion
Bill Hunt – Keyboards
Hugh McDowell – Cello
Nick Pentelow – Saxophone
Rick Price – Bass and Vocals
Keith Smart – Drums
Roy Wood – Guitar and Vocals

Wu Tang Clan
Genius
Ghostface Killah
Inspectah Deck
Masta Killa
Method Man
Ol' Dirty Bastard
Raekwon
RZA
U-God

X-Ray Spex
Jak 'Airport' Stafford – Guitar
Paul Dean – Bass
Glyn Johns – Saxophone
Paul 'BP' Hurding – Drums
Lora Logic – Saxophone
Steve 'Rudi' Thompson – Saxophone
Poly Styrene – Vocals

Yardbirds
Jeff Beck – Lead Guitar
(replaced Eric Clapton in 1965)
Eric Clapton – Lead Guitar
(replaced Top Topham in 1963)
Chris Dreja – Guitar
(became bass after Samwell-Smith left)
Jim McCarty – Drums
Jimmy Page – Lead Guitar
(replaced Samwell-Smith in 1966)
Keith Relf – Lead Vocals and Harmonica
Paul Samwell-Smith – Bass
Anthony 'Top' Topham – Lead Guitar

Yazoo
Vince Clarke – Drum Machine, Guitar and Keyboards
Alison 'Alf' Moyet – Vocals

Yes
Jon Anderson – Vocals
(left briefly in 1980 but rejoined 1983)
Peter Banks – Guitar
Bill Bruford – Drums
Geoff Downes – Keyboards
(replaced Rick Wakeman 1980)
Trevor Horn – Guitar and Vocals
(replaced Anderson in 1980)
Steve Howe – Guitar
(replaced Peter Banks in 1970)
Tony Kaye – Organ
(1968–71 and then rejoined in 1983)
Patrick Moraz – Keyboards
(replaced Rick Wakeman 1974)
Trevor Rabin – Guitar joined in 1983)
Chris Squire – Bass
(remained with the band throughout)
Rick Wakeman – Keyboards
(1971–4, rejoined 1976–80)
Alan White – Drums (replaced Bill Bruford in 1972)

Zombies
Rod Argent – Clarinet, Keyboards, Violin and Vocals
Paul Atkinson – Guitar, Violin and Harmonica
Colin Blunstone – Guitar, Percussion and Vocals
Hugh Grundy – Drums
Chris White – Bass and Vocals

ZZ Top
Frank Beard – Drums
Billy Gibbons – Vocals, Guitar
Dusty Hill – Bass
Ironically both Dusty Hill and Billy Gibbons sported
beards but Frank Beard was clean-shaven

General Information

album charts: first No. 1 *South Pacific, Original Soundtrack*.

album charts: started 1958.

Beatles Joint holders, with Elvis Presley, of most No. 1 records (17), including 11 consecutive No. 1s

B sides: famous 'I Talk to the Trees' by Clint Eastwood, B side of 'Wand'rin Star'; 'I Do it For You' by Fatima Mansions, B side of 'Theme from Mash' by Manic Street Preachers.

bongo player on 'Apache' Cliff Richard.

Booker T. and the M.G.s MG stands for Memphis Group.

charts: symbol indicating rise or fall Bullet.

cover crowd: 'Ferry 'Cross the Mersey' Christians, Holly Johnson, Paul McCartney, Gerry Marsden and Stock Aitken Waterman.

David Bowie First TV appearance on *Gadzooks! It's All Happening* in 1965 with the Manish Boys who were nearly banned because of the length of Bowie's hair. Other groups he formed included King Bees, Kon-Rads, Feathers, Hype, and the Lower Third.

Five Star: family name Pearson.

Madonna: father of children Carlos Leon, actor and personal trainer, Guy Ritchie, film director (husband).

Missing star Richey Edwards of Manic Street Preachers went missing in 1995.

Monkees Advertisement in the Los Angeles *Daily Vanity* in September 1965 by Bob Rafelson and Bert Schneider led to the formation of the band. Of the 437 hopefuls who were auditioned, Stephen Stills, Charles Manson and Danny Hutton (later of Three Dog Night) were among those turned down.

most weeks on LP charts *Bat Out of Hell* (472 weeks to date but only reached No. 9).

No. 1 in LP charts throughout year *South Pacific, Original Soundtrack* (1959).

pop star thrown off plane in Germany Keith Flint of Prodigy.

Single charts: first No. 1 'Here in My Heart' by Al Martino (November 1952).

Single charts: started 14 November 1952 (12 records).

Single: wrong name on label 'Elizabethan Reggae' by Boris Gardiner originally had 'Byron Lee' on label.

Spice Girls: nicknames Emma Bunton – Baby Spice, Mel Brown – Scary Spice, Mel Chisholm – Sporty Spice, Victoria Adams – Posh Spice, Geri Halliwell – Ginger Spice.

Spice Girls: No. 1s Four of the five original members have had solo No. 1s, although Victoria Beckham's highest chart entry is at number two.

That's What Friends Are For Dionne Warwick and Friends featuring Elton John, Stevie Wonder and Gladys Knight.

Top of the Pops: theme tunes 'Whole Lotta Love', 'Yellow Pearl' (Phil Lynott), 'The Wizard' (Paul Hardcastle), 'Get out of That' (Tony Gibber).

Vice-President of USA wrote: No. 1 Hit Charles Dawes adapted his 'Melodie' with Carl Sigman, which became 'It's all in the game'.

Vince Clarke: bands involved with Depeche Mode, Yazoo (with Alison Moyet) and Erasure (with Andy Bell).

Westlife: No. 1s First seven records all reached No. 1.

Previous Names of Groups

The Alarm Toilets, 17

America Daze

Applejacks Jaguars, Crestas

Badfinger Iveys

Bangles Supersonic Bangs, The Bangs

Bauhaus Bauhaus 1919

Beachboys Carl and the Passions

Beatles Silver Beatles, Quarrymen, Beatals, Beat Brothers

Black Sabbath Earth

Boomtown Rats Nightlife Thugs

The Christians Natural High

The Commodores Mighty Mystics

The Cult Southern Death Cult

Culture Club In Praise of Lemmings, Sex Gang Children

The Cure The Easy Cure

Deep Purple Roundabout

Depeche Mode Composition of Sound

Dire Straits Cafe Racers

Doobie Brothers Pud

Dr Hook Chocolate Papers

Eurythmics The Catch, Tourists

Faces Quiet Melon, Small Faces

Family Farinas

Fifth Dimension Versatiles

The Fixx Portraits, The Fix

The Fourmost Blue Jays, Four Jays

The Four Seasons Variatones, Four Lovers

The Four Tops Four Aims

Frankie Goes to Hollywood Hollycaust

Freddie and the Dreamers Kingfishers

Genesis Garden Wall

Gerry and the Pacemakers Mars Bars

The Grateful Dead Warlocks

Herman's Hermits Heartbeats

Hollies Fourtones, Deltas

Human League Dead Daughters, Future

Icehouse Flowers

INXS Farriss Brothers

Led Zeppelin New Yardbirds, Birmingham Water Buffalo Society

Madness The Invaders

Mamas and the Papas The New Journeymen, Mugwumps

Manfred Mann Mann-Hugg Blues Brothers

Marillion Silmarillion

The Mission Sisters of Mercy

Mothers of Invention Muthers, Mothers

Mott the Hoople Silence

New Order Joy Division

Orchestral Manoeuvres in the Dark (OMD) VCL XL

Pogo Poco

Pogues Pogue Mahone

Procol Harum Paramounts

Righteous Brothers Paramours

Shadows Drifters
Simon and Garfunkel Tom and Jerry
Simply Red Frantic Elevators
Slade Ambrose Slade, 'N' Betweens
Sonny and Cher Caesar and Cleo
Spice Girls Touch (without Emma Bunton)
Split Enz Split Ends
Starship Jefferson Airplane, Jefferson Starship
Status Quo Spectres, Traffic Jam
Stone Roses Patrol, English Rose
Stranglers Guildford Stranglers
Strawbs Strawberry Hill Boys

Supremes Primettes
Sweet Wainwright's Gentlemen, Sweetshop
Swinging Blue Jeans Bluegenes
Talking Heads Portable Crushers, Vague Dots
Ten Years After Jaybirds
T Rex Tyrannosaurus Rex
Ultravox Zips, Innocents, London Soundtrack, Fire of London
Wham Executive (Paul Ridgeley and David Mortimer in line-up)
The Who High Numbers

Dubbed Singing Voice of Well-Known Actors

Actor	*Voice and film*
Ann Blyth	Gogi Grant *(Both Ends of the Candle)*
Audrey Hepburn	Marni Nixon *(My Fair Lady)*
Christopher Plummer	Bill Lee *(Sound of Music)*
Cyd Charisse	India Adams *(The Band Wagon)*
Deborah Kerr	Marni Nixon *(King and I)*
Diahann Carroll	Bernice Peterson *(Carmen Jones)*
Dorothy Dandridge	Marilyn Horne *(Carmen Jones)*
Edmund Purdom	Mario Lanza *(The Student Prince)*
Franco Nero	Gene Merlina *(Camelot)*
Harry Belafonte	LeVerne Hutcherson *(Carmen Jones)*
Jean Seberg	Anita Gordon *(Paint Your Wagon)*
Jeanne Crain	Anita Ellis *(Gentlemen Marry Brunettes)*
Joan Leslie	Louanne Hogan *(Rhapsody in Blue)*
Joe Adams	Marvin Hayes *(Carmen Jones)*
John Kerr	Bill Lee *(South Pacific)*
Juanita Hall	Muriel Smith *(South Pacific)*
Larry Parks	Al Jolson *(The Jolson Story)*
Lucille Bremer	Trudy Erwin *(Till the CloudsRoll By)*
Natalie Wood	Marni Nixon *(West Side Story)*
Ned Beatty	Vernon Midgley *(Hear My Song)*
Peter O'Toole	Simon Gilbert *(Man of La Mancha)*
Richard Beymer	Jim Bryant *(West Side Story)*
Rita Moreno	Leona Gordon *(King and I)*
Rita Moreno	Betty Wand *(West Side Story)*
Rossano Brazzi	Giorgio Tozi *(South Pacific)*
Sophia Loren	Renata Tebaldi *(Aida)*
Susan Hayward	Jane Froman *(With a Song inMy Heart)*
Vera-Ellen	Carole Richards *(Call Me Madam)*

UK Pop Top Tens

UK's Top Ten Singles of 2002

1 'Anything Is Possible'/'Evergreen' – Will Young
2 'Unchained Melody' – Gareth Gates
3 'Hero' – Enrique Iglesias
4 'Little Less Conversation' – Elvis v JXL
5 'Dilemma' – Nelly/Kelly Rowland
6 'Anyone of Us' – Gareth Gates
7 'Whenever Wherever' – Shakira
8 'Just a Little' – Liberty X
9 'Without Me' – Eminem
10 'The Ketchup Song (Asereje)' – Las Ketchup

UK Top Ten Albums of 2002

1 *Escape* – Enrique Iglesias
2 *Missundaztood* – Pink
3 *Rush of Blood to the Head* – Coldplay
4 *Escapology* – Robbie Williams
5 *By the Way* – Red Hot Chili Peppers

6 *Eminem Show* – Eminem
7 *Heathen Chemistry* – Oasis
8 *One Love* – Blue
9 *Silver Side Up* – Nickelback
10 *Come Away With Me* – Norah Jaones

MYTHOLOGY AND LEGEND

Deities

Role	Greek	Roman	Egyptian	Norse	Sumerian
Principal god	Zeus	Jupiter	Am(m)on	Odin	An
Principal goddess	Hera	Juno	Mut	Frigg	Inanna
Messenger of the gods	Hermes	Mercury	Thoth	Hermod	Uncertain
God of agriculture	Cronus	Saturn	Osiris	Uncertain	Emesh
Goddess of agriculture	Demeter	Ceres	Renenutet	Rindr	Nisaba
Goddess of childbirth	Eileithyia	Juno	Apet	Uncertain	Ninhursaga
Goddess of the dawn	Eos	Aurora	Uncertain	Uncertain	Anahita
God of the dead	Thanatos	Mors	Anubis	Odin	Nergal
Goddess of death	Hecate	Libitina	Nephthys	Hel	Uncertain
God of destruction	Ares	Mars	Seth	Uncertain	Uncertain
God of dreams	Morpheus	Morpheus	Uncertain	Uncertain	Uncertain
God of the Earth	Aesculapius	Aesculapius	Geb	Uncertain	Uncertain
Goddess of the Earth	Gaia	Tellus	Maat	Nerthus	Ki
God of fertility	Priapus	Faunus	Ing	Frey	Ninurta
Goddess of fertility	Artemis	Diana	Bastet	Gefjon	Inanna
God of fire	Hephaestus	Vulcan	Ptah	Loki	Gerra
Goddess of flowers	Hestia	Flora	Qudshu	Nanna	Uncertain
Goddess of health	Hygeia	Salus	Meresger	Uncertain	Nininsina Dazimus
Goddess of the hearth	Hestia	Vesta	Uncertain	Sigyn	Uncertain
God of heaven	Zeus	Jupiter	Ptah	Uncertain	An
Goddess of the hunt	Artemis	Diana	Neith	Skadi	Uncertain
Goddess of justice	Themis	Uncertain	Maat	Forseti	Uncertain
God of love	Eros	Cupid	Uncertain	Uncertain	Uncertain
Goddess of love	Aphrodite	Venus	Hathor	Freya	Inanna
Goddess of magic/ witchcraft	Hecate	Uncertain	Isis	Uncertain	Uncertain
God of marriage	Hymen	Hymen	Bes	Uncertain	Uncertain
God of the Moon	Apollo	Apollo	Neferhotep	Uncertain	Nanna
Goddess of the Moon	Selene	Luna	Isis	Mani	Ningal
Goddess of motherhood	Rhea	Ops	Taweret	Uncertain	Uncertain
God of music	Apollo	Apollo	Uncertain	Bragi	Uncertain
Goddess of night	Nyx	Uncertain	Nephthys	Nott	Uncertain
Goddess of peace	Irene	Pax	Uncertain	Uncertain	Uncertain
God of poetry	Apollo	Apollo	Thoth	Odin/Bragi	Uncertain
Goddess of the rainbow	Iris	Uncertain	Uncertain	Uncertain	Uncertain
God of the sea	Poseidon	Neptune	Nun	Aegir/Njord	Apsu
Goddess of the sea	Amphitrite	Salacia	Tefenet	Ran	Nammu
God of the sky	Uranus	Jupiter	Uncertain	Odin	An
Goddess of the sky	Hera	Juno	Nut	Uncertain	Inanna
God of sleep	Hypnos	Somnus	Uncertain	Uncertain	Uncertain
Goddess of spring	Persephone	Proserpine	Renpet	Uncertain	Ninkasi
God of the sun	Helios	Sol	Ra (Re)	Sol	Utu
God of thunder	Hephaestus	Jupiter	Seth	Thor	Adad
Goddess of truth	Themis	Justitia	Maat	Uncertain	Uncertain
God of the Underworld	Pluto/Hades	Orcus/Dis	Osiris	Villi	Endugukka
Goddess of the Underworld	Hecate	Proserpine	Hathor	Hel	Ereshkigal
Goddess of victory	Nike	Victoria	Apet	Uncertain	Uncertain
God of war	Ares	Mars	Seth	Tyr/Odin	Ninurta
Goddess of war	Athene	Minerva	Sekhmet	Uncertain	Inanna
God of water	Ganymede	Uncertain	Hapi	Uncertain	Enki
God of wine	Dionysus	Bacchus/Liber	Bes	Uncertain	Uncertain
God of wisdom	Apollo	Apollo	Thoth	Odin	Enki
Goddess of wisdom	Athene	Minerva	Neith	Uncertain	Hea
God of woods	Pan	Silvanus	Min	Uncertain	Ashnan
Goddess of youth	Hebe	Juventas	Renpet	Uncertain	Uncertain

Deities of Other Mythologies

Role	Babylonian	Hindu	Phoenician	Celtic	Aztec
King of the gods	Marduk	Indra	Kumarbi/El	Dagda	Tezcatlipoca
God of agriculture	Tammuz	Sita	Telepinu	Amaethon	Centeotl
Goddess of childbirth	Uncertain	Shashti	Ashtaroth	Brigit	Chihuacoatl
Goddess of the dawn	Aja	Ushas	Shachar	Uncertain	Uncertain
God of the Dead	Uncertain	Yama	Mot	Dagda	Mictlantecuhtli
Goddess of death	Uncertain	Kali	Uncertain	Morrígan	Mictlantecuhtli
God of destruction	Uncertain	Shiva	Uncertain	Balor	Itzlacoliuhqui
God of the Earth	Apsu	Uncertain	Uncertain	Dagda	Ometecuhtli
Goddess of the Earth	Tiamat	Pitthivi	Beruth	Danu	Coatlicue
God of fertility	Hadad	Dyaus	Baal	Cernunnos	Tlaloc
Goddess of fertility	Ishtar	Prithivi	Anath/Astarte	Danu	Chalchiuhtlicue
God of fire	Uncertain	Agni	Uncertain	Belenus	Xiuhtecuhtli
Goddess of flowers	Uncertain	Uncertain	Uncertain	Olwen	Xochiquetzal
God of heaven	Apsu	Dyaus	Anu	Uncertain	Ometeotl
Goddess of the hunt	Uncertain	Minakshi	Uncertain	Abnoba	Uncertain
God of love	Uncertain	Kama	Uncertain	Angus	Huehuecoyotl
Goddess of love	Ishtar	Rati	Astarte	Aine	Xochiquetzal
Goddess of magic/witchcraft	Uncertain	Dursa	Kamrusepa	Bodhbh	Malinalxochi
God of the Moon	Sin	Chandra	Yarikh	Uncertain	Uncertain
Goddess of the Moon	Anunitu	Candi	Nikkal	Arianrhod	Coyolxauhqui
Goddess of motherhood	Nintur	Devi	Hannahanna	Danu	Chalchiuhtlicue
God of music	Uncertain	Uncertain	Uncertain	Maponus	Macuilxochitl
Goddess of night	Uncertain	Ratri	Shalim	Uncertain	Itzlacoliuhqui
God of poetry	Uncertain	Uncertain	Uncertain	Ogma	Huitzilopochtli
God of the sea	Uncertain	Varuna	Yamm	Manannan	Uncertain
Goddess of the sea	Tiamat	Uncertain	Asherat	Don	Chalchiuhtlicue
God of the sky	Anu	Dyaus	Teshub	Camulus	Tlaloc
Goddess of the sky	Tiamat	Aditi	Shapash	Don	Uncertain
God of the sun	Shamash	Surya	Nergal	Lug	Tonatiuh
God of thunder	Hadad	Indra	Taru	Taranis	Tlaloc
God of war	Uncertain	Karttikeya	Astabis	Uncertain	Huitzilopochtli
Goddess of war	Ishtar	Durga	Astarte	Morrígan	Clhvacoatl
God of water	Ea	Varuna	Uncertain	Nechtan	Tlaloc
God of wine	Uncertain	Uncertain	Uncertain	Uncertain	Tepoztecatl
God of wisdom	Ea	Ganes(h)a	Uncertain	Uncertain	Uncertain
Goddess of wisdom	Uncertain	Uncertain	Uncertain	Sul	Uncertain

NB: There are a number of points that should be borne in mind when studying the above tables.

First, it should be remembered that in many instances there would be more than one representation of a god for a particular subject. For example, as well as Aegir, both Njord and Vili are often described as Norse gods of the sea. In all cases I have listed the main god who is usually identified with the subject.

Second, there is often a transposition of gods in some mythologies, and in particular the Middle East should be treated with some care. Babylonian mythology is often called Assyrian, Akkadian or Persian, while Phoenician can also be called Hittite as well as Assyrian and Akkadian.

Third, where there is controversy over an entry or there is no god who represents a subject, the word 'Uncertain' has been entered; this does not mean, for instance, that there was no Egyptian god of love but merely that there is not a single god who unequivocally fits the criteria of being both universally accepted and identifiable.

Groups

Muses (9)	of	Literal meaning	Pleiades (7)	7 against Thebes
Thalia	Comedy	Good cheer/plenty	Maia	Polynices
Clio	History	Fame	Taygete	Tydeus
Melpomene	Tragedy	Singing	Elektra	Adrastus
Urania	Astronomy	Celestial	Alkyone	Capaneus
Polyhymnia	Song and mime	Many songs	Asterope	Hippomedon
Erato	Love poetry	Lovely	Kelaino	Parthenopaeus
Euterpe	Lyric poetry	Joy	Merope	Amphiarus
Calliope	Epic poetry	Beautiful voice		
Terpsichore	Dance	Joyful dance		

MYTHOLOGY AND LEGEND

Sages of India (7)

Atri
Bharadvaja
Gautama
Jamadagni
Kashyapa
Vasistha
Vishvamitra

Hills of Rome (7)

Capitoline
Quirinal
Viminal
Esquiline
Caelian
Aventine
Palatine

Useful mnemonic:
Can Queen Victoria Eat
Cold Apple Pie?

Titans (12)

Brontes
Atlas
Astraeus
Cronus
Hyperion
Oceanus
Phoebe
Coeus
Helios
Arges
Rhea
Thema

Useful mnemonic:
BAA CHOP CHART

Underworld Rivers (5)

Cocytus (wailing)
Lethe (forgetfulness)
Acheron (grief)
Styx (hate)
Phlegethon (fire)

Useful mnemonic:
CLASP

Furies (3) (Erinyes or Eumenides)

Tisiphone (avenger of murder)
Alecto (relentless)
Megaera (resentful)

Useful mnemonic:
Furies aren't TAMe

Graces (3) (Charites)

Euphrosyne (good cheer)
Aglaia (splendour or bright one)
Thaleia (jollity)

Useful mnemonic:
Say Grace before you EAT

Fates (3) (Moerae)

Clotho (spun the thread of life)
Atropos (cut off the thread of life)
Lachesis (measured out the thread of life)

Useful mnemonic:
CALI the fates in times of trouble

Gorgons (3)

Medusa
Euryale
Stheno

Useful mnemonic:
Medusa's hair was a MESs

Twelve Labours of Heracles

The killing of the Nemean lion Heracles beat the lion senseless and throttled it; he then skinned the lion with its own claws and donned the pelt to render himself invulnerable.

The killing of the Lernaean Hydra Iolaus cauterised the neck of the Hydra to prevent the two new heads growing each time that Heracles chopped off one of its nine heads.

The capture of the Hind on Mt Ceryneia Heracles chased the Hind for a year, for its golden horns and bronze hoofs. He blamed Eurystheus for its capture so as not to bring the wrath of Artemis on himself.

The capture of the Boar of Mt Erymanthus Heracles returned with the Boar to Tiryns, and Eurystheus hid in an urn at the sight of it.

The cleansing of the Augean stables Heracles cleaned the stables, which had not been cleaned in 30 years, by diverting the rivers Alpheus and Peneus through them.

The killing of the Birds of Lake Stymphalos Heracles scared the Birds from the trees with bronze castanets and shot them with arrows one by one.

The capture of the Cretan Bull Heracles captured the Bull and returned it to Greece.

The capture of the Mares of Diomedes Heracles slew Diomedes, fed him to the Mares and tamed them.

The capture of the Girdle of Hippolyte Heracles slew the queen of the Amazons and took the Girdle for Eurystheus' daughter.

The capture of Geryon's Cattle Heracles slew Geryon and returned to Greece with the Cattle.

The capture of the Apples of the Hesperides Heracles slew Ladon, the dragon that guarded the tree tended by the Hesperides, and took the Golden Apples (later returned by Athene).

The capture of Cerberus Heracles entered the underworld to capture the 3-headed dog.

General Information

Abderus Friend of Heracles in whose care Heracles left the mares of Diomedes. The horses ate him and Heracles founded a town in Thrace in his honour.

Abnoba The goddess of the hunt in the mythology of Gaul. Identified with the Roman Diana.

Acheloüs Greek river god, the son of Oceanus and Tethys.

Achilles Greek hero, born in Thessaly, son of Peleus and the goddess Thetis. When he was a baby his mother dipped him in the Styx, making him invulnerable save for his right heel, by which she held him.

Actaeon Greek hero, grandson of Cadmus, changed into a stag by Artemis and killed by his own hounds because he spied her bathing.

Admetus In Greek mythology the king of Pherae in Thessaly. Apollo served him for a year and introduced him to Alcestis.

Adonis Syrian god, the son of Myrrha and her father Cinyras. He was born from the bark of a tree and brought up by Persephone and forced to spend a third of his time with her and a third with Aphrodite. He was mortally wounded by a wild boar sent by a hostile god or goddess.

Aeacus Son of Zeus and Aegina and king of the Myrmidones. The Myrmidones were originally ants, transformed into men by Zeus at the request of Aeacus. He had two sons, Peleus and Telamon, by his wife Endeis and was also the father of Phocus by a Nereid. Aeacus was one of the three judges of the Underworld.

Aeëtes In Greek mythology, the king of Colchis and possessor of the Golden Fleece sought by Jason.

Aegeus Greek king of Athens and father of Theseus by Aethra, daughter of Pittheus, king of Troezen. Aethra brought Theseus up secretly at her father's court, during which time Aegeus married Medea. When Theseus finally returned to his father's court, Medea fled. Before Theseus went to slay the Minotaur he and Aegeus agreed that he would hoist a white sail when returning to Athens to signal his success. On returning, Theseus forgot to do this and Aegeus, seeing a black sail on his son's ship, supposed him dead and, in grief, threw himself into the sea, henceforth called the Aegean.

Aegisthus In Greek mythology the seducer of Clytemnestra, the wife of his cousin Agamemnon, whom the two lovers conspired to kill. Agamemnon's son Orestes avenged the assassination by killing Aegisthus and Clytemnestra.

Aeneas Trojan hero, son of Aphrodite and Anchises, bravest of the Trojans after Hector and, according to some Roman lines of mythology, the founder of Rome. Aeneas was the lover of Dido, queen of Carthage.

Aeneid Virgil's unfinished epic poem in 12 volumes recounting the deeds of Aeneas, supposed ancestor of Emperor Augustus of Rome. The epic begins after the fall of Troy and ends with the defeat of Turnus the Rutulian prince and the subsequent marriage of Aeneas and Lavinia, the Latin princess.

Aeolus Greek god of the winds and son of Poseidon who gave Odysseus a sack containing all the winds.

Aesculapius Roman god of medicine. Greek counterpart is Asclepius.

Aesir Norse race of warlike gods, who lived in Asgardthey included Odin, Thor, Tyr, Baldu and Frigg (see Vanir).

Aetolus Conqueror of Aetolia. The son of Endymion, king of Elis, he was banished across the Corinthian Gulf after accidentally killing Apis in a chariot race.

Agamemnon Greek king of Argos, murdered by his wife Clytemnestra.

Aganippe Fountain at the foot of Mt Helicon, sacred to the Muses, who are sometimes called the Aganippides.

Ajax (the greater) Greek hero, a giant of a man, the son of Telamon. Killed himself in fury at not receiving Achille's armour after his death.

Ajax (the lesser) Greek hero, son of Oileus. Raped King Priam's daughter Cassandra on the altar of Athene.

Alcestis Greek heroine who saved her husband Admetus by offering her own life.

Alcheringa According to Australian aboriginal mythology, the Golden Age when the first ancestors were created.

Alcides Another name for Heracles, whose grandfather was reputed to be Alcaeus.

Alcmene Wife of Amphitrion, son of Alcaeus. Alcmene mothered Heracles by Zeus in the guise of her husband. Married Rhadamanthus after Amphitrion's death.

Alphito Greek barley goddess of Argos.

Amalthea She-goat. Zeus broke off one of Amalthea's horns to make the Cornucopia (Horn of Plenty).

Amazons Warrior women of Greek mythology who removed a breast to give free play to bow arm.

Amphitrion In Greek mythology king of Tiryns and husband of Alcmene.

Amphitrite Daughter of Nereus, leader of the Nereids. Mothered Triton by Poseidon.

Anchises According to Greek and Roman mythology, the Trojan father of Aeneas by Aphrodite.

Androcles Roman slave who aided and befriended a lion that later saved his life when he was thrown to the lions for attempting to escape.

Andromache In Greek mythology, the wife of Hector and slave of Neoptolemus.

Andromeda According to Greek mythology, daughter of king Cepheus and queen Cassiopeia; she was rescued by Perseus from a sea-monster and subsequently married him.

Angels Nine choirs divided into three ranks: Seraphim, Cherubim and Thrones; Dominions, Powers and Virtues; Principalities, Archangels and Angels.

Antaeus Libyan giant, son of Poseidon and Ge, who was an invincible wrestler until Hercules – realising he drew his strength from his mother, Earth – held him in the air and squeezed him to death.

Antigone In Greek mythology the daughter of Oedipus and Jocasta and sister of Ismene.

Anubis Egyptian god who guides souls to the world beyond. Often depicted with the head of a jackal.

Aphrodite Greek goddess of love and beauty and wife of Hephaestus.

Apis In Egyptian mythology, the sacred bull of Memphis, seen as an incarnation of Osiris.

Apollo Greek and Roman god of prophecy, music, youth, archery and healing, and son of Zeus and Leto (Jupiter and Latona in Roman myth).

Arachne According to Greek mythology, a weaver from Lydia who was changed into a spider by Athena.

Ares Greek god of war, son of Zeus and Hera and lover of Aphrodite.

Arethusa Greek goddess of springs and fountains.

Argo The 50-oared longship which carried Jason and the Argonauts to Colchis in their quest for the Golden Fleece.

Argonauts The band of heroes chosen by Jason to man the Argo and sail in search of the Golden Fleece. The Argonauts included Argus, Atalanta, Calais, Castor and Polydeuces, Heracles, Meleager, Orpheus, Peleus, Telamon and Zetes.

Argus (1) Greek watchman with 100 eyes who watched over Io but was killed by Hermes. His eyes were placed in the peacock's tail by Hera. (2) The faithful hound of Odysseus/Ulysses. (3) The builder of the *Argo*.

MYTHOLOGY AND LEGEND

Ariadne   In Greek mythology, the daughter of King Minos of Crete and wife of Dionysus after Theseus abandoned her.

Arjuna   The Hindu god of dawn and charioteer of the sun, often identified with the Greek and Roman goddesses Eos and Aurora. Ajuna was also known as Rumra (lit. rosy).

Artemis   Greek goddess of fertility and the hunt, daughter of Zeus and Leto and twin sister of Apollo.

Arthur   Legendary British king, son of Uther Pendragon and Igraine, said to have lived in the 6th century. He was born in Tintagel and buried in Glastonbury; Arthur's court was at Camelot (Winchester, according to Malory's *Morte d'Arthur*).

Aruru   One of the names of the Sumerian goddess of childbirth, Ninhursaga (lit. germ loosener).

Asclepius   Greek god of healing.

Asgard   In Norse mythology the realm of the gods in heaven and connected to the earth by the rainbow bridge, Bifrost, which was guarded by Heimdall.

Ask   In Norse mythtology the ash tree from which man was hewn.

Asphodel, Plain of   That part of Hades reserved for the great proportion of the dead. There they continued a shadowy existence in continuance of their former lives since they were bodiless. Contrast Elysium and Tartarus.

Ataentsic   According to Iroquois and Huron mythology, the first woman and ancestor of the human race.

Atalanta   Greek heroine who refused to marry any man unless he could beat her in a foot race. Milanion became her husband after Aphrodite helped him defeat her. Atalanta was the sole female Argonaut.

Aten   Egyptian god; took the form of a solar disc.

Athene   According to Greek mythology, the daughter of Zeus and Metis who sprang from her father's head fully armed. Among her titles was Parthenos (Virgin), from which the Parthenon was named.

Atlas   Titan that bears up the earth. Son of Iapetus and Clymene and brother of Prometheus.

Attis   Greek god of vegetation.

Autolycus   Son of Hermes and Chione and grandfather of Odysseus.

Baba Yaga   Witch or ogress in Slav mythology.

Bacchae   Female followers of the cult of Bacchus or Dionysus.

Bacchus   Roman mythological counterpart of the Greek Dionysus, god of wine and ecstasy.

Baldur   Norse favourite of the gods and son of Odin and Frigg. Baldur was invulnerable to everything except mistletoe, and Loki tricked the blind god Hoder into throwing a mistletoe dart that killed him.

Balmung   Siegfried's sword, according to the *Nibelungenlied*.

Basilisk   Greek monster also called a Cockatrice, that killed with a stare.

Bastet   According to Egyptian mythology, the cat-headed goddess of fertility, love and sex.

Befana   Good fairy of Italian children who is supposed to fill their stockings with toys on Twelfth Night.

Belenus   The Celtic god of healing and light, referred to as 'The Shining One'. He was in charge of the welfare of sheep and cattle. His wife is the goddess Belisama; they are often compared to the Roman Apollo and Minerva.

Bellerophon   Greek hero who tamed Pegasus and killed the Chimera.

Bellona   Greek goddess of war.

Beowulf   Norse warrior prince who killed the man-eating monster Grendel in a wrestling match.

Bifrost   In Norse mythology, the rainbow bridge that led from Asgard to Earth. Literally means quivering path.

Biton and Cleobis   Sons of a priestess of Hera in Argos who drew their mother's chariot several miles to the goddess's temple when no oxen could be found.

Bor (Burr)   Norse god who married the giantess Bestla. She bore him three sons, Odin, Villi and Vé.

Boreas   Greek god of the north wind.

Bragi   Norse god of poetry and music, son of Odin.

Briareus   One of the Hecatoncheires. Aka Aegaeon.

Brigit   Celtic goddess of the poetic arts, childbirth and divination.

Bunyip   In Australian aboriginal mythology, monster who was the source of evil.

Cadmus   In Greek mythology, the son of Agenor, king of Phoenicia and grandson of Poseidon. When Zeus carried off his sister Europa, he went to look for her but was told by the Delphic oracle to relinquish the search and to follow a magical cow. Where the cow lay down he was to found a city, the future city of Thebes. Cadmus married Harmonia.

Caishen   Chinese god of wealth.

Calais   Twin brother of Zetes. The winged sons of Boreas and Oreithyia, they accompanied the Argonauts and drove off the Harpies.

Calchas   Renegade Trojan seer who helped the Greeks at Troy and foretold that Troy would not fall without Achilles' presence and that the sacrifice of Iphigenia was necessary to secure a favourable wind.

Callisto   Daughter of Lycaon, who became one of Artemis's huntresses. She bore Arcas to Zeus, who sought to conceal their affair from his wife Hera by turning Callisto into a bear.

Calypso (Hidden)   Nymph of the island of Ogygia who tended Odysseus there for 8 years until Zeus ordered him home to Ithaca.

Cassandra   Greek heroine given the gift of prophecy by Apollo with the proviso that, although telling the truth, she would not be believed.

Cassiopeia   Wife of Cepheus and mother of Andromeda.

Castor and Pollux   Roman counterpart of Castor and Polydeuces.

Castor and Polydeuces   Aka the Dioscuri, sons of Zeus and Leda. Castor was an expert horseman and Polydeuces was the best boxer in Greece. Some versions have the mortal Castor as son of Tyndareus (Leda lay with both Zeus and Tyndareus). They were transformed into the Gemini constellation

Centaur   In Greek mythology the hybrid offspring of

Centaurus, son of Ixion, and the mares of Mt Pelion in Thessaly.

Cepheus In Greek mythology, the husband of Cassiopeia and father of Andromeda.

Cerberus According to Greek mythology, the three-headed dog that guards the entrance to the Underworld. Offspring of Echidna and Typhon.

Chac Maya god of rain and lightening.

Chaos In Greek creation myth, Chaos was the infinite space existing before creation, from which Ge (the Earth) sprang.

Charon According to Greek mythology, the ferryman of the underworld. Offspring of Erebos and Nyx. Greeks to this day place a coin in the mouth of corpses to pay for the ferry charge.

Charybdis Greek mythological monster resembling a giant whirlpool which infested the Strait of Messina together with Scylla.

Chimera Greek monster with the head of lion, the body of a goat and the tail of a serpent. Offspring of Echidna and Typhon.

Chiron Centaur who was untypically wise and civilised. When Chiron died he became the constellation Sagittarius.

Circe Greek sorceress who turned Odysseus's men into swine. Daughter of Helios and Perse.

Clytemnestra Greek twin sister of Helen and wife of Agamemnon.

Conán the Bald According to Celtic mythology, a warrior and follower of the hero Finn Mac Cumhall. Conán was the son of Morna and brother of Goll.

Conchobar Celtic king of Ulster and illegitimate son of Nessa, queen of Ulster, and the druid Cathbhadh.

Consus Roman god of seed sowing.

Cressida According to Greek mythology, she deserted Troilus, a Trojan prince, for Diomedes.

Cretan bull Magnificent white bull sent by Poseidon to Minos for sacrifice. Minos's wife Pasiphaë so admired the bull that she had Daedalus construct a hollow cow for her to get inside and mate with the bull – that was how she came to bear the Minotaur. The bull was captured by Heracles, freed by Eurystheus and finally recaptured by Theseus at Marathon and sacrificed to Athene.

Croesus Last king of Lydia, famous for his vast wealth.

Cronus Greek god of agriculture and father of Zeus.

Cuchulainn In Celtic mythology the legendary Irish hero, called the 'Hound of Culann' because, having accidentally slain the watchdog of the smith, Culann, he subsequently took the animal's place as penance. He was brought up in the court of King Conchobar of Ulster, whose kingdom he defended against all invaders. Cuchulainn's parents were the sun god Lug, and Dechtire, the wife of an Ulster chieftain. Although Cuchulainn was a handsome youth, in battle he would turn into a frenzied monster, with one eye receding into his head while the other stood out huge and red on his cheek. Cuchulainn's wife was Emer, daughter of the chieftain Forgall. Women continued to fall in love with Cuchulainn after his marriage, and his eventual death was as a result of rebuffing the war goddess Morrigan, who assaulted him with innumerable foes.

Cupay In the mythology of the Peruvian Inca people, the god of death. He is sometimes known as Supay.

Cybele Greek goddess of the earth and lover of Attis.

Cyclops One-eyed giants descended from Gaia and Uranus. Polyphemus is most famous for his capture of Odysseus, who blinded him.

Daedalus In Greek mythology the greatest of mortal craftsmen who made wings out of wax and feathers for himself and his son Icarus to escape imprisonment in the Cretan labyrinth. However, Icarus flew too near the sun and fell to his death when the wax melted.

Damocles Member of the court of Dionysius I, tyrant of Syracuse. Cicero tells how the tyrant had him eat a sumptuous dinner while a sword was suspended by a hair over his head, to show him the limits of rank and power.

Danu (Dana) The Celtic earth-mother goddess, also identified with fertility, wisdom and the wind. In Welsh versions she is known as Don and is associated with the air and the sea.

Daphne Greek heroine turned into a laurel bush to evade Apollo.

Daphnis Son of Hermes and a nymph. The originator of pastoral poetry.

Deianeira Greek princess, the daughter of King Oenus and Queen Althaea of Aetolia, and the second wife of Heracles, whom she killed by mistake when she smeared his garment with a centaur's poisonous blood, thinking it was a love charm.

Deidamia Maiden who fell in love with Achilles and bore him Neoptolemus.

Deirdre According to Irish legend, she killed herself after being forced to marry King Conchobar.

Delphi Site of Apollo's Dorian shrine and oracle, the most famous centre of his worship.

Deucalion Greek hero, son of Prometheus, who repopulated the earth with his wife Pyrrha after Zeus's flood.

Devi (Mahadevi) In Hindu mythology the wife of S(h)iva. Originally there were several goddesses acknowledged as the wives of S(h)iva by different Hindu castes, but eventually they merged into the one manifestation, Devi. Other forms of Devi include, Bhairavi, Chandi, Durga, Gauri (Jagadgauri), Jaganmata, Kali, Parvati, Sati and Uma.

Dian-Cecht The Celtic god of medicine and healing, and the grandfather of the sun god Lug.

Dido Greek heroine, daughter of the King of Tyre, who founded Carthage. Virgil told of her suicide when abandoned by her lover, Aeneas.

Dioscuri (sons of Zeus) Zeus had intercourse with Leda in the form of a swan and she produced two eggs. From one came Castor and Clytemnestra and from the other came Polydeuces and Helen.

Draupnir Odin's magic ring.

Dryad In classical mythology a tree-nymph, sometimes called a hamadryad, which was supposed to die when the tree died. Oak trees were usually favoured by dryads.

Durga In Hindu mytholog a fierce form of Devi who was born fully grown and beautiful; she was immediately armed by the gods and sent forth against the buffalo demon Mahisha. Although

MYTHOLOGY AND LEGEND

blessed with beautiful golden skin, Durga had a fixed, menacing expression and rode upon a tiger. In each of her 10 hands she held one of the god's weapons, i.e. Agni's flaming dart, Indra's thunderbolt, Kubera's club, Shesha's garland of snakes, S(h)iva's trident, Surya's quiver and arrow, Varuna's conch shell, Vayu's bow, Vishnu's discus and Yama's iron rod.

Echidna In Greek mythology, she was the offspring of the earth goddess Gaia and her brother Tartarus. Echidna had the upper body of a nymph and the lower body of a serpent.

Echo Greek nymph who pined away till she was only a voice for the love of Narcissus.

Edda Norse collection of mythological and heroic lays. Also the title of a manual of mythology compiled by the Icelandic historian Snorri Sturluson (1178–1241).

Egeria Roman goddess of fountains and childbirth.

Electra Daughter of Agamemnon and Clytemnestra, and sister of Orestes and Iphegenia.

Electryon Son of Perseus and Andromeda, king of Mycenae and father of Alcmene, the wife of Amphitrion.

Elysian Fields (Elysium) Greek mythological paradise to which the great and virtuous went after death.

Embla In Norse mythology the elm tree from which woman was hewn.

Endymion King of Elis who was visited by Selene while sleeping in a cave and forced into an endless sleep so she could admire his beauty.

Enlil In Sumerian mythology one of the triad of creator-gods with Enki and An.

Epeius Cowardly son of Panopeus who built the Trojan horse.

Epigoni Greek sons of the 7 against Thebes who succeeded in destroying the city.

Epimetheus In Greek mythology, the brother of Prometheus and husband of Pandora.

Epona Roman goddess of horses.

Erebus (Darkness) Son of Chaos and father of Aether and Hemera by Night, his sister.

Eros (Desire) Greek god of love, the offspring of Aphrodite and Ares.

Eshmun The Phoenician god of healing, identified with the Greek Asclepius and Roman Aesculapius.

Europa According to Greek mythology, the daughter of King Agenor and Queen Telephassa of Phoenicia. Zeus wooed Europa as a bull and had intercourse with her in the guise of an eagle. She bore him three sons: Minos, Rhadamanthus and Sarpedon. Europa married the Cretan king Asterius.

Eurus South-east wind, son of Astraeus and Eos.

Eurydice Greek dryad, wife of Orpheus. She was lost forever after Orpheus looked back to make sure she was following as he led her out of Hades.

Eurystheus King of the Argolid region of the Peloponnese, son of King Sthenelus and Queen Nicippe of Mycenae. Heracles was sentenced to serve him for 12 years as penance for killing his wife, Megara. Eurystheus subsequently set him the twelve labours.

Fafnir In Germanic mythology a dragon who guarded the Nibelung hoard of treasure.

Fauna Roman goddess of fertility.

Faunus Roman god of crops, herds and woodlands.

Fenrir In Norse mythology a monstrous wolf who was the offspring of Loki.

Ferghus Irish hero of superhuman size and strength. King of Ulster before Conchobar, Ferghus was the lover of Nessa, the mother of Conchobar.

Feronia Roman goddess of spring flowers.

Fides Roman god of honesty.

Finn mac Cumhal Irish hero who possessed the gift of foresight when biting his thumb.

Fintan In Irish mythology the salmon of knowledge, which Finn mac Cumhal tasted accidentally. He burned his thumb on the flesh as he turned it on a spit. Once he sucked the thumb he became a sage.

Fjorgyn Norse goddess, mother of Thor.

Fortuna Roman goddess of chance and fate.

Frey Norse god of fertility.

Freyja Norse goddess of love, twin sister of Frey.

Frigg Norse goddess of fertility, wife of Odin.

Ganesha Hindu god depicted with the head of an elephant; the offspring of Parvati, the wife of S(h)iva.

Ganymede Greek god of rain and cupbearer to the gods; the son of King Tros of Troy.

Garang The first man according to the Dinka people of the Sudan.

Genius Roman protective god, one for every individual, group and State.

Geryon Three-bodied monster living on the island of Erythia who owned cattle guarded by Eurytion.

Gilgamesh Sumerian king of Uruk, son of the goddess Ninsun and a mortal. His story is told in the Gilgamesh epic, the oldest extant work of literature (c. 2000 BC), which tells of his search for the secret of eternal life.

Gimli In Norse mythology the highest heavenly abode that was not consumed in Ragnarok.

Ginnungagap In Norse mythology the 'Yawning Gap' or primeval emptiness, which held all the potential energy of creation.

Glaucus (1) King of Corinth, son of Sisyphus and Merope and father of Bellerophon. He fed his horses on human flesh but Aphrodite caused them to devour Glaucus himself because he mocked her.

Glaucus (2) Grandson of Bellerophon who fought for the Trojans and was slain by Ajax.

Glaucus (3) Son of Minos and Pasiphaë who was drowned in a barrel of honey.

Glaucus (4) Boeotian fisherman who pursued Scylla and was turned into a sea god on eating a magic herb.

Golden Age Concept of the Greek poet Hesiod, who listed Golden, Silver, Bronze and Iron as the four ages of man in his *Works and Days*.

Golden Bough A gift Aeneas had to take to Proserpina before he could enter the underworld.

Golden Fleece Fleece of the golden ram of Colchis, kept by King Aeëtes of Colchis and guarded by an unsleeping dragon.

Gorgons Three sisters – Eurydale, Medusa and Scheno – offspring of Phorcys and Ceto. Medusa was the mortal sister killed by Perseus. The Gorgons were the sisters of the Graiae.

Götterdämmerung Literally means 'Twilight of the Gods'; in Germanic mythology the equivalent of the Norse final battle, Ragnarok.

Graces Daughters of Zeus and the sea nymph Eurynome.

Graiae In Greek mythology, three sisters who had one eye and one tooth between them; sisters of the Gorgons.

Great Mother of the Gods Oriental and Greco-Roman deity, known as Cybele in Latin literature. Her full Roman name was Mater Deum Magna Idaea (Great Idaean Mother of the Gods). Her Phrygian name was Agdistis or Dindymus.

Griffin Greek monster with lion's body and eagle's head and wings.

Gula In Babylonian mythology the goddess of healing corresponding to the Sumerian Bau.

Hades In Greek mythology the son of Cronus and Rhea, and brother of Zeus and Poseidon. The three brothers drew lots for their realms and Hades drew the underworld. Although this nether world was not originally given a name, it became known by the name of its chief god Hades (unseen). The god Hades was also known as Pluto (rich), and the Roman equivalent was Dis or Orcus. The realm of Hades can be sub-divided into Elysium, Tartarus and the Plain of Asphodel.

Hamadryad See Dryad.

Hanuman In Indian mythology the monkey that became the most loyal companion of Rama and his consort Sita.

Harpies Greek spirits with heads of women and bodies of birds.

Hebe Greek goddess of youth and spring, daughter of Zeus and Hera, and wife of Heracles after his death.

Hecate Greek goddess of the underworld and daughter of Coeus and Phoebe.

Hector According to Greek mythology, the bravest Trojan and son of Priam; the brother of Paris and husband of Andromache. Killed by Achilles.

Hecuba Wife of King Priam of Troy and mother of Hector, Paris, Troilus and Cassandra.

Heimdall Norse god, and guardian of the bridge, Bifrost. Born of nine mothers.

Hekatoncheires (100 hands) In Greek mythology, the name of three giants with 100 hands and 50 heads each: Briareus, Cottus and Gyges. They were the offspring of Gaia and Uranus.

Helen Greek heroine, daughter of Zeus and Leda, sister of Clytemnestra and Castor and Pollux.

Hephaestus Son of Zeus and Hera who was thrown from Olympia by his mother and landed in the sea. Hephaestus made the armour for Achilles.

Hera Greek goddess of marriage and childbirth and queen of the gods.

Heracles Greek hero who performed the Twelve Labours of Eurystheus. Offspring of Zeus and Alcmene.

Hercules Roman equivalent of Heracles.

Hermaphroditus Son of Hermes and Aphrodite. Salmacis embraced him so closely that they became fused as one, with a woman's breasts and a man's genitals.

Hermes Son of Zeus and Maia. Hermes invented the lyre soon after birth.

Hermione Daughter of Helen and Menelaus.

Hermod Norse god, son of Odin.

Hero Greek high priestess and lover of Leander, who swam the Hellespont every night to see her but was eventually drowned causing Hero to throw herself in the sea.

Hesperides In Greek mythology, the daughters of the evening star who guarded the Golden Apples together with the dragon Ladon.

Hindu myth and religion Of all the world's leading mythologies, by far the most complex and expansive are Hindu beliefs. Even the term 'mythology' does not sit easily with a body of culture that is still revered today. It is beyond the scope of this work to trace the roots of Hindu beliefs and philosophy with its many tributaries, which themselves form a whole, separate strata of mythology. Many of the gods have personifications under differing names, and others have re-incarnations (avatars), which may bring with them a whole new substrata of mythology. Hindu mythology does not lend itself to fall comfortably within the table of comparative gods, indeed, the choice of Indra as principal god, or king of the gods, can only be loosely adhered to as a comparative to Zeus or Jupiter. Hindu mythology can be further divided into pre-Vedic, late-Vedic, post-Vedic, pre-Aryan post-Aryan and Classical, all of which has its own version of the creation. In the late-Vedic period, c.1200 BC, Brahma might have been considered the most important Hindu god, but he was gradually eclipsed by Vishnu and S(h)iva. Strict adherence to the Veda would place Prajapati (Lord of Creatures) as the creator god. In another version, the Prajapatis are the 10 'mind-born' children of Brahma. The traditional Trimurti of Brahma, Vishnu and S(h)iva, would be considered the most important Hindu gods, but it is true to say that Indra is the equivalent of Zeus in Greek mythology or Jupiter in Roman.

Hippolyte Queen of the Amazons and sister of Antiope.

Hoder Blind Norse god who killed Baldur.

Horus Egyptian god of light with a falcon's head, son of Osiris and Isis.

Huitzilopochtli Chief Aztec god, linked with the sun, fire, war and human sacrifice.

Hyacinthus Peloponnesian youth loved by Apollo who was killed when the jealous Zephyrus diverted a discus to hit him.

Hydra Greek monster usually depicted with 9 heads; slain by Heracles.

Hyperion Greek Titan, son of Uranus and Gaia.

Iapetus Greek Titan, father of Prometheus and Atlas, grandfather of Deucalion.

Icarus Son of Daedalus; he flew too near the sun while escaping from Crete and fell into the Aegean Sea and drowned.

Idavold In Norse mythology the playground of the gods.

Idomeneus King of Crete who contributed 100 ships to the expedition against Troy.

Idunn Norse goddess of the golden apples of youth, wife of Bragi.

MYTHOLOGY AND LEGEND

Iliad Homer's epic poem on the siege of Troy.

Imhotep The Egyptian god of medicine and healing.

Io Greek heroine turned into a heifer by Zeus to save her from the wrath of Hera.

Iphigenia Daughter of Agamemnon and Clytemnestra, sacrificed by her father at Aulis to gain a favourable wind for the Greek fleet sailing to Troy.

Isis Egyptian goddess of magic and mother of Horus.

Ismene Daughter of Oedipus and Jocasta. She followed her father and her sister, Antigone, into exile.

Isthmian Games Quadrennial games held at Corinth in honour of Poseidon.

Ithaca Island home of Odysseus, one of the Ionian Islands.

Ixion Greek king of Thessaly who was the first to murder a kinsman, his father-in-law; he was bound to a wheel of fire in Tartarus for trying to rape Hera.

Janus Roman god of entrances, travel and the dawn, depicted as a man with two faces.

Jason Son of Aeson, the Aeolian King of Iolcos. Aeson's half-brother Pelias usurped the throne and Queen Alcimede was forced to smuggle her son to safety, entrusting him to the care of Chiron, the centaur. Jason returned to Iolcos to regain his father's kingdom and was told by Pelias that he would step down in return for the golden fleece of a ram, which hung from a tree in Colchis, and was guarded by a dragon. Jason engaged Argus to build a large galley for the journey and successfully attained his goal with the help of some legendary Greek heroes. During his adventures he married the sorceress Medea, but whether he ever attained the throne of Iolcos is doubtful. Jason eventually died when the decaying prow of the Argo fell on him.

Jimmu-tenno Legendary first Emperor of Japan, aka Kamu-yamato-iware-biko.

Jocasta Wife of King Laius and mother of Oedipus.

Jotunheim In Norse mythology the land of the race of giants, said to lie among the roots of Yggdrasil.

Jumala Finnish supreme god.

Juno Roman goddess of marriage, childbirth and light, and queen of the gods.

Jupiter Originally a Roman sky god, but then regarded by the Romans as *Dies Pater* (Father Day), and later still became the Roman equivalent of Zeus.

Kama Hindu god of love and pleasure.

Khnum Egyptian goddess of creation.

Khonsou Egyptian god, son of Ammon.

Kvasir Norse god of wisdom.

Laertes King of Ithaca and father of Odysseus by Anticleia.

Lakshmi In Hindu mythology, also known as Sri, attained importance as the consort of Vishnu under each of his incarnations; when he became Rama she was faithful Sita, and when he became Krishna she became his wife, Rukmini.

Lapithes Mythological race that fought a famous war with the centaurs.

Lares Roman gods of the house and fertility.

Leander Mythical youth of Abydos who drowned while swimming the Hellespont to meet Hero.

Leda Seduced by Zeus in the form of a swan and gave birth to Helen and Polydeuces in one egg and Castor and Clytemnestra in another. Other versions record that Helen and Polydeuces were children of Zeus and that Castor and Clytemnestra were children of her husband, Tyndareus.

Leviathan Sea monster mentioned in the book of Job, resembling a crocodile.

Liber Pater Roman god of agriculture and human fertility.

Libitina Roman goddess of funeral rites.

Lilith Demonic first wife of Adam in Hebrew mytholgy.

Lohengrin In Germanic legend, the son of Parsifal.

Loki Norse god of mischief.

Lorelei In German mythology a siren said to dwell on a rock at the edge of the Rhine, south of Koblenz, who lures boatmen to destruction.

Lud(d) Mythical king of Britain whose temple in Roman London was near St Paul's Cathedral. Ludd was also the name of a Celtic god of the sea.

Llyr (Lir) A Celtic god of waters and the sea; the father of Manannan.

Maat Egyptian goddess of sterility, truth and justice.

Mabinogion A collection of stories written in Welsh in medieval times, the principal source of ancient Welsh and British myths.

Macha In Celtic mythology a collective name for the trinity of war goddesses Macha, Morrígan and Nemain. As an individual, Macha was sometimes known as Dana (crow) or Badb (raven).

Mahabharata Sanskrit verse epic composed between 400 BC and AD 400. It relates a dynastic feud between the Pandavas and their cousins the Kauravas, respectively gods and demons.

Maia Roman goddess of fertility.

Manasa Serpent goddess of Hindu mythology.

Manitou Supreme deity of the Algonquian people of North America.

Manticore A fabulous monster with the body of a lion, the head of a man, porcupine's quills, and the tail or sting of a scorpion.

Marduk Supreme god of Babylon.

Mazda Persian god of wisdom.

Medea In Greek mythology a princess of Colchis and powerful sorceress; deserted by Jason after helping him to steal the Golden Fleece, she killed their two children.

Megara Daughter of King Creon of Thebes and first wife of Heracles, who killed her in a fit of madness caused by the goddess Hera.

Megingjord Name of Thor's belt, which magnifies his strength.

Meleager In Greek mythology the heir of King Oeneus of Calydon. The Fates appeared to his mother, Althaea, when he was seven days old, they pointed to a burning stick in the fireplace and told her that her son's life would last as long as the stick would burn. Althaea snatched the stick from the fire and hid it away. His father incurred the wrath of Artemis and she sent a wild boar to Calydon to ravage his crops. Meleager offered the boar's pelt and tusks to anyone who could deliver the death blow. Many of his fellow Argonauts joined the hunt, including Atalanta, who he was besotted by. Although Meleager himself delivered the final death thrust, he gave the pelt to Atalanta, which upset his two uncles. In a rage he killed them both, and his mother, seeing the corpses of her brothers, threw the stick into the fire, and Meleager's life drained away

Menelaus King of Sparta, younger brother of Agamemnon and husband of Helen.

Merope A Pleiad and wife of Sisyphus.

Metis In Greek mythology the daughter of Oceanus and Tethys and first wife of Zeus.

Mictlan Aztec land of the dead.

Midas Mythical king of Phygian. In one story, Apollo burdens him with ass's ears for fudging badly in a music contest. In another, he receives but manages to shed the gift of turning all he touches to gold.

Midgard In Norse mythology the dwelling place of mankind, formed from the body of the giant Ymir and linked to Asgard by Bifrost, the rainbow bridge.

Milo Champion wrestler in Greek mythology.

Mimir Norse giant who guarded the well of wisdom near the roots of Yggdrasil.

Minos In Greek mythology the son of Europa and Zeus and brother to Sarpedon and Rhadamanthys. Following a dispute with his two brothers, Minos succeeded to the throne of Crete. The issue of the succession was decided when, having prayed for a divine sign, Poseidon sent Minos a magnificent bull from the sea. However, because Minos neglected to sacrifice the bull, Poseidon cursed him, causing his wife, Pasiphaë, to fall madly in love with the creature. With the help of the craftsman Daedalus, Pasiphaë was able to satisfy her lust by hiding in a decoy cow. The offspring of this union was the Minotaur, a monster with the head of a bull but the body of a man. Minos commissioned Daedalus to construct a labyrinth to house the Minotaur, and each year 9 boys and 9 girls were brought from Athens as food for the monster. One year the Greek hero Theseus was chosen for sacrifice and slew the Minotaur with the help of Minos's daughter Ariadne, who supplied him with a thread to enable him to retrace his steps after the slaying. King Minos followed Daedalus to Sicily with his mind set on revenge, but Daedalus was warned of his presence and arranged for boiling oil to kill the king when he took a bath at Kamikos.

Minotaur Greek monster, son of Pasiphaë and a bull, kept in a labyrinth on Crete by King Minos.

Mithra(s) Persian god of light, justice and war.

Mjollnir Thor's hammer, said to cause lightning.

Mnemosyne Greek Titan who was the mother of all the Muses.

Morrígan Irish war goddess whose name means phantom queen; also the collective name of the trinity of war goddesses Macha, Morrígan and Nemain.

Muses Sacred to Mount Helicon. See listing on p. 993.

Myrmidons People of Aegina, created by Zeus for King Aeacus; some of them fought for Achilles at Troy.

Myth The term was first used by the Greek historian Herodotus (c.484 BC – c.420 BC) to describe a body of knowledge or beliefs that have no foundation in fact and so must be distinguished from history although recorded fact can take mythical proportions due to historical interpretation.

Nabu (Nebo) In Babylonian mythology, son of Marduk, and the scribe and herald of the gods.

Naiads Freshwater nymphs in Greek mythology.

Nanna Norse goddess, wife of Baldur.

Narcissus Greek hero whom Nemesis caused to fall in love with his own reflection.

Nataraja Title of the Hindu god S(h)iva, meaning lord of the dance.

Nehallenia Norse goddess of plenty.

Nemesis Greek goddess of destiny, the daughter of Oceanus.

Nereids Fifty beautiful sea nymphs, the daughters of Nereus and Doris, of whom the most famous were Amphitrite and Thetis.

Nereus Greek god of the sea.

Nessus Greek centaur whose blood caused the death of his killer, Heracles.

Nestor King of Pylos and only one of Neleus's 12 sons spared by Heracles. The oldest of the Greeks at Troy and the only one to return home without mishap.

Nibelung In German legend, any of the race of dwarfs who possessed a treasure hoard stolen by Siegfried.

Nibelungenlied Heroic epic of unknown authorship written in the early 13th centruy and based on German history and legend.

Niflheim In Norse mythology the abode of the dead, sometimes identified with hell.

Niobe In Greek mythology, queen of Thebes, wife of King Amphion and daughter of Tantalus and Dione.

Njord Norse god, father of Frey and Freyja.

Norns Norse goddesses of destiny: Urdr – the past, Verdandi – the present, and Skuld – the future.

Notus Greek mythology. South-west wind known to the Romans as Auster. Son of Astraeus and Eos.

Numa Pompilius Legendary second King of Rome who succeeded Romulus.

Nun In Egyptian mythology, the dark primeval ocean of chaos, which existed before the first gods.

Nymph Any one of a class of mythological, youthful female divinities inhabiting woods, springs, mountains or the sea. Although nymphs were not immortal, their life span was usually several thousand years.

Oceanid(e)s Greek sea-nymphs, daughters of Oceanus and Tethys.

Oceanus Greek god of the River Oceanus and son of Gaia and Uranus.

Odysseus (aka Ulysses) Greek hero, the son of Laertes and Anticlea, king and queen of Ithaca, a key figure in Homer's *Iliad* and central in the *Odyssey*.

Oedipus (swollen foot) Greek hero, king of Thebes, who inadvertently killed his father and married his mother.

Oisin In Celtic mythology, a warrior and poet, son of Finn mac Cumhall and Sadb.

Ops Roman goddess of the harvest, and consort of Saturn.

Oread A Greek mountain-nymph.

Orestes In Greek mythology the king of Argos and

MYTHOLOGY AND LEGEND

Sparta, son of Agamemnon and Clytemnestra.

Orion In Greek mythology a giant hunter, son of Poseidon and Euryale.

Orpheus Greek musician and poet, son of King Oeagrus of Thrace and Calliope. He married Eurydice, failed to rescue her from Hades after she was killed by a snake, and was finally torn to pieces by the women of Thrace.

Osiris Egyptian god of vegetation, brother of Seth and husband of Isis.

Otr Norse otter god.

Otus and Ephialtes Twin sons of Iphimedeia and Poseidon.

Pales Roman goddess of flocks.

Palladium Mythical statue of Athene given to Dardanus by Zeus to ensure the protection of Troy.

Pan Greek god of male sexuality, herds and woods.

Pandora In Greek mythology the first woman on earth. When her dowry box was opened it released all the world's ill and retained only hope.

Paris A prince of Troy, the son of Priam. He abducted Helen, the wife of Menelaus, so causing the Trojan War.

Parvati In Hindu mythology Parvati (the mountaineer) was one of the forms of Devi and as such, the mother of the elephant-headed god of wisdom, Ganes(h)a. Parvati became the golden-skinned Gauri.

Pasiphaë In Greek mythology the daughter of Helios and mother of the Minotaur.

Patroclus Greek warrior who, while wearing Achilles' armour, was killed by Hector during the siege of Troy.

Pegasus Greek winged horse that sprang from the body of Medusa after her death.

Pelasgus The first man, according to one version of the Greek creation myth.

Peleus In Greek mythology the King of Phythia in Thessaly. He married Thetis and fathered Achilles.

Penates Roman gods of food and drink.

Penelope The wife of Odysseus. During his long absence after the Trojan war, she tricked the suitors who were plaguing her to marry by unravelling a shroud every night, having promised to make her decision when she had finished weaving it.

Persephone Greek goddess of the underworld, corn and the spring.

Perse Daughter of Oceanus and wife of Helios, to whom she bore Circe, Pasiphaë, Aeëtes and Perses.

Perses (1) Son of Perseus and Andromeda. Said to have given his name to Persia.

Perses (2) Son of Helios and Perse and father of Hecate.

Perseus Greek hero, son of Zeus and Danaë; he slew the Gorgon Medusa and married Andromeda.

Phaeton Greek hero, son of Helios and Clymene. Killed by a thunderbolt from Zeus after losing control of the sun-chariot and endangering the safety of the world. Phaeton's body fell into the river Eridanus (Po).

Philoctetes Greek hero who killed Paris.

Pleiades In Greek mythology the 7 daughters of Atlas and Pleione.

Plutus Greek god of wealth.

Polybus In Greek mythology the king of Corinth, husband of Merope and adoptive father of Oedipus.

Pomona Roman goddess of fruit trees.

Portunus Roman god of husbands and harbours.

Poseidon Greek god of the sea and earthquakes.

Priam In Greek mythology the king of Troy, son of King Laomedon and Queen Strymo.

Priapus Son of Dionysus and Aphrodite, a fertility god, often portrayed with a grotesquely large phallus.

Procrustes (Stretcher) In Greek mythology an innkeeper who killed travellers on the road between Athens and Eleusis by lopping or stretching their bodies to fit his bed. Theseus killed him by decapitation.

Prometheus In Greek mythology a Titan, sometimes credited with making mankind out of clay. Because he stole fire from the gods and gave it to man, Zeus bound him to a rock for an eagle to peck out his liver, which always regrew because Prometheus was immortal.

Proserpine Roman goddess of the Underworld, corn and the spring.

Proteus Sea god, the son of Oceanus and Tethys. Proteus was a seer but would take any form to avoid questioning.

Psyche In Greek mythology the soul, often portrayed as a butterfly. Personified as a woman, she fell in love with Eros and suffered many ordeals before they were united.

Ptah Egyptian god of creation.

Pygmalion In Greek mythology the king of Cyprus who fell in love with Aphrodite and, because she would not lie with him, made an ivory image of her and laid it in his bed. Aphrodite brought the statue to life as Galatea.

Pyrrha Daughter of Epimetheus and Pandora and wife of Deucalion with whom she repopulated the earth after the flood.

Quetzalcoatl Toltec and Aztec god of vegetation and the wind, sometimes depicted as a bearded man wearing a mask, sometimes as a feathered serpent..

Quirinus Roman god of war, after whom a hill of Rome was named.

Ragnarok Final destruction of the Norse gods in a battle to the death with evil.

Ramayana One of the two great Sanskrit verse epics (along with the *Mahabharata*) dating back to the 3rd century BC, the story of Prince Rama, his struggle for the throne of Ajodhya, and his war with the demon Ravana to rescue his abducted wife Sita, with Hanuman's help

Remus See Romulus and Remus.

Rhadamanthus Son of Europa and Zeus and brother to Minos and Sarpedon. After death he became a judge in the underworld.

Rhea Greek goddess of motherhood; sister and wife of Cronus.

Rhesus Thracian king who helped the Trojans but was slain by Odysseus.

Rhiannon In Welsh Celtic mythology, the daughter of the King of the Otherworld and wife of Pwyll, prince of Dyfed.

Romulus and Remus Twin sons of Mars, and legendary founders of Rome.

Round Table In Arthurian legend the great table of Camelot that seated King Arthur's knights. The Siege Perilous (dangerous seat) remained vacant because only the bringer of the Holy Grail could use it without coming to harm.

Rumina Roman goddess of nursing mothers.

Sarpedon In Greek mythology the son of Europa and Zeus and brother to Minos and Rhadamanthus.

Satyr A Greek mythological creature, part man, part goat; the satyrs were followers of Dionysus.

Scaean (Left-Hand) Gate Situated in the walls of Troy; the spot where Achilles fell.

Scylla Greek sea monster; originally the daughter of Poseidon, she was turned into a monster by Amphitrite. In Strait of Messina located opposite Charybdis and depicted as snake with 6 heads that lived in a cave.

Sekmet Egyptian goddess of power and battle, depicted with the head of a lioness.

Selene Greek goddess of the moon, daughter of Hyperion and Thea; she was most notably the lover of Endymion.

Semiramis In Assyrian mythology the wife of Ninus and co-founder with him of Nineveh.

Set Egyptian god of evil.

Seven against Thebes Greek champions – Adrasius, Amphiaraüs, Capaneus, Hippomedon, Parthenopaeus, Polynices and Tydeus – who failed to overthrow Eteocles from his Kingship.

Seven Kings of Rome Romulus (753–715 BC), Numa Pompilius (715–673 BC), Tullius Hostilius (673–642 BC), Ancus Marcius (642–616 BC), Tarquin the Elder (616–579 BC), Servius Tullius (579–534 BC), Tarquinius Superbus (Proud Tarquin) (534–510 BC).

Shu Egyptian god of Air.

Sibyl Roman prophetess.

Sibylline Books Roman tradition tells how a sibyl offered Tarquinius Priscus 9 prophetic books which he refused to buy at the price. She destroyed three and he still refused them; she burned three more and he took the remaining three at the price demanded for the nine. Special priests kept them and they were consulted only when the Senate authorised it in time of need. In 83 BC the originals were destroyed by fire. The original books instructed the Romans to convey the sacred stone of Cybele to Rome.

Sif Norse goddess, wife of Thor.

Sigmund In Germanic legend the son of Volsung who won the divine sword Gram by extracting it from a tree trunk.

Sigurd In Germanic legend the son of Sigmund and Hjordis and owner of the horse, Grani.

Sigyn Norse goddess, wife of Loki.

Silvanus Roman god of trees and forests.

Siren In Homer's *Odyssey* one of a group of creatures, half woman and half bird, who lure sailors to their death by their singing. Odysseus and the Argonauts withstood their fatal charms, the latter because Orpheus outsang them.

Sisyphus In Greek mythology a Corinthian king destined in Hades to roll a large stone up a hill for evermore, only for it to keep rolling back when it reaches the top.

Skadi In Norse mythology the wife of Njord.

Skan Lakota god embodying the sky.

Sleipnir Odin's 8-legged horse.

Sobek Egyptian crocodile god.

Soma In Hindu mythology an intoxicating drink. Soma was also an early god of the moon.

Spartoi (sown men) Sprang up fully armed when Cadmus sowed the dragon's teeth and killed each other until five remained: Echion, Udaeus, Chthonius, Hyperenor and Pelorus.

Sphinx Greek monster with a woman's head and lion's body.

Stentor Greek herald during the Trojan War, famous for his very loud voice.

Stymphalian birds In Greek mythology a flock of man-eating birds, which infested Lake Stymphalos in Arcadia. Killed by Heracles.

Surabhi In Indian mythology a divine cow of plenty.

Syrinx Greek nymph of Arcadia. She was pursued by Pan, who made the first pan-pipes from her embodiment, as turning into a bed of reeds was the only way she could escape him.

Tantalus Greek mythological king of Sipylos in Lydia, who stole the food of the gods and was condemned to stand thirsty and hungry forever in a pool that receded when he bent down to drink, beneath fruit trees whose branches retreated when he reached to pick their fruit.

Tarpeian Rock Named after Tarpeia, the traitor daughter of the keeper of the Roman citadel. Became the rock from which Roman traitors were thrown.

Tartarus That part of Hades reserved for those that offended the gods during their lifetime.

Taweret Egyptian protector goddess of women and children, often depicted as part crocodile, part lion and part hippopotamus.

Telamon Son of Aeacus and brother of Peleus; Telamon fathered Ajax by Periboea.

Telemachus Greek hero, son of Odysseus and Penelope.

Tenes Son of Apollo who gave his name to the Greek island of Tenedos.

Themis Daughter of Ge and Uranus and sister of Cronus. The wife of Zeus before Hera.

Theseus Mythical Greek hero, king of Athens and son of King Aegeus and Queen Aethra; it was Theseus who defeated the Minotaur in its labyrinth home in Crete.

Thetis Greek goddess and mother of Achilles.

Thunderbird Totem figure of Native Americans from the north-west. Aka Skyamsen.

Tiresias Legendary blind prophet of Thebes who had been both male and female and estimated that women had 9 times more pleasure during intercourse than men.

Tonalpohualli Aztec sacred calendar consisting of 260 days which were divided into 20 weeks of 13 days.

Trimurti Trinity of Hindu gods: Brahma(n) the Creator, Vishnu the Preserver and S(h)iva the

MYTHOLOGY AND LEGEND

Destroyer.

Tristan and Isolde Celtic legend. Tristan was a harpist and Isolde was the daughter of the king of Ireland. They drank a love potion together by mistake and fell irretrievably in love.

Triton Son of Poseidon and Amphitrite. He was a merman, the upper half human, the lower half fish. Triton used a conch shell trumpet to calm the waves.

Troilus In Greek mythology, the young son of Priam, slain by Achilles. His romance with Cressida is a medieval invention.

Ull Norse god and stepson of Thor.

Valhalla In Norse mythology the great hall of Odin in Asgard, where warriors who died as heroes in battle dwelled eternally.

Valkyries Norse warrior handmaidens to Odin.

Vanir Norse race of benevolent gods including Njörd, Frey and Freyja. The Vanir warred with the Aesir and were eventually absorbed into their number.

Varuna In Hindu mythology Varuna was at one time the upholder of heaven and earth and often associated with Surya as the creator of the sun. In post-Vedic mythology he became god of the seas and rivers.

Vertumnus Roman god of fertility.

Vestal virgins College of priestesses of the Roman cult of Vesta, the hearth goddess. Originally four of them; later 6 (generally considered as the number); and finally 7.

Vidar Norse god, a son of Odin and slayer of the wolf Fenir.

Vishnu's Incarnations The 10 avatars of Vishnu are 1. Matsya, 2. Kurma, 3. Varaha, 4. Narasinha, 5. Vamana 6. Paras(h)urama, 7. Ramachandra (Rama), 8. Krishna, 9. Buddha, 10. Kalki.

Völund In Norse mythology, a smith and artificer and king of the elves. In Germanic legends he appears as Wieland; in English folklore as Wayland Smith.

Wyvern Mythical beast with a dragon's head, a serpent's tail and a body with wings and two legs.

Yggdrasil In Norse mythology, the ash tree that binds the heavens, earth and the underworld with its roots and branches. It shelters the remnants of humanity when Raganrok destroys the gods and sets the world on fire.

Ymir The first being and forefather of all the Norse giants. Slain by Odin, who made the earth from his flesh, the water from his blood and the sky from his skull.

Zephyrus West Wind, the son of Astraeus and Eus and father of Xanthus and Balius, the talking horses of Achilles. Roman counterpart was Favonius.

Zetes Twin brother of Calais. Winged sons of Boreas and Oreithyia, they accompanied the Argonauts and drove off the Harpies.

Zeus's conquests The supreme god of the Greek parthenon took many forms in his amorous pursuit of goddesses, nymphs and humans. See below.

Zeus's Conquests

Conquest	Form	Offspring
Alcmene	Amphitryon	Heracles
Antiope	Satyr	Amphion and Zetheus
Danaë	Shower of gold	Perseus
Demeter	Himself	Persephone
Europa	Bull and eagle	Minos, Sarpedon and Rhadamanthus
Eurynome	Himself	Graces
Ganymede	Eagle	None
Io	Cloud	Epaphos
Leda	Swan	Helen, Clytemnestra, Castor and Pollux
Leto	Quail	Apollo and Artemis
Maia	Himself	Hermes
Mnemosyne	Himself	Moses
Rhea	Serpent	None
Semele	Mortal	Dionysus
Thetis	Himself	None

Famous Horses of Myth and History

Name	Owner	Horse's owner's identity	Name	Owner	Horse's owner's identity
Arvak	Sol	Norse maiden	Harpagus	Castor and Pollux	Roman mythological twins
Abaster	Pluto	Greek god			
Abatos	Pluto	Greek god			
Abraxa	Aurora	Roman goddess	Hercules	The Steptoes	TV creation
Actaeon	Helios	Greek sun god	Hippocampus	Neptune	Roman god
Aethon	Helios	Greek sun god	Hrimfaxi (Frost Mane)	Nott	Horse of Night (Norse myth)
Aeton	Pluto	Greek god			
Al Borak	Mohammed	Founder of Islam	Incitatus	Caligula	Roman emperor
Alfana	Gradasso	Literary creation	Kantanka	Prince Gautama	The Buddha
Alsvid	Sol	Norse maiden	Lampon	Diomedes	Mythological king of Argos
Amethea	Helios	Greek sun god			
Arion	Hercules	Mythological hero			
Arundel	Bevis of Hampton	Literary creation	Lampos	Helios	Greek sun god
Babieca	El Cid	Spanish hero	Lamri	King Arthur	Legendary Anglo-Saxon king
Balios	Achilles	Greek hero			
Barbary Roan	Richard II	English king			
Bayard	Renaud de Montauban	Legendary Frankish knight	Marengo	Napoleon	French emperor
			Marocco	Mr Banks	Elizabethan horseman
Black Agnes	Mary Queen of Scots	Scottish queen			
Black Bess	Dick Turpin	Literary creation	Marsala	Garibaldi	Italian patriot
Brigliadoro	Orlando	Legendary character	Nonios	Pluto	Greek god
			Pegasus	Bellerophon	Greek hero
Bronte	Helios	Greek sun god	Phaeton	Aurora	Roman goddess
Bucephalus (Ox-Head)	Alexander the Great	Macedonian ruler	Phallus (stallion)	Heraclius	Byzantine emperor
Carman	Chevalier de Bayard	French knight	Phlegon	Helios	Greek sun god
Celer	Lucius Verus	Roman emperor	Phrenicos	Hiero of Syracuse	Winner of 73rd olympiad
Cerus	Adrastus	Mythological king of Argos			
			Podarge (Swift Foot)	Hector	Trojan hero
Champion	Gene Autry	TV cowboy			
Comanche	US cavalry	Only survivor of Little Big Horn	Purocis	Helios	Greek sun god
			Ronald	Lord Cardigan	British soldier
Copenhagen	Duke of Wellington	Soldier and statesman	Rosabelle	Mary Queen of Scots	Scottish queen
Cyllaros	Castor and Pollux	Roman mythological twins	Rosinante	Don Quixote	Literary creation
			Savoy	Charles VIII	French king
			Scout	Tonto	TV creation
Dapple	Sancho Panza	Literary character	Sefton	British Army	Bomb victim
			Shadowfax	Gandalf	Wizard in *Lord of the Rings*
Diablo	Cisco Kid	Literary creation			
Dinos	Diomedes	Mythological king of Argos	Shibdiz	Chosroes II	Persian ruler
			Silver	Lone Ranger	TV creation
			Skinfaxi (Shining Mane)	Dagr	Horse of Day (Norse myth)
Doublet	Princess Anne	Royal Olympian			
Eos	Aurora	Roman goddess			
Erythreos	Helios	Greek sun god	Sleipnir	Odin	Norse supreme god
Ethon	Hector	Trojan hero			
Fadda (mule)	Mohammed	Founder of Islam	Sorrel	William III	British king
Ferrant d'Espagne	Oliver	Legendary Frankish knight	Strymon	Xerxes	Persian king
			Tachebrune	Ogier the Dane	Hero of chansons de geste
Foxhunter	Colonel Harry Llewellyn	Olympic champion			
Galathe	Hector	Trojan hero	Tony	Tom Mix	Film cowboy
Grani	Siegfried	German legendary character	Topper	Hopalong Cassidy	Film cowboy
			Trebizond	Guarinos	French knight at Roncesvalles
Gringolet	Sir Gawain	Arthurian Knight	Trigger	Roy Rogers	TV cowboy
			White Surrey	Richard III	English king
Grizzle	Dr Syntax	Literary creation	Xanthus	Achilles	Greek hero
Haizum	Gabriel	Archangel			

M
Y
T
H
O
L
O
G
Y

A
N
D

L
E
G
E
N
D

Famous Dogs   (Fact and Fiction)

Name	Owner or details
Arctophonos	Orion's dog (bear-killer)
Argos	Ulysses
Asta	*Thin Man* series
Blondie	Hitler
Boatswain	Lord Byron
Boot	Old English sheepdog in *The Perishers* (cartoon strip)
Bounce	Alexander Pope
Boy	Prince Rupert's dog, killed at Marston Moor
Bran	Finn mac Cumhal
Brutus	Landseer's greyhound (invader of the larder)
Cabal (Cavall)	King Arthur's favourite hound
Cerberus	Three-headed dog that guards Hades
Checkers	Richard Nixon
Daisy	Blondie
Danny	2003 Supreme Champion at Crufts. The Kennel name of the Pekinese is Yakee A Dangerous Liaison
Dash	Charles Lamb
Diamond	Isaac Newton
Digby	Biggest dog in the world in 1973 film
Dizzie	Michael Foot
Dougal	Character in *Magic Roundabout*
Dragon	Aubry of Montdidier
Flush	Elizabeth Barrett Browning
Freeway	Jonathan and Jennifer Hart
Gargittios	One of Geryon's dogs slain by Hercules
Geist	Matthew Arnold's dachshund
Gelert	Prince Llewellyn's greyhound
Giallo	Walter Savage Landor
Gnasher	Dennis the Menace
Goofy	Disney cartoon dog
Greyfriars Bobby	Watched over owner's grave for 14 years
Hamlet	Sir Walter Scott's black greyhound
Hodain (aka Leon)	Tristan
K9	Robot in *Dr Who*
Kaiser	Matthew Arnold's dachshund
Katmir	Dog of the Seven Sleepers
Laelaps	Procris
Laika	Fox terrier that was the first dog in space

Name	Owner or details
Lassie	Actually a female dog named Pal
Luath	Cuchulainn
Luath	Robert Burns
Lucy	David Blunkett
Lufra	Douglas's hound in Scott's *Lady of the Lake*
Maera (Glistener)	Icarius
Maida	Sir Walter Scott's deerhound
Mathe	Richard II's greyhound
Montmorency	Three Men in a Boat
Nana	Darling family (*Peter Pan*)
Nigger	Guy Gibson
Nipper	Fox terrier logo for His Master's Voice (HMV)
Offa	David Blunkett
Olaf	Snoopy's brother
Orthos	One of Geryon's dogs slain by Hercules
Paddy	Harold Wilson
Pearl	Beryl the Peril
Peritas	Alexander the Great
Petra	*Blue Peter*
Pickles	Found the World Cup
Pluto	Disney cartoon dog
Ptoophagos	Orion's dog (glutton of Ptoon, in Boeotia)
Rin Tin Tin	Died in Jean Harlow's arms
Rufus	Sir Winston Churchill's poodle
Sandy	Little Orphan Annie
Scamper	Secret Seven
Sceolang	Finn mac Cumhal
Shep	John Noakes
Snoopy	Beagle in *Peanuts* (cartoon strip)
Snowy	Tintin
Soda	Chris Patten
Spike	Snoopy's brother
Spottie	*The Woodentops*
Theron	Roderick the Goth
Timmy	Famous Five member
Toby	Punch
Well'ard	Originally owned by Robbie Jackson in Eastenders. Dogs real name is Kyte
Whisky	Chris Patten
Won Ton Ton	Saved Hollywood in 1976 film

NATURE

Living Creatures (except birds)

aardvark nocturnal mammal, inhabiting the grasslands of Africa south of the Sahara and feeding on ants and termites. It is the sole member of its family (Orycteropodidae) and order (Tubulidentata). Research by British, Chinese and South African scientists in 2003 reveals that the aardvark has the greatest number of features in common with other mammals, which makes it the closest living relative of our common ancestor. The aardvark is also called an ant bear. Sp.: *Orycteropus afer.*

aardwolf nocturnal mammal, inhabiting the plains of east and southern Africa, feeding on termites and insect larvae. Family: Hyaenidae (Hyenas) and Order: Carnivora. Sp.: *Proteles cristatus.*

abalone gastropod mollusc with a shallow, ear-shaped shell lined with mother-of-pearl. Gen.: *Haliotis.*

albacore long-finned tunny fish. Sp.: *Thunnus alalunga.*

alewife fish of the north-west Atlantic related to the herring. Sp.: *Alosa pseudoharengus.*

alligator either of two crocodilian reptiles of the family Alligatoridae (alligators and caymans) and distinguished from true crocodiles by their shorter and broader snouts. The American alligator (*Alligator mississippiensis*), the larger of the two species, can grow to a length of almost 6 metres, and the Chinese alligator (*Alligator sinensis*) to about a quarter of that length.

alpaca South American herbivore mammal of the Andes with long shaggy hair, related to the llama. Sp.: *Lama pacos.*

anchovy small marine food fish of the herring family. Sp.: *Engraulis encrasicholus.*

ant small social insect of the order Hymenoptera, typically living in organised colonies of winged males (drones), wingless sterile females (workers) and fertile females (queens). The body of an ant has three segments, i.e. head, abdomen and thorax. Family: Formicidae.

ant: Amazon ant which captures pupae of other ant species to raise as slaves. Gen.: *Polyergus.*

antelope bovid mammals of Africa and Asia that include bushbucks, elands, gnus, gazelles, impalas, springboks, dik-diks, blackbucks, oryxes, gerenuks and nilgai. Antelopes have unbranched horns, which they do not shed. Family: Boridae.

ape primates characterised by long arms and the absence of a tail. Great apes are the chimpanzee, gorilla and orang-utan (Family: Pongidae). Lesser apes are the various gibbons (Family: Hylobatidae).

argalis large Asiatic wild sheep with massive horns. Sp.: *Ovis ammon.*

armadillo nocturnal insect-eating but generally omnivorous edentate mammal native to the southern USA and Central and S. America, with large claws for digging and a body covered in bony plates, often rolling itself into a ball when threatened. They range from 3- to as many as 13-banded. Burmeister's and pink fairy armadillos are endangered species. Family: Dasypodidae.

axolotl aquatic newt-like salamander from Mexico, which in natural conditions retains its larval form for

life but is able to breed. Name means 'water servant'. Sp.: *Ambystoma mexicanum.*

aye-aye nocturnal arboreal prosimian primate of Madagascar related to the lemurs. Sp.: *Daubentonia madagascariensis.*

babirusa wild hog with upturned tusks native to the Malay archipelago. Sp.: *Babyrousa babyrussa.*

baboon primate of the family Cercopithecidae, characterised by its fox-like muzzle and long tail. Gen.: *Papio.*

badger (American) stout-bodied carnivore with greyish to reddish coat and black facial stripes. Sp.: *Taxidea taxus.*

badger (Eurasian) stout-bodied carnivore with greyish coat and black and white facial stripes. All badgers are members of the family Mustelidae. Sp.: *Meles meles.*

badger (honey) aka ratel. Musteline mammal inhabiting wooded regions of Africa and Asia. Sp.: *Mellivora capensis.*

bandicoot any small, agile terrestrial marsupial of the family Peramelidae of Australia and New Guinea. Bandicoots typically have long, pointed muzzles, large ears and long tails, and feed mainly on small invertebrates.

bandicoot rat large, dark brown, burrowing rat of the family Muridae, order Rodentia, of India and Sri Lanka, sometimes known as a mole rat. The bandicoot rat makes a grunting noise similar to that of a pig. Sp.: *Bandicota indica.*

barnacle small marine crustacean of the subclass Cirripedia that, as an adult, lives head-down attached to rocks or the bottom of the hull of a ship.

barnacle: goose common barnacle found worldwide, living attached by a stalk to driftwood. Gen.: *Lepas.*

bear large plantigrade, omnivorous mammal of the family Ursidae, order Carnivora. The smallest species is the Malaysian sun bear (*Helarctos malayanus*), and the largest is the Kodiak bear (*Ursus arctos middendorffi*).

beluga large kind of Russian sturgeon from which caviar is obtained. Sp.: *Huso huso.*

bib light brown European marine gadoid food fish. Aka pout. Sp.: *Gadus luscus.*

binturong arboreal civet of southern. Asia with a shaggy black coat and a prehensile tail. Sp.: *Arctictis binturong.*

bison: American ox-like grazing mammal with short-haired body and longer, darker hair on its head. Aka plains buffalo. Sp.: *Bison bison.*

black widow any venomous spider of the family Theridiidae, inhabiting warm climates throughout the world. The venom of the spider causes sharp pain and some muscle cramping but is usually only temporary and never fatal. The female is characterised by its dark colour and red hourglass marking on its abdomen. The males are rarely seen as they are often eaten by the female after mating. Black widows are known as button spiders in South Africa, redbacks in Australia and katipos in New Zealand. Gen.: *Latrodectus.*

bobcat small Northern American lynx with a

spotted, reddish-brown coat and a short tail. Sp.: *Felis rufus*.

bonito   one of several small, tuna-like marine food fishes of the family Scombridae (tunnies and mackerels) inhabiting warm Atlantic and Pacific waters. Gen.: *Sarda*.

boomslang   venomous tree-snake native to sub-Saharan Africa. Sp.: *Dispholidus typus*.

brachiosaurus   herbivorous dinosaurs, probably the largest land animals ever known (80 tons+). Gen.: *Brachiosaurus*.

brandling   red earthworm with rings of a brighter colour, which is often found in manure and used as fishing bait. Sp.: *Eisenia foetida*.

brown recluse   North American venomous spider with a dark brown body about 3 centimetres long with a distinct violin-shaped design on its back. Sp.: *Loxosceles reclusa*.

buffalo (African)   large, black, sparsely haired animal weighing up to 700kg. Sp.: *Syncerus caffer*.

buffalo (Indian)   aka water buffalo or carabao. South-east Asian domestic beast of burden weighing up to 1200kg. Sp.: *Bubalus bubalis*.

bullfrog   large frog native to North America and Mexico and known for its loud croak. Sp.: *Rana cateseiana*.

bumble-bee   large social bee with a loud hum. Aka humble-bee. Gen.: *Bombus*.

bummalo   small fish of south Asian coasts, dried and used as food, especially Bombay duck. Sp.: *Harpodon nehereus*.

bush baby   small nocturnal tree-dwelling African primate with very large eyes. Aka galago. Six species of the family Lorisidae.

cacomistle   raccoon-like animal of North America with a dark ringed tail. Sp.: *Bassariscus sumichrasti*.

callop   gold-coloured freshwater fish of Australia. Aka golden perch. Sp.: *Plectroplites ambiguus*.

camel: Arabian   camel with one hump native to the deserts of North Africa and the Near East (aka dromedary). Sp.: *Camelus dromedarius*.

camel: Bactrian   camel with two humps native to central Asia. Sp.: *Camelus bactrianus*.

capelin   small smeltlike fish of the North Atlantic used as food and as bait for catching cod. Sp.: *Mallotus villosus*.

capuchin   monkey of the family Cebidae, characterised by its head hair suggestive of a cowl. Gen.: *Cebus*.

capybara   very large, semi-aquatic rodent (up to 65 kg) native to South America east of the Andes. Sp.: *Hydrochoerus hydrochaeris*.

caracal   lynx native to Norht Africa and south-west. Asia. Sp.: *Felis caracal*.

caribou   large deer of Arctic regions of North America, having large branched antlers in the male and female, the only species of deer to do so. The caribou is known as a reindeer in Eurasia. Sp.: *Rangifer tarandus*.

carpenter ant   large ant which bores into wood to nest. Gen.: *Camponotus*.

cat: domestic   small feline mammal often kept as household pet. The cat is thought to have originated in Egypt. Unusual breeds include the Angora, which is usually deaf, the Manx, which is tailless, and the Siamese, which has blue eyes. Cats move in the same way as the camel and giraffe, i.e. by moving first the front and back legs on one side, then the front and back legs on the other side. Most cats have 18 toes, 5 on the front foot and 4 on the back. Sp.: *Felis domesticus*.

cat: wild   feline mammal living in the wild. Sp.: *Felis silvestris*.

cattle   dairy breeds include Ayrshire, Danish Red, Friesian, Guernsey, Jersey and Kerry. Beef cattle include Aberdeen Angus, Blonde d'Aquitaine, Blue Grey, Charolais, Chianina, Devon, Galloway, Hereford, Highland, Limousin, Lincoln Red, Luing, Maine-Anjou, Shorthorn and Sussex. Dual-purpose breeds include Dexter, Meuse-Rhine-Ijssel, Red Poll, Dairy Shorthorn, Simmental, South Devon and Welsh Black. Gen.: *Bos*.

cavy   any small South American rodent of the family Caviidae, especially of the genus *Cavia*.

cayman (caiman)   reptile of the family Alligatoridae (alligators and caymans), inhabiting riverbanks of Central and South America.

centipede   carnivorous arthropod, having a body of between 14 and 190 segments, each bearing one pair of legs. The common house centipede, order Scutigerida, is 25 millimetres (1 inch) long with a black striped body and 15 pairs of legs. Class: Chilopoda.

chamois   agile goat-antelope native to the mountains of Europe and Asia. Sp.: *Rupicapra rupicapra*.

cheese-fly   small black fly that breeds in cheese. Sp.: *Piophila casei*.

cheetah   fastest-running feline with a leopard-like spotted coat and non-retractable claws. Sp.: *Acinonyx jubatus*.

chigger   tropical flea of which females burrow under people's skin, causing painful sores. Aka chigoe, sand flea and jigger. Sp.: *Tunga penetrans*.

chimpanzee   tailless primate of the family Pongidae, inhabiting forests and savannahs of tropical west and central Africa. The two species are the common chimpanzee (*Pan troglodytes*) and the pygmy chimpanzee (*Pan paniscus*).

chinchilla   small South American rodent of the family Chinchillidae, which is bred in captivity for its soft grey fur. Chinchillas resemble long-tailed rabbits, although their ears are smaller. Sp.: *Chinchilla laniger*.

Chinese water deer   along with the musk deer, one of only two species of deer that do not have antlers. Sp.: *Hyfropotes inermis*.

chipmunk   North American ground squirrel having alternate light and dark stripes running down the body. Gen.: *Tamias*.

cicada   any of 1,500 varieties of winged-insects of the order Homoptera. The dog-day cicada of the genus *Tibicen*, is typically 3 centimetres long with greenish head and wings, acting as a canopy over its abdomen and thorax. The so-called periodic cicadas of the genus *Magicicada*, including the 17-year and 13-year cicadas, are darker in colour and have red eyes.

civet   cat-like mammals of Africa and Southern Asia with spotted fur, noted for the powerful-smelling fluid from their anal glands from which they bear their name. Family: Viverridae.

clouded leopard   large spotted arboreal cat of South-east Asia. Sp.: *Neofelis nebulosa*.

coati   raccoon-like, omnivorous mammals of Central and South America with a long flexible snout and a long, usually ringed, tail. Gen.: *Nasua* and *Nasuella*.

coelacanth   primitive lobe-finned fish of the Indian Ocean, thought to be many millions of years extinct until a living specimen was caught in 1938. Sp.: *Latimeria chalumnae*.

colugo   see flying lemur.

coral any of a variety of invertebrate marine organisms of the phylum Cnidaria, class Anthozoa, characterised by having spikey, leathery or stonelike skeletons. Stony coral, of the order Madreporaria, form reefs and islands. Red coral, of the genus *Corallium*, also known as precious coral, is used to make ornaments and jewellery.

cougar see puma.

coyote aka prairie wolf. Predatory canine mammal of North America, smaller than the wolf. Sp.: *Canis latrans*.

crane-fly large two-winged flies with very long legs. Aka daddy-long-legs or leatherjacket. Family: Tipulidae.

crayfish small lobster-like freshwater crustacean. Aka spiny lobster. Gen.: *Astacus*.

cribo large, non-venomous American snake. Aka indigo snake or gopher snake. Sp.: *Drymarchon corais*.

crocodile any reptile of the family Crocodilidae, typically having a broad head, tapering snout, massive jaws, and a thick outer covering of boney scales. The salt water crocodile may grow up to 7 metres long and is the world's largest reptile. The sex of a crocodile is decided during incubation: a male is born if the egg is maintained at a constant 31.6 ° Celsius; hotter or colder and the sex is female. Gen.: *Crocodilus*.

crown of thorns starfish that feeds on coral polyps and has increasingly threatened Australia's Great Barrier Reef. The species can grow up to 50 centimetres, has numerous red spines and may have up to 19 arms. Sp.: *Acanthaster planci*.

dace freshwater fish related to the carp. Sp.: *Leuciscus leuciscus*.

death's-head hawk-moth Large dark hawk-moth with yellowish underwings and skull-like markings on the back of the thorax. Sp.: *Acherontia atropos*.

death-watch beetle small beetle which makes a sound like a watch ticking, once supposed to portend death, and whose larva bores in dead wood. Sp.: *Xestobium rufovillosum*.

deer any ruminant quadruped of the family Cervidae, distinguished in the male by the presence of deciduous branching horns or antlers, and in the young by the presence of spots. The furry covering of the newly formed antlers is given the name velvet.

devil's coach-horse large rove beetle. Sp.: *Ocypus olens*.

devil's darning needle alternative name for a dragonfly or damselfly. Order: Odonata.

dhole fierce canine pack-hunting mammal of the forests of central and South-east Asia. Sp.: *Cuon alpinus*.

dik-dik dwarf antelope native to Africa. Gen.: *Madoqua*.

dingo wild dog of the family Canidae, generally light brown in colour with long muzzle and bushy tail. The dingo, also known as the warrigal, can be found throughout mainland Australia and Tasmania. It is a scavenging carnivore and has a distinct howl but does not bark. Sp.: *Canis dingo*.

diplodocus four-legged plant-eating dinosaur with the longest known tail of all dinosaurs (11 metres). Gen.: *Diplodocus*.

dog domesticated carnivorous mammal. Sp.: *Canis familiaris*.

dolphin any of various marine cetacean mammals of the family Delphinidae, which are typically larger than porpoises but smaller than whales. The common dolphin is *Delphinus delphis*.

dolphin: bottle-nosed inhabiting all the world's oceans and named after its beak-like snout, which is shaped like a bottle and gives the impression of having a permanent smile. Sp.: *Tursiops truncatus*.

dormouse: common nocturnal squirrel-like rodent with bushy tail. Sp.: *Muscardinus avellanarius*.

dormouse (edible) aka fat dormouse. Largest of the dormice, once prized as food by the Romans. Sp.: *Glis glis*.

douroucouli nocturnal monkey of South America having large, staring eyes. Aka night monkey or owl monkey. Sp.: *Aotus trivirgatus*.

dragonet Any scaleless, spiny marine fish of the family Callionymidae, the males of which are brightly coloured.

dragonfly predatory insect of the suborder Anisoptera, order Odonata, having a large head and eyes, long slender body and two pairs of iridescent wings, which may have a span in excess of 15 centimetres. Sp.: *Libellula forensis*. Alternative names of the dragonfly include devil's darning needle and devil's arrow.

drosophila small fruit fly used extensively in genetic research because of its large chromosomes, numerous varieties and rapid rate of reproduction. Gen.: *Drosophila*.

duck-billed platypus amphibious egg-laying mammal of eastern Australia, having dense fur, a broad flat bill and tail and webbed feet. The platypus and echidna are the only two members of the order Monotremata, i.e. mammals that lay eggs. The male has a toxic horny spur on both hind legs, the venom of which is powerful enough to kill a dog and cause excruciating pain to humans. An excellent swimmer, the platypus has a buoyant body so always swims in a downward tract and is capable of being submerged for up to 10 minutes if resting. Sp.: *Ornithorhynchus anatinus*.

dugong large marine mammal of the order Sirenia, closely related to the manatee; the sole extant member of the family Dugongidae. The dugong is shorter than the manatee and darker skinned but has the same body shape. Manatees inhabit the waters of the Caribbean, South America and West Africa, while the dugongs are found in East African and Australian waters. Like the manatee, the dugong is also sometimes called a sea cow because of its grass-eating habits. Sightings of dugongs and manatees by early explorers gave rise to the mythology of mermaids and sirens. Sp.: *Dugong dugon*.

duiker mostly forest-dwelling African antelopes having a crest of long hair between their horns. Gen.: *Cephalophus* and *Sylvicapra*.

eagle ray large ray with long pointed pectoral fins. Family: Myliobatidae.

earth worm any of various species of ground worms of the phylum Annelida, class Oligochaeta, especially members of the genera *Lumbricus*, *Allolobophora* and *Eisenia*.

echidna egg-laying insectivorous mammals native to Australia and New Guinea, with a covering of spines, a long snout and long claws. Aka spiny anteater. Family: Tachyglossidae.

eel teleost fish having long, snake-like body, smooth slimy skin and reduced fins. Gen.: *Anguilla*.

eland antelope native to Africa, having spirally twisted horns. The giant eland is the largest of living antelopes. Gen.: *Taurotragus*.

NATURE

elephant: African larger of the two species of elephant. Sp.: *Loxodonta africana*.

elephant: Indian smaller of the two species of elephant. Gen.: *Elephas maximus*.

emperor moth large moth related to the silk moths with eye-spots on all four wings. Sp.: *Saturnia pavonia*.

eyra reddish-brown variety of jaguarondi. Sp.: *Felis yagouaroundi*.

fallfish freshwater fish of North America resembling the chub. Sp.: *Semotilus corporalis*.

fallow deer small deer having a white-spotted reddish-brown coat in the summer. Sp.: *Dama dama*.

false gavial (gharial) Southeast Asian reptile of the family Crocodilidae with long straight snout, giving the impression of being a gavial. Sp.: *Tomistoma schlegeli*.

fennec smallest fox, native to North Africa and Arabia, having large pointed ears. Sp.: *Vulpes zerda*.

fer-de-lance large, highly venomous pit viper of tropical South America and the West Indies. Sp.: *Bothrops atrox*.

ferret domesticated albino variety of the polecat, bred for hunting rats and rabbits. Sp.: *Mustela putorius*.

fly member of the insect order Diptera, containing over 85,000 species divided into the suborders Nematocera (midges, gnats, crane flies and mosquitoes), Brachycera (bee flies, robber flies and horse flies) and Cyclorrhapha (house flies, fruit flies, blow flies, and leafminers). Dipterans are distinguished from other insects (such as dragonflies and mayflies) by their wing structure, the so-called 'true' flies being characterised by the use of only one pair of wings for flight, the second pair becoming fixed and being used for balance. The smallest two-winged flies are midges, and the largest are robber flies of the family Asilidae, which can attain lengths of up to 8 centimetres.

flying fish warm-water fish with wing-like pectoral fins for gliding through the air. Family: Exocoetidae.

flying fox fruitbats with fox-like heads, largest species with wingspan approaching 2 metres. Family: Pteropodidae.

flying lemur either of two lemur-like mammals of South-east Asia, having a membrane between the fore and hind limbs for gliding from tree to tree. Aka colugo. Gen.: *Cynocephalus*.

flying lizard long-tailed lizard of S.E. Asia with elongated ribs supporting membranes for gliding. Gen.: *Draco*.

flying squirrel any squirrel with skin joining the fore and hind limbs for gliding from tree to tree. Gen.: *Aeromys, Belomys, Eupetdurus, Glaucomys, Hylopetes, Petaurista, Petinomys, Pteromys, Pteromyscus, Trogopterus*.

fox various members of the dog family, Canidae, typically small in stature with a bushy tail known as a brush. They include the African Sand, Bat-eared, Bengal, Black, Blanford's, Brant, Chama, Corsac, Hoary, Indian, Kit, Pale, Rüppell's, Samson, Sand, Silver, Steppe, Swift and Tibetan Sand. Gen.: *Vulpes, Dusicyon, Alopex, Otocyon*.

frog several families of the order Anura, mainly insectivorous amphibians having a short, tailless body with long hind legs for hopping. The European common frog is Sp.: *Rana temporaria*.

furniture beetle beetle whose larvae bore into wood and are known as 'woodworm'. Sp.: *Anobium punctatum*.

galago see bush baby.

galliwasp West Indian lizard. Sp.: *Diploglossus monotropis*.

garfish marine fish having long, beak-like jaws with sharp teeth. Aka needlefish. Family: Belonidae.

gavial (gharial) long-snouted reptile of the order Crocodilia, and the only species of the family Gavialidae. The gavial inhabits the rivers of northern India and grows to a length of up to 5 metres. Sp.: *Gavialis gangeticus*.

gazelle antelope of Asia or Africa. Gen.: *Gazella, Antilope, Antidoreas, Procapra, Ammodoreas, Litocranius*.

gecko nocturnal lizards found in warm climes, with adhesive feet for climbing purposes, the only lizards with voices. Family: Gekkonidae.

gelada brownish baboon with a bare red patch on its chest, native to Ethiopia. Sp.: *Theropithecus gelada*.

gemsbok large antelope of south-west and east Africa. Sp.: *Oryx gazella*.

genet (genette) cat-like mammal native to Africa and Southern Europe with spotted fur and a long, ringed, bushy tail. Gen.: *Genetta*.

gerbil various genera of mouse-like desert rodents. The species often kept as a pet is *Meriones unguiculatus*, the Mongolian gerbil.

gerenuk antelope native to east Africa, with a very long neck and small head. Sp.: *Litocranius walleri*.

giant anteater edentate (toothless) mammal of Central and South America with long snout used for feeding on termites. Sp.: *Myrmecophaga tridactyla*.

gila monster venomous lizard of southwest USA and northwestern Mexico. The gila monster is stout-bodied with black and pink markings and grows to about 45 centimetres (18 inches). Sp.: *Heloderma suspectum*.

giraffe ruminant mammal of Africa with a long neck and forelegs and a skin of dark patches separated by lighter lines. It is the tallest living animal (over 5 metres). Sp.: *Giraffa camelopardalis*.

gnu two antelope species of the genus *Connochaetes*, native to southern Africa, Kenya, Tanzania and Zambia, with a large, erect head and brown stripes on the neck and shoulders. Aka wildebeest.

goat males are called rams or billies and females are does or nannies. Domesticated breeds include Angora, Kashmir, Nubian, Saanen and Toggenburg. Sp.: *Capra hircus*.

goldfish freshwater cyprinid fish of eastern Europe and Asia, especially China. Sp.: *Carassius auratus*.

gopher burrowing rodents of the family Geomyidae native to North America, having food pouches on the cheeks. Aka pocket gopher.

gopher tortoise tortoise native to southern USA, that excavates tunnels to shelter from the sun. Gen.: *Gopherus*.

gorilla largest anthropoid ape, native to central Africa. Sp.: *Gorilla gorilla*.

gourami large freshwater fish native to South-east Asia. Aka labyrinth fish. Sp.: *Osphronemus goramy*.

grampus dolphin with a blunt snout and long, pointed black flippers. Aka Risso's dolphin. Sp.: *Grampus griseus*.

grasshopper any orthopterous insect of the families Acrididae (short-horned grasshoppers) and Tettigoniidae (long-horned grasshoppers). The grasshopper frequents semi-arid regions and grasslands. Many species are green in colour, although some are brownish-grey with red or yellow markings. The upper hind legs of a grasshopper are elongated, and the males tend to produce a buzzing sound by rubbing the femur against its wings. The young of a grasshopper is called a nymph.

grayling silver-grey freshwater fish with a long, high dorsal fin. Gen.: *Thymallus*.

grayling butterfly having wings with grey undersides and bright eye-spots on the upper side. Sp.: *Hipparchia semele*.

greenbottle fly of the genus *Lucilia*, which lays eggs in the flesh of sheep.

grunion slender Californian silverside fish, which spawns on beaches. Sp.: *Leuresthes tenuis*.

gudgeon: common small European freshwater fish, often used as bait. Sp.: *Gobio gobio*.

guinea pig domesticated Southern American cavy kept as a pet or for research in biology. Sp.: *Cavia porcellus*.

haddock edible marine fish of the north Atlantic, similar to cod but smaller. Sp.: *Melanogrammus aeglefinus*.

hairstreak species of butterfly of the family Lycaenidae, distinguished by the hair-like markings on the underside of their wings. Usually brown or grey in colour but occasionally red and black. Gen.: *Callophrys*.

hamadryas large, powerful monkey of the plains and open-rock areas of southern Arabia and northeast Africa. Aka sacred baboon or Arabian baboon. Sp.: *Papio hamadryas*.

hamster: common Eurasian rodent of the subfamily Cricetinae, having a short tail and large cheek pouches for storing food. Sp.: *Cricetus cricetus*.

hamster: golden Eurasian rodent of the subfamily Cricetinae, having a short tail and large cheek pouches for storing food and often kept as a pet or as a laboratory animal. Sp.: *Mesocricetus auratus*.

hanuman Indian langur venerated by Hindus. Aka wanderoo. Sp.: *Semnopithecus entellus*.

hare larger than a rabbit, with longer ears, its habitat is called a form. Sp.: *Lepus europaeus*.

harp seal earless seal of the family Phocidae, found in the North Atlantic and Arctic oceans. The typical male is golden-grey with dark markings on its back and face and can grow up to 2 metres long and weigh in excess of 200 kilograms (440 pounds). A young harp seal is variously named bedlamer, beater or greyback, depending on its age and development. Sp.: *Pagophilus groenlandicus*.

hartebeest large African antelope with ringed horns bent back at the tips. Gen.: *Alcelaphus*.

harvest mouse small mouse with a prehensile tail, which nests in the stalks of growing grain. Sp.: *Micromys minutus*.

hedgehog Old World mammal of the order Insectivora with spiny back and very small tail. The common western European species is *Erinaceus europaeus*.

hellbender large, brownish-grey North American salamander measuring up to 75 centimetres in length, with a flat head, short stout legs and a wrinkled fold of skin down its sides. Sp.: *Cryptobranchus alleganiensis*.

hercules beetle large South American beetle with two horns extending from its head. Sp.: *Dynastes hercules*.

herring soft-finned fish of northern seas with elongated scaled body and smooth head. Sp.: *Clupea harengus*.

horned toad South-east Asian toads with horn-shaped extensions over the eyes. Family: Pelobatidae.

horned toad American lizard covered with spiny scales. Gen.: *Phrynosoma*.

hornet large wasp with brown and yellow striped body, capable of inflicting a severe sting. Sp.: *Vespa crabro*.

horseshoe bat bat of the Old World with a horseshoe-shaped ridge on the nose. Family: Rhinolophidae.

horseshoe crab large marine arthropod with a horseshoe-shaped shell and a long tail-spine. Gen.: *Limulus*.

house mouse very common grey mouse, which scavenges around human dwellings. Often kept as pets or used in laboratory experiments. Sp.: *Mus musculus*.

housefly fly of the family Muscidae, breeding in decaying organic matter and often entering houses. Sp.: *Musca domestica*.

hyena (spotted) long-legged, carnivorous, dog-like mammal of Africa. Aka laughing hyena. Sp.: *Crocuta crocuta*.

ibex wild goat of mountainous areas of Europe, north Africa and Asia, with a beard and thick, curved, ridged horns. Sp.: *Capra ibex*.

iguanodon large, herbivorous, long-tailed bipedal dinosaur of the Cretaceous period. Gen.: *Iguanodon*.

impala medium-size antelope of South and East Africa capable of long high jumps. Sp.: *Aepyceros melampus*.

indigo snake see cribo.

jackal four species of African or South Asian canine mammals of the genus *Canis*.

jackrabbit North American hare with long hind legs and large ears. The white-tailed jackrabbit is *Lepus townsendii*.

jaguar large feline mammal of south-west USA and Central and South America, similar to the leopard but with a shorter tail and larger spots on its coat. Sp.: *Panthera onca*.

jaguarondi North and South American small grey cat with short legs and long tail. Sp.: *Felis yagouaroundi*.

jellyfish marine coelenterate of the class Scyphozoa having an umbrella-shaped, jelly-like body and stinging tentacles.

kalong fruit-eating bat. Aka flying fox. Sp.: *Pteropus edulis*.

kangaroo any of up to 50 species of Australasian marsupial mammals of the family Macropodidae. Kangaroos may grow to a height in excess of 2.5 metres and leap a distance of over 13 metres in a single bound at a speed of 50 km per hour.

katipo venomous spider of New Zealand, usually black with a red or orange stripe on its abdomen. Sp.: *Latrodectus katipo*.

katydid orthopterous insect of the family Tettigoniidae (long-horned grasshopper). The katydid is usually coloured green and lives among the foliage of North American trees. Its name derives from the cry of 'katydid, katy didn't' which is heard throughout the night and produced by the insect rubbing its wings together.

kiang wild ass of a race native to Tibet with a thick furry coat, a subspecies of the Asiatic ass, *Equus hemionus*.

NATURE

killer whale   actually a kind of dolphin, with a black back, white belly and prominent dorsal fin. Sp.: *Orcinus orca*.

king cobra   world's largest venomous snake (up to 5.5 metres), found from southern China to the Philippines and Indonesia. Aka hamadryad. Sp.: *Ophiophagus hannah*.

kinkajou   nocturnal fruit-eating mammal of Central and South America, with a prehensile tail and a very long tail. Sp.: *Potos flavus*.

kissing gourami   small, brightly coloured freshwater fish, a popular aquarium pet. Sp.: *Helostoma temminckii*.

koala   slow-moving, arboreal marsupial of eastern Australia, having grey fur and feeding on eucalyptus leaves and bark. The koala is also known as a koala bear, although not related to the Ursidae family. It is the only animal apart from humans with unique fingerprints. Sp.: *Phascolarctos cinereus*.

kolinsky   Siberian and Asian weasel with a rich brown coat. Sp.: *Mustela sibirica*.

Komodo dragon   predatory lizard native to the East Indies, largest of all surviving lizards, reaching over 3 metres long. Sp.: *Varanus komodoensis*.

kouprey   rare grey ox, native to forests in Indo-China. Sp.: *Bos sauveli*.

krait   any venomous snake of the Asiatic genus *Bungarus*.

lamprey   mostly parasitic, eel-like fish of the family Petromyzontidae, without scales, paired fins or jaws, but having a sucker mouth with horny teeth and a rough tongue.

land crab   crab that lives in burrows inland and migrates in large numbers to the sea to breed. Sp.: *Cardisoma guanhumi*.

langur   any of various agile arboreal Old World monkeys of the family Cercopithecidae.

laughing hyena   see hyena (spotted).

leafcutter ant   ant of tropical America, which cuts pieces from leaves to cultivate fungus. Gen.: *Atta*.

leafcutter bee   solitary bee, which lines its nest with leaf fragments. Family: Megachilidae.

lemon sole   flatfish of the plaice family. Sp.: *Microstomus kitt*.

lemur   any Madagascan prosimian primate of the family Lemuridae.

leopard   large African or Asian feline mammal with either a black-spotted yellowish fawn or all-black coat. Aka panther. Sp.: *Panthera pardus*.

limpet   marine gastropod mollusc with a shallow conical shell and a broad muscular foot that sticks tightly to rocks. The common limpet is *Patella vulgata*.

lion   large predatory feline mammal of Africa and north-west India, often called the king of beasts. Sp.: *Panthera leo*.

llama   South American ruminant related to the camel, kept as a beast of burden and for its soft woolly fleece. Sp.: *Lama glama*.

loach   small, edible freshwater fish of the family Cobitidae.

locust   orthopterous insect of the family Acrididae (short-horned grasshopper), which is prone to multiply quickly and migrate long distances in destructive swarms billions strong.

loris: slender and slow   small slow-moving nocturnal tree-dwelling primates with small ears and a very short tail. The slender loris, *Loris tardigradus*, is found in southern India. The slow loris, *Nycticebus coucang*, is found in south-west Asia and the East Indies.

louse   wingless insect parasitic on a wide range of birds and mammals. Those that infest the human hair and skin and transmit various diseases are *Pediculus humanus*.

lynx   short-tailed cat inhabiting forests of Europe, Asia and North America. The lynx is distinguished by its tufted ears, hairy soles, broad short head and mottled fur. Sp.: *Felis lynx*.

macaque   medium-sized monkey of the Old World genus *Macaca*, including the rhesus monkey and barbary ape, typically having a rather long face with cheek pouches.

mackerel (common)   North Atlantic marine fish with a greenish-blue body, used for food. Sp.: *Scomber scombrus*.

magpie moth   white geometrid moth with black and yellow markings whose caterpillars feed on fruit bushes. Sp.: *Abraxas grossulariata*.

Malayan stink badger   aka teledu or skunk badger. Strong-smelling dark coat is key feature. Sp.: *Mydaus javanensis*.

mamba   any venomous African snake of the genus *Dendroaspis*, especially the green and black mambas, *Dendroaspis angusticeps* and *Dendroaspis polylepis*.

mammoth   large, extinct elephant of the Pleistocene period. Gen.: *Mammuthus*.

mammoth (woolly)   large extinct elephant of the Pleistocene period having a hairy coat and long tusks. Sp.: *Mammuthus primigenius*.

manatee   large, aquatic, plant-eating, sirenian mammal with paddle-like forelimbs, no hind limbs and a powerful tail. Aka sea cow. Gen.: *Trichechus*.

mandrill   large West African baboon, the adult of which has a brilliantly coloured face and blue-coloured buttocks. Sp.: *Papio sphinx*.

mangabey   various small long-tailed West and Central African monkeys of the genus *Cercocebus*. Named after a region of Madagascar.

marbled white   whitish butterfly with black markings. Sp.: *Melanargia galathea*.

margay   small wild Central and South American cat. Sp.: *Felis wiedii*.

markhor   large, spiral-horned wild goat of Central Asia. Sp.: *Capra falconeri*.

marmoset   tropical American monkeys having a long silky coat and a bushy tail. Gen.: *Callithrix*.

marmot   burrowing, hibernating rodents of the squirrel family with a heavy-set body and short bushy tail, living in colonies in Europe, Asia and the Americas. Gen.: *Marmota*.

marten   any weasel-like carnivore of the genus *Martes*, having valuable fur.

massasauga   small North American rattlesnake named from corruption of Mississagi River, Ontario. Sp.: *Sistrurus catenatus*.

mastodon   extinct, elephant-like proboscidean mammal common in the Miocene period. Gen.: *Mammut*.

mayfly   insects with an acquatic nymph and a fragile-winged adult, which lives only briefly in spring. Aka green drake. Order: Ephemeroptera.

meadow brown   common brown butterfly with eye-spots on the upper wing. Sp.: *Maniola jurtina*.

megaloceros   giant deer whose antlers had a 3.5 metre span; it lived in Eurasia during the last Ice Age. Gen.: *Megaloceros*.

megalosaurus flesh-eating dinosaur, the first to receive a scientific name. Gen.: *Megalosaurus*.

Mexican bearded lizard related to the gila monster and inhabiting the same territory, the Mexican bearded lizard is similar in colour but grows to about 80 centimetres (32 inches). Together they are the only species of poisonous lizards. Sp.: *Heloderma horridum*.

miller's thumb small, spiny, freshwater fish with a large head. Aka bullhead. Sp.: *Cottus gobio*.

millipede herbivorous arthropod of the class Diplopoda, which can have up to 200 pairs of legs.

mink: American semi-aquatic musteline mammal having slightly webbed feet, often hunted for their valuable fur. Sp.: *Mustela vison*.

mink: European slightly smaller version of the American mink. Sp.: *Mustela lutreola*.

mite small parasitic arachnid of the order Acarina, similar to ticks but distinguished by the lack of a sensory pit, known as Haller's organ, on the end segment of the first of four pairs of legs.

mola (ocean sunfish, headfish) large grey heavy ocean fish with short body, flattened sideways. Aka Sp.: *Mola mola*.

mole small burrowing mammals of the order Insectivora, family Talpidae, found in Europe, Asia and North America. The British mole is *Talpa europaeus*.

mongoose small predatory mammals of Africa, southern Europe and Asia, having long tail and brindled coat. Two sub-families: Galidinae and Herpestinae.

monkey any of numerous primates of a group including the families Cebidae (capuchins), Callithricidae (marmosets and tamarins) and Cercopithecidae (baboons and macaques), especially any of the long-tailed varieties.

moonfish see opah.

moose North American elk. Sp.: *Alces alces*.

mouf(f)lon wild mountain sheep of South Europe. Sp.: *Ovis musimon*.

mud puppy large, grey, neotenous aquatic salamander of eastern USA with conspicuous red feathery gills. Sp.: *Necturus maculosus*.

mudskipper any small goby of the family Periophthalmidae, found along the coasts of the Indian and Pacific oceans, able to leave the water and scramble over mud.

mulloway large Australian marine fish used as food. Sp.: *Argyrosomos hololepidotus*.

muntjac any small deer of the genus *Muntiacus*, native to South-east Asia, the male having tusks and small antlers.

musk deer three species of small Asian deer of the genus *Moschus*, having no antlers and in the male having long protruding canine teeth. The musk gland of the male is valued for its use in perfume and medicines.

musk ox large goat-antelope native to North America with a thick, shaggy coat and small, curved horns. Sp.: *Ovibos moschatus*.

muskellunge large North American pike particularly inhabiting the Great Lakes. Aka maskinonge. Sp.: *Esox masquinongy*.

muskrat large aquatic rodent of the vole tribe, native to North America, having a musky smell. Aka musquash. Gen.: *Ondata zibethicus*.

narwhal small Arctic whale, the male of which has a long, straight, spirally twisted tusk developed from one of its teeth. Sp.: *Monodon monoceros*.

natterjack toad of western Eurasia with a bright yellow stripe down its back and moving by running not hopping. Sp.: *Bufo calamita*.

newt any of more than 40 species of tailed amphibian of the order Urodela and family Salamandridae. Aquatic newts have smooth moist skins, while terrestrial species have rough skin and are known as efts. British newts are of the genera *Triturus* (tritons), the most common being the smooth newt (*Triturus vulgaris*).

nilgai large short-horned Indian antelope. Sp.: *Boselaphus tragocamelus*.

Norway lobster small European lobster or scampi. Aka Dublin Bay prawn. Sp.: *Nephrops norvegicus*.

numbat small western Australian termite-eating marsupial with a bushy tail and black and white striped back. Sp.: *Myrmecobius fasciatus*.

ocelot medium-size cat native to the Americas, having a deep yellow or orange coat with black striped and spotted markings. Sp.: *Felis pardalis*.

octopus any cephalopod mollusc of the order Octopoda, varying in size from 1 centimetre to almost 6 metres, with an armspan of almost 9 metres. Octopuses (or octopi) have 8 tentacles and eject an inky fluid when attacked. The largest species is the North Pacific octopus (*Octopus dofleini*) and the smallest is the Californian octopus (*Octopus micropyrsus*).The common octopus (*Octopus vulgaris*) reaches an average size of 1 metre. The octopus has the most complex brain of any invertebrate, having both long-term and short-term memories.

opah large, rare, deep-sea fish having a silver-blue back with white spots and crimson fins. Aka moonfish. Sp.: *Lampris guttatus*.

opossum any mainly tree-living marsupial of the family Didelphidae, native to North and South America, and having a prehensile tail and hind feet with an opposable thumb.

orang-utan large, red, long-haired, tree-living ape native to Borneo and Sumatra. Aka wild man of the woods. Sp.: *Pongo pygmaeus*.

orfe freshwater cyprinid fish of Europe that occurs in two colour varieties i.e. golden and silver. Orfes are often called goldfish. Sp.: *Idus idus*.

oribi small African grazing antelope having reddish-fawn back and white underparts. Sp.: *Ourebia ourebi*.

oryx large African antelope having long straight nearly upright horns. Gen.: *Oryx*.

otter freshwater carnivorous mammals of Europe, Asia, Africa and the Americas, with smooth fur and webbed feet. Sub-family Lutrinae.

ounce see snow leopard.

paddlefish primitive bony fish of the Mississippi and Yangtze rivers, leaden grey, with a long flat snout. Sp.: *Polyodon spathula* and *Psephurus gladius*.

paddymelon (pademelon) small wallaby of coastal scrubby regions of Australia. Gen.: *Thylogale*.

painted lady orange-red butterfly with black and white spots. Sp.: *Cynthia cardui*.

panda: giant large, rare, bear-like mammal native to certain mountain bamboo forests of China, having characteristic black and white markings. Sp.: *Ailuropoda melanoleuca*.

panda: red Himalayan raccoon-like mammal with reddish-brown fur and a long, bushy tail. Sp.: *Ailurus fulgens*.

pangolin various mammal species native to Asia and

NATURE

Africa covered with overlapping horny scales and having a small head with elongated snout and tongue, with which they feed on ants, and a tapering tail. Aka scaly anteater. Gen.: *Manus*.

peacock butterfly butterfly with eye-like markings on its wings. Sp.: *Inachis io*.

pearl-oyster any of various marine bivalve molluscs of the genus *Pinctada*, bearing pearls.

peccary three species of American, wild, pig-like mammals of the family Tayassuidae. Sp.: *Tayassu tajacu*, *Tayassu pecari* and *Catagonus wagneri*.

Père David's deer large, slender-antlered deer, named after Father A David, French missionary and naturalist (d. 1900). Sp.: *Elaphurus davidiensis*.

phalanger any of various species of Australasian marsupial mammals of the family Phalangeridae, also known as possums on the Australian mainland and Tasmania.

plaice European flatfish having a brown back with orange spots and a white underside, much used for food. Sp.: *Pleuronectes platessa*.

polar bear white carnivorous bear of coastal regions of the North Pole. Sp.: *Ursus maritimus*.

polecat (European) small, brownish-black, fetid flesh-eating mammal of the weasel family. Sp.: *Mustela putorius*.

porpoise any of various marine cetacean mammals of the families Delphinidae and Phocoenidae, which are typically smaller than dolphins and with chubbier shape and blunter snout. Sp.: *Phocoena phocoena*.

possum any member of the Phalangeridae family of marsupial mammals native to Australasia. Possums are tree-dwellers. The brush-tailed possum (*Trichosurus vulpecula*) is the most common marsupial in Australia.

potto short-tailed prosimian primate, of the family Lorisidae, having vertebral spines protruding through its neck. The potto is often confused with the kinkajou, as it is a slow-moving, nocturnal, arboreal mammal.

prawn any of various marine decapod crustaceans of the genera *Palaemon* and *Penaeus*, similar to shrimps but having two pairs of pincers.

pterodactyl extinct flying reptile of the late Jurassic, having membranous wings supported on an elongated 4th digit. Gen.: *Pterodactylus*.

puma largest American feline mammal, resembling a lion. It is the best jumper of the cat family. Aka cougar or mountain lion. Sp.: *Felis concolor*.

pygmy white-toothed shrew smallest member of the mouse-like, long-snouted mammals of the family Soricidae. Sp.: *Suncus etruseus*.

quokka small marsupial resembling a wallaby, primarily inhabiting Rottnest Island off the coast of Perth, Western Australia. Sp.: *Setonix brachyurus*.

rabbit burrowing leporid mammal which is smaller than a hare and has much shorter ears. The European rabbit is *Oryctolagus cuniculus*.

raccoon omnivorous mammal of the genus *Procyon* occupying diverse habitats in North and South America. It has a pointed muzzle, long tail and greyish-black fur with black bands around the tail and across the face. The common raccoon of North America is *Procyon lotor*.

ratel see badger (honey).

red deer forest-dweller of Europe and western to central Asia. Males are called harts and females, hinds. Harts with 12 tines are known as 'Royal' and one with 14 tines is a 'Wilson'. Sp.: *Cervus elaphus*.

reindeer see caribou.

ring-tailed lemur rock-dwelling lemur with elongated hind legs and a long tail with brown and white ringed markings. Sp.: *Lemur catta*.

Rocky Mountain goat massive, yellowish-white goat-antelope inhabiting mountains in western North America. Sp.: *Oreamnos americanus*.

roe deer small, graceful woodland deer of Eurasia, the males having small antlers and a reddish-brown summer coat. Sp.: *Capreolus capreolus*.

sable marten of northern Asian and Japanese forests, with dark brown luxuriant fur. Sp.: *Martes zibellina*.

sabre-toothed tiger extinct, lion-size mammal of the cat family (only distantly related to the tiger) with long, curved, upper canine teeth. Aka sabre-toothed cat. Gen.: *Smilodon*.

salamander any tailed amphibian of the order Urodela that most commonly inhabit freshwater and damp woodlands. Salamanders resemble lizards but are related to newts in the family Salamandridae, and can be aquatic, semi-aquatic, or terrestrial. They are generally very small (10–15 centimetres) but giant salamanders may attain a length of up to 180 centimetres. The semi-aquatic Chinese giant salamander (*Andrias davidianus*) grows in excess of 1 metre but the largest salamander is the Japanese giant salamander (*Andrias japonicus*).

sand lizard small, green-grey-brown Eurasian lizard with long clawed digits. Sp.: *Lacerta agilis*.

scorpion arachnid of the order Scorpionida, having an elongated body and a segmented, upwardly curving tail that is tipped with a venomous stinger. During mating the male and female perform a courtship dance and after copulation the female often devours the male.

seal: eared carnivorous pinniped (paddle-footed) aquatic mammal of the family Otariidae, which comes to shore to breed. Eared seals swim by 'rowing' with their front flippers and can turn their hindflippers forward to walk on land.

seal: elephant large seal, the male having an inflatable snout. Aka sea elephant. Gen.: *Mirounga*.

seal: true carnivorous pinniped (paddle-footed) aquatic mammal of the family Phocidae, which comes to shore to breed. They are earless, swim with their hindflippers, and hump along on land, unable to use their hindflippers as support.

sea lion any of five species of eared seal of the South Atlantic and Pacific. The Californian sea lion (*Zalophus californianus*) is the species trained for circus performances.

sea squirt any small primitive marine animal of the class Ascidiacea, having a sac-like body with openings through which water enters and leaves. Sea squirts are sedentary and sessile and can be found on coral reefs, pier pilings, ships' hulls, rocks and seashells. Peculiarly, they can be found on the backs of some species of crabs, while other species of crabs may dwell inside the cavities of a sea squirt.

serval slender feline mammal of the African savanna, having an orange-brown coat with black spots, large ears and long legs. Sp.: *Felis serval*.

sheep any of various bovid mammals having ribbed horns and a narrow face. Domesticated breeds, genus *Ovis*, include Border Leicester, Cheviot, Clun Forest, Cobb 101, Cotswold, Dartmoor, Devon Longwool, Dorset Down, Dorset Horn, Exmoor Horned, Hampshire, Herdwick, Ile-de-France,

Karakul, Kerry Hill, Leicester, Lincoln, The Lonk, Masham, Merino, Oxford, Rambouillet, Romney, Roscommon, Ryeland, Scottish Blackface, Shropshire, Southdown, Suffolk, Swaledale, Welsh Mountain, Wensleydale and Wiltshire Horned.

shrew small, mouse-like, long-snouted mammals of the order Insectivora, family Soricidae. The European common shrew is *Sorex araneus*. Aka shrewmouse.

shrew: elephant small, insect-eating mammals native to Africa, having a long snout and long hind limbs Family: Macroscelididae.

shrimp any of various marine decapod crustaceans of the genus *Crangon*, having a slender flattened body, long tail and a single pair of pincers. Although large shrimps in excess of 5 millimetres are sometimes called prawns, this is misleading as a prawn is a distinct species with two sets of pincers. The two most important shrimps are the common shrimp (*Crangon vulgaris*) and the edible shrimp (*Peneus setiferus*).

skunk American musteline mammals of the sub-family Mephitinae, typically having a black and white coat and bushy tail. They eject a foul-smelling fluid from the anal gland when attacked. The familiar striped skunk is *Mephitis mephitis*.

slender-tailed meerkat see suricate.

sloth shaggy-coated, arboreal edentate mammals of Central and South America that hang upside down by their arms. Three-toed sloths, genus *Bradypus*; two-toed sloths, genus *Choloepus*.

slow worm Eurasian legless lizard with brownish-grey, snake-like body. Sp.: *Anguis fragilis*.

snake (grass) non-venomous European snake having brownish-green body. Sp.: *Natrix natrix*.

snow leopard large, feline, mammal of mountainous regions of central Asia, having a long, pale brown coat marked with black rosettes. Aka ounce. Sp.: *Panthera uncia*.

solenodon rare, shrew-like, nocturnal mammal of the West Indies, having a long hairless tail and an elongated snout. Cuban species, *Solenodon cubanus*; Hispaniola species, *Solenodon paradoxus*.

spectacled bear solitary South American species of the family Ursidae and inhabiting mountainous terrain, which gives it an alternative name of Andean bear. It grows up to 180 centimetres long (6 feet) and has a dark brown coat, with whitish markings around its eyes and facial circumference. Sp.: *Tremarctos ornatus*.

sponge any member of primitive multicellular aquatic animals of the phylum Porifera, which have porous, baglike bodies with a skeleton of hard spicules or elastic fibres. The dried skeleton of sponges are procured for commercial purposes as bathroom sponges because of their ability to hold water.

squirrel (grey) grey-furred squirrel native to eastern North America but found worldwide. Sp.: *Sciurus carolinensis*.

squirrel (red) reddish-brown squirrel inhabiting woodlands of Europe and Asia. Sp.: *Sciurus vulgaris*.

starfish any echinoderm of the classes Asteroidea (sea stars) and Ophiuroidea (brittle stars), typically having a flat body and 5 tentacles, although some species may have many more.

stoat small, long-bodied carnivorous mammal of the weasel family having reddish-brown upper parts and a black-tipped tail and in northern areas turning white in winter, when it is known as ermine. Sp.: *Mustela erminea*.

sturgeon primitive bony fish of temperate waters of the northern hemisphere, valued as a source of caviar and isinglass. Family: Acipenseridae.

sugar glider Australian possum that glides from tree to tree by means of a fold of skin that joins its front and hind legs. The sugar glider is also known as the flying possum or flying phalanger. Sp.: *Petaurus breviceps*.

suricate southern African mongoose which has a lemur-like face. Aka slender-tailed meerkat. Sp.: *Suricata suricatta*.

swallowtail butterfly member of the subfamily Papilioninae, order Lepidoptera. Swallowtails are found worldwide and are named for the tail-like extensions of their hindwings. Gen.: *Papilio*.

taipan large highly venomous snake of north-east Australia, dark brown with a creamy-coloured head. Sp.: *Oxyuranus scutellatus*.

tapeworm any of various parasitic flatworms of the order Cestoda, which attack the liver and digestive tract of vertebrates.

tapir four species of forest-dwelling perissodactyl mammals of South and Central America and South-east Asia, having an elongated snout, three-toed hind legs and four-toed forelegs. Genus *Tapirus*.

tarpon large, silvery, game fish of warm Atlantic waters, having a compressed, scaled body. *Tarpon atlanticus* is the best-known species.

Tasmanian devil small, ferocious, carnivorous marsupial having black fur with pale markings, strong jaws and short legs. Aka ursine dasyure. Sp.: *Sarcophilus harrisi*.

Tasmanian wolf see thylacine.

tayra large, arboreal, musteline mammal of Central and South America, having a dark brown body and paler head. Sp.: *Eira barbata*.

teledu see Malayan stink badger.

tenrec: tailless small mammal of Madagascar (but largest insectivore), resembling a hedgehog or shrew. Sp.: *Tenrec ecaudatus*.

termite whitish, ant-like insect of the order Isoptera. The two main species are 'ground' termites and 'drywood' termites. Termites feed on cellulose, which is found in wood and wood products. They are social insects, and a typical colony would include workers, soldiers, winged reproductives, and a king and queen. The alternative name for a termite is 'white ant', although there are subtle differences between the body shape of an ant and a termite. An ant has a tapered abdomen, while that of a termite is straight. The ant also has bent antennae whereas the termites are straight. The winged reproductives are similar to flying ants, although their double wings are even in size while the ant's double wings are uneven in size.

terrapin web-footed chelonian reptile that lives on land or in fresh water. Family: Emydidae.

thylacine presumed extinct, dog-like carnivorous marsupial of Tasmania, having greyish-brown fur with dark vertical stripes on the back. Aka Tasmanian wolf. Sp.: *Thylacinus cynocephalus*.

tick small parasitic arachnid of the families Ixodidae and Nuttalliellidae (hard ticks) and Argasidae (soft ticks). Ticks dwell on the skin of warm-blooded animals and feed on the blood and tissues of their hosts.

tiger large Asian feline mammal with yellowy coat and black stripes. Sp.: *Panthera tigris*.

timber rattlesnake heavy-bodied snake with a broad head that is distinct from its narrow neck. The

NATURE

rattlesnake inhabits the prairies of North America, where it feeds on a variety of small mammals, which are killed by its venomous bite. Humans are not under threat from rattlesnakes as 60 per cent of all bites are dry, and even venomous bites rarely cause more than temporary discomfort. The rattlesnake is generally golden-brown with black markings except for the head, which is plain brown, and its rattler, at the tip of its tail, which is dark black. Sp.: *Crotalus horridus*.

toad anuran amphibian, secreting a poisonous fluid, similar to frogs but more terrestrial, having drier, warty skin. The Eurasian common toad is *Bufo bufo*.

tokay large (35 cm) grey gecko with orange and deep blue spots, of South-east Asia. Sp.: *Gekko gecko*.

tortoise herbivorous chelonian reptile found in warm regions worldwide except Australia. Family: Testudinidae.

tree frog arboreal frog of the family Hylidae, with sucker-like pads to aid in climbing. Tree frogs are also known as tree toads.

triceratops rhinoceros-like herbivorous dinosaur of the Cretaceous period, up to 9 metres long, having three horns and a short armoured neck frill. Gen.: *Triceratops*.

turtle aquatic chelonian reptiles with a flattened shell and flipper-like limbs for swimming. Several families of the order Chelonia.

Tyrannosaurus rex 14 metres long, 6 metres tall, flesh-eating dinosaur with relatively small 2-fingered hands. Gen.: *Tyrannosaurus*.

unau aka Linné's two-toed sloth. Sp.: *Choloepus didactylus*.

vervet small, yellowish-grey, African, long-tailed monkey. Sp.: *Cercopithecus aethiops*.

vicuña South American mammal of the high Andes related to the llama, with fine silky wool. Sp.: *Vicugna vicugna*.

viscacha large South American burrowing rodent related to the chinchillas. Gen.: *Lagidium* and *Lagostomus*.

vole (field) small, rodent of the family Cricetidae with stocky body, short tail and small ears. Sp.: *Microtus agrestis*.

vole (water) large amphibious vole of Eurasian river banks. Sp.: *Arvicola terrestris*.

wallaby (hare) small rodent-like herbivorous marsupial of Australia and New Guinea, family Macropodidae. Gen.: *Lagorchestes*.

wallaby (rock) herbivorous marsupial of Australia and New Guinea, resembling a small kangaroo, of the family Macropodidae. Gen.: *Protemnodon*.

walrus large, tusked, aquatic mammal of the Arctic, a bottom feeder – mainly on molluscs – related to the eared seals. Its family, Odobenidae, has only one species: *Odobenus rosmarus*.

wapiti big North American deer, which is now considered as a larger race of the red deer. Sp.: *Cervus canadensis*.

warble fly any of various flies of the genus *Hypoderma*, whose larvae infest the skin of cattle and horses.

warthog African wild pig with a large head, warty lumps on its face and large curved tusks. Sp.: *Phacochoerus aethiopicus*.

wasp stinging insect of the order Hymenoptera, with black and yellow stripes and a very thin waist.

water moccasin (cottonmouth) poisonous, semi-aquatic pit viper of south-eastern USA. Sp.: *Agkistrodon piscivorus*.

water opossum semi-aquatic tropical American opossum with dark-banded grey fur. Aka yapok. Sp.: *Chironectes minimus*.

weasel (European common) small, brown and white carnivorous mammal with a slender body, related to the stoat. Gen.: *Mustela nivalis*.

whale any of the larger marine mammals of the order Cetacea, having a streamlined body and horizontal tail, and breathing air through a blowhole on the head. Gen.: *Cetacea*.

whale shark large, tropical whale-like shark feeding close to the surface. Sp.: *Rhincodon typus*.

white admiral mottled brown butterfly with a white splashed band down its wings. Sp.: *Limenitis camilla*.

wildcat wild cat of Eurasia and Africa with a grey and black coat and a bushy tail. Sp.: *Felis silvestris*.

wildebeest see gnu.

wisent the European bison. Sp.: *Bison bonasus*.

witch North Atlantic flatfish resembling the lemon sole. Sp.: *Glyptocephalus cynoglossus*.

wobbegong (spotted) carpet shark of the family Orectolobidae, inhabiting Australian waters and having a richly patterned brown and white skin. Sp.: *Orectolobus maculatus*.

wolf (grey) wild, flesh-eating mammal of the northern hemisphere, ancestor of the domestic dog. Gen.: *Canis lupus*.

wolf-fish large, voracious blenny of the North Atlantic. Family: Anarhichadidae.

wolverine large, musteline mammal of northern forests of Eurasia and North America, a predator and scavenger, having dark very thick water-resistant fur. Aka glutton. Sp.: *Gulo gulo*.

wombat (common) Australian bear-like terrestrial marsupial with coarse dark hair and small ears. Sp.: *Vombatus ursinus*.

wombat (hairy nosed) two marsupial species of Queensland and central south Australia, with fine grizzled fur and longer ears than the common wombat. Sp.: *Lasiorhinus krefftii* and *Lasiorhinus latifrons*.

woodchuck reddish-brown and grey North American burrowing marmot. Aka groundhog. Sp.: *Marmota monax*.

woodlouse small, terrestrial, isopod crustacean of the order Oniscoidea, feeding on rotten wood and plant matter, some of them (pill bugs) able to roll into a ball. The common woodlouse is *Oniscus asellus*.

yapok see water opossum.

yellowfin tuna fish of warm seas with yellowish fins, widely fished for food. Sp.: *Thunnus albacares*.

yellowtail game fish of coastal waters of southern California and Mexico, having a yellow tail fin. Sp.: *Seriola dorsalis*.

zebra (plains) African quadruped related to the ass and horse, with black and white stripes. Sp.: *Equus burchelli*.

zebu domestic humped ox of India, East Asia and Africa. Sp.: *Bos indicus*.

zorilla flesh-eating African mammal of the weasel family, aka African polecat. Sp.: *Ictonyx striatus*.

Miscellaneous Information

abranchiate having no gills.

amphibian: largest Japanese giant salamander.

anadromous of a fish (e.g. the salmon), swimming up a river from the sea to spawn.

anthrax fatal bacterial disease of sheep and cattle, transmissible to humans and affecting the skin and lungs; aka wool-sorters' disease.

ants: noses five.

apatosaurus: aka Brontosaurus.

ape: smallest gibbon (apes have no tails).

artiodactyl any placental ungulate mammal whose hoofs have an even number of toes – e.g. pigs, sheep, camels, deer, cattle, antelope and hippopotamuses.

batrachian of or relating to frogs or toads.

bees: eyes five.

braxy acute and usually fatal bacterial disease of sheep characterised by high fever, coma and inflammation of the fourth stomach, caused by infection with *Clostridium septicum.*

butterfly: largest Queen Alexandra's birdwing of Papua New Guinea has a wingspan of up to 25 centimetres (10 inches).

butterfly: tastes with back feet.

carnivore: largest the dinosaur Tyrannosaurus is the largest so far known; today the Kodiak bear is largest. The badger is the largest British carnivore.

carnivores: largest molars giant panda.

catadromous of a fish (e.g. the eel), swimming down a river from the sea to spawn.

chelonian reptiles including turtles, terrapins and tortoises, having upper and lower shells of bony plates – the carapace and plastron – covered with horny scales.

cladistics method of classifying animals and plants on the basis of shared characteristics that indicate the relative recency of common ancestry.

class major taxonomic division of animals that contain one or more orders e.g. Amphibia, Mammalia and Reptilia. The class Mammalia includes the orders Carnivora, Primates and Rodentia.

coarse fish any freshwater fish other than salmon and trout.

crab: lives in cast-off mollusc shell hermit crab.

cricket: ears situated on front legs.

crops: damage boll weevil (cotton); Colorado beetle (potato); locust (most vegetation); phylloxera (vine).

daddy-long-legs: aka cranefly or harvestman (US); the larvae are called leatherjackets.

death-watch beetle the ticking is caused by knocking its head against wood.

dinosaur: heaviest Brachiosaurus (up to 100 tons).

dinosaur: longest Diplodocus (up to 30 metres).

dog licences: year abolished 1988.

droppings deer – crotties, hare – currants, otter – spraints.

elephant: teeth number four.

elytron either of the two wing cases of a beetle.

family major taxonomic division of animals that contain one or more genera e.g. Canidae (dogs) and Felidae (cats). The family Canidae includes the genus *Vulpes* (foxes).

fish: fastest cosmopolitan sailfish.

fish: most poisonous stone fish.

fly: wings trues flies (including craneflies, gnat, mosquitos) have two; the four-winged caddis flies, dragonflies, etc., are not true flies.

genus major taxonomic division of animals that contain one or more species e.g. *Vulpes* (foxes). The genus *Vulpes* (foxes) includes the species *Vulpes bengalensis* (Bengal fox).

giant panda: related to raccoons (family Procyonidae).

glanders contagious and fatal disease of horses, mules and donkeys, caused by the bacterium *Actinobacillus mallei* and characterized by swellings below the jaw and mucous discharge from the nostrils.

hedgehog: fleas one hedgehog may have up to 500 fleas, but the hedgehog flea (*Archaeopsylla erinacei*) does not bite humans.

hedgehog: no. of spines usually about 5,000.

hinny offspring of a female donkey and a male horse.

horse: colours bay – brown with black mane and legs; chestnut – reddish-brown; dun – sandy with black mane; palomino – golden with pale mane; piebald – black and white; skewbald – brown and white; strawberry roan – chestnut and white.

insect: heaviest goliath beetle.

insects: segments head, abdomen, thorax (mnemonic: insects wear HATs).

invertebrate: largest giant squid.

kangaroo: name means 'I don't understand'.

kingdom any of the three groups into which natural objects may be divided i.e. animals, plants and minerals.

koala: name means 'no drink' (feeds on eucalyptus leaves).

lobster: colour Bluish but goes red when cooked.

louping-ill viral disease of animals, especially sheep, transmitted by ticks and causing staggering and jumping.

males give birth seahorse, from a pouch where the female deposits her eggs.

mallenders dry, scabby eruption behind a horse's knee.

metazoan any animal of the subkingdom Metazoa, having multicellular and differentiated tissues and comprising all animals except Protozoa and Parazoa (sponges).

mirror: response to the chimpanzee is the only animal, apart from humans, able to recognise itself in a mirror.

mule cross between a male horse and a donkey.

murrain infectious disease of cattle caused by parasites.

octopus: hearts three.

omasum the third stomach of a ruminant.

ophidian reptile of the suborder Serpentes, comprising snakes.

order Major taxonomic division of animals that contain one or more families e.g. Carnivora, Primates and Rodentia. The order Carnivore includes the families Canidae (dogs) and Felidae (cats).

pandas: born January (feed on bamboo shoots).

perissodactyl any placental ungulate mammal whose hoofs have an odd number of toes – e.g. horses, tapirs and rhinoceroses.

pets: legal age to buy in Britain 12 years old is the minimum legal age to purchase a pet.

NATURE

phylum major taxonomic division of animals that contains one or more classes, e.g. Arthropoda and Chordata. The phylum Arthropoda includes the classes, Arachnids, Centipedes, Crustaceans and insects. The phylum Chordata includes the classes, Amphibia, Aves, Mammalia and Reptilia.

pinnipeds: definition carnivorous aquatic mammals with flippers for feet (name means wing-foot).

pismire Middle English name for an ant deriving from the smell of an anthill.

reproduces: young axolotl often reproduces before reaching adult stage itself.

rhinoceros: number of horns Indian and Javan, one; Black, Sumatran and White, two.

rodents: largest capybara (in world), beaver (in Europe), coypu (in UK).

ruminant herbivorous animal that chews the cud.

scrapie fatal disease of sheep and goats, a spongiform encephalopathy producing degeneration of the central nervous system, caused by changes in prion proteins.

sex: changes annually oyster.

silkworm: food mulberry leaves.

snake: heaviest South American anaconda.

spavin disease of a horse's hock with a hard bony swelling or excrescence.

species any of the taxonomic groups into which a genus is divided; e.g. the genus *Vulpes* (foxes) has many different species, such as *Vulpes bengalensis* (Bengal fox) and *Vulpes pallida* (pale fox). Species are denoted by two words, the first being the genus and the second the species.

spider: eyes eight.

stomach: turns inside out starfish.

strangles acute bacterial disease of horses caused by infection with *Streptococcus equi*, characterised by inflammation of the mucous membranes of the respiratory tract. Aka equine distemper.

sunburn: suffers from the pig is the only non-human animal to suffer from sunburn.

taxonomy the branch of biology concerned with the classification of organisms into groups based on similarities of structure, origin and type. Carolus Linnaeus (1707–78) was the first person to structure principles for defining genera and species of organsims and to create a uniform system for naming them. The seven tiers of the hierarchy are kingdom, phylum, class, order, family, genus and species. The first six ranks use a single word to describe their members, but the names of species are binomial. Various intermediary divisions of the seven main ranks have been necessitated by the continuing discovery of new species: the prefixes sub-, super- and infra- are often applied to create new categories, and further tiers are established by using headings such as tribe or cohort. All intermediary divisions use a single word to describe their members, but subspecies become trinomial. Conventionally, the names of superfamilies end in 'oidea', families in idae', subfamilies in 'inae' and tribes in 'ini'.

taxonomy: mnemonic Kingdom, Phylum, Class, Order, Family, Genus, Species (Kent Play Cricket On Fridays, Girls Spectate).

turning sickness affliction of wildebeest whereby loss of balance faculties causes a never-ending walking in circles until death; it happens when bot-flies lay eggs in their nose and larvae find their way into the brain.

twins: consistent production armadillos and salamanders always give birth to twins.

ungulates all mammals with hoofs; they are divided into odd-toed (perissodactyl) and even-toed (artiodactyl).

vision: rear-view giraffes have ability to see behind them without turning.

woodlouse: legs fourteen.

WWF: symbol World Wide Fund for Nature symbol is a giant panda.

zoophyte plantlike animal, e.g. coral, sea anemone or sponge.

Gestation Periods

Animal	Days	Animal	Days	Animal	Days
aardvark	210	chimpanzee	235	goat	150
alpaca	345	civet	80	gorilla	260
anteater, giant	190	coati	77	guinea pig	63
antelope	280	coyote	63	hamster	25
armadillo	60–120	deer, fallow	230	hare	32
ass	350	deer, musk	170	hare, mountain	50
baboon	180	dhole	61	hedgehog	30
badger	100–360	dingo	63	hippopotamus	240
bear, grizzly	230	dog, domestic	60	horse	350
polar bear	240	dog, African wild	72	hyena	93
beaver	105	dolphin	350	jackal	63
bison	280	dormouse	30	jaguar	100
boar, wild	115	dromedary	400	kangaroo	180–335
bobcat	63	elephant, Asiatic	608	koala	36
buffalo	310	ermine	28	lemming	21
bush baby	110–193	ferret	60	lemur	60–160
capybara	150	fox, red	63	leopard	100
cat, domestic	52	gazelle	188	lion	110
cattle	283	gerbil	28	llama	360
chamois	165	gibbon	230	lynx	63
cheetah	95	giraffe	460	macaque	180

Animal	Days	Animal	Days	Animal	Days
marmoset	150	puma	93	tiger	103
mink	50	rabbit	30	vole	90
mole	35	raccoon	63	wallaby	40
mongoose	60	rat, black	21	walrus	460
moose	264	reindeer	225	warthog	172
mouse	25	rhinoceros, black	450	weasel	40
narwhal	435	seal, common	245	whale	350
ocelot	70	seal, eared	360	whale, beluga	435
opossum	12	sea lion	350	whale, sperm	435
orang-utan	240	sheep	148	wolf	62
otter	55	shrew	18	wolverine	270
panda, giant	138	skunk	63	yak	258
pig	115	sloth	180–340	zebra	340
porcupine	210	squirrel	40	zorilla	43
porpoise	183	tapir	370		

Maximum Life Spans

Species	Years	Species	Years	Species	Years
Marion's tortoise	152	slow-worm	54	giant panda	27
quahog	150	gorilla	53	red deer	26
man	123	domestic goose	50	tiger	26
spur thighed tortoise	116	Indian rhinoceros	49	grey squirrel	23
deep sea clam	100	European brown bear	47	domestic goat	20
killer whale	90	grey seal	46	blue sheep	20
sea anemone	90	blue whale	45	queen ant	18
European eel	88	goldfish	41	common rabbit	18
lake sturgeon	82	common boa	40	hedgehog	16
freshwater mussel	80	common toad	40	land snail	15
Asiatic elephant	78	Cape giraffe	36	guinea pig	14
tuatara	77	Bactrian camel	35	capybara	12
Andean condor	72	Hoffmann's sloth	34	tree shrew	11
African elephant	70	domestic cat	34	giant centipede	10
great eagle owl	68	canary	34	golden hamster	10
American alligator	66	American bison	33	fat dormouse	8
blue macaw	64	bobcat	32	millipede	7
horse	62	red kangaroo	30	house mouse	6
ostrich	62	domestic dog	29	moonrat	4
orang-utan	57	budgerigar	29	monarch butterfly	1
chimpanzee	56	lion	29	bedbug	0.5
pike	55	theraphosid spider	28	house fly	0.04
hippopotamus	54	domestic pig	27		

NATURE

Animal Cries

Animal	Cry	Animal	Cry	Animal	Cry
apes	gibber	chickens	peep	frogs	croak
asses	bray	cocks	crow	geese	cackle, hiss
bears	growl	cows	moo, low	grasshoppers	chirp, pitter
bees	hum	crows	caw	guineafowls	come back
beetles	drone	cuckoos	cuckoo	guineapigs	squeak
bitterns	boom	deer	bell	grouse	drum
blackbirds	whistle	dogs	bark, bay,	hares	squeak
blackcaps	chick-chack		howl, yelp	hawks	scream
bulls	bellow	doves	coo	hens	cackle,
calves	bleat	ducks	quack		cluck
cats	mew, purr,	eagles	scream	horses	neigh,
	caterwaul,	falcons	chant		whinny
	swear	flies	buzz	hyenas	laugh
chaffinches	chirp, pink	foxes	bark, yelp	jays	chatter

Animal	Cry	Animal	Cry	Animal	Cry
kittens	mew	owls	hoot,	sheep	bleat, baa
lambs	bleat, baa		screech	snakes	hiss
linnets	chuckle	oxen	low, bellow	sparrows	chirp
lions	roar, growl	parrots	talk	stags	bellow, call
magpies	chatter	peacocks	scream	swallows	twitter
mice	squeak,	peewits	peewit	swans	cry, sing
	squeal	pigs	grunt,	(before death)	
monkeys	chatter,		squeak,	thrushes	whistle
	gibber		squeal	tigers	roar, growl
nightingales	pipe,	pigeons	coo	turkeys	gobble
	warble,	ravens	croak	vultures	scream
	jug-jug	rooks	caw	whitethroat	chirr
				wolves	howl

Animal Habitations

Animal	Habitation	Animal	Habitation	Animal	Habitation
ant	formicary,	hare	form, down	squirrel	drey
	ant-hill	horse	stable	tiger	lair
ape	tree-nest	lion	den	wasp	vespiary,
badger	set, earth	mole	fortress		nest
bear	den, lair	mouse	hole, nest	wolf	lair
beaver	lodge	otter	holt		
bee	apiary, hive	penguin	rookery		
bird	nest, aviary	rabbit	burrow,		
eagle	eyrie		warren		
fox	earth, lair	spider	web		

Animals: Young

Animal	Young	Animal	Young	Animal	Young
ass	foal, hinny	fox	cub	pigeon	squab
bear	cub	frog	tadpole,	pike	jack
beaver	kitten		froglet	rabbit	kit
cat	kitten	gnat	bloodworm	roe deer	kid
cod	codling	goat	kid	salmon	parr, smolt,
cow	calf, heifer	goose	gosling		grilse
crane-fly	leather	grouse	poult	seal	pup
	jacket	hare	leveret	sheep	lamb
deer	fawn	hippopotamus	calf	squirrel	kitten
duck	duckling	horse	foal	swan	cygnet
eagle	eaglet	kangaroo	joey	whale	calf
eel	elver	lion	cub	zebra	foal
elephant	calf	otter	whelp		
fish	fry	pig	piglet		

Plants and Trees

abele the white poplar. Sp.: *Populus alba*.

alder betulaceous tree having toothed leaves and cone-like fruits. The bark is used in dying and tanning and the wood for bridges (as it resists underwater rot). Gen.: *Alnus*.

alfalfa leguminous plant with clover-like leaves and flowers, grown for fodder and as a salad vegetable. Aka lucerne. Sp.: *Medicago sativa*.

almond small rosaceous tree native to western Asia with pink flowers and green fruit containing edible nut. Sp.: *Prunus amygdalus*.

aloe vera Caribbean aloe yielding a gelatinous substance used in cosmetics as an emollient. Sp.: *Aloe vera*.

alsike species of clover named after Swedish town. Sp.: *Trifolium hybridum*.

anise umbelliferous plant having aromatic seeds. Sp.: *Pimpinella anisum*.

arum lily tall, lily-like, aroid plant found mainly in Southern Africa. Sp.: *Zantedeschia aethiopica*.

ash oleaceous tree with compound leaves, winged seeds and clusters of greenish flowers. Gen.: *Fraxinus*.

aspen poplar tree with especially tremulous leaves. Sp.: *Populus tremula*.

balsa bombacaceous tree of tropical America, distinguished by its very light wood. Sp.: *Ochroma lagopus*.

banyan moraceous tree of tropical India and the East Indies, having aerial roots that grow down from the branches into the soil, forming additional trunks. Sp.: *Ficus benghalensis*.

baobab African tree with an enormously thick trunk and large, edible, pulpy fruit hanging down on stalks. Sp.: *Adansonia digitata*.

barley erect, annual, temperate grass with short leaves and bristly flowers used for grain. Sp.: *Hordeum vulgares*.

bayberry North American shrub having aromatic leaves and bearing berries covered in a wax coating. Sp.: *Myrica cerifera and Myrica cerifera*.

beech hardwood tree having smooth, greyish bark. Gen.: *Fagus*.

bee orchid European and North Africa orchid with bee-shaped flowers. Sp.: *Ophrys apifera*.

betony purple-flowered plant. Sp.: *Stachys officinalis*.

bilberry hardy dwarf shrub of North Europe growing on heaths and mountains and having red drooping flowers and dark blue berries. Sp.: *Vaccinium myrtillus*.

birch hardwood, close-grained tree with thin, peeling bark. Gen.: *Betula*.

black bryony climbing plant with dark tubers and poisonous red berries. Sp.: *Tamus communis*.

black-eyed Susan flower with yellow petals and a dark centre. Gen.: *Rudbeckia*.

bladderwort aquatic plant whose leaves have small bladders for trapping and digesting insects. Gen.: *Utricularia*.

bladderwrack common brown seaweed with fronds containing air bladders that give buoyancy. Sp.: *Fucus vesiculosus*.

bleeding heart plant with heart-shaped, rose pink flowers hanging from an arched stem. Sp.: *Dicentra spectabilis*.

borage plant with bright blue flowers and hairy leaves used as flavouring. Sp.: *Borago officinalis*.

brookweed small, white-flowered plant of the primrose family growing in wet ground. Sp.: *Samolus valerandi*.

buckbean bog plant with white or pinkish hairy flowers. Sp.: *Menyanthes trifoliata*.

buckthorn (common) thorny shrub with berries formerly used as a cathartic. Sp.: *Rhamnus cathartica*.

buckwheat cereal plant with seeds used for fodder and for flour to make bread. Sp.: *Fagopyrum esculentum*.

burdock plant with prickly flowers and dock-like leaves. Gen.: *Arctium*.

busy Lizzie East African plant with abundant red, pink or white flowers, often grown as bedding or house plants. Sp.: *Impatiens walleriana*.

butterbur waterside plant with pale purple flowers and large, soft leaves formerly used to wrap butter. Gen.: *Petasites*.

buttercup yellow-flowered meadow plant of Europe and North America. Gen.: *Ranunculus*.

butterfly bush common name given to buddleia bush. Sp.: *Buddleia davidii*.

calabash tree evergreen tree, bearing fruit in the form of large gourds, native to tropical America. Sp.: *Crescentia cujete*.

calluna common heather native to Europe and North Africa. Sp.: *Calluna vulgaris*.

carambola small tree native to South-east Asia bearing golden-yellow ribbed fruit. Aka star fruit. Sp.: *Averrhoa carambola*.

cashew bushy evergreen tree native to Central and North America bearing kidney-shaped nuts attached to fleshy fruits. Sp.: *Anacardium occidentale*.

cassava (bitter) plant of the spurge family having starchy tuberous roots. Aka manioc tapioca. Sp.: *Manihot esculenta*.

catmint plant with downy leaves, purple-spotted white flowers, and a mint-like smell attractive to cats. Sp.: *Nepeta cataria*.

cedar coniferous tree having spreading branches, needle-like evergreen leaves and cones. Gen.: *Cedrus*.

celery pine Australasian tree with branchlets like celery leaves. Sp.: *Phyllocladus trichomanoides*.

charlock a wild mustard with yellow flowers. Sp.: *Sinapis arvensis*.

checkerberry North American evergreen shrub of the health family with spiny, scented leaves, white flowers and crimson fruits. Aka wintergreen. Sp.: *Gaultheria procumbens*.

cherry plum tree native to south-western Asia with solitary white flowers and red fruit. Sp.: *Prunus cerasifera*.

chervil umbelliferous plant with small white flowers; its aniseed flavoured leaves used as a herb for flavouring soup and salads. Sp.: *Anthriscus cereifolium*.

chestnut broad-leaved tree, which produces flowers in long catkins and nuts in a prickly bur. Gen.: *Castanea*.

chickpea leguminous plant with short, swollen pods containing yellow-beaked edible seed. Aka garbanza. Sp.: *Cicer arietinum*.

chicory blue-flowered plant cultivated for its salad leaves and its root, which is ground for coffee. Sp.: *Cichorium intybus*.

Chinese water chestnut sedge with rushlike leaves arising from a corm, which is used as food. Sp.: *Eleocharis tuberosa*.

chives small allium with purple-pink flowers and dense tufts of long tubular leaves, which are used as a herb. Sp.: *Allium schoenoprasum*.

Christmas rose small, white-flowered, winter-blooming plant. Sp.: *Helleborus niger*.

cinchona evergreen trees of South America, of the madder family, having fragrant flowers; the bark of this tree contains quinine. Gen.: *Cinchona*.

cineraria plant cultivated for its bright flowers. Sp.: *Pericallis cruenta*.

cloudberry small mountain bramble with a white flower and an orange-coloured fruit. Sp.: *Rubus chamaemorus*.

coco de mer palm tree of the Seychelles producing a large fruit containing a two-lobed, edible nut (world's largest seed). Sp.: *Lodoicea maldivica*.

coltsfoot plant of the daisy family with large leaves and yellow flowers. Sp.: *Tussilago farfara*.

columbine an aquilegia with purple-blue flowers. Sp.: *Aquilegia vulgaris*.

cork oak evergreen Mediterranean oak. Sp.: *Quercus suber*.

cowbane poisonous plant found in marshes. Sp.: *Cicuta virosa*.

cow parsley hedgerow plant having lacelike umbels of flowers. Sp.: *Anthriscus sylvestris*.

NATURE

cowslip   primula with fragrant yellow flowers, which grows in pastures and meadows. Sp.: *Primula veris.*

cranesbill   any of various plants of the genus *Geranium*, having pink or purple flowers and long, slender, beaked fruit.

cuckoo flower   meadow plant with pale lilac flowers. Aka lady's smock. Sp.: *Cardamine pratensis.*

cuckoo pint   wild arum with arrow-shaped leaves and scarlet berries. Sp.: *Arum maculatum.*

daffodil   bulbous plant with a yellow, trumpet-shaped corona. Sp.: *Narcissus pseudonarcissus.*

daisy   small, low-growing European plant having a rosette of white leaves and yellow centre. Sp.: *Bellis perennis.*

dawn redwood   Chinese deciduous coniferous tree of a genus first known only from fossils. Sp.: *Metasequoia glyptostroboides.*

dead man's fingers   species of orchid, *Orchis mascula.*

deadly nightshade   highly poisonous plant with drooping purple flowers and black, cherry-like fruit. Sp.: *Atropa belladonna.*

death cap   poisonous toadstool of deciduous woodland. Sp.: *Amanita phalloides.*

deodar   Himalayan cedar with drooping branches bearing large barrel-shaped cones. Tallest of the cedar family. Sp.: *Cedrus deodara.*

destroying angel   poisonous white toadstool. Sp.: *Amanita virosa.*

dewberry   shrub with bluish fruit similar to a blackberry. Sp.: *Rubus caesius.*

dill   umbelliferous herb with yellow flowers and aromatic seeds. Sp.: *Anethum graveolens.*

divi-divi   tree native to tropical America, bearing curved pods, which are a source of tannin. Sp.: *Caesalpinia coriaria.*

dog's tooth violet   plant of the Liliaceae family with speckled leaves, purple flowers and a toothed perianth. Sp.: *Erythronium dens-canis.*

Douglas fir   large conifer over 100m tall of western North America. Sp.: *Pseudotsuga menziesii.*

doum   palm tree with edible fruit. Sp.: *Hyphaene thebaica.*

dove's foot   type of cranesbill. Sp.: *Geranium molle.*

dragon tree   palm-like tree of the Canary Islands. Sp.: *Dracaena draco.*

durian   large tree native to South-east Asia, bearing oval spiny fruit containing a creamy pulp with a fetid smell but an agreeable taste. Sp.: *Durio zibethinus.*

Dutchman's breeches   plant of eastern North America with white flowers and finely divided leaves. Sp.: *Dicentra cucullaria.*

Dutchman's pipe   climbing vine of eastern North America with hooked tubular flowers. Sp.: *Aristolochia durior.*

ebony   tree with hard, dark wood often used for cabinetwork. Sometimes called persimmon. Sp.: *Diospyros ebenum.*

eglantine   wild rose with small fragrant leaves and flowers. Sp.: *Rosa eglanteria.*

elm   tree with serrated leaves and winged fruits (samaras), the wood being hard and heavy. Gen.: *Ulmus.*

endive   curly-leaved plant used in salads. Sp.: *Cichorium endivia.*

eucalyptus   myrtaceous tree native to Australia; species include blue gum and ironbark. Gen.: *Eucalyptus.*

false acacia   the locust tree, often grown for ornament. Sp.: *Robinia pseudoacacia.*

felwort   purple-flowered gentian. Sp.: *Gentianella amarella.*

fennel   yellow-flowered umbelliferous plant with fragrant seeds and fine leaves used as flavourings. Sp.: *Foeniculum vulgare.*

fenugreek   leguminous plant with aromatic seeds, which are often used in curry powder. Sp.: *Trigonella foenum-graecum.*

fern   pteridophyte plant having roots, stems and fronds and reproducing by spores formed in structures (sori) on the fronds. Division: Pteridophyta (syn. Filicinophyta).

fever tree   yellow-flowered southern African tree. Sp.: *Acacia xanthophloea.*

feverfew   aromatic, bushy plant with feathery leaves and white, daisy-like flowers, used to treat migraine and formerly to reduce fever. Sp.: *Tanacetum parthenium.*

figwort   plant of the genus *Scrophularia* with dull, purplish-brown flowers, once believed to be useful against scrofula.

flax-lily   New Zealand plant of the agave family yielding valuable fibre. Sp.: *Phormium tenax.*

forget-me-not   plant with small, yellow-eyed, bright blue flowers. Gen.: *Myosotis.*

foxglove   tall plant with erect spikes of purple or white bell-shaped flowers. Sp.: *Digitalis purpurea.*

fraxinella   aromatic plant of rue family having foliage that emits an ethereal inflammable oil. Aka burning bush. Sp.: *Dictamnus albus.*

gentian   plants found in mountainous regions, having violet or blue trumpet-shaped flowers. Gen.: *Gentiana.*

gerbera   any plant of the genus *Gerbera*, of Africa or Asia, especially the Transvaal daisy. Gen.: *Gerbera.*

germander   any of various plants of the genus *Teucrium*, typically a mildly aromatic, white-felted perennial shrublet with a compact domed shape. The flowers, which appear between April and July, are reddish or purplish in colour. Germander was used in Cypriot folk-medicine as a cure for stomach ailments and jaundice.

germander speedwell   creeping plant with germander-like leaves and blue flowers. US name: bird's-eye speedwell. Sp.: *Veronica chamaedrys.*

ginger   hot, spicy root, which can be powdered for use in cooking, or preserved in syrup, or candied. Sp.: *Zingiber officinale.*

gladiolus   plants of *Iridaceae* family with sword-shaped leaves and brightly coloured flower spikes. Gen.: *Gladiolus.*

goatsbeard   Eurasian plant with woolly stems and large heads of yellow-rayed flowers surrounded by large, green bracts. Sp.: *Tragopogon pratensis.*

goatsbeard   American rosaceous plant with long spikes of small white flowers. Gen.: *Aruncus.*

goat's-rue   Eurasian leguminous plant cultivated for its white, mauve or pinkish flowers. Sp.: *Galega officinalis.*

goat's-rue   North American leguminous plant with pink-and-yellow flowers. Sp.: *Tephrosia virginiana.*

good King Henry   weed of the goosefoot family. Sp.: *Chenopodium bonus-henricus.*

goosefoot   plant that has small greenish flowers and leaves like the foot of a goose. Gen.: *Chenopodium.*

gopher   North American tree, yielding yellowish timber aka yellowwood. Not to be confused with the field gopher tree from which Noah's Ark was reputedly built. Sp.: *Cladrastis lutea*.

grass monocotyledonous plants encompassing all the cereal plants as well as reeds and bamboos. Family *Gramineae*.

greenheart tropical American evergreen tree of the laurel family. Gen.: *Ocotea rodiaei*.

guaiacum trees native to tropical America with hard, dense, oily timber. Gen.: *Guaiacum*.

guava small tropical American tree bearing an edible, pale orange fruit with pinky, juicy flesh. Sp.: *Psidium guajava*.

guelder rose deciduous shrub with round bunches of creamy-white flowers. Sp.: *Viburnum opulus*.

guernsey lily nerine, originally from South Africa, with large, pink, lily-like flowers. Sp.: *Nerine sarniensis*.

hare's-foot clover with soft hair around the flowers. Sp.: *Trifolium arvense*.

hart's tongue fern with narrow undivided fronds. Sp.: *Phyllitis scolopendrium*.

hawthorn thorny shrub or tree with white, red or pink blossom and small, dark red fruit or haws. Sp.: *Crataegus monogyna*.

hazel small tree bearing round brown edible nuts. Sp.: *Corylus avellana*.

henbane poisonous herbaceous plant with sticky hairy leaves and an unpleasant smell. Sp.: *Hyoscyamus niger*.

henna tropical shrub having small pink, red or white flowers; the reddish dye from its shoots and leaves is used to colour hair. Sp.: *Lawsonia inermis*.

herb Christopher white-flowered baneberry. Sp.: *Actaea spicata*.

herb Paris plant with a single flower and four leaves in a cross shape on an unbranched stem. Sp.: *Paris quadrifolia*.

herb Robert common cranesbill with red-stemmed leaves and pink flowers. Sp.: *Geranium robertianum*.

holly evergreen tree with prickly leaves and red berries, often used as Christmas decorations. Gen.: *Ilex*.

hop climbing plant cultivated for the cones borne by the female, used in brewing. Sp.: *Humulus lupulus*.

hornbeam tree of the genus *Carpinus* with a smooth bark and a hard tough wood. Gen.: *Carpinus*.

horse chestnut Eurasian tree with palmate leaves and inedible nuts enclosed in a spiky bur (conkers). Sp.: *Aesculus hippocastanum*.

horse mushroom large, edible mushroom. Sp.: *Agaricus arvensis*.

horseradish cruciferous plant with long, lobed leaves. Sp.: *Armoracia rusticana*.

hortensia kind of hydrangea (distinct from lacecap) with large, round, infertile flower heads. Sp.: *Hydrangea macrophylla*.

huckleberry North American shrub with blue or black soft fruit. Gen.: *Gaylussacia*.

Iceland poppy Arctic poppy with white or yellow flowers. Sp.: *Papaver nudicaule*.

Indian hemp strong-smelling Asian moraceous plant. Aka marijuana, Cannabis. Sp.: *Cannabis indica*.

ivy climbing plants having lobed evergreen leaves and black, berry-like fruits. Gen.: *Hedera*.

jack-by-the-hedge white-flowered cruciferous plant of shady places. Sp.: *Alliaria petiolata*.

jackfruit East Indian tree bearing fruit resembling breadfruit. Sp.: *Artocarpus heterophyllus*.

japonica flowering shrub with round white, green or yellow, edible fruit and bright red flowers. Sp.: *Chaenomeles speciosa*.

jarrah the Western Australian mahogany gum tree. Sp.: *Eucalyptus marginata*.

jasmine oleaceous shrub or climbing plant whose fragrant flowers are used in perfumery. Gen.: *Jasminum*.

kangaroo paw Australian plant with irregular woolly flowers. Floral emblem of Western Australia. Sp.: *Anigozanthos manglesii*.

kangaroo vine evergreen climbing plant with serrated leaves. Sp.: *Cissus antarctica*.

kidney vetch yellow-flavoured leguminous plant found in grassland. Aka lady's finger. Sp.: *Anthyllis vulneraria*.

knotweed fast-growing Japanese plant. Sp.: *Fallopia japonica*.

ladino large type of white clover native to Italy and cultivated for fodder. Sp.: *Trifolium repens*.

lamb's ears garden plant with whitish, woolly leaves. Sp.: *Stachys byzantina*.

lemon balm bushy plant with leaves smelling and tasting of lemon. Sp.: *Melissa officinalis*.

lemon geranium lemon-scented pelargonium. Sp.: *Pelargonium crispum*.

lemon verbena shrub with lemon-scented leaves. Aka lemon plant. Sp.: *Aloysia triphylla*.

leopard's bane any plant of the genus *Doronicum* with large, yellow, daisy-like flowers. Sp.: *Doronicum*.

live oak American evergreen tree. Sp.: *Quercus virginiana*.

loquat tree of the Rosaceae family, bearing small, yellow, egg-shaped fruit. Sp.: *Eriobotrya japonica*.

love-in-a-mist blue-flowered garden plant with many delicate green bracts. Sp.: *Nigella damascena*.

love-lies-bleeding garden plant with drooping spikes of purple-red blooms. Sp.: *Amaranthus caudatus*.

lungwort Eurasian plant with spotted leaves and clusters of blue or purple flowers. Sp.: *Pulmonaria officinalis*.

lungwort (sea) boraginaceous plant of the northern temperate genus *Mertensia*, with drooping clusters of tubular, usually blue flowers. Aka oyster plant. Gen.: *Mertensia maritima*.

madder plant with small yellow flowers and a red fleshy root. Gen.: *Rubia*.

mahogany tropical tree yielding a hard, reddish-brown wood used for furniture making. Sp.: *Swietenia mahagoni*.

mandrake poisonous plant with white, or purple flowers and large yellow fruit, having emetic and narcotic properties and possessing a root once thought to resemble the human form and to shriek when plucked. Sp.: *Mandragora officinarum*.

mangosteen Malaysian tree bearing a white juicy-pulped fruit with a thick, reddish-brown rind. Sp.: *Garcinia mangostana*.

mangrove any tropical tree or shrub of the genus *Rhizophora* growing in shore-mud with many tangled roots above ground. Gen.: *Rhizophora*.

Manila hemp Philippine plant with a strong fibre used for rope-making. Sp.: *Musa textilis*.

manuka small New Zealand tree with aromatic leaves and hard timber. Sp.: *Leptospermum scoparium*.

maple any tree or shrub of the genus *Acer*, grown for shade, ornament, wood, or sugar.

NATURE

marsh mallow herbaceous plant, the roots of which were formerly used to make a sweet confection. Sp.: *Althaea officinalis.*

marsh marigold golden-flowered plant, which grows in moist pastures. Sp.: *Caltha palustris.*

martagon lily with small, purple, turban-like flowers. Sp.: *Lilium martagon.*

marvel of Peru showy garden plant with flowers opening at dusk. Sp.: *Mirabilis jalapa.*

mayapple American herbaceous plant bearing a yellow, egg-shaped fruit in May. Sp.: *Podophyllum peltatum.*

mayflower In North America trailing arbutus that blooms in May. Sp.: *Epigaea repens.*

maz(z)ard the wild sweet cherry of Europe. Sp.: *Prunus avium.*

meadow rue plants of the buttercup family with small yellow or purple flowers. Gen.: *Thalictrum.*

meadow saffron meadow plant resembling a crocus and producing lilac flowers in autumn, while still leafless. Sp.: *Colchicum autumnale.*

meadowsweet plant of the Rosaceae family, common in meadows and damp places, with creamywhite fragrant flowers. Also the name of a North American plant of the genus *Spiraea.* Sp.: *Filipendula ulmaria.*

medlar tree of the rose family bearing small brown apple-like fruits, which are best eaten when overripe. Sp.: *Mespilus germanica.*

mignonette plants of the genus *Reseda,* some having aromatic grey-green flowers.

mimosa Leguminous shrub having globular yellow flowers and sensitive leaflets, which droop when touched. Sp.: *Mimosa pudica.*

mistletoe parasitic plant growing on apple and other trees and bearing white, glutinous berries in winter. Americans have a related plant of the genus *Phoradendron.* Sp.: *Viscum album.*

mock pennyroyal North American aromatic plant. Sp.: *Hedeoma pulegioides.*

moneywort trailing evergreen plant with round glossy leaves and yellow flowers. Sp.: *Lysimachia nummularia.*

monkey flower short creeping plant with bright yellow flowers. Sp.: *Mimulus guttatus.*

monkey-puzzle coniferous tree native to Chile with downward-pointing branches and small, close-set leaves. Aka Chile pine. Sp.: *Araucaria araucana.*

montbretia hybrid plant of genus *Crocosmia* with bright, orange-yellow, trumpet-shaped flowers.

morning glory any of various twining plants, with trumpet-shaped flowers, of the genus *Ipomoea.*

mother-in-law's tongue plant with long, erect, pointed leaves. Sp.: *Sansevieria trifasciata.*

mung bean leguminous plants of the genus *Vigna,* native to India and yielding a small bean used as food.

musk-rose rambling rose with large, white flowers smelling of musk. Sp.: *Rosa moschata.*

musk thistle nodding thistle whose flowers have a musky fragrance. Sp.: *Carduus nutans.*

musk tree Australian tree with a musky smell. Sp.: *Olearia argyrophylla.*

mustard plant eaten at the seedling stage, often with cress, and whose seeds are crushed and made into a paste and used as a spicy condiment. Sp.: *Sinapis alba.*

mustard plant with slender pods and yellow flowers. Sp.: *Brassica nigra.*

myrtle evergreen shrub with aromatic foliage and white flowers with purple-black ovoid berries. Sp.: *Myrtus communis.*

narcissus yellow, orange or white flowered plants with crown surrounded by spreading segments. Gen.: *Narcissus*

nardoo clover-like plant of Australian origin. Sp.: *Marsilea drummondii.*

nasturtium Any cruciferous plant of the genus Nasturtium, including watercress. Trailing plants of the Americas with rounded edible leaves and bright orange, yellow or red flowers of the genus *Tropaeolum.*

nopal cactus having yellow flowers and purple fruits, sometimes called prickly pear. Gen.: *Opuntia.*

oak any tree of the genus *Quercus,* having lobed leaves and bearing acorns.

obeche West African tree. Sp.: *Triplochiton scleroxylon.*

okra African edible plant of the mallow family. Aka gumbo or ladies' fingers. Sp.: *Abelmoschus esculentus.*

orpin(e) succulent, herbaceous, purple-flowered plant. Sp.: *Sedum telephium.*

ox-eye daisy plant of the daisy family, with large white flowers with yellow centres. Sp.: *Leucanthemum vulgare.*

oxlip woodland primula. Sp.: *Primula elatior.*

ox-tongue plant of the daisy family with bright yellow flowers. Gen.: *Picris.*

palmyra Asian palm with fan-shaped leaves used for matting. Sp.: *Borassus flabellifer.*

parsley biennial herb with white flowers and crinkly aromatic leaves. Sp.: *Petroselinum crispum.*

parsley fern fern with leaves like parsley. Sp.: *Cryptogramma crispa.*

passion flower any climbing plant of the genus *Passiflora* with a flower that was supposed to suggest the instruments of the Crucifixion.

patchouli strongly scented south Asian shrub from which a perfume is made. Gen.: *Pogostemon.*

peanut leguminous plant bearing pods that ripen underground and contain seeds used as food and yielding oil. Sp.: *Arachis hypogaea.*

pedunculate oak a common oak in which clusters of acorns are borne on long stalks. Sp.: *Quercus robur.*

peepul (pipal) moraceous tree of tropical India and the East Indies, resembling the banyan, and thought of as sacred by Buddhists because the founder of the religion is said to have found enlightenment while sitting under its branches. Sp.: *Ficus religiosa.*

pennyroyal creeping mint cultivated for its supposed medicinal properties. Sp.: *Mentha pulegium.*

periwinkle tropical shrub native to Madagascar. Sp.: *Catharanthus roseus.*

periwinkle any of several Eurasian apocynaceous evergreen plants of the genus *Vinca,* having trailing stems and blue flowers. Aka creeping myrtle or trailing myrtle (USA).

pine coniferous evergreen with long, needle-shaped leaves and brown cones. Gen.: *Pinus.*

pinkster flower the pink azalea. Sp.: *Rhododendron periclymenoides.*

piripiri plant of the rose family native to New Zealand and having prickly burs. Sp.: *Acaena anserinifolia.*

poplar salicaceous tree with triangular leaves, light, soft wood and flowers borne in catkins. Gen.: *Populus.*

prickly pear cactus of the genus *Opuntia*, native to arid regions of America and bearing barbed bristles and large, pear-shaped, prickly fruits.

ragged robin pink-flowered campion with spiky, tattered-looking petals. Aka cuckoo flower. Sp.: *Lychnis flos-cuculi.*

rose shrub or climbing plant having prickly stems and fragrant flowers. Gen.: *Rosa.*

rowan tree with delicate pinnate leaves and scarlet berries. Sp.: *Sorbus aucuparia.*

rue dwarf shrub with bipinnate or tripinnate glaucous leaves and yellow flowers. Gen.: *Ruta.*

salsify Mediterranean plant having grass-like leaves, purple flower heads and a long, white edible taproot. Aka oyster plant or vegetable oyster. Sp.: *Tragopogon porrifolius.*

shaddock tree named after Captain Shaddoch who brought the seed to Barbados. Aka pomelo. Sp.: *Citrus maxima.*

shamrock most common shamrock is the wood sorrel, *Oxalis acetosella*, and this is the plant worn on St Patrick's Day. Other trifoliate shamrocks include black medic (*Medicago lupulina*) and white clover (*Trifolium repens*).

snake's head bulbous plant with bell-shaped, pendent flowers. Sp.: *Fritillaria meleagris.*

southernwood bushy kind of wormwood. Sp.: *Artemisia abrotanum.*

sweet marjoram one of two aromatic herbs (the other being wild marjoram) whose fresh dried leaves are used as a flavouring in cookery. Sp.: *Majorana hortensis.*

teak large, verbenaceous tree of East Indies yielding a hard, valuable yellow-brown wood. Sp.: *Tectona grandis.*

tobacco solanaceous plant having hairy leaves, and funnel-shaped, fragrant flowers. Gen.: *Nicotiana.*

tomatillo Mexican ground cherry bearing purplish, edible fruit. Sp.: *Physalis philadelphica.*

tomato plant of the nightshade family bearing glossy red or yellow pulpy edible fruit. Sp.: *Lycopersicon esculentum.*

toothwort parasitic plant with toothlike, root scales. Sp.: *Lathraea squamaria.*

toquilla palm-like tree native to South America. Sp.: *Carludovica palmata.*

trailing arbutus see mayflower.

Transvaal daisy plant of the Asteraceae family. Gen.: *Gerbera.*

traveller's joy wild clematis. Aka old man's beard. Sp.: *Clematis vitalba.*

tree mallow tall, woody-stemmed European mallow of cliffs and rocks. Sp.: *Lavatera arborea.*

tree tomato South American shrub with egg-shaped, red fruit. Sp.: *Cyphomandra betacea.*

tulip bulbous, spring-flowering plant of a variety of colours. The word tulip is derived from the Turkish *Tülbend*, meaning turban, from the shape of the expanded flower. Gen.: *Tulipa.*

tulip tree North American tree with tulip-like flowers and lobed leaves. Gen.: *Liriodendron tulipifera.*

tumbleweed plant of arid areas of North America and Australia. Its globular bush breaks off in late summer and is tumbled about by the wind, spreading its seed. Gen.: *Amaranthus alba.*

turmeric tropical Asian plant of the Zingiberaceae family, yielding aromatic rhizomes used as a spice and for yellow dye. Sp.: *Curcuma longa.*

umbrella plant African sedge having large umbrella-like whorls of slender leaves and widely grown as an ornamental water plant. Sp.: *Cyperus alternifolius.*

umbrella tree North American magnolia having long leaves clustered into an umbrella formation at the ends of the branches and unpleasant-smelling, white flowers. Sp.: *Magnolia tripetala.*

vetch plant largely used for silage and fodder. Sp.: *Vicia sativa.*

violet low-growing plant characterised by horizontal petals and purple, cordate leaves. Gen.: *Viola.*

viper's bugloss stiff bristly blue-flowered plant. Sp.: *Echium vulgare.*

wall fern an evergreen polypody with very large leaves. Sp.: *Polypodium vulgare.*

wallflower spring-flowering garden plant with fragrant yellow, orange-red or dark red flowers. Sp.: *Cheiranthus cheiri.*

wall germander European germander having two-lipped pinkish-purple flowers with a very small upper lip. Sp.: *Teucrium chamaedrys.*

wall rue small fern with leaves like rue, growing on walls and rocks. Aka spleewort. Sp.: *Asplenium ruta-muraria.*

walnut tree having aromatic leaves and drooping catkins, the nut of which contains a wrinkled edible kernel in two halves and enclosed in a green fruit. Gen.: *Juglans.*

wandering jew climbing plant with stemless, variegated leaves. Gen.: *Tradescantia albiflora.*

water chestnut aquatic plant bearing an edible seed. Sp.: *Trapa natans.*

water hyacinth tropical American aquatic plant which is a serious weed of waterways in warm countries. Sp.: *Eichhornia crassipes.*

watercress hardy perennial cress growing in running water, with pungent leaves used in salad. Sp.: *Nasturtium officinale.*

wayfaring tree white-flowered European and Asian shrub, common along roadsides, with berries turning from green through red to black. Sp.: *Viburnum lantana.*

wild marjoram one of two aromatic herbs (the other being sweet marjoram) whose fresh dried leaves are used as a flavouring in cookery. Sp.: *Origanum vulgare.*

wild pansy Eurasian plant having purple, yellow, and pale mauve spurred flowers, aka heartsease, love-in-idleness. Sp.: *Viola tricolor.*

willow white-wood tree with graceful flexible branches and catkins. Gen.: *Salix.*

wintergreen low-growing plants with drooping spikes of white, bell-shaped flowers. Gen.: *Pyrola.*

witch alder American shrub with leaves like that of the alder. Sp.: *Fothergilla gardenii.*

witch hazel North American shrub with yellow flowers, the leaves and bark used to treat bruises. Gen.: *Hamamelis virginiana.*

woad glaucous, yellow-flowered cruciferous plant formerly grown for its blue dye. Sp.: *Isatis tinctoria.*

wolfsbane various ranunculaceous plants with hooded purple or yellow flowers. Aka aconite, monkshood. Gen.: *Aconitum.*

wood anemone wild spring-flowering, anemone. Sp.: *Anemone nemorosa.*

woodruff white-flowered plant grown for the fragrance of its whorled leaves when dried or crushed. Sp.: *Galium odoratum.*

NATURE

woody nightshade scrambling woody Eurasian plant with purple flowers and recurved petals with protruding cone of yellow anthers and poisonous, red, berry-like fruits. Aka bittersweet. Sp.: *Solanum dulcamara*.

wych elm Eurasian elm with large rough leaves and pliant branches. Sp.: *Ulmus glabra*.

yellow archangel Eurasian yellow-flowered nettle. Sp.: *Lamiastrum galeobdolon*.

yellow flag yellow-flowered iris with slender, sword-shaped leaves. Sp.: *Iris pseudacorus*.

yellow rattle yellow-flowered herb, which is partly parasitic. Sp.: *Rhinanthus minor*.

yellow toadflax plant with narrow leaves like flax and spurred yellow flowers. Sp.: *Linaria vulgaris*.

yerba buena (good herb) North American trailing plant with lilac flowers formally used by Californian

Americans to make a medicinal tea. Sp.: *Satureja douglasii*.

yerba santa North American shrub whose leaves are used medicinally. Lit. 'holy herb'. Sp.: *Eriodictyon californicum*.

yew Dark-leaved evergreen coniferous tree having seeds enclosed in a fleshy red aril, and often planted in churchyards. Gen.: *Taxus*.

yiang-ylang / ilang-ilang. Malaysian tree from which a fragrant perfume is distilled. Sp.: *Cananga odorata*.

Yorkshire fog fodder grass. Sp.: *Holcus lanatus*.

yucca plant of Agavaceae family with woody stem and sword-shaped leaves. Aka Adam's needle. Gen.: *Yucca*.

Miscellaneous Information

agriculture: soilless hydroponics.

allogamy cross-fertilisation in plants.

angiosperm flower-producing plants that reproduce by seeds enclosed within a carpel, including herbaceous plants, herbs, shrubs, grasses and most trees.

carnations: types of self (one colour), fancy (multi-coloured), picotee (pale with darker edge).

carnivorous plants pitcher plant, sundew, venus fly trap.

deciduous conifer larch, swamp cypress.

Dutch elm disease disease of elms, often fatal, caused by the fungus *Ceratocystis ulmi* and spread by bark beetles.

entomophily pollination by insects.

entophyte plant growing inside a plant or animal.

epiphyte plant growing on another but not parasitic on it, e.g. a moss on a tree trunk.

fastest growth bamboo (about 38 cm, 15 inches a day).

flower parts female part: pistil male part: stamen Perfect flower: contains male and female parts. Stigma: mouth of the pistil, which receives the pollen in impregnation. Style: neck of the pistil, which contains the stigma. Ovary: swollen basal part of the pistil containg the ovules.

frond the compound leaf of a fern or a palm.

garden city: First Letchworth in Herts (1903), founded by Ebenezer Howard.

gymnosperm any of various plants having seeds unprotected by an ovary, including conifers, cycads and ginkgo.

halophyte plant adapted to saline conditions.

largest living thing a Californian redwood tree, *Sequoia sempervirens*, nicknamed the General Sherman (275 feet high and 1,385 tons in weight).

leaves: types of bract, stipule and pinnate.

mulch half-rotten vegetable matter used to prevent soil erosion.

nettle sting: cause formic acid.

oak apples: caused by wasp eggs.

oldest tree a bristlecone pine (*Pinus longaera*) nicknamed Old Methuselah. Approx 5,000 years old and situated in the White Mountains, California.

osmosis the passage of a solvent through a semi-permeable membrane from a less concentrated to a more concentrated solution until both solutions are of the same concentration. Wilhelm Pfeffer, a

German plant physiologist, first studied osmosis in 1877, although the term was introduced by the British chemist Thomas Graham in 1854. Osmosis is the method used by plants for water absorption.

pergola arbour or covered walk, formed of growing plants trained over trellis-work.

plant families apple – rose (Rosaceae); ash – olive (Oleaceae); asparagus – lily (Liliaceae); aubergine – nightshade (Solanum); avocado – laurel (Lauraceae); bamboo - grass (Gramineae); barley – grass (Gramineae); blackberry – rose (Rosaceae); bluebell – lily (Liliaceae); breadfruit – mulberry (Moraceae); broccoli – cabbage (Brassica); brussels sprout – cabbage (Brassica); buckwheat – dock (Polygonaceae); camellia – tea (Theaceae); carrot – parsley (Apiaceae); cauliflower – cabbage (Brassica); celery – parsley (Apiaceae); cherry – rose (Rosaceae); chives – lily (Liliaceae); cinnamon – laurel (Lauraceae); coffee – madder (Rubiaceae); cork oak – beech (Fagacrab); cotton – mallow (Malvaceae); dandelion – daisy (Compositae); elder – honeysuckle (Caprifoliaceae); fig – mulberry (Moraceae); garlic – lily (Liliaceae); gooseberry – Grossulariaceae); guelder Rose – (Caprifoliaceae); hemlock – parsley (Apiaceae); hemp - mulberry (Moraceae); hop – mulberry (Moraceae); hyacinth – lily (Liliaceae); jasmine –olive (Oleaceae); Jerusalem artichoke – daisy (Compositae); knot-grass (Aka Allseed) – dock (Polygonaceae); leek – lily (Liliaceae); lemon – rue (Rutaceae); lettuce – daisy (Compositae); lilac – olive (Oleaceae); lime – rue (Rutaceae); maize – grass (Gramineae); mari-juana – mulberry (Moraceae); mustard – cabbage (Brassica); okra – mallow (Malvaceae); onion – lily (Liliaceae); orange – rue (Rutaceae); parsnip – parsley (Apiaceae); peach – rose (Rosaceae); pear – rose (Rosaceae); plum – rose (Rosaceae); potato – nightshade (Solanum); privet – olive (Oleaceae); radish – cabbage (Brassica); rape – cabbage (Brassica); raspberry – rose (Rosaceae); rhubarb – dock (Polygonaceae); rye – grass (Gramineae); shallot – lily (Liliaceae); sorrel – dock (Polygonaceae); strawberry – rose (Rosaceae); swede – cabbage (Brassica); thistle – daisy (Compositae); tobacco – nightshade (Solanum); tomato – nightshade (Solanum); tulip – lily (Liliaceae); turnip – cabbage (Brassica); vanilla – orchid (Orchidaceae); wheat – grass (Gramineae).

plants: products from agar agar – seaweed; amber – pine tree resin; aspirin – willow tree (originally);

atropine – deadly nightshade; cocaine – coca plant; cochineal – beetles; copra – coconut; digitalis – foxglove; frankincense (*Olibanum*) – tree bark resin (*Boswellia*); henna dye – leaves of henna plant; heroin – opium poppy; hessian – plant root; linen – spun flax; linseed oil – seeds of flax plant; madder – plant root; morphine – opium poppy; myrrh – myrrh tree resin; opium – opium poppy (*Papaver somniferum*); quinine – cinchona bark; raffia – palm; saffron – crocus; semolina – wheat; tapioca – cassava root; turmeric – curcuma plant; turpentine – coniferous trees (especially pine).

pomegranate: varieties   paper-shell, Spanish ruby, wonderful.

roots: types of   adventitious, aerial, climbing, contralie, lateral, pneumatophore, prop.

Royal Horticultural Society   Founded in 1804 and in its centenary year of 1904 established Wisley as its Show Garden.

sacking: fibre used for   jute.

scandents   climbing plants.

sweet pea: from   Sicily.

tallest tree   Douglas fir.

taxonomy   classification of living organisms into groups in an organised hierarchy. The largest group is the kingdom – e.g. Plants (Plantae); Animals (Animalia). Below the Kingdom; in descending order, come: Phylum, Class, Subclass; Order, Family, Genus, Species.

toadstool: most poisonous   deathcap.

tomato: original name   love apple.

tudor rose   conventionalized 5-lobed figure of a rose; the white and the red rose were adopted as the symbols of the Houses of York and Lancaster during the Wars of the Roses.

tulip: named from   the Turkish turban *Tülbend*.

underwater: grows   rice.

vanilla: family   orchid family.

variegation   different colourings of a leaf.

xerophyte   plant, such as cacti, that grows in dry conditions.

yucca tree: pollination   only by the yucca moth, *Pronuba* (Tegetierila) *yuccasella*.

Alternative Names of Flowers, Plants and Trees

Aaron's beard	rose of Sharon	clematis	traveller's joy
	althaea	columbine	aquilegia
adder's tongue	dogtooth violet	cow parsley	Queen Anne's
abele	white poplar		lace
abelmosk	musk mallow	cowbane	water hemlock
althaea	Aaron's beard	cowslip	marsh marigold
amaryllis	belladonna lily		(USA)
antirrhinum	snapdragon	cranberry	fen-berry
aquilegia	columbine	creeping myrtle	periwinkle
arum lily	calla lily	cuckoo flower	ragged Robin
Australian sword lily	kangaroo paw		lady's smock
autumn crocus	meadow saffron	cuckoo pint	jack-in-the-pulpit
baby's breath	gypsophila		lords and ladies
baobab	monkey bread		wake-Robin
	tree	dasheen	elephant's ear
bayberry	wax myrtle	deadly nightshade	belladonna
bergenia	elephant's ear	delphinium	larkspur
belladonna lily	amaryllis	dittany	Fraxinella
belladonna	deadly	dogtooth violet	adder's tongue
	nightshade	dwale	belladonna
	dwale	eddo	elephant's ear
bluebell	wild hyacinth	eglantine	sweet brier
bog myrtle	sweet gale		bergenia
bo tree	peepul		Chinese eddo
bogbean	buckbean	elephant's ear	eddo
buckbean	bogbean		dasheen
burning bush	Fraxinella		taro
calla lily	arum lily	fen-berry	cranberry
cardinal flower	scarlet lobelia	field mustard	charlock
carnation	gillyflower	fleur-de-lis	iris
catmint	catnip	fraxinella	dittany
catnip	catmint		burning bush
charlock	field mustard		gas plant
checkerberry	wintergreen	French lilac	goat's-rue
Chile pine	monkey puzzle		(Eurasian
Chinese eddo	elephant's ear		plant)
chionodoxa	glory-of-the-	gas plant	fraxinella
	snow	gillyflower	carnation
chlorophytum	spider plant	ginkgo	maidenhair tree

gladiolus — sword lily
glory-of-the-snow — chionodoxa
goatsbeard (Eurasian plant) — Jack-go-to-bed-at-noon
goat's-rue (Eurasian plant) — French lilac
golden chain — laburnum
guaiacum — lignum vitae
guelder Rose — snowball tree
gumbo — okra
gypsophilia — baby's breath
hawthorn — may / quickthorn / whitethorn

Johnny-jump-up (USA) — love-in-idleness / wild pansy

heartsease — nasturtium?

Indian cress — nasturtium
iris — fleur-de-lis
Jack-go-to-bed-at-noon — goatsbeard (Eurasian plant)

Jack-in-the-pulpit — cuckoo pint
Japanese quince — japonica
japonica — Japanese quince

Johnny-jump-up (USA) — heartsease
kangaroo paw — Australian sword lily

kidney vetch — lady's finger
kingcup — marsh marigold
laburnum — golden chain
ladies' fingers — okra
lady's finger — kidney vetch
lad's love — southernwood
lady's smock — cuckoo flower
larkspur — delphinium
lignum vitae — guaiacum
lime tree — linden tree
linden tree — lime tree
livelong — orpin(e)
lords and ladies — cuckoo pint
love-in-idleness — heartsease
lungwort — oyster-plant
maidenhair tree — ginkgo
mandrake — may apple
marsh marigold — kingcup
marsh marigold (USA) — cowslip
may — hawthorn
may apple — mandrake
mayflower — trailing arbutus
meadow saffron — autumn crocus / naked ladies / naked boys

moneywort — wandering sailor
monkey bread tree — baobab
monkey puzzle — Chile pine
mountain ash — rowan

musk mallow — abelmosk
naked boys — meadow saffron
naked ladies — meadow saffron
nasturtium — Indian cress
okra — gumbo / ladies' fingers

old man's beard — traveller's joy
orpin(e) — livelong
oyster-plant — lungwort / salsify

pandanus — screw-pine
peepul — bo tree
periwinkle — creeping myrtle / trailing myrtle

pink azalea — pinkster flower
pinkster flower — pink azalea
Queen Anne's lace — cow parsley
quickthorn — hawthorn
ragged Robin — cuckoo flower
Rose of Sharon — Aaron's beard / althaea

rowan — mountain ash
salsify — oyster-plant / vegetable oyster

scarlet lobelia — cardinal flower
screw – pine — pandanus
snapdragon — antirrhinum
snowball tree — guelder rose
southernwood — lad's love
spider plant — chlorophytum
sweet brier — eglantine
sweet gale — bog myrtle
sword lily — gladiolus
taro — elephant's ear
trailing arbutus — mayflower
trailing myrtle — periwinkle
traveller's joy — clematis
vegetable oyster — salsify
Virginia creeper — woodbine (USA)
wake-Robin — cuckoo pint
wandering sailor — moneywort
water hemlock — cowbane
wax myrtle — bayberry
white poplar — abele
whitethorn — hawthorn
wild honeysuckle — woodbine
wild hyacinth — bluebell
wild pansy — heartsease
winter cress — yellow rocket
wintergreen — checkerberry
woodbine — wild honeysuckle

woodbine (USA) — Virginia creeper
yellow rocket — winter cress

NB: All the alternatives have been listed alphabetically for ease of reference.

Birds

alcid bird of the auk famil, Sp.: *Alcidae*.

Andean condor world's largest bird of prey with a wingspan of 3 metres and body weight of up to 15 kilograms. Sp.: *Vultur gryphus*.

avadavat: green and red South Asian waxbills (aka amadavat). Sp.: *Amandava formosa* and *Amandava amandava*.

avocet white bird with black-patterned head and back; its most notable feature is the upcurved bill. Sp.: *Recurvirostra avosetta*.

bateleur short-tailed African eagle. Sp.: *Terathopius ecaudatus*.

bean goose similar to the pink-footed goose but distinguished by its orange bill and feet. Sp.: *Anser fabalis*.

bee-eater exotic European bird with yellow throat and multi-coloured plumage. Sp.: *Merops apiaster*.

bittern bird of the heron family with a brown and buff plumage barred with black, and famous for its booming call. Sp.: *Botaurus stellaris*.

black grouse spectacular bird with a lyre-shaped tail, the cocks having black plumage and the hens, grey. The black grouse is famous for its courtship display during the mating season. Sp.: *Lyrurus tetrix*.

blackbird black bird of the thrush family having a yellow beak, the female having a dark brown plume. Sp.: *Turdus merula*.

blackcap small songbird, nicknamed 'the monk' in Germany because of its grey plumage and distinct black cap. Sp.: *Sylvia atricapilla*.

bobolink North American oriole originally called Bob o' Lincoln. Sp.: *Dolichonyx oryzivorus*.

boobook brown spotted owl, native to Australia and New Zealand. Sp.: *Ninox novaeseelandiae*.

booby tropical marine bird, similar to a gannet, with a straight, stout bill and white plumage with darker markings. Gen.: *Sula*.

bowerbird bird native to Australia and New Guinea; the males construct elaborate bowers of feathers, grasses and shells. Family *Ptilonorhynchidae*.

budgerigar small, green parakeet native to Australia, bred in coloured varieties and often kept as cage birds. Sp.: *Melopsittacus undulatus*.

bulbul Asian or African songbird of dull plumage with contrasting bright patches. Family *Pycnonotidae*.

bullfinch small plump finch with black head, grey-blue back and red breast. Sp.: *Pyrrhula pyrrhula*.

bunting: corn. seed-eating bird related to the finches with a streaked, sparrow-like plumage. Sp.: *Emberiza calandra*.

bustard: great large, mainly terrestrial bird with long neck, long legs and stout tapering body. Sp.: *Otis tarda*.

buzzard predatory bird of the hawk family with broad wings, well adapted for soaring flight. Sp.: *Buteo buteo*.

capercaillie largest of the grouse family and extinct in Britain from the late 18th until mid-19th century. Sp.: *Tetrao urogallus*.

cassowary large, flightless bird of Australia and the Malay Archipelago, with heavy body, stout legs, a wattled neck and a bony crest on its forehead. Gen.: *Casuarius*.

chaffinch common European finch, the male of which has a blue-grey head with pinkish cheeks and breast. Sp.: *Fringilla coelebs*.

chough large black bird of the crow family, seen in Europe, Asia and Africa, with a long, downward-curving red bill and red legs. Sp.: *Pyrrhocorax pyrrhocorax*.

chukar red-legged Eurasian partridge. Sp.: *Alectoris chukar*.

collared turtle dove similar to the turtle dove but with a black half moon on the back of its neck, which gives rise to the name. Sp.: *Streptopelia decaocto*.

coot resembles an oversized moorhen, although the breast is grey-black and the beak is white rather than yellow and red. Sp.: *Fulica atra*.

cormorant diving seabird with lustrous black plumage. Sp.: *Phalacrocorax carbo*.

corncrake rail with a rasping call, inhabiting grassland and nesting on the ground. Sp.: *Crex crex*.

cotinga any member of the large and varied New World tropical family Cotingidae, many with vivid plumage and unusually modified heel feathers.

cowbird North American oriole which often eats insects stirred up by grazing cattle and is known to lay its eggs in other birds' nests. Gen.: *Molothrus*.

crane long-legged, long-necked wading bird, which inhabits marshes and plains in most parts of the world except South America. Sp.: *Grus grus*.

crested lark often kept as a cage bird, not only for its own song but also for its ability to imitate the calls and cries of other birds. Sp.: *Galerida cristata*.

crossbill finch having a bill with crossed mandibles with which it opens pine cones. Gen.: *Loxia curvirostra*.

crow: carrion common predatory and scavenging European crow, similar to the rook but having a pure black bill. Sp.: *Corvus corone*.

crow: hooded highly intelligent bird with jet black and ashen grey plumage. Sp.: *Corvus cornix*.

cuckoo known as the harbinger of spring, the adult birds are slate blue-grey above, white underneath with dark grey barring. The cuckoo builds no nest of its own but parasitises other birds by laying in their nests. Sp.: *Cuculus canorus*.

curlew bird with brownish plumage that is barred and patterned, and bill that is long and slightly curved downwards. Sp.: *Numenius arquata*.

demoiselle small crane native to Asia and North Africa. Sp.: *Anthropoides virgo*.

dipper diving bird of mountain streams. Aka water ouzel. Gen.: *Cinclus*.

dotterel small migratory plover named from the ease with which it is caught (word supposedly signifying stupidity). Sp.: *Eudromias morinellus*.

dowitcher wading bird breeding in North America and related to sandpipers. Gen.: *Limnodromus*.

drongo any insect-eating bird of the family Dicruridae, possessing a long, forked tail, native to Asia, Africa and Australia.

duiker long-tailed cormorant. Sp.: *Phalacrocorax africanus*.

dunlin long-billed sandpiper. Sp.: *Calidris alpina*.

dunnock small European songbird with brown and grey plumage. Sp.: *Prunella modularis*.

eagle large bird of prey with keen vision and powerful flight. Family Accipitridae.

eider sea duck of which the female's brownish plumage is the source of eiderdown, while the male plumage is white and black. Sp.: *Somateria mollissima*.

NATURE

emu Australian flightless bird, second in size only to the ostrich, which it resembles, although the emu has three-toed feet as opposed to the ostriches' two-toed. Sp.: *Dromaius novaehollandiae*.

falcon any diurnal bird of prey of the family Falconidae, having long pointed wings and sometimes trained to hunt small game for sport.

fieldfare large Old World thrush having a pale grey head and rump, brown wings and back and a blackish tail. Sp.: *Turdus pilaris*.

finch any small seed-eating songbird of the family Fringillidae, including canaries, crossbills and chaffinches.

finch: zebra small Australian waxbill with black and white stripes on face, popular as a cage bird. Sp.: *Poephila guttata*.

frigate bird: magnificent seabird found in tropical seas, with a wide wingspan and deeply forked tail. Sp.: *Fregata magnificens*.

fulmar gull-like seabird, Britain's longest-lived bird, often reaching 40 years of age. Sp.: *Fulmarus glacialis*.

gadwall brownish-grey freshwater duck. Sp.: *Anas strepera*.

gannet heavily built marine bird, a spectacular diver for fish, having a long stout bill and typically white plumage with dark markings. Sp.: *Sula bassana*.

garganey small duck, the drake of which has a white stripe from the eye to the neck. Sp.: *Anas querquedula*.

gerfalcon (gyrfalcon) large falcon of cold northern regions. Sp.: *Falco rusticolus*.

glaucous gull large gull with typical brown and white speckled plumage, of Arctic coasts. Sp.: *Larus hyperboreus*.

go-away bird any of several touracos of the genus *Corythaixoides*.

godwit wading bird with long legs and a long, straight or slightly upcurved bill. Gen.: *Limosa*.

goldcrest smallest British and European bird, usually growing to a maximum of about 9cm (3½in), with an olive green plumage and yellow or orange crest. Sp.: *Regulus regulus*.

golden eagle large eagle with yellow-tipped head-feathers. Sp.: *Aquila chrysaetos*.

golden-eye black-and-white diving duck of northern waters. Sp.: *Bucephala clangula*.

golden-eye black-and-white diving duck, slightly larger than the above. Sp.: *Bucephala islandica*.

goldfinch exotically coloured bird with an unusual tinkling, twittering song, often compared to little bells. Sp.: *Carduelis carduelis*.

goosander large diving duck with a narrow serrated bill. Sp.: *Mergus merganser*.

goose any of various large waterbirds of the family Anatidae, with short legs, webbed feet and a broad bill.

goose: barnacle an Arctic goose which winters in northern Europe. Sp.: *Branta leucopsis*.

goose: Brent small migratory Arctic-breeding goose with black, grey and white plumage. Sp.: *Branta bernicla*.

goose: Canada wild goose with brownish-grey plumage and white cheeks and breast, native to northern America. Sp.: *Branta canadensis*.

goshawk large, short-winged hawk often used in falconry. Sp.: *Accipiter gentilis*.

great crested grebe large Old World grebe with a crest and ear-tufts. Sp.: *Podiceps cristatus*.

greenfinch finch with green and yellow plumage. Sp.: *Carduelis chloris*.

greylag goose native to Europe. Sp.: *Anser anser*.

grosbeak Any of various finches and cardinals having stout conical bills and brightly coloured plumage. The largest species is the pine grosbea,. *Pinicola enucleator*.

guillemot narrow-billed auk, nesting on cliffs or islands. Sp.: *Uria aalge*.

guinea fowl African fowl with slate-coloured white-spotted plumage. Sp.: *Numida meleagris*.

hammerhead heron-like African and Arabian marsh bird with a heavy black bill and an occipital crest. Sp.: *Scopus umbretta*.

harpy eagle South American crested bird of prey, one of the largest of eagles. Sp.: *Harpia harpyja*.

harrier any bird of prey of the genus *Circus* with long wings for swooping over the ground.

hawk any of various diurnal birds of prey of the family Accipitridae, having a characteristic curved beak, rounded short wings and a long tail.

heron: grey long-necked wading bird with a blue-grey plumage and yellow beak. Sp.: *Ardea cinerea*.

herring gull becomes progressively greyer as it matures and also changes colour from winter to summer. Sp.: *Larus argentatus*.

hobby small, long-winged falcon, which catches prey on the wing. Sp.: *Falco subbuteo*.

hoopoe Eurasian bird whose crest is held erect at moments of excitement. Sp.: *Upupa epops*.

hornbill tropical Old World bird with a horn-like excrescence on its large curved bill. Family Bucerotidae.

house martin black and white swallow-like bird, which builds a mud nest under the eaves of houses. Sp.: *Delichon urbica*.

ibis any wading bird of the family Threskiornithidae, with a long down-curved bill, long neck and long legs, and nesting in colonies.

Iceland gull although many spend the winter in Iceland the Iceland gull breeds in Greenland and north Alaska. Sp.: *Larus glaucoides*.

jabiru large black-necked stork of Central and South America, with mainly white plumage. Sp.: *Ephippiorhynchus mycteria*.

jacamar small insect-eating bird with partly iridescent plumage, of the tropical South American family Galbulidae.

jacana tropical wading bird with elongated toes and hind claws, which enable them to walk on floating leaves. Family Jacanidae.

jack snipe small snipe often seen in marshy areas. Sp.: *Lymnocryptes minimus*.

jackdaw small grey-headed crow often frequenting rooftops and nesting in tall buildings and noted for its inquisitiveness and magpie tendencies to thieve bright objects. Sp.: *Corvus monedula*.

Java sparrow waxbill native to Java and Bali. Sp.: *Padda oryzivora*.

jay brownish-pink bird of crow family, whose wings are decorated with flashes of blue. Sp.: *Garrulus glandarius*.

kaka large New Zealand parrot with olive-brown plumage. Sp.: *Nestor meridionalis*.

kestrel a resident of Great Britain and our most common true falcon; often mistaken for a sparrowhawk, but is a hoverer rather than a glider and is far less ferocious. Sp.: *Falco tinnunculus*.

killdeer large North American plover with a plaintive song. Sp.: *Charadrius vociferus*.

kingfisher slightly larger than the house sparrow and brilliantly plumed, the kingfisher is a swift flying, swooping bird that feeds on insects and small fish. Sp.: *Alcedo atthis*.

kittiwake small gull that nests on sea cliffs of the north Atlantic and Arctic oceans. Sp.: *Rissa tridactyla*.

kiwi flightless New Zealand birds with hairlike feathers and a long bill, nesting in burrows. Gen.: *Apteryx*.

knot small northern sandpiper with a short bill and grey plumage. Sp.: *Calidris canutus*.

lammergeier large vulture of Africa, central Asia and southern Europe, with a very large wingspan and dark, beard-like feathers on either side of its beak. Sp.: *Gypaetus barbatus*.

lapwing plover with black and white plumage, crested head, and a shrill cry. Sp.: *Vanellus vanellus*.

lesser whitethroat slightly smaller than its namesake and tends to be somewhat shyer. Sp.: *Sylvia curruca*.

limpkin wading marsh bird of the Americas whose name derives from its limping gait. Aka courlan. Sp.: *Aramus guarauna*.

linnet small European songbird; grey-brown plumage with red forehead and breast in summer; famous for its wide range of singing voice. Sp.: *Acanthis cannabina*.

little auk small Arctic auk. Sp.: *Plautus alle*.

little grebe small waterbird of the grebe family. Sp.: *Tachybaptus ruficollis*.

lory any of various brightly coloured Australasian and South-east Asian parrots of the subfamily Loriinae.

lorikeet any of various small brightly coloured parrots of the subfamily Loriinae.

lovebird any of various African and Madagascan parrots. Gen.: *Agapornis*.

lyre-bird either of two Australian birds of the family Menuridae, the male of which has a lyre-shaped tail.

macaw any long-tailed, brightly coloured parrot of the genus *Ara* or *Anodorhynchus*, native to South and Central America.

magpie black and white plumed bird of the crow family, often regarded as a pest by farmers as it has thieving tendencies, especially for bright shiny objects. Sp.: *Pica pica*.

magpie lark Australian bird of the family Grallinidae, in particular a common long-legged black and white bird, Sp.: *Grallina cyanoleuca*.

mallard duck which is common over most of the northern hemisphere, the drake having a bottle green head and rufous markings. The mallard is thought to be the ancestor of all domestic breeds of duck. Sp.: *Anas platyrhynchos*.

mandarin duck originally from eastern Asia but introduced in many other regions; although the female has typical looks, the drake is exotically coloured. Sp.: *Aix galericulata*.

Manx shearwater European oceanic bird with long slender wings and black and white plumage. Sp.: *Puffinus puffinus*.

marabou large West African stork whose down is used as a trimming for hats. Sp.: *Leptoptilos crumeniferus*.

meadow pipit common pipit native to Europe, Asia and Africa. Sp.: *Anthus pratensis*.

meadowlark North American songbirds with a yellow breast. Sp.: *Sturnella magna* and slightly smaller *Sturnella reglecta*.

merganser any of various diving fish-eating northern ducks of the genus *Mergus*, with a long narrow serrated hooked bill.

merlin small European or N. American falcon that hunts small birds. Sp.: *Falco columbarius*.

mistle (missel) thrush large thrush with a spotted breast that feeds on mistletoe berries. Sp.: *Turdus viscivorus*.

mockingbird long-tailed songbirds of the American family Mimidae noted as mimics of other birds' calls. The common mockingbird of the eastern USA is *Mimus polyglottos*.

Montagu's harrier slender migratory Eurasian bird of prey named after George Montagu 1751–1815, a British naturalist. Sp.: *Circus pygargus*.

moorhen waterside bird having black plumage with blue-green breast and a white line along the flanks. Sp.: *Gallinula chloropus*.

Muscovy musk duck tropical American duck, having a small crest and red markings on its head. Sp.: *Cairina moschata*.

musk duck Australian duck, having a musky smell. Sp.: *Biziura lobata*.

mutton-bird various southern hemisphere birds of the genus *Puffinus*, especially the short-tailed shearwater. Sp.: *Puffinus tenuirostris*.

nightingale loud songbird with dark brown plumage and lighter underparts. Sp.: *Luscinia megarhynchos*.

nightjar nocturnal birds with a cryptic plumage and large eyes, which feed on insects. Sp.: *Caprimulgus*.

nutcracker forest-dwelling Old World bird of the crow family, having speckled plumage. Sp.: *Nucifraga caryocatactes*.

nuthatch small songbird that climbs up and down tree trunks and feeds on nuts and insects. Sp: Sitta europaea.

oriole: golden yellow-plumed Eurasian bird with black wings and red beak. Sp.: *Oriolus oriolus*.

osprey bird of prey with a dark back and whitish head and underparts praying on fish. Sp.: *Pandion haliaetus*.

ostrich world's largest living bird can weigh in excess of 180 kilograms and stand 2.5 metres high. The ostrich can attain running speed of 40 mph, which it can sustain for up to 30 minutes. The ostrich lays the largest egg, weighing up to 2 kg and measuring 15 cm in diameter. Sp.: *Struthio camelus*.

ovenbird any Central or South American bird of the family Furnariidae, which build domed nests out of clay or tunnel underground to lay their eggs.

owl: barn type of owl that likes to nest in barns and other accessible rural buildings. Sp.: *Tyto alba*.

owl: eagle large Eurasian owl with long ear-tufts. Sp.: *Bubo bubo*.

owl: horned North American owl with hornlike feathers over the ears. Sp.: *Bubo virginianus*.

owl: little small owl of Africa and Eurasia, with speckled plumage. Sp.: *Athene noctua*.

owl: long-eared known for its peculiar barking cry, broken by 'yaps'; its long ears are in reality tufts of feathers. Sp.: *Asio otus*.

owl: tawny familiar owl with rich brown plumage, barred and checked with darker bars and streaks. Sp.: *Strix aluco*.

oystercatcher wading bird with black and white plumage and long laterally compressed orange-red bill. Sp.: *Haematopus ostralegus*.

partridge game bird with light grey plumage, barred and streaked with chestnut. Sp.: *Perdix perdix*.

NATURE

penguin flightless seabird of the southern hemisphere with black upper parts and white underparts, and wings developed into scaly flippers for swimming underwater. Family Spheniscidae.

penguin: Adélie Most common species of penguin. Sp.: *Pygoscelis adeliae.*

penguin: emperor largest species of penguin, which can grow to a height of 120 cm (4 ft). Sp.: *Aptenodytes forsteri.*

penguin: fairy smallest species of penguin, average height of 41 cm (16 in). Aka little blue penguin. Sp.: *Eudyptula minor.*

penguin: Galápagos unlike the emperor and the Adélie, the Galápagos penguin is confined to the tropics of South America. Sp.: *Spheniscus mendiculus.*

penguin: gentoo abundant in the Falkland and other Atlantic islands. Sp.: *Pygoscelis papua.*

peregrine falcon powerful falcon, breeding on coastal cliffs and much used for falconry. Sp.: *Falco peregrinus.*

petrel small wave-hanging seabirds, blackish with a white rump. Family: Hydrobihdar.

petrel: Wilson's common petrel that breeds around Antarctica but is often seen in the Atlantic. Sp.: *Oceanites oceanicus.*

phalarope any small wading bird or swimming bird of the family Phalaropodidae, with a straight bill and lobed feet.

pheasant game bird introduced to Britain from its native home in south-eastern Europe and central Asia; the cock birds show a wide colour variation, with brown and buff common specimens, although some almost black birds have been sighted in recent years. Sp.: *Phasianus colchicus.*

pipit: tree light brown plumed bird of the wagtail family. Sp.: *Anthus trivialis.*

plover: golden a wader noted for its musical but sad rising whistle, the golden plover is a golden speckled colour with a white or sometimes black underparts. Sp.: *Pluvialis apricaria.*

plover: ringed small chunky wader with brown plumage, white underparts and a black ring round the neck. Sp.: *Charadrius hiaticula.*

pochard familiar diving duck, the male having silvery plumage with chestnut head and black underparts whilst the females are silvery-brown. Sp.: *Aythya ferina.*

ptarmigan high mountain grouse whose grey-brown and black plumage changes to white in the winter. Sp.: *Lagopus mutus.*

puffin Britain's most recognisable seabird, with its large multicoloured bill and awkward movement; the main colonies are in north Scotland, the largest on St Kilda, west of the Outer Hebrides. Sp.: *Fratercula arctica.*

quail game bird, which looks like a miniature partridge although its plumage is a red-buff carrying streaks of cream and black. The quail is rarely sighted, due largely to its habit of taking refuge in grassland when spotted. Sp.: *Coturnix coturnix.*

quetzal spectacular tree bird of central America, a member of the trogon family, with green back and crimson and white under parts; the male's green tail plumes grow to 60 cm (2 feet). Sp.: *Pharomachons mocinno.*

raven large passerine bird of the crow family, having a large,straight, black bill, long, wedge-shaped tail and black plumage. Sp.: *Corvus corax.*

razorbill common auk of the north Atlantic which typically nests in colonies on cliffs. Sp.: *Alca torda.*

red kite once a common scavenger in the streets during Elizabethan and the early Stuart period, this bird of prey gradually died out but has been reintroduced into England and Wales. Sp.: *Milvus milvus.*

redpoll soft striped brown plumed songbird of the finch family. Sp.: *Acanthis flammea.*

redstart similar in size and habit to the robin, with a grey plumage and black throat. Sp.: *Phoenicurus phoenicurus.*

redstart: black darker than its namesake but has similar feeding habits of taking insects, mainly on the wing. Sp.: *Phoenicurus ochruros.*

redwing small European thrush, having a speckled breast, reddish flanks and brown back. Sp.: *Turdus iliacus.*

rhea either of two large flightless birds of South Africa, *Rhea americana* and *Pterocieia pennara*, similar to ostrich but hairy, three-toed feet.

ring ouzel thrush with a white crescent across its breast. Sp.: *Turdus torquatus.*

robin well-loved bird with brown plumage and red breast with yellow throat. Sp.: *Erithacus rubecula.*

roller beautifully coloured migrant from Africa. The plumage shows a brown back, with blue wing coverts, greenish-blue head, blue undersurface and purplish tail and wings. Sp.: *Coracias garrulus.*

rook most common member of the crow family, notable for its jet black plumage and depredations among the eggs of smaller birds. Sp.: *Corvus frugilegus.*

ruff Eurasian member of the sandpiper family. The males' communal dancing display is called 'lekking'. The female is called a reeve. Sp.: *Philomachus pugnax.*

Sabine's gull fork-tailed seabird breeding on islets and marshy tundra in Arctic Greenland, Alaska and northern Siberia. Sp.: *Larus sabini.*

sanderling small busy sandpiper of the genus *Calidris* that frequents sandy shores. Sp.: *Calidris alba.*

sand martin slightly smaller than the house martin, with dark brown plumage and a brown band across its white breast. Sp.: *Riparia riparia.*

sandpiper various smallish members of the family Scolopacidae, walkers with long legs and long slender bills, which includes the curlew, dunlin and snipe.

shag very similar to the cormorant but smaller and darker green, no white marking on face and more of a crest. Sp.: *Phalacrocorax aristotelis.*

shoveler duck with spoon-shaped bill, a blue patch on each wing, and in the male a green head, white breast and reddish-brown body. Sp.: *Anas clypeata.*

shrike: red-backed chestnut-backed bird with grey head and rump and black ear coverts. Aka butcher bird because it impales its prey on thorn-bushes for storage. Sp.: *Lanius collurio.*

siskin small finch with brownish-green back with yellow shades and black cap. Sp.: *Carduelis spinus.*

skua: Arctic smaller member of this predatory seabird genus with dark plumage and a hooked bill, all of them famous for harassing terns or gulls into dropping or disgorging fish they have caught. Sp.: *Stercorarius parasiticus.*

skua: great heavy, broad-winged seabird with brown plumage and wings with white bar on wings. Sp.: *Stercorarius skua.*

skylark like the cuckoo, this ground-dwelling song-bird is often thought of as a harbinger of spring; it has a dull brown plumage with white ribbing. Sp.: *Alauda arvensis*.

smew merganser of north Europe and Asia with white plumage with black markings. Sp.: *Mergus albellus*.

snipe bird of the sandpiper family inhabiting marshy areas. Collective noun is a 'wisp'. Sp.: *Gallinago gallinago*.

snow bunting bunting of northern and arctic regions having a white plumage with dark markings on the wings, back and tail. Sp.: *Plectrophenax nivalis*.

social weaver small gregarious Old World passerine songbird of the chiefly African family Ploceidae, having a short thick bill and a dull plumage. The name derives from the bird's characteristic of building covered nests in trees and living in communities of hundreds. Sp.: *Philetairus socius*.

song thrush song bird with brown plumage and white underparts speckled with brown; its repetitive refrain sounds rather like 'Come out, come out, come out'. Sp.: *Turdus philomelos*.

sparrowhawk fiercest of our native hawks, identified by its rapid flight with long gliding intervals and sudden swoops on prey. Sp.: *Accipiter nisus*.

sparrow: house small common brown and grey bird which nests in the eaves and roofs of houses. Sp.: *Passer domesticus*.

spoonbill wading bird of warm regions, having white plumage and a long, horizontally flattened bill. Sp.: *Platalea leucorodia*.

spotted flycatcher sparrow-sized grey-brown bird with a whitish breast, able to catch insects in flight. Sp.: *Muscicapa striata*.

starling distinctly coloured bird with black, iridescently green-tinged plumage, white flecks throughout its cover, and a yellow beak. Sp.: *Sturnus vulgaris*.

stock dove similar to the wood-pigeon but smaller. Sp.: *Columba oenas*.

storm(y) petrel small petrel of the north Atlantic, Europe's smallest seabird. Sp.: *Hydrobates pelagicus*.

swallow streamlined insect-hunter with a distinctive blue sheen on the back and wings, chestnut throat and white breast. Sp.: *Hirunda rustica*.

swan: Bewick's smallest swan, rarely seen in England outside the Slimbridge Wildfowl Trust and the Ouse Washes. Sp.: *Cygnus columbianus*.

swan: mute commonest Eurasian swan, having white plumage and an orange-red bill with a swollen black base. Sp.: *Cygnus olor*.

swan: trumpeter large North American wild swan. Sp.: *Cygnus buccinator*.

swan: whooper black bill with yellow nose, most of Britain's winter whoopers are from Iceland. Sp.: *Cygnus cygnus*.

swift fast-flying bird with dark brown plumage; it is a summer bird in Britain and spends its winters in Africa. Sp.: *Apus apus*.

teal smallest of Europe's wintering ducks, appearing like a smaller wigeon. Sp.: *Anas crecca*.

tern graceful, slender-winged seabird that dives headlong after small fish. Gen.: *Sterna*.

tern: Arctic greyer than the common or sandwich tern, can be seen at close hand on the Farne Islands. Sp.: *Sterna paradisaea*.

tern: common most familiar tern, with grey-white plumage, black cap and red bill. Sp.: *Sterna hirundo*.

tern: little small tern distinguished from other terns by its yellow bill. Sp.: *Sterna albifrons*.

tern: roseate rare bird with white plumage, black cap and extremely long tail streamers. Sp.: *Sterna dougallii*.

tern: Sandwich largest of the terns found regularly in Britain, distinguished from other terns by its pale white plumage and black bill with yellow tip. Sp.: *Sterna sandvicensis*.

tit: bearded Eurasian songbird common in reed beds; it has a tawny back and tail and, in the male, a grey and black head. Sp.: *Panurus biarmicus*.

tit: blue gymnastic bird with bright blue cap and yellow underparts, often seen hanging upside down while hunting for food. Sp.: *Parus caeruleus*.

tit: crested chubby bird with dull brown plumage and white crest marked with black, in Britain restricted to the Scottish Highlands but more common on the Continent. Sp.: *Parus cristatus*.

tit: great Eurasian songbird with black-and-white head markings. Sp.: *Parus major*.

tit: long-tailed black and white plumed tit distinguished from other tits by its long tail. Sp.: *Aegithalos caudatus*.

tit: marsh grey-backed tit that inhabits woods and hedges. Sp.: *Parus palustris*.

tit: penduline southern European bird that derives its name from the hanging nest characteristic of the species. Sp.: *Remiz pendulinis*.

tit: willow Eurasian black-capped tit. Sp.: *Parus montanus*.

touraco (turaco) any brightly coloured crested arboreal African bird of the family Musophagidae.

tragopan tree-dwelling Asian pheasant; the male displays erect fleshy horns on its head. Gen.: *Tragopan*.

tree sparrow two distinct species. *Passer montanus* is a Eurasian sparrow inhabiting agricultural land. *Spizella arborea* is a North American sparrow-like bird of the bunting family, breeding on the edge of the tundra.

treecreeper small passerine songbirds of the family Certhiidae of the northern hemisphere, having a brown-and-white plumage and slender downward-curving bill. Named from their characteristic of creeping up trees to feed on insects. Gen.: *Certhia*.

turkey buzzard American vulture, unrelated to the Old World vultures, so called because of its bare reddish head and dark plumage. Sp.: *Cathartes aura*.

turtle dove small slim dove with thin neck, protruding round white head, deep chest and brownish-grey plumage with black marks. Sp.: *Streptopelia turtur*.

umbrella bird cotinga of tropical America, with a large, black, overhanging crest and a long feathered wattle. Gen.: *Cephalopterus*.

Victoria crowned pigeon large blue-crested pigeon of New Guinea. Sp.: *Goura victoria*.

vulture any of various large birds of prey of the distinct Old and New World families Accipitridae and Cathartidae, with the head and neck more or less bare of feathers, feeding mainly on carrion and reputed to gather with others in anticipation of a death.

wagtail: white terrestrial bird, named from the up and down waggings of the tail at each halt that accompany its short darting rushes in a zigzag course. Sp.: *Motacilla alba alba*.

wandering albatross very large white albatross of southern oceans, having very long and narrow black-tipped wings. Sp.: *Diomedea exulans*.

NATURE

warbler: barred arrives in Europe, from Africa, later than the other warblers and rarely visits Britain. Sp.: *Sylvia nisoria.*

warbler: Cetti's named after an 18th-century Italian Jesuit; it is the only European passerine with 10 tail feathers, rather than 12. Sp.: *Cettia cetti.*

warbler: Dartford until recently Britain's only resident warbler; it was first described from Bexley Heath, near Dartford in Kent, in 1773. Sp.: *Sylvia undata.*

warbler: great reed migrant bird seen frequently in the reed beds of East Anglia and the southern coast. Sp.: *Acrocephalus arundinaceus.*

warbler: icterine migratory warbler with brownish plumage and olive green underparts. Sp.: *Hippolais icterina.*

warbler: reed inconspicuous bird with overall brown colouring with lighter underparts. Sp.: *Acrocephalus scirpaceus.*

water ouzel see dipper.

water rail highly nervous and secretive bird, more often heard than seen; it hides in its reed-bed home at the slightest disturbance. Sp.: *Rallus aquaticus.*

wattlebird various Australian honeyeaters with a wattle hanging from each cheek. Gen.: *Anthochaera* and *Melidectes.* Also various New Zealand songbirds of the family Callaeidae, with wattles hanging from the base of the bill, e.g. the saddleback. Sp.: *Creadion carunculatus.*

waxbill any small finch-like bird of the family Estrildidae, with a red bill resembling sealing wax in colour.

waxwing any of three species of crested perching birds of the genus *Bombycilla*, with small tips like red sealing wax to some wing feathers.

weka large flightless New Zealand rail. Sp.: *Gallirallus australis.*

whale-headed stork grey African stork with a large bill shaped like a clog. Sp.: *Balaeniceps rex.*

wheatear small northern thrush having a grey back, black wings and tail, white rump and pale brown underparts. Sp.: *Oenanthe oenanthe.*

whimbrel small migratory curlew with a striped crown and trilling call. Sp.: *Numenius phaeopus.*

whinchat Old World songbird having mottled brown-and-white plumage with pale cream underparts; it is a member of the subfamily of thrushes. Sp.: *Saxicola rubetra.*

white stork widely protected in Europe, a pure white bird with black wing tips and long red beak and legs. Sp.: *Ciconia ciconia.*

whitethroat warbler with greyish plumage, rusty wings and white underparts. Sp.: *Sylvia communis.*

wi(d)geon gregarious duck, the male of which has a reddish-brown head and chest, and grey and white back and wings. Sp.: *Anas penelope.*

woodchat shrike shrike of southern Europe, north Africa and the Middle East, having black and white plumage with a chestnut head. Sp.: *Lanius senator.*

woodcock any game bird of the genus *Scolopax* that inhabits woodlands. The common Eurasian species is *Scolopax rusticola.*

woodpecker any bird of the family Picidae that climbs and taps tree trunks in search of insects.

woodpecker: black largest of the European woodpeckers; the jet-black plumage is broken only by its red cap. Sp.: *Dryocopus martius.*

woodpecker: great spotted black and white plumage with a large red patch on the nape of the neck (male only); noted for its repeated drumming on the trunks of trees. Sp.: *Dendrocopos major.*

woodpecker: green large green and yellow European woodpecker with a red crown. Sp.: *Picus viridis.*

woodpecker: pileated large North American woodpecker with a red-topped head. Sp.: *Dryocopus pileatus.*

wood pigeon large pigeon, having white patches like a ring round its neck. Sp.: *Columba palumbus.*

wren small light brown bird famous for its building of more than one nest, the hen making her choice and the 'spares' used as roosting spots in bad weather. Sp.: *Troglodytes troglodytes.*

wryneck small bird of the woodpecker family, able to turn its head over its shoulder. Sp.: *Jynx torquilla.*

yellowhammer bunting of which the male has a yellow head, neck and breast. Sp.: *Emberiza citrinella.*

yellowlegs: greater and lesser two migratory sandpipers with yellow legs. Sp.: *Tringa melanoleuca* and *Tringa flavipes.*

Birds: Miscellaneous Information

altricial of a young bird or animal requiring care and feeding by the parents after hatching or birth

arctic tern: migrates to Antarctica

backwards-flying the hummingbird is the only bird that can fly backwards

beaks: characteristics insect-eating birds usually have pointed bills while carnivorous birds have hooked bills

bird: smallest bee hummingbird

bird of paradise: from New Guinea and nearby islands (birds of paradise hang upside down)

bird of prey: largest Andean condor

bird of prey: largest UK golden eagle

British bird: biggest mute swan

British bird: fastest runner pheasant (up to 21 mph)

British bird: highest flier whooper swans on migration have been sighted at 27,000 feet

British bird: largest egg mute swan

British bird: longest-lived Manx shearwater (29.82 years)

British bird: most common wren

British bird: smallest goldcrest

British bird: smallest egg goldcrest

British Isles: exclusive to red grouse and Scottish crossbill do not migrate and are found only in the UK

carinate of a bird having a keeled breastbone; opposite of ratite

deepest diving bird emperor penguin

drops bones on rocks to break the bearded vulture (lammergeyer)

ducks: sex that quacks only females

egg: smallest hummingbird

extinct birds dodo lived on the island of Mauritius and became extinct in the late 17th century; great auk or Atlantic pigeon became extinct in the mid-19th century; moa of New Zealand became totally extinct by early 19th century

falconry breeding and training of hawks for sporting purposes. The female is called a falcon, the male is a tiercel

fastest bird peregrine falcon has been timed at 217 mph during swoop as part of the courtship display. The golden eagle has reached speeds exceeding 150 mph during a vertical dive, but the fastest bird in level flight, with recorded speeds exceeding 110 mph, is the Alpine swift

fastest runner ostrich

first known bird archaeopteryx (name means 'ancient wing')

gizzard muscular thick-walled part of a bird's stomach, used for grinding food, usually with the help of grit

grallatorial of or relating to long-legged wading birds e.g. flamingos and storks (from Latin *grallator*, 'stiltwalker')

guano excrement of seabirds found on islands off South America, Africa and the West Indies and used as manure

hangs upside down birds of paradise of Papua New Guinea frequently adopt this position

largest birds ostrich is clearly the largest living bird (moas extinct); the largest flying bird is more contentious but is possibly the kori bustard of sub-Saharan Africa

longest migration Arctic tern (11,222 miles from Anglesey to Australia)

nests at end of riverbank tunnels kingfisher

nests in water crested grebe

New World: definition term used to differentiate between the time before and after the Americas were discovered. New World relates to the Americas: the western hemisphere

nostrils at tip of beak kiwi

Old World: definition term used to differentiate between the time before and after the Americas were discovered. The Old World consists of Europe, Asia and Africa: the eastern hemisphere

owl: smallest elf owl

painter of USA birds John Audubon

palmiped web-footed bird

ratite of a bird having a keelless breastbone and therefore unable to fly; opposite of carinate

sacred birds quetzal (Aztecs), ibis (Egyptians)

seabird: largest emperor penguin

smells when excited the hoopoe raises its crest when excited and emits a foul-smelling liquid

smell: keenest sense of kiwi

snail shells: breaks with stone thrush

sonar-equipped the guacharo, or oilbird, is capable of flying in total darkness in a similar way to bats

steals food in flight skua often steals food from other birds while in flight

strigiformes order of birds that solely includes owls

underwater: longest emperor penguin (up to 18 minutes)

underwater: walks dipper

web-footed bird: smallest petrel

white stork: UK breeding in 1416 a nest was found on St Giles Cathedral, Edinburgh, the only known UK breeding occurrence

wingspan: longest albatross, although the largest wings belong to the Andean condor

NATURE

Alternative or Poetic Names of Birds

adjutant bird	stork	fish hawk (North America)	osprey
aepyornis	elephant bird	frigate bird	man-of-war bird
apteryx	kiwi	goatsucker	nightjar
ash-coloured falcon	Montagu's harrier	goldcrest	woodcock pilot
barn owl	yellow owl		golden-crested wren
	white owl	golden-crested wren	goldcrest
bearded tit	reedling	gowk	cuckoo
blackbird	merle	grackle	crow blackbird
blackcap	monk	great grey shrike	white whisky john
black guillemot	puffinet	great skua	bonxie
blue tit	tinnock	green cormorant	shag
	tom tit	greenfinch	green linnet
bonxie	great skua	green linnet	greenfinch
	skua	green plover	lapwing
bullbat	nighthawk	green woodpecker	yaffle
bullfinch	nope	halcyon	kingfisher
butcher bird	shrike (esp. red-backed)	hedge sparrow	dunnock
chaffinch	sheld apple	horned grebe	Slavonian grebe
corncrake	land rail	kestrel	windhover
crow blackbird	grackle	kingfisher	halcyon
cuckoo	gowk	kiwi	apteryx
cushat	wood pigeon	kotuku	white heron
	ring dove	land rail	corncrake
dabchick	little grebe	lapwing	peewit (pewit)
dipper	water crake		green plover
dunnock	hedge sparrow	lark	laverock
elephant bird	aepyornis		

laverock	lark	sheld apple	chaffinch
little grebe	dabchick	shrike	butcher bird (esp. red-backed)
man-of-war bird	frigate bird	shoebill	whale-headed stork
mavis	song thrush	skua	bonxie
merganser	sawbill	Slavonian grebe	horned grebe
merle	blackbird	smew	white nun
mock nightingale	sedge warbler	song thrush	mavis
monk	blackcap		throstle
Montagu's harrier	ash-coloured falcon	stork	adjutant bird
moorhen	water hen	storm petrel	Mother Carey's chicken
mosquito hawk	nighthawk		witch
Mother Carey's chicken	storm petrel	tawny owl	wood owl
mountain Linnet	twite	throstle	song thrush
nighthawk	bullbat	tinnock	blue tit
	mosquito hawk	tit lark	pipit
nightingale	philomel	tom tit	blue tit
nightjar	goatsucker (North America)	turkey buzzard	turkey vulture
nope	bullfinch	turkey vulture	turkey buzzard
osprey	fish hawk	twite	mountain linnet
peewit (pewit)	lapwing	water crake	dipper
philomel	nightingale	water hen	moorhen
pipit	tit lark	whale-headed stork	shoebill
puffin	sea parrot	white heron	kotuku
puffinet	black guillemot	white nun	smew
reedling	bearded tit	white owl	barn owl
ring dove	cushat	white whisky john	great grey shrike
robin	ruddock	windhover	kestrel
ruddock	robin	witch	storm petrel
sawbill	merganser	woodcock pilot	goldcrest
Scotch nightingale	sedge warbler	wood owl	tawny owl
sea parrot	puffin	wood pigeon	cushat
sedge warbler	Scotch nightingale	yaffle	green woodpecker
	mock nightingale	yellow bunting	yellowhammer
shag	green cormorant	yellowhammer	yellow bunting
		yellow owl	barn owl

NB: For ease of reference, the alternatives have been listed alphabetically.

Collective Nouns

BY GROUPS

actors cast, company, troupe
aeroplanes flight, squadron, wing
angels host
antelopes herd
ants colony, army
apes shrewdness
arms pile
arrows sheaf, quiver
asparagus bundle
asses pace
badgers cete
barley crop
barracuda battery
baseball team
bass fleet
bears sleuth, sloth
beaters squad
beauties galaxy
beavers colony
bees swarm, grist

bells peal
birds flock
bishops bench
bitterns sedge, siege
bloodhounds sute
boars sounder
books library
bowls set
boy scouts jamboree
boys blush
bread batch, caste
bucks brace, leash
budgerigars chatter
butlers draught
camels caravan, flock
capercaillie tok
capitalists syndicate
cards pack, deck
cars fleet
cats clowder
cattle herd, drove
chickens brood

children class
chocolates box
choughs chattering
cigarettes packet
clams bed
clergy assemblage, convocation
clothes outfit
colts rag
coots covert
corn sheaf
cranes sedge, siege
cricket team eleven
crockery service
crows murder
cubs litter
curlews herd
dancers troupe
deer herd
dogs show, kennel
donkeys drove
dottrel trip

ducks (in flight) flush, pump, team
ducks (on ground) badelynge
ducks (in water) paddling
dunlins flight
eagles convocation
eels swarm
eggs clutch
elk gang
falcons cast
ferrets fesnyng, business
finches charm
firewood bundle
fish shoal
flamingos flurry, regiment
flies swarm
flowers bunch, bouquet, nosegay, posy
foresters stalk

foxes skulk, earth
frogs army, colony
fruit orchard
geese (in flight)
  skein
geese (on ground)
  gaggle
girls bevy
gnats swarm, cloud
goats herd, tribe, trip
goldfinches charm
goldfish troubling
golf-clubs set
grapes bunch, cluster
grass tuft
grouse (several broods)
  pack
grouse (single brood)
  covey
guardians board
guillemots bazaar
gulls colony
guns battery, park
hares down, husk
harpists melody
hawks cast
hay truss
hedgehogs array
hermits observance
herons sedge, siege
hooligans gang
horses haras
hounds pack, mute
hunters blast
hunting dogs cry
ibis crowd
islands archipelago,
  chain
jellyfish smuck
kangaroos troop
kittens kindle
knaves rayful

labourers gang
lapwings deceit
larks exaltation
leopards leap
lions pride
magistrates bench
magpies tiding, tittering
majors morbidity
mallards flush
mares stud
martens richesse
mice nest
minstrels troupe
moles labour
monkeys troop
mules barren
music library
musicians band,
  orchestra
nightingales watch
onions rope
owls parliament
oxbirds fling
oxen yoke, team
papers budget
parrots company
partridges covey
passenger pigeons
  roost
peacocks muster
pearls string, rope
peas pod
penguins rookery,
  colony
people assembly,
  clique, audience, com-
  munity, congregation
pheasants nye
pictures exhibition
pigs litter, drove
plovers congregation,
  wing

plums basket
pochards rush
polecats chine
police posse. detach-
  ment
politicians caucus
porpoises school
poultry run
pups litter
quail bevy
rabbits nest
race horses string
rags bundle
ravens unkindness
rhinoceros crash
roes bevy
rooks clamour, building
ruffs hill
runners field
sailors crew, deck,
  watch
sails outfit
saints community
sandpipers fling
sardines family
savages horde
seals herd, pod
sergeants subtiltie
servants staff
sheep flock
sheldrakes dopping
ships fleet, flotilla
slaves gang
smelt quantity
snakes den, pit
snipe wisp, walk
soldiers detachment
spiders cluster, clutter
stamps collection
starlings murmuration
stars cluster, constella-

tion
steps flight
sticks faggot
strawberries punnet
subalterns simplicity
swans herd, bevy
swifts flock
swine sounder, drift,
  dryet
swine (tame) doylt
teals spring
thieves gang
thrush mutation
tigers ambush
toads knot, knab
trees clump, orchard,
  spinney, thicket
troops brigade, division
trout hover
turkeys rafter
turtles bale, dole
turtle doves pitying
wasps nest
whales school, pod,
  gam
whelps litter
whiskey case
whiting pod
wigeon company
wild cats dout
wildfowl plump, sord,
  sute
wine vintage
witches coven
wolves pack
women bevy
woodcock fall, plump
woodpeckers descent
worshippers congrega-
  tion.

N
A
T
U
R
E

BY NAMES

ambush tigers
archipelago islands
army frogs, ants
array hedgehogs
assemblage clergy
assembly people
audience people
badelynge ducks (on
  ground)
bale turtles
band musicians
barren mules
basket plums
batch bread
battery guns, barracuda
bazaar guillemots
bed clams
bench magistrates,
  bishops

bevy quail, girls,
  women, roes, swans
blast hunters
blush boys
board guardians
bouquet flowers
box chocolates
brace bucks
brigade troops
brood chickens
budget papers
building rooks
bunch grapes,
  flowers
bundle firewood,
  asparagus, rags
business ferrets
caravan camels
case whiskey

cast hawks, actors,
  falcons
caste bread
caucus politicians
cete badgers
chain islands
charm goldfinches
chatter budgerigars
chattering choughs
chine polecats
clamour rooks
class children
clique people
cloud gnats
clowder cats
clump trees
cluster grapes, spiders,
  stars
clutch eggs

clutter spiders
collection stamps
colony gulls, frogs, penguins, ants, beavers
community people,
  saints
company actors,
  wigeon, parrots
congregation people,
  plovers, worshippers
constellation stars
convocation eagles,
  clergy
coven witches
covert coots
covey partridges,
  grouse (single brood)
crew sailors
crash rhinoceros

crew sailors
crop barley
crowd ibis
cry hunting dog
deceit lapwings
deck cards, sailors
den snakes
descent woodpeckers
detachment soldiers, police
division troops
dole turtles
dopping sheldrakes
dout wild cats
down hares
doylt swine (tame)
draught butlers
drift swine
drove donkeys, cattle, pigs
dryet swine
earth foxes
eleven cricket team
exaltation larks quiver
exhibition pictures
faggot sticks
fall woodcock
family sardines
fesnyng ferrets
field runners
fleet cars, ships
flight dunlins, aeroplanes, steps
fling oxbirds, sandpipers
flock swifts, birds, sheep
flotilla ships
gaggle geese (on ground)
galaxy beauties
gam whales
gang labourers, hooligans, thieves, slaves, elk
gleam herring
grist bees
haras horses
herd deer, goats, cattle, curlews, antelopes, seals, swans
hill ruffs
horde savages
host angels
hover trout
husk hares
jamboree boy scouts
kennel dogs

kindle kittens
knab toads
knot toads
labour moles
leap leopards
leash bucks
library music, books
litter pups, whelps, pigs, cubs
melody harpists
morbidity majors
murder crows
murmuration starlings
muster peacocks
mutation thrush
mute hounds
nest mice, rabbits, wasps
nosegay flowers
nye pheasants
observance hermits
orchard fruit, trees
orchestra musicians
outfit sails, clothes
pace asses
pack hounds, cards, wolves, grouse (several broods)
packet cigarettes
paddling ducks (in water)
park guns
parliament owls
peal bells
pile arms
pit snakes
pitying turtle doves
plump woodcock, wildfowl
pod peas, whiting, whales, seals
posse police
posy flowers
pride lions
pump ducks (in flight)
punnet strawberries
quantity smelt
quiver arrows
rafter turkeys
rag colts
rayful knaves
richesse martens
rookery penguins
roost passenger pigeons
rope onions, pearls
run poultry

rush pochards
school porpoises, whales
sedge cranes, bitterns, herons
service cockery
set golf-clubs, bowls
sheaf corn, arrows
shoal fish
show dogs
shrewdness apes
siege bitterns, cranes, herons
simplicity subalterns
skein geese (in flight)
skulk foxes
sleuth bears
sloth bears
smuck jellyfish
sord wildfowl
sounder swine, boars
spinney trees
spring teals
squad beaters
squadron aeroplanes
staff servants
stalk foresters
string race horses, pearls
stud mares
subtiltie sergeants
sute bloodhounds, wildfowl
swarm gnats, bees, flies
syndicate capitalists
team ducks (in flight), baseball, oxen
thicket trees
tiding magpies
tittering magpies
tok capercaillie
tribe goats
trip goats
troop kangaroos, monkeys
troubling goldfish
troupe minstrels, actors, dancers
truss hay
tuft grass
unkindness ravens
vintage wine
walk snipe
watch sailors, nightingales
wing aeroplanes, plovers
wisp snipe
yoke oxen

NEWSPAPERS

National Newspapers

Name	Location	Founded	Details
Belfast News Letter	Belfast	1737	Britain's oldest surviving daily newspaper
Courier	Dundee	1816	Founded as the *Dundee Courier and Argus*
Daily Courant	London	1702	First successful daily newspaper
Daily Express	London	1900	Founded by C Arthur Pearson
Daily Herald	London	1911	Merged into the *Sun* in 1964
Daily Mail	London	1896	Founded by Alfred Harmsworth (Lord Northcliffe)
Daily Mirror	London	1903	Founded by Alfred Harmsworth (Lord Northcliffe). Address: 1 Canada Square, Canary Wharf, London E14 5AP. Tel: 020 7293 3000
Daily Record	Glasgow	1895	Scottish equivalent of the *Daily Mirror*
Daily Sketch	London	1909	Merged into the *Daily Mail* in 1971
Daily Star	London	1978	Owned by United Newspapers (Express Group)
Daily Telegraph	London	1855	Amalgamated in 1937 with the *Morning Post*. Address: 1 Canada Square, Canary Wharf, London E14 5AP. Tel: 0161 848 0610
European	London	1990	Founded by Robert Maxwell and sold on Thursdays
Evening Standard	London	1827	Part of the 'Mail' Group of Newspapers
Financial News	London	1884	Merged with *Financial Times* in 1945
Financial Times	London	1888	Adopted its pink paper in 1893
Guardian	London	1821	Founded as the *Manchester Guardian* and became a daily in 1855
Herald	Glasgow	1783	Founded as *Glasgow Advertiser*, changed name to *Glasgow Herald* 1802–1992
Independent	London	1986	Originally part of the Mirror Group and founded by three *Daily Telegraph* journalists. Address: Independent House, 191 Marsh Wall, London E14 9RS. Tel: 020 7005 2000
Independent on Sunday	London	1990	Originally part of the Mirror Group
Mail on Sunday	London	1982	Sister paper to the *Daily Mail*
News of the World	London	1843	Founded by John Browne Bell. Address: 1 Virginia St, London E1 9XR. Tel: 020 7782 4000
Observer	London	1791	Founded by Irishman W S Bourne
People	London	1881	Founded to support the Conservative cause originally. Address: 1 Canada Square, Canary Wharf, London E14 5AP. Tel: 020 7293 3000
Press and Journal	Aberdeen	1748	Founded by James Chalmers as *Aberdeen's Journal*
Scotland on Sunday	Edinburgh	1988	Sister paper to the *Scotsman*
Scotsman	Edinburgh	1817	First non-London newspaper to open an office in Fleet Street
Sun	London	1964	Founded in 1911 as the *Daily Herald*. Address: 1 Virginia St, London E1 9XR. Tel: 020 7782 4100
Sunday Express	London	1918	Founded by Lord Beaverbrook
Sunday Mirror	London	1963	Founded by Harold Harmsworth as the *Sunday Pictorial* in 1915
Sunday Post	Glasgow	1914	Launched as the *Post Sunday Special*, it is the leading Scottish Sunday paper
Sunday Telegraph	London	1961	Sister paper to the *Daily Telegraph*. Address: 1 Canada Square, Canary Wharf, London E14 5AP. Tel: 0161 876 8000
Sunday Times	London	1822	Launched as *The New Observer* and then *The Independent Observer* in 1821
Times	London	1785	Founded by John Walter. Address: 1 Pennington St, London E1 9XN. Tel: 020 7782 5000
Today	London	1986	Founded by Eddie Shah

International Newspapers
(location and date founded)

ABC Madrid 1905
Al-Akhbar Cairo 1944
Apogevmatini Athens 1952
Avriani Athens 1980
Berlingske Tidende Copenhagen 1749
Bild am Sonntag Hamburg 1956
Boston American Boston 1904
B.T. Copenhagen 1916
Chicago Sun Chicago 1941
Corriere della Sera Milan 1876
Diario Popular Lisbon 1942
Ethnos Athens 1891
Evening Herald Dublin 1891
Evening Press Dublin 1954
Le Figaro Paris 1828
L'Humanité Paris 1904
Irish Independent Dublin 1905
Irish Times Dublin 1859
Izvestiya Petrograd 1917

La Lanterne Brussels 1944
La Libre Brussels 1884
Il Messaggero Rome 1878
Le Monde Paris 1944
Morgunbladid Reykavik 1913
Die Neue Zeitung Munich 1945
Neue Zürcher Zeitung Zurich 1789
New York Post New York 1801
New York Times New York 1851
New York World New York 1860
L'Osservatore Romano Vatican 1929
El Pais Madrid 1976
Plain Dealer Cleveland 1842
Politiken Copenhagen 1884
Pravda Moscow 1912
La Repubblica Rome 1976
Le Soir Brussels 1887
La Stampa Turin 1867

Süddeutsche Zeitung Munich 1945
Sunday Independent Dublin 1905
Sunday Press Dublin 1949
Sunday World Dublin 1973
Svenska Dagbladet Stockholm 1884
Tagesspiegel Berlin 1945
Tägliche Rundschau Berlin 1945
De Telegraaf Amsterdam 1893
Tribune Chicago 1847
La Vanguardia Barcelona 1881
Wall Street Journal New York 1889
Washington Post Washington DC 1877
Die Welt Hamburg 1945
Ya Madrid 1935

Regional Newspapers

Name	Location	Name	Location	Name	Location
Argus	Brighton	**Evening Mail**	Birmingham	**Evening Telegraph**	
Burton Mail	Burton-on-Trent	**Evening News**	Bolton	**Mercury**	Leicester
			Cambridge	**News and Star**	Carlisle
Chronicle	Bath		Edinburgh	**The News**	Portsmouth
Chronicle and Echo	Northamptons		Manchester	**Northern Echo**	Darlington
			Norwich	**Northamptonshire Evening Telegraph**	Kettering
Courier and Advertiser	Dundee		Scarborough	**Observer**	Crawley
Citizen	Gloucester	**Evening Post**	Bristol	**Oxford Mail**	Oxford
Daily Echo	Bournemouth		Nottingham	**Paisley**	Glasgow
Daily Examiner	Huddersfield		Reading	**Daily Express**	
Daily Mail	Hull		Wigan	**Post**	Birmingham
Daily Post	Liverpool	**Evening Telegraph**	Coventry	**Sentinel**	Stoke
Daily Record	Glasgow		Derby	**Shropshire Star**	Telford
Dorset Echo	Weymouth		Dundee	**South Wales Evening Post**	Swansea
East Anglian Daily Times	Ipswich		Grimsby	**Southern Daily Echo**	Southampton
Eastern Daily Press	Norwich		Peterborough		
			Scunthorpe	**Star**	Sheffield
Echo	Liverpool	**Evening Times**	Glasgow		Barnsley
	Lincoln	**Express and Echo**	Exeter		Doncaster
	Sunderland	**Express Star**	Wolverhampton	**Telegraph**	Belfast
Essex Chronicle	Chelmsford	**The Gazette**	Blackpool	**Telegraph and Argus**	Bradford
Evening Advertiser	Swindon		South Shields	**Western Daily Press**	Bristol
Evening Chronicle	Oldham	**Gloucestershire Echo**	Cheltenham		
	Newcastle	**Greenock Telegraph**	Dunfermline (head office)	**Western Mail**	Cardiff
Evening Courier	Halifax	**Heartland Evening News**	Nuneaton	**Western Morning News**	Plymouth
Evening Echo	Weymouth	**Herald Express**	Torquay	**Yorkshire Evening Post**	Leeds
	Basildon	**Kent Today**	Aylesford	**Yorkshire Post**	Leeds
Evening Express	Aberdeen	**The Journal**	Newcastle		
Evening Gazette	Colchester	**Lancashire Evening Post**	Preston		
	Middlesbrough	**Lancashire**	Blackburn		
Evening Herald	Plymouth				

Editors (as at February 2003)

Daily Mail   Paul Dacre
Daily Mirror   Piers Morgan
Daily Record   Peter Cox
Daily Sport   Jeff McGowan
Daily Star   Peter Hill (previously Phil Walker)
Daily Telegraph   Charles Moore
Evening Standard   Veronica Wadley (previously Max Hastings)
Express   Christopher Williams (previously Rosie Boycott)
Guardian   Alan Rusbridger
Independent   Simon Kelner (previously Andrew Marr)
Independent on Sunday   Tristan Davies (previously Janet Street Porter)
Mail on Sunday   Peter Wright (previously Jonathan Holborow)
Metro   Kenny Campbell
News of the World   Andy Coulson (previously Rebekah Wade)

Observer   Roger Alton (previously Will Hutton, now Editor-in-Chief)
People   Acting Editor Alan Edwards (previously Neil Wallis)
Racing Post   Chris Smith (previously Alan Byrne)
Radio Times   Gill Hudson
Spectator   Boris Johnson
Sun   Rebekah Wade (previously David Yelland)
Sunday Express   Martin Townshend (previously Michael Pilgrim)
Sunday Mirror   Tina Weaver (previously Colin Myler)
Sunday Star   Hugh Whittow
Sunday Telegraph   Dominic Lawson
Sunday Times   John Witherow
Times   Robert Thomson
Tribune   Mark Seddon
Vogue   Alexandra Shulman

Agony Aunts, Horoscopes, Crosswords

Agony Aunts

Virginia Ironside   *Independent*
Jane O'Gorman   *Daily Star*
Just Joan   *Daily Record*
Eve Pollard   *Daily Mirror*
Deidre Sanders   *Sun*
Kate Saunders   *Express*
Miriam Stoppard   *Daily Mirror*

Horoscopes

Jonathan Cainer   *Daily Mirror*
Lynne Ewart   *Daily Record*
Russell Grant   *Daily Mirror*
Sally Kirkman   *Daily Star*
Marjorie Orr   *Express*
Mystic Meg   *Sun*
Shelley von Strunckel   *Evening Standard; Sunday Times*
Justin Toper   *Daily Express; Daily Star*
Peter Watson   *Daily Mail*

Crosswords

Peter Watson   *Daily Mail*
Aelred   *Independent*
Aquila   *Independent*
Araucaria   *Guardian*
Auctor   *Times*
Azed   *Observer*
Beelzebub   *Sunday Independent*
Bunthorne   *Guardian*
Columba   *Independent*
Enigmatist   *Guardian*
Gemini   *Guardian*
Mod   *Times*
Monk   *Independent*
Pasquale   *Guardian*
Paul   *Guardian*
Phi   *Independent*
Quixote   *Sunday Independent*
Rufus   *Guardian*
Spurios   *Independent*

Chess

Leonard Barden   *Evening Standard*
Raymond Keene   *Times*
Jon Speelman   *Independent*

Newspaper Cartoons and Cartoonist(s)

Alisdair   *Times*   Pugh and Way
Andy Capp   *Daily Mirror* and *Sunday Mirror*   Reg Smythe
As If   *Independent*   Sally Ann Lasson
Augusta   *Evening Standard*   Angus McGill and Dominic Poelsma
Austin   *Guardian*   Austin
Badlands   *Sun*   Steve McGarry
Beau Peep   *Daily Star*   Kettle and Christine
Ben and Katie   *Daily Star*   Doug Baker and Roca
Bill Caldwell (cartoonist)   *Daily Star*
Bogart   *Daily Mail*   Peter Plant
Bristow   *Evening Standard*   Frank Dickens

Clogger F.C.   *Daily Star*   Bill Caldwell
Colonel Blimp   *Evening Standard*   David Low
Dilbert   *Daily Telegraph* and *Express*   Scott Adams
Doonesbury   *Guardian*   Garry Trudeau
Dreadnoughts, The   *Sun*   Martin Fish
Faith, Hope and Sue   *Express*   Lisa Wild
Flatmates   *Daily Record*   Michael Atkinson
Flook (1949–84)   *Daily Mail*   Trog (Wally Fawkes)
Fred Basset   *Daily Mail*   Alex Graham
Gambols   *Express*   Barry Appleby
Garfield   *Evening Standard* and *Express*   Jim Davis
George & Lynne   *Sun*   Conrad and Gual
Giles   Daily and Sunday *Express*   Carl Ronald Giles

NEWSPAPERS

Grandad and the Lad *Daily Record* Bryan Walker
Griffin *Express* Griffin
Hagar the Horrible *Sun* Chris Browne
Heath *Daily Telegraph* Heath
Hector Breeze *Express* Hector Breeze
Horace *Daily Mirror* Kettle and Christine
I Don't Believe It *Daily Mail* Dick Millington
If *Guardian* Steve Bell
Jane *Daily Mirror* Norman Pett (originally)
The Johnsons *Daily Express* Peter Plant
Judge Dredd of 2000 AD *Daily Star* Smith and Rennie
Kipper Williams (cartoonist) *Guardian*
Liberty Meadows *Express* Frank Cho
Livvy *Sun* Bob Maher
Mandy Capp *Daily Mirror* Carla Ostrer and Mahoney
Matt *Daily Telegraph* Matt Pritchett
Modesty Blaise (1963–2001) *Evening Standard* Peter O'Donnell

Paul Thomas *Express* Paul Thomas (untitled cartoon)
Peanuts *Daily Mail* Charles Schulz
Perishers *Daily Mirror* Bill Mevin and Maurice Dodd
Peter Brookes *Times* Peter Brookes (untitled cartoon)
Potto *Evening Standard* Frank Dickens
Psycops *Sun* Wilbur
Real Life *Daily Mirror* Johnston
Rupert Bear *Express* Mary Tourtel (1920–48)
Scorer *Daily Mirror* Tomlinson, Gillat and Pugh
Shuggie and Duggie *Daily Record* Bullimore and Anderson
Steve Bell (cartoonist) *Guardian*
Striker *Sun* Pete Marsh
The Stringalongs *Times* (originally) Mark Boxer
Teenage Mum *Daily Star* Graham Hey
Tim *Independent*
Up and Running *Daily Telegraph* Gray and Shack
Weber Family *Guardian* Posy Simmonds
Wizard of Id *Evening Standard* Parker and Hart

General Information

Asahi Shimbun Japan's leading newspaper has been produced 'untouched by human hands' since 24 September 1980.

Avanti: **famous editor** Benito Mussolini edited the Milan-based socialist paper from 1912 to 1914. Mussolini subsequently founded the newspaper *Il Popolo d'Italia* in 1914.

Beachcomber Column Began in the *Daily Express* in 1917 under the name 'By the Way' its author inheriting the name 'Beachcomber', J B Morton wrote the column from 1924 to 1975 and the present author is William Hartston.

Boy's Own: **founded** in 1879 by the Religious Tract Society and ceased in 1967.

cartoon: first drawn by John Wesley Jarvis in 1814 for the Washington Federal Republican.

cartoon: first UK 'The Unknown Tongue' (printed in *Bell's New Weekly Messenger*) 8 Jan. 1832.

Children's Newspaper founded by Arthur Mee in 1919.

Christian Science Monitor: **founder** Mary Baker Eddy in Boston 1908.

clock on *Times* **Diary page** always set on 4.30.

colour supplement: first four-page section of the *New York World* 19 November 1893.

colour supplement: first UK Sunday Times Colour Section (became Sunday Times Magazine) 4 February 1962.

comic strip: first *Yellow Kid* by R F Outcault (published in the *New York World* in 1896).

Corriere della Sera although this newspaper translates as 'Evening Courier', it is a morning daily newspaper.

crossword puzzle: first compiled by Liverpool-born Arthur Wynne (published in *New York World* Sunday 21 December 1913).

crossword puzzle: first UK *Sunday Express* 2 November 1924.

crossword puzzle: first *Times* 1 February 1930 and compiled by Adrian Bell (father of ex-MP Martin Bell).

crusader logo introduced on the *Express* by Lord Beaverbrook in 1930.

Daily Express **column: famous** 'By the Way' (J B Morton under the name of 'Beachcomber').

famous sale Max Aitken sold the Express group to Trafalgar House on 30 June 1977 (subsequently sold to United Newspapers 1985).

daily newspaper: first UK *The Perfect Diurnall* Feb. 1660 (*Daily Courant* of 1702 was first successful daily).

daily poem *Independent*.

Daily Sketch: **merger** in May 1971 the *Daily Sketch* merged into the *Daily Mail*.

Daily Telegraph **editor: former** W F (Bill) Deedes.

Daily Telegraph: **news first published on front page** 1969.

Daily Worker Communist newspaper founded in 1932. Name changed to *Morning Star* in 1966 but *Daily Worker* revived in 1992.

Der Spiegel the German news magazine was founded in 1947.

Edinburgh Gazette Scottish equivalent of the *London Gazette*, founded in 1699 and appearing twice a week.

Evening News: **merger** on 31 October 1980 the *Evening News* was merged into the *Evening Standard*.

evening newspaper: first *Dawks's News-Letter* (published in London) 23 June 1696.

famous columnists *Daily Mirror* political cartoonist Vicky and columnist Cassandra.

Foreign newspapers *El Pais* – Argentina, *Avanti* – Milan, *Exame* – Brazil, *Feral Tribune* – Croatia, *Hihon Keizai Shimbun* – Japan, *La Presse* – Quebec, *Moderna Tider* – Stockholm, *Qianshao* – Hong Kong.

founded as women's paper *Daily Mirror*.

Globe the British paper was suppressed in November 1915 for spreading false rumours about Lord Kitchener's resignation.

Good Housekeeping: **founded** the British magazine was founded in 1922, although the US version was founded much earlier.

Harijan: **founder** Mahatma Gandhi founded the Indian weekly publication in 1933.

Hearst, William Randolph: famous castle San Simeon, California.

Hearst: famous newspapers *Examiner* (1887 his first), *Morning Journal* (1895 later became *Journal-American*).

Hitler diaries extracts published by *Stern* magazine in May 1983 and considered authentic by historian Hugh Trevor-Roper, but later exposed as a fake produced by a dealer in Nazi memorabilia.

Independent: launched by Andreas Whittam-Smith and associates on 7 Oct. 1986 and subsequently acquired by a consortium led by Mirror Group Newspapers, 18 March 1994.

***John Bull:* date commenced** 1906, although the character first appeared in 1712 in a pamphlet by John Arbuthnot (1667–1735).

The Liberator influential anti-slavery weekly newspaper of Abolitionist crusader William Lloyd Garrison between 1831 and 1865, published in Boston.

***Life* magazine: first published** 1936 by Henry Luce, publisher of *Time*. *Life* magazine ceased on 29 December 1972 but was relaunched in October 1978.

***Listener:* founded** by the BBC in 1929 and closed in January 1991.

***London Daily News:* founded by** Robert Maxwell in February 1987 but it folded in July when the *Evening News* was temporarily relaunched.

London Gazette Government's bulletin in which official announcements are made. Founded in 1665 as the *Oxford Gazette* and appearing 4 times a week.

magazine: shortest title *Ms*, the American feminist magazine founded in 1972, may lay claim to that title.

***Manchester Guardian:* renamed** In 1960 the *Manchester Guardian* was renamed *The Guardian*.

***Marie-Claire:* founded** the French women's magazine was founded in 1954.

Messenger Group: launched by The free newspapers were launched by Eddie Shah in Warrington in 1983 and produced by non-union workers.

***New Republic:* founded by** the American paper was founded by H D Croly in 1914.

***New Society:* founded** the weekly sociology magazine was founded in 1962 and merged into the *New Statesman* in 1988.

newspaper: best-selling *News of the World* is Britain's largest-selling newspaper (approx 4.8 million).

newspaper: first *Acta Diurna* (Daily Events) dating from 59 BC and attributed to Julius Caesar.

newspaper: first surviving English *Weekly News* 1622. (Newspapers were printed before this date but none survive.)

***New Statesman:* founded by** Beatrice and Sidney Webb in 1913 and aided by leading Fabians such as G B Shaw.

***Now:* founder** the magazine was founded by James Goldsmith in September 1979 and ceased in March 1981.

page 3 girls: year started 1970.

***People:* famous libel case** an article in 1909 alleged that chancellor David Lloyd George had committed adultery and had paid £20,000 to keep the case out of court.

***Picture Post:* first published** 1938 and founded by Edward Hulton. It closed in 1957.

***Playboy:* founded by** Hugh Hefner, December 1953.

***Post:* launched by** Eddie Shah in November 1988 and folded after 33 issues.

Press Council: founded 1953 (replaced by the Press Complaints Commission 1 January 1991).

***Private Eye:* founded** In February 1962 and saved from financial ruin by Peter Cook in April 1962.

Punch first published in 1841 and ceased production on 8 Aril 1992. Aka *The London Charivari*.

***Radio Times:* founded** 1923.

***Radio Times:* first woman editor** Sue Robinson.

***Reader's Digest:* founded** DeWitt Wallace and his wife Lila Acheson published the first issue in Greenwich Village, New York 5 February 1922.

***Scottish Daily News:* founded** launched by a workers' co-operative 5 May 1975 but closed in Oct. 1975 despite intervention by Robert Maxwell.

***Sun:* founded** 15 September 1964 when the TUC sold its shares in the *Daily Herald*.

***Sunday Correspondent:* launched** on 17 September 1989 and closed in Nov. 1990.

***Sunday Herald:* founded** in 1915 and subsequently renamed the *Sunday Graphic*; closed down in 1960.

Tatler: founded by Richard Steele in 1709 and assisted by Joseph Addison until its closure in 1711. It was replaced by the non-political *Spectator* in 1711 but the name was revived in 1901 for an illustrated monthly magazine which is still published today.

Telegraph Group moved from Fleet Street to Docklands in 1987 and printed in London and new site (1986) in Manchester.

***Time* magazine: founded by** Henry A Luce and Briton Hadden in 1923.

***Times:* previous name** *Daily Universal Register* until 1788.

***Times:* nickname** *The Thunderer* (the nickname of Thomas Barnes, editor of the *Times* 1817–41).

***Times:* news first appeared on front page** 3 May 1966.

***Today:* date commenced** launched by Eddie Shah 4 March 1986 as Britain's first full-colour, low-cost tabloid, its sales failed to achieve targets and it was subsequently sold to Tiny Rowland's Lonrho Co.

Wapping: exodus to *Times*, *Sunday Times*, *Sun* and *News of the World* moved overnight to a new plant in Wapping 25 Jan. 1986.

yellow journalism term coined to describe the sensationalistic reporting and frenzied promotional schemes adopted in the fierce circulation wars between William Randolph Hearst's *Journal* and Joseph Pulitzer's *World*.

NEWSPAPERS

NOBEL PRIZE WINNERS

	Physics	Chemistry	Literature	Medicine	Peace	Economics
1901	Wilhelm Röntgen (Ger.) Discovery of X-rays	Jacobus van't Hoff (Neth.) Laws of chemical dynamics and osmotic pressure	René Sully-Prudhomme (Fr.) Poet	Emil von Behring (Ger.) Work on serum therapy Pioneer in immunology	Jean Henri Dunant (Switz.) Frédéric Passy (Fr.)	
1902	Hendrik Lorentz (Neth.) Pieter Zeeman (Neth.) Magnetism on radiation	Emil Fischer (Ger.) Work on sugar and purine syntheses	Theodor Mommsen (Ger.) Historian	Sir Ronald Ross (Brit.) Discovery of how malaria enters an organism	Elie Ducommun (Switz.) Charles Gobat (Switz.)	
1903	Antoine-Henri Becquerel (Fr.) Pierre and Marie Curie (Fr.) Radioactivity	Svante Arrhenius (Swed.) Theory of electrolytic dissociation	Björnsterne Björnson (Nor.) Novelist, poet, dramatist	Niels Finsen (Den.) Phototherapy	Sir William Cremer (Brit.) Founder of Workmen's Peace Association	
1904	Lord Rayleigh (Brit.) Discovery of argon	Sir William Ramsay (Brit.) Discovery of inert gases	Frédéric Mistral (Fr.) Poet J Echegaray Eizaguirre (Sp.)	Ivan Pavlov (Russ.) Physiology of digestion	Institute of International Law (founded 1873)	
1905	Philipp Lenard (Ger.) Research on cathode rays	Adolf von Baeyer (Ger.) Work on organic dyes	H Sienkiewicz (Pol.) Novelist	Robert Koch (Ger.) Tuberculosis research	Bertha von Suttner (Austria)	
1906	Sir J J Thomson (Brit.) Research into electrical conductivity of gases	Henri Moissan (Fr.) Isolation of fluorine Moissan furnace	Giosuè Carducci (Ita.) Poet	Camillo Golgi (Ita.) and S Ramon y Cajal (Sp.) Structure of nervous system	Theodore Roosevelt (US)	
1907	A A Michelson (US) Spectroscopic and metrological investigations	Eduard Buchner (Ger.) Discovery of non-cellular fermentation	Rudyard Kipling (Brit.) Poet and novelist	Alphonse Laveran (Fr.) Discovery of the role of protozoa in diseases	Ernesto T Moneta (Ita.) Louis Renault (Fr.)	
1908	Gabriel Lippman (Fr.) Photographic reproduction of colours	Lord Rutherford (Brit.) Disintegration of elements Chemistry of radioactivity	Rudolf Eucken (Ger.) Philosopher	Paul Ehrlich (Ger.) Ilya Mechnikov (Russ.) Work on immunity	Klas P Arnoldson (Swed.) Fredrik Bajer (Den.)	
1909	Guglielmo Marconi (Ita.) Karl Braun (Ger.) Wireless telegraphy	Wilhelm Ostwald (Ger.) Pioneer work on catalysis, chemical equilibrium and reaction velocities	Selma Lagerlöf (Swed.) Novelist	Emil Kocher (Switz.) Physiology, pathology and surgery of thyroid gland	Baron d'Estournelles de Constant (Fr.) Auguste Beernaert (Belg.)	
1910	J van Der Waals (Neth.) Gas and liquid equation	Otto Wallach (Ger.) Alicyclic combinations	Paul von Heyse (Ger.) Poet and novelist	Albrecht Kossel (Ger.) Cellular chemistry research	International Peace Bureau (founded 1891)	

	Physics	Chemistry	Literature	Medicine	Peace	Economics
1911	Wilhelm Wien (Ger.) Discoveries regarding laws governing heat radiation	Marie Curie (Fr.) Discovered/isolated radium Discovered Polonium	Maurice Maeterlinck (Belg.) Dramatist	Allvar Gullstrand (Swed.) Work on dioptrics of the eye	Tobias Asser (Neth.) Alfred Fried (Austria)	
1912	Nils Gustaf Dalén (Swed.) Invention of automatic regulators for lighting coastal beacons and light buoys	Victor Grignard (Fr.) Paul Sabatier (Fr.) Discovery of Grignard reagents and hydrogenating organic compounds	Gerhart Hauptmann (Ger.) Dramatist	Alexis Carrel (Fr.) Work on vascular suture Transplantation of organs	Elihu Root (US)	
1913	H Kamerlingh Onnes (Neth.) Liquid helium production Low temperature properties	Alfred Werner (Switz.) Work on the linkage of atoms in molecules	Sir R Tagore (India) Poet	Charles Richet (Fr.) Work on anaphylaxis	Henri Lafontaine (Belg.)	
1914	Max von Laue (Ger.) Discovery of diffraction of X-rays by crystals	Theodore Richards (US) Accurate determination of atomic weights of elements	no award	Robert Barany (Austria) Work on vestibular apparatus	no award	
1915	Sir William Bragg (Brit.) Sir Lawrence Bragg (Brit.) Analysis of crystals by means of X-rays	Richard Willstätter (Ger.) Pioneer researches on plant pigments, especially chlorophyll	Romain Rolland (Fr.) Novelist	no award	no award	
1916	no award	no award	V von Heidenstam (Swed.) Poet	no award	no award	
1917	Charles Barkla (Brit.) Discovery of characteristic X-radiation of elements	no award	Karl Gjellerup (Den.) H Pontoppidan (Den.) Novelists	no award	International Red Cross Committee (founded 1863)	
1918	Max Planck (Ger.) Elemental quantum theory	Fritz Haber (Ger.) Synthesis of ammonia	no award	no award	no award	
1919	Johannes Stark (Ger.) Doppler effect in positive ions and spectral line division	no award	Carl Spitteler (Switz.) Poet and novelist	Jules Bordet (Belg.) Discoveries in regard to immunity	Woodrow Wilson (US)	
1920	Charles Guillaume (Switz.) Discovery of anomalies in alloys	Walther Nernst (Ger.) Work in thermochemistry	Knut Hamsun (Nor.) Novelist	August Krogh (Den.) Discovery of capillary motor regulating mechanism	Léon Bourgeois (Fr.)	

NOBEL PRIZE WINNERS

	Physics	Chemistry	Literature	Medicine	Peace	Economics
1921	Albert Einstein (Switz.) Services to theoretical physics	Frederick Soddy (Brit.) Chemistry of radioactive substances and occurrence and nature of isotopes	Anatole France (Fr.) Novelist	no award	Karl Branting (Swed.) Christian Louis Lange (Nor.)	
1922	Niels Bohr (Den.) Investigation of atomic structure and radiation	Francis Aston (Brit.) Work with mass spectrograph	Jacinto Benavente y Martinez (Spa.) Dramatist	Archibald Hill (Brit.) Discovery relating to heat production in muscles	Fridtjof Nansen (Nor.)	
1923	Robert Millikan (US) Work on elementary electric charge	Fritz Pregl (Austria) Method of microanalysis of organic substances	W B Yeats (Ire.) Poet	Sir F G Banting (Can.) J J R Macleod (Brit.) Discovery of insulin	no award	
1924	Karl Siegbahn (Swed.) Work in X-ray spectroscopy	no award	Wladyslaw Reymont (Pol.) Novelist	Willem Einthoven (Neth.) Discovery of electro-cardiogram mechanism	no award	
1925	James Franck (Ger.) Gustav Hertz (Ger.) Discovery of laws governing impact of electrons upon an atom	Richard Zsigmondy (Austria) Elucidation of hetero-geneous nature of colloidal solutions	George Bernard Shaw (Ire.) Dramatist	no award	Austen Chamberlain (Brit.) Charles G Dawes (US)	
1926	Jean-Baptiste Perrin (Fr.) Work on discontinuous structure of matter	Theodor Svedberg (Swed.) Work on disperse systems	Grazia Deledda (Ita.) Novelist	Johannes Fibiger (Den.) Contributions to cancer research	Aristide Briand (Fr.) Gustav Stresemann (Ger.)	
1927	Arthur Holly Compton (US) Discovery of wave change in diffused X-rays Charles Wilson (Brit.) Visibility of electric particles	Heinrich Wieland (Ger.) Researches into the constitution of bile acids	Henri Bergson (Fr.) Philosopher	J Wagner-Jauregg (Austria) Work on malaria inoculation in dementia paralytica	Ferdinand Buisson (Fr.) Ludwig Quidde (Ger.)	
1928	Owen Richardson (Brit.) Richardson's Law	Adolf Windaus (Ger.) Sterols + vitamin connection	Sigrid Undset (Nor.) Novelist	Charles Nicolle (Fr.) Work on typhus	no award	
1929	Louis de Broglie (Fr.) Discovery of the wave nature of electrons	Sir Arthur Harden (Brit.) H von Euler-Chelpin (Swed.) Fermentation of sugars and connective enzymes	Thomas Mann (Ger.) Novelist	Christiaan Eijkman (Neth.) Antineuritic vitamin Sir F Hopkins (Brit.) Growth stimulating vitamins	Frank B Kellogg (US)	
1930	Sir C Raman (India) Work on light diffusion	Hans Fischer (Ger.) Chlorophyll research	Sinclair Lewis (US) Novelist	Karl Landsteiner (US) Human blood grouping	Nathan Söderblom (Swed.)	

	Physics	Chemistry	Literature	Medicine	Peace	Economics
1931	no award	Karl Bosch (Ger.) Friedrich Bergius (Ger.) High pressure methods	Erik Axel Karlfeldt (Swed.) Poet	Otto Warburg (Ger.) Discovery of nature and action of respiratory enzyme	Jane Addams (US) Nicholas Murray Butler (US)	
1932	Werner Heisenberg (Ger.) Indeterminacy principle of quantum mechanics	Irving Langmuir (US) Discoveries in surface chemistry	John Galsworthy (Brit.) Novelist	Edgar D Adrian (Brit.) Sir C Sherrington (Brit.) Neuron investigations	no award	
1933	P A M Dirac (Brit.) Erwin Schrödinger (Austria) Intro of wave equations in quantum mechanics	no award	Ivan Bunin (USSR) Novelist	Thomas Hunt Morgan (US) Heredity transmission functions of chromosomes	Sir Norman Angell (Brit.)	
1934	no award	Harold Urey (US) Discovery of heavy hydrogen	Luigi Pirandello (Ita.) Dramatist	George R Minot (US) William P Murphy (US) George H Whipple (US) Anaemia treatments	Arthur Henderson (Brit.)	
1935	Sir James Chadwick (Brit.) Discovery of the neutron	Frédéric Joliot-Curie (Fr.) Irène Joliot-Curie (Fr.) Radioactive element theory	no award	Hans Spemann (Ger.) Organizer effect in embryo	Carl von Ossietzky (Ger.)	
1936	Victor Hess (Austria) Cosmic radiation discovery Carl Anderson (US) Positron discovery	Peter Debye (Neth.) Work on dipole moments and diffraction of X-rays and electrons in gases	Eugene O'Neill (US) Dramatist	Sir H H Dale (Brit.) Otto Loewi (Ger.) Work on chemical transmission of nerve impulses	Carlos S Lamas (Arg.)	
1937	Clinton Davisson (US) George P Thomson (Brit.) Interference phenomenon in crystals irradiated by electrons	Walter Haworth (Brit.) Research on carbohydrates and vitamin C Paul Karrer (Switz.) Research on Carotenoids	Roger Martin du Gard (Fr.) Novelist	Albert Szent-Györgyi (Hung.) Work on biological combustion	Viscount Cecil of Chelwood (Brit.)	
1938	Enrico Fermi (Ita.) Artificial radioactive element by neutron irradiation	Richard Kuhn (Ger.) Research on carotenoids (declined)	Pearl Buck (US) Novelist	Corneille Heymans (Belg.) Discovery of sinus role in respiration regulation	Nansen International Office for Refugees (founded 1931)	
1939	Ernest Lawrence (US) Invented cyclotron	Adolf Butenandt (Ger.) Work on sexual hormones (declined) Leopold Ružička (Switz.) Polymethylenes research	Frans Eemil Sillanpää (Fin.) Novelist	Gerhard Domagk (Ger) Antibacterial effect of Prontosil (declined)	no award	

NOBEL   PRIZE   WINNERS

	Physics	Chemistry	Literature	Medicine	Peace	Economics
1940	no award	no award	no award	no award	no award	
1941	no award	no award	no award	no award	no award	
1942	no award	no award	no award	no award	no award	
1943	Otto Stern (US) Discovery of the magnetic moment of the proton	George de Hevesy (Hung.) Use of isotopes as tracers in chemical research	no award	Henrik Dam (Den.) Discovery of vitamin K Edward A Doisy (US) Chemical nature of vitamin K	no award	
1944	Isidor Rabi (US) Resonance method for registration of magnetic properties of atomic nuclei	Otto Hahn (Ger.) Discovery of the fission of heavy nuclei	J V Jensen (Den.) Novelist	Joseph Erlanger (US) Herbert S Gasser (US) Research on differentiated functions of nerve fibres	International Red Cross Committee (founded 1863)	
1945	Wolfgang Pauli (Austria) Discovery of the exclusion principle	Artturi Virtanen (Fin.) Invention of fodder preservation method	Gabriela Mistral (Chile) Poet	Sir Alexander Fleming (Brit.) Ernst B Chain (Brit.) Lord Florey (Aus.) Penicillin discovery	Cordell Hull (US)	
1946	Percy Bridgman (US) Discoveries in the domain of high-pressure physics	James Sumner (US) Wendell Stanley (US) John Northrop (US) Enzyme research	Herman Hesse (Switz.) Novelist	Hermann J Muller (US) Production of mutations by X-ray irradiation	Emily Greene Balch (US) John R Mott (US)	
1947	Edward Appleton (Brit.) Discovery of Appleton layer in upper atmosphere	Robert Robinson (Brit.) Investigations on alkaloids and other plant products	André Gide (Fr.) Novelist and essayist	Carl F Cori (US) Gerty T Cori (US) Bernardo Houssay (Arg.) Glycogen conversion	American Friends Service Committee (US) Friends Service Council (London)	
1948	Patrick Blackett (Brit.) Discoveries in the domain of nuclear physics	Arne Tiselius (Swed.) Researches on electro-phoresis and adsorption	T S Eliot (Brit.) Poet and critic	Paul Müller (Switz.) Properties of DDT	no award	
1949	Yukawa Hideki (Jap.) Prediction of the existence of mesons	William Giauque (US) Behaviour of substances at extremely low temps	William Faulkner (US) Novelist	Walter Rudolf Hess (Switz.) Middle brain function Antonio Egas Moniz (Port.) Leucotomy research	Lord Boyd-Orr (Brit.)	
1950	Cecil Powell (Brit.) Photographic method of studying nuclear processes; discoveries about mesons	Otto Diels (Ger.) Kurt Alder (Ger.) Discovery and development of diene synthesis	Bertrand Russell (Brit.) Philosopher	Philip S Hench (US) Edward C Kendall (US) Tadeus Reichstein (Switz.) Cortex hormones research	Ralph Bunche (US)	

	Physics	Chemistry	Literature	Medicine	Peace	Economics
1951	John Cockcroft (Brit.) Ernest Walton (Ire.) Atomic nuclei research	Edwin McMillan (US) Glenn Seaborg (US) Transuranium element work	Pär Lagerkvist (Swed.) Novelist	Max Theiler (SA) Yellow fever research	Léon Jouhaux (Fr.)	
1952	Felix Bloch (US) Edward Purcell (US) Discovery of nuclear magnetic resonance in solids	Archer Martin (Brit.) Richard Synge (Brit.) Development of partition chromatography	François Mauriac (Fr.) Poet, novelist, dramatist	Selman A Waksman (US) Discovery of streptomycin	Albert Schweitzer (Alsace)	
1953	Frits Zernike (Neth.) Method of phase contrast microscopy	Hermann Staudinger (Ger.) Work on macromolecules	Winston Churchill (Brit.) Historian and orator	Fritz A Lipman (US) H A Krebs (Brit.) Discovery of coenzyme A	George C Marshall (US)	
1954	Max Born (Brit.) Wave functions studies Walther Bothe (Ger.) Coincidence method	Linus Pauling (US) Study of the nature of the chemical bond	Ernest Hemingway (US) Novelist	John F Enders (US) Thomas H Weller (US) Frederick Robbins (US) Polio virus in tissue culture	Office of the UN High Commissioner for Refugees (founded 1951)	
1955	Willis Lamb Jnr (US) Hydrogen spectrum study Polykarp Kusch (US) Magnetic electron study	Vincent du Vigneaud (US) First synthesis of a polypeptide hormone	Halldór Laxness (Ice.) Novelist	Axel Hugo Theorell (Swed.) Nature and mode of action of oxidation enzymes	no award	
1956	William Shockley (US) John Bardeen (US) Walter Brattain (US) Discovery of transistor effect	Nikolay Semyonov (USSR) Cyril Hinshelwood (Brit.) Work on the kinetics of chemical reactions	Juan Ramon Jimenez (Spa.) Poet	Werner Forssman (Ger.) Dickinson Richards (US) André F Cournand (US) Heart catheterisation	no award	
1957	Tsung-Dao Lee (China) Chen Ning Yang (China) Principle of parity research	Alexander Todd (Brit.) Work on nucleotides and nucleotide coenzymes	Albert Camus (Fr.) Novelist and dramatist	Daniel Bovet (Ita.) Production of curare	Lester B Pearson (Can.)	
1958	Pavel A Cherenkov (USSR) Ilya M Frank (USSR) Igor Y Tamm (USSR) Discovery and interpretation of Cherenkov effect	Frederick Sanger (Brit.) Determination of structure of the insulin molecule	Boris Pasternak (USSR) Novelist and poet (declined)	George W Beadle (US) Edward L Tatum (US) Joshua Lederberg (US) Research in genetics	Dominique G Pire (Belg.)	
1959	Emilio Segrè (US) Owen Chamberlain (US) Antiproton research	Jaroslav Heyrovsky (Czech) Discovery + development of polarography	Salvatore Quasimodo (Ita.) Poet	Severo Ochoa (US) Arthur Kornberg (US) Nucleic acids research	Philip Noel-Baker (Brit.)	

	Physics	Chemistry	Literature	Medicine	Peace	Economics
1960	Donald Glaser (US) Development of the bubble chamber	Willard Libby (US) Development of radio-carbon dating	Saint-John Perse (Fr.) Poet	Macfarlane Burnet (Aus.) Peter B Medawar (Brit.) Tissue transplant research	Albert Lutuli (SA)	
1961	Robert Hofstadter (US) Atomic nucleon research Rudolf Mössbauer (Ger.) Mössbauer effect	Melvin Calvin (US) Study of chemical steps that take place during photosynthesis	Ivo Andrić (Yug) Novelist	Georg von Békésy (US) Functions of the inner ear	Dag Hammarskjöld (Swed.)	
1962	Lev D Landau (USSR) Research into condensed state of matter	John C Kendrew (Brit.) Max F Perutz (Brit.) Hemoprotein research	John Steinbeck (US) Novelist	Francis H C Crick (Brit.) James D Watson (US) Maurice Wilkins (Brit.) DNA molecular structure	Linus Pauling (US)	
1963	J H D Jensen (Ger.) Maria Goeppert Mayer (US) Eugene Paul Wigner (US) Atomic nuclei research	Giulio Natta (Ita.) Karl Ziegler (Ger.) Research into polymers in the field of plastics	George Seferis (Gre.) Poet	Sir John Eccles (Aus.) Alan Lloyd Hodgkin (Brit.) Andrew Huxley (Brit.) Nerve fibre research	International Red Cross and League of Red Cross (HQ of both in Geneva)	
1964	Charles H Townes (US) Nikolay G Basov (USSR) Aleksandr Prokhorov (USSR) Maser/laser research	Dorothy Hodgkin (Brit.) Determining the structure of biochemical compounds used to control pernicious anaemia	Jean-Paul Sartre (Fr.) Philosopher and dramatist (declined)	Konrad Bloch (US) Feodor Lynen (Ger.) Cholesterol research	Martin Luther King Jr (US)	
1965	Julian Schwinger (US) Richard Feynman (US) Tomonaga Shin'ichiro (Jap.) Quantum electrodynamics	Robert B Woodward (US) Synthesis of chlorophyll	Mikhail Sholokhov (USSR) Novelist	François Jacob (Fr.) Jacques Monod (Fr.) André Lwolf (Fr.) Body cells research	UN Children's Fund (founded 1946)	
1966	Alfred Kastler (Fr.) Optical methods for studying Hertzian resonances in atoms	Robert S Mulliken (US) Research into electronic structure of molecules	Shmuel Yosef Agnon (Isr.) Nelly Sachs (Swed.) Novelist and poet	Charles B Huggins (US) Francis Peyton Rous (US) Cancer research	no award	
1967	Hans A Bethe (US) Discoveries concerning the energy production of stars	Manfred Eigen (Ger.) Ronald G W Norrish (Brit.) George Porter (Brit.) Chemical reaction research	Miguel Angel Asturias (Guat.) Novelist	Haldan Keffer Hartline (US) George Wald (US) Ragnar A Granit (Swed.) Eye research	no award	
1968	Luis W Alvarez (US) Discovered resonance states	Lars Onsager (US) Work on theory of thermo-dynamics of irreversible processes	Kawabata Yasunari (Jap.) Novelist	Robert W Holley (US) H Gobind Khorana (US) Marshall Nirenberg (US) Genetic code deciphering	René Cassin (Fr.)	

	Physics	Chemistry	Literature	Medicine	Peace	Economics
1969	Murray Gell-Mann (US) Discoveries concerning the classification of elementary particles	Derek H R Barton (Brit.) Odd Hassel (Nor.) Organic compound research	Samuel Beckett (Ire.) Novelist and dramatist	Max Delbrück (US) Alfred D Hershey (US) Salvador E Luria (US) Research of viruses	International Labour Organization (founded 1919)	Ragnar Frisch (Nor.) Jan Tinbergen (Neth.) Work in econometrics
1970	Hannes Alfvén (Swed.) Louis Néel (Fr.) Work in magnetohydro-dynamics and magnetism	Luis Leloir (Arg.) Discovery of sugar nucleo-tides and their role in the biosynthesis of carbohydrates	A Solzhenitsyn (USSR) Novelist	Julius Axelrod (US) Bernard Katz (Brit.) Ulf von Euler (Swed.) Nerve transmission research	Norman Borlaug (US)	Paul Samuelson (US) Work in scientific analysis of economic theory
1971	Dennis Gabor (Brit.) Holography invention	Gerhard Herzberg (Can.) Molecule structure research	Pablo Neruda (Chile) Poet	Earl W Sutherland Jr (US) Action of hormones	Willy Brandt (Ger.)	Simon Kuznets (US) Economic growth of nations
1972	John Bardeen (US) Leon N Cooper (US) John R Schrieffer (US) Superconductivity theory	Christian B Anfinsen (US) Stanford Moore (US) William H Stein (US) Enzyme chemistry research	Heinrich Böll (Ger.) Novelist	Gerald M Edelman (US) Rodney Porter (Brit.) Research on the chemical structure of antibodies	no award	John Hicks (Brit.) Kenneth J. Arrow (US) Welfare theory and economic equilibrium theory
1973	Leo Esaki (Jap.) Ivar Giaever (US) Brian Josephson (Brit.) Superconductivity research	Ernst Fischer (Ger.) Geoffrey Wilkinson (Brit.) Organometallic chemistry	Patrick White (Aus.) Novelist	Karl von Frisch (Austria) Konrad Lorenz (Austria) Nikolaas Tinbergen (Neth.) Animal behaviour patterns	Henry Kissinger (US) Le Duc Tho (N. Viet.) (declined)	Wassily Leontief (US) Input analysis
1974	Sir Martin Ryle (Brit.) Antony Hewish (Brit.) Work in radio astronomy	Paul J Flory (US) Studies of long-chain molecules	Eyvind Johnson (Swed.) Harry Martinson (Swed.) Novelist and poet	Albert Claude (US) Christian R de Duve (Belg.) George E Palade (US) Cell structure research	Sato Eisaku (Jap.) Sean MacBride (Ire.)	Gunnar Myrdal (Swed.) Friedrich von Hayek (Brit.) Economic, social and institutional phenomena
1975	Aage Bohr (Den.) Ben R Mottelson (Den.) L James Rainwater (US) Atomic nucleus research paved way for nuclear fusion	J W Cornforth (Brit.) Vladimir Prelog (Switz.) Work in stereochemistry	Eugenio Montale (Ita.) Poet	Renato Dulbecco (US) Howard M Temin (US) David Baltimore (US) Tumour viruses research	Andrey D Sakharov (USSR)	Leonid Kantorovich (USSR) Tjalling Koopmans (US) Contribution to the theory of optimum allocation of resources
1976	Burton Richter (US) Samuel C C Ting (US) Elementary particles research	William Lipscomb (US) Structure of boranes	Saul Bellow (US) Novelist	Baruch Blumberg (US) D Carleton Gajdusek (US) Infectious diseases research	Mairead Corrigan (N. Ire.) Betty Williams (N. Ire.)	Milton Friedman (US) Consumption analysis and monetary theory

Year	Physics	Chemistry	Literature	Medicine	Peace	Economics
1977	Philip W Anderson (US) Sir Nevill Mott (Brit.) John H Van Vleck (US) Studies into behaviour of electrons in magnetic non-crystalline solids	Ilya Prigogine (Belg.) Widening the scope of thermodynamics	Vicente Aleixandre (Spa.) Poet	Rosalyn S Yalow (US) Roger Guillemin (US) Andrew Schally (US) Development of radio-immunoassay, research on pituitary hormones	Amnesty International (founded 1961)	Bertil Ohlin (Swed.) James Meade (Brit.) Contributions to theory of International trade
1978	Pyotr L Kapitsa (USSR) Invention of helium liquefier Robert W Wilson (US) Arno A Penzias (US) Discovery of cosmic micro-wave background radiation	Peter D Mitchell (Brit.) Formulation of a theory of energy transfer processes in biological systems	Isaac Bashevis Singer (US) Novelist	Werner Arber (Switz.) Daniel Nathans (US) Hamilton O Smith (US) Discovery of enzymes that fragment DNAs	Menachem Begin (Isr.) Anwar Sadat (Egy.)	Herbert A Simon (US) Decision-making processes in economic organisations
1979	Sheldon Glashow (US) Abdus Salam (Pak.) Steven Weinberg (Ger.) Establishment of analogy between electromagnetism and subatomic particles	Herbert C Brown (US) Georg Wittig (Ger.) Introduction of compounds of boron and phosphorus in the synthesis of organic substances	Odysseus Elytis (Greece) Poet	Allan M Cormack (US) Godfrey N Hounsfield (Brit.) Development of computed axial tomography scan	Mother Teresa of Calcutta (India)	W Arthur Lewis (Brit.) Theodore W. Schultz (US) Analyses of economic processes in developing nations
1980	James W Cronin (US) Val L Fitch (US) Demonstration of simultaneous violation of both charge-conjugation + parity inversion symmetries	Paul Berg (US) 1st preparation of hybrid DNA Walter Gilbert (US) Frederick Sanger (Brit.) Development of chemical analysis of DNA structure	Czeslaw Milosz (US) Poet	Baruj Benacerraf (US) George D Snell (US) Jean Dausset (Fr.) Investigations of genetic control of the response of immunological system to foreign substances	Adolfo Pérez Esquivel (Arg.)	Lawrence R Klein (US) Development and analysis of empirical models of business fluctuations
1981	Kai M Siegbahn (Swed.) Nicolaas Bloembergen (US) Electron spectroscopy for chemical analysis Arthur L Schawlow (US) Applications of lasers in spectroscopy	Fukui Kenichi (Jap.) Roald Hoffmann (US) Orbital symmetry interpretation of chemical reactions	Elias Canetti (Bulg.) Novelist and essayist	Roger W Sperry (US) Functions of the cerebral hemispheres Torsten N Wiesel (Swed.) David H Hubel (US) Processing of visual information by the brain	Office of the United Nations High Commissioner for Refugees (founded 1951)	James Tobin (US) Empirical macro-economic theories
1982	Kenneth G Wilson (US) Analysis of continuous phase transitions	Aaron Klug (Brit.) Determination of structure of biological substances	Gabriel G Márquez (Col.) Novelist, journalist and social critic	Sune K Bergström (Swe.) Bengt I Samuelsson (Swe.) John R Vane (Brit.) Prostaglandins research	Alva Myrdal (Swed.) Alfonso G. Robles (Mex.)	George Stigler (US) Economic effects of governmental regulation

	Physics	Chemistry	Literature	Medicine	Peace	Economics
1983	S Chandrasekhar (US) William A Fowler (US) Research into stars	Henry Taube (Can.) Study of electron transfer reactions	William Golding (Brit.) Novelist	Barbara McLintock (US) Discovery of mobile plant genes affecting heredity	Lech Walesa (Pol.)	Gerard Debreu (US) Mathematical proof of supply and demand theory
1984	Carlo Rubbia (Ita.) Simon van der Meer (Neth.) Discovery of subatomic particles W and Z which supports electro weak theory	Bruce Merrifield (US) Development of a method of polypeptide synthesis	Jaroslav Seifert (Czech.) Poet	Niels K Jerne (Den.) Georges J F Kohler (Ger.) Cesar Milstein (Arg.) Study of monoclonal antibodies	Desmond Tutu (SA)	Richard Stone (Brit.) Development of national income accounting system
1985	Klaus von Klitzing (Ger.) Discovery of quantised Hall effect concerning exact measurement of electrical resistance	Herbert A Hauptman (US) Jerome Karle (US) Mapping chemical structure of small molecules	Claude Simon (Fr.) Novelist	Michael S Brown (US) Joseph L Goldstein (US) Cholesterol metabolism cell receptors	International Physicians for the Prevention of Nuclear War (founded 1980)	Franco Modigliani (US) Financial market theory and household savings
1986	Ernst Ruska (Ger.) Gerd Binnig (Ger.) Heinrich Rohrer (Switz.) Electron microscopes	Dudley Herschbach (US) Yuan T Lee (US) John C Polyani (Can.) Analytical methodology	Wole Soyinka (Nigeria) Playwright and poet	Stanley Cohen (US) Rita Levi-Montalcini (Ita.) Discovery of regulatory agents concerning cell growths	Elie Wiesel (Fr.)	James M Buchanan (US) Political theories advocating limited government role in the economy
1987	J Georg Bednorz (Ger.) K Alex Müller (Switz.) Discovery of new superconducting materials	Charles J Pedersen (US) Donald J Cram (US) Jean-Marie Lehn (Fr.) molecule development	Joseph Brodsky (US) Poet and essayist	Tonegawa Susumu (Jap.) Study of genetic aspects of antibodies	Oscar Arias Sanchez (Costa Rica)	Robert M Solow (US) Economic growth theory
1988	Leon Lederman (US) Melvin Schwartz (US) Jack Steinberger (US) Subatomic particle research	Johann Deisenhofer (Ger.) Robert Huber (Ger.) Hartmut Michel (Ger.) Photosynthesis research	Naguib Mahfouz (Egypt) Novelist	James W Black (Brit.) Gertrude B Elion (US) George H Hitchings (US) Drug research	UN Peacekeeping Forces	Maurice Allais (Fr.) Market theory
1989	Hans Dehmelt (US) Wolfgang Paul (Ger.) Norman Ramsey (US)	Sydney Altman (US) Thomas Cech (US) RNA research	Camilo Jose Cela (Spa.) Poet and novelist	J Michael Bishop (US) Harold E Varmus (US)	Tenzin Gyatso (Tib.) Dalai Lama XIV	Trygve Haavelmo (Nor.) Quantitative economics
1990	Jerome Friedman (US) Henry Kendall (US) Richard Taylor (Can.) Quark model theory	Elias James Corey (US) Retrosynthetic analysis	Octavio Paz (Mex.) Poet	Joseph E Murray (US) E Donnall Thomas (US)	Mikhail Gorbachev (Rus.)	Harry M Markowitz (US) Merton Miller (US) William Sharpe (US) Financial economic theory

	Physics	Chemistry	Literature	Medicine	Peace	Economics
1991	Pierre-Gilles de Gennes (Fr.) Superconductivity theory	Richard R Ernst (Switz.) Spectroscopy development	Nadine Gordimer (SA)	Erwin Neher (Ger.) Bert Sakmann (Ger.) Patch-clamp technique	Aung San Suu Kyi (Burma)	Ronald Coase (Brit.) Transaction cost theory
1992	George Charpak (Fr.) Elementary particle study	Rudolph A Marcus (US) Electron transfer	Derek Walcott (St Lucia) Poet	Edmond H Fischer (US) Edwin G Krebs (US) Protein regulation	Rigoberta Menchú (Guat.)	Gary S Becker (US) Microeconomic analysis
1993	Russell Hulse (US) Joseph Hooton Taylor (US) Discovery of new type of pulsar	Kary Banks Mullis (US) Polymerase chain reaction Michael Smith (Can.) Mutagenesis theory	Toni Morrison (US) Novelist	Richard Roberts (Brit.) Phillip Allen Sharp (US) Mosaic genes discovery	Nelson Mandela (SA) F W de Klerk (SA)	Robert Fugel (US) Douglas North (US) Quantitative methods as reasons for economic change
1994	Clifford Shull (US) Bertram Brockhouse (Can.) Study of neutron beams	George Olah (US) Carbocations	Kenzaburo Oe (Jap.) Novelist	Martin Rodbell (US) Alfred G Gilman (US) Discovery of G protein	Yasser Arafat (Pal.) Shimon Peres (Isr.) Yitzhak Rabin (Isr.)	John Nash (US) John Harsanyi (US) Reinhard Selten (Ger.) Games theory
1995	Martin L Pearl (US) Tau lepton discovery Frederick Reines (US) Neutrino detection	F Sherwood Rowland (US) Mario Molina (Mex.) Paul Crutzen (Ned.) Ozone layer research	Seamus Heaney (Ire.) Poet	Edward B Lewis (US) Eric F Wieschaus (US) C Nüsslein-Volhard (Ger.) Genes theory	Joseph Rotblat (Brit.) Pugwash Conferences on Science and World Affairs	Robert E Lucas (US) Macroeconomic analysis
1996	David M Lee (US) Douglas D Osheroff (US) Robert C Richardson (US) Discovery of superfluidity in helium-3	Harry Kroto (Brit.) Robert Curl (US) Richard Smalley (US) Discovery of C_{60} molecule	Wislawa Szymborska (Pol.) Poet	Peter C Doherty (Aus.) Rolf M Zinkernagel (Switz.)	Jose Ramos-Horta (E. Timor) Bishop Carlos Belo of Dili	James Mirrlees (Brit.) William Vickrey (Can.)
1997	Steven Chu (US) Claude Cohen-Tannoudji (Fr.) William D Phillips (US) Atom research	John Walker (Brit.) Paul Boyer (US) Jens Skou (Den.) Molecular biology research	Dario Fo (Ita.) Playwright	Stanley B Prusiner (US) Discovery of prions	Ms Jodie Williams (US) and International Campaign to Ban Landmines	Robert Merton (US) Myron Scholes (US) Fischer Black (US) Contribution to economic theory
1998	Robert B Laughlin (US) Horst L Stormer (Ger.) Daniel C Tsui (US) Quantum fluids	John Pople (Brit.) Walter Kohn (US) Quantum theory application to molecules	José Saramago (Port.) Novelist	Robert S Furghgott (US) Louis J Ignarro (US) Ferid Murad (US) Cardiovascular research	John Hume (N. Ire.) David Trimble (N. Ire.) For 'Good Friday' Agreement	Amartya Sen (India) Welfare economics
1999	Gerardus T Hooft (Neth.) Martinus J G Veltman (Neth.) Study of electro-weak interactions	Ahmed Zewail (Egypt) Femtosecond spectroscopy	Günter Grass (Ger.) Novelist	Günter Blobel (Ger.) Study of proteins	Médecins Sans Frontières (Belg.)	Robert A Mundell (Can.) Fiscal policy analysis

	Physics	Chemistry	Medicine	Literature	Peace	Economics
2000	Herbert Kroemer (Ger.) Zhores Alferov (Ger.) Developing semiconductor heterostructures Jack S Kilby (US) Invention of the integrated circuit	Alan J Heeger (US) Alan G MacDiarmid (US) Hideki Shirakawa (Japan) Discovery of conductive polymers	Arvid Carlsson (Sweden) Paul Greengard (US) Eric Kandel (US) Research into signal transduction in the nervous system	Gao Xingjian (China)	Kim Dae Jung (S. Korea) Work in reconciliation with North Korea	James J Heckman (Ger.) Daniel L McFadden (US) Contribution to economic theory and analysis
2001	Eric A Cornell (US) Wolfgang Ketterle (Ger.) Carl E Wieman (US) Bose-Einstein condensation in dilute gases of alkali atoms and studies of the properties of the condensates	William S Knowles (US) Ryoji Noyori (Jap.) Work on chirally catalysed hydrogenation reactions K Barry Sharpless (US) Work on chirally catalysed oxidation reactions	Leland H Hartwell (US) R Timothy Hunt (Brit.) Sir Paul M Nurse (Brit.) Discoveries of key regulators of the cell cycle	V S Naipaul (Trin.)	United Nations Kofi Annan (Gha.) for their work for a better-organised and more peaceful world	George A Akerlof (US) A Michael Spence (US) Joseph E Stiglitz (US) Analyses of markets with asymmetric information
2002	Raymond Davis Jr (US) Masatoshi Koshiba (Jap.) Detection of cosmic neutrinos Riccardo Giacconi (US) Discovery of cosmic X-ray sources	John B Fenn (US) Koichi Tanaka (Jap.) Soft desorption ionisation methods Kurt Wüthrich (Switz.) Nuclear magnetic resonance spectroscopy	Sydney Brenner (Brit.) H Robert Horvitz (US) John E Sulston (Brit.) Study of genetic regulation of organ development and programmed cell death	Imre Kertész (Hung.)	Jimmy Carter (US) for his efforts to find peaceful solutions to international conflicts	Daniel Kahneman (Isr.) Application of psychological research into economic science Vernon L Smith (US) Experiments in the study of alternative market mechanisms

NB: Many of the award winners listed above have dual nationalities. The nationality given is therefore not necessarily the country of birth.

General Information

Royal Swedish Academy of Sciences awards the Physics, Chemistry and Economics Prizes.

Swedish Karolinska Institute awards the Medicine Prize.

Swedish Academy of Arts awards the Literature Prize.

The Peace Prize is awarded by a committee of 5 members of the Norwegian Storting.

Nils Dalen, the 1912 Nobel Prizewinner for Physics, was blinded in 1913 by an explosion whilst conducting an experiment.

William and Lawrence Bragg were the only father and son to win a prize when they were joint winners of the 1915 Physics Prize.

A woman has never won the Economics Prize.

ORGANISATIONS

Chief Executives or Chairmen (as at February 2003)

Abbey National Luqman Arnold (CE); Lord Burns (C)

Aberdeen Football Club Stuart Milne (C)

Adidas-Salomon Herbert Hainer (CE)

Alfred McAlpine Oliver Whitehead (C)

Allders Brian Fidler (C)

Alliance & Leicester John R Windeler (C)

Allied Domecq Philip Bowman (CE); G J Robinson (C)

Antisoma Dr Barry Price (C); Glyn Edwards (CE)

AOL Time Warner Dick Parsons (C); Dick Parsons (CE)

AorTech International Eddie McDaid (CE); Eddie McDaid (C)

Arena Leisure Roger Withers (C)

Arsenal Football Club P D Hill-Wood (C)

Arts Council Gerry Robinson (C); P Hewitt (CE)

Associated British Foods Harold W Bailey (C); Peter J Jackson (CE)

Aston Villa Football Club Herbert Douglas Ellis (C & CE);

Astra Zeneca P Barnevik (C); Dr T F W McKillap (CE)

Austin Reed Roger Jennings (CE)

BAA M Agius (C); Mike S Hodgkinson (CE)

BAE Systems Richard Evans (C); M J Turner (CE)

Barclays Sir Peter Middleton (C); Matthew W Barrett (CE)

BAT (British American Tobacco) Martin F Broughton (C)

BG Group Frank Chapman (CE); Richard V Giordano (C)

BHP Billiton D R Argus (C); P M Anderson (CE)

Bhs Allan Leighton (C)

BMW Helmut Panke (CE)

BOC Tony Isaac (CE); R J Margetts (C)

Body Shop Peter Saunders (CE); Adrian Bellamy (C)

Boeing Phil Condit (C & CE)

Boosey & Hawkes Richard Holland (CE); Gerry Mortimer (C)

Boots John McGrath (C); Steve G Russell (CE)

BP P D Sutherland (C); Lord Browne of Madingley (CE)

Bradford & Bingley Lindsay MacKinlay (C); Christopher Rodrigues (CE)

British Airways Rod Eddington (CE); Lord Marshall of Knightsbridge (C)

British Banker's Association Ian Mullen (CE)

British Energy Adrian Montague (C)

British Midland Sir Michael Bishop (C)

British Telecom Sir Christopher Bland (C)

British Tourist Authority David Quarmby (C)

Brown & Jackson Johan Visser (CE)

BSkyB Tony Ball (CE); K R Murdoch (C)

Budgens Clive T Clague (C); Martin Hyson (CE)

BUPA Bryan Nicholson (C)

Burger King John Dasburg (C); John Dasburg (CE)

Cable & Wireless Richard Lapthorne (C); Graham Wallace (CE)

Cadbury Schweppes Derek Bonham (C); John Sunderland (CE)

Camelot Michael Grade (C)

Cannons Allan Leighton (C); Harm Tegelaars (CE)

Carpetright Lord Philip Charles Harris of Peckham (C)

Carlton Communications Michael Green (C)

Centrica Roy Gardner (CE); Sir Michael Perry (C)

CGNU Insurance Richard Harvey (CE)

Channel 4 Mark Thompson (CE); Vanni Treves (C)

Chelsea Village Trevor Birch (CE); Ken Bates (C)

Chelsfield Elliott Bernerd (C)

Chrysalis Group Richard Huntingford (CE); Chris Wright (C)

Chubb Jonathan P Findler (CE)

Cisco Systems John Chambers (CE)

Claims Direct Colin Poole (CE); Tony Sullman (C)

Clearstream André Lussi (CE)

CNN Jim Walton (C)

Coca Cola Douglas N Daft (C)

Compass Mike Bailey (CE); Francis MacKay (C)

Co-operative Bank Graham Bennett (C); Mervyn Pedelty (CE)

Coral Eurobet Robert Scott (CE)

Cordiant Communications Michael Bungey (CE); Charles

Scott (C)

Corus (formerly British Steel) Sir Brian Moffatt (C)

Coutts and Company Lord Home (C)

Daily Mail Viscount Rothermere IV (C); Charles Sinclair (CE)

Debenhams Belinda Earl (CE); Peter Jarvis (C)

De La Rue Brandon Gough (C); Ian Much (CE)

Deutsche Bank Rolf Breuer (C)

De Vere Group Lord Daresbury (C); Paul Dermody (CE)

Diageo (Guinness & Grand Met) Lord Blyth (C); Paul Walsh (CE)

Dixons John Clare (CE); Sir Stanley Kalms (C)

Easyjet Andrew Clark (C); Ray Webster (CE)

Economist Group, The Dominic Cadbury (C)

Egg Paul Gratton (CE); Roberto Mendoza (C)

Elementis Geoff Gaywood (CE); Jonathan Fry (C)

EMAP Kevin Hand (CE); Robin Miller (C)

EMI Eric L Nicoli (C & CE)

Energis Archie Norman (C)

Equitable Life Assurance Society Charles Thomson (CE); Vanni Treves (C)

Eurotunnel PLC Richard Shirrefs (CE); Charles MacKay (C)

Excel PLC J F Devaney (C); J M Allan (CE)

Express Dairies David Naish (C)

Financial Times Group David Bell (C); Olivier Fleurot (CE)

Findel K Chapman (C); D Johnson (CE)

First Choice Holidays Ian Clubb (C); Peter Long (CE)

FirstGroup Martin Gilbert (C); Moir Lockhead (CE)

Fitness First Mike Balfour (CE)

France Telecom Michel Bon (C)

Freeserve John Charles Clare (C)

Fremantle Media (formerly Pearson Television) Alan Boyd (CE)

Friends Provident D K Newbigging (C); K Satchell (CE)

Friends Reunited Stephen Pankhurst, Jason Porter, Julie Pankhurst (joint founders)

Galen Holdings John King (C); Roger Biossonneault (CE)

Geest R Ian Menzies-Gow (C)

George Wimpey Peter Johnson (C); John Robinson (C)

GKN Kevin Smith (CE); Sir David Lees (C)

GlaxoSmithKline Jean-Pierre Garnier (CE); Sir Richard Sykes (C)

Goshawk Insurance David Hooker (C)

Granada Group Charles Lamb Allen (C); S R Morrison (CE)

Greene King Timothy Bridge (CE); David McCall (C)

GUS Sir Victor Blank (C); John Peace (CE)

Habitat Terence Conran (C)

Halifax James Crosby (CE); Lord Stevenson of Coddenham (C)

Hamleys Simon Burke (C)

Hanson PLC C D Collins (C); A J H Dougal (CE)

Harland and Wolff Bryngulv Mugaas (CE)

Harrods Mohamed Al Fayed (C)

Hays R A Lawson (C); Colin Matthews (CE)

Hilton Group Sir Ian Robinson (C); David Michels (CE)

HMV Media Group Alan Giles (CE); Timothy Waterstone (C)

Homebase John Lovering (C); Rob Templeman (CE)

Hornby Frank Martin (CE)

House of Fraser John Coleman (CE); Michael Wemms (C)

HSBC John Bond (C); Keith Whitson (CE)

Imperial Chemical Industries Lord Trotman (C); Brendan O'Neill (CE)

I Feel Good Holdings J K H Brown (CE); Felix Dennis (C)

Imperial Tobacco Derek Bonham (C); Gareth Davis (CE)

Independent Television Commission (ITC) Patricia Hodgson (CE)

Invensys Lord Marshall of Knightsbridge (C); R N Haythornthwaite (CE)

J D Wetherspoon Tim Martin (C)

J J B Sports David Whelan (C)

Johnson Matthey H Michael P Miles (C); C R N Clark (CE)

John Lewis Partnership Stuart Hampson (C & CE)

John Menzies David MacKay (CE); Gavin Reed (C)

J Sainsbury George Bull (C); Sir Peter Davis (CE)

Kellogg Carlos Gutierrez (C)

Kenwood Appliances Colin Gordon (CE)

Kingfisher F H MacKay (C); Sir Geoffrey Mulcahy (CE)

Lastminute.com Allan Leighton (C)

Laura Ashley Khoo Kay Peng

(C); Ng Kwan Cheong (CE)

Legal & General R J Margetts (C)

Lego Kjeld Kristiansen (CE)

Leicester City Football Club Rodney Walker (C)

LIFFE Hugh Freedberg (CE); R Brian Williamson (C)

Littlewoods J M Barry Gibson (CE); James Ross (C)

Lloyd's of London Nicholas E T Prettejohn (CE); Saxon Riley (C)

Lloyds - TSB Peter Ellwood (CE); Maarten A van den Bergh (C)

London Bridge Software Gordon Crawford (C)

London Scottish Bank P T Furlong (C); Roy Reese (CE)

London Stock Exchange Don Cruickshank (C). Stands down at 2003 AGM

London Transport Sir Malcolm Bates (C)

LucasVarity Victor Rice (CE)

Luminar Keith Hamill (C); Steven Thomas (CE)

LVMH Bernard Arnault (C)

Man Group PLC H A McGrath (C); S Fink (CE)

Manchester City David Bernstein (C)

Manchester United PLC Peter Kenyon (CE); Sir Roland Smith (C)

Marconi John Mayo (CE); Lord Simpson (C)

Marks & Spencer Luc Vandevelde (C); Roger Holmes (CE)

Matalan John Hargreaves (C); Paul Mason (CE)

Méridien Hotels Juergen Bartels (CE); Guy Hands (C)

Merrill Lynch HSBC Margaret Barrett (CE)

Microsoft Bill Gates (CE)

Money Channel PLC T H Hobman (C); Paul Killik (C)

Mothercare Ben Gordon (CE)

Motorola Christopher B Galvin (C & CE)

My Travel (formerly Airtours) David Crossland (C)

NASDAQ Wick Simmons (CE)

National Air Traffic Services Sir Roy McNulty (C)

National Lottery Commission Mark Harris (CE); Helena Shovelton (C)

National Power Keith Henry (CE)

National Westminster Bank Sir David Rowland (C)

Nationwide Building Society Charles Nunneley (C); Philip Williamson (C)

N Brown David Alliance (C); Jim Martin (CE)

Newcastle United PLC Alfred Olding Fletcher (CE)

News Corp K R Murdoch (C & CE)

Next Sir Brian Pitman (C); Simon Wolfson (CE)

Nottingham Forest PLC M A Arthur (CE); E M Barnes (C)

Novartis Healthcare Daniel Vasella (C & CE)

Odeon Cinemas John Lovering (C)

Old Mutual PLC M J Levett (C); J H Sutcliffe (CE)

ONdigital Stuart Prebble (CE)

Orchestream Alan Bates (C); Ashley Ward (CE)

Peacock Group John Lovering (C); Richard Kirk (CE)

Pearson PLC Marjorie Scardino (CE); Lord Stevenson of Coddenham (C)

Persimmon Duncan Davidson (C)

Pilkington Nigel Rudd (C); Stuart Chambers (CE)

Pizza Express Ian Eldridge (CE); David Page (C)

Podia Scott Poulter (CE); David Giampaolo (C)

Post Office (formerly Consignia) John Roberts (CE)

Powderject Pharmaceuticals Paul Drayson (C); Paul Drayson (CE)

Powergen Nick Baldwin (CE); Edmund Wallis (C)

Preston North End PLC B M Gray (C); A J Scholes (CE)

Prison Reform Trust Lord Hurd (C)

Prudential Jonathan Bloomer (CE); Sir Roger Hurn (C)

Rangers Football Club PLC John McClelland (C)

Rank Mike Smith (CE)

Ranks Hovis McDougall Paul Wilkinson (C)

Reed Elsevier PLC Morris Tabakslat (C); C H L Davis (CE)

Rentokil Initial Henry E St L King (C); Sir Clive Thompson (CE)

Reuters Group Sir Christopher Hogg (C); T H Glocer (CE)

Rio Tinto R Leigh Clifford (CE); Robert Wilson (C)

Rolls-Royce PLC John Rose (CE); Sir Ralph Robins (C)

Royal & Sun Alliance John Napier (C); Andy Haste (CE)

Royal Bank of Scotland Fred Goodwin (CE); Sir George Mathewson (C)

Royal Doulton Hamish Grossart (C)

Royal Opera House Sir Colin Southgate (C)

Ryanair Michael O'Leary (CE)

Safeway Carlos Criado-Perez (CE); David Webster (C)

Sage Group   Michael Jackson (C); Paul Walker (CE)

Sainsbury PLC   Sir George Bull (C); Sir Peter Davis (CE)

Schroders   M W R Dobson (CE); I Peter Sedgwick (C)

Scoot.com   Richard Eykel (C)

Scottish & Newcastle   Brian Stewart (C)

Scottish Power   Ian Russell (CE); Charles Miller Smith (C)

Selfridges   W Alun Cathcart (C); Peter Williams (CE)

Severn Trent Water   T David G Arculus (C); Robert Walker (CE)

Shaftesbury   Jonathan Lane (CE); Peter Levy (C)

Shell Transport & Trading   Phil Watts (C)

Signet Group   James McAdam (C)

Six Continents   Sir Ian Prosser (C); T Clarke (CE)

Slough Estates   Sir Nigel Mobbs (C); Derek Wilson (CE)

Somerfield   Alan Smith (CE); John von Spreckelsen (C)

Stagecoach Holdings   Keith Cochrane (CE); Brian Souter (C)

Standard Chartered   Sir Patrick Gillam (C); E M Davies (CE)

Sun Life & Provincial   Lord Douro (C); Mark Wood (CE)

Tate and Lyle   David Lees (C); Larry Pillard (CE)

Taylor Woodrow   Keith Egerton (CE); Robert Hawley (C)

Telewest Communications   Adam Singer (CE); Anthony Stenham (C)

Tesco   Terry Leahy (CE); John Gardiner (C)

Thomas Cook Holdings   John Donaldson (C); John Donaldson (CE)

3i Group   Brian P Larcombe (CE); Sir George Russell (C); Baroness Hogg (C)

Tote   Peter Jones (C)

Tottenham Hotspur PLC   Daniel Levy (C)

Tussauds Group   Eric L Nicoli (C); Peter Phillipson (CE)

Ultraframe   David Moore (CE); Rod Sellers (C)

Unilever   Niall FitzGerald (C)

United Biscuits Holdings   Malcolm Ritchie (C & CE)

Virgin Group   Sir Richard Branson (C)

Viridian Group   Patrick Haren (CE); Philip Rogerson (C)

Vodafone   Chris Gent (CE); Lord MacLaurin of Knebworth (C)

Wal-Mart   Lee Scott (CE); S

Robson Walton (C)

Weetabix   Richard George (C)

Wellcome Trust   Sir Dominic Cadbury (C)

Welsh Water (Glas Cymru)   Lord Burns (C)

Wembley PLC   Claes Hultman (C)

West Bromwich Albion PLC   Jeremy Peace (C)

W H Smith   Richard Handover (CE); Martin Taylor (C)

Whitbread   Sir John Banham (C); David Thomas (CE)

William Hill Organization   John Brown (C); David Harding (CE)

Wireless Group   Kelvin Mackenzie (C); Kelvin Mackenzie (CE)

Wolseley   Charlie Banks (CE); R Ireland (C)

Woolwich   Lynne Peacock (CE)

Woolworths   Trevor Bish-Jones (CE)

Xenova Group   John Jackson (C); David Oxlade (CE)

Yahoo! Inc.   Terry S Semel (C)

Yorkshire-Tyne Tees TV   Ward Thomas (C)

Zara   Amancio Ortega (C)

Zeneca   Sir David Barnes (CE); Sir M S Lipworth (C)

Key

CE = Chief Executive

Organisations, Movements and Bodies

ACP   the 68 African, Caribbean and Pacific countries which have special trade relations with the European Union.

Action Directe   leftwing French revolutionary group formed in 1979 and responsible for numerous bombings.

Agenda 21   blueprint for action adopted at the 1992 Earth Summit in Rio setting out requirements for sustainable development.

Aipac   American Israel Public Affairs Committee, Israel's official lobbying arm in the USA and as such part of the influential US Jewish lobby. Based in Washington, DC.

Akali Dal   supreme political organisation of the Indian Sikh community. Founded in December 1920 and based in the Punjab.

Alawi   Islamic sub-sect signifying followers of the Caliph Ali, revered by Shias. Prominent in Syria, Lebanon and Turkey.

Alfaro Vive Carajo!   translates as 'Alfaro Lives, Dammit!' Ecuadorean left-wing nationalist guerrilla group named in memory of the President 1895–1901, 1906–11.

Al-Fatah   (Arabic: victory) Movement for the National Liberation of Palestine. Mainstream component of the PLO founded by Yasser Arafat in 1958.

Alpha 66   paramilitary group of anti-Castroites based in Miami. Formed in 1962 and named after its 66 founder members.

Al-Qaeda   international terrorist group formed in the

late 1980s by Osama bin Laden and Muhammad Atef and dedicated to opposing non-Islamic governments with force and violence.

Amazon Pact   signed in July 1978 by Bolivia, Brazil, Colombia, Ecuador, Guyana, Peru, Surinam and Venezuela. Committed to preserving ecological balance of the Amazon region.

Amnesty International   founded in 1961 by Peter Benenson and Sean Macbride Kropotkin, it campaigns for the release of prisoners of conscience.

ANC   African National Congress, South Africa's principal anti-apartheid organisation, banned 1960–90 but now the majority party in ruling coalition.

Angry Brigade   small anarchistic group in the UK in existence in 1968–71, which carried out several bombings.

Anti-Nazi League   leftwing organisation in the UK formed in the 1970s to combat racist parties and more recently the British National Party.

Anzus   security pact between Australia, NZ and the USA signed in San Francisco on 1 September 1951. Initially formed as deterrent to Japan but no longer operational.

Apostles   Cambridge University Conversation Society founded in 1820. Guy Burgess and Anthony Blunt were recruited from the Apostles by Soviet Intelligence.

Arab League   organisation formed in 1945 originally for mutual economic aid but more recently dealing with the Middle East peace process.

ASEAN Association of South East Asian Nations. Founded in 1967, members include Indonesia, Malaysia, Singapore, Thailand, Philippines and Brunei.

Baader-Meinhof Gang extremist leftwing terrorist group active in Germany in the late 1960s; later became the Rote Armee Fraktion (RAF).

Ba'ath movement founded in Syria in the 1940s by Michel Aflaq with the aim of creating a single social-ist Arab nation.

Band Aid charity formed by Bob Geldof and Midge Ure in December 1984 for the purpose of famine relief in Ethiopia.

BCCI Bank of Credit and Commerce International which collapsed in July 1991. Lord Justice Bingham criticised the Bank of England's supervisory role.

Benelux grouping of Belgium, Netherlands and Luxembourg for a mutually advantageous economic climate. Founded in 1932 by the Convention of Ouchy.

Black Berets élite paramilitary police force formed by the Soviet Interior Ministry in 1987. Aka Omon, they had a reputation for ruthlessness, especially in the Baltic States.

Black Sash South African liberal women's anti-apartheid organisation originally formed in 1955 as the Women's Defence of the Constitution League in response to the removal of the vote for coloureds. The black sash was worn as a peaceful protest against violation of rights.

Black September Palestinian terrorist group, named in memory of the Jordanian expulsion of Palestinians in Sepember 1970. Responsible for the Munich Olympic massacre of Israeli athletes.

B'Nai B'rith international Jewish organisation found-ed in 1843 and based in Washington, DC.

BND the German Federal Intelligence Service, founded in 1956 under the ex-Nazi Reinhard Gehlen and based in Munich.

Boss Bureau of State Security, a now defunct branch of the South African Intelligence Service. Founded in 1969 by PM J B Vorster.

Boundaries Commission UK body responsible for defining the boundaries of parliamentary constituen-cies.

Boys Brigade founded by William Smith in 1883.

Boys' Clubs although boys' clubs were in existence in major British cities in the 19th century, the National Association was founded in 1925.

BRA Bougainville Revolutionary Army, a guerrilla force fighting for independence for the mineral-rich island of Bougainville from the state of Papua New Guinea.

Brigate Rosse (Red Brigades) leftwing urban guer-rillas responsible for a spate of kidnappings and bombings in the 1970s culminating in the murder of former PM Aldo Moro in 1978.

British Academy Established in 1901; its full title is 'British Academy for the Promotion of Historical, Philosophical and Philological Studies'.

British Council Established in 1934 and funded by the government for the purpose of representing British culture abroad. With offices in more than 80 countries, it arranges for visits by British artists, lec-turers and performers, mounts exhibitions, teaches English and provides libraries of British books.

Brookings Institution Influential US think-tank based in Washington, DC, and comprised of distin-guished figures from various fields.

Bruges Group Informal Conservative grouping of 'Eurosceptics', named from a speech made in the Belgian city of Bruges on 20 September 1988 by Margaret Thatcher.

Camorra Network of groups engaged in organised crime in the Naples region.

Caricom Caribbean Community and Common Market, an alliance of English-speaking Caribbean countries promoting economic, political and cultural unity.

Central African Federation Federation of the British colonies of Northern Rhodesia (Zambia), Southern Rhodesia (Zimbabwe) and Nyasaland (Malawi). Established in 1953 and dissolved in 1963.

Central Committee Leading organ in the Communist Party of the Soviet Union whose full members elected the powerful Politburo and secretariat.

CERM Centre d'Exploitation du Renseignement Militaire (Centre for Exploitation of Military intelli-gence). French internal security agency, formerly called Deuxième Bureau until 10 Dec. 1971.

CERN European Centre for Nuclear Research, a co-operative agency with 12 member countries founded in 1952 and located outside Geneva.

Charter 88 Pressure group in the UK that demands a new constitutional settlement guaranteeing politi-cal, civil and human rights.

Chetniks Serbian nationalist army of resistance led by Draza Mihailovic, which occupied parts of east and south Yugoslavia during the second world war. Term now applies to all Serb irregulars.

CHOGM Commonwealth Heads of Government Meeting, the main policy-making body of the Commonwealth. A CHOGM is convened every 2 years.

CIA Central Intelligence Agency, often referred to inter-nally as 'The Company'. Its HQ is at Langley, Virginia.

Civic Forum Czech coalition of parties formed during the Velvet Revolution in November 1989 as the focus of democratic opposition to the communist regime.

Club of Rome non-governmental association of industrialists, policy analysts and scientists, seeking to bring their different perspectives to bear on prob-lems of the global economy.

CND Campaign for Nuclear Disarmament, a British organisation which mobilised mass opposition to nuclear weapons in general and the UK's independ-ent nuclear deterrent in particular. Founder mem-bers in 1958 include Bertrand Russell.

Comecon Informal name for the Council for Mutual Economic Assistance (CMEA), founded in 1949 as a response to the USA's Marshall Plan. Members included Warsaw Pact countries (excluding Albania) and Cuba, Mongolia and Vietnam.

Committee of 100 Militant offshoot of CND, formed in 1960 and headed by Bertrand Russell; its main weapon was 'sit down' protests.

Commonwealth of Nations Voluntary association of 53 independent states (Mozambique being latest member) which evolved from the British Empire, lat-terly concerned with postcolonial economic and cul-tural development. Originated with the 1931 Statute of Westminster. Elizabeth II is head of 16 Commonwealth states.

Confederation of British Industry CBI, formed in 1965 via merger of Federation of British Industries, British Employers' Confederation and National Association of British Manufacturers.

Congress Bicameral legislature of the USA consist-ing of a 100-member senate elected for 6 years,

ORGANISATIONS

with one third being renewed every 2 years, and a 435-member House of Representatives (lower chamber) elected for 2 years. Each state sends 2 senators to the upper house.

Contadora Group Latin American peace initiative in Central America set up by Colombia, Mexico, Panama and Venezuela in January 1983; controversially recognises Nicaraguan Sandinistas.

Contras Nicaraguan counter-revolutionary forces financed during the 1980s by the US Reagan administration, in part illegally, as revealed by the Iran–Contra affair. Many Contras offered allegiance to the dictator Anastasio Somoza, ousted in 1979.

Council of Europe Intergovernmental organisation with its HQ in Strasbourg. Founded on 5 May 1949 to promote civil society and human rights.

CPLA Cordillera People's Liberation Army, a guerrilla group operating in the Philippines until it signed a ceasefire with President Corazon Aquino on 13 Sept. 1986.

Creep Committee to Re-elect the President. Established in advance of the November 1972 US Presidential elections, its aim was to re-elect Richard Nixon by orchestrating a dirty tricks campaign against his Democratic opponents, which ultimately led to the Watergate scandal.

Dáil Éireann   166-seat lower house of the legislature of Eire. Members are elected for 5-year term on the basis of proportional representation. Translates as 'Assembly of Ireland'.

Death Squads Rightwing paramilitary groups often associated with conniving governments who assassinate those deemed a threat to the state. Term was coined in the 1960s in Brazil, when the police force used such squads, perhaps financed by the CIA.

Dergue Military ruling body in Ethiopia between 1973 and 1991, most closely associated with the Marxist-Leninist regime of Lt-Col. Mengistu Haile Mariam.

Deuxième Bureau French internal security agency run by the Ministry of the Interior and Administative Reform. Changed its name to CERM in 1971.

DGSE Direction Générale de la Sécurité Extérieure (General Directorate for External Security), the French foreign secret service established on 4 April 1982.

Diet Japanese bicameral legislature consisting of a House of Representatives (lower chamber) elected for a 4-year term and a House of Councillors (upper chamber), half of whose members are elected every years.

Dina Chilean secret police serving the military junta during the 1970s.

DST Direction de la Surveillance du Territoire. The French counterpart to the FBI or MI5.

Duma The name of the parliament of Imperial Russia but now referring to the lower house of the new Russian parliament or Federal Assembly.

Earth Day Annual worldwide effort on 22 April by pressure groups to focus public attention on environmental issues.

Earth Summit World environmental conference also known as the UN Conference on Environment and Development (UNCED), held in Rio de Janeiro on 3–14 June 1992 and billed as the largest-ever gathering of world leaders.

EBRD European Bank for Reconstruction and Development, founded in May 1990 by 39 countries (including USA and Soviet Union), plus the European Commission and the European Investment Bank. Conceived by French president

François Mitterrand to aid the Eastern European transition to a market economy.

Economic and Social Council ECOSOC, one of the 6 principal organs of the UN, established under Chapter X of the UN Charter, responsible for co-ordination of UN specialised agencies.

ECSC European Coal and Steel Community, which brought Italy and Benelux countries into Franco-German co-operation framework of 1950 Schuman Plan, forerunner of EEC.

EEC European Economic Community, founded under Treaty of Rome in March 1957 by France, Germany, Italy and Benelux countries; came into operation in January 1958.

EFTA European Free Trade Association, set up in 1960 under the Stockholm Convention. Its 7 original members were UK, Denmark (left in 1973 to join the EC), Portugal (left 1986), Austria, Switzerland, Norway and Sweden.

EMS European Monetary System, an arrangement for closer monetary co-operation within the EC, operational from March 1979.

EMU European Monetary Union, dating back to the Werner report of 1971; works to promote the smooth operation of capital transfers within participating countries.

EOKA National Organisation of Cypriot Fighters, Greek Cypriot movement which from 1955 until the independence of Cyprus in 1960 fought a guerrilla campaign against British rule.

ERM Exchange Rate Mechanism, regarded as the core of the EMS but badly damaged when the UK and Italy pulled out as a result of Black Wednesday in September 1992.

ESA European Space Agency, formed in 1973 as a result of the merger of the European Space Research Organisation and the European Launcher Development Organisation and committed to a European Space policy.

ETA Basque Fatherland and Freedom, militant separatist organisation which fights for the independence of the Basque country from Spain.

EU European Union, currently existing of 15 member states, the original 6 (Belgium, France, West Germany, Italy, Luxembourg, The Netherlands) plus Denmark, Eire, UK, Portugal, Spain, Greece, Austria, Sweden and Finland.

European Communities more generally referred to as the EU since 1 November 1993, the date on which the Maastricht Treaty on the European Union came into force.

European Court of Justice set up in Luxembourg under 1958 Treaty of Rome and responsible for ruling on whether EU member countries are acting in accord with Community Law.

European Parliament one of 3 principal institutions of the EU, with the Council of Ministers and European Commission. Elections held every 5 years and parliament meets in Strasbourg.

Falange Spain's rightwing nationalist party formed in 1937 by General Francisco Franco and formally abolished on 1 April 1977.

Falashas name assigned to Ethiopian Jews, which they themselves reject in favor of the name Beta Israel (House of Israel).

FAO Food and Agricultural Organisation, one of the largest of the UN specialised agencies founded in 1945, it aims to combat malnutrition and hunger.

Fascism a 20th-century ideology which has been interpreted as rightwing or centrist in orientation.

Derived from the Latin fasces (bundle of rods sometimes including an axe used by Roman magistrates as a symbol of authority), term became prominent following Mussolini's 'March on Rome' in 1922.

FBI Federal Bureau of Investigation, part of the US Justice Department and deals with violations of federal law; has its HQ in Washington DC.

FCO Foreign and Commonwealth Office, UK government department responsible for external relations and representation. The FCO was created in 1968 through the merger of the original Foreign Office (formed in 1782) and the Commonwealth Office.

FLN Front de Libération Nationale (National Liberation Front), political organisation during Algeria's independence struggle (1954–62). Founded 1954 under leadership of Ahmed Ben Bella.

FLNC Front de Libération Nationale de la Corse (Corsican National Liberation Front). Formed in May 1976, it is a clandestine extremist group fighting for self-determination from France.

Force de Frappe independent French nuclear weapons strike force instigated by Charles de Gaulle in December 1960 as a protest at the special relationship between the UK and USA.

Four D's democratisation, disarmament, decartelisation and denazification, implemented against the defeated Germans by the Allies and agreed at Potsdam.

Friends of the Earth international environmental pressure group, originating in the USA as an offshoot of the Sierra Club. It supports research on environmental issues, lobbies policy makers, and has been most successful in increasing public awareness.

G7 Group of 7 most powerful industrialised countries: Canada, France, Germany, Italy, Japan, USA and the UK.

GCHQ Government Communications Headquarters, part of the UK intelligence machinery which provides government departments and military commands with signals intelligence. Established in 1946 as the successor to the Government Code and Cipher School.

Geneva Conventions body of international humanitarian laws adopted in Geneva on 12 August 1949 and endorsed by the UN, which are intended to protect and assist war victims.

Gleneagles Agreement the 1977 decision by Commonwealth heads of government to ban official sporting links with South Africa until the dismantling of apartheid. Named after the golf club in Scotland which was the venue for the meeting.

Gosplan Soviet Union's State Planning Committee established in 1921 to work out a single state economic plan and methods and means of implementing it.

Greenpeace environmental pressure group whose members, now organised internationally with a headquarters in Amsterdam, engage in non-violent action to disrupt environmentally damaging projects. Founded in 1971 when nuclear tests on Amchitka Island, Alaska were disrupted.

Grey Panthers US pressure group organised to promote the interests of the elderly and retired. Name derived humorously from the Black Panthers.

Guardian Angels US volunteer group founded in 1979 to fight crime in New York City. Wearing red berets, they have been accused of being vigilantes.

Gulag Soviet acronym, Chief Directorate of Labour Camps. Established in 1930, estimates put number of inmates in the 1940s at over 8 million, of whom 85% were political prisoners.

Haganah Jewish defence force which operated from 1920 until the creation of Israel in 1948 to defend Jewish settlements in Palestine.

Hallstein Doctrine West German policy in 1950s and 1960s of severing diplomatic relations with any state recognising East Germany and refusing relations with any communist country except the Soviet Union.

Hamas acronym for Islamic Resistance Movement, a radical islamic group operating in Israeli-occupied territories. Founded in February 1988 by Sheikh Ahmed Ismail Yassin.

harkis Algerian Muslim auxiliary soldiers in the service of the French army during the French occupation of Algeria 1938–62.

Hezbollah Party of God. The main fundamentalist, Shia movement in Lebanon, operating in the south against Israel.

Human Rights Watch US-based international human rights organisation, the second largest worldwide after Amnesty International. Originated in 1978 with HQ in New York.

IAEA International Atomic Energy Agency, autonomous organisation within the UN which aims to promote the peaceful use of nuclear energy; founded in 1957, and based in Vienna.

IBRD International Bank for Reconstruction and Development, a UN specialised agency more commonly known as the World Bank. Based in Washington, DC, and established in 1945 following the Bretton Woods conference, it is the largest single source of lending for development by its worldwide members.

ICAO International Civil Aviation Organisation, UN specialised agency which aims to establish international standards necessary for the safety and security of air transport.

ICRC International Committee of the Red Cross, founded in 1863 by Swiss philanthropist Henry Dunant after witnessing the battle of Solferino in 1859.

IMF International Monetary Fund, usually deemed synonymous with the World Bank, but to gain access to IBRD funds, member states must be members of the IMF.

Inkatha Zulu word meaning 'Mystical Coil', a reference to the coil worn by African women to help them carry heavy weights on their heads. Conservative South African organisation led by Chief Mangosuthu Buthelezi, founded in 1976 and based in Kwazulu-Natal.

International Court of Justice based at The Hague and founded in 1946, the ICJ is the principal judicial organ of the UN and is authorized to resolve disputes between UN member states. It is assisted by a governing body composed of 15 judges of differing nationalities, elected for a 9-year term.

Interpol International Criminal Police Organisation established in 1923 and based in Lyon.

IRA Irish Republican Army, currently the main militant republican movement in Northern Ireland, originally formed in 1919 to fight for Irish independence.

John Birch Society extreme rightwing group founded in the USA in 1958 by Robert H W Welch, its name deriving from an American intelligence worker killed by Chinese communists in 1945.

ORGANISATIONS

KGB Komitet Gosudarstvennoy Bezopasnosti (Committee of State Security), Soviet Union's security police established in 1954. The KGB was scrapped after the August coup of 1991 and replaced in Russia in Jan. 1994 by the Federal Counterintelligence Service.

Knesset The Israeli unicameral legislature, located in Jerusalem.

KNU Karen National Union, a guerrilla organisation in Myan Mar (Burma), which has fought for a separate Karen state since the late 1940s.

Ku Klux Klan US white racist paramilitary organisation with long history of violence against blacks. Established in Tennessee at the end of the US Civil War in 1865 and still active.

Lok Sabha lower house of the Indian Parliament; the upper chamber is the Rajya Sabah.

Mafia in Italy, the network of organised crime, including the Sicilian Mafia, the Neapolitan Camorra and the Calabrian 'Ndrangheta.

Matrix Churchill UK machine tool company at the centre of the events that led to the Scott inquiry established on 15 February 1996, into defence-related exports to Iraq. Paul Henderson, Trevor Abrahams and Peter Allen, executives of the Iraqi-owned Matrix Churchill, were arrested in October 1990 and charged with illegally exporting machine tools to Iraq. All three were acquitted and it emerged that Henderson had acted as an MI6 agent.

Mau Mau secret political society in Kenya which developed into a violent anti-colonial rebellion in the 1950s.

Médecins Sans Frontières founded in Paris by a group of French doctors in 1971 to provide emergency medical aid worldwide, it is funded by donations. MSF has offices in 20 countries worldwide, the international office being in Brussels.

MI5 the UK Security Service. The counterintelligence service was originally established in 1909 to assess and combat threats to UK security.

MI6 UK's Secret Intelligence Service. Formed in 1909, its role is to gather intelligence abroad in support of the government's security, defence, foreign and economic policies.

Monday Club right-wing grouping of the UK Conservative Party, formed in 1960. Established in reaction to Harold Macmillan's wind of change speech, the Club was characterised by support for the South African regime, and subsequently the Rhodesian UDI regime, by advocacy of voluntary repatriation of black Commonwealth immigrants, and by opposition to anti-apartheid activities such as sporting boycotts.

Moral Rearmament revivalist movement established in the UK in 1938 by the US-born Lutheran pastor Frank Buchman, which succeeded Buchman's previous 'Oxford Movement', based its teachings on the 4 absolutes of purity, unselfishness, honesty and love, and on the importance of 'life-change'.

Mossad the most important, powerful and prominent of the Israeli intelligence agencies. Founded in 1951 by Isser Harel, who served as its director until 1963, it concerns itself with matters of espionage, intelligence gathering and covert political operations in foreign countries.

Mujaheddin-I-Khalq lay guerrilla organisation representing leftwing Muslim groups in Iran. Founded in the early 1970s, it was banned after the Islamic Revolution for its espousal of a variant of Islamic socialism and its criticism of the regime of Ayatollah Khomeini.

NASA National Aeronautics and Space Administration, the US government agency created in 1958 to co-ordinate civilian activities in space.

National Front fringe UK racist party founded in 1967 from small neo-fascist groups, including League of Empire Loyalists, British National Party, and Racial Preservation Society.

National Health Service UK's state health care system. The architect of the service was Aneurin Bevan, health minister in the Labour government of Clement Attlee, drawing on the Beveridge Report of 1942 on the welfare state. The NHS was officially inaugurated on 5 July 1948.

National Trust National Trust for Places of Historic Interest or Natural Beauty, founded by Octavia Hill in 1895.

Nato North Atlantic Treaty Organisation, based in Brussels and formed in April 1949. Nato came into being during the Soviet blockade of Berlin, taking as its basic tenet that an armed attack on any Nato country would be seen as an attack on them all.

New Jewel Movement leftwing party founded in Grenada in 1973 which in 1979 overthrew the government of Sir Eric Gairy and set up a People's Revolutionary Government under PM Maurice Bishop.

1922 Committee body consisting of all Conservative back-bench MPs in the UK House of Commons. The name commemorates the decision in 1922, forced on the party leadership by Tory backbenchers, to bring down Lloyd George's coalition government. Sir Michael Spicer is the chairman as at the time of writing.

Non-Proliferation Treaty arms control agreement approved by the UN in June 1968 and effective from March 1970.

OECD Organisation for Economic Co-Operation and Development, formed in 1961 as the instrument for international co-operation among industrialised member states on economic and social policies. HQ in Paris.

Oireachtas bicameral legislature of the Republic of Ireland, comprising the 166-seat lower house, the Dáil Éireann, and the 60-seat upper house or Senate, the Seanad Éireann.

OPEC Organisation of Petroleum Exporting Countries, Established in Sept. 1960 by Iran, Iraq, Kuwait, Saudi Arabia and Venezuela, subsequently enlarged to include Qatar, Indonesia, Libya, Abu Dhabi, Algeria, Nigeria, Ecuador and Gabon. It aims to unify petroleum policies among member countries in order to ensure stable prices. Ecuador left OPEC in 1993.

Organisation of African Unity established in 1963 by 32 African countries to promote continental unity and solidarity of African states. Headquarters are in Addis Ababa, Ethiopia.

OSS Office for Strategic Services, US intelligence organisation which was the predecessor of the CIA. Established in June 1942.

Oxfam Oxford Committee for Famine Relief, founded in 1942 to aid women and children in Nazi-occupied Greece and based in Oxford, it now has 40 overseas field offices.

PDSA People's Dispensary for Sick Animals, founded by Mary Dickin in 1917.

Pearce Commission UK government body established in Nov. 1971 to investigate whether proposals to settle the dispute with Rhodesia over UDI (Unilateral Declaration of Independence) were acceptable to the Rhodesian people.

Pentagon HQ, in Arlington, VA, of the US Defense Department and the Departments of the Army, Navy and Airforce.

Phalange main rightwing Maronite Christian movement in Lebanon. The Phalangist Party and its militias spearheaded the Christian side in the Lebanese civil war 1975–91, during which they were allied with Israel.

PLO Palestine Liberation Organisation, founded in 1964 as spokesman for all matters concerning the Palestinian people. Yasser Arafat has led the PLO since 1969.

Politburo key committee in the leadership structures of most communist parties, elected in the case of the Soviet Union by the central committee of the CPSU.

Quai d'Orsay term used for the French Ministry of Foreign Affairs, whose HQ is located in this street alongside the River Seine in Paris.

Radio Free Europe broadcasting operation covering the countries of Eastern and Central Europe, funded by the US government and operating from Munich under US management. Founded in 1949, it merged with Radio Liberty in 1976 and its aims are to broadcast non-partisan information.

Red Army Russian army formed in 1917 by the Bolsheviks and organised by Leon Trotsky to fight the anti-communist white armies.

Red Guards groups composed of students and schoolchildren in China who as 'Red Guards of the Cultural Revolution' had the task of unmasking revisionists and promoting Maoism. Emerging in 1966, the Red Guard operated for over a year before being disbanded.

Risorgimento the 19th-century movement for the political unification of Italy.

Royal Academy (of Arts) founded in 1768 at Somerset House but eventually moved to Burlington House. First president was Joshua Reynolds.

Royal Automobile Club founded in 1897 and responsible for many aspects of motoring safety and control.

Royal Exchange founded by Thomas Gresham in 1568 and home to various financial institutions. The present building was built by William Tite in 1844.

Royal Geographical Society founded in 1830 as the Geographical Society of London, it has been sited at Kensington Gore since 1912 in a house designed by Norman Shaw.

Royal Horticultural Society established in 1804 and awarded its royal charter in 1861, the RHS holds many shows but is primarily concerned with the Chelsea Flower Show held in Ranelagh Gardens since 1913. The Society has gardens at Wisley, Rosemoor near Great Torrington, Devon, and Hyde Hall, Essex.

Royal Institute of British Architects founded in 1834 under the patronage of William IV and given its Royal Charter in 1837. Membership in excess of 30,000; headquarters at Portland Place, London.

Royal Institution (of GB) established in 1799 by Count Rumford (Benjamin Thompson), this scientific organisation still has its headquarters in Albemarle St, London W1.

Royal Scottish Academy founded in 1826 and occupying a Greek Revival building in Edinburgh built by William Playfair.

Royal Society founded in 1660, early members

included Christopher Wren and Samuel Pepys. Isaac Newton was president 1703–27.

SALT Strategic Arms Limitation Talks, held between USSR and USA 1969–79. Salt I, 1969–72, and Salt II, 1973–4, were between Nixon and Brezhnev and Salt II talks were concluded in 1979 by Carter and Brezhnev in Vienna, after which the SALT talks were renamed START.

Samaritans Founded by the Rev Chad Varah in November 1953. At this time Varah was Vicar of St Paul's, Clapham Junction, as well as being the scientific and astronautical consultant to Dan Dare in the *Eagle* comic strip. He was haunted by the suicide of a 14-year-old girl, who killed herself in 1935 when her periods started because she thought she had VD, and when the opportunity arose the helpline phone number of MAN 9000 was set up on 2 November 1953. In 1974 Chad Varah set up Befrienders International, the overseas equivalent of the Samaritans.

Sandinista leftwing Nicaraguan revolutionary movement that overthrew President Anastasio Somoza in 1979. Founded in 1961 and named in honour of Augusto César Sandino, the leader of a small peasant army that waged a campaign (1926–33) against the US occupation of Nicaragua.

SAVAK defunct Iranian security organisation established in 1957 with the aid of USA and Israeli intelligence services, and used to crush opposition to Mohammad Reza Shah Pahlavi.

Save the Children Fund founded by Eglantyne Jebb, an Englishwoman, who saw starving children in Austria (1919). The Princess Royal is the President.

Schengen Group European mainland countries within the EU which are party to the Schengen Agreement on abolishing border controls between their territories while improving police co-operation. The original group which met in Schengen in Luxembourg in June 1985 consisted of the Benelux countries and France and Germany; Spain and Portugal soon ratified the treaty, followed by Italy, Greece and Austria.

Securitate communist Romania's security police which mounted a brutal defence of the regime of Nicolae Ceausescu during the December 1989 revolution.

Sejm the lower house of the Polish National Assembly, comprising 460 directly elected members.

SHAPE Supreme Headquarters Allied Powers Europe, the NATO military HQ of Allied Command Europe. SHAPE was moved from Paris to near Mons in Belgium in 1967, after De Gaulle's decision to withdraw France from NATO.

Shin Bet the Israeli internal security agency, aka the General Security Service.

Sierra Club probably the world's first environmental pressure group, formed in the 1892 in California by naturalist John Muir.

Sinn Fein (ourselves alone) prominent revolutionary party fighting initially for the republican independence of Ireland, and, since partition, for the reunification of the country.

Snowdrop Campaign founded after the killing of 16 children in Dunblane on 13 March 1996 and named after the only flower in bloom that day. The campaign, backed by international film star Sean Connery, aims to ban civilian ownership of firearms.

Solidarity Polish trade union and opposition movement founded in 1980 by striking workers at the Gdansk shipyard. Its first leader was the future President Lech Walesa.

Stasi the Ministry of State Security of communist East Germany, which operated from 1950 to 1990.

Stern Gang British name for the Zionist guerrilla group founded in Palestine in 1940 by Abraham Stern and responsible till 1949 for several terrorist attacks.

Stormont the Northern Ireland parliament buildings in Belfast, the seat of the N.I. parliament from 1932 until the introduction of direct rule in 1972.

Tamil Tigers militant organisation formed in 1976 aiming to achieve and independent Tamil state in northern Sri Lanka.

TASS Soviet Union's state news agency.

Tontons Macoutes (from a Creole word meaning 'Uncle Knapsack', a bogeyman), the notorious Haitian right-wing secret police, set up in 1958 by Papa Doc Duvalier.

TUC Trades Union Congress, the key umbrella employees' organisation in the UK, founded in 1868.

Tupamaros Uruguayan guerrilla group named after an 18th-century Peruvian Indian chief Tupac Amarú, and founded in 1962 by Raúl Antonaccio, an activist in sugar cane cutters' strikes. The group is still active today under the name 'National Liberation Movement'.

Tynwald parliament of the Isle of Man, a UK Crown Dependency. The principal chamber of Tynwald is the 24-member directly elected House of Keys. Tynwald celebrated its millennium in 1979; only the Althing of Iceland claims to be older (dating back to at least 930).

UN General Assembly established under Chapter IV of the UN Charter to act as the organisation's plenary body, representing all member states, it oversees the work of the UN's subsidiary bodies.

UN Secretariat listed in Chapter III of its Charter, the Secretariat, and the functions of the Secretary-General, are covered in detail in Chapter XV of the Charter. Elected by the Security Council. Secretariatship is usually for a term of 5 years with an automatic option to carry on unless vetoed by a member of the Council. Trygve Lie of Norway took office in Feb. 1946 and his term was extended until he resigned in November 1952, despite a Soviet veto. Other holders have been Dag Hammarskjöld of Sweden (April 1953 until his death in the Congo in September 1961), U Thant of Burma (1961–71), Kurt Waldheim of Austria (1972–81), Javier Pérez de Cuéllar of Peru (1982–91), Boutros Boutros-Ghali of Egypt (1 January 1992 – 1 January 1997, US vetoed continuation) and the incumbent Kofe Anan of Ghana.

UN Security Council established under Chapter V of the Charter, the Security Council has primary responsibility for the maintenance of international peace and security. It presently has 15 member states, 10 non-permanent members plus China, France, Russia, UK and USA, which are permanent members and carry power of veto.

UNESCO Paris-based UN Educational, Scientific and Cultural Organisation, founded in 1946 to promote

international collaboration in those fields of endeavour. USA, UK and Singapore are not members at present after suggestions of financial mismanagement.

UNITA National Union for the Total Independence of Angola. Founded by Jonas Savimbi in March 1966, UNITA fought alongside the Popular Movement for the Liberation of Angola during the struggle against colonial rule, but following the Portuguese withdrawal in 1975 it began a rivalry with the MPLA, backed by South Africa and the USA and not yet concluded. Since the death of Savimbi in February 2002, UNITA has been led by Paulo Lukamba Gato.

United Arab Republic political union of Egypt and Syria proclaimed between 1958 and 1961. Egypt retained the title of UAR until 1971, when it took the name Arab Republic of Egypt.

United Nations Established on 24 Oct. 1945 with its HQ completed in New York in 1952, the UN replaced the inter-war League of Nations, and its 111 articles of the Charter were proposed at the San Francisco Conference from 25 April – 25 June 1945. Its 6 principal organs are the General Assembly, Security Council, Economic and Social Council, Trusteeship Council, International Court of Justice and the Secretariat. Membership has risen from 51 at inception to 188 as at 30 September 1998.

United Nations Budget Top 7 countries contributing to the UN are USA (25%), Japan (18%), Germany (9.6%), Russia (2.9%), France (6.5%), UK (5.1%) and Italy (5.4%) as at 30 September 1998.

Universal Postal Union UN specialised agency based in Berne, Switzerland, first established in 1875 and taken over by the UN in 1948, charged with promoting international collaboration in postal services.

UNPROFOR UN Protection Force, established in January 1992 and dispatched to Croatia in March 1992 to monitor a ceasefire between Croatia and Krajina Serbs.

Velvet Revolution near-bloodless overthrow of Czech communist regime in November–December 1989 resulting in the ousting of the leader, Milos Jakes, and subsequent presidency of Vaclav Havel.

Warsaw Pact Warsaw Treaty Organisation, which was the communist counterpart to NATO during the cold war. Original signatories in May 1955 were Albania, Bulgaria, Czechoslovakia, East Germany, Hungary, Poland, Romania and the USSR. Albania withdrew in 1968 and following the collapse of communism in central and Eastern Europe the Warsaw Pact was dissolved in February 1991.

Women's Institute founded in 1897 at Stoney Creek, Canada.

World Health Organisation UN specialised agency based in Geneva and founded in 1948 with the aim of attaining the highest level of health for mankind.

World Wide Fund for Nature known until 1988 as the World Wildlife Fund, it was formed in 1961 and raises funds for a variety of conservation projects.

Yakuza Japanese criminal organisation comparable to US mafia-type syndicates.

PERFUME

Animal Sources

ambergris found floating on the sea (particularly the Indian Ocean) in oily grey lumps. It is excreted by the sperm whale after feeding on cuttlefish and is used as a base for perfumes.

castoreum comes from the follicles in the genital areas of both male and female beavers; used as a fixative.

civet comes from a pouch beneath the tails of both male and female civet cats; used as a fixative.

hyraceum excreted by the hyrax, a small rabbit-like animal found in the Middle East. It was used in ancient Arabic perfumes but is rarely used nowadays.

musk comes from the preputial follicle of the male musk deer. It is used as a fixative and is also thought to be an aphrodisiac. Chinese courtesans were fed bland foods perfumed with musk, so that when aroused the warmth of their bodies released the scent.

propolis a sticky brown fixative which bees collect from trees to use as a cement in their hives.

sweet hoof or onycha an ingredient of incense that comes from the shells of marine snails found around India and the Red Sea.

Plant, Mineral and Synthetic Sources

angelica root of the holy ghost (*Angelica archangelica*). It has a strong musky aroma.

bdellium myrrh (see also opoponax), an aromatic gum.

ben oil an essential oil from the winged seeds of the horseradish tree, used as a base oil for perfumes.

burning bush white dittany. The oil from the plant can vaporise in hot weather and catch fire without harming the plant itself. The fragrant essential oil is used in pot-pourri.

cherry pie heliotrope, used in pot-pourri and in modern perfumes such as 'Lou Lou' (Cacharel).

coumarin a white crystalline substance with a scent of new-mown hay, found in withered herbs and fruits. It is also manufactured synthetically from coal tar.

devil's dung asafoetida, a tall evil-smelling plant used as a fixative.

farnesol manufactured synthetically, but also found in musk. It gives a scent of lily of the valley.

frangipani the first plant to be named after a perfume. In 15th-century Rome, one of the Frangipani family made the perfume from orris, spices, civet and musk digested in wine alcohol. Later, French colonists in the West Indies found a bush (*Plumeria alba*) which had the same smell and named it frangipani.

galbanum small drops of it ooze from the stems of the giant fennel. It is mentioned in the Old Testament. It has a spicy-green scent with a hint of musk and is used in the 'top notes' of quality perfumes like Chanel No. 19.

handflower wallflower. The name 'handflower' comes from the practice, stemming from ancient Greece, of carrying the flowers in the hand as a nosegay during festivals.

indole the synthetic material derived from coal tar used to produce the scent of jasmine and neroli.

ionone the synthetic material used to make the scent of violets.

isoeugenol the synthetic material used to make the scent of carnations.

labdanum comes from rock-rose shrubs found around the Mediterranean; often gathered by combing the beards of goats which have browsed on the bushes. It was thought to have aphrodisiac qualities. Assyrian kings liked young women who had spent time soaking during a six-month period in baths of labdanum or bdellium, after six months soaking in myrrh.

linalol the synthetic material used to make the scents of lilac, lily and honeysuckle.

love-in-the-mist nigella, a hardy annual which grows to a height of about 1.5 m and has a fragrance of ambrette seeds.

malabathrum a dried aromatic leaf from a species of cinnamon, used by the Romans in the making of unguents.

muguet lily of the valley. It is used in many 'quality' perfumes such as 'Opium' (Yves St Laurent), and 'Florissa' (Floris). Its fragrance is manufactured synthetically as farnesol.

olibanum frankincense, a fragrant gum resin often used as an incense and, in perfumes, as a fixative.

opoponax myrrh (probably the Biblical myrrh collected from the land of Punt). Its oil, with a scent of fenugreek, is distilled from the yellowish lumps which occur on the plant. It is used mainly for incense and pot-pourri.

orris comes from iris roots; has a violet-like scent.

storax originally from the bark of the liquidamber tree which grows in Turkey, Asia Minor and Rhodes, but now manufactured synthetically. It has a smell of cinnamon, and is used as a fixative.

syringa lilac. The flowers are used mainly in pot-pourri, and its oil is used in 'quality' perfumes such as 'Chamade' (Guerlain), 'Florissa' (Floris) and 'Soir de Paris' (Bourjois).

verbena holy wort. The leaves have a lemon scent. It is used mainly in cosmetics and soaps and the leaves are sometimes dried for use in sachets.

Perfumes and Perfume Houses

Alliage	Estée Lauder (1972)	Knowing	Estée Lauder (1988)
Amarige	Givenchy (1991)	L'Aimant	Coty (1927)
Anaïs Anaïs	Cacharel (1978)	L'Air du Temps	Nina Ricci (1948)
Arpège	Lanvin (1927; relaunched 1994)	L'Egoïste	Chanel (1990)
		Le Jardin	Max Factor (1986)
Bal à Versailles	Jean Desprez (1962)	Lou Lou	Cacharel (1987)
Beautiful	Estée Lauder (1985)	Ma Griffe	Carven (1946)
Brut	Fabergé (1964)	Mon Parfum	Paloma Picasso / L'Oréal (1984)
Cabochard	Grès (1959)		
Calandre	Paco Rabanne (1969)	Must	Cartier (1981)
Chamade	Guerlain (1969)	Obsession	Calvin Klein (1985)
Charlie	Revlon (1973)	Old Spice	Shulton (1937)
Cheap and Chic	Moschino (1996)	Only	Julio Iglesias / Myrurgia (1989)
Chlöe	Lagerfeld (1975)		
Chypre	Coty (1917)	Opium	Yves St Laurent (1977)
CKOne	Calvin Klein (1994)	Paris	Yves St Laurent (1983)
Devin	Aramis (1978)	Parure	Guerlain (1975)
Diva	Ungaro (1983)	Pleasures	Estée Lauder (1996)
Drakkar Noir	Guy Laroche (1982)	Poême	Lancôme (1995)
Dune	Christian Dior (1991)	Poison	Christian Dior (1985)
Eau de Bonpoint	Annick Goutal (1989)	Polo	Ralph Lauren (1978)
Eau Sauvage	Dior (1966)	Red	Giorgio Beverly Hills (1989)
Eden	Cacharel (1994)		
Escape	Calvin Klein (1991)	Red Door	Elizabeth Arden (1990; relaunched 1996)
Eternity	Calvin Klein (1988)		
Fahrenheit	Dior (1988)	Rive Gauche	Yves St Laurent (1971)
Femme	Rochas (1944)	Samsara	Guerlain (1989)
Fidgi	Guy Laroche (1962)	Shalimar	Guerlain (1925)
Fleurs de Fleurs	Nina Ricci (1980)	Shocking	Schiaparelli (1936)
Gentleman	Givenchy (1974)	So Pretty	Cartier (1995)
Imprévu	Coty (1965)	Special No. 127	Floris (1890)
Intimate	Revlon (1955)	Trésor	Lancôme (1990)
Ivoire	Balmain (1979)	Tweed	Lenthéric (1933)
Jardins de Bagatelle	Guerlain (1983)	Vent Vert	Balmain (1947)
Je Reviens	Worth (1932)	Youth Dew	Estée Lauder (1953)
Jicky	Guerlain (1889)	Ysatis	Givenchy (1984)
Joy	Patou (1930)		

Notable Perfumes

aqua angeli a perfumed water made from aloewood, nutmeg, clove, storax, benzoin and rosewater, first made for scenting the shirts of Louis XIV of France.

eau-de-Cologne first developed by Paul Feminis in Cologne in the early 18th century. Its main ingredients were lavender and citrus, neroli, bergamot and lemon. 4711 Mullhens of Cologne still uses the original formula.

Chanel No. 5 named because the fragrance chosen by Coco Chanel from specimens supplied by Ernest Beauxs was sample No. 5. The first aldehyde perfume.

Chanel No. 19 named for Coco Chanel's birthday (19 August).

damask water popular in 16th-century England. It is made mainly from rosewater.

Eau de Bonpoint by Annick Goutal (1989). The first fragrance for babies.

Imperial Leather first made in 1768 by Bayleys, the court perfumers in London, as a result of a challenge by the Russian Count Orloff, to make a perfume with the scent of worn leather. It became a favourite of Catherine the Great, under the name 'Eau de Cologne Impériale Russe'. Cussons took over Bayleys and renamed the perfume Imperial Russian Leather, but dropped 'Russian' in 1939.

L'Interdit launched for Audrey Hepburn in 1957. It was Givenchy's first perfume. The name means 'the forbidden one' – forbidden, at first, to all but Audrey Hepburn, whose face graced the advertisement.

Jicky the first 'modern' perfume, created in 1889 by Aimé Guerlain.

Joy the most expensive perfume on the market soon after its manufacture by Jean Patou in 1930.

Only launched in 1989 by Myrurgia in association with singer Julio Iglesias.

Special No. 127 created by Floris in 1890 for Grand Duke Orloff of Russia. No. 127 was the page in Floris' Book where he wrote formulae which were created uniquely for individual customers.

Vent Vert launched in 1947 by Balmain. It was the first 'green' perfume.

Notable Perfumers

Baur Albert Baur was patenter of the first synthetic musk perfume, Musk Baur, in 1988.

Beaux Ernest Beaux developed the first aldehyde-based perfume, Chanel No. 5.

Carles Jean Carles, of Grasse, insured his nose for $1 million. His creations include 'Canoe' in 1935 (for Dana) and 'Shocking' in 1936 (for Schiaparelli). He founded the School of Perfumery in Grasse, Provence.

Farina Jean-Marie Farina opened a shop in Paris in 1806 to sell eau-de-Cologne. He sold his business in 1840 to Léonce Collas, who passed it on in 1862 to his cousins, Messrs Roger & Gallet.

Floris the oldest perfume house in the world, founded in 1730 as a barber's shop in Jermyn Street, London, by Juan Floris from Minorca.

Hermès arose from a harness-making, then glove-making business. Many of its perfumes are named after horse and carriage parts, for example 'Calèche' (a four-wheeled horse-drawn carriage).

Perkin William Perkin found out how to synthesise coumarin from coal tar, a much-used ingredient with a new-mown-hay fragrance. This was one of the first major discoveries in synthetic perfumery.

Miscellaneous

Abir perfumed powder used in India, usually sprinkled on linen. Its ingredients include sandalwood, aloes, cardamon, cloves, civet and rose.

Aldehyde a group of alcohol-derived chemicals which form other groups of chemicals known as benzoid compounds. Their discovery led to the manufacture of synthetic perfume ingredients.

chypre originally a famous Roman perfume made in Cyprus (hence the name). Nowadays used to describe perfumes with fresh top notes of bergamot, with other citrus ingredients such as neroli, lemon and orange, with middle notes of jasmin and rose and a base of oakmoss, with labdanum, storax, civet, patchouli and musk. The first modern chypre perfume was 'Chypre by Coty' (1917).

khaluq an unguent made by early Arabs which men were forbidden to use.

kyphi an incense made by the ancient Egyptians, based on wine, honey, raisins, herbs, frankincense, myrrh and juniper berries.

kypros an ancient Greek perfume which contained wine and cardamon and a sweet-scented substance called aspalathus.

magma the dried dregs from unguent bottles which the ancient Greeks and Romans added to scented powders.

olla-podrida pot-pourri made by perfume-makers from their waste materials with which they mixed herbs and lavender and rose petals.

perfumer's organ not his or her nose! It is the work bench and surrounding ingredients and equipment.

pomander a solid ball of perfumed material, such as crushed petals bound with a gum. In Tudor times they were carried to mask unpleasant smells and to ward off infection. In the 16th century it became popular to make them from oranges with cloves pushed into them, then baked. People fastened them to their belts or wrists. Nowadays they are sometimes used to perfume wardrobes.

tussie-mussie a nosegay dating from Elizabethan times, when it was originally made from flowers and herbs chosen for their symbolic meanings, e.g. rosemary for remembrance, daisy for faithfulness etc.

unguent cone cone made from perfumed fat (usually ox-tallow), which was fixed on to the hair or head-dress so that it melted and ran down the hair and body, perfuming them as it did so.

Strengths and Forms of Perfume in Descending Order According to Strength

Concentration	Name
15–30% in high-grade alcohol	extrait
15–18% in 80–90% grade alcohol	eau de parfum
4–8% in alcohol	eau de toilette
3–5% in 70% alcohol/water	eau de Cologne
3% in 80% pure alcohol	eau fraiche

Containers

acerra small box used by the Romans to contain incense burned in temples.

alabastrum pot, usually made from alabaster, agate or onyx, used by the Romans to contain perfumed oils.

aryballos / ampulla small flask used by the ancient Greeks to contain perfumed oils, often carried hanging from the wrist by a small strap.

pouncet box box used since Elizabethan times to contain perfumed powders placed between bedlinen. Originally used to hold pumice stone which was needed in the preparation of parchment for writing.

vinaigrette small metal box whose inner lid was pierced, popular in 18th/19th-century Europe. It held a sponge soaked in aromatic vinegar and was used as a smelling bottle.

Founders

Amouage The Hamood family of the Sultanate of Oman (1983).

Avon David McConnell (1886), Suffern, California. He was a travelling book-salesman who liked to give his customers free gifts of inexpensive perfume. Originally called the California Perfume Co., its name changed to Avon (after Stratford-on-Avon) in 1959.

Cacharel Jean Bosquet (1962), Paris. The name comes from a wild duck found in Provence.

Charles of the Ritz Charles Jundt (1934), New York.

Coty François Sputorno (1905), Paris.

Elizabeth Arden Florence Graham (1910), New York. Name derived from the title of the book *Elizabeth and Her German Garden* by Elizabeth von Arnim.

Fragonard Eugene Fuchs (1783), Grasse, Provence. Named after the painter Fragonard.

Lancôme Armand Petitjean (1935), Paris.

Mary Chess Grace Mary Chess Robinson (1932), London.

Revlon Charles and Joseph Revson and Charles Lachmann (1932), Boston, originally to market nail varnish.

Perfume Families or Classification

Perfumes are usually classified according to seven 'family' groups which form a continuum from floral to fougère.

floral mainly made from flower oils. These are light, daytime perfumes, e.g. 'Anaïs Anaïs' (Cacharel), 'L'Air du Temps' (Nina Ricci).

green giving an impression of new-mown grass. Fresh-smelling perfumes which include among their ingredients mosses, ferns, citrus fruits and herbs, e.g. 'Alliage' (Estée Lauder), 'Chanel No. 19' (Chanel).

aldehydic based on synthetic aldehydes. They range from floral through woody to powdery, e.g. 'Chanel No. 5' (Chanel), 'White Linen' (Estée Lauder).

chypre their fragrance is floral or green but with a heavy base such as ambergris, e.g. 'Cabochard' (Grès), 'Chypre' (Coty).

oriental their fragrance is spicy, strong and exotic and has a heavy sweetness which comes from ingredients such as musk, vanilla and sandalwood, e.g. 'Poison' (Christian Dior) and 'Opium' (Yves St Laurent).

tobacco / leather they have a hint of tobacco, leather and woody aromas, e.g. 'Antaeus' (Chanel) and 'Cuir de Russie' (Chanel).

fougère their fragrance is fresh, with a note of lavender, herbs, oakmoss, coumarin and new-mown hay, e.g. 'Drakkar Noir' (Guy Laroche), 'Brut' (Fabergé).

Photography and Cinematography

Ansel Easton Adams (1902–84) American photographer who co-founded Group f/64 with Edward Weston (1932) and helped set up the Department of Photography at the New York Museum of Modern Art (1940). His publications include *Taos Pueblo* (1930) and *Born Free and Equal* (1944).

Diane Arbus (1923–71) American photographer famous for her intense portraits of American social outcasts.

Eugène Atget (1857–1927) French photographer famous for recording the streets and scenes of old Paris; his unusual images of the commonplace inspired the Surrealists.

Richard Avedon (1923–) Photographer who made his name as a fashion photographer with *Harper's Bazaar*. His first sitter was Russian pianist-composer Sergei Rachmaninov.

David Royston Bailey (1938–) English photographer who started his professional life as a fashion photographer but developed as a portraitist during the 1960s, specialising in nudes. His 1965 collection *David Bailey's Box of Pin-ups* (1965) included pictures of celebrities of the day, from the Beatles to the Krays.

Billy Bitzer (1874–1944) US motion picture cameraman who, in partnership with the pioneer director D W Griffiths, developed camera techniques that set the standard for all future motion pictures. He was the first cameraman to use artificial lighting for his work, and his other innovations included the use of soft-focus photography, using a light-diffusion screen in front of the camera lens, the fade-out, and the iris shot, in which the frame is either gradually blacked out in a shrinking circle, thereby ending a scene, or gradually opened in a widening circle, beginning a scene.

Margaret Bourke-White (1904–71) American photojournalist who was employed by *Fortune* magazine in 1929 and subsequently became staff photographer and associate editor on *Life* magazine (1936). She was the first woman photographer to be attached to the US armed forces, producing outstanding reports of the siege of Moscow in 1941, and the opening of the concentration camps in 1944. Bourke-White married the American author Erskine Caldwell in 1939 but was divorced in 1942.

Mathew Brady (1823–96) New York-born photographer famous for his record of the American Civil War with the Union armies.

Bill Brandt (1904–83) English photographer who studied with Man Ray in London before working for the Ministry of Information and recording conditions during the Blitz. Brandt subsequently found fame with his landscapes and nudes. His publications include *The English at Home* (1936), *Perspective of Nudes* (1961) and *Shadows of Light* (1966).

Brassaï (1899–1984) Professional name of Gyula Halász, the Hungarian-born French painter and photographer. His photography included the nightlife of 1930s Paris.

Henri Cartier–Bresson (1908–) French photographer who initially studied painting with André Lhote before working as an assistant to film director Jean Renoir. His publications include *The Decisive Moment* (1952) and *The Europeans* (1955).

Julia Margaret Cameron (1815–79) British photographer who pioneered portrait photography.

Louis Jacques Mandé Daguerre (1787–1851) French painter and physicist who invented the daguerreotype, i.e. the first practical process of photography. Though the first permanent photograph was made in 1826 by Niépce, it was of poor quality and required about 8 hours exposure time as opposed to Daguerre's process which took 20 to 30 minutes.

Terence Donovan (1936–96) London-born photographer and film director whose work covered a wide spectrum of contemporary life. He worked for *Vogue*, *Harpers & Queen*, *Elle*, and *Marie Claire*.

George Eastman (1854–1932) US manufacturer who introduced the Kodak camera (1888) and Brownie camera (1900). Contrary to popular belief he was unrelated to Linda Eastman.

Walker Evans (1903–75) American photographer who produced a powerful record of the faces, homes and lives of America's 1930s rural poor.

Roger Fenton (1819–69) English photographer who was famous for his Crimean War pictures.

William Henry Fox Talbot (1800–77) English chemist, linguist and photographer who in 1839 invented the photographic negative and whose *The Pencil of Nature* (1844) was the first photographic book.

William Friese-Greene (1855–1921) British photographer who is often credited with the invention of cinematography, although Thomas Edison would appear to have a stronger claim. Friese-Greene did however pioneer stereoscopic and colour cinematography, but once again lacked the technical knowledge necessary to bring his ideas to fruition. A 1951 feature film, *The Magic Box*, was based on his life.

John Heartfield (1891–1968) Originally named Helmut Herzfelde, German pioneer of the photomontage, e.g. *Hurrah, the Butter is Finished* (1935).

Lewis Wickes Hine (1874–1940) American photographer who studied sociology before making a photographic study of Ellis Island immigrants and child labourers. Hine worked for the American Red Cross in WW1 and recorded the construction of the Empire State Building in his survey *Men at Work* (1932).

James Wong Howe (1899–1976) Chinese-born American cinematographer who started work in 1917 as assistant cameraman to Cecil B De Mille and in 1922 became chief cameraman for *Famous Players*. Howe favoured the use of the wide-angle lens, deep focus, and ceilinged sets to replicate shipboard claustrophobia. He won Oscars for his work on *The Rose Tattoo* (1955) and *Hud* (1963).

Yousuf Karsh (1908–2002) Armenian-born Canadian photographer who was appointed official portrait photographer to the Canadian government in 1935. His reputation was made with a 1941 portrait of Sir Winston Churchill, and he continued to photograph all the world's leading statesmen.

André Kertész (1894–1985) Hungarian-born American photographer famous for his pioneering use of the small hand-held camera, the well-observed social scene, the surreal figure study, still life, and later the fashion image.

Edwin Herbert Land (1909–91) US inventor and physicist whose invention of the Polaroid (one-step) process for developing and printing photographs culminated in a revolution in photography unparalleled since the advent of roll film.

Dorothea Lange (1895–1965) US photographer who started as a society photographer but became famous for her social records of migrant workers during the 1930s depression.

Lord Patrick Lichfield (1939–) British aristocratic photographer whose reputation was built around his royal photographs and his nude calendars.

Auguste Lumière (1862–1954), Louis Lumière (1864–1948) French chemist brothers who invented the first successful cine camera and projector (1895) and a process of colour photography. They also produced the first film newsreels, and the first movie, *La Sortie des usines Lumière* (1895).

László Moholy-Nagy (1895–1946) Hungarian-born American photographer famous for his constructivist-inspired, semi-abstract images, and his inspiring teaching at the Bauhaus.

Eadweard Muybridge (1830–1904) Original name Edward James Muggeridge. English photographer famous for his early experiments in capturing motion in photographic images and for his landscapes of the American West. Muybridge was employed by the railroad magnate Leland Stanford in 1872 to prove that during a particular moment in trotting, all four legs of a horse are off the ground simultaneously. His studies were interrupted while he was tried for the murder of his wife's lover, but after his acquittal he developed a special shutter that gave an exposure of 2/1,000 of a second which proved Stanford's theory.

Nadar (1820–1910) Professional name of Gaspard-Félix Tournachon, French artist and photographer whose Paris studio became a favourite haunt of the intelligentsia. In 1886 he produced the first photo interview, a series of 21 photographs of the centenarian scientist Eugène Chevreul, each captioned with the sitter's replies to Nadar's questions. He pioneered the use of aerial photographs for map-making and in 1858 took the first pictures from a balloon.

Joseph-Nicéphore Niépce (1765–1833) French inventor who was the first to make a permanent photographic image (1826).

Man Ray (1890–1976) American photographer, painter and film-maker, born Emanuel Rabinovich, who was a leading light in the development of Modernism. He founded the New York Dadaist movement with Marcel Duchamp and Francis Picabia before moving to Paris and working with René Clair. Man Ray pioneered the use of photographic images made without a camera, 'Rayographs'.

Henry Peach Robinson (1830–1901) English photographer who opened a studio at Leamington Spa in 1857 and specialised in images of costumed models and painted settings. He was a founder member of the Linked Ring (1892), a group of photographers seeking to excel in artistic creation.

Alexander Rodchenko (1891–1956) Soviet photographer and photomontagist who introduced 'New Photography' to post-revolutionary Russia.

Erich Salomon (1886–1944) German photojournalist who was master of the candid shot whereby he caught politicians and celebrities off guard for new magazines of the 1920s. He died in Auschwitz.

August Sander (1876–1964) German photographer celebrated for his ambitious project 'Man in the Twentieth Century', a picture of the doomed Weimar Republic through the faces of its people.

Aaron Siskind (1903–) American photographer who began his career while teaching English in New York (1932). His subjects showed the usual American depiction of the depression of the 1930s, but unlike other documentaries of the period his *Dead End: The Bowery* and *Harlem Document* show as much concern for pure design as for the plight of the subjects. Siskind developed an abstract approach to his art and began photographing mundane subjects and architectural ruins. He became professor of photography at the Institute of Design of the Illinois Institute of Technology in Chicago (1951–71) and held a similar post at Rhode Island School of Design from 1971.

W Eugene Smith (1918–78) US photojournalist noted for his impassioned documentary photographs from around the world, seen mostly in *Life* magazine in the 1940s and 50s.

Edward Steichen (1879–1973) Luxembourg-born American photographer who became a member of the Linked Ring in England and made his reputation with his studies of the nude. In 1902 he co-founded the American Photo-Secession Group with Alfred Stieglitz. In WW1 he served as commander of the photographic division of the US army. In the 1920s Steichen developed a New Realism style and became heavily involved in fashion photography. He was head of US Naval Film Services during WW2, and director of photography at the New York Museum of Modern Art from 1945 to 1962, where he put on the 'Family of Man' exhibition in 1955.

Alfred Stieglitz (1864–1946) American photographer who founded the Photo-Secession Group in 1902 with Edward Steichen. He was a major figure in establishing photography as an art form and his gallery of modern art at 291 Fifth Avenue, NY, was the linchpin of his work.

Paul Strand (1890–1976) US photographer and documentary film-maker who studied under Lewis Hine. In 1933 he was appointed chief of photography and cinematography in the government Secretariat of Education in Mexico. Known for his still lifes, architectural studies and photographic books on regions of the world.

Edward Weston (1886–1958) American photographer who made his reputation in his Glendale studio but moved to Mexico in 1923, where he developed his modernist style. In 1932 he joined Ansel Adams and others in forming the 'straight photography' purists Group f/64 in California. His close-up studies of inanimate objects such as shells and vegetables exemplified his vision of detailed form and the richness of his control of tone. He produced notable landscapes of the Mojave Desert, and in 1937, with the first-ever award of a Guggenheim Fellowship to a photographer, travelled the American West before touring the Eastern States to illustrate an edition of Walt Whitman's *Leaves of Grass*.

Minor White (1908–76) American photographer and editor who was greatly influenced by Edward Weston and Alfred Stieglitz. In 1946 he moved to San Francisco and worked with Ansel Adams, whom he followed as director of the photographic department in the California School of Fine Art (1947–52). White was appointed professor of creative photography at the Massachusetts Institute of Technology

(1965–76) and founded the periodicals *Aperture* and
Image.

Garry Winogrand (1928–84) American photographer who created a highly influential brand of urban
street photography, fusing the 'snapshot' approach
with a sense of energy and crowded events in his
images.

POLITICS

Country – Name of Governmental Chambers – Type of Government

NB The upper chambers of bicameral parliaments are listed first in this table, and the name of parliaments are the most commonly accepted, e.g. the parliament of Algeria is bicameral, the upper house being the Majlis el-Umma and the lower house the National Assembly. The combined assemblies are generally referred to as the Majlis (council). Parliaments are generally elected for a term of years but in some bicameral assemblies the two chambers may have differing lengths of term. In our example of Algeria, the lower house is elected for a five-year term but the upper house has a third of its members elected for six years, a third elected for three years, and the remaining third at the president's discretion. The membership is the statutory capacity as at January 2003.

Country	Name of Governmental Chambers	Name of Parliament	Years of Office
Afghanistan	Shura (Ruling Council) (10 members)	Shura	varies
Albania	National Assembly (155 members)	People's Assembly	4
Algeria	Majlis el-Umma (Council of the Nation) (144 members)	Majlis	varies
	National Assembly (389 members)		5
Andorra	General Council of the Valleys (28 members)	General Council of the Valleys	4
Angola	National Assembly (223 members)	National Assembly	2–4
Antigua and Barbuda	Senate (17 members)	Parliament	varies
	House of Representatives (17 members)		5
Argentina	Senate (72 members)	Congress	varies
	Chamber of Deputies (257 members)		varies
Armenia	Azgayin Zhoghov (National Assembly) (131 members)	Azgayin Zhoghov	4
Australia	Senate (76 members)	Federal Parliament	6
	House of Representatives (150 members)		3
Austria	Bundesrat (Federal Council) (64 members)	National Assembly	varies
	Nationalrat (National Council) (183 members)		4
Azerbaijan	Milli-Mejlis (National Council) (125 members)	Milli-Mejlis	varies
Bahamas	Senate (16 members)	Parliament	varies
	House of Assembly (40 members)		5
Bahrain	Consultative Council (40 members)	Majlis al-Shura	4
Bangladesh	Jatiya Sangsad (house of the nation) (300 members)	Jatiya Sangsad	5
Barbados	Senate (21 members)	Parliament	5
	House of Assembly (28 members)		5
Belarus	Council of the Republic (64 members)	National Assembly	5
	House of Representatives (110 members)		5
Belgium	Senate (71 members)	Federal Parliament	varies
	Chamber of Representatives (150 members)		4
Belize	Senate (8 members)	National Assembly	varies
	House of Representatives (29 members)		5
Benin	National Assembly (83 members)	National Assembly	4
Bhutan	Tshogdu (National Assembly) (154 members)	Tshogdu	3
Bolivia	Senate (27 members)	Congress	5
	Chamber of Deputies (130 members)		5
Bosnia-Herzegovina	Chamber of Peoples (15 members i.e. 5 Croat, 5 Muslim, 5 Serb)	National Assembly	2
	Chamber of Representatives (42 members)		2
Botswana	House of Chiefs (15 members)	National Assembly	5
	National Assembly (47 members)		5
Brazil	Senate (81 members)	Congress	8
	Chamber of Deputies (513 members)		4
Brunei	There are no political parties or elections, the Sultan ruling since a revolt in December 1962.		
Bulgaria	National Assembly (240 members)	National Assembly	4
Burkina Faso	Assembly of People's Deputies (111 members)	National Assembly	5
	Chamber of Representatives (178 members)		3
Burundi	National Assembly (170 members)	National Assembly	5
Cambodia	Senate (61 members)	National Assembly	5
	National Assembly (122 members)		5
Cameroon	National Assembly (180 members)	National Assembly	5
Canada	Senate (105 members)	Federal Parliament	varies
	House of Commons (301 members)		5
Cape Verde	National Assembly (72 members)	National Assembly	5

Country	Name of Governmental Chambers	Name of Parliament	Years of Office
Central African Republic	National Assembly (109 members)	National Assembly	5
Chad	National Assembly (155 members)	National Assembly	4
Channel Islands (less Sark)	States of Deliberation (132 members)	The States	4
– Sark	Chief Pleas (5 members)	Chief Pleas	4
Chile	Senate (48 members)	Congress	8
	Chamber of Deputies (120 members)		4
China	National People's Congress (2,984 members)	National People's Congress	5
Colombia	Senate (102 members)	Congress	4
	House of Representatives (165 members)		4
Comoros	Senate (15 members)	Federal Assembly	6
	Legislative Council (42 members)		4
Congo, Dem. Rep. of the	New constitution yet to be finalised.	To be arranged	T. B. A.
Congo, Republic of the	Supreme Council of the Republic (153 members)	Supreme Council	T. B. A.
Costa Rica	Legislative Assembly (57 members)	Legislative Assembly	4
Côte d'Ivoire	National Assembly (225 members)	National Assembly	5
Croatia	Chamber of Counties (65 members)	Sabor (parliament)	4
	House of Representatives (151 members)		4
Cuba	National Assembly of People's Power (601 members)	National Assembly	5
Cyprus	House of Representatives (80 members)	Parliament	5
Czech Republic	Senate (81 members)	Federal Assembly	6
	Chamber of Deputies (200 members)		4
Denmark	Folketing (179 members including 2 for Greenland and the Faroes)	Folketing (parliament)	4
Djibouti	Chamber of Deputies (65 members)	National Assembly	5
Dominica	House of Assembly (30 members)	National Assembly	5
Dominican Republic	Senate (30 members)	Congress	4
	Chamber of Deputies (149 members)		4
East Timor	National Assembly (88 members)	National Assembly	T. B. A.
Ecuador	National Congress (121 members)	Congress	4
Egypt	Majlis Ash-Sha'Ab (People's Assembly) (454 members)	Majlis	5
El Salvador	Legislative Assembly (84 members)	Legislative Assembly	3
Equatorial Guinea	National Assembly (80 members)	National Assembly	5
Eritrea	Hagerawi Baito (National Assembly) (150 members)	Hagerawi Baito	4
Estonia	Riigikogu (National Assembly) (101 members)	Riigikogu	4
Ethiopia	Federation Council (108 members)	Parliament	5
	Council of People's Representatives (548 members)		5
Fiji Islands	Senate (32 members)	Parliament	varies
	House of Representatives (71 members)		5
Finland	Eduskunta (parliament) (200 members)	Eduskunta	4
France	Senate (321 members)	Parliament	varies
	National Assembly (577 members)		5
Gabon	Senate (91 members)	Parliament	6
	National Assembly (120 members)		5
Gambia	National Assembly (53 members)	National Assembly	5
Georgia	Parliament (235 members)	Parliament	4
Germany	Bundesrat (Federal Council) (69 members)	Parliament	varies
	Bundestag (Federal Assembly) (669 members)		4
Ghana	Parliament (200 members)	Parliament	4
Greece	Vouli Ton Ellinon (Chamber of Deputies) (300 members)	Vouli	4
Grenada	Senate (13 members)	Parliament	5
	House of Representatives (15 members)		5
Guatemala	National Congress (113 members)	Congress	4
Guinea	National Assembly (114 members)	National Assembly	5
Guinea-Bissau	National People's Assembly (102 members)	National People's Assembly	4
Guyana	National Assembly (65 members)	National Assembly	5
Haiti	Senate (27 members)	National Assembly	6
	Chamber of Deputies (83 members)		4
Honduras	National Congress (128 members)	Congress	4
Hong Kong	Legislative Council (60 members)	Legislative Council	4
	Executive Council (19 members)		varies

POLITICS

Country	Name of Governmental Chambers	Name of Parliament	Years of Office
Hungary	Országgyülés (National Assembly) (386 members)	Országgyülés	4
Iceland	Althingi (Parliament) (63 members)	Althingi	4
India	Rajya Sabha (Council of States) (245 members)	Sansad (Parliament)	6
	Lok Sabha (House of the People) (545 members)		5
Indonesia	Dewan Perwakilan Rakyat (H. of Representatives) (500 members)	Dewan Perwakilan Rakyat	5
Iran	Majles Shoraye Eslami (Islamic Ruling Council) (290 members)	Majles	4
Iraq	Majlis Watani (Council of the Nation) (250 members)	Majlis	4
Ireland	Seanad Eireann (Senate) (60 members)	Oireachtas (parliament)	5
	Dáil Eireann (House of Representatives) (166 members)		5
Israel	Knesset (Assembly) (120 members)	Knesset	4
Italy	Senate (315 members)	Parliament	5
	Chamber of Deputies (630 members)		5
Jamaica	Senate (21 members)	Parliament	5
	House of Representatives (60 members)		5
Japan	Sangiin (House of Councillors) (247 members)	Kokkai (Diet)	6
	Shugiin (House of Representatives) (480 members)		4
Jordan	Al-Aayan (Senate) (40 members)	Majlis Al-Umma	4
	Al-Nuwaab (House of Representatives) (80 members)		4
Kazakhstan	Senate (39 members)	Mazhilis	5
	Mazhilis (Council) (77 members)		5
Kenya	Bunge (National Assembly) (210 members)	Bunge	5
Kiribati	Maneaba Ni Maungatabu (House of Assembly) (41 members)	Unicameral	4
Korea South	Kuk Hoe (National Assembly) (273 members)	Kuk Hoe	4
Korea North	Supreme People's Assembly (687 members)	National Assembly	5
Kuwait	Majlis Al-Umma (Council of the Nation) (50 members)	Majlis	4
Kyrgyzstan	Myizam Chygaru Palatasay (Legislative Assembly) (60 members)	Jogorku Kenesh (High Council)	5
	El Okuldor Palatasay (People's Assembly) (45 members)		5
Laos	Sapha Heng Xat (National Assembly) (109 members)	Sapha Heng Xat	5
Latvia	Saeima (Supreme Council) (100 members)	Saeima	4
Lebanon	Majlis Al-Nuwwab (Council of Deputies) (128 members)	Majlis	4
Lesotho	Senate (33 members)	Parliament	5
	National Assembly (120 members)		5
Liberia	Senate (26 members)	National Assembly	9
	House of Representatives (64 members)		6
Liechtenstein	Landtag (25 members)	Landtag	4
Lithuania	Seimas (Supreme Council) (141 members)	Seimas	4
Luxembourg	Chamber of Deputies (60 members)	Parliament	5
Macedonia	Sobranie (Assembly) (120 members)	Sobranie	4
Madagascar	National Assembly (150 members)	National Assembly	5
Malawi	National Assembly (193 members)	National Assembly	5
Malaysia	Dewan Negara (Senate) (69 members)	Majlis	3
	Dewan Rakyat (House of Representatives) (193 members)		5
Maldives	Majlis (50 members)	Majlis	5
Mali	National Assembly (147 members)	National Assembly	5
Malta	Il-Kamra Tad-Deputati (House of Representatives) (65 members)	Il-Kamra Tad-Deputati	5
Marshall Islands	Nitijela (House of Assembly) (33 members)	Nitijela	4
Mauritania	Majlis-Al-Chouyoukh (Senate) (56 members)	National Assembly	6
	Al Jamiya-Al-Wataniya (National Assembly) (81 members)		5
Mauritius	National Assembly (70 members)	National Assembly	5
Mexico	Senate (128 members)	Congress	6
	Chamber of Deputies (500 members)		3

Country	Name of Governmental Chambers	Name of Parliament	Years of Office
Micronesia (Federated States)	Congress (14 members, four of whom are elected for four years)	Congress	2
Moldova	Parliament (101 members)	Parliament	4
Monaco	National Council (18 members)	National Council	5
Mongolia	Ulsyn Ikh Khural (The Great Hural) (76 members)	Ulsyn Ikh Khural	4
Montenegro	National Assembly (85 members)	National Assembly	5
Morocco	Majlis Nawab (Chamber of Representatives) (325 members)	Majlis	6
	Majlis al-Mustacharin (Chamber of Counsellors) (270 members)		9
Mozambique	People's Assembly (250 members)	National Assembly	5
Myanmar (Burma)	Constitutional Convention (706 members)	Constitutional Convention	T. B. A.
Namibia	National Council (26 members)	Parliament	6
	National Assembly (72 members)		5
Nauru	Parliament (18 members)	Parliament	3
Nepal	Rastriya Sabha (National Council) (60 members)	Parliament	6
	Pratinidhi Sabja (House of Representatives) (205 members)		5
Netherlands	First Chamber (75 members)	States General	4
	Second Chamber (150 members)		4
New Zealand	House of Representatives (120 members)	Parliament	3
Nicaragua	National Assembly (90 members)	National Assembly	6
Niger	National Assembly (83 members)	National Assembly	5
Nigeria	Senate (109 members)	National Assembly	4
	House of Representatives (360 members)		4
Norway	Lagting (25% of Storting membership)	Storting(et) (165 members)	4
	Odelsting (75% of Storting membership)		4
Oman	Majlis al Shura (Council of State) (41 members)	Majlis	varies
Pakistan	Senate (87 members)	Majlis	3
	Majlis as-Shoora (National Assembly) (237 members)		5
Palau	Senate (14 members)	Olbiil Era Kelulau (Congress)	4
	House of Delegates (16 members)		4
Panama	Legislative Assembly (71 members)	Legislative Assembly	5
Papua New Guinea	National Parliament (109 members)	Parliament	5
Paraguay	Senate (45 members)	Congress	5
	Chamber of Deputies (80 members)		5
Peru	National Congress (120 members)	Congress	5
Philippines	Senate (24 members)	Congress	6
	House of Representatives (250 members)		3
Poland	Senate (100 members)	Sejm	4
	Sejm (Parliament) (460 members)		4
Portugal	Assembly of the Republic (230 members)	Assembly of the Republic	4
Qatar	No established parliament although the Amir is advised by a 30-member Council of Ministers		
Romania	Senate (140 members)	Parliament	4
	Chamber of Deputies (345 members)		4
Russia	Soviet Federation (178 members)	Federal Assembly	varies
	Duma (450 members)		4
Rwanda	National Transitional Assembly (74 members)	National Transitional Assembly	5
Saint Kitts and Nevis	National Assembly (15 members)	National Assembly	5
Saint Lucia	Senate (11 members)	National Assembly	5
	National Assembly (18 members)		5
Saint Vincent and Grenadines	National Assembly (21 members)	National Assembly	5
Samoa	Legislative Assembly (49 members)	Legislative Assembly	5
San Marino	Consiglio grande e generale (60 members)	Consiglio grande e generale	5
São Tomé and Principe	National Assembly (55 members)	National Assembly	4
Saudi Arabia	Majlis al Shura (Council of State) (121 members)	Majlis	varies
Senegal	National Assembly (120 members)	National Assembly	5
Serbia	National Assembly (250 members)	National Assembly	5
Seychelles	National Assembly (34 members)	National Assembly	5
Sierra Leone	Parliament (68 members)	Parliament	5
Singapore	Parliament (93 members)	Parliament	5
Slovakia	National Council (150 members)	National Council	4

POLITICS

Country	Name of Governmental Chambers	Name of Parliament	Years of Office
Slovenia	State Council (40 members)	National Assembly	5
	National Assembly (90 members)		4
Solomon Islands	Parliament (50 members)	Parliament	4
Somalia	National Assembly (245 members)	National Assembly	varies
South Africa	National Council of Provinces (90 members)	Volksraad	5
	Volksraad (National Assembly) (400 members)		5
Spain	Congress Senate (259 members)	Cortes Generales	4
	Congress of Deputies (350 members)		4
Sri Lanka	Parliament (225 members)	Parliament	6
Sudan	Majlis Watani (Council of the Nation) (360 members)	Majlis	4
Suriname	National Assembly (51 members)	National Assembly	5
Swaziland	Senate (30 members)	Libandla (Parliament)	5
	House of Assembly (65 members)		5
Sweden	Riksdag (349 members)	Riksdag(en)	4
Switzerland	Council of States (46 members)	Federal Assembly	4
	National Council (200 members)		4
Syria	Majlis Al-Chaab (250 members)	Majlis	4
Tadzhikstan	Majlisi Milliy (34 members)	Majlis Oli (Supreme Council)	5
	Majlisi Namoyandogon (63 members)		5
Taiwan	Yuan (225 members)	Yuan	3
Tanzania	Bunge (National Assembly) (296 members)	Bunge	5
Thailand	Wuthisapha (Senate) (200 members)	Rathasapha (Parliament)	6
	Saphaphuthan Ratsadon (National Assembly) (500 members)		4
Togo	National Assembly (81 members)	National Assembly	5
Tonga	Fale Alea (Legislative Assembly) (30 members)	Fale Alea	3
Trinidad and Tobago	Senate (31 members)	Parliament	5
	House of Representatives (36 members)		5
Tunisia	Majlis Al-Nuwwab (Council of Deputies) (182 members)	Majlis	5
Turkey	Millet Meclisi (National Assembly) (550 members)	Millet Meclisi	5
Turkmenistan	Mejlis (Council) (50 members)	Mejlis	5
Tuvalu	Parliament (15 members)	Parliament	4
Uganda	Parliament (276 members)	Parliament	5
Ukraine	Verkhovna Rada (Supreme Council) (450 members)	Verkhovna Rada	4
United Arab Emirates	Majlis Watani Itihad (Federal National Council) (360 members)	Majlis	2
United Kingdom	House of Lords (688 members as at 31 July 2002)	Parliament	varies
	House of Commons (659 members)		5
USA	Senate (Upper House of 100 members serve for 6 yrs)	Congress	6
	House of Representatives (435 members serve for 2 yrs)		2
Uruguay	Senate (31 members)	Congress	5
	Chamber of Deputies (99 members)		5
Uzbekistan	Oliy Majlis (Supreme Assembly) (250 members)	Majlis	5
Vanuatu	Parliament (52 members)	Parliament	4
Venezuela	National Assembly (165 members)	National Assembly	5
Vietnam	Quoc Hoi (National Assembly) (500 members)	Quoc Hoi	5
Yemen	Majlis Annowab (Council of Representatives) (301 members)	Majlis	4
Yugoslavia	Vece Republika (Chamber of the Republics) (40 members)	Skupstina SRJ	5
	Vece Gradjana (Chamber of Citizens) (138 members)		4
Zambia	House of Assembly (150 members)	National Assembly	5
Zimbabwe	House of Assembly (150 members)	National Assembly	5

British Prime Ministers

Name	Term of Office	Party	Education	Constituency	Marriage(s)	Buried
1 Sir Robert Walpole (earl of Orford) (1676–1745)	1721–1742	Whig	Eton & Cambridge (King's)	Castle Rising (1701–2), King's Lynn (1702–42)	Catherine Shorter, Maria Skerrett	Houghton, Norfolk
2 Sir Spencer Compton (earl of Wilmington) (1673–1743)	1742–1743	Whig	St Pauls & Oxford (Trinity)	Eye (Suffolk) (1698–1710), East Grinstead (1713–15), Sussex (1715–28)	Unmarried	Compton Wynates, Warwickshire
3 Henry Pelham (1695–1754)	1743–1754	Whig	Westminster & Oxford (Hart Hall)	Seaford (1717–22), Sussex (1722–54)	Catherine Manners	Laughton Church, nr Lewes, E. Sussex
4 Thomas Pelham-Holles (duke of Newcastle) (1693–1768)	1754–1756	Whig	Westminster & Cambridge (Clare)	House of Lords	Henrietta Godolphin	Laughton Church, nr Lewes, E. Sussex
5 William Cavendish (duke of Devonshire) (1720–1764)	1756–1757	Whig	private education	Derbyshire (1741–51)	Baroness Clifford	Derby Cathedral
6 Thomas Pelham-Holles (duke of Newcastle) (1693–1768)	1757–1762	Whig	Westminster & Cambridge (Clare)	House of Lords	Henrietta Godolphin	Laughton Church, nr Lewes, E. Sussex
7 John Stuart (earl of Bute) (1713–1792)	1762–1763	Tory	Eton	House of Lords	Mary Wortley-Montagu	Rothesay, Bute
8 George Grenville (1712–1770)	1763–1765	Whig	Eton & Oxford (Christ Church)	Buckingham (1741–70)	Elizabeth Wyndham	Wotton, Bucks
9 Charles Watson Wentworth (marquis of Rockingham) (1730–1782)	1765–1766	Whig	Westminster & Cambridge (St John's)	House of Lords	Mary Bright	York Minster
10 Augustus Henry Fitzroy (duke of Grafton) (1735–1811)	1766–1770	Whig	Westminster & Cambridge (Peterhouse)	Bury St Edmunds (1756)	Anne Liddell, Elizabeth Wrottesley	Euston, Suffolk
11 Lord Frederick North (earl of Guildford) (1732–1792)	1770–1782	Tory	Eton, Oxford (Trinity), Leipzig	Banbury (1754–90)	Anne Speke	All Saints, Wroxton, Oxfordshire
12 Charles Watson Wentworth (marquis of Rockingham) (1730–1782)	1782	Whig	Westminster & Cambridge (St John's)	House of Lords	Mary Bright	York Minster
13 William Petty (earl of Shelburne) (1737–1805)	1782–1783	Whig	Oxford (Christ Church)	Chipping Wycombe (1760–61)	Sophia Carteret, Louisa FitzPatrick	High Wycombe
14 William Henry Cavendish-Bentinck (duke of Portland) (1738–1809)	1783	Coalition	Eton & Oxford (Christ Church)	Weobly, Herefordshire (1761–2) (as Whig)	Dorothy Cavendish	St Marylebone, London
15 William Pitt the Younger (1759–1806)	1783–1801	Tory	Cambridge (Pembroke Hall)	Appleby (1781–1806)	Unmarried	Westminster Abbey
16 Henry Addington (Viscount Sidmouth) (1757–1844)	1801–1804	Tory	Cheam, Winchester, Lincoln's Inn & Oxford (Brasenose)	Devizes (1784–1805)	Ursula Mary Hammond, Marianne Townshend	Mortlake
17 William Pitt the Younger (1759–1806)	1804–1806	Tory	Cambridge (Pembroke Hall)	Appleby (1781–1806)	Unmarried	Westminster Abbey
18 William Wyndham Grenville (1759–1834)	1806–1807	Coalition	Eton, Oxford (Christ Church), Lincoln's Inn	Buckingham (1782–4), Buckinghamshire (1784–90)	Anne Pitt	Burnham, Bucks
19 William Henry Cavendish-Bentinck (duke of Portland) (1738–1809)	1807–1809	Tory	Westminster & Oxford (Christ Church)	Weobly, Herefordshire (1761–2) (as Whig)	Dorothy Cavendish	St Marylebone, London
20 Spencer Perceval (1762–1812)	1809–1812	Tory	Harrow & Cambridge (Trinity)	Northampton	Jane Spencer-Wilson	Charlton

POLITICS

Name	Term of Office	Party	Education	Constituency	Marriage(s)	Buried
21 Robert Banks Jenkinson (earl of Liverpool) (1770–1828)	1812–1827	Tory	Charterhouse & Oxford (Christ Church)	Rye (1791–1803) elected for Appleby 1790 too young see note 4 below	Louisa Theodosia Hervey Mary Chester	Hawkesbury
22 George Canning (1770–1827)	1827	Tory	Eton, Oxford (Christ Church), Lincoln's Inn		Joan Scott	Westminster Abbey
23 Frederick John Robinson (Viscount Goderich) (1782–1859)	1827–1828	Tory	Harrow, Cambridge (St John's), Lincoln's Inn	Carlow (1806–7) & Ripon (1807–27)	Sarah Hobart	Nocton, Lincs
24 Arthur Wellesley (duke of Wellington) (1769–1852)	1828–1830	Tory	Browns Seminary, King's Rd, Chelsea, Eton, Brussels & Angers Military Acad.	Rye (1806), Newport IOW (1807–9) St Michael (1807)	Catherine Pakenham	St Paul's Cathedral
25 Charles Grey (Earl Grey) (1764–1845)	1830–1834	Whig	Eton, Cambridge (Trinity) & Middle Temple	Northumberland (1786–1807) Appleby (1807), Tavistock (1807)	Mary Elizabeth Ponsonby	Howick House, Northumberland
26 Henry William Lamb (Viscount Melbourne) (1779–1848)	1834	Whig	Eton, Cambridge (Trinity), Glasgow, Lincoln's Inn	see n. 4 below	Caroline Ponsonby	Hatfield
27 Robert Peel (1788–1850)	1834–1835	Tory	Harrow, Oxford (Christ Church), Lincoln's Inn	see n. 4 below	Julia Floyd	Drayton Bassett
28 Henry William Lamb (Viscount Melbourne) (1779–1848)	1835–1841	Whig	Eton, Cambridge (Trinity), Glasgow, Lincoln's Inn	see n. 4 below	Caroline Ponsonby	Hatfield
29 Robert Peel (1788–1850)	1841–1846	Conservative	Harrow, Oxford (Christ Church), Lincoln's Inn	see n. 4 below	Julia Floyd	Drayton Bassett
30 John Russell (Earl Russell) (1792–1878)	1846–1852	Whig	Westminster & Edinburgh	see n. 4 below	Abigail Lister Lady Frances Elliot	Chenies, Bucks
31 Edward George Stanley (earl of Derby) (1799–1869)	1852	Conservative	Eton & Oxford (Christ Church)	see n. 4 below	Emma Wilbraham-Bootle	Knowsley, Lancs
32 George Hamilton Gordon (earl of Aberdeen) (1784–1860)	1852–1855	Conservative (Peelite)	Harrow & Cambridge (St John's)	House of Lords	Catherine Hamilton Harriet Douglas	Stanmore, Gtr London
33 Henry John Temple (Viscount Palmerston) (1784–1865)	1855–1858	Liberal	Harrow, Edinburgh, Cambridge (St John's)	see n. 4 below	Emile Lamb the Dowager Countess Cowper	Westminster Abbey
34 Edward George Stanley (earl of Derby) (1799–1869)	1858–1859	Conservative	Eton & Oxford (Christ Church)	see n. 4 below	Emma Wilbraham-Bootle	Knowsley, Lancs
35 Henry John Temple (Viscount Palmerston) (1784–1865)	1859–1865	Liberal	Harrow, Edinburgh, Cambridge (St John's)	see n. 4 below	Emile Lamb the Dowager Countess Cowper	Westminster Abbey
36 John Russell (Earl Russell) (1792–1878)	1865–1866	Liberal	Westminster & Edinburgh	see n. 4 below	Abigail Lister Lady Frances Elliot	Chenies, Bucks
37 Edward George Stanley (earl of Derby) (1799–1869)	1866–1868	Conservative	Eton & Oxford (Christ Church)	see n. 4 below	Emma Wilbraham-Bootle	Knowsley, Lancs

Name	Term of Office	Party	Education	Constituency	Marriage(s)	Buried
38 Benjamin Disraeli (earl of Beaconsfield) (1804–1881)	1868	Conservative	Lincoln's Inn	Maidstone (1837–41), Shrewsbury (1841–7), Buckinghamshire (1847–76)	Mrs Wyndham Lewis née Mary Ann Evans	Hughenden Manor, Buckinghamshire
39 William Ewart Gladstone (1809–1898)	1868–1874	Liberal	Seaforth Vicarage, Eton, Oxford (Christ Church)	see n. 4 below	Catherine Glynne	Westminster Abbey
40 Benjamin Disraeli (earl of Beaconsfield) (1804–1881)	1874–1880	Conservative	Lincoln's Inn	Maidstone (1837–41), Shrewsbury (1841–7), Buckinghamshire (1847–76)	Mrs Wyndham Lewis née Mary Ann Evans	Hughenden Manor, Buckinghamshire
41 William Ewart Gladstone (1809–1898)	1880–1885	Liberal	Seaforth Vicarage, Eton, Oxford (Christ Church)	see n. 4 below	Catherine Glynne	Westminster Abbey
42 Robert Arthur Talbot Cecil (marquis of Salisbury) (1830–1903)	1885–1886	Conservative	Eton & Oxford (Christ Church)	Stamford (1853–68)	Georgiana Alderson	Hatfield
43 William Ewart Gladstone (1809–1898)	1886	Liberal	Seaforth Vicarage, Eton, Oxford (Christ Church)	see n. 4 below	Catherine Glynne	Westminster Abbey
44 Robert Arthur Talbot Cecil (marquis of Salisbury) (1830–1903)	1886–1892	Conservative	Eton & Oxford (Christ Church)	Stamford (1853–68)	Georgiana Alderson	Hatfield
45 William Ewart Gladstone (1809–1898)	1892–1894	Liberal	Seaforth Vicarage, Eton, Oxford (Christ Church)	see n. 4 below	Catherine Glynne	Westminster Abbey
46 Archibald Philip Primrose (earl of Rosebery) (1847–1929)	1894–1895	Liberal	Eton & Oxford (Christ Church)	House of Lords	Hannah de Rothschild	Dalmeny
47 Robert Arthur Talbot Cecil (marquis of Salisbury) (1830–1903)	1895–1902	Conservative	Eton & Oxford (Christ Church)	Stamford (1853–68)	Georgiana Alderson	Hatfield
48 Arthur Balfour (earl of Balfour) (1848–1930)	1902–1905	Conservative	Eton & Cambridge (Trinity)	Hertford (1874–85), E. Manchester (1885–1906), London (1906–22)	Unmarried	Whittinghame, East Lothian
49 Henry Campbell-Bannerman (1836–1908)	1905–1908	Liberal	Glasgow & Cambridge (Trinity)	Stirling (1868–1908)	Sarah Charlotte Bruce	Meigle, Scotland
50 Herbert Henry Asquith (earl of Oxford) (1852–1928)	1908–1916	Liberal	City of London & Oxford (Balliol)	East Fife (1886–1918), Paisley (1920–4)	Helen Kelsall Melland Emma Tennant	Sutton Courtney Church, Bucks
51 David Lloyd George (earl of Dwyfor) (1863–1945)	1916–1922	Coalition	Llanystumdwy Church School	Caernarvon (1890–1945)	Margaret Owen Frances Stevenson	Bank of River Dwyfor
52 Andrew Bonar Law (1858–1923)	1922–1923	Conservative	Gilbertfield in Hamilton & Glasgow High School	see n. 4 below	Annie Pitcairn Robley	Westminster Abbey
53 Stanley Baldwin (1867–1947) (Earl Baldwin of Bewdley)	1923–1924	Conservative	Harrow & Cambridge (Trinity)	Bewdley, Worcs (1908–37)	Lucy Ridsdale	Worcester Cathedral
54 James Ramsay MacDonald (1866–1937)	1924	Labour	Drainie Parish Board School	see n. 4 below	Margaret Gladstone	Spynie Churchyard, Lossiemouth
55 Stanley Baldwin (1867–1947) (Earl Baldwin of Bewdley)	1924–1929	Conservative	Harrow & Cambridge (Trinity)	Bewdley, Worcs (1908–37)	Lucy Ridsdale	Worcester Cathedral

POLITICS

Name	Term of Office	Party	Education	Constituency	Marriage(s)	Buried
56 James Ramsay MacDonald (1866–1937)	1929–1935	Labour	Drainie Parish Board School	see n. 4 below	Margaret Gladstone	Spynie Churchyard, Lossiemouth
57 Stanley Baldwin (1867–1947) (Earl Baldwin of Bewdley)	1935–1937	National	Harrow & Cambridge (Trinity)	Bewdley, Worcs (1908–37)	Lucy Ridsdale	Worcester Cathedral
58 Neville Chamberlain (1869–1940)	1937–1940	National	Rugby & Mason College (later Birmingham University)	Ladywood, Birmingham (1918–29) Edgbaston (1929–40)	Annie Vere Cole	Westminster Abbey (ashes)
59 Winston Leonard Spencer Churchill (1874–1965)	1940–1945	Coalition	Harrow & Royal Military College, Sandhurst	see n. 4 below	Clementine Ogilvy Hozier	Bladon, Oxfordshire
60 Clement Attlee (1883–1967)	1945–1951	Labour	Haileybury Coll. & Oxford (University)	Limehouse, Stepney (1922–50) West Walthamstow (1950–5)	Violet Millar	Westminster Abbey
61 Winston Leonard Spencer Churchill (1874–1965)	1951–1955	Conservative	Harrow & Royal Military College, Sandhurst	see n. 4 below	Clementine Ogilvy Hozier	Bladon, Oxfordshire
62 Anthony Eden (earl of Avon) (1897–1977)	1955–1957	Conservative	Eton & Oxford (Christ Church)	Warwick & Leamington (1923–57)	Beatrice Beckett Anne Spencer-Churchill	Alvediston, Wiltshire
63 Maurice Harold Macmillan (earl of Stockton) (1894–1986)	1957–1963	Conservative	Eton & Oxford (Balliol)	Stockton on Tees (1924–9 & 1931–45), Bromley (1945–64)	Dorothy Cavendish	Horsted Keynes
64 Alexander Frederick Douglas-Home (Lord Home of the Hirsel) (1903–1995)	1963–1964	Conservative	Eton & Oxford (Christ Church)	S. Lanark (1931–45), Lanark (1950–1), Kinross & West Perthshire (1963–74)	Elizabeth Alington	Coldstream
65 James Harold Wilson (1916–1995) (Lord Wilson of Rievaulx)	1964–1970	Labour	Milnsbridge, Royds Hall, Wirral, Oxford (Jesus)	Ormskirk (1945–50), Huyton (1950–83)	Gladys Mary Baldwin	Scilly Isles
66 Edward Heath (1916–)	1970–1974	Conservative	Chatham House, Ramsgate, Oxford (Balliol)	Bexley (1950–74), Bexley–Sidcup (1974–83), Old Bexley and Sidcup (1983–2001)	Unmarried	
67 James Harold Wilson (1916–1995) (Lord Wilson of Rievaulx)	1974–1976	Labour	Milnsbridge, Royds Hall, Wirral, Oxford (Jesus)	Ormskirk (1945–50), Huyton (1950–83)	Gladys Mary Baldwin	Scilly Isles
68 Leonard James Callaghan (Lord Callaghan of Cardiff) (1912–)	1976–1979	Labour	Portsmouth Northern Sec.	South Cardiff (1945–50), SE Cardiff (1950–83), Cardiff South and Penarth (1983–87)	Audrey Moulton	
69 Margaret Hilda Thatcher (1925–) (Baroness Thatcher of Kesteven)	1979–1990	Conservative	Kesteven & Grantham, Oxford (Somerville)	Finchley (1959–74), Barnet, Finchley (1974–92)	Denis Thatcher	
70 John Major (1943–)	1990–1997	Conservative	Rutlish Grammar	Huntingdon (1983 to present)	Norma Johnson	
71 Tony Blair (1953–)	1997–	Labour	Durham Choristers, Fettes (Edinburgh), Oxford (St John's)	Sedgefield (1983 to present)	Cherie Booth	

Notes

1 Prime Minister Although the office of prime minister is traditionally stated as commencing in 1721, in fact there were chief ministers given this label long before this date, and conversely there have been chief ministers subsequent to this date who did not bear the title of prime minister, e.g. William Pitt the Elder and Charles James Fox, in the mid- and late 18th century. To confuse matters further, Walpole was designated First Lord of the Treasury until 1730, as were some other future prime ministers of the 18th and 19th centuries. It was not until 1905 that the title of prime minister became official.

2 Party A second point of conjecture concerns the designation of the ruling party of the day. Until the first Electoral Reform Act of 1832 and the subsequent rise of the Conservative and Liberal parties, the government of the day was often a coalition of sorts, and the ruling party is given as the party of the prime minister in power, unless unaffiliated.

3 Chief ministers not listed above Sir William Pulteney, earl of Bath, actually kissed the hand of George II on 10 Feb. 1746, but within three days was unable to form a government. James Waldegrave kissed the hand of George II on 8 June 1757 but returned seals on 12 June, unable to form a ministry. Charles James Fox and his erstwhile enemy Lord North were the de facto heads of government in 1783, while the duke of Portland was merely the nominal prime minister. William Pitt the Elder, earl of Chatham, although not included in the table above, was in effect the prime minister from 1756 to 1761 during most of the Seven Years' War, although never taking up official office. From 1766 to 1768 Pitt was also Head of the Government but chose the secondary post of Lord Privy Seal; gout prevented him serving in anything but name for this second term.

4 Constituencies: See numbers in table above

(22) George Canning's constituencies: Newport IOW (1793–6 & 1806–7), Wendover (1796–1802), Tralee (1802–6), Hastings (1807–12), Liverpool (1812–23), Harwich (1823–6), Newport IOW (1826–7) & Seaford (1827).

(26) Viscount Melbourne's constituencies: Leominster (1806), Haddington Borough (1806–7), Portarlington (1807–12), Peterborough (1816–19), Hertfordshire (1819–26) Newport IOW (1827), Bletchingley (1827–8).

(27) Robert Peel's constituencies: Cashel (Tipperary) (1809–12), Chippenham (1812–17), Oxford University (1817–29), Westbury (1829–30), Tamworth (1830–50).

(30) Earl Russell's constituencies: Tavistock (1813–17, 1818–20, 1830–1), Huntingdonshire (1820–6), Bandon (1826–30), Devon (1831–2), South Devon (1832–5), Stroud (1835–41), London (1841–61).

(31) Earl of Derby's constituencies: Stockbridge (1822–6), Preston (1826–30), Windsor (1831–2), North Lancs (1832–44).

(33) Viscount Palmerston's constituencies: Newport IOW (1807–11), Cambridge University (1811–31), Bletchingley (1831–2), South Hants (1832–4), Tiverton (1835–65).

(39) William Gladstone's constituencies: Newark (1832–45 as Tory), Oxford University (1847–65 as Peelite until 1859 then Liberal), South Lancs (1865–8), Greenwich (1868–80), Midlothian (1880–95).

(52) Andrew Bonar Law's constituencies: Blackfriars, Glasgow (1900–6), Dulwich (1906–10), Bootle (1911–18), Central Glasgow (1918–23).

(54) Ramsay MacDonald's constituencies: Leicester (1906–18), Aberavon (1922–9), Seaham, Co. Durham (1929–31), Scottish Universities (1936–7).

(59) Winston Churchill's constituencies: Oldham (1900–6, Conservative until 1904 then Liberal), NW Manchester (1906–8), Dundee (1908–22), Epping (1924–45), Woodford, Essex (1945–64 as Conservative).

5 Miscellaneous information

(2) Sir Spencer Compton was a Tory until 1704.

(8) George Grenville was nicknamed the Gentle Shepherd.

(9) Charles Watson Wentworth repealed the Stamp Act.

(10) Augustus Henry Fitzroy, the duke of Grafton, was a victim of the pseudonymous Junius letters which attacked various government ministers in the London *Public Advertiser* (1769–72), although the identity of Junius remains unknown. Sir Philip Francis is a possible candidate. He was also a direct descendant of the illegitimate son of Charles II.

(11) Lord Frederick North became a Whig in 1783.

(13) William Petty, the earl of Shelburne, was nicknamed Malagrida, after a notorious scheming Jesuit. He sat in the English House of Lords in his father's English title of Baron Wycombe.

(18) William Wyndham Grenville's administration of February 1806–March 1807 was known as 'The Ministry of All the Talents' and comprised followers of Charles James Fox. Its greatest achievement was the abolition of slavery in March 1807. He was the son of George Grenville (PM 1763–65).

(20) Spencer Perceval was assassinated by John Bellingham in the lobby of the Commons.

(21) Robert Banks Jenkinson was created Lord Hawkesbury in 1803 and earl of Liverpool in 1808.

(22) George Canning fought a duel with Viscount Castlereagh on Putney Heath in September 1809 but was only slightly wounded.

(24) Arthur Wellesley, duke of Wellington, was known as Arthur Wesley until 1804.

(27) Robert Peel created the Metropolitan Police Force in 1829 and drafted the 'Tamworth Manifesto' which laid down the ideology and objectives of the party which became the Conservatives. He died after a fall from a horse.

(30) Abigail Lister, the wife of Lord John Russell, became Baroness Ribblesdale.

(31) Edward George Stanley, the earl of Derby, became a Tory in 1835 (previously a Whig).

(33) Henry John Temple, Viscount Palmerston, was a Tory until 1829, then a Whig, and finally a Liberal. He was the last Prime Minister to die in office.

(42) Robert Arthur Talbot Gascoyne-Cecil was also known as Viscount Cranborne.

(48) Arthur James Balfour was the son of James Balfour MP and his wife, the sister of the third marquess of Salisbury, later the Conservative Prime Minister.

POLITICS

(49) Henry Campbell-Bannerman died at 10 Downing Street, three weeks after resigning.
(50) Herbert Henry Asquith's administration was a coalition from 1915.
(52) Andrew Bonar Law was born in New Brunswick, Canada. His term of office was 209 days.
(53) Stanley Baldwin was related to Rudyard Kipling and Sir Edward Burne-Jones.
(59) Winston Churchill's first administration became Conservative from 23 May 1945.
(62) Anthony Eden's second wife was the niece of the former Prime Minister Winston Churchill.

6 William Pitt (the Elder) (1708–1778) Educated at Eton and Trinity College, Oxford. In 1735 he entered the House of Commons as member for the family borough of Old Sarum. In 1756 Pitt became nominally Secretary of State but was de facto Prime Minister from 1756 until October 1761. The King invited him to form a further government between 1766 and 1768 but he chose the secondary title of Lord Privy Seal while performing Prime Ministerial duties. Chronic gout caused a severe decline in his mental health and he died after making a speech in the House of Lords on 2 April 1778. His second son was William Pitt the Younger.

Members of Cabinet

(as at 12 June 2003)

Note: The Cabinet restructure of 12 June created a new Department for Constitutional Affairs which will include the Scottish and Welsh offices.

Tony Blair	Prime Minister, First Lord of the Treasury and Minister for the Civil Service
John Prescott	Deputy Prime Minister and First Minister of State
Gordon Brown	Chancellor of the Exchequer
Jack Straw	Secretary of State for Foreign and Commonwealth Affairs
	Previous incumbent Robin Cook (May 1997 to June 2001)
Lord Falconer of Thoroton	Lord Chancellor and Secretary of State for Constitutional Affairs
David Blunkett	Secretary of State for the Home Department
	Previous incumbent Jack Straw (May 1997 to June 2001)
Charles Clarke	Secretary of State for Education and Skills
	Previous incumbents David Blunkett (May 1997 to June 2001 when Education and Employment) and Estelle Morris (June 2001 to Oct. 2002)
Peter Hain	Leader of the House of Commons and Lord Privy Seal
	Previous incumbents Ann Taylor (May 1997 to July 1998), Margaret Beckett (July 1998 to June 2001) and Robin Cook (June 2001 to March 2003)
Alistair Darling	Secretary of State for Scotland
	Previous incumbents Donald Dewar (1997 to 1999) and Dr John Reid (1999 to 2001)
Geoff Hoon	Secretary of State for Defence
	Previous incumbent Lord George Robertson (May 1997 to Oct. 1999)
Dr John Reid	Secretary of State for Health
	Previous incumbents Frank Dobson (May 1997 to Oct. 1999) and Alan Milburn (Oct. 1999 to June 2003)
Hilary Armstrong	Chief Whip (Parliamentary Secretary to the Treasury)
	Previous incumbent Nick Brown (May 1997 to July 1998) and Ann Taylor (July 1998 to June 2001)
Tessa Jowell	Secretary of State for Culture, Media and Sports
	Previous incumbent Chris Smith (May 1997 to June 2001)
Andrew Smith	Secretary of State for Work and Pensions
	Previous incumbent Harriet Harman (May 1997 to July 1998 when Social Security) and Alistair Darling (July 1998 to June 2001 when Social Security)
Paul Murphy	Secretary of State for Northern Ireland
	Previous incumbents Mo Mowlam (May 1997 to Oct. 1999), Peter Mandelson (Oct. 1999 to Jan. 2001) and Dr John Reid (Jan. 2001 to Oct. 2002)
Peter Hain	Secretary of State for Wales
	Previous incumbents Ron Davies (May 1997 to 1998), Alun Michael (1998 to 1999) and Paul Murphy (1999 to 2002)
Baroness Amos	Secretary of State for International Development
	Previous incumbent Clare Short (June 2001 to May 2003)
Lord Williams of Mostyn	Leader of the House of Lords and Lord President of the Council
	Previous incumbents Lord Richard of Ammanford (May 1997 to July 1998) and Baroness Jay of Paddington (July 1998 to June 2001)
Patricia Hewitt	Secretary of State for Trade and Industry
	Previous incumbents Margaret Beckett (May 1997 to July 1998), Peter Mandelson (July to Dec. 1998) and Stephen Byers (Dec. 1998 to June 2001)
Paul Boateng	Chief Secretary to the Treasury
	Previous incumbents Alistair Darling (May 1997 to July 1998), Stephen Byers (July to Dec. 1998) and Alan Milburn (Dec. 1998 to Oct. 1999)
Margaret Beckett	Secretary of State for Environment, Food and Rural Affairs
	Previous incumbents Jack Cunningham (May 1997 to July 1998) when Agriculture,

Fisheries and Food and Nick Brown (July 1998 to June 2001) when Agriculture,
Fisheries and Food

Alistair Darling   Secretary of State for Transport, Local Government and the Regions
                          Previous incumbent Dr John Reid as Minister for Transport (1998 to 1999)
Ian McCartney   Minister Without Portfolio and Party Chairman
                          Previous incumbent Dr John Reid (Oct. 2002 to March 2003)

also attending Cabinet meetings
Lord Grocott   Lords Chief Whip and Captain of the Gentlemen at Arms
Sir Andrew Turnbull   Secretary of the Cabinet and Head of the Home Civil Service

Departments of State and Ministers

Defence

Secretary of State – The Rt. Hon. Geoff Hoon, MP
Minister of State – The Rt. Hon. Adam Ingram, MP
Parliamentary Under-Secretaries of State – The Lord Bach and Ivor Caplin, MP

Education and Skills

Secretary of State – The Rt. Hon. Charles Clarke, MP
Minister of State for Schools – David Miliband, MP
Minister of State for Children – Margaret Hodge, MP
Minister of State for Lifelong Learning and Higher Education – Alan Johnson
Parliamentary Under-Secretaries of State – Ivan Lewis, MP, Stephen Twigg, MP, and
    Baroness Ashton of Upholland

Environment, Food and Rural Affairs

Secretary of State – The Rt. Hon. Margaret Beckett, MP
Minister for the Environment – The Rt. Hon. Elliot Morley, MP
Minister for Rural Affairs – The Rt. Hon. Alun Michael, MP
Parliamentary Under-Secretaries of State – The Lord Whitty and Ben Bradshaw, MP

Foreign and Commonwealth Office

Secretary of State – The Rt. Hon. Jack Straw, MP
Minister of State for the Middle East – Baroness Symons of Vernham Dean
Minister for Europe – Dr Denis MacShane, MP
Ministers of State – Mike O'Brien, MP, Bill Rammell, MP, and Chris Mullin, MP

Health

Secretary of State – The Rt. Hon. Dr John Reid, MP
Minister of State – John Hutton, MP
Parliamentary Secretary of State – Rosie Winterton, MP
Parliamentary Under-Secretaries of State – Melanie Johnson, MP, Stephen Ladyman,
    MP, and Lord Warner

Home Office

Secretary of State – The Rt. Hon. David Blunkett, MP
Minister of State for Crime Reduction – Hazel Blears, MP
Minister of State (Criminal Justice System) – Baroness Scotland of Ashtal
Minister of Asylum and Immigration – Bev Hughes, MP
Parliamentary Under-Secretaries of State – Caroline Flint, Paul Goggins, Fiona
    Mactaggart, Michael Wills

International Development

Secretary of State – The Rt. Hon. Baroness Amos
Parliamentary Secretary – Gareth Thomas, MP
Minister of State – Hilary Benn, MP

Law Officers' Department

Attorney General – Lord Goldsmith, QC
Solicitor General – The Rt. Hon. Harriet Harman, MP
Advocate General for Scotland – Dr Lynda Clark, QC, MP

Culture, Media and Sports

Secretary of State – The Rt. Hon. Tessa Jowell, MP
Minister of State for Sport – The Rt. Hon. Richard Caborn, MP
Minister of State for the Arts – The Rt. Hon. Estelle Morris, MP
Parliamentary Secretary – Lord McIntosh of Haringey

Northern Ireland Office

Secretary of State – The Rt. Hon. Paul Murphy, MP

POLITICS

Minister of State for Security, Prisons and Policing – Jane Kennedy, MP
Parliamentary Under-Secretaries – Ian Pearson, MP, and Angela Smith, MP
Minister of State – John Spellar, MP

Constitutional Affairs

Lord Chancellor – Lord Falconer of Thoroton, QC
Secretary of State – Lord Falconer of Thoroton, QC
Parliamentary Under-Secretaries – Christopher Leslie, MP, David Lammy, MP, Anne
    McGuire, MP, Don Touhig, MP, and Lord Filkin

Cabinet Office

Minister and Chancellor of the Duchy of Lancaster – The Rt. Hon. Douglas Alexander,
    MP
Previous incumbents David Clark (May 1997 to July 1998), Dr Jack Cunningham (July
    1998 to Oct. 1999) and Mo Mowlam (Oct. 1999 to June 2001)
Minister Without Portfolio and Party Chairman – The Rt. Hon. Ian McCartney, MP
Secretary of the Cabinet and Head of the Home Civil Service – Sir Andrew Turnbull

Privy Council Office

Leader of the House of Commons, Lord Privy Seal, and Secretary of State for Wales –
    Peter Hain, MP
Deputy Leader of the House of Commons – Philip Woolas, MP

Office of the Deputy Prime Minister

Deputy Prime Minister – The Rt. Hon. John Prescott, MP
Minister of State for Local Government and the Regions – Nick Raynsford, MP
Minister of State – Lord Rooker
Minister of State for Housing and Planning – Keith Hill, MP
Under-Secretary of State – Yvette Cooper, MP

Work and Pensions

Secretary of State for Work and Pensions – Rt. Hon. Andrew Smith, MP
Minister for Work – Desmond Browne, MP
Minister for Pensions – Malcolm Wicks, MP
Parliamentary Secretary of State – The Baroness Hollis of Heigham
Parliamentary Under-Secretaries of State – Maria Eagle, MP, and Chris Pond, MP

Transport, Local Government and the Regions

Secretary of State for Transport, Local Government and the Regions – Rt. Hon. Alistair
    Darling, MP
Minister for Transport – Kim Howells, MP
Under-Secretary of State – David Jamieson, MP, and Tony McNulty, MP

Trade and Industry

Secretary of State and Minister for Women – The Rt. Hon. Patricia Hewitt, MP
Minister for E-Commerce and Competitiveness – Stephen Timms, MP
Minister for Trade – Mike O'Brien, MP
Under-Secretaries of State – Lord Sainsbury of Turville, Nigel Griffiths, MP, and Gerry
    Sutcliffe, MP
Minister of State – Jacqui Smith, MP

Treasury

Prime Minister, First Lord of the Treasury and Minister for Civil Service – Rt. Hon. Tony
    Blair, MP
Chancellor of the Exchequer – Rt. Hon. Gordon Brown, MP
Financial Secretary – Ms Ruth Kelly, MP
Paymaster General – Dawn Primarolo, MP
Economic Secretary – John Healey, MP
Parliamentary Secretary and Government Chief Whip – Rt. Hon. Hilary Armstrong, MP
Lords Commissioners – John Heppell, MP, Nick Ainger, MP, Ian Pearson, MP, Jim
    Fitzpatrick, MP, Philip Woolas, MP
Assistant Whips – Fraser Kemp, MP, Bridget Prentice, MP, Jim Murphy, MP, Dan Norris,
    MP, Derek Twigg, MP, Joan Ryan, MP, Gillian Merron, MP, Margaret Moran, MP,
    Charlotte Atkins, MP, Vernon Coaker, MP, and Paul Clarke, MP
Prime Minister's Parliamentary Private Secretary – David Hanson, MP

Her Majesty's Household

Lord Chamberlain – Rt. Hon. Lord Luce, GCVO
Lord Steward – The Duke of Abercorn
Master of the Horse – The Lord Vestey
Mistress of the Robes – The Duchess of Grafton, GCVO
Deputy Chief Whip and Treasurer – Keith Hill, MP
Comptroller – Thomas McAvoy, MP

Vice-Chamberlain – Gerry Sutcliffe, MP
Lord Chief Whip and Capt of the Honourable Corps of Gentlemen-At-Arms – Rt. Hon.
   The Lord Grocott
Deputy Chief Whip and Captain of the Queen's Yeoman of the Guard – The Lord
   Davies of Oldham
Lords-in-Waiting – Lord Bassam of Brighton, and Lord Evans of Temple Guiting
Baronesses-in-Waiting – Baroness Farrington of Ribbleton, Baroness Andrews and
   Baroness Crawley

Downing Street Staff

Chief of Staff – Jonathan Powell
Prime Minister's Principal Private Secretary – Jeremy Heywood
Director of Communications and Strategy – Alastair Campbell
Head of Government Relations – The Baroness Margaret Morgan of Huyton
Political Secretary – Robert Hill
Prime Minister's Official Spokesmen – Godric Smith and Tom Kelly

NB From 1 April 2003, the basic salary of Cabinet ministers is £127,791.
The Prime Minister's basic salary was increased to £175,414.
The First Minister of Scotland is Jack McConnell, representing Motherwell and Wishaw in the Scottish Parliament.
The First Minister of Wales is Rhodri Morgan, representing Cardiff West in the Welsh Assembly.
The Northern Ireland Assembly was dissolved on 28 April 2003.

General Election Results by Candidate: 7 June 2001

Abbott, Diane	Hackney North & Stoke Newington	Labour
Adams, Gerry	Belfast West	Sinn Fein
Adams, Irene	Paisley North	Labour
Ainger, Nick	Carmarthen West & Pembrokeshire South	Labour
Ainsworth, Bob	Coventry North East	Labour
Ainsworth, Peter	Surrey East	Conservative
Alexander, Douglas	Paisley South	Labour Co-Op
Allan, Richard	Sheffield Hallam	Liberal Democrat
Allen, Graham	Nottingham North	Labour
Amess, David	Southend West	Conservative
Ancram, Michael	Devizes	Conservative
Anderson, Donald	Swansea East	Labour
Anderson, Janet	Rossendale & Darwen	Labour
Arbuthnot, James	Hampshire North East	Conservative
Armstrong, Hilary	Durham North West	Labour
Atherton, Candy	Falmouth & Camborne	Labour
Atkinson, David	Bournemouth East	Conservative
Atkinson, Peter	Hexham	Conservative
Atkins, Charlotte	Staffordshire Moorlands	Labour
Austin, John	Erith & Thamesmead	Labour
Bacon, Richard	Norfolk South	Conservative
Bailey, Adrian	West Bromwich West	Labour Co-Op
Baird, Vera	Redcar	Labour
Baker, Norman	Lewes	Liberal Democrat
Baldry, Tony	Banbury	Conservative
Banks, Tony	West Ham	Labour
Barker, Greg	Bexhill & Battle	Conservative
Barnes, Harry	Derbyshire North East	Labour
Baron, John	Billericay	Conservative
Barrett, John	Edinburgh West	Liberal Democrat
Barron, Kevin	Rother Valley	Labour
Battle, John	Leeds West	Labour
Bayley, Hugh	York, City of	Labour
Beard, Nigel	Bexleyheath & Crayford	Labour
Beckett, Margaret	Derby South	Labour
Beggs, Roy	Antrim East	Ulster Unionist
Begg, Anne	Aberdeen South	Labour
Beith, Alan	Berwick-upon-Tweed	Liberal Democrat
Bellingham, Henry	Norfolk North West	Conservative
Bell, Stuart	Middlesborough	Labour
Bennett, Andrew	Denton & Reddish	Labour
Benn, Hilary	Leeds Central	Labour
Benton, Joe	Bootle	Labour

Bercow, John	Buckingham	Conservative
Beresford, Sir Paul	Mole Valley	Conservative
Berry, Roger	Kingswood	Labour
Best, Harold	Leeds North West	Labour
Betts, Clive	Sheffield Attercliffe	Labour
Blackman, Elizabeth	Erewash	Labour
Blair, Tony	Sedgefield	Labour
Blears, Hazel	Salford	Labour
Blizzard, Bob	Waveney	Labour
Blunkett, David	Sheffield Brightside	Labour
Blunt, Crispin	Reigate	Conservative
Boateng, Paul	Brent South	Labour
Borrow, David	Ribble South	Labour
Boswell, Tim	Daventry	Conservative
Bottomley, Peter	Worthing West	Conservative
Bottomley, Virginia	Surrey South West	Conservative
Bradley, Keith	Manchester Withington	Labour
Bradley, Peter	Wrekin, The	Labour
Bradshaw, Ben	Exeter	Labour
Brady, Graham	Altrincham & Sale West	Conservative
Brake, Tom	Carshalton and Wallington	Liberal Democrat
Brazier, Julian	Canterbury	Conservative
Breed, Colin	Cornwall South East	Liberal Democrat
Brennan, Kevin	Cardiff West	Labour
Brinton, Helen	Peterborough	Labour
Brooke, Annette	Dorset Mid & Poole North	Liberal Democrat
Browne, Des	Kilmarnock & Loudoun	Labour
Browning, Angela	Tiverton & Honiton	Conservative
Brown, Gordon	Dunfermline East	Labour
Brown, Nick	Newcastle upon Tyne East & Wallsend	Labour
Brown, Russell	Dumfries	Labour
Bruce, Malcolm	Gordon	Liberal Democrat
Bryant, Chris	Rhondda	Labour
Buck, Karen	Regent's Park & Kensington	Labour
Burden, Richard	Birmingham Northfield	Labour
Burgon, Colin	Elmet	Labour
Burnett, John	Devon West & Torridge	Liberal Democrat
Burnham, Andrew	Leigh	Labour
Burnside, David	Antrim South	Ulster Unionist
Burns, Simon	Chelmsford West	Conservative
Burstow, Paul	Sutton and Cheam	Liberal Democrat
Burt, Alastair	Bedfordshire North East	Conservative
Butterfill, John	Bournemouth West	Conservative
Byers, Stephen	Tyneside North	Labour
Cable, Dr Vincent	Twickenham	Liberal Democrat
Caborn, Richard	Sheffield Central	Labour
Cairns, David	Greenock & Inverclyde	Labour
Calton, Patsy	Cheadle	Liberal Democrat
Cameron, David	Witney	Conservative
Campbell, Alan	Tynemouth	Labour
Campbell, Anne	Cambridge	Labour
Campbell, Gregory	Londonderry East	Democratic Unionist
Campbell, Menzies	Fife North East	Liberal Democrat
Campbell, Ronnie	Blyth Valley	Labour
Cann, Jamie	Ipswich	Labour
Caplin, Ivor	Hove	Labour
Carmichael, Alistair	Orkney & Shetland	Liberal Democrat
Casale, Roger	Wimbledon	Labour
Cash, William	Stone	Conservative
Caton, Martin	Gower	Labour
Cawsey, Ian	Brigg & Goole	Labour
Challen, Colin	Morley & Rothwell	Labour
Chapman, Ben	Wirral South	Labour
Chapman, Sir Sydney	Chipping Barnet	Conservative
Chaytor, David	Bury North	Labour
Chidgey, David	Eastleigh	Liberal Democrat
Chope, Christopher	Christchurch	Conservative
Clapham, Michael	Barnsley West and Penistone	Labour
Clappison, James	Hertsmere	Conservative
Clarke, Charles	Norwich South	Labour
Clarke, Kenneth	Rushcliffe	Conservative
Clarke, Paul	Gillingham	Labour

Clarke, Tom	*Coatbridge & Chryston*	Labour
Clark, Lynda	*Edinburgh Pentlands*	Labour
Clark, Tony	*Northampton South*	Labour
Clelland, David	*Tyne Bridge*	Labour
Clifton-Brown, Geoffrey	*Cotswold*	Conservative
Clwyd, Ann	*Cynon Valley*	Labour
Coaker, Vernon	*Gedling*	Labour
Coffey, Ann	*Stockport*	Labour
Cohen, Harry	*Leyton & Wanstead*	Labour
Coleman, Iain	*Hammersmith & Fulham*	Labour
Collins, Tim	*Westmorland & Lonsdale*	Conservative
Colman, Tony	*Putney*	Labour
Connarty, Michael	*Falkirk East*	Labour
Conway, Derek	*Old Bexley & Sidcup*	Conservative
Cook, Frank	*Stockton North*	Labour
Cook, Robin	*Livingston*	Labour
Cooper, Yvette	*Pontefract & Castleford*	Labour
Corbyn, Jeremy	*Islington North*	Labour
Cormack, Sir Patrick	*Staffordshire South*	Conservative
Corston, Jean	*Bristol East*	Labour
Cotter, Brian	*Weston-Super-Mare*	Liberal Democrat
Cousins, Jim	*Newcastle upon Tyne Central*	Labour
Cox, Tom	*Tooting*	Labour
Cranston, Ross	*Dudley North*	Labour
Cran, James	*Beverley & Holderness*	Conservative
Crausby, David	*Bolton North East*	Labour
Cruddas, Jon	*Dagenham*	Labour
Cryer, Ann	*Keighley*	Labour
Cryer, John	*Hornchurch*	Labour
Cummings, John	*Easington*	Labour
Cunningham, Jack	*Copeland*	Labour
Cunningham, Jim	*Coventry South*	Labour
Cunningham, Tony	*Workington*	Labour
Curry, David	*Skipton & Ripon*	Conservative
Curtis-Thomas, Claire	*Crosby*	Labour
Daisley, Paul	*Brent East*	Labour
Dalyell, Tam	*Linlithgow*	Labour
Darling, Alistair	*Edinburgh Central*	Labour
Davey, Edward	*Kingston & Surbiton*	Liberal Democrat
Davey, Valerie	*Bristol West*	Labour
David, Wayne	*Caerphilly*	Labour
Davidson, Ian	*Glasgow Pollok*	Labour Co-Op
Davies, Denzil	*Llanelli*	Labour
Davies, Geraint	*Croydon Central*	Labour
Davies, Quentin	*Grantham & Stamford*	Conservative
Davis, David	*Haltemprice & Howden*	Conservative
Davis, Terry	*Birmingham Hodge Hill*	Labour
Dawson, Hilton	*Lancaster & Wyre*	Labour
Dean, Janet	*Burton*	Labour
Denham, John	*Southampton Itchen*	Labour
Dhanda, Parmjit	*Gloucester*	Labour
Dismore, Andrew	*Hendon*	Labour
Djanogly, Jonathan	*Huntingdon*	Conservative
Dobbin, Jim	*Heywood & Middleton*	Labour Co-Op
Dobson, Frank	*Holborn & St Pancras*	Labour
Dodds, Nigel	*Belfast North*	Democratic Unionist
Doherty, Pat	*Tyrone West*	Sinn Fein
Donaldson, Jeffrey	*Lagan Valley*	Ulster Unionist
Donohoe, Brian	*Cunninghame South*	Labour
Doran, Frank	*Aberdeen Central*	Labour
Dorrell, Stephen	*Charnwood*	Conservative
Doughty, Sue	*Guildford*	Liberal Democrat
Dowd, Jim	*Lewisham West*	Labour
Drew, David	*Stroud*	Labour Co-Op
Drown, Julia	*Swindon South*	Labour
Duncan Smith, Iain	*Chingford & Woodford Green*	Conservative
Duncan, Alan	*Rutland & Melton*	Conservative
Duncan, Peter	*Galloway & Upper Nithsdale*	Conservative
Dunwoody, Gwyneth	*Crewe & Nantwich*	Labour
Eagle, Angela	*Wallasey*	Labour
Eagle, Maria	*Liverpool Garston*	Labour
Edwards, Huw	*Monmouth*	Labour

POLITICS

Efford, Clive	Eltham	Labour
Ellman, Louise	Liverpool Riverside	Labour
Ennis, Jeff	Barnsley East & Mexborough	Labour
Etherington, Bill	Sunderland North	Labour
Evans, Nigel	Ribble Valley	Conservative
Ewing, Annabelle	Perth	Scottish Nationalists
Fabricant, Michael	Lichfield	Conservative
Fallon, Michael	Sevenoaks	Conservative
Farrelly, Paul	Newcastle-under-Lyme	Labour
Field, Frank	Birkenhead	Labour
Field, Mark	Cities of London & Westminster	Conservative
Fisher, Mark	Stoke-on-Trent Central	Labour
Fitzpatrick, Jim	Poplar & Canning Town	Labour
Fitzsimons, Lorna	Rochdale	Labour
Flight, Howard	Arundel & South Downs	Conservative
Flint, Caroline	Don Valley	Labour
Flook, Adrian	Taunton	Conservative
Flynn, Paul	Newport West	Labour
Follett, Barbara	Stevenage	Labour
Forth, Eric	Bromley & Chislehurst	Conservative
Foster, Derek	Bishop Auckland	Labour
Foster, Don	Bath	Liberal Democrat
Foster, Michael	Worcester	Labour
Foster, Michael	Hastings & Rye	Labour
Foulkes, George	Carrick, Cumnock & Doon	Labour Co-Op
Fox, Dr Liam	Woodspring	Conservative
Francis, Hywel	Aberavon	Labour
Francois, Mark	Rayleigh	Conservative
Gale, Roger	Thanet North	Conservative
Galloway, George	Glasgow Kelvin	Labour
Gapes, Mike	Ilford South	Labour Co-Op
Gardiner, Barry	Brent North	Labour
Garnier, Edward	Harborough	Conservative
George, Andrew	St Ives	Liberal Democrat
George, Bruce	Wallsall South	Labour
Gerrard, Neil	Walthamstow	Labour
Gibb, Nick	Bognor Regis & Littlehampton	Conservative
Gibson, Dr Ian	Norwich North	Labour
Gidley, Sandra	Romsey	Liberal Democrat
Gildernew, Michelle	Fermanagh & South Tyrone	Sinn Fein
Gillan, Cheryl	Chesham & Amersham	Conservative
Gilroy, Linda	Plymouth Sutton	Labour Co-Op
Godsiff, Roger	Birmingham Sparkbrook & Small Heath	Labour
Goggins, Paul	Wythenshawe & Sale East	Labour
Goodman, Paul	Wycombe	Conservative
Grayling, Chris	Epsom and Ewell	Conservative
Gray, James	Wiltshire North	Conservative
Greenway, John	Ryedale	Conservative
Green, Damien	Ashford	Conservative
Green, Matthew	Ludlow	Liberal Democrat
Grieve, Dominic	Beaconsfield	Conservative
Griffiths, Jane	Reading East	Labour
Griffiths, Nigel	Edinburgh South	Labour
Griffiths, Win	Bridgend	Labour
Grogan, John	Selby	Labour
Gummer, John	Suffolk Coastal	Conservative
Hague, William	Richmond (Yorks)	Conservative
Hain, Peter	Neath	Labour
Hall, Mike	Weaver Vale	Labour
Hall, Patrick	Bedford	Labour
Hamilton, David	Midlothian	Labour
Hamilton, Fabian	Leeds North East	Labour
Hammond, Philip	Runnymede & Weybridge	Conservative
Hancock, Mike	Portsmouth South	Liberal Democrat
Hanson, David	Delyn	Labour
Harman, Harriet	Camberwell & Peckham	Labour
Harris, Dr Evan	Oxford West & Abingdon	Liberal Democrat
Harris, Tom	Glasgow Cathcart	Labour
Harvey, Nick	Devon North	Liberal Democrat
Haselhurst, Sir Alan	Saffron Walden	Conservative
Havard, Dai	Merthyr Tydfil & Rhymney	Labour
Hawkins, Nicholas	Surrey Heath	Conservative

Hayes, John	South Holland & The Deepings	Conservative
Heald, Oliver	Hertfordshire North East	Conservative
Healey, John	Wentworth	Labour
Heal, Sylvia	Halesowen & Rowley Regis	Labour
Heathcoat-Amory, David	Wells	Conservative
Heath, David	Somerton & Frome	Liberal Democrat
Henderson, Doug	Newcastle upon Tyne North	Labour
Henderson, Ivan	Harwich	Labour
Hendrick, Mark	Preston	Labour Co-Op
Hendry, Charles	Wealden	Conservative
Hepburn, Stephen	Jarrow	Labour
Heppell, John	Nottingham East	Labour
Hermon, Sylvia	Down North	Ulster Unionist
Hesford, Stephen	Wirral West	Labour
Hewitt, Patricia	Leicester West	Labour
Heyes, David	Ashton-under-Lyne	Labour
Hill, Keith	Streatham	Labour
Hinchcliffe, David	Wakefield	Labour
Hoban, Mark	Fareham	Conservative
Hodge, Margaret	Barking	Labour
Hoey, Kate	Vauxhall	Labour
Hogg, Douglas	Sleaford & North Hykeham	Conservative
Holmes, Paul	Chesterfield	Liberal Democrat
Hood, Jimmy	Clydesdale	Labour
Hoon, Geoff	Ashfield	Labour
Hope, Phil	Corby	Labour Co-Op
Hopkins, Kelvin	Luton North	Labour
Horam, John	Orpington	Conservative
Howard, Michael	Folkestone & Hythe	Conservative
Howarth, Alan	Newport East	Labour
Howarth, George	Knowsley North & Sefton East	Labour
Howarth, Gerald	Aldershot	Conservative
Howells, Dr Kim	Pontypridd	Labour
Hoyle, Lindsay	Chorley	Labour
Hughes, Beverley	Stretford & Urmston	Labour
Hughes, Kevin	Doncaster North	Labour
Hughes, Simon	Southwark North & Bermondsey	Liberal Democrat
Humble, Joan	Blackpool North & Fleetwood	Labour
Hume, John	Foyle	SDLP
Hunter, Andrew	Basingstoke	Conservative
Hurst, Alan	Braintree	Labour
Hutton, John	Barrow & Furness	Labour
Iddon, Brian	Bolton South East	Labour
Illsley, Eric	Barnsley Central	Labour
Ingram, Adam	East Kilbride	Labour
Jackson, Glenda	Hampstead and Highgate	Labour
Jackson, Helen	Sheffield Hillsborough	Labour
Jackson, Robert	Wantage	Conservative
Jack, Michael	Fylde	Conservative
Jamieson, David	Plymouth Devonport	Labour
Jenkins, Brian	Tamworth	Labour
Jenkin, Bernard	Essex North	Conservative
Johnson, Alan	Hull West & Hessle	Labour
Johnson, Boris	Henley	Conservative
Johnson, Melanie	Welwyn Hatfield	Labour
Jones, Dr Lynne	Birmingham Selly Oak	Labour
Jones, Helen	Warrington North	Labour
Jones, Kevan	Durham North	Labour
Jones, Martyn	Clwyd South	Labour
Jones, Nigel	Cheltenham	Liberal Democrat
Jowell, Tessa	Dulwich and West Norwood	Labour
Joyce, Eric	Falkirk West	Labour
Kaufman, Gerald	Manchester Gorton	Labour
Keeble, Sally	Northampton North	Labour
Keen, Alan	Feltham & Heston	Labour Co-Op
Keen, Ann	Brentford & Isleworth	Labour
Keetch, Paul	Hereford	Liberal Democrat
Kelly, Ruth	Bolton West	Labour
Kemp, Fraser	Houghton & Washington East	Labour
Kennedy, Charles	Ross, Skye & Inverness West	Liberal Democrat
Kennedy, Jane	Liverpool Wavertree	Labour
Key, Robert	Salisbury	Conservative

P
O
L
I
T
I
C
S

Khabra, Piara	Ealing Southall	Labour
Kidney, David	Stafford	Labour
Kilfoyle, Peter	Liverpool Walton	Labour
King, Andy	Rugby & Kenilworth	Labour
King, Oona	Bethnal Green & Bow	Labour
Kirkbride, Julie	Bromsgrove	Conservative
Kirkwood, Archy	Roxburgh & Berwickshire	Liberal Democrat
Knight, Greg	Yorkshire East	Conservative
Knight, Jim	Dorset South	Labour
Kumar, Dr Ashok	Middlesborough South & Cleveland East	Labour
Ladyman, Dr Stephen	Thanet South	Labour
Laing, Eleanor	Epping Forest	Conservative
Lait, Jacqui	Beckenham	Conservative
Lamb, Norman	Norfolk North	Liberal Democrat
Lammy, David	Tottenham	Labour
Lansley, Andrew	Cambridgeshire South	Conservative
Lawrence, Jackie	Preseli Pembrokeshire	Labour
Laws, David	Yeovil	Liberal Democrat
Laxton, Bob	Derby North	Labour
Lazarowicz, Mark	Edinburgh North & Leith	Labour
Leigh, Edward	Gainsborough	Conservative
Lepper, David	Brighton Pavilion	Labour Co-Op
Leslie, Christopher	Shipley	Labour
Letwin, Oliver	Dorset West	Conservative
Levitt, Tom	High Peak	Labour
Lewis, Dr Julian	New Forest East	Conservative
Lewis, Ivan	Bury South	Labour
Lewis, Terry	Worsley	Labour
Liddell-Grainger, Ian	Bridgwater	Conservative
Liddell, Helen	Airdrie and Shotts	Labour
Lidington, David	Aylesbury	Conservative
Lilley, Peter	Hitchen & Harpenden	Conservative
Linton, Martin	Battersea	Labour
Lloyd, Tony	Manchester Central	Labour
Llwyd, Elfyn	Meirionnydd Nant Conwy	Plaid Cymru
Lord, Michael	Suffolk Central & Ipswich North	Conservative
Loughton, Tim	Worthing East & Shoreham	Conservative
Love, Andy	Edmonton	Labour Co-Op
Lucas, Ian	Wrexham	Labour
Luff, Peter	Worcestershire Mid	Conservative
Luke, Iain	Dundee East	Labour
Lyons, John	Strathkelvin & Bearsden	Labour
MacDonald, Calum	Western Isles	Labour
MacDougall, John	Fife Central	Labour
Mackay, Andrew	Bracknell	Conservative
MacKinlay, Andrew	Thurrock	Labour
MacLean, David	Penrith & The Border	Conservative
MacShane, Denis	Rotherham	Labour
MacTaggart, Fiona	Slough	Labour
Mahmood, Khalid	Birmingham Perry Barr	Labour
Mahon, Alice	Halifax	Labour
Malins, Humfrey	Woking	Conservative
Mallaber, Judy	Amber Valley	Labour
Mallon, Seamus	Newry & Armagh	SDLP
Mandelson, Peter	Hartlepool	Labour
Mann, John	Bassetlaw	Labour
Maples, John	Stratford-on-Avon	Conservative
Marris, Robert	Wolverhampton South West	Labour
Marsden, Gordon	Blackpool South	Labour
Marsden, Paul	Shrewsbury & Atcham	Labour
Marshall-Andrews, Robert	Medway	Labour
Marshall, David	Glasgow Shettleston	Labour
Marshall, Jim	Leicester South	Labour
Martin, Michael	Glasgow Springburn	Labour
Martlew, Eric	Carlisle	Labour
Mates, Michael	Hampshire East	Conservative
Maude, Francis	Horsham	Conservative
Mawhinney, Sir Brian	Cambridgeshire North West	Conservative
May, Theresa	Maidenhead	Conservative
McAvoy, Tommy	Glasgow Rutherglen	Labour Co-Op
McCabe, Stephen	Birmingham Hall Green	Labour
McCafferty, Christine	Calder Valley	Labour

McCartney, Ian	Makerfield	Labour
McDonagh, Siobhain	Mitcham & Morden	Labour
McDonnell, John	Hayes & Harlington	Labour
McFall, John	Dumbarton	Labour Co-Op
McGrady, Eddie	Down South	SDLP
McGuinness, Martin	Ulster Mid	Sinn Fein
McGuire, Anne	Stirling	Labour
McIntosh, Anne	Vale of York	Conservative
McIsaac, Shona	Cleethorpes	Labour
McKechin, Ann	Glasgow Maryhill	Labour
McKenna, Rosemary	Cumbernauld & Kilsyth	Labour
McLoughlin, Patrick	Derbyshire West	Conservative
McNamara, Kevin	Hull North	Labour
McNulty, Tony	Harrow East	Labour
McWalter, Tony	Hemel Hempstead	Labour Co-Op
McWilliam, John	Blaydon	Labour
Meacher, Michael	Oldham West & Royton	Labour
Meale, Alan	Mansfield	Labour
Mercer, Patrick	Newark	Conservative
Merron, Gillian	Lincoln	Labour
Michael, Alun	Cardiff South & Penarth	Labour Co-Op
Milburn, Alan	Darlington	Labour
Miliband, David	South Shields	Labour
Miller, Andrew	Ellesmere Port & Neston	Labour
Mitchell, Andrew	Sutton Coldfield	Conservative
Mitchell, Austin	Great Grimsby	Labour
Moffatt, Laura	Crawley	Labour
Moonie, Lewis	Kirkcaldy	Labour Co-Op
Moore, Michael	Tweeddale, Ettrick & Lauderdale	Liberal Democrat
Moran, Margaret	Luton South	Labour
Morgan, Julie	Cardiff North	Labour
Morley, Elliot	Scunthorpe	Labour
Morris, Estelle	Birmingham Yardley	Labour
Moss, Malcolm	Cambridgeshire North East	Conservative
Mountford, Kali	Colne Valley	Labour
Mudie, George	Leeds East	Labour
Mullin, Chris	Sunderland South	Labour
Munn, Meg	Sheffield Heeley	Labour
Murphy, Denis	Wansbeck	Labour
Murphy, Jim	Eastwood	Labour
Murphy, Paul	Torfaen	Labour
Murrison, Andrew	Westbury	Conservative
Naysmith, Doug	Bristol North West	Labour Co-Op
Norman, Archie	Tunbridge Wells	Conservative
Norris, Dan	Wansdyke	Labour
O'Brien, Mike	Warwickshire North	Labour
O'Brien, Stephen	Eddisbury	Conservative
O'Brien, William	Normanton	Labour
O'Hara, Eddie	Knowsley South	Labour
O'Neill, Martin	Ochil	Labour
Oaten, Mark	Winchester	Liberal Democrat
Olner, Bill	Nuneaton	Labour
Opik, Lembit	Montgomeryshire	Liberal Democrat
Organ, Diana	Forest of Dean	Labour
Osborne, George	Tatton	Conservative
Osborne, Sandra	Ayr	Labour
Ottaway, Richard	Croydon South	Conservative
Owen Jones, John	Cardiff Central	Labour Co-Op
Owen, Albert	Yns Mon	Labour
Page, Richard	Hertfordshire South West	Conservative
Paice, James	Cambridgeshire South East	Conservative
Paisley, Rev. Ian	Antrim North	Democratic Unionist
Palmer, Nick	Broxtowe	Labour
Paterson, Owen	Shropshire North	Conservative
Pearson, Ian	Dudley South	Labour
Perham, Linda	Ilford North	Labour
Picking, Anne	East Lothian	Labour
Pickles, Eric	Brentwood & Ongar	Conservative
Pickthall, Colin	Lancashire West	Labour
Pike, Peter	Burnley	Labour
Plaskitt, James	Warwick & Leamington	Labour
Pollard, Kerry	St Albans	Labour

POLITICS

Pond, Chris	Gravesham	Labour
Pope, Greg	Hyndburn	Labour
Portillo, Michael	Kensington & Chelsea	Conservative
Pound, Stephen	Ealing North	Labour
Powell, Sir Raymond	Ogmore	Labour
Prentice, Bridget	Lewisham East	Labour
Prentice, Gordon	Pendle	Labour
Prescott, John	Hull East	Labour
Price, Adam	Carmarthen East & Dinefwr	Plaid Cymru
Primarolo, Dawn	Bristol South	Labour
Prisk, Mark	Hertford & Stortford	Conservative
Prosser, Gwynn	Dover	Labour
Pugh, John	Southport	Liberal Democrat
Purchase, Ken	Wolverhampton North East	Labour Co-Op
Purnell, James	Stalybridge & Hyde	Labour
Quinn, Lawrie	Scarborough & Whitby	Labour
Quin, Joyce	Gateshead East & Washington West	Labour
Rammell, Bill	Harlow	Labour
Randall, John	Uxbridge	Conservative
Rapson, Syd	Portsmouth North	Labour
Raynsford, Nick	Greenwich & Woolwich	Labour
Redwood, John	Wokingham	Conservative
Reed, Andy	Loughborough	Labour
Reid, Alan	Argyll & Bute	Liberal Democrat
Reid, Dr John	Hamilton North & Bellshill	Labour
Rendel, David	Newbury	Liberal Democrat
Robathan, Andrew	Blaby	Conservative
Robertson, Angus	Moray	Scottish Nationalist
Robertson, Hugh	Faversham & Kent Mid	Conservative
Robertson, John	Glasgow Aniesland	Labour
Robertson, Laurence	Tewkesbury	Conservative
Robinson, Geoffrey	Coventry North West	Labour
Robinson, Iris	Strangford	Democratic Unionist
Robinson, Peter	Belfast East	Democratic Unionist
Roche, Barbara	Hornsey & Wood Green	Labour
Roe, Marion	Broxbourne	Conservative
Rooney, Terry	Bradford North	Labour
Rosindell, Andrew	Romford	Conservative
Ross, Ernie	Dundee West	Labour
Roy, Frank	Motherwell & Wishaw	Labour
Ruane, Chris	Vale of Clwyd	Labour
Ruddock, Joan	Lewisham Deptford	Labour
Ruffley, David	Bury St Edmunds	Conservative
Russell, Bob	Colchester	Liberal Democrat
Russell, Christine	Chester, City of	Labour
Ryan, Joan	Enfield North	Labour
Salmond, Alex	Banff & Buchan	Scottish Nationalist
Salter, Martin	Reading West	Labour
Sanders, Adrian	Torbay	Liberal Democrat
Sarwar, Mohammad	Glasgow Govan	Labour
Savidge, Malcolm	Aberdeen North	Labour
Sawford, Philip	Kettering	Labour
Sayeed, Jonathan	Bedfordshire Mid	Conservative
Sedgemore, Brian	Hackney South & Shoreditch	Labour
Selous, Andrew	Bedfordshire South West	Conservative
Shaw, Jonathan	Chatham & Aylesford	Labour
Sheerman, Barry	Huddersfield	Labour Co-Op
Shephard, Gillian	Norfolk South West	Conservative
Shepherd, Richard	Aldridge-Brownhills	Conservative
Sheridan, James	Renfrewshire West	Labour
Shipley, Debra	Stourbridge	Labour
Short, Clare	Birmingham Ladywood	Labour
Simmonds, Mark	Boston & Skegness	Conservative
Simon, Sion Llewelyn	Birmingham Erdington	Labour
Simpson, Alan	Nottingham South	Labour
Simpson, Keith	Norfolk Mid	Conservative
Singh, Marsha	Bradford West	Labour
Skinner, Dennis	Bolsover	Labour
Smith, Andrew	Oxford East	Labour
Smith, Angela	Basildon	Labour Co-Op
Smith, Chris	Islington South & Finsbury	Labour
Smith, Geraldine	Morecambe & Lunesdale	Labour

Smith, Jacqui	*Redditch*	Labour
Smith, John	*Vale of Glamorgan*	Labour
Smith, Llew	*Blaenau Gwent*	Labour
Smith, Sir Robert	*Aberdeenshire West & Kincardine*	Liberal Democrat
Smyth, Rev. Martin	*Belfast South*	Ulster Unionist
Soames, Nicholas	*Sussex Mid*	Conservative
Soley, Clive	*Ealing Acton & Shepherd's Bush*	Labour
Southworth, Helen	*Warrington South*	Labour
Spellar, John	*Warley*	Labour
Spelman, Caroline	*Meriden*	Conservative
Spicer, Sir Michael	*Worcestershire West*	Conservative
Spink, Robert	*Castle Point*	Conservative
Spring, Richard	*Suffolk West*	Conservative
Squire, Rachel	*Dunfermline West*	Labour
Stanley, Sir John	*Tonbridge & Malling*	Conservative
Starkey, Phyllis	*Milton Keynes South West*	Labour
Steen, Sir Anthony	*Totnes*	Conservative
Steinberg, Gerry	*Durham, City of*	Labour
Stevenson, George	*Stoke-on-Trent South*	Labour
Stewart, David	*Inverness East, Nairn & Lochaber*	Labour
Stewart, Ian	*Eccles*	Labour
Stinchcombe, Paul	*Wellingborough*	Labour
Stoate, Howard	*Dartford*	Labour
Strang, Dr Gavin	*Edinburgh East & Musselburgh*	Labour
Straw, Jack	*Blackburn*	Labour
Streeter, Gary	*Devon South West*	Conservative
Stringer, Graham	*Manchester Blackley*	Labour
Stuart, Gisela	*Birmingham Edgbaston*	Labour
Stunell, Andrew	*Hazel Grove*	Liberal Democrat
Sutcliffe, Gerry	*Bradford South*	Labour
Swayne, Desmond	*New Forest West*	Conservative
Swire, Hugo	*Devon East*	Conservative
Syms, Robert	*Poole*	Conservative
Tami, Mark	*Alyn & Deeside*	Labour
Tapsell, Sir Peter	*Louth & Horncastle*	Conservative
Taylor, Ann	*Dewsbury*	Labour
Taylor, Dari	*Stockton South*	Labour
Taylor, David	*Leicestershire North West*	Labour
Taylor, Ian	*Esher & Walton*	Conservative
Taylor, John	*Solihull*	Conservative
Taylor, Matthew	*Truro & St Austell*	Liberal Democrat
Taylor, Richard	*Wyre Forest*	Independent
Taylor, Sir Teddy	*Rochford & Southend East*	Conservative
Thomas, Gareth	*Harrow West*	Labour
Thomas, Gareth	*Clwyd West*	Labour
Thomas, Simon	*Ceredigion*	Plaid Cymru
Thurso, John	*Caithness, Sunderland & Easter Ross*	Liberal Democrat
Timms, Stephen	*East Ham*	Labour
Tipping, Paddy	*Sherwood*	Labour
Todd, Mark	*Derbyshire South*	Labour
Tonge, Dr Jenny	*Richmond Park*	Liberal Democrat
Touhig, Don	*Islwyn*	Labour Co-Op
Tredinnick, David	*Bosworth*	Conservative
Trend, Michael	*Windsor*	Conservative
Trickett, Jon	*Hemsworth*	Labour
Trimble, David	*Upper Bann*	Ulster Unionist
Truswell, Paul	*Pudsey*	Labour
Turner, Andrew	*Isle of Wight*	Conservative
Turner, Dennis	*Wolverhampton South East*	Labour Co-Op
Turner, Desmond	*Brighton Kemptown*	Labour
Turner, Neil	*Wigan*	Labour
Twigg, Derek	*Halton*	Labour
Twigg, Stephen	*Enfield Southgate*	Labour
Tyler, Paul	*Cornwall North*	Liberal Democrat
Tynan, Bill	*Hamilton South*	Labour
Tyrie, Andrew	*Chichester*	Conservative
Vaz, Keith	*Leicester East*	Labour
Viggers, Peter	*Gosport*	Conservative
Vis, Rudi	*Finchley & Golders Green*	Labour
Walley, Joan	*Stoke-on-Trent North*	Labour
Walter, Robert	*Dorset North*	Conservative
Ward, Claire	*Watford*	Labour

POLITICS

Wareing, Robert	*Liverpool West Derby*	Labour
Waterson, Nigel	*Eastbourne*	Conservative
Watkinson, Angela	*Upminster*	Conservative
Watson, Tom	*West Bromwich East*	Labour
Watts, Dave	*St Helens North*	Labour
Webb, Professor Steven	*Northavon*	Liberal Democrat
Weir, Michael	*Angus*	Scottish Nationalist
Whitehead, Alan	*Southampton Test*	Labour
White, Brian	*Milton Keynes North East*	Labour
Whittingdale, John	*Maldon & Chelmsford East*	Conservative
Wicks, Malcolm	*Croydon North*	Labour
Widdecombe, Ann	*Maidstone & The Weald*	Conservative
Wiggin, Bill	*Leominster*	Conservative
Wilkinson, John	*Ruislip Northwood*	Conservative
Willetts, David	*Havant*	Conservative
Williams, Alan	*Swansea West*	Labour
Williams, Betty	*Conwy*	Labour
Williams, Hywel	*Caernarfon*	Plaid Cymru
Williams, Roger	*Brecon & Radnorshire*	Liberal Democrat
Willis, Phil	*Harrogate & Knaresborough*	Liberal Democrat
Wills, Michael	*Swindon North*	Labour
Wilshire, David	*Spelthorne*	Conservative
Wilson, Brian	*Cunninghame North*	Labour
Winnick, David	*Walsall North*	Labour
Winterton, Ann	*Congleton*	Conservative
Winterton, Nicholas	*Macclesfield*	Conservative
Winterton, Rosie	*Doncaster Central*	Labour
Wishart, Peter	*Tayside North*	Scottish Nationalist
Woodward, Shaun	*St Helens South*	Labour
Wood, Mike	*Batley & Spen*	Labour
Woolas, Phil	*Oldham East & Saddleworth*	Labour
Worthington, Tony	*Clydebank & Milngavie*	Labour
Wray, Jimmy	*Glasgow Baillieston*	Labour
Wright, David	*Telford*	Labour
Wright, Dr Anthony	*Cannock Chase*	Labour
Wright, Tony	*Great Yarmouth*	Labour
Wyatt, Derek	*Sittingbourne & Sheppey*	Labour
Yeo, Tim	*Suffolk South*	Conservative
Younger-Ross, Richard	*Teignbridge*	Liberal Democrat
Young, Sir George	*Hampshire North West*	Conservative

General Election Results by Constituency: 7 June 2001

Aberavon	Francis, Hywel	*Labour*
Aberdeen Central	Doran, Frank	*Labour*
Aberdeen North	Savidge, Malcolm	*Labour*
Aberdeen South	Begg, Anne	*Labour*
Aberdeenshire West & Kincardine	Smith, Sir Robert	*Liberal Democrat*
Airdrie and Shotts	Liddell, Helen	*Labour*
Aldershot	Howarth, Gerald	*Conservative*
Aldridge-Brownhills	Shepherd, Richard	*Conservative*
Altrincham & Sale West	Brady, Graham	*Conservative*
Alyn & Deeside	Tami, Mark	*Labour*
Amber Valley	Mallaber, Judy	*Labour*
Angus	Weir, Michael	*Scottish Nationalist*
Antrim East	Beggs, Roy	*Ulster Unionist*
Antrim North	Paisley, Rev. Ian	*Democratic Unionist*
Antrim South	Burnside, David	*Ulster Unionist*
Argyll & Bute	Reid, Alan	*Liberal Democrat*
Arundel & South Downs	Flight, Howard	*Conservative*
Ashfield	Hoon, Geoff	*Labour*
Ashford	Green, Damien	*Conservative*
Ashton-under-Lyne	Heyes, David	*Labour*
Aylesbury	Lidington, David	*Conservative*
Ayr	Osborne, Sandra	*Labour*
Banbury	Baldry, Tony	*Conservative*
Banff & Buchan	Salmond, Alex	*Scottish Nationalist*
Barking	Hodge, Margaret	*Labour*
Barnsley Central	Illsley, Eric	*Labour*
Barnsley East & Mexborough	Ennis, Jeff	*Labour*

Barnsley West and Penistone	Clapham, Michael	*Labour*
Barrow & Furness	Hutton, John	*Labour*
Basildon	Smith, Angela	*Labour Co-Op*
Basingstoke	Hunter, Andrew	*Conservative*
Bassetlaw	Mann, John	*Labour*
Bath	Foster, Don	*Liberal Democrat*
Batley & Spen	Wood, Mike	*Labour*
Battersea	Linton, Martin	*Labour*
Beaconsfield	Grieve, Dominic	*Conservative*
Beckenham	Lait, Jacqui	*Conservative*
Bedford	Hall, Patrick	*Labour*
Bedfordshire Mid	Sayeed, Jonathan	*Conservative*
Bedfordshire North East	Burt, Alastair	*Conservative*
Bedfordshire South West	Selous, Andrew	*Conservative*
Belfast East	Robinson, Peter	*Democratic Unionist*
Belfast North	Dodds, Nigel	*Democratic Unionist*
Belfast South	Smyth, Rev. Martin	*Ulster Unionist*
Belfast West	Adams, Gerry	*Sinn Fein*
Berwick-upon-Tweed	Beith, Alan	*Liberal Democrat*
Bethnal Green & Bow	King, Oona	*Labour*
Beverley & Holderness	Cran, James	*Conservative*
Bexhill & Battle	Barker, Greg	*Conservative*
Bexleyheath & Crayford	Beard, Nigel	*Labour*
Billericay	Baron, John	*Conservative*
Birkenhead	Field, Frank	*Labour*
Birmingham Edgbaston	Stuart, Gisela	*Labour*
Birmingham Erdington	Simon, Sion Llewelyn	*Labour*
Birmingham Hall Green	McCabe, Stephen	*Labour*
Birmingham Hodge Hill	Davis, Terry	*Labour*
Birmingham Ladywood	Short, Clare	*Labour*
Birmingham Northfield	Burden, Richard	*Labour*
Birmingham Perry Barr	Mahmood, Khalid	*Labour*
Birmingham Selly Oak	Jones, Dr Lynne	*Labour*
Birmingham Sparkbrook & Small Heath	Godsiff, Roger	*Labour*
Birmingham Yardley	Morris, Estelle	*Labour*
Bishop Auckland	Foster, Derek	*Labour*
Blaby	Robathan, Andrew	*Conservative*
Blackburn	Straw, Jack	*Labour*
Blackpool North & Fleetwood	Humble, Joan	*Labour*
Blackpool South	Marsden, Gordon	*Labour*
Blaenau Gwent	Smith, Llew	*Labour*
Blaydon	McWilliam, John	*Labour*
Blyth Valley	Campbell, Ronnie	*Labour*
Bognor Regis & Littlehampton	Gibb, Nick	*Conservative*
Bolsover	Skinner, Dennis	*Labour*
Bolton North East	Crausby, David	*Labour*
Bolton South East	Iddon, Brian	*Labour*
Bolton West	Kelly, Ruth	*Labour*
Bootle	Benton, Joe	*Labour*
Boston & Skegness	Simmonds, Mark	*Conservative*
Bosworth	Tredinnick, David	*Conservative*
Bournemouth East	Atkinson, David	*Conservative*
Bournemouth West	Butterfill, John	*Conservative*
Bracknell	Mackay, Andrew	*Conservative*
Bradford North	Rooney, Terry	*Labour*
Bradford South	Sutcliffe, Gerry	*Labour*
Bradford West	Singh, Marsha	*Labour*
Braintree	Hurst, Alan	*Labour*
Brecon & Radnorshire	Williams, Roger	*Liberal Democrat*
Brent East	Daisley, Paul	*Labour*
Brent North	Gardiner, Barry	*Labour*
Brent South	Boateng, Paul	*Labour*
Brentford & Isleworth	Keen, Ann	*Labour*
Brentwood & Ongar	Pickles, Eric	*Conservative*
Bridgend	Griffiths, Win	*Labour*
Bridgwater	Liddell-Grainger, Ian	*Conservative*
Brigg & Goole	Cawsey, Ian	*Labour*
Brighton Kemptown	Turner, Desmond	*Labour*
Brighton Pavilion	Lepper, David	*Labour Co-Op*
Bristol East	Corston, Jean	*Labour*
Bristol North West	Naysmith, Doug	*Labour Co-Op*
Bristol South	Primarolo, Dawn	*Labour*

POLITICS

Bristol West	Davey, Valerie	*Labour*
Bromley & Chislehurst	Forth, Eric	*Conservative*
Bromsgrove	Kirkbride, Julie	*Conservative*
Broxbourne	Roe, Marion	*Conservative*
Broxtowe	Palmer, Nick	*Labour*
Buckingham	Bercow, John	*Conservative*
Burnley	Pike, Peter	*Labour*
Burton	Dean, Janet	*Labour*
Bury North	Chaytor, David	*Labour*
Bury South	Lewis, Ivan	*Labour*
Bury St Edmunds	Ruffley, David	*Conservative*
Caernarfon	Williams, Hywel	*Plaid Cymru*
Caerphilly	David, Wayne	*Labour*
Caithness, Sunderland & Easter Ross	Thurso, John	*Liberal Democrat*
Calder Valley	McCafferty, Christine	*Labour*
Camberwell & Peckham	Harman, Harriet	*Labour*
Cambridge	Campbell, Anne	*Labour*
Cambridgeshire North East	Moss, Malcolm	*Conservative*
Cambridgeshire North West	Mawhinney, Sir Brian	*Conservative*
Cambridgeshire South	Lansley, Andrew	*Conservative*
Cambridgeshire South East	Paice, James	*Conservative*
Cannock Chase	Wright, Dr Anthony	*Labour*
Canterbury	Brazier, Julian	*Conservative*
Cardiff Central	Owen Jones, John	*Labour Co-Op*
Cardiff North	Morgan, Julie	*Labour*
Cardiff South & Penarth	Michael, Alun	*Labour Co-Op*
Cardiff West	Brennan, Kevin	*Labour*
Carlisle	Martlew, Eric	*Labour*
Carmarthen East & Dinefwr	Price, Adam	*Plaid Cymru*
Carmarthen West & Pembrokeshire South	Ainger, Nick	*Labour*
Carrick, Cumnock & Doon	Foulkes, George	*Labour Co-Op*
Carshalton and Wallington	Brake, Tom	*Liberal Democrat*
Castle Point	Spink, Robert	*Conservative*
Ceredigion	Thomas, Simon	*Plaid Cymru*
Charnwood	Dorrell, Stephen	*Conservative*
Chatham & Aylesford	Shaw, Jonathan	*Labour*
Cheadle	Calton, Patsy	*Liberal Democrat*
Chelmsford West	Burns, Simon	*Conservative*
Cheltenham	Jones, Nigel	*Liberal Democrat*
Chesham & Amersham	Gillan, Cheryl	*Conservative*
Chesterfield	Holmes, Paul	*Liberal Democrat*
Chester, City of	Russell, Christine	*Labour*
Chichester	Tyrie, Andrew	*Conservative*
Chingford & Woodford Green	Duncan Smith, Iain	*Conservative*
Chipping Barnet	Chapman, Sir Sydney	*Conservative*
Chorley	Hoyle, Lindsay	*Labour*
Christchurch	Chope, Christopher	*Conservative*
Cities of London & Westminster	Field, Mark	*Conservative*
Cleethorpes	McIsaac, Shona	*Labour*
Clwyd South	Jones, Martyn	*Labour*
Clwyd West	Thomas, Gareth	*Labour*
Clydebank & Milngavie	Worthington, Tony	*Labour*
Clydesdale	Hood, Jimmy	*Labour*
Coatbridge & Chryston	Clarke, Tom	*Labour*
Colchester	Russell, Bob	*Liberal Democrat*
Colne Valley	Mountford, Kali	*Labour*
Congleton	Winterton, Ann	*Conservative*
Conwy	Williams, Betty	*Labour*
Copeland	Cunningham, Jack	*Labour*
Corby	Hope, Phil	*Labour Co-Op*
Cornwall North	Tyler, Paul	*Liberal Democrat*
Cornwall South East	Breed, Colin	*Liberal Democrat*
Cotswold	Clifton-Brown, Geoffrey	*Conservative*
Coventry North East	Ainsworth, Bob	*Labour*
Coventry North West	Robinson, Geoffrey	*Labour*
Coventry South	Cunningham, Jim	*Labour*
Crawley	Moffatt, Laura	*Labour*
Crewe & Nantwich	Dunwoody, Gwyneth	*Labour*
Crosby	Curtis-Thomas, Claire	*Labour*
Croydon Central	Davies, Geraint	*Labour*
Croydon North	Wicks, Malcolm	*Labour*
Croydon South	Ottaway, Richard	*Conservative*

Cumbernauld & Kilsyth	McKenna, Rosemary	*Labour*
Cunninghame North	Wilson, Brian	*Labour*
Cunninghame South	Donohoe, Brian	*Labour*
Cynon Valley	Clwyd, Ann	*Labour*
Dagenham	Cruddas, Jon	*Labour*
Darlington	Milburn, Alan	*Labour*
Dartford	Stoate, Howard	*Labour*
Daventry	Boswell, Tim	*Conservative*
Delyn	Hanson, David	*Labour*
Denton & Reddish	Bennett, Andrew	*Labour*
Derby North	Laxton, Bob	*Labour*
Derby South	Beckett, Margaret	*Labour*
Derbyshire North East	Barnes, Harry	*Labour*
Derbyshire South	Todd, Mark	*Labour*
Derbyshire West	McLoughlin, Patrick	*Conservative*
Devizes	Ancram, Michael	*Conservative*
Devon East	Swire, Hugo	*Conservative*
Devon North	Harvey, Nick	*Liberal Democrat*
Devon South West	Streeter, Gary	*Conservative*
Devon West & Torridge	Burnett, John	*Liberal Democrat*
Dewsbury	Taylor, Ann	*Labour*
Don Valley	Flint, Caroline	*Labour*
Doncaster Central	Winterton, Rosie	*Labour*
Doncaster North	Hughes, Kevin	*Labour*
Dorset Mid & Poole North	Brooke, Annette	*Liberal Democrat*
Dorset North	Walter, Robert	*Conservative*
Dorset South	Knight, Jim	*Labour*
Dorset West	Letwin, Oliver	*Conservative*
Dover	Prosser, Gwynn	*Labour*
Down North	Hermon, Sylvia	*Ulster Unionist*
Down South	McGrady, Eddie	*SDLP*
Dudley North	Cranston, Ross	*Labour*
Dudley South	Pearson, Ian	*Labour*
Dulwich and West Norwood	Jowell, Tessa	*Labour*
Dumbarton	McFall, John	*Labour Co-Op*
Dumfries	Brown, Russell	*Labour*
Dundee East	Luke, Iain	*Labour*
Dundee West	Ross, Ernie	*Labour*
Dunfermline East	Brown, Gordon	*Labour*
Dunfermline West	Squire, Rachel	*Labour*
Durham, City of	Steinberg, Gerry	*Labour*
Durham North	Jones, Kevan	*Labour*
Durham North West	Armstrong, Hilary	*Labour*
Ealing Acton & Shepherd's Bush	Soley, Clive	*Labour*
Ealing North	Pound, Stephen	*Labour*
Ealing Southall	Khabra, Piara	*Labour*
Easington	Cummings, John	*Labour*
East Ham	Timms, Stephen	*Labour*
East Kilbride	Ingram, Adam	*Labour*
East Lothian	Picking, Anne	*Labour*
Eastbourne	Waterson, Nigel	*Conservative*
Eastleigh	Chidgey, David	*Liberal Democrat*
Eastwood	Murphy, Jim	*Labour*
Eccles	Stewart, Ian	*Labour*
Eddisbury	O'Brien, Stephen	*Conservative*
Edinburgh Central	Darling, Alistair	*Labour*
Edinburgh East & Musselburgh	Strang, Dr Gavin	*Labour*
Edinburgh North & Leith	Lazarowicz, Mark	*Labour*
Edinburgh Pentlands	Clark, Lynda	*Labour*
Edinburgh South	Griffiths, Nigel	*Labour*
Edinburgh West	Barrett, John	*Liberal Democrat*
Edmonton	Love, Andy	*Labour Co-Op*
Ellesmere Port & Neston	Miller, Andrew	*Labour*
Elmet	Burgon, Colin	*Labour*
Eltham	Efford, Clive	*Labour*
Enfield North	Ryan, Joan	*Labour*
Enfield Southgate	Twigg, Stephen	*Labour*
Epping Forest	Laing, Eleanor	*Conservative*
Epsom and Ewell	Grayling, Chris	*Conservative*
Erewash	Blackman, Elizabeth	*Labour*
Erith & Thamesmead	Austin, John	*Labour*
Esher & Walton	Taylor, Ian	*Conservative*

Essex North	Jenkin, Bernard	Conservative
Exeter	Bradshaw, Ben	Labour
Falkirk East	Connarty, Michael	Labour
Falkirk West	Joyce, Eric	Labour
Falmouth & Camborne	Atherton, Candy	Labour
Fareham	Hoban, Mark	Conservative
Faversham & Kent Mid	Robertson, Hugh	Conservative
Feltham & Heston	Keen, Alan	Labour Co-Op
Fermanagh & South Tyrone	Gildernew, Michelle	Sinn Fein
Fife Central	MacDougall, John	Labour
Fife North East	Campbell, Menzies	Liberal Democrat
Finchley & Golders Green	Vis, Rudi	Labour
Folkestone & Hythe	Howard, Michael	Conservative
Forest of Dean	Organ, Diana	Labour
Foyle	Hume, John	SDLP
Fylde	Jack, Michael	Conservative
Gainsborough	Leigh, Edward	Conservative
Galloway & Upper Nithsdale	Duncan, Peter	Conservative
Gateshead East & Washington West	Quin, Joyce	Labour
Gedling	Coaker, Vernon	Labour
Gillingham	Clarke, Paul	Labour
Glasgow Aniesland	Robertson, John	Labour
Glasgow Bailliestown	Wray, Jimmy	Labour
Glasgow Cathcart	Harris, Tom	Labour
Glasgow Govan	Sarwar, Mohammad	Labour
Glasgow Kelvin	Galloway, George	Labour
Glasgow Maryhill	McKechin, Ann	Labour
Glasgow Pollok	Davidson, Ian	Labour Co-Op
Glasgow Rutherglen	McAvoy, Tommy	Labour Co-Op
Glasgow Shettleston	Marshall, David	Labour
Glasgow Springburn	Martin, Michael	Labour
Gloucester	Dhanda, Parmjit	Labour
Gordon	Bruce, Malcolm	Liberal Democrat
Gosport	Viggers, Peter	Conservative
Gower	Caton, Martin	Labour
Grantham & Stamford	Davies, Quentin	Conservative
Gravesham	Pond, Chris	Labour
Great Grimsby	Mitchell, Austin	Labour
Great Yarmouth	Wright, Tony	Labour
Greenock & Inverclyde	Cairns, David	Labour
Greenwich & Woolwich	Raynsford, Nick	Labour
Guildford	Doughty, Sue	Liberal Democrat
Hackney North & Stoke Newington	Abbott, Diane	Labour
Hackney South & Shoreditch	Sedgemore, Brian	Labour
Halesowen & Rowley Regis	Heal, Sylvia	Labour
Halifax	Mahon, Alice	Labour
Haltemprice & Howden	Davis, David	Conservative
Halton	Twigg, Derek	Labour
Hamilton North & Bellshill	Reid, Dr John	Labour
Hamilton South	Tynan, Bill	Labour
Hammersmith & Fulham	Coleman, Iain	Labour
Hampshire East	Mates, Michael	Conservative
Hampshire North East	Arbuthnot, James	Conservative
Hampshire North West	Young, Sir George	Conservative
Hampstead and Highgate	Jackson, Glenda	Labour
Harborough	Garnier, Edward	Conservative
Harlow	Rammell, Bill	Labour
Harrogate & Knaresborough	Willis, Phil	Liberal Democrat
Harrow East	McNulty, Tony	Labour
Harrow West	Thomas, Gareth	Labour
Hartlepool	Mandelson, Peter	Labour
Harwich	Henderson, Ivan	Labour
Hastings & Rye	Foster, Michael	Labour
Havant	Willetts, David	Conservative
Hayes & Harlington	McDonnell, John	Labour
Hazel Grove	Stunell, Andrew	Liberal Democrat
Hemel Hempstead	McWalter, Tony	Labour Co-Op
Hemsworth	Trickett, Jon	Labour
Hendon	Dismore, Andrew	Labour
Henley	Johnson, Boris	Conservative
Hereford	Keetch, Paul	Liberal Democrat
Hertford & Stortford	Prisk, Mark	Conservative

Hertfordshire North East	Heald, Oliver	Conservative
Hertfordshire South West	Page, Richard	Conservative
Hertsmere	Clappison, James	Conservative
Hexham	Atkinson, Peter	Conservative
Heywood & Middleton	Dobbin, Jim	Labour Co-Op
High Peak	Levitt, Tom	Labour
Hitchen & Harpenden	Lilley, Peter	Conservative
Holborn & St Pancras	Dobson, Frank	Labour
Hornchurch	Cryer, John	Labour
Hornsey & Wood Green	Roche, Barbara	Labour
Horsham	Maude, Francis	Conservative
Houghton & Washington East	Kemp, Fraser	Labour
Hove	Caplin, Ivor	Labour
Huddersfield	Sheerman, Barry	Labour Co-Op
Hull East	Prescott, John	Labour
Hull North	McNamara, Kevin	Labour
Hull West & Hessle	Johnson, Alan	Labour
Huntingdon	Djanogly, Jonathan	Conservative
Hyndburn	Pope, Greg	Labour
Ilford North	Perham, Linda	Labour
Ilford South	Gapes, Mike	Labour Co-Op
Inverness East, Nairn & Lochaber	Stewart, David	Labour
Ipswich	Cann, Jamie	Labour
Isle of Wight	Turner, Andrew	Conservative
Islington North	Corbyn, Jeremy	Labour
Islington South & Finsbury	Smith, Chris	Labour
Islwyn	Touhig, Don	Labour Co-Op
Jarrow	Hepburn, Stephen	Labour
Keighley	Cryer, Ann	Labour
Kensington & Chelsea	Portillo, Michael	Conservative
Kettering	Sawford, Philip	Labour
Kilmarnock & Loudoun	Browne, Des	Labour
Kingston & Surbiton	Davey, Edward	Liberal Democrat
Kingswood	Berry, Roger	Labour
Kirkcaldy	Moonie, Lewis	Labour Co-Op
Knowsley North & Sefton East	Howarth, George	Labour
Knowsley South	O'Hara, Eddie	Labour
Lagan Valley	Donaldson, Jeffrey	Ulster Unionist
Lancashire West	Pickthall, Colin	Labour
Lancaster & Wyre	Dawson, Hilton	Labour
Leeds Central	Benn, Hilary	Labour
Leeds East	Mudie, George	Labour
Leeds North East	Hamilton, Fabian	Labour
Leeds North West	Best, Harold	Labour
Leeds West	Battle, John	Labour
Leicester East	Vaz, Keith	Labour
Leicester South	Marshall, Jim	Labour
Leicester West	Hewitt, Patricia	Labour
Leicestershire North West	Taylor, David	Labour
Leigh	Burnham, Andrew	Labour
Leominster	Wiggin, Bill	Conservative
Lewes	Baker, Norman	Liberal Democrat
Lewisham Deptford	Ruddock, Joan	Labour
Lewisham East	Prentice, Bridget	Labour
Lewisham West	Dowd, Jim	Labour
Leyton & Wanstead	Cohen, Harry	Labour
Lichfield	Fabricant, Michael	Conservative
Lincoln	Merron, Gillian	Labour
Linlithgow	Dalyell, Tam	Labour
Liverpool Garston	Eagle, Maria	Labour
Liverpool Riverside	Ellman, Louise	Labour
Liverpool Walton	Kilfoyle, Peter	Labour
Liverpool Wavertree	Kennedy, Jane	Labour
Liverpool West Derby	Wareing, Robert	Labour
Livingston	Cook, Robin	Labour
Llanelli	Davies, Denzil	Labour
Londonderry East	Campbell, Gregory	Democratic Unionist
Loughborough	Reed, Andy	Labour
Louth & Horncastle	Tapsell, Sir Peter	Conservative
Ludlow	Green, Matthew	Liberal Democrat
Luton North	Hopkins, Kelvin	Labour
Luton South	Moran, Margaret	Labour

Macclesfield	Winterton, Nicholas	*Conservative*
Maidenhead	May, Theresa	*Conservative*
Maidstone & The Weald	Widdecombe, Ann	*Conservative*
Makerfield	McCartney, Ian	*Labour*
Maldon & Chelmsford East	Whittingdale, John	*Conservative*
Manchester Blackley	Stringer, Graham	*Labour*
Manchester Central	Lloyd, Tony	*Labour*
Manchester Gorton	Kaufman, Gerald	*Labour*
Manchester Withington	Bradley, Keith	*Labour*
Mansfield	Meale, Alan	*Labour*
Medway	Marshall-Andrews, Robert	*Labour*
Meirionnydd Nant Conwy	Llwyd, Elfyn	*Plaid Cymru*
Meriden	Spelman, Caroline	*Conservative*
Merthyr Tydfil & Rhymney	Havard, Dai	*Labour*
Middlesborough	Bell, Stuart	*Labour*
Middlesborough South & Cleveland East	Kumar, Dr Ashok	*Labour*
Midlothian	Hamilton, David	*Labour*
Milton Keynes North East	White, Brian	*Labour*
Milton Keynes South West	Starkey, Phyllis	*Labour*
Mitcham & Morden	McDonagh, Siobhain	*Labour*
Mole Valley	Beresford, Sir Paul	*Conservative*
Monmouth	Edwards, Huw	*Labour*
Montgomeryshire	Opik, Lembit	*Liberal Democrat*
Moray	Robertson, Angus	*Scottish Nationalist*
Morecambe & Lunesdale	Smith, Geraldine	*Labour*
Morley & Rothwell	Challen, Colin	*Labour*
Motherwell & Wishaw	Roy, Frank	*Labour*
Neath	Hain, Peter	*Labour*
New Forest East	Lewis, Dr Julian	*Conservative*
New Forest West	Swayne, Desmond	*Conservative*
Newark	Mercer, Patrick	*Conservative*
Newbury	Rendel, David	*Liberal Democrat*
Newcastle-under-Lyme	Farrelly, Paul	*Labour*
Newcastle upon Tyne Central	Cousins, Jim	*Labour*
Newcastle upon Tyne East & Wallsend	Brown, Nick	*Labour*
Newcastle upon Tyne North	Henderson, Doug	*Labour*
Newport East	Howarth, Alan	*Labour*
Newport West	Flynn, Paul	*Labour*
Newry & Armagh	Mallon, Seamus	*SDLP*
Norfolk Mid	Simpson, Keith	*Conservative*
Norfolk North	Lamb, Norman	*Liberal Democrat*
Norfolk North West	Bellingham, Henry	*Conservative*
Norfolk South	Bacon, Richard	*Conservative*
Norfolk South West	Shephard, Gillian	*Conservative*
Normanton	O'Brien, William	*Labour*
Northampton North	Keeble, Sally	*Labour*
Northampton South	Clark, Tony	*Labour*
Northavon	Webb, Professor Steven	*Liberal Democrat*
Norwich North	Gibson, Dr Ian	*Labour*
Norwich South	Clarke, Charles	*Labour*
Nottingham East	Heppell, John	*Labour*
Nottingham North	Allen, Graham	*Labour*
Nottingham South	Simpson, Alan	*Labour*
Nuneaton	Olner, Bill	*Labour*
Ochil	O'Neill, Martin	*Labour*
Ogmore	Powell, Sir Raymond	*Labour*
Old Bexley & Sidcup	Conway, Derek	*Conservative*
Oldham East & Saddleworth	Woolas, Phil	*Labour*
Oldham West & Royton	Meacher, Michael	*Labour*
Orkney & Shetland	Carmichael, Alistair	*Liberal Democrat*
Orpington	Horam, John	*Conservative*
Oxford East	Smith, Andrew	*Labour*
Oxford West & Abingdon	Harris, Dr Evan	*Liberal Democrat*
Paisley North	Adams, Irene	*Labour*
Paisley South	Alexander, Douglas	*Labour Co-Op*
Pendle	Prentice, Gordon	*Labour*
Penrith & The Border	MacLean, David	*Conservative*
Perth	Ewing, Annabelle	*Scottish Nationalist*
Peterborough	Brinton, Helen	*Labour*
Plymouth Devonport	Jamieson, David	*Labour*
Plymouth Sutton	Gilroy, Linda	*Labour Co-Op*
Pontefract & Castleford	Cooper, Yvette	*Labour*

Pontypridd	Howells, Dr Kim	Labour
Poole	Syms, Robert	Conservative
Poplar & Canning Town	Fitzpatrick, Jim	Labour
Portsmouth North	Rapson, Syd	Labour
Portsmouth South	Hancock, Mike	Liberal Democrat
Preseli Pembrokeshire	Lawrence, Jackie	Labour
Preston	Hendrick, Mark	Labour Co-Op
Pudsey	Truswell, Paul	Labour
Putney	Colman, Tony	Labour
Rayleigh	Francois, Mark	Conservative
Reading East	Griffiths, Jane	Labour
Reading West	Salter, Martin	Labour
Redcar	Baird, Vera	Labour
Redditch	Smith, Jacqui	Labour
Regent's Park & Kensington	Buck, Karen	Labour
Reigate	Blunt, Crispin	Conservative
Renfrewshire West	Sheridan, James	Labour
Rhondda	Bryant, Chris	Labour
Ribble South	Borrow, David	Labour
Ribble Valley	Evans, Nigel	Conservative
Richmond Park	Tonge, Dr Jenny	Liberal Democrat
Richmond (Yorks)	Hague, William	Conservative
Rochdale	Fitzsimons, Lorna	Labour
Rochford & Southend East	Taylor, Sir Teddy	Conservative
Romford	Rosindell, Andrew	Conservative
Romsey	Gidley, Sandra	Liberal Democrat
Rossendale & Darwen	Anderson, Janet	Labour
Ross, Skye & Inverness West	Kennedy, Charles	Liberal Democrat
Rother Valley	Barron, Kevin	Labour
Rotherham	MacShane, Denis	Labour
Roxburgh & Berwickshire	Kirkwood, Archy	Liberal Democrat
Rugby & Kenilworth	King, Andy	Labour
Ruislip Northwood	Wilkinson, John	Conservative
Runnymede & Weybridge	Hammond, Philip	Conservative
Rushcliffe	Clarke, Kenneth	Conservative
Rutland & Melton	Duncan, Alan	Conservative
Ryedale	Greenway, John	Conservative
Saffron Walden	Haselhurst, Sir Alan	Conservative
Salford	Blears, Hazel	Labour
Salisbury	Key, Robert	Conservative
Scarborough & Whitby	Quinn, Lawrie	Labour
Scunthorpe	Morley, Elliot	Labour
Sedgefield	Blair, Tony	Labour
Selby	Grogan, John	Labour
Sevenoaks	Fallon, Michael	Conservative
Sheffield Attercliffe	Betts, Clive	Labour
Sheffield Brightside	Blunkett, David	Labour
Sheffield Central	Caborn, Richard	Labour
Sheffield Hallam	Allan, Richard	Liberal Democrat
Sheffield Heeley	Munn, Meg	Labour
Sheffield Hillsborough	Jackson, Helen	Labour
Sherwood	Tipping, Paddy	Labour
Shipley	Leslie, Christopher	Labour
Shrewsbury & Atcham	Marsden, Paul	Labour
Shropshire North	Paterson, Owen	Conservative
Sittingbourne & Sheppey	Wyatt, Derek	Labour
Skipton & Ripon	Curry, David	Conservative
Sleaford & North Hykeham	Hogg, Douglas	Conservative
Slough	MacTaggart, Fiona	Labour
Solihull	Taylor, John	Conservative
Somerton & Frome	Heath, David	Liberal Democrat
South Holland & The Deepings	Hayes, John	Conservative
South Shields	Miliband, David	Labour
Southampton Itchen	Denham, John	Labour
Southampton Test	Whitehead, Alan	Labour
Southend West	Amess, David	Conservative
Southport	Pugh, John	Liberal Democrat
Southwark North & Bermondsey	Hughes, Simon	Liberal Democrat
Spelthorne	Wilshire, David	Conservative
St Albans	Pollard, Kerry	Labour
St Helens North	Watts, Dave	Labour
St Helens South	Woodward, Shaun	Labour

St Ives	George, Andrew	*Liberal Democrat*
Stafford	Kidney, David	*Labour*
Staffordshire Moorlands	Atkins, Charlotte	*Labour*
Staffordshire South	Cormack, Sir Patrick	*Conservative*
Stalybridge & Hyde	Purnell, James	*Labour*
Stevenage	Follett, Barbara	*Labour*
Stirling	McGuire, Anne	*Labour*
Stockport	Coffey, Ann	*Labour*
Stockton North	Cook, Frank	*Labour*
Stockton South	Taylor, Dari	*Labour*
Stoke-on-Trent Central	Fisher, Mark	*Labour*
Stoke-on-Trent North	Walley, Joan	*Labour*
Stoke-on-Trent South	Stevenson, George	*Labour*
Stone	Cash, William	*Conservative*
Stourbridge	Shipley, Debra	*Labour*
Strangford	Robinson, Iris	*Democratic Unionist*
Stratford-on-Avon	Maples, John	*Conservative*
Strathkelvin & Bearsden	Lyons, John	*Labour*
Streatham	Hill, Keith	*Labour*
Stretford & Urmston	Hughes, Beverley	*Labour*
Stroud	Drew, David	*Labour Co-Op*
Suffolk Central & Ipswich North	Lord, Michael	*Conservative*
Suffolk Coastal	Gummer, John	*Conservative*
Suffolk South	Yeo, Tim	*Conservative*
Suffolk West	Spring, Richard	*Conservative*
Sunderland North	Etherington, Bill	*Labour*
Sunderland South	Mullin, Chris	*Labour*
Surrey East	Ainsworth, Peter	*Conservative*
Surrey Heath	Hawkins, Nicholas	*Conservative*
Surrey South West	Bottomley, Virginia	*Conservative*
Sussex Mid	Soames, Nicholas	*Conservative*
Sutton and Cheam	Burstow, Paul	*Liberal Democrat*
Sutton Coldfield	Mitchell, Andrew	*Conservative*
Swansea East	Anderson, Donald	*Labour*
Swansea West	Williams, Alan	*Labour*
Swindon North	Wills, Michael	*Labour*
Swindon South	Drown, Julia	*Labour*
Tamworth	Jenkins, Brian	*Labour*
Tatton	Osborne, George	*Conservative*
Taunton	Flook, Adrian	*Conservative*
Tayside North	Wishart, Peter	*Scottish Nationalist*
Teignbridge	Younger-Ross, Richard	*Liberal Democrat*
Telford	Wright, David	*Labour*
Tewkesbury	Robertson, Laurence	*Conservative*
Thanet North	Gale, Roger	*Conservative*
Thanet South	Ladyman, Dr Stephen	*Labour*
Thurrock	MacKinlay, Andrew	*Labour*
Tiverton & Honiton	Browning, Angela	*Conservative*
Tonbridge & Malling	Stanley, Sir John	*Conservative*
Tooting	Cox, Tom	*Labour*
Torbay	Sanders, Adrian	*Liberal Democrat*
Torfaen	Murphy, Paul	*Labour*
Totnes	Steen, Sir Anthony	*Conservative*
Tottenham	Lammy, David	*Labour*
Truro & St Austell	Taylor, Matthew	*Liberal Democrat*
Tunbridge Wells	Norman, Archie	*Conservative*
Tweeddale, Ettrick & Lauderdale	Moore, Michael	*Liberal Democrat*
Twickenham	Cable, Dr Vincent	*Liberal Democrat*
Tyne Bridge	Clelland, David	*Labour*
Tynemouth	Campbell, Alan	*Labour*
Tyneside North	Byers, Stephen	*Labour*
Tyrone West	Doherty, Pat	*Sinn Fein*
Ulster Mid	McGuinness, Martin	*Sinn Fein*
Upminster	Watkinson, Angela	*Conservative*
Upper Bann	Trimble, David	*Ulster Unionist*
Uxbridge	Randall, John	*Conservative*
Vale of Clwyd	Ruane, Chris	*Labour*
Vale of Glamorgan	Smith, John	*Labour*
Vale of York	McIntosh, Anne	*Conservative*
Vauxhall	Hoey, Kate	*Labour*
Wakefield	Hinchcliffe, David	*Labour*
Wallasey	Eagle, Angela	*Labour*

Wallsall South	George, Bruce	Labour
Walsall North	Winnick, David	Labour
Walthamstow	Gerrard, Neil	Labour
Wansbeck	Murphy, Denis	Labour
Wansdyke	Norris, Dan	Labour
Wantage	Jackson, Robert	Conservative
Warley	Spellar, John	Labour
Warrington North	Jones, Helen	Labour
Warrington South	Southworth, Helen	Labour
Warwick & Leamington	Plaskitt, James	Labour
Warwickshire North	O'Brien, Mike	Labour
Watford	Ward, Claire	Labour
Waveney	Blizzard, Bob	Labour
Wealden	Hendry, Charles	Conservative
Weaver Vale	Hall, Mike	Labour
Wellingborough	Stinchcombe, Paul	Labour
Wells	Heathcoat-Amory, David	Conservative
Welwyn Hatfield	Johnson, Melanie	Labour
Wentworth	Healey, John	Labour
West Bromwich East	Watson, Tom	Labour
West Bromwich West	Bailey, Adrian	Labour Co-Op
West Ham	Banks, Tony	Labour
Westbury	Murrison, Andrew	Conservative
Western Isles	MacDonald, Calum	Labour
Westmorland & Lonsdale	Collins, Tim	Conservative
Weston-Super-Mare	Cotter, Brian	Liberal Democrat
Wigan	Turner, Neil	Labour
Wiltshire North	Gray, James	Conservative
Wimbledon	Casale, Roger	Labour
Winchester	Oaten, Mark	Liberal Democrat
Windsor	Trend, Michael	Conservative
Wirral South	Chapman, Ben	Labour
Wirral West	Hesford, Stephen	Labour
Witney	Cameron, David	Conservative
Woking	Malins, Humfrey	Conservative
Wokingham	Redwood, John	Conservative
Wolverhampton North East	Purchase, Ken	Labour Co-Op
Wolverhampton South East	Turner, Dennis	Labour Co-Op
Wolverhampton South West	Marris, Robert	Labour
Woodspring	Fox, Dr Liam	Conservative
Worcester	Foster, Michael	Labour
Worcestershire Mid	Luff, Peter	Conservative
Worcestershire West	Spicer, Sir Michael	Conservative
Workington	Cunningham, Tony	Labour
Worsley	Lewis, Terry	Labour
Worthing East & Shoreham	Loughton, Tim	Conservative
Worthing West	Bottomley, Peter	Conservative
Wrekin, The	Bradley, Peter	Labour
Wrexham	Lucas, Ian	Labour
Wycombe	Goodman, Paul	Conservative
Wyre Forest	Taylor, Richard	Independent
Wythenshawe & Sale East	Goggins, Paul	Labour
Yeovil	Laws, David	Liberal Democrat
Yns Mon	Owen, Albert	Labour
Yorkshire East	Knight, Greg	Conservative
York, City of	Bayley, Hugh	Labour

POLITICS

Miscellaneous Information: After 2001 General Election

Composition of the House of Commons (541 men, 118 women = 659)	Labour 412 (317 men, 95 women), Conservatives 166 (152 men, 14 women). Liberal Democrats 52 (47 men, 5 women), Ulster Unionists 6 (5 men, 1 woman). Scottish Nationalists 5 (4 men, 1 woman), Dem. Unionists 5 (4 men, 1 woman). Plaid Cymru 4 (4 men), Sinn Fein 4 (3 men, 1 woman), SDLP 3 (3 men). Independent 1 (man) and Michael Martin (speaker) who does not vote in divisions except when the voting is tied.
husband and wife MPs	Ann and Nicholas Winterton; Julie Kirkbride and Andrew Mackay.
largest majority	John Cummings (Easington) had a majority of 21,949.
mother and son MPs	Ann Cryer (Keighley) is the mother of John Cryer (Hornchurch).
Muslim MP: first	Mohammad Sarwar (first elected in 1997). Khalid Mahmood (first in England).
overseas-born MPs	Paul Beresford (NZ), Gisella Stuart (Germany), Rudi Vis (Holland).
quickest result	South Sunderland result announced at 10.42 pm, the fastest ever.
smallest majority	Patsy Calton (LD) defeated Stephen Day (C) by 33 votes.
sons of ex MP	Dominic Grieve is the son of Percy Grieve, former MP for Solihull. Hilary Benn is the son of Tony Benn, former MP for Chesterfield.
twins	Angela and Maria Eagle, MPs for Wallasey and Liverpool Garston.

PROVERBS

Biblical Proverbs (from the Book of Proverbs)

A wise man will hear, and will increase learning: and a man of understanding shall attain unto wise counsels (1.5).

Listen to the discipline of your father and do not forsake the law of your mother (1.8).

Happy is the man that has found wisdom, and the man that has discernment (3.13).

Do not hold back good from those to whom it is owing, when it happens to be in the power of your hand to do [it] (3.27).

Do not fabricate against your fellow man anything bad, when he is dwelling in a sense of security with you (3.29).

Do not quarrel with a man without cause, if he has rendered no bad to you (3.30).

Do not become envious of a man of violence, nor choose any of his ways (3.31).

Into the path of wicked ones do not enter, and do not walk straight on into the way of bad ones (4.14).

Remove from yourself the crookedness of speech, and the deviousness of lips put far away from yourself (4.24).

Smooth out the course of your foot, and may all your own ways be firmly established (4.26).

Go to the ant, see its ways and become wise (6.6).

Do not reprove a ridiculer, that he may not hate you. Give a reproof to a wise person and he will love you (9.8).

A wise son is one that makes a father rejoice, and a stupid son is the grief of his mother (10.1).

He that is walking in integrity will walk in security, but he that is making his ways crooked will make himself known (10.9).

Hatred is what stirs up contentions, but love covers over even all transgressions (10.12).

The tongue of the righteous person is choice silver, whilst the heart of the wicked one is worth little (10.20).

Deception is in the heart of those fabricating mischief, but those counselling peace have rejoicing (12.20).

A prudent man concealeth knowledge (12.23).

He that walketh with wise men shall be wise: but a companion of fools shall be destroyed (13.20).

He that spareth his rod hateth his son (13.24).

Pride goeth before destruction, and an haughty spirit before a fall (16.18).

General Proverbs

All roads lead to Rome.

An old poacher makes the best keeper.

Beauty is potent but money is omnipotent.

Better be stung by a nettle than pricked by a rose.

Between two stools one falls to the ground.

A bird in the hand is worth two in the bush.

Caesar's wife must be above suspicion.

Cards are the devil's books.

All cats are grey in the dark.

Caveat emptor (Let the buyer beware).

Diligence is the mother of good luck.

A drowning man will catch at a straw.

Enough is as good as a feast.

Every cloud has a silver lining.

Experience is the mistress of fools.

Faint heart never won fair lady.

A fair exchange is no robbery.

Fair words butter no parsnips.

Far fowls have fair feathers.

The folly of one man is the fortune of another.

A fool may ask more questions in an hour than a wise man can answer in seven years.

The fool wanders, the wise man travels.

Give a dog a bad name and hang him.

Go to bed with the lamb, and rise with the lark.

The hand that rocks the cradle rules the world.

He is a fool who makes his doctor his heir.

He should have a long spoon that sups with the devil.

He that sings on Friday will weep on Sunday.

He was a bold man that first ate an oyster.

A heavy purse makes a light heart.

A hedge between keeps friendship green.

If ifs and ans were pots and pans, there'd be no trade for tinkers.

If St Vitus's day [15 June] be rainy weather, it will rain for 30 days together.

If you run after two hares, you will catch neither.

If you sing before breakfast, you'll cry before night.

If you swear, you'll catch no fish.

Keep a thing seven years and you will find a use for it.

Knowledge is power.

A light purse makes a heavy heart.

Lose an hour in the morning and you'll be all day hunting for it.

A mackerel sky is never long dry.

Magpies: one's sorrow, two's mirth, three's a wedding, four's a birth, five's a christening, six a dearth, seven's heaven, eight is hell, and nine's the devil his ane sel'.

March comes in like a lion and goes out like a lamb.

Mighty oaks from little acorns grow.

Monday's child is fair of face,/Tuesday's child is full of grace,/Wednesday's child is full of woe,/Thursday's child has far to go,/Friday's child is loving and giving,/Saturday's child works hard for living. But the child who is born on the Sabbath day is lucky and happy and good and gay.

Nature abhors a vacuum.

Necessity is the mother of invention.

Needs must when the devil drives.

Never is a long day.

Never trouble trouble till trouble troubles you.

A nod is as good as a wink to a blind horse.

Out of debt, out of danger.

Penny wise, pound foolish.

Prevention is better than cure.

Procrastination is the thief of time

Promises and pie-crusts are made to be broken.

The proof of the pudding is in the eating.

Providence is better than rent.

Rain before seven, fine before eleven.

Red sky at night shepherd's delight, red sky in the morning shepherd's warning.

The road to hell is paved with good intentions.

Salmon and sermon have their season in Lent.

Save your breath to cool your porridge.

Sloth is the key to poverty.

Sneeze on a Monday you sneeze for danger, sneeze on a Tuesday you kiss a stranger, sneeze on a Wednesday you sneeze for a letter, sneeze on a Thursday for something better, sneeze on a Friday you sneeze for sorrow, sneeze on a Saturday see your sweetheart tomorrow, sneeze on a Sunday your safety seek, the devil will have you the whole of the week.

Spare the rod and spoil the child.

Speak well of your friend, of your enemy say nothing.

Still waters run deep.

A tale twice told is cabbage twice sold.

Talk of the devil, and he'll appear.

Tell that to the marines.

Thrift is good revenue.

Time and tide wait for no man.

Virtue is its own reward.

Virtue never grows old.

What can't be cured must be endured.

When the sun is highest he casts the least shadow.

When the wind is in the east it's good for neither man nor beast./When the wind is in the north the skilful fisher goes not forth./When the wind is in the south it blows the bait in the fish's mouth./When the wind is in the west the weather is at the best.

Who knows most says least.

Whom God wishes to destroy, he first makes mad *(Quos Deus vult perdere, prius dementat)*.

A wild goose never laid a tame egg.

A wonder lasts but nine days.

You cannot make an omelette without breaking eggs.

You cannot make a silk purse out of a sow's ear.

You cannot teach an old dog new tricks.

Young men may die, old men must.

Zeal without knowledge is fire without light.

Zeal without prudence is frenzy.

NB Some of the proverbs above are corruptions of biblical proverbs. Others were coined by great thinkers and philosophers, and yet others have simply come into general usage through time.

QUOTATIONS

Quotations (in Alphabetical Order)

All Gaul is divided into three parts.	Julius Caesar
All hope abandon ye who enter. (from *Divine Comedy*)	Dante Alighieri
All is for the best in the best of possible worlds. (from *Candide*)	Voltaire
An archaeologist is the best husband any woman can have – the older she gets the more interested he is in her.	Agatha Christie
And so to bed.	Samuel Pepys
And therefore never send to know for whom the bell tolls; It tolls for thee.	John Donne
Arms and the man I sing. (from the *Aeneid*)	Virgil
Art for art's sake.	Victor Cousin
Attila the hen. (speaking about Margaret Thatcher)	Clement Freud
Balance of power.	Sir Robert Walpole
A bank is a place that will lend you money if you can prove that you don't need it.	Bob Hope
Because it's there. (when asked why he wanted to climb Mt Everest)	George Mallory
Better to err with Pope, than shine with Pye.	Lord George Byron
The bigger they come the harder they fall.	Robert Fitzsimmons
Blood is thicker than water.	Commodore Tattnall
The boy stood on the burning deck. (from 'Casablanca')	Felicia Hemans
Bread and circuses. (*Panem et circenses*, alluding to what the people desired)	Juvenal
The buck stops here.	Harry S Truman
A bumping pitch and a blinding light, an hour to play and the last man in.	Sir Henry Newbolt
Candy is dandy. But liquor is quicker.	Ogden Nash
Carthage must be destroyed.	Senator Cato
Cauliflower is nothing but cabbage with a college education. (from Pudd'nhead Wilson's calendar)	Mark Twain
The child is father of the man.	William Wordsworth
Claret is the liquor for boys, Port for men, but he who aspires to be a hero must drink brandy.	Dr Samuel Johnson
A classic is something that everybody wants to have read and nobody wants to read.	Mark Twain
A comedian does funny things; a good comedian does things funny.	Buster Keaton
The cook was a good cook as cooks go; and as cooks go she went.	Saki
Cough and the world coughs with you. Fart and you stand alone.	Trevor Griffiths
A desiccated calculating machine. (writing about Hugh Gaitskell)	Aneurin Bevan
The die is cast. (on crossing the Rubicon in 49 BC)	Julius Caesar
Don't count your chickens before they are hatched.	Aesop
Don't get mad, get even.	Senator Everett Dirksen
Don't one of you fire until you see the whites of their eyes. (at Bunker Hill in 1775)	US General Israel Putnam
Each man kills the thing he loves. (from *The Ballad of Reading Gaol*)	Oscar Wilde
Ears made him look like a taxi cab with both doors open. (writing about Clark Gable)	Howard Hughes
East is East and West is West and never the twain shall meet.	Rudyard Kipling
England is a nation of shopkeepers.	Napoleon Bonaparte
Eureka (I have found it).	Archimedes
Every man over forty is a scoundrel.	G B Shaw
Experience is the name everyone gives to his mistakes. (from *Lady Windermere's Fan*)	Oscar Wilde
Fair stood the wind for France.	Michael Drayton
Father, I cannot tell a lie, I did it with my little hatchet.	George Washington
The female of the species is more deadly than the male.	Rudyard Kipling
For fools rush in where angels fear to tread.	Alexander Pope
From the sublime to the ridiculous there is only one step. (after the retreat from Moscow in 1812)	Napoleon Bonaparte
Generals January and February. (referring to his chief allies against Britain and France in the Crimea)	Tsar Nicholas I
Genius is one per cent inspiration and ninety-nine per cent perspiration.	Thomas Alva Edison
The ghost in the machine.	Gilbert Ryle
Give a man a free hand and he'll run it all over you.	Mae West
Give me a lever long enough and I will move the world.	Archimedes
Give us the tools and we will finish the job.	Winston Churchill
Go and catch a falling star.	John Donne
Go West, young man, and grow up with the country.	Horace Greeley
God made the country, and man made the town.	William Cowper
God moves in a mysterious way, his wonders to perform.	William Cowper
God's in his heaven – all's right with the world.	Robert Browning
Golf is a good walk spoiled.	Mark Twain
The gondola of London. (referring to the hansom cab)	Benjamin Disraeli
Good Americans, when they die, go to Paris.	Thomas Gold Appleton

A grain, which in England is generally given to horses but in Scotland supports the people. (definition of oats)	Dr Samuel Johnson
That Great Cham of literature Samuel Johnson. (in a letter to John Wilkes)	Tobias Smollett
Great fleas have little fleas upon their backs to bite 'em, and little fleas have lesser fleas and so ad infinitum.	Augustus De Morgan
The greatest happiness of the greatest number.	Jeremy Bentham
He can run but he can't hide.	Joe Louis
He makes no friend who never made a foe.	Lord Alfred Tennyson
He nothing common did, or mean, Upon that memorable scene. ('An Horatian Ode upon Cromwell's Return from Ireland')	Andrew Marvell
He speaks to me as if I were a public meeting. (referring to William Gladstone)	Queen Victoria
Heaven has no rage like love to hatred turned, Nor hell a fury like a woman scorned.	William Congreve
Hell is other people.	Jean-Paul Sartre
Here Skugg lies snug as a bug in a rug.	Benjamin Franklin
History is bunk.	Henry Ford
The history of the world is but the biography of great men.	Thomas Carlyle
Hope springs eternal in the human breast.	Alexander Pope
How can they tell? (on being told Calvin Coolidge was dead)	Dorothy Parker
I am his Highness' dog at Kew; Pray tell me sir, whose dog are you?	Alexander Pope
I am just going outside and may be some time.	Capt. Lawrence Oates
I am the State (*L'État, c'est moi*).	Louis XIV
I awoke one morning and found myself famous.	Lord George Byron
I beseech you in the bowels of Christ, think it possible you may be mistaken.	Oliver Cromwell
I can resist everything except temptation. (from *Lady Windermere's Fan*)	Oscar Wilde
I fear the Greeks even when they bring gifts. (from the *Aeneid*)	Virgil
I have always thought that every woman should marry, and no man.	Benjamin Disraeli
I have been poor and I have been rich. Rich is better.	Sophie Tucker
I have nothing to declare but my genius. (at US customs)	Oscar Wilde
I have nothing to offer but blood, toil, tears and sweat.	Winston Churchill
I know I have the body of a weak and feeble woman, but I have the heart and stomach of a King.	Elizabeth I
I look upon the world as my parish.	John Wesley
I married beneath me, all women do.	Nancy Astor
I never trust a man unless I've got his pecker in my pocket.	Lyndon B Johnson
I think, therefore I am (*cogito ergo sum*).	René Descartes
I want to be the white man's brother, not his brother-in-law.	Martin Luther King
Ich bin ein Berliner.	John F Kennedy
I'd like that translated, if I may. (reacting to Nikita Khrushchev's banging of shoe on table at the UN)	Harold Macmillan
If God did not exist, it would be necessary to invent him.	Voltaire
If I have seen further it is by standing on the shoulders of giants.	Isaac Newton
If you can keep your head when all about you are losing theirs and blaming it on you. (from 'If')	Rudyard Kipling
If you can meet with triumph and disaster and treat those two impostors just the same (from 'If')	Rudyard Kipling
If you pay peanuts, you get monkeys.	Sir James Goldsmith
Ignorance is bliss.	Thomas Gray
Ignorance, Madam, pure ignorance. (when asked why he defined pastern as a knee of a horse in his dictionary).	Dr Samuel Johnson
I'm going to spend, spend, spend.	Viv Nicholson
I'm not really a Jew, just Jew-ish, not the whole hog. (*Beyond the Fringe* sketch)	Dr Jonathan Miller
I'm only a beer teetotaller not a champagne teetotaller. (from *Candida*)	G B Shaw
In my sport the quick are too often listed among the dead.	Jackie Stewart
In the future everyone will be famous for fifteen minutes.	Andy Warhol
In the long run we are all dead.	J M Keynes
In this country [England] it is good to kill an admiral from time to time, to encourage the others. (re: shooting of Byng)	Voltaire
In two words, Impossible.	Sam Goldwyn
Include me out.	Sam Goldwyn
Indomitable in retreat; invincible in advance; insufferable in victory. (writing of Field-Marshal Montgomery)	Winston Churchill
Into each life some rain must fall.	Henry Wadsworth Longfellow
Into the valley of death rode the six hundred.	Lord Alfred Tennyson
It is better to die on your feet than to live on your knees.	La Pasionaria
It is magnificent but it is not war. (referring to the Charge of the Light Brigade)	General Pierre Bousquet
It is true that liberty is precious – so precious that it must be rationed.	Lenin
It matters not how a man dies, but how he lives.	Dr Samuel Johnson
It's not the size of the dog in the fight – it's the size of the fight in the dog.	Dwight D Eisenhower
Keep a diary and one day it'll keep you.	Mae West
Kind hearts are more than coronets.	Lord Alfred Tennyson
Knowledge is Power.	Francis Bacon

The lady's not for turning.	Margaret Thatcher
The lamps are going out all over Europe.	Edward Gray
Laugh and the world laughs with you; Weep and you weep alone. (from her poem 'Solitude')	Ella Wheeler Wilcox
Let them eat cake.	Marie Antoinette
Let us never negotiate out of fear, but let us never fear to negotiate.	John F Kennedy
Lies, damned lies and statistics.	Benjamin Disraeli
The lion and the calf shall lie down together, but the calf won't get much sleep.	Woody Allen
A little learning is a dangerous thing.	Alexander Pope
Love is like the measles, we all have to go through it.	Jerome K Jerome
Love's young dream.	Thomas Moore
Macmillan's role as a poseur was itself a pose.	Harold Wilson
Mad is he? Then I hope he will bite some of my other generals. (on being told General Wolfe was mad)	George II
Man is born free; and everywhere he is in chains. (first line of *The Social Contract*)	Jean-Jacques Rousseau
Man is by nature a civic animal.	Aristotle
A man is only as old as the woman he feels.	Groucho Marx
Man is the hunter, woman is his game.	Lord Alfred Tennyson
A man who knows the price of everything and the value of nothing. (definition of a cynic)	Oscar Wilde
Manners maketh man.	William of Wykeham
Marriage is a wonderful invention, but then again, so is the bicycle repair kit.	Billy Connolly
The medium is the message.	Marshall McLuhan
The meek shall inherit the earth, but not its mineral rights.	J Paul Getty
Men seldom make passes at girls who wear glasses.	Dorothy Parker
A modest little man with much to be modest about. (writing of Clement Attlee)	Winston Churchill
The moving finger writes and having writ moves on.	Omar Khayyam
Mr Balfour's poodle. (referring to the House of Lords)	Lloyd George
Music hath charms to soothe a savage breast.	William Congreve
Never in the field of human conflict was so much owed by so many to so few. (referring to Battle of Britain pilots)	Winston Churchill
Never trust a man with short legs – brains too near their bottom.	Noël Coward
Nice guys finish last. (referring to his baseball team)	Leo Durocher
The night has a thousand eyes and the day but one.	Francis Bourdillon
No man but a blockhead ever wrote except for money.	Dr Samuel Johnson
No man is an island.	John Donne
No man is justified in doing evil on the ground of expediency.	Theodore Roosevelt
None but the brave deserves the fair.	John Dryden
Nothing is certain but death and taxes.	Benjamin Franklin
Nuts! (replying to von Manteuffel's surrender call during the Battle of the Bulge)	Brigadier General McAuliffe
O what a tangled web we weave when first we practise to deceive.	Sir Walter Scott
Oh liberty! what crimes are committed in your name!	Madame Roland
Old soldiers never die, they simply fade away.	General MacArthur
Once upon a midnight dreary, while I pondered weak and weary. (from 'The Raven')	Edgar Allan Poe
One man's wage rise is another man's price increase.	Harold Wilson
One swallow does not make a summer.	Aristotle
The only good Indians I ever saw were dead.	General Philip Sheridan
The only reason so many people showed up was to make sure that he was dead. (of Louis Mayer's funeral)	Sam Goldwyn
The only thing we have to fear is fear itself.	F D Roosevelt
Open my heart and you will see graved inside of it, 'Italy'.	Robert Browning
Patriotism is not enough. I must have no hatred or bitterness towards anyone.	Edith Cavell
Patriotism is the last refuge of a scoundrel.	Dr Samuel Johnson
Peace for our time. (on returning from Munich in 1938)	Neville Chamberlain
Peccavi. ('I have sinned' from a telegram sent after capturing Sind in 1834)	Sir Charles Napier
The pen is mightier than the sword.	Bulwer Lytton
A penny Punch and Judy show. (referring to television)	Winston Churchill
Politics is the art of the possible.	R A Butler
Power tends to corrupt and absolute power corrupts absolutely.	Lord Acton
Power without responsibility, the privilege of the harlot throughout the ages (referring to the press)	Stanley Baldwin
Procrastination is the thief of time.	Edward Young
Property is theft.	Pierre-Joseph Proudhon
The public be damned.	Cornelius Vanderbilt
Publish and be damned.	Duke of Wellington
Put your trust in God and keep your powder dry.	Oliver Cromwell
Quoth the Raven, 'Nevermore'. (from 'The Raven')	Edgar Allan Poe
Religion is the opium of the people.	Karl Marx
The remedy is worse than the disease.	Francis Bacon
Remember that time is money.	Benjamin Franklin

Reports of my death have been greatly exaggerated.	Mark Twain
A riddle wrapped in a mystery inside an enigma. (referring to the Soviet Union)	Winston Churchill
A Rose is a Rose is a Rose.	Gertrude Stein
The seagreen incorruptible. (referring to Robespierre)	Thomas Carlyle
The secret of success is sincerity, once you can fake that you've got it made.	Arthur Bloch
Seize the present day. (*carpe diem*)	Horace
She is the best man in England. (referring to Margaret Thatcher)	Ronald Reagan
A sheep in sheep's clothing. (writing of Clement Attlee)	Winston Churchill
Sic transit gloria mundi (So passes away the glory of the world).	Thomas à Kempis
A single death is a tragedy, a million deaths is a statistic.	Joseph Stalin
Speak softly and carry a big stick.	Theodore Roosevelt
Speech is silvern, Silence is golden.	Thomas Carlyle
Stone walls do not a prison make, Nor iron bars a cage. (from 'To Althea from Prison')	Richard Lovelace
Sweet Swan of Avon. (referring to William Shakespeare)	Ben Jonson
Television is an invention that permits you to be entertained in your living room by people you wouldn't have in your home.	Sir David Frost
Tell me the old, old story.	Katherine Hankey
There are two things no man will admit he can't do well: drive and make love.	Stirling Moss
There is no terror in a bang – only in the anticipation of it.	Alfred Hitchcock
There is properly no history; only biography.	Ralph Waldo Emerson
There never was a good war or a bad peace.	Benjamin Franklin
There's a sucker born every minute.	P T Barnum
There's no such thing as a free lunch. (also used by J K Galbraith)	Milton Friedman
They also serve who only stand and wait.	John Milton
Thy need is greater than mine. (on giving his water to a soldier at Zutphen)	Sir Philip Sydney
'Tis better to have loved and lost, than never to have loved at all. (from 'In Memoriam')	Lord Alfred Tennyson
To err is human, to forgive, divine.	Alexander Pope
The trouble with Freud is that he never played the Glasgow Empire Saturday night.	Ken Dodd
Turn on, Tune in, Drop out.	Timothy Leary
Unpleasant and unacceptable face of Capitalism. (referring to Lonrho)	Edward Heath
The unspeakable in pursuit of the uneatable. (referring to foxhunting)	Oscar Wilde
Variety's the spice of life.	William Cowper
Veni, Vidi, Vici (I came, I saw, I conquered). (from a letter written after his victory at Zela in Asia Minor)	Julius Caesar
A verbal contract isn't worth the paper it's written on.	Sam Goldwyn
War is hell.	General Sherman
Warts and everything.	Oliver Cromwell
We are American at puberty. We die French.	Evelyn Waugh
We are not amused.	Queen Victoria
We must indeed all hang together or, most assuredly, we shall all hang separately (on signing the Declaration of Independence)	Benjamin Franklin
A week is a long time in politics.	Harold Wilson
What you said hurt me very much. I cried all the way to the bank. (replying to critics)	Liberace
When a man is tired of London he is tired of life.	Dr Samuel Johnson
When a man knows he is to be hanged in a fortnight it concentrates his mind wonderfully.	Dr Samuel Johnson
When the eagles are silent the parrots begin to jabber.	Winston Churchill
Where law ends, tyranny begins.	William Pitt (1st Earl of Chatham)
Whoever is not against us is with us.	Janos Kadar
Will no one rid me of this turbulent priest? (referring to Thomas à Becket)	Henry II
The wind of change is blowing through the continent. (speaking to South African Parliament in 1960)	Harold Macmillan
Winning is not everything. It's the only thing.	Vince Lombardi
The wisest fool in Christendom. (speaking of James I of England and VI of Scotland)	Henry IV of France
A woman is only a woman, but a good cigar is a smoke. (from 'The Betrothed')	Rudyard Kipling
Women should be obscene and not heard.	John Lennon
Wonders will never cease.	Sir Henry Bate Dudley
The world must be made safe for democracy.	Woodrow Wilson
Worth seeing, yes; but not worth going to see. (speaking about the Giant's Causeway)	Dr Samuel Johnson
Would you buy a second-hand car from this man? (writing about Richard Nixon)	Mort Sahl
A writer of dictionaries, a harmless drudge. (definition of a lexicographer)	Dr Samuel Johnson
Ye distant spires, ye antique towers. (from 'Ode on a Distant Prospect of Eton')	Thomas Gray
You can fool all the people some of the time, and some of the people all the time, but you cannot fool all the people all of the time.	Abraham Lincoln
You can have it any colour as long as it's black.	Henry Ford
You can make a throne from bayonets but you can't sit on it long.	Boris Yeltsin
You're either part of the solution or part of the problem.	Eldridge Cleaver
You're not drunk if you can lie on the floor without holding on.	Dean Martin
Youth is wasted on the young.	G B Shaw

NB Details of the quotation are given in brackets above but will need to be cross-referenced if the alphabetical table by person is being used. The same caveat as in the 'Dying Sayings' applies. It is doubtful that many of these utterances were original thoughts; for instance, the Milton Friedman entry may have been a corruption of a phrase from a Robert Heinlein novel *The Moon Is a Harsh Mistress* and the MacArthur entry was almost certainly from a popular song of the 1920s. Some popular attributions, e.g. 'An Iron Curtain Descending', have also been omitted because of doubts about their origins.

Quotations (in Alphabetical Order by Person)

Acton, Lord	Power tends to corrupt and absolute power corrupts absolutely.
Aesop	Don't count your chickens before they are hatched.
Allen, Woody	The lion and the calf shall lie down together, but the calf won't get much sleep.
Antoinette, Marie	Let them eat cake.
Appleton, Thomas Gold	Good Americans, when they die, go to Paris.
Archimedes	*Eureka* (I have found it).
	Give me a lever long enough and I will move the world.
Aristotle	Man is by nature a civic animal.
	One swallow does not make a summer.
Astor, Nancy	I married beneath me, all women do.
Bacon, Francis	Knowledge is Power.
	The remedy is worse than the disease.
Baldwin, Stanley	Power without responsibility, the privilege of the harlot throughout the ages.
Barnum, P T	There's a sucker born every minute.
Bentham, Jeremy	The greatest happiness of the greatest number.
Bevan, Aneurin	A desiccated calculating machine.
Bloch, Arthur	The secret of success is sincerity, once you can fake that you've got it made.
Bonaparte, Napoleon	England is a nation of shopkeepers.
	From the sublime to the ridiculous there is only one step.
Bourdillon, Francis	The night has a thousand eyes and the day but one.
Bousquet, General Pierre	It is magnificent but it is not war.
Browning, Robert	God's in his heaven – all's right with the world.
	Open my heart and you will see graved inside of it, 'Italy'.
Butler, R A	Politics is the art of the possible.
Byron, Lord George	Better to err with Pope, than shine with Pye.
	I awoke one morning and found myself famous.
Caesar, Julius	All Gaul is divided into three parts.
	The die is cast.
	Veni, Vidi, Vici (I came, I saw, I conquered).
Carlyle, Thomas	Speech is silvern, Silence is golden.
	The history of the world is but the biography of great men.
	The seagreen incorruptible.
Cato, Senator	Carthage must be destroyed.
Cavell, Edith	Patriotism is not enough. I must have no hatred or bitterness towards anyone.
Chamberlain, Neville	Peace for our time.
Christie, Agatha	An archaeologist is the best husband any woman can have – the older she gets the more interested he is in her.
Churchill, Winston	A modest little man with much to be modest about.
	A penny Punch and Judy show.
	A riddle wrapped in a mystery inside an enigma.
	A sheep in sheep's clothing.
	Give us the tools and we will finish the job.
	I have nothing to offer but blood, toil, tears and sweat.
	Indomitable in retreat; invincible in advance; insufferable in victory.
	Never in the field of human conflict was so much owed by so many to so few.
	When the eagles are silent the parrots begin to jabber.
Cleaver, Eldridge	You're either part of the solution or part of the problem.
Congreve, William	Heaven has no rage like love to hatred turned, Nor hell a fury like a woman scorned.
	Music hath charms to soothe a savage breast.
Connolly, Billy	Marriage is a wonderful invention, but then again, so is the bicycle repair kit.
Cousin, Victor	Art for art's sake.
Coward, Noël	Never trust a man with short legs – brains too near their bottom.
Cowper, William	God made the country, and man made the town.
	God moves in a mysterious way, his wonders to perform.
	Variety's the spice of life.
Cromwell, Oliver	I beseech you in the bowels of Christ, think it possible you may be mistaken.
	Put your trust in God and keep your powder dry.
	Warts and everything.
Dante Alighieri	All hope abandon ye who enter.

De Morgan, Augustus	Great fleas have little fleas upon their backs to bite 'em, and little fleas have lesser fleas and so ad infinitum.
Descartes, René	I think, therefore I am (*cogito ergo sum*).
Dirksen, Senator Everett	Don't get mad, get even.
Disraeli, Benjamin	I have always thought that every woman should marry, and no man.
	Lies, damned lies and statistics.
	The gondola of London.
Dodd, Ken	The trouble with Freud is that he never played the Glasgow Empire Saturday night.
Donne, John	And therefore never send to know for whom the bell tolls; it tolls for thee.
	Go and catch a falling star.
	No man is an island.
Drayton, Michael	Fair stood the wind for France.
Dryden, John	None but the brave deserves the fair.
Dudley, Sir Henry Bate	Wonders will never cease.
Durocher, Leo	Nice guys finish last.
Edison, Thomas Alva	Genius is one per cent inspiration and ninety-nine per cent perspiration.
Eisenhower, Dwight D	It's not the size of the dog in the fight – it's the size of the fight in the dog.
Elizabeth I	I know I have the body of a weak and feeble woman, but I have the heart and stomach of a King.
Emerson, Ralph Waldo	There is properly no history; only biography.
Fitzsimmons, Robert	The bigger they come the harder they fall.
Ford, Henry	History is bunk.
	You can have it any colour as long as it's black.
Franklin, Benjamin	Here Skugg lies snug as a bug in a rug.
	Nothing is certain but death and taxes.
	Remember that time is money.
	There never was a good war or a bad peace.
	We must indeed all hang together or, most assuredly, we shall all hang separately.
Freud, Clement	Attila the hen.
Friedman, Milton	There's no such thing as a free lunch.
Frost, Sir David	Television is an invention that permits you to be entertained in your living room by people you wouldn't have in your home.
George II	Mad is he? Then I hope he will bite some of my other generals.
George, Lloyd	Mr Balfour's poodle.
Getty, J Paul	The meek shall inherit the earth, but not its mineral rights.
Goldsmith, Sir James	If you pay peanuts, you get monkeys.
Goldwyn, Sam	A verbal contract isn't worth the paper it's written on.
	In two words, Impossible.
	Include me out.
	The only reason so many people showed up was to make sure that he was dead.
Gray, Thomas	Ignorance is bliss.
	Ye distant spires, ye antique towers.
Greeley, Horace	Go West, young man, and grow up with the country.
Grey, Edward	The lamps are going out all over Europe.
Griffiths, Trevor	Cough and the world coughs with you. Fart and you stand alone.
Hankey, Katherine	Tell me the old, old story.
Heath, Edward	Unpleasant and unacceptable face of Capitalism.
Hemans, Felicia	The boy stood on the burning deck.
Henry II	Will no one rid me of this turbulent priest?
Henry IV of France	The wisest fool in Christendom.
Hitchcock Alfred	There is no terror in a bang – only in the anticipation of it.
Hope, Bob	A bank is a place that will lend you money if you can prove that you don't need it.
Horace	Seize the present day (*carpe diem*).
Hughes, Howard	Ears made him look like a taxi cab with both doors open.
Jerome, Jerome K	Love is like the measles, we all have to go through it.
Johnson, Dr Samuel	A grain, which in England is generally given to horses but in Scotland supports the people.
	A writer of dictionaries, a harmless drudge.
	Claret is the liquor for boys, Port for men, but he who aspires to be a hero must drink brandy.
	Ignorance, Madam, pure ignorance.
	It matters not how a man dies, but how he lives.
	No man but a blockhead ever wrote except for money.
	Patriotism is the last refuge of a scoundrel.
	When a man is tired of London he is tired of life.
	When a man knows he is to be hanged in a fortnight it concentrates his mind wonderfully.
	Worth seeing, yes; but not worth going to see.
Johnson, Lyndon B	I never trust a man unless I've got his pecker in my pocket.
Jonson, Ben	Sweet Swan of Avon.
Juvenal	Bread and circuses (*Panem et circenses*).
Kadar, Janos	Whoever is not against us is with us.

Keaton, Buster	A comedian does funny things; a good comedian does things funny.
Kempis, Thomas à	*Sic transit gloria mundi* (so passes away the glory of the world).
Kennedy, John F	Ich bin ein Berliner.
	Let us never negotiate out of fear, but let us never fear to negotiate.
Keynes, J M	In the long run we are all dead.
Khayyam, Omar	The moving finger writes and having writ moves on.
King, Martin Luther	I want to be the white man's brother, not his brother-in-law.
Kipling, Rudyard	A woman is only a woman, but a good cigar is a smoke.
	East is East and West is West and never the twain shall meet.
	If you can keep your head when all about you are losing theirs and blaming it on you.
	If you can meet with triumph and disaster and treat those two impostors just the same.
	The female of the species is more deadly than the male.
Leary, Timothy	Turn on, Tune in, Drop out.
Lenin	It is true that liberty is precious – so precious that it must be rationed.
Lennon, John	Women should be obscene and not heard.
Liberace	What you said hurt me very much. I cried all the way to the bank.
Lincoln, Abraham	You can fool all the people some of the time, and some of the people all of the time, but you cannot fool all the people all the time.
Lombardi, Vince	Winning is not everything. It's the only thing.
Longfellow, Henry Wadsworth	Into each life some rain must fall.
Louis XIV	I am the State (*L'État, c'est moi*).
Louis, Joe	He can run but he can't hide.
Lovelace, Richard	Stone walls do not a prison make, Nor iron bars a cage.
Lytton, Bulwer	The pen is mightier than the sword.
MacArthur, General	Old soldiers never die, they simply fade away. (originally from a First World War song)
Macmillan, Harold	I'd like that translated, if I may.
	The wind of change is blowing through the continent.
Mallory, George	Because it's there.
Martin, Dean	You're not drunk if you can lie on the floor without holding on.
Marvell, Andrew	He nothing common did, or mean, Upon that memorable scene.
Marx, Groucho	A man is only as old as the woman he feels.
Marx, Karl	Religion is the opium of the people.
McAuliffe, Brigadier General	Nuts!
McLuhan, Marshall	The medium is the message.
Miller, Dr Jonathan	I'm not really a Jew, just Jew-ish, not the whole hog.
Milton, John	They also serve who only stand and wait.
Moore, Thomas	Love's young dream.
Moss, Stirling	There are two things no man will admit he can't do well: drive and make love.
Napier, Sir Charles	Peccavi (I have sinned).
Nash, Ogden	Candy is dandy. But liquor is quicker.
Newbolt, Sir Henry	A bumping pitch and a blinding light, an hour to play and the last man in.
Newton, Isaac	If I have seen further it is by standing on the shoulders of giants.
Nicholas I, Tsar	Generals January and February.
Nicholson, Viv	I'm going to spend, spend, spend.
Oates, Capt. Lawrence	I am just going outside and may be some time.
Parker, Dorothy	How can they tell?
	Men seldom make passes at girls who wear glasses.
Pasionaria, La	It is better to die on your feet than to live on your knees.
Pepys, Samuel	And so to bed.
Pitt, William (1st Earl of Chatham)	Where law ends, tyranny begins.
Poe, Edgar Allan	Once upon a midnight dreary, while I pondered weak and weary.
	Quoth the Raven, 'Nevermore'.
Pope, Alexander	A little learning is a dangerous thing.
	For fools rush in where angels fear to tread.
	Hope springs eternal in the human breast.
	I am his Highness' dog at Kew; Pray tell me sir, whose dog are you?
	To err is human, to forgive, divine.
Proudhon, Pierre-Joseph	Property is theft.
Putnam, US General Israel	Don't one of you fire until you see the whites of their eyes.
Reagan, Ronald	She is the best man in England.
Roland, Madame	Oh liberty! what crimes are committed in your name!
Roosevelt, F D	The only thing we have to fear is fear itself.
Roosevelt, Theodore	No man is justified in doing evil on the ground of expediency.
	Speak softly and carry a big stick.
Rousseau, Jean-Jacques	Man is born free, and everywhere he is in chains.
Ryle, Gilbert	The ghost in the machine.
Sahl, Mort	Would you buy a second-hand car from this man?
Saki	The cook was a good cook as cooks go; and as cooks go she went.

Sartre, Jean-Paul	Hell is other people.
Scott, Sir Walter	O what a tangled web we weave when first we practise to deceive.
Shaw, G B	Every man over forty is a scoundrel.
	I'm only a beer teetotaller not a champagne teetotaller.
	Youth is wasted on the young.
Sheridan, General Philip	The only good Indians I ever saw were dead.
Sherman, General	War is hell.
Sidney, Sir Philip	Thy need is greater than mine.
Smollett, Tobias	That great Cham of literature Samuel Johnson.
Stalin, Joseph	A single death is a tragedy, a million deaths is a statistic.
Stein, Gertrude	A Rose is a Rose is a Rose.
Stewart, Jackie	In my sport the quick are too often listed among the dead.
Tattnall, Commodore	Blood is thicker than water.
Tennyson, Lord Alfred	He makes no friend who never made a foe.
	Into the valley of death rode the six hundred.
	Kind hearts are more than coronets.
	Man is the hunter, woman is his game.
	'Tis better to have loved and lost, than never to have loved at all.
Thatcher, Margaret	The lady's not for turning.
Truman, Harry S	The buck stops here.
Tucker, Sophie	I have been poor and I have been rich. Rich is better.
Twain, Mark	A classic is something that everybody wants to have read and nobody wants to read.
	Cauliflower is nothing but cabbage with a college education.
	Golf is a good walk spoiled.
	Reports of my death have been greatly exaggerated.
Vanderbilt, Cornelius	The public be damned.
Queen Victoria	We are not amused.
	He speaks to me as if I were a public meeting.
Virgil	Arms and the man I sing.
	I fear the Greeks even when they bring gifts.
Voltaire	All is for the best in the best of possible worlds.
	If God did not exist, it would be necessary to invent him.
	In this country [England] it is good to kill an admiral from time to time, to encourage the others.
Walpole, Sir Robert	Balance of power.
Warhol, Andy	In the future everyone will be famous for fifteen minutes.
Washington, George	Father, I cannot tell a lie, I did it with my little hatchet.
Waugh, Evelyn	We are American at puberty. We die French.
Wellington, Duke of	Publish and be damned.
Wesley, John	I look upon the world as my parish.
West, Mae	Give a man a free hand and he'll run it all over you.
	Keep a diary and one day it'll keep you.
Wilcox, Ella Wheeler	Laugh and the world laughs with you; Weep and you weep alone.
Wilde, Oscar	A man who knows the price of everything and the value of nothing.
	Each man kills the thing he loves.
	Experience is the name everyone gives to his mistakes.
	I can resist everything except temptation.
	I have nothing to declare but my genius.
	The unspeakable in pursuit of the uneatable.
William of Wykeham	Manners maketh man.
Wilson, Harold	A week is a long time in politics.
	Macmillan's role as a poseur was itself a pose.
	One man's wage rise is another man's price increase.
Wilson, Woodrow	The world must be made safe for democracy.
Wordsworth, William	The child is father of the man.
Yeltsin, Boris	You can make a throne from bayonets but you can't sit on it long.
Young, Edward	Procrastination is the thief of time.

Nursery Rhymes

As I was going to St Ives I met a man with seven wives, each wife had seven sacks, each sack had seven cats, each cat had seven kits, kits, cats, sacks and wives, how many going to St Ives?

Baa baa black sheep have you any wool? Yes sir, yes sir, three bags full; one for the master, and one for the dame, and one for the little boy who lives down the lane.

Bobby Shafto's gone to sea, silver buckles on his knee,

he'll come back and marry me, bonny Bobby Shafto.

Dance to your daddy, my little babby, dance to your daddy, my little lamb; you shall have a fishy, in a little dishy, you shall have a fishy, when the boat comes in.

Ding, dong, bell, pussy's in the well. Who put her in? Little Johnny Green. Who pulled her out? Little Tommy Stout.

Doctor Foster went to Gloucester, in a shower of rain;

he stepped in a puddle, right up to his middle, and never went there again.

Georgie Porgie pudding and pie, kissed the girls and made them cry; when the boys came out to play, Georgie Porgie ran away.

Goosey, goosey gander, where shall I wander? Upstairs and downstairs, in my lady's chamber. There I met an old man who would not say his prayers, I took him by the left leg and threw him down the stairs.

Hark, hark, the dogs do bark, the beggars are coming to town; some in rags, and some in jags, and one in a velvet gown.

Hey diddle diddle, the cat and the fiddle, the cow jumped over the moon; the little dog laughed to see such sport, and the dish ran away with the spoon.

Hickory, dickory dock, the mouse ran up the clock. The clock struck one, the mouse ran down, hickory, dickory dock.

Humpty Dumpty sat on a wall, Humpty Dumpty had a great fall; all the king's horses and all the king's men couldn't put Humpty together again.

I had a little nut tree, nothing would it bear, but a silver nutmeg, and a golden pear.

If all the world were paper, and all the sea were ink, if all the trees were bread and cheese, what should we have to drink?

Jack be nimble, Jack be quick, Jack jump over the candle stick.

Jack Sprat could eat no fat, his wife could eat no lean, and so between them both, you see, they licked the platter clean.

Little Bo-Peep has lost her sheep, and doesn't know where to find them; leave them alone and they will come home, dragging their tails behind them.

Little Boy Blue, come blow your horn, the sheep's in the meadow, the cow's in the corn. Where is the boy who looks after the sheep? He's under a haystack fast asleep.

Little Jack Horner sat in the corner, eating a Christmas pie; he put in his thumb, and pulled out a plum, and said, What a good boy am I.

Little Miss Muffet sat on a tuffet, eating her curds and whey; along came a spider, who sat down beside her, and frightened Miss Muffet away.

Little Polly Flinders, sat among the cinders, warming her pretty little toes; her mother came and caught her, and whipped her little daughter, for spoiling her nice new clothes.

Little Tommy Tucker sings for his supper; what shall we give him? White bread and butter. How shall he cut it without a knife? How will he marry without a wife?

Lucy Locket lost her pocket, Kitty Fisher found it; not a penny was there in it, only ribbon round it.

Mary had a little lamb, its fleece was white as snow; and everywhere that Mary went the lamb was sure to go.

Mary, Mary, quite contrary, how does your garden grow? With silver bells and cockle shells, and pretty maids all in a row.

Old King Cole was a merry old soul, and a merry old soul was he; he called for his pipe, and he called for his bowl, and he called for his fiddlers three.

Old Mother Hubbard went to the cupboard, to fetch her poor dog a bone; but when she came there, the cupboard was bare, and so the poor dog had none.

On the twelfth day of Christmas my true love sent to me twelve lords a-leaping, eleven ladies dancing, ten pipers piping, nine drummers drumming, eight maids a-milking, seven swans a-swimming, six geese a-laying, five gold rings, four colly birds, three French hens, two turtle doves, and a partridge in a pear tree.

One, two, three, four, five, once I caught a fish alive; six, seven, eight, nine, ten, then I let it go again. Why did you let it go? Because it bit my finger so. Which finger did it bite? This little finger on the right.

Oranges and lemons, say the bells of St Clement's. You owe me five farthings, say the bells of St Martin's. When will you pay me? say the bells of Old Bailey. When I grow rich, say the bells of Shoreditch. When will that be? say the bells of Stepney. I'm sure I don't know, says the great bell at Bow. Here comes the candle to light you to bed, here comes a chopper to chop off your head.

Pat-a-cake, pat-a-cake baker's man, bake me a cake as fast as you can; pat it and prick it and mark it with B, put it in the oven for baby and me.

Pease porridge hot, pease porridge cold, pease porridge in the pot, nine days old.

Polly put the kettle on, Polly put the kettle on, Polly put the kettle on, we'll all have tea. Sukey take it off again, Sukey take it off again, Sukey take it off again, they've all gone away.

Pussy cat, pussy cat, where have you been? I've been to London to visit the Queen. Pussy cat, pussy cat, what did you there? I frightened a little mouse under her chair.

Ride a cock horse to Banbury Cross, to see a fine lady upon a white horse; rings on her fingers and bells on her toes, and she shall have music wherever she goes.

Ring-a-ring o'roses, a pocket full of posies, A-tishoo, A-tishoo, we all fall down.

Rub-a-dub-dub, three men in a tub, and how do you think they got there? The butcher, the baker, the candlestick maker, they all jumped out of a rotten potato, 'twas enough to make a man stare.

See-saw Margery Daw, Johnny shall have a new master; Johnny shall have but a penny a day, because he can't work any faster.

Simple Simon met a pieman, going to the fair; said Simple Simon to the pieman, let me taste your ware. Said the pieman to Simple Simon, show me first your penny; said Simple Simon, indeed I have not any.

Sing a song of sixpence, a pocket full of rye; four and twenty blackbirds baked in a pie. When the pie was opened the birds began to sing; wasn't that a dainty dish to set before the king? The king was in his counting-house, counting out his money, the queen was in the parlour, eating bread and honey, the maid was in the garden, hanging out the clothes, along came a blackbird and pecked off her nose.

Solomon Grundy, born on Monday, christened on Tuesday, married on Wednesday, took ill on Thursday, worse on Friday, died on Saturday, buried on Sunday, this is the end of Solomon Grundy.

Taffy was a Welshman, Taffy was a thief, Taffy came to my house and stole a leg of beef. I went to Taffy's house, Taffy wasn't in, I jumped upon his Sunday hat, and poked it with a pin.

The Grand Old Duke of York, he had ten thousand men, he marched them up to the top of the hill, and he marched them down again; and when they were up they were up, and when they were down they were down, and when they were only halfway up, they were neither up nor down.

The man in the moon came down too soon, and asked

the way to Norwich; he went by the south, and burnt his mouth, with supping cold plum porridge.

The north wind doth blow, and we shall have snow, and what will poor Robin do then, poor thing? He'll sit in a barn, and keep himself warm, and hide his head under his wing, poor thing.

The Queen of Hearts she made some tarts, all on a summer's day. The Knave of Hearts he stole the tarts, and took them clean away. The King of Hearts called for the tarts, and beat the knave full sore. The Knave of Hearts brought back the tarts, and vowed he'd steal no more.

There was a crooked man, who walked a crooked mile, he found a crooked sixpence against a crooked stile, he bought a crooked cat, which caught a crooked mouse, and they all lived together in a little crooked house.

There was a man lived in the moon, lived in the moon, lived in the moon, and his name was Aiken Drum, and he played upon a ladle, a ladle, a ladle.

There was an old woman who lived in a shoe, she had so many children she didn't know what to do; she gave them some broth without any bread, she whipped them all soundly and sent them to bed.

This little piggy went to market, this little piggy stayed at home, this little piggy had roast beef, this little piggy had none, and this little piggy went wee-wee-wee, all the way home.

Tom, Tom, the piper's son, stole a pig and away he run; the pig was eat, and Tom was beat, and Tom went howling down the street.

Twinkle, twinkle, little star, how I wonder what you are! Up above the world so high, like a diamond in the sky.

Wee Willie Winkie runs through the town, upstairs and downstairs in his night-gown, rapping at the window, crying through the lock, are the children all in bed, it's past eight o' clock.

What are little boys made of? . . . Snips and snails and puppy-dog tails. What are little girls made of? . . . Sugar and spice and all things nice.

Who killed Cock Robin? I, said the sparrow, with my bow and arrow, I killed Cock Robin. Who saw him die? I, said the fly, with my little eye, I saw him die.

Yankee Doodle came to town, riding on a pony; stuck a feather in his cap, and called it macaroni.

NB There are slight corruptions of wording in some nursery rhymes, usually dependent on region. For example, little boys can be made of 'frogs and snails'.

RELIGION

Popes

*Popes and antipopes		Dates	Original name, feast day or miscellaneous information
1	St Peter	To 64	feast day 29 June
2	St Linus	c. 67–76/79	feast day 23 September
3	St Anacletus	c. 76/79–88/91	feast day 26 April
4	St Clement I	c. 88/92–97/101	feast day 23 November
5	St Evaristus	c. 97–c107	feast day 6 October
6	St Alexander I	c. 105/9–115/19	feast day 3 May
7	St Sixtus I	c. 115–c125	feast day 3 April
8	St Telesphorus	c. 125–c136	feast day 5 January (Greek)
9	St Hyginus	c. 136–c140	feast day 11 January (Greek)
10	St Pius I	c. 140–c155	feast day 11 July
11	St Anicetus	c. 155–c166	feast day 17 April (Syria)
12	St Soter	c. 166–c175	feast day 22 April
13	St Eleutherius	c. 175–c189	feast day 26 May
14	St Victor I	c. 189–c199	feast day 28 July (African)
15	St Zephyrinus	c. 199–c217	feast day 26 August
16	St Calixtus I	217–222	feast day 14 October
17	Hippolytus	217–235	first antipope
18	St Urban I	222–230	feast day 25 May
19	St Pontian	230–235	feast day 19 November
20	St Anterus	235–236	feast day 3 January (Greek)
21	St Fabian	236–250	feast day 20 January
22	St Cornelius	251–253	feast day 16 September
23	Novatian	251	Novatianus (antipope)
24	St Lucius I	253–254	feast day 4 March
25	St Stephen I	254–257	feast day 2 August
26	St Sixtus II	257–258	feast day 6 August (Greek)
27	St Dionysius	259–268	feast day 6 December (Greek)
28	St Felix I	269–274	feast day 30 May
29	St Eutychian	275–283	feast day 7 December
30	St Gaius	283–296	feast day 22 April (Dalmatian)
31	St Marcellinus	296–304	feast day 26 April
32	St Marcellus I	308–309	feast day 16 January
33	St Eusebius	309–310	feast day 17 August (Greek)
34	St Miltiades	311–314	feast day 10 December
35	St Sylvester I	314–335	feast day 31 December
36	St Mark	336	feast day 7 October
37	St Julius I	337–352	feast day 12 April
38	Liberius	352–366	
39	Felix II	355–358	antipope 357–8
40	St Damasus I	366–384	feast day 11 December (Latin Mass)
41	Ursinus	366–367	Antipope
42	St Siricius	384–399	feast day 26 November
43	St Anastasius I	399–401	feast day 19 December
44	St Innocent I	401–417	feast day 28 July
45	St Zosimus	417–418	feast day 26 December (Greek)
46	St Boniface I	418–422	feast day 4 September
47	Eulalius	418–419	antipope
48	St Celestine I	422–432	feast day 27 July
49	St Sixtus III	432–440	feast day 28 March
50	St Leo I	440–461	feast day 11 April (Leo the Great)
51	St Hilary	461–468	feast day 28 February
52	St Simplicius	468–483	feast day 10 March
53	St Felix III	483–492	feast day 1 March
54	St Gelasius I	492–496	feast day 21 November
55	Anastasius II	496–498	
56	St Symmachus	498–514	feast day 19 July
57	Laurentius	498	antipope
58	Laurentius	501–505	antipope
59	St Hormisdas	514–523	feast day 6 August
60	St John I	523–526	feast day 27 May
61	Felix IV	526–530	feast day 30 January
62	Dioscorus	530	Egyptian
63	Boniface II	530–532	
64	John II	533–535	Mercurius (first pope to change name)

Popes and antipopes	Dates	Original name, feast day or miscellaneous information
65 St Agapetus I	535–536	feast day 22 April
66 St Silverius	536–537	feast day 20 June
67 Vigilius	537–555	
68 Pelagius I	556–561	
69 John III	561–574	Catelinus
70 Benedict I	575–579	
71 Pelagius II	579–590	
72 St Gregory I	590–604	feast day 12 March
73 Sabinian	604–606	
74 Boniface III	607	
75 St Boniface IV	608–615	
76 St Deusdedit	615–618	feast day 8 November (aka Adeodatus I)
77 Boniface V	619–625	
78 Honorius I	625–638	
79 Severinus	638–640	
80 John IV	640–642	Dalmatian
81 Theodore I	642–649	Jerusalem
82 St Martin I	649–655	feast day 12 November
83 St Eugenius I	654–657	feast day 2 June
84 St Vitalian	657–672	
85 Adeodatus II	672–676	
86 Donus	676–678	
87 St Agatho	678–681	feast day 10 January
88 St Leo II	681–683	feast day 3 July
89 St Benedict II	684–685	feast day 8 May
90 John V	685–686	Syrian
91 Conon	686–687	
92 St Sergius I	687–701	feast day 8 September
93 Theodore	687	antipope
94 Paschal	687	antipope
95 John VI	701–705	Greek
96 John VII	705–707	Greek
97 Sisinnius	708	
98 Constantine	708–715	
99 St Gregory II	715–731	feast day 11 February
100 St Gregory III	731–741	feast day 28 November (Syrian)
101 St Zacharias	741–752	feast day 15 March
102 Stephen II	752	died after two days
103 Stephen III	752–757	Papal States founder
104 St Paul I	757–767	feast day 28 June
105 Constantine II	767–768	antipope
106 Philip	768	antipope
107 Stephen IV	768–772	
108 Adrian I	772–795	
109 St Leo III	795–816	feast day 12 June (Crowned Charlemagne)
110 Stephen V	816–817	
111 St Paschal I	817–824	feast day 14 May
112 Eugenius II	824–827	
113 Valentine	827	feast day 14 February
114 Gregory IV	827–844	created 1 November All Saints day
115 John	844	antipope
116 Sergius II	844–847	
117 St Leo IV	847–855	feast day 17 July
118 Benedict III	855–858	
119 Anastasius	855	Anastasius the Librarian (antipope)
120 St Nicholas I	858–867	
121 Adrian II	867–872	
122 John VIII	872–882	crowned Charles the Fat Emperor
123 Marinus I	882–884	
124 St Adrian III	884–885	feast day 8 July
125 Stephen VI	885–891	
126 Formosus	891–896	
127 Boniface VI	896	
128 Stephen VII	896–897	
129 Romanus	897	
130 Theodore II	897	
131 John IX	898–900	
132 Benedict IV	900–903	
133 Leo V	903	
134 Christopher	903–904	antipope
135 Sergius III	904–911	

Popes and antipopes	Dates	Original name, feast day or miscellaneous information
136 Anastasius III	911–913	
137 Lando	913–914	
138 John X	914–928	
139 Leo VI	928	
140 Stephen VIII	929–931	
141 John XI	931–935	
142 Leo VII	936–939	
143 Stephen IX	939–942	
144 Marinus II	942–946	
145 Agapetus II	946–955	
146 John XII	955–964	Ottaviano (crowned Emperor Otto)
147 Leo VIII	963–965	
148 Benedict V	964–966	Benedict the Grammarian
149 John XIII	965–972	
150 Benedict VI	973–974	
151 Boniface VII	974	Franco (first term)
152 Benedict VII	974–983	
153 John XIV	983–984	Pietro Canepanova
154 Boniface VII	984–985	Franco (second term)
155 John XV	985–996	
156 Gregory V	996–999	Bruno of Carinthia (first German pope)
157 John XVI	997–998	Giovanni Filagato (antipope)
158 Sylvester II	999–1003	Gerbert of Aurillac (French)
159 John XVII	1003	Secco
160 John XVIII	1004–1009	Fasano
161 Sergius IV	1009–1012	Pietro Buccaporci
162 Gregory VI	1012	antipope
163 Benedict VIII	1012–1024	Teofilatto
164 John XIX	1024–1032	Romano (crowned Emperor Conrad II)
165 Benedict IX	1032–1044	Teofilatto (12 yrs old)
166 Sylvester III	1045	John of Sabina
167 Benedict IX	1045	Teofilatto (second term)
168 Gregory VI	1045–1046	Giovanni Graziano
169 Clement II	1046–1047	Suidger
170 Benedict IX	1047–1048	Teofilatto (third term)
171 Damasus II	1048	Poppo (Bavarian)
172 St Leo IX	1049–1054	feast day 19 April (aka Bruno of Egisheim)
173 Victor II	1055–1057	Gebhard of Hirschberg
174 Stephen X	1057–1058	Frederick of Lorraine
175 Benedict X	1058–1059	Giovanni Mincio (antipope)
176 Nicholas II	1058–1061	Gerard of Burgundy
177 Alexander II	1061–1073	Anselm of Baggio
178 Honorius II	1061–1072	Cadelo (antipope)
179 St Gregory VII	1073–1085	feast day 25 May 25 (aka Hildebrand)
180 Clement III	1080–1100	Guibert (antipope)
181 Victor III	1086–1087	feast day 16 September
182 Urban II	1088–1099	Odo of Lagery
183 Paschal II	1099–1118	Raniero
184 Theodoric	1100–1102	antipope
185 Albert/Aleric	1102	antipope
186 Sylvester IV	1105–1111	Maginulfo (antipope)
187 Gelasius II	1118–1119	Giovanni da Gaetan
188 Gregory VIII	1118–1121	Maurice Bourdin (antipope)
189 Calixtus II	1119–1124	Guy of Burgundy
190 Honorius II	1124–1130	Lamberto Scannabecchi
191 Celestine II	1124	Theobald Buccapecus
192 Innocent II	1130–1143	Gregorio Papareschi
193 Anacletus II	1130–1138	Pietro Pierleoni (antipope)
194 Victor IV	1138	Gregory Conti (antipope)
195 Celestine II	1143–1144	Guido de Castellis
196 Lucius II	1144–1145	Gherardo Caccianemici
197 Eugenius III	1145–1153	feast day 8 July (aka Bernard of Pisa)
198 Anastasius IV	1153–1154	Corrado di Suburra
199 Adrian IV	1154–1159	Nicholas Breakspear (only English pope)
200 Alexander III	1159–1181	Rolando Bandinelli
201 Victor IV	1159–1164	Ottaviano de Monticello (antipope)
202 Paschal III	1164–1168	Guido da Crema (antipope)
203 Calixtus III	1168–1178	John of Struma (antipope)
204 Innocent III	1179–1180	Lando di Sezze (antipope)
205 Lucius III	1181–1185	Ubaldo Allucingoli
206 Urban III	1185–1187	Uberto Crivelli

RELIGION

Popes and antipopes		Dates	Original name, feast day or miscellaneous information
207	Gregory VIII	1187	Alberto de Morra
208	Clement III	1187–1191	Paolo Scolari
209	Celestine III	1191–1198	Giacinto Bobo-Orsini
210	Innocent III	1198–1216	Lothair di Segni
211	Honorius III	1216–1227	Cencio Savelli
212	Gregory IX	1227–1241	Ugolino di Segni (excommunicated Frederick II)
213	Celestine IV	1241	Goffredo Castiglioni
214	Innocent IV	1243–1254	Sinibaldo Fieschi
215	Alexander IV	1254–1261	Rinaldo Deisegni
216	Urban IV	1261–1264	Jacques Pantaleon
217	Clement IV	1265–1268	Guido Fulcodi
218	Gregory X	1271–1276	Tebaldo Visconti
219	Innocent V	1276	feast day June 22nd (first Dominican pope)
220	Adrian V	1276	Ottobono Fieschi
221	John XXI	1276–1277	Pedro Hispano (Portuguese)
222	Nicholas III	1277–1280	Giovanni Orsini
223	Martin IV	1281–1285	Simon de Brion
224	Honorius IV	1285–1287	Giacomo Savelli
225	Nicholas IV	1288–1292	Girolamo Masci
226	St Celestine V	1294	feast day 19 May (first pope to abdicate)
227	Boniface VIII	1294–1303	Benedict Caetani
228	Benedict XI	1303–1304	feast day 7 July
229	Clement V	1305–1314	Bertrand de Got (Avignon from 1309)
230	John XXII	1316–1334	Jacques Duese (Babylonian Captivity 1309–77)
231	Nicholas V	1328–1330	Pietro Rainalducci (antipope)
232	Benedict XII	1334–1342	Jacques Fournier (Avignon)
233	Clement VI	1342–1352	Pierre Roger (Avignon)
234	Innocent VI	1352–1362	Etienne Aubert (Avignon)
235	Urban V	1362–1370	feast day 19 December (Avignon)
236	Gregory XI	1370–1378	Pierre de Beaufort (Avignon till 1377)
237	Urban VI	1378–1389	Bartolomeo Prignano (Western Schism 1378–1417)
238	Clement VII	1378–1394	Robert of Geneva (antipope)
239	Boniface IX	1389–1404	Pietro Tomacelli
240	Benedict XIII	1394–1423	Pedro de Luna (antipope)
241	Innocent VII	1404–1406	Cosimo de Migliorati
242	Gregory XII	1406–1415	Angelo Correr
243	Alexander V	1409–1410	Peter of Candia (antipope)
244	John XXIII	1410–1415	Baldassare Cossa (antipope)
245	Martin V	1417–1431	Oddone Colonna
246	Clement VIII	1423–1429	Gil Sanchez Munoz (antipope)
247	Benedict XIV	1425–1433	The Hidden Pope (counter antipope)
248	Eugenius IV	1431–1447	Gabriele Condulmer
249	Felix V	1439–1449	Amadeus VIII the Peaceful (antipope)
250	Nicholas V	1447–1455	Tommaso Parentucelli
251	Calixtus III	1455–1458	Alfonso di Borgia (uncle of Rodrigo)
252	Pius II	1458–1464	Enea Piccolomini
253	Paul II	1464–1471	Pietro Barbo
254	Sixtus IV	1471–1484	Francesco Dellarovere
255	Innocent VIII	1484–1492	Giovanni Battista Cibo
256	Alexander VI	1492–1503	Rodrigo Borgia (father of Lucretia)
257	Pius III	1503	Francesco Piccolomini
258	Julius II	1503–1513	Giuliano Dellarovere (patron of Michelangelo)
259	Leo X	1513–1521	Giovanni de Medici (excommunicated Luther 1521)
260	Adrian VI	1522–1523	Adrian Florenz Boeyens (only Dutch pope)
261	Clement VII	1523–1534	Giulio de Medici
262	Paul III	1534–1549	Alessandro Farnese (called Council of Trent)
263	Julius III	1550–1555	Giovanni del Monte
264	Marcellus II	1555	Marcello Cervini
265	Paul IV	1555–1559	Gian Pietro Carafa
266	Pius IV	1559–1565	Giovanni de Medici (concluded Council of Trent)
267	St Pius V	1566–1572	Antonio Ghislieri (excommunicated Elizabeth I 1570)
268	Gregory XIII	1572–1585	Ugo Boncompagni (Gregorian calendar)
269	Sixtus V	1585–1590	Felice Peretti (excommunicated Henry of Navarre)
270	Urban VII	1590	Giambattista Castagna
271	Gregory XIV	1590–1591	Niccolo Sfondrato
272	Innocent IX	1591	Giovanni Facchinetti
273	Clement VIII	1592–1605	Ippolito Aldobrandini
274	Leo XI	1605	Alessandro de Medici
275	Paul V	1605–1621	Camillo Borghese
276	Gregory XV	1621–1623	Alessandro Ludovisi
277	Urban VIII	1623–1644	Maffeo Barberini (patron of sculptor Bernini)

Popes and antipopes		Dates	Original name, feast day or miscellaneous information
278	Innocent X	1644–1655	Giovanni Pamphili
279	Alexander VII	1655–1667	Fabio Chigi
280	Clement IX	1667–1669	Giulio Rospiglioso
281	Clement X	1670–1676	Emilio Altieri
282	Innocent XI	1676–1689	feast day 13 August
283	Alexander VIII	1689–1691	Pietro Ottoboni
284	Innocent XII	1691–1700	Antonio Pignatelli
285	Clement XI	1700–1721	Giovanni Albani
286	Innocent XIII	1721–1724	Michelangelo dei Conti (recognised Old Pretender)
287	Benedict XIII	1724–1730	Pietro Maria Orsini
288	Clement XII	1730–1740	Lorenzo Corsini (condemned Freemasonry)
289	Benedict XIV	1740–1758	Prospero Lambertini
290	Clement XIII	1758–1769	Carlo Rezzonico
291	Clement XIV	1769–1774	Giovanni Ganganelli (dissolved Jesuits 1773)
292	Pius VI	1775–1799	Giannangelo Braschi
293	Pius VII	1800–1823	Barnaba Chiaramonti (revived Jesuits 1814)
294	Leo XII	1823–1829	Annibale Della Genga
295	St Pius VIII	1829–1830	Francesco Castiglioni
296	Gregory XVI	1831–1846	Bartolomeo Cappellari (Austrian)
297	Pius IX	1846–1878	Giovanni Mastai-Ferretti (longest reign, 32 yrs)
298	Leo XIII	1878–1903	Vincenzo Pecci
299	St Pius X	1903–1914	feast day 3 September (last to be canonised)
300	Benedict XV	1914–1922	Giacomo Della Chiesa
301	Pius XI	1922–1939	Ambrogio Damiano Ratti
302	Pius XII	1939–1958	Eugenio Maria Pacelli
303	John XXIII	1958–1963	Angelo Giuseppe Roncalli (second Vatican Council)
304	Paul VI	1963–1978	Giovanni Battista Montini (first to visit Asia)
305	John Paul I	1978	Albino Luciani (reigned 34 days)
306	John Paul II	1978–	Karol Wojtyla (Polish: first non-Italian since Adrian VI)

Popes: Miscellaneous Information

antipope	an alternative claimant to the bishop of Rome who has just cause in disputing the papacy.
assassinated	26
boy pope	Benedict IX (12 yrs old)
Britain: first to visit	John Paul II (1982)
British Pope	Adrian IV (Nicholas Breakspear)
Cadaver Synod	Formosus (896) tried and executed after his death!
Celestine II	Theobald Buccapecus, elected pope in 1124, resigned after a few days and is often omitted in lists, hence the duplication.
Council of Trent	19th ecumenical council of RC Church; 1545–63 in northern Italy
crushed to death	John XXI; ceiling of papal palace at Viterbo collapsed
directives called	Papal Bull
double name: first	John Paul I (named after two predecessors)
female pope	Joan (fictional)
Humanae Vitae	encyclical of Paul VI condemning birth control (1968)
Infallibility	doctrine promulgated in July 1870, reaffirmed 1973
John Paul II	archbishop of Cracow
last antipope	the count of Savoy took holy orders and set himself up as Clement XV in 1969 but was never recognised outside his own small circle.

last non-Italian	Adrian VI (1522) Dutch
last to be canonised	Pius X on 29 May 1954
letters to churches	encyclicals
longest reign	Pius IX (32 yrs)
new pope: how known	White smoke from Vatican chimney
non-existent pope	John XX, due to error in numbering in 10th century
Pacem in Terris	encyclical of John XXIII (Peace on Earth)
Pilgrim Pope	Paul VI (because of his great travelling)
pope's blessing	Urbi et Orbi (To the city and the world)
pope: also called	Sovereign of Vatican City Vicar of Christ on Earth Bishop of Rome Patriarch of the West Primate of Italy
pope: elected by	College of Cardinals: two-thirds majority required
pope: means	father
Redemptor Hominus	encyclical of John Paul II about respect for man
Sacerdotalis Caelibatus	encyclical of Paul VI concerning priestly celibacy
throne	Sedes Gestatoria
Vatican Council: first	1869–70 (convoked by Pius IX)
Vatican Council: second	1962–65 (convoked by John XXIII)

	Felix X was the last elected antipope.

RELIGION

Popes (Alphabetical Order)

1	Adeodatus II	672–676	69	Clement I	c. 88/92–97/101
2	Adrian I	772–795	70	Clement II	1046–1047
3	Adrian II	867–872	71	Clement III	1080–1100
4	Adrian III	884–885	72	Clement III	1187–1191
5	Adrian IV	1154–1159	73	Clement IV	1265–1268
6	Adrian V	1276	74	Clement V	1305–1314
7	Adrian VI	1522–1523	75	Clement VI	1342–1352
8	Agapetus I	535–536	76	Clement VII	1378–1394
9	Agapetus II	946–955	77	Clement VII	1523–1534
10	Agatho	678–681	78	Clement VIII	1423–1429
11	Albert/Aleric	1102	79	Clement VIII	1592–1605
12	Alexander I	c. 105/9–115/19	80	Clement IX	1667–1669
13	Alexander II	1061–1073	81	Clement X	1670–1676
14	Alexander III	1159–1181	82	Clement XI	1700–1721
15	Alexander IV	1254–1261	83	Clement XII	1730–1740
16	Alexander V	1409–1410	84	Clement XIII	1758–1769
17	Alexander VI	1492–1503	85	Clement XIV	1769–1774
18	Alexander VII	1655–1667	86	Conon	686–687
19	Alexander VIII	1689–1691	87	Constantine	708–715
20	Anacletus	c. 76/79–88/91	88	Constantine II	767–768
21	Anacletus II	1130–1138	89	Cornelius	251–253
22	Anastasius	855	90	Damasus I	366–384
23	Anastasius I	399–401	91	Damasus II	1048
24	Anastasius II	496–498	92	Deusdedit	615–618
25	Anastasius III	911–913	93	Dionysius	259–268
26	Anastasius IV	1153–1154	94	Dioscorus	530
27	Anicetus	c. 155–c. 166	95	Donus	676–678
28	Anterus	235–236	96	Eleutherius	c. 175–c. 189
29	Benedict I	575–579	97	Eugenius I	654–657
30	Benedict II	684–685	98	Eugenius II	824–827
31	Benedict III	855–858	99	Eugenius III	1145–1153
32	Benedict IV	900–903	100	Eugenius IV	1431–1447
33	Benedict V	964–966	101	Eulalius	418–419
34	Benedict VI	973–974	102	Eusebius	309–310
35	Benedict VII	974–983	103	Eutychian	275–283
36	Benedict VIII	1012–1024	104	Evaristus	c. 97–c. 107
37	Benedict IX	1032–1044	105	Fabian	236–250
38	Benedict IX	1045	106	Felix I	269–274
39	Benedict IX	1047–1048	107	Felix II	355–358
40	Benedict X	1058–1059	108	Felix III	483–492
41	Benedict XI	1303–1304	109	Felix IV	526–530
42	Benedict XII	1334–1342	110	Felix V	1439–1449
43	Benedict XIII	1394–1423	111	Formosus	891–896
44	Benedict XIII	1724–1730	112	Gaius	283–296
45	Benedict XIV	1425–1433	113	Gelasius I	492–496
46	Benedict XIV	1740–1758	114	Gelasius II	1118–1119
47	Benedict XV	1914–1922	115	Gregory I	590–604
48	Boniface I	418–422	116	Gregory II	715–731
49	Boniface II	530–532	117	Gregory III	731–741
50	Boniface III	607	118	Gregory IV	827–844
51	Boniface IV	608–615	119	Gregory V	996–999
52	Boniface V	619–625	120	Gregory VI	1012
53	Boniface VI	896	121	Gregory VI	1045–1046
54	Boniface VII	974	122	Gregory VII	1073–1085
55	Boniface VII	984–985	123	Gregory VIII	1118–1121
56	Boniface VIII	1294–1303	124	Gregory VIII	1187
57	Boniface IX	1389–1404	125	Gregory IX	1227–1241
58	Calixtus I	217–222	126	Gregory X	1271–1276
59	Calixtus II	1119–1124	127	Gregory XI	1370–1378
60	Calixtus III	1168–1178	128	Gregory XII	1406–1415
61	Calixtus III	1455–1458	129	Gregory XIII	1572–1585
62	Celestine I	422–432	130	Gregory XIV	1590–1591
63	Celestine II	1124	131	Gregory XV	1621–1623
64	Celestine II	1143–1144	132	Gregory XVI	1831–1846
65	Celestine III	1191–1198	133	Hilary	461–468
66	Celestine IV	1241	134	Honorius I	625–638
67	Celestine V	1294	135	Honorius II	1061–1072
68	Christopher	903–904	136	Honorius II	1124–1130

137	Honorius III	1216–1227	209	Marinus II	942–946
138	Honorius IV	1285–1287	210	Mark	336
139	Hormisdas	514–523	211	Martin I	649–655
140	Hyginus	c. 136–c. 140	212	Martin IV	1281–1285
141	Innocent I	401–417	213	Martin V	1417–1431
142	Innocent II	1130–1143	214	Miltiades	311–314
143	Innocent III	1179–1180	215	Nicholas I	858–867
144	Innocent III	1198–1216	216	Nicholas II	1058–1061
145	Innocent IV	1243–1254	217	Nicholas III	1277–1280
146	Innocent V	1276	218	Nicholas IV	1288–1292
147	Innocent VI	1352–1362	219	Nicholas V	1328–1330
148	Innocent VII	1404–1406	220	Nicholas V	1447–1455
149	Innocent VIII	1484–1492	221	Novatian	251
150	Innocent IX	1591	222	Paschal	687
151	Innocent X	1644–1655	223	Paschal I	817–824
152	Innocent XI	1676–1689	224	Paschal II	1099–1118
153	Innocent XII	1691–1700	225	Paschal III	1164–1168
154	Innocent XIII	1721–1724	226	Paul I	757–767
155	John	844	227	Paul II	1464–1471
156	John I	523–526	228	Paul III	1534–1549
157	John II	533–535	229	Paul IV	1555–1559
158	John III	561–574	230	Paul V	1605–1621
159	John IV	640–642	231	Paul VI	1963–1978
160	John V	685–686	232	Pelagius I	556–561
161	John VI	701–705	233	Pelagius II	579–590
162	John VII	705–707	234	Peter	to c. 64
163	John VIII	872–882	235	Philip	768
164	John IX	898–900	236	Pius I	c. 140–c. 155
165	John X	914–928	237	Pius II	1458–1464
166	John XI	931–935	238	Pius III	1503
167	John XII	955–964	239	Pius IV	1559–1565
168	John XIII	965–972	240	Pius V	1566–1572
169	John XIV	983–984	241	Pius VI	1775–1799
170	John XV	985–996	242	Pius VII	1800–1823
171	John XVI	997–998	243	Pius VIII	1829–1830
172	John XVII	1003	244	Pius IX	1846–1878
173	John XVIII	1004–1009	245	Pius X	1903–1914
174	John XIX	1024–1032	246	Pius XI	1922–1939
175	John XXI	1276–1277	247	Pius XII	1939–1958
176	John XXII	1316–1334	248	Pontian	230–235
177	John XXIII	1410–1415	249	Romanus	897
178	John XXIII	1958–1963	250	Sabinian	604–606
179	John Paul I	1978	251	Sergius I	687–701
180	John Paul II	1978–	252	Sergius II	844–847
181	Julius I	337–352	253	Sergius III	904–911
182	Julius II	1503–1513	254	Sergius IV	1009–1012
183	Julius III	1550–1555	255	Severinus	638–640
184	Lando	913–914	256	Silverius	536–537
185	Laurentius	498	257	Simplicius	468–483
186	Laurentius	501–505	258	Siricius	384–399
187	Leo I	440–461	259	Sisinnius	708
188	Leo II	681–683	260	Sixtus I	c115–c125
189	Leo III	795–816	261	Sixtus II	257–258
190	Leo IV	847–855	262	Sixtus III	432–440
191	Leo V	903	263	Sixtus IV	1471–1484
192	Leo VI	928	264	Sixtus V	1585–1590
193	Leo VII	936–939	265	Soter	c. 166–c. 175
194	Leo VIII	963–965	266	Stephen I	254–257
195	Leo IX	1049–1054	267	Stephen II	752
196	Leo X	1513–1521	268	Stephen III	752–757
197	Leo XI	1605	269	Stephen IV	768–772
198	Leo XII	1823–1829	270	Stephen V	816–817
199	Leo XIII	1878–1903	271	Stephen VI	885–891
200	Liberius	352–366	272	Stephen VII	896–897
201	Linus	c. 67–76/79	273	Stephen VIII	929–931
202	Lucius I	253–254	274	Stephen IX	939–942
203	Lucius II	1144–1145	275	Stephen X	1057–1058
204	Lucius III	1181–1185	276	Sylvester I	314–335
205	Marcellinus	296–304	277	Sylvester II	999–1003
206	Marcellus I	308–309	278	Sylvester III	1045
207	Marcellus II	1555	279	Sylvester IV	1105–1111
208	Marinus I	882–884	280	Symmachus	498–514

RELIGION

281	Telesphorus	c. 125–c. 136
282	Theodore	687
283	Theodore I	642–649
284	Theodore II	897
285	Theodoric	1100–1102
286	Urban I	222–230
287	Urban II	1088–1099
288	Urban III	1185–1187
289	Urban IV	1261–1264
290	Urban V	1362–1370
291	Urban VI	1378–1389
292	Urban VII	1590
293	Urban VIII	1623–1644

294	Ursinus	366–367
295	Valentine	827
296	Victor I	c. 189–c. 199
297	Victor II	1055–1057
298	Victor III	1086–1087
299	Victor IV	1138
300	Victor IV	1159–1164
301	Vigilius	537–555
302	Vitalian	657–672
303	Zacharias	741–752
304	Zephyrinus	c. 199–c. 217
305	Zosimus	417–418

General Information

Adam's first wife Lilith (according to Jewish folklore).

Adulterer's Bible edition of the Bible of 1631, with the misprinted commandment 'thou shalt commit adultery'. Aka Wicked Bible.

ahimsa law of Reverence for, and non-violence to, every form of life (Hindu, Buddhist and Jainist philosophy).

Angels: hierarchy of
1 Seraphim
2 Cherubim
3 Thrones
4 Dominations/Dominions
5 Virtues
6 Powers
7 Principalities
8 Archangels
9 Angels

Black Friars Dominicans (Friar Preachers are a mendicant order founded in 1215).

Black Monks Benedictines (established c. AD 535–540).

Buddhism founded by Siddhartha Gautama in the sixth century BC. Buddha means 'Enlightened One'.
Two main divisions are Theravada Buddhism and Mahayana Buddhism.
The third minor division is Vajrayana or Tantric Buddhism.
The Buddha's teachings are described as the Four Noble Truths.
The Middle or Noble Eightfold Path is the finding of truth and leads to Nirvana.
The ten precepts include five for laymen, i.e. prohibiting killing, stealing, lying, sexual misconduct and drinking intoxicating liquor, and five for monastic novices, i.e. not to eat at certain hours, not to take part in festivals, not to use garlands or perfumes, not to use a luxurious bed and not to accept money for oneself. The birth of the Buddha is celebrated in the festival of Vesak/Wesak. The Buddha's first sermon is celebrated in the festival of Dhamma-cakka.

Cathari Manichean order that flourished in western Europe during the 12th and 13th centuries. The name derives from the Greek 'Katharos' meaning pure.

Christadelphians founded by John Thomas in 1848, although the name was adopted during the US Civil War.

Christian Scientists founded in Boston, Massachusetts, by Mary Baker Eddy (1879).

Church Army founded by Wilson Carlile (1882) in the slums of London.

Grey Friars Franciscans (founded c. 1207 and affiliated with the Poor Clares since 1212).

Hinduism originated about 4,000 years ago in the land of the Indus River.
The Veda is the most ancient body of religious literature.
The power of the Brahmans (priest class) is central to the belief.
Ahimsa is the doctrine of non-injury or the absence of the desire to harm.
Brahma (creator), Vishnu (protector) and Siva (destroyer and restorer) constitute the Trimurti.

Islam founded by Mohammed in AD 622 when he fled from Mecca to Medina (flight known as the Hegira).
Koran (Qur'ān) is regarded as the word of God given to Mohammed by the angel Gabriel.
Five pillars of Islamic faith are: the Shahādah – there is no god but God and Mohammed is the prophet of God; the salat – the five daily prayer sessions; the zakat – the tax that constitutes the giving of alms; the saum – fasting during daylight hours of Ramadan; hajj – the pilgrimage to Mecca that every Muslim should take at least once in their lifetime. The two major branches of Islam are the Sunnites (largest) and the Shi'ites.

Jainism founded in India in the sixth century BC by Mahavira. Jains practise Ahimsa.

Jehovah's Witnesses founded by Charles Taze Russell (1881).

Jerusalem centre of Islam, Judaism and Christianity. The Wailing Wall is sacred to the Jews, the Dome of the Rock is sacred to Muslims and Church of the Holy Sepulchre is sacred to Christians.

Jesse son of Obed, and father of David.

Judaism the body of Jewish civil and ceremonial law is contained in the Talmud, which comprises the Mishnah and the Gemara. The Hebrew Bible comprises 24 books. The civil calendar begins with the month of Tishri, the first day of which is the holiday of Rosh Hashana (New Year). Other Jewish holidays include Shavuot or Pentecost, which commemorates the revelation of the Torah (Law) at Sinai; Yom Kippur (Day of Atonement), which ends the ten days of penitence from Rosh Hashana; and Sukkot (Tabernacles), in remembrance of the Israelites' wanderings after the Exodus. Yom Kippur, Rosh Hashana, and Sukkot are celebrated in the Jewish month of Tishri. Purim celebrates the story of Esther and is celebrated in the month of Adar.
Israeli Jews are divided equally among Ashkenazi (Germanic) and Sephardic (strictly speaking, descendants of Spanish Jews pre-1492; more

loosely, non-Ashkenazi), although the Ashkenazim constitute more than 80% of all Jews in the world.

Koran (Qur'an)   Sacred book of Islam, regarded by Muslims as the final revelation of God to humankind, passed by the archangel Gabriel in Arabic to Muhammmad, the last of the prophets. It consists of 114 chapters (sūras) containing Christian and Arabic legend as well as Old and New Testament stories. The first translation into English was by George Sale in 1734, although Alexander Ross translated the Koran into English in 1649, but this was from a French translation.

Manich(a)eism   religious order founded by the Persian prophet Mani (c. 216–274) based on the conflict between goodness and evil. Manicheism also describes any heretical philosophy involving dualistic doctrines.

Menorah   seven-branched candelabrum that is now an emblem of Judaism and badge of Israel.

Methodism   founded by John Wesley (1738).

Mormons   aka Church of Jesus Christ of Latter-Day Saints, founded by Joseph Smith in 1830 and not Brigham Young, who merely led them to Salt Lake City, Utah, in 1847.

Panchen Lama   one of the two great Lamas of Tibet. (The other is the Dalai Lama.)

Penitential Psalms   seven psalms (i.e. 6, 32, 38, 51, 102, 130, 143' xpressing penitence.

Plymouth Brethren   founded in Dublin by the Reverend John Nelson Darby (1827) and named after the Devon town.

Potiphar   Pharaoh's official who bought Joseph as a slave.

Premonsu. .tensians   religious sect founded in the twelfth century by St Norbert.

religious journals   Christian Scientists – *Citadel, Monitor*, Jehovah's Witnesses – *Watchtower*, Roman Catholics – *Tablet, Universe, Herald*; Salvation Army – *War Cry*.

Salvation Army   founded by William Booth (1865) as the New Christian Mission; name changed in 1878. Motto: Blood and Fire.

Seven Sorrows of Mary

1 The prophecy of Simeon (that a sword would pierce her soul).

2 The flight into Egypt.

3 The loss of the holy child in Jerusalem.

4 Meeting with the Lord on the road to Calvary.

5 The Crucifixion (when she stood at the foot of the cross).

6 The Deposition (taking down of Christ from the cross).

7 The Entombment (burial of Christ).

Shakers   founded by James Wardley and Jane Wardley (1747).

Shinto   founded in Japan in the eighth century AD and

divided into groups of which the best-known are Jinja and Kyoha.

The sacred texts are *Kojiki* and *Nihonshoki*.

Shinto literally means 'the teaching' or 'the way of the Gods'.

Sikhism   founded by the Guru Nanak in the fifteenth century; the holy book is the Adi Granth.

Society of Friends   founded by George Fox (1650); aka Quakers.

Society of Jesus   founded by Ignatius Loyola (1534).

Stations of the Cross   There are fourteen Stations of the Cross (aka Way of the Cross). They depict the final events in the Passion of Christ. Usually seen portrayed in churches but may also be found in cemeteries, hospitals and on mountainsides.

1 Jesus is condemned to death.

2 Jesus is made to bear his cross.

3 Jesus falls the first time.

4 Jesus meets his mother.

5 Simon of Cyrene is made to bear the cross.

6 Veronica wipes Jesus' face.

7 Jesus falls the second time.

8 Women of Jerusalem weep over Jesus.

9 Jesus falls the third time.

10 Jesus is stripped of his garments.

11 Jesus is nailed to the cross.

12 Jesus dies on the cross.

13 Jesus is taken down from the cross.

14 Jesus is placed in the sepulchre.

Ten Commandments   listed in Exodus and Deuteronomy.

1 Thou shalt have no other gods before me.

2 Thou shalt not make any graven images or likeness of anything in Heaven.

3 Thou shalt not take the name of the Lord thy God in vain.

4 Remember the Sabbath day, to keep it holy.

5 Honour thy father and thy mother.

6 Thou shalt not kill.

7 Thou shalt not commit adultery.

8 Thou shalt not steal.

9 Thou shalt not bear false witness against thy neighbour.

10 Thou shalt not covet thy neighbour's house, wife, manservant, ox or ass.

Unification Church   founded by the Reverend Sun Myung Moon (1954).

Visitation   the visit of the Virgin Mary to her cousin Elizabeth, mother of John the Baptist.

White Friars   Carmelites (mendicant order established c. 1155 and approved in 1226 by Pope Honorius III).

White Monks   Cistercians (founded in 1098).

R E L I G I O N

Archbishops of York

734	Egberht	928	Hrothweard	1041	Æthelric
767	Æthelberht	931	Wulfstan I	1051	Cynesige
780	Eanbald I	956	Osketel	1061	Ealdred
796	Eanbald II	971	Oswald	1070	Thomas I of Bayeux
808	Wulfsige	971	Edwald	1100	Gerard
837	Wigmund	992	Ealdwulf	1109	Thomas II
854	Wulfhere	1003	Wulfstan II	1119	Thurstan
900	Æthalbald	1023	Ælfric Puttoc	1143	William Fitzherbert

1147	Henry Murdac
1153	William Fitzherbert
1154	Roger of Pont l'Eveque
1191	Geoffrey Plantagenet
1215	Walter de Gray
1256	Sewal de Bovill
1258	Godfrey Ludham
1266	Walter Giffard
1279	William Wickwane
1286	John Romanus
1298	Henry Newark
1300	Thomas Corbridge
1306	William Greenfield
1317	William Melton
1342	William de la Zouche
1352	John Thoresby
1374	Alexander Neville
1388	Thomas Arundel
1396	Robert Waldby
1398	Richard le Scrope
1407	Henry Bowet
1426	John Kempe
1452	William Booth
1464	George Nevill

1476	Lawrence Booth
1480	Thomas Rotherham
1501	Thomas Savage
1508	Christopher Bainbridge
1514	Thomas Wolsey
1531	Edward Lee
1545	Robert Holgate
1555	Nicholas Heath
1561	Thomas Young
1570	Edmund Grindal
1577	Edwin Sandys
1589	John Piers
1595	Matthew Hutton
1606	Tobias Matthew
1628	George Montaigne
1629	Samuel Harsnett
1632	Richard Neile
1641	John Williams
1660	Accepted Frewen
1664	Richard Sterne
1683	John Dolben
1688	Thomas Lamplugh
1691	John Sharp
1714	William Dawes

1724	Lancelot Blackburn
1743	Thomas Herring
1747	Matthew Hutton
1757	John Gilben
1761	Roben Hay Drumond
1777	William Markham
1808	Edward Venables Vernon Harcourt
1847	Thomas Musgrave
1860	Charles Thomas Longley
1863	William Thomson
1891	William Connor Magee
1891	William Dalrymple Maclagan
1909	Cosmo Gordon Lang
1929	William Temple
1942	Cyril Forster Garbett
1956	Arthur Michael Ramsey
1961	Frederick Donald Coggan
1975	Stuart Yarwonh Blanch
1983	John Stapylton Habgood
1995	David Michael Hope

Patron Saints

accountants	Matthew
actors	Genesius, Vitus
advertising	Bernardino of Siena
airmen	Our Lady of Loretto, Theresa
animals	Francis of Assisi
archers	Sebastian
architects	Thomas, Barbara
Argentina	Our Lady of Lujan
army	Maurice
artists	Luke
astronauts	Joseph of Cupertino
astronomers	Dominic
athletes	Sebastian
Australia	Our Lady Help of Christians
Austria	Leopold
authors	Francis of Sales
bakers	Elizabeth of Hungary, Nicholas of Torentino, Zita
bankers	Matthew
barbers	Cosmas, Damian, Louis
bastards	John Francis Regis
battle	Archangel Michael
beekeepers	Ambrose
beggars	Martin of Tours
Belgium	Joseph
blacksmiths	Dunstan
Bolivia	Our Lady of Capucclana
bookkeepers	Matthew
booksellers	John of God
Brazil	Peter of Alcantara
brewers	Augustine of Hippo, Luke, Nicholas of Myra
bricklayers	Stephen
brides	Nicholas of Myra
bridges	John Nepomucen
broadcasters	Archangel Gabriel
Brussels	Michael
butchers	Anthony the Abbot, Luke, Adrian of Nicomedia
button-makers	Louis
builders	Vincent Ferrer, Barbara, Thomas
cab-drivers	Fiacre

Canada	Joseph, Anne (mother of Mary)
cancer victims	Peregrine Laziosi
caretakers	Joseph of Arimathea
candle-makers	Ambrose
cavalry	Martin of Tours
chaplains	John of Capistrano
charcoal burners	Alexander
childbirth	Gerard Majella, Margaret of Antioch
choirboys	Dominic Savio
church	Joseph
carpenters	Joseph
children	Nicholas
chorea	Vitus
civil servants	Thomas More
clergy	Gabriel Possenti
coffin bearers	Joseph of Arimathea
colleges	Thomas Aquinas
comedians	Vitus
condemned criminals	Dismas
cooks	Lawrence, Martha
craftsmen	Elegius
crippled	Giles
Cuba	Our Lady of Charity
Cyprus	Barnabas
Czech Republic	Wenceslas
dairy workers	Bridgid of Ireland
dancers	Vitus
deacons	Stephen
deaf	Francis of Sales
death	Archangel Michael, Margaret of Antioch
Denmark	Asgar/Canute
dentists	Apollonia
dieticians	Martha
disabled	Giles
disasters	Genevieve
doctors	Luke
domestics	Zita
Dominican Republic	Our Lady of Mercy
doubters	Thomas
drunkards	Martin of Tours
dyers	Maurice

earthquakes	Francis Borgia, Gregory the Wonderworker
ecologists	Francis of Assisi
eczema	Anthony the Abbot
Edinburgh	Giles
editors	John Bosco
Egypt	Mark
El Salvador	Our Lady of Peace
engineers	Patrick, Ferdinand III
England	George
epilepsy	Dympna, Vitus
Europe	Cyril, Benedict
examination candidates	Joseph of Cupertino
farmers	George, Isidore
fathers	Joseph
Finland	Henry
firemen	Florian
flying	Joseph of Cupertino
fishermen	Peter, Andrew
Florence	John the Baptist
florists	Dorothea, Therese
France	Denis
funeral directors	Joseph of Arimathea, Dismas
gardeners	Adelard, Phocas, Tryphon, Dorothea, Fiacre
Germany	Boniface
Glasgow	Kentigern (aka Mungo)
goldsmiths	Dunstan
gravediggers	Anthony, Joseph
Greece	Andrew, Nicholas, Paul
grocers	Michael
Guatemala	James the Greater
gunners	Barbara
haemorrhoids	Fiacre
hairdressers	Martin of Porres
Haiti	Our Lady of Perpetual Help
headaches	Teresa of Avila, Denis
heart patients	John of God
hernia sufferers	Cathal
Holland	Willibrord
horseriders	Martin of Tours
horses	Eligius, Hippolytus
hospitals	John of God, Camillus de Lellis, Vincent de Paul
hoteliers	Gentian, Amand
housewives	Anne, Martha, Zita
Hungary	Stephen
hunters	Eustace, Hubert
ice skaters	Edwina
Iceland	Olaf
India	Our Lady of the Assumption
infantrymen	Maurice
innkeepers	Amand, Martin of Tours, Gentian
Ireland	Patrick
Italy	Francis of Assisi
jewellers	Eligius (Eloi)
Jordan	John the Baptist
journalists	Francis of Sales
judges	John of Capistrano
jumping	Venantius
lame	Giles
lawyers	Genesius, Ivo, Thomas More
lepers	Giles
librarians	Jerome, Catherine of Alexandria
lighthouse keepers	Clement, Venerius
Lisbon	Vincent
London	Paul
lost articles	Anthony of Padua
lost causes	Jude
lovers	Valentine
Madagascar	Vincent de Paul

Madrid	Isidore
magistrates	Ferdinand III of Castile
Malta	Paul
marriage	John Francis Regis
masons	Thomas
mental illness	Dymphna
messengers	Archangel Gabriel
metalworkers	Anastasius, Eligius
Mexico	Joseph
midwives	Raymond Nonnatus
milliners	James the Greater
miners	Barbara, Anne (mother of Mary)
Moscow	Boris
motorcyclists	Our Lady of Grace
motorists	Christopher, Frances of Rome
motorways	John the Baptist
musicians/singers	Cecilia, Dunstan, Gregory
neurological disorders	Vitus
New Zealand	Our Lady Help of Christians
Norway	Olaf
numismatists	Eligius
nurses	Agatha, Raphael, Camillus of Lellis
orphans	Ivo of Kermartin
Oslo	Halivard
painters	Luke
Pakistan	Thomas, Francis Xavier
pallbearers	Joseph of Arimathea
Papua New Guinea	Archangel Michael
paralysed	Giles
paratroopers	Archangel Michael
Paris	Geneviève
pawnbrokers	Nicholas
perfumers	Nicholas of Myra
Peru	Joseph, Rose of Lima
pilots	Mary, Our Lady of Loreto
physicians	Luke
pig herders	Anthony
plasterers	Bartholomew
poets	Cecilia, David, Columbia
Poland	Stanislaus, Casimir
policemen	Michael
politicians	Thomas More
poor	Anthony of Padua, Lawrence
Portugal	George, Anthony
postal workers	Archangel Gabriel
pregnancy	Gerard Majella, Raymond Nonnatus
printers	Augustine of Hippo, John of God
prison officers	Hippolytus
quantity surveyors	Thomas
Quebec	John the Baptist
rabies victims	Hubert
radio	Archangel Gabriel
radiologists	Archangel Michael
Ripon	Wilfred
Rome	Peter
Russia	Andrew, Nicholas
sailors	Christopher, Cuthbert, Francis of Paolo, Dhocas
scholars	Bede, Bridgit, Jerome
scientists	Albert
Scotland	Andrew
scouts	George
sculptors	Claude
secretaries	Genesius
shoemakers	Crispin
singers	Gregory
skiers	Bernard of Montjoux
skin diseases	Anthony

RELIGION

soldiers	George, Joan of Arc, Sebastian
South Africa	Our Lady of the Assumption
Spain	James
speleologists	Benedict
stamp collectors	Archangel Gabriel
statesmen	Thomas More
students	Thomas Aquinas
surgeons	Cosmas, Damian
Sweden	Bridget, Eric
swimmers	Adjutor
Switzerland	Nicholas
tailors	Homobonus
tax collectors	Matthew
teachers	Catherine, Gregory
teenagers	Maria Goretti
telecommunications	Archangel Gabriel
telephone	Gabriel
television	Clare
thieves	Dismas
throat disorders	Blaise
toothache	Apollonia
travellers	Christopher
undertakers	Dismas
unmarried women	Nicholas of Myra
venereal disease	Fiacre
Venice	Mark
vets	Eligius (Eloi)
Vietnam	Joseph
volcanoes	Agatha
Wales	David
West Indies	Gertrude
wine merchants	Amand, Vincent
wine growers	Vincent
wool combers	Blaise
workers	Joseph
writers	Francis of Sales
yachtsmen	Adjutor

NB Almost everyone, everything and everywhere can be included under the auspices of a patron saint. Sometimes the affiliation lies in historical events and sometimes in ancient folklore and, more frequently still, homage is often paid to a particular saint for convenience, for example, cab-drivers call on St Fiacre as their protector because the Hotel St Fiacre in Paris was the first establishment to offer coaches for hire. Confusion often arises in this field as to why a particular saint has been adopted by a particular group. For example, St Martin of Tours is identified with innkeepers and drunks but is often depicted as a young mounted soldier. It should also be noted that many occupations have more than one recognised patron saint, and extra care should therefore be taken when compiling questions on this subject. For example, do not ask who is the patron saint of soldiers unless you are prepared to accept any of the three possible answers.

Archbishops of Canterbury

1	Augustine	597–604		37	Ralph d'Escures	1114–22
2	Lawrence (Laurentius)	604–619		38	William of Corbeil	1123–36
3	Mellitus	619–624		39	Theobald	1138–61
4	Justus	624–627		40	Thomas à Becket	1162–70
5	Honorius	627–653		41	Richard of Dover	1174–84
6	Deusdedit	655–664		42	Baldwin	1184–90
7	Theodore (Theodorus) of Tarsus	668–690		43	Hubert Walter	1193–1205
				44	Stephen Langton	1206–28
8	Berhtwald (Beorhtweald)	693–731		45	Richard le Grant	1229–31
9	Tatwine	731–734		46	Edmund Rich	1233–40
10	Nothelm	735–739		47	Boniface of Savoy	1241–70
11	Cuthbert (Cuthbeorht)	740–760		48	Robert Kilwardby	1272–78
12	Bregowine (Breguwine)	761–764		49	John Pecham	1279–92
13	Jaenberht (Jaenbeorht)	765–792		50	Robert Winchelsey	1293–1313
14	Aethelheard	793–805		51	Walter Reynolds	1313–27
15	Wulfred	805–832		52	Simon Mepham	1327–33
16	Feologild	832		53	John Stratford	1333–48
17	Ceolnoth	833–870		54	Thomas Bradwardine	1348–49
18	Aethelred	870–889		55	Simon Islip	1349–66
19	Piegmund	890–914		56	Simon Langham	1366–68
20	Aethelhelm	914–923		57	William Whittlesey	1368–74
21	Wulfhelm	923–942		58	Simon Sudbury	1375–81
22	Oda	942–958		59	William Courtenay	1381–96
23	Aelfsige	959		60	Thomas Arundel	1396–97
24	Beorhthelm	959		61	Roger Walden	1397–99
25	Dunstan	960–988		60	Thomas Arundel (restored)	1399–1414
26	Aethelgar	988–990		62	Henry Chichele	1414–43
27	Sigeric Serio	990–994		63	John Stafford	1443–52
28	Aelfric	995–1005		64	John Kempe	1452–54
29	Aelfheah	1005–12		65	Thomas Bourchier	1454–86
30	Lyfing	1013–20		66	John Morton	1486–1500
31	Aethelnoth	1020–38		67	Henry Deane	1501–03
32	Eadsige	1038–50		68	William Warham	1503–32
33	Robert of Jumièges	1051–52		69	Thomas Cranmer	1533–56
34	Stigand	1052–70		70	Reginald Pole	1556–58
35	Lanfranc	1070–89		71	Matthew Parker	1559–75
36	Anselm	1093–1109		72	Edmund Grindal	1575–83

73	John Whitgift	1583–1604		89	Charles Manners Sutton	1805–28
74	Richard Bancroft	1604–10		90	William Howley	1828–48
75	George Abbot	1611–33		91	John Bird Sumner	1848–62
76	William Laud	1633–45		92	Charles Thomas Longley	1862–68
77	William Juxon	1660–63		93	Archibald Campbell Tait	1868–82
78	Gilbert Sheldon	1663–77		94	Edward White Benson	1883–96
79	William Sancroft	1677–90		95	Frederick Temple	1896–1902
80	John Tillotson	1691–94		96	Randall Thomas Davidson	1903–28
81	Thomas Tenison	1694–1715		97	Cosmo Gordon Lang	1928–42
82	William Wake	1715–37		98	William Temple	1942–44
83	John Potter	1737–47		99	Geoffrey Francis Fisher	1945–61
84	Thomas Herring	1747–57		100	Arthur Michael Ramsey	1961–74
85	Matthew Hutton	1757–58		101	Frederick Donald Coggan	1974–80
86	Thomas Secker	1758–68		102	Robert Alexander Runcie	1980–90
87	Frederick Cornwallis	1768–83		103	George Carey	1990–2002
88	John Moore	1783–1805		104	Rowan Williams	2002–

Miscellaneous Information

Archbishop of Canterbury: 100th	Arthur Michael Ramsey
Archbishop: remained bishop	Stigand remained bishop of Worcester
Aristotle philosophies: taught at Oxford	Edmund of Abingdon: first to do so
Augustine landed: where	Isle of Thanet AD 597
buried	SS Peter and Paul (later St Augustine's), Canterbury
converted King	King Aethelbert of Kent
founded church	Christ Church Canterbury
order of monks	Benedictines
Roman prior of	St Andrews Benedictine monastery
welcomed by	King Aethelbert of Kent
Bishop of London	Richard Chartres (132nd) since 26 January 1996
Book of Common Prayer: drew up	Thomas Cranmer
born on Greek island	Frederick Temple
Carthusian monk	Boniface of Savoy
Catholic archbishop: last	Reginald Pole
Charles I: ministered on scaffold	William Juxon
Edmund Rich: also known as	Edmund of Abingdon
English-born archbishop: first	Berhtwald
Father and son: only holders	Frederick and William Temple
Henry Chichele: founded	St John's and All Souls colleges at Oxford 1437
heresy: convicted of	Thomas Cranmer (burned at stake)
high treason: accused of	William Laud (beheaded on Tower Hill)
investiture controversy: resolved by	Synod of Rockingham (temporarily)
Lambeth Conference	decennial meeting of Anglican bishops
Lanfranc: originally trained as	lawyer
secured Crown for	William II (Rufus)
Laurentius' dream	dream of St Peter reminded him of his mission
Lombardy: born	Lanfranc and Anselm
Maidstone Hospital: founder	Boniface of Savoy
married Oliver Cromwell's niece	John Tillotson 1664
Mellitus: prayer legend	caused wind to divert fire from Canterbury church
Morton's Fork:	rich pay taxes; poor are considered to be concealing wealth
murdered in Canterbury Cathedral	Thomas à Becket
murdered during Peasant's Revolt	Simon Sudbury (first beheading on Tower Hill)
nicknames: John Whitgift	Little black husband (by Elizabeth I)
Matthew Parker	Nosey Parker
official residence	Lambeth Palace, and Old Palace Canterbury
ordination of women	promulgated in the General Synod in Feb. 1994.
pallium	a mantle, and symbol of papal approval of archiepiscopal appointment
Piers Gaveston excommunicated by	Robert Winchelsey
plague: died of	Thomas Bradwardine
plot against William I: detected	Lanfranc
position created by	Pope Gregory I
Primate of	All England
prior of Bec Benedictine monastery	Lanfranc, Anselm, Theobald
Protestant archbishop: first	Thomas Cranmer
published *Antiquities of Greece*	John Potter
Queen Elizabeth II: crowned	Geoffrey Fisher
refused oath of allegiance	William Sancroft: to William and Mary
Repton School: former headmasters	William Temple and Geoffrey Fisher

RELIGION

Richard I: governor in absentia — Hubert Walter
Rochester: first bishop of — St Justus
Scholasticism: founder of — St Anselm
Sheldonian Theatre, Oxford: built — Gilbert Sheldon
son-in-law of Archbishop Tait — Randall Thomas Davidson
St Dunstan: secured crown for — St Edward the Martyr AD 975
Stigand: excommunicated by — Pope Nicholas II 1059. Uncanonical behaviour caused Pope to support William I's invasion
succeeded Thomas Arnold at Rugby — Archibald Campbell Tait
Synod of Whitby 663/664 — Northumbria decided to follow Roman Church
Tarsus: born in — Theodore
Theobald: patron of — Thomas à Becket, John of Salisbury, Vacarius
Thomas à Becket: also known as — Thomas of London
　　　　　　　　born — Cheapside, London
　　　　　　　　shrine despoiled by — Henry VIII
York: first bishop of — St Paulinus

The Bible

Genesis　God creates Adam from dust.
Garden of Eden planted.
Trees of Life and Knowledge.
Adam names all living beasts.
Eve is created from Adam's rib.
Serpent deceives Eve into eating forbidden fruit.
Birth of Cain and Abel.
Cain becomes tiller of the soil, and Abel a shepherd.
Cain kills Abel and when asked by the Lord as to his whereabouts replies, 'Am I my brother's keeper?'
Cain is 'marked' by God and flees to the land of Nod.
Cain's wife gives birth to a son, Enoch, and builds a city in his name.
Adam's third son Seth is fathered at the age of 130 and Adam dies at age 930.
Methuselah is sired by Enoch (descendant of Seth, not Cain) and lives for 969 years.
Methuselah sires Lamech who subsequently sires Noah.
Noah begets three sons: Shem, Ham, and Japheth. He was 500 years old.
God destroys man by bringing great flood but reprieves Noah.
Noah (aged 600) builds an ark of gopher wood (300 x 50 cubits, and 30 cubits high), three storeys in total.
God directs Noah to take aboard seven of each type of clean beast but just two of each unclean.
There were eight humans on the ark, i.e. Noah and his sons plus their wives.
Ark comes to rest on Mt Ararat.
Noah sends forth a raven and then a dove, which comes back with an olive leaf to show that the rains have ceased.
Noah becomes the first 'drunken man' after planting a vineyard.
Noah lives for 350 years after the flood and dies aged 950.
Noah's great grandson, Nimrod, begins to be a mighty one on the earth.
Nimrod's kingdom begins with Babel, Erech, Accad, Calneh and Shinar.
The whole earth is of one language, one speech.
After the tower of Babel is built, the Lord scatters the people abroad to confound their language.
The Lord calls unto Abram and blesses him.
Abram, with his wife Sarai and nephew Lot, journey into the land of Canaan.
Abram and Lot return from Egypt, after Sarai is taken by the Pharaoh.
Lot moves to live in Sodom, but the men of Sodom are wicked and sinners.
Then comes the 'Battle of the Kings'.
At the battle in the vale of Siddim, the kings of Sodom and Gomorrah are beaten and fall into slimepits.
Lot is taken prisoner by the victors.
Abram attacked at Hobah, and gains the release of Lot, all his goods, the women and the people.
Abram's wife Sarai cannot bear him children; she therefore gives Abram her maid Hagar, who bears him a child, Ishmael.
Abram is 86 years old when he fathers Ishmael.
The Lord renames Abram – Abraham.
The Lord makes a covenant with Abraham which states that every male child is to be circumcised at eight days old.
The Lord renames Sarai – Sarah.
At the age of 90, Sarah bears Abraham a son, Isaac.
Two angels come to see Lot at the gates of Sodom.
The men of Sodom are struck blind.
Lot, his wife and two daughters leave Sodom.
They are told not to look behind them.
Sodom and Gomorrah are destroyed by the Lord.
Lot's wife looks behind her and is turned into a pillar of salt.

Lot's two daughters get him drunk so that they may 'lie' with him to preserve his seed.

Lot's elder daughter has a son, Moab.

Lot's younger daughter also has a son called Ben-ammi.

Abraham tells Abimelech, king of Gerar, that Sarah is his sister, and she is taken by Abimelech.

Abraham casts Hagar and his son Ishmael away.

Abimelech makes a covenant with Abraham and returns to the land of the Philistines.

Abraham has his faith tested by the Lord.

Sarah dies at the age of 127.

A wife is sought for Isaac.

Abraham's servant finds and meets Rebekah.

Rebekah consents to go to Isaac; she then becomes his wife.

Abraham takes a second wife, Keturah.

Keturah bears him Zimran, Jokshan, Medan, Midian, Ishbak and Shuah.

Abraham dies aged 175.

Ishmael dies aged 137.

Ishmael has twelve sons – Nebajoth, Kedar, Adbeel, Mibsam, Mishma, Dumah, Massa, Hadar, Tems, Jetur, Naphish and Kedemah.

Rebekah gives birth to twins – Esau (a hunter) and Jacob (a tent-maker).

Esau sells his birthright to Jacob for a mess of pottage (bread and lentil stew).

Jacob deceives his father, Isaac, into believing that he is his brother Esau.

When Esau finds out about the deceit he threatens Jacob.

While searching for a wife, Jacob dreams of the ladder reaching from earth to the heavens.

Jacob dreams of the Angels of God ascending and descending on the ladder.

Jacob meets Rachel.

Jacob works for seven years in order to win Rachel.

Jacob takes both Rachel and her younger sister Leah as his wives.

Rachel is barren, but Leah bears Jacob a son, Reuben.

Leah later bears Simeon, Levi and Judah.

Rachel gives Jacob her handmaiden, Bilhah, to take as a wife.

Bilhah bears Dan and Naphtali.

Leah gives her maid, Zilpah, to Jacob to take as a wife.

Zilpah bears Gad and Asher.

Leah bears Jacob a fifth son, Issachar, a sixth, Zebulun, and a daughter, Dinah.

Rachel herself then conceives and bears a son, Joseph.

Jacob becomes very rich, with many cattle, maidservants, menservants, camels and asses.

Jacob has a vision at Mahanaim.

Jacob sends messengers to Esau, requesting his return to Laban.

Esau comes to meet him with 400 men.

Jacob sends a present to Esau of various animals.

When Jacob meets Esau, Jacob bows seven times.

Esau runs to meet Jacob, and embraces him. They both weep.

Jacob builds an altar at Shalem, and calls it El-elohe-Israel.

Dinah is defiled by Shechem, son of Hamor, the Hivite.

Simeon and Levi slay all the males of the city, and take Dinah from Shechem's house.

Jacob is unhappy with his sons, because the Canaanites and Perizzites will now rise against him.

God tells Jacob to move to Beth-el.

Jacob and his household journey to Beth-el, build an altar and call it El-beth-el.

Jacob is renamed Israel.

Rachel dies while giving birth to Benjamin.

While away from his household, Reuben lies with Bilhah, his father's concubine.

Jacob's sons now number twelve.

Jacob goes to his father, Isaac, at Hebron, where Isaac dies, aged 180.

Jacob favours Joseph over his brothers.

Joseph has dreams which cause his brothers to hate him.

At first Joseph's brothers plot to kill him.

Joseph's brothers sell him into slavery with the Ishmaelites.

The brothers dip Joseph's long garment in goat's blood, and take it to Jacob.

Jacob mourns his son's death.

Judah meets and takes the daughter of a Canaanite, named Shuah.

Shuah bears three sons: Er, Onan and Shelah.

Judah takes a wife for Er, whose name is Tamar.

Er displeases the Lord and He slays him.

Judah tells Onan to marry Tamar, his brother's widow.

Onan spills his seed on the ground; this displeases the Lord also and He slays Onan.

Judah tells Tamar to live in his house and wait until Shelah is grown.

Tamar deceives Judah into thinking she is a harlot.

When Judah hears that Tamar is pregnant, he orders her to be burnt.

She is spared when Judah realises he is the father of her child.

Tamar has twins, Pharez and Zarah.

Joseph is sold in Egypt to Potiphar, an officer of the Pharaoh.

Joseph is promoted to overseer.

Joseph's master's wife asks him to lie with her, but Joseph refuses.

She later pulls his garment off him and Joseph flees.
She lies to Potiphar, saying that Joseph came to her to force her to lie with him.
Joseph is imprisoned in the King's prison.
He interprets the dreams of the Pharaoh's officers.
After being in prison for two years, the Pharaoh has a dream and is told of Joseph.
Joseph interprets the Pharaoh's dream.
Joseph foretells the famine.
Joseph is released from prison and lives in the Pharaoh's house.
The famine is worldwide, but Egypt has stockpiled corn.
All the countries of the world come to Egypt to buy corn.
Jacob sends Joseph's brothers to Egypt to buy corn.
Joseph is now governor of the land.
His brothers come and bow before him.
Joseph recognises his brothers but they not him.
Joseph accuses his brothers of being spies.
Joseph supplies them with food and returns all their money to them.
At an inn the brothers realise that Joseph has returned their money.
Joseph insists that his brothers bring Benjamin to him.
Israel sends all the brothers to Egypt.
All the brothers are taken to Joseph's house for a feast.
Again Joseph fills their sacks with food and also returns their money.
Joseph puts his silver cup in the sack of Benjamin, the youngest brother.
Joseph's stewards find the silver cup and accuse the brothers of theft.
Judah petitions Joseph, asking that Benjamin be allowed to return to his father.
Joseph weeps and makes himself known to his brothers.
Pharaoh commands the brothers to bring back to Egypt all their families.
They tell Israel that Joseph is alive, but Israel does not believe them.
When Israel sees the wagons that Pharaoh has given to them, he believes.
Israel and his entire family return to Egypt to see Joseph.
Joseph meets his father at Goshen.
Israel is given Goshen by Pharaoh.
When people run out of money to buy bread, Joseph sells bread in exchange for livestock.
Joseph buys all the land of Egypt, except the land of the priests.
Joseph gives the people seed to grow their own crops.
The people must give one-fifth of their crops to Pharaoh.
Joseph takes his two sons, Manasseh and Ephraim, to Israel, where Israel blesses them.
Israel prophesies to his twelve sons, then dies, aged 147.
Israel insists that he be buried with his ancestors.
Pharaoh allows Joseph to travel to Canaan for the burial.
Afterwards Joseph and his brothers return to Egypt.
The brothers think that now Israel is dead, Joseph may seek retribution.
Joseph reassures them.
Joseph dies aged 110 and is buried in Egypt.

Exodus   Israel and his sons enter Egypt, each with his household.
Joseph is already in Egypt.
Their offspring multiply at an extraordinary rate until the land is filled with them.
A new king of Egypt becomes worried that the sons of Israel are growing so numerous.
The sons of Israel are oppressed.
The more they are oppressed, the more they multiply.
Eventually the Egyptians make the sons of Israel slaves.
The king of Egypt orders the Hebrew midwives, Shiphrah and Puah, to put to death any male child at birth.
Fearing God, the midwives disobey the Egyptian king.
Finally Pharaoh orders all his people to throw every newborn son into the River Nile.
A man from the house of Levi takes a daughter of Levi, and she becomes pregnant.
She conceals her son for three months.
She then places him in a basket, in the reeds, on the River Nile.
Pharaoh's daughter finds him, and realises he is a child of the Hebrews.
The child grows up and becomes a son to the daughter of Pharaoh.
She names him Moses.
Moses sees an Egyptian striking a Hebrew; he strikes the Egyptian down and kills him.
Pharaoh hears about it and tries to kill Moses.
Moses runs away to the land of Midian.
Moses meets the priest of Midian, who gives his daughter Zipporah to him.
Zipporah bears Moses a son, Gershom.
Moses becomes a shepherd.
While with the flock, Moses comes to Horeb. Here, an Angel appears to him in a flaming bush.
God speaks to Moses, instructing him to bring the sons of Israel out of Egypt.
Moses wants a sign that this is God.
God tells Moses to throw his rod on to the ground and it becomes a serpent.
God then tells Moses to grab the serpent by its tail, and it becomes a rod.
God gives Moses other signs, turning his hand into a leper's hand and restoring it and turning water from

the Nile into blood.

Moses meets Aaron, his brother.

Moses returns to Egypt with his wife and family.

Moses and Aaron meet with the elders of the sons of Israel.

Moses and Aaron meet with Pharaoh and ask that the Hebrews may go into the wilderness for a festival.

Pharaoh refuses permission for the Hebrews to go into the wilderness.

Pharaoh makes the sons of Israel work harder.

The officers of the sons of Israel blame Moses and Aaron for this harsh treatment.

Moses promises to deliver the sons of Israel from this oppression.

Moses and Aaron again meet with Pharaoh; Moses is now 80 years old and Aaron 83.

Aaron throws down his rod in front of Pharaoh and it becomes a serpent.

The magic-practising priests of Egypt do the same thing.

Aaron's rod swallows their rods.

Moses meets Pharaoh on the bank of the Nile, strikes the water with his rod and turns the water into blood.

The magic-practising priests proceed to do the same thing.

Moses tells Pharaoh that unless the people are allowed to go into the wilderness, there will be a plague of frogs. Aaron waves his staff over the Nile and a plague of frogs come to land.

The magic-practising priests do the same thing.

Aaron strikes the dust of Egypt, and it all becomes a swarm of gnats.

The magic practising priests attempts to do the same but they fail.

Moses tells Pharaoh that if the people are not released into the wilderness, gadfly will infest every house.

Gadfly infest every house in Egypt.

Finally Pharaoh calls Moses and Aaron and tells them to take their people into the wilderness.

The gadfly disappear, so Pharaoh does not allow the people to go into the wilderness.

Moses tells Pharaoh that if the people are not released, a pestilence will strike every animal in Egypt.

Moses takes a handful of soot, throws it in the air, in sight of Pharaoh, and it becomes boils and blisters upon man and beast.

The magic-practising priests are unable to attempt to copy this because the boils are affecting them.

Moses again goes to Pharaoh and promises a hailstorm that will kill every man and beast in the field .

The next day, a storm of hail, thunder and lightning strikes Egypt.

Pharaoh now calls Moses and Aaron and release the people to go into the wilderness.

Once the storm stops, Pharaoh again refuses to release the people into the wilderness.

Moses and Aaron see Pharaoh and tell him that a plague of locusts will appear tomorrow unless the people are released.

Locusts covers all of the land of Egypt.

Moses stretches out his arm and darkness falls all over Egypt.

The firstborn of every family in Egypt is threatened with death.

Instructions for the feast of the Passover are given to Moses by the Lord.

At midnight, the firstborn of every man and every beast dies.

Finally Pharaoh tells the people to leave.

The exodus takes place.

The people of Israel reach the Red Sea.

A pillar of cloud by daytime and a pillar of fire by night lead them into the wilderness.

Pharaoh proceeds to give chase when he realises that the people are escaping.

When Pharaoh reaches the people they are camped by the sea.

Moses stretches his hand over the sea and it parts, allowing the sons of Israel to walk through the Red Sea.

The Egyptians follows them into the Red Sea.

Moses again stretches his hand over the sea and the water returns to its normal state, drowning the Egyptians.

Moses leads the people into the wilderness for three days; they reach Marrah, but cannot drink the water because it is bitter.

The Lord directs Moses to a tree, which he throws into the water and the water becomes sweet.

At the wilderness of Sin, the sons of Israel begin to murmur against Moses and Aaron.

Quails arrive in the evening, and in the morning the wilderness is covered in bread.

By collecting double bread on the sixth day, and resting on the seventh, the Sabbath law is observed.

The sons of Israel eat the manna for 40 years.

At Massah, Moses is instructed to strike a stone with his rod, and water comes out of the rock.

The Amalekites attack the sons of Israel.

Moses instructs Joshua to choose men to go and fight the Amalekites.

Moses watches from the top of a hill.

When Moses lifts his rod, the Israelites are superior.

When Moses lowers his rod, the Amalekites are superior.

Moses' father-in-law, Jethro, along with his wife Zipporah, his two children, Gershom and Eliezer, and Moses' two sons, visits Moses in the wilderness.

Jethro adviseds Moses to appoint Judges.

Moses takes his advice.

The people go to meet their God on Mount Sinai.

The Lord calls Moses to the top of the mountain.

Moses then returns down the mountain to take Aaron back to the top with him.

Moses is given the Ten Commandments.

RELIGION

Rules on how slaves are treated, including 'eye for eye'.
Further rules covering theft, seduction, sorcery, bestiality, bribery and many more are given to Moses.
Three times a year the Israelites must celebrate a festival to the Lord.
Boundary of the 'promised land' is set, from the Red Sea to the Sea of the Philistines and from the wilderness to the river.
Moses goes up the mountain to receive the stone tablets.
Moses stays on the mountain for 40 days and 40 nights.
The people are instructed to build an ark of acacia wood, two and a half cubits in length, and one and a half cubits deep.
The ark must be overlaid with gold, both inside and outside.
The ark must have four gold rings, two either side.
The people must make two poles of acacia wood and overlay them with gold.
These poles go through the rings in order for the ark to be carried.
The poles must not be removed from the rings.
The commandments must be placed within the ark.
The people are instructed to build a tabernacle, with all its utensils.
The design of the garments to be worn by priests is given to Moses.
Instructions for the installation of priests are given.
Instructions for keeping the Sabbath are given.
When the Lord finishes speaking with Moses on Mount Sinai, he gives to Moses two tablets of stone.
The people are frustrated because Moses is on Mount Sinai for so long.
The people persuade Aaron to make a 'God' for them.
After melting down the people's jewellery, he makes a golden calf.
The making of the golden calf angers the Lord.
When Moses sees the golden calf, he is so angry he smashes the two tablets and destroys the golden calf.
Moses seeks out the loyal people and the sons of Levi gather themselves to him.
Moses sends the sons of Levi back into the camp to kill the sinners; they kill about 3,000.
Moses moves his tent outside the camp and calls it a tent of meeting.
Whenever Moses enters the tent, a pillar of cloud descends and stands at the entrance.
The Lord instructs Moses to carve out two tablets of stone and the Lord will rewrite the commandments.
The Lord will not allow Moses to see his face.
The Lord repeats the terms of the covenant between himself and the people of Israel.
Moses again comes down from Mount Sinai with the two tablets.
The people contribute gifts to the Lord.
Bezalel and Oholiab are selected for special teachings and wisdom.
The people begin to make the cloth and other finery for the tabernacle.
Once completed, the Lord's glory fills the tabernacle.

Leviticus Instructions for offerings of animals and grain are given to the people of Israel.
All grain offerings must be seasoned with salt.
A young bull must be sacrificed for a sin of a priest.
A young goat must be sacrificed for a sin of a chieftain.
Other sins demand other offerings.
Even unintentional sins must be paid for with offerings.
The eating of fat or blood is forbidden.
Aaron and his sons are installed as priests.
Nadab and Abihu, sons of Aaron, make an offering to the Lord that was not prescribed.
Fire from heaven consumes both.
Instructions as to which animals and fish are clean or unclean are given.
Instructions for the purification of women are given.
Priests are to make leprosy tests; anybody with leprosy is declared unclean.
Garments worn by lepers are also unclean.
Instructions for offerings in the case of a cleansed leper are given.
Uncleanliness in the case of male and female discharges is explained.
Atonement Day procedures are given.
The laws regarding incest are given.
Similarly laws regarding sodomy and bestiality are given.
Laws regarding gleaning of crops are given.
Laws regarding slander, interbreeding, fruit trees and magic are given.
Similarly, laws regarding spiritism, respect of parents and adultery are given.
The law that priests are to be undefiled is explained.
Laws regarding Sabbath, Pentecost, Day of Atonement, festival of Booths and loaves of showbread explained.
The fiftieth year is to become a Jubilee.
The Jubilee year is also a year of restorations. For example, if a man sells his house, he must repurchase it in the fiftieth year.
Laws regarding the help to be given to the poor are explained.
Regarding the poor, money given must bear no usury or interest charges.
No idols or images of the Lord are to be worshipped.
The Lord explains the blessings that the people will enjoy if they keep his laws and commandments.
The Lord explains the chastisements that the people will suffer if they do not keep his laws and commandments.

Values are put on sanctifying your soul, animal, house, field, etc. to the Lord.

Numbers   (Numbers is Bemidbar in Hebrew and means 'In the wilderness'.)
The Lord tells Moses to register every male over 20 years of age.
The Lord also names the assembly; all are chieftains of the tribes of Israel.
The tribes are registered for the army.
All are registered except the Levites.
Moses is told to appoint the Levites over the tabernacle and all the utensils.
When the people set up camp, each tribe must camp with its (three-tribe) division.
Each tribe is designated a place to camp, starting with the (three-tribe) division of Judah eastmost.
The other tribes are designated a place in camp working westwards.
The tribe of Levi must minister to Aaron, and must keep their obligation to him.
Moses registers all the male Levites from the age of one month upwards.
Each of the families of Levi are given a task to perform regarding the tabernacle and the utensils.
Following instructions from Moses, all lepers, persons with discharges and anyone unclean are sent out of the camp.
A water test is explained, to test for jealousy.
If a man or woman takes a special vow to live as a Nazirite, they must stay away from grapes, wine and intoxicating liquor.
Also during the time of living as a Nazirite, no razor should touch a hair.
The further rules of the special vows of living as a Nazirite are explained.
The wording of the Lord's blessing is given to Moses. It is: May the Lord bless you and keep you, May the Lord make his face shine toward you and may he favour you, May the Lord lift up his face toward you and assign peace to you.
Having had all the laws and commandments explained to him, Moses now anoints the tabernacle.
All the chieftains make offerings of grain and cattle, of silver bowls, of other animals, which Moses accepts.
These offerings continue for eleven days.
On the twelfth day an offering by Naphtali is made; this is the inaugural offering at the altar.
The Lord tells Moses to instruct Aaron to light the seven lamps.
Moses is instructed to take the Levites among the people and cleanse them.
Instructions for the cleansing are given.
The Lord explains to Moses the preparation for the Passover.
The Lord instructs Moses to make two trumpets of silver.
These are to be used for convening the assembly or breaking up the camp.
If one trumpet is blown, the chieftains meet with Moses.
If two trumpets are blown, the whole assembly must meet with Moses.
On the twentieth day of the second month, of the third year, the cloud lifts and the people begin to leave the wilderness.
Moses asks Hobab to join the people going to Israel, but Hobab says that he wants to return to his own people.
Moses pleads with Hobab, and he joins Moses and the people.
Some of the people begin to complain about being in the wilderness.
This angers the Lord, and He sends down fire.
The people begin to cry for meat and fish.
Moses asks the Lord for help, because he feels he cannot cope.
The Lord tells Moses to select 70 of the oldest men, take them to the meeting tent, and He will place some of the spirit on them.
The spirit also falls on Eldad and Medad, who were not in the meeting tent, and they begin acting as prophets.
A wind blows quails from the coast to the camp.
Those people who showed selfish craving are slaughtered by the Lord.
Miriam and Aaron begin opposing Moses.
The Lord tells Moses to take Miriam and Aaron to the meeting tent, where He will speak with them.
The Lord is so angry that Miriam is struck with leprosy.
Moses pleads for mercy, and after seven days in quarantine, she is allowed back into the camp.
Moses sends out a man from each tribe, each a chieftain, to spy out the land of Canaan.
After 40 days they return to Moses; ten spies give bad reports.
The people begin to rebel.
The Lord is very angry that the people do not respect Him; He tells Moses that He will strike them with pestilence.
Moses pleads on their behalf.
The punishment for rebellion is to remain in the wilderness for 40 years.
Some of the people decide to leave the camp without Moses and the ark.
These people are defeated by the Amalekites and Canaanites.
Moses is instructed to tell the people of Isreal how they must render up burnt offerings on entering the promised land.
Moses is instructed to tell the people how they must atone for a sin by mistake.
Anyone who commits a deliberate sin must die.
A man collecting pieces of wood on the Sabbath is stoned to death.
Korah, Dathan and Abiram, together with 250 rebels, rise against Moses.
All the rebels are instructed to attend a meeting, each carrying a fire holder.

The earth swallows up Korah, Dathan and Abiram, their households and anything belonging to them.
A fire comes from the Lord and consumes the 250 rebels.
Some of the people still complain, so the Lord brings forth a scourge on them.
Moses tells Aaron to go among them and atone for their sins.
This Aaron does, and eventually stops the scourge.
This scourge kills 14,700 people.
A rod is taken from each of the twelve houses of Israel, placed in the meeting tent, and the Lord chooses
     one rod to bud.
Aaron's rod, for the house of Levi, has budded.
The Lord explains to Aaron the obligations of Levi.
Moses is instructed again regarding cleansing, especially regarding a man who dies in a tent.
The people move into the wilderness of Zin.
Here Miriam dies and is buried.
The people now have no water and reproach Moses and Aaron.
The Lord instructs Moses to strike a rock and water will come forth.
Moses strikes the rock twice and water enough for all the people and beasts comes forth.
These waters are called the Waters of Meribah.
Moses sends messengers to the king of Edom, to seek permission to pass through his land.
The king of Edom refuses.
The people turn away and travel to Mount Hor.
On Mount Hor, Moses strips Aaron of his clothes and places them on Eleazar (Aaron's son).
Aaron then dies.
The people weep for Aaron for 30 days.
The Canaanite king of Arad begins to attack the people and takes some captives.
The Lord intervenes and strikes down the Canaanites.
The people continue to trek around the land of Edom, but are not happy.
Some of the people rebel, so the Lord sends poisonous serpents among them and many die.
Moses is instructed to make a copper serpent and place it on a pole.
Anyone who was bitten by the serpents will look at the copper serpent and will live.
Moses sends messengers to Sihon, king of the Amorites, requesting permission to pass through his land.
Sihon refuses, and gathers his people and begins to fight the Israelites at Jahaz.
Sihon is defeated and the Israelites take possession of his land.
The Israelites now attack Ogm, the king of Bashan; they defeat him and take possession of his land.
Moab now grows very frightened of the Israelites.
Balak, the king of Moab, sends messengers to Balaam.
Balaam refuses to help.
Balak sends more messengers, more important messengers than at first.
Balaam goes with them to Balak, but on the journey meets with the Lord's angel, which only Balaam's
     she-ass sees.
Balaam beats his she-ass, and passes by the angel by walking in a field.
The angel reappears at a narrow place; again only Balaam's she-ass sees the angel.
Balaam beats his she-ass and he passes the angel by walking alongside the wall.
The angel reappears at a place where he cannot pass by; the she-ass lies down in the road.
Balaam beats his she-ass again.
The Lord makes the she-ass speak.
She asks Balaam, 'Why have you beaten me three times?'
Balaam says that if he had a sword he would have killed her.
The angel appears to Balaam and asks why he beats his she-ass.
Balaam continues his journey to Moab.
Balaam begins to speak the words that the Lord has put into his mouth.
He orders Balak to build seven altars.
He also orders him to provide seven bulls and seven rams.
A bull and a ram are offered on each altar.
Balaam refuses to help Balak.
Balaam proceeds to utter four proverbial statements, all the word of the Lord.
Balak is foiled.
Israel abides in Shittim and the people begin to commit whoredom with the daughters of Moab.
Israel joins himself unto Baal-peor and the anger of the Lord is blazed against him.
The Lord tells Moses to take the heads of the people and hang them up before him.
Zimri, a child of Israel, brings a Midianite woman into the sight of Moses.
Phinehas, son of Eleazar, son of Aaron, pierces both the man and woman and the plague is scourged.
The Lord tells Moses to vex the Midianites and smite them.
After the plague the Lord tells Moses and Eleazar to take the children of Israel, from 20 years
     onwards, out of Egypt.
Reuben and his descendants, numbering 250, are swallowed by the earth and become a sign.
The sons of Korah do not die.
Census is taken of eight more tribes and the land is divided.
Josnua is appointed to succeed Moses.
The procedures for various feast days and solemn days are established.
Moses equips an army to slay the Midianites.
The Lord speaks to Moses on the plains of Moab, by the Jordan at Jericho, and tells him to dwell in
     Canaan.

Deuteronomy	The fifth book of the Old Testament is written in the form of a farewell address by Moses to the Israelites before they enter the Promised Land of Canaan. The speeches recall Israel's past, reiterate laws and emphasise that observance of these laws is essential for the well-being of the people. The title Deuteronomy derives from the Greek meaning 'copy', although the Hebrew translation means 'words'.
Joshua	The book of Joshua was written while the people of Israel were exiles in Babylonia. It can be divided into three sections, i.e. the conquest of Canaan, the distribution of the land and Joshua's farewell address and death. This book contains the destruction of the Wall of Jericho.
Judges	The book of Judges was written at about the same time as the book of Joshua and the Judges were the leaders of Israel. Noteworthy events are the death of Joshua and the birth and death of Samson.
Ruth	The central character is a Moabite woman who marries the son of a Judaean couple living in Moab. Ruth moves to Judah with her mother-in-law, Naomi, and becomes the wife of Boaz. She bears Obed, the grandfather of David, although these events are thought to be doubtful.
Samuel, first book	Samuel anoints Saul as the first King of Israel and the book tells further of the exploits of his son Jonathan. The book continues with the story of David conquering Goliath and his great friendship with Jonathan. The book concludes with Abigail giving good counsel to David, Saul visiting the Witch of Endor, and the ultimate death of both Saul and Jonathan on Mount Gilboa.
Samuel, second book	David is anointed king at age 30. He rules for a further 40 years. David commits adultery with Bathsheba, the wife of Uriah the Hittite, and plots his death so he can marry her himself. The Lord sends Nathan, the anointer of David, to reprove him for his deed by telling him a parable of a ewe lamb. The Lord takes the life of the first-born of David and Bathsheba as penance. David and Bathsheba soon have another child, Solomon, and he is loved by the Lord. David's son Absalom plots the death of his brother Amnon, for forcing his sister Tamar. Absalom is killed during the civil war and is mourned by David.
Kings, first book	Zadok the Priest anoints Solomon as king. David eventually dies. The Lord appears to Solomon in a dream and grants a request and is pleased that he asks for wisdom. Solomon builds a great temple as a place of worship to the Lord and also a great house for himself. Queen of Sheba visits King Solomon and is impressed by his demeanour and they exchange gifts. Solomon's heart moves away from the Lord in his old age and he is told the kingship will be removed from his son. Solomon dies and is succeeded by his son, Rehoboam. The Lord's words come true as Jeroboam replaces Rehoboam as king of all Israel except Judah. The divided kingdom of Israel is eventually ruled by Ahab, son of Omri. Ahab takes Jezebel for a wife and sets up an altar to Baal in Samaria. Elijah the Tishbite informs Ahab there will be a drought and indeed no rain falls for 3½ years. Ahab tries to buy the vineyard of Naboth the Jezreelite but is refused. Ahab's wife Jezebel plots the death of Naboth to gain possession of his vineyard. Ahab is slain in battle with the Syrians.
Kings, second book	Elijah is taken up into heaven by a whirlwind and is succeeded by his pupil, Elisha. Jezebel is thrown out of a window and killed. Elisha dies and is buried; a dead man laid on his bones comes to life. The Lord is incensed by the Israelites and removes them, leaving only the tribe of Judah. Nebuchadnezzar II, the king of Babylon, destroys Jerusalem.
Chronicles, first book	The first book of Chronicles details genealogies from Adam up to and including the reign of David. The chronicler used the books of Samuel and Kings as his main source, although modifications were made.
Chronicles, second book	The second book of Chronicles details the reign of Solomon to the end of the Babylonian exile. The chronicler has ignored the northern kingdom of Samaria.
Ezra	Ezra continues the history of Israel from the end of the Babylonian exile. The chronicler details the rising of the Persian Empire from its first king, Cyrus the Great.
Nehemiah	The chronicler continues the story of Israel in the time of another Jewish leader, Nehemiah, who was released from captivity in *c.* 444 BC, during the reign of Artaxerxes, king of Persia. The rebuilding of Jerusalem is highlighted and the great wall is built.

R
E
L
I
G
I
O
N

Esther
Esther is the Jewish wife of the Persian King Ahasuerus (Xerxes I).
Esther persuades the king to retract an order for the general annihilation of Jews throughout the Empire.
The book explains how the feast of Purim came to be celebrated by the Jews, although the story is largely apocryphal.

Job
The book of Job is written in the form of a series of speeches whereby Job disputes with three friends and the Lord.
Job proclaims his innocence and injustice of his suffering while his friends (Job's comforters) blame his sin.
Job personifies poverty and patience.

Psalms
The book of Psalms consists of 150 sacred poems, which are meant to be sung.
Usually divided into five sections, i.e. psalms 1–41, 42–72, 73–89, 90–106, 107–150.
The best-known psalm is no. 23, 'The Lord is my Shepherd'.
Psalm 51 is often called the 'Neck' verse as its recitation would save the neck of those claiming Benefit of Clergy.
Although the authors are of doubtful origin, 73 psalms are attributed to David.

Proverbs
Book of wisdom with moral and ethical relevance, in a similar vein to the book of Job but with more finite thoughts.
At the start of the text the proverbs are attributed to Solomon but it is known that many of them were written after his time.

Ecclesiastes
Another book of wisdom, which takes a fatalistic view of life and asks man not to question God's love.
Once again the book alludes to Solomon as being the author, but this is doubtful because of chronologies in the text.

Song of Solomon
Collection of love poems spoken alternately by a man and a woman.
This book is the festival scroll for Passover, which celebrates the Exodus of the Israelites from Egypt.
The authorship is unknown and Solomon's name was added at a later date.

Isaiah
The prophet Isaiah, son of Amos, reflects on the blasphemy of his people in the eyes of the Lord.
Isaiah calls for a return to the worship of the Lord and talks of 'beating swords into ploughshares'.
Isaiah talks further of peace and his vision of the wolf residing with the lamb.
Isaiah's prophecy of the falling of Babylon comes true.

Jeremiah
The Judaean prophet Jeremiah lived during the reign of King Josiah and his ministry lasted until the Babylonian conquest.
Chapters 1–25 consist of prophecies against Judah and Jerusalem.
Chapters 26–45 consist of narratives about Jeremiah and may have been composed by Baruch.
Chapters 46–51 consist of prophecies against foreign nations and chapter 52 is a historical appendix.

Lamentations
The poems are laments over the destruction of Judah, Jerusalem and the Temple by the Babylonians in 586 BC.
Lamentations is often called 'Lamentations of Jeremiah', although authorship is uncertain.

Ezekiel
The prophet Ezekiel was active during the first quarter of the sixth century BC.
The book was written in exile and is valuable for understanding the lives of exiles in Babylon.

Daniel
Daniel interprets Nebuchadnezzar's dream.
Nebuchadnezzar throws Shadrach, Meshach and Abednego into a fiery furnace but the Lord sends an angel to help them.
Belshazzar holds a feast and Daniel interprets the writing on the wall, 'mene, mene, tekel, parsin'.
The interpretation means that the Lord has numbered the days of the Babylonian kingdom and it is to be divided.
King Darius reluctantly throws Daniel into the lions' den but the Lord sends an angel to help Daniel

Hosea
The last twelve books of the Old Testament bear the name of the minor prophets and are sometimes known as 'the Twelve'.
The first chapter is a biographical report of the prophet Hosea's marriage to Gomer, a harlot.
A similar marriage is described in Chapter 3, which is thought to allude to the Lord's love for Israel.

Joel
Joel reiterates the concept that salvation will come to Judah and Jerusalem only when the people turn to the Lord.

Amos
Amos, a Judaean prophet from Tekoa, was active during the reign of Jeroboam II.
Most of the chapters form a collection of individual sayings and reports of visions.
Much of the rest of the text is by way of a moral judgement on the rich and self-indulgent.

The book ends with a promise of restoration for Israel.

Obadiah
Shortest book of the Bible, with one chapter of 21 verses.
The book announces that the Day of Judgement is nigh for all nations and that Jews will be restored to their native land.

Jonah
The book of Jonah recounts the story of the prophet.
The Lord calls for Jonah to go to the Assyrian city of Nineveh to prophesy.
Jonah is concerned that the city will repent and be forgiven, and tries to escape his bidding.
Jonah is caught in a storm at sea while escaping and is thrown overboard at his own request.
The Lord appoints a great fish to swallow Jonah and he remains in the fish's maw for three days and nights.
Jonah prays for deliverance and is vomited out of the fish and once again told to go to Nineveh.
Jonah becomes angry as his fears of repentance are realised and he sits outside the city awaiting its destruction.
A plant springs up overnight to give him shelter from the heat but it is destroyed by a great worm.
Jonah is bitter about the destruction but the Lord chastises him for his care for a plant rather than people.

Micah
The Judaean prophet Micah was active during the last half of the eighth century BC.
Micah's threats and promises are a reiteration of many of the other minor prophets.

Nahum
The book is an oracle concerning Nineveh and is attributed to the vision of Nahum of Elkosh.
The fall of the city of Nineveh is the theme of the prophetic oracle.

Habakkuk
Similar to the book of Nahum; it is written in a liturgical style and portrays a moral theme.

Zephaniah
The dominant theme of the book is the 'Day of the Lord', which the prophet sees as imminent due to the sins of Judah.
The 'Humble' and 'Lowly' will be saved through purification by judgement.

Haggai
The book comprises four prophecies delivered over a four-month period in the second year of the reign of Darius I.

Zechariah
Chapters 1–8 contain the prophecies of Zechariah; the rest of the book is of unknown attribution.
Zechariah was active from 520 to 518 BC and was a contemporary of Haggai.
He shared the concern of Haggai that the Temple of Jerusalem must be rebuilt.

Malachi
Last of the twelve Old Testament books that bear the name of the minor prophets and, indeed, the last book of the OT.
The book comprises four chapters, each in the form of a question-and-answer discussion.
Malachi was probably written in the first half of the fifth century BC and its authorship is unknown.

NB The first five books of the Old Testament are usually called the Pentateuch, or Books of Moses. The contents of the first four of these books have been catalogued in the order that the events took place in the text of the Bible. The remaining books have important events highlighted but have no other great detail about them. The New Testament has been dealt with in a similar manner. The author does not wish to upset any religious denomination and it should be noted that texts can differ slightly from Bible to Bible. There are 39 books of the Old Testament and 27 of the New Testament, totalling 66 in all.

New Testament

Matthew
The first of the four New Testament Gospels recounting the life and death of Jesus Christ.
Matthew, Mark and Luke are known as Synoptic Gospels, as they share a similar general view.
The Gospel was composed in Greek c. AD 70 and is traditionally attributed to the Apostle Matthew the tax-collector.
Chapters 5–7 describe Jesus's Sermon on the Mount, which includes the Beatitudes and the Lord's Prayer.

Mark
The Gospel is attributed to John Mark (Acts 12:12; 15:37), a disciple of Peter and associate of Paul.
Mark is the shortest and earliest of the four Gospels and was probably used by Matthew and Luke to compose their accounts.
More than 90 per cent of the content of Mark's Gospel appears in Matthew's and more than 50 per cent in the Gospel of Luke.

Luke
Luke was known as the beloved physician and was a close associate of the Apostle Paul.
Luke gives details of Jesus' infancy and the Ascension as well as Caesar Augustus' census.
Parables include the Good Samaritan and the Prodigal Son.

John
John was known as the beloved disciple of Jesus.

RELIGION

John's Gospel covers a different time span than the others, concentrating on Jesus' ministry in Judea.

John's account differs in that it does not record many of the symbolic acts of Jesus but rather portrays Jesus as God's son.

Acts of the Apostles

Acts was traditionally written by Luke, whose Gospel concludes where Acts begins, that is, with Christ's Ascension into heaven.

The early chapters describe the descent of the Holy Spirit on the Apostles at Pentecost, which was the birth of the Church.

Chapter 3 describes Peter's healing of a lame man and chapter 5 the death of Ananias for his false tongue.

Chapter 7 describes the stoning of Stephen.

Chapter 9 describes the healing of Aeneas by Peter and the conversion of Saul to Paul on the road to Damascus.

Chapters 27 and 28 describe Paul's shipwreck in Malta and his successful teaching in Rome.

The underlying theme is the spreading of Christianity to the Gentile world under the influence of the Holy Spirit.

Romans

The proper and full title of this book is 'The Epistle of Paul the Apostle to the Romans'.

The book was probably composed at Corinth in c. AD 57 and was addressed to the Christian Church at Rome.

The letter is largely a morality and cautionary tale but is considered important in Lutheran teaching.

Corinthians, first book

The proper and full title of this book is 'The First Letter of Paul the Apostle to the Corinthians'.

Written c. AD 53 at Ephesus, Asia Minor, and addresses the problems of the early years of the Church.

Paul begins his letter with a reminder that all are servants of Christ and stewards of the mysteries of God.

Paul goes on to address questions of immorality, marriage and celibacy as well as the worthy reception of the Eucharist.

In chapter 13 Paul explains that no gift of God has meaning unless accompanied by love.

Corinthians, second book

The proper and full title of this book is 'The Second Letter of Paul the Apostle to the Corinthians'.

Written c. AD 55 in Macedonia, possibly after an unsatisfactory visit by Paul to Corinth.

Paul urges the Corinthians to assist the poor of Jerusalem and is gratified when Titus reveals their repentance.

Galatians

The proper and full title of this book is 'The Letter of Paul the Apostle to the Galatians'.

In this book, Paul defends his credentials as a true Apostle of Jesus Christ.

Ephesians

The proper and full title of this book is 'The Letter of Paul the Apostle to the Ephesians'.

Traditionally supposed to have been written while Paul was in prison, but this is doubtful.

The text is in the form of an affirmation that there is one Lord, one faith, one baptism, one God and father of us all.

Philippians

The proper and full title of this book is 'The Letter of Paul the Apostle to the Philippians'.

There is more evidence that this letter was in fact written by Paul in prison (c. AD 62) than in the case of his letter to the Ephesians.

His address to the Macedonian people was probably stirred by thoughts of his own mortality as he pondered execution.

Colossians

The proper and full title of this book is 'The Letter of Paul the Apostle to the Colossians'.

Addressed to Christians at Colossae, Asia Minor, whose congregation was founded by Epaphras.

The letter is in the form of a reminder of God's love and a call for repentance for their wayward ways.

Thessalonians, first book

The proper and full title of this book is 'The First Letter of Paul the Apostle to the Thessalonians'.

First letter was written after his co-worker, Timothy, returned from Thessalonia to report that the new converts were steadfast.

Thessalonians, second book

The proper and full title of this book is 'The Second Letter of Paul the Apostle to the Thessalonians'.

The second letter explains that the final day will not come until after the Antichrist appears and proclaims himself God.

Timothy, first book

The proper and full title of this book is 'The First Letter of Paul the Apostle to Timothy'.

The book deals with Church administration and the growth of heresies.

Timothy, second book

The proper and full title of this book is 'The Second Letter of Paul the Apostle to Timothy'.

The letter urges Timothy to 'guard the truth that has been entrusted to you by the Holy Spirit'.

The letter urges Timothy to visit soon, although the writer believes he is 'on the point of being sacrificed'.

Titus	The proper and full title of this book is 'The Letter of Paul the Apostle to Titus'. Titus was a close friend of Paul and was the organiser of the Church in Crete. The letter urges Titus to appoint worthy elders to positions of responsibility and to preach sound doctrine. The letter also warns against the disruptive influence of 'Jewish myths', especially those of the 'circumcision party'.
Philemon	The proper and full title of this book is 'The Letter of Paul the Apostle to Philemon'. The letter was written to Philemon, a wealthy Christian from Colossae, on behalf of Onesimus, Philemon's former slave.
Hebrews	The proper and full title of this book is 'The Letter of Paul the Apostle to the Hebrews'. The letter was addressed to a Christian community whose faith was faltering because of strong Jewish influences. The author concludes that Christianity is superior to Judaism.
James	The letter of James, a Christian Jew, is a moralistic reflection on early Jewish Christianity. The letter covers topics such as cursing, boasting, oaths, prayers, poverty and endurance under persecution.
Peter, first book	The first letter urges persecuted Christians to emulate the suffering Christ in their distress. He reminded them that after his Passion and death, Jesus rose from the dead and is now in glory.
Peter, second book	The second letter is principally concerned with the Second Coming of Christ. Peter also warns against false teachers, whose conduct is as immoral as their words are deceptive.
John, first book	The John in question is the disciple John the Evangelist, son of Zebedee. His first letter urges the Christian community to repudiate heretical teachings.
John, second book	The writer of both the second and the third letters calls himself 'presbyter', i.e. elder.
John, third book	Addressed to a certain Gaius and complaining of Diotrephes, who lies to put himself first.
Jude	The letter of Jude, brother of James and a servant of Jesus Christ, warns against false gods.
Revelation	The proper and full title of this book is 'The Revelation of St John the Divine'. Attributed to John, the beloved disciple, and possibly written at Patmos in the Aegean Sea. The number 7 is used in a symbolic sense to represent totality or perfection. Chapter 6 describes the Four Horsemen of the Apocalypse. Chapter 7 describes the 12 tribes of Israel, which were sealed 12,000 of each, totalling 144,000. Chapter 13 gives the number of the beast, i.e. 666. Chapter 14 describes the 144,000 virgins who will have their place in heaven.

RELIGION

SCIENCE

Chemical Elements

Name	Symbol	No.	Name source	Discovered or isolated by
actinium	Ac	89	beam	André-Louis Debierne 1899
aluminium	Al	13	alum	Hans Christian Oersted 1825
americium	Am	95	America	Glenn Seaborg, Ralph James, Leon Morgan and Albert Ghiorso at the University of Chicago 1944
antimony	Sb	51	antimonium	known to the ancients, its extraction from stibnite was first discovered by Basil Valentine c.1450, although its properties were first described by Nicholas Lémery in 1707
argon	Ar	18	inactive	Lord Rayleigh and W Ramsay 1894
arsenic	As	33	yellow orpiment	Albertus Magnus in the 13th century
astatine	At	85	unstable	Berkeley University, California, 1940
barium	Ba	56	heavy	Humphry Davy 1808
berkelium	Bk	97	university	Berkeley University, California, 1949
beryllium	Be	4	beryl	Nicolas Louis Vauquelin 1797
bismuth	Bi	83	uncertain	Basil Valentine 1450
boron	B	5	Arabic, buraq	Gay-Lussac, Thenard and Davy 1808
bromine	Br	35	stench	Antoine-Jérôme Balard 1826
cadmium	Cd	48	zinc ore	Friedrich Stromeyer 1817
caesium	Cs	55	silvery white	Robert Bunsen and G Kirchhoff 1860
calcium	Ca	20	lime	Humphry Davy 1808
californium	Cf	98	California	Berkeley University, California, 1950
carbon	C	6	charcoal	prehistoric
cerium	Ce	58	asteroid Ceres	Hisinger, Klaproth and Berzelius 1803
chlorine	Cl	17	greenish yellow	Humphry Davy 1810
chromium	Cr	24	colour	Nicolas Louis Vauquelin 1797
cobalt	Co	27	goblin	Georg Brandt 1735
copper	Cu	29	Cyprus	prehistoric
curium	Cm	96	Pierre and Marie Curie	Berkeley University, California, 1944
dysprosium	Dy	66	hard to get at	P E Lecoq de Boisbaudran 1886
einsteinium	Es	99	Einstein	Albert Ghiorso, Berkeley 1952
erbium	Er	68	Ytterby (Sweden)	Carl Gustav Mosander 1843
europium	Eu	63	Europe	Eugène-Anatole Demarçay 1901
fermium	Fm	100	Enrico Fermi	Albert Ghiorso, Berkeley 1952
fluorine	F	9	flowing	Henri Moissan 1886
francium	Fr	87	France	Marguerite Perey 1939
gadolinium	Gd	64	Johan Gadolin	P E Lecoq de Boisbaudran 1886
gallium	Ga	31	cock	P E Lecoq de Boisbaudran 1875
germanium	Ge	32	Germany	Clemens Winkler 1886
gold	Au	79	colour gold	prehistoric
hafnium	Hf	72	Copenhagen	Dirk Coster and G von Hevesy 1923
hahnium	Ha	105	Otto Hahn	disputed by Russia and USA
helium	He	2	sun	William Ramsay 1895
holmium	Ho	67	Stockholm	Soret, Delafontaine and Cleve 1878/9
hydrogen	H	1	water-producing	Cavendish 1766 but Lavoisier named it
indium	In	49	indigo	Ferdinand Reich and Theo Richter 1863
iodine	I	53	violet	Bernard Courtois 1811
iridium	Ir	77	rainbow (iris)	Smithson Tennant 1804
iron	Fe	26	Anglo-Saxon word	prehistoric
krypton	Kr	36	hidden	W Ramsay and Morris W Travers 1898
lanthanum	La	57	lie unseen	Carl Gustav Mosander 1839
lawrencium	Lr	103	Ernest Lawrence	Berkeley University, California, 1961
lead	Pb	82	Anglo-Saxon word	prehistoric
lithium	Li	3	stone	Johan August Arfvedson 1817
lutetium	Lu	71	Paris	Carl Auer von Welsbach and G Urbain 1907/8
magnesium	Mg	12	magnesia	Humphry Davy 1808
manganese	Mn	25	magnet	Carl W Scheele and Johan Gahn 1774
mendelevium	Md	101	D I Mendeleyev	Berkeley University, California, 1955
mercury	Hg	80	planet Mercury	prehistoric
molybdenum	Mo	42	lead	Peter Jacob Hjelm 1782
neodymium	Nd	60	new twin	Carl Auer von Welsbach 1885
neon	Ne	10	new	W Ramsay and Morris W Travers 1898
neptunium	Np	93	planet Neptune	Edwin McMillan and Philip Abelson 1940
nickel	Ni	28	copper demon	Baron Axel Frederik Cronstedt 1751

Name	Symbol	No.	Name source	Discovered or isolated by
niobium	Nb	41	Tantalus's daughter	discovered by Charles Hatchett 1801; first isolated by C W Blomstrand
nitrogen	N	7	nitre-forming	Daniel Rutherford 1772
nobelium	No	102	Nobel Inst. Stockholm	Berkeley University, California, 1958
osmium	Os	76	smell	Smithson Tennant 1804
oxygen	O	8	acid-producing	Scheele/Priestley 1772/4; Lavoisier name
palladium	Pd	46	asteroid Pallas	William Hyde Wollaston 1803
phosphorus	P	15	light-bringer	Hennig Brand 1669
platinum	Pt	78	silvery element	known to the ancients; first reported by A de Ulloa in South America 1736
plutonium	Pu	94	planet Pluto	Berkeley University, California, 1940
polonium	Po	84	Poland	Marie Curie 1898
potassium	K	19	potash	Humphry Davy 1807
praseodymium	Pr	59	green twin	Carl Auer von Welsbach 1885
promethium	Pm	61	Prometheus	Marinsky, Glendenin and Coryell 1947
protactinium	Pa	91	first actinium	Kasmir Fajans and D Göhring 1913
radium	Ra	88	ray	Pierre and Marie Curie and G Bemont 1898
radon	Rn	86	radium	F Dorn 1901
rhenium	Re	75	rhine	I Tacke, W Noddack and O Berg 1925
rhodium	Rh	45	rose	William Hyde Wollaston 1803
rubidium	Rb	37	dark red	R Bunsen and Gustav Kirchhoff 1861
ruthenium	Ru	44	Russia	Karl Klaus 1844 but named by G Osann in its impure form in 1827
rutherfordium	Rf	104	Ernest Rutherford	disputed by Soviet and US scientists
samarium	Sm	62	samarskite	P E Lecoq de Boisbaudran 1879
scandium	Sc	21	Scandinavia	Lars Nilson and Per Teodor Cleve 1879
selenium	Se	34	moon	Jons Jacob Berzelius 1817
silicon	Si	14	hard stone	Jons Jacob Berzelius 1824
silver	Ag	47	colour silver	prehistoric
sodium	Na	11	soda	Humphry Davy 1807
strontium	Sr	38	Strontian (Scotland)	Humphry Davy 1808
sulphur	S	16	sulphur	known to the ancients; first recognised as an element by Antoine Lavoisier 1777
tantalum	Ta	73	Tantalus	Anders Gustaf Ekeberg 1802
technetium	Tc	43	man-made	discovered by C Perrier and E G Segrè of Italy in a sample of molybdenum at Berkeley University, California, 1937
tellurium	Te	52	Earth	Franz J Müller von Reichenstein 1782
terbium	Tb	65	Ytterby (Sweden)	Carl Gustav Mosander 1843
thallium	Tl	81	green shoot	discovered by Sir William Crookes 1861
thorium	Th	90	Thor	Jons Jacob Berzelius 1828
thulium	Tm	69	Thule	Per Teodor Cleve 1879
tin	Sn	50	Anglo-Saxon word	prehistoric
titanium	Ti	22	Titans	discovered by William Gregor 1771; rediscovered by Martin Heinrich Klaproth (who gave it its present name) 1795
tungsten	W	74	heavy stone	Juan Jose and Fausto Elhuyar 1783
uranium	U	92	planet Uranus	Martin Heinrich Klaproth 1789
vanadium	V	23	Norse goddess	Nils Gabriel Sefström 1830
xenon	Xe	54	stranger	W Ramsay and Morris W Travers 1898
ytterbium	Yb	70	Ytterby (Sweden)	J C G de Marignac 1878
yttrium	Y	39	Ytterby (Sweden)	Johan Gadolin 1794
zinc	Zn	30	German word	known in China and India before 1500
zirconium	Zr	40	golden	discovered by Martin Heinrich Klaproth 1789; isolated by J J Berzelius in 1824

SCIENCE

Periodic Table of Elements

No.	Name	Symbol	Form	No.	Name	Symbol	Form
1	hydrogen	H	gas	10	neon	Ne	gas
2	helium	He	gas	11	sodium	Na	metallic solid
3	lithium	Li	metallic solid	12	magnesium	Mg	metallic solid
4	beryllium	Be	metallic solid	13	aluminium	Al	metallic solid
5	boron	B	metallic solid	14	silicon	Si	metallic solid
6	carbon	C	non-metallic solid	15	phosphorus	P	non-metallic solid
7	nitrogen	N	gas	16	sulphur	S	non-metallic solid
8	oxygen	O	gas	17	chlorine	Cl	gas
9	fluorine	F	gas	18	argon	Ar	gas

No.	Name	Symbol	Form		No.	Name	Symbol	Form
19	potassium	K	metallic solid		62	samarium	Sm	metallic solid
20	calcium	Ca	metallic solid		63	europium	Eu	metallic solid
21	scandium	Sc	metallic solid		64	gadolinium	Gd	metallic solid
22	titanium	Ti	metallic solid		65	terbium	Tb	metallic solid
23	vanadium	V	metallic solid		66	dysprosium	Dy	metallic solid
24	chromium	Cr	metallic solid		67	holmium	Ho	metallic solid
25	manganese	Mn	metallic solid		68	erbium	Er	metallic solid
26	iron	Fe	metallic solid		69	thulium	Tm	metallic solid
27	cobalt	Co	metallic solid		70	ytterbium	Yb	metallic solid
28	nickel	Ni	metallic solid		71	lutetium	Lu	metallic solid
29	copper	Cu	metallic solid		72	hafnium	Hf	metallic solid
30	zinc	Zn	metallic solid		73	tantalum	Ta	metallic solid
31	gallium	Ga	metallic liquid		74	tungsten	W	metallic solid
32	germanium	Ge	metalloid solid		75	rhenium	Re	metallic solid
33	arsenic	As	metalloid solid		76	osmium	Os	metallic solid
34	selenium	Se	non-metallic solid		77	iridium	Ir	metallic solid
35	bromine	Br	non-metallic liquid		78	platinum	Pt	metallic solid
36	krypton	Kr	gas		79	gold	Au	metallic solid
37	rubidium	Rb	radioactive semi-solid		80	mercury	Hg	metallic liquid
					81	thallium	Tl	metallic solid
38	strontium	Sr	metallic solid		82	lead	Pb	metallic solid
39	yttrium	Y	metallic solid		83	bismuth	Bi	metallic solid
40	zirconium	Zr	metallic solid		84	polonium	Po	radioactive solid
41	niobium	Nb	metallic solid		85	astatine	At	from bismuth
42	molybdenum	Mo	metallic solid		86	radon	Rn	gas
43	technetium	Tc	from molybdenum		87	francium	Fr	radioactive liquid
44	ruthenium	Ru	metallic solid		88	radium	Ra	radioactive solid
45	rhodium	Rh	metallic solid		89	actinium	Ac	from uranium
46	palladium	Pd	metallic solid		90	thorium	Th	metallic solid
47	silver	Ag	metallic solid		91	protactinium	Pa	from thorium
48	cadmium	Cd	metallic solid		92	uranium	U	metallic solid
49	indium	In	metallic solid		93	neptunium	Np	from plutonium
50	tin	Sn	metallic solid		94	plutonium	Pu	from uranium-238
51	antinomy	Sb	metallic solid		95	americium	Am	from plutonium
52	tellurium	Te	non-metallic solid		96	curium	Cm	from plutonium
53	iodine	I	solid but sublimates		97	berkelium	Bk	from americium
54	xenon	Xe	gas		98	californium	Cf	from cerium
55	caesium	Cs	metallic liquid		99	einsteinium	Es	from plutonium
56	barium	Ba	metallic solid		100	fermium	Fm	from plutonium
57	lanthanum	La	metallic solid		101	mendelevium	Md	from einsteinium
58	cerium	Ce	metallic solid		102	nobelium	No	from cerium
59	praseodymium	Pr	metallic solid		103	lawrencium	Lr	from californium
60	neodymium	Nd	metallic solid		104	rutherfordium	Rf	synthetic metal
61	promethium	Pm	from uranium		105	hahnium	Ha	from californium

Chemistry: General Information

atom and molecule: difference atoms are the smallest part of an element that can take part in a chemical reaction; molecules are the smallest particle of either an element or compound that can exist independently and at the same time keep the properties of the original substance, e.g. the smallest unit of water is the water molecule, which is made up of two atoms of hydrogen and one of oxygen.

atom: meaning indivisible.

chemical bonds there are two main types of chemical bonding, covalent and ionic, and two more specialised types, metallic and hydrogen bonding.

chemical groups there are various ways elements can be subdivided, the most common being metallic and non-metallic. Metallic elements, or their oxides, dissolve in acids to form positively charged ions called cations. Non-metallic elements can be further subdivided into the unreactive noble gases, the reactive halogens, and others.

chemical matter: three types compound, mixture or element.

chemistry: definition chemistry is the scientific study of substances.

isotopes atoms of a given element which have the same number of protons and electrons and the same chemical properties, but have a different number of neutrons in their nuclei, and consequently different atomic masses. Isotopes may be either stable or radioactive.

organic compounds all compounds that contain carbon. All other compounds are inorganic.

polymers polymers are long-chain molecules in which a group of atoms are repeated. They can be natural – e.g. cellulose, DNA, fats, proteins and starches – or artificial – e.g. nylon, polystyrene, polythene, PVC, and in fact all by-products of 'plastics'.

states of matter solid, liquid or gas.

sub-atomic particles chemical properties of elements depend on the structure of their atoms, which are made up of three sub-atomic particles, protons (positive charge), neutrons and electrons (negative charge). Protons and neutrons are situated in the nucleus of the atom and the electrons orbit this nucleus. The number of protons in the nucleus of an element determines the atomic number used in the periodic table.

sublimation occurs when chemical matter changes directly from a solid to a gas without first melting into a liquid.

valency property of atoms or groups, equal to the number of atoms of hydrogen that the atom or group will combine with or displace in forming compounds.

Geochemical Abundances of the Elements

		%		Mohs scale of hardness
Lithosphere	oxygen	46.60	1	talc
	silicon	27.72	2	gypsum
	aluminium	8.13	3	calcite
	iron	5.00	4	fluorite
			5	apatite
Hydrosphere	oxygen	85.70	6	orthoclase
	hydrogen	10.80	7	quartz
	chlorine	1.935	8	topaz
	sodium	1.078	9	corundum
			10	diamond
Halogens*	fluorine	**Noble gases†**		helium
	astatine			argon
	bromine			radon
	iodine			krypton
	chlorine			xenon
				neon

* Mnemonic: Fab(r)ic all end ine.

† Also called inert or rare gases.

NB The table listing the chemical elements in alphabetical order contains the name of the person who discovered or first isolated the element. This may be different from the person who first prepared the chemical, e.g. chlorine was first prepared (from hydrochloric acid and manganese dioxide) by Carl Wilhelm Scheele in 1774 and was considered a compound until Sir Humphry Davy showed that it could not in fact be decomposed and that muriatic (hydrochloric) acid consists of hydrogen and another true element that he named chlorine.

S
C
I
E
N
C
E

Mathematics: General Information

algebra method of solving mathematical problems by the use of symbols when figures are inadequate due to their size or unknown nature.

angles less than 90° = acute; more than 90° = obtuse; more than 180° = reflex.

Archimedes' principle physical law of buoyancy stating that any body submerged in a fluid at rest is acted upon by an upward force equal to the weight of the fluid displaced.

binary numbers a comparison of decimal and binary numbers (decimal first) 1 = 1, 2 = 10, 3 = 11, 4 = 100, 5 = 101, 6 = 110, 7 = 111, 8 = 1000, 9 = 1001, 10 = 1010.

books Euclid – *Elements*; Bertrand Russell (in collaboration with A N Whitehead) – *Principia Mathematica*; Sir Isaac Newton – *Principia*.

calculus branch of mathematics that permits the manipulation of continuously varying quantities. It is subdivided into integral and differential. Calculus (which is Latin for pebble) was independently invented by Gottfried Leibniz and Isaac Newton.

circle: parts of *chord* = a line that joins two points of a circle; *diameter* = the longest chord of a circle; *radius* = point from centre of circle to perimeter; *sector* = portion of circle between centre and two points on perimeter; *segment* = portion of a circle between a chord and the perimeter (it is important to know the distinction between a sector and a segment as this is an often-asked question). Circumference of a circle = 2 × pi × the radius (or pi × the diameter); the area of a circle = pi × radius².

complex number number having a real and an imaginary part, e.g. 5 + 3i is a complex number.

coordinates the technical names for graph coordinates are abscissa (the horizontal x coordinate) and ordinate (the vertical y coordinate).

cylinder solid figure with straight sides and a circular section.
The area of a cylinder = 2 × pi × radius × height + 2 × pi × radius squared.
The volume = the area of the base × the height.

ellipse an ellipse is a closed conic section with the appearance of a flattened circle. It is formed by an inclined plane that does not intersect the base of the cone.

factorial the factorial of a number is the product of all the whole numbers inclusive between 1 and the number itself; the symbol is ! e.g. 6! = 1×2×3×4×5×6 = 720.

factors a factor is a number that divides exactly into another number, e.g. 6 divides exactly into 48 eight times; thus both 6 and 8 are factors of 48.

Fibonacci numbers   sequence of numbers in which each number is the sum of its two predecessors, e.g. 1, 1, 2, 3, 5, 8, 13, etc.

game theory   branch of mathematics used to analyse competitive situations whose outcomes depend not only on one's own choices, and perhaps chance, but also on the choices made by other parties, or 'players'. Modern game theory was created practically at one stroke by the publication in 1944 of *Theory of Games and Economic Behaviour* by the mathematician John von Neumann and the economist Oskar Morgenstern.

geometry   branch of mathematics concerned with the properties and relations of points, lines, surfaces, and solids. Euclid's *Elements*, written about 330 BC, is the definitive origin of the subject.

hexadecimal system   base 16, uses digits 0–9 plus letters A–F to denote numbers 10 to 15.

imaginary number   the square root of –1 is denoted by the letter i, so $i^2 = -1$; real multiples of i, such as 3i, 2.3i, etc., are known as imaginary numbers.

line: definition   a line is length without breadth.

logarithms   system invented by John Napier whereby multiplication and division of large numbers are made simple by substituting the operations of addition and subtraction.

matrix   set of numbers arranged in rows and columns so as to form a rectangular array.
The numbers are called the elements, or entries, of the matrix.
The term matrix was introduced by the 19th-century English mathematician Arthur Cayley, who developed the algebraic aspect of matrices.

mean   in a series of values in a distribution the mean is the average value of all the values: e.g. in a series such as 1, 4, 4, 5, 7, 9, 12 the mean would be 6.

median   in a series of values in a distribution the median is the middle value in order of size: e.g. in a series such as 1, 4, 4, 5, 7, 9, 12 the median would be 5.

mode   in a series of values in a distribution the mode is the most frequently occurring value: e.g. in a series such as 1, 4, 4, 5, 7, 9, 12 the mode would be 4.

numbers   chiliad – 1,000; myriad – 10,000; lakh – 100,000; crore – 10,000,000; billion – 1,000,000,000,000 (USA 1,000,000,000); googol – one followed by a hundred noughts; googolplex – one followed by a googol of noughts.

octal system   base 8; uses digits 0–7: e.g. 31 in base 10 would be 37 in base 8.

parabola   curve formed by cutting a right circular cone with a plane parallel to the sloping side of the cone.

parallelogram   quadrilateral with opposite pairs of sides equal in length and parallel. When all sides are of the same length it is known as a rhombus. The area of a parallelogram is base × height.

perfect numbers   perfect numbers are equal to the sum of all their factors excluding the number itself, e.g. 6, whose factors are 1, 2, and 3. The first five perfect numbers are 6, 28, 496, 8,128, and 33,550,336.

pi (π)   pi has been measured to many thousands of decimal places but to six places = 3.141592. It is a transcendental number.

polygons   the sum of the interior angles = $(2n - 4) \times 90°$ where n = the number of sides. The sum of the exterior angles of any polygon = 360° regardless of the number of sides (an exterior angle of a polygon

is the angle between one side extended and the adjacent side): e.g. triangle = 180°; quadrilateral = 360°; pentagon = 540°; hexagon = 720°; octagon = 1080°; nonagon = 1260°; decagon = 1440°; hendecagon = 1620°; dodecagon = 1800°; icosagon = 3240°.

polyhedron   solid figure with four or more plane faces.

prime number   a natural number (over 1) that has no proper factors, i.e. which cannot be divided by any natural numbers other than itself and 1 – e.g. 2, 3, 5, 7, 11, 13, 17 ...

prism   solid figure (polyhedron) with two equal polygonal faces in parallel planes, other faces being parallelograms. The volume of a prism = the area of either end × the perpendicular distance between the ends.

pyramid   a solid figure whose base is a polygon and whose apex is joined to each vertex of the base. Therefore all its faces, apart from the base, are triangles. Any pyramid can be fitted inside a prism so that the base of the pyramid is one end of the prism, and the apex of the pyramid is on the other end of the prism. The volume of a pyramid on a rectangular base = ⅓ length × breadth × height.

Pythagoras' theorem   in a right-angled triangle, the square of the hypotenuse is equal to the sum of the squares of the other two sides.

quadratic equation   equation containing as its highest power the square of a single unknown variable.
General formula is $ax^2 + bx + c = 0$, in which a, b, and c are constants and only the coefficient a cannot equal 0.

rational number   number that can be written in the form % (a over b), where a and b are integers and b is not equal to zero.

reciprocal   of a quantity, that quantity divided into 1; thus the reciprocal of 2 is ½.

rhombus   diamond-shaped plane figure, a parallelogram with four equal sides and no right angles. The area of a rhombus = ½ the product of the diagonals.

simultaneous equations   two or more algebraic equations that contain two or more unknown quantities and are simultaneously true, e.g. x + 3y = 6 and 3y – 2x = 4. The solution is to eliminate one of the variables by multiplying the first equation by 2 and adding the two equations to give 9y = 16.

sine   in trigonometry, of an angle in a right-angled triangle, the ratio of the length of the side opposite the angle to the length of the hypotenuse.

sphere   circular solid with all points on its surface the same distance from its centre. The surface area = 4 × pi × radius squared. Volume = ⅔ pi × radius cubed A little-known fact about the sphere is that the area of any zone of its curved surface lying between two parallel planes is exactly equal to the curved surface of the surrounding cylinder between the same two planes.

standard deviation   in statistics, a measure of the variability (dispersion or spread) of any set of numerical values about their arithmetic mean. It is specifically defined as the square root of the arithmetic mean of the squared deviations.

tetrahedron   solid figure with four triangular faces, i.e. a pyramid on a triangular base. The volume of a tetrahedron = ⅓ (the area of the triangular base x height).

topology   branch of geometry which deals with those

properties of a figure which remain unchanged even when the figure is continuously transformed. A famous topological problem was to prove that only three colours are needed to produce a map to give adjoining areas different colours.

transcendental number real number that is not a root of a polynomial equation with integer coefficients.

trapezium four-sided plane figure quadrilateral with two parallel sides of unequal length. The area of a trapezium = ½ the sum of the parallel sides x the perpendicular distance between them. To find the area three measurements have to be taken, i.e. the height between the pair of parallel sides and the length of both of the parallel sides. If a and b are the two parallel sides the formula would be ½ (a + b)h.

triangle Three-sided plane figure; *scalene* triangles have no two sides equal; *isosceles* triangles have two equal sides and angles, *equilateral* triangles have three equal sides and angles. The area of a triangle = ½ base × height, however it is possible to calculate the area from the length of its sides using an Archimedean formula square root of (s(s − a) (s − b) (s − c)) where s = half the sum of the sides.

trigonometry branch of mathematics which solves problems relating to plane and spherical triangles.

vector physical quantity that has both magnitude and direction, such as velocity or acceleration of an object.

Venn diagrams diagram representing a set or sets and the logical relationships between them. Sets are drawn as circles whose overlap contains elements that are common to both sets and thus represent a third set.

NB The information on mathematics is merely an overview of basic relevant information on the subject. No attempt has been made to show functions of matrices or calculus, for example, as these are beyond the scope of this book.

Physics: SI Units
(*Système International d'Unités*)

Base units

Quantity	Unit	Symbol	Definition
length	metre	m	1,650,763.73 wavelengths in vacuum of the red-orange light given out by the krypton-86 isotope.
mass	kilogram	kg	Mass of international prototype of the kilogram, at the Bureau International des Poids et Mesures at Sèvres, near Paris.
time	second	s	Duration of 9,192,631,770 periods of the radiation corresponding to the transition between the two hyperfine levels of the ground state of the caesium-133 atom.
electric current	ampere	A	That constant current which, if maintained in two straight parallel conductors of infinite length of negligible circular cross-section, and placed 1 metre apart in a vacuum, would produce between these conductors a force equal to 2×10^{-7} newtons per metre of length.
thermodynamic temperature	kelvin	K	The fraction $1/273.16$ of the thermodynamic temperature of the triple point of water. The triple point of water is the point where water, ice and water vapour are in equilibrium.
luminous intensity	candela	cd	The luminous intensity, in a given direction, of a source that emits monochromatic radiation of frequency 540×10^{12} Hz, and has a radiant intensity in that direction of $1/683$ watts per steradian.
amount of substance	mole	mol	Amount of substance of a system that contains as many elementary entities (atoms, molecules, ions, etc.) as there are atoms in 0.012 kilogram of carbon-12.

Supplementary units

plane angle	radian	rad	The plane angle between two radii of a circle that cut off on the circumference an arc equal in length to the radius.
solid angle	steradian	sr	The solid angle that, having its vertex in the centre of a sphere, cuts off an area of the surface of the sphere equal to that of a square having sides of length equal to the radius of the sphere.

SCIENCE

Derived Units

Quantity	Unit	Symbol	Other SI Units
area	square metre	m^2	
volume	cubic metre	m^3	
velocity	metre per second	$m·s^{-1}$	
angular velocity	radian per second	$rad\ s^{-1}$	
acceleration	metre per second squared	$m·s^{-2}$	
angular acceleration	radian per second squared	$rad\ s^{-2}$	
frequency	hertz	Hz	s^{-1}
density	kilogram per cubic metre	$kg·m^{-3}$	
momentum	kilogram metre per second	$kg·m·s^{-1}$	
angular momentum	kilogram metre squared per second	$kg·m^2·s^{-1}$	
moment of inertia	kilogram metre squared	$kg·m^2$	
force	newton	N	$kg·m·s^{-2}$
pressure (stress)	pascal	Pa	$N·m^{-2} = kg·m^{-1}·s^{-2}$
work (energy)	joule	J	$N·m = kg·m^2·s^{-2}$
power	watt	W	$J·s^{-1} = kg·m^2·s^{-3}$
surface tension	newton per metre	$N·m^{-1}$	$kg·s^{-2}$
dynamic viscosity	newton second per metre squared	$N·s·m^{-2}$	$kg·m^{-1}·s^{-1}$
kinematic viscosity	metre squared per second	$m^2·s^{-1}$	
temperature	degree Celsius	$°C$	
thermal coefficient of linear expansion	per degree Celsius (or kelvin)	$°C^{-1}, K^{-1}$	
thermal conductivity	watt per metre degree Celsius	$W·m^{-1}·°C^{-1}$	$kg·m·s^{-3}·°C^{-1}$
heat capacity	joule per kelvin	$J·K^{-1}$	$kg·m^2·s^{-2}·K^{-1}$
specific heat capacity	joule per kilogram kelvin	$J·kg^{-1}·K^{-1}$	$m^2·s^{-2}K^{-1}$
specific latent heat	joule per kilogram	$J·kg^{-1}$	$m^2\ s^{-2}$
electrical charge	coulomb	C	$A·s$
electromotive force (potential difference)	volt	V	$W·A^{-1} = kg·m^2·s^{-3}·A^{-1}$
electrical resistance	ohm	Ω	$V·A^{-1} = kg·m^2·s^{-3}·A^{-2}$
electrical conductance	siemens	S	$A·V^{-1} = kg^{-1}·m^{-2}·s^3·A^2$
electrical capacitance	farad	F	$A·s·V^{-1} = kg^{-1}·m^{-2}·s^4·A^2$
inductance	henry	H	$V·s·A^{-1} = kg·m^2·s^{-2}·A^{-2}$
magnetic flux	weber	Wb	$V·s = kg·m^2·s^{-2}·A^{-1}$
magnetic flux density	tesla	T	$Wb·m^{-2} = kg·s^{-2}·A^{-1}$
magnetomotive force	ampere	A	
luminous flux	lumen	Lm	$cd·sr$
illumination	lux	Lx	$lm·m^{-2} = cd·sr·m^{-2}$
radiation activity	becquerel	Bq	s^{-1}
radiation absorbed dose	gray	Gy	$J·kg^{-1} = m^2·s^{-2}$

Physics: General Information

Avogadro's law law stating that equal volumes of gases at the same temperature and pressure contain equal numbers of molecules.

Avogadro's constant the number of atoms or molecules in one mole of a substance.

baryon subatomic particle that has a mass equal to or greater than that of a proton.

Bernoulli's principle the principle that in a liquid flowing through a pipe the pressure difference that accelerates the flow when the bore changes is equal to the product of half the density times the change of the square of the speed, provided friction is negligible. Named after Daniel Bernoulli, Swiss mathematician and physician 1700–82.

Coriolis effect an effect whereby a mass moving in a rotating system is accelerated perpendicular to its motion and to the axis of rotation, which helps to explain why wind patterns are clockwise in the northern hemisphere and anticlockwise in the southern. Named after French engineer G G Coriolis 1792–1843.

Doppler effect phenomenon observed for sound waves and electromagnetic radiation, characterised by a change in the apparent frequency of a wave as a result of relative motion between the observer and the source.

entropy measure of the unavailability of a system's thermal energy for conversion into mechanical work, often interpreted as a measure of the degree of disorder or randomness in the system.

fermion any of several subatomic particles with half-integral spin, e.g. nucleons.

Feynman diagram diagram of interactions between subatomic particles. Named after Richard Feynman, US physicist (1918–88).

Foucault's pendulum pendulum which rotates in relation to the Earth's surface and thus changes its plane in relation to the position of the Earth's rotational plane. The pendulum swings in a clockwise plane in the northern hemisphere and anticlockwise in the southern, and on the equator would therefore be stationary. This mathematical effect explains the trajectory of moving objects through the air. Named after Jean Bernard Foucault (1819–68), who set up the first pendulum.

General relativity   Einstein's theory that the effects of acceleration and gravity were equivalent.

Heisenberg uncertainty principle   principle that the momentum and position of a particle cannot both be precisely determined at the same time.

Latent heat   heat required to convert a solid into a liquid or vapour, or a liquid into vapour, without change of temperature.

Matter: four fundamental forces   interactions between matter can be explained by four forces.

1) Gravitational: weakest of the four forces, whereby masses mutually attract. Gravity is the force that holds solar systems and galaxies together.

2) Electromagnetic: force maintaining the magnetic field and the electron-nucleus structure of an atom.

3) Strong: about 100 times stronger than the electromagnetic force, it holds together the protons and neutrons within an atomic nucleus.

4) Weak: force associated with the radioactive beta-decay of some nuclei.

Matter: three fundamental states   gas, solid, liquid.

Newton's three laws of motion   1) A body will remain stationary or travelling at a constant velocity unless it is acted upon by an external force.

2) The resultant force exerted on a body is directly proportional to the acceleration produced by the force and takes place in the direction of the force.

3) To every action there is an equal and opposite reaction.

Pauli exclusion principle   the assertion that no two electrons in an atom can occupy the same energy state simultaneously, or in other words, that no two fermions can have the same quantum number. Named after Wolfgang Pauli, Austrian physicist (1900–58).

Physics: definition   physics is the study of the basic laws that govern matter.

Quantum theory   describes the behaviour of particles within atoms and the absorption and emission of electromagnetic radiation by matter in its various states.

Schrödinger's cat   hypothetical situation whereby a cat is placed inside a box for one hour with a radioactive atom whose probability of decay is 50% per hour. If the atom decays a Geiger counter triggers a mechanism breaking a cyanide capsule and killing the cat. If the atom does not decay the cat remains alive. Quantum theory suggests that until the box is opened at the end of the hour, the cat is neither alive nor dead.

Special relativity   states that nothing can exceed the speed of light, which is the same in all inertial time frames, and that all inertial time frames are equally good for carrying out experiments.

Thermodynamics: three laws   1) First law states that the total amount of energy in any closed system always remains the same.

2) Second law states that heat will always flow from a hotter object to a colder one and not the other way round.

3) Third law states that on approaching absolute zero, extracting energy from a system becomes increasingly harder.

Venturi tube   device for measuring fluid flow, consisting of a tube so constricted that the pressure differential produced by fluid flowing through the constriction gives a measure of the rate of flow.

Wheatstone bridge   apparatus for measuring electrical resistances by equalising the potential at two points of a circuit.

Young's modulus   measure of elasticity equal to the ratio of the stress acting on a substance to the strain produced. Named after Thomas Young, English scientist (1773–1829).

Zeeman effect   the splitting of the spectrum line into several components by a magnetic field. Named after Pieter Zeeman, Dutch physicist (1865–1943).

SCIENCE

SHAKESPEARE

Plays

1 All's Well That Ends Well

The Persons of The Play

The Dowager COUNTESS of Roussillon
BERTRAM, Count of Roussillon, her son
HELEN, an orphan, attending the Countess
LAVATCH, a clown, the Countess's servant
REYNALDO, the Countess's steward
PAROLES, Bertram's companion
LAFEU, an old lord
The KING of France

FIRST LORD DUMAINE
SECOND LORD DUMAINE, his brother
INTERPRETER, a French soldier
The DUKE of Florence
WIDOW Capilet
DIANA, her daughter
MARIANA, a friend of the widow
Lords, attendants, soldiers, citizens

Quotations

	Spoken by
A young man married is a man that's marr'd.	Paroles
From lowest place when virtuous things proceed.	King of France
I have an answer will serve all men.	Lavatch
Love all, trust a few, do wrong to none.	Countess of Roussillon
Oft expectation fails and most oft there where most it promises.	Helen
Our remedies oft in ourselves do lie which we ascribe to heaven.	Helen
Praising what is lost makes the remembrance dear.	King of France
The hind that would be mated by the lion must die for love.	Helen
The web of our life is of a mingled yarn.	First Lord Dumaine
There's a place and means for every man alive.	Paroles
'Twere all one that I should love a bright particular star.	Helen

Précis of plot

Helen, the daughter of a poor physician, Gerard de Narbonne, falls in love with Bertram, son of her guardian the Countess of Roussillon. Helen uses her magic to cure the King of France and as a reward he brings about the marriage of Helen and Bertram. The marriage is doomed to fail when Bertram takes flight to the Tuscan wars, and it is only consummated when Bertram seduces Helen in the guise of the Florentine maiden Diana.

Setting

France and Italy in the 14th century

2 Antony and Cleopatra

Mark ANTONY, Triumvir of Rome
Friends and followers of Antony:
VENTIDIUS
SILIUS
EROS
CAMIDIUS
SCARUS
DECRETAS
Domitius ENOBARBUS
DEMETRIUS
PHILO
SELEUCUS
Octavius CAESAR, Triumvir of Rome
OCTAVIA, his sister
Friends and followers of Caesar:
MAECENAS
AGRIPPA
TAURUS
DOLABELLA
THIDIAS
GALLUS
PROCULEIUS

LEPIDUS, Triumvir of Rome
Sextus POMPEY (Pompeius)

Friends of Pompey:
MENECRATES
MENAN
VARRIUS

CLEOPATRA, Queen of Egypt
Cleopatra's attendants:
CHARMIAN
IRAS
ALEXAS
DIOMED

MARDIAN, a eunuch

SOOTHSAYER
AMBASSADOR
MESSENGERS
BOY who sings
SENTRY and men of his WATCH
Men of the GUARD
EGYPTIAN
CLOWN
SERVANTS
SOLDIERS
Attendants, eunuchs, soldiers

Quotations

	Spoken by
Age cannot wither her, nor custom stale her infinite variety.	Enobarbus
Celerity is never more admired than by the negligent.	Cleopatra
Come thou monarch of the vine, plumpy Bacchus with pink eyne!	Boy (sung)
Dost thou not see my baby at my breast.	Cleopatra
Finish, good lady; the bright day is done, and we are for the dark.	Iras

Give me my robe, put on my crown; I have immortal longings in me.	Cleopatra
He wears the rose of youth upon him.	Antony
His biting is immortal; those that do die of it seldom or never recover.	Clown
His legs bestrid the ocean: his rear'd arm crested the world: his voice was propertied.	Cleopatra
I am dying, Egypt, dying; only I here importune death a while until of many thousand kisses the poor last I lay upon thy lips.	Antony
I found you as a morsel cold upon dead Caesar's trencher.	Antony
I have yet room for six scotches more.	Scarus
I saw her once hop forty paces through the public street; and having lost her breath, she spoke, and panted, that she did make defect perfection.	Enobarbus
I wish you joy o' the worm.	Clown
If thou and nature can so gently part, the stroke of death is as a lover's pinch.	Cleopatra
In nature's infinite book of secrecy little can I read.	Soothsayer
In time we hate that which we often fear.	Charmian
It is well done, and fitting for a princess descended of so many royal kings.	Charmian
Let's have one other gaudy night.	Antony
My salad days, when I was green in judgement, cold in blood.	Cleopatra
Now boast thee, death, in thy possession lies a lass unparalleled.	Charmian
Out, fool – I forgive thee for a witch.	Charmian
O, wither'd is the garland of the war. The soldier's pole is fall'n: young boys and girls are level now with men. The odds is gone.	Cleopatra
Sometime we see a cloud that's dragonish, a vapour sometime like a bear or lion, a towered citadel, a pendant rock, a fork'd mountain, or blue promontory with trees upon't.	Antony
The barge she sat in, like a burnish'd throne, burn'd on the water.	Enobarbus
The nature of bad news infects the teller.	Messenger
There's beggary in the love that can be reckon'd.	Antony
Though I am mad I will not bite him. Call!	Cleopatra
Though it be honest, it is never good to bring bad news.	Cleopatra
To business that we love we rise betime, and go to't with delight	Antony
Unarm, Eros; the long day's task is done, and we must sleep	Antony
What's brave, what's noble, let's do it after the high Roman fashion, and make death proud to take us.	Cleopatra
Where's my serpent of old Nile.	Cleopatra

Précis of plot
The second triumvirate is disintegrating and Mark Antony becomes infatuated with Cleopatra, Queen of Egypt. The play tells of the sea fight between Antony and Octavius near Actium and Antony's subsequent suicide, believing Cleopatra dead. Cleopatra too commits suicide rather than be captured by Octavius.

Setting
Rome and Alexandria in the 1st century BC.

3 As You Like It

DUKE SENIOR, living in banishment	ORLANDO, Oliver's brother
ROSALIND, his daughter, later disguised as Ganymede	ADAM, a former servant of Sir Rowland
AMIENS, Lord attending on Duke Senior	DENIS, Oliver's servant
JAQUES, Lord attending on Duke Senior	SIR OLIVER MARTEXT, a country clergyman
TWO PAGES	CORIN, an old shepherd
DUKE FREDERICK	SILVIUS, a young shepherd, in love with Phoebe
CELIA, his daughter, later disguised as Aliena	PHOEBE, a shepherdess
LE BEAU, a courtier attending on Duke Frederick	WILLIAM, a countryman, in love with Audrey
CHARLES, Duke Frederick's wrestler	AUDREY, a goatherd, betrothed to Touchstone
TOUCHSTONE, a jester	HYMEN, God of marriage
OLIVER, eldest son of Sir Rowland de Bois	Lords, pages, and other attendants
JAQUES, Oliver's brother	

Quotations

	Spoken by
All the world's a stage, and all the men and women merely players. They have their exits and their entrances and one man in his time plays many parts, his acts being seven ages.	Jaques
And rail'd on Lady Fortune in good terms	Jaques
And so, from hour to hour, we ripe and ripe, and then from hour to hour, we rot and rot; and thereby hangs a tale.	Jaques
An ill-favoured thing, sir, but mine own.	Touchstone
Ay, now am I in Ardenne; the more fool I. When I was at home I was in a better place; but travellers must be content.	Touchstone
Beauty provoketh thieves sooner than gold.	Rosalind
Blow, blow, thou winter wind, thou are not so unkind as man's ingratitude.	Amiens (sung)
But whate'er you are that in this desert inaccessible under the shade of melancholy boughs, lose and neglect the creeping hours of time.	Orlando

Chewing the food of sweet and bitter fancy.	Oliver
Dead shepherd, now I find thy saw of might, 'Who ever loved that loved not at first sight?'	Phoebe (quoting Marlowe's 'Hero and Leander')
Down on your knees, and thank heaven, fasting, for a good man's love.	Rosalind
Do you not know I am a woman? when I think I must speak, sweet, say on.	Rosalind
Every one fault seeming monstrous till his fellow-fault came to match it.	Rosalind
Fleet the time carelessly, as they did in the golden world.	Charles
For in my youth I never did apply hot and rebellious liquors to my blood	Adam
Hast any philosophy in thee, shepherd?	Touchstone
He that wants money, means and content is without three good friends.	Corin
He uses his folly like a stalking-horse and under the presentation of that he shoots his wit.	Duke Senior
How now, wit! whither wander you?	Celia
I am not a slut, though I thank the gods I am foul.	Audrey
I can suck melancholy out of a song, as a weasel sucks eggs.	Jaques
I do desire we may be better strangers.	Orlando
If ever – as that ever may be near – you meet in some fresh cheek the power of fancy, then shall you know the wounds invisible that love's keen arrows make.	
If it be true that good wine needs no bush 'tis true that a good play needs no epilogue.	Rosalind
If thou remember'st not the slightest folly that ever love did make thee run into, thou hast not loved.	Silvius
I had rather have a fool to make me merry than experience to make me sad.	Rosalind
I must have liberty withal, as large a charter as the wind, to blow on whom I please.	Jaques
It is a melancholy of mine own, compounded of many simples, extracted from many objects, and indeed the sundry contemplation of my travels, in which my often rumination wraps me in a most humorous sadness.	Jaques
It is meat and drink to me to see a clown.	Touchstone
It is to be all made of faith and service.	Silvius
It is to be all made of fantasy, all made of passion.	Silvius
It is to be all made of sighs and tears.	Silvius
Men are April when they woo, December when they wed, maids are May when they are maids, but the sky changes when they are wives.	Rosalind
Men have died from time to time and worms have eaten them, but not for love.	Rosalind
Most friendship is feigning, most loving mere folly.	Amiens (sung)
Motley's the only wear.	Jaques
My lungs began to crow like chanticleer, that fools should be so deep-contemplative, and I did laugh sans intermission an hour by his dial.	Jaques
My pride fell with my fortunes.	Rosalind
'No sir,' quoth he, 'Call me not fool till heaven hath sent me fortune' and then he drew a dial from his poke, and, looking on it with lack-lustre eye, says very wisely 'it is ten o' clock thus we may see,' quoth he, 'how the world wags.'	Jaques
No sooner met but they looked; no sooner looked but they loved; no sooner loved but they sighed; no sooner sighed but they asked one another the reason, no sooner knew the reason but they sought the remedy.	Rosalind
O, how bitter a thing it is to look into happiness through another man's eyes!	Orlando
O, how full of briers is this working-day world!	Rosalind
O Sir, we quarrel in print, by the book; as you have books for good manners. I will name you the degrees. The first, the Retort Courteous; the second, the Quip Modest; the third, the Reply Churlish; the fourth, the Reproof Valiant; the fifth, the Countercheck Quarrelsome; the sixth, the Lie with Circumstance; the seventh, the Lie Direct.	Touchstone
O wonderful, wonderful, and most wonderful! and yet again wonderful, and after that, out of all whooping!	Celia
Sans teeth, sans eyes, sans taste, sans everything.	Jaques
Speak, sad brow and true maid.	Rosalind
Sweep on, you fat and greasy citizens.	First Lord
Sweet are the uses of adversity, which like the toad, ugly and venomous, wears yet a precious jewel in its head; and this our life exempt from public haunt, finds tongues in trees, books in the running brooks, sermons in stones, and good in everything.	Duke Senior
The big round tears coursed one another down his innocent nose in piteous chase.	First Lord
The fair, the chaste and unexpressive she.	Orlando
The horn, the horn, the lusty horn is not a thing to laugh to scorn.	Lords (sung)
Therefore my age is as a lusty winter, frosty, but kindly.	Adam
The 'why' is plain as way to parish church.	Jaques
This is the very false gallop of the verses.	Touchstone
Thou mak'st a testament as worldlings do, giving thy sum of more to that which had too much.	First Lord
Time travels in divers paces with divers persons.	Rosalind

Truly, I would the gods had made thee poetical.	Touchstone
Truly thou art damned, like an ill-roasted egg all on one side.	Touchstone
Under the greenwood tree, who loves to lie with me, and turn his merry note, unto the sweet bird's throat, Come hither, come hither, come hither. Here shall he see: no enemy, but winter and rough weather.	Amiens (sung)
Very good orators, when they are out, they will spit.	Rosalind
We'll have a swashing and a martial outside, as many other mannish cowards have, that do outface it with their semblances.	Rosalind
Well said: that was laid on with a trowel.	Celia
We that are true lovers run into strange capers.	Touchstone
Who doth ambition shun and loves to live i' the sun seeking the food he eats and pleased with what he gets.	Chorus
Your 'if' is the only peacemaker; much virtue in 'if'.	Touchstone

Précis of plot
The story of the love between a high-born maiden, Rosalind, oppressed by her uncle Duke Frederick, who has usurped his elder brother's dukedom, and Orlando, the third and youngest son of Duke Frederick's enemy Sir Rowland de Bois, himself oppressed by his tyrannical elder brother Oliver. Sub-plots include the romantic liaisons between Touchstone and Audrey, Celia and Oliver, and Silvius and Phoebe.

Setting
The Forest of Arden (possibly Ardenne).

4 The Comedy of Errors
Solinus, DUKE of Ephesus
EGEON, father of the Antipholus twins
ANTIPHOLUS OF EPHESUS, Egeon's son
ANTIPHOLUS OF SYRACUSE, twin brother
DROMIO OF EPHESUS
DROMIO OF SYRACUSE, his twin brother
ADRIANA, wife of Antipholus of Ephesus
LUCIANA, her sister
NELL, Adriana's kitchen-maid

ANGELO, a goldsmith
BALTHASAR, a merchant
A COURTESAN
Doctor PINCH, a schoolmaster and exorcist
MERCHANT OF EPHESUS
SECOND MERCHANT, Angelo's creditor
EMILIA, an abbess at Ephesus
Officers and attendants
Jailer, messenger, headsman

Quotations	Spoken by
A wretched soul, bruised with adversity.	Adriana
The pleasing punishment that women bear.	Egeon

Précis of plot
The Comedy of Errors is a true farce, in as much as the unlikely situations stretch the imagination of the audience. But the play itself is probably the most classically constructed of any of Shakespeare's works. The action all takes place within a few hours and revolves around the mistaken identity of twin brothers and their bondmen, who also happen to be twins. The audience are further tested intellectually by the long-lost brothers sharing the same names as do their servants.

Setting
Ephesus circa 14th century.

5 Coriolanus
Caius MARTIUS, later surnamed CORIOLANUS
MENENIUS Agrippa
Titus LARTIUS, a General
COMINIUS, a General
VOLUMNIA, Coriolanus' mother
VIRGILIA, his wife
YOUNG MARTIUS, his son
VALERIA, a chaste lady of Rome
SICINIUS Velutus, tribune
Junius BRUTUS, tribune
CITIZENS of Rome
SOLDIERS in the Roman army
Tullus AUFIDIUS, General of the Volscian army

His LIEUTENANT
His SERVINGMEN
CONSPIRATORS with Aufidius
Volscian LORDS
Volscian CITIZENS
SOLDIERS in the Volscian army
ADRIAN, a Roman
NICANOR, a Volscian
A Roman HERALD
MESSENGERS
AEDILES
Gentlewoman, usher, Volscian Senators, Roman Captains, officers and lictors

Quotations	Spoken by
Bid them wash their faces and keep their teeth clean.	Coriolanus
Chaste as the icicle that's candied by the frost from purest snow and hangs on Diana's temple.	Coriolanus
Hear you this Triton of the minnows?	Coriolanus
His nature is too noble for the world. He would not flatter Neptune for his trident.	Menenius
If you have writ your annals true, 'tis there that, like an eagle in a dove-cote, I fluttered your Volscians in Corioles. Alone I did it. 'Boy'!	Coriolanus

I thank you for your voices, thank you, your most sweet voices.	Third citizen
Look, sir, my wounds, I got them in my country's service when some certain of your brethren roar'd and ran from the noise of our own drums.	Coriolanus
My gracious silence, hail!	Coriolanus
O, a kiss long as my exile, sweet as my revenge!	Coriolanus
You common cry of curs! whose breath I hate.	Coriolanus

Précis of plot
Caius Marcius is granted the cognomen of Coriolanus for his fearlessness in the Roman struggle against the neighbouring Volsci, but this brave but tyrannical warrior ultimately rebels and the subsequent intrigues form the basis of the plot.

Setting
Rome circa 5th century BC, Corioli, Antium.

6 Cymbeline, King of Britain

CYMBELINE, King of Britain
Princess INNOGEN, his daughter
GUIDERIUS, Cymbeline's son, known as Polydore
ARVIRAGUS, Cymbeline's son, known as Cadwal
QUEEN, Cymbeline's wife, Innogen's stepmother
Lord CLOTEN, the Queen's son
BELARIUS, a banished Lord, calling himself Morgan
CORNELIUS, a physician
HELEN, a lady attending on Innogen
Two LORDS, attending on Cloten
Two GENTLEMEN
Two British CAPTAINS
Two JAILERS
POSTHUMUS Leonatus, Innogen's husband
PISANIO, his servant
FILARIO, a friend of Posthumus

Filario's friends:
FRENCHMAN
DUTCHMAN
SPANIARD
GIACOMO, an Italian

Caius LUCIUS, ambassador, later General
Two Roman SENATORS
Roman TRIBUNES
Philharmonus, a SOOTHSAYER
JUPITER
Ghost of SICILIUS Leonatus, father of Posthumus
Ghost of the MOTHER of Posthumus
Ghosts of the BROTHERS of Posthumus
Lords attending Cymbeline, ladies attending the
Queen, musicians, messengers, soldiers

Quotations

	Spoken by
Fear no more the heat o' th' sun, nor the furious winter' rages. Thou thy worldly task hast done, home art gone and ta'en thy wages. Golden lads and girls all must, as chimney-sweepers, come to dust.	Guiderius
Hark, hark! the lark at heaven's gate sings, and Phoebus gins arise.	Musician (sung)
I have not slept one wink.	Pisanio
Prouder than rustling in unpaid-for silk.	Belarius
Slander, whose edge is sharper than the sword, whose tongue outvenoms all the worms of Nile, whose breath rides on the posting winds and doth belie all corners of the world.	Pisanio
The natural bravery of your isle, which stands as Neptune's park, ribbed and paled in, with banks unscalable and roaring waters.	Queen
There will be many Caesars, ere such another Julius. Britain's a world by itself, and we will nothing pay for wearing our own noses.	Cloten
Thersites body is as good as Ajax when neither is alive	Guiderius
The sceptre, learning, physic, must all follow this, and come to dust	Arviragus
Weariness can snore upon the flint, when resty sloth finds the down pillow hard.	Belarius
With fairest flowers whilst summer lasts and I live here Fidele, I'll sweeten thy sad grave; thou shalt not lack the flower that's like thy face, pale primrose, nor the azured harebell, like thy veins, no, nor the leaf of eglantine, whom not to slander, out-sweeten'd not thy breath.	Arviragus

Précis of plot
Cymbeline is a tragicomedy full of intrigues and sub-plots, the most notable concerning the wager between Giacomo and Posthumus regarding the chastity of Posthumus' wife Innogen. The subsequent 'death' and awakening of Innogen are central to the events that happily conclude this fantasy.

Setting
Britain and Rome circa 1st century AD.

NB Cymbeline's daughter's name is given in the folio as Imogen, but this is thought to be a misprint.

7 Hamlet

Prince HAMLET, son of King Hamlet and Queen Gertrude	Courtiers:
GHOST of Hamlet, late King of Denmark	VALTEMAND
KING CLAUDIUS, his brother	CORNELIUS
QUEEN GERTRUDE of Denmark, wife of Claudius	OSRIC
POLONIUS, a Lord	GENTLEMEN
LAERTES, son of Polonius	
OPHELIA, a daughter of Polonius	SAILOR
REYNALDO, servant of Polonius	PRIEST
FORTINBRAS, Prince of Norway	
A CAPTAIN in his army	HORATIO
AMBASSADORS from England	ROSENCRANTZ
PLAYERS, who play the Prologue, King and Queen, and	GUILDENSTERN
Lucianus, in 'The Mousetrap'	Soldiers:
Lords, messengers, attendants, guards, soldiers	FRANCISCO
followers of Laertes, sailors	BARNARDO
Two CLOWNS, gravedigger and his companion	MARCELLUS

Quotations	Spoken by
A beast, that wants discourse of reason, would have mourned longer.	Hamlet
A certain convocation of political worms are e'en at him.	Hamlet
A countenance more in sorrow than in anger.	Horatio
A king of shreds and patches.	Hamlet
Alas, poor Yorick. I knew him, Horatio – a fellow of infinite jest, of most excellent fancy.	Hamlet
A little more than kin, and less than kind.	Hamlet
A man may fish with the worm that hath eat of a king, and eat of the fish that hath fed of that worm.	Hamlet
A man that fortune's buffets and rewards, hath ta'en with equal thanks.	Hamlet
And then it started like a guilty thing upon a fearful summons.	Horatio
And these few precepts in thy memory keep.	Polonius
And to my mind – though I am native here, and to the manner born, it is a custom more honoured in the breach than the observance.	Hamlet
Angels and ministers of grace defend us.	Hamlet
Assume a virtue, if you have it not.	Hamlet
A was a man. Take him for all in all, I shall not look upon his like again.	Hamlet
Ay, springes to catch woodcocks.	Polonius
Be all my sins remembered.	Hamlet
Beggar that I am, I am even poor in thanks.	Hamlet
Be somewhat scanter of your maiden presence.	Polonius
Be thou as chaste as ice, as pure as snow, thou shalt not escape calumny. Get thee to a nunnery, go, farewell.	Hamlet
Beware of entrance to a quarrel, but being in, bear't that the opposed may be aware of thee.	Polonius
Brevity is the soul of wit.	Polonius
But I am pigeon-liver'd and lack gall to make oppression bitter.	Hamlet
But I have that within which passeth show – these but the trappings and the suits of woe.	Hamlet
But in the gross and scope of my opinion, this bodes some strange eruption to our state.	Horatio
But, look, the morn, in russet mantle clad, walks o'er the dew of yon high eastern hill.	Horatio
But soft! methinks I scent the morning air.	Ghost
But that I am forbid to tell the secrets of my prison-house, I could a tale unfold.	Ghost
Come, give us a taste of your quality.	Hamlet
Cudgel thy brains no more about it.	First Clown
Cut off even in the blossoms of my sin.	Ghost
Do not, as some ungracious pastors do, show me the steep and thorny way to heaven.	Ophelia
Doubt thou the stars are fire; doubt that the sun doth move; doubt truth to be a liar; but never doubt I love.	Polonius
For this relief much thanks; tis bitter cold and I am sick at heart.	Francisco
Frailty thy name is woman.	Hamlet
Give it an understanding but no tongue.	Hamlet
Give me that man that is not passion's slave, and I will wear him in my heart's core, ay, in my heart of heart, as I do thee.	Hamlet
God's bodykins, man, much better. Use every man after his desert, and who should 'scape whipping?	Hamlet
Hath oped his ponderous and marble jaws.	Hamlet
His greatness weighed, his will is not his own.	Laertes
How now, a rat? dead for a ducat, dead.	Hamlet
I am but mad north-north-west; when the wind is southerly, I know a hawk from a handsaw.	Hamlet
I do not set my life at a pin's fee.	Hamlet
I doubt some foul play.	Hamlet

S H A K E S P E A R E

I have heard of your paintings too, well enough. God hath given you one face, and you make yourselves another.	Hamlet
I have thought some of nature's journeymen had made men and not made them well, they impersonated humanity so abominably.	Hamlet
Imperious Caesar, dead, and turn'd to clay. Might stop a hole to keep the wind away.	Hamlet
I must be cruel only to be kind.	Hamlet
In my mind's eye, Horatio.	Hamlet
In the dead waste and middle of the night.	Horatio
It goes so heavily with my disposition that this goodly frame, the earth, seems to me a sterile promontory.	Hamlet
It is not nor it cannot come to good. But break, my heart, for I must hold my tongue.	Hamlet
It out-Herods Herod.	Hamlet
It was as I have seen it in his life, a sable silver'd.	Horatio
It will discourse most excellent music.	Hamlet
I will speak daggers to her, but use none.	Hamlet
Look with what courteous action, it wafts you to a more removed ground.	Marcellus
Marry, this is miching *malhecho*. That means mischief.	Hamlet
More matter, with less art.	Queen Gertrude
Murder most foul, as in the best it is.	Ghost
Must, like a whore, unpack my heart with words.	Hamlet
My words fly up, my thoughts remain below.	King Claudius
Neither a borrower, nor a lender be.	Polonius
Now cracks a noble heart. Goodnight, sweet prince, and flight of angels sing thee to thy rest.	Horatio
O Hamlet, what a falling off was there!	Ghost
O, my offence is rank! it smells to heaven.	King Claudius
O my prophetic soul! mine uncle?	Hamlet
On fortune's cap we are not the very button.	Guildenstern
O, that this too too solid flesh would melt, thaw and resolve itself into a dew	Hamlet
O villain, villain, smiling, damned villain!	Hamlet
O, what a noble mind is here o'erthrown!	Ophelia
O, what a rogue and peasant slave am I.	Hamlet
Rest, rest, perturbed spirit!	Hamlet
Seems, madam? nay, it is; I know not 'seems'.	Hamlet
So excellent a king, that was, to this, Hyperion to a satyr: so loving to my mother, that he might not beteem the winds of heaven visit her face too roughly.	Hamlet
Some say that ever 'gainst that season comes, wherein our saviour's birth is celebrated, the bird of dawning singeth all night long.	Marcellus
Something is rotten in the state of Denmark.	Marcellus
Speak the speech, I pray you, as I pronounced it to you.	Hamlet
Still harping on my daughter.	Polonius
Suit the action to the word, the word to the action.	Hamlet
Take these again; for to the noble mind, rich gifts wax poor when givers prove unkind.	Ophelia
Tear a passion to tatters, to very rags, to split the ears of the groundlings.	Hamlet
That he is mad, 'tis true; 'tis true 'tis pity and pity 'tis 'tis true.	Polonius
The best actors in the world, either for tragedy, comedy, history pastoral, pastorical-comical, historical-pastoral, tragical-historical, tragical-comical-historical-pastoral, scene individable, or poem unlimited. Seneca cannot be too heavy, nor Plautus too light.	Polonius
The chariest maid is prodigal enough if she unmask her beauty to the moon.	Laertes
The glow-worm shows the matin to be near.	Ghost
The lady doth protest too much, methinks.	Queen Gertrude
The mobled queen.	Hamlet
The play, I remember, pleased not the million; 'twas caviare to the general.	Hamlet
The play's the thing wherein I'll catch the conscience of the King.	Hamlet
There are more things in heaven and earth, Horatio, than are dreamt of in your philosophy.	Hamlet
There is nothing either good or bad, but thinking makes it so.	Hamlet
There's rosemary, that's for remembrance. Pray, love, remember. And there is pansies; that's for thoughts.	Ophelia
The rest is silence. O, O, O, O!	Hamlet
These are but wild and whirling words, my lord.	Horatio
The time is out of joint. O cursed spite, that ever I was born to set it right.	Hamlet
They are the abstract and brief chronicles of the time.	Hamlet
This is the very coinage of your brain.	Queen Gertrude
This sweaty haste doth make the night joint-labourer with the day.	Marcellus
Though this be madness, yet there is method in't.	Polonius
Thou know'st 'tis common; all that lives must die.	Queen Gertrude
Thrift, thrift, Horatio! the funeral baked meats did coldly furnish forth the marriage tables.	Hamlet
'Tis now the very witching time of night, when churchyards yawn and hell itself breathes out contagion to this world.	Hamlet
To be, or not to be; that is the question: whether 'tis nobler in the mind to suffer the slings and arrows of outrageous fortune, or to take arms against a sea of troubles, and,	Hamlet

by opposing, end them. To die, to sleep – no more, and by a sleep to say we end the heartache and the thousand natural shocks that flesh is heir to – 'tis a consummation devoutly to be wished. To die, to sleep. To sleep, perchance to dream. Ay, there's the rub, for in that sleep of death what dreams may come when we have shuffled off this mortal coil must give us pause.

Unhand me, gentlemen; by heaven, I'll make a ghost of him that lets me.	Hamlet
Very like a whale.	Polonius
We do it wrong, being so majestical, to offer it the show of violence.	Marcellus
We know what we are, but know not what we may be.	Ophelia
What, frighted with false fire?	Hamlet
What may this mean, that thou, dead corpse, again in complete steel, revisit'st thus the glimpses of the moon, making night hideous.	Hamlet
What's Hecuba to him or he to Hecuba, that he should weep for her?	Hamlet
What should such fellows as I do, crawling between earth and heaven.	Hamlet
When sorrows come, they come not single spies, but in battalions.	King Claudius
Whether in sea or fire, in earth or air, the extravagant and erring spirit hies to his confine.	Horatio
While memory holds a seat in this distracted globe.	Hamlet
While one with moderate haste might tell a hundred.	Horatio
Whose sore task does not divide the Sunday from the week.	Marcellus
Why, let the stricken deer go weep, the hart ungalled play, for some must watch, while some must sleep, so runs the world away.	Hamlet
Why, she would hang on him, as if increase of appetite had grown by what it fed on.	Hamlet
With devotion's visage and pious action we do sugar o'er the devil himself.	Polonius
With one auspicious and one dropping eye, with mirth in funeral and with dirge in marriage.	King Claudius

Précis of plot

King Hamlet has been murdered by his brother Claudius, who has usurped the throne and married Gertrude, the King's widow. Prince Hamlet gains his revenge by feigning madness and ultimately killing his would-be assassins and Claudius.

Setting

Denmark.

8 Henry IV Part 1

KING HENRY IV	SIR JOHN Oldcastle
PRINCE HARRY, Prince of Wales, Henry's son	Edward (Ned) POINS
Lord JOHN OF LANCASTER, Henry's son	RUSSELL
Earl of WESTMORLAND	HARVEY
Sir Walter BLUNT	Earl of DOUGLAS
Earl of WORCESTER	FRANCIS, a drawer
Percy, Earl of NORTHUMBERLAND, his brother	VINTNER
Henry Percy, known as HOTSPUR, Northumberland's son	GADSHILL
Kate, LADY PERCY, Hotspur's wife	CARRIERS
Lord Edmund MORTIMER, called Earl of March	CHAMBERLAIN
LADY MORTIMER, his wife	OSTLER
OWAIN GLYNDWR, Lady Mortimer's father	TRAVELLERS
Mistress Quickly, HOSTESS of an Eastcheap inn	SHERIFF
Sir Richard VERNON	MESSENGERS
Scrope, ARCHBISHOP of York	SERVANT
SIR MICHAEL, member of the Archbishop's household	Lords and soldiers

Quotations

	Spoken by
A fellow of no mark nor likelihood.	King Henry
And such a deal of skimble-skamble stuff.	Hotspur
A plague of all cowards, I say.	Sir John
A plague of sighing and grief, it blows a man up like a bladder.	Sir John
Banish plump Jack, and banish all the world.	Sir John
By heaven, methinks it were an easy leap.	Hotspur
Came there a certain lord, neat and trimly dressed, fresh as a bridegroom, and his chin, new reaped, showed like a stubble-land at harvest-home. He was perfumed like a milliner, and 'twixt his finger and his thumb he held a pouncet-box, which ever and anon he gave his nose and took't away again.	Hotspur
Company, villainous company hath been the spoil of me.	Sir John
Domesday is near: die all, die merrily.	Hotspur
Farewell, the latter spring; farewell, All-hallown summer.	Prince Harry
He made me mad, to see him shine so brisk, and smell so sweet, and talk so like a waiting-gentlewoman, of guns and drums, and wounds, God save the mark! and telling me the sovereign'st thing on earth was parmacity for an inward bruise.	Hotspur
He was but as the cuckoo is in June, heard, not regarded.	King Henry
I am bewitched by the rogue's company.	Sir John
I am not in the role of common men.	Glyndwr

I am not yet of Percy's mind, the Hotspur of the North – he that kills me some six or seven dozen of Scots at a breakfast, washes his hands, and says to his wife, 'Fie upon this quiet life! I want work.'	Prince Harry
I could brain him with his lady's fan.	Hotspur
If all the year were playing holidays, to sport would be as tedious as to work.	Prince Harry
If reasons were as plentiful as blackberries.	Sir John
In those holy fields, over whose acres walk'd those blessed feet; which fourteen hundred years ago were nailed, for our advantage, on the bitter cross.	King Henry
I saw young Harry, with his beaver on.	Vernon
It would be argument for a week, laughter for a month, and a good jest forever.	Prince Harry
I understand thy kisses, and thou mine.	Mortimer
Let us be Diana's foresters, gentlemen of the shade, minions of the moon.	Sir John
Look down into the pomegranate, Ralph!	Francis
O, the blood more stirs to rouse a lion than to start a hare!	Hotspur
Old father antic, the law.	Sir John
So shaken as we are, so wan with care.	King Henry
O, thou hast damnable iteration, and art indeed able to corrupt a saint.	Sir John
O, monstrous! eleven buckram men grown out of two!	Prince Harry
Tell truth and shame the devil.	Hotspur
There lives not three good men unhanged in England, and one of them is fat and grows old.	Sir John
There's neither honesty, manhood, nor good fellowship in thee.	Sir John
'Tis my vocation, Hal. 'Tis no sin for a man to labour in his vocation.	Sir John
Two stars keep not their motion in one sphere.	Prince Harry
What, in thy quips and thy quiddities.	Sir John
You rogue, they were bound every man of them, or I am a jew else, an Hebrew jew.	Sir John

Précis of plot
The main plot tells of the rebellions against King Henry by Worcester, Hotspur and Glyndwr. However, the sub-plots highlighting the characters of the young Prince Hal and the reprobate Sir John Oldcastle (Falstaff) lend the real substance to the play.

Setting
England in the early 15th century.

9 Henry IV Part 2

KING HENRY IV	Ensign PISTOL
PRINCE HARRY, later crowned King Henry V	PETO
PRINCE JOHN of Lancaster, Henry IV's son	DOLL TEARSHEET, a whore
SIR JOHN Falstaff	GOWER, a messenger
Bardolf	Sir John Blunt
Poins	Sir John Coleville
Falstaff's Page	Lord Hastings
Humphrey, Duke of GLOUCESTER, Henry IV's son	SNARE, a sergeant
Thomas, Duke of CLARENCE, Henry IV's son	FANG, a sergeant
Percy, Earl of NORTHUMBERLAND, of the rebels' party	Neville, Earl of WARWICK
NORTHUMBERLAND'S WIFE	Earl of SURREY
KATE, their son Hotspur's widow	Earl of WESTMORLAND
TRAVERS, Northumberland's servant	HARCOURT
MORTON, a bearer of news from Shrewsbury	Ralph MOULDY
Scrope, ARCHBISHOP of York	Simon SHADOW
Thomas, Lord MOWBRAY, the Earl Marshal	Thomas WART
MISTRESS QUICKLY, hostess of a tavern	Francis FEEBLE
PORTER of Northumberland's household	Peter BULLCALF
Robert SHALLOW, a country justice	DRAWERS
DAVY, Shallow's servant	BEADLES
SILENCE, a country justice	GROOMS
Sneak and other musicians	MESSENGER
Lord Chief Justice's men, soldiers and attendants	

Quotations

	Spoken by
A foutre for the world and worldlings base! I speak of Africa and golden joys.	Pistol
A joint of mutton, and any pretty little tiny kickshaws.	Shallow
A man can die but once.	Feeble
A rascally yea-forsooth knave.	Sir John
An habitation giddy and unsure, hath he that buildeth on the vulgar heart.	Archbishop of York
Away, you scullion, you rampallian, you fustilarian! I'll tickle your catastrophe.	Page
By my troth, captain, these are very bitter words.	Mistress Quickly
Death, as the psalmist saith, is certain to all; all shall die. How a good yoke of bullocks at Stamford fair?	Shallow
Even such a man, so faint, so spiritless, so dull, so dead in look, so woe-begone, drew Priam's curtain in the dead of night.	Northumberland
For my voice, I have lost it with hallowing and singing of anthems.	Sir John

He hath eaten me out of house and home.	Mistress Quickly
He was indeed the glass wherein the noble youth did dress themselves.	Lady Percy
I am not only witty in myself, but the cause that wit is in other men.	Sir John
I beseek you now, aggravate your choler.	Mistress Quickly
I can get no remedy against this consumption of the purse. Borrowing only lingers and lingers it out, but the disease is incurable.	Sir John
If I do, fillip me with a three-man beetle.	Sir John
Is it not strange that desire should so many years outlive performance.	Poins
I know thee not old man, fall to thy prayers.	King Harry
It was always yet the trick of our English nation, if they have a good thing, to make it too common.	Sir John
Let the end try the man.	Prince Harry
Lord, Lord, how subject we old men are to this vice of lying.	Sir John
O, sleep, O gentle sleep, nature's soft nurse, how have I frighted thee, that thou no more wilt weigh my eyelids down, and steep my senses in forgetfulness.	King Henry
Past and to come seems best; things present, worst.	Archbishop of York
Thou didst swear to me, upon a parcel-gilt goblet, sitting in my Dolphin-chamber, at the round table, by a sea coal fire, upon Wednesday in Wheeson week.	Mistress Quickly
Under which king, Besonian? speak, or die.	Pistol
Uneasy lies the head that wears a crown.	King Henry
We have heard the chimes at midnight, Master Shallow.	Sir John
We that are in the vanguard of our youth, I must confess, are wags too.	Sir John
Wilt thou upon the high and giddy mast, seal up the ship-boy's eyes, and rock his brains.	King Henry
With all appliances, and means to boot.	King Henry
Yet the first bringer of unwelcome news hath but a losing office, and his tongue sounds ever after as a sullen bell remembered knolling a departing friend.	Northumberland

Précis of plot

The plot of the first part of Henry IV is continued, although there are subtle changes made to certain characters and the historical content is not so highlighted. Hal is still plagued with rebellions, albeit from different spheres, but his anxieties over Prince Harry's behaviour are eventually alleviated in a touching scene, and this change of character is shown to the full in Harry's rejection of Sir John after his crowning.

Setting

England in the early 15th century.

10 Henry V

KING HARRY V of England, claimant to French throne	Sir Thomas ERPINGHAM
Duke of GLOUCESTER, the King's brother	John BATES
Duke of CLARENCE, the King's brother	Alexander COURT
Duke of EXETER, his uncle	Michael WILLIAMS
KING CHARLES VI of France	HERALD
ISABEL, his wife and queen	Duke of YORK
The DAUPHIN, their son and heir	SALISBURY
CATHERINE, their daughter	WESTMORLAND
Archbishop of CANTERBURY	WARWICK
ALICE, an old gentlewoman	Bishop of ELY
Richard, Earl of CAMBRIDGE	Sir Thomas GREY
Henry, Lord SCROPE of Masham	Duke of BOURBON
The CONSTABLE of France	Duke of ORLÉANS
MONTJOY, the French Herald	Duke of BERRI
GOVERNOR of Harfleur	Lord RAMBURES
French AMBASSADORS to England	Lord GRANDPRÉ
BOY, formerly Falstaff's page	Duke of BURGUNDY
HOSTESS, formerly Mistress Quickly, now Pistol's wife	PISTOL
Captain GOWER, an Englishman	NIM
Captain FLUELLEN, a Welshman	BARDOLPH
Captain MACMORRIS, an Irishman	CHORUS
Captain JAMY, a Scot	

Quotations

	Spoken by
All hell shall stir for this.	Pistol
And gentlemen in England now abed, shall think themselves accursed they were not here, and hold their manhoods cheap while any speaks, that fought with us upon Saint Crispin's day.	King Harry
And make your chronicle as rich with praise, as is the ooze and bottom of the sea.	Canterbury
As 'tis ever common that men are merriest when they are from home.	King Harry
Base is the slave that pays.	Pistol
But if it be a sin to covet honour, I am the most offending soul alive.	King Harry
Can this cock-pit hold the vasty fields of France? or may we cram, within this wooden O the very casques that did affright the air at Agincourt?	Chorus
Consideration like an angel came, and whipp'd the offending Adam out of him.	Canterbury
Cry, 'God for Harry! England and Saint George.'	King Harry

SHAKESPEARE

Every subject's duty is the king's; but every subject's soul is his own.	King Harry
For so work the honey-bees, creatures that by a rule in nature teach the act of order to a peopled kingdom.	Canterbury
For these fellows of infinite tongue, that can rhyme themselves into ladies' favours, they do always reason themselves out again.	King Harry
From camp to camp through the foul womb of night.	Chorus
He's in Arthur's bosom, if ever man went to Arthur's bosom.	Hostess
I dare not fight, but I will wink and hold out mine iron.	Nim
I see you stand like greyhounds in the slips.	King Harry
If he be not fellow with the best king, thou shalt find the best king of good fellows.	King Harry
If we are marked to die, we are enough to do our country loss; and if to live, the fewer men, the greater share of honour.	King Harry
I thought upon one pair of English legs did march three Frenchmen.	King Harry
Men of few words are the best men.	Boy
Now all the youth of England are on fire, and silken dalliance in the wardrobe lies.	Chorus
O that we now had here, but one ten thousand of those men in England that do no work today!	Warwick
Old men forget, yet all shall be forgot; but he'll remember with advantages, what feats he did that day.	King Harry
Once more unto the breach, dear friends, once more.	King Harry
On, on, you noblest English, whose blood is fet from fathers of war-proof. Fathers that, like so many Alexanders, have in these parts from morn til even fought, and sheathed their swords for lack of argument.	King Harry
Self love, my liege, is not so vile a sin as self neglecting.	Dauphin
Tennis balls, my liege.	Exeter
Then shall our names, familiar in his mouth as household words – Harry the King, Bedford and Exeter, Warwick and Talbot, Salisbury and Gloucester – be in their flowing cups, freshly remember'd.	King Harry
There is occasions and causes why and wherefore in all things.	Fluellen
There is some soul of goodness in these evils.	King Harry
This day is called the feast of Crispian. He that outlives this day and comes safe home will stand a-tiptoe when this day is named, and rouse him of the name of Crispian.	King Harry
Though patience be a tired mare, yet she will plod.	Nim
Trust none, for oaths are straws, men's faiths are wafer-cakes, and hold-fast is the only dog, my duck.	Pistol
Turn him to any cause of policy, the Gordian knot of it he will unloose.	Canterbury
We few, we happy few, we band of brothers.	King Harry

Précis of plot
The war against France dominates the play, although Shakespeare stayed loyal to many characters from the two parts of Henry IV to create comic diversion.

Setting
England and France 1414 to 1420.

11 Henry VI Part 1

KING HENRY VI	BASSET
Duke of GLOUCESTER, Lord Protector, uncle of Henry	A LAWYER
Duke of BEDFORD, regent of France	A LEGATE
Duke of EXETER	Earl of WARWICK
Bishop of WINCHESTER (later Cardinal), uncle of Henry	Earl of SALISBURY
Duke of SOMERSET	Earl of SUFFOLK
RICHARD PLANTAGENET, later DUKE OF YORK	Edmund MORTIMER
Duke of BURGUNDY, uncle of King Henry	Duke of ALENÇON
GENERAL of the French garrison at Bordeaux	BASTARD of Orléans
RENÉ, Duke of Anjou, King of Naples	Lord TALBOT
MARGARET, his daughter	JOHN Talbot
Sir William GLASDALE	COUNTESS of Auvergne
Sir Thomas GARGRAVE	MASTER GUNNER of Orléans
Sir John FASTOLF	A BOY, his son
Sir William LUCY	JOAN la Pucelle
CHARLES, Dauphin of France	A SHEPHERD, father of Joan
WOODVILLE, Lieutenant of the Tower of London	MAYOR of London
Porter, French sergeant, sentinels, scout, herald, officers	VERNON
Governor of Paris, fiends and soldiers, servingmen	
Messengers and keepers of the Tower of London	

Quotations	**Spoken by**
And while I live, I'll ne'er fly from a man.	Joan
Between two hawks, which flies the higher pitch.	Warwick
Between two dogs, which hath the deeper mouth.	
Between two blades, which bears the better temper.	
Between two horses, which doth bear him best.	

Between two girls, which hath the merriest eye.   Joan
I have perhaps some shallow spirit of judgement.
Christ's mother helps me, else I were too weak.   Bedford
Unbidden guests are often welcomest when they are gone.

Précis of plot
The first part of Henry VI covers the period between the funeral of Henry V and the end of the Hundred Years War, between England and France. As in many of the Shakespearian plays, the historical accuracy comes second to the plot.

Setting
England 1422 to 1453.

12 Henry VI Part 2

KING HENRY VI and QUEEN MARGARET	Gloucester's SERVANTS
William de la Pole, Marquis, later Duke of SUFFOLK	Two SHERIFFS of London
Duke Humphrey of GLOUCESTER, the Lord Protector	Sir John STANLEY
Dame Eleanor Cobham, the DUCHESS of Gloucester	HERALD
CARDINAL BEAUFORT, Bishop of Winchester	Two MURDERERS
Duke of BUCKINGHAM	COMMONS
Duke of SOMERSET	CAPTAIN of a ship
Old Lord CLIFFORD and YOUNG CLIFFORD, his son	MASTER of that ship
Duke of YORK	The Master's MATE
EDWARD, Earl of March, the Duke's son	Walter WHITMORE
Crookback RICHARD, the Duke's son	Two GENTLEMEN
Earl of SALISBURY and Earl of WARWICK, his son	Jack CADE, a Kentishman
Emmanuel, the CLERK of Chatham	Dick the BUTCHER
Two or three PETITIONERS	Smith the WEAVER
Thomas HORNER, an armourer	A sawyer
PETER Thump, his man	JOHN
Three NEIGHBOURS, who drink to Horner	REBELS
Three PRENTICES, who drink to Peter	Sir Humphrey STAFFORD
Sir John HUME, a priest	STAFFORD'S BROTHER
John SOUTHWELL, a priest	Lord SAYE
Margery Jordan, a WITCH	Lord SCALES
Roger BOLINGBROKE, a conjurer	Matthew Gough
ASNATH, a spirit	A SERGEANT
Three or four CITIZENS of London	A BEADLE of Saint Albans
Simon SIMPCOX and SIMPCOX'S WIFE	Townsmen of Saint Albans
The MAYOR of Saint Albans	VAUX, a messenger
Alexander IDEN, who kills Cade	A POST
Aldermen of Saint Albans	MESSENGERS
Attendants, guards, servants, soldiers, falconers	A SOLDIER

Quotations

	Spoken by
Could I come near your beauty with my nails, I'd set my ten commandments in your face.	Duchess
Is not this a lamentable thing that of the skin of an innocent lamb should be made parchment? that parchment being scribbled o'er should undo a man?	Cade
Sir, he made a chimney in my father's house, and the bricks are alive at this day to testify.	Weaver
Smooth runs the water where the brook is deep.	Suffolk
The first thing we do let's kill all the lawyers.	Dick the Butcher
The gaudy, blabbing, and remorseful day, is crept into the bosom of the sea.	Captain
There shall be in England seven halfpenny loaves sold for a penny, the three-hooped pot shall have ten hoops and I will make it a felony to drink small beer.	Cade
Thou hast most traitorously corrupted the youth of the realm in erecting a grammar school; and, whereas before, our forefathers had no books but the score and tally, thou hast caused printing to be used and, contrary to the King, his crown and dignity, thou hast built a paper mill.	Cade
What stronger breastplate than a heart untainted.	King Henry

Précis of plot
The original title of this play was *The First Part of the Contention of the Two Famous Houses of York and Lancaster*, and Shakespeare has stayed true, to a great extent, to this period of history, which includes the Kentish rebellion led by Jack Cade, and ultimately leads to the Wars of the Roses.

Setting
England 1445 to 1455.

13 Henry VI Part 3

KING HENRY VI
QUEEN MARGARET
PRINCE EDWARD, their son
Duke of SOMERSET
Duke of EXETER
Earl of NORTHUMBERLAND
Earl of WESTMORLAND
Lord CLIFFORD
Lord Stafford
SOMERVILLE
Henry, young Earl of Richmond
A SOLDIER who has killed his father
A HUNTSMAN who guards King Edward
The divided House of Neville:
Earl of WARWICK
Marquis of MONTAGUE, his brother
Earl of OXFORD, their brother-in-law
Lord HASTINGS, their brother-in-law
Of the Duke of York's party:
Richard Plantagenet, Duke of YORK
EDWARD, Earl of March, his son, later KING EDWARD IV
LADY GRAY, a widow, later Edward's wife and queen
Earl RIVERS, Lady Gray's brother

GEORGE, later DUKE OF CLARENCE
RICHARD, later DUKE OF GLOUCESTER
Earl of RUTLAND, Edward's brother
Rutland's TUTOR, a chaplain
SIR JOHN Mortimer, York's uncle
Sir Hugh Mortimer, his brother
Duke of NORFOLK
Sir William Stanley
Earl of Pembroke
Sir John MONTGOMERY
A NOBLEMAN
Two GAMEKEEPERS
Three WATCHMEN
LIEUTENANT of the Tower

The French:
KING LOUIS
LADY BONA, his sister-in-law
Lord Bourbon, the French High Admiral

A SOLDIER who has killed his son
Mayor of Coventry
MAYOR of York
Aldermen of YORK
Soldiers, messengers and attendants

Quotations

	Spoken by
Didst thou never hear that things ill got had ever bad success?	King Henry
Down, down to hell, and say I sent thee thither.	Richard of Gloucester
Gives not the hawthorn bush a sweeter shade, to shepherds looking on their seely sheep, than doth a rich embroider'd canopy, to Kings that fear their subjects' treachery?	King Henry
My crown is in my heart, not on my head.	King Henry
O God! methinks it were a happy life, to be no better than a homely swain, to sit upon a hill, as I do now; to carve out dials quaintly, point by point, thereby to see the minutes how they run. How many makes the hour full complete, how many hours bring about the day, how many days will finish up the year, how many years a mortal man may live.	King Henry
Oh tiger's heart wrapp'd in a woman's hide!	York
Suspicion always haunts the guilty mind, the thief doth fear each bush an officer.	Richard of Gloucester

Précis of plot

This play chronicles the substantive episodes in the War of the Roses, although the usual Shakespearian anachronisms do not detract from the play's subtleties.

Setting

England 1455 to 1471.

14 Henry VIII (All Is True)

PROLOGUE
KING HENRY VIII
Duke of BUCKINGHAM
Lord ABERGAVENNY
Earl of SURREY
Duke of NORFOLK
Duke of SUFFOLK
LORD CHAMBERLAIN
LORD CHANCELLOR
Lord SANDS (aka Sir William Sands)
Sir Thomas LOVELL
Sir Anthony DENNY
Sir Henry GUILDFORD
CARDINAL WOLSEY
Two SECRETARIES
Buckingham's SURVEYOR
CARDINAL CAMPEIUS
GARDINER, King's secretary, later Bishop of Winchester
His PAGE
Thomas CROMWELL
CRANMER, Archbishop of Canterbury
QUEEN KATHERINE, later KATHERINE, Princess Dowager
GRIFFITH, her gentleman usher
PATIENCE, her waiting woman

Archbishop of Canterbury
Bishop of LINCOLN
Bishop of Ely
Bishop of Rochester
Bishop of Saint Asaph
Two priests
Serjeant-at-arms
Two noblemen
A CRIER
Appearing in the Coronation:
Three GENTLEMEN
Two judges
Choristers
Lord Mayor of London
Garter King of Arms
Marquis of Dorset
Four Barons of the Cinque Ports
Stokesley, Bishop of London
Old Duchess of Norfolk
Countesses

A MESSENGER
Lord CAPUTIUS
ANNE Boleyn

Other WOMEN
Six spirits who dance before Katherine in a vision
At Cranmer's trial:
A DOOR-KEEPER
Doctor BUTTS, the King's physician
Pursuivants, pages, footboys, grooms
BRANDON
SERJEANT-AT-ARMS
Sir Nicholas VAUX
Tipstaves, Halberdiers and common people
Appearing at the Legatine Court:
Two vergers
Ladies, gentlemen, a SERVANT, attendants

An OLD LADY
At the Christening:
A PORTER
His MAN
Two aldermen
Lord Mayor of London
GARTER King of Arms
Six noblemen
Old Duchess of Norfolk, godmother
Princess Elizabeth, the child
Marchioness Dorset, godmother

EPILOGUE
Two SCRIBES

Quotations

	Spoken by
A peace above all earthly dignities, a still and quiet conscience.	Cardinal Wolsey
Cromwell, I charge thee, fling away ambition. By that sin fell the angels.	Cardinal Wolsey
Had I but serv'd my God with half the zeal I served my King, he would not in mine age have left me naked to mine enemies.	Cardinal Wolsey
Heaven is above all yet – there sits a judge that no king can corrupt.	Queen Katherine
He gave his honours to the world again, his blessed part to heaven, and slept in peace.	Griffith
He was a man of an unbounded stomach.	Katherine
Love thyself last. Cherish those hearts that hate thee.	Cardinal Wolsey
He was a scholar, and a ripe and good one.	Griffith
Men's evil manners live in brass; their virtues we write in water	Griffith
So farewell – to the little good you bear me. Farewell, a long farewell, to all my greatness!	Cardinal Wolsey
So may he rest, his faults lie gently on him.	Katherine
Those twins of learning that he raised in you, Ipswich and Oxford.	Griffith
'Tis better to be lowly born, and range with humble livers in content, than to be perk'd up in a glistering grief and wear a golden sorrow.	Anne
Vain pomp and glory of this world, I hate ye!	Cardinal Wolsey

Précis of plot
The reign of Henry VIII from the opening description of the Field of the Cloth of Gold, of 1520, to the christening of Princess Elizabeth, in 1533.

Setting
England 1521 to 1533.

15 Julius Caesar

Julius CAESAR
CALPURNIA, his wife
Marcus BRUTUS, a noble Roman, opposed to Caesar
PORTIA, his wife
LUCIUS, his servant
Officers and soldiers in Brutus' army:
LUCILLIUS
MESSALA
VARRUS
CLAUDIO
YOUNG CATO
STRATO
VOLUMNIUS
FLAVIUS
DARDANIUS
CLITUS
Rulers of Rome after Caesar's death:
Mark ANTONY
OCTAVIUS Caesar
LEPIDUS

PINDARUS, Cassius' bondman
TITINIUS, an officer in Cassius' army
POPILLIUS Laena, a Senator
Senators, soldiers and attendants

ARTEMIDORUS
CINNA the Poet
Opposed to Caesar:
Caius CASSIUS
CASCA
TREBONIUS
DECIUS Brutus
METELLUS Cimber
CINNA
Caius LIGARIUS

FLAVIUS, a tribune
MURELLUS, a tribune
CICERO, a Senator
PUBLIUS, a Senator

A POET
GHOST of Caesar
A COBBLER
A CARPENTER
Other PLEBEIANS
A MESSENGER
SERVANTS
SOOTHSAYER

Quotations

	Spoken by
As Caesar loved me, I weep for him.	Brutus
As proper men as ever trod upon neat's leather have gone upon my handiwork.	Cobbler

SHAKESPEARE

Between the acting of a dreadful thing and the first motion, all the interim is like a phantasma, or a hideous dream.	Brutus
Beware the ides of March.	Soothsayer
But for your words, they rob the Hybla bees, and leave them honeyless.	Cassius
But I am constant as the Northern Star, of whose true fixed and resting quality, there is no fellow in the firmament.	Caesar
But when I tell him he hates flatterers; he says he does being then most flattered.	Decius
But yesterday the word of Caesar might have stood against the world. Now lies he there, and none so poor to do him reverence.	Antony
Caesar said to me 'Darest thou, Cassius, now leap in with me into this angry flood, and swim to yonder point?' Upon the word, accoutred as I was I plunged in and bade him follow.	Cassius
Cowards die many times before their deaths; the valiant never taste of death but once.	Caesar
Cry 'havoc' and let slip the dogs of war.	Antony
Et tu, Brute? – then fall Caesar.	Caesar (last words)
Fierce fiery warriors fight upon the clouds, in ranks and squadrons and right form of war.	Calpurnia
For Brutus is an honourable man; so are they all, all honourable men.	Antony
For he will never follow anything that other men begin.	Brutus
For I have neither wit, nor words, nor worth, action nor utterance, nor the power of speech, to stir men's blood.	Antony
Friends, Romans, countrymen, lend me your ears.	Antony
He reads much, he is a great observer, and he looks quite through the deeds of men.	Caesar
His life was gentle, and the elements so mixed in him that nature might stand up and say to all the world, 'This was a man'.	Antony
How hard it is for women to keep counsel!	Portia
How many ages hence, shall this our lofty scene be acted over, in states unborn and accents yet unknown.	Cassius
I am no orator as Brutus is; but as you know me all, a plain blunt man.	Antony
I am not gamesome; I do lack some part of that quick spirit that is in Antony.	Brutus
If you have tears, prepare to shed them now.	Antony
I had rather be a dog and bay the moon than such a Roman.	Brutus
Let me have men about me who are fat.	Caesar
Let's carve him as a dish fit for the gods.	Brutus
Lowliness is young ambition's ladder, whereto the climber upward turns his face; but when he once attains the upmost round, he then unto the ladder turns his back, looks in the clouds, scorning the base degrees by which he did ascend.	Brutus
Now in the name of all the gods at once, upon what meat doth this our Caesar feed, that he is grown so great?	Cassius
O judgement, thou art fled to brutish beasts, and men have lost their reasons!	Antony
O pardon me, thou bleeding piece of earth, that I am meek and gentle with these butchers!	Antony
See what a rent the envious Casca made.	Antony
Set honour in one eye and death i'th'other, and I will look on both indifferently.	Brutus
There is a tide in the affairs of men, which, taken at the flood, leads on to fortune.	Brutus
There was a Brutus once that would have brooked the eternal devil to keep his state in Rome, as easily as a king.	Cassius
This was the most unkindest cut of all.	Antony
This was the noblest Roman of them all.	Antony
Well, honour is the subject of my story. I cannot tell what you and other men think of this life; but, for my single self, I had as lief not be, as live to be in awe of such a thing as I myself.	Cassius
When beggars die, there are no comets seen; the heavens themselves blaze forth the death of princes.	Calpurnia
When love begins to sicken and decay, it useth an enforced ceremony.	Brutus
Why, he that cuts off twenty years of life, cuts off so many years of fearing death.	Casca
Why, man, he doth bestride the narrow world like a Colossus.	Cassius
Yet Brutus says he was ambitious, and Brutus is an honourable man.	Antony
Yond Cassius has a lean and hungry look. He thinks too much. Such men are dangerous.	Caesar
You are my true and honourable wife, as dear to me as are the ruddy drops that visit my sad heart.	Brutus
You blocks, you stones, you worse than senseless things!	Murellus

Précis of plot

The play depicts the events that led to the assassination of Julius Caesar and the aftermath thereof. As in many Shakespearian History plays, facts are often altered and rearranged in the interests of dramatic economy and effectiveness.

Setting

Rome, Sardis and near Philippi 44 to 42 BC.

16 King John

KING JOHN of England
QUEEN ELEANOR, his mother
LADY FALCONBRIDGE
Philip the BASTARD, later knighted as Richard Plantagenet,
her illegitimate son by King Richard I
Robert FALCONBRIDGE, her legitimate son
James GURNEY, her attendant
Lady BLANCHE of Spain, niece of King John
PRINCE HENRY, son of King John
HUBERT, a follower of King John
KING PHILIP of France
LOUIS THE DAUPHIN, his son
ARTHUR, Duke of Brittaine, nephew of King John
Lady CONSTANCE, his mother
Duke of AUSTRIA (Limoges)
CHÂTILLON, ambassador
Cardinal PANDOLF, a legate from the Pope
PETER OF POMFRET, a prophet
Lords, soldiers, attendants

Earl of SALISBURY
Earl of PEMBROKE
Earl of ESSEX
Lord BIGOT
A CITIZEN of Angers
HERALDS
EXECUTIONERS
MESSENGERS
SHERIFF

Quotations

	Spoken by
And oftentimes excusing of a fault doth make the fault the worser by th' excuse.	Pembroke
Another lean unwashed artificer cuts off his tale, and talks of Arthur's death.	Hubert
For courage mounteth with occasion.	Duke of Austria
Heat me these irons hot.	Hubert
Here is my throne; bid kings come bow to it.	Constance
How oft the sight of means to do ill deeds, make deeds ill done!	King John
Life is as tedious as a twice-told tale, vexing the dull ear of a drowsy man.	Louis the Dauphin
Lord of thy presence, and no land beside?	Queen Eleanor
Saint George that swinged the dragon, and e'er since sits on his horseback at mine hostess' door.	Bastard
This England never did, nor never shall, lie at the proud foot of a conqueror.	Bastard
To gild refined gold, to paint the lily.	Salisbury
When Fortune means to men most good, she looks upon them with a threatening eye.	Pandolf
Zounds! I was never so bethumped with words, since first I called my brother's father, dad.	Bastard

Précis of plot

Selected events from King John's reign are portrayed, although Shakespeare concentrates on Philip Falconbridge, the illegitimate son of Richard I, for his sub-plot; and significant events such as Magna Carta are ignored.

Setting

England and France 1199 to 1216.

17 King Lear

LEAR, King of Britain
GONERIL, Lear's eldest daughter
Duke of ALBANY, her husband
REGAN, Lear's second daughter
Duke of CORNWALL, her husband
CORDELIA, Lear's youngest daughter
King of FRANCE, a suitor of Cordelia
Duke of BURGUNDY, a suitor of Cordelia
Earl of KENT, later disguised as Caius
Earl of GLOUCESTER

EDGAR, later disguised as Tom o' Bedlam
EDMOND, bastard son of Gloucester
OLD MAN, Gloucester's tenant
Lear's FOOL
OSWALD, Goneril's steward
A SERVANT of Cornwall
A KNIGHT
A HERALD
A CAPTAIN
Gentlemen, servants, soldiers, attendants

Quotations

	Spoken by
And my poor fool is hanged. No, No, no life? Why should a dog, a horse, a rat have life and thou no breath at all?	Lear
As flies to wanton boys are we to the gods, they kill us for their sport	Gloucester
A still soliciting eye, and such a tongue.	Cordelia
Blow, winds, and crack your cheeks! rage, blow, you cataracts and hurricanoes, spout.	Lear
Drinks the green mantle of the standing pool.	Edgar
Fie, foe, and fum; I smell the blood of a British man.	Edgar
Fortune, good night; smile once more; turn thy wheel.	Kent
Howl, howl, howl, howl! O, you are men of stones.	Lear
How sharper than a serpent's tooth it is to have a thankless child.	Lear
I am a man more sinned against than sinning.	Lear
I have seen better faces in my time than stands on any shoulder that I see before me at this instant.	Kent

S
H
A
K
E
S
P
E
A
R
E

I have seen the day, with my good biting falchion.	Lear
I'll talk a word with this same learned Theban.	Lear
Ingratitude, thou marble-hearted fiend.	Lear
I tax you not, you elements, with unkindness.	Lear
Mastiff, greyhound, mongrel grim.	Edgar
My cue is villainous melancholy, with a sigh like Tom o' Bedlam.	Edmond
O, that way madness lies. Let me shun that.	Lear
Out-paramoured the Turk.	Edgar
Poor naked wretches, whereso'er you are.	Lear
Poor Tom's a-cold.	Edgar
So young and so untender?	Lear
Take physic, pomp, expose thyself to feel what wretches feel.	Lear
The gods are just, and of our pleasant vices, make instruments to plague us.	Edgar
The little dogs and all, Tray, Blanch, and sweetheart see, they bark at me.	Lear
The prince of darkness is a gentleman.	Edgar
These late eclipses in the sun and moon portend no good to us.	Gloucester
The wheel has come full circle.	Edmond
The worst is not so long as we can say 'This is the worst'.	Edgar
Things that love night, love not such nights as these.	Kent
This is the excellent foppery of the world; that when we are sick in fortune – often the surfeits of our own behaviour – we make guilty of our disasters the sun, the moon, and stars, as if we were villains by necessity, fools by heavenly compulsion, knaves, thieves, and treachers by spherical predominance, drunkards, liars, and adulterers by an enforced obedience of planetary influence; and all that we are evil in by a divine thrusting on.	Edmond
This is the foul fiend Flibbertigibbet; he begins at curfew, and walks 'til the first cock.	Edgar
Thou whoreson Z, thou unnecessary letter.	Kent
'Tis a naughty night to swim in.	Fool
Vex not his ghost, O let him pass.	Kent
You are not worth the dust which the rude wind blows in your face.	Albany

Précis of plot
The story of a king who, angry with the failure of his virtuous youngest daughter, Cordelia, to compete for his favour in a love-test, divides his kingdom between her two malevolent sisters. The sub-plot depicts Lear's madness and the blinding of Gloucester, as well as Edgar's loyalty to his father.

Setting
Britain.

18 Love's Labour's Lost

Ferdinand, KING of Navarre	BOYET
Lords attending on the King:	Two other LORDS
BIRON	COSTARD, a Clown
LONGUEVILLE	JAQUENETTA, a country wench
DUMAINE	Sir NATHANIEL, a curate
	HOLOFERNES, a schoolmaster
	Anthony DULL, a constable
PRINCESS of France	MERCADÉ, a messenger
Ladies attending on the Princess:	A FORESTER
ROSALINE	Don Adriano de ARMADO, a Spanish
KATHERINE	braggart
MARIA	MOTE, his page

Quotations

	Spoken by
A jest's prosperity lies in the ear of him that hears it, never in the tongue of him that makes it.	Rosaline
A lover's eyes will gaze an eagle blind; a lover's ear will hear the lowest sound.	Biron
At Christmas I no more desire a rose, than wish a snow in May's new-fangled mirth.	Biron
A very beadle to a humorous sigh.	Biron
Devise wit, write pen, for I am for whole volumes, in folio.	Armado
He draweth out the thread of his verbosity finer than the staple of his argument.	Holofernes
He hath never fed of the dainties that are bred in a book.	Nathaniel
In the posteriors of this day, which the rude multitude call the afternoon.	Armado
Light, seeking light, doth light of light beguile.	Biron
Remuneration – O, that's the Latin word for three-farthings.	Costard
Spite of cormorant devouring time.	King
Study is like the heavens' glorious sun, that will not be deep-searched with saucy looks. Small have continual plodders ever won, save base authority from others' books.	Biron
This wimpled, whining, purblind, wayward boy.	Biron
Why, all delights are vain; but that most vain, which with pain purchased, doth inherit pain.	Biron

Précis of plot
The young King of Navarre, and three of his friends, vow to devote the following three years to austere self-improvement, forgoing the company of women. The ensuing farce is both sophisticated and cleverly staged.

Setting
Navarre circa 14th century.

19 Macbeth

KING DUNCAN of Scotland
MALCOLM, King Duncan's son
DONALBAIN, King Duncan's son
A CAPTAIN in Duncan's army
MACBETH, Thane of Glamis, later Thane Cawdor,
　　then King of Scotland
LADY MACBETH, Macbeth's wife
A DOCTOR, attending on Lady Macbeth
A Waiting-GENTLEWOMAN, attending on Lady Macbeth
BANQUO, a Scottish Thane
FLEANCE, his son
MACDUFF, Thane of Fife
LADY MACDUFF, his wife
MACDUFF'S SON
SIWARD, Earl of Northumberland
YOUNG SIWARD, his son
HECATE, Queen of the Witches
A PORTER at Macbeth's castle
Three MURDERERS attending on Macbeth
SEYTON, servant of Macbeth
A show of eight kings, Lords and Thanes

Scottish Thanes:
LENNOX
ROSS
ANGUS
CAITHNESS
MENTEITH

Six WITCHES
An English DOCTOR
A SPIRIT LIKE A CAT
Three APPARITIONS:
an armed head
a bloody child
a child crowned
Other SPIRITS
An OLD MAN
A MESSENGER
MURDERERS
SERVANTS
soldiers, drummers

Quotations

	Spoken by
All the perfumes of Arabia will not sweeten this little hand.	Lady Macbeth
Angels are bright still, though the brightest fell.	Malcolm
Be innocent of the knowledge, dearest chuck.	Macbeth
Blow wind, come wrack, at least we'll die with harness on our back.	Macbeth
But screw your courage to the sticking-place, and we'll not fail.	Lady Macbeth
By the pricking of my thumbs, something wicked this way comes.	Second Witch
Canst thou not minister to a mind diseased.	Macbeth
Come what, come may, time and the hour runs through the toughest day.	Macbeth
Consider it not so deeply.	Lady Macbeth
Double, double, toil and trouble, fire burn, and cauldron bubble.	Three Witches
Hang out our banners on the outward walls.	Macbeth
How now, you secret, black, and midnight hags.	Macbeth
I am in blood stepped in so far that, should I wade no more, returning were as tedious as go o'er.	Macbeth
I dare do all that may become a man; who dares do more is none.	Macbeth
If you can look into the seeds of time, and say which grain will grow and which will not.	Banquo
I 'gin to be aweary of the sun.	Macbeth
I had most need of blessing, and Amen stuck in my throat.	Macbeth
I must become a borrower of the night, for a dark hour or twain.	Banquo
Infirm of purpose! give me the daggers.	Lady Macbeth
Is this a dagger which I see before me? the handle towards my hand? come let me clutch thee.	Macbeth
It was the owl that shrieked, the fatal bellman.	Lady Macbeth
I would applaud thee to the very echo.	Macbeth
Look like the innocent flower, but be the serpent under't.	Lady Macbeth
Might be the be-all and the end-all here.	Macbeth
Now good digestion wait on appetite, and health on both.	Macbeth
O, I could play the woman with mine eyes, and braggart with my tongue!	Macduff
Or have we eaten on the insane root, that takes the reason prisoner.	Banquo
Out, damned spot; out, I say.	Lady Macbeth
Shake off this downy sleep, death's counterfeit, and look on death itself!	Macduff
Sleep shall neither night nor day, hang upon his pent-house lid.	First Witch
Stands not within the prospect of belief.	Macbeth
That no compunctious visitings of nature shake my fell purpose.	Lady Macbeth
That which hath made them drunk hath made me bold.	Lady Macbeth
The attempt and not the deed confounds us.	Lady Macbeth
The earth hath bubbles, as the water has, and these are of them.	Banquo
The labour we delight in physics pain.	Macbeth
There's husbandry in heaven, their candles are all out.	Banquo
The Thane of Cawdor lives; why do you dress me in borrow'd robes.	

SHAKESPEARE

The weird sisters hand in hand.	Three Witches
This castle hath a pleasant seat; the air nimbly and sweetly recommends itself unto our gentle senses.	King Duncan
Throw physic to the dogs; I'll none of it.	Macbeth
To-morrow, and to-morrow, and to-morrow, creeps in this petty pace from day to day, to the last syllable of recorded time, and all our yesterdays have lighted fools the way to dusty death. Out, out, brief candle! Life's but a walking shadow, a poor player that struts and frets his hour upon the stage and then is heard no more: It is a tale told by an idiot, full of sound and fury, signifying nothing.	Macbeth
We have scotched the snake, not killed it.	Macbeth
What, all my pretty chickens and their dam, at one fell swoop.	Macduff
What are these, so wither'd and so wild in their attire, that look not like the inhabitants o' the earth, and yet are on't.	Banquo
What bloody man is that?	King Duncan
Who can be wise, amazed, temperate and furious, loyal and neutral, in a moment?	Macbeth
Yet I do fear thy nature; it is too full o'th' milk of human kindness.	Lady Macbeth
Yet who would have thought the old man to have had so much blood in him.	Lady Macbeth
Your face, my thane, is as a book where men may read strange matters.	Lady Macbeth

Précis of plot

A story of witchcraft, murder, and retribution, which can also be seen as a study in the philosophy and psychology of evil.

Setting

Scotland and England 1039 to 1057.

20 Measure for Measure

Vincentio, the DUKE of Vienna	A PROVOST
ANGELO, appointed his deputy	ELBOW, a simple constable
ESCALUS, an old Lord	A JUSTICE
CLAUDIO, a young gentleman	ABHORSON, an executioner
JULIET, betrothed to Claudio	BARNARDINE, a dissolute condemned
ISABELLA, Claudio's sister	prisoner
LUCIO, 'a fantastic'	MARIANA, betrothed to Angelo
Two other such GENTLEMEN	A BOY, attendant on Mariana
FROTH, a foolish gentleman	FRIAR PETER
MISTRESS OVERDONE, a bawd	FRANCESCA, a nun
POMPEY, her clownish servant	VARRIUS, a Lord, friend to the Duke
	Lords, officers, citizens, servants

Quotations	**Spoken by**
Ay, but to die, and go we know not where; to lie in cold obstruction, and to rot.	Claudio
But man, proud man, dressed in a little brief authority, most ignorant of what he's most assured, his glassy essence, like an angry ape, plays such fantastic tricks before high heaven as makes the angels weep.	Isabella
Condemn the fault, and not the actor of it.	Angelo
Every true man's apparel fits your thief.	Abhorson
Heaven doth with us as we with torches do.	Duke of Vienna
If I must die, I will encounter darkness as a bride, and hug it in my arms.	Claudio
I hold you as a thing enskied and sainted.	Lucio
No ceremony that to great ones 'longs. Not the king's crown, nor the deputed sword, the marshal's truncheon, nor the judge's robe, become them with one half so good a grace, as mercy does.	Isabella
O, it is excellent to have a giant's strength, but it is tyrannous to use it like a giant.	Isabella
Our doubts are traitors, and makes us lose the good we oft might win.	Lucio
Some rise by sin, and some by virtue fall.	Escalus
That in the captain's but a choleric word, which in the soldier is flat blasphemy.	Isabella
The jury passing on the prisoner's life, may in the sworn twelve have a thief or two, guiltier than him they try.	Angelo
The miserable have no other medicine; but only hope.	Claudio
They say, best men are moulded out of faults; and for the most, become much more the better, for being a little bad.	Mariana
This will last out a night in Russia, when nights are longest there.	Angelo
Virtue is bold, and goodness never fearful	Duke of Vienna

Précis of plot

The central action revolves around the dilemma of Isabella, a novice nun, whose brother is to be executed unless she succumbs to the attentions of Angelo. *Measure for Measure* is a morality play with similar sentiments to *The Merchant of Venice*, but is far more explicitly concerned with sex, and death.

Setting

Vienna circa 1500.

21 The Merchant of Venice

ANTONIO, a merchant of Venice
BASSANIO, his friend and Portia's suitor
LEONARDO, Bassanio's servant
LANCELOT, a clown and servant
GOBBO, his father
Prince of MOROCCO, Portia's suitor
Prince of ARAGON, Portia's suitor
PORTIA, an heiress
NERISSA, her waiting-gentlewoman
BALTHASAR, Portia's servant
STEFANO, Portia's servant
Jailer, attendants, servants, magnificoes of Venice

SHYLOCK, a Jew
JESSICA, his daughter
LORENZO
GRAZIANO
SALERIO
SOLANIO
DUKE of Venice
TUBAL, a Jew

Quotations

	Spoken by
A Daniel come to judgement, yea, a Daniel!	Shylock
All that glisters is not gold.	Morocco
And when I ope my lips, let no dog bark.	Graziano
But love is blind and lovers cannot see.	Jessica
But ships are but boards, sailors but men. There be land rats and water rats, water thieves and land thieves.	Shylock
How like a fawning publican he looks. I hate him for he is a Christian.	Shylock
How sweet the moonlight sleeps upon this bank!	Lorenzo
I am never merry when I hear sweet music	Jessica
I dote on his very absence.	Portia
If you prick us do we not bleed? If you tickle us do we not laugh? If you poison us do we not die? and if you wrong us shall we not revenge?	Shylock
It is a wise father that knows his own child.	Lancelot
I would not have given it for a wilderness of monkeys.	Shylock
Mislike me not for my complexion, the shadowed livery of the burnished sun.	Morocco
The quality of mercy is not strained. It droppeth as the gentle rain from heaven, upon the place beneath.	Portia
You call me misbeliever, cut-throat, dog, and spit upon my Jewish gaberdine.	Shylock
You taught me first to beg, and now methinks, you teach me how a beggar should be answered.	Portia

Précis of plot

The central plot involves an irascible Jewish money-lender and his efforts to exact full payment for a debt. The sub-plot involves the method of an heiress, Portia, of testing her suitors. The comedy is created by Shylock, the Jew's, strict adherence to the letter of the law and his ultimate downfall by being hoist by his own petard.

Setting

Venice and Belmont circa 14th century.

22 The Merry Wives of Windsor

MISTRESS Margaret PAGE
Master George PAGE, her husband
ANNE and WILLIAM Page, their children
MISTRESS Alice FORD
Master Frank FORD, her husband
Doctor CAIUS, a French physician
MISTRESS QUICKLY, his housekeeper
John RUGBY, his servant
Master FENTON, in love with Anne Page
Master Abraham SLENDER
Robert SHALLOW, his uncle, a justice
The HOST of the Garter Inn
Sir Hugh EVANS, a Welsh parson
Peter SIMPLE, Slender's servant
Children of Windsor, appearing as fairies

ROBIN, Sir John's page
JOHN, a servant
ROBERT, a servant
SIR JOHN Falstaff
BARDOLPH
PISTOL
NIM

Quotations

	Spoken by
A man of my kidney.	Sir John
Faith, thou hast some crotchets in thy head now.	Mistress Ford
Here will be an old abusing of God's patience and the King's English.	Mistress Quickly
I cannot tell what the dickens his name is.	Mistress Page
I have a kind of alacrity in sinking.	Sir John
I hope good luck lies in odd numbers.	Sir John
I will make a Star Chamber matter of it.	Shallow
O, what a world of vile ill-favoured faults.	Anne
There was the rankest compound of villainous smell that ever offended nostril.	Sir John
Vengeance of Jenny's case!	Mistress Quickly

S
H
A
K
E
S
P
E
A
R
E

We burn daylight. Here: read, read.   Mistress Ford
Why then, the world's mine oyster, which I with sword will open.   Pistol

Précis of plot
The central plot tells of Sir John Falstaff's unsuccessful attempts to seduce Mistress Page and Mistress Ford, and of the unfounded jealousy of Master Ford. The sub-plot revolves around the wooing of Anne Page and ultimate success of Master Fenton.

Setting
Windsor mid-15th century.

23 A Midsummer Night's Dream

THESEUS, Duke of Athens   SNUG, a joiner
HIPPOLYTA, Queen of the Amazons   Tom SNOUT, a Tinker
EGEUS, father of Hermia
HERMIA, daughter of Egeus   Four Fairies:
LYSANDER, loved by Hermia   COBWEB
DEMETRIUS, suitor to Hermia   MOTE
HELENA, in love with Demetrius   MUSTARDSEED
OBERON, King of the Fairies   PEASEBLOSSOM
TITANIA, Queen of the Fairies
ROBIN GOODFELLOW, a puck
Peter QUINCE, a carpenter
Nick BOTTOM, a weaver
Francis FLUTE, a bellows-mender
Robin STARVELING, a tailor
Attendant Lords and fairies

Quotations   **Spoken by**

Quotation	Spoken by
A calendar, a calendar! look in the almanac; find out moonshine, find out moonshine.	Bottom
A lion among ladies is a most dreadful thing; for there is not a more fearful wild-fowl than your lion living.	Bottom
A part to tear a cat in.	Bottom
A proper man, as one shall see in a summer's day.	Quince
And the imperial votaress passed on, in maiden meditation, fancy-free, yet marks I where the bolt of Cupid fell: It fell upon a little western flower, before milk-white, now purple with love's wound, and maidens call it love-in-idleness.	Oberon
Bless thee, Bottom! bless thee! thou art translated.	Quince
But earthlier happy is the rose distilled than that which, withering on the virgin thorn, grows, lives, and dies in single blessedness.	Theseus
He bravely broach'd his boiling bloody breast.	Quince (as prologue)
I am slow of study.	Snug
I have a reasonable good ear in music. Let's have the tongs and the bones.	Bottom
I have an exposition of sleep come upon me.	Bottom
I know a bank where the wild thyme blows, where oxlips and the nodding violet grows, quite over-canopied with luscious woodbine, with sweet musk-roses and with eglantine.	Oberon
Ill met by moonlight, proud Titania.	Oberon
I'll put a girdle round the earth in forty minutes.	Puck
I will roar you as gently as any sucking dove; I will roar you as 'twere any nightingale.	Bottom
Lord, what fools these mortals be.	Puck
Love looks not with the eyes, but with the mind; and therefore is wing'd Cupid painted blind.	Helena
Masters, spread yourselves.	Bottom
My hounds are bred out of the Spartan kind, so flew'd, so sanded, and their heads are hung, with ears that sweep away the morning dew; crook-knee'd, and dew-lapp'd like Thessalian bulls; slow in pursuit, but match'd in mouth like bells.	Theseus
Oh hell! to choose love by another's eyes.	Hermia
Or in the night, imagining some fear, how easy is a bush supposed a bear.	Theseus
She was a vixen when she went to school; and though she be but little, she is fierce.	Helena
Since once I sat upon a promontory, and heard a mermaid on a dolphin's back uttering such dulcet and harmonious breath that the rude sea grew civil at her song and certain stars shot madly from their spheres, to hear the sea-maid's music.	Oberon
So we grew together, like to a double cherry, seeming parted, but yet an union in partition; two lovely berries moulded on one stem.	Helena
Swift as a shadow, short as any dream, brief as the lightning in the collied night, that, in a spleen, unfolds both heaven and earth, and ere a man hath power to say 'Behold' the jaws of darkness do devour it up.	Lysander
That is the true beginning of our end.	Quince (as prologue)
The best in this kind are but shadows; and the worst are no worse, if imagination amend them.	Theseus
The course of true love never did run smooth.	Lysander

The iron tongue of midnight hath told twelve.	Theseus
The jaws of darkness do devour it up: so quick bright things come to confusion.	Lysander
The lover, all as frantic, sees Helen's beauty in a brow of Egypt. The poet's eye, in a fine frenzy rolling, doth glance from heaven to earth, from earth to heaven.	Theseus
The lunatic, the lover and the poet, are of imagination all compact.	Theseus
This is 'erc'les' vein.	Bottom
Very tragical mirth.	Lysander (reads)
What hempen homespuns have we swaggering here.	Puck

Précis of plot
Theseus, Duke of Athens, prepares to marry Hippolyta, Queen of the Amazons. The sub-plots include the tangled web of love between Lysander, Hermia, Demetrius and Helena, and the production of a play, *Pyramus and Thisbe* (based on Ovid's *Metamorphoses*), for the Duke's wedding.

Setting
Athens and a nearby wood.

24 Much Ado About Nothing

DON PEDRO, Prince of Aragon	BENEDICK, of Padua
BALTHASAR, attendant on Don Pedro, a singer	CLAUDIO, of Florence
DON JOHN, the bastard brother of Don Pedro	FRIAR Francis
BORACHIO, follower of Don John	A SEXTON
CONRAD, follower of Don John	WATCHMEN
LEONATO, Governor of Messina	A BOY, serving Benedick
HERO, his daughter	Attendants and messengers
BEATRICE, an orphan, his niece	
ANTONIO, an old man, brother of Leonato	
MARGARET, attendant on Hero	
URSULA, attendant on Hero	
DOGBERRY, constable in charge of Watch	
VERGES, the Headborough, Dogberry's partner	

Quotations

Quotations	Spoken by
Are you good men and true?	Dogberry
But then there was a star danced, and under that was I born.	Beatrice
Comparisons are odorous.	Dogberry
Disdain and scorn ride sparkling in her eyes.	Hero
Flat burglary, as ever was committed.	Dogberry
For there was never yet philosopher, that could endure the toothache patiently.	Leonato
Friendship is constant in all other things, save in the office and affairs of love.	Claudio
He hath indeed better bettered expectation.	Messenger
He is a very valiant trencherman, he has an excellent stomach.	Beatrice
He wears his faith but as the fashion of his hat.	Beatrice
I have a good eye, uncle, I can see a church by daylight.	Beatrice
I was not born under a rhyming planet.	Benedick
O that he were here to write me down an ass!	Dogberry
O, what men dare do! what men may do! what men daily do, not knowing what they do!	Claudio
Patch grief with proverbs, make misfortune drunk.	Leonato
Taming my wild heart to thy loving hand.	Beatrice
To be a well-favoured man is the gift of fortune, but to write and read comes by nature.	Dogberry
Well, everyone can master a grief but he that has it.	Benedick
What, my dear Lady Disdain! are you yet living?	Benedick
Yes, I thank God, I am as honest as any man living that is an old man and no honester than I.	Verges

Précis of plot
The central plot concerns Don John's deception whereby Claudio believes his beloved Hero unfaithful. However, the sub-plot of the relationship between Beatrice and Benedick adds the real substance to the play, and the gradual realisation of their love for each other has spawned countless works.

Setting
Messina in Sicily.

25 Othello

OTHELLO, the Moor of Venice	The DUKE of Venice
DESDEMONA, his wife	SENATORS of Venice
Michael CASSIO, his lieutenant	A HERALD
BIANCA, a courtesan, in love with Cassio	A MESSENGER
IAGO, the Moor's Ensign	
EMILIA, Iago's wife	
A CLOWN, servant of Othello	
BRABANZIO, Desdemona's father, a senator	

GRAZIANO, Brabanzio's brother
LODOVICO, kinsman of Brabanzio
RODERIGO, Venetian in love with Desdemona
MONTANO, Governor of Cyprus
Attendants, officers, sailors, gentlemen, musicians

Quotations	Spoken by
A fellow almost damned in a fair wife, that never set a squadron in the field.	Iago
Alas, what ignorant sin have I committed?	Desdemona
And of the cannibals that each other eat, the Anthropophagi, and men whose heads do grow beneath their shoulders.	Othello
Be sure thou prove my love a whore. Be sure of it. Give me the ocular proof.	Othello
But I will wear my heart upon my sleeve, for daws to peck at.	Iago
But men are men, the best sometimes forgot.	Iago
But this denoted a foregone conclusion.	Othello
Excellent wretch! Perdition catch my soul.	Othello
He hath a daily beauty in his life that makes me ugly.	Iago
He that is robbed, not wanting what is stol'n, let him not know it and he's not robbed at all.	Othello
How poor are they that ha' not patience! what wound did ever heal but by degrees?	Iago
I am not merry, but I do beguile.	Desdemona
I do perceive here a divided duty.	Desdemona
If she be black, and thereto have a wit; she'll find a white that shall her blackness fit.	Iago
I have very poor and unhappy brains for drinking, I could well wish courtesy would invent some other custom of entertainment.	Cassio
I would have him nine years a-killing. A fine woman, a fair woman, a sweet woman.	Othello
Keep up your bright swords, for the dew will rust 'em.	Othello
My story being done, she gave me for my pains a world of kisses.	Othello
No hinge, nor loop to hang a doubt on.	Othello
O beware, my lord, of jealousy; it is the green-eyed monster which doth mock the meat it feeds on.	Iago
O God, that men should put an enemy in their mouths to steal away their brains.	Cassio
O most lame and impotent conclusion.	Desdemona
On horror's head horrors accumulate.	Othello
Potations pottle-deep.	Iago
Pride, pomp and circumstance of glorious war!	Othello
Reputation, reputation, reputation! O, I have lost my reputation! I have lost the immortal part of myself, and what remains is bestial.	Cassio
Silence that dreadful bell – It frights the isle from her propriety.	Othello
Take note, take note, O world, to be direct and honest is not safe.	Iago
Then must you speak of one that loved not wisely but too well.	Othello
'Tis neither here nor there.	Emilia
To mourn a mischief that is past and gone, is the next way to draw new mischief on.	Duke of Venice
To suckle fools, and chronicle small beer.	Iago
Your daughter and the Moor are now making the beast with two backs.	Iago
You are one of those that will not serve God, if the devil bids you.	Iago

Précis of plot
The story of a Moorish commander deluded by his ensign into believing that his young wife has been unfaithful to him with another soldier. By subtle innuendo and apparent physical proof, Iago convinces Othello that Desdemona has slept with Cassio, his lieutenant; his deceit results in tragedy.

Setting
Venice and Cyprus circa 1570.

26 Pericles, Prince of Tyre

John GOWER, the Presenter
ANTIOCHUS, King of Antioch
His DAUGHTER
PERICLES, Prince of Tyre
MARINA, Pericles' daughter
CLEON, governor of Tarsus
DIONIZA, his wife
LEONINE, a murderer
CERIMON, a physician of Ephesus
PHILEMON, his servant
KING SIMONIDES of Pentapolis
THAISA, his daughter
Three FISHERMEN, his subjects
Five PRINCES, suitors of Thaisa
LYSIMACHUS, Governor of Mytilene
Lords, ladies, pages, messengers, sailors and gentlemen

THALIART, a villain
HELICANUS
AESCHINES
A MARSHAL
LICHORIDA, Thaisa's nurse
A BAWD
A PANDER
BOULT, a leno
DIANA, Goddess of chastity

Quotations

	Spoken by
Master, I marvel how the fishes live in the sea.	Third Fisherman
Why, as men do a-land; the great ones eat up the little ones.	First Fisherman (reply)
O you gods! why do you make us love your goodly gifts and snatch them straight away?	Pericles
See where she comes, apparell'd like the spring!	Pericles
'Tis time to fear when tyrants seem to kiss.	Pericles

Précis of plot

Pericles, Prince of Tyre, flees from the court of the King of Antioch after solving a riddle that incriminates the King in an incestuous relationship with his daughter. The play chronicles the ensuing travels of Pericles and culminates in his reunion with his long lost daughter, Marina.

Setting

Antioch, Tyre, Tarsus, Pentapolis, Ephesus, Mitylene.

27 Richard II

KING RICHARD II
The QUEEN, his wife
JOHN OF GAUNT, Duke of Lancaster, Richard's uncle
Harry BOLINGBROKE, his son, later HENRY IV
DUCHESS OF GLOUCESTER
Duke of YORK, King Richard's uncle
DUCHESS OF YORK
Duke of AUMERLE, their son
Thomas MOWBRAY, Duke of Norfolk

Of Bolingbroke's party:
Percy, Earl of NORTHUMBERLAND
HARRY PERCY, his son
Lord ROSS
Of King Richard's party:
Earl of SALISBURY
BISHOP OF CARLISLE
Sir Stephen SCROPE

KEEPER of the prison at Pomfret
GROOM of King Richard's stable

Followers of King Richard:
GREEN
BAGOT
BUSHY

Lord BERKELEY
Lord FITZWATER
Duke of SURREY
Lord WILLOUGHBY
ABBOT OF WESTMINSTER
Sir Piers EXTON
LORD MARSHAL
HERALDS
CAPTAIN of the Welsh army
LADIES attending the Queen
GARDENER
Gardener's MEN
Exton's MEN
Lords, soldiers, attendants

Quotations

	Spoken by
A jewel in a ten-times barred-up chest is a bold spirit in a loyal breast	Mowbray
Can sick men play so nicely with their names?	King Richard
For God's sake let us sit upon the ground, and tell sad stories of the death of kings: how some have been deposed; some slain in war; some haunted by the ghost they have deposed; some poisoned by their wives; some sleeping kill'd; all murder'd.	King Richard
How long a time lies in one little word!	Bolingbroke
Methinks I am a prophet new-inspired.	John of Gaunt
Mount, mount, my soul; thy seat is up on high, whilst my gross flesh sinks downward, here to die.	Richard (last words)
Not all the water in the rude rough sea, can wash the balm from an anointed king.	King Richard
O call back yesterday, bid time return.	Salisbury
Of comfort no man speak. Let's talk of graves, of worms and epitaphs.	King Richard
Peace shall go sleep with Turks and infidels.	Bishop of Carlisle
That which in mean men we entitle patience is pale cold cowardice in noble breasts.	Duchess of Gloucester
The daintiest last, to make the end most sweet.	Bolingbroke
Things sweet to taste prove in digestion sour.	John of Gaunt
This must my comfort be: the sun that warms you here shall shine on me.	Bolingbroke
This royal throne of kings, this sceptred isle, this earth of majesty, this seat of Mars, this other Eden, demi-paradise, this fortress built by nature for herself against infection and the hand of war, this happy breed of men, this little world, this precious stone set in the silver sea, which serves it in the office of a wall, or as a moat defensive to a house against the envy of less happier lands; this blessed plot, this earth, this realm, this England.	John of Gaunt
Truth hath a quiet breast.	Mowbray
We were not born to sue, but to command.	King Richard
You may my glories and my state depose, but not my griefs; still am I king of those.	Richard

Précis of plot

This tragical history play centres around the time of Richard's enforced abdication. The substance of the play is historically accurate, although elements of fiction do exist to some degree, for example, the murder of Richard by Sir Piers Exton.

Setting

England and Wales at the turn of the 15th century.

SHAKESPEARE

28 Richard III

KING EDWARD IV
DUCHESS OF YORK, his mother
PRINCE EDWARD, Edward IV's son
Richard, the young Duke of YORK, Edward IV's son
George, Duke of CLARENCE
RICHARD, Duke of Gloucester, later KING RICHARD
Clarence's SON
Clarence's DAUGHTER
QUEEN ELIZABETH, King Edward's wife
Anthony Woodville, Earl RIVERS, her brother
Marquis of DORSET, her son
Lord GRAY, her son
Sir Thomas VAUGHAN
GHOST OF KING HENRY the Sixth
QUEEN MARGARET, his widow
GHOST OF PRINCE EDWARD, his son
LADY ANNE, Prince Edward's widow
William, LORD HASTINGS, Lord Chamberlain
Lord STANLEY, Earl of Derby, his friend
HENRY EARL OF RICHMOND, later KING HENRY VII
Sir Robert BRACKENBURY, Lieutenant of the Tower

Sir James BLUNT
Sir Walter HERBERT
Duke of BUCKINGHAM
Duke of NORFOLK
Sir Richard RATCLIFF
Sir William CATESBY
Sir James TIRREL
Two MURDERERS
A PAGE
CARDINAL
Bishop of ELY
John, a PRIEST
CHRISTOPHER, a priest
Earl of OXFORD
Lord MAYOR of London
A SCRIVENER
Hastings, a PURSUIVANT
SHERIFF
Aldermen and citizens
Attendants, two bishops,
messengers and soldiers

Quotations

	Spoken by
A horse, a horse, my kingdom for a horse!	King Richard
And thus I clothe my naked villainy, with odd old ends stol'n forth of holy writ, and seem a saint, when I most play the devil.	Richard Gloucester
But soft, here come my executioners.	Richard Gloucester
High-reaching Buckingham grows circumspect.	King Richard
Now is the winter of our discontent, made glorious summer by this son of York.	Richard Gloucester
O coward conscience, how dost thou afflict me?	King Richard
Slave, I have set my life upon a cast, and I will stand the hazard of the die. I think there be six Richmonds in the field. Five have I slain today, instead of him. A horse, a horse, my kingdom for a horse.	King Richard (last words)
So wise so young, they say, do never live long.	Richard Gloucester
Their lips were four red roses on a stalk, and in their summer beauty kissed each other.	Tyrrell
Was ever woman in this humour wooed?	Richard Gloucester
Was ever woman in this humour won?	

Précis of plot

In this play, Shakespeare demonstrates a more complete artistic control of his historical material than in its predecessors, and historical events are freely manipulated in the interests of an overriding design. The play chronicles the period of about twelve years before Richard's reign, highlighting his bloody progress to the crown and his short two-year reign, culminating in his defeat at Bosworth.

Setting

England 1471 to 1485.

29 Romeo and Juliet

CHORUS
ROMEO
MONTAGUE, his father
MONTAGUE'S WIFE
BENVOLIO, Montague's nephew
ABRAHAM, Montague's servingman
BALTHASAR, Romeo's man
JULIET
CAPULET, her father
CAPULET'S WIFE
TYBALT, her nephew
His page
Escalus, PRINCE of Verona
Other CITIZENS OF THE WATCH
Masquers, guests, gentlewomen, followers

PETER
SAMSON
GREGORY
Other SERVINGMEN
MUSICIANS
PETRUCCIO
MERCUTIO
PARIS
PAGE to Paris
FRIAR LAURENCE
FRIAR JOHN
An APOTHECARY
CHIEF WATCHMAN
CAPULET'S COUSIN
Juliet's NURSE

Quotations

	Spoken by
A pair of star-crossed lovers take their life.	Chorus
A plague o' both your houses.	Mercutio
For you and I are past our dancing days.	Capulet
I do not bite my thumb at you sir, but I bite my thumb, sir.	Samson
Nay, I am the very pink of courtesy.	Mercutio
O happy dagger, this is thy sheath! there rust, and let me die.	Juliet (last words)

One pain is lessened by another's anguish.	Benvolio
O Romeo, Romeo, wherefore art thou Romeo.	Juliet
O then I see Queen Mab hath been with you.	Mercutio
Parting is such sweet sorrow.	Juliet
See how she leans her cheek upon her hand. O, that I were a glove upon that hand, that I might touch that cheek.	Romeo
Thus with a kiss I die.	Romeo (last words)
True, I talk of dreams, which are the children of an idle brain, begot of nothing but vain fantasy.	Mercutio
What's in a name? That which we call a rose by any other word would smell as sweet.	Juliet
When well-apparelled April on the heel of limping winter treads.	Capulet
With Rosaline, my ghostly father? No, I have forgot that name and that name's woe.	Romeo

Précis of plot

This play tells of the bitter feud between the Montagues and Capulets. Romeo, a Montague, falls in love with Juliet, a Capulet, but their love is doomed from the outset as death and tragedy befall both families.

Setting

Verona and Mantua early in the 14th century.

30 The Taming of the Shrew

In the Induction:	GREMIO, suitor of Bianca
CHRISTOPHER SLY, beggar and tinker	HORTENSIO, another suitor
A HOSTESS	TRANIO, a servant
A LORD	BIONDELLO, a servant
BARTHOLOMEW, his page	GRUMIO, a servant
HUNTSMEN, SERVANTS AND PLAYERS	CURTIS, a servant
In the play-within-the-play:	A WIDOW
BAPTISTA Minola, a gentleman of Padua	A TAILOR
KATHERINE, his elder daughter	A HABERDASHER
BIANCA, his younger daughter	An OFFICER
PETRUCHIO, a gentleman of Verona, suitor of Katherine	NATHANIEL, a servingman
VINCENTIO, Lucentio's father	PHILIP, a servingman
A PEDANT, schoolmaster from Mantua	JOSEPH, a servingman
Other servants of Baptista and Petruchio	PETER, a servingman
LUCENTIO, disguised as Cambio, a teacher	

Quotations

	Spoken by
And as the sun breaks through the darkest clouds, so honour peereth in the meanest habit.	Petruccio
A woman moved is like a fountain troubled, muddy, ill seeming, thick, bereft of beauty.	Katherine
No profit grows where is no pleasure ta'en.	Tranio
This is a way to kill a wife with kindness.	Petruccio

Précis of plot

The play has three main strands. The first shows how a drunken tinker, Christopher Sly, is made to believe himself a lord for whose entertainment a play is to be presented. The second strand is the central plot of the play performed for Sly, in which the shrewish Katherine is wooed, won, and tamed by the fortune-hunting Petruchio. The third strand involves Lucentio, Gremio, and Hortensio, all of them suitors for the hand of Katherine's sister, Bianca.

Setting

Padua and Petruchio's house circa 14th century.

31 The Tempest

PROSPERO, the rightful Duke of Milan	The MASTER of a ship
MIRANDA, his daughter	BOATSWAIN
ANTONIO, his brother, the usurping Duke of Milan	MARINERS
ALONSO, King of Naples	SPIRITS
SEBASTIAN, his brother	*The Masque*
FERDINAND, Alonso's son	Spirits appearing as:
GONZALO, an honest old counsellor of Naples	IRIS
ADRIAN, a Lord	CERES
FRANCISCO, a Lord	JUNO
ARIEL, an airy spirit attendant upon Prospero	Nymphs and reapers
CALIBAN, a savage and deformed native, who is also Prospero's slave	
TRINCULO, Alonso's jester	
STEFANO, Alonso's drunken butler	

Quotations

	Spoken by
A very ancient and fish-like smell.	Trinculo
Be not afeard. The isle is full of noises, sounds and sweet airs, that give delight and hurt not.	Caliban

SHAKESPEARE

Fie, what a spendthrift is he of his tongue!	Antonio
Full fathom five thy father lies. Of his bones are coral made.	Ariel (sung)
He that dies pays all debts.	Stefano
How beauteous mankind is! O brave new world, that has such people in't!	Miranda
In the dark backward and abyss of time?	Prospero
Knowing I loved my books, he furnished me from mine own library with volumes that I prize above my dukedom.	Prospero
Misery acquaints a man with strange bedfellows.	Trinculo
My library was dukedom large enough.	Prospero
They'll take suggestions as a cat laps milk.	Antonio
We are such stuff as dreams are made on, and our little life is rounded with a sleep.	Prospero
Where the bee sucks, there suck I.	Ariel
You taught me language, and my profit on't is I know how to curse.	Caliban

Précis of plot

The central plot of *The Tempest* is one of witchcraft and connivance. The action takes place on an island after a shipwreck, as Prospero explains to his daughter, Miranda, how they came to the island, some twelve years earlier, and how the shipwreck has brought his enemies, Alonso, King of Naples, and Prospero's own brother, Antonio, face to face with their wrongdoings. The action takes place within a few hours, as in *The Comedy of Errors*.

Setting

A small island off the coast of Tunis.

32 Timon of Athens

TIMON of Athens	FOOL
LUCILIUS, a servant	PAGE
An OLD ATHENIAN	CAPHIS
LORDS and SENATORS of Athens	ISIDORE'S SERVANT
VENTIDIUS, one of Timon's false friends	POET
ALCIBIADES, an Athenian Captain	PAINTER
APEMANTUS, a churlish philosopher	JEWELLER
One dressed as CUPID in the Masque	MERCHANT
LADIES dressed as Amazons in the Masque	Mercer
FLAVIUS, Timon's steward	LUCULLUS' SERVANT
FLAMINIUS, a servant	LUCIUS' SERVANT
SERVILIUS, a servant	TITUS' SERVANT
Other SERVANTS of Timon	HORTENSIUS' SERVANT
LUCULLUS, a flattering Lord	PHILOTUS' SERVANT
LUCIUS, a flattering Lord	PHRYNIA, a whore
SEMPRONIUS, a flatterring Lord	TIMANDRA, a whore
Three STRANGERS, one called Hostilius	The banditti, THIEVES
SOLDIER of Alcibiades' army	
Two of VARRO'S SERVANTS	
Messengers, attendants, soldiers	

Quotations	Spoken by
I wonder men dare trust themselves with men.	Apemantus
'Tis not enough to help the feeble up, but to support him after.	Timon

Précis of plot

Timon is a misanthrope because his friends flattered and sponged on him in prosperity but abandoned him in poverty. Timon finds gold once more and his friends return.

Setting

Athens and neighbouring woods.

33 Titus Andronicus

SATURNINUS, later Emperor	CAPTAIN
BASSIANUS, his brother	AEMILIUS
TITUS ANDRONICUS, general against the Goths	Sons of Titus:
SEMPRONIUS, kinsman of Titus	LUCIUS
VALENTINE, kinsman of Titus	QUINTUS
TAMORA, Queen of the Goths, wife of Saturninus	MARTIUS
Her sons:	MUTIUS
ALARBUS	
DEMETRIUS	NURSE
CHIRON	CLOWN
AARON, a Moor, her lover	
LAVINIA, daughter of Titus	
YOUNG LUCIUS, a boy, son of Lucius	
MARCUS ANDRONICUS, a tribune, Titus' brother	

PUBLIUS, his son
Senators, tribunes, Romans, Goths, soldiers and attendants

Quotations   **Spoken by**
She is a woman, therefore may be wooed; she is a woman, therefore may be won;   Demetrius
she is Lavinia, therefore must be loved.
Sweet mercy is nobility's true badge.   Tamora

Précis of plot
Tamora, Queen of the Goths, seeks revenge on her captor, Titus, for the ritual slaughter of her son, Alarbus; she achieves it when her other sons, Chiron and Demetrius, rape and mutilate Titus' daughter, Lavinia. Later, Titus himself seeks revenge on Tamora and her husband Saturninus, after Tamora's black lover, Aaron, has falsely led him to believe that he can save his sons' lives by allowing his own hand to be chopped off. Though he is driven to madness, Titus, with his brother Marcus and his last surviving son, Lucius, achieves a spectacular sequence of vengeance in which he cuts Tamora's sons' throats, serves their flesh baked in a pie to their mother, kills Lavinia to save her from her shame, and stabs Tamora to death. Then in rapid succession, Saturninus kills Titus and is himself killed by Lucius, who, as the new Emperor, is left with Marcus to bury the dead, to punish Aaron, and to 'heal' Rome.

Setting
Rome 4th century AD.

34 Troilus and Cressida

HELEN, wife of Menelaus, now living with Paris
ALEXANDER, servant of Cressida
Servants of Troilus, musicians
soldiers and attendants
Greeks:
AGAMEMNON, Commander-in-Chief
MENELAUS, his brother
NESTOR
ULYSSES
ACHILLES
PATROCLUS, his companion
DIOMEDES
AJAX
THERSITES
MYRMIDONS, soldiers of Achilles
Servants of Diomedes, soldiers
CASSANDRA, Priam's daughter, a prophetess
ANDROMACHE, wife of Hector
AENEAS, a commander
ANTENOR, a commander
PANDARUS, a Lord
CRESSIDA, his niece
CALCHAS, her father, who has joined the Greeks

PROLOGUE
Trojans:
PRIAM, King of Troy
His sons:
HECTOR
DEIPHOBUS
HELENUS, a priest
PARIS
TROILUS
MARGARETON, a bastard

Quotations   **Spoken by**
For to be wise and love exceeds man's might.   Cressida
I am giddy. Expectation whirls me round. The imaginary relish is so sweet, that it   Troilus
enchants my sense.
I have had my labour for my travail.   Pandarus
One touch of nature makes the whole world kin.   Ulysses
The baby figure of the giant mass of things to come at large.   Nestor
Welcome ever smiles, and farewell goes out sighing.   Ulysses

Précis of plot
The war between Greece and Troy has been provoked by the abduction of the Greek, Helen, by the Trojan hero Paris, son of King Priam. Shakespeare's play opens when the Greek forces, led by Menelaus' brother Agamemnon, have already been besieging Troy for seven years. Shakespeare concentrates on the opposition between the Greek hero Achilles and the Trojan Hector. Shakespeare also shows how the war, caused by one love affair, destroys another. The story of the love between the Trojan, Troilus, and the Grecian, Cressida, encouraged by her uncle Pandarus, and of Cressida's desertion of Troilus for the Greek Diomedes.

Setting
Troy and the Greek camp during the Trojan War.

35 Twelfth Night

ORSINO, Duke of Illyria
VALENTINE, attending Orsino
CURIO, attending Orsino
VIOLA, a lady, later disguised as Cesario

SIR ANDREW AGUECHEEK
MALVOLIO, Olivia's steward
FABIAN, a member of Olivia's household
FESTE, the clown, her jester
FIRST OFFICER

SHAKESPEARE

SEBASTIAN, her twin brother
ANTONIO, a sea-captain
OLIVIA, a Countess
MARIA, her waiting-gentlewoman
SIR TOBY BELCH, Olivia's kinsman

SECOND OFFICER
CAPTAIN
PRIEST
SERVANT of Olivia
Musicians, sailors, lords, attendants

Quotations

	Spoken by
Be not afraid of greatness. Some are born great, some achieve greatness, and some have greatness thrust upon 'em.	Malvolio
Cressida was a beggar.	Feste
Farewell, fair cruelty.	Viola
He does it with a better grace, but I do it more natural.	Sir Andrew
He plays o'th' viol-de-gamboys, and speaks three or four languages word for word without book.	Sir Toby
I am a great eater of beef, and I believe that does harm to my wit.	Sir Andrew
I am all the daughters of my father's house, and all the brothers too.	Viola
I am sure care's an enemy to life.	Sir Toby
If music be the food of love, play on.	Orsino
Is it a world to hide virtues in?	Sir Toby
Love sought is good, but given unsought, is better.	Olivia
Many a good hanging prevents a bad marriage.	Feste
My purpose is indeed a horse of that colour.	Maria
No more cakes and ale.	Sir Toby
Not to be a-bed after midnight is to be up betimes.	Sir Toby
O world, how apt the poor are to be proud!	Olivia
Still you keep o'th' windy side of the law.	Fabian
What is the opinion of Pythagoras concerning wildfowl?	Feste
Wherefore are these things hid?	Sir Toby
Why, this is very midsummer madness.	Olivia

Précis of plot

The main plot is of a shipwrecked girl, Viola, who, disguised as a boy, Cesario, serves a young Duke, Orsino, and undertakes love-errands on his behalf to a noble lady, Olivia, who falls in love with her but mistakenly betrothes herself to her twin brother Sebastian.

Setting

Illyria.

36 The Two Gentlemen of Verona

DUKE of Milan
SILVIA, his daughter
PROTEUS, a gentleman of Verona
LANCE, his clownish servant
VALENTINE, a gentleman of Verona
SPEED, his clownish servant
THURIO, a foolish rival to Valentine
EGLAMOUR, agent for Silvia in her escape

ANTONIO, father of Proteus
PANTHINO, his servant
JULIA, beloved of Proteus
LUCETTA, her waiting-woman
HOST, where Julia lodges
OUTLAWS
Servants and musicians

Quotations

	Spoken by
How use doth breed a habit in a man!	Valentine
I have no other but a woman's reason, I think him so because I think him so.	Lucetta
O heaven, were man but constant, he were perfect.	Proteus
Who is Silvia? What is she, that all our swains commend her?	Host (sung)

Précis of plot

This play tells of the friendship of Valentine and Proteus and the strain their relationship is put under when they both fall in love with Silvia, the daughter of the Duke of Milan.

Setting

Verona, Milan, and Mantua.

37 The Two Noble Kinsmen

THESEUS, Duke of Athens
HIPPOLYTA, Queen of the Amazons
EMILIA, her sister
PIRITHOUS, friend of Theseus
PALAMON, a noble kinsman
ARCITE, a noble kinsman
Hymen, God of marriage
ARTESIUS, an Athenian soldier
Three QUEENS, widows of kings killed in Thebes
VALERIUS, a Theban

PROLOGUE
A SERVANT
A BOY, who sings
A HERALD
MESSENGERS
A DOCTOR
EPILOGUE

WOMAN, attending Emilia
An Athenian GENTLEMAN
Six KNIGHTS, attending Arcite and Palamon
A JAILER, in charge of Theseus' prison
The WOOER of the jailer's daughter
Two FRIENDS of the jailer
Six COUNTRYMEN, one dressed as a baboon
GERALD, a schoolmaster
NELL, a country wench
Four other country wenches:
Fritz, Madeleine, Luce and Barbara
Timothy, a TABORER

Quotations	Spoken by
New plays and maidenheads are near akin.	Prologue
Your grief is written on your cheek.	Emilia

Précis of plot
This play is based on Chaucer's Knight's Tale, on which Shakespeare had already drawn for episodes of *A Midsummer Night's Dream*. It tells of the conflicting claims of love and friendship between Palamon and Arcite, the Two Noble Kinsmen of the title, who, as in *The Two Gentlemen of Verona*, both fall in love with the same woman, but unlike the earlier play, decide to fight for their love. The play is sometimes not listed as a Shakespearian play, as there is a body of thought that believes it to be, at best, a collaboration with John Fletcher; unlike *Henry VIII*, their other joint work, it was not listed in the 1623 folio of Shakespeare's works.

Setting
Athens.

38 The Winter's Tale

LEONTES, King of Sicily	A JAILER
HERMIONE, his wife	A MARINER
MAMILLIUS, his son	CAMILLO, a Lord
PERDITA, his daughter	ANTIGONUS, a Lord
POLIXENES, King of Bohemia	CLEOMENES, a Lord
FLORIZEL, his son, in love with Perdita, aka Doricles	DION, a Lord
ARCHIDAMUS, a Bohemian Lord	CLOWN, his son
AUTOLYCUS, a rogue, once in the service of Florizel	
PAULINA, Antigonus's wife	Other shepherds and shepherdesses
EMILIA, a lady attending on Hermione	Twelve countrymen disguised as satyrs
MOPSA, a shepherdess	Other Lords and gentlemen, ladies,
DORCAS, a shepherdess	Officers and servants at Leontes' court
SERVANT of the old shepherd	TIME, as chorus

S
H
A
K
E
S
P
E
A
R
E

Quotations	Spoken by
A sad tale's best for winter.	Mamillius
A snapper up of unconsidered trifles.	Autolycus
Exit, pursued by a bear.	Stage direction
For you there's rosemary and rue.	Perdita
Good sooth, she is the queen of curds and cream.	Camillo
I would there were no age between ten and three-and twenty, or that youth would sleep out the rest; for there is nothing in the between but getting wenches with child, wronging the ancientry, stealing, fighting.	Old Shepherd
Jog on, jog on, the footpath way.	Autolycus (sung)
Lawn as white as driven snow.	Autolycus (sung)
Let me have no lying. It becomes none but tradesmen.	Autolycus
We were as twinned lambs that did frisk i' th' sun, and bleat the one at th' other.	Polixenes
When daffodils begin to peer.	Autolycus (sung)

Précis of plot
The improbable tale of King Leontes' suspicions of his wife's adultery with King Polixenes, his childhood friend. Leontes expels his new-born daughter, Perdita, thinking her the fruit of this unholy alliance, and she is brought up as a shepherdess. Perdita falls in love with Florizel, son of Polixenes, her supposed father, but she is eventually re-united with her true father.

Setting
Sicily and Bohemia circa 14th century.

Chronology of Shakespeare's Plays

1589–92	Henry VI Parts 1, 2, and 3
1592–93	Richard III, The Comedy of Errors
1593–94	Titus Andronicus, The Taming of the Shrew
1594–95	The Two Gentlemen of Verona, Love's Labour's Lost, Romeo and Juliet
1595–96	Richard II, A Midsummer Night's Dream
1596–97	King John, The Merchant of Venice
1597–98	Henry IV Parts 1 and 2
1598–99	Much Ado About Nothing, Henry V
1599–1600	Julius Caesar, As You Like It
1600–01	Hamlet, The Merry Wives of Windsor
1601–02	Twelfth Night, Troilus and Cressida
1602–03	All's Well That Ends Well
1604–05	Measure for Measure, Othello
1605–06	King Lear, Macbeth
1606–07	Antony and Cleopatra
1607–08	Coriolanus, Timon of Athens
1608–09	Pericles
1609–10	Cymbeline
1610–11	The Winter's Tale
1611–12	The Tempest
1612–13	Henry VIII, The Two Noble Kinsmen

Other Works

1592–93	Venus and Adonis (narrative poem)
1593–94	The Rape of Lucrece (narrative poem)
1593–1600	Sonnets (154 in total)
1600–01	The Phoenix and the Turtle (67-line elegy)
1609 circa	A Lover's Complaint (329-line poem)
	Various poems (attributed)

Original Titles

Henry VI Part 2 – The First Part of the Contention
Henry VI Part 3 – Richard Duke of York
Henry VIII – All Is True

Full Titles

Cymbeline, King of Britain
Hamlet, Prince of Denmark
Othello, the Moor of Venice
Pericles, Prince of Tyre
Twelfth Night, or What You Will

NB Shakespeare is generally credited with having penned 37 plays, but it can be argued that this figure could perhaps be just as easily 36, or 38, depending on the treatment given to the final two works, Henry VIII and The Two Noble Kinsmen. These plays are thought to be collaborations between Shakespeare and John Fletcher, although only Henry VIII appears in the First Folio of 1623. Therefore, when one is asked which was the last play Shakespeare wrote, it is true to say that it would be impossible to give an unqualified answer unless the question is very specific. The last play wholly credited to Shakespeare is The Tempest; the last play cited in the First Folio is Henry VIII; and the last play that Shakespeare wrote ignoring these two provisos is The Two Noble Kinsmen. The author of this work was asked this question by Anne Robinson on The Weakest Link and she was not impressed when I informed her there were three possible answers. I referred her to my book but was quickly voted off.

It should also be noted that as well as doubts as to the degree of Shakespeare's involvement in one or two of the plays, there are also doubts as to their chronological order. There is evidence to suggest, for instance, that Shakespeare's first play was probably not Henry VI Part 1, but, Henry VI Part 2. However, an answer of Henry VI would seem to be the most equitable solution to this one.

Films Based on Shakespearian Works

All Night Long – 1961	based on Othello directed by Basil Dearden
An Honourable Murder – 1959	based on Julius Caesar directed by Godfrey Grayson
Chimes at Midnight – 1966	based on Henry V directed by Orson Welles
Forbidden Planet – 1956	based on The Tempest directed by Fred M Wilcox
Kiss Me Kate – 1953	musical based on The Taming of the Shrew directed by George Sidney
Men of Respect – 1990	based on Macbeth directed by William Reilly
Prospero's Books – 1991	based on The Tempest directed by Peter Greenaway
Ran – 1985	Japanese version of King Lear three sons cast instead of three daughters written and directed by Akiro Kurosawa
Rosencrantz and Guildenstern Are Dead – 1990	based on Hamlet written and directed by Tom Stoppard
The Boys from Syracuse – 1940	musical based on The Comedy of Errors directed by Edward A Sutherland
Throne of Blood – 1957	Japanese version of Macbeth

West Side Story – 1961

directed by Akiro Kurosawa
based on *Romeo and Juliet*
directed by Robert Wise

NB The list above includes only films that do not specifically mention the title of the Shakespeare work: e.g. *Joe Macbeth* is a gangster film that follows a very similar plot to *Men of Respect* but includes a reference to *Macbeth* in the title. There are many films that allude to characters in Shakespeare but do not follow the plot closely enough to be included here. The Orson Welles film *Chimes at Midnight* is sometimes called *Falstaff*.

General Information

As You Like It	seven ages of man: 1) infant; 2) schoolboy; 3) lover; 4) soldier; 5) justice; 6) old age; 7) second childhood.
born	23 April 1564 in Stratford-upon-Avon. This may or may not be the actual date, but St George's Day seemed apt.
children	three: Susanna, Judith and Hamnet. Susanna born 1582, and twins Hamnet and Judith born 1585. Hamnet died in 1596, aged 11½. Susanna married Dr John Hall and Judith married Thomas Quiney. Shakespeare's line ended in 1670 with the death of Elizabeth, Susanna's daughter.
christened	26 April 1564 at Holy Trinity Church, Stratford-upon-Avon.
chronicler	Francis Meres' *Palladis Tamia* listed Shakespeare's works up to 1598.
collaborators	John Fletcher and various others.
death	23 April 1616 in Stratford-upon-Avon. Shakespeare therefore, traditionally, died on his birthday, aged 52. There are no names on Shakespeare's gravestone, but these words: Good friend, for Jesus' sake forbear To dig the dust enclosed here. Blest be the man that spares these stones, And curst be he that moves my bones. Shakespeare's family erected a monument in Holy Trinity church, Stratford, 1623.
dedicatee	Henry Wriothesley, the 3rd Earl of Southampton, had the narrative poems *Venus and Adonis* and *The Rape of Lucrece* dedicated to him.
Falstaff, Sir John	based on Sir John Oldcastle, the Protestant martyr. Shakespeare was forced to change the name from Oldcastle to Falstaff after complaints from relatives. *Henry IV* Part 1 is here quoted using the original name. The original names of Sir John's associates Bardolph and Peto have also been listed in *Henry IV* Part 1 in their original form, i.e. Russell and Harvey.
father	John Shakespeare, a glover, wool dealer, and sometime Mayor; died 1601.
First Folio	John Heminges and Henry Condell produced First Folio 1623.
first play	*Henry VI* (see notes at end of plays).
great tragedy	the 'four great tragedies' are often listed as *Hamlet*, *King Lear*, *Macbeth*, and *Othello*.
home	bought 'New Place' Stratford in 1597 Bishopsgate, and also lived with a French Huguenot family called Mountjoy for a short while during 1604, at Cripplegate.
July: takes place in	*Romeo and Juliet*.
kin	William was one of eight children of which he was the third child and first son. Only three brothers and a sister survived infancy. William's brother Edmund was also an actor.
last play	*The Tempest*, *Henry VIII*, or *The Two Noble Kinsmen* (see notes at end of plays).
lines: most	Hamlet has the most lines spoken by any one character in a single play but is only third on the overall list if one takes into consideration other plays that a character may appear in. Richard III has more lines taking into account his appearances in *Henry VI*, but the most lines are spoken by Sir John Falstaff, if one considers that Shakespeare's folio of 1623 had by then changed the name of Sir John Oldcastle in *Henry IV* Part 1.
longest play	this can be contentious due to disputed passages, but taking the 1623 folio as the basis of the question, then *Hamlet* is longest followed by *Richard III*.
married	Anne Hathaway, a farmer's daughter, from Shottery, near Stratford, 28 November 1582. He was 18, she 26 and pregnant. Anne died in 1623.
mother	Mary Arden, from Wilmcote, Warwickshire; died in 1609.
portraits	Martin Droeshout's engraving of Shakespeare, first published on the title-page of the First Folio 1623, is one of only two likenesses of Shakespeare; the other is the bust of Shakespeare in his monument, designed by Gheerart Janssen. It is unclear whether these are true likenesses, as it was common practice of many artists to use stencils, and it is thought possible that Droeshout may have used a common stencil of the day, possibly that of Elizabeth I.
shortest play	given the criteria used for deciding the longest play, the shortest play is clearly *The Comedy of Errors*.
sobriquet	the Sweet Swan of Avon, coined by Ben Jonson.
sonnets	published in 1609 by Thomas Thorpe, and dedicated to 'Mr W.H.' The sonnets pertain to a young man, a dark lady, and a rival poet. Sonnets 1 to 17 exhort a young man to marry; Sonnets 1 to 126 are all about a young man; Sonnets 127 to 154 are about the dark lady; Sonnet 126 is not in sonnet form, as it has only 12 lines.
theatres	Globe was built in 1599 on Bankside, south of the Thames. James Burbage founded the Lord Chamberlain's Company within the Globe and his son Richard Burbage was the principal

SHAKESPEARE

actor. Shakespeare bought an interest in the Globe, and also a half share in the Blackfriars Theatre, in 1608, and from then on Shakespeare produced winter plays at the Blackfriars and summer plays at the Globe. The Lord Chamberlain's Men became the King's Men on James I's accession. Opposition to the King's Men came mainly from Edward Alleyne's 'Admiral's Men'. John Fletcher became chief dramatist of the King's Men after Shakespeare. Will Kempe was the leading comedy actor of the King's Men. Richard Tarleton was the leading comedy actor of the rival Admiral's Men. Forerunners of the Lord Chamberlain's Men were the Queen's Men. The Chamberlain's Men first performed at the 'Theatre', in Shoreditch, and then at the 'Curtain'. The Globe caught fire and was destroyed in 1613 during performance of *Henry VIII*.

First Lines of Shakespeare's Plays

(C = Comedy   H = History   T = Tragedy)

Play	First line	Spoken by
C **All's Well That Ends Well**	In delivering my son from me I bury a second husband.	Dowager Countess of Roussillon
T **Antony and Cleopatra**	Nay, but this dotage of our General's o'erflows the measure.	Philo
C **As You Like It**	As I remember, Adam, it was upon this fashion.	Orlando
C **The Comedy of Errors**	Proceed, Solinus, to procure my fall.	Egeon
T **Coriolanus**	Before we proceed any further, hear me speak.	first Citizen
C **Cymbeline, King of Britain**	You do not meet a man but frowns.	first Gentleman
T **Hamlet**	Who's there?	Barnardo
H **Henry IV Part 1**	So shaken as we are, so wan with care.	King Henry IV
H **Henry IV Part 2**	Open your ears; for which of you will stop.	Rumour
H **Henry V**	O for a muse of fire.	Chorus (as Prologue)
H **Henry VI Part 1**	Hung be the heavens with black!	Bedford
H **Henry VI Part 2**	As by your high imperial majesty.	Suffolk
H **Henry VI Part 3**	I wonder how the King escaped our hands.	Warwick
H **Henry VIII (All Is True)**	I come no more to make you laugh.	Prologue
T **Julius Caesar**	Hence, home, you idle creatures, get you home.	Flavius
H **King John**	Now say, Châtillon, what would France with us?	King John
T **King Lear**	I thought the King had more affected the Duke of Albany than Cornwall.	Earl of Kent
C **Love's Labour's Lost**	Let fame, that all hunt after in their lives.	King Ferdinand
T **Macbeth**	When shall we three meet again? In thunder, lightning, or in rain?	First Witch
C **Measure for Measure**	Escalus.	Vincentio, Duke of Vienna
C **The Merchant of Venice**	In sooth, I know not why I am so sad.	Antonio
C **The Merry Wives of Windsor**	Sir Hugh, persuade me not. I will make a Star Chamber matter of it.	Shallow
C **A Midsummer Night's Dream**	Now, fair Hippolyta, our nuptial hour draws on apace.	Theseus
C **Much Ado About Nothing**	I learn in this letter that Don Pedro of Aragon comes this night to Messina.	Leonato
T **Othello**	Tush, never tell me!	Roderigo
C **Pericles, Prince of Tyre**	To sing a song that old was sung.	Gower, as Chorus
H **Richard II**	Old John of Gaunt, time-honoured Lancaster.	King Richard II
H **Richard III**	Now is the winter of our discontent.	Richard Gloucester
T **Romeo and Juliet**	Two households, both alike in dignity in fair Verona.	Chorus (as Prologue)
C **The Taming of the Shrew**	I'll feeze you, in faith.	Christopher Sly
C **The Tempest**	Boatswain!	Master of a ship
T **Timon of Athens**	Good day, sir.	Poet
T **Titus Andronicus**	Noble patricians, patrons of my right.	Saturninus
C **Troilus and Cressida**	In Troy there lies the scene. From isles of Greece.	Prologue
C **Twelfth Night**	If music be the food of love, play on.	Orsino
C **The Two Gentlemen of Verona**	Cease to persuade, my loving Proteus.	Valentine
C **The Two Noble Kinsmen**	New plays and maidenheads are near akin.	Prologue
C **The Winter's Tale**	If you shall chance, Camillo, to visit Bohemia.	Archidamus

Play	Last line	Spoken by
C **All's Well That Ends Well**	The bitter past, more welcome is the sweet.	The King of France (N.B. Epilogue follows)
T **Antony and Cleopatra**	High order in this great solemnity.	Octavius Caesar
C **As You Like it**	Proceed, proceed. We'll so begin these rites as we do trust they'll end, in true delights.	Duke Senior (N.B. Epilogue follows)
C **The Comedy of Errors**	And now let's go hand in hand, not one before another.	Dromio of Ephesus
T **Coriolanus**	Yet he shall have a noble memory. Assist.	Aufidius
C **Cymbeline, King of Britain**	Ere bloody hands were washed, with such a peace.	Cymbeline
T **Hamlet**	Go, bid the soldiers shoot.	Fortinbras
H **Henry IV Part 1**	Let us not leave till all our own be won.	King Henry IV
H **Henry IV Part 2**	Come, will you hence?	Prince John (N.B. Epilogue follows)
H **Henry V**	And may our oaths well kept and prosp'rous be.	King Harry (N.B. Epilogue follows)
H **Henry VI Part 1**	But I will rule both her, the King, and realm.	Suffolk
H **Henry VI Part 2**	And more such days as these to us befall!	Warwick
H **Henry VI Part 3**	For here, I hope, begins our lasting joy.	King Edward IV
H **Henry VIII (All Is True)**	This little one shall make it holiday.	King Henry VIII (nb Epilogue follows)
T **Julius Caesar**	To part the glories of this happy day.	Octavius
H **King John**	If England to itself do rest but true.	Philip the Bastard
T **King Lear**	Shall never see so much, nor live so long.	Edgar
C **Love's Labour's Lost**	The words of Mercury are harsh after the songs of Apollo. You that way, we this way.	Armado
T **Macbeth**	Whom we invite to see us crowned at Scone.	Malcolm
C **Measure for Measure**	What's yet behind that's meet you all should know.	Vincentio, Duke of Vienna
C **The Merchant of Venice**	Well, while I live I'll fear no other thing so sore as keeping safe Nerissa's ring.	Graziano
C **The Merry Wives of Windsor**	For he tonight shall lie with Mistress Ford.	Master Ford
C **A Midsummer Night's Dream**	Meet me all by break of day.	Oberon (N.B. Epilogue follows)
C **Much Ado About Nothing**	Think not on him till tomorrow, I'll devise thee brave punishments for him. Strike up, pipers.	Benedick
T **Othello**	This heavy act with heavy heart relate.	Lodovico
C **Pericles, Prince of Tyre**	New joy wait on you. Here our play has ending.	Gower
H **Richard II**	In weeping after this untimely bier.	King Henry IV
H **Richard III**	That she may long live here, God say 'Amen'.	King Henry VII
T **Romeo and Juliet**	For never was a story of more woe than this of Juliet and her Romeo.	Escalus
C **The Taming of the Shrew,**	'Tis a wonder, by your leave, she will be tamed so.	Lucentio
C **The Tempest**	Please you, draw near.	Prospero (N.B. Epilogue follows)
T **Timon of Athens**	Let our drums strike.	Alcibiades
T **Titus Andronicus**	And being dead, let birds on her take pity.	Lucius
C **Troilus and Cressida**	Hope of revenge shall hide our inward woe.	Troilus
C **Twelfth Night**	And we'll strive to please you every day.	Feste
C **The Two Gentlemen of Verona**	One feast, one house, one mutual happiness.	Valentine
C **The Two Noble Kinsmen**	And bear us like the time.	Theseus (N.B. Epilogue follows)
C **The Winter's Tale**	We were dissevered. Hastily lead away.	Leontes

Shakespearian Characters

Character	Play
AARON, a Moor	*Titus Andronicus*
ABERGAVENNY, Lord	*Henry VIII*
ABHORSON, an executioner	*Measure for Measure*
ABRAHAM, Montague's servingman	*Romeo and Juliet*
ACHILLES	*Troilus and Cressida*
ADAM, a former servant of Sir Rowland	*As You Like It*
ADRIAN, a Lord	*The Tempest*
ADRIAN, a Roman	*Coriolanus*
ADRIANA	*The Comedy of Errors*
AEDILES	*Coriolanus*
AEMILIUS	*Titus Andronicus*
AENEAS, a commander	*Troilus and Cressida*
AESCHINES	*Pericles, Prince of Tyre*
AGAMEMNON, commander in chief	*Troilus and Cressida*
AGRIPPA	*Antony and Cleopatra*
AGUECHEEK, Sir Andrew	*Twelfth Night*
AJAX	*Troilus and Cressida*
ALARBUS, son of Tamora	*Titus Andronicus*
ALBANY, Duke of, Goneril's husband	*King Lear*
ALCIBIADES, an Athenian	*Timon of Athens*

Character	Play	Character	Play
Captain		BARDOLPH	Henry IV Part 2 and
ALENÇON, Duke of	Henry VI Part 1		Henry V
ALEXANDER, servant of	Troilus and Cressida		The Merry Wives of
Cressida			Windsor
ALEXAS	Antony and Cleopatra	BARNARDINE	Measure for Measure
ALICE, an old gentlewoman	Henry V	BARNARDO	Hamlet
ALONSO, King of Naples	The Tempest	BARTHOLOMEW, a page	The Taming of the
AMIENS, Lord attending on	As You Like It		Shrew
Duke Senior		BASSANIO	The Merchant of Venice
ANDROMACHE, wife of	Troilus and Cressida	BASSET	Henry VI Part 1
Hector		BASSIANUS, Saturninus'	Titus Andronicus
ANGELO, a goldsmith	The Comedy of Errors	brother	
ANGELO, appointed	Measure for Measure	BASTARD of Orleans	Henry VI Part 1
Vincentio's deputy		BATES, John	Henry V
ANGUS, a Thane	Macbeth	BAWD	Pericles, Prince of Tyre
ANNE, Lady	Richard III	BEADLE of Saint Albans	Henry VI Part 2
ANTENOR, a commander	Troilus and Cressida	BEATRICE, an orphan	Much Ado About
ANTIGONUS, a Lord	The Winter's Tale		Nothing
ANTIOCHUS, King of	Pericles, Prince of Tyre	BEAUFORT, Cardinal	Henry VI Part 2
Antioch		Bishop of Winchester	
ANTIPHOLUS OF	The Comedy of Errors	BEDFORD, Duke of, regent	Henry VI Part 1
EPHESUS		of France	
ANTIPHOLUS OF	The Comedy of Errors	BELARIUS, a banished Lord	Cymbeline, King of
SYRACUSE			Britain
ANTONIO, a merchant of	The Merchant of Venice	BELCH, Sir Toby, Olivia's	Twelfth Night
Venice		kinsman	
ANTONIO, a sea-captain	Twelfth Night	BENEDICK, of Padua	Much Ado About
ANTONIO, an old man	Much Ado About		Nothing
	Nothing	BENVOLIO, Montague's	Romeo and Juliet
ANTONIO, father of Proteus	The Two Gentlemen of	nephew	
	Verona	BERKELEY, Lord	Richard II
ANTONIO, Prospero's	The Tempest	BERRI, Duke of	Henry V
brother		BIANCA, a courtesan	Othello
ANTONY, Mark	Antony and Cleopatra,	BIANCA, Baptista's	The Taming of the
	Julius Caesar	youngest daughter	Shrew
APEMANTUS, a churlish	Timon of Athens	BIGOT, Lord	King John
philosopher		BIONDELLO, a servant	The Taming of the
APOTHECARY	Romeo and Juliet		Shrew
ARAGON, Prince of	The Merchant of Venice	BIRON	Love's Labour's Lost
ARCHBISHOP of York,	Henry IV Parts 1 and 2	BLANCHE, Lady, of Spain	King John
Scrope		BLUNT, Sir James	Richard III
ARCHIDAMUS, a	The Winter's Tale	BLUNT, Sir Walter	Henry IV Part 1
Bohemian Lord		BOATSWAIN	The Tempest
ARCITE, a noble kinsman	The Two Noble Kinsmen	BOLEYN, Anne	Henry VIII
ARIEL, an airy spirit	The Tempest	BOLINGBROKE, Harry,	Richard II
ARMADO, Don Adriano de	Love's Labour's Lost	Duke of Hereford	
ARTEMIDORUS	Julius Caesar	BOLINGBROKE, Roger,	Henry VI Part 2
ARTESIUS, an Athenian	The Two Noble Kinsmen	a conjurer	
soldier		BONA, Lady	Henry VI Part 3
ARTHUR, Duke of Brittaine	King John	BORACHIO, follower of	Much Ado About
ARVIRAGUS	Cymbeline, King of	Don John	Nothing
	Britain	BOTTOM, a weaver	A Midsummer Night's
ASNATH, a spirit	Henry VI Part 2		Dream
AUDREY, a goatherd	As You Like It	BOULT	Pericles, Prince of Tyre
AUFIDIUS, General	Coriolanus	BOURBON, Duke of	Henry V
AUMERLE, Duke of	Richard II	BOY who sings	Antony and Cleopatra
AUSTRIA (Limoges),	King John	BOY who sings	The Two Noble Kinsmen
Duke of		BOY, attendant on Mariana	Measure for Measure
AUSTRINGER	All's Well That Ends Well	BOY, formerly Falstaff's page	Henry V
AUTOLYCUS, a rogue	The Winter's Tale	BOY, serving Benedick	Much Ado About
BAGOT	Richard II		Nothing
BALTHASAR, a merchant	The Comedy of Errors	BOYET	Love's Labour's Lost
BALTHASAR, a singer	Much Ado About	BRABANZIO, a senator	Othello
	Nothing	of Venice	
BALTHASAR, Portia's	The Merchant of Venice	BRACKENBURY, Sir Robert	Richard III
servant		BRANDON	Henry VIII
BALTHASAR, Romeo's man	Romeo and Juliet	BRUTUS, Marcus, a noble	Julius Caesar
BANDITTI, thieves	Timon of Athens	Roman	
BANQUO, a Scottish Thane	Macbeth	BRUTUS, tribune	Coriolanus
BAPTISTA MINOLA	The Taming of the	BUCKINGHAM, Duke of	Henry VIII
	Shrew	BUCKINGHAM, Duke of	Henry VI Part 2 and

Character	Play
	Richard III
BULLCALF, Peter	Henry IV Part 2
BURGUNDY, Duke of	Henry V and
	Henry VI Part I
BURGUNDY, Duke of	King Lear
BUSHY	Richard II
BUTTS, the King's physician	Henry VIII
CADE, Jack	Henry VI Part 2
CAITHNESS, a Thane	Macbeth
CAIUS, a French physician	The Merry Wives of
	Windsor
CALCHAS, Cressida's father	Troilus and Cressida
CALIBAN, a deformed	The Tempest
savage	
CALPURNIA	Julius Caesar
CAMBRIDGE, Richard,	Henry V
Earl of	
CAMIDIUS	Antony and Cleopatra
CAMILLO, a Lord	The Winter's Tale
CANTERBURY,	Henry V
Archbishop of	
CANTERBURY,	Henry VIII
Archbishop of	
CAPHIS	Timon of Athens
CAPTAIN	King Lear
CAPTAIN	Titus Andronicus
CAPTAIN	Twelfth Night
CAPTAIN in Duncan's army	Macbeth
CAPTAIN of a ship	Henry VI Part 2
CAPTAIN of the Welsh army	Richard II
CAPULET'S COUSIN	Romeo and Juliet
CAPULET'S WIFE	Romeo and Juliet
CAPULET, Juliet's father	Romeo and Juliet
CAPUTIUS, Lord	Henry VIII
CARDINAL	Richard III
CARDINAL CAMPEIUS	Henry VIII
CARDINAL WOLSEY	Henry VIII
CARLISLE, Bishop of	Richard II
CARPENTER	Julius Caesar
CARRIERS	Henry IV Part 1
CASCA	Julius Caesar
CASSANDRA, a prophetess	Troilus and Cressida
CASSIO, Michael, a	Othello
Lieutenant	
CASSIUS	Julius Caesar
CATESBY, Sir William	Richard III
CATHERINE	Henry V
CELIA, later disguised as	As You Like It
Aliena	
CERES, a spirit	The Tempest
CERIMON, a physician	Pericles, Prince of Tyre
of Ephesus	
CHAMBERLAIN	Henry IV Part 1
CHARLES, Dauphin	Henry VI Part 1
of France	
CHARLES, Duke	As You Like It
Frederick's wrestler	
CHARMIAN	Antony and Cleopatra
CHÂTILLON, an	King John
ambassador	
CHIEF WATCHMAN	Romeo and Juliet
CHILDREN of WINDSOR	The Merry Wives of
	Windsor
CHIRON, son of Tamora	Titus Andronicus
CHRISTOPHER, a priest	Richard III
CICERO, a senator	Julius Caesar
CINNA the conspirator	Julius Caesar
CINNA the poet	Julius Caesar
CITIZENS OF THE WATCH	Romeo and Juliet
CLARENCE, Duke of	Henry V
CLARENCE, Duke of	Richard III

Character	Play
CLAUDIO	Julius Caesar
CLAUDIO, a young	Measure for Measure
gentleman	
CLAUDIO, of Florence	Much Ado About
	Nothing
CLEOMENES, a Lord	The Winter's Tale
CLEON, Governor of	Pericles, Prince of Tyre
Tarsus	
CLEOPATRA, Queen of	Antony and Cleopatra
Egypt	
CLIFFORD, Lord	Henry VI Part 3
CLIFFORD, Old Lord	Henry VI Part 2
CLIFFORD, the younger	Henry VI Part 2
CLITUS	Julius Caesar
CLOTEN, the Queens' son	Cymbeline, King of
	Britain
CLOWN	Antony and Cleopatra
CLOWN	Titus Andronicus
CLOWN, Autolycus' son	The Winter's Tale
CLOWN, servant of Othello	Othello
CLOWNS	Hamlet
COBBLER	Julius Caesar
COBHAM, Dame Eleanor	Henry VI Part 2
COBWEB	A Midsummer Night's
	Dream
COLEVILLE, Sir John	Henry IV Part 2
COMINIUS, a General	Coriolanus
CONRAD	Much Ado About
	Nothing
CONSTABLE of France	Henry V
CONSTANCE, Lady	King John
CORDELIA	King Lear
CORIN, an old shepherd	As You Like It
CORIOLANUS	Coriolanus
CORNELIUS	Hamlet
CORNELIUS, a physician	Cymbeline, King of
	Britain
CORNWALL, Duke of	King Lear
COSTARD, a Clown	Love's Labour's Lost
COUNTESS of Auvergne	Henry VI Part 1
COURT, Alexander	Henry V
COURTESAN	The Comedy of Errors
CRANMER, Archbishop	Henry VIII
of Canterbury	
CRESSIDA, Pandarus'	Troilus and Cressida
niece	
CRIER	Henry VIII
CROMWELL, Thomas	Henry VIII
CUPID	Timon of Athens
CURIO, attending Orsino	Twelfth Night
CURTIS, a servant	The Taming of the
	Shrew
CYMBELINE, King of Britain	Cymbeline, King of
	Britain
DARDANIUS	Julius Caesar
DAUPHIN, of France	Henry V
DAVY, Shallow's servant	Henry IV Part 2
DE LA POLE, William	Henry VI Part 2
DECIUS BRUTUS	Julius Caesar
DECRETAS	Antony and Cleopatra
DEIPHOBUS, son of Priam	Troilus and Cressida
DEMETRIUS	A Midsummer Night's
	Dream
DEMETRIUS	Antony and Cleopatra
DEMETRIUS	Titus Andronicus
DENIS, Oliver's servant	As You Like It
DENNY, Sir Anthony	Henry VIII
DESDEMONA	Othello
DIANA	All's Well That Ends Well
DIANA, Goddess of chastity	Pericles, Prince of Tyre
DICK the BUTCHER	Henry VI Part 2

Character	Play
DIOMED	Antony and Cleopatra
DIOMEDES	Troilus and Cressida
DION, a Lord	The Winter's Tale
DIONIZA, wife of Cleon	Pericles, Prince of Tyre
DOCTOR to Lady Macbeth	Macbeth
DOCTOR, an Englishman	Macbeth
DOGBERRY, the constable	Much Ado About Nothing
DOLABELLA	Antony and Cleopatra
DOLL TEARSHEET, a whore	Henry IV Part 2
DONALBAIN	Macbeth
DON JOHN	Much Ado About Nothing
DON PEDRO, Prince of Aragon	Much Ado About Nothing
DOOR-KEEPER	Henry VIII
DORCAS, a shepherdess	The Winter's Tale
DORSET, Marchioness of	Henry VIII
DORSET, Marquis of	Henry VIII
DORSET, Marquis of	Richard III
DOUGLAS, Earl of	Henry IV Part 1
DROMIO OF EPHESUS	The Comedy of Errors
DROMIO OF SYRACUSE	The Comedy of Errors
DULL, Anthony, a constable	Love's Labour's Lost
DUMAINE	Love's Labour's Lost
DUNCAN, King of Scotland	Macbeth
DUTCHMAN	Cymbeline, King of Britain
EDGAR, aka Tom o' Bedlam	King Lear
EDMOND	King Lear
EDWARD IV, King	Richard III
EDWARD, Earl of March	Henry VI Parts 2 and 3
EGEON, merchant of Syracuse	The Comedy of Errors
EGEUS, father of Hermia	A Midsummer Night's Dream
EGLAMOUR	The Two Gentlemen of Verona
EGYPTIAN	Antony and Cleopatra
ELBOW, a simple constable	Measure for Measure
ELIZABETH, Princess	Henry VIII
ELY, Bishop of	Henry V
ELY, Bishop of	Henry VIII
ELY, Bishop of	Richard III
EMILIA	The Two Noble Kinsmen
EMILIA, a lady	The Winter's Tale
EMILIA, an abbess	The Comedy of Errors
EMILIA, Iago's wife	Othello
EMMANUEL, Clerk of Chatham	Henry VI Part 2
ENOBARBUS, Domitius	Antony and Cleopatra
EROS	Antony and Cleopatra
ERPINGHAM, Sir Thomas	Henry V
ESCALUS, an old Lord	Measure for Measure
ESCALUS, Prince of Verona	Romeo and Juliet
ESSEX, Earl of	King John
EVANS, Sir Hugh, a Welsh parson	The Merry Wives of Windsor
EXETER, Duke of	Henry V
EXETER, Duke of	Henry VI Part 1
EXETER, Duke of	Henry VI Part 3
EXTON, Sir Piers	Richard II
FABIAN	Twelfth Night
FALCONBRIDGE, Lady	King John
FALCONBRIDGE, Robert	King John
FALSTAFF, Sir John	Henry IV Part 2
	The Merry Wives of Windsor
FANG, a sergeant	Henry IV Part 2
FASTOLF, Sir John	Henry VI Part 1

Character	Play
FEEBLE, Francis	Henry IV Part 2
FENTON, Master	The Merry Wives of Windsor
FERDINAND	The Tempest
FERDINAND, King of Navarre	Love's Labour's Lost
FESTE, the clown	Twelfth Night
FILARIO	Cymbeline, King of Britain
FIRST LORD DUMAINE	All's Well That Ends Well
FIRST OFFICER	Twelfth Night
FITZWATER, Lord	Richard II
FIVE PRINCES	Pericles, Prince of Tyre
FLAMINIUS, a servant	Timon of Athens
FLAVIUS	Timon of Athens
FLAVIUS, a tribune	Julius Caesar
FLEANCE	Macbeth
FLORENCE, Duke of	All's Well That Ends Well
FLORIZEL, aka Doricles	The Winter's Tale
FLUELLEN, Captain, a Welshman	Henry V
FLUTE, a bellows-mender	A Midsummer Night's Dream
FOOL	King Lear
FOOL	Timon of Athens
FORD, Master Frank	The Merry Wives of Windsor
FORD, Mistress Alice	The Merry Wives of Windsor
FORESTER	Love's Labour's Lost
FORTINBRAS, Prince of Norway	Hamlet
FRANCESCA, a nun	Measure for Measure
FRANCIS, a drawer	Henry IV Part 1
FRANCISCO	Hamlet
FRANCISCO, a Lord	The Tempest
FREDERICK, Duke	As You Like It
FRENCHMAN	Cymbeline, King of Britain
FRIAR FRANCIS	Much Ado About Nothing
FRIAR JOHN	Romeo and Juliet
FRIAR LAURENCE	Romeo and Juliet
FRIAR PETER	Measure for Measure
FROTH	Measure for Measure
GADSHILL	Henry IV Part 1
GALLUS	Antony and Cleopatra
GARDENER	Richard II
GARDINER, later Bishop of Winchester	Henry VIII
GARGRAVE, Sir Thomas	Henry VI Part 1
GARTER King of Arms	Henry VIII
GENERAL of French garrison	Henry VI Part 1
GEORGE, Duke of Clarence	Richard III
GEORGE, later Duke of Gloucester	Henry VI Part 3
GERALD, a schoolmaster	The Two Noble Kinsmen
GERTRUDE, Queen of Denmark	Hamlet
GHOST of Caesar	Julius Caesar
GHOST of Hamlet	Hamlet
GHOST of King Henry VI	Richard III
GHOST of Mother of Posthumus	Cymbeline, King of Britain
GHOST of Prince Edward	Richard III
GHOST of Sicilius Leonatus	Cymbeline, King of Britain
GHOSTS of brothers of Posthumus	Cymbeline, King of Britain

Character	Play	Character	Play
GIACOMO, an Italian	Cymbeline, King of Britain	HERMIA	A Midsummer Night's Dream
GLASDALE, Sir William	Henry VI Part 1	HERMIONE	The Winter's Tale
GLOUCESTER, Duchess of	Richard II	HERO	Much Ado About Nothing
GLOUCESTER, Duke Humphrey of	Henry VI Part 2	HIPPOLYTA, Queen of the Amazons	A Midsummer Night's Dream
GLOUCESTER, Duke of	Henry V	HIPPOLYTA, Queen of the Amazons	The Two Noble Kinsmen
GLOUCESTER, Duke of	Henry VI Part 1	HOLOFERNES, a schoolmaster	Love's Labour's Lost
GLOUCESTER, Earl of	King Lear
GLOUCESTER, Humphrey, Duke of	Henry IV Part 2	HORATIO	Hamlet
GOBBO	The Merchant of Venice	HORNER, Thomas, an armourer	Henry VI Part 2
GONERIL	King Lear	HORTENSIO, a teacher	The Taming of the Shrew
GONZALO	The Tempest
GOODFELLOW, Robin, a puck	A Midsummer Night's Dream	HORTENSIUS' SERVANT	Timon of Athens
GOUGH, Matthew	Henry VI Part 2	HOST of the Garter Inn	The Merry Wives of Windsor
GOVERNOR of Harfleur	Henry V
GOWER, a messenger	Henry IV Part 2	HOST, where Julia lodges	The Two Gentlemen of Verona
GOWER, Captain, an Englishman	Henry V
GOWER, John, the Presenter	Pericles, Prince of Tyre	HOSTESS, formerly Mistress Quickly	Henry V
GRANDPRÉ, Lord	Henry V	HOTSPUR, Henry Percy	Henry IV Part 1
GRAY, Lady	Henry VI Part 3	HUBERT	King John
GRAY, Lord	Richard III	HUME, Sir John, a priest	Henry VI Part 2
GRAZIANO	Othello	HUNTSMAN	Henry VI Part 3
GRAZIANO	The Merchant of Venice	HYMEN, God of marriage	The Two Noble Kinsmen
GREEN	Richard II	HYMEN, God of marriage	As You Like It
GREGORY	Romeo and Juliet	IAGO, the Moor's ensign	Othello
GREMIO	The Taming of the Shrew	IDEN, Alexander	Henry VI Part 2
		INNOGEN, Princess	Cymbeline, King of Britain
GREY, Sir Thomas	Henry V
GRIFFITH, a gentleman usher	Henry VIII	INTERPRETER, a French soldier	All's Well That Ends Well
GROOM of King Richard's stable	Richard II	IRAS	Antony and Cleopatra
		IRIS, a spirit	The Tempest
GRUMIO, a servant	The Taming of the Shrew	ISABEL	Henry V
		ISABELLA	Measure for Measure
GUIDERIUS, known as Polydore	Cymbeline, King of Britain	ISIDORE'S SERVANT	Timon of Athens
GUILDENSTERN	Hamlet	JAILER	The Two Noble Kinsmen
GUILDFORD, Sir Henry	Henry VIII	JAILER'S BROTHER	The Two Noble Kinsmen
GURNEY, James	King John	JAILER'S DAUGHTER	The Two Noble Kinsmen
HABERDASHER	The Taming of the Shrew	JAMY, Captain, a Scot	Henry V
		JAQUENETTA, a country wench	Love's Labour's Lost
HAMLET, Prince	Hamlet	JAQUES, Lord	As You Like It
HARCOURT	Henry IV Part 2	JESSICA	The Merchant of Venice
HARVEY	Henry IV Part 1	JEWELLER	Timon of Athens
HASTINGS, a pursuivant	Richard III	JOAN la Pucelle	Henry VI Part 1
HASTINGS, Lord	Henry IV Part 2	JOHN	Henry VI Part 2
HASTINGS, Lord	Henry VI Part 3	JOHN OF GAUNT, Duke of Lancaster	Richard II
HECATE, Queen of Witches	Macbeth
HECTOR	Troilus and Cressida	JOHN OF LANCASTER	Henry IV Part 1
HELEN	Cymbeline, King of Britain	JOHN, a priest	Richard III
		JOHN, a servant	The Merry Wives of Windsor
HELEN	Troilus and Cressida
HELEN, an orphan	All's Well That Ends Well	JOHN, King of England	King John
HELENA	A Midsummer Night's Dream	JOSEPH, a servingman	The Taming of the Shrew
HELENUS, a priest	Troilus and Cressida	JULIA	The Two Gentlemen of Verona
HELICANUS	Pericles, Prince of Tyre
HENRY IV, King	Henry IV Parts 1 and 2	JULIET	Measure for Measure
HENRY V, King	Henry V	JULIET	Romeo and Juliet
HENRY VI, King	Henry VI Parts 1, 2 and 3	JULIUS CAESAR	Julius Caesar
		JUNO, a spirit	The Tempest
HENRY VIII, King	Henry VIII	JUPITER	Cymbeline, King of Britain
HENRY, Earl of Richmond	Richard III
HENRY, Lord Scrope of Masham	Henry V	JUSTICE	Measure for Measure
		KATE	Henry IV Part 2
HERBERT, Sir Walter	Richard III	KATE, Lady Percy	Henry IV Part 1

SHAKESPEARE

Character	Play	Character	Play
KATHERINE	Love's Labour's Lost	MACBETH, Lady	Macbeth
KATHERINE	The Taming of the Shrew	MACBETH, Thane of Glamis	Macbeth
KEEPER of the prison	Richard II	MACDUFF, Lady	Macbeth
KENT, Earl of	King Lear	MACDUFF, Thane of Fife	Macbeth
KING CHARLES VI of France	Henry V	MACDUFF'S SON	Macbeth
		MACMORRIS, Captain	Henry V
KING CLAUDIUS	Hamlet	MAECENAS	Antony and Cleopatra
KING of France	All's Well That Ends Well	MALCOLM, King	Macbeth
KING of France	King Lear	MALVOLIO, Olivia's steward	Twelfth Night
KING PHILIP of France	King John	MAMILLIUS	The Winter's Tale
KING SIMONIDES of Pentapolis	Pericles, Prince of Tyre	MARCELLUS	Hamlet
		MARCUS ANDRONICUS, a tribune	Titus Andronicus
LAERTES	Hamlet		
LAFEU, an old lord	All's Well That Ends Well	MARDIAN, a eunuch	Antony and Cleopatra
LANCE	The Two Gentlemen of Verona	MARGARET	Henry VI Part 1
		MARGARET	Much Ado About Nothing
LANCELOT, a clown	The Merchant of Venice		
LARTIUS, a General	Coriolanus	MARGARETON, a bastard	Troilus and Cressida
LAVATCH, a clown	All's Well That Ends Well	MARIA	Love's Labour's Lost
LAVINIA	Titus Andronicus	MARIA, a waiting-gentlewoman	Twelfth Night
LEAR, King of Britain	King Lear		
LE BEAU	As You Like It	MARIANA	All's Well That Ends Well
LEGATE	Henry VI Part 1	MARIANA	Measure for Measure
LENNOX, a Thane	Macbeth	MARINA	Pericles, Prince of Tyre
LEONARDO	The Merchant of Venice	MARINER	The Winter's Tale
LEONATO, governor of Messina	Much Ado About Nothing	MARSHAL	Pericles, Prince of Tyre
		MARTEXT, Sir Oliver, a clergyman	As You Like It
LEONINE, a murderer	Pericles, Prince of Tyre	MARTIUS	Titus Andronicus
LEONTES, King of Sicily	The Winter's Tale	MASTER of a ship	Henry VI Part 2
LEPIDUS	Antony and Cleopatra, Julius Caesar	MASTER of a ship	The Tempest
		MASTER GUNNER of Orleans	Henry VI Part 1
LICHORIDA, Thaisa's nurse	Pericles, Prince of Tyre		
LIEUTENANT of the Tower	Henry VI Part 3	MATE of a ship	Henry VI Part 2
LIGARIUS	Julius Caesar	MAYOR of London	Henry VI Part 1
LINCOLN, Bishop of	Henry VIII	MAYOR of Saint Albans	Henry VI Part 2
LODOVICO	Othello	MAYOR of York	Henry VI Part 3
LONGUEVILLE	Love's Labour's Lost	MELUN, Count	King John
LORD CHAMBERLAIN	Henry VIII	MENAN	Antony and Cleopatra
LORD CHANCELLOR	Henry VIII	MENECRATES	Antony and Cleopatra
LORD CHIEF JUSTICE	Henry IV Part 2	MENELAUS	Troilus and Cressida
LORD MARSHAL	Richard II	MENENIUS Agrippa	Coriolanus
LORD MAYOR OF LONDON	Henry VIII	MENTEITH, a Thane	Macbeth
LORD MAYOR OF LONDON	Richard III	MERCADE, a messenger	Love's Labour's Lost
LORENZO	The Merchant of Venice	MERCHANT OF EPHESUS	The Comedy of Errors
LOUIS THE DAUPHIN	King John	MERCUTIO	Romeo and Juliet
LOUIS, King	Henry VI Part 3	MESSALA	Julius Caesar
LOVELL, Sir Thomas	Henry VIII	METELLUS CIMBER	Julius Caesar
LUCENTIO, from Pisa	The Taming of the Shrew	MICHAEL, Sir	Henry IV Part 1
		MILAN, Duke of	The Two Gentlemen of Verona
LUCETTA, a waiting-woman	The Two Gentlemen of Verona		
		MIRANDA	The Tempest
LUCIANA	The Comedy of Errors	MONTAGUE, Marquis of	Henry VI Part 3
LUCILIUS, a servant	Timon of Athens	MONTAGUE, Romeo's father	Romeo and Juliet
LUCILLIUS	Julius Caesar		
LUCIO, 'a fantastic'	Measure for Measure	MONTAGUE'S WIFE	Romeo and Juliet
LUCIUS	Titus Andronicus	MONTANO, Governor of Cyprus	Othello
LUCIUS, a flattering Lord	Timon of Athens		
LUCIUS, a servant	Julius Caesar	MONTGOMERY, Sir John	Henry VI Part 3
LUCIUS, an ambassador	Cymbeline, King of Britain	MONTJOY, the French Herald	Henry V
LUCIUS' SERVANT	Timon of Athens	MOPSA, a shepherdess	The Winter's Tale
LUCULLUS, a flattering Lord	Timon of Athens	MOROCCO, Prince of	The Merchant of Venice
		MORTIMER, aka Earl of March	Henry IV Part 1
LUCULLUS' SERVANT	Timon of Athens		
LUCY, Sir William	Henry VI Part 1	MORTIMER, Edmund	Henry VI Part 1
LYSANDER	A Midsummer Night's Dream	MORTIMER, Lady	Henry IV Part 1
		MORTIMER, Sir Hugh	Henry VI Part 3
LYSIMACHUS, Governor of Mytilene	Pericles, Prince of Tyre	MORTIMER, Sir John	Henry VI Part 3
		MORTON	Henry IV Part 2

Character	Play	Character	Play
MOTE	A Midsummer Night's Dream	PANDOLF, Cardinal	King John
		PANTHINO, a servant	The Two Gentlemen of Verona
MOTE, a page	Love's Labour's Lost		
MOULDY, Ralph	Henry IV Part 2	PARIS	Romeo and Juliet
MOWBRAY, Thomas, Duke of Norfolk	Richard II	PARIS	Troilus and Cressida
		PAROLLES	All's Well That Ends Well
MURELLUS, a tribune	Julius Caesar		
MUSTARDSEED	A Midsummer Night's Dream	PATIENCE, a waiting woman	Henry VIII
MUTIUS	Titus Andronicus	PATROCLUS	Troilus and Cressida
MYRMIDONS	Troilus and Cressida	PAULINA	The Winter's Tale
NATHANIEL, a servingman	The Taming of the Shrew	PEASEBLOSSOM	A Midsummer Night's Dream
NATHANIEL, Sir, a curate	Love's Labour's Lost	PEDANT, schoolmaster from Mantu	The Taming of the Shrew
NELL, a country wench	The Two Noble Kinsmen	PEMBROKE, Earl of	King John
NELL, a kitchen-maid	The Comedy of Errors	PERCY, Earl of Northumberland	Henry IV Parts 1 and 2
NERISSA, a waiting-gentlewoman	The Merchant of Venice		
		PERCY, Earl of Northumberland	Richard II
NESTOR	Troilus and Cressida		
NICANOR, a Volscian	Coriolanus	PERCY, Harry	Richard II
NIM	Henry V	PERDITA	The Winter's Tale
NIM	The Merry Wives of Windsor	PERICLES, Prince of Tyre	Pericles, Prince of Tyre
NORFOLK, Duke of	Henry VIII	PETER	Romeo and Juliet
NORFOLK, Duke of	Henry VI Part 3 and Richard III	PETER, a servingman	The Taming of the Shrew
NORFOLK, old Duchess of	Henry VIII	PETER OF POMFRET, a prophet	King John
NORTHUMBERLAND, Earl of	Henry VI Part 3	PETER THUMP	Henry VI Part 2
NORTHUMBERLAND'S WIFE	Henry IV Part 2	PETO	Henry IV Part 2
OBERON, King of the Fairies	A Midsummer Night's Dream	PETRUCCIO	Romeo and Juliet
		PETRUCHIO, a gentleman of Verona	The Taming of the Shrew
OCTAVIA	Antony and Cleopatra		
OCTAVIUS Caesar	Julius Caesar	PHILEMON, Cerimon's servant	Pericles, Prince of Tyre
OCTAVIUS CAESAR	Antony and Cleopatra		
OLD ATHENIAN	Timon of Athens	PHILIP, a servingman	The Taming of the Shrew
OLDCASTLE, Sir John	Henry IV Part 1		
OLD MAN	Macbeth	PHILIP the BASTARD	King John
OLD MAN, Gloucester's tenant	King Lear	PHILO	Antony and Cleopatra
		PHILOTUS' SERVANT	Timon of Athens
OLIVER	As You Like It	PHOEBE, a shepherdess	As You Like It
OLIVIA, a Countess	Twelfth Night	PHRYNIA, a whore	Timon of Athens
OPHELIA	Hamlet	PINCH, Doctor, a schoolmaster	The Comedy of Errors
ORLANDO	As You Like It		
ORLÉANS, Duke of	Henry V	PINDARUS	Julius Caesar
ORSINO, Duke of Illyria	Twelfth Night	PIRITHOUS	The Two Noble Kinsmen
OSRIC	Hamlet	PISANIO, a servant	Cymbeline, King of Britain
OSTLER	Henry IV Part 1		
OSWALD, Goneril's steward	King Lear	PISTOL, Ensign	Henry V
			The Merry Wives of Windsor
OTHELLO, the Moor of Venice	Othello		Henry IV Part 2
OVERDONE, Mistress, a bawd	Measure for Measure	POET	Julius Caesar
		POET	Timon of Athens
OWAIN GLYNDWR	Henry IV Part 1	POINS, Edward	Henry IV Parts 1 and 2
OXFORD, Earl of	Henry VI Part 3 and Richard III	POLIXENES, King of Bohemia	The Winter's Tale
PAGE, Anna	The Merry Wives of Windsor	POLONIUS, a Lord	Hamlet
		POMPEY (Pompeius)	Antony and Cleopatra
PAGE, Master George	The Merry Wives of Windsor	POMPEY, a clownish servant	Measure for Measure
PAGE, Mistress Margaret	The Merry Wives of Windsor	POPILIUS Laena, a senator	Julius Caesar
PAGE, William	The Merry Wives of Windsor	POLONIUS POPILIUS POMPEY	
		PORTER	Henry IV Part 2
PAINTER	Timon of Athens	PORTER at Macbeth's castle	Macbeth
PALAMON, a noble kinsman	The Two Noble Kinsmen	PORTER, at the christening	Henry VIII
PANDARUS, a Lord	Troilus and Cressida	PORTIA, an heiress	The Merchant of Venice
PANDER	Pericles, Prince of Tyre	PORTIA, Brutus's wife	Julius Caesar

Character	Play	Character	Play
POSTHUMUS Leonatus	Cymbeline, King of Britain	SAMSON	Romeo and Juliet
PRIAM, King of Troy	Troilus and Cressida	SANDS, Lord	Henry VIII
PRIEST	Hamlet	SATURNINUS	Titus Andronicus
PRIEST	Twelfth Night	SAWYER	Henry VI Part 2
PRINCE EDWARD	Henry VI Part 3 and Richard III	SAYE, Lord	Henry VI Part 2
		SCALES, Lord	Henry VI Part 2
PRINCE HAL	Henry IV Parts 1 and 2	SCARUS	Antony and Cleopatra
PRINCE HENRY	King John	SCRIVENER	Richard III
PRINCE JOHN of Lancaster	Henry IV Part 2	SCROPE, Sir Stephen	Richard II
PRINCESS of France	Love's Labour's Lost	SEBASTIAN	The Tempest
PROCULEIUS	Antony and Cleopatra	SEBASTIAN	Twelfth Night
PROSPERO	The Tempest	SECOND LORD DUMAINE	All's Well That Ends Well
PROTEUS, a gentleman of Verona	The Two Gentlemen of Verona	SECOND MERCHANT	The Comedy of Errors
		SECOND OFFICER	Twelfth Night
PROVOST	Measure for Measure	SELEUCUS	Antony and Cleopatra
PUBLIUS	Titus Andronicus	SEMPRONIUS	Titus Andronicus
PUBLIUS, a senator	Julius Caesar	SEMPRONIUS, a flattering Lord	Timon of Athens
QUEEN, Cymbeline's wife	Cymbeline, King of Britain	SENIOR, Duke	As You Like It
QUEEN, wife of Richard II	Richard II	SENTRY and men of his WATCH	Antony and Cleopatra
QUEEN ELEANOR	King John		
QUEEN ELIZABETH	Richard III	SERGEANT	Henry VI Part 2
QUEEN KATHERINE	Henry VIII	SERJEANT-AT-ARMS	Henry VIII
QUEEN MARGARET	Henry VI Parts 2 and 3	SERVANT of Cornwall	King Lear
QUEEN MARGARET	Richard III	SERVANT of Olivia	Twelfth Night
QUICKLY, Mistress	Henry IV Parts 1 and 2	SERVANT of the old shepherd	The Winter's Tale
QUICKLY, Mistress	The Merry Wives of Windsor	SERVILIUS, a servant	Timon of Athens
		SEXTON	Much Ado About Nothing
QUINCE, a carpenter	A Midsummer Night's Dream	SEYTON, servant of Macbeth	Macbeth
QUINTUS	Titus Andronicus	SHADOW, Simon	Henry IV Part 2
RAMBURES, Lord	Henry V	SHALLOW, Robert, a country justice	Henry IV Part 2
RATCLIFF, Sir Richard	Richard III		The Merry Wives of Windsor
REGAN	King Lear		
RENÉ, King of Naples	Henry VI Part 1	SHEPHERD, father of Joan	Henry VI Part 1
REYNALDO, a servant	Hamlet	SHERIFF	Henry IV Part 1
REYNALDO, a steward	All's Well That Ends Well	SHERIFF	King John
RICHARD II, King	Richard II	SHERIFF	Richard III
RICHARD PLANTAGENET	Henry VI Parts 1, 2 and 3	SHYLOCK, a Jew	The Merchant of Venice
RICHARD, Duke of Gloucester, afterwards King Richard III	Richard III	SICINIUS Velutus, tribune	Coriolanus
		SILENCE, a country justice	Henry IV Part 2
		SILIUS	Antony and Cleopatra
RICHARD, the young	The Merry Wives of Windsor	SILVIA	The Two Gentlemen of Verona
RIVERS, LORD	Henry VI Part 3	SILVIUS, a young shepherd	As You Like It
ROBIN, Sir John's page	The Merry Wives of Windsor	SIMPCOX, Simon	Henry VI Part 2
		SIMPCOX'S WIFE	Henry VI Part 2
ROCHESTER, Bishop of	Henry VIII	SIMPLE, Peter, Slender's servant	The Merry Wives of Windsor
RODERIGO, a Venetian gentleman	Othello	SIWARD, Earl of Northumberland	Macbeth
ROMEO	Romeo and Juliet		
ROSALIND	As You Like It	SIWARD, the younger	Macbeth
ROSALINE	Love's Labour's Lost	SIX COUNTRYMEN	The Two Noble Kinsmen
ROSENCRANTZ	Hamlet	SIX KNIGHTS	The Two Noble Kinsmen
ROSS, a Thane	Macbeth	SIX SPIRITS	Henry VIII
ROSS, Lord	Richard III	SIX WITCHES	Macbeth
ROUSILLON, Bertram, Count of	All's Well That Ends Well	SLENDER, Master Abraham	The Merry Wives of Windsor
ROUSILLON, Countess of	All's Well That Ends Well	SLY, Christopher, beggar and tinker	The Taming of the Shrew
RUGBY, John	The Merry Wives of Windsor		
		SMITH the WEAVER	Henry VI Part 2
RUMOUR, the Presenter	Henry IV Part 2	SNARE, a sergeant	Henry IV Part 2
RUSSELL	Henry IV Part 1	SNOUT, a tinker	A Midsummer Night's Dream
RUTLAND, Earl of	Henry VI Part 3		
SAINT ASAPH, Bishop of	Henry VIII	SNUG, a joiner	A Midsummer Night's Dream
SALERIO	The Merchant of Venice		
SALISBURY	Henry V	SOLANIO	The Merchant of Venice
SALISBURY, Earl of	Henry VI Parts 1 and 2	SOLDIER of Alcibiades' army	Timon of Athens
SALISBURY, Earl of	King John		
SALISBURY, Earl of	Richard II	SOLDIER who has killed	Henry VI Part 3

Character	Play
his father	
SOLDIER who has killed his son	Henry VI Part 3
SOLINUS, Duke of Ephesus	The Comedy of Errors
SOMERSET, Duke of	Henry VI Parts 1, 2 and 3
SOMERVILLE	Henry VI Part 3
SOOTHSAYER	Antony and Cleopatra
SOOTHSAYER	Julius Caesar
SOOTHSAYER, called Philarmonus	Cymbeline, King of Britain
SOUTHWELL, John, a priest	Henry VI Part 2
SPANIARD	Cymbeline, King of Britain
SPEED	The Two Gentlemen of Verona
SPIRIT LIKE A CAT	Macbeth
STAFFORD, Sir Humphrey	Henry VI Part 2
STAFFORD'S BROTHER	Henry VI Part 2
STANLEY, Lord, Earl of Derby	Richard III
STANLEY, Sir John	Henry VI Part 2
STARVELING, a tailor	A Midsummer Night's Dream
STEFANO, Alonso's drunken butler	The Tempest
STEFANO, Portia's servant	The Merchant of Venice
STOKESLEY, Bishop of London	Henry VIII
STRATO	Julius Caesar
SUFFOLK, Duke of	Henry VIII
SUFFOLK, Earl of	Henry VI Part 1
SURREY, Duke of	Richard II
SURREY, Earl of	Henry IV Part 2
SURREY, Earl of	Henry VIII
TABORER, called Timothy	The Two Noble Kinsmen
TAILOR	The Taming of the Shrew
TALBOT, John	Henry VI Part 1
TAMORA, Queen of the Goths	Titus Andronicus
TAURUS	Antony and Cleopatra
THAISA	Pericles, Prince of Tyre
THALIART, a villain	Pericles, Prince of Tyre
THERSITES	Troilus and Cressida
THESEUS, Duke of Athens	A Midsummer Night's Dream
THESEUS, Duke of Athens	The Two Noble Kinsmen
THIDIAS	Antony and Cleopatra
THOMAS, Duke of Clarence	Henry IV Part 2
THOMAS, Lord Mowbray	Henry IV Part 2
THREE APPARITIONS	Macbeth
THREE FISHERMEN	Pericles, Prince of Tyre
THREE MURDERERS	Macbeth
THREE NEIGHBOURS	Henry VI Part 2
THREE PRENTICES	Henry VI Part 2
THREE QUEENS	The Two Noble Kinsmen
THREE STRANGERS	Timon of Athens
THURIO	The Two Gentlemen of Verona
TIMANDRA, a whore	Timon of Athens
TIME, as chorus	The Winter's Tale
TIMON of Athens	Timon of Athens
TIRREL, Sir James	Richard III
TITANIA, Queen of the Fairies	A Midsummer Night's Dream
TITINIUS, a Roman officer	Julius Caesar
TITUS ANDRONICUS	Titus Andronicus
TITUS' SERVANT	Timon of Athens
TOUCHSTONE, a jester	As You Like It

Character	Play
TRANIO, a servant	The Taming of the Shrew
TRAVERS, Northumberland's servant	Henry IV Part 2
TREBONIUS	Julius Caesar
TRINCULO, Alonso's jester	The Tempest
TROILUS	Troilus and Cressida
TUBAL, a Jew	The Merchant of Venice
TUTOR, of Rutland, a chaplain	Henry VI Part 3
TWELVE COUNTRYMEN	The Winter's Tale
TYBALT	Romeo and Juliet
ULYSSES	Troilus and Cressida
URSULA, attendant on Hero	Much Ado About Nothing
VALENTINE, a gentleman of Verona	The Two Gentlemen of Verona
VALENTINE, attending Orsino	Twelfth Night
VALENTINE, kinsman of Titus	Titus Andronicus
VALERIA	Coriolanus
VALERIUS, a Theban	The Two Noble Kinsmen
VALTEMAND	Hamlet
VARRIUS	Antony and Cleopatra
VARRIUS, a Lord	Measure for Measure
VARRUS	Julius Caesar
VAUGHAN, Sir Thomas	Richard III
VAUX, a messenger	Henry VI Part 2
VAUX, Sir Nicholas	Henry VIII
VENICE, Duke of	Othello
VENICE, Duke of	The Merchant of Venice
VENTIDIUS	Antony and Cleopatra
VENTIDIUS	Timon of Athens
VERGES, the Headborough	Much Ado About Nothing
VERNON	Henry VI Part 1
VERNON, Sir Richard	Henry IV Part 1
VINCENTIO, Lucentio's father	The Taming of the Shrew
VINCENTIO, The Duke of Vienna	Measure for Measure
VINTNER	Henry IV Part 1
VIOLA, a lady	Twelfth Night
VIRGILIA	Coriolanus
VOLUMNIA	Coriolanus
VOLUMNIUS	Julius Caesar
WAITING-GENTLEWOMAN	Macbeth
WART, Thomas	Henry IV Part 2
WARWICK	Henry V
WARWICK, Earl of	Henry VI Parts 1, 2 and 3
WARWICK, Neville, Earl of	Henry IV Part 2
WATCHMEN	Much Ado About Nothing
WESTMINSTER, Abbot of	Richard II
WESTMORLAND	Henry V
WESTMORLAND, Earl of	Henry IV Parts 1, 2 and 3
WHITMORE, Walter	Henry VI Part 2
WIDOW	The Taming of the Shrew
WIDOW CAPILET	All's Well That Ends Well
WILLIAM, a countryman	As You Like It
WILLIAM, Lord Hastings	Richard III
WILLIAMS, Michael	Henry V
WILLOUGHBY, Lord	Richard II
WINCHESTER, Bishop of	Henry VI Part 1
WITCH, Margery Jordan	Henry VI Part 2
WOMAN, attending Emilia	The Two Noble Kinsmen
WOODVILLE, Anthony,	Richard III

S
H
A
K
E
S
P
E
A
R
E

Character	Play	Character	Play
Earl RIVERS		YORK, Duchess of	*Richard III*
WOODVILLE, Lieutenant of Tower	*Henry VI Part 1*	YORK, Duke of	*Henry V*
		YORK, Duke of	*Henry VI Part 2*
WOOER of the jailer's daughter	*The Two Noble Kinsmen*	YORK, Duke of	*Richard II*
		YOUNG CATO	*Julius Caesar*
WORCESTER, Earl of	*Henry IV Part 1*	YOUNG LUCIUS, a boy	*Titus Andronicus*
YORK, Duchess of	*Richard II*	YOUNG MARTIUS	*Coriolanus*

First Lines of Shakespearian Sonnets

No.

1 From fairest creatures we desire increase
2 When forty winters shall besiege thy brow
3 Look in thy glass, and tell the face thou viewest
4 Unthrifty loveliness, why dost thou spend
5 Those hours that with gentle work did frame
6 Then let not winter's ragged hand deface
7 Lo, in the orient when the gracious light
8 Music to hear, why hear'st thou music sadly?
9 Is it for fear to wet a widow's eye
10 For shame deny that thou bear'st love to any
11 As fast as thou shalt wane, so fast thou grow'st
12 When I do count the clock that tells the time
13 O that you were yourself! But, love, you are
14 Not from the stars do I my judgement pluck
15 When I consider every thing that grows
16 But wherefore do not you a mightier way
17 Who will believe my verse in time to come
18 Shall I compare thee to a summer's day?
19 Devouring time, blunt thou the lion's paws
20 A woman's face with nature's own hand painted
21 So is it not with me as with that muse
22 My glass shall not persuade me I am old
23 As an unperfect actor on the stage
24 Mine eye hath played the painter, and hath steeled
25 Let those who are in favour with their stars
26 Lord of my love, to whom in vassalage
27 Weary with toil I haste me to my bed
28 How can I then return in happy plight
29 When, in disgrace with fortune and men's eyes
30 When to the sessions of sweet silent thought
31 Thy bosom is endeared with all hearts
32 If thou survive my well-contented day
33 Full many a glorious morning have I seen
34 Why didst thou promise such a beauteous day
35 No more be grieved at that which thou hast done
36 Let me confess that we two must be twain
37 As a decrepit father takes delight
38 How can my muse want subject to invent
39 O, how thy worth with manners may I sing
40 Take all my loves, my love, yea, take them all
41 Those pretty wrongs that liberty commits
42 That thou hast her, it is not all my grief
43 When most I wink, then do mine eyes best see
44 If the dull substance of my flesh were thought
45 The other two, slight air and purging fire
46 Mine eye and heart are at a mortal war
47 Betwixt mine eye and heart a league is took
48 How careful was I when I took my way
49 Against that time – if ever that time come
50 How heavy do I journey on the way
51 Thus can my love excuse the slow offence
52 So am I as the rich whose blessed key
53 What is your substance, whereof are you made
54 O how much more doth beauty beauteous seem
55 Not marble nor the gilded monuments
56 Sweet love, renew thy force. Be it not said

57 Being your slave, what should I do but tend
58 That god forbid, that made me first your slave
59 If there be nothing new, but that which is
60 Like as the waves make towards the pebbled shore
61 Is it thy will thy image should keep open
62 Sin of self-love possesseth all mine eye
63 Against my love shall be as I am now
64 When I have seen by time's fell hand defaced
65 Since brass, nor stone, nor earth, nor boundless sea
66 Tired with all these, for restful death I cry
67 Ah, wherefore with infection should he live
68 Thus is his cheek the map of days outworn
69 Those parts of thee that the world's eye doth view
70 That thou are blamed shall not be thy defect
71 No longer mourn for me when I am dead
72 O, lest the world should task you to recite
73 That time of year thou mayst in me behold
74 But be contented when that fell arrest
75 So are you to my thoughts as food to life
76 Why is my verse so barren of new pride
77 Thy glass will show thee how thy beauties wear
78 So oft have I invoked thee for my muse
79 Whilst I alone did call upon thy aid
80 O, how I faint when I of you do write
81 Or I shall live your epitaph to make
82 I grant thou wert not married to my muse
83 I never saw that you did painting need
84 Who is it that says most which can say more
85 My tongue-tied muse in manners holds her still
86 Was it the proud full sail of his great verse
87 Farewell – thou art too dear for my possessing
88 When thou shalt be disposed to set me light
89 Say that thou didst forsake me for some fault
90 Then hate me when thou wilt, if ever, now
91 Some glory in their birth, some in their skill
92 But do thy worst to steal thyself away
93 So shall I live supposing thou art true
94 They that have power to hurt and will do none
95 How sweet and lovely dost thou make the shame
96 Some say thy fault is youth, some wantonness
97 How like a winter hath my absence been
98 From you have I been absent in the spring
99 The forward violet thus did I chide
100 Where art thou, muse, that thou forget'st so long
101 O truant muse, what shall be thy amends
102 My love is strengthened, though more weak in seeming
103 Alack, what poverty my muse brings forth
104 To me, fair friend, you never can be old
105 Let not my love be called idolatry
106 When in the chronicle of wasted time
107 Not mine own fears nor the prophetic soul
108 What's in the brain that ink may character
109 O never say that I was false of heart
110 Alas, 'tis true, I have gone here and there

First Lines of Sonnets: Alphabetical Order

SOVEREIGNS

General Information on Sovereigns of England and Great Britain

William I

Domesday Book of 1086 contained details of the land settlement of England and its purpose was to maximise the land tax yield. It received its name in the 12th century to signify that, like the day of judgement, there could be no appeal from its verdict.

Hereward the Wake ('Watchful One'), a Lincolnshire squire, raided Peterborough Abbey in 1070 as a protest against William's appointment of a Norman abbot. He took refuge on the Isle of Ely and eventually escaped through the Fens.

Bishop Odo of Bayeux was William's half-brother and it was he who commissioned the Bayeux Tapestry (embroidery).

Of William's four sons, Robert became duke of Normandy and Richard died in infancy.

William was Edward the Confessor's cousin by way of his mother Emma, who was the sister of William's grandfather, Count Richard II. Edward the Confessor was Harold II's brother-in-law by way of his marriage to Edith, Harold's sister.

William's invasion forces assembled at the mouth of the Dives river in September 1066 but adverse winds prevented a due-north sailing to the Isle of Wight, so he regrouped at St Valéry on Somme and sailed on 27 September to the south coast of England and took Pevensey and Hastings. unchallenged. Harold was victorious against Tostig and Harald Hardraade at Stamford Bridge, near York, on 25 September and met William at the Battle of Hastings on 14 October. William only had about 7,000 troops but his archers won the day and, when Harold was killed, the English gave up.

William II

William was called Rufus because of his ruddy complexion.

Malcolm III of Scotland (Malcolm Canmore, aka Great Head) became king of Scotland in 1057 on the death of Macbeth, who had killed Malcolm's father, Duncan, in 1040. He invaded England five times between 1061 and 1093 and was killed at Alnwick in Northumberland. Four of his sons succeeded him – Duncan, Edgar, Alexander and David.

Traditionally William was shot by an arrow fired by a Norman knight called Walter Tirel, although many believe that William's younger brother Henry was the instigator.

Henry I

Henry was the only English-born son of William I.

His brother Robert was paid a pension of 3,000 marks to resign his claim to the English throne and concentrate his attentions on Normandy, but in 1105–6 Henry was forced to make war against his brother's maladministration. Robert was defeated at Tinchebrai in 1106, and was kept a prisoner for life.

In 1120, Henry's only legitimate son, William, was drowned on his way from Normandy to England in what is now known as the *White Ship* disaster.

Matilda

Matilda was pledged the throne in 1127 but Stephen became king in 1135. Matilda invaded the kingdom in 1139, landed at Arundel and established a stronghold in the West Country with her half-brother Robert of Gloucester. She captured Stephen at Lincoln and pronounced herself 'Lady of the English'. Her forces were defeated September 14 1141 while besieging the royalist-held Wolvesey Castle in what is known as the 'Rout of Winchester'. Robert Earl of Gloucester was taken prisoner and exchanged for King Stephen. Matilda was never crowned and her six months' reign is often disregarded.

Stephen

Stephen usurped the crown by declaring Matilda illegitimate, as her father had remarried.

Henry II

Henry was the first Plantagenet king of England.

He systematically destroyed the adulterine (unlicensed) castles which had sprung up during the reign of his predecessor.

Henry's conflict with Thomas à Becket was over a written statement made by Henry at Clarendon, near Salisbury, on 30 January 1164 whereby he wanted the benefit of clergy to be lifted and have lay authorities try clerks taking holy orders.

The English pope, Adrian IV, gave Henry authority over the whole of Ireland.

Incited by Queen Eleanor, Prince John and Richard rebelled against Henry and their cause was espoused by the kings of France and Scotland. William the Lion of Scotland was taken prisoner at Alnwick and forced to sign the Treaty of Falaise, 1174, thereby swearing allegiance to Henry.

Henry, the first son of Henry II, died in 1183 and his second son, Geoffrey, was killed in a tournament in Paris in 1185.

Henry's mistress, the fair Rosamond, daughter of Walter Clifford, was said to have borne him two sons – William Longsword, earl of Salisbury, and Geoffrey, archbishop of York – but this is unlikely.

Henry and his two sons were known as Angevin kings, and although Plantagenet was the other name for this royal House, subsequent members are not Angevin. To confuse matters further, although Richard II was traditionally the last king of the House of Plantagenet, the Yorkist Richard III was the last of the direct line.

Henry's second son, Henry (aka FitzHenry), was crowned on 14 June 1170, to rule in association with his father, and was known as Henry III or Henry the Young King; he died of dysentery in 1183.

Richard I   Richard was given the Duchy of Aquitaine aged 11, and was enthroned as duke of Aquitaine at Poitiers in 1172.

He departed for the Holy Land to fight the third Crusade in 1190.

Richard made a truce for three years with Saladin but was captured on his way home by Duke Leopold in December 1192. He was imprisoned at the duke's castle at Durnstein on the Danube and then handed over to Henry VI of Germany. Richard was released in February 1194 after paying a ransom of nearly 150,000 marks.

Richard left Hubert Walter as virtual ruler of England while he was away.

John   John became count of Mortain on Richard's accession in 1189.

When Richard recognised his nephew, Arthur, duke of Brittany, as his heir in October 1190, John broke his oath to Richard not to enter England while he was away at the Crusades.

Richard finally accepted John as his heir in 1196.

John's first marriage to Isabella of Gloucester was dissolved on the grounds of consanguinity, both parties being great-grandchildren of Henry I. John's second marriage, to Isabella of Angoulême, was largely responsible for the loss of many French territories.

Pope Innocent III excommunicated John in November 1209 because of his refusal to accept Stephen Langton as archbishop of Canterbury.

The Barons' War of 1215–17 ensued after John sealed the Magna Carta of 15 June 1215 but did not abide by it. Magna Carta comprises a preamble and 63 clauses. The most famous clauses are (39), guaranteeing every free man security from illegal interference in his person or property, (40), which guaranteed justice to all, and (12), which stated that the king was not to levy taxes without reference to the 'common council'.

Henry III   Henry was 9 years old when he became king, so William Marshal, First Earl of Pembroke and Striguil, acted as his regent for the first three years, followed by Hubert de Burgh for the next eight years.

Henry was forced to agree to the Provisions of Oxford, 1258, which created a council of fifteen barons and formed the first judicial Parliament.

The civil war between Henry III and his barons, led by Simon de Montfort, was called the Second Baron's War (1264–7).

Edward I   Edward won great renown as a knight on the eigth, and last, Crusade of 1270 and did not return home for his coronation until 1274.

He campaigned against Llewelyn ap Gruffud, of Gwynedd, and finally forced him into submission in 1276; and after his death in 1282 the principality was formally annexed to the English Crown by the Statute of Wales, 1284.

In 1289 Edward betrothed his infant son to Margaret, the infant Queen of Scotland (Maid of Norway), in order to unite England and Scotland, but Margaret died the following year.

Edward called the 'Model Parliament' of 1295 to allay discontent at home and the following year marched north, stripped John Balliol of his crown and carried the Stone of Scone back to England.

He had a setback at Stirling Bridge in 1297, but the following year he trounced William Wallace at Falkirk.

Edward II   In 1301 Edward became the first English Prince of Wales.

His favourite was Piers Gaveston, whom he made duke of Cornwall. When Gaveston was executed in 1312, Edward chose Hugh le Despenser and his son as his new favourites, and they aided in the overthrow of Thomas, earl of Lancaster, in 1321.

Edward was defeated by Robert the Bruce at Bannockburn, 24 June 1314.

Edward's wife, Isabella, despised him and took a lover in Roger de Mortimer. In 1326 she landed on the coast of Suffolk, executed the Despensers and forced Edward to abdicate on 25 January 1327, in favour of his son. He was murdered later that year in Berkeley Castle, Gloucestershire, probably by Isabella and Roger de Mortimer. Edward III was crowned in January 1327, eight months before his father died.

Edward III   In 1328 Edward married Phillipa of Hainault and two years later put Mortimer to death and banished his mother to Castle Rising.

Charles IV of France died without a son in 1328 and Edward claimed his kingdom by right of his mother, who was Charles's sister. He declared war against Philip VI in 1337, which was in effect the start of the Hundred Years War.

Accompanied by his eldest son, Edward the Black Prince, Edward had a great victory at Crécy in 1346 and another at Poitiers in 1356, where it is said the Black Prince gained his spurs.

Edward's mistress from 1366 onwards was Alice Perrers, his wife's lady-in-waiting, who let the government slip into the hands of Edward's fourth son, John of Gaunt.

The Black Prince died in 1376 and his son by Joan, the Fair Maid of Kent, succeeded Edward III, as Richard II.

Richard II   Although a council of twelve was officially entrusted to govern during Richard's minority, in effect John of Gaunt was the regent.

Poll tax of 1380 created national unrest and led to the Peasants' Revolt of 1381, when rebels under Wat Tyler took Rochester Castle in Kent and then marched on London with fellow radicals from Essex. Richard saw the Essex men at Mile End and made extensive promises, and the next day, 14 June, met Wat Tyler's men at Smithfield. Tyler was struck down by the mayor of London, William Walworth, in revenge for the atrocities of the previous day when the archbishop of Canterbury, Simon of Sudbury, was murdered.

John of Gaunt died in 1399 and his son succeeded him as duke of Lancaster. Richard went to Ireland in May 1399 and on 4 July Henry, duke of Lancaster, landed back in England. Although Richard hurried back to England, he submitted to his cousin at Flint on 19 August and was put in the Tower. On 29 September 1399 he resigned the Crown in favour of Henry and he seems to have been murdered at Pontefract Castle, Yorkshire, early in 1400.

Henry IV   Henry was the first king of the House of Lancaster.

His surname of Bolingbroke came from his birthplace in Lincolnshire.

Henry defeated Harry Hotspur at Shrewsbury on 21 July 1403, when Hotspur was slain.

Henry V   Henry had Richard II's body buried in Westminster Abbey.

Henry thought he had a good claim to the French crown through his great-grandfather, Edward III.

Henry's famous victory at Agincourt was on 25 October 1415.

In 1420 Henry became regent of France via the 'Perpetual Peace' of Troyes.

Henry persecuted the Lollards, would-be Church reformers who had become the first group of English heretics to represent a political threat.

Henry VI   Henry was less than a year old when he became king of England, and on the death of his maternal grandfather, King Charles VI, he became king of France when just over 1 year of age. He was officially crowned king of England in 1429 and of France in 1431.

By 1453 the Hundred Years War was effectively over, with England expelled from all France except Calais.

Cade's Rebellion of 1450 was a revolt by Kentish gentry against the high taxes and alleged corruption in Henry's council. On 18 June Cade defeated a royal army at Sevenoaks and then marched on London. He was eventually killed attempting to evade arrest at Heathfield, Sussex.

Edward IV   Richard, duke of York, became protector while Henry VI suffered temporary madness in 1454. Richard had in fact a better title to the crown than Henry, as he was descended from Lionel, duke of Clarence, third son of Edward III. When Henry recovered, Richard refused to hand back the throne. He defeated Henry at St Albans on 22 May 1455, thereby starting the Wars of the Roses. Although in the ascendant, York did not claim the Crown until 1460, when he became Henry's heir, resulting in Edward Prince of Wales being disinherited. Richard was killed at Wakefield soon after but his son claimed the Crown as Edward IV, after his victory at Mortimer's Cross, and the second battle at St Albans. After a series of victories at Towton, Hedgeley Moor and Hexham, Edward married Elizabeth Woodville and the opposition to this family briefly restored Henry VI to the throne in 1470. Undeterred, Edward regrouped and with only 2,000 men, defeated the Lancastrians and killed Warwick at Barnet on 14 April 1471. Edward carried on to Tewkesbury and on 4 May 1471 his decisive victory and the death of Edward, Prince of Wales, effectively ended the Lancastrian resistance. Henry VI was killed soon after in the Tower of London.

Edward V   The 12-year-old King Edward V was escorted from Ludlow by Earl Rivers but Richard, duke of Gloucester, the future Richard III, intercepted him at Northampton, brought him to London on 4 May 1483 and was then made protector. In June, Edward's brother, Richard, duke of York, joined him in the Tower of London and they were never seen again. In 1674 some bones were found and re-interred as theirs in Westminster Abbey.

Richard III   Richard became duke of Gloucester in 1461.

On the death of Edward IV on 9 April 1483, Richard became Protector of the Realm for Edward's son and successor, the 12-year-old King Edward V, whom he imprisoned in the Tower of London along with his younger brother Richard on the premise that Edward IV's marriage was invalid and therefore his sons were illegitimate. Richard was proclaimed king in June 1483.

It is possible that Richard had a hand in the murder of Henry VI in the Tower of London on the night of 21 May 1471.

Richard's chief supporter had been Henry Stafford, 2nd duke of Buckingham, but soon after Richard's coronation he entered into a plot with friends of Henry, earl of Richmond, the future Henry VII. The attempt failed and Buckingham was executed. Henry landed at Milford Haven on 7 August 1485. Richard met him at Bosworth on 22 August, and there lost his kingdom and his life. He was the last British monarch to die in battle.

Henry VII   Henry was the first Tudor monarch of England. His claim to the throne became definite on the

SOVEREIGNS

deaths of Henry VI's only son, Edward, and Henry VI himself, which made Henry Tudor the last surviving male heir of the House of Lancaster.

Henry's victory at Bosworth owed a great deal to his stepfather, Lord Stanley, deserting to him. Henry united the houses of York and Lancaster by way of his marriage to Elizabeth of York.

In 1487 Lambert Simnel, the son of a baker, under the influence of a priest named William Symonds, claimed to be Edward Plantagenet, son of George, duke of Clarence. He was crowned in Dublin in 1487, but his followers were defeated at Stoke and Henry gave Simnel a job in his kitchens. In 1491 Perkin Warbeck impersonated Richard, duke of York, one of the princes presumed dead in the Tower. Warbeck invaded south-west England in 1498 but was caught by Henry and eventually hanged.

Henry VIII   The six wives of Henry VIII were:

Catherine of Aragon (1485–1536), daughter of Ferdinand II of Spain and Isabella I of Castile. Married 11 June 1509, Chapel of the Observant Friars.

Anne Boleyn (1507–36), marchioness of Pembroke, daughter of Thomas Boleyn. Married 25 January 1533.

Jane Seymour (1509–37), daughter of Sir John Seymour. Married 30 May 1536, Queen's Closet, York Place, London.

Anne of Cleves (1515–57), daughter of John, duke of Cleves. Married 6 January 1540, Greenwich.

Catherine Howard (1521–42), daughter of Lord Edmund Howard. Married 28 July 1540, Oatlands.

Catherine Parr (1512–48), daughter of Sir Thomas Parr. Married 12 July 1543, Hampton Court.

Henry met Francis I in a field near Calais in June 1520, and although the display of friendship was short-lived, the lavish ceremonies became known as the Field of the Cloth of Gold.

Henry accused Thomas Wolsey (1475–1530), Lord Chancellor England 1515–29, of high treason for failing to obtain the pope's permission for the king's divorce from Catherine of Aragon. Wolsey died on the journey from York to London and was succeeded by Thomas More (1478–1535), who was executed in 1535 for refusing to swear the oath to the Act of Succession and thereby denying papal supremacy. Thomas Cromwell now became Henry's most trusted aide. After arranging Henry's divorce from Catherine in 1533 he organised the dissolution of the monasteries, 1536–9, but was ultimately executed on a trumped-up charge of treason in 1540.

Edward VI   Edward was 10 years old when he became king and his uncle, Edward Seymour, duke of Somerset, acted as his first Lord Protector, followed by John Dudley, earl of Warwick.

Lady Jane Grey Jane was married against her will to the son of the Lord Protector, John Dudley, earl of Warwick, who connived to put her on the throne because she was the great-granddaughter of Henry VII, through her mother Lady Frances Brandon, whose own mother was Mary, the younger of King Henry VIII's two sisters. Jane ruled for only nine days and was beheaded with her husband on 12 February 1554 after her father was found to be involved in the Wyatt Rebellion.

Mary I   Mary was known as Bloody Mary because of her policy of burning heretics.

After she lost Calais in 1554 she was reported to have said that when she died, Calais would be found writ on her heart.

Elizabeth I   Elizabeth was linked romantically with Robert Dudley, earl of Leicester, and later in life with Robert Devereux, earl of Essex, whom she was forced to execute for treason.

Two important conspiracies against Elizabeth were the Ridolfi Plot (1571) and the Babington Plot (1586), which ultimately caused the execution of Mary, Queen of Scots, in 1587.

Elizabeth's chief minister for most of her reign was William Cecil, Lord Burghley.

Elizabeth had a first-class intelligence network which was the envy of Europe; her minister in charge was Francis Walsingham.

James I   James was also James VI of Scotland (1567–1625), after his mother, Mary, Queen of Scots, was forced to abdicate.

James's slogan was 'No Bishop, No King', which was used to reassure the people that Elizabethan Church settlements were to be maintained and that he believed the Anglican Church and the monarchy to be interdependent.

The leader of the Gunpowder Plot of 5 November 1605 was Robert Catesby, and his fellow conspirators included Thomas Winter, John Wright and Guido/Guy Fawkes, all staunch Roman Catholics. The plot was against James's stance on religion, and the aim was to blow up him, his family and all the lords present. The plot failed when Francis Tresham, a newly enrolled conspirator, warned his brother-in-law, Lord Monteagle, not to attend parliament that day.

James's parliament of April–June 1614 was called the 'Addled' because it was dissolved without passing any bills.

Before he became king of England, James was thought to be having a homosexual affair with Esmé Stuart.

The 'Main' plot of 1603 was an attempt to put Arabella Stuart on the throne.

Charles I   The 'Five Members' that Charles attempted to arrest on 4 January 1642 were John Pym, John Hampden, Denzil Holles, Arthur Hesilrige and William Strode.

Charles's parliaments were: the 'Short', 13 April–5 May 1640, in which he demanded money for the Bishops' War against the Scottish covenanters, and the 'Long', in which Charles impeached Strafford and Laud and which ran from 1640 to 1660 but became the 'Rump' after Pride's purge of about 140 royalist MPs on 6 December 1648.

The Bishops' Wars of 1639–40 were provoked by the attempts of Charles to impose Anglicanism on Scotland. The English prayer book was refused and episcopacy was abolished in Scotland. Charles summoned the Short Parliament in order to obtain supplies for the resumption of the war.

After the 'Grand Remonstrance', whereby parliament voiced its dissatisfaction with the monarchy, and the incident of the 'Five Members', civil war was imminent and Charles eventually raised his standard at Nottingham on 22 August 1642. After the indecisive battle of Edgehill, 23 October 1642, Charles was forced to retreat at Turnham Green, London, and for the duration of the Civil War based his capital at Oxford. After many more indecisive battles, the formation of the New Model Army in February 1645, commanded by Fairfax and Cromwell, and the royalist defeat at Naseby, June 1645, spelt the end for Charles.

Charles II   James, duke of Monmouth, was the illegitimate son of Charles II and Lucy Walter.

The incident of Charles hiding up an oak tree to escape capture occurred during the Battle of Worcester in 1651.

General George Monk organised the restoration of the monarchy, and Charles entered London in triumph on his birthday, 29 May 1660, after issuing his Declaration of Breda promising a general amnesty and liberty of conscience.

In 1678 anti-Catholic feeling was stoked to fever-point by the trumped-up revelations of Titus Oates about a supposed Popish plot to murder Charles. In 1683 the Rye House Plot was a conspiracy to murder Charles and his brother James, duke of York, as they travelled from Newmarket races to London past Rye House in Hertfordshire. Monmouth, Algernon, Sidney and several prominent Whigs were implicated.

James II   In 1685 the Monmouth Rebellion was crushed and Judge Jeffreys' Bloody Assizes followed.

James was forced to abdicate because of his Catholic tendencies and was succeeded by the Protestant William of Orange.

Aided by a small body of French troops, James invaded Ireland and made an abortive attempt to reclaim his throne, but was defeated at the battle of the Boyne, 1690, and returned to St Germain.

William III   William landed at Torbay on 5 November 1688, following an invitation from the 'Immortal Seven' noblemen to protect the Protestant religion. When James fled to France, William and Mary were declared joint sovereigns. Jacobite resistance was ended by the battles of Killiecrankie, July 1689, and the Boyne, 1690.

William died after his horse stumbled at seeing a mole run out from his hill, causing him to fall and break his right collarbone. Complications set in when William caught an infection and he died on 8 March 1702.

Anne   Only one of Anne's children survived infancy, William, duke of Gloucester, who died in 1700 at the age of 12.

Sarah Churchill, later duchess of Marlborough, was the lifelong friend and confidante of Anne, and when corresponding they often used the names Mrs Freeman and Mrs Morley. Sarah Churchill's cousin, Abigail Masham, née Hill, later became Anne's favourite.

In 1704 a fund was set up by Anne for the benefit of the poorer clergy and this 'Queen Anne's Bounty' was amalgamated into the Church Commissioners when it was set up in 1948.

George I   The Act of Settlement of 1701 ensured the Crown for George.

George married his cousin Sophia Dorothea of Zell in 1682, but divorced her in 1694 for adultery with a Swedish nobleman and kept her imprisoned in the castle of Ahlden until her death in 1726.

The '15' rebellion (1715) was an attempt by Jacobites to put James Edward Stuart, the Old Pretender (son of James II and Mary of Modena), on the throne.

George's unpopularity was not helped by the fact that he never learnt to speak fluently in English.

George II   George was the last British sovereign to lead an army into battle, in 1743 at Dettingen, which he won.

The '45' rebellion (1745) was an attempt to put Charles Edward Stuart, the Young Pretender (son of James Edward Stuart), on the British throne. It was ruthlessly put down by William Augustus, the duke of Cumberland, the second son of George, at Culloden.

George III   George is said to have had a child by Hannah Lightfoot, a Quaker, and it is possible he even married her, although this is extremely doubtful.

George had long periods of insanity and the Prince of Wales, later George IV, was appointed Regent from 1811 onwards.

George IV   George had a much-publicised affair with an actress, Mrs Robinson, when aged 18; his ceremony of marriage with Mrs Maria Fitzherbert, when aged 23, was deemed unlawful in England.

William IV   William was called the Sailor King.

He lived with an actress, Dorothy Jordan, from 1790 to 1811 and she bore him ten children.

S
O
V
E
R
E
I
G
N
S

Victoria	Under Salic law, Victoria could not claim her dominion over Hanover, and this title passed to her uncle, Ernest Augustus, duke of Cumberland.
	She became Empress of India in 1876, although officially this title was conferred on her on 1 January 1877.
	Victoria published *Leaves from the Journal of our Life in the Highlands (1869)* and *More Leaves (1884)*.
	Victoria was the first monarch to live in Buckingham Palace.
Edward VII	Edward's Christian name was Albert but he used his second name in deference to Queen Victoria.
	Edward was cited in a divorce scandal of 1870.
George V	George instigated the monarch's Christmas Day broadcasts to the nation in 1932.
Edward VIII	Abdicated to marry a divorcee and became Governor of the Bahamas in WW2.
George VI	George was a keen tennis player and played in the Wimbledon Championships of 1926.
	He substituted the title of Head of the Commonwealth for Emperor of India in 1947.
	George's Christian name was Albert but he used his fourth name in deference to Queen Victoria.
Elizabeth II	On 13 June 1996, Elizabeth II had ruled longer than Elizabeth I.
	Elizabeth was in Kenya when she heard she was Queen.
	The Queen's actual birthday is 21 April; her official birthday falls on the second Saturday in June.

NB The list above contains information on sovereigns since the Norman invasion, which tends to be 90 per cent of any school history curriculum; other sovereigns, either of the whole or part of England, are listed below.

House of Wessex

802–839	Egbert (became ruler of all the English kingdoms from 829–30)
839–858	Aethelwulf (son of Egbert)
858–860	Aethelbald (son of Aethelwulf)
860–865	Aethelbert (brother of Aethelbald)
865–871	Aethelred I (brother of Aethelbert)
871–899	Alfred (the Great, brother of Aethelred I)
899–924	Edward (the Elder, son of Alfred)
924–924	Aelfweard (son of Edward)
924–939	Aethelstan (brother of Aelfweard)
939–946	Edmund I (brother of Aethelstan)
946–955	Eadred (brother of Edmund)
955–959	Eadwig (son of Edmund)
959–975	Edgar (the Peaceful, brother of Eadwig)
975–978	St Edward (the Martyr, son of Edgar)
978–1016	Aethelred II (the Unready or Ill-Advised, brother of St Edward)
1013–1014	Swein Forkbeard (deposed Aethelred II in this year)
1016–1016	Edmund II (Ironside, son of Aethelred II)
1042–1066	St Edward (the Confessor, son of Aethelred II)
1066–1066	Harold II (Godwinson)

House of Denmark

1016–1035	Cnut (the Great, son of Swein Forkbeard)
1037–1040	Harold I (Harefoot, son of Cnut)
1040–1042	Harthacnut (brother of Harold)

Kings and Queens of England and Great Britain

	Reign	Date of accession	Born	Died	Marriage(s)
William I aka the Bastard, the Conqueror	1066–1087	25 Dec.	Falaise, France, c. 1028, illegitimate son of Robert I, 6th duke of Normandy, by Herleva/Arlette, daughter of Fulbert the Tanner.	Abdominal injury while riding via Mantes, died 5 weeks later on 9 Sept. 1087 at Rouen. Buried at the Abbey of St Stephen, Caen.	Matilda (died 1083), daughter of Baldwin V, count of Flanders; 4 sons, 5 daughters. Married at Eu c. 1053.
William II Rufus	1087–1100	26 Sept.	Normandy, c. 1056, 3rd son of William I and Matilda.	Arrow wound while hunting in the New Forest, nr Brockenhurst, Hants, 2 Aug. 1100. Buried in Winchester Cathedral.	Unmarried.
Henry I Beauclerc	1100–1135	5 Aug.	Selby, Yorkshire, 1068, 4th son of William I and Matilda. Buried at Reading Abbey. 1 Dec. 1135.	Fever, St Denis-le-Ferment, Grisors. Aged 67, 1 Dec. 1135.	Edith (aka Matilda), died 1118, daughter of Malcolm III and Margaret. Wed Westminster Abbey, Nov. 1100. Adela, died 1151, daughter of Godfrey VII, count of Louvaine (granddaughter of Edmund Ironside); 1 son, 1 daughter.
Matilda 'Empress Maud'	1141		London, Feb. 1102, only legitimate daughter of Henry I.	Natural causes, Rouen, Normandy. Buried at Fontevraud Abbey church, Anjou.	Henry V, Emperor of Germany, married in 1114, died in 1125. Geoffrey V, count of Anjou; 3 sons. Married 1128, died 1151.
Stephen	1135–1154	22 Dec.	Blois, France, c. 1096, 3rd son of Stephen aka Henry, count of Blois, and Adela, 5th daughter of William I.	Heart attack, St Martin's Priory, Dover, 25 Oct. 1154. Buried at Faversham Abbey.	Matilda, died 1151, daughter of count of Boulogne and Mary, sister of Matilda (wife of Henry I); 3 sons, 2 daughters. Married 1125.
Henry II Plantagenet Fitzempress Curtmantle	1154–1189	19 Dec.	Le Mans, France, 5 March 1133, eldest son of Geoffrey V, count of Anjou, and Matilda, only daughter of Henry I.	Fever, castle of Chinon, Tours, 6 July 1199. Buried at Fontevraud Abbey in Anjou, reburied Westminster Abbey.	Eleanor (1122–1204), daughter of duke of Aquitaine and divorced wife of Louis VII of France; 5 sons, 3 daughters. Married at Bordeaux, 1152.
Richard I aka Lionheart	1189–1199	3 Sept.	Oxford, 8 Sept. 1157, 3rd son of Henry II and Eleanor.	Arrow wound while besieging the castle of Chalus, Limousin, France, 6 April 1199. Buried at Fontevraud Abbey in Anjou, reburied Westminster Abbey.	Berengaria died c.1230, daughter of Sancho VI of Navarre. No issue. Married at Limassol, Cyprus, 1191.
John aka Lackland	1199–1216	27 May	Beaumont Palace, Oxford, 24 Dec. 1167, 5th son of Henry II and Eleanor.	Dysentery, Newark Castle, Notts, Oct. 1216. Buried at Worcester Cathedral.	Isabel, died 1217. Married 1191 at Marlborough, Wilts; no issue. Isabella, died 1246, daughter of count of Angoulême; 2 sons, 3 daughters. Married at Angoulême, Aug. 1200.

	Reign	Date of accession	Born	Died	Marriage(s)
Henry III aka the Builder	1216–1272	28 Oct.	Winchester, 1 Oct. 1207, elder son of John and Isabella of Angoulême.	Natural causes, Westminster, aged 65, 16 Nov. 1272. Buried Westminster Abbey Church.	Eleanor, died 1291, daughter of count of Provence, Raymond Berengar. Married at Canterbury, 1236; 2 sons, 3 daughters.
Edward I aka Longshanks, Hammer of the Scots	1272–1307	20 Nov.	Westminster, 17 June 1239; eldest son (to survive infancy) of Henry III and Eleanor of Provence. Buried at Westminster Abbey.	Natural causes, Burgh-on-the-Sands nr Carlisle, 7 July 1307, aged 68.	Eleanor, died 1290, daughter of king of Castile, Ferdinand III, 4 sons, 7 daughters. Married Las Huelgas, Oct. 1254. Margaret (1282–1317), daughter of King Philip III of France; 2 sons, 1 daughter. Married Canterbury Sept. 1299.
Edward II	1307–1327	8 July	Caernarfon Castle, Wales, 25 April 1284; 4th and only surviving son of Edward I and Eleanor of Castile.	Murdered Berkeley Castle, Sept. 1327. Buried Gloucester Cathedral.	Isabella (1292–1358), daughter of King Philip IV of France; 2 sons, 2 daughters. Married Boulogne, Jan. 1308.
Edward III	1327–1377	25 Jan.	Windsor Castle, 13 Nov. 1312; elder son of Edward II and Isabella.	Natural causes, Sheen, 21 June 1377. Buried at Westminster Abbey.	Philippa (1314–69) daughter of count of Hainault and Holland; 7 sons, 5 daughters. Married at York, 24 June 1328.
Richard II	1377–1399	22 June	Bordeaux, France, 6 Jan. 1367; 2nd but only surviving son of Edward, the Black Prince, and Joan, the Fair Maid of Kent (granddaughter of Edward I).	Neurasthenia, Pontefract Castle. Buried at Westminster Abbey.	Anne of Bohemia (1366–94), daughter of Emperor Charles I. No issue. Wed St Stephens Chapel, 1382. Isabelle (1389–1409), daughter of Charles VI of France. No issue. Wed St Nicholas, Calais, 1396.
Henry IV aka Bolingbroke	1399–1413	30 Sept.	Bolingbroke Castle, Lincolnshire, April 1366; eldest son of John of Gaunt, 4th son of Edward III and Blanche, great-granddaughter of Henry III.	Eczema and gout, Jerusalem Chamber, Westminster. Buried at Westminster Abbey.	Mary de Bohun (1368–94), daughter of Humphrey of Hereford; 5 sons, 2 daughters. Wed Rochford, Essex, 1380. Joan (1370–1437), 2nd daughter of King Charles II of Navarre. No issue. Married Winchester, Feb. 1403.
Henry V aka Harry	1413–1422	21 March	Monmouth, Wales, 16 Sept. 1387; 2nd and eldest surviving son of Henry IV and Lady Mary de Bohun.	Dysentery, Bois de Vincennes, aged 34. Buried in Chapel of the Confessor, Westminster Abbey.	Catherine of Valois (1401–37), daughter of Charles VI of France; 1 son. Wed church of St John, Troyes, 2 June 1420.

	Reign	Date of accession	Born	Died	Marriage(s)
Henry VI	1422–1461	1 Sept.	Windsor, 6 Dec. 1421; only son of Henry V and Catherine of Valois.	Murdered by stabbing, Tower of London, 21 May 1471. Buried at Windsor.	Margaret (1430–82), daughter of René, duke of Anjou; 1 son. Wed Tichfield Abbey, April 1445.
Edward IV	1461–1470	4 March	Rouen, France, 28 April 1442; eldest son of Richard, 3rd duke of York and the Lady Cecily Nevill, daughter of Ralph, earl of Westmorland.	Pneumonia, Westminster, April 1483. Buried at Windsor.	Elizabeth (1437–92), daughter of Sir Richard Woodville; 3 sons, 7 daughters. Wed Grafton, Northants, 1464.
Henry VI	1470–1471	6 Oct.	As above.		
Edward IV	1471–1483	11 April	As above.		
Edward V	1483	9 April	Westminster, 2 Nov. 1470, eldest son of Edward IV and Elizabeth Woodville.	Tower of London?	Unmarried.
Richard III aka Crookback	1483–1485	26 June	Fotheringay, Northants, 2 Oct. 1452; 4th and only surviving son of Richard, 3rd duke of York (the Protector), and Cecily Nevill.	Killed Bosworth 22 Aug. 1485. Buried at the Abbey of the Grey Friars, Leicester.	Anne (1456–85), daughter of Richard Nevill, earl of Warwick, and widow of Edward, prince of Wales; 1 son. Married 12 July 1472.
Henry VII	1485–1509	22 Aug.	Pembroke Castle, 27 Jan. 1457; only child of Edmund Tudor, 1st earl of Richmond, and Margaret Beaufort, great-great-granddaughter of Edward III.	Rheumatoid arthritis and gout, 21 April, at Richmond. Buried in his own chapel at Westminster.	Elizabeth (1466–1503), daughter of Edward IV; 3 sons, 4 daughters. Wed Westminster, Jan. 1486.
Henry VIII aka Bluff King Hal, Old Copper Nose	1509–1547	22 April	Greenwich, 28 June 1491; 2nd and only surviving son of Henry VII and Elizabeth.	Sinusitis and periostitis of the leg at Whitehall, 28 Jan. 1547. Buried at Windsor.	See separate entry.
Edward VI	1547–1553	28 Jan.	Hampton Ct, 12 Oct. 1537; only surviving son of Henry VIII by Jane Seymour.	Tuberculosis at Greenwich. Buried in Henry VII's Chapel, Westminster Abbey.	Unmarried.
Jane aka Nine-Day Queen	1553	10 July	Bradgate Park, Leics, Oct. 1537; eldest daughter of Henry Grey, 3rd marquess of Dorset, and Frances, daughter of Mary Tudor, sister of Henry VIII.	Beheaded Tower of London Feb. 1554. Buried St Peter ad Vincula within the Tower.	Guilford Dudley, son of John Dudley, duke of Northumberland. Wed Durham Hse, London, May 1533.
Mary I aka Bloody Mary	1553–1558	19 July	Greenwich, 18 Feb. 1516; only surviving child of Henry VIII and Catherine of Aragon.	Influenza in London. Buried Westminster Abbey.	Philip, son of Emperor Charles V and later king of Spain in 1554.
Elizabeth I aka Virgin Queen	1558–1603	17 Nov.	Greenwich, 7 Sept. 1533; daughter of Henry VIII and Anne Boleyn.	Sepsis from tonsillar abscess at Richmond. Buried Westminster Abbey.	Unmarried.

SOVEREIGNS

	Reign	Date of Accession	Born	Died	Marriage(s)
James I	1603–1625	26 March	Edinburgh Castle, 19 June 1566; son of Mary queen of Scots (daughter of James V) and Henry Darnley.	Bright's disease, Theobalds Park, Herts. Buried Westminster Abbey.	Anne, daughter of Frederick II of Denmark. Married 20 Aug. 1589, by proxy.
Charles I	1625–1649	27 March	Dunfermline Palace, 19 Nov. 1600; only surviving son of James I and Anne of Denmark.	Beheaded at Whitehall, Jan 1649. Buried at Windsor.	Henrietta Maria, daughter of Henry IV of France. Paris, 1 May 1625, by proxy.
Charles II aka Old Rowley	1660–1685	29 May	St James's Palace, 29 May 1630; eldest son of Charles I and Henrietta Maria.	Uraemia and mercurial poisoning, Whitehall. Buried Henry VII's Chapel, Westminster.	Catherine of Braganza, daughter of John. Wed Portsmouth, 21 May 1662.
James II	1685–1688	6 Feb.	St James's Palace, 14 Oct. 1633; only surviving son of Charles I and Henrietta Maria.	Cerebral haemorrhage, St Germain, France. Remains were interred at 5 different venues in France. All are now lost except for those at the parish church at St Germain.	Anne Hyde, daughter of Edward Hyde, Worcester Hse, Strand, 3 Sept. 1660. Mary D'este, daughter of duke of Modena. Wed Modena, 30 Sept. 1673, by proxy.
William III	1688–1702	13 Feb.	The Hague, 4 Nov. 1650; only son of William II, Prince of Orange, and Mary Stuart, daughter of Charles I.	Pleuro-pneumonia following fracture of right collarbone after falling from his horse near Kensington. Buried Henry VII's Chapel, Westminster.	Mary, daughter of James II and Anne Hyde. Wed St James's Palace, 4 Nov. 1677.
Mary II	1688–1694	13 Feb.	St James's Palace, 30 April 1662.	Smallpox at Kensington, 28 Dec. 1694. Buried Henry VII's Chapel, Westminster.	William III.
Anne aka Brandy Nan	1702–1714	8 March	St James's Palace, 6 Feb. 1665, daughter of James II and Anne Hyde.	Brain haemorrhage, Kensington. Buried Henry VII's Chapel, Westminster.	George of Denmark (1653–1708), son of Frederick III of Denmark. Chapel Royal, St James's Palace, 1683.
George I	1714–1727	1 Aug.	Osnabrück, 28 May 1660; son of Ernest, duke of Brunswick-Lüneburg and elector of Hanover, and Sophia, daughter of Elizabeth, queen of Bohemia, eldest daughter of James I.	Thrombosis, Ibbenburen. Buried Hanover.	Sophia Dorothea, daughter of George William, duke of Lüneburg-Celle. Wed 21 Nov. 1682, divorced 1694.
George II	1727–1760	11 Jun.	Hanover, 30 Oct. 1683; son of George I and Sophia Dorothea.	Thrombosis, Palace of Westminster. Buried Henry VII's Chapel, Westminster.	Wilhelmina Charlotte Caroline of Ansbach (1683–1737), daughter of John Frederick, margrave of Brandenburg-Ansbach, 22 Aug. 1705.
George III aka Farmer George	1760–1820	25 Oct.	Norfolk House, London, 24 May 1738; son of Frederick Lewis, prince of Wales, and Princess Augusta of Saxe-Gotha.	Senility, Windsor. St George's Chapel, Windsor.	Charlotte Sophia (1744–1818), daughter of Charles Louis Frederick, duke of Mecklenburg-Strelitz, 8 Sept. 1761.

	Reign	Date of Accession	Born	Died	Marriage(s)
George IV	1820–1830	29 Jan.	St James's Palace, 12 Aug. 1762; eldest son of George III and Charlotte.	Stomach rupture and dropsy, Windsor. Buried St George's Chapel, Windsor.	Maria Fitzherbert, 1785, without king's consent and denied by George IV. Caroline of Brunswick, 8 April 1795, Chapel Royal, St James's Palace.
William IV aka Sailor King	1830–1837	26 June	Buckingham Palace, 21 Aug. 1765; son of George III and Charlotte.	Pneumonia/cirrhosis, Windsor. Buried St George's Chapel, Windsor.	Adelaide, daughter of duke of Saxe-Meiningen, 11 July 1818, Kew.
Victoria	1837–1901	20 June	Kensington Palace, 24 May 1819; daughter of Edward duke of Kent, 4th son of George III, and Victoria, daughter of Francis of Saxe-Coburg-Saalfeld.	Senility, Osborne House, IoW. Buried at Frogmore nr Windsor.	Francis Albert (1819–61), 2nd son of Ernest I of Saxe-Coburg-Gotha, 10 Feb. 1840, St James's Palace.
Edward VII aka Denmark, Peacemaker	1901–1910	22 Jan.	Buckingham Palace, 9 Nov. 1841; eldest son of Victoria and Albert.	Bronchitis, Buckingham Palace. Buried at St George's Chapel, Windsor.	Alexandra, daughter of Christian IX of Denmark, 10 March 1863, St George's Chapel.
George V	1910–1936	6 May	Marlborough House, London, 3 June 1865; 2nd son of Edward and Alexander.	Bronchitis, Sandringham. Buried at St George's Chapel, Windsor.	Mary, daughter of Francis, duke of Teck, 6 July 1893, St James's Palace.
Edward VIII aka People's King,	1936	20 Jan.	White Lodge, Richmond Park, 23 June 1894; eldest son of George V and Mary.	Throat cancer, Paris, 28 May 1972. Buried at Frogmore, Windsor.	Wallis Simpson née Warfield, 3 June 1937, Château de Candé, near Tours, France
George VI	1936–1952	11 Dec.	York Cottage, Sandringham, 14 Dec. 1895; second son of George V and Mary.	Lung cancer, Sandringham. Buried at St George's Chapel, Windsor.	Elizabeth Bowes-Lyon, daughter of 14th earl of Strathmore and Kinghorne, 26 April 1922.
Elizabeth II	1952–	6 Feb.	17 Bruton St, London, 21 April 1926; elder daughter of George VI and Elizabeth.	Reigned since 6 Feb. 1952.	Philip, son of Prince Andrew of Greece and Princess Alice. Married in Westminster Abbey, 20 Nov. 1947.

SOVEREIGNS

British Royalty: Miscellaneous Details

abdicated: first   Edward II (25 January 1327)

Alexandra, Princess   (the Hon. Lady Ogilvy)
full name: Alexandra Helen Elizabeth Olga Christabel
born: 25 December 1936
relationship to Queen: Cousin (sister of Edward, Duke of Kent)
husband: The Rt Hon. Sir Angus Ogilvy (born 14 September 1928)
children: James Robert Bruce Ogilvy (born 29 February 1964)
Marina Victoria Alexandra Mowatt (born 31 July 1966)
house: Thatched House Lodge, Richmond Park, Surrey

Alexandra Rose Day   inaugurated in 1912 by Queen Alexandra

Angevin kings   Henry II, Richard I, John

Andrew, Prince   married Sarah Ferguson in 1986
born: 19 February 1960
full name: Andrew Albert Christian Edward
titles: The Duke of York, Earl of Inverness and Baron Killyleagh
schools: Heatherdown, nr Ascot; Gordonstoun, Morayshire; Lakefield College School, Ontario
children: Beatrice Elizabeth Mary, born 8 August 1988
Eugene Victoria Helena, born 23 March 1990
houses: Sunninghill Park, Ascot; Buckingham Palace, London

Anne, Princess   Princess Royal since 1987
born: 15 August 1950
full name: Anne Elizabeth Alice Louise
school: Benenden, Kent
children: Peter Mark Andrew Phillips, born 15 November 1977
Zara Anne Elizabeth Phillips, born 15 May 1981
marriages: Captain Mark Phillips (1973–92)
Captain Tim Lawrence (1992–)
attempted kidnapping: by Ian Ball in 1974 in the Mall
house: Gatcombe Park, Gloucestershire

annus horribilis   Queen Elizabeth's name for 1992

anti-smoking tract: published   James I

Babington Plot   Roman Catholic plot against Elizabeth I in 1586

bald as a young woman   Elizabeth I

baldness revealed after execution   Mary, queen of Scots

bathed every three months   Elizabeth I

battle: died in; last sovereign   Richard III

battle: led troops in; last   George II (Dettingen)

bigamist   George IV

Bill of Rights   Act barring Catholics from succession

bodyguard scandal   Commander Michael Trestrail resigned as the Queen's bodyguard (19 July 1982) after admitting to his part in a sexual scandal

breast: extra   Anne Boleyn

Buckingham Palace: first to live in   Queen Victoria
bought by   George III in 1762

burnt the cakes (traditionally)   King Alfred

Cabal   advisers to Charles II: Clifford, Ashley, Buckingham, Arlington and Lauderdale

Cabinet meetings: attended most   Queen Anne

Cavalier Parliament   Charles II (aka Pensionary Parliament) first English Parliament 8 May 1661

Charles II: illegitimate son   Duke of Monmouth, son of Lucy Walter

Charles, Prince   married 1981, divorced 1996
full name: Charles Philip Arthur George
born: 14 November 1948
titles: Duke of Cornwall, Earl of Carrick and Baron Renfrew, Lord of the Isles, Duke of Rothsay, Prince and Great Steward of Scotland
children: William Arthur Philip Louis, born 21 June 1982
Henry Charles Albert David, born 15 September 1984
Prince of Wales: title bestowed in 1958; inaugurated in 1969
houses: St James's Palace, London and Highgrove, Gloucestershire
Cherry B incident of 1963: Charles bought while under-age, in Outer Hebrides
aka: Lord of the Isles, Steward of Scotland, Duke of Cornwall
children's nanny: Tiggy Legge-Bourke

cherry brandy drinker   George IV

children: most   Henry I (20 acknowledged bastards plus two legitimate)
most legitimate   Edward I (18)

Christian: first   Ethelbert

Clarence, duke of: last   Albert, eldest son of Edward VII

commoner; first to wed   Henry IV

crowned: battlefield   Henry VII

crowned: twice   Charles II

Defender of the Faith: first   Henry VIII

deposed   James II

divorced: first   John

dukes: royal   Cornwall, Edinburgh, Gloucester, Kent, York

education   *Prince Charles* Cheam, Gordonstoun, Cambridge. The Prince of Wales also spent the 1966 school year as an exchange student at the Geelong Church of England Grammar School in Melbourne, Australia.
Prince William Mrs Mynors' Nursery School, London, Wetherby School, London, Ludgrove School, Wokingham, Eton College, Berkshire, St Andrews University
Prince Harry Eton College
Princess Beatrice St George's School for Girls, Ascot, Berkshire

Edward, Prince   full name: Edward Antony Richard Louis
born: 10 March 1964
titles: Earl of Wessex, Viscount Severn
marriage: Sophie Helen Rhys-Jones (19 June 1999)
house: Bagshot Park, Surrey
schools: Gibbs Preparatory School, Kensington; Heatherdown Preparatory School, nr Ascot; Gordonstoun, Morayshire; Jesus College, Cambridge

Edward VII: House of Lords speech   housing speech given while Prince of Wales

Edward VIII   abdication speech written by Walter Monckton

Eleanor Crosses: 12   Marking resting place of Eleanor of Castile's cortege; crosses at Lincoln, Grantham, Stamford, Stratford, Woburn, Dunstable, St Albans, Cheapside, Northampton Geddington and Waltham still standing; last, Charing Cross, is a replica

Elizabeth I: favourite Robert Dudley, Earl of Leicester
Elizabeth II coronation day 2 June 1953
  biographer Sarah Bradford (1996)
  royal arms insignia Dieu et Mon Droit
  aka Lord High Admiral of England
  married 20 Nov. 1947
fattest king George IV
finger: extra Anne Boleyn
Five Members Pym, Hampden, Heselrige, Holles
  and Strode, whom Charles I attempted to arrest on 4
  Jan. 1642, as well as Lord Mandeville
gilded coach used by the new Sovereign during
  Coronation ceremony
Gloucester, Duke of full name: Richard Alexander
  Walter George
  born: 26 August 1944
  relationship to Queen: cousin (his father Henry, Duke
    of Gloucester (1900–74) was the brother of the
    Queen's father)
  wife: Birgitte Eva Van Deurs (born 20 June 1946)
  children: Earl of Ulster (Alexander Patrick, born 24
    October 1974)
    Lady Davina Windsor, born 19 November
    1977
    Lady Rose Windsor, born 1 March 1980
  house: Kensington Palace, London
heirs to throne males are heirs apparent; females
  are heirs presumptive
Henry VIII: fate of wives divorced, beheaded, died,
  divorced, beheaded, survived
honours: awarded on New Year's Day and the
  Queen's official birthday
immoral queen Caroline of Brunswick
Irish state coach used by British monarchs for State
  Opening of Parliaments and by family members at
  Coronations
jewellers, Crown Garrards
Kent, Duke of full name: Edward George Nicholas
  Paul Patrick
  born: 9 October 1935
  relationship to Queen: cousin (his father George,
    Duke of Kent (1902–42), was the brother of the
    Queen's father)
  wife: Katharine Worsley (born 22 Feb. 1933)
  children: Earl of St Andrews (George Philip Nicholas,
    born 26 June 1962)
    Lady Helen Taylor, born 28 April 1964
    Lord Nicholas Windsor, born 25 July 1970
  house: Wren House, Palace Green, London
king over the water Jacobite term for pretenders
Lancaster: House of Henry IV, V, VI
Lollards: suppressed Henry V
mad king George III
madness: bouts of Henry VI
Margaret, Princess married 1960 to Anthony
  Armstrong Jones
married kings of England and France Eleanor of
  Aquitaine (Louis VII and Henry II)
Michael of Kent, Prince full name: Michael George
  Charles Franklin
  born: 4 July 1942
  relationship to Queen: cousin (brother of Edward,
    Duke of Kent)
  wife: Baroness Marie-Christine Agnes Hedwig Ida
    von Reibnitz (born 15 January 1945)
  children: Lord Frederick Michael George David Louis
    Windsor, born 6 April 1979
    Lady Gabriella Marina Alexandra Ophelia,
    born 23 April 1981

houses: Kensington Palace, London
  Nether Lypiatt Manor, Gloucestershire
murdered by queen and her lover Edward II
nicknames *Elizabeth II* 'Lilibet' (name originated
  because she could not pronounce Elizabeth when a
  child)
  Princess Margaret 'Bud' (coined by her sister
  Elizabeth as a play on her second name of Rose)
oldest on accession William IV (64)
oldest royal residence Windsor Castle
Parliament: first; in the reign of Henry III
pawned Crown jewels Richard II (to pay for wedding)
Philip, Prince born: 10 June 1921
  titles: Duke of Edinburgh, Earl of Merioneth, Baron
    Greenwich
  schools: Cheam, Salem School, Germany,
    Gordonstoun, Morayshire
Plantagenet: first Henry II
  last Richard II, although later kings from
  Plantagenet line
pot-smoking Prince: Prince Harry (sent to drug
  rehabilitation clinic to warn him of dangers)
Popish Plot fictitious Jesuit plot of Titus Oates and
  Israel Tonge against Charles II resulting in the
  execution of Oliver Plunket, primate of Ireland
premier Duke of Scotland Dukes of Hamilton
pretenders: Henry VII's reign Perkin Warbeck
  (1498), hanged for treason; Lambert Simnel (1487),
  became kitchen hand
prince of Wales: longest Edward VII (59 yrs)
  last before Charles Edward VIII
  last Welsh Llewellyn
Prince Philip: parents Prince Andrew and Princess
  Alice of Greece
queen never set foot in England Berengaria, wife
  of Richard I
Richards all died violently
Ridolfi Plot Catholic plot against Elizabeth I in 1571
Roman Catholic monarch: last James II
royal allowance Civil List
rugby Peter Phillips, son of the Princess Royal,
  played rugby for Scottish schools
Rye House Plot plot to murder Charles II and his
  brother on the way home from Newmarket races
Sarah Armstrong-Jones daughter of Princess
  Margaret, born 1 May 1964, married Daniel Chatto
shortest queen Matilda, wife of William I
spoke little English George I
stammered George VI
St Edward's crown made for Charles II's coronation
toilet: died on George II
two queens: father of James II (Mary and Anne)
urinated in font Ethelred the Unready
USA: first to go to George VI
Victoria's gillie John Brown
Viscount Linley son of Princess Margaret, born 3
  November 1961
  married: Hon. Serena Stanhope
***White Ship* disaster** William, son of Henry I,
  drowned at Barfleur, 25 Nov. 1120
wife: met at altar George III (Charlotte Sophia)
Wimbledon: played at George VI
wisest fool in Christendom James I (coined by
  Henry IV of France)
write name: first to do so Richard II
York, House of Edward IV, V, Richard III

Order of Precedence (England and Wales)

The sovereign	Lord President of the Council
The Prince Philip, duke of Edinburgh	Speaker of the House of Commons
The Prince of Wales	Lord Privy Seal
The sovereign's younger sons	Ambassadors and High Commissioners
The sovereign's grandsons	Lord Great Chamberlain
The sovereign's cousins	Earl Marshal
Archbishop of Canterbury	Lord Steward of the Household
Lord High Chancellor	Lord Chamberlain of the Household
Archbishop of York	Master of the Horse
The Prime Minister	Then dukes, marquesses, earls, viscounts, barons

NB The order of precedence has been included in this section purely to show the distinction between order of precedence and succession. Precedence is a traditional ceremonial observation and, although closely following the order of succession in some areas, it is in fact a separate and distinct list.

Order of Succession

1	HRH Prince Charles, The Prince of Wales	11	Viscount Linley, David Armstrong-Jones
2	HRH Prince William of Wales	12	Hon. Charles Armstrong-Jones
3	HRH Prince Henry of Wales	13	Lady Sarah Chatto (née Armstrong-Jones)
4	HRH Prince Andrew, duke of York	14	Samuel Chatto
5	HRH Princess Beatrice of York	15	Arthur Chatto
6	HRH Princess Eugenie of York	16	HRH Richard, duke of Gloucester
7	HRH Prince Edward	17	The earl of Ulster
8	HRH Princess Anne, Princess Royal	18	Lady Davina Windsor
9	Peter Phillips, son of Princess Anne	19	Lady Rose Windsor
10	Zara Phillips, daughter of Princess Anne	20	HRH Edward, duke of Kent

The earl of St Andrews and HRH Prince Michael of Kent, who would usually be in the line of succession at numbers 21 and 29 respectively, forfeited their right through marriage to a Roman Catholic.

Rulers of the British Isles

Kings and Queens of Scotland

House of Alpin

842–858	Kenneth I (MacAlpin)
858–862	Donald I
862–877	Constantine I
877–878	Aed
878–889	Giric and Eochaid
889–900	Donald II
900–943	Constantine II
943–954	Malcolm I
954–962	Indulf
962–966	Duf
966–971	Culén
971–995	Kenneth II
995–997	Constantine III
997–1005	Kenneth III
1005–1034	Malcolm II

House of Dunkeld

1034–1040	Duncan I

House of Moray

1040–1057	Macbeth
1057–1058	Lulach

House of Dunkeld

1058–1093	Malcolm III (Canmore, aka Big Head)
1093–1097	Donald III
1094	Duncan II
1097–1107	Edgar
1107–1124	Alexander I (the Fierce)
1124–1153	David I (the Saint)
1153–1165	Malcolm IV (the Maiden)
1165–1214	William I (the Lion)
1214–1249	Alexander II
1249–1286	Alexander III

House of Norway

1286–1290	Margaret (Maid of Norway)
1290–1292	interregnum (disputed by 13 competitors)

House of Balliol

1292–1296	John Balliol
1296–1306	interregnum

House of Bruce

1306–1329	Robert I (the Bruce)
1329–1371	David II

House of Balliol

1332–1356	Edward (son of John, abdicated)

House of Stewart

1371–1390	Robert II (Stewart)
1390–1406	Robert III
1406–1437	James I
1437–1460	James II
1460–1488	James III
1488–1513	James IV
1513–1542	James V
1542–1567	Mary
1567–1625	James VI

Rulers of the Principality of Wales

Kingdom of Gwynedd

825–844	Merfyn the Freckled
844–878	Rhodri I (the Great)
878–916	Anarawd
916–942	Idwal the Bald
942–950	Hywel I (the Good)
950–979	Iago I

979–985	Hywel II
985–986	Cadwallon
986–999	Maredudd
999–1005	Cynan I
1005–1023	Llywelyn I
1023–1039	Iago II
1039–1063	Gruffydd I
1081–1137	Gruffydd II
1137–1170	Owain
1170–1174	Cynan II
1174–1194	David I (East Gwynedd)
1174–1195	Rhodri II (West Gwynedd)
1174–1200	Gruffydd III (South Gwynedd)
1194–1240	Llywelyn II (The Great)
1240–1246	David II

Principality of Wales

1246–1282	Llywelyn III (ap Gruffydd)
1282–1283	David III

NB Although Llywelyn ap Gruffydd is invariably quoted as the last native prince of Wales, in fact it is true to say that his brother, David ap Gruffydd, was the last native prince of Wales. This confusion arises simply because England did not recognise anyone except Llywelyn as ruler. The Welsh would recognise David as their last prince, and the English Llywelyn. In 1301 the future Edward II became prince of Wales, and subsequently the eldest son of the reigning monarch has been given this title.

The High Kingship of Ireland

House of Ui Néill

445–452	Niall of the Nine Hostages
819–833	Conchobar
1002–1014	Brian Bóruma (king of Munster)
1166–1186	Ruaidri

NB The short list above includes the first and last kings of Ireland and two other famous kings. Many of the other rulers are obscure and were not recognised as such until at least the 9th century.

Other Important Historical Rulers

Israel

1020–1010 BC	Saul
1010–970 BC	David
970–931 BC	Solomon

Kingdom of Judah

930–914 BC	Rehoboam (son of Solomon)

Kingdom of Israel

931–910 BC	Jeroboam I (son of Solomon)

Lydia: last king

560–547 BC	Croesus

Persian Empire

559–530 BC	Cyrus the Great
529–522 BC	Cambyses
522 BC	Smerdis (Bardiya)
521–486 BC	Darius I (The Great)
485–465 BC	Xerxes I
464–424 BC	Artaxerxes I
424 BC	Xerxes II
424 BC	Sogdianus
423–405 BC	Darius II
404–359 BC	Artaxerxes II
358–338 BC	Artaxerxes III
337–336 BC	Arses
335–330 BC	Darius III

Macedonia (selected kings)

399–397 BC	Orestes
359–336 BC	Philip II
336–323 BC	Alexander III (the Great)
179–168 BC	Perseus (the last king)

Visigoth kingdom

395–410	Alaric I (first king of the Visigoths)
711–714	Agila II (last king of the Visigoths)

Anglo-Saxon kingdoms

455–488	Hengest (first ruler of kingdom of Kent)
823–825	Baldred (last ruler of kingdom of Kent)
547–559	Ida (first ruler of Bernicia)
585–592	Hussa (last ruler of Bernicia)
569–599	Aelle (first ruler of Deira)
599–604	Aethelric (last ruler of Deira)
592–616	Aethelfrith (Northumberland: Bernicia and Deira)
913–927	Aldred (last ruler of Northumberland)
633–655	Penda (first ruler of Mercia)
757–796	Offa (kingdom of Mercia)
918–919	Aelfwyn (last ruler of Mercia)
519–534	Cerdic (first ruler of Wessex)
802–839	Egbert (last ruler of Wessex)

Kingdom of France (selected)
Carolingian House

751–768	Pepin the Short (first king of France)
768–814	Charlemagne (Holy Roman Emperor, 800)
840–877	Charles I (the Bald)
877–879	Louis II (the Stammerer)
885–888	Charles II (the Fat)
893–923	Charles III (the Simple)
986–987	Louis V (the Sluggard)

Capetian House

987–996	Hugh Capet
996–1031	Robert II (the Pious)
1108–1137	Louis VI (the Fat)
1137–1180	Louis VII (the Younger)
1223–1226	Louis VIII (the Lion)
1285–1314	Philip IV (the Fair)
1314–1316	Louis X (the Stubborn)
1316–1322	Philip V (the Tall)
1322–1328	Charles IV (the Fair)

House of Valois

1328–1350	Philip VI
1350–1364	John II (the Good)
1364–1380	Charles V (the Wise)
1380–1422	Charles VI (the Mad)
1422–1461	Charles VII (the Victorious)
1483–1498	Charles VIII

House of Angoulême

1515–1547	Francis I
1547–1559	Henry II
1559–1560	Francis II (husband of Mary of Scots)
1560–1574	Charles IX
1574–1589	Henry III

House of Bourbon

1589–1610	Henry IV (Paris is worth a mass)
1610–1643	Louis XIII
1643–1715	Louis XIV (the Sun King)
1715–1774	Louis XV
1774–1792	Louis XVI

First Empire

1804–1814	Napoleon I (king of Italy, 1805)

Second Empire

1852–1870	Napoleon III

Kingdom of Italy

1849–1878	Victor Emmanuel II
1878–1900	Humbert I
1900–1946	Victor Emmanuel III
1946–1946	Humbert II

NB Although Victor Emmanuel III is often thought to be the last king of Italy, in fact, he was the last 'crowned' king. Humbert II (Umberto) was the last incumbent.

Kingdom of Spain (selected)
House of Habsburg

1516–1556	Charles I (Holy Roman Emperor, 1519–58)
1556–1598	Philip II (husband of Bloody Mary)

House of Bourbon

1700–1724	Philip V (grandson of Louis XIV of France)

House of Bonaparte

1808–1813	Joseph Napoleon

House of Bourbon

1975–	Juan Carlos I

Kingdom of Portugal (selected)

1139–1185	Afonso I

House of Avis

1385–1433	John I (the Bastard)
1578–1580	Henry (the Cardinal)

House of Braganza

1640–1656	John IV
1706–1750	John V (the Magnanimous)
1834–1853	Maria II

House of Saxe-Coburg-Gotha

1853–1861	Pedro V
1908–1910	Manuel II

Kingdom of Norway (selected)

858–928	Harald I
1957–1991	Olav V
1991–	Harald V

Kingdom of Denmark (selected)

940–986	Harald I
1972–	Margaret II

Kingdom of Sweden (selected)

980–995	Erik the Victorious

House of Vasa

1523–1560	Gustavus I
1560–1568	Erik XIV
1568–1592	John III
1592–1599	Sigismund

House of Bernadotte

1818–1844	Charles XIV
1973–	Charles XVI Gustavus

Kingdom of Netherlands (selected)

1572–1584	William I (the Silent)
1806–1810	Louis Napoleon
1890–1948	Wilhelmina
1948–1980	Juliana
1980–	Beatrix

Tsars/Tsarinas of Russia

1533–1584	Ivan IV (the Terrible)
1598–1605	Boris Godunov
1462–1505	Ivan III (the Great)
1613–1645	Michael Romanov
1682–1725	Peter I (the Great)
1725–1727	Catherine I (Martha)
1762–1796	Catherine II (the Great, born Sophie of Anhalt)
1894–1917	Nicholas II

Inca Empire

1532–1533	Atauhualpa
1571–1572	Tupac Amaru

Aztec Empire

1372–1391	Acamapichtli
1427–1440	Itzcoatl

Japanese Empire

0–10 BC	Jimmu
1623–1651	Iemitsu
1713–1716	Ietsugu
1853–1858	Iesada
1867–1868	Keiki (Yoshinobu)

Chinese dynasties

18th–12th cent. BC	Shang
1111–255 BC	Chou
770–221 BC	Tung
221–206 BC	Ch'in
206–220 AD	Han
581–618	Sui
618–907	T'ang
960–1279	Sung
1206–1368	Yüan
1368–1644	Ming
1644–1912	Manchu (Ch'ing)

Last kings/queens of

Romania	Michael (1940–47)
Bulgaria	Simeon II (1943–46)
Albania	Zog I (1928–39)
Afghanistan	Muhammad Zahir Shah (1933–73)
Korea	Sunjong (1907–10)
Burma	Thibaw (1878–85)
Laos	SavangVatthana (1959–75)
Cambodia	Sihanouk (1941–55) Monarchy re-established on 23 Sept. 1993

Ethiopia	Asfa Wossen (1974–75)	Hungary	John Sigismund (1540–70)
Madagascar	Ranavalona (1883–96)	Poland	Stanislas II Augustus (1764–95)
Zululand	Dinuzulu (1884–87)	Bohemia	Ferdinand I (1526–64)
Hawaii	Liliuokalani (1891–93)		

Holy Roman Emperors

Charlemagne (Charles I)	800–814	William of Holland	1247–1256
Louis I (the Pious)	814–840	Conrad IV	1250–1254
civil war	840–843	great interregnum	1254–1273
Lothair I	843–855	Richard	1257–1272
Louis II	855–875	Alfonso	1257–1275
Charles II (the Bald)	875–877	Rudolf I	1273–1291
interregnum	877–881	Adolf	1292–1298
Charles III (the Fat)	881–887	Albert I	1298–1308
interregnum	887–891	Henry VII	1308–1313
Guido of Spoleto	891–894	Frederick III	1314–1326
Lambert of Spoleto	892–898	Louis IV	1314–1346
Arnulf	898–899	Charles IV	1346–1378
Louis III (the Blind)	901–905	Wenceslas	1378–1400
Conrad I	911–918	Rupert	1400–1410
Berengar	915–924	Jobst	1410–1411
Henry I	919–936	Sigismund	1410–1437
Otto I (the Great)	936–973	Albert II	1438–1439
Otto II	973–983	Frederick III	1440–1493
Otto III	983–1002	Maximillian I	1493–1519
Henry II (the Saint)	1002–1024	Charles V	1519–1556
Conrad II	1024–1039	Ferdinand I	1556–1564
Henry III (the Black)	1039–1056	Maximillian II	1564–1576
Henry IV	1056–1106	Rudolf II	1576–1612
Rudolf	1077–1080	Matthias	1612–1619
Hermann	1081–1093	Ferdinand II	1619–1637
Conrad	1093–1101	Ferdinand III	1637–1657
Henry V	1106–1125	Leopold I	1658–1705
Lothair II	1125–1137	Joseph I	1705–1711
Conrad III	1138–1152	Charles VI	1711–1740
Frederick I (Barbarossa)	1152–1190	interregnum	1740–1742
Henry VI	1190–1197	Charles VII	1742–1745
Philip	1198–1208	Francis I	1745–1765
Otto IV	1198–1214	Joseph II	1765–1790
Frederick II	1215–1250	Leopold II	1790–1792
Henry VII	1220–1235	Francis II	1792–1806
Henry Raspe	1246–1247		

SOVEREIGNS

Roman Kings

Romulus	753–715 BC	Tarquinius Priscus	616–578 BC
Numa Pompilius	715–673 BC	Servius Tullius	578–534 BC
Tullus Hostilius	673–642 BC	Tarquinius Superbus	534–509 BC
Ancus Marcius	642–616 BC		

NB The traditional seven kings of Rome as listed above are of extremely dubious authenticity and nowadays are only observed as truth in the context of being a very popular quiz question, and to this end the ones to remember are the first, Romulus, and the last, Tarquinius Superbus (Proud Tarquin).

Roman Emperors

Augustus	27 BC–AD 14	Vespasian	69–79
Tiberius	14–37	Titus	79–81
Caligula	37–41	Domitian	81–96
Claudius	41–54	Nerva	96–98
Nero	54–68	Trajan	98–117
Galba	68–69	Hadrian	117–138
Otho	69	Antoninus Pius	138–161
Vitellius	69	Marcus Aurelius	161–180

Commodus	180–192	Tetricus (Gaul)	271–274
Pertinax	193	Diocletian (see below)	284–305
Didius Julianus	193	Maximian (see below)	286–305
Septimius Severus	193–211	Constantius I (see below)	305–306
Geta	211	Galerius (see below)	305–311
Caracalla	211–217	Severus (west)	306–307
Macrinus	217–218	Maxentius (west)	307–312
Diadumenian	218	Constantine I (west until 324)	307–337
Elagabalus	218–222	Licinius (Pannonia and east)	308–324
Severus Alexander	222–235	Maximinus II (east)	310–313
Maximinus the Thracian	235–238	Valerius Valens	316–317
Gordian I	238	Martinian	324
Gordian II	238	Constantine II (Gaul, Britain, Spain)	337–340
Balbinus	238	Constans (west)	337–350
Pupienus Maximus	238	Constantius II (east)	337–361
Gordian III	238–244	Magnentius (west)	350–353
Philip I the Arabian	244–249	Julian the Apostate (Gaul until 361)	360–363
Philip II	247–249	Jovian	363–364
Decius	249–251	Valentinian I (west)	364–375
Herennius Etruscus	251	Valens (east)	364–378
Hostilian	251	Gratian (west)	375–383
Trebonianus Gallus (co-ruler with		Valentinian II	375–392
Misson Volusian)	251–253	Theodosius I (the Great) (east)	379–395
Volusian	251–253	Maximus (west)	383–388
Aemilian	253	Victor (west)	387–388
Valerian (east)	253–260	Eugenius (west)	392–394
Gallienus (west)	253–268		
Saloninus	260		
Claudius II	268–270		
Quintillus	270		
Aurelian	270–275		
Tacitus	275–276		
Florian	276		
Probus	276–282		
Carus	282–283		
Numerian (east)	283–284		
Carinus (west)	283–285		
Postumus (Gaul)	260–269		
Laelian (Gaul)	269		
Marius (Gaul)	269		
Victorinus (Gaul)	269–271		

After a short interregnum the Empire split into east and west. Selected entries are as follows:

Western Roman Emperors

Honorius	395–423 (the first)
Romulus Augustus	475–476 (the last)

Eastern Roman Emperors

Arcadius	395–408 (the first)
Justinian I (the Great)	527–565
Constantine XI	1449–1453 (the last)

Turkish capture of Constantinople ultimately ended the Byzantine Empire.

NB The names used in the above table are the ones familiarly adopted by history. The full names are complex and can be depicted in an imperial style or in Latin. It became increasingly impractical to rule over the whole of the Roman Empire and although the empire was not officially split until AD 395, many joint emperors divided their territories between east and west, with further subdivisions into Gaul, Britain, Illyria etc. To use the Diocletian tetrarchy as an example, Galerius, residing in Sirmium, administered Illyria, Achaea, and the Danubian provinces; Maximian, residing in Milan, administered Italy, Sicily, and Africa; Constantius I, residing in Trier, governed Gaul, Spain, and Britain; and Diocletian, residing in Nicomedia, watched over Thrace, Asia, and Egypt.

AD 69 is often referred to as the year of the four emperors but in AD 238 there were six emperors. Maximinus became the first soldier who had started from the ranks to become Roman emperor, he was replaced by the aged proconsul Gordian, who ruled jointly with his son. Gordian committed suicide on learning of the death of his son in a battle with Capellianus, governor of Numidia. The Roman Senate then proclaimed two elderly senators Balbinus and Pupienus Maximus joint emperors. The imperial guards murdered the Senate's nominees and the grandson of Gordian became emperor as Gordian III, at the age of 13. Valentinian II was proclaimed emperor in Budapest (Aquincum) at the age of 4, and ruled Italy, Africa, Illyricum, through his mother. He was found dead in his palace at Vienna, probably murdered by agents of Arbogast, the usurper in Gaul. In areas likely to confuse, I have added the administrative area in parenthesis. I have omitted usurpers such as Vetranio (abdicated in AD 351) and Procopius (reigned in Constantinople AD 365–6), as this would only confuse matters further.

American Football

	Superbowl winners				*Runners up*
1967	Green Bay Packers	NFC	35-10		Kansas City Chiefs
1968	Green Bay Packers	NFC	33-14		Oakland Raiders
1969	New York Jets	AFC	16-7		Baltimore Colts
1970	Kansas City Chiefs	AFC	23-7		Minnesota Vikings
1971	Baltimore Colts	AFC	16-13		Dallas Cowboys
1972	Dallas Cowboys	NFC	24-3		Miami Dolphins
1973	Miami Dolphins	AFC	14-7		Washington Redskins
1974	Miami Dolphins	AFC	24-7		Minnesota Vikings
1975	Pittsburgh Steelers	AFC	16-6		Minnesota Vikings
1976	Pittsburgh Steelers	AFC	21-7		Dallas Cowboys
1977	Oakland Raiders	AFC	32-14		Minnesota Vikings
1978	Dallas Cowboys	NFC	27-10		Denver Broncos
1979	Pittsburgh Steelers	AFC	35-31		Dallas Cowboys
1980	Pittsburgh Steelers	AFC	31-19		Los Angeles Raiders
1981	Oakland Raiders	AFC	27-10		Philadelphia Eagles
1982	San Francisco 49ers	NFC	26-21		Cincinnati Bengals
1983	Washington Redskins	NFC	27-17		Miami Dolphins
1984	Los Angeles Raiders	AFC	38-9		Washington Redskins
1985	San Francisco 49ers	NFC	38-16		Miami Dolphins
1986	Chicago Bears	NFC	46-10		New England Patriots
1987	New York Giants	NFC	39-20		Denver Broncos
1988	Washington Redskins	NFC	42-10		Denver Broncos
1989	San Francisco 49ers	NFC	20-16		Cincinnati Bengals
1990	San Francisco 49ers	NFC	55-10		Denver Broncos
1991	New York Giants	NFC	20-19		Buffalo Bills
1992	Washington Redskins	NFC	37-24		Buffalo Bills
1993	Dallas Cowboys	NFC	52-17		Buffalo Bills
1994	Dallas Cowboys	NFC	30-13		Buffalo Bills
1995	San Francisco 49ers	NFC	49-28		San Diego Chargers
1996	Dallas Cowboys	NFC	27-17		Pittsburgh Steelers
1997	Green Bay Packers	NFC	35-21		New England Patriots
1998	Denver Broncos	AFC	31-24		Green Bay Packers
1999	Denver Broncos	AFC	34-19		Atlanta Falcons
2000	St Louis Rams	NFC	23-16		Tennessee Titans
2001	Baltimore Ravens	AFC	34-7		New York Giants
2002	New England Patriots	AFC	20-17		St Louis Rams
2003	Tampa Bay Buccaneers	NFC	48-21		Oakland Raiders

(AFC = American Football Conference. NFC = National Football Conference.)

American Football: General Information

field goals: points score	3
most valuable player award	Jim Thorpe Trophy
players: number	11 a side on pitch at any one time
playing area	grid iron
playing period	60 minutes
rules played	Harvard Rules
safety touch: points score	2
Super Bowl	championship game of the National Football League played by the winners of league's American Football Conference and National Football Conference
touchdown: points score	6
trophy played for	Vince Lombardi trophy
World Bowl 2000 winner	Rhein Fire beat Scottish Claymores 13-10
World League: teams	Barcelona Dragons, London Monarchs, Amsterdam Admirals, Scottish Claymores, Frankfurt Galaxy, Rhein Fire

Angling: British Freshwater Records (as at February 2003)

Barbel	17 lb 4oz	Ray Walton	Rudd	4 lb 8oz		Rev. E C Alston
Bleak	4oz 9dm	Dennis Flack	Salmon	64 lb		Georgina Ballatine
Bream	16 lb 10oz	Lee McManus	Tench	14 lb 7oz		Gordon Beaven
Carp (Mary)	56 lb 6oz	Kevin Cummins	Natural Trout:			
Carp: Crucian	4 lb 5oz 8dm	Adrian Eves	Brown	25 lb 5oz 12dm	A Finlay
Carp: Grass	31 lb	Derek Smith	Cultivated Trout:			
Catfish	62 lb	Rob Garner	Brown	28 lb 1oz		D Taylor
Chub	8 lb 10oz	Peter Smith	Natural Trout:			
Dace	1 lb 4oz 4dm	J. Gasson	Rainbow	36 lb 14oz 8dm	C White
Eel	11 lb 2oz	Steve Terry	Cultivated Trout:			
Golden Orfe	7 lb 14oz 8dm	Mick Pardoe	Rainbow	24 lb 1oz 4dm	J Hammond
Perch	5 lb 9oz	John Shayler	Trout: Sea	28 lb 5oz		J Farrent
Pike	46 lb 13oz	Ray Lewis	Zander	19 lb 5oz 8dm	Dave Lavender
Roach	4 lb 3oz	Ray Clarke				

Angling: Freshwater Champions

	Individual	*Team*
1959	Robert Tesse (France)	France
1960	Robert Tesse (France)	Belgium
1961	Ramon Legogue (France)	E. Germany
1962	Raimondo Tedasco (Italy)	Italy
1963	William Lane (England)	France
1964	Joseph Fontanet (France)	France
1965	Robert Tesse (France)	Romania
1966	Henri Guiheneuf (France)	France
1967	Jacques Isenbaert (Belgium)	Belgium
1968	Gunter Grebenstein (W. Germany)	France
1969	Robin Harris (England)	Holland
1970	Marcel Van den Eynde (Belgium)	Belgium
1971	Dino Bassi (Italy)	Italy
1972	Hubert Levels (Netherlands)	France
1973	Pierre Michiels (Belgium)	Belgium
1974	Aribert Richter (W. Germany)	France
1975	Ian Heaps (England)	France
1976	Dino Bassi (Italy)	Italy
1977	Jean Mainil (Belgium)	Luxembourg
1978	Jean-Pierre Fourgeat (France)	France
1979	Gérard Heulard (France)	France
1980	Wolf-Rudiger Kremkus (W. Germany)	W. Germany
1981	Dave Thomas (England)	France
1982	Kevin Ashurst (England)	Holland
1983	Wolf-Rudiger Kremkus (W. Germany)	Belgium
1984	Bobby Smithers (Ireland)	Luxembourg
1985	Dave Roper (England)	England
1986	Lud Wever (Netherlands)	Italy
1987	Clive Branson (Wales)	England
1988	Jean-Pierre Fourgeat (France)	England
1989	Tom Pickering (England)	Wales
1990	Bob Nudd (England)	France
1991	Bob Nudd (England)	England
1992	David Wesson (Australia)	Italy
1993	Mario Barros (Portugal)	Italy
1994	Bob Nudd (England)	England
1995	Paul Jean (France)	France
1996	Alan Scotthorne (England)	Italy
1997	Alan Scotthorne (England)	Italy
1998	Alan Scotthorne (England)	England
1999	Bob Nudd (England)	Spain
2000	Jacopo Falsini (Italy)	Italy
2001	Umberto Balabeni (Italy)	England
2002	G Blasco (Spain)	Portugal

World Fly Fishing Champions

	Individual	Team		Individual	Team
1981	C Wittkamp (Netherlands)	Netherlands	1992	Perluigi Coccito (Italy)	Italy
1982	Viktor Diez (Spain)	Italy	1993	Russell Owens (Wales)	England
1983	S Fernandez (Spain)	Italy	1994	Pascal Cognard (France)	Czechoslovakia
1984	Tony Pawson (England)	Italy	1995	Jeremy Herrmann (England)	England
1985	Leslaw Frasik (Poland)	Poland	1996	Perluigi Coccito (Italy)	Czecholsovakia
1986	Slivoj Svoboda (Czechoslovakia)	Italy	1997	Pascal Cognard (France)	France
1987	Brian Leadbetter (England)	England	1998	T Starychfolta (Czechoslovakia)	Czechoslovakia
1988	John Pawson (England)	England	1999	Ross Steward (Australia)	Australia
1989	Wladislaw Trzebuinia (Poland)	Poland	2000	Pascal Cognard (France)	France
1990	Franciszek Szajnik (Poland)	Czechoslovakia	2001	Vladimir Sedivy (Czechoslovakia)	France
1991	Brian Leadbetter (England)	NZ	2002	Jerome Brossutti (France)	France

Archery: Target World Champions

	Men	Team	Women	Team
1931	M Sawicki (Poland)	France	J Kurkowska (Poland)	—
1932	L Reith (Belgium)	Poland	J Kurkowska (Poland)	—
1933	D McKenzie (USA)	Belgium	J Kurkowska (Poland)	Poland
1934	H Kjellson (Sweden)	Sweden	J Kurkowska (Poland)	Poland
1935	A van Kohlen (Belgium)	Belgium	Ina Catani (Sweden)	GB
1936	E Heilborn (Sweden)	Czechoslovakia	J Kurkowska (Poland)	Poland
1937	G de Rons (Belgium)	Poland	Ingo Simon (GB)	GB
1938	F Hadas (Czechoslovakia)	Czechoslovakia	N Weston Martyr (GB)	Poland
1939	R Beday (France)	France	J Kurkowska (Poland)	Poland
1946	E T Holbek (Denmark)	Denmark	N de Wharton Burr	GB
1947	H Deutgen (Sweden)	Czechoslovakia	J Kurkowska (Poland)	Denmark
1948	H Deutgen (Sweden)	Sweden	N de Wharton Burr	Czechoslovakia
1949	H Deutgen (Sweden)	Czechoslovakia	B Waterhouse (GB)	GB
1950	H Deutgen (Sweden)	Denmark	Jean Lee (USA)	Finland
1952	S Andersson (Sweden)	Sweden	Jean Lee (USA)	USA
1953	B Lundgren (Sweden)	Sweden	Jean Richards (USA)	Finland
1955	N Andersson (Sweden)	Sweden	K Wisniowska (Poland)	GB
1957	O Smathers (USA)	USA	C Meinhart (USA)	USA
1958	S Thysell (Sweden)	Finland	S Johansson (Sweden)	USA
1959	J Caspers (USA)	USA	Ann Corby (USA)	USA
1961	J Thornton (USA)	USA	N Vanderheide (USA)	USA
1963	C Sandlin (USA)	USA	V Cook (USA)	USA
1965	M Haikonen (Finland)	USA	M Lindholm (Finland)	USA
1967	Ray Rogers (USA)	USA	M Maczynska (Poland)	Poland
1969	Hardy Ward (USA)	USA	D Lidstone (Canada)	USSR
1971	J Williams (USA)	USA	E Gapchenko (USSR)	Poland
1973	V Sidoruk (USSR)	USA	Linda Myers (USA)	USSR
1975	Darrell Pace (USA)	USA	Z Rustamova (USSR)	USSR
1977	R McKinney (USA)	USA	Luann Ryon (USA)	USA
1979	Darrell Pace (USA)	USA	Kim Jin-ho (Korea)	Korea
1981	K Laasonen (Finland)	USA	N Butuzova (USSR)	USSR
1983	R McKinney (USA)	USA	Kim Jin-ho (Korea)	Korea
1985	R McKinney (USA)	Korea	I Soldatova (USSR)	USSR
1987	V Yesheyev (USSR)	W. Germany	Ma Xiaojun (China)	USSR
1989	S Zabrodskiy (USSR)	USSR	Kim Soo-nyung (Korea)	Korea
1991	S Fairweather (Australia)	Korea	Kim Soo-nyung (Korea)	Korea
1993	Kyung Mo Park (Korea)	France	K Hyo-Jung (Korea)	Korea
1995	Lee Kyung-Chul (Korea)	Korea	N Valeeva (Moldovia)	Korea
1997	Kim Kyung-Ho (Korea)	Korea	Kim Du-Ri (Korea)	Korea
1999	Chil Hong Sung (Korea)	Italy	Lee Eun Kyung (Korea)	Italy
2001	J K Yeon (Korea)	Korea	S H Park (Korea)	China

SPORT&LEISURE

Athletics: Olympic Games 1996

Men			Women		
100m	Donovan Bailey (Canada)	9.84	100m	Gail Devers (USA)	10.94
	Frankie Fredericks (Namibia)	9.89		Merlene Ottey (Jamaica)	10.94
	Ato Boldon (Trinidad)	9.90		Gwen Torrance (USA)	10.96
200m	Michael Johnson (USA)	19.32	200m	Marie-José Pérec (France)	22.12
	Frankie Fredericks (Namibia)	19.68		Merlene Ottey (Jamaica)	22.24
	Ato Boldon (Trinidad)	19.80		Mary Onyali (Nigeria)	22.38
400m	Michael Johnson (USA)	43.49	400m	Marie-José Pérec (France)	48.25
	Roger Black (GB)	44.41		Cathy Freeman (Australia)	48.63
	Davis Kamoga (Uganda)	44.53		Falilat Ogunkoya (Nigeria)	49.10
800m	Vebjorn Rodal (Norway)	1:42.58	800m	Svetlana Masterkova (Russia)	1:57.73
	Hezekiel Sepeng (SA)	1:42.74		Ana Fidelia Quirot (Cuba)	1:58.11
	Fred Onyancha (Kenya)	1:42.79		Maria Lurdes Mutola (Zambia)	1:58.71
1,500m	Noureddine Morceli (Algeria)	3:35.78	1,500m	Svetlana Masterkova (Russia)	4:00.83
	Fermin Cacho (Spain)	3:36.40		Gabriela Szabo (Romania)	4:01.54
	Stephen Kipkorir (Kenya)	3:36.72		Theresia Kiesl (Austria)	4:03.02
5,000m	Venuste Niyongabo (Bur)	13:07.96	5,000m	Wang Junxia (China)	14:59.88
10,000m	Haile Gebrselassie (Ethiopia)	27:07.34	10,000m	Fernando Ribeiro (Portugal)	31:01.63
Marathon	Josia Thugwane (SA)	2:12.36	Marathon	Fatuma Roba (Ethiopia)	2:26.05
3,000m S/chase	Joseph Keter (Kenya)	8:07.12	100m Hurdles	Lyudmila Engquist (Sweden)	12.58
			400m Hurdles	Deon Hemmings (Jamaica)	52.82
110m Hurdles	Allen Johnson (USA)	12.95	High Jump	Stefka Kostadinova (Bulgaria)	2.05m
400m Hurdles	Derrick Adkins (USA)	47.54	Long Jump	Chioma Ajunwa (Nigeria)	7.12m
Pole Vault	Jean Galfione (France)	5.92m	Triple Jump	Inessa Kravets (Ukraine)	15.33m
High Jump	Charles Austin (USA)	2.39m	Shot Putt	Astrid Kumbernuss (Germany)	20.56m
Long Jump	Carl Lewis (USA)	8.50m	Discus	Ilke Wyludda (Germany)	69.66m
Triple Jump	Kenny Harrison (USA)	18.09m	Javelin	Heli Rantanen (Finland)	67.94m
Shot Putt	Randy Barnes (USA)	21.62m	Heptathlon	Ghada Shouaa (Syria)	6780
Discus	Lars Riedel (Germany)	69.40m	10k Walk	Yelena Nikolayeva (Russia)	41.49
Hammer	Balazs Kiss (Hungary)	81.24m	800m Wheelchair:	Louise Sauvage (Australia)	1:54.90
Javelin	Jan Zelezny (Czechoslovakia)	88.16m			
Decathlon	Dan O'Brien (USA)	8824	4x100	United States	41.95
20k Walk	Jefferson Perez (Ecuador)	1:20.07	4x400	United States	3:20.91
50k Walk	Robert Korzeniowski (Poland)	3:43.30			
1,500m Wheelchair:	Claude Issorat (France)	3:15.18			
4x100	Canada	37.69			
4x400	United States	2:55.99			

Athletics: Olympic Games 2000

Men			Women		Team
100m	M Greene (US)	9.87	100m	M Jones (US)	10.75
	A Boldon (Tri)	9.99		E Thanou (Gr)	11.12
	O Thompson (Bar)	10.04		T Lawrence (Jam)	11.18
200m	K Kenderis (Gr)	20.09	200m	M Jones (US)	21.84
	D Campbell (GB)	20.14		P Davis-Thompson (Bah)	22.27
	A Boldon (Tri)	20.20		S Jayasinghe (S. Lanka)	22.28
400m	M Johnson (US)	43.84	400m	C Freeman (Aus)	49.11
	A Harrison (US)	44.40		L Graham (Jam)	49.58
	G Haughton (Jam)	44.70		K Merry (GB)	49.72
800m	N Schumann (Ger)	1:45.08	800m	M Mutola (Moz)	1:56.15
	W Kipketer (Den)	1:45.14		S Graf (Aus)	1:56.64
	A D Said-Guerni (Alg)	1:45.16		K Holmes (GB)	1:56.80
1500m	N Ngeny (Ken)	3:32.07	1500m	N Merah-Benida (Alg)	4:05.10
	H El Guerrouj (Mor)	3:32.32		V Szekely (Rom)	4:05.15
	B Lagat (Ken)	3:32.44		G Szabo (Rom)	4:05.27
5000m	M Wolde (Eth)	13:35.49	5000m	G Szabo (Rom)	14:40.79
	A Saidi-Sief (Alg)	13:36.20		S O' Sullivan (Ire)	14:41.02
	B Lahlafi (Mor)	13:36.47		G Wami (Eth)	14:42.23
10000m	H Gebrselassie (Eth)	27:18.20	10000m	D Tulu (Eth)	30:17.49
	P Tergat (Ken)	27:18.29		G Wami (Eth)	30:22.48
	A Mezgebu (Eth)	27:19.75		F Ribeiro (Por)	30:22.88
Marathon	G Abera (Eth)	2:10:11	Marathon	N Takahashi (Jap)	2:23:14
	E Wainaina (Ken)	2:10:31		L Simon (Rom)	2:23:22
	T Tola (Eth)	2:11:10		J Chepchumba (Ken)	2:24:45

Men			Women		Team
3,000m S/Chase	R Kosgei (Ken)	8:21.43	100m Hurdles	O Shishigina (Kaz)	12.65
	W B Kipketer (Ken)	8:21.77		G Alozie (Nig)	12.68
	A Ezzine (Mor)	8:22.15		M Morrison (US)	12.76
110m Hurdles	A Garcia (Cub)	13.00	400m Hurdles	I Privalova (Rus)	53.02
	T Trammell (US)	13.16		D Hemmings (Jam)	53.45
	M Crear (US)	13.22		N Bidouane (Mor)	53.57
400m Hurdles	A Taylor (US)	47.50	Pole Vault	S Dragila (US)	4.60
	H S Somayli (Saudi)	47.53		T Grigorieva (Aus)	4.55
	L Herbert (SA)	47.81		V Flosadottir (Ice)	4.50
Pole Vault	N Hysong (US)	5.90	High Jump	Y Yelesina (Rus)	2.01
	L Johnson (US)	5.90		H Cloete (SA)	2.01
	M Tarasov (Rus)	5.90		K Bergqvist (Swe)	1.99
High Jump	S Kliugin (Rus)	2.35		O Pantelimon (Rom)	1.99
	J Sotomayor (Cub)	2.32	**note**	Joint gold medallists	
	A Hammad (Alg)	2.32		and joint bronze medallists	
Long Jump	I Pedroso (Cub)	8.55	Long Jump	H Drechsler (Ger)	6.99
	J Taurima (Aus)	8.49		F May (Ita)	6.92
	R Schurenko (Ukr)	8.31		M Jones (US)	6.92
Triple Jump	J Edwards (GB)	17.71	Triple Jump	T Marinova (Bul)	15.20
	Y Garcia (Cub)	17.47		T Lebedeva (Rus)	15.00
	D Kasputin (Rus)	17.46		O Hovorova (Ukr)	14.96
Shot Putt	A Harju (Fin)	21.29	Shot Putt	Y Korolchik (Bela)	20.56
	A Nelson (US)	21.21		L Peleshenko (Rus)	19.92
	J Godina (US)	21.20		A Kumbernuss (Ger)	19.62
Discus	V Alekna (Lith)	69.30	Discus	E Zvereva (Bela)	68.40
	L Riedel (Ger)	68.50		A Kelesidou (Gr)	65.71
	F Kruger (SA)	68.19		I Yatchenko (Bela)	65.20
Hammer	S Ziolkowski (Pol)	80.02	Hammer	K Skolimowska (Pol)	71.16
	N Vizzoni (Ita)	79.64		O Kuzenkova (Rus)	69.77
	I Astapkovich (Bela)	79.17		K Muenchow (Ger)	69.28
Javelin	J Zelezny (Cz)	90.17	Javelin	T Hattestad (Nor)	68.91
	S Backley (GB)	89.85		M Maniani-Tzelili (Gr)	67.51
	S Makarov (Rus)	88.67		O Menendez (Cub)	66.18
Decathlon	E Nool (Est)	8641	Heptathlon	D Lewis (GB)	6584
	R Sebrle (Cz)	8606		Y Prokhorova (Rus)	6531
	C Huffins (US)	8595		N Sazanovich (Bela)	6527
20 Walk	R Korzeniowski (Pol)	1:18:59	20k Walk	Wang Liping (China)	1:29:05
	N Hernandez (Mex)	1:19:03		K Plaetzer (Nor)	1:29:33
	V Andreyev (Rus)	1:19:27		M Vasco (Esp)	1:30:23
50 Walk	R Korzeniowski (Pol)	3:42.22			
	A Fadejevs (Lat)	3:43.40			
	J Sanchez (Mex)	3:44.36			
4x100	USA	37.61	4x100	Bahamas	41.95
	Brazil	37.90		Jamaica	42.13
	Cuba	38.04		USA	42.20
4x400	USA	2:56.35	4x400	United States	3:22.62
	Nigeria	2:58.35		Jamaica	3:23.25
	Jamaica	2:58.78		Russia	3:23.46

SPORT & LEISURE

Athletics: General Information

Amateur Athletic Association AAA founded in 1880 from the Amateur Athletic Club of 1866.

decathlon: order of events 100m, Long Jump; Shot; High Jump; 400m; 110m Hurdles; Discus; Pole Vault; Javelin; 1,500m.

discus: weight and dimensions Men's: 2kg (4 lb 6½ oz), Women's: 1kg   Circle: 2½m (8 feet 2½ in).

5,000m: first under 13 minutes Said Aouita (Morocco).

four-minute mile: first Roger Bannister wearing No. 41 ran 3 mins 59.4 secs at Iffley Rd, Oxford (6 May 1954).

four-minute mile: second John Landy.

hammer: weight 16 lb.

heptathlon: order of events 100m Hurdles; High Jump; Shot; 200m (first day); Long Jump; Javelin and 800m (second day).

high jump: first to 2m (woman) Rosie Ackerman (Germany).

first to 6′ (man) Marshall Jones Brooks (1876).

first to 6′ (woman) Debbie Brill (1970).

first to 7′ (man) Charles Dumas (1956).

100m: first (man) under 10 seconds Armin Hary (1960).

100 yards: first (man) under 10 seconds J P Tennent (1868).

110 hurdles: first (man) under 13 seconds Renaldo Nehemiah.

hurdles men's 110m H: 3′ 6″ (106.7 cm). Women's 100 H: 2′ 9″ (83.8 cm). Men's 400 H: 3′ high (91.4cm) and 35m between. Women's 400 H: 2′ 6″ high (26.2cm) 35m between.

javelin: weight and dimensions Men's: 800 grams

(1 lb 12 oz), minimum length 260 cm. Women's: 600 grams (1lb 5oz), minimum length 220 cm.

marathon: distance   26 miles 385 yards.

marathon: origin   distance run by Pheidippides to relay news of battle of Marathon (extra 385 yards added in 1908 Olympics so as to finish race in front of Royal Box).

mile: first man under 3 minutes 50 seconds   John Walker (1975).

mile: first woman under 5 minutes   Diane Leather (1955).

pentathlon: ancient   running, jumping, discus, javelin, wrestling.

pentathlon: modern   riding, fencing, shooting, swimming, cross country run.

pentathlon: women   200m; 100 Hurdles; Shot; High Jump; Long Jump (800m and Javelin added for Heptathlon).

pole vault: first man over 6m   Sergey Bubka (1985).

shot: dimensions   Men's: 7.26 kg (16 lb). Women's: 4kg (8 lb 13 oz). Circle: 2.134m (7 feet).

steeplechase: waterjump   not jumped on first lap so seven times in all.

tattoo   British sprinter Mark Lewis-Francis sports a tattoo of the name of his illegitimate son Romeo (b. 2002) on his left arm.

World Championships: won first six   Sergey Bubka won the first six World Championship pole vault events (1983, 1987, 1991, 1993, 1995, 1997).

world record holders: became MPs   Chris Chataway and Sebastian Coe.

world records: five in a day   Jesse Owens (1935).

world records: not broken at Olympics   only the Men's Discus record has never been broken at an Olympic Games.

World Record Holders (as at 30/04/03)

Men

100m	Tim Montgomery (USA)	9.78
200m	Michael Johnson (USA)	19.32
300m	Michael Johnson (USA)	30.85
400m	Michael Johnson (USA)	43.18
800m	Wilson Kipketer (Ken)	1:41.11
1,000m	Noah Ngeny (Ken)	2:11.96
1,500m	Hicham El Guerrouj (Mor)	3:26.00
Mile	Hicham El Guerrouj (Mor)	3:43.13
2 Miles	Daniel Komen (Ken)	7:58.61
2,000m	Hicham El Guerrouj (Mor)	4:44.79
3,000m	Daniel Komen (Ken)	7:20.67
5,000m	Haile Gebrselassie (Eth)	12:39.36
10,000m	Haile Gebrselassie (Eth)	26:22.75
20,000m	Arturo Barrios (Mex)	56:55.60
1 Hour	Arturo Barrios (Mex)	21,101m
Half Marathon	Paul Tergat (Ken)	59:17
25,000m (road)	Rodgers Rop (Ken)	1:13.14
30,000m (road)	Toshihiko Seko (Jap)	1:29:18.80
Marathon	Khalid Khannouchi (Mor)	2:05:38
3,000m S/Chase	Brahim Boulami (Mor)	7:53.17
110m Hurdles	Colin Jackson (GB)	12.91
400m Hurdles	Kevin Young (USA)	46.78
Pole Vault	Sergey Bubka (UKR)	6.14
High Jump	Javier Sotomayor (Cub)	2.45
Long Jump	Mike Powell (USA)	8.95
Triple Jump	Jonathan Edwards (GB)	18.29
Shot Putt	Randy Barnes (USA)	23.12
Discus	Jürgen Schult (Ger)	74.08
Hammer	Yury Sedykh (URS)	86.74
Javelin	Jan Zelezny (CZ)	98.48
Decathlon	Roman Sebrle (Czech)	9026
4x100	USA	37.40
4x200	Santa Monica Track Club	1:18.68
4x400	USA	2:54.20
4x800	GB (Eliott, Cook, Cram, Coe)	7:03.89
4x1500	Germany	14:38.80

Women

100m	Florence Griffith-Joyner (USA)	10.49
200m	Florence Griffith-Joyner (USA)	21.34
400m	Marita Koch (Ger)	47.60
800m	Jarmila Kratochvilova (TCH)	1:53.28
1,000m	Svetlana Masterkova (RUS)	2:28.98
1,500m	Qu Yunxia (Chn)	3:50.46
2,000m	Sonia O'Sullivan (Ire)	5:25.36
Mile	Svetlana Masterkova (RUS)	4:12.56

Women

3,000m	Wang Junxia (Chn)	8:06.11
5,000m	Jiang Bo (China)	14:28.09
10,000m	Wang Junxia (Chn)	29:31.78
20,000m	Tegla Loroupe (Ken)	1:05:26.06
25,000m	Tegla Loroupe (Ken)	1:27:05.90
3,000m S/chase	Alesya Turova (Blr)	9:16.51
1 Hour	Silvana Cruciata (Ita)	18,084m
Half Marathon	I. Kristiansen (Nor)	1:06:40
Marathon	Paula Radcliffe (GB)	2:15:25
30,000m	Karolina Szabo (Hung)	1:47:05.06
100m Hurdles	Yordanka Donkova (Bul)	12.21
400m Hurdles	Kim Batten (USA)	52.61
Pole Vault	Stacy Dragila (USA)	4.81
High Jump	Stefka Kostadinova (Bul)	2.09
Long Jump	Galina Chistyakova (URS)	7.52
Triple Jump	Inessa Kravets (UKR)	15.50
Shot Putt	Natalya Lisovskaya (URS)	22.63
Discus	Gabriele Reinsch (Ger)	76.80
Hammer	Mihaela Melinte (Rom)	76.07
Javelin (pre 1999)	Petra Felke (Ger)	80.00
Javelin (post 1999)	Osleidys Menéndez (Cub)	71.54
Heptathlon	Jackie Joyner-Kersee (USA)	7291
4x100	East Germany	41.37
4x200	USA	1:27.46
4x400	Soviet Union	3:15.17
4x800	Soviet Union	7:50.17

NB Marathon and half marathon records are officially 'World Bests' rather than World Records due to the non-standardisation of courses.

Baseball: World Series

	Winners		Runners-up
1903	Boston Red Sox (AL)	5–3	Pittsburgh Pirates (NL)
1904	no series		
1905	New York Giants (NL)	4–1	Philadelphia Athletics (AL)
1906	Chicago White Sox (AL)	4–2	Chicago Cubs (NL)
1907	Chicago Cubs (NL)	4–0	Detroit Tigers (AL)
1908	Chicago Cubs (NL)	4–1	Detroit Tigers (AL)
1909	Pittsburgh Pirates (NL)	4–3	Detroit Tigers (AL)
1910	Philadelphia Athletics (AL)	4–1	Chicago Cubs (NL)
1911	Philadelphia Athletics (AL)	4-2	New York Giants (NL)
1912	Boston Red Sox (AL)	4–3	New York Giants (NL)
1913	Philadelphia Athletics (AL)	4–1	New York Giants (NL)
1914	Boston Braves (NL)	4–0	Philadelphia Athletics (AL)
1915	Boston Red Sox (AL)	4–1	Philadelphia Phillies (NL)
1916	Boston Red Sox (AL)	4–1	Brooklyn Dodgers (NL)
1917	Chicago White Sox (AL)	4–2	New York Giants (NL)
1918	Boston Red Sox (AL)	4–2	Chicago Cubs (NL)
1919	Cincinnati Reds (NL)	5–3	Chicago White Sox (AL)
1920	Cleveland Indians (AL)	5–2	Brooklyn Dodgers (NL)
1921	New York Giants (NL)	5–3	New York Yankees (AL)
1922	New York Giants (NL)	4–0	New York Yankees (AL)
1923	New York Yankees (AL)	4–2	New York Giants (NL)
1924	Washington Senators (AL)	4–3	New York Giants (NL)
1925	Pittsburgh Pirates (NL)	4–3	Washington Senators (AL)
1926	St Louis Cardinals (NL)	4–3	New York Yankees (AL)
1927	New York Yankees (AL)	4–0	Pittsburgh Pirates (NL)
1928	New York Yankees (AL)	4–0	St Louis Cardinals (NL)
1929	Philadelphia Athletics (AL)	4–1	Chicago Cubs (NL)
1930	Philadelphia Athletics (AL)	4–2	St Louis Cardinals (NL)
1931	St Louis Cardinals (NL)	4–3	Philadelphia Athletics (AL)
1932	New York Yankees (AL)	4–0	Chicago Cubs (NL)
1933	New York Giants (NL)	4–1	Washington Senators (AL)
1934	St Louis Cardinals (NL)	4–3	Detroit Tigers (AL)
1935	Detroit Tigers (AL)	4–2	Chicago Cubs (NL)
1936	New York Yankees (AL)	4–2	New York Giants (NL)
1937	New York Yankees (AL)	4–1	New York Giants (NL)

	Winners		*Runners-up*
1938	New York Yankees (AL)	4–0	Chicago Cubs (NL)
1939	New York Yankees (AL)	4–0	Cincinnati Reds (NL)
1940	Cincinnati Reds (NL)	4–3	Detroit Tigers (AL)
1941	New York Yankees (AL)	4–1	Brooklyn Dodgers (NL)
1942	St Louis Cardinals (NL)	4–1	New York Yankees (AL)
1943	New York Yankees (AL)	4–1	St Louis Cardinals (NL)
1944	St Louis Cardinals (NL)	4–2	St Louis Browns (AL)
1945	Detroit Tigers (AL)	4–3	Chicago Cubs (NL)
1946	St Louis Cardinals (NL)	4–3	Boston Red Sox (AL)
1947	New York Yankees (AL)	4–3	Brooklyn Dodgers (NL)
1948	Cleveland Indians (AL)	4–2	Boston Braves (NL)
1949	New York Yankees (AL)	4–1	Brooklyn Dodgers (NL)
1950	New York Yankees (AL)	4–0	Philadelphia Phillies (NL)
1951	New York Yankees (AL)	4–2	New York Giants (NL)
1952	New York Yankees (AL)	4–3	Brooklyn Dodgers (NL)
1953	New York Yankees (AL)	4–2	Brooklyn Dodgers (NL)
1954	New York Giants (NL)	4–0	Cleveland Indians (AL)
1955	Brooklyn Dodgers (NL)	4–3	New York Yankees (AL)
1956	New York Yankees (AL)	4–3	Brooklyn Dodgers (NL)
1957	Milwaukee Braves (NL)	4–3	New York Yankees (AL)
1958	New York Yankees (AL)	4–3	Milwaukee Braves (NL)
1959	Los Angeles Dodgers (NL)	4–2	Chicago White Sox (AL)
1960	Pittsburgh Pirates (NL)	4–3	New York Yankees (AL)
1961	New York Yankees (AL)	4–1	Cincinnati Reds (NL)
1962	New York Yankees (AL)	4–3	San Francisco Giants (NL)
1963	Los Angeles Dodgers (NL)	4–0	New York Yankees (AL)
1964	St Louis Cardinals (NL)	4–3	New York Yankees (AL)
1965	Los Angeles Dodgers (NL)	4–3	Minnesota Twins (AL)
1966	Baltimore Orioles (AL)	4–0	Los Angeles Dodgers (NL)
1967	St Louis Cardinals (NL)	4–3	Boston Red Sox (AL)
1968	Detroit Tigers (AL)	4–3	St Louis Cardinals (NL)
1969	New York Mets (NL)	4–1	Baltimore Orioles (AL)
1970	Baltimore Orioles (AL)	4–1	Cincinnati Reds (NL)
1971	Pittsburgh Pirates (NL)	4–3	Baltimore Orioles (AL)
1972	Oakland Athletics (AL)	4–3	Cincinnati Reds (NL)
1973	Oakland Athletics (AL)	4–3	New York Mets (NL)
1974	Oakland Athletics (AL)	4–1	Los Angeles Dodgers (NL)
1975	Cincinnati Reds (NL)	4–3	Boston Red Sox (AL)
1976	Cincinnati Reds (NL)	4–0	New York Yankees (AL)
1977	New York Yankees (AL)	4–2	Los Angeles Dodgers (NL)
1978	New York Yankees (AL)	4–2	Los Angeles Dodgers (NL)
1979	Pittsburgh Pirates (NL)	4–3	Baltimore Orioles (AL)
1980	Philadelphia Phillies (NL)	4–2	Kansas City Royals (AL)
1981	Los Angeles Dodgers (NL)	4–2	New York Yankees (AL)
1982	St Louis Cardinals (NL)	4–3	Milwaukee Brewers (AL)
1983	Baltimore Orioles (AL)	4–1	Philadelphia Phillies (NL)
1984	Detroit Tigers (AL)	4–1	San Diego Padres (NL)
1985	Kansas City Royals (AL)	4–3	St Louis Cardinals (NL)
1986	New York Mets (NL)	4–3	Boston Red Sox (AL)
1987	Minnesota Twins (AL)	4–3	St Louis Cardinals (NL)
1988	Los Angeles Dodgers (NL)	4–1	Oakland Athletics (AL)
1989	Oakland Athletics (AL)	4–0	San Francisco Giants (NL)
1990	Cincinnati Reds (NL)	4–0	Oakland Athletics (AL)
1991	Minnesota Twins (AL)	4–3	Atlanta Braves (NL)
1992	Toronto Blue Jays (AL)	4–2	Atlanta Braves (NL)
1993	Toronto Blue Jays (AL)	4–2	Philadelphia Phillies (NL)
1994	no series		
1995	Atlanta Braves (NL)	4–2	Cleveland Indians (AL)
1996	New York Yankees (AL)	4–2	Atlanta Braves (NL)
1997	Florida Marlins (NL)	4–3	Cleveland Indians (AL)
1998	New York Yankees (AL)	4–0	San Diego Padres (NL)
1999	New York Yankees (AL)	4–0	Atlanta Braves (NL)
2000	New York Yankees (AL)	4–1	New York Mets (NL)
2001	Arizona Diamondbacks (NL)	4–3	New York Yankees (AL)
2002	Anaheim Angels (AL)	4–3	San Francisco Giants (NL)

(AL = American League.   NL = National League.)

Baseball: General Information

ball: weight between 5 and 5¼ oz.

bat: dimensions maximum length of 42 inches, maximum thickness of 2¾ inches.

Black Sox scandal eight members of the Chicago White Sox were accused of accepting bribes to throw the 1919 World Series. Although subsequently found not guilty the players were suspended for life from the 1921 season onwards.

Black Sox scandal: judge Kenesaw Mountain Landis.

commissioner: first Kenesaw Mountain Landis.

Continental League: inaugurated 27 July 1959.

first match under Cartwright Rules (1846) New York Nine (23) v Knickerbocker Club (1).

Hall of Fame founded in 1936 in Cooperstown, NY.

innings per game nine.

inventor of game Abner Doubleday, a Civil War general, credited with invention in 1839 although it was more likely derived from the game of rounders in the 18th century.

number in team nine.

playing area diamond.

rules codified by Alexander Joy Cartwright (1845).

Ruth: George Herman nicknamed 'Babe' and 'The Sultan of Swat'.

umpires four umpires run a game positioned near the home plate and the three bases.

World Series: contestants winners of the American League and National League.

Boxing Champions (as at end 2002)

International Boxing Federation (IBF), World Boxing Association (WBA),
World Boxing Council (WBC), World Boxing Organization (WBO)

	IBF	WBA Super	WBA	WBC	WBO
Heavyweight	Chris Byrd		John Ruiz	Lennox Lewis	Wladimir Klitschko
Cruiserweight (190 pounds)	Vassily Jirov		Jean Mark Mormeck	Wayne Braithwaite	Johnny Nelson
Light Heavyweight (175 pounds)	Roy Jones Jr	Roy Jones Jr	Bruno Girard	Roy Jones Jr	Dariusz Michalczewski
Super Middleweight (168 pounds)	Sven Ottke		Byron Mitchell	Eric Lucas	Joe Calzaghe
Middleweight (160 pounds)	Bernard Hopkins	Bernard Hopkins	William Joppy	Bernard Hopkins	Harry Simon
Junior Middleweight (154 pounds)	Winky Wright		Oscar De La Hoya	Oscar De La Hoya	Daniel Santos
Welterweight (147 pounds)	Michele Piccirillo		Ricardo Mayorga	Vernon Forrest	Antonio Margarito
Junior Welterweight (140 pounds)	Kostya Tszyu	Kostya Tszyu	Vivian Harris	Kostya Tszyu	Demarcus Corley
Lightweight (135 pounds)	Paul Spadafora		Leonard Dorin	Floyd Mayweather Jr	Artur Grigorian
Junior Lightweight (130 pounds)	vacant	Acelino Freitas	Yodsanan Nanthachai	Sirimongkol Singmanussuk	Acelino Freitas
Featherweight (126 pounds)	Johnny Tapia		Derrick Gainer	Erik Morales	Scott Harrison
Junior Featherweight (122 pounds)	Manny Pacquiao		Salim Medjkoune	Oscar Larios	Joan Guzman
Bantamweight (118 pounds)	Tim Austin		Johnny Bredahl	Veeraphol Sahaprom	Cruz Carbajal
Junior Bantamweight (115 pounds)	Felix Machado		Alexander Munoz	Masanori Tokuyama	Fernando Montiel
Flyweight (112 pounds)	Irene Pacheco		Eric Morel	Pongsaklek Wonjongkam	Omar Narvaez
Junior Flyweight (108 pounds)	Ricardo Lopez		Rosendo Alvarez	Jorge Arce	Nelson Dieppa
Strawweight (105 pounds)	Miguel Barrera		Noel Arambulet	Jose Antonio Aguirre	Kermin Guardia

SPORT & LEISURE

Cricket – Trophy Winners from 1946

	County Championship	Sunday League	Benson and Hedges Cup	Cheltenham and Gloucester Trophy (C & G) (Gillette Cup 1963–81; NatWest Trophy 1982–2000)
1946	Yorkshire	–	–	–
1947	Middlesex	–	–	–
1948	Glamorgan	–	–	–
1949	Middlesex/Yorkshire	–	–	–
1950	Lancashire/Surrey	–	–	–
1951	Warwickshire	–	–	–
1952	Surrey	–	–	–
1953	Surrey	–	–	–
1954	Surrey	–	–	–
1955	Surrey	–	–	–
1956	Surrey	–	–	–
1957	Surrey	–	–	–
1958	Surrey	–	–	–
1959	Yorkshire	–	–	–
1960	Yorkshire	–	–	–
1961	Hampshire	–	–	–
1962	Yorkshire	–	–	–
1963	Yorkshire	–	–	Sussex
1964	Worcestershire	–	–	Sussex
1965	Worcestershire	–	–	Yorkshire
1966	Yorkshire	–	–	Warwickshire
1967	Yorkshire	–	–	Kent
1968	Yorkshire	–	–	Warwickshire
1969	Glamorgan	Lancashire	–	Yorkshire
1970	Kent	Lancashire	–	Lancashire
1971	Surrey	Worcestershire	–	Lancashire
1972	Warwickshire	Kent	Leicestershire	Lancashire
1973	Hampshire	Kent	Kent	Gloucestershire
1974	Worcestershire	Leicestershire	Surrey	Kent
1975	Leicestershire	Hampshire	Leicestershire	Lancashire
1976	Middlesex	Kent	Kent	Northamptonshire
1977	Kent/Middlesex	Leicestershire	Gloucestershire	Middlesex
1978	Kent	Hampshire	Kent	Sussex
1979	Essex	Somerset	Essex	Somerset
1980	Middlesex	Warwickshire	Northamptonshire	Middlesex
1981	Nottinghamshire	Essex	Somerset	Derbyshire
1982	Middlesex	Sussex	Somerset	Surrey
1983	Essex	Yorkshire	Middlesex	Somerset
1984	Essex	Essex	Lancashire	Middlesex
1985	Middlesex	Essex	Leicestershire	Essex
1986	Essex	Hampshire	Middlesex	Sussex
1987	Nottinghamshire	Worcestershire	Yorkshire	Nottinghamshire
1988	Worcestershire	Worcestershire	Hampshire	Middlesex
1989	Worcestershire	Lancashire	Nottinghamshire	Warwickshire
1990	Middlesex	Derbyshire	Lancashire	Lancashire
1991	Essex	Nottinghamshire	Worcestershire	Hampshire
1992	Essex	Middlesex	Hampshire	Northamptonshire
1993	Middlesex	Glamorgan	Derbyshire	Warwickshire
1994	Warwickshire	Warwickshire	Warwickshire	Worcestershire
1995	Warwickshire	Kent	Lancashire	Warwickshire
1996	Leicestershire	Surrey	Lancashire	Lancashire
1997	Glamorgan	Warwickshire	Surrey	Essex
1998	Leicestershire	Lancashire	Essex	Lancashire
1999	Surrey	Lancashire	Gloucestershire	Gloucestershire
2000	Surrey	Gloucestershire	Gloucestershire	Gloucestershire
2001	Yorkshire	Kent	Surrey	Somerset
2002	Surrey	Glamorgan	Warwickshire	Yorkshire

Wisden One-Day Cricketers of all time (as at 31.12.2002)

Batsmen (minimum 2,500 runs)

1 IVA Richards (WI)
2 SR Tendulkar (Ind)
3 BC Lara (WI)
4 DM Jones (Aus)
5 MG Bevan (Aus)
6 SC Ganguly (Ind)
7 ME Waugh (Aus)
8 Zaheer Abbas (Pak)
9 JH Kallis (SA)
10 Saeed Anwar (Pak)

Bowlers (minimum 100 wickets)

1 Wasim Akram (Pak)
2 AA Donald (SA)
3 Waqar Younis (Pak)
4 GD McGrath (Aus)
5 J Garner (WI)
6 Saqlain Mushtaq (Pak)
7 M Muralitharan (SL)
8 SM Pollock (SA)
9 SK Warne (Aus)
10 DK Lillee (Aus)

Wisden Test Cricketers of all time (as at 31.12.2002)

Batsmen

1 Don Bradman (Aus)
2 Sachin Tendulkar (Ind)
3 Viv Richards (WI)
4 Garfield Sobers (WI)
5 Allan Border (Aus)
6 Jack Hobbs (Eng)
7 Ken Barrington (Eng)
8 Sunil Gavaskar (Ind)
9 Greg Chappell (Aus)
10 Brian Lara (WI)

Bowlers

1 Mutthiah Muralitharan (SL)
2 Richard Hadlee (NZ)
3 Sidney Barnes (Eng)
4 Shane Warne (Aus)
5 Clarrie Grimmett (Aus)
6 Glenn McGrath (Aus)
7 Dennis Lillee (Aus)
8 Malcolm Marshall (WI)
9 Imran Khan (Pak)
10 Courtney Walsh (WI)

Wisden Test Cricketers of the Century

(chosen by a panel of 100 cricketers and experts)

1 Don Bradman (Aus)
2 Garfield Sobers (WI)
3 Jack Hobbs (Eng)
4 Shane Warne (Aus)
5 Viv Richards (WI)
6 Dennis Lillee (Aus)
7 Frank Worrell (WI)
8 Wally Hammond (Eng)
9 Dennis Compton (Eng)
10 Richard Hadlee (NZ)

Cricket: General Information

ball: weight Between 5½ and 5¾ ounces (159.9–163g).

bat throwing controversy Dermot Reeves (Warks) threw bat away to avoid bat and pad catch.

Benson and Hedges Cup in 1999, the Benson and Hedges Super Cup replaced the old format, but the original format was reverted to in 2000.

best Test Match bowling figures Jim Laker 19 for 90, England v Australia at Old Trafford (1956). (Tony Locke took other wicket).

best Test Match bowling figures in single innings Jim Laker 10 for 53 v Australia at Old Trafford (1956).

Bodyline Series of 1932/3 (Australia v England) the leading bowler was Harold Larwood (33 wickets) and the England captain was Douglas Jardine, who instructed Larwood to bowl at the leg stump and into the batsman's body.

Bosie Aussie name for googly (named after its inventor B J T Bosanquet, father of newsreader Reginald).

brothers: seven played for Worcestershire Foster brothers: Basil, Henry, Maurice, Neville, Reginald, Geoffrey, Wilfrid.

captain of England also Olympic boxing gold medallist J W H T Douglas.

Chinaman googly bowled by a left-hander, i.e. ball that breaks from off to leg.

county captain: longest tenure W G Grace for Gloucester (1871–99).

county championship officially constituted in 1890, although counties existed prior to that date and claimed a sort of unofficial title. The 1890 championship was contested by eight counties, Gloucestershire, Kent, Lancashire, Middlesex, Nottinghamshire, Surrey, Sussex, and Yorkshire. The title was won in 1890, and the following two seasons, by Surrey. The sponsors for the 2003 season are Liverpool Victoria and will be branded under their affinity name of Frizzell. Previous sponsors included Schweppes (1977–83), Britannic Assurance (1984–98), PPP Healthcare (1999–2000) and Cricinfo 2001–02. The only two counties to join the championship since World War One are Glamorgan (1921) and Durham (1992).

County Cricket: Grounds Derbyshire – Nottingham Road, Derby; Durham – Riverside Ground, Chester-le-Street; Essex – New Writtle St, Chelmsford;

Glamorgan – Sophia Gardens, Cardiff; Gloucestershire – Nevil Road, Bristol; Hampshire – Rose Bowl, Southampton; Kent – St Lawrence Ground, Canterbury; Lancashire – Old Trafford, Manchester; Leicestershire – Grace Road, Leicester; Middlesex – Lord's, London; Northants – Wantage Road, Northampton; Nottinghamshire – Trent Bridge, Nottingham; Somerset – St James's Street, Taunton; Surrey – Foster's Oval, Kennington; Sussex – Eaton Road, Hove; Warwickshire – Edgbaston, Birmingham; Worcestershire – New Road, Worcester; Yorkshire – Headingley, Leeds.

CGU National League nicknames Derbyshire (Scorpions), Durham (Dynamos), Essex (Eagles), Glamorgan (Dragons), Gloucestershire (Gladiators), Hampshire (Hawks), Lancashire (Lightning), Leicestershire (Foxes), Middlesex (Crusaders), Northamptonshire (Steelbacks), Nottinghamshire (Outlaws), Somerset (Sabres), Surrey (Lions), Sussex (Sharks), Warwickshire (Bears), Worcestershire (Royals), Yorkshire (Phoenix).

dismissal: methods bowled, caught, handled the ball, hit the ball twice, hit wicket, leg before wicket (lbw), obstructing the field, run out, stumped, timed out.

double: first to complete (1000 runs and 100 wickets in a season) W.G. Grace.

Douglas, J W H T : nickname Johnny Won't Hit Today. Douglas also won a gold medal for Great Britain in the 1908 Olympics at Middleweight Boxing.

Duckworth/Lewis System used to determine the winning score in rain-interrupted one-day matches.

ECB (England and Wales Cricket Board): chairman Lord MacLaurin of Knebworth.

fifty: slowest first class Trevor Bailey.

googly off break bowled with a leg-break action.

highest scorer in first class cricket Brian Lara 501 not out v Durham.

highest scorer in test cricket Brian Lara 375 v England.

hundred: first recorded John Minshull, 107 for Duke of Dorset's XI v Wrexham (1769).

last man to take hattrick in Test Match for England Darren Gough v Australia at Sydney (1998–99).

Lords: three locations present site: St John's Wood, London.

monarch made cricket illegal Edward IV in 1477 (revoked in 1748).

Olympic champions Great Britain.

one day internationals: fastest century Shahid Afridi (Pakistan) scored 100 in 37 balls against Sri Lanka in 1997.

run: distance for completion of 58ft (17.68m).

six 6's in over: first Gary Sobers (for Notts v Glamorgan, bowler: Malcolm Nash); Ravi Shastri was the second man to accomplish the feat.

stumps: height 28 inches (71.1cm).

Sunday League CGU National League 1999 and 2000, Norwich Union League since 2001. Scotland will be playing in the National Cricket League Division Two in 2003.

Sunday League: double century Ally Brown of Surrey.

swearing incident Mike Gatting at umpire Shakoor Rana (1987).

TCCB: name change in 1996 ECB (England and Wales Cricket Board).

Test cricket: oldest player Wilfred Rhodes (52).

Test cricket: youngest English player Brian Close (18).

Test cricket: youngest player Hasan Raza (Pakistan) was 14 yrs 227 days old when he played against Zimbabwe in 1996–97.

Test Match century: fewest balls Viv Richards (56) against England at St John's in 1985–86.

Test Match double century: fewest balls Nathan Astle (153) for New Zealand against England at Christchurch in March 2002. The first hundred took 114 balls and the second hundred only 39 balls.

Test Match: first Australia v England, Melbourne Cricket Ground 1877.

Test Match: tied Australia v West Indies (1960) and Australia v India (1986).

university grounds Cambridge – Fenner's Oxford – The Parks.

West Indies: three Ws Weekes, Worrell, Walcott.

Wisden: colour yellow.

World Cup football winner played County Cricket Geoff Hurst.

World Cup winners West Indies beat Australia (1975); West Indies beat England (1979); India beat West Indies (1983); Australia beat England (1987); Pakistan beat England (1991); Sri Lanka beat Australia (1996); Australia beat Pakistan (1999).

World Cup: defeated West Indies Kenya bowled West Indies out for 93 in group match of 1996 World Cup.

Darts: World Champions

	Winner		Runner-up
1978	Leighton Rees (Wal)	11–7	John Lowe (Eng)
1979	John Lowe (Eng)	5–0	Leighton Rees (Wal)
1980	Eric Bristow (Eng)	5–3	Bobby George (Eng)
1981	Eric Bristow (Eng)	5–3	John Lowe (Eng)
1982	Jocky Wilson (Sco)	5–3	John Lowe (Eng)
1983	Keith Deller (Eng)	6–5	Eric Bristow (Eng)
1984	Eric Bristow (Eng)	7–1	Dave Whitcombe (Eng)
1985	Eric Bristow (Eng)	6–2	John Lowe (Eng)
1986	Eric Bristow (Eng)	6–0	Dave Whitcombe (Eng)
1987	John Lowe (Eng)	6–4	Eric Bristow (Eng)
1988	Bob Anderson (Eng)	6–4	John Lowe (Eng)
1989	Jocky Wilson (Sco)	6–4	Eric Bristow (Eng)
1990	Phil Taylor (Eng)	6–1	Eric Bristow (Eng)
1991	Dennis Priestley (Eng)	6–0	Eric Bristow (Eng)

	Winner			*Runner-up*
1992	Phil Taylor (Eng)	6–5		Mike Gregory (Eng)
1993	John Lowe (Eng)	6–3		Alan Warriner (Eng)
1994	John Part (Can)	6–0		Bobby George (Eng)
	Dennis Priestley (Eng)	6–1		Phil Taylor (Eng)
1995	Richie Burnett (Wal)	6–3		Ray Barneveld (Ned)
	Phil Taylor (Eng)	6–2		Rod Harrington (Eng)
1996	Steve Beaton (Eng)	6–3		Richie Burnett (Wal)
	Phil Taylor (Eng)	6–4		Dennis Priestley (Eng)
1997	Les Wallace (Sco)	6–3		Marshall James (Wal)
	Phil Taylor (Eng)	6–3		Dennis Priestley (Eng)
1998	Ray Barneveld (Ned)	6–5		Richie Burnett (Wal)
	Phil Taylor (Eng)	6–0		Dennis Priestley (Eng)
1999	Ray Barneveld (Ned)	6–5		Ronnie Baxter (Sco)
	Phil Taylor (Eng)	6–2		Peter Manley (Eng)
2000	Ted Hankey (Eng)	6–0		Ronnie Baxter (Sco)
	Phil Taylor (Eng)	7–3		Dennis Priestley (Eng)
2001	John Walton (Eng)	6–2		Ted Hankey (Eng)
	Phil Taylor (Eng)	7–0		John Part (Can)
2002	Tony David (Aust)	6–4		Mervyn King (Eng)
	Phil Taylor (Eng)	7–0		Peter Manley (Eng)
2003	Ray Barneveld (Ned)	6–3		Ritchie Davies (Wal)
	John Part (Can)	7–6		Phil Taylor (Eng)

NB First named winners are Embassy BDO champions. Second named winners are WDC champions (now called PDC).

Darts: General Information

BDO: stands for	British Darts Organization
News of the World Competition	1991–7 suspended sponsorship
News of the World: best of legs	best of three throughout competition
PDC: stands for	Professional Darts Council
venues: Embassy	Lakeside CC, Frimley Green, Surrey
	Heart of Midlands Club, Notts (1978)
	Jollees Night Club, Stoke (1979–85)
venue: PDC	Circus Tavern, Purfleet
WDC: stands for	World Darts Council
World Champions: nine-dart legs	John Lowe won £102,000 for achieving the first nine-dart 501 leg
	Paul Lim (USA) was second man to achieve a nine-dart leg

Darts: News of the World Champions

1948	Harry Leadbetter	1960	Tom Reddington	1972	Brian Netherton	1982	Roy Morgan
1949	Jack Boyce	1961	Alec Adamson	1973	Ivor Hodgkinson	1983	Eric Bristow
1950	Dixie Newberry	1962	Eddie Brown	1974	Peter Chapman	1984	Eric Bristow
1951	Harry Perryman	1963	Robbie Rumney	1975	Derek White	1985	Dave Lee
1952	Tommy Gibbons	1964	Tom Barrett	1976	Bill Lennard	1986	Bobby George
1953	Jimmy Carr	1965	Tom Barrett	1977	Mick Norris	1987	Mike Gregory
1954	Oliver James	1966	Wilf Ellis	1978	Stefan Lord	1988	Mike Gregory
1955	Tom Reddington	1967	Wally Seaton		(Sweden)	1989	Dave Whitcombe
1956	Trevor Peachey	1968	Bill Duddy	1979	Bobby George	1990	Paul Cook
1957	Alwyn Mullins	1969	Barry Twomlow	1980	Stefan Lord	1997	Phil Taylor
1958	Tommy Gibbons	1970	Henry Barney		(Sweden)		
1959	Albert Welch	1971	Dennis Filkins	1981	John Lowe		

Football: English League Winners

	Division 1	Division 2	Division 3	Division 3 South
1889	Preston North End	—	—	—
1890	Preston North End	—	—	—
1891	Everton	—	—	—
1892	Sunderland	—	—	—
1893	Sunderland	Small Heath	—	—
1894	Aston Villa	Liverpool	—	—
1895	Sunderland	Bury	—	—
1896	Aston Villa	Liverpool	—	—
1897	Aston Villa	Notts County	—	—
1898	Sheffield United	Burnley	—	—
1899	Aston Villa	Manchester City	—	—
1900	Aston Villa	The Wednesday	—	—
1901	Liverpool	Grimsby Town	—	—
1902	Sunderland	West Bromwich Albion	—	—
1903	The Wednesday	Manchester City	—	—
1904	The Wednesday	Preston North End	—	—
1905	Newcastle United	Liverpool	—	—
1906	Liverpool	Bristol City	—	—
1907	Newcastle United	Nottingham Forest	—	—
1908	Manchester United	Bradford City	—	—
1909	Newcastle United	Bolton Wanderers	—	—
1910	Aston Villa	Manchester City	—	—
1911	Manchester United	West Bromwich Albion	—	—
1912	Blackburn Rovers	Derby County	—	—
1913	Sunderland	Preston North End	—	—
1914	Blackburn Rovers	Notts County	—	—
1915	Everton	Derby County	—	—
1916	not held	not held	—	—
1917	not held	not held	—	—
1918	not held	not held	—	—
1919	not held	not held	—	—
1920	West Bromwich Albion	Tottenham Hotspur	—	—
1921	Burnley	Birmingham City	Crystal Palace	—

	Division 1	Division 2	Division 3 North	Division 3 South
1922	Liverpool	Nottingham Forest	Stockport County	Southampton
1923	Liverpool	Notts County	Nelson	Bristol City
1924	Huddersfield Town	Leeds United	Wolverhampton Wanderers	Portsmouth
1925	Huddersfield Town	Leicester City	Darlington	Swansea Town
1926	Huddersfield Town	The Wednesday	Grimsby Town	Reading
1927	Newcastle United	Middlesbrough	Stoke City	Bristol City
1928	Everton	Manchester City	Bradford Park Avenue	Millwall
1929	The Wednesday	Middlesbrough	Bradford City	Charlton Athletic
1930	Sheffield Wednesday	Blackpool	Port Vale	Plymouth Argyle
1931	Arsenal	Everton	Chesterfield	Notts County
1932	Everton	Wolverhampton Wanderers	Lincoln City	Fulham
1933	Arsenal	Stoke City	Hull City	Brentford
1934	Arsenal	Grimsby Town	Barnsley	Norwich City
1935	Arsenal	Brentford	Doncaster Rovers	Charlton Athletic
1936	Sunderland	Manchester United	Chesterfield	Coventry City
1937	Manchester City	Leicester City	Stockport County	Luton Town
1938	Arsenal	Aston Villa	Tranmere Rovers	Millwall
1939	Everton	Blackburn Rovers	Barnsley	Newport County
1940	not held	not held	not held	not held
1941	not held	not held	not held	not held
1942	not held	not held	not held	not held
1943	not held	not held	not held	not held
1944	not held	not held	not held	not held
1945	not held	not held	not held	not held
1946	not held	not held	not held	not held
1947	Liverpool	Manchester City	Doncaster Rovers	Cardiff City
1948	Arsenal	Birmingham City	Lincoln City	Queen's Park Rangers
1949	Portsmouth	Fulham	Hull City	Swansea Town
1950	Portsmouth	Tottenham Hotspur	Doncaster Rovers	Notts County
1951	Tottenham Hotspur	Preston North End	Rotherham United	Nottingham Forest
1952	Manchester United	Sheffield Wednesday	Lincoln City	Plymouth Argyle

1953	Arsenal	Sheffield United	Oldham Athletic	Bristol Rovers
1954	Wolverhampton Wanderers	Leicester City	Port Vale	Ipswich Town
1955	Chelsea	Birmingham City	Barnsley	Bristol City
1956	Manchester United	Sheffield Wednesday	Grimsby Town	Leyton Orient
1957	Manchester United	Leicester City	Derby County	Ipswich Town
1958	Wolverhampton Wanderers	West Ham United	Scunthorpe United	Brighton & Hove Albion

	Division 1	**Division 2**	**Division 3**	**Division 4**
1959	Wolverhampton Wanderers	Sheffield Wednesday	Plymouth Argyle	Port Vale
1960	Burnley	Aston Villa	Southampton	Walsall
1961	Tottenham Hotspur	Ipswich Town	Bury	Peterborough United
1962	Ipswich Town	Liverpool	Portsmouth	Millwall
1963	Everton	Stoke City	Northampton Town	Brentford
1964	Liverpool	Leeds United	Coventry City	Gillingham
1965	Manchester United	Newcastle United	Carlisle United	Brighton & Hove Albion
1966	Liverpool	Manchester City	Hull City	Doncaster Rovers
1967	Manchester United	Coventry City	Queen's Park Rangers	Stockport County
1968	Manchester City	Ipswich Town	Oxford United	Luton Town
1969	Leeds United	Derby County	Watford	Doncaster Rovers
1970	Everton	Huddersfield Town	Orient	Chesterfield
1971	Arsenal	Leicester City	Preston North End	Notts County
1972	Derby County	Norwich City	Aston Villa	Grimsby Town
1973	Liverpool	Burnley	Bolton Wanderers	Southport
1974	Leeds United	Middlesbrough	Oldham Athletic	Peterborough United
1975	Derby County	Manchester United	Blackburn Rovers	Mansfield Town
1976	Liverpool	Sunderland	Hereford United	Lincoln City
1977	Liverpool	Wolverhampton Wanderers	Mansfield Town	Cambridge United
1978	Nottingham Forest	Bolton Wanderers	Wrexham	Watford
1979	Liverpool	Crystal Palace	Shrewsbury Town	Reading
1980	Liverpool	Leicester City	Grimsby Town	Huddersfield Town
1981	Aston Villa	West Ham United	Rotherham United	Southend United
1982	Liverpool	Luton Town	Burnley	Sheffield United
1983	Liverpool	Queen's Park Rangers	Portsmouth	Wimbledon
1984	Liverpool	Chelsea	Oxford United	York City
1985	Everton	Oxford United	Bradford City	Chesterfield
1986	Liverpool	Norwich City	Reading	Swindon Town
1987	Everton	Derby County	Bournemouth	Northampton Town
1988	Liverpool	Millwall	Sunderland	Wolverhampton Wanderers
1989	Arsenal	Chelsea	Wolverhampton Wanderers	Rotherham United
1990	Liverpool	Leeds United	Bristol Rovers	Exeter City
1991	Arsenal	Oldham Athletic	Cambridge United	Darlington
1992	Leeds United	Ipswich Town	Brentford	Burnley

	Premier League	**Division 1**	**Division 2**	**Division 3**
1993	Manchester United	Newcastle United	Stoke City	Cardiff City
1994	Manchester United	Crystal Palace	Reading	Shrewsbury Town
1995	Blackburn Rovers	Middlesbrough	Birmingham City	Carlisle United
1996	Manchester United	Sunderland	Swindon Town	Preston North End
1997	Manchester United	Bolton Wanderers	Bury	Wigan Athletic
1998	Arsenal	Nottingham Forest	Watford	Notts County
1999	Manchester United	Sunderland	Fulham	Brentford
2000	Manchester United	Charlton	Preston North End	Swansea City
2001	Manchester United	Fulham	Millwall	Brighton
2002	Arsenal	Manchester City	Brighton & Hove	Plymouth Argyle
2003	Manchester United	Portsmouth	Wigan	Rushden and Diamonds

Football: English League Clubs

Club	League debut	Nickname(s)	Ground	Previous name(s)
Arsenal	1893	Gunners	Arsenal Stadium, Highbury	Dial Square, Royal Arsenal, Woolwich Arsenal
Aston Villa	1888	Villans	Villa Park	none
Barnsley	1898	Tykes, Reds, Colliers	Oakwell	Barnsley St Peter's
Birmingham City	1892	Blues	St Andrew's	Small Heath Alliance, Small

				Heath, Birmingham
Blackburn Rovers	1888	Rovers	Ewood Park	none
Blackpool	1896	Seasiders	Bloomfield Road	Blackpool St Johns, Blackpool South Shore
Bolton Wanderers	1888	Trotters	The Reebok Stadium	Christ Church FC
Boston United	2002	Pilgrims	York Street Stadium	none
AFC Bournemouth	1923	Cherries	Fitness First Stadium, Dean Court	Boscombe St John's, Boscombe, Bournemouth & Boscombe Athletic
Bradford City	1903	Bantams	The Pulse Stadium, Valley Parade	none
Brentford	1920	Bees	Griffin Park	none
Brighton & Hove Albion	1920	Seagulls	Withdean Stadium	Brighton & Hove Rangers, Brighton & Hove United
Bristol City	1901	Robins	Ashton Gate	Bristol South End
Bristol Rovers	1920	Pirates (originally The Purdown Poachers)	Memorial Ground	Black Arabs, Eastville Rovers, Bristol Eastville Rovers
Burnley	1888	Clarets	Turf Moor	Burnley Rovers
Bury	1894	Shakers	Gigg Lane	none
Cambridge United	1970	The 'U's'	Abbey Stadium	Abbey United
Cardiff City	1920	Bluebirds	Ninian Park	Riverside, Riverside Albion
Carlisle United	1928	Cumbrians, Blues	Brunton Park	amalgamation of Shaddongate United and Carlisle Red Rose
Charlton Athletic	1921	Addicks, Valiants, Robins	The Valley	none
Chelsea	1905	Blues	Stamford Bridge	none
Cheltenham Town	1999	Robins	Whaddon Road	none
Chesterfield	1899	Spireites, Blues	Recreation Ground, Saltergate	Chesterfield Town
Colchester United	1950	The 'U's'	Layer Road	Colchester Town
Coventry City	1919	Sky Blues	Highfield Road	Singers FC
Crewe Alexandra	1892	Railwaymen	Gresty Road	none
Crystal Palace	1920	Eagles	Selhurst Park	none
Darlington	1921	Quakers	Feethams Ground	none
Derby County	1888	Rams	Pride Park	none
Everton	1888	Toffees	Goodison Park	St Domingo FC
Exeter City	1920	Grecians	St James Park	amalgamation of St Sidwell's United and Exeter United
Fulham	1907	Cottagers	Loftus Road	Fulham St Andrew's
Gillingham	1920	Gills	Priestfield Stadium	Excelsior, New Brompton
Grimsby Town	1892	Mariners	Blundell Park	Grimsby Pelham
Hartlepool United	1921	Pool	Victoria Park	Hartlepools United, Hartlepool
Huddersfield Town	1910	Terriers	Alfred McAlpine Stadium, Leeds Rd	none
Hull City	1905	Tigers	Kingston Communications Stadium	none
Ipswich Town	1938	Blues, Town, Tractor Boys	Portman Road	Ipswich Association FC
Kidderminster Harriers	2000	Harriers	Aggborough Stadium	none
Leeds United	1920	United, The Whites, The Peacocks	Elland Road	formed after Leeds City disbanded by FA order
Leicester City	1894	Foxes, Filberts	City Stadium, Filbert Street	Leicester Fosse
Leyton Orient	1905	The 'O's'	Leyton Stadium, Brisbane Road	Glyn Cricket & Football Club, Eagle FC, Orient, Clapton Orient
Lincoln City	1892	Red Imps	Sincil Bank	none
Liverpool	1893	Reds, Pool	Anfield	none
Luton Town	1897	Hatters	Kenilworth Road	amalgamation of Luton Town Wanderers and Excelsior
Macclesfield Town	1997	Silkmen	Moss Rose	none
Manchester City	1892	Citizens, Blues	Maine Road	Ardwick FC
Manchester United	1892	Red Devils	Old Trafford	Newton Heath
Mansfield Town	1931	Stags	Field Mill	Mansfield Wesleyans
Middlesbrough	1899	Boro	Riverside Stadium	none
Millwall	1920	Lions	New Den	Millwall Rovers, Millwall Athletic
Newcastle United	1893	Magpies	St James' Park	Stanley, Newcastle East End
Northampton Town	1920	Cobblers	Sixfields Stadium	none
Norwich City	1920	Canaries	Carrow Road	none
Nottingham Forest	1892	Forest, Reds	City Ground	none
Notts County	1888	Magpies	County Ground, Meadow Lane	Notts FC
Oldham Athletic	1907	Latics	Boundary Park	Pine Villa
Oxford United	1962	The 'U's'	Kassam Stadium,	Headington, Headington United

Club	League debut	Nickname(s)	Ground	Previous name(s)
			Grenoble Road	
Peterborough United	1960	Posh	London Road	formed after Peterborough and Fletton disbanded
Plymouth Argyle	1920	Pilgrims	Home Park	Argyle Athletic Club
Portsmouth	1920	Pompey	Fratton Park	none
Port Vale	1892	Valiants	Vale Park	Burslem Port Vale
Preston North End	1888	Lilywhites, North End	Deepdale	none
Queen's Park Rangers	1920	Rangers, 'R's'	Rangers Stadium, Loftus Road	St Jude's
Reading	1920	Royals, Biscuitmen	Madejski Stadium	none
Rochdale	1921	Dale	Spotland	none
Rotherham United	1893	Merry Millers	Millmoor	Thornhill United, Rotherham County, Rotherham Town
Rushden and Diamonds	2001	Diamonds	Nene Park	formed from a merger between Rushden Town and Diamonds in 1992
Scunthorpe United	1950	The Iron	Glanford Park	Scunthorpe & Lindsey United
Sheffield United	1892	Blades	Bramall Lane	none
Sheffield Wdnesday	1892	Owls	Hillsborough	The Wednesday
Shrewsbury Town	1950	Shrews, Town	Gay Meadow	none
Southampton	1920	Saints	St Mary's Stadium	Southampton St Mary's
Southend United	1920	Shrimpers, Blues	Roots Hall	none
Stockport County	1900	County, Hatters	Edgeley Park	Heaton Norris Rovers
Stoke City	1888	Potters	The Britannia Stadium	Stoke
Sunderland	1890	Rokerites, Black Cats	The Stadium of Light	Sunderland and District Teachers Association FC
Swansea City	1920	Swans	Vetch Field	Swansea Town
Swindon Town	1920	Robins	County Ground	Spartans and St Mark's Young Men's Friendly Society (amalgamation)
Torquay United	1927	Gulls	Plainmoor	Torquay Town
Tottenham Hotspur	1908	Spurs	White Hart Lane	Hotspur FC
Tranmere Rovers	1921	Rovers	Prenton Park	Belmont AFC
Walsall	1892	Saddlers	Bescot Stadium	Walsall Town Swifts
Watford	1920	Hornets	Vicarage Road	West Herts
West Bromwich Albion	1888	Throstles, Baggies, Albion	The Hawthorns	West Bromwich Strollers
West Ham United	1919	Hammers, Irons	Boleyn Ground, Upton Park	Thames Ironworks FC
Wigan Athletic	1978	Latics	JJB Stadium	none
Wimbledon	1977	Dons	Selhurst Park	Wimbledon Old Centrals
Wolverhampton Wanderers	1888	Wolves	Molineux	St Luke's
Wrexham	1921	Robins	Racecourse Ground	none
Wycombe Wanderers	1993	Chairboys, Blues	Adams Park	North Town Wanderers
York City	1929	Minstermen	Bootham Crescent	none

Football: Scottish League Clubs

Club	Ground	Nickname(s)
Aberdeen	Pittodrie Stadium	The Dons
Airdrie United (formerly Airdrieonians)	New Broomfield Park	The Diamonds/Waysiders
Albion Rovers	Cliftonhill Stadium, Coatbridge	The Wee Rovers
Alloa Athletic	Recreation Park	The Wasps
Arbroath	Gayfield Park	The Red Lichties
Ayr United	Somerset Park	The Honest Men
Berwick Rangers	Shielfield Park	The Borderers
Brechin City	Glebe Park	City
Celtic	Celtic Park (formerly Parkhead)	The Bhoys
Clyde	Broadwood Stadium	The Bully Wee
Clydebank	Cappielow Park	The Bankies
Cowdenbeath	Central Park	Blue Brazil
Dumbarton	Strathclyde Homes Stadium	The Sons
Dundee	Dens Park	The Dark Blues/Dee
Dundee United	Tannadice Park	The Terrors

Dunfermline Athletic	East End Park	The Pars
East Fife	Bayview Park, Methil	The Fifers
East Stirling	Firs Park, Falkirk	The Shire
Elgin City	Borough Briggs	City/Black & Whites
Falkirk	Brockville Park	The Bairns
Forfar Athletic	Station Park	The Loons/Sky Blues
Greenock Morton	Cappielow Park	The Ton
Hamilton Academical	New Douglas Park	The Accies
Heart of Midlothian	Tynecastle Park	The Jam Tarts
Hibernian	Easter Road	The Hi-Bees
Inverness Caledonian Thistle	Caledonian Stadium, East Longman	Caley/The Jags
Kilmarnock	Rugby Park	The Killies
Livingston	West Lothian Courier Stadium	Livi Lions
Montrose	Links Park	The Gable Endies
Motherwell	Fir Park	The Well
Partick Thistle	Firhill Park	The Jags
Peterhead	Balmoor Stadium	Blue Toon
Queen of the South	Palmerston Park, Dumfries	The Doonhamers/Queens
Queen's Park	Hampden Park	The Spiders
Raith Rovers	Stark's Park, Kirkcaldy	The Rovers
Rangers	Ibrox Stadium	The Blues/Gers
Ross County	Victoria Park, Dingwall	County
St Johnstone	McDiarmid Park, Perth	The Saints
St Mirren	St Mirren Park, Love Street, Paisley	The Buddies
Stenhousemuir	Ochilview Park	The Warriors
Stirling Albion	Forthbank Stadium	The Binos/The Albion
Stranraer	Stair Park	The Blues

NB Elgin City are now the most northerly club in the Football League.

European Nations Championship

Date	Venue	Winners		Runners-up
1960	Paris	Soviet Union	2–1	Yugoslavia
1964	Madrid	Spain	2–1	Soviet Union
1968	Rome	Italy	2–0	Yugoslavia (replay after 1–1 draw)
1972	Brussels	West Germany	3–0	Soviet Union
1976	Belgrade	Czechoslovakia	2–2	West Germany (5–3 on penalties)
1980	Rome	West Germany	2–1	Belgium
1984	Paris	France	2–0	Spain
1988	Munich	Holland	2–0	Soviet Union
1992	Gothenburg	Denmark	2–0	Germany
1996	London	Germany	2–1	Czech Republic (golden goal after 1–1)
2000	Rotterdam	France	2–1	Italy (golden goal after 1–1)

PFA Young Player of the Year

Kevin Beattie (Ipswich)	1974
Mervyn Day (West Ham)	1975
Peter Barnes (Manchester City)	1976
Andy Gray (Aston Villa)	1977
Tony Woodcock (Notts Forest)	1978
Cyrille Regis (WBA)	1979
Glenn Hoddle (Tottenham)	1980
Gary Shaw (Aston Villa)	1981
Steve Moran (Southampton)	1982
Ian Rush (Liverpool)	1983
Paul Walsh (Luton)	1984
Mark Hughes (Manchester Utd)	1985
Tony Cottee (West Ham)	1986
Tony Adams (Arsenal)	1987
Paul Gascoigne (Newcastle)	1988
Paul Merson (Arsenal)	1989
Matt Le Tissier (Southampton)	1990
Lee Sharpe (Manchester Utd)	1991
Ryan Giggs (Manchester Utd)	1992
Ryan Giggs (Manchester Utd)	1993
Andy Cole (Newcastle)	1994

PFA Player of the Year

Norman Hunter (Leeds)	
Colin Todd (Derby County)	
Pat Jennings (Tottenham)	
Andy Gray (Aston Villa)	
Peter Shilton (Notts Forest)	
Liam Brady (Arsenal)	
Terry McDermott (Liverpool)	
John Wark (Ipswich)	
Kevin Keegan (Southampton)	
Kenny Dalglish (Liverpool)	
Ian Rush (Liverpool)	
Peter Reid (Everton)	
Gary Lineker (Everton)	
Clive Allen (Tottenham)	
John Barnes (Liverpool)	
Mark Hughes (Manchester Utd)	
David Platt (Aston Villa)	
Mark Hughes (Manchester Utd)	
Gary Pallister (Manchester Utd)	
Paul McGrath (Aston Villa)	
Eric Cantona (Manchester Utd)	

Robbie Fowler (Liverpool)	1995	Alan Shearer (Blackburn)	
Robbie Fowler (Liverpool)	1996	Les Ferdinand (Newcastle)	
David Beckham (Manchester Utd)	1997	Alan Shearer (Newcastle)	
Michael Owen (Liverpool)	1998	Dennis Bergkamp (Arsenal)	
Nicolas Anelka (Arsenal)	1999	David Ginola (Tottenham Hotspur)	
Harry Kewell (Leeds)	2000	Roy Keane (Manchester Utd)	
Steven Gerrard (Liverpool)	2001	Teddy Sheringham (Manchester Utd)	
Craig Bellamy (Newcastle)	2002	Ruud van Nistelrooy (Manchester Utd)	

FIFA World Footballer of the Year

Lothar Matthäus (Germany and Inter Milan) (1991)
Marco Van Basten (Holland and AC Milan) (1992)
Robert Baggio (Italy and Juventus) (1993)
Romario (Brazil and Barcelona) (1994)
George Weah (Liberia and AC Milan (1995)
Ronaldo (Brazil and Inter Milan) (1996)

Ronaldo (Brazil and Inter Milan) (1997)
Zinédine Zidane (France and Juventus) (1998)
Rivaldo (Brazil and Barcelona) (1999)
Zinédine Zidane (France and Juventus) (2000)
Luis Figo (Portugal and Real Madrid) (2001)
Ronaldo (Brazil and Real Madrid) (2002)

Football Writers' Player of the Year

1948	Stanley Matthews (Blackpool)	1975	Alan Mullery (Fulham)
1949	Johnny Carey (Manchester Utd)	1976	Kevin Keegan (Liverpool)
1950	Joe Mercer (Arsenal)	1977	Emlyn Hughes (Liverpool)
1951	Harry Johnston (Blackpool)	1978	Kenny Burns (Notts Forest)
1952	Billy Wright (Wolves)	1979	Kenny Dalglish (Liverpool)
1953	Nat Lofthouse (Bolton)	1980	Terry McDermott (Liverpool)
1954	Tom Finney (Preston North End)	1981	Frans Thijssen (Ipswich)
1955	Don Revie (Manchester City)	1982	Steve Perryman (Tottenham)
1956	Bert Trautmann (Manchester City)	1983	Kenny Dalglish (Liverpool)
1957	Tom Finney (Preston North End)	1984	Ian Rush (Liverpool)
1958	Danny Blanchflower (Tottenham)	1985	Neville Southall (Everton)
1959	Syd Owen (Luton)	1986	Gary Lineker (Everton)
1960	Bill Slater (Wolves)	1987	Clive Allen (Tottenham)
1961	Danny Blanchflower (Tottenham)	1988	John Barnes (Liverpool)
1962	Jimmy Adamson (Burnley)	1989	Steve Nicol (Liverpool)
1963	Stanley Matthews (Stoke City)	1990	John Barnes (Liverpool)
1964	Bobby Moore (West Ham)	1991	Gordon Strachan (Leeds)
1965	Bobby Collins (Leeds)	1992	Gary Lineker (Tottenham)
1966	Bobby Charlton (Manchester Utd)	1993	Chris Waddle (Sheffield Wednesday)
1967	Jackie Charlton (Leeds)	1994	Alan Shearer (Blackburn Rovers)
1968	George Best (Manchester Utd)	1995	Jürgen Klinsmann (Tottenham)
1969	Tony Book (Manchester City) and	1996	Eric Cantona (Manchester Utd)
	Dave Mackay (Derby County)	1997	Gian Franco Zola (Chelsea)
1970	Billy Bremner (Leeds)	1998	Dennis Bergkamp (Arsenal)
1971	Frank McLintock (Arsenal)	1999	David Ginola (Tottenham)
1972	Gordon Banks (Stoke City)	2000	Roy Keane (Manchester Utd)
1973	Pat Jennings (Tottenham)	2001	Teddy Sheringham (Manchester Utd)
1974	Ian Callaghan (Liverpool)	2002	Robert Pires (Arsenal)

SPORT & LEISURE

European Footballer of the Year

1956	Stanley Matthews (Blackpool)	1971	Johann Cruyff (Ajax)
1957	Alfredo Di Stefano (Real Madrid)	1972	Franz Beckenbauer (Bayern Munich)
1958	Raymond Kopa (Real Madrid)	1973	Johann Cruyff (Barcelona)
1959	Alfredo Di Stefano (Real Madrid)	1974	Johann Cruyff (Barcelona)
1960	Luis Suarez (Barcelona)	1975	Oleg Blokhin (Dynamo Kiev)
1961	Omar Sivori (Juventus)	1976	Franz Beckenbauer (Bayern Munich)
1962	Josef Masopust (Dukla Prague)	1977	Allan Simonsen (Borussia
1963	Lev Yashin (Moscow Dynamo)		Moenchengladbach)
1964	Denis Law (Manchester Utd)	1978	Kevin Keegan (SV Hamburg)
1965	Eusebio (Benfica)	1979	Kevin Keegan (SV Hamburg)
1966	Bobby Charlton (Manchester Utd)	1980	Karl-Heinz Rummenigge (Bayern Munich)
1967	Florian Albert (Ferencvaros)	1981	Karl-Heinz Rummenigge (Bayern Munich)
1968	George Best (Manchester Utd)	1982	Paolo Rossi (Juventus)
1969	Gianni Rivera (AC Milan)	1983	Michel Platini (Juventus)
1970	Gerd Muller (Bayern Munich)	1984	Michel Platini (Juventus)

1985	Michel Platini (Juventus)	1994	Hristo Stoichkov (Barcelona)
1986	Igor Belanov (Dynamo Kiev)	1995	George Weah (AC Milan)
1987	Ruud Gullit (AC Milan)	1996	Matthias Sammer (Borussia Dortmund)
1988	Marco Van Basten (AC Milan)	1997	Ronaldo (Inter Milan)
1989	Marco Van Basten (AC Milan)	1998	Zinédine Zidane (Juventus)
1990	Lothar Matthäus (Inter Milan)	1999	Rivaldo (Barcelona)
1991	Jean-Pierre Papin (Marseille)	2000	Luis Figo (Real Madrid)
1992	Marco Van Basten (AC Milan)	2001	Michael Owen (Liverpool)
1993	Roberto Baggio (Juventus)	2002	Ronaldo (Real Madrid)

NB In 1955–1994 the award was restricted to Europeans. Since 1995 it is for all players in European clubs regardless of nationality.

Football: General Information

Arsenal tube station: former name — Gillespie Road (one of the innovative Herbert Chapman's ideas).
artificial turf: 1st team to use — Queen's Park Rangers (1981). Luton followed soon after.
ball: circumference — between 27 and 28 inches (69–71cm).
Black: 1st English international — Viv Anderson (1978).
caps 1st awarded for internationals — 1886.
city that never had Premier (Div. 1) team — Hull.
crossbar introduced — 1875.
England team from one club — In 1894 Corinthians supplied all eleven players for England v Wales at Wrexham.
England: 1st home loss to foreign side — In 1953 Hungary defeated England 6–3.
England: 1st loss to foreign side — In 1929 Spain beat England 4–3 in Madrid.
European Footballer of the Year: 1st — Stanley Matthews.
FA Charity Shield: contestants — FA Cup winners v League winners.
FA Cup Final: 1st monarch to attend — King George V (1914).
FA Cup: 15 original teams — Barnes, Civil Service, Clapham Rovers, Crystal Palace (not the present one), Donnington School (Spalding), Great Marlow, Hampstead Heathens, Harrow Chequers, Hitchin, Maidenhead, Queen's Park, Reigate Priory, Royal Engineers (Chatham), Upton Park, Wanderers.
FA Cup: 1st floodlit tie — Kidderminster v Brierley Hill (1955).
1st player sent off in final — Kevin Moran of Manchester Utd (1985).
1st replay (Wembley) — 1970 (draw at Wembley, replayed at Old Trafford).
1st scorer — M P Betts (a Harrow Chequer) scored the first goal in an FA Cup tie.
broke neck in final — Bert Trautmann of Manchester City (1956).
horse cleared pitch — PC George Storey on a white horse cleared overcrowded pitch at Wembley's first Cup Final (1923).
non-League winner — Tottenham Hotspur (1901).
played every year — Great Marlow (now Marlow) and Maidenhead have played in every FA Cup since 1872.
stolen — 1895 (from a Birmingham shop).
floodlit game: 1st — 1887.
floodlit: international 1st — England v Spain at Wembley (1955).
Football Association: address — 16 Lancaster Gate, London W2 3LW; Tel: 020 7 262 4542.
Football Association: set up at — Freemason's Tavern, Lincoln's Inn Fields (1863).
goal nets: used for 1st time — 1891 (North v South match).
goal: dimensions — height: 8 feet (2.4m), width: 8 yards (7.3m).
home internationals: 1st played — 1883 (Scotland v Ireland was the first match).
home internationals: last played — 1984 (Ireland won on goal difference after all four teams finished on 3 points).
international: first official — England v Scotland (1872).
Irish club: lst founded — Cliftonville (1879).
Irish FA: when formed — 1880.
League and Cup double: 1st — Preston North End won FA Cup without conceding a goal and League without losing a game (1889).
numbering of players — introduced by Herbert Chapman, manager of Arsenal (1928).
oldest club: when founded — Sheffield (1857).
oldest League club: when founded — Notts County (1862).
oldest Scottish club: when founded — Queen's Park (1867).
Olympic Games: UK victory — White City (1908) and Stockholm (1912).
penalty kick introduced — 1891 (at request of the Irish FA).
penalty spot: distance from goal — 12 yards (11m).
points: first club to score over 100 in League — York City (101) 1983/4 season.
points: League record — Sunderland (105) 1998/9.
Rangers: won every league match — 1898/9 season.
religious support: Glasgow — traditionally Catholics follow Celtic and Protestants follow Rangers.

rules: codified	at Cambridge University (1846).
Scottish FA: when formed	1873.
shinguards introduced	1874.
stadiums: famous world football	Amsterdam Arena, Amsterdam (Ajax); Azteca Stadium, Mexico; Bernabeu, Madrid (Real Madrid); Giuseppe Meazza, San Siro (AC and Inter Milan); Lansdowne Rd, Dublin; Maracana, Rio de Janeiro; Noucamp, Barcelona; Olympic Stadium, Munich (Bayern Munich); Parc des Princes, Paris (St Germain); Stade de France, St Denis; Stadio Delle Alpi, Torino (Juventus); Stadium of Light, Lisbon (Benfica); Windsor Park, Belfast (Linfield).
stadium: largest capacity	Maracana Stadium, Rio de Janeiro.
Sunday football: 1st League game	20 Jan. 1974 (Millwall v Fulham).
televised football: 1st	29 Aug. 1936 (Arsenal v Everton). BBC showed same evening.
televised football: 1st live	30 April 1938, Wembley FA Cup final, shown by BBC.
3 points: 1st played	1981/2 season.
3 points: 1st played Scotland	1994/5 season.
tragedies: Bolton	9 March 1946 (wall and barrier collapsed, 33 killed) Bolton v Stoke.
Bradford	11 May 1985 (3rd Division game between Bradford City and Lincoln City), fire in main stand, 56 died.
Heysel (Brussels)	29 May 1985 (European Cup final Liverpool v Juventus), Liverpool fans on rampage, 41 died.
Hillsborough	15 April 1989 (Notts Forest v Liverpool, FA Cup semi-final), Leppings Lane end, 96 died.
Ibrox	5 April 1902 (stand collapsed, 25 killed) Scotland v England. 2 Jan. 1971 (Celtic v Rangers who equalised in final minute, causing mayhem, 66 died).
transfer: 1st £1,000	A Common from Sunderland to Middlesbrough (1905).
1st £10,000	D Jack from Bolton to Arsenal (1928).
1st £50,000	D Law from Huddersfield to Manchester City (1960).
1st £100,000	D Law from Torino to Manchester Utd (1962).
1st £100,000 (English clubs)	A Ball from Blackpool to Everton (1966) (actual transfer price £110,000).
1st £200,000	M Peters from West Ham to Spurs (1970).
1st £500,000	G McQueen from Leeds to Manchester Utd (1978).
1st £1 million	T Francis from Birmingham to Nottingham Forest (1979).
1st £2 million	P Gascoigne from Newcastle to Spurs (1988).
1st £5 million	C Sutton from Norwich City to Blackburn Rovers (1994).
1st £10 million and £15 million	A Shearer from Blackburn to Newcastle (1996).
1st £30 million	R Ferdinand from Leeds to Manchester Utd (2002).
two-handed throw introduced	1895.
war started by football match	El Salvador v Honduras (1969).
Welsh FA: when formed	1876.
white ball legalised	1950.
World Cup: England 1st played	in 1950 (England were beaten in the qualifying competition in Brazil).
World Cup: most tournaments	Antonio Carbajal, the Mexican goalkeeper (5). Lothar Matthäus, Germany (5).
World Cup: top scorer in single tournament	Just Fontaine of France (13), 1958.

Football Association Cup

Date	Winner		Runner-up
1872	Wanderers	1–0	Royal Engineers
1873	Wanderers	2–0	Oxford University
1874	Oxford University	2–0	Royal Engineers
1875	Royal Engineers	1–1, 2–0	Old Etonians
1876	Wanderers	1–1, 3–0	Old Etonians
1877	Wanderers	2–1 aet	Oxford University
1878	Wanderers	3–1	Royal Engineers
1879	Old Etonians	1–0	Clapham Rovers
1880	Clapham Rovers	1–0	Oxford University
1881	Old Carthusians	3–0	Old Etonians
1882	Old Etonians	1–0	Blackburn Rovers (first appearance of a Northern club in the final)
1883	Blackburn Olympic	2–1 aet	Old Etonians (last appearance of English amateur finalists)
1884	Blackburn Rovers	2–1	Queen's Park

Date	Winner		Runner-up
1885	Blackburn Rovers	2–0	Queen's Park
1886	Blackburn Rovers	0–0, 2–0	West Bromwich Albion
1887	Aston Villa	2–0	West Bromwich Albion
1888	West Bromwich Albion	2–1	Preston North End
1889	Preston North End	3–0	Wolverhampton Wanderers
1890	Blackburn Rovers	6–1	The Wednesday
	William Townley scored first-ever Cup Final hat-trick		
1891	Blackburn Rovers	3–1	Notts County
1892	West Bromwich Albion	3–0	Aston Villa
1893	Wolverhampton Wanderers	1–0	Everton
1894	Notts County (first 2nd Division team to win the FA Cup)	4–1	Bolton Wanderers
1895	Aston Villa	1–0	West Bromwich Albion
	trophy was stolen on 11/9/95 and was never recovered		
1896	The Wednesday	2–1	Wolverhampton Wanderers
	new trophy was an exact replica of the original		
1897	Aston Villa (second team to do 'the double')	3–2	Everton
1898	Nottingham Forest	3–1	Derby County
1899	Sheffield United	4–1	Derby County
1900	Bury	4–0	Southampton
1901	Tottenham Hotspur	2–2, 3–1	Sheffield United
	Tottenham – only non-League team to win the FA Cup since the League started in 1888/9 – also started the tradition of decorating the cup with ribbons in the colours of the winning team		
1902	Sheffield United	1–1, 2–1	Southampton
1903	Bury (record winning margin in FA Cup Final)	6–0	Derby County
1904	Manchester City	1–0	Bolton Wanderers
1905	Aston Villa	2–0	Newcastle United
1906	Everton	1–0	Newcastle United
1907	The Wednesday	2–1	Everton
1908	Wolverhampton Wanderers	3–1	Newcastle United
1909	Manchester United	1–0	Bristol City
1910	Newcastle United	1–1, 2–0	Barnsley
	after this final it was discovered that the trophy had not been copyrighted and it had been copied for another tournament, so the trophy was presented to Lord Kinnaird and a new one was commissioned		
1911	Bradford City	0–0, 1–0	Newcastle United
	first winners of new (present) trophy made by Fattorini & Sons of Bradford		
1912	Barnsley	0–0, 1–0 aet	West Bromwich Albion
1913	Aston Villa	1–0	Sunderland
1914	Burnley	1–0	Liverpool
1915	Sheffield United	3–0	Chelsea
1916	not held		
1917	not held		
1918	not held		
1919	not held		
1920	Aston Villa	1–0 aet	Huddersfield Town
1921	Tottenham Hotspur	1–0	Wolverhampton Wanderers
1922	Huddersfield Town	1–0	Preston North End
1923	Bolton Wanderers	2–0	West Ham United
	first Wembley Final – official crowd figure 126,047 – actual figure 180,000–200,000		
1924	Newcastle United	2–0	Aston Villa
1925	Sheffield United	1–0	Cardiff City
1926	Bolton Wanderers	1–0	Manchester City (1st team to reach the Cup Final and be relegated in same season)
1927	Cardiff City (only non-English team to win the Cup)	1–0	Arsenal
1928	Blackburn Rovers	3–1	Huddersfield Town
1929	Bolton Wanderers	2–0	Portsmouth
1930	Arsenal	2–0	Huddersfield Town
1931	West Bromwich Albion	2–1	Birmingham City
1932	Newcastle United	2–1	Arsenal
1933	Everton	3–0	Manchester City
1934	Manchester City	2–1	Portsmouth
1935	Sheffield Wednesday	4–2	West Bromwich Albion
1936	Arsenal	1–0	Sheffield United
1937	Sunderland	3–1	Preston North End
1938	Preston North End	1–0 aet	Huddersfield Town
1939	Portsmouth	4–1	Wolverhampton Wanderers

Date	Winner		Runner-up
1940	not held		
1941	not held		
1942	not held		
1943	not held		
1944	not held		
1945	not held		
1946	Derby County	4–1 aet	Charlton Athletic
	the ball burst during the final – also this was the only season when two-legged matches were played in the FA Cup – prior to the semi-final stage		
1947	Charlton Athletic	1–0 aet	Burnley
	the ball burst again		
1948	Manchester United	4–2	Blackpool
	only time winners have played against a team from top flight in every round		
1949	Wolverhampton Wanderers	3–1	Leicester City
1950	Arsenal	2–0	Liverpool
1951	Newcastle United	2–0	Blackpool
1952	Newcastle United	1–0	Arsenal
1953	Blackpool	4–3	Bolton Wanderers
	'The Matthews Final' – Stan Mortensen hat-trick – winner scored by Bill Perry		
1954	West Bromwich Albion	3–2	Preston North End
1955	Newcastle United	3–1	Manchester City
1956	Manchester City	3–1	Birmingham City
1957	Aston Villa	2–1	Manchester United
1958	Bolton Wanderers	2–0	Manchester United
1959	Nottingham Forest	2–1	Luton Town
1960	Wolverhampton Wanderers	3–0	Blackburn Rovers
1961	Tottenham Hotspur (3rd team to do 'the double' – first in 20th century	2–0	Leicester City
1962	Tottenham Hotspur	3–1	Burnley
1963	Manchester United	3–1	Leicester City
1964	West Ham United	3–2	Preston North End
	Howard Kendall was the then youngest finalist in 20th century)		
1965	Liverpool	2–1 aet	Leeds United
1966	Everton	3–2	Sheffield Wednesday
1967	Tottenham Hotspur	2–1	Chelsea
	first all-London Wembley final		
1968	West Bromwich Albion	1–0 aet	Everton
1969	Manchester City	1–0	Leicester City
1970	Chelsea	2–2, 2–1 aet	Leeds United
1971	Arsenal (4th team to do 'the double')	2–1 aet	Liverpool
1972	Leeds United	1–0	Arsenal
1973	Sunderland (first 2nd division team to win the Cup since West Brom in 1931)	1–0	Leeds United
1974	Liverpool	3–0	Newcastle United
1975	West Ham United	2–0	Fulham
	Bobby Moore played for Fulham against West Ham		
1976	Southampton	1–0	Manchester United
1977	Manchester United	2–1	Liverpool
1978	Ipswich Town (only team to play in every round of Cup including preliminary)	1–0	Arsenal
1979	Arsenal	3–2	Manchester United
1980	West Ham United (most recent 2nd Division Cup winners Paul Allen beat Howard Kendall's 20th century record as youngest player)	1–0	Arsenal
1981	Tottenham Hotspur	1–1, 3–2	Manchester City
1982	Tottenham Hotspur	1–1, 1–0	Queen's Park Rangers
1983	Manchester United	2–2, 4–0	Brighton & Hove Albion
1984	Everton	2–0	Watford
1985	Manchester United	1–0 aet	Everton
1986	Liverpool	3–1	Everton
1987	Coventry City	3–2 aet	Tottenham Hotspur
1988	Wimbledon	1–0	Liverpool
1989	Liverpool	3–2 aet	Everton
1990	Manchester United	3–3, 1–0	Crystal Palace
1991	Tottenham Hotspur	2–1 aet	Nottingham Forest
1992	Liverpool	2–0	Sunderland
1993	Arsenal	1–1, 2–1 aet	Sheffield Wednesday
	Arsenal also beat Sheffield Wednesday in the League Cup final		

SPORT & LEISURE

Date	Winner		Runners-up	Venue
1994	Manchester United (6th team to do 'the double')	4–0		Chelsea
1995	Everton	1–0		Manchester United
1996	Manchester United (1st team to do a second 'double')	1–0		Liverpool
	Eric Cantona 1st foreign player to captain the FA Cup winners			
1997	Chelsea	2–0		Middlesbrough
1998	Arsenal	2–0		Newcastle United
1999	Manchester United (3rd double – also 1st team to do a	2–0		Newcastle United
	'treble' of League, FA Cup and European Champions Cup)			
2000	Chelsea	1–0		Aston Villa
2001	Liverpool	2–1		Arsenal
2002	Arsenal	2–0		Chelsea
2003	Arsenal	1–0		Southampton

European Cup Winners' Cup

Date	Winner		Runners-up	Venue
1961	Fiorentina	4–1 on agg.	Glasgow Rangers	Glasgow, Florence
1962	Atletico Madrid	1–1, 3–0	Fiorentina	Glasgow, Stuttgart
1963	Tottenham Hotspur	5–1	Atletico Madrid	Rotterdam
1964	Sporting Lisbon	3–3,1–0	MTK Budapest	Brussels, Antwerp
1965	West Ham United	2–0	Munich 1860	Wembley
1966	Borussia Dortmund	2–1 aet	Liverpool	Glasgow
1967	Bayern Munich	1–0 aet	Glasgow Rangers	Nuremberg
1968	AC Milan	2–0	SV Hamburg	Rotterdam
1969	Slovan Bratislava	3–2	Barcelona	Basle
1970	Manchester City	2–1	Gornik Zabrze	Vienna
1971	Chelsea	1–1, 2–1 aet	Real Madrid	Athens, Athens
1972	Glasgow Rangers	3–2	Dynamo Moscow	Barcelona
1973	AC Milan	1–0	Leeds United	Salonika
1974	Magdeburg	2–0	AC Milan	Rotterdam
1975	Dynamo Kiev	3–0	Ferencvaros	Basle
1976	Anderlecht	4–2	West Ham United	Brussels
1977	SV Hamburg	2–0	Anderlecht	Amsterdam
1978	Anderlecht	4–0	Austria Vienna	Paris
1979	Barcelona	4–3 aet	Fortuna Düsseldorf	Basle
1980	Valencia	0–0, 5–4 on pens	Arsenal	Brussels
1981	Dynamo Tbilisi	2–1	Carl Zeiss Jena	Düsseldorf
1982	Barcelona	2–1	Standard Liège	Barcelona
1983	Aberdeen	2–1 aet	Real Madrid	Gothenburg
1984	Juventus	2–1	FC Porto	Basle
1985	Everton	3–1	Rapid Vienna	Rotterdam
1986	Dynamo Kiev	3–0	Atletico Madrid	Lyon
1987	Ajax	1–0	Lokomotiv Leipzig	Athens
1988	Mechelen	1–0	Ajax	Strasbourg
1989	Barcelona	2–0	Sampdoria	Berne
1990	Sampdoria	2–0	Anderlecht	Gothenburg
1991	Manchester United	2–1	Barcelona	Rotterdam
1992	Werder Bremen	2–0	AS Monaco	Lisbon
1993	Parma	3–1	Royal Antwerp	London (Wembley)
1994	Arsenal	1–0	Parma	Copenhagen
1995	Real Zaragoza	2–1	Arsenal	Paris
1996	Paris St-Germain	1–0	Rapid Vienna	Brussels
1997	Barcelona	1–0	Paris St-Germain	Rotterdam
1998	Chelsea	1–0	VFB Stuttgart	Stockholm
1999	Lazio	2–1	Real Majorca	Birmingham

NB The European Cup Winners' Cup was established in 1960 and is contested by national Cup winners or the runners-up if the winners were in the European Cup. 1999 was the last competition. As from 1999/2000 national Cup winners will compete in an expanded UEFA Cup.

European Champion Clubs' Cup

Date	Winner		Runners-up	Venue
1956	Real Madrid	4–3	Stade de Reims	Paris
1957	Real Madrid	2–0	Fiorentina	Madrid
1958	Real Madrid	3–2, aet	AC Milan	Brussels
1959	Real Madrid	2–0	Stade de Reims	Stuttgart

Date	Winner		Runners-up	Venue
1960	Real Madrid	7–3	Eintracht Frankfurt	Glasgow
1961	Benfica	3–2	Barcelona	Berne
1962	Benfica	5–3	Real Madrid	Amsterdam
1963	AC Milan	2–1	Benfica	London
1964	Inter Milan	3–1	Real Madrid	Vienna
1965	Inter Milan	1–0	Benfica	Milan
1966	Real Madrid	2–1	Partizan Belgrade	Brussels
1967	Celtic	2–1	Inter Milan	Lisbon
1968	Manchester United	4–1, aet	Benfica	London
1969	AC Milan	4–1	Ajax	Madrid
1970	Feyenoord	2–1, aet	Celtic	Milan
1971	Ajax	2–0	Panathinaikos	London
1972	Ajax	2–0	Inter Milan	Rotterdam
1973	Ajax	1–0	Juventus	Belgrade
1974	Bayern Munich	1–1, 4–0	Atletico Madrid	Brussels
1975	Bayern Munich	2–0	Leeds United	Paris
1976	Bayern Munich	1–0	St Etienne	Glasgow
1977	Liverpool	3–1	Borussia Moenchengladbach	Rome
1978	Liverpool	1–0	FC Bruges	London
1979	Nottingham Forest	1–0	Malmo	Munich
1980	Nottingham Forest	1–0	SV Hamburg	Madrid
1981	Liverpool	1–0	Real Madrid	Paris
1982	Aston Villa	1–0	Bayern Munich	Rotterdam
1983	SV Hamburg	1–0	Juventus	Athens
1984	Liverpool	1–1, 4–2 on pens	AS Roma	Rome
1985	Juventus	1–0	Liverpool	Brussels
1986	Steaua Bucharest	0–0, 2–0 on pens	Barcelona	Seville
1987	FC Porto	2–1	Bayern Munich	Vienna
1988	PSV Eindhoven	0–0, 6–5 on pens	Benfica	Stuttgart
1989	AC Milan	4–0	Steaua Bucharest	Barcelona
1990	AC Milan	1–0	Benfica	Vienna
1991	Red Star Belgrade	0–0, 5–3 on pens	Marseille	Bari
1992	Barcelona	1–0, aet	Sampdoria	London
1993	Marseille*	1–0	AC Milan	Munich
1994	AC Milan	4–0	Barcelona	Athens
1995	Ajax	1–0	AC Milan	Vienna
1996	Juventus	1–1, 4–2 on pens	Ajax	Rome
1997	Borussia Dortmund	3–1	Juventus	Munich
1998	Real Madrid	1–0	Juventus	Amsterdam
1999	Manchester United	2–1	Bayern Munich	Barcelona
2000	Real Madrid	3–0	Valencia	Paris
2001	Bayern Munich	1–1, 5–4 on pens	Valencia	Milan
2002	Real Madrid	2–1	Bayer Leverkusen	Glasgow

*Marseille were subsequently stripped of title following bribery scandal concerning Bernard Tapié, the club president.

NB The European Cup was established in 1955 and was contested by the respective League champions of the member countries of the Union of European Football Associations (UEFA).

In recent seasons, clubs finishing second, third and fourth in the League of those countries with the highest UEFA points coefficients can qualify for the European Champions Cup.

Since 1992/3 season the European Cup has changed its format to include a qualifying competition, two group stages and a final knockout phase of quarter-finals, semi-finals, played over two legs, and a single-match final. The competition since the rule changes is more properly called the UEFA Champions League.

European Super Cup

1972	Ajax	1983	Aberdeen
1973	Ajax	1984	Juventus
1974	not contested	1985	not contested
1975	Kiev Dynamo	1986	Steaua
1976	Anderlecht	1987	FC Porto
1977	Liverpool	1988	Mechelen
1978	Anderlecht	1989	Milan
1979	Notts Forest	1990	Milan
1980	Valencia	1991	Manchester Utd
1981	not contested	1992	Barcelona
1982	Aston Villa	1993	Parma

1994	Milan	1999	Lazio
1995	Ajax	2000	Galatasaray
1996	Juventus	2001	Liverpool
1997	Barcelona	2002	Real Madrid
1998	Chelsea		

NB The European Super Cup was for the winners of the UEFA Champions League and the European Cup Winners Cup. With the demise of the latter trophy the opponents have been the UEFA Cup winners.

Original 12 Football League Clubs

Accrington	Everton
Aston Villa	Notts County
Blackburn Rovers	Preston North End
Bolton Wanderers	Stoke City
Burnley	West Bromwich Albion
Derby County	Wolverhampton Wanderers

Women's World Championship

1991	USA
1995	Norway
1999	USA

Asian Cup

Date	Winner	Date	Winner	Date	Winner
1956	South Korea	1972	Iran	1988	Saudi Arabia
1960	South Korea	1976	Iran	1992	Japan
1964	Israel	1980	Kuwait	1996	Saudi Arabia
1968	Iran	1984	Saudi Arabia	2000	Japan

African Champions Cup

Date	Winner	Date	Winner
1964	Oryx Douala (Cameroon)	1984	Zamalek (Egypt)
1965	not held	1985	FAR Rabat (Morocco)
1966	Stade Abidjan (Ivory Coast)	1986	Zamalek (Egypt)
1967	TP Englebert (Zaïre)	1987	Al Ahly (Egypt)
1968	TP Englebert (Zaïre)	1988	EP Setif (Algeria)
1969	Al Ismaili (Egypt)	1989	Raja Casablanca (Morocco)
1970	Asante Kotoko (Ghana)	1990	JS Kabylie (Algeria)
1971	Canon Yaoundé (Cameroon)	1991	Club Africain (Algeria)
1972	Hafia Conakry (Ghana)	1992	Wydad Casablanca (Morocco)
1973	AS Vita Kinshasa (Zaïre)	1993	Zamalek (Egypt)
1974	CARA Brazzaville (Congo)	1994	Esperance (Tunisia)
1975	Hafia Conakry (Ghana)	1995	Orlando Pirates (South Africa)
1976	MC Algiers (Algeria)	1996	Zamalek (Egypt)
1977	Hafia Conakry (Ghana)	1997	Raja Casablanca (Morocco)
1978	Canon Yaoundé (Cameroon)	1998	ASEC Abidjan (Ivory Coast)
1979	Union Douala (Cameroon)	1999	Raja Casablanca (Morocco)
1980	Canon Yaoundé (Cameroon)	2000	Hearts of Oak (Ghana)
1981	JE Tizi-Ouzou (Algeria)	2001	Al Ahly (Egypt)
1982	Al Ahly (Egypt)	2002	Zamalek (Egypt)
1983	Asante Kotoko (Ghana)		

African Nations Cup

1957	Egypt		
1959	Egypt	1982	Ghana
1962	Ethiopia	1984	Cameroon
1963	Ghana	1986	Egypt
1965	Ghana	1988	Cameroon
1968	Zaïre	1990	Algeria
1970	Sudan	1992	Ghana
1972	Congo	1994	Nigeria
1974	Zaïre	1996	South Africa
1976	Morocco	1998	Egypt
1978	Ghana	2000	Cameroon
1980	Nigeria	2002	Cameroon

World Club Intercontinent Cup

Date	Winner		Date	Winner
1960	Real Madrid		1982	Peñarol (Montevideo)
1961	Peñarol (Montevideo)		1983	Gremio (Porto Alegre, Brazil)
1962	Santos (São Paulo)		1984	Independiente (Argentina)
1963	Santos (São Paulo)		1985	Juventus (Turin)
1964	Internazionale (Milan)		1986	River Plate (Buenos Aires)
1965	Internazionale (Milan)		1987	FC Porto (Oporto)
1966	Peñarol (Montevideo)		1988	Nacional (Montevideo)
1967	Racing Club (Arg)		1989	AC Milan
1968	Estudiantes (La Plata, Argentina)		1990	AC Milan
1969	AC Milan		1991	Red Star Belgrade
1970	Feyenoord (Rotterdam)		1992	São Paulo
1971	Nacional (Montevideo)		1993	São Paulo
1972	Ajax (Amsterdam)		1994	Velez Sarsfield (Argentina)
1973	Independiente (Argentina)		1995	Ajax (Amsterdam)
1974	Atletico Madrid		1996	Juventus (Turin)
1975	not played		1997	Borussia Dortmund
1976	Bayern Munich		1998	Real Madrid
1977	not played		1999	Manchester United
1978	Boca Juniors (Buenos Aires)		2000	Boca Juniors (Buenos Aires)
1979	Olimpia (Paraguay)		2001	Bayern Munich
1980	Nacional (Montevideo)		2002	Real Madrid
1981	Flamengo (Rio)			

NB From 1960 to 1979 the competition was decided on points, not goal difference. From 1980 it was played as a single match in Tokyo. In 2000 the inaugural FIFA Club World Championship took place in Brazil and was won by the Brazilian side Corinthians.

Copa America
South American Championship

Date	Winner		Date	Winner
1910	Argentina		1949	Brazil
1916	Uruguay		1953	Paraguay
1917	Uruguay		1955	Argentina
1919	Brazil		1956	Uruguay
1920	Uruguay		1957	Argentina
1921	Argentina		1959	Argentina
1922	Brazil			Uruguay
1923	Uruguay		1963	Bolivia
1924	Uruguay		1967	Uruguay
1925	Argentina		1975	Peru
1926	Uruguay		1979	Paraguay
1927	Argentina		1983	Uruguay
1929	Argentina		1987	Uruguay
1935	Uruguay		1989	Brazil
1937	Argentina		1991	Argentina
1939	Peru		1993	Argentina
1941	Argentina		1995	Uruguay
1942	Uruguay		1997	Brazil
1945	Argentina		1999	Brazil
1946	Argentina		2001	Colombia
1947	Argentina			

Copa Libertadores
South American Club Cup

Date	Winner	Date	Winner
1960	Peñarol (Montevideo, Uruguay)	1989	Atlético Nacional (Medellín, Colombia)
1964	Independiente (Buenos Aires, Argentina)	1990	Olimpia (Asunción, Paraguay)
1965	Independiente (Buenos Aires, Argentina)	1991	Colo Colo (Santiago, Chile)
1969	Estudiantes (La Plata, Argentina)	1995	Gremio (Pôrto Alegre, Brazil)
1970	Estudiantes (La Plata, Argentina)	1996	River Plate (Buenos Aires, Argentina)
1972	Independiente (Buenos Aires, Argentina)	1997	Cruzeiro (Belo Horizonte, Brazil)
1974	Independiente (Buenos Aires, Argentina)	1998	Vasco Da Gama (Rio, Brazil)
1975	Independiente (Buenos Aires, Argentina)	1999	Palmeiras (São Paulo, Brazil)
1976	Cruzeiro (Belo Horizonte, Brazil)	2001	Boca Juniors (Buenos Aires, Argentina)
1985	Argentinos Juniors (Buenos Aires, Argentina)	2002	Olimpia (Asunción, Paraguay)
1987	Peñarol (Montevideo, Uruguay)		

NB The competition has been held every year since 1960. Only the winners that did not go on to win the World Club Cup are listed.

Scottish Cup Finals

Winners			*Runners-up*	*Winners*			*Runners-up*
1874	Queen's Park	2–0	Clydesdale	1917	not held		
1875	Queen's Park	3–0	Renton	1918	not held		
1876	Queen's Park	1–1, 2–0	Third Lanark	1919	not held		
1877	Vale of Leven	0–0,1–1, 3–2	Rangers	1920	Kilmarnock	3–2	Albion Rovers
1878	Vale of Leven	1–0	Third Lanark	1921	Partick Thistle	1–0	Rangers
1879	Vale of Leven	1–1, walkover	Rangers	1922	Morton	1–0	Rangers
1880	Queen's Park	3–0	Thornlibank	1923	Celtic	1–0	Hibernian
1881	Queen's Park	3–1	Dumbarton	1924	Airdrieonians	2–0	Hibernian
1882	Queen's Park	2–2, 4–1	Dumbarton	1925	Celtic	2–1	Dundee
1883	Dumbarton	2–2, 2–1	Vale of Leven	1926	St Mirren	2–0	Celtic
1884	Queen's Park	walkover	Vale of Leven	1927	Celtic	3–1	East Fife
1885	Renton	0–0, 3–1	Vale of Leven	1928	Rangers	4–0	Celtic
1886	Queen's Park	3–1	Renton	1929	Kilmarnock	2–0	Rangers
1887	Hibernian	2–1	Dumbarton	1930	Rangers	0–0, 2–1	Partick Thistle
1888	Renton	6–1	Cambuslang	1931	Celtic	2–2, 4–2	Motherwell
1889	Third Lanark	2–1	Celtic	1932	Rangers	1–1, 3–0	Kilmarnock
1890	Queen's Park	1–1, 2–1	Vale of Leven	1933	Celtic	1–0	Motherwell
1891	Hearts	1–0	Dumbarton	1934	Rangers	5–0	St Mirren
1892	Celtic	5–1	Queen's Park	1935	Rangers	2–1	Hamilton
1893	Queen's Park	2–1	Celtic	1936	Rangers	1–0	Third Lanark
1894	Rangers	3–1	Celtic	1937	Celtic	2–1	Aberdeen
1895	St Bernard's	2–1	Renton	1938	East Fife	1–1, 4–2	Kilmarnock
1896	Hearts	3–1	Hibernian	1939	Clyde	4–0	Motherwell
1897	Rangers	5–1	Dumbarton	1940	not held		
1898	Rangers	2–0	Kilmarnock	1941	not held		
1899	Celtic	2–0	Rangers	1942	not held		
1900	Celtic	4–3	Queen's Park	1943	not held		
1901	Hearts	4–3	Celtic	1944	not held		
1902	Hibernian	1–0	Celtic	1945	not held		
1903	Rangers	0–0, 1–1, 2–0	Hearts	1946	not held		
1904	Celtic	3–2	Rangers	1947	Aberdeen	2–1	Hibernian
1905	Third Lanark	0–0, 3–1	Rangers	1948	Rangers	1–1, 1–0	Morton
1906	Hearts	1–0	Third Lanark	1949	Rangers	4–1	Clyde
1907	Celtic	3–0	Hearts	1950	Rangers	3–0	East Fife
1908	Celtic	5–1	St Mirren	1951	Celtic	1–0	Motherwell
1909	cup withheld (see below)			1952	Motherwell	4–0	Dundee
				1953	Rangers	1–1, 1–0	Aberdeen
1910	Dundee	2–2, 0–0, 2–1	Clyde	1954	Celtic	2–1	Aberdeen
1911	Celtic	0–0, 2–0	Hamilton	1955	Clyde	1–1, 1–0	Celtic
1912	Celtic	2–0	Clyde	1956	Hearts	3–1	Celtic
1913	Falkirk	2–0	Raith Rovers	1957	Falkirk	1–1, 2–1	Kilmarnock
1914	Celtic	0–0, 4–1	Hibernian	1958	Clyde	1–0	Hibernian
1915	not held			1959	St Mirren	3–1	Aberdeen
1916	not held			1960	Rangers	2–0	Kilmarnock

Winners			Runners-up	Winners			Runners-up
1961	Dunfermline	0–0, 2–0	Celtic	1984	Aberdeen	2–1 aet	Celtic
1962	Rangers	2–0	St Mirren	1985	Celtic	2–1	Dundee
1963	Rangers	1–1, 3–0	Celtic				United
1964	Rangers	3–1	Dundee	1986	Aberdeen	3–0	Hearts
1965	Celtic	3–2	Dunfermline	1987	St Mirren	1–0 aet	Dundee
1966	Rangers	0–0, 1–0	Celtic				United
1967	Celtic	2–0	Aberdeen	1988	Celtic	2–1	Dundee
1968	Dunfermline	3–1	Hearts				United
1969	Celtic	4–0	Rangers	1989	Celtic	1–0	Rangers
1970	Aberdeen	3–1	Celtic	1990	Aberdeen	0–0, 9–8 pens	Celtic
1971	Celtic	1–1, 2–1	Rangers	1991	Motherwell	4–3 aet	Dundee
1972	Celtic	6–1	Hibernian				United
1973	Rangers	3–2	Celtic	1992	Rangers	2–1	Airdrieonians
1974	Celtic	3–0	Dundee	1993	Rangers	2–1	Aberdeen
			United	1994	Dundee United	1–0	Rangers
1975	Celtic	3–1	Airdrieonians	1995	Celtic	1–0	Airdrieonians
1976	Rangers	3–1	Hearts	1996	Rangers	5–1	Hearts
1977	Celtic	1–0	Rangers	1997	Kilmarnock	1–0	Falkirk
1978	Rangers	2–1	Aberdeen	1998	Hearts	2–1	Rangers
1979	Rangers	0–0, 0–0, 3–2	Hibernian	1999	Rangers	1–0	Celtic
1980	Celtic	1–0	Rangers	2000	Rangers	4–0	Aberdeen
1981	Rangers	0–0, 4–1	Dundee	2001	Celtic	3–0	Hibernian
			United	2002	Rangers	3–2	Celtic
1982	Aberdeen	4–1 aet	Rangers	2003	Rangers	1–0	Dundee
1983	Aberdeen	1–0 aet	Rangers				

NB In 1879 Vale of Leven awarded cup as Rangers failed to appear for replay after 1–1 draw.
In 1881 Dumbarton protested the first result in which Queen's Park won 2–1.
In 1884 Queen's Park awarded the cup after Vale of Leven failed to appear.
In 1889 Scottish FA ordered a replay because of playing conditions after Third Lanark won match 3–0.
In 1892 both teams protested about first game in which Celtic won 1–0.
In 1909 Celtic v Rangers 2–2, 1–1 with riot in extra time – clubs refused to play a third match – cup was withheld by Scottish FA.

World Cup

	Winner		Runners-up		Venue
1930	Uruguay	4–2	Argentina		Uruguay
1934	Italy	2–1	Czechoslovakia	after extra time	Italy
1938	Italy	4–2	Hungary		France
1950	Uruguay	2–1	Brazil	deciding match of pool	Brazil
1954	West Germany	3–2	Hungary		Switzerland
1958	Brazil	5–2	Sweden		Sweden
1962	Brazil	3–1	Czechoslovakia		Chile
1966	England	4–2	West Germany	after extra time	England
1970	Brazil	4–1	Italy		Mexico
1974	West Germany	2–1	Holland		West Germany
1978	Argentina	3–1	Holland	after extra time	Argentina
1982	Italy	3–1	West Germany		Spain
1986	Argentina	3–2	West Germany		Mexico
1990	West Germany	1–0	Argentina		Italy
1994	Brazil	0–0	Italy	Brazil won 3–2 on penalties	USA
1998	France	3–0	Brazil		France
2002	Brazil	2–0	Germany		Japan

Inter-Cities Cup (became UEFA Cup in 1972)

	Winners		Runners-up
1955–58	Barcelona	8–2 agg.	London
1958–60	Barcelona	4–1 agg.	Birmingham City
1961	AS Roma	4–2 agg.	Birmingham City
1962	Valencia	7–3 agg.	Barcelona
1963	Valencia	4–1 agg.	Dynamo Zagreb
1964	Real Zaragoza	2–1 (in Barcelona)	Valencia
1965	Ferencvaros	1–0 (in Turin)	Juventus
1966	Barcelona	4–3 agg.	Real Zaragoza

	Winners		Runners-up
1967	Dynamo Zagreb	2–0 agg.	Leeds United
1968	Leeds United	1–0 agg.	Ferencvaros
1969	Newcastle United	6–2 agg.	Ujpest Dozsa
1970	Arsenal	4–3 agg.	Anderlecht
1971	Leeds United	3–3 agg., away goals	Juventus
1972	Tottenham Hotspur	3–2 agg.	Wolverhampton Wanderers
1973	Liverpool	3–2 agg.	Borussia Moenchengladbach
1974	Feyenoord	4–2 agg.	Tottenham Hotspur
1975	Borussia Moenchengladbach	5–1 agg.	Twente Enschede
1976	Liverpool	4–3 agg.	FC Bruges
1977	Juventus	2–2 agg., away goals	Athletic Bilbao
1978	PSV Eindhoven	3–0 agg.	Bastia
1979	Borussia Moenchengladbach	2–1 agg.	Red Star Belgrade
1980	Eintracht Frankfurt	3–3 agg., away goals	Borussia Moenchengladbach
1981	Ipswich Town	5–4 agg.	AZ67 Alkmaar
1982	IFK Gothenburg	4–0 agg.	SV Hamburg
1983	Anderlecht	2–1 agg.	Benfica
1984	Tottenham Hotspur	2–2 agg., 4–3 on pens	Anderlecht
1985	Real Madrid	3–1 agg.	Videoton
1986	Real Madrid	5–3 agg.	Cologne
1987	IFK Gothenburg	2–1 agg.	Dundee United
1988	Bayer Leverkusen	3–3 agg., 3–2 on pens	Espanol
1989	Napoli	5–4 agg.	Stuttgart
1990	Juventus	3–1 agg.	Fiorentina
1991	Inter Milan	2–1 agg.	AS Roma
1992	Ajax	2–2 agg., away goals	Torino
1993	Juventus	6–1 agg.	Borussia Dortmund
1994	Inter Milan	2–0 agg.	Casino Salzburg
1995	Parma	2–1 agg.	Juventus
1996	Bayern Munich	5–1 agg.	Bordeaux
1997	Schalke 04	1–1 agg., 4–1 on pens	Inter Milan
1998	Inter Milan	3–0 (Paris)	Lazio
1999	Parma	3–0 (Moscow)	Marseille
2000	Galatasaray	0–0, 4–1 on pens	Arsenal
2001	Liverpool	5–4 on golden goal (Dortmund)	Alavés
2002	Feyenoord	3–2 (Rotterdam)	Borussia Dortmund
2003	FC Porto	3–2 on golden goal (Seville)	Celtic

NB The 1998 UEFA Cup in Paris was held over one leg for the first time.
Between 1967 and 1971 the competition was known as the European Fairs Cup.

Football League Cup (since 1998/9 known as the Worthington Cup)

	Winners		Runners-up
1961	Aston Villa	3–2 on agg. aet	Rotherham United
1962	Norwich City	4–0 on agg.	Rochdale
1963	Birmingham City	3–1 on agg.	Aston Villa
1964	Leicester City	4–3 on agg.	Stoke City
1965	Chelsea	3–2 on agg.	Leicester City
1966	West Bromwich Albion	5–3 on agg.	West Ham United
1967	Queen's Park Rangers	3–2	West Bromwich Albion
1968	Leeds United	1–0	Arsenal
1969	Swindon Town	3–1	Arsenal
1970	Manchester City	2–1	West Bromwich Albion
1971	Tottenham Hotspur	2–0	Aston Villa
1972	Stoke City	2–1	Chelsea
1973	Tottenham Hotspur	1–0	Norwich City
1974	Wolverhampton Wanderers	2–1	Manchester City
1975	Aston Villa	1–0	Norwich City
1976	Manchester City	2–1	Newcastle United
1977	Aston Villa	0–0, 1–1, 3–2 aet	Everton
1978	Nottingham Forest	0–0, 1–0 aet	Liverpool
1979	Nottingham Forest	3–2	Southampton
1980	Wolverhampton Wanderers	1–0	Nottingham Forest
1981	Liverpool	1–1, 2–1	West Ham United
1982	Liverpool	3–1 aet	Tottenham Hotspur
1983	Liverpool	2–1 aet	Manchester United
1984	Liverpool	0–0, 1–0 aet	Everton
1985	Norwich City	1–0	Sunderland
1986	Oxford United	3–0	Queen's Park Rangers
1987	Arsenal	2–1	Liverpool

	Winners				Runners-up
1988	Luton Town	3–2			Arsenal
1989	Nottingham Forest	3–1			Luton Town
1990	Nottingham Forest	1–0			Oldham Athletic
1991	Sheffield Wednesday	1–0			Manchester United
1992	Manchester United	1–0			Nottingham Forest
1993	Arsenal	2–1			Sheffield Wednesday
1994	Aston Villa	3–1			Manchester United
1995	Liverpool	2–1			Bolton Wanderers
1996	Aston Villa	3–0			Leeds United
1997	Leicester City	1–1, 1–0 aet			Middlesbrough
1998	Chelsea	1–0			Middlesbrough
1999	Tottenham	1–0			Leicester City
2000	Leicester	2–1			Tranmere Rovers
2001	Liverpool	1–1, 5–4 on pens.			Birmingham
2002	Blackburn Rovers	2–1			Tottenham
2003	Liverpool	2–0			Manchester United

NB In 1982 the League Cup became the Milk Cup following sponsorship by the Milk Marketing Board. Over the next few seasons it became the Littlewoods, Rumbelows and Coca Cola Cup.

Scottish League Cup

	Winners		Runners-up		Winners		Runners-up
1947	Rangers	4–0	Aberdeen	1977	Aberdeen	2–1	Celtic
1948	East Fife	1–1, 4–1	Falkirk	1978	Rangers	2–1	Celtic
1949	Rangers	2–0	Raith Rovers	1979	Rangers	2–1	Aberdeen
1950	East Fife	3–0	Dunfermline	1980	Dundee Utd	0–0, 3–0	Aberdeen
1951	Motherwell	3–0	Hibernian	1981	Dundee Utd	3–0	Dundee
1952	Dundee	3–2	Rangers	1982	Rangers	2–1	Dundee Utd
1953	Dundee	2–0	Kilmarnock	1983	Celtic	2–1	Rangers
1954	East Fife	3–2	Partick Thistle	1984	Rangers	3–2	Celtic
1955	Hearts	4–2	Motherwell	1985	Rangers	1–0	Dundee Utd
1956	Aberdeen	2–1	St Mirren	1986	Aberdeen	3–0	Hibernian
1957	Celtic	0–0, 3–0	Partick Thistle	1987	Rangers	2–1	Celtic
1958	Celtic	7–1	Rangers	1988	Rangers	3–3, 5–3 on penalties	Aberdeen
1959	Hearts	5–1	Partick Thistle				
1960	Hearts	2–1	Third Lanark	1989	Rangers	3–2	Aberdeen
1961	Rangers	2–0	Kilmarnock	1990	Aberdeen	2–1	Rangers
1962	Rangers	1–1, 3–1	Hearts	1991	Rangers	2–1	Celtic
1963	Hearts	1–0	Kilmarnock	1992	Hibernian	2–0	Dunfermline
1964	Rangers	5–0	Morton	1993	Rangers	2–1	Aberdeen
1965	Rangers	2–1	Celtic	1994	Rangers	2–1	Hibernian
1966	Celtic	2–1	Rangers	1995	Raith Rovers	2–2, 6–5 on penalties	Celtic
1967	Celtic	1–0	Rangers				
1968	Celtic	5–3	Dundee	1996	Aberdeen	2–0	Dundee
1969	Celtic	6–2	Hibernian	1997	Rangers	4–3	Hearts
1970	Celtic	1–0	St Johnstone	1998	Celtic	3–0	Dundee Utd
1971	Rangers	1–0	Celtic	1999	Rangers	2–1	St Johnstone
1972	Partick Thistle	4–1	Celtic	2000	Celtic	2–0	Aberdeen
1973	Hibernian	2–1	Celtic	2001	Celtic	3–0	Kilmarnock
1974	Dundee	1–0	Celtic	2002	Rangers	4–0	Ayr United
1975	Celtic	6–3	Hibernian	2003	Rangers	2–1	Celtic
1976	Rangers	1–0	Celtic				

Scottish League Champions

		1904	Third Lanark	1917	Celtic	
1892	Dumbarton	1905	Celtic	1918	Rangers	
1893	Celtic	1906	Celtic	1919	Celtic	
1894	Celtic	1907	Celtic	1920	Rangers	
1895	Hearts	1908	Celtic	1921	Rangers	
1896	Celtic	1909	Celtic	1922	Celtic	
1897	Hearts	1910	Celtic	1923	Rangers	
1898	Celtic	1911	Rangers	1924	Rangers	
1899	Rangers	1912	Rangers	1925	Rangers	
1900	Rangers	1913	Rangers	1926	Celtic	
1901	Rangers	1914	Celtic	1927	Rangers	
1902	Rangers	1915	Celtic	1928	Rangers	
1903	Hibernian	1916	Celtic	1929	Rangers	

1930	Rangers	1960	Hearts	1982	Celtic
1931	Rangers	1961	Rangers	1983	Dundee Utd
1932	Motherwell	1962	Dundee	1984	Aberdeen
1933	Rangers	1963	Rangers	1985	Aberdeen
1934	Rangers	1964	Rangers	1986	Celtic
1935	Rangers	1965	Kilmarnock	1987	Rangers
1936	Celtic	1966	Celtic	1988	Celtic
1937	Rangers	1967	Celtic	1989	Rangers
1938	Celtic	1968	Celtic	1990	Rangers
1939	Rangers	1969	Celtic	1991	Rangers
1947	Rangers	1970	Celtic	1992	Rangers
1948	Hibernian	1971	Celtic	1993	Rangers
1949	Rangers	1972	Celtic	1994	Rangers
1950	Rangers	1973	Celtic	1995	Rangers
1951	Hibernian	1974	Celtic	1996	Rangers
1952	Hibernian	1975	Rangers	1997	Rangers
1953	Rangers	1976	Rangers	1998	Celtic
1954	Celtic	1977	Celtic	1999	Rangers
1955	Aberdeen	1978	Rangers	2000	Rangers
1956	Rangers	1979	Celtic	2001	Celtic
1957	Rangers	1980	Aberdeen	2002	Celtic
1958	Hearts	1981	Celtic	2003	Rangers
1959	Rangers				

Golf: Majors

Year	British Open	US Open	US PGA	US Masters
1860	W Park	—	—	—
1861	T Morris Snr	—	—	—
1862	T Morris Snr	—	—	—
1863	W Park	—	—	—
1864	T Morris Snr	—	—	—
1865	A Strath	—	—	—
1866	W Park	—	—	—
1867	T Morris Snr	—	—	—
1868	T Morris Jnr	—	—	—
1869	T Morris Jnr	—	—	—
1870	T Morris Jnr	—	—	—
1871	not held	—	—	—
1872	T Morris Jnr	—	—	—
1873	T Kidd	—	—	—
1874	M Park	—	—	—
1875	W Park	—	—	—
1876	R Martin	—	—	—
1877	J Anderson	—	—	—
1878	J Anderson	—	—	—
1879	J Anderson	—	—	—
1880	R Ferguson	—	—	—
1881	R Ferguson	—	—	—
1882	R Ferguson	—	—	—
1883	W Fernie	—	—	—
1884	J Simpson	—	—	—
1885	R Martin	—	—	—
1886	D Brown	—	—	—
1887	W Park Jnr	—	—	—
1888	J Burns	—	—	—
1889	W Park Jnr	—	—	—
1890	J Ball	—	—	—
1891	H Kirkcaldy	—	—	—
1892	H Hilton	—	—	—
1893	W Auchterlonie	—	—	—
1894	J Taylor	—	—	—
1895	J Taylor	H Rawlins	—	—
1896	H Vardon	J Foulis	—	—
1897	H Hilton	J Lloyd	—	—
1898	H Vardon	F Herd	—	—
1899	H Vardon	W Smith	—	—
1900	J Ball	H Vardon	—	—
1901	H Kirkcaldy	W Anderson	—	—

Year	British Open	US Open	US PGA	US Masters
1902	A Herd	L Auchterlonie	—	—
1903	H Vardon	W Anderson	—	—
1904	J White	W Anderson	—	—
1905	J Braid	W Anderson	—	—
1906	J Braid	A Smith	—	—
1907	A Massy (France)	A Ross	—	—
1908	J Braid	F McLeod	—	—
1909	J Taylor	G Sargent	—	—
1910	J Braid	A Smith	—	—
1911	H Vardon	J McDermott	—	—
1912	Ted Ray	J McDermott	—	—
1913	J Taylor	F Ouimet	—	—
1914	H Vardon	W Hagen	—	—
1915	not held	J Travers	—	—
1916	not held	C Evans Jnr	J Barnes	—
1917	not held	not held	not held	—
1918	not held	not held	not held	—
1919	not held	W Hagen	J Barnes	—
1920	G Duncan	Ted Ray (GB)	J Hutchison	—
1921	J Hutchison	J Barnes	W Hagen	—
1922	W Hagen	G Sarazen	G Sarazen	—
1923	A G Havers	B Jones	G Sarazen	—
1924	W Hagen	C Walker	W Hagen	—
1925	J Barnes	W McFarlane	W Hagen	—
1926	B Jones	B Jones	W Hagen	—
1927	B Jones	T Armour	W Hagen	—
1928	W Hagen	J Farrell	L Diegel	—
1929	W Hagen	B Jones	L Diegel	—
1930	B Jones	B Jones	T Armour	—
1931	T Armour	B Burke	T Creavy	—
1932	G Sarazen	G Sarazen	O Dutra	—
1933	D Shute	J Goodman	G Sarazen	—
1934	T Cotton	O Dutra	P Runyan	H Smith
1935	A Perry	S Parks Jnr	J Revolta	G Sarazen
1936	A Padgham	T Manero	D Shute	H Smith
1937	T Cotton	R Guldahl	D Shute	B Nelson
1938	R Whitcombe	R Guldahl	P Runyan	H Picard
1939	R Burton	B Nelson	H Picard	R Guldahl
1940	not held	L Little	B Nelson	J Demaret
1941	not held	C Wood	V Ghezzi	C Wood
1942	not held	not held	S Snead	B Nelson
1943	not held	not held	not held	not held
1944	not held	not held	B Hamilton	not held
1945	not held	not held	B Nelson	not held
1946	S Snead	L Mangrum	B Hogan	H Keiser
1947	F Daly	L Worsham	J Ferrier	J Demaret
1948	T Cotton	B Hogan	B Hogan	C Harmon
1949	B Locke	C Middlecoff	S Snead	S Snead
1950	B Locke	B Hogan	C Harper	J Demaret
1951	M Faulkner	B Hogan	S Snead	B Hogan
1952	B Locke	J Boros	J Turnesa	S Snead
1953	B Hogan	B Hogan	W Burkemo	B Hogan
1954	P Thompson	E Furgol	C Harbert	S Snead
1955	P Thompson	J Fleck	D Ford	C Middlecoff
1956	P Thompson	C Middlecoff	J Burke	J Burke Jnr
1957	B Locke	D Mayer	L Hebert	D Ford
1958	P Thompson	T Bolt	D Finsterwald	A Palmer
1959	G Player	W Casper	B Rosburg	A Wall Jnr
1960	K Nagle	A Palmer	J Hebert	A Palmer
1961	A Palmer	G Littler	J Barber	G Player
1962	A Palmer	J Nicklaus	G Player	A Palmer
1963	R Charles	J Boros	J Nicklaus	J Nicklaus
1964	T Lema	K Venturi	B Nicholls	A Palmer
1965	P Thompson	G Player	D Marr	J Nicklaus
1966	J Nicklaus	W Casper	A Geiberger	J Nicklaus
1967	R de Vicenzo	J Nicklaus	D January	G Brewer
1968	G Player	L Trevino	J Boros	B Goalby
1969	A Jacklin	O Moody	R Floyd	G Archer
1970	J Nicklaus	A Jacklin	D Stockton	W Caspar
1971	L Trevino	L Trevino	J Nicklaus	C Coody
1972	L Trevino	J Nicklaus	G Player	J Nicklaus

Year	The Open	US Open	US PGA	US Masters
1973	T Weiskopf	J Miller	J Nicklaus	T Aaron
1974	G Player	H Irwin	L Trevino	G Player
1975	T Watson	L Graham	J Nicklaus	J Nicklaus
1976	J Miller	J Pate	D Stockton	R Floyd
1977	T Watson	H Green	L Wadkins	T Watson
1978	J Nicklaus	A North	J Mahaffey	G Player
1979	S Ballesteros	H Irwin	D Graham (Australia)	F Zoeller
1980	T Watson	J Nicklaus	J Nicklaus	S Ballesteros
1981	W Rogers	D Graham (Australia)	L Nelson	T Watson
1982	T Watson	T Watson	R Floyd	C Stadler
1983	T Watson	L Nelson	H Sutton	S Ballesteros
1984	S Ballesteros	F Zoeller	L Trevino	B Crenshaw
1985	S Lyle	A North	H Green	B Langer (Germany)
1986	G Norman	R Floyd	B Tway	J Nicklaus
1987	N Faldo	S Simpson	L Nelson	L Mize
1988	S Ballesteros	C Strange	J Sluman	S Lyle
1989	M Calcavecchia	C Strange	P Stewart	N Faldo
1990	N Faldo	H Irwin	W Grady (Australia)	N Faldo
1991	I Baker-Finch	P Stewart	J Daly	I Woosnam
1992	N Faldo	T Kite	N Price	F Couples
1993	G Norman	L Janzen	P Azinger	B Langer
1994	N Price	E Els	N Price	J M Olazabal
1995	J Daly	C Pavin	S Elkington	B Crenshaw
1996	T Lehman	S Jones	M Brooks	N Faldo
1997	J Leonard	E Els	D Love III	T Woods
1998	M O'Meara	L Janzen	V J Singh	M O'Meara
1999	P Lawrie	P Stewart	T Woods	J M Olazabal
2000	T Woods	T Woods	T Woods	V J Singh
2001	D Duval	R Goosen	D Toms	T Woods
2002	E Els	T Woods	R Beem	T Woods
2003		J Furyk		M Weir

Golf: World Matchplay Championship

	Winner	Runner-up		Winner	Runner-up
1964	Arnold Palmer	Neil Coles	1984	Severiano Ballesteros	Bernhard Langer
1965	Gary Player	Peter Thomson	1985	Severiano Ballesteros	Bernhard Langer
1966	Gary Player	Jack Nicklaus	1986	Greg Norman	Sandy Lyle
1967	Arnold Palmer	Peter Thomson	1987	Ian Woosnam	Sandy Lyle
1968	Gary Player	Bob Charles	1988	Sandy Lyle	Nick Faldo
1969	Bob Charles	Gene Littler	1989	Nick Faldo	Ian Woosnam
1970	Jack Nicklaus	Lee Trevino	1990	Ian Woosnam	Mark McNulty
1971	Gary Player	Jack Nicklaus	1991	Severiano Ballesteros	Nick Price
1972	Tom Weiskopf	Lee Trevino	1992	Nick Faldo	Jeff Sluman
1973	Gary Player	Graham Marsh	1993	Corey Pavin	Nick Faldo
1974	Hale Irwin	Gary Player	1994	Ernie Els	Colin Montgomerie
1975	Hale Irwin	Al Geiberger	1995	Ernie Els	Steve Elkington
1976	David Graham	Hale Irwin	1996	Ernie Els	Vijay Singh
1977	Graham Marsh	Ray Floyd	1997	Vijay Singh	Ernie Els
1978	Isao Aoki	Simon Owen	1998	Mark O'Meara	Tiger Woods
1979	Bill Rogers	Isao Aoki	1999	Colin Montgomerie	Mark O'Meara
1980	Greg Norman	Sandy Lyle	2000	Lee Westwood	Colin Montgomerie
1981	Severiano Ballesteros	Ben Crenshaw	2001	Ian Woosnam	Padraig Harrington
1982	Severiano Ballesteros	Sandy Lyle	2002	Ernie Els	Sergio Garcia
1983	Greg Norman	Nick Faldo			

Golf: Ryder Cup

	Winner	Venue		Winner	Venue
1927	USA	Worcester, Massachusetts	1937	USA	Southport & Ainsdale, Lancashire
1929	GB	Moortown, North Yorkshire			
1931	USA	Scioto, Ohio	1947	USA	Portland, Oregon
1933	GB	Southport & Ainsdale, Lancashire	1949	USA	Ganton, Yorkshire
			1951	USA	Pinehurst, North Carolina
1935	USA	Ridgewood, New Jersey	1953	USA	Wentworth, Surrey

1955	USA	Thunderbird G & C, California	1979	USA	Greenbrier, Virginia
1957	GB	Lindrick, Yorkshire	1981	USA	Walton Heath
1959	USA	Eldorado CC, California	1983	USA	Palm Beach
1961	USA	Royal Lytham, Lancashire	1985	Europe	Belfry
1963	USA	Atlanta, Georgia	1987	Europe	Muirfield Village
1965	USA	Royal Birkdale, Lancashire	1989	tie	Belfry
1967	USA	Houston, Texas	1991	USA	Kiawah Island
1969	tie	Royal Birkdale, Lancashire	1993	USA	Belfry
1971	USA	St Louis, Missouri	1995	Europe	Oak Hill CC
1973	USA	Muirfield, Scotland	1997	Europe	Valderrama
1975	USA	Laurel Valley, Pennsylvania	1999	USA	Boston, Massachusetts
1977	USA	Royal Lytham, Lancashire	2002	Europe	Belfry

NB Since 1979 the Ryder Cup has been contested by USA and Europe.
The 2001 event was cancelled due to the terrorist attack of 11 September.

Golf: General Information

British Open: correct title	The Open Championship (as it was the first championship open to the world)
oldest winner	Old Tom Morris (46)
youngest winner	Young Tom Morris (17)
youngest winner 20th century	Seve Ballesteros (22)
clubs: maximum allowed	14
Curtis Cup	Biennial tournament instituted in 1932 and played between amateur ladies' teams from the United States and Great Britain and Ireland. Teams consist of six players, two substitutes and a captain.
golf balls: pimples	332
Ryder Cup: father and sons played	Percy and Peter Alliss, Antonio and Ignacio Garrido
Samuel Ryder: profession	seed-merchant
Solheim Cup	Biennial tournament instituted in 1990 and played between professional ladies teams from the United States and Europe. It takes its name from Karsten Solheim, owner of golf club manufacturer Ping. Teams consist of 12 players and a non-playing captain.
US Masters: oldest winner	Jack Nicklaus (46)
youngest winner	Tiger Woods (21)
US Open: oldest winner	Hale Irwin (45)
youngest winner	John McDermott (19)
US PGA: oldest winner	Julius Boros (48)
youngest winner	Gene Sarazen (20)
US Women's Open: first UK winner	Laura Davies (1987)
Walker Cup	Inaugurated in 1921 and played between amateur teams from the United States and the British Isles. It was proposed by George Walker, the then president of the USGA, as the International Challenge Trophy but took its present name in 1922. It became a biennial event in 1924. Teams consist of eight players, two substitutes and a captain.
yips: coined by	Scottish professional Tommy Armour in the 1920s. Term describing inability to release the putter through the ball.

SPORT & LEISURE

Greyhound Racing

Derby Winners

1980	Indian Joe	1992	Farloe Melody
1981	Parkdown Jet	1993	Ringa Hustle
1982	Laurie's Panther	1994	Moral Standards
1983	I'm Slippy	1995	Moaning Lad
1984	Whisper Wishes	1996	Shanless Slippy
1985	Pagan Swallow	1997	Some Picture
1986	Tico	1998	Tom's the Best
1987	Signal Spark	1999	Chart King
1988	Hit the Lid	2000	Rapid Ranger
1989	Lartigue Note	2001	Rapid Ranger
1990	Slippy Blue	2002	Allen Gift
1991	Ballinderry Ash		

Horse Racing: British Classics and Grand National Winners

Year	St Leger Horse	St Leger Jockey	Oaks Horse	Oaks Jockey	Derby Horse	Derby Jockey
1776	Allabaculia	J Singleton	—	—	—	—
1777	Bourbon	J Cade	—	—	—	—
1778	Hollandaise	G Hearon	—	—	—	—
1779	Tommy	G Lowrey Snr	Bridget	R Goodison	—	—
1780	Ruler	J Mangle	Teetotum	R Goodison	Diomed	S Arnull
1781	Serina	R Forster	Faith	R Goodison	Young Eclipse	C Hindley
1782	Imperatrix	G Searle	Ceres	S Chifney Snr	Assassin	S Arnull
1783	Phoenomenon	A Hall	Maid of Oakes	S Chifney Snr	Saltram	C Hindley
1784	Omphale	J Kirton	Stella	C Hindley	Sergeant	J Arnull
1785	Cowslip	G Searle	Trifle	J Bird	Aimwell	C Hindley
1786	Paragon	J Mangle	Perdita by Tanden	J Edwards	Noble	J White
1787	Spadille	J Mangle	Annette	Fitzpatrick	Sir Peter Teazle	S Arnull
1788	Young Flora	J Mangle	Nightshade	Fitzpatrick	Sir Thomas	W South
1789	Pewett	J Singleton	Tag	S Chifney Snr	Skyscraper	S Chifney Snr
1790	Ambidexter	G Searle	Hippolyta	S Chifney Snr	Rhadamanthus	J Arnull
1791	Young Traveller	J Jackson	Portia	J Singleton	Eager	Stephenson
1792	Tartar	J Mangle	Volante	C Hindley	John Bull	F Buckle
1793	Ninety-three	W Peirse	Caelia	J Singleton	Waxy	W Clift
1794	Beningborough	J Jackson	Hermione	S Arnull	Daedalus	F Buckle
1795	Hambletonian	Boyes	Platina	Fitzpatrick	Spreadeagle	A Wheatley
1796	Ambrosio	J Jackson	Parissot	J Arnull	Didelot	J Arnull
1797	Lounger	J Shepherd	Nike	F Buckle	Brown c by fidget	J Singleton
1798	Symmetry	J Jackson	Bellissima	F Buckle	Sir Harry	S Arnull
1799	Cockfighter	T Fields	Bellina	F Buckle	Archduke	J Arnull
1800	Champion	F Buckle	Ephemera	Fitzpatrick	Champion	W Clift
1801	Quiz	J Shepherd	Eleanor	Saunders	Eleanor	Saunders
1802	Orville	J Singleton Jnr	Scotia	F Buckle	Tyrant	F Buckle
1803	Remembrancer	B Smith	Theophania	F Buckle	Ditto	W Clift
1804	Sancho	F Buckle	Pellisse	W Clift	Hannibal	W Arnull
1805	Staveley	J Jackson	Meteora	F Buckle	Cardinal Beaufort	Fitzpatrick
1806	Fyldener	T Carr	Bronze	W Edwards	Paris	J Shepherd
1807	Paulina	W Clift	Briseis	S Chifney	Election	J Arnull
1808	Petronius	B Smith	Morel	W Clift	Pan	Collinson
1809	Ashton	B Smith	Maid of Orleans	J Moss	Pope	T Goodison
1810	Octavian	W Clift	Oriana	W Peirse	Whalebone	W Clift
1811	Soothsayer	B Smith	Sorcery	S Chifney	Phantom	F Buckle
1812	Ottrington	R Johnson	Manuella	W Peirse	Octavius	W Arnull
1813	Altisidora	J Jackson	Music	T Goodison	Smolensko	T Goodison
1814	William	J Shepherd	Medora	Barnard	Blucher	W Arnull
1815	Filho da Puta	J Jackson	Minuet	T Goodison	Whisker	T Goodison
1816	The Duchess	B Smith	Landscape	S Chifney	Prince Leopold	W Wheatley
1817	Ebor	R Johnson	Neva	F Buckle	Azor	J Robinson
1818	Reveller	R Johnson	Corinne	F Buckle	Sam	S Chifney Jnr
1819	Antonio	J Nicholson	Shoveler	S Chifney	Tiresias	W Clift
1820	St Patrick	J Johnson	Caroline	H Edwards	Sailor	S Chifney Jnr
1821	Jack Spiggot	W Scott	Augusta	J Robinson	Gustavus	S Day
1822	Theodore	J Jackson	Pastille	H Edwards	Moses	T Goodison
1823	Barefoot	T Goodison	Zinc	F Buckle	Emilius	F Buckle
1824	Jerry	B Smith	Cobweb	J Robinson	Cedric	J Robinson
1825	Memnon	W Scott	Wings	S Chifney	Middleton	J Robinson
1826	Tarrare	G Nelson	Lilias	T Lye	Lap-dog	G Dockeray
1827	Matilda	J Robinson	Gulnare	F Boyce	Mameluke	J Robinson
1828	The Colonel	W Scott	Turquoise	J B Day	Cadland	J Robinson
1829	Rowton	W Scott	Green Mantle	G Dockeray	Frederick	Forth
1830	Birmingham	P Conolly	Variation	G Edwards	Priam	S Day
1831	Chorister	J B Day	Oxygen	J B Day	Spaniel	W Wheatley
1832	Margrave	J Robinson	Galata	P Conolly	St Giles	W Scott
1833	Rockingham	S Darling	Vespa	J Chapple	Dangerous	J Chapple
1834	Touchstone	G Calloway	Pussy	J B Day	Plenipotentiary	P Conolly
1835	Queen of Trumps	T Lye	Queen of Trumps	T Lye	Mundig	W Scott
1836	Elis	J B Day	Cyprian	W Scott	Bay Middleton	J Robinson
1837	Mango	S Day Jnr	Miss Letty	J Holmes	Phosphorus	G Edwards
1838	Don John	W Scott	Industry	W Scott	Amato	J Chapple
1839	Charles the Twelfth	W Scott	Deception	J B Day	Bloomsbury	S Templeman
1840	Launcelot	W Scott	Crucifix	J B Day	Little Wonder	Macdonald

	St Leger		Oaks		Derby	
Year	Horse	Jockey	Horse	Jockey	Horse	Jockey
1841	Satirist	W Scott	Ghuznee	W Scott	Coronation	P Conolly
1842	Blue Bonnett	T Lye	Our Nell	T Lye	Attila	W Scott
1843	Nutwith	J Marson	Poison	F Butler	Cotherstone	W Scott
1844	Foig a Ballagh	H Bell	The Princess	F Butler	Orlando	E Flatman
1845	The Baron	F Butler	Refraction	H Bell	The Merry Monarch	F Bell
1846	Sir Tatton Sykes	W Scott	Mendicant	S Day	Pyrrhus the First	S Day
1847	Van Tromp	J Marson	Miami	S Templeman	Cossack	S Templeman
1848	Surplice	E Flatman	Cymba	S Templeman	Surplice	S Templeman
1849	Flying Dutchman	Marlow	Lady Evelyn	F Butler	Flying Dutchman	Marlow
1850	Voltigeur	J Marson	Rhedycina	F Butler	Voltigeur	J Marson
1851	Newminster	S Templeman	Iris	F Butler	Teddington	J Marson
1852	Stockwell	J Norman	Songstress	F Butler	Daniel O'Rourke	F Butler
1853	West Australian	F Butler	Catherine Hayes	Marlow	West Australian	F Butler
1854	Knight of St George	Basham	Mincemeat	Charlton	Andover	A Day
1855	Saucebox	J Wells	Marchioness	S Templeman	Wild Dayrell	R Sherwood
1856	Warlock	E Flatman	Mincepie	A Day	Ellington	Aldcroft
1857	Imperieuse	E Flatman	Blink Bonny	Charlton	Blink Bonny	Charlton
1858	Sunbeam	L Snowden	Governess	Ashmall	Beadsman	J Wells
1859	Gamester	Aldcroft	Summerside	G Fordham	Musjid	J Wells
1860	St Albans	L Snowden	Butterfly	J Snowden	Thormanby	H Custance
1861	Caller Ou	T Challoner	Brown Duchess	L Snowden	Kettledrum	Bullock
1862	The Marquis	T Challoner	Feu de Joie	T Challoner	Caractacus	J Parsons
1863	Lord Clifden	J Osborne	Queen Bertha	Aldcroft	Macaroni	T Challoner
1864	Blair Atholl	J Snowden	Fille de l'Air	A Edwards	Blair Atholl	J Snowden
1865	Gladiateur	H Grimshaw	Regalia	Norman	Gladiateur	H Grimshaw
1866	Lord Lyon	H Custance	Tormentor	J Mann	Lord Lyon	H Custance
1867	Achievement	T Challoner	Hippia	J Daley	Hermit	J Daley
1868	Formosa	T Challoner	Formosa	G Fordham	Blue Gown	J Wells
1869	Pero Gomez	J Wells	Brigantine	T Cannon	Pretender	J Osborne
1870	Hawthornden	J Grimshaw	Gamos	G Fordham	Kingcraft	T French
1871	Hannah	C Maidment	Hannah	C Maidment	Favonius	T French
1872	Wenlock	C Maidment	Reine	G Fordham	Cremorne	C Maidment
1873	Marie Stuart	T Osborne	Marie Stuart	T Cannon	Doncaster	F Webb
1874	Apology	J Osborne	Apology	J Osborne	George Frederick	H Custance
1875	Craig Millar	T Challoner	Spinaway	F Archer	Galopin	Morris
1876	Patriarch	J Goater	Enguerrande	Hudson	Kisber	C Maidment
1877	Silvio	F Archer	Placida	H Jeffrey	Silvio	F Archer
1878	Jannette	F Archer	Jannette	F Archer	Sefton	H Constable
1879	Rayon d'Or	J Goater	Wheel of Fortune	F Archer	Sir Bevys	G Fordham
1880	Robert the Devil	T Cannon	Jenny Howlet	J Snowden	Bend Or	F Archer
1881	Iroquois	F Archer	Thebais	G Fordham	Iroquois	F Archer
1882	Dutch Oven	F Archer	Geheimnis	T Cannon	Shotover	T Cannon
1883	Ossian	J Watts	Bonny Jean	J Watts	St Blaise	C Wood
1884	The Lambkin	J Watts	Busybody	T Cannon	St Gatien/ Harvester	C Wood/Loates
1885	Melton	F Archer	Lonely	F Archer	Melton	F Archer
1886	Ormonde	F Archer	Miss Jummy	J Watts	Ormonde	F Archer
1887	Kilwarlin	W Robinson	Reve d'Or	C Wood	Merry Hampton	J Watts
1888	Seabreeze	W Robinson	Seabreeze	W Robinson	Ayrshire	F Barrett
1889	Donovan	F Barrett	L'Abbesse de Jouarre	J Woodburn	Donovan	T Loates
1890	Memoir	J Watts	Memoir	J Watts	Sainfoin	J Watts
1891	Common	G Barrett	Mimi	F Rickaby	Common	G Barrett
1892	La Fleche	J Watts	La Fleche	G Barrett	Sir Hugo	Allsopp
1893	Isinglass	T Loates	Mrs Butterwick	J Watts	Isinglass	T Loates
1894	Throstle	M Cannon	Amiable	W Bradford	Ladas	J Watts
1895	Sir Visto	S Loates	La Sagesse	S Loates	Sir Visto	S Loates
1896	Persimmon	J Watts	Canterbury Pilgrim	F Rickaby	Persimmon	J Watts
1897	Galtee More	C Wood	Limasol	W Bradford	Galtee More	C Wood
1898	Wildfowler	C Wood	Airs and Graces	W Bradford	Jeddah	O'Madden
1899	Flying Fox	M Cannon	Musa	O Madden	Flying Fox	M Cannon
1900	Diamond Jubilee	H Jones	La Roche	M Cannon	Diamond Jubilee	H Jones
1901	Doricles	K Cannon	Cap and Bells II	M Henry	Volodyovski	L Reiff
1902	Sceptre	F W Hardy	Sceptre	H Randall	ard Patrick	J Martin
1903	Rock Sand	D Maher	Our Lassie	M Cannon	Rock Sand	D Maher

	St Leger		Oaks		Derby	
Year	Horse	Jockey	Horse	Jockey	Horse	Jockey
1904	Pretty Polly	W Lane	Pretty Polly	W Lane	St Amant	K Cannon
1905	Challacombe	O Madden	Cherry Lass	H Jones	Cicero	D Maher
1906	Troutbeck	G Stern	Keystone II	D Maher	Spearmint	D Maher
1907	Wool Winder	W Halsey	Glass Doll	H Randall	Orby	J Reiff
1908	Your Majesty	W Griggs	Signorinetta	W Bullock	Signorinetta	W Bullock
1909	Bayardo	D Maher	Perola	F Wootton	Minoru	H Jones
1910	Swynford	F Wootton	Rosedrop	C Trigg	Lemberg	B Dillon
1911	Prince Palatine	F O'Neill	Cherimoya	F Winter	Sunstar	G Stern
1912	Tracery	G Bellhouse	Mirska	J Childs	Tagalie	J Reiff
1913	Night Hawk	E Wheatley	Jest	F Rickaby Jnr	Aboyeur	E Piper
1914	Black Jester	W Griggs	Princess Dorrie	W Huxley	Durbar II	M MacGee
1915	Pommern	S Donoghue	Snow Marten	Walter Griggs	Pommern	S Donoghue
1916	Hurry On	C Childs	Fifinella	J Childs	Fifinella	J Childs
1917	Gay Crusader	S Donoghue	Sunny Jane	O Madden	Gay Crusader	S Donoghue
1918	Gainsborough	J Childs	My Dear	S Donoghue	Gainsborough	J Childs
1919	Keysoe	B Carslake	Bayuda	J Childs	Grand Parade	F Templeman
1920	Caligula	A Smith	Charlebelle	A Whalley	Spion Kop	F O'Neill
1921	Polemarch	J Childs	Love in Idleness	J Childs	Humorist	S Donoghue
1922	Royal Lancer	R Jones	Pogram	E Gardner	Captain Cuttle	S Donoghue
1923	Tranquil	T Weston	Brownhylda	V Smyth	Papyrus	S Donoghue
1924	Salmon-Trout	B Carslake	Straitlace	F O'Neill	Sansovino	T Weston
1925	Solario	J Childs	Saucy Sue	F Bullock	Manna	S Donoghue
1926	Coronach	J Childs	Short Story	R A Jones	Coronach	J Childs
1927	Book Law	H Jellis	Beam	T Weston	Call Boy	C Elliot
1928	Fairway	T Weston	Toboggan	T Weston	Felstead	H Wragg
1929	Trigo	M Beary	Pennycomequick	H Jelliss	Trigo	J Marshall
1930	Singapore	G Richards	Rose of England	G Richards	Blenheim	H Wragg
1931	Sandwich	H Wragg	Brulette	E C Elliot	Cameronian	F Fox
1932	Firdaussi	F Fox	Udaipur	M Beary	April the Fifth	F Lane
1933	Hyperion	T Weston	Chatelaine	S Wragg	Hyperion	T Weston
1934	Windsor Lad	C Smirke	Light Brocade	B Carslake	Windsor Lad	C Smirke
1935	Bahram	C Smirke	Quashed	H Jelliss	Bahram	F Fox
1936	Boswell	P Beasley	Lovely Rosa	T Weston	Mahmoud	C Smirke
1937	Chulmleigh	G Richards	Exhibitionist	S Donoghue	Mid-day Sun	M Beary
1938	Scottish Union	B Carslake	Rockfel	H Wragg	Bois Roussel	C Elliot
1939	no race held		Galatea II	R A Jones	Blue Peter	E Smith
1940	Turkhan	G Richards	Godiva	D Marks	Pont L'Eveque	S Wragg
1941	Sun Castle	G Bridgland	Commotion	H Wragg	Owen Tudor	W Nevett
1942	Sun Chariot	G Richards	Sun Chariot	G Richards	Watling Street	H Wragg
1943	Herringbone	H Wragg	Why Hurry	C E Elliot	Straight Deal	T Carey
1944	Tehran	G Richards	Hycilla	G Bridgland	Ocean Swell	W Nevett
1945	Chamossaire	T Lowrey	Sun Stream	H Wragg	Dante	W Nevett
1946	Airborne	T Lowrey	Steady Aim	H Wragg	Airborne	T Lowrey
1947	Sayajirao	E Britt	Imprudence	W R Johnstone	Pearl Diver	G Bridgland
1948	Black Tarquin	E Britt	Masaka	W Nevett	My Love	W Johnstone
1949	Ridge Wood	M Beary	Musidora	E Britt	Nimbus	C Elliot
1950	Scratch II	W R Johnstone	Asmena	W R Johnstone	Galcador	W R Johnstone
1951	Talma II	W R Johnstone	Neasham Belle	S Clayton	Arctic Prince	C Spares
1952	Tulyar	C Smirke	Frieze	E Britt	Tulyar	C Smirke
1953	Premonition	E Smith	Ambiguity	J Mercer	Pinza	G Richards
1954	Never Say Die	C Smirke	Suncap	W R Johnstone	Never Say Die	L Piggott
1955	Meld	W H Carr	Meld	W H Carr	Phil Drake	F Palmer
1956	Cambremer	F Palmer	Sicarelle	F Palmer	Lavandin	W R Johnstone
1957	Ballymoss	T P Burns	Carrozza	L Piggott	Crepello	L Piggott
1958	Alcide	W Carr	Bella Paola	M Garcia	Hard Ridden	C Smirke
1959	Cantelo	E Hide	Petite Etoile	L Piggott	Parthia	W Carr
1960	St Paddy	L Piggott	Never Too Late	R Poincelet	St Paddy	L Piggott
1961	Aurelius	L Piggott	Sweet Solera	W Rickaby	Psidium	R Poincelet
1962	Hethersett	W Carr	Monade	Y Saint-Martin	Larkspur	N Sellwood
1963	Ragusa	G Bougoure	Noblesse	G Bougoure	Relko	Y Saint-Martin
1964	Indiana	J Lindley	Homeward Bound	G Starkey	Santa Claus	A Breasley
1965	Provoke	J Mercer	Long Look	J Purtell	Sea Bird II	T P Glennon
1966	Sodium	F Durr	Valoris	L Piggott	Charlottown	A Breasley
1967	Ribocco	L Piggott	Pia	E Hide	Royal Palace	G Moore
1968	Ribero	L Piggott	La Lagune	G Thiboeuf	Sir Ivor	L Piggott
1969	Intermezzo	R Hutchinson	Sleeping Partner	J Gorton	Blakeney	E Johnson
1970	Nijinsky	L Piggott	Lupe	A Barclay	Nijinsky	L Piggott
1971	Athens Wood	L Piggott	Altesse Royale	G Lewis	Mill Reef	G Lewis
1972	Boucher	L Piggott	Ginevra	A Murray	Roberto	L Piggott
1973	Peleid	F Durr	Mysterious	G Lewis	Morston	E Hide

	St Leger		Oaks		Derby	
Year	Horse	Jockey	Horse	Jockey	Horse	Jockey
1974	Bustino	J Mercer	Polygamy	P Eddery	Snow Knight	B Taylor
1975	Bruni	A Murray	Juliet Marny	L Piggott	Grundy	P Eddery
1976	Crow	Y Saint-Martin	Pawneese	Y Saint-Martin	Empery	L Piggott
1977	Dunfermline	W Carson	Dunfermline	W Carson	The Minstrel	L Piggott
1978	Julio Mariner	E Hide	Fair Salinia	G Starkey	Shirley Heights	G Starkey
1979	Son of Love	A Lequeux	Scintillate	P Eddery	Troy	W Carson
1980	Light Cavalry	J Mercer	Bireme	W Carson	Henbit	W Carson
1981	Cut Above	J Mercer	Blue Wind	L Piggott	Shergar	W Swinburn
1982	Touching Wood	P Cook	Time Charter	W Newmes	Golden Fleece	P Eddery
1983	Sun Princess	W Carson	Sun Princess	W Carson	Teenoso	L Piggott
1984	Comanche Run	L Piggott	Circus Plume	L Piggott	Secreto	C Roche
1985	Oh So Sharp	S Cauthen	Oh So Sharp	S Cauthen	Slip Anchor	S Cauthen
1986	Moon Madness	P Eddery	Midway Lady	R Cochrane	Shahrastani	W Swinburn
1987	Reference Point	S Cauthen	Unite	W Swinburn	Reference Point	S Cauthen
1988	Minster Son	W Carson	Diminuendo	S Cauthen	Kayhasi	R Cochrane
1989	Michelozzo	S Cauthen	Snow Bride	S Cauthen	Nashwan	W Carson
1990	Snurge	A Quinn	Salsabil	W Carson	Quest for Fame	P Eddery
1991	Toulon	P Eddery	Jet Ski Lady	C Roche	Generous	A Munro
1992	User Friendly	G Duffield	User Friendly	G Duffield	Dr Devious	J Reid
1993	Bobs Return	P Robinson	Intrepidity	M Roberts	Commander-in-Chief	M J Kinane
1994	Moonax	P Eddery	Balanchine	L Dettori	Erhaab	W Carson
1995	Classic Cliché	L Dettori	Moonshell	L Dettori	Lammtarra	W Swinburn
1996	Shantou	L Dettori	Lady Carla	P Eddery	Shaamit	M Hills
1997	Silver Patriarch	P Eddery	Reams of Verse	K Fallon	Benny the Dip	W Ryan
1998	Nedawi	J Reid	Shahtoush	M J Kinane	High Rise	O Peslier
1999	Mutafaweq	R Hills	Ramruma	K Fallon	Oath	K Fallon
2000	Millenary	T Quinn	Love Divine	T Quinn	Sinndar	J Murtagh
2001	Milan	M J Kinane	Imagine	M J Kinane	Galileo	M J Kinane
2002	Bollin Eric	K Darley	Kazzia	L Dettori	High Chaparral	J Murtagh
2003			Casual Look	M Dwyer	Kris Kin	K Fallon

	2000 Guineas		1000 Guineas		Grand National	
Year	Horse	Jockey	Horse	Jockey	Horse	Jockey
1809	Wizard	W Clift	—	—	—	—
1810	Hephestion	F Buckle	—	—	—	—
1811	Trophonius	S Barnard	—	—	—	—
1812	Cwrw	S Chifney	—	—	—	—
1813	Smolensko	H Miller	—	—	—	—
1814	Olive	W Arnold	Charlotte	W Clift	—	—
1815	Tigris	W Arnold	Brown foal by Selim	W Clift	—	—
1816	Nectar	W Arnold	Rhoda	S Barnard	—	—
1817	Manfred	W Wheatley	Neva	W Arnold	—	—
1818	Interpreter	W Clift	Corinne	F Buckle	—	—
1819	Antar	E Edwards	Catgut	F Buckle	—	—
1820	Pindarrie	F Buckle	Rowena	F Buckle	—	—
1821	Reginald	F Buckle	Zeal	F Buckle	—	—
1822	Pastille	F Buckle	Whizgig	F Buckle	—	—
1823	Nicolo	W Wheatley	Zinc	F Buckle	—	—
1824	Schariar	W Wheatley	Cobweb	J Robinson	—	—
1825	Enamel	J Robinson	Tontine	W Alkover	—	—
1826	Dervise	J B Day	Problem	J Day	—	—
1827	Turcoman	F Buckle	Arab	F Buckle	—	—
1828	Cadland	J Robinson	Zoe	J Robinson	—	—
1829	Patron	F Boyce	B foal by Godolphin	Arnull	—	—
1830	Augustus	P Conolly	Charlotte West	J Robinson	—	—
1831	Riddlesworth	J Robinson	Galantine	P Conolly	—	—
1832	Archibald	Pavis	Galata	Arnull	—	—
1833	Clearwell	J Robinson	Tarantella	Wright	—	—
1834	Glencoe	J Robinson	May-Day	J Day	—	—
1835	Ibrahim	J Robinson	Preserve	E Flatman	—	—
1836	Bay Middleton	J Robinson	Destiny	J Day	—	—
1837	Achmet	E Edwards	Chapeau d'Espagne	J Day	The Duke (Maghull)	Mr Potts
1838	Grey Momus	J B Day	Barcarolle	E Edwards	Sir Henry (Maghull)	T Olliver
1839	The Corsair	Wakefield	Cara	G Edwards	Lottery (Liverpool)	Jem Mason
1840	Crucifix	J B Day	Crucifix	J Day	Jerry	Mr Bretherton
1841	Ralph	J B Day	Potentia	J Robinson	Charity	Mr Powell
1842	Meteor	W Scott	Firebrand	S Rogers	Gaylad	T Olliver

	2000 Guineas		1000 Guineas		Grand National	
Year	Horse	Jockey	Horse	Jockey	Horse	Jockey
1843	Cotherstone	W Scott	Extempore	S Chifney	Vanguard	T Olliver
1844	The Ugly Buck	J Day Jnr	Sorella	J Robinson	Discount	Crickmere
1845	Idas	E Flatman	Pic-nic	W Abdale	Cure-all	W G Loft
1846	Sir Tatton Sykes	W Scott	Mendicant	S Day	Pioneer	Taylor
1847	Conyngham	J Robinson	Clementina	E Flatman	Matthew	D Wynne
1848	Flatcatcher	J Robinson	Canezou	F Butler	Chandler	Capt Little
1849	Nunnykirk	F Butler	Flea	A Day	Peter Simple	T Cunningham
1850	Pitsford	A Day	Chestnut foal by Slane	F Butler	Abdel Kader	C Green
1851	Hernandez	E Flatman	Aphrodite	J Marson	Abdel Kader	T Abbot
1852	Stockwell	Norman	Kate	A Day	Miss Mowbray	Mr A Goodman
1853	West Australian	F Butler	Mentmore Lass	Charlton	Peter Simple	T Olliver
1854	The Hermit	A Day	Virago	J Wells	Bourton	Tasker
1855	Lord of the Isles	Aldcroft	Habena	S Rogers	Wanderer	J Hanlon
1856	Fazzaletto	E Flatman	Manganese	J Osborne	Freetrader	G Stevens
1857	Vedette	J Osborne	Imperieuse	E Flatman	Emigrant	C Boyce
1858	Fitz-Roland	J Wells	Governess	Ashmall	Little Charley	W Archer
1859	The Promised Land	A Day	Mayonnaise	G Fordham	Half Caste	C Green
1860	The Wizard	Ashmall	Sagitta	Aldcroft	Anatis	Mr Thomas
1861	Diophantus	A Edwards	Nemesis	G Fordham	Jealousy	J Kendall
1862	The Marquis	Ashmall	Hurricane	Ashmall	Huntsman	H Lamplugh
1863	Macaroni	T Challoner	Lady Augusta	A Edwards	Emblem	G Stevens
1864	General Peel	Aldcroft	Tomato	J Wells	Emblematic	G Stevens
1865	Gladiateur	H Grimshaw	Siberia	G Fordham	Alcibiade	Capt Coventry
1866	Lord Lyon	Thomas	Repulse	T Cannon	Salamander	Mr A Goodman
1867	Vauban	G Fordham	Achievement	H Custance	Cortolvin	J Page
1868	Moslem	T Challoner	Formosa	G Fordham	The Lamb	Mr Edwards
1869	Pretender	J Osborne	Scottish Queen	G Fordham	The Colonel	G Stevens
1870	Macgregor	J Daley	Hester	J Grimshaw	The Colonel	G Stevens
1871	Bothwell	J Osborne	Hannah	C Maidment	The Lamb	Mr Thomas
1872	Prince Charlie	J Osborne	Reine	H Parry	Casse Tete	J Page
1873	Gang Forward	T Challoner	Cecilia	J Morris	Disturbance	J M Richardson
1874	Atlantic	F Archer	Apology	J Osborne	Reugny	J M Richardson
1875	Camballo	J Osborne	Spinaway	F Archer	Pathfinder	Mr Thomas
1876	Petrarch	Luke	Camelia	T Glover	Regal	J Cannon
1877	Chamant	J Goater	Belphoebe	H Jeffery	Austerlitz	Mr F G Hobson
1878	Pilgrimage	T Cannon	Pilgrimage	T Cannon	Shifnal	J Jones
1879	Charibert	F Archer	Wheel of Fortune	F Archer	The Liberator	G Moore
1880	Petronel	G Fordham	Elizabeth	C Wood	Empress	T Beasley
1881	Peregrine	F Webb	Thebais	G Fordham	Woodbrook	T Beasley
1882	Shotover	T Cannon	St Marguerite	C Wood	Seaman	Lord Manners
1883	Galliard	F Archer	Hauteur	G Fordham	Zoedone	Count Kinsky
1884	Scot-free	Platt	Busybody	T Cannon	Voluptuary	Mr E P Wilson
1885	Paradox	F Archer	Farewell	G Barrett	Roquefort	Mr E P Wilson
1886	Ormonde	G Barrett	Miss Jummy	J Watts	Old Joe	T Skelton
1887	Enterprise	T Cannon	Reve d'Or	C Wood	Gamecock	W Daniells
1888	Ayrshire	J Osborne	Briar-root	W Warne	Playfair	Mawson
1889	Enthusiast	T Cannon	Minthe	J Woodburn	Frigate	T Beasley
1890	Surefoot	Liddiard	Semolina	J Watts	Ilex	A Nightingall
1891	Common	G Barrett	Mimi	F Rickaby	Come Away	H Beasley
1892	Bonavista	W Robinson	La Fleche	G Barrett	Father O'Flynn	Capt Owen
1893	Isinglass	T Loates	Siffleuse	T Loates	Cloister	Dollery
1894	Ladas	J Watts	Amiable	W Bradford	Why Not	A Nightingall
1895	Kirkconnel	J Watts	Galeottia	F Pratt	Wildman From Borneo	J Widger
1896	St Frusquin	T Loates	Thais	J Watts	The Soarer	D Campbell
1897	Galtee More	C Wood	Chelandry	J Watts	Manifesto	T Kavanagh
1898	Disraeli	S Loates	Nun Nicer	S Loates	Drogheda	J Gourley
1899	Flying Fox	M Cannon	Sibola	J T Sloan	Manifesto	G Williamson
1900	Diamond Jubilee	H Jones	Winifreda	S Loates	Ambush II	A Anthony
1901	Handicapper	W Halsey	Aida	D Maher	Grudon	A Nightingall
1902	Sceptre	H Randall	Sceptre	H Randall	Shannon Lass	D Read
1903	Rock Sand	J H Martin	Quintessence	H Randall	Drumcree	P Woodland
1904	St Amant	K Cannon	Pretty Polly	W Lane	Moifaa	A Birch
1905	Vedas	H Jones	Cherry Lass	G McCall	Kirkland	F Mason
1906	Gorgos	H Jones	Flair	B Dillon	Ascetic's Silver	Hon A Hastings
1907	Slieve Gallion	W Higgs	Witch Elm	B Lynham	Eremon	A Newey
1908	Norman III	O Madden	Rhodora	L Lyne	Rubio	H B Bletsoe
1909	Minoru	H Jones	Electra	B Dillon	Lutteur III	G Parfrement

Year	2000 Guineas Horse	Jockey	1000 Guineas Horse	Jockey	Grand National Horse	Jockey
1910	Neil Gow	D Maher	Winkipop	B Lynham	Jenkinstown	R Chadwick
1911	Sunstar	G Stern	Atmah	F Fox	Glenside	J R Anthony
1912	Sweeper II	D Maher	Tagalie	L H Hewitt	Jerry M	E Piggott
1913	Louvois	J Reiff	Jest	F Rickaby Jnr	Covetcoat	P Woodland
1914	Kennymore	G Stern	Princess Dorrie	W Huxley	Sunloch	W J Smith
1915	Pommern	S Donoghue	Vaucluse	F Rickaby Jnr	Ally Sloper	J R Anthony
1916	Clarissimus	J Clark	Canyon	F Rickaby Jnr	Vermouth	J Reardon
1917	Gay Crusader	S Donoghue	Diadem	F Rickaby Jnr	Ballymacad	E Driscoll
1918	Gainsborough	J Childs	Ferry	B Carslake	Poethlyn	E Piggott
1919	The Panther	R Cooper	Roseway	A Whalley	Poethlyn	E Piggott
1920	Tetratema	B Carslake	Cinna	W Griggs	Troytown	J R Anthony
1921	Craig An Eran	J Brennan	Bettina	G Bellhouse	Shaun Spadah	F B Rees
1922	St Louis	G Archibald	Silver Urn	B Carslake	Music Hall	F B Rees
1923	Ellangowan	C Elliot	Tranquil	E Gardner	Sgt Murphy	Capt Bennet
1924	Diophon	G Hulme	Plack	E C Elliott	Master Robert	R Trudgill
1925	Manna	S Donoghue	Saucy Sue	F Bullock	Double Chance	Major Wilson
1926	Colorado	T Weston	Pillion	R Perryman	Jack Horner	W Watkinson
1927	Adam's Apple	J Leach	Cresta Run	A Balding	Sprig	T E Leader
1928	Flamingo	C Elliot	Scuttle	J Childs	Tipperary Tim	W P Dutton
1929	Mr Jinks	H Beasley	Taj Mah	W Sibbritt	Gregalach	R Everett
1930	Diolite	F Fox	Fair Isle	T Weston	Shaun Goilin	T Cullinan
1931	Cameronian	J Childs	Four Course	E C Elliott	Grakle	R Lyall
1932	Orwell	R Jones	Kandy	E C Elliott	Forbra	J Hamey
1933	Rodosto	R Brethes	Brown Betty	J Childs	Kellsboro Jack	D Williams
1934	Colombo	W Johnstone	Campanula	H Wragg	Golden Miller	G Wilson
1935	Bahram	F Fox	Mesa	W R Johnstone	Reynoldstown	F C Furlong
1936	Pay Up	R Dick	Tide-Way	R Perryman	Reynoldstown	F T Walwyn
1937	Le Ksar	C Semblat	Exhibitionist	S Donoghue	Royal Mail	E Williams
1938	Pasch	G Richards	Rockfel	S Wragg	Battleship	Bruce Hobbs
1939	Blue Peter	E Smith	Galatea II	R A Jones	Workman	T Hyde
1940	Djebel	C Elliot	Godiva	D Marks	Bogskar	M Jones
1941	Lambert Simnel	C Elliot	Dancing Time	R Perryman	no race	—
1942	Big Game	G Richards	Sun Chariot	G Richards	no race	—
1943	Kingsway	S Wragg	Herringbone	H Wragg	no race	—
1944	Garden Path	H Wragg	Picture Play	E C Elliott	no race	—
1945	Court Martial	C Richards	Sun Stream	H Wragg	no race	—
1946	Happy Knight	T Weston	Hypericum	D Smith	Lovely Cottage	Capt R Petre
1947	Tudor Minstrel	G Richards	Imprudence	W R Johnstone	Caughoo	E Dempsey
1948	My Babu	C Smirke	Queenpot	G Richards	Sheila's Cottage	A P Thompson
1949	Nimbus	C Elliot	Musidora	E Britt	Russian Hero	L McMorrow
1950	Palestine	C Smirke	Camaree	W R Johnstone	Freebooter	J Power
1951	Ki Ming	A Breasley	Belle Of All	G Richards	Nickel Coin	J A Bullock
1952	Thunderhead II	R Poincelet	Zabara	K Gethin	Teal	A P Thompson
1953	Nearula	E Britt	Happy Laughter	E Mercer	Early Mist	B Marshall
1954	Darius	E Mercer	Festoon	A Breasley	Royal Tan	B Marshall
1955	Our Babu	D Smith	Meld	W H Carr	Quare Times	P Taaffe
1956	Gilles de Retz	F Barlow	Honeylight	E Britt	E.S.B.	D V Dick
1957	Crepello	L Piggott	Rose Royale II	C Smirke	Sundew	F Winter
1958	Pall Mall	D Smith	Bella Paola	S Boullenger	Mr What	A R Freeman
1959	Taboun	G Moore	Petite Etoile	D Smith	Oxo	M Scudamore
1960	Martial	R Hutchinson	Never Too Late	R Poincelet	Merryman II	G Scott
1961	Rockavon	N Stirk	Sweet Solera	W Rickaby	Nicolaus Silver	R Beasley
1962	Privy Councillor	W Rickaby	Abermaid	W Williamson	Kilmore	F Winter
1963	Only For Life	J Lindley	Hula Dancer	R Poincelet	Ayala	P Buckley
1964	Baldric II	W Pyers	Pourparler	G Bougoure	Team Spirit	W Robinson
1965	Niksar	D Keith	Night Off	W Williamson	Jay Trump	T Smith
1966	Kashmir II	J Lindley	Glad Rags	P Cook	Anglo	T Norman
1967	Royal Palace	G Moore	Fleet	G Moore	Foinavon	J Buckingham
1968	Sir Ivor	L Piggott	Caergwrle	A Barclay	Red Alligator	B Fletcher
1969	Right Tack	G Lewis	Full Dress II	R Hutchinson	Highland Wedding	E Harty
1970	Nijinsky	L Piggott	Humble Duty	L Piggott	Gay Trip	P Taaffe
1971	Brigadier Gerard	J Mercer	Altesse Royale	Y Saint-Martin	Specify	J Cook
1972	High Top	W Carson	Waterloo	E Hide	Well To Do	G Thorner
1973	Mon Fils	F Durr	Mysterious	G Lewis	Red Rum	B Fletcher
1974	Nonoalco	Y Saint-Martin	Highclere	J Mercer	Red Rum	B Fletcher
1975	Bolkonski	G Dettori	Nocturnal Spree	J Roe	L'Escargot	T Carberry
1976	Wollow	G Dettori	Flying Water	Y Saint-Martin	Rag Trade	J Burke
1977	Nebbiolo	G Curran	Mrs McArdy	E Hide	Red Rum	T Stack
1978	Roland Gardens	F Durr	Enstone Spark	E Johnson	Lucius	R Davies
1979	Tap on Wood	S Cauthen	One in a Million	J Mercer	Rubstic	M Barnes

Year	2000 Guineas		1000 Guineas		Grand National	
	Horse	Jockey	Horse	Jockey	Horse	Jockey
1980	Known Fact	W Carson	Quick as Lightning	B Rouse	Ben Nevis	C Fenwick
1981	To-Agori-Mou	G Starkey	Fairy Footsteps	L Piggott	Aldaniti	R Champion
1982	Zino	F Head	On the House	J Reid	Grittar	R Saunders
1983	Lomond	P Eddery	Ma Biche	F Head	Corbiere	B De Haan
1984	El Gran Señor	P Eddery	Pebbles	P Robinson	Hallo Dandy	N Doughty
1985	Shadeed	L Piggott	Oh So Sharp	S Cauthen	Last Suspect	H Davies
1986	Dancing Brave	G Starkey	Midway Lady	R Cochrane	West Tip	R Dunwoody
1987	Don't Forget Me	W Carson	Miesque	F Head	Maori Venture	S Knight
1988	Doyoun	W Swinburn	Ravinella	G Moore	Rhyme 'n Reason	B Powell
1989	Nashwan	W Carson	Musical Bliss	W Swinburn	Little Polveir	J Frost
1990	Tirol	M Kinane	Salsabil	W Carson	Mr Frisk	Mr M Armytage
1991	Mystiko	M Roberts	Shadayid	W Carson	Seagram	N Hawke
1992	Rodrigo De Triano	L Piggott	Hatoof	W Swinburn	Party Politics	C Llewellyn
1993	Zafonic	P Eddery	Sayyedati	W Swinburn	no race	—
1994	Mr Baileys	J Weaver	Las Meninas	J Reid	Minnehoma	R Dunwoody
1995	Pennekamp	T Jarnet	Harayir	R Hills	Royal Athlete	J Titley
1996	Mark of Esteem	L Dettori	Bosra Sham	P Eddery	Rough Quest	M Fitzgerald
1997	Entrepreneur	M J Kinane	Sleepytime	K Fallon	Lord Gyllene	A Dobbin
1998	King of Kings	M J Kinane	Cape Verdi	L Dettori	Earth Summit	C Llewellyn
1999	Island Sands	L Dettori	Wince	K Fallon	Bobbyjo	P Carberry
2000	King's Best	K Fallon	Lahan	R Hills	Papillon	R Walsh
2001	Golan	K Fallon	Ameerat	P Robinson	Red Marauder	R Guest
2002	Rock of Gibraltar	J Murtagh	Kazzia	L Dettori	Bindaree	J Culloty
2003	Refuse to Bend	P Smullen	Russian Rhythm	K Fallon	Monty's Pass	B Geraghty

Horse Racing: General Information

all weather tracks: UK	Lingfield, Southwell, Wolverhampton
autumn double	Cesarewitch and Cambridgeshire
champion jockey: 13 times in a row	E Flatman (1840–52) and Fred Archer (1874–86)
champion jockey: shot himself	Fred Archer (aged 29)
Cheltenham Gold Cup: won five times in row	Golden Miller (1932–36)
classics: jockey won most	Lester Piggott (30)
crash helmets: made compulsory	1924
Derby: inaugurated by	Sir Charles Bunbury
Derby: longest winning distance	Shergar (10 lengths)
Derby: where run during WW2	Newmarket (1940–45)
flat jockey: champion most times	Gordon Richards (26)
Fred Archer: nickname	The Tinman
French Derby: run	Chantilly
Gary Bardwell: nickname	The Angry Ant
Grand National winner: future monarch owned	Ambush II (King Edward VII in 1900)
Grand National: 1st woman jockey	Charlotte Brew (1977)
Grand National: 1st woman jockey to complete	Geraldine Rees
Grand National: number of fences	30
Grand National: royal horse that collapsed	Devon Loch, ridden by Dick Francis
Grand National: where run during WW1	Gatwick (1916–18) as 'War National Chase' (1917–18), and 'Race Course Association Chase' 1916
Grand National: youngest winning rider	Bruce Hobbs on Battleship in 1938 aged 17
harness racing: gaits	trotting (striding with horse's left front and right rear leg synchronised) pacing (moving both legs on one side of body at the same time)
harness racing: vehicle pulled	sulky
Harry Wragg: nickname	The Head Waiter
Irish Classics: run	all at the Curragh
Irish Grand National: run	Fairyhouse
Irish Grand National: woman jockey won	Ann Ferris
jockey: 1st knighted	Gordon Richards
Lester Piggott: 1st winner	The Chase (1948)
Lester Piggott: nickname	The Long Fellow
mare: age filly becomes	five
Melbourne Cup: run	Flemington Park
Oaks: where run during WW2	Newmarket (1940–45)
pacing: US Triple Crown	William H Cane Futurity (1955); Messenger Stake (1957); Little Brown Jug (1946)

racehorse birthdays	1 January (Northern Hemisphere) and 1 August (Southern Hemisphere)
racehorses: maximum letters in name	18
racing colours: Her Majesty the Queen	purple, gold braid, scarlet sleeves, black velvet cap with gold fringe
racing colours: Queen Elizabeth the Queen Mother	blue, buff stripes, blue sleeves, black cap, gold tassel
Scottish Grand National: run	Ayr
spring double	Lincoln and Grand National
stallion: age colt becomes	five
starting stalls: 1st used in UK	Newmarket in 1965 (8 July)
thoroughbred: ancestry	Darley Arabian, Byerly Turk, Godolphin Arabian (aka barb)
trotting: US Triple Crown	Hambleton (commenced 1926); Yonkers Futurity (1958); Kentucky Futurity (1893)
US Triple Crown	Kentucky Derby (1st of the season), Preakness Stakes, Belmont Stakes (last of the season)
virtual racetracks	Portman Park (Flat) Steepledown (Jumps)
Welsh Grand National: run	Chepstow

Motor Racing: Formula 1 World Champions

Year	Winning driver	Country	Car	Runner-up	Constructor Championship
1950	Giuseppe Farina	Italy	Alfa Romeo	Juan Manuel Fangio	—
1951	Juan Manuel Fangio	Argentina	Alfa Romeo	Alberto Ascari	—
1952	Alberto Ascari	Italy	Ferrari	Giuseppe Farina	—
1953	Alberto Ascari	Italy	Ferrari	Juan Manuel Fangio	—
1954	Juan Manuel Fangio	Argentina	Maserati/Mercedes	Jose Gonzalez (Argentina)	—
1955	Juan Manuel Fangio	Argentina	Mercedes-Benz	Stirling Moss (GB)	—
1956	Juan Manuel Fangio	Argentina	Lancia-Ferrari	Stirling Moss (GB)	—
1957	Juan Manuel Fangio	Argentina	Maserati	Stirling Moss (GB)	—
1958	Mike Hawthorn	UK	Ferrari	Stirling Moss (GB)	Vanwall
1959	Jack Brabham	Australia	Cooper-Climax	Tony Brooks (GB)	Cooper-Climax
1960	Jack Brabham	Australia	Cooper-Climax	Bruce McLaren (NZL)	Cooper-Climax
1961	Phil Hill	USA	Ferrari	Wolfgang von Trips (W. Germany)	Ferrari
1962	Graham Hill	UK	BRM	Jim Clark	BRM
1963	Jim Clark	UK	Lotus-Climax	Graham Hill	Lotus-Climax
1964	John Surtees	UK	Ferrari	Graham Hill	Ferrari
1965	Jim Clark	UK	Lotus-Climax	Graham Hill	Lotus-Climax
1966	Jack Brabham	Australia	Brabham-Repco	John Surtees	Brabham-Repco
1967	Denny Hulme	New Zealand	Brabham-Repco	Jack Brabham	Brabham-Repco
1968	Graham Hill	UK	Lotus-Ford	Jackie Stewart	Lotus-Ford
1969	Jackie Stewart	UK	Matra-Ford	Jacky Ickx (Belgium)	Matra-Ford
1970	Jochen Rindt	Austria	Lotus-Ford	Jacky Ickx (Belgium)	Lotus-Ford
1971	Jackie Stewart	UK	Tyrrell-Ford	Ronnie Peterson (Sweden)	Tyrrell-Ford
1972	Emerson Fittipaldi	Brazil	Lotus-Ford	Jackie Stewart	Lotus-Ford
1973	Jackie Stewart	UK	Tyrrell-Ford	Emerson Fittipaldi	Lotus-Ford
1974	Emerson Fittipaldi	Brazil	McLaren-Ford	Clay Regazzoni (Switzerland)	McLaren-Ford
1975	Niki Lauda	Austria	Ferrari	Emerson Fittipaldi	Ferrari
1976	James Hunt	UK	McLaren-Ford	Niki Lauda	Ferrari
1977	Niki Lauda	Austria	Ferrari	Jody Scheckter	Ferrari
1978	Mario Andretti	USA	Lotus-Ford	Ronnie Peterson (Sweden)	Lotus-Ford
1979	Jody Scheckter	South Africa	Ferrari	Gilles Villeneuve (Canada)	Ferrari
1980	Alan Jones	Australia	Williams-Ford	Nelson Piquet	Williams-Ford
1981	Nelson Piquet	Brazil	Brabham-Ford	Carlos Reutemann (Argentina)	Williams-Ford
1982	Keke Rosberg	Finland	Williams-Ford	J Watson (GB) and D Pironi (France)	Ferrari
1983	Nelson Piquet	Brazil	Brabham-BMW	Alain Prost	Ferrari
1984	Niki Lauda	Austria	McLaren-TAG	Alain Prost	McLaren-TAG
1985	Alain Prost	France	McLaren-TAG	Michele Alboreto (Italy)	McLaren-TAG
1986	Alain Prost	France	McLaren-TAG	Nigel Mansell	Williams-Honda
1987	Nelson Piquet	Brazil	Williams-Honda	Nigel Mansell	Williams-Honda
1988	Ayrton Senna	Brazil	McLaren-Honda	Alain Prost	McLaren-Honda
1989	Alain Prost	France	McLaren-Honda	Ayrton Senna	McLaren-Honda
1990	Ayrton Senna	Brazil	McLaren-Honda	Alain Prost	McLaren-Honda
1991	Ayrton Senna	Brazil	McLaren-Honda	Nigel Mansell	McLaren-Honda
1992	Nigel Mansell	UK	Williams-Renault	Ricardo Patrese (Italy)	Williams-Renault
1993	Alain Prost	France	Williams-Renault	Ayrton Senna	Williams-Renault
1994	Michael Schumacher	Germany	Benetton-Ford	Damon Hill	Williams-Renault
1995	Michael Schumacher	Germany	Benetton-Renault	Damon Hill	Williams-Renault
1996	Damon Hill	UK	Williams-Renault	Jacques Villeneuve	Williams-Renault
1997	Jacques Villeneuve	Canada	Williams-Renault	Michael Schumacher	Williams-Renault

SPORT & LEISURE

Year	Winning driver	Country	Car	Runner-up	Constructor Championship
1998	Mika Hakkinen	Finland	McLaren-Mercedes	Michael Schumacher	McLaren-Mercedes
1999	Mika Hakkinen	Finland	McLaren-Mercedes	Eddie Irvine	Ferrari
2000	Michael Schumacher	Germany	Ferrari	Mika Hakkinen	Ferrari
2001	Michael Schumacher	Germany	Ferrari	David Coulthard (UK)	Ferrari
2002	Michael Schumacher	Germany	Ferrari	Rubens Barrichello (Brazil)	Ferrari

Motor Racing: General Information

circuits: Formula 1	Argentinian – Buenos Aires; Australian – Adelaide, Melbourne; Austrian – A1 Ring, Spielberg; Belgian – Spa-Francorchamps, Zolder; Brazilian – São Paolo, Interlagos (Rio de Janeiro); British – Silverstone; Canadian – Montreal; Dutch – Zandvoort; French – Magny Cours, Dijon; German – Hockenheim; Hungarian – Budapest; Italian – Monza; Japanese – Suzuka; Luxembourg – Nurburgring, Germany; Malaysian – Sepang; Mexican – Mexico City; Monaco – Monte Carlo; Portuguese – Estoril; San Marino – Imola; Spanish – Catalunya Montjuich (Barcelona); US – Detroit, Long Beach, Indianapolis. Nurburgring is no longer used for German GP but has been the venue of the European GP in recent years. Similarly, Aida in Japan is no longer used for its own GP but has been the venue for Pacific GP.
Formula 1: flags	black – disqualification of a driver; black and white chequered – end of race; blue – car about to overtake; red – premature end of race; yellow – danger, no overtaking; yellow and red diagonal stripes – oil on track.
Formula 1: most consecutive wins	Alberto Ascari (9).
Formula 1: oldest champion	Juan Manuel Fangio (46).
Formula 1: points system	For the 2003 season points are awarded for the top eight finishers thus: 10, 8, 6, 5, 4, 3, 2, 1.
Formula 1: posthumous champion	Jochen Rindt (1970).
Formula 1: woman driver first	Maria Teresa de Filippis (1958)
fuel: used in Formula 1	pre 1961 nitro-methane, but since 1961 ordinary commercial fuel has been compulsory, although Indianapolis still uses nitro-methane.
Indianapolis 500: first winner	Ray Harroun in Marmon Wasp (1911).
Indianapolis 500: laps	200, (although the race is 500 miles in length, hence the name).
Indianapolis 500: Formula 1 winners	Jim Clark (1965), Graham Hill (1966), Mario Andretti (1969), E Fittipaldi (1989 and 1993), J Villeneuve (1995).
land speed record: holder	Andy Green in Thrust SSC (714 mph). first over 100 mph: Louis Rigolly in 1904.
Monaco GP: five times winner	Graham Hill.
motor cycling: nine championships	Giacomo Agostini of Italy (eight consecutive 1965–72 and 1975 in the 500 cc class).
speedway championships	raced over four laps, the short track world championships commenced in 1936 and long track in 1971.
UK motor racing circuit: first	Brooklands.

Olympic Games: Venues

1896	Athens, Greece		1960	Rome, Italy
1900	Paris, France		1964	Tokyo, Japan
1904	St Louis, USA		1968	Mexico City
1908	London, UK		1972	Munich, Germany
1912	Stockholm, Sweden		1976	Montreal, Canada
1920	Antwerp, Belgium		1980	Moscow, USSR
1924	Paris, France		1984	Los Angeles, USA
1928	Amsterdam, Holland		1988	Seoul, South Korea
1932	Los Angeles, USA		1992	Barcelona, Spain
1936	Berlin, Germany		1996	Atlanta, USA
1948	London, UK		2000	Sydney, Australia
1952	Helsinki, Finland		2004	Athens, Greece
1956	Melbourne, Australia		2008	Beijing, China

Winter Olympics: Venues

1924	Chamonix, France	1972	Sapporo, Japan
1928	St Moritz, Switzerland	1976	Innsbruck, Austria
1932	Lake Placid, NY, USA	1980	Lake Placid, NY, USA
1936	Garmisch Partenkirchen, Germany	1984	Sarajevo, Yugoslavia
1948	St Moritz, Switzerland	1988	Calgary, Canada
1952	Oslo, Norway	1992	Albertville, France
1956	Cortina, Italy	1994	Lillehammer, Norway
1960	Squaw Valley, California, USA	1998	Nagano, Japan
1964	Innsbruck, Austria	2002	Salt Lake City, USA
1968	Grenoble, France	2006	Turin, Italy

Olympics: General Information

ancient Olympics: in honour of	Zeus.
appearances: most	Raymondo d'Inzeo (8).
black power salute	Tommie Smith and John Carlos 1968. (Other man on rostrum was Peter Norman of Australia.)
Briton took part in Summer and Winter Olympics	Derek Allhusen.
British peer gold medallist	The Marquess of Exeter (Lord Burghley) 1928, 400m Hurdles.
cancelled games: intended hosts	1916 – Berlin; 1940 – Tokyo (then Helsinki); 1944 – London.
champions: father and son	Imre Nemeth (Hammer) and Miklos Nemeth (Javelin).
champion: five times in row	Steve Redgrave (Rowing 1984–2000).
champion: four times in row	Al Oerter (Discus 1956–68).
cheat: Modern Pentathlon	Boris Onischenko in Fencing discipline (1976).
country contested every games	UK (both Summer and Winter).
diplomas awarded to	fourth to eighth places.
equestrian events: 1956	held in Stockholm.
extra lap run in error	Steeplechase 1932.
father and son rowing gold medallists	Charles and Richard Burnell.
flag: colours	blue, yellow, black, green, red rings on a white background. (Rings represent the five major continents.)
gold medals: last given	1912 was the last time solid gold medals were given.
gold medal: received by post	Harold Abrahams (1924).
golds: most in single games	Mark Spitz (7) (Swimming 1972).
high jump: youngest champion	Ulrike Mayfarth (16), who was also the oldest winner aged 28.
host country: no golds	Canada (1976).
IOC: presidents	Dimitrios Vikélas (1894–96); Baron de Coubertin (1896–1925); Henri de Baillet-La Tour (1925–42); J. Sigfrid Edström (1946–52); Avery Brundage (1956–72); Michael Morris, Lord Killanin (1972–80); Juan António Samaranch (1980–2001).
marathon: barefoot winner	Abebe Bikila (1960).
marathon: distance standardised	1924 (although first run as 26 miles 385 yds in 1908).
medal withheld for professionalism	Jim Thorpe in 1912 (he was reinstated in 1973).
modern Olympics: instigator	Baron Pierre de Coubertin.
Munich massacre	Black September terrorists killing of Israeli athletes (1972).
oldest Briton to win gold medal	Jerry Milner (60 years old in 1908 when winning Shooting gold).
Olympiad: definition	in ancient Greece the time between games was an Olympiad (four years).
Olympic motto	Citius Altius Fortius (Faster, Higher, Stronger).
opening parade	always led by Greece and completed by the host country.
original location	Olympia (776 BC–AD 393, abolished by Emperor Theodosius I).
POW in World War Two	Harold Cassells (1920 Hockey gold medallist).
sex testing: year began	1968.
swimming: first 100m under 1 minute	Johnny Weismuller (1924) (59 seconds).
walkover: champion	Wyndham Halswelle in the 400m (1908).
woman gold medallist: first	Charlotte Cooper (GB) when she won Tennis Singles (1900).
woman: running, throwing, jumping medals	Mildred 'Babe' Didrikson won gold in 80m Hurdles and Javelin and silver medal in High Jump (1932).
Zatopek gold medal treble	In 1952 Emil Zatopek won 5k, 10k and Marathon.

SPORT & LEISURE

Summer Olympics: British Gold Medal Winners

Name	Date	Sport	Event
Abrahams, Harold	1924	Athletics	4 x 100m Relay
Ainslie, Ben	2000	Sailing	Laser Class
Ainsworth-Davis, Jack	1920	Athletics	4 x 400m Relay
Allhusen, Derek	1968	Equestrian	3-Day Event – Team
Amoore, Edward	1908	Shooting	Small-Bore Rifle Team
Applegarth, Willie	1912	Athletics	4 x 100m Relay
Aspin, John	1908	Yachting	12 Metres Class
Astor, J J	1908	Rackets	Doubles
Atkin, Charles	1920	Hockey	
Attrill, Louis	2000	Rowing	Coxed Eight
Bacon, Stanley	1908	Wrestling	Middleweight Freestyle
Badcock, Felix	1932	Rowing	Coxless Fours
Bailey, Horace	1908	Football	
Baillon, Louis	1908	Hockey	
Barber, Paul	1988	Hockey	
Barrett, Edward	1908	Tug of War	
Barrett, Frederick	1920	Polo	
Barrett, Roper	1908	Lawn Tennis	Indoor Men's Doubles
Barridge, J E	1900	Football	
Bartlett, Charles	1908	Cycling	100km Track Race
Batchelor, Steve	1988	Hockey	
Beachcroft, Charles	1900	Cricket	
Beesly, Richard	1928	Rowing	Coxless Fours
Belville, Miles	1936	Yachting	6 Metres Class
Bennett, Charles	1900	Athletics	1500m
	1900	Athletics	5000m Team
Bennett, John	1920	Hockey	
Bentham, Isaac	1912	Swimming	Water Polo Team
Beresford, Jack	1924	Rowing	Single Sculls
	1932	Rowing	Coxless Fours
	1936	Rowing	Double Sculls
Beresford, John	1900	Polo	
Berry, Arthur	1908	Football	
	1912	Football	
Bevan, Edward	1928	Rowing	Coxless Fours
Bhaura, Kulbir	1988	Hockey	
Bingley, Norman	1908	Yachting	7 Metres Class
Birkett, Arthur	1900	Cricket	
Blackstaffe, Harry	1908	Rowing	Single Sculls
Boardman, Chris	1936	Yachting	6 Metres Class
Boardman, Chris	1992	Cycling	4000m Pursuit
Bond, David	1948	Yachting	Swallow Class
Bowerman, Alfred	1900	Cricket	
Braithwaite, Bob	1968	Shooting	Clay Pigeon
Brasher, Chris	1956	Athletics	3000m Steeplechase
Brebner, Ron	1912	Football	
Brown, Godfrey	1936	Athletics	4 x 400m Relay
Buchanan, John	1908	Yachting	12 Metres Class
Buckenham, Claude	1900	Football	
Buckley, George	1900	Cricket	
Bucknall, Henry	1908	Rowing	Eights
Budgett, Richard	1984	Rowing	Coxed Fours
Bugbee, Charlie	1912	Swimming	Water Polo Team
	1920	Swimming	Water Polo Team
Bullen, Jane	1968	Equestrian	3-Day Event Team
Bunten, James	1908	Yachting	12 Metres Class
Burchell, Francis	1900	Cricket	
Burgess, Edgar	1912	Rowing	Eights
Burghley, Lord David	1928	Athletics	400m Hurdles
Burn, Tom	1912	Football	
Burnell, Charles	1908	Rowing	Eights
Burnell, Richard	1948	Rowing	Double Sculls
Bushnell, Bertie	1948	Rowing	Double Sculls
Butler, Guy	1920	Athletics	4 x 400m Relay
Campbell, Charles	1908	Yachting	8 Metres Class
Campbell, Colin	1920	Hockey	
Canning, George	1920	Tug of War	

Name	Date	Sport	Event
Carnell, Arthur	1908	Shooting	Small-Bore Rifle
Cassels, Harold	1920	Hockey	
Chalk, Alfred	1900	Football	
Chapman, Frederick	1908	Football	
Christian, Fred	1900	Cricket	
Christie, Linford	1992	Athletics	100m
Clift, Robert	1988	Hockey	
Clive, Lewis	1932	Rowing	Coxless Pairs
Coales, Bill	1908	Athletics	3 Miles Team
Cochrane, Blair	1908	Yachting	8 Metres Class
Coe, Sebastian	1980	Athletics	1,500m
	1984	Athletics	1,500m
Coe, Tom	1900	Swimming	Water Polo Team
Coleman, Robert	1920	Yachting	7 Metres Class
Cook, Stephanie	2000	Modern Pentathlon	Individual Event
Cooke, Harold	1920	Hockey	
Cooper, Charlotte	1900	Lawn Tennis	Women's Singles
	1900	Lawn Tennis	Mixed Doubles
Cooper, Malcolm	1984	Shooting	Small-Bore Rifle, three positions
	1988	Shooting	Small-Bore Rifle, three positions
Corbett, Walter	1908	Football	
Corner, Harry	1900	Cricket	
Cornet, George	1908	Swimming	Water Polo Team
	1912	Swimming	Water Polo Team
Cracknell, James	2000	Rowing	Coxless Fours
Crichton, Charles	1908	Yachting	6 Metres Class
Crockford, Eric	1920	Hockey	
Cross, Martin	1984	Rowing	Coxed Fours
Crummack, Rex	1920	Hockey	
Cudmore, Collier	1908	Rowing	Coxless Fours
Cuming, Fred	1900	Cricket	
Currie, Lorne	1900	Yachting	Open Class
	1900	Yachting	0.5–1 Ton Class
Daly, Denis	1900	Polo	
D'Arcy, Vic	1912	Athletics	4 x 100m Relay
Davies, Chris	1972	Yachting	Flying Dutchman Class
Davies, Lynn	1964	Athletics	Long Jump
De Relwyskow, George	1908	Wrestling	Lightweight Freestyle
Deakin, Joe	1908	Athletics	3 Miles Team Race
Dean, Billy	1920	Swimming	Water Polo Team
Dennis, Simon	2000	Rowing	Coxed Eight
Derbyshire, Rob	1900	Swimming	Water Polo Team
	1908	Swimming	4 x 200m Freestyle Relay
Dines, Joe	1912	Football	
Dixon, Charles	1912	Lawn Tennis	Indoor Mixed Doubles
Dixon, Richard	1908	Yachting	7 Metres Class
Dod, William (brother of Lottie)	1908	Archery	York Round
Dodds, Richard	1988	Hockey	
Doherty, Laurie	1900	Lawn Tennis	Men's Singles
	1900	Lawn Tennis	Men's Doubles
Doherty, Reggie	1900	Lawn Tennis	Men's Doubles
(brother of Laurie Doherty)	1900	Lawn Tennis	Mixed Doubles
	1908	Lawn Tennis	Men's Doubles
Donne, William	1900	Cricket	
Douglas, Johnny	1908	Boxing	Middleweight
Douglas, Rowley	2000	Rowing	Coxed Eight
Downes, Arthur	1908	Yachting	12 Metres Class
Downes, Henry (Arthur's brother)	1908	Yachting	12 Metres Class
Dunlop, David	1908	Yachting	12 Metres Class
Easte, Philip	1908	Shooting	Clay Pigeon Team
Eastlake-Smith, Gladys	1908	Lawn Tennis	Indoor Women's Singles
Edwards, Jonathan	2000	Athletics	Triple Jump
Edwards, Jumbo	1932	Rowing	Coxless Pairs
	1932	Rowing	Coxless Fours
Eley, Maxwell	1924	Rowing	Coxless Fours
Elliot, Launceston	1896	Weightlifting	One-Handed Lift
Ellison, Adrian	1984	Rowing	Coxed Fours (cox)
Etherington-Smith, Raymond	1908	Rowing	Eights
Exshaw, William	1900	Yachting	2–3 Ton Class
Faulds, Richard	2000	Shooting	Double Trap
Faulkner, David	1988	Hockey	

Name	Date	Sport	Event
Fenning, John	1908	Rowing	Coxless Pairs
Field-Richards, John	1908	Motor Boating	8 Metres Class
Finnegan, Chris	1968	Boxing	Middleweight
Fleming, John	1908	Shooting	Small-Bore Rifle, moving target
Fleming, Philip	1912	Rowing	Eights
Fletcher, Jennie	1912	Swimming	4 x 100m Freestyle Relay
Forsyth, Charlie	1908	Swimming	Water Polo Team
Foster, Bill	1908	Swimming	4 x 200m Freestyle Relay
Foster, Tim	2000	Rowing	Coxless Fours
Fox, Jim	1976	Modern Pentathlon	Team Event
Freeman, Harry	1908	Hockey	
Garcia, Russell	1988	Hockey	
Garton, Stanley	1912	Rowing	Eights
George, Rowland	1932	Rowing	Coxless Fours
Gillan, Angus	1908	Rowing	Coxless Fours
	1912	Rowing	Eights
Gladstone, Albert	1908	Rowing	Eights
Glen-Coats, Thomas	1908	Yachting	12 Metres Class
Godfree, Kitty	1920	Lawn Tennis	Women's Doubles
Goodfellow, Fred	1908	Tug of War	
Goodhew, Duncan	1980	Swimming	100m Breaststroke
Gordon-Watson, Mary	1972	Equestrian	3-Day Event Team
Gore, Arthur	1908	Lawn Tennis	Indoor Men's Singles
	1908	Lawn Tennis	Indoor Men's Doubles
Gosling, William	1900	Football	
Grace, Fred	1908	Boxing	Lightweight
Green, Eric	1908	Hockey	
Green, Tommy	1932	Athletics	50km Walk
Gretton, John (serving MP)	1900	Yachting	Open Class
	1900	Yachting	0.5–1 Ton Class
Griffiths, Cecil	1920	Athletics	4 x 400m Relay
Grimley, Martyn	1988	Hockey	
Grinham, Judy	1956	Swimming	100m Backstroke
Grubor, Luka	2000	Rowing	Coxed Eight
Gunn, Dick	1908	Boxing	Featherweight
Gunnell, Sally	1992	Athletics	400m Hurdles
Halswelle, Wyndham	1908	Athletics	400m
Hampson, Tommy	1932	Athletics	800m
Hannam, Edith	1912	Lawn Tennis	Indoor Women's Singles
	1912	Lawn Tennis	Indoor Mixed Doubles
Hanney, Ted	1912	Football	
Hardman, Harry	1908	Football	
Harmer, Russell	1936	Yachting	6 Metres Class
Harrison, Audley	2000	Boxing	Super Heavyweight
Haslam, A	1900	Football	
Haslam, Harry	1920	Hockey	
Hawkes, Robert	1908	Football	
Hemery, David	1968	Athletics	400m Hurdles
Herbert, Garry	1992	Rowing	Coxed Pairs (cox)
Hill, Albert	1920	Athletics	800m
	1920	Athletics	1,500m
Hill, Arthur	1912	Swimming	Water Polo Team
Hill, Bertie	1956	Equestrian	3-Day Event Team
Hillyard, George	1908	Lawn Tennis	Men's Doubles
Hirons, Bill	1908	Tug of War	
Hoare, Gordon	1912	Football	
Hodge, Percy	1920	Athletics	3,000m Steeplechase
Holman, Fred	1908	Swimming	200m Breaststroke
Holmes, Andy	1984	Rowing	Coxed Fours
	1988	Rowing	Coxless Pairs
Holmes, Fred	1920	Tug of War	
Horsfall, Ewart	1912	Rowing	Eights
Humby, Harry	1908	Shooting	Small-Bore Rifle Team
Humphreys, Fred	1908	Tug of War	
	1920	Tug of War	
Hunt, Kenneth	1908	Football	
Hunt-Davis, Ben	2000	Rowing	Coxed Eight
Ireton, Albert	1908	Tug of War	
Jacobs, David	1912	Athletics	4 x 100m Relay
Jarvis, John Arthur	1900	Swimming	1,000m Freestyle
	1900	Swimming	4,000m Freestyle

Name	Date	Sport	Event
Johnson, Victor	1908	Cycling	One-Lap Race
Johnstone, Banner	1908	Rowing	Eights
Jones, Ben	1908	Cycling	5,000m Track Race
	1908	Cycling	Three-Lap Pursuit
Jones, Ben	1968	Equestrian	3-Day Event Team
Jones, Chris	1920	Swimming	Water Polo Team
Jones, J H	1900	Football	
Keene, Foxhall	1900	Polo	
Kelly, Fred	1908	Rowing	Eights
Kemp, Peter	1900	Swimming	Water Polo Team
Kerly, Sean	1988	Hockey	
Kingsbury, Clarrie	1908	Cycling	20km Track Race
	1908	Cycling	Three-Lap Pursuit
Kinnear, Wally	1912	Rowing	Single Sculls
Kirby, Alister	1912	Rowing	Eights
Kirkwood, Jimmy	1988	Hockey	
Knight, Arthur	1912	Football	
Lambert-Chambers, Dolly	1908	Lawn Tennis	Women's Singles
Lance, Tommy	1920	Cycling	2,000m Tandem
Lander, John	1928	Rowing	Coxless Fours
Larner, George	1908	Athletics	3,500m and 10 Mile Walk
Laurie, Ran	1948	Rowing	Coxless Pairs
Laws, Gilbert	1908	Yachting	6 Metres Class
Leaf, Charles	1936	Yachting	6 Metres Class
Leighton, Arthur	1920	Hockey	
Leman, Richard	1988	Hockey	
Lessimore, Edward	1912	Shooting	Small-Bore Rifle Team, 50m
Lewis, Denise	2000	Athletics	Heptathlon
Liddell, Eric	1924	Athletics	400m
Lindsay, Andrew	2000	Rowing	Coxed Eight
Lindsay, Robert	1920	Athletics	4 x 400m Relay
Lister, Bill	1900	Swimming	Water Polo Team
Littlewort, Henry	1912	Football	
Llewellyn, Sir Harry (Foxhunter)	1952	Equestrian	Prix des Nations Team
Lockett, Vivian	1920	Polo	
Logan, Gerald	1908	Hockey	
Lonsbrough, Anita	1960	Swimming	200m Breaststroke
Lowe, Douglas	1924	Athletics	800m
	1928	Athletics	800m
McBryan, Jack	1920	Hockey	
MacDonald-Smith, Iain	1968	Yachting	Flying Dutchman Class
McGrath, George	1920	Hockey	
Macintosh, Henry	1920	Athletics	4 x 100m Relay
McIntyre, Mike	1988	Yachting	Star Class
Mackay, Frank (USA born)	1900	Polo	
McKenzie, John	1908	Yachting	12 Metres Class
MacKinnon, Duncan	1908	Rowing	Coxless Fours
Mackworth-Praed, Cyril	1924	Shooting	Running Deer (double shot)
MacLagen, Gilchrist	1908	Rowing	Eights
McMeekin, Tom	1908	Yachting	6 Metres Class
Macnabb, James	1924	Rowing	Coxless Fours
McNair, Winifred	1920	Lawn Tennis	Women's Doubles
McTaggart, Dick	1956	Boxing	Lightweight
McWhirter, Douglas	1912	Football	
Maddison, W.J.	1920	Yachting	7 Metres Class
Mallin, Harry	1920	Boxing	Middleweight
(retired undefeated 300 fights)	1924	Boxing	Middleweight
Marcon, Sholto	1920	Hockey	
Martin, Albert	1908	Yachting	12 Metres Class
Martin, Leonard	1936	Yachting	6 Metres Class
Martin, Steve (played 1 minute)	1988	Hockey	
Matthews, Ken	1964	Athletics	20km Walk
Matthews, M K	1908	Shooting	Small-Bore Rifle Team
Maunder, Alex	1908	Shooting	Clay Pigeon Team
Meade, Richard	1968	Equestrian	3-Day Event Team
	1972	Equestrian	3-Day Event and Team
Melvill, Tim	1920	Polo	
Meredith, Leon	1908	Cycling	Three-Lap Pursuit
Merriman, Fred	1908	Tug of War	
Miller, Charles	1908	Polo	
Miller, George (brother of Charles)	1908	Polo	

SPORT&LEISURE

Name	Date	Sport	Event
Millner, Jerry	1908	Shooting	Free Rifle
Mills, Edwin	1908	Tug of War	
	1920	Tug of War	
Mitchell, Harry	1924	Boxing	Light-Heavyweight
Moore, Bella	1912	Swimming	4 x 100m Freestyle Relay
Moore, F W	1908	Shooting	Clay Pigeon Team
Moorhouse, Adrian	1988	Swimming	100m Breaststroke
Morris, Stewart	1948	Yachting	Swallow Class
Morrison, Robert	1924	Rowing	Coxless Fours
Morton, Lucy	1924	Swimming	200m Breaststroke
Murray, Robert	1912	Shooting	Small-Bore Rifle Team
Neame, Philip	1924	Shooting	Running Deer (double shot)
(only man to be awarded Victoria Cross, knighthood and Olympic gold)			
Nevinson, George	1908	Swimming	Water Polo Team
Newall, Queenie	1908	Archery	National Round
Nicholas, J	1900	Football	
Nickalls, Guy	1908	Rowing	Eights
Nickalls, Patteson	1908	Polo	
Nightingale, Danny	1976	Modern Pentathlon	Team Event
Noble, Alan	1908	Hockey	
Noel, Evan	1908	Rackets	Singles
O'Kelly, Con	1908	Wrestling	Heavyweight, Freestyle
Oldman, Albert	1908	Boxing	Heavyweight
Osborn, John	1976	Yachting	Tornado Class
Ovett, Steve	1980	Athletics	800m
Packer, Ann	1964	Athletics	800m
Page, Edgar	1908	Hockey	
Palmer, Charles	1908	Shooting	Clay Pigeon Team
Pappin, Veryan	1988	Hockey	
Parker, Adrian	1976	Modern Pentathlon	Team Event
Parker, Bridget	1972	Equestrian	3-Day Event Team
Pattisson, Rodney	1968	Yachting	Flying Dutchman Class
	1972	Yachting	Flying Dutchman Class
Payne, Ernest	1908	Cycling	Three-Lap Pursuit
(known as the Worcester Wonder, Payne changed sports to become a Manchester Utd footballer)			
Peacock, Bill	1920	Swimming	Water Polo Team
Pennell, Vane	1908	Rackets	Doubles
Pepe, Joseph	1912	Shooting	Small-Bore Rifle Team, 50m
Percy, Iain	2000	Sailing	Finn Class
Perry, Herbert	1924	Shooting	Running Deer (double shot)
Peters, Mary	1972	Athletics	Pentathlon
Phillips, Mark	1972	Equestrian	3-Day Event Team
Pike, J F	1908	Shooting	Clay Pigeon Team
Pimm, William	1908	Shooting	Small-Bore Rifle Team
	1912	Shooting	Small-Bore Rifle Team, 50m
Pinsent, Matthew	1992	Rowing	Coxless Pairs
	1996	Rowing	Coxless Pairs
	2000	Rowing	Coxless Fours
Postans, J M	1908	Shooting	Clay Pigeon Team
Potter, Jonathan	1988	Hockey	
Powlesland, Alfred	1900	Cricket	
Pridmore, Reggie	1908	Hockey	
Purcell, Noel	1920	Swimming	Water Polo Team
(Purcell was also an Irish rugby international)			
Purnell, Clyde	1908	Football	
Quash, Bill	1900	Football	
Queally, Jason	2000	Cycling	Kilometre Sprint
Radmilovic, Paul	1908	Swimming	Water Polo Team
	1908	Swimming	4 x 200m Freestyle Relay
	1912	Swimming	Water Polo Team
	1920	Swimming	Water Polo Team
Rampling, Godfrey	1936	Athletics	4 x 400m Relay
Rand, Mary	1964	Athletics	Long Jump
(Mary won the full set of medals with silver in Pentathlon and bronze in the relay)			
Rawlinson, Alfred	1900	Polo	
Rawson, Ronald	1920	Boxing	Heavyweight

Name	Date	Sport	Event
Redgrave, Steve	1984	Rowing	Coxed Fours
	1988	Rowing	Coxless Pairs
	1992	Rowing	Coxless Pairs
	1996	Rowing	Coxless Pairs
	2000	Rowing	Coxless Fours
Redwood, Bernard	1908	Motor Boating	8 Metres Class
	1908	Motor Boating	Under 60-Foot Class
Rees, Percy	1908	Hockey	
Rhodes, John	1908	Yachting	8 Metres Class
Rimmer, J T	1900	Athletics	4,000m Steeplechase
	1900	Athletics	5,000m Team Race
Ritchie, Major	1908	Lawn Tennis	Men's Singles
Rivett-Carnac, Charles	1908	Yachting	7 Metres Class
Rivett-Carnac, Frances	1908	Yachting	7 Metres Class
(wife of Charles)			
Roberts, Bill	1936	Athletics	4 x 400m Relay
Robertson, Arthur	1908	Athletics	Three Miles Team Race
Robertson, Arthur	1900	Swimming	Water Polo Team
Robertson, Shirley	2000	Sailing	Europe Dinghy Class
Robinson, Eric	1900	Swimming	Water Polo Team
Robinson, John	1908	Hockey	
Robinson, Sidney	1900	Athletics	5,000m Team Race
Rook, Laurence	1956	Equestrian	3-Day Event Team
Russell, Arthur	1908	Athletics	3,200m Steeplechase
Ryan, Harry	1920	Cycling	2,000m Tandem
Sanders, Terence	1924	Rowing	Coxless Fours
Sanderson, Ronald	1908	Rowing	Eights
Sanderson, Tessa	1984	Athletics	Javelin
Scarlett, Fred	2000	Rowing	Coxed Eight
Searle, Greg	1992	Rowing	Coxed Pairs
Searle, Jonny	1992	Rowing	Coxed Pairs
Sewell, John	1912	Tug of War	
	1920	Tug of War	
Sharpe, Ivan	1912	Football	
Sheen, Gillian	1956	Fencing	Individual Foil
Shepherd, John	1908	Tug of War	
	1920	Tug of War	
Sherwani, Imran	1988	Hockey	
Shoveller, Stanley	1908	Hockey	
	1920	Hockey	
Smith, Charles	1908	Swimming	Water Polo Team
	1912	Swimming	Water Polo Team
	1920	Swimming	Water Polo Team
Smith, Faulder	1920	Hockey	
Smith, Herbert	1908	Football	
Somers-Smith, John	1908	Rowing	Coxless Fours
Southwood, Dick	1936	Rowing	Double Sculls
Spackman, F G	1900	Football	
Spiers, Annie	1912	Swimming	4 x 100m Freestyle Relay
Spinks, Terry	1956	Boxing	Flyweight
Stamper, Harry	1912	Football	
Stapley, Henry	1908	Football	
Steer, Irene	1912	Swimming	4 x 100m Freestyle Relay
Stewart, Douglas	1952	Equestrian	Prix des Nations Team
(only British man to have competed at			
Olympic eventing and show jumping competitions)			
Stiff, Harry	1920	Tug of War	
Strode-Jackson, Arnold	1912	Athletics	1,500m
Styles, William	1908	Shooting	Small-Bore disappearing target
Sutton, Henry	1908	Yachting	8 Metres Class
Swann, Sidney	1912	Rowing	Eights
Symes, John	1900	Cricket	
Tait, Gerald	1908	Yachting	12 Metres Class
Taylor, Henry	1908	Swimming	400m Freestyle
	1908	Swimming	1,500m Freestyle
	1908	Swimming	4 x 200m Freestyle Relay
Taylor, Ian	1988	Hockey	
Thomas, Harry	1908	Boxing	Bantamweight
Thompson, Daley	1980	Athletics	Decathlon
	1984	Athletics	Decathlon
Thompson, Don	1960	Athletics	50km Walk

Name	Date	Sport	Event
Thomson, Gordon	1908	Rowing	Coxless Pairs
Thorne, Ernie	1920	Tug of War	
Thornycroft, Tom	1908	Motor Boating	8 Metres Class
	1908	Motor Boating	Under 60-Foot Class
Thould, Tom	1908	Swimming	Water Polo Team
	1912	Swimming	Water Polo Team
Toller, Montague	1900	Cricket	
Trapmore, Steve	2000	Rowing	Coxed Eight
Turnbull, Noel	1920	Lawn Tennis	Men's Doubles
Turner, R R	1900	Football	
Tysoe, Alf	1900	Athletics	800m
	1900	Athletics	5,000m Team Race
Vaile, Bryn	1988	Yachting	Star Class
Voigt, Emil	1908	Athletics	Five Miles
Walden, Harry (also music-hall comic)	1912	Football	
Warriner, Michael	1928	Rowing	Coxless Fours
Weldon, Frank	1956	Equestrian	Three-Day Event Team
(born in India, Weldon was the only			
British Olympic gold medal winner to escape from Colditz)			
Wells, Allan	1980	Athletics	100m
Wells, Henry	1912	Rowing	Eights (cox)
West, Kieran	2000	Rowing	Coxed Eight
White, Reg	1976	Yachting	Tornado Class
White, Wilf	1952	Equestrian	Prix des Nations Team
Whitlock, Harold	1936	Athletics	50km Walk
Whitty, Allen	1924	Shooting	Running Deer (double shot)
Wilkie, David	1976	Swimming	200m Breaststroke
Wilkinson, Cyril	1920	Hockey	
Wilkinson, George	1900	Swimming	Water Polo Team
	1908	Swimming	Water Polo Team
	1912	Swimming	Water Polo Team
Wilson, Herbert	1908	Polo	
Wilson, Jack	1948	Rowing	Coxless Pairs
Wodehouse, Lord John	1920	Polo	
Wolff, Freddie	1936	Athletics	4 x 400m Relay
Wood, Arthur	1908	Yachting	8 Metres Class
Wood, Harvey	1908	Hockey	
Woodward, Vivian	1908	Football	
	1912	Football	
Woosnam, Max	1920	Lawn Tennis	Men's Doubles
(also played football for England and			
golf and cricket for Cambridge)			
Wormald	1912	Rowing	Eights
Wright, Cyril	1920	Yachting	7 Metres Class
Wright, Dorothy	1920	Yachting	7 Metres Class
(wife of Cyril)			
Wright, Gordon	1912	Football	
Zealey, Jim	1900	Football	

Rugby League Challenge Cup Winners

Year	Winners		Runners Up		Venue	Att	Man of Match
1897	Batley	10	St Helens	3	Leeds	13,492	(First awarded in 1946)
1898	Batley	7	Bradford	0	Leeds	27,941	
1899	Oldham	19	Hunslet	9	Manchester	15,763	
1900	Swinton	16	Salford	8	Manchester	17,864	
1901	Batley	6	Warrington	0	Leeds	29,563	
1902	Broughton R	25	Salford	0	Rochdale	15,006	
1903	Halifax	7	Salford	0	Leeds	32,507	
1904	Halifax	8	Warrington	3	Salford	17,041	
1905	Warrington	6	Hull KR	0	Leeds	19,638	
1906	Bradford	5	Salford	0	Leeds	15,834	
1907	Warrington	17	Oldham	3	Broughton	18,500	
1908	Hunslet	14	Hull	0	Huddersfield	18,000	
1909	Wakefield T	17	Hull	0	Leeds	23,587	
1910	Leeds	7	Hull	7	Huddersfield	19,413	
replay	Leeds	26	Hull	12	Huddersfield	11,608	
1911	Broughton R	4	Wigan	0	Salford	8,000	

1912	Dewsbury	8	Oldham	5	Leeds	15,271	
1913	Huddersfield	9	Warrington	5	Leeds	22,754	
1914	Hull	6	Wakefield T	0	Halifax	19,000	
1915	Huddersfield	37	St Helens	3	Oldham	8,000	
1920	Huddersfield	21	Wigan	10	Leeds	14,000	
1921	Leigh	13	Halifax	0	Broughton	25,000	
1922	Rochdale H	10	Hull	9	Leeds	32,596	
1923	Leeds	28	Hull	3	Wakefield	29,335	
1924	Wigan	21	Oldham	4	Rochdale	41,831	
1925	Oldham	16	Hull KR	3	Leeds	28,335	
1926	Swinton	9	Oldham	3	Rochdale	27,000	
1927	Oldham	26	Swinton	7	Wigan	33,448	
1928	Swinton	5	Warrington	3	Wigan	33,909	
1929	Wigan	13	Dewsbury	2	Wembley	41,500	
1930	Widnes	10	St Helens	3	Wembley	36,544	
1931	Halifax	22	York	8	Wembley	40,368	
1932	Leeds	11	Swinton	8	Wigan	29,000	
1933	Huddersfield	21	Warrington	17	Wembley	41,874	
1934	Hunslet	11	Widnes	5	Wembley	41,280	
1935	Castleford	11	Huddersfield	8	Wembley	39,000	
1936	Leeds	18	Warrington	2	Wembley	51,250	
1937	Widnes	18	Keighley	5	Wembley	47,699	
1938	Salford	7	Barrow	4	Wembley	51,243	
1939	Halifax	20	Salford	3	Wembley	55,453	
1941	Leeds	19	Halifax	2	Bradford	28,500	
1942	Leeds	15	Halifax	10	Bradford	15,250	
1943	Dewsbury	16	Leeds	9	Dewsbury	10,470	
	Dewsbury	0	Leeds	6	Leeds	16,000	
	(Dewsbury win 16–15 on aggregate)						
1944	Bradford N	0	Wigan	3	Wigan	22,000	
	Bradford N	8	Wigan	0	Bradford	30,000	
	(Bradford win 8–3 on aggregate)						
1945	Huddersfield	7	Bradford N	4	Huddersfield	9,041	
	Huddersfield	6	Bradford N	5	Bradford	17,500	
	(Huddersfield win 13–9 on aggregate)						
1946	Wakefield T	13	Wigan	12	Wembley	54,730	Billy Stott
1947	Bradford N	8	Leeds	4	Wembley	77,605	Willie Davies
1948	Wigan	8	Bradford N	3	Wembley	91,465	Frank Whitcombe
1949	Bradford N	12	Halifax	0	Wembley	95,050	Ernest Ward
1950	Warrington	19	Widnes	0	Wembley	94,249	Gerry Helme
1951	Wigan	10	Barrow	0	Wembley	94,262	Cec Mountford
1952	Workington T	18	Featherstone R	10	Wembley	72,093	Billy Ivison
1953	Huddersfield	15	St Helens	10	Wembley	89,588	Peter Ramsden
1954	Warrington	4	Halifax	4	Wembley	81,841	
replay	Warrington	8	Halifax	4	Bradford	102,569	Gerry Helme
1955	Barrow	21	Workington T	12	Wembley	66,513	Jack Grundy
1956	St Helens	13	Halifax	2	Wembley	79,341	Alan Prescott
1957	Leeds	9	Barrow	7	Wembley	76,318	Jeff Stevenson
1958	Wigan	13	Workington T	9	Wembley	66,109	Rees Thomas
1959	Wigan	30	Hull	13	Wembley	79,811	Brian McTigue
1960	Wakefield T	38	Hull	5	Wembley	79,773	Tommy Harris
1961	St Helens	12	Wigan	6	Wembley	94,672	Dick Huddart
1962	Wakefield T	12	Huddersfield	6	Wembley	81,263	Neil Fox
1963	Wakefield T	25	Wigan	10	Wembley	84,492	Harold Poynton
1964	Widnes	13	Hull KR	5	Wembley	84,488	Frank Collier
1965	Wigan	20	Hunslet	16	Wembley	89,016	Ray Ashby & Brian Gabbitas
1966	St Helens	21	Wigan	2	Wembley	98,536	Len Killeen
1967	Featherstone R	17	Barrow	12	Wembley	76,290	Carl Dooler
1968	Leeds	11	Wakefield T	10	Wembley	87,100	Don Fox
1969	Castleford	11	Salford	6	Wembley	97,939	Mal Reilly
1970	Castleford	7	Wigan	2	Wembley	95,255	Bill Kirkbride
1971	Leigh	24	Leeds	7	Wembley	85,514	Alex Murphy
1972	St Helens	16	Leeds	13	Wembley	89,495	Kel Coslett
1973	Featherstone R	33	Bradford N	14	Wembley	72,395	Steve Nash
1974	Warrington	24	Featherstone R	9	Wembley	77,400	Derek Whitehead
1975	Widnes	14	Warrington	7	Wembley	85,098	Ray Dutton
1976	St Helens	20	Widnes	5	Wembley	89,982	Geoff Pimblett
1977	Leeds	16	Widnes	7	Wembley	80,871	Steve Pitchford
1978	Leeds	14	St Helens	12	Wembley	96,000	George Nicholls
1979	Widnes	12	Wakefield T	3	Wembley	94,218	Dave Topliss
1980	Hull KR	10	Hull	5	Wembley	95,000	Brian Lockwood

1981	Widnes	18	Hull KR	9	Wembley	92,496	Mick Burke
1982	Hull	14	Widnes	14	Wembley	92,147	Eddie Cunningham
replay	Hull	18	Widnes	9	Leeds	41,171	
1983	Featherstone R	14	Hull	12	Wembley	84,969	David Hobbs
1984	Widnes	19	Wigan	6	Wembley	80,116	Joe Lydon
1985	Wigan	28	Hull	25	Wembley	97,801	Brett Kenny
1986	Castleford	15	Hull KR	15	Wembley	82,134	Bob Beardmore
1987	Halifax	19	St Helens	18	Wembley	91,267	Graham Eadie
1988	Wigan	32	Halifax	12	Wembley	94,273	Andy Gregory
1989	Wigan	27	St Helens	0	Wembley	78,000	Ellery Hanley
1990	Wigan	36	Warrington	14	Wembley	77,729	Andy Gregory
1991	Wigan	13	St Helens	8	Wembley	75,532	Denis Betts
1992	Wigan	28	Castleford	12	Wembley	77,286	Martin Offiah
1993	Wigan	20	Widnes	14	Wembley	77,684	Dean Bell
1994	Wigan	26	Leeds	16	Wembley	78,348	Martin Offiah
1995	Wigan	30	Leeds	10	Wembley	78,550	Jason Robinson
1996	St Helens	40	Bradford B	32	Wembley	75,994	Robbie Paul
1997	St Helens	32	Bradford B	22	Wembley	78,022	Tommy Martyn
1998	Sheffield E	17	Wigan W	6	Wembley	60,699	Mark Aston
1999	Leeds R	52	London B	16	Wembley	73,242	Leroy Rivett
2000	Bradford N	22	Leeds R	18	Edinburgh	75,356	Henry Paul
2001	St Helens	13	Bradford B	6	Twickenham	68,250	Sean Long
2002	Wigan W	21	St Helens	12	Edinburgh	62,140	Kris Radlinski
2003	Bradford B	22	Leeds R	20	Cardiff	71,212	Gary Connolly

Rugby League – Man of Steel

1977	David Ward (Leeds)	1989	Ellery Hanley (Wigan)
1978	George Nicholls (St Helens)	1990	Shaun Edwards (Wigan)
1979	Doug Laughton (Widnes)	1991	Gary Schofield (Leeds)
1980	George Fairbairn (Wigan)	1992	Dean Bell (Wigan)
1981	Ken Kelly (Warrington)	1993	Andy Platt (Wigan)
1982	Mick Morgan (Carlisle)	1994	Jonathan Davies (Warrington)
1983	Allan Agar (Featherstone Rovers)	1995	Denis Betts (Wigan)
1984	Joe Lydon (Widnes)	1996	Andy Farrell (Wigan)
1985	Ellery Hanley (Bradford Northern)	1997	James Lowes (Bradford Bulls)
1986	Gavin Miller (HKR)	1998	Iestyn Harris (Leeds Rhinos)
1987	Ellery Hanley (Wigan)	1999	Adrian Vowles (Castleford Tigers)
1988	Martin Offiah (Widnes)	2000	Sean Long (St Helens)

Rugby Union Six Nations Championships

1977	France	1991	England
1978	Wales	1992	England
1979	Wales	1993	France
1980	England	1994	Wales
1981	France	1995	England
1982	Ireland	1996	England
1983	France / Ireland	1997	France
1984	Scotland	1998	France
1985	Ireland	1999	Scotland (last Five Nations Championship)
1986	France / Scotland	2000	England
1987	France	2001	England
1988	France / Wales	2002	France
1989	France	2003	England
1990	Scotland		

Tennis: Wimbledon Champions

	Men	Women	Men's Doubles	Women's Doubles
1877	S W Gore (GB)	—	—	—
1878	P F Hadow (GB)	—	—	—
1879	J T Hartley (GB)	—	—	—
1880	J T Hartley (GB)	—	—	—
1881	W Renshaw (GB)	—	—	—

	Men	Women	Men's Doubles	Women's Doubles
1882	W Renshaw (GB)	—	—	—
1883	W Renshaw (GB)	—	—	—
1884	W Renshaw (GB)	M Watson (GB)	W Renshaw / E Renshaw	—
1885	W Renshaw (GB)	M Watson (GB)	W Renshaw / E Renshaw	—
1886	W Renshaw (GB)	B Bingley (GB)	W Renshaw / E Renshaw	—
1887	H FLawford (GB)	C Dod (GB)	W Wilberforce / P BLyon	—
1888	E Renshaw (GB)	C Dod (GB)	W Renshaw / E Renshaw	—
1889	W Renshaw (GB)	B Bingley Hillyard (GB)	W Renshaw / E Renshaw	—
1890	W J Hamilton (GB)	H Rice (GB)	J Pim / F O Stoker	—
1891	W Baddeley (GB)	C Dod (GB)	W Baddeley / H Baddeley	—
1892	W Baddeley (GB)	C Dod (GB)	E W Lewis / H S Barlow	—
1893	J Pim (GB)	C Dod (GB)	J Pim / F O Stoker	—
1894	J Pim (GB)	B Hillyard (GB)	W Baddeley / H Baddeley	—
1895	W Baddeley (GB)	C Cooper (GB)	W Baddeley / H Baddeley	—
1896	H S Mahony (GB)	C Cooper (GB)	W Baddeley / H Baddeley	—
1897	R F Doherty (GB)	B Hillyard (GB)	R F Doherty / L H Doherty	—
1898	R F Doherty (GB)	C Cooper (GB)	R F Doherty / L H Doherty	—
1899	R F Doherty (GB)	B Hillyard (GB)	R F Doherty / L H Doherty	—
1900	R F Doherty (GB)	B Hillyard (GB)	R F Doherty / L H Doherty	—
1901	A W Gore (GB)	C Cooper Sterry (GB)	R F Doherty / L H Doherty	—
1902	L H Doherty (GB)	M E Robb (GB)	S H Smith / F L Riseley	—
1903	L H Doherty (GB)	D K Douglass (GB)	R F Doherty / L H Doherty	—
1904	L H Doherty (GB)	D K Douglass (GB)	R F Doherty / L H Doherty	—
1905	L H Doherty (GB)	M Sutton (US)	R F Doherty / L H Doherty	—
1906	L H Doherty (GB)	D K Douglass (GB)	S Smith / F Riseley	—
1907	N E Brookes (Aus)	M Sutton (US)	N E Brookes / A F Wilding	—
1908	A W Gore (GB)	C Sterry (GB)	A F Wilding / M J G Ritchie	—
1909	A W Gore (GB)	D P Boothby (GB)	A W Gore / H Roper Barrett	—
1910	A F Wilding (NZ)	D K Douglass Chambers (GB)	A F Wilding / M J G Ritchie	—
1911	A F Wilding (NZ)	D K Douglass Chambers (GB)	A H Gobert / M Decugis	—
1912	A F Wilding (NZ)	E W Larcombe (GB)	H Roper Barrett / C P Dixon	—
1913	A F Wilding (NZ)	D K Douglass Chambers (GB)	H Roper Barrett / C P Dixon	R J McNair / D P Boothby
1914	N E Brookes (Aus)	D K Douglass Chambers (GB)	N E Brookes / A F Wilding	E Ryan / A M Morton
1915	not held	not held	not held	not held
1916	not held	not held	not held	not held
1917	not held	not held	not held	not held
1918	not held	not held	not held	not held
1919	G L Patterson (Aus)	S Lenglen (Fr)	R V Thomas / P O'Hara Wood	S Lenglen / E Ryan
1920	W T Tilden (US)	S Lenglen (Fr)	R N Williams / C S Garland	S Lenglen / E Ryan
1921	W T Tilden (US)	S Lenglen (Fr)	R Lycett / M Woosnam	S Lenglen / E Ryan
1922	G L Patterson (Aus)	S Lenglen (Fr)	J O Anderson / R Lycett	S Lenglen / E Ryan
1923	W M Johnston (US)	S Lenglen (Fr)	L A Godfree / R Lycett	S Lenglen / E Ryan
1924	J Borotra (Fr)	K McKane (GB)	F T Hunter / V Richards	H Wightman / H N Wills
1925	R Lacoste (Fr)	S Lenglen (Fr)	J Borotra / R Lacoste	S Lenglen / E Ryan
1926	J Borotra (Fr)	K McKane Godfree (GB)	J Brugnon / H Cochet	M K Browne / E Ryan
1927	H Cochet (Fr)	H N Wills (US)	F T Hunter / W T Tilden	H N Wills / E Ryan
1928	R Lacoste (Fr)	H N Wills (US)	J Brugnon / H Cochet	P Saunders / M Watson
1929	H Cochet (Fr)	H N Wills (US)	W L Allison / J Van Ryn	P Saunders Michell/ M Watson
1930	W T Tilden (US)	H N Wills Moody (US)	W L Allison / J Van Ryn	H N Wills Moody/ E Ryan
1931	S B Wood (US)	C Aussem (Ger)	G M Lott / J Van Ryn	P Mudford / D Shepherd-Barron
1932	H E Vines (US)	H N Wills Moody (US)	J Borotra / J Brugnon	D Metaxa / J Sigart
1933	J H Crawford (Aus)	H N Wills Moody (US)	J Borotra / J Brugnon	E Ryan / R Mathieu
1934	F J Perry (GB)	D E Round (GB)	G M Lott / L R Stoefen	E Ryan / R Mathieu
1935	F J Perry (GB)	H N Wills Moody (US)	J H Crawford / A K Quist	F James / K E Stammers
1936	F J Perry (GB)	H H Jacobs (US)	G P Hughes / C R D Tuckey	F James / K E Stammers
1937	J D Budge (US)	D E Round (GB)	J D Budge / G Mako	S Mathieu / B Yorke
1938	J D Budge (US)	H N Wills Moody (US)	J D Budge / G Mako	S Palfrey Fabyan / A Marble
1939	R L Riggs (US)	A Marble (US)	E T Cooke / R L Riggs	S Palfrey Fabyan / A Marble
1940	not held	not held	not held	not held
1941	not held	not held	not held	not held

SPORT & LEISURE

	Men	Women	Men's Doubles	Women's Doubles
1942	not held	not held	not held	not held
1943	not held	not held	not held	not held
1944	not held	not held	not held	not held
1945	not held	not held	not held	not held
1946	Y Petra (Fr)	P M Betz (US)	T Brown / J A Kramer	L A Brough / M Osborne
1947	J Kramer (US)	M E Osborne (US)	R Falkenburg / J A Kramer	R B Todd / D J Hart
1948	B Falkenburg (US)	A L Brough (US)	J E Bromwich / F A Sedgman	A L Brough / M E Osborne du Pont
1949	T Schroeder (US)	A L Brough (US)	R A Gonzales / F A Parker	A L Brough / M du Pont
1950	B Patty (US)	A L Brough (US)	J E Bromwich / A K Quist	A L Brough / M du Pont
1951	D Savitt (US)	D J Hart (US)	K B McGregor / F A Sedgman	D J Hart / S J Fry
1952	F Sedgman (Aus)	M Connolly (US)	K B McGregor / F A Sedgman	D J Hart / S J Fry
1953	V Seixas (US)	M Connolly (US)	L A Hoad / K R Rosewall	D J Hart / S J Fry
1954	J Drobny (Cze)	M Connolly (US)	R N Hartwig / M G Rose	A L Brough / M du Pont
1955	M A Trabert (US)	A L Brough (US)	R N Hartwig / L A Hoad	A Mortimer / J A Shilcock
1956	L A Hoad (Aus)	S J Fry (US)	L A Hoad / K R Rosewall	A Buxton / A Gibson
1957	L A Hoad (Aus)	A Gibson (US)	J E Patty / G Mulloy	A Gibson / D R Hard
1958	A J Cooper (Aus)	A Gibson (US)	S Davidson / U Schmidt	M E Bueno / A Gibson
1959	A Olmedo (Per)	M E Bueno (Braz)	R Emerson / N A Fraser	J Arth / D R Hard
1960	N A Fraser (Aus)	M E Bueno (Braz)	R H Osuna / R D Ralston	M E Bueno / D R Hard
1961	R G Laver (Aus)	A Mortimer (GB)	R Emerson / N A Fraser	K Hantze / B J Moffitt
1962	R G Laver (Aus)	K Hantze Susman (US)	R A J Hewitt / F S Stolle	B J Moffitt / K Hantze Susman
1963	C R McKinley (US)	M Smith (Aus)	R H Osuna / A Palafox	M E Bueno / D R Hard
1964	R S Emerson (Aus)	M E Bueno (Braz)	R A J Hewitt / F S Stolle	M Smith / L R Turner
1965	R S Emerson (Aus)	M Smith (Aus)	J D Newcombe / A D Roche	M E Bueno / B J Moffitt
1966	M Santana (Spa)	B J Moffitt King (US)	K N Fletcher / J D Newcombe	M E Bueno / N Richey
1967	J D Newcombe (Aus)	B J King (US)	R A J Hewitt / F D McMillan	R Casals / B J Moffitt King
1968	R G Laver (Aus)	B J King (US)	J D Newcombe / A D Roche	R Casals / B J King
1969	R G Laver (Aus)	A Haydon Jones (GB)	J D Newcombe / A D Roche	M Smith Court / J A M Tegart
1970	J D Newcombe (Aus)	M Smith Court (Aus)	J D Newcombe / A D Roche	R Casals / B J King
1971	J D Newcombe (Aus)	E F Goolagong (Aus)	R S Emerson / R G Laver	R Casals / B J King
1972	S R Smith (US)	B J King (US)	R A J Hewitt / F D McMillan	B J King / B Stove
1973	J Kodes (Cze)	B J King (US)	J S Connors / I Nastase	R Casals / B J King
1974	J S Connors (US)	C M Evert (US)	J D Newcombe / A D Roche	E F Goolagong / M Michel
1975	A R Ashe (US)	B J King (US)	V Gerulaitis / A Mayer	A Kiyomura / K Sawamatsu
1976	B Borg (Swe)	C M Evert (US)	B E Gottfried / R Ramirez	C M Evert / M Navratilova
1977	B Borg (Swe)	S V Wade (GB)	R L Case / G Masters	H Gourlay Cawley / J C Russell
1978	B Borg (Swe)	M Navratilova (Cze)	R A J Hewitt / F D McMillan	K Reid / W Turnbull
1979	B Borg (Swe)	M Navratilova (US)	J P McEnroe / P Fleming	B J King / M Navratilova
1980	B Borg (Swe)	E F Goolagong Cawley (Aus)	P McNamara / P McNamee	K Jordan / A E Smith
1981	J P McEnroe (US)	C M Evert Lloyd (US)	J P McEnroe / P Fleming	M Navratilova / P H Shriver
1982	J S Connors (US)	M Navratilova (US)	P McNamara / P McNamee	M Navratilova / P H Shriver
1983	J P McEnroe (US)	M Navratilova (US)	J P McEnroe / P Fleming	M Navratilova / P H Shriver
1984	J P McEnroe (US)	M Navratilova (US)	J P McEnroe / P Fleming	M Navratilova / P H Shriver
1985	B Becker (Ger)	M Navratilova (US)	H P Gunthardt / B Taroczy	K Jordan / E Smylie
1986	B Becker (Ger)	M Navratilova (US)	J Nystrom / M Wilander	M Navratilova / P H Shriver
1987	P Cash (Aus)	M Navratilova (US)	R Seguso / K Flach	C Kohde-Kilsch / H Sukova

	Men	Women	Men's Doubles	Women's Doubles
1988	S Edberg (Swe)	S Graf (Ger)	R Seguso / K Flach	S Graf / G Sabatini
1989	B Becker (Ger)	S Graf (Ger)	J B Fitzgerald / A Jarryd	J Novotna / H Sukova
1990	S Edberg (Swe)	M Navratilova (US)	R Leach / J Pugh	J Novotna / H Sukova
1991	M Stich (Ger)	S Graf (Ger)	J B Fitzgerald / A Jarryd	L Savchenko / N Zvereva
1992	A Agassi (US)	S Graf (Ger)	J P McEnroe / M Stich	G Fernandez / N Zvereva
1993	P Sampras (US)	S Graf (Ger)	T Woodbridge / M Woodforde	G Fernandez / N Zvereva
1994	P Sampras (US)	C Martinez (Spa)	T Woodbridge / M Woodforde	G Fernandez / N Zvereva
1995	P Sampras (US)	S Graf (Ger)	T Woodbridge / M Woodforde	J Novotna / A Sanchez-Vicario
1996	R Krajicek (Ned)	S Graf (Ger)	T Woodbridge / M Woodforde	M Hingis / H Sukova
1997	P Sampras (US)	M Hingis (Swi)	T Woodbridge / M Woodforde	G Fernandez / N Zvereva
1998	P Sampras (US)	J Novotna (Cze)	J Eltingh / P Haarhuis	M Hingis / J Novotna
1999	P Sampras (US)	L Davenport (US)	M Bhupathi / L Paes	L Davenport / C Morariu
2000	P Sampras (US)	V Williams (US)	T Woodbridge/M Woodforde	V Williams / S Williams
2001	G Ivanisevic (Cro)	V Williams (US)	D Johnson / J Palmer	L Raymond / R Stubbs
2002	L Hewitt (Aus)	S Williams (US)	J Bjorkman / T Woodbridge	V Williams / S Williams

Tennis: US Open

	Men	Women	Men's Doubles	Women's Doubles
1881	R D Sears (US)	—	C M Clark / F W Taylor	—
1882	R D Sears (US)	—	R D Sears / J Dwight	—
1883	R D Sears (US)	—	R D Sears / J Dwight	—
1884	R D Sears (US)	—	R D Sears / J Dwight	—
1885	R D Sears (US)	—	R D Sears / J S Clark	—
1886	R D Sears (US)	—	R D Sears / J Dwight	—
1887	R D Sears (US)	E Hansell (US)	R D Sears / J Dwight	—
1888	H W Slocum (US)	B L Townsend (US)	O S Campbell / V G Hall	—
1889	H W Slocum (US)	B L Townsend (US)	H W Slocum / H A Taylor	M Ballard / B L Townsend
1890	O S Campbell (US)	E C Roosevelt (US)	V G Hall / C Hobart	E C Roosevelt / G W Roosevelt
1891	O S Campbell (US)	M E Cahill (US)	O S Campbell / R P Huntington	M E Cahill / W F Morgan
1892	O S Campbell (US)	M E Cahill (US)	O S Campbell / R P Huntington	M E Cahill / A M McKinley
1893	R D Wrenn (US)	A M Terry (US)	C Hobart / F H Hovey	A M Terry / H Butler
1894	R D Wrenn (US)	H R Hellwig (US)	C Hobart / F H Hovey	H R Hellwig / J P Atkinson
1895	F H Hovey (US)	J P Atkinson (US)	M G Chace / R D Wrenn	H R Hellwig / J P Atkinson
1896	R D Wrenn (US)	E H Moore (US)	C B Neel / S R Neel	E H Moore / J P Atkinson
1897	R D Wrenn (US)	J P Atkinson (US)	L E Ware / G P Sheldon	J P Atkinson / K Atkinson
1898	M D Whitman (US)	J P Atkinson (US)	L E Ware / G P Sheldon	J P Atkinson / K Atkinson
1899	M D Whitman (US)	M Jones (US)	H Ward / D F Davis	J W Craven / M McAteer
1900	M D Whitman (US)	M McAteer (US)	H Ward / D F Davis	E Parker / H Champlin
1901	W A Larned (US)	E H Moore (US)	H Ward / D F Davis	J P Atkinson / M McAteer
1902	W A Larned (US)	M Jones (US)	R F Doherty / H L Doherty	J P Atkinson / M Jones
1903	H L Doherty (GB)	E H Moore (US)	R F Doherty / H L Doherty	E H Moore / C B Neely
1904	H Ward (US)	M G Sutton (US)	H Ward / B C Wright	M G Sutton / M Hall
1905	B C Wright (US)	E H Moore (US)	H Ward / B C Wright	H Homans / C B Neely
1906	W J Clothier (US)	H Homans (US)	H Ward / B C Wright	L S Coe / D S Platt
1907	W A Larned (US)	Evelyn Sears (US)	F B Alexander / B C Wright	M Wimer / C B Neely
1908	W A Larned (US)	M Barger-Wallach (US)	F B Alexander / H H Hackett	Evelyn Sears / M Curtis
1909	W A Larned (US)	H Hotchkiss (US)	F B Alexander / H H Hackett	H V Hotchkiss / E E Rotch
1910	W A Larned (US)	H Hotchkiss (US)	F B Alexander / H H Hackett	H V Hotchkiss / E E Rotch
1911	W A Larned (US)	H Hotchkiss (US)	R D Little / G F Touchard	H V Hotchkiss /

	Men	Women	Men's Doubles	Women's Doubles
				Eleanora Sears
1912	M E McLoughlin (US)	K Browne (US)	M E McLoughlin / T C Bundy	D Greene / MK Browne
1913	M E McLoughlin (US)	M K Browne (US)	M E McLoughlin / T C Bundy	M K Browne / L Williams
1914	R N Williams (US)	M K Browne (US)	M E McLoughlin / T C Bundy	M K Browne / L Williams
1915	W M Johnston (US)	M Bjurstedt (Nor)	W M Johnston / C J Griffin	H V Hotchkiss Wightman / Eleanora Sears
1916	R N Williams (US)	M Bjurstedt (Nor)	W M Johnston / C J Griffin	M Bjurstedt / Eleanora Sears
1917	R L Murray (US)	M Bjurstedt (Nor)	F B Alexander / H A Throckmorton	M Bjurstedt / Eleanora Sears
1918	R L Murray (US)	M Bjurstedt (Nor)	W T Tilden / V Richards	M Zinderstein / E E Goss
1919	W M Johnston (US)	H Hotchkiss Wightman (US)	N E Brookes / G L Patterson	M Zinderstein / E E Goss
1920	W T Tilden (US)	M Bjurstedt Mallory (US)	W M Johnston / C J Griffin	M Zinderstein / E E Goss
1921	W T Tilden (US)	M Mallory (US)	W T Tilden / V Richards	M K Browne / L Williams
1922	W T Tilden (US)	M Mallory (US)	W T Tilden / V Richards	M Zinderstein Jessup / H N Wills
1923	W T Tilden (US)	H N Wills (US)	W T Tilden / B I C Norton	K McKane / P L Howkins Covell
1924	W T Tilden (US)	H N Wills (US)	H O Kinsey / R G Kinsey	H Wightman / H N Wills
1925	W T Tilden (US)	H N Wills (US)	R N Williams / V Richards	M K Browne / H N Wills
1926	R Lacoste (Fr)	M Mallory (US)	R N Williams / V Richards	E Ryan / E E Goss
1927	R Lacoste (Fr)	H N Wills (US)	W T Tilden / F T Hunter	K McKane Godfree / E H Harvey
1928	H Cochet (Fr)	H N Wills (US)	G M Lott / J F Hennessey	H Wightman / H N Wills
1929	W T Tilden (US)	H N Wills (US)	G M Lott / J H Doeg	P Watson / P Michel
1930	J H Doeg (US)	B Nuthall (GB)	G M Lott / J H Doeg	B Nuthall / S Palfrey
1931	H E Vines (US)	H N Wills Moody (US)	W L Allison / J Van Ryn	B Nuthall / E Bennett Whittingstall
1932	H E Vines (US)	H H Jacobs (US)	H E Vines / K Gledhill	H H Jacobs / S Palfrey
1933	F J Perry (GB)	H H Jacobs (US)	G M Lott / L R Stoefen	B Nuthall / F James
1934	F J Perry (GB)	H H Jacobs (US)	G M Lott / L R Stoefen	H H Jacobs / S Palfrey
1935	W L Allison (US)	H H Jacobs (US)	W L Allison / J Van Ryn	H H Jacobs / S Palfrey Fabyan
1936	F J Perry (GB)	A Marble (US)	J D Budge / G Mako	M Van Ryn / C A Babcock
1937	J D Budge (US)	A Lizana (Chile)	G Von Cramm / H Henkel	S Palfrey Fabyan / A Marble
1938	J D Budge (US)	A Marble (US)	J D Budge / G Mako	S Palfrey Fabyan / A Marble
1939	R L Riggs (US)	A Marble (US)	A K Quist / J E Bromwich	S Palfrey Fabyan / A Marble
1940	W D McNeill (US)	A Marble (US)	J A Kramer / F R Schroeder	S Palfrey Fabyan / A Marble
1941	R L Riggs (US)	S Palfrey Cooke (US)	J A Kramer / F R Schroeder	S Palfrey Cooke / M E Osborne
1942	F R Schroeder (US)	P M Betz (US)	G Mulloy / W F Talbert	A L Brough / M E Osborne
1943	J R Hunt (US)	P M Betz (US)	J A Kramer / F A Parker	A L Brough / M E Osborne
1944	F A Parker (US)	P M Betz (US)	W D McNeill / R Falkenburg	A L Brough / M E Osborne
1945	F A Parker (US)	S Palfrey Cooke (US)	G Mulloy / W F Talbert	A L Brough / M E Osborne
1946	J A Kramer (US)	P M Betz (US)	G Mulloy / W F Talbert	A L Brough / M E Osborne
1947	J A Kramer (US)	A L Brough (US)	J A Kramer / F R Schroeder	A L Brough / M E Osborne
1948	R A Gonzales (US)	M E Osborne du Pont (US)	G Mulloy / W F Talbert	A L Brough / M E Osborne du Pont
1949	R A Gonzales (US)	M E du Pont (US)	J Bromwich / O W Sidwell	A L Brough / M E du Pont
1950	A Larsen (US)	M E du Pont (US)	J Bromwich / F A Sedgeman	A L Brough / M E du Pont
1951	F A Sedgeman (Aus)	M Connolly (US)	K B McGregor / F A Sedgeman	D J Hart / S J Fry
1952	F A Sedgeman (Aus)	M Connolly (US)	M G Rose / E V Seixas	D J Hart / S J Fry
1953	M A Trabert (US)	M Connolly (US)	R N Hartwig / M G Rose	D J Hart / S J Fry
1954	E V Seixas (US)	D J Hart (US)	E V Seixas / M A Trabert	D J Hart / S J Fry
1955	M A Trabert (US)	D J Hart (US)	K Kamo / A Miyagi	A L Brough / M E du Pont
1956	K R Rosewall (Aus)	S J Fry (US)	L A Hoad / K R Rosewall	A L Brough /

	Men	Women	Men's Doubles	Women's Doubles
				M E du Pont
1957	M J Anderson (Aus)	A Gibson (US)	A J Cooper / N A Fraser	A L Brough / M E du Pont
1958	A J Cooper (Aus)	A Gibson (US)	A Olmedo / H Richardson	J M Arth / D R Hard
1959	N A Fraser (Aus)	M E Bueno (Braz)	N A Fraser / R S Emerson	J M Arth / D R Hard
1960	N A Fraser (Aus)	D R Hard (US)	N A Fraser / R S Emerson	M E Bueno / D R Hard
1961	R S Emerson (Aus)	D R Hard (US)	C McKinley / R D Ralston	D R Hard / L Turner
1962	R G Laver (Aus)	M Smith (Aus)	R H Osuna / A Palafox	M E Bueno / D R Hard
1963	R H Osuna (Mex)	M E Bueno (Braz)	C McKinley / R D Ralston	R Ebbern / M Smith
1964	R S Emerson (Aus)	M E Bueno (Braz)	C McKinley / R D Ralston	B J Moffitt / K Hantze Susman
1965	M Santana (Spa)	M Smith (Aus)	R S Emerson / F S Stolle	C A Graebner / N Richey
1966	F S Stolle (Aus)	M E Bueno (Braz)	R S Emerson / F S Stolle	M E Bueno / N Richey
1967	J D Newcombe (Aus)	B J Moffitt King (US)	J D Newcombe / A D Roche	R Casals / B J Moffitt King
1968	A R Ashe (US)	S V Wade / B M Smith Court (Aus)	R C Lutz / S R Smith	M E Bueno / B M Smith Court
1969	R G Laver (Aus) / S R Smith (US)	B M Court (Aus)	K R Rosewall / F S Stolle	F Durr / D R Hard
			D Crealy / A Stone	B M Court / S V Wade
1970	K R Rosewall (Aus)	B M Court (Aus)	P Barthes / N Pilic	B M Court / J A M Dalton
1971	S R Smith (US)	B J King (US)	J D Newcombe / R Taylor	R Casals / J A M Dalton
1972	I Nastase (Rom)	B J King (US)	C E Drysdale / R Taylor	F Durr / B Stove
1973	J D Newcombe (Aus)	B M Court (Aus)	O K Davidson / J D Newcombe	B M Court / S V Wade
1974	J S Connors (US)	B J King (US)	R C Lutz / S R Smith	R Casals / B J King
1975	M Orantes (Spa)	C M Evert (US)	J S Connors / I Nastase	B M Court / S V Wade
1976	J S Connors (US)	C M Evert (US)	T S Okker / M C Riessen	L Boshoff / I Kloss
1977	G Vilas (Arg)	C M Evert (US)	R A J Hewitt / F D McMillan	M Navratilova / B Stove
1978	J S Connors (US)	C M Evert (US)	R C Lutz / S R Smith	B J King / M Navratilova
1979	J P McEnroe (US)	T A Austin (US)	J P McEnroe / P Fleming	W M Turnbull / B Stove
1980	J P McEnroe (US)	C M Evert Lloyd (US)	R C Lutz / S R Smith	B J King / M Navratilova
1981	J P McEnroe (US)	T A Austin (US)	J P McEnroe / P Fleming	K Jordan / A Smith
1982	J S Connors (US)	C M Evert Lloyd (US)	K Curren / S Denton	R Casals / W M Turnbull
1983	J S Connors (US)	M Navratilova (US)	J P McEnroe / P Fleming	M Navratilova / P H Shriver
1984	J P McEnroe (US)	M Navratilova (US)	J B Fitzgerald / T Smid	M Navratilova / P H Shriver
1985	I Lendl (Cze)	H Mandlikova (Cze)	K Flach / R Seguso	C Kohde-Kilsch / H Sukova
1986	I Lendl (Cze)	M Navratilova (US)	A Gomez / S Zivojinovic	M Navratilova / P H Shriver
1987	I Lendl (Cze)	M Navratilova (US)	S Edberg / A Jarryd	M Navratilova / P H Shriver
1988	M Wilander (Swe)	S Graf (Ger)	S Casal / E Sanchez	G Fernandez / R White
1989	B Becker (Ger)	S Graf (Ger)	J P McEnroe / M Woodforde	H Mandlikova / M Navratilova
1990	P Sampras (US)	G Sabatini (Arg)	P Aldrich / D Visser	G Fernandez / M Navratilova
1991	S Edberg (Swe)	M Seles (Yug)	J B Fitzgerald / A Jarryd	P H Shriver / N Zvereva
1992	S Edberg (Swe)	M Seles (Yug)	J Grabb / R Reneberg	G Fernandez / N Zvereva
1993	P Sampras (US)	S Graf (Ger)	K Flach / R Leach	A Sanchez-Vicario / H Sukova
1994	A Agassi (US)	A Sanchez-Vicario (Spa)	J Eltingh / P Haarhuis	J Novotna / A Sanchez-Vicario
1995	P Sampras (US)	S Graf (Ger)	T Woodbridge / M Woodforde	G Fernandez / N Zvereva
1996	P Sampras (US)	S Graf (Ger)	T Woodbridge / M Woodforde	G Fernandez / N Zvereva
1997	P Rafter (Aus)	M Hingis (Swi)	Y Kafelnikov / D Vacek	J Novotna / L Davenport
1998	P Rafter (Aus)	L Davenport (US)	S Stolle / C Suk	M Hingis / J Novotna
1999	A Agassi (US)	S Williams (US)	S Lareau / A O'Brien	S Williams / V Williams
2000	M Safin (Rus)	V Williams (US)	L Hewitt / M Mirnyi	A Sugiyama / J Halard-Decugis
2001	L Hewitt (Aus)	V Williams (US)	W Black / K Ullyett	L Raymond / R Stubbs
2002	P Sampras (US)	S Williams (US)	Mahesh Bhupathi / Max Myrnyi	Virginia Ruano Pascual / Paola Suarez

SPORT & LEISURE

Tennis: Australian Open

	Men	Women		Men	Women
1905	R W Heath (Aus)	—	1957	A J Cooper (Aus)	S J Fry (US)
1906	A F Wilding (NZ)	—	1958	A J Cooper (Aus)	A Mortimer (GB)
1907	H M Rice (Aus)	—	1959	A Olmedo (Per)	M Carter Reitano (Aus)
1908	F B Alexander (US)	—			
1909	A F Wilding (NZ)	—	1960	R G Laver (Aus)	M Smith (Aus)
1910	R W Heath (Aus)	—	1961	R S Emerson (Aus)	M Smith (Aus)
1911	N E Brookes (Aus)	—	1962	R G Laver (Aus)	M Smith (Aus)
1912	J C Parke (GB)	—	1963	R S Emerson (Aus)	M Smith (Aus)
1913	E F Parker (Aus)	—	1964	R S Emerson (Aus)	M Smith (Aus)
1914	A O'Hara Wood (Aus)	—	1965	R S Emerson (Aus)	M Smith (Aus)
1915	F G Lowe (GB)	—	1966	R S Emerson (Aus)	M Smith (Aus)
1916	not held	—	1967	R S Emerson (Aus)	N Richey (US)
1917	not held	—	1968	W W Bowrey (Aus)	B J Moffitt King (US)
1918	not held	—			
1919	A R F Kingscote (GB)	—	1969	R G Laver (Aus)	M Smith Court (Aus)
1920	P O'Hara Wood (Aus)	—			
1921	R H Gemmell (Aus)	—	1970	A R Ashe (US)	M Court (Aus)
1922	J O Anderson (Aus)	M Molesworth (Aus)	1971	K R Rosewall (Aus)	M Court (Aus)
			1972	K R Rosewall (Aus)	V S Wade (GB)
1923	P O'Hara Wood (Aus)	M Molesworth (Aus)	1973	J D Newcombe (Aus)	M Court (Aus)
			1974	J S Connors (US)	E Goolagong (Aus)
1924	J O Anderson (Aus)	S Lance (Aus)	1975	J D Newcombe (Aus)	E Goolagong (Aus)
1925	J O Anderson (Aus)	D S Akhurst (Aus)	1976	M Edmondson (Aus)	E Goolagong Cawley (Aus)
1926	J B Hawkes (Aus)	D S Akhurst (Aus)			
1927	G L Patterson (Aus)	E F Boyd (Aus)	1977 (Jan)	R Tanner (US)	K Reid (Aus)
1928	J Borotra (Fr)	D S Akhurst (Aus)	1977 (Dec)	V Gerulaitis (US)	E Cawley (Aus)
1929	J C Gregory (GB)	D S Akhurst (Aus)	1978	G Vilas (Arg)	C O'Neill (Aus)
1930	E F Moon (Aus)	D S Akhurst (Aus)	1979	G Vilas (Arg)	B Jordan (US)
1931	J H Crawford (Aus)	C Buttsworth (Aus)	1980	B Teacher (US)	H Mandlikova (Cze)
1932	J H Crawford (Aus)	C Buttsworth (Aus)	1981	J Kriek (SA)	M Navratilova (US)
1933	J H Crawford (Aus)	J Hartigan (Aus)	1982	J Kriek (SA)	C M Evert Lloyd (US)
1934	F J Perry (GB)	J Hartigan (Aus)			
1935	J H Crawford (Aus)	D E Round (GB)	1983	M Wilander (Swe)	M Navratilova (US)
1936	A K Quist (Aus)	J Hartigan (Aus)	1984	M Wilander (Swe)	C M Evert Lloyd (US)
1937	V B McGrath (Aus)	N M Wynne (Aus)			
1938	J D Budge (US)	D M Bundy (US)	1985	S Edberg (Swe)	M Navratilova (US)
1939	J E Bromwich (US)	E Westacott (Aus)	1986	not held	not held
1940	A K Quist (Aus)	N M Wynne Bolton (Aus)	1987	S Edberg (Swe)	H Mandlikova (Cze)
			1988	M Wilander (Swe)	S Graf (Ger)
1941	not held	not held	1989	I Lendl (Cze)	S Graf (Ger)
1942	not held	not held	1990	I Lendl (Cze)	S Graf (Ger)
1943	not held	not held	1991	B Becker (Ger)	M Seles (Yug)
1944	not held	not held	1992	J Courier (US)	M Seles (Yug)
1945	not held	not held	1993	J Courier (US)	M Seles (Yug)
1946	J E Bromwich (US)	N M Bolton (Aus)	1994	P Sampras (US)	S Graf (Ger)
1947	D Pails (Aus)	N M Bolton (Aus)	1995	A Agassi (US)	M Pierce (Fra)
1948	A K Quist (Aus)	N M Bolton (Aus)	1996	B Becker (Ger)	M Seles (US)
1949	F A Sedgman (Aus)	D J Hart (US)	1997	P Sampras (US)	M Hingis (Swi)
1950	F A Sedgman (Aus)	L A Brough (US)	1998	P Korda (Cze)	M Hingis (Swi)
1951	R Savitt (US)	N M Bolton (Aus)	1999	Y Kafelnikov (Rus)	M Hingis (Swi)
1952	K B McGregor (Aus)	T Long (Aus)	2000	A Agassi (US)	L Davenport (US)
1953	K R Rosewall (Aus)	M Connolly (US)	2001	A Agassi (US)	J Capriati (US)
1954	M G Rose (Aus)	T Long (Aus)	2002	T Johansson (Swe)	J Capriati (US)
1955	K R Rosewall (Aus)	B Penrose (Aus)	2003	A Agassi (US)	S Williams (US)
1956	L G Hoad (Aus)	M Carter (Aus)			

Tennis: French Open

	Men	Women		Men	Women
1891	H Briggs	—	1950	J E Patty (US)	D J Hart (US)
1892	J Schopfer (Fr)	—	1951	J Drobny (Cze)	S J Fry (US)
1893	L Riboulet (Fr)	—	1952	J Drobny (Cze)	D J Hart (US)
1894	A Vacherot (Fr)	—	1953	K R Rosewall (Aus)	M Connolly (US)
1895	A Vacherot (Fr)	—	1955	M A Trabert (US)	M Connolly (US)
1896	A Vacherot (Fr)	—	1955	M A Trabert (US)	A Mortimer (GB)
1897	P Aymé (Fr)	C Masson (Fr)	1956	L A Hoad (Aus)	A Gibson (US)
1898	P Aymé (Fr)	C Masson (Fr)	1957	S Davidson (Swe)	S J Bloomer (GB)
1899	P Aymé (Fr)	C Masson (Fr)	1958	M Rose (Aus)	S Kormoczy (Hung)
1900	P Aymé (Fr)	Y Prévost (Fr)			
1901	A Vacherot (Fr)	P Girod (Fr)	1959	N Pietrangeli (Ita)	C C Truman (GB)
1902	A Vacherot (Fr)	C Masson (Fr)	1960	N Pietrangeli (Ita)	D R Hard (US)
1903	M Decugis (Fr)	C Masson (Fr)	1961	M Santana (Spa)	A S Haydon (GB)
1904	M Decugis (Fr)	K Gillou (Fr)	1962	R G Laver (Aus)	M Smith (Aus)
1905	M Germot (Fr)	K Gillou (Fr)	1963	R S Emerson (Aus)	L R Turner (Aus)
1906	M Germot (Fr)	K Fenwick	1964	M Santana (Spa)	M Smith (Aus)
1907	M Decugis (Fr)	M de Kermel (Fr)	1965	F S Stolle (Aus)	L R Turner (Aus)
1908	M Decugis (Fr)	K Fenwick	1966	A D Roche (Aus)	A S Haydon Jones (GB)
1909	M Decugis (Fr)	J Mattey (Fr)			
1910	M Germot (Fr)	J Mattey (Fr)	1967	R S Emerson (Aus)	F Durr (Fr)
1911	A H Gobert (Fr)	J Mattey (Fr)	1968	K R Rosewall (Aus)	N Richey (US)
1912	M Decugis (Fr)	J Mattey (Fr)	1969	R G Laver (Aus)	M Smith Court (Aus)
1913	M Decugis (Fr)	M Broquedis (Fr)	1970	J Kodes (Cze)	M Court (Aus)
1914	M Decugis (Fr)	M Broquedis (Fr)	1971	J Kodes (Cze)	E Goolagong (Aus)
1915	not held	not held	1972	A Gimeno (Spa)	B J Moffitt King (US)
1916	not held	not held	1973	I Nastase (Rom)	M Court (Aus)
1917	not held	not held	1974	B Borg (Swed)	C M Evert (US)
1918	not held	not held	1975	B Borg (Swed)	C M Evert (US)
1919	not held	not held	1976	A Panatta (Ita)	S Barker (GB)
1920	A H Gobert (Fr)	S Lenglen (Fr)	1977	G Vilas (Arg)	M Jausovec (Yug)
1921	J Samazeuilh (Fr)	S Lenglen (Fr)	1978	B Borg (Swed)	V Ruzici (Rom)
1922	H Cochet (Fr)	S Lenglen (Fr)	1979	B Borg (Swed)	C M Evert Lloyd (US)
1923	P Blanchy (Fr)	S Lenglen (Fr)	1980	B Borg (Swed)	C M Evert Lloyd (US)
1924	J Borotra (Fr)	D Vlasto (Fr)	1981	B Borg (Swed)	H Mandlikova (Cze)
1925	R Lacoste (Fr)	S Lenglen (Fr)	1982	M Wilander (Swe)	M Navratilova (US)
1926	H Cochet (Fr)	S Lenglen (Fr)	1983	Y Noah (Fr)	C M Evert Lloyd (US)
1927	R Lacoste (Fr)	K Bouman (Ned)	1984	I Lendl (Cze)	M Navratilova (US)
1928	H Cochet (Fr)	H N Wills (US)	1985	M Wilander (Swe)	C M Evert Lloyd (US)
1929	R Lacoste (Fr)	H N Wills (US)	1986	I Lendl (Cze)	C M Evert Lloyd (US)
1930	H Cochet (Fr)	H N Wills Moody (US)	1987	I Lendl (Cze)	S Graf (Ger)
			1988	M Wilander (Swe)	S Graf (Ger)
1931	J Borotra (Fr)	C Aussem (Ger)	1989	M Chang (US)	A Sanchez-Vicario (Spa)
1932	H Cochet (Fr)	H N Wills (US)			
1933	J H Crawford (Aus)	M C Scriven (GB)	1990	A Gomez (Ecu)	M Seles (Yug)
1934	G von Cramm (Ger)	M C Scriven (GB)	1991	J Courier (US)	M Seles (Yug)
1935	F J Perry (GB)	H Sperling (Den)	1992	J Courier (US)	M Seles (Yug)
1936	G von Cramm (Ger)	H Sperling (Den)	1993	S Bruguera (Spa)	S Graf (Ger)
1937	H Henkel (Ger)	H Sperling (Den)	1994	S Bruguera (Spa)	A Sanchez-Vicario (Spa)
1938	J D Budge (US)	S Mathieu (Fr)			
1939	W D McNeill (US)	S Mathieu (Fr)	1995	T Muster (Aut)	S Graf (Ger)
1940	not held	not held	1996	Y Kafelnikov (Rus)	S Graf (Ger)
1941	not held	not held	1997	G Kuerten (Braz)	I Majoli (Croat)
1942	not held	not held	1998	C Moya (Spa)	A Sanchez-Vicario (Spa)
1943	not held	not held			
1944	not held	not held	1999	A Agassi (US)	S Graf (Ger)
1945	not held	not held	2000	G Kuerten (Braz)	M Pierce (Fra)
1946	M Bernard (Fr)	M E Osborne (US)	2001	G Kuerten (Braz)	J Capriati (US)
1947	J Asboth (Hung)	P Todd (US)	2002	A Costa (Spa)	S Williams (US)
1948	F A Parker (US)	N Landry (Belg)	2003	J C Ferrero (Spa)	J Henin-Hardenne (Belg)
1949	F A Parker (US)	M E Osborne du Pont (US)			

Tennis: General Information

Australian Open: venue	Melbourne Park (formerly known as Flinders Park).
Davis Cup: inaugurated	1900.
most wins	USA.
official title	The International Men's Team Championship of the World.
Federation Cup	women's equivalent of the Davis Cup. Inaugurated in 1963. The United States defeated Australia 2–1 in the first final.
'Four Musketeers'	Jean Borotra, Jacques ('Toto') Brugnon, Henri Cochet, René Lacoste.
French Championships: made Open	before 1925 the French Championships were open only to members of French clubs.
French Open: venue	Roland Garros Stadium, Paris, since 1928.
Grand Slam: definition	winning the four major titles consecutively irrespective of calendar year (formerly had to be achieved in the calendar year).
holders	Donald Budge, Maureen Connolly, Margaret Court, Steffi Graf, Rod Laver (twice) and Martina Navratilova.
junior winner	Earl Buchholz won all four junior titles in 1958 followed by Stefan Edberg in 1983.
Hopman Cup	international mixed teams event first held between 28 December 1988 and 1 January 1989, Czechoslovakia beating Australia in the first championship.
net: height in middle	3 feet (91cm).
nicknames: Bounding Basque	Jean Borotra.
Poker Face	Helen Wills Moody.
Rocket	Rod Laver.
The Ghost	Harold Mahony.
The Two Helens	Helen Wills Moody and Helen Jacobs (great rivals and born on the same street in Berkeley, California).
Olympic champions: 1996	Lindsay Davenport (US) and André Agassi (US).
Olympic Games: ice hockey player	Jaroslav Drobny (Cze, 1948).
tennis challenge: battle of the sexes	Bobby Riggs had beaten Margaret Court but was then beaten by Billie Jean King (and famously presented with a pig).
tennis: original name	sphairistiké.
'Three Musketeers'	Jean Borotra, Henri Cochet, René Lacoste.
US Open: venue	Flushing Meadows, New York, since 1978. Finals showcourt named after Arthur Ashe.
Wimbledon champion: 1st black man	Arthur Ashe (1975).
1st black person	Althea Gibson (1957).
Mixed Doubles: brother and sister	John and Tracy Austin won the 1981 Championship.
man and wife	Mr and Mrs L A Godfree won the 1926 Championship.
boycott year	1973 (due to suspension of Nikki Pilic of Yugoslavia).
champion at first and only attempt	Bobby Riggs (1939) won all three titles on his only appearance at the Championships.
first professional champion	Rod Laver (1968).
last amateur champion	John Newcombe (1967).
longest match	5 hours 12 minutes: Pancho Gonzales beat Charlie Pasarell (22–24, 1–6, 16–14, 6–3, 11–9) in 1969 (this match hastened the need for the tie-break system).
oldest men's champion	Arthur Gore (41).
champion later represented Brazil in Davis Cup	Robert Falkenburg.
unseeded champion	Boris Becker (1985).
unseeded player in two finals	Kurt Nielsen (Den) beaten in 1953 and 1955.
youngest champion	Lottie Dod (GB) aged 15.
youngest men's champion	Boris Becker (Ger) aged 17.

Sporting Trophies

Name	Sport	Details	First held
Admirals Cup	yachting	biennial international competition for sailing yachts	1957
Air Canada Silver Broom	curling	formerly the Scotch Whisky Cup, became Air Canada in 1959	1968
America's Cup	yachting	originally called 100 Guineas Cup and raced around the Isle of Wight	1851
Ashes	cricket	England v Australia test matches (since 1882 called 'Ashes')	1877
Baron Matsui Inter-Club Cup	judo	club competition named after the Japanese Ambassador	1928
Beefeater's Gin	rowing	Oxford and Cambridge Boat Race	1829
Bledisloe Cup	rugby union	New Zealand v Australia	1931
Bologna Trophy	swimming	England v Scotland v Wales speed swimming contest	1929
Borg-Warner Trophy	motor racing	winner of the Indianapolis 500	1932
Bowring Bowl	rugby union	annual Oxbridge Varsity match	1872
Britannia Cup	yachting	for small yachts (under 32ft) of any country to challenge the holder	1951
Britannia Shield	speedway	inter-club challenge competition	1957
Calcutta Cup	rugby union	England v Scotland	1870
Camanachd Cup	shinty	championship of Scotland	1896
Canada Cup	golf	world team championship (two per team)	1953
Cole Cup	fencing	men's sabre	1922
Cowdray Park Gold Cup	polo	international competition	1956
Currie Cup	cricket	South African Provincial competition	1889
Currie Cup	rugby union	South African Provincial Championship	1892
Curtis Cup	golf	amateur women – USA v Great Britain and Ireland	1932
Davis Cup	tennis	The International Lawn Tennis Challenge Trophy	1900
Dewar Cup	rifle shooting	small-bore shooting competition	1909
Diamond Challenge	rowing	blue riband of single sculling	1884
Doggetts Coat & Badge	rowing	sculling contest on the Thames between ex-passenger skiffs	1715
Eisenhower Trophy	golf	biennial international competition	1958
Federation Cup	tennis	women's world amateur team championship	1963
George Hearn Cup	diving	awarded to England's most successful diver	1954
Goldberg-Vass Memorial Trophy	judo	London open competition	1956
Gordon Bennett Trophy	motor racing	forerunner of the Grand Prix	1901
Grand Challenge Cup	rowing	Henley Regatta – eights	1839
Grey Cup	Canadian football	championship game between winners of Eastern and Western Conferences	1909
G. Melville Clark Trophy	diving	awarded to England's most successful diving club	1951
Harry Sunderland Trophy	rugby league	man of the Premiership final. T Fogarty of Halifax first winner	1965
Heisman Memorial Trophy	American football	awarded annually by the Downtown Athlete Club of New York City to the outstanding college football player of the United States	1935
Henry Benjamin Trophy	swimming and water polo	awarded to England's most successful swimming and water polo club	1910
Iroquois Cup	lacrosse	English club championship	1890
Jules Rimet Trophy	football	world cup	1930
King George V Gold Cup	showjumping	men's international competition at Hickstead	1934
Kinnaird Cup	Eton fives	public schools' competition	1926
Lance Todd Award	rugby league	man of the match award in Challenge Cup final	1897
Lapham Trophy	squash	Canada v USA	1921
Londonderry Cup	squash	public schools' Old Boys' competition	1934
Lonsdale Belt	boxing	British title – won outright for winning three title fights at the same weight	1909
Lugano Trophy	walking	world championship of race walking	1961
MacRobertson International Shield	croquet	international competition	1925
Manuel Avila Camacho Cup	polo	Mexico v USA	1941
Marcel Corbillon Cup	table tennis	women's world table tennis team championships	1934
Marchant Cup	rugby fives	London grammar schools competition	1929
Middleton Cup	bowls	inter-county championship	1911
Philadelphia Gold Cup	rowing	Olympic single sculling trophy	1908
Pilkington Cup	rugby union	English club knockout cup (prev. National Cup)	1972

Presidents Trophy	golf	USA v Rest of World (Men)	1994
Prince of Wales Cup	yachting	international 14 ft dinghy championship	1927
Prince Rainier Cup	fencing	awarded tothe nation with best results in World Championships	1950
Princess Elizabeth Cup	rowing	Henley Regatta – eights for public schools	1946
Queen Elizabeth II Cup	showjumping	women's international competition at Hickstead	1949
Queen's Prize	rifle shooting	open competition first competed for at Wimbledon	1860
Ranfurly Shield	rugby union	NZ rugby trophy for provincial teams	1902
Regal Trophy	rugby league	formerly sponsored by John Player, became Regal Trophy in 1989	1971
Ryder Cup	golf	men – USA v Europe (USA v GB and I before 1979)	1927
Scottish Tennant's Cup	rugby union	Scottish club knockout cup	1996
Seawanhaka Cup	yachting	For small yachts (under 25ft) of any country to challenge the holder	1895
Silver Goblets & Nickalls Cup	rowing	Henley Regatta: coxless pairs amateur international	1845
Sir William Burton Trophy	yachting	national 12 ft dinghy championship	1936
Solheim Cup	golf	women – USA v Europe	1990
Stanley Cup	ice hockey	North American ice hockey championship	1894
Strathcona Cup	curling	Canada v Scotland international competition	1903
Subalterns' Cup	polo	inter-services competition	1896
Super 12 Trophy	rugby union	Southern Hemisphere provincial championship	1995
SWALEC Cup	rugby union	Welsh club knockout cup (prev. Welsh Cup, Schweppes Cup)	1972
Swaythling Cup	table tennis	men's world table tennis team championships	1927
Talbot Handicap	crown green bowls	Blackpool-based open competition	1882
Thomas Cup	badminton	men's world badminton team championship	1949
Über Cup	badminton	women's world badminton team championships	1957
Val Barker Trophy	boxing	most stylish boxer at an Olympic Games	1904
Vince Lombardi Trophy	American football	superbowl	1967
Volvo World Cup	showjumping	world championship competition	1979
Walker Cup	golf	amateur men – USA v Great Britain and Ireland	1922
Waterloo Cup	coursing	the 'Derby' of coursing, named after a Liverpool hotel	1836
Waterloo Cup	crown green bowls	Blackpool-based open competition	1907
Webb Ellis Trophy	rugby union	world cup	1987
Westchester Cup	polo	Great Britain v USA	1886
Wheeler-Schebber	motor racing	awarded to the leader of the Indianapolis 500 after 400 miles (160 laps), replaced in 1932 by the Borg-Warner Trophy	
Wightman Cup	tennis	annual team competition between USA and England	1923
Wolfe-Noel Cup	squash	USA v GB women's match	1933
Worrell Trophy	cricket	West Indies v Australia	1931
Wyfold Challenge Cup	rowing	Henley Regatta	1847
Yeaden Memorial Trophy	swimming	awarded to the English swimmer whose performance is adjudged the best	1938

NB The inaugural dates given are for the competition; in some cases the trophy has been renamed.

Sporting Trophies: Supplements

Britannia Cup	rowing	James Norris Trophy	ice hockey
Camrose Trophy	yachting	Leekes British Open	squash
Corble Cup	fencing	Leonard Trophy	bowls
Courtney Trophy	rugby League	Little Brown Jug	harness racing
Eden Cup	fencing	Melrose Trophy	rugby union
Espirito Santo Trophy	golf	Peall Trophy	car rallying
Gordon Bennett Cup	ballooning	Prince Philip Cup	rowing
Halford Hewitt Cup	golf	Prince Philip Trophy	showjumping
Hambleton	harness racing	Russell-Cargill Trophy	rugby union
Harmsworth Trophy	powerboat racing	Sam McGuire Trophy	Gaelic football
Hummel Super Cup	handball	Sheffield Shield	cricket
Hummel Super League	handball	Stewards Cup	rowing
Hurlingham Champion Cup	polo	Veuve Cliquot Gold Cup	polo
Ipswich Cup	fencing	Yetton Trophy	bowls

Television Sports Personality of the Year

Chris Chataway	1954	Sebastian Coe	1979
Gordon Pirie	1955	Robin Cousins	1980
Jim Laker	1956	Ian Botham	1981
Dai Rees	1957	Daley Thompson	1982
Ian Black	1958	Steve Cram	1983
John Surtees	1959	Torvill and Dean	1984
David Broome	1960	Barry McGuigan	1985
Stirling Moss	1961	Nigel Mansell	1986
Anita Lonsbrough	1962	Fatima Whitbread	1987
Dorothy Hyman	1963	Steve Davis	1988
Mary Rand	1964	Nick Faldo	1989
Tommy Simpson	1965	Paul Gascoigne	1990
Bobby Moore	1966	Liz McColgan	1991
Henry Cooper	1967	Nigel Mansell	1992
David Hemery	1968	Linford Christie	1993
Ann Jones	1969	Damon Hill	1994
Henry Cooper	1970	Jonathan Edwards	1995
HRH Princess Anne	1971	Damon Hill	1996
Mary Peters	1972	Greg Rusedski	1997
Jackie Stewart	1973	Michael Owen	1998
Brendan Foster	1974	Lennox Lewis	1999
David Steele	1975	Steve Redgrave	2000
John Curry	1976	David Beckham	2001
Virginia Wade	1977	Paula Radcliffe	2002
Steve Ovett	1978		

Commonwealth Games: Venues

Hamilton, Canada	1930	Christchurch, NZ	1974
London, England	1934	Edmonton, Canada	1978
Sydney, Australia	1938	Brisbane, Australia	1982
Auckland, NZ	1950	Edinburgh, Scotland	1986
Vancouver, Canada	1954	Auckland, NZ	1990
Cardiff, Wales	1958	Victoria, Canada	1994
Perth, Australia	1962	Kuala Lumpur, Malaysia	1998
Kingston, Jamaica	1966	Manchester, England	2002
Edinburgh, Scotland	1970	Melbourne, Australia	2006

Number of Players in a Team

		Details
polo	4	Up to 8 chukkas of $7^{1}/_{2}$ min
basketball	5	4 periods
ice hockey	6	3 periods of 20 min
volleyball	6	Court size: 30ft x 60ft
kabaddi	7	2 halves of 20 minutes each
netball	7	4 periods of 15 min
water polo	7	blue or white caps (red for goalkeepers)
baseball	9	9 innings
rounders	9	2 innings
American football	11	1 hour
football	11	2 halves of 45 min
cricket	11	see relevant section
hockey	11	field size: 100 yd x 60 yd (goal 4 yd x 7 ft high) men's, 2 halves of 35 min; women's, 2 of 30 min
stoolball	11	girls' game resembling cricket
lacrosse (men's)	10	4 periods of 15 min
lacrosse (women's)	12	4 periods of 15 min
Canadian football	12	field size: 110 yd x 65 yd
shinty	12	field size: 160 yd x 80 yd
rugby league	13	no wing forwards
rugby union	15	2 halves of 40 min
Gaelic football	15	2 periods of 30 min
hurling	15	women's version called 'camogie'
Australian rules	18	4 periods of 25 min

SPORT & LEISURE

Sportspeople

Ackland, Janet	bowls	Cadalora, Luca (Ita)	motor cycling (250cc and 125cc)
Adams, Neil	judo		
Alexander, Wayne	boxing	Caira, Philip Mario	weightlifting
Allahgreen, Diane	athletics	Callender, Simone	judo
Allan, Alister	shooting	Capirossi, Loris (Ita)	motor cycling (125cc and 250cc)
Alsop, Fred	triple jump		
Altwegg, Jeannette	figure skating	Carnill, Denys	hockey
Angus, Howard	rackets and real tennis	Cazelet, Victor	squash
Aoki, Haruchika (Jpn)	motor cycling (125cc)	Chambers, Dwayne	athletics
Appleyard, Bob	cricket	Chapman, Vera	hockey
Armstrong, Gary	rugby union	Cheape, Leslie	polo
Ashton, Eric	rugby league	Cheeseborough, Susan	gymnastics
Aspinall, Nigel	croquet	Chester, Frank	cricket
Astbury, Andrew	swimming	Chifney, Sam	horse racing
Atkins, Geoffrey	rackets	Childs, Joe	horse racing
Atkins, John	cyclo cross	Clark, Gillian	badminton
Baddeley, Steve	badminton	Clark, Roger	rallying
Baddeley, Wilfred and Herbert	tennis	Clarke, Chris	croquet
Baerlein, Edgar	rackets and real tennis	Cobb, John	motor racing
		Cockett, John	hockey
Baggaley, Andrew	table tennis	Colclough, Maurice	rugby union
Bailey, Bill	cycling	Colledge, Cecilia	figure skating
Bailey, McDonald	athletics	Collett, Rebecca	figure skating
Bailey, William James	cycling	Collins, Peter (1931–58)	motor racing
Baillieu, Chris	rowing	Collins, Peter (1954–)	speedway
Baird, Charlotte	surfing	Cooke, Rebecca	swimming
Baker, Edwin Percy	bowls	Cooper, Charlotte	tennis
Baker, Philip Noel	athletics (1959 Nobel Peace Prize)	Cooper, Malcolm	shooting
		Cotter, Edmond	croquet
Baker, Zoe	swimming	Covey, Fred	real tennis
Bakewell, Enid	cricket	Craven, Peter	speedway
Balashov, Alexandr (Rus)	ice speedway	Creus, Julian	weightlifting
Balding, Gerald	polo	Cripps, Norwood	rackets and real tennis
Balding, Gerald Matthews	polo		
Ball, John	golf	Cronshey, John Dennis	speed skating
Barber, Paul	hockey	Crooks, Lee	rugby league
Barnato, Woolf	motor racing	Crooks, Tim	rowing
Barrichello, Rubens (Braz)	motor racing (Formula 1)	Culvert, David	shooting
		Cumming, Arthur	figure skating
Barry, Ernest	rowing	Curry, Joan	squash and tennis
Barton, Pam	golf	Cutler, David	bowls
Beamish, George	rugby union	Daly, Fred	golf
Beck, Margaret	badminton	Datoo, Camille	fencing
Bedell-Sivright, Darkie	rugby union	Davidge, Chris	rowing
Bell, Diane	judo	Davies, Terry	rugby union
Beresford, Jack	rowing	Davis, Howard	hockey
Besford, Jack	swimming	Dawes, Alison	show jumping
Biaggi, Massimiliano (Ita)	motor cycling (250cc)	De Beaumont, Charles	fencing
Bickers, Dave	motocross	De Wharton Burr, Nilla	archery
Black, Ian	swimming	Dear, Jim	rackets, real tennis, squash
Blenkinsop, Ernie	football		
Bond-Williams, Louise	fencing	Deaton, Nicola	table tennis
Boocock, Nigel	speedway	Dempsey, Jack 'Nonpareil'	boxing
Boone, Willie	rackets	Denny, Doreen	ice dancing
Bourne, Teddy	fencing	Disley, John	steeplechaser
Bowman, George	carriage driving	Dixon, Charles	tennis
Bradley, Caroline	show jumping	Dixon, Karen	three-day event
Bradshaw, Harry	golf	Dixon, Robin	bobsleigh
Braid, James	golf	Dod, Willie	archery
Braithwaite, Bob	shooting	Doherty, Reggie	tennis
Briggs, Johnny	cricket	Donaldson, Walter	snooker
Briggs, Karen	judo	Doohan, Michael (Aus)	motor cycling (500cc)
Brinkley, Brian	swimming	Doyle, Tony	cycling
Brittin, Janette	cricket	Driffield, Leslie	billiards
Brockway, John	swimming	Drummond, Des	rugby league
Bromfield, Percy	table tennis	Drummond-Hay, Anneli	show jumping
Bullen, Jane	three-day event	Duke, Geoff	motor cycling (500cc)
Butcher, Don	squash	Dugard, Martin	speedway

Eastman, Howard	boxing	Hatfield, Jack	swimming
Edwards, Hugh 'Jumbo'	rowing	Hathorn, Gina	skiing
Edwards, Margaret	swimming	Hatton, Ricky	boxing
Egan, Joe	rugby league	Haughton, Colin	badminton
Elford, Vic	motor racing	Havelock, Gary	speedway
Ellaby, Alf	rugby league	Hawke, Lord Martin	cricket
Elliot, Douglas	rugby union	Healey, Donald	rallying
Elliot, Helen	table tennis	Heaney, Julz	water skiing
Elliot, Launceston	weightlifting	Heaney, Nick	water skiing
Elwell, Keith	rugby league	Heatley, Basil	marathon
Erhardt, Carl	ice hockey	Heatly, Peter	diving
Evans, Mal	bowls	Helme, Gerry	rugby league
Everts, Stefan (Bel)	motocross	Hendren, Patsy	cricket
Fairbrother, Nicola	judo	Herriott, Maurice	steeplechaser
Fairs, Punch	real tennis	Hicks, Humphrey	croquet
Fallon, Craig	judo	Hide, Molly	cricket
Farndon, Tom	speedway	Hill, Albert	athletics
Farr, Judy	walking	Hiller, Bob	rugby union
Ferris, Liz	diving	Hilton, Elliot	ice skating
Ferris, Sam	marathon	Hipwood, Julian	polo
Figg, James	boxing	Hocking, Gary (Zim)	motor cycling (500cc)
Flockhart, Ron	motor racing		
Fogarty, Carl	superbike racing	Hodgson, Neil	superbike racing
Ford, Bernard	ice dancing	Holden, Jack	marathon
Ford, Horace	archery	Holmes, Andrea	trampolining
Ford, Trevor	football	Holmes, Terry	rugby union
Fordham, George	football	Horgan, Denis	shot putter
Foster, Jimmy	ice hockey	Hoskyns, Bill	fencing
Fox, Jim	modern pentathlon	Hoy, Chris	cycling
Fox, Neil	rugby league	Howland, Bonzo	shot putter
Fox, Richard	canoeing	Hume, Donald	badminton
Fox-Pitt, William	equestrianism	Inman, Melbourne	billiards
Freeman, Alfred 'Tich'	cricket	Ireland, Innes	motor racing
Frentzen, Heinz-Harold (Ger)	motor racing (Formula 1)	Ivy, Bill	motor cycling (125cc)
		Jackson, Kanukai	gymnastics
Frith, Frederick	motor cycling	James, Carwyn	rugby union
Fulford, Robert	croquet	Jameson, Andrew	swimming
Fulton, Arthur	shooting	Jameson, Tommy	squash
Funnell, Pippa	equestrianism	Jarrett, Keith	rugby union and league
Furrer, Carl	trampolining		
Galica, Davina	skiing and motor racing	Jarvis, John	swimming
		Jay, Allan	fencing
Gallie, Christine	judo	Jeeps, Dickie	rugby union
Gardner, Jason	athletics	Johnson, Ralph	fencing
Gault, Michael	shooting	Johnson, Tebbs Lloyd	walking
Gee, Kenneth	rugby league	Jones, Cliff (1914–90)	rugby union
George, Walter	athletics	Jones, Cliff (1935–)	football
Giles, Jack	squash	Jones, Courtney	ice dancing
Glen Haig, Mary	fencing	Jones, Mandy	cycling
Goddard, James	swimming	Jordan, Tony	badminton
Gordon, Winston	judo	Kane, Peter	boxing
Gower, Lily	croquet	Karalius, Vince	rugby league
Grace, Edward Mills	cricket	Keane, Moss	rugby union
Green, Tommy	walking	Keenan, Peter	boxing
Greenwood, Giles	weightlifting	Kelly, Sean	cycling
Guthrie, Jimmy	motor cycling	Kelly-Hohmann, Margaret	swimming
Haining, Peter	rowing	Kelsey, Jack	football
Hale, Jack	swimming	Kendall-Carpenter, John	rugby union
Hall, Darren	badminton	Kerly, Sean	hockey
Hallam, Ian	cycling	Kershaw, Cecil	rugby union
Hallard, Steve	archery	King, Norman	bowls
Halliday, Jim	weightlifting	King, Shayne (NZ)	motocross
Hamill, Billy (USA)	speedway	Kitchen, Bill	speedway
Hancock, Greg (USA)	speedway	Knight, Billy	tennis
Hand, Tony	ice hockey	Kocinski, John (USA)	motor cycling (250cc and superbikes)
Harding, Phyllis	swimming		
Hardisty, Alan	rugby league	Laidlaw, Roy	rugby union
Hardstaff, Joe	cricket	Langton, Eric	speedway
Harlow, Greg	bowls	Larcombe, Ethel	tennis
Harper, Ernie	marathon	Larner, George	walking
Harris, Lord George	cricket	Latham, Peter	rackets and real tennis
Harris, Reg	cycling		

Lawler, Ivan	canoeing	Milford, David	rackets
Lawton, Barbara	high jumper	Millar, Robert	cycling
Leather, Diane	athletics	Miller, David	bowls
Leden, Judy	hang gliding	Miller, Sammy	motor cycling
Lee, George	gliding	Millward, Roger	rugby league
Lee, Michael	speedway	Minter, Derek	motor cycling
Lee, Sidney	billiards	Mitchell, Abe	golf
Legh, Alice	archery	Mitchell, Beryl	rowing
Leman, Richard	hockey	Mitchell, William	billiards
Le Moignan, Martine	squash	Monaghan, Terry	speed skating
Lennox, Avril	gymnastics	Montgomerie, Robert	fencing
Lerwill, Alan	long jumper	Moore, Ann	show jumping
Lessing, Simon	triathlon	Moore, Steve	water skiing
Lewis-Francis, Mark	athletics	Morgan, Janet	squash
Line, Peter	bowls	Morris, Stewart	yachting
Lloyd, Emrys	fencing	Morton, Lucy	swimming
Long, Liz	swimming	Moss, Pat	rallying
Lorum, Mark	speedway	Mould, Marion	show jumping
Loris, Chris	speedway	Muckelt, Ethel	figure skating
Lowe, Samantha	judo	Murphy, Catherine	athletics
Lucas, Muriel	badminton	Mynn, Alfred	cricket
Lumb, Margot	squash	Nash, Tony	bobsleigh
Lumley, Penny	real tennis	Neale, Denis	table tennis
Lunn family	skiing	Neligan, Gwen	fencing
Lunn, Gladys	athletics	Nettleton, Louise	archery
Lycett, Randolph	tennis	Nevett, Bill	jockey
Lynch, Benny	flyweight boxer	Neville, Gary	football
Mace, Jem	middleweight boxer	Neville, Phil	football
Mack, Curly	badminton	Neville, Tracey	netball (sister of Gary
Mackey, Mick	hurling		& Phil)
Mackinnon, Esmé	skiing	Newall, Queenie	archery
Maduaka, Joice	athletics	Newman, Tom	billiards
Mahoney, Harold	tennis	Nicholas, Alison	golf
Male, James	rackets and real	Nielsen, Hans (Den)	speedway
	tennis	Nieto, Angel (Esp)	motor cycling (125cc)
Mallin, Frederick	middleweight boxer	Noel, Susan	squash
Mallin, Harry	middleweight boxer	Norman, Wendy	modern pentathlon
Mann, Julia	badminton	Obolensky, Alex	rugby union
Mannion, Wilf	football	Obree, Graeme	cycling
Mansergh, Terence	hockey	O'Dell, George	motor cycling
Mapple, Andy	water skiing	O'Keefe, Dan	Gaelic football
Marques, David	rugby union	Oliver, Alan	show jumping
Marshall, Peter	squash	Oliver, Eric	sidecar racing
Martin, Louis	weightlifting	Opie, Lisa	squash
Martin, Stephen	hockey	O'Reilly, Wilf	speed skating
Matthews, Ken	walking	Ottley, Dave	javelin
McAuliffe, Jack	lightweight boxer	Paish, Geoff	tennis
McAvoy, Jock	light-heavyweight	Palmer, Charles	judo
	boxer	Palmer, Thomas 'Pedlar'	bantamweight boxer
McCoig, Robert	badminton	Panis, Olivier (Fra)	motor racing
McConnell, William	hockey		(Formula 1)
McEvoy, Freddie	bobsleigh	Parke, James	tennis and rugby union
McGregor, Yvonne	cycling	Parker, Jack	speedway
McIntyre, Bob	motor cycling	Paterson, Alan	high jumper
McKechnie, Neil	swimming	Pattisson, Rodney	yachting
McKenzie, George	Wrestling	Patton, Peter	ice hockey
McKiernan, Catherina	athletics	Paul, René	fencing
McKinlay, Ken	speedway	Payne, Howard	hammer thrower
McLean, William	hockey	Payne, Rosemary	discus thrower
McLeod, Hugh	rugby union	Paynter, Eddie	cricket
McNeill, Carol	orienteering	Peall, W J	billiards
McQueen, Delroy	weightlifting	Peck, Geoff	orienteering
McRae, Alister	rallying	Petersen, Jack	light-heavyweight
McRae, Colin	rallying		boxer
McRae, Jimmy	rallying	Phelps, Brian	diving and
McTigue, Mike	boxing		trampolining
Meade, Richard	three-day event	Phelps, Richard	modern pentathlon
Menu, Alain (Switz)	touring cars	Phelps, Ted	rowing
Meredith, Billy	football	Phillips, Mollie	figure skating
Meredith, Leon	cycling	Pickering, Jean	long jumper
Miles, Eustace	rackets and real	Pickering, Karen	swimming
	tennis	Pilch, Fuller	cricket

Pinching, Evie	skiing	Sekjer, Martyn	bowls
Platt, Susan	javelin	Seligman, Edgar	fencing
Porter, Hugh	cyclist	Sharpe, Graham	figure skating
Potter, Jon	hockey	Shaw, Norma	bowls
Potter, Martin	surfing	Sheen, Gillian	fencing
Prenn, John	rackets	Sheil, Norman	cycling
Price, Berwyn	athletics	Sheppard, Alison	swimming
Price, Sarah	swimming	Sheridan, Eileen	cycling
Price, Tommy	speedway	Shilcock, Anne	tennis
Probyn, Jeff	rugby union	Shotton, Sue	trampolining
Pullin, John	rugby union	Shoveller, Stanley	hockey
Radford, Peter	athletics	Shrubb, Alf	athletics
Radmilovic, Paul	swimming and water polo	Simmers, Max	rugby union
		Simmonds, Dave	motor cycling (125cc)
Rainey, Wayne (USA)	motor cycling (500cc)		
Randall, Graeme	judo	Simmonite, Rachael	rallying
Ray, Ted	golf	Simmonite, Stephanie	rallying
Read, Phil	motor cycling (125cc and 250cc)	Simpson, Cyril	rackets
		Simpson, Tommy	cycling
Redman, Jim (Zim)	motor cycling (250cc)	Singleton, Georgina	judo
Reece, Tom	billiards	Singleton, Joey	boxing
Rendle, Sharon	judo	Sixsmith, Janet	hockey
Renshaw, William	tennis	Slawinski, Kendra	netball
Rhodes, Ronald	canoeing	Small, Ruth	bowls
Richards, Gordon W (1930–98)	horse racing	Smith, Charles	water polo
		Smith, Lawrie	yachting
Richards, Sir Gordon (1904–86)	horse racing	Smith, Sydney	tennis
		Smithies, Karen	cricket
Richards, Tom	marathon	Snode, Chris	diving
Richardson, Peter	cricket	Snow, John	cricket
Richardson, T D	figure skating	Snow, Julian	real tennis
Richmond, Ken	wrestling and judo	Snowball, Betty	cricket
Ring, Christy	hurling	Solomon, John	croquet
Ringer, Anthony	shooting	Sopwith, Sir Tommy	yachting
Riseley, Frank	tennis	Springman, Sarah	triathlon
Ritchie, Margaret	discus	Stammers, Kay	tennis
Roberts, John	billiards	Starbrook, Dave	judo
Roberts, Karen	judo	Steel, Dorothy	croquet
Roberts, Philippa	water skiing	Steele, Mavis	bowls
Robinson, Brian	cycling	Stevens, Ray	badminton
Robinson, Jem	horse racing	Stewart-Wood, Jeannette	water skiing
Robinson, Val	hockey	Stoop, Adrian	rugby union
Rogers, Iris	badminton	Sturgess, Colin	cycling
Rogers, Michelle	judo	Sturgess, William	walking
Ronaldson, Chloe	roller skating	Surtees, William	rackets
Rooney, Wayne	football	Talbot, Derek	badminton
Rose, Justin	golf	Tancred, Bill	discus
Ross, Jonathan	bowls	Tanner, Haydn	rugby union
Round, Dorothy	tennis	Tarleton, Nelson	boxing
Rowe, Arthur	shot putter	Tate, Maurice	cricket
Rowe, Diana	table tennis	Tatum, Kelvin	speedway
Rowe, Rosalind	table tennis	Taylor, Ian	hockey
Russell-Vick, Mary	hockey	Terry, Simon	archery
Rutherford, Monica	gymnastics	Thomas, Neil	gymnastics
Salo, Mika (Fin)	motor racing (Formula 1)	Thompson, Don	walking
		Thompson, Ian	marathon
Salvadori, Roy	motor racing	Thomson, Andy	bowls
Sandford, Cecil	motor cycling (125cc and 250cc)	Thorpe, Dave	motocross
		Tisdall, Bob	400m hurdler
Saunders, Vivien	golf	Tomes, Alan	rugby union
Savage, David	hockey	Tomlins, Freddie	figure skating
Saville, Sammy	hockey	Tortelli, Sébastien (USA)	motocross
Schofield, Garry	rugby league	Towler, Diane	ice dancing
Schwantz, Kevin (USA)	motor cycling (500cc)	Tredgett, Mike	badminton
		Tredgold, Roger	fencing
Scotland, Ken	rugby union	Trew, Billy	rugby union
Scott, Peter	yachting and gliding	Troke, Helen	badminton
Scriven, Peggy	tennis	Tucker, Andrew	shooting
Seaman, Dick	motor racing	Tucker, Sam	rugby union
Searle, Greg and Johnny	rowing	Tuckey, Raymond	tennis
Seaton, Paul	water skiing	Tweddle, Elisabeth	gymnastics
Segrave, Henry	motor racing	Tyler, Dorothy	high jumper

SPORT & LEISURE

Ubbiali, Carlo (Ita)	motor cycling (125cc and 250cc)	Westwood, Jean	ice dance
Uber, Betty	badminton	White, Belle	diving
Ulyett, George	cricket	White, Wilf	show jumping
Usher, Georgina	fencing	Whitehead, Adam	swimming
Verstappen, Jos (Neth)	motor racing (Formula 1)	Whiteley, Johnny	rugby league
Vickers, Stan	walking	Whitford, Arthur	gymnastics
Wagstaff, Harold	rugby league	Whitlock, Harold	walking
Walker, Stefanie	ice dancing	Whittle, Harry	athletics
Wallace, Shaun	cycling	Whyte, Jamie	ice dancing
Warburg, David	real tennis	Wigg, Simon	speedway
Ward, David	bowls	Wilkinson, Diana	swimming
Ward, Pat	tennis	Wilkinson, George	water polo
Wardrop, Jack	swimming	Williams, Freddie	speedway
Warner, Sir Pelham	cricket	Wills, Philip	gliding
Warren, James	judo	Wonderful Terrific Mons III (USA)	baseball
Waterman, Split	speedway	Wooderson, Sydney	athletics
Watson, Maud	tennis	Woodgate, W.B.	rowing
Watson, Willie	cricket and football	Woodward, Clive	rugby union
Webster, Steve	motor cycling (sidecars)	Woodward, Vivian	football
Weetman, Harry	golf	Wooller, Wilf	rugby union
Welsh, Freddie	boxing	Woosnam, Max	tennis and football
		Yardley, Norman	cricket

NB The table above is merely a list of perhaps less well-known sports people, due either to their practising a minority sport or to the time elapsed since their success. A more thorough record of their achievements is beyond the scope of this book. Sportspeople listed are British unless stated otherwise.

Sporting Terms

adolph *trampolining* three-and-a-half front twisting somersault.

airshot *golf* complete missing of ball which constitutes a stroke (unless mulligan awarded).

albatross *golf* score of 3 under par on a particular hole.

appel *fencing* beating or stamping of foot during contest.

apron *golf* grass cut short between fairway and approach to the green.

Arab spring *gymnastics* cartwheel with a quarter turn.

assist *basketball* final pass given to shooter of a basket.

axel *ice skating* a one-and-a-half turn jump from the forward outside edge of one skate to the backward outside edge of the other (named after Norwegian skater Axel Rudolph Paulser).

back alley *badminton* the area at the back of the court.

bai-hou *karate* white crane stance with one knee raised high (popularised in *Karate Kid* films).

balestra *fencing* attack after an appel.

barani *trampolining* front somersault with half twist.

battery *baseball* originally a term for the pitcher but now incorporates the pitcher and catcher.

baulk *billiards* line from which game begins.

ba(u)lk *baseball* illegal action by a pitcher.

beamer *cricket* ball bowled higher than a full toss so endangering the batsman.

Bernouilli effect *hang-gliding* see venturi effect.

besom *curling* type of broom used to sweep the ice to gain more distance.

bib *netball* tie-up over top with player's position labelled.

birdie *golf* score of 1 under par on a hole.

blind side *rugby* short side between scrum and touch line.

block *volleyball* basic return at the net to counter the opponent's spike.

blocking *basketball* illegal personal contact that impedes the progress of an opponent who does not have the ball.

bogey *golf* score of 1 over par on a hole.

bonk *cycling* tiredness caused by lack of food.

bonspiel *curling* term used for an important match.

boom *yachting* long spar or pole hinged at one end, securing the bottom of a ship's sail.

bosey / bosie *cricket* Australian name for a googly (named after B J T Bosanquet 1877–1936, an English cricketer).

Boston crab *wrestling* manoeuvre whereby one fighter sits on the back of the other with legs tucked under his arms.

bouncer *cricket* ball bowled short and fast in order to cause batsman to take evasive action.

bowling crease *cricket* line extended from the stumps sideways and four feet behind the popping crease; the ball must be delivered between these two lines.

brakeman *bobsleigh* person who operates the brakes in the sleigh.

Brill bend *high jumping* named after Debbie Brill, equivalent to the Fosbury flop.

brush *curling* implement for sweeping the ice, thereby causing the stone to travel further.

bunt *baseball* to let the ball hit the bat without swinging at it.

burgee *yachting* ornamental flag which serves no other purpose.

buttonhook *American football* type of pass for the receiver running straight downfield and then doubling back a few steps to receive it.

bye *cricket* extra gained by batting side when the batsmen run or the ball crosses the boundary after no contact with bat has taken place.

calx *Eton wall game* area behind the goal-line.

caman *shinty* stick used for striking.

cannon *billiards* object ball hitting opponent's ball and the red ball (scores 3 points).

capriole *dressage* horse jumps straight upward with its forelegs drawn in, kicking back with its hind legs horizontal.

catch *real tennis* obsolete former name for the game.

catch a crab *rowing* to get an oar trapped underwater or to miss the water with a stroke.

catenaccio system *football* sweeper system.

checking *ice hockey* legal manoeuvre of physical contact to gain control of puck.

chicane *motor racing* sharp double-bend.

chinaman *cricket* left-handed bowler's googly to a right-handed batsman.

chistera *pelota / jaii alaii* curved glove with a chestnut or ash frame, aka Cesta.

christiania *skiing* turn in which the skis are kept in parallel, used for stopping short. Aka christie.

Christmas tree *drag racing* starting system.

Christmas tree *football* descriptive formation.

chui *judo* warning with 3 points deducted.

chukka *polo* each of the 7½-minute periods into which a game is divided. Also spelt 'chucker' or 'chukker'.

close-hauled *wind surfing* area 45 degrees each side of wind direction.

conversion *Canadian football* method of adding to score after touchdown has been scored.

conversion *rugby* method of adding to score after try has been scored (2 points score).

courbet / curvet *dressage* jump forward at the levade.

cover *cricket* fielding position midway between infield and outfield in which a good fielder may save a single.

cover point *cricket* fielding position on the off side and nearer the batsman than the non-striker.

crampon *curling* device formerly used to enable a steady delivery but now obsolete.

crampon *rock-climbing* frame with 10 or 12 metal spikes, strapped to boots to give a firmer footing.

cross buttock *wrestling* throw in which a wrestler throws an opponent head first over his or her hip.

crosse *lacrosse* stick between 40–72 inches long and 4–10 inches wide.

crucifix *gymnastics (rings)* basic position with the arms held outstretched to the sides.

curve ball *baseball* ball which deviates from the path it would otherwise take, because of the spin imparted by the pitcher.

cut line *squash* line above which a served ball must strike the wall.

dan *martial arts* each of the numbered grades of the advanced level of proficiency in many martial arts.

diamond *baseball* the area formed by the four bases within the infield.

dig *volleyball* defensive motion of digging the ball up from below the net height with two hands to counter a spike.

ditch *bowls* the channel around the rink.

dog-leg *golf* hole that bends sharply to one side, so ensuring a positional shot is played.

domestiques *cycling* team members of tour teams who will sacrifice their position for team leaders.

double eagle *golf* score of 3 under par on a particular hole (US term).

down *American football* each of a fixed number of attempts to advance the ball 10 yards.

drop-kick *rugby* kick made by dropping the ball and kicking it as it rebounds from the ground.

drop-out *rugby* a drop-kick made from within the defending team's 22-metre (formerly 25yds) line in order to restart play after the ball has gone dead.

drop-line *angling* weighted fishing-line for fishing near the bottom of a waterway.

dropped goal *rugby* goal scored with a drop-kick that propels the ball over the crossbar.

dummy, sell a *rugby* to successfully feign a pass.

dunk *basketball* shoot a basket by jumping so that the hands are above the ring and the ball is dunked down through the hoop.

eagle *American football* defensive formation.

eagle *golf* score of 2 under par on a hole.

egg position *skiing* tucked position that ensures a good fast glide.

en garde *fencing* call to a fencer to adopt a defensive stance in readiness for an attack or bout.

end *bowls* division of a match whereby after all woods are bowled the next 'end' is played from the other end of the rink.

end *curling* division of a match whereby after all stones are bowled the next 'end' is played from the other end of the rink.

English *pool* north American term for using 'side' on the cueball.

Eskimo roll *canoeing* a 360-degree roll starting and finishing above water but 180 degrees of which is underwater.

expedite *table tennis* rule whereby a match is brought to a conclusion after a series of long rallies or deuces by setting a limit to the number of strokes per point.

extras *cricket* generic name for all types of byes and penalty runs scored other than by the batsman hitting the ball.

face-off *ice hockey* start of game.

fairway *golf* part of golf course between tee and green in which the grass is cut short to reward accuracy.

feng taidu *kung fu* phoenix stance keeping low on one leg ready to rise.

fine leg *cricket* fielding position between wicket keeper and square leg but deeper.

flèche *archery* obsolete name for an arrow.

flèche *fencing* a running attack.

flic flac *gymnastics* simple back flip.

fliffis *trampolining* double front somersault with twist.

flying mare *wrestling* throw in which one wrestler throws the other over his or her back using the other's arm as a lever.

Fosbury flop *high jumping* technique named after Dick Fosbury, whereby head and shoulders are thrown over the bar first, chest upwards and with legs pulled back to ensure economical clearance.

free throw *basketball* free shot at basket due to an infringement by the opposition.

fukuro shinai *kendo* wooden sword often covered in cloth or leather.

full-nelson *wrestling* two-handed hold whereby the

SPORT & LEISURE

arms are placed under the arms of the opponent and interlocked behind his neck, immobilising the upper body.

gaff *yachting* spar situated on the after side of a mast and supporting the head of a fore-and-aft sail.

garryowen *rugby* another name for an up and under.

genoa *yachting* large jib with a low foot.

gojo-ryu *karate* hard / soft technique.

gokuhi *martial arts* techniques and 'secrets' of masters relayed to gifted students.

googly *cricket* off-break ball bowled with apparent leg-break action.

goosewinged *yachting* square-rigged boats having the topsail spread for scudding under when the wind is strong, the bunt of the sail being hauled up to the yard.

gridiron *American football* the field of play.

gully *cricket* fielding position a little wider than the slips.

gybe *yachting* of a fore-and-aft sail or its boom, to swing from one side of a vessel to the other.

hack *curling* notch made in the ice used to steady the foot when delivering a stone.

hackamore *horse racing* bitless bridle with a hard oval noseband which allows pressure to be exerted on the nose by means of the reins attached just in front of a heavy counterbalancing knot.

half-nelson *wrestling* hold whereby the arm of the opponent is bent behind his back and pushed upwards.

halyard *yachting* rope or tackle for raising or lowering a sail.

hammer grip *table tennis* rarely used method of holding the bat whereby no fingers touch its face.

hand-in *squash* the server.

hand-out *squash* when player loses a point on his service he becomes hand-out.

haute école *dressage* advanced training methods (high school).

head *bowls* the grouping of the woods around the jack.

hecht *gymnastics* dismount from the asymmetric bars head and body first between bars.

held ball *basketball* called when two opponents have one or two hands so firmly upon the ball that neither can gain possession.

herringboning *skiing* method of climbing a slope by walking with the skis pointing outwards.

hikiwake *kendo* a draw in a competitive match.

hog line *curling* line behind which the stone must be delivered.

hog's back *equestrianism* sharp-ridged natural mound for jumping.

honk *cycling* cycling out of the saddle.

hooker *rugby* front row of scrum position player supported between the two props who attemps to hook ball back with his feet to be used by his team.

hoop *basketball* the metal ring of the 'basket'.

hoop *croquet* arch through which the ball must be driven.

house *curling* the round target area of concentric circles.

I formation *American football* offensive formation.

in touch *rugby* out of play.

ippon *judo* full point in Japan (scores 10 points in competition).

Irish whip *wrestling* one-handed throw whereby the arm is whipped back and forth forcing a somersault in the air by the opponent.

jack *bowls* white ball which is the target for the woods.

jib *yachting* triangular staysail stretching from the outer end of the jib-boom to the fore-topmast.

judoka *judo* judo player.

jugogi *judo* judo suit.

jump ball *basketball* method of putting the ball into play whereby the referee tosses it up between two opponents who try to tap it to a teammate.

katame-waza *judo* basic hold.

keikoku *judo* judge's warning with 7 points deducted.

kinsa *judo* 3 point scoring technique.

kip *gymnastics* movement whereby the body is straightened from a piked position by pushing the hips forward and the legs back.

knock-on *rugby* illegal move that knocks the ball forward and on to the ground with hand or arm.

koka *judo* hold between 10 and 20 seconds.

kyu *martial arts* student.

laundry *drag racing* the parachute that slows the cars down.

leg-bye *cricket* run scored after the ball has touched any part of the batsman but his hand.

leg side *cricket* the side of the wicket on which the receiving batsman stands.

levade *dressage* horse raises and draws in its forelegs, standing balanced on its bent hind legs.

line-out *rugby* method of throwing ball back into play between two lines of opposing forwards after it has gone out over the touchline.

lock *rugby* one of two forwards in second row of scrum.

long bomb *roller hockey* long pass from defence to set up sudden counter-attack.

long dong *kung fu* eastern dragon position with one hand in front of forehead (palm out) and the other covering abdomen (palm down).

long hop *cricket* ball that is bowled flat and short so as to almost bounce twice before reaching batsman.

luff *yachting* the edge of a fore-and-aft sail next to the mast or stay (among other definitions it is also a term for obstructing the opposition attempting to pass on the windward side by sailing closer to the wind).

lutz *ice skating* jump in which the skater takes off from the outside back edge of one skate and lands, after full rotation, on the outside back edge of the other.

maiden *cricket* an over in which no runs have been scored.

mallet *croquet* the striking implement used to manoeuvre the ball through the hoops.

mashie *golf* obsolete colloquial name for a no. 5 iron.

mashie-niblick *golf* obsolete colloquial name for a no. 7 iron.

mata *judo* break of a hold.

maul *rugby* distinguished from ruck by ball being held off the ground.

men *kendo* the armour that covers the head and face.

mid-off *cricket* fielding position on the side opposite to where the facing batsman stands; in the case of a right-handed batsman, to the left of the bowler during his run-up.

mid-on *cricket* fielding position on the side where

the facing batsman stands; in the case of a right-handed batsman, to the right of the bowler during his run-up.

mid-wicket *cricket* self-explanatory fielding position whereby if an equilateral triangle was plotted using the 22 yards between the stumps, mid-wicket would lie on the apex.

monkey climb *wrestling* move whereby one wrestler climbs up and wraps himself around the other to immobilise him.

mulligan *golf* free stroke awarded informally after a poor shot, usually an air shot.

nage-waza *judo* basic throw.

niblick *golf* obsolete colloquial name for a sand wedge or sometimes a wedge.

night watchman *cricket* lower-order batsman who comes in up the order to protect a key player if a wicket is lost near close of play.

no side *rugby* official name for end of the game, no longer commonly used.

nock *archery* notch at end of bow to run string through.

nocking point *archery* point of a bowstring to which the notch of an arrow is applied.

Notre Dame shift *American football* offensive move whereby the backs move just before the snap of the ball from their T-formation.

nunchaku *kung fu* rice flail used in exhibitions.

nutmeg *football* to play the ball between the legs of a defender and run around him to collect it.

O'Brien shift *shot putting* common gliding technique named after Parry O'Brien.

Oklahoma *American football* defensive formation.

oxer *equestrianism* brush fence with a guard rail on one side.

ozeki *sumo* the second rank after yokozuna (means 'great barrier').

painter *yachting* short rope or chain by which the shank of an anchor is held fast.

parallelogram *Gaelic football* playing area.

parry *fencing* warding off an attack especially with a counter.

passage *dressage* cadenced high-stepping trot.

pebble *curling* another name for a stone.

penholder grip *table tennis* method of holding the bat like a pencil popularised by the Chinese; quick footwork is essential as backhands are impossible to play. Aka eastern grip.

penthouse *real tennis* sloping roof of the corridor or gallery running around three sides of the court.

piaffe *dressage* a trot in place.

pick *basketball* action of a player who, without causing contact, delays or prevents an opponent from reaching his desired position.

pick-up *sprinting* second phase of race after the start during which the head is raised and relaxation starts.

pile-driver *wrestling* up-ending the opponent and driving his head into the canvas.

pinch-hitter *baseball* less technically accomplished player capable of hitting out forcefully.

piste *fencing* total fencing area.

piste *skiing* total skiing area.

pitcher *baseball* specialist thrower of the ball towards the opposing batter.

piton *rock-climbing* eye peg hammered into rock so that a rope can be attached.

pivot *basketball* movement in which a player with the ball steps once or more in any direction with the

same foot while the other foot is kept at its point of contact with the floor.

plastron *fencing* padded, leather-covered breastplate.

point *cricket* off-side fielding position wide of gully.

popping crease *cricket* line four feet in front of and parallel to the wicket within which the batsmen must remain unless the ball is dead or they are running.

press *basketball* defensive technique of harassing players into hurried play.

prop *rugby* one of the two forwards in the front row of the scrum who support hooker.

puck *ice hockey* flat rubber disc used in place of ball.

puissance *show jumping* high jump event.

punt *rugby* kick made by dropping the ball and kicking before it hits the ground.

putout *baseball* self-explanatory term meaning to cause a batter or base runner to be out.

quarterback *American football* player stationed behind the centre who directs a team's attacking play.

rack *pool* implement used for setting the red balls at the start of a frame (also the name used for an individual frame).

randolph (randi) *trampolining* two-and-a-half twisting front somersault.

repechage *rowing* a second chance for the best of the losing rowers in eliminating heats to progress to a final.

return crease *cricket* the lines either side of the wicket at right angles to the bowling crease.

riposte *fencing* a lunge or quick thrust after parrying.

rocker *ice skating* a skate with a curved blade.

roquet *croquet* to strike another player's ball with your own.

rover *American football* defensive linebacker assigned to move about to anticipate opponents' plays.

rover *archery* target chosen at random and at an undetermined range (also a mark for long-distance shooting).

rover *Australian rules football* player forming part of the ruck.

rover *croquet* ball that has passed through all the hoops but not pegged out (also a name for a player whose ball has done this).

ruck *rugby* occurs when progress of the ball is checked and two or more players struggle to gain possession. Distinguished from maul by ball being on the ground and legally playable only with the feet.

rush *ice hockey* sudden attack on goal often from a defensive position.

salchow *ice skating* full-turn jump from the inside back edge of one skate to the outside back edge of the other.

schuss *skiing* starting gate or housing.

scissors *high jump* training technique of clearing bar with legs only and no rotation of hips.

scissors *rugby* change of direction of attack by player running in diagonally opposite to the line of attacking play when receiving ball.

screen *basketball* another name for 'pick'.

scrimmage *American football* offense and defense facing each other.

scrum *rugby* formed by eight forwards of each side in three ranks for purpose of gaining possession with the feet. Note: rugby league scrummages contain six players.

serpentine *dressage* series of half-circles alternately to right and left.

shido *judo* judge's warning with no point deducted.

shime-waza *judo* strangulation technique.

shinai *kendo* sword made up of four bamboo sticks bound together.

shobu-ari *kendo* the end of a match.

shopping, going *billiards* potting your opponent's ball.

short leg *cricket* fielding position close to the batsman and on the leg side.

shotgun *American football* offensive formation.

shroud *yachting* set of ropes supporting the mainsail.

shukokai *karate* a karate school.

shuriken *karate* one of various designs of small throwing weapons often eight-sided and sharp.

side *billiards* off-centre striking of the cueball to make false angle in positional play.

silly mid-off *cricket* close fielding position short of mid-off.

silly mid-on *cricket* close fielding position short of mid-on.

sleeper *wrestling* application of pressure on the nerves in the neck which can cause loss of consciousness.

slip *cricket* fielding position next to the wicket-keeper.

snap *American football* put the ball into play on the ground by a quick backward movement.

soigneur *cycling* general dogsbody of team responsible for its physical and mental preparation.

soop *curling* assist the progress of a curling stone by sweeping the ice in front of it.

southpaw *boxing* boxer who leads with his right hand.

space lob *roller hockey* use of end boards to pass to team mates.

spare *ten pin bowling* knocking down all the pins with two successive bowls.

spider *billiards, snooker* implement used when bridging directly over a ball.

spider *darts* wire frame around the board.

spike *volleyball* one-handed attacking shot from above and across the net. Spike serves are common at the higher levels.

spinnaker *yachting* large triangular sail carried forward of or opposite the mainsail.

spinner *angling* real or artificial bait or lure fixed so as to revolve when pulled through the water.

spinnerama *roller hockey* complicated tactical move to deceive opposition.

spinning *cycling* US term for twiddling now commonly used in UK.

split *ten pin bowling* attempt to knock down pins which are wide apart.

split *weightlifting* action of thrusting forward with one foot and backward with the other to aid leverage during lift.

split T *American football* offensive formation.

spoon *angling* artificial bait in the shape of the bowl of a spoon, used in spinning or trolling.

spoon *golf* any club with a slightly concave wooden head, but often refers to a 3 wood specifically.

stealing bases *baseball* reaching bases without the striker hitting the ball.

stone *curling* the heavy 'top' with a handle which is aimed at the house.

straddle *high jump* similar to western roll, but the straddle jumper keeps legs wide apart and body straight.

strike *baseball* complete miss of the ball.

strike *ten pin bowling* knocking all the pins down with one ball.

suicide squad *American football* specialist players who deliberately block attacks.

sulky *harness racing* vehicle used in harness racing.

sweeper *curling* team member who sweeps the ice to gain distance for stone.

swingtime *trampolining* a series of different moves performed between bounces.

switch-hitting *boxing* changing from orthodox to southpaw during a bout.

tack *equestrianism* saddle, bridle and bit.

tack *yachting* zigzag movement of a boat.

tagged out *baseball* self-explanatory term.

tame-shiwari *karate* exercise for toughening using breaking techniques.

taw *marbles* line from which a player shoots; also another name for the actual game and formerly a name for a large marble.

tee *curling* centre point of the house.

tee *golf* small peg on which to rest the ball when driving; also the name for the area where the initial drive is made.

T formation *American football* offensive formation.

third man *cricket* fielding position deep behind the slip area.

tice *cricket* obsolete term for a yorker.

tice *croquet* stroke tempting an opponent to aim at one's ball.

tiger country *golf* deep rough usually on high ground.

tin *squash* the lower line on the wall above which all shots must be played.

tkachyov *gymnastics* one-handed 360-degree swing on horizontal (high) bar.

tolley *marbles* portmanteau word from 'taw' and 'alley'.

touchdown *American football* equivalent of a try in rugby, except that the ball need not touch the ground when carried or received inside the opponents' end zone (6 points score).

touché *fencing* an acknowledgment that a scoring hit has been made in a bout.

toucher *bowls* wood that has touched the jack in its travels.

tram lines *tennis* the outer lines at each side of the court which become part of the court in doubles matches.

trapeze *yachting* sliding support used for outboard balancing on a yacht.

travelling *basketball* running with the ball without bouncing it.

triangle *angling* set of three hooks fastened together so that the barbs form a triangle.

triangle *snooker* implement used for setting the red balls at the start of a frame.

troll *angling* fish by drawing bait along in the water.

try *rugby* scoring method by means of touching the ball down in the opponents' goal area behind their goal line (5 points score).

tsuba *kendo* guard of the sword.

tsuka *kendo* handle of the sword.

tsukahara *gymnastics* vault consisting of a quarter

or half turn on to the horse followed by one and half somersaults off.

turkey *ten pin bowling* gaining three strikes in successive bowls.

turnover *basketball* loss of possession of the ball by a team before any member has been able to try for a basket.

twiddling *cycling* pedalling fast in a gear with no pressure asserted.

up and under *rugby* kicking the ball up field high and long to make time for the kicker and attacking players to reach the point where it comes down.

uwate-dashi-nage *sumo* one-handed throw.

uwate-nage *sumo* hip throw using both hands.

veer attack *American football* offensive formation.

Venturi effect *hang-gliding* basis for wing design, explaining that air flowing over the upper part of a wing moves faster than the air on the underside of the wing, so that the pressure underneath is greater and hence creates lift. Aka Bernouilli effect.

volley *volleyball* two-handed shot that may go over the net or to another team member to spike.

vorlage *skiing* position in which the skier leans forward without lifting the heels from the skis. It is also a common name for skiing trousers when pluralized.

vorlaufer *skiing* literally meaning 'run on ahead' in German, it is a term used for the pre-competition skiers who test the safety and degree of difficulty of a ski course.

walkover *horse racing* horse having the formality of walking over the line as it is the only entrant in a race.

wall pass *football* pass from one player to another and back to save having to face a defender (also called one-two).

warner single wing *American football* offensive formation.

wazari-ni-chikai-waza *judo* 5-point score (two make an ippon).

wazari *judo* almost point in Japanese (scores 7 points in competition).

western grip *table tennis* traditional method of holding a bat with fingers on face of bat.

western roll *high jumping* technique, rarely used today, whereby the front leg is thrown high over the bar and the body and other leg roll over and parallel to the bar.

wicket maiden *cricket* an over during which no runs have been scored and a wicket has been taken.

wide *cricket* extra given to batting side due to ball being bowled too wide of the batsman.

wipe out *surfing* tumbling off the board, often due to unforeseen wave.

wired *croquet* prevented from taking a particular course by an intervening hoop or peg.

wishbone *yachting* boom composed of two halves that curve outward from the mast on either side of the sail and in again, the clew of the sail between them being attached to the point where they meet aft.

yamashita *gymnastics* flat handspring over the vaulting horse.

yokozuna *sumo* grand champion.

yori kiri *sumo* strong forward push.

yorker *cricket* ball bowled at feet of batsman whether playing back or forward.

yuko *judo* hold between 20 and 25 seconds.

NB This is far from being an exhaustive listing of sporting terminology. Dictionaries of terms are available on many individual sports and so it would be impossible to catalogue all known terms. What I have tried to do is give a good cross-section of technical terms over many sports. I should also point out that some terms will relate to other sports, e.g. billiards-based sports or running ball sports.

Other Sports: World's Strongest Man

The World's Strongest Man competition has been covered by BBC Television almost since the beginning and is based on all aspects of strength and not just the lifting of weights, although most of the very best competitors have also been champion weight-lifters. Geoff Capes of Great Britain ushered in a new breed of athlete: not only very large but also very fit and very quick. The competitions have had many great personalities over the years, from the great bullish Kazmaier to the very extrovert Sigmarsson (sadly no longer with us), with his 'Viking' chant, and of course the other great Icelander Magnusson. The present champion, Pudzianowski, showed outstanding aerobic abilities and strength that belied his relatively small frame.

1977	Bruce Wilhelm (United States)	1990	Jon Pall Sigmarsson (Iceland)
1978	Bruce Wilhelm (United States)	1991	Magnus Ver Magnusson (Iceland)
1979	Don Reinhoudt (United States)	1992	Ted Van Der Parre (Holland)
1980	Bill Kazmaier (United States)	1993	Gary Taylor (Great Britain)
1981	Bill Kazmaier (United States)	1994	Magnus Ver Magnusson (Iceland)
1982	Bill Kazmaier (United States)	1995	Magnus Ver Magnusson (Iceland)
1983	Geoff Capes (Great Britain)	1996	Magnus Ver Magnusson (Iceland)
1984	Jon Pall Sigmarsson (Iceland)	1997	Jouko Ahola (Finland)
1985	Geoff Capes (Great Britain)	1998	Magnus Samuelsson (Sweden)
1986	Jon Pall Sigmarsson (Iceland)	1999	Jouko Ahola (Finland)
1987	*Jon Pall Sigmarsson (Iceland)	2000	Janne Virtanen (Finland)
1988	Jon Pall Sigmarsson (Iceland)	2001	Sven Karlssen (Norway)
1989	Jamie Reeves (Great Britain)	2002	Mariusz Pudzianowski (Poland)

*Competition known as Pure Strength

Other Sports: The Superstars

The World Superstars competition ran for six years on the BBC and made stars of athletes such as Brian Budd, who treated the competition with the same professional approach as his own sport of soccer. Although Brian Hooper won the last of the competitions, the domestic Superstars was won by fine athletes such as Lynn Davies, Andy Ripley, John Conteh, David Hemery, Keith Fielding, and the most famous of all, judo player Brian Jacks, he of the dip-bar records. And who can ever forget the painful demise of Kevin Keegan on a bike. Austin Healey won the 2001 one-off special. The champions are listed together with their original sport.

1977 Bob Seagren, USA, Pole Vault	1980 Brian Budd, CAN, Soccer
1978 Brian Budd, CAN, Soccer	1981 Jody Sheckter, RSA, Racing
1979 Brian Budd, CAN, Soccer	1982 Brian Hooper, GBR, Pole Vault

The USA maintain the tradition to this day and their winners are as follows:

1973 Bob Seagren, Pole Vault	1987 Herschel Walker, American Football
1974 Kyle Rote, Jr, Soccer	1988 Herschel Walker, American Football
1975 O J Simpson, American Football	1989 Willie Gault, American Football
1976 Kyle Rote, Jr, Soccer	1990 Willie Gault, American Football
1977 Kyle Rote, Jr, Soccer	1991 Kelly Gruber, Baseball
1978 Wayne Grimditch, Water Skiing	1992 Mike Powell, Long Jump
1979 Greg Pruitt, American Football	1993 Dave Johnson, Decathlon
1980 Charles White, American Football	1994 Dave Johnson, Decathlon
1981 Renaldo Nehemiah, Hurdles	1998 Jason Sehorn, American Football
1982 Renaldo Nehemiah, Hurdles	1999 Jason Sehorn, American Football
1983 Renaldo Nehemiah, Hurdles	2000 Jason Sehorn, American Football
1984 Tom Petranoff, Javelin	2001 Hermann Maier, Alpine Skiing
1985 Mark Gastineau, American Football	2002 Bode Miller, Alpine Skiing
1986 Renaldo Nehemiah, American Football	

Miscellaneous Information: Sport

Acque Minerale and Tamburello	features of Imola and San Marino motor racing circuits.
archery: target colours	gold (centre), red, blue, black, white.
Australian rules football: inventor	George Ligowsky.
backwards: sports where competitors move	back-stroke swimming; rowing; tug of war.
badminton: All-England champion seven successive years	Rudy Hartono (1968–74).
badminton: family won 35 All-England titles	Frank Devlin and his daughters Judy and Sue.
badminton: origin	originally called Shuttlecock and Battledore and named after the country estate of the Duke of Beaufort, where it originated in 1873. It was popularized by army officers in India who played it as an outdoor game.
bagatelle: brief description	similar to bar billiards but board has nine holes and nine balls are used (four red, four white and a black ball that scores double).
bagatelle: variations	cannon game; Mississippi; sans égal.
basketball: court size	50' × 94'.
basketball: famous US teams	Boston Celtics; Houston Rockets; Los Angeles Lakers; Milwaukee Bucks; New York Knickerbockers; Philadelphia 76ers; Phoenix Suns; Portland Trail Blazers; Seattle Supersonics; St Louis Hawks; Washington Bullets.
basketball: inventor	Dr James Naismith invented basketball at the YMCA training school in Springfield, Mass. (1891).
beard: not allowed	jockeys.
billiards: World Matchplay champion 1998	Mike Russell of England defeated Peter Gilchrist of England 8–5.
boat race: dead heat	1877 (although Oxford are said to have won by about six feet). The actual closest winning margin being the official one foot

victory by Oxford in the 2003 race.

boat race: first woman cox Susan Brown in 1981.

boat race: reserve crews Cambridge – Goldie, Oxford – Isis.

bowls: first world champion in 1966 David Bryant (Eng).

bowls: invented by flat green bowls in its modern form began in 1848 when William Mitchell, a Glasgow solicitor, drew up the rules.

bowls: 2002 world indoor champion Tony Allcock (Eng).

boxing: amateur weight limits light fly – 106lb/48kg; fly – 112lb/51kg; bantam – 119lb/54kg; feather – 126lb/57kg; light – 132lb/60kg; light welter – 140lb/63.5kg; welter – 148lb/67kg; light middle – 157lb/71kg; middle – 165lb/75kg; light heavy – 179lb/81kg; heavy – 201lb/91kg; super heavy – 201lb+/91kg+.

champion at five weights Sugar Ray Leonard.
first champion James Figg is generally regarded as the first modern champion when he set up his school in 1719.
first East European professional Laszlo Papp.
first fight with gloves Gentleman Jim Corbett defeated John L Sullivan in 1892.
first million dollar gate Jack Dempsey v Georges Carpentier in 1921.
four main governing bodies World Boxing Association (WBA), founded 1920; World Boxing Council (WBC), founded 1963; International Boxing Federation (IBF), founded 1983; World Boxing Organization (WBO), founded 1988.
heavyweight champion longest reign Joe Louis (1937–49).
last bareknuckle champion John L Sullivan.
oldest and youngest world champions light heavyweight, Archie Moore (48); light welterweight, Wilfredo Benitez (17).
professional weight limits straw/mini-fly – 105lb/48kg; light fly/jnr fly – 108lb/49kg; fly – 112lb/51kg; super fly/jnr bantam – 115lb/52kg; bantam – 118lb/54kg; super bantam/jnr feather – 122lb/55kg; feather – 126lb/57kg; super feather/jnr light – 130lb/59kg; light – 135lb/61kg; super light/jnr welter – 140lb/64kg; welter – 147lb/67kg; super welter/jnr middle – 154lb/70kg; middle – 160lb/73kg; super middle – 168lb/76kg; light heavy – 175lb/79kg; jnr heavy/cruiser – 190lb/86kg; heavy – 190lb+/86kg+.
Queensberry Rules: first fight under Jim Corbett beat John L Sullivan (1892).
initiated by Jack Broughton devised first rules in 1743, but they were not codified until 1867 by 8th marquess of Queensberry.
undefeated heavyweight champion Rocky Marciano (49 fights).
undisputed heavyweight champions John L Sullivan (1882); James J Corbett (1892); Bob Fitzsimmons (1897); James J Jeffries (1899); Marvin Hart (1905); Tommy Burns (1906); Jack Johnson (1908); Jess Willard (1915); Jack Dempsey (1919); Gene Tunney (1926); Max Schmeling (1930); Jack Sharkey (1932); Primo Carnera (1933); Max Baer (1934); James J Braddock (1935); Joe Louis (1937); Ezzard Charles (1949); Jersey Joe Walcott (1951); Rocky Marciano (1952); Floyd Patterson (1956); Ingemar Johansson (1959); Floyd Patterson (1960); Sonny Liston (1962); Cassius Clay (1964); Joe Frazier (1970); George Foreman (1973); Muhammad Ali (1974); Leon Spinks (1978); Mike Tyson (1987).
youngest world heavyweight champion Mike Tyson.

bullfighting: barbed sticks banderillas.
cape muleta (red one side and yellow the other).
term used for a pass veronica.
terms for fighters matador – principal fighter appointed to kill the bull; picador – horseman who pricks the bull with a banderilla to weaken it; toreador – stock name for any fighter.

chess: mens world champions 2002 Ruslan Ponomatiov (FIDE); Vladimir Kramnik (PCA World Champion).

croquet four balls used; two to a team; red and yellow play against blue and black; six hoops are used.

curling: 2002 world championships Women: Scotland beat Sweden 6–5.
Men: Canada beat Norway 10–5.

cycling: oldest British sprint champion Reg Harris (aged 54).
terms honking – cycling off the saddle; spinning – turning an easy gear very quickly with no effort.

Tour de France, first non-European

SPORT & LEISURE

winner	Greg Lemond of USA in 1986.
Tour de France, five times winners	Eddie Merckx, Jacques Anquetil, Bernard Hinault.
Tour de France Winner 2002	Lance Armstrong (USA).
Tour of Italy Winner 2002	Gilberto Simoni (Italy).
Tour of Spain Winner 2002	Aitor Gonzalez (Spain).
UCI Rankings 2002	1) Erik Zabel (Germany) 2) Paolo Bettini (Italy) 3) Lance Armstrong (USA)

darts: sponsors
Embassy sponsor the BDO World Championship while Skol sponsor the WDC Championship.

Eton fives: 2002 county champions
Kent beat Warwickshire 3–0.

fatalities: sport with highest rate of
angling (fish rather than folk!).

fencing: caught cheating
Boris Onischenko of USSR in Modern Pentathlon (1976).
heaviest weapon
épée.
target areas
foil – body only; épée – no restriction; sabre – over waist.
technical term for guard
coquille.
weapons used by women
traditionally foil only but nowadays championships exist for sabre and épée.

frisbee: two forms of
Ultimate and Guts.

golf: British amateur champion 2002
Alejandro Larrazabal.

gong: banged for J Arthur Rank
Bombardier Billy Wells (1889–1967), British heavyweight boxing champion, was succeeded by Ken Richmond, the wrestling gold medalist at the 1954 Commonwealth Games.

Greyhound Grand National: triple winner
Sherry's Prince.

greyhound racing: most consecutive wins
Ballyregan Bob (32).
trap colours
red – 1; blue – 2; white – 3; black – 4; orange – 5; black and white striped – 6.

grouse shooting: season
Glorious Twelfth (August) to 10 December.

gymnastics: exercises for men
floor, horizontal bar, parallel bars, pommel horse, rings, vault (lengthwise).
exercises for women
floor, asymmetric bars, beam, vault (widthwise).
first perfect score of 10
Nadia Comaneci in 1976.

ice hockey: 2002 world champions
Slovakia beat Russia 4–3.
Stanley Cup 2002
Detroit Red Wings beat Carolina Hurricanes 3–1.

ice skating: British champions 2001
Elliot Hilton (men) and Maria Butyrskaya (women).
world champions 2002
Alexei Yagudin (men), Irina Slutskaya (women), Xue Shen and Hongbo Zhao (pairs), and Irina Lobacheva and Ilia Averbukh (dance).

judo: 2002 British open champion
Samantha Lowe (middleweight), Sarah Clark (welter), Georgina Singleton (junior lightweight), Craig Fallon (bantamweight).

London Marathon organisers
John Disley and Chris Brasher organised first London Marathon in 1981.

martial arts: meanings
tae kwon do – way of the foot and fist; judo – gentle way; aikido – way of spirit harmony; karate – way of the empty hand; kyudo – way of the bow; kung fu – leisure time/hobby.

Olympic Games: famous competitors
Philip Noel Baker was an Olympic finalist at 1,500m in 1912 and silver medallist in 1920 before winning the Nobel Peace Prize in 1959. Noel Harrison, who took part in Skiing in 1952, is the actor son of Rex Harrison. Harry Llewellyn, who won gold medal for Equestrianism in 1952, is father of Roddy Llewellyn. Charles Simmons, who took part in Gymnastics 1952, is father of Jean Simmons. John Kelly, who won gold medal for Rowing in 1920, was father of Grace Kelly. Prince Albert of Monaco took part in bobsleigh events in 1988. Godfrey Rampling, who ran in the 4 x 400m Relay in 1936, was the father of Charlotte Rampling. Bill Nankeville who ran in the 1500m in 1948, is the father of Bobby Davro. Ioannis Theodoracopulous, who was a hurdler in 1936, was the father of Taki. Arthur Porritt, who accompanied Harold Abrahams in the 1924 Games, was father of Jonathon Porritt the Green politician.

pelota vasca (jai alai): origins
invented in Italy as 'longue paume' and introduced to France in 13th century. It is the fastest ball game in the world.

pheasant shooting: season	1 October to 1 February.
polo: pitch dimensions	polo has the largest pitch of any sport with a maximum length of 300 yards and width of 200 yards.
rackets: 2001 world champion	James Male (GB) defeated N Smith (GB).
racketball: inventors	American racketball devised by Joe Sobek in 1949; British racketball was devised by Ian Wright in 1976.
real tennis: origins	developed from 'jeu de paume' (game of the palm) and played in Australia, England, France, Scotland and USA. First world champion in 1740 was a Frenchman named Clergé. World champion since 1994: Robert Fahey (Aus).
roller skating: first rink opened	Newport, Rhode Island, in 1866.
rowing: skimming of oar across water	feathering.
rugby league: nicknames	Australia – Kangaroos; New Zealand – Kiwis; Widnes – Chemics; Warrington – Wires.
rugby union: jersey colours	Australia – gold; Barbarians – black and white hoops; England – white; France – blue; Ireland – green; New Zealand – black; Scotland – blue; Wales – red.
nicknames	Argentina – Pumas; Australia – Wallabies; New Zealand – All Blacks; South Africa – Springboks.
played both codes at same time	Martin Offiah left Wigan August 1996 to play union for Bedford and league for London Broncos.
skiing: Olympic champions who won all titles	Toni Sailer (1956) and Jean-Claude Killy (1968).
piste grading	black – difficult run; red – intermediate run; blue – easy run; green – beginners' slope.
snooker: first televised 147 maximum by	Steve Davis (1982 Lada Classic).
first to make 147 in World Championships	Cliff Thorburn (1983).
women's Embassy World Champion 2002	Kelly Fisher (GB) beat Lisa Quick (GB) 4–1.
world champions at the Crucible	John Spencer (1977), Ray Reardon (1978), Terry Griffiths (1979), Cliff Thorburn (1980), Steve Davis (1981), Alex Higgins (1982), Steve Davis (1983–84), Dennis Taylor (1985), Joe Johnson (1986), Steve Davis (1987–89), Stephen Hendry (1990), John Parrott (1991), Stephen Hendry 1992–96), Ken Doherty (1997), John Higgins (1998), Stephen Hendry (1999), Mark Williams (2000), Ronnie O'Sullivan (2001), Peter Ebdon (2002).
softball: inventor	George Hancock invented the indoor version of baseball in 1887 in Chicago.
speedway: laps	four
2002 world champion	Tony Rickardsson of Sweden.
squash: origins	Harrow school.
world champion sixteen years running	Heather McKay Blundell of Australia.
stop on line: competitors do not pass finishing line	swimming.
substitutes: allowed while game in play	ice hockey.
suicides: famous sportsmen	Fred Archer (1857–86), champion jockey for 13 years 1874–86, shot himself aged 29. George O'Dell (1945–81), a double world champion in side-car racing, took his own life aged 35. Recent sporting suicides include the Yorkshire cricketer David Bairstow and footballer Justin Fashanu.
table tennis: ball dimensions	from 2001 season ball diameter increased to 40mm.
expedite rule	comes into play in long game and means point must be won within so many strikes or receiver is awarded the point.
2001 world champions: men's	Wang Liqin
women's	Wang Nam
ten pin bowling: maximum score in one game	300.
tennis champs: British, venue	Telford.
Vasaloppet	Swedish marathon ski race over 85km between Sälen and Mora, first run in 1922.
volleyball: former name	invented in 1895 by William Morgan of Massachusetts and

S
P
O
R
T
&
L
E
I
S
U
R
E

	called 'Mintonette'.
weightlifting: Olympic lifts	clean and jerk, snatch.
weightlifting: power lifts	bench press, dead lift, squat.
wrestling: two styles	freestyle and Greco-Roman.
yachting: famous champion	Peter Scott, son of explorer Robert Falcon Scott, won bronze medal in 1936 Olympics and became British gliding champion in 1963.
Olympic classes	Europe, Finn (solo class), 470, Laser, Mistral, Star, Tornado (catamaran), Soling (three-man crew).

Games: Miscellaneous

baccarat

gambling card game the object of which is to hold cards with values as near to nine as possible.

backgammon

dice number: 5; counters: 15 per player; points on board: 24.

bezique

played with a 64-card double piquet deck, i.e. all cards below 7, except the ace, are removed from two standard 52-card decks.

bingo calls

The origins of Bingo can be traced back to Italy in the year 1530, when a State-run lottery game Lo Giuoco del Lotto d'Italia was originated. 'Le Lotto' migrated to France in the late 1700s in a form similar to the Bingo we know today, with a playing card, tokens and numbers read aloud. Throughout the 1800s these lottery type of games spread quickly throughout Europe and many offshoots of the game were created. In 1929, a game called 'Beano' was played at a carnival near Atlanta, Georgia. A New York toy salesman named Edwin Lowe observed the game, where players exclaimed 'BEANO!' if they filled a line of numbers on their card. Lowe introduced the game to his friends and one of them mistakenly yelled 'BINGO!' in her excitement . 'Lowe's Bingo' was soon very popular and the name stuck.

1   Kelly's eye, Buttered scone, At the beginning, Little Jimmy, Nelson's column, B1 Baby of bingo
2   One little duck, Baby's done it, Doctor Who, Me and you, Little boy blue
3   Dearie me, I'm free, Debbie McGee, You and me, Goodness me, One little flea, Cup of tea
4   The one next door, On the floor, Knock at the door, B4 Crowd says 'and after'
5   Man alive, Jack's alive, Dead alive
6   Tom Mix, Tom's tricks, Chopsticks
7   Lucky seven, God's in heaven, One little crutch
8   Garden gate, Golden gate, Harry Tate, One fat lady
9   Doctor's orders
10 Downing street (UK prime minister's address), Cock and hen (rhyming), Uncle Ben (rhyming), Tony's Den (or whoever is the PM of the day)
11 Legs eleven, Legs – they're lovely, Kelly's Legs Number eleven
12 One dozen, One and two – a dozen, Monkey's cousin (rhymes with 'a dozen')
13 Unlucky for some, Devil's number, Baker's dozen
14 Valentine's day
15 Rugby team, Young and keen
16 Sweet sixteen, She's lovely, Never been kissed
17 Often been kissed, Old Ireland, Dancing queen, The age to catch 'em
18 Key of the door, Now you can vote, Coming of age
19 Goodbye teens
20 One score, Getting plenty, Blind 20
21 Royal salute, Key of the door
22 Two little ducks (suggesting the necks of two swans), Ducks on a pond, Dinky doo, All the twos
23 A duck and a flea, Thee and me, The Lord's My Shepherd (based on 23rd Psalm)
24 Two dozen, Hours from Tulsa
25 Duck and dive
26 Bed and breakfast (traditional price was 2 shillings 6 pence), Half a crown (equivalent to 2 shillings 6 pence), Pick and mix
27 Little duck with a crutch, Gateway to heaven
28 In a state, The old brags, Over weight
29 You're doing fine, Rise and shine
30 Burlington Bertie, Dirty Gertie, Speed limit (in built-up area, UK), Blind 30, Flirty thirty
31 Get up and run

32 Buckle my shoe
33 Dirty knees, All the feathers, All the threes, Gertie Lee, Two little fleas, Sherwood forest (all the trees)
34 Ask for more
35 Jump and jive
36 Three dozen
37 A flea in heaven, More than eleven
38 Christmas cake
39 Those famous steps, All the steps
40 Two score, Life begins at, Blind 40, Naughty 40
41 Life's begun, Time for fun
42 That famous street in Manhattan, Winnie the Poo
43 Down on your knees
44 Droopy drawers, All the fours, Open two doors
45 Halfway house, Halfway there
46 Up to tricks
47 Four and seven
48 Four dozen
49 PC (Police Constable), Copper, Nick nick, Rise and shine
50 Bulls eye, Bung hole, Blind 50, Half a century
51 I love my mum, Tweak of the thumb, The Highland Div[ision]
52 Weeks in a year, The Lowland Div[ision], Danny La Rue
53 Stuck in the tree, The Welsh Div[ision]
54 Clean the floor
55 Snakes alive, All the fives
56 Was she worth it?
57 Heinz varieties, All the beans (Heinz 57 varieties of canned beans)
58 Make them wait, Choo choo Thomas
59 Brighton line
60 Three score, Blind 60, Five dozen
61 Bakers bun
62 Tickety boo, Turn of the screw
63 Tickle me
64 The Beatles number, Red raw
65 Old age pension, Stop work (retirement age)
66 Clickety click, All the sixes
67 Made in heaven, Argumentative number
68 Saving grace
69 The same both ways, your place or mine?, Any way up, Either way up, Any way round, Meal for two
70 Three score and ten, Blind 70
71 Bang on the drum
72 A crutch and a duck, Six dozen, Par for the course (golf)
73 Crutch with a flea, Queen B
74 Candy store
75 Strive and strive
76 Trombones
77 Sunset strip, All the sevens, Two little crutches
78 Heaven's gate
79 One more time
80 Gandhi's breakfast, Blind 80, Eight and blank
81 Fat lady and a little wee, Stop and run
82 Fat lady with a duck, Straight on through
83 Fat lady with a flea, Time for tea, Ethel's Ear
84 Seven dozen
85 Staying alive
86 Between the sticks
87 Fat lady with a crutch, Torquay in Devon
88 Two fat ladies, Wobbly wobbly, All the eights
89 Nearly there, All but one
90 Top of the shop, Top of the house, Blind 90, As far as we go, End of the line

canasta   played with two standard decks of 52 cards, plus four jokers, totalling 108 cards. Hands are played until one partnership reaches 5000 points.

Canasta was developed in Uruguay and passed via Argentina to the USA in 1949.

card games: names   beggar my neighbour, boston, briscola, calabrasella, donkey, écarté, imperial, klaberjass, loo, michigan, napoleon, oh hell, old maid, Persian pasha, Pope Joan, skat, vint.

cards: Queen depicted   Elizabeth of York (wife of Henry VII).

charades   parlour game whereby one person mimes and the other players guess the title.

SPORT & LEISURE

chess: right-hand corner	the right-hand corner square as white sets up is white (important to remember).
chicane	bridge hand without trumps or without cards of any one suit.
Cluedo: characters	Colonel Mustard, Professor Plum, Reverend Green, Mrs Peacock, Miss Scarlet, Mrs White, Dr Black (victim).
weapons	knife, revolver, spanner, lead pipe, rope, and candlestick.
crambo	game in which a player gives a word or verse line to which each of the others must find a rhyme.
cribbage	developed by poet, Sir John Suckling, in the early 17th century and usually played to 121 points.
dominoes	28 tiles in a set with a total of 168 pips (seven doubles).
El Gordo	Spanish National Lottery (largest in the world).
euchre	played with a 32-card deck (cards below 7 are removed).
fan-tan	chinese gambling game in which players try to guess the remainder after the banker has divided a number of hidden objects into four groups.
faro	gambling card game in which bets are placed on the order of appearance of the cards. This is the game in which Count Rostov lost a fortune in Tolstoy's *War and Peace*.
frisbee: original name	Pluto Platter.
go	Japanese board game using terms: false eyes, eyes and armies. Played on a grid of 19 horizontal and 19 vertical lines forming 361 interactions.
jai alai	South American version of pelota played with large curved wicker baskets.
mah jongg	Chinese game using terms: pung, kong and chow. 144 tiles are usually used (36 bamboos, 36 circles, 36 characters, 12 honours, 16 winds, 8 flowers and seasons). The name was coined and copyrighted by Joseph P Babcock.
Monopoly: inventor	Charles Darrow, a heating engineer.
properties	brown: Old Kent Road (cheapest), Whitechapel; light blue: Angel Islington (pub), Euston Road, Pentonville Road; mauve: Pall Mall, Whitehall, Northumberland Avenue; orange: Bow Street, Marlborough Street, Vine Street (statistically the most 'landed on' square); red: Strand, Fleet Street, Trafalgar Square; yellow: Leicester Square, Coventry Street, Piccadilly; green: Regent Street, Oxford Street, Bond Street; dark blue: Park Lane, Mayfair (most expensive).
stations	King's Cross, Marylebone, Fenchurch Street, Liverpool Street.
corners	Go, Just Visiting, Free Parking, Go to Jail.
USA version	Atlantic City, New Jersey, is used, with 'Boardwalk' the most expensive property.
ombre	card game for three players that was popular throughout Europe in the 17th and 18th centuries.
pall-mall	game in which a ball is driven by a mallet along an alley and through an iron ring.
patzer	poor player at chess.
pelota	Basque and Spanish game played in a walled court with a ball and 'basket-like' rackets attached to the hand. Pelota is thought to be the fastest of ball sports outside golf.
pinochle	pronounced 'pea knuckle', and played with 48 cards (two decks stripped of cards below 9). Within the game, pinochle stands for the Jack of Diamonds and Queen of Spades. The 9 of trumps is called the dix. Winner is player who first reaches 1000 points.
piquet	given the name by Charles I of England to honour Henrietta Maria, his French wife. Piquet deck is 32 cards with all cards below 7 stripped from deck.
poker: best hand	royal flush (ace to 10 in the same suit).
roulette: numbers	European wheels have 37 divisions (0–36), American wheels have 38 including a double zero.
Scrabble: inventor	James Brunot in 1949, first used the name scrabble.
made by	Spear Games.
tile values	highest Q and Z (10), J and X (8), K (5), Y H V W F (4), P M C B (3), D G (2), others 1 point except blank (0).
original name	criss cross (designed by Alfred M Butts, an architect, in 1931).
vigoro	Australian ball game combining elements of cricket and baseball.
Yarborough	whist or bridge hand with no card above a 9. Named afer the earl of Yarborough who died in 1897, and was said to have bet against its occurrence.
tarot	originally 22 cards (the Major Arcana: see below). The Venetians added 56 cards (the Minor Arcana) split into 4 suits: the clubs, symbolising money matters; cups (hearts), symbolising love and friendship; swords (spades), symbolising ill fortune; denari (diamonds), symbolising business and travel.

0	Fool/Joker	11	Fortitude / Strength
1	Magician / Mountebank	12	Hanged Man
2	High Priestess / Popess	13	Death
3	Empress	14	Temperance
4	Emperor	15	Devil
5	Hierophant / Pope	16	Tower
6	Lovers	17	Star
7	Chariot	18	Moon
8	Justice	19	Sun
9	Hermit	20	Judgement
10	Wheel of Fortune	21	World / Universe

NB In some versions of the Major Arcana nos. 8 and 11 are reversed.

Stamps: First Issues

Country	Year	Country	Year	Country	Year
Aden	1937	Georgia	1919	Northern Rhodesia	1925
Afghanistan	1870	Germany	1872	Norway	1855
Andorra	1928	Ghana	1875	Orange Free State	1868
Antigua and Barbuda	1862	Gibraltar	1886	Pakistan	1947
Argentina	1858	Great Britain	1840	Palestine	1918
Armenia	1920	Greece	1861	Panama	1878
Ascension	1922	Greenland	1938	Papua	1901
Australia	1902	Grenada	1861	Papua New Guinea	1952
Austria	1850	Guatemala	1871	Paraguay	1870
Azerbaijan	1919	Guyana	1850	Philippines	1854
Bahamas	1859	Haiti	1881	Pitcairn Isles	1940
Bahrain	1933	Hawaii	1851	Portugal	1853
Bangladesh	1971	Heligoland	1867	Queensland	1860
Barbados	1852	Honduras	1866	Rhodesia	1890
Barbuda	1922	Hong Kong	1862	Rhodesia and Nyasaland	1954
Belgium	1849	Hungary	1871	Russia	1857
Belize	1866	Iceland	1873	Sabah (North Borneo)	1883
Bermuda	1865	India	1852	San Marino	1877
Bolivia	1866	Ionian Isles	1859	Sarawak	1869
Bosnia-Hercegovina	1879	Ireland	1922	Saudi Arabia	1916
Botswana	1886	Isle of Man	1973	Serbia	1866
Brazil	1843	Israel	1948	Seychelles	1890
British Indian Ocean Territory	1968	Italy	1862	Sierra Leone	1860
		Jamaica	1860	South Africa	1910
British Solomon Isles	1907	Japan	1871	South Australia	1855
Brunei	1906	Jordan	1920	Southern Rhodesia	1924
Bulgaria	1879	Kenya	1890	South West Africa	1923
Burma/Myanmar	1937	Kiribati	1911	South Yemen	1963
Canada	1851	Latvia	1918	Spain	1850
Cape of Good Hope	1853	Lebanon	1924	Sri Lanka	1857
Cayman Islands	1900	Leeward Isles	1890	St Helena	1856
Channel Isles	1941	Liberia	1860	Sudan	1897
Chile	1853	Liechtenstein	1912	Swaziland	1889
China	1878	Lithuania	1918	Sweden	1855
Cook Isles	1892	Luxembourg	1852	Switzerland	1843
Crete	1900	Malawi	1891	Syria	1919
Cuba	1855	Malaysia	1867	Tasmania	1853
Cyprus	1880	Maldives	1906	Thailand	1883
Czech Republic	1918	Malta	1860	Tokelau Isles	1948
Danish West Indies	1855	Mauritius	1847	Tonga	1886
Danzig	1920	Mexico	1856	Transvaal	1869
Denmark	1851	Monaco	1885	Turkey	1863
Dominica	1874	Mongolia	1924	Uganda	1895
Dominican Republc	1865	Montserrat	1876	Uruguay	1856
Ecuador	1865	Natal	1857	USA	1845
Egypt	1866	Nauru	1915	USA: Confederacy	1861
El Salvador	1867	Nepal	1881	Victoria	1850
Estonia	1918	Netherlands	1852	Western Australia	1854
Ethiopia	1894	New Guinea	1914	Yemen	1926
Faroe Isles	1940	New South Wales	1850	Zambia	1964
Fiji	1870	New Zealand	1855	Zanzibar	1895
Finland	1856	Nicaragua	1862	Zimbabwe	1979
France	1849	Nigeria	1914	Zululand	1888
Gambia	1869	Norfolk Isles	1947		

SPORT & LEISURE

TELEVISION

Programmes

A For Andromeda Julie Christie (Christine/A for Andromeda).

Absolutely Fabulous Jennifer Saunders (Edina Monsoon), Joanna Lumley (Patsy Stone), Julia Sawalha (Saffron), Jane Horrocks (Bubble), June Whitfield (Mother). Shopped at Harvey Nichols and based on Lynne Franks.

Adam Adamant Lives! Gerald Harper (Adam Llewellyn De Vere Adamant), Juliet Harmer (Georgina Jones), Peter Ducrow (the Face). Entombed from 1902 to 1966.

Addams Family, The Carolyn Jones (Morticia), John Astin (Gomez), Jackie Coogan (Uncle Fester Frump), Ted Cassidy (Lurch and Thing), Blossom Rock, sister of Jeanette McDonald (Grandmama). Lived in Cemetery Ridge with assortment of pets including octopus called Aristotle, black widow spider called Homer, man-eating African strangler called Cleopatra.

Adventures of Black Beauty, The Judi Bowker (Victoria Gordon), William Lucas (Dr James Gordon).

Adventures of Robin Hood, The Richard Greene (Robin), Bernadette O'Farrell and Patricia Driscoll (Maid Marian), Archie Duncan and Rufus Cruikshank (Little John), Alexander Gauge (Friar Tuck), Alan Wheatley (Sheriff of Nottingham). Theme sung by Dick James.

Adventures of Tugboat Annie, The Minerva Urecal (Tugboat Annie Brennan, Capt. of *Narcissus*), Walter Sande (Capt. Bullwinkle).

Adventures of William Tell, The Conrad Phillips (Tell), Jennifer Jayne (Hedda), Willoughby Goddard (Landburgher Gessler).

After Henry Prunella Scales (Sarah France), Joan Sanderson (Eleanor Prescott). Originally a BBC radio series, it was transferred to television with the same two stars.

Agony Maureen Lipman (Jane Lucas), Simon Williams (Laurence Lucas). Magazine: *Person Series*. Created by Anna Raeburn and Len Richmond.

Airwolf Jan-Michael Vincent (Stringfellow Hawke, a keen cellist), Ernest Borgnine (Dominic Santini).

Alf Alien Life Form (Michu Meszaros wore furry suit and Paul Fusco was the voice of ALF), Max Wright (Willie Tanner). Home planet: Melmac. Neighbours: Ochmoneks. Tanners' pet cat was called Lucky.

Alias Smith and Jones Pete Duel (Hannibal Heyes/Joshua Smith), Ben Murphy (Jed 'Kid' Curry/Thaddeus Jones). Roger Davis was narrator of first series but took over from Pete Duel after he committed suicide and Ralph Story took over voice-overs.

All Creatures Great and Small Christopher Timothy (James Herriot), Robert Hardy (Siegfried Farnon), Tricki Woo (Pekinese), Peter Davison (Tristan Farnon), Carol Drinkwater and Lynda Bellingham (Helen Alderson/Herriot).

All Gas and Gaiters Derek Nimmo (Rev. Mervyn Noote), William Mervyn (Bishop), Robertson Hare (Archdeacon).

All in the Family Carroll O'Connor (Archie Bunker), Jean Stapleton (Edith 'Dingbat' Bunker), Rob Reiner (Mike 'Meathead' Stivic the Pole), Sally Struthers (Gloria). America's answer to Alf Garnett.

All Our Yesterdays Presenters: James Cameron, Brian Inglis, Bernard Braden.

'Allo 'Allo Gorden Kaye (René Artois), Carmen Silvera (Edith), Vicki Michelle (Yvette), Guy Siner (Lt Gruber), Nicholas Frankou (Flying Officer Carstairs), John D. Collins (Flying Officer Fairfax), Kirsten Cooke (Michelle), Richard Gibson (Herr Flick), Richard Marner (Colonel Von Strohm), Kim Hartman (Helga Geerhart). Created by Jeremy Lloyd and David Croft.

Ally McBeal Calista Flockhart (Ally McBeal), Gil Bellows (Billy Thomas), Courtney Thorne-Smith (Georgia Thomas), Greg Germann (Richard Fish), Peter MacNicol (John Cage), Lucy Liu (Ling Woo).

And Mother Makes Three Wendy Craig (Sally Harrison/Redway). Follow-up series called *And Mother Makes Five*.

Andromeda Breakthrough, The Susan Hampshire (Christine/A for Andromeda). Follow-on series from *A For Andromeda*.

Andy Pandy Created by Freda Lingstrom and Maria Bird. Friends: Teddy and Looby Loo.

Angels Fiona Fullerton (Patricia Rutherford), Julie Dawn Cole (Jo Longhurst), Shirley Cheriton (Kathy Betts), Pauline Quirke (Vicky Smith). Hospital: St Angela's, Battersea.

Animal Hospital Rolf Harris, Shauna Lowry (Hamden Veterinary Hospital in Aylesbury).

Animal Magic Presenters: Johnny Morris, Terry Nutkins.

Antiques Roadshow Presenters: Angela Rippon, Bruce Parker, Arthur Negus, Hugh Scully. See *Going For A Song*.

Aquarius Presenters: Humphrey Burton, Russell Harty, Peter Hall.

Are You Being Served? John Inman (Mr Humphries), Mollie Sugden (Mrs Slocombe), Arthur Brough (Mr Grainger), Frank Thornton (Capt. Peacock), Nicholas Smith (Mr Rumbold), Arthur English (Mr Harman), Wendy Richard (Miss Brahms), Mike Berry (Mr Spooner), Trevor Bannister (Mr Lucas). Sequel: *Grace and Favour*.

Army Game, The William Hartnell (CSM Bullimore), Bill Fraser (Sgt Claude Snudge), Michael Medwin (Corporal Springer), Harry Fowler (Corporal 'Flogger' Hoskins), Charles Hawtrey (Pte 'Prof' Hatchett), Bernard Bresslaw (Pte 'Popeye' Popplewell), Alfie Bass (Pte 'Excused Boots' Bisley), Norman Rossington (Pte 'Cupcake' Cook), Frank Williams (Capt. Pocket), Mario Fabrizi (Lance Corporal Ernest 'Moosh' Merryweather), Dick Emery (Pte 'Chubby' Catchpole). Base: Hut 29 of the Surplus Ordnance Depot at Nether Hopping, Staffordshire.

Around the World in 80 Days Michael Palin's reconstruction of Phileas Fogg's journey.

Arthur of the Britons Oliver Tobias (Arthur), Rupert Davies (Cerdig), Jack Watson (Llud), Brian Blessed (Mark of Cornwall), Michael Gothard (Kai).

A-Team, The George Peppard (Col. John 'Hannibal' Smith), Lawrence 'Mr T' Tureaud (Sgt Bosco 'BA'

Baracus), Dwight Schultz (Capt. H M 'Howling Mad' Murdock), Dirk Benedict (Lt Templeton 'Faceman' Peck), Melinda Culea (Amy Amanda Allen alias Triple A). 'BA' stood for Bad Attitude.

At Last the 1948 Show   John Cleese, Tim Brooke-Taylor, Graham Chapman, Marty Feldman, Aimi Macdonald.

Auf Wiedersehen Pet   Tim Healy (Denis Patterson), Jimmy Nail ('Oz' Osbourne), Kevin Whately (Neville Hope), Gary Holton (Wayne), Pat Roach (Bomber), Timothy Spall (Barry Taylor), Christopher Fairbank (Moxey). Gary Holton died during filming of the follow-up series in Spain.

Avengers, The   Patrick MacNee (John Steed), Honor Blackman (Cathy Gale), Diana Rigg (Emma Peel), Linda Thorson (Tara King), Patrick Newell (Mother). Steed lived at 3 Duchess Mews, London. Originally called *Police Surgeon*, starring Ian Hendry as Dr David Keel.

A J Wentworth, BA   Arthur Lowe played the absent-minded teacher.

Bagpuss   Bagpuss owned by Emily. Narrator and writer: Oliver Postgate.

Ballykissangel   Niall Tobin (Father MacAnally), Gary Whelan (Brendan Kearney), Peter Caffrey (Padraig Kelly), Deirdre Donnelly (Siobhan Mehigan), Birdy Sweeney (Eamon), Victoria Smurfit (Orla), Don Wycherley (Father Aidan), Aine Ni Mhuiri (Kathleen), Joe Savino (Liam), Tina Kellegher (Niamh Egan), Lorcan Cranitch (Sean Dillon), Frankie McCafferty (Donal). Original series starred Stephen Tompkinson (Father Clifford) and Dervla Kirwan (Assumpta Fitzgerald) and the late Tony Doyle.

Banacek   George Peppard (Thomas Banacek).

Banana Splits, The   Voices: Fleegle (Paul Winchell), Bingo (Daws Butler), Drooper (Allan Melvin), Snorky (Don Messick).

Batman   Adam West (Batman/Bruce Wayne), Burt Ward (Robin/Dick Grayson), Frank Gorshin and John Astin (Riddler), Julie Newmar, Eartha Kitt, Lee Meriwether (Catwoman), Vincent Price (Egg Head), Tallulah Bankhead (Black Widow), Burgess Meredith (Penguin), Carolyn Jones (Queen of Diamonds), Liberace (Chandel), Cliff Robertson (Shame), Van Johnson (Minstrel), Shelley Winters (Ma Parker), Ida Lupino (Dr Cassandra), Otto Preminger, George Sanders and Eli Wallach (Mr Freeze), Cesar Romero (Joker), Yvonne Craig (Batgirl alias Barbara Gordon).

Battlestar Galactica   Lorne Greene (Commander Adama), Dirk Benedict (Lt Starbuck).

Baywatch   David Hasselhoff (Lt Mitch Bucannon), Pamela Denise Anderson (C J Parker), Erika Eleniak (Shauni McLain), Nicole Eggert (Summer Quinn), Yasmin Bleeth (Caroline Holden). Story of Los Angeles County Lifeguards working on Malibu Beach. Spin-off from 1989 TV film *Panic at Malibu Beach,* starring David Hasselhoff.

Beadle's About   Popular hidden-camera show starring Jeremy Beadle and still shown regularly on Challenge TV. Little-known fact: Jeremy is a trivia buff par excellence and entered the 2002 British Quiz Championships, placing a very respectable 30th.

Beauty and the Beast   Vincent (Ron Perlman), Assistant DA Catherine Chandler (Linda Hamilton), Roy Dotrice (Father), Stephen McHattie (Gabriel).

Beiderbecke Affair   James Bolam (Trevor Chaplin), Barbara Flynn (Jill Swinburne). The Beiderbecke of

the title was Bix Beiderbecke the jazz great, whose music was played by Kenny Baker. Sequels were *The Beiderbecke Tapes* and *The Beiderbecke Connection.*

Ben Casey   Vince Edwards (Ben), Sam Jaffe (Dr David Zorba), Ben Piazza (Dr Mike Rogers). Hospital: County General. Produced by Bing Crosby Productions, which discovered Vince Edwards.

Bergerac   John Nettles (Det. Sgt Jim Bergerac), Terence Alexander (Charlie Hungerford), Lisa Goddard (Philippa Vale). Story of an alcoholic policeman in Jersey.

Beverly Hillbillies   Buddy Ebsen (Jed Clampett), Irene Ryan (Daisy Moses alias Granny), Donna Douglas (Elly May), Max Baer Jnr (Jethro Bodine and Jethrene Bodine), Nancy Kulp (Jane Hathaway), Sharon Tate (Janet Trego).

Beverly Hills 90210   Shannen Doherty (Brenda Walsh), Jason Priestley (Brandon Walsh). Title is a Zip code.

Bewitched   Elizabeth Montgomery (Samantha Stephens), Dick York and Dick Sargent (Darren), Agnes Moorhead (Endora), Marion Lorne (Aunt Clara), David White (Larry Tate).

Big Big Talent Show, The   Jonathan Ross hosts the star-spotting talent show.

Big Break   Snooker-based game show hosted by Jim Davidson and John Virgo.

Big Brother   Launched in July 2000. The original ten housemates were Anna, Andrew, Caroline, Craig, Darren, Melanie, Nick, Nichola, Sada and Thomas. Nick Bateman was evicted for cheating and replaced by Claire Strutton. The three finalists were Craig Philips, Anna Nolan and Darren Ramsey. The winner of the £70,000 first prize was Craig. Marjorie was the pet chicken, Juanita the toy baby, and Davina McCall the presenter.

Birds of a Feather   Pauline Quirke (Sharon Theodopolopoudos), Linda Robson (Tracey Stubbs), Lesley Joseph (Dorien Green), Peter Polycarpou and David Cardy (Chris Theodopolopoudos). Series created by Laurence Marks and Maurice Gran.

Blackadder   Various series written by Rowan Atkinson, Richard Curtis and Ben Elton. Characters included Baldrick (Tony Robinson), Queen Elizabeth I (Miranda Richardson), Melchett (Stephen Fry), Captain Darling/Percy (Tim McInnerny).

Blake's 7   Gareth Thomas (Blake), Paul Darrow (Kerr Avon), Sally Knyvette (Jenna Stannis), Michael Keating (Vila Restal), Jan Chappell (Cally from Auron), Josette Simon (Dayna Mellanby), David Jackson (Gan Olag), Steven Pacey (Capt. Del Tarrant), Peter Tuddenham (voice of Zen and Orac), Glynis Barber (Soolin), Jacqueline Pearce (Servalan). Spacecraft: Liberator and Scorpio Penal Colony, Cygnus Alpha. Dictatorship name: The Federation. Creator: Terry Nation. Gan Olag was implanted with a 'Brain Limiter' to stop him killing.

Blooming Marvellous   Sarah Lancashire (Liz), Clive Mantle (Jack).

Blott on the Landscape   David Suchet (Blott), George Cole (Sir Giles Lynchwood MP), Simon Cadell (Dundridge). Adaption by Malcolm Bradbury of Tom Sharpe's black comic novel. Filmed at Stanage Park, near Ludlow.

Blue Peter   Original presenters in 1958: Leila Williams and Christopher Trace. Other presenters include Valerie Singleton, Peter Purves, John Noakes, Lesley Judd, Simon Groom, Sarah Greene, Peter Duncan, Janet Ellis, Michael Sundin, Anthea

T
E
L
E
V
I
S
I
O
N

Turner, Diane-Louise Jordan, Caron Keating, John Leslie, Mark Curry and Yvette Fielding.

Bonanza Lorne Greene (Ben Cartwright), Michael Landon (Little Joe Cartwright), Dan Blocker (Eric 'Hoss' Cartwright, Norwegian for good luck), Pernell Roberts (Adam), Victor Sen Yung (Hop Sing), Ray Teal (Sheriff Ray Coffee), David Canary (Mr 'Candy' Canaday), Tim Matheson (Griff King). The three sons had different mothers.

Boon Michael Elphick (Ken Boon), Neil Morrissey (Rocky Cassidy).

Boss Cat Cartoon characters include: Benny the Ball, Choo Choo, Spook, The Brain, Fancy-Fancy, Officer Dibble. Series called *Top Cat* outside UK.

Bottom Rik Mayall (Richie Richard), Adrian Edmondson (Eddie Hitler).

Bouquet of Barbed Wire Frank Finlay (Peter Manson), Sheila Allen (Cassie), Susan Penhaligon (Prue), James Aubrey (Gavin Sorenson).

Boyd QC Michael Denison.

Boys from the Blackstuff Bernard Hill (Yosser Hughes), Michael Angelis (Chrissie Todd), Julie Walters (Angie Todd). Written by Alan Bleasdale. Famous catchphrase: Gi's a job.

Boys from the Bush Tim Healy (Reg Toomer), Chris Haywood (Dennis Tontine).

Brains Trust, The Chairmen: Hugh Ross Willliams, Michael Flanders.

Branded Chuck Connors (Jason McCord), only survivor of Indian massacre at the Battle of Bitter Creek in Wyoming and thought therefore to be a coward. Opening court martial scene is memorable.

Brass Timothy West (Bradley Hardacre), Caroline Blakiston (Patience), Geoffrey Hinsliff and Geoffrey Hutchings (George Fairchild). Set in Utterley.

Bread Peter Howitt and Graham Bickley (Joey Boswell), Jean Boht (Nellie), Ronald Forfar (Freddie), Victor McGuire (Jack), Gilly Coman and Melanie Hill (Aveline), Jonathan Morris (Adrian), Nick Conway (Billy), Rita Tushingham (Celia Higgins). Series created by Carla Lane.

Brideshead Revisited Anthony Andrews (Lord Sebastian Flyte), Jeremy Irons (Charles Ryder), Diana Quick (Lady Julia Flyte), Laurence Olivier (Lord Marchmain), John Gielgud (Edward Ryder), Claire Bloom (Lady Ryder).

Brittas Empire, The Chris Barrie (Gordon), Pippa Heywood (Helen), Julia St John (Laura Lancing). Leisure centre: Whitbury Newtown Leisure Centre.

Brothers, The Jean Anderson (Mary Hammond), Glyn Owen and Patrick O'Connell (Edward Hammond), Gabrielle Drake (Jill Hammond), Colin Baker (Paul Merroney), Liza Goddard (April Merroney), Kate O' Mara (Jane Maxwell). Type of business: haulage.

Brush Strokes Karl Howman (Jacko), Mike Walling (Eric), Nicky Croydon (Jean), Howard Lew Lewis (Elmo Putney), Gary Waldhorn (Lionel Bainbridge).

Buck Rogers in the 25th Century Gil Gerard (Buck), Felix Silla (Twiki: voiced by Mel Blanc, Bob Elyea), Henry Silva and Michael Ansara (Kane), Wilfred Hyde-White (Dr Goodfellow), Pamela Hensley (Princess Ardala). Year 2491. Space capsule: Ranger 3, launched in 1987. City: New Chicago. Rivals: Draconians.

Budgie Adam Faith (Budgie Bird), Iain Cuthbertson (Charlie Endell), Lynn Dalby (Hazel), Georgina Hale (Jean Bird), John Rhys-Davies (Laughing Spam Fritter), Rio Fanning (Grogan). Writers: Keith Waterhouse and Willis Hall.

Buffy the Vampire Slayer Sarah Michelle Gellar (Buffy Summers), Alyson Hannigan (Willow Rosenberg), Nicholas Brendon (Xander Harris), Anthony Head (Rupert Giles), Emma Caulfield (Anya), Seth Green (Oz), Marc Blucas (Riley Finn), David Boreanaz (Angel), Charisma Carpenter (Cordelia), James Marsters (Spike).

Bulman Don Henderson (George Bulman). Character first appeared in *The XYY Man* and then in *Strangers*. His quirky nature included his wearing of fingerless gloves, constant use of an inhaler and carrying of a plastic bag whose contents we rarely saw.

Busman's Holiday Presenters: Julian Pettifer, Sarah Kennedy, Elton Welsby.

Butterflies Wendy Craig (Ria Parkinson), Geoffrey Palmer (Ben Parkinson, a dentist), Andrew Hall (Russell Parkinson), Nicholas Lyndhurst (Adam Parkinson). Series created by Carla Lane.

By the Sword Divided Sharon Mughan (Anne Lacey/Fletcher), Julian Glover (Sir Martin Lacey), Tim Bentinck (Sir Thomas Lacey). Plot: a family is torn apart by the English Civil War.

Cagney and Lacey Tyne Daly (Mary Beth Lacey), Meg Foster and Sharon Gless (Christine Cagney).

Call My Bluff Presenters: Robert Robinson, Bob Holness.

Callan Edward Woodward (Callan), Russell Hunter (Lonely), Ronald Radd, Michael Goodliffe, Derek Bond, William Squire (Hunter), Anthony Valentine (Toby Meres), Patrick Mower (Cross). Series started as an Armchair Theatre production, *A Magnum For Schneider,* with Peter Bowles playing Toby Meres.

Camberwick Green Took over Monday *Watch with Mother* slot from 'Picture Box'. Characters included Capt. Snort, Sgt Major Grout, Windy Miller of Colley's Mill, Mickey Murphy the baker, Dr Mopp, Thomas Tripp the milkman, Mrs Dingle the postmistress, Mrs Honeyman, PC McGarry (No. 452).

Campion Peter Davison (Albert Campion), Brian Glover (Magersfontein Lugg, Campion's manservant).

Candid Camera Presenters: Bob Monkhouse, Jonathan Routh, Peter Dulay.

Captain Pugwash Characters included Capt. Horatio Pugwash (Skipper of the *Black Pig*), Able Seamen Barnabas and Willy, Master Mate (occasionally referred to as Master Bate), Tom and Cutthroat Jake. Theme music 'The Hornblower', performed by Tommy Edmondson. Narrator: Peter Hawkins.

Captain Scarlet and the Mysterons Voices: Francis Matthews (Paul Metcalfe/Capt. Scarlet), Donald Gray (Charles Gray/Col. White), Ed Bishop (Adam Svenson/Capt. Blue), Paul Maxwell (Bradley Holden/Capt. Grey), Sylvia Anderson (Magnolia Jones/Melody Angel), Liz Morgan (Juliette Pointon/Destiny Angel), Janna Hill (Karen Wainwright/Symphony Angel), Liz Morgan (Diane Sims/Rhapsody Angel), Lian-Shin (Chan Kwan/Harmony Angel), Donald Gray (Conrad Turner/Capt. Black), Charles Tingwell (Edward Wilkie/Dr Fawn), Gary Files (Patrick Donaghue/Capt. Magenta), Jeremy Wilkin (Richard Frazier/Capt. Ochre), Cy Grant (Seymour Griffiths/Lt Green), Paul Maxwell (World President). Year: 2068. Spectrum base: Cloudbase Angel. Interceptor aircraft codeword: SIG Spectrum is Green.

Casey Jones Alan Hale Jnr (John Luther 'Casey' Jones). Worked for Illinois Central Railroad. Engine name: Cannonball Express. His faithful dog was called Cinders.

Cathy Come Home Carol White (Cathy Ward), Ray Brooks (Reg Ward). Written by Jeremy Sandford, directed by Ken Loach. This drama brought Shelter, a campaign for the homeless, to the awareness of many.

Catweazle Geoffrey Baildon (Catweazle), Robin Davis (Carrot Bennett). Story of an 11th-century wizard stranded in the 20th century.

Celeb Harry Enfield (Gary), Amanda Holden (Debs), Leo Bill (Troy), Rupert Vansittart (Johnson). Sit-com set in the home of a rock superstar. Based on a cartoon in *Private Eye* magazine.

Champions Stuart Damon (Craig Stirling), William Gaunt (Richard Barrett), Alexandra Bastedo (Sharon McCready). Worked for Nemesis, based in Geneva.

Changing Rooms Hosted by Carol Smillie. Designers include Graham Wynne and Linda Barker. DIY expert: Andy Kane.

Charlie's Angels Kate Jackson (Sabrina Duncan), Farrah Fawcett-Majors (Jill Munroe), Jaclyn Smith (Kelly Garrett), Cheryl Ladd (Kris Munroe), Shelley Hack (Tiffany Welles), Tanya Roberts (Julie Rogers). Voice of Charlie Townshend: John Forsythe.

Cheers Ted Danson (Sam Malone), Shelley Long (Diane Chambers), Rhea Perlman (Carla Tortelli/Le Bec), Georg Wendt (Norm the accountant), John Ratzenberger (Cliff the mailman), Kelsey Grammer (Frasier Crane the psychiatrist), Woody Harrelson (Woody), Kirstie Alley (Rebecca Howe).

Chef Lenny Henry (Gareth Blackstock), Caroline Lee Johnson (Janice), Roger Griffiths (Everton). Chef of Le Château Anglais in the Oxfordshire Cotswolds.

Cheyenne Clint Walker (Cheyenne Bodie). Replaced for short time by Ty Hardin as Bronco Lane, who eventually gained his own series.

Chigley Described as a hamlet near Camberwick Green, Trumptonshire. Characters included Mr Clutterbuck the Builder, Chipppy Minton the Carpenter, Lord Belborough, Mr Cresswell the owner of the biscuit factory, Harry Farthing the Potter, Mr Brackett the Butler.

Chinese Detective, The David Yip (Det. Sgt Johnny Ho).

Chips Erik Estrada (Francis 'Ponch' Poncherello), Larry Wilcox (Jonathan Baker). Story of two Los Angeles police motorcyclists working for the California Highway Patrol (Chips).

Circus Boy Notable for the casting of Mickey Braddock (formerly and latterly Dolenz) as Corky.

Cisco Kid, The Duncan Renaldo (Cisco), Leo Carrillo (Pancho). Cisco's horse: Diablo. Pancho's horse: Loco. Pancho was expert with a whip. Based on stories by O'Henry.

Citizen James Sid James (Sidney Balmoral James), Bill Kerr (William 'Bill' Kerr), Liz Fraser (Liz Fraser).

Citizen Smith Robert Lindsay (Walter Henry 'Wolfie' Smith), Mike Grady (Ken), Tony Millan (Tucker), Cheryl Hall (Shirley), Peter Vaughan and Tony Steedman (Charlie Johnson). Leader of the Tooting Popular Front with his catchphrase 'Power to the People'.

Clangers, The Clangers were the pink and woolly, mouse-like creatures who took their names from the sound made when they battened down their dustbin-lid hatches and retreated underground. Other inhabitants of the planet were the Froglets, Soup Dragon and Iron Chicken.

Cleopatras, The Actresses who played the Cleopatras included Michelle Newell, Elizabeth Shepherd, Caroline Mortimer, Sue Holderness, Amanda Boxer, Prue Clarke, Pauline Moran.

Colditz Jack Hedley (Lt Col. John Preston), Robert Wagner (Flt Lt/Major Phil Carrington), David McCallum (Flt Lt Simon Carter), Bernard Hepton (Kommandant), Anthony Valentine (Major Horst Mohn).

Come Dancing Presenters include McDonald Hobley, Angela Rippon, David Jacobs, Terry Wogan, Rosemarie Ford, Noel Edmonds, Judith Chalmers, Keith Fordyce, Michael Aspel, Peter West and Peter Dimmock.

Compact Ronald Allen (Ian Harmon), Carmen Silvera (Camilla Hope), Vincent Ball (David Rome). Created by Hazel Adair and Peter Ling of *Crossroads* fame.

Cool For Cats Britain's first pop music show in 1956 and hosted by Ker Robertson and then Kent Walton.

Cosby Show Bill Cosby (Heathcliff Huxtable, an obstetrician), Phylicia Ayres-Allen/Rashad (Clair, a lawyer). Their children: Sondra, Rudy, Denise, Theo, Vanessa.

Countdown Words-and-numbers game hosted by Richard Whiteley and Carol Vorderman. First programme on Channel 4. *Countdown* has the most professional production team of any show on the box – it includes three *Countdown* champions and producer Mark Nyman is a former World Scrabble Champion. The author has happy memories of the show although beaten on the conundrum on his second appearance.

Cracker Robbie Coltrane (Eddie 'Fitz' Fitzgerald). Created by Jimmy McGovern.

Crackerjack Hosts: Eamonn Andrews, Leslie Crowther, Michael Aspel, Ed Stewart, Stu Francis. Stooges: Peter Glaze, Don Maclean, Leslie Crowther. Game: Double or Drop.

Crime Traveller Michael French (David Wicks in *EastEnders*) starred in this time machine series.

Criss Cross Quiz Popular quiz show hosted by Jeremy Hawk (father of actress Belinda Lang). Derived its format from the American *Tic Tac Dough*.

C.A.T.S. Eyes Jill Gascoigne (Maggie Forbes), Rosalyn Landor (Pru Standfast), Leslie Ash (Frederica 'Fred' Smith). C.A.T.S. stood for Covert Activities Thames Section.

Dad's Army Arthur Lowe (Capt. George Mainwaring, a bank manager), John Le Mesurier (Sgt Arthur Wilson), Clive Dunn (L/Corporal Jack Jones, a butcher), John Laurie (Pte James Frazier, an undertaker), James Beck (Pte James Walker, a spiv), Ian Lavender (Pte Frank Pike, a silly boy), Arnold Ridley (Pte Charles Godfrey), Bill Pertwee (ARP Warden William Hodges, a greengrocer), Frank Williams (the vicar), Colin Bean (Pte Sponge), Pamela Cundell (Mrs Fox). Created by Jimmy Perry and David Croft and set in Walmington-on-Sea (supposedly Bexhill).

Dalziel and Pascoe Warren Clarke (Det. Supt Andrew Dalziel), Colin Buchanan (Det. Insp. Peter Pascoe). Written by Stephen Lowe and based on Reginald Hill's books.

Dangermouse Voices: Dangermouse (David Jason), Penfold (Terry Scott), Stiletto Mafioso (Brian Trueman), Baron Greenback (Edward Kelsey). Created by Mike Harding and Brian Trueman. Written by Brian Trueman and Angus Allen. Narrated by David Jason.

Darling Buds of May, The David Jason (Sidney

TELEVISION

Charles 'Pop' Larkin), Pam Ferris (Ma Larkin), Catherine Zeta-Jones (Mariette Larkin/Charlton), Philip Franks (Cedric 'Charley' Charlton).

Defenders, The   E G Marshall (Lawrence Preston), Robert Reed (Kenneth Preston). Father and son lawyers.

Dempsey and Makepeace   Michael Brandon (Lt James Dempsey), Glynis Barber (Det. Sgt Harriet Makepeace). Dept: S110.

Department S   Peter Wyngarde (Jason King), Joel Fabiani (Stewart Sullivan), Rosemary Nichols (Annabelle Hurst). Department S was a department of Interpol.

Desmond's   Norman Beaton (Desmond Ambrose), Carmen Munroe (Shirley Ambrose), Ram John Holder (Pork Pie). Life in a Peckham barber's shop.

Detectives, The   Jasper Carrott (Bob Louis), Robert Powell (Dave Briggs), George Sewell (Supt Frank Cottam).

Dial 999   Robert Beatty (Canadian Mountie Mike Maguire), seconded to London on work experience.

Dick Van Dyke Show, The   Dick Van Dyke (Rob Petrie), Mary Tyler Moore (Laura), Larry Matthews (Ritchie), Rose Marie (Sally Rogers), Carl Reiner (Alan Brady), Morey Amsterdam (Maurice 'Buddy' Sorrell).

Dinnerladies   Victoria Wood (Bren), Thelma Barlow (Dolly), Celia Imrie (Philippa), Maxine Peake (Twinkle), Anne Reid (Jean), Duncan Preston (Stan), Andrew Dunn (Tony), Shobna Gulati (Anita), Julie Walters (Petula), Christopher Greet (Mr Michael), Jane Hazlegrove (Lisa), Sue Devaney (Secretary).

Doctor Finlay   Tannochbrae 20 years on (real-life Auchtermuchty in Fife), with Dr Finlay played by David Rintoul and the character's Christian name changed to John.

Dr Finlay's Casebook   Bill Simpson (Dr Alan Finlay), Andrew Cruickshank (Dr Angus Cameron), Barbara Mullen (Janet). Set in 1920s Tannochbrae (real-life Callander), the base for practice was Arden House. The stories were based on *The Adventures of a Black Bag* by A J Cronin.

Doctor in the House   Barry Evans (Michael Upton), Robin Nedwell (Duncan Waring), Geoffrey Davies (Dick Stuart-Clark), George Layton (Paul Collier). Based on the books by Richard Gordon.

Don't Wait Up   Nigel Havers (Dr Tom Latimer), Tony Britton (Dr Toby Latimer). Writer: George Layton.

Doomwatch   John Paul (Dr Spencer Quist), Simon Oates (Dr John Ridge), Robert Powell (Tobias 'Toby' Wren).

Dotto   Game show hosted by Robert Gladwell, Jimmy Hanley and Shaw Taylor during its two-year run. Based on American show which was taken off as part of the 'Quiz Show Scandal'.

Dr Kildare   Richard Chamberlain (Dr James Kildare), Raymond Massey (Dr Leonard Gillespie). Based on Max Brand books. Richard Chamberlain had a hit with the vocal version of the theme tune, 'Three Stars Will Shine Tonight'. Hospital: Blair General.

Dr Who   First Dr Who was William Hartnell, followed by Patrick Troughton, Jon Pertwee, Tom Baker, Peter Davison, Colin Baker, Sylvester McCoy. Other Dr Who's have included Richard Hurndall, who took William Hartnell's part in *The Five Doctors*, Paul McGann who played the Doctor in a television film, and Peter Cushing, who appeared as the Doctor in two feature films. The original crew were William Russell (Ian Chesterton), Jacqueline Hill (Barbara

Wright) and Carole Ann Ford (Susan Foreman, the Doctor's granddaughter). Other assistants included Peter Purves (Steven Taylor), Nicola Bryant (Perpugilliam 'Peri' Brown), Sophie Aldred (Ace), Louise Jameson (Leela), Frazer Hines (Jamie McCrimmon), Janet Fielding (Tegan Jovanka), Elizabeth Sladen (Sarah Jane Smith), Katy Manning (Jo Grant), Sarah Sutton (Nyssa). The Doctor is from the planet Gallifrey. The five actors who played the Master were (1) Roger Delgado (2) Peter Pratt (3) Geoffrey Beevers (4) Anthony Ainley (5) Eric Roberts. Tardis: Time And Relative Dimension In Space.

Dragnet   Jack Webb (Joe Friday). Episodes began: 'The story you are about to see is true, only the names have been changed to protect the innocent.' Set in Los Angeles. Badge no.: 714.

Drop the Dead Donkey   Robert Duncan (Gus), Neil Pearson (Dave), Jeff Rawle (George), Stephen Tompkinson (Damien), David Swift (Henry), Victoria Wicks (Sally). Written by Andy Hamilton and Guy Jenkin. Original working title for the show was 'Dead Belgians Don't Count'.

Duchess of Duke Street, The   Gemma Jones (Louisa Trotter), Christopher Cazenove (Charles Tyrrell). Loosely based on the life story of Rosa Lewis, a kitchen maid who became manageress of the Cavendish Hotel in Jermyn Street. Hotel in series: Bentinck.

Dukes of Hazzard, The   Catherine Bach (Daisy Duke), Tom Wopat (Luke Duke), John Schneider (Bo Duke), Sorrell Booke (Jefferson Davis 'Boss' Hogg). The Dukes were the Robin Hoods of Hazzard County, driving around in their 1969 Dodge Charger named The General Lee. Narration and theme tune by Waylon Jennings.

Dustbinmen, The   John Woodvine and Brian Wilde (Bloody Delilah), Bryan Pringle (Cheese and Egg), Graham Haberfield (Winston Platt), Trevor Bannister (Heavy Breathing). Created and produced by Jack Rosenthal. Lorry called Thunderbird Three.

Edge of Darkness   Bob Peck (Ronald Craven), Joanne Whalley (Emma Craven), Joe Don Baker (Darius Jedburgh). Music by Eric Clapton.

Edward and Mrs Simpson   Edward Fox (Edward), Cynthia Harris (Mrs Wallis Warfield Simpson), Peggy Ashcroft (Queen Mary), David Waller (Stanley Baldwin).

Edward the Seventh   Timothy West (Edward as an adult), Charles Sturridge (Edward as a teenager), Annette Crosbie (Queen Victoria), Robert Hardy (Prince Albert).

Elizabeth R   Glenda Jackson (Elizabeth), Robert Hardy (Robert Dudley), Ronald Hines (William Cecil), Daphne Slater (Mary Tudor), Vivian Pickles (Mary, Queen of Scots), John Woodvine (Sir Francis Drake), Nicholas Selby (Sir Walter Raleigh).

Emergency Ward 10   Jill Browne (Carole Young), Charles Tingwell (Dr Alan Dawson), Desmond Carrington (Dr Chris Anderson), John Carlisle (Mr Lester Large), Ray Barrett (Dr Don Nolan), Jane Rossington (Nurse Kate Ford), Paul Darrow (Mr Verity), John Alderton (Dr Richard Moone), Pik-Sen Lim (Nurse Kwai).

Empire Road   Norman Beaton (Everton Bennett).

Equalizer, The   Edward Woodward (Robert McCall).

ER   George Clooney (Dr Douglas Ross), Noah Wyle (Dr John Carter), Eriq La Salle (Dr Peter Benton), Julianna Margulies (Nurse Hathaway), Alex Kingston (Dr Elizabeth Corday), Anthony Edwards (Dr Mark

Greene), Paul McCrane (Dr Robert Romano), Ming-Na (Dr Jing-Mai Chen), Michael Michele (Dr Cleo Finch), Maura Tiernay (Nurse Abby Lockheart), Laura Innes (Dr Kerry Weaver), Goran Visnjie (Dr Luka Kovac), Erik Palladino (Dr Dave Malucci). Set in Cook County Hospital, Chicago.

Ever-Decreasing Circles Richard Briers (Martin Brice), Penelope Wilton (Ann Brice), Stanley Lebor (Howard Hughes). Creators: John Esmonde and Bob Larbey.

Expert, The Marius Goring (Dr John Hardy).

Face to Face Presenter: John Freeman.

Fairly Secret Army Geoffrey Palmer (Major Harry Kitchener Wellington Truscott). Army called Queen's Own West Mercian Lowlanders.

Fall and Rise of Reginald Perrin, The Leonard Rossiter (Reginald Iolanthe Perrin/Martin Wellbourne), Pauline Yates (Elizabeth), John Barron (CJ), Sue Nicholls (Joan Greengross), Geoffrey Palmer (Jimmy), John Horsley (Doc Morrissey), Bruce Bould (David Harris-Jones). Created by David Nobbs. Companies: Sunshine Desserts/Grot.

Fame Debbie Allen (Lydia Grant), Erica Gimpel (Coco Hernandez), Gene Anthony Ray (Leroy Johnson), Lori Singer (Julie Miller), Janet Jackson (Cleo Hewitt).

Fame Academy BBC programme showcasing new talent. The first winner in 2002 was David Sneddon, with Ireland's Sinead Quinn runner-up.

Family at War, A Colin Douglas (Edwin Ashton), Barbara Flynn (Freda Ashton), Coral Atkins (Sheila Ashton), John Nettles (Ian McKenzie).

Family Fortunes Presenters include Bob Monkhouse, Max Bygraves and Les Dennis.

Family, The Fly-on-the-wall look at the Wilkins family from Reading.

Fantasy Football Presenters: Frank Skinner and David Baddiel.

Fantasy Island Ricardo Montalban (Mr Roarke), Herve Villechaize (Tattoo).

Far Pavilions, The Ben Cross (Ashton Pelham-Martyn), Amy Irving (Princess Anjuli), Christopher Lee (Kaka-Ji-Rao), Omar Sharif (Koda Dad), John Gielgud (Cavagnari), Rossano Brazzi (the Rana of Bhithor).

Father Dear Father Patrick Cargill (Patrick Glover), Natasha Pyne (Anna Glover), Ann Holloway (Karen Glover), Noel Dyson (Matilda 'Nanny' Harris).

Fawlty Towers John Cleese (Basil), Prunella Scales (Sybil), Andrew Sachs (Manuel), Connie Booth (Polly Sherman), Ballard Berkeley (Major Gowen). Set in Torquay.

FBI, The Efrem Zimbalist Jnr (Inspector Lewis Erskine).

Fifteen to One General knowledge quiz hosted by William G Stewart. Series winners include Jon Goodwin, Anthony Martin, Kevin Ashman, Mal Collier, Thomas Dyer, Andrew Francis, Barbara Thompson, Leslie Booth, Julian Allen, Martin Riley, Ian Potts, Arnold O'Hara, Trevor Montague, Stanley Miller, Glen Binnie, Bill Francis, Mike Kirby, Nick Terry, Doug Griffiths and Bill McKaig. Mal Collier won the Champion of Champions event held at Christmas 1997. The author was sued by William G Stewart for the return of his prizes and all his expenses incurred during his eight appearances on the show. The suit was brought by Mr Stewart because a breach of his rules took place whereby contestants are not allowed to take part a second time unless he invites them. The judge commented

that 'Mr Stewart was very easily upset'.

Filthy, Rich and Catflap Nigel Planer (Filthy Ralph), Rik Mayall (Richard Rich), Adrian Edmondson (Eddie Catflap). Written by Ben Elton.

Fire Crackers Joe Baker (Jumbo). Inept local firemen working in Cropper's End.

Fireball XL5 Characters include Colonel Steve Zodiac, Professor Matthew Matic, Venus Commander Zero, Lt 90, Zoonie, Robert the Robot.

Flintstones Characters include Fred, Wilma and Pebbles Flintstone, Barney, Betty and Bamm Bamm Rubble, and Dino the pet dinosaur.

Flipper Luke Halpin (Sandy Ricks), Brian Kelly (Porter Ricks). Last star dolphin of seven, called Bebe, died 4 May 1997, aged 40.

Flowerpot Men, The Characters included Bill and Ben, Little Weed and Slowcoach the Tortoise.

Follyfoot Gillian Blake (Dora), Arthur English (Slugger), Desmond Llewellyn (the Colonel), Steve Hodson (Steve).

Food and Drink Presenters include Chris Kelly, Henry Kelly, Susan Grossman, Jilly Goolden, Michael Barry, Oz Clarke, Paul Heiney.

Forsyte Saga, The Kenneth More (Jolyon Forsyte), Eric Porter (Soames Forsyte), Nyree Dawn Porter (Irene Heron/Forsyte).

Fortunes of War Kenneth Branagh (Guy Pringle), Emma Thompson (Harriet Pringle).

Fosters, The Notable for an early performance by Lenny Henry as Sonny Foster.

Four Feather Falls Voice of Tex Tucker: Nicholas Parsons. One feather allowed Tex's dog Dusty to speak; another gave speech to his horse, Rocky; the last two controlled the accuracy of his pistols.

Four Just Men, The Jack Hawkins (Ben Manfred MP), Dan Dailey (Tim Collier), Richard Conte (Jeff Ryder), Vittorio De Sica (Ricco Poccari).

Frasier Kelsey Grammer (Frasier Crane), David Hyde Pierce (Niles Crane), Bebe Neuwirth (Lilith), John Mahoney (Martin Crane), Jane Leeves (Daphne Moon), Peri Gilpin (Roz Doyle).

Friends Lisa Kudrow (Phoebe), Matt Le Blanc (Joey), Courtney Cox (Monica), Jennifer Aniston (Rachel Green), David Schwimmer (Ross), Matthew Perry (Chandler).

F Troop Ken Berry (Captain Wilton Parmenter), Forrest Tucker (Sgt Morgan O'Rourke), Larry Storch (Corporal Randolph Agarn), John Mitchum (Trooper Hoffenmuller).

Fugitive, The David Janssen (Dr Richard Kimble), Barry Morse (Lt Philip Gerard), Bill Raisch (Fred Johnson alias the one-armed man).

Game for a Laugh Presenters include Matthew Kelly, Henry Kelly, Sarah Kennedy, Jeremy Beadle, Rustie Lee, Martin Daniels, Debbie Rix, Lee Peck.

Generation Game Hosts include Bruce Forsyth, Larry Grayson and Jim Davidson.

Gentle Touch, The Jill Gascoigne (DI Maggie Forbes), Derek Thompson (Det. Sgt Jimmy Fenton).

Get Smart Don Adams (Maxwell Smart, Agent 86), Barbara Feldon (Agent 99). Cover: salesman for Pontiac Greeting Card Co. Series created by Mel Brooks.

Girl From Uncle, The Stefanie Powers (April Dancer), Noel Harrison (Mark Slate), Leo G Carroll (Mr Waverly).

Girls on Top Tracey Ullman (Candice), Dawn French (Amanda), Jennifer Saunders (Jennifer), Ruby Wax (Shelley), Joan Greenwood (Lady Carlton).

TELEVISION

Give Us a Break Robert Lindsay (Mickey Noades), Paul McGann (Mo Morris).

Gladiators Presenters: John Fashanu, Jeremy Guscott, Ulrika Jonsson.

Gnomes of Dulwich Terry Scott and Hugh Lloyd continuing their partnership as a big and small gnome. John Clive played the third 'old' gnome.

Going For a Song Presenter: Max Robertson.

Golden Girls, The Beatrice Arthur (Dorothy Zbornak), Rue McClanahan (Blanche Devereaux), Betty White (Rose Nylund), Estelle Getty (Sophia Petrillo).

Golden Shot, The Presenters included Jackie Rae, Bob Monkhouse, Norman Vaughan, Charlie Williams.

Good Afternoon Channel 5 daytime programme featuring the hospital documentary series Liverpool Mums, Pets Go Public, where contestants have to match pets with their owners, and Cryptogram, a general knowledge and word game of which the author has pleasant memories.

Good Life, The Richard Briers (Tom Good), Felicity Kendall (Barbara), Penelope Keith (Margo Leadbeatter), Paul Eddington (Jerry Leadbeatter). Goat: Geraldine.

Goodness Gracious Me Sanjeev Bhaskar, Meera Syal, Kulvinder Ghir, Nina Wadia. Irreverent sketch show that takes a light-hearted look at the Anglo-Asian community.

Goodnight Sweetheart Nicholas Lyndhurst (Gary Sparrow), Dervla Kirwan (Phoebe Bamford), Victor McGuire (Ron Wheatcroft), Christopher Ettridge (PC Reg Deadman), Michelle Holmes (Yvonne Sparrow). Elizabeth Carling and Emma Amos took over leading female roles.

Good Old Days, The Transmitted from the Leeds City Varieties Theatre, compered by Leonard Sachs (originally Don Gemmell). Every show ended with a rendition of 'Down at the Old Bull and Bush'.

Grange Hill Todd Carty (Peter 'Tucker' Jenkins), Susan Tully (Suzanne Ross), Letitia Dean (Lucinda), Peter Moran (Pogo Patterson), Gwyneth Powell (Bridget McCluskey), Mark Savage (Gripper Stebson), Sean Maguire (Tegs Ratcliffe).

Great Antiques Hunt, The Host: Jilly Goolden.

Grimleys, The Brian Conley (Digby), Amanda Holden (Geraldine), Noddy Holder, James Bradshaw.

Gunsmoke/Gun Law James Arness (Matt Dillon), Amanda Blake (Kitty Russell), Milburn Stone (Dr Galen 'Doc' Adams), Dennis Weaver (Chester Goode), Burt Reynolds (Quint Asper).

Happy Days Henry Winkler (Arthur Fonzarelli), Ron Howard (Richie Cunningham), Scott Baio (Charles 'Chachi' Arcola), Suzi Quattro (Leather Tuscadero), Robin Williams (Mork).

Hark at Barker Ronnie Barker (Lord Rustless), David Jason (Dithers).

Harry Enfield Show Characters include the Slobs: Wayne and Waynetta and children Frogmella and Spudulike.

Hart to Hart Robert Wagner (Jonathan Hart), Stefanie Powers (Jennifer Hart), Lionel Stander (Max), Freeway the dog. Occupations: businessman and journalist.

Have Gun Will Travel Richard Boone (Paladin), Kam Tong (Hey Boy), Lisa Lu (Hey Girl).

Have I Got News for You Hosted by Angus Deayton. Team captains are Paul Merton and Ian Hislop.

Hawaii Five-O Jack Lord (Steve Garrett), James MacArthur ('Danno' Williams), Kam Fong (Chin Ho Kelly).

Hawkeye and the Last of the Mohicans John Hart (Nat 'Hawkeye' Cutler), Lon Chaney Jnr (Chingachgook).

Hazell Nicholas Ball (James Hazell), Roddy McMillan (Choc Minty). Created by Terry Venables and Gordon Williams.

Heartbeat Nick Berry (PC Nick Rowan), Derek Fowlds (Sgt Oscar Blaketon), Bill Maynard (Claude Jeremiah Greengrass). Set in 1964 Yorkshire.

Hector's House Adventures of a dog (Hector), a cat (Zaza) and a frog (Mrs Kiki).

Herbs, The Garden owners: Sir Basil and Lady Rosemary. Other characters include Constable Knapweed, Mr Onion the schoolteacher and his pupils, the Chives, Bayleaf the gardener, Aunt Mint, Sage the owl, Tarragon the dragon, Pashana Bedi the snake-charmer, and Belladonna. The real stars were Dill the dog and Parsley the lion. Gordon Rollings was the narrator and the magic word that opened the gate was 'Herbidacious'.

Here's Lucy Lucille Ball (Lucy Carter), Gale Gordon (Harrison Carter).

Hergé's Adventures of Tin Tin Narrator: Peter Hawkins. Characters include Snowy the white fox-terrier, Captain Haddock, the Thompson Twins, Professor Calculus and General Alcazar.

Hi-De-Hi Paul Shane (Ted Bovis), Ruth Madoc (Gladys Pugh), Simon Cadell (Jeffrey Fairbrother), David Griffin (Squadron Leader Clive Dempster), Jeffrey Holland (Spike Dixon), Su Pollard (Peggy Ollerenshaw). Holiday camp: Maplins at Crimpton-on-Sea.

Highway to Heaven Michael Landon (Jonathan Smith), Victor French (Mark Gordon).

Hill Street Blues Daniel J Travanti (Captain Frank Furillo), Veronica Hamel (Joyce Davenport), Robert Prosky (Sgt Stanislaus Jablonski).

Hitch-Hiker's Guide to the Galaxy, The Simon Jones (Arthur Dent), David Dixon (Ford Prefect), Sandra Dickinson (Trillian), David Learner (Marvin), Stephen Moore (Marvin's voice), Mark Wing-Davey (Zaphod Beeblebrox), Peter Jones (the book voice).

Hogan's Heroes Bob Crane (Colonel Robert Hogan), Werner Klemperer (Colonel Wilhelm Klink), John Banner (Sgt Hans Schulz), Larry Hovis (Sgt Andrew Carter), Ivan Dixon (Corporal James Kinchloe).

Holiday Presenters include Frank Bough, Des Lynam, Cliff Michelmore, Joan Bakewell, Jill Dando, Anneka Rice, Eamonn Holmes.

House of Cards Ian Richardson (Francis Urquhart). Based on Michael Dobbs's novel.

How/How 2 Presenters include Fred Dineage, Jack Hargreaves, Jon Miller, Bunty James, Marian Davies, Carol Vorderman, Gareth Jones.

Howard's Way Maurice Colbourne (Tom Howard), Jan Harvey (Jan Howard), Glyn Owen (Jack Rolfe), Stephen Yardley (Ken Masters), Tony Anholt (Charles Frere), Nigel Davenport (Sir Edward Frere), Kate O'Mara (Laura Wilde). Created by Gerard Glaister and Allan Prior. Yard name: Mermaid.

How Do They Do That? Presenters: Esther McVeigh and Eamonn Holmes.

HR Pufnstuff Jack Wild (Jimmy), Billie Hayes (Witchiepoo).

Huckleberry Hound Show, The Characters included Pixie and Dixie, Jinks the Cat, Yogi Bear and Boo Boo, Hokey Wolf and Ding a Ling. Huckleberry used to sing 'Clementine' constantly.

Human Jungle, The Herbert Lom (Dr Roger Corder), Sally Smith (Jennifer Corder), Mary Yeomans (Nancy Hamilton).

I Claudius Derek Jacobi (Claudius), Siân Phillips (Livia), Brian Blessed (Octavian/Augustus), George Baker (Tiberius), John Hurt (Caligula), Patrick Stewart (Sejanus), Chris Biggins (Nero).

I Love Lucy Lucille Ball (Lucy Ricardo), Desi Arnaz (Ricky Ricardo), Vivian Vance (Ethel Mertz), William Frawley (Fred Mertz). First sit-com to be filmed live in front of a studio audience.

In at the Deep End Chris Searle and Paul Heiney took it in turn to learn new skills.

Inside George Webley Roy Kinnear played the depressive character created by Keith Waterhouse and Willis Hall.

Inspector Alleyn Mysteries, The Patrick Malahide (Chief Insp. Roderick Alleyn). Character created by Ngaio Marsh.

Inspector Morse John Thaw (Chief Insp. Endeavour Morse), Kevin Whately (Det. Sgt Robbie Lewis).

Interpol Calling Charles Korvin (Insp. Paul Duval), Edwin Richfield (Insp. Mornay).

Invaders, The Roy Thinnes (David Vincent, an architect). Narrator: William Conrad.

Invisible Man, The In the original series Dr Peter Brady's voice was that of Tim Turner although no actor was billed. David McCallum played the character of Daniel Westin in the 1975 series.

I Spy Robert Culp (Kelly Robinson, tennis pro), Bill Cosby (Alexander Scott, tennis trainer).

It Ain't Half Hot Mum Windsor Davies (RSM B L Williams), Melvyn Hayes (Bombardier 'Gloria' Beaumont), George Layton (Bombardier Solomons), Michael Bates (Rangi Ram), Don Estelle (Gunner 'Lofty' Sugden).

It Takes a Thief Robert Wagner (Alexander Mundy), Fred Astaire (Alister Mundy).

Ivor the Engine Narrated by David Edwards, Anthony Jackson, Olwen Griffiths and Oliver Postgate, who also wrote the stories. Railway: Merioneth and Llantissily Rail Traction Company. Driver: Jones the Steam. Other characters included Owen the Signal and Dai Station, the man who looked after Llaniog Station. Ivor's boiler was fired by Idris the dragon. Jones always aspired to sing in the choir like his pal Evans the Song. Peter Firmin drew all the pictures.

Jackanory First story told by Lee Montague ('Cap of Rushes'). Most prolific story teller: Bernard Cribbins.

The Jamie Kennedy Experiment Actor/comedian Jamie Kennedy, nicknamed JKX for the purposes of this show, combines hidden-camera pranks with sketch comedy to see how everyday people and celebrities behave in unusual situations. JKX is often disguised, and when the joke has run its course he delivers the immortal tag line 'You've been X-ed'. First aired in January 2002 on Channel 4.

Jane Glynis Barber played the wartime cartoon character in the 1982 television adaption.

Jemima Shore Investigates Patricia Hodge played the TV reporter created by Lady Antonia Fraser.

Jesus of Nazareth Robert Powell (Jesus as an adult), Immad Cohen (Jesus as a boy), Olivia Hussey (Virgin Mary), Anne Bancroft (Mary Magdalene), Ian McShane (Judas Iscariot), Rod Steiger (Pontius Pilate), James Mason (Joseph of Arimathea), Peter Ustinov (Herod the Great), Michael York (John the Baptist), Stacy Keach (Barabbas), Laurence Olivier (Nicodemus).

Jetsons, The Jetsons lived in the 21st century in Orbit City. George Jetson worked at Spacely Space Sprockets. The family pet dog was Astro.

Jewel in the Crown, The Peggy Ashcroft (Barbie Batchelor), Geraldine James (Sarah Layton), Stuart Wilson (Major Clark), Tim Pigott-Smith (Ronald Merrick), Art Malik (Hari Kumar), Susan Wooldridge (Daphne Manners), Charles Dance (Sgt Guy Perron), Josephine Welcome (Mira). Based on Paul Scott's novels.

Joe 90 Joe McClaine, alias Joe 90, worked for WIN, the World Intelligence Network, using his father's invention BIGRAT (Brain Impulse Galvanoscope Record And Transfer).

Joking Apart Robert Bathurst (Mark Taylor), Tracie Bennett (Tracy), Fiona Gillies (Becky Taylor).

Jonathan Creek Alan Davies (Jonathan Creek), Caroline Quentin (Madeline Magellan), Julia Sawahla (Carla Borrego).

Juke Box Jury First panel: Alma Cogan, Susan Stranks, Gary Miller and Pete Murray. The three presenters were David Jacobs, Noel Edmonds and Jools Holland.

Juliet Bravo Stephanie Turner (Insp. Jean Darblay), Anna Carteret (Insp. Kate Longton). Fictional town: Hartley in Lancashire.

Junior Criss Cross Quiz Hosts included Jeremy Hawk, Bob Holness, Mike Sarne, Bill Grundy and Danny Blanchflower.

Just Good Friends Paul Nicholas (Vince Pinner), Jan Francis (Penny Warrender).

Kavanagh QC John Thaw (James Kavanagh QC), Geraldine James (Eleanor Harker QC).

Keeping Up Appearances Patricia Routledge (Hyacinth Bucket), Geoffrey Hughes (Onslow). Created by Roy Clarke.

Knight Rider David Hasselhoff (Michael Knight, formerly Michael Long), William Daniels (voice of Kitt, the Knight Industries Two Thousand).

Kojak Telly Savalas (Lt Theo Kojak), Dan Frazer (Capt. Frank McNeil), Kevin Dobson (Lt Bobby Crocker), George Savalas (Stavros), Mark Russell (Saperstein). Worked in Manhattan South 13th Precinct.

Krypton Factor, The Tough quiz testing both physical and mental faculties. Gordon Burns's name was synonymous with the series.

The Kumars at No. 42 Sanjeev (Sanjeev Bhaskar), Dad (Vincent Ebrahim), Mum (Indira Joshi), Granny Sushila (Meera Syal). Spoof chat show following the pretext that the Kumars have bulldozed their back garden to build a studio on the back of their house to indulge their spoilt son, Sanjeev, who fancies himself as a celebrity chat-show host.

Kung Fu David Carradine (Kwai Chang Caine), Keye Luke (Master Po), Radames Pera (Caine as a boy). Bruce Lee was rejected for the role and died soon after.

KYTV Angus Deayton (Mike Channel), Geoffrey Perkins (Mike Flex), Helen Atkinson Wood (Anna Daptor).

LA Law Richard Dysart (Leland McKenzie), Harry Hamlin (Michael Kuzak), Corbin Bernsen (Arnie Becker), Michael Tucker (Stuart Markowitz), Diana Muldaur (Rosalind Shays).

Laramie John Smith (Slim Sherman), Robert Fuller (Jess Harper), Hoagy Carmichael (Jonesy), Spring

TELEVISION

Byington (Daisy Cooper).

Larry Sanders Show, The Garry Shandling (Larry Sanders), Rip Torn (Arthur), Jeffrey Tambor (Hank Kingsley).

Last of the Summer Wine Peter Sallis (Norman Clegg), Bill Owen (Compo Seminite), Michael Bates (Blamire), Brian Wilde (Foggy Dewhurst), Michael Aldridge (Seymour Utterthwaite), Kathy Staff (Nora Batty), Jean Alexander (Auntie Wainwright). Filmed in Holmfirth in Yorkshire. Written by Roy Clarke.

League of Gentlemen, The Jeremy Dyson, Mark Gatiss, Steve Pemberton, Reece Shearsmith. Set in Royston Vazey (the real name of comedian Roy 'chubby' Brown).

Life and Loves of a She Devil, The Julie T Wallace (Ruth Patchett), Dennis Waterman (Bobbo Patchett), Patricia Hodge (Mary Fisher).

Likely Lads, The James Bolam (Terry Collier), Bob Ferris (Rodney Bewes), Sheila Fearn (Audrey Collier), Brigit Forsyth (Thelma Ferris). Written by Dick Clement and Ian La Frenais. Sequel: *Whatever Happened to the Likely Lads.*

Little House on the Prairie Michael Landon (Charles Ingalls), Karen Grassle (Caroline Ingalls), Melissa Gilbert (Laura Ingalls/Wilder), Melissa Sue Anderson (Mary Ingalls/Kendall).

Liver Birds, The Polly James (Beryl Hennessey), Nerys Hughes (Sandra Hutchinson/Paynton), Pauline Collins (Dawn, the original flatmate of Beryl), Elizabeth Estensen (Carol Boswell), Mollie Sugden (Mrs Hutchinson), John Nettles (Paul), Jonathan Lynn (Robert).

London's Burning Mark Arden (Roland 'Vaseline' Cartwright), Glen Murphy (George Green), James Hazeldine (Mike 'Bayleaf' Wilson), Richard Walsh (Bert 'Sicknote' Quigley), Gerard Horan (Leslie 'Charisma' Appleby), Ben Onwukwe (Stuart 'Recall' Mackenzie), Heather Peace (Sally 'Gracie' Fields), Edward Peel (John Coleman), Michael Garner (Geoffrey 'Poison' Pearce), Fuman Dar (Ronnie 'Hi-Ho' Silver), Connor Byrne (Rob 'Hyper' Sharpe), Sam Callis (Adam Benjamin), Al Hunter Ashton (Pit bull). Firefighters of Blue Watch B25, Blackwall, created by Jack Rosenthal.

Lone Ranger, The Initially played by Clayton Moore and then by John Hart before he left to play Hawkeye. Jay Silverheels always played the faithful Tonto. Lone Ranger's horse: Silver. (He would often say 'Hi-ho, Silver, away' when in a hurry.) Tonto's horse: Scout. (Tonto would often call his friend Kemo Sabe, which meant Trusty Scout.) The Lone Ranger's real name was John Reid, a Texas Ranger ambushed and left for dead. It is often said that if you can listen to Rossini's 'William Tell Overture' without thinking of the Lone Ranger (same tune) then you are a real classical music aficionado.

Lord Peter Wimsey Ian Carmichael (Lord Peter Wimsey), Glyn Houston (Bunter, his manservant).

Lost in Space Guy Williams (Professor John Robinson), Jonathan Harris (Zachary Smith), Bob May (the robot), Dick Tufeld (voice of the robot). Spaceship: Jupiter 11. Pet space monkey: the Bloop.

Lotus Eaters, The Ian Hendry (Erik Shepherd), Wanda Ventham (Ann Shepherd). Drama set on Crete.

Lou Grant Edward Asner (Lou), Robert Walden (Joe Rossi). Spin-off from the *Mary Tyler Moore Show.* Newspaper: *Los Angeles Tribune.*

Love Hurts Adam Faith (Frank Carver), Zoë Wanamaker (Tessa Piggott), Jane Lapotaire (Diane Warburg), Tony Selby (Max Taplow).

Love Me Do Game show in which three couples vie for the chance to wed. Host: Shane Richie.

Love Thy Neighbour Jack Smethurst (Eddie Booth), Kate Williams (Joan), Rudolph Walker (Bill Reynolds), Nina Baden Semper (Barbie), Keith Marsh (Jacko Jackson). Jacko's famous saying: 'I'll 'ave 'alf.'

Lovejoy Ian McShane (Lovejoy), Dudley Sutton (Tinker Deal), Chris Jury (Eric Catchpole), Phyllis Logan (Lady Jane Felsham). Lovejoy's Morris Minor: Miriam.

Lovers, The Richard Beckinsale (Geoffrey), Paula Wilcox (Beryl).

Lucy Show, The Lucille Ball (Lucy Carmichael), Gale Gordon (Theodore J Mooney), Vivian Vance (Vivian Bagley).

Lytton's Diary Peter Bowles (Neville Lytton). Incidents in the life of a newspaper diarist.

Magic Roundabout Characters include Dougal (the dog), Ermintrude (the cow), Brian (the snail), Mr Rusty, Mr McHenry, Zebedee, Dylan (the rabbit), Florence. Created by Serge Danot and narrated by Eric Thompson and Nigel Planer.

Magnificent Evans, The Ronnie Barker (Plantagenet Evans), Dyfed Thomas (Home Rule O'Toole), Myfanwy Talog (Bron).

Magnum PI Tom Selleck (Thomas Sullivan Magnum), John Hillerman (Jonathan Quayle Higgins III), Roger E Mosley (Theodore 'TC' Calvin), Orson Welles (voice of Robin Masters).

Magpie Presenters include Susan Stranks, Pete Brady, Tony Bastable, Mick Robertson, Jenny Hanley, Tommy Boyd, Douglas Rae.

Main Chance, The John Stride (David Main), Kate O'Mara (Julia Main). Story of a young, successful lawyer.

Making Out Margi Clarke (Queenie), Shirley Stelfox (Carol May), Tracie Bennett (Norma), Melanie Kilburn (Jill), Keith Allen (Rex), Brian Hibbard (Chunky).

Man About the House Richard O'Sullivan (Robin Tripp), Paula Wilcox (Chrissy Plummer), Sally Thomsett (Jo), Brian Murphy (George Roper), Yootha Joyce (Mildred Roper). Spin-off series were *Robin's Nest* and *George and Mildred.*

Man at the Top Kenneth Haigh (Joe Lampton). Feature film of the same name followed.

Man Called Ironside, A Raymond Burr (Chief Robert T Ironside), Don Galloway (Det. Sgt Ed Brown), Barbara Anderson (Eve Whitfield), Don Mitchell (Mark Sanger), Elizabeth Baur (Fran Belding).

Man From Atlantis Patrick Duffy (Mark Harris; had green eyes), Belinda J Montgomery (Dr Elizabeth Merrill), Victor Buono (Mr Schubert), Robert Lussier (Brent). Submersible name: Cetacean.

Man From Uncle, The Robert Vaughn (Napoleon Solo, agent no. 11), David McCallum (Ilya Kuryakin, agent no. 2), Leo G Carroll (Alexander Waverly, agent no. 1). UNCLE: United Network Command for Law and Enforcement. Secret office: behind Del Floria's Tailor Shop. Enemy: Thrush.

Manhunt Alfred Lynch (Jimmy Porter), Peter Barkworth (Vincent), Cyd Hayman (Nina). Heroic tales of French Resistance in WW2. Theme tune: Beethoven's Fifth Symphony.

Man in a Suitcase Richard Bradford (McGill).

Man in Room 17, The   Richard Vernon (Oldenshaw), Michael Aldridge (Dimmock). Criminologists working in an office near the Houses of Parliament.

Marcus Welby MD   Robert Young (Welby), James Brolin (Dr Steven Kiley).

Mark Saber   Donald Gray (Saber), Michael Balfour (Barny O'Keefe). Story of the one-armed detective.

Marriage Lines   Richard Briars (George Starling), Prunella Scales (Kate).

Mary Tyler Moore Show   Mary Tyler Moore (Mary Richards), Ed Asner (Lou Grant), Valerie Harper (Rhoda Morgenstern), Cloris Leachman (Phyllis Lindstrom). Based in TV Station WJM-TV.

M.A.S.H.   Alan Alda (Capt. Benjamin Franklin 'Hawkeye' Pierce), Wayne Rogers (Capt. 'Trapper John' McIntyre), Loretta Swit (Maj. Margaret 'Hot Lips' Houlihan), Larry Linville (Maj. Frank Burns), Gary Burghoff (Corporal Walter 'Radar' O'Reilly), William Christopher (Father Francis Mulcahy), Jamie Farr (Corporal Maxwell Klinger). Hawkeye's tent known as the Swamp. M.A.S.H.: Mobile Army Surgical Hospital.

Mastermind   Ran from 1972 to 1997 with Magnus Magnusson as 'Interrogator' throughout the run. Producer/director David Mitchell. Other producers include Bill Wright, Roger MacKay, Peter Massey, Penelope Cowell Doe. Main researcher: Dee Wallace. Winners: Nancy Wilkinson (1972), Patricia Owen (1973), Elizabeth Horrocks (1974), John Hart (1975), Roger Pritchard (1976), Sir David Hunt (1977), Rosemary James (1978), Dr Philip Jenkins (1979), Fred Housego (1980), Leslie Grout (1981), Sir David Hunt (1982), Christopher Hughes (1983), Margaret Harris (1984), Ian Meadows (1985), Jennifer Keaveney (1986), Dr Jeremy Bradbrooke (1987), David Beamish (1988), Mary-Elizabeth Raw (1989), David Edwards (1990), Stephen Allen (1991), Steve Williams (1992), Gavin Fuller (1993), George Davidson (1994), Kevin Ashman (1995), Richard Sturch (1996), Anne Ashurst (1997). The format transferred to Radio 4 for three years and was hosted by Peter Snow. The winners were Robert Gibson (1998), Rev Kit Carter (1999), Stephen Follows (2000). The Discovery Channel then took over for one season in 2001. The winner was Michael Penrice.

Maverick   James Garner (Brett Maverick), Jack Kelly (Bart Maverick), Roger Moore (Cousin Beau).

May to December   Anton Rodgers (Alec Callender), Eve Matheson/Lesley Dunlop (Zoe Angell/Callender).

McCloud   Dennis Weaver (Sam McCloud), seconded to New York from Taos, New Mexico.

McMillan and Wife   Rock Hudson (Commissioner Stewart McMillan), Susan Saint James (Sally McMillan). Based in San Francisco.

Me and My Girl   Richard O'Sullivan (Simon Harrap), Joanne Ridley (Samantha Harrap), Joan Sanderson (Nell Cresset), Tim Brooke-Taylor (Derek Yates). Advertising agency: Eyecatchers. Theme song sung by Peter Skellern.

Meet the Wife   Thora Hird (Thora Blacklock), Freddie Frinton (Freddie Blacklock). Stemmed from a Comedy Playhouse production called *The Bed*.

Me Mammy   Milo O'Shea (Bunjy Kennefick), Anna Manahan (Mrs Kennefick), Yootha Joyce (Miss Argyll), David Kelly (Cousin Enda), Ray McAnally (Father Patrick).

Men Behaving Badly   Martin Clunes (Gary), Neil Morrissey (Tony), Leslie Ash (Deborah), Caroline

Quentin (Dorothy). The first series featured Harry Enfield as Dermot but Neil Morrissey replaced him for series two Although originally an ITV series, by series three it was screened on BBC 1. The writer was Simon Nye, who also created Frank Stubbs.

Metal Mickey   The robot Mickey was invented by Ken Wilberforce and played by Ashley Knight. This series is best remembered for the fact that Mickey Dolenz was the producer/director.

Miami Vice   Don Johnson (James 'Sonny' Crockett), Philip Michael Thomas (Ricardo Tubbs), Edward James Olmos (Lt Martin Castillo), Sheena Easton (Caitlin Davies).

Midnight Caller   Gary Cole (Jack 'Nighthawk' Killian).

Millennium   Lance Henriksen (Frank Black), Megan Gallagher (Catherine Black), Chris Ellis (Penseyres). Created by Chris Carter of *X Files* fame.

Minder   George Cole (Arthur Daly), Dennis Waterman (Terry McMann), Glynn Edwards (Dave), Patrick Malahide (Det. Sgt Albert 'Charlie' Chisholm), Peter Childs (Sgt Rycott). The theme tune, 'I Could Be So Good For You', was sung by Dennis Waterman.

Mind Your Language   Barry Evans (Jeremy Brown), François Pascal (Danielle Favre), Pik-Sen-Lim (Chung Su-Lee).

Miss Marple   Joan Hickson (Miss Marple).

Mission Impossible   Peter Graves (Jim Phelps), Leonard Nimoy (Paris), Barbara Bain (Cinnamon Carter), Martin Landau (Rollin Hand), Greg Morris (Barney Collier), Steven Hill (Daniel Briggs), Lesley Ann Warren (Dana Lambert), Peter Lupus (Willie Armitage). Voice on the tape: Bob Johnson. Catchprase: 'This tape will self-destruct in five seconds' (occasionally ten seconds).

Mister Ed   Alan Young (Wilbur Post). Story of a talking horse.

Mogul   Series about an oil company, which later changed it's title to *The Troubleshooters*.

Moment of Truth   Cilla Black hosted the show in which three contestants have a week to master a given task.

Monkees, The   TV Series about a pop group. Micky Dolenz, Mike Nesmith, Peter Tork and Davy Jones.

Monty Python's Flying Circus   Messrs Cleese, Idle, Gilliam, Jones, Palin, Chapman and Carol Cleveland.

Moonlighting   Bruce Willis (David Addison), Cybill Shepherd (Maddie Hayes). Detective agency: Blue Moon.

Mork and Mindy   Robin Williams (Mork from Ork), Pam Dawber (Mindy McConnell), Jonathan Winters (Mearth). Mork gave birth to Mearth, who called Mindy 'Shoe' and Mork 'Mommy'. Series was a spin-off from an episode of *Happy Days*.

Moviedrome   Presenters Alex Cox, Mark Cousins.

Mr and Mrs   The alternating presenters were Alan Taylor and Derek Batey.

Mr Magoo   Voice of Magoo (Jim Backus); Waldo was his nephew.

Mr Pastry   Richard Hearne, an actor, acrobat and dancer, invented this character. Popular for over 20 years.

Muffin the Mule   Presenter: Annette Mills. Puppeteer: Ann Hogarth.

Munsters, The   Fred Gwynne (Herman), Yvonne De Carlo (Lily), Al Lewis (Grandpa), Butch Patrick (Eddie), Beverley Owen/Pat Priest (Marilyn). Lived

TELEVISION

at: 1313 Mockingbird Lane, Mockingbird Heights.

Muppet Show, The Characters include Miss Piggy Lee, Kermit T Frog, Statler and Waldorf, Animal, Gonzo, Fozzie Bear, Zoot, Swedish Chef, Dr Teeth, Robin the Frog. First seen in *Sesame Street*. Created by Jim Henson and Frank Oz.

My Favorite Martian Ray Walston (Uncle Martin), Bill Bixby (Tim O'Hara).

Nearest and Dearest Hylda Baker (Nellie Pledge), Jimmy Jewel (Eli), Madge Hindle (Lily), Edward Malin (Walter).

Never the Twain Donald Sinden (Simon Peel), Windsor Davies (Oliver Smallbridge), Honor Blackman (Veronica).

New Avengers Joanna Lumley (Purdey), Gareth Hunt (Mike Gambit), Patrick MacNee (John Steed).

New Statesman, The Rik Mayall (Alan Beresford B'Stard), Terence Alexander (Sir Greville), Marsha Fitzalan (Sarah).

Nice Time Germaine Greer, Jonathan Routh and Kenny Everett in wacky sketch show produced by John Birt.

Night Fever Channel 5 karaoke programme hosted by Suggs.

99–1 Leslie Grantham (Mick Raynor), Robert Stephens (Commander Oakwood).

No Hiding Place Sequel to *Crimesheet* and *Murder Bag*. Raymond Francis (Superintendent Lockhart), Eric Lander (Sergeant Baxter), Johnny Briggs (Det. Sgt Russell).

No, Honestly John Alderton (Charles 'CD' Danby), Pauline Collins (Clara Danby).

No Place Like Home William Gaunt (Arthur Crabtree), Martin Clunes (Nigel Crabtree), Patricia Garwood (Beryl).

No – That's Me Over Here Ronnie Corbett (Ronnie), Rosemary Leach (Rosemary), Henry McGee (Henry).

Not in Front of the Children Wendy Craig (Jennifer Corner), Paul Daneman/Ronald Hines (Henry Corner).

Not Only But Also Peter Cook and Dudley Moore.

Not the Nine O'Clock News Rowan Atkinson, Chris Langham (replaced by Griff Rhys-Jones), Mel Smith, Pamela Stephenson.

NYPD Blue Dennis Franz (Det. Andy Sipowicz), Rick Schroder (Det. Danny Sorenson), James McDaniel (Lt. Arthur Fancy), Nicholas Turturro (Det. James Martinez), Sharon Lawrence (Asst. DA Sylvia Costas Sipowicz), Gordon Clapp (Det. Greg Medavoy), Mark-Paul Gosselaar (Det. John Clark Jr), Henry Simmons (Det. Baldwin Jones), Bill Brochtrup (PAA John Irvin), Esai Morales (Lt. Tony Rodriguez), Charlotte Ross (Det. Connie McDowell), Garcelle Beauvais-Nilon (ADA Valerie Haywood), Jacqueline Obradors (Det. Rita Ortiz), Sherry Stringfield (Laura Michaels Kelly). Co-created by Steven Bochco and David Milch. NYPD is New York Police Department.

Office, The Ricky Gervais (David Brent), Martin Freeman (Tim Canterbury), Mackenzie Crooke (Gareth Keenan), Lucy Davis (Dawn Tynsley), Ewan Macintosh (Keith), Ralph Ineson (Chris 'Finchy' Finch), Oliver Chris (Ricky), Joel Beckett (Lee), Sally Bretton (Donna), Patrick Baladi (Neil Godwin), Steve Merchant (Nathan aka The Oggmonster or Oggy). Co-written and directed by Ricky Gervais and Steve Merchant. Theme tune: 'Handbags and Gladrags', written by Mike D'abo and arranged and performed by Big George.

Oh Brother/Oh Father Derek Nimmo (Brother/Father Dominic), Felix Aylmer (Father Anselm).

Oh, Doctor Beeching! Su Pollard (Ethel Schumann), Paul Shane (Jack Skinner), Jeffrey Holland (Cecil Parkin), Stephen Lewis (Harry Lambert), Julia Deakin (May Skinner).

Old Grey Whistle Test/Whistle Test Bob Harris, Anne Nightingale, Andy Kershaw, Mark Ellen, Ian Whitcomb, Richard Skinner.

One Foot in the Grave Richard Wilson (Victor Meldrew), Annette Crosbie (Margaret), Angus Deayton (Patrick).

Onedin Line, The Peter Gilmore (Capt. James Onedin), Jane Seymour (Emma Callon), Jill Gascoigne (Letty Gaunt). First ship: *Charlotte Rose*.

Only Fools and Horses David Jason (Del Boy Trotter), Nicholas Lyndhurst (Rodney), Lennard Pearce (Grandad), Buster Merryfield (Uncle Albert), Tessa Peake-Jones (Raquel), Gwyneth Strong (Cassandra), Roger Lloyd Pack (Trigger), John Challis (Boycie), Sue Holderness (Marlene). Pub: Nag's Head. Trotters' address: 368 Nelson Mandela House, Peckham. Company name: Trotter's Independent Trading. Transport: features Del's yellow Reliant Regal Van Mk II. Title from the adage 'Only fools and horses work'. Writer: John Sullivan.

Only When I Laugh James Bolam (Roy Figgis), Peter Bowles (Archie Glover), Richard Wilson (Dr Gordon Thorpe).

On Safari Presenters Armand and Michaela Denis.

On the Buses Reg Varney (Stan Butler), Stephen Lewis (Blakey), Anna Karen (Olive), Michael Robbins (Arthur), Bob Grant (Jack). Bus company: Luxtons.

On the Move Bob Hoskins (Alf), Donald Gee (Bert).

On the Up Dennis Waterman (Tony Carpenter), Sam Kelly (Sam), Joan Sims (Mrs Fiona Wembley).

Opportunity Knocks Presenters: Hughie Green, Bob Monkhouse, Les Dawson.

Other 'Arf, The Lorraine Chase (Lorraine Watts), John Standing (Charles Lattimer), Pat Hodge (Sybil Howarth).

OTT (Over The Top) Adult version of *TISWAS*, with variations such as the three naked balloon dancers.

Our Man at St Mark's Leslie Phillips (Rev. Andrew Parker), Donald Sinden (Rev. Stephen Young).

Outside Edge Robert Daws (Roger Dervish), Brenda Blethyn (Miriam, 'Mim'), Timothy Spall (Kevin Costello), Josie Lawrence (Maggie).

Pallisers, The Susan Hampshire (Lady Glencora McCluskie/Palliser), Philip Latham (Plantagenet Palliser), Jeremy Irons (Frank Tregear), Anthony Andrews (Earl of Silverbridge), Derek Jacobi (Lord Fawn).

Panorama Presenters include Pat Murphy, Richard Dimbleby, Malcolm Muggeridge, David Dimbleby.

Paradise Club Leslie Grantham (Danny Kane), Don Henderson (Frank Kane).

Partridge Family Shirley Jones (Shirley), David Cassidy (Keith), Susan Dey (Laurie), Danny Bonaduce (Chris).

Peak Practice Kevin Whately (Dr Jack Kerruish), Amanda Burton (Dr Beth Glover), Gray O'Brien (Tom Deneley), Gary Mavers (Andrew Attwood), Maggie O'Neill (Alex Redman), Joseph Millson (Sam Morgan). Set in Cardale, Peak District.

Pebble Mill at One Presenters: Bob Langley, Donny MacLeod, Jan Leeming, Anna Ford, Paul

Coia, Magnus Magnusson. Pebble Mill was revived after a short break with presenters including Judi Spiers, Alan Titchmarsh, Gloria Hunniford and Ross King.

Pennies From Heaven Bob Hoskins (Arthur Parker), Cheryl Campbell (Eileen), Gemma Craven (Joan Parker). Written by Dennis Potter.

Perfect Scoundrels Peter Bowles (Guy Buchanan), Bryan Murray (Harry Cassidy). Series created by its stars.

Perry Mason Raymond Burr (Perry Mason), Barbara Hale (Della Street), William Hopper (Paul Drake), William Talman (Hamilton Burger), Ray Collins (Lt Tragg). Set in Los Angeles.

Persuaders, The Tony Curtis (Danny Wilde), Roger Moore (Lord Brett Sinclair), Laurence Naismith (Judge Fulton).

Peter Principle, The Jim Broadbent (Peter), Claire Skinner (Susan), Stephen Moore (Geoffrey), Tracy Keating (Brenda), David Schneider (Bradley), Daniel Flynn (Dave), Janette Legge (Iris). Tale of inept bank manager.

Petrocelli Barry Newman (Tony Petrocelli), Susan Howard (Maggie). Set in fictional San Remo.

Peyton Place Ryan O'Neal (Rodney Harrington), Mia Farrow (Allison McKenzie), Ed Nelson (Dr Mike Rossi), Dorothy Malone (Constance McKenzie), Christopher Connelly (Norman Harrington).

Phil Silvers Show Phil Silvers (Master Sgt Ernest Bilko), Maurice Gosfield (Pte Duane Doberman), Joe E. Ross (Sgt Rupert Ritzik), Billy Sands (Pte Dino Paparelli), Paul Ford (Colonel John Hall), Allan Melvin (Cpl Henshaw), Harvey Lembeck (Cpl Rocco Barbella), Elizabeth Fraser (Joan). Rocco Barbella was the real name of boxer Rocky Graziano, the casting director.

Phoenix Nights Peter Kay plays club boss Brian Potter, who was disabled after being crushed by a fruit machine during a flood, as well as doorman Max and Chorley FM's mullet-haired DJ Paul Le Roy. Series developed from one-off *The Club* and other characters include resident compere Jerry St Clair, real name Jerry Dignan (Dave Spikey), Kenny Senior (Archie Kelly), Kenny Junior (Justin Moorhouse), Holy Mary (Janice Connolly). Resident band: Les Alanos with Alan (Steve Edge) on keyboards and Les (Toby Foster) on drums. Written by Peter Kay, Dave Spikey and Neil Fitzmaurice.

Pie in the Sky Richard Griffiths stars as masterchef and ace detective Henry Crabbe.

Pinky and Perky Creators: Jan and Vlasta Dalibor.

Plane Makers, The Patrick Wymark (John Wilder), Barbara Murray/Ann Firbank (Pamela Wilder), Jack Watling (Don Henderson). Aircraft factory name: Scott Furlong. Follow-on series was called *The Power Game*.

Please Sir John Alderton (Bernard 'Privet' Hedges), Deryck Guyler (Norman Potter), Peter Cleall (Eric Duffy), Joan Sanderson (Doris Ewell), David Barry (Frankie Abbott), Richard Davies (Mr Price), Jill Kerman (Penny Wheeler/Hedges), Spin-off series: *The Fenn Street Gang*.

Poldark Robin Ellis (Ross Poldark), Angharad Rees (Demelza), Ralph Bates (George Warleggan). Based on novels by Winston Graham.

Police Woman Angie Dickinson (Sgt Suzanne 'Pepper' Anderson), Earl Holliman (Lt Bill Crowley).

Popstars Auditions of thousands of young budding pop stars in the quest to put together a five-piece all singing and dancing supergroup. The five winners were Danny Foster, Myleene Klass, Noel Sullivan, Kym Marsh and Suzanne Shaw who became Hear'Say. The show's executive producer was 'Nasty' Nigel Lythgoe.

Porridge Ronnie Barker (Norman Stanley Fletcher), Richard Beckinsale (Lennie Godber), Fulton MacKay (Mr MacKay), Peter Vaughan (Groutie), David Jason (Blanco), Brian Wilde (Mr Barrowclough), Patricia Brake (Ingrid), Chris Biggins (Lukewarm), Maurice Denham (Judge Rawley), Tony Osoba (McLaren), Sam Kelly (Warren). Prison setting: HMP Slade. Sentence: five years. Sequel: *Going Straight*.

Porterhouse Blue David Jason (Skullion), Ian Richardson (Sir Godber Evans), Griff Rhys-Jones (Cornelius Carrington).

Postman Pat Characters include Jess the cat, Mrs Goggins the postmistress and twins Katie and Tom Pottage.

Pot Black Half-hour snooker programme which popularised the game as a television medium. Ran from 1969 to 1986, Ray Reardon was the first champion and Jimmy White the last. The theme tune was 'Ivory Rag'. *Pot Black* was briefly revived for one series. A *Masters Pot Black* was held in 1997, the winner being Joe Johnson.

Potter Arthur Lowe (Redvers Potter), replaced by Robin Bailey when Arthur Lowe died between series.

Price is Right, The Presenters: Leslie Crowther and Bruce Forsyth.

Pride and Prejudice Colin Firth (Fitzwilliam Darcy), Jennifer Ehle (Elizabeth Bennet), Alison Steadman (Mrs Bennet), Julia Sawalha (Lydia Bennet).

Prisoner, The Patrick McGoohan (No. 6). Filmed in Portmeirion, Wales.

Professionals, The Gordon Jackson (George Cowley), Lewis Collins (William Bodie), Martin Shaw (Ray Doyle).

Protectors, The Robert Vaughn (Harry Rule), Nyree Dawn Porter (Contessa di Contini), Tony Anholt (Paul Buchet).

Quantum Leap Scott Bakula (Dr Sam Beckett), Dean Stockwell (Al Calavicci).

Quatermass Reginald Tate/André Morell/John Robinson/John Mills (Professor Bernard Quatermass). Written by Nigel Kneale.

Question of Sport, A Presenters: David Vine, David Coleman, Sue Barker.

Rab C Nesbit Gregor Fisher's character first appeared in *Naked Video*. Children are Gash and Burney.

Rag Trade, The Peter Jones (Mr Fenner), Reg Varney (Reg), Miriam Karlin (Paddy), Sheila Hancock (Carole), Esma Cannon (Little Lil), Barbara Windsor (Judy), Wanda Ventham (Shirley). A revival series starred Anna Karen as the character she played in *On the Buses*.

Randall and Hopkirk (Deceased) Mike Pratt (Jeff Randall), Kenneth Cope (Marty Hopkirk), Annette Andre (Jean Hopkirk). Revived in the 1990s with Reeves and Mortimer playing Marty and Jeff.

Rawhide Eric Fleming (Gil Favor), Clint Eastwood (Rowdy Yates), Paul Brinegar (Wishbone), Sheb Wooley (Pete Nolan), James Murdock (Harkness 'Mushy' Mushgrove).

Ready Steady Go Presenters Keith Fordyce, Cathy McGowan, David Gell, Michael Aldred.

Red Dwarf Chris Barrie (Arnold J Rimmer BSc,

TELEVISION

SSC), Craig Charles (Dave Lister), Danny John-Jules (Cat), Norman Lovett/Hattie Hayridge (Holly), David Ross/Robert Llewellyn (Kryten).

Remington Steele   Pierce Brosnan, Stephanie Zimbalist (Laura Holt, the owner of Remington Steele Investigations).

Rhoda   Valerie Harper (Rhoda Morgenstern/Gerard), Julie Kavner (Brenda Morgenstern), Lorenzo Musoc (Carlton the doorman, voice only). Spin-off from the *Mary Tyler Moore Show*.

Rich Man Poor Man   First of the TV 'Best Sellers', based on an Irwin Shaw novel and starring Peter Strauss and Nick Nolte.

Rifleman, The   Chuck Connors (Lucas McCain), Johnny Crawford (Mark McCain).

Right to Reply   Presenters include: Gus MacDonald, Linda Agran, Brian Hayes, Rory McGrath, Sheena McDonald, Roger Bolton.

Rings on Their Fingers   Martin Jarvis (Oliver Pryde), Diane Keen (Sandy Bennett/Pryde).

Rising Damp   Leonard Rossiter (Rigsby), Richard Beckinsale (Allan), Frances de la Tour (Miss Jones), Don Warrington (Philip), Vienna the cat. Based on a one-act play, *The Banana Box*.

Robin Hood   Short-lived series of 1953 in which Patrick Troughton (second Dr Who) took the lead role.

Robin of Sherwood   Michael Praed (Robin of Loxley), Jason Connery (Robert of Huntingdon), Clive Mantle (Little John), Ray Winstone (Will Scarlet), Judi Trott (Maid Marian). Music by Clannad.

Robin's Nest   Richard O'Sullivan (Robin Tripp), Tessa Wyatt (Victoria Nicholls), Tony Britton (James Nicholls), David Kelly (Albert Riddle, the one-armed washer-up), Honor Blackman/Barbara Murray (Marion).

Rock Follies   Charlotte Cornwell, Julie Covington (Devonia Dee Rhoades), Rula Lenska. Group name: The Little Ladies.

Rockford Files, The   James Garner, Noah Beery Jnr (Joseph 'Rocky' Rockford), Joe Santos (Det. Sgt Dennis Becker).

Room 101   Original presenter Nick Hancock, who was followed by Paul Merton.

Roseanne   Roseanne Barr (Roseanne Conner), John Goodman (Dan), George Clooney (Booker Brooks).

Royle Family, The   Caroline Aherne (Denise Best), Ricky Tomlinson (Jim Royle), Sue Johnston (Barbara Royle), Craig Cash (Dave Best), Ralf Little (Anthony Royle), Liz Smith (Norma Speakman).

Rumpole of the Bailey   Leo McKern (Horace Rumpole), Patricia Hodge (Phyllida Trant/Erskine-Brown), Peter Bowles (Guthrie Featherstone), Bill Fraser (Justice Bullingham). Wife: Hilda (She who must be obeyed). Winebar: Pomeroy's. Drink: Château Fleet Street).

Saint, The   Roger Moore (Simon Templar alias the Saint). Car: Volvo P1800S. Inspector: Claude Eustace Teal. Sequel: *Return of the Saint*, starring Ian Ogilvy.

Sea Hunt   Lloyd Bridges (Mike Nelson). Boat: the *Argonaut*.

Secret Army   Jan Francis (Lisa Colbert; codename Yvette), Bernard Hepton (Albert Foiret), Clifford Rose (Sturmbannführer Ludwig Kessler). Underground movement: Lifeline.

Secret Diary of Adrian Mole, Aged 13¾   Gian Sammarco (Adrian), Stephen Moore (Mr Mole), Julie Walters and Lulu (Pauline Mole), Lindsey Stagg (Pandora). Based on the Sue Townsend novels.

Seinfeld   Jerry Seinfeld (Jerry), Jason Alexander (George), Michael Richards (Kramer), Julia Louis Dreyfus (Elaine).

September Song   Michael Williams (Billy Balsam), Russ Abbot (Ted Fenwick), Michael Angelis (Arnie).

77 Sunset Strip   Efrem Zimbalist Jnr (Stuart Bailey), Roger Smith (Jeff Spencer), Ed Byrnes (Kookie). Much of the action took place outside Dean Martin's restaurant, Dino's.

Sex and the City   Sarah Jessica Parker (Carrie Bradshaw), Kim Cattrall (Samantha Jones), Kristin Davis (Charlotte York), Cynthia Nixon (Miranda Hobbes), John Corbett (Aidan), Christopher Orr (Alexander).

Sexton Blake   Laurence Payne (Sexton Blake), Roger Foss (Tinker), Dorothea Phillips (Mrs Bardell). Bloodhound: Pedro. White Rolls Royce nicknamed the Grey Panther.

Sharpe   Sean Bean (Richard Sharpe), Daragh O'Malley (Sgt Pat Harper), Peter Postlewaite (Hakeswill), Philip Whitchurch (Frederickson), Liz Hurley (Isabella), Assumpta Sema (Teresa, the first Mrs Sharpe), Abigail Cruttenden (Lady Jane, the second Mrs Sharpe), Cecile Paoli (Lucille Dubert, the third Mrs Sharpe), Louise Germaine (Sally Clayton), John Tams (Hagman) also co-wrote the music. Based on novels by Bernard Cornwell.

Shillingbury Tales   Robin Nedwell (Peter Higgins), Diane Keen (Sally Higgins), Lionel Jeffries (Major Langton), Bernard Cribbins (Cuffy), Jack Douglas (Jake).

Shine On Harvey Moon   Kenneth Cranham/Nicky Henson (Harvey Moon), Linda Robson (Maggie Moon), Nigel Planer (Lou Lewis), Elizabeth Spriggs (Nan), Pauline Quirke (Veronica), Maggie Steed (Rita Moon). Harvey's occupation: professional footballer.

Simpsons, The   Characters include: Homer and Marge Simpson and their children Bart, Lisa and Maggie. The pet dog is called Santa's Little Helper. Other characters include Montgomery Burns, Waylon Smithers, Professor John Frink, Millhouse van Houten, Sideshow Bob, Krusty the Clown, and Chief Wiggum and his son Ralph. Series is set in Springfield and started life as a cartoon short on the *Tracy Ullman Show*.

Singing Detective, The   Michael Gambon (Philip E Marlow), Joanne Whalley (Nurse Mills/Carlotta), Patrick Malahide (Mark Binney/Mark Finney/Raymond Binney), Jim Carter (Mr Marlow), Alison Steadman (Beth Marlow/Lili). Hospital ward: Sherpa Tensing. Illness: psoriasis. Written by Dennis Potter.

Sir Francis Drake   Terence Morgan (Drake), Jean Kent (Queen Elizabeth), Michael Crawford (John Drake).

Six-Five Special   Presenters: Pete Murray, Josephine Douglas, Freddie Mills, Jim Dale. Jack Good was the original producer and Adam Faith made his debut on his way to stardom.

Six Million Dollar Man   Lee Majors (Steve Austin), Richard Anderson (Oscar Goldman), Lyndsay Wagner (Jaime Sommers). The opening sequence showing Steve Austin's crash in the Mojave Desert was in fact Donald Campbell's fatal accident while attempting the world water-speed record on Coniston Water.

64,000 Dollar Question, The Questions were guarded every week by Detective Fabian. Bob Monkhouse hosted the British version.

Six Wives of Henry VIII, The Keith Michell (Henry), Annette Crosbie (Catherine of Aragon), Dorothy Tutin (Anne Boleyn), Anne Stallybrass (Jane Seymour), Elvi Hale (Anne of Cleves), Angela Pleasance (Catherine Howard), Rosalie Crutchley (Catherine Parr), Patrick Troughton (Duke of Norfolk). Narrator: Anthony Quayle.

Sliders John Rhys-Davies (Maximillian Arturo), Jerry O'Connell (Quinn Mallory), Sabrina Lloyd (Wade Wells), Cleavant Derricks (Rembrandt Brown). Sliding is the term used for entering parallel universes.

Slinger's Day Bruce Forsyth (Cecil Slinger). The untimely death of Leonard Rossiter precipitated the arrival of Bruce Forsyth to take over the role of the put-upon supermarket manager, his name changed from Tripper to Slinger.

Soap Katherine Helmond (Jessica Tate), Cathryn Damon (Mary Dallas Campbell), Billy Crystal (Jodie Dallas), Robert Guillaume (Benson Dubois), Robert Mandan (Chester Tate).

Soldier, Soldier Jerome Flynn (Paddy Garvey), Robson Green (Dave Tucker), David Haig (Mjr Tom Cadman).

Some Mothers Do 'Ave 'Em Michael Crawford (Frank Spencer), Michele Dotrice (Betty). Daughter: Jessica.

Sopranos, The James Gandolfini (Tony Soprano), Edie Falco (Carmela Soprano), Nancy Marchand (Livia Soprano), Lorraine Bracco (Dr Jennifer Melfi), Jamie-Lynn Sigler (Meadow Soprano), Robert Iler (A J Soprano), Aida Turturro (Janice 'Parvati' Soprano), Dominic Chianese (Corrado Soprano), Tony Sirico (Paulie Walnuts), Steve van Zandt (Silvio Dante), John Ventimiglia (Artie Bucco). Theme tune: 'Woke Up This Morning' by Alabama 3.

Sorry! Ronnie Corbett (Timothy Lumsden, a librarian), Barbara Lott (Mrs Phyllis Lumsden).

South Park Adult cartoon series. Characters include Kenny (who is invariably killed), Kyle, Stan, Cartman, Chef, Mr Garrison, Ned, Uncle Jimbo and Officer Barbrady.

Space: 1999 Martin Landau (John Koenig), Barbara Bain (Dr Helena Russell), Catherine Schell (Maya), Barry Morse (Professor Victor Bergman). Crew of Moonbase Alpha stranded in space.

Space Patrol Voices: Capt. Larry Dart (Dick Vosburgh), Husky and Slim (Ronnie Stevens), Gabblerdictum (Libby Morris), Colonel Raeburn (Murray Kash). Ship: Galasphere 347. Year: 2100. The Space Patrol was the active unit of the United Galactic Organization. Libby Morris was Raeburn's super-efficient blonde secretary from Venus; fortunately there is no such thing as a dumb blonde on Venus.

Special Branch George Sewell (Det. Chief Insp. Alan Craven), Patrick Mower (Det. Chief Insp. Tom Haggerty), Derren Nesbitt (Det. Insp. Jordan), Fulton Mackay (Det. Supt Inman).

Spender Jimmy Nail, Sammy Johnson (Stick), Paul Greenwood (Supt Yelland).

Spenser For Hire Robert Urich (Spenser), Avery Brooks (Hawk), Barbara Stock (Susan Silverman).

Spitting Image Created by Peter Fluck, Roger Law and Michael Lambie-Martin.

St Elsewhere Ed Flanders (Donald Westphall), William Daniels (Mark Craig), Ed Begley Jnr (Victor Ehrlich). Hospital: St Elegius, Boston.

Star Trek William Shatner (James Tiberius Kirk), Leonard Nimoy (Mr Spock – his mother is T'Pau, a Vulcan), De Forest Kelly (Dr Leonard 'Bones' McCoy), James Doohan (Scottie), George Takei (Mr Sulu), Nichelle Nichols (Lt Uhura), Walter Koenig (Ensign Pavel Chekov), Majel Barrett (Nurse Chapel). Crew size: 430. Decks: 8. Five-year mission to boldly go where no man has gone before. Enterprise no.: NCC 1701A. Shuttle: Galileo. Spock's blood colour: green (T positive).

Star Trek: The Next Generation Patrick Stewart (Captain Jean-Luc Picard), Jonathan Frakes (Commander William Ryker), LeVar Burton (Lt Geordi La Forge), Michael Dorn (Lt Worf), Denise Crosby (Lt Tasha Yar), Gates McFadden (Dr Bev Crusher), Marina Sirtis (Deanna Troi), Brent Spiner (Lt Cmdr Data), Wil Wheaton (Wesley), Diana Muldaur (Dr Katherine Pulaski), Whoopi Goldberg (Guinan). Original *Star Trek* set in the 23rd century; this series was set 78 years later. Enterprise no.: NCC 1701D.

Stars in Their Eyes Presenters: Leslie Crowther, Matthew Kelly.

Starsky and Hutch David Soul (Ken Hutchinson), Paul Michael Glaser (Dave Starsky), Antonio Fargas (Huggie Bear).

Steptoe and Son Harry H Corbett (Harold), Wilfred Bramble (Albert), Hercules the horse. American spin-off: *Sandford and Son*.

Stingray Troy Tempest, George 'Phones' Sheridan, Atlanta Shore, Titan, Agent X20. Marina was the mute daughter of Emperor Aphony from Pacifica and her pet seal was called Oink. Organisation: WASP, World Aquanaut Security Patrol, in Marineville. Year: 2000.

Streets of San Francisco, The Karl Malden (Det. Lt Mike Stone), Michael Douglas (Insp. Steve Keller).

Sunday Night at the London Palladium Comperes included: Tommy Trinder, Bruce Forsyth, Des O'Connor, Jimmy Tarbuck, Norman Vaughan, Jim Dale, Hughie Green, Alfred Marks, Robert Morley, Dave Allen, Roger Moore, Don Arrol, Arthur Haynes, Dickie Henderson.

Supercar Mike Mercury, Professor Popkiss, Dr Beaker, Masterspy, Mitch the monkey, Zarin.

Supergran Gudrun Ure (Granny Smith), Iain Cuthbertson (Scunner Campbell). Set in Chisleton.

Superman Original series starred George Reeves, who committed suicide after being typecast in this role. The more recent series stars Dean Cain as Superman and Teri Hatcher as Lois Lane.

Surgical Spirit Nichola McAuliffe (Dr Sheila Sabatini), Duncan Preston (Dr Jonathan Haslam). Gillies Hospital.

Sutherland's Law Iain Cuthbertson played Procurator Fiscal Sutherland.

Sweeney, The John Thaw (Det. Inspector Jack Regan), Dennis Waterman (Det. Sgt George Carter).

Sykes Eric Sykes and Hattie Jacques (lived at Sebastopol Terrace), Derek Guyler (Korky), Richard Wattis (Mr Brown).

Sylvania Waters Australian fly-on-the-wall story of the Baker-Donaher family by Paul Watson (*The Family*).

Taggart Mark McManus (Det. Chief Insp. Jim Taggart), Neil Duncan (Det. Sgt Peter Livingstone), Blythe Duff (Det. Sgt. Jackie Reid).

Take Three Girls Angela Down, Liza Goddard,

T
E
L
E
V
I
S
I
O
N

Susan Jameson.

Take Your Pick Presenters: Michael Miles, Des O'Connor. Original man with the gong: Alec Dane.

Taxi Judd Hirsch (Alex Reiger), Jeff Conaway (Bobby Wheeler), Danny de Vito (Louis de Palma), Marilu Henner (Elaine Nardo), Tony Danza (Tony Banta), Andy Kaufman (Latka Gravas), Christopher Lloyd (Reverend Jim 'Iggie' Ignatowski). Cab company: Sunshine Cabs.

Teletubbies Tinky Winky, Dipsy, Laa Laa, Po. Babygros open to reveal televisions. Created by Anne Wood. Looked after by a vacuum cleaner called Noo Noo. Voices include Eric Sykes and Toyah Wilcox.

Tenko Stephanie Beacham (Rose Millar), Stephanie Cole (Dr Beatrice Mason), Bert Kwouk (Yamauchi).

Thank Your Lucky Stars Presenters: Brian Matthews, Jim Dale and Keith Fordyce.

Third Man Michael Rennie (Harry Lime). Popular theme tune played on the zither by Shirley Abicaire.

This Morning Popular daytime magazine hosted live by Richard Madeley and Judy Finnegan.

Thomas the Tank Engine Narrators: Ringo Starr, Michael Angelis. Thomas is a blue engine; Gordon is green. Written by the Reverend Awdry. The Fat Controller became Sir Topham Hat.

1000 to One Quiz show hosted by Dale Winton in which, over five weeks, 1000 contestants were whittled down to one winner who scooped 1000 prizes. Your author was one of the five winners but alas narrowly failed to hit the jackpot.

Thunderbirds Thunderbird I pilot Scott Tracy (usually first at the scene because of its high-speed capability); Thunderbird 2 pilot Virgil (pod carrier for Thunderbird 4 and any special equipment required); Thunderbird 3 pilot Alan (rocket back-up) – Alan manned the Spacestation occasionally; Thunderbird 4 pilot Gordon (underwater machine which had great versatility); Thunderbird 5 pilot John (the stationery Spacestation). Jeff Tracy was the father and co-ordinator and Kyrano was his oriental assistant. GB agent was Lady Penelope Creighton-Ward and her butler was Parker. Her Rolls Royce had the registration FAB1; her yacht was FAB2. Technical expert was Hiram Hackenbacker (Brains). Set in the year 2063. The Hood (Kyrano's half-brother) was the arch-enemy who regularly appeared.

Till Death Us Do Part Warren Mitchell (Alf Garnett), Anthony Booth (Mike), Dandy Nichols (Else), Una Stubbs (Rita), Patrica Hayes (Min Reed). Written by Johnny Speight.

Time Tunnel, The James Darren (Dr Tony Newman), Robert Colbert (Dr Doug Phillips), Lee Meriwether (Dr Ann McGregor).

Tinker Tailor Soldier Spy Alec Guinness (George Smiley), Bernard Hepton (Toby Esterhase), Beryl Reid (Connie Sachs).

TISWAS Today is Saturday, Watch (wear a) and Smile. Presenters included Chris Tarrant, John Asher, Trevor East, Sally James, Lenny Henry, John Gorman, Clive Webb, Sylvester McCoy, Frank Carson, Fogwell Flax and Bob Carolgees and Spit the dog.

Today's the Day Current affairs quiz programme hosted by Martyn Lewis. Your author, with his chum, won the 1997 series.

To the Manor Born Penelope Keith (Audrey Fforbes-Hamilton), Peter Bowles (Richard de Vere), Michael Bilton (Ned), Angela Thorne (Marjory

Frobisher), John Rudling (Brabinger), Daphne Heard (Mrs Polouvicka).

Tonight Presenter: Cliff Michelmore. Catchphrase: The next Tonight will be tomorrow night. Notable reporters included Trevor Philpott, Julian Pettifer, Magnus Magnusson, Alan Whicker and the hugely popular Fyfe Robertson.

Top Gear Presenters include William Woolard, Angela Rippon, Barrie Gill, Noel Edmonds, Sue Baker, Jeremy Clarkson, Quentin Willson, Tiff Needell, Chris Goffey, Tony Mason, Janet Trewin, Michele Newman.

Triangle Kate O'Mara (Katherine Laker), Michael Craig (John Anderson), Larry Lamb (Matt Taylor). Company: Triangle Lines. Short-lived soap notable for the bikini-clad posing of its star.

Tripper's Day Leonard Rossiter (Norman Tripper); see *Slinger's Day*.

Trumpton Spin-off series from *Camberwick Green* but the action moved from Pippin Fort. Captain Flack's local firemen: Hugh, Pugh, Barney McGrew, Cuthbert, Dibble and Grubb.

Tutti Frutti Robbie Coltrane (Danny McGlone), Emma Thompson (Suzie Kettles). Band: The Majestics.

TW3 That Was The Week That Was, presented by David Frost and produced by Ned Sherrin.

Twin Peaks Kyle MacLachlan (Agent Dale Cooper), Michael Ontkean (Sheriff Harry S Truman), Ray Wise (Leland Palmer), Sheryl Lee (Laura Palmer/Madeleine Ferguson), Piper Laurie (Catherine Martell), Dana Ashbrook (Bobby Briggs), Sherilyn Fenn (Audrey Horne). Characters included a dwarf who talked backwards, the Log Lady and Audrey, who tied knots in cherry stalks with her tongue. Killer was Laura's father, Leland, possessed by 'Bob'.

Two Fat Ladies Jennifer Paterson and Clarissa Dickson Wright. Oversize chefs who ride in a combination motorcycle.

2 Point 4 Children Belinda Lang (Bill Porter), Gary Olsen (Ben Porter).

Two's Company Elaine Stritch (Dorothy McNab), Donald Sinden (Robert Hiller).

UFO Ed Bishop (Commander Edward Straker), George Sewell (Colonel Alec Freeman), Peter Gordeno (Peter Karlin, the captain of the Vipers), Gabrielle Drake (Lt Gay Ellis), Michael Billington (Colonel Paul Foster), Wanda Ventham (Colonel Virginia Lake). Defence unit: SHADO (Supreme Headquarters Alien Defence Organization). Reconnaissance satellite: S.I.D. (Space Intruder Detector). Location: beneath the Harlington-Straker film studios just outside London (and Moonbase).

University Challenge Began in 1962 with Bamber Gascoigne as the presenter. After he bowed out in 1987 the series was resumed in 1995 with Jeremy Paxman as the new presenter. The highest winning score was in a first-round match in 1987 when University College, Oxford, defeated Reading 520-35. Series winners are as follows: 1963 Leicester, 1964 no series this year, 1965 New College, Oxford, 1966 Oriel College, Oxford, 1967 Sussex, 1968 Keele, 1969 Sussex, 1970 Churchill College, Cambridge, 1971 Sidney Sussex College, Cambridge, 1972 University College, Oxford, 1973 Fitzwilliam College, Cambridge, 1974 Trinity College, Cambridge, 1975 Keble College, Oxford, 1976 University College, Oxford, 1977 Durham,

1978 Sidney Sussex College, Cambridge, 1979 Bradford, 1980 Merton College, Oxford, 1981 Queen's University, Belfast, 1982 St Andrews, 1983 Dundee, 1984 Open University 1985 No series this year, 1986 Jesus College, Oxford, 1987 Keble College, Oxford, 1995 Trinity College, Cambridge, 1996 Imperial College, London, 1997 Magdalen College, Oxford, 1998 Magdalen College, Oxford, 1999 Open University, 2000 Durham, 2001 Imperial College, London, 2002 Somerville College, Oxford.

Upstairs Downstairs Gordon Jackson (Mr Angus Hudson), Angela Baddeley (Mrs Kate Bridges), Jean Marsh (Rose), David Langton (Lord Richard Bellamy), Simon Williams (Capt. James Bellamy), Nicola Pagett (Elizabeth Bellamy/Kirkbridge), Lesley-Anne Down (Georgina Worsley), Jacqueline Tong (Daisy), Christopher Beeny (Edward), Pauline Collins (Sarah), John Alderton (Thomas). Address: 165 Eaton Place. Spin-off series: *Thomas and Sarah*.

V Marc Singer (Mike Donovan), Jane Badler (Diana: famous scene where she swallowed a mouse), Jenny Beck and Jennifer Cooke (Elizabeth), Michael Ironside (Ham Tyler), Blair Tefkin (Robin Maxwell, who gave birth to Elizabeth).

Very Peculiar Practice, A Peter Davison (Dr Stephen Daker), David Troughton (Dr Bob Buzzard), Barbara Flynn (Dr Rose Marie), Michael J Shannon (Jack B Daniels). Set at Lowlands University. Written by Andrew Davies.

Vicar of Dibley, The Dawn French (Geraldine Granger), Emma Chambers (Alice Tinker), Gary Waldhorn (David Horton), James Fleet (Hugo Horton), Roger Lloyd Pack (Owen Newitt), Trevor Peacock (Jim Trott), John Bluthal (Frank Pickle). Written by Paul Mayhew-Archer and Richard Curtis.

Virginian, The James Drury (Virginian), Doug McClure (Trampas), Lee J Cobb (Judge Henry Garth), Gary Clarke (Steve Hill), John McIntire (Clay Grainger), Stewart Grainger (Alan MacKenzie), Lee Majors (Roy Tate). Series set on the Shiloh Ranch, Medicine Bow, Wyoming.

Vision On Presenters include Tony Hart, Larry Parker, Sylvester McCoy, Pat Keysell, Ben Benison, Wilf Lunn, David Cleveland.

Voyage to the Bottom of the Sea Richard Basehart (Admiral Harriman Nelson), David Hedison (Captain Lee Crane). Nuclear submarine: the *Seaview*. Set in the year 1984.

Wacky Races Eleven cars lined up to win the title 'The World's Wackiest Racer'. Car 1: Boulder Mobile; Rock and Gravel Slag. Car 2: Creepy Coupé; Big and Little Gruesome. Car 3: Ring-a-Ding Convert-a-Car; Prof. Pat Pending. Car 4: Crimson Haybailer; Red Max. Car 5: Compact Pussycat; Penelope Pitstop. Car 6: Army Surplus Special; Gen. Sgt and Private Pinkley. Car 7: Bulletproof Bomb; Clyde and Anthill Mob. Car 8: Arkansas Chugabug; Luke and Blubber Bear. Car 9: Turbo Terrific; All-American Peter Perfect. Car 10: Buzz Wagon; Rufus Ruffcut and Sawtooth. Car 00: Mean Machine driven by Dick Dastardly and his dog Muttley. Spin-off series were *The Perils of Penelope Pitstop* and *Dastardly and Muttley in their Flying Machines*, in which they tried to 'Stop the Pigeon'.

Waltons, The Ralph Waite (John), Michael Learned (Olivia), and their seven children: Richard Thomas and Robert Wightman (John Boy), Judy Norton Taylor (Mary Ellen), Jon Walmsley (Jason), Mary Elizabeth McDonough (Erin), David W Harper (J Robert 'Jim Bob'), Eric Scott (Ben), Kami Cotler

(Elizabeth). Their grandparents were played by Will Geer (Zeb) and Ellen Corby (Esther).

Washington Behind Closed Doors Jason Robards (President Richard Monckton).

Watch With Mother Original five: Picture Book (Patricia Driscoll), Andy Pandy, Bill and Ben, Rag, Tag and Bobtail, The Woodentops. Ran from 1952 to 1980. Others included Tales of the Riverbank, Pogles Wood, Bizzy Lizzy and Barnaby.

Watchdog Presenters include Nick Ross, Lynn Faulds Wood, John Stapleton, Anne Robinson, Alice Beer.

Water Margin, The Set in the water margins of Lian Shan Po. The hero was Lin Chung who, with his wife Hsiao, warred against evil in 14th-century China.

Weakest Link, The Presenter Anne Robinson's catchphrase of 'You are the weakest link, goodbye' soon became the ultimate put-down. The popular daytime BBC2 quiz show was given a prime-time slot on BBC1 due to its record viewing figures. Highlights include Ms Robinson's strange pronunciation and inability to cope with answers not exactly corresponding to what's on her card. Your author lasted a mere two rounds and was voted off after answering all his questions correctly. Please refer to the Shakespeare section for further details.

West Wing, The Martin Sheen (President Josiah Bartlet), Allison Janney (C J Cregg), Rob Lowe (Sam Seaborn), John Spencer (Leo McGarry), Janel Maloney (Donna Moss), Richard Schiff (Toby Ziegler), Dulé Hill (Charlie Young), Bradley Whitford (Josh Lyman), Stockard Channing (Abigail Bartlet).

Whack-O! Jimmy Edwards (Prof. James Edwards), Arthur Howard and Julian Orchard (Mr Oliver Pettigrew). School name: Chiselbury.

What's My Line Presenters include Eamonn Andrews, Emma Forbes, Penelope Keith, David Jacobs. Original panel: Isobel Barnett, David Nixon, Gilbert Harding, Barbara Kelly.

What the Papers Say Presenters include Kingsley Martin, Brian Inglis and Stuart Hall.

When the Boat Comes In James Bolam (Jack Ford), Susan Jameson (Jessie Seaton).

Whiplash Peter Graves (Christopher Cobb). Set in the outback of Australia with a memorable theme tune.

Who Wants to Be a Millionaire? Presenter Chris Tarrant's catchphrases include 'D'you wanna phone a friend?', '50/50', and 'Ask the audience'. The first winner was Judith Keppel and the first man to win the million was David Edwards.

Whoops! Apocalypse Barry Morse (Johnny Cyclops), Richard Griffiths (Premier Dubienkin), Ed Bishop (Jay Garrick), Alexei Sayle (Commissar Solzhenitsyn), Peter Jones (Kevin Pork), John Cleese (Lacrobat).

Wind in the Willows, The Voices were Michael Hordern (Badger), David Jason (Toad), Peter Sallis (Rat), Richard Pearson (Mole).

Winds of War, The Robert Mitchum (Commander Victor 'Pug' Henry), Victoria Tennant (Pamela Tudsbury), Ali MacGraw (Natalie Jastrow), Jan-Michael Vincent (Byron Henry), Ben Murphy (Warren Henry), Howard Lang (Winston Churchill), Gunter Meisner (Hitler). Written by Herman Wouk.

Winston Churchill – The Wilderness Years Robert Hardy (Winston), Siân Phillips (Clementine), Peter Barkworth (Stanley Baldwin), Eric Porter (Neville Chamberlain).

TELEVISION

Win, Lose or Draw Hosts: Danny Baker, Shane Richie, Bob Mills.

WKRP in Cincinnati Gary Sandy (Andy Travis), Gordon Jump (Arthur Carlson, 'Big Guy'), Loni Anderson (Jennifer Marlowe), Tim Reid (Gordon Sims, 'Venus Flytrap'), Howard Hesseman (Johnny Caravella, 'Dr Johnny Fever').

Woodentops, The Characters included Daddy and Mummy Woodentop, their twin children Jenny and Willy, Baby Woodentop, Mrs Scrubbit, Sam (the man who helped out in the garden), Buttercup the cow and Spotty the mischievous dog.

World at War World War Two history researched by Noble Frankland, produced by Jeremy Isaacs and narrated by Laurence Olivier.

World's End Short-lived soap opera set around the Mulberry public house, Chelsea, and starring Harry Fowler, Michael Angelis, Paul Brooke, Neville Smith, Primi Townsend.

Worzel Gummidge Jon Pertwee (Worzel), Una Stubbs (Aunt Sally), Geoffrey Bayldon (the Crowman), Lorraine Chase (Dolly Clothes-Peg), Joan Sims (Mrs Bloomsbury-Barton). Written by Keith Waterhouse and Willis Hall from an adaption of Barbara Euphan Todd novels. Worzel was found in Ten Acre Field on Scatterbrook Farm by John and Sue Peters.

Wyatt Earp, The Life and Legend of Hugh O'Brian (Wyatt Earp), Mason Alan Dinehart III (Bat Masterson, Earp's deputy), Douglas Fowley and Myron Healey (Doc Holliday), Lash La Rue (Sheriff John Behan).

Wycliffe Jack Shepherd (Det. Supt Wycliffe), Helen Masters (Det. Insp. Lane), Jimmy Yuill (Det. Insp. Kersey).

Xena: Warrior Princess Lucy Lawless (Xena), New Zealand-made off-shoot series from *Hercules*.

X Files, The David Duchovny (Fox Mulder), Gillian Anderson (Dana Scully), Mitch Pileggi (Skinner), William B Davis (the Cigarette-Smoking Man [C G B Spender]).

XYY Man, The Stephen Yardley (William 'Spider' Scott, who had an extra 'Y' chromosome which appeared to give him a liking for dangerous pursuits, sometimes criminal), Don Henderson (Det. Sgt George Bulman).

Year in Provence, A John Thaw (Peter Mayle), Lindsay Duncan, Christian Luciani.

Yes Minister/Prime Minister Paul Eddington (Jim Hacker, Minister of Administrative Affairs/Prime Minister), Nigel Hawthorne (Sir Humphrey Appleby), Derek Fowlds (Bernard Wooley). Created by Antony Jay and Jonathan Lynn.

You Rang, M'Lord Paul Shane (Alf Stokes), Su Pollard (Ivy Teesdale), Jeffrey Holland (James Twelvetrees). Title song sung by Paul Shane and Bob Monkhouse.

Young Ones, The Rik Mayall (Rick), Nigel Planer (Neil), Adrian Edmondson (Vyvyan), Christopher Ryan (Mike), Alexei Sayle (Jerzy Balowski, and his family). Saying: For Cliff's sake.

You've Been Framed Presenters include Jeremy Beadle and Lisa Riley.

Z Cars Stratford Johns (Det. Chief Insp. Barlow), Frank Windsor (Det. Sgt John Watt), Brian Blessed (PC William 'Fancy' Smith), Joseph Brady (PC John 'Jock' Weir), James Ellis (Sgt Herbert 'Bert' Lynch), Jeremy Kemp (PC Bob Steele), Terence Edmond (PC Ian Sweet), Colin Welland (PC David Graham), Leonard Rossiter (Det. Insp. Bamber), John Slater (Det. Sgt Tom Stone), Alison Steadman (WPC Bayliss). Theme tune based on folk song 'Johnny Todd'. Spin-off series *Softly Softly*, set in Wyvern.

Zoo Gang, The John Mills (Tommy Devon), Brian Keith (Stephen Halliday), Barry Morse (Alec Marlowe), Lili Palmer (Manouche Roget).

Zoo Time Presenters were Desmond Morris, Chris Kelly and Harry Watt.

Zorro Guy Williams (Don Diego de la Vega, 'Zorro'), Gene Sheldon (Bernardo). Zorro means fox in Spanish.

Soap Operas: Cast of Characters

Character	Actor	Character	Actor
Albion Market		Roy Harrison	Jonathan Barlow
(set in Manchester; aired between August 1985 and		Sita Sharma	Seeta Indrani
August 1986) ITV		Ted Pilkington	Anthony Booth
Alan Curtis	Simon Rouse	Terry Flynn	Alistair Walker
Anita Rai	Souad Faress	Tony Fraser	John Michie
Carol Broadbent	Barbara Wilshere	Viv Harker	Helen Shapiro
Colette Johnson	Nimmy March		
Debbie Taylor	Jane Hazlegrove	**The Bill**	
Derek Owen	David Hargreaves	(set in Sun Hill and first aired in 1983) ITV	
Geoff Travis	Geoffrey Leesley	ADI Samantha Nixon	Lisa Maxwell
Janet Owen	Hetta Charnley	Chief Insp Cato	Philip Whitchurch
Jaz Sharma	Paul Bhattacharjee	Chief Insp Derek Conway	Ben Roberts
Keith Naylor	Derek Hicks	Chief Supt Charles Brownlow	Peter Ellis
Larry Rigg	Peter Benson	DC Alfred 'Tosh' Lines	Kevin Lloyd
Lisa O'Shea	Sally Baxter	DC Danny Glaze	Karl Collins
Louise Todd	Kelly Lawrence	DC Eva Sharpe	Diane Parish
Ly Nhu Chan	Pik-Sen Lim	DS Mickey Webb	Chris Simmons
Lynne Harrison	Noreen Kershaw	DC Mike Dashwood	Jon Iles
Miriam Ransome	Carol Kaye	DC Woods	Tom Cotcher
Morris Ransome	Bernard Spear	DCI Jack Meadows	Simon Rouse
Narya Vyas	Rashid Karapiet	Det Chief Insp Kim Reid	Carolyn Pickles
Paul O'Donnell	Paul Beringer	Det Insp Chris Deakin	Shaun Scott
Peggy Sagar	Maria Vega	Det Insp Frank Burnside	Christopher Ellison
Phil Smith	Burt Caesar	Det Insp Roy Galloway	John Salthouse
Ralph Friend	David Boyce	Det Sgt Danny Pearce	Martin Marquez

Character	Actor/Actress	Character	Actor/Actress
Det Sgt Don Beech	Billy Murray		Chambers
Det Sgt Ted Roach	Tony Scannell	Georgia Simpson	Helen Grace
DS Debbie McAllister	Natalie Roles	Heather Huntington /	Amanda Burton
DS Phil Hunter	Scott Maslen	Haversham / Black	
FDO Roberta Cryer	Moya Brady	Jackie Corkhill	Sue Jenkins
Insp Gina Gold	Roberta Taylor	Jacqui Dixon / Farnham	Alexandra Fletcher
PC Barry Stringer	Jonathan Dow	Jerome Johnson	Leon Lopez
PC Cameron Tait	Daniel MacPherson	Jimmy Corkhill	Dean Sullivan
PC Cathy Bradford	Connie Hyde	Julia Brogan	Gladys Ambrose
PC Dave Litten	Gary Olsen	Karen Grant	Shelagh O'Hara
PC Dave Quinnan	Andrew Paul	Katie Rogers	Diane Burke
PC Des Taviner	Paul Usher	Katrina Evans	Ann Marie Davies
PC Francis 'Taffy' Edwards	Colin Blumenau	Lance Powell	Mickey Poppins
PC Gary Best	Ciaran Griffiths	Leanne Powell	Vickie Gates
PC Gemma Osbourne	Jane Danson	Leo Johnson	Steven Cole
PC George Garfield	Huw Higginson	Luke Smith	Callum Giblin
PC Jarvis	Stephen Beckett	Madge Richmond	Shirley Stelfox
PC Jim Carver (former DC)	Mark Wingett	Mandy Jordache	Sandra Maitland
PC Kerry Young	Beth Cordingly	Marty Murray	Neil Caple
PC Luke Ashton	Scott Neal	Max Farnham	Steve Pinder
PC Nick Klein	Rene Zagger	Mick Johnson	Louis Emerick
PC Reg Hollis	Jeff Stewart	Mike Dixon	Paul Byatt
PC Robin Frank	Ashley Gunstock	Nat Simpson	John Sandford
PC Ron Smollett	Nick Stringer	Nicholas Black	Alan Rothwell
PC Ruby Buxton	Nicola Alexis	Nikki Shadwick	Suzanne Collins
PC Steve Loxton	Tom Butcher	Ollie Simpson	Michael J Jackson
PC Timothy Able	Mark Haddigan	Peter Phelan	Sam Kane
PC Tony Stamp	Graham Cole	Rachel Dixon	Tiffany Chapman
PC Tony 'Yorkie' Smith	Robert Hudson	Ray Hilton	Kenneth Cope
Sgt Bob Cryer	Eric Richard	Robbie Moffat	Neil Davies
Sgt Craig Gilmore	Hywel Simons	Rod Corkhill	Jason Hope
Sgt Matthew Boyden	Tony O'Callaghan	Roger Huntington	Rob Spendlove
Supt Adam Okaro	Cyril Nri	Ron Dixon	Vince Earl
TDC Brandon Kane	Pal Aron	Ruth Smith	Lynsey McCaffrey
Viv Martella	Nula Conwell	Sean Smith	Barry Sloane
WPC Cathy Marshall	Lynne Miller	Sheila Grant / Corkhill	Sue Johnston
WPC Claire Brind	Kelly Lawrence	Steve Murray	Steven Fletcher
WPC June Ackland	Trudie Goodwin	Stuart Gordon	David Lyon
WPC Norika Datta	Seeta Indrani	Susannah Farnham / Morrisey	Karen Drury
WPC Polly Page	Lisa Geoghan	Thomas 'Sinbad' Sweeney	Michael Starke
		Tim 'Tinhead' O'Leary	Philip Oliver

Brookside
(set in Liverpool and first aired in 1982; created by Phil Redmond) C4

		Tracy Corkhill	Justine Kerrigan
		Trevor Jordache	Brian Murray
Adele Murray	Katy Lamont		
Alan Gordon	John Burton	**Casualty**	
Ali Gordon	Kristopher Mochrie	(set in Holby City Hospital; first aired in Sept 1986) BBC1	
Annabelle Collins	Doreen Sloane	Adam Osman	Pal Aron
Anthea Dixon	Barbara Hatwell	Amy Howard	Rebecca Wheatley
Anthony Murray	Raymond Quinn	Anna Paul	Zita Sattar
Barry Grant	Paul Usher	Baz Fairhead	Julia Watson
Bel Simpson	Lesley Nightingale	Beth Harper	Lynda Rooke
Beth Jordache	Anna Friel	Charlie Fairhead	Derek Thompson
Bev McLoughlin	Sarah White	Chloe Hill	Jan Anderson
Billy Corkhill	John McArdle	Clive King	George Harris
Bobby Grant	Ricky Tomlinson	Colette Kierney	Adjoa Andoh
Brigid McKenna	Meg Johnson	Comfort Jones	Martina Laird
Chrissy Rogers	Eithne Browne	Dillon Cahill	Dan Rymer
Christy Murray	Glyn Pritchard	Dr Barbara 'Baz' Samuels Hayes	Julia Watson
Damon Grant	Simon O'Brien	Dr Ewart Plimmer	Bernard Gallagher
Dan Morrisey	Matthew Crompton	Dr Mike Barratt	Clive Mantle
Dan Simpson	Andrew Butler	Elizabeth Straker	Maureen O'Brien
David 'Bing' Crosbie	John Burgess	Eve Montgomery	Barbara Marten
D-D Dixon	Irene Marot	Finlay Newton	Kwame Kwei-Armah
Debbie Gordon	Annette Ekblom		
Diane Murray	Bernie Nolan	Harry Harper	Simon MacCorkindale
Diana Spence / Corkhill	Paula Frances		
Doreen Corkhill	Kate Fitzgerald	Holly Miles	Sandra Huggett
Dr Gary Parr	Ben Hull	Jack Hathaway	Peter Birch
Emily Shadwick / O'Leary	Jennifer Ellison	Jack Vincent	Will Mellor
Gabby Parr	Stephanie	Jan Goddard	Judy Loe

Character	Actor/Actress	Character	Actor/Actress
Jimmy Powell	Robson Green	Chris Collins	Matthew Marsden
Josh Griffiths	Ian Bleasedale	Ciaran McCarthy	Keith Duffy
Jude Korcanik	Lisa Coleman	Concepta Hewitt / Regan / Riley	Doreen Keogh
Lisa 'Duffy' Duffin	Catherine Shipton	Customer in Sylvia's Separates	Joanne Whalley
Liz Harker	Sue Devaney	David Barlow	Alan Rothwell
Matt Hawley	Jason Merrells	David Platt	Jack P Shepherd
Max Gallagher	Robert Gwilym	Deirdre Hunt / Langton / Barlow /	Anne Kirkbride
Megan Roach	Brenda Fricker	Rachid	
Mel Dyson	Michelle Butterly	Dennis Tanner	Philip Lowrie
Merlin	Orlando Seale	Derek Wilton	Peter Baldwin
Nikki Marshall	Kelly Harrison	Des Barnes	Philip Middlemiss
Patrick Spiller	Ian Kelsey	Detective Sergeant Cross	Peter Postlethwaite
Penny Hutchens	Donna Alexander	Dev Alahan	Jimmi Harkishin
Philip Hall	Dominic Guard	Don Brennan	Geoff Hinsliff
Roxanne Bird	Loo Brealey	Doreen Heavey	Prunella Gee
Ryan Johnson	Russell Boulter	Dr Graham	Fulton MacKay
Sandra Nicholl	Maureen Beattie	Duggie Ferguson	John Bowe
Sean Maddox	Gerald Kyd	Eddie Yeats	Geoffrey Hughes
Simon Kaminski	Christopher	Eileen Grimshaw	Sue Cleaver
	Colquhoun	Eileen Hughes	Prunella Scales
Tina Seabrook	Claire Goose	Elaine Perkins	Joanna Lumley
Tony Vincent	Lee Warburton	Elsie Grimshaw / Tanner / Howard	Pat Phoenix
Tony Walker	Eamonn Boland	Emily Nugent / Swain / Bishop	Eileen Derbyshire
		Emma Watts	Angela Lonsdale

The Colbys
(spin-off from Dynasty set in Los Angeles; aired between 1985 and 1987) BBC1

Character	Actor/Actress	Character	Actor/Actress
Bliss Colby	Claire Yarlett	Ena Sharples	Violet Carson OBE
Constance Colby	Barbara Stanwyck	Ernest Bishop	Stephen Hancock
Fallon Carrington / Colby	Emma Samms	Fiona Middleton	Angela Griffin
Francesca Scott Colby	Katherine Ross	Fiz Brown	Jennie McAlpine
Jason Colby	Charlton Heston	Florrie Lindley	Betty Alberge
Miles Colby	Maxwell Caulfield	Frank Roper	Paul Shane
Monica Colby	Tracy Scoggins	Fred Elliott	John Savident
Sable Scott Colby	Stephanie	Fred Gee	Fred Feast
	Beacham	Gail Potter / Tilsley / Platt /	Helen Worth
Zachary Powers	Ricardo Montalban	Hillman	
		Gary Mallett	Ian Mercer
		Geena Gregory	Jennifer James

Coronation Street
(set in Weatherfield; first aired in 1960) ITV

Character	Actor/Actress	Character	Actor/Actress
Aidan Critchley	Dean Ashton	George Barton	Patrick Troughton
Alan Bradley	Mark Eden	Gordon Clegg	Bill Kenwright CBE
Alan Howard	Alan Browning	Harry Flagg	Iain Rogerson
Alan McKenna	Glenn Hugill	Harry Hewitt	Ivan Beavis
Albert Tatlock	Jack Howarth MBE	Hayley Patterson / Cropper	Julie
Alec Gilroy	Roy Barraclough		Hesmondhalgh
Alf Roberts OBE	Bryan Mosley	Hilda Ogden	Jean Alexander
Alma Halliwell / Sedgewick /	Amanda Barrie	Himself	Sir Trevor
Baldwin			McDonald
Andy McDonald	Nicholas Cochrane	Irma Ogden / Barlow	Sandra Gough
Angie Freeman	Deborah McAndrew	Ivy Nelson / Tilsley / Brennan	Lynne Perrie
Annie Walker	Doris Speed MBE	Jack Duckworth	Bill Tarmey
Archie Shuttleworth	Roy Hudd	Jack Walker	Arthur Leslie
Arthur Stokes	Stan Richards	Janice Battersby	Vicky Entwistle
Arthur Watts	Kenneth Waller	Jed Stone	Kenneth Cope
Ashley Peacock	Steven Arnold	Jeff Bateman	Peter Dean
Audrey Potter / Roberts	Sue Nicholls	Jerry Booth	Graham Haberfield
Bernard Bulter	Gorden Kaye	Jez Quigley	Lee Boardman
Bernard Evans (Dave the Rave)	Paul Shane	Jim McDonald	Charles Lawson
Bet Lynch / Gilroy	Julie Goodyear	Joe Carter	Jonathan Wrather
	MBE	John Arnley	Paul Warriner
Betty Turpin / Williams	Betty Driver MBE	Judy Mallett	Gaynor Faye
Bill Fielding	John Junkin	Karen Phillips / McDonald	Suranne Jones
Bill Webster	Peter Armitage	Ken Barlow	William Roache
Billy Walker	Ken Farrington		MBE
Bingo checker	Tim Healy	Kevin (a lorry driver)	Kevin Whately
Blanche Hunt	Maggie Jones	Kevin Webster	Michael Le Vell
Brian Tilsley	Christopher	Leanne Battersby / Tilsley	Jane Danson
	Quentin	Len Fairclough	Peter Adamson
Candice Stowe	Nikki Sanderson	Leonard Swindley	Arthur Lowe
Charlie Dickinson	Bill Owen	Les Battersby	Bruce Jones
		Lillian Spencer	Maureen Lipman
		Linda Sykes / Baldwin	Jacqueline Pirie
		Liz McDonald	Beverley Callard
		Lorraine Mason	Samantha

Character	Actor/Actress	Character	Actor/Actress
	Beckinsale	Tyrone Dobbs	Alan Halsall
Lucille Hewitt	Jennifer Moss	Valerie Barlow	Anne Reid
Maggie Clegg	Irene Sutcliffe	Vera Duckworth	Elizabeth Dawn
Malcolm Nutall	Michael Ball	Vera Hopkins	Kathy Staff
Maria Sutherland	Samia Ghadie	Vicky Arden / McDonald	Chloe Newsome
Martha Longhurst	Lynne Carol	Vikram Desai	Chris Bisson
Martin Platt	Sean Wilson	Vinnie Sorrell	James Gaddas
Maud Grimes	Elizabeth Bradley		
Maureen Grimes / Naylor /	Sherrie Hewson	**Crossroads**	
Holdsworth / Elliot		(set in Kings Oak, nr Birmingham; on its third	
Mavis Riley / Wilton	Thelma Barlow	generation 1964–88; 2001–02; 2003–) ITV	
Maxine Heavey / Peacock	Tracy Shaw	Adam Chance	Tony Adams
Mickey Malone	Bill Maynard	Amy Turtle	Ann George
Mike Baldwin	Johnny Briggs	Angel Samson	Jane Asher
Minnie Caldwell	Margot Bryant	Anne-Marie Wade	Dee Hepburn
Mrs Chadwick	Sue Johnston	Anthony Mortimer	Jeremy Sinden
Mrs Snape	Patricia Routledge	Arthur Brownlow	Peter Hill
Myra Dickenson / Booth	Susan Jameson	Barbara Brady / Hunter	Sue Lloyd
Natalie Horrocks / Barnes	Denise Welch	Beena Shah	Rebecca
Nellie Harvey	Mollie Sugden		Hazlewood
Nick(y) Tilsley	Warren Jackson	Belle Wise	Jessica Fox
	Adam Rickitt	Benny Hawkins	Paul Henry
Norman 'Curly' Watts	Kevin Kennedy	Betty Waddell	Anne Charleston
Norris Cole	Malcolm Hebden	Bradley Clarke	Luke Walker
PC Wilcox	Richard Beckinsale	Carlos Raphael	Anthony Morton
Percy Sugden	Bill Waddington	Carol Sands	Joanne Good
Peter Barlow	John Heanneau	Caroline Winthrop	Elaine Page
	Mark Duncan	Chris Hunter	Stephen Hoye
	Linus Roache	Cleopatra Samson	Clare Wilkie
	Christopher	Clifford Leyton	Johnny Briggs
	Dormerr	Daniel Freeman	Philip Goodhew
	Joseph McKenna	Dave Stocks	Jim Dunk
	David Lonsdale	David Hunter	Ronald Allen
	Chris Gascoine	Diane Lawton / Hunter / Parker	Susan Hanson
Phyllis Pearce	Jill Summers	Dick Jarvis	Brian Kent
Ralph Lancaster	Kenneth Watson	Doris Luke	Kathy Staff
Raquel Wolstenholme / Watts	Sarah Lancashire	Glenda Banks	Lynette
Ravi Desai	Saeed Jaffrey OBE		McMorrough
Ray Harrison	Kenneth Cranham	Holly Brown	Stephanie De
Ray Langton	Neville Buswell		Sykes
Reg Holdsworth	Ken Morley	Hugh Mortimer	John Bentley
Richard Hillman	Brian Capron	J Henry Pollard	Michael Turner
Rita Littlewood / Fairclough /	Barbara Knox	Jill Richardson / Harvey / Chance	Jane Rossington
Sullivan		Jim Baines	John Forgeham
Ron Jenkins	Ben Kingsley	Jimmy Gudgeon	Jimmy Hanley
Roy Cropper	David Neilson	Jimmy Samson	Graham McGrath
Sally Webster	Sally Whittaker	Joe Lacey	Richard Burke
Samantha Failsworth	Tina Hobley	Joe McDonald	Carl Andrews
Samia Ghadie	Maria Sutherland	Josefina Raphael	Gillian Betts
Samir Rachid	Al Nedjari	Kate Loring	Kate Robbins
Sarah Louise Platt	Leah King	Kate Russell	Jane Gurnett
	Lyndsey King	Kath Brownlow	Pamela Vezey
	Tina O'Brien	Kevin Banks	David Moran
Spider (Geoffrey) Nugent	Martin Hancock	Kevin McArthur	Vincent Ball
Stan Ogden	Bernard Youens	Lady Alice Fox	Kate O'Mara
Stan Potter	Noddy Holder	Lola Wise	Freema Agyeman
Stanley Fairclough	Peter Noone	Louise Dixon (aka Sarah Jane)	Joanne Farrell
Steve McDonald	Simon Gregson	Mandy Dobbs	Natasha Marquiss
Susan Barlow / Baldwin	Katie Heanneau	Marilyn Gates / Hope	Sue Nicholls
	Wendy Jane Walker	Max Samson	Stuart Milligan
	Suzy Patterson	Meg Richardson / Mortimer	Noele Gordon
	Joanna Foster	Miranda Pollard	Claire
Tanya Pooley	Eva Pope		Faulkenbridge
Ted Sullivan	William Russell	Myrtle Cavendish	Gretchen Franklin
Terry Duckworth	Nigel Pivaro	Nicola Freeman	Gabrielle Drake
Todd Grimshaw	Bruno Langley	Oona Stocks	Di Sherlock
Tommy Nelson	Thomas Craig	Patrick Russell	Neil McCaul
Toyah Battersby	Georgia Taylor	Paul Ross	Sandor Elès
Tracy Langton / Preston / Barlow	Christabel Finch	Reg Lamont	Reginald Marsh
	Holly Chamarette	Rocky Wesson	Roger Sloman
	Dawn Acton	Rosemary Hunter	Janet Hargreaves

Character	Actor/Actress
Roy Lambert	Steven Pinder
Ryan Samson	Luke Roberts
Sam Benson	Norman Bowler
Sandra Gould	Diane Keen
Sandy Richardson	Roger Tonge
Sarah Jane Harvey	Sophie Cook
Sharon Metcalfe	Carolyn Jones
Shughie McFee	Angus Lennie
Sid Hooper	Stan Stennett
Stafford Wynter	Paul Shelley
Stan Harvey	Edward Clayton
Stevie	Wendy Padbury
Suzie Samson	Emma Noble
Tish Hope	Joy Andrews
Tom Curtis	Toby Sawyer
Tracey Booth	Cindy Marshall-Day
Valerie Pollard	Heather Chasen
Vera Downend	Zeph Gladstone
Vince Parker	Peter Brookes
Virginia Raven	Sherrie Hewson
Wally Soper	Max Wall
Wedding Car Chauffeur	Larry Grayson

Dallas
(main location Southfork Ranch, Dallas; aired from 1978 to 1991) BBC1

Character	Actor/Actress
Ben Stivers / Wes Parmalee	Steve Forrest
Bobby Ewing	Patrick Duffy
Carter McKay	George Kennedy
Clayton Farlow	Howard Keel
Cliff Barnes	Ken Kercheval
Don Lockwood	Ian McShane
Dusty Farlow	Jared Martin
Eleanor Southworth Ewing / Farlow (Miss Ellie)	Barbara Bel Geddes and Donna Reed
Gary Ewing	David Ackroyd and Ted Shackelford
Jenna Wade	Morgan Fairchild, Francine Tacker, Priscilla Presley
Jock Ewing	Jim Davis
John Ross 'JR' Ewing	Larry Hagman
Katherine Wentworth	Morgan Brittany
Kristin Shepard	Colleen Camp and Mary Crosby
LeeAnn De La Vega	Barbara Eden
Lucy Ewing / Cooper	Charlene Tilton
Pamela Barnes / Ewing	Victoria Principal
Ray Krebbs	Steve Kanaly
Stephanie Rogers	Lesley Anne Down
Sue Ellen Ewing	Linda Gray
Valene Ewing	Joan Van Ark
Willard 'Digger' Barnes	David Wayne and Keenan Wynn

Dawson's Creek
(set in Capeside, Massachusetts) C4

Character	Actor/Actress
Andrea 'Andie' McPhee	Meredith Monroe
Audrey Liddell	Busy Philipps
Dawson Leery	James Van Der Beek
Evelyn 'Grams' Ryan	Mary Beth Peil
Gail Leery	Mary-Margaret Humes
Jack McPhee	Kerr Smith
Jennifer 'Jen' Lindley	Michelle Williams
Josephine 'Joey' Potter	Katie Holmes
Mitchell 'Mitch' Leery	John Wesley Shipp
Pacey Witter	Joshua Jackson

Dynasty
(set in Denver, Colorado; aired from 1981 to 1989) BBC1

Character	Actor/Actress
Adam Carrington / Michael Torrance	Gordon Thomson
Alexis Carrington / Colby / Dexter	Joan Collins
Amanda Carrington	Catherine Oxenburg and Karen Cellini
Ben Carrington	Christopher Cazenove
Blake Carrington	John Forsythe
Caress Morell	Kate O'Mara
Dominique Deveraux	Diahann Carroll
Dr Nick Toscanni	James Farentino
Fallon Carrington / Colby	Pamela Sue Martin and Emma Samms
Jeff Colby	John James
Krystle Jennings / Carrington	Linda Evans
Monica Colby	Tracy Scoggins
Prince Michael	Michael Praed
Sable Colby	Stephanie Beacham
Sammy Jo	Heather Locklear
Steven Carrington	Al Corley and Jack Coleman

EastEnders
(set in Walford, E20; and first aired in 1985) BBC1

Character	Actor/Actress
Aidan Brosnan	Sean Maguire
Alan Jackson	Howard Anthony
Alex Healy	Richard Driscoll
Alfie Moon	Shane Richie
Ali Osman	Nejdet Salih
Andy O'Brien	Ross Davidson
Angel	Goldie
Angie Watts	Anita Dobson
Annie Palmer	Nadia Sawalha
Anthony Trueman, Dr	Nicholas R Bailey
Arthur Fowler	Bill Treacher
Barry Evans	Shaun Williamson
Beppe di Marco	Michael Greco
Bianca Butcher	Patsy Palmer
Big Ron	Ron Tarr
Billy Mitchell	Perry Fenwick
Charlie Slater	Derek Martin
Carol Jackson	Lindsay Coulson
Cindy Beale	Michelle Collins
Dan Sullivan	Craig Fairbrass
David Wicks	Michael French
Debbie Wilkins	Shirley Cheriton
Dennis 'Dirty Den' Watts	Leslie Grantham
Derek Harkinson	Ian Lavender
Diane Butcher	Sophie Lawrence
Doris Moisey	Marcia Ashton
Dot Cotton / Branning	June Brown
Eddie Royle	Michael Melia
Ethel Skinner	Gretchen Franklin
Frank Butcher	Mike Reid
Fred Fonseca, Dr	Jimi Mistry
Garry Hobbs	Ricky Groves
George Palmer	Paul Moriarty
George 'Lofty' Holloway	Tom Watt
Gianni di Marco	Marc Bannerman
Gita Kapoor	Shobu Kapoor
Grant Mitchell	Ross Kemp
Harold Legg, Dr	Leonard Fenton
Harry Slater	Michael Elphick
Hattie Tavernier	Michelle Gayle
Ian Beale	Adam Woodyatt
Irene Hills / Raymond	Roberta Taylor
Jamie Mitchell	Jack Ryder
Janine Butcher	Rebecca Michael

Character	Actor
	Alexia Demetriou
	Charlie Brooks
Jim Branning	John Bardon
Joanne Ryan	Tara Lynne O'Neill
Joe Wicks	Paul Nicholls
Kat Slater	Jessie Wallace
Kate Tyler	Jill Halfpenny
Kathy Beale / Mitchell	Gillian Taylforth
Kelly Taylor	Brooke Kinsella
Laura Dunn / Beale	Hannah Waterman
Lisa Shaw / Fowler	Lucy Benjamin
Little Mo Slater / Mitchell	Kacey Ainsworth
Lorraine Wicks	Jacqueline Leonard
Lou Beale	Anna Wing
Lynne Slater / Hobbs	Elaine Lordan
Mark Fowler	David Scarboro and Todd Carty
Martin Fowler	Jon Peyton Price and James Alexandrou
Matthew Rose	Joe Absolom
Melanie Healy / Owen	Tamzin Outhwaite
Michelle Fowler / Holloway	Susan Tully
Mo Harris	Laila Morse
Natalie Evans	Lucy Speed
Nick Cotton	John Altman
Nigel Bates	Paul Bradley
Nina	Troy Titus-Adams
Pat Butcher / Evans	Pam St Clement
Patrick Trueman	Rudolph Walker
Paul Trueman	Gary Beadle
Pauline Fowler	Wendy Richard
Peggy Mitchell / Butcher / Mitchell	Jo Warne and Barbara Windsor
Pete Beale	Peter Dean
Phil Mitchell	Steve McFadden
Polly Becker	Victoria Gould
Rick Peterson	Cliff Parisi
Ricky Butcher	Sid Owen
Robbie Jackson	Dean Gaffney
Roy Evans	Tony Caunter
Sadie Banks	Isobel Middleton
Sam Mitchell / Butcher / Mitchell	Daniella Westbrook and Kim Medcalf
Sandra di Marco	Clare Wilkie
Sanjay Kapoor	Deepak Verma
Sarah Hills	Daniela Denby-Ashe
Sharon Watts / Mitchell / Watts	Letitia Dean
Simon Wicks	Nick Berry
Sonia Jackson	Natalie Cassidy
Spencer Moon	Christopher Parker
Steve Owen	Martin Kemp
Sue Osman	Sandy Ratcliff
Terry Hills	Brian Croucher
Terry Raymond	Gavin Richards
Tiffany Raymond / Mitchell	Martine McCutcheon
Tom Banks	Colm O Maonlai
Tom Clements	Donald Tandy
Tony Hills	Mark Homer
Trevor Morgan	Alex Ferns
Vicki Fowler	Samantha Crown and Scarlett Johnson
Wellard	Robbie Jackson's Dog
Willy	Ethel Skinner's Dog
Winston	Ulric Browne
Zoe Slater	Michelle Ryan

Eldorado

(set in Los Barcos and first aired on 6 July 1992) BBC1

Character	Actor
Blair Lockhead	Josh Nathan
Dieter Schultz	Kai Maurer
Drew Lockhead	Campbell Morrison
Gwen Lockhead	Patricia Brake
Joy Slater	Leslee Udwin
Marcus Tandy	Jesse Birdsall
Nessa Lockhead	Julie Fernandez
Stanley Webb	William Lucas
Trish Valentine	Polly Perkins

Emmerdale Farm

(set in Beckindale; first aired 16 October 1972; since 1989 the series has been known as Emmerdale) ITV

Character	Actor
Adam Forrester	Tim Vincent
Alan Turner	Richard Thorp
Albert Dingle	Bobby Knutt
Amos Brearly	Ronald Magill
Andy Hopwood / Sugden	Kelvin Fletcher
Angie Reynolds	Freya Copeland
Annie Sugden / Kempinski / Brearly	Sheila Mercier
Bernice Blackstock	Samantha Giles
Betty Eagleton	Paula Tilbrook
Biff Fowler	Stuart Wade
Bob Hope	Antony Audenshaw
Brian Addyman	Martin Reeve
Butch Dingle	Paul Loughran
Cain Dingle	Jeff Hordley
Carlos Diaz	Gary Turner
Charity Tate / Dingle	Emma Atkins
Chloe Atkinson	Amy Nuttall
Christopher Tate	Peter Amory
Danny Daggert	Cleveland Campbell
Dave Glover	Ian Kelsey
Des Bartenshaw	Tony Barton
Diane Blackstock	Elizabeth Estensen
Dolly Arcaster / Skilbeck	Katherine Barker and Jean Rogers
Donna Windsor	Sophie Jeffery and Verity Rushworth
Edna Birch	Shirley Stelfox
Emily Wylie / Dingle / Kirk	Kate McGregor
Eric Pollard	Christopher Chittell
Frank Tate	Norman Bowler
Gloria Weaver / Pollard	Janice McKenzie
Glynis Hardy	Christine Cox
Henry Wilks	Arthur Pentelow
Jack Sugden	Andrew Burt and Clive Hornby
Jan Glover	Roberta Kerr
Jarvis Skelton	Richard Moore
Jason Kirk	James Carlton
Jerry 'Mack' Mackinley	Rob Dixon
Joe Sugden	Frazer Hines
Kathy Bates/Merrick/Tate/Glover	Malandra Burrows
Katie Addyman	Sammy Winward
Kelly Windsor / Glover	Adele Silva
Kim Barker / Tate / Marchant	Claire King
Laurel Potts	Charlotte Bellamy
Len Reynolds	Peter Martin
Linda Glover / Fowler	Tonicha Jeronimo
Lisa Clegg / Dingle	Jane Cox
Louise Appleton	Emily Symons
Luke McAllister	Noah Huntley
Mandy Dingle / Kirk	Lisa Riley
Marc Reynolds	Anthony Lewis
Marlon Dingle	Mark Charnock
Matt Skilbeck	Jo Kendall
Ned Glover	Johnny Leeze

TELEVISION

Nick Bates
Nicola Blackstock
Olivia 'Ollie' Reynolds
Pat Merrick / Sugden
Patricia 'Tricia' Stokes
Patrick 'Paddy' Kirk
Rachel Hughes
Rev Ashley Thomas
Rev Donald Hinton
Robert Sugden
Rodney Blackstock
Roy Glover
Sam Dingle
Sarah Sugden
Scott Windsor

Sean Reynolds
Seth Armstrong
Sophie Wright
Steve Marchant
Syd Woolfe
Tara Oakwell / Thornfield /
  Cockburn
Terry Woods
Tina Dingle
Vic Windsor
Viv Windsor / Hope
Zak Dingle
Zoe Tate

Falcon Crest
(set in winery in Tuscany Valley, California; aired
between 1981 and 1990)
Angela Channing / Stavros
Apollonia

Chase Gioberti
Diana Hunter
Dr Michael Ranson
Emma Channing
Francesca Gioberti
Frank Agretti
Greg Reardon

Jacqueline Perrault
Jordan Roberts
Kit Marlowe
Lance Cumson
Maggie Gioberti / Channing
Nick Hogan
Peter Stavros
Phillip Erikson
Tony Cumson

Family Affairs
(aired at launch of C5 in March 1997)
Albie Leach
Amir Sadati
Angus Hart
Anna Gregory
Annie Hart
Becky Scott
Ben Galloway
Benji McHugh
Cameron Davenport
Cat Webb
Chris Hart
Chris Jacobs
Claire Callan / Toomey

Dan Wilkinson
Darren Scott
Dave Matthews

Cy Chadwick
Nicola Wheeler
Vicky Binns
Helen Weir
Sheree Murphy
Dominic Brunt
Glenda McKay
John Middleton
Hugh Manning
Karl Davies
Patrick Mower
Nicky Evans
James Hooton
Alyson Spiro
Toby Cockerell and
  Ben Freeman
Stephen McGann
Stan Richards
Jane Cameron
Paul Opacic
Nathan Gladwell
Anna Brecon

Billy Hartman
Jacqueline Pirie
Alun Lewis
Deena Payne
Steve Halliwell
Leah Bracknell

Jane Wyman
Patricia 'Apollonia'
  Kotero
Robert Foxworth
Shannon Tweed
Cliff Robertson
Margaret Ladd
Gina Lollobrigida
Rod Taylor
Simon
  MacCorkindale
Lana Turner
Morgan Fairchild
Kim Novak
Lorenzo Lamas
Susan Sullivan
Roy Thinnes
Cesar Romero
Mel Ferrer
John Saxon

Martin Herdman
Kayvan Novak
Ian Cullen
Martha Cope
Liz Crowther
Chandra Ruegg
Peter England
Mark McLean
Rupert Hill
Nicola Duffett
Ian Ashpitel
Gemma Wardle
Tina Hall (formerly
  Russell)
Charlie Watts
Ike Hamilton
Richard Hawley

David Cash
Duncan Hart
Eddie Harris
Eileen Day
Elsa Gates
Gemma Craig
Geri Evans
Ginny Davenport
Grace Ellis

Holly Hart
Jack Gates
Jamie Hart
Jim Webb
Joe Thorn
Karen Ellis
Kelly Hurst
Kim Davies
Lucy Day
Maria Simons
Matt Ellis
Melanie Hart
Nick Trip
Nikki Warrington
Paul Webb
Pete Callan
Sadie Hargreaves
Samantha Cockerill
Tim Webster
Vince Farmer
Yasmin Matthews

Flamingo Road
(set in Truro County, Florida; aired between January
1981 and May 1982)
Claude Weldon
Constance Weldon / Carlyle
Elmo Tyson
Eudora Flowers Weldon
Fielding Carlyle
Lane Ballou Curtis
Lute-Mae Sanders
Michael Tyronne
Sam Curtis
Sheriff Titus Semple
Skipper Weldon

General Hospital
(set in Midland General; aired between Sept 1972 and
Jan 1979) ITV
Dr Gregory Knight
Dr Guy Wallman
Dr Martin Baxter
Dr Matthew Armstrong
Dr Neville Bywaters
Dr Peter Ridge
Dr Robert Thorne
Jeffrey Burstall
Mr William Parker-Brown
Nurse Hilda Price
Principal Nursing Officer
  Ruth Milner
Sister Ellen Chapman
Sister Holland
Sister Washington
Student Nurse Katy Shaw

Holby City (spin-off from *Casualty* and set in the
same hospital; first aired in January 1999) BBC1
Adrian Townsend
Alex Adams

James Gaddas
Rocky Marshall
Tony Scannell
Rosie Rowell
Delena Kidd
Angela Hazeldine
Anna Acton
Joanna Foster
Amber and Jade
  Montague
  (the author is
  their great-uncle)
Sandra Huggett
Ken Farrington
Michael Cole
Jo Dow
Les Dennis
Tanya Franks
Nicky Talacko
Troy Titus-Adams
Julia Lee Smith
Annie Miles
Matthew Jay Lewis
Cordelia Bugeja
Barry McCormick
Rebecca Blake
Martin Delaney
David Easter
Barbara Young
Tessa Wyatt
Idris Elba
Stephen Yardley
Ebony Thomas

Kevin McCarthy
Morgan Fairchild
Peter Donat
Barbara Rush
Mark Harmon
Cristina Raines
Stella Stevens
David Selby
John Beck
Howard Duff
Woody Brown

Carl Rigg
Tom Adams
James Kerry
David Garth
Tony Adams
Ian White
Ronald Leigh-Hunt
Ray Lonnen
Lewis Jones
Lynda Bellingham
Kathleen Byron

Peggy Sinclair
Pippa Rowe
Carmen Munroe
Judy Buxton

Ian Ashpitel
Jeremy Sheffield

Ben Saunders
Carole Townsend
Chrissie Williams
Christian Connolly

Damien Weatherall
Danny Shaughnessy
David Keelan
Deborah Sandford
Diane Lloyd
Ed Keating
Elaine Sandford
Guy Morton
Jan Goddard
Jane Archer
Jasmine Hopkins
Jess Griffin
Joanne Townsend
Karen Gilham
Kath Shaughnessy
Kirsty Shaw
Lisa Fox

Mubbs Hussein
Natalie Anderson
Nick Jordan
Owen Davis
Pam McGrath
Patricia Kennedy
Paul Eccles
Ray Sykes
Ric Griffin
Roger Sandford
Samantha Kennedy
Sandy Harper
Stan Ashleigh
Steve Waring
Terry Fox
Tom Campbell-Gore
Tony Vincent
Victoria Merrick

Hollyoaks
(set in Hollyoaks, Chester, and first aired in 1995) C4
Abby Davies
Adam Morgan
Alex Bell
Andy Morgan
Anna Green
Bazz FM
Becca Hayton
Ben Davies
Beth Morgan

Bombhead
Brian Drake
Carol Groves
Chloe Bruce
Cindy Cunningham

Dan Hunter
Darren Osborne

Dawn Cunningham
Debbie Dean
Ellie Hunter
Eve Crawford
Geri Hudson / Cunliffe
Gina Patrick
Gordon Cunningham
Helen Richardson / Cunningham

David Paisley
Kate Rutter
Tina Hobley
Michael
 Fassbender
Matt Dempsey
Jeremy Edwards
Pascal Langdale
Tracy Whitwell
Patricia Potter
Rocky Marshall
Gillian Bevan
Paul Blackthorne
Judy Loe
Christine Entwistle
Angela Griffin
Verona Joseph
Lucy Gaskell
Indra Ove
Jan Pearson
Natalie Blades
Luisa Bradshaw-
 White
Ian Aspinall
Sophie Shaw
Michael French
Mark Moraghan
Denise Welch
Lois Baxter
Leroy Liburd
Ian Curtis
Hugh Quarshie
Richard Hope
Colette Brown
Laura Sadler
Paul Shane
Peter De Jersey
Miles Anderson
Denis Lawson
Lee Warburton
Lisa Faulkner

Helen Noble
David Brown
Martino Lazzeri
Ross Davidson
Lisa M Kay
Toby Sawyer
Ali Bastian
Marcus Patric
Elizabeth O'Grady
 and Kate Baines
Lee Otway
Jonathon Le Billon
Nathalie Casey
Mikyla Dodd
Laura Crossley and
 Stephanie Waring
Andy McNair
Adam Booth and
 Ashley Taylor
 Dawson
Lisa Williamson
Jodi Albert
Sarah Baxendale
Natasha Lund
Joanna Taylor
Danielle Brent
Bernard Latham
Kathryn George

Izzy Cornwell
Jack Osborne
Jake Dean
Jambo Bolton
Jamie Nash
Jasmine Bates
Jason Cunliffe
Jill Patrick / Osborne
Jodie Nash
Jude Cunningham
Kate Patrick
Kerry
Kurt Benson
Laura Burns
Lee Hunter
Les Hunter

Lewis Richardson
Lisa Hunter
Lucy Benson
Luke Morgan
Mandy Richardson
Matt Musgrove
Max Cunningham

Nick O'Connor
Nikki Sullivan
Norman Sankofa
Ollie Benson
Rob Hawthorn
Rory 'Finn' Finnegan
Ruth Osborne / Benson
Sally Hunter

Sam 'OB' O'Brien
Sam Smallwood
Scott Anderson
Sol Patrick
Steph Dean
Sue Morgan
Theo
Toby Mills
Tony Hutchinson
Will Davies
Zara Morgan
Locations include Dan's Pit Stop (a motor accessories shop), Gnosh Village (bistro), The Loft (nightclub) and The Dog in the Pond pub.

Home and Away
(set in Summer Bay nr Sydney) C5
Adam Cameron
Ailsa Hogan Stewart
Al Simpson
Alf Stewart
Angel Brooks / Parish
Blake Dean
Bobby Simpson / Morgan /
 Marshall
Brad Cooper
Carly Morris / Lucini
Celia Stewart
Chloe Richards / Fraser
Colleen Smart
Curtis Reed
Damian Roberts
Dani Sutherland
David Croft
Donald 'Flathead' Fisher
Emma Jackson
Finlay Roberts
Floss McPhee

Elize Du Toit
James McKenna
Kevin Sacre
Will Mellor
Stefan Booth
Elly Fairman
Alex Thorne
Lynda Rooke
Kate McEnery
Davina Taylor
Natasha Symms
Sarah Vandenburgh
Jeremy Edwards
Lesley Johnston
Alex Carter
John Graham
 Davies
Ben Hull
Gemma Atkinson
Kerrie Taylor
Gary Lucy
Sarah Dunn
Kristian Ealey
Ben Sheriff
 and Matt Littler
Darren Bransford
Wendy Glenn
Jamie Luke
Paul Leyshon
Warren Derosa
James Redmond
Terri Dwyer
Katherine Dow-
 Blyton
Darren Jefferies
Tim Downie
Daniel Hyde
Paul Danan
Carley Stenson
Eve White
Andrew Somerville
Henry Luxemburg
Nick Pickard
Barney Clevely
Kelly Greenwood

Mat Stevenson
Judy Nunn
Terence Donovan
Ray Meagher
Melissa George
Les Hill
Nicolle Dickson

Bruce Samazan
Sharyn Hodgson
Fiona Spence
Kristy Wright
Lyn Collingwood
Shane Ammann
Matt Doran
Tammin Sursok
Guy Pearce
Norman Coburn
Dannii Minogue
Tina Thomsen
Angela Keep

Frank Morgan
Grant Mitchell
Greg Marshall
Gypsy Nash
Hayley Smith

Irene Roberts
Jack Wilson
Jade Sutherland
Jesse McGregor
Joel Nash
Joey Rainbow
Jude Lawson
Kirsty Sutherland
Lachlan 'Lachie' Fraser, Dr
Lance Smart
Leah Poulos
Marilyn Chambers / Fisher
Martin Dibble
Matt Wilson
Natalie Nash

Neville McPhee
Nick Parrish
Nick Smith
Noah Lawson
Peter 'Tug' O'Neale
Pippa Fletcher
Pippa Fletcher / Ross
Rebecca Fisher

Rebecca Fisher / Nash
Rhyss Sutherland
Ruth 'Roo' Stewart
Sally Keating Fletcher
Sam Nicholls Marshall
Sarah Thompson
Sebastion 'Seb' Miller
Selina Cook / Roberts
Shane Parrish
Shannon Reed
Shauna Bradley
Shelley Sutherland
Simon Fitzgerald
Sophie Simpson

Steven Matheson
Tom Nash
Tom Fletcher
Travis Nash
Vincent 'Vinnie' Patterson
Will Smith

Knots Landing
(spin-off from *Dallas* set in California)
Abby Cunningham / Ewing / Sumner
Charles Scott
Gary Ewing
Gregory Sumner
Joshua Rush
Karen Fairgate / MacKenzie
Patrick 'Mack' MacKenzie
Peter Hollister
Ruth Galveston
Valene Ewing / Gibson / Waleska

Neighbours
(set in Erinsborough, Melbourne; first aired in 1986)
BBC1
Amy Greenwood
Annalise Hartman

Alex Papps
Craig McLachlan
Ross Newton
Kimberley Cooper
Rebecca Cartwright
Lynne McGranger
Daniel Amalm
Kate Garven
Ben Unwin
David Woodley
Alex O'Han
Ben Steel
Christie Hayes
Richard Grieve
Peter Vroom
Ada Nicodemou
Emily Symons
Craig Thompson
Greg Benson
Angelica La Bozzetta and Antoinette Byron
Frank Lloyd
Bruce Roberts
Christopher Egan
Beau Brady
Tristan Bancks
Vanessa Downing
Debra Lawrance
Jane Hall and Danielle Carter
Belinda Emmett
Michael Beckley
Justine Clarke
Kate Ritchie
Ryan Clark
Laura Vazquez
Mitch Firth
Tempany Deckert
Dieter Brummer
Isla Fisher
Kylie Watson
Paula Forrest
Richard Norton
Rebekah Elmaloglou
Adam Willits
Graeme Squires
Roger Oakley
Nic Testoni
Ryan Kwanten
Zac Drayson

Donna Mills

Michael York
Ted Shackleford
William Devane
Alec Baldwin
Michele Lee
Kevin Dobson
Hunt Block
Ava Gardner
Joan Van Ark

Jacinta Stapleton
Kimberley Davies

Anne Wilkinson
Beth Brennan / Willis
Beverly Marshall, Dr

Billy Kennedy
Boyd Hoyland
Brad Willis
Bronwyn Davies
Caroline Alessi
Charlene Mitchell / Robinson
Cheryl Stark / Carpenter
Christina Alessi / Robinson
Clive Gibbons, Dr
Connor O'Neill
Danni Stark
Darcy Tyler
Debbie Martin
Des Clarke
Dione Bliss
Dorothy Burke
Doug Willis
Drew Kirk
Felicity 'Flick' Scully
Gaby Willis
Gail Lewis / Robinson
Hannah Martin
Harold Bishop
Helen Daniels
Henry Mitchell
Jane Harris
Jim Robinson
Joanna Hartman
Joe Mangel
Joe Scully
Joel Samuels
Julie Robinson / Martin

Karl Kennedy, Dr
Kerry Bishop
Lance Hails Wilkinson
Lauren Carpenter
Libby Kennedy / Kirk
Lou Carpenter
Lucy Robinson

Lyn Scully
Madge Mitchell / Ramsey / Bishop
Malcolm Kennedy
Mark Gottlieb
Max Ramsay
Melanie Pearson / Mangel
Michelle Scully
Mike Young
Nell Mangel / Worthington
Pam Willis
Paul McClain
Paul Robinson
Phoebe Bright
Philip Martin

Rick Alessi
Rosemary Daniels
Ruth Wilkinson
Sam Kratz
Sarah Beaumont
Scott Robinson

Shane Ramsay
Sky Bishop / Mangel
Stephanie Scully
Susan Kennedy

Brooke Satchwell
Natalie Imbruglia
Lisa Armytage and Shaunna O'Grady
Jesse Spencer
Kyal Marsh
Scott Michaelson
Rachel Friend
Gillian Blakeney
Kylie Minogue
Caroline Gillmer
Gayle Blakeney
Geoff Paine
Patrick Harvey
Eliza Szonert
Mark Raffety
Mandy Storvik
Paul Keane
Madeleine West
Maggie Dence
Terence Donovan
Dan Paris
Holly Valance
Rachel Blakely
Fiona Corke
Rebecca Ritters
Ian Smith
Anne Haddy
Craig McLachlan
Annie Hones
Alan Dale
Emma Harrison
Mark Little
Shane Connor
Daniel Macpherson
Vikki Blanche and Julie Mullins
Alan Fletcher
Linda Hartley
Andrew Bibby
Sarah Vandenbergh
Kym Valentine
Tom Oliver
Kylie Flinker
Sascha Close
Melissa Bell
Janet Andrewartha
Anne Charleston
Benji McNair
Bruce Samazan
Francis Bell
Lucinda Cowden
Kate Keltie
Guy Pearce
Vivean Gray
Sue Jones
Jansen Spencer
Stefan Dennis
Simone Robertson
Christopher Milne and Ian Rawlings
Dan Falzon
Joy Chambers
Ailsa Piper
Richard Grieve
Nicola Charles
Darius Perkins and Jason Donovan
Peter O'Brien
Miranda Fryer
Carla Bonner
Jackie Woodburne

Tadpole 'Tad' Reeves — Jonathon Dutton
Teresa Bell — Krista Vendy
Toadfish Rebecchi — Ryan Moloney
Toby Mangel — Finn Greentree-Keane
Todd Landers — Kristian Schmid
Tom Ramsay — Gary Files

The Newcomers
(set in Angleton; aired from 1965 to 1969) BBC1

Andrew Kerr — Robin Bailey
Ellis Cooper — Alan Browning
Joyce Harker — Wendy Richard
Julie Robertson — Deborah Watling
Maria Cooper — Judy Geeson
Robert Malcolm — Conrad Phillips
Vivienne Cooper — Maggie Fitzgibbon

The Sullivans
(made between 1976 and 1982) ITV (set during World War Two)

Alice Watkins / Sullivan (Maggie's daughter) — Megan Williams
Anna Kauffmann (John's 1st wife) — Ingrid Mason
Bert Duggan (killed in the war) — Peter Hehir
Cara — Kylie Minogue
Caroline Sullivan (Terry's wife) — Genevieve Picot
Christopher Merchant — John Waters
Dave Sullivan — Paul Cronin
Detective Sgt Shearer — Noel Trevarthen
Dr Donovan Sullivan — Keith Eden

Ernest 'Erger' O'Keefe — Peter Harvey Wright
Flynn Errol (flying ace) — Peter Ford
Frank Errol — Damon Herriman
Geoff Johnson/Sullivan (adopted son) — Jamie Higgins
Grace Sullivan (killed in London) — Lorraine Bayly
Harry Sullivan — Michael Caton
Horace 'Orrible' Brown — Nick Waters
Ida Jessup / Pike — Vivean Gray
Jack Fletcher — Reg Gorman
Jim Sullivan (Alice's husband) — Andy Anderson
John Sullivan — Andrew McFarlane
Juliana Sleven — Saski Post
Kate Meredith — Ilona Rodgers
Kitty Sullivan — Susan Hannaford
Leslie 'Magpie' Maddern — Gary Sweet
Lou Sullivan (Harry's 2nd wife) — Annie Byron
Maggie Baker (Norm's 2nd wife) — Vikki Hammond
Maureen Sullivan — Fiona Paul
Melina Baker (Norm's 1st wife) — Chantel Contouri
Norm Baker — Norman Yemm
Patty Spencer / Sullivan (Tom's wife) — Penny Downie
Robbie McGovern (Kitty's husband) — Graham Harvey
Rose Sullivan (Harry's 1st wife) — Maggie Dence
Sally Meredith — Lisa Crittenden
Terry Sullivan — Richard Morgan
Tom Sullivan — Steven Tandy

Television, Radio and Media Adverts

A diamond is forever De Beer Consolidated Mines
A little dab'll do ya Brylcreem
Aah . . . Bisto
All human life is there News of the World
All the news that's fit to print *New York Times*
And all because the lady loves . . . Milk Tray
Any time, any place, anywhere Martini (coined by Barry Day)
Appliance of science Zanussi
Are you with . . . No, I'm with the Woolwich
Ask the man from the . . . Pru (Prudential Assurance Co. Ltd)
A . . . works wonders Double Diamond
Australians wouldn't give a xxxx for anything else Castlemaine xxxx lager
Bank that likes to say Yes TSB
Beanz meanz . . . Heinz
Beats as it sweeps as it cleans Hoover vacuum cleaners
Because I'm worth it L'oriel
Because life's complicated enough Abbey National
Beer that made Milwaukee famous Schlitz
Bet you can't eat three Shredded Wheat
B . . . O . . . Lifebuoy soap
Bread with nowt taken out Allinson's bread
. . . Brings express relief Settlers
Builds bonny babies Glaxo
Buy some for Lulu Smarties
. . . calling! Avon
Can you tell . . . from butter? Stork margarine

Central heating for kids Ready Brek
Chocolates with the less fattening centres Maltesers
Chocolates? No . . . Maltesers
Cleans a big, big carpet for less than half a crown 1001
Cleans and polishes in one go Pledge
Clunk click, every trip Jimmy Savile's seat belt campaign (from 1971)
Cool as a mountain stream Consulate cigarettes
Cuts cleaning time in half Flash
Does she or doesn't she? Clairol hair colouring (coined by Shirley Polykoff)
Don't ask the price. It's a penny Marks & Spencer (when first opened)
Don't be vague, ask for . . . Haig whisky
Don't leave home without it American Express
Don't say brown, say . . . Hovis
Don't you just love being in control British Gas, and Mrs Merton and her son, Malcolm
Eveninks and morninks I drink . . . Warninks
Everything you want from a store, and a little bit more Safeways
Finger of Fudge is just enough to give your kids a treat
Fingerlickin' good Kentucky Fried Chicken
First truly feminine cigarette Eve
Fly the flag British Airways
For men who don't have to try too hard Old Spice
Forces grey out, forces white in Fairy Snow
Fortifies the over forties Phyllosan
Fresh as the moment when the pod went pop

Birds Eye peas
Full of Eastern promise　Fry's Turkish Delight
Genuine article　Budweiser
Getting there is half the fun　Cunard Steamship Line
Gives a meal man appeal　Oxo
Good to the last drop　Maxwell House coffee
Gordon's gin (first scented advert)　Shown in May 1997 when juniper berries could be smelt in cinema
Go to work on an . . .　Egg (slogan is often attributed to Fay Weldon)
Graded grains make finer flour　Homepride
Great way to fly　Singapore Airlines
Hands that do dishes are as soft as your face　with mild, green Fairy Liquid
Have a break, bave a . . .　KitKat
Helps you work, rest and play　A Mars a day (possibly attributed to Murray Walker)
Hold it up to the light, not a stain and shining bright　Surf
I dreamed I . . . in my　Maidenform bra
I think you probably are　Cockburns Port
I was so impressed I bought the company　Remington (said by Victor Kyam)
If you see Sid, tell him　British Gas slogan during privatisation
I'm only here for the beer　Double Diamond
I'm . . . fly me　National Airlines
. . . is good for you　Guinness
I never knew it had so much in it　TV Times
Is it live, or is it . . .　Memorex
Is she or isn't she?　Harmony hair spray
It could be you　National Lottery
It's for yoo-hoo!　British Telecom
It's the real thing　Coca-Cola
It's what your right arm's for　Courage beer
Keep going well, keep going　Shell
Keep your schoolgirl complexion　Palmolive
Keynsham – spelt K-E-Y-N-S-H-A-M　Horace Batchelor's phrase on Luxembourg's pools advisory service
Kills 99% of all household germs　Domestos
King of beers　Budweiser
Let's face the music and dance　Allied Dunbar
Let your fingers do the walking　Yellow Pages (Kirsty MacColl's version of 'Days' was popular theme)
Lion goes from strength to strength　Peugeot
Liquid engineering　Castrol Motor Oil
Listening Bank　The Midland
Looks good, tastes good and by golly it does you good　Mackeson
Lot less bovver than a hover　Qualcast
Loudest noise comes from the electric clock　Rolls Royce
Made by robots, driven by humans　Nissan
Made in Scotland from girders　Irn Bru
Made to make your mouth water　Opal Fruits
Make tea bags make tea　Tetley's
Make yourself heard　Ericsson
Makes exceedingly good cakes　Mr Kipling
Means happy motoring　Esso (sign)
Melts in your mouth, not in your hands　Treets
Milk from contented cows　Carnation
Mint with the hole　Polo
Minty bit stronger　Trebor Mints

Naughty but nice　Original advert about cream cakes (Salman Rushdie coined the phrase)
Never knowingly undersold　John Lewis Stores
Nice 'ere 'innit?　Campari (Lorraine Chase)
Nice face, shame about the breath　Listerine mouthwash
Nice one, Cyril　Wonderloaf
Nicole . . . Papa　Renault Clio
99 44/100 % Pure　Ivory soap
Nissan Almira　Parodies of *The Sweeney* and *The Professionals*
Nissan Micra　'No No No' by Nancy Nova
Not everything in black and white makes sense　Guinness
Nothing acts faster than . . .　Anadin
Nuts! Whole hazelnuts　Cadbury's Wholenut
Often a bridesmade – but never a bride　Listerine mouthwash
One degree under? Try . . .　Aspro
Pizza Hut: appeared in adverts　Jonathan Ross, Caprice, Gareth Southgate, Damon Hill, Mikhail Gorbachev, Pamela Anderson
Plink plink fizz　Alka Seltzer
Prevents that sinking feeling　Bovril
Probably the best lager in the world　Carlsberg
Prolongs active life　Pal dog food
Promise her anything, but give her . . .　Arpège (coined by Edouard Cournand, president of Lanvin Perfumes)
Pure genius　Guinness
Put a tiger in your tank　Esso
Puts the 'T' in Britain　Typhoo tea
Refreshes the parts other beers cannot reach　Heineken (coined by Terry Lovelock)
Ring of confidence　Colgate toothpaste
. . . satisfy　Senior Service cigarettes
Schhh . . . you know who　Schweppes
Seven pieces of heaven　Fry's Chocolate Cream
Simply years ahead　Philips
'Singing in the Rain' (rap version)　McDonald's
Snap! crackle! and pop!　Kellogg's Rice Crispies
Solutions for a small planet　IBM
Splash it on all over　Brut
Spreads straight from the fridge　Blueband margarine
Station of the Nation　Radio Caroline
Stays sharp till the bottom of the glass　Harp lager
Stop me and buy one　Wall's ice cream
Sweet you can eat between meals　Milky Way (without spoiling your appetite)
Takes good care of you　BOAC
Tastes as good as it smells　Maxwell House Coffee
Tested by dummies, driven by the intelligent　Volvo
That's the wonder of ...　Woollies (Woolworths)
The appetizer　Tizer
The bank that listens　Midland
The bright one, the right one, it's . . .　Martini
The cereal that's shot from guns　Quaker Puffed Wheat
The drive of your life　Peugeot 106
The real smell of . . .　Brut
The shirt you don't iron　Rael Brook Toplin
The soluble aspirin　Disprin
They came in search of paradise　Bounty
They grow on you　Roses chocolates

They're bootiful   Bernard Matthews's turkeys

They're grrrreat!   Frosties

Things go better with . . .   Coke (Coca-Cola)

To fly, to serve   British Airways

Too good to hurry mints   Murray Mints

To our members we're the fourth emergency service   Automobile Association

Top breeders recommend it   Pedigree Chum dog food

Top people read the . . .   Times

Try a little VC 10derness   British Airways

Vorsprung durch Technik   Audi

Watch out there's a Humphrey about   Milk

We never forget you have a choice   British Caledonian

We sell more cars than Ford, Chrysler, Chevrolet and Buick combined   Matchbox toys

We try harder   Avis Car Rentals (coined by Doyle, Dane & Bernbach)

We'll take more care of you   British Airways

Were you truly wafted here from Paradise? Nah! Luton Airport   Campari (Lorraine Chase)

When you fancy a fruity treat, unzip a . . .   Banana

When you've got it, flaunt it   Braniff Airways

Where do you want to go today   Microsoft

Which twin has the Toni?   Toni Home Perms

Why does the man in the mask drink . . .   Metz

Wodka from Warrington   Vladivar

World's favourite airline   British Airways

World's finest blade   Wilkinson Sword

Wot a lot I got   Smarties

Would you give me your last . . .?   Rolo

You know what comes between me and my Calvins?   Calvin Klein jeans (15-year-old Brooke Shields in 1980)

You'll look a little lovelier each day   with fabulous pink Camay soap

You'll wonder where the yellow went . . .   when you brush your teeth with Pepsodent

You make it what it is   BBC

You press the button, we do the rest   Kodak

You too can have a body like mine   Charles Atlas (Angelo Siciliano)

Your country needs you   WW1 army recruitment poster (Kitchener pointing with right hand)

Your flexible friend   Access credit card

You're never alone with a . . .   Strand (coined by John May)

Television and Radio: Miscellaneous Information

advertisement: first   Gibbs SR toothpaste.

advertisement: shown after death   Yul Brynner made anti-smoking advert with the message, 'Hullo, I'm dead; smoking killed me.'

Any Questions/Answers   Presenters: Freddy Grisewood, David Jacobs.

Archers   First broadcast on BBC on 1 January 1951, although first heard on a local station in the Midlands in 1950. The Archers lived on Brookfield Farm in Ambridge, just south of Borchester, Borsetshire. Many weddings during the series have been recorded at Hanbury Church in Worcestershire. Princess Margaret as President of the NSPCC visited Ambridge for a fashion show (1984). Eddie Grundy famously got drunk in Britt Ekland's dressing room at the Christmas pantomime (1992). Billing: Everyday story of country folk. Local pub: The Bull.

aspect ratio   Normal: 4 x 3. Wide screen: 16 x 9.

BAFTA TV Awards: 2002

Best Actress   Julie Walters (*My Beautiful Son*)

Best Actor   Michael Gambon (*Perfect Strangers*)

Best Light Entertainment Performance   Graham Norton (*So Graham Norton*)

Best Comedy Performance   Ricky Gervais (*The Office*)

Best Single Drama   *When I Was 12*

Best Drama Serial   *The Way We Live Now*

Best Factual Series   *Horizon*

Best Comedy Programme   *The Sketch Show*

Best Situation Comedy   *The Office*

Best Soap   *EastEnders*

BBC announcer: first   Leslie Mitchell.

BBC Choice   First new BBC channel for 34 years (Clive Anderson opened the proceedings on 23 September 1998).

BBC Director General: first   Lord Reith.

BBC Director of Radio   Jenny Abramsky took over

from Matthew Bannister on 19 November 1998.

BBC1   Commenced broadcasting from Alexandra Palace in 1936.

BBC Radio controllers   Radio 5 Live – Bob Shennan; Radio 4 – Helen Boaden; Radio 3 – Roger Wright; Radio 2 – James Moir; Radio 1 – Andy Parfitt.

BBC Television controllers   BBC 1 – Lorraine Heggessey; BBC 2 – Jane Root.

BBC Television executives   Chairman is Gavin Davies and Director General is Greg Dyke.

BBC3   Digital station. Commenced 9 February 2003 and launched by Johnny Vaughan.

BBC 2   Commenced 20 April 1964; mascots were Hullabaloo and Custard (two kangaroos).

Beyond Our Ken   Billed as 'A sort of radio show' and starred Kenneth Horne.

Brain of Britain   Hosted by Robert Robinson and produced by Richard Edis. Questions set by Kevin Ashman (Jorkins). Winners: Martin Dakin (1954), Arthur Maddock (1955), Anthony Carr (1956), Rosemary Watson (1957), David Keys (1958), Dr Reginald Webster (1959), Patrick Bowing (1960), Irene Thomas (1961), Henry Button (1962), Ian Barton (1963), Ian Gillies (1964), Robert Crampsey (1965), Richard Best (1966), Lt Cmdr Loring (1967), Ralph Raby (1968), T D Thomson (1969), Ian Matheson (1970), Fred Morgan (1971), A Lawrence (1972), Glyn Court (1973), Roger Pritchard (1974), Winifred Lawson (1975), Thomas Dyer (1976), Martin Gostelow (1977), James Nesbitt (1978), Arthur Gerard (1979), Tim Paxton (1980), Peter Barlow (1981), John Pusey (1982), Sue Marshall (1983), Peter Bates (1984), Richard Fife (1985), Stephen Gore (1986), Ian Sutton (1987), Paul Monaghan (1988), Barbara Thompson (1989), Jim Eccleson (1990), Chris Wright (1991), Mike Billson (1992), Geoffrey Colton (1993), Ian Wynn-Mackenzie (1994), Ian Kinloch (1995), Kevin

Ashman (1996), Daphne Fowler (1997), Guy Herbert (1998), Leslie Duncalf (1999), Mike Smith-Rawnsley (2000), Tom Corfe (2001), Dr David Jones (2002).

Brains Trust The first panel were Julian Huxley, C E M Joad and Cmdr A B Campbell. The chairman was Donald McCullough, who was replaced by Gilbert Harding.

Breakfast Television Started 17 January 1983 (*BBC Breakfast Time*).

Broadcasting Standards Authority: first chairman Lord Rees Mogg.

BSkyB: controller Elizabeth Murdoch.

Byker Grove: setting Newcastle upon Tyne.

Carlton TV: fine Carlton Television was fined £2m for faking the documentary *The Connection*.

Channel 4 Started in 1982 (first programme: *Countdown*).

Channel 4: chief executive Mark Thompson (chairman: Vanni Treves).

Channel 5 Launched on 30 March 1997 by Dawn Airey and the Spice Girls.

Channel 5: chief executive Dawn Airey.

chefs on television Jane Asher, Susan Brooks, Robert Carrier, Fanny Craddock, Anton Edelman, Keith Floyd, Philip Harbin, Ainsley Harriott, Graham Kerr, Anton Mossiman, Jamie Oliver, Paul Rankin, Gary Rhodes, Delia Smith, Rick Stein, Brian Turner, Antony Worrall Thompson.

Classic FM: chief executive Roger Lewis.

colour television Started in 1967.

Crookes Tube: function Produced cathode rays.

Desert Island Discs: first guest Vic Oliver.

Desert Island Discs: presenters Roy Plomley, Michael Parkinson, Sue Lawley.

digital television: advantages Traditional broadcasting is based on electronic signals that rise and fall to represent the shades of black, white and colour in the TV picture. The continuously varying signal is a direct analogue of the image it represents, just as the variations in the grooves of an LP, picked up by the stylus, are an analogue of the music. Analogue broadcasting is spendthrift in its use of the radio spectrum. There is a limited range of frequencies that can be used for TV transmissions, and each analogue station needs a healthy chunk of that space (approx 8 megahertz). Transmitters using the same frequency must be a long way apart, otherwise they interfere with one another, so transmitters closer than a few hundred kilometres to each other must employ different frequencies. As a result, it takes 44 frequencies in the UHF band to provide the four terrestrial channels. Digital broadcasting alters the rules. Instead of representing the image by a continuously variable signal, digital TV encodes it in the same language used by computers, a long stream of binary digits, or 'bits', each of which is either 0 or 1, a pulse or a non-pulse. It takes an enormous number of such bits to encode a TV picture, but it is easier to distinguish a pulse from a non-pulse than it is to discern the varying waveform of an analogue signal. This means that transmitters can be run at a much lower signal strength and still provide a decent picture. This in turn reduces the interference problem for terrestrial broadcasters so that better use can be made of the available frequencies, and picture quality is greatly improved. A full TV picture requires about 216 million bits per second but only the changes from one picture to the next are encoded so as to enable the data to fit into the frequency band.

Golden Rose of Montreux: 2002 *Pop Idol* (ITV 1).

Hamish Macbeth: setting Plockton, on the west coast of Scotland.

House of Lords: first televised 1985.

iconoscope: inventor Vladimir Zworykin (1923).

ITMA (It's That Man Again) Tommy Handley was the title character and Dorothy Summers played Mrs Mopp.

ITN newscaster: first Chris Chataway.

ITV: managing director David Liddiment.

Just a Minute Chairman Nicholas Parsons. Panellists have included: Kenneth Williams, Derek Nimmo, Peter Jones, Clement Freud, Paul Merton, Graham Norton, Lance Percival and Sheila Hancock. The aim is to talk for one minute on a given topic without Hesitation, Deviation or Repetition.

Life with the Lyons Ben Lyon and Bebe Daniels and their children Barbara and Richard.

local radio stations Aire – Leeds, Arrow – Hastings, Beacon – Wolverhampton, BRMB – Birmingham, The Beach – Lowestoft, Broadland – Norwich, Cat – Cheltenham, Centre – Leicester, Chiltern – Luton/Bedford, City – Liverpool, Dream – Colchester, Hallam – Sheffield, Hereward – Peterborough, Kestrel – Basingstoke, Mercia – Coventry, Mercury – Crawley, Oak – Loughborough, Orwell – Ipswich, Pennine – Bradford, Piccadilly – Manchester, Ram – Derby, Silk – Macclesfield, Trent – Nottingham, 2CR – Bournemouth, Viking – Hull, West – Bristol, Wire – Warrington, Wish – Wigan, Wyvern – Hereford and Worcester.

Men from the Ministry, The Wilfrid Hyde Whyte (Roland Hamilton-Jones), Richard Murdoch (Richard Lamb).

Nielsens US equivalent of BARB showing American audience ratings.

OnDigital TV service 30-channel service launched by Ulrika Jonsson on 15 November 1998.

pirate radio station: first Radio Caroline, from 1964 to 1967.

radio play: caused panic Orson Welles's *War of the Worlds* broadcast in 1938.

radio stations: formerly called Radio 4 (Home), Radio 3 (Third), Radio 2 (Light). These were the three main stations. Radio 1 commenced in 1967.

Round Britain Quiz Hosted by Nick Clarke.

satellite TV: reception areas Known as Footprints.

S4C: full name Sianel Pedwar Cymru.

SkyDigital Launched on 1 October 1998.

soap opera: first on television *The Appleyards* ran from 1952 to 1957 and is truly the first example of a televised British soap opera. The first adult British soap opera was *The Grove Family* (1954–7). The first daily soap opera was *Sixpenny Corner* (set in the new town of Springwood). This is another controversial area that requires careful attention. *The Appleyards* was shown fortnightly and was a children's soap, while *The Groves* was broadcast weekly and was for adults.

soap opera: why called Term derived from the American radio of the 1930s when soap and detergent companies sponsored the 15-minute daily radio programmes. Proctor and Gamble were a leading light in this field.

Sony Radio Academy Awards 2002
  Comedy Award *I'm Sorry I Haven't A Clue* (Radio 4). Humphrey Lyttelton, Graeme Garden, Tim

Brooke-Taylor, Barry Cryer, Colin Sell.

Drama Award *A Woman In Waiting* (Radio 4). Performer: Thembi Mtshali.

Station of the Year BBC Radio 2.

Gold Award John Peel for four decades of quality broadcasting.

Sports Award *Chiles on Saturday* (BBC Radio News For Five Live)

Interactive Award The *Stephen Nolan Show* (Belfast City Beat).

Feature Award *Roots of Homophobia* (BBC Radio 4).

News Broadcaster Award Peter Allen and Jane Garvey (BBC Radio News For Five Live).

Breakfast Music Award *Wake Up to Wogan* (BBC Radio 2).

Music Broadcaster Award *Big George* (BBC Three Counties Radio). Big George Webley.

Steve Coogan Creations Alan Partridge, Paul Calf, Pauline Calf, Tony Farino.

stripping Showing of programme at the same time every day of every week.

swear word: first to use Kenneth Tynan was the first to use the 'f' word on television.

Teletext BBC – Ceefax; ITV – Oracle.

television companies Anglia TV, based in Norwich, started in 1959 (logo is a series of triangles in shape of an 'A'). Associated Television (ATV) first broadcast in September 1955, at weekends only. The BBC formed in London in 1922 as a radio station and in 1936 started television broadcasts. BSkyB formed in 1990 by merger of Sky TV and British Satellite Broadcasting. Border Television formed in 1961 (logo is ovoid shape with an inverted 'Y' running through the centre). Carlton Television formed in 1992. Central Television formed in 1982 and is now part of the Carlton Network (logo is a 12-part sphere). Grampian Television formed in 1961 (logo is a saltire cross on a television screen). Granada Television formed in 1955 and is the only original franchise holder still broadcasting. Harlech Television formed in 1968. ITC (Independent Television Corporation) formed as an alternative to the BBC. LWT (London Weekend Television) started in 1967 from Fridays at 6.00 p.m. to Sunday nights.

Meridian Television replaced TVS as franchise holder for the south and south-east on 1 January 1993 (logo is a sunny face). Rediffusion started broadcasting on weekdays only in September 1955. Scottish Television formed in 1957. Southern Television formed in 1958. Thames Television formed when ABC merged with Associated Rediffusion in the late 1960s. Tyne Tees formed in 1959 and is now owned by Granada Media. Ulster Television formed in 1959. Westcountry Television formed in 1993 and is owned by Carlton Communications. Yorkshire Television formed in 1968 and is owned by Granada Media.

television: inventor John Logie Baird created his first televisor, a contraption made from a tea-chest, a biscuit box and darning needles, in 1923, and gave a first public demonstration in 1926. In 1928 he produced a crude colour system.

television licences: first Licences were first issued in 1946 at £2 each. Cost of a colour licence at February 2003 is £112 but increasing to £116 in April. Black and white is £37.50.

test card girl: famous Carol Hersey (billed as the most seen person on television).

TV am: launched by David Frost, Michael Parkinson, Robert Kee, Anna Ford, Angela Rippon.

Twenty Questions: **presenters** Stewart McPherson, Gilbert Harding, Kenneth Horne, Cliff Michelmore.

Twenty Questions: **mystery voice** Norman Hackforth.

Ulster TV: chairman John B McGuckian.

Ulster TV: location Havelock House, Belfast.

Variety Playhouse: **MC** Vic Oliver.

weather Laura Greene (ITV), Ian McCaskill, Bill Giles, Suzanne Charlton, Helen Young, John Ketley, Peter Cockcroft, Michael Fish (BBC).

weather: hurricane announcement Michael Fish gave us the good news on 15 October 1987 that the person who rang up saying a hurricane was likely for tomorrow was completely wrong!

Wogan: **appeared drunk on in 1990** George Best.

World Service Radio: controller Mark Byford.

World Service Television BBC channel launched in 1991.

T
E
L
E
V
I
S
I
O
N

TRANSPORT: AIRCRAFT

Chronology

1300   Marco Polo reports man-carrying kites in use in China.

1500   Leonardo da Vinci designs helicopters and ornithopters.

1709   A model hot-air balloon demonstrated by Father Laurenço de Gusmao at the court of King John V of Portugal (8 Aug.).

1783   First manned balloon flight by Pilâtre de Rozier and the marquis d'Arlandes in the Bois de Boulogne (21 Nov.). First flight of hydrogen balloon by Professor Jacques Charles (1 Dec.).

1784   First British balloon flight (4 Oct.).

1785   First crossing of the English Channel by balloon piloted by Jean-Pierre Blanchard and John Jeffries (7 Jan.).

1799   Sir George Cayley designs his first glider.

1810   Cayley publishes a paper on the theory of the airplane.

1843   The 'Steam Airplane' patented by William Samuel Henson.

1849   Cayley's 'Boy-Lifter' glider succeeds in lifting a small boy off the ground.

1852   Henri Giffard makes first semi-controlled powered flight in airship (24 Sept.).

1853   Cayley succeeds in making his coachman fly his glider.

1861   Balloons used by Union forces in American Civil War.

1870   Leon Gambetta escapes from a besieged Paris by balloon (7 Oct.).

1890   Clément Ader's *Eole* aircraft makes a short 'hop' near Paris (9 Oct.).

1891   Otto Lilienthal makes his first glider flight.

1894   Sir Hiram Maxim's biplane makes brief uncontrolled ascent (31 July).

1896   Otto Lilienthal dies after glider crash (10 Aug.).

1899   Glider pioneer Percy Pilcher dies following glider crash (2 Oct.).

1900   LZ1 makes first rigid airship flight (Count Zeppelin) (2 July).

1900   Wright brothers begin glider experiments (1 Dec.).

1903   Lebaudy airship makes first fully controlled flight in history (8 May). Samuel Langley's *Aerodrome* aircraft narrowly fails to make first powered flight (7 Oct.). Wright brothers make first powered flight (Orville at the controls) in *Flyer* (17 Dec.).

1906   Alberto Santos-Dumont makes first powered flight in Europe (23 Oct.). French company, Voisin Frères, established for the production of powered aircraft (Nov.).

1907   Breguet gyroplane makes first helicopter 'hop' (19 Sept.). Paul Cornu's helicopter makes first 'hop' (13 Nov.). Lt Thomas W Selfridge becomes first person killed in a plane crash when he and Orville Wright crash at Fort Meyer, Virginia (17 Sept.).

1908   Samuel Cody makes first powered flight in Britain (16 Oct.).

1909   Louis Blériot makes first flight across the English Channel (25 July).

1910   Harry Houdini, the celebrated escapologist and illusionist, makes the first successful flight on the Australian continent in a Voisin biplane (18 March).

1911   Eugene Ely lands Curtiss biplane on USS *Pennsylvania* (18 Jan.). First mail carried by air in UK (9 Sept.). First aerial warfare by Italian Army Aviation Corps over Libya (23 Oct.). Lt Giulio Gavotti makes the first air raid by dropping a 4½ lb bomb on Turks at Ain Zara (1 Nov.). Aircraft used in Mexican Revolution.

1912   Royal Flying Corps (RFC) formed (13 April). Death of Wilbur Wright (30 May). Bulgarian M Popoff becomes first pilot killed in warfare, during a reconnaissance flight (3 Nov.).

1914   Lts V Waterfall and C G G Bayley first British fliers killed in action (22 Aug.). Paris becomes the first capital city to be bombed from the air (30 Aug.). Japanese seaplanes attack the Austro-German fleet at Kiaochow, causing the first ship to be sunk from the air (17 Sept.). HMS *Ark Royal* becomes the world's first aircraft carrier (9 Dec.).

1915   LZ38 airship makes the first air raid on London (31 May). Flt Sub-Lt R A Warneford (VC) downs the LZ37, the first Zeppelin to be shot down (7 June). Katherine Stinson becomes first woman to loop the loop (18 July). Roland Garros is captured in Belgium (20 April). Garros was the first Frenchman to cross the Mediterranean by air, and working with Raymond Saulnier invented deflector plates to enable him to fire a machine gun through the propeller.

1916   Death of Ernst Mach (19 Feb.). Boeing formed as Pacific Aero Products Co (15 July). SL11 airship shot down in North London by Lt W Leefe-Robinson (VC) (2 Sept.). World's first flying bomb, the Hewitt-Sperry, built by Curtiss, is tested (12 Sept.). The airship ace Heinrich Mathy is killed when LZ72 is shot down over Potters Bar (2 Oct.). First British airline, Aircraft Transport &Travel Ltd, registered (5 Oct.).

1917   Baron von Richthofen awarded the 'Pour le Mérite' medal (16 Jan.). Death of Count von Zeppelin (8 March). Billy Mitchell became the first US Army officer to fly over German lines (24 April). Albert Ball killed in France (7 May), awarded posthumous VC (3 June). Sopwith Camel goes into service with Royal Flying Corps (RFC) in France (July). First flight of the Vickers Vimy (30 Nov.).

1918   Air Ministry established and Lord Rothermere is first Sec. of State for Air (2 Jan.). Royal Flying Corps and Royal Naval Air Service combine to create the Royal Air Force (1 April). Baron von Richthofen shot down (21 April). Hermann Goering takes over as leader of

Richthofen's squadron (7 July). HMS *Furious*, adapted from cruiser to aircraft carrier, launched six Sopwith Camels against Zeppelin sheds (19 July). Peter Strasser, German commander of airships, shot down in L70 off Cromer (5 Aug.). Roland Garros killed when his SPAD XIII breaks up during a dogfight (5 Oct.). Handley Page 0/400 becomes first plane to fly from Egypt to India (12 Dec.).

1919 Britain's first scheduled air service inaugurated (10 May). US Navy Curtiss flying boat flown by Lt Cmdr Albert Read becomes first aircraft to fly the Atlantic (in stages) (27 May). Alcock and Brown make first non-stop crossing of the Atlantic in a Vickers Vimy (15 June). German Zeppelin fleet scuttled (23 June). First flight of Junkers F13, the first all-metal monoplane airliner (25 June). London's first airport opens at Hounslow Heath (1 July). British airship R34 makes first two-way Atlantic crossing (13 July). Edward Mannock, Britain's most successful ace, posthumously awarded VC (18 July). First flight over the Canadian Rockies by Capt. Ernest Hoy (7 Aug.). KLM founded (7 Oct.). Handley Page Transport provide first in-flight meals (11 Oct.). Ross and Keith Smith make first flight from Britain to Australia in a Vickers Vimy (10 Dec.) .

1920 First flight from Britain to South Africa (20 March). Croydon Airport begins operations, taking over from Hounslow (29 March). Juan de la Cierva is granted a patent for the Autogiro (27 Aug.). Dayton-Wright RB Racer aircraft flown with retractable landing gear. Qantas (Queensland and Northern Territory Aerial Services) founded (16 Nov.). First British airline disaster: Handley Page 0/400 crashes at Cricklewood, killing four (14 Dec.). Airline AT & T goes into liquidation (15 Dec.).

1921 First free flight of a helicopter since 1907, assisted by a balloon (15 Jan.). Orly aerodrome opened in Paris (1 March). Croydon Airport officially opened (31 March). Vickers Vernon, first troop-carrying aircraft, delivered to RAF (1 Aug.). First aerial crop-dusting takes place in Ohio, USA, by Lt John B Macready in a Curtiss JN6 (3 Aug.). Airship R38 crashes in Hull, killing many of Britain's most experienced airshipmen (24 Aug.).

1922 Formation of RAF reserve announced (9 Feb.). Jack Sanderson became first airline steward (2 April). First mid-air collision, between Farman Goliath and Daimler DH18, over Poix in northern France (7 April). First night flight by Grands Express from Le Bourget to Croydon (9 June). First air crossing of South Atlantic by S Cabral and G Coutinho of Portugal (16 June). Dr Albert Taylor and Leo Young make first successful detections of objects by radio observation (23 Sept.). QANTAS flies its first scheduled service, the first passenger being Mr A Kennedy (2 Nov.). First instance of skywriting 'Smoke Lucky Strikes' (28 Nov.).

1923 First public flight of Juan de la Cierva's Autogyro (9 Jan.). First drop tank used (Boeing MB-3A) (5 March). First air troop-transport took place during Kurdish uprising when 280 Sikhs were flown from Kingarban to Kirkuk (April).

Etienne Ochmichen makes world's first helicopter closed-circuit flight (1 May). Amelia Earhart receives pilot's certificate from NAA, the first woman to do so (16 May). Sabena Airlines formed in Belgium (23 May). Formation of New Zealand Air Force (14 June). First flight of US airship *Shenandoah* (3 Sept.). Dixmunde disaster over the Mediterranean: 52 killed in airship explosion (21 Dec.).

1924 Royal Canadian Air Force formed (1 April). First sustained forward flight of a helicopter made by Etienne Ochmichen (14 April). Fleet Air Arm established (April). Start of first aeroplane flight round the world by Lts L H Smith and Erik Nelson (24 April–28 Sept.). Formation of Imperial Airways (28 April). First circumnavigation of Australia: Goble and McIntyre in a Fairey IIID (19 May). First flight around Japan: Goto and Yonezawa in a Kawanishi K-6 (31 July). First aerial circumnavigation by two Douglas world cruisers of the US Army Air Service: Smith and Arnold in *Chicago*, Nelson and Harding in *New Orleans* (28 Sept.).

1925 First production DH60 Moth delivered (21 July), maiden flight 22 Feb. First flight of M-17 ELLO, the first Messerschmitt aircraft (16 Aug.). *Shenandoah* breaks up in mid-air over Ohio; 29 dead (3 Sept.).

1926 Alan Cobham flies his DH-50 over Victoria Falls on the way to Cape Town (24 Jan.). Robert Goddard launches first liquid-fuelled rocket (16 March). Formation of Deutsche Luft Hansa A.G. (6 April). Richard E Byrd flies over North Pole in Fokker F.VII (9 May). Amundsen makes first flight over North Pole in an airship (14 May). US Army Air Service becomes US Army Air Corps (2 July). First aircraft launched and recovered by submarine, US *S-1* (28 July). Alan Cobham completes epic flight from London to Australia and back (1 Oct.).

1927 Lindbergh makes first non-stop solo Atlantic crossing in *Spirit of St Louis* (21 May). Lt Dick Bentley makes first solo flight from Britain to Cape Town (28 Sept.).

1928 Inauguration of Flying Doctor service in Australia (15 May). Nobile's *Italia* airship crashes in the Arctic (25 May). Charles Kingsford Smith flies Pacific in *Southern Cross* (9 June). Amelia Earhart becomes first woman to fly the Atlantic (as passenger 18 June). JAL formed in Japan (30 Oct.).

1929 Formation of LOT in Poland (1 Jan.). First scheduled passenger flight from London to India (6 April). First stowaway on transatlantic flight (journalist Arthur Shreiber, 14 June). *Graf Zeppelin* completes first circumnavigation of the globe (29 Aug.). Schneider Trophy retained by Britain, Flying Officer H R D Waghorn in Supermarine S-6B (7 Sept.). Testing of first wireless guidance system for aircraft (1 Oct.). R101 unveiled at Cardington (2 Oct.). First flight of R100 from Howden (16 Nov.).

1930 Whittle applies for patent for his turbojet (16 Jan.). Jack Northrop flies experimental 'Flying Wing', with tail boom (1 May). Ellen Church, a registered nurse from Iowa, became the first air hostess (15 May). Amy Johnson makes first

TRANSPORT AIRCRAFT

solo flight to Australia by a woman (24 May). Formation of TWA (16 July). Death of Glen Curtiss (23 July). R101 receives Certificate of Airworthiness (2 Oct.). R101 crashes and explodes at Beauvais, France, on way to India (5 Oct.). First demonstration of Handley Page HP42 (17 Nov.).

1931 Iraqi airforce makes inaugural flight (8 April). Wiley Post makes flight around Northern Hemisphere in Lockheed Vega *Winnie Mae* (1 July). 400 mph barrier broken by Flt Lt George Stainforth in Supermarine SGB (29 Sept.). USS *Akron* aircraft carrier airship commissioned (2 Nov.).

1932 Asian mainland attacked from the air for the first time by Japanese bombers (26 Feb.). Aeroflot formed in Moscow (25 March). Amy Johnson and Jim Mollison announce their engagement (9 May). Amelia Earhart becomes first woman to fly Atlantic non-stop solo (21 May). Santos-Dumont commits suicide (23 July). First flight of Model 17, Beech Aircraft Corporation's first aircraft (4 Nov.).

1933 Maiden flight of Boeing 247 (8 Feb.). Formation of Indian airforce (1 April). French Armée de l'Air created (1 April). First flight over Everest (Westland PV3 piloted by marquis of Douglas and Westland Wallace piloted by David McIntyre (3 April). USS *Akron* crashes into the Atlantic off New Jersey; 70 killed (5 April). USS *Macon* (*Akron*'s replacement) commissioned (23 June). First flight of Douglas DC-1 (1 July). Air France inaugurated (31 Oct.).

1934 Deutsche Luft Hansa becomes Lufthansa (1 Jan.). First flight of Boeing P-26 (10 Jan.). DC-2 goes into service with TWA (11 May). De Havilland Comet wins England–Australia air race (24 Oct.).

1935 Amelia Earhart becomes first woman to fly the Pacific alone (12 Jan.). Death of Hugo Junkers (3 Feb.). USS *Macon* crashes into the sea off California (12 Feb.). Goering named as chief of the new Luftwaffe (10 March). First flight of Messerschmitt BF 109 (28 March). Swissair begins regular scheduled service to London (1 April). First flight of privately funded Bristol 142 (Blenheim) (12 April). Successful radar experiment in Suffolk (24 July). First flight of Boeing 299 (Flying Fortress) (28 July). Deaths of Wiley Post and Will Rogers in Alaskan air crash (15 Aug.). First flight of Hurricane (6 Nov.). Charles Kingsford Smith disappears over Indian Ocean (9 Nov.). First air traffic control centre opens in US (1 Dec.). First flight of Douglas DST (DC-3) (12 Dec.).

1936 Death of Billy Mitchell (19 Feb.). Maiden flight of *Hindenburg* (4 March). Supermarine Spitfire makes first flight piloted by Mutt Summers (5 March). Gatwick Airport officially opened (6 June). First flight of Westlander Lysander (10 June). First flight of Vickers Wellington (by Mutt Summers) (15 June). Formation of RAF Volunteer Reserve (30 July). Death of Blériot (8 Aug.). First Short Empire C-Class flying boat goes into service (30 Oct.). DC-2 crashes at Croydon killing 14 including Juan de la Cierva (9 Dec.).

1937 Saab established (2 April). First trials of

Whittle's turbojet (13 April). Guernica bombed (26 April). *Hindenburg* explodes at Lakehurst; 36 killed (6 May). Death of R J Mitchell (11 June). Amelia Earhart disappears over the Pacific while attempting a round-the-world flight (navigator: Fred Noonan) (2 July).

1938 First in-flight refuelling of an airliner (Short Empire Flying Boat) (20 Jan.). Short-Mayo composite aircraft separates in flight for the first time (6 Feb.). First flight of Bell XP-3A Airacobra, the first US fighter to feature a cannon (6 April). First flight of Douglas DC-4 (7 June). Spitfire goes into RAF service (4 Aug.). Japanese aircraft shoot down a Chinese DC-2 airliner, the first civil airliner to be lost to hostile air attack (24 Aug.). First flight of Westland Whirlwind (11 Oct.). Germany launches its first aircraft carrier, *Graf Zeppelin* (8 Dec.). First flight of Boeing Stratoliner, the first pressurised airliner (31 Dec.).

1939 First flight of XP-38, Lockheed Lightning (27 Jan.). First flight of Mitsubishi Zero (1 April). Chain Home radar system goes online (4 April). First flight of Short Stirling (14 May). First flight of Focke-Wulf FW 190 (1 June). First flight of rocket-powered Heinkel He 176 at Peenemünde (20 June). Formation of Women's Auxiliary Air Force (28 June). First flight of Bristol Beaufighter (17 July). Formation of BOAC from British Airways and Imperial Airways (4 Aug.). First flight of jet aircraft, Heinkel He 178 (23 Aug.). RAF mobilised (1 Sept.). German paratroops make first-ever offensive parachute drop in Poland (3 Sept.). First 'bombing' raid (of leaflets) by RAF against Germany (4 Sept.). First 'kills' by RAF against German bombers (16 Oct.). First German bomber brought down on British soil since 1918 (28 Oct.). First flight of Heinkel He 177 (19 Nov.). First flight of Consolidated XB-24, Liberator (29 Dec.).

1940 First flight of Hawker Typhoon (24 Feb.). Sikorsky VS-300 helicopter makes first free flight (13 May). First flight of North American B-25 Mitchell (19 Aug.). First RAF raid on Berlin (25 Aug.). Caproni-Campini N.I. experimental jet makes first flight (28 Aug.). Battle of Britain Day; entire strength of RAF Fighter Command committed against Luftwaffe attack (15 Sept.). Eagle Squadron of RAF formed by US volunteer pilots at Church Fenton (19 Sept.). First flight of North American NA-73 (P-51 Mustang) (20 Oct.). First major Italian air raid on Britain (11 Nov.). Twenty Fairy Swordfish from HMS *Eagle* and HMS *Illustrious* successfully attack Italian fleet at Taranto (12 Nov.). Coventry bombed (14 Nov.). First flight of DH 98 Mosquito (25 Nov.). First test flight of HS-293A guided bomb (18 Dec.).

1941 Death of Amy Johnson when her Airspeed Oxford crashes in Thames Estuary (5 Jan.). First flight of Avro Lancaster (9 Jan.). First flight of the Heinkel He 280, the world's first multi-jet aircraft (2 April). First flight of Republic P-47 Thunderbolt (6 May). Rudolf Hess parachutes into Scotland from a Messerschmitt Me110 (10 May). First British jet aircraft, a Gloster E-28/39, makes its maiden flight (15

May). Opening of Washington National Airport (16 June). First successful rocket assisted take-off in California (July). Heini Dittmar pilots a Messerschmitt Me 163A Komet at a speed of 623.85 mph (2 Oct.). Japanese attack Pearl Harbor (7 Dec.).

1942 Arthur Harris takes charge of Bomber Command (22 Feb.). First Lancaster mission (3 March). Doolittle raid against Japanese B 25s from USS *Hornet* (21 April). Battle of the Coral Sea (8 May). Battle of Midway (6 June). First flight of Grumman Hellcat (26 June). First flight of Me 262 jet fighter (18 July). First flight of Hawker Tempest (2 Sept.). First flight of B29 Super Fortress (21 Sept.). First flight of Bell XP-59 Airacomet, the first US jet aircraft (1 Oct.). Brabazon Committee (postwar airliners) established (23 Dec.).

1943 First flight of Gloster Meteor, the first British jet fighter (5 March). RAF breaches Mohne and Eder dams using 'bouncing' bomb designed by Barnes Wallis (16 May). Leslie Howard shot down in KLM DC-3 over the Biscay Channel (1 June). First flight of Arado Ar 234, the world's first jet bomber (15 June). *Memphis Belle* becomes first B-17 to complete 25 missions in Europe (19 June). First use by RAF of 'Window', the strips of metal foil dropped to jam radar systems (24 July).

1944 First B29 raid (on Bangkok) (5 June). First V1 hits London (13 June). Marianas Turkey Shoot – Japanese lose 480 aircraft and 3 carriers (20 June). First use of napalm (by Lockheed Lightnings against Coutances, France (17 July). International Civil Aviation conference in Chicago; 52 countries attend. Gives rise to Chicago Convention (1 Nov.–7 Dec.). *Tirpitz* sunk by RAF Lancasters of 617 Squadron (12 Nov.). Glenn Miller disappears in a UC-64 over the English Channel (5 Dec.).

1945 22,000 lb Grand Slam, the heaviest bomb ever dropped, used successfully against the Bielefeld Viaduct (14 March). International Air Transport Association (IATA) formed in Havana (19 April). Atomic bomb tested at Alamogordo (16 July). Atomic bomb 'Little Boy' dropped on Hiroshima by B29 *Enola Gay* (6 Aug.). Atomic bomb 'Fat Man' dropped on Nagasaki by B29 *Bock's Car* (9 Aug.). First flight of turboprop-powered aircraft, a modified Gloster Meteor (20 Sept.). Absolute speed record taken to 606 mph by Gloster Meteor (7 Nov.).

1946 Civil Aviation Act establishes BOAC, BEA and BSAA (British South American Airways), their first commercial departure, made from London Heathrow, a BSAA Lancastrian (1 Jan.). First Pan-Am flight to London from New York (1 June). Air India formed from TATA airlines (29 July). Scandinavian Airline Systems (SAS) formed (31 July). First flight of Convair B-36 (8 Aug.). Aerolinee Italiane Internazionali (Alitalia) established (16 Sept.). Cathay Pacific Airways formed in Hong Kong (24 Sept.). First artificial snowstorm caused by cloud seeding (13 Nov.).

1947 Last DC-3 built by Douglas; it is sold to Sabena but on 2 March 1948 it crashes at Heathrow with loss of 19 lives. First round-the-world air service operated by Pan-Am (12 June).

Kenneth Arnold sees nine aircraft moving 'as a saucer would if you skimmed it over the water' at high speed near Mt Rainier, Washington (24 June). First flight of Boeing Stratocruiser (8 July). Last DC-4 built by Douglas delivered to South African Airways (and still in service) (9 Aug.). USAF established as a separate armed service (18 Sept). Captain Charles Yeager becomes first man to break the sound barrier flying at Mach 1.015 at 42,000′ in Bell X-1 (14 Oct.). BEA makes last scheduled flight from Croydon Airport (1 Nov.). Hughes H-4 Hercules (*Spruce Goose*), the largest aircraft in the world, is flown for the first and only time by Howard Hughes, for one mile (2 Nov.).

1948 Death of Orville Wright (30 Jan.). Thirty killed when a Pan-Am Lockheed Constellation crashes near Shannon (15 April). First action by Israeli airforce (20 May). Start of Operation Vittles – the Berlin Airlift (26 June). Thirty-nine killed at Northolt when an RAF Avro York collides with an SAS DC-6 (4 July). First flight of Vickers Viscount (16 July). Idlewild Airport (now JFK) opens in New York (31 July). John Derry breaks sound barrier in UK in a DH 108 (6 Sept.). El Al comes into being (15 Nov.). Wright Flyer goes on display at the Smithsonian Institute (17 Dec.).

1949 Israeli airforce Messerschmitt 109s shoot down four RAF Spitfires near the Egyptian border (7 Jan.). First non-stop round-the-world flight completed by USAF B-50A *Lucky Lady II* (2 March). First flight of English Electric Canberra (13 May). First flight of De Havilland Comet, the world's first jet airliner (27 July). BOAC absorbs BSAA (30 July). First flight of Bristol Brabazon, largest aircraft ever built in Britain (4 Sept.).

1950 World's worst aircrash: 80 killed when Avro Tudor carrying rugby fans crashes in a field near Cardiff (12 March). First glider crossing of the English Channel (Lorne Welch, 12 April). HMS *Ark Royal* launched (3 May). First North Korean aircraft shot down in Korean war by Twin Mustang (27 June). First helicopter rescue of downed pilot behind enemy lines in Korea (4 Sept.). First flight of Lockheed Super Constellation (13 Oct.). Twenty-eight killed as BEA Viking crashes in fog at Heathrow (31 Oct.). World's first jet-against-jet dogfight, F-80 versus Mig-15, the F-80 being successful (8 Nov.). Bell Model 47 helicopters arrive at MASH units in Korea (1 Dec.).

1951 First non-stop unrefuelled crossing of Atlantic by jet, RAF Canberra (21 Feb.). First flight of Vickers Valiant (18 May). First in-flight refuelling under combat conditions in Korea (6 July). First in-flight sweeping of wings – Bell X-5 research aircraft (16 July). JAL reformed in Tokyo (1 Aug.). First flight of Supermarine Swift (5 Aug.). USAF orders nuclear-powered aircraft from Convair (5 Sept.). First mass movement of troops to battlefront by helicopter, in Korea (21 Sept.). Last DC-6 completed and delivered to Braniff Airways (2 Nov.). First flight of Gloster Javelin (26 Nov.). First interception of aircraft by missile at White Sands, New Mexico (27 Nov.). First turbine-engined helicopter,

Kaman K-225, makes its maiden flight (10 Dec.). First airline flight over North Pole by Alaska Air (12 Dec.).

1952 First flight of Bristol type 173 twin rotor helicopter (3 Jan.). De Havilland Comet 1 gets first certificate of airworthiness for a jet airliner (22 Jan.). First flight of B-52 (15 April). First successful landing of an aircraft at the North Pole (USAF C-47) (3 May). First scheduled passenger jet service: BOAC Comet 1 from London (3 May). BOAC begins a weekly service from London to Colombo with Comet 1 (11 Aug.). First flight of Bristol Britannia (16 Aug.). First flight of Avro Vulcan (30 Aug.). John Derry and 28 spectators killed when his DH110 crashes at Farnborough (6 Sept.). First doubts about Comet safety after take-off accident in Rome (26 Oct.). First flight of Handley Page Victor (24 Dec.).

1953 Lufthansa revived in Germany (6 Jan.). BOAC Comet crashes near Calcutta killing 43 (2 May). First flight of DC-7 (18 May). Dan-Air established (21 May). 129 killed when USAF C-124 Globemaster II crashes on take-off in Japan (18 June). Neville Duke breaks absolute speed record (727.48 mph) in Hawker Hunter (7 Sept.).

1954 First flight of Lockheed Starfighter (7 Jan.). BOAC Comet *Yoke Peter* crashes off Elba, killing 35 (10 Jan.). Last operational flight of a RAF Spitfire (1 April). South African Airways Comet crashes off Stromboli (8 April). Churchill orders the grounding of all Comets (12 April). First flight of Jet Provost (26 June). First flight of Boeing Model 367-80, prototype of the 707 (15 July). First flight of the Rolls Royce Thrust Measuring Rig, 'The Flying Bedstead' (3 Aug.). First flight of Lockheed Hercules (23 Aug.). Court of Inquiry into Comet crashes concludes that metal fatigue is to blame (19 Oct.).

1955 Pakistan International Airlines (PIA) established (10 Jan.). First operational departure from the central complex at Heathrow (17 April). Fifty-eight killed when a Lockheed Constellation of El Al is shot down by Bulgarian Airforce Mig-15s near the Greek border (27 July). First flight of Republic Thunderchief (22 Oct.). Forty-four killed aboard a United Airlines DC-6B after it blows up in mid-air. It is subsequently proven that the explosion was caused by a bomb, planted to perpetrate an insurance fraud. (Arthur Hailey's *Airport* was based on this incident) (1 Nov.). First flight of Fokker Friendship (24 Nov.).

1956 Death of Lord Trenchard (10 Feb.). Peter Twiss flies Fairey Delta 2 at 1,131.76 mph to take official airspeed record (10 March). First flight of Dassault Super Mystère (15 May). 128 killed when a United Airlines DC-3 collides with a TWA Constellation over the Grand Canyon (30 June). First flight of Fiat G-91 (9 Aug.). First human flight over 100,000': Iven Kincheloe in Bell X-2 (125,907') (7 Sept.). Luftwaffe re-established (24 Sept.). First flight of Convair B-58 Hustler (11 Oct.). UK's first atomic bomb dropped in Australia (11 Oct.). Last RAF Lancaster retired (15 Oct.). First aircraft landing at the South Pole: US Navy R4D-5

Skytrain *Que Sera Sera* (31 Oct.). First flight of Dassault Mirage III (17 Nov.).

1957 World's first long-haul airliner, Bristol Britannia, enters service with BOAC (1 Feb.). Death of Richard Byrd (12 March). First flight of Short SC-1 (2 April). UK's first hydrogen bomb dropped near Christmas Island (15 May). First flight of Fairey Rotodyne (6 Nov.). First flight of Boeing 707 (production model) (21 Dec.).

1958 Death of Ernst Heinkel (Jan.). Munich air crash: seven Manchester Utd players killed (6 Feb.). First flight of De Havilland Comet 4 (27 April). First flight of Blackburn Buccaneer (30 April). First flight of McDonnell F-4 Phantom (27 May). First flight of DC-8 (30 May). New Gatwick Airport opens (9 June). First flight of Westland Wessex (20 June). Death of Henri Farman (17 July). NASA created (29 July). Last flying boat operations in UK (Aquila Airways: Southampton to Madeira) (30 Sept.). First jet airliner on Atlantic route (BOAC Comet 4: London–New York–London) (4 Oct.). Last DC-6 built delivered to JAT (Jugoslavian Airlines) (17 Nov.). First production Fokker Friendship delivered to Aer Lingus (29 Nov.).

1959 First flight of A.W. Argosy (8 Jan.). First flight of Convair 880 (27 Jan.). Buddy Holly, Richie Valens and the Big Bopper killed when their Beechcraft Bonanza crashes in Mason City, Iowa (3 Feb.). First flight of Alouette III (28 Feb.). First scheduled passenger flight of Sud-Aviation Caravelle (6 May). Last operational flight of RAF Sunderland (15 May). First flight of X-15 (8 June). First flight of Mirage IV A (17 June). First flight of Northrop F-5 (30 July). Jacqueline Auriol becomes first woman to exceed Mach 2 (in Mirage III) (26 Aug.). Croydon Airport closed (30 Sept.). De Havilland merges with Hawker Siddeley (17 Dec.).

1960 First flight of Grumman A-6 Intruder (19 April). Gary Powers shot down in Lockheed U-2 over Siberia (1 May). Captain Joseph Kittinger free-falls from 102,800' to 17,500', the highest parachute jump ever (16 Aug.). First flight of Hawker P-1127 (prototype of Harrier) (21 Oct.). 132 killed when TWA Super Constellation and United DC-8 collide over New York (16 Dec.).

1961 Seventy-three killed when Sabena 707 crashes in Brussels (15 Feb.). VIASA begins operations in Caracas (1 April). Yuri Gagarin becomes first man in space (12 April). X-15 flown at 3,074 mph and 105,100' by Major Robert White (21 April). Alan Shepherd becomes first US astronaut (5 May). First flight across the Channel by VTOL aircraft, Short SC-1 (27 May). First flight of Aviation Traders ATL-98 Carvair (21 June). Air Congo established (28 June). First flight of Handley Page HP-115 (17 Aug.). Mirage III jet slices through a cable car wire killing six at Chamonix (30 Aug.). Dag Hammarskjöld's DC-6B crashes near Ndola, Northern Rhodesia (18 Sept.).

1962 First flight of Hawker Siddeley Trident (9 Jan.). First use of Agent Orange in defoliant raids in SE Asia (12 Jan.). First US helicopter shot down in Vietnam (4 Feb.). 111 killed when British Caledonian DC-7C crashes at Douala,

Cameroon (4 Mar). First flight of Bristol T-188 (14 April). Death of Sir Frederick Handley Page (21 April). First flight of A-12 (prototype of SR-71 Blackbird) (26 April). 130 killed when Air France 707 crashes at Orly (3 June). Air France 707 crashes in Guadeloupe, killing 113 (21 June). X-15A flies at 4,159 mph (27 June). First flight of Vickers VC-10 (29 June). X-15 goes into space: Major Robert White flies it to 314,750', earning himself 'Astronauts' Wings' (17 July). First flight of HS 125 (13 Aug.). First flight of Aerospace Lines 'Pregnant Guppy' (19 Sept.).

1963   First reference to Anglo-French supersonic airliner as 'Concorde', in speech by De Gaulle (13 Jan.). First flight of Boeing 727 (2 Feb.). BEA introduces first stand-by fares (1 April). Last RAF Mosquitoes retired (8 May). First flight of BAC III (20 Aug.). First flight of HS-748 (21 Dec.). Idlewild Airport renamed John F. Kennedy (24 Dec.).

1964   First flight of Short Belfast (5 Jan.). Death of Maurice Farman (25 Feb.). Jerrie Mock completes first solo aerial circumnavigation by a woman (17 April). VC-10 enters airline service (29 April). First flight of BAC 221 (Concorde research aircraft) (1 May). Actor Roger Moore becomes Air France's 8,000,000th passenger (21 May). First flight of North American XB-70 Valkyrie (21 Sept.). First flight of BAC TSR2 (27 Sept.). First flight of General Dynamics F-111 (21 Dec.). First flight of Lockheed SR-71 (22 Dec.).

1965   First flight of Mirage III V-01 (VTOL aircraft) (12 Feb.). First flight of Douglas DC-9 (25 Feb.). TSR2 cancelled by Wilson government (6 April). Death of Sir Geoffrey De Havilland (26 May).

1966   Four hydrogen bombs fall from a B-52 over southern Spain following a collision with KC-135 tanker; all four are recovered (17 Jan.). Laker Airways launched (8 Feb.). France leaves NATO (7 March). Death of Sir Sydney Camm (12 March). North American XB-70 crashes after colliding with a chase aircraft (8 June). Sheila Scott completes first round-the-world solo flight by a British woman (20 June). X-15 flies at 4,250 mph (Mach 6.33) (18 Nov.).

1967   First flight of Saab 37 Viggen (8 Feb.). Wrecked oil tanker the Torrey Canyon bombed by RAF and Royal Navy aircraft (18 March). First flight of Boeing 737 (9 April). First flight of HS Nimrod (23 May). DC-4 charter plane crashes in the Pyrenees, killing 88 (3 June). British Midland Argonaut crashes at Manchester, killing 72 (4 June). Six-day war begins with Israeli air strikes against Egypt, Syria and Jordan (5 June). X-15 attains its fastest speed, 4,534 mph (Mach 6.72), flown by Major William Knight (3 Oct.). Concorde rolled out at Toulouse (11 Dec.).

1968   Last Handley Page Hastings retires from RAF (5 Jan.). Yuri Gagarin is killed when his Mig-15 crashes near Moscow (27 March). 121 survive crash of BOAC 707 at Heathrow (8 April). Last Avro Anson retires from RAF after 32 years (28 June). First flight of Sepecat Jaguar (8 Sept.). First flight of TU-144 'Concordski' (31 Dec.).

1969   First flight of Boeing 747 (9 Feb.). First flight of Concorde (001 at Toulouse) (2 March). First flight of Concorde (002 in UK) (9 April). RAF Strike Command formed from Bomber and Fighter Command (30 April). Concorde goes supersonic for the first time (1 Oct.). Nigeria Airways VC-10 crashes in the jungle; 87 killed (20 Nov.).

1970   First wide-bodied airliner landing at Heathrow (Boeing 747 of Pan-Am) (12 Jan.). Death of Mikhail Mil (31 Jan.). Death of Lord Hugh Dowding (15 Feb.). Last Dakota retires from RAF service (4 April). Tullamarine Airport in Melbourne opens (1 July). First flight of McDonnell Douglas DC-10 (29 Aug.). Black September blow up TWA 707, Swissair DC-8 and BOAC VC-10 at Dawson's Field, and a Pan-Am 747 at Cairo (12 Sept.). Concorde 002 lands at Heathrow (13 Sept.). Concorde 001 flies at Mach 2 (4 Nov.). First flight of Lockheed Tristar (16 Nov.). Death of Artem Mikoyan (15 Dec.). Airbus Industrie formally established (18 Dec.). Jeanne M Holm becomes first USAF female general (31 Dec.).

1971   Four members of the Red Arrows killed when two Folland Gnats collide at RAF Kemble (20 Jan.). London Air Traffic Control Centre opens at West Drayton (31 Jan.). First flight of Westland Lynx (21 March). Federal Express founded (17 April). Southwest Airlines begin operations (18 June). 162 killed when ANA Boeing 707 collides with a fighter in Japan (30 July). DC-10 enters airline service (5 Aug.). Civil Aviation Authority established in London (5 Aug.). First flight of Shackleton AEW (30 Sept.). BEA Vanguard breaks up over Belgium; 55 killed (2 Oct.). D B Cooper successfully hijacks a Northwest Boeing 727, demands $200,000 and escapes by parachute (24 Nov.).

1972   President Nixon announces that the space shuttle will be developed (5 Jan.). British Airways Board takes over BOAC, BEA and their subsidiaries (1 April). Lockheed Tristar enters airline service (26 April). First fly-by-wire in the USA: Phantom II (29 April). First flight of Fairchild A-10 (10 May). Japanese terrorists kill 25 at Lod Airport (30 May). 118 killed at Staines when BEA Trident crashes after take-off, Britain's worst air disaster until Lockerbie (18 June). First flight of McDonnell Douglas F15 Eagle (27 July). Ilyushin IL-62 crashes in Berlin; 156 killed (14 Aug.). Prince William of Gloucester is killed when his Piper Cherokee crashes during the Goodwood Trophy air race at Wolverhampton (28 Aug.). Death of Igor Sikorsky (26 Oct.). Death of Andrei Tupolev (23 Dec.).

1973   Libyan Airlines 727 shot down by Israeli fighters over Sinai; 74 killed (21 Feb.). TU-144 crashes at the Paris Air Show following mid-air breakup; 14 killed (3 June). 123 die at Orly when a Varig 707 burns after an emergency landing (11 July). Death of Sir Alan Cobham (21 Oct.). First flight of Dassault-Bregeu Dornier Alpha jet (26 Oct.).

1974   First flight of General Dynamics F-16 (2 Feb.). Last Comet in airline service retires (12 Feb.). World's worst air disaster: 346 killed when a

Turkish Airlines DC-10 crashes near Paris (worst until 27 March 1977) (3 March). Airbus A300 enters airline service (23 May). Death of Charles Lindbergh (26 Aug.). First flight of Panavia Tornado (14 Aug.). Fifty-nine killed when Lufthansa 747 crashes in Nairobi, the first ever 747 crash (20 Nov.). First flight of Rockwell B-1 Bomber (23 Dec.).

1975   Death of Air Chief Marshal Sir Keith Park (6 Feb.). Death of Adrienne Bolland (18 March). First flight of DHC Dash 7 (27 March). US helicopters airlift last personnel from embassy roof in Saigon (30 April). First flight of Boeing 747 SP (4 July). Last Lockheed Constellation in airline service retires (16 July). Concorde becomes first aircraft to make four Atlantic crossings in one day (1 Sept.). Graham Hill killed when his aircraft crashes near Elstree (29 Nov.).

1976   First commercial flight of Concorde (Paris–Rio and London–Bahrain) (21 Jan.). Death of Howard Hughes (5 April). Air France and British Airways Concordes land together at Dulles Airport, Washington (24 May). Israeli commandos rescue over 100 passengers from Palestinian terrorists at Entebbe, Uganda (4 July). Viktor Belenko defects to the West in a Mig-25 in Japan (6 Sept.). Worst ever mid-air collision: 176 killed when BA Trident and Yugoslav DC-9 collide over Croatia (10 Sept.).

1977   Death of Sergei Ilyushin (7 Feb.). World's worst ever aircraft disaster: two 747s (KLM and Pan-Am) collide on the ground in Tenerife, 575 killed (27 March). Death of Werner von Braun (16 June). Rockwell B-1 cancelled by President Carter (30 June). First gliding flight of space shuttle *Enterprise* (released from 747) (13 Aug.). Bryan Allen flies *Gossamer Condor*, the first successful man-powered aircraft (23 Aug.). Freddie Laker launches his Skytrain service from London to New York (26 Sept.). GSG 9 successfully storm a hijacked Lufthansa 737 at Mogadishu; 86 saved (17 Oct.).

1978   213 killed when Air India Boeing 747 explodes in mid-air over Bombay (1 Jan.). British Aerospace takes control of British Aircraft Corporation, Hawker Siddeley and Scottish Aviation (1 Jan.). Narita Airport opens in Tokyo amid environmental protests (22 May). First crossing of Atlantic by balloon: *Double Eagle II* (17 Aug.). Death of German aircraft engineer Willy Messerschmitt (15 Sept.). Collision between Pacific Southwest 727 and Cessna in San Diego; 144 killed (25 Sept.). Icelandair DC-8 crashes in Sri Lanka; 202 killed (16 Nov.).

1979   All DC-10 aircraft grounded following crash at Chicago on 25 May which killed 279 (6 June). Bryan Allen flies man-powered aircraft, *Gossamer Albatross*, across the Channel (13 June). Death of Emile Dewoitine (5 July). Death of Sir Barnes Wallis (30 Oct.). 257 killed in Antarctica when Air New Zealand DC-10 crashes near Mt Erebus (29 Nov.).

1980   Air UK formed from British Island Airways and Air Anglia (16 Jan.). Air Zimbabwe created from Air Rhodesia (18 April). Operation Eagle Claw aborted in Iranian desert following collision of CH-53 helicopter with Hercules transport. The operation was intended to free US hostages in Tehran (25 April). HMS *Ark Royal* makes its final voyage, to the breakers yard (22 Sept.). Last commercial flight of Comet 4, a round trip for enthusiasts (9 Nov.).

1981   Last Boeing 707 in Pan-Am service retires (3 Jan.). Death of Donald Douglas (1 Feb.). Death of Jack Northrop (18 Feb.). First flight of Rockwell Space Shuttle *Columbia* (12 April). Israeli airforce bombs Iraqi nuclear reactor at Osirak (7 June). Gulf of Sirte/Sidra incident: two US Navy F-14s shoot down two Libyan SU-22s (19 Aug.). First flight of Boeing 767 (26 Sept.). First flight of Hughes Notar helicopter, i.e. No Tail Rotor (17 Dec.).

1982   Eighty killed when Air Florida 737 crashes into the icy Potomac River in Washington, after wings ice up before take-off (13 Jan.). First flight of Boeing 757 (19 Feb.). First flight of Airbus A310 (3 April). RAF Vulcans take part in the longest bombing runs in history (7,860 miles) from Ascension Island against targets in the Falklands (April–May). Braniff International Airlines files for bankruptcy (13 May). Last Boeing 707 in British Airways service retires (24 May). Last Boeing 707 in Air France service retires (28 Oct.). Last British V-Bomber Squadron disbanded (21 Dec.).

1983   269 killed when a Soviet SU-15 shoots down a Korean Airlines 747 over Sakhalin Island (2 Sept.).

1984   Inaugural flight of Virgin Atlantic Airways (22 June). Last Boeing 727 completed (14 Aug.). First flight of ATR 42 feeder airliner (16 Aug.). First flight of Rockwell B-1B (18 Oct.). First flight of MD-83 (17 Dec.).

1985   TWA 727 hijacked in Rome by AMAL guerrillas; all bar one of the hostages are subsequently released (15 June). 329 killed after an Air India 747 explodes over the Atlantic en route to London (23 June). 520 when JAL 747 crashes into a mountain in Japan (13 Aug). Fifty-four killed at Manchester when a British Airtours 737 catches fire (22 Aug.).

1986   Armed police begin patrolling Heathrow Airport (8 Jan.). *Challenger* disaster: all seven crew are killed when space shuttle explodes shortly after launch (28 Jan.). Terminal 4 opens at Heathrow (12 April). USAF F-IIIs execute air strikes against targets in Libya (15 April). Death of Marcel Bloch (18 April). BA privatised (21 Oct.). Forty-five killed when a BA Chinook ferrying oil workers crashes in the Shetlands (6 Nov.). Dick Rutan and Jeana Yeager fly around the world non-stop and unrefuelled, in specially designed aircraft *Voyager* (23 Dec.).

1987   First flight of Airbus A320 (22 Feb.). Last airworthy Bristol Blenheim crashes at Denham (21 June). BAA privatised (16 July). Richard Branson and Per Lindstrand complete first hot-air balloon crossing of the Atlantic (3 July). BA takes over British Caledonian (16 July). BA takes on first female pilots (31 Oct.). London City Airport opens (5 Nov.).

1988   First ever aircraft registration number retired by FAA, i.e. Amelia Earhart's Lockheed Electra which vanished in July 1937 (8 Feb.). North Terminal opens at Gatwick Airport (18 March). First flight of 'Super-Jumbo' Boeing 747-400 (29 April). Airbus A320 crashes in trees at Mulhouse air show; four killed (26 June). 290 killed when USS Vincennes shoots down Iranian Airbus (3 July). Thirty-three killed at Ramstein when Frecce Tricolori (Italian National Aerobatic Team) aircraft collide above spectators at air show (28 Aug.). Death of Sheila Scott (20 Oct.). F-117A Stealth aircraft formally unveiled by USAF (10 Nov.). Lockerbie disaster: 270 killed after bomb causes Pan-Am Jumbo to crash on houses; worst air disaster in British history (21 Dec.).

1989   Thirty-two killed when British Midland 737 crashes on to the M1 at Kegworth (8 Jan.). First flight of Northrop B-2 Spirit Flying Wing Stealth Bomber (17 July). 107 killed at Sioux City, Iowa, when United Airlines DC-10 crashes on landing (19 July). Death of Alexander Yakovlev (22 Aug.). Bell/Boeing Vertol V-22 Osprey tilt rotor aircraft makes first transition to level flight (14 Sept.).

1990   First flight of Northrop/McDonnell Douglas YF-23 (subsequently dropped in favour of Lockheed YF-22) (27 Aug.). First flight of

Rockwell/MBB X-31A low-speed experimental aircraft (11 Oct.). United Airlines takes over Pan-Am's London routes (23 Oct.). Osaka Airport opens in Japan (9 Nov.).

1991   First Boeing 727 retires after 27 years with United Airlines (13 Jan.). Air Europe, based at Gatwick Airport, ceases to operate (17 Jan.). Operation Desert Storm makes large-scale use of Stealth aircraft for the first time (Jan.). First scheduled United Airlines flight to London (4 April). Boeing finally ends production of 707 after 37 years (1 Sept.). First flight of McDonnell Douglas C-17 (15 Sept.). First flight of Airbus A-340 (25 Oct.). First MD-11 delivered (to Finnair) (29 Nov.). Pan-Am ceases operations (4 Dec.).

1992   TWA announces that it is bankrupt (11 Jan.). Piper declared bankrupt (1 April). Plans for MD-12 (4-engine, 600-seat airliner) announced (30 April). BAA announces plans for Terminal 5 at Heathrow (12 May).

1995   First Boeing 777 begins operations at Heathrow (United Airlines) (July).

2003   Air France announced it is to chop its fleet of Concordes on 31 May while British Airways will close down its fleet of seven Concordes at the end of October.

Airports: UK

Airport	Location	Airport	Location	Airport	Location
Aldergrove	Belfast	(formerly Speke)		Southampton	Hampshire
Baltasound	Unst, Shetlands	Kidlington	Oxford	Stansted	NE London
Barton	Manchester	Kirkwall	Orkneys	Stapleford	Essex
Benbecula	Hebrides	Leeds Bradford	West Yorkshire	Staverton	Gloucestershire
Booker	Wycombe, Bucks	Leuchars	Fife (RAF Station)	Stornoway	Hebrides
				Stronsay	Orkneys
Bournemouth	Dorset	Linley Hill	Beverley	Sumburgh	Shetlands
Brize Norton	Oxford (RAF Station)	Lulsgate	Bristol	Sywell	Northampton
		Manchester	Manchester	Teeside	Cleveland
Brough	East Yorkshire	(formerly Ringway)		Tingwall	Lerwick, Shetlands
City	Belfast	Manston	Kent		
City	London	North Bay	Barra, Hebrides	Tiree	Hebrides
Compton Abbas	Dorset	North Denes	Great Yarmouth	Tresco	Scillies
Conington	Peterborough	North Ronaldsay	Orkneys	Turnhouse	Edinburgh
Coventry	West Midlands	Papa Westray	Orkneys	Unst	Shetlands
Dalcross	Inverness	Port Ellen	Islay, Hebrides	Walney Island	Barrow, Cumbria
Dyce	Aberdeen	Prestwick	Ayrshire		
East Midlands	Derbyshire	Rhoose	Cardiff	West Freugh	Dumfries
Eday	Orkneys	Roborough	Plymouth	West Midlands	Birmingham
Eglinton	Londonderry	Ronaldsway	Isle of Man	Westray	Orkneys
Exeter	Devon	St Angelo	Enniskillen, Fermanagh	Whalsay	Shetlands
Fair Isle	Shetlands			Wick	Caithness
Flotta	Orkneys	St Just	Land's End	Wickenby	Lincolnshire
Gatwick	West Sussex	St Mary's	Scilly Isles	Woodford	Greater Manchester
Glasgow	Glasgow	Sanday	Orkneys		
Glenegedale	Islay	Sandown	Isle of Wight	Woodvale	Merseyside (RAF Station)
Goodwood	Chichester	Scatsa	Shetlands		
Grimsetter	Orkney	Scone	Perth	Yeovilton	Somerset (private airfield)
Hatfield	Hertfordshire	Shoreham	East Sussex		
Heathrow	London	Sibson	Peterborough		
John Lennon	Liverpool	Silverstone	Northants		

TRANSPORT AIRCRAFT

Airlines

Name	Country	Name	Country	Name	Country
ACES	Colombia	**Delta Airlines**	USA	**Norontair**	Canada
Aer Lingus	Ireland	**DETA**	Mozambique	**Northwest Airlines**	USA
Aeroflot	Russia	**Dragonair**	Hong Kong	**Olympic**	Greece
Aerolineas	Argentina	**Eastern Airlines**	USA	**Pan-Am**	USA
Air Littoral	France	**El Al**	Israel	**PIA**	Pakistan
Air UK	UK (Stansted)	**Flitestar**	South Africa	**Qantas**	Australia
Alia	Jordan	**Frontie Airlines**	USA	**Republic Airlines**	USA
Alitalia	Italy	**Garuda**	Indonesia	**RyanAir**	Ireland
American Airlines	USA	**Gronlandsfly**	Greenland	**Sabena**	Belgium
ANA	All Nippon Airways	**Iberia**	Spain	**Sansa**	Costa Rica
Augusta Airways	Australia	**Interflug**	East Germany	**SAS**	Denmark, Norway, Sweden
Avianca	Colombia	**JAL**	Japanese Airlines		
Bell-Air	New Zealand	**JAT**	Yugoslavia	**TAP**	Portugal
Britannia	UK (Luton)	**KLM**	Netherlands	**THY**	Turkey
British Airways	UK	**Kyrnair**	Corsica	**Tower Air**	USA
Cathay Pacific	Hong Kong	**Ladeco**	Chile	**Transavia Airlines**	Netherlands
Continental Airlines	USA	**LAP**	Paraguay	**Transworld Airlines**	USA
		Linjeflyg	Sweden	**United Airlines**	USA
CP Air	Canada	**LOT**	Poland	**Varig**	Brazil
Crossair	Switzerland	**Lufthansa**	Germany	**VIASA**	Venezuela
CSA	Czech Republic	**Malev**	Hungary	**Virgin**	UK (Gatwick)
		NFD	Germany	**Western Airlines**	USA

Airport Codes

Code	Airport	Location	Code	Airport	Location	Code	Airport	Location
ABD	Abadan	Iran	**BKO**	Bamako	Mali	**DUS**	Düsseldorf	Germany
ABJ	Abidjan	Ivory Coast	**BLZ**	Blantyre	Malawi	**DXB**	Dubai	UAE
ABS	Abu Simnel	Egypt	**BRN**	Berne	Switzerland	**DYU**	Dushanbe	Tadzhikstan
ABZ	Aberdeen	Scotland	**BSL**	Basle	Switzerland	**EGC**	Bergerac	France
ACE	Arecife	Lanzarote	**BTZ**	Bursa	Turkey	**EVN**	Yerevan	Armenia
ACI	Alderney	Channel Islands	**BUH**	Bucharest	Romania	**EWR**	Newark, NJ	USA
ACK	Nantucket, MA	USA	**BXO**	Bissau	Guinea-Bissau	**EYW**	Key West	Florida
ACT	Waco, Texas	USA				**FAO**	Faro	Portugal
ADD	Addis Ababa	Ethiopia	**BZV**	Brazzaville	Congo	**FBU**	Fornebu	Oslo
AGP	Malaga	Spain	**CAJ**	Cairo	Egypt	**FCO**	Fiumicino	Rome
AKL	Auckland	New Zealand	**CCS**	Caracas	Venezuela	**FIE**	Fair Isle	Scotland
			CCU	Calcutta	India	**FIH**	Kinshasa	Dem Rep. of Congo
ALC	Alicante	Spain	**CDG**	Charles de Gaulle	Paris			
ALH	Albany, WA	Australia	**CER**	Cherbourg	France	**FNA**	Freetown	Sierra Leone
ALP	Aleppo	Syria	**CFN**	Donegal	Eire			
ALY	Alexandria	Egypt	**CFR**	Caen	France	**FNC**	Funchal	Madeira Islands
AMA	Amarillo, Texas	USA	**CFU**	Kerkyra	Greece	**FNI**	Nîmes	France
ANR	Antwerp	Belgium	**CHC**	Christchurch	New Zealand	**FRA**	Frankfurt	Germany
ASD	Andros	Bahamas				**GBE**	Gaborone	Botswana
AUH	Abu Dhabi	UAE	**CMN**	Casablanca	Morocco	**GCI**	Guernsey	UK
BBQ	Barbuda	Leeward Isles	**CPT**	Cape Town	South Africa	**GNB**	Grenoble	France
			CXI	Christmas Island	Kiribati	**GOA**	Genoa	Italy
BEB	Benbecula	Scotland				**GOH**	Nuuk (Godthaab)	Greenland
BEY	Beirut	Lebanon	**DCA**	Washington	USA			
BFS	Belfast	N. Ireland	**DLH**	Duluth	Minnesota	**GOI**	Goa	India
BGO	Bergen	Norway	**DOL**	Deauville	France	**GPS**	Galapagos Isles	Ecuador
BHX	Birmingham	England	**DTM**	Dortmund	Germany			
BJL	Bangui	Gambia	**DUD**	Dunhedin	New Zealand	**HAJ**	Hanover	Germany
BKK	Bangkok	Thailand				**HBA**	Hobart	Tasmania

Code	Airport	Location	Code	Airport	Location	Code	Airport	Location
HDO	Hyderabad	Pakistan	LHR	Heathrow	London	ORD	O'Hare	Chicago
HFA	Haifa	Israel	LIG	Limoges	France	ORK	Cork	Eire
HKT	Phuket	Thailand	LTN	Luton	Bedfordshire	ORN	Oran	Algeria
HLZ	Hamilton	New Zealand	LUN	Lusaka	Zambia	PAP	Port au Prince	Haiti
			LWK	Lerwick	Shetlands	PFO	Paphos	Cyprus
HND	Haneda	Tokyo	LXR	Luxor	Egypt	PGF	Perpignan	France
HYD	Hyderabad	India	MAA	Madras	India	PID	Paradise Island	Bahamas
IAD	Dulles International	Washington	MBJ	Montego Bay	Jamaica	PMO	Palermo	Italy
			MCM	Monte Carlo	Monaco	PNQ	Poona	India
IBZ	Ibiza	Spain	MDL	Mandalay	Burma (Myanmar)	PPG	Pago Pago	American Samoa
IEV	Kiev	Ukraine						
IOM	Isle of Man	UK	MEB	Melbourne	Australia	PRJ	Capri	Italy
IOR	Inishmore	Eire	MFN	Milford Sound	New Zealand	PRY	Pretoria	South Africa
IPC	Easter Island	Chile				RBA	Rabat	Morocco
JDH	Jodhpur	India	MLH	Mulhouse	France	REK	Reykjavik	Iceland
JFK	John F. Kennedy	New York	MMA	Malmö	Sweden	RUH	Riyadh	Saudi Arabia
			MME	Teesside	England			
JNU	Juneau	Alaska	MOW	Moscow	Russia	SEL	Seoul	South Korea
JRS	Jerusalem	Israel	MPM	Maputu	Mozambique	SNN	Shannon	Eire
KEF	Keflavik	Iceland	MRS	Marseille	France	SPK	Sapporo	Japan
KEL	Kiel	Germany	MXL	Mexicali	Mexico	STR	Stuttgart	Germany
KHI	Karachi	Pakistan	NBO	Nairobi	Kenya	THR	Tehran	Iran
KLU	Klagenfurt	Austria	NCE	Nice	France	TIA	Tirana	Albania
KRK	Krakow	Poland	NCL	Newcastle	England	URO	Rouen	France
KTP	Kingston	Jamaica	NDY	Sanday	Scotland	VRN	Verona	Italy
KTW	Katowice	Poland	NQY	Newquay	England	WAW	Warsaw	Poland
LAS	McCarran	Las Vegas	NRT	Narita	Tokyo	WLG	Wellington	New Zealand
LAX	Los Angeles	California	NSI	Nsimalen, Yaoundé	Cameroon			
LCA	Larnaca	Cyprus				YXY	Whitehorse	Canada
LEH	Le Havre	France	NTE	Nantes	France	YYC	Calgary	Canada
LFW	Lomé	Togo	NTY	Sun City	South Africa	YZF	Yellowknife	Canada
LGW	Gatwick	London	ODE	Odense	Denmark	ZAZ	Zaragosa	Spain
LHE	Lahore	Pakistan	OPO	Oporto	Portugal	ZRH	Zurich	Switzerland

NB The airport codes above are a small-cross section of the thousands of abbreviations used internationally. Most of the codes represent the location of the airport but others denote the name.

Airports: International

Name	Location	Name	Location	Name	Location
Abadan	Iran	Baneasa	Bucharest	Butmir	Sarajevo
Adana	Turkey	Barajas	Madrid	Byrd Field	Richmond, Virginia
Agno	Lugano, Switzerland	Basle-Mulhouse (Euro Airport)	Basle, Switzerland	Cairns	Queensland
Albany County	New York	Beira	Mozambique	Calabar	Nigeria
Alexander Hamilton	St Croix, W. Indies	Ben Gurion	Tel Aviv	Cancun	Mexico
		Benina	Benghazi, Libya	Cannon	Reno, Nevada
Alfonso Bonilla Aragon	Cali, Colombia	Benito Juarez	Mexico City	Canton	Akron, Ohio
		Bierset	Liège, Belgium	Capodichino	Naples
Amborovy	Majunga, Madagascar	Bilund	Denmark	Cardiff	Rhoose
		Blackburne/ Plymouth	Montserrat	Carrasco	Montevideo
Amilcar Cabral	Cape Verde			Cebu	Philippines
Aminu	Kano, Nigeria	Blagnac	Toulouse	Changi	Singapore
Arlanda	Stockholm	Bole	Addis Ababa	Charleroi	Belgium
Arnos Vale	St Vincent	Bonriki	Kiribati	Charles de Gaulle	Paris
Arrecife	Lanzarote	Boukhalef	Tangier, Morocco		
Arturo Marino Benitez	Santiago, Chile	Bourgas	Bulgaria	Charlotte	North Carolina
		Bradley	Hartford, Connecticut	Chek Lap Kok	Hong Kong (New)
Atuona	Hiva Oa, French Polynesia	Brnik	Ljubljana	Chiang Kai Shek	Taipei, Taiwan
Augusto Co Sandino	Managua, Nicaragua	Bromma	Stockholm	Ciampino	Rome
Balice	Kracow, Poland	Bulawayo	Zimbabwe	Cointrin	Geneva

Name	Location	Name	Location	Name	Location
Collinstown	Dublin	Haneda	Tokyo		(Gothenburg)
Congonhas	São Paulo, Brazil	Hartsfield	Atlanta, Georgia		Sweden
Coolidge	Antigua	Hato	Curaçao	Larnaca	Cyprus
Costa Smeralda	Olbia, Sardinia	Hellenikon	Athens	Las Americas	Dominican
Cotonou	Benin	Henderson Field	Honiara,		Republic
Cristoforo	Genoa		Solomon Isles	Las Palmas	Gran Canaria
Colombo		Heraklion	Crete	Le Bourget	Paris
Crown Point	Scarborough,	Hewanorra	St Lucia	Le Lamentin	Martinique
	Tobago	Hongqiao	Shanghai	Leonardo da	Rome
Cuscatlan	El Salvador	Hopkins	Cleveland, Ohio	Vinci (Fiumicino)	
Dalaman	Turkey	Indira Gandhi	New Delhi	Le Raizet	Guadeloupe
Deurne	Antwerp	Inezgane	Agadir, Morocco	Les Angades	Oujda, Morocco
D F Malan	Cape Town	Isla Verde	San Juan,	Lesquin	Lille, France
Domodedovo	Moscow		Puerto Rico	Lester B	Toronto
Dorval	Montreal	Ivanka	Bratislava	Pearson	
Douala	Cameroon	Ivato	Antananarivo,	Linate	Milan
Dulles	Washington		Madagascar	Lindbergh	San Diego,
Dum Dum	Calcutta	Izmir	Turkey		California
Eagle Farm	Brisbane	Jackson Field	Port Moresby,	Logan	Boston,
Ecterdingen	Stuttgart		PNG		Massachusetts
Eduardo Gomes	Manaus, Brazil	James M Cox	Dayton, Ohio	Long Beach	California
El Alto	La Paz, Bolivia	J F Kennedy	La Paz	Loshitsa	Minsk,
El Dorado	Bogotá, Colombia	John F Kennedy	New York		Byelorussia
Elat	Israel	John Foster	Washington DC	Louis Botha	Durban
Elmas	Cagliari	Dulles		Lourdes/Tarbes	Juillan, France
Eppley Airfield	Omaha,	John Wayne	Los Angeles,	Lubbock	Texas
	Nebraska		California	Lungi	Freetown, Sierra
Esenboga	Ankara	Jorge Chavez	Lima, Peru		Leone
Ezeiza	Buenos Aires	Jose Martí	Havana, Cuba	Lupepau'u	Tonga
Faaa	Tahiti	Kai Tak	Hong Kong (old)	Luqa	Malta
Faleolo	Apia, Samoa	Kamazu	Lilongwe, Malawi	Mactan	Cebu,
F D Roosevelt	St Eustatius,	Kastrup	Copenhagen,		Philippines
	W. Indies		Denmark	Mahon	Menorca
Ferihegy	Budapest	Katunayake	Colombo, Sri	Mais Gate	Haiti
Findel	Luxembourg		Lanka	Malpensa	Milan
Fiumicino		Keflavik	Reykjavik,	Marco Polo	Venice
(Leonardo da	Rome		Iceland	Mariscal Sucre	Quito, Ecuador
Vinci)		Kent County	Grand Rapids,	Marsh Harbour	Abaco Island,
Flamingo Field	Bonaire		Michigan		Bahamas
Flesland	Bergen, Norway	Kerkyra	Corfu	Matsapha	Manzini,
Fontanarossa	Catania, Sicily	Khoramaksar	Aden		Swaziland
Fornebu	Oslo	Khwaja Rawash	Kabul,	Maturin	Venezuela
Fort Myers	Florida		Afghanistan	Maxglan	Salzburg, Austria
Fort Worth	Dallas, Texas	Kimpo	Seoul, South	Maya Maya	Brazzaville,
Freeport	Bahamas		Korea		Congo
Fua'amotu	Tonga	King Khaled	Riyadh, Saudi	McCarran	Las Vegas
Fuenterrabia	San Sebastián		Arabia	McCoy	Orlando, Florida
Fuerteventura	Canary Islands	Kingsford Smith	Sydney, Australia	McNary Field	Salem, Oregon
Fuhlsbüttel	Hamburg	Kitsap	Washington,	Meenambakkam	Madras, India
Galileo Galilei	Pisa		USA	Mehrabad	Tehran, Iran
G'Bessia	Conakry	Klagenfurt	Austria	Melita	Djerba, Tunisia
General Manuel		Kloten	Zurich	Melsbroek	Brussels
Marquez de	Mexico	Kota Kinabulu	Sabah, Malaysia	Melville Hall	Dominica
Leon		Kotoka	Accra, Ghana	Menara	Marrakesh,
General Mitchell	Milwaukee	Kranebitten	Innsbruck		Morocco
Gillot	Réunion	Kuching	Sarawak,	Mercedita	Puerto Rico
G. Marconi	Bologna		Malaysia	Midway	Chicago
Golden Rock	St Kitts	Kungsangen	Norrköping,	Ministro Pistarini	Buenos Aires
Grantley Adams	Barbados		Sweden	Mirabel	Montreal
Hahaya	Moroni, Comoros	La Aurora	Guatemala	Monroe County	Rochester, NY
Halim	Djakarta	La Coruña	Spain	Morelos	Mexico
Perdanakusama		La Guardia	New York	Münster/	
Hanan	Niue	La Mesa	San Pedro Sula,	Osnabrück	Germany
Hancock Field	Syracuse, NY		Honduras	Murtala	Lagos,
		Landvetter	Göteborg,	Muhammed	Nigeria

Name	Location	Name	Location	Name	Location
Nadi	Fiji	Punta Raisi	Palermo, Sicily	St Thomas	Virgin Islands
Naha	Okinawa (Japan)	Queen Alia	Jordan	Sturup	Malmö, Sweden
Narita	Tokyo	Ras Al Khaimah	United Arab	Subang	Malaysia
Narssarsuaq	Greenland		Emirates	Sunan	North Korea
N'Djili	Kinshasa, Congo	Rebiechowo	Gdansk, Poland	Sylmet	Dhaka,
	Democratic	Reina Beatrix	Aruba		Bangladesh
	Republic	Reina Sofia	Tenerife	Tacoma	Seattle
Nejrab	Aleppo, Syria	Riem	Munich	Tamatve	Madagascar
Newark	New York	Robert Mueller	Austin, Texas	Tarbes (Lourdes)	Juillan, France
Newcastle	Nevis Island	Roberts	Monrovia, Liberia	Tegal	Berlin
Ninoy Aquino	Manila,	Rochambau	French Guiana	Tempelhof	Berlin
	Philippines	Ruzyne	Prague	Thalerhof	Graz, Austria
Nis	Yugoslavia	Sainte Foy	Quebec	Theodore	
Norman Manley	Kingston,	Sale	Rabat, Morocco	Francis Green	Rhode Island
	Jamaica	Salgado Filho	Brazil	Timehri	Georgetown,
North Front	Gibraltar	Salote Pilolevu	Tonga		Guyana
Nouadhibou	Mauritania	Sangster	Montego Bay,	Toncontin	Tegucigalpa,
Oakland	California		Jamaica		Honduras
O'Hare	Chicago	San Pablo	Seville	Tontouta	New Caledonia
Okecie	Warsaw	Santa Caterina	Funchal, Madeira	Torslanda	Göteborg
Olaya Herrera	Medellín,	Santa Cruz	Bombay		(Gothenburg)
	Colombia	Santa Isabel	Malabo, Guinea	Totegegie	Gambier Island
Oran	Algeria	Santos Dumont	Rio	Townsville	Australia
Orebro	Sweden	Schipol	Amsterdam	Treasure Cay	Abaco Island,
Orly	Paris	Schwechat	Vienna		Bahamas
Osaka	Japan	Seeb	Oman	Tribhuyan	Nepal
Osnabrück	Germany	Seewoosagur	Mauritius	Trivandrum	India
(Münster)		Ramgoolam		Truax Field	Wisconsin
Osvaldo Vieira	Guinea Bissau	Senou	Mali	Tullamarine	Melbourne
Otopeni	Bucharest	Sfax	Tunisia	Turku	Finland
Owen Roberts	Grand Cayman	Sharjah	United Arab	Ulemiste	Estonia
Paphos	Cyprus		Emirates	Unokovo	Moscow
Paradisi	Rhodes	Sheremetyevo	Moscow	Uplands	Ottawa
Patenga	Bangladesh	Silvio Pettirossi	Paraguay	V.C. Bird	Antigua
Patrick Henry	Norfolk, Virginia	Simon Bolivar	Ecuador	Vagar	Faeroe Islands
Pearson	Toronto	Simon Bolivar	Caracas,	Vantaa	Helsinki
Pekoa	Vanuatu		Venezuela	Vigie	St Lucia
Peretola	Florence	Sir Seretse		Viracopos	São Paulo, Brazil
Peshawar	Pakistan	Khama	Botswana	Wall Blake	Anguilla
Peterson Field	Colorado	Skanes	Morocco	Washington	Baltimore,
Piarco	Trinidad	Sky Harbour	Phoenix, Arizona		Maryland
Pochentong	Cambodia	Snilow	Ukraine	Wattay	Laos
Point Noire	Congo	Sola	Stavanger,	West End	Bahamas
Point Salines	Grenada		Norway	Wichita	Kansas
Polonia	Indonesia	Sondica	Bilbao	Will Rogers	Oklahoma
Port Bouet	Ivory Coast	Søndre		William B	Atlanta,
Port Harcourt	Nigeria	Srømfjord	Greenland	Hartsfield	Georgia
Portland	Maine	Spilve	Latvia	William P Hobby	Houston, Texas
Princess Beatriz	Aruba	Spokane	Washington	Yoff	Senegal
Provence	Marseille	Standiford Field	Louisville,	Yundam	Gambia
Pula	Yugoslavia		Kentucky	Zaventem	Brussels
Pulkovo	St Petersburg	Stapleton	Denver,	Zia	Bangladesh
			Colorado		

TRANSPORT AIRCRAFT

Transport: Cars

Makes and Models

AC Cars Ace, Aceca, Cobra Sportster

Alfa Romeo GTV, 156, Spider

Aston Martin DB5, DB7 (David Brown), V8

Audi A3, 80, Cabriolet, Quattro

Austin A90, Healey, Maestro, Metro

Bentley Arnage Mulsanne, Brooklands, Continental T

BMW 528i, M3, 328i, Z3

Cadillac Allante, Evoq, Fleetwood, La Salle

Citroën Berlingo, Dyane, Mehari, Saxo 2CV, VTS, Xantia, Xsara

Daewoo (Korea) Cielo, Espero, Lanos, Leganza, Matiz, Nexia, Nubira

Daihatsu (Japan) Applause, Cuore, Move

Dodge Charger, Coronet, Power Wagon, Viper

Ferrari Berlinetta, F355, Maranello, 360 Modena, 360 Spider, Testarossa

Fiat Barchetta, Brava, Bravo, Cinquecento, Doblo, Ducato, Fiorino, Marea, Multipla, Punto, Scudo, Seicento, Spider, Stilo, Tempra, Tipo, Ulysse, Uno

Ford Aerostar, Anglia, Aspire, Bronco, Capri, Contour, Cortina, Cougar, Edsel, Escort, Explorer, Fiesta, Focus, Galaxy, Granada, Ka, Maverick, Model T, Mondeo, Mustang, Pinto, Probe, Ranger, Sapphire, Scorpio, Taurus, Torino, Thunderbird, Victoria

Honda Accord, Aerodeck, Civic, CR-V, J-VX, Legend, Odyssey, Passport, Prelude

Hyundai (Korea) Accent, Avatar, Elantra, Santa Fe, Sonata, Tiburon

Jaguar E-Type, S-Type, XJ12, XK120, XK8

Lada Niva, Riva, Samara

Landrover Defender, Discovery, Freelander

Lincoln Blackwood, Navigator

Lotus Elan, Elise, Esprit, Exige

Maserati Ghibil

Mercedes C180, CLK, Malaya, Necar 3, SLK Roadster, Vision SLR

Mitsubishi Diamante, Eclipse, Mirage, Montero, Salent, Shogun

Nissan Almira, Frontier, Maxima, Micra, Pathfinder, Patrol, Primera, Quest, QX, Serena, Skyline, 300 ZX, Tirano

Peugeot Boxer, 406, Partner, 205

Porsche Boxster, Carrera, 911, 924, Varrera minivan

Proton Perdana, Persona, Satria

Renault Clio, Espace, Extra, Fuego, Kangoo, Laguna, Master, Mégane Alizé, Mégane Scenic, Safranes, Spider, Trafic, Twingo

Rolls Royce Camargue, Corniche, Phantom, Silver Cloud, Silver Dawn, Silver Ghost, Silver Seraph, Silver Shadow, Silver Spirit, Silver Wraith

Rover Ascot, 800, Relax, 200

Saab Carlsson, Sonett

Seat Alhambra, Arosa, Malaga, Marbella

Skoda Felicia

Subaru Justy, Legacy, Loyale

Suzuki Alto, Baleno, Capuccino, Swift, Vitaras

Toyota Avalon, Camry Solara, Celica, Corolla, Highlander, Lexus, Prius, RAV4, Sequoia, Sienna, Supra, Tacoma, Tercel, Tundra

TVR Cerbera, Chimaera

Vauxhall Astra SRi, Belmont SRi, Calibra, Carlton, Cavalier (became Vectra), Chevette, Corsa, Frontera, Monterrey, Nova, Omega, Senator, Tigra Bermuda, Vectra

Vauxhall (van) Arena, Astravan, Brava, Combo, Corsavan

Volkswagen Beetle, Cabrio, Cabriolet, Corrado, Fox, Golf GTi, Jetta, Passat, Polo, Scirocco, Sharan, Thing, Vento

Volvo C70, 850, 340, S60, S80, V40, V70

Yugo 55A GL

Motorways

M1	London to Leeds	M32	Bristol to M4	M66	Manchester to Rochdale
M2	Rochester to Faversham	M40	London to Birmingham	M67	Hyde Bypass
M3	Sunbury to Southampton	M41	London to West Cross	M69	Coventry to Leicester
M4	London to Swansea	M42	Bromsgrove to Measham	M73	Glasgow
M5	Birmingham to Exeter	M45	M1 to A45 (Coventry)	M74	Glasgow to Lesmahagow
M6	Rugby to Carlisle	M50	Ross to Tewkesbury	M77	Ayr
M8	Edinburgh to Erskine Bridge	M53	Chester to Birkenhead	M80	Stepps Bypass
M9	Edinburgh to Dunblane	M54	M6 to Telford	M90	Dunfermline to Perth, Bonnybridge to Kincardine Bridge
M10	M1 to St Albans	M55	Preston to Blackpool		
M11	London to Cambridge	M56	Manchester to Queensferry	M180	M18 to Humber Bridge
M18	Rotherham to Goole	M57	Liverpool outer ring road		
M20	Swanley to Folkestone	M58	Liverpool to Wigan		
M23	Hooley (Surrey) to Crawley (Sussex)	M61	Manchester to Preston		
		M62	Liverpool to Hull		
M25	London Orbital	M63	Manchester south ring road		
M26	Sevenoaks to Tonbridge				
M27	Southampton Bypass	M65	Calder Valley from M6		

NB The first UK motorway was the Preston Bypass in 1958, now part of the M6.

International Registration Plates

A	Austria	ETH	Ethiopia	MA	Morocco	RSM	San Marino
AFG	Afghanistan	F	France	MAL	Malaysia	RU	Burundi
AL	Albania	FJI	Fiji	MC	Monaco	RWA	Rwanda
AND	Andorra	FL	Liechtenstein	MEX	Mexico	S	Sweden
AUS	Australia	FR	Faeroe	MS	Mauritius	SD	Swaziland
B	Belgium		Islands	MW	Malawi	SF	Finland
BD	Bangladesh	GB	United	N	Norway	SGP	Singapore
BDS	Barbados		Kingdom	NA	Netherlands	SME	Surinam
BG	Bulgaria	GBA	Alderney		Antilles	SN	Senegal
BH	Belize	GBG	Guernsey	NIC	Nicaragua	SWA	Namibia
BR	Brazil	GBJ	Jersey	NL	Netherlands	SY	Seychelles
BRN	Bahrain	GBM	Isle of Man	NZ	New Zealand	SYR	Syria
BRU	Brunei	GBY	Malta	P	Portugal	T	Thailand
BS	Bahamas	GBZ	Gibraltar	PA	Panama	TG	Togo
BUR	Burma	GCA	Guatemala	PAK	Pakistan	TN	Tunisia
	(Myanmar)	GH	Ghana	PE	Peru	TR	Turkey
C	Cuba	GR	Greece	PL	Poland	TT	Trinidad and
CDN	Canada	GUY	Guyana	PNG	Papua New		Tobago
CH	Switzerland	H	Hungary		Guinea	USA	USA
CI	Ivory Coast	HK	Hong Kong	PY	Paraguay	V	Vatican City
CL	Sri Lanka	HKJ	Jordan	RA	Argentina	VN	Vietnam
CO	Colombia	I	Italy	RB	Botswana	WAG	Gambia
CR	Costa Rica	IL	Israel	RC	Taiwan	WAL	Sierra Leone
CS	Czech Republic	IND	India	RCA	Central	WAN	Nigeria
CY	Cyprus	IR	Iran		African Rep.	WD	Dominica
D	Germany	IRL	Ireland	RCB	Congo	WG	Grenada
DK	Denmark	IRQ	Iraq	RCH	Chile	WL	St Lucia
DOM	Dominican	IS	Iceland	RH	Haiti	WS	Western
	Republic	J	Japan	RI	Indonesia		Samoa
DY	Benin	JA	Jamaica	RIM	Mauritania	WV	St Vincent and
DZ	Algeria	K	Cambodia	RL	Lebanon		Grenadines
E	Spain	KWT	Kuwait	RM	Madagascar	YU	Yugoslavia
EAK	Kenya	L	Luxembourg	RMM	Mali	YV	Venezuela
EAT	Tanzania	LAO	Laos	RN	Niger	Z	Zambia
EAZ	Zanzibar	LAR	Libya	RO	Romania	ZA	South Africa
EC	Ecuador	LB	Liberia	ROK	Korea	ZRE	Dem. Rep. of
ES	El Salvador	LS	Lesotho	ROU	Uruguay		Congo
ET	Egypt	M	Malta	RP	Philippines	ZW	Zimbabwe

Vehicle Number Plates

A new registration mark system was introduced on 1 September 2001. The new plates will comprise seven characters: the first two letters to denote the registered office; the next two a numeric age identifier; the final three letters a random element to differentiate vehicles. The age identifier will be subject to change every six months. The tables are reproduced below and the example given by the DVLA is as follows: BD51 SMR where BD indicates the vehicle was registered in the Birmingham office and the 51 indicates a registration date between Sept 2001 and Feb 2002. The typeface was also standardised from 1 September 2001 and only regular block capitals are now allowable.

Letter	Region	Local Offices	DVLA Local Office Identifier
A	Anglia	Peterborough	AA AB AC AD AE AF AG AH AJ AK AL AM AN
		Norwich	AO AP AR AS AT AU
		Ipswich	AV AW AX AY
B	Birmingham	Birmingham	BA – BY
C	Cymru	Cardiff	CA CB CC CD CE CF CG CH CJ CK CL CM CN CO
		Swansea	CP CR CS CT CU CV
		Bangor	CW CX CY
D	Deeside to Shrewsbury	Chester	DA DB DC DD DE DF DG DH DJ DK
		Shrewsbury	DL DM DN DO DP DR DS DT DU DV DW DX DY
E	Essex	Chelmsford	EA – EY
F	Forest & Fens	Nottingham	FA FB FC FD FE FF FG FH FJ FK FL FM FN FP

TRANSPORT CARS

		Lincoln	FR FS FT FV FW FX FY
G	Garden of England	Maidstone	GA GB GC GD GE GF GG GH GJ GK GL GM GN GO
		Brighton	GP GR GS GT GU GV GW GX GY
H	Hampshire & Dorset	Bournemouth	HA HB HC HD HE HF HG HH HJ
		Portsmouth	HK HL HM HN HO HP HR HS HT HU HV HW HX HY
			(HW will be used exclusively for Isle of Wight residents)
K		Luton	KA KB KC KD KE KF KG KH KJ KK KL
		Northampton	KM KN KO KP KR KS KT KU KV KW KX KY
L	London	Wimbledon	LA LB LC LD LE LF LG LH LJ
		Stanmore	LK LL LM LN LO LP LR LS LT
M	Manchester & Merseyside	Manchester	MA – MY
N	North	Newcastle	NA NB NC ND NE NG NH NJ NK NL NM NN NO
		Stockton	NP NR NS NT NU NV NW NX NY
O	Oxford	Oxford	OA – OY
P	Preston	Preston	PA PB PC PD PE PF PG PH PJ PK PL PM PN PO PP PR PS PT
		Carlisle	PU PV PW PX PY
R	Reading	Reading	RA – RY
S	Scotland	Glasgow	SA SB SC SD SE SF SG SH SJ
		Edinburgh	SK SL SM SN SO
		Dundee	SP SR SS ST
		Aberdeen	SU SV SW
		Inverness	SX SY
V	Severn Valley	Worcester	VA – VY
W	West of England	Exeter	WA WB WC WD WE WF WG WH WJ
		Truro	WK WL
		Bristol	WM WN WO WP WR WS WT WU WV WW WX WY
Y	Yorkshire	Leeds	YA YB YC YD YE YF YG YH YJ YK
		Sheffield	YL YM YN YO YP YR YS YT YU
		Beverley	YV YW YX YY

Age Identifiers

Code	Date	Code	Date
		51	Sept 2001 – Feb 2002
O2	March 2002 – Aug 2002	52	Sept 2002 – Feb 2003
O3	March 2003 – Aug 2003	53	Sept 2003 – Feb 2004
O4	March 2004 – Aug 2004	54	Sept 2004 – Feb 2005
O5	March 2005 – Aug 2005	55	Sept 2005 – Feb 2006
O6	March 2006 – Aug 2006	56	Sept 2006 – Feb 2007
O7	March 2007 – Aug 2007	57	Sept 2007 – Feb 2008
O8	March 2008 – Aug 2008	58	Sept 2008 – Feb 2009
O9	March 2009 – Aug 2009	59	Sept 2009 – Feb 2010
10	March 2010 – Aug 2010	60	Sept 2010 – Feb 2011
11	March 2011 – Aug 2011	61	Sept 2011 – Feb 2012

General Information

Automobile Association founded in 1905; originally formed to warn members of police patrols.

Breathalyser introduced in 1967 by Minister of Transport, Barbara Castle.

car founders and designers: Fiat – Agnelli family; Jaguar – William Lyons; Lotus – Colin Chapman.

driving test initiated in 1935 and L-plates issued in the same year.

Mini introduced in 1959 and designed by Alex Issigonis.

MoT (Ministry of Transport) testing established in 1960 and compulsory for vehicles over three years old.

number plates first issued in 1903, the first being A1 to Lord Russell.

parking meters first seen in the UK in 1958, the same year that London saw its first traffic wardens.

petrol pumps were first used in 1919 in the UK.

Route 66 runs from Chicago (Illinois) to Los Angeles (California).

Royal Automobile Club founded in 1897, the second largest motoring organisation after the AA.

veteran cars are those built up to the end of 1918; contrast Vintage cars, 1919–30.

Famous Ships – Miscellaneous

Aaron Manby   first iron steamship, launched in 1822.

Achille Lauro   formerly *Willem Ruys*, Italian cruise ship dogged by disaster. Collided with a fishing boat 1971, one crew member killed; fire broke out on board 1981, two passengers killed; hijacked between Alexandria and Port Said by the PLO Oct. 1985, one passenger murdered; gutted by fire and sank in the Indian Ocean Nov. 1994, two passengers killed.

Amoco Cadiz   super-tanker that ran aground off the coast of Brittany (March 1978) spilling 220,000 tons of crude oil.

Ancon   first ship through the Panama Canal.

Andrea Doria   Italian ship which collided with a Swedish ship and sank (1956).

Archimedes   first large sea-going steamship driven by a screw-propeller, it weighed 237 tons (Nov. 1838).

Argonaut   first submarine to navigate extensively in the open sea. Built in 1897 by the US engineer and naval architect Simon Lake, it was fitted with wheels for travel on the bottom of the sea. In 1898 the *Argonaut* travelled from Norfolk, Virginia, to New York, through heavy storms, proving the seaworthiness of this type of submarine construction.

Black Pig   vessel captained by Captain Pugwash in the children's series.

Braer   oil tanker that ran aground off the Shetlands (Jan. 1993) spilling 85,000 tons of crude oil.

Britannia   launched in April 1953, the Royal Yacht *Britannia* was finally laid to rest in December 1997.

Britannic   sister ship of the *Titanic*, sank after hitting a mine in 1916 in the Aegean while employed as a hospital ship.

Californian   Leyland liner, accused of ignoring *Titanic*'s distress calls but subsequently found to have no radio operator on duty.

Canberra   P&O cruise ship, affectionately nicknamed 'The Great White Whale'; entered service 1961; served as a hospital ship in the Falklands 1982; last cruise 1997.

Carnival Destiny   largest passenger ship in history: 893' long, 116' wide, gross registered tonnage 101,353 tons and too wide to go through Panama Canal.

Carpathia   ship that came to the rescue of the *Titanic* when it sank.

Charlotte Dundas   first commercially successful paddle-steamer launched in Scotland, 1802, by William Symington for Lord Dundas.

Charlotte Rhodes   James Onedin's ship in the TV series *The Onedin Line*.

Christina   Aristotle Onassis' yacht named after his daughter.

Cutty Sark   famous tea and wool clipper built in 1869, the name deriving from the witch in Burns's *Tam O'Shanter*. It has been on display at Greenwich since 1957.

Don Juan   boat in which Percy Bysshe Shelley was drowned in 1822.

Dona Paz   Philippine ferry that collided with the tanker *Vector* in the Sibuyan Sea, 20 December 1987. In the subsequent fire both ships sank and a total of 4,386 people lost their lives, only 24 surviving from the *Dona Paz* and two from the *Vector*. The worst-ever peacetime maritime disaster.

Elise   first steamboat to cross the English Channel (1816).

ENZA   New Zealand catamaran with eight-man crew led by Peter Blake and Robin Knox-Johnston which won the Jules Verne Trophy for sailing non-stop round the world in a record time of 74 days 22 hrs 17 mins, returning on 1 April 1994.

Estonia   Swedish-owned ferry that sank in the Baltic in September 1994 when the bow doors broke open, costing 852 lives.

Exxon Valdez   super-tanker that ran aground off Alaskan coast (March 1989) spilling 12,000,000 gallons of crude oil.

Forfarshire   steamer wrecked off the Farne Islands in 1838, Grace Darling famously helping in the rescue.

Francis Smith   first British steamboat fitted with screw-propellers and built by Francis Pettit Smith, a farmer from Hendon (1836). It was 25' long and weighed 5 tons.

Grand Princess   the P&O liner is currently being built in Fincantieri, Italy, and is expected to be 951' long with a gross registered tonnage of 109,000 tons exceeding the *Carnival Destiny* as the largest-ever passenger ship.

Great Britain   built by Isambard Kingdom Brunel (1843), it was the first iron-hulled screw-propeller steamship. Since being towed from the Falklands in 1970, where it had been scuttled in 1937, it has been on display in Bristol.

Great Eastern   built by Isambard Kingdom Brunel (1858). At 666' long, it was the world's largest ship until 1899. In 1866, it laid the transatlantic cable. Sold for scrap in 1888.

Great Western   built by Isambard Kingdom Brunel (1838), it was the first wooden steamship to make regular transatlantic crossings.

Gypsy Moth IV   Francis Chichester became the first Englishman to sail single-handed round the world in this yacht (1966/7). Now on display at Greenwich.

Happy Giant   formerly named the *Seawise Giant* and with a deadweight tonnage of 564,763 tons, this was the largest ship afloat, but after extensive damage in the Gulf in Dec. 1987 and May 1988 has been refitted and reduced to 420,000 tons.

Helias Fos   this steam-turbine oil tanker is the current largest ship afloat at a deadweight tonnage of 550,051 tons.

Herald of Free Enterprise   Townsend Thoresen-owned cross-Channel ferry which capsized near the Belgian port of Zeebrugge due to the bow doors being insecure (6 March 1987); 193 lives were lost as a result.

Hispaniola   fictional ship in Robert Louis Stevenson's *Treasure Island*, skippered by Captain Smollet and owned by Squire Trelawney.

Lady Ghislaine   yacht owned by Robert Maxwell and named after his daughter, from which he went overboard and drowned (Nov. 1991).

Lake Champlain   first British liner with ship's radio (1901), it communicated with the SS *Lucania* mid-Atlantic.

Lenin first nuclear-powered ship. This Soviet naval ice-breaker was launched in 1957.

Little Juliana first steamboat fitted with screw-propellers (May 1804).

Lively Lady yacht in which Alec Rose sailed single-handed round the world, returning to Portsmouth after nearly a year (4 July 1968).

Lusitania Cunard liner sunk by German torpedo off the Irish coast (7 May 1915) with the loss of about 1,200 lives. This was a major factor in the USA's entry into the First World War.

Maiden British yacht with all-female crew skippered by Tracy Edwards; won its class in Whitbread Round the World Race (1989).

Marchioness Thames pleasure steamer rammed and sunk by the dredger *Bowbelle* at Southwark (August 1989); 51 lives were lost.

Mary Celeste US brigantine under command of Ben Briggs, found in Atlantic (1872) with no sign of crew or struggle; cargo was secure.

Mauretania sister ship of the *Lusitania*, built in 1907.

Mayflower carried the 102 Pilgrim Fathers from Plymouth to Cape Cod, Massachusetts (1620), to found the first New England colony. Oceanus Hopkins was born on board the *Mayflower*.

Morning Cloud yacht owned and captained by Edward Heath.

Nautilus Captain Nemo's submarine in Jules Verne's novel *20,000 Leagues Under the Sea*.

Normandie passenger liner destroyed by fire in New York harbour in 1941.

Norway longest passenger liner ever built (formerly called *France*): overall length 1035′ 2″.

Olympic sister ship of the *Titanic*.

Pequod whaling ship captained by Captain Ahab and destroyed by Moby Dick in Melville's novel.

Pyroscaphe first practical steamboat. Built near Lyon in 1783, it was a 138′-long paddle steamer and weighed 182 tons.

Queen Anne's Revenge Edward Teach's (Blackbeard) ship captured in the Caribbean in 1717 and used for piracy until Jan. 1718.

Queen Elizabeth built in 1938, the *Queen Elizabeth* (Seawise University) was destroyed in Hong Kong Harbour in Jan. 1972.

QEII built in 1968, it is the largest passenger liner in service between Southampton and New York.

Queen Mary now a floating hotel in Long Beach, California, it was built in 1936 and was the flagship of the Cunard line.

Rainbow Warrior Greenpeace ship which was sunk in Auckland Harbour in July 1985 by French intelligence agents, killing one member of the crew.

Rising Star first ship to cross the Atlantic from east to west (1821/2).

Savannah first steamship to cross the Atlantic (1819).

Savannah first commercially successful nuclear-powered ship, launched 1959.

Sea Empress oil tanker which ran aground off Milford Haven (Feb. 1996) spilling 72,000 tons of crude oil.

Speedwell sister ship of the *Mayflower* which left Southampton for New England but was forced into harbour at Plymouth, Devon.

Suhaili yacht in which Robin Knox-Johnston became first man to circumnavigate the world non-stop and single-handed; he returned in April 1969.

Talitha G motor yacht owned by John Paul Getty.

Thomas W Lawson US schooner; the only seven-masted sailing vessel on record. Designed by Bowdoin B Crowninshield and built by the Fore River Ship and Engine Building Co in 1902 for Coastwise Transportation Co. The seven masts were Fore, Main, Mizzen, Number 4, Number 5, Number 6 and Spanker.

Titanic White Star's unsinkable flagship which hit an iceberg on its maiden voyage on the night of 14 April 1912 and capsized in the early hours of 15 April with the loss of 1,513 lives. Wreck was found in 1985.

Torrey Canyon ran aground off Land's End (March 1967) spilling its cargo of 100,000 tons of crude oil.

Turbinia built and demonstrated by Charles Parsons at Spithead (1897), it was the first ship to use turbine engines.

Victoria and Albert name given to three royal yachts; the first was a paddle-steamer of 1843; the last was built in 1899 and used until replaced by *Britannia*.

Famous Ships – Naval

Agamemnon 64-gun ship launched in 1781, commanded by Nelson from 1793 and his favourite ship. Abandoned in 1809 when it ran aground at Maldonado Bay.

Amethyst frigate which in July 1949 escaped under cover of night along the flooded Yangtze.

Arethusa launched 1849; last Royal Navy ship to go into action entirely under sail, at Sebastopol in 1855. From 1874 to 1933 it was a training ship at Greenhithe.

Argus first aircraft carrier, completed in 1918.

Arizona said to be the first US battleship sunk at Pearl Harbor on 7 Dec. 1941.

Ark Royal many ships have had the name but the most famous were probably the flagship of the British Fleet against the Spanish Armada (1588), although it was only the nickname, the aircraft carrier sunk by an Italian torpedo in November 1941, and the present aircraft carrier which is the Royal

Navy's largest fighting ship.

Association flagship of Sir Cloudesley Shovell, wrecked off the Scilly Isles in 1707 with all hands lost.

Belfast Europe's largest surviving WW2 warship, displacing 11,500 tons. Commissioned 1939, paid off 1971. The cruiser is now on display on the Thames.

Bellerophon Napoleon Bonaparte surrendered to the British aboard this ship (15 July 1815) after the Battle of Waterloo.

Birmingham US light cruiser from which Eugène Ely took off in a 50 hp Curtiss pusher biplane (10 Nov. 1910) while it was at anchor in Chesapeake Bay, so making it the first ship with a temporary flight-deck.

Bismarck German battleship sunk in the North Atlantic after it had sunk the British battle cruiser HMS *Hood* (May 1941).

Bonhomme Richard John Paul Jones's 40-gun

warship, blown in two off Flamborough Head in 1779.

Bounty ship that while carrying breadfruit trees from Tahiti was the scene of a mutiny (28 April 1789) by Fletcher Christian (settled on Pitcairn Island). Captain William Bligh and 18 crew were set adrift in the Pacific.

Captain experimental British turret ship of 1870 designed by Captain Cowper Coles; sank in the Bay of Biscay shortly after commissioning with the loss of 472 lives.

Constitution American ship of the line, launched 1798. Nicknamed 'Old Ironsides'; on display in Boston.

Coventry sister ship of the *Sheffield* and also sunk by an Argentinian Exocet missile during the Falklands War.

Devastation launched 1871; first British capital ship which did not require sails.

Dreadnought British battleship launched 1906 which revolutionised naval warfare in the early decades of the 20th century.

Dreadnought Britain's first nuclear submarine, launched in 1960.

Elizabeth Bonaventure Drake's flagship in the raid on Cadiz in 1587.

Enterprise first nuclear-powered aircraft carrier.

Excellent home to the naval gunnery school established in 1830; since 1891, a shore base on Whale Island, Portsmouth.

Ganges last British ship of the line; launched 1821, paid off 1861. From 1866 a training ship. Name passed to a shore base near Ipswich in 1905; closed 1976.

General Belgrano Argentine cruiser sunk by the British submarine *Conqueror* during Falklands War (2 May 1982).

Graf Spee German pocket battleship scuttled by her captain off Montevideo Harbour after being harried across the River Plate by the cruisers, *Ajax*, *Achilles* and *Exeter* (Dec. 1939).

Henry, Grâce de Dieu Henry VIII's flagship, built 1514 and carried 186 guns.

Hermes aircraft carrier, last of the old-style carriers operated by the Royal Navy, which was flagship during the Falklands War.

Invincible the second aircraft carrier that was sent to the Falklands after the Argentine invasion (2 April 1982).

Lightning first purpose-built torpedo boat (1877).

Long Beach first nuclear warship, launched in Quincy, Massachusetts (14 July 1959).

Maine American armoured cruiser of 1886; blew up in Havana 1898, resulting in the Spanish-American War.

Mary Rose Henry VIII's favourite ship, launched 1509, sank 1545 but was raised in 1982 and is still being restored at Portsmouth.

Merrimack steam frigate scuttled in Norfolk harbour by Union forces, then raised by the Confederates, converted to an ironclad and renamed *Virginia*; fought a draw with the *Monitor* in Hampton Roads in 1862 and destroyed by her own captain shortly afterwards.

Missouri Japanese surrender terms were signed aboard this ship in Tokyo Bay (2 Sept. 1945).

Monarch First British turret-gunned ship, launched 1868.

Monitor US iron-hulled warship with single gun turret, fought *Merrimack* in Hampton Roads 1862; capsized in a gale shortly after.

Nautilus world's first nuclear-powered submarine, launched by the USA in 1954. The name derived from an early submarine designed by Robert Fulton for Napoleon (1800).

Northumberland third-rate ship of the line which took Napoleon Bonaparte to St Helena in 1815.

PT 109 John F Kennedy's torpedo boat during World War II.

Revenge Drake's ship used during the attack by the Spanish Armada (1588). In 1591, captained by Sir Richard Grenville, fought a fifteen-hour battle single-handedly against 53 Spanish ships off Flores.

Royal George 100-gun ship of 1756; carried Hawke's flag at Quiberon Bay in 1759; capsized at Spithead in 1782 with loss of 900 lives.

Royal Oak British battleship sunk at Scapa Flow (Orkneys) by a German torpedo (Oct. 1939) with the loss of 833 lives.

Scharnhorst German battlecruiser which escaped from Brest with the *Gneisenau* and *Prinz Eugen* (Feb. 1942) but was sunk at the Battle of North Cape (Dec. 1943).

Sheffield British destroyer hit by an Exocet missile on 4 May 1982 with the loss of 20 lives.

Squirrel Sir Humphrey Gilbert's ship used during the attack by the Spanish Armada (1588).

Temeraire 98-gun ship launched in 1798; fought at Trafalgar; broken up on the Thames 1838 and immortalised on canvas by Turner.

Tiger the ship used by Harold Wilson and Ian Smith during their UDI discussions (1966).

Tirpitz German battleship sunk by RAF bombers in April 1944.

Trincomalee built 1817, renamed *Foudroyant* in 1892 and a training ship in Portsmouth Harbour until 1987 when she was towed to Hartlepool for restoration and given back her original name.

Vanguard iron-hulled frigate accidentally rammed and sunk by her sister ship *Iron Duke* in 1875.

Vanguard Britain's largest battleship. Decommissioned 1960 and ran aground on leaving Portsmouth to be scrapped.

Vasa flagship of Gustavus Adolphus of Sweden. Sank in harbour in 1628; recovered intact from seabed and now on display.

Victoria launched 1859; last wooden battleship built for the Royal Navy. Paid off 1867; name used by British battleship of 1887 which sank off Tripoli in 1893 when flagship of Admiral George Tryon. It was accidentally rammed by *Camperdown*, flagship of Tryon's second-in-command, Alfred Markham.

Victory launched at Chatham 1765, Horatio Nelson's flagship at the battle of Trafalgar (21 Oct. 1805); flagship of C-in-C Portsmouth since 1835. Dry-docked and restored in 1922, the *Victory* is now on display at Portsmouth.

Warrior first iron-hulled battleship (and last surviving); built at Blackwall on the Thames (1859/60). When commissioned in 1861, it made every other naval vessel obsolete. On display in Portsmouth since 1987.

Wilton first plastic warship, launched in Southampton 18 Jan. 1972.

TRANSPORT SHIPS

Famous Ships – Voyages of Exploration

Adventure James Cook's consort ship to the *Resolution* during his Antarctic voyage 1772–5; converted from a Whitby collier.

Arktika first ship to reach the North Pole, in 1977.

Beagle Charles Darwin's ship which surveyed South American islands and in particular Galapagos (1831–6). Darwin was the science officer, the captain was Robert Fitzroy.

Calypso most famous survey ship of Jacques Cousteau.

Challenger Royal Navy survey ship, sailed 79,000 miles from 1872 to 1876, adding greatly to knowledge of the seas. Most recent RN ship of that name also an oceanographic vessel.

Discovery Captain James Cook sought the Northwest Passage in 1776–9 with the *Resolution* and the *Discovery*. He was slain on the beach at Kealakekua, Hawaii, by Polynesian natives (1779).

Discovery Robert Falcon Scott's ship used in his British National Antarctic Expedition of 1901–4 in which he was accompanied by Ernest Shackleton. Now on display in Dundee.

Endeavour James Cook's voyage to Australia and New Zealand (1768–71), on which Joseph Banks was chief scientist, was carried out on this converted collier, originally called *Earl of Pembroke*.

Endurance Ernest Shackleton's ship on his Antarctic voyage of 1914–16; sank in the Weddell Sea but since raised and on display in Dundee.

Erebus one of the two ill-fated ships (the other was the *Terror*) used by Sir John Franklin in his search for the Northwest Passage (1845–6).

Fram Norwegian explorer Fridtjof Nansen's ship used on his Arctic explorations (1893–6). Roald Amundsen sailed in *Fram* (which meant 'Forward') on his successful expedition of 1911–12 to the South Pole.

Gjöa Roald Amundsen's ship in which he sailed the Northwest Passage (1902–6) and found the magnetic North Pole.

Golden Hind ship on which Francis Drake became first Englishman to circumnavigate the globe (1580); originally called *Pelican*.

Grenville the schooner that James Cook commanded while surveying the coast of Newfoundland 1763–68.

Kon Tiki Thor Heyerdahl's single-sailed balsa-wood raft on which he crossed the Pacific (1947).

Matthew John Cabot discovered Newfoundland and Nova Scotia (1497) in this 50-ton ship.

Mazurek carried Krystyna Choynowska-Liskievicz on the first female solo circumnavigation of the globe in 1978.

Morning Supply ship that accompanied the *Discovery* in Scott's Antarctic expedition of 1901–4.

Ernest Shackleton was invalided home on this ship.

Nimrod Ernest Shackleton's ship on the voyage (1907–9) in which he located the magnetic South Pole, and climbed Mt Erebus but only came within 97 miles of the South Pole.

Quest ship on which Ernest Shackleton died during his third Antarctic voyage (Grytviken, South Georgia 1922).

RA II Thor Heyerdahl's papyrus raft on which he crossed the Atlantic (1970).

Resolute one of Edward Belcher's ships sent to seek the missing (and already dead) John Franklin in 1852; abandoned in 1854 after being locked in ice off Melville Island; found 1,000 miles away in Davis Strait in 1855, still perfectly seaworthy.

Resolution James Cook's flagship during his voyage to Antarctica 1772–5. Cook sought the Northwest Passage 1776–9 in this ship.

Roebuck William Dampier's ship on his voyage to Australia and New Guinea (1699–1700).

Santa Maria Christopher Columbus's flagship during his expedition to the New World (1492–3), accompanied by the caravels *Niña* and *Pinta*.

Spray Joshua Slocum's boat in which he circumnavigated the Earth, the first man to do so solo (1895–8).

Terra Nova Captain Robert Falcon Scott's ship used on his ill-fated Antarctic expedition 1910–12.

Terror one of the two ships (the other was *Erebus*) used by Sir John Franklin in his search for the Northwest Passage (1845–6).

Theodore Roosevelt Robert Peary's ship used when he became first person to reach the North Pole (6 April 1909). Peary's former friend, Frederick Cook, was found to have fraudulently reported his own earlier reaching of the Pole.

Tigris Thor Heyerdahl's third raft.

Trieste bathysphere submarine which holds the record for the deepest descent (10,916 m) on 23 Jan. 1960.

Vega first ship to achieve the Northeast Passage, in 1878–9, under Nils Nordenskjöld.

Victoria first ship to circumnavigate the globe (1519–22). Although Ferdinand Magellan set out with five ships (the flagship *Trinidad, San Antonio, Concepción, Santiago* and *Victoria*) four were lost and he himself was killed in the Philippines (1521). The circumnavigation was completed by the Basque seaman Juan Sebastián del Cano.

Viking Norwegian explorer Fridtjof Nansen's first exploratory ship (1888) in which he first sailed to Greenland.

Windward British Arctic explorer Frederick Jackson's ship on which Fridtjof Nansen briefly journeyed back to Norway in Aug. 1896.

Ships – General Information

binnacle the casing in which the ship's compass is kept.

box the compass to name the points of the compass in proper order.

breeches buoy life-saving device run on a rope stretched from a wrecked vessel to a place of safety.

bulwark that part of the sides of a ship which rises above the upper deck.

caïque long, narrow, light rowing skiff used on the Bosporus.

clipper ship: first *Rainbow* (1845).

dahabeah/dahabeeyah houseboat used on the Nile (from Arabic: the Golden One).

dhow single-masted ship with a very long yard and a lateen sail, used on the Arabian sea.

diesel-powered ship: first *Petit-Pierre*.

distress signals SOS – Morse (formerly CQD, Come Quickly Danger); Mayday – vocal distress shout.

extremities of ship front – bow; back – stern; left side looking front – port (formerly larboard); right side looking front – starboard.

felucca small vessel used in the Mediterranean, propelled by oars or lateen sails, or both.

flotsam goods lost in shipwreck and found floating.

gondola long, narrow Venetian boat with peaked ends, propelled by one oar.

gunwale upper edge of a ship's side next to the bulwarks.

hull: plank types clinker-built – built with overlapping planks fastened with clinched nails; carvel-built – having the planks flush at the edges.

hydrofoil invented by Comte de Lambert in 1897 and developed by Enrico Forlanini in 1898.

jetsam goods thrown overboard in order to lighten a ship in distress, and subsequently washed ashore.

junk flat-bottomed vessel with lugsails, used in the Chinese seas.

kayak Inuit and Alaskan canoe, made of sealskins stretched on a light wooden framework.

kitchen or cook-house galley.

knot one nautical mile per hour. The British nautical mile was 6,080 feet but in 1970 the International nautical mile of 1,852 metres was adopted. The measurement was devised by Richard Norwood in 1673.

lighthouses: UK authority Trinity House.

lights starboard – green; port – red; top at night – white.

masts: how many sloop and cutter (1); ketch, brig, brigantine, yawl (2); barque (3 or more); schooner (2 or more).

oldest surviving ships *Khufu I* and *Khufu II*, built *c.* 2600 BC and buried in pits outside the Great Pyramid of Khufu in Egypt. *Khufu I*, first to be excavated after discovery in 1954, is plank-built and 43 metres long.

P&O: meaning Peninsular and Oriental.

pipe down naval colloquialism derived from the boatswain's call of this name, meaning 'Hands turn in', i.e. 'Lights out'.

piping the side traditional ceremony of blowing the boatswain's pipe when royalty arrive or depart from battleship.

plimsoll line maximum loading mark on hull of ship, named after Samuel Plimsoll (1824–98), promoter of the Merchant Shipping Act 1876.

ports: famous Athens – Piraeus; London – Tilbury; Rome – Ostia.

ports: general biggest – New York; busiest – Rotterdam; largest inland – Montreal.

PT Boat: meaning Patrol Torpedo Boat.

Q-ship merchant ship with concealed guns, used to decoy enemy ships into the range of its weapons. Q stood for 'Query'.

rudder: invented by Chinese, 1st century BC.

sails lateen – triangular.

ships: register of Lloyd's.

ship: largest oil tanker *Jahre Viking* at 1,504′ long and weighing over 564,000 tonnes.

steam turbine: inventor Charles Parsons (1897).

V-shaped hull: pioneer Uffa Fox (who instructed HRH Prince Philip, the Duke of Edinburgh, in the finer points of yachting).

Venice: water bus vaporetto.

watches at sea first watch – 8pm to midnight; middle watch – midnight to 4am; morning watch – 4am to 8am; forenoon – 8am to midday; afternoon watch – midday to 4pm; first dog watch – 4pm to 6pm; second dog watch – 6pm to 8pm.

xebec/zebec small three-masted Mediterranean vessel with both square and lateen sails, formerly used by Algerian pirates.

yachts: famous *Talitha G* – John Paul Getty; *Saratoga* – Humphrey Bogart; *Saxara* – Mohamed Al Fayed.

TRANSPORT SHIPS

TRANSPORT: TRAINS

Railway Tunnels: World's Longest

	Span	Built	Railway	Length (mile)
Seikan	Honshu–Hokkaido	1988	Japan Rail	33.5
Channel	Cheriton–Fréthun	1994	BR/French National	30.7
Daishimizu	Jōmō-Kogen–Echigo	1980	Japan Rail	13.9
Simplon No. 2	Brig–Iselle	1922	Swiss Federal	12.4
Simplon No. 1	Brig–Iselle	1906	Swiss Federal	12.3
Shin Kanmon	Honshu–Kyushu	1975	Japan Rail	11.6
Apennine	Florence–Bologna	1934	Italian State	11.5
Rokko	Osaka–Shinkobe	1972	Japan Rail	10.1
Furka Base	Oberwald–Realp	1982	Furks-Oberalp Switzerland	9.6
Haruna	Jōmō-Kogen–Echigo	1982	Japan Rail	9.5
Gotthard	Göschenen–Airolo	1882	Swiss Federal	9.3
Mt Macdonald	Selkirk Mts–British Columbia	1989	CP Rail, Canada	9.1

Longest railway tunnel on the Indian sub-continent is the Kojak Tunnel at Shelabagh, Pakistan (2½ miles). The Lyttelton Tunnel (1.6 miles) was the first railway tunnel in NZ and the only one through an extinct volcano. Longest overland railway tunnel in the UK is the Severn Tunnel.

Railway Bridges: World's Longest

	Location	Opened	Length (ft)
Huey P Long	New Orleans, USA	1935	23,235
Yangtze River	Nanjing, China	1968	22,218
Hell Gate	New York, USA	1917	19,233
Greenwich	London, England	1836	19,000
Orvieto Viaduct	Paglia River	1980	17,634
Savannah River	S. Carolina, USA	1909	13,000
Lower Zambesi	Mozambique	1934	12,064
Venice Viaduct	Italy	1846	11,821
Tay	Scotland	1887	11,653
Storstrom	Denmark	1937	10,537

World's oldest railway bridge is the Tanfield Arch in County Durham, designed by Ralph Wood and built in 1727. World's highest railway bridge, above water, is the Hanging Bridge above the Arkansas River, Colorado, at 1,053′.

London Underground Stations: Name Changes

Current name	Previous name
Acton Town	Mill Hill Park
Arsenal	Gillespie Road
Becontree	Gale Street Halt
Charing Cross	Strand
Debden	Chigwell Road
Embankment	Charing Cross
Euston Square	Gower Street
Fulham Broadway	Walham Green
Green Park	Dover Street
Kensington (Olympia)	Addison Road
Ladbroke Grove	Notting Hill
Marylebone	Great Central
Moor Park	Sandy Lodge
Oakwood	Enfield West
Ravenscourt Park	Shaftesbury Road
South Woodford	George Lane
St Paul's	Post Office
Tooting Bec	Trinity Road
Tower Hill	Mark Lane
West Kensington	North End (Fulham)
White City	Wood Lane
Woodside Park	Torrington Park, Woodside

Rail Companies: Since BR Privatised

Anglia Railway
Cardiff Railway Co.
Central Trains
Chiltern Railway Co.
Connex South Central
Connex South Eastern
Eurostar
Gatwick Express

Island Line
LTS Rail (London, Tilbury South)
Mersey Rail
Midland Mainline
North London Rail
North Western Trains
Regional Railways North East
Scot Rail

South Wales and West
South West Trains
South West Trains (Stagecoach)
Thames
Thameslink
Virgin West
West Anglia Great Northern
West Coast Railway Co.

Railway Stations: Locations

Anhalter	Berlin	**King's Cross**	London	**Saint Lazare**	Paris
Bank Top	Darlington	**Lime Street**	Liverpool	**Shrub Hill**	Worcester
Buchanan Street	Glasgow	**Liverpool Street**	London	**Snow Hill**	Birmingham
Charing Cross	London	**London Rd**	Leicester	**Spa**	Bath
Citadel	Carlisle	**Low Level**	Wolverhampton	**St David's**	Exeter
Connolly	Dublin	**Marine**	Dover	**St Enoch**	Glasgow
Euston	London	**Midland**	Derby	**Temple Meads**	Bristol
Foregate Street	Worcester	**Mumps**	Oldham	**Thorpe**	Norwich
Forster Square	Bradford	**New Street**	Birmingham	**Trent Valley**	Nuneaton
Gare du Nord	Paris	**Paddington**	London	**Union**	Washington
Grand Central	New York	**Paragon**	Hull	**Victoria**	London,
Harbour	Folkestone, Portsmouth	**Parkway**	Bristol		Manchester, Bombay
		Piccadilly	Manchester		
Haymarket	Edinburgh	**Priory**	Dover	**Waterloo**	London
High Level	Wolverhampton	**Queen Street**	Cardiff, Glasgow	**Waverley**	Edinburgh
High Street	Swansea			**Yaroslavl**	Moscow

Railways: General Information

accident: first caused by moving train Rt Hon William Huskisson MP was run down by the *Rocket* at the opening of the Liverpool & Manchester Railway 15 Sept. 1830. He was rushed to Eccles Hospital on the *Northumbrian*. A runaway wagon caused the death of two boys in a Tyne coalpit in 1650. Unfortunately numerous incidents of this kind took place but were not really the work of trains in the accepted sense of the word.

air-brake: designer George Westinghouse (1846–1914) developed the air-brake from the simple non-automatic system of 1866 into the fully automatic (i.e. the brakes are automatically applied should any break in the train air pipe occur). System still in use in most countries. Most British railways used the vacuum brake, which had nothing to do with Westinghouse.

APT BR Advanced Passenger Train ran from London to Glasgow in 3 hrs 52 mins 45 secs at an average speed of 103 mph (12 Dec. 1984). This service was abandoned in 1986 due to numerous problems.

broad-gauge railway: last train the *Cornishman* was the last broad-gauge passenger train to run, on 21 May 1892, from Paddington to Penzance.

Chicago rail system nicknamed the 'El', which is short for elevated (several other cities, notably New York, also had elevated railways known as 'Els').

diesel locomotive: first the first diesel locomotive to go into regular service was a Swedish-built metre-gauge Bo Bo type put into operation by Tunisian Railways in 1921.

dining car: first first buffet cars were put into service on the Philadelphia, Wilmington & Baltimore Railroad in 1863.

electric railway: first Brighton seafront, built by Magnus Volk (1851–1937), still known as Volk's Electric Railway.

electrification of railways modern standard system of railway electrification at 25 kV 50 Hz was first used in France in 1950 and in England on the Colchester– Clacton–Walton lines in 1959.

fare-paying customers: first to carry Oystermouth Railway built a railway from Swansea to Mumbles

and on 25 March 1807 became first to convey fare-paying passengers. This railway closed in 1960.

father of railways George Stephenson.

father of the locomotive Richard Trevithick.

horse-drawn railways Middleton Railway, Leeds, in 1758 was the first to be built under its own Act of Parliament, although other horse-worked railways had been operating in the Tyne coalfield on private land for many years previously.

horse-drawn railways: public the Surrey Iron Railway from Wandsworth to Croydon (opened 26 July 1803) was the first horse-drawn railway opened to the public, inasmuch as it accepted consignments. Passengers were not carried (at least not officially!).

locomotive railway: first Stockton and Darlington, opened in 1825.

locomotive railway: first passenger line Liverpool to Manchester, opened in 1830.

London railway: first Spa Road to Deptford, part of London & Greenwich Railway, opened 8 Feb. 1836.

London Underground: first automatic barrier Stamford Brook.

London Underground: first line Metropolitan Line, from Bishop's Road to Farringdon Street, 10 Jan. 1863.

longest platform in Great Britain Colchester, at 1981′.

Mallard LNER 'A4' Class Pacific No. 4468 *Mallard* reached a speed of just over 126 mph for a few seconds on a brake-test trial run between Grantham and Peterborough (3 July 1938). *Mallard* can be seen at the National Railway Museum, York.

monorail: first Charles Lartique's monorail system was used on a short demonstration line in France and then on the Listowel and Ballybunion Railway in Ireland, 1883. It was not a true monorail but comprised a single rail raised about 4′ above the ground on an A-frame with two guiding rails about 1′ off the ground.

National Railway Museum museum opened in York in 1975 and combining the holdings of the British Transport Commission's museum at Clapham and the LNER museum at York.

nationalisation railways were nationalised from 1 Jan. 1948 and were divided into five regions: 1) Scottish, 2) North Eastern, 3) London Midland, 4) Eastern, 5) Western and Southern. (The Eastern and North Eastern were amalgamated on 1 Jan. 1967.)

platforms: most UK Waterloo main line.

Puffing Billy world's first steam locomotive running on smooth rails instead of the previous rack rails. Designed by William Hedley and first put into operation in 1813 from Wylam colliery in Northumberland to the river Tyne. The *Wylam Dilly* was made at much the same time. Note: Trevithick's Penydarren engine had smooth iron wheels running on smooth cast-iron tram plates!

railcar: designer William Bridges Adams designed the 6-wheeled steam railcar *Fairfield* (named after the road in Bow, London, where he operated from).

railtrack: longest in straight line Nullarbor Plain, Australia.

railway: first private opened in June 1789 by the Loughborough & Nanpanton Railway Co.

railway king George Hudson.

Railways Act 1921 from 1 Jan. 1923 the amalgamation of the railways meant that four major companies were formed: 1) The Great Western Railway, 2) The London, Midland & Scottish Railway, 3) The London and North Eastern Railway, 4) The Southern Railway.

railways: USA operating co. Amtrak.

Rainhill Trials competition held on 6–14 Oct. 1829 near Liverpool to choose the design of locomotive for Liverpool & Manchester Railway. Robert Stephenson's *Rocket* won the £500 prize by beating Timothy Hackworth's *Sans Pareil* and John Braithwaite and John Ericsson's *Novelty*.

RKB code: meaning the code RKB refers to a single item of rolling stock containing a restaurant seating portion, a buffet counter and a kitchen.

San Francisco rail system BART (Bay Area Rapid Transit).

Schools-Class locomotives introduced by Southern Railway in 1930 and named after famous schools, first being called *Eton*.

Scottish railway: first Kilmarnock and Troon Railway was the first 'proper' railway in Scotland. Opened 6 July 1812.

sleeping cars: European wagons lits.

sleeping car: first the *Chambersburg*, introduced by the Cumberland Valley Railroad on its Pennsylvanian Harrisburg–Chambers route, was the first example of a sleeping car (1836).

standard gauge first used on Willington Colliery wagonway near Newcastle upon Tyne in 1764 and set at 4′ 8½″ or 1,435 mm, this being an average of the wagon ways in this area. It is thought that the average gauge of between 4′ 6″ and 4′ 9″ was the width of the track required for two horses abreast.

station: largest Grand Central, New York.

station: largest UK Clapham Junction.

station: most northerly in Great Britain Thurso.

steam locomotive: first Richard Trevithick built the first locomotive and ran it on the Penydarren Railway, near Merthyr Tydfil, on 6 Feb. 1804.

TGV Train à Grande Vitesse (High-Speed Train); began a regular hourly service between Paris and Lyon, the 265-mile journey taking 2 hrs 40 mins.

third-class travel redesignated as second class by British Rail in 1956. (The old second class had largely fallen out of use by the turn of the century.)

timetable: national *Bradshaw's Railway Companion* was the first national railway timetable in 1839.

underground: British four British cities with underground railways: London, Glasgow, Liverpool and Newcastle (Metro).

most passengers Moscow.

most stations New York.

names Berlin – U Bahn; Rome – Metropolitana; Stockholm – T-Bana; Paris – Métro.

USSR: terms for first and second class Soft and Hard class.

wheel configurations: nicknames Atlantic (4-4-2): name originally applied to a batch of 4-4-2s built by Baldwin of Philadelphia for the Atlantic Coast Railroad in 1894. In the UK, Atlantics were in use for hauling express passenger trains on the Great Northern, North Eastern, North British and London, Brighton & South Coast Railways. It should be borne in mind that the term 'Atlantic' properly describes a 4-4-2 locomotive with a separate tender; thus 4-4-2 tank engines, such as were in widespread use in the UK, are not true Atlantics but are more analogous to a 4-4-0 with an additional axle to support a rear bunker. **Mogul (2-6-0):** first true Mogul, with a leading two-wheel Bissell truck, was built by Baldwin of Philadelphia for the Louisville & Nashville Railroad in 1860. In the UK in the twentieth century Moguls were in extensive use on all four of the post-1923 mainline railways, and after 1948, in all regions of British Railways. The term Mogul properly applies to a 2-6-0 with outside cylinders, so that the inside-cylindered 2-6-0s of the Caledonian, and Glasgow and South Western Railways were not true Moguls, being essentially large 0-6-0-s with a leading truck for increased front-end stability. **Pacific (4-6-2):** name seems to have originated because the engines concerned were obviously bigger than Atlantics. In the UK, Pacifics were in general express service on the LNER from the mid-Twenties, the LMS from 1933 and the Southern Railway from 1941. The Great Western Railway had actually built the first UK Pacific (No. 111 *The Great Bear*) in 1908 but found it something of a white elephant. It was scrapped in 1924, and various mechanical components were incorporated in a new 'Castle' class 4-6-0, No. 111 *Viscount Churchill*. **Baltic (4-6-4):** name appears to be of Germanic origin. (To an American, a 4-6-4 is a Hudson.) Only one 4-6-4 tender engine ever ran in the UK. This was Gresley's experimental high-pressure water-tube boiler 4-cylinder compound No. 10000, built for the LNER in 1929. It was rebuilt as a conventional 3-cylinder simple expansion engine and ran until 1959, latterly as British Railways No. 60700. This engine was not a true Baltic, since the rear carrying axles were disposed as a Cartazzi axle and a separate two-wheel radial truck, making the engine technically a 4-6-2-2. Around 1920, however, there was a vogue, particularly on the London Brighton & South Coast, Lancashire & Yorkshire and Glasgow & South Western Railways, for extremely large 4-6-4 tank engines, which, while not true Baltics (*vide supra* under Atlantic), were referred to as Baltics consistently enough to legitimise the usage. **Prairie (2-6-2):** name applied in the American Midwest after first examples were built in 1900 for the Chicago, Burlington & Quincy Railroad. Apart from one curious 8-cylinder experimental engine built as a semi-private venture by Cecil Paget at Derby in 1908, the only 2-6-2 tender engines to run in the UK were Gresley's extremely successful V2-class built from

1936 onwards for the LNER, and his lightweight V4 design of 1941, of which only two examples were built before his death. In the 20th century, several hundred 2-6-2 tank engines were built in the UK, particularly by the Great Western Railway, and, although not true Prairies (being actually Moguls with a rear bunker), they were generally referred to as Prairie tanks. **Consolidation (2-8-0):** name is that carried by the first example of this type, built in 1865 for the Lehigh & Mahanoy Railroad. The name was not much used to describe British 2-8-0s, but it does seem to have attached itself to the 2-8-0 freight locomotives built at Swindon for the Great Western Railway by G J Churchward and his successors. This may be due to Churchward's close following of American locomotive practice resulting in an essentially American designation attaching itself to his engines of the 2-8-0 type. **Mikado (2-8-2):** so named because the first examples were made in the USA for export to Japan. In the UK, the only 2-8-2 tender engines were built by Gresley for the LNER. First, the two heavy freight engines of class P1, built in 1925. These were mechanically a cross between an A1-class Pacific and an O2-class Consolidation. As a small, non-standard class they were both withdrawn in 1945. Second was the magnificent class P2, six examples of which were built 1934–36, for working express passenger trains to Scotland. They were rebuilt as very mediocre Pacifics after Gresley's death. **Decapod:** a curiosity – to an American, a Decapod is a 2-10-0. The only two classes of engines of this type to run in the UK were the 251 examples of the standard-class 9F, built by British Railways between 1954 and 1960, and 25

examples bought secondhand from the Ministry of Supply after WW2. These, however, were never referred to as Decapods (except, presumably, by Americans!). The Decapod, however, was a huge 0-10-0 tank engine built by the Great Eastern Railway in 1903 as part of an experiment in the drastic acceleration of suburban trains. It did everything which was expected of it, but was far too heavy for the track and bridges. It was broken up shortly afterwards and a few components incorporated in a 0-8-0 goods engine. **NB** The following type names are largely in American use only, generally because no locomotives of the type referred to ever ran in the UK. **American (4-4-0):** applies only to the classic outside-cylindered, bar-framed three-point suspension locomotive familiar from countless Western films. **Ten Wheeler (4-6-0):** strictly an American term only. (Casey Jones was driving Illinois Central ten-wheeler No. 382 when he met his death at Vaughan, Mississippi, on 29 April 1900.) **Mastodon (4-8-0):** there were actually two 4-8-0 tender engines on the narrow-gauge Londonderry & Lough Swilly Railway in Ireland. They were used on the desolate Burtonport extension line in north-west Donegal, where I doubt if anyone ever referred to them as Mastodons. **Berkshire (2-8-4):** pronounced 'BurkSHIRE'. **Mountain (4-8-4) Santa Fe (2-10-2):** introduced by the Atchison, Topeka & Santa Fe Railroad in 1903, for working over the Raton Pass. **Texas (2-10-4):** called this in the USA but called 'Selkirk' in Canada.

World's longest railway: Trans-Siberian running from Moscow (Yaroslavl Station) to Vladivostok (5,801 miles); opened 3 Nov. 1901.

UNITED STATES

Presidents

	President		Birthplace	Life span	Party	In office
1	**Washington**	George	Virginia	1732–1799	Federalist	1789–1797
2	**Adams**	John	Massachusetts	1735–1826	Federalist	1797–1801
3	**Jefferson**	Thomas	Virginia	1743–1826	Republican	1801–1809
4	**Madison**	James	Virginia	1751–1836	Republican	1809–1817
5	**Monroe**	James	Virginia	1758–1831	Republican	1817–1825
6	**Adams**	John Quincy	Massachusetts	1767–1848	Republican	1825–1829
7	**Jackson**	Andrew	South Carolina	1767–1845	Democratic	1829–1837
8	**Van Buren**	Martin	New York	1782–1862	Democratic	1837–1841
9	**Harrison**	William Henry	Virginia	1773–1841	Whig	1841
10	**Tyler**	John	Virginia	1790–1862	Whig	1841–1845
11	**Polk**	James Knox	North Carolina	1795–1849	Democratic	1845–1849
12	**Taylor**	Zachary	Virginia	1784–1850	Whig	1849–1850
13	**Fillmore**	Millard	New York	1800–1874	Whig	1850–1853
14	**Pierce**	Franklin	New Hampshire	1804–1869	Democratic	1853–1857
15	**Buchanan**	James	Pennsylvania	1791–1868	Democratic	1857–1861
16	**Lincoln**	Abraham	Kentucky	1809–1865	Republican	1861–1865
17	**Johnson**	Andrew	North Carolina	1808–1875	Union	1865–1869
18	**Grant**	Ulysses Simpson	Ohio	1822–1885	Republican	1869–1877
19	**Hayes**	Rutherford Birchard	Ohio	1822–1893	Republican	1877–1881
20	**Garfield**	James Abram	Ohio	1831–1881	Republican	1881
21	**Arthur**	Chester Alan	Vermont	1830–1886	Republican	1881–1885
22	**Cleveland**	Stephen Grover	New Jersey	1837–1908	Democratic	1885–1889
23	**Harrison**	Benjamin	Ohio	1833–1901	Republican	1889–1893
24	**Cleveland**	Grover	New Jersey	1837–1908	Democratic	1893–1897
25	**Mckinley**	William	Ohio	1843–1901	Republican	1897–1901
26	**Roosevelt**	Theodore	New York	1858–1919	Republican	1901–1909
27	**Taft**	William Howard	Ohio	1857–1930	Republican	1909–1913
28	**Wilson**	Thomas Woodrow	Virginia	1856–1924	Democratic	1913–1921
29	**Harding**	Warren Gamaliel	Ohio	1865–1923	Republican	1921–1923
30	**Coolidge**	Calvin	Vermont	1872–1933	Republican	1923–1929
31	**Hoover**	Herbert Clark	Iowa	1874–1964	Republican	1929–1933
32	**Roosevelt**	Franklin Delano	New York	1882–1945	Democratic	1933–1945
33	**Truman**	Harry S	Missouri	1884–1972	Democratic	1945–1953
34	**Eisenhower**	Dwight David	Texas	1890–1969	Republican	1953–1961
35	**Kennedy**	John Fitzgerald	Massachusetts	1917–1963	Democratic	1961–1963
36	**Johnson**	Lyndon Baines	Texas	1908–1973	Democratic	1963–1969
37	**Nixon**	Richard Milhous	California	1913–1995	Republican	1969–1974
38	**Ford**	Gerald Rudolph	Nebraska	1913–	Republican	1974–1977
39	**Carter**	James Earl	Georgia	1924–	Democratic	1977–1981
40	**Reagan**	Ronald Wilson	Illinois	1911–	Republican	1981–1989
41	**Bush**	George Herbert Walker	Massachusetts	1924–	Republican	1989–1993
42	**Clinton**	William Jefferson	Arkansas	1946–	Democratic	1993–2001
43	**Bush**	George Walker	Connecticut	1946–	Republican	2001–

Vice Presidents

Vice President		Birthplace	In office	Vice President to
Adams	John	Massachusetts	1789–1797	Washington
Jefferson	Thomas	Virginia	1797–1801	Adams
Burr	Aaron	New Jersey	1801–1805	Jefferson
Clinton	George	New York	1805–1812	Jefferson/Madison
Gerry	Elbridge	Massachusetts	1813–1814	Madison
Tompkins	Daniel D	New York	1817–1825	Monroe
Calhoun	John Caldwell	South Carolina	1825–1832	Adams/Jackson
Van Buren	Martin	New York	1833–1837	Jackson
Johnson	Richard Mentor	Kentucky	1837–1841	Van Buren
Tyler	John	Virginia	1841	Harrison
Dallas	George Mifflin	Pennsylvania	1845–1849	Polk
Fillmore	Millard	New York	1849–1850	Taylor
King	William Rufus De Vane	North Carolina	1853	Pierce
Breckinridge	John Cabell	Kentucky	1857–1861	Buchanan
Hamlin	Hannibal	Maine	1861–1865	Lincoln
Johnson	Andrew	North Carolina	1865	Lincoln
Colfax	Schuyler	New York	1869–1873	Grant

Vice President		Birthplace	In office	Vice President to
Wilson	Henry	New Hampshire	1873–1875	Grant
Wheeler	William A	New York	1877–1881	Hayes
Arthur	Chester A	Vermont	1881	Garfield
Hendricks	Thomas A	Ohio	1885	Arthur
Morton	Levi Parsons	Vermont	1889–1893	Harrison
Stevenson	Adlai E	Kentucky	1893–1897	Cleveland
Hobart	Garret A	New Jersey	1897–1899	McKinley
Roosevelt	Theodore	New York	1901	McKinley
Fairbanks	Charles Warren	Ohio	1905–1909	Roosevelt
Sherman	James Schoolcraft	New York	1909–1912	Taft
Marshall	Thomas R	Indiana	1913–1921	Wilson
Coolidge	Calvin	Vermont	1921–1923	Harding
Dawes	Charles Gates	Ohio	1925–1929	Coolidge
Curtis	Charles	Kansas	1929–1933	Hoover
Garner	John Nance	Texas	1933–1941	Roosevelt
Wallace	Henry Agard	Iowa	1941–1945	Roosevelt
Truman	Harry S	Missouri	1945	Roosevelt
Barkley	Alben W	Kentucky	1949–1953	Truman
Nixon	Richard Milhous	California	1953–1961	Eisenhower
Johnson	Lyndon Baines	Texas	1961–1963	Kennedy
Humphrey	Hubert H	South Dakota	1965–1969	Johnson
Agnew	Spiro T	Maryland	1969–1973	Nixon
Ford	Gerald Rudolph	Nebraska	1973–1974	Nixon
Rockefeller	Nelson Aldrich	Maine	1974–1977	Ford
Mondale	Walter F	Minnesota	1977–1981	Carter
Bush	George Herbert Walker	Massachusetts	1981–1989	Reagan
Quayle	J Danforth	Indiana	1989–1993	Bush, G H W
Gore	Albert	Washington DC	1993–2001	Clinton
Cheney	Richard B	Nebraska	2001	Bush, G W

Presidents and Vice Presidents: Miscellaneous Information

assassinated Lincoln, Garfield, McKinley, Kennedy.

attempts Jackson (Richard Lawrence 1835), Truman (Griselio Torresola and Oscar Collazo 1950), Ford (5 Sept 1975, Lynette 'Squeaky' Frome; 22 Sept 1975, Sarah Jane More), Reagan (John Hinckley) 1981.

bachelor James Buchanan.

bald Martin Van Buren and Dwight Eisenhower.

bath: got stuck in William Howard Taft.

born in a log cabin Andrew Jackson

broccoli: hated George Bush.

Camelot: nickname of John F Kennedy's regime.

China: first to visit Richard Nixon.

Clinton's cat: named Socks (belonged to daughter Chelsea).

Confederate states: president Jefferson Davis.

cried on television during campaign Edmund Muskie.

Declaration of Independence: drafted by Thomas Jefferson.

Democrat-turned-Republican: first Ronald Reagan.

Democratic Party Headquarters Tammany Hall, New York.

Democratic Party symbol Donkey.

Democratic split during Vietnam War Hawks and Doves.

died in office W Harding, W Harrison, F D Roosevelt, Z Taylor.

divorced: first Ronald Reagan.

duel: killed opponent in Andrew Jackson killed Charles Dickinson in a pistol duel, 30 May 1806.

elected for four terms F D Roosevelt.

elected unanimously by Electoral College George Washington.

elected with one vote against James Monroe.

ex-director of the CIA George Bush.

father and son John Adams and his son John Quincy Adams.

father was UK ambassador John F Kennedy's father Joseph.

fireside chats: radio broadcasts F D Roosevelt.

four freedoms Speech, worship, freedom from fear and want. Roosevelt's basis for UN Charter, San Francisco 1945.

Fourteen Points Woodrow Wilson.

Garfield: assassinated by Charles Guiteau 1881.

Gettysburg Address Lincoln's speech of 1863.

grandfather and grandson William Harrison and Benjamin Harrison.

Grand Old Party (GOP) Republican party nickname.

Great Triumvirate of statesmen John Calhoun, Henry Clay, Daniel Webster.

hospital: first born in Jimmy Carter.

illegitimate child: accused of having Stephen Grover Cleveland.

impeachment: two In 1868 Andrew Johnson was cleared of breaching Tenure of Office Act. Senate vote fell one short of two-thirds majority. In 1999 Bill Clinton was cleared of high crimes and misdemeanours by the Senate vote on both Articles I and II.

imprisoned by British Andrew Jackson (during War of Independence).

Jefferson: holiday retreat Poplar Row.

Kennedy's attorney general Robert Kennedy, his brother.

Kennedy: assassinated by Lee Harvey Oswald, 1963 (shot by Jack Ruby).

kitchen cabinet Andrew Jackson's unofficial advisers.

knighted by Britain Eisenhower.

Lincoln assassinated by John Wilkes Booth (an actor), 1865. Samuel Mudd jailed for setting Booth's leg. Lincoln died in Peterson House, Washington DC.

longest term F D Roosevelt, 12 years.

male model: former Gerald Ford.

McKinley assassinated by Leon Czolgosz, 1901.

minister to Great Britain: first John Adams.

Monroe Doctrine: allegedly drafted by John Quincy Adams.

Monroe: lived Oak Hill.

New Deal F D Roosevelt's 1930s recovery plan.

newspaper publisher Warren Harding – Marion *Star*.

nicknames J Carter – Hot Shot & Toadsy; G Bush – Wimp; Andrew Jackson – Old Hickory; Clinton – Comeback Kid.

Nobel Peace Prize Theodore Roosevelt, 1906; Woodrow Wilson, 1919.

not elected as President Gerald Ford (was also not elected Vice President).

occupation: most common lawyer.

oldest to take office Ronald Reagan, aged 69.

pneumonia: died of William Henry Harrison.

President for the day David Atchison – Zachary Taylor would not be sworn in on a Sunday.

prison; presidential candidate ran from Eugene Debs in 1912.

Quakers Herbert Hoover, Richard Nixon.

qualifications required native born, 14 years' residence, 35 years old.

re-elected: after losing office Stephen Grover Cleveland.

Republican Party symbol elephant.

residence White House.

resigned Richard Nixon.

resigned as Vice President Spiro Agnew; income tax evasion charge.

Roman Catholic: first John F Kennedy.

Roughriders Roosevelt second in command to Col. Leonard Wood.

Secretary of State Eisenhower's – John Foster Dulles; Nixon's – Henry Kissinger; Carter's – Cyrus Robert Vance.

shirt advertisement: appeared in Ronald Reagan.

shortest term William Henry Harrison, about a month.

slogans: presidential Full Dinner Pail – McKinley; Great Society – Lyndon Johnson; New Deal – F D Roosevelt; New Frontier – Kennedy.

slogans: other 'Would you buy a used car from this man?' – said by anti-Nixon protesters. 'The buck stops here' – Truman. 'No taxation without representation' – during dispute with Britain over taxation.

State of the Union presidential speech given annually in January.

stood against Bush – Michael Dukakis; Clinton – Ross Perot and George Bush; Hayes – Samuel Tilde; Hoover – Al Smith; Truman – Thomas Dewey.

terms limitation two, under the 22nd Amendment to Constitution.

Vice President: born James Colbath Henry Wilson.

    Crédit Mobilier scandal Schuyler Colfax.

    Confederate general John Cabell Breckinridge.

    killed Alexander Hamilton Aaron Burr.

    letters from London George Mifflin Dallas.

    lives at Admiralty Building, Washington.

    Nobel Peace Prize 1925 Charles Dawes.

    treason trial Aaron Burr.

    wrote no. 1 hit single Charles Dawes ('It's all in the Game').

vice-presidential candidate: first female Geraldine Ferraro in 1984.

Virginia plan James Madison.

Washington: lived Mount Vernon.

Watergate scandal burglary of Democratic HQ in Washington on 17 June 1972.

White House: architect James Hoban.

White House: first occupier John Adams.

wives of presidents George Washington – Martha Custis; Abraham Lincoln – Mary Todd; F D Roosevelt – Eleanor Roosevelt; J F Kennedy – Jacqueline Bouvier; Ronald Reagan – Nancy Davis; George Bush – Barbara Pierce; Bill Clinton – Hilary Rodham.

youngest elected president John F Kennedy.

youngest president Theodore Roosevelt (took office following assassination of McKinley).

States

State	Nickname	Motto	State tree	State bird	State flower	State capital	Zip code
Alabama (Ala.)	Cotton Yellowhammer Heart of Dixie	We dare defend our rights	southern pine	yellowhammer	camelia	Montgomery	AL
Alaska (Alas.)	Last Frontier Land of the Midnight Sun	North to the future	Sitka spruce	willow ptarmigan	forget-me-not	Juneau	AK
Arizona (Ariz.)	Grand Canyon Apache	God enriches	paloverde	cactus wren	saguaro cactus blossom	Phoenix	AZ
Arkansas (Ark.)	Land of Opportunity Bear Wonder	The people rule	pine	mockingbird	apple blossom	Little Rock	AR
California (Cal.)	Golden	I have found it	Californian redwood	Californian valley quail	golden poppy	Sacramento	CA
Colorado (Colo.)	Centennial	Nothing without providence	Colorado blue spruce	lark bunting	Rocky Mountain columbine	Denver	CO
Connecticut (Conn.)	Constitution Nutmeg	He who transplanted still sustains	white oak	American robin	mountain laurel	Hartford	CT
District of Columbia	DC	Justice for all	scarlet oak	woodthrush	American beauty rose		
Delaware (Del.)	First Diamond	Liberty and independence	American holly	blue hen chicken	peach blossom	Dover	DE
Florida (Fla.)	Sunshine Peninsular	In God we trust	sabal palm	mockingbird	orange blossom	Tallahassee	FL
Georgia (Ga.)	Empire State of the South Peach	Wisdom, justice and moderation	live oak	brown thrasher	Cherokee rose	Atlanta	GA
Hawaii (Hi.)	Aloha	The life of the land is perpetuated in righteousness	kukui (candlenut)	nene (Hawaiian goose)	hibiscus	Honolulu	HI
Idaho (Ida.)	Gem Gem of the Mountains	Let it be perpetual	western white pine	mountain bluebird	syringa	Boise	ID
Illinois (Ill.)	Prairie Land of Lincoln	State sovereignty – national union	white oak	cardinal	native violet	Springfield	IL
Indiana (Ind.)	Hoosier	Crossroads of America	tulip tree (yellow poplar)	cardinal	peony	Indianapolis	IN
Iowa (Ia.)	Hawkeye Corn	Our liberties we prize and our rights we will maintain	oak	eastern goldfinch	wild rose	Des Moines	IA
Kansas (Kan.)	Sunflower Jayhawker	To the stars through difficulties	cottonwood	western meadowlark	native sunflower	Topeka	KS
Kentucky (Ky.)	Blue Grass	United we stand, divided we fall	tulip tree (yellow poplar)	cardinal	goldenrod	Frankfort	KY

UNITED STATES

State	Nickname	Motto	State tree	State bird	State flower	State capital	Zip code
Louisiana (La.)	Pelican Creole Sugar Bayou	Union, justice and confidence	bald cypress	eastern brown pelican	magnolia	Baton Rouge	LA
Maine (Me.)	Pine Tree	I direct	eastern white pine	chickadee	white pine cone and tassel	Augusta	ME
Maryland (Md.)	Free Old Line	Manly deeds, womanly words	white oak	Baltimore oriole	black-eyed Susan	Annapolis	MD
Massachusetts (Mass.)	Bay Old Colony	By the sword we seek peace, but peace only under liberty	American elm	chickadee	mayflower (trailing arbutus)	Boston	MA
Michigan (Mich.)	Wolverine Water Wonderland	If you seek a pleasant peninsula, look about you	white pine	robin	apple blossom	Lansing	MI
Minnesota (Minn.)	North Star Gopher Land of 10,000 Lakes Land of Sky-Blue Waters	The North Star	red, or Norway pine	loon	pink and white lady's slipper	St Paul	MN
Mississippi (Miss.)	Magnolia	By valor and arms	magnolia	mockingbird	magnolia	Jackson	MS
Missouri (Mo.)	Show Me	The welfare of the people shall be the supreme law	dogwood	bluebird	hawthorn	Jefferson City	MO
Montana (Mont.)	Treasure Big Sky Country	Gold and silver	Ponderosa pine	western meadowlark	bitterroot	Helena	MT
Nebraska (Nebr.)	Cornhusker Beef Tree Planters	Equality before the law	cottonwood	western meadowlark	goldenrod	Lincoln	NB
Nevada (Nev.)	Sagebrush Silver Battle Born	All for our country	single-leaf piñon	mountain bluebird	sagebrush	Carson City	NV
New Hampshire (NH)	Granite	Live free or die	white birch	purple finch	purple lilac	Concord	NH
New Jersey (NJ)	Garden	Liberty and prosperity	red oak	eastern goldfinch	purple violet	Trenton	NJ
New Mexico (N. Mex)	Land of Enchantment Sunshine	It grows as it goes	piñon (nut pine)	roadrunner	yucca flower	Santa Fe	NM
New York (NY)	Empire	Ever upward	sugar maple	bluebird	rose	Albany	NY
North Carolina (NC)	Tar Heel Old North	To be rather than to seem	longleaf pine	cardinal	dogwood	Raleigh	NC
North Dakota (N. Dak.)	Flickertail Sioux	Liberty and union, now and forever, one and inseparable	American elm	western meadowlark	wild prairie rose	Bismarck	ND

State	Nickname	Motto	State tree	State bird	State flower	State capital	Zip code
Ohio (Oh.)	Buckeye	With God, all things are possible	buckeye	cardinal	scarlet carnation	Columbus	OH
Oklahoma (Okla.)	Sooner	Labor conquers all things	redbud	scissor-tailed flycatcher	mistletoe	Oklahoma City	OK
Oregon (Oreg.)	Beaver	The Union	Douglas fir	western meadowlark	Oregon grape	Salem	OR
Pennsylvania (Pa.)	Keystone	Virtue, liberty, and independence	hemlock	ruffed grouse	mountain laurel	Harrisburg	PA
Rhode Island (RI)	Little Rhody Plantation	Hope	red maple	Rhode Island red	violet	Providence	RI
South Carolina (SC)	Palmetto	Prepared in mind and resources While I breathe, I hope	cabbage palmetto	Carolina wren	yellow jessamine	Columbia	SC
South Dakota (S. Dak.)	Coyote Sunshine	Under God the people rule	Black Hills spruce	ring-necked pheasant	pasqueflower	Pierre	SD
Tennessee (Tenn.)	Volunteer	Agriculture and commerce	tulip poplar	mockingbird	iris	Nashville	TN
Texas (Tex.)	Lone Star	Friendship	pecan	mockingbird	bluebonnet	Austin	TX
Utah (Ut.)	Beehive	Industry	blue spruce	sea gull	sego lily	Salt Lake City	UT
Vermont (Vt.)	Green Mountain	Freedom and unity	sugar maple	hermit thrush	red clover	Montpelier	VT
Virginia (Va.)	Mother of Presidents Old Dominion Cavalier	Thus always to tyrants	flowering dogwood	cardinal	dogwood	Richmond	VA
Washington (Wash.)	Evergreen Chinook	By and by	western hemlock	willow goldfinch	western rhododendron	Olympia	WA
West Virginia (W. Va.)	Mountain Panhandle	Mountaineers are always free	sugar maple	cardinal	big rhododendron	Charleston	WV
Wisconsin (Wis.)	Badger America's Dairyland	Forward	sugar maple	robin	wood violet	Madison	WI
Wyoming (Wyo.)	Equality	Equal rights	cottonwood	meadowlark	Indian paintbrush	Cheyenne	WY

UNITED STATES

State: Bordered by

Alabama Tennessee, Georgia, Mississippi, Florida.

Alaska None.

Arizona California, Nevada, Utah, New Mexico, Colorado.

Arkansas Tennessee, Mississippi, Louisiana, Missouri, Texas, Oklahoma.

California Arizona, Nevada, Oregon.

Colorado Utah, Wyoming, Arizona, New Mexico, Nebraska, Kansas, Oklahoma.

Connecticut Massachusetts, Rhode Island, New York.

Delaware Pennsylvania, New Jersey, Maryland.

Florida Georgia, Alabama.

Georgia South Carolina, Florida, Alabama, Tennessee, North Carolina.

Hawaii None.

Idaho Utah, Nevada, Washington, Wyoming, Oregon, Montana.

Illinois Kentucky, Missouri, Indiana, Wisconsin, Iowa.

Indiana Illinois, Michigan, Ohio, Kentucky.

Iowa Nebraska, Missouri, Illinois, Wisconsin, Minnesota, South Dakota.

Kansas Colorado, Oklahoma, Missouri, Nebraska.

Kentucky Tennessee, Illinois, Virginia, West Virginia, Missouri, Ohio, Indiana.

Louisiana Mississippi, Arkansas, Texas.

Maine New Hampshire.

Maryland Pennsylvania, Virginia, West Virginia, Delaware.

Massachusetts Vermont, New Hampshire, Rhode Island, New York, Connecticut.

Michigan Indiana, Ohio, Wisconsin.

Minnesota North Dakota, South Dakota, Iowa, Wisconsin.

Mississippi Louisiana, Arkansas, Tennessee, Alabama.

Missouri Iowa, Illinois, Kentucky, Tennessee, Arkansas, Oklahoma, Kansas, Nebraska.

Montana Idaho, Wyoming, North Dakota, South Dakota.

Nebraska Colorado, Wyoming, Iowa, South Dakota, Kansas, Missouri.

Nevada California, Utah, Arizona, Idaho, Oregon.

New Hampshire Maine, Massachusetts, Vermont.

New Jersey New York, Pennsylvania, Delaware.

New Mexico Colorado, Oklahoma, Texas, Arizona, Utah.

New York Vermont, Massachusetts, Connecticut, New Jersey, Pennsylvania.

North Carolina South Carolina, Virginia, Georgia, Tennessee.

North Dakota Montana, Minnesota, South Dakota.

Ohio Michigan, Indiana, Kentucky, West Virginia, Pennsylvania.

Oklahoma Texas, Arkansas, Kansas, Missouri, New Mexico, Colorado.

Oregon Washington, Idaho, California, Nevada.

Pennsylvania Delaware, New Jersey, New York, Maryland, West Virginia, Ohio.

Rhode Island Connecticut, Massachusetts.

South Carolina North Carolina, Georgia.

South Dakota North Dakota, Minnesota, Iowa, Nebraska, Wyoming, Montana.

Tennessee Kentucky, Alabama, Mississippi, Missouri, Arkansas, Georgia, Virginia, North Carolina.

Texas Louisiana, New Mexico, Oklahoma, Arkansas.

Utah Colorado, New Mexico, Arizona, Nevada, Wyoming, Idaho.

Vermont Massachusetts, New York, New Hampshire.

Virginia Maryland, West Virginia, Kentucky, Tennessee, North Carolina.

Washington Oregon, Idaho.

West Virginia Virginia, Kentucky, Ohio, Pennsylvania, Maryland.

Wisconsin Illinois, Michigan, Minnesota, Iowa.

Wyoming Montana, South Dakota, Nebraska, Colorado, Utah, Idaho.

Statistical Information

Order of Admission to the Union

1st	Delaware (1787)	18th	Louisiana (1812)	35th	West Virginia (1863)
2nd	Pennsylvania (1787)	19th	Indiana (1816)	36th	Nevada (1864)
3rd	New Jersey (1787)	20th	Mississippi (1817)	37th	Nebraska (1867)
4th	Georgia (1788)	21st	Illinois (1818)	38th	Colorado (1876)
5th	Connecticut (1788)	22nd	Alabama (1819)	39th	North Dakota (1889)
6th	Massachusetts (1788)	23rd	Maine (1820)	40th	South Dakota (1889)
7th	Maryland (1788)	24th	Missouri (1821)	41st	Montana (1889)
8th	South Carolina (1788)	25th	Arkansas (1836)	42nd	Washington (1889)
9th	New Hampshire (1788)	26th	Michigan (1837)	43rd	Idaho (1890)
10th	Virginia (1788)	27th	Florida (1845)	44th	Wyoming (1890)
11th	New York (1788)	28th	Texas (1845)	45th	Utah (1896)
12th	North Carolina (1789)	29th	Iowa (1846)	46th	Oklahoma (1907)
13th	Rhode Island (1790)	30th	Wisconsin (1848)	47th	New Mexico (1912)
14th	Vermont (1791)	31st	California (1850)	48th	Arizona (1912)
15th	Kentucky (1792)	32nd	Minnesota (1858)	49th	Alaska (1959)
16th	Tennessee (1796)	33rd	Oregon (1859)	50th	Hawaii (1959)
17th	Ohio (1803)	34th	Kansas (1861)		

Largest: by size

1st	Alaska	18th	North Dakota	35th	Tennessee
2nd	Texas	19th	Oklahoma	36th	Virginia
3rd	California	20th	Missouri	37th	Kentucky
4th	Montana	21st	Washington	38th	Indiana
5th	New Mexico	22nd	Wisconsin	39th	Maine
6th	Arizona	23rd	Georgia	40th	South Carolina
7th	Nevada	24th	Florida	41st	West Virginia
8th	Colorado	25th	Illinois	42nd	Maryland
9th	Wyoming	26th	Iowa	43rd	Vermont
10th	Michigan	27th	Arkansas	44th	New Hampshire
11th	Oregon	28th	New York	45th	Massachusetts
12th	Minnesota	29th	North Carolina	46th	Hawaii
13th	Utah	30th	Alabama	47th	New Jersey
14th	Idaho	31st	Louisiana	48th	Connecticut
15th	Kansas	32nd	Mississippi	49th	Delaware
16th	Nebraska	33rd	Pennsylvania	50th	Rhode Island
17th	South Dakota	34th	Ohio		

Largest: by population

1st	California	18th	Maryland	35th	New Mexico
2nd	New York	19th	Washington	36th	Utah
3rd	Texas	20th	Louisiana	37th	Nebraska
4th	Florida	21st	Minnesota	38th	Maine
5th	Pennsylvania	22nd	Alabama	39th	Hawaii
6th	Illinois	23rd	Kentucky	40th	New Hampshire
7th	Ohio	24th	Arizona	41st	Nevada
8th	Michigan	25th	South Carolina	42nd	Idaho
9th	New Jersey	26th	Colorado	43rd	Rhode Island
10th	North Carolina	27th	Oklahoma	44th	Montana
11th	Georgia	28th	Connecticut	45th	South Dakota
12th	Virginia	29th	Iowa	46th	North Dakota
13th	Massachusetts	30th	Oregon	47th	Delaware
14th	Indiana	31st	Mississippi	48th	Alaska
15th	Missouri	32nd	Kansas	49th	Vermont
16th	Tennessee	33rd	Arkansas	50th	Wyoming
17th	Wisconsin	34th	West Virginia		

U
N
I
T
E
D

S
T
A
T
E
S

General Information

Alamo: killed in siege of 1836   Davy Crockett and Jim Bowie. **site of siege**   Franciscan Mission Hall in San Antonio, Texas. **dates of siege**   23 February to 6 March 1836. **Mexican leader**   Santa Anna. **meaning of**   poplar (Spanish) or cottonwood tree.

Alaska: purchased from   Russia, 1867; known as Seward's Folly.

America: named after   Amerigo Vespucci.

anti-communist witch hunts 1950s   Senator Joseph McCarthy.

Back to Africa Movement leader   Marcus Garvey.

Bay Area Rapid Transit (BART)   San Francisco.

Black Muslims: developed movement   Elijah Muhammad 1934.

borders with eight other states   Missouri and Tennessee.

Boss Tweed   Corrupt leader of Tammany Hall Democrats, New York.

Boston Mountains   Arkansas and Oklahoma (Ozarks).

Boston Tea Party: date of   16 December 1773. **reason for destruction of tea**   protest against British tea tax. **owners of tea**   British East India Company. **British retaliation**   Intolerable Acts (shut down port, pending payment).

Bretton Woods Conference, NH, 1944: formed   IMF and International Bank for Reconstruction.

bus boycott of Montgomery, Alabama: caused by   Rosa Parks refusing to give up seat in Dec. 1955.

California: largest city   Los Angeles.

Californian gold rush: first prospector   James Wilson Marshall, 1848.

first major strike   J A Sutter, a Swiss settler, 1849.

capital of America before Washington DC   Philadelphia, 1783–9.

Central Park: designers   Frederick Law Olmstead and Calvert Vaux.

child: first born of English parents   Virginia Dare.

civil rights demo: troops called in   Selma, Alabama,1956; Autherine Lucy expelled.

Civil War: dates of outbreak and surrender   15 April 1861 to 9 April 1865. **started: where**   Fort Sumter in Charleston Harbour, SC, April 1861. **Lee surrender to Grant: where**   Appomattox

Court House, Virginia, 9 April 1865. **official ending: on surrender of** Gen. Richard Taylor, 4 May 1865. **first state to secede from Union** South Carolina, December 1860. **second state to secede** Mississippi, January 1861. **antebellum: meaning of** period before the war. **battle above the clouds** Lookout Mountain, Chattanooga, Tennessee. **Confederate capital** Richmond, Virginia.

Colin Powell: autobiography *My American Journey.*

commonwealths: officially called Massachusetts, Kentucky and Virginia.

commonwealth: self-styled Pennsylvania.

Confederate states: antebellum Alabama, Florida, Georgia, Louisiana, Mississippi, South Carolina, Texas. **four joined at outbreak of Civil War** Arkansas, North Carolina, Tennessee, Virginia. **President** Jefferson Davis.

Congress: first woman Jeanette Rankin, 1916.

Constitution of the USA: ratified by New Hampshire's ninth vote, 1788.

constitutional amendments Abolition of Slavery, 13th. Presidential Terms, 22nd. Prohibition, 18th. Votes for Blacks, 15th. Votes for Women, 19th.

coterminous states: high and low point Mt Whitney and Death Valley, both in California.

Coxey's Army unemployed march to Washington DC, 1894.

Dakota: named after Sioux Indian tribe.

Declaration of Independence 4 July 1776.

Delaware: three counties New Castle, Kent, Sussex.

Delaware: largest city Wilmington.

District of Columbia: ceded by Maryland, 1791.

Emancipation proclamation freeing of slaves during Civil War.

Essex Junto: leader Timothy Pickering. **term coined by** John Hancock, 1778. **supported** Alexander Hamilton. **based** Massachusetts.

first state to join Union Delaware, 7 Dec. 1787.

Florida: largest city Jacksonville.

four corners touching Utah, Colorado, New Mexico, Arizona.

Gadsden purchase of land for USA in 1853 land bought from Mexico, now New Mexico and Arizona.

Georgia: marched through during Civil War General Sherman.

gold on land caused rush 1849 John Sutter.

good neighbour policy 1928 Latin American policy of F D Roosevelt.

Grape Workers Union leader led boycott Cesar Chavez, 1968.

Hartford Convention of 1814–15 began demise of Federalist Party.

Hawaii: European discoverer Captain James Cook, 1778.

Hawaii: former name Sandwich Islands.

Haymarket Massacre of 1886 police fire on crowd at May Day Rally in Chicago.

Homestead Act 1862: Lincoln's aim to provide land free to settlers to cultivate.

Honolulu: island situated Oahu.

honorary citizenship Winston Churchill.

Indian chief surrendered to General Miles Geronimo.

Intolerable Acts enforced embargo of Boston until compensation paid.

Irangate scandal: USA accused of arms for Iran in return for funds to Nicaraguan Contras. **famous**

testimony Oliver North.

Ivy League: nickname for The top eight universities and colleges of USA. **members** Harvard (1636), Yale (1701), Pennsylvania (1740), Princeton (1746), Columbia (1754), Brown (1764), Dartmouth (1769), Cornell (1853).

Kent State University, Ohio, 1970 National Guard shot dead four students during anti-war demo.

Ku Klux Klan: formed Pulaski, Tennessee, 1866.

Lend-lease Pact: March 1941 Roosevelt signed with Britain for WW2 aid.

Lewis and Clark expedition 1804–6 exploration of western America.

Lewis and Clark: state governors of Louisiana and Missouri Territory respectively.

Los Angeles: name when founded, 1781 the Town of the Queen of the Angels.

Louisiana purchase Mississippi valley bought from France 1803; 828,000 sq miles cost $15 million!

Louisiana: largest city New Orleans.

Louisiana: named in honour of Louis XIV.

Mammoth Cave Kentucky.

Manhattan Island: bought from Indian tribes for trinkets worth 60 guilders.

Manhattan Island: purchaser Peter Minuit.

mapped America Samuel de Champlain, 1605; John Smith, 1614.

Maryland named in honour of wife of Charles I: Henrietta Maria.

Mason–Dixon line: boundaries Pennsylvania– Maryland; border of North and South.

Mason–Dixon line: why drawn disputes of Penn and Calvert families in 1760s.

Mayflower: **sister ship** *Speedwell;* deemed unseaworthy.

Mexican ceded states of 1848 Texas, New Mexico, California.

Mexican ceded states: clerk responsible Nicholas Trist.

Michigan: two land masses joined by Mackinac Bridge (Big Mac), built 1957.

Michigan: borders on Great Lakes all except Ontario.

Mississippi University: first black to enter James Meredith.

Montana: name means mountain (Spanish).

Mormon Church: founded at Fayette, New York, in 1830.

mountain: highest in America Mount McKinley, Alaska, 20,320′ (6,194 m).

Nat Turner insurrection 1831 slave uprising in Virginia.

Naval Academy Annapolis, Maryland.

Nebraska: name means flat water.

Nevada: name means snow-clad (Spanish).

New England: named by John Smith, 1614. **six states** Connecticut, Maine, Massachusetts, New Hampshire, Rhode Island, Vermont.

New Hampshire: named after English county of Hampshire, 1629.

New Orleans: same parallel as Cairo, Delhi, Shanghai.

New York named in honour of duke of York, later James II.

New York City: five boroughs Queens, Bronx, Manhattan, Brooklyn, Staten Island.

New York State: capital's former name Fort

Orange, 1624; became Albany.

New York: political differences   upstate is Conservative, downstate is Liberal.

North Dakota: largest city   Fargo.

Oklahoma: name means   red people.

oldest American town   St Augustine, Florida, 1565.

Pilgrim Fathers: ship   *Mayflower*. **landed** Provincetown in Massachusetts, November 1620. **first to land**   John Alden. **established**   Plymouth Colony. **Indian interpreter**   Squanto. **Indian welcomed them**   Samoset, a Pemaquid from Maine.

Portsmouth, New Hampshire   treaty ended Russo-Japanese war, 1905.

presidential primary: earliest   New Hampshire.

rectangular-shaped states   Wyoming and Colorado.

Rhode Island: official name   The State of Rhode Island and Providence Plantations.

Richmond County: named in honour of   Charles Lennox, duke of Richmond, son of Charles II.

Russia: closest point to   Diomede Islands, Bering Strait.

San Francisco meeting of United Nations   April 1945.

school integration: Federal troops enforced   Little Rock, Arkansas, 1957.

Sea Islands: sub-tropical islands of   South Carolina.

senator: first black   Edward Brooke.

Seneca Falls Convention, 1848   Women's Rights' Movement began.

size of USA doubled by   Louisiana purchase.

slave abolitionist leader   Harriet Tubman, former slave.

slavery: abolished   1863. **escape network to the North**   underground railroad. **last state to abolish** Mississippi.

Spindletop oil well, Texas   blew 1901.

Tammany Hall (New York)   byword for municipal corruption.

Tarpon Springs, Florida   centre for Greek Orthodox religion and sponge industry.

Teapot Dome Affair, aka Elk Hills Scandal   Sec. of Interior Albert Fall jailed for corruption.

territories: overseas   American Virgin Islands, Commonwealth of Puerto Rico, Guam, Samoa.

terrorism: executed 1927 but pardoned 1977 Sacco and Vanzetti.

Texas: annexed by America, in   1845. **former capital**   Houston, until 1839, then Austin. **largest city** Houston.

Townshend Acts 1767   British taxes that sparked revolt.

Vietnam: secret documents   Pentagon papers showed USA involvement. **secret documents revealed by**   Daniel Ellsberg, 1971.

Virginia: named in honour of   Elizabeth I.

War of Independence: started   Lexington, Massachusetts, April 1775. **ended**   Yorktown, Virginia, October 1781. **rode to warn of British approach**   Paul Revere. **traitor for British** Benedict Arnold. **American general**   George Washington. **British general**   Charles Cornwallis. **Washington's ally**   Marquis of Lafayette.

Washington: capital since   1789.

Watts riots   Los Angeles, 1965.

witchcraft trials   Salem, Massachusetts, 1692 (20 executed).

wobblies   Industrial Workers of the World, trade union.

Yellowstone National Park: three states   Wyoming, Montana, Idaho.

NB More detailed information pertaining to rivers, mountains and other geographical features of the USA can be found in the Geography section.

U
N
I
T
E
D

S
T
A
T
E
S

Miscellaneous Items of Interest

Units of Length

link (surveying)	7.92 inches (100th part of chain)
span	9 inches (approx span of hand)
hand	4 inches (horse measurement)
cubit	18 inches (biblical measurement)
pace	30 inches (from the stride)
cable	120 fathoms (720 feet; a fathom equals six feet)
nautical mile	6,080 feet (1 sec of arc at Equator) (now 1,852 metres)

Book Sizes

Crown Quarto	246 × 189 mm
Crown Octavo	186 × 123 mm
Demy Quarto	276 × 219 mm
Demy Octavo	216 × 138 mm
Royal Quarto	312 × 237 mm
Royal Octavo	234 × 156 mm

Paper Sizes

A0	841 x 1189 mm (33⅛ × 46¾ inches)
A1	594 x 841 mm (23⅜ × 33⅛ inches)
A2	420 x 594 mm (16½ × 23⅜ inches)
A3	297 x 420 mm (11¾ × 16½ inches)
A4	210 x 297 mm (8¼ × 11¾ inches)
A5	148 x 210 mm (5⅞ × 8¼ inches)
A6	105 x 148 mm (4⅛ × 5⅞ inches)
A7	74 x 105 mm ($2\frac{15}{16}$ × 4⅛ inches)
A8	52 x 74 mm ($2\frac{1}{16}$ × $2\frac{15}{16}$ inches)
A9	37 x 52 mm ($1\frac{15}{32}$ × $2\frac{1}{16}$ inches)
A10	26 x 37 mm ($1\frac{1}{32}$ × $1\frac{15}{32}$ inches)
Elephant	584 x 711 mm (23 × 28 inches)

Morse Code

A	dot dash	**H**	dot dot dot dot	**O**	dash dash dash	**V**	dot dot dot dash
B	dash dot dot dot	**I**	dot dot	**P**	dot dash dash dot	**W**	dot dash dash
C	dash dot dash dot	**J**	dot dash dash dash	**Q**	dash dash dot dash	**X**	dash dot dot dash
D	dash dot dot	**K**	dash dot dash	**R**	dot dash dot	**Y**	dash dot dash dash
E	dot	**L**	dot dash dot dot	**S**	dot dot dot	**Z**	dash dash dot dot
F	dot dot dash dot	**M**	dash dash	**T**	dash		
G	dash dash dot	**N**	dash dot	**U**	dot dot dash		

Mnemonics

Types of cedars Atlas – Ascending branches, deodar – drooping branches, Lebanon – level branches.

Can Queen Victoria eat cold apple pie? The seven hills of Rome: Capitoline, Quirinal, Viminal, Esquiline, Caelian, Aventine, Palatine.

Did Mary ever visit Brighton Beach? Order of Nobility: Duke, Marquess, Earl, Viscount, Baron, Baronet.

Bless my dear Aunt Sally Order of operations in algebraic expressions: Brackets, Multiply, Divide, Add, Subtract.

BROM 4689 (Duke of Marlborough's Telephone No.) Marlborough's battles: Blenheim (1704), Ramilies (1706), Oudenarde (1708), Malplaquet (1709).

Men very easily make jugs serve useful nocturnal purposes Planets from the sun: Mercury, Venus, Earth, Mars, Jupiter, Saturn, Uranus, Neptune, Pluto.

Spring forward, fall back Mnemonic to remember whether to put clock forward or back.

Virgins are rare Ohm's Law: Volts = Amps × Resistance.

How I want a drink alcoholic of course after the heavy chapters involving quantum mechanics Mnemonic for remembering pi to 14 places: 3.14159265358979.

No plan like yours to study history wisely British ruling houses: Norman, Plantagenet, Lancaster, York, Tudor, Stuart, Hanover, Windsor

Richard of York gave battle in vain Rainbow colours in order: red, orange, yellow, green, blue, indigo, violet

NB This last little section on mnemonics is a reminder in itself that a sound general knowledge base can only be achieved if facts are committed to memory. There is no shortcut to success in the quiz world; of course, a keen interest taken in things going on around you is desirable, as is a basic level of intelligence, but given that most people share those basic requirements then the secret of success is the amount of data consumed and the way that data is processed. The rate at which information is consumed varies depending on the level of commitment of the reader, but the way that information is stored can be the vital edge required to recall that seemingly long-forgotten nugget or that either/or situation so often encountered by quiz buffs. Mnemonics are an invaluable aid to quiz players, and should be used in some form or other when memorising lists. It does not matter how silly, rude, outlandish or downright inarticulate the mnemonic is, all that matters is that it works.

Colours

alabaster	White	**ebony**	Brownish-Black		browny yellow)
amaranth	Purple	**elephant**	Grey	**olive**	Greyish-Green
amber	Yellow	**emerald**	Green	**or**	Gold
argent	Silver	**fallow**	Yellow	**peridot**	Green (yellowish-green)
ash	Pale Grey	**fawn**	Yellowish-Brown		
auburn	Reddish-Brown	**flame**	Orangey-Red	**pillar-box**	Bright Red
aureate	Golden	**foxy**	Reddish-Brown	**plum**	Reddish-Purple
azure	Sky Blue	**gamboge**	Yellow	**primrose**	Pale Yellow
bamboo	Yellowish-Brown	**gentian**	Violet	**puce**	Purple-Brown
bay	Reddish-Brown	**gridelin**	Grey-Violet	**russet**	Reddish-Brown
bice	Blue	**grizzly**	Grey	**rust**	Reddish-Brown
bistre	Brown	**gules**	Red	**sable**	Black
bronze	Yellowish-Brown	**hazel**	Reddish-Brown	**saffron**	Orange-Yellow
brunette	Dark Brown	**heliotrope**	Mauve (light purple)	**sandy**	Yellowish-Red
buff	Pale Yellow			**sanguine**	Blood Red
cardinal	Red (scarlet)	**honey**	Yellow	**sapphire**	Blue
carmine	Red (crimson)	**indigo**	Violet Blue	**scarlet**	Bright Red tinged with Orange
carnation	Rosy Pink	**ivory**	Creamy-White		
celandine	Yellow	**jonquil**	Yellow		
cerise	Red	**jupiter**	Blue	**sepia**	Reddish-Brown
cerulean	Blue	**khaki**	Brownish-Yellow	**sienna**	Yellowish-Brown
chestnut	Reddish-Brown	**lake**	Crimson	**solferino**	Crimson
chocolate	Brown	**lapis lazuli**	Blue	**sorrel**	Reddish-Brown
chrome	Yellow	**lavender**	Pale Blue (with a trace of red)	**straw**	Pale Yellow
cinereous	Ash-Grey			**tan**	Yellowish-Brown
cinnabar	Vermilion	**lilac**	Pinkish-Violet	**teak**	Reddish-Brown
cinnamon	Yellowish-Brown	**lily**	White	**teal**	Greenish-Blue
citrine	Lemon Yellow	**livid**	Bluish-Purple	**topaz**	Yellow
cobalt	Blue	**magenta**	Mauve (mauvish-crimson)	**turquoise**	Greenish-Blue
cochineal	Scarlet			**ultramarine**	Blue
cornelian	Reddish-White	**malachite**	Green	**umber**	Reddish-Brown
cornflour	Blue	**maroon**	Brownish-Crimson	**verd-antique**	Green
crimson	Purplish-Red	**mazarine**	Blue	**vermilion**	Red
damask	Pinkish-Red	**moon**	White	**violet**	Bluish-Purple
duck-egg	Blue	**murrey**	Purplish-Red	**viridescent**	Green
dun	Greyish-Brown	**nacarat**	Orangey-Red	**xanthin**	Yellow
		ochre	Yellow (light		

MISCELLANEOUS

Angles

	Angles in regular polygon	Total angles	Sides	Formula
triangle	60°	180°	3	$(2 \times 3 - 4) \times 90 = 180$
quadrilateral	90°	360°	4	$(2 \times 4 - 4) \times 90 = 360$
pentagon	108°	540°	5	$(2 \times 5 - 4) \times 90 = 540$
hexagon	120°	720°	6	$(2 \times 6 - 4) \times 90 = 720$
heptagon	129°	900°	7	$(2 \times 7 - 4) \times 90 = 900$
octagon	135°	1080°	8	$(2 \times 8 - 4) \times 90 = 1080$
nonagon	140°	1260°	9	$(2 \times 9 - 4) \times 90 = 1260$
decagon	144°	1440°	10	$(2 \times 10 - 4) \times 90 = 1440$
dodecagon	150°	1800°	12	$(2 \times 12 - 4) \times 90 = 1800$
hendecagon	162°	3240°	20	$(2 \times 20 - 4) \times 90 = 3240$

NB Sum of the interior angles of a polygon = $(2n - 4) \times 90$ degrees where n = the number of sides.

Adjectives

Objects

acicular	needle-like	hastate	spear-shaped
acinaciform	scimitar-shaped	lenticular	lens-shaped
		ligneous	wood-like
aciniform	grape-like	linguiform	tongue-shaped
alaric	wing-shaped		
allantoic	sausage-shaped	lunate	crescent-shaped
		marmoreal	marble-like
amygdaloid	almond-shaped	navicular	boat-shaped
		oculiform	eye-shaped
annular	ring-shaped	odontoid	tooth-shaped
arcuate	bow-shaped	oviform	egg-shaped
baculiform	rod-like	palmate	palm-shaped
cancroid	crab-like	pinnate	feather-like
clavate	club-shaped	pyriform	pear-like
cordate	heart-shaped	reniform	kidney-shaped
cricoid	ring-shaped	sagittate	arrow-shaped
crinoidal	lily-like	saponaceous	soap-like
cuneal	wedge-shaped	scutate	shield-shaped
cyprinoid	carp-like	stellate	star-shaped
decussate	cross-shaped	toroid	doughnut-shaped
dendroid	tree-shaped	trochal	wheel-shaped
dentoid	tooth-shaped	unciform	hook-shaped
ethmoid	sieve-like	verticillate	whorl-shaped
falciform	sickle-shaped	xiphoid	sword-shaped
ganoid	scale-like		

Animals

anguine	snake-like	lupine	wolf-like
anserine	goose-like	murine	mouse-like
apian	bee-like	ovine	sheep-like
aquiline	eagle-like	ophidian	snake-like
asinine	ass-like	passerine	sparrow-like
avian	bird-like	pavanine	peacock-like
bovine	ox-like	piscine	fish-like
canine	dog-like	porcine	pig-like
caprine	goat-like	psittacine	parrot-like
cervine	deer-like	saurian	lizard-like
columbine	dove-like	simian	ape-like
corvine	crow-like	squaloid	shark-like
equine	horse-like	taurine	bull-like
feline	cat-like	turdine	thrush-like
hircine	goat-like	ursine	bear-like
leonine	lion-like	vaccine	cow-like
leporine	hare-like	vulpine	fox-like

Alphabets

	No. of characters	Description
Albanian	36	based on the Tosk language since 1945.
Arabic	28	all consonants; written from right to left.
Aramaic	22	all consonants; written from right to left.
Armenian	38	31 consonants and 7 vowels.
Balinese	27	the Latin alphabet is now used in Bali.
Bassa	29	formerly used in Liberia.
Batak	30	20 consonants, 10 vowels, written from bottom to top.
Braille	63	each made up of 1–6 raised dots arranged in six-position matrix.
Buhid	48	used to write the Tagalog language of the Philippines.
Bulgarian	30	adaptation of the Cyrillic alphabet.
Cyrillic	32	nowadays synonymous with the Russian alphabet.
Ethiopic	26	all consonants; 7 variations of each letter.
Etruscan	20	16 consonants, 4 vowels written left to right then right to left.
Gaelic	18	no J, K, Q, V, W, X, Y, Z.
Georgian	33	used by about 3.5 million people.
Gothic	27	original Gothic alphabet had 25 letters.
Grantha	35	30 consonants and 5 vowels; written left to right.
Greek	24	17 consonants and 7 vowels.
Gujarati	41	34 consonants, 7 vowels each having two variants.
Hebrew	22	all consonants; written from right to left.
Latin (Roman)	26	alphabet used by English speakers. J, U, W not in original Roman alphabet.
Mongolian	33	adaptation of the Cyrillic alphabet.
Ogham	29	also known as beth luis, or beth luis nion.
Phoenician	22	no vowels.
Runic	24	also known as fu(th)ark from its first six letters.
Russian	33	adaptation of the Cyrillic alphabet.
Serbian	29	adaptation of the Cyrillic alphabet.
Tamil	36	24 consonants, 12 vowels.
Telugo	51	35 consonants, 16 vowels.
Ugaritic	30	cuneiform alphabet of 27 consonants and 3 vowels.
Ukrainian	33	adaptation of the Cyrillic alphabet.

Roman Roads

Aemilian Way	Rimini to Milan	**Fosse Way**	Lincoln to Exeter
Akeman Street	Alchester to Cirencester	**Icknield Way**	Wash to Salisbury Plain
Appian Way	Rome to Brindisi	**Salarian Way**	Rome to Ancona
Aurelian Way	Rome to Genoa	**Stane Street (1)**	London to Chichester
Casinge Street	Dover to London	**(2)**	Braughing in Hertfordshire to Colchester
Cassian Way	Rome to Florence		
Dere Street	Risingham to Hadrian's Wall	**Watling Street (1)**	London to Wroxeter via St Albans
Ermine Street	London to York		
Flaminian Way	Rome to Rimini	**Watling Street (2)**	Wroxeter to Abergavenny

US Money

All US bills have a portrait of a famous American on the front and a design on the back as follows:

	Front	Back		Front	Back
$1	Washington	Great Seal of USA	$100	Franklin	Independence Hall
$2	Jefferson	Signers of Declaration	$500	McKinley	Ornate Design
$5	Lincoln	Lincoln Memorial	$1,000	Cleveland	Ornate Design
$10	Hamilton	US Treasury	$5,000	Madison	Ornate Design
$20	Jackson	White House	$10,000	Chase	Ornate Design
$50	Grant	US Capitol	$100,000	Wilson	Ornate Design

British Money

Until 1943 there were white bank notes for values of £10, £20, £50, £100, £500 and £1,000 but these ceased to be legal tender in 1945. The old white £5 note issued between 1945 and 1956 ceased to be legal tender in 1961. The £5 note issued between 1957 and 1963 that coincided with the term of office of Harold MacMillan, and bearing a portrait of Britannia, ceased to be legal tender in 1967. The £5 note issued between 1963 and 1971 was the first of the series to bear a portrait of the Queen. The first note with a portrait of the Queen on the front was a £1 note issued in 1960. The 10 shilling note was replaced by the 50p coin in 1969 and ceased to be legal tender in 1970 (they could however be redeemed if presented at the Head Office of the Bank of England). The £1 note was replaced by a coin in 1983 and ceased to be legal tender in 1988, although the Scottish £1 note is still acceptable in Scotland.

The current notes as at August 2001 portray famous people as follows:

£5	Elizabeth Fry (1780–1845)
£10	Charles Darwin (1809–82) and the *Beagle*
£20	Sir Edward Elgar (1857–1934) and Worcester Cathedral
£50	Sir John Houblon (1632–1712) the Bank of England gatekeeper. The current Chief Cashier of the Bank of England is Merlyn Lowther, who replaced G E A Kentfield.

Previous portraits on notes are as follows:

£5	George Stephenson and before him The Duke of Wellington
£10	Charles Dickens and before him Florence Nightingale
£20	Michael Faraday and before him William Shakespeare
£50	Sir Christopher Wren

British coins ceased to be legal tender as follows:

Farthing (¼d)	1960
Pre-decimal halfpenny	1969
Half-crown (2s 6d)	1970
Threepenny bit	1971
Sixpence (6d = 2½p)	1980
Decimal halfpenny	1984

Confusion often arises when one considers which was the first decimal coin brought into circulation. In 1968 the shilling and two shilling coins were replaced by a new 5p and 10p coin. This pre-empted decimalisation in 1971 and was an exercise in the public becoming used to the new system. The coins were of the same value as previously and did not alter the public perception in any way. In 1969 the new 50p coin was introduced, replacing the ten-shilling note which of course was a vastly different form, hence it often being considered as the first decimal coin introduced.

In 1971 the ½p, 1p, and 2p coins were introduced and in 1982 the 20p coin followed. In 1983 the £1 coin replaced the £1 note and in 1986 the first £2 coin was minted. Decimal coins minted before 1982 had their value in 'New' pence.

UK Telephone STD Codes

0121 Birmingham
0131 Edinburgh
0141 Glasgow
0151 Liverpool
0161 Manchester
0191 Newcastle upon Tyne

Recent changes to STD codes

Cardiff was 01222 now 02920
Coventry was 01203 now 02476
London was 0171 now 0207
London was 0181 now 0208
Portsmouth was 01705 now 02392
Southampton was 01703 now 02380

NB All Northern Ireland numbers have been changed to six-digit numbers, all of which begin 028.

British Quiz Championships
Annual competition first held at Olympia in 1999

1999   (1) Kevin Ashman, (2 joint) Daphne Fowler and Geoff Thomas
2000   (1) Kevin Ashman, (2) Roger Mortimore, (3 joint) Geoff Thomas and Daphne Fowler
2001   (1) Ian Bayley, (2) Kevin Ashman, (3) John Wilson
2002   (1) Kevin Ashman, (2) John Wilson, (3) Trevor Montague

A British team championship was held for the first time in 2002.
The winning team were Kevin Ashman, Mark Bytheway, Eric Kilby and Tim Westcott.

Top-ten Ranked British Quiz Players (as at 30 June 2003)

1 John Wilson
2 Kevin Ashman
3 Ray Oakes
4 Dag Griffiths
5 Karl Whelan

6 Andy Page
7 Stephen Pearson
8 Tom Farley
9 David Stainer
10 Pat Gibson

and finally

A few well-known people whose name belies their gender:

Colley Cibber (dramatist) male
Wilkie Collins (novelist) male
Richmal Crompton (novelist) female
Keri Hulme (novelist) female
Ngaio Marsh (novelist) female
Julian of Norwich (mystic) female
Harper Lee (novelist) female
Laurie Lee (novelist) male
Marilyn Manson (pop star) male

Joan Miro (painter) male
Nelly (rapper) male
Andrea Palladio (architect) male
Caryl Phillips (novelist) male
Carol Reed (film director) male
Vesta Tilley (music hall star) female
Reese Witherspoon (actress) female
Evelyn Waugh (novelist) male
George Sand (novelist) female